National Student Nurses'
Association, Inc.

NCLEX-RN™
REVIEW

Fourth Edition

EDITORS

Alice M. Stein, EdD, RN
Associate Dean for Continuing Education
School of Nursing
MCP Hahnemann University

Judith C. Miller, RN, MSN
President, Nursing Tutorial and Consulting Services

Delmar Thomson Learning

NOTICE TO THE READER

Delmar Staff:

Publisher: William Brottmiller
Acquisitions Editor: Marion S. Waldman
Developmental Editor: Patricia A. Gaworecki
Art & Design Coordinator: Jay Purcell

COPYRIGHT © 2000 Delmar
a division of Thomson Learning. Thmoson Learning is a trademark
used herein under license

Printed in the United States of America

For more information, contact:

Delmar Thomson Learning
3 Columbia Circle, Box 15015
Albany, New York 12212-5015

International Thomson Publishing Europe
Berkshire House
168-173 High Holborn
London, WC1V 7AA
England

Thomas Nelson Australia
102 Dodds Street
South Melbourne 3205
Victoria, Australia

Nelson Canada
1120 Birchmont Road
Scarborough, Ontario
Canada M1K 5G4

International Thomson Editores
Campos Eliseos 385, Piso 7
Col Polonco
11560 Mexico D F Mexico

International Thomson Publishing GmbH
Konigswinterer Str. 418
53227 Bonn
Germany

International Thomson Publishing Asia
221 Henderson Road
#05 - 10 Henderson Building
Singapore 0315

International Thomson Publishing Japan
Kyowa Building, 3F
2-2-1 Hirakawa-cho
Chiyoda-ku, Tokyo 102
Japan

2 3 4 5 6 7 8 9 10 XXX 02 01 00 99

Library of Congress Cataloging-in-Publication Data
NSNA, NCLEX-RN review / editors, Alice M. Stein, Judith C. Miller.—
  4th ed.
     p. cm.
   Includes bibliographical references and index.
   ISBN 0-7668-1443-2
   1. Nursing Examinations, questions, etc.   I. Stein, Alice M.
 II. Miller, Judith C.   III. National Student Nurses' Association
 (U.S.)   IV. Title: NCLEX-RN review.
   [DNLM: 1.   Nursing Examination Questions.   2. Nursing Process
 Examination Questions.   WY 18.2 N961   2000 / WY 18.2 N961   2000]
RT55.N73   2000
610.73'076—dc2l
DNLM/DLC
for Library of Congress   00-12882
                                                      CIP

A Message from the National Student Nurses' Association

The National Student Nurses' Association, NSNA, is pleased to bring you the *NSNA NCLEX-RN™ REVIEW*. Whether you use this book alone or in conjunction with the *NSNA/NCLEX Excel!™* courses presented by the MCP Hahnemann University, you will be better prepared to meet the challenge of passing the exam the first time around.

NSNA is committed to the professional development of today's nursing student. We recognize the challenges of succeeding in today's complex health care environment. This outstanding book maintains high standards both in content and in presentation. The contributing experience of the clinicians and educators will help you achieve NCLEX success!

Contents

Message from the National Student Nurses'
  Association   iii
Index of Tables   x
Contributors   xi
Preface   xiv
List of Abbreviations   xvi

UNIT 1   PREPARING FOR THE NCLEX EXAMINATION   1

Understanding the NCLEX Examination   2
The Test Plan   2
How the Test Is Constructed   3
How the Test Is Scored   3
How Candidates Are Notified of Results   4

Preparation and Test Taking   4
Using the Test Plan to Your Best Advantage   4
Final Preparation for Test Taking   5
Taking the Test   6
How to Use This Book   7

References and Suggested Readings   7

UNIT 2   DRUGS AND NURSING IMPLICATIONS   9

Factors Affecting Drug Action   10
Definition of a Drug   10
Factors Affecting Drug Action   10

Drug Administration   12
Assessments Appropriate to All Medication
   Administration   12
Analysis   12
Planning and Implementation   12
Techniques of Drug Administration   12
Medication Calculations   20

Central Nervous System Drugs   26
Local Anesthetics   26
Nonnarcotic Analgesics and Antipyretics   27
Narcotic Analgesics   28
Narcotic Antagonists   30
Sedatives and Hypnotics   30
Anticonvulsants   32
Skeletal Muscle Relaxants   33
Antipsychotic Agents   34

Autonomic Nervous System Drugs   38
Adrenergic Drugs   38
Adrenergic-Blocking Agents   41
Cholinergics   43
Anticholinergics   44
Antiparkinson Agents   45

Drugs Affecting the Endocrine System   47
Antidiabetic Agents   47
Pituitary Hormones   49
Corticosteroids   50
Thyroid Hormones   51

Thyroid Antagonists   51
Progestagens (Progestins)   52
Oxytocics   53

Eye Drugs   54
Mydriatics and Cycloplegics   54
Miotics   54

Cardiovascular Drugs   55
Cardiac Glycosides   55
Antianginal Drugs   56
Peripheral Vasodilators   59
Antiarrhythmics   60
Beta Blockers   62
Cardiac Stimulants   62
Anticoagulants   63
Thrombolytic Drugs   64
Antilipemic Agents   65
Antihypertensives   66

Renal Drugs   69
Diuretics   69
Potassium-Removing Resin   72

Respiratory Drugs   73
Antiasthmatic Drugs   73
Antihistamines   74
Mucolytics   75
Expectorants and Antitussives   75

Gastrointestinal Tract Drugs   76
Histamine (H_2) Antagonists   76
Gastrointestinal (GI) Anticholinergics   77
Antacids   77
Antidiarrheal Agents   79
Laxatives   80
Antiemetics   80
Emetics   82
Sucralfate (Carafate)   82

Arthritis Drugs   83
Arthritis Drugs   83
Antigout Drugs   84

Antimicrobials   85
General Information   85
Aminoglycosides   86
Penicillins   86
Cephalosporins   87
Erythromycins   89
Tetracyclines   89
Chloramphenicol   90
Sulfonamides   90
Urinary Anti-infectives   91
Vancomycin Hydrochloride (Vancocin)   92
Ciprofloxacin (Cipro)   92
Antitubercular Drugs   93

Antiviral Agents   94
Acyclovir (Zovirax)   94

Antifungal Agents   95
Antifungals   95

Antihelmintics   96
    Antihelmintics   96

Antineoplastic Agents   97
    Antineoplastic Agents   97
    Alkylating Agents   97
    Antimetabolites   98
    Antibiotic Antineoplastic Agents   98
    Antineoplastics Affecting Hormonal Balance   100
    Vinca Alkaloids   101
    Miscellaneous Antineoplastic Agents   102

Immunosuppressants   103
    Azathioprine (Imuran)   103
    Cyclosporine (Sandimmune)   103

Vitamins and Minerals   104
    Vitamins   104
    Minerals   104
    Heavy Metal Antagonists   105

Vaccines and Toxoids   105
    Vaccines and Toxoids   105
    Immune Serums   106

References and Suggested Readings   107

UNIT 3   UNIVERSAL PRINCIPLES OF NURSING CARE MANAGEMENT   109

Nursing Practice Standards   110
    Standards of Nursing Practice   110
    Standard I   110
    Standard II   110
    Standard III   111
    Standard IV   111
    Standard V   111
    Standard VI   112
    Standard VII   112
    Standard VIII   112

Legal and Ethical Aspects of Nursing   113
    Overview   113
    Code for Nurses (ANA, 1985)   113

Managing Client Care   115
    Priorities of Client Care   115
    Assignment Methods for Delivery of Care   116

Safety   117
    Fire Safety/Preparedness Practices   117
    Equipment   117
    Restraints   118

Principles and Interventions for Specific Aspects of Care   118
    Body Mechanics   118
    Transfer and Movement Principles and Techniques   118
    Positioning of the Client   119
    Cold Application   121
    Application of External Heat   122
    Asepsis   122
    Pressure Sore   123

References and Suggested Readings   127

UNIT 4   ADULT NURSING   129

Multisystem Stressors   130
    Stress and Adaptation   130
    Inflammatory Response   130
    Immune Response   130
    Nutrition   132
    Infection   140
    Pain   141
    Fluids and Electrolytes   144
    Acid-Base Balance   146
    Intravenous Therapy   147
    Shock   149
    Multiple Trauma   150

Aging   154
    General Information   154
    Patterns of Health and Disease in the Elderly   156
    Assessment   156
    Analysis   157
    Planning and Implementation   158
    Evaluation   158
    Elder Abuse and Neglect   159

Perioperative Nursing   161
    Overview   161
    Preoperative Period   162
    Intraoperative Period   163
    Postoperative Period   164

Oncologic Nursing   168
    Pathophysiology and Etiology of Cancer   168
    Diagnosis of Cancer   168
    Treatment of Cancer   169

The Neurosensory System   174
    Overview of Anatomy and Physiology   174
    Assessment   178
    Analysis   181
    Planning and Implementation   182
    Evaluation   185
    Disorders of the Nervous System   185
    Disorders of the Eye   199
    Disorders of the Ear   202

The Cardiovascular System   205
    Overview of Anatomy and Physiology   205
    Assessment   207
    Analysis   209
    Planning and Implementation   209
    Evaluation   211
    Disorders of the Cardiovascular System   211

The Hematologic System   227
    Overview of Anatomy and Physiology   227
    Assessment   231
    Analysis   232
    Planning and Implementation   232
    Evaluation   233
    Disorders of the Hematologic System   234

The Respiratory System   243
    Overview of Anatomy and Physiology   243
    Assessment   244
    Analysis   246
    Planning and Implementation   246

Evaluation   251
Disorders of the Respiratory System   251

The Gastrointestinal System   262
Overview of Anatomy and Physiology Assessment   262
Assessment   264
Analysis   267
Planning and Implementation   267
Evaluation   267
Disorders of the Gastrointestinal System   269
Disorders of the Liver   281
Disorders of the Gallbladder   286
Disorders of the Pancreas   287

The Genitourinary System   290
Overview of Anatomy and Physiology   290
Assessment   293
Analysis   294
Planning and Implementation   294
Evaluation   297
Disorders of the Genitourinary System   297

The Musculoskeletal System   306
Overview of Anatomy and Physiology   306
Assessment   307
Analysis   308
Planning and Implementation   308
Evaluation   311
Disorders of the Musculoskeletal System   311

The Endocrine System   321
Overview of Anatomy and Physiology   321
Assessment   322
Analysis   324
Planning and Implementation   324
Evaluation   325
Disorders of the Endocrine System   325

The Integumentary System   340
Overview of Anatomy and Physiology   340
Assessment   341
Analysis   342
Planning and Implementation   342
Evaluation   342
Disorders of the Integumentary System   343

References and Suggested Readings   348

UNIT 5   PEDIATRIC NURSING   349

Growth and Development   350
General Principles   350
Assessment   350
Analysis   358
Planning and Implementation   358
Evaluation   359
Growth and Development Issues   360
Death and Dying   363

Multisystem Stressors   365
Genetic Disorders   365
Fluid and Electrolyte, Acid-Base Balances   368
Accidents, Poisonings, and Ingestion   370

The Neurosensory System   373
Variations from the Adult   373

Assessment   374
Analysis   375
Planning and Implementation   375
Evaluation   376
Disorders of the Nervous System   376

The Cardiovascular System   385
Variations from the Adult   385
Assessment   386
Analysis   387
Planning and Implementation   387
Evaluation   388
Disorders of the Cardiovascular System   388

The Hematologic System   394
Variations from the Adult   394
Assessment   394
Analysis   394
Planning and Implementation   394
Evaluation   394
Disorders of the Hematologic System   395

The Respiratory System   400
Variations from the Adult   400
Assessment   400
Analysis   401
Planning and Implementation   401
Evaluation   402
Disorders of the Respiratory System   402

The Gastrointestinal System   409
Variations from the Adult   409
Assessment   409
Analysis   409
Planning and Implementation   410
Evaluation   410
Disorders of the Gastrointestinal System   410

The Genitourinary System   416
Variations from the Adult   416
Assessment   417
Analysis   417
Planning and Implementation   417
Evaluation   417
Disorders of the Genitourinary System   417

The Musculoskeletal System   421
Variations from the Adult   421
Assessment   422
Analysis   422
Planning and Implementation   422
Evaluation   423
Disorders of the Musculoskeletal System   423

The Endocrine System   428
Variations from the Adult   428
Analysis   428
Planning and Implementation   428
Evaluation   428
Disorders of the Endocrine System   428

The Integumentary System   430
Variations from the Adult   430
Assessment   431
Analysis   431
Planning and Implementation   431
Evaluation   431
Disorders of the Integumentary System   431

Pediatric Oncology   433
  Overview   433
  Assessment   434
  Interventions   434
  Stages of Cancer Treatment   436
  Cancers   437

References and Suggested Readings   443

UNIT 6	MATERNITY AND FEMALE REPRODUCTIVE NURSING 445

Overview of Anatomy and Physiology of the Female Reproductive System   446
  Anatomy   446
  Physiology   448

The Childbearing Cycle   450
  Conception   450
  Nidation (Implantation)   450
  Developmental Stages   450
  Special Structures of Pregnancy   451
  Physical and Psychologic Changes of Pregnancy   452

The Antepartal Period   455
  Assessment   455
  Analysis   456
  Planning and Implementation   456
  Evaluation   459
  Complications of Pregnancy   459
  Pre- and Coexisting Diseases of Pregnancy   463

Labor and Delivery   468
  Overview   468
  Assessment During Labor   471
  First Stage of Labor   473
  Second Stage of Labor   474
  Third Stage of Labor   474
  Fourth Stage of Labor   475
  Complications of Labor and Delivery   475
  Analgesia and Anesthesia   479
  Operative Obstetrical Procedures   481

The Postpartum Period   485
  Overview   485
  Postpartal Psychosocial Changes   486
  Assessment   486
  Analysis   487
  Planning and Implementation   487
  Evaluation   488
  Complications of the Postpartum Period   489

The Newborn   492
  Physiologic Status of the Newborn   492
  Assessment   494
  Analysis   495
  Planning and Implementation   495
  Evaluation   496
  Variations from Normal Newborn Assessment Findings   496

The High-Risk Infant   499
  Overview   499
  Assessment   499
  Analysis   499
  Planning and Implementation   499
  Evaluation   499

  High-Risk Disorders   499
  Special Conditions in the Neonate   501

Conditions of the Female Reproductive System   506
  Fertility and Infertility   506
  Menstrual Disorders   509
  Infectious Disorders   510
  Female Reproductive System Neoplasia   511
  Menopause   513

References and Suggested Readings   516

UNIT 7	PSYCHIATRIC-MENTAL HEALTH NURSING 517

Overview of Psychiatric-Mental Health Nursing   519
  Theoretical Basis   519
  Nursing Process   522
  Analysis   523
  Planning and Implementation   523
  Evaluation   526
  Behaviors Related to Emotional Distress   526

Psychiatric Disorders (DSM IV)   530
  Disorders of Infancy, Childhood, and Adolescence   530
  Pervasive Developmental Disorders   532
  Delirium, Dementia, and Other Cognitive Disorders   534
  Substance Use Disorders   536
  Psychoactive Substance-Induced Organic Mental Disorders   536
  Schizophrenia and Other Psychotic Disorders   541
  Mood Disorders   544
  Neurotic Disorders   549
  Anxiety Disorders   549
  Somatoform Disorders   552
  Dissociative Disorders   553
  Personality Disorders   554

Psychologic Aspects of Physical Illness   556
  Stress-Related Disorders   556
  Victims of Abuse   557
  Critical Illness   559
  Chronic Illness   560
  AIDS   561
  Death and Dying   562
  Grief and Mourning   563

References and Suggested Readings   563

Appendix: Special Diets   565

Practice Tests: 577
  1   578
  2   607
  3   634
  4   663
  5   690
  6   716
  7   741
  8   769

Review Tests   799
  Universal Principles of Nursing Care Management   800
  Adult Health   815
  Pediatric Nursing   922
  Maternity and Female Reproductive System   946
  Psychiatric Nursing   977

Index   1003

REVIEW TESTS   799

**Review Test 1   Universal Principles
of Nursing Care Management**   **800**

Legal and Ethical Aspects
   of Nursing   #1-10   800
Managing Client Care   #11-15   801
Safety   #16-20   801
Principles and Interventions
   for Specific Aspects of Care   # 21-65   802

Review Test 2   Adult Health   **815**

Multisystem Stressors   #1-35   815
Aging   #36-45   818
Perioperative Nursing   #46-60   819
Oncologic Nursing   #61-75   821
The Neurosensory System   #76-120   823
The Cardiovascular System   #121-165   826
The Hematologic System   #166-185   830
The Respiratory System   #186-220   832
The Gastrointestinal System   #221-260   836
The Genitourinary System   #261-290   839
The Musculoskeletal System   #291-325   843
The Endocrine System   #326-365   847
The Integumentary System   #366-385   850

Review Test 3   Pediatric Nursing   **922**

Growth and Development   #1-15   922
Multisystem Stressors   #16-25   923
The Neurosensory System   #26-35   924
The Cardiovascular System   #36-45   925
The Hematologic System   #46-50   926
The Respiratory System   #51-60   926
The Gastrointestinal System   #61-70   927
The Genitourinary System   #71-75   928
The Musculoskeletal System   #76-85   929
The Integumentary System   #86-90   930
Pediatric Oncology   #91-100   930

**Review Test 4   Maternity and
Female Reproductive Nursing**   **946**

The Antepartal Period   #1-25   946
Labor and Delivery   #26-45   949
The Postpartum Period   #46-55   951
The Newborn   #56-70   952
The High-Risk Infant   #71-80   953
Conditions of the Female
   Reproductive System   #81-100   954

**Review Test 5   Psychiatric-Mental
Health Nursing**   **977**

Overview of Psychiatric-Mental
   Health Nursing   #1-20   977
Psychiatric Disorders   #21-90   979
Psychologic Aspects
   of Physical Illness   #91-100   985

Index of Tables

2.1 Apothecary units of weight and volume   21
2.2 Household units of liquid measure   21
2.3 Approximate equivalents to remember   21
2.4 Local anesthetics   26
2.5 Nonsteroidal anti-inflammatory drugs (NSAIDs) (NSAIDs are prostaglandin inhibitors)   28
2.6 Narcotic analgesics   29
2.7 Barbiturates   31
2.8 Benzodiazepines   32
2.9 Phenothiazines   39
2.10 Anticholinergics   44
2.11 Antiparkinson agent (Anticholinergic)   45
2.12 Antiparkinson agents (Dopaminergic agents)   46
2.13 Oxytocin-related drugs   53
2.14 Review of antiarrhythmic drugs   57
2.15 Direct-acting vasodilators   60
2.16 Drugs related to lidocaine   61
2.17 Review of antihypertensive drugs   68
2.18 Other H_2 antagonists   77
2.19 Antacids   78
2.20 Antidiarrheals   79
2.21 Laxatives   81
2.22 Urinary anti-infectives   92
2.23 Drugs commonly used to treat tuberculosis   94
2.24 Antihelmintics   96
2.25 Alkylating agents   98
2.26 Antibiotic antineoplastic agents   99
2.27 Estrogens   100
2.28 Androgens   100
2.29 Vinca alkaloids   101

3.1 Examples of crimes and torts   114
3.2 Maslow's hierarchy of needs   115
3.3 Fire hazards and prevention   118

4.1 Alterations in immune functioning   131
4.2 Minerals   134
4.3 Vitamins   135
4.4 Pain assessment   142
4.5 Fluid and electrolyte imbalances   145
4.6 Acid-base imbalances   147
4.7 Complications of IV therapy   148
4.8 Classification of shock   149
4.9 Drugs used to treat shock   150
4.10 Physical changes of aging   155

4.11 Chronic disease vs acute disease   157
4.12 Stages of anesthesia   163
4.13 Regional anesthesia   164
4.14 Seven warning signs of cancer (CAUTION)   169
4.15 Cranial nerves   176
4.16 Effects of autonomic nervous system activity   177
4.17 Complications of blood transfusion   230
4.18 Classification system for HIV infection   239
4.19 Drug therapy for peptic ulcer   275
4.20 Bowel surgeries   279
4.21 Preventing complications of immobility   308
4.22 Hormone functions   322
4.23 Characteristics of insulin preparations   335
4.24 Oral hypoglycemic agents   336
4.25 Guidelines and formulas for fluid replacement for burns   346

5.1 Recommended schedule for immunization, American Academy of Pediatrics, Committee on Infectious Disease, January 1994   359
5.2 Communicable childhood diseases   361
5.3 Types of seizures   379

6.1 Markers in fetal development   452
6.2 Methods of childbirth   458
6.3 Nonstress test (NST)   458
6.4 Contraction stress test (CST)   459
6.5 Common discomforts during pregnancy   459
6.6 Danger signals of pregnancy   460
6.7 Apgar scoring   475
6.8 Emergency delivery of an infant   479
6.9 Tips for successful breast-feeding   488

7.1 Types of therapeutic groups   525
7.2 Defense mechanisms   527
7.3 Groups at increased risk for suicide   529
7.4 Lethality assessment   530
7.5 Commonly abused drugs   537
7.6 Phases of alcohol addiction   539
7.7 Antipsychotic medications   542
7.8 Antidepressant medications   546
7.9 Types of stress-related disorders   557
7.10 Symptoms of child abuse   557
7.11 Stages of dying   562

Contributors

EDITORS

Alice M. Stein, EdD, RN
Associate Dean for Continuing Education
School of Nursing
MCP Hahnemann University
Philadelphia, Pennsylvania

Judith C. Miller, RN, MSN
President, Nursing Tutorial and Consulting Services
Clifton, Virginia

CONTRIBUTORS TO THE FOURTH EDITION

Nancy Clarkson, RN, C, MEd
Associate Professor of Nursing
Finger Lakes Community College
Canandaigua, New York

Deborah L. Dalrymple, RN, MSN, CRNI
Associate Professor of Nursing
Montgomery County Community College
Blue Bell, Pennsylvania

Jeanne Gelman, RN, MA, MSN
Professor Emeritus, Psychiatric-Mental Health Nursing
Widener University
Chester, Pennsylvania

Judith M. Hall, RNC, MSN, IBCLC, LCCE
Lactation Consultant and Childbirth Educator
Mary Washington Hospital
Fredericksburg, Virginia

Marilyn Herbert-Ashton, RN, C, MS
Director, Wellness Center
F.F. Thompson Health Systems, Inc.
Adjunct Professor of Nursing
Finger Lakes Community College
Canandaigua, New York

Nancy H. Jacobson, RN, CS, MSN
Senior Manager
The Whitman Group
Huntington Valley, Pennsylvania

Mary Lou Manning, RN, PhD, CPNP
Director, Infection Control and Occupational Health
The Children's Hospital of Philadelphia
Adjunct Assistant Professor
University of Pennsylvania School of Nursing
Philadelphia, Pennsylvania

Anne Robin Waldman, RN, C, MSN, AOCN
Clinical Nurse Specialist
Albert Einstein Medical Center
Philadelphia, Pennsylvania

CONTRIBUTORS TO PREVIOUS EDITIONS

Margaret Ahearn-Spera, RN, C, MSN
Director, Medical Patient Care Services
Danbury Hospital
Danbury, Connecticut
Assistant Clinical Professor
Yale University School of Nursing
New Haven, Connecticut

Margaret Brenner, RN, MSN
Senior Consultant, Pinnacle Healthcare Group, Inc.
Paoli, Pennsylvania

Judy Donlen, RN, DNSc
Executive Director, Southern New Jersey
Perinatal Cooperative
Pennsauken, New Jersey

Theresa M. Giglio, RD, MS
Instructor, LaSalle University
Philadelphia, Pennsylvania

Holly Hillman, RN, MSN
Assistant Professor
Montgomery County Community College
Blue Bell, Pennsylvania

Charlotte D. Kain, RN, C, EdD
Professor Nursing, Health Care of Women
Montgomery County Community College
Blue Bell, Pennsylvania

Constance O. Kolva Taylor, RN, MSN
Kolva Consulting
Harrisburg, Pennsylvania

Eileen Moran, RN, C, MSN
Clinical Educator
Abington Memorial Hospital
Abington, Pennsylvania

Marie O'Toole, RN, EdD
Associate Professor, College of Nursing
Rutgers, The State University of New Jersey
Newark, New Jersey

Janice Selekman, RN, DNSc
Professor and Chair
Department of Nursing
University of Delaware
Newark, Delaware

TEST ITEM WRITERS

Frances Amorim, RN, MSN
Clinical Lecturer
University of Pennsylvania, School of Nursing
Philadelphia, Pennsylvania

Eileen B. Augente, RN, MA, CDE
Instructor, Long Island University
Brooklyn, New York
Clinical Nurse Specialist, Diabetes
Amityville, New York

Pamela Bellefeuille, RN, CS, CEN, TRNCCP, MN
Clinical Nurse Specialist, Manager
Emergency Department, Kaiser
Santa Rosa, California

Jean E. Berry, MSN, RN
Assistant Professor
Bloomsburg University
Bloomsburg, Pennsylvania

Janice Caie-Lawrence, MSN, RN
Assistant Professor
University of Detroit Mercy
Detroit, Michigan

Susan Chaney, RN, C, MSE
Staff Nurse, Harbor View Mercy Hospital
Psychiatric Division of St. Edward Mercy Medical Center
Fort Smith, Arkansas

Jane A. Claffy, MSN, RN, C
St. Vincent's Hospital School of Nursing
New York City, New York

H. Allethaire Cullen, RNP, CS, MSN, CEN
Director of Education
Education Empowerment
Coventry, Rhode Island

Janet Curley, RN, CEN, EdD(C)
Adjunct Lecturer
Pace University
New York, New York

Sandra H. Faria, DSN, RN
Florida State University School of Nursing
Tallahassee, Florida-

Elizabeth A. Fisk, RN, MS
Associate Professor
Fitchburg State College
Fitchburg, Massachusetts

Judith M. Hall, RNC, MSN, IBCLC, LCCE
Lactation Consultant and Childbirth Educator
Mary Washington Hospital
Fredericksburg, Virginia

Shirley Sullivan Hall, RN, MS
Assistant Professor
School of Nursing Hampton University
Hampton, Virginia

Janice L. Hinkle, RN, MSN, CNRN
Instructor
Thomas Jefferson University
Philadelphia, Pennsylvania

Susan Jaskowski, RN, MSN, CCRN, CRNP
Pediatric Neurosurgery Nurse Practitioner
Penn State University Hershey Medical Center
Hershey, Pennsylvania

Nancy Kirk, RN, MSN
Lead Instructor, Medical Surgical Nursing and Pharmacology
The Health Institute of Tampa Bay
St. Petersburg, Florida

Kathleen I. Marchiondo, RN, MSN
Assistant Professor
Research College of Nursing
Kansas City, Missouri

Cheryl Martin, RNC, MSN
Associate Professor of Nursing
Bethel College
Mishawaka, Indiana

Patricia A. Middlemiss, RN, MSN
Assistant Professor of Nursing
Gwynedd-Mercy College
Gwynedd Valley, Pennsylvania

Anna P. Moore, RN, MS
Assistant Professor
Southside Regional Medical Center
School of Nursing
Petersburg, Virginia

Patricia A. Mynaugh, RN, PhD
Associate Professor
Villanova University College of Nursing
Villanova, Pennsylvania

Joan Opelia, RN, MSN
Consultant
Nursing Tutorial and Consulting Services
Clifton, Virginia

Lynda C. Opdyke, RN, MSN
Facilitator, Academic Affairs
Mercy School of Nursing
Charlotte, North Carolina

Deborah L. Panning, RN, C, MSN
Unit Manager
Brandywine Hospital School of Nursing
Coatesville, Pennsylvania

Carol Park, RN, CS, MSN
School of Nursing
Sentara Norfolk General Hospital
Norfolk, Virginia

Mary Reuland, RN, MS
College of St. Catherine
Minneapolis Campus
Minneapolis, Minnesota

Kathy Rodgers, RN, MSN, CNS, CCRN, CEN
Critical Care Clinical Nurse Specialist
St. Elizabeth Hospital
Beaumont, Texas

Mary Jean Ricci, MSN, RN, C
Holy Family College
Philadelphia, Pennsylvania

Nancy G. Runton, MSN, CPNP
Pediatric Nurse Practitioner
Virginia Pediatric Group, LTD
Fairfax, Virginia

Linda F. Samson, PhD, RNC, CNAA
Dean, School of Health Sciences
Clayton State College
Morrow, Georgia

Fran Schuda, MSN, RN, CCRN
Director, Training and Development
Episcopal Hospital
Philadelphia, Pennsylvania

Ruth Schumacher, RN, MSN
Lecturer, Department of Maternal-Child Nursing
College of Nursing
The University of Illinois at Chicago
Chicago, Illinois

Cheryl J. Smally, RN, MSN, MSS
St. Luke's College of Nursing and Health Sciences
Sioux City, Iowa

Lorry L. Smith, RN, MSN
Clinical Instructor, Baccalaureate Nursing
Eastern Kentucky University
Richmond, Kentucky

Diane L. Spatz, PhD, RN, C
University of Pennsylvania
Philadelphia, Pennsylvania

Martha L. Tanicala, MSN, RN, CPN
Instructor
St. Vincent Medical Center School of Nursing
Toledo, Ohio

Susanne M. Tracy, RN, MN, MA
Associate Professor
Rivier—St. Joseph School of Nursing
Nashua, New Hampshire

Rosemarie Trouton, MSN, RN
Clinical Nurse Educator, Pediatrics
Hershey Medical Center
Hershey, Pennsylvania

Wanda May Webb, MSN, RN, CS
Level Coordinator
Brandywine School of Nursing
Coatesville, Pennsylvania

Mary Jo Westien, APRN, CS, MS
Brigham Young University
Provo, Utah

Diane Wieland, RN, CS, MSN
Assistant Professor
Thomas Jefferson University
College of Allied Health Sciences
Department of Nursing
Philadelphia, Pennsylvania

Judy Winterhalter, DNSc, RN, CS
Associate Professor
Gwynedd-Mercy College
Gwynedd Valley, Pennsylvania
Psychotherapist
North Penn Counseling Center
Lansdale, Pennsylvania

Evelyn Wolynies, RN, MSN
Clinical Nurse Specialist
Neuropsych Huntington's Disease
University of Medicine and Dentistry of New Jersey
Cooper Hospital
Camden, New Jersey

Catherine Y. Zion, RN, MS
Clinical Instructor
Macon College School of Nursing
Macon, Georgia

Preface

This book has been developed expressly to meet your needs as you study and prepare for the all-important NCLEX-RN™ examination. Taking this exam is always a stressful event in the best of circumstances: It constitutes a major career milestone, and NCLEX success is the key to your future ability to practice as a registered nurse.

ORGANIZATION, CONTENT, AND FEATURES

The content and design of this revised edition have been carefully crafted to conform to the NCLEX-RN™ test plan effective April 1998, beginning with an introductory unit on how to prepare for NCLEX-RN™. This includes:
- Explanation of the test plan
- Information on how the test is constructed
- Information on the new CAT examination
- Data on scoring and notification of results
- Tips on how to plan your study and prepare successfully

The highly acclaimed unit "Drugs and Nursing Implications" groups drugs by classification and similarities to aid you in consolidating this pertinent but sometimes overwhelming information. This unit includes:
- Case studies that apply relevant drug content
- Prototypes for most drug classification
- Mechanism of drug action
- Uses
- Adverse effects
- Nursing implications
- Discharge teaching
- Related drugs and their variance from the prototype
- Practice test questions

The recently added unit on *Universal Principles of Nursing Care Management* includes:
- Nursing practice standards;
- Legal and ethical aspects of nursing;
- Client care management issues such as determining priorities, working with the health care team, making assignments, and coordinating client care;
- Safety considerations regarding fire, electricity, equipment, and the use of physical restraints;
- Principles and interventions for specific aspects of care, including: body mechanics; transfer and movement principles and techniques; positioning; application of cold and external heat; asepsis; and pressure sores.

The units that follow concentrate on adult nursing, pediatric nursing, maternity and female reproductive nursing, and psychiatric-mental health nursing. The *Psychiatric-Mental Health Nursing* unit has been *updated to reflect DSM IV changes*. A section on aging is included in the unit on adult nursing.

Each unit includes:
- The nursing process (utilizing all five steps) integrated with a body-systems approach
  - Assessment: reviews both history and physical examination
  - Analysis: includes appropriate NANDA nursing diagnoses
  - Planning: discusses client goals
  - Implementation: provides interventions to achieve client goals
  - Evaluation: lists outcome criteria
- Introductory review of anatomy and physiology, and basic theories/principles
- Review of pertinent disorders for each system including:
  - General characteristics
  - Pathophysiology/psychopathology
  - Medical management
  - Assessment data
  - Nursing intervention/client education
- Sample test questions, structured like those on the NCLEX-RN™, so you can evaluate yourself as you study. *This edition contains hundreds of additional questions.* The *expanded rationales* follow the questions so you can easily check your answers.
- References and Suggested Readings—at the end of each unit—further supplement your studying.
- Updated and expanded information on selected disorders, theories, and therapies

There are eight *100-question* practice tests. These tests include:
- Practice questions similar to the NCLEX-RN™
- Correct answers with *expanded rationales* and a key to categorize each question according to the test plan, including phases of the nursing process, client needs classification, and levels of cognitive ability.
- Practice tests and sample questions feature the *stand-alone questions* now included on the NCLEX exam.

New to this edition are five review tests containing an additional 750 NCLEX style questions. Each test corresponds to one of the book's units.

Within each review test, the questions are grouped by specific topics.

A guide depicting the review test breakdown can be found on page ix.

The five tests are:
- Universal Principles of Nursing Care Management
- Maternity and Female Reproductive Nursing
- Pediatric Nursing
- Psychiatric-Mental Health Nursing
- Adult Nursing

The appendix provides readily accessible information on special diets.

The practice disk included at the back of the book features two 100-question tests that you may take either in test mode or learning mode. These are *additional* review questions that simulate the computerized exam, using the same keys used on the actual NCLEX exam. The two test options are as follows:

1. You may take the practice tests with immediate answers and rationales, in which you will be given immediate feedback after each question. The feedback consists of an explanation for the correct answer as well as an explanation for each of the incorrect choices.
2. Or you may take the practice tests without this feedback. If you choose this option, after you have completed the questions in the tests, you will receive a

score. You can also review all questions answered incorrectly.

This experience enables them to organize and present, clearly and concisely, what seems to be an overwhelming amount of information. They have used an easy-to-follow outline format that emphasizes key content and frequently tested areas, as well as areas that tend to present difficulty for the graduate nurse.

We are all committed, through continuing education, to help you reach your fullest professional potential. Collectively, the authors and editors of this book have many years of experience helping nurses to pass their NCLEX-RN™ exams. The publisher views helping you to pass the NCLEX-RN™ as a major commitment. We believe that our experience has enabled us to produce a book that will fully meet your needs.

We thank the MCP Hahnemann University for granting us permission to use selected test items from the RN/MCP Home Study Program. Use of these items has enhanced the quality of this work substantially.

Alice M. Stein
Judith C. Miller
Editors

List of Abbreviations

AA	Alcoholics Anonymous	CHO	carbohydrate
ABGs	arterial blood gases	Cl	chloride
ABE	acute bacterial endocarditis	CL	cognitive level
ac	before meals	cm	centimeter
ACOA	Adult Children of Alcoholics	CN	client need
ACE	angiotensin-converting enzyme	CNM	certified nurse midwife
ACh	acetylcholine	CNS	central nervous system
ACTH	adrenocorticotropic hormone	Co	comprehension
ADA	American Dietetic Association	CO_2	carbon dioxide
ADH	antidiuretic hormone	COPD	chronic obstructive pulmonary disease
ADL	activities of daily living	CP	cerebral palsy
AFB	acid-fast bacillus	CPAP	continuous positive airway pressure
AIDS	acquired immune deficiency syndrome	CPD	cephalopelvic disproportion
AK	above the knee	CPK	creatine phosphokinase
ALG	antilymphocytic globulin	CPR	cardiopulmonary resuscitation
ALL	acute lymphocytic leukemia	C&S	culture and sensitivity
ALT	alanine aminotransferase	CSF	cerebrospinal fluid
An	analysis	CST	contraction stress test
ANA	American Nurses Association *or* antinuclear antibodies	CT	computed tomography
		CTZ	chemoreceptor trigger zone
ANLL	acute nonlymphocytic leukemia	CV	cardiovascular
ANS	autonomic nervous system	CVA	cerebrovascular accident
Ap	application	CVP	central venous pressure
A-P	anterior-posterior	CVS	chorionic villi sampling
APTT	activated partial thromboplastin time	D&C	dilatation and currettage
ARC	AIDS-related complex	DDAVP	desmopressin
ARDS	adult respiratory distress syndrome	DDST	Denver Developmental Screening Test
As	assessment	DES	diethylstilbestrol
ASA	acetylsalicyclic acid (aspirin)	DIC	disseminated intravascular coagulation
ASD	atrial septal defect	dl	deciliter
ASO	antistreptolysin	DMT	a hallucinogen
AST	aspartate aminotransferase	DNA	deoxyribonucleic acid
ATG	antithymocytic globulin	DPT	diphtheria, pertussis, and tetanus toxoid
ATN	acute tubular necrosis	dr	dram
ATP	adenosine triphosphate	DT	diphtheria and tetanus toxoid
AV	atrial-ventricular	DTs	delirium tremens
AZT	Zidovudine	DTaP	diphtheria-tetanus-acellular pertussis vaccine
BCG	Bacillus Calmette-Guérin		
BID	twice a day	DTP	diphtheria, tetanus, and pertussis toxoid
BK	below the knee	DVT	deep vein thrombosis
BMR	basal metabolic rate	ECG	electrocardiogram
B&O	suppositories containing belladonna	ECT	electroconvulsive therapy
BP	blood pressure	EDC	estimated date of confinement
BPD	bronchopulmonary dysplasia	EEG	electroencephalogram
BPH	benign prostatic hypertrophy	EKG	electrocardiogram
BSE	breast self-examination	EMG	electromyography
BUN	blood urea nitrogen	ENT	ear, nose, throat
CABG	coronary artery bypass graft	EP	erythrocyte protoporphyrin
C	Celsius	ERT	estrogen replacement therapy
Ca	calcium	ESR	erythrocyte sedimentation rate
CAD	coronary artery disease	ETOH	ethyl alcohol
CAT	computerized adaptive testing	Ev	evaluation
CBC	complete blood count	fl dr	fluid dram
cc	cubic centimeter	fl oz	fluid ounce
CCK-PZ	cholecystokinin and pancreozymin	F	Farenheit
CCU	coronary care unit	FAD	flavin adenine dinucleotide
CDC	Centers for Disease Control and Prevention	FDA	Food and Drug Administration
		FHT	fetal heart tracing
CEA	carcinoembryonic antigen	FHR	fetal heart rate
CF	cystic fibrosis	FSH	follicle-stimulating hormone
CHD	congenital heart disease	FSP	fibrin split products
CHF	congestive heart failure	ft	feet

FTT	failure to thrive
g	gauge *or* gram
GI	gastrointestinal
gr	grain
gtts	drops
GTT	glucose tolerance test
GU	genitourinary
GVHD	graft versus host disease
h	hour
H_2	histamine 2
HBIG	hepatitis B immunoglobulin
HBV	hepatitis B vaccine
HCG	human chorionic gonadotropin
HCl	hydrochloric acid *or* hydrochloride
HCO_3	bicarbonate
HCS/HPL	human chorionic somatomammotropin/ human placental lactogen
He	health promotion/maintenance
HELLP	hemolysis, elevated liver enzymes, lowered platelets
Hct	hematocrit
Hg	mercury
Hgb	hemoglobin
$HgbA_{1c}$	Hemoglobin A_{1c}
HgbS	abnormal hemoglobin seen in sickle-cell anemia
Hib	*Haemophilus influenzae* type B
HIV	human immunodeficiency virus
HLA	human leukocyte antigen
HMD	hyaline membrane disease
HNP	herniated nucleus pulposus
H_2O	water
H_2O_2	hydrogen peroxide
hrs	hours
HS	hour of sleep
HSV_2	herpes simplex virus type 2
I & O	intake and output
I&Os	intake and outputs
IA	intra-arterial
ICP	intracranial pressure
ICU	intensive care unit
ID	identification
IDDM	insulin-dependent diabetes mellitus
IDM	infant of diabetic mother
IgG	immunoglobulin G
IM	intramuscular
Im	implementation
IMV	intermittent mandatory ventilation
in	inch
INH	isoniazid
IPPB	intermittent positive pressure breathing
IQ	intelligence quotient
ISG	immune serum globulin
ITP	idiopathic thrombocytopenic purpura
IU	international units
IUD	intrauterine devices
IUGR	intrauterine growth retardation
IV	intravenous
IVP	intravenous pyelogram
JRA	juvenile rheumatoid arthritis
K	potassium or knowledge (in question code at back of book)
kcal	kilocalories
KCl	potassium chloride
kg	kilogram
KUB	kidney, ureter, bladder
L	liter
lb	pound
LDH	lactic dehydrogenase
LE	lupus erythematosus
LGA	large for gestational age
LH	luteinizing hormone
LOA	left occiput anterior
LOC	level of consciousness
LOP	left occiput posterior
LP	lumbar puncture
LPN	licensed practical nurse
L/S	lecithin/sphingomyelin
LSD	lysergic acid diethylamide
LVN	licensed vocational nurse
m	meter *or* minim
min	minim *or* minutes
MAO	monamine oxidase
MAOI	monamine oxidase inhibitors
MAR	medication administration record
mcg	microgram
MCT	medium chain triglycerides
MD	medical doctor
mEq	milliequivalent
mg	milligram
Mg	magnesium
MI	myocardial infarction
ml	milliliter
MLC	mixed leukocyte culture
mm	millimeter
MMR	measles, mumps, rubella
MOM	milk of magnesia
MRI	magnetic resonance imaging
MSH	melanocyte-stimulating hormone
mU	milliunit
Na	sodium
NANDA	North American Nursing Diagnosis Association
NEC	necrotizing enterocolitis
ng	nannograms
NG	nasogastric
NIDDM	non–insulin-dependent diabetes mellitus
NP	nursing process
NPO	nothing by mouth
NS	normal saline
NSAIDs	nonsteroidal anti-inflammatory drugs
NSS	normal saline solution
NST	nonstress test
O_2	oxygen
OB-Gyn	obstetrics-gynecology
OBS	organic brain syndrome
OCD	obsessive-compulsive disorder
OCT	oxytocin challenge test
OD	right eye
OMD	organic mental disorder
OOB	out of bed
OPV	oral polio vaccine
OR	operating room
OS	left eye
OTC	over-the-counter
OU	both eyes
oz	ounce
P	pulse
PA	pulmonary artery
PABA	paraaminobenzoic acid
PACU	postanesthesia care unit
PAP	pulmonary artery pressure
Pap	Papanicoleau
PCA	patient-controlled analgesia
pCO_2	partial pressure of carbon dioxide

PCP	*Pneumocystis carinii* pneumonia *or* phencyclidine		ROM	range of motion
PCWP	pulmonary capillary wedge pressure		ROP	right occiput posterior
PDA	patient ductus arteriosus		S_3	third heart sound
PEEP	positive-end expiratory pressure		SA	sinoatrial
PG	phosphatidylglycerol		Sa	safe, effective care environment
PGE_2	prostaglandin E_2		SBE	subacute bacterial endocarditis
Ph	physiological integrity		SC	subcutaneous
PICCs	peripherally implanted central catheters		SGA	small for gestational age
PID	pelvic inflammatory disease		SGOT	serum glutamic-oxylacetic transaminase
PIH	pregnancy-induced hypertension		SGPT	serum glutamic-pyruvic transaminase
PKU	phenylketonuria		SIDS	sudden infant death syndrome
Pl	planning		SL	sublingual
PMI	point of maximal impulse		SLE	systemic lupus erythematosus
PND	paroxysmal noctural dyspnea		STD	sexually transmitted disease
PNS	parasympathetic nervous system *or* peripheral nervous system		T	temperature or thoracic
			TB	tuberculosis
PO	by mouth		TBI	total body irradiation
pO_2	partial pressure of oxygen		tbsp	tablespoon
post-op	postoperative (after surgery)		TCAs	tricyclic antidepressants
PPD	purified protein derivative		Td	adult tetanus toxoid and diphtheria toxoid
PPN	peripheral parenteral nutrition		TEF	tracheoesophageal fistula
pre-op	preoperative		TENS	transcutaneous electrical nerve stimulator
prep	preparation			
prn	as needed		TET	tetralogy
Ps	psychosocial integrity		THC	tetrahydrocannabinol
PSA	prostate-specific antigen		TIA	transient ischemic attack
PT	prothrombin time		TID	three times a day
PTCA	percutaneous transluminal coronary angioplasty		TPN	total parenteral nutrition
			TPP	thiamin pyrophosphate
PTH	parathormone		TSE	testicular self-examination
PTSD	posttraumatic stress disorder		TSH	thyroid-stimulating hormone
PTT	partial thromboplastin time		tsp	teaspoon
PTU	propylthiouracil		TUR	transurethral resection
PUBS	percutaneous umbilical blood sampling		TURP	transurethral prostatectomy
PUC	pediatric urine collector		u	units
PVC	premature ventricular contraction *or* polyvinyl chloride		UC	ulcerative colitis
			µg	microgram
PVD	peripheral vascular disease		URI	upper respiratory infection
q	every		UTI	urinary tract infection
QID	four times a day		VBAC	vaginal birth after cesarean
R	respirations		VDRL	Venereal Disease Reactive Laboratory
RA	rheumatoid arthritis		VER	visual evoked response
RAIU	radioactive iodine uptake		VF	ventricular fibrillation
RBC	red blood cell		VMA	vanillylmandelic acid
RDA	recommended daily allowances		VS	vital signs
RDS	respiratory distress syndrome		VSD	ventricular septal defect
RF	rheumatic fever		VT	ventricular tachycardia
RIA	radioimunoassay		WBC	white blood count or white blood cell
RN	registered nurse		WBCs	white blood cells
RNA	ribonucleic acid		wk	week
ROA	right occiput anterior		<	less than
			>	greater than

Unit 1

Preparing for the NCLEX Examination

Anne Robin Waldman, RN, C, MSN, OCN

This first unit of the NCLEX-RN™ REVIEW will provide you with the important information you need to know about the construction of the National Council Licensure Examination for Registered Nurses (NCLEX-RN™, often referred to as "State Boards"), with tips on how to study and with test-taking techniques you can use to improve your success when writing the examination.

UNIT OUTLINE

2 Understanding the NCLEX Examination

4 Preparation and Test Taking

Understanding the NCLEX Examination

THE TEST PLAN

The NCLEX-RN™ examination questions are based on a test plan comprising the categories of client needs with concepts and processes fundamental to the practice of nursing integrated throughout the categories.

Categories of Client Needs

The health care needs of the client are grouped under four broad categories with several subcategories.

A. Safe, Effective Care Environment
1. Management of care includes 7–13% of test items. This includes but is not limited to the following:
    a. advanced directives
    b. advocacy
    c. case management
    d. client rights
    e. concepts of management
    f. confidentiality
    g. continuity of care
    h. continuous quality improvement
    i. delegation
    j. ethical practice
    k. incident/irregular occurrence reports
    l. informed consent
    m. legal responsibilities
    n. organ donation
    o. consultation and referrals
    p. resource management
    q. supervision
2. Safety and infection control comprises 5–11% of test items. This includes but is not limited to the following:
    a. accident prevention
    b. disaster planning
    c. use of restraints
    d. standard (universal) and other precautions
    e. medical and surgical asepsis
    f. error prevention
    g. handling hazardous and infectious materials

B. Health Promotion and Maintenance
3. Growth and development through the life span comprises 7–13% of test questions and includes but is not limited to the following:
    a. aging process
    b. ante/intra/postpartum and newborn
    c. expected body image changes
    d. developmental stages and transitions
    e. family planning
    f. family systems
    g. human sexuality
4. Prevention and Early Detection of Disease comprises 5–11% of test questions and includes but is not limited to the following:
    a. disease prevention
    b. health and wellness
    c. health promotion programs
    d. health screening
    e. lifestyle changes
    f. immunizations
    g. techniques of physical assessment

C. Psychosocial Integrity
5. Coping and Adaptation comprises 5–11% of test questions and includes but is not limited to:
    a. coping mechanisms
    b. sensory/perceptual alterations
    c. counseling techniques
    d. situational role changes
    e. grief and loss
    f. stress management
    g. mental health concepts
    h. support systems
    i. unexpected body image changes
    j. religious and spiritual influences on health
6. Psychosocial Adaptation comprises 5–11% of test questions and includes but is not limited to:
    a. behavioral interventions
    b. elder abuse/neglect
    c. chemical dependency
    d. psychopathology
    e. child abuse/neglect
    f. sexual abuse
    g. crisis intervention
    h. therapeutic milieu
    i. domestic violence

D. Physiological Integrity
7. Basic care and comfort comprises 7–13% of test questions and includes but is not limited to:
    a. assistive devices
    b. nutrition and oral hydration
    c. elimination
    d. mobility/immobility
    e. personal hygiene
    f. rest and sleep
    g. non-pharmacological comfort interventions
8. Pharmacological and parenteral therapies comprise 5–11% of test questions and includes but is not limited to:
    a. central venous access devices

     b. total parenteral nutrition
     c. parenteral fluids
     d. intravenous therapy
     e. medication administration
     f. chemotherapy
     g. pharmacological agents
     h. expected effects
     i. pharmacological actions
     j. side effects
     k. untoward effects
     l. administration of blood and blood products

9. Reduction of risk potential comprises 12–18% of test question and includes but is not limited to:
     a. alteration in body systems
     b. pathophysiology
     c. diagnostic tests
     d. lab values
     e. therapeutic procedures
     f. potential complications of diagnostic tests, procedures, surgery, and health alterations

10. Physiological Adaptation comprises 12–18% of test questions and includes but is not limited to:
     a. alterations in body systems
     b. pathophysiology
     c. fluid and electrolyte imbalances
     d. radiation therapy
     e. hemodynamics
     f. infectious diseases
     g. respiratory care
     h. unexpected response to therapies
     i. medical emergencies

E. Integrated concepts and processes include nursing process, caring, communication, cultural awareness, documentation, self-care, and teaching/learning.

The majority of questions are written at the application and/or analysis level of cognitive ability.

Levels of Cognitive Ability

The test also evaluates four of the cognitive abilities defined by Bloom et al. (1956): recall, comprehension, application, and analysis. While all four of these levels are evaluated, emphasis is placed on the higher functions of application and analysis. The four are defined as

A. Knowledge base: involves the ability to recall information.
B. Comprehension: involves the ability to understand what is being communicated and make use of the information without necessarily relating it to other information.
C. Application: requires the ability to remember and apply principles, procedures, and theories.
D. Analysis: requires the ability to break down a communication into the hierarchy of its parts and recognize the relationship among the ideas.

HOW THE TEST IS CONSTRUCTED

A. The National Council of State Boards of Nursing Inc. is the central organization for the independent member boards of nursing, which includes the 50 states, the District of Columbia, Guam, and the Virgin Islands. The member boards are divided into four regional areas, which supervise the selection of test item writers (representing educators and clinicians), whose names are suggested by the individual state boards of nursing. This provides for regional representation in the testing of nursing practice.
B. The National Council contracts with a professional testing service to supervise writing and validation of test items by the item writers. This professional service works closely with the Examination Committee of the National Council in the test development process. The National Council and the state boards are responsible for the administration and security of the test.
C. The exam is a computer exam known as CAT, which stands for Computerized Adaptive Testing. The exam is taken on a computer utilizing state-of-the-art technology. All questions are multiple choice. The computer screen will display the question and the answer choices (see Figure 1.1). Computer skills are not essential. Only two keys are used during the exam. Each candidate is oriented to the computer before the exam starts. Because the exam is geared to the candidate's skill level, each candidate will have a unique exam. Each exam will include some experimental questions. The experimental questions are interspersed throughout the examination so the candidate will answer all questions with equal effort. Some candidates will be finished in a little over an hour; others will take up to five hours. A break is scheduled during the exam.
D. The exam is given at Sylvan Technology Centers across the United States. The candidate submits credentials to the State Board of Nursing in the state in which licensure is desired. Once the credentials are accepted, the candidate calls the testing service for an appointment, which will be scheduled within 30 days.

HOW THE TEST IS SCORED

A. The NCLEX-RN™ is scored by computer and a pass/fail grade is reported.
B. A criterion-referenced approach is used to set the passing score. This provides for the

candidate's test performance to be compared with a consistent standard of criteria.

HOW CANDIDATES ARE NOTIFIED OF RESULTS

A. Approximately two to three weeks after administration of the CAT test, candidates are notified of their success or failure by the board of nursing of the state in which they wrote the examination.
B. Successful candidates are notified that they have passed.
C. Unsuccessful candidates are provided with a diagnostic profile that describes their overall performance on a scale from low to high, and their performance on the questions testing their abilities to meet client needs.

Question 1

Background	Question
Harold Sorenson, a 19-year-old unmarried college student is admitted unconscious following a car accident. He is hemorrhaging from severe internal injuries.	Which statement is true concerning obtaining informed consent for treating Mr. Sorenson? Answers (1) Emergency care can be given because his injuries are life threatening. (2) He can sign his own consent form because he is over 18. (3) Parental consent must be obtained before treatment is started. (4) The hospital must obtain a court order before treating Mr. Sorenson.

Question 2

Question	Answers
An adult client is to have abdominal surgery this morning. Immediately preoperatively the nurse must ensure that he:	(1) is comfortable. (2) has an empty bowel. (3) practices coughing. (4) voids.

FIGURE 1.1   Sample screen displays for computerized adaptive testing

Preparation and Test Taking

USING THE TEST PLAN TO YOUR BEST ADVANTAGE

Performing a Self-needs Analysis

The first step to take when preparing to study for the NCLEX-RN™ is to perform a self-needs analysis to identify your knowledge base in relation to the information provided in the test plan.
A. Look carefully at the elements of the test plan (Categories of Client Needs) that are reported to those failing the test.
B. Go through your notes and text references. Select what is important and star, underline, or highlight this information.
C. Categorize this information in terms of material that needs to be learned or material that needs only to be reviewed.

Planning for Study

A. Look at the period of time available to you for study between now and when you are scheduled to take the NCLEX-RN™. Ideally, plan to study up to four nights before the test, allow three nights for review, and the night before the test for relaxation. If you have limited time for study, plan your time so that you have at least one night for nothing but review.

B. Identify your maximum concentration time for profitable study. It is better to block out short periods of time (45–60 minutes, interspersed with planned breaks) that can be quality study time, rather than setting aside three hours of time to study, which may only produce 90 minutes of quality study time.

C. When you decide what your maximum time for profitable study is, then that is the block of time you should set aside on a regular basis for study purposes. Within the confines of your allocated study time, make sure you establish a schedule that permits you to cover completely all the material to be learned.

How to Study

A. To promote maximum concentration, ensure that your study materials are your prime area of focus.

B. Make sure you are mentally alert and in a room where you will be free from outside interruptions. If possible, choose a room with no telephone.

C. Do not smoke, do not nibble on snacks, and do not answer the telephone. This will allow you to direct your energy to the study activity.

D. Proceed with your planned study periods in an organized manner by choosing an approach that will be meaningful to you. Some content lends itself to study using concepts, while other content is best studied using systems.

E. Use methods of memory improvement that will work for you. Mnemonic devices (where a letter represents the first letter of each item in a sequence) are an effective means of retrieving material. Mental imagery is the technique of forming pictures in your mind to help you remember details of the sequence of events, such as the administration of an injection. Try practicing self-recitation to improve your study habits. Reciting to yourself the material being learned will promote retention of information being studied. Concentrate on the information you identified in your self-needs analysis as needing to be learned.

F. The final step of your study program involves organizing the material so that you will be able to learn all the "need to learn" and review all the "need to review" information within the allotted study time period. Your schedule should have allowed you to complete your review so you can close your books and do something relaxing on the night before the examination.

FINAL PREPARATION FOR TEST TAKING

In addition to having studied appropriately to assure yourself of a good knowledge base, there are measures you can take to be in prime physiologic and psychologic shape for writing the examination.

Physiologic Readiness

To prime yourself physiologically, you should meet your own needs for nutrition, sleep, and comfort.

A. You will function best if you are well nourished.
  1. Plan to eat three well-balanced meals a day for at least three days prior to the examination.
  2. Be careful when choosing the food you consume within 24 hours of the examination.
    a. Avoid foods that will make you thirsty or cause intestinal distress.
    b. Minimize the potential of a full bladder midway through the examination by limiting the amount of fluids you drink and by allowing sufficient time at the test site to use the bathroom before entering the room.

B. Assess your sleep needs.
  1. Determine the minimal amount of sleep you need in order to function effectively.
  2. Plan to allow sufficient time in your schedule the week before the examination to provide yourself with the minimum sleep you need to function effectively for at least three days prior to the examination.

C. Plan your wardrobe ahead of time.
  1. Shoes and clothes that fit you comfortably will not distract your thought processes during the examination.
  2. Include a comfortable sweater.
  3. Your clothes for the test day should be ready to wear by the night before the examination.

D. If you wear glasses or contact lenses, take along an extra pair of glasses.

E. If you are taking medications on a regular basis, continue to do so during this period of time. Introduction of new medications should be avoided until after completion of the examination.

Reducing Psychologic Stress

While a certain amount of anxiety will stimulate your nervous system to focus keenly on the examination, excess anxiety will interfere with your ability to concentrate on the examination and, indeed, hinder your success. You must approach the examination with a positive attitude. You have graduated from a school of nursing that has prepared you to provide safe and effective nursing care to your clients. Trust that the curriculum in your school of nursing was designed to include all the important concepts and principles necessary for safe nursing practice. Most of the tests you wrote while in school were developed in the style used for the NCLEX-RN™. Keeping these points in mind will enable you to approach the examination with a positive frame of reference for success.

Minimize the anxiety-producing situations related to writing the examination by carefully planning your pre-examination activities. Make a list of the important things you need to accomplish.

A. Rehearse the route or means of transportation you plan to take to the test location, preferably at the same time of the day on which you actually will be going. Check your local resources for road conditions that might necessitate altering your planned route. In your time assessment, include parking your car, locating where you are to report for registration, and locating the bathrooms. To ensure adequate travel time and to minimize stress related to getting to the test site on time the morning of the test, add an extra 30 minutes to the total time needed for the rehearsal run.

B. Have your admission materials readily available.

C. If you are staying overnight near the test site, be sure you pack everything you will need. Before retiring for the night, make your rehearsal run to the test location in preparation for the next day.

D. Plan to use relaxation exercises to control your anxiety level. If you have been using a specific method of relaxation successfully, then continue using it during this period of time. If you have not, consider trying one of the following.
   1. Active progressive relaxation (Flynn, 1980): requires a quiet environment, a comfortable sitting position, and progressive tension and relaxation of individual muscle groups.
   2. Guided imagery: requires using your imagination to create a relaxing sensory scene on which to concentrate.
   3. Breathing exercises.
   4. Relaxation response (Benson, 1975): requires a quiet environment, a mental device, a passive attitude, and a comfortable position.

E. For any of the methods to achieve the desired results, you must be willing to commit the time necessary to implement their prescribed protocols.

TAKING THE TEST

While having a good knowledge base is important for success in test-taking situations, the following strategies can be used to maximize your skill in choosing the correct answers.

A. Take your seat and give yourself an opportunity to implement the method of relaxation you have been practicing.

B. Read the directions carefully, and then be sure to follow them carefully.

C. Plan to manage your time effectively. While taking the CAT test, work steadily. You do not have to answer a specific number of questions in a given time period. If you take the maximum length of time, your score will reflect the number of questions you have completed. Depending on how you answer questions, your test may be completed in a little over an hour, or it may take up to five hours to complete.

D. Read the stem of the question carefully. This is the part of the question that describes what is being asked.

E. Read the stem a second time to be clear about what the question is asking.

F. Move to the four answer choices. One will be correct and three incorrect. Incorrect answers are called distractors.

G. Carefully evaluate the answer choices for key words. Be sure to appreciate the universality of words such as *each, all, never,* and *none;* the limitations of words such as *rarely, most,* and *least;* and the latitude offered by words such as *usually, frequently,* and *often.*

H. Read each option twice. Use the space bar on the keyboard to highlight each answer choice.

I. Answer it by saying to yourself
   1. *Yes,* it answers what is being asked.
   2. *No,* it does not answer what is being asked.
   3. *Maybe* it answers what is being asked.

J. Use this procedure for all four answer choices. When you first read the question, if an obvious answer comes to mind, restrain your desire to look for it in the answer choices. Read all four choices to make sure your thought was indeed the only *yes* answer. If you are fortunate enough to have only one *yes* answer, then you have eliminated the three distractors.

K. If you identified more than one *yes* option, then evaluate those in terms of which is more *yes* than *maybe.* If you have no *yes* answer, then evaluate the *maybe* choices for one that leans more toward *yes.*

L. Always choose the answer that has the highest likelihood for being *yes* (correct). Look critically at the answer choices for clues. If you see choices that are opposites, frequently one is the correct answer. For example

---

During insertion of a central venous catheter, the patient should be in
   1. a supine position.
   2. Trendelenburg's position.

3. reverse Trendelenburg's position.
4. a high-Fowler's position.

Choices 2 and 3 are opposites, and in this case 2 is the correct answer.

M. If you have an answer that contains more than one option, all of the options must be correct for that choice to be correct. If you can eliminate one of the options in an answer, you can automatically eliminate the other answer choices with that option. For example

Metabolic complications from the administration of TPN include
1. hyperglycemia and hypocalcemia.
2. hyperglycemia and hyperkalemia.
3. hypoglycemia and hypercalcemia.
4. hyperkalemia and hypercalcemia.

Hypercalcemia and hyperkalemia are distractors. Eliminate the choices with these options and there is only one correct choice remaining.

N. Look for options that do not meet the requirements of the stem. For example

A drug that is used to lyse (break up) already formed clots is
1. warfarin sodium (Coumadin).
2. heparin sodium (Lipo-Hepin).
3. streptokinase (Kabikinase).
4. vitamin K.

Choices 1, 2, and 3 are all used in the treatment of formed clots. Choice 4 is necessary for clot formation and therefore does not meet the requirements for the stem and must be eliminated as a possibility. Now choose among the remaining options. 3 is correct.

O. If the stem asks for the exception or which choice is not the answer, you are looking for the *no* answer rather than the *yes* answer. For example

Individuals at risk of getting TB include all of the following EXCEPT
1. lower socioeconomic groups.
2. malnourished and debilitated individuals.
3. individuals on steroid therapy.
4. white females with a history of alcohol abuse.

Choices 1, 2, and 3 are all at risk and therefore, *yes* responses. Choice 4 is the *no* response and, therefore, the correct answer.

P. Be careful to avoid reading elements into the question that are not specifically included in the stem and answer choices.

Q. When you have decided on an answer, press the return key. The computer will ask if this is your desired answer choice. If it is, then press the enter key again and your choice will be recorded. If you wish to review the answer choices again, use the space bar to do so and then press the enter key when you have made your decision. The computer will again ask if this is your desired answer choice. If it is, then press the enter key again to record your choice.

HOW TO USE THIS BOOK

As you go through each unit of this book, use it to perform your self-needs analysis and as a basis for study. You will make the best use of both your time and the book if you use the study skills suggested earlier in this unit.

A. For more detailed information on the particular subjects you feel need extra study, review those subjects in current textbooks, and scan the list of suggested readings at the end of each unit for further resources.
B. The questions interspersed throughout Units 2 through 7 are typical of the board questions, and they will help you to become more familiar with the style of questions found in the NCLEX-RN™.
C. When setting up your study time include time to take the practice tests on the enclosed disk in the back of this book. You may take these tests once, before you start studying, to help you with your needs analysis. When you have completed studying, you may take them again, to evaluate for test performance.
D. While taking the practice tests, apply the test-taking strategies discussed earlier in this unit.

References and Suggested Readings

Benson, H. (1975). *The relaxation response.* New York: Morrow.
Benson, H., & Proctor, W. (1985). *Beyond the relaxation response.* New York: Berkley.
Bloom, B., et al. (Eds.) (1956). Taxonomy of educational objections. *Handbook I, The cognitive domain.* New York: Longmans, Green.
Carpenito, L. (1996). *Nursing diagnosis: Application to clinical practice.* Philadelphia: J. B. Lippincott Co.
Flynn, P. (1980). *Holistic health: The art and science of care.* Bowie, MD: Brady.
Levy, J. (1989). *The fine arts of relaxation and meditation.* New York: Wisdom Publications.

Unit 2

Drugs and Nursing Implications

Nancy E. Clarkson, RN, C, MEd
Marilyn J. Herbert-Ashton, RN, C, MS
Deborah L. Dalrymple, RN, MSN, CRNI

Today's nurse needs to have a firm foundation in pharmacology. Important aspects of current nursing practice deal with effectiveness of medications, detecting adverse effects, drug interactions, and incorporating client teaching concerning drug use. Clients, including pregnant women and nursing mothers, should be taught adverse effects of drugs and not to take OTC drugs while on prescribed medication without consulting their physician.

This unit, Drugs and Nursing Implications, provides a review of all major drug classifications. The first part of the unit contains a review of pharmacokinetics, drug administration, and calculations. Keep in mind that pediatric drug doses typically are calculated per kilograms of body weight. Following these introductory concepts, case studies with multiple choice questions for each drug classification are reviewed.

Each major drug classification is represented by a prototype drug. A review of action, use, adverse effects, nursing implications, discharge teaching (where applicable), and related drugs is in chart form when appropriate or otherwise listed with pertinent comments. At times, a prototype drug may not be used because one particular drug might not represent a drug group. For example, in the laxative drug group, there is not one single representative or prototype drug. If no prototype drug is used, this is indicated under the drug classification.

UNIT OUTLINE

10 Factors Affecting Drug Action
12 Drug Administration
26 Central Nervous System Drugs
38 Autonomic Nervous System Drugs
47 Drugs Affecting the Endocrine System
54 Eye Drugs
55 Cardiovascular Drugs
69 Renal Drugs
73 Respiratory Drugs
76 Gastrointestinal Tract Drugs
83 Arthritis Drugs
85 Antimicrobials
94 Antiviral Agents
95 Antifungal Agents
96 Anthelmintic Agents
97 Antineoplastic Agents
103 Immunosuppressants
104 Vitamins and Minerals
105 Vaccines and Toxoids

Factors Affecting Drug Action

DEFINITION OF A DRUG

A. According to the Food and Drug Administration (FDA), a drug is any substance used to diagnose, cure, mitigate, treat, or prevent a condition or disease.

B. Drugs come from three main sources: plants (e.g., digoxin), animals (e.g., insulin), and synthetic chemicals (e.g., meperidine).

C. Most of the drugs used today are synthetic chemicals and are associated with fewer allergic reactions.

FACTORS AFFECTING DRUG ACTION

Absorption

A. Absorption refers to the time the drug enters the body until it enters the bloodstream.

B. Many factors affect the rate and amount of absorption.
   1. Dosage form
   2. Route of administration
      a. Parenteral: absorption generally rapid
      b. Intravenous (IV) and intra-arterial (IA): most rapid absorption
      c. Intramuscular (IM) and subcutaneous (SC)
         1) absorption is relatively fast if given in an aqueous base but can be delayed if given in an oil base
         2) speed of absorption depends on condition of blood flow
         3) impaired peripheral circulation and shock will delay absorption
      d. Intradermal: absorption is slow and confined to area injected (e.g., purified protein derivative—PPD)
      e. Oral: rate and degree of absorption can vary depending on GI motility, presence of food in stomach, gastric pH, and use of other drugs
   3. Lipid solubility: affects absorption as it passes through gastric intestinal mucosa.
   4. Gastrointestinal (GI) motility
      a. Stomach empties more slowly with food and will delay oral drug absorption.
      b. Most oral drugs are best absorbed if given before meals or between meals.
         1) diarrhea can cause drugs not to be absorbed
         2) constipation may delay drug absorption, potentially causing toxicity

Distribution

A. Once in bloodstream, drugs are distributed around body. Distribution can take as long as several hours, depending on blood flow (in various areas of the body) and cardiac output.

B. Plasma-protein binding
   1. Medications connect with plasma proteins (primarily albumin) in vascular system.
   2. Strong attachments have a longer period of drug action.
   3. Clients with reduced plasma proteins such as in kidney or liver disease could receive a heightened drug effect.

C. Volume of distribution
   1. Client with edema has an enlarged area in which a drug can be distributed and may need an increased dose.
   2. Smaller dose may be needed for client with dehydration.

D. Barriers to drug distribution: prevent some medications from entering certain body organs.
   1. Blood-brain barrier
      a. Helps preserve homeostasis in brain.
      b. To pass through this barrier, drug must be lipid soluble and loosely attached to plasma protein.
   2. Placental barrier
      a. Shields fetus from possibility of adverse drug effects
      b. Many substances (drugs, nicotine, alcohol) do cross placental barrier.

E. Obesity: body weight plays a role in drug distribution because blood flows through fat slowly, thus increasing time before drug is released.

F. Receptor combination
   1. A receptor is an area on a cell where drug attaches and response takes place.
      a. Receptor is usually protein or nucleic acid.
      b. Other substances that can be receptors are enzymes, lipids, and carbohydrate residues.
   2. Drugs can have an agonist or antagonist effect.
      a. Agonist will connect itself to the receptor site and cause pharmacological response.

       b. Antagonist will attempt to attach, but because attachment is uneven, there is no drug response.

    3. There can be competition at receptor site when more than one drug tries to occupy it.

Metabolism

A. Process of metabolism is a sequence of chemical events that change a drug after it enters the body.

B. Liver is principal site of drug metabolism.

C. Oral medications
    1. Go directly to the liver via the portal circulation before entering systemic circulation.
    2. Many medications become entirely inactivated by the liver the first time they go through it.

D. Age
    1. Age of an individual influences metabolism of drugs.
    2. Infants and elderly have reduced ability to metabolize some drugs.

E. Nutrition: liver enyzmes involved in metabolism rely on adequate amounts of amino acids, lipids, vitamins, and carbohydrates.

F. Insufficient amounts of major body hormones such as insulin or adrenal corticosteroids can reduce metabolism of drugs in liver.

Excretion

A. Process by which drugs are eliminated from body.
    1. Drugs can be excreted by kidneys, intestines, lungs, and mammary, sweat, and salivary glands.
    2. Most important route of excretion for most drugs is kidneys.

B. Renal excretion
    1. Carried out by glomerular filtration and tubular secretion, which increase quantity of drug excreted.
    2. Another renal process that results in excretion is tubular reabsorption.
        a. Drug metabolites in urine can be reverted back into bloodstream.
        b. Decreases quantity of drug excreted.

C. Drugs can affect elimination of other drugs
    1. Example: Probenecid is sometimes administered with penicillin to prevent excretion of penicillin and thus increase effects of penicillin.
    2. Example: antacids increase elimination of aspirin, thus decreasing its effects.

D. Blood concentration levels
    1. Affect drug elimination
    2. When peak blood level of drug is reached, excretion becomes greater than absorption and blood levels of drug begin to drop.

E. Half-life: time required for total amount of drug to decrease by 50%.

Accumulation

A. Therapeutic levels
    1. Important goal is for drug to reach therapeutic levels and maintain therapeutic level.
    2. Can be maintained when liver or renal function remain unchanged.

B. Loading dose
    1. Sometimes given to raise therapeutic level quickly before drug has chance to be eliminated.
    2. For client safety, loading doses are given in several smaller doses over short periods of time.
    3. Once therapeutic level is achieved, a smaller daily maintenance dose is given to maintain therapeutic levels; digoxin may be given this way.

C. Toxicity: occurs when drug is eliminated more slowly than it is absorbed, causing excessive drug concentration.

Underlying Disease

A. Disease can lead to variable drug response.

B. Diseases that may affect drug response
    1. Cardiovascular disease
    2. Gastrointestinal disease
    3. Liver disease
    4. Kidney disease

Client's Age

A. Pediatric: drug dosages are based on body weight—milligrams per kilogram (mg/kg)

B. Geriatric: careful drug history should be obtained, including over-the-counter (OTC) drugs to determine if there are drug interactions or adverse effects.

SAMPLE QUESTIONS

1. Taking antibiotics with food will
    1. delay rate of absorption.
    2. increase rate of absorption.
    3. prevent side effects.
    4. enhance action of drug.

2. The elderly tend to have decreased serum albumin levels, which may cause
    1. enhanced absorption.
    2. toxic drug effects.
    3. enhanced drug distribution.
    4. an increase in the therapeutic effects.

3. The nurse needs to be aware that if a central nervous system (CNS) depressant is

administered to an infant, toxic effects can occur primarily due to
1. increased drug absorption.
2. increased drug distribution.
3. decreased drug half-life.
4. decreased drug excretion.

ANSWERS AND RATIONALES

1. The correct answer is 1. Taking food will decrease the rate of absorption. Furthermore, taking dairy products with an antibiotic such as tetracycline will cause calcium (Ca+) to bind to drug and decrease absorption.
2. The correct answer is 2. Toxic drug effects occur because there is less albumin or protein for the drug to bind to in the elderly.
3. The correct answer is 2. The blood-brain barrier is not fully developed in infants and CNS depressants can readily penetrate.

Drug Administration

ASSESSMENTS APPROPRIATE TO ALL MEDICATION ADMINISTRATION

A. Confirm client diagnosis and appropriateness of medication.
B. Identify all concurrent medications.
C. Identify any potential contraindications or allergies.
D. Identify client's knowledge of medications.

ANALYSIS

Nursing diagnoses for the client receiving medications may include
A. Potential for injury related to side effects of medications.
B. Knowledge deficit: drug effects related to lack of previous experience.
C. Noncompliance related to side effects, financial, or other difficulties limiting ability to take medications.

PLANNING AND IMPLEMENTATION

A. Identify appropriate goals such as, "Client will explain rationale for medication prior to discharge."
B. Prepare and administer medications according to the following principles.

TECHNIQUES OF DRUG ADMINISTRATION

General Principles for All Medications

A. Verify all new or questionable orders on the medication administration record (MAR) against physician orders for completeness.
B. Prepare medications in a quiet environment.
C. Wash your hands. Observe universal precautions, as appropriate.
D. Collect all necessary equipment including straws, juice or water, stethoscope.
E. Review MAR for each client carefully to ensure safety: note medication, dosage, route, expiration date, and frequency.
F. Research drug compatibilities, action, purpose, contraindications, side effects, and appropriate routes.
G. Find medication for individual client and calculate dosage accurately. Confirm normal range of dose, particularly in pediatrics.
H. Check expiration date on medication and look for any changes that may indicate decomposition (color, odor, and clarity).
I. Compare label three times with the medication to decrease risk of error.
   1. When removing package from drawer
   2. Before preparing medication
   3. After preparing medication
J. Check need for prn medications.
K. Be sure medications are identified for each client.
L. Check for any allergies and perform all special assessments before administration.

M. Confirm client's identity by checking at least two of the three possible mechanisms for identification to ensure safety.
  1. Ask client his name.
  2. Check client's identi-band.
  3. Check bed tag (this is least reliable method).
N. Provide privacy, if needed.
O. Inform client of medication, any procedure, technique, purpose, and client teaching as applicable.
P. Stay with client until medication is gone; do not leave medication at bedside.
Q. Assist client as needed, and leave in position of comfort.
R. Give medication within 30 minutes of prescribed time.
S. Chart administration immediately in ink, marking your initials in the appropriate space.
T. Circle initials and document rationale if drug not administered.
U. Report any errors immediately and complete appropriate institutional documentation.
V. Liquid medications—all routes of administration—must *not* be mixed together unless compatibility is verified.
W. Observe for any reactions and document both positive and negative responses.
X. Observe the five "rights": give the right *dose* of the right *drug* to the right *client* at the right *time* by the right *route*.
Y. To ensure safety do not give a medication that someone else prepared. Institution policies may require having a colleague double check medications such as insulin and heparin. If you are unsure in any way, have a colleague verify.

Administration of Oral Medications

A. Special assessment: assess client's knowledge level, diet status, oral cavity, and ability to swallow medication.
B. Use mortar and pestle to crush tablets, if appropriate. In general, enteric-coated tablets should not be crushed. Only scored tablets can be broken.
C. With the exception of time-release capsules, capsule contents may be mixed with food to enhance swallowing.
D. Unless contraindicated (e.g., cough syrup) give medication with 60–100 ml water or juice to aid in swallowing and to increase intake.
E. Prepare solid medications (tablets, capsules, etc.).
  1. All solid medications can be placed in one medicine cup unless an assessment needs to be made before administering a particular medication (e.g., blood pressure, apical pulse)
  2. Unit dose containers can remain in original individual package.

  3. To reduce chance of contamination, place any removable lids open side up; place necessary medications into cap of container; transfer to med cup; replace lid and container.
F. Prepare liquid medications.
  1. Shake liquid medications, if necessary, to mix.
  2. Pour away from bottle label.
  3. Read liquid amount at meniscus of med cup at eye level to ensure accuracy.
  4. If needed, a syringe may be used to measure and administer liquid medications.
  5. Wipe lip of bottle with damp towel to prevent stickiness.
  6. Replace lid and container.
  7. Do not administer alcohol-based products, such as elixirs, to alcohol-dependent persons.
G. Sit client upright to enhance swallowing.
H. Have client swallow medication except with the following
  1. Sublingual (SL) route: have client place medication under tongue (high rate of absorption). Do not allow fluids for 30 minutes following administration.
  2. Buccal route: have client place medication between gum and cheek. Do not allow fluids for 30 minutes following administration.
  3. Iron or HCl: have client use straw to prevent staining teeth.
I. Stay with client until medication is gone. Use gloves if you place your finger in client's mouth.
J. Special concerns
  1. Use a calibrated dropper, nipple, or syringe to give medications to an infant.
  2. Keep infant at 45° angle.
  3. See if medication is available in liquid form if client is a child or unable to swallow solid medication.
  4. Be sure not to use a child's favorite food, as this may result in distrust.
  5. If using an NG or stomach tube for medication administration, check for correct placement before administration and follow medication with water. Be sure to check for food interaction.

Administration of Rectal Drugs

A. Special assessment: assess client's bowel function and ability to retain suppository/enema.
B. Remove suppository from refrigerator.
C. Provide privacy.
D. Position client left laterally.
E. Put on glove or finger cot.
F. Moisten suppository with water-soluble lubricant.

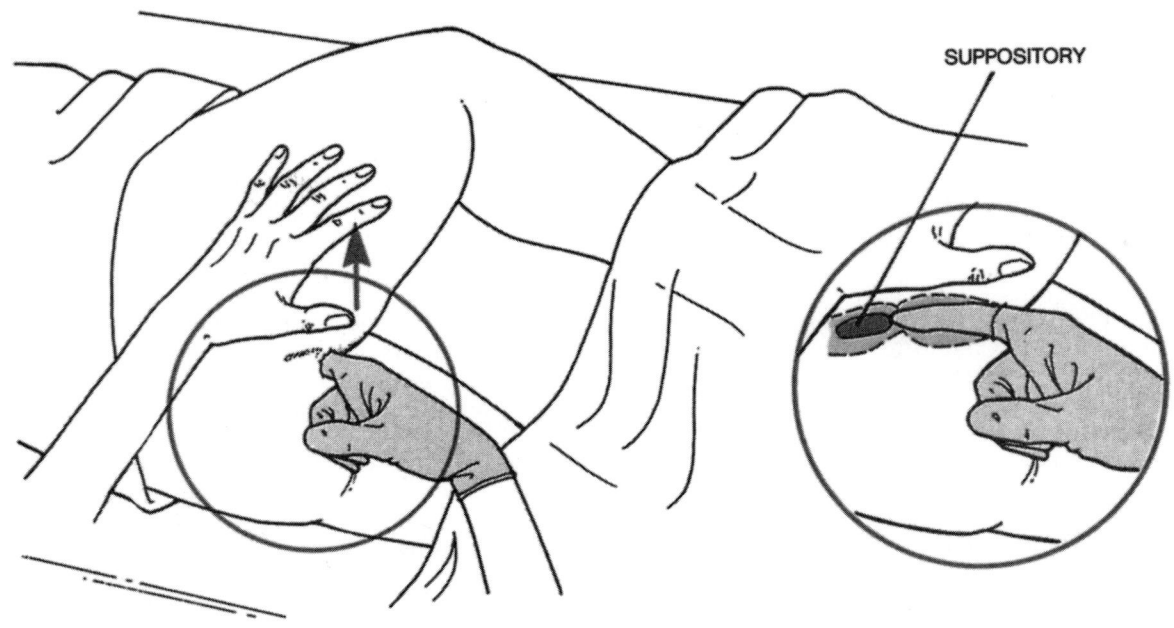

SUPPOSITORY

FIGURE 2.1 A rectal suppository is inserted about 2 inches in adults so it will be placed in the internal anal sphincter. (Delmar Publishers)

G. Insert suppository, tapered end first, approximately 2 inches (to pass internal sphincter), Figure 2.1.
H. Hold buttocks together.
I. Encourage client to retain suppository for 10–20 minutes to allow suppository to melt.
J. If drug administered via enema, have client retain solution 20–30 minutes.

Administration of Nasal Medications

A. Have client blow nose to clear mucus.
B. Position client so that head can be tilted back to aid in gravitational flow or in specific position to reach sinuses.
C. Push up on tip of nostril.
D. Place dropper or atomizer angled slightly upward just inside nostril; be careful not to touch nose with applicator.
E. Squeeze atomizer quickly and firmly or instill correct number of drops.
F. Remind client to keep head tilted for 5 minutes.
G. Inform client the drops may produce an unpleasant taste.
H. Leave tissues with client; instruct just to wipe nose, not blow, to allow for absorption.
I. Special concerns
   1. If client aspirates and begins to cough, sit client upright, stay until client's distress is relieved.
   2. If client is an infant, lay infant on its back.

Administration of Inhalants

A. Special assessment: monitor vital signs before and after treatments.
B. Have client inhale and exhale deeply.
C. Have client place lips around mouthpiece without touching and inhale medication until lungs are fully inflated. A specially designed spacer device is available to assist the client who may have difficulty with this.
D. Have client remove mouthpiece, hold breath as long as able, and then exhale completely.
E. If necessary, repeat procedure until medication is gone.
F. Wash mouthpiece with warm water.
G. Special concerns
   1. Have tissues handy; encourage expectoration of sputum.
   2. Be sure client is aware that coughing is expected after treatment.
   3. If mouth is placed directly on inhaler, it is possible that the tongue will absorb medication, resulting in inadequate dosing and tongue irritation.

Administration of Ophthalmic Medications

A. Check solution for color and clarity before administering.
B. Warm solution in hands before administration.
C. Have client lie on back or sit with head turned to affected side to aid in gravitational flow.

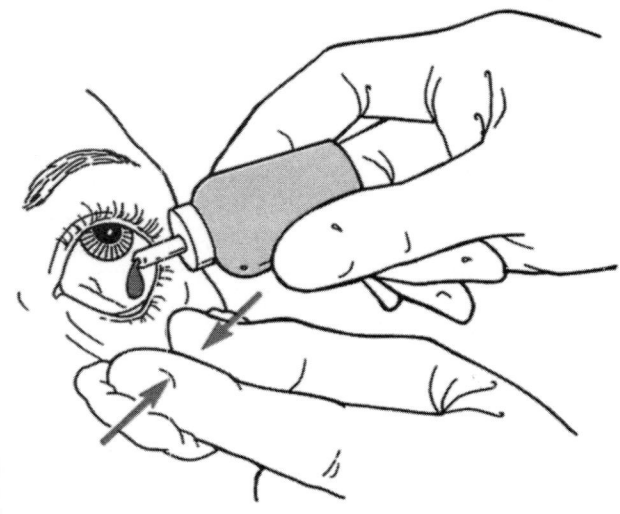

FIGURE 2.2 Instilling eye drops (Delmar Publishers)

J. Wipe away any excess medication starting from inner canthus.
K. Repeat if necessary using clean tissue.
L. Special concerns
    1. Ophthalmic medications are for individual clients; droppers and ointments should not be shared.
    2. Restrain infants and children if necessary.

Administration of Otic Medications

A. Warm medication in hands prior to administration.
B. Have client turn to unaffected side to aid gravitational flow.
C. Clean outer ear using a wet gauze pad. Assess ear condition.
D. Straighten ear canal by pulling pinna up and back for adults or down and back for infants and children under 3, Figure 2.4.
E. Instill necessary number of drops along side of canal without touching ear with dropper.

D. Cleanse eyelid and eyelashes with sterile gauze pad soaked with physiologic saline. Assess eye condition.
E. Have client look up.
F. Assist client in keeping eye open by pulling down on cheekbone with thumb or forefinger and pulling up on eyelid. Be sure lower conjunctiva is exposed, Figure 2.2.
G. Place necessary number of drops into lower conjunctiva near outer canthus (less sensitive than cornea).
H. If using ointment, squeeze into lower conjunctiva moving from inner to outer canthus, Figure 2.3.
    1. Do not touch eye with applicator.
    2. Twist tube to break medication stream.
I. Have client blink 2–3 times.

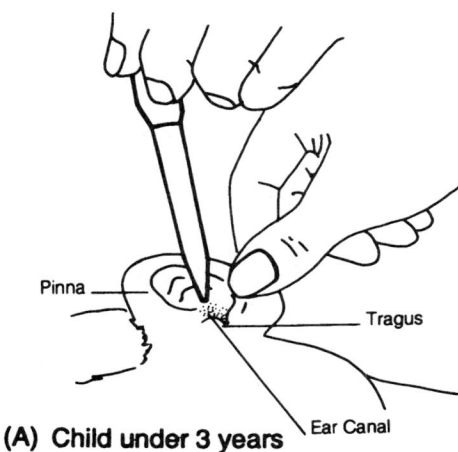

(A) **Child under 3 years**

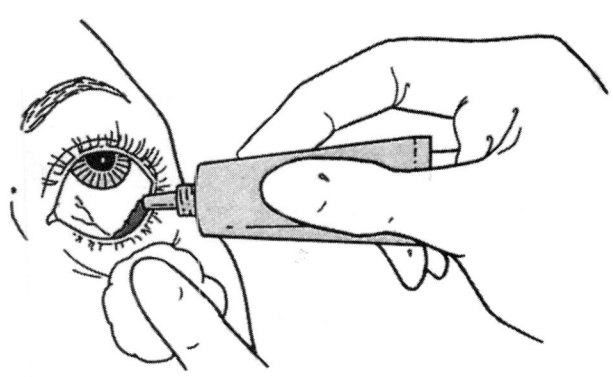

FIGURE 2.3 Instilling eye ointment (Delmar Publishers)

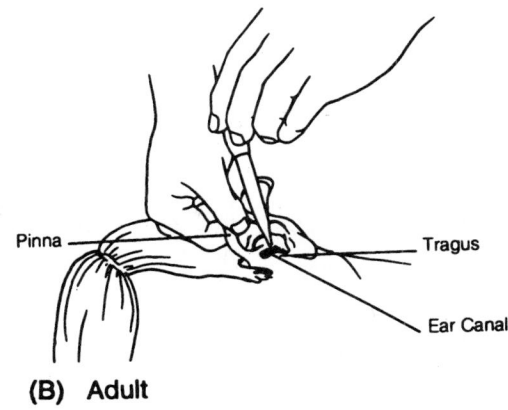

(B) **Adult**

FIGURE 2.4 Administering ear drops (Delmar Publishers)

F. Maintain position of ear until medication has totally entered canal.

G. Have client remain on side for 5–10 minutes to allow medication to reach inner ear.

H. Cotton may be used to keep medication in canal, but only if it is premoistened with medication.

I. Repeat procedure for other ear if necessary.

J. Special concern: restrain infants and children if necessary.

Administration of Topical Agents

A. Provide privacy and expose only appropriate area to promote comfort.

B. Cleanse area of old medications using gauze pads with soap and warm water.

C. Use gloves and gauze, tongue depressor, or sterile applicator, if integument broken.

D. Assess area for any changes or contraindications of application.

E. Spread medication over site evenly and thinly.

F. If necessary, cover area loosely with a dressing.

G. Special concerns
1. Clients often receive topical agents for image-altering problems. Applying the medication offers a good opportunity to talk about these problems and to share information about improvements.
2. When applying nitroglycerin ointment, take client's blood pressure 5 minutes before and after application. (See page 58.)
3. Wash hands after administration to prevent self-absorption.
4. When using transderm patches, use gloves to avoid inadvertent drug absorption. Remove backing and place patch in area with little hair. Press edges down to secure patch.

Administration of Vaginal Medications

A. Provide privacy.

B. Put on gloves.

C. Have client void.

D. Place client on a bedpan in dorsal recumbent position with hips and knees flexed, Figure 2.5.

E. Cleanse perineum with warm, soapy water, working from outer to inner position.

F. Moisten applicator tip with water-soluble lubricant.

G. Separate labia to insert applicator approximately 2 inches, angled downward and back.

H. Instill medication.

I. If giving douche, dry client's buttocks; otherwise have client remain in position approximately 15–20 minutes (there is no sphincter to hold suppository in place).

J. Wash applicator with warm, soapy water.

K. Provide client with pads if needed.

Administration of Parenteral Medications

General Principles

A. Special assessments for parenteral medications:
1. Assess area for presence of lesions, rashes, or abscesses prior to administration.
2. Assess for discomfort or impaired mobility, which may affect site selection.
3. Assess client ability for self-injection, if appropriate.

B. Select appropriate needle size and syringe.
1. Use tuberculin 1 ml syringe for volumes less than 1 ml.
2. Needle lumen must be larger for solutions with increased viscosity.

C. When medication comes in a vial, cleanse rubber stopper with alcohol pledget.

D. Without contaminating plunger, draw up air equal to the amount of medication needed.

E. Inject the air into the vial to prevent negative pressure and aid in aspirating medication.

F. Remove the appropriate amount of medication (the vial may be multidose).

G. Check to ensure no air bubbles are present; if bubbles are a problem, draw up slightly more medication than is needed, return all medication to vial, and withdraw medication again or tap syringe until air is all collected at top of barrel and can be expelled.

H. When using an ampule: tap neck to force medication into ampule, wrap neck with alcohol

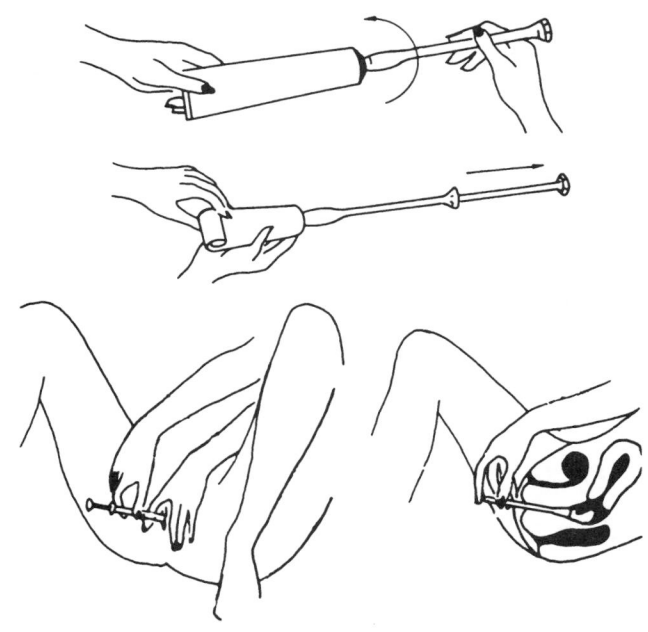

FIGURE 2.5 The client should be in a dorsal recumbent position for the administration of vaginal creams. (Delmar Publishers)

pledget, snap off top toward self, place needle into ampule to withdraw medication. A filter needle should be used to avoid glass shards.

I. When mixing a powder, use a filter needle when drawing up medication. Reconstitute according to manufacturer's recommendations.

J. Replace protective cover on needle before proceeding.

K. Select appropriate site, avoiding bruised or tender areas; rotate sites as much as possible.

L. Cleanse site with alcohol pledget to decrease contamination. Use gloves to avoid contact with blood.

M. Insert needle quickly with bevel up, leaving a small amount of needle showing, and release hold (to decrease pain).
   1. With the exception of heparin, aspirate to check for blood.
   2. If blood present, remove needle and start again.
   3. When giving medications IV, a blood return is desired.

N. Inject medication slowly.

O. Place alcohol pledget over site with gentle pressure.

P. Remove needle and massage area; do not massage area if giving heparin or a Z-track injection.

Q. Dispose of syringe in appropriate manner.

R. Record site when documenting medication administration to assist in site rotation and avoid tissue atrophy.

S. Variations on preparing medications

1. Disposable injection systems have already-prepared cartridges with attached needle appropriate to route and viscosity. To add medication, add sterile air from cartridge to vial, then add medication from vial to cartridge.

2. When combining two medications from an ampule and a vial, first determine appropriate volumes, as well as total volume. Withdraw appropriate volume of medication from vial, followed by medication in ampule.

3. When combining medications from two vials, determine appropriate volume for each drug and total volume. Inject air into vial A, then into vial B. Withdraw medication from vial B, then return to vial A.

Subcutaneous (SC) Administration

A. Use size 25 g to 27 g, ½–1-inch needle, maximum volume 1.5 ml.

B. Pinch skin to form SC fold.

C. Insert needle at 45° angle in thigh or arm or 90° angle in abdomen (to avoid entering muscle), Figure 2.6—for insulin, see Unit 4, page 336.

D. Possible sites
   1. Lateral aspect of upper arm
   2. Anterior thigh
   3. Abdomen: 1 inch away from umbilicus
   4. Back, in scapular area

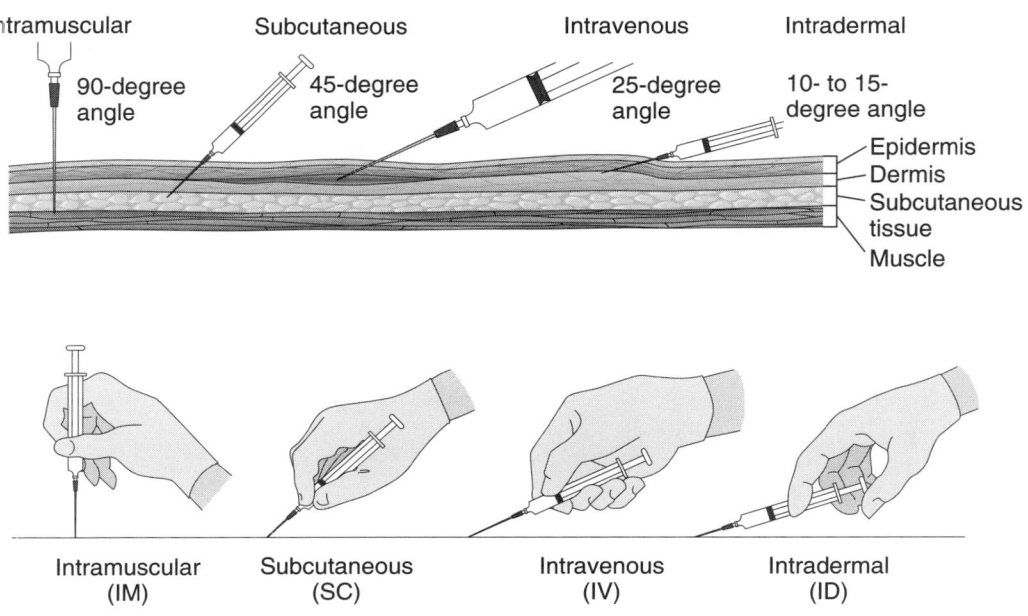

FIGURE 2.6 Angles of injections (Delmar Publishers)

Hypodermoclysis

A. A method of giving large volume solutions SC at a slow rate.
B. Reserved for patients unable to receive fluids IV.

Intradermal Administration

A. Use size 26 g to 27 g, 1-inch needle on a 1 ml or tuberculin syringe (volume will be approximately 0.1 ml).
B. Stretch skin taut.
C. Insert needle at 10°–15° angle approximately 1–2 mm depth with needle bevel upward.
D. Possible sites
    1. Ventral forearm
    2. Scapula
    3. Upper chest
E. When wheal appears, remove needle; do not massage site.

Intramuscular (IM) Administration

A. Use size 18 g to 23 g, 1–2-inch needle, maximum volume 5 ml.
B. Stretch skin taut.
C. Insert needle at 90° angle.
D. Possible sites
    1. Gluteus minimus (ventrogluteal): landmarks are anterior superior iliac spine, iliac crest, greater trochanter of femur.
    2. Vastus lateralis (anterior thigh), Figure 2.7: a handbreadth above the knee and below greater trochanter; good site for children.
    3. Rectus femoris (medial thigh): a handbreadth above knee and below

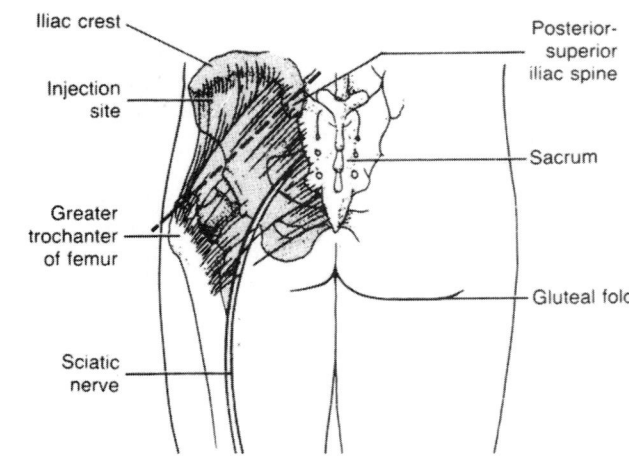

FIGURE 2.8 When using the dorsogluteal site, injection is made into the gluteus medius muscle (Delmar Publishers)

greater trochanter; good site for infants and self-injection.
    4. Gluteus medius (dorsogluteal), Figure 2.8: landmarks are posterior superior iliac spine, iliac crest, greater trochanter of femur.
    5. Deltoid, Figure 2.9: landmarks are acromium process, axilla base; for small doses less than 2 ml only.
E. Z-track injection (IM variation) for irritating solutions.
    1. Needle size: replace needle used to draw up medication with one 2–3 inches long, 20–22 g.
    2. Pull skin away from site laterally with nondominant hand to ensure medication enters muscle.
    3. Wait 10 seconds after injecting medication before withdrawing needle.
    4. Release skin; do not massage (seals needle track).
    5. Encourage physical activity.
    6. Possible sites: gluteus medius best, but may use any IM site except deltoid.
F. A 45° angle may be sufficient for infants and children.

Administration of Intravenous (IV) Medications

A. General principles
    1. Check site for complications (redness, swelling, tenderness).
    2. Check for blood return.
    3. Prepare medication according to manufacturer's specifications.
    4. Appropriate tubing selection varies according to institution policy. Generally,

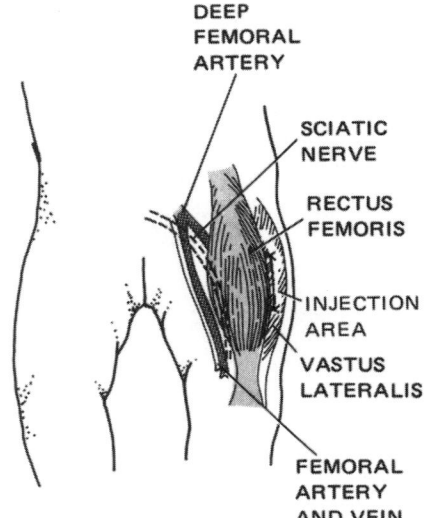

FIGURE 2.7 Anterior view of the location of the vastus lateralis muscle in a young child (Delmar Publishers)

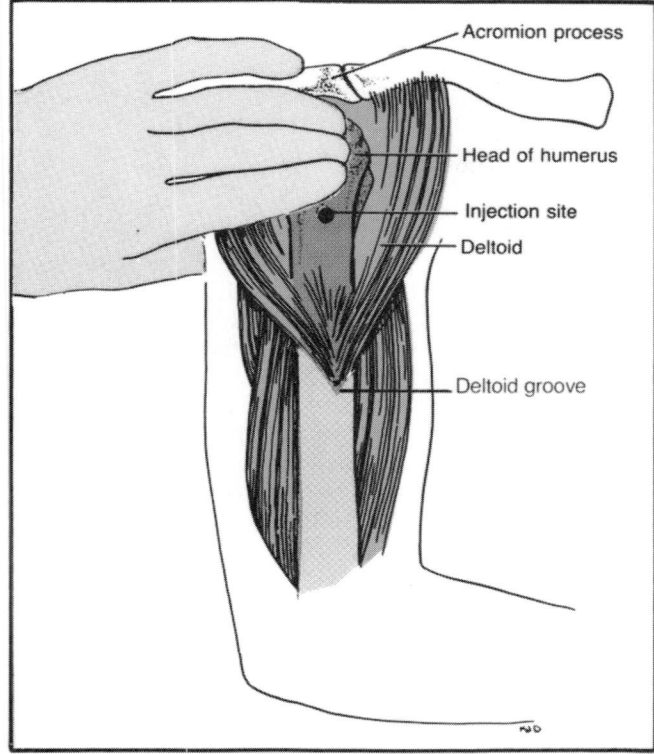

FIGURE 2.9   Deltoid injection site (Delmar Publishers)

4. If using add-a-line tubing, lower main IV bag on hanger provided, otherwise hang bag at same level as primary bag.
5. Swab most proximal port with alcohol for add-a-line systems, otherwise lower port is acceptable.
6. Attach 20 g 1-inch needle to tubing, if a needleless system is not being used.
7. Insert needle into injection port.
8. Regulate rate with control and watch to count drops.
9. When medication absorbed, main line will start to drip again.
10. Turn off secondary tubing.
11. Return main bag to original position.
12. Special concerns
   a. Be sure to label tubing with date.
   b. Use new tubing every 24–72 hours (according to institution policy).
D. Intravenous push medications
  1. Using an appropriately sized needle, prepare medication as ordered.
  2. Cleanse injection port with alcohol or other appropriate cleanser.

rates greater than or equal to 12 hours require microtubing (60 gtts/ml), all others require macrotubing (10, 15, or 20 gtts/ml).
B. Intermittent therapy (also known as heparin well, INT, male adaptor, capped jelco, or heparin lock)
  1. Swab injection port with alcohol at each step.
  2. Use SASH method to give medication.
   a. S: flush with 2 ml saline.
   b. A: administer medication at prescribed rate using a short needle with a gauge equal to or smaller than catheter (25 g, ½ in).
   c. S: flush with 2 ml saline (maintain positive pressure to prevent blood back-up into catheter). Not required if drug compatible with heparin.
   d. H: flush with 10–100 units heparin if required by facility policy.
C. Secondary piggyback/add-a-line (added to an existing IV line), Figure 2.10.
  1. With regulator turned off, spike tubing into IV bag with medication.
  2. Squeeze drip chamber; fill halfway with solution.
  3. Run fluid through tubing.

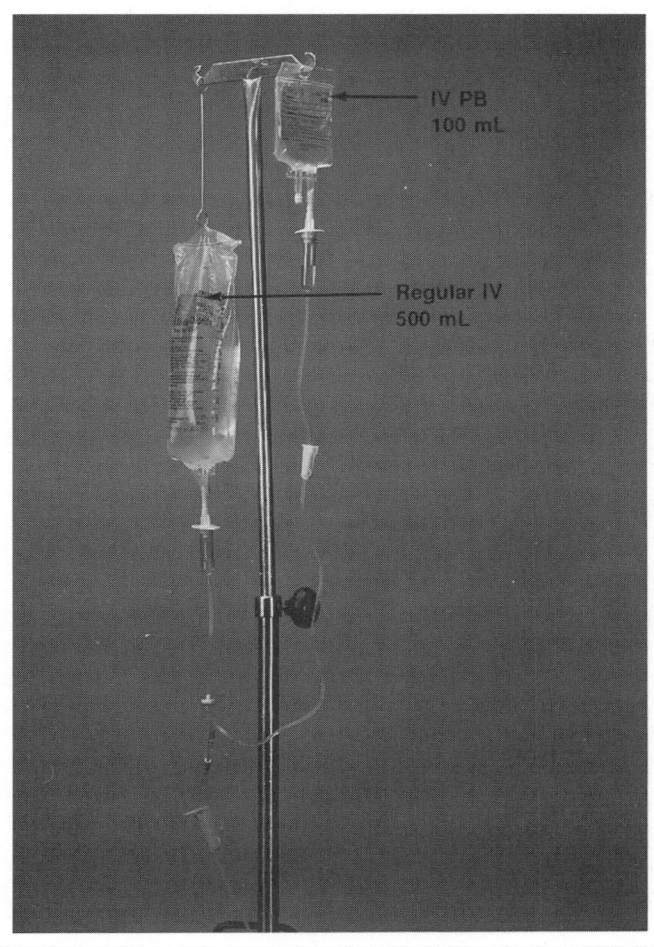

FIGURE 2.10   IV with Piggyback (IV PB) (Delmar Publishers)

3. Unless otherwise recommended, turn off primary IV bag; flush with saline if indicated.
4. Insert needle and administer medication at prescribed rate.
E. Electronic regulators
   1. Syringe infusers
      a. Check for drug compatibility, flush with saline if necessary.
      b. Place syringe into infuser and prime appropriate tubing with prepared medication.
      c. Secure unit and activate unit according to manufacturer's recommendations.
   2. Pumps and controllers
      a. Prime tubing according to manufacturer's recommendations; do not purge when attached to client.
      b. Prior to connecting IV to client, check to determine if tubing allows gravity free-flow. If it does be sure to turn off regulator.
      c. Connect tubing to client and turn on electronic regulator.
      d. Confirm alarm function by keeping tubing clamped while machine is turned on. Do not turn off alarms.
      e. Follow manufacturer's directions for deactivating alarm and starting IV flow.
      f. Explain regulator and alarms to client.
      g. Confirm flow rate with hourly checks on client, fluid, and regulator.

MEDICATION CALCULATIONS

Conversions

Conversions need to be made within systems (from one measurement to another) and also among systems (from apothecary to metric or household to metric).

Conversions within Systems

A. Metric system
   1. Based on decimal system, basic unit is 10.
   2. Units of measurement are
      a. Meter (m) for length
      b. Gram (g) for weight
      c. Liter (l or L) for volume
   3. Multiples and fractions of 10 are identified by prefixes, Figure 2.11.

a. 0.001 liter would then be equal to 1 milliliter (ml).
b. 1000 grams would be equal to a kilogram (kg).
4. Commonly used terms of weight include kilogram, gram, milligram, and microgram.
5. Commonly used terms of volume include liter and milliliter. *Note:* A cube measuring 1 cm per side holds one milliliter, so a cubic centimeter (cc) equals a milliliter (ml): *1 cc = 1 ml.*
6. To convert within the metric system, set up a ratio with the conversion factor on the right and the desired information on the left, cross multiply, divide to find X, and complete needed math. Remember to keep ratios equal: whatever is done to one side must be done to the other.
7. Example: convert 5000 mg to g
   a. 1000 mg = 1 g
   b. $\dfrac{5000 \text{ mg}}{X} = \dfrac{1000 \text{ mg}}{1 \text{ g}}$
   c. (X) (1000 mg) = (5000 mg) (1 g)
   d. $\dfrac{(X)(1000 \text{ mg})}{(1000 \text{ mg})} = \dfrac{(5000 \text{ mg})(g)}{(1000 \text{ mg})}$
   e. X = (5) (1 g)
   f. X = 5 g
   g. 5000 mg = 5 g

B. Apothecary system (No longer an approved system; however markings are still on medication containers.)
   1. Based on arbitrary measure.
   2. Basic unit of weight is a grain (gr), basic unit of volume is minim (m or min), Table 2.1.
   3. Small Roman numerals are often used to identify drug dosages (gr xvi = 16 grains) as are fractions (⅓ gr); $\overline{ss}$ is abbreviation for ½ and is used with Roman numerals (v$\overline{ss}$ = 5½).
   4. Grain is only common term for weight.
   5. Common terms for volume include minim, fluidram (f ʒ), fluid ounce (f ℥), pints (pt), quarts (qt), and gallons (gal).
   6. Conversions within the apothecary system are made the same way as conversions within the metric system.
   7. Example: convert 360 min to fluidrams
      a. 60 min = 1 f ʒ
      b. $\dfrac{360 \text{ min}}{X} = \dfrac{60 \text{ min}}{1 \text{ f ʒ}}$

	Multiples			Measure		Fractions		Micro
Decimal Metric	1000 Thousands Kilo-	100 Hundreds Hecto-	10 Tens Deka-	L G M	0.1 Tenths Deci-	0.01 Hundredths Cent-	0.001 Thousandths Cent-	.000001 Millionths Micro

FIGURE 2.11 Metric Prefixes denoting multiples and fractions of 10

TABLE 2.1   Apothecary Units of Weight and Volume

Weight	Volume
60 grains (gr) = 1 dram (ℨ)	60 minims
8 = 1 ounce (ℨ)	(ℳ or min) = 1 fluidram (fℨ)
12 = 1 pound (lb)	8fℨ = 1 fluidounce (fℨ)
	16fℨ = 1 pint (pt)
	2 pt = 1 quart (qt)
	4 qt = 1 gallon (gal)

TABLE 2.3   Approximate Equivalents to Remember

Household	Apothecary	Metric
1 drop (gtt)	= 1 minim (ℳ or min)	= .06 milliliter (ml)
15 drops (gtts)	= 15 min	= 1 ml [1 cc]
1 teaspoon (tsp)	= 1 fluidram (fℨ) [60 min]	= 5 (4) ml
1 tablespoon (tbsp)	= 4 fℨ	= 15 ml
2 tbsp.	= 1 fluidounce (fℨ)	= 30 ml
1 ounce (oz)	= 1 fℨ	= 30 ml
1 teacup	= 6 fℨ	= 180 ml
1 glass	= 8 fℨ	= 240 ml
1 measuring cup	= 8 fℨ	= 240 ml
2 measuring cups	= 1 pint (pt)	= 500 ml

    c. (60 min) (X) = (360 min) (1 fℨ)

    d. $\dfrac{(60 \text{ min}) (X)}{60 \text{ min}} = \dfrac{(360 \text{ min}) (1\,fℨ)}{60 \text{ min}}$

    e. X = 6 fℨ

C. Household system

  1. Approximate measures that vary according to manufacturer, temperature.

  2. Common units include teaspoon (tsp), tablespoon (tbsp), ounce (oz), cup, and drop, Table 2.2.

  3. Conversions within the system are the same.

  4. Example: convert 3 tsp to drops

    a. 60 drops = 1 tsp

    b. $\dfrac{3 \text{ tsp}}{X} = \dfrac{1 \text{ tsp}}{60 \text{ gtts}}$

    c. (1 tsp) (X) = (3 tsp) (60 gtts)

    d. $\dfrac{(1 \text{ tsp}) (X)}{1 \text{ tsp}} = \dfrac{(3 \text{ tsp}) (60 \text{ gtts})}{1 \text{ tsp}}$

    e. X = 180 gtts

Conversions from One System to Another

A. Conversions are done in the same manner. Some of the equivalents must be memorized, Table 2.3.

B. Example: convert 90 gtts to ml

  1. 15 gtts = 1 ml

  2. $\dfrac{90 \text{ gtts}}{X} = \dfrac{15 \text{ gtts}}{1 \text{ ml}}$

  3. (15 gtts (X) = (90 gtts) (1 ml)

  4. $\dfrac{(15 \text{ gtts}) (X)}{15 \text{ gtts}} = \dfrac{(90 \text{ gtts}) (1 \text{ ml})}{15 \text{ gtts}}$

  5. X = 6 ml

TABLE 2.2   Household Units of Liquid Measure

60 drops (gtts) = 1 teaspoon (tsp)
3 tsp = 1 tablespoon (tbsp)
6 tsp = 1 ounce (oz)
2 tbsp = 1 oz
6 oz = 1 teacup
8 oz = 1 glass
8 oz = 1 measuring cup

Dosage Calculations

A. Calibrated containers are available for oral liquids, Figure 2.12, and liquid injectables, Figure 2.13.

B. Formula for calculations

$$\frac{\text{desired amount of drug}}{\text{amount of drug on hand}} = \frac{\text{unknown quantity needed (X)}}{\text{known quantity of drug}}$$

C. Be sure all conversions are done first. The technique of using ratios is the same.

Technique

A. Dosage calculation for scored tablet

  1. 30 gr of a drug is ordered; it is available in scored tablets, 4 g per tablet.

  2. Calculations

    a. 15 gr = 1 g

    b. $\dfrac{30 \text{ gr}}{X} = \dfrac{15 \text{ gr}}{1 \text{ g}}$

    c. (15 gr) (X) = (30 gr) (1 g)

    d. $\dfrac{(15 \text{ gr})}{15 \text{ gr}} = \dfrac{(30 \text{ gr}) (1 \text{ g})}{15 \text{ gr}}$

    e. X = 2 g

    f. Desired amount of drug is 2 g; amount of drug on hand is 4 g.

    g. Unknown quantity is X; known quantity is 1 tablet

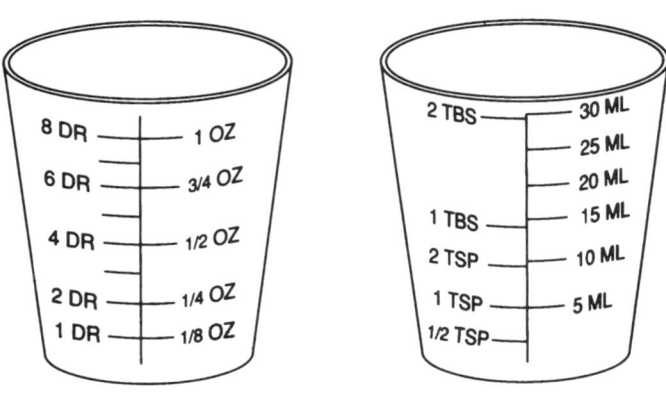

FIGURE 2.12   Disposable medicine containers (Delmar Publishers)

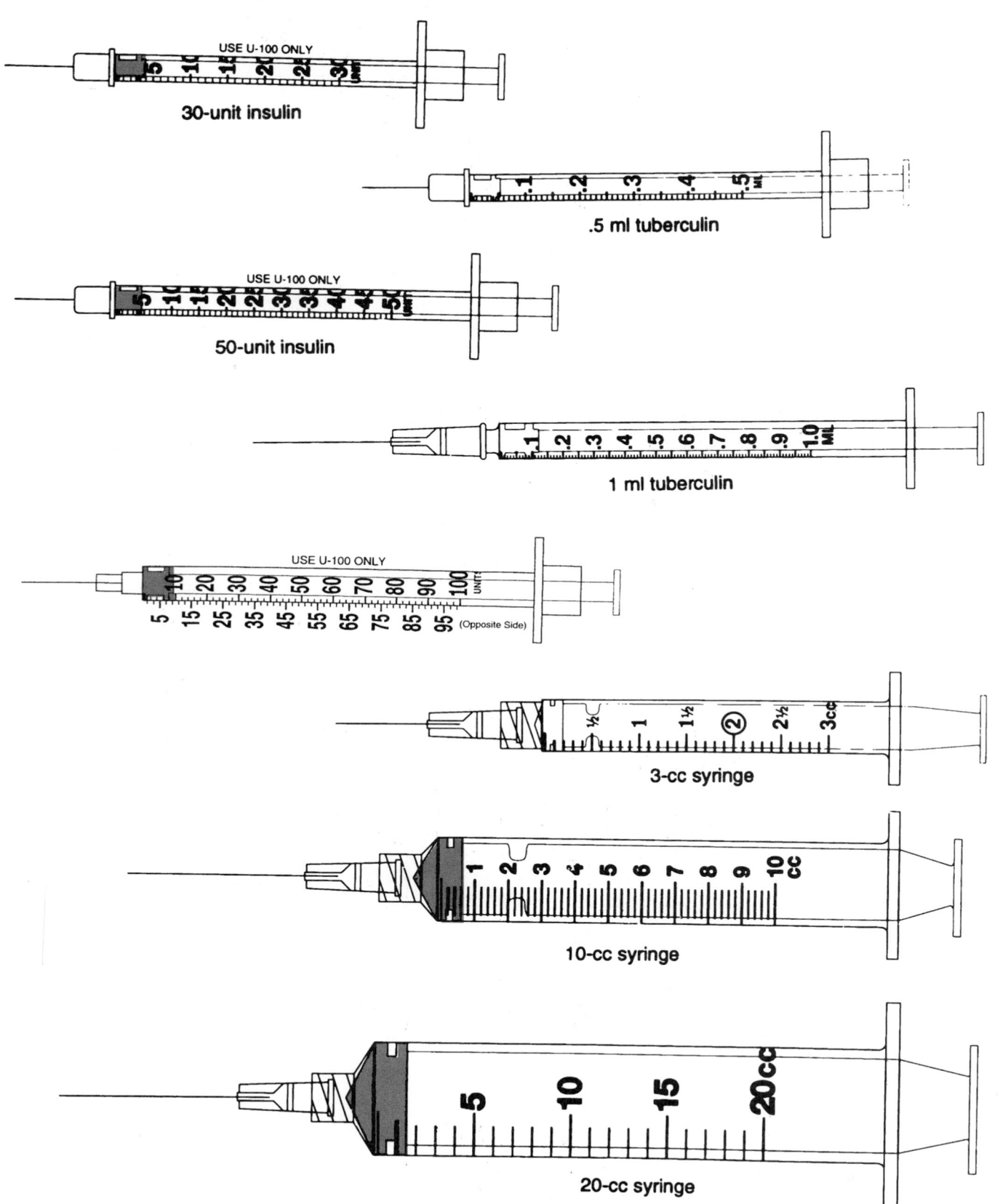

FIGURE 2.13 Commonly used syringes, not to scale (Delmar Publishers)

1) $\dfrac{2g}{4g} = \dfrac{X}{1 \text{ tablet}}$

2) $(4 \text{ g}) (X) = (2 \text{ g}) (1 \text{ tab})$

3) $\dfrac{(4 \text{ g}) (X)}{4 \text{ g}} = \dfrac{(2 \text{ g}) (1 \text{ tab})}{4 \text{ g}}$

4) $X = 0.5$ tablet

3. Give ½ tablet.

B. Dosage calculation for liquid
  1. The order is for potassium chloride (KCl) 20 mEq. The bottle is labeled KCl elixir 10 mEq/ml. How many ml will be given?
     a. Desired amount of drug is 20 mEq; amount of drug on hand is 10 mEq.
     b. Unknown quantity is X; known quantity of drug on hand is 1 ml.
  2. Calculations
     a. $\dfrac{20 \text{ mEq}}{10 \text{ mEq}} = \dfrac{X}{1 \text{ ml}}$
     b. $(10 \text{ mEq}) (X) = (20 \text{ mEq}) (1 \text{ ml})$
     c. $\dfrac{(10 \text{ mEq}) (X)}{10 \text{ mEq}} = \dfrac{(20 \text{ mEq}) (1 \text{ ml})}{10 \text{ mEq}}$
     d. $X = 2$ ml
  3. Give 2 ml potassium chloride.

C. Dosage calculation for a capsule
  1. The order is for Nembutal gr iss. The bottle contains Nembutal 100 mg/capsule. How many capsules will be given?
  2. Calculations
     a. First, convert to equal measurements
        1) 1 gr = 60 mg
        2) $\dfrac{1 \text{ gr}}{60 \text{ mg}} = \dfrac{1.5 \text{ gr}}{X}$
        3) $(X) (1 \text{ gr}) = (60 \text{ mg}) (1.5 \text{ gr})$
        4) $\dfrac{(X) (1 \text{ gr})}{1 \text{ gr}} = \dfrac{(60 \text{ mg}) (1.5 \text{ gr})}{1 \text{ gr}}$
        5) $X = 90$ mg
     b. Desired amount of drug is 90 mg; amount of drug on hand is 100 mg
     c. Unknown quantity is X; known quantity on hand is 1 capsule
     d. Now you can calculate dosage
        1) $\dfrac{90 \text{ mg}}{100 \text{ mg}} = \dfrac{X}{1 \text{ capsule}}$
        2) $(100 \text{ mg}) (X) = (90 \text{ mg}) (1 \text{ capsule})$
        3) $\dfrac{(100 \text{ mg}) (X)}{100 \text{ mg}} = \dfrac{(90 \text{ mg}) (1 \text{ capsule})}{100 \text{ mg}}$
        4) $X = 0.9$ capsule
  3. Since part of a capsule, drop, or suppository cannot be given, give 1 capsule.

D. Dosage calculation for parenteral medications
  1. The order reads codeine gr s̄s̄. The vial reads codeine 60 mg/cc. How many ml should be given?
  2. Calculations
     a. First, convert to like units of measure
        1) 60 mg = 1 gr
        2) $\dfrac{60 \text{ mg}}{X} = \dfrac{60 \text{ mg}}{1 \text{ gr}}$
        3) $(60 \text{ mg}) (X) = (60 \text{ mg}) (1 \text{ gr})$
        4) $\dfrac{(60 \text{ mg}) (X)}{60 \text{ mg}} = \dfrac{(60 \text{ mg}) (1 \text{ gr})}{60 \text{ mg}}$
        5) $X = 1$ gr
     b. Desired amount of drug is 0.5 gr; amount on hand is 1 gr.
     c. Unknown quantity is X; known quantity on hand is 1 ml.
     d. Then calculate dosage
        1) $\dfrac{.5 \text{ gr}}{1 \text{ gr}} = \dfrac{X}{1 \text{ ml}}$
        2) $(X) (1 \text{ gr}) = (.5 \text{ gr}) (1 \text{ ml})$
        3) $\dfrac{(X) (1 \text{ gr})}{1 \text{ gr}} = \dfrac{(5 \text{ gr}) (1 \text{ ml})}{1 \text{ gr}}$
        4) $X = 0.5$ ml
  3. Give 0.5 ml codeine.

E. Dosage calculation for units (some medications such as heparin and penicillin are ordered in units)
  1. The order is penicillin 750,000 units. The vial reads 300,000 u/2 ml. How many ml will be given?
  2. Desired amount of drug is 750,000 units; amount of drug on hand is 300,000 units.
  3. Unknown quantity is X; known quantity is 2 ml.
  4. Calculations
     a. $\dfrac{750{,}000 \text{ units}}{300{,}000 \text{ units}} = \dfrac{X}{2 \text{ ml}}$
     b. $(300{,}000 \text{ units}) (X) = (750{,}000 \text{ units}) (2 \text{ ml})$
     c. $\dfrac{(300{,}000 \text{ units}) (X)}{300{,}000 \text{ units}} = \dfrac{(750{,}000 \text{ units}) (2 \text{ ml})}{300{,}000 \text{ units}}$
     d. $X = 5$ ml
  5. Give 5 ml penicillin.

F. Dosage calculation for powders that need to be reconstituted by adding sterile water or normal saline solution (the total amount of solution is used for calculations)
  1. Mefoxin 1 g is ordered; mefoxin 2 g is on hand. Add 4.3 ml to equal 5 ml solution.
  2. Desired amount of drug is 1 g; amount of drug on hand is 2 g.
  3. Unknown quantity is X; known quantity is 5 ml.
  4. Calculations
     a. $\dfrac{1 \text{ g}}{2 \text{ g}} = \dfrac{X}{5 \text{ ml}}$
     b. $(2 \text{ g}) (X) = (5 \text{ ml}) (1 \text{ g})$
     c. $\dfrac{(2.0 \text{ g}) (X)}{2 \text{ g}} = \dfrac{(5 \text{ ml}) (1 \text{ g})}{2 \text{ g}}$
     d. $X = 2.5$ ml
  5. Give 2.5 ml mefoxin.

G. Dosage calculation in children (pediatric dosages)
  1. Body surface area (BSA): most accurate method for calculating pediatric dosages
     a. *West nomogram,* Figure 2.14, if BSA is not known: draw a line from height on the nomogram; the point of intersection on surface area is the BSA.

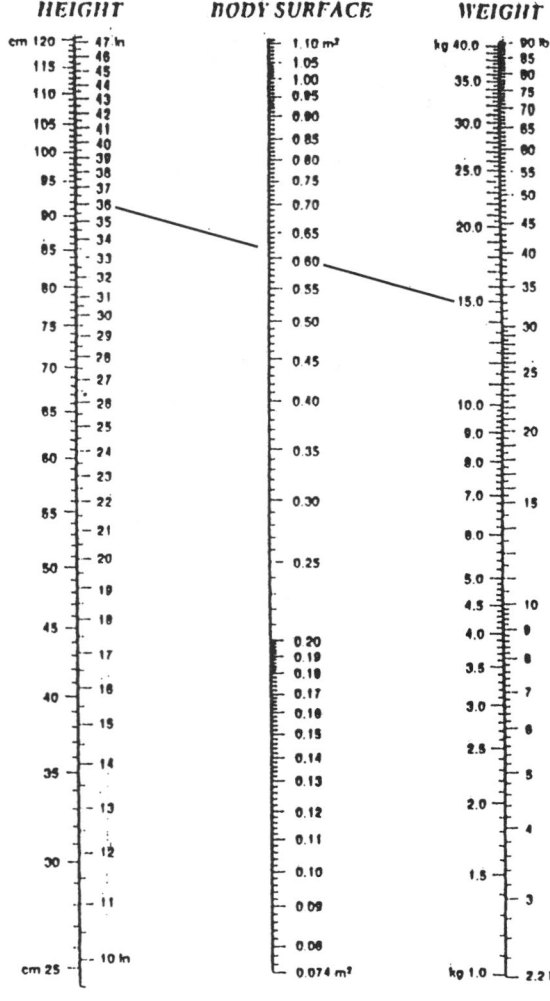

HEIGHT   **BODY SURFACE**   **WEIGHT**

Nomogram for determining body surface of children from height and weight. ($S = W^{0.425} \times H^{0.725} \times 71.84$, or log S = log $W \times 0.425$ + log $H \times 0.725$ + 1.8564 [S = body surface in cm^2; W = weight in kg; H = height in cm]).

FIGURE 2.14 Nomogram. In the example, a child who weighs 15 Kilograms and is about 92 centimeters in height has a body surface area of .60 square meters (From the formula of Du Bois and Du Bois. Modified from *Arch. of Intern. Med.* 17:863, 1926).

b. Formula using surface area (m²)

$$\frac{\text{surface area (m}^2)}{1.73 \text{ m}^2} \times \text{adult dose} = \text{child dose}$$

c. Example of calculating a pediatric dosage using BSA
  1) the adult dose is 100 mg Demerol; the child weighs 20 kg and is 40 inches tall.
  2) BSA is .77 m²
  3) Calculations
    a) $\dfrac{.77 \text{ m}^2}{1.73 \text{ m}^2} \times 100 \text{ mg} = X$

    b) $0.45 \times 100 \text{ mg} = X$
    c) 45 mg = X
  4) Child's dose is 45 mg.
2. Pediatric dosages may also be calculated by weight (mg/kg)
  a. Example: the order is for phenobarbital 2 mg/kg of body weight; the patient weighs 25 kg.
  b. Calculations
    1) $\dfrac{2 \text{ mg}}{X} = \dfrac{1 \text{ kg}}{25 \text{ kg}}$
    2) (1 kg) (X) = (2 mg) (25 kg)
    3) $\dfrac{(1 \text{ kg}) (X)}{1 \text{ kg}} = \dfrac{(2 \text{ mg}) (25 \text{ kg})}{1 \text{ kg}}$
    4) X = 50 mg
  c. Give 50 mg of phenobarbital.
3. Other, less frequently used formulas include
  a. Fried's rule (birth to 12 months)
    $\dfrac{\text{age in months}}{150} \times \text{adult dose} = \text{infant's dose}$
  b. Young's rule (1–12 years)
    $\dfrac{\text{age in years}}{\text{age in years} + 12} \times \text{adult dose} = \text{child's dose}$
  c. Clark's rule
    $\dfrac{\text{weight of child in lb}}{150 \text{ lb}} \times \text{adult dose} = \text{child's dose}$

H. Dosage calculation for IV medications
  1. In order to calculate the flow rate, need to know drop factor: 10, 15, or 20 gtts/ml depending on manufacturer.
  2. Microdrop drop factor is always 60 gtts/ml.
  3. Formula for calculation
    $\dfrac{\text{amount of solution in ml}}{\text{time in minutes}} \times \text{drop factor} \left[\dfrac{\text{gtts}}{\text{ml}}\right] = \text{gtts/minute}$
  4. Example: the order is for 1000 ml NSS over 8 hours; drop factor is 10 gtts/ml
  5. Calculation
    a. $\dfrac{1000 \text{ ml}}{480 \text{ min}} \times \dfrac{10 \text{ gtts}}{\text{ml}} = X$
    b. $\dfrac{1000 \text{ ml}}{480 \text{ min}} \times \dfrac{10 \text{ gtts}}{\text{ml}} = X$
    c. $\dfrac{1000 \text{ gtts}}{48 \text{ min}} = 20.8$
    d. X = 20.8 gtts/min
  6. A partial drop cannot be given so run IV at 21 gtts/min.
  7. The same formula can be used for IVs requiring microdrop rates, or the following formula can be used
    ml/hour = microdrops/min
    This formula works because the drop factor for microdrop tubing is always 60 microgtts/ml and an hour is 60 minutes.
  a. Example: order is for 1000 ml D$_5$NS over 24 hours. Drop factor is 60 gtts/ml.
  b. Calculation with the first formula
    1) $\dfrac{1000 \text{ ml}}{1440 \text{ min}} \times \dfrac{60 \text{ gtts}}{\text{ml}} = X$

2) $\dfrac{1000 \text{ ml}}{1440 \text{ min}} \times \dfrac{60 \text{ gtts}}{\text{ml}} = X$

3) $X = 41.66$

   c. Cannot give a partial drop, so rate is 42 gtts/min.

   d. Calculation with the second formula

     1) first determine the ml/hour:

$$\dfrac{\text{total volume}}{\text{total hours}}$$

     2) $\dfrac{1000 \text{ ml}}{24 \text{ hours}} = 42 \text{ ml/hour} = 42 \text{ gtts/min}$

8. Readjusting IV rates may be necessary when the prescribed rate for an existing IV is changed

   a. Formula for calculation

$$\dfrac{\text{amount of solution remaining}}{\text{remaining hours in minutes}} \times \text{drop factor}$$

   b. Example: the order is to infuse remaining 700 ml over 3 hours; drop factor is 15 gtts/ml.

   c. Calculation

     1) $\dfrac{700 \text{ ml}}{180 \text{ min}} = \dfrac{15 \text{ gtts}}{\text{ml}} = X$

     2) $\dfrac{700 \text{ ml}}{180 \text{ min}} = \dfrac{15 \text{ gtts}}{\text{ml}} = X$

     3) $\dfrac{700 \text{ gtts}}{12 \text{ min}} = 58.3 \text{ gtts/min}$

   d. Cannot give partial drop, so run IV at 58 gtts/min.

Sample Questions

4. The order is dilaudid gr 1/8. The bottle reads dilaudid 15 mg/tablet. Give _____ tablet.
5. The order is chloral hydrate 200 mg. The bottle reads chloral hydrate 0.1 g/capsule. Give _____ capsules.
6. The order is penicillin 50,000 units. The vial reads penicillin 500,000 units. Add 4.3 ml to yield 5 ml. Give _____ ml.
7. The order is ampicillin 0.4 mg/kg. Patient weighs 38.5 pounds. The bottle reads ampicillin 10 mg/ml. Give _____ ml.
8. The adult dose is Dilantin 150 mg. Give _____ mg to a 6-year-old child.
9. Average adult dose is 200 mg. What is dose for a 4-year-old who weighs 40 kg and is 100 cm tall?
10. Order is for 2500 ml D_5W over 24 hours. Drop factor is 15 gtts/ml. Run IV at _____ gtts/minute.
11. Order is for 2000 ml D_5W over 24 hours. Drop factor is 60 gtts/ml. Run IV at _____ gtts/minute.
12. Average adult dose is 250 mg. What is dose for 12-month-old infant?
13. Average adult dose is 500 mg. What is dose for 30-lb child?
14. Mrs. Michy is on continuous IV heparin therapy for her thrombophlebitis. The IV contains 15,000 units of heparin in 500 cc of 5% dextrose (D_5W) at the rate of 20 cc per hr. How many units per hour is Mrs. Michy receiving?
   1. 60 units.
   2. 25 units.
   3. 600 units.
   4. 700 units.
15. The order is for Ancef 1 gram IV in 50 cc 5% dextrose (D_5W) to run in over 30 minutes every 6 hours. The administration set delivers 10 gtts/cc. What should the drip rate be?
   1. 8 gtts/min.
   2. 15 gtts/min.
   3. 17 gtts/min.
   4. 25 gtts/min.

Answers and Rationales

4. ½ tablet
5. 2 capsules
6. 0.5 ml
7. 0.7 ml
8. 50 mg
9. 129 mg
10. 26 gtts/min
11. 83 gtts/min
12. 20 mg
13. 100 mg
14. The correct answer is 3. Divide 500 cc by 20 cc to determine the number of hours of the infusion: 25 hours. Next, divide 15,000 units into 25 hours to get units/hour: 600 units of heparin/hour.
15. The correct answer is 3.

$$\dfrac{\text{Total volume infused}}{\text{Time in minutes}} \times \text{drop factor}$$
$$= \text{gtts per minute}$$
$$\dfrac{50 \text{ cc}}{30 \text{ minutes}} \times \dfrac{10 \text{ gtts}}{1 \text{ cc}} = 16.6 = 17 \text{ gtts/min}$$

Central Nervous System Drugs

LOCAL ANESTHETICS

A. Case Study
   Steve Austin is a 20-year-old college student with two impacted wisdom teeth. The oral surgeon injects lidocaine (Xylocaine) to anesthetize and facilitate removal of the wisdom teeth. Steve has no history of allergies.
B. Prototype—Lidocaine (Xylocaine)
   1. Action. Amide-type anesthetic that blocks nerve conduction; metabolized by hepatic enzymes; produces temporary loss of sensation and motion in a limited area of the body.
   2. Use. Topical anesthesia, regional anesthesia (Unit 4), antiarrhythmic (discussed in Cardiovascular Drugs).
   3. Adverse Effects. Drowsiness, dizziness, light-headedness, restlessness, numbness of lips and tongue; headache with spinal anesthesia; hypotension, bradycardia, cardiovascular collapse; convulsions; tinnitus; muscle weakness; anaphylaxis; respiratory depression.
   4. Nursing Implications
      a. Force fluids with spinal anesthesia.
      b. When used for spinal or epidural anesthesia, should be preservative free.
      c. Monitor VS, and keep siderails up.
      d. Epinephrine, a vasoconstrictor, may be added to lidocaine (Xylocaine).
      e. May interfere with swallowing reflex.
      f. Discard drug without preservatives after immediate use.
      g. Due to adverse effects, elderly clients should be closely monitored.
      h. Do not use discolored, cloudy solutions.
C. Related Drugs. See Table 2.4.

Sample Questions

16. Epinephrine is added to local anesthetic preparations to
    1. prolong anesthetic action.
    2. lower blood pressure.
    3. prevent arrhythmias.
    4. increase blood flow to injection site.
17. Steve Austin complains of a severe sore throat after the extraction of his two wisdom teeth. Viscous lidocaine (Xylocaine) is ordered. Which of the following should be included in client teaching concerning the use of viscous lidocaine (Xylocaine)?
    1. Take viscous lidocaine (Xylocaine) with fluids to soothe sore throat.
    2. Instruct client to use a humidifier while taking viscous lidocaine (Xylocaine).
    3. Advise client to wait 60 minutes before eating after drug application.
    4. Encourage client to take viscous lidocaine (Xylocaine) with food to reduce GI distress.

TABLE 2.4 Local Anesthetics

Drug	Use	Adverse Effects	Nursing Implications
Procaine (Novocain)	Nerve block Spinal anesthesia Infiltration anesthesia	Anaphylaxis is seen more with ester-type anesthetics	• Procaine is an ester-type anesthetic metabolized by esterase found in plasma • Emergency resuscitation equipment should be available • Monitor VS (see lidocaine [Xylocaine])
Benzocaine (Americaine)	Topical anesthesia	See procaine (Novocain) and lidocaine (Xylocaine)	• Benzocaine (Americaine) is similar to procaine (Novocain) and is an ester-type anesthetic • Commonly found in OTC preparations to treat sunburn, rashes, sore throats, and hemorrhoids
Mepivacaine (Carbocaine)	Infiltration nerve block anesthesia	See lidocaine (Xylocaine)	• Amide-type local anesthetic that has two times the potency and toxicity of lidocaine

Answers and Rationales

16. The correct answer is 1. Epinephrine prolongs anesthetic action, while shortening the onset of action and reducing blood flow to injection site.

17. The correct answer is 3. Viscous lidocaine (Xylocaine) can interfere with swallowing reflex and clients should wait at least 60 minutes after use before eating.

NONNARCOTIC ANALGESICS AND ANTIPYRETICS

A. Case Study
   Hazel George is a 50-year-old registered nurse with rheumatoid arthritis. Ms. George is taking aspirin without much relief. The physician decides to start Ms. George on indomethacin (Indocin).
B. Prototype—Salicylates
   Acetylsalicylic Acid (aspirin) (ASA)
   1. Action.
      a. Analgesia: Inhibits formation of prostaglandins involved with pain. Analgesia also occurs by action of hypothalamus and blocking generation of pain impulses.
      b. Antipyretic: Inhibits formation of prostaglandins in production of fever. Aspirin acts on the hypothalamus to produce vasodilation.
      c. Anti-inflammatory: Inhibits prostaglandin synthesis causing anti-inflammatory action.
      d. Antiplatelet action occurs when aspirin inhibits prostaglandin derivative, thromboxane A_2.
   2. Use. Mild to moderate pain; control of fever; inflammatory conditions; reduce TIA occurrence; reduce risk of MI in men with unstable angina.
   3. Adverse Effects. Tinnitus, confusion, dizziness—all are symptoms of salicylism; drowsiness; epistaxis, bleeding, bruising; edema, hypertension; nausea, vomiting, diarrhea, gastritis; hypersensitivity; hypoglycemia, sweating; impaired renal function; respiratory alkalosis and metabolic acidosis are associated with aspirin toxicity.
   4. Nursing Implications
      a. Clients with history of nasal polyps, asthma, rhinitis, chronic urticaria have high incidence of aspirin hypersensitivity.
      b. Clients with diabetes should have glucose monitored.
      c. Monitor CBC, prothrombin time, kidney and liver function studies for clients on long-term therapy.
      d. Additive effect for clients on anticoagulant.
      e. Stop therapy one week before surgery.
   5. Discharge Teaching
      a. Drink plenty of fluids to prevent salicylate crystalluria.
      b. Take with glass of water, antacid, milk, or food to reduce gastric irritation.
      c. Parents should not give to children or adolescents with flu or chickenpox because Reye's syndrome may occur.
      d. Report signs of bleeding and bruising to physician.
      e. Discontinue use if tinnitus, dizziness, or GI distress occur.
      f. Pregnant women should not use.
      g. Do not crush enteric-coated tablets.
      h. Do not ingest large amounts of alcohol as this increases risk of GI bleeding.
C. Related Drugs. See Table 2.5.
D. Prototype—Acetaminophen (Tylenol)
   1. Action. Analgesic and antipyretic action (see aspirin); does not have anti-inflammatory or antiplatelet action.
   2. Use. Mild to moderate pain, fever control.
   3. Adverse Effects. Rash, thrombocytopenia, liver toxicity. Toxicity can occur 2–24 hours after ingestion.
   4. Nursing Implications
      a. Monitor liver and kidney function, and CBC periodically for clients on long-term therapy.
      b. Can cause psychologic dependence.
      c. Antidote: acetylcysteine (Mucomyst)
   5. Discharge Teaching
      Notify physician if no relief of symptoms within 5 days of therapy.

Sample Questions

18. Which of the following should be included in Ms. George's teaching concerning the administration of indomethacin (Indocin)?
    1. Have periodic ophthalmic examinations.
    2. Take on an empty stomach.
    3. Take aspirin for headache relief.
    4. Eat high-fiber foods to prevent constipation.
19. In comparing aspirin to acetaminophen (Tylenol), acetaminophen (Tylenol)
    1. is contraindicated in clients with peptic ulcer disease.
    2. is contraindicated in asthmatic clients.
    3. is as effective as aspirin for reducing fever.
    4. has a stronger anti-inflammatory effect than aspirin.

TABLE 2.5　Nonsteroidal Anti-Inflammatory Drugs (NSAIDs) (NSAIDs are Prostaglandin Inhibitors)

Drug	Use	Adverse Effects	Nursing Implications
Ibuprofen (Motrin, Advil)	Relief of mild to moderate pain Primary dysmenorrhea Rheumatoid and osteoarthritis	May cause sodium or water retention Thrombocytopenia, hemolytic anemia Acute renal failure, hematuria Can elevate liver enzymes	• Do not take with aspirin • Take with food or with milk to decrease GI distress • Monitor liver enzymes
Naproxen (Naprosyn)	Rheumatoid and osteoarthritis Ankylosing spondylitis Primary dysmenorrhea Acute gout attacks Juvenile diabetes	See aspirin and ibuprofen (Motrin)	• See aspirin and ibuprofen (Motrin)
Indomethacin (Indocin)	Close patent ductus arteriosus in premature infant Acute gouty arthritis Moderate severe refractory rheumatoid and osteoarthritis Ankylosing spondylitis	GI distress, anorexia Severe headache Corneal cloudiness, visual field changes	• Clients need to have periodic ophthalmic examinations • Do not take aspirin. See aspirin
Piroxicam (Feldene)	Acute or long-term management of rheumatoid or osteoarthritis	Higher incidence of GI bleeding	• See aspirin, indomethacin (Indocin), and ibuprofen (Motrin)
Ketorolac (Toradol)	Short term pain management	Risk of renal impairment and GI bleeding in prolonged use	• Do not give longer than 5 days • Anaphylaxis can occur with first dose

20. Which condition is an indication for aspirin use?
    1. Asthma.
    2. TIA.
    3. Gout.
    4. Nasal polyps.
21. Which drug is the drug of choice used to treat primary dysmenorrhea?
    1. Acetaminophen (Tylenol).
    2. Piroxicam (Felene).
    3. Indomethacin (Indocin).
    4. Ibuprofen (Motrin).

Answers and Rationales

18. The correct answer is 1. Indomethacin (Indocin) may cause visual field changes or corneal cloudiness. Clients should have periodic ophthalmic examinations to monitor for visual change.
19. The correct answer is 3. Acetaminophen (Tylenol) is as effective as aspirin in reducing fever. Both have similar antipyretic actions.
20. The correct answer is 2. Due to aspirin's antiplatelet effect, aspirin can be used to decrease TIA.
21. The correct answer is 4. Ibuprofen (Motrin) is the drug of choice to treat primary dysmenorrhea.

NARCOTIC ANALGESICS

A. Case Study
    Mrs. Linda Boyd, age 48, is admitted to the local hospital for an abdominal hysterectomy. Postoperatively she is placed on meperidine (Demerol) 100 mg IM every 4 hours prn.
B. Prototype—Morphine Sulfate
    1. Action. Acts on opioid receptors in CNS and induces sedation, analgesia, and euphoria.
    2. Use. Relief of moderate to severe pain, preoperative medication, pain relief in MI, relief of dyspnea occurring in pulmonary edema or acute left ventricular failure.
    3. Adverse Effects. Sedation, confusion, euphoria, impaired coordination, dizziness; urinary retention; hyperglycemia; respiratory depression; hypotension, tachycardia, bradycardia; nausea, vomiting, constipation; decreased uterine contractility; allergic reactions; tolerance, physical and psychological dependence; pupil constriction.
    4. Nursing Implications
        a. Assess client's pain before giving medication.
        b. Evaluate effectiveness of analgesic including onset and duration of response to medication.

c. Observe for signs of tolerance with prolonged use.
 1) Tolerance means that a larger dose of narcotic analgesic is required to produce the original effect.
 2) The first sign of tolerance is usually a decreased duration of effect of the analgesic.
d. Monitor respiratory rate and depth before giving drug, and periodically thereafter.
e. Encourage sighing, coughing, and deep breathing.
f. Warn ambulatory clients to avoid activities that require alertness.
g. Advise client to change position slowly.
h. Check for signs of urinary retention.
i. Keep stool record and institute measures to prevent constipation; e.g., fluids, foods high in fiber, and activity as tolerated; administer stool softeners and laxatives as ordered.
j. Have narcotic antagonist (naloxone [Narcan]) available for reversal of effects if necessary.
k. Teach client not to drink alcoholic beverages while taking narcotics.
l. Monitor for withdrawal symptoms and decrease dose slowly since these drugs may produce physical dependence.
m. Use special caution with clients with increased intracranial pressure, chronic obstructive pulmonary disease (COPD), alcoholism, severe hepatic or renal disease, and in elderly or debilitated clients who may not metabolize the drug efficiently.
 5. Discharge Teaching
a. Take before pain intensifies to receive fullest analgesic effect.
b. No alcohol or CNS depressants should be taken.
c. No smoking or ambulating alone after drug has been taken.
d. Avoid activities requiring alertness.
C. Related Drugs. See Table 2.6.
D. Narcotic Agonists/Antagonists
 1. Examples: pentazocine (Talwin), nalbuphine (Nubain), butorphanol (Stadol), buprenorphine (Buprenex)
 2. Mechanism of action
a. Term "agonist" refers to the fact that they bind to opioid receptors to produce analgesia.
b. Term "antagonist" refers to the fact that they counteract the effects of the pure narcotic agonists (i.e., morphine, meperidine [Demerol]).
 3. Use. Relief of moderate to severe pain; may be used for clients who cannot tolerate pure narcotic agonists. Caution: May produce withdrawal in a client who has been taking pure narcotic agonists for a week or more.
 4. Adverse Effects. Drowsiness, nausea, psychotomimetic effects, e.g., hallucinations; respiratory depression and constipation but less of a risk than with pure narcotic agonists such as butorphanol (Stadol), nalbuphine (Nubain), pentazocine (Talwin)
E. Combination Drugs
 1. Some narcotics can be combined with other drugs.
 2. Examples of this would be codeine combined with Empirin, Fiorinal, or Tylenol.

Sample Questions

22. Mrs. Boyd is one day post-op. She tells the nurse that she's worried she will become addicted to painkillers so she wants to wait for the pain to become very intense before she takes anything. The best response to her statement by the nurse is:
 1. "Meperidine (Demerol) is very addicting. You shouldn't request pain medication unless you really need it."

TABLE 2.6 Narcotic Analgesics

Drug	Use	Comments
Codeine	Moderate to severe pain, cough relief	• Less potential for dependence than morphine sulfate • Take oral form with food • Monitor for cough suppression • Smoking can reduce pain relief • Cautious use with client on MAO inhibitor
Hydromorphone (Dilaudid)	Moderate to severe pain	• Take oral form with food • Mix with 5 ml of sterile water or normal saline for IV use • Smoking reduces pain relief
Meperidine (Demerol)	Moderate to severe pain, preoperative medication	• Take oral form with food • PO dose <50% as effective as parenteral • IM preferred route for duplicate doses
Methadone (Dolophine)	Severe pain, narcotic withdrawal	• IM preferred route
Oxycodone Hydrochloride (Percocet, Percodan)	Moderate to severe pain	• Monitor liver and blood studies • Give oral form with food • High abuse potential

2. "Meperidine (Demerol) is not appropriate for you. I'll ask the doctor to order a nonnarcotic pain medication for you."
3. "Meperidine" (Demerol) will be most effective if you take it before your pain becomes severe. This will decrease your needing excess amounts of a narcotic."
4. "Meperidine (Demerol) is ordered for you to help manage your pain. You really should take it."

23. Before administering meperidine (Demerol) to Mrs. Boyd, which assessment is most important for the nurse to make?
1. Apical pulse rate.
2. Respiratory rate.
3. Blood pressure.
4. Level of consciousness.

24. Which adverse effect would the nurse NOT expect to observe in a client receiving a narcotic analgesic?
1. Urine retention.
2. Constipation.
3. Hypoglycemia.
4. Hypotension.

Answers and Rationales

22. The correct answer is 3. Narcotic drugs should be taken before pain becomes intense so the client can receive the fullest analgesic effects. By adhering to this, the client will have good pain control and will not be requesting additional doses.
23. The correct answer is 2. Respiratory rate needs to be assessed before giving the client a narcotic as narcotics can have a life-threatening effect.
24. The correct answer is 3. An adverse effect of narcotic analgesics is hyperglycemia. The nurse would not expect to see hypoglycemia.

NARCOTIC ANTAGONISTS

A. Case Study
Mr. Donald Jones, age 55, is in the recovery room after a laminectomy. The recovery room nurse is concerned about his respiratory status. Mr. Jones' respirations were initially stable at 16 per minute but have been steadily decreasing. The anesthetist is called in to examine Mr. Jones and orders naloxone hydrochloride (Narcan).
B. Prototype—Naloxone Hydrochloride (Narcan)
1. Action. Occupies opiate receptor sites and prevents or reverses effects of agonists such as morphine sulfate.
2. Use. Postoperative respiratory depression caused by narcotics, therapy in suspected or confirmed narcotic overdose.

3. Adverse Effects. Excess dosage in narcotic depression: hypertension, tremors, reversal of analgesia, hyperventilation, increases PTT. In too quick reversal: nausea, vomiting; sweating, tachycardia.
4. Nursing Implications
   a. Emergency resuscitative equipment needs to be available.
   b. Monitor VS, especially respirations.
   c. Monitor client closely as activity of some narcotics last longer than that of naloxone hydrochloride (Narcan).
   d. Monitor surgical clients for bleeding.
   e. Withdrawal symptoms will be seen in client addicted to narcotics.
C. Related Drug—Naltrexone (Trexan)
1. Used in narcotic detoxification and to prevent readdiction in drug users.
2. Initial treatment of overdose is naloxone hydrochloride (Narcan) and then naltrexone (Trexan) is given as it has a longer duration of action.

Sample Questions

25. Which of the following observations by the nurse indicates an adverse effect of naloxone hydrochloride (Narcan) on Mr. Jones?
1. Hypotension.
2. Bradycardia.
3. Tremors.
4. Increased urine output.
26. Which client should have cautious use of naloxone hydrochloride (Narcan)?
1. Meperidine (Demerol) addict.
2. Brittle diabetic.
3. Asthmatic.
4. Postoperative radical neck.

Answers and Rationales

25. The correct answer is 3. Tremors are an adverse effect of naloxone hydrochloride (Narcan) and indicate an overdose of the drug.
26. The correct answer is 1. If naloxone hydrochloride (Narcan) is given to a client who is addicted to narcotics, the client will experience withdrawal syndrome. Thus, narcotic addicts should use this drug cautiously.

SEDATIVES AND HYPNOTICS

A. Case Study
Mr. Jack Williams, age 56, a regional sales manager, visits his family physician with

complaints of abdominal pain, recent weight loss of 8 pounds, and change in bowel habits. The physician has been having Mr. Williams undergo diagnostic tests to determine what is wrong with him. As the days have passed without a firm diagnosis from the physician, Mr. Williams has been unable to sleep at night. The physician orders the following medications for Mr. Williams:

Diazepam (Valium) 5 mg PO TID prn
Pentobarbital (Nembutal) 100 mg PO HS prn

B. Prototype for the Barbiturates—Phenobarbital Sodium (Luminal)
   1. Action. Hinders movement of impulses from the thalamus to the brain cortex, thus creating depression in the CNS, which can range from mild to severe. Considered a long-acting barbiturate.
   2. Use. Sedation, hypnosis, seizure disorders.
   3. Adverse Effects. Dizziness, ataxia, drowsiness, "hangover," anxiety, irritability, hand tremors, vision difficulties, insomnia; bradycardia, low blood pressure; chest tightness, wheezing, apnea, respiratory depression; nausea, vomiting, constipation; hypersensitivity reactions.
   4. Nursing Implications
      a. High doses for long periods of time can cause physical dependence.
      b. Drug has extended half-life so steady plasma level may take 3–4 weeks of medication before occurring.
      c. Give reconstituted solutions within 30 minutes of mixing.
      d. Give IM deeply in large muscle mass and observe IM sites.
      e. IV administration: client must be monitored constantly: take VS frequently; have emergency equipment available; monitor for extravasation at infusion site.
      f. Pill can be crushed and mixed with food or fluid.
      g. Will cause restlessness in client in pain.
      h. Geriatric, pediatric, and debilitated clients can have paradoxical reactions.
      i. Monitor liver and blood studies with long-term therapy.
      j. Schedule IV drug under Federal Controlled Substances Act.
      k. Many drug interactions.
   5. Discharge Teaching
      a. Drowsiness occurs in first few weeks of therapy and will decrease.
      b. Avoid potentially dangerous activities until response to drug is known.
      c. Alcohol is prohibited.
      d. Do not alter dosing schedule or amount.

   e. Do not stop abruptly.
   f. Teratogenic. Prolonged use necessitates alternative contraception methods if taking birth control pills.
   g. Do not keep at bedside due to potential for overdosing.

C. Related Drugs. See Table 2.7.
   Note: Actions, adverse effects, and nursing implications are similar to phenobarbital sodium (Luminal).

D. Prototype for Benzodiazepines (antianxiety agents)—Diazepam (Valium)
   1. Action. Not fully understood. Depresses the CNS at the limbic system and reticular formation.
   2. Use. Anxiety disorders, acute alcohol withdrawal, muscle relaxant, tetanus, convulsive disorders, preoperative medication.
   3. Adverse Effects. Dry mouth, constipation, urinary retention, photophobia and blurred vision; for other effects see adverse effects listed under pentobarbital sodium (Luminal).
   4. Nursing Implications
      a. Adverse effects typically dose related.
      b. Two weeks of therapy needed before steady plasma levels seen.
      c. Tablet can be crushed.
      d. Do not mix with other drugs in the same syringe.
      e. Cautious IV use as drug can precipitate in IV solutions.
      f. IM should be deep into large muscle mass; rotate IM sites.
      g. Parenteral administration can cause low blood pressure, increased heart rate, muscle weakness, and respiratory depression.
      h. For extended therapy, monitor liver and blood studies.

TABLE 2.7 Barbiturates

Drug	Use
Amobarbital sodium (Amytal) (intermediate acting)	Sedation, hypnosis, preoperative medication, labor, chronic and acute seizures
Butabarbital sodium (Butisol) (intermediate acting)	Sedation, hypnosis, preoperative medication
Pentobarbital sodium (Nembutal) (short acting)	Sedation, hypnosis, preoperative medication
Secobarbital sodium (Seconal) (short acting)	Hypnosis, preoperative medication
Thiopental sodium (Pentothal Sodium) (ultrashort acting)	Induction of general anesthesia, acute seizures, decrease of intracranial pressure in neurosurgery, narcoanalysis and narcosynthesis in psychiatry

TABLE 2.8 Benzodiazepines

Drug	Use
Alprazolam (Xanax)	Anxiety
Clorazepate (Tranxene)	Anxiety
Flurazepam (Dalmane)	Hypnosis
Midazolam (Versed)	Preoperative Medication, Conscious Sedation
Triazolam (Halcion)	Hypnosis

  i. Adverse effects more likely in geriatric clients.
  j. Monitor I&O.
  k. Schedule IV drug under Federal Controlled Substances Act.
 5. Discharge Teaching
  a. Avoid alcohol.
  b. Avoid potentially dangerous activities until response to drug is known.
  c. Smoking decreases drug effect.
  d. Avoid abrupt discontinuance of drug.
  e. If pregnant or planning a pregnancy, discuss ending drug therapy with physician.
  f. Long-term high dose use can cause physical dependence.
E. Related Drugs. See Table 2.8.
 Note: Actions, adverse effects, and nursing implications are similar to diazepam (Valium).
F. Nonbenzodiazepines
 1. Small number of drugs with similar actions, uses, adverse effects, and nursing implications to the barbiturates.
 2. Examples
  a. Chloral hydrate (Noctec): mainly used as a hypnotic.
  b. Paraldehyde (Paral): used as hypnotic and in delirium tremors.

Sample Questions

27. The nurse tells Mr. Williams that adverse effects of pentobarbital sodium (Nembutal) include all the following except
 1. respiratory depression.
 2. anxiety and hand tremors.
 3. hypotension and bradycardia.
 4. dry mouth and urinary retention.
28. Which group should not receive barbiturates?
 1. Children < 5 years of age.
 2. Pregnant women.
 3. Nursing mothers.
 4. Adults with bleeding ulcers.

Answers and Rationales

27. The correct answer is 4. Adverse effects of pentobarbital sodium (Nembutal) do not

include dry mouth and urinary retention. These effects are more typical of an anticholinergic drug.
28. The correct answer is 2. Barbiturates are teratogenic and are contraindicated for pregnant women.

ANTICONVULSANTS

A. Case Study
 Emily Converse, age 15, has been admitted to the medical surgical unit of the hospital with tonic-clonic seizures. She is started on phenytoin (Dilantin) 100 mg PO TID.
B. Prototype
 Several categories of drugs are used to treat seizure activity. Each group will be addressed and there will be no prototype.
 1. Barbiturates (Phenobarbital)
  a. Used for generalized and absence seizures.
  b. Refer to discussion under sedatives and hypnotics on barbiturates.
 2. Benzodiazepines (Diazepam [Valium])
  a. Drug of choice for status epilepticus. Also used for absence seizures.
  b. Refer to discussion under sedatives and hypnotics on benzodiazepines.
 3. Hydantoins (Phenytoin [Dilantin])
  a. Action: prevents dissemination of electrical discharges in motor cortex area of the brain.
  b. Use: Tonic-clonic and complex partial seizures, status epilepticus, prevention of seizures that accompany neurosurgery.
  c. Adverse Effects. Confusion, slurred speech, slow physical movement; blood dyscrasias; nausea, vomiting, constipation; gingival hyperplasia; hirsutism; rash; acne; hypotension, circulatory collapse, cardiac arrest.
  d. Nursing Implications
   1) May take 7–10 days to achieve therapeutic serum concentration.
   2) Tablet can be crushed and should be mixed with food or fluid.
   3) Suspension must be shaken well.
   4) Can turn urine pink, red, or red-brown.
   5) IM route not recommended.
   6) Do not mix with other drugs.
   7) Monitor CBC, liver, thyroid, and urine tests.
   8) Gingival hyperplasia seen most often in children and adolescents.
   9) Stop drug immediately if a measles-like rash occurs.
  e. Discharge Teaching

1) Relate signs of fatigue, dry skin, deepening voice with extended therapy as drug can mask decreased thyroid reserve.
2) Report jaundice as drug is metabolized in the liver and liver dysfunction causes elevated blood levels of drug.
3) Abrupt drug withdrawal can cause seizures or status epilepticus.
4) Withdraw gradually.
5) Avoid potentially dangerous activities until drug response is known.
6) Alcohol use can cause drug toxicity.
7) Cautious use in pregnancy and lactation.
8) Flu shot during therapy can increase seizure occurrence.
9) Family members need instruction in care of client during a seizure.
4. Succinimides (Ethosuximide [Zarontin]) Used in treatment of absence seizures.
5. Acetazolamide (Diamox) Diuretic used as an adjunct or alone in treatment of absence, tonic-clonic, or myoclonic seizures.
6. Carbamazepine (Tegretol)
   a. Chemically similar to tricyclic antidepressants.
   b. Used in treatment of tonic-clonic, complex partial, and mixed seizures.
7. Valporic Acid (Depakene)
   a. Used in treatment of absence seizures.
   b. Low incidence of side effects as compared to other anticonvulsants.

Sample Questions

29. The nurse should teach Emily and her parents to watch for which common adverse effect of phenytoin (Dilantin)?
    1. Alopecia.
    2. Edema.
    3. Gingival hyperplasia.
    4. Hallucinations.
30. The drug of choice for status epilepticus is
    1. Phenytoin (Dilantin).
    2. Carbamazepine (Tegretol).
    3. Phenobarbital (Luminal).
    4. Diazepam (Valium).

Answers and Rationales

29. The correct answer is 3. Gingival hyperplasia is a common adverse effect of phenytoin (Dilantin) seen most often in children and adolescents.

30. The correct answer is 4. Diazepam (Valium) is the drug of choice for status epilepticus.

SKELETAL MUSCLE RELAXANTS

A. Case Study
   Ms. Kathy Smith, age 41, has multiple sclerosis. She is experiencing muscle spasticity. The physician prescribes baclofen (Lioresal).
B. Prototype
   Various drugs used to treat musculoskeletal problems. Three common drugs will be discussed. There will be no prototype drug.
   1. Baclofen (Lioresal)
      a. Mechanism of action not known but drug inhibits nerve activity in the spinal cord thus decreasing spasms of skeletal muscles.
      b. Used in multiple sclerosis and spinal cord injuries.
      c. Adverse effects. CNS depression ranging from sedation to coma and seizures; urinary frequency; hirsutism, photosensitivity, acne-like rash; nausea and vomiting.
      d. Nursing implications include: may be taken with food, monitor ambulation, depressant effects will be increased if mixed with other CNS depressants, monitor VS, client should avoid potentially dangerous activities until response is known, do not abruptly withdraw.
   2. Carisoprodol (Soma)
      a. Mechanism of action not known but is believed due to drug's central depressant action.
      b. Used in cerebral palsy, muscle stiffness, and spasm found in various musculoskeletal disorders.
      c. Adverse effects. Sedation; headache; syncope, tachycardia, postural hypotension; nausea, vomiting; hiccups, allergic reactions.
      d. Nursing implications. May be taken with food, drowsiness is common effect and client may need dosage reduced, client should not take alcohol or other CNS depressants, do not abruptly stop, allergic reactions usually occur from the first to the fourth dose.
   3. Dantrolene (Dantrum)
      a. Interferes with calcium release from the muscle, which causes a decrease in muscle contraction.
      b. Used for muscle spasms associated with cerebral vascular accident, spinal cord injury, cerebral palsy, and multiple sclerosis. Also given intravenously for malignant hyperthermia.

c. Adverse effects. Drowsiness; malaise, diarrhea; hepatotoxicity (in extended use at high doses).

d. Nursing implications include: capsule can be opened and contents can be mixed with juice or other liquid, monitor ambulation, liver and kidney function tests should be monitored, monitor IV site for extravasation, should be withdrawn after 45 days if no improvement has been seen.

Sample Questions

31. Which statement by Ms. Smith indicates a need for more teaching about baclofen (Lioresal) by the nurse?
    1. "I'll take my pills with my meals."
    2. "I'll drive myself to work each day."
    3. "I won't have wine with dinner anymore."
    4. "I'll use sunscreen when I go outside."

Answers and Rationales

31. The correct answer is 2. Due to the depressant effects of baclofen (Lioresal), the client should not engage in any potentially dangerous activities until the client response to the drug is known.

ANTIPSYCHOTIC AGENTS

A. Case Study
Alice Benson, a 22-year-old student, has become withdrawn from social interaction, has had delusions and hallucinations, and is no longer attending to personal hygiene needs. Her parents take her to the mental health clinic, where Alice is diagnosed with schizophrenia. Alice is to start chlorpromazine (Thorazine).

B. Prototype—Phenothiazines (Chlorpromazine [Thorazinel])
1. Action. Not fully understood, but is thought to block dopamine receptors in the brain. Chlorpromazine causes a sedative effect known as a neuroleptic effect and antipsychotic effect. Also causes an anti-emetic effect by depressing the chemo-receptor trigger zone (CTZ). Potentiates the effects of other CNS depressant drugs. Blocks peripheral acetylcholine (Ach) receptors, histamine (H_1) receptors, and alpha-adrenergic receptors. These actions cause anticholinergic, alpha-anti-adrenergic, and antihistamine effects that can produce adverse effects.

2. Use. Management of acute and chronic schizophrenia, manic phase of bipolar disorder, management of nausea and vomiting, control of excessive anxiety before surgery, treatment of acute intermittent porphyria, treatment of intractable hiccups, tetanus.

3. Adverse Effects. Extrapyramidal symptoms; dizziness, sedation, seizures; orthostatic hypotension, tachycardia, arrhythmias; cholestatic jaundice; agranulocytosis; photosensitivity; anticholinergic effects: "Red, Hot, Dry, Blind, Mad"; urticaria; changes in menses and libido; potentiates CNS effects of narcotic analgesics, sedatives, hypnotics, and alcohol; neuroleptic malignant syndrome.

4. Nursing Implications
   a. Monitor blood pressure (standing, lying, and sitting), pulse, respirations, and I&O.
   b. Wear gloves when handling parenteral or liquid form to prevent contact dermatitis.
   c. Give deep IM injection into gluteal muscle and massage well.
   d. Monitor client for extrapyramidal symptoms, which can occur 1–60 days after therapy is begun. Tardive dyskinesia can occur several months or years after therapy.
   e. Monitor CBC, liver function studies, glucose levels, and urinalysis and encourage periodic ocular examinations.
   f. Supervise ambulation to prevent falls until client develops a tolerance.
   g. Protect drug from light.

5. Discharge Teaching
   a. Take with food or milk to decrease GI distress.
   b. Take drug at bedtime.
   c. Wear protective clothing and/or sunscreen before exposure to sun.
   d. With initial therapy, change positions gradually to reduce orthostatic hypotension.
   e. Report fever, sore throat to physician.
   f. Stop or reduce cigarette smoking, as this shortens the half-life and higher doses may be needed.
   g. Mix liquid form in juice, water, milk, or baby food.
   h. With long-term therapy, drug is gradually reduced before discontinuing therapy.
   i. Incompatible with many drugs. Note: Also review the anticholinergic drug atropine sulfate for nursing implications and discharge teaching.

C. Related Drugs. See Table 2.9.

TABLE 2.9 Phenothiazines

Drug	Use	Comments
Promethazine (Phenergan)	Pre- and postoperative sedation Prophylaxis for nausea, vomiting, motion sickness Adjunct to analgesics Allergic conditions	• Rarely causes extrapyramidal symptoms
Thioridazine (Mellaril)	Psychotic disorders Short-term use in depression Attention deficit disorder	• Rarely causes extrapyramidal symptoms
Fluphenazine (Prolixin) (Prolixin Decanoate)	Psychotic disorders	• Clients at great risk for extrapyramidal symptoms • Most potent phenothiazine
Haloperidol (Haldol)	Psychotic disorders Tourette's syndrome Short-term treatment in hyperactive children	• Clients at great risk for extrapyramidal symptoms • Causes less sedation and hypotension

Sample Questions

32. The psychiatrist orders chlorpromazine (Thorazine) IM for Alice Benson. The nurse should handle the medication carefully to prevent
    1. skin discoloration.
    2. skin irritation.
    3. headache.
    4. dizziness.
33. Which of the following interventions should be included in Alice's care plan concerning chlorpromazine (Thorazine) therapy?
    1. Supervise ambulation.
    2. Take a hot bath to reduce agitation.
    3. Restrict fluid intake to prevent edema.
    4. Discontinue drug if sedation occurs.
34. Which phenothiazine is used specifically as an antiemetic and rarely causes extrapyramidal symptoms?
    1. Thioridazine (Mellaril).
    2. Fluphenazine (Prolixin).
    3. Promethazine (Phenergan).
    4. Chlorpromazine (Thorazine).
35. Which antipsychotic agent is also used to treat Tourette's syndrome and causes less sedation than other phenothiazines?
    1. Haloperidol (Haldol).
    2. Thioridazine (Mellaril).
    3. Fluphenazine (Prolixin).
    4. Chlorpromazine (Thorazine).

Answers and Rationales

32. The correct answer is 2. Handling the parenteral or liquid forms of chlorpromazine (Thorazine) may cause contact dermatitis.
33. The correct answer is 1. Chlorpromazine (Thorazine) during initial use can cause orthostatic hypotension; ambulation should be supervised to prevent falls until tolerance develops.
34. The correct answer is 3. Promethazine (Phenergan) is used as an antiemetic, and rarely causes extrapyramidal symptoms.
35. The correct answer is 1. Haloperidol (Haldol) is also used to treat Tourette's syndrome and causes fewer sedative effects than other phenothiazines.

Antipsychotic Agents (Continued)

A. Case Study
   John Hall, aged 38, is diagnosed with bipolar disorder and is in the manic phase. John is started on lithium therapy.
B. Prototype—Lithium (Lithium carbonate [Eskalith])
   1. Action. Exact mode of action unknown. Thought to alter neurotransmitters in CNS that produce antidepressant and antimanic effects.
   2. Use. Treatment and prophylaxis of manic phase of bipolar disorder.
   3. Adverse Effects. Confusion, restlessness, fatigue, weakness, hand tremors; arrhythmias, circulatory collapse, palpitations, hypotension; blurred vision; dry mouth, thirst, weight gain; nausea, diarrhea; leukocytosis.
   4. Nursing Implications
      a. Monitor serum lithium levels (blood tests usually done monthly).
      b. Monitor for lithium intoxication.
      c. Treatment for lithium intoxication includes IV therapy with normal saline, diuretics, and hemodialysis.
      d. Monitor thyroid function studies periodically.
      e. May take 1–2 weeks to achieve therapeutic effects.
   5. Discharge Teaching
      a. Drink 2.5–3 liters of fluid per day to relieve thirst and dry mouth.
      b. Maintain sodium intake of 6–10 g daily to reduce lithium toxicity.
      c. Take with food to decrease GI distress.
      d. Do not drive or operate machinery until drug response established.
      e. Report to physician: nausea, vomiting, edema, weight gain, tremors, and

drowsiness (may be signs of lithium toxicity or hypothyroidism).
f. Record weight on a weekly basis.
C. Related Drugs
Lithium citrate (Cibalith-S): available in liquid form

Sample Questions

36. Which of the following interventions should the nurse stress to John Hall while on lithium therapy?
    1. Weigh self once a month.
    2. Restrict fluid intake to prevent edema.
    3. Do not restrict sodium intake.
    4. Avoid eating cheese and bananas and drinking wine.

Answers and Rationales

36. The correct answer is 3. Clients need to maintain sodium intake (usually 6–10 g daily) to prevent lithium toxicity.

Antipsychotic Agents (Continued)

A. Case Study
Peter Lutz is a 42-year-old airline pilot who recently lost his job. Peter has become despondent, complains of constant fatigue, and has been contemplating suicide. Peter is referred to the mental health clinic with endogenous depression and is started on imipramine (Tofranil) therapy.
B. Prototype—Tricyclic Antidepressants (Imipramine [Tofranil])
    1. Action. Structurally related to phenathiazines. Blocks reuptake of the neurotransmitters norepinephrine and serotonin at the neuronal membrane, which increases and prolongs the response of the neurotransmitters.
    2. Use. Endogenous and reactive depression; childhood enuresis.
    3. Adverse Effects. Sedation, confusion; anticholinergic effects; orthostatic hypotension, arrhythmias; clients recovering from an acute MI should not take drug; blood dyscrasias; extrapyramidal symptoms; gynecomastia; jaundice.
    4. Nursing Implications
        a. May take 2–4 weeks to achieve therapeutic effects. Monitor for suicidal tendencies.
        b. Monitor CBC for clients on long-term therapy.
        c. Monitor I&O.

d. Drug therapy is discontinued gradually.
5. Discharge Teaching
Take with food to decrease GI distress
Note: Review the anticholinergic atropine sulfate for further nursing implications and discharge teaching as imipramine (Tofranil) has anticholinergic adverse effects.
C. Related Drugs
    1. Amitriptyline (Elavil)
    2. Noritriptyline (Aventyl): more useful in elderly clients due to fewer anticholinergic effects.

Sample Questions

37. Which of the following is included in Peter Lutz's teaching concerning imipramine (Tofranil)?
    1. Expect to see improvement of depression in 2–3 days.
    2. Stop taking drug if dizziness occurs.
    3. Do not drive or operate machinery.
    4. Take drug on an empty stomach.
38. When should Mr. Lutz expect to see improvement of depression while on imipramine (Tofranil)?
    1. 1–2 days.
    2. 1 week.
    3. Several weeks.
    4. Immediately after first dose.

Answers and Rationales

37. The correct answer is 3. Imipramine (Tofranil) can cause drowsiness; the client should avoid driving or operating machinery.
38. The correct answer is 3. It takes several weeks (2–4 weeks) before clients may see improvement of depression.

Antipsychotic Agents (Continued)

A. Case Study
Leo Smith has been withdrawn and very depressed since his wife passed away 6 weeks ago. His physician starts Mr. Smith on phenelzine (Nardil) 15 mg PO TID.
B. Prototype—Monoamine Oxidase Inhibitors (MAO Inhibitors) (Phenelzine [Nardil])
    1. Action. Inhibits MAO, which increases neurotransmitter levels (dopamine, norepinephrine, serotonin).
    2. Use. Neurotic and atypical depression.
    3. Adverse Effects. Orthostatic hypotension; dry mouth, blurred vision, constipation; hypertensive crisis; liver dysfunction; leukopenia.

4. Nursing Implications
    a. Monitor blood pressure standing, sitting, and supine.
    b. Interacts with many drugs.
    c. Monitor I&O.
    d. Therapeutic effectiveness takes 2–4 weeks.
    e. Monitor liver function studies, glucose, and CBC.
5. Discharge Teaching
    a. Avoid foods or beverages containing tyramine or tryptophan including: caffeine beverages, soy sauce, red wine, beer, cheese, yogurt, sour cream, raisins, bananas, avocado, herring, beef and chicken liver, Italian green beans.
    b. Change position slowly.
C. Related Drugs
    1. Tranylcypromine (Parnate): contraindicated in clients over age 60.

Sample Questions

39. Which foods/beverages should Mr. Smith avoid while taking phenelzine (Nardil)?
    1. Cheese.
    2. Apples.
    3. Pasta.
    4. Cereal.

Answers and Rationales

39. The correct answer is 1. Foods such as cheese that contain tyramine or tryptophan should be avoided while taking MAO inhibitors to prevent hypertensive crisis.

Antipsychotic Agents (Continued)

A. Case Study
    Jose Cruz, a 20-year-old college student, has stopped attending classes and is unable to get out of bed and perform his ADL's. His parents are notified and they take him to a psychiatrist who starts him on fluoxetine (Prozac) therapy.

B. Prototype-Selective Serotonin Reuptake Inhibitors (Fluoxetine [Prozac])
    1. Action. Blocks serotonin reuptake and increases transmission at serotonergic synapses.
    2. Use. Major depression; obsessive-compulsive disorder.
    3. Adverse Effects. CNS stimulation, sexual dysfunction, nausea, headache, anorexia, weight loss, skin rash.
    4. Nursing Implications
        a. Can take up to 4 weeks to achieve therapeutic effects.
        b. Interacts with warfarin (Coumadin).
        c. Cannot be combined with Monoamine Oxidase Inhibitors.
    5. Discharge Teaching
        a. Take in the morning.
        b. Report skin rash immediately.
C. Related Drugs
    1. Paroxetine (Paxil)
    2. Sertraline (Zoloft)
D. Miscellaneous Antidepressants
    1. Bupropion (Wellbutrin)
    2. Venlafaxine (Effexor)

Sample Questions

40. Which statement by Jose indicates a need for more teaching by the nurse concerning fluoxetine (Prozac) therapy?
    1. "I will take this medication in the morning."
    2. "I will use calamine lotion if I get a skin rash."
    3. "It will take a month before I feel better."
    4. "I will check with my doctor before I take any other medications."

Answers and Rationales

40. The correct answer is 2. A skin rash resulting from use of fluoxetine (prozac) indicates an allergic reaction and should be reported to the physician immediately.

Autonomic Nervous System Drugs

ADRENERGIC DRUGS

A. Case Study

Mr. Lloyd Baker, age 61, is brought to the cardiac care unit in cardiogenic shock. He is placed on an intravenous infusion of dopamine hydrochloride (Intropin).

B. Prototype

Adrenergic drugs are divided into two groups, direct-acting and mixed-acting. The direct-acting contain most of the adrenergic drugs.

Direct-acting Adrenergics

Nonselective (Alpha and Beta) Agonists

Prototype—Epinephrine (Adrenalin Chloride)

1. Action. Epinephrine (Adrenalin Chloride) has the same actions stimulated as the sympathetic nervous system. It increases the force of myocardial contraction; increases systolic blood pressure, cardiac rate and output; relaxes bronchial smooth muscle; inhibits histamine release; increases tidal volume and vital capacity; prevents insulin release and raises blood sugar; prevents uterine contractions and relaxes uterine smooth muscle; lowers intraocular pressure and decreases formation of aqueous humor; constricts arterioles in kidneys, mucous membranes, and skin; and dilates blood vessels in skeletal muscle.

2. Use. Treatment of anaphylaxis and bronchospasm, cardiac resuscitation, control or prevention of low blood pressure during spinal anesthesia, lengthening effects of local anesthesia, promotion of mydriasis, treatment of acute hypotension.

3. Adverse Effects. Systemic: anxiety, headache, fear, arrhythmias, hypertension, cerebral/subarachnoid hemorrhage, hemiplegia, pulmonary edema, insomnia, anginal pain in clients with angina pectoris, tremors, vertigo, sweating, nausea, vomiting, agitation, disorientation, paranoid delusions; prolonged use at high doses causes increased serum lactic acid levels, metabolic acidosis, and increased blood glucose. Local injection: necrosis at sites when injections are repeated. Nasal solution: stinging and burning locally, rebound congestion. Ophthalmic solutions: stinging on initial use, eye pain, headache, browache, blurred vision, photophobia, problems with night vision, pigment deposits in conjunctiva, cornea, and eyelids with prolonged use.

4. Nursing Implications
   a. Use great caution in preparing and calculating doses as this is a potent drug.
   b. Tolerance occurs with extended use.
   c. Solutions should be clear and colorless (except suspension for injection). Protect solutions from light, heat, and freezing.
   d. Suspension for injection must be shaken well.
   e. Rotate SC sites and monitor for necroses.
   f. Have a fast-acting alpha-adrenergic blocker such as phentolamine (Regitine) or vasodilator such as nitrite available for excessive hypertensive reaction.
   g. Have an alpha-adrenergic blocker available for pulmonary edema.
   h. Have a beta-adrenergic blocker available for cardiac arrhythmias.
   i. Monitor VS.

5. Discharge Teaching
   a. For inhalation products: do not exceed recommended dosage; take drug during second half of inspiration, take second inhalation 3–5 minutes after first dose.
   b. For nasal solutions: do not use for more than 3–5 days; burning and stinging may occur initially but are transient.
   c. For ophthalmic solution: slight stinging may occur initially but is usually transient; headache and browache are also transient.
   d. Do not take any OTC medications without physician approval.

Prototype—Norepinephrine Bitartrate (Levophed)

1. Action. Norepinephrine bitartrate (Levophed) is an alpha and beta-1 receptor agonist and has no effect on beta-2 receptors. Its biggest action is seen on the cardiovascular system, where the following happens: an increase in total peripheral resistance (vasopressor response); and increased force, rate, and impulse conduction of the heart, which is usually overridden by activation of baroreceptors, thus causing bradycardia. Other actions are mydriasis and elevated blood glucose and insulin.

2. Use. Revives blood pressure in acute hypotensive states (sympathectomy, spinal anesthesia, poliomyelitis, septicemia, blood transfusion, drug reactions); adjunct in treatment of cardiac arrest.
3. Adverse Effects. Bradycardia; cardiac arrhythmias; headache.
4. Nursing Implications
   a. Do not mix drug in 100% saline solutions (NS) as oxidation will occur. Mix in 5% dextrose solution or 5% dextrose in saline solution.
   b. Give into large vein to prevent extravasation.
   c. Do not infuse in femoral vein in elderly clients or those with occlusive vascular disease.
   d. Check blood pressure every 2 minutes after start of infusion until desired blood pressure is attained; then check blood pressure every 5 minutes if infusion continued.
   e. Monitor IV site for extravasation.
   f. Have phentolamine (Regitine) available in case of extravasation. 5–10 mg of phentolamine (Regitine) in 10–15 ml of saline should be infiltrated into area.
   g. Drug solution should be clear and colorless.

Selective Alpha Agonists

Prototype—Phenylephrine (Neo-Synephrine)
1. Action. Phenylephrine (Neo-Synephrine) produces vasoconstriction and increased blood pressure. Topical application produces vasoconstriction of mucous membranes. Application to eye causes mydriasis and vasoconstriction and promotes flow of aqueous humor.
2. Use. Stabilizes blood pressure during anesthesia; vascular failure in shock; subdues paroxysmal supraventricular tachycardia; rhinitis of allergy and common cold; sinusitis; wide-angle glaucoma; ophthalmoscopic examination or surgery; uveitis.
3. Adverse Effects. Eye tearing and stinging, headache, browache, blurred vision, increased sensitivity to light; nasal rebound congestion; nasal burning, stinging, dryness, and sneezing; palpitations, tachycardia, bradycardia (overdose); hypertension; trembling, sweating, feeling of fullness in the head; sleeplessness, dizziness, light-headedness, tingling in extremities.
4. Nursing Implications
   a. For IV infusion, check blood pressure, pulse, and central venous pressure every 2–5 minutes.
   b. IV overdose can cause ventricular arrhythmias.
   c. Phentolamine (Regitine) should be available for hypertensive crisis seen in IV administration.
   d. Levodopa (L-Dopa) is used to decrease excess mydriatic effect.
   e. If systemic adverse effects are seen from nasal and eye use, stop drug and notify physician.
   f. Apply pressure to lacrimal sac of eye during and for 1–2 minutes after administration of eye drops.
   g. Incompatible with Butacaine, oxidizing agents, ferric salts, metals, and alkalies.
   h. Wash hands after handling drug as blurred vision and unequal pupil size can result if drug-contaminated finger rubs eye.
5. Discharge Teaching
   a. Client should not change dose in any way.
   b. If drug has been taken for 5 days without relief, notify physician.
   c. Clear nasal passages before using nasal preparations.
   d. Wear sunglasses after eye administration if eyes sensitive to light.
   e. Call physician if eye sensitivity lasts more than 12 hours after drug has been given.
   f. Ophthalmic solutions can stain contact lenses.
   g. Tips and droppers of nasal solutions should be cleaned with hot water after each use.
   h. Do not touch droppers of eye solutions.
6. Related Drugs
   a. Methoxamine (Vasoxyl): used for treating acute hypotension seen during surgery. It is given IV for immediate effect or IM for longer lasting effects.
   b. Agents found in OTC cough, cold, and allergy remedies and in eye decongestant products include naphazoline, oxymetazoline, tetrahydrozoline, xylometazoline.

Nonselective Beta (Beta-1 and Beta-2) Agonists

Prototype—Isoproterenol (Isuprel)
1. Action. Isoproterenol (Isuprel) has cardiovascular actions of vasodilation, which decreases diastolic blood pressure and peripheral resistance, and actions of increased cardiac output. Other actions are bronchodilation; raising levels of blood glucose, insulin, and free fatty acids; and causing release of renin from the kidney.
2. Use. Acute heart failure; management of intraoperative bronchospasm; additive

treatment in cardiac arrest, AV heart block, Stokes-Adams syndrome; treatment of chronic bronchoconstriction; management of syncope; treatment of bronchospasm in COPD and asthma.

3. Adverse Effects. Restlessness, anxiety, CNS stimulation, hyperkinesia, insomnia, tremors, irritability, vertigo, headache; arrhythmias, tachycardia, angina, blood pressure changes; pulmonary edema, respiratory difficulties; flushing, pallor, sweating; nausea, vomiting, heartburn.

4. Nursing Implications
   a. Tolerance can develop with prolonged use.
   b. A beta-adrenergic blocker should be available if arrhythmias occur.
   c. Client needs continuous EKG monitoring during IV administration.
   d. IV infusion must be given via infusion pump with guidelines from the physician.

5. Discharge Teaching
   a. Client should not alter dosage.
   b. Inhalation form should be taken during second half of inspiration; second inhalation should be taken 3–5 minutes later.
   c. Client should not chew or swallow sublingual tablets.
   d. Avoid OTC drugs unless approved by physician.

6. Related Drugs
   a. Ethylnorepinephrine (Bronkephrine) is used to treat acute bronchospasm and is given SC or IM to both adults and children.
   b. Isorsuprine hydrochloride (Vasodilan) is used in cerebrovascular insufficiency and peripheral vascular disease. It is given to adults via IM or PO.
   c. Nylidrin hydrochloride (Arlidin) is used in peripheral vascular disease and ischemic disorders of inner ear. It is given orally to adults.

Selective Beta-1 Agonists

Prototype—Dopamine Hydrochloride (Intropin)
1. Action. Dopamine hydrochloride (Intropin) increases cardiac output and systolic blood pressure. In low doses it reduces renal vascular resistance, which increases glomerular filtration rate and urinary output.
2. Use. Corrects hemodynamic imbalance in shock caused by myocardial infarction, trauma, septicemia, congestive heart failure, and open heart surgery.
3. Adverse Effects. Tachycardia, palpitations, hypotension, vasoconstriction; nausea, vomiting; dyspnea, headache; piloerection.

4. Nursing Implications
   a. Must be administered cautiously as even small errors can produce deleterious effects.
   b. Always dilute drug if not prediluted.
   c. Dose must be decreased by 1/10 in clients who have been receiving MAO inhibitors.
   d. Do not mix with other drugs.
   e. Protect drug from light.
   f. Infuse into large vein.
   g. Monitor for extravasation and have phentolamine (Regitine) available if this occurs.
   h. Closely check blood pressure, urine output, and cardiac output.

5. Related Drugs
   Dobutamine (Dobutrex) is used in treatment of acute heart failure. It is given to adults via IV infusion.

Selective Beta-2 Agonists

All drugs in this group are similar so there will be no prototype. Two representative examples will be mentioned.

1. Metaproterenol sulfate (Alupent) is used to treat bronchial asthma and bronchospasm that accompanies emphysema and bronchitis. It is given orally and via metered-dose inhaler or inhalant solution to adults. Children 60 pounds or less receive syrup orally and children > 12 years can receive inhalation therapy. Adverse effects include CNS stimulation; cardiac arrhythmias, tachycardia, palpitations, changes in blood pressure; respiratory difficulties; sweating, pallor, flushing; nausea, vomiting, and heartburn. Nursing implications are: tolerance can occur with prolonged use; have a beta-adrenergic blocker available in case of arrhythmia; give inhalant during second half of inspiration; and teach clients to not alter dose and not to take any OTC drugs without physician approval.

2. Terbutaline sulfate (Brethine): refer to data on metaproterenol sulfate (Alupent). It is given PO, SC, and via inhaler to adults and children > 12 years.

Mixed-acting Adrenergics

Prototype—Ephedrine (various products)
1. Action. Ephedrine's actions are similar to the peripheral autonomic effects of norepinephrine. The main effects of the drug are reduced nasal congestion, increased blood pressure, bronchodilation, cardiac stimulation, and stimulation of the central nervous system.
2. Use. Relief of allergies and mild asthma; therapy in shock and hypotension.

3. Adverse Effects. Systemic with increased doses: headache, insomnia, nervousness; palpitations, tachycardia, arrhythmias, urinary retention; nausea, vomiting, anorexia; sweating, thirst. Topical use: burning, stinging, sneezing, dry nasal mucosa, rebound congestion. Overdose: confusion, delirium, convulsions, pyrexia, coma; hypertension; respiratory depression; paranoid psychosis; auditory and visual hallucinations.
4. Nursing Implications
   a. Parenteral solution must be clear and should be protected from light.
   b. Monitor urine output.
   c. Clients with cardiovascular problems need monitoring of cardiac response and blood pressure.
   d. Client receiving IV ephedrine needs close monitoring of vital signs.
5. Discharge Teaching
   a. Client should not use nasal decongestant longer than 5 days.
   b. Anxiety reaction can occur with extended use of systemic ephedrine.
   c. Ephedrine is commonly abused. Client needs to be aware of adverse effects and proper use.
   d. Client should not take any OTC preparations without consulting physician.
   e. Insomnia is a common effect and doses should be spaced accordingly.
6. Related Drugs
   Metaraminol (Aramine): used for acute hypotension and can be given preoperatively to prevent hypotension; given SC, IM, or IV; given to adults and children.

Sample Questions

41. Mr. Baker is started out on a low dose level of dopamine hydrochloride (Intropin) intravenously. Which of the following can the nurse expect?
    1. A decrease in glomerular filtration rate.
    2. A decrease in the force of myocardial contractions.
    3. An increase in urine output.
    4. An increase in tactile sensation.
42. Which nursing action is NOT appropriate for Mr. Baker while receiving IV dopamine hydrochloride (Intropin)?
    1. The nurse will monitor vital signs frequently.
    2. The nurse will check the IV infusion site frequently for extravasation.
    3. The nurse will infuse the drug via macrodrip tubing and will adjust the rate manually.
    4. The nurse will check client extremities for temperature and color.
43. Mr. Baker experiences extravasation at the insertion site of dopamine hydrochloride (Intropin) IV. The infusion is stopped. What should be done next?
    1. Warm compresses should be applied to the IV site.
    2. An ice pack should be applied to the IV site.
    3. The extremity with the IV site should be elevated on two pillows.
    4. The IV site should be infiltrated with phentolamine (Regitine).
44. When high doses of dopamine hydrochloride (Intropin) are given IV for treatment of shock, what effect would the nurse be looking for?
    1. Increased blood pressure.
    2. Decreased heart rate.
    3. Increased respirations.
    4. Elevated body temperature.
45. Which drug produces effects that closely mimic high doses of dopamine hydrochloride (Intropin)?
    1. Atropine sulfate.
    2. Ephedrine.
    3. Isoproterenol (Isuprel).
    4. Norepinephrine (Levophed).

Answers and Rationales

41. The correct answer is 3. Dopamine hydrochloride (Intropin) at low doses causes dilation of renal and mesenteric arteries, which in turn causes increased urine output.
42. The correct answer is 3. Dopamine hydrochloride (Intropin) needs to be infused via a minidrip tubing and attached to an infusion pump for accurate administration.
43. The correct answer is 4. If extravasation occurs when dopamine hydrochloride (Intropin) is administered, the IV site should be infiltrated with phentolamine (Regitine) immediately after discontinuing the infusion.
44. The correct answer is 1. High doses of dopamine hydrochloride (Intropin) stimulate alpha-adrenergic activity, which causes increased blood pressure.
45. The correct answer is 4. Dopamine hydrochloride (Intropin) given in high doses has effects that closely mimic norepinephrine (Levophed).

ADRENERGIC BLOCKING AGENTS

A. Case Study
   Mrs. Ruth Gardener is 43 years old and has a history of migraine headaches. She has tried

various drug therapies without success. The physician has now decided to start her on ergotamine tartrate (Ergomar).

B. Prototype for Alpha-Adrenergic Blocking Agents—Phentolamine (Regitine)
   1. Action. Phentolamine (Regitine) blocks alpha-1 receptors, thus causing blood vessel dilation; decreased blood pressure; increased cardiac output; miosis; increased tearing, mucous secretion, gastric acid secretion, and gastrointestinal motility.
   2. Use. Diagnosis of pheochromocytoma; management of hypertensive episodes in pheochromocytoma; treatment of extravasation from norepinephrine (Levophed) or dopamine hydrochloride (Intropin); adjunctive therapy in cardiogenic shock or other situations of decreased cardiac output.
   3. Adverse Effects. Hypotension, orthostatic hypotension; MI, cerebrovascular occlusion (these effects can occur with hypotensive states that can occur after parenteral administration); tachycardia, arrhythmias; dizziness, weakness, flushing; nausea, vomiting, diarrhea; nasal stuffiness.
   4. Nursing Implications
      a. For parenteral administration client must be in supine position. Blood pressure and pulse should be checked every 2 minutes until stable.
      b. Use reconstituted solutions immediately.
      c. Have client lie down or put head down if feeling dizzy or light-headed.
      d. Treatment for overdose: keep client lying down with head lowered, supportive measures, IV infusion of Levarterenol (norepinephrine).
C. Related Drug—Ergotamine tartrate (Ergomar)
   1. Along with adrenergic blocking activity, has a direct stimulatory effect on smooth muscle. It also decreases pulsation in cranial arteries and has emetic and oxytocic effects.
   2. Used for treatment of vascular headaches such as migraines or cluster headaches.
   3. Given to adults via sublingual or inhalation route.
   4. Adverse effects: nausea, vomiting; numbness, tingling, and muscle pain in extremities; pulselessness in legs; precordial pain; transient tachycardia or bradycardia; ergotism (ergot poisoning); dependency and abuse.
   5. Nursing implications: take drug at beginning of migraine attack, avoid prolonged use, give antiemetics for nausea and vomiting; monitor extremities; pregnant client should not receive this drug; client should not increase dose of

drug without consulting physician; and use lowest effective dose.

Beta-Adrenergic Blocking Agents

Note: Refer to Beta Blockers in the section on Cardiovascular Drugs.

Timolol maleate (Timoptic) is an optic beta-adrenergic blocker. It decreases intraocular pressure whether glaucoma is present or not. It also decreases aqueous humor formation and increases aqueous humor outflow. It is used to treat glaucoma and hypertension. It is given orally and via eye drops to adult clients.

Sample Questions

46. Mrs. Gardener calls the physician's office and states that she has vomited each time she has taken ergotamine tartrate (Ergomar). The nurse's best response is:
    1. "Vomiting is a common adverse effect. Tell the physician so he can prescribe an antiemetic for you."
    2. "Stop taking the drug immediately. Vomiting is a toxic drug effect."
    3. "You must be allergic to the drug. Notify the physician."
    4. "Vomiting is a transient effect and it will eventually go away."
47. Which group of individuals should not receive ergotamine tartrate (Ergomar)?
    1. Diabetic clients.
    2. Asthmatic clients.
    3. Alcoholic clients.
    4. Pregnant women.
48. The nurse should relate all of the following information about ergotamine tartrate (Ergomar) to Mrs. Gardener EXCEPT
    1. take the drug as soon as you feel a migraine headache coming on.
    2. have your blood pressure checked routinely when taking this drug.
    3. increase the dose as needed to help control your migraines.
    4. tell the physician if you have any numbness or tingling in your toes and fingers.

Answers and Rationales

46. The correct answer is 1. Ergotamine tartrate (Ergomar) has emetic effects; vomiting is a common side effect. The client needs an antiemetic to help control this problem.
47. The correct answer is 4. Ergotamine tartrate (Ergomar) has oxytocic effects; it is contraindicated in pregnant women.
48. The correct answer is 3. Ergotamine tartrate (Ergomar) is a drug that is abused by clients

by altering dosage amount. Only the physician should change the dose of the drug.

CHOLINERGICS

A. Case Study
Faye Nesbitt is a 62-year-old woman who is scheduled for a right (OD) cataract extraction. The physician orders acetylcholine chloride (Miochol) topically to the right eye to produce miosis.

B. Prototype—Acetylcholine Chloride (Miochol)
1. Action. A neurotransmitter that mediates synaptic activity in the nervous system; stimulates the vagus nerve and parasympathetic nervous system (PNS) causing vasodilation and cardiac depression; causes miosis of the eye as it contracts the iris sphincter muscle; contracts and relaxes the urinary bladder, causing micturition. Acetylcholine chloride (Miochol) is identical to synthesized acetylcholine (Ach).
2. Use. To produce miosis in eye surgery.
3. Adverse Effects. Systemic absorption: hypotension, bradycardia; bronchospasm; flushing, sweating.
4. Nursing Implications
   a. Reconstitute vial just before use and discard unused portion.
   b. Shake vial gently to mix drug.

C. Related Drugs—Bethanechol Chloride (Urecholine)
1. Used to treat postoperative urinary retention.
2. See acetylcholine chloride (Miochol); also: nausea, vomiting, diarrhea, abdominal cramping, dizziness, faintness; cholinergic crisis can occur with overdose.
3. Nursing Implications
   a. Monitor VS, breath sounds, and I&O.
   b. PO drug should be given one hour before meals or two hours after meals.
   c. Never give IM or IV as drug may cause life-threatening effects.
   d. Atropine sulfate is antidote.
4. Discharge Teaching
   a. Encourage client not to drive or operate heavy machinery while taking drug.
   b. Teach client to change positions slowly. Note: carbachol (Isopto Carbachol) and pilocarpine (Almocarpine) are discussed under Miotics in section on Eye Drugs.

D. Prototype—Acetylcholinesterase Inhibitors—Neostigmine (Prostigmin)
1. Action. Neostigmine (Prostigmin) inhibits the neurotransmitter acetylcholine, which produces a cholinergic response, and produces reversible cholinesterase inactivation, which permits a prolonged effect of acetylcholine at cholinergic synapses.
2. Use. Treatment and diagnosis of myasthenia gravis; prevention of postoperative abdominal distension; treatment and prevention of postoperative bladder distension; postoperative reversal of nondepolarizing muscle relaxants.
3. Adverse Effects. Nausea, vomiting, cramping, diarrhea, increased salivation; muscle tremor and weakness; dyspnea, bronchospasm, increased bronchial secretions, respiratory depression; hypo- or hypertension, arrhythmias, bradycardia; miosis; cholinergic crisis.
4. Nursing Implications
   a. Keep atropine and emergency resuscitation equipment readily available, especially for parenteral use.
   b. Monitor vital signs, breath sounds, I&O.
   c. Report to physician if client does not void within one hour after receiving dose.
5. Discharge Teaching
   a. Encourage client to take drug with food or milk if GI distress occurs.
   b. Instruct client to keep a record of response to drug.
   c. Instruct client to monitor and report adverse effects.
   d. Advise client to wear a medic alert bracelet (for myasthenia gravis).
   e. Instruct client to cough, breathe deeply, and perform range of motion exercises regularly.

E. Related Drugs
1. Pyridostigmine (Mestinon, Regonol): used to treat myasthenia gravis and postoperative reversal of nondepolarizing skeletal muscle relaxants.
   Additional adverse effects: rash; thrombophlebitis with IV use.
2. Edrophonium chloride (Tensilon): used to diagnose myasthenia gravis.
3. Tacrine (Cognex): used to treat mild to moderate Alzheimer's Disease.

Sample Questions

49. When preparing the drug bethanechol chloride (Urecholine) the nurse knows that
   1. IM or IV is the preferred route.
   2. bethanichol chloride (Urecholine) should be given with food.
   3. breath sounds should be monitored.
   4. constipation is a frequent adverse effect.
50. Which drug would be given to treat neostigmine (Prostigmin) overdose?

1. Acetylcholine acetate (Miochol).
2. Atropine sulfate.
3. Bethanechol (Urecholine).
4. Lidocaine (Xylocaine).

Answers and Rationales

49. The correct answer is 3. Breath sounds should be monitored to assess for wheezing and bronchospasm.
50. The correct answer is 2. Atropine sulfate, an anticholinergic, is the antidote for neostigmine (Prostigmin).

ANTICHOLINERGICS

A. Case Study
   Dennis Greene, a 42-year-old former professional football player, is scheduled for a right total knee replacement. The anesthesiologist orders atropine sulfate 1 mg IM 30 minutes before surgery.
B. Prototype—Atropine Sulfate
   1. Action. Atropine sulfate is a plant alkaloid derived from the atropa belladonna plant that blocks the neurotransmitter acetylcholine and inhibits parasympathetic actions.
   2. Use. To produce mydriasis and cycloplegia for eye examinations; treat uveitis; preoperative medication to reduce secretions and bradycardia; treat sinus bradycardia or asystole; hypermotility of GU tract; adjunct in treating asthmatic bronchospasm; GI disorders, peptic ulcer, GI hypermotility and biliary colic; antidote for overdoses of parasympathomimetic drugs; prevention of adverse effects when reversing neuromuscular blockade post-operatively with acetylcholine inhibitor; antidote to organophosphate pesticides.
   3. Adverse Effects. Disorientation, restlessness, hallucinations, headache, dizziness; palpitation, hypertension or hypotension, ventricular tachycardia; blurred vision, photophobia; suppression of sweating; urinary hesitancy and retention, constipation; dry mouth; flushed, dry skin.
   4. Nursing Implications
      a. Do not give to clients with myasthenia gravis, acute glaucoma, prostatic hypertrophy.
      b. Monitor VS, especially pulse and blood pressure and I&O.
      c. Monitor for constipation and check bowel sounds.

TABLE 2.10 Anticholinergics

Drug	Use	Comments
Scopolamine (Hydrolromide)	Preanesthetic medication (Transderm-scop) used for prophylaxis of motion sickness Mydriatic and cyclo-plegic for eye exam Irritable bowel syndrome, diverticulitis Management of postencephalitic parkinsonism	• Place transderm scop patch behind ear the night before trip. Replace patch after three days if more prolonged effects are needed.
Glycopyrrolate (Robinul)	Preanesthetic medication Adjunct in peptic ulcer disease therapy Reverse neuromuscular blockade	• Has fewer CNS effects than atropine. Do not mix with barbiturates or alkaline drugs.

      d. Monitor geriatric clients for CNS stimulation and heat stroke (infants and small children should also be monitored for heat stroke).
      e. Note: smaller doses usually are given to geriatric clients due to adverse effects.
   5. Discharge Teaching
      a. Take drug 30 minutes before meals.
      b. Eat foods high in fiber and drink plenty of liquids to overcome consti-pation.
      c. Keep dental appointments as decreased salivation makes clients more prone to tooth decay.
      d. Use good oral hygiene, i.e., rinse mouth, brush teeth, hard candy, saliva substitute, fluids.
      e. Maintain periodic eye appointments to monitor for increased intraocular pressure.
      f. Avoid hot baths and showers, sun, and heat to prevent heat stroke.
      g. Change position gradually.
      h. Do not drive or operate machinery.
C. Related Drugs. See Table 2.10.

Sample Questions

51. Which of the following effects of atropine sulfate would the nurse expect Mr. Greene to exhibit?
    1. Dry mouth.
    2. Increased bronchial secretions.
    3. Tachycardia.
    4. Miosis.

52. Which statement indicates that the client needs more teaching concerning the use of atropine sulfate?
    1. "I will brush my teeth and see my dentist regularly."
    2. "I will eat low-residue foods to prevent diarrhea."
    3. "I will take my medication at least a half hour before meals."
    4. "I will stay in my air conditioned house on hot and humid days."

Answers and Rationales

51. The correct answer is 1. Atropine sulfate causes dry mouth and decreases secretions, which is why it is given as a preanesthetic.
52. The correct answer is 2. Atropine sulfate can cause constipation; high-fiber foods and fluids should be encouraged.

ANTIPARKINSON AGENTS

General Considerations

There are 2 major categories of antiparkinson's agents:
    1. Anticholinergics
    2. Dopaminergic agents
    Antiparkinson drugs control rather than cure symptoms of Parkinson's.
    Antiparkinson agents can cause or worsen other disorders, and clients, especially the elderly, need to be closely monitored for adverse effects. Antiparkinson drugs are initiated and discontinued gradually. Drugs should not be abruptly withdrawn.
    Antiparkinson agents are contraindicated in clients with glaucoma, prostatic hypertrophy, duodenal ulcers, tachycardia, and biliary obstruction.
A. Case Study
    Mrs. Janet Lyons, aged 68, has noticed gradual muscle weakness and hand tremors with pill-rolling finger motion. After a complete history and physical and an EEG, the physician starts Mrs. Lyons on trihexyphenidyl HCl (Artane). Mrs. Lyons' symptoms begin to improve and the physician makes the diagnosis of Parkinson's disease.
B. Prototype—Anticholinergics (Trihexyphenidyl HCl [Artane]) This drug is similar to atropine sulfate.
    1. Action. Blocks the neurotransmitter acetylcholine at certain cerebral synapses and inhibits parasympathetic responses.
    2. Use. Treat Parkinson's disease, prevent or control antipsychotic drug-induced extrapyramidal tract symptoms.
    3. Adverse Effects. Note phrase "Red, hot, dry, mad"; dry mouth; constipation; tachycardia, hypotension; dizziness, drowsiness, confusion; decreased bronchial secretions; blurred vision, photophobia, acute glaucoma; urinary retention; suppression of sweating.
    4. Nursing Implications
        a. Drug can be taken before or after meals.
        b. See atropine sulfate.
        c. Drug should be gradually withdrawn.
    5. Discharge Teaching. See atropine.
C. Related Drugs. See Table 2.11.
D. Prototype—Dopaminergic Agents (Levodopa [Larodopa])
    1. Action. Levodopa (Larodopa) is a metabolic precursor of the catecholamine neurotransmitter dopamine that readily crosses the blood-brain barrier and restores dopamine levels in extrapyramidal centers.
    2. Use. Treat Parkinson's disease (except drug-induced Parkinson's).
    3. Adverse Effects. Anorexia, nausea, vomiting; orthostatic hypotension, dizziness, headache; constipation, dry mouth; mydriasis; urinary retention, darkened urine; increase BUN AST (SGOT), ALT (SGPT), LDH, bilirubin, alkaline phosphatase; decreased WBCs, hemoglobin, and hematocrit, decreased glucose tolerance; blurred vision; muscle twitching, blepharospasm, ataxia, increased hand tremors; disturbed breathing; confusion, anxiety, agitation.
    4. Nursing Implications
        a. Monitor vital signs and client for adverse effects.
        b. Monitor client for behavior changes.
        c. Monitor CBC, glucose, and kidney and liver function studies.
        d. With long-term therapy levodopa (Levopa) may lose its effectiveness and adjunctive drugs may be used.

TABLE 2.11 Antiparkinson Agent (Anticholinergic)

Drug	Use	Comments
Benztropine Mesylate (Cogentin)	Treat Parkinson's disease and as adjunct with trihexyphenidyl HCl (Artane) Prevent or control drug-induced extrapyramidal tract symptoms	• Longer lasting sedative effects and muscle relaxation than trihexyphenidyl HCl (Artane)

TABLE 2.12   Antiparkinson Agents (Dopaminergic Agents)

Drug	Use	Comments
Carbidopa/ Levodopa (Senemet)	Treatment of Parkinson's disease	• Carbidopa prevents metabolism of levodopa and allows more levodopa for transport to brain • Adverse CNS effects may occur sooner • Levodopa (Levopa) should be discontinued 8 hours before starting Senemet
Bromocriptine (Parlodel)	Parkinson's Treatment of amenorrhea, galactorrhea Female infertility Suppression of postpartum lactation Acromegaly	• Treat Parkinson's • Often given with levodopa (Levopa) or carbidopa/levodopa (Senemet) • Give with food or milk • Contraindicated in clients with hypersensitivity to ergot alkaloids • Oral contraceptives antagonize effects of bromocriptine (Parlodel). Advise client to use another method of contraception. • This drug causes increased fertility • Hypotension is a frequently seen adverse effect.

5. Discharge Teaching
   a. Restrict foods high in Vitamin B_6 (pyridoxine) (i.e., liver, green vegetables, fortified cereals, whole grain cereals). Vitamin B_6 reverses therapeutic effects of levadopa (Levopa).
   b. Change positions gradually.
   c. Do not abruptly stop taking drug as sudden withdrawal can lead to parkinsonian crisis.
   d. Do not take OTC medications without consulting physician.
   e. Take drug between meals.
6. Related Drugs. See Table 2.12.

Sample Questions

53. Which adverse effect would the nurse NOT expect to see with trihexyphenidyl HCl (Artane) therapy?
    1. Dizziness.
    2. Dry mouth.
    3. Diarrhea.
    4. Suppression of sweating.
54. Janet Lyons' symptoms are not improving so the physician starts her on levodopa (Larodopa) as an adjunct with trihexyphenidyl HCl (Artane). Which statement by Janet indicates understanding of proper use of levodopa (Levopa)?
    1. "If my symptoms get worse I will stop taking this drug."
    2. "I will not eat liver or boxed cereals."
    3. "If I have a cold I will take aspirin or a cold remedy."
    4. "I will eat foods low in residue to prevent diarrhea."
55. Which instruction should the nurse give to clients taking bromocriptine (Parlodel)?
    1. "Take one hour before meals."
    2. "Do not use birth control pills as contraceptives."
    3. "This drug causes infertility and use of contraceptives will not be necessary."
    4. "Adverse effects will be reduced if taken during the day."

Answers and Rationales

53. The correct answer is 3. Trihexylphenidyl HCl (Artane) is an anticholinergic that can cause constipation, not diarrhea.
54. The correct answer is 2. Vitamin B_6 (pyridoxine) reverses the therapeutic effects of levodopa (Levopa); clients should restrict their intake of foods high in vitamin B_6 such as whole-grain cereals, fortified cereals, liver, green vegetables.
55. The correct answer is 2. Oral contraceptives antagonize the effects of bromocriptine (Parlodel). Another method of birth control should be used.

Drugs Affecting the Endocrine System

Refer to Table 4.22, Hormone Functions, as part of review for Unit 2.

ANTIDIABETIC AGENTS

A. Case Study
   Mrs. Grace Baker, age 54, is admitted to the hospital with Type I diabetes. The doctor prescribes regular humulin insulin 12 units SC and NPH humulin insulin 25 units SC every morning before breakfast.
B. Prototype—Insulin
   1. Action. Hormone that increases glucose transport across cell membranes; transforms glycogen into glucose, prevents breakdown of fats to fatty acids, and inhibits protein breakdown.
   2. Use. Type I diabetic clients; Type II diabetics not controlled with oral hypoglycemic agents, diet, and exercise; Type II diabetics undergoing stressful situations: infection or surgery; pregnant diabetic women; emergency management of diabetic coma.
   3. Adverse Effects. Allergic reaction: local or systemic; hypoglycemia; ketoacidosis.
   4. Nursing Implications
      a. There is a difference between insulin injection and insulin injection concentrated, for which 500 units = 1 milliliter.
      b. Human insulins should only be mixed with each other.
      c. IV insulin can be absorbed by the container or tubing.
      d. Stable at room temperature for 1 month.
      e. Do not inject cold insulin, causes lipodystrophy.
      f. Drug solution should not be used if discolored or contains precipitate. Do not shake vial. Gently roll (all except regular insulin) vial between palms before drawing up medicine.
      g. Check expiration date.
      h. When mixing two insulins, rapid-acting insulin should be drawn up first.
      i. Syringe must coordinate with strength of insulin.
      j. Injection sites must be rotated.
      k. Treat severe hypoglycemic reaction with glucagon or 10%–50% IV glucose.
      l. Treat ketoacidosis with IV insulin and IV fluids.
      m. Diet is prescribed by physician.
      n. Monitor blood glucose levels.
      o. Premixed insulin called "70/30 insulin" is available. Contains 70% NPH and 30% regular insulin. "50/50 insulin" is also available and contains 50% NPH and 50% regular insulin.
      p. Insulin Analog: Insulin lispro (Humalog) is a synthetic insulin with a faster onset and shorter duration of action than human insulin.
      q. Injections should be given immediately after mixing two insulins.
   5. Discharge Teaching
      a. Available without a prescription (except insulin injection, concentrated). Prescription is needed for needles and syringes (depending on state law).
      b. Change of insulin brand, type, etc., is done by physician.
      c. In initial period of dosage regulation client may have visual problems. Should not get lens changes until vision is balanced.
      d. Remove prefilled syringes from refrigerator 1 hour before administration.
      e. Inject at a 90° angle if you can pinch an inch, otherwise inject at a 45° angle.
      f. Report symptoms of reactions at injection site.
      g. Know symptoms of hypoglycemic reaction and have some type of fast-acting carbohydrate at all times.
      h. If ill, continue taking insulin and drink freely noncaloric liquids. Notify physician if diet cannot be followed.
      i. Monitor blood glucose at home and instruct on use.
      j. Smoking decreases insulin absorption.
      k. When traveling, needs to have necessary supplies.
      l. Carry a medical identification card.
C. Refer to Table 4.23, Characteristics of Insulin Preparations, Unit 4.

Sample Questions

56. The nurse is teaching Mrs. Baker about insulin injections. Which statement is correct?
    1. Insulin needs to be shaken well before being drawn up into the syringe.
    2. Long-acting insulins are clear in color.
    3. When putting regular and NPH insulin in the same syringe, draw regular insulin up first.

4. NPH is compatible with regular and lente insulin.
57. The nurse tells Mrs. Baker that she can minimize local skin reactions to insulin by
   1. injecting it slowly.
   2. always refrigerating it.
   3. giving it in divided doses.
   4. bringing it to room temperature before administering.
58. Which statement by Mrs. Baker indicates a need for further teaching by the nurse?
   1. "I will inject my insulin at a 90° angle."
   2. "I will take more insulin when I go to my exercise class."
   3. "I will always have some kind of sugar with me in case I have a hypoglycemic reaction."
   4. "I will carefully draw up my doses of insulin."

Answers and Rationales

56. The correct answer is 3. Regular insulin should be drawn up before NPH insulin when putting the two together in one syringe.
57. The correct answer is 4. Insulin should be at room temperature before injecting to decrease occurrence of lipodystrophy.
58. The correct answer is 2. Exercise increases glucose use in the body, so a decreased dose of insulin may be needed.

Oral Hypoglycemic Agents

A. Case Study
   Mr. Ben Bowerman, age 69, has a history of hypertension and obesity. He has controlled his blood sugars by diet for two years but now is having difficulty doing this. The doctor prescribes an oral hypoglycemic agent.
B. Prototype—Tolbutamide (Orinase)
   1. Action. Lowers blood glucose concentrations by stimulating secretion of endogenous insulin from beta cells in the pancreas. Increases peripheral sensitivity to insulin. From the class of sulfonylureas.
   2. Use. Type II diabetes: not controlled by diet and exercise, used with insulin in Type II diabetic when neither insulin nor oral hypoglycemic agents work well alone.
   3. Adverse Effects. Hypoglycemia; increased chance of cardiovascular disease; anorexia, nausea, vomiting, diarrhea; hemolytic anemia; allergic skin rashes; photosensitivity; inappropriate ADH secretion.
   4. Nursing Implications
      a. Tablet can be crushed.
      b. Monitor closely during initial therapy.
      c. If client stabilized on tolbutamide (Orinase) is exposed to stress (infection, surgery), the oral agent may be discontinued and replaced by insulin.
      d. Can transfer from one sulfonylurea to another easily.
      e. Monitor and teach symptoms of hypoglycemic reactions and how to treat.
      f. Monitor blood and urine glucose levels.
   5. Discharge Teaching
      a. Reinforce that drug is not "oral" insulin and will control diabetes.
      b. Use form of birth control other than oral contraceptives.
      c. Alcohol can trigger a hypoglycemic reaction.
      d. Cover body in sunshine. Use sunscreen.
      e. Weigh weekly and report progressive gain.
      f. Carry medical identification.
C. Refer to Table 4.24, Oral Hypoglycemic Agents, Unit 4.

Sample Questions

59. Mr. Bowerman tells the nurse that his brother has Type I diabetes and he takes insulin. Mr. Bowerman asks the nurse why his brother cannot take an oral antidiabetic agent. The nurse explains that oral antidiabetic agents are not effective in Type I diabetes because people with Type I diabetes
   1. have little or no endogenous insulin that can be released.
   2. are allergic to oral antidiabetic agents.
   3. would need so much of an oral antidiabetic agent that it would be financially prohibitive for them to take one.
   4. would have more episodes of hypoglycemia with oral antidiabetic agents.
60. A person should not take tolbutamide (Orinase) if allergic to
   1. penicillin.
   2. insulin.
   3. sulfa.
   4. caffeine.
61. Mr. Bowerman will need more teaching about tolbutamide (Orinase) if he makes the following statement.
   1. "I will get a medic alert bracelet that says I'm a diabetic taking tolbutamide (Orinase)."
   2. "I'm glad I can still have wine with my meals."
   3. "If I go outside, I'll stay out of the sun or use sunscreen."

4. "I know that tolbutamide (Orinase) will help control my diabetic condition."

Answers and Rationales

59. The correct answer is 1. Oral antidiabetic agents can only work when the client has endogenous insulin, which is not the case in Type I diabetes.
60. The correct answer is 3. Clients who are allergic to sulfa cannot take tolbutamide (Orinase), which is a sulfonylurea.
61. The correct answer is 2. Alcohol combined with an oral hypoglycemic agent can trigger a hypoglycemic reaction.

PITUITARY HORMONES

A. Prototype—Hormone Corticotropin (ACTH) (Cosyntropin [Cortrosyn])
   1. Action. Synthetic corticotropin that stimulates corticosteroid release from functional adrenal cortex.
   2. Use. As a diagnostic test to diagnose adrenal insufficiency.
   3. Adverse Effects. (see corticosteroids) Cushing's syndrome if given over a period of time, hypersensitivity reactions.
   4. Nursing Implications. (see corticosteroids) Administer deep IM.
B. Related Drugs. Long-acting preparations.
C. Case Study
   Robert Smith, age 51, develops diabetes insipidus following the removal of a pituitary tumor and is started on vasopressin (Pitressin).
D. Prototype—ADH (Antidiuretic Hormone) (Vasopressin [Pitressin]).
   1. Action. Hormone released by posterior pituitary gland that regulates water metabolism and prevents dehydration. Has vasoconstrictor effect that elevates blood pressure. In diabetes insipidus a deficiency in ADH is characterized by polyuria and polydipsia. Vasopressing (Pitressin) acts as a replacement for ADH.
   2. Use. Replacement therapy for diabetes insipidus.
   3. Adverse Effects. Hypersensitivity, anaphylaxis; water intoxication, hyponatremia; nausea, diarrhea, cramping; hypertension; nasal irritation, headache.
   4. Nursing Implications
      a. Monitor BP, weight, and I&O.
      b. Vasopressins are given IM or SC. Desmopressin (DDAVP) is given IV.
   5. Discharge Teaching
      a. Keep record of I&O, weight.
      b. If URI and use drug intranasally, absorption may be affected.
      c. Report sudden changes in output.
      d. Drink water with dose to reduce GI distress.
E. Related Drugs
   1. Desmopressin (DDAVP)
      a. Can be given IV or SC, monitor for extravasation.
      b. Keep refrigerated.
   2. Lypressin spray (Diapid) Given intranasally.

Sample Questions

62. Which of the following is the desired response of vasopressin (Pitressin)?
   1. Lower urine specific gravity.
   2. Lower urine output.
   3. Treat hypotension.
   4. Control polyphagia.
63. Mr. Smith complains of GI distress following administration of vasopressin (Pitressin). The nurse should instruct Mr. Smith to
   1. eat crackers after taking the dose.
   2. take a warm bath to reduce abdominal cramping.
   3. lie down for 30 minutes following administration.
   4. drink a glass of water with each dose.

Answers and Rationales

62. The correct answer is 2. The goal of vasopressin (Pitressin) is to lower urine output; replacement for the ADH hormone.
63. The correct answer is 4. Drinking a glass of water with each dose will decrease GI distress.

F. Case Study
   Danny Fine is a 9-year-old with a somatotropin deficiency. After evaluation, Danny is started on somatropin (Humatrope) replacement therapy.
G. Prototype—Somatotropin (Growth Hormone) (Somatropin [Humatrope])
   1. Action. Somatotropin stimulates growth of skin, connective tissue, and long bones.
   2. Use. Replacement therapy in children with growth retardation caused by lack of somatotropin.
   3. Adverse Effects. Hyperglycemia; pain at injection site; myalgia; headache; hypercalciuria; allergic reactions.
   4. Nursing Implications
      a. Record height.
      b. Monitor blood glucose.
      c. Rotate IM sites. Do not give SC.
      d. Store in refrigerator.
      e. Discontinue if epiphyses have fused.

5. Discharge Teaching
Annual bone age assessment test.

CORTICOSTEROIDS

General Information

The adrenal cortex secretes 3 natural steroids: glucocorticoids, mineralcorticoids, and adrenal androgens and estrogens.

    1. Glucocorticoids (Cortisol)
      a. Have anti-inflammatory effects.
      b. Regulate carbohydrate, protein, and fat metabolism.
    2. Mineralcorticoids (Aldosterone, Desoxycorticosterone)
    Regulate water and electrolyte metabolism.
    3. Adrenal androgens and estrogens
      a. Supplement sex hormones from gonads.
      b. Corticosteroids suppress immune response and affect all body systems.

A. Case Study
Adam White is a 20-year-old college student with a three-year history of ulcerative colitis (UC). Adam is taking hydrocortisone (Cortisol) to alleviate symptoms.

B. Prototype—Hydrocortisone (Cortisol)
    1. Action. Glucocorticoid, mineralcorticoid, and immunosuppressive actions.
    2. Use. Replacement therapy for adrenocorticoid insufficiency; anti-inflammatory for many allergic, inflammatory, or immunoreactive disorders.
    3. Adverse Effects. Increased susceptibility to infection; hypokalemia, hypocalcemia; sodium and fluid retention; increased appetite, nausea, peptic ulcer; headache, hypertension, congestive heart failure; osteoporosis; acne, impaired wound healing, hirsutism, skin thinning; ecchymosis, petechiae; hyperglycemia, impaired glucose metabolism, growth retardation, menstrual disorders; glaucoma, cataract formation; mental disturbances, insomnia; thrombophlebitis; masks symptions of infection.
    4. Nursing Implications
      a. Observe for mental changes.
      b. Monitor BP, weight, I&O, blood glucose, and serum potassium.
      c. IM use: inject deep IM. Do not give SC.
      d. Corticosteroid doses are not interchangeable.
      e. Corticosteroids are not abruptly withdrawn. Doses are tapered to allow the adrenal gland to function independently.
    5. Discharge Teaching
      a. Take drug before 9 A.M. (This causes less suppression on the adrenal cortex.)
      b. Take with food or milk to decrease GI effects.
      c. Never abruptly stop taking. This could precipitate acute adrenal crisis.
      d. Eat foods high in potassium.
      e. Avoid individuals with infections.
      f. Restrict sodium, alcohol, and caffeine intake.
      g. Carry medic alert card.
      h. Follow directions for topical use. Do not use an occlusive dressing, and apply ointment sparingly.
      i. Rinse mouth after using inhaled steroids.

C. Related Drugs
    1. Dexamethasone (Decadron)
      a. Given IV to treat cerebral edema or allergic symptoms.
      b. Betamethasone (Celestone)
      c. Dexamethasone and betamethasone are 10–30 times more potent than hydrocortisone.
      d. Both drugs can be inhaled to treat asthma.
    2. Methylprednisolone (Solu-Medrol) (has little mineralcorticoid action)
      a. Prednisone (Deltasone)
      b. Prednisolone (Delta-Cortef)
      All of these drugs are 4–5 times as potent as hydrocortisone. Prednisone and prednisolone have half the mineral-corticoid action of hydrocortisone.
    3. Desoxycorticosterone acetate (DOCA) (Percorten)
      a. Mineralcorticosteroid used to treat Addison's disease.
      b. Given IM or by SC pellet.
      c. Administer deep IM.
    4. Fludrocortisone (Florinef)
    An oral mineralcorticosteroid.

Sample Questions

64. Which statement should be included in Mr. White's teaching concerning hydrocortisone (Cortisol) therapy?
    1. Take aspirin to treat fever.
    2. Take hydrocortisone (Cortisol) before meals.
    3. Restrict caffeine and alcohol intake.
    4. Restrict potassium intake.
65. Hydrocortisone (Cortisol) is discontinued gradually to prevent
    1. anaphylaxis.
    2. diabetic coma.

3. adrenal insufficiency.
4. cardiovascular collapse.

Answers and Rationales

64. The correct answer is 3. Hydrocortisone (Cortisol) can cause GI distress and even lead to a peptic ulcer with long-term use. Caffeine and alcohol can further increase GI distress and should be restricted.
65. The correct answer is 3. Adrenal insufficiency can occur with abrupt removal of cortico-steroids. Corticosteroids are gradually discontinued so that the adrenal glands can begin to secrete corticosteroids independently.

THYROID HORMONES

A. Case Study
   Mrs. Ann Tan, age 64, has a subtotal thyroidectomy. After surgery she develops mild hypothyroidism. The doctor prescribes levothyroxine (Synthroid).
B. Prototype
   1. Various agents are used to treat hypothyroid conditions. There is not a single prototype drug. Important drugs include: desiccated thyroid; thyroglobulin (Proloid); levothyroxine (Synthroid); liothyronine sodium (Cytomel).
   2. Use. Replacement or substitution of diminished or absent thyroid function due to thyroid disease or thyroidectomy.
   3. Adverse Effects. Headache, nervousness, insomnia, irritability; palpitations, increased blood pressure, tachycardia, dysrhythmias, angina; weight loss, nausea, vomiting; menstrual irregularities; allergic skin reaction; heat intolerance.
   4. Nursing Implications
      a. Baseline weight and thyroid studies.
      b. Avoid aspirin use.
      c. Protect from light.
      d. Check pulse before taking.
   5. Discharge Teaching
      a. Do not alter dosage.
      b. Medic alert card.

Sample Questions

66. Before administering levothyroxine (Synthroid) to Mrs. Tan, the nurse should
   1. check Mrs. Tan's pulse.
   2. listen to Mrs. Tan's chest.
   3. take Mrs. Tan's temperature.
   4. assess Mrs. Tan's neuro status.

Answers and Rationales

66. The correct answer is 1. An adverse effect of levothyroxine (Synthroid) is tachycardia; the nurse should check the client's pulse before administration.

THYROID ANTAGONISTS

A. Case Study
   Mrs. Karen Grant, age 30, is diagnosed with hyperthyroidism. The physician prescribes propylthiouracil (PTU).
B. Prototype—Propylthiouracil (PTU)
   1. Action. Prevents synthesis of thyroid hormones. Partially prevents peripheral conversion of T_4 to T_3.
   2. Use. Management of hyperthyroidism.
   3. Adverse Effects. Hypothyroidism; agranulocytosis, thrombocytopenia, bleeding; nausea, vomiting, loss of taste; rash, urticaria, skin pigmentation; jaundice, hepatitis; nephritis.
   4. Nursing Implications
      a. Take same time daily with respect to meals. Food can change absorption rate.
      b. Drug response occurs 2–3 weeks after starting drug.
      c. Therapy may last 6 months to several years with remission in 25% of clients.
      d. Can be given during pregnancy. Stopped 2–3 weeks before delivery.
      e. Do not nurse baby.
      f. Check pulse daily.
   5. Discharge Teaching
      a. Report signs of agranulocytosis (fever, chills, sore throat).
      b. Report signs of bleeding promptly.
      c. Ask physician about use of iodized salt and seafood in diet.
C. Related Drugs
   1. Methimazole (Tapazole): Similar to propylthiouracil (PTU) except it is 10 times more potent. Given once daily due to long duration of action. Risk of hepatotoxicity is less.
   2. Iodines: Cause dose-related effects on thyroid function. Low doses necessary for thyroid function. High amounts inhibit thyroid function. Used to decrease size and vascularity of the thyroid before thyroid surgery, management of thyroid storm, treatment of hyperthyroidism, and treatment of thyroid cancer. Adverse effect GI distress.

Sample Questions

67. Mrs. Grant calls the physician's office and complains of chills, fever, and sore throat. Which nursing action is appropriate?
    1. Tell Mrs. Grant it sounds like she has the flu and that she should drink lots of fluids, take aspirin, and get extra rest.
    2. Tell her to come in immediately for a throat culture and blood work as this may be a serious drug reaction.
    3. Expect the physician to prescribe another thyroid antagonist drug as this is an allergic reaction.
    4. Tell Mrs. Grant that these are expected drug reactions and that they will subside in a few days.

Answers and Rationales

67. The correct answer is 2. Symptoms of chills, fever, and sore throat while receiving propylthiouracil (PTU) require throat culture and blood work right away.

PROGESTAGENS (PROGESTINS)

A. Case Study
   Ms. Carol Barr, a college freshman, has come to the gynecology clinic for birth control pills. After being examined by the nurse practitioner, Ms. Barr is given a prescription for Ortho-Novum birth control pills.
B. Prototype—Progesterone (Progestin)
   1. Action. Changes a proliferative endometrium into a secretory one; causes a change in consistency of cervical mucus; stops spontaneous uterine contractions.
   2. Use. Amenorrhea; abnormal uterine bleeding; endometrial cancer; prevention of conception.
   3. Adverse Effects
      a. In parenteral administration: Breakthrough bleeding, spotting, dysmenorrhea, breast tenderness; headache, dizziness; edema, thromboembolism, hypertension; nausea, vomiting, bloating, weight gain; jaundice; rash, hirsutism, acne, oily skin; vision changes.
      b. Other effects: Hypertension; reduced glucose tolerance; thromboembolism in high doses in specific groups of women.
   4. Nursing implications
      a. Take oral forms with food.
      b. Monitor weight.
      c. Monitor BP.

      d. For intramuscular injection
         1) Inject deeply into gluteal muscle.
         2) Rotate injection sites.
         3) Shake vial to insure uniform dispersion.
   5. Discharge Teaching
      a. Should not smoke.
      b. Should have regular Pap tests and should do breast self-exam.
      c. Report calf pain, breast lumps, or severe headache.
C. Related Drugs
   1. Hydroxyprogesterone (Delalutin) and medroxyprogesterone (Provera).
   2. Oral contraceptives
      a. Estrogen-Progestin Combinations
         1) Action. Suppress ovulation by preventing release of follicle-stimulating hormone (FSH) and luteinizing hormone (LH). Act directly on reproductive organs.
         2) Use. Prevention of pregnancy; amenorrhea; functional bleeding; endometriosis.
         3) Adverse Effects. Same as for progesterone.
         4) Nursing Implications. Stop taking one week before surgery to decrease risk of thromboembolism. If one menstrual period is missed and tablets were taken correctly, continue pills; if two periods are missed, stop pills and have pregnancy test; will need additional birth control method for first month of drug therapy; smoking increases risk of thromboembolism; may take longer to conceive after stopping pills. See Nursing Implications for progesterone.
      b. Progestin-Only Preparations
         1) Referred to as "minipills."
         2) Less effective than estrogen-progestin combinations.
         3) Action not understood.
         4) Adverse effects and nursing implications are same as for estrogen-progestin combinations.
         5) If two consecutive doses are missed, client must stop drug, use alternative birth control, wait until menses occurs, and start therapy again.

Sample Questions

68. Ms. Barr calls the gynecology clinic and states she thinks she is pregnant even though she has consistently taken her birth control pills. The nurse tells her to

1. continue taking the pills and see the physician.
2. stop taking the pills and see the physician.
3. continue taking the pills and see if menses occurs in the next cycle.
4. stop taking the pills for this cycle; wait 28 days and start them again.
69. The "minipill" oral contraceptive contains
1. estrogen.
2. progestin.
3. estrogen and progestin.
4. none of the above.

Answers and Rationales

68. The correct answer is 2. If the client is taking birth control pills and believes she is pregnant, she should stop taking the pills and see the physician.
69. The correct answer is 2. The "minipill" oral contraceptive contains only progestin.

OXYTOCICS

A. Case Study
Mrs. Kathy Bute, 35 years old, a gravida 2, para 1, is 42 weeks pregnant and is admitted for induction of labor. An oxytocin (Pitocin) infusion is started at 1 mU/min (mU = milliunit). Mrs. Bute is connected to an external fetal monitor.
B. Prototype—Oxytocin (Pitocin)
 1. Action. Posterior pituitary gland hormone that may initiate labor by stimulating uterine smooth muscle contractions. Releases milk from breast in breast-feeding women.
 2. Use. Labor induction; control postpartum bleeding; treatment of incomplete abortion; stimulate breast milk ejection.
 3. Dose. IV infusion: 1 mU/min and increase 1 mU/min every 15 minutes until contraction pattern. Dose not to exceed 1–2 mU/min every 15–30 minutes.

IV for uterine bleeding: 10–40 units to 1 liter of dextrose or electrolyte solution. IM: 10 units after delivery of placenta.
 4. Adverse Effects. Water intoxication, hypotension; postpartum hemorrhage; PVCs, cardiac arrhythmias; uterine rupture; nausea, vomiting; hypertension, cardiovascular collapse; fetus: bradycardia, hypoxia, intracranial hemorrhage, death; anaphylactic reactions.
 5. Nursing Implications
   a. Infusion pump for IV infusion.
   b. Monitor BP, heart rate, I&O.
   c. Use fetal monitor to monitor fetal heart rate and uterine contractions.
   d. Notify physician and stop infusion if fetal or maternal distress. Place mother on left side.
   e. Drug IV line should be piggybacked into a primary infusion line.
   f. Physician should be readily available to manage maternal or fetal complications.
C. Related Drugs. See Table 2.13.

Sample Questions

70. The nurse sets up Mrs. Bute's oxytocin (Pitocin) infusion. Which of the following are nursing considerations in caring for clients receiving oxytocin infusions?
1. The nurse should increase the infusion by 3 U/min every 15 minutes until there is a pattern of contractions.
2. Time-tape the solution and use a microdrop tubing to monitor the rate.
3. Use an infusion pump and piggyback infusion into primary infusion line.
4. Monitor client's temperature every 15 minutes.
71. Which statements concerning methylergonovine (Methergine) is correct? Methylergonovine is given
1. to induce labor.
2. in the first stage of labor.

TABLE 2.13 Oxytocin-Related Drugs

Drug	Use	Adverse Effects	Nursing Implications
Ergonovine (Ergotrate) Ergot Alkaloid (produce vasoconstriction and intense oxytocic effects)	Control late postpartum bleeding Treatment and prevention of postpartum and postabortion bleeding	Severe hypertension; bradycardia; nausea, vomiting; diarrhea	• Monitor BP, heart rate, and fundus • Notify physician if BP increases • Contraindicated to induce labor
Methylergonovine (Methergine) Ergot Alkaloid (See above)	Prophylaxis after delivery of placenta Management of postpartum bleeding	Fewer adverse effects than ergonovine. See above.	• Never administer before delivery of placenta • See above

3. after placental delivery.
4. IV prophylactically to prevent postpartum hemorrhage.

Answers and Rationales

70. The correct answer is 3. Oxytocin (Pitocin) infusion should be administered on an infusion pump and piggybacked into a primary infusion line to control rate of infusion and to minimize/prevent potentially dangerous adverse effects of oxytocin (Pitocin).
71. The correct answer is 3. Is given after placental delivery because methylergonovine (Methergine) can cause uterine tetany.

Eye Drugs

MYDRIATICS AND CYCLOPLEGICS

A. Case Study
   John Adams, a 75-year-old male, is at the opthalmologist's office for a routine eye check-up. The nurse instills 2 drops of 0.5% solution of atropine (Isopto-Atropine) in each eye (OU) to dilate the pupils, paralyze the eye muscles, and facilitate the eye examination. The examination reveals bilateral cataracts, and Mr. Adams is scheduled for surgery in one month.
B. Prototype—Atropine (Isopto Atropine)
   1. Action. An anticholinergic that causes mydriasis (dilation) of the pupil and cycloplegia, which paralyzes the lens and eye muscles.
   2. Use. Facilitate eye exams and treat uveitis.
   3. Adverse Effects. Photophobia, reduced lacrimation, impaired distant vision, increased intraocular pressure, eye pain, blurred vision.
   4. Nursing Implications
      a. Sunglasses to reduce photophobia.
      b. Artificial tears for reduced lacrimation.
      c. Elderly clients should be screened prior to receiving atropine—can increase intraocular pressure.
      d. Should not drive until drug effects have worn off.
C. Related Drugs
   1. Homatropine (Isopto Homatropine)
   2. Cyclopentolate (Cyclogyl)

Sample Questions

72. To reduce the chance of Mr. Adams having systemic effects related to atropine, the nurse will
   1. place a warm compress over both eyes.
   2. rinse the eye with water following instillation.
   3. maintain pressure on inner canthus for 1–2 minutes.
   4. have client wipe eyes with gauze after instillation.
73. Which of the following conditions should Mr. Adams be assessed for prior to topical atropine application?
   1. Cataracts.
   2. Glaucoma.
   3. Uveitis.
   4. Conjunctivitis.
74. Which statement by Mr. Adams indicates that he understands the instructions given following instillation of atropine?
   1. "My son will drive me home after the exam."
   2 "If my eyes itch it's OK to rub them."
   3. "I plan to go to the beach after this appointment."
   4. "I will mow the lawn as soon as I get home."

Answers and Rationales

72. The correct answer is 3. Applying pressure to the inner canthus (lacrimal sac) will reduce systemic effects.
73. The correct answer is 2. Atropine can raise intraocular pressure. Clients with glaucoma have increased intraocular pressure and a further increase in intraocular pressure could lead to an acute crisis and blindness.
74. The correct answer is 1. Vision is temporarily impaired following the examination. This client should not drive, as distant vision is impaired.

MIOTICS

A. Case Study
   Mrs. Martha Fuller, a 67-year-old retired registered nurse, goes to the eye doctor with a

complaint of reduced peripheral vision. After a thorough eye examination, the doctor makes a diagnosis of open-angle glaucoma. Mrs. Fuller is prescribed pilocarpine eye drops.

B. Prototype—Acetylcholine (Miochol)
  1. Action. A cholinergic drug that causes miosis (contraction) of the pupil and contraction of the ciliary muscle in the eye.
  2. Use. Decreases intraocular pressure in glaucoma and achieves miosis in cataract surgery.
  3. Adverse Effects. Low toxicity after systemic absorption; transient hypotension, decreased heart rate; bronchospasm; flushing, sweating.
  4. Nursing Implications
     a. Reconstitute just before use due to instability of solution.
     b. Systemic reactions treated with intravenous atropine.
C. Related Drugs
  1. Carbachol (Isopto Carbachol): Tell client of brief stinging in eye after use; symptoms of eye and brow pain, photophobia, and blurred vision will usually be lessened with prolonged use.
  2. Echothiophate (Phospholine Iodine): Solutions are unstable, client must wash hands before use.
  3. Pilocarpine (Pilocar, Isopto Carpine): Causes blurred vision and focusing difficulty. Client needs to understand that glaucoma treatment is long and needs adherence to prevent blindness; eyedropper tip should not be contaminated; clients with asthma and lung disorders should be observed for respiratory difficulties.

Sample Questions

75. Glaucoma is treated with eye medication that is
    1. both mydriatic and miotic.
    2. mydriatic.
    3. miotic.
    4. none of the above.
76. Which statement made by Mrs. Fuller indicates a need for more teaching about pilocarpine?
    1. "I know a side effect of pilocarpine is blurred vision."
    2. "I won't touch the eyedropper tip of the pilocarpine to my eye when instilling the drops."
    3. "I will stop the pilocarpine as soon as my vision improves."
    4. "I know that pilocarpine can cause side effects in my eye as well in other areas of my body."

Answers and Rationales

75. The correct answer is 3. Miotic eye medication causes a contraction of the eye pupil and contraction of the ciliary muscle, which helps to decrease intraocular pressure.
76. The correct answer is 3. Treatment for glaucoma will continue throughout the client's life. Eye medication should not be discontinued.

Cardiovascular Drugs

CARDIAC GLYCOSIDES

A. Case Study
   Jeremy Stevens is a 2-month-old male born with a ventricular septal defect (VSD). Jeremy currently has CHF and is being treated with digoxin (Lanoxin). Jeremy is seen in the pediatrician's office to evaluate the effectiveness of digoxin therapy as he was digitalized the week before.
B. Prototype—Digoxin (Lanoxin)
  1. Action. Increases force of myocardial contraction (positive inotropic effect). Decreases rate of conduction (negative chronotropic effect) while increasing refractory period of the AV node. Positive inotropic effect improves blood supply to vital organs and kidneys, providing a diuretic effect. Has a slow onset and shorter duration of action than other cardiac glycosides. Is eliminated through the kidneys. Digoxin elixir is better absorbed by the GI tract than digoxin tablets.
  2. Use. Congestive heart failure (CHF); atrial fibrillation; atrial flutter; paroxysmal atrial tachycardia.
  3. Adverse Effects. Cumulative with a narrow margin of safety. With toxicity there are

many symptoms that make it difficult to distinguish from the condition being treated. Arrhythmias, bradycardia: arrhythmias more frequently seen in children; anorexia, nausea, vomiting, diarrhea; headaches, fatigue, confusion, insomnia, convulsions; visual disturbances: blurred vision, green or yellow tint or halos; hypersensitivity. Toxicity occurs more quickly in presence of a low serum potassium. Quinidine-digoxin reaction may occur. When digoxin is stabilized in clients receiving quinidine, serum digoxin levels could double, leading to possible toxicity.

4. Nursing Implications
   a. Half-life is longer in elderly.
   b. Monitor CBC, serum electrolytes, liver and renal function studies, and ECG.
   c. Hold if apical rate is below 60 or greater than 120 beats per minute in adults, below 90 beats per minute in infants, or below 70 beats per minute in children up to adolescence.
   d. Monitor I&O and daily weights; potassium levels. Encourage foods high in potassium.
   e. Monitor serum digoxin levels therapeutic range (0.5–2.0 ng/ml).
   f. Give after meals if GI distress.
   g. Do not confuse digoxin with digitoxin (Crystodigin) as they are not the same.
   h. IM injections are painful and absorption is erratic. Avoid IM injections if possible and give in large muscle mass.
   i. Digoxin antidote: Digoxin Immune Fab (Digi-bind)
5. Discharge Teaching
   a. Take radial pulse and notify physician if toxicity symptoms occur.
   b. Take dose the same time each day and do not skip or double up on dose.
   c. Daily weights.
   d. Avoid high-sodium foods. Increase dietary intake of potassium.
   e. Separate digoxin from other pills in pillbox.
C. Related Drugs. See Table 2.14.

Sample Questions

77. What is most important for the nurse to teach Mrs. Stevens?
    1. Take Jeremy's apical pulse before giving digoxin.
    2. Take Jeremy's weight daily.
    3. Provide foods high in potassium.
    4. Monitor Jeremy's intake and output.

78. Which of the following cardiac glycosides is preferred for clients who have renal failure?
    1. Digoxin (Lanoxin).
    2. Digitoxin (Crystodigin).
    3. Deslanoside (Cedilanid-D).
    4. Amrinone (Inocor).
79. Mrs. Stevens asks the nurse which pulse rate indicates a dose of digoxin should be withheld for Jeremy. The nurse responds, "Hold the digoxin if the pulse rate is
    1. below 60 beats/minute."
    2. below 70 beats/minute."
    3. below 90 beats/minute."
    4. below 120 beats/minute."
80. The nurse would know that Mrs. Stevens understands teaching about adverse effects of digoxin if she said:
    1. "I'll call the physician if Jeremy's pulse is below 120 beats/minute."
    2. "If Jeremy develops a rash I'll use A&D ointment."
    3. "I will call the physician daily to report Jeremy's weight and daily intake and output."
    4. "I will notify the physician if Jeremy vomits or develops diarrhea."

Answers and Rationales

77. The correct answer is 1. Children and infants are prone to arrhythmias, which are a toxic effect of digoxin. Teaching Mrs. Stevens to take an apical pulse will help to identify if there is a potential for arrhythmias.
78. The correct answer is 2. Digitoxin is eliminated and metabolized through the hepatic system and not the kidneys; is considered safer to use in clients with renal failure.
79. The correct answer is 3. Fewer than 90 beats/minute in an infant is a sign of bradycardia, which could indicate digoxin toxicity.
80. The correct answer is 4. Vomiting and diarrhea are adverse effects of digoxin therapy and may also be symptoms of digoxin toxicity; should be reported to physician for follow-up.

ANTIANGINAL DRUGS

A. Case Study
Frank Ashworth, a 50-year-old airline mechanic, is complaining of chest pain after strenuous activity that is relieved by rest. Mr. Ashworth has a 20-year history of hypertension, and his father and maternal grandfather both died from myocardial

TABLE 2.14 Review of Antiarrhythmic Drugs

Drug	Action	Adverse Effects	Nursing Implications
Quinidine	Depresses myocardial excitability; slows conduction time in atria and ventricles, prolongs P-R interval and QRS complex; prolongs refractory period; depresses myocardial contractility, reduces vagal tone. Used in atrial fibrillation and flutter ventricular tachycardia..	Hematologic/Dermatologic: Agranulocytosis; thrombocytopenia purpura; urticaria CNS: vertigo; blurred vision; diplopia; confusion, syncope GI: vomiting; cramping CV: AV heart block; atrial or ventricular arrhythmias; hypotension; severe bradycardia; arterial embolism	• Administer drug with food to minimize GI symptoms (nausea and vomiting) • Carefully monitor electrolyte levels, blood counts, and kidney and liver function • Advise clients that diarrhea is common in early therapy and should disappear • Encourage client to report dizziness or faintness immediately • Instruct patient to avoid fatigue, excessive caffeine, alcohol, smoking, heavy meals, stressful situations, OTC medications
Procainamide (Pronestyl)	Depresses ectopic pacemakers; action on the heart similar to quinidine. Used to treat PVCs, ventricular tachycardia, and some atrial arrhythmias.	Same as quinidine, plus severe hypotension with parenteral use, possible development of a erythematosus-like syndrome in some clients.	• Inform client that drug may cause lightheadedness and dizziness • Periodic ECG determinations and blood counts in clients on prolonged therapy
Lidocaine (Xylocaine)	Suppresses automaticity of ectopic pacemaker; shortens refractory period; decreases duration of action potential in Purkinje fibers; local anesthetic action Used for acute ventricular arrhythmias	CNS: dizziness; slurred speech; apprehension; muscle twitching; tremors; convulsions. CV: hypotension, bradycardia. Dermatologic: urticaria, peripheral edema	• Closely monitor IV flow rate to ensure maintenance of adequate plasma levels • Observe carefully for signs of CNS toxicity (e.g., confusion, tremors), particularly during IV infusion • Monitor cardiac function and blood pressure closely. IM use may increase CPK (creatine phosphokinase) levels.
Disopyramide (Norpace)	Increases action potential duration and effective refractory period of the atria and ventricles which decreases automaticity and conduction velocity. Useful for PVCs and episodes of ventricular tachycardia.	CV: hypotension; precipitation or aggravation of CHF GU: urinary hesitancy CNS: dry mouth; blurred vision; fatigue, headache, malaise, dizziness GI: nausea, constipation	• Caution client to avoid driving until effects of drug are known because dizziness may occur • Monitor intake and output because urinary retention may occur. • Encourage use of hard candy to relieve dry mouth.
Verapamil (Calan, Isoptin) Nifedipine (Procardia) Diltiazem (Cardizem)	Calcium channel blockers inhibit the influx of extracellular calcium ions into cardiac and smooth muscle cells. Antianginal effects include dilation of coronary arteries and arterioles. Verapamil also decreases the influx of calcium into the cardiac contractile and conduction cells of the SA and AV node. Useful in management of chronic, stable angina and treatment of supraventricular tachyrhythmias	CV: hypotension, bradycardia; palpitations, peripheral edema CNS: flushing; weakness; dizziness; lightheadedness. GI: nausea; cramping; heartburn; constipation with Verapamil Respiratory: dyspnea; cough; wheezing	• Carefully monitor blood pressure during initial therapy and whenever dosage changes are made because hypotension may occur • Monitor liver enzymes periodically during therapy • Be alert for signs of CHF, which can occur especially if client is also receiving a beta blocker
Digitalis	Stimulates the force of cardiac contraction with improvement of cardiac output. Decreases cardiac oxygen demands, diastolic heart size, and heart rate. Useful in treatment of CHF and certain arrhythmias, such as atrial fibrillation and atrial flutter.	Digitalis toxicity: CNS: headache, fatigue, malaise, drowsiness, muscle weakness, insomnia, agitation, seizures, paresthesias of hands and feet, personality changes, impaired memory, hallucinations CV: arrhythmias (all types are possible) ENT: yellow-green halos GI: anorexia, nausea and vomiting, abdominal distension and pain	• Closely observe client for signs of toxicity • Check with physician regarding what pulse rates (both high and low) should be used as indicators for withholding medication • Watch for changes in pulse rate (sudden increase above 120 or fall below 60) • Recognize signs of hypokalemia, which increases the incidence of digitalis toxicity • Encourage client to take digitalis at prescribed times only • Advise client that protracted diarrhea or vomiting can create an electrolyte imbalance and lead to digitalis toxicity • Recommend adherence to prescribed diet

infarction. After a complete physical and exercise treadmill test a diagnosis of angina is made. The physician orders nitroglycerin 0.15 mg SL prn for chest pain and verapamil (Isoptin) 80 mg TID.

B. Prototype—Nitrites and Nitroglycerin (Nitro-bid, Nitrodur, Nitrostat IV)
   1. Action. Dilates the peripheral vascular smooth muscles of smaller vessels, which decreases cardiac preload and afterload leading to decreased myocardial oxygen needs. Selectively dilates large coronary arteries, which helps to decrease anginal pain and hypoxia of the myocardium. Given by many different routes of administration including PO, SL, buccal, topical, transdermal. Tolerance may develop with continued use.
   2. Use. Treatment and prophylaxis of angina pectoris. IV nitroglycerin manages congestive heart failure associated with acute myocardial infarction and controls intraoperative hypotension or manages hypertension.
   3. Dose
      Adult:
      SL: 0.15–0.6 mg at onset of attack or anticipation of attack.
      PO: Sustained release 2.5–2.6 mg TID or QID.
      Topical ointment: 1–2 inches every 8 hours up to 4–5 inches every 4 hours.
      Transdermal: 5 mg/24 hours and can be titrated to higher doses.
      IV: 5 mcg/min in 5% dextrose in water or 0.9% sodium chloride and titrate every 3–5 minutes until response.
   4. Adverse Effects. Headache, usually disappears with long-term therapy; flushing; hypotension, dizziness; reflex tachycardia; skin rash with ointment.
   5. Nursing Implications
      a. No more than 3 tablets should be taken in a 15-minute period (one tablet every 5 minutes). If pain not relieved by 3 tablets over 15 minutes, could indicate an acute MI and physician should be contacted.
      b. Leave tablets at bedside and allocate a specific number of tablets in container. Instruct client to tell nurse when having an attack and number of tablets taken.
      c. Sustained release tablets or capsules should be taken one hour before meals or two hours after meals.
      d. Nitroglycerin ointment should be applied to a hairless or shaved area to promote absorption. New site should be used with each new dose. Use ruled applicator paper that comes with ointment to measure dose. Wear gloves when applying ointment to applicator.

Leave applicator paper on site. Cover the applicator paper with plastic wrap and secure with tape.
      e. Transdermal nitroglycerin has aluminum backing and patch. Remove before defibrillation. Avoid standing near microwave ovens to prevent burns. Patches are usually applied in morning and removed in evening to prevent tolerance.
      f. Dilute IV nitroglycerin in 5% dextrose or 0.9% sodium chloride. Avoid using polyvinyl chloride (PVC) plastic as it can absorb nitroglycerin. Non-PVC is provided by the manufacturer. IV use requires continuous hemodynamic monitoring.
   6. Discharge Teaching
      a. Rise slowly to prevent dizziness.
      b. Store in original dark glass container in a cool place. Date bottle when opening and discard after 3 months.
      c. Headache will discontinue with long-term use.
      d. Keep diary of the number of anginal attacks and tablets taken.
      e. Do not drink alcohol.

C. Related Drugs
   Isosorbide dinitrate (Isordil): used to treat and prevent anginal attacks; given SL or PO in chewable tablets.

Sample Questions

81. Mr. Ashworth states that he is getting headaches after taking nitroglycerin. The nurse is aware that this is a
   1. toxic effect.
   2. symptom of tolerance.
   3. hypersensitivity reaction.
   4. adverse effect.
82. The physician decides to order nitroglycerin transdermal patches. Which instruction is important for Mr. Ashworth?
   1. Remove patch when showering.
   2. Replace the transdermal patch every 8 hours.
   3. Do not stand near microwave ovens while in use.
   4. Put on an extra transdermal patch if chest pain occurs.
83. Which of the following should the nurse include in teaching Mr. Ashworth about taking sublingual nitroglycerin?
   1. To replace tablets on a yearly basis.
   2. Keep tablets in a moist warm environment.
   3. Take the tablet before exercise to prevent angina.
   4. Notify physician if after 5 consecutive doses the chest pain persists.

Answers and Rationales

81. The correct answer is 4. A headache is a frequently seen adverse effect that usually disappears with long-term therapy. The physician may order aspirin or acetaminophen for headache relief.
82. The correct answer is 3. The back of a transdermal nitroglycerin patch contains aluminum, which could cause burns to clients standing near microwave ovens or if defibrillation is needed.
83. The correct answer is 3. Nitroglycerin should be taken before exercise to prevent an anginal attack.

D. Prototype for Calcium Channel Blockers— Verapamil (Calan, Isoptin)
   1. Action. Inhibits myocardial oxygen demand by inhibiting the influx of calcium through muscle cell, which leads to reduced afterload and coronary vasodilation. Decreases myocardial contractility, causing peripheral vasodilation leading to decreased heart workload.
   2. Use. Angina; essential hypertension (PO form); cardiac arrhythmias (IV use).
   3. Adverse Effects. Constipation; nausea and vomiting; hypotension; bradycardia; AV block; dizziness.
   4. Nursing Implications
      a. Monitor VS, I&O, and ECG.
      b. Encourage high-fiber foods and increased fluid intake (condition permitting).
   5. Discharge Teaching
      a. Take radial pulse before taking verapamil.
      b. Avoid caffeine.
      c. Avoid driving or operating machinery/heavy equipment until response to drug is established.
      d. Change positions slowly to decrease orthostatic hypotension.
      e. Do not abruptly discontinue verapamil therapy as rebound angina could occur. Dose is generally tapered.
      f. Continue with nitroglycerin therapy if prescribed.
   6. Related Drugs. See Table 2.14.

Sample Questions

84. Since Mr. Ashworth is taking nitroglycerin with verapamil (Isoptin), the nurse should observe for
    1. hyperkalemia.
    2. hypotension.
    3. seizures.
    4. insomnia.

85. Which statement by Mr. Ashworth indicates understanding concerning the use of verapamil (Isoptin)?
    1. "If I get dizzy I will stop taking the pills and call the physician."
    2. "I'm glad that I can continue to drink coffee."
    3. "I will only have to take the pills for a couple of weeks."
    4. "I will take my pulse before taking my pill."

Answers and Rationales

84. The correct answer is 2. Verapamil (Isoptin) reduces afterload and with concurrent use of nitroglycerin can cause hypotension.
85. The correct answer is 4. Clients should take pulse before taking verapamil (Isoptin) as this drug can cause bradycardia.

PERIPHERAL VASODILATORS

A. Case Study
   Marilyn Hill, age 39, has a 15-year history of Raynaud's disease. She is currently taking isoxsuprine HCl (Vasodilan) 10 mg PO three times a day as part of her treatment for this condition.
B. Prototype
   Group of direct-acting vasodilators have same action of relaxation of the smooth muscle of blood vessels. Direct-acting vasodilators are used to treat peripheral vascular disorders such as Raynaud's and Buerger's disease (thromboangitis obliterans), diabetic vascular disease, and varicose ulcers. See Table 2.15.
C. Related Drugs
   1. Dipyridamole (Persantine): Potent vasodilator that also decreases platelet aggregation and clotting time. Selectively dilates small resistance vessels of coronary vascular bed. Use to treat chronic angina attacks; prevention of thromboembolism in cardiac valve replacement surgery. Adverse effects: headaches, dizziness, weakness, hypotension, GI distress, flushing, and skin rashes. Monitor BP.

Sample Questions

86. Ms. Hill complains of nausea while taking isoxsuprine HCl (Vasodilan). The nurse should tell her to
    1. stop taking the medication and report this to the physician.
    2. take an antacid with the isoxsuprine HCl (Vasodilan).

TABLE 2.15   Direct-Acting Vasodilators

Drug	Adverse Effects	Nursing Implications
Cyclandelate (Cyclospasmol)	Flushing; headache; weakness; heartburn; eructation; tachycardia	• Take with meals if GI upset occurs • Improvement occurs gradually and prolonged therapy may be necessary • Change position slowly • Stop smoking
Isoxsuprine HCl (Vasodilan)	Hypotension, tachycardia, chest pain; nausea, vomiting, abdominal distress; weakness; rash	• Adverse effects should be reported promptly as they are dose related • Client should change position slowly • Therapeutic effect takes several weeks • Monitor blood pressure and pulse with parenteral administration
Papaverine HCl (Pavabid, Vasospan)	Malaise; dizziness, hypertension, flushing of face, tachycardia; nausea, abdominal distress; anorexia; rash	• Monitor VS & liver studies. • Limit alcohol intake • May have feeling of warmth in extremities • Missed dose should not be doubled at next dosing time • IV administration incompatible with Ringer's lactate solution

3. keep taking the drug as this effect is only transient.
4. report this to the physician so he can reduce the dose of isoxsuprine HCl (Vasodilan).

Answers and Rationales

86. The correct answer is 4. Adverse effects of isoxsuprine HCl (Vasodilan) are dose related and can be dealt with by reduction of the dose.

ANTIARRHYTHMICS

A. Case Study
   Mrs. Francis North is a 76-year-old retired secretary with a history of mitral stenosis. Recently she states she has not felt well and is complaining of heart palpitations. Her heart rate is 130 beats per minute and ECG reveals atrial fibrillation. Mrs. Francis is started on quinidine 200 mg TID PO.

B. Prototype—Quinidine (Quinaglute) Class 1A
   1. Action. Alkaloid from the bark of the cinchona tree. Related to quinine, an antimalarial drug. Decreases myocardial excitability and slows conduction velocity, while prolonging the refractory period. PR interval and QRS complex may be prolonged. Has anticholinergic effects that reduce vagus nerve activity, which slows AV conduction.
   2. Use. Atrial arrhythmias, atrial fibrillation, and atrial flutter; ventricular dysrhythmias.
   3. Adverse Effects. Cinchonism: GI distress, tinnitus, visual disturbances, dizziness, headache; AV block, hypotension; thrombocytopenia; hypersensitivity; nausea, vomiting, diarrhea.
   4. Nursing Implications
      a. Monitor ECG and VS, serum electrolytes, CBC, kidney and liver function.
      b. Monitor serum quinidine levels. Normal range 3–6 mcg/ml.
      c. Take an apical pulse.
      d. Take with food if GI upset.
      e. Clients taking digoxin and quinidine are more prone to digitalis toxicity.
   5. Discharge Teaching
      a. Take radial pulse before taking.
      b. Report symptoms of cinchonism, palpitations, faintness, or breathlessness.
C. Related Drugs. See Table 2.14.
   1. Procainamide
   2. Disopyramide

Sample Questions

87. Which of the following adverse effects is unique to quinidine (Quinaglute)?
   1. SLE (systemic lupus erythematosus).
   2. Agranulocytosis.
   3. Cinchonism.
   4. Hypoglycemia.
88. Client teaching for Mrs. North concerning quinidine administration includes
   1. drink plenty of orange juice.
   2. maintain a fiber diet.
   3. take Pepto Bismol if diarrhea occurs.
   4. take medication with meals.

Answers and Rationales

87. The correct answer is 3. Cinchonism is a syndrome seen specifically when using

quinidine; manifested by tinnitus, GI distress, dizziness, visual disturbances, and headache.

88. The correct answer is 4. Taking quinidine with meals will decrease GI distress.

Prototype

A. Case Study
Don Jamison is a 52-year-old married business executive admitted to CCU with acute MI. While in CCU Mr. Jamison develops frequent PVCs and a lidocaine drip is started.

B. Prototype—Lidocaine (Xylocaine) Class 1C
   1. Action. Prolongs refractory period in the myocardium and Purkinje fibers. Has little effect on atria. Depresses automaticity but therapeutic doses do not depress myocardial contractility. Also used as a local anesthetic.
   2. Use. Ventricular arrhythmias, i.e., VT; VF; PVCs.
   3. Dose: (given parenterally only)
   Adult
   IV Bolus: 50–100 mg at a rate of 25–50 mcg/kg/minute; once arrhythmia controlled continue infusion of 1–4 mg/minute.
   IM: 200–300 mg and repeat in 60–90 minutes if needed.
   Pediatric
   IV: 1 mg/kg followed by an infusion of 30 mcg/kg/minute.
   4. Adverse Effects. Drowsiness; CNS stimulation can develop leading to seizures; ventricular tachycardia, heart block, hypertension, bradycardia.
   5. Nursing Implications
      a. Monitor ECG, VS, neurologic status, and serum lidocaine levels.
      b. Therapeutic lidocaine levels range between 1.5–5 mcg/ml.

   c. Use an infusion pump.
   d. Cardiac IV lidocaine should not contain preservatives or epinephrine.
   e. Deltoid muscle is preferred for IM use.
   f. Do not mix with other drugs.
C. Related Drugs. See Table 2.16.

Sample Questions

89. Which of the following statements is correct concerning the administration of phenytoin (Dilantin)?
   1. Phenytoin is administered by continuous infusion.
   2. Phenytoin can be mixed in dextrose solutions.
   3. 0.9% normal saline should be used to flush IV line and site before and after administration.
   4. Phenytoin is given by rapid IV push.

Answers and Rationales

89. The correct answer is 3. Phenytoin (Dilantin) has a high alkalinity and can precipitate easily. Flushing the IV line and site with 0.9% normal saline will minimize venous irritation and prevent precipitation.

Prototype

A. Case Study
Bill Walker is a 65-year-old, single, retired naval officer admitted to ICU after having coronary artery bypass graft surgery (CABG). Twelve hours post-op Mr. Walker develops ventricular fibrillation that is unresponsive to

Table 2.16 Drugs Related to Lidocaine

Drug	Action	Use	Adverse Effects	Nursing Implications
Tocainide (Tonocard)	Oral analog of lidocaine (Xylocaine)	Ventricular arrhythmias	Drug-induced SLE; dyspnea; GI distress; see lidocaine	• Give with food to reduce GI distress • Avoid driving or operating heavy machinery until drug response known • Take radial pulse
Phenytoin Sodium (Dilantin)	Also an anti-epileptic drug. See lidocaine	Ventricular and supra-ventricular arrhythmias unresponsive to lidocaine or procainamide. Also used to treat digitalis-induced arrhythmias.	Drowsiness; slurred speech; ataxia; nystagmus; hypotension; agranulocytosis; rash; nausea, vomiting	• Should not be given with other antiarrhythmics • IV: do not mix with dextrose as crystallization can occur. Flush IV line with saline before and after administration. • Do not mix with other drugs • Monitor CBC • Therapeutic levels range between 10–20 mcg/ml

lidocaine therapy and bretylium (Bretylol) therapy is initiated.

B. Prototype—Bretylium (Bretylol) Class III
1. Action. An antifibrillatory drug. Initially releases norepinephrine to increase conduction velocity and strengthen the heartbeat.
2. Use. Life-threatening arrhythmias.
3. Adverse Effects. Hypotension, dizziness; worsening arrhythmias, hypertension; nausea, vomiting, diarrhea.
4. Nursing Implications
    a. Monitor ECG, vital signs, I&O.
    b. Gradually reduce dose.
    c. Change position slowly.
C. Related Drugs
1. Amiodarone (Cordarone)
    a. Given orally to treat chronic recurrent ventricular tachycardia or ventricular fibrillation that is unresponsive to other drugs.

Sample Questions

90. Which adverse effect should the nurse monitor Mr. Walker for while on maintenance bretylium therapy?
    1. Hypotension.
    2. Tachycardia.
    3. Insomnia.
    4. Hearing loss.

Answers and Rationales

90. The correct answer is 1. Hypotension occurs because after the initial release of norepinephrine, bretylium blocks further release of norepinephrine.

BETA BLOCKERS (Class II)

A. Case Study
Ms. Betty Lewis, a 56-year-old magazine editor, is admitted to the telemetry unit with atrial tachycardia. Ms. Lewis is started on propranolol (Inderal) 30 mg QID. Ms. Lewis also has a history of diabetes mellitus.
B. Prototype—Propranolol (Inderal)
1. Action. Beta-adrenergic blocker that decreases heart rate, force of contraction, myocardial irritability, and conduction velocity, and depresses automaticity.
2. Use. Cardiac arrhythmias caused by excessive cardiac stimulation of sympathetic nerve impulse; digitalis-induced arrhythmias; essential hypertension; angina pectoris;

preoperative management of pheochromocytoma; prevention of migraine headaches.
3. Adverse Effects. Dizziness, drowsiness, insomnia, depression; hypoglycemia; bronchospasm; bradycardia, heart block, hypotension; rash.
4. Nursing Implications
    a. Take apical pulse.
    b. Monitor I&O, daily weights.
    c. Gradually reduce dose before discontinuing.
    d. Pulse rate may not rise following exercise or stress, due to beta-blocking effects.
5. Discharge Teaching
    a. Take radial pulse before administering drug.
    b. Avoid alcoholic beverages.
    c. Avoid cold exposure to extremities.
    d. Change positions slowly.
C. Related Drugs
Note: "olol" is present in generic names.
1. Esmolol (Brevibloc): used to treat tachycardia, supraventricular tachycardia, atrial fibrillation, and atrial flutter.
2. Nadolol (Corgard): used to treat essential hypertension and angina.
3. Pinolol (Visken): used to treat essential hypertension.
4. Timolol (Blocadren): used to treat essential hypertension.

Sample Questions

91. Which adverse effect should Ms. Lewis be monitored for while on propranolol (Inderal) therapy?
    1. Hyperglycemia.
    2. Hypoglycemia.
    3. Diplopia.
    4. Seizure activity.

Answers and Rationales

91. The correct answer is 2. Mrs. Lewis is diabetic and is more prone to developing hypoglycemia. Hypoglycemia is an adverse effect associated with propranolol (Inderal) use.

CARDIAC STIMULANTS

A. Are autonomic nervous system drugs. The autonomic nervous system drugs are discussed in more detail in Unit 7.
B. Representative Drugs

1. Atropine Sulfate
   a. Blocks vagal stimulation of the SA node in the heart, thus increasing heart rate. Acts systemically to block cholinergic activity throughout the body.
   b. Cardiac uses: Treatment of sinus bradycardia or asystole; management of symptomatic sinus bradycardia; diagnosis of sinus node dysfunction.
   c. Adverse effects are related to blocking of cholinergic activity in the body.
2. Isoproteronol (Isuprel)
   a. Stimulates beta-1 adrenergic receptors in heart to increase cardiac output. Is also a bronchodilator.
   b. Cardiac uses: Cardiac standstill; carotid sinus hypersensitivity; Stokes-Adams syndrome; ventricular arrhythmias.
   c. Adverse effects: headache, palpitations, dry mouth, flushing, sweating, and bronchial edema.

ANTICOAGULANTS

A. Case Study
   Mr. Steve Miller, age 52, is admitted to the medical/surgical unit for treatment of acute thrombophlebitis of left calf. An initial dose of 5000 units of heparin is given intravenously and he is started on an IV infusion of 1000 units of heparin per hour. On the fourth day of hospitalization, Mr. Miller is started on warfarin sodium (Coumadin) in conjunction with heparin. Mr. Miller will be discharged in three days.
B. Prototype
   Anticoagulants hinder one or more steps of the coagulation process. They do not dissolve existing blood clots but prevent further coagulation from occurring.

Heparin	Warfarin Sodium (Coumadin)
Action: Blocks conversion of prothrombin to thrombin and fibrinogen to fibrin. Immediate action.	*Action:* Blocks prothrombin synthesis. Action takes 2–5 days to occur.
Use: a. Prophylaxis and treatment of thrombosis and embolism. b. Anticoagulation for vascular and cardiac surgery. c. Prevention of clotting in heparin lock sets, blood samples, and during dialysis. d. Treatment of disseminated intravascular clotting syndrome (DIC). e. Adjunctive treatment of coronary occlusion with acute MI.	*Use:* a. Prophylaxis and treatment of thrombosis and embolism. b. Atrial fibrillation with embolization. c. Adjunct in treatment of coronary occlusion.

Heparin	Warfarin Sodium (Coumadin)
Dose: Adult: SC (deep, intrafat): initially, 10,000–20,000 units, then 8,000–10,000 units every 8 hours or 15,000–20,000 units every 12 hours or as determined by coagulation test results. Intermittent IV injection: 10,000 units initially followed by 5,000–10,000 units every 6 hours. Continuous IV infusion: inject 5,000 units initially followed by infusing 1,000 units per hour. Pediatric: IV: Initially 50 units per kilogram. Maintenance: 50–100 units per kilogram IV drip every 4 hours.	*Dose:* Adult: Oral: 10–15 mg PO initially, then 2–10 mg PO per day. Can also be given IM, IV.
Adverse Effects: a. Hemorrhage, bruising, thrombocytopenia. b. Alopecia c. Osteoporosis d. Suppression of renal function with long-term high-dose use. e. Allergic reactions: fever, chills, urticaria, bronchospasm. f. Elevated AST (SGOT), ALT (SGPT).	*Adverse Effects:* a. Hemorrhage from any tissue or organ. b. Anorexia, nausea, vomiting, diarrhea. c. Hypersensitivity: dermatitis, urticaria, fever d. Jaundice, hepatitis e. Overdosage: paralytic ileus; skin necrosis of toes (purple toes syndrome), tip of nose, buttocks, thighs, abdomen
Antidote: Protamine Sulfate	*Antidote:* Vitamin K
Laboratory test used to monitor therapy: Partial thromboplastin time (PTT)	*Laboratory tests used to monitor therapy:* Prothrombin time (PT), INR
Nursing Implications: • Read label carefully as drug is supplied in differing strengths. • Do not give IM. • Subcutaneous injection: given in fatty layer of abdomen or just above iliac crest; use 25–26 gauge 1/2–5/8-inch needle; change needle after drawing heparin into syringe; do not inject within 2 inches of umbilicus, scars, or bruises; do not aspirate; apply pressure to injection site for 5–10 seconds after injection; do not massage injection site; rotate injection sites and keep a record of this. • Continuous IV infusion should be given via IV volume control device. • Observe needle sites daily for signs of hematoma. • Monitor PTT and other coagulation tests. • Test stool for occult blood daily. • Have antidote protamine sulfate available. • Monitor VS.	*Nursing Implications:* • Tablet can be crushed and taken with any fluid. • Monitor prothrombin time (PT) and INR. • Have antidote vitamin K available. • Many drug interactions. • Smoking increases dose requirement. *Discharge Teaching:* • Client will need to report frequently for blood tests. • Client shouldn't take any medication without checking with physician first. • Client should report signs of bleeding. • Use soft toothbrush; floss teeth with waxed floss. • Shave with electric razor. • Client should tell other health care personnel such as dentists, dental hygienists, etc., that he is taking Coumadin.

Heparin	Warfarin Sodium (Coumadin)
• Report: hematuria, bloody stools, hematemesis, bleeding gums, petechiae, nose bleed, bloody sputum. • Alcohol and smoking alter drug response. • Aspirin, antihistamines, and guaifenesin (found in cough syrups) shouldn't be taken while on heparin therapy as these agents may cause platelet function interference. • Do not abruptly withdraw. • Generally followed with oral anticoagulant therapy.	• Client should carry medical identification (Medic Alert) stating name of drug, name of physician, etc. • Teach client measures to avoid venous stasis.

Sample Questions

92. Which action should the nurse perform while Mr. Miller is on IV heparin?
    1. Protect the medication from light.
    2. Use IM route if there are frequent intravenous site changes.
    3. Attach the IV heparin to an infusion pump.
    4. Regulate intravenous flow with macrotubing.
93. What should the nurse have readily available if Mr. Miller receives a heparin overdose?
    1. Platelets.
    2. Urokinase.
    3. Protamine sulfate.
    4. Vitamin K.
94. Mr. Miller requests pain medication for a headache. The physician has ordered aspirin X grains PO every 4 hours for pain. The nurse should
    1. substitute Tylenol for the aspirin.
    2. give the aspirin as ordered.
    3. call the physician for a different pain reliever.
    4. give Mr. Miller 5 grains of aspirin now and 5 grains in 2 hours.
95. The nurse is teaching Mr. Miller about his warfarin sodium (Coumadin) therapy. Which statement by the nurse is incorrect?
    1. "If you miss your daily dose of Coumadin, take 2 tablets the next day."
    2. "Use waxed dental floss while on Coumadin therapy."
    3. "Notify your physician before taking any other medication."
    4. "Avoid drinking alcohol in any form while on Coumadin therapy."

Answers and Rationales

92. The correct answer is 3. Continuous intravenous infusion of heparin needs constant monitoring to ensure accuracy in dose. An infusion pump or volume controller should be used for this purpose.
93. The correct answer is 3. Protamine sulfate is the antidote for heparin overdose.
94. The correct answer is 3. A client on heparin therapy should not take aspirin due to increased potential for bleeding. The nurse needs to notify the physician for a different pain medication.
95. The correct answer is 1. Changing dose of warfarin sodium (Coumadin) by missing a dose on one day and doubling the dose on the following day is unacceptable as it will negatively affect blood coagulation.

THROMBOLYTIC DRUGS

A. Case Study
   Mr. Doug Manning, age 45, arrives at the emergency room with severe, crushing chest pain. A 12-lead electrocardiogram reveals acute anterior wall MI. Mr. Manning is given streptokinase (Streptase) intravenously.
B. Prototype—Streptokinase (Streptase)
   1. Action. Transforms plasminogen to plasmin which degrades fibrinogen, fibrin clots, and other plasma proteins.
   2. Use. Pulmonary emboli; coronary artery thrombosis; deep venous thrombosis; arteriovenous cannula occlusion.
   3. Adverse Effects. Bleeding; allergic reaction; arrhythmias.
   4. Nursing Implications
      a. Start therapy as soon as possible after thrombus appears as thrombi older than 7 days react poorly to streptokinase.
      b. When used in treatment of an acute MI, start therapy within 6 hours of attack.
      c. Heparin is discontinued before streptokinase is started.
      d. Corticosteroids can be given to decrease allergic reaction.
      e. Reconstitute streptokinase with normal saline (preferred solution) or 5% dextrose solution.
      f. IM injections are contraindicated.
      g. Monitor blood coagulation studies and VS.
      h. Maintain bed rest while receiving drug.
      i. Monitor for excessive bleeding every 15 minutes for the first hour of treatment, every 30 minutes for second to eighth hours, then every 8 hours.
      j. Keep whole blood available.
      k. Aminocaproic acid is the antidote for streptokinase.

C. Related Drugs
Two thrombolytic agents similar to streptokinase (Streptase): alteplase (Activase) and urokinase (Abbokinase).

Sample Questions

96. During and after Mr. Manning's streptokinase treatment the nurse needs to assess him for
    1. urticaria.
    2. diarrhea.
    3. sore throat.
    4. peripheral edema.

Answers and Rationales

96. The correct answer is 1. Streptokinase (Streptase) is a foreign protein and does cause allergic reactions. Urticaria would be a sign of this.

ANTILIPEMIC AGENTS

A. Case Study
Mike Small, age 38, returns to the clinic for a second visit. At his first visit, the doctor diagnosed Mr. Small with Type IIa hyperlipoproteinemia and advised him to decrease cholesterol and triglycerides in his diet and increase exercise. Even though Mr. Small has carried out these instructions, his cholesterol and triglyceride levels remain elevated. The physician prescribes cholestyramine (Questran).

B. Prototype—Cholestyramine (Questran)
1. Action. Prevents the metabolism of cholesterol in the body.
2. Use. Type IIa hyperlipoproteinemia; pruritus caused by partial biliary obstruction.
3. Adverse Effects. Constipation, nausea, and vomiting; deficiencies in fat-soluble vitamins A, D, K; rash and skin irritation; osteoporosis; headache, dizziness, syncope; arthritis; fever.
4. Nursing Implications
   a. Monitor cholesterol and serum triglyceride levels.
   b. Assess preexisting constipation problems.
   c. Long-term use increases bleeding tendencies: oral vitamin K may be given prophylactically.
5. Discharge Teaching
   a. Take with water or preferred liquid and dissolve.
   b. Take before meals.
   c. Eat a high-bulk diet low in cholesterol and saturated fats with increased fluids.
   d. Do not omit doses or change dose intervals.
   e. Do not take cholestyramine (Questran) at the same time as other medications as there will be interference with absorption.
   f. Encourage exercise and weight loss.
   g. Give for several months or years if it is effective.

C. Related Drugs
1. Colestipol (Colestid) is similar in action, use, adverse effects, and nursing implications to cholestyramine (Questran).
2. Lovastatin (Mevacor) decreases cholesterol levels by stopping the body from making its own cholesterol. Used to treat hypercholesterolemia types IIa and IIb. Adverse effects include headache; insomnia, fatigue, cataracts, nausea, hepatotoxicity, elevated CPK, alkaline phosphatase and transaminase. Nursing implications: periodic eye exam, monitor renal and hepatic studies; take with meals to increase absorption.
3. Gemfibrozil (Lopid) decreases triglycerides and increases HDL cholesterol. May cause diarrhea or GI upset.
4. Niacin—Vitamin B_3 (Nicobid)—reduces liver synthesis and reduces cholesterol and total lipid levels. Used in treatment of hyperlipidemia. Adverse effects: tingling, flushing, jaundice, GI upset, pruritus. Nursing implications: dosage is individualized. Niacin is an OTC preparation that should be taken under a physician's care.

Sample Questions

97. Which statement by Mr. Small indicates a need for more teaching about cholestyramine (Questran) by the nurse?
    1. "I will continue going to exercise class."
    2. "I will take the drug with meals."
    3. "I will dissolve the drug in liquid before taking it."
    4. "I will increase the fiber in my diet."

Answers and Rationales

97. The correct answer is 2. Cholestyramine (Questran) should be taken before meals for better absorption.

ANTIHYPERTENSIVES

General Information for Administration of Antihypertensives

1. Primary objective of antihypertensive therapy is to control essential hypertension and maintain BP with minimal adverse effects.
2. "Stepped care" approach, recommended by the Joint National Committee on Detection, Evaluation and Treatment of Hypertension, is used by physicians as a guide to treat essential hypertension, which includes 4 steps.
   Step I: Thiazide diuretics, and/or beta blockers, calcium channel blockers, or ACE inhibitors. Usually small doses of 1 or 2 drugs are used to treat mild essential hypertension.
   Step II: Thiazide diuretics, beta blockers, calcium channel blockers, ACE inhibitors, alpha blockers, or centrally acting antihypertensives. Usually a combination of 2 drugs is used if hypertension is not controlled. Steps II and III may be used to treat moderate essential hypertension.
   Step III: Add or replace with direct-acting vasodilators.
   Step IV: ACE inhibitors, MAO inhibitor, adrenergic blockers. Step III and IV clients have severe essential hypertension.
3. Antihypertensives reduce peripheral resistance and decrease volume of circulating blood.
4. Orthostatic hypotension is a common adverse effect for all antihypertensives.
5. Should not be abruptly discontinued as rebound hypertension could occur.
6. Discharge instructions for all antihypertensives:
   a. Have adverse effects that may affect client compliance in taking medication. It is important for client to receive thorough teaching and support to maintain compliance.
   b. Do not abruptly discontinue or skip doses of medications.
   c. Change positions gradually; avoid alcohol and hot showers and baths.
   d. Do not take OTC drugs without consulting physician.
   e. Monitor weight and eat low-sodium foods.
   f. Take BP and record in diary. Report changes to physician.
   g. Do not drive or operate heavy machinery until drug effects are established.
   Note: Thiazide diuretics are discussed under Renal Drugs; MAO (monamine oxidase inhibitors) are discussed under Central Nervous System Drugs; beta blockers are discussed under Antiarrhythmics; and calcium channel blockers are discussed under Antianginal Drugs.

A. Case Study
Mr. Edward Simon, a 50-year-old married accountant, was diagnosed with essential hypertension 8 years ago. Mr. Simon has a positive family history of hypertension and heart disease. Mr. Simon has followed an exercise program, low-sodium diet, and has taken captopril (Capoten). His blood pressure has constantly ranged around 150/98. Mr. Simon is started on an additional antihypertensive agent.

B. Prototype—Central Acting Antihypertensives (Clonidine [Catapress])
   1. Action. Blocks sympathetic nerve impulses in brain, which causes decreased sympa-thetic outflow leading to decreased BP, vasoconstriction, heart rate, and cardiac contractility.
   2. Use. Moderate hypertension not responding to thiazide diuretics or beta blockers.
   3. Adverse Effects. Orthostatic hypotension; drowsiness, behavior changes; peripheral edema, CHF; Raynaud's phenomenon; impotence, urinary retention; dry mouth, constipation.
   4. Nursing Implications
      a. Monitor I&O, weight, and BP.
      b. Monitor clients with a history of mental depression.
   5. Discharge Teaching
      Take last dose of medication in the evening to minimize drowsiness during the day.

C. Related Drugs
   Methyldopa (Aldomet): may cause blood dyscrasias and hepatotoxicity; monitor blood work and liver function tests.

D. Prototype—Alpha-Adrenergic Receptor Blocker (Prazosin [Minipress])
   1. Action. Blocks alpha receptors in arterial smooth-muscle vasculature and mediates vasoconstriction.
   2. Use. Hypertension caused by pheochrom-ocytoma; Step II antihypertensive usually in combination with a thiazide diuretic.
   3. Adverse Effects. Postural hypotension and syncope with initial therapy; reflex tachycardia. See clonidine (Catapress).
   4. Nursing Implications. Monitor vital signs.
   5. Discharge Teaching
      a. Take with food to reduce dizziness, light-headedness.
      b. Take initial dose at bedtime to reduce effects of syncope.
      c. Report sexual difficulties.

E. Prototype—Peripheral-acting Adrenergic Neuron Blockers (Reserpine [Serpasil])
   1. Action. Lowers BP by blocking norepinephrine in CNS and peripherally.
   2. Use. Rarely used due to its adverse effects and availability of other antihypertensives; agitated psychosis; essential hypertension with a diuretic in Step II or Step III; parenteral use to treat hypertensive emergencies.
   3. Adverse Effects. Suicidal depression, drowsiness; nasal obstruction; increased incidence of breast cancer in women; impotence; decreased cardiac output, postural hypotension; diarrhea, increased gastric secretions.
   4. Nursing Implications
      a. Monitor for depression; obtain a mental health history for depression.
      b. Assess for family history of breast cancer.
      c. Administer with meals to reduce GI distress.
      d. Monitor BP and I&O.
      e. Rinse mouth or use hard candy for dry mouth.
   5. Related Drugs
      Guanethidine (Ismelin): step IV antihypertensive agent rarely used due to its adverse effect; affects sympathetic nerve endings by releasing norepinephrine; and then interferes with release of norepinephrine; with initial use may see transient hypertension and elevated heart rate.
F. Prototype—ACE Inhibitor (Angiotensin-Converting Enzyme Inhibitor) (Captopril [Capoten])
   1. Action. Lowers BP by inhibiting angiotensin-converting enzyme, which inhibits angiotensin II (vasoconstrictor) and indirectly reduces serum aldosterone levels.
   2. Use. Initial therapy of essential hypertension in clients with normal renal function; severe hypertension in clients with renal dysfunction; CHF.
   3. Adverse Effects. Blood dyscrasias; hypotension; proteinuria; hyperkalemia; rash; loss of taste perception.
   4. Nursing Implications
      a. Monitor CBC, electrolytes, and urinalysis.
      b. Administer one hour before meals.
   5. Discharge Teaching
      a. Report fever, sore throat, and rash.
      b. Use salt substitutes only if prescribed (many substitutes contain K+).
   6. Related Drugs
      a. Enalapril (Vasotec)
      b. Lisinopril (Zestril)
         Both used to treat essential hypertension and not CHF.

   c. Losarten (Cozaar)—Angiotensin II receptor antagonist.
G. Prototype—Direct-acting Vasodilators (Hydralazine [Apresoline])
   1. Action. Direct relaxation of arteriolar smooth muscle causing vasodilation.
   2. Use. Step III antihypertensive; parenteral hydralazine (Apresoline) is used in hypertensive emergencies.
   3. Adverse Effects. Headache, dizziness, depression; tachycardia, angina, palpitations; lupus-like syndrome, rash, fever; weight gain, sodium retention; nausea, vomiting, anorexia.
   4. Nursing Implications
      a. Monitor CBC, ANA titer, and LE preparation.
      b. Clients receiving parenteral hydralazine (Apresoline) check BP and pulse every 5 minutes until stable while on parenteral agent.
   5. Related Drugs
      a. Minoxidil (Loniten)
         1) Has more adverse effects than hydralazine. May cause cardiac muscle lesions and hirsutism.
         2) Topical preparation (Rogaine) is available to treat baldness.
      b. Nitroprusside (Nipride)
         1) Given IV to treat hypertensive emergencies.
         2) Should be administered in an infusion pump. IV tubing and container should be wrapped in aluminum foil to protect from light. VS, neuro checks, and I&O should be closely monitored.
      c. Diazoxide (Hyperstat)
         1) Given IV to treat hypertensive emergencies.
         2) May cause hyperglycemia.
      d. See Table 2.17.

Sample Questions

98. Mr. Simon is started on prazosin (Minipress) 1 mg PO daily. Which client teaching instructions should the nurse stress?
   1. Rise slowly from a lying or sitting position.
   2. Take the drug on an empty stomach.
   3. Force fluids to 2 liters/day.
   4. Take the medication in the morning.
99. Which of the following should the nurse specifically assess for prior to clients starting on captopril (Capoten) therapy?
   1. Depression.
   2. Renal dysfunction.
   3. Liver disease.
   4. Hyperglycemia.

TABLE 2.17   Review of Antihypertensive Drugs

Drug	Action	Adverse Effects	Nursing Implications

Diuretics
   Thiazide diuretics
      Chlorothiazide
      (Diuril)
      Hydrochlorothiazide
      (Esidrex, Hydro
      Diuril, Oretic)
      Chlorthalidone
      (Hygroton)
      Metolazone
      (Zaroxolyn)
	Block sodium reabsorption in ascending tubule of kidney; water excreted with sodium, producing decreased blood volume	Hyperuricemia, hyperglycemia, hypercalcemia, elevated BUN; hypokalemia, orthostatic hypotension, anorexia, nausea, vomiting, light-headedness, headache, drowsiness, rash	• Monitor intake and output and observe for excessive diuresis.
			• Encourage client to make positional changes slowly to decrease occurrence of orthostatic hypotension.
			• Perform baseline and periodic determinations of electrolytes, BUN, uric acid, blood sugar, weight, and blood pressure.
			• If possible, administer in the morning to avoid nocturia.
			• Administer with food to minimize gastric distress.
			• Encourage inclusion of high-potassium foods in diet to decrease possibility of hypokalemia. Advise client to avoid high-sodium foods.
			• Stress the importance of taking the drugs regularly as prescribed.

Loop (High-Ceiling) diuretics
   Furosemide (Lasex)
   Ethacrynic acid
   (Edecrin)
   Bumetanide (Bumex)
	Inhibit reabsorption of sodium and chloride at the proximal portion of ascending loop of Henle	Similar to thiazides but intensity differs. Hypocalcemia, hearing loss.	See above.

Potassium-sparing diuretic
   Spironolactone
   (Aldactone)
	Antagonizes the effect of aldosterone on the tubular cells of the kidney; sodium excreted in exchange for potassium	Hyperkalemia, gynecomastia, hirsutism, irregular menses, rash, drowsiness or confusion	• Monitor I&O, blood pressure, and weight regularly.
			• Instruct client to be alert for signs of hyponatremia.
			• Inform client that swelling and tenderness of the breasts occur most often with prolonged therapy.
			• Monitor serum potassium levels daily during early stages of therapy.
			• Advise client to avoid excessive intake of potassium-rich foods.

Drugs acting on the CNS Methyldopa (Aldomet)	Metabolized into a false neurotransmitter displacing norepinephrine from its receptor sites; sympathetic activity reduced	Orthostatic hypotension, sedation, weakness, drowsiness, dry mouth, liver damage	• Advise slow positional changes and avoid prolonged standing in one position. • Inform client the drug may darken urine. • Advise client to observe for signs of liver dysfunction.
Clonidine (Catapress)	Stimulates alpha-adrenergic receptor in brain, causing inhibition of sympathetic vasoconstriction	Orthostatic hypotension, sedation, drowsiness, dry mouth, anxiety, depression	• Closely observe clients with prior history of mental depression because the drug may cause depressive episodes. • Advise slow positional changes. • Encourage client to dangle feet for a few minutes before standing.

Beta-Adrenergic Blockers
   Propranolol (Inderal)
   Nadolol (Corgard)
	Reversible competitive blocking action at beta-adrenergic receptor sites. Results in decreased heart rate and force of contraction, slowed AV conduction, decreased plasma renin, and lowered blood pressure	Drowsiness, light-headedness, lethargy, cramping, nausea, and bradycardia	• Record intake and output and client's weight and notify physician of any significant changes.
			• Advise client to rise slowly, avoid prolonged standing, and be careful when operating machinery.
			• Inform client that smoking may reduce effectiveness of drug.
			• Evaluate heart rate and rhythm before administration of the drug.
			• Warn client that alcohol may enhance the hypotensive effect of the drug.

TABLE 2.17   Review of Antihypertensive Drugs (continued)

Drug	Action	Adverse Effects	Nursing Implications
Drugs acting on renin-angiotensin system Captopril (Capoten) Enalapril (Vasotec)	Depresses the functioning of the renin-angiotensin-aldosterone mechanism by inhibiting angiotensin-converting enzyme (ACE) in the plasma	Rash, pruritus, proteinuria (mainly captopril), agranulocytosis (mainly captopril), excessive hypotension, blood dyscrasias	• Perform urinary protein estimates prior to therapy and at monthly intervals thereafter. • Administer (captopril) one hour before meals. • Instruct client to report blood dyscrasias (sore throat, fever) and excessive hypotension (dizziness) and rashes immediately.
Vasodilators Hydralazine (Apresoline)	Direct relaxation of arteriolar smooth muscle producing decreased peripheral resistance	Headache, nausea, vomiting, diarrhea, sweating, palpitations, and tachycardia. Systemic lupus-like symptoms (high doses).	• Advise client that headache and palpitations may occur during early stages of therapy. • Perform periodic blood counts, LE cell preparations, and antinuclear antibody titer determinations. • Advise client to make positional changes slowly. • Observe clients receiving large amounts of hydralazine closely for signs of developing lupus-like reaction.

100. Which antihypertensive drug may be linked to breast cancer and may cause suicidal depression?
1. Guanethidine (Ismelin).
2. Hydralazine (Apresoline).
3. Reserpine (Serpasil).
4. Clonidine (Catapress).

101. Which of the following actions should the nurse take when administering nitroprusside (Nipride)?
1. Mix the solution in normal saline.
2. Administer the drug by IV push.
3. Monitor neuro checks and VS every hour.
4. Wrap IV bottle and tubing with aluminum foil.

102. Which side effect should Mr. Simon be aware of when taking clonidine (Catapress)?
1. Anxiety.
2. Diarrhea.
3. Dry mouth.
4. Irritability.

Answers and Rationales

98. The correct answer is 1. As with most antihypertensives, initial therapy of prazosin (Minipress) may produce orthostatic hypotension; client should rise slowly.

99. The correct answer is 2. Renal damage is an adverse response to captopril (Capoten) that is more apt to occur in clients with renal dysfunction.

100. The correct answer is 3. Reserpine (Serpasil) has been known to cause suicidal depression; an increased incidence of breast cancer has also been noted with this drug.

101. The correct answer is 4. Nitroprusside (Nipride) is sensitive to light and becomes less active; therefore the IV tubing and container should be covered.

102. The correct answer is 3. Clonidine (Catapress) can cause dry mouth due to decreased salivary flow.

Renal Drugs

DIURETICS

A. Case Study
Mrs. Wendy Miller is a 60-year-old bank teller with a 3-year history of hypertension. Recently Mrs. Miller has complained of dyspnea and a 10-lb weight gain. After seeing her physician, a diagnosis of congestive heart failure (CHF) is made and Mrs. Miller is started on hydrochlorothiazide therapy.

B. Prototype—Thiazide Diuretics (Hydrochlorothiazide [Hydrodiuril])
1. Action. Blocks sodium reabsorption in the distal convoluted tubule, which prevents

water reabsorption, increases urine output, and decreases blood volume. Potassium is also excreted.
2. Use. Essential hypertension; edema associated with CHF.
3. Adverse Effects. Hypokalemia, hyponatremia; drowsiness; hyperglycemia; photosensitivity, hypersensitivity—thiazides are chemically related to sulfonamides; orthostatic hypotension, arrhythmias; anorexia, nausea, vomiting, diarrhea; agranulocytosis.
4. Nursing Implications
   Monitor I&O, weights, and serum electrolytes, glucose, and BUN.
5. Discharge Teaching
   a. Take medication in the early morning and after meals to prevent GI distress.
   b. Report symptoms of agranulocytosis such as fever, sore throat.
   c. Change positions slowly.
   d. Eat foods high in potassium (i.e., oranges, bananas, strawberries).
   e. Take daily weights.
C. Related Drugs
   1. Metolazone (Zaroxolyn)
   2. Chlorathiazide (Diuril)
   3. Chlorthalidone (Hygroton)

Sample Questions

103. Which statement by Mrs. Miller indicates that she needs more client teaching in regard to hydrochlorothiazide (Hydrodiuril) therapy?
   1. "I will take my medication with orange juice."
   2. "I will take my medication before going to bed."
   3. "I will take my medication after meals."
   4. "I will notify the physician if I have a sore throat."

Answers and Rationales

103. The correct answer is 2. Taking hydrochlorothiazide (Hydrodiuril) before going to bed may cause nocturia and interrupted sleep. Mrs. Miller needs to be taught to take the medication in the morning as the diuretic effect begins in 2 hours and peaks in 4 hours.

D. Prototype—Loop Diuretics (Furosemide [Lasix])
   1. Action. Acts by inhibiting reabsorption of sodium and chloride at the proximal portion of the ascending loop of Henle, increasing water excretion. This drug is considered to be potent.

2. Use. Hypertension, pulmonary edema, edema seen with congestive heart failure, cirrhosis, and renal disease.
3. Adverse Effects. Fluid and electrolyte imbalances—hypokalemia, hypochloremic alkalosis, hyperuricemia, hyponatremia, hypocalcemia, hypomagnesemia, hyperglycemia; nausea, vomiting, anorexia, constipation; diarrhea in children given high doses with sorbitol as the vehicle; jaundice, acute pancreatitis; polyuria, nocturia, urinary bladder spasm; dizziness, paresthesias, headache, blurred vision, irreversible hearing loss; leukopenia, anemia; orthostatic hypotension, cardiac arrhythmias; muscle spasms; photosensitivity, rash, pruritus.
4. Nursing Implications
   a. Can take with food.
   b. Monitor CBC, serum and urine electrolytes, BUN, blood glucose, uric acid.
   c. Monitor VS closely when patient receiving IM or IV administration. Client should be switched to oral preparation when practical.
   d. IM injection is painful; use Z-track technique.
   e. Infusion rate must be closely monitored. Should not be more than 4 mg per minute.
   f. Elderly require close monitoring during active diuresis. Watch for fluid and electrolyte imbalances.
   g. Monitor I&O.
   h. Weigh client daily.
   i. Monitor for hearing loss.
   j. Monitor diabetic clients closely.
   k. Tablets slightly discolored are still considered potent; discolored parenteral solutions should be discarded.
   l. Compatible with 5% dextrose in water, sodium chloride, and lactated Ringer's; use solution mixed with furosemide (Lasix) within 24 hours.
5. Discharge Teaching
   a. Take dose early in day to avoid nocturia.
   b. Usually allowed liberal salt intake; consult physician.
   c. Caution client about orthostatic hypotension if on high dose of furosemide (Lasix) or on other antihypertensive agents.
   d. Needs diet high in potassium and maybe a potassium supplement.
   e. Stay out of the sun and use sunscreen.
6. Related Drugs
   Ethacrynic acid (Edecrin) and bumetanide (Bumex) are similar to furosemide (Lasix). Both drugs are used for treating edema and can be given orally and parenterally.

Sample Questions

104. Which group of clients needs special monitoring by the nurse while receiving furosemide (Lasix) therapy?
    1. Premature infants.
    2. Diabetics.
    3. Asthmatics.
    4. Clients with peripheral vascular disease (PVD).

Answers and Rationales

104. The correct answer is 2. Furosemide (Lasix) can cause hyperglycemia. Diabetics need close monitoring of urine and blood glucose while on furosemide therapy.

E. Prototype—Carbonic Anhydrase Inhibitors (Acetazolamide [Diamox])
    1. Action. Promotes renal excretion of sodium, potassium, bicarbonate, and water via reduction of hydrogen ion secretion in the renal tubule cells of the kidney.
    2. Use. Adjunct ion treating congestive heart failure; adjunct in treating open-angle glaucoma to decrease intraocular pressure; acute mountain sickness; epilepsy.
    3. Adverse Effects. Nausea, vomiting, anorexia, melena, constipation; hematuria, renal colic, renal calculi, crystalluria; liver damage; fatigue, nervousness, drowsiness, dizziness, depression, headache, tremor, convulsions; transient myopia; bone marrow depression; urticaria, pruritus, rash, photosensitivity; weight loss, fever, acidosis; increased excretion of calcium, potassium, magnesium, and sodium; hyperglycemia; hyperuricemia.
    4. Nursing Implications
        a. Can be taken with food.
        b. Tablets (regular, only not sustained release) can be crushed or dissolved in hot water. Will not dissolve in fruit juice.
        c. Give in morning to avoid interrupting sleep.
        d. Avoid IM route; alkalinity of solution causes pain.
        e. Monitor clients for metabolic acidosis.
        f. Monitor I&O and weight when using drug for edema.
        g. Maintain fluid intake to prevent kidney stones.
        h. Many adverse effects are dose related.
        i. Monitor diabetic clients.
        j. Potassium loss greatest in early treatment.
        k. Observe for signs of hypokalemia; those at high risk for this are clients receiving other diuretics or digitalis glycosides, and the elderly.
        l. Client may need a potassium supplement.
        m. Monitor serum electrolytes, blood gases, urinalysis.
        n. Parenteral solution should be used within 24 hours after reconstitution.
    5. Discharge Teaching
        a. Do not interchange brands without asking physician.
        b. Avoid excess salt intake.
        c. Report any adverse effects.
        d. Do not drive or perform other activities if experiencing CNS effects.
        e. If taken in high doses or for long periods of time, client will need a diet high in potassium.

F. Prototype—Potassium-sparing Diuretics (Spironolactone [Aldactone])
    1. Action. Acts by blocking aldosterone receptors in the kidney tubule, thus causing excretion of water and sodium and potassium retention.
    2. Use. Primary hyperaldosteronism; edema; treatment and prevention of hypokalemia; essential hypertension.
    3. Adverse Effects. Hyperkalemia; hyponatremia; gynecomastia; thirst, dry mouth, diarrhea; impotence, irregular menses, hirsutism; headache, dizziness, drowsiness, confusion; rash, urticaria.
    4. Nursing Implications
        a. Give with food.
        b. Tablet can be crushed.
        c. Monitor serum electrolytes.
        d. Duiretic effect may take until third day of therapy and may last 2–3 days after drug is stopped.
        e. Monitor I&O and check for edema.
        f. Weigh client daily.
        g. Monitor blood pressure.
        h. Adverse effects usually reversible if drug discontinued.
    5. Discharge Teaching
        a. Teach signs of electrolyte imbalance and when to report.
        b. Consult physician concerning potassium and sodium intake. Usually client should avoid a high-potassium diet.
    6. Related Drugs
        a. Triamterene (Dyrenium): prevents sodium reabsorption in the distal tubule of the kidney, which causes retention of potassium and sodium and water. It is used to treat edema, hypertension, and hypokalemia. Adverse effects are: hyperkalemia, renal calculi, nausea, vomiting, anorexia, diarrhea, headache, fatigue,

rash, photosensitivity, and blood dyscrasias. Nursing implications include giving the drug with food to decrease GI upset; give the drug in the morning, monitor I&O, body weight, serum electrolytes, and BUN; client should avoid foods high in potassium.

    b. Amiloride (Midamor): resembles triamterene. The biggest difference is that it is much more potent than triamterene.

G. Prototype—Osmotic Diuretics (Mannitol [Osmitrol])

   1. Action. Acts by increasing the osmotic pressure of the glomerular filtrate inside the renal tubules. This causes less reabsorption of fluid and electrolytes by the tubules and increased loss of fluid, chloride, and sodium.

   2. Use. Prevention and treatment of acute renal failure; reduction of intracranial pressure; reduction of intraocular pressure; urinary excretion of drug overdoses.

   3. Adverse Effects. Nausea, anorexia, thirst; diuresis, urinary retention; dizziness, headache, convulsions; pulmonary congestion; tachycardia, chest pain, high or low blood pressure; metabolic acidoses; hypokalemia, hyponatremia, hypochloremia, dehydration.

   4. Nursing Implications
    a. Test dose given to clients with advanced oliguria.
    b. Monitor serum and urine electrolytes, central venous pressure, and renal function.
    c. Accurate I&O every 30 minutes.
    d. Monitor VS.
    e. Monitor for signs of electrolyte imbalance.
    f. Weigh client daily.
    g. Avoid extravasation.
    h. Drug may crystallize if exposed to low temperatures. Warm solution to dissolve crystals.
    i. Solutions above 15% have tendency to crystallize. IV filter must be used for infusing solutions 15% and above.

Sample Questions

105. Which nursing action is NOT appropriate while caring for a client receiving intravenous mannitol?

   1. Using an intravenous filter when giving the client a concentration of mannitol of 15% or higher.
   2. Placing the bottle of mannitol in warm water to dissolve crystals appearing in the drug solution.
   3. Using the drug solution if at least half of the crystals are dissolved.
   4. Monitoring the intravenous flow rate to keep the urine output at 30–50 ml per hour.

Answers and Rationales

105. The correct answer is 3. If crystals are present in the solution of mannitol (Osmitrol), the solution should be placed in a warm water bath, then cooled to body temperature prior to administration.

POTASSIUM-REMOVING RESIN

A. There is one drug in this category, sodium polystyrene sulfonate (Kayexalate).

B. Characteristics of polystyrene sulfonate (Kayexalate)

   1. A resin that exchanges sodium ions for potassium ions in the large intestine.
   2. Used in the treatment of hyperkalemia.
   3. Given orally or rectally via high enema to both adults and children.
   4. Nursing implications
    a. Retain rectal suspension for at least 30–60 minutes.
    b. Monitor for electrolyte deficiency.
     1) Hypokalemia can occur.
     2) Magnesium and calcium can also be lost.
     3) Sodium may be retained.
    c. Constipation can occur with oral administration.
    d. Rectal administration helps prevent constipation.
    e. Mix resin with sorbitol and water (never with oil).
    f. Stop administration when serum potassium is 4–5 milliequivalents.

Respiratory Drugs

ANTIASTHMATIC DRUGS

A. Case Study

Nicholas Lewis is a 5-year-old male who has recently been diagnosed with extrinsic asthma. His asthma seems to be exacerbated during hay fever season. Nicholas has undergone skin testing and is allergic to many environmental factors such as smoke and ragweed. Nicholas's father had extrinsic asthma as a child. Nicholas is taking theophylline and cromolyn sodium (Intal).

B. Prototype—Theophylline
   1. Action. Classified as a methylexanthine; a bronchodilator that relaxes the bronchial smooth muscle cells. It also increases renal blood flow, thus producing a diuretic effect, and acts as a CNS stimulant.
   2. Use. Emphysema; chronic bronchitis; asthma; CHF.
   3. Adverse Effects. CNS stimulation: irritability, nervousness, restlessness (note: children are more susceptible to developing CNS stimulation effects); tachycardia, hypotension, palpitations (note: shouldn't be used in clients with cardiovascular disease); tachypnea, flushing; nausea, vomiting, GI distress (note: should not be used in clients with peptic ulcer disease or hyperthyroidism); rectal irritation with rectal suppository use.
   4. Nursing Implications
      a. Monitor theophylline levels (10–20 mcg/ml).
      b. Monitor vital signs and symptoms of toxicity.
      c. Clients who smoke tobacco and marijuana require higher doses of theophylline.
      d. Administer with milk or meals if GI distress is present, otherwise give 1–2 hours before meals with water.
   5. Discharge Teaching
      a. Consult with the physician before taking OTC drugs.
      b. Avoid excessive caffeine use.
      c. Do not crush or chew time-released or enteric-coated preparations.
C. Related Drugs
   (See prototype theophylline for adverse effects)
   1. Aminophylline (Somophyllin)
      a. Can be given PO, rectal, IV, or IM.
      b. IM injection is painful and generally avoided.
      c. IV infusion should not exceed 25 milligrams per minute.

d. Vital signs should be monitored.
e. Often used to treat severe bronchoconstriction.
f. Avoid mixing with other medications as it is incompatible with many medications.
   2. Theo-dur
   3. Slow-Bid Gyrocaps
   4. Quibron
   5. Elixophylline
      All of the above are derivatives of theophylline. Note: they are less potent than theophylline and dosage adjustments may be needed.
   6. Dyphylline (Dilor) is a synthetic chemical derivative of theophylline. Theophylline levels do not monitor Dyphylline.
D. Prototype—Antiasthmatic (Cromolyn Sodium [Intal, Nasalcrom])
   1. Action. Acts on lung mucosa to prevent histamine release. Classified as a mast cell stabilizer.
   2. Use. Prophylactically to reduce the number of asthmatic attacks. It is not used in the treatment of acute asthmatic attacks; to treat allergic rhinitis; ophthalmically to treat allergic disorders.
   3. Adverse Effects. Bronchoconstriction; cough; nasal congestion; rash.
   4. Discharge Teaching
      a. Proper use of inhaler:
         1) With spinhaler place capsule in container and exhale fully.
         2) Place mouthpiece between lips.
         3) Tilt head back.
         4) Inhale deeply and rapidly to cause the propeller to turn.
         5) Remove the inhaler.
         6) Hold breath a few seconds.
         7) Slowly exhale.
      b. Capsules should not be swallowed or opened.
      c. Rinsing or gargling may reduce irritation in the mouth.
      d. Discontinue use if an allergic reaction occurs.
E. Leukotriene Inhibitors: Zileuton (Zyflo) used to prevent asthma attacks.

Sample Questions

106. Which statement by Nicholas's mother best indicates her understanding of the use of cromolyn sodium?

1. "I will have Nicholas take this medication during an asthma attack."
2. "I will open the capsule and dilute it in juice."
3. "I will tell Nicholas to take a puff of medication upon exhalation."
4. "I will have Nicholas use this medication to prevent asthma attacks."

107. Which adverse effect should Mrs. Lewis be alert for when administering theophylline to Nicholas?
    1. Drowsiness.
    2. Irritability and restlessness.
    3. Constipation.
    4. Bradycardia.

108. Which of the following fluids should be avoided while Nicholas is taking theophylline?
    1. Ginger ale.
    2. Apple juice.
    3. Hot chocolate.
    4. Milk.

109. Mrs. Lewis asks the nurse the purpose of offering theophylline. The nurse's best response is:
    1. "This drug decreases inflammation in the bronchi."
    2. "Theophylline's antihistamine effect will counteract bronchospasm."
    3. "This drug will help to facilitate removal of secretions."
    4. "Theophylline dilates the bronchial tree and will make breathing easier."

Answers and Rationales

106. The correct answer is 4. Cromolyn sodium is effective in preventing asthma attacks because it prevents histamine release.

107. The correct answer is 2. Irritability and restlessness are symptoms of CNS stimulation, which could lead to seizures. Children are very prone to CNS stimulation with this drug.

108. The correct answer is 3. Hot chocolate contains caffeine, which can further increase CNS effects of theophylline.

109. The correct answer is 4. Theophylline dilates the smooth muscle cells in the bronchi, which enhances breathing and counteracts bronchial constriction.

ANTIHISTAMINES

1. Antihistamines reduce histamine activity by blocking histamine receptor sites. They act within 15–30 minutes after administration but are eliminated slowly from the body. Antihistamines are used to suppress symptoms of histamine release in allergy and are also indicated during the first stage of a cold. It is important to remember to administer any antihistamine before an allergy attack to prevent histamine from occupying receptor sites and thus decreasing the severity of the attack. There are a few classes of drugs that contain antihistamine properties. Sedation is the most common adverse effect of antihistamines. Paradoxical excitation has been seen in children taking these drugs, and symptoms such as dizziness, confusion, sedation, and hypotension are seen in the elderly. There are also anticholinergic effects from antihistamines, which include dry nose, mouth, and throat; urinary retention; constipation; tachycardia; and blurred vision.

2. Chlorpheniramine maleate (Chlor-Trimeton): given PO, IM, SC, and IV. Available in a sustained-release form. There are increased depressant effects if taken with alcohol or other CNS depressants. Give oral forms with food if GI upset occurs.

3. Diphenhydramine HCl (Benadryl): given PO, IM, and IV. IM should be given deeply in a large muscle mass. Hypersensitivity reactions occur more with parenteral administration than with PO.

4. Promethazine HCl (Phenergan): given PO, IM, rectally, and IV. Can be taken with food. Oral administration for allergy usually given before meals (ac) or at bedtime (hs) as a single dose. Monitor respiratory function especially in children as drug can suppress cough reflex and thicken bronchial secretions. Can cause photosensitivity.

5. Second generation non-sedating antihistamines (Prescription drugs)
    a. Loratadine (Claritin)
    b. Astemizole (Hismanal)

Sample Questions

110. What would the nurse teach the client to do to lessen the sedation effects of antihistamines?
    1. Increase caffeine intake during the day.
    2. Take the antihistamine when going to bed.
    3. Take the antihistamine with a vitamin.
    4. Have a 2-hour nap in the morning and afternoon.

111. An adverse effect that is more often seen in children than adults who are taking antihistamines is
    1. dizziness.
    2. dry mucous membranes.

3. constipation.
4. CNS excitement.

Answers and Rationales

110. The correct answer is 2. The sedation effects of antihistamines will be decreased if the client takes the drug at bedtime.
111. The correct answer is 4. A side effect of antihistamines that is seen more commonly in children than adults is excitation of the central nervous system.

MUCOLYTICS

A. Acetylcysteine (Mucomyst)
   1. Action. Reduces the viscosity of mucus in the bronchial tree.
   2. Use. Cystic fibrosis; acute and chronic bronchopulmonary diseases such as pneumonia, bronchitis, and emphysema; acetylcysteine is the antidote for acetaminophen (Tylenol) overdose.
   3. Adverse Effects. May cause bronchospasm in asthmatic clients and should be discontinued; stomatitis, nausea, vomiting.
   4. Nursing Implications
      a. Suction equipment should be readily available.
      b. Has a foul odor of "rotten eggs."
      c. Should rinse mouth after treatment.

Sample Questions

112. Which of the following should be available for clients receiving acetylcysteine?
   1. A glass of water.
   2. Tracheostomy set-up.
   3. Suction set-up.
   4. Room deodorizer.

Answers and Rationales

112. The correct answer is 3. Acetylcysteine (Mucomyst) can cause an outpouring of copious secretions, which may cause gagging. Suction may be needed to facilitate the removal of secretions to prevent aspiration.

EXPECTORANTS AND ANTITUSSIVES

A. Case Study
   Jeff Allyn, a college freshman, for five days has had nasal discharge, malaise, headache, and nonproductive cough. The student health physician orders guaifenesin (Robitussin) for Jeff.
B. Expectorants
   1. Expectorants reduce the viscosity of bronchial secretions, which allows for their removal from the lungs. They are used in the management of cough associated with the common cold and in the treatment of bronchitis.
   2. Guaifenesin (Robitussin): can be given to adults and children. It increases the respiratory tract fluid thus reducing viscosity of secretions. It is the most frequently used OTC expectorant medication. Client should be told to increase fluid intake and add humidification. A common adverse effect is gastric upset, which is caused by its stimulatory effect on gastric secretions.
   3. Terpin Hydrate Elixir: directly stimulates the bronchial secretory glands. Is often used as a vehicle for other cough medications. Terpin hydrate has a high alcohol content and shouldn't be given to alcoholics. Also shouldn't be given to children under 12 years.
C. Antitussives
   1. Antitussives are given to reduce the force and amount of coughing. They can act centrally by suppressing the cough center in the brain or peripherally to reduce the susceptibility of irritant receptors to activity. Some antitussives contain narcotics. The antitussives are given for the symptomatic relief of nonproductive cough.
   2. Dextromethorphan (Benylin DM, Pertussin): This is the most frequently used non-narcotic antitussive. Because of its safety record, it is used for children as well as adults. Common adverse effects are dizziness, drowsiness, and nausea. It shouldn't be given to clients receiving MAO inhibitors.
   3. Codeine: Due to its addicting capabilities, it should be given in the smallest dose possible to decrease adverse effects and tolerance. The client needs to be watched for signs of dependency. Common adverse effects are nausea, vomiting, and constipation. Encourage clients to increase fluid intake and take a laxative if constipation occurs. Provide for client safety due to codeine's sedative effects. If the client is taking other CNS depressants with codeine there is an increased chance of CNS effects. Respiratory depression occurs at high doses. Observe respiratory rate and use cautiously in clients with asthma or emphysema.

Sample Questions

113. Which of the following points should be made to Jeff regarding guaifenesin by the nurse?
    1. Guaifenesin has a high incidence of adverse effects.
    2. Increase fluid intake to help liquefy and loosen secretions while taking guaifenesin.
    3. Guaifenesin has a large alcohol content.
    4. This drug can cause blood glucose level to rise.

114. After a week, Jeff returns to the student health center and states he feels better but his cough is interfering with his sleep. The physician now orders an antitussive for Jeff. In which situation would the use of an antitussive be inappropriate?
    1. The client's cough is interfering with eating meals.
    2. The client's cough is associated with a suppurative lung disorder.
    3. The client's cough is the source of a complication such as a rib fracture.
    4. The client's cough is irritating to the respiratory tract.

115. Which adverse effect is associated with the use of high doses of codeine as an antitussive?
    1. Diarrhea.
    2. Nasal congestion.
    3. Respiratory depression.
    4. Skin rash.

Answers and Rationales

113. The correct answer is 2. Clients taking guaifenesin (Robitussin) need to increase fluid intake daily to help thin and loosen secretions. This allows the drug to be more effective.

114. The correct answer is 2. An antitussive is not appropriate for a client with lung disease accompanied by increased sputum as pneumonia or atelectasis could occur.

115. The correct answer is 3. Respiratory depression is an adverse effect associated with use of codeine. It is a life-threatening effect.

Gastrointestinal Tract Drugs

HISTAMINE (H₂) ANTAGONISTS

A. Case Study
Mr. Stan Clark is a 40-year-old recently divorced business executive who likes to "live on the edge." His history is remarkable in that he smokes 1 pack of cigarettes per day; drinks 6 cups of coffee per day, and drinks 3 scotches every night to "unwind." He is currently taking 800 mg of motrin (Ibuprofen) TID for a recent knee injury.
   One week into his motrin (Ibuprofen) therapy, Mr. Clark complains of severe burning epigastric pain in the early morning. The burning sensation is somewhat relieved after eating, but after 2 days of discomfort, Mr. Clark sees his internist. An endoscopy is ordered and reveals a duodenal ulcer. Medication ordered: cimetedine (Tagamet) 300 mg QID, with meals and at bedtime for 4 weeks.

B. Prototype—Cimetidine (Tagamet)
    1. Action. Decreases stomach acidity by impeding the action of histamine. Competes with histamine for occupancy of histamine (H₂) receptor sites on the parietal cells in the stomach and suppresses the release of gastric acid.
    2. Use. Short-term treatment of active duodenal ulcer and benign gastric ulcer; decreased dose after ulcer has healed to inhibit reappearance; pathologic hypersecretory conditions, e.g., Zollinger-Ellison syndrome.
    3. Adverse Effects. Diarrhea, muscle pain, rash; CNS effects of dizziness, confusion, drowsiness, headache; changes in liver function studies; agranulocytosis and neutropenia; reversible impotence.
    4. Nursing Implications
        a. Oral form should be taken with meals.
        b. Antacids decrease absorption; give antacid one hour before or after administration.
        c. Usual course of treatment for ulcer disease is 4–6 weeks.
        d. Many drug interactions.
        e. Watch for CNS changes particularly in the elderly as confusion is a major toxic effect.

TABLE 2.18   Other H₂ Antagonists

Drug	Nursing Implications
Ranitidine (Zantac)	See cimetidine
Famotidine (Pepcid)	• May be given with antacid dose. • Dosage modifications not necessary in elderly except with renal impairment.
Nizatidine (Axid)	• Can elevate serum salicylate levels in clients taking high doses of aspirin.

   f. Use cautiously with clients who have impaired renal or hepatic function.
   g. Monitor CBC and liver function studies.
   5. Discharge Teaching. Smoking decreases effectiveness of cimetidine.
   6. Related drugs. See Table 2.18.
C. Proton Pump Inhibitor
   1. Omeprazole (Prilosec)
   2. Used to decrease gastric acid concentration in peptic ulcer and gastroesophageal reflux disease.
   3. Nursing Implications
      a. Do not chew, crush, or open capsule.
      b. Can be administered with antacids.
D. Peptic ulcers caused by *Helicobacter pylori* are commonly treated with a combination of two antibiotics, a bismuth compound and a histamine antagonist or proton pump inhibitor.

Sample Questions

116. The primary action of cimetidine is to
   1. suppress the action of acetylcholine at the receptor responsible for histamine release.
   2. decrease the pH of gastric fluids.
   3. antagonize the action of histamine at its H₂ receptor site.
   4. neutralize gastric secretions.
117. An antacid is also ordered for Mr. Clark in conjunction with the cimetidine. What instruction should the nurse give to Mr. Clark concerning concurrent use of an antacid with cimetidine?
   1. Take both drugs together.
   2. Take both drugs with milk.
   3. Take both drugs with meals.
   4. Take the drugs one hour apart.
118. Which statement made by Mr. Clark best indicates his understanding of cimetidine therapy?
   1. "I will stop taking cimetidine when my stomach pain is gone."
   2. "I will stop smoking."
   3. "I will take cimetidine on an empty stomach."

4. "I know that cimetidine will turn my stools black."
119. In elderly clients taking cimetidine, which adverse effect should the nurse be most concerned with?
   1. Confusion.
   2. Diarrhea.
   3. Muscle pain.
   4. Constipation.

Answers and Rationales

116. The correct answer is 3. Cimetidine (Tagamet) competes with histamine for occupancy of histamine (H₂) receptor sites on the parietal cells in the stomach.
117. The correct answer is 4. Antacids decrease cimetidine absorption.
118. The correct answer is 2. Smoking decreases the effectiveness of cimetidine (Tagamet) and is also contraindicated in ulcer disease.
119. The correct answer is 1. Confusion is a major toxic effect in the elderly.

GASTROINTESTINAL (GI) ANTICHOLINERGICS

With the advent of H₂ antagonists, gastrointestinal anticholinergics are rarely used. H₂ antagonists have a more prolonged action and fewer side effects, and are considered more effective in treating gastric ulcers. Gastrointestinal anticholinergics delay gastric emptying time, which prolongs the action of antacids.

ANTACIDS

A. Case Study
   Mrs. Laurie Lopez is a 60-year-old homemaker who was recently diagnosed as having a hiatal hernia. Her chief complaint was heartburn after meals. The physician ordered an upper gastrointestinal series and a subsequent diagnosis was made.
   Orders include Maalox 30 ml one hour pc and hs and prn for heartburn; high-protein, low-fat diet with small frequent meals, no caffeine, chocolate, or alcohol; rest in a supine position 2–3 hours after eating and no heavy lifting.
B. Prototype
   1. Action. There are 5 antacid categories with the same action of neutralizing gastric acid. There are significant differences between each of the 5 categories; therefore no individual antacid is considered a prototype.

2. Use. Control ulcer pain; peptic ulcer; esophageal reflux; prophylaxis for Curling's ulcer.
3. Adverse Effects. See Table 2.19.
4. Nursing Implications for All Antacids
   a. Shake liquid antacids prior to use.
   b. Liquids tend to be more effective than tablets.
   c. Tablets must be chewed completely before swallowing.
   d. Take a sip of water following antacid administration to ensure passage to the stomach.
   e. Large amounts of water will dilute the antacid.
   f. Aluminum and magnesium combinations to reduce the side effects of diarrhea and constipation.
   g. Do not take other oral drugs within 1–2 hours of an antacid.
   h. Can interfere with the intended response of enteric-coated medications.

Sample Questions

120. Which antacid is LEAST LIKELY to cause adverse effects?

1. Magnesium hydroxide (Milk of Magnesia).
2. Aluminum hydroxide (Amphogel).
3. Aluminum/magnesium combination (Maalox).
4. Calcium carbonate (Tums).
121. The nurse tells Mrs. Lopez that the first effect she should expect from taking Maalox is
1. constipation.
2. decrease of gastric acid secretion.
3. alleviation of burning pain.
4. diarrhea.

Answers and Rationales

120. The correct answer is 3. Antacid combinations containing aluminum and magnesium have reduced adverse effects as aluminum antacids cause constipation and magnesium antacids cause diarrhea.
121. The correct answer is 3. Antacids such as Maalox neutralize gastric acidity, thus reducing pain. Maalox does not decrease gastric acid secretions. Constipation and diarrhea are adverse effects when taking antacids. They are decreased when taking a combination antacid acid such as Maalox.

TABLE 2.19   Antacids

Drug Categories	Adverse Effects	Nursing Implications
Magnesium-containing antacids Magnesium Hydroxide (Milk of Magnesia)	Diarrhea	• Doses greater than 1.5 ml may have a laxative effect. • Contraindicated in clients with renal failure. • Monitor for symptoms of hypermagnesemia, CNS changes, hypotension, nausea, vomiting.
Aluminim-containing antacids Aluminum Hydroxide (Amphogel)	Constipation	• Check serum for hypophosphatemia. • Monitor for fecal impaction and intestinal obstruction in elderly. • Aluminum can accumulate in CNS causing toxic effects; not given over a long period of time.
Sodium Carbonate/Bicarbonate Dihydroxy- aluminum Sodium Carbonate (Rolaids)	Constipation, sodium retention	• Must chew tablet • Not for long-term use
Sodium Bicarbonate (Baking Soda)	Systemic alkalosis, bloating, sodium retention	• Contraindicated in congestive heart failure, hypertension, or sodium-restricted diets. • Monitor for milk-alkali syndrome, nausea, vomiting, headache, hypercalcemia, hypercalcuria, hypophosphatemia.
Calcium Carbonate (Tums)	Acid rebound, milk-alkali syndrome, hypercalcemia, constipation	• Monitor for milk-alkali syndrome. • Not to be taken with milk or foods high in vitamin D.
Aluminum Magnesium combinations Magaldrate (Riopan)	Constipation or diarrhea, hypermagnesemia	• Other common antacids in this group are Maalox, DiGel, Gelusil. • Use cautiously in clients with impaired renal function and monitor magnesium levels.

ANTIDIARRHEAL AGENTS

A. Case Study

Mrs. Lucy Pike is a 75-year-old widow who enjoys dining out nightly. One evening after eating a Caesar salad and roast turkey, Mrs. Pike developed severe abdominal cramping, distention, and frequent watery diarrhea. For 4 days Mrs. Pike used home remedies to treat the diarrhea, including yogurt and Pepto-Bismol. On the fifth day Mrs. Pike's daughter finds her in bed, dehydrated, lethargic, and confused. Mrs. Pike is taken to the emergency room via ambulance and admitted with a diagnosis of salmonella. Lab values reveal serum potassium 3.2 mEq/l, sodium 134 mEq/l.

B. Prototype

1. Action. There are 2 categories of drugs to treat diarrhea. Adsorbents act by binding substances such as bacteria, toxins, and digestive enzymes, which could be the cause of diarrheal conditions. They tend to absorb other oral drugs and should not be taken together. The second category, opiates, decrease gastrointestinal motility and slow intestinal propulsion promoting dehydration of intestinal contents. Within these two categories there is not an individual prototype.

2. Related Drugs. See Table 2.20.

Sample Questions

122. The physician orders Lomotil 5 mg PO QID for Mrs. Pike's diarrhea. What adverse effect of Lomotil must the nurse be alert for?
    1. Urinary retention.
    2. Decreased peristalsis.
    3. Tinnitus.
    4. Diarrhea.
123. Mrs. Pike's daughter mentions to the nurse that her 6-year-old son often takes Pepto-Bismol for an upset stomach. The nurse should reinforce that Pepto-Bismol could cause a potential problem in children because it
    1. interacts with multivitamins.
    2. will cause anorexia.
    3. has an antibiotic effect.
    4. contains salicylate.

Answers and Rationales

122. The correct answer is 1. Lomotil contains atropine, which is an anticholinergic that cause cause urinary retention.
123. The correct answer is 4. Pepto-Bismol contains small amounts of salicylate. Salicylates are connected with Reye's syndrome and are not recommended in children under the age of 12.

TABLE 2.20 Antidiarrheals

Category	Drug	Adverse Effects	Nursing Implications
Adsorbent	Bismuth subsalicylate (Pepto-Bismol)	Salicylate poisoning, impaction, darkening of stool and tongue	• Over-the-counter (OTC) preparation • Use cautiously with aspirin or other aspirin-containing drugs
	Kaolin and Pectin (Kaopectate)	Constipation, fecal impaction	• OTC preparation • Regular and concentrated suspensions • Extended use can cause disruption of nutrient absorption in body.
Opiate	Loperamide Hydrochloride (Imodium)	Toxic megacolon in clients with ulcerative colitis; drowsiness, dizziness, abdominal discomfort, constipation	• Synthetically related to meperidine (Demerol) • Shouldn't be taken together with other CNS depressants • Treat overdose with slurry of activated charcoal and watch for CNS depression.
	Diphenoxylate Hydrochloride with Atropine (Lomotil)	Sedation, flushing, palpitations, blurred vision, dry mouth, urinary retention	• Withhold in severe dehydration or electrolyte imbalance • Addition possible in high doses and with prolonged use
	Opium Tincture (Paregoric)	Respiratory depression, physical and psychological dependence, mental impairment	• Reduced dose for elderly and clients with respiratory problems • Safety precautions • Give with 2–3 swallows of water to ensure passage to stomach

LAXATIVES

A. Case Study
Mrs. Isabelle Sherwood is an 85-year-old widow who lives with her daughter. Mrs. Sherwood is very concerned about her bowel function. She thinks that if she doesn't have a bowel movement every day she will become constipated. Her daily routine consists of eating one bowl of 100% bran and one 8-ounce glass of prune juice. If she doesn't have a bowel movement after breakfast each morning, she takes one dose of Ex-Lax. On this particular day, Mrs. Sherwood took an additional dose of Ex-Lax. During that evening she developed diarrhea and after her sixth stool, she fainted. Her daughter found her on the floor and immediately called an ambulance, which took Mrs. Sherwood to the local emergency room.

B. Prototype
1. Used to promote movement of feces through the bowel. Usually given to prepare clients for diagnostic tests and/or surgery, to prevent straining during defecation, and to prevent or treat constipation. There are five categories of laxatives based on their different actions. There is no prototype drug for this group.
2. Saline cathartics attract and hold large amounts of fluids thereby increasing the bulk of stools. The nurse needs to encourage fluid intake to prevent dehydration.
3. Bulk-forming laxatives increase the bulk of the feces by stimulating mechanical peristalsis and are considered the safest of all the laxative groups.
4. Lubricant laxatives coat the feces with an oil film and prevent the colon from reabsorbing water from the feces.
5. Stool softeners prevent straining during defecation and prevent constipation by decreasing surface tension of feces.
6. Stimulant laxatives stimulate peristalsis.
7. Should not be given to clients with symptoms of nausea, vomiting, abdominal pain, symptoms of appendicitis, or intestinal obstruction.
8. Used for a week or less to prevent rebound constipation and dependence.
9. Appropriate fluid intake and a diet high in fiber will help promote proper bowel function.
Related drugs. See Table 2.21.

Sample Questions

124. The nurse tells Mrs. Sherwood that the group of laxatives that is considered the safest and most natural is the

1. saline-cathartics group.
2. lubricant-laxative group.
3. stool-softener group.
4. bulk-forming laxative group.
125. The nurse should not administer a laxative to a client who states he has
1. nausea.
2. excess body weight.
3. increase in appetite.
4. painful defecation.

Answers and Rationales

124. The correct answer is 4. Bulk-forming laxatives are considered the safest and most natural of all laxative groups because they are natural or semisynthetic substances, they produce stools that are formed normally, and are not absorbed systemically.
125. The correct answer is 1. A client with nausea should never be given a laxative because this person is at risk for fluid and electrolyte imbalance.

ANTIEMETICS

A. Case Study
Nancy Pelcher, age 40, married with two children, went on a cruise of the eastern Caribbean for seven days. She had never been on a cruise ship before but didn't think she would have trouble with motion sickness. The first night at sea was extremely rough and Nancy felt dizzy and nauseous and vomited several times. She had packed dimenhydrinate (Dramamine) but didn't take the first dose until well after her symptoms were quite acute. The next day she took 100 mg of dimenhydrinate (Dramamine) every 6 hours and felt drowsy and sedated; all she did was sleep in her cabin. By the third day of her trip, she had her "sea-legs" and stopped taking the dimenhydrinate (Dramamine).

B. Prototype
1. To treat and prevent nausea and vomiting (more effective in prevention than treatment). There are three categories of antiemetics.
2. The phenothiazines group is primarily used to treat psychoses, but also acts on the chemoreceptor trigger zone (CTZ) and vomiting center to relieve nausea and vomiting. Most commonly used as anti-emetics are prochlorperazine (Compazine) and promethazine (Phenergan). Used for treating nausea and vomiting especially in pre- and postoperative clients. The major adverse effects of the phenothiazines are orthostatic hypotension, anticholinergic

TABLE 2.21   Laxatives

Category	Drug	Adverse Effects	Nursing Implications
Saline	Magnesium citrate (Citroma)	Hypermagnesia in renal failure, nausea	• Laxation in 2–6 hrs • Available in effervescent form • Most effective on empty stomach and followed with a glass of water
	Magnesium hydroxide (Milk of Magnesia)	See magnesium citrate	• Lower doses act as antacid • Shake bottle before taking
	Glycerin (Glycerol)	Abdominal cramps, rectal discomfort	• Evacuation occurs in 15–30 minutes after enema/suppository.
Bulk Forming	Methylcellulose (Citrucel, Cologel)	Fecal impaction, esophageal obstruction, nausea	• Laxation in 12–72 hrs • Take with 1 glass of water to prevent fecal impaction • Must not chew tablet form or take in dry powder form as it may cause esophageal obstruction.
	Psyllium hydrophilic muciloid (Metamucil)	See above	See above
Lubricant	Mineral oil	Impairs absorption of fat-soluble vitamins and nutrients, lipid pneumonia	• Administer in an upright position • Do not take with meals, first given in evening • Retention enema is usually followed by a cleansing enema. • Keep in refrigerator
Stool softener	Ducosate sodium (Colace)	Rare—rash, abdominal cramps	• Effective in 12–72 hrs • Take with plenty of fluids • Use caution with clients on sodium-restricted diets.
Stimulant	Bisacodyl (Dulcolax)	Rare	• Effect in 12 hr PO, and 15 min.–1 hour in rectal form • PO drug given before breakfast or at bedtime • Do not take tablets within 1 hour of antacid or milk administration.
	Cascara Sagrada	Large doses can cause hypokalemia, glucose intolerance, calcium deficiency, anorexia	• Could discolor urine • Effect in 6–12 hrs • Prolonged use can cause rebound constipation
	Castor Oil (Emulsoil, Neoloid)	Rebound constipation, abdominal cramps, nausea, vomiting	• Effect in 2–3 hrs • Do not schedule within 2 hours of taking other oral drugs • Shake emulsion well • Give with juice or carbonated beverage to mask castor oil's unpleasant odor and taste
	Phenolphthalein (Ex-Lax, Feen-a-Mint, Correctol)	Rash, lupus-like syndrome	• Effect in 6–8 hrs • Urine/feces may have reddish discoloration • Usually given at bedtime • Effect could last 3–4 days • Discontinue if rash occurs
	Senna (Senokot)	Abdominal cramps, nausea	• Laxation in 6–10 hrs • Administer at bedtime • Urine/feces may have yellowish-brown or reddish-brown discoloration

symptoms, cardiac stimulation, and parkinsonian movement disorders also referred to as extrapyramidal effects.

3. The antihistamine drugs block the action of acetylcholine in the brain and alleviate nausea and vomiting. Antihistamines are quite efficient in treating and preventing motion sickness. Common examples from this group are dimenhydrinate (Dramamine), hydroxyzine (Vistaril), and meclizine (Antivert). Adverse effects of antihistamines are CNS depression and anticholinergic effects.

4. The third group of antiemetic drugs is a group of miscellaneous agents. The newest drug from this category is metoclopramide (Reglan). Reglan blocks dopamine receptors in the CTZ of the brain, thus

treating nausea and vomiting. An important use is to decrease symptoms from cancer chemotherapy. Adverse effects include drowsiness, restlessness, weakness, sleeplessness, headache, and extrapyramidal effects.

Sample Questions

126. Which statement by Nancy demonstrates her understanding of dimenhydrinate therapy?
     1. "I'm glad I'll still be able to have wine with my meals while I'm taking Dramamine."
     2. "I'll have my husband drive the rental car while I'm taking Dramamine."
     3. "I know the ship's doctor is very busy so I'll just go ahead and take my other prescription drugs with the Dramamine before checking with him."
     4. "My mouth has become so dry since I started taking Dramamine. I must be allergic to this drug."

Answers and Rationales

126. The correct answer is 2. There is a high incidence of drowsiness with dimenhydrinate (Dramamine); clients need to refrain from driving and operating dangerous machinery while taking this medication.

EMETICS

A. Case Study
   Johnny Lewis is a very active 2-year-old who has a tendency to put everything into his mouth. One afternoon Johnny climbed up onto the kitchen counter and opened a cabinet where his children's liquid Tylenol was located. He opened the container and swallowed the contents. Just after Johnny swallowed the Tylenol, his mother saw him with the empty container and some of the Tylenol on his face. Mrs. Lewis immediately called the poison control center and administered syrup of ipecac per instructions.

B. Prototype—Ipecac Syrup
   1. Action. Not fully known but probably stimulates the CTZ and irritates the GI tract to induce vomiting, thus delaying the absorption time of toxic substances. Emesis should occur within 20–30 minutes.
   2. Use. Stimulate vomiting for clients who have taken toxic doses of oral medications, and poisons.
   3. Adverse Effects. Fluid and electrolyte imbalance; stimulated and then suppressed

nervous system; hypotension; persistent vomiting; aspiration.
   4. Nursing Implications
      a. Should not be given after charcoal administration as it antagonizes the effects.
      b. Administer with water and monitor vital signs.
      c. Repeat dose once if vomiting does not occur.
      d. If a client is less than age 10 only one dose should be given.
      e. Should not be given to semiconscious or unconscious clients or clients having seizures.
      f. Should not be given if substance ingested is corrosive, petroleum based, or cyanide.
      g. Teach parents proper use of ipecac at home and follow-up care after use.

C. Prototype—Apomorphine HCl.
   A CNS depressant and a controlled substance that is given subcutaneously. In adults is usually effective in 5–15 minutes. Clients who are allergic to morphine or other opiates should not take apomorphine.

Sample Questions

127. Mrs. Lewis has been instructed that to enhance the effectiveness of ipecac syrup she should:
     1. give with milk.
     2. repeat dose every 15 minutes until vomiting occurs.
     3. give after a dose of activated charcoal.
     4. follow dose with water.

Answers and Rationales

127. The correct answer is 4. Water helps to facilitate the action of ipecac syrup.

SUCRALFATE (CARAFATE)

A. Case Study
   Georgia Delbert, age 54, is diagnosed as having a duodenal ulcer. Her physician prescribes sucralfate (Carafate), 1 gram PO QID before meals and at bedtime. She is to call her physician in two weeks to let him know how she is doing.

B. Prototype—Sucralfate (Carafate)
   1. Action. Reacts with gastric acid to form a substance that adheres to the ulcer site to protect the ulcer from bile salts, pepsin, and acid. This permits healing.

2. Use. Treatment of duodenal ulcer—short term (up to 8 weeks).
3. Adverse Effects. Diarrhea, constipation; gastric discomfort; dry mouth; pruritus, rash; back pain; dizziness, sleeplessness.
4. Nursing Implications
   a. Separate administration from other drugs by 2 hours to decrease chance of interaction.
   b. Take on an empty stomach.
   c. Antacids should not be given within 1/2 hour before or after sucralfate dose.

Sample Questions

128. The nurse explains to Ms. Delbert that sucralfate enables her ulcer to heal by
    1. coating the stomach mucosa, thus preventing gastric acid irritation.
    2. forming a paste-like substance at the ulcer site that serves as a protective barrier.
    3. binding with all gastric contents to inactivate their function in the stomach.
    4. attracting white and red blood cells to the stomach to increase circulation.

129. Which of the following teaching points about sucralfate should the nurse emphasize with Ms. Delbert to ensure success with the therapy?
    1. Discontinue the drug if indigestion occurs.
    2. Use the drug on an as-needed basis if future ulcer problems occur.
    3. Constipation may occur with long-term use.
    4. Take the drug 1 hour before meals or 2 hours after meals and at bedtime.

Answers and Rationales

128. The correct answer is 2. Sucralfate (Carafate) reacts with gastric acid and becomes a paste-like substance that forms a protective barrier at the ulcer site.

129. The correct answer is 4. Sucralfate is more active in the lower-pH environment of an empty stomach. By taking the drug 1 hour before meals or 2 hours after meals, the stomach is empty and optimal results will be obtained from the drug.

Arthritis Drugs

ARTHRITIS DRUGS

A. Case Study
Mrs. Vana Carley, age 50, has noticed an increase in generalized joint pain and morning stiffness over the past few weeks. Her left knee and both hands are swollen and she is unable to wear her wedding ring. Her joint pain has forced her to take a leave of absence from her job as a computer operator. A physical examination with accompanying lab work reveals the diagnosis of rheumatoid arthritis. The physician orders aspirin 15 grains PO QID for Mrs. Carley. A week later there is no improvement in the joint pain and stiffness so she is placed on ibuprofen (Motrin) 400 mg PO QID. After one month of Motrin therapy, Mrs. Carley is experiencing some improvement in joint pain and stiffness but still cannot work. The doctor now prescribes a gold salt auranofin (Ridaura) 6 mg PO QID.

B. Prototype—Auranofin (Ridaura)
1. Action. Mechanism of action is unclear. This is the only group of drugs that may partially reverse or stop joint destruction.
2. Use. These drugs are most effective early in rheumatoid arthritis.
3. Adverse Effects. Nitroid crisis is an anaphylactic reaction that resembles effects of a large dose of nitroglycerin: i.e., flushing, severe hypotension, tachycardia, light-headedness. Nitroid crisis not common with oral gold salt therapy; diarrhea; pruritic skin rashes, dermatitis, stomatitis; blood dyscrasia; glomerulonephritis.
4. Nursing Implications
   a. Gold salts should not be given to clients with hepatic and renal disorders, hypertension, uncontrolled diabetes, or heart failure, or to clients receiving radiation therapy.
   b. Baseline CBC must be checked prior to administration and checked throughout therapy.
   c. Nitroid crisis is more apt to occur with IM injection of gold salts; therefore a test dose is given.
   d. VS should be monitored and

resuscitation equipment should be readily available with test dose.

    e. Diarrhea is more severe with oral gold salts.

    f. Oral auranofin is less toxic and better tolerated than IM.

    g. Overdose of gold salts can be treated with dimercaprol (BAL).

    h. Gold salts given IM are best given in the gluteal muscle.

  5. Discharge Teaching. Be aware that therapeutic effects may not be seen for several months.

C. Other Gold Salts
  1. Aurothioglucose (Solganol)
  2. Gold sodium thiomalate (Myochrysine)
  3. Both drugs are given IM only. Noncompliance can be a problem with both drugs as weekly injections may be needed for several months.

D. Antimalarials
  1. Chloroquine (Aralen)
  2. Hydroxychloroquine (Plaquenil)
  3. These drugs are used to treat malaria and rheumatoid arthritis that is unresponsive to NSAIDs.
  4. Nursing Implications
    a. The nurse needs to remind clients that frequent ophthalmic examinations are required as visual impairment can occur.
    b. The nurse must be alert for blood dyscrasia, GI distress, and dermatologic reactions.

Sample Questions

130. Based on the side effects of gold salt therapy, when Mrs. Carley comes to the office for her monthly visits the nurse should do all of the following EXCEPT
  1. assess Mrs. Carley's skin.
  2. examine Mrs. Carley's oral cavity.
  3. question Mrs. Carley about any itching.
  4. check her blood sugar levels.

131. Mrs. Carley has been receiving auranofin for 2 months and is showing little clinical response to it. She is experiencing the following adverse effects of the drug: abdominal cramps, vomiting, diarrhea, and stomatitis. The physician decides to continue her on auranofin. What is the reason for this?
  1. Side effects of auranofin are rare and will pass quickly.
  2. It will take several months of therapy with auranofin to achieve therapeutic effects.
  3. The physician is not sure of the best effects from auranofin because it is such a new form of treatment.

  4. Side effects of auranofin always occur just before the beginning of a therapeutic response to the drug.

Answers and Rationales

130. The correct answer is 4. Skin rashes, pruritus, and mouth lesions are all adverse effects of gold salts and need to be monitored frequently. Hyperglycemia has not been associated with gold salt therapy.

131. The correct answer is 2. It can take 6 months or longer for the gold salts to show a therapeutic response. Because of this, clients are left on gold salt therapy even though they are experiencing adverse effects before therapeutic response.

ANTIGOUT DRUGS

A. Case Study
  Mrs. Carley visits her internist complaining of a red, swollen, and painful right great toe. After examination and lab tests are completed, she is diagnosed with acute gouty arthritis, and is started on colchicine and allopurinal.

B. Prototype—Allopurinal (Zyloprim)
  1. Action. Prevents the production of uric acid by inhibiting the enzyme xanthine oxidose.
  2. Use. Used to manage primary or secondary gout and to prevent attacks; used to treat clients with recurrent calcium oxalate calculi.
  3. Adverse Effects. GI symptoms: nausea, vomiting, diarrhea; skin rash, maculopapular; hepatomegaly; drowsiness.
  4. Nursing Implications
    a. Discontinue use at first sign of skin rash.
    b. Force fluids (1–2 liters) to help prevent formation of uric acid kidney stones.
    c. Monitor liver function tests and CBC throughout therapy.
    d. Administer drug after meals.
  5. Discharge Teaching. Advise client not to drive.

C. Prototype—Colchicine (Novocolchine)
  1. Action. Drug of choice to treat acute gout attacks and prophylaxis of recurrent gout. It decreases the inflammatory response to deposition of monosodium urate crystals.
  2. Adverse Effects. Nausea, vomiting, diarrhea, abdominal pain; bone marrow depression; hair loss; rash; thrombophlebitis if given IV.
  3. Nursing Implications

a. Do not give intramuscularly or subcutaneously as this causes severe irritation.
b. Monitor IV site.
c. Assess for rash.
d. Monitor CBC.
e. Take drug after meals.
f. Hair loss is reversible when drug is stopped.
g. During an acute attack is usually given every 1–2 hours until pain is relieved and should be stopped if nausea, vomiting, or diarrhea occurs.
h. No more than 12 tablets should be given in a 24-hour period.

Sample Questions

132. What should the nurse teach Mrs. Carley in regards to colchicine therapy?
    1. The drug will be absorbed better if you take it on an empty stomach.
    2. You should limit your fluid intake while you're on this drug.
    3. No more than 12 colchicine tablets should be taken in a 24-hour period.
    4. If you have another gout attack, you need to wait 12 hours before taking colchicine.
133. The nurse knows that colchicine should be discontinued when
    1. the client becomes dizzy.
    2. diarrhea or vomiting occurs.
    3. stools turn black.
    4. serum uric acid level is below normal.
134. In addition to treating gouty arthritis, which drug is also used to treat calcium oxalate stones?
    1. Allopurinol (Zyloprim)
    2. Colchicine (Novocholchine)
    3. Naproxen (Naprosyn)
    4. Sulindac (Clinoril)

Answers and Rationales

132. The correct answer is 3. In order for the client to be treated safely with colchicine (Novocolchine), not more than 12 tablets should be taken in a 24-hour period.
133. The correct answer is 2. Diarrhea and vomiting are both early signs of colchicine toxicity. Other signs of early toxicity are anorexia, nausea, abdominal discomfort, and weakness. Colchicine should be stopped immediately before more serious toxicity occurs.
134. The correct answer is 1. Allopurinol (Zyloprim) is used to manage and prevent gout attacks. A new use for this drug is treatment of calcium oxalate stones.

Antimicrobials

GENERAL INFORMATION

A. Terminology
    1. Bacteriostatic: prevents multiplication and growth of bacterial organisms.
    2. Bactericidal: kills bacterial organisms.
B. Cultures need to be obtained before initiating therapy.
C. Sites of Action
    1. Agents that suppress bacterial cell wall synthesis; action creates a defect in bacterial cell wall structure and death of organism;
    2. Agents that suppress protein synthesis within the bacterial cell: Action interferes with normal growth and reproduction of bacterial cell, which eventually causes its eradication.
    3. Agents that interfere with bacterial cell membrane permeability: Action causes intracellular parts to escape and leads to bacterial cell death.
    4. Agents with antimetabolite action: Action causes interference with a necessary metabolic process that the bacterial cell needs for normal growth and function.
D. Need to be administered at regular intervals so therapeutic blood levels can be maintained. This will prevent development of resistant strains of organisms. An order for QID administration means giving the drug at 6-hour intervals.
E. Peak and trough levels
    1. Blood levels need to be high enough to be therapeutic but not so high that severe toxicity is caused.
    2. Peak: Client's blood is drawn 1 hour after IM or 30 minutes after IV administration.
    3. Trough: Client's blood is drawn just before next dose of antibiotic is given.
F. Superinfection

1. Infection occurring when client is receiving or has recently been given antibiotic treatment.
2. Develops when normal bacterial flora are changed by the use of an antibiotic. Allows growth of bacteria that are resistant to the antibiotic being used.
3. Clients more susceptible when placed on broad-spectrum antibiotics.

AMINOGLYCOSIDES

A. Case Study
Georgia Dean, a 42-year-old schoolteacher, is admitted to the hospital with a diagnosis of rule out appendicitis. Mrs. Dean is taken to the operating room for an appendectomy. The surgeon discovers that Mrs. Dean's appendix has ruptured. After the surgery, her orders include gentamicin (Garamycin) 80 mg IV piggyback every 8 hours.
B. Prototype—Gentamicin (Garamycin)
　1. Action. Acts by suppressing protein synthesis in bacterial cell. Bactericidal.
　2. Use. Serious gram-negative bacterial infections, eye infections.
　3. Adverse Effects. Ototoxicity, nephrotoxicity, neuromuscular blockade, hypersensitivity, photosensitivity with topical preparations.
　4. Nursing Implications
　　a. Cautious use in clients with decreased renal function, reduced hearing, dehydration, neuromuscular disorders.
　　b. Monitor hearing and balance.
　　c. Monitor renal function tests and I&O.
　　d. Client needs adequate hydration.
　　e. Safety precautions if there are vestibular nerve effects.
　　f. Monitor drug levels.
　5. Discharge Teaching
　　a. Full course of treatment is essential.
　　b. Report problems with balance or hearing changes.
　　c. Avoid sunlight.
C. Related Drugs. Amikacin (Amikin), kanamycin (Kantrex), neomycin (Neobiotic), streptomycin, tobramycin (Nebcin). Kanamycin (Kanrex) and neomycin (Neobiotic) are given orally to prepare the bowel for surgery. Neomycin (Neobiotic) is given to persons in hepatic failure to reduce ammonia levels.

Sample Questions

135. The nurse knows that the antibacterial action of gentamicin is
　1. anti-inflammatory.
　2. bacteriostatic.
　3. bactericidal.
　4. antihelminic.
136. The nurse will assess Mrs. Dean daily for which of the following adverse effects of gentamicin?
　1. Constipation.
　2. Hearing loss.
　3. Tetany.
　4. Bradycardia.
137. The nurse needs to monitor Mrs. Dean daily for the presence of superinfection. A superinfection can be defined as an infection that
　1. is resistant to the currently used antibiotic.
　2. necessitates increased amount of antibiotics for treatment.
　3. occurs if antibiotic therapy is abruptly stopped.
　4. develops when an antibiotic alters the normal bacterial flora.

Answers and Rationales

135. The correct answer is 3. Gentamicin (Garamycin) acts by suppressing protein synthesis in the bacterial cell. This effect is bactericidal.
136. The correct answer is 2. Gentamicin (Garamycin) can cause auditory and vestibular damage. The nurse must assess the client daily for hearing loss while on this drug.
137. The correct answer is 4. A superinfection occurs when normal bacterial flora are changed by the use of an antibiotic. This allows growth of bacteria that are resistant to the antibiotic currently being used.

PENICILLINS

A. Case Study
Pat Leonard, age 30, is 1 month postpartum and is nursing her baby. She notices her right breast has an area that is red, hot, and very firm to the touch. She goes to see her physician where a diagnosis of cellulitis of the right breast is made. The nurse gives her an IM injection of 1 million units of penicillin G and she is started on a course of penicillin V potassium (Pen Vee K) 500 mg PO every 6 hours for 10 days.
B. Prototype—Penicillin G Potassium (Pentids)
　1. Action. Inhibits cell wall synthesis of microorganisms. Bactericidal. Natural penicillin.
　2. Use. Systemic infections caused by gram-positive cocci; syphilis; prophylaxis for rheumatic fever and bacterial endocarditis.
　3. Adverse Effects. Hypersensitivity reactions; GI upset; anemia,

thrombocytopenia, leukopenia; nephritis; potassium poisoning; irritation at injection site.
   4. Nursing Implications
      a. Monitor client for allergic reactions. Have emergency equipment available.
      b. Clients with questionable serious penicillin allergy may be skin tested.
      c. Give oral form on empty stomach.
      d. Oral form should be taken with a full glass of water.
      e. Monitor CBC, BUN, and creatinine.
      f. Probenecid (Benemid) may be given to increase blood levels of penicillins.
      g. Monitor IV and IM injection sites.
      h. IV solutions are stable at room temperature for 24 hours only.
   5. Discharge Teaching
      a. Complete the therapy even if you feel well before the medicine is finished.
      b. Oral doses should be taken around the clock.
      c. Don't take for other infections.
C. Related Drugs
   1. Penicillinase-resistant Penicillins
      a. Used to treat infections caused by penicillinase-producing organisms.
      b. Examples: Methicillin sodium (Staphcillin), nafcillin sodium (Nafcil, Unipen)
   2. Aminopenicillins
      a. Increased effectiveness against gram-negative organisms.
      b. Examples: Ampicillin (Amcill, Polycillin), amoxicillin trihydrate (Amoxil)
   3. Extended-spectrum Penicillins
      a. Structurally similar to ampicillin but have an increased spectrum of activity against gram-negative bacteria.
      b. Examples: Carbenicillin sodium (Geocillin), piperacillin sodium (Pipracil)
   4. Penicillin/Beta-Lactamase Inhibitor Combinations
      a. Combination of penicillin with beta-lactamase inhibitor which prevents destruction of penicillin by enzymes and extends the penicillin's spectrum of antimicrobial activity.
      b. Examples: Amoxicillin/potassium clavulanate (Augmentin), Piperacillin/tazobactam (Zosyn)

Sample Questions

138. Before giving Mrs. Leonard her prescription for penicillin V potassium, the nurse reviews basic information about penicillins. Which of the following statements is true?

   1. Penicillins are well absorbed from the gastrointestinal tract after oral ingestion.
   2. Penicillins have a long half-life due to their extended excretion time.
   3. Extended-spectrum penicillins have an increased ability to penetrate outer membranes of gram-negative bacteria.
   4. Penicillins easily enter bacterial cell membranes due to their lipid solubility.
139. Penicillin is ordered for a client. The physician also orders probenecid therapy. The nurse tells the client that the probenecid will
   1. prevent a hypersensitivity reaction to the penicillin.
   2. enhance metabolism of the penicillin.
   3. stimulate the immune system.
   4. increase blood levels of the penicillin.

Answers and Rationales

138. The correct answer is 3. Extended-spectrum penicillins enter the membranes of gram-negative organisms more readily than other penicillin groups.
139. The correct answer is 4. Probenecid (Benemid) is given with penicillin to enhance therapeutic blood levels of the penicillin.

CEPHALOSPORINS

A. Case Study
   Mr. Jack Lacy, age 58, had developed a wound infection after abdominal surgery. The physician orders cefazolin sodium (Ancef) 1 g IV every 8 hours. Mr. Lacy is also diabetic.
B. Prototype for First-generation Cephalosporins—Cefazolin Sodium (Ancef) (Note: The cephalosporins are divided into three groups or "generations" based on their spectrums of activity.)
   1. Action. Inhibits bacterial cell wall synthesis. Bactericidal.
   2. Use. Infections caused by gram-positive cocci; septicemia; bone, joint, and skin infections; prophylactic use in surgery; serious intra-abdominal infection.
   3. Adverse Effects. Phlebitis at IV site; diarrhea, pseudomembranous colitis; hypersensitivity reactions; fungal overgrowth; discomfort at IM injection site; nephrotoxicity; hepatotoxicity; bone marrow depression.
   4. Nursing Implications
      a. Give IM injections deeply into large muscle masses; rotate sites.
      b. Assess for history of penicillin allergy as there is a cross allergy between cephalosporins and penicillin.

c. Dose will be reduced with renal impairment and decreased liver function.
d. Increased risk of renal toxicity if given with other nephrotoxic drugs.
e. Monitor renal, liver function studies, and I&O.
f. Prolonged IV administration can cause thrombophlebitis. Assess and rotate IV sites.
g. Probenecid therapy will increase blood levels of cephalosporin.
5. Discharge Teaching
   a. Finish full course of therapy even if you feel well.
   b. Promptly report diarrhea, rash, hives, difficulty breathing, unusual bleeding.
   c. Report signs of superinfection.
6. Related Drugs. Cephalexin (Keflex), cephalothin sodium (Keflin), cephapirin sodium (Cefadyl), cepharadine (Velosef).
C. Prototype for Second-generation Cephalosporins—Cefoxitin Sodium (Mefoxin)
   1. Action. See action for cefazolin sodium (Ancef).
   2. Use. Infections caused by gram-negative and gram-positive bacteria; septicemia; pelvic, skin, and soft-tissue infections; prophylaxis in abdominal or pelvic surgery; gonorrhea.
   3. Adverse Effects. See adverse effects for cefazolin sodium (Ancef).
   4. Nursing Implications. Lidocaine used as diluent for IM injection and helps reduce pain of IM injection. See Nursing Implications and Discharge Teaching for cefazolin sodium (Ancef).
   5. Related Drugs. Cefaclor (Ceclor), cefamandole naftate (Mandol), cefuroxime sodium (Ceftin)
D. Prototype for Third-generation Cephalosporins—Cefotaxime (Claforan)
   1. Action. See action for cefazolin sodium (Ancef).
   2. Use. Serious infections caused by gram-negative and gram-positive bacteria; meningitis, especially in neonates; uncomplicated gonorrhea.
   3. Adverse Effects. See adverse effects for cefazolin sodium (Ancef).
   4. Nursing Implications
      a. Do not mix with aminoglycoside solutions. Give these drugs separately.
      b. Protect IV solutions from light. See Nursing Implications and Discharge Teaching for cefazolin sodium (Ancef).
   5. Related Drugs. Ceftazidime (Fortaz), ceftizoxime sodium (Cefizox), ceftriaxone sodium (Rocephin).
E. Prototype for Fourth-generation Cephalosporins—Cefepine (Maxipine).
   1. Action. See action for cefazolin sodium (Ancef).

2. Use. Urinary tract infections caused by *E. coli* or *Klebsiella*; skin infections caused by *S. aureus*; pneumonia caused by *Streptococcus pneumoniae, Pseudomonas aeruginosa* or *Enterobacter*.
3. Adverse Effects. See adverse effects for cefazolin sodium (Ancef).
4. Nursing Implications. Have Vitamin K available if hypoprothrombinemia develops. See Nursing Implications and Discharge Teaching for cefazolin sodium (Ancef).

Sample Questions

140. The nurse knows that both penicillins and cephalosporins act on bacteria by
    1. inhibiting bacterial cell wall synthesis.
    2. preventing bacterial protein synthesis.
    3. increasing permeability of bacterial membranes.
    4. inhibiting metabolic processes in the bacterial cell.
141. Mr. Lacy will have an increased chance of developing nephrotoxicity if he takes cefazolin sodium along with
    1. an antacid.
    2. vitamin D.
    3. dimenhydrinate (Dramamine).
    4. an aminoglycoside.
142. Which statement by Mr. Lacy indicates a need for more teaching about cephalosporins by the nurse?
    1. "I will take every bit of this medication even if I feel better."
    2. "I will tell the doctor if I have diarrhea, a rash, or any difficulty breathing."
    3. "I will continue to test my urine for glucose with Clinitest tablets."
    4. "I will tell the dentist that I'm taking a cephalosporin when I go for my appointment."
143. Which lab result is indicative of an adverse effect of cephalosporins?
    1. Increased potassium.
    2. Decreased AST (SGOT) and ALT (SGPT).
    3. Elevated hemoglobin.
    4. Increased BUN and creatinine.

Answers and Rationales

140. The correct answer is 1. Penicillins and cephalosporins have the same action on bacteria: inhibition of bacterial cell wall synthesis.
141. The correct answer is 4. There is an increased risk of renal toxicity when cephalosporins are given with other nephrotoxic drugs such as diuretics and aminoglycosides.

142. The correct answer is 3. A diabetic client who is taking a cephalosporin drug will get a false-positive glucose reaction if Clinitest tablets are used in urine testing. The client needs to use Clinistix or Tes Tape for urine testing.
143. The correct answer is 4. Cephalosporins can cause renal toxicity for which an elevated BUN and creatinine would be indicative.

ERYTHROMYCINS

A. Case Study
   Bruce Arthur, age 35, is outside working in his yard when he is stung on the arm by a bee. He is unable to remove the stinger. Two days after this episode, his arm is swollen, red, and hot to the touch in the area of the sting. He goes to the emergency room where the physician diagnoses Mr. Arthur with a staph infection of the skin and starts him on E-Mycin 500 mg PO every 6 hours for 10 days.
B. Prototype—Erythromycin Base (E-Mycin)
   1. Action. Inhibits protein synthesis in bacterial cell. Bacteriostatic. Has broad spectrum of activity.
   2. Use. Persons allergic to penicillin; Legionnaire's disease; mycoplasma pneumonia; intestinal dysenteric amebiasis; acne; staphylococcal and streptococcal infections.
   3. Adverse Effects. Gastrointestinal irritation, reversible hearing loss, hepatitis, allergic reactions, superinfections.
   4. Nursing Implications
      a. Do not crush enteric-coated tablet.
      b. Take on empty stomach with a full glass of water.
      c. Do not give with acids.
      d. Monitor liver function tests.
      e. GI symptoms are dose related.
      f. Give IM deeply into a large muscle mass.
      g. IV must be diluted sufficiently and administered slowly to avoid venous irritation and thrombophlebitis.
C. Related Drugs. Erythromycin estolate (Ilosone), erythromycin gluceptate (Ilotycin), erythromycin stearate.

Sample Questions

144. Mr. Arthur states he is allergic to penicillin. The nurse knows that clients who are allergic to penicillin can be given erythromycin because
   1. erythromycin is more easily absorbed from the GI tract than penicillin.
   2. erythromycin has a spectrum of activity that is similar to penicillin.

3. erythromycin has fewer adverse effects than penicillin.
   4. erythromycin is not as toxic to the body as penicillin.
145. Which statement by Mr. Arthur indicates a need for more teaching about erythromycin?
   1. "If I notice any change in my hearing I will call the doctor."
   2. "I will take the erythromycin with orange juice."
   3. "I won't take the erythromycin with meals."
   4. "I won't crush the erythromycin tablets, I'll swallow them whole."

Answers and Rationales

144. The correct answer is 2. Erythromycin and penicillin have a similar spectrum of activity; so individuals who are allergic to penicillin can take erythromycin.
145. The correct answer is 2. Acidity decreases the activity of erythromycin; it should not be taken with acids such as fruit juices.

TETRACYCLINES

A. Case Study
   John Hess, a 17-year-old high school senior, has severe acne vulgaris. An appointment is made with the dermatologist and John is started on tetracycline therapy.
B. Prototype—Tetracycline Hydrochloride (Achromycin V)
   1. Action. Broad-spectrum drug with bacteriostatic action and, at higher doses, bactericidal action. Inhibits bacterial wall synthesis. Reduces free fatty acids from triglycerides, thus reducing acne lesions.
   2. Use. Chlamydia, mycoplasma, rickettsia, acne vulgaris, gonorrhea, spirochetes.
   3. Adverse Effects. Headache, dizziness; neutropenia; nausea, vomiting, diarrhea, colitis, abdominal cramping; hepatotoxicity; photosensitivity; hypersensitivity; superinfections; chelating to teeth and new bone.
   4. Nursing Implications
      a. Avoid use during pregnancy, in nursing women, and in children under age 8 as drug binds to calcium in teeth and new bone growth, which results in tooth discoloration of permanent teeth and retarded bone growth.
      b. Give deep IM.
      c. Monitor CBC and signs of liver toxicity.
   5. Discharge Teaching
      a. Take one hour before or two hours after meals and avoid taking with dairy

products, antacids, vitamins, and minerals.
- b. Avoid the sun while taking drug and for a few days after therapy is terminated.
- c. Use meticulous hygiene to reduce superinfections.
- d. Complete prescribed course.
- C. Related Drugs
  1. Doxycycline (Vibramycin): Can be administered with food. Safe to use in clients with renal impairment.
  2. Minocycline (Minocin): Can be taken with food. Dizziness and fatigue may occur.

Sample Questions

146. Which of the following should the nurse include in teaching John Hess about taking tetracycline HCl?
    1. Take tetracycline HCl with milk.
    2. Take tetracycline with food.
    3. Encourage John to sit in sun to enhance tetracycline's effects.
    4. Take tetracycline before meals.
147. Which of the following adverse effects should John Hess report to the physician while taking tetracycline?
    1. Constipation.
    2. Hypertension.
    3. Tachycardia.
    4. Diarrhea.

Answers and Rationales

146. The correct answer is 4. Tetracycline is best absorbed on an empty stomach. Taking tetracycline with food or milk impairs absorption.
147. The correct answer is 4. Diarrhea should be reported to the physician, who can rule out diarrhea as a symptom of superinfection or an adverse effect.

CHLORAMPHENICOL

- A. Case Study
  Larry Leonard, age 18 months, has developed *Haemophilus influenzae* meningitis and has been admitted to the hospital. The pediatrician orders IV chloramphenicol (Chloromycetin).
- B. Prototype—Chloramphenicol (Chloromycetin)
  1. Action. A synthetic broad-spectrum agent. Primarily bacteriostatic but is bactericidal in higher doses. Inhibits protein synthesis.

2. Use. *Haemophilus influenzae* meningitis, rickettsia, salmonella typhi, mycoplasma, bacteroides, typhoid fever. Note: Chloramphenicol (Chloromycetin) used only in severe infections when other antibiotics cannot be used due to its severe adverse effect of aplastic anemia.
3. Adverse Effects. Aplastic anemia; neurotoxicity; gray-baby syndrome (seen in premature infants, newborns, and children less than 2 years old. Abdominal distention, vomiting, pallor, irregular respirations, circulatory collapse, and death can occur due to the infant's immature liver function); hypersensitivity; nausea, vomiting, enterocolitis; superinfections; bitter taste especially after IV injection.
4. Nursing Implications
   - a. Obtain and monitor baseline CBC, platelets, and serum iron.
   - b. Monitor children less than 2 years old for gray-baby syndrome.
   - c. Do not give by IM injection.
5. Discharge Teaching
   - a. Inform physician immediately of fever, fatigue, sore throat, or bruising.
   - b. Take drug on an empty stomach unless GI upset.
   - c. Notify physician and discontinue drug if symptoms of hypersensitivity occur.

Sample Questions

148. Which of the following changes in Larry should the nurse immediately report to the physician?
    1. Vomiting.
    2. Constipation.
    3. Flushing.
    4. Dry skin.

Answers and Rationales

148. The correct answer is 1. Abdominal distention and vomiting are early symptoms of gray-baby syndrome and should be reported immediately as this syndrome is life threatening.

SULFONAMIDES

- A. Case Study
  Lindsey Bennett, age 3, is taken to the pediatrician for a recheck of her ears following

a case of acute otitis media. This was her third ear infection in four months. Mrs. Bennett asks the pediatrician if anything can be done for Lindsey so she won't have so many ear infections. The pediatrician prescribes sulfisoxazole (Gantrisin) for Lindsey.

B. Prototype—Sulfisoxazole (Gantrisin)
  1. Action. Prevents conversion of para-aminobenzoic acid (PABA) to folic acid, which is required for bacterial growth. Effects are usually bacteriostatic but can be bactericidal in high urinary concentrations.
  2. Use. Urinary tract infections, otitis media, nocardiosis (occurs in the lungs and spreads to skin, brain, and other areas), systemic infections, vaginitis, superficial eye infections.
  3. Adverse Effects. Hypersensitivity; Stevens-Johnson syndrome (acute onset of fever, bullae on skin and ulcers on mucous membranes of lips, eyes, mouth, nasal passages, and genitalia. Pneumonia, joint pain, and prostration are also seen); fever 7–10 days after starting therapy may indicate sensitization or hemolytic anemia; renal dysfunction; hematologic reaction; GI reaction; photosensitivity.
  4. Nursing Implications
    a. Give oral form on empty stomach with full glass of water.
    b. Observe skin for presence of rash, ulcers.
    c. Monitor temperature.
    d. Monitor I&O; force fluids; check urine pH; cautious use in clients with renal dysfunction; monitor renal function tests.
    e. Monitor CBC.
  5. Discharge Teaching
    a. Avoid direct sunlight.
    b. Complete full course of treatment.
    c. Diabetics who take oral hypoglycemic agents need to be aware of increased chance of hypoglycemic reactions with use of sulfonamides.
    d. Oral contraceptives may be unreliable while client is receiving sulfonamides. Alternate method of contraception should be used.
C. Related Drugs
  1. Sulfasalazine (Azulfidine) used in treatment of ulcerative colitis. Contains aspirin, so is contraindicated in clients allergic to salicylates.
  2. Sulfamethorazole (Gantanol) can be given in combination with trimethoprim (Proloprim) as Septra or Bactrim. Used in treating urinary tract infections, bronchitis, and pneumocystis pneumonia.

Sample Questions

149. Eight days after taking the sulfisoxazole, Lindsey develops a fever. When Mrs. Bennett calls the pediatrician's office about this, the nurse advises Mrs. Bennett to:
    1. reduce the dose of the sulfisoxazole.
    2. have Lindsey rest in bed.
    3. call the pediatrician if more symptoms develop.
    4. stop the sulfisoxazole and bring Lindsey in to see the pediatrician today.

Answers and Rationales

149. The correct answer is 4. A fever 7–10 days after starting sulfisoxazole is an adverse effect of the drug that could indicate a sensitization to the drug or hemolytic anemia. The drug should be stopped and the client should see the physician as soon as possible.

URINARY ANTI-INFECTIVES

A. Case Study
  Chris Pinto, 37, goes to the physician with complaints of urinary frequency, urgency, and burning on urination for two days. A clean-catch urine specimen for culture and sensitivity is obtained. Mrs. Pinto is allergic to sulfonamides. The physician orders nitrofurantoin (Macrodantin) 50 mg QID for 10 days.
B. Prototype
  1. Urinary anti-infectives are structurally different so there will be no prototype drug identified.
  2. See Table 2.22.

Sample Questions

150. Mrs. Pinto should be taught which of the following points about nitrofurantoin?
    1. Take it on an empty stomach.
    2. You may experience nausea and vomiting.
    3. You can crush the tablet if it's too hard to swallow whole.
    4. It doesn't interact with any other drugs.

Answers and Rationales

150. The correct answer is 2. GI irritation is the most frequent adverse effect of nitrofurantoin (Macrodantin).

TABLE 2.22 Urinary Anti-Infectives

Drug	Action	Adverse Effects	Nursing Implications
Methenamine (Hiprex; Mandelamine)	Converted to formaldehyde (which is bactericidal) in the presence of acidic urine.	Nausea, vomiting, diarrhea, abdominal discomfort.	• Give with food or milk to prevent GI upset. • Avoid foods, fluids, and medications that alkalinize urine. • Monitor I&O. • Increase fluid intake. • Monitor liver function tests.
Nalidixic Acid (Neg Gram)	Bactericidal effect on gram-negative bacteria by preventing transmission of genetic information.	Headache, dizziness, vertigo, visual disturbances, photosensitivity.	• Minor CNS reactions are common and should decrease in 48 hours. • Client should wear sunglasses if bothered by bright lights. • Client should avoid sun exposure, wear sunscreen and appropriate clothing. • Give with food to decrease GI upset.
Nitrofurantoin (Macrodantin)	Interferes with carbohydrate metabolism of bacteria. Is bacteriostatic in low concentrations and bactericidal in high concentrations.	Pulmonary hypersensitivity, nausea, vomiting, lower extremity paresthesias.	• Monitor pulmonary status. • Give drug with milk or meals. • Monitor neurologic status. • Avoid tooth staining by not crushing tablets, dilute suspension, and rinse mouth after taking drug.
Phenazopyridine (Pyridium)	An azo dye excreted in the urine which provides a topical analgesic effect to the urinary tract.	Rash, headache, GI disturbances, reddish-orange discoloration of urine.	• Give after meals to prevent GI upset. • Tell client urine may turn reddish-orange and can stain fabrics. • Stop drug if skin or sclera turn yellow which is a sign of drug accumulation.

VANCOMYCIN HYDROCHLORIDE (VANCOCIN)

A. Case Study

Mrs. Nancy Stewart is a 58-year-old executive secretary who has had a history of recurring venous stasis ulcers. Currently the ulcer on her right ankle has become infected. A culture and sensitivity reveals a staphylococcal infection. Mrs. Stewart is resistant to other antibiotics and is admitted to the hospital for IV vancomycin therapy.

B. Prototype—Vancomycin Hydrochloride (Vancocin)
1. Action. Interferes with cell membrane synthesis and exhibits a bactericidal and bacteriostatic effect.
2. Use. Staphylococcus infections, pseudomembranous colitis, gram-positive organisms.
3. Adverse Effects. Ototoxicity, nephrotoxicity, hypersensitivity, thrombophlebitis, red-neck syndrome (flushing and hypotension from rapid IV infusion), superinfections.
4. Nursing Implications
   a. Monitor I&O.
   b. Obtain and monitor renal and auditory function tests.
   c. Administer IV slowly to prevent phlebitis, extravasation, red-neck syndrome.
   d. Do not swim.

Sample Questions

151. Which of the following is an important nursing consideration for the nurse to follow when administering IV vancomycin hydrochloride?
   1. Mix the dose in 50 ml of dextrose in water.
   2. Infuse over 30 minutes.
   3. Infuse over 60 minutes.
   4. Administer IV push.

Answers and Rationales

151. The correct answer is 3. IV vancomycin hydrochloride (Vancocin) should be given over 1 hour to help prevent thrombophlebitis and red-neck syndrome.

CIPROFLOXACIN (CIPRO)

A. Case Study
Ms. Anne Blake is a 34-year-old nurse who has

developed a UTI. A urine culture and sensitivity indicates that Ms. Blake has a pseudomonas infection. She is treated with ciprofloxacin (Cipro).

B. Prototype—Ciprofloxacin (Cipro)
   1. Action. Inhibits DNA-gyrase (an enzyme needed for replication of bacterial DNA). Bactericidal effect.
   2. Use. Pseudomonas infections, gram-negative urinary tract infections or gram-negative systemic infections.
   3. Adverse Effects. Nausea, vomiting, diarrhea, flatulence; headache, tremors, confusion, dizziness, insomnia; fever; rash; elevated BUN, AST (SGOT), ALT (SGPT), creatinine; decreased WBC, hematocrit.
   4. Nursing Implications
     a. Administer with a large glass of water to prevent crystalluria.
     b. Do not give with antacids.
     c. Give 2 hours after meals.
C. Related Drugs. Norfloxacin (Noroxin). Used to treat urinary tract infections only.

Sample Questions

152. Which statement by Ms. Blake indicates that she understands correct use of ciprofloxacin?
   1. "I will take this drug with Maalox to prevent GI upset."
   2. "I will stop taking this drug when I no longer have pain upon urination."
   3. "I will drink an 8-oz glass of water with this drug."
   4. "I will take this drug with a cup of tea or coffee, as caffeinated beverages make this drug work more quickly."

Answers and Rationales

152. The correct answer is 3. Taking an 8-oz glass of water will help to prevent crystalluria.

ANTITUBERCULAR DRUGS

A. Case Study
Maureen Gilbert, age 31, has been diagnosed as having pulmonary tuberculosis. Her physician prescribes the following drug therapy: Isoniazid (INH) 300 mg PO daily; rifampin (Rimactane) 600 mg PO daily; pyridoxine (vitamin B_6) 10 mg PO daily.

B. Prototype—Isoniazid (INH)
   1. Action. Bacteriostatic and in high concentrations becomes bactericidal. Mechanism of action not known but is believed to interfere with lipid and nucleic acid biosynthesis in tubercle bacilli that are actively growing.
   2. Use. Initial treatment of tuberculosis; prophylactic treatment of tuberculosis in high-risk groups.
   3. Adverse Effects. Peripheral neuritis; jaundice, elevation in liver function tests; nausea, vomiting; blood dyscrasias.
   4. Nursing Implications
     a. Assess neuromuscular function and give pyridoxine (vitamin B_6) to treat and/or prevent problems.
     b. Regularly scheduled baseline liver function studies.
     c. Monitor for hepatic dysfunction.
     d. Take drug on empty stomach in a single daily dose.
     e. Give drug with meals and divide daily dose into 3 equal parts if GI upset occurs.
     f. Assess for bruising, bleeding, fever, sore throat.
     g. Monitor CBC.
   5. Discharge Teaching
     a. Tyramine-containing foods may cause hypertensive crises, so should be avoided.
     b. Avoid histamine-containing foods as may cause an exaggerated drug response.
     c. Avoid use of alcohol.
     d. May cause a feeling of euphoria. Plan rest periods and don't overdo.
     e. Drug therapy must not be interrupted and must be continued for prescribed time.
C. Related Drugs. See Table 2.23.

Sample Questions

153. The nurse needs to tell Mrs. Gilbert which fact about rifampin?
   1. Rifampin increases the effectiveness of oral contraceptives.
   2. Rifampin will turn urine, sweat, tears, and feces an orange-red color.
   3. Rifampin will increase the activity of coumarin-type oral anticoagulants.
   4. Rifampin is taken in the usual adult dose of 60 mg daily.

Answers and Rationales

153. The correct answer is 2. Rifampin (Rimactane) discolors body secretions such as sweat, urine, feces, and tears a red-orange color.

TABLE 2.23   Drugs Commonly Used to Treat Tuberculosis

Drug and Dosage	Adverse Effects	Nursing Implications
Isoniazid (INH) 10 to 20 mg/kg (up to 300 mg) PO or IM daily, or 15 mg/kg PO or IM twice a week	Peripheral neuritis, a numbness and tingling in hands and feet. Vitamin B$_6$ (pyridoxine) may be given to prevent or treat this condition. Hepatitis, with the risk increasing with age. Liver enzymes may be routinely monitored in elderly or symptomatic clients. Hyperexcitability may occur with single 300 mg dose.	• Tell client to report signs of neuritis and hepatitis (anorexia, nausea, vomiting, jaundice, malaise, or dark urine). • Isoniazid may interfere with phenytoin (Dilantin) metabolism, requiring a lower dose of the TB medication; should be taken on an empty stomach, and the client should not drink alcohol while on therapy.
Ethambutol (Myambutol) 15 to 25 mg/kg PO daily, or 50 mg/kg PO twice weekly	Optic neuritis, a loss of red-green color discrimination, and decreased visual acuity can occur with dosages of 25 mg/kg. Reversible, if medication discontinued. Skin rash.	• Tell client to notify physician if vision blurs or if unable to see red or green. • Use the drug with caution if a visual exam cannot be done and in clients with renal impairment.
Rifampin (Rifadin, Rimactane) 10 to 20 mg/kg (up to 600 mg) PO daily, or 600 mg PO twice a week	Body fluids (urine, tears, saliva, etc.) may turn orange. Hepatitis Flu-like syndrome Purpura (rare)	• Tell clients to expect orange-tinged body fluids. • Tell clients to report anorexia, nausea, vomiting, jaundice, malaise, or dark urine. • Use the drug with caution in cases of liver disease. • Rifampin affects the actions of other drugs, including anticoagulants, oral hypoglycemics, corticosteroids, oral contraceptives, and methadone.
Streptomycin 15 to 20 mg/kg (up to 1 gm) IM daily or 25 to 30 mg/kg IM twice a week	Damage to cranial nerve VIII (vestibulocochlear). Damage to the vestibular portion causes dizziness, vertigo, tinnitus, and roaring in ears. Auditory damage causes loss of hearing at high frequency ranges. Renal toxicity.	• Baseline renal and audiology studies may be obtained before therapy begins. • Tell client to report any ringing, roaring, or fullness in ears. • Help coordinate outpatient arrangements for IM injections, if necessary.
Pyrazinamide 20 to 40 mg/kg (up to 2 gm) PO daily	Excess uric acid levels, which can cause gout or hepatitis.	• Baseline uric acid and liver enzyme levels may be obtained; monitor uric acid and liver enzymes. • Instruct patient to report any signs of gout (painful swelling in joints, chills, fever) and hepatitis (anorexia, nausea, vomiting, jaundice, malaise, and dark urine). • Use with caution in clients who have liver disease, gout, or renal impairment.

Other drugs used: capreomycin (Capastat), kanamycin (Kantrex), ethionamide (Trecator-SC), para-amino-salicylic acid, and cycloserine (Seromycin). From Coleman, D., T.B.: The disease that's not dead yet. RN, September, 1984, 49–59.

Antiviral Agents

ACYCLOVIR (ZOVIRAX)

A. Case Study
Ms. Gina Leonard is a sexually active 20-year-old college junior seen at the venereal disease clinic for genital herpes. Ms. Leonard is started on acyclovir (Zovirax).

B. Prototype—Acyclovir (Zovirax)
 1. Action. Inhibits viral DNA replication. Does not cure herpes infections but decreases the severity and duration of herpes.
 2. Use. Herpes simplex virus 1 and 2, initial treatment of genital herpes infection.

 3. Adverse Effects. Nausea, vomiting, diarrhea; rash; headache, vertigo; crystalluria; phlebitis at injection site; transient burning with topical use.
 4. Nursing Implications
   a. Do not give IV bolus. Give IV over one hour to prevent crystalluria and phlebitis.
   b. Clients should drink plenty of fluids.
 5. Discharge Teaching
   a. Use topical preparation sparingly, and use rubber gloves when applying.
   b. Avoid sexual contact while lesions are visible.

c. Drug does not cure herpes nor prevent transmission to others.
C. Related Drugs
 1. Ribavirin (Virazole). Given by inhalation to treat respiratory syncytial virus (RSV) in hospitalized infants and small children. Inhalation of aerosol can be teratogenic.
 2. Zidovudine (AZT, Retrovir). Developed to control AIDS or ARC (AIDS-related complex) with *Pneumocystis carinii*. Causes leukocytopenia; monitor blood work.

Sample Questions

154. Which statement concerning the use of acyclovir is correct?

1. Sexual relations can be resumed while using topical acyclovir.
2. Acyclovir can be used for repeated genital herpes infections.
3. Acyclovir should be given IV over one hour.
4. Acyclovir prevents the recurrence of genital herpes.

Answers and Rationales

154. The correct answer is 3. IV acyclovir (Zovirax) should be given over one hour to prevent phlebitis and crystalluria.

Antifungal Agents

ANTIFUNGALS

A. Case Study
 Mr. Jerry Logan, a 45-year-old chicken farmer, has complained of fever, cough, and lymphadenopathy. Mr. Logan is admitted to the hospital with a diagnosis of histoplasmosis and started on IV amphotericin B (Fungizone) therapy.
B. Prototype—Amphotericin B (Fungizone)
 1. Action. Fungicidal or fungistatic. Alters the fungal cell membrane permeability by binding to sterols. Clients must be monitored due to many toxic effects.
 2. Use. Candida infections, histoplasmosis, coccidiomycoses, blastomycosis, cryptococcoses.
 3. Adverse Effects. Febrile reactions, nausea, vomiting; nephrotoxicity, hypokalemia, azotemia; thrombophlebitis; hypotension, tachycardia, or cardiovascular collapse with rapid infusion; blood dyscrasia; hypersensitivity.
 4. Nursing Implications
  a. Monitor CBC, BUN, creatinine, electrolytes.
  b. Administer analgesics, antihistamines, prior to infusion to minimize febrile reactions.
  c. Infuse drug slowly.
  d. Monitor VS frequently.
  e. Monitor I&O.
  f. Administer potassium supplements.
  g. Do not mix with other drugs.
C. Related Drugs
 1. Nystatin (Mycostatin). Used to treat candida infections.
 2. Griseofulvin (Grisactin). Used to treat ringworm infections. Adverse effects: headaches, blood dyscrasias, GI upset, rash from sunlight. Give on full stomach. Clients allergic to penicillin should use this drug with caution.

Sample Questions

155. Which electrolyte imbalance should the nurse monitor Mr. Logan for while on amphotericin B therapy?
 1. Hyponatremia.
 2. Hypokalemia.
 3. Hyperkalemia.
 4. Hypercalcemia.

Answers and Rationales

155. The correct answer is 2. Hypokalemia can occur due to nephrotoxocity of this drug.

Anthelmintic Agents

ANTHELMINTICS

A. Case Study
Mrs. Schwartz brings her 4-year-old son, Andy, to the pediatrician because he has lost weight, is quite irritable, and has perianal pruritus that causes continuous scratching. A lab test confirms the diagnosis of enterobiasis (pinworm infection). The pediatrician orders mebendazole (Vermox) 100 mg PO as single dose.

B. Prototype
1. The anthelmintics are a group of drugs that affect various systems within the worms causing them to die. Most of these drugs are poorly absorbed in the gastrointestinal tract. Approximately 98% of the drug remains effective as it passes through the GI tract and is excreted in the feces.
2. See Table 2.24.

Sample Questions

156. Mebendazole is quite effective against pinworms because
    1. it is active in the stomach where the pinworm eggs hatch.
    2. it is poorly absorbed in the GI tract and kills the pinworms that infect the intestines.
    3. its systemic activity kills pinworms all over the body.
    4. it stimulates peristalsis causing the pinworms to be expelled before they reproduce.

Answers and Rationales

156. The correct answer is 2. Pinworms infect the intestines. Mebendazole (Vermox) is poorly absorbed in the GI tract and therefore is quite effective against these helminths.

TABLE 2.24 Anthelmintics

Drug	Action	Use	Adverse Effects	Nursing Implications
Pyrantel (Antiminth)	Paralyzes intestinal tract of worm.	Roundworm, pinworm, hookworm	Nausea, vomiting, anorexia, abdominal cramps, diarrhea.	• Give with milk or fruit juice. • Entire dose must be taken at once. • Offer frequent, small meals.
Mebendazole (Vermox)	Inhibits glucose and other nutrient uptake of helminth.	Pinworm, roundworm, threadworm, hookworm	Abdominal cramping, occasional fever.	• Can be taken with or without food. • Tablet can be chewed or crushed. • Examine stool for presence of worms.
Thiabendazole (Mintezol)	Interferes with parasitic metabolism.	Threadworm, pinworm	Dizziness, drowsiness, headache, anorexia, nausea, malodor of urine.	• Give with food. • Chew tablets before swallowing. • Avoid activities such as driving and working with machinery.

Antineoplastic Agents

ANTINEOPLASTIC AGENTS

A. General Considerations
   1. Combination of antineoplastic agents usually used to destroy cancer cells.
   2. Clients must be closely monitored due to many toxic adverse effects.
   3. Agents destroy cancer cells and may also kill normal cells.
B. General Adverse Effects. Nausea, vomiting, anorexia; diarrhea and constipation; stomatitis; alopecia; bone marrow depression (leukopenia, anemia, and thrombocytopenia); hepatic toxicity; hyperuricemia; fatigue.
C. Nursing Implications
   1. Handle antineoplastic agents carefully—mutagenic and possibly carcinogenic.
   2. Nurses should wear gloves, long-sleeved cover gown, protective goggles, and mask as appropriate.
   3. Monitor IV site closely to assess for extravasation and stop IV if it occurs.
   4. Treat used equipment as hazardous waste.
   5. Administer antiemetic if ordered prior to chemotherapy and up to 48 hours afterwards.
   6. Monitor CBC.
   7. Monitor I&O.
   8. Monitor liver and renal function studies.
   9. Inspect oral cavity daily.
D. Discharge Teaching
   1. Eat frequent, small portions of high-calorie, high-protein, bland, low-residue foods.
   2. Avoid highly seasoned foods, drink clear liquids if nauseated.
   3. Frequent rest periods.
   4. Expect alopecia and purchase scarves or wigs.
   5. Report fever, use good hand-washing technique, avoid individuals with upper respiratory infections.
   6. Use soft toothbrush and baking soda rinse to minimize stomatitis.
   7. Use progressive relaxation exercises or guided imagery to help cope with nausea.

ALKYLATING AGENTS

A. Case Study
   Ms. Linda Levin is a 48-year-old accountant diagnosed with breast cancer. Ms. Levin is starting cyclophosphamide (Cytoxan) therapy in combination with another antineoplastic agent. This is Ms. Levin's first experience with chemotherapy.
B. Prototype—Cyclophosphamide (Cytoxan)
   1. Action. Produces cytoxic effects by damaging DNA and interfering with cell replication. Most effective against rapidly dividing cells.
   2. Use. Leukemias; multiple myeloma; neuroblastoma; ovarian, breast, lung cancers; Hodgkin's disease; Ewing's sarcoma.
   3. Adverse Effects. Gonadal suppression, hemorrhagic and nonhemorrhagic cystitis.
   4. Nursing Implications
      a. Force fluids.
      b. Assess for signs and symptoms of unexplained bleeding.
      c. Assess leukocyte count frequently.
      d. Monitor CBC, uric acid, electrolytes, thrombocytes, and hepatic and renal function at least twice a week.
      e. Instruct client to report hematuria or dysuria immediately.
C. Related Drugs. See Table 2.25.

Sample Questions

157. Which of the following should be included in teaching Ms. Levin about cyclophosphamide (Cytoxan) therapy?
   1. Omit dose if anorexic or nauseated.
   2. Drink plenty of water.
   3. Take cyclophosphamide with meals.
   4. Take cyclophosphamide before going to bed.
158. Which of the following medications might the physician order along with cyclophosphamide?
   1. Metoclopramide (Reglan).
   2. Diphenhydramine HCl (Benadryl).
   3. Minoxidil (Loniten).
   4. Dexamethasone (Decadron).

Answers and Rationales

157. The correct answer is 2. Hemorrhagic and nonhemorrhagic cystitis are related to cyclophosphamide (Cytoxan) therapy. Drinking plenty of water and fluids reduces the risk of developing both types of cystitis.
158. The correct answer is 1. Metaclopramide (Reglan) is an antiemetic used to treat the

TABLE 2.25 Alkylating Agents

Drug	Use	Comments
Cisplatin (Platinol)	Lymphoma; myeloma; melanoma; osteosarcoma; cervical, ovarian, testicular, lung, esophageal, prostatic cancers.	• Causes nephrotoxicity and ototoxicity, ensure adequate hydration and give diuretics prior to therapy. • Have client void every hour or insert Foley catheter before initiating treatment. • Assess for hearing deficits.
Busulfan (Myleran)	Polycythermia vera, chronic myelogenous leukemia.	• Discontinue drug when white blood cells (WBC) reach 15,000 mm^3. • Monitor CBC as this drug can cause severe bone marrow depression.
Mechlorethamine HCl (Mustargen)	Hodgkin's disease, non-Hodgkin's lymphomas; lung cancer.	• Assess for edema, ascites, weight gain. • Assess for signs and symptoms of dehydration. • Wear gloves if applying solid preparation.
Thiotepa	Bladder, breast, and ovarian cancers.	• Decreased dose for renal or hepatic impairment and bone marrow depression. • Only given parenterally.
Chlorambucil (Leukeran)	Breast and ovarian cancer; non-Hodgkin's lymphomas; chronic lymphocytic leukemia.	• Assess CBC, WBC, and serum uric acid levels routinely. • Avoid IM injections when platelet count is low. • Urge client to drink 10–12 glasses of fluid per day. • Provide urine alkalinization if uric acid levels are increased.

nausea and vomiting that are adverse effects seen with cyclophosphamide (Cytoxan) therapy.

ANTIMETABOLITES

A. Case Study
Mrs. Jenny Johnson is a 28-year-old secretary diagnosed with choriocarcinoma following a hydatid mole. Mrs. Johnson is started on methotrexate with leucovorin rescue therapy.
B. Prototype—Methotrexate with leucovorin rescue
 1. Action. Leucovorin calcium is a folic acid analog that interferes with mitotic process by blocking folinic acid.
 2. Use. Acute lymphoblastic leukemia; cancer of breast, lung, testes, ovary, head, and neck; choriocarcinoma.
 3. Adverse Effects. See General Considerations. Intrathecal use may cause fever, headache, and vomiting.
 4. Nursing Implications. Leucovorin calcium is frequently given to prevent toxicity when high doses of methotrexate are given.
 5. Discharge Teaching. See General Considerations. Instruct client to avoid self-medication with over-the-counter vitamins (folic acid and derivatives may alter drug response).
C. Related Drugs.
 1. 5-Fluorouracil (5-FU)
 2. Mercaptopurine (Purinethol)
 3. Cytarabine (Cytosar-U)

Sample Questions

159. Which of the following drugs is given to prevent methotrexate toxicity?
 1. Trimethobenzamide HCl (Tigan)
 2. Prednisone
 3. Allopurinol (Zyloprim)
 4. Leucovorin calcium
160. Which of the following agents should be avoided by clients on methotrexate therapy?
 1. Folic acid
 2. Vitamin C
 3. Iron
 4. Vitamin D

Answers and Rationales

159. The correct answer is 4. Leucovorin calcium is a reduced form of folic acid that takes up binding sites to prevent methotrexate toxicity.
160. The correct answer is 1. Folic acid can alter methotrexate response.

ANTIBIOTIC ANTINEOPLASTIC AGENTS

A. Case Study
Mr. Alan Holt, age 54, is diagnosed with cancer of the bladder. He is receiving a combination of antineoplastic agents that includes doxorubicin HCl (Adriamycin).

B. Prototype—Doxorubicin HCl (Adriamycin)
  1. Action. Attaches to DNA and prevents DNA synthesis in vulnerable cells.
  2. Use. Cancer of thyroid, lung, bladder, breast, and ovary; acute leukemia; sarcoma; Ewing's sarcoma; neuroblastoma; lymphomas.
  3. Adverse Effects. Nausea, vomiting, stomatitis; EKG changes; agranulocytosis, leukopenia, thrombocytopenia; hyper-pigmentation of skin and nails; alopecia.
  4. Nursing Implications
      a. Do not give SC or IM—local reaction and skin necrosis can occur.
      b. IV use: reconstitute with normal saline or sterile water; reconstituted solution stable for 24 hours at room temperature or 48 hours if refrigerated; protect from sunlight; do not infuse in less than 5 minutes; red streaking over vein and facial flushing are signs of too-rapid administration.
      c. Do not mix with other drugs.
      d. Monitor IV site; for local extravasation pour normal saline on area, apply a cold compress; infiltration with corticosteroid may be ordered.
      e. Monitor CBC, serum uric acid levels, cardiac output (listen for S_3), weight.
      f. Frequent mouth care.
      g. Client needs sufficient fluids to prevent hyperuricemia.
      h. Assist client with information on wigs and head coverings before hair loss starts.
      i. Offer support to client to deal with drug therapy and diagnosis.
      j. Wear gloves to prepare this drug. Wash skin with soap and water if powder or solution contacts skin.
      k. Urine is red colored for 1–2 days after administration. Clears within 48 hours.
C. Related Drugs. See Table 2.26.

Sample Questions

161. While Mr. Holt is receiving intravenous doxorubicin the nurse should monitor which of the following?
    1. Chest X-rays.
    2. Sodium levels.
    3. Liver function studies.
    4. Electrocardiograms.
162. The nurse should stop the infusion of doxorubicin if Mr. Holt complains of
    1. headache and dizziness.
    2. burning and pain at the infusion site.
    3. upset stomach and heartburn.
    4. light-headedness and confusion.
163. Which nursing action is NOT appropriate for the client receiving doxorubicin?
    1. Provide frequent mouth care for the client.
    2. Tell the client his urine will be red-tinged for the first couple of days after administration of the drug.
    3. Put the client on fluid restriction.
    4. Explain to the client he will lose his hair.

TABLE 2.26 Antibiotic Antineoplastic Agents

Drug	Action	Uses	Comments
Bleomycin Sulfate (Blenoxane)	Prevents DNA, RNA, and protein synthesis in cells. Cell cycle specific in G2 and M phases.	Lymphomas, melanoma, cancers of head, neck, esophagus, lung, skin, penis, testes, vulva, cervix, anus.	• Pulmonary side effects of dyspnea, fever, rales, cough. • Febrile reaction usually occurs on first day of therapy. • Monitor respiratory status.
Dactinomycin (Actinomycin D)	Prevents synthesis of messenger RNA; cell cycle nonspecific.	Testicular cancer, melanoma, choriocarinoma, Wilm's tumor, neuroblastoma, retinoblastoma, Ewing's sarcoma, Kaposi's sarcoma.	• Monitor IV site carefully. • Do not expose drug solution to direct sunlight.
Daunorubicin (Daunomycin)	Inhibits DNA synthesis; cell cycle specific in S-phase of cell cycle.	Acute myelocytic and lymphocytic leukemia.	• EKG changes can occur. • Urine turns red on day of administration. • Monitor IV site carefully • Never give IM or SC. • Do not mix with heparin.
Mitomycin (Mutamycin)	Prevents DNA and protein synthesis in cells; cell cycle nonspecific	Cancer of gastrointestinal tract, breast, lung, bladder, cervix.	• See Prototype Drug
Plicamycin (Mithramycin)	Prevents DNA synthesis; decreases serum calcium by unknown action; blocks action of parathyroid hormone.	Testicular cancer, hypercalcemia.	• Side effect of bleeding. • Monitor blood coagulation studies. • Monitor client for signs of hypocalcemia.

TABLE 2.27 Estrogens

Drug	Use	Adverse Effects	Nursing Implications
Diethylstilbestrol (DES)	Breast and prostate cancer.	Headache; vertigo; insomnia; nausea; weight changes; phlebitis; edema; uterine bleeding; feminization in males; changes in calcium and folic acid metabolism	• Monitor calcium levels. • Monitor males for signs of feminization. • Monitor salt intake and keep it reduced. • Weigh client daily.
Ethinyl Estradiol (Estinyl)	Breast and prostate cancer.	See Diethylstilbestrol (DES)	See Diethylstilbestrol (DES)

Answers and Rationales

161. The correct answer is 4. Doxorubicin (Adriamycin) can cause EKG changes; the nurse should monitor electrocardiograms while the client is receiving this drug.
162. The correct answer is 2. Intravenous infusion of doxorubicin (Adriamycin) should be stopped if the client complains of burning and pain at the infusion site. These signs are indicative of extravasation, which could lead to skin necrosis.
163. The correct answer is 3. Fluids should not be restricted for a client receiving doxorubicin; this drug can cause hyperuricemia if fluid intake is not sufficient.

ANTINEOPLASTICS AFFECTING HORMONAL BALANCE

A. Case Study
   Mr. Irving Heeley, age 68, has metastatic cancer of the prostate gland. He receives diethylstilbestrol (DES) as treatment for his disease.
B. Mechanism of action of hormonal agents.
   1. Exact mechanism is not completely understood.
   2. Believed that hormonal agents hinder use of steroids necessary for cell growth.

   3. Hormonal therapy keeps cancer cells in resting phase, thus decreasing growth of tumor.
   4. No direct cytotoxic effect of hormonal agents so they are unable to cure cancer.
C. Estrogens (Female Hormones). See Table 2.27.
D. Androgens (Male Hormones)
   Androgens are also used as replacement therapy for growth and development of male sex organs and secondary sex characteristics in androgen-deficient males. See Table 2.28.
E. Antihormonal Agents
   1. Antiestrogen—Tamoxifen (Nolvadex)
      a. Use. Advanced breast cancer in pre- and postmenopausal women.
      b. Adverse Effects. Most common are similar to signs of menopause (hot flashes and flushing); nausea, vomiting; temporary bone and tumor pain; temporary drop in WBC count.
      c. Nursing Implications. Monitor WBC count; tell premenopausal women to use contraception as short-term therapy causes ovulation.
   2. Antiadrenal—Aminoglutethamide (Cytadren)
      a. Use. Adrenal and metastatic breast cancer.
      b. Adverse Effects. Drowsiness; anorexia, nausea; vomiting, severe pancytopenia; rash; and adrenal insufficiency.
      c. Nursing Implications. Possible replacement therapy with hydrocortisone and

TABLE 2.28 Androgens

Drug	Use	Adverse Effects	Nursing Implications
Fluoxymesterone (Halotestin)	Breast and renal cancer	Nausea; vomiting; weight gain; edema and fluid retention; vaginal dryness and itching; acne; hypercalcemia if bone cancer present; masculinization of females	• Monitor client for masculinizing effects. • Monitor weight. • Low salt intake. • Restrict fluids if necessary. • Monitor blood pressure.
Testosterone Cypionate (Depo-Testosterone)	Breast cancer	See Fluoxymesterone (Halotestin)	• IM must be given deeply into gluteal muscle. • See Fluoxymesterone (Halotestin)

mineralocorticoids; monitor blood pressure, thyroid studies, and CBC; tell client that drug may cause drowsiness and orthostatic hypotension.
3. Gonadotropin Releasing Hormone—Leuprolide (Lupron)
   a. Use. Prostate cancer.
   b. Adverse Effects. Hot flashes, transient bone pain, rash, alopecia, cardiac arrhythmias, breathing difficulty, and hematuria.
   c. Nursing Implications. Monitor and rotate injection sites; only use syringes provided with drug; provide comfort measures.

Sample Questions

164. Which diagnostic test should the nurse monitor when the client is receiving diethylstilbestrol?
   1. Arterial blood gases.
   2. Liver enzymes.
   3. Serum potassium.
   4. Serum calcium.
165. Which statement about diethylstilbestrol made by the nurse to Mr. Heeley is incorrect?
   1. "You may develop signs of increased masculinity while taking diethylstilbestrol."
   2. "You need to decrease your salt intake while taking diethylstilbestrol."
   3. "You will need to weigh yourself each day while taking diethylstilbestrol."
   4. "You can experience vascular problems while taking diethylstilbestrol."

Answers and Rationales

164. The correct answer is 4. Diethylstilbestrol (DES) can cause hypercalcemia; serum calcium levels need to be monitored.

165. The correct answer is 1. Diethylstilbestrol (DES) can cause signs of feminization in males, not increased masculinity in males.

VINCA ALKALOIDS

A. Case Study
   Mr. Jerry Newman, age 38, suddenly develops a high fever and petechiae on his chest and arms. Following bone marrow aspiration, the diagnosis is acute lymphocytic leukemia. The physician puts Mr. Newman on a regime that contains vincristine (Oncovin).
B. Prototype—Vincristine (Oncovin)
   1. Action. Acts on cells undergoing mitosis, thus stopping cell division.
   2. Use. Acute leukemia; lymphomas; cancer of brain, breast, cervix, testes; Wilm's tumor.
   3. Adverse Effects. Peripheral neuropathy; paresthesias; loss of deep tendon reflexes; jaw pain; cramps; muscle weakness; constipation; nausea, vomiting, stomatitis; phlebitis; alopecia; hyponatremia; leukopenia; photosensitivity.
   4. Nursing Implications
      a. Do not give IM or SC as tissue necrosis can occur.
      b. For IV use, inject solution directly into vein or into tubing of running IV infusion. Infusion can be given over 1 minute.
      c. Monitor bowel function.
      d. Frequent neuro checks.
      e. Monitor CBC and platelets.
      f. Advise client to avoid overexposure to sun.
C. Related Drugs. See Table. 2.29.

TABLE 2.29 Vinca Alkaloids

Drug	Use	Adverse Effects	Nursing Implications
Etoposide (VP-16; VePesid)	Lymphomas; acute nonlymphocytic leukemia; cancer of lung, testes, bladder, prostate, liver, uterus	Myelotoxic; nausea; vomiting; diarrhea; somnolence; peripheral neuropathy; hepatotoxicity	• Do not give IM or SC as will cause tissue necrosis. • Do not give IV push. • Avoid skin contact with this drug. • Hypotension can occur during administration; monitor blood pressure.
Vinblastine (Velban)	Lymphomas; cancer of testes, breast, kidney, head and neck, Kaposi's sarcoma	Peripheral neuropathies, parethesias, neuritis, muscle pain and weakness, pain in tumor site, urinary retention	• Monitor CBC and platelets. • Frequent neuro checks. • Monitor for extravasation. • Monitor I&O.

Sample Questions

166. Mr. Newman requests information about the adverse effects of vincristine. The nurse tells him all of the following EXCEPT:
    1. "You may experience muscle cramps and muscle weakness."
    2. "You won't lose any hair."
    3. "You may have constipation."
    4. "You won't have any breathing problems."

Answers and Rationales

166. The correct answer is 2. Alopecia is an adverse effect of vincristine (Oncovin).

MISCELLANEOUS ANTINEOPLASTIC AGENTS

A. L-Asparaginase (Elspar)
    1. Action. Enzyme that destroys asparagine, an amino acid necessary for protein synthesis of leukemia cells. Causes death to leukemia cells.
    2. Use. Acute lymphocytic leukemia.
    3. Adverse Effects. Anorexia, nausea, vomiting, azotemia, hemorrhagic pancreatitis, rash, hyperglycemia, increased serum ammonia, anaphylaxis, and hepatotoxicity.
    4. Nursing Implications
        a. Monitor CBC, platelets, renal and pancreatic enzymes, coagulation studies, uric acid, blood glucose, and serum albumin.
        b. Don't shake vial.
        c. Only give drug in a clear solution; chance of hypersensitivity is increased with each dose.
B. Hydroxyurea (Hydrea)
    1. Action. Urea derivative that kills granulocytes. Prevents DNA synthesis in cell cycle.
    2. Use. Chronic myelogenous leukemia; malignant melanoma and cancers of the head, neck, ovary, and colon.
    3. Adverse Effects. Anemia, leukopenia, megaloblastosis, thrombocytopenia, anorexia, nausea, vomiting, and diarrhea.
    4. Nursing Implications. Monitor CBC, platelets, liver and renal enzymes; encourage fluids.

C. Procarbazine (Matulane)
    1. Action. Similar to alkylating agents; inhibits RNA, DNA, and protein synthesis in the cell.
    2. Use. Hodgkin's disease, multiple myeloma, malignant melanoma, lung cancer, and brain tumors.
    3. Adverse effects. Anorexia, nausea, vomiting, leukopenia, thrombocytopenia, and altered reproductive potential.
    4. Nursing Implications
        a. Advise client to avoid alcohol, sedatives, narcotics, and tricyclic antidepressants (drug is an MAO inhibitor).
        b. Restrict foods high in tyramines.
        c. Monitor CBC, platelets, and liver enzymes.
D. Paclitaxel (Taxol)
    1. Action. Inhibits cell replication by interfering with miosis.
    2. Use. Advanced ovarian cancer.
    3. Adverse effects. Severe allergic reactions, bone marrow suppression, peripheral neuropathy, muscle pain.
    4. Nursing Implications
        a. Wear gloves when handling drug.
        b. Premedicate client with a steroid and an H-1 and H-2 antagonist before administration.
        c. Check blood pressure and pulse during administration.

Sample Questions

167. Your client is receiving L-asparaginase (Elspar) and complains of stomach pain. You will need to evaluate which laboratory test?
    1. Platelet count.
    2. BUN.
    3. Serum amylase.
    4. Serum potassium.

Answers and Rationales

167. The correct answer is 3. Stomach pain may be a sign of pancreatitis, which is an adverse effect of L-asparaginase (Elspar). The nurse should monitor serum amylase as an elevation of this enzyme indicates a need to discontinue the drug.

Immunosuppressants

AZATHIOPRINE (IMURAN)

A. Case Study
Ted Neft, a 35-year-old teacher, is about to undergo renal transplant surgery. Azathioprine (Imuran) is started five days before surgery.

B. Prototype—Azathioprine (Imuran)
1. Action. Purine analog and derivative of mercaptopurine that antagonizes purine metabolism, interferes with nucleic acid synthesis, and alters antibody production. Immunosuppressant action not fully understood.
2. Use. Adjunct to prevent rejection of renal transplants; severe rheumatoid arthritis.
3. Adverse Effects. Hypotension, pulmonary edema; hepatotoxicity; nausea, vomiting, diarrhea, stomatitis, anorexia; alopecia; bone marrow suppression, leukopenia, thrombocytopenia; hypersensitivity pancreatitis, skin rash; secondary infection.
4. Nursing Implications
   a. Monitor CBC, liver and kidney function studies.
   b. Monitor for symptoms of infection.
   c. Monitor for symptoms of rejection.
5. Discharge Teaching
   a. Take with food.
   b. Report signs of infection and bruising.
   c. Use good handwashing and hygiene and avoid individuals with URIs.

C. Related Drugs
1. Mycophenolate (CellCept)
   a. Used to prevent and treat rejection of renal transplants.
   b. Given orally.

Sample Questions

168. Which statement by Mr. Neft indicates a need for further teaching in regard to azathioprine therapy?
   1. "I will take one daily dose one hour before breakfast."
   2. "I should avoid individuals who have the flu or a cold."
   3. "I will notify the physician if I notice any bruising."
   4. "I will try to maintain good personal hygiene."

Answers and Rationales

168. The correct answer is 1. Azathioprine (Imuran) should be taken with food and in divided doses to reduce GI upset.

CYCLOSPORINE (SANDIMMUNE)

A. Prototype—Cyclosporine (Sandimmune)
1. Action. Exact immunosuppressant action unknown. Interferes with T-lymphocyte activity.
2. Use. Prophylaxis for recipients of kidney, heart, and liver transplants to prevent organ rejection.
3. Adverse Effects. Nephrotoxicity; hepatotoxicity; hypertension; infections; tremors; leukopenia; diarrhea, nausea, vomiting; anaphylaxis in IV use; gum hyperplasia.
4. Nursing Implications
   a. Monitor CBC, liver and kidney function studies.
   b. With IV use epinephrine; resuscitation equipment should be available.
   c. Protect IV infusion from light.
   d. Mix PO medication in milk or orange juice at room temperature. Stir and drink immediately and rinse glass with more milk or juice to ensure that entire dose has been taken.
   e. Notify physician if bruising present or oliguria.
5. Discharge Teaching. See Azathioprine (Imuran).

B. Related Drugs
1. Tacrolimus (Prograf)
   a. Used to prevent rejection with kidney, heart, and liver transplants.
   b. Given orally or IV.

Sample Questions

169. Which lab values should be monitored in clients receiving cyclosporine?
   1. Electrolytes.
   2. Glucose.
   3. BUN and creatinine.
   4. Serum amylase.

Answers and Rationales

169. The correct answer is 3. Cyclosporine (Sandimmune) has nephrotoxic effects, therefore BUN and creatinine levels should be monitored.

Vitamins and Minerals

Vitamins and some minerals are vital substances needed by the human body. Because nutrition plays an important role, they are primarily discussed in the nutrition section, Unit 4. Excessive quantities of vitamins can cause adverse effects. Treatment of poisonous minerals is included here as is fluoride, a treatment for prevention of dental caries.

VITAMINS

A. Case Study
   Mr. George Washington is 67 years old and retired from his electric motor business. He has been reading many books and magazine articles on vitamins and organic foods. For the past year, he has been taking megadoses of both water- and fat-soluble vitamins. Today he comes to the physician's office for his annual physical.
B. General considerations related to vitamins and minerals
   1. Vitamins are necessary for body metabolism of carbohydrates, protein, and fat. Minerals are essential components of living tissues.
   2. Dosage of vitamins and minerals is stated in RDAs—recommended daily allowances.
   3. Fat-soluble vitamins accumulate in the body; therefore excessive amounts should not be taken.
C. See Table 4.3, Vitamins, Unit 4.

Sample Questions

170. Mr. Washington admits to taking Vitamin A in excess of 50,000 units daily. The nurse explains that this is considered an overdose and that he can get adequate amounts of vitamin A in his diet. A good dietary source of vitamin A is
    1. spinach.
    2. pork.
    3. nuts.
    4. tomatoes.

Answers and Rationales

170. The correct answer is 1. Dark green vegetables such as spinach are good food sources of vitamin A.

MINERALS

A. Case Study
   Kristen Buttel, a 15-year-old sophomore in high school, recently joined the tennis team. Lately Kristen has been complaining of increased fatigue and difficulty concentrating in class. Her parents take her to the physician where physical exam reveals pale mucous membranes and spoon-shaped nails. After ordering a CBC, the physician diagnoses iron deficiency anemia and prescribes an iron preparation.
   Later that day, Kristen has a dentist appointment and two cavities are found. The dentist suggests that since Kristen lives in a rural area where fluoride has not been added to the water supply that she take fluoride tablets to help prevent tooth decay. Fluoride reduces tooth decay and strengthens bones. While found in certain foods, it is often added to community water supplies.
B. See Table 4.2, Minerals, Unit 4.

Sample Questions

171. The nurse should instruct Kristen that iron should be taken
    1. with milk.
    2. with meals.
    3. after meals with an antacid.
    4. with orange juice between meals.

Answers and Rationales

171. The correct answer is 4. Orange juice contains vitamin C which helps to absorb iron. Iron should be taken between meals for maximum absorption. Note: sometimes iron is given with meals to decrease GI side effects, but absorption is reduced.

HEAVY METAL ANTAGONISTS

A. Heavy metals such as lead, iron, arsenic, gold, and mercury can have toxic effects. Heavy metal antagonists prevent or reverse poisoning by neutralizing the heavy metals. Toxic effects or poisoning can occur from drug overdose (e.g., gold salts or iron), or accidental ingestion of lead chips from lead-containing paint, or pesticide ingestion.

B. Examples of Heavy Metal Antagonists
  1. Deferoxamine mesylate for iron intoxication
     a. May turn urine red.
     b. When given IV, use an infusion pump and monitor blood pressure frequently.
     c. May cause hypotension, tachycardia, allergic reactions, and pain on injection.

  2. Ededate calcium disodium (Calcium EDTA). For lead poisoning; can cause renal toxicity. May increase intracranial pressure—do not give IV if lead encephalopathy.
  3. Dimercaprol (BAL in oil). Given IM in combination with calcium EDTA to treat lead poisoning. Also used to treat arsenic, mercury, and gold toxicity. Painful on injection and can cause hypertension and tachycardia in large doses.
  4. Edetate disodium (Disodium EDTA) for hypercalcemic crisis.

Sample Questions

172. The nurse is aware that when administering calcium EDTA for lead poisoning to monitor
   1. liver function studies.
   2. kidney function.
   3. hemoglobin and hematocrit.
   4. glucose levels.

Answers and Rationales

172. The correct answer is 2. Calcium EDTA can cause renal toxicity.

Vaccines and Toxoids

VACCINES AND TOXOIDS

A. Case Study
   Two-month-old Grant Tomey is brought to the clinic for diphtheria, tetanus toxoid, and pertussis vaccine (DPT) and oral polio vaccine (OPV) immunizations.

B. Vaccines and Toxoids—General Information
   1. Given to prevent some infectious diseases and diseases transferred by animal bites and injuries.
   2. Vaccine is composed of weakened or dead microorganisms that cause antibody formation.
   3. Toxoid is a bacterial toxin that has reduced toxicity but can cause antibody formation.
   4. Immunity is the ability to fight or conquer infection.

   a. Natural immunity exists from birth and is a basic form of resistance to disease.
   b. Acquired immunity occurs after birth. Can be active or passive. Involves the manufacture of antibodies against antigens in the body. Takes time to develop and considered to be permanent. Acquired by the person having a specific disease or by inoculation with toxoid or vaccines. Passive immunity involves the individual receiving antibodies against antigens that have been formed someplace other than within the person. Is immediate but effects are short-lived. Is acquired through injection of serum containing antibodies.

5. If immunosuppressed, receiving corticosteroid therapy, or has an active infection, should not be inoculated.
C. Specific Vaccines and Toxoids
   1. DPT (Diphtheria, Tetanus Toxoid, and Pertussis Vaccine). Produces active immunity by forming antibodies.
      a. DT (Diphtheria and Tetanus Toxoid) Vaccine. Available for children with contraindications to pertussis vaccine. Three doses are given at 2-month intervals starting at 2 months of age followed by a booster 6–12 months after the third dose. Booster is given at age 4–6 years when starting school.
      b. Pertussis vaccine contraindicated in children with nervous system disorders as the pertussis component has led to occasional neurological reactions. Pertussis vaccine not given to children above age 7.
   2. MMR (Measles, Mumps, Rubella). Contains live attenuated virus. Made from chick embryos. Should not be given to persons allergic to eggs.
      a. Give at 15 months and again at age 11–12.
      b. DPT and OPV can be given with MMR.
   3. Oral Polio Vaccine (OPV) trivalent contains live attenuated virus that causes three types of polio. Give at age 2 and 4 months. Third dose is not indicated in U.S. Booster is given between 12–24 months and again at age 4–6.
   4. Bacillus Calmette-Guerin Vaccine (BCG). Produces active immunity to tuberculosis (TB). Give to infants in countries where TB is endemic. Persons who have had BCG will have a positive purified protein derivative (PPD) test.
      a. Also used to stimulate the immune system in treating cancer.
      b. Should not be given to persons taking antituberculosis drugs.
   5. Hepatitis B Vaccine (Engerix-B). Effective against all types of hepatitis B and recommended for individuals at risk to contract hepatitis B. Now recommended for all children.
      a. Does not prevent an unrecognized infection already present.
      b. Two IM doses are given 1 month apart and a third dose is given six months after the first dose.
   6. Hemophilus Influenza B (Hibtiter). Given at 2, 4, and 6 months and booster at 15 months.
   7. Td (Adult Tetanus Toxoid and Diphtheria Toxoid). Give at age 14–16 years and repeated every ten years.
   8. Refer to Table 5.1, Recommended Schedule for Immunization, Unit 5.

Sample Questions

173. Grant is now 4 months old. His mother brings him to the clinic for his next set of immunizations. Which of the following would contraindicate Grant receiving immunizations at this time?
    1. Delayed development.
    2. Weight loss.
    3. Anorexia.
    4. Active infection.

Answers and Rationales

173. The correct answer is 4. Any evidence of an active infection contraindicates immunization. Other contraindications for immunization are immunosuppression and corticosteroid therapy.

IMMUNE SERUMS

A. Case Study
   Sue Jones is a third-semester nursing student currently involved in an advanced medical/surgical nursing course. Her client assignment is a man with hepatitis B. After giving this client an IM injection, Sue accidentally stabs her left index finger with the contaminated needle from the used syringe.
B. Immune Serums
   1. Provide passive immunity. They are antibodies that are formed in another person or animal and then given to the client. Offer immediate immunity but duration is short. Treatment considered to be only moderately effective.
   2. Hepatitis B immune globulin, human. Given as a prophylactic treatment after exposure to hepatitis B. Needs to be given to adults within seven days of exposure and repeated in 28–30 days. Newborns are immunized at birth and then again at 3 and 6 months. Cautious use in persons with hypersensitivity to immune globulins. Adverse effects: tenderness at injection site and urticaria.
   3. Immune serum globulin (immunoglobulin). Given to nonimmunized persons to prevent or reduce severity of various infectious diseases and prophylactically in primary immune deficiencies. Adverse effects: pain and redness at the injection site.
   4. Tetanus immune globulin, human (Hypertet). Used if wound more than 24 hours old or if client has fewer than two previous tetanus toxoid injections. Is considered to be better than antitoxin.

Adverse effect: discomfort at the injection site.

5. Rho (D) immune globulin, human (RhoGam). Given to Rh-negative mothers with Rh-positive fetus, and also given to Rh-negative women who have miscarriages or abortions. Must be given within 72 hours of delivery. Contra-indicated in hypersensitivity to immune globulin. Adverse effect: local tenderness.

Sample Questions

174. Sue is given the hepatitis B immune globulin serum, which will provide her with passive immunity. One advantage of passive immunity is that it
   1. has effects that last a long time.
   2. is highly effective in treatment of disease.
   3. offers immediate protection.
   4. encourages the body to produce antibodies.

175. The nurse tells Sue common adverse effects that she may experience after being given hepatitis B immune globulin are
   1. tachycardia and chest tightness.
   2. heartburn and diarrhea.
   3. dyspnea and upper respiratory infection.
   4. pain and tenderness at the injection site.

Answers and Rationales

174. The correct answer is 3. Passive immunity provides immediate protection. Passive immunity is also short-lived, is limited in effectiveness, and does not stimulate the body to produce antibodies.
175. The correct answer is 4. The most common adverse effects of hepatitis B immune globulin are pain and tenderness at the injection site.

References and Suggested Readings

Abrams, A. (1998) *Clinical drug therapy; Rationales for nursing practice* (5th ed.). Philadelphia: Lippincott.

Karch, A. (1998) *1998 Lippincott's nursing drug guide.* Philadelphia: Lippincott.

Kuhn, M. (1998) *Pharmacotherapeutics: A nursing process approach* (3rd ed.). Philadelphia: F. A. Davis Company.

Lehne, R., et al. (1998) *Pharmacology for nursing care.* Philadelphia: Saunders.

Lilley, L., et al. (1996) *Pharmacology and the nursing process.* St. Louis: Mosby.

McKenry, L. and Salerno, E. (1998) *Pharmacology in Nursing.* St. Louis: Mosby.

Reiss, B., and Evans, M. (1996) *Pharmacologic aspects of nursing care* (4th ed.). Albany: Delmar Publishers.

Unit 3

Universal Principles of Nursing Care Management

Nancy H. Jacobson, RN, CS, MSN

Nurses must frequently apply various management principles while caring for their clients in various health care settings. This unit has been crafted to clarify these issues. It begins with a comprehensive view of nursing practice standards as well as legal and ethical aspects of nursing.

Client care management issues such as determining priorities, working with the health care team, making assignments, and coordinating client care as the client progresses from admission through discharge have been described along with valuable principles to facilitate the nurse's application of this information.

Safety considerations regarding fire, electricity, equipment, and the use of physical restraints have been incorporated.

This unit also includes selected principals and interventions related to specific aspects of care such as body mechanics, transfer techniques, positioning, application of cold and heat, asepsis, and the care of clients who develop or are at risk for pressure ulcers.

UNIT OUTLINE
110 Nursing Practice Standards
113 Legal and Ethical Aspects of Nursing
115 Managing Client Care
117 Safety

Nursing Practice Standards

STANDARDS OF NURSING PRACTICE*1

Nursing practice is a direct service that is goal directed and adaptable to the needs of the individual, family, and community during health and illness. Professional practitioners of nursing bear primary responsibility and accountability for the nursing care clients receive. The purpose of the Standards of Nursing Practice is to fulfill the profession's obligation to provide and improve this practice.

The Standards focus on practice. They provide a means for determining the quality of nursing a client receives regardless of whether such services are provided solely by a professional nurse or by a professional nurse and nonprofessional assistants.

The Standards are stated according to a systematic approach to nursing practice: the assessment of the client's status, the plan of nursing actions, the implementation of the plan, and the evaluation. These specific divisions are not intended to imply that practice consists of a series of discrete steps, taken in strict sequence, beginning with assessment and ending with evaluation. The processes described are used concurrently and recurrently. Assessment, for example, frequently continues during implementation; similarly, evaluation dictates reassessment and replanning.

These Standards for Nursing Practice apply to nursing practice in any setting. Nursing practice in all settings must possess the characteristics identified by these Standards if clients are to receive a high quality of nursing care. Each Standard is followed by a rationale and assessment factors. Assessment factors are to be used in determining achievement of the standard.

STANDARD I

The collection of data about the health status of the client is systematic and continuous. The data are accessible, communicated, and recorded.

Rationale

Comprehensive care requires complete and ongoing collection of data about the client. All

health status data about the client must be available for all members of the health care team.

Assessment Factors

A. Health status data include:
   1. Growth and development
   2. Biophysical status
   3. Emotional status
   4. Cultural, religious, socioeconomic background
   5. Performance of activities of daily living
   6. Patterns of coping
   7. Interaction patterns
   8. Client's perception of and satisfaction with his health status
   9. Client health goals
   10. Environment (physical, social, emotional, ecological)
   11. Available and accessible human and material resources
B. Data are collected from:
   1. Client
   2. Health care personnel
   3. Individuals within the immediate environment and/or the community
C. Data are obtained by:
   1. Interview
   2. Examination
   3. Observation
   4. Reading records, reports, etc.
D. There is a format for the collection of data that:
   1. Provides for a systematic collection of data
   2. Facilitates the completeness of data collection
E. Continuous collection of data is evident by:
   1. Frequent updating
   2. Recording of changes in health status
F. The data are:
   1. Accessible on the client records
   2. Retrievable from record-keeping systems
   3. Confidential when appropriate

STANDARD II

Nursing diagnoses are derived from health status data.

Rationale

The health status of the client is the basis for determining the nursing care needs. The data are analyzed and compared to norms when possible.

---

*Reprinted with permission from *Standards of Nursing Practice,* © 1973, Kansas City, American Nurses' Association.
1Standards of Nursing Practice and Legal and Ethical Aspects of Nursing contributed by Jeanne Gelman, RN, MSN.

Assessment Factors

A. The client's health status is compared to the norm in order to determine if there is a deviation from the norm and the degree and direction of deviation.
B. The client's capabilities and limitations are identified.
C. The nursing diagnoses are related to and congruent with the diagnoses of all other professionals caring for the client.

STANDARD III

The plan of nursing care includes goals derived from the nursing diagnosis.

Rationale

The determination of the results to be achieved is an essential part of planning care.

Assessment Factors

A. Goals are mutually set with the client and pertinent others.
   1. They are congruent with other planned therapies.
   2. They are stated in realistic and measurable terms.
   3. They are assigned a time period for achievement.
B. Goals are established to maximize functional capabilities and are congruent with:
   1. Growth and development
   2. Biophysical status
   3. Behavioral patterns
   4. Human and material resources

STANDARD IV

The plan of nursing care includes priorities and the prescribed nursing approaches or measures to achieve the goals derived from the nursing diagnoses.

Rationale

Nursing actions are planned to promote, maintain, and restore the client's well-being.

Assessment Factors

A. Physiological measures are planned to manage (prevent or control) specific client problems and are related to the nursing diagnoses and goals of care, e.g., ADL, use of self-help devices, etc.
B. Psychosocial measures are specific to the client's nursing care problem and to the nursing care goals, e.g., techniques to control aggression, motivation.
C. Teaching-learning principles are incorporated into the plan of care and objectives for learning stated in behavioral terms, e.g., specification of content for learner's level, reinforcement, readiness, etc.
D. Approaches are planned to provide for a therapeutic environment.
   1. Physical environmental factors are used to influence the therapeutic environment, e.g., control of noise, control of temperature, etc.
   2. Psychosocial measures are used to structure the environment for therapeutic ends, e.g., paternal participation in all phases of the maternity experience.
   3. Group behaviors are used to structure interaction and influence the therapeutic environment, e.g., conformity, ethos, territorial rights, locomotion, etc.
E. Approaches are specified for orientation of the client to:
   1. New roles and relationships
   2. Relevant health (human and material) resources
   3. Modifications in plan of nursing care
   4. Relationship of modifications in nursing care plan to the total care plan
F. The plan of nursing care includes the utilization of available and appropriate resources:
   1. Human resources—other health personnel
   2. Material resources
   3. Community
G. The plan includes an ordered sequence of nursing actions.
H. Nursing approaches are planned on the basis of current scientific knowledge.

STANDARD V

Nursing actions provide for client participation in health promotion, maintenance, and restoration.

Rationale

The client and family are continually involved in nursing care.

Assessment Factors

A. The client and family are kept informed about:
   1. Current health status
   2. Changes in health status
   3. Total health care plan
   4. Nursing care plan
   5. Roles of health care personnel
   6. Health care resources
B. The client and family are provided with the information needed to make decisions and choices about:

1. Promoting, maintaining, and restoring health
2. Seeking and utilizing appropriate health care personnel
3. Maintaining and using health care resources

STANDARD VI

Nursing actions assist the client to maximize his health capabilities.

Rationale

Nursing actions are designed to promote, maintain, and restore health.

Assessment Factors

A. Nursing actions:
   1. Are consistent with the plan of care.
   2. Are based on scientific principles.
   3. Are individualized to the specific situation.
   4. Are used to provide a safe and therapeutic environment.
   5. Employ teaching-learning opportunities for the client.
   6. Include utilization of appropriate resources.
B. Nursing actions are directed by the client's physical, physiological, psychological, and social behavior associated with:
   1. Ingestion of food, fluid, and nutrients
   2. Elimination of body wastes and excesses in fluid
   3. Locomotion and exercise
   4. Regulatory mechanisms—body heat, metabolism
   5. Relating to others
   6. Self-actualization

STANDARD VII

The client's progress or lack of progress toward goal achievement is determined by the client and the nurse.

Rationale

The quality of nursing care depends upon comprehensive and intelligent determination of nursing's impact upon the health status of the client. The client is an essential part of this determination.

Assessment Factors

A. Current data about the client are used to measure his progress toward goal achievement.
B. Nursing actions are analyzed for their effectiveness in the goal achievement of the client.
C. The client evaluates nursing actions and goal achievement.
D. Provision is made for nursing follow-up of a particular client to determine the long-term effects of nursing care.

STANDARD VIII

The client's progress or lack of progress toward goal achievement directs reassessment, reordering of priorities, new goal setting, and revision of the plan of nursing care.

Rationale

The nursing process remains the same, but the input of new information may dictate new or revised approaches.

Assessment Factors

A. Reassessment is directed by goal achievement or lack of goal achievement.
B. New priorities and goals are determined and additional nursing approaches are prescribed appropriately.
C. New nursing actions are accurately and appropriately initiated.

Legal and Ethical Aspects of Nursing

OVERVIEW

It is important for nurses to recognize that nursing practice is guided by legal restrictions and professional obligations. Legal responsibilities are regulated by state nurse-practice acts and may vary from state to state. In addition, general standards for the practice of nursing have been developed and published by the American Nurses' Association, which has also developed a code of ethics.

Nurses need to be aware of these standards, as well as legal and ethical concepts and principles, since nurses are accountable for their actions in all these areas in their professional role.

Ethical Concepts That Apply to Nursing Practice

A. *Ethics:* rules and principles that guide nursing decisions or conduct in terms of the rightness/wrongness of that decision or action.
B. *Morals:* personally held beliefs, opinions, and attitudes that guide our actions.
C. *Values:* appraisal of what is "good."
   1. Dilemmas may occur when different values conflict.
   2. Example: client's right to refuse treatment may be in conflict with nurse's obligation to benefit client and to carry out treatment.
D. *Ethical dilemma:* a problem in making a decision because there is no clearly correct or right choice. This may result in having to choose an action that violates one principle or value in order to promote another.
E. *Autonomy:* an individual has the right to make his or her own decision regarding treatment and care.
F. *Paternalism:* another person makes decisions about what is right or best for the individual.
G. *Beneficence:* promoting good or doing no harm to another.
H. *Right to know:* right to knowledge necessary or helpful in making an informed decision.
I. *Principle of double effect:* promoting good may involve some expected harm, such as adverse side effects of medication.
J. *Distributive justice:* allocation of goods and services and how or to whom they are distributed.
   1. Equality: everyone receives the same.
   2. Need: greater services go to those with greater needs (e.g., critically ill client receives more intensive nursing care).
   3. Merit: services go to more deserving (used as a criterion for transplant recipients).

CODE FOR NURSES (ANA, 1985)*

1. The nurse provides services with respect for human dignity and the uniqueness of the client, unrestricted by considerations of social or economic status, personal attributes, or the nature of health problems.
2. The nurse safeguards the client's right to privacy by judiciously protecting information of a confidential nature.
3. The nurse acts to safeguard the client and the public when health care and safety are affected by the incompetent, unethical, or illegal practice of any person.
4. The nurse assumes responsibility and accountability for individual nursing judgments and actions.
5. The nurse maintains competence in nursing.
6. The nurse exercises informed judgment and uses individual competence and qualifications as criteria in seeking consultation, accepting responsibilities, and delegating nursing activities to others.
7. The nurse participates in activities that contribute to the ongoing development of the profession's body of knowledge.
8. The nurse participates in the profession's efforts to implement and improve standards of nursing.
9. The nurse participates in the profession's efforts to establish and maintain conditions of employment conducive to high-quality nursing care.
10. The nurse participates in the profession's efforts to protect the public from misinformation and misrepresentation and to maintain the integrity of nursing.
11. The nurse collaborates with members of the health professions and other citizens in promoting community and national efforts to meet the health needs of the public.

Legal Concepts That Apply to Nursing Practice

A. *Standards:* identify the minimal knowledge and conduct expected from a professional practitioner. Standards are applied as they relate to a practitioner's experience and

---

*Reprinted with permission from *American Nurses' Association, Code for Nurses with Interpretive Statements,* Kansas City, American Nurses' Association, 1985.

educational preparation. For example, any nurse would be expected to be certain that an ordered medication was being given to the correct client. However, more complex nursing actions, such as respirator monitoring, would require supervised experience and/or continuing education.

B. *Negligence:* lack of reasonable conduct or care. Omitting an action expected of a prudent person in a particular circumstance is considered negligence, as is committing an action that a prudent person would not.

C. *Malpractice:* professional negligence, misconduct, or unreasonable lack of skill resulting in injury or loss to the recipient of the professional services.

D. *Competence:* ability or qualification to make informed decisions.

E. *Informed consent:* agreement to the performance of a procedure/treatment based on knowledge of facts, risks, and alternatives.
   1. Simple: having capacity to give consent for the treatment or procedure.
   2. Valid: having capacity to give consent and also demonstrating an understanding of the nature of the treatment, expected effects, possible side effects, and alternatives to treatment.

F. *Assault:* unjustifiable threat or attempt to touch or injure another.

G. *Battery:* unlawful touching or injury to another.

H. *Crime:* act that is a violation of duty or breach of law, punishable by the state by fine or imprisonment (see Table 3.1).

I. *Tort:* a legal wrong committed against a person, his or her rights, or property; intentional, wilfully committed without just cause (see Table 3.1). The person who commits a tort is liable for damages in a civil action.
   1. Negligence and malpractice are torts.
   2. Victims of malpractice are entitled to receive monetary awards (damages) to compensate for their injury or loss.

J. *Good Samaritan doctrine:* rescuer is protected from liability when assisting in an emergency situation or rescuing a person from imminent and serious peril, if attempt is not reckless and person's condition is not made worse.

K. *Licensure:* Granted by states to protect public
   1. Purposes
      a. Standards for entry into practice
      b. Defines what licensed person can do (e.g., Nurse Practice Acts)
   2. License revocation/suspension
      a. Criteria vary in each state.
      b. Licensed nurses should be aware of their state's nurse practice act.
      c. Nurses who are disciplined in one state may also be disciplined in another state in which they hold a license.

Legal Concepts Related to Psychiatric-Mental Health Nursing

A. *Voluntary commitment:* client consents to hospital admission.
   1. Client must be released when he or she no longer chooses to remain in the hospital.
   2. State laws govern how long a client must remain hospitalized prior to release.
   3. Client has the right to refuse treatment.

B. *Involuntary commitment:* client is hospitalized without consent.
   1. Most states require that the client be mentally ill and be a danger to others/self (includes being unable to meet own basic needs such as eating or protection from injury).
   2. In most states the client who has been involuntarily committed may *not* refuse treatment.

C. *Insanity:* a legal term for mental illness where an individual cannot be held responsible for or does not understand the nature of his or her acts.

D. *Insanity defenses:* not guilty by reason of insanity.
   1. M'Naghten rule ("right and wrong test"): the accused is not legally responsible for an act if, at the time the act was committed, the person did not, because of mental defect or illness, know the nature of the act or that the act was wrong.
   2. Irresistible impulse: the accused, because of mental illness, did not have the will to resist an impulse to commit the act, even

TABLE 3.1 Examples of Crimes and Torts

Crimes	Torts
Assault and battery	Assault and battery
Involuntary manslaughter: committing a lawful act that results in the death of a client	False imprisonment: intentional confinement of a client without consent
Illegal possession or sale of a controlled substance	Fraud
	Negligence/malpractice:
	• Medication errors
	• Carelessness resulting in loss of client's property
	• Burns from hot water bottles, heating pads, hot soaks
	• Failure to prevent falls by not using bed rails
	• Incompetence in assessing symptoms (shock, chest pain, respiratory distress)
	• Administering treatment to wrong client

though able to differentiate between right and wrong.
3. Individuals who commit crimes and successfully plead insanity defenses may be involuntarily committed to psychiatric hospitals under civil commitment laws. There is presently a trend toward finding individuals insane and guilty.
E. *Rights of clients:* rights that each state may grant to its residents committed to a psychiatric hospital.
   1. Right to receive treatment and not just be confined
   2. Right to the least restrictive alternative (locked vs unlocked units, inpatient vs outpatient care)
   3. Right to individualized treatment plan and to participation in the development of that plan and to an explanation of the treatment
   4. Right to confidentiality of records
   5. Right to visitors, mail, and use of telephone
   6. Right to refuse to participate in experimental treatments
   7. Right to freedom from seclusion or restraints

8. Right to an explanation of rights and assertion of grievances
9. Right to due process

Legal Responsibilities of the Nurse

A nurse is expected to
A. Be responsible for his or her own acts
B. Protect the rights and safety of patients
C. Witness, but not obtain, informed consent for medical procedures
D. Document and communicate information regarding client care and responses
E. Refuse to carry out orders that the nurse knows/believes harmful to the client
F. Perform acts allowed by that nurse's state nurse practice act
G. Reveal client's confidential information only to appropriate persons
H. Perform acts for which the nurse is qualified by either education or experience
I. Witness a will (this is not a legal obligation, but the nurse may choose to do so)
J. Restrain clients only in emergencies to prevent injury to self/others. Clients have the right to be free from unlawful restraint.

Managing Client Care

PRIORITIES OF CLIENT CARE

For One Client

A. Maslow's Hierarchy of Needs (1954) (see Table 3.2)
   1. Principles
      a. An individual's needs are depicted in ascending levels on the hierarchy.
      b. Needs on one level must be (at least partially) met before one can focus on a higher-level need
   2. Levels of Maslow's Hierarchy
      a. Physiologic/survival needs: basic human needs (e.g., oxygen, water, food, elimination, physical and mental rest, activity, and avoidance of pain)
      b. Safety and security needs
         1) Protection from physical harm (e.g., mechanical, thermal, chemical, or infectious)
         2) Interpersonal, economic, and emotional security

c. Affection or belonging needs
   1) Giving and receiving of affection
   2) Sense of belonging (e.g., including client/family in planning of care)
d. Self-esteem/respect needs
   1) Feeling of self-worth
   2) Need for recognition

TABLE 3.2   Maslow's Hierarchy of Needs

e. Self-actualization
   1) Highest level: not reached by all
   2) Independence
   3) Feeling of achievement or competency

B. Application of Maslow's Hierarchy in health care
   1. Client Care
      a. Basic physiologic needs should take precedence over higher-level needs and on up the continuum accordingly.
      b. Professional nurse often delivers care at multiple levels simultaneously (e.g., while feeding a client, you position them to prevent aspiration and converse with them).
      c. Tool to guide decision making of priorities in emergencies and time management of care.
   2. Also applies to families, staff, and yourself

For Multiple Clients

A. Maslow's Hierarchy applies (e.g., more critically ill clients will require more care to meet their physiologic/survival needs)
B. Organizing multiple client assignments
   1. Analyze and plan for entire shift.
   2. Develop a working plan so that priorities get accomplished and all clients receive optimal care.
   3. First consider schedules for nursing activities (e.g., meds, treatments, VS, mealtimes, client appointments, I&Os, etc.).
   4. Then work in the nonscheduled activities that need to be accomplished to meet care plan goals (e.g., supporting family, teaching client, meeting with other departments about scheduling, writing care plan, discharge planning).

ASSIGNMENT METHODS FOR DELIVERY OF CARE

Principles

A. RN is the decision maker/delegator
   1. Assesses each client. Determines appropriate plan of care.
   2. Assesses available staff and their job descriptions. Decides how to use human resources to accomplish care.
B. Typical levels of staff
   1. Nursing Assistants
      a. Least-skilled workers
      b. Assign to majority of the "routine" procedures (e.g., baths, bed making, routine VS, etc.)
   2. Licensed Practical Nurse (LPN)/Licensed Vocational Nurse (LVN)

      a. LPN/LVN is the technical doer.
      b. Assign to physical care of clients with more complex conditions, selected treatments, and perhaps some medications.
   3. Registered Nurse (RN)
      a. Performs the most complex procedures (e.g., starting IVs, developing the plan of care, interpreting EKGs, correlating laboratory results with client status)
      b. Applies the nursing process for each client
      c. Coordinates the medical plan with the nursing care plan
      d. Coordinates client activities
         1) Other departments
         2) Health care workers
         3) Community
      e. Performs client/family teaching
      f. Ensures documentation of care and outcomes
      g. Directs and supervises care given by LPNs and ancillary personnel
      h. Acts as a client advocate Supporting, pleading, or arguing in favor of the client
         1) Client rights
         2) Facility policy
         3) Treatment/care issues
         4) Personnel issues

Admission of Client to Hospital

A. Room assignment
   1. Check available data (e.g., diagnosis, age, pertinent history)
   2. Does client need to be close to nurses' station for optimal monitoring?
   3. Does client need isolation or special precautions?
   4. Who will be the client's roommate?
   5. Consider the physical layout of available rooms and bathrooms. What would be best for the client based on his or her functional status?
B. Perform a baseline admission assessment per facility procedure.
C. Obtain needed equipment (e.g., urinal, denture cup, etc.).
D. Record on clothing record and explain/ document the disposition of valuables per facility policy.
E. Orient to facility/policies (e.g., visiting hours, parking, telephone, chaplaincy services, TV, mealtimes, electrical equipment, etc.).
F. Orient to unit (e.g., layout, lounges, smoking policy, activities, menu selection, medication times, straight vs. prn orders, mealtimes, unit personnel, etc.).
G. Orient to room (e.g., roommate; bedside stand, table, and closet; call light, bathroom call system, bed operation, TV, telephone, etc.).

Caring for the Client Who Leaves the Unit

A. Coordinate scheduling to consider client's diagnosis, activity/test to be performed, and client's other therapeutic goals.
B. Prepare client physically and psychologically as indicated.
C. Consider the client's condition; medication, diet, and treatment regimes; as well as specific precautions and adjust the client's schedule as needed.
D. Communicate pertinent information to other departments/personnel.

Discharge of Client from the Hospital

A. Discharge to home
   1. Begin discharge plan on admission.
   2. Teach client/significant other about disease process, needed precautions, restrictions, treatments, and medications.
   3. Assess and document knowledge of disease and home-care regimen and ability to perform safely.
   4. Make referrals as needed for added support and care (e.g., community/home health nurses, home health aide, community support groups, other disciplines, i.e., social worker, physical therapist, etc.).
   5. Arrange for client to obtain needed equipment/supplies (e.g., bedside commode, ostomy supplies, dressings, etc.).
   6. Ensure that client has needed prescriptions.
   7. Provide written/audio educational materials at the level of the client's ability.
   8. Schedule or direct client to arrange for appropriate follow-up.
   9. Communicate with individuals/agency(ies) responsible for follow-up care.
B. Discharge of Client to Long-term Care Facility Communicate with facility nursing staff
   1. Client's functional abilities and limitations
   2. Present medical regime and schedule
   3. Mental and behavioral status
   4. Family support/involvement
   5. Nursing care plan and response
   6. Existing advance directives
   7. Recent medication administration records
   8. History and Physical
   9. Pertinent diagnostic reports
   10. Other: requirements per insurance

Safety

FIRE SAFETY/PREPAREDNESS PRACTICES

A. Be aware of hazards and report immediately.
B. Locate and remember
   1. Escape routes
   2. Fire drill procedures.
   3. Use of available equipment
      a. Fire escapes
      b. Fire doors
      c. Fire alarms
      d. Fire sprinkler controls
      e. Fire extinguishers
      f. Shut off valves for O_2 and/or medical air
   4. Keep fire exits clear.
C. Fire Safety
   1. Prevention is everyone's responsibility.
   2. Three elements needed for a fire to start
      a. Fuel—substance that will burn
      b. Heat—flame or spark
      c. Oxygen—room air contains 21% O_2.
   3. See Table 3.3.
D. In the event of a fire
   1. Move clients to safety if in immediate vicinity of fire
   2. Sound the alarm
   3. Close all windows and doors
      a. If selected clients need continuous O_2 or medical air, attach to emergency provisions once they are removed from vicinity of fire
      b. Shut off piped-in O_2 and/or medical air
   4. Follow institutional policy concerning announcing the fire and location and notifying fire company
   5. Avoid use of elevators
   6. Follow institutional evacuation plan as needed.

EQUIPMENT

A. Follow facility procedure when using various equipment.
B. Unfamiliar equipment

TABLE 3.3 Fire Hazards and Prevention

Fire Hazards	Fire Prevention
Faulty electrical equipment and wiring	Report frayed or exposed electrical wires Report sparks or excessive heat coming from electrical equipment
Overloaded circuits	Avoid overloaded circuits Don't use adaptors or extension cords
Plugs that are not properly grounded	Use only 3-pronged grounded plugs Do not allow electrical equipment from outside the institution to be used until it is checked by the maintenance department
Clutter	Avoid clutter
Unsafe practices when O_2 in use	No open flames or smoking in the area Remove flammable liquids from the area Post "Oxygen in Use" signs as per institutional policy Secure O_2 storage per institutional policy
Smoking	Remove cigarettes and matches from room Report suspicious odors of smoke or burning immediately Control smoking practices per institutional policy Limit smoking to designated areas No smoking in bed Directly supervise smoking of selected clients Ensure use of safe ashtrays/metal receptacles
Spontaneous combustion	Dispose of chemicals, rags, and combustible substances in proper containers

1. Contact your staff development department or supervisor for information.
2. Read available manufacturer's literature.
C. Suspected malfunction (e.g., equipment that: 1) doesn't do its task consistently or correctly, 2) makes unusual noises, 3) gives off an unusual odor or extreme temperature)
   1. Don't try to repair.
   2. Replace it immediately.
   3. Contact maintenance department so that it can be checked out safely and repaired.

RESTRAINTS

A. Physical restraints should be used only if necessary to prevent injury to the client or others.

1. Signed, dated, physician's order needs to be written specifying the form of restraint and a time limit for restraint use. (At that time the client will be reevaluated for restraint need to determine if a less restrictive method is appropriate.)
2. Least restrictive form of restraint should be used
   a. Maintain functional abilities
   b. Decrease risk of complications
   c. Minimize behavioral reaction
3. Remove restraints for 10 min q2h for ROM, repositioning/ambulation, toileting, and preventative skin care.
4. Document rationale for restraint, other measures tried in lieu of restraint (e.g., pillows, environmental modifications, etc.), client response, and preventative care.

PRINCIPLES AND INTERVENTIONS FOR SPECIFIC ASPECTS OF CARE

Body Mechanics

A. Safe and efficient use of appropriate muscle groups to do the job
B. Principles for the safe movement of clients
   1. Keep your back straight.
   2. Ensure a wide base of support (keep your feet separated).
   3. Bend from the hips and knees (not the waist).
   4. Use the major muscle groups (strongest).
   5. Use your body weight to help push or pull.
   6. Avoid twisting. (Pivot the whole body.)
   7. Hold heavy objects close to your body.
   8. Push or pull objects instead of lifting.
   9. Ask for help as needed.
   10. Synchronize efforts with client and other staff.
   11. Use turning or lifting sheets as needed.
   12. Use mechanical devices as needed.

Transfer and Movement Principles and Techniques

A. From bed to chair or wheelchair
   1. Identify client's strongest side.
   2. Place chair beside bed, on same side as client's strongest side, so it faces the foot of bed. Stabilize chair and lock wheels.
   3. Lower bed, lock wheels, and elevate head of bed.
   4. If assistance is needed:
      a. Place one arm under client's shoulders. The other arm should be placed over and around the knees.
      b. Bring legs over the side of bed while raising the client's shoulders off of the bed.

c. Dangle client and watch for signs of fainting or dizziness. (Stand in front of client for protection in case of balance problems.)
d. Protect paralyzed arm during transfer. (Use sling or clothing for support.)
e. Place client's feet flat on the floor. (If client has a weak leg, use your leg and foot to brace the weak foot and knee.)
f. Face the client and grasp firmly by placing your arms under the arm pits. Have client lean forward so that your control of the client's upper body is stabilized.
g. Using a wide base of support and bending at your knees, coach the client to assist as much as possible by using verbal instruction and counting.
h. Stand client (if weight bearing is permitted) by pivoting the feet, legs, and hips to a standing position.
i. Continue the slow pivotal movement until client is positioned over chair. Lower client into chair.

B. Log Rolling
1. Performed when spinal column must be kept straight (post-injury or surgery).
2. Two or more persons needed
   a. Both staff should be on side opposite where client is to be turned.
      1) One staff places hands under client's head and shoulders.
      2) One staff places hands under client's hips and legs.
      3) Move client as a unit toward you.
      4) Cross arms over chest and place pillow between legs.
      5) Raise side rail.
   b. Both staff move to side of bed to which client is being turned.
      1) One staff should be positioned to keep client's shoulders and hips straight.
      2) One staff should be positioned to keep thighs and lower legs straight.
      3) At the same time the client is drawn toward both staff in a single unified motion. The client's head, spine and legs are kept in a straight position.
   c. Position with pillows for support and raise side rails.

Positioning of the Client

A. General principles
1. Privacy/draping
2. Universal precautions as needed
3. Knowledge of client's condition when moving client (e.g., paresis or paralysis of a limb; need to support joints or limbs in a specific manner; awareness of pressure points)

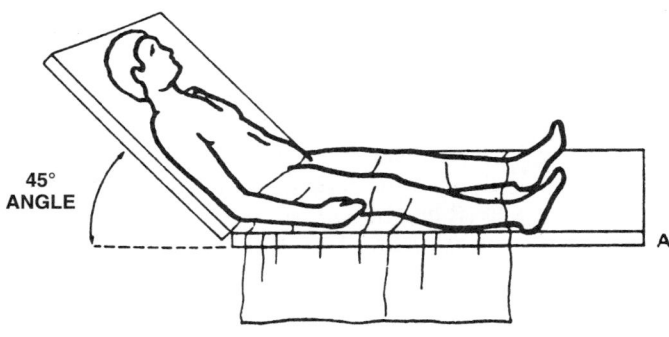

FIGURE 3.1a Semi-Fowler's position (Delmar Publishers)

4. Good posture and body alignment
5. Use of added supports as needed (e.g., pillows, wedge cushions, handrolls, foot boards, etc.)
6. Comfort—reduce pressure and strain on body parts
7. Safety
8. Bed in a low position once repositioned
9. Access to personal items and care (e.g., call bell, drinking water, tissues, telephone, etc.)
10. Clients should change position fairly frequently (at least every 2 hours).

B. Positions
1. Semi-Fowler's (see Figure 3.1a)
   a. Backrest elevated at 45° angle
   b. Knees supported in slight flexion
   c. Arms rest at sides
2. High Fowler's (see Figure 3.1b)
   a. Backrest elevated at 90° angle (right angle)
   b. Knees slightly flexed
   c. Arms supported on pillows or bedside table

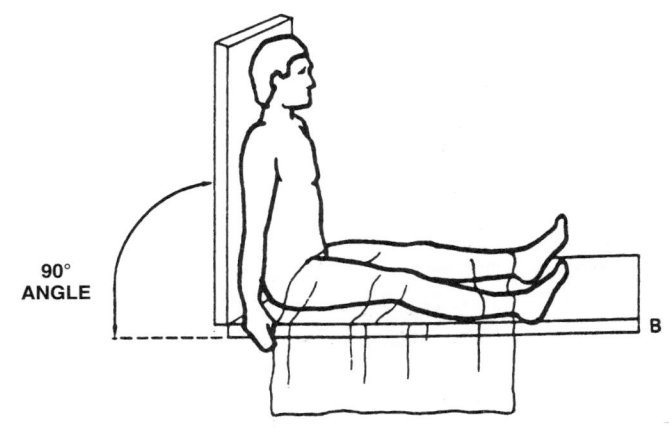

FIGURE 3.1b High Fowler's position (Delmar Publishers)

d. Allows for good chest expansion in clients with cardiac or respiratory problems

3. Supine (dorsal/horizontal recumbent)
   a. Client lies on his back.
   b. Client's head and shoulders slightly elevated with pillow (modified per client condition, physician order or agency policy regarding spinal injury/surgery or post spinal anesthesia)
   c. Small pillow under lumbar curvature
   d. Prevent external rotation of legs with supports placed laterally to trocanters
   e. Knees slightly flexed
   f. Prevent footdrop with foot board, rolled pillow or high top sneakers (depends on persistence of client condition)

4. Prone (see Figure 3.2)
   a. Client lies on his abdomen.
   b. Head turned to one side on *small* pillow or on flat surface.
   c. Small pillow just below diaphragm to support lumbar curve, facilitate breathing, and decrease pressure on female breasts.
   d. Pillow under lower legs to reduce plantar flexion and flex knees.
   e. May be modified in amputees where flexion of hips and knees may be contraindicated.

5. Trendelenburg
   a. Client lies on back with head lower than rest of body.
   b. Enhances circulation to the heart and brain. Sometimes used when shock is present.
   c. In emergencies, the entire lower bed may be elevated on "shock blocks."
   d. May be used for prolapsed cord outside of the hospital.

6. Modified Trendelenburg
   a. Client is positioned with legs elevated to an angle of approximately 20°, knees

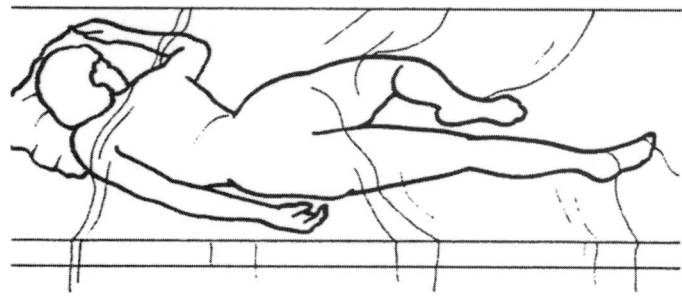

FIGURE 3.3 Sim's position (Delmar Publishers)

straight, trunk horizontal, and head slightly elevated.
   b. Used for persons in shock to improve cerebral circulation and venous return to the heart without compromising respiration. (Contraindicated when head injury is present.)

7. Lateral (side-lying)
   a. Client lies on his side.
   b. Pillow under head to prevent lateral neck flexion and fatigue.
   c. Both arms are slightly flexed in front of the body. Pillow under the upper arm and shoulder provides support and permits easier chest expansion.
   d. Pillow under upper leg and thigh prevents internal rotation and hip adduction.
   e. Rolled pillow behind client's back.

8. Sims' (semiprone; see Figure 3.3)
   a. Similar to lateral, but with weight supported on *anterior* aspects of the ilium, humerous, and clavicle.
   b. Used for vaginal and rectal exams, enema administration, and drainage of oral secretions from the unconscious client. Comfortable for the client in the last trimester of pregnancy.
   c. Client placed on side (left side for enema or rectal exam) with head turned to side on a pillow.
   d. Lower arm is extended behind the body.
   e. Upper arm flexed in front of body and supported by a pillow.
   f. Upper leg is sharply flexed over pillow with the lower leg slightly bent.

9. Knee-chest (see Figure 3.4)
   a. Client first lies on abdomen with head turned to one side on a pillow.
   b. Arms flexed on either side of head.
   c. Finally the client is assisted to flex and draw knees up to meet the chest.
   d. Difficult position to be maintained—do not leave client alone. Used for rectal and vaginal exams.

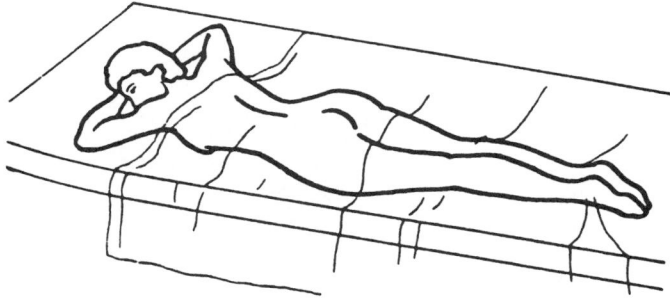

FIGURE 3.2 Prone position (Delmar Publishers)

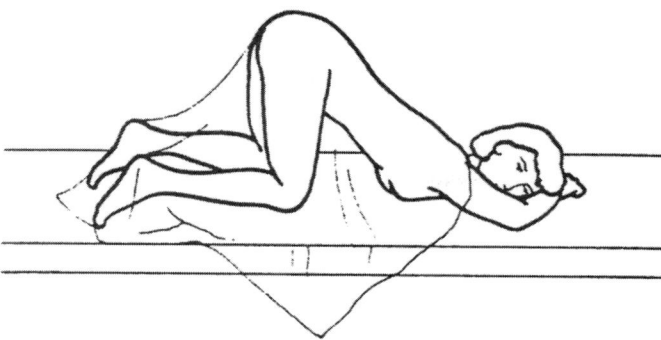

FIGURE 3.4 The knee-chest position (Delmar Publishers)

10. Dorsal lithotomy (see Figure 3.5)
    a. Used for female pelvic exam.
    b. Have client void before assuming this position.
    c. Client lies on back with the knees well flexed and separated.
    d. Frequently stirrups are used. (Adjust for proper feet and lower leg support.)
    e. If prolonged use of stirrups, be alert to signs of clot formation in the pelvis and lower extremities.

Cold Application

A. Systemic
   1. Lowers metabolic rate
      a. Client lies on top of one, or between two, cooling blankets. Blanket(s) are attached to a machine that circulate(s) coolant solution.
         1) Follow agency policy/procedure for care of client treated with hypothermia blanket(s).
         2) Monitor VS (T, P, R, and BP) regularly and frequently.

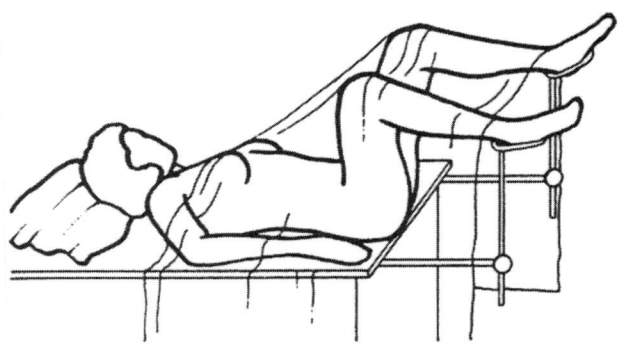

FIGURE 3.5 Dorsal lithotomy position (Delmar Publishers)

      3) Attention to skin hygiene and protection with oil as required.
      4) Frequent repositioning and assessment of body surface areas.
      5) Observe for signs of tissue damage and frostbite (pale areas).
      6) Assist client in basic needs (e.g., hygiene, elimination, nutrition, etc.).
      7) Identify client temperature at which to cease the treatment (temperature may continue to drift downward). Monitor VS frequently until stable for 72 hours.
   2. Alcohol or sponge bath (tepid solutions, 85°–100° F)
      a. Alcohol bath—combination of alcohol and water (alcohol has a drying effect on skin—used less frequently). Alcohol increases heat loss by evaporation.
      b. Sponge bath—cool or tepid (not cold) water.
      c. Frequent and regular VS monitoring (T, P, R, and BP).
      d. Large areas sponged at one time allowing for transfer of body heat to the cooling solution.
      e. Wet cloths applied to forehead, ankles, wrists, armpits, and groin where blood circulates close to skin surface.
      f. Identify temperature to cease treatment due to potential for continued downward temperature drift.
   3. Discontinue systemic cold applications and report and document findings if:
      a. shivering occurs (this mechanism will raise body temperature);
      b. cyanosis of the lips or nails occurs; or
      c. accelerated weak pulse occurs.
B. Local
   1. Purposes
      a. Control bleeding by constriction of blood vessels.
      b. Reduce inflammation;
         1) inhibit swelling;
         2) decrease pain; and
         3) reduce loss of motion at site of inflammation.
      c. Control accumulation of fluid.
      d. Reduce cellular activity (e.g., check bacterial growth in local infections).
      e. Effective *initial* treatment after trauma (24–48 hours). This application of cold is then frequently followed by a phase of application of heat.
   2. Ice caps or ice collars
      a. Covered with cotton cloth, flannel, or towel to absorb moisture from condensation. Change as needed.
      b. Not left on for longer than 1 hour.
      c. Cease treatment and report if client complains of cold or numbness, or if area appears mottled.

3. Cold compresses
   a. Use sterile technique for open wounds. Check site of application after 5–10 minutes for signs of intolerance (cyanosis, blanching, mottling, maceration, or blisters).
   b. Remove after prescribed treatment period (usually 20 minutes).
C. Special considerations
   1. Elderly clients and clients with impaired circulation have decreased tolerance to cold.
   2. Moist application of cold penetrates better than dry application.

Application of External Heat

A. Rationale
   1. Relaxes muscles in spasm.
   2. Softens exudates for easy removal.
   3. Hastens healing due to vasodilation.
   4. Localization of infection. (Note: Do not apply heat to the abdomen with suspected appendicitis as it may precipitate rupture.)
   5. Hastens suppuration.
   6. Warms a body part.
   7. Reduces congestion of an underlying organ.
   8. Increases peristalsis.
   9. Reduces pressure from accumulated fluids.
   10. Comforts and relaxes.
B. Dry heat
   1. Hot water bottle/bag, electric heating pad, lamp, cradle, or aquamatic pad.
   2. Deeper tissue penetration modes—ultrasound, and shortwave and microwave diathermy (administered by Licensed Physical Therapist).
   3. Follow agency policy for heat application mode ordered:
      a. check temperature of water and machine setting carefully;
      b. assess site of application frequently for signs of tissue damage or burns; and
      c. be alert to potential bleeding resulting from vasodilation.
C. Moist heat
   1. Soaks, compresses, hot packs
      a. Follow agency policy.
      b. Check temperature of application.
      c. Use sterile technique for open wounds.
      d. Assess skin condition after 5 minutes for increased swelling, excessive redness, blistering, maceration, pronounced pallor, or if the client reports pain or discomfort.
      e. Remove the device after 15–25 minutes or as ordered/necessary.
D. Special considerations
   1. Moist heat penetrates deeper than dry and is usually better tolerated.

2. The skin area involved may vary in any individual depending on the number of heat receptors present.
3. Heat is less tolerated in the very young, elderly, and clients with circulatory problems.

Asepsis

A. Defined as the absence of disease-producing organisms.
B. Medical asepsis
   1. Practices to reduce the number of microorganisms after they leave the body or to reduce transmission.
   2. Often referred to as *clean technique*.
   3. Includes:
      a. Hand washing
      b. Universal or standard precautions
      c. Isolation technique (see Unit 4)
      d. Cleaning/disinfecting of equipment.
C. Surgical asepsis
   1. Practices aimed at destroying pathological organisms before they enter the body through an open wound.
   2. Referred to as *sterile technique*.
   3. Includes:
      a. Physical barriers—gloves, masks, gowns, drapes.
      b. High risk procedures:
         1) Catheter insertion
         2) Surgical wound dressing changes
         3) Administration of injections.
      c. Associated with populations with high risk for infection. The clients in this category are:
         1) Transplant recipients
         2) Burns
         3) Neonates
         4) Immunosuppressed/AIDS, cancer clients receiving chemotherapy.
   4. Principles of surgical asepsis
      a. Sterile field—area where sterile materials for a sterile procedure are placed (e.g., a table covered with sterile drape).
      b. Sterile field remains sterile throughout procedure.
      c. Movement in and around field must not contaminate it.
      d. Keep hands in front of you and above your waist (never reach across the field with unsterile items).
      e. Barrier techniques (gown, gloves, masks, and drapes are used as indicated to decrease transmission).
      f. Edges of sterile containers are not sterile once opened.
      g. Dry field is necessary to maintain sterility of field.

Pressure Sore (Bedsore, Dermal Ulcer, Decubitis Ulcer)

A. Any lesion caused by unrelieved pressure that causes local interference with circulation and subsequent tissue damage.
B. Risk factors
   1. Immobility (e.g., bed and chair-bound clients as well as those with impaired ability to reposition themselves)
   2. Incontinence
   3. Impaired nutritional status/intake
   4. Impaired level of consciousness
   5. Impaired physical condition (e.g., stability of condition, chronicity, and severity)
   6. Skin condition impaired (e.g., nourishment, turgor, integrity)
   7. Predisposing conditions (e.g. diabetes mellitus, neuropathy, vascular disease, anemia, cortisone therapy, etc.)
C. General prevention, care, and treatment
   1. Inspect skin and document status and interventions daily.
   2. Cleanse when soiling occurs (e.g., avoid hot water, harsh, or drying cleansing agents).
   3. Minimize dry skin (e.g., avoid cold or dry air and use moisturizers as needed).
   4. Minimize moisture from irritating substances (urine, feces, perspiration, wound drainage).
      a. Cleanse immediately and apply protective barrier as indicated.
   5. Avoid massage over bony prominences. (Massage around but not directly over pressure sites.)
   6. Change position frequently, every 15 minutes to two hours, to decrease prolonged pressure.
   7. Reduce friction and shearing (e.g., promote lifting rater than dragging).
   8. Pressure reducing mattresses/beds (e.g., foam, air, gel, or water)
   9. Positioning devices
   10. Nutritional intake (especially calories, protein and fluids if not contraindicated). Also vitamin A and C, iron and zinc
   11. ROM, ambulation, or activities as appropriate to promote increased circulation
   12. Avoid pressure from appliances and care equipment.
D. Staging of pressure ulcers
   1. Stage I
      a. Observable pressure-related alteration of intact skin as compared to adjacent or opposite area on body
      b. May include changes in color (red, blue, purple tones), temperature (warmth or coolness), skin stiffness (hardness, edema) and/or sensation (pain) (Temporary blanching from pressure can last up to 30 minutes.)
   2. Stage II
      a. Partial thickness loss of skin involving epidermis and/or dermis.
      b. Superficial breakdown characterized by blister, abrasion, or shallow crater. Wound base is pink and moist, painful, and free from necrosis.
   3. Stage III
      a. Full thickness skin loss involving subcutaneous damage or necrosis. May extend to but not through underlying fascia.
      b. Infection is generally present.
      c. Characterized by deep crater or eschar. May include undermining and exudate. Wound base is not usually painful.
   4. Stage IV
      a. Full thickness loss of skin with severe destruction, tissue necrosis, or damage to muscle, bone, or supporting structures (e.g., tendon or joint capsule).
      b. Infection, undermining, and sinus tracts are frequently present.
   5. If wound contains necrotic tissue or eschar, accurate staging cannot be confirmed until wound base is visible.
E. Specific wound care treatments
   1. Goals
      a. Support moist wound healing.
      b. Prevent or treat infection.
      c. Avoid trauma of tissue and surrounding skin.
      d. Comfort
   2. Solutions
      a. Cleansing products
      b. Control of bacteria
   3. Dressings or coverings
      a. Damp to dry dressing (e.g., gauze dressing put on damp and removed at tacky dry status) debrides slough and eschar.
         1) If dries completely and adheres to *viable* tissue, moisten dressing before removal.
      b. Non-adherent dressing impregnated with sodium chloride to draw in wound exudate and decrease bacteria.
         1) Change at least daily.
      c. Transparent films, semipermeable membrane to promote moist healing by gas exchange and prevention of bacterial and fluid penetration.
         1) Change when seal is lost or excessive amount of fluid collected underneath.
      d. Hydrocolloid wafers contain water-loving colloids. Wound exudate mixes

with wafer to form a gel, moist environment and nonsurgical debridement.

    1) Wafers are occlusive and should not be used on infected wounds.

  e. Gels/Hydrogels available in sheets or gels and are nonadherent. They provide a moist environment and some absorption of bacteria and exudate from the wound.

    1) Not highly absorptive

      a) Do not use on wounds with copious exudate.

      b) Be alert to maceration of peri wound areas. (Use moisture barriers.)

  f. Exudate absorptive dressings, beads, pastes, or powders which when mixed conform to the wound shape. Attracts debris, exudate, and bacteria via osmosis.

    1) Removed only by irrigation. Do not use with deeply undermined wounds or tracts.

  g. Foams create a moist environment and absorption.

    1) Nonadherent to wound. Many require a secondary dressing to secure.

  h. Calcium alginates pads or ropes made from seaweed that convert to a firm substance when mixed with exudate.

    1) Highly absorptive—will dry out wounds that have little exudate.

  i. Moisture barrier (e.g., A & D ointment) protects high risk skin from moisture and breakdown.

  j. Skin sealant protects high risk skin from moisture and/or chemical breakdown.

4. Debridement—Removal of necrotic devitalized tissue (eschar or slough). Necrotic tissue provides nutrients for bacterial growth and needs to be removed for healing to occur.

  a. Methods of debridement

    1) Enzymatic

    2) Mechanical

    3) Surgical

    4) Physiologic/autolytic

  b. Be alert to bleeding and damage to adjacent viable tissue.

5. Miscellaneous

  a. Whirlpool—for cleansing.

  b. Hyperbaric O_2—application of high O_2 concentration for healing.

  c. Electrical stimulation—stimulates healing.

  d. Growth factor—cell growth stimulation.

F. Documentation

1. Interventions and response to interventions

2. Address:

  a. Location of lesions.

  b. Dimensions—measure and record size (length, width, and depth in cm).

    1) Measuring guides with concentric circles available.

    2) Use sterile applicator to determine accurate depth.

    3) Photographs—need client's written permission.

  c. Stage

  d. Undermining, pockets, or tracts (e.g., undermining from 7:00 to 10:00 measuring 3 cm).

  e. Condition of tissue

    1) Granulation—red, moist, beefy.

    2) Epithelialized—new pink, shiny epidermis.

    3) Necrotic tissue—avascular.

      a) Slough—yellow, green, gray, brown.

      b) Eschar—hard, black, leathery.

  f. Drainage

    1) Volume (scant, small, moderate, copious, number of soaked dressings)

    2) Color

    3) Consistency

    4) Odor

  g. Periwound condition and wound margins (e.g., errythema, crepitus, induration, maceration, hematoma, desiccation, blistering, denudation, pustule, tenderness, temperature).

  h. Pain—related to procedures or constant, location, severity.

Sample Questions

1. Helen, a 24-year-old secretary, has suffered a fractured pelvis in an automobile accident. She has been hospitalized for three days when she tells her primary nurse that she has something to tell her but she does not want the nurse to tell anyone. Helen says that she had tried to donate blood and tested positive for HIV. What is the best action for the nurse to take?

  1. Document this information on Helen's chart.

  2. Tell Helen's physician.

  3. Inform the health care team who will come in contact with Helen.

  4. Encourage Helen to disclose this information to her physician.

2. Helen tells her nurse that she has had many sexual partners. She has been on an oral

contraceptive and frequently had not requested that her partners use condoms. She denies IV drug use. She tells her nurse that she believes that she will die soon. What would be the best response for the nurse to make?
1. "Where there's life there's hope."
2. "Would you like to talk to the nurse who works with HIV-positive clients?"
3. "You are a long way from dying, Helen."
4. "Not everyone who is HIV positive will develop AIDS and die."

3. Helen agrees to talk to the HIV/AIDS nurse. After recommending another blood test, which is positive, the nurse justifies her actions by referring to which of the Standards of Practice?
1. Standard I
2. Standard II
3. Standard III
4. Standard VII

4. Helen is offered the opportunity to participate in research on a new therapy. The researcher asks the nurse to obtain Helen's consent. What is the most appropriate action for the nurse to take?
1. Be sure Helen understands the project before she signs the consent form.
2. Read the consent form to Helen and give her an opportunity to ask questions.
3. Refuse to be the one to obtain Helen's consent.
4. Give the form to Helen and tell her to read it carefully before she signs it.

5. Helen decides not to participate in the research project. She has signed the consent form, but she has changed her mind. The nurse tells Helen that she has the right to change her mind based upon which of the following principles?
1. Paternalism and justice.
2. Autonomy and informed consent.
3. Beneficence and double effect.
4. Competence and right to know.

6. The nurse is preparing to move an adult who has right-sided paralysis from the bed into a wheelchair. Which statement describes the best action for the nurse to take?
1. Position the wheelchair on the left side of the bed.
2. Keep the head of the bed elevated 10°.
3. Protect the client's left arm with a sling during the transfer.
4. Bend at the waist while helping the client into a standing position.

7. Mr. K. has experienced a cerebrovascular accident that has resulted in right-sided weakness. The nurse is preparing to move Mr. K. to the right side of the bed so that he may then be turned to his left side. The nurse knows that an important principle when moving the client is

1. to keep the feet close together.
2. to bend from the waist.
3. to use body weight when moving objects.
4. a twisting motion will save steps.

8. Which statement by the nurse best indicates a correct understanding of "log rolling" when moving a client?
1. One nurse may perform this task alone.
2. Pillows are needed for positioning in order to provide support.
3. The legs should be moved before the head is moved.
4. Keeping the neck in a straight position is the primary concern.

9. The nurse is caring for a client who has a temperature of 105°F (40.5°C). The physician orders the application of a cooling blanket. The nurse should know that which of the following statements is true about the use of a cooling blanket?
1. Cold application will increase the metabolic rate.
2. Vital signs should be monitored every eight hours.
3. The client should remain in one position to conserve energy.
4. Skin hygiene and protection of body surface areas is essential.

10. Topical heat is ordered for all of the following clients. The order should be questioned for which client?
1. A teenager who is active and rapidly growing.
2. A new mother who is breast feeding.
3. A middle aged adult with a cardiac dysrhythmia.
4. An adult with arteriosclerosis obliterans.

11. The nurse is preparing to administer a sponge bath to an infant with a high fever. Administration of the bath should include
1. large amounts of alcohol to increase evaporation of heat.
2. adjustment of the water temperature to 60°–70°F.
3. wet cloths applied to all areas where blood circulates close to skin surfaces.
4. small areas of the body sponged at a time to avoid rapid heat loss.

12. The nurse is instructing the family of a homebound bedridden client in the general prevention of pressure sores. Measures to include in the teaching include
1. promoting lifting rather than dragging when turning the client.
2. massaging directly over pressure sites.
3. changing the client's position every 4 hours.
4. cleaning soiled areas with hot water.

13. Which of the following findings would the nurse note when assessing a client with a stage I pressure ulcer? The ulcer displays

1. superficial skin breakdown.
2. deep pink, red, or mottled skin.
3. subcutaneous damage or necrosis.
4. damage to muscle or bone.

14. An adult has developed a stage II pressure ulcer. He is scheduled to receive wet to dry dressings every shift. The nurse realizes that the purpose of receiving this type of dressing is to
    1. draw in wound exudate and decrease bacteria.
    2. debride slough and eschar.
    3. promote healing by gas exchange.
    4. promote a moist environment and soften exudate.

15. The nurse is performing a wound irrigation and dressing change. Which action, if taken by the nurse, would be a break in technique?
    1. Consistently facing the sterile field.
    2. Washing hands before opening the sterile set.
    3. Opening the bottle of irrigating solution and pouring directly into a container on the sterile field.
    4. Opening the sterile set so that the initial flap is opened away from the nurse.

Answers and Rationales

1. The correct answer is 4. A nurse is legally obliged to protect a client's right to privacy. ANA Code #2 is the ethical obligation. Documenting the information on a chart, telling the physician, or informing other health care workers is neither legal nor ethical unless a state law mandates reporting.

2. The correct answer is 2. This provides Helen with expert care. Standard V provides for client participation in gaining knowledge; Standard VI provides for promotion of health; ANA Code #6 applies. Response 1 is a cliché. Responses 3 and 4 offer inappropriate reassurance to Helen and will not be helpful.

3. The correct answer is 1. Standard I provides for the collection of data. Standards II, III, and VII are the steps of the nursing process that flow from assessment data.

4. The correct answer is 3. Nurses cannot obtain consent. They may legally witness consent to medical procedures. In research, the research team is responsible for obtaining consent. The other choices are not in the realm of the nurse's legal responsibilities.

5. The correct answer is 2. Autonomy is the ethical right to decide what treatment you will or will not receive. Informed consent can be withdrawn; it includes the right to know and competence. Paternalism is making a decision for another person. Beneficence and the principle of double effect do not

have priority over autonomy and informed consent.

6. The correct answer is 1. Place the wheelchair beside the bed, on the client's strongest side, so that it faces the foot of the bed. The head of the bed should be in an upright position. There is no need to give special protection to the unaffected arm during the transfer. The nurse should always bend at the knees, not the waist.

7. The correct answer is 3. Objects should be pushed or pulled instead of lifted. Using the body weight to push or pull prevents strain to muscles and joints. The feet should be kept apart to provide a broad base of support. The nurse should bend from the knees, not the waist. Twisting puts the nurse at risk for muscle pulls.

8. The correct answer is 2. A pillow should be placed between the knees/legs for support while the client is being turned. It takes two or three nurses to do log rolling. The whole spinal column should be kept straight and the entire body moved at once.

9. The correct answer is 4. Cold application lowers the metabolic rate and causes vasoconstriction in the area. Therefore, assessment of the skin, protection of the skin surfaces with oil, and repositioning are all vital to prevent skin breakdown. The temperature will be monitored continually with a rectal probe and blood pressure, pulse, and respirations will be monitored frequently.

10. The correct answer is 4. Heat is not well tolerated in clients with circulatory impairment. If topical heat application is to be carried out in a client with circulatory impairment, the nurse should assess the site frequently for signs of tissue damage. Topical heat is not a problem for healthy teenagers and is indicated to help relieve breast engorgement in breast-feeding women. A cardiac dysrhythmia is not a contraindication for topical heat. Saunas may be contraindicated because of the rapid increase in metabolic rate.

11. The correct answer is 3. Wet cloths should be applied to forehead, ankles, wrists, axilla, and groin. These are the areas where blood circulates closest to the skin surface. If alcohol is used, small amounts are indicated. Large amounts of alcohol are very drying to the skin and toxic to inhale. The temperature should be 85°–100°F. Rapid heat loss is desired so large areas of the body are sponged.

12. The correct answer is 1. Promoting lifting rather than dragging when turning or moving the client will reduce friction and shearing. This will assist in preventing pressure sores. The caregiver should massage around—but not directly over—pressure sites. The client's position should be changed every two hours.

Soiled areas should be cleaned with warm—not hot—water.

13. The correct answer is 2. Stage I pressure ulcers show discoloration of skin to a deep pink, red, or mottled appearance. Temporary blanching of the area from pressure can last several minutes due to poor circulation in the area. Choice 1, superficial skin breakdown, is characteristic of a stage II pressure ulcer. Choice 3, subcutaneous damage or necrosis, is characteristic of a stage II pressure ulcer. Choice 4, damage to muscle or bone, is characteristic of a stage IV pressure ulcer.

14. The correct answer is 2. In a wet to dry dressing, the wet gauze dressing either covers the wound or is packed into the wound and is covered with a dry dressing. The dry layer creates a wick and pulls moisture (drainage) from the wound, thus debriding slough and bacteria. Answer 1 is not correct because the exudate is drawn out, not in.

15. The correct answer is 3. After opening a sterile bottle the edge of the bottle is considered to be contaminated. The nurse should pour a little solution out first to wash away organisms on the lip of the opening and then pour from the same side of the bottle into the sterile container on the sterile field. The nurse should always face the sterile field. Hands should be washed before opening the sterile set. The sterile set should be opened so that the initial flap is opened away from the nurse. This means that the final flap will be opened toward the nurse and the nurse will not have to reach across the sterile field.

References and Suggested Readings

Bandman, E., & Bandman, B. (1990). *Nursing ethics through the life span* (2nd ed.). Norwalk, CT: Appleton & Lange.

Benjamin, A., & Curtis, J. (1986). *Ethics in nursing* (2nd ed.). New York: Oxford University Press.

Bernzweig, E. (1990). *The nurse's liability for malpractice* (5th ed.). St. Louis: Mosby.

Creighton, H. (1986). *Law every nurse should know.* Philadelphia: Saunders.

Comprehensive accreditation Manual for Hospitals (1996), The Joint Commission on Accreditation of Healthcare Organizations, Chicago: Joint Commission.

ET Nurse Certification Review Course Book (1997), Mechanicsburg: Wicks Educational Associates, Inc.

Federal Requirements for Medicare/Medicaid Interpretive Guidelines (1995), Department of Health and Human Services, Health Care Financing Administration.

Gillies, D. (1994). *Nursing management: a systems approach* (3rd ed.). Philadelphia: Saunders.

Guido, G. (1988). *Legal issues in nursing: a source book for practice.* Norwalk, CT: Appleton & Lange.

Hegner, B., Caldwell, E., and Needham, J. (1995). *The nursing assistant: A nursing process approach* (7th ed.) New York: Delmar Publishers.

Laben, J., & MacLean, C. (1989). *Legal issues and guidelines for nurses who care for the mentally ill* (2nd ed.). Owings Mills, MD: National Health Publishing.

Maslow, A.H. (1970). Motivation and personality (2nd ed.). New York: Harper & Row Publishers, Inc.

Miedema, F. (1991). A practical approach to ethical decisions. *American Journal of Nursing,* 91(12), 20–25.

National Pressure Ulcer Advisory Panel Fifth National Conference (1997), Buffalo: NPUAP.

Northrop, C., & Kelly, M. (1987). *Legal issues in nursing.* St. Louis: Mosby.

Pence, T., & Cantrell, J. (1990). *Ethics in nursing: an anthology.* New York: National League for Nursing.

Unit 4

Adult Nursing

Margaret B. Brenner, RN, MSN*
Judith Miller, RN, MSN

Nursing care of the adult client in today's changing health care environment is a challenge to the skill and knowledge of the professional nurse. Holistic care requires that nurses not only meet a client's physical needs through technical skills and sound clinical judgment, they also must be aware of a client's psychosocial needs. The role of client advocate puts the nurse in a unique position to help clients achieve the highest level of wellness.

This unit presents a comprehensive review of nursing care of adult clients with specific health problems. It begins with a section on multisystem stressors (such as infection, pain, and surgery). These stressors are common to many areas of nursing practice and may be applied to clients with various levels of health care needs. Issues related to aging are also presented.

The unit is further divided according to specific body systems. For each system there is a review of anatomy and physiology. Each step of the nursing process (assessment, analysis, planning, intervention, and evaluation) is then reviewed for the system, followed by consideration of the major health problems of that system. Congenital disorders will be discussed in Unit 5.

UNIT OUTLINE

130 Multisystem Stressors
154 Aging
161 Perioperative Nursing
168 Oncologic Nursing
174 The Neurosensory System
205 The Cardiovascular System
227 The Hematologic System
243 The Respiratory System
262 The Gastrointestinal System
290 The Genitourinary System
306 The Musculoskeletal System
321 The Endocrine System
340 The Integumentary System

---

*Also contributed selected charts and nursing interventions to Unit 2.

Multisystem Stressors

STRESS AND ADAPTATION

Definitions

A. Stress: tension resulting from changes in the internal or external environment; either physiologic, psychologic, or social
B. Stressors: agents or forces threatening an individual's ability to meet his or her needs
C. Adaptation: an individual's (or the body's) reaction to and attempt to deal with stress

General Characteristics

A. A certain amount of stress is necessary for life and growth, but excessive and continuous stress can be detrimental.
B. Success of adaptation depends on perception of stressor(s), the individual's coping mechanisms, and biologic adaptive resources.
C. Types of stressors: physical, chemical, microbiologic, psychologic, social.

General Adaptation Syndrome (Hans Selye)

Response to Stress

A. Caused by release of certain adaptive hormones
B. Three Stages
   1. Alarm Reaction
      a. Sympathetic nervous system is activated (fight-or-flight response)
      b. Results in increased heart rate, blood pressure, and respirations; dilated pupils; increased state of alertness; increased blood sugar and coagulability; increased tension of skeletal muscles
   2. Resistance: body adapts to stressor; uses physical, physiologic, and psychologic coping mechanisms.
   3. Exhaustion: adaptive resources are depleted, overwhelmed, or insufficient; if stress is excessive and continues, death will occur without support.

Stress Management/Nursing Responsibilities

A. Instruct the client concerning ways to manage stress
   1. Eat a well-balanced diet.
   2. Get sufficient amount of rest.
   3. Exercise regularly.
   4. Use relaxation methods and techniques: e.g., deep breathing, guided imagery, progressive muscle relaxation, relaxation response, meditation, yoga, biofeedback.
   5. Engage in a social support system.

INFLAMMATORY RESPONSE

A reaction of the tissues of the body to injury in order to destroy or dilute an injurious agent, to prevent the spread of injury, and to promote repair of damaged tissue.

Causes

A. Physical irritants (e.g., trauma or a foreign body)
B. Chemical irritants (e.g., strong acids or alkalis)
C. Microorganisms (e.g., bacteria and viruses)

Components

A. Vascular response: transitory period of localized vasoconstriction, followed by vasodilatation, increased capillary permeability, and blood stasis
B. Formation of inflammatory exudate
   1. Composition: water, colloids, ions, and defensive cells
   2. Functions: dilution of toxins, transportation of nutrients to area of injury for tissue repair, transportation of protective cells that phagocytize and destroy bacteria
C. Defense cell response: migration of leukocytes to affected area for phagocytosis of foreign bodies and dead cells
D. Healing: resolution of inflammation and regeneration of tissue or replacement with scar tissue

Assessment Findings

A. Local: pain, swelling, heat, redness, and impaired function of part (five cardinal signs of inflammation)
B. Systemic (appear with moderate to severe response): fever, leukocytosis, chills, sweating, anorexia, weight loss, general malaise

IMMUNE RESPONSE

Essence of immune response is to recognize foreign substances and to neutralize, eliminate, or metabolize them with or without injury to the body's own tissues.

Functions of the Immune System

A. Defense: protection against antigens. An *antigen* is a protein or protein complex recognized as nonself.
B. Homeostasis: removal of worn out or damaged components (e.g., dead cells)
C. Surveillance: ability to perceive or destroy mutated cells or nonself cells.

Alterations in Immune Functioning

See Table 4.1.

Types of Immunity

There are two major types of immunity: natural (or innate) and acquired.
A. *Natural (innate) immunity:* immune responses that exist without prior exposure to an immunologically active substance. Genetically acquired immunity is natural immunity.
B. *Acquired immunity*
  1. Immune responses that develop during the course of a person's lifetime.
  2. Acquired immunity may be further classified as naturally or artificially acquired, active or passive. Active immunity results when the body produces its own antibodies in response to an

antigen. Passive immunity results when an antibody is transferred artificially.
  a. *Naturally acquired active immunity:* results from having the disease and recovering successfully
  b. *Naturally acquired passive immunity:* antibodies obtained through placenta or breast milk
  c. *Artificially acquired active immunity:* conferred by immunization with an antigen
  d. *Artificially acquired passive immunity:* antibodies transferred from sensitized person (e.g., immune serum globulin [gamma globulin])

Components of Immune Response

A. Located throughout the body
B. Organs include thymus, bone marrow, lymph nodes, spleen, tonsils, appendix, Peyer's patches of small intestine.
C. Main cell types are WBCs (especially lymphocytes, plasma cells, and macrophages); all originate from the same stem cell in bone marrow, then differentiate into separate types.
  1. Granulocytes
    a. Eosinophils: increase with allergies and parasites
    b. Basophils: contain histamine and increase with allergy and anaphylaxis
    c. Neutrophils: involved in phago-cytosis
  2. Monocytes (macrophages) (e.g., histiocytes, Kupffer cells): involved in phagocytosis
  3. Lymphocytes (T cells and B cells): involved in cellular and humoral immunity

Classification of Immune Responses

Cellular Immunity

A. Mediated by T cells: persist in tissues for months or years
B. Functions: transplant rejection, delayed hypersensitivity, tuberculin reactions, tumor surveillance/destruction, intracellular infections

Humoral Immunity

A. Mediated by B cells
  1. Production of circulating antibodies (gamma globulin)
  2. Only survive for days
B. Functions: bacterial phagocytosis, bacterial lysis, virus and toxin neutralization, anaphylaxis, allergic hay fever and asthma

TABLE 4.1 Alterations in Immune Functioning

Immune Function	Hypofunction	Hyperfunction
Defense	Immunosuppression with increased susceptibility to infection; includes disorders such as neutropenia, AIDS, immunosuppression secondary to drugs and hypo- or agammaglobulinemia.	Inappropriate and abnormal response to external antigens; an allergy
Homeostasis	No known effect	Abnormal response where antibodies react against normal tissues and cells; an *autoimmune disease.*
Surveillance	Inability of the immune system to perceive and respond to mutated cells, suspected mechanism in cancer.	No known effect

NUTRITION*

Basic Concepts

Principles

A. Essential nutrients: carbohydrates, fats, proteins, minerals, vitamins, and water that must be supplied to the body in specified amounts.
B. Foods: the sources of nutrients, provide energy to help build, repair, and maintain tissue and regulate body processes.
C. Malnutrition: results from deficiency, excess, or imbalance of required nutrients.

Carbohydrates (Sugars and Starches)

A. Major source of food energy; 4 kcal/g; composed of carbon, hydrogen, and oxygen
B. Classification
   1. Monosaccharides: simplest form of carbohydrate
      a. Glucose (dextrose): found chiefly in fruits and vegetables; oxidized for immediate energy
      b. Fructose: found in honey and fruits
      c. Galactose: not free in nature; part of milk sugar
   2. Disaccharides: double sugars
      a. Sucrose: found in table sugar, syrups, and some fruits and vegetables
      b. Lactose: found in milk
      c. Maltose: intermediate product in the hydrolysis of starch
   3. Polysaccharides: composed of many glucose molecules
      a. Starch: found in cereal grains, potatoes, root vegetables, and legumes
      b. Glycogen: synthesized and stored in the liver and skeletal muscles
      c. Cellulose, hemicellulose, pectins, gums, and mucilages: indigestible polysaccharides
   4. Dietary fiber: includes several polysaccharides plus other substances that are not digestible by GI enzymes.
      a. Dietary fiber (roughage) holds water so that stools are soft and bulky; increases motility of the small and large intestine and decreases transit time; reduces intraluminal pressure in the colon.
      b. Sources: wheat bran, unrefined cereals, whole wheat, raw fruits and vegetables, dried fruits
C. Functions of carbohydrates
   1. Cheapest and most abundant source of energy; only source of energy for central nervous system
   2. To spare protein for tissue building when sufficient carbohydrate is present
   3. Necessary for the complete oxidation of fats (to prevent ketosis)
D. Dietary sources: grains, fruits, vegetables, nuts, milk, sugars ("empty calories," contain few nutrients)

Lipids (Fats)

A. Most concentrated source of energy in foods; 9 kcal/g; contain carbon, hydrogen, oxygen
B. Include fats, oils, resins, waxes, and fatlike substances such as glycerides, phospholipids, sterols, and lipoproteins
C. Fatty acids
   1. Saturated fatty acids: usually solid at room temperature; predominantly present in animal fats
   2. Monounsaturated fatty acids: present in oleic acid found in olive oil, peanut oil
   3. Polyunsaturated fatty acids: usually liquid at room temperature; predominantly present in plant fats and fish
   4. Essential fatty acids: cannot be manufactured by the body (e.g., linoleic fatty acid)
   5. Nonessential fatty acids: can be synthesized by the body
D. Functions of lipids
   1. Most concentrated source of energy
   2. Insulation and padding of body organs
   3. Component of the cell membrane
   4. Carrier of the fat-soluble vitamins A, D, E, K
   5. Help maintain body temperature
E. Dietary sources: oil from seeds of grains, nuts, vegetables; milk fat, butter, cream cheese; fat in meat; lard, bacon fat; fish oil; egg yolk
F. *Cholesterol*: essential constituent of body tissues
   1. A component of cell membranes
   2. A precursor of steroid hormones
   3. Can be manufactured in the body
   4. Present in animal fats
   5. Dietary sources: egg yolk, brains, liver, butter, cream, cheese, shellfish
G. Indications for low fat diet (see Appendix for fat-restricted diet)
   1. Cardiovascular disease
   2. Gallbladder disease
   3. Malabsorption syndromes, cystic fibrosis, pancreatitis

Proteins

A. Organic compounds that may be composed of hundreds of amino acids; 4 kcal/g; contain

---

*The section on nutrition was contributed by Theresa Giglio, RD, MS, and revised by Judith C. Miller, RN, MSN.

nitrogen in addition to carbon, hydrogen, and oxygen

B. Classification
   1. Complete protein: contains all the essential amino acids; usually from animal food sources.
   2. Incomplete protein: lacks one or more essential amino acids; usually from plant food sources

C. Amino acids
   1. Essential amino acids: eight amino acids that cannot be synthesized in the body and must be taken in food.
   2. Nonessential amino acids: 12 amino acids that can be synthesized in the body.

D. Functions of proteins
   1. Necessary for growth and continuous replacement of cells throughout life
   2. Play a role in the immune processes
   3. Participate in regulating body processes such as fluid balance, muscle contraction, mineral balance, iron transport, buffer actions
   4. Provide energy if necessary

E. Dietary sources: meat, fish, eggs, milk, cheese, poultry, grains, nuts, legumes (soybeans, lentils, peanuts, peanut butter)

F. Deficiencies
   1. Conditions
      a. Kwashiorkor
      b. Hypoproteinemia
      c. Marasmus (protein-kilocalorie malnutrition)
   2. Manifestations
      a. Generalized weakness
      b. Weight loss
      c. Lowered resistance to infection
      d. Slow wound healing and prolonged recovery from illness
      e. Growth failure
      f. Brain damage to fetus or infant
      g. Edema due to decreased albumin in blood
      h. Anemia in severe deficiency
      i. Fatty infiltration of liver and liver damage
   3. Risk factors
      a. Chronically ill
      b. Elderly on fixed incomes
      c. Low-income families
      d. Strict vegetarians

G. Indications for high-protein diet
   1. Burns, massive wounds when tissue building desired
   2. Mild to moderate liver disease for organ repair when liver is still functioning
   3. Malabsorption syndromes such as cystic fibrosis
   4. Undernutrition
   5. Pregnancy to meet needs of mother and developing fetus

   6. Pregnancy-induced hypertension to replace protein lost in urine
   7. Nephrosis to replace protein lost in urine
   8. Deficiencies

H. Indications for low-protein diet
   1. Liver failure (liver does not metabolize protein causing nitrogen toxicity to brain)
   2. Kidney failure (kidneys can no longer excrete nitrogenous waste products causing toxic nitrogen levels in the brain)

I. Nursing interventions for clients needing low-protein diet
   1. Increase carbohydrates so energy needs will be met by carbohydrates, not by breakdown of proteins
   2. Protein intake that is allowed will be complete proteins (animal sources)

Energy Metabolism

A. Measurement of energy expressed in terms of heat units called kilocalories (kcal): amount of heat required to raise 1 kg water by 1°C

B. Energy expenditure
   1. Basal metabolism
      a. Amount of energy expended to carry on the involuntary work of the body while at rest
      b. Factors influencing basal metabolic rate (BMR): body surface area, sex, age, body temperature, hormones, pregnancy, fasting, malnutrition
   2. Physical activity: amount of energy expended depends upon the type of activity, the length of time involved, and the weight of the person

C. Factors determining total energy needs
   1. Amount necessary for BMR
   2. Amount required for physical activity
   3. Specific dynamic action of food ingested
   4. Growth
   5. Climate

Minerals

Inorganic compounds that yield no energy; essential structural components involved in many body processes (see Table 4.2).

Vitamins

Organic compounds necessary in small quantities for cellular functions of the body; do not give energy; necessary in many enzyme systems (see Table 4.3).

A. Fat-soluble vitamins (A, D, E, K): can be stored in body; toxic in large amounts.

B. Water-soluble vitamins (B_1 [thiamin]; B_2 [riboflavin]; B_6 [pyridoxine]; B_{12} [hydroxycobalamin]; C [ascorbic acid]; folacin; niacin): cannot be stored in body so must be

TABLE 4.2   Minerals

Mineral	Functions	Deficiency Syndrome	Food Sources	Comments
Calcium	Development of bones and teeth Transmission of nerve impulses Muscle contraction Permeability of cell membrane Catalyze thrombin formation Maintenance of normal heart rhythm	Rickets, osteoporosis, osteomalacia, stunted growth, fragile bones, tetany, occurs when parathyroids removed	Milk, cheese, ice cream, broccoli, collard greens, kale, oysters, shrimp, salmon, clams, sardines	Needs vitamin D and parathormone for utilization. Acid, lactose, and vitamin D favor absorption.
Phosphorus	Development of bones and teeth Transfer of energy in cells (ATP) Cell permeability Buffer salts Component in phospholipids	Rickets, stunted growth, poor bone mineralization	Milk, cheese, meat, fish, poultry, eggs, legumes, nuts, whole-grain cereals	Factors that affect calcium absorption also affect phosphorus. Inverse relationship to calcium.
Magnesium	Constituent of bones and teeth Cation in intracellular fluid Muscle and nerve irritability Activate enzymes in carbohydrate metabolism	Tremor observed in severe alcoholism, diabetic acidosis, severe renal disease	Milk, cheese, meat, nuts, legumes, green leafy vegetables, whole-grain cereals	Absorption similar to calcium.
Sulfur	Constituent of keratin in hair, skin, and nails Detoxification reactions Constituent of thiamin, biotin, insulin, coenzyme A, melanin, glutathione	None	Protein foods, eggs, meat, fish, poultry, milk, cheese, nuts	Diet adequate in protein provides sufficient sulfur.
Iron	Constituent of hemoglobin, myoglobin, oxidative enzymes	Anemia	Liver, organ meats, meat, poultry, egg yolk, whole-grain cereals, legumes, dark green vegetables, dried fruit	Ascorbic acid enhances absorption.
Iodine	Constituent of thyroxine Regulate rate of energy metabolism	Simple goiter, creatinism, myxedema	Iodized salt, seafood	Allergies to iodine-rich foods may indicate allergy to iodine dyes used in diagnostic tests.
Sodium	Principle cation of extracellular fluid Osmotic pressure Water balance Regulate nerve irritability and muscle contraction Pump for active transport of glucose	Rare, seen in persons with Addison's disease.	Table salt, protein foods, processed foods, baking soda	Diet usually provides excess. Increase in clients with cystic fibrosis and persons taking lithium. Decrease intake in clients with hypertension, congestive heart failure, renal failure, and edema.
Potassium	Principle cation of extracellular fluid Osmotic pressure Water balance Acid-base balance Regular heart rhythm Nerve irritability and muscle contraction	Muscle weakness, arrhythmias Deficiency may occur with diabetic acidosis Deficiency may occur with thiazide and loop diuretics.	Oranges, bananas, dried fruits, melons, apricots, most fruits and vegetables, whole-grain cereals	Readily absorbed. Increase intake in clients taking thiazide and loop diuretics. Decrease intake for clients in renal failure.
Chlorine	Chief anion of extracellular fluid Constituent of gastric juice Acid-base balance Activate salivary amylase	Seen only after prolonged vomiting	Table salt, processed meats	Rapidly absorbed.

TABLE 4.3 Vitamins

Vitamin	Function	Deficiency Syndrome	Food Sources	Comments
Fat Soluble				
Vitamin A (retinol)	Maintenance of mucous membranes Visual acuity in dim light, growth and bone development	Night blindness, xerophthalmia, keratinization of epithelium, poor bone and tooth development	Fish liver oils, liver, butter, cream, whole milk, egg yolk, dark green vegetables, yellow vegetables, yellow fruits, fortified margarine	Bile necessary for absorption. Large amounts are toxic.
Vitamin D (cholecalciferol)	Increase absorption of calcium and phosphorus Bone mineralization	Rickets, osteomalacia, enlarged joints, muscle spasms, delayed dentition	Fish liver oils, fortified milk	Synthesized in skin by activity of ultraviolet light. Large amounts are toxic.
Vitamin E (tocopherol)	Reduces oxidation of vitamin A, phospholipids, and polyunsaturated fatty acids	Hemolysis of red blood cells, deficiency not likely	Vegetable oils, wheat germ, nuts, legumes, green leafy vegetables	Not toxic.
Vitamin K (phylloquinone)	Formation of prothrombin and other clotting proteins	Prolonged clotting time, hemorrhagic disease in newborn and liver disease	Green leafy vegetables, cabbage, liver, alfalfa	Bile necessary for absorption; injectable form may be given in gallbladder and liver disease. Large amounts are toxic.
Water Soluble				
Vitamin B_1 (thiamine)	Involved in carbohydrate metabolism Thiamine pyrophosphate (TPP)	Beriberi, mental depression, polyneuritis, cardiac failure	Enriched cereals, whole grains, meat, organ meats, pork, fish, poultry, legumes, nuts	Very little storage.
Vitamin B_2 (riboflavin)	Coenzyme for transfer and removal of hydrogen Flavin adenine dinucleotide (FAD)	Cheilosis, photophobia, burning and itching of eyes, sore tongue and mouth	Milk, eggs, organ meats, green leafy vegetables	Limited storage.
Vitamin B_6 (pyridoxine, pyridoxal, pyridoxamine)	Coenzyme for transamination, transsulfuration, and decarboxylation	Convulsions, dermatitis, nervous irritability	Meat, poultry, fish, vegetables, potatoes	Converts glycogen to glucose. Given with isoniazid (INH) to prevent INH side effect of peripheral neuropathy
Vitamin B_{12} (hydroxycobalamin)	Formation of mature red blood cells Synthesis of DNA and RNA	Pernicious anemia, neurologic degeneration, macrocytic anemia	Animal foods only	Intrinsic factor is necessary for absorption.
Vitamin C (ascorbic acid)	Synthesis of collagen Formation of intercellular cement Facilitation of iron absorption	Scurvy, bleeding gums, poor wound healing, cutaneous hemorrhage, capillary fragility	Citrus fruits, tomatoes, melon, raw cabbage, broccoli, strawberries	Most easily destroyed vitamin. Very little storage in body.
Folacin (folic acid)	Maturation of red blood cells, interrelated with vitamin B_{12}	Megaloblastic anemia, tropical sprue	Organ meats, muscle meats, poultry, fish, eggs, green leafy vegetables	Ascorbic acid necessary for utilization.
Niacin (nicotinamide)	Coenzyme to accept and transfer hydrogen, coenzyme for glycolysis	Pellagra, dermatitis, neurologic degeneration, glossitis, diarrhea	Meat, poultry, fish, whole grains, enriched breads, nuts, legumes	Amino acid tryptophan is a precursor.

ingested daily; dissolve in cooking water, toxicity unlikely.

Water

A. Distribution: present in all body tissues; accounts for 50%–60% total body weight in adults and 70%–75% in infants.
   1. Intracellular fluid: exists within the cells.
   2. Extracellular fluid: includes plasma fluid, interstitial fluid, lymph, and secretions.
B. Functions: the medium of all body fluids
   1. Necessary for many biologic reactions
   2. Acts as a solvent.
   3. Transports nutrients to cells and eliminates waste.
   4. Body lubricant.
   5. Regulates body temperature.
C. Sources
   1. Ingestion of water and other beverages
   2. Water content of food eaten
   3. Water resulting from food oxidation
D. Recommended daily intake
   1. Replacement of losses through the kidneys, lungs, skin, and bowel
   2. Thirst usually a good guide
   3. Approximately 48 oz/day of water from all sources is adequate; requirement is higher if physical activity is strenuous or if sweating is profuse.

Dietary Guides

A. Food Pyramid
   1. New recommendations replace four food groups.
   2. Foods are grouped by composition and nutrient value: grains; vegetable group; fruit group; meat, poultry, fish, dry beans, eggs and nut group; and milk, yogurt and cheese group.
   3. Greater emphasis on fruits and vegetables with less emphasis on meats and fats than with basic four.
   4. Recommends using fats and sweets sparingly (see Special Diets, Appendix).
B. Recommended daily allowances: established by the Food and Nutrition Board of the National Academy of Science; recommended nutrient intake is provided for infants, children, men, women, pregnant and lactating women; recommendations are stated for protein, kcal, and most vitamins and minerals.
C. Food composition tables: helpful in calculating the nutritive value of the daily diet; list nutrient content of foods.
D. Height and weight charts: ideal or desirable body weight for both men and women at specified heights with a small, medium, or large frame.
E. Exchange lists for meal planning
   1. Foods are separated into six exchange lists.

2. Specific foods on each list are approximately equal in carbohydrate, protein, fat, and kcal content.
3. Individual foods on the same list may be exchanged for each other at the same meals.
4. Food lists are helpful in planning diets for weight control or diabetes (see Special Diets, Appendix).

Nutritional Assessment

Health History

A. Presenting problem
   1. Weight changes
      a. Usual body weight 20% above or below normal standards.
      b. Recent loss or gain of 10% of usual body weight.
   2. Appetite changes: may be increase or decrease from usual.
   3. Food intolerances: allergies, fluids, fat, salt, seafood
   4. Difficulty swallowing
   5. Dyspepsia or indigestion
   6. Bowel dysfunction: record frequency, consistency, color of stools.
      a. Constipation
      b. Diarrhea
B. Lifestyle: eating behaviors such as fast foods, "junk foods," and skipping meals; cultural/religious concerns (vegetarian, kosher foods, exclusion of certain food groups); alcohol, socioeconomic status, living conditions (alone or with family).
C. Use of medications: vitamin supplements, antacids, antidiarrheals, laxatives, diuretics, antihypertensives, immunosuppressants, oral contraceptives, antibiotics, antidepressants, digitalis, anti-inflammatory agents, catabolic steroids.
D. Medical history: gastrointestinal diseases; endocrine diseases; hyperlipidemia; coronary artery disease; malabsorption syndrome; circulatory problems or heart failure; cancer; radiation therapy; chronic lung, renal, or liver disease; food allergies; recent major surgery; eating disorders; obesity.
E. Family history: obesity, allergies, cardio-vascular diseases, diabetes, thyroid disease.
F. Dietary history: Evaluation of the nutritional adequacy of diet
   1. 24-hour recall
   2. Food diary for a given number of days

Physical Examination

A. Assess for alertness and responsiveness
B. Record weight in relation to height, body build, and age
C. Inspect posture, muscle tone, skeleton for deformities

D. Elicit reflexes
E. Auscultate heart rate, rhythm; blood pressure
F. Inspect hair, skin, nails, oral mucosa, tongue, teeth
G. Inspect for swelling of legs or feet
H. Anthropometric measurements: indicators of available stores in muscle and fat compartments of body
   1. Height/weight ratio
   2. Midarm muscle circumference
   3. Skinfold thickness (triceps, biceps, subscapular, abdominal, hip, pectoral, or calf)

Laboratory/Diagnostic Tests

A. Blood studies: serum albumin, iron-binding capacity, hemoglobin, hematocrit, lymphocyte count, blood sugar, total cholesterol, high-density lipids, low-density lipids, triglycerides, serum electrolytes
B. Urine studies, urinalysis, glucose, ketones, albumin, 24-hour creatinine
C. Nitrogen balance studies
D. Feces, hair
E. Intradermal delayed hypersensitivity testing

Analysis

Nursing diagnoses for the client with a nutritional dysfunction may include:
A. Alteration in nutrition: less than body requirements
B. Alteration in nutrition: more than body requirements
C. Alteration in nutrition: high risk for more than body requirements
D. Altered oral mucous membrane
E. Self-care deficit, feeding
F. Sensory/perceptual alterations: gustatory, olfactory
G. Actual or high risk for impairment of skin integrity
H. Impaired swallowing
I. Impaired tissue integrity
J. Activity intolerance
K. Body image disturbance
L. Constipation
M. Diarrhea
N. Fluid volume deficit
O. Fluid volume excess
P. Altered growth and development
Q. High risk for infection
R. Knowledge deficit
S. Noncompliance

Planning and Implementation

Goals

A. Normal weight will be achieved and maintained.
B. Integrity of oral cavity will be maintained.
C. Client will feed self or receive help with feeding.
D. Normal skin integrity will be achieved/maintained.
E. Client will not aspirate.
F. Normal tissue integrity will be achieved/maintained.
G. Client will be able to exercise normally.
H. Client will maintain/develop satisfactory self-image.
I. Normal bowel functioning will be maintained.
J. Fluid and electrolyte balance will be achieved/maintained.
K. Client will have normal growth and development patterns.
L. Client will not develop infection.
M. Client will demonstrate knowledge of special dietary needs/prescriptions.
N. Client will comply with special diet.

Interventions

Care of the Client on a Special Diet

A. General information: therapeutic diets involve modifications of nutritional components necessitated by a client's disease state or nutritional status or to prepare a client for a procedure.
B. Nursing care in relation to special diets
   1. Assess client's mental, emotional, physical, and economic status; appropriateness of diet to client's condition; and ability to understand diet and comply with it.
   2. Maintain appropriate diet and teach client.
   3. Changing diet means changing lifelong patterns.
   4. Teach client importance of adhering to special diets that are long term.

Weight Control Diets

A. Underweight: 10% or more below individual's ideal weight
   1. Causes: failure to ingest enough kcal, excess energy expenditure, irregular eating habits, GI disturbances, mouth sores, cancer, endocrine disorders, emotional disturbances, lack of education, economic problems.
   2. Treatment: diet counseling, correction of underlying disease, nutritional supplements, behavioral therapy, social service referral.
B. Overweight: 10% or more above individual's ideal weight
C. Obesity: 20% or more above individual's ideal weight
   1. Causes: overeating, underactivity, genetic factors, fat cell theory, alteration in

hypothalamic function, endocrine disorders, emotional disturbances.
2. Treatment: diet counseling, nutritionally balanced diet, behavior modification, increased physical activity, medical treatment of any underlying disease, appropriate referrals.
D. Nursing care
1. Explain dietary instructions (see Appendix: Special Diets, 1500-Kilocalorie Diet).
   a. Reducing fats and "empty calories" reduces caloric intake without sacrificing nutritional intake
   b. Increasing exercise increases metabolism
2. Caution against fad diets that may be nutritionally inadequate.
3. Encourage support groups if indicated.

Diabetic Diet

A. Prescribed for clients with diabetes mellitus.
B. Purposes include: attain or maintain ideal body weight, ensure normal growth, maintain plasma glucose levels as close to normal as possible.
C. Principles
1. Distribution of kcal: protein 12–20%; carbohydrates 55–60%; fats (unsaturated) 20–25%.
2. Daily distribution of kcal: equally divided among breakfast, lunch, supper, snacks.
3. Use foods high in fiber and complex carbohydrates.
4. Avoid simple sugars, jams, honey, syrup, frosting.
D. Teach client to utilize exchange lists (see Appendix: Special Diets, Exchange Lists for Meal Planning).
E. New recommendations include low fat, high fiber diet.

Protein-modified Diets

A. Gluten-free diet
1. Purpose is to eliminate gluten (a protein) from the diet.
2. Indicated in malabsorption syndromes such as sprue and celiac disease.
3. Eliminate all barley, rye, oats, and wheat (BROW).
4. Avoid: cream sauces, breaded foods, cakes, breads, muffins.
5. Allow corn, rice, and soy flour.
6. Teach client to read labels of prepared foods.
B. PKU (Phenylketonuria) diet
1. Purpose is to control intake of phenylalanine, an amino acid that cannot be metabolized.

2. Diet will be prescribed until at least age 6 to prevent brain damage and mental retardation.
3. Avoid: breads, meat, fish, poultry, cheeses, legumes, nuts, eggs.
4. Give Lofenalac formula.
5. Teach family to use low-protein flour for baking.
6. Sugar substitutes such as Nutrasweet contain phenylalanine and must not be used.
C. Low-purine diet
1. Indicated for gout, uric acid kidney stones, and uric acid retention.
2. Purpose is to decrease the amount of purine, a precursor to uric acid.
3. Teach client to avoid: organ meats, other meats, fowl, fish and lobster, lentils, dried peas and beans, nuts, oatmeal, whole wheat.
4. Eggs are not high in purine.

Fat-restricted Diets (See Appendix: Special Diets, 20-Gram Fat-restricted Diet and Fat-controlled Diet)

Purpose is to restrict amount of fats ingested for clients with chronic pancreatitis, malabsorption syndromes, gallbladder disease, cystic fibrosis, and hyperlipidemia, and to control weight.

Consistency Modifications

A. Clear liquid diet
1. Purpose is to rest GI tract and maintain fluid balance.
2. Indications include difficulty chewing or swallowing; before certain diagnostic tests to reduce fecal material; immediate postoperative period (until bowel sounds have returned) to maintain electrolyte balance; and nausea, vomiting, and diarrhea.
3. Foods allowed: "see-through foods" include water, tea, broth, jello, apple juice, clear carbonated beverages, and frozen ice pops.
4. Not nutritionally adequate.
B. Full liquid diet
1. Used as a transition diet between clear liquid and soft diet; usually short term.
2. Foods allowed: clear liquids, milk and milk products, all fruit juices, cooked and strained cereals.
3. Can be nutritionally adequate.
C. Soft diet
1. Used as a transition diet between full liquid and regular diet.
2. Indications include postoperatively, mild GI disturbances, chewing difficulties from lack of teeth or oral surgery.

3. Foods allowed: foods low in fiber, connective tissue and fat (full liquid diet, pureed vegetables, eggs cooked any way except fried, tender meat, potatoes, cooked fruit).
4. Nutritionally adequate.
D. Bland diet (see Appendix: Special Diets, Bland Diet)
   1. Promotes healing of the gastric mucosa and is chemically and mechanically nonstimulating.
   2. Foods allowed: soft diet without spices.
E. Low-residue diet (see Appendix: Special Diets, Low-residue Diet)
   1. Residue is the indigestible substances left in digestive tract after food has been digested.
   2. Indications include colon, rectal, or perineal surgery to reduce pressure on the operative site; prior to examination of the lower bowel to enhance visualization; internal radiation for cancer of the cervix; Crohn's disease or regional enteritis; ulcerative colitis to reduce irritation of the large bowel; and diarrhea.
   3. Teach client to avoid foods high in fiber, foods having skins and seeds, and milk and milk products.

Evaluation

A. Client's weight is within normal limits.
B. No lesions in oral cavity.
C. Client feeds self or receives needed assistance with feeding.
D. Skin and tissue integrity is maintained.
E. Client demonstrates ability to exercise.
F. Client makes positive statements about self-image.
G. Client's bowel functioning is normal.
H. Serum electrolytes are within normal limits.
I. Client will exhibit growth and development patterns appropriate for age.
J. Client shows no evidence of infection.
K. Client states reason for special diet.
L. Client describes foods allowed and not allowed on prescribed diet.
M. Client adheres to prescribed diet.

Enteral Nutrition

Preferred method for nutritional support for the malnourished client whose GI system is intact.

Oral Feeding

A. Always the first choice
B. Oral formula supplements may be used between meals to provide added kcal and nutrients.
   1. Offer small quantities several times a day.

2. Vary flavors, avoid taste fatigue.
3. Chill and serve over ice.

Tube Feeding

A. Used for clients who have a functioning GI tract but cannot ingest food orally
   1. Feeding tubes
      a. Short term: nasogastric tube
      b. Long term: esophagostomy, gastrostomy, or enterostomy tube
   2. Formulas: nutritionally adequate, tolerated by client, easily prepared, easily digested, usual concentration 1 kcal/ml
   3. Feeding schedules
      a. Intermittent: usually 4–6 times/day, volumes up to 400 ml, by slow gravity drip over 30–60 minutes
      b. Continuous: usually administered by pump through a duodenal or proximal jejunostomy feeding tube
   4. Nursing responsibilities
      a. Administer formulas at room temperature (refrigerate unused portion).
      b. Gradually increase rate and concentration until desired amount is attained if there are no signs of intolerance (e.g., gastric residual greater than 120 ml, nausea, vomiting, diarrhea, distention, diaphoresis, increased pulse, glycosuria, aspiration).
      c. Check tube placement and elevate head of bed (see also Nasogastric Tubes, page 000).
      d. Monitor I&O, serum electrolytes, fractional urines, serum glucose, daily weights; keep a stool record as well as an ongoing assessment of tolerance.

Parenteral Nutrition

Nutrients are infused directly into a vein for clients who are unable to eat or digest food through the GI tract, who refuse to eat, or who have inadequate oral intake.

Total Parenteral Nutrition (TPN)

A. Involves the infusion of nutrients through a central vein catheter. A central vein is needed because its larger caliber and higher blood flow will quickly dilute the hypertonic hyperalimentation solution to isotonic concentrations.
B. Hyperalimentation solutions
   1. Hypertonic glucose of 20%–70%, amino acids, water, vitamins, and minerals with lipid emulsions given in a separate solution.
   2. Three-in-one solutions

a. Lipids mixed with dextrose and amino acids in pharmacy.
b. Comes in a three liter container and administered over 24 hours.

C. Nursing responsibilities
1. For details of nursing care of the client with a central venous line, see IV Therapy, page 147.
2. Inspect solution before hanging.
   a. Check for correct solution and additives against physician's order.
   b. Check expiration date.
   c. Observe fluid for cloudiness or floating particulate matter.
3. Control flow rate of solution.
   a. Calculate correct rate.
   b. Administration via pump is preferable.
   c. Monitor flow rate.
   d. Never attempt to speed up or slow down infusion rate.
      1) speeding up infusion causes large amounts of glucose to enter body, causing hyperosmolar state.
      2) slowing down infusion can cause hypoglycemic state, as it takes time for the pancreas to adjust to reduced glucose level.
4. Monitor fluid balance.
5. Obtain fractional urines or Accu-checks every 6 hours.
6. Use Testape to detect hyperglycemia (some additives may cause false positive if Clinitest is used); cover with sliding scale insulin as ordered.
7. Provide psychologic support.
8. Encourage exercise regimen.

IV Lipid Emulsions

A. May be given through a central vein or peripherally in order to prevent essential fatty acid deficiency in long-term TPN clients, or to provide supplemental kcal IV.
B. Nursing care
1. Protect the stability of the emulsion.
   a. Administer in its own separate IV bottle and IV tubing, and piggyback the emulsion into the Y connector closest to the catheter insertion. Follow hospital policy and manufacturer's recommendations for specific products.
   b. Inspect solution for evidence of separation of oil, frothiness, inconsistency, particulate matter; discard solution if any of these signs of instability occur.
   c. Do not shake the bottle; this might cause aggregation of fat globules.
   d. Discard partially used bottles.
2. Control the infusion rate accurately and safely.
   a. If using gravity method, lipid emulsion must hang higher than hyperalimentation to prevent back flow.
   b. Pump is preferred but may not be possible due to viscous nature of emulsion.
3. Prevent and assess for adverse reactions.
   a. Administer slowly according to package insert over first 30 minutes; if no adverse reactions, increase rate to complete infusion over the specified number of hours.
   b. Obtain baseline vital signs; repeat after first 30 minutes, and then every 1–2 hours until completion.
   c. Acute reactions may include: fever, chills, dyspnea, nausea, vomiting, headache, lethargy, syncope, chest or back pain, hypercoagulability, thrombocytopenia.
4. Evaluate tolerance and patient response.

Peripheral Vein Parenteral Nutrition (PPN)

A. Can be used for short-term support, when the central vein is not available, and as a supplemental means of obtaining nutrients. Client must be able to tolerate a relatively high fluid volume.
B. Solution contains the same components as central vein therapy, but lower concentrations (less than 20% glucose).
C. Care is the same as for the client receiving hyperalimentation centrally.
D. Phlebitis and thrombosis are common and IV sites will need frequent changing.

INFECTION

Infection is an invasion of the body by pathogenic organisms that multiply and produce injurious effects. Communicable disease is an infectious disease that may be transmitted from one person to another.

Chain of Events

A. *Causative agent:* invading organism (e.g., bacteria, virus)
B. *Reservoir:* environment in which the invading organism lives and multiplies
C. *Portal of exit:* mode of escape from reservoir (e.g., respiratory tract, GI tract)
D. *Mode of transmission:* method by which invading organism is transported to new host (e.g., direct contact, air, food)
E. *Portal of entry:* means by which organism enters new host (e.g., respiratory tract, broken skin)

F. *Susceptible host:* susceptibility determined by factors such as number of invading organisms, duration of exposure, age, state of health, nutritional status.

Nursing Responsibilities in Prevention of Spread of Infection

A. Maintain an environment that is clean, dry, and well ventilated.
B. Use proper handwashing before and after client contact and after contact with contaminated material.
C. Disinfect and handle wastes and contaminated materials properly.
D. Prevent transmission of infectious droplets.
   1. Teach clients to cover mouth and nose when sneezing or coughing.
   2. Place contaminated tissues and articles in paper bag before disposing.
E. Institute proper isolation techniques as required by specific disease
F. Use surgical aseptic technique when appropriate: caring for open wounds, irrigating, or entering sterile cavities.
G. Practice universal precautions when caring for all clients regardless of their diagnosis in order to minimize contact with blood and body fluids and prevent the transmission of specific infections such as hepatitis B and human immunodeficiency virus (HIV).
   1. Hands must always be washed before and after contact with clients even when gloves have been used.
   2. If hands come in contact with blood, body fluids, or human tissue they should be immediately washed with soap and water.
   3. Gloves should be worn before touching blood or body fluids, mucous membranes, or nonintact skin.
   4. Gloves should be changed between each client contact and as soon as possible if torn.
   5. Wear masks and protective eyewear during procedures that are likely to generate splashes of blood or other body fluids.
   6. Wear gowns during procedures that are likely to generate splashes of blood or other body fluids and when cleaning spills from incontinent clients or changing soiled linen.
   7. Disposable masks should be used when performing CPR.
   8. Dispose of used needles properly. They should be promptly placed in a puncture-resistant container. They *should not* be recapped, bent, broken, or removed from syringes.

PAIN

Pain is an unpleasant sensation, entirely subjective, that produces discomfort, distress, or suffering.

Gate Control Theory

A. Substantia gelatinosa in the dorsal horn of the spinal cord acts as a gate mechanism that can close to keep pain impulses from reaching the brain, or can open to allow pain impulses to ascend to the brain.
B. Most pain impulses are conducted over small-diameter nerve fibers; if predominant nerve message is pain, the gate opens and allows pain impulses to reach the brain.
C. The gate can be closed by conflicting impulses from the skin conducted over large-diameter nerve fibers, by impulses from the reticular formation in the brainstem, or by impulses from the entire cerebral cortex or thalamus.

Acute Pain and Chronic Pain

A. Acute pain
   1. Short duration; may last from split second to about six months.
   2. Serves the purpose of warning the client that damage or injury has occurred in the body that requires treatment.
   3. Subsides as healing occurs.
   4. Usually associated with autonomic nervous system symptoms, e.g., increased pulse and blood pressure, sweating, pallor.
B. Chronic pain
   1. Prolonged duration; lasts for six months or longer.
   2. Serves no useful purpose.
   3. Persists long after injury has healed.
   4. Rarely accompanied by autonomic nervous system activity.

Assessment of Pain

See Table 4.4.

General Nursing Interventions

A. Establish nurse-client relationship.
   1. Let the client know that you believe that his pain is real.
   2. Respect the client's attitudes and behavioral responses to his pain.
B. Assess characteristics of pain and evaluate client's response to interventions.
C. Promote rest and relaxation.
   1. Prevent fatigue.
   2. Teach relaxation techniques, e.g., slow, rhythmic breathing, guided imagery.
D. Institute comfort measures.
   1. Positioning: support body parts.

TABLE 4.4   Pain Assessment

Influencing factors
- Past experience with pain
- Age (tolerance generally increases with age)
- Culture and religious beliefs
- Level of anxiety
- Physical state (fatigue or chronic illness may decrease tolerance)

Characteristics of pain
- Location
- Quality
- Intensity
- Timing and duration
- Precipitating factors
- Aggravating factors
- Alleviating factors
- Interference with activities of daily living
- Patterns of response

2. Decrease noxious stimuli such as noise or bright lights.
E. Provide cutaneous stimulation: massage, pressure, baths, vibration, heat, cold packs; increased input of large-diameter fibers closes gate.
F. Relieve anxiety and fears.
 1. Spend time with client.
 2. Offer reassurance, explanations.
G. Provide distraction and diversion, e.g., music, puzzles.
H. Administer pain medication as needed.
 1. Administer pain medication in early stages before pain becomes severe.
 2. If pain is present most of the day, a preventative approach may be used, e.g., an around-the-clock schedule may be ordered in place of a prn schedule.
I. Teach client about pain and pain control measures, e.g., relaxation techniques, cutaneous stimulation.

Specific Medical and Surgical Therapies for Pain

See also Narcotic and Nonnarcotic Analgesics in Unit 2.

Nonnarcotic Analgesics

A. Salicylates
 1. Examples: Acetylsalicylic acid (ASA, aspirin (Ecotrin), choline magnesium trisalicylate (Trilisate), diflunisal (Dolobid), salsalate (Disalcid)
 2. Mechanism of action
  a. Analgesic action: produced by action on the hypothalamus and inhibition of prostaglandin synthesis
  b. Antipyretic action: acts on hypothalamus to produce peripheral vasodilation, which causes sweating and heat loss (diflunisal [Dolobid] has minimal antipyretic effect)
  c. Anti-inflammatory action: caused by inhibition of prostaglandin formation
  d. Antiplatelet activity: inhibits platelet aggregation (Trilisate, Dolobid, and Disalcid have no effect on platelet aggregation)
 3. Uses
  a. Relief of mild to moderate pain
  b. Reduction of elevated body temperature
  c. Symptomatic treatment of numerous inflammatory disorders
 4. Side effects
  a. Allergic reaction: varies from rash to anaphylaxis
  b. Anemia, decreased platelet aggregation, prolonged bleeding time (not with Trilisate, Dolobid, or Disalcid)
  c. Nausea, vomiting, gastritis, occult GI bleeding
  d. Renal failure with high doses
  e. Toxicity: tinnitus, visual changes, alterations in mental status
 5. Nursing interventions
  a. Give with food, milk, or antacid to decrease GI irritation; contraindicated in clients with ulcer disease.
  b. Check auditory and visual status periodically.
  c. Instruct client to watch for any signs of bleeding.
  d. Monitor renal function tests in clients receiving high doses or those in ASA toxicity.
B. Acetaminophen (Datril, Tylenol) (see Unit 2, p.27).
C. Nonsteroidal anti-inflammatory drugs (NSAIDs: ibuprofen [Motrin], indomethacin [Indocin], piroxicam [Feldene])
 1. Nursing interventions
  a. Administer with food or milk to prevent GI upset.
  b. Teach client to observe for and report signs of bleeding.
  c. Caution client that drowsiness and dizziness may occur and may impair ability to perform mechanical tasks.

Adjuvants

A. Includes several classes of drugs that may either:
 1. Potentiate the effects of narcotic or nonnarcotic analgesics, e.g., hydroxyzine (Vistaril, Atarax)
 2. Have independent analgesic properties in certain situations, e.g., tricyclic antidepressants such as amitriptyline (Elavil) for neuropathic pain.

3. Help control signs and symptoms associated with pain, e.g., anxiety, depression, nausea, and insomnia

Patient-controlled Analgesia (PCA)

A. Type of intravenous pump that allows the client to administer his own narcotic analgesic (e.g., morphine) on demand within preset dose and frequency limits.
B. Goal is to achieve more constant level of analgesia as compared to prn IM injections; also, in general, causes less sedation and lower risk of pulmonary depression.
C. Used most often for postoperative pain management; also used for intractable pain in terminal illness.
D. PCA pump may be used solely on PCA mode or may be combined with a continuous basal mode where client is receiving continuous infusion of narcotic in addition to self-administered bolus injections.
E. The dose of the analgesic bolus and the time interval between boluses (lockout period) is preset on the pump by the RN according to physician's orders.
F. Nursing Interventions
  1. Instruct client in use of PCA pump
    a. Demonstrate how to push control button.
    b. Explain concept of patient-controlled analgesia.
  2. Assess client's level of consciousness, respiratory rate, and degree of pain relief frequently.

Intraspinal Narcotic Infusion

A. Involves intraspinal infusion of narcotics or local anesthetic agents for relief of acute or chronic pain.
B. Medication is infused through catheter placed in the subarachnoid (intrathecal) or epidural space in the thoracic or lumbar area.
C. Repeated injections of narcotics produce analgesia without many of the side effects associated with systemic narcotics, e.g., sedation.
D. Indications
  1. Temporary intraspinal narcotic therapy is used most frequently for postoperative pain.
  2. For chronic pain, e.g., chronic cancer pain, the catheter may be tunneled under the skin and implanted subcutaneously in the abdomen; an implantable infusion device may be used to provide continuous narcotic infusion.
E. Nursing Interventions
  1. Monitor client closely for respiratory depression especially during initiation of treatment.

2. Assess for other side effects:
  a. urinary retention: Foley catheter may be used in post-op client until infusion is discontinued
  b. pruritus: may be reversed with naloxone (Narcan)
  c. nausea and vomiting
3. Check insertion site frequently for signs of infection.

Electrical Stimulation Techniques for Pain Control

A. *Transcutaneous electrical nerve stimulator (TENS)*
  1. Noninvasive alternative to traditional methods of pain relief
  2. Used in treating acute pain (e.g., post-op pain) and chronic pain (e.g., chronic low back pain)
  3. Consists of impulse generator connected by wires to electrodes on skin; produces tingling, buzzing sensation in the area.
  4. Mechanism based on gate-control theory: electrical impulse stimulates large diameter nerve fibers to "close the gate."
  5. Nursing responsibilities
    a. Do not place electrodes over incision site, broken skin, carotid sinus, eyes, laryngeal or pharyngeal muscles.
    b. Do not use in client with cardiac pacemaker.
    c. Provide skin care.
      1) remove electrodes once a day; wash area with soap and water and air dry.
      2) wipe area with skin prep pad before reapplying electrode.
      3) assess area for signs of redness; reposition electrodes if redness persists for more than 30 minutes.
B. *Dorsal column stimulator*
  1. Used in selected clients for whom conventional methods of pain relief have not been effective
  2. Electrode is surgically placed over the dorsal column of the spinal cord via laminectomy; connected by wires to a transmitter that may be worn externally or be implanted subcutaneously.

Neurosurgical Procedures for Pain Control

A. Performed for persistent intractable pain of high intensity
B. Involves surgical destruction of nerve pathways to block transmission of pain
C. Types
  1. *Neurectomy:* interruption of cranial or peripheral nerves by incision or injection
  2. *Rhizotomy:* interruption of posterior nerve root close to the spinal cord

      a. Laminectomy is necessary.
      b. Results in permanent loss of sensation and position sense in affected parts.
   3. *Chordotomy:* interruption of pain-conducting pathways within the spinal cord
      a. Laminectomy usually required.
      b. May be done by percutaneous needle insertion.
      c. Interrupts conduction of pain and temperature sense in affected parts.
   4. *Sympathectomy:* interruption of afferent pathways in the sympathetic division of the autonomic nervous system; used to control pain from causalgia and peripheral vascular disease.
D. Nursing responsibilities
   1. Provide pre- and post-op care for a laminectomy (see page 317).
   2. Assess extremities for sensation (e.g., touch, pain, temperature, pressure, position sense) and movement.
   3. Provide safety measures to protect client from injury and carefully monitor skin for signs of damage or pressure.
   4. Teach client ways to compensate for loss of sensation in affected parts.
      a. Visually inspect skin for signs of injury or pressure.
      b. Check temperature of bath water.
      c. Avoid use of hot water bottles, heating pads.
      d. Avoid extremes of temperature.

Acupuncture

A. A Chinese technique of pain control by insertion of fine needles at various points on the body
B. Based on Eastern philosophy where insertion of needles is thought to block energy flow and restore the body's harmony
C. Mechanism of action: two theories
   1. Trigger points: the needles stimulate hypersensitive areas in muscle that produce local and referred pain. Extinction of the trigger point alleviates the referred pain.
   2. Endorphin system: needle insertion activates production of endorphins (body's natural opiates).
D. Acupressure: a less invasive variation; uses finger pressure and massage

Hypnosis

A. Has been used in dental procedures, labor and delivery, pain control in cancer.
B. Mechanism is thought to be that positive suggestions alter client's perception of pain.

Behavioral Techniques

A. Types
   1. *Operant conditioning:* based on decreasing positive reinforcement for pain behaviors
   2. *Biofeedback:* teaches clients to control physiologic responses to pain (e.g., muscle tension, heart rate, blood pressure) and to replace them with a state of relaxation.
B. Work best in conjunction with other types of pain management and stress reduction techniques.

FLUIDS AND ELECTROLYTES

Basic Principles

Fluids

A. Water constitutes over 50% of individual's weight; largest single component.
B. Body water divided into two compartments
   1. Intracellular: within cells
   2. Extracellular: outside cells, further divided into interstitial and intravascular fluid
C. Fluids in two compartments move among cells, tissue spaces, and plasma

Electrolytes

A. Salts or minerals in extracellular or intracellular body fluids
B. If positively charged, called *cations*; if negatively charged, called *anions*
C. Common electrolytes and normal blood values
   1. Sodium (Na)—135–148 mEq/liter
   2. Potassium (K)—3.5–5 mEq/liter
   3. Calcium (Ca)—4.5–5.3 mEq/liter, 9–11 mg/dl
   4. Magnesium (Mg)—1.3–2.1 mEq/liter
   5. Chloride (Cl)—98–106 mEq/liter

Movement of Fluids and Electrolytes

A. Diffusion: movement of particles from an area of greater concentration to an area of lesser concentration as part of random activity
B. Active transport: movement across cell membranes requiring energy from an outside source
C. Osmosis: movement of water through a semipermeable membrane

Fluid and Electrolyte Imbalances

See Table 4.5.
A. *Hypovolemia:* extracellular fluid volume deficit
B. *Hypervolemia:* extracellular fluid volume excess
C. *Water excess:* hypo-osmolar imbalances; water intoxication or solute deficit

TABLE 4.5   Fluid and Electrolyte Imbalances

Imbalance	Causes	Assessment Findings	Nursing Interventions
Hypovolemia (extracellular fluid volume deficit)	Hemorrhage, diarrhea, vomiting, kidney disease, diaphoresis, burns, fever, draining fistulas, sequestration of fluids (peritonitis, edema associated with burns)	Nausea and vomiting, weakness, weight loss, anorexia, longitudinal wrinkles of the tongue, dry skin and mucous membranes, decreased fullness of neck veins, postural hypotension, oliguria to anuria, shock	Measure I&O. Weigh daily. Monitor closely and regulate isotonic IV infusion. Monitor blood pressure (determine lying down, sitting, and standing). Report urine output less than 30 ml/hr. Carefully assess skin and mucous membranes. Monitor for signs of shock.
Hypervolemia (extracellular fluid volume excess)	Excess or too rapid administration of any isotonic solution; side effect of corticosteroid administration; cardiac, liver, or renal disease; cerebral damage; stress	Weight gain, pitting edema, dyspnea, cough, diaphoresis, frothy or pink-tinged sputum, edema of the eyelids, distended neck veins, elevated blood pressure, moist rales (crackles)	Weigh daily. Measure I&O. Regulate IV fluids/administration of diuretics strictly and monitor carefully. Monitor abdominal girth. Assess for pitting edema. Restrict sodium and water intake.
Water excess syndromes	Excessive intake of water, inability to excrete water due to kidney or brain damage, excessive administration of electrolyte-free solutions, poor salt intake, use of diuretics, irrigation of nasogastric tube with plain water, administration of excessive amount of ice chips to a vomiting client or one with a nasogastric tube	Polyuria (in absence of renal disease), oliguria (with renal disease), twitching, hyperirritability, disorientation, coma, convulsions, abdominal cramps	Measure I&O. Weigh daily. Restrict oral and IV intake. Replace fluid losses with isotonic solutions. Use normal saline solution for nasogastric tube irrigation.
Water deficit syndromes	Increased water output due to watery diarrhea, diabetic acidosis, excess TPN; dysphagia; impaired thirst mechanism; coma; general debility; diaphoresis; excess protein intake without sufficient water intake	Thirst, poor skin turgor, dry skin and mucous membranes, dry furrowed tongue, sunken eyeballs, weight loss, elevated temperature, apprehension, oliguria to anuria	Measure I&O. Weigh daily. Assess skin frequently. Ensure that clients with a high solute intake receive adequate water. Assess vital signs frequently, particularly temperature. Monitor TPN infusions accurately.
Hyperkalemia	Renal insufficiency, adrenocortical insufficiency, cellulose damage (burns), infection, acidotic states, rapid infusion of IV solutions with potassium, overzealous administration of potassium-conserving diuretics	Thready, slow pulse; shallow breathing; nausea and vomiting; diarrhea; intestinal colic, irritability; muscle weakness, numbness, flaccid paralysis; tingling; difficulty with phonation, respiration	Administer Kayexalate as ordered. Administer/monitor IV infusion of glucose and insulin. Control infection. Provide adequate calories and carbohydrates. Discontinue IV or oral sources of potassium.
Hypokalemia	Anorexia, alcoholism, gastric and intestinal suction, GI surgery, vomiting, diarrhea, laxative abuse, thiazide diuretics, steroid therapy, stress, alkalotic states	Thready, rapid, weak pulse; faint heart sounds; decreased blood pressure; skeletal muscle weakness; decreased or absent reflexes; shallow respirations; malaise; apathy; lethargy; loss of orientation; anorexia, vomiting, weight loss, gaseous intestinal distention	Be especially cautious if administering drugs that are not potassium sparing. Administer potassium supplements to replace losses. Monitor acid-base balance. Monitor pulse, blood pressure, and ECG.
Hypernatremia	Excessive/rapid IV administration of normal saline solution, inadequate water intake, kidney disease	Dry, sticky mucous membranes; flushed skin; rough, dry tongue; firm skin turgor; intense thirst; edema; oliguria to anuria	Weigh daily. Assess degree of edema frequently. Measure I&O. Assess skin frequently and institute nursing measures to prevent breakdown. Encourage sodium-restricted diet.

TABLE 4.5   Fluid and Electrolyte Imbalances (continued)

Imbalance	Causes	Assessment Findings	Nursing Interventions
Hyponatremia	Decreased sodium intake, increased sodium excretion through diaphoresis or GI suctioning, adrenal insufficiency	Nausea and vomiting; abdominal cramps; weight loss; cold, clammy skin; decreased skin turgor; fingerprinting over the sternum; shrunken tongue; apprehension; headache; convulsions; confusion; weakness; fatigue; postural hypotension; rapid, thready pulse	Provide foods high in sodium. Administer normal saline solution IV. Assess blood pressure frequently (measure lying down, sitting, and standing).
Hypercalcemia	Hyperparathyroidism, immobility, increased vitamin D intake, osteoporosis and osteomalacia (early stages)	Nausea and vomiting, anorexia, constipation, headache, confusion, lethargy, stupor, decreased muscle tone, deep bone and/or flank pain	Encourage mobilization. Limit vitamin D and calcium intake. Administer diuretics. Protect from injury.
Hypocalcemia	Acute pancreatitis, diarrhea, hypoparathyroidism, lack of vitamin D in diet, long-term steroid therapy	Painful tonic muscle spasms, facial spasms, fatigue, laryngospasm, positive Trousseau's and Chvostek's signs, convulsions, dyspnea	Administer oral calcium lactate or IV calcium chloride or gluconate. Provide safety by padding side rails. Administer dietary sources of calcium. Provide quiet environment.
Hypermagnesemia	Renal insufficiency, dehydration, excessive use of magnesium-containing antacids or laxatives	Lethargy, somnolence, confusion, nausea and vomiting, muscle weakness, depressed reflexes, decreased pulse and respirations	Withhold magnesium-containing drugs/foods. Increase fluid intake (unless contraindicated).
Hypomagnesemia	Low intake of magnesium in diet, prolonged diarrhea, massive diuresis, hypoparathyroidism	Paresthesias, confusion, hallucinations, convulsions, ataxia, tremors, hyperactive deep reflexes, muscle spasm, flushing of the face, diaphoresis	Provide good dietary sources of magnesium.

D. *Water deficit:* hyperosmolar imbalances; water depletion or solute excess
E. *Hyperkalemia:* potassium excess, serum potassium above 5.5 mEq/liter
F. *Hypokalemia:* potassium deficit, serum potassium below 3 mEq/liter
G. *Hypernatremia:* sodium excess, serum sodium level above 145 mEq/liter
H. *Hyponatremia:* sodium deficit, serum sodium level below 135 mEq/liter
I. *Hypercalcemia:* calcium excess, serum calcium level above 5.8 mEq/liter
J. *Hypocalcemia:* calcium deficit, serum calcium level below 4.5 mEq/liter
K. *Hypermagnesemia:* magnesium excess, serum magnesium level above 3 mEq/liter
L. *Hypomagnesemia:* magnesium deficit, serum magnesium level below 1.5 mEq/liter

ACID-BASE BALANCE

Basic Principles

A. Normal pH of the body is 7.35–7.45.
B. Buffer or control systems maintain normal pH. Kidneys excrete acids and reabsorb bicarbonate while the respiratory system gives off carbon dioxide in acidic states. In alkalotic states, the kidneys excrete bicarbonate and the respiratory system retains carbonic acid.

Acid-Base Imbalances

See Table 4.6.
A. *Metabolic acidosis:* a primary deficit in the concentration of base bicarbonate in the extracellular fluid; decreased pH and bicarbonate, decreased pCO_2 (if lung compensation)
B. *Metabolic alkalosis:* a primary excess of base bicarbonate in the extracellular fluid; elevated pH and bicarbonate, elevated pCO_2 (if lung compensation)
C. *Respiratory acidosis:* a primary excess of carbonic acid in the extracellular fluid; decreased pH, elevated pCO_2 and bicarbonate (if renal compensation)
D. *Respiratory alkalosis:* a primary deficit of carbonic acid in the extracellular fluid; elevated pH, decreased pCO_2 and bicarbonate (if renal compensation)

TABLE 4.6 Acid-Base Imbalances

Imbalance	Causes	Assessment Findings	Nursing Interventions
Metabolic acidosis	Diabetic ketoacidosis, uremia, starvation, diarrhea, severe infections, renal tubular acidosis	Headache, nausea and vomiting, weakness, lethargy, disorientation, tremors, convulsions, coma	Administer sodium bicarbonate as ordered and monitor for signs of excess. Monitor for signs of hyperkalemia. Provide alkaline mouthwash (baking soda and water) to neutralize acids. Lubricate lips to prevent dryness from hyperventilation. Measure I&O. Institute seizure precautions. Monitor arterial blood gases and electrolytes.
Metabolic alkalosis	Severe vomiting, nasogastric suctioning, diuretic therapy, excessive ingestion of sodium bicarbonate, biliary drainage	Nausea and vomiting, diarrhea, numbness and tingling of extremities, tetany, bradycardia, decreased respirations	Replace fluid and electrolyte losses (potassium and chloride). Institute seizure precautions. Measure I&O. Assess for signs of hypokalemia. Monitor arterial blood gases and electrolytes.
Respiratory acidosis	COPD, barbiturate or sedative overdose, acute airway obstruction, weakness of respiratory muscles	Headache, weakness, visual disturbances, rapid respirations, confusion, drowsiness, tachycardia, coma	Position in semi-Fowler's. Maintain patent airway. Turn, cough, and deep breathe. Perform postural drainage. Administer fluids to help liquefy secretions (unless contraindicated). Administer low-concentration oxygen therapy. Monitor arterial blood gases and electrolytes. Administer prophylactic antibiotics as ordered.
Respiratory alkalosis	Hyperventilation, mechanical overventilation, encephalitis	Numbness and tingling of mouth and extremities, inability to concentrate, rapid respirations, dry mouth, coma	Offer reassurance. Encourage breathing into a paper bag or voluntary breath holding. Ensure adequate rest. Provide sedation as ordered. Monitor mechanical ventilation, arterial blood gases, and electrolytes.

INTRAVENOUS THERAPY

Purposes

A. Maintenance of fluid and electrolyte balance
B. Replacement of fluid and electrolyte loss
C. Provision of nutrients
D. Provision of a route for medications

Nursing Interventions

A. Select correct solution after checking physician's order.
B. Note clarity of solution.
C. Calculate flow rate (Intravenous Calculations, Unit 2). Time-tape bag to assist in monitoring flow rate.
D. Assess infusion rate and site at least hourly.
E. Use infusion pump if administering medications (e.g., aminophylline, heparin, insulin).
F. Maintain I&O record.
G. Provide tubing change and IV site change according to hospital policy. Intravenous Nurses Society standards recommend IV site and tubing change every 48 hours.
H. Discontinue IV if complications occur.

Complications of Intravenous Therapy

See Table 4.7.

Central Lines

Uses

A. Administration of TPN
B. Measurement of central venous pressure (CVP)
C. IV therapy when suitable peripheral veins are not available
D. Long-term antibiotic therapy
E. Chemotherapy

Types

A. Nontunneled catheters: inserted into subclavian vein for short-term access
  1. Subclavian catheters: single lumen

TABLE 4.7 Complications of IV Therapy

Complication	Manifestation	Nursing Interventions
Infiltration	Blanching of skin, swelling, pain at site; cool to touch; decreased infusion rate	Discontinue IV. Restart in a new site. May apply warm compresses to increase fluid absorption.
Phlebitis	Redness, heat, and swelling at site; possible pain and red line along course of vein	Discontinue IV. Restart in new site. Apply warm compresses to site.
Pyrogenic reaction	Fever, chills, general malaise, nausea, vomiting, headache, backache	Discontinue infusion immediately. Monitor vital signs and notify physician. Retain IV equipment for culture/lab study
Air embolism	Dyspnea, cyanosis, hypotension, tachycardia, loss of consciousness	Stop infusion immediately. Turn client on left side with his head down. Administer oxygen. Notify physician.
Circulatory overload	Apprehension, shortness of breath, coughing, frothy sputum, crackles, engorged neck veins, increased blood pressure and pulse	Slow down IV rate. Monitor vital signs. Notify physician.

  2. Multilumen catheters: double, triple, or quadruple lumens for simultaneous infusion of fluids or for blood drawing with fluid infusion.
B. Tunneled catheters: long, silicone catheter threaded through subcutaneous layer to prevent infection with long-term use; catheter tip is located in the superior vena cava.
  1. Hickman/Broviac catheters: single- or double-lumen catheters with external presentation; need to be flushed daily with a heparinized saline solution and must be clamped when not in use; repair kit available.
  2. Groshong catheters: similar to Hickman/Broviac; difference is in valve at closed distal end of catheter that opens when used and remains closed at other times, preventing blood back-up into catheter; no clamping is necessary; flushing is done daily with saline in a vigorous manner.
  3. Implantable ports: totally internal device consists of subcutaneous self-sealing injection port and a tunneled catheter; flushing is done with a heparinized saline solution every 28 days; access must be with a special noncoring needle.

  4. Peripherally inserted central lines (PICC): short-term long lines that can be inserted by qualified nurses; inserted via a vessel in the antecubital fossa (median or cephalic); flushing is with a heparinized saline solution.

Care of the Client with a Central Venous Line

A. Assist physician with placement; catheters should initially be flushed with saline. Have fluids or cap and heparin flush ready.
B. Confirm placement in superior vena cava by x-ray prior to catheter use.
C. Institute nursing measures to prevent infection (particularly important with TPN since high concentration of glucose encourages growth of bacteria).
  1. Change dressings
    a. Usually 3 times/week and as needed (e.g., when loose or wet) but agency policies may vary
    b. Use sterile technique and apply sterile occlusive dressing.
  2. Monitor for signs of infection: redness, drainage, odor at site, or elevated temperature.
  3. Do not piggyback anything into a TPN infusion line except intralipids.
D. Monitor for infiltration: check for swelling of neck, face, and shoulder, and pain in upper arm.
E. Prevent catheter occlusion.
  1. Keep infusion continuous.
  2. Use infusion pump.
  3. Check for kinks in tubing.
  4. Evaluate for catheter migration or dislodgment.
F. Prevent air embolism.
  1. Tighten and tape all tubing connections to prevent accidental disconnection of tubing.
  2. Clamp catheter (except Groshong) and instruct client to perform Valsalva maneuver when changing or detaching tubing.
  3. Check tubing for cracks or perforations.
G. Maintain proper infusion rate.
  1. Monitor rate closely to prevent clotting, fluid depletion, or fluid overload.
  2. Never attempt to speed up or slow down infusion.
H. With a multilumen catheter, flush ports not being used to prevent clotting (per agency's protocol).
I. With Hickman/Broviac catheters, Groshongs, PICCs, and implanted port provide other specific care according to agency protocol.
J. If clotting occurs, try to aspirate or add a declotting agent according to agency protocol. Do not irrigate.

1. Streptokinase requires 1 hour waiting time.
   2. Urokinase requires 10 minutes waiting time.
K. When drawing blood specimens, discard initial sample of 5–10 ml prior to drawing required volume for specimens. Flush with saline prior to flushing with heparinized saline solution or continuing fluids.

Blood Transfusions

See page 232.

SHOCK

An abnormal physiologic state where an imbalance between the amount of circulating blood volume and the size of the vascular bed results in circulatory failure and oxygen and nutrient deprivation of tissues. See Table 4.8 for classification of shock.

Body's Response to Shock

A. Hyperventilation leading to respiratory alkalosis
B. Vasoconstriction: shunts blood to heart and brain
C. Tachycardia

D. Fluid shifts: intracellular to extracellular shift to maintain circulating blood volume
E. Impaired metabolism: tissue anoxia leads to anaerobic metabolism causing lactic acid buildup, resulting in metabolic acidosis
F. Impaired organ function
   1. Kidney: decreased perfusion can result in renal failure.
   2. Lung: shock lung (adult respiratory distress syndrome [ARDS])

Assessment Findings

A. Skin
   1. Cool, pale, moist in hypovolemic and cardiogenic shock
   2. Warm, dry, pink in septic and neurogenic shock
B. Pulse
   1. Tachycardia, due to increased sympathetic stimulation
   2. Weak and thready
C. Blood pressure
   1. Early stages: may be normal due to compensatory mechanisms
   2. Later stages: systolic and diastolic blood pressure drops.
D. Respirations: rapid and shallow, due to tissue anoxia and excessive amounts of CO_2 (from metabolic acidosis)

TABLE 4.8   Classification of Shock

Type	Characteristics	Causes
Hypovolemic	Decreased circulating blood volume	Blood loss Plasma loss (e.g., burns) Fluid loss (e.g., excessive vomiting or diarrhea)
Cardiogenic	Failure of the heart to pump properly	Myocardial infarction Congestive heart failure Cardiac arrhythmias Pericardial tamponade Tension pneumothorax
Septic	Factors favoring septic shock • development of antibiotic-resistant organisms • invasive procedures such as urinary tract instrumentation • immunosuppression and old age • trauma: presence of blood in peritoneal cavity greatly increases likelihood of peritonitis	Release of bacterial toxins that act directly on the blood vessels producing massive vasodilation and pooling of blood; results most frequently from gram-negative septicemia.
Neurogenic	Failure of arteriolar resistance, leading to massive vasodilation and pooling of blood	Interruption of sympathetic impulses from • exposure to unpleasant circumstances • extreme pain • spinal cord injury • high spinal anesthesia • vasomotor depression • head injury
Anaphylactic	Massive vasodilation resulting from allergic reaction causing release of histamine and related substances	Allergic reaction to • insect venom • medications • dyes used in radiologic studies

E. Level of consciousness: restlessness and apprehension, progressing to coma
F. Urinary output: decreases due to impaired renal perfusion
G. Temperature: decreases in severe shock (except septic shock).

Nursing Interventions

A. Maintain patent airway and adequate ventilation.
   1. Establish and maintain airway.
   2. Administer oxygen as ordered.
   3. Monitor respiratory status, blood gases.
   4. Start resuscitative procedures as necessary.
B. Promote restoration of blood volume; administer fluid and blood replacement as ordered
   1. Crystalloid solutions: Ringer's lactate, normal saline
   2. Colloid solutions: albumin, plasmanate, dextran
   3. Blood products: whole blood, packed red blood cells, fresh frozen plasma
C. Administer drugs as ordered (see Table 4.9).
D. Minimize factors contributing to shock.
   1. Elevate lower extremities to 45° to promote venous return to heart, thereby improving cardiac output.
   2. Avoid Trendelenburg's position: increases respiratory impairment.
   3. Promote rest by using energy-conservation measures and maintaining as quiet an environment as possible.
   4. Relieve pain by cautious use of narcotics.
      a. Since narcotics interfere with vasoconstriction, give only if absolutely necessary, IV and in small doses.
      b. If given IM or subcutaneously, vasoconstriction may cause incomplete absorption; when circulation improves, client may get overdose.
   5. Keep client warm.
E. Maintain continuous assessment of the client.
   1. Check vital signs frequently.
   2. Monitor urine output: report urine output of less than 30 ml/hour.
   3. Observe color and temperature of skin.
   4. Monitor CVP.
   5. Monitor ECG.
   6. Check lab studies: CBC, electrolytes, BUN, creatinine, blood gases.
   7. Monitor other parameters such as arterial blood pressures, cardiac output, pulmonary artery pressures, pulmonary artery wedge pressures.
F. Provide psychologic support: reassure client to relieve apprehension, and keep family advised.

TABLE 4.9 Drugs Used to Treat Shock

Generic (Trade) Name	Action
Dopamine (Intropin)	*Low dosage:* Dilates renal, mesenteric, and splanchnic vessels, which in turn increases perfusion of kidneys and urine output. *High dosage:* Increases cardiac contractility; causes vasoconstriction (often given with nitroprusside [Nipride]).
Dobutamine (Dobutrex)	Increases myocardial contractility; vasodilator
Isoproterenol (Isuprel)	Increases myocardial contractility; decreases peripheral resistance by dilating peripheral vascular bed; usefulness is limited by the tachycardia it produces
Norepinephrine (Levophed)	Improves cardiac contractility and cardiac output; potent vasoconstrictor
Sodium nitroprusside (Nipride)	Vasodilator; decreases peripheral resistance and workload of heart, thereby increasing cardiac output; used in cardiogenic shock and hypertensive emergencies.
Digitalis preparations	Improve cardiac performance.
Corticosteroids	Used especially in septic shock; help to protect cell membranes and decrease the inflammatory response to stress.
Antibiotics	Used in treating infectious processes related to septic shock.

NOTE: Vasopressors such as Levophed can cause almost complete occlusion of arterioles, causing a decrease of blood flow to larger tissue areas. Therefore, if blood pressure is adequate, a vasodilator such as Nipride could probably be given as well, to modify the vasoconstrictor effects.

MULTIPLE TRAUMA

Assessment and Emergency Care

Airway

A. Assess, establish, and maintain an adequate airway.
   1. Do not hyperextend the neck in a client with suspected cervical spine injury.
   2. Use jaw thrust instead.
B. Administer artificial resuscitation if necessary.
C. Observe for chest trauma such as open sucking wounds or flail chest (see Chest Trauma, page 254).
D. Administer oxygen at 5 liters/minute unless client has history of COPD; lower oxygen levels needed for those with COPD.
E. Draw blood samples for ABGs.

Hemorrhage and Shock

A. Deep wounds with pulsating blood flow

1. Apply firm pressure over the wound with a sterile dressing.
2. If wound is on a limb, elevate the extremity.
3. Apply pressure with three fingers over appropriate pressure point.
4. Once bleeding is controlled, apply a pressure dressing.
5. Tourniquets should be used only when all other methods have failed.

B. Venous bleeding: apply direct pressure to bleeding site.
C. Never remove any foreign object, such as a knife, from the client; immobilize the object with packing.
D. Assess for and treat shock (see Shock, pages 149–150).
E. Administer tetanus booster as ordered.

Neurologic Injuries

A. Inspect the scalp, head, face, and neck for abrasions, hematomas, and lacerations.
B. Gently palpate the head for any injuries.
C. Inspect the nose and ears for leakage of cerebrospinal fluid.
D. Assess the level of consciousness.
E. Evaluate pupillary size, shape, equality, and reaction to light.
F. Assess for sensation and motor abilities.
G. Observe for signs of increased intracranial pressure (see page 182).
H. For additional details of care see Head Injury and Spinal Cord Injury, pages 195–197).

Abdominal Injuries

A. Keep client NPO.
B. Assist with insertion of nasogastric tube (for assessment of stomach bleeding and aspiration of stomach contents, which prevents vomiting).
C. Inspect abdomen for injuries.
D. Auscultate bowel sounds.
E. Do not palpate the abdomen (could aggravate possible internal injuries).
F. Prepare client for peritoneal lavage if indicated.
G. Insert Foley catheter.
  1. Measure urine output every 15 minutes.
  2. Assess for hematuria.

Musculoskeletal Injuries

A. Observe for sign of fracture: pain, swelling, tenderness, ecchymosis, crepitation (grating sound), loss of function, exposed bone fragments.
B. Cover open fracture with sterile dressing to prevent infection.
C. Immobilize any suspected fractures by splinting the joint above and below the injury.

D. Perform neurovascular check of area distal to fracture: assess for color, temperature, capillary refill, sensation, movement, pulses.

Sample Questions

1. A 27-year-old adult male is admitted for treatment of Crohn's disease. Which information is most significant when the nurse assesses his nutritional health?
   1. Anthropometric measurements.
   2. Bleeding gums.
   3. Dry skin.
   4. Facial rubor.
2. Total parenteral nutrition (TPN) is ordered for an adult client. The nurse expects the solution will contain all of the following nutrients except
   1. dextrose 10%.
   2. trace minerals.
   3. electrolytes.
   4. amino acids.
3. The nurse caring for an adult client who is receiving TPN will need to monitor him for which of the following metabolic complications?
   1. hypoglycemia and hypercalcemia.
   2. hyperglycemia and hypokalemia.
   3. hyperglycemia and hyperkalemia.
   4. hyperkalemia and hypercalcemia.
4. Acetylsalicylic acid is being administered to an adult client. The nurse understands that the most common mechanism of action for nonnarcotic analgesics is their ability to
   1. inhibit prostaglandin synthesis.
   2. alter pain perception in the cerebellum.
   3. directly affect the central nervous system.
   4. target the pain-producing effect of kinins.
5. An adult has been taking acetylsalicylic acid (ASA) 650 mg four times a day for chronic back pain. The nurse assessing this client knows that a common side effect of high doses of ASA is
   1. renal failure.
   2. paralytic ileus.
   3. gastrointestinal bleeding.
   4. retinal detachment.
6. Ibuprofen (Motrin) is prescribed for an adult with chronic pain. The nurse must teach the client to observe which dietary precaution while taking ibuprofen?
   1. Eat a high-fiber diet.
   2. Drink citrus juices daily.
   3. Take the medication with milk.
   4. Omit spinach and other green leafy vegetables from her diet.
7. A 48-year-old woman has just returned to her room after having had a hysterectomy. She has patient-controlled analgesia (PCA). To

reduce anxiety regarding receiving adequate pain relief, the client was most likely told that
1. PCA is almost always effective.
2. comfort will be assessed frequently.
3. additional IM medication will be available.
4. most therapies are better than frequent IM injections.

8. Preoperative teaching for an adult who is to have patient controlled analgesia following surgery includes telling her:
1. "You will not be drowsy."
2. "You will experience no pain."
3. "Pain control will be adequate."
4. "You will not have incisional pain but you may have muscle pain."

9. What protective mechanism prevents drug overdose with PCA?
1. The nurse controls the amount administered.
2. Extensive client teaching precedes its use.
3. The client can stop drug administration but not initiate it.
4. After a bolus is administered, there is a mandatory waiting period.

10. The nurse is the first professional to arrive at the scene of a multivehicle accident. Mr. R. was riding a motorcycle. Upon impact, he fell off the bike and it fell back on his legs. Priority care for Mr. R. should be directed toward
1. assessing blood loss.
2. monitoring respiratory status.
3. obtaining vital signs.
4. organizing lay people on the scene.

11. The nurse is at the scene of a multivehicle accident. A young man was injured when his motorcycle was hit by a car. He fell off the bike and then it fell back on his legs. He is bleeding profusely from a 4-inch gash on his left leg. Which of the following is the best approach for the nurse to take to stop the bleeding?
1. Apply direct pressure to the wound.
2. Move the motorcycle off his legs.
3. Raise the extremity.
4. Wrap a tourniquet above the wound.

12. The nurse is caring for a client who is receiving IV fluids. Which observation the nurse makes best indicates the IV has infiltrated?
1. Pain at the site.
2. A change in flow rate.
3. Coldness around the insertion site.
4. Redness around the insertion site.

13. The nurse is caring for a client whose arterial blood gases indicate metabolic acidosis. The nurse knows that causes of metabolic acidosis include all of the following except
1. cardiac arrest.
2. diabetic ketoacidosis.
3. hypokalemia.
4. renal failure.

14. An adult woman is admitted with metabolic acidosis. Which set of arterial blood gases should the nurse expect to find in a client with metabolic acidosis?
1. pH 7.28; PCO_2 - 55; HCO_3 - 26.
2. pH 7.50; PCO_2 - 40; HCO_3 - 31.
3. pH 7.48; PCO_2 - 30; HCO_3 - 22.
4. pH 7.30; PCO_2 - 36; HCO_3 - 18.

15. A 93-year-old woman is hospitalized for the treatment of gastroenteritis complicated by dehydration and hyponatremia. The nurse expects that an early symptom of hyponatremia exhibited by the client was
1. ataxia.
2. hunger.
3. thirst.
4. weakness.

Answers and Rationales

1. The correct answer is 1. Anthropometric measurements are the prime parameters used to evaluate fat and muscle stores in the body. Bleeding gums and dry skin are associated with several systemic problems and can be signs of micronutrient deficiencies as well. Facial rubor is not a parameter used to evaluate the client's nutritional status.

2. The correct answer is 1. The concentration of dextrose in TPN solutions is at least 30%. Trace minerals such as zinc, copper, chromium, and manganese are usually added. Electrolytes and amino acids are part of TPN solutions.

3. The correct answer is 2. Metabolic complications from administration of TPN include hyperglycemia, hypoglycemia, hypocalcemia, hypokalemia, hypomagnesemia, hyponatremia, and hypophosphatemia. Hyperglycemia is the most common complication of TPN. Hypoglycemia can occur when TPN is suddenly withdrawn. Electrolyte deficiencies can occur. The addition of electrolytes is individualized based on the client's metabolism and on the underlying condition.

4. The correct answer is 1. Nonnarcotic analgesics inhibit prostaglandin synthesis. Prostaglandins increase the sensitivity of peripheral pain receptors to endogenous pain-producing substances. There is no direct action on the central nervous system or change in pain perception.

5. The correct answer is 3. High doses of aspirin are associated with GI bleeding. Renal failure, paralytic ileus, and retinal detachment are not complications associated with aspirin therapy.

6. The correct answer is 3. NSAIDs are very irritating to the GI tract and should always be taken with milk or food to minimize the

possibility of bleeding. It is not necessary to add or eliminate food from the diet unless the individual is experiencing some specific food intolerances. Spinach may be omitted from the diet of a person taking coumadin.

7. The correct answer is 2. Pain is an individual experience. It is important to reassure the client that assessments will be made on a frequent basis and that drug dosages will be adjusted according to the amount of pain the client is perceiving. IM boosts are generally not needed when PCA is in use. PCA is effective when used with clients who are able to follow the directions for use.

8. The correct answer is 3. Clients should be told that they will be able to control their pain. They should not be told that there will be no pain. The client receiving PCA will have few side effects. Incisional and muscle pain may both be present to some degree following surgery.

9. The correct answer is 4. Immediately after a bolus dose of medication is administered, the device enters the mandatory lock-out mode where no other boluses of medication can be delivered. The nurse may program the amount of medication administered but it is the mandatory lock-out that prevents overdose. The client chooses whether or not to initiate the administration or abstain from using the drug. Pre-op teaching is always important but it is not the protective device to prevent drug overdose.

10. The correct answer is 2. In the presence of multiple trauma, maintenance of a patent airway must always be the priority in the sequence of care delivery. Assessing blood loss would be the second priority of care. Obtaining vital signs would be the next action. Organizing lay people on the scene would be a later action.

11. The correct answer is 1. Direct pressure to the wound will aid in the development of a blood clot, which is the first step in wound healing. The extremity should be elevated while applying direct pressure. A tourniquet would be a last resort if elevation and direct pressure did not stop the bleeding.

12. The correct answer is 3. Coldness and swelling around the insertion site are the best indicators that the fluid has infiltrated into the subcutaneous tissue. Pain at the site can be a sign of a phlebitis. A change in the flow rate can also be a sign of an infiltrated IV. Redness around the insertion site is a sign of phlebitis.

13. The correct answer is 3. Untreated hypokalemia will eventually lead to metabolic alkalosis. Potassium shifts from the serum into the cells in exchange for H+ ions. The absence of H+ ions causes a base excess, thus metabolic alkalosis. Hyperkalemia is seen in metabolic acidosis. Cardiac arrest causes metabolic acidosis because of the buildup of lactic acid. Diabetic ketoacidosis causes metabolic acidosis from the buildup of ketone bodies, which are a byproduct of fat breakdown. Renal failure causes metabolic acidosis because hydrogen ions (acid) are reabsorbed by the kidney.

14. The correct answer is 4. The pH is below the normal range of 7.35–7.45. The PCO_2 is within the normal range of 35–45 and the HCO_3 is below the normal limits of 21–28. These values indicate a metabolic problem because the PCO_2 is within normal limits. And the problem is acidosis because the pH is below normal. This is uncompensated metabolic acidosis because the HCO_3 level is below normal and the pH is below normal.
Choice 1 is respiratory acidosis because the pH is below normal (acidosis) and the PCO_2 is above normal, indicating the CO_2 (acid) is trapped in the respiratory tract.
Choice 2 is metabolic alkalosis because the pH is above normal (alkalosis), the CO_2 is within normal limits, and the HCO_3 (base) is above normal, indicating a base excess.
Choice 3 is respiratory alkalosis because the pH is above normal (alkalosis) and the PCO_2 is below normal, indicating a deficit of CO_2 in the respiratory tract.

15. The correct answer is 3. Thirst is the body's attempt to restore blood volume depletion that occurs in hyponatremia. Ataxia might be a sign of a neurological disorder. Hunger might be a sign of hypoglycemia. Weakness could be a sign of abnormal potassium levels or hypoglycemia.

Aging

GENERAL INFORMATION

Aging is a normal developmental process that occurs throughout the life span, causing a progressive decrease in functional capabilities. The elderly client is generally regarded as one who is 65 years of age or older.

Biologic Theories of Aging

A. Immunity theory
  1. Primary organs of the immune system (bone marrow and thymus) are affected by the aging process, causing decreased numbers of T cells and a decline in humoral cell mediated responses.
  2. Increase in the incidence of infections, autoimmunity, and cancer with aging.
B. Crosslinkage theory
  1. Crosslinking is a chemical reaction that produces irreparable, spontaneous damage to DNA and results in cell death.
  2. Crosslinking over a lifetime causes interference with normal cell functioning and impedes intracellular transport.
  3. Irreversible aging of proteins such as collagen is responsible for ultimate failure of tissues and organs—especially lungs, heart, muscle, and lining of vessel walls.
C. Free radical theory
  1. Free radicals oxidatively attack adjacent molecules.
  2. Chemical and structural changes are progressive.
  3. Free radicals do not contain useful biographical information and replace genetic order with randomness, causing faulty molecules as person ages.
D. Stress theory
  1. Old age is determined by the amount of wear and tear to which one has been exposed, not chronological age.
  2. Currently stress theory is receiving little support from aging theorists.
E. Error theory
  1. Cell nucleus emits inappropriate information that interferes with normal cell functioning and causes cell mutations.
  2. Mutated cells are less able to perform normal functions and organs become inefficient and senescent.

  3. Cellular mutations are thought to result from extracellular influences such as radiation.
F. Biological programming
  1. Senescence occurs at the cellular level.
  2. Cellular reproduction is a programmed event under genetic control.

Physical Changes of Aging

See Table 4.10

Psychosocial Changes in the Elderly

A. Aging process is not just physical; psychologic, social, and cultural factors play a crucial role.
  1. Some cultures revere the elderly.
  2. American culture places a high value on youth.
B. Developmental tasks of the elderly
  1. Ego integrity vs despair (Erikson)
    a. Ego integrity results when the individual accepts own life as having been meaningful and appropriate.
    b. Despair results from the lack of ego integration and the feeling that time is too short to start another life and to find new means toward integrity.
  2. Other developmental tasks
    a. Successfully adjusting to retirement
    b. Making satisfactory living arrangements
    c. Adjusting to reduced income
    d. Keeping socially active
    e. Maintaining contact with friends and family members
    f. Adjusting to death of spouse
    g. Viewing own death as an appropriate outcome of life

Psychologic/Social Theories of Aging

A. Activity theory
  1. The relationship between society and the aging individual remains fairly stable as the person passes from middle age to old age.
  2. If roles are relinquished (e.g., retirement from job) the person will substitute new roles.
B. Developmental or continuity theory
  1. As a person grows older, he or she is likely to maintain continuity in habits, preferences, commitments, etc., that are a part of personality.

The section on aging was contributed by Judith C. Miller, RN, MSN.

TABLE 4.10 Physical Changes of Aging

System	Physical Change	Nursing Interventions
Special Senses		
Sight	Diminished visual acuity Reduction in visual fields Reduced accommodation to light changes Decreased ability to distinguish colors Major eye problems: presbyopia (difficulty seeing clearly at close range), cataracts, glaucoma, retinal detachment, senile macular degeneration	Provide increased illumination without glare. Provide safe environment by orienting client to surroundings and removing potential hazards. Use sunglasses outdoors Use large print books Avoid night driving Use contrasting colors for color coding
Hearing	Decreased hearing acuity Presbycusis: hearing impairment especially in higher frequencies	Look directly at person when speaking and speak clearly and slowly; low-pitched voice heard best. Decrease background noise
Taste/Smell	Decrease in sense of smell and number of taste buds	Provide attractive meals in comfortable social setting. Vary taste, textures, and colors of food. Be alert for difficulty chewing and swallowing when selecting foods.
Nervous	Progressive loss of number of neurons in brain and spinal cord Loss of total bulk of brain substance Slowed speed of nerve impulse and conduction; slowed reaction time Decreased blood flow to brain Change in sleep patterns Impaired thermoregulation Behavioral changes: diminished emotional responses; lessened adaptability; decreased short-term memory; narrowed interests; confusion/disorientation	Promote independence in daily activities. Allow ample time for completion of tasks. Use sleeping medications with caution. Provide adequate warmth. Maintain social functioning by providing recreational and diversional activities. Prevent translocation shock, minimizing frequency of transfers. Orient to reality to prevent and treat confusion/disorientation.
Integumentary	Skin: thinning, wrinkling, loss of elasticity, dryness Decreased perspiration Increased sensitivity to cold Hair: loss of pigment (graying), thinning Increased vascular fragility (senile purpura) Subcutaneous drugs absorbed more slowly	Observe and assess the skin frequently. Protect the skin against trauma. Avoid overexposure to sun. Maintain adequate hydration. Keep skin clean, dry, lubricated, and pressure free. Provide adequate humidity and heat in environment. Lower bath water temperature to 100–105°F. Decrease frequency of complete baths.
Musculoskeletal	Atrophy of muscles with decreased strength, endurance, and agility Bones more porous and lighter through calcium loss; falls are dangerous Enlarged, stiff joints Stooped posture	Encourage exercise program to help minimize age-related changes. Promote optimum physical activity within level of ability. Maintain optimum nutrition, especially intake of protein, calcium, and vitamins. Encourage use of appropriate adaptive or assistive devices to enhance mobility.
Cardiovascular	Decreased cardiac output Decreased endurance Arteriosclerosis, edema Increased systolic blood pressure Orthostatic hypotension	Assess symptoms and make appropriate modifications in care. Minimize edema and fatigue with rest periods and elevation of legs. Encourage exercise as tolerated. Teach energy conservation methods in daily activities. Teach person to change position slowly to avoid falls.
Respiratory	Impaired ventilation and diffusion Reduced vital capacity Reduced cough Impaired pulmonary circulation Diminished lung capacity Increased risk of pneumonia	Manipulate environment to enhance ventilation. Position to promote optimum ventilation. Maintain tone and efficiency of respiratory muscles by encouraging exercises and prescribed pulmonary exercises. Encourage person to get influenza vaccines.

TABLE 4.10 Physical Changes of Aging (continued)

System	Physical Change	Nursing Interventions
Gastrointestinal	Reduced gastric motility and impaired absorption Diminished food appeal Reduced peristalsis and decreased excretory efficiency Decreased gastric acid Decreased liver size Decreased saliva Loss of teeth common Constipation common problem	Assess condition of teeth and mouth, fit and comfort of dentures, and ability to chew. Encourage fluids and foods high in bulk and fiber. Encourage optimal activity. Promote independence and privacy in use of bathroom. Keep stool record and observe for constipation.
Urinary	Decreased kidney function Common problems: frequency, dysuria, incontinence Enlargement of prostate in males	Assess voiding patterns. Provide adequate fluids. Encourage independence in use of bathroom. Establish voiding schedule or bladder program as needed to control incontinence (assist to bathroom or offer bedpan every 2–3 hours). Avoid catheterization unless no other alternative.

Reproductive
  Female
 	
  Male
	Decreased production of estrogens/progesterone at menopause
	Atrophy and drying of vaginal canal
	Impaired ability to achieve full penile erection; reduced frequency of ejaculation
	Sexual responses slower and less intense
		Promote good perineal care, treat with prescribed creams.
		Use vaginal lubricant as needed.
		Provide encouragement and discuss modifications in sexual expression as necessary; rest before and after sexual activity.

Endocrine	Decreased function of pituitary, thyroid, adrenal cortex, pancreas, parathyroid, and gonads	Assess for endocrine deficiency conditions such as diabetes mellitus and hypothyroidism

2. Because these factors are very complex and individualized, this theory implies that there are many possible adaptations to aging.

C. Disengagement theory
   1. Aging is an inevitable mutual withdrawal or disengagement of the aging person and society from each other.
   2. The number of interrelationships with others is reduced, those remaining are altered in quality.

PATTERNS OF HEALTH AND DISEASE IN THE ELDERLY

A. Diseases that occur to varying degrees in all aging persons
   1. Cataracts
   2. Arteriosclerosis
   3. Benign prostatic hypertrophy (males)
B. Diseases with increased incidence with advancing age but which do not occur universally
   1. Neoplastic disease
   2. Diabetes mellitus
   3. Dementing disorders
C. Diseases that have more serious consequences in the elderly and more difficulty maintaining homeostasis
   1. Pneumonia
   2. Influenza
   3. Trauma

D. Chronic disease very common
   1. 86% of the elderly have at least one chronic disease
   2. 60% of doctor visits among the elderly due to chronic disease
   3. Most hospital visits for persons over 65 are for chronic diseases
   4. Elderly account for 30% of hospital cases but are only 14% of the population
   5. 99% of nursing home residents have at least one chronic disease; average is 3.9 chronic conditions per resident
E. Functional disability (inability to perform activities of daily living [ADL])
   1. 41–60% of persons over 65 have some limitation of functions
   2. 2–18% of persons over 65 require help with ADL
F. Chronic vs acute diseases
   See Table 4.11

ASSESSMENT

Health History

A. Assessment of the elderly is complex and time consuming
   1. Information processing slows in aging; allow enough time for processing.
   2. Assessment takes more than one session.
B. Presenting problem
   1. Assess client systematically depending upon presenting problem.

TABLE 4.11   Chronic Disease vs Acute Disease

Characteristic	Chronic Diseases	Acute Diseases
Cause	Multiple causes; often related to life-style	Specific etiologies
Onset	Slow, insidious	Rapid
Duration	Indeterminate; remissions and exacerbations	Short
Understanding of disease	Often difficult because of indeterminate course, remissions, and exacerbations	Simpler because symptoms more overt
Outcomes	Somewhat predictable but often debilitating and associated with long periods of illness Management of condition Life-style changes required Individual with disease must assume control of disease	Symptoms resolve with cure of disease Outcomes usually favorable; cures Health care provider directs care and cure

2. Manifestations of illness change with age (i.e., aging clients often do not have dysuria with a urinary tract infection).
3. Multidimensionality of problems in the aging
   a. Each problem is likely to have several contributing factors.
   b. Each problem is likely to affect other aspects of life.
C. Life-style: emphasis on functional changes rather than structural changes
   1. There is often no 1:1 correlation between altered structure and function.
   2. Functional assessment is an attempt to measure performance in physical health, ADL, psychologic and social status.
   3. There is a lack of definitive health standards for the aging; comparing older persons' previous patterns of health and functioning with current ability is often helpful.
   4. Have the person demonstrate ADL whenever possible (i.e., observe client dress self, drink a glass of water, walk, etc.)
D. Use of medications
   1. Inquire about drug prescriptions.
   2. Determine client's understanding of purpose of drugs, treatment regimen, side effects.
   3. Determine if client is taking prescribed drugs; cost of drugs may cause client to skip doses or stop taking medications.
   4. Inquire about use of nonprescription drugs, especially analgesics and laxatives.
   5. Polypharmacy often present.
E. Nutrition
   1. Obtain food intake profile (24 hours or 3 days).
   2. Determine if client has difficulty ingesting food (chewing, salivation, swallowing, manual dexterity, tremors)
   3. Are there any foods the client is unable to eat such as dairy products, sodium-containing foods, or foods the client must

eat, such as those containing potassium or calcium?
   4. Can the client purchase and prepare food?
   5. Can the client afford to buy food?
F. Past medical history
   1. Determine presence of chronic diseases; client may have several conditions he/she lives with and does not consider important.
   2. Inquire about previous illnesses and surgeries.

Physical Examination

A. Assess body systems as indicated.
B. Note physical changes in elderly (Table 4.10)

Laboratory/Diagnostic Tests

A. Laboratory tests as indicated according to symptoms of individual client.
B. Interpret lab tests with aging client in mind.

ANALYSIS

Nursing diagnoses for aging clients may include:
A. Activity intolerance
B. Alterations in bowel elimination: constipation, impaction, and incontinence
C. Alteration in bowel elimination: diarrhea
D. Alteration in comfort: acute or chronic pain
E. Anxiety
F. Impaired verbal communication
G. Fluid volume deficit
H. Risk for infection
I. Knowledge deficit
J. Impaired physical mobility
K. Alteration in oral mucous membranes
L. Noncompliance
M. Alterations in nutrition: less than body requirements
N. Alterations in respiratory function: ineffective airway clearance, ineffective

breathing pattern, and impaired gas exchange

O. Self-care deficits: feeding, bathing, dressing, grooming, toileting
P. Disturbance in self-concept: body image, self-esteem, role performance
Q. Sensory perceptual alterations
R. Sexual dysfunction
S. Alteration in skin integrity
T. Sleep pattern disturbance
U. Alteration in thought processes
V. Alteration in peripheral tissue perfusion
W. Alteration in patterns of urinary elimination
X. Diversional activity deficit
Y. Impaired home maintenance management related to sensory losses
Z. Sensory-perceptual alterations: visual, auditory, kinesthetic, gustatory, tactile, olfactory related to aging processes
AA. Impaired social interaction
BB. Risk for violence directed at others related to sensory-perceptual alterations

PLANNING AND IMPLEMENTATION

Goals

A. Maximum independence in self-care activities will be maintained.
B. Client will maintain normal bowel and bladder elimination patterns.
C. Client will maintain ability to communicate.
D. Client will maintain positive self-concept.
E. Client will remain free from injury.
F. Optimal cognitive functioning will be maintained.
G. Skin integrity will be maintained.
H. Client will maintain adequate nutritional status and fluid balance.
I. Client will maintain social contacts.
J. Client will follow treatment regimens as prescribed.

Interventions

Pharmacotherapy in the Elderly

A. General information
1. Decreased body weight, dehydration, and slowed organ functioning may cause higher concentrations of drugs in tissues and slower excretion of drugs, resulting in a greater likelihood of accumulation of overdosage than in a younger person.
2. The elderly often have multiple chronic diseases, which may affect metabolism and excretion of drugs.
3. Rate of medication errors among the elderly estimated to be between 25 to 50% for those living in the community.

4. Elderly often take several drugs and may have more than one physician prescribing drugs, increasing risk of drug-drug interaction.

B. Nursing care
1. Perform a drug inventory with client; determine all prescription and over-the-counter drugs the client is taking.
2. Assess client's perceptions of purpose of drug therapy.
3. Assess client's ability to administer medications safely; vision, reading ability, memory, judgment, motivation, and fine motor coordination.
4. Provide aids if indicated; large-print instructions, memory aids, daily drug dose containers, premeasured syringes, unit dose, etc.
5. Be alert for the possibility of drug-drug interactions. Check with pharmacist if in doubt.
6. Determine baseline measures of vital signs, mental status, bladder and bowel function, and vision before starting drug therapy.
7. Common drug-induced pathology includes confusion, falls, incontinence, and immobility.
8. Determine if client needs assistance to pay for prescriptions.
9. Teach family proper techniques for administering oral medication. Client should be positioned with head forward and neck slightly flexed to facilitate swallowing. Head back with neck hyperextended puts client at risk for difficulty swallowing and aspiration.
10. Liquid rather than tablet forms of drugs may be indicated for clients who have difficulty swallowing medication.
11. Monitor client for effectiveness of medications and for adverse reactions.
12. Teach family members about client's medication regime if indicated.

EVALUATION

A. Client performs self-care activities; if client is unable to perform these, caregiver provides needed assistance.
B. Client is continent of feces and urine; voids in adequate amounts and has regular bowel elimination.
C. Client is able to communicate needs and concerns.
D. Client makes positive statements about self.
E. Client/caregiver modifies environment as needed to provide safety.
F. Client is alert and oriented.
G. Skin is intact with no decubiti.
H. Client eats nutritionally balanced diet and maintains stable weight.

I. Client maintains friends and social interactions.
J. Client describes and adheres to treatment regimen.

Conditions

Senile Dementia, Alzheimer's Type

(See also Delirium, Dementia and Other Cognitive Disorders, p.534)

A. General information
   1. Dementia is defined as an impairment of intellectual function, usually accompanied by memory loss and personality change.
   2. Pathology for presenile and senile dementia is the same; presenile dementia starts before senescence; senile dementia starts at an older age.
   3. Alzheimer's disease is a chronic, progressive degenerative illness for which no cure or treatment has yet been found.
B. Medical management
   1. Rule out other conditions that might be causing the symptoms; Alzheimer's can only be diagnosed with absolute certainty upon autopsy.
   2. Symptom management
C. Assessment findings
   1. Stage one
      a. Lasts from 2 to 4 years
      b. Memory loss, especially recent memory
      c. Difficulty with abstract thinking and mathematical tasks
      d. Lack of spontaneity
      e. Loss of sense of humor
      f. Subtle personality changes; accentuation or caricature of previous personality
      g. Disorientation to time and date
      h. Lack of energy
   2. Stage two
      a. May last several years
      b. Impaired cognition and abstract thinking
      c. Restlessness and agitation
      d. Wandering, "sundowning" (wandering in the late afternoon and evening)
      e. Inability to carry out activities of daily living
      f. Impaired judgment
      g. Impaired impulse control
      h. Inappropriate social behavior
      i. Lack of insight, abstract thinking
      j. Repetitive behavior
      k. Voracious appetite, often for junk food
      l. Depression if client aware of loss of abilities
   3. Stage three
      a. Usually lasts 1 to 2 years but may be as long as 10 years
      b. Emaciation, indifference to food
      c. Inability to communicate
      d. Urinary and fecal incontinence
      e. Seizures
D. Nursing interventions
   1. Institute safety measures
      a. Keep side rails up and bed in low position.
      b. Check client frequently, especially at night.
      c. Use restraints only when no other choice and only with physician order.
      d. Assist with ambulation if needed.
      e. Never leave anything at the bedside that could harm client.
   2. Approach client with friendly relaxed manner; persons with Alzheimer's mirror the affect of those around them.
   3. Facilitate effective communication
      a. Speak in clear, low-pitched voice
      b. Use short, simple words and sentences
      c. Ask only one question at a time; use yes/no questions and avoid questions that require choices.
   4. Orient client to person, time, and place frequently.
   5. Label items, using visual cues such as pictures.
   6. Maintain mobility and exercise as much as possible given the client's level of fitness: walking if able; range of motion exercises if bedridden.
   7. Avoid isolating the client; provide stimulation such as television or soft music.
   8. Promote bowel and bladder continence by offering bedpan and urinal at regular intervals, offering fluids during day, and limiting fluids at bedtime.
   9. Prevent constipation by encouraging high-fiber diet and activity.
   10. Provide high-calorie diet to clients who are hyperactive; provide finger foods if necessary.
   11. Encourage clients to stay awake during day so they can sleep at night.
   12. Avoid overstimulation at bedtime; schedule tests and activities for morning and early afternoon.

ELDER ABUSE AND NEGLECT

A. General information
   1. Elder abuse is the willful infliction of physical pain, injury, or debilitating mental anguish, unreasonable confinement, or the willful deprivation by a caretaker of services that are necessary to maintain physical and mental health.
   2. Elder neglect refers to an elderly person who is living alone and not able to provide for him/herself or to an elderly person who is not receiving necessary services from the responsible caretaker.

3. Abuse can be physical (i.e., beatings or withholding medical care); psychological (i.e., instilling fear through verbal assaults or isolating the elder); material (i.e., theft of money or personal belongings); or violation of rights (i.e., being forced out of one's home).
4. Problem is widespread and occurs in the home and in health care facilities.

B. Assessment findings
1. Identify individuals at risk.
   a. Persons who are dependent and have a limited informal support network.
   b. Persons whose primary caregivers express frustration or high stress levels.
   c. Persons who come from families with a history of abuse.
   d. Individuals who are substance abusers or whose family includes substance abusers.
   e. Persons who have disorders that have multiple physical and emotional disabilities such as Parkinson's disease, Alzheimer's disease, and CVA.
2. Signs and symptoms may include
   a. Signs of malnutrition
   b. Poor hygiene and grooming
   c. Omission of medication or overmedication
   d. Decubiti
3. When assessing for abuse the nurse should consider:
   a. Is the person in immediate danger of bodily harm?
   b. Is the person competent to make decisions regarding his/her care?
   c. What is the degree and significance of the person's functional impairments?
   d. What specific services might help to meet the unmet needs?
   e. Who in the family is involved and to what extent?
   f. Are the client and family willing to accept intervention?

C. Nursing interventions
1. Report suspected abuse according to state laws.
2. Obtain client's consent for treatment.
3. Document nursing assessments of client's physical and emotional status.
4. Refer client and family to support services.
5. Remove client from setting if necessary.
6. Provide for careful follow-up as potential for further abuse is high.

OSTEOPOROSIS (See page 514)

CEREBRAL VASCULAR ACCIDENT (See page 187)

BENIGN PROSTATIC HYPERTROPHY (See page 303)

CATARACTS (See page 199)

GLAUCOMA (See page 200)

Sample Questions

16. An 87-year-old woman has come to the medical clinic for her annual physical examination. The nurse assessing her knows that pulmonary function in elderly clients often shows
   1. a reduced vital capacity.
   2. a decrease in residual volume.
   3. an increase in functional alveoli.
   4. blood gases that reflect mild acidosis.
17. A normal sign of aging in the renal system is
   1. incontinence.
   2. concentrated urine.
   3. microscopic hematuria.
   4. a decreased glomerular filtration rate.
18. An elderly woman reports that she has been using more salt on her food than she used to. This is because
   1. her taste buds are dulled.
   2. she is confused because of her advanced age.
   3. sodium is needed to ensure adequate renal function.
   4. her body is attempting to compensate for lost fluids.
19. Which assessment finding in the elderly is caused by decreased vessel elasticity and increased peripheral resistance?
   1. Confusion.
   2. An erratic pulse rate.
   3. An increase in blood pressure.
   4. Wide QRS complexes on the ECG.
20. Which notation on the nursing care plan reflects inappropriate care of the elderly client with a hearing problem?
   1. Face the client when speaking.
   2. Examine the ears for cerumen accumulation.
   3. Assess the function of the client's hearing aid daily.
   4. Shout loudly and clearly when talking to the client.

Answers and Rationales

16. The correct answer is 1. Residual volume increases with age, probably related to the loss of elastic forces in the lung. This

increased residual volume reduces the vital capacity. Arterial pH does not change with age. The functional alveoli decrease in the elderly due to the thinning of alveolar walls, resulting in the loss of alveolar septal tissue. There are also fewer capillaries present.

17. The correct answer is 4. The glomerular filtration rate is decreased dramatically in the elderly because of changes in the renal tubules. The person loses the ability to concentrate urine as aging occurs. Microscopic hematuria is a symptom of pathology, not normal aging. Incontinence is not an expected outcome of aging.

18. The correct answer is 1. The taste buds begin to atrophy at age 40 and insensitivity to taste qualities occurs after 60. Studies related to diminished taste indicate that there are changes in the salt threshold for some elderly individuals. People lose the ability to compensate for fluid losses as they age. Extra sodium is not needed for renal function. Confusion can cause a wide variety of behaviors but most elderly individuals do not experience confusion.

19. The correct answer is 3. The blood pressure increases in response to the thickening of vessels and less-distensible arteries and veins. There is also an impedance to blood flow and increased systemic vascular resistance, contributing to hypertension. Confusion could be caused by decreased oxygenation to the brain or by the interaction of multiple medications. An erratic pulse rate is not caused by decreased vessel elasticity and increased peripheral resistance. An erratic pulse could be a sign of cardiac disease, a side effect of a prescribed medication, or a sign of the interaction of multiple medications. A wide QRS complex on an ECG is present in arrhythmias arising in the ventricles or in the presence of conduction defects in the ventricles.

20. The correct answer is 4. Raising the voice to shout loudly only increases the emission of higher frequency sounds, which the elderly client with presbycusis (a progressive bilateral perceptive loss of hearing in the older individual that occurs with the aging process) will have difficulty hearing. Facing the client when speaking allows the client to read lips as well as listen to the words. It is important to examine the ears for cerumen, which could be obstructing the auditory canal. Assessing the function of the client's hearing aid is important because the hearing aid batteries could be losing power.

Perioperative Nursing

OVERVIEW

Effects of Surgery on the Client

Physical Effects

A. Stress response (neuroendocrine response) is activated.
B. Resistance to infection is lowered due to surgical incision.
C. Vascular system is disturbed due to severing of blood vessels and blood loss.
D. Organ function may be altered due to manipulation.

Psychologic Effects

Common fears: pain, anesthesia, loss of control, disfigurement, separation from loved ones, alterations in roles or life-style

Factors Influencing Surgical Risk

A. *Age:* very young and elderly are at increased risk.
B. *Nutrition:* malnutrition and obesity increase risk of complications.
C. *Fluid and electrolyte balance:* dehydration, hypovolemia, and electrolyte imbalances can pose problems during surgery.
D. *General health status:* infection, cardiovascular disease, pulmonary problems, liver dysfunction, renal insufficiency, or metabolic disorders create increased risk.
E. *Medications*
   1. Anticoagulants (including aspirin and NSAIDS) predispose to hemorrhage; discontinue 2 weeks before surgery.
   2. Tranquilizers (e.g., phenothiazines) may cause hypotension and potentiate shock.
   3. Antibiotics: aminoglycosides may intensify

neuromuscular blockade of anesthesia with resultant respiratory paralysis.

   4. Diuretics: may cause electrolyte imbalances.
   5. Antihypertensives: can cause hypotension and contribute to shock.
   6. Long-term steroid therapy: causes adrenocortical suppression; may need increased dosage during perioperative period.

F. *Type of surgery planned:* major surgery (e.g., thoractomy) poses greater risk than minor surgery (e.g., dental extraction).

G. *Psychologic status of client:* excessive fear or anxiety may have adverse effect on surgery.

PREOPERATIVE PERIOD

Psychologic Support

A. Assess client's fears, anxieties, support systems, and patterns of coping.
B. Establish trusting relationship with client and significant others.
C. Explain routine procedures, encourage verbalization of fears, and allow client to ask questions.
D. Demonstrate confidence in surgeon and staff.
E. Provide for spiritual care if appropriate.

Preoperative Teaching

A. Frequently done on an outpatient basis.
B. Assess client's level of understanding of surgical procedure and its implications.
C. Answer questions, clarify and reinforce explanations given by surgeon.
D. Explain routine pre- and post-op procedures and any special equipment to be used.
E. Teach coughing and deep-breathing exercises, splinting of incision, turning side to side in bed, and leg exercises; explain their importance in preventing complications; provide opportunity for return demonstration.
F. Assure client that pain medication will be available post-op.

Physical Preparation

A. Obtain history of past medical conditions, surgical procedures, allergies, dietary restrictions, and medications.
B. Perform baseline head-to-toe assessment, including vital signs, height, and weight.
C. Ensure that diagnostic procedures are performed as ordered: common tests are
   1. CBC (complete blood count)
   2. Electrolytes
   3. PT/PTT (prothrombin time; partial thromboplastin time)
   4. Urinalysis
   5. ECG (electrocardiogram)
   6. Type and crossmatch
D. Prepare client's skin.
   1. Shower with antibacterial soap to cleanse skin if ordered; client may do this at home the night before surgery if outpatient admission.
   2. Skin prep if ordered: shave or clip hairs and cleanse appropriate areas to reduce bacteria on skin and minimize chance of infection.
E. Administer enema if ordered (usually for surgery on GI tract, gynecologic surgery).
F. Promote adequate rest and sleep.
   1. Provide back rub, clean linens.
   2. Administer bedtime sedation.
G. Instruct client to remain NPO after midnight to prevent vomiting and aspiration during surgery.

Legal Responsibilities

A. Surgeon obtains operative permit (*informed consent*).
   1. Surgical procedure, alternatives, possible complications, disfigurements, or removal of body parts are explained.
   2. It is part of the nurse's role as client advocate to confirm that the client understands information given.
B. Informed consent is necessary for each operation performed, however minor. It is also necessary for major diagnostic procedures, e.g., bronchoscopy, thoracentesis, etc., where a major body cavity is entered.
C. Adult client (over 18 years of age) signs own permit unless unconscious or mentally incompetent.
   1. If unable to sign, relative (spouse or next of kin) or guardian will sign.
   2. In an emergency, permission via telephone or telegram is acceptable; have a second listener on phone when telephone permission being given.
   3. Consents are not needed for emergency care if all four of the following criteria are met.
      a. There is an immediate threat to life.
      b. Experts agree that it is an emergency.
      c. Client is unable to consent.
      d. A legally authorized person cannot be reached.
D. Minors (under 18) must have consent signed by an adult (i.e., parent or legal guardian). An emancipated minor (married, college student living away from home, in military service) may sign own consent.
E. Witness to informed consent may be nurse, another physician, clerk, or other authorized person.

F. If nurse witnesses informed consent, specify whether witnessing explanation of surgery or just signature of client.

Preparation Immediately Before Surgery

A. Obtain baseline vital signs; report any elevated temperature.
B. Provide oral hygiene and remove dentures.
C. Remove client's clothing and dress in clean gown.
D. Remove nail polish, cosmetics, hair pins, prostheses.
E. Instruct client to empty bladder.
F. Check identification band.
G. Administer pre-op medications as ordered.
   1. Narcotic analgesics (meperidine [Demerol], morphine sulfate) relax client, reduce anxiety, and enhance effectiveness of general anesthesia.
   2. Sedatives (secobarbital sodium [Seconal]), sodium pentobarbital [Nembutal] decrease anxiety and promote relaxation and sleep.
   3. Anticholinergics (atropine sulfate, scopolamine [Hyoscine]) and glycopyrrolate (Robinul) decrease tracheobronchial secretions to minimize danger of aspirating secretions in lungs, decrease vagal response to inhibit undesirable effects of general anesthesia (bradycardia).
   4. Droperidol, fentanyl or a combination may be ordered; should not be given with sedatives because of danger of respiratory depression; also helpful in control of postoperative nausea and vomiting.
H. Elevate side rails and provide quiet environment.
I. Prepare client's chart for OR including operative permit and complete pre-op check list.

INTRAOPERATIVE PERIOD

Anesthesia

General Anesthesia

A. General information
   1. Drug-induced depression of CNS; produces decreased muscle reflex activity and loss of consciousness.
   2. Balanced anesthesia: combination of several anesthetic drugs to provide smooth induction, appropriate depth and duration of anesthesia, sufficient muscle relaxation, and minimal complications.
B. Stages of general anesthesia: induction, excitement, surgical anesthesia, and danger stage (see Table 4.12).
C. Agents for general anesthesia
   1. Inhalation agents
      a. Gas anesthetics
         1) nitrous oxide: induction agent; component of balanced anesthesia; used alone for short procedures; always given in combination with oxygen
         2) cyclopropane: obstetric anesthesia; clients with cardiovascular complications; highly flammable and explosive
      b. Liquid anesthetics
         1) halothane (Fluothane): widely used; rapid induction, low incidence of post-op nausea and vomiting; may cause bradycardia and hypotension; contraindicated in clients with liver disease.
         2) enflurane (Ethrane): effects similar to halothane, but muscle relaxation is stronger and hepatotoxicity not a problem; use cautiously in clients with cardiac disease.
         3) methoxyflurane (Penthrane): very potent agent with slow onset and

TABLE 4.12 Stages of Anesthesia

Stage	From	To	Client Status
Stage I (induction)	Beginning administration of anesthetic agent	Loss of consciousness	May appear euphoric, drowsy, dizzy.
Stage II (delirium or excitement)	Loss of consciousness	Relaxation	Breathing irregular; may appear excited; very susceptible to external stimuli.
Stage III (surgical anesthesia)	Relaxation	Loss of reflexes and depression of vital functions	Regular breathing pattern; corneal reflexes absent; pupillary constriction.
Stage IV (danger stage)	Vital functions depressed	Respiratory arrest; possible cardiac arrest	No respirations; absent or minimal heartbeat; dilated pupils

recovery; circulatory depression at high concentrations; associated with liver and kidney damage; rarely used.

    4) isoflurane (Forane): rapid induction and recovery; potentiates muscle relaxants; causes profound respiratory depression; monitor respirations carefully.

  2. IV anesthetics: used primarily as induction agents; produce rapid, smooth induction; may be used alone in short procedures such as dental extractions.

    a. Common IV anesthetics: methohexital (Brevital), sodium thiopental (Pentathol)

    b. Disadvantages: poor relaxation; respiratory and myocardial depression in high doses; bronchospasm, laryngospasm; hypotension, respiratory depression

  3. Dissociative agents: produce state of profound analgesia, amnesia, and lack of awareness without loss of consciousness; used alone in short surgical and diagnostic procedures or for induction prior to administration of more potent general anesthetics.

    a. Agent: ketamine (Ketalar)

    b. Side effects: tachycardia, hypertension, respiratory depression, hallucinations, delirium

    c. Precautions: decrease verbal, tactile, and visual stimulation during recovery period

  4. Neuroleptics: produce state of neuroleptic analgesia characterized by reduced motor activity, decreased anxiety, and analgesia without loss of consciousness; used alone for short surgical and diagnostic procedures, as premedication or in combination with other anesthetics for longer anesthesia.

    a. Agent: fentanyl citrate with droperidol (Innovar)

    b. Side effects: hypotension, bradycardia, respiratory depression, skeletal muscle rigidity, twitching

    c. Precautions: reduce narcotic doses by ½ to ⅓ for at least 8 hours postanesthesia as ordered to prevent respiratory depression.

D. Adjuncts to general anesthesia: neuro-muscular blocking agents: used with general anesthetics to enhance skeletal muscle relaxation.

  1. Agents: gallamine (Flaxedil), pancuronium (Pavulon), succinylcholine (Anectine), tubocurarine, atracurium besylate (Tubarine), vecuronium bromide (Norcuron)

TABLE 4.13 Regional Anesthesia

Types	Method
Topical	Cream, spray, drops, or ointment applied externally, directly to area to be anesthetized.
Local infiltration block	Injected into subcutaneous tissue of surgical area.
Field block	Area surrounding the surgical site injected with anesthetic.
Nerve block	Injection into a nerve plexus to anesthetize part of body.
Spinal	Anesthetic introduced into subarachnoid space of spinal cord producing anesthesia below level of diaphragm.
Epidural	Anesthetic injected extradurally to produce anesthesia below level of diaphragm; used in obstetrics.
Caudal	Variation of epidural block; produces anesthesia of perineum and occasionally lower abdomen; commonly used in obstetrics.
Saddle block	Similar to spinal, but anesthetized area is more limited; commonly used in obstetrics.

  2. Precaution: monitor client's respirations for at least 1 hour after drug's effect has worn off.

Regional Anesthesia

A. General information (see also Table 4.13).

  1. Produces loss of painful sensation in one area of the body; does not produce loss of consciousness.

  2. Uses: biopsies, excision of moles and cysts, endoscopies, surgery on extremities; childbirth

  3. Agents: lidocaine (Xylocaine), procaine (Novocain), tetracaine (Pontocaine)

POSTOPERATIVE PERIOD

Postoperative Care

Recovery Room (Immediate Postoperative Care)

A. Assess for and maintain patent airway.

  1. Position unconscious or semiconscious client on side (unless contraindicated) or on back with head to side and chin extended forward.

  2. Check for presence/absence of gag reflex.

  3. Maintain artificial airway in place until gag and swallow reflex have returned.

B. Administer oxygen as ordered.

C. Assess rate, depth, and quality of respirations.

D. Check vital signs every 15 minutes until stable, then every 30 minutes.
E. Note level of consciousness; reorient client to time, place, and situation.
F. Assess color and temperature of skin, color of nailbeds, and lips.
G. Monitor IV infusions: condition of site, type, and amount of fluid being infused and flow rate.
H. Check all drainage tubes and connect to suction or gravity drainage as ordered; note color, amount, and odor of drainage.
I. Assess dressings for intactness, drainage, hemorrhage.
J. Monitor and maintain client's temperature; may need extra blankets.
K. Encourage client to cough and deep breathe after airway is removed.
L. If spinal anesthesia used, maintain flat position and check for sensation and movement in lower extremities.

Care on Surgical Floor

A. Monitor respiratory status and promote optimal functioning.
   1. Encourage client to cough (if not contraindicated) and deep breathe every 1–2 hours.
   2. Instruct client to splint incision while coughing.
   3. Assist client to turn in bed every 2 hours.
   4. Encourage early ambulation.
   5. Encourage use of incentive spirometer every 2 hours: causes sustained, maximal inspiration that inflates the alveoli.
   6. Assess respiratory status and auscultate lungs every 4 hours; be alert for any signs of respiratory complications.
B. Monitor cardiovascular status and avoid post-op complications.
   1. Encourage leg exercises every 2 hours while in bed.
   2. Encourage early ambulation.
   3. Apply antiembolism stockings as ordered.
   4. Assess vital signs, color and temperature of skin every 4 hours.
C. Promote adequate fluid and electrolyte balance.
   1. Monitor IV and ensure adequate intake.
   2. Measure I&O.
   3. Irrigate NG tube properly, using normal saline solution.
   4. Observe for signs of fluid and electrolyte imbalances.
D. Promote optimum nutrition.
   1. Maintain IV infusion as ordered.
   2. Assess for return of peristalsis (presence of bowel sounds and flatus).
   3. Add progressively to diet as ordered and note tolerance.
E. Monitor and promote return of urinary function.

   1. Measure I&O.
   2. Assess client's ability to void.
   3. Report to surgeon if client has not voided within 8 hours after surgery.
   4. Check for bladder distention.
   5. Use measures to promote urination (e.g., assist male to sit on side of bed, pour warm water over female's perineum).
F. Promote bowel elimination.
   1. Encourage ambulation.
   2. Provide adequate food and fluid intake when tolerated.
   3. Keep stool record and note any difficulties with bowel elimination.
G. Administer post-op analgesics as ordered; provide additional comfort measures.
H. Encourage optimal activity, turning in bed every 2 hours, early ambulation if allowed (generally client will be out of bed within 24 hours; have client dangle legs before getting out of bed).
I. Provide wound care.
   1. Check dressings frequently to ensure they are clean, dry, and intact.
   2. Observe aseptic technique when changing dressings.
   3. Encourage diet high in protein and vitamin C.
   4. Report any signs of infection: redness, drainage, odor, fever.
J. Provide adequate psychologic support to client/significant others.
K. Provide appropriate discharge teaching: dietary restrictions, medication regimen, activity limitations, wound care, and possible complications.

Postoperative Complications

Respiratory System

Common post-op complications of respiratory tract are atelectasis and pneumonia (for additional information on these disorders see pages 255 and 256).
A. Predisposing factors
   1. Type of surgery (e.g., thoracic or high abdomen surgery)
   2. Previous history of respiratory problems
   3. Age: greater risk over age 40
   4. Obesity
   5. Smoking
   6. Respiratory depression caused by narcotics
   7. Severe post-op pain
   8. Prolonged post-op immobility
B. Prevention: see Care on Surgical Floor, above.

Cardiovascular System

Common post-op complications of the cardiovascular system are deep vein thrombosis, pulmonary embolism, and shock (for additional information on these disorders see pages 223, 224, and 149.

A. Predisposing factors to deep vein thrombosis (DVT)
1. Lower abdominal surgery or septic diseases (e.g., peritonitis)
2. Injury to vein by tight leg straps during surgery
3. Previous history of venous problems
4. Increased blood coagulability due to dehydration, fluid loss
5. Venous stasis in the extremity due to decreased movement during surgery
6. Prolonged post-op immobilization

B. Predisposing factors to pulmonary embolism: may occur as a complication of DVT.

C. Most common causes of shock during post-op period
1. Hemorrhage
2. Sepsis
3. Myocardial infarction and cardiac arrest
4. Drug reactions
5. Transfusion reactions
6. Pulmonary embolism
7. Adrenal failure

D. Prevention of DVT, pulmonary embolism, and shock: see Care on Surgical Floor, page 165.

Genitourinary System

Post-op complications of the genitourinary system often include urinary retention and urinary tract infection (for additional information on these disorders see pages 191 and 299).

A. Predisposing factors to urinary retention include
1. Anxiety
2. Pain
3. Lack of privacy
4. Narcotics and certain anesthetics that diminish client's sense of a full bladder

B. Prevention and nursing interventions for urinary retention: see Care on Surgical Floor, page 165.

C. Post-op urinary tract infections are most commonly caused by catheterization; prevention consists of using strict sterile technique when inserting a catheter, and appropriate catheter care (every 8 hours or according to agency protocol).

Gastrointestinal System

An important GI post-op complication is paralytic ileus (paralysis of intestinal peristalsis).

A. Predisposing factors
1. Temporary: anesthesia, manipulation of bowel during abdominal surgery
2. Prolonged: electrolyte imbalance, wound infection, pneumonia

B. Assessment findings
1. Absent bowel sounds
2. No passage of flatus
3. Abdominal distention

C. Nursing interventions
1. Assist with insertion of nasogastric or intestinal tube with application of suction as ordered.
2. Keep client NPO.
3. Maintain IV therapy as ordered.
4. Assess for bowel sounds every 4 hours; check for abdominal distention, passage of flatus.
5. Encourage ambulation if appropriate.

Wound Complications

A. Wound infection
1. Predisposing factors
   a. Obesity
   b. Diabetes mellitus
   c. Malnutrition
   d. Elderly clients
   e. Steroids and immunosuppressive agents
   f. Lowered resistance to infection, as found in clients with cancer
2. Assessment findings: redness, tenderness, drainage, heat in incisional area; fever; usually occurs 3–5 days after surgery.
3. Prevention: see Care on Surgical Floor, page 165.
4. Nursing interventions
   a. Obtain culture and sensitivity of wound drainage (*S. aureus* most frequently cultured).
   b. Perform cleansing and irrigation of wound as ordered.
   c. Administer antibiotic therapy as ordered.

B. Wound dehiscence and evisceration
1. Dehiscence: opening of wound edges
2. Evisceration: protrusion of loops of bowel through incision; usually accompanied by sudden escape of profuse, pink serous drainage
3. Predisposing factors to wound dehiscence and evisceration
   a. Wound infection
   b. Faulty wound closure
   c. Severe abdominal stretching (e.g., coughing, retching)
4. Nursing interventions for wound dehiscence
   a. Apply Steri-Strips to incision.
   b. Notify physician.
   c. Promote wound healing.
5. Nursing interventions for wound evisceration
   a. Place client in supine position.

b. Cover protruding intestinal loops with moist normal saline soaks.
c. Notify physician.
d. Check vital signs.
e. Observe for signs of shock.
f. Start IV line.
g. Prepare client for OR for surgical closure of wound.

Sample Questions

21. A 56 year old man is in the postanesthesia care unit (PACU) following a hemicolectomy. While in the PACU, the nurse will monitor his vital signs
    1. continuously.
    2. every 5 minutes.
    3. every 15 minutes.
    4. on a prn basis.
22. An adult who has had general anesthesia for major surgery is in the PACU. One of the signs that may indicate that his artificial airway should be removed is
    1. gagging.
    2. restlessness.
    3. an increase in pain.
    4. clear lungs on auscultation.
23. An adult is 6 days post abdominal surgery. Which sign alerts the nurse to wound evisceration?
    1. Acute bleeding.
    2. Pink serous drainage.
    3. Purple drainage.
    4. Severe pain.
24. An adult client's wound has eviscerated. The nurse assesses his respiratory status because
    1. dehiscence elevates the diaphragm.
    2. coughing increases the risk of evisceration.
    3. respiratory arrest commonly accompanies wound dehiscence.
    4. splinting the wound will compromise respiratory status.
25. A 26 year old has acute leukemia and is scheduled for a Hickman catheter insertion under local anesthesia. A MAJOR advantage of regional anesthesia is that the client
    1. retains all reflexes.
    2. remains conscious.
    3. has retroactive amnesia.
    4. is in the OR for a short period of time.

Answers and Rationales

21. The correct answer is 3. While in the PACU, client's vital signs are assessed every 15 minutes.
22. The correct answer is 1. The return of the gag reflex often indicates that the client is able to manage his own secretions and maintain a patent airway. Restlessness can indicate cerebral anoxia due to a blockage of the tube. Changes in the perception of pain are unrelated to intubation. It is expected that the client who is intubated will have clear lungs.
23. The correct answer is 2. A sudden gush of serosanguineous drainage that looks like "pink lemonade" is usually the major symptom of wound dehiscence. Clients usually complain of a ripping sensation, not pain, when the wound edges separate. Acute bleeding is not a common sign.
24. The correct answer is 2. Coughing increases intraabdominal pressure, which could force loops of bowel out through the open wound. It is essential to splint the wound to prevent evisceration. Wound dehiscence will not elevate the diaphragm or cause respiratory distress.
25. The correct answer is 2. The client receiving regional anesthesia has nerve impulses blocked but does not lose consciousness. Reflexes may be lost or diminished in the area that is anesthetized since sensory and motor functions are impaired. Retroactive amnesia does not occur unless the anesthesia is supplemented with other drugs. The length of time a client is in the operating room depends on the surgical procedure, not the type of anesthesia.

Oncologic Nursing

PATHOPHYSIOLOGY AND ETIOLOGY OF CANCER

Evolution of Cancer Cells

A. All cells constantly change through growth, degeneration, repair, and adaptation. Normal cells must divide and multiply to meet the needs of the organism as a whole, and this cycle of cell growth and destruction is an integral part of life processes. The activities of the normal cells in the human body are all coordinated to meet the needs of the organism as a whole, but when the regulatory control mechanisms of normal cells fail, and growth continues in excess of the body's needs, neoplasia results.

B. The term neoplasia refers to both benign and malignant growths, but malignant cells behave very differently from normal cells and have special features characteristic of the cancer process.

C. Since the growth control mechanism of normal cells is not entirely understood, it is not clear what allows the uncontrolled growth, therefore no definitive cure has been found.

Characteristics of Malignant Cells

Differentiation

A. Cancer cells are mutated stem cells that have undergone structural changes so that they are unable to perform the normal functions of specialized tissue (un- or dedifferentiation).

B. They may function in a disorderly way or cease normal function completely, only functioning for their own survival and growth.

C. The most undifferentiated cells are also called *anaplastic*.

Rate of Growth

A. Cancer cells have uncontrolled growth or cell division.

B. Rate at which a tumor grows involves both increased cell division and increased survival time of cells.

C. Malignant cells do not form orderly layers, but pile on top of each other to eventually form tumors.

Spread (Invasion and Metastasis)

A. Cancer cells are less adhesive than normal cells, more easily dissociated from their location.

B. Lack of adhesion and loss of contact inhibition make it possible for a cancer to spread to distant parts of the body (*metastasis*).

C. Malignant tumors are not encapsulated and expand into surrounding tissue (*invasion*).

Etiology (Carcinogenesis)

Actual cause of cancer is unknown but there are a number of theories; it is currently thought that there are probably multiple etiologies.

Environmental Factors

A. Majority (over 80%) of human cancers related to environmental carcinogens

B. Types
1. Physical
   a. Radiation: x-rays, radium, nuclear explosion or waste, ultraviolet
   b. Trauma or chronic irritation
2. Chemical
   a. Nitrites and food additives, polycyclic hydrocarbons, dyes, alkylating agents
   b. Drugs: arsenicals, stilbestrol, urethane
   c. Cigarette smoke
   d. Hormones

Genetics

A. Some cancers show familial pattern.

B. May be caused by inherited genetic defects.

Viral Theory

A. Viruses have been shown to be the cause of certain tumors in animals.

B. Oncoviruses (RNA-type viruses) thought to be culprit.

C. Viruses (HTLV-I, Epstein-Barr, Human Papilloma Virus) linked to human tumors.

Immunologic Factors

A. Failure of the immune system to respond to and eradicate cancer cells

B. Immunosuppressed individuals more susceptible to cancer

DIAGNOSIS OF CANCER

Classification and Staging

Tissue of Origin

A. *Carcinoma:* arises from surface, glandular, or parenchymal epithelium.

1. *Squamous cell carcinoma:* surface epithelium
2. *Adenocarcinoma:* glandular or parenchymal tissue

B. *Sarcoma:* arises from connective tissue.
C. *Leukemia, lymphoma,* and *multiple myeloma:* separate categories for each

Stages of Tumor Growth

A. Several staging systems, important in selection of therapy
  1. TNM system: uses letters and numbers to designate the extent of the tumor.
     a. T: stands for primary growth; 1–4 with increasing size. T1S indicates carcinoma in situ.
     b. N: stands for lymph node involvement; 0–4 indicates progressively advancing nodal disease.
     c. M: stands for metastasis; 0 indicates no distant metastases, 1 indicates presence of metastases.
  2. Stages 0-IV: all cancers divided into five stages incorporating size, nodal involvement, and spread.
B. Cytologic diagnosis of cancer (e.g., Pap smear)
  1. Involves study of shed cells
  2. Classified by degree of cellular abnormality
     a. Normal
     b. Probably normal (slight changes)
     c. Doubtful (more severe changes)
     d. Probably cancer or precancerous
     e. Definitely cancer

Client Factors

Early detection of cancer is crucial in reducing morbidity and mortality. Clients need to be taught about
A. Seven warning signs of cancer (see Table 4.14).
B. Breast self-examination (BSE) (see page 512).
C. Importance of rectal exam for those over age 40
D. Hazards of smoking
E. Oral self-examination as well as annual exam of mouth and teeth
F. Hazards of excess sun exposure
G. Importance of Pap smear
H. Physical exam with lab work-up: every 3 years ages 20–40; yearly age 40 and over

TABLE 4.14   Seven Warning Signs of Cancer (Caution)

C — Change in bowel or bladder habits
A — A sore that doesn't heal
U — Unusual bleeding or discharge
T — Thickening or lump in breast (or elsewhere)
I — Indigestion or dysphagia
O — Obvious change in wart or mole
N — Nagging cough or hoarseness

I. Testicular self-examination (TSE)
  1. *Testicular Cancer:* Most common cancer in young men between the ages of 15 and 34. Most testicular cancers are found by men themselves, by accident or when doing TSE.
  2. *Testicular Self-Examination:* Ideally, should be performed monthly, after a warm shower or bath, when the skin of the scrotum is relaxed. Standing in front of a mirror, the man should gently roll each testicle between the thumb and fingers of both hands. The testes are smooth, oval-shaped, and rather firm.
  3. *Warning Signs That Men Should Look For:*
     a. Painless swelling
     b. Feeling of heaviness
     c. Hard lump (size of a pea)
     d. Sudden collection of fluid in the scrotum
     e. Dull ache in the lower abdomen or in the groin
     f. Pain in a testicle or in the scrotum
     g. Enlargement or tenderness of the breasts

TREATMENT OF CANCER

Chemotherapy

Principles

A. Based on ability of drug to kill cancer cells; normal cells may also be damaged, producing side effects discussed below. Effect is greatest on rapidly dividing cells, such as bone marrow cells, the GI tract and hair.
B. Different drugs act on tumor cells in different stages of the cell growth cycle.

Types of Chemotherapeutic Drugs

See Tables 2.25–2.29 in Unit 2.
A. Antimetabolites: foster cancer cell death by interfering with cellular metabolic process.
B. Alkylating agents: act with DNA to hinder cell growth and division.
C. Plant alkaloids: obtained from the periwinkle plant; makes the host's body a less favorable environment for the growth of cancer cells.
D. Antitumor antibiotics: affect RNA to make environment less favorable for cancer growth.
E. Steroids and sex hormones: alter the endocrine environment to make it less conducive to growth of cancer cells.

Major Side Effects and Nursing Interventions

A. GI system
  1. Nausea and vomiting
     a. Administer antiemetics routinely every

4–6 hours as well as prophylactically before chemotherapy is initiated.
   b. Withhold foods/fluids 4–6 hours before chemotherapy.
   c. Provide bland foods in small amounts after treatments.
2. Diarrhea
   a. Administer antidiarrheals.
   b. Maintain good perineal care.
   c. Give clear liquids as tolerated.
   d. Monitor potassium, sodium, and chloride levels.
3. Stomatitis
   a. Provide and teach the client good oral hygiene, including avoidance of commercial mouthwashes.
   b. Rinse with viscous lidocaine before meals to provide an analgesic effect.
   c. Perform a cleansing rinse with plain water or dilute a water-soluble lubricant such as hydrogen peroxide after meals.
   d. Apply water-soluble lubricant such as K-Y jelly to lubricate cracked lips.
   e. Advise client to suck on Popsicles to provide moisture.
B. Hematologic system
   1. Thrombocytopenia
      a. Teach client the importance of avoiding bumping or bruising the skin.
      b. Protect client from physical injury.
      c. Avoid aspirin or aspirin products.
      d. Avoid giving IM injections.
      e. Monitor blood counts carefully.
      f. Assess for and teach signs of increased bleeding tendencies (epistaxis, petechiae, ecchymoses).
   2. Leukopenia
      a. Use careful handwashing technique.
      b. Maintain reverse isolation if white blood cell count drops below 1000/mm^3.
      c. Assess for signs of respiratory infection.
      d. Instruct client to avoid crowds/persons with known infection.
   3. Anemia
      a. Provide for adequate rest periods.
      b. Monitor hemoglobin and hematocrit.
      c. Protect client from injury.
      d. Administer oxygen as necessary.
C. Integumentary system—Alopecia
   1. Explain that hair loss is not permanent.
   2. Offer support and encouragement.
   3. Scalp tourniquets or scalp hypothermia via ice pack may be ordered to minimize hair loss with some agents.
   4. Advise client to obtain a wig before initiating treatments.
D. Renal System
   1. May cause direct damage to kidney by excretion of metabolites; encourage fluids and frequent voiding to prevent accumulation of metabolites in bladder.
   2. Increased excretion of uric acid may damage kidneys.
   3. Administer allopurinol (Zyloprim) as ordered to prevent uric acid formation; encourage fluids when administering allopurinol.
E. Reproductive System
   1. Damage may occur to both men and women resulting in infertility and/or mutagenic damage to chromosomes.
   2. Banking sperm often recommended for men before chemotherapy.
   3. Patients and partners advised to use reliable methods of contraception during chemotherapy.
F. Neurologic System
   1. Plant alkaloids (vincristine) cause neurologic damage with repeated doses.
   2. Peripheral neuropathies, hearing loss, loss of deep tendon reflexes, and paralytic ileus may occur.

Radiation Therapy

Principles

A. Radiation therapy uses ionizing radiation to kill or limit the growth of cancer cells, may be internal or external.
B. It not only injures the cell membrane, but destroys or alters DNA so that the cells cannot reproduce.
C. Like chemotherapy, effect cannot be limited to cancer cells only; all exposed cells, including normal ones, will be injured, causing side effects discussed below. Localized effects are related to area of body being treated; generalized effects may be related to cellular breakdown products.
D. Types of energy emitted
   1. Alpha: particles cannot pass through skin, rarely used
   2. Beta: particles cannot pass through skin, somewhat more penetrating than alpha, generally emitted from radioactive isotopes, used for internal source
   3. Gamma rays (electromagnetic or x-rays): penetrate deeper areas of body, most common form of external radiotherapy.

Methods of Delivery

A. External radiation therapy: beams high-energy rays directly to the affected area.
B. Internal radiation therapy: radioactive material is injected or implanted in the client's body for a designated period of time.
   1. Sealed implants: a radioisotope enclosed in a container so it does not circulate in the

body; client's body fluids should not become contaminated with radiation.
  2. Unsealed sources: a radioisotope that is not encased in a container and does circulate in the body and contaminate body fluids.

Factors Controlling Exposure

A. Half-life: time required for half of radioactive atoms to decay
  1. Each radioisotope has a different half-life.
  2. At the end of the half-life, the danger from exposure decreases.
B. Time: the shorter the duration, the less the exposure
C. Distance: the greater the distance from the radiation source the less the exposure
D. Shielding: all radiation can be blocked; rubber gloves stop alpha and usually beta rays; thick lead or concrete stops gamma rays
E. These factors affect health care worker's exposure as well as client's.
  1. Health care worker at greater risk from internal than external sources
  2. Film badge can measure the amount of exposure received
  3. No pregnant nurses or visitors permitted near radiation source

Side Effects of Radiation Therapy and Nursing Interventions

A. Skin: itching, redness, burning, oozing, sloughing
  1. Keep skin free from foreign substances.
  2. Avoid use of medicated solutions, ointments, or powders that contain heavy metals such as zinc oxide.
  3. Avoid pressure, trauma, infection to skin; use bed cradle.
  4. Wash affected areas with plain water and pat dry; avoid soap.
  5. Use cornstarch, olive oil for itching; avoid talcum powder.
  6. If sloughing occurs, use a sterile dressing with micropore tape.
  7. Teach client to avoid exposing skin to heat, cold, or sunlight and to avoid constricting or irritating clothing.
B. Anorexia, nausea, and vomiting
  1. Arrange mealtimes so they do not directly precede or follow therapy.
  2. Encourage bland foods.
  3. Provide small, attractive meals.
  4. Avoid extremes of temperature.
  5. Administer antiemetics as ordered before meals.
C. Diarrhea
  1. Encourage low-residue, bland, high-protein foods.
  2. Administer antidiarrheal drugs as ordered.

  3. Provide good perineal care.
  4. Monitor electrolytes, particularly sodium, potassium, and chloride.
D. Anemia, leukopenia, and thrombocytopenia
  1. Isolate from those with known infections.
  2. Provide frequent rest periods.
  3. Encourage high-protein diet.
  4. Instruct client to avoid injury.
  5. Assess for bleeding.
  6. Monitor CBC, leukocytes, and platelets.

Bone Marrow Transplant

A. General information
  1. Treatment alternative for a variety of diseases
    a. Malignancies including several types of leukemias
    b. Blood disorders including severe aplastic anemia, thalassemia
    c. Solid tumors such as breast cancer and brain tumors; treatment for these diseases frequently causes bone marrow destruction; autologous bone marrow transplant may be indicated (Bone marrow harvested before chemotherapy or radiation destroys it and infused after therapy completed)
    d. Other conditions including malignant infantile osteopetrosis, some inherited metabolic disorders
  2. Types
    a. Autologous: client transplant with own harvested marrow
    b. Syngeneic: transplant between identical twins
    c. Allogeneic: transplant from a genetically nonidentical donor
      1) most common transplant type
      2) sibling most common donor
  3. Procedure
    a. Donor suitability determined through tissue antigen typing; includes human leukocyte antigen (HLA) and mixed leukocyte culture (MLC) typing.
    b. Donor bone marrow is aspirated from multiple sites along the iliac crests under general anesthesia.
    c. Donor marrow is infused IV into the recipient.
  4. Early evidence of engraftment seen during the second week posttransplant; hematologic reconstitution takes 4–6 weeks; immunologic reconstitution takes months.
  5. Hospitalization of 2 or 3 months required.
  6. Prognosis is highly variable depending on indication for use.
B. Complications
  1. Failure of engraftment
  2. Infection: highest risk in first 3–4 weeks

3. Pneumonia: nonbacterial or interstitial pneumonias are principal cause of death during first 3 months posttransplant
4. *Graft vs host disease (GVHD):* principal complication; caused by an immunologic reaction of engrafted lymphoid cells against the tissues of the recipient
   a. Acute GVHD: develops within first 100 days posttransplant and affects skin, gut, liver, marrow, and lymphoid tissue
   b. Chronic GVHD: develops 100–400 days post-transplant; manifested by multiorgan involvement
5. Recurrent malignancy
6. Late complications such as cataracts, endocrine abnormalities
C. Nursing care: pretransplant
1. Recipient immunosuppression attained with total body irradiation (TBI) and chemotherapy to eradicate existing disease and create space in host marrow to allow transplanted cells to grow.
2. Provide protected environment.
   a. Client should be in a laminar air flow room or on strict reverse isolation; surveillance cultures done twice a week.
   b. Objects must be sterilized before being brought into the room.
   c. When working with children introduce new people where they can be seen, but outside child's room so child can see what they look like without isolation garb.
3. Monitor central lines frequently; check patency and observe for signs of infection (fever, redness around site).
4. Provide care for the client receiving chemotherapy and radiation therapy to induce immunosuppression.
   a. Administer chemotherapy as ordered, assist with radiation therapy if required.
   b. Monitor side effects and keep client as comfortable as possible.
   c. Monitor carefully for potential infection.
   d. Client will become very ill; prepare client and family.
D. Nursing care: posttransplant
1. Prevent infection.
   a. Maintain protective environment.
   b. Administer antibiotics as ordered.
   c. Assess all mucous membranes, wounds, catheter sites for swelling, redness, tenderness, pain.
   d. Monitor vital signs frequently (every 1–4 hours as needed).
   e. Collect specimens for cultures as needed and twice a week.
   f. Change IV set-ups every 24 hours.
2. Provide mouth care for stomatitis and mucositis (severe mucositis develops about 5 days after irradiation).
   a. Note tissue sloughing, bleeding, changes in color.
   b. Provide mouth rinses, viscous lidocaine, and antibiotic rinses.
   c. Do not use lemon and glycerin swabs.
   d. Administer parenteral narcotics as ordered if necessary to control pain.
   e. Provide care every 2 hours or as needed.
3. Provide skin care: skin breakdown may result from profuse diarrhea from the TBI.
4. Monitor carefully for bleeding.
   a. Check for occult blood in emesis and stools.
   b. Observe for easy bruising, petechiae on skin, mucous membranes.
   c. Monitor changes in vital signs.
   d. Check platelet count daily.
   e. Replace blood products as ordered (all blood products should be irradiated).
5. Maintain fluid and electrolyte balance and promote nutrition.
   a. Measure I&O carefully.
   b. Provide adequate fluid, protein, and caloric intake.
   c. Weigh daily.
   d. Administer fluid replacement as ordered.
   e. Monitor hydration status: check skin turgor, moisture of mucous membranes, urine output.
   f. Check electrolytes daily.
   g. Check urine for glucose, ketones, protein.
   h. Administer antidiarrheal agents as needed.
6. Provide client teaching and discharge planning concerning
   a. Home environment (e.g., cleaning, pets, visitors)
   b. Diet modifications
   c. Medication regimen: schedule, dosages, effects, and side effects
   d. Communicable diseases and immunizations
   e. Daily hygiene and skin care
   f. Fever
   g. Activity

Sample Questions

26. A 43 year old woman is undergoing chemotherapy treatment for uterine cancer. She asks the nurse how chemotherapeutic drugs work. The most accurate explanation would include which statement?
    1. They affect all rapidly dividing cells.
    2. Molecular structure of the DNA segment is altered.

3. Chemotherapy stimulates cancer cells to divide.
4. The cancer cells are sensitive to drug toxins.

27. An adult experiences severe vomiting from cancer chemotherapy drugs. Which acid-base imbalance should the nurse anticipate?
1. Ketoacidosis.
2. Metabolic acidosis.
3. Metabolic alkalosis.
4. Respiratory alkalosis.

28. A woman loses most of her hair as a result of cancer chemotherapy. The nurse understands that which of the following is true about chemotherapy-induced alopecia?
1. New hair will be gray.
2. Avoid the use of wigs.
3. The hair loss is temporary.
4. Pre-chemo hair texture will return.

29. A 24 year old is diagnosed with Hodgkin's disease Stage 1A. He is being treated with radiation therapy. To minimize skin damage from radiation therapy, the nursing care plan should include which of the following?
1. Avoid washing with water.
2. Apply a heating pad to the site.
3. Cover the area with an airtight dressing.
4. Avoid applying creams and powders to the area.

30. An adult develops a second-degree or second-level skin reaction from radiation therapy. When evaluating his symptoms, the nurse can expect to find all of the following except
1. scaly skin.
2. an itchy feeling.
3. dry desquamation.
4. reddening of the skin.

31. An adult client is receiving radiation therapy. The nurse is teaching the client about signs of radiation-induced thrombocytopenia, which include
1. fatigue.
2. shortness of breath.
3. elevated temperature.
4. a tendency to bruise easily.

32. The nurse is caring for a client who is receiving radiation therapy. Which activity by the client indicates he does NOT understand the side effects of radiation therapy?
1. Using an electric razor.
2. Eating a high-protein diet.
3. Taking his children to see Santa at the mall.
4. Calling the doctor for a temperature of 101°F (38.3°C).

Answers and Rationales

26. The correct answer is 1. There are numerous mechanisms of action for chemotherapeutic drugs, but most affect rapidly dividing cells. Cancer cells are characterized by rapid division. Some, but not all, chemotherapeutic drugs affect molecular structure. Chemotherapy slows, not stimulates, cell division. All cells are sensitive to drug toxins, but not all chemotherapeutic drugs are toxins; there are several different mechanisms of action.

27. The correct answer is 3. Severe vomiting results in a loss of hydrochloric acid and acids from extracellular fluids, leading to metabolic alkalosis. It is rare that a loss of base intestinal fluids results in metabolic acidosis.

28. The correct answer is 3. Alopecia from chemotherapy is only temporary. While hair color and texture may change following loss due to chemotherapy, the returning color will not necessarily be gray. Hair loss is a serious threat to self-esteem in the client receiving chemotherapeutic drugs. Clients who will be receiving medications known to cause hair loss should be encouraged to purchase a wig while they still have hair to allow for matching.

29. The correct answer is 4. Creams and powders, many of which contain heavy metals, will further irritate skin sensitized by radiation therapy and reduce the effectiveness of therapy by blocking radiation. The client may wash with water only, but must take care not to wash off the radiation markings. It would not be desirable to further heat the area. Covering the area is not desirable. The area should be left open to the air as much as possible.

30. The correct answer is 4. Reddening of the skin will not be seen in a second-level or second-degree skin reaction. A second-degree skin reaction would be evidenced by scaly skin, an itchy feeling, and dry desquamation.

31. The correct answer is 4. Clients with decreased platelet counts (thrombocytopenia) have a tendency to bruise easily. Fatigue could indicate anemia. Shortness of breath could be evidence of fluid overload, respiratory disease, or decreased red cells. Elevated temperature could indicate infection due to decreased white cells.

32. The correct answer is 3. People being treated with radiation therapy should avoid crowds because of the increased risk of infection. Crowds at Christmastime can be very large and children are frequent carriers of infection. Use of an electric razor would be preferable to using a safety razor because of the danger of cutting the skin and causing prolonged bleeding due to the thrombocytopenia. The client should eat a high-protein diet. The client should call his doctor for a temperature of 101°F.

The Neurosensory System

OVERVIEW OF ANATOMY AND PHYSIOLOGY

The Nervous System

The functional unit of the nervous system is the nerve cell, or neuron. The nervous system consists of the central nervous system (CNS), which includes the brain and spinal cord, and the peripheral nervous system (PNS), which includes the cranial nerves and the spinal nerves. The autonomic nervous system (ANS) is a subdivision of the PNS that automatically controls body functions such as breathing and heartbeat. It is further divided into the sympathetic and parasympathetic nervous systems. The special senses of vision and hearing are also covered in this section.

Neuron

A. Primary component of the nervous system; composed of cell body (gray matter), axon, and dendrites
B. *Axon:* elongated process or fiber extending from the cell body; transmits impulses (messages) away from the cell body to dendrites or directly to the cell bodies of other neurons; neuron usually has only one axon.
C. *Dendrites:* short, branching fibers that receive impulses and conduct them toward the nerve cell body. Neurons may have many dendrites.
D. *Synapse:* junction between neurons where an impulse is transmitted
E. *Neurotransmitters:* chemical agents (e.g., acetylcholine, norepinephrine) involved in the transmission of impulse across synapse
F. *Myelin sheath:* a wrapping of myelin (a whitish, fatty material) that protects and insulates nerve fibers and enhances the speed of impulse conduction
   1. Both axons and dendrites may or may not have a myelin sheath (myelinated/unmyelinated)
   2. Most axons leaving the CNS are heavily myelinated by *Schwann cells*

Functional Classification

A. *Afferent (sensory) neurons:* transmit impulses from peripheral receptors to the CNS
B. *Efferent (motor) neurons:* conduct impulses from CNS to muscles and glands
C. *Internuncial neurons (interneurons):* connecting links between afferent and efferent neurons

Central Nervous System: Brain and Spinal Cord

Brain

A. *Cerebrum:* outermost area (cerebral cortex) is gray matter; deeper area is composed of white matter
   1. Two hemispheres: right and left
   2. Each hemisphere divided into four lobes; many of the functional areas of the cerebrum have been located in these lobes (see Figure 4.1).
      a. *Frontal lobe*
         1) personality, behavior
         2) higher intellectual functioning
         3) precentral gyrus: motor function
         4) Broca's area: specialized motor speech area
      b. *Parietal lobe*
         1) postcentral gyrus: registers general sensation (e.g., touch, pressure)
         2) integrates sensory information
      c. *Temporal lobe*
         1) hearing, taste, smell
         2) Wernicke's area: sensory speech area (understanding/formulation of language)
      d. *Occipital lobe:* vision
   3. *Corpus callosum:* large fiber tract that connects the two cerebral hemispheres
   4. *Basal ganglia:* islands of gray matter within white matter of cerebrum
      a. Regulate and integrate motor activity originating in the cerebral cortex
      b. Part of extrapyramidal system

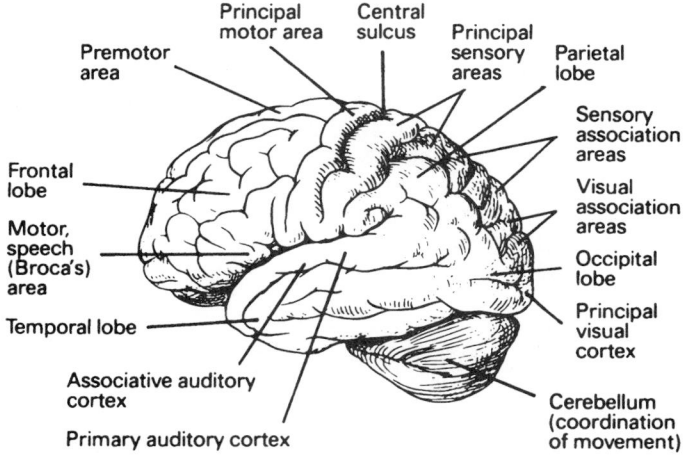

FIGURE 4.1 Side view of the brain, showing principal functional areas

B. *Diencephalon:* connecting part of the brain, between the cerebrum and the brain stem. Contains several small structures; the thalamus and hypothalamus are most important
   1. *Thalamus*
      a. Relay station for discrimination of sensory signals (e.g., pain, temperature, touch)
      b. Controls primitive emotional responses (e.g., rage, fear).
   2. *Hypothalamus*
      a. Found immediately beneath the thalamus.
      b. Plays major role in regulation of vital functions such as blood pressure, sleep, food and water intake, and body temperature.
      c. Acts as control center for pituitary gland and affects both divisions of the autonomic nervous system.
C. *Brain stem*
   1. Contains midbrain, pons, and medulla oblongata.
   2. Extends from the cerebral hemispheres to the foramen magnum at the base of the skull.
   3. Contains nuclei of the cranial nerves and the long ascending and descending tracts connecting the cerebrum and the spinal cord.
   4. Contains vital centers of respiratory, vasomotor, and cardiac functions.
D. *Cerebellum:* coordinates muscle tone and movements and maintains position in space (equilibrium).

Spinal Cord

A. Serves as a connecting link between the brain and the periphery.
B. Extends from foramen magnum to second lumbar vertebra.
C. H-shaped gray matter in the center (cell bodies) surrounded by white matter (nerve tracts and fibers).
D. *Gray matter*
   1. Anterior horns: contain cell bodies giving rise to efferent (motor) fibers
   2. Posterior horns: contain cell bodies connecting with afferent (sensory) fibers from dorsal root ganglion
   3. Lateral horns: in thoracic region, contain cells giving rise to autonomic fibers of sympathetic nervous system
E. *White matter*
   1. Ascending tracts (sensory pathways)
      a. Posterior columns: carry impulses concerned with touch, pressure, vibration, and position sense.
      b. Spinocerebellar: carry impulses concerned with muscle tension and position sense to cerebellum.

      c. Lateral spinothalamic: carry impulses resulting in pain and temperature sensations.
      d. Anterior spinothalamic: carry impulses concerned with crude touch and pressure.
   2. Descending tracts (motor pathways)
      a. Corticospinal (pyramidal, upper motor neuron): conduct motor impulses from motor cortex to anterior horn cells (cross in the medulla).
      b. Extrapyramidal: help to maintain muscle tone and to control body movement, especially gross automatic movements such as walking.
F. *Reflex arc*
   1. Reflex consists of an involuntary response to a stimulus occurring over a neural pathway called a reflex arc.
   2. Not relayed to and from brain; takes place at cord levels.
   3. Components
      a. Sensory receptor: receives/reacts to a stimulus.
      b. Afferent pathway: transmits impulses to spinal cord.
      c. Interneuron: synapses with a motor neuron (anterior horn cell).
      d. Efferent pathway: transmits impulses from motor neuron to effector.
      e. Effector: muscle or organ that responds to stimulus.

Supporting Structures

A. Skull
   1. Rigid; numerous bones fused together
   2. Protects and supports the brain.
B. Spinal column
   1. Consists of 7 cervical, 12 thoracic, and 5 lumbar vertebrae, as well as sacrum and coccyx.
   2. Supports the head and protects the spinal cord.
C. Meninges
   1. Membranes between the skull and brain and the vertebral column and spinal cord
   2. Layers
      a. *Dura mater:* outermost layer, tough, leathery
      b. *Arachnoid mater:* middle layer, web-like
      c. *Pia mater:* innermost layer, delicate, clings to surface of brain
   3. Area between arachnoid and pia mater is called *subarachnoid space.*
D. Ventricles
   1. Four fluid-filled cavities connecting with one another and the spinal canal
   2. Produce and circulate cerebrospinal fluid.
E. *Cerebrospinal fluid (CSF)*
   1. Surrounds brain and spinal cord.

2. Offers protection by functioning as a shock absorber.
3. Allows fluid shifts from the cranial cavity to the spinal cavity.
4. Carries nutrients to and waste products away from nerve cells.

F. Vascular supply
   1. Two *internal carotid arteries* anteriorally
   2. Two *vertebral arteries* leading to basilar artery posteriorally
   3. These arteries communicate at the base of the brain through the *circle of Willis.*
   4. Anterior, middle, and posterior cerebral arteries are the main arteries for distributing blood to each hemisphere of the brain.
   5. Brain stem and cerebellum are supplied by branches of the vertebral and basilar arteries.
   6. Venous blood drains into dural sinuses and then into internal jugular veins.

G. *Blood-brain barrier:* protective barrier preventing harmful agents from entering the capillaries of the CNS; protects brain and spinal cord.

Peripheral Nervous System

Spinal Nerves

A. 31 pairs: carry impulses to and from spinal cord.
B. Each segment of the spinal cord contains a pair of spinal nerves (one for each side of the body).
C. Each nerve is attached to the spinal cord by two roots.
   1. Dorsal (posterior) root: contains afferent (sensory) nerve whose cell body is in the dorsal root ganglion.
   2. Ventral (anterior) root: contains efferent (motor) nerve whose nerve fibers originate in the anterior horn cell of the spinal cord (lower motor neuron).

Cranial Nerves

A. 12 pairs: carry impulses to and from brain (see Table 4.15).
B. May have sensory, motor, or mixed functions.

Autonomic Nervous System

A. Part of the peripheral nervous system
B. Includes those peripheral nerves (both cranial and spinal) that regulate functions occurring automatically in the body; ANS regulates smooth muscle, cardiac muscle, and glands.
C. Components
   1. *Sympathetic nervous system:* generally accelerates some body functions in response to stress

TABLE 4.15 Cranial Nerves

Name and Number	Function
Olfactory: cranial nerve I	Sensory: carries impulses for sense of smell
Optic: cranial nerve II	Sensory: carries impulses for vision
Oculomotor: cranial nerve III	Motor: muscles for pupillary constriction, elevation of upper eyelid; 4 out of 6 extraocular movements
Trochlear: cranial nerve IV	Motor: muscles for downward, inward movement of eye
Trigeminal: cranial nerve V	Mixed: impulses from face, surface of eyes (corneal reflex); muscles controlling mastication
Abducens: cranial nerve VI	Motor: muscles for lateral deviation of eye
Facial: cranial nerve VII	Mixed: impulses for taste from anterior tongue; muscles for facial movement
Acoustic: cranial nerve VIII	Sensory: impulses for hearing (cochlear division) and balance (vestibular division)
Glossopharyngeal: cranial nerve IX	Mixed: impulses for sensation to posterior tongue and pharynx; muscles for movement of pharynx (elevation) and swallowing
Vagus: cranial nerve X	Mixed: impulses for sensation to lower pharynx and larynx; muscles for movement of soft palate, pharynx, and larynx
Spinal accessory: cranial nerve XI	Motor: movement of sternomastoid muscles and upper part of trapezius muscles
Hypoglossal: cranial nerve XII	Motor: movement of tongue

   2. *Parasympathetic nervous system:* controls normal body functioning
D. Effects of ANS activity: see Table 4.16.

Vision

External Structures of Eye

A. Eyelids (palpebrae) and eyelashes: protect the eye from foreign particles
B. *Conjunctiva*
   1. Palpebral conjunctiva: pink; lines inner surface of eyelids.
   2. Bulbar conjunctiva: white with small blood vessels, covers anterior sclera.
C. *Lacrimal apparatus* (lacrimal gland and its ducts and passages): produces tears to lubricate the eye and moisten the cornea; tears drain into the nasolacrimal duct, which empties into nasal cavity.
D. Movement of the eye is controlled by six extraocular muscles.

TABLE 4.16   Effects of Autonomic Nervous System Activity

Effector	Sympathetic (Adrenergic) Effects	Parasympathetic (Cholinergic) Effects
Eye	Dilates pupil (mydriasis)	Constricts pupil (miosis)
Glands of head		
Lacrimal	No effect	Stimulates secretion
Salivary	Scanty thick, viscous secretions; dry mouth	Copious thin, watery secretions
Heart	Increases rate and force of contraction	Decreases rate
Blood vessels	Constricts smooth muscles of skin, abdominal blood vessels, and cutaneous blood vessels	No effect
	Dilates smooth muscle of bronchioles, blood vessels of heart, and skeletal muscles	
Lungs	Bronchodilation	Bronchoconstriction
GI tract	Decreases motility	Increases motility
	Constricts sphincters	Relaxes sphincters
	Possibly inhibits secretions	Stimulates secretion
	Inhibits activity of gallbladder and ducts	Stimulates activity of gallbladder and ducts
	Inhibits glycogenolysis in liver	
Adrenal gland	Stimulates secretion of epinephrine and norepinephrine	No effects
Urinary tract	Relaxes detrusor muscle	Contracts detrusor muscle
	Contracts trigone sphincter (prevents voiding)	Relaxes trigone sphincter (allows voiding)

Internal Structures of Eye

A. Three layers of the eyeball
   1. Outer layer
      a. *Sclera:* tough, white connective tissue ("white of the eye"); located anteriorly and posteriorly
      b. *Cornea:* transparent tissue through which light enters the eye; located anteriorly
   2. Middle layer
      a. *Choroid:* highly vascular layer, nourishes retina; located posteriorly
      b. *Ciliary body:* anterior to choroid, secretes aqueous humor; muscles change shape of lens
      c. *Iris:* pigmented membrane behind cornea, gives color to eye; located

anteriorly. *Pupil* is a circular opening in the middle of the iris that constricts or dilates to regulate amount of light entering eye.
   3. Inner layer: *retina*
      a. Light-sensitive layer composed of rods and cones (visual cells)
         1) cones: specialized for fine discrimination and color vision
         2) rods: more sensitive to light than cones, aid in peripheral vision
      b. *Optic disk:* area in retina for entrance of optic nerve, has no photoreceptors
B. *Lens:* transparent body that focuses image on retina.
C. Fluids of the eye
   1. *Aqueous humor:* clear, watery fluid in anterior and posterior chambers in anterior part of eye; serves as refracting medium and provides nutrients to lens and cornea; contributes to maintenance of intraocular pressure.
   2. *Vitreous humor:* clear, gelatinous material that fills posterior cavity of eye; maintains transparency and form of eye.

Visual Pathways

A. Retina (rods and cones) translates light waves into neural impulses that travel over the optic nerves.
B. Optic nerves for each eye meet at the optic chiasm.
   1. Fibers from median halves of the retinas cross here and travel to the opposite side of the brain.
   2. Fibers from lateral halves of retinas remain uncrossed.
C. Optic nerves continue from optic chiasm as optic tracts and travel to the cerebrum (occipital lobe), where visual impulses are perceived and interpreted.

Hearing

External Ear

A. Auricle (pinna): outer projection of ear composed of cartilage and covered by skin; collects sound waves.
B. *External auditory canal:* lined with skin; glands secrete cerumen (wax), providing protection; transmits sound waves to tympanic membrane.
C. *Tympanic membrane (eardrum):* at end of external canal; vibrates in response to sound and transmits vibrations to middle ear.

Middle Ear

A. *Ossicles*
   1. 3 small bones: *malleus (hammer)* attached

to tympanic membrane, *incus (anvil),
stapes (stirrup)*
2. Ossicles are set in motion by sound waves
from tympanic membrane.
3. Sound waves are conducted by vibration to
the footplate of the stapes in the *oval
window* (an opening between the middle
ear and the inner ear).
B. *Eustachian tube:* connects nasopharynx and
middle ear; brings air into middle ear, thus
equalizing pressure on both sides of eardrum.

Inner Ear

A. *Cochlea*
1. Contains *organ of Corti,* the receptor end-
organ for hearing
2. Transmits sound waves from the oval
window and initiates nerve impulses
carried by cranial nerve VIII (acoustic
branch) to the brain (temporal lobe of
cerebrum).
B. *Vestibular apparatus*
1. Organ of balance
2. Composed of three semicircular canals and
the utricle.

ASSESSMENT

Health History

Nervous System

A. Presenting problem: symptoms may include
behavior changes, memory loss, mood
changes, nervousness or anxiety, headache,
seizures, syncope, vertigo, loss of
consciousness; problems with speech, vision,
or smell; motor problems (paralysis, tremor);
sensory problems (pain, paresthesias)
B. Life-style: drug and alcohol intake, exposure to
toxins, recent travel, employment, stressors
C. Use of medications: prescribed and over-the-
counter (OTC)
D. Past medical history
1. Perinatal exposure to toxic agents, x-rays;
difficult labor and delivery
2. Childhood and adult: history of systemic
diseases; seizures; loss of consciousness;
head trauma
E. Family history: may uncover diseases with
hereditary or congenital background.

Eye

A. Presenting problem: symptoms may include
blurred vision, decreased vision, or blind spots;
pain, redness, excessive tearing; double vision
(diplopia); drainage
B. Use of eyeglasses, contact lenses; date of last
eye exam.

C. Life-style: occupation (exposure to fumes,
smoke, or eye irritant); use of safety glasses
D. Use of medications: cortisone preparations
may contribute to formation of glaucoma and
cataracts
E. Past medical history: systemic diseases;
previous childhood or adult eye disorders, eye
trauma
F. Family history: many eye disorders may be
inherited.

Ear

A. Presenting problem: symptoms may include
hearing loss, tinnitus (ringing in ear), dizziness
or vertigo, pain, drainage
B. Life-style: occupation (exposure to excessive
noise levels), swimming habits
C. Use of medications: ototoxic drugs; aspirin
(tinnitus)
D. Past medical history
1. Perinatal: rubella in first trimester of
pregnancy
2. Childhood and adult: otitis media,
perforated eardrum, measles, mumps,
allergies, tonsillectomy, and
adenoidectomy
E. Family history: hearing loss in family members.

Physical Examination

Nervous System

A. Neurologic examination
1. Mental status exam (cerebral function); see
also Psychiatric-Mental Health Nursing,
page 522
a. General appearance and behavior
b. Level of consciousness; see Neuro
Check, below.
c. Intellectual function: memory (recent
and remote), attention span, cognitive
skills
d. Emotional status
e. Thought content
f. Language/speech
1) *expressive aphasia:* inability to speak
2) *receptive aphasia:* inability to
understand spoken words
3) *dysarthria:* difficult speech due to
impairment of muscles involved
with production of speech
2. Cranial nerves (see Table 4.15)
3. Cerebellar function: posture, gait, balance,
coordination
4. Motor function: muscle size, tone,
strength; abnormal or involuntary
movements
5. Sensory function: light touch, superficial
pain, temperature, vibration, and position
sense
6. Reflexes

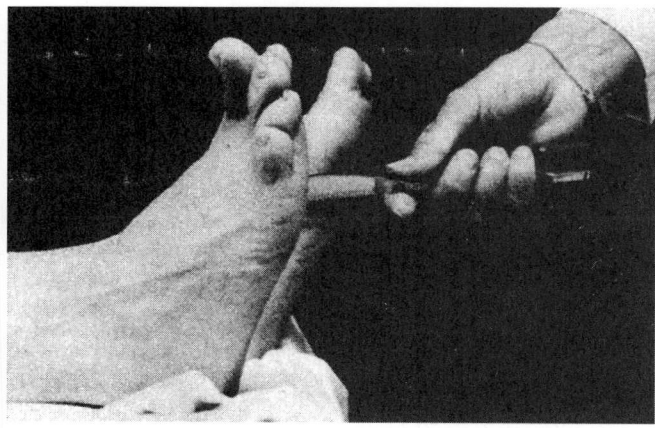

FIGURE 4.2 Pathologic Reflex (Babinski)

a. Deep tendon: grade from 0 (no response) to 4 (hyperactive); 2 is normal
b. Superficial
c. Pathologic: *Babinski's reflex* (dorsiflexion of great toe with fanning of other toes) indicates damage to corticospinal tracts (see Figure 4.2)

B. Neuro check
  1. *Level of consciousness (LOC)*
    a. Orientation to time, place, and person
    b. Speech: clear, garbled, rambling
    c. Ability to follow commands
    d. If client does not respond to verbal stimuli, apply a painful stimulus (e.g., pressure on nailbeds, squeeze trapezius muscle); note response to pain
      1) appropriate: withdrawal, moaning
      2) inappropriate: nonpurposeful
    e. Abnormal posturing (may occur spontaneously or in response to stimulus)
      1) *decorticate posturing:* extension of legs, internal rotation and adduction of arms with flexion of elbows, wrists, and fingers (damage to corticospinal tracts; cerebral hemispheres)
      2) *decerebrate posturing:* back arched, rigid extension of all four extremities with hyperpronation of arms and plantar flexion of feet (damage to upper brainstem, midbrain, or pons)
  2. *Glasgow coma scale* (see Figure 4.3)
    a. Objective evaluation of LOC, motor/verbal response; a standardized system for assessing the degree of neurologic impairment in critically ill clients.
    b. Cannot replace a complete neurologic check, but can be used as an aid in evaluation and to eliminate ambiguous terms such as stupor and lethargy.

Subscale	Response	Score
Best eye opening (E)	Spontaneous	4
	To voice	3
	To pain	2
	None	1
Best verbal response (V)	Oriented	5
	Confused conversation	4
	Inappropriate words	3
	Incomprehensible sounds	2
	None	1
Best motor response, upper limb (M)	Obeys commands	6
	Localizes to pain	5
	Flexor withdrawal (decorticate posturing)	4
	Abnormal flexion (decerebrate posturing)	3
	Extension	2
	Flaccid	1

FIGURE 4.3 Glasgow Coma Scale (From "What the comatose patient can tell you" by A. Stolarik, RN, 48(4), 32)

    c. A score of 15 indicates client is awake and oriented; the lowest score, 3, is deep coma; a score of 7 or below is considered coma.
  3. Pupillary reaction and eye movements
    a. Observe size, shape, and equality of pupils (note size in millimeters)
    b. Reaction to light: pupillary constriction
    c. Corneal reflex: blink reflex in response to light stroking of cornea
    d. Oculocephalic reflex (doll's eyes): present in unconscious client with intact brainstem
  4. Motor function
    a. Movement of extremities (paralysis)
    b. Muscle strength
  5. Vital signs: respiratory patterns (may help localize possible lesion)
    a. *Cheyne-Stokes respiration:* regular, rhythmic alternating between hyperventilation and apnea; may be caused by structural cerebral dysfunction or by metabolic problems, such as diabetic coma.
    b. *Central neurogenic hyperventilation:* sustained, rapid, regular respirations (rate of 25/minute) with normal blood oxygen levels; usually due to brain stem dysfunction.
    c. *Apneustic breathing:* prolonged inspiratory phase, followed by a 2- to 3-second pause; usually indicates dysfunction of respiratory center in pons.

d. *Cluster breathing:* clusters of irregular breathing, irregularly followed by periods of apnea; usually caused by a lesion in upper medulla and lower pons.

e. *Ataxic breathing:* breathing pattern completely irregular; indicates damage to respiratory centers of the medulla.

Eye

A. Visual acuity: Snellen chart
B. Visual fields (peripheral vision)
 1. Confrontation method
 2. Perimetry: more precise method
C. External structures
 1. Position and alignment of eyes
 2. Eyebrows, eyelids, lacrimal apparatus, conjunctiva, sclera, cornea, iris, pupils (size, shape, equality, and reaction to light)
D. Extraocular movements; note paralysis, nystagmus (rapid, abnormal movement of the eyeball)
E. Corneal reflex

Ear

A. Inspection and palpation of auricle, preauricular area, and mastoid area
B. Hearing acuity
 1. Whispered voice or ticking watch tests: gross estimation
 2. Audiometry: more precise method
C. Tuning fork tests distinguish between sensorineural and conductive deafness.
 1. Conductive hearing loss: secondary to problem in external or middle ear; transmission of sound waves to inner ear impaired
 2. Sensorineural (perceptive) hearing loss: disease of inner ear or cranial nerve VIII (acoustic branch)
 3. *Weber's test:* handle of vibrating tuning fork placed on midline of client's skull, sound should be heard equally in midline or in both ears; in conductive hearing loss, sound is louder in poorer ear; in sensorineural hearing loss, sound is louder in better ear.
 4. *Rinne's test:* tuning fork placed on mastoid process (bone conduction) until sound no longer heard, then placed in front of the ear (air conduction); sound should be heard longer (almost twice as long) with air conduction than with bone conduction; bone conduction greater than air conduction indicates conductive hearing deficit.

Laboratory/Diagnostic Tests

Nervous System

A. Lumbar puncture (LP)
 1. A hollow spinal needle introduced into subarachnoid space of spinal canal between L_4/L_5 for diagnostic or therapeutic reasons
 2. Purposes
  a. Measures CSF pressure (normal opening pressure 60–150 mm H_2O)
  b. Obtain specimens for lab analysis (protein [normally not present], sugar [normally present], cytology, C&S)
  c. Check color of CSF (normally clear) and check for blood
  d. Inject air, dye, or drugs into the spinal canal
 3. Nursing care: pretest
  a. Have client empty bladder.
  b. Position client in lateral recumbent position with head and neck flexed onto the chest and knees pulled up.
  c. Explain the need to remain still during the procedure.
 4. Nursing care: posttest
  a. Ensure labeling of CSF specimens in proper sequence.
  b. Keep client flat for 12–24 hours as ordered.
  c. Force fluids.
  d. Check puncture site for bleeding, leakage of CSF.
  e. Assess sensation and movement in lower extremities.
  f. Monitor vital signs.
  g. Administer analgesics for headache as ordered.
B. X-rays of skull and spine
 1. Used to detect atrophy, erosion, or fractures of bones; calcifications
 2. Pretest nursing care: remove hairpins, glasses, hearing aids.
C. Computerized tomography (CT scan)
 1. Skull/spinal cord are scanned in successive layers by a narrow beam of x-rays; computer uses information obtained to construct a picture of the internal structure of the brain; contrast medium may or may not be used.
 2. Used to detect intracranial and spinal cord lesions and monitor effects of surgery or other therapy.
 3. Nursing care
  a. Explain appearance of scanner.
  b. Instruct client to lie still during procedure.
  c. Check for allergy to iodine if contrast material is used.
  d. Remove hairpins, etc.
D. Magnetic resonance imaging (MRI)
 1. Also known as nuclear magnetic resonance (NMR)
 2. Computer-drawn, detailed pictures of structures of the body through use of large magnet, radio waves
 3. Used to detect intracranial and spinal abnormalities associated with disorders

such as cerebrovascular disease, tumors, abscesses, cerebral edema, hydrocephalus, multiple sclerosis
    4. Nursing care
       a. Instruct client to remove jewelry, hairpins, glasses, wigs (with metal clips), and other metallic objects.
       b. Be aware that this test cannot be performed on anyone with orthopedic hardware, intrauterine devices, pacemaker, internal surgical clips, or other fixed metallic objects in the body.
       c. Inform client of need to remain still while completely enclosed in scanner throughout the procedure, which lasts 45–60 minutes.
       d. Teach relaxation techniques to assist client to remain still and to help prevent claustrophobia.
       e. Warn client of normal audible humming and thumping noises from the scanner during test.
       f. Have client void before test.
       g. Sedate client if ordered.
 E. Brain scan
    1. Injection of radioactive isotope, followed by scanning of head; isotopes will accumulate in abnormal lesions and be recorded by the scanner.
    2. Used to detect intracranial masses, vascular lesions, infarcts, hemorrhage
    3. Nursing care: check for allergy to iodine.
 F. Myelography (see page 307)
 G. Cerebral angiography
    1. Injection of radiopaque substance into the cerebral circulation via carotid, vertebral, femoral, or brachial artery followed by x-rays
    2. Used to visualize cerebral vessels and detect tumors, aneurysms, occlusions, hematomas, or abscesses
    3. Nursing care: pretest
       a. Explain that client may have warm, flushed feeling and salty taste in mouth during procedure.
       b. Check for allergy to iodine.
       c. Keep NPO after midnight or offer clear liquid breakfast only.
       d. Take baseline vital signs and neuro check.
       e. Administer sedation if ordered.
    4. Nursing care: posttest
       a. Maintain pressure dressing over site if femoral or brachial artery used; apply ice as ordered.
       b. Maintain bed rest until next morning as ordered.
       c. Monitor vital signs and neuro checks frequently; report any changes immediately.
       d. Check site frequently for bleeding or hematoma; if carotid artery used,

assess for swelling of neck, difficulty swallowing or breathing.
       e. Check pulse, color, and temperature of extremity distal to site used.
       f. Keep extremity extended and avoid flexion.
 H. Echoencephalography: use of ultrasound to detect midline shift of intracranial contents due to brain tumors, hematomas.
 I. Electroencephalography (EEG)
    1. Graphic recording of electrical activity of the brain by several small electrodes placed on the scalp
    2. Used to detect focus or foci of seizure activity and to quantitatively evaluate level of brain function (determine brain death)
    3. Pretest nursing care: withhold sedatives, tranquilizers, stimulants for 2–3 days.
    4. Posttest nursing care: remove electrode paste with acetone and shampoo hair.

Eye

 A. Ophthalmoscopic exam
 B. Refraction: detects refractive errors and provides information for prescription of eyeglasses and contact lenses
 C. Perimetry: assesses peripheral vision, visual fields
 D. Tonometry: measures intraocular pressure (normal: 12–20 mm Hg)

Ear

 A. Otoscopic exam
 B. Audiometry: screening test for hearing loss and diagnostic test to determine degree and type of hearing loss
 C. Vestibular function
    1. Caloric test
    2. Electronystagmography (ENG)

ANALYSIS

Nursing diagnoses for clients with disorders of the neurosensory system may include
 A. Altered nutrition: less than body requirements
 B. Risk for altered body temperature
 C. Dysreflexia
 D. Constipation
 E. Bowel incontinence
 F. Altered urinary elimination
    1. Reflex incontinence
    2. Total incontinence
    3. Urinary retention
 G. Altered tissue perfusion: cerebral
 H. Ineffective airway clearance
 I. Ineffective breathing pattern
 J. Risk for injury
 K. Risk for aspiration
 L. Risk for disuse syndrome

M. Risk for impaired skin integrity
N. Impaired verbal communication
O. Sexual dysfunction
P. Impaired physical mobility
Q. Feeding self-care deficit
R. Impaired swallowing
S. Bathing/hygiene self-care deficit
T. Dressing/grooming self-care deficit
U. Toileting self-care deficit
V. Sensory perceptual alterations: visual, auditory, kinesthetic, gustatory, tactile, olfactory
W. Unilateral neglect
X. Altered thought processes

PLANNING AND IMPLEMENTATION

Goals

A. Nutritional state will be optimal.
B. Normal body temperature will be maintained.
C. Complications will be recognized early and treated promptly.
D. Adequate bowel and bladder elimination will be maintained.
E. Cerebral perfusion will be improved.
F. Adequate respiratory function will be maintained.
G. Client will remain free from any injury resulting from neurosensory deficits.
H. Client's skin integrity will be maintained.
I. Client's ability to communicate will be improved.
J. Sexual health will return to optimal level.
K. Mobility will be restored to optimal level.
L. Maximum independence in self-care activities will be attained.
M. Sensory perception will be improved.
N. Optimal cognitive functioning will be attained.

Interventions

Care of the Unconscious Client

A. Maintain a clear, patent airway.
   1. Place client in a side-lying or three-quarters prone position to prevent tongue from obstructing airway.
   2. If tongue is obstructing, insert oral airway.
   3. Prepare for insertion of a cuffed endotracheal or tracheostomy tube as the client's condition requires.
   4. Suction as needed.
   5. Check respiratory rate, depth, and quality every 1–2 hours and as needed.
   6. Auscultate breath sounds for crackles (rales), rhonchi, or absent breath sounds every 4 hours and before and after suctioning.

B. Take vital signs and perform neuro checks at specified intervals as ordered; report any significant changes immediately.
C. Maintain fluid and electrolyte balance and ensure adequate nutrition.
   1. Administer IV fluids, nasogastric tube feedings as ordered.
   2. Maintain accurate I&O.
   3. Assess client's hydration status: skin turgor, check for dry mucous membranes.
   4. Provide mouth care to keep mucous membranes clean, moist, and intact.
D. Provide for client's safety.
   1. Keep side rails up at all times.
   2. Avoid restraints if at all possible.
   3. Observe client carefully for seizures and intervene to avoid precipitating factors: fever, hypoxia, electrolyte imbalance.
   4. Protect client if seizure occurs.
   5. Speak softly and use client's name during nursing care.
   6. Touch client as gently as possible.
   7. Protect client's eyes from corneal irritation.
      a. Check for corneal reflex.
      b. Instill artificial tears as ordered; patch eye.
E. Prevent complications of immobility.
   1. Keep skin clean, dry, and pressure free.
   2. Turn and reposition client every 2 hours.
   3. Perform passive range-of-motion (ROM) exercises every 4 hours.
   4. Use nursing measures to prevent deformities: footboard/high-topped sneakers to prevent foot drop, splint to prevent wrist drop.
F. Maintain adequate bladder and bowel elimination.
   1. Urinary: indwelling catheter (may use external device in male)
   2. Bowel: stool softeners and suppositories as ordered

Care of the Client with Increased Intracranial Pressure (ICP)

A. General information
   1. An increase in intracranial bulk due to an increase in any of the major intracranial components: brain tissue, CSF, or blood
   2. Increased ICP may be caused by tumors, abscesses, hemorrhage, edema, hydrocephalus, inflammation.
   3. Untreated increased ICP can lead to displacement of brain tissue (herniation).
   4. Presents life-threatening situation because of pressure on vital structures in the brain stem, nerve tracts, and cranial nerves.
B. Assessment findings
   1. Earliest sign: decrease in LOC; progresses from restlessness to confusion and disorientation to lethargy and coma

2. Changes in vital signs (may be a late sign)
    a. Systolic blood pressure rises while diastolic pressure remains the same (widening pulse presence)
    b. Pulse slows
    c. Abnormal respiratory patterns (e.g., Cheyne-Stokes respirations)
    d. Elevated temperature
3. Pupillary changes
    a. Ipsilateral (same side) dilation of pupil with sluggish reaction to light from compression of cranial nerve III
    b. Pupil eventually becomes fixed and dilated.
4. Motor abnormalities
    a. Contralateral (opposite side) hemiparesis from compression of corticospinal tracts
    b. Decorticate or decerebrate rigidity
5. Headache, projectile vomiting, papilledema (edema of the optic disc)

C. Nursing care
1. Maintain patent airway and adequate ventilation.
    a. Prevention of hypoxia and hypercarbia (increased CO_2) important: hypoxia may cause brain swelling and hypercarbia causes cerebral vasodilation, which increases ICP.
    b. Before and after suctioning, hyperventilate the client with a resuscitator bag connected to 100% oxygen. Limit suctioning to 15 seconds.
    c. Assist with mechanical hyperventilation as indicated: produces hypocarbia (decreased CO_2) causing cerebral vasoconstriction and decreased ICP.
2. Monitor vital sign and neuro checks frequently to detect rises in ICP.
3. Maintain fluid balance: fluid restriction to 1200–1500 ml/day may be ordered.
4. Position client with head of bed elevated to 30°–45° and neck in neutral position unless contraindicated (improves venous drainage from brain).
5. Prevent further increases in ICP.
    a. Maintain quiet, comfortable environment.
    b. Avoid use of restraints.
    c. Prevent straining at stool; administer stool softeners and mild laxatives as ordered.
    d. Prevent vomiting; administer antiemetics as ordered.
    e. Prevent excessive coughing.
    f. Avoid clustering nursing care activities together.
6. Prevent complications of immobility.
7. Administer medications as ordered.
    a. Hyperosmotic agents (mannitol [Osmitrol]) to reduce cerebral edema; monitor urine output every hour (should increase).
    b. Corticosteroids (dexamethasone [Decadron]); anti-inflammatory effect reduces cerebral edema
    c. Diuretics (furosemide [Lasix]) to reduce cerebral edema.
    d. Anticonvulsants (phenytoin [Dilantin]) to prevent seizures.
    e. Analgesics for headache as needed
        1) small doses of codeine
        2) stronger opiates are contraindicated since they potentiate respiratory depression, alter LOC, and cause pupillary changes.
8. Assist with ICP monitoring when indicated.
    a. ICP monitoring records the pressure exerted within the cranial cavity by the brain, cerebral blood, and CSF.
    b. Types of monitoring devices
        1) Intraventricular catheter: inserted in lateral ventricle to give direct measurement of ICP; also allows for drainage of CSF if needed
        2) Subarachnoid screw (bolt): inserted through skull and dura mater into subarachnoid space
        3) Epidural sensor: least invasive method; placed in space between skull and dura mater for indirect measurement of ICP
    c. Monitor ICP pressure readings frequently and prevent complications.
        1) Normal ICP reading is 0–10 mm Hg; a sustained increase above 15 mm Hg is considered abnormal.
        2) Use strict aseptic technique when handling any part of the monitoring system.
        3) Check insertion site for signs of infection; monitor temperature.
        4) Assess system for CSF leakage, loose connections, air bubbles in lines, and occluded tubing.
9. Provide intensive nursing care for client treated with barbiturate therapy or administration of paralyzing agents.
    a. Intravenous administration of barbiturates may be ordered to induce coma artificially in the client who has not responded to conventional treatment
    b. Pancuronium (Pavulon) may be administered to paralyze client.
    c. Reduces cellular metabolic demands that may protect the brain from further injury
    d. Constant monitoring of the client's ICP, arterial blood pressures, pulmonary

pressures, arterial blood gases, serum barbiturate levels, and ECG is necessary
   e. Provide appropriate nursing care for the client on a ventilator (see page 249).
   10. Observe for hyperthermia secondary to hypothalamus damage.

Care of the Client with Hyperthermia

A. General information
   1. Abnormal elevation of body temperation to 41°C (106°F) or above
   2. Caused by dysfunction of hypothalamus (temperature regulating center) from edema, head injury, hemorrhage, CVA, brain tumor, or intracranial surgery
   3. Hyperthermia increases cerebral metabolism; predisposes to seizures; may cause neurologic damage if prolonged.
B. Nursing care
   1. Remove blankets and excess clothing if temperature rises above 38.4°C (101°F).
   2. Maintain room temperature at 21.1°C (70°F).
   3. Administer antipyretic drugs (acetaminophen [Tylenol]) orally or rectally every 4 hours as ordered.
   4. Increase fluid intake to 3000 ml/day unless contraindicated (in increased ICP).
   5. Monitor vital signs, especially temperature, every 2–4 hours (more often if hypothermia is used).
   6. Monitor urine output and assess for signs of dehydration.
   7. Observe for seizure activity and protect client if seizures occur.
   8. Change linen frequently if client is diaphoretic (sweating profusely).
   9. Apply methods for inducing hypothermia as ordered: cool or tepid sponge baths, fans, hypothermia blanket. (See also Cold Application p. 121.)
   10. Provide special care for the client with a hypothermia blanket. (See also Cold Application p. 121.)
      a. Reduce temperature gradually to prevent shivering and serious dysrhythmias; chlorpromazine (Thorazine) may be given for shivering.
      b. Provide frequent skin care to prevent breakdown.
         1) check every hour for signs of tissue damage or frostbite.
         2) apply lotion to skin to prevent drying.
         3) turn every 2 hours.
      c. Monitor temperature with rectal probe.

Care of the Client with Diminished Eyesight

A. Always speak and identify yourself upon entering the room to prevent startling the client.

B. Orient the client to his surroundings.
   1. Walk the client around the room and have him touch the objects in the room, e.g., table, chair.
   2. Keep personal belongings and objects in the room in the same place in order to increase client's independence and sense of security.
   3. Explain noises or other activities going on in the room.
C. Provide safety measures.
   1. Keep call bell nearby.
   2. Keep at least one side rail up.
   3. If client smokes, supervise smoking.
   4. Keep the room orderly and free of clutter.
D. Assist the client in walking by having him take your arm; walk a half step in front of the client.
E. Offer explanations to the client and tell him what to expect next.
F. Provide mental stimulation and prevent sensory deprivation by providing frequent contacts with the staff, visitors, use of radio, TV, etc.

Communicating with the Client with Impaired Hearing

A. Attract the client's attention by raising an arm or hand.
B. Face the client directly when speaking.
C. Do not obscure the client's view of your mouth in any way.
D. Initially state the topic or subject of your conversation to give the client clues as to what you are going to say.
E. Speak slowly and distinctly, but do not overaccentuate words.
F. Speak in a normal tone of voice; do not shout.
G. If you are not certain that the client has understood you, check to be sure that he has.

Irrigation of the Ear

A. Introduction of fluid into external auditory canal for cleansing purposes; may be used to apply antiseptic solutions.
B. Nursing care
   1. Explain procedure to the client.
   2. Prepare supplies needed: irrigating solution (about 500 ml normal saline at body temperature), irrigating syringe, basin, towel, cotton-tipped applicators, cotton balls.
   3. Assist client to a sitting or lying position with head tilted toward the affected ear.
   4. Straighten ear canal by pulling auricle upward and backward (down and backward on a child under 3 years).
   5. Insert tip of syringe into auditory meatus and direct the solution gently upward toward the top of the canal.
   6. Collect returning fluid in basin.

7. Dry the outer ear with cotton balls.
8. Instruct client to lie on affected side to encourage drainage of solution.
9. Record the procedure and results.

EVALUATION

A. Client maintains normal weight; no evidence of malnutrition.
B. Client's temperature is maintained within normal limits.
C. Dysreflexia will be prevented or recognized early and treated promptly.
D. Client has regular bowel movements.
E. Client has adequate patterns of urinary elimination.
F. Neuro checks are within normal limits.
G. Client maintains patent airway and has effective respiratory patterns.
H. Client remains free from injuries.
I. Client remains free from aspiration and complications of immobility.
J. Client's skin remains clear and intact.
K. Client communicates effectively, responds appropriately to others.
L. Client experiences satisfying sexual activity/ expression.
M. No contractures or limitations in motor function have occurred or loss of mobility has been kept to a minimum.
N. Client attains independence in self-care activities; uses assistive devices as necessary.
O. Sensory dysfunction is corrected or compensated for.
P. Client is oriented to time, place, and person; memory is intact; able to evaluate reality.

DISORDERS OF THE NERVOUS SYSTEM

Headache

A. General information
1. Diffuse pain in different parts of the head
2. Types
   a. Functional
      1) tension (muscle contraction): associated with tension or anxiety
      2) migraine: recurrent throbbing headache
         a) often starts in adolescence
         b) affects women more than men
         c) vascular origin: vasoconstriction or spasm of cerebral blood vessels (producing an aura) then vasodilation
      3) cluster: similar to migraine (vascular origin); recur several times a day over a period of weeks followed by remission lasting for weeks or months
   b. Organic: secondary to intracranial or systemic disease (e.g., brain tumor, sinus disease)
B. Assessment findings
1. Tension headache: pain usually bilateral, often occurring in the back of the neck and extending diffusely over top of head
2. Migraine headache: severe, throbbing pain, often in temporal or supraorbital area, lasting several hours to days; may be an aura (e.g., visual disturbance) preceding the pain; nausea and vomiting; pallor; sweating; irritability
3. Cluster headache: intense, throbbing pain, usually affecting only one side of face and head; abrupt onset, lasts 30–90 minutes; eye and nose water on side of pain; skin reddens
4. Diagnostic tests may be used to rule out organic causes.
C. Nursing interventions
1. Carefully assess details regarding the headache.
2. Provide quiet, dark environment.
3. Administer medications as ordered.
   a. Symptomatic during acute attack
      1) nonnarcotic analgesics (aspirin, acetaminophen [Tylenol])
      2) Fiorinal (analgesic-sedative/ tranquilizer combination)
      3) for migraines, ergotamine tartrate (Gynergen) or ergotamine with caffeine (Cafergot); vasoconstrictors given during aura may prevent the headache
      4) Midrin (vasoconstrictor and sedative)
      5) Sumatriptan (Imitrex) causes vasoconstriction in cerebral arteries; given via cutaneous injection.
   b. Prophylactic to prevent migraine attacks
      1) methysergide maleate (Sansert): after 6 months' use, drug should be discontinued for a 2-month period before resuming
      2) propranolol (Inderal) and amytriptyline (Elavil): have also been used in migraine prevention
4. Provide additional nursing interventions for pain (see page 141–142).
5. Provide client teaching and discharge planning concerning
   a. Identification of factors including diet that appear to precipitate attacks
   b. Examination of life-style, identification of stressors, and development of more positive coping behaviors

c. Importance of daily exercise and relaxation periods
   d. Relaxation techniques
   e. Use and side effects of prescribed medications
   f. Alternative ways of handling the pain of headache: meditation, relaxation, self-hypnosis, yoga.

Meningitis

A. General information
   1. Inflammation of the meninges of the brain and spinal cord
   2. Caused by bacteria, viruses, or other microorganisms
   3. May reach CNS
      a. Via the blood, CSF, lymph
      b. By direct extension from adjacent cranial structures (nasal sinuses, mastoid bone, ear, skull fracture)
      c. By oral or nasopharyngeal route
   4. Most common organisms: meningococcus, pneumococcus, *H. influenzae,* streptococcus
B. Assessment findings
   1. Headache, photophobia, malaise, irritability
   2. Chills and fever
   3. Signs of meningeal irritation
      a. Nuchal rigidity: stiff neck
      b. *Kernig's sign:* contraction or pain in the hamstring muscle when attempting to extend the leg when the hip is flexed
      c. Opisthotonos: head and heels bent backward and body arched forward
      d. *Brudzinski's sign:* flexion at the hip and knee in response to forward flexion of the neck
   4. Vomiting
   5. Possible seizures and decreasing LOC
   6. Diagnostic test: lumbar puncture (measurement and analysis of CSF shows increased pressure, elevated WBC and protein, decreased glucose and culture positive for specific microorganism)
C. Nursing interventions
   1. Administer large doses of antibiotics IV as ordered.
   2. Enforce respiratory isolation for 24 hours after initiation of antibiotic therapy for some types of meningitis (consult hospital's infection control manual for specific directions).
   3. Provide nursing care for increased ICP, seizures, and hyperthermia if they occur.
   4. Provide nursing care for delirious or unconscious client as needed.
   5. Provide bed rest; keep room quiet and dark if client has headache or photophobia.
   6. Administer analgesics for headache as ordered.
   7. Maintain fluid and electrolyte balance.
   8. Prevent complications of immobility.
   9. Monitor vital signs and neuro checks frequently.
   10. Provide client teaching and discharge planning concerning
      a. Importance of good diet: high protein, high calorie with small, frequent feedings
      b. Rehabilitation program for residual deficits.

Encephalitis

A. General information
   1. Inflammation of the brain caused by a virus, e.g., herpes simplex (type I) or arbovirus (transmitted by mosquito or tick)
   2. May occur as a sequela of other diseases such as measles, mumps, chickenpox.
B. Assessment findings
   1. Headache
   2. Fever, chills, vomiting
   3. Signs of meningeal irritation
   4. Possibly seizures
   5. Alterations in LOC
C. Nursing interventions
   1. Monitor vital signs and neuro checks frequently.
   2. Provide nursing measures for increased ICP, seizures, hyperthermia if they occur.
   3. Provide nursing care for confused or unconscious client as needed.
   4. Provide client teaching and discharge planning: same as for meningitis.

Brain Abscess

A. General information
   1. Collection of free or encapsulated pus within the brain tissue
   2. Usually follows an infectious process elsewhere in the body (ear, sinuses, mastoid bone).
B. Assessment findings
   1. Headache, malaise, anorexia
   2. Vomiting
   3. Signs of increased ICP
   4. Focal neurologic deficits (hemiparesis, seizures)
C. Nursing interventions
   1. Administer large doses of antibiotics as ordered.
   2. Monitor vital signs and neuro checks.
   3. Provide symptomatic and supportive care.
   4. Prepare client for surgery if indicated (see Craniotomy, page 194).

Brain Tumors

A. General information

1. Tumor within the cranial cavity; may be benign or malignant
2. Types
   a. Primary: originates in brain tissue (e.g., glioma, meningioma)
   b. Secondary: metastasizes from tumor elsewhere in the body (e.g., lung, breast)
B. Medical management
   1. Craniotomy: to remove the tumor when possible
   2. Radiation therapy and chemotherapy: may follow surgery; also for inaccessible tumors and metastatic tumors
   3. Drug therapy: hyperosmotic agents, corticosteroids, diuretics to manage increased ICP
C. Assessment findings
   1. Headache: worse in the morning and with straining and stooping
   2. Vomiting
   3. Papilledema
   4. Seizures (focal or generalized)
   5. Changes in mental status
   6. Focal neurologic deficits (e.g., aphasia, hemiparesis, sensory problems)
   7. Diagnostic tests
      a. Skull x-ray, CT scan, MRI, brain scan: reveal presence of tumor
      b. Abnormal EEG
      c. Brain biopsy
D. Nursing interventions
   1. Monitor vital signs and neuro checks; observe for signs and symptoms of increased ICP.
   2. Administer medications as ordered.
      a. Drugs to decrease ICP, e.g., dextromethasone (Decadron)
      b. Anticonvulsants, e.g., phenytoin (Dilantin)
      c. Analgesics for headache, e.g., acetaminophen (Tylenol)
   3. Provide supportive care for any neurologic deficit (see Cerebrovascular Accident).
   4. Prepare client for surgery (see Craniotomy, page 194).
   5. Provide care for effects of radiation therapy or chemotherapy (see Oncologic Nursing, page 168).
   6. Provide psychologic support to client/ significant others.
   7. Provide client teaching and discharge planning concerning
      a. Use and side effects of prescribed medications.
      b. Rehabilitation program for residual deficits.

Cerebrovascular Accident (CVA)

A. General information
   1. Destruction (infarction) of brain cells caused by a reduction in cerebral blood flow and oxygen
   2. Affects men more than women; incidence increases with age
   3. Caused by thrombosis, embolism, hemorrhage
   4. Risk factors
      a. Hypertension, diabetes mellitus, arteriosclerosis/atherosclerosis, cardiac disease (valvular disease/ replacement, chronic atrial fibrillation, myocardial infarction)
      b. Life-style: obesity, smoking, inactivity, stress, use of oral contraceptives
   5. Pathophysiology
      a. Interruption of cerebral blood flow for 5 minutes or more causes death of neurons in affected area with irreversible loss of function
      b. Modifying factors
         1) cerebral edema: develops around affected area causing further impairment
         2) vasospasm: constriction of cerebral blood vessel may occur, causing further decrease in blood flow
         3) collateral circulation: may help to maintain cerebral blood flow when there is compromise of main blood supply
   6. Stages of development
      a. *Transient ischemic attack (TIA)*
         1) warning sign of impending CVA
         2) brief period of neurologic deficit: visual loss, hemiparesis, slurred speech, aphasia, vertigo
         3) may last less than 30 seconds, but no more than 24 hours with complete resolution of symptoms
      b. *Stroke in evolution:* progressive development of stroke symptoms over a period of hours to days
      c. *Completed stroke:* neurologic deficit remains unchanged for a 2- to 3-day period.
B. Assessment findings
   1. Headache
   2. Generalized signs: vomiting, seizures, confusion, disorientation, decreased LOC, nuchal rigidity, fever, hypertension, slow bounding pulse, Cheyne-Stokes respirations
   3. Focal signs (related to site of infarction): hemiplegia, sensory loss, aphasia, homonymous hemianopsia
   4. Diagnostic tests
      a. CT and brain scan: reveal lesion
      b. EEG: abnormal changes
      c. Cerebral arteriography: may show occlusion or malformation of blood vessels
C. Nursing interventions: acute stage

1. Maintain patent airway and adequate ventilation.
2. Monitor vital signs and neuro checks and observe for signs of increased ICP, shock, hyperthermia, and seizures.
3. Provide complete bed rest as ordered.
4. Maintain fluid and electrolyte balance and ensure adequate nutrition.
   a. IV therapy for the first few days
   b. Nasogastric tube feedings if client unable to swallow
   c. Fluid restriction as ordered to decrease cerebral edema
5. Maintain proper positioning and body alignment.
   a. Head of bed may be elevated 30°–45° to decrease ICP
   b. Turn and reposition every 2 hours (only 20 minutes on the affected side)
   c. Passive ROM exercises every 4 hours.
6. Promote optimum skin integrity: turn client and apply lotion every 2 hours
7. Maintain adequate elimination.
   a. Offer bedpan or urinal every 2 hours, catheterize only if absolutely necessary.
   b. Administer stool softeners and suppositories as ordered to prevent constipation and fecal impaction.
8. Provide a quiet, restful environment.
9. Establish a means of communicating with the client.
10. Administer medications as ordered.
    a. Hyperosmotic agents, corticosteroids to decrease cerebral edema
    b. Anticonvulsants to prevent or treat seizures
    c. Thrombolytics given to dissolve clot (hemorrhage must be ruled out)
       1) tissue plasminogen activator (tPA, Alteplase)
       2) streptokinase, urokinase
       3) must be given within 2 hours of episode
    d. Anticoagulants for stroke in evolution or embolic stroke (hemorrhage must be ruled out)
       1) heparin
       2) warfarin (Coumadin) for long-term therapy
       3) aspirin and dipyridamole (Persantine) to inhibit platelet aggregation in treating TIAs
    e. Antihypertensives if indicated for elevated blood pressure
D. Nursing interventions: rehabilitation
   1. *Hemiplegia:* results from injury to cells in the cerebral motor cortex or to corticospinal tracts (causes contralateral hemiplegia since tracts cross in medulla)
      a. Turn every 2 hours (20 minutes only on affected side).
      b. Use proper positioning and repositioning to prevent deformities (foot drop, external rotation of hip, flexion of fingers, wrist drop, abduction of shoulder and arm).
      c. Support paralyzed arm on pillow or use sling while out of bed to prevent subluxation of shoulder.
      d. Elevate extremities to prevent dependent edema.
      e. Provide active and passive ROM exercises every 4 hours.
   2. Susceptibility to hazards
      a. Keep side rails up at all times.
      b. Institute safety measures.
      c. Inspect body parts frequently for signs of injury.
   3. *Dysphagia* (difficulty swallowing)
      a. Check gag reflex before feeding client.
      b. Maintain a calm, unhurried approach.
      c. Place client in upright position.
      d. Place food in unaffected side of mouth.
      e. Offer soft foods.
      f. Give mouth care before and after meals.
   4. *Homonymous hemianopsia:* loss of half of each visual field
      a. Approach client on unaffected side.
      b. Place personal belongings, food, etc., on unaffected side.
      c. Gradually teach client to compensate by scanning, i.e., turning the head to see things on affected side.
   5. Emotional lability: mood swings, frustration
      a. Create a quiet, restful environment with a reduction in excessive sensory stimuli.
      b. Maintain a calm, nonthreatening manner.
      c. Explain to family that the client's behavior is not purposeful.
   6. *Aphasia:* most common in right hemiplegics; may be receptive/expressive
      a. Receptive aphasia
         1) give simple, slow directions.
         2) give one command at a time; gradually shift topics.
         3) use nonverbal techniques of communication (e.g., pantomime, demonstration).
      b. Expressive aphasia
         1) listen and watch very carefully when the client attempts to speak.
         2) anticipate client's needs to decrease frustration and feelings of helplessness.
         3) allow sufficient time for client to answer.
   7. *Sensory/perceptual deficits:* more common in left hemiplegics; characterized by

impulsiveness, unawareness of disabilities, visual neglect (neglect of affected side and visual space on affected side)
   a. Assist with self-care.
   b. Provide safety measures.
   c. Initially arrange objects in environment on unaffected side.
   d. Gradually teach client to take care of the affected side and to turn frequently and look at affected side.
8. *Apraxia:* loss of ability to perform purposeful, skilled acts
   a. Guide client through intended movement (e.g., take object such as washcloth and guide client through movement of washing).
   b. Keep repeating the movement.
9. Generalizations about clients with left hemiplegia versus right hemiplegia and nursing care
   a. Left hemiplegia
      1) Perceptual, sensory deficits; quick and impulsive behavior
      2) Use safety measures, verbal cues, simplicity in all areas of care
   b. Right hemiplegia
      1) Speech-language deficits; slow and cautious behavior
      2) Use pantomime and demonstration

Cerebral Aneurysm

A. General information
   1. Dilation of the walls of a cerebral artery, resulting in a sac-like outpouching of vessel
   2. Caused by congenital weakness in the vessel, trauma, arteriosclerosis, hypertension
   3. Pathophysiology
      a. Aneurysm compresses nearby cranial nerves or brain substance, producing dysfunction
      b. Aneurysm may rupture, causing subarachnoid hemorrhage or intracerebral hemorrhage
      c. Initially a clot forms at the site of rupture, but fibrinolysis (dissolution of the clot) tends to occur within 7–10 days and may cause rebleeding.
B. Assessment findings
   1. Severe headache and pain in the eyes
   2. Diplopia, tinnitus, dizziness
   3. Nuchal rigidity, ptosis, decreasing LOC, hemiparesis, seizures
C. Nursing interventions
   1. Maintain a patent airway and adequate ventilation.
      a. Instruct client to take deep breaths but to avoid coughing.
      b. Suction only with a specific order.
   2. Monitor vital signs and neuro checks and

observe for signs of vasospasm, increased ICP, hypertension, seizures, and hyperthermia.
   3. Enforce strict bed rest and provide complete care.
   4. Keep head of bed flat or elevated to 20°–30° as ordered.
   5. Maintain a quiet, darkened environment.
   6. Avoid taking temperature rectally and instruct client to avoid sneezing, coughing, and straining at stool.
   7. Enforce fluid restriction as ordered; maintain accurate I&O.
   8. Administer medications as ordered.
      a. Antihypertensive agents to maintain normotensive levels
      b. Corticosteroids to prevent increased ICP
      c. Anticonvulsants to prevent seizures
      d. Stool softeners to prevent straining
      e. Aminocaproic acid (Amicar) to decrease fibrinolysis of the clot (administered IV).
   9. Prevent complications of immobility.
   10. Institute seizure precautions.
   11. Provide nursing care for the unconscious client if needed.
   12. Prepare the client for surgery if indicated (see Craniotomy, page 194).

Parkinson's Disease

A. General information
   1. A progressive disorder with degeneration of the nerve cells in the basal ganglia resulting in generalized decline in muscular function; disorder of the extrapyramidal system
   2. Usually occurs in the older population
   3. Cause unknown; predominantly idiopathic, but sometimes disorder is postencephalitic, toxic, arteriosclerotic, traumatic, or drug induced (reserpine, methyldopa [Aldomet], haloperidol [Haldol], phenothiazines)
   4. Pathophysiology
      a. Disorder causes degeneration of the dopamine-producing neurons in the substantia nigra in the midbrain
      b. Dopamine influences purposeful movement
      c. Depletion of dopamine results in degeneration of the basal ganglia.
B. Assessment findings
   1. Tremor: mainly of the upper limbs, "pill-rolling," resting tremor; most common initial symptom
   2. Rigidity: cogwheel type
   3. Bradykinesia: slowness of movement
   4. Fatigue
   5. Stooped posture; shuffling, propulsive gait (see Figure 4.4)

 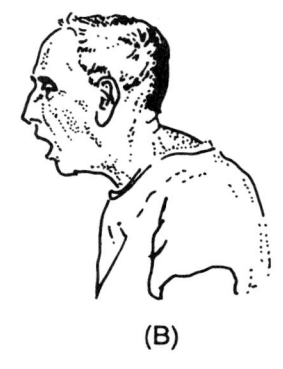 

(A)

(B)   (C)

FIGURE 4.4 The shuffling gait and early postural changes of Parkinson's disease shown in (A). (B) and (C) show an advanced stage of the disease with head held forward, mouth open, and inability to stand. (Delmar Publishers)

6. Difficulty rising from sitting position
7. Masklike face with decreased blinking of eyes
8. Quiet, monotone speech
9. Emotional lability, depression
10. Increased salivation, drooling
11. Cramped, small handwriting
12. Autonomic symptoms: excessive sweating, seborrhea, lacrimation, constipation; decreased sexual capacity

C. Nursing interventions
  1. Administer medications as ordered
    a. Levodopa (L-dopa)
      1) increases level of dopamine in the brain; relieves tremor, rigidity, and bradykinesia
      2) side effects: anorexia; nausea and vomiting; postural hypotension; mental changes such as confusion, agitation, and hallucinations; cardiac arrhythmias; dyskinesias.
      3) contraindications: narrow-angle glaucoma; clients taking MAO inhibitors, reserpine, guanethidine, methyldopa, antipsychotics; acute psychoses.
      4) avoid multiple vitamin preparations containing vitamin B_6 (pyridoxine) and foods high in vitamin B_6.
      5) be aware of any worsening of symptoms with prolonged high-dose therapy: "on-off" syndrome.
      6) administer with food or snack to decrease GI irritation.
      7) inform client that urine and sweat may be darkened.
    b. Carbidopa-levodopa (Sinemet): prevents breakdown of dopamine in

the periphery and causes fewer side effects.
    c. Amantadine (Symmetrel): used in mild cases or in combination with L-dopa to reduce rigidity, tremor, and bradykinesia.
    d. Anticholinergic drugs: benztropine mesylate (Cogentin), procyclidine (Kemadrin), trihexyphenidyl (Artane)
      1) inhibit action of acetylcholine
      2) used in mild cases or in combination with L-dopa
      3) relieve tremor and rigidity
      4) side effects: dry mouth, blurred vision, constipation, urinary retention, confusion, hallucinations, tachycardia
    e. Antihistamines: diphenhydramine (Benadryl)
      1) decrease tremor and anxiety
      2) side effect: drowsiness
    f. Bromocriptine (Parlodel)
      1) stimulates release of dopamine in the substantia nigra.
      2) often employed when L-dopa loses effectiveness.
    g. Eldepryl (Selegilene) a MAO Inhibitor inhibits dopamine breakdown and slows progression of disease
    h. Tricyclic antidepressants given to treat depression commonly seen in Parkinson's disease
  2. Provide a safe environment.
    a. Side rails on bed; rails and handlebars in toilet, bathtub, and hallways; no scatter rugs
    b. Hard-back or spring-loaded chair to make getting up easier

3. Provide measures to increase mobility.
    a. Physical therapy: active and passive ROM exercises; stretching exercises; warm baths
    b. Assistive devices
    c. If client "freezes," suggest thinking of something to walk over.
4. Encourage independence in self-care activities: alter clothing for ease in dressing; use assistive devices; do not rush client.
5. Improve communication abilities: instruct client to practice reading aloud, to listen to own voice, and enunciate each syllable clearly.
6. Refer for speech therapy when indicated.
7. Maintain adequate nutrition.
    a. Cut food into bite-sized pieces.
    b. Provide small, frequent feedings.
    c. Allow sufficient time for meals, use warming tray.
8. Avoid constipation and maintain adequate bowel elimination.
9. Provide psychologic support to client/ significant others; depression is common due to changes in body image and self-concept.
10. Provide client teaching and discharge planning concerning
    a. Nature of the disease
    b. Use of prescribed medications and side effects
    c. Importance of daily exercise: walking, swimming, gardening as tolerated; balanced activity and rest
    d. Activities/methods to limit postural deformities: firm mattress with a small pillow; keep head and neck as erect as possible; use broad-based gait; raise feet while walking
    e. Promotion of active participation in self-care activities.

Multiple Sclerosis (MS)

A. General information
    1. Chronic, intermittently progressive disease of the CNS, characterized by scattered patches of demyelination within the brain and spinal cord
    2. Incidence
        a. Affects women more than men
        b. Usually occurs from 20–40 years of age
        c. More frequent in cool or temperate climates
    3. Cause unknown; may be a slow-growing virus or possibly of autoimmune origin
    4. Signs and symptoms are varied and multiple, reflecting the location of demyelination within the CNS
    5. Characterized by remissions and exacerbations

B. Assessment findings
    1. Visual disturbances: blurred vision, scotomas (blind spots), diplopia
    2. Impaired sensation: touch, pain, temperature, or position sense; paresthesias such as numbness, tingling
    3. Euphoria or mood swings
    4. Impaired motor function: weakness, paralysis, spasticity
    5. Impaired cerebellar function: scanning speech, ataxic gait, nystagmus, dysarthria, intention tremor
    6. Bladder: retention or incontinence
    7. Constipation
    8. Sexual impotence in the male
    9. Diagnostic tests:
        a. CSF studies: increased protein and IgG (immunoglobulin)
        b. Visual evoked response (VER) determined by EEG: may be delayed
        c. CT scan: increased density of white matter
        d. MRI: shows areas of demyelination
C. Nursing interventions
    1. Assess the client for specific deficits related to location of demyelinization.
    2. Promote optimum mobility.
        a. Muscle-stretching and strengthening exercises
        b. Walking exercises to improve gait: use wide-based gait
        c. Assistive devices: canes, walker, rails, wheelchair as necessary
    3. Administer medications as ordered.
        a. For acute exacerbations: corticosteroids (ACTH [IV], prednisone) to reduce edema at sites of demyelinization
        b. For spasticity: baclofen (Lioresal), dantrolene (Dantrium), diazepam (Valium)
        c. Beta interferon (Betaseron) to alter immune response
    4. Encourage independence in self-care activities.
    5. Prevent complications of immobility.
    6. Institute bowel program.
    7. Maintain urinary elimination.
        a. Urinary retention
            1) administer bethanecol chloride (Urecholine) as ordered.
            2) perform intermittent catheterization as ordered.
        b. Urinary incontinence
            1) establish voiding schedule.
            2) administer propantheline bromide (Pro-Banthine) if ordered.
        c. Force fluids to 3000 ml/day.
        d. Promote use of acid-ash foods like cranberry or grape juice (see page 299).
    8. Prevent injury related to sensory problems.
        a. Test bath water with thermometer.

b. Avoid heating pads, hot-water bottles.
   c. Inspect body parts frequently for injury.
   d. Make frequent position changes.
9. Prepare client for plasma exchange (to remove antibodies) if indicated.
10. Provide psychologic support to client/significant others.
   a. Encourage positive attitude and assist client in setting realistic goals.
   b. Provide compassion in helping client adapt to changes in body image and self-concept.
   c. Do not encourage false hopes during remission.
   d. Refer to multiple sclerosis societies and community agencies.
11. Provide client teaching and discharge planning concerning
   a. General measures to ensure optimum health
      1) balance between activity and rest
      2) regular exercise such as walking, swimming, biking in mild cases
      3) use of energy conservation techniques
      4) well-balanced diet
      5) fresh air and sunshine
      6) avoiding fatigue, overheating or chilling, stress, infection
   b. Use of medications and side effects
   c. Alternative methods for sexual gratification; refer for sexual counseling if indicated.

Myasthenia Gravis

A. General information
   1. A neuromuscular disorder in which there is a disturbance in the transmission of impulses from nerve to muscle cells at the neuromuscular junction, causing extreme muscle weakness
   2. Incidence
      a. Highest between ages 15–35 for women, over 40 for men.
      b. Affects women more than men
   3. Cause: thought to be autoimmune disorder whereby antibodies destroy acetylcholine receptor sites on the postsynaptic membrane of the neuromuscular junction.
   4. Voluntary muscles are affected, especially those muscles innervated by the cranial nerves.
B. Medical management
   1. Drug therapy
      a. Anticholinesterase drugs: ambenonium (Mytelase), neostigmine (Prostigmin), pyridostigmine (Mestinon)
         1) block action of cholinesterase and increase levels of acetylcholine at the neuromuscular junction

         2) side effects: excessive salivation and sweating, abdominal cramps, nausea and vomiting, diarrhea, fasciculations (muscle twitching)
      b. Corticosteroids: prednisone
         1) used if other drugs are not effective
         2) suppress autoimmune response
   2. Surgery (*thymectomy*)
      a. Surgical removal of the thymus gland (thought to be involved in the production of acetylcholine receptor antibodies)
      b. May cause remission in some clients especially if performed early in the disease
   3. Plasma exchange
      a. Removes circulating acetylcholine receptor antibodies
      b. Use in clients who do not respond to other types of therapy
C. Assessment findings
   1. Diplopia, dysphagia
   2. Extreme muscle weakness, increased with activity and reduced with rest
   3. Ptosis, masklike facial expression
   4. Weak voice, hoarseness
   5. Diagnostic tests
      a. Tensilon test: IV injection of Tensilon provides spontaneous relief of symptoms (lasts 5–10 minutes)
      b. Electromyography (EMG): amplitude of evoked potentials decreases rapidly
      c. Presence of antiacetylcholine receptor antibodies in the serum
D. Nursing interventions
   1. Administer anticholinesterase drugs as ordered.
      a. Give medication exactly on time.
      b. Give with milk and crackers to decrease GI upset.
      c. Monitor effectiveness of drugs: assess muscle strength and vital capacity before and after medication.
      d. Avoid use of the following drugs: morphine and strong sedatives (respiratory depressant effect), quinine, curare, procainamide, neomycin, streptomycin, kanamycin and other aminoglycosides (skeletal muscle blocking effects).
      e. Observe for side effects.
   2. Promote optimal nutrition.
      a. Mealtimes should coincide with the peak effects of the drugs: give medications 30 minutes before meals.
      b. Check gag reflex and swallowing ability before feeding.
      c. Provide a mechanical soft diet.
      d. If the client has difficulty chewing and swallowing, do not leave alone at mealtimes; keep emergency airway and suction equipment nearby.

3. Monitor respiratory status frequently: rate, depth; vital capacity; ability to deep breathe and cough
4. Assess muscle strength frequently; plan activity to take advantage of energy peaks and provide frequent rest periods.
5. Observe for signs of myasthenic or cholinergic crisis.
   a. *Myasthenic crisis*
      1) abrupt onset of severe, generalized muscle weakness with inability to swallow, speak, or maintain respirations
      2) caused by undermedication, physical or emotional stress, infection
      3) symptoms will improve temporarily with Tensilon test.
   b. *Cholinergic crisis*
      1) symptoms similar to myasthenic crisis and, in addition, the side effects of anticholinesterase drugs (e.g., excessive salivation and sweating, abdominal cramps, nausea and vomiting, diarrhea, fasciculations)
      2) caused by overmedication with the cholinergic (anticholinesterase) drugs
      3) symptoms worsen with Tensilon test; keep atropine sulfate and emergency equipment on hand.
   c. Nursing care in crisis
      1) maintain tracheostomy or endotracheal tube with mechanical ventilation as indicated (see Mechanical Ventilation, page 249).
      2) monitor arterial blood gases and vital capacities.
      3) administer medications as ordered.
         a) *myasthenic crisis:* increase doses of anticholinesterase drugs as ordered.
         b) *cholinergic crisis:* discontinue anticholinesterase drugs as ordered until the client recovers.
      4) establish a method of communication.
      5) provide support and reassurance.
6. Provide nursing care for the client with a thymectomy.
7. Provide client teaching and discharge planning concerning
   a. Nature of the disease
   b. Use of prescribed medications, their side effects and signs of toxicity
   c. Importance of checking with physician before taking any new medications including OTC drugs
   d. Importance of planning activities to take advantage of energy peaks and of scheduling frequent rest periods
   e. Need to avoid fatigue, stress, people with upper-respiratory infections
   f. Use of eye patch for diplopia (alternate eyes)
   g. Need to wear Medic-Alert bracelet
   h. Myasthenia Gravis Foundation and other community agencies

Epilepsy

See Seizure Disorders, page 378.

Head Injury

A. General information
   1. Usually caused by car accidents, falls, assaults
   2. Types
      a. *Concussion:* severe blow to the head jostles brain, causing it to strike the skull; results in temporary neural dysfunction
      b. *Contusion:* results from more severe blow that bruises the brain and disrupts neural function
      c. Hemorrhage
         1) *epidural hematoma:* accumulation of blood between the dura mater and skull; commonly results from laceration of middle meningeal artery during skull fracture; blood accumulates rapidly
         2) *subdural hematoma:* accumulation of blood between the dura and arachnoid; venous bleeding that forms slowly; may be acute, subacute, or chronic
         3) *subarachnoid hematoma:* bleeding in subarachnoid space
         4) *intracerebral hematoma:* accumulation of blood within the cerebrum
      d. Fractures: linear, depressed, comminuted, compound
B. Assessment findings (depend on type of injury)
   1. Concussion: headache, transient loss of consciousness, retrograde or posttraumatic amnesia, nausea, dizziness, irritability
   2. Contusion: neurologic deficits depend on the site and extent of damage; include decreased LOC, aphasia, hemiplegia, sensory deficits
   3. Hemorrhages
      a. Epidural hematoma: brief loss of consciousness followed by lucid interval; progresses to severe headache, vomiting, rapidly deteriorating LOC, possible seizures, ipsilateral pupillary dilation
      b. Subdural hematoma: alterations in LOC, headache, focal neurologic

deficits, personality changes, ipsilateral pupillary dilation

    c. Intracerebral hematoma: headache, decreased LOC, hemiplegia, ipsilateral pupillary dilation

  4. Fractures

    a. Headache, pain over fracture site

    b. Compound fractures: rhinorrhea (leakage of CSF from nose); otorrhea (leakage of CSF from ear)

  5. Diagnostic tests

    a. Skull x-ray: reveals skull fracture or intracranial shift

    b. CT scan: reveals hemorrhage

C. Nursing interventions (see also Care of the Unconscious Client [page 182] and Care of the Client with Increased ICP [page 182])

  1. Maintain a patent airway and adequate ventilation.

  2. Monitor vital signs and neuro checks; observe for changes in neurologic status, signs of increased ICP, shock, seizures, and hyperthermia.

  3. Observe for CSF leakage.

    a. Check discharge for positive Testape or Dextrostix reaction for glucose; bloody spot encircled by watery, pale ring on pillowcase or sheet.

    b. Never attempt to clean the ears or nose of a head-injured client or use nasal suction unless cleared by physician

  4. If a CSF leak is present

    a. Instruct client not to blow nose.

    b. Elevate head of bed 30° as ordered.

    c. Observe for signs of meningitis and administer antibiotics to prevent meningitis as ordered.

    d. Place a cotton ball in the ear to absorb otorrhea; replace frequently.

    e. Gently place a sterile gauze pad at the bottom of the nose for rhinorrhea; replace frequently.

  5. Prevent complications of immobility.

  6. Prepare the client for surgery if indicated.

    a. Depressed skull fracture: surgical removal or elevation of splintered bone; debridement and cleansing of area; repair of dural tear if present; cranioplasty (if necessitated for large cranial defect)

    b. Epidural or subdural hematoma: evacuation of the hematoma

  7. Provide psychologic support to client/significant others.

  8. Observe for hemiplegia, aphasia, and sensory problems, and plan care accordingly (see Cerebrovascular Accident, page 187)

  9. Provide client teaching and discharge planning concerning rehabilitation for neurologic deficits; note availability of community agencies.

Intracranial Surgery

A. Types

  1. *Craniotomy:* surgical opening of skull to gain access to intracranial structures; used to remove a tumor, evacuate blood clot, control hemorrhage, relieve increased ICP

  2. *Craniectomy:* excision of a portion of the skull; sometimes used for decompression

  3. *Cranioplasty:* repair of a cranial defect with a metal or plastic plate

B. Nursing interventions: preoperative

  1. Routine pre-op care (see Perioperative Nursing, page 161).

  2. Provide emotional support; explain post-op procedures and that client's head will be shaved, there will be a large bandage on head, possibly temporary swelling and discoloration around the eye on the affected side, and possible headache.

  3. Shampoo the scalp and check for signs of infection.

  4. Shave hair.

  5. Evaluate and record baseline vital signs and neuro checks.

  6. Avoid enemas unless directed (straining increases ICP).

  7. Give pre-op steroids as ordered to decrease brain swelling.

  8. Insert Foley catheter as ordered.

C. Nursing interventions: postoperative

  1. Provide nursing care for the unconscious client (page 182).

  2. Maintain a patent airway and adequate ventilation.

    a. Supratentorial incision: elevate head of bed 15°–45° as ordered; position on back (if intubated or conscious) or on unaffected side; turn every 2 hours to facilitate breathing and venous return.

    b. Infratentorial incision: keep head of bed flat or elevate 20°–30° as ordered; do not flex head on chest; turn side to side every 2 hours using a turning sheet; check respirations closely and report any signs of respiratory distress.

    c. Instruct the conscious client to breathe deeply but not to cough; avoid vigorous suctioning.

  3. Check vital signs and neuro checks frequently; observe for decreasing LOC, increased ICP, seizures, hyperthermia.

  4. Monitor fluid and electrolyte status.

    a. Maintain accurate I&O.

    b. Restrict fluids to 1500 ml/day or as ordered to decrease cerebral edema.

    c. Avoid overly rapid infusions.

    d. Watch for signs of diabetes insipidus (severe thirst, polyuria, dehydration) and inappropriate ADH secretion (decreased urine output, hunger, thirst, irritability, decreased LOC, muscle weakness).

    e. For infratentorial surgery: may be NPO for 24 hours due to possible impaired swallowing and gag reflexes.

5. Assess dressings frequently and report any abnormalities.

    a. Reinforce as needed with sterile dressings.

    b. Check dressings for excessive drainage, CSF, infection, displacement and report to physician.

    c. If surgical drain is in place, note color, amount, and odor of drainage.

6. Administer medications as ordered.

    a. Corticosteroids: to decrease cerebral edema

    b. Anticonvulsants: to prevent seizures

    c. Stool softeners: to prevent straining

    d. Mild analgesics

7. Apply ice to swollen eyelids; lubricate lids and areas around eyes with petrolatum jelly.

8. Refer client for rehabilitation for residual deficits.

Spinal Cord Injuries

A. General information

    1. Occurs most commonly in young adult males between ages 15 and 25

    2. Common traumatic causes: motor vehicle accidents, diving in shallow water, falls, industrial accidents, sports injuries, gunshot or stab wounds

    3. Nontraumatic causes: tumors, hematomas, aneurysms, congenital defects (spina bifida)

    4. Classified by extent, level, and mechanism of injury

        a. Extent of injury

            1) may affect the vertebral column: fracture, fracture/dislocation

            2) may affect anterior or posterior ligaments, causing compression of spinal cord

            3) may be to the spinal cord and its roots: concussion, contusion, compression or laceration by fracture/dislocation or penetrating missiles

        b. Level of injury: cervical, thoracic, lumbar

        c. Mechanisms of injury

            1) hyperflexion

            2) hyperextension

            3) axial loading (force exerted straight up or down spinal column as in a diving accident)

            4) penetrating wounds

    5. Pathophysiology: hemorrhage and edema cause ischemia, leading to necrosis and destruction of the cord

B. Medical management: immobilization and maintenance of normal spinal alignment to promote fracture healing

    1. Horizontal turning frames (Stryker frame)

    2. Skeletal traction: to immobilize the fracture and maintain alignment of the cervical spine

        a. *Cervical tongs (Crutchfield, Gardner-Wells, Vinke):* inserted through burr holes; traction is provided by a rope extended from the center of tongs over a pulley with weights attached at the end.

        b. *Halo traction*

            1) stainless steel halo ring fits around the head and is attached to the skull with four pins; halo is attached to plastic body cast or plastic vest

            2) permits early mobilization, decreased period of hospitalization and reduces complications of immobility

    3. Surgery: decompression laminectomy, spinal fusion

        a. Depends on type of injury and the preference of the surgeon

        b. Indications: unstable fracture, cord compression, progression of neurologic deficits

C. Assessment findings

    1. Spinal shock

        a. Occurs immediately after the injury as a result of the insult to the CNS

        b. Temporary condition lasting from several days to three months

        c. Characterized by absence of reflexes below the level of the lesion, flaccid paralysis, lack of temperature control in affected parts, hypotension with bradycardia, retention of urine and feces

    2. Symptoms depend on the level and the extent of the injury.

        a. Level of injury

            1) *quadriplegia:* cervical injuries (C_1–C_8) cause paralysis of all four extremities; respiratory paralysis occurs in lesions above C_6 due to lack of innervation to the diaphragm; (phrenic nerves at the C_4–C_5 level).

            2) *paraplegia:* thoraco/lumbar injuries (T_1–L_4) cause paralysis of the lower half of the body involving both legs

        b. Extent of injury

            1) complete cord transection

                a) loss of all voluntary movement and sensation below the level of the injury; reflex activity below the level of the lesion may return after spinal shock resolves.

                b) lesions in the conus medullaris

or cauda equina result in permanent flaccid paralysis and areflexia.
   2) incomplete lesions: varying degrees of motor or sensory loss below the level of the lesion depending on which neurologic tracts are damaged and which are spared.
  3. Diagnostic test: spinal x-rays may reveal fracture.
D. Nursing interventions: emergency care
  1. Assess airway, breathing, circulation
    a. Do not move the client during assessment.
    b. If airway obstruction or inadequate ventilation exists: do not hyperextend neck to open airway, use jaw thrust instead.
  2. Perform a quick head-to-toe assessment: check for LOC, signs of trauma to the head or neck, leakage of clear fluid from ears or nose, signs of motor or sensory impairment.
  3. Immobilize the client in the position found until help arrives.
  4. Once emergency help arrives, assist in immobilizing the head and neck with a cervical collar and place the client on a spinal board; avoid any movement during transfer, especially flexion of the spinal column.
  5. Have suction available to clear the airway and prevent aspiration if the client vomits; client may be turned slightly to the side if secured to a board.
  6. Evaluate respiration and observe for weak or labored respirations.
E. Nursing interventions: acute care
  1. Maintain optimum respiratory function.
    a. Observe for weak or labored respirations; monitor arterial blood gases.
    b. Prevent pneumonia and atelectasis: turn every 2 hours; cough and deep breathe every hour; use incentive spirometry every 2 hours.
    c. Tracheostomy and mechanical ventilation may be necessary if respiratory insufficiency occurs.
  2. Maintain optimal cardiovascular function.
    a. Monitor vital signs; observe for bradycarida, arrhythmias, hypotension.
    b. Apply thigh-high elastic stockings or Ace bandages.
    c. Change position slowly and gradually elevate the head of the bed to prevent postural hypotension.
    d. Observe for signs of deep-vein thrombosis.
  3. Maintain fluid and electrolyte balance and nutrition.

    a. Nasogastric tube may be inserted until bowel sounds return.
    b. Maintain IV therapy as ordered; avoid overhydration (can aggravate cord edema).
    c. Check bowel sounds before feeding client (paralytic ileus is common).
    d. Progress slowly from clear liquid to regular diet.
    e. Provide diet high in protein, carbohydrates, calories.
  4. Maintain immobilization and spinal alignment always.
    a. Turn every hour on turning frame.
    b. Maintain cervical traction at all times if indicated.
  5. Prevent complications of immobility; use footboard/high-topped sneakers to prevent foot drop; provide splint for quadriplegic client to prevent wrist drop.
  6. Maintain urinary elimination.
    a. Provide intermittent catheterization or maintain indwelling catheter as ordered.
    b. Increase fluids to 3000 ml/day.
    c. Provide acid-ash foods/fluids to acidify urine and prevent infection (see page 299).
  7. Maintain bowel elimination: administer stool softeners and suppositories to prevent impaction as ordered.
  8. Monitor temperature control.
    a. Check temperature every 4 hours.
    b. Regulate environment closely.
    c. Avoid excessive covering or exposure.
  9. Observe for and prevent infection.
    a. Observe tongs or pin site for redness, drainage.
    b. Provide tong- or pin-site care. Cleanse with antiseptic solution according to agency policy.
    c. Observe for signs of respiratory or urinary infection.
  10. Observe for and prevent stress ulcers.
    a. Assess for epigastic or shoulder pain.
    b. If corticosteroids are ordered, give with food or antacids; administer cimetidine (Tagamet) as ordered.
    c. Check nasogastric tube contents and stools for blood.
F. Nursing interventions: chronic care
  1. *Neurogenic bladder*
    a. Reflex or upper motor neuron bladder; reflex activity of the bladder may occur after spinal shock resolves; the bladder is unable to store urine very long and empties involuntarily
    b. Nonreflexive or lower motor neuron bladder: reflex arc is disrupted and no reflex activity of the bladder occurs, resulting in urine retention with overflow

         c. Management of reflex bladder
            1) intermittent catheterization every 4
               hours and gradually progress to
               every 6 hours.
            2) regulate fluid intake to 1800–2000
               ml/day.
            3) bladder taps or stimulating trigger
               points to cause reflex emptying of
               the bladder.
         d. Management of nonreflexive bladder
            1) intermittent catheterization every 6
               hours.
            2) Credé maneuver or rectal stretch.
            3) regulate intake to 1800–2000 ml/day
               to prevent overdistention of bladder.
         e. Management depends on life-style,
            age, sex, home care, and availability of
            care giver.
      2. *Spasticity*
         a. Return of reflex activity may occur
            after spinal shock resolves; severe
            spasticity may be detrimental
         b. Drug therapy: baclofen (Lioresal),
            dantrolene (Dantrium), diazepam
            (Valium)
         c. Physical therapy: stretching exercises,
            warm tub baths, whirlpool
         d. Surgery: chordotomy
      3. *Autonomic dysreflexia*
         a. Rise in blood pressure, sometimes to
            fatal levels
         b. Occurs in clients with cord lesions
            above T_6 and most commonly in clients
            with cervical injuries
         c. Reflex response to stimulation of the
            sympathetic nervous system
         d. Stimulus may be overdistended bladder
            or bowel, decubitus ulcer, chilling,
            pressure from bedclothes
         e. Symptoms: severe headache,
            hypertension, bradycardia, sweating,
            goose bumps, nasal congestion,
            blurred vision, convulsions
         f. Interventions
            1) raise client to sitting position to
               decrease BP.
            2) check for source of stimulus
               (bladder, bowel, skin).
            3) remove offending stimulus (e.g.,
               catheterize client, digitally remove
               impacted feces, reposition client).
            4) monitor blood pressure.
            5) administer antihypertensives (e.g.,
               hydralazine HCl [Apresoline]) as
               ordered.
G. Nursing interventions: general rehabilitative
   care
   1. Provide psychologic support to client/
      significant others.
      a. Support during grieving process.
      b. Assist client to adjust to effects of
         injury.

         c. Encourage independence.
         d. Involve the client in decision making.
      2. Provide sexual counseling.
         a. Work with the client and partner.
         b. Explore alternative methods of sexual
            gratification.
      3. Initiate rehabilitation program.
         a. Physical therapy.
         b. Vocational rehabilitation
         c. Psychologic counseling
         d. Use of braces, electronic wheelchair,
            and other assistance devices to
            maximize independence.

Specific Disorders of the Peripheral Nervous System

Trigeminal Neuralgia (Tic Douloureux)

A. General information
   1. Disorder of cranial nerve V causing
      disabling and recurring attacks of severe
      pain along the sensory distribution of
      one or more branches of the trigeminal
      nerve
   2. Incidence increased in elderly women
   3. Cause unknown
B. Medical management
   1. Anticonvulsant drugs: carbamazepine
      (Tegretol), phenytoin (Dilantin)
   2. Nerve block: injection of alcohol or phenol
      into one or more branches of the
      trigeminal nerve; temporary effect, lasts
      6–18 months
   3. Surgery
      a. Peripheral: avulsion of peripheral
         branches of trigeminal nerve
      b. Intracranial
         1) retrogasserian rhizotomy: total
            severance of the sensory root of the
            trigeminal nerve intracranially;
            results in permanent anesthesia,
            numbness, heaviness, and stiffness
            in affected part; loss of corneal
            reflex
         2) microsurgery: uses more precise
            cutting and may preserve facial
            sensation and corneal reflex
         3) percutaneous radio-frequency
            trigeminal gangliolysis: current
            surgical procedure of choice;
            thermally destroys the trigeminal
            nerve in the area of the ganglion;
            provides permanent pain relief with
            preservation of sense of touch,
            proprioception, and corneal reflex;
            done under local anesthesia
         4) microvascular decompression of
            trigeminal nerve: decompresses the
            trigeminal nerve; craniotomy
            necessary; provides permanent pain

relief while preserving facial sensation

C. Assessment findings
1. Sudden paroxysms of extremely severe shooting pain in one side of the face
2. Attacks may be triggered by a cold breeze, foods/fluids of extreme temperature, toothbrushing, chewing, talking, or touching the face
3. During attack: twitching, grimacing, and frequent blinking/tearing of the eye
4. Poor eating and hygiene habits
5. Withdrawal from interactions with others
6. Diagnostic tests: x-rays of the skull, teeth, and sinuses may identify dental or sinus infection as an aggravating factor.

D. Nursing interventions
1. Assess characteristics of the pain including triggering factors, trigger points, and pain management techniques.
2. Administer medications as ordered; monitor response.
3. Maintain room at an even, moderate temperature, free from drafts.
4. Provide small, frequent feedings of lukewarm, semiliquid, or soft foods that are easily chewed.
5. Provide the client with a soft washcloth and lukewarm water and perform hygiene during periods when pain is decreased.
6. Prepare the client for surgery if indicated.
7. Provide client teaching and discharge planning concerning
   a. Need to avoid outdoor activities during cold, windy, or rainy weather
   b. Importance of good nutrition and hygiene
   c. Use of medications, side effects, and signs of toxicity
   d. Specific instructions following surgery for residual effects of anesthesia and loss of corneal reflex
      1) protective eye care
      2) chew on unaffected side only
      3) avoid hot fluids/foods
      4) mouth care after meals to remove particles
      5) good oral hygiene; visit dentist every 6 months
      6) protect the face during extremes of temperature.

Bell's Palsy

A. General information
1. Disorder of cranial nerve VII resulting in the loss of ability to move the muscles on one side of the face
2. Cause unknown; may be viral or autoimmune
3. Complete recovery in 3–5 weeks in majority of clients

B. Assessment findings
1. Loss of taste over anterior two-thirds of tongue on affected side
2. Complete paralysis of one side of face
3. Loss of expression, displacement of mouth toward unaffected side, and inability to close eyelid (all on affected side)
4. Pain behind the ear

C. Nursing interventions
1. Assess facial nerve function regularly (see Table 4.15, page 176).
2. Administer medications as ordered.
   a. Corticosteroids: to decrease edema and pain
   b. Mild analgesics as necessary
3. Provide soft diet with supplementary feedings as indicated.
4. Instruct to chew on unaffected side, avoid hot fluids/foods, and perform mouth care after each meal.
5. Provide special eye care to protect the cornea.
   a. Dark glasses (cosmetic and protective reasons) or eyeshield
   b. Artificial tears to prevent drying of the cornea
   c. Ointment and eye patch at night to keep eyelid closed
6. Provide support and reassurance.

Guillain-Barré Syndrome

A. General information
1. Symmetrical, bilateral, peripheral polyneuritis characterized by ascending paralysis
2. Can occur at any age; affects women and men equally
3. Cause unknown; may be an autoimmune process
4. Precipitating factors: antecedent viral infection, immunization
5. Progression of disease is highly individual; 90% of clients stop progression in 4 weeks; recovery is usually from 3–6 months; may have residual deficits

B. Medical Management
1. Mechanical ventilation if respiratory problems present
2. Plasmapheresis to reduce circulating antibodies
3. Continuous ECG monitoring to detect alteration in heart rate and rhythm
4. Propranolol to prevent tachycardia
5. Atropine may be given to prevent episodes of bradycardia during endotracheal suctioning and physical therapy.

C. Assessment findings
1. Mild sensory changes; in some clients severe misinterpretation of sensory stimuli resulting in extreme discomfort
2. Clumsiness: usually first symptom

3. Progressive motor weakness in more than one limb (classically is ascending and symmetrical)
4. Cranial nerve involvement (dysphagia)
5. Ventilatory insufficiency if paralysis ascends to respiratory muscles
6. Absence of deep tendon reflexes
7. Autonomic dysfunction
8. Diagnostic tests
   a. CSF studies: increased protein
   b. EMG: slowed nerve conduction
D. Nursing interventions
1. Maintain adequate ventilation.
   a. Monitor rate and depth of respirations; serial vital capacities.
   b. Observe for ventilatory insufficiency.
   c. Maintain mechanical ventilation as needed; keep airway free of secretions and prevent pneumonia.
2. Check individual muscle groups every 2 hours in acute phase to check for progression of muscle weakness.
3. Assess cranial nerve function: check gag reflex and swallowing ability; ability to handle secretions; voice.
4. Monitor vital signs and observe for signs of autonomic dysfunction such as acute periods of hypertension fluctuating with hypotension, tachycardia, arrhythmias.
5. Administer corticosteroids to suppress immune reaction as ordered.
6. Administer antiarrhythmic agents as ordered.
7. Prevent complications of immobility.
8. Promote comfort (especially in clients with sensory changes): foot cradle, sheepskin, guided imagery, relaxation techniques.
9. Promote optimum nutrition.
   a. Check gag reflex before feeding.
   b. Start with pureed foods.
   c. Assess need for nasogastric tube feedings if unable to swallow.
10. Provide psychologic support and encouragement to client/significant others.
11. Refer for rehabilitation to regain strength and to treat any residual deficits.

Amyotrophic Lateral Sclerosis (Lou Gehrig's Disease)

A. General information
1. Progressive motor neuron disease, which usually leads to death in 2–6 years
2. Onset usually between ages 40–70; affects men more than women
3. Cause unknown
4. There is no cure or specific treatment; death usually occurs as a result of respiratory infection secondary to respiratory insufficiency.
B. Assessment findings

1. Progressive weakness and atrophy of the muscles of the arms, trunk, or legs
2. Dysarthria, dysphagia
3. Fasciculations
4. Respiratory insufficiency
5. Diagnostic tests: EMG and muscle biopsy can rule out other diseases.
C. Nursing interventions
1. Provide nursing measures for muscle weakness and dysphagia.
2. Promote adequate ventilatory function.
3. Prevent complications of immobility.
4. Encourage diversional activities; spend time with the client.
5. Provide compassion and intensive support to client/significant others.
6. Provide or refer for physical therapy as indicated.
7. Promote independence for as long as possible.

DISORDERS OF THE EYE

Cataracts

A. General information
1. Opacity of the ocular lens
2. Incidence increases with age
3. May be caused by changes associated with aging ("senile" cataract); may be congenital; or may develop secondary to trauma, radiation, infection, certain drugs (corticosteroids)
B. Assessment findings
1. Blurred vision
2. Progressive decrease in vision
3. Glare in bright lights
4. Pupil may develop milky-white appearance
5. Diagnostic test: ophthalmoscopic exam confirms presence of cataract
C. Nursing interventions: prepare client for cataract surgery.

Cataract Surgery

A. General information
1. Performed when client can no longer remain independent because of reduced vision
2. Surgery performed on one eye at a time; usually in a same-day surgery unit
3. Local anesthesia and intravenous sedation usually used
4. Types
   a. *Extracapsular extraction:* lens capsule is excised and the lens is expressed; posterior capsule is left in place (may be used to support new artificial lens implant).
   b. *Phacoemulsification:* a type of extracapsular extraction; a hollow

needle capable of ultrasonic vibration is inserted into lens, vibrations emulsify the lens, which is then aspirated.

   c. *Intracapsular extraction:* lens is totally removed within its capsule, may be delivered from eye by *cryoextraction* (lens is frozen with a metal probe and removed).

  5. *Peripheral iridectomy* may be performed at the time of surgery; small hole cut in iris to prevent development of secondary glaucoma

  6. *Intraocular lens implant* often performed at the time of surgery.

B. Nursing interventions: preoperative (see also Perioperative Nursing, page 161)

  1. Assess vision in the unaffected eye since the affected eye will be patched post-op.

  2. Provide pre-op teaching regarding measures to prevent increased intraocular pressure post-op.

  3. Administer medications as ordered.

   a. Topical mydriatics and cycloplegics to dilate the pupil

   b. Topical antibiotics to prevent infection

   c. Acetazolamide (Diamox) and osmotic agents (oral glycerin or IV mannitol) to decrease intraocular pressure to provide a soft eyeball for surgery

C. Nursing interventions: postoperative

  1. Reorient the client to surroundings.

  2. Provide safety measures: elevate side rails, provide call bell, assist with ambulation when fully recovered from anesthesia.

  3. Prevent increased intraocular pressure and stress on the suture line.

   a. Elevate head of bed 30°–40°.

   b. Have client lie on back or unaffected side.

   c. Avoid having client cough, sneeze, bend over, or move head too rapidly.

   d. Treat nausea with antiemetics as ordered to prevent vomiting.

   e. Give stool softeners as ordered to prevent straining.

   f. Observe for and report signs of increased intraocular pressure: severe eye pain, restlessness, increased pulse.

  4. Protect eye from injury.

   a. Dressings are usually removed the day after surgery.

   b. Eyeglasses or eye shield used during the day.

   c. Always use eye shield during the night.

  5. Administer medications as ordered.

   a. Topical mydriatics and cycloplegics to decrease spasm of ciliary body and relieve pain

   b. Topical antibiotics and corticosteroids

   c. Mild analgesics as needed

  6. Provide client teaching and discharge planning concerning

   a. Technique of eyedrop administration

   b. Use of eye shield at night

   c. No bending, stooping, or lifting

   d. Report signs or symptoms of complications immediately to physician: severe eye pain, decreased vision, excessive drainage, swelling of eyelid.

   e. Cataract glasses/contact lenses

    1) if a lens implant has not been performed, the client will need glasses or contact lenses.

    2) temporary glasses are worn for 1–4 weeks, then permanent glasses fitted.

    3) cataract glasses magnify objects by ⅓ and distort peripheral vision; have client practice manual coordination with assistance until new spatial relationships become familiar; have client practice walking, using stairs, reaching for articles.

    4) contact lenses cause less distortion of vision; prescribed at one month.

Glaucoma

A. General information

  1. Characterized by increased intraocular pressure resulting in progressive loss of vision; may cause blindness if not recognized and treated

  2. Risk factors: age over 40, diabetes, hypertension, heredity; history of previous eye surgery, trauma, or inflammation

  3. Types

   a. *Chronic (open-angle) glaucoma:* most common form, due to obstruction of the outflow of aqueous humor, in trabecular meshwork or canal of Schlemm

   b. *Acute (closed-angle) glaucoma:* due to forward displacement of the iris against the cornea, obstructing the outflow of the aqueous humor; occurs suddenly and is an emergency situation; if untreated, blindness will result

   c. *Chronic (closed-angle) glaucoma:* similar to acute (closed-angle) glaucoma, with the potential for an acute attack

  4. Early detection is very important; regular eye exams including tonometry for persons over age 40 is recommended.

B. Medical management

  1. Chronic (open-angle) glaucoma

   a. Drug therapy: one or a combination of the following

    1) miotic eyedrops (pilocarpine) to increase outflow of aqueous humor

    2) epinephrine eyedrops to decrease

aqueous humor production and increase outflow

    3) acetazolamide (Diamox): carbonic anhydrase inhibitor to decrease aqueous humor production

    4) timolol maleate (Timoptic): topical beta-adrenergic blocker to decrease intraocular pressure

  b. Surgery (if no improvement with drugs)

    1) filtering procedure (trabeculectomy, trephining) to create artificial openings for the outflow of aqueous humor

    2) laser trabeculoplasty: noninvasive procedure performed with argon laser that can be done on an outpatient basis; produces similar results as trabeculectomy

2. Acute (closed-angle) glaucoma

  a. Drug therapy (before surgery)

    1) miotic eyedrops (e.g., pilocarpine) to cause pupil to contract and draw iris away from cornea

    2) osmotic agents (e.g., glycerin [oral], mannitol [IV]) to decrease intraocular pressure

    3) narcotic analgesics for pain

  b. Surgery

    1) peripheral iridectomy: portion of the iris is excised to facilitate outflow of aqueous humor

    2) argon laser beam surgery: noninvasive procedure using laser that produces same effect as iridectomy; done on an outpatient basis

    3) iridectomy usually performed on second eye later since a large number of clients have an acute attack in the other eye

3. Chronic (closed-angle) glaucoma

  a. Drug therapy: miotics (pilocarpine)

  b. Surgery: bilateral peripheral iridectomy to prevent acute attacks

C. Assessment findings

1. Chronic (open-angle) glaucoma: symptoms develop slowly; impaired peripheral vision (tunnel vision); loss of central vision if unarrested; mild discomfort in the eyes; halos around lights

2. Acute (closed-angle) glaucoma: severe eye pain; blurred, cloudy vision; halos around lights; nausea and vomiting; steamy cornea; moderate pupillary dilation

3. Chronic (closed-angle) glaucoma: transient blurred vision; slight eye pain; halos around lights

4. Diagnostic tests

  a. Visual acuity: reduced

  b. Tonometry: reading of 24–32 mm Hg suggests glaucoma; may be 50 mm Hg or more in acute (closed-angle) glaucoma

  c. Ophthalmoscopic exam: reveals narrowing of small vessels of optic disk, cupping of optic disk

  d. Perimetry: reveals defects in visual fields

  e. Gonioscopy: examine angle of anterior chamber

D. Nursing interventions

1. Administer medications as ordered.

2. Provide quiet, dark environment.

3. Maintain accurate I&O with the use of osmotic agents.

4. Prepare the client for surgery if indicated.

5. Provide post-op care (see Cataract Surgery, page 199).

6. Provide client teaching and discharge planning concerning

  a. Self-administration of eyedrops

  b. Need to avoid stooping, heavy lifting, or pushing, emotional upsets, excessive fluid intake, constrictive clothing around the neck

  c. Need to avoid the use of antihistamines or sympathomimetic drugs (found in cold preparations) in closed-angle glaucoma since they may cause mydriasis

  d. Importance of follow-up care

  e. Need to wear Medic-Alert tag

Detached Retina

A. General information

1. Detachment of the sensory retina from the pigment epithelium of the retina

2. Caused by trauma, aging process, severe myopia, postcataract extraction, severe diabetic retinopathy

3. Pathophysiology: tear in the retina allows vitreous humor to seep behind the sensory retina and separate it from the pigment epithelium

B. Medical management

1. Bed rest with eyes patched and detached areas dependent to prevent further detachment

2. Surgery: necessary to repair detachment

  a. *Photocoagulation:* light beam (argon laser) through dilated pupil creates an inflammatory reaction and scarring to heal the area

  b. *Cryosurgery* or *diathermy:* application of extreme cold or heat to the external globe; inflammatory reaction causes scarring and healing of area

  c. *Scleral buckling:* shortening of sclera to force pigment epithelium close to retina

C. Assessment findings

1. Flashes of light, floaters

2. Visual field loss, veil-like curtain coming across field of vision
3. Diagnostic test: ophthalmoscopic examination confirms diagnosis.
D. Nursing interventions: preoperative
   1. Maintain bed rest as ordered with head of bed flat and detached area in a dependent position.
   2. Use bilateral eye patches as ordered; elevate side rails to prevent injury.
   3. Identify yourself when entering the room.
   4. Orient the client frequently to time, date, and surroundings; explain procedures.
   5. Provide diversional activities to provide sensory stimulation.
E. Nursing interventions: postoperative (see also Cataract Surgery, page 199)
   1. Check orders for positioning and activity level.
      a. May be on bed rest for 1–2 days.
      b. May need to position client so that detached area is in dependent position.
   2. Administer medications as ordered: topical mydriatics, analgesics as needed.
   3. Provide client teaching and discharge planning concerning
      a. Technique of eyedrop administration
      b. Use of eye shield at night
      c. No bending from waist; no heavy work or lifting for 6 weeks
      d. Restriction of reading for 3 weeks or more
      e. May watch television
      f. Need to check with physician regarding combing and shampooing hair and shaving
      g. Need to report complications such as recurrence of detachment

Eye Injuries/Emergency Care

A. Removal of loose foreign body from conjunctiva
   1. Foreign bodies, e.g., sand, dust, may cause pain and lacrimation.
   2. Instruct client to look upward.
   3. Evert lower lid to expose the conjunctival sac.
   4. Gently remove the particle with a cotton applicator dipped in sterile normal saline using a twisting motion.
   5. If particle is not found, examine the upper lid.
   6. Place cotton applicator stick or tongue blade horizontally on outer surface of upper lid; grasp under eyelashes with fingers of other hand and pull the upper lid outward and upward over the applicator stick.
   7. Gently remove the particle as above.
B. Penetrating injuries to the eye
   1. Examples: darts, scissors, flying metal

2. Do not attempt to remove object.
3. Do not allow client to apply pressure to the eye.
4. Cover eye lightly with sterile eye patch for embedded objects, e.g., metal; apply protective shield, e.g., paper cup, for impaled objects such as darts.
5. Cover uninjured eye to prevent excessive movement of injured eye.
6. Refer the client to an emergency room immediately.
C. Chemical burns
   1. Flush eye immediately with copious amounts of water for 15–20 minutes.
      a. Have client hold head under faucet to let water run over eye to thoroughly wash it out; may need to forcibly separate eyelids during flush
      b. If available, flush eye with syringe
   2. After flushing, refer client to an emergency room immediately

DISORDERS OF THE EAR

Otosclerosis

A. General information
   1. Formation of new spongy bone in the labyrinth of the ear causing fixation of the stapes in the oval window; this prevents transmission of auditory vibration to the inner ear
   2. Found more often in females
   3. Cause unknown, but there is a familial tendency
B. Medical management: stapedectomy is the procedure of choice.
C. Assessment findings
   1. Progressive loss of hearing
   2. Tinnitus
   3. Diagnostic tests
      a. Audiometry: reveals conductive hearing loss
      b. Weber's and Rinne's tests: show bone conduction is greater than air conduction
D. Nursing interventions: see Stapedectomy.

Stapedectomy

A. General information
   1. Removal of diseased portion of stapes and replacement with a prosthesis to conduct vibrations from the middle ear to inner ear; usually performed under local anesthesia
   2. Used to treat otosclerosis
B. Nursing interventions: preoperative
   1. Provide general pre-op nursing care, including an explanation of post-op expectations.

2. Explain to the client that hearing may improve during surgery and then decrease due to edema and packing.
C. Nursing interventions: postoperative
1. Position the client according to the surgeon's orders (possibly with operative ear uppermost to prevent displacement of the graft).
2. Have client deep breathe every 2 hours while in bed, but no coughing.
3. Elevate side rails; assist the client with ambulation and move slowly (may have some vertigo).
4. Administer medications as ordered: analgesics, antibiotics, antiemetics, anti-motion-sickness drugs.
5. Check dressings frequently for excessive drainage or bleeding.
6. Assess facial nerve function, i.e., ask client to wrinkle forehead, close eyelids, puff out cheeks, smile and show teeth; check for any asymmetry.
7. Question client about pain, headache, vertigo, and unusual sensations in the ear; report existence to physician.
8. Provide client teaching and discharge planning concerning
   a. Warnings against blowing nose or coughing; sneeze with the mouth open
   b. Need to keep ear dry in the shower; no shampooing until allowed
   c. No flying for 6 months, especially if an upper respiratory tract infection is present
   d. Placement of cotton ball in auditory meatus after packing is removed; change twice a day.

Ménière's Disease

A. General information
1. Disease of the inner ear resulting from dilation of the endolymphatic system and increased volume of endolymph; characterized by recurrent and usually progressive triad of symptoms: vertigo, tinnitus, and hearing loss
2. Incidence highest between ages 30 and 60
3. Cause unknown; theories include allergy, toxicity, localized ischemia, hemorrhage, viral infection, or edema.
B. Medical management
1. Acute: atropine (decreases autonomic nervous system activity), diazepam (Valium), fentanyl, and droperidol (Innovar)
2. Chronic
   a. Drug therapy: vasodilators (nicotinic acid), diuretics, mild sedatives or tranquilizers (diazepam [Valium]), antihistamines (diphenhydramine [Benadryl], meclizine [Antivert])
   b. Low-sodium diet, restricted fluid intake, restrict caffeine and nicotine.
3. Surgery
   a. Surgical destruction of labyrinth causing loss of vestibular and cochlear function (if disease is unilateral)
   b. Intracranial division of vestibular portion of cranial nerve VIII
   c. Endolymphatic sac decompression or shunt to equalize pressure in endolymphatic space
C. Assessment findings
1. Sudden attacks of vertigo lasting hours or days; attacks occur several times a year
2. Nausea, tinnitus, progressive hearing loss
3. Vomiting, nystagmus
4. Diagnostic tests
   a. Audiometry: reveals sensorineural hearing loss
   b. Vestibular tests: reveal decreased function
D. Nursing interventions
1. Maintain bed rest in a quiet, darkened room in position of choice; elevate side rails as needed.
2. Only move the client for essential care (bath may not be essential).
3. Provide an emesis basin for vomiting.
4. Monitor IV therapy; maintain accurate I&O.
5. Assist with ambulation when the attack is over.
6. Administer medications as ordered.
7. Prepare the client for surgery as indicated (post-op care includes using above measures).
8. Provide client teaching and discharge planning concerning
   a. Use of medication and side effects
   b. Low-sodium diet and decreased fluid intake
   c. Importance of eliminating smoking

Sample Questions

33. An adult has a medical diagnosis of increased intracranial pressure and is being cared for on the neurology unit. The nursing care plan includes elevating the head of the bed and positioning the client's head in proper alignment. The nurse recognizes that these actions are effective because they act by
1. making it easier for the client to breathe.
2. preventing a Valsalva maneuver.
3. promoting venous drainage.
4. reducing pain.
34. A client begins to have Cheyne-Stokes respirations. This type of breathing pattern is best explained as

1. completely irregular breathing pattern with random deep and shallow respirations.
2. prolonged inspirations with inspiratory and/or expiratory pauses.
3. rhythmic waxing and waning of both rate and depth of respiration with brief periods of interspersed apnea.
4. sustained, regular, rapid respirations of increased depth.

35. Which of the following reduces cerebral edema by constricting cerebral veins?
1. Dexamethasone (Decadron).
2. Mechanical hyperventilation.
3. Mannitol (Osmitrol).
4. Ventriculostomy.

36. The nurse is caring for an adult client who was admitted unconscious. The initial assessment utilized the Glasgow Coma Scale. The nurse knows that the Glasgow Coma Scale is a systematic neurologic assessment tool that evaluates all of the following EXCEPT
1. eye opening.
2. motor response.
3. pupillary reaction.
4. verbal performance.

37. An adult's Glasgow Coma Scale score is indicative of coma. Her score is
1. zero.
2. two.
3. six.
4. ten.

38. When the nurse tested an unconscious client for noxious stimuli, the client responded with decorticate rigidity or posturing. This is best described as
1. flexion of the upper and lower extremities into a fetal-like position.
2. rigid extension of the upper and lower extremities and plantar flexion.
3. complete flaccidity of both upper and lower extremities and hyperextension of the neck.
4. flexion of the upper extremities, extension of the lower extremities, and plantar flexion.

39. A 42 year old male is receiving cryotherapy for repair of a detached retina. When taking a history from him, which symptom should the nurse expect him to have?
1. Diplopia.
2. Severe eye pain.
3. Sudden blindness.
4. Bright flashes of light.

40. An adult who has a detached retina asks the nurse what may have contributed to the development of his detached retina. The nurse explains that the client at greatest risk for development of a retinal tear usually has
1. hypertension.
2. near-sightedness.

3. cranial tumors.
4. sinusitis.

41. The nurse is explaining cryotherapy to a client who has a detached retina. The nurse should explain that the MAJOR purpose of cryotherapy in the treatment of detached retina is to
1. create a scar that promotes healing.
2. disintegrate debris in the eye.
3. freeze small blood vessels.
4. halt secretions of the lacrimal duct.

42. An adult client has a stapedectomy. Which of the following is most important for the nurse to include in the post-op care plan?
1. Checking the gag reflex.
2. Encouraging independence.
3. Instructing the client not to blow her nose.
4. Positioning the client on the operative side.

Answers and Rationales

33. The correct answer is 3. It has been demonstrated that positioning the client with the head elevated to 30° decreases ICP. Gravity aids in venous drainage from the head. Pronounced angulation of the neck can obstruct venous return. Pain, airway problems, and a Valvalsa maneuver will all increase ICP and will not directly benefit from proper head alignment.

34. The correct answer is 3. Cheyne-Stokes respirations are a pattern of breathing in which phases of hyperpnea regularly alternate with apnea. The pattern waxes (crescendo) and wanes (decrescendo). Ataxis breathing is a completely irregular breathing pattern. Apneustic breathing is a pattern of prolonged inspiration with pauses. Central neurogenic hyperventilation is a sustained, regular, rapid respiratory pattern of increased depth.

35. The correct answer is 2. Mechanical hyperventilation to reduce CO_2 levels to 25 mm Hg produces cerebral vasoconstriction and thereby decreases ICP. Dexamethasone is an anti-inflammatory agent. Mannitol is an osmotic diuretic. While the actions of both drugs will reduce cerebral edema, neither constricts cerebral veins. Ventriculostomy is a surgical procedure where a catheter is placed into a cerebral ventricle to drain excess cerebrospinal fluid.

36. The correct answer is 3. The Glasgow Coma Scale is a practical scale that independently evaluates three features: eye opening, motor response, and verbal performance. It does not evaluate pupillary reaction.

37. The correct answer is 3. A score of seven or less defines coma. The lowest achievable score is three, which indicates deep coma. Fifteen is a perfect score.

38. The correct answer is 4. Decorticate rigidity or posturing is best described as an abnormal flexor response in the arm with extension and plantar flexion in the lower extremities. Decerebrate rigidity involves rigid extensions of the arms and legs with plantar flexion. Flexion of the upper and lower extremities into a fetal-like position is a complication of bed rest.

39. The correct answer is 4. Momentary bright flashes of light are a common symptom of retinal detachment. Retinal detachment is usually partial at first; however, if the disorder goes untreated and the entire retina becomes involved, blindness may occur. Diplopia does not accompany retinal detachment. Retinal detachment is a painless process.

40. The correct answer is 2. Myopia or near-sightedness is a predisposing factor in the development of a retinal tear. Hypertension, cranial tumors, and sinusitis are not causes of retinal tears unless they result in eye trauma.

41. The correct answer is 1. Cryotherapy is used to produce a chorioretinal adhesion or scar that allows the retina to return to its normal position. It does not involve the freezing of blood vessels or affect material in the vitreous. It will not halt the action and function of the lacrimal duct.

42. The correct answer is 3. The client should be taught to avoid blowing her nose because this action could increase the pressure in the eustachian tube and dislodge the surgical graft. A stapedectomy is done under local anesthesia, which will have no affect on the gag reflex. Encouraging independence is not a priority nursing approach at this time. The client should be positioned on the unoperative side.

The Cardiovascular System

OVERVIEW OF ANATOMY AND PHYSIOLOGY

The cardiovascular system consists of the heart, arteries, veins, and capillaries. The major functions are circulation of blood, delivery of oxygen and other nutrients to the tissues of the body, and removal of carbon dioxide and other products of cellular metabolism.

Heart

The heart is a muscular pump that propels blood into the arterial system and receives blood from the venous system.

Heart Wall

A. *Pericardium:* composed of fibrous (outermost layer) and serous pericardium (parietal and visceral); a sac that functions to protect the heart from friction.
B. *Epicardium:* covers surface of heart, becomes continuous with visceral layer of serous pericardium.
C. *Myocardium:* middle, muscular layer.
D. *Endocardium:* thin, inner membranous layer lining the chambers of the heart.
E. *Papillary muscles:* arise from the endocardial and myocardial surface of the ventricles and attach to the chordae tendinae.
F. *Chordae tendinae:* attach to the tricuspid and mitral valves and prevent eversion during systole.

Chambers

A. *Atria:* two chambers, function as receiving chambers, lie above the ventricles
　　1. Right atrium: receives systemic venous blood through the superior vena cava, inferior vena cava, and coronary sinus.
　　2. Left atrium: receives oxygenated blood returning to the heart from the lungs through the pulmonary veins.
B. *Ventricles:* two thick-walled chambers; major responsibility for forcing blood out of the heart; lie below the atria.
　　1. Right ventricle: contracts and propels deoxygenated blood into the pulmonary circulation via the pulmonary artery.
　　2. Left ventricle: propels blood into the systemic circulation via the aorta during ventricular systole.

Valves

See Figure 4.5.
A. Atrioventricular (AV) valves
　　1. *Mitral valve:* located between the left atrium and left ventricle; contains two leaflets attached to the chordae tendinae.

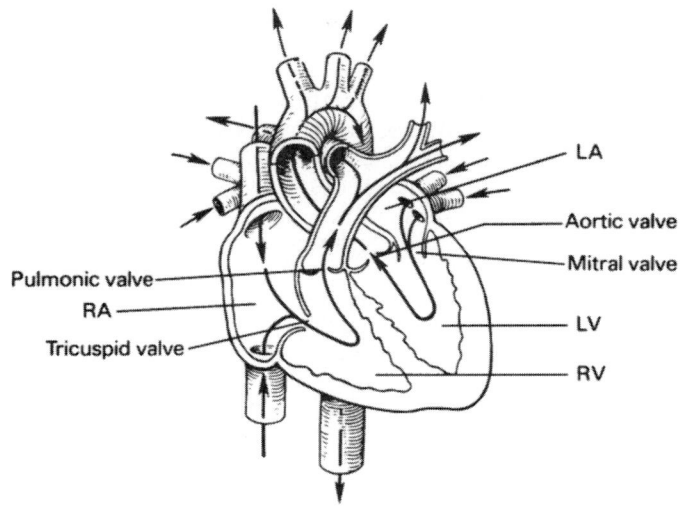

FIGURE 4.5 The valves of the heart; arrows indicate the direction of blood flow.

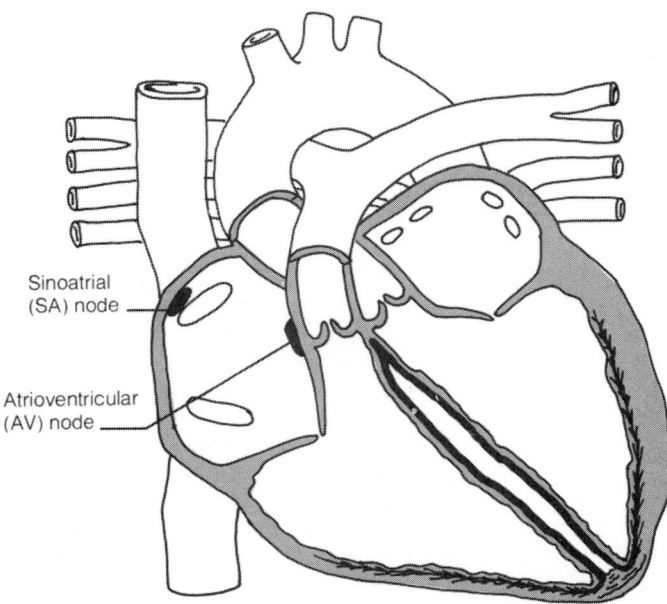

FIGURE 4.6 Conduction system of the heart (Delmar Publishers)

2. *Tricuspid valve:* located between the right atrium and right ventricle; contains three leaflets attached to the chordae tendinae.
3. Functions
   a. Permit unidirectional flow of blood from specific atrium to specific ventricle during ventricular diastole
   b. Prevent reflux flow during ventricular systole
   c. Valve leaflets open during ventricular diastole and close during ventricular systole; valve closure produces *first heart sound* (S_1).
B. Semilunar valves
   1. *Pulmonary valve:* located between right ventricle and pulmonary artery
   2. *Aortic valve:* located between left ventricle and aorta
   3. Functions
      a. Permit unidirectional flow of blood from specific ventricle to arterial vessel during ventricular systole
      b. Prevent reflux blood flow during ventricular diastole.
      c. Valves open when ventricles contract and close during ventricular diastole; valve closure produces *second heart sound* (S_2).

Conduction System

See Figure 4.6.
A. *Sinoatrial (SA) node:* the pacemaker of the heart; initiates the cardiac impulse, which spreads across the atria and into AV node.
B. *Atrioventricular (AV) node:* delays the impulse from the atria while the ventricles fill.
C. *Bundle of His:* arises from the AV node and conducts impulse to the bundle branch system.
   1. Right bundle branch: divided into anterior, lateral, and posterior; transmits impulses down the right side of the interventricular septum toward the right ventricular myocardium
   2. Left bundle branch: divided into anterior and posterior
      a. Anterior portion transmits impulses to the anterior endocardial surface of the left ventricle.
      b. Posterior portion transmits impulses over the posterior and inferior endocardial surfaces of the left ventricle.
D. *Purkinje fibers:* transmit impulses to the ventricles and provide for depolarization after ventricular contraction.
E. Electrical activity of heart can be visualized by attaching electrodes to the skin and recording activity by electrocardiograph (see page 208).

Coronary Circulation

See Figure 4.7.
A. Coronary arteries: branch off at the base of the aorta and supply blood to the myocardium and the conduction system; two main coronary arteries are *right* and *left;*
B. Coronary veins: return blood from the myocardium back to the right atrium via the coronary sinus.

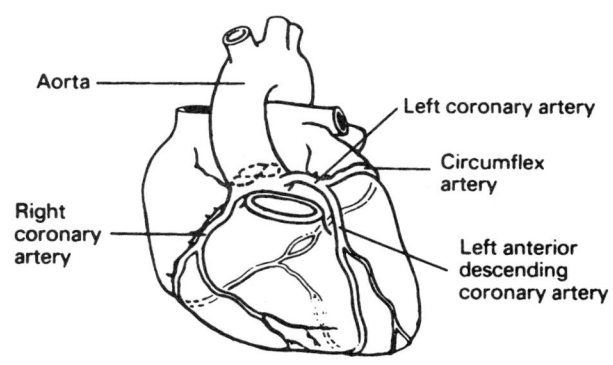

FIGURE 4.7 Coronary circulation

Vascular System

The major function of the blood vessels is to supply the tissues with blood, remove wastes, and carry unoxygenated blood back to the heart.

Types of Blood Vessels

A. *Arteries:* elastic-walled vessels that can stretch during systole and recoil during diastole; they carry blood away from the heart and distribute oxygenated blood throughout the body.
B. *Arterioles:* small arteries that distribute blood to the capillaries and function in controlling systemic vascular resistance and, therefore, arterial pressure.
C. *Capillaries:* the following exchanges occur in the capillaries
   1. Oxygen and carbon dioxide
   2. Solutes between the blood and tissues
   3. Fluid volume transfer between the plasma and interstitial spaces
D. *Venules:* small veins that receive blood from the capillaries and function as collecting channels between the capillaries and veins.
E. *Veins:* low-pressure vessels with thin walls and less muscle than arteries; most contain valves that prevent retrograde blood flow; they carry deoxygenated blood back to the heart. When skeletal muscles surrounding veins contract, the veins are compressed, promoting movement of blood back to the heart.

ASSESSMENT

Health History

A. Presenting problem
   1. Nonspecific symptoms may include fatigue, shortness of breath, cough, dizziness, syncope, headache, palpitations, weight loss/gain, anorexia, difficulty sleeping.
   2. Specific signs and symptoms
      a. Chest pain: note character, quality, location, radiation, frequency, and whether it is associated with precipitating factors (exertion, eating, excitement).
      b. Dyspnea (shortness of breath): note kind and extent of precipitating activities.
      c. Orthopnea (form of dyspnea that develops when client lies down): determine how many pillows are used when sleeping; note any paroxysmal nocturnal dyspnea (PND) (client awakens suddenly in the night, breathing with difficulty).
      d. Palpitations (awareness of heartbeat, fluttering feeling): assess precipitating factors (anxiety, caffeine, nicotine, stress); ask client to tap out the rhythm.
      e. Edema (abnormal accumulation of fluid in tissues): note whether unilateral/bilateral, location, time of day when most apparent.
      f. Cyanosis (dusky, bluish coloration to the skin): note whether peripheral or central.
B. Lifestyle: occupation, hobbies, financial status, stressors, unusual life patterns, relaxation time, exercise, living conditions, smoking, sleep habits
C. Use of medications: OTC drugs, contraceptives, cardiac drugs
D. Personality profile: Type A, manic-depressive, anxieties
E. Nutrition: dietary habits; calorie, cholesterol, salt intake; alcohol consumption
F. Past medical history
   1. Heart murmurs, rheumatic fever, sexually transmitted diseases, angina, myocardial infarction (MI), hypertension, CVA, alcoholism, obesity, hyperlipidemia, varicose veins, claudication
   2. Pregnancies, contraceptive use
G. Family history: heart disease (congenital, acute, chronic); risk factors (diabetes, hypertension, obesity)

Physical Examination

A. Skin and mucous membranes: note color/texture, temperature, hair distribution on extremities, atrophy or edema, venous pattern, petechiae, lesions, ulcerations or gangrene; examine nails.
B. Peripheral pulses: palpate and rate all arterial pulses (temporal, carotid, brachial, radial, femoral, popliteal, dorsalis pedis, and posterior tibial) on scale of: 0 = absent, 1 = palpable, 2 = normal, 3 = full, 4 = full and bounding.
C. Assess for arterial insufficiency and venous impairment.
D. Measure and record blood pressure.

E. Inspect and palpate the neck vessels.
   1. Jugular veins: note location, characteristics; measure jugular venous pressure.
   2. Carotid arteries: note location, characteristics
F. Precordium
   1. Inspect and palpate sternoclavicular, aortic, pulmonic, Erb's point, tricuspid, apical, epigastric sites.
   2. Note point of maximum impulse (PMI), pulsations, thrills.
G. Auscultate aortic, pulmonic, Erb's point, tricuspid, mitral or apical, xiphoid areas; note heart rate and rhythm (see Figure 4.8).
   1. Normal heart sounds (S_1 and S_2): note location, intensity, splitting.
   2. Abnormal heart sounds (S_3, S_4): note location, occurrence in cardiac cycle
   3. Murmurs: note location, occurrence in cardiac cycle
   4. Friction rubs

Laboratory/Diagnostic Tests

A. Blood chemistry and electrolyte analysis
   1. Cardiac enzymes: will be elevated with myocardial infarction
      a. creatine phosphokinase (CPK) 50–325 mU/ml
      b. CPK-MB 0%
      c. lactic acid dehydrogenase (LDH) 100–225 mU/ml
         1) LDH_1 20%–35%
         2) LDH_2 25%–40%
      d. aspartate aminotransferase (AST), also called serum glutamic-oxalacetate (SGOT) 7–40 U/ml
   2. Electrolytes
      a. Sodium (Na): 135–148 mEq/l; reflects relative fluid balance, hyponatremia indicates fluid excess and hypernatremia indicates fluid deficit
      b. Potassium (K): 3.5–5 mEq/l; increased and decreased levels can cause dysrhythmias
      c. Magnesium (Mg): 1.3–2.1 mEq/l; decreased levels can cause dysrhythmias
      d. Calcium (Ca): 4.5–5.3 mEq/l, 9–11 mg/dl; calcium necessary for blood clotting and neuromuscular activity, decreased levels cause tetany, increased levels cause muscle atony, increased and decreased levels can cause dysrhythmias
   3. Serum lipids
      a. Total cholesterol: 150–200 mg/dl; elevated levels predispose to atherosclerotic heart disease
      b. High density lipids (HDL): 30–85 mg/dl; low levels predispose to cardiovascular disease
      c. Low density lipids (LDL): 50–140 mg/dl; high levels predispose to atherosclerotic plaque formation
      d. Triglycerides: 10–150 mg/dl; high levels increase risk of atherosclerotic heart disease
B. Hematologic studies
   1. CBC (see Hematologic system for values)
   2. Coagulation time: 5–15 min.; increased levels indicate bleeding tendency, used to monitor heparin therapy
   3. Prothrombin time (PT) 9.5–12 sec.; INR 1.0, increased levels indicate bleeding tendency, used to monitor warfarin therapy
   4. Activated partial thromboplastin time (APTT) 20–45 sec., increased levels indicate bleeding tendency, used to monitor heparin therapy
   5. Erythrocyte sedimentation rate (ESR) <20 mm/hr; increased level indicate inflammatory process
C. Urine studies: routine urinalysis
D. Electrocardiogram (ECG or EKG)
   1. Noninvasive test that produces a graphic record of the electrical activity of the heart. In addition to determining cardiac rhythm, pattern variations may reveal pathologic processes (MI and ischemia, electrolyte and acid-base imbalance, chamber enlargement, block of the right or left bundle branch); see also Cardiac Monitoring, page 210
   2. Portable recorder (Holtor monitor) provides continuous recording of ECG for up to 24 hours; client keeps a diary noting presence of symptoms or any unusual activities.

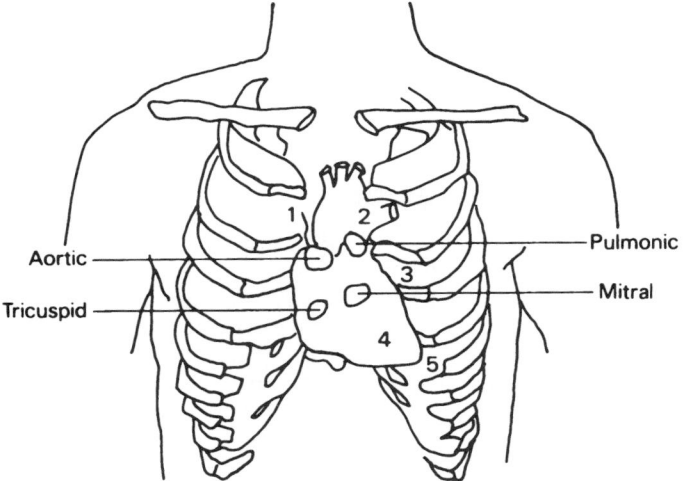

FIGURE 4.8 Heart valves and areas of auscultation: (1) aortic area; (2) pulmonic area; (3) Erb's point; (4) tricuspid area; (5) mitral area

E. *Exercise ECG* (*stress test*): the ECG is recorded during prescribed exercise such as climbing a set of stairs, walking a treadmill, or riding a stationary bicycle; stress tests may show heart disease when resting ECG does not.

F. *Phonocardiogram:* noninvasive device to amplify and record heart sounds and murmurs.

G. *Echocardiogram:* noninvasive recording of the cardiac structures using ultrasound.

H. *Cardiac catheterization:* invasive, but often definitive test for diagnosis of cardiac disease.
   1. A catheter is inserted into the right or left side of the heart to obtain information.
      a. Right-sided catheterization: the catheter is inserted into an antecubital vein and advanced into the vena cava, right atrium, and right ventricle with further insertion into the pulmonary artery.
      b. Left-sided catheterization: performed by inserting the catheter into a brachial or femoral artery; the catheter is passed retrograde up the aorta and into the left ventricle.
   2. Purpose: to measure intracardiac pressures and oxygen levels in various parts of the heart; with injection of a dye, it allows visualization of the heart chambers, blood vessels, and course of blood flow (*angiography*).
   3. Nursing care: pretest
      a. Confirm that informed consent has been signed.
      b. Ask about allergies, particularly to iodine, if dye being used.
      c. Keep client NPO for 8–12 hours prior to test.
      d. Record height and weight, take baseline vital signs, and monitor peripheral pulses.
      e. Inform client that a feeling of warmth and fluttering sensation as catheter is passed is common.
   4. Nursing care: posttest
      a. Assess circulation to the extremity used for catheter insertion.
      b. Check peripheral pulses, color, sensation of affected extremity every 15 minutes for 4 hours.
      c. If protocol requires, keep affected extremity straight for approximately 8 hours.
      d. Observe catheter insertion site for swelling and bleeding; a sandbag or pressure dressing may be placed over insertion site.
      e. Assess vital signs and report significant changes from baseline.

I. *Aortography*
   1. Injection of radiopaque contrast medium into the aorta to visualize the aorta, valve leaflets, and major vessels on a movie film.
   2. Purpose: to determine and diagnose aortic valve incompetence, aneurysms of the ascending aorta, abnormalities of major branches of the aorta.
   3. Nursing care: pretest
      a. Confirm that informed consent has been signed.
      b. Inform client that a dye will be injected and to report any dyspnea, numbness, or tingling.
   4. Nursing care: posttest
      a. Assess the puncture site frequently for bleeding or inflammation.
      b. Assess peripheral pulses distal to the injection site every hour for 4–8 hours posttest.

J. *Coronary arteriography*
   1. Visualization of coronary arteries by injection of radiopaque contrast dye and recording on a movie film.
   2. Purpose: evaluation of heart disease and angina, location of areas of infarction and extent of lesions, ruling out coronary artery disease in clients with myocardial disease
   3. Nursing care: same as for Aortography (above).

ANALYSIS

Nursing diagnoses for the client with a cardiovascular dysfunction may include
A. Fluid volume excess
B. Decreased cardiac output
C. Altered cardiopulmonary tissue perfusion
D. Altered peripheral tissue perfusion
E. Impairment of skin integrity
F. Risk for activity intolerance
G. Pain
H. Ineffective individual coping
I. Fear
J. Anxiety

PLANNING AND IMPLEMENTATION

Goals

A. Fluid imbalance will be resolved, edema minimized.
B. Cardiac output will be improved.
C. Cardiopulmonary and peripheral tissue perfusion will be improved.
D. Adequate skin integrity will be maintained.
E. Activity tolerance will progressively increase.
F. Pain in the chest or in the affected extremity will be diminished.
G. Client will use effective coping techniques.
H. Client's level of fear and anxiety will be decreased.

Interventions

Cardiac Monitoring

A. The cardiac monitor provides continuous information regarding the cardiac rhythm and rate (ECG). Constant surveillance and understanding of the basic electrocardiographic system is imperative to avoid/treat arrhythmias (see Figure 4.9).
1. ECG strip: each small square represents 0.04 seconds, each large square 0.2 seconds.
2. P wave: produced by atrial depolarization; indicates SA node function.
3. P-R interval
   a. Indicates atrioventricular conduction time or the time it takes an impulse to travel from the atria down and through the AV node
   b. Measured from beginning of P wave to beginning of QRS complex
   c. Normal: 0.12–0.20 seconds.
4. QRS complex
   a. Indicates ventricular depolarization
   b. Measured from onset of Q wave to end of S wave
   c. Normal: 0.06–0.10 seconds
5. ST segment
   a. Indicates time interval between complete depolarization of ventricles and repolarization of ventricles
   b. Measured after QRS complex to beginning of T wave
6. T wave
   a. Represents ventricular repolarization
   b. Follows ST segment

Hemodynamic Monitoring (Swan-Ganz Catheter)

A. A multilumen catheter with a balloon tip that is advanced through the superior vena cava into the right atrium, right ventricle, and pulmonary artery. When it is wedged it is in the distal arterial branch of the pulmonary artery.

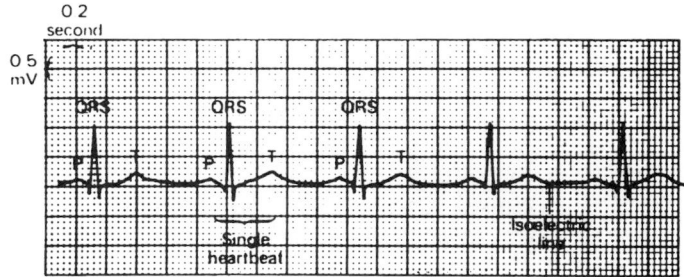

FIGURE 4.9 A typical ECG; all beats appear as a similar pattern, equally spaced, and have three major units: P wave, QRS complex, and T wave.

B. Purposes
1. Proximal port: measures right atrial pressure
2. Distal port
   a. Measures pulmonary artery (PA) pressure (reflects left and right heart pressures) and pulmonary capillary wedge pressure (PCWP) (reflects left atrial and left ventricular end diastolic pressure).
   b. Normal values: PA systolic and diastolic less than 20 mm Hg; PCWP 4–12 mm Hg
3. Balloon port: inflated with 1–2 cc air to obtain PCWP
4. Thermistor lumen: used to measure cardiac output if ordered

C. Nursing care
1. A sterile dry dressing should be applied to site and changed every 24 hours; inspect site daily and report signs of infection.
2. If catheter is inserted via an extremity, immobilize extremity to prevent catheter dislodgment or trauma.
3. Observe catheter site for leakage.
4. Ensure that balloon is deflated with a syringe attached, except when PCWP is read.
5. Continuously monitor PA systolic and diastolic pressures and report significant variations.
6. Irrigate line before each reading of PCWP.
7. Maintain client in same position for each reading.
8. Maintain pressure bag at 300 mm Hg.
9. Record PA systolic and diastolic readings at least every hour and PCWP as ordered, noting position of client.

Central Venous Pressure (CVP)

A. Obtained by inserting a catheter into the external jugular, antecubital, or femoral vein and threading it into the vena cava. The catheter is attached to an IV infusion and H_2O manometer by a three-way stopcock.
B. Purposes
1. Reveals right atrial pressure, reflecting alterations in the right ventricular pressure
2. Provides information concerning blood volume and adequacy of central venous return
3. Provides an IV route for drawing blood samples, administering fluids or medication, and possibly inserting a pacing catheter
C. Normal range is 4–10 cm H_2O; elevation indicates hypervolemia, decreased level indicates hypovolemia.
D. Nursing care
1. Ensure client is relaxed.

2. Maintain zero point of manometer always at level of right atrium (midaxillary line).
3. Determine patency of catheter by opening IV infusion line.
4. Turn stopcock to allow IV solution to run into manometer to a level of 10–20 cm above expected pressure reading.
5. Turn stopcock to allow IV solution to flow from manometer into catheter; fluid level in manometer fluctuates with respiration.
6. Stop ventilatory assistance during measurement of CVP.
7. After CVP reading, return stopcock to IV infusion position.
8. Record CVP reading and position of client.

EVALUATION

A. Resolution of peripheral edema and neck vein distention; weight stable; lungs clear.
B. Capillary refill is less than 3 seconds; balanced I&O with urine output at least 30 ml/hour; hemodynamic measurements within normal range; usual mental status.
C. Stable vital signs; skin warm and dry; peripheral pulses present, equal, and strong; absence of edema; increased tolerance to activity; usual mentation; absence of pain.
D. Client's skin warm and dry, shows absence of redness and irritation; healing of lesions.
E. Progressive increase in tolerance for activity with heart rate and blood pressure stable; absence of pain.
F. Client expresses relief from pain; relaxed facial expression; stable vital signs; progressive increase in activity tolerance.
G. Demonstrates the use of effective coping skills and problem-solving techniques.
H. Verbalizes awareness of feelings of fear and anxiety. Client reports fear/anxiety as reduced/controlled.

DISORDERS OF THE CARDIOVASCULAR SYSTEM

The Heart

Coronary Artery Disease (CAD)

A. General information
1. CAD refers to a variety of pathologic conditions that cause narrowing or obstruction of the coronary arteries, resulting in decreased blood supply to the myocardium.
2. *Atherosclerosis* (deposits of cholesterol and lipids within the walls of the artery) is the major causative factor.
3. Occurs most often between ages 30 and 50;

men affected more often than women; nonwhites have higher mortality rates.
4. May manifest as angina pectoris or MI.
5. Risk factors: family history of CAD, elevated serum lipoproteins, cigarette smoking, diabetes mellitus, hypertension, obesity, sedentary and/or stressful/competitive life-style, elevated serum uric acid levels
B. Medical management, assessment findings, and nursing interventions: see Angina Pectoris (below) and Myocardial Infarction (page 213).

Angina Pectoris

A. General information
1. Transient, paroxysmal chest pain produced by insufficient blood flow to the myocardium resulting in myocardial ischemia.
2. Risk factors: CAD, atherosclerosis, hypertension, diabetes mellitus, thromboangiitis obliterans, severe anemia, aortic insufficiency
3. Precipitating factors: physical exertion, consumption of a heavy meal, extremely cold weather, strong emotions, cigarette smoking, sexual activity
B. Medical management
1. Drug therapy: nitrates, beta-adrenergic blocking agents, and/or calcium-blocking agents, lipid reducing drugs if cholesterol elevated
2. Modification of diet and other risk factors
3. Surgery: coronary artery bypass surgery (page 214)
C. Assessment findings
1. Pain: substernal with possible radiation to the neck, jaw, back, and arms; relieved by rest
2. Palpitations, tachycardia
3. Dyspnea
4. Diaphoresis
5. Increased serum lipid levels
6. Diagnostic tests
   a. ECG may reveal ST segment depression and T-wave inversion during chest pain
   b. Stress test may reveal an abnormal ECG during exercise.
D. Nursing interventions
1. Administer oxygen.
2. Give prompt pain relief with nitrates or narcotic analgesics as ordered.
3. Monitor vital signs, status of cardiopulmonary function.
4. Monitor ECG.
5. Place client in semi- to high-Fowler's position.
6. Provide emotional support.
7. Provide client teaching and discharge planning concerning

a. Proper use of nitrates
 1) nitroglycerin tablets (sublingual)
  a) allow tablet to dissolve.
  b) relax for 15 minutes after taking tablet to prevent dizziness.
  c) if no relief with 1 tablet, take additional tablets at 5-minute intervals, but no more than 3 tablets within a 15-minute period.
  d) know that transient headache is a frequent side effect.
  e) keep bottle tightly capped and prevent exposure to air, light, heat.
  f) ensure tablets are within reach at all times.
  g) check shelf life, expiration date of tablets.
 2) nitroglycerin ointment (topical)
  a) rotate sites to prevent dermal inflammation.
  b) remove previously applied ointment.
  c) avoid massaging/rubbing as this increases absorption and interferes with the drug's sustained action.
b. Ways to minimize precipitating events
 1) reduce stress and anxiety (relaxation techniques, guided imagery)
 2) avoid overexertion and smoking
 3) maintain low-cholesterol, low-saturated fat diet and eat small, frequent meals
 4) avoid extremes of temperature
 5) dress warmly in cold weather
c. Gradual increase in activities and exercise
 1) participate in regular exercise program
 2) space exercise periods and allow for rest periods
8. Instruct client to notify physician immediately if pain occurs and persists, despite rest and medication administration.

Dysrhythmias

An arrhythmia is a disruption in the normal events of the cardiac cycle. It may take a variety of forms. Treatment varies depending on the type of dysrhythmia; commonly used drugs are summarized in Unit 2, Table 2.14.

Sinus Tachycardia

A. General information
 1. A heart rate of over 100 beats/minute, originating in the SA node
 2. May be caused by fever, apprehension, physical activity, anemia, hyperthyroidism, drugs (epinephrine, theophylline), myocardial ischemia, caffeine
B. Assessment findings
 1. Rate: 100–160 beats/minute
 2. Rhythm: regular
 3. P wave: precedes each QRS complex with normal contour
 4. P-R interval: normal (0.08 second)
 5. QRS complex: normal (0.06 second)
C. Treatment: correction of underlying cause, elimination of stimulants; sedatives, propranolol (Inderal).

Sinus Bradycardia

A. General information
 1. A slowed heart rate initiated by SA node
 2. Caused by excessive vagal or decreased sympathetic tone, MI, intracranial tumors, meningitis, myxedema, cardiac fibrosis; a normal variation of the heart rate in well-trained athletes
B. Assessment findings
 1. Rate: less than 60 beats/minute
 2. Rhythm: regular
 3. P wave: precedes each QRS with a normal contour
 4. P-R interval: normal
 5. QRS complex: normal
C. Treatment: usually not needed; if cardiac output is inadequate, atropine and isoproterenol (Isuprel) are usually prescribed; if drugs are not effective, a pacemaker may need to be inserted (see page 216).

Atrial Fibrillation

A. General information
 1. An arrhythmia in which ectopic foci cause rapid, irregular contractions of the heart
 2. Commonly seen in clients with rheumatic mitral stenosis, thyrotoxicosis, cardiomyopathy, hypertensive heart disease, pericarditis, and coronary heart disease
B. Assessment findings
 1. Rate
  a. Atrial: 350–600 beats/minute
  b. Ventricular: varies between 100–160 beats/minute
 2. Rhythm: atrial and ventricular regularly irregular
 3. P wave: no definite P wave; rapid undulations called fibrillatory (f) waves
 4. P-R interval: not measurable
 5. QRS complex: generally normal
C. Treatment: digitalis preparations, propranolol, verapamil in conjunction with digitalis; direct-current cardioversion

Premature Ventricular Contractions (PVCs)

A. General information
1. Irritable impulses originate in the ventricles
2. Caused by electrolyte imbalance (hypokalemia); digitalis drug therapy; myocardial disease; stimulants (caffeine, epinephrine, isoproterenol); hypoxia; congestive heart failure

B. Assessment findings
1. Rate: varies according to number of PVCs
2. Rhythm: irregular because of PVCs
3. P wave: normal; however, often lost in QRS complex
4. P-R interval: often not measurable
5. QRS complex: wide and distorted in shape, greater than 0.12 seconds

C. Treatment
1. IV push of lidocaine (50–100 mg) followed by IV drip of lidocaine at rate of 1–4 mg/minute
2. Procainamide (Pronestyl), quinidine
3. Treatment of underlying cause

Ventricular Tachycardia

A. General information
1. A run of three or more consecutive PVCs; occurs from repetitive firing of an ectopic focus in the ventricles
2. Caused by acute MI, CAD, digitalis intoxication, hypokalemia

B. Assessment findings
1. Rate
   a. Atrial: 60–100 beats/minute
   b. Ventricular: 110–250 beats/minute
2. Rhythm: atrial (regular), ventricular (occasionally irregular)
3. P wave: often lost in QRS complex
4. P-R interval: usually not measurable
5. QRS complex: greater than 0.12 seconds, wide

C. Treatment
1. IV push of lidocaine (50–100 mg), then IV drip of lidocaine 1–4 mg/minute
2. Procainamide via IV infusion of 2–6 mg/minute
3. Direct-current cardioversion
4. Bretylium, propranolol (Inderal)

Myocardial Infarction (MI)

A. General information
1. The death of myocardial cells from inadequate oxygenation, often caused by a sudden complete blockage of a coronary artery; characterized by localized formation of necrosis (tissue destruction) with subsequent healing by scar formation and fibrosis.

2. Risk factors: atherosclerotic CAD, thrombus formation, hypertension, diabetes mellitus

B. Assessment findings (see also Angina Pectoris, page 211)
1. Pain usually substernal with radiation to the neck, arm, jaw, or back; severe, crushing, viselike with sudden onset; *unrelieved by rest or nitrates*
2. Nausea and vomiting
3. Dyspnea
4. Skin: cool, clammy, ashen
5. Elevated temperature
6. Initial increase in blood pressure and pulse, with gradual drop in blood pressure
7. Restlessness
8. Occasional findings: rales or crackles; presence of S_4; pericardial friction rub; split S_1, S_2
9. Diagnostic tests
   a. Elevated WBC
   b. Elevated CPK and CPK-MB
   c. Elevated SGOT or AST
   d. Elevated LDH, LDH_1, and LDH_2
   e. ECG changes (specific changes dependent on location of myocardial damage and phase of the MI; inverted T wave and ST segment changes seen with myocardial ischemia
   f. Increased ESR, elevated serum cholesterol

C. Nursing interventions
1. Establish a patent IV line
2. Provide pain relief; morphine sulfate IV (given IV because after an infarction there is poor peripheral perfusion and because serum enzymes would be affected by IM injections) as ordered.
3. Administer oxygen as ordered to relieve dyspnea and prevent arrhythmias.
4. Provide bed rest with semi-Fowler's position to decrease cardiac workload.
5. Monitor ECG and hemodynamic procedures.
6. Administer antiarrhythmias as ordered.
7. Perform complete lung/cardiovascular assessment.
8. Monitor urinary output and report output of less than 30 ml/hour; indicates decreased cardiac output.
9. Maintain full liquid diet with gradual increase to soft; low sodium.
10. Maintain quiet environment.
11. Administer stool softeners as ordered to facilitate bowel evacuation and prevent straining.
12. Relieve anxiety associated with coronary care unit (CCU) environment.
13. Administer anticoagulants, as ordered.
14. Administer thrombolytics (tissue-type plasminogen activator or t-pa and

streptokinase) and monitor for side effects; bleeding.

15. Provide client teaching and discharge planning concerning
    a. Effects of MI, healing process, and treatment regimen
    b. Medication regimen including name, purpose, schedule, dosage, side effects
    c. Risk factors, with necessary lifestyle modifications
    d. Dietary restrictions: low sodium, low cholesterol, avoidance of caffeine
    e. Importance of participation in a progressive activity program
    f. Resumption of sexual activity according to physician's orders (usually 4–6 weeks)
    g. Need to report the following symptoms: increased persistent chest pain, dyspnea, weakness, fatigue, persistent palpitations, light-headedness
    h. Enrollment of client in a cardiac rehabilitation program

Percutaneous Transluminal Coronary Angioplasty

A. General information
   1. Percutaneous transluminal coronary angioplasty (PTCA) can be performed instead of coronary artery bypass graft surgery in various clients with single-vessel coronary artery disease.
   2. The aim of PTCA is to revascularize the myocardium, decrease angina, and increase survival.
   3. PTCA is performed in the cardiac catheterization lab and is accomplished by insertion of a balloon-tipped catheter into the stenotic, diseased coronary artery. The balloon is inflated with a controlled pressure and thereby decreases the stenosis of the vessel.
B. Nursing interventions
   Preoperative and postoperative care is similar to the care of the client undergoing cardiac catheterization.

Coronary Artery Bypass Surgery

A. General information
   1. A coronary artery bypass graft is the surgery of choice for clients with severe CAD.
   2. New supply of blood brought to diseased/occluded coronary artery by bypassing the obstruction with a graft that is attached to the aorta proximally and to the coronary artery distally.
   3. Several bypasses can be performed depending on the location and extent of the blockage.

4. Procedure requires use of extracorporeal circulation (heart-lung machine, cardiopulmonary bypass)
B. Nursing interventions: preoperative
   1. Explain anatomy of the heart, function of coronary arteries, effects of CAD
   2. Explain events of the day of surgery: length of time in surgery, length of time until able to see family.
   3. Orient to the critical and coronary care units and introduce to staff.
   4. Explain equipment to be used (monitors, hemodynamic procedures, ventilator, endotracheal tube, drainage tubes).
   5. Demonstrate activity and exercises (turning from side to side, dangling, sitting in a chair, ROM exercises for arms and legs, effective deep breathing, and coughing).
   6. Reassure client that pain medication is available.
C. Nursing interventions: postoperative
   1. Maintain patent airway.
   2. Promote lung reexpansion.
      a. Monitor drainage from chest/mediastinal tubes, and check patency of chest drainage system.
      b. Assist client with turning, coughing, and deep breathing.
   3. Monitor cardiac status.
      a. Monitor vital signs and cardiac rhythm and report significant changes, particularly temperature elevation.
      b. Perform peripheral pulse checks.
      c. Carry out hemodynamic monitoring.
      d. Administer anticoagulants as ordered and monitor hematologic test results carefully.
   4. Maintain fluid and electrolyte balance.
      a. Maintain accurate I&O with hourly outputs; report if less than 30 ml/hour urine.
      b. Assess color, character, and specific gravity of urine.
      c. Daily weights.
      d. Assess lab values, particularly BUN, creatinine, sodium, and potassium levels.
   5. Maintain adequate cerebral circulation: frequent neuro checks.
   6. Provide pain relief.
      a. Administer narcotics cautiously and monitor effects.
      b. Assist with positioning for maximum comfort.
      c. Teach relaxation techniques.
   7. Prevent abdominal distension.
      a. Monitor nasogastric drainage and maintain patency of system.
      b. Assess for bowel sounds every 2–4 hours.
      c. Measure abdominal girths if necessary.

8. Monitor for and prevent the following complications.
   a. Thrombophlebitis/pulmonary embolism
   b. Cardiac tamponade (see page 219)
   c. Arrhythmias
      1) maintain continuous ECG monitoring and report changes.
      2) assess electrolyte levels daily and report significant changes, particularly potassium.
      3) administer antiarrhythmics as ordered.
   d. Congestive heart failure (see below)
9. Provide client teaching and discharge planning concerning
   a. Limitation with progressive increase in activities
      1) encourage daily walking with gradual increase in distance weekly
      2) avoid heavy lifting and activities that require continuous arm movements (vacuuming, playing golf, bowling)
      3) avoid driving a car until physician permits
   b. Sexual intercourse: can usually be resumed by third or fourth week post-op; avoid sexual positions in which the client would be supporting weight
   c. Medical regimen: ensure client/family are aware of drugs, dosages, proper times of administration, and side effects
   d. Meal planning with prescribed modifications (decreased sodium, cholesterol, and possibly carbohydrates)
   e. Wound cleansing daily with mild soap and H_2O and report signs of infection
   f. Symptoms to be reported: fever, dyspnea, chest pain with minimal exertion.

Congestive Heart Failure (CHF)

A. General information: inability of the heart to pump an adequate supply of blood to meet the metabolic needs of the body.
B. Types
   1. *Left-sided heart failure*
      a. Left ventricular damage causes blood to back up through the left atrium and into the pulmonary veins. Increased pressure causes transudation into the interstitial tissues of the lungs with resultant pulmonary congestion.
      b. Caused by left ventricular damage (usually due to an MI), hypertension, ischemic heart disease, aortic valve disease, mitral stenosis
      c. Assessment findings
         1) dyspnea, orthopnea, PND, tiredness, muscle weakness, cough

         2) tachycardia, PMI displaced laterally, possible S_3, bronchial wheezing, rales or crackles, cyanosis, pallor
         3) decreased pO_2, increased pCO_2
         4) diagnostic tests
            a) chest x-ray: shows cardiac hypertrophy
            b) PAP and PCWP usually increased; however, this is dependent on the degree of heart failure
         5) Echocardiography: shows increased size of cardiac chambers
   2. *Right-sided heart failure*
      a. Weakened right ventricle is unable to pump blood into the pulmonary system; systemic venous congestion occurs as pressure builds up.
      b. Caused by left-sided heart failure, right ventricular infarction, atherosclerotic heart disease, COPD, pulmonic stenosis, pulmonary embolism.
      c. Assessment findings
         1) anorexia, nausea, weight gain
         2) dependent pitting edema, jugular venous distension, bounding pulses, hepatomegaly, cool extremities, oliguria
         3) elevated CVP, decreased pO_2, increased ALT (SGPT)
         4) diagnostic tests
            a) chest x-ray: reveals cardiac hypertrophy
            b) echocardiography: indicates increased size of cardiac chambers
   3. *High-output failure*
      a. Cardiac output is adequate but exceeded by the metabolic needs of the tissues; the exorbitant demands made on the heart eventually cause ventricular failure.
      b. Caused by hyperthyroidism, anemia, AV fistula, pregnancy
C. Medical management (all types)
   1. Determination and elimination/control of underlying cause
   2. Drug therapy: digitalis preparations, diuretics, vasodilators
   3. Sodium-restricted diet to decrease fluid retention
   4. If medical therapies unsuccessful, mechanical assist devices (intra-aortic balloon pump), cardiac transplantation, or mechanical hearts may be employed.
D. Nursing interventions
   1. Monitor respiratory status and provide adequate ventilation (when CHF progresses to pulmonary edema).
      a. Administer oxygen therapy.
      b. Maintain client in semi- or high-Fowler's position.

    c. Monitor ABGs.

    d. Assess for breath sounds, noting any changes.

  2. Provide physical and emotional rest.

    a. Constantly assess level of anxiety.

    b. Maintain bed rest with limited activity.

    c. Maintain quiet, relaxed environment.

    d. Organize nursing care around rest periods.

  3. Increase cardiac output.

    a. Administer digitalis as ordered and monitor effects.

    b. Monitor ECG and hemodynamic monitoring.

    c. Administer vasodilators as ordered.

    d. Monitor vital signs.

  4. Reduce/eliminate edema.

    a. Administer diuretics as ordered.

    b. Daily weights.

    c. Maintain accurate I&O.

    d. Assess for peripheral edema.

    e. Measure abdominal girths daily.

    f. Monitor electrolyte levels.

    g. Monitor CVP and Swan-Ganz readings.

    h. Provide sodium-restricted diet as ordered.

    i. Provide meticulous skin care.

  5. Provide client teaching and discharge planning concerning

    a. Need to monitor self daily for signs and symptoms of CHF (pedal edema, weight gain of 1–2 kg in a 2-day period, dyspnea, loss of appetite, cough)

    b. Medication regimen including name, purpose, dosage, frequency, and side effects (digitalis, diuretics)

    c. Prescribed dietary plan (low sodium; small, frequent meals)

    d. Need to avoid fatigue and plan for rest periods.

Pulmonary Edema

A. General information

  1. A medical emergency that usually results from left-sided heart failure. The capillary pressure within the lungs becomes so great that fluid pours from the blood into the alveoli, bronchi, and bronchioles. Death occurs by suffocation if this condition is untreated.

  2. Caused by left-sided heart failure, rapid administration of IV fluids.

B. Medical management

  1. Oxygen therapy

  2. Endotracheal/nasotracheal intubation (possible)

  3. Drug therapy

    a. Morphine sulfate to induce vasodilation and decrease anxiety; 5 mg IV, administer slowly

    b. Digitalis to improve cardiac output

    c. Diuretics (furosemide [Lasix] is drug of choice) to relieve fluid retention

    d. Aminophylline to relieve bronchospasm and increase cardiac output; 250–500 mg IV, administer slowly

    e. Vasodilators (nitroglycerin, isosorbide dinitrate) to dilate the vessels, thereby reducing amount of blood returned to the heart

  4. Rotating tourniquets or phlebotomy

C. Assessment findings

  1. Dyspnea

  2. Cough with large amounts of blood-tinged sputum

  3. Tachycardia, pallor, wheezing, rales or crackles, diaphoresis

  4. Restlessness, fear/anxiety

  5. Jugular vein distension

  6. Decreased pO_2, increased pCO_2, elevated CVP

D. Nursing interventions

  1. Assist with intubation (if necessary) and monitor mechanical ventilation.

  2. Administer oxygen by mask in high concentrations (40%–60%) if not intubated.

  3. Place client in semi-Fowler's position or over bedside table to ease dyspnea.

  4. Administer medications as ordered.

  5. Apply and monitor *rotating tourniquets*.

    a. Occlude vessels of each limb for no more than 45 minutes at a time.

    b. Rotate in a clockwise fashion every 15 minutes.

    c. Assess continuously for presence of arterial pulses.

    d. Observe skin for signs of irritation.

    e. When discontinuing, remove 1 tourniquet every 15 minutes to avoid rapid influx of fluid to the heart.

  6. Assist with phlebotomy (removal of 300–500 ml of blood from a peripheral vein) if performed.

  7. CVP/hemodynamic monitoring.

  8. Provide client teaching and discharge planning concerning

    a. Prescribed medications, including name, purpose, schedule, dosage, and side effects

    b. Dietary restrictions: low sodium, low cholesterol

    c. Importance of adhering to planned rest periods with gradual progressive increase in activities

    d. Daily weights

    e. Need to report the following symptoms to physician immediately: dyspnea, persistent productive cough, pedal edema, restlessness

Pacemakers

A. General information

1. A pacemaker is an electronic device that provides repetitive electrical stimulation to the heart muscle to control the heart rate.
2. Artificial pacing system consists of a battery-powered generator and a pacing wire that delivers the stimulus to the heart.

B. Indications for use
1. Adams-Stokes attack
2. Acute MI with Mobitz II AV block
3. Third-degree AV block with slow ventricular rate
4. Right bundle branch block
5. New left bundle branch block
6. Symptomatic sinus bradycardia
7. Sick sinus syndrome
8. Arrhythmias (during or after cardiac surgery)
9. Drug-resistant tachyarrhythmia

C. Modes of pacing
1. Fixed rate: pacemaker fires electrical stimuli at preset rate, regardless of the client's rate and rhythm.
2. Demand: pacemaker produces electrical stimuli only when the client's own heart rate drops below the preset rate per minute on the generator.

D. Types of pacemakers
1. Temporary
   a. Used in emergency situations and performed via an endocardial (transvenous) or transthoracic approach to the myocardium.
   b. Performed at bedside or using fluoroscopy.
2. Permanent
   a. Endocardial or transvenous procedure involves passing endocardial lead into right ventricle with subcutaneous implantation of pulse generator into right or left subclavian areas. Usually done under local anesthesia.
   b. Epicardial or myocardial method involves passing the electrode transthoracically to the myocardium where it is sutured in place. The pulse generator is implanted into the abdominal wall.

E. Nursing interventions
1. Assess pacemaker function
   a. Monitor heart rate, noting deviations from the preset rate.
   b. Observe the presence of pacemaker spikes on ECG tracing or cardiac monitor; spike before P wave with atrial pacemaker; spike before QRS complex with ventricular pacemaker
   c. Assess for signs of pacemaker malfunction, such as weakness, fainting, dizziness, or hypotension.
2. Maintain the integrity of the system

a. Ensure that catheter terminals are attached securely to the pulse generator (temporary pacemaker)
b. Attach pulse generator to client securely to prevent accidental dislodgment (temporary pacemaker)
3. Provide safety and comfort
   a. Provide safe environment by properly grounding all equipment in the room.
   b. Monitor electrolyte level periodically, particularly potassium.
4. Prevent infection
   a. Assess vital signs, particularly temperature changes.
   b. Assess catheter insertion site daily for signs of infection.
   c. Maintain sterile dressing over catheter insertion site.

F. Provide client teaching and discharge planning concerning
1. Fundamental concepts of cardiac physiology
2. Daily pulse check for one minute
3. Need to report immediately any sudden slowing or increase in pulse rate
4. Importance of adhering to weekly monitoring schedule during first month after implantation and when battery depletion is anticipated (depending on type of battery)
5. Wear loose-fitting clothing around the area of the pacemaker for comfort
6. Notify physician of any pain or redness over incision site
7. Avoid trauma to area of pulse generator
8. Avoid heavy contact sports
9. Carry an identification card/bracelet that indicates physician's name, type and model number of pacemaker, manufacturer's name, pacemaker rate
10. Display identification card and request scanning by hand scanner when going through weapons detector at airport
11. Remember that periodic hospitalization is necessary for battery changes/pacemaker unit replacement

Cardiac Arrest

A. General information: sudden, unexpected cessation of breathing and adequate circulation of blood by the heart
B. Medical management
1. Cardiopulmonary resuscitation (CPR); see below
2. Drug therapy
   a. Lidocaine, procainamide, verapamil
   b. Dopamine (Intropin), isoproterenol (Isuprel), norepinephrine (Levophed): see also Drugs Used to Treat Shock, Table 4.9

c. Epinephrine to enhance myocardial automaticity, excitability, conductivity, and contractility
d. Atropine sulfate to reduce vagus nerve's control over the heart, thus increasing the heart rate
e. Sodium bicarbonate: administered during first few moments of a cardiac arrest to correct respiratory and metabolic acidosis
f. Calcium chloride: calcium ions help the heart beat more effectively by enhancing the myocardium's contractile force
3. Defibrillation (electrical countershock)
C. Assessment findings: unresponsiveness, cessation of respiration, pallor, cyanosis, absence of heart sounds/blood pressure/palpable pulses, dilation of pupils, ventricular fibrillation (if client on a monitor)
D. Nursing interventions: monitored arrest caused by ventricular fibrillation
1. Begin precordial thump and, if successful, administer lidocaine.
2. If unsuccessful, defibrillation.
3. If defibrillation unsuccessful, initiate CPR immediately.
4. Assist with administration of and monitor effects of additional emergency drugs.

Cardiopulmonary Resuscitation (CPR)

A. General information: process of externally supporting the circulation and respiration of a person who has had a cardiac arrest
B. Nursing interventions: unwitnessed cardiac arrest
1. Assess LOC.
   a. Shake victim's shoulder and shout.
   b. If no response, summon help.
2. Position victim supine on a firm surface.
3. Open airway.
   a. Use head tilt, chin lift maneuver.
   b. Place ear over nose and mouth.
      1) look to see if chest is moving.
      2) listen for escape of air.
      3) feel for movement of air against face.
   c. If no respiration, proceed to #4.
4. Ventilate twice, allowing for deflation between breaths.
5. Assess circulation: palpate for carotid pulse; if not present, proceed to #6.
6. Initiate external cardiac compressions
   a. Proper placement of hands: lower half of the sternum
   b. Depth of compressions: 1½–2 inches for adults
   c. One rescuer: 15 compressions (at rate of 80–100 per minute) with 2 ventilations

d. Two rescuers: 5 compressions (at rate of 80–100 per minute) with 1 ventilation

Endocarditis

A. General information
1. Inflammation of the endocardium; platelets and fibrin deposit on the mitral and/or aortic valves causing deformity, insufficiency, or stenosis.
2. Caused by bacterial infection: commonly *S. aureus, S. viridans,* B-hemolytic streptococcus, gonococcus
3. Precipitating factors: rheumatic heart disease, open-heart surgery procedures, GU/Ob-Gyn instrumentation/surgery, dental extractions, invasive monitoring, septic thrombophlebitis
B. Medical management
1. Drug therapy
   a. Antibiotics specific to sensitivity of organism cultured
   b. Penicillin G and streptomycin if organism not known
   c. Antipyretics
2. Cardiac surgery to replace affected valve
C. Assessment findings
1. Fever, malaise, fatigue, dyspnea and cough (if extensive valvular damage), acute upper quadrant pain (if splenic involvement), joint pain
2. Petechiae, murmurs, edema (if extensive valvular damage), splenomegaly, hemiplegia and confusion (if cerebral infarction), hematuria (if renal infarction)
3. Elevated WBC and ESR, decreased Hgb and Hct
4. Diagnostic tests: positive blood culture for causative organism
D. Nursing interventions
1. Administer antibiotics as ordered to control the infectious process.
2. Control temperature elevation by administration of antipyretics.
3. Assess for vascular complications (see Thrombophlebitis, page 223, and Pulmonary Embolism, page 224).
4. Provide client teaching and discharge planning concerning
   a. Types of procedures/treatments (e.g., tooth extractions, GU instrumentation) that increase the chances of recurrences
   b. Antibiotic therapy, including name, purpose, dose, frequency, side effects
   c. Signs and symptoms of recurrent endocarditis (persistent fever, fatigue, chills, anorexia, joint pain)
   d. Avoidance of individuals with known infections.

Pericarditis

A. General information
1. An inflammation of the visceral and parietal pericardium
2. Caused by a bacterial, viral, or fungal infection; collagen diseases; trauma; acute MI; neoplasms; uremia; radiation therapy; drugs (procainamide, hydralazine, doxorubicin HCl [Adriamycin])
B. Medical management
1. Determination and elimination/control of underlying cause
2. Drug therapy
a. Medication for pain relief
b. Corticosteroids, salicylates (aspirin), and indomethacin (Indocin) to reduce inflammation
c. Specific antibiotic therapy against the causative organism may be indicated.
C. Assessment findings
1. Chest pain with deep inspiration (relieved by sitting up), cough, hemoptysis, malaise
2. Tachycardia, fever, pleural friction rub, cyanosis or pallor, accentuated component of S_2, pulsus paradoxus, jugular vein distension
3. Elevated WBC and ESR, normal or elevated AST (SGOT)
4. Diagnostic tests
a. Chest x-ray may show increased heart size if effusion occurs
b. ECG changes: ST elevation (precordial leads and 2- or 3-limb heads), T wave inversion
D. Nursing interventions
1. Ensure comfort: bed rest with semi- or high-Fowler's position.
2. Monitor hemodynamic parameters carefully.
3. Administer medications as ordered and monitor effects.
4. Provide client teaching and discharge planning concerning
a. Signs and symptoms of pericarditis indicative of a recurrence (chest pain that is intensified by inspiration and position changes, fever, cough)
b. Medication regimen including name, purpose, dosage, frequency, side effects.

Cardiac Tamponade

A. General information
1. An accumulation of fluid/blood in the pericardium that prevents adequate ventricular filling; without emergency treatment client will die in shock.
2. Caused by blunt or penetrating chest trauma, malignant pericardial effusion; can be a complication of cardiac surgery

B. Medical management: emergency treatment of choice is *pericardiocentesis* (insertion of a needle into the pericardial sac to aspirate fluid/blood and relieve the pressure on the heart)
C. Assessment findings
1. Chest pain
2. Hypotension, distended neck veins, tachycardia, muffled or distant heart sounds, paradoxical pulse, pericardial friction rub
3. Elevated CVP, decreased Hgb and Hct if massive hemorrhage
4. Diagnostic test: chest x-ray reveals enlarged heart and widened mediastinum.
D. Nursing interventions
1. Administer oxygen therapy
2. Monitor CVP/IVs closely
3. Assist with pericardiocentesis.
a. Monitor ECG, blood pressure, and pulse.
b. Assess aspirated fluid for color, consistency.
c. Send specimen to lab immediately.

Cardiogenic Shock

See page 149.

The Blood Vessels

Hypertension

A. General information
1. According to the World Health Organization, hypertension is a persistent elevation of the systolic blood pressure above 140 mm Hg and of the diastolic above 90 mm Hg.
2. Types
a. Essential (primary, idiopathic): marked by loss of elastic tissue and arteriosclerotic changes in the aorta and larger vessels coupled with decreased caliber of the arterioles
b. Benign: a moderate rise in blood pressure marked by a gradual onset and prolonged course
c. Malignant: characterized by a rapid onset and short dramatic course with a diastolic blood pressure of more than 150 mm Hg
d. Secondary: elevation of the blood pressure as a result of another disease such as renal parenchymal disease, Cushing's disease, pheochromocytoma, primary aldosteronism, coarctation of the aorta
3. Essential hypertension usually occurs between ages 35 and 50; more common in men over 35, women over 45; African-

American men affected twice as often as white men/women

4. Risk factors for essential hypertension include positive family history, obesity, stress, cigarette smoking, hyper-cholesteremia, increased sodium intake

B. Medical management
1. Diet and weight reduction (restricted sodium, kcal, cholesterol)
2. Life-style changes: alcohol moderation, exercise regimen, cessation of smoking
3. Antihypertensive drug therapy (see Table 2.17)

C. Assessment findings
1. Pain similar to anginal pain; pain in calves of legs after ambulation or exercise (*intermittent claudication*); severe occipital headaches, particularly in the morning; polyuria; nocturia; fatigue; dizziness; epistaxis; dyspnea on exertion
2. Blood pressure consistently above 140/90, retinal hemorrhages and exudates, edema of extremities (indicative of right-sided heart failure)
3. Rise in systolic blood pressure from supine to standing position (indicative of essential hypertension)
4. Diagnostic tests; elevated serum uric acid, sodium, cholesterol levels

D. Nursing interventions
1. Record baseline blood pressure in three positions (lying, sitting, standing) and in both arms.
2. Continuously assess blood pressure and report any variables that relate to changes in blood pressure (positioning, restlessness).
3. Administer antihypertensive agents as ordered; monitor closely and assess for side effects.
4. Monitor intake and hourly outputs.
5. Provide client teaching and discharge planning concerning
   a. Risk factor identification and development/implementation of methods to modify them
   b. Restricted sodium, kcal, cholesterol diet; include family in teaching (see Appendix)
   c. Antihypertensive drug regimen (include family); see Table 2.17
      1) names, actions, dosages, and side effects of prescribed medications
      2) take drugs at regular times and avoid omission of any doses
      3) never abruptly discontinue the drug therapy
      4) supplement diet with potassium-rich foods if taking potassium-wasting diuretics
      5) avoid hot baths, alcohol, or strenuous exercise within 3 hours of taking medications that cause vasodilation
   d. Development of a graduated exercise program
   e. Importance of routine follow-up care

Arteriosclerosis Obliterans

A. General information
1. A chronic occlusive arterial disease that may affect the abdominal aorta or the lower extremities. The obstruction to blood flow with resultant ischemia usually affects the femoral, popliteal, aortal, and iliac arteries.
2. Occurs most often in men ages 50–60
3. Caused by atherosclerosis
4. Risk factors: cigarette smoking, hyperlipidemia, hypertension, diabetes mellitus

B. Medical management
1. Drug therapy
   a. Vasodilators: papaverine, isoxsuprine HCl (Vasodilan), nylidrin HCl (Arlidin), nicotinyl alcohol (Roniacol), cyclandelate (Cyclospasmol), tolazoline HCl (Priscoline) to improve arterial circulation; effectiveness questionable
   b. Analgesics to relieve ischemic pain
   c. Anticoagulants to prevent thrombus formation
   d. Lipid-reducing drug: cholestyramine (Questran), colestipol HCl (Cholestid), dextrothyroxine sodium (Choloxin), clofibrate (Atromid-S), gemfibrozil (Lopid), niacin, lovastatin (Mevacor) (see Unit 2)
2. Surgery: bypass grafting, endarterectomy, balloon catheter dilation; lumbar sympathectomy (to increase blood flow), amputation may be necessary

C. Assessment findings
1. Pain, both intermittent claudication and rest pain, numbness or tingling of the toes
2. Pallor after 1–2 minutes of elevating feet, and dependent hyperemia/rubor; diminished or absent dorsalis pedis, posterior tibial and femoral pulses; trophic changes; shiny, taut skin with hair loss on lower legs
3. Diagnostic tests
   a. Oscillometry may reveal decrease in pulse volume
   b. Doppler ultrasound reveals decreased blood flow through affected vessels
   c. Angiography reveals location and extent of obstructive process
4. Elevated serum triglycerides; sodium

D. Nursing interventions
1. Encourage slow, progressive physical activity (out of bed at least 3–4 times/day, walking 2 times/day).

2. Administer medications as ordered.
3. Assist with Buerger-Allen exercises q.i.d.
   a. Client lies with legs elevated above heart for 2–3 minutes
   b. Client sits on edge of bed with legs and feet dependent and exercises feet and toes—upward and downward, inward and outward—for 3 minutes
   c. Client lies flat with legs at heart level for 5 minutes
4. Assess for sensory function and trophic changes.
5. Protect client from injury.
6. Provide client teaching and discharge planning concerning
   a. Restricted kcal, low-saturated-fat diet; include family (see Appendix)
   b. Importance of continuing with established exercise program
   c. Measures to reduce stress (relaxation techniques, biofeedback)
   d. Importance of avoiding smoking, constrictive clothing, standing in any position for a long time, injury
   e. Importance of foot care, immediately taking care of cuts, wounds, injuries
7. Prepare client for surgery if necessary.

Thromboangiitis Obliterans (Buerger's Disease)

A. General information
   1. Acute, inflammatory disorder affecting medium/smaller arteries and veins of the lower extremities. Occurs as focal, obstructive process; results in occlusion of a vessel with subsequent development of collateral circulation.
   2. Most often affects men ages 25–40
   3. Disease is idiopathic; high incidence among smokers.
B. Medical management: see Arteriosclerosis Obliterans, above; only really effective treatment is cessation of smoking.
C. Assessment findings
   1. Intermittent claudication, sensitivity to cold (skin of extremity may at first be white, changing to blue, then red)
   2. Decreased or absent peripheral pulses (posterior tibial and dorsalis pedis), trophic changes, ulceration and gangrene (advanced)
   3. Diagnostic tests: same as in Arteriosclerosis Obliterans except no elevation in serum triglycerides
D. Nursing interventions
   1. Prepare client for surgery.
   2. Provide client teaching and discharge planning concerning
      a. Drug regimen (vasodilators, anticoagulants, analgesics) to include

names, dosages, frequency, and side effects
   b. Need to avoid trauma to the affected extremity
   c. Need to maintain warmth, especially in cold weather
   d. Importance of stopping smoking.

Raynaud's Phenomenon

A. General information
   1. Intermittent episode of arterial spasms, most frequently involving the fingers
   2. Most often affects women between the teenage years and age 40
   3. Cause unknown
   4. Predisposing factors: collagen diseases (systemic lupus erythematosus, rheumatoid arthritis), trauma (e.g., from typing, piano playing, operating a chain saw)
B. Medical management: vasodilators, catecholamine-depleting antihypertensive drugs (reserpine, guanethidine monosulfate [Ismelin])
C. Assessment findings
   1. Coldness, numbness, tingling in one or more digits; pain (usually precipitated by exposure to cold, emotional upsets, tobacco use)
   2. Intermittent color changes (pallor, cyanosis, rubor); small ulcerations and gangrene at tips of digits (advanced)
D. Nursing interventions
   1. Provide client teaching concerning
      a. Importance of stopping smoking
      b. Need to maintain warmth, especially in cold weather
      c. Need to use gloves when handling cold objects/opening freezer or refrigerator door
      d. Drug regimen

Aneurysms

An aneurysm is a sac formed by dilation of an artery secondary to weakness and stretching of the arterial wall. The dilation may involve one or all layers of the arterial wall.

Classification

A. *Fusiform:* uniform spindle shape involving the entire circumference of the artery
B. *Saccular:* outpouching on one side only, affecting only part of the arterial circumference
C. *Dissecting:* separation of the arterial wall layers to form a cavity that fills with blood
D. *False:* the vessel wall is disrupted, blood escapes into surrounding area but is held in place by surrounding tissue.

Thoracic Aortic Aneurysm

A. General information
   1. An aneurysm, usually fusiform or dissecting, in the descending, ascending, or transverse section of the thoracic aorta.
   2. Usually occurs in men ages 50–70
   3. Caused by arteriosclerosis, infection, syphilis, hypertension
B. Medical management
   1. Control of underlying hypertension
   2. Surgery: resection of the aneurysm and replacement with a Teflon/Dacron graft; clients will need extracorporeal circulation (heart-lung machine).
C. Assessment findings
   1. Often asymptomatic
   2. Deep, diffuse chest pain; hoarseness; dysphagia; dyspnea
   3. Pallor, diaphoresis, distended neck veins, edema of head and arms
   4. Diagnostic tests
      a. Aortography shows exact location of the aneurysm
      b. X-rays: chest film reveals abnormal widening of aorta; abdominal film may show calcification within walls of aneurysm
D. Nursing interventions: see Cardiac Surgery, page 214.

Abdominal Aortic Aneurysm

A. General information
   1. Most aneurysms of this type are saccular or dissecting and develop just below the renal arteries but above the iliac bifurcation
   2. Occur most often in men over age 60
   3. Caused by atherosclerosis, hypertension, trauma, syphilis, other types of infectious processes
B. Medical management: surgical resection of the lesion and replacement with a graft (extracorporeal circulation not needed)
C. Assessment findings
   1. Severe mid- to low-abdominal pain, low-back pain
   2. Mass in the periumbilical area or slightly to the left of the midline with bruits heard over the mass
   3. Pulsating abdominal mass
   4. Diminished femoral pulses
   5. Diagnostic tests: same as for thoracic aneurysms
D. Nursing interventions: preoperative
   1. Prepare client for surgery: routine pre-op care.
   2. Assess rate, rhythm, character of the peripheral pulses and mark all distal pulses.
E. Nursing interventions: postoperative

1. Provide routine post-op care
2. Monitor the following parameters
   a. Hourly circulation checks noting rate, rhythm, character of all pulses distal to the graft
   b. CVP/PAP/PCWP
   c. Hourly outputs through Foley catheter (report less than 30 ml/hour)
   d. Daily BUN/creatinine/electrolyte levels
   e. Presence of back pain (may indicate retroperitoneal hemorrhage)
   f. IV fluids
   g. Neuro status including LOC, pupil size and response to light, hand grasp, movement of extremities
   h. Heart rate and rhythm via monitor
3. Maintain client flat in bed without sharp flexion of hip/knee (avoid pressure on femoral/popliteal arteries).
4. Auscultate lungs and encourage turning, coughing, and deep breathing.
5. Assess for signs and symptoms of paralytic ileus (see page 277).
6. Prevent thrombophlebitis.
   a. Encourage client to dorsiflex foot while in bed.
   b. Use elastic stockings or sequential compression boots as ordered.
   c. Assess for signs and symptoms (see Thrombophlebitis, page 223).
7. Provide client teaching and discharge planning concerning
   a. Importance of changes in color/temperature of extremities
   b. Avoidance of prolonged sitting, standing, and smoking
   c. Need for a gradual progressive activity regimen
   d. Adherence to low-cholesterol, low-saturated-fat diet

Femoral-Popliteal Bypass Surgery

A. General information
   1. Most common type of surgery to correct arterial obstructions of the lower extremities
   2. Procedure involves bypassing the occluded vessel with a graft, such as Teflon, Dacron, or an autogenous artery or vein (saphenous).
B. Nursing interventions: preoperative
   1. Provide routine pre-op care.
   2. Monitor and correct potassium imbalances to prevent cardiac arrhythmias.
   3. Assess for focus of infection (infected tooth) or infectious processes (urinary tract infections).
   4. Mark distal peripheral pulses.
C. Nursing interventions: postoperative
   1. Provide routine post-op care.
   2. Assess the following

a. Circulation, noting rate, rhythm, and quality of peripheral pulses distal to the graft; color; temperature; and sensation
b. Signs and symptoms of thrombophlebitis (see page below)
c. Neuro checks
d. Hourly outputs
e. CVP
f. Wound drainage, noting amount, color, and characteristics
3. Elevate legs above the level of the heart.
4. Encourage turning, coughing, and deep breathing while splinting incision.

Venous Stasis Ulcers

A. General information
1. Usually a complication of thrombophlebitis and varicose veins.
2. Ulcers result from incompetent valves in the veins, causing high pressure with rupture of small skin veins and venules.
B. Medical management
1. Antibiotic therapy (specific to organism cultured); topical bacteriocidal solutions
2. Skin grafting
3. Enzymatic or surgical debridement
C. Assessment findings
1. Pain in the limb in dependent position or during ambulation
2. Skin of leathery texture, brownish pigment around ankles; positive pulses but edema makes palpation difficult.
D. Nursing interventions
1. Provide bed rest, elevating extremity.
2. Provide a balanced diet with added protein and vitamin supplements.
3. Administer antibiotics as ordered to control infection.
4. Promote healing by cleansing ulcer with prescribed agents.
5. Provide client teaching and discharge planning concerning
a. Importance of avoiding trauma to affected limb
b. Skin care regimen
c. Use of elastic support stockings (after ulcer is healed)
d. Need for planned rest periods with elevation of the extremities
6. Adherence to balanced diet with vitamin supplements.

Thrombophlebitis

A. General information
1. Inflammation of the vessel wall with formation of a clot (thrombus); may affect superficial or deep veins.
2. Most frequent veins affected are the saphenous, femoral, and popliteal.

3. Can result in damage to the surrounding tissues, ischemia, and necrosis.
4. Risk factors: obesity, CHF, prolonged immobility, MI, pregnancy, oral contraceptives, trauma, sepsis, cigarette smoking, dehydration, severe anemias, venous cannulation, complication of surgery
B. Medical management
1. Anticoagulant therapy
a. Heparin
1) blocks conversion of prothrombin to thrombin and reduces formation or extension of thrombus
2) side effects: spontaneous bleeding, injection site reactions, ecchymoses, tissue irritation and sloughing, reversible transient alopecia, cyanosis, pain in arms or legs, thrombocytopenia
b. Warfarin (coumadin)
1) blocks prothrombin synthesis by interfering with vitamin K synthesis
2) side effects
a) GI: anorexia, nausea and vomiting, diarrhea, stomatitis
b) hypersensitivity: dermatitis, urticaria, pruritus, fever
c) other: transient hair loss, burning sensation of feet, bleeding complications
2. Surgery
a. Vein ligation and stripping (see page 224)
b. *Venous thrombectomy:* removal of a clot in the iliofemoral region
c. *Plication of the inferior vena cava:* insertion of an umbrella-like prosthesis into the lumen of the vena cava to filter incoming clots
C. Assessment findings
1. Pain in the affected extremity
2. Superficial vein: tenderness, redness, induration along course of the vein
3. Deep vein: swelling, venous distension of limb, tenderness over involved vein, positive Homan's sign, cyanosis
4. Elevated WBC and ESR
5. Diagnostic tests
a. Venography (phlebography): increased uptake of radioactive material
b. Doppler ultrasonography: impairment of blood flow ahead of thrombus
c. Venous pressure measurements: high in affected limb until collateral circulation is developed
D. Nursing interventions
1. Provide bed rest, elevating involved extremity to increase venous return and decrease edema.
2. Apply continuous warm, moist soaks to decrease lymphatic congestion.

3. Administer anticoagulants as ordered
    a. Heparin
        1) monitor PTT; dosage should be adjusted to keep PTT between 1.5–2.5 times normal control level.
        2) use infusion pump to administer IV heparin.
        3) ensure proper injection technique.
            a) use 26- or 27-gauge syringe with ½–⅝-in needle, inject into fatty layer of abdomen above iliac crest.
            b) avoid injecting within 2 inches of umbilicus.
            c) insert needle at 90° to skin.
            d) do not withdraw plunger to assess blood return.
            e) apply gentle pressure after removal of needle, avoid massage.
        4) assess for increased bleeding tendencies (hematuria; hematemesis; bleeding gums; petechiae of soft palate, conjunctiva, retina; ecchymoses, epistaxis, bloody sputum, melena) and instruct patient to observe for and report these.
        5) have antidote (protamine sulfate) available.
        6) instruct client to avoid aspirin, antihistamines, and cough preparations containing glyceryl guaiacolate, and to obtain physician's permission before using other OTC drugs.
    b. Warfarin (Coumadin)
        1) assess PT daily; dosage should be adjusted to maintain PT at 1.5–2.5 times normal control level; INR of 2.
        2) obtain careful medication history (there are many drug-drug interactions).
        3) advise client to withhold dose and notify physician immediately if bleeding or signs of bleeding occur (see Heparin, above).
        4) instruct client to use a soft toothbrush and to floss gently.
        5) have antidote (vitamin K) available.
        6) alert client to factors that may affect the anticoagulant response (high-fat diet or sudden increases in vitamin K-rich foods).
        7) instruct client to wear Medic-Alert bracelet.
4. Assess vital signs every 4 hours.
5. Monitor for chest pain or shortness of breath (possible pulmonary embolism).
6. Measure thighs, calves, ankles, and instep every morning.

7. Provide client teaching and discharge planning concerning
    a. Need to avoid standing, sitting for long periods; constrictive clothing; crossing legs at the knees; smoking; oral contraceptives
    b. Importance of adequate hydration to prevent hypercoagulability
    c. Use of elastic stockings when ambulatory
    d. Importance of planned rest periods with elevation of the feet
    e. Drug regimen
    f. Plan for exercise/activity
        1) begin with dorsiflexion of the feet while sitting or lying down
        2) swim several times weekly
        3) gradually increase walking distance
    g. Importance of weight reduction if obese

Pulmonary Embolism

A. General information
    1. Most pulmonary emboli arise as detached portions of venous thrombi formed in the deep veins of the legs, right side of the heart, or pelvic area.
    2. Distribution of emboli is related to blood flow; emboli involve the lower lobes of the lung because of higher blood flow.
    3. Embolic obstruction to blood flow increases venous pressure in the pulmonary artery and pulmonary hypertension.
    4. Rick factors: venous thrombosis, immobility, pre- and post-op states, trauma, pregnancy, CHF, use of oral contraceptives, obesity
B. Medical management
    1. Drug therapy
        a. Anticoagulants (see Thrombophlebitis, page 223)
        b. Thrombolytics: streptokinase or urokinase
        c. Dextran 70 to decrease blood viscosity and aggregation of blood cells
        d. Narcotics for pain relief
        e. Vasopressors (in the presence of shock)
    2. Surgery: *embolectomy* (surgical removal of an embolus from the pulmonary arteries)
C. Assessment findings
    1. Chest pain (pleuritic), severe dyspnea, feeling of impending doom
    2. Tachypnea, tachycardia, anxiety, hemoptysis, shock symptoms (if massive)
    3. Decreased pCO_2; increased pH (due to hyperventilation)
    4. Increased temperature
    5. Intensified pulmonic S_2; rales or crackles
    6. Diagnostic tests

a. Pulmonary angiography: reveals location/extent of embolism
b. Lung scan reveals adequacy/ inadequacy of pulmonary circulation

D. Nursing interventions
1. Administer medications as ordered; monitor effects and side effects.
2. Administer oxygen therapy to correct hypoxemia.
3. Assist with turning, coughing, deep breathing, and passive ROM exercises.
4. Provide adequate hydration to prevent hypercoagulability.
5. Offer support/reassurance to client/family.
6. Elevate head of bed to relieve dyspnea
7. Provide client teaching and discharge planning: same as for thrombophlebitis.

Varicose Veins

A. General information
1. Dilated veins that occur most often in the lower extremities and trunk. As the vessel dilates, the valves become stretched and incompetent with resultant venous pooling/edema
2. Most common between ages 30 and 50
3. Predisposing factor: congenital weakness of the veins, thrombophlebitis, pregnancy, obesity, heart disease

B. Medical management: vein ligation (involves ligating the saphenous vein where it joins the femoral vein and stripping the saphenous vein system from groin to ankle)

C. Assessment findings
1. Pain after prolonged standing (relieved by elevation)
2. Swollen, dilated, tortuous skin veins
3. Diagnostic tests
   a. Trendelenburg test: varicose veins distend very quickly (less than 35 seconds)
   b. Doppler ultrasound: decreased or no blood flow heard after calf or thigh compression

D. Nursing interventions
1. Elevate legs above heart level.
2. Measure circumference of ankle and calf daily.
3. Apply knee-length elastic stockings.
4. Provide adequate rest.
5. Prepare client for vein ligation, if necessary.
   a. Provide routine pre-op care.
   b. In addition to routine post-op care
      1) keep affected extremity elevated above the level of the heart to prevent edema.
      2) apply elastic bandages and stockings, which should be removed every 8 hours for short periods and reapplied.

3) assist out of bed within 24 hours, ensuring that elastic stockings are applied.
4) assess for increased bleeding, particularly in the groin area.
6. Provide client teaching and discharge planning: same as for thrombophlebitis, page 223.

Amputation

A. General information
1. Surgical procedure done for peripheral vascular disease if medical management is ineffective and the symptoms become worse.
2. The level of amputation is determined by the extent of the disease process.
   a. Above knee (AK): performed between the lower third to the middle of the thigh
   b. Below knee (BK): usually done in middle third of leg, leaving a stump of 12.5–17.5 cm

B. Nursing interventions: preoperative
1. Provide routine pre-op care.
2. Offer support/encouragement and accept client's response of anger/grief.
3. Discuss
   a. Rehabilitation program and use of prosthesis
   b. Upper extremity exercises such as push-ups in bed
   c. Crutch walking
   d. Amputation dressings/cast
   e. Phantom limb sensation as a normal occurrence

C. Nursing interventions: postoperative
1. Provide routine post-op care.
2. Prevent hip/knee contractures
3. Avoid letting client sit in chair with hips flexed for long periods of time.
4. Have client assume prone position several times a day and position hip in extension (unless otherwise ordered).
5. Avoid elevation of the stump after 12–24 hours.
6. Observe stump dressing for signs of hemorrhage and mark outside of dressing so rate of bleeding can be assessed.
7. Administer pain medication as ordered.
8. Ensure that stump bandages fit tightly and are applied properly to enhance prosthesis fitting.
9. Initiate active ROM exercises of all joints (when medically advised), crutch walking, and arm/shoulder exercises.
10. Provide stump care.
   a. Inspect daily for signs of skin irritation.

b. Wash thoroughly daily with warm water and bacteriostatic soap; rinse and dry thoroughly.

c. Avoid use of irritating substances such as lotions, alcohol, powders.

Sample Questions

43. Ms. H. is admitted to the coronary care unit to rule out a myocardial infarction. She tells the nurse she is sure it is just angina and cannot understand what the difference is between angina and infarct pain. Which response is most appropriate for the nurse to make?
    1. Anginal pain usually lasts only 3–5 minutes.
    2. Anginal pain produces clenching of the fists over the chest while acute MI pain does not.
    3. Anginal pain requires morphine for relief.
    4. Anginal pain radiates to the left arm while acute MI pain does not.

44. Mrs. J. is admitted to the cardiac care unit with a myocardial infarction. The morning after admission she and her husband tell the nurse that she must be home tonight to care for the children when Mr. J. goes to work. The problem identified at this point would be
    1. anxiety related to physical limitations.
    2. alteration in cardiac output.
    3. inability of client/family to understand disease process.
    4. safety needs related to inability to cope.

45. The nurse is caring for an adult admitted to the coronary care unit with a myocardial infarction. During the second night in the CCU, the client develops congestive heart failure. A Swan-Ganz catheter is inserted to monitor the client for left ventricular function because
    1. it provides information about pulmonary resistance.
    2. it measures myocardial oxygen consumption.
    3. it controls renal blood flow.
    4. it controls afterload.

46. The acute nursing management of a client with CHF will include all of the following goals except
    1. an increase in cardiac output.
    2. an elevation in renal blood flow.
    3. a reduction in the heart's workload.
    4. a decrease in myocardial contractility.

47. The nurse is caring for an adult who is being treated for a myocardial infarction. Oxygen is ordered. Administering oxygen to this client is related to which of the following client problems?
    1. Anxiety.
    2. Chest pains.
    3. Alteration in myocardial perfusion.
    4. Alteration in heart rate, rhythm, or conduction.

48. The nurse reading an ECG rhythm strip notes that there are 8 QRS complexes in a 6-second strip. The heart rate is
    1. 48.
    2. 64.
    3. 80.
    4. 120.

49. Mr. J., 57 years old, is being treated in the clinic for hypertension. His blood pressure is 170/92 and he is complaining of fatigue and lassitude. He has been taking propranolol (Inderal) 80 mg bid. The best indication that previous teaching about this drug has been successful is that he
    1. checks his pulse for bradycardia.
    2. makes an appointment as soon as he notices fatigue.
    3. stops the drug when he experiences chest pain.
    4. takes the drug with breakfast and dinner.

50. A 56-year-old obese man is recovering from a bowel resection for cancer of the colon. On his third post-op day he complains that the area around the calf of his leg is warm and tender. Suspecting he may have developed a thrombus, the nurse performs a thorough assessment. When assessing for common clinical manifestations of deep vein thrombosis, the nurse will observe the client for
    1. absence of a pulse distal to the clot.
    2. cyanosis distal to the clot.
    3. pain on dorsiflexion.
    4. reddened area around the clot.

51. Mr. D., 68 years old, has been treated over the years for chronic venous insufficiency. Today he came to the medical clinic complaining of severe pain in his legs. They were swollen and covered with deep, draining, foul-smelling ulcers. He is admitted to the hospital for aggressive treatment. The nurse caring for Mr. D. reminds him that the underlying cause of his venous insufficiency is
    1. congestive heart failure.
    2. hypertrophied leg muscles.
    3. decreased hemoglobin levels.
    4. poor blood return to the heart.

52. A 65-year-old man is admitted with venous stasis ulcers and chronic venous insufficiency. A goal of care for this client is the control of swelling. The primary mechanism for achieving this is to
    1. exercise vigorously.
    2. restrict fluid intake.
    3. promote gravity drainage.
    4. eat a high-protein, low-salt diet.

Answers and Rationales

43. The correct answer is 1. Anginal pain is of short duration. It is usually relieved by rest. The usual treatment for anginal pain is nitroglycerin. Anginal pain and the pain of an acute MI can both radiate to other locations.

44. The correct answer is 3. The nurse should assess both Mr. and Mrs. J.'s understanding of the disease and rehabilitation processes. They both exhibit the need for information in order to be able to make rational decisions.

45. The correct answer is 1. The Swan-Ganz catheter measures pulmonary artery and capillary wedge pressures, which are good indicators of pulmonary pathology. The Swan-Ganz catheter does not measure myocardial oxygen consumption and does not control renal blood flow.

46. The correct answer is 4. Improving the force and strength of ventricular contraction is a goal in the care of clients with congestive heart failure. Decreased contractility will worsen the failure. Elevation of renal blood flow, increased cardiac output, and reducing the heart's workload are all realistic goals in caring for the client with CHF.

47. The correct answer is 3. With acute myocardial infarction there is an alteration in myocardial perfusion resulting in a decrease in the amount of oxygen available for tissue perfusion. Therefore, oxygen is administered to improve tissue perfusion in these clients. Nursing interventions for alteration in heart rate, rhythm, or conduction are implemented by monitoring ECGs and administering antiarrhythmics. Anxiety requires nursing implementation of explanation of care as well as environmental control. Pain leads to nursing interventions of analgesia and drug administration.

48. The correct answer is 3. A regular heart rate is determined by multiplying the number of QRS complexes in 6 seconds (8 QRS complexes) by 10 (because there are 60 seconds in one minute). Therefore the heart rate is 80. This method would not determine an accurate pulse if the client's heart rate was irregular.

49. The correct answer is 1. A common side effect of propranolol is a slowed pulse rate because the drug is a beta blocker. Propranolol will cause some fatigue. Follow-up appointments should be kept on a regular basis. The doctor should be notified, but the medication should not be stopped. Propranolol does not have to be taken with meals.

50. The correct answer is 3. Pain on dorsiflexion is a common manifestation of deep vein thrombosis. Arterial pulse would be normal and palpable, except in presence of marked edema. There might be slight cyanosis distal to the clot. Area around clot would be warm but not necessarily reddened.

51. The correct answer is 4. Venous insufficiency is stasis of venous blood flow. The leg muscles that normally compress the veins to force blood upward are not effective. Congestive heart failure does not cause venous insufficiency. The leg muscles are not contracting effectively. They are probably not hypertrophied. Decreased hemoglobin is seen in anemia.

52. The correct answer is 3. Swelling is minimized by promoting gravity drainage. This could be accomplished by elevating the extremities. The client would not be able to exercise vigorously. Fluid retention is not the cause of venous insufficiency, so fluid restriction is not necessary. Dietary changes will not control the swelling.

The Hematologic System

This section contributed by Margaret Ahearn Spera, RNC, MSN.

OVERVIEW OF ANATOMY AND PHYSIOLOGY

The structures of the hematologic or hemato-poietic system include the blood, blood vessels, and blood-forming organs (bone marrow, spleen, liver, lymph nodes, and thymus gland). The major function of blood is to carry necessary materials (oxygen, nutrients) to cells and to remove carbon dioxide and metabolic waste products. The hematologic system also plays an important role in hormone transport, the inflammatory and immune responses, temperature regulation, fluid-electrolyte balance, and acid-base balance.

Bone Marrow

A. Contained inside all bones, occupies interior of spongy bones and center of long bones; collectively one of the largest organs of the body (4%–5% of total body weight)
B. Primary function is hematopoiesis (the formation of blood cells)
C. Two kinds of bone marrow, red and yellow
   1. Red (functioning) marrow
      a. Carries out hematopoiesis; production site of erythroid, myeloid, and thrombocytic components of blood; one source of lymphocytes and macrophages
      b. Found in ribs, vertebral column, other flat bones
   2. Yellow marrow: red marrow that has changed to fat; found in long bones; does not contribute to hematopoiesis
D. All blood cells start as stem cells in the bone marrow; these mature into the different, specific types of cells, collectively referred to as formed elements of blood or blood components: erythrocytes, leukocytes, and thrombocytes.

Blood

A. Composed of plasma (55%) and cellular components (45%)
B. *Hematocrit*
   1. Reflects portion of blood composed of red blood cells
   2. Centrifugation of blood results in separation into top layer of plasma, middle layer of leukocytes and platelets, and bottom layer of erythrocytes.
   3. Majority of formed elements is erythrocytes; volume of leukocytes and platelets is negligible.
C. Distribution
   1. 1300 ml in pulmonary circulation
      a. 400 ml arterial
      b. 60 ml capillary
      c. 840 ml venous
   2. 3000 ml in systemic circulation
      a. 550 ml arterial
      b. 300 ml capillary
      c. 2150 ml venous

Plasma

A. Liquid part of blood; yellow in color because of pigments
B. Consists of serum (liquid portion of plasma) and fibrinogen
C. Contains plasma proteins such as albumin, serum globulins, fibrinogen, prothrombin, plasminogen
   1. Albumin: largest of plasma proteins, involved in regulation of intravascular plasma volume and maintenance of osmotic pressure
   2. Serum globulins: alpha, beta, gamma
      a. Alpha: role in transport of steroids, lipids, bilirubin
      b. Beta: role in transport of iron and copper
      c. Gamma: role in immune response, function of antibodies
   3. Fibrinogen, prothrombin, plasminogen (see Coagulation, see page 229)

Cellular Components

Cellular components or formed elements of blood are erythrocytes (red blood cells [RBCs]), which are responsible for oxygen transport; leukocytes (white blood cells [WBCs]), which play a major role in defense against microorganisms; and thrombocytes (platelets), which function in hemostasis.

A. *Erythrocytes*
   1. Bioconcave disc shape, no nucleus, chiefly sacs of hemoglobin
   2. Cell membrane is highly diffusible to O_2 and CO_2
   3. RBCs are responsible for oxygen transport via *hemoglobin* (*Hgb*)
      a. Two portions: iron carried on heme portion; second portion is protein
      b. Normal blood contains 12–18 g Hgb/100 ml blood; higher (14–18 g) in men than in women (12–14 g)
   4. Production
      a. Start in bone marrow as stem cells, released as reticulocytes (immature cells), mature into erythrocytes
      b. Erythropoietin stimulates differentiation; produced by kidneys and stimulated by hypoxia
      c. Iron, vitamin B_{12}, folic acid, pyridoxine (vitamin B_6), and other factors required for erythropoiesis
   5. Hemolysis (destruction)
      a. Average life span 120 days
      b. Immature RBCs destroyed in either bone marrow or other reticuloendothelial organs (blood, connective tissue, spleen, liver, lungs, and lymph nodes)
      c. Mature cells removed chiefly by liver and spleen
      d. *Bilirubin:* byproduct of Hgb released when RBCs destroyed, excreted in bile
      e. Iron: freed from Hgb during bilirubin formation; transported to bone marrow via transferrin and reclaimed for new Hgb production
      f. Premature destruction: may be caused by RBC membrane abnormalities, Hgb abnormalities, extrinsic physical

factors (such as the enzyme defects found in G6PD)

    g. Normal age RBCs may be destroyed by gross damage as in trauma or extravascular hemolysis (in spleen, liver, bone marrow)

B. *Leukocytes:* granulocytes and mononuclear cells: involved in protection from bacteria and other foreign substances

  1. Granulocytes: eosinophils, basophils, and neutrophils

    a. *Eosinophils:* involved in phagocytosis and allergic reactions

    b. *Basophils:* involved in prevention of clotting in microcirculation and allergic reactions

    c. Eosinophils and basophils are reservoirs of histamine, serotonin, and heparin

    d. *Neutrophils:* involved in short-term phagocytosis

      1) mature neutrophils: polymorphonuclear leukocytes

      2) immature neutrophils: band cells (bacterial infection usually produces increased numbers of band cells)

  2. Mononuclear cells: monocytes and lymphocytes: large nucleated cells

    a. *Monocytes:* involved in long-term phagocytosis; play a role in immune response

      1) largest leukocyte

      2) produced by bone marrow: give rise to histiocytes (Kupffer cells of liver), macrophages, and other components of reticuloendothelial system

    b. *Lymphocytes:* immune cells; produce substances against foreign cells; produced primarily in lymph tissue (B cells) and thymus (T cells) (see also Immune Response, page 131)

C. *Thrombocytes* (*platelets*)

  1. Fragments of megakaryocytes formed in bone marrow

  2. Production regulated by thrombopoietin

  3. Essential factor in coagulation via adhesion, aggregation, and plug formation

  4. Release substances involved in coagulation

Blood Groups

A. Erythrocytes carry antigens, which determine the different blood groups.

B. Blood-typing systems are based on the many possible antigens, but the most important are the antigens of the ABO and Rh blood groups because they are most likely to be involved in transfusion reactions.

  1. ABO typing

    a. Antigens of system are labelled A and B.

    b. Absence of both antigens results in type O blood.

    c. Presence of both antigens is type AB.

    d. Presence of either A or B results in type A and type B respectively.

    e. Nearly half the population is type O, the *universal donor*.

    f. Antibodies are automatically formed against the ABO antigens not on person's own RBCs; transfusion with mismatched or incompatible blood results in a transfusion reaction (Table 4.17).

  2. Rh typing

    a. Identifies presence or absence of Rh antigen (Rh positive or Rh negative).

    b. Anti-Rh antibodies not automatically formed in Rh-negative person, but if Rh-positive blood is given, antibody formation starts and a second exposure to Rh antigen will trigger a transfusion reaction.

    c. Important for Rh-negative woman carrying Rh-positive baby; first pregnancy not affected, but in a subsequent pregnancy with an Rh-positive baby, mother's antibodies attack baby's RBCs (see Hemolytic Disease of the Newborn, page 502).

Blood Coagulation

Conversion of fluid blood into a solid clot to reduce blood loss when blood vessels are ruptured.

A. Systems that initiate clotting

  1. *Intrinsic system:* initiated by contact activation following endothelial injury ("intrinsic" to vessel itself)

    a. Factor XII initiates as contact made between damaged vessel and plasma protein

    b. Factors VIII, IX, and XI activated

  2. *Extrinsic system*

    a. Initiated by tissue thromboplastins, released from injured vessels ("extrinsic" to vessel)

    b. Factor VII activated

B. Common pathway: activated by either intrinsic or extrinsic pathways

  1. Platelet factor 3 (PF3) and calcium react with factors X and V.

  2. Prothrombin converted to thrombin via thromboplastin.

  3. Thrombin acts on fibrinogen, forming soluble fibrin.

  4. Soluble fibrin polymerized by factor XIII to produce a stable, insoluble fibrin clot.

C. Clot resolution: takes place via fibrinolytic system by plasmin and proteolytic enzymes; clot dissolves as tissue repairs.

TABLE 4.17   Complications of Blood Transfusion

Type	Causes	Mechanism	Occurrence	Signs and Symptoms	Intervention
Hemolytic	ABO incompatibility; Rh incompatibility; use of dextrose solutions; wide temperature fluctuations	Antibodies in recipient plasma react with antigen in donor cells. Agglutinated cells block capillary blood flow to organs. Hemolysis (Hgb into plasma and urine).	*Acute:* first 5 min after completion of transfusion *Delayed:* days to 2 weeks after	Headache, lumbar or sternal pain, nausea, vomiting, diarrhea, fever, chills, flushing, heat along vein, restlessness, anemia, jaundice, dyspnea, signs of shock, renal shutdown, DIC	Stop transfusion. Continue saline IV. Send blood unit and client blood sample to lab. Watch for hemoglobinuria. Treat or prevent shock, DIC, and renal shutdown.
Allergic	Transfer of an antigen or antibody from donor to recipient; allergic donors	Immune sensitivity to foreign serum protein	Within 30 min of start of transfusion	Urticaria, laryngeal edema, wheezing, dyspnea, bronchospasm, headache, anaphylaxis	Stop transfusion. Administer antihistamine and/or epinephrine. Treat life-threatening reactions.
Pyrogenic	Recipient possesses antibodies directed against WBCs; bacterial contamination; multitransfused clients; multiparous clients	Leukocyte agglutination Bacterial organisms	Within 15–90 min after initiation of transfusion	Fever, chills, flushing, palpitations, tachycardia, occasional lumbar pain	Stop transfusion. Treat temperature. Transfuse with leukocyte-poor blood or washed RBCs. Administer antibiotics prn.
Circulatory overload	Too rapid infusion in susceptible clients	Fluid volume overload	During and after transfusion	Dyspnea, tachycardia, orthopnea, increased blood pressure, cyanosis, anxiety	Slow infusion rate. Use packed cells instead of whole blood. Monitor CVP through a separate line.
Air embolism	Blood given under air pressure following severe blood loss	Bolus of air blocks pulmonary artery outflow	Anytime	Dyspnea, increased pulse, wheezing, chest pain, decreased blood pressure, apprehension	Clamp tubing. Turn client on left side.
Thrombocytopenia	Use of large amounts of banked blood	Platelets deteriorate rapidly in stored blood	When large amounts of blood given over 24 hr	Abnormal bleeding	Assess for signs of bleeding. Initiate bleeding precautions. Use fresh blood.
Citrate intoxication	Large amounts of citrated blood in clients with decreased liver function	Citrate binds ionic calcium	After large amounts of banked blood	Neuromuscular irritability Bleeding due to decreased calcium	Monitor/treat hypocalcemia. Avoid large amounts of citrated blood. Monitor liver function.
Hyperkalemia	Potassium levels increase in stored blood	Release of potassium into plasma with red cell lysis	In clients with renal insufficiency	Nausea, colic, diarrhea, muscle spasms, ECG changes (tall peaked T-wave, short Q-T segment)	Administer blood less than 5–7 days old in clients with impaired potassium excretion.

Spleen

A. Largest lymphatic organ: functions as blood filtration system and reservoir
B. Vascular, bean shaped; lies beneath the diaphragm, behind and to the left of the stomach; composed of a fibrous tissue capsule surrounding a network of fiber
C. Contains two types of pulp
   1. Red pulp: located between the fibrous strands, composed of RBCs, WBCs, and macrophages
   2. White pulp: scattered throughout the red pulp, produces lymphocytes and sequesters lymphocytes, macrophages, and antigens
D. 1%–2% of red cell mass or 200 ml blood/minute stored in spleen; blood comes via the splenic artery to the pulp for cleansing, then passes into splenic venules that are lined with phagocytic cells, and finally to the splenic vein to the liver.
E. Important hematopoietic site in fetus; postnatally produces lymphocytes and monocytes
F. Important in phagocytosis; removes misshapen erythrocytes, unwanted parts of erythrocytes
G. Also involved in antibody production by plasma cells and iron metabolism (iron released from Hgb portion of destroyed erythrocytes returned to bone marrow)
H. In the adult, functions of the spleen can be taken over by the reticuloendothelial system.

Liver

See also Gastrointestinal Tract, page 262.
A. Involved in bile production (via erythrocyte destruction and bilirubin production) and erythropoiesis (during fetal life and when bone marrow production is insufficient).
B. Kupffer cells of liver have reticuloendothelial function as histiocytes; phagocytic activity and iron storage.
C. Liver also involved in synthesis of clotting factors, synthesis of antithrombins.

ASSESSMENT

Health History

A. Presenting problem
   1. Nonspecific symptoms may include chills, fatigue, fever, weakness, weight loss, night sweats, delayed wound healing, malaise, lethargy, depression, cold/heat intolerance
   2. Note specific signs and symptoms
      a. Skin: prolonged bleeding, petechiae, jaundice, ecchymosis, pruritus, pallor
      b. Eyes: visual disturbance, yellowed sclera
      c. Ears: vertigo, tinnitus
      d. Mouth and nose: epistaxis; gingival bleeding, ulceration, pain; dysphagia, hoarseness
      e. Neck: nuchal rigidity, lymphadenopathy
      f. Respiratory: dyspnea, orthopnea, palpitations, chest discomfort or pain, cough (productive or dry), hemoptysis
      g. GI: melena, abdominal pain, change in bowel habits
      h. GU: hematuria, recurrent infection, amenorrhea, menorrhagia
      i. CNS: confusion, headache, paresthesias, syncope
      j. Musculoskeletal: joint, back, or bone pain
B. Life-style: exposure to chemicals, occupational exposure to radiation
C. Use of medications
   1. Iron, vitamins (B_6, B_{12}, folic acid)
   2. Corticosteroids
   3. Anticoagulants
   4. Antibiotics
   5. Aspirin or aspirin-containing compounds
   6. Cold or allergy preparations
   7. Antiarrhythmics
   8. Blood transfusions (cryoprecipitates)
   9. Cancer chemotherapy drugs
   10. Immunosuppressant drugs
D. Medical history
   1. Surgery: splenectomy, tumor resection, cardiac valve replacement, GI tract resection
   2. Allergies: multiple transfusions with whole blood or blood products, other known allergies
   3. Mononucleosis; radiation therapy; recurrent infections; malabsorption syndrome; anemia; delayed wound healing; thrombophlebitis, pulmonary embolism, deep vein thrombosis (DVT); liver disease, ETOH abuse, vitamin K deficiency; angina pectoris, atrial fibrillation
E. Family history; jaundice, anemia, bleeding disorders (hemophilia, polycythemia), malignancies, congenital blood dyscrasias

Physical Examination

A. Auscultate for heart murmurs; bruits (cerebral, cardiac, carotid); pericardial or pleural friction rubs; bowel sounds.
B. Inspect for
   1. Flush or pallor of mucous membranes, nail beds, palms, soles of feet
   2. Infection or pallor of sclera, conjunctiva
   3. Cyanosis

    4. Jaundice of skin, mucous membranes, conjunctiva
    5. Signs of bleeding, petechiae, ecchymoses, oral mucosal bleeding (especially gums), epistaxis, hemorrhage from any orifice
    6. Ulcerations or lesions
    7. Swelling or erythema
    8. Neurologic changes: pain and touch, position and vibratory sense, superficial and deep tendon reflexes
C. Palpate lymph nodes; note location, size, texture, sensation, fixation; palpate the ribs for sternal, bone tenderness.
D. Evaluate joint range of motion and tenderness.
E. Percuss for lung excursion, splenomegaly, hepatomegaly.

Laboratory/Diagnostic Tests

A. Blood
    1. Complete blood count (CBC) with differential and peripheral smear
      a. White blood cell count (WBC) with differential
      b. Hgb and hct
      c. Platelet and reticulocyte count
      d. Red blood cell count (RBC) with peripheral smear
    2. Coagulation studies
      a. Prothrombin time (PT)
      b. Partial thromboplastin time (PTT)
      c. Fibrin split products (FSP)
      d. Lee-White clotting time (whole blood clotting time)
    3. Blood chemistry
      a. Blood urea nitrogen (BUN)
      b. Creatinine
      c. Bilirubin: direct and indirect
      d. Uric acid
    4. Miscellaneous
      a. Erythrocyte sedimentation rate (ESR)
      b. Serum protein electrophoresis
      c. Serum iron and total iron-binding capacity
      d. Plasma protein assays
      e. Direct and indirect Coombs' tests
B. Urine and stool
    1. Urinalysis
    2. Hematest
    3. Bence-Jones protein assay (urine)
C. Radiologic
    1. Chest or other x-ray as indicated by history and physical exam
    2. Radionuclide scans (e.g., bone scan)
    3. Lymphangiography
D. *Bone marrow aspiration and biopsy*
    1. Puncture of iliac crest (preferred site), vertebrae body, sternum, or tibia (in infants) to collect tissue from bone marrow
    2. Purpose: study cells involved in blood production

    3. Nursing care
      a. Confirm that consent form has been signed
      b. Allay client anxiety; prepare client for a sharp, brief pain when bone marrow is aspirated into syringe
      c. Position client and assist physician to maintain sterile field
      d. Immediately after the aspiration, apply pressure to the site for at least 5 minutes and longer, if necessary.
      e. Check the site frequently for signs of bleeding or infection.
      f. Send specimen to laboratory.

ANALYSIS

Nursing diagnoses for clients with disorders of the hematologic system may include
A. Altered nutrition: less than body requirements
B. High risk for infection
C. Altered tissue perfusion: cerebral, peripheral
D. Impaired gas exchange
E. Altered protection
F. High risk for impaired skin integrity
G. Altered oral mucous membrane
H. High risk for activity intolerance
I. Pain
J. Anxiety

PLANNING AND IMPLEMENTATION

Goals

A. Optimal nutrition will be maintained.
B. Client will be free from infection.
C. Adequate cerebral and peripheral tissue perfusion will be maintained.
D. Client will maintain optimal respiratory function.
E. Client will maintain adequate protective mechanisms.
F. Optimal skin integrity will be maintained.
G. Client maintains optimal health of oral mucous membranes.
H. Client will have increased strength and endurance.
I. Client's pain will be relieved/controlled.
J. Client's anxiety will be relieved/reduced.

Interventions

Blood Transfusion and Component Therapy

A. Purpose: improve oxygen transport (RBCs); volume expansion (whole blood, plasma, albumin); provision of proteins (fresh frozen plasma, albumin, plasma protein fraction); provision of coagulation factors (cryoprecipitate, fresh frozen plasma, fresh whole blood); provision of platelets (platelet concentrate, fresh whole blood)

B. Blood and blood products
  1. Whole blood; provides all components
     a. Large volume can cause difficulty: 12–24 hours for Hgb and hct to rise
     b. Complications: volume overload, transmission of hepatitis or AIDS, transfusion reaction, infusion of excess potassium and sodium, infusion of anticoagulant (citrate) used to keep stored blood from clotting, calcium binding and depletion (citrate) in massive transfusion therapy
  2. Red blood cells
     a. Provide twice the amount of Hgb as an equivalent amount of whole blood
     b. Indicated in cases of blood loss, pre- and post-op clients, and those with incipient congestive failure
     c. Complications: transfusion reaction (less common than with whole blood due to removal of plasma proteins)
  3. Fresh frozen plasma
     a. Contains all coagulation factors including V and VIII
     b. Can be stored frozen for 12 months; takes 20 minutes to thaw
     c. Hang immediately upon arrival to unit (loses its coagulation factors rapidly)
  4. Platelets
     a. Will raise recipient's platelet count by 10,000/mm³
     b. Pooled from 4–8 units of whole blood
     c. Single-donor platelet transfusions may be necessary for clients who have developed antibodies; compatibility testing may be necessary
  5. Factor VIII fractions (cryoprecipitate): contains Factors VIII, fibrinogen, and XIII
  6. Granulocytes
     a. Do not increase WBC; increase marginal pool (at tissue level) rather than circulating pool
     b. Premedication with steroids, antihistamines, and acetaminophen
     c. Respiratory distress with shortness of breath, cyanosis, and chest pain may occur; requires cessation of transfusion and immediate attention
     d. Shaking chills or rigors common, require brief cessation of therapy, administration of meperidine IV until rigors are diminished, and resumption of transfusion when symptoms relieved
  7. Volume expanders: albumin; percentage concentration varies (50–100 ml/unit);

hyperosmolar solutions should not be used in dehydrated clients.

C. Nursing care
  1. Assess client for history of previous blood transfusions and any adverse reactions.
  2. Ensure that the adult client has an 18- or 19-gauge IV catheter in place.
  3. Use 0.9% sodium chloride.
  4. At least two nurses should verify the ABO group, Rh type, client and blood numbers, and expiration date.
  5. Take baseline vital signs before initiating transfusion.
  6. Start transfusion slowly (2 ml/minute).
  7. Stay with the client during the first 15 minutes of the transfusion and take vital signs frequently.
  8. Maintain the prescribed transfusion rate.
     a. Whole blood: approximately 3–4 hours
     b. RBCs: approximately 2–4 hours
     c. Fresh frozen plasma: as quickly as possible
     d. Platelets: as quickly as possible
     e. Cryoprecipitate: rapid infusion
     f. Granulocytes: usually over 2 hours
     g. Volume expanders: volume-dependent rate
  9. Monitor for adverse reactions (see Table 4.17, page 230).
  10. Document the following
     a. Blood component unit number (apply sticker if available)
     b. Date infusion starts and ends
     c. Type of component and amount transfused
     d. Client reaction and vital signs
     e. Signature of transfusionist

EVALUATION

A. Client maintains normal weight; no evidence of malnutrition.
B. Client's temperature is within normal range; no signs of infection.
C. Client neuro status is within normal limits.
D. Client demonstrates adequate peripheral capillary refill, sensation, and movement; palpable peripheral pulses; skin warm, dry, and usual color.
E. Client's respirations are of normal rate, rhythm, and depth; lungs clear to auscultation.
F. Client verbalizes signs and symptoms of infection and preventive measures; reports signs and symptoms of infection immediately.
G. Client's skin remains clear and intact.
H. Client's oral mucous membranes are healthy and intact.
I. Client experiences increased strength and endurance.

J. Client reports relief/control of pain.

K. Client expresses relief/reduction in anxiety.

DISORDERS OF THE HEMATOLOGIC SYSTEM

Anemias

Iron-deficiency Anemia

A. General information
1. Chronic microcytic, hypochromic anemia caused by either inadequate absorption or excessive loss of iron
2. Acute or chronic bleeding principal cause in adults (chiefly from trauma, excessive menses, and GI bleeding)
3. May also be caused by inadequate intake of iron-rich foods or by inadequate absorption of iron (from chronic diarrhea, malabsorption syndromes, high cereal-product intake with low animal protein ingestion, partial or complete gastrectomy, pica)
4. Incidence related to geographic location, economic class, age group, and sex
   a. More common in developing countries and tropical zones (blood-sucking parasites)
   b. Women between ages 15–45 and children affected more frequently, as are the poor
5. In iron-deficiency states, iron stores are depleted first, followed by a reduction in Hgb formation.

B. Assessment findings
1. Mild cases usually asymptomatic
2. Palpitations, dizziness, and cold sensitivity
3. Brittleness of hair and nails; pallor
4. Dysphagia, stomatitis, and atrophic glossitis
5. Dyspnea, weakness
6. Laboratory findings
   a. RBCs small (microcytic) and pale (hypochromic)
   b. Hgb markedly decreased
   c. Hct moderately decreased
   d. Serum iron markedly decreased
   e. Hemosiderin absent from bone marrow
   f. Serum ferritin decreased
   g. Reticulocyte count decreased

C. Nursing interventions
1. Monitor for signs and symptoms of bleeding through hematest of all elimination including stool, urine, and gastric contents.
2. Provide for adequate rest: plan activities so as not to overtire.
3. Provide a thorough explanation of all diagnostic tests used to determine sources of possible bleeding (helps allay anxiety and ensure cooperation).
4. Administer iron preparations as ordered.
   a. Oral iron preparations: route of choice
      1) give following meals or a snack.
      2) dilute liquid preparations well and administer using a straw to prevent staining teeth.
      3) when possible administer with orange juice as vitamin C (ascorbic acid) enhances iron absorption.
      4) warn clients that iron preparations will change stool color and consistency (dark and tarry) and may cause constipation.
   b. Parenteral: used in clients intolerant to oral preparations, who are noncompliant with therapy, or who have continuing blood losses.
      1) use one needle to withdraw and another to administer iron preparations as tissue staining and irritation are a problem.
      2) use the Z-track injection technique to prevent leakage into tissues (see page 18)
      3) do not massage injection site but encourage ambulation as this will enhance absorption; advise against vigorous exercise and constricting garments.
      4) observe for local signs of complications: pain at the injection site, development of sterile abscesses, lymphadenitis as well as fever, headache, urticaria, hypotension, or anaphylactic shock.
5. Provide dietary teaching regarding foods high in iron.
6. Encourage ingestion of roughage and increase fluid intake to prevent constipation if oral iron preparations are being taken.

Pernicious Anemia

A. General information
1. Chronic progressive, macrocytic anemia caused by a deficiency of intrinsic factor; the result is abnormally large erythrocytes and hypochlorhydria (a deficiency of hydrochloric acid in gastric secretions)
2. Characterized by neurologic and GI symptoms; death usually results if untreated
3. Lack of intrinsic factor is caused by gastric mucosal atrophy (possibly due to heredity, prolonged iron deficiency, or an autoimmune disorder); can also result in clients who have had a total gastrectomy if vitamin B_{12} not administered

4. Usually occurs in men and women over age 50, with an increase in blue-eyed persons of Scandinavian descent
5. Pathophysiology
   a. Intrinsic factor is necessary for the absorption of vitamin B_{12} into the small intestine.
   b. B_{12} deficiency diminishes DNA synthesis, which results in defective maturation of cells (particularly rapidly dividing cells such as blood cells and GI tract cells).
   c. B_{12} deficiency can alter structure and function of peripheral nerves, spinal cord, and the brain.

B. Medical management
   1. Drug therapy
      a. Vitamin B_{12} injections: monthly maintenance
      b. Iron preparations (if Hgb level inadequate to meet increased numbers of erythrocytes)
      c. Folic acid
         1) controversial
         2) reverses anemia and GI symptoms but may intensify neurologic symptoms
         3) may be safe if given in small amounts in addition to vitamin B_{12}
   2. Transfusion therapy

C. Assessment findings
   1. Anemia, weakness, pallor, dyspnea, palpitations, fatigue
   2. GI symptoms: sore mouth; smooth, beefy, red tongue; weight loss; dyspepsia; constipation or diarrhea; jaundice
   3. CNS symptoms; tingling, paresthesias of hands and feet, paralysis, depression, psychosis
   4. Laboratory tests
      a. Erythrocyte count decreased
      b. Blood smear: oval, macrocytic erythrocytes with a proportionate amount of Hgb
      c. Bone marrow
         1) increased megaloblasts (abnormal erythrocytes)
         2) few normoblasts or maturing erythrocytes
         3) defective leukocyte maturation
      d. Bilirubin (indirect): elevated unconjugated fraction
      e. Serum LDH elevated
      f. Positive *Schilling test*
         1) measures absorption of radioactive vitamin B_{12} both before and after parenteral administration of intrinsic factor
         2) definitive test for pernicious anemia
         3) used to detect lack of intrinsic factor
         4) fasting client is given radioactive vitamin B_{12} by mouth and nonradioactive vitamin B_{12} IM to saturate tissue binding sites and to permit some excretion of radioactive vitamin B_{12} in the urine if it is absorbed
         5) 24–48 hour urine collection is obtained; client is encouraged to drink fluids
         6) if indicated, second stage Schilling test performed 1 week after first stage. Fasting client is given radioactive vitamin B_{12} combined with human intrinsic factor and test is repeated.
      g. Gastric analysis: decreased free hydrochloric acid
      h. Large numbers of reticulocytes in the blood following parenteral vitamin B_{12} administration

D. Nursing interventions
   1. Provide a nutritious diet high in iron, protein, and vitamins (fish, meat, milk/milk products, and eggs).
   2. Avoid highly seasoned, coarse, or very hot foods if client has mouth sores.
   3. Provide mouth care before and after meals using a soft toothbrush and nonirritating rinses.
   4. Bed rest may be necessary if anemia is severe.
   5. Provide safety when ambulating (especially if carrying hot items, etc.)
   6. Provide client teaching and discharge planning concerning
      a. Dietary instruction
      b. Importance of lifelong vitamin B_{12} therapy
      c. Rehabilitation and physical therapy for neurologic deficits, as well as instruction regarding safety

Aplastic Anemia

A. General information
   1. Pancytopenia or depression of granulocyte, platelet, and erythrocyte production due to fatty replacement of the bone marrow
   2. Bone marrow destruction may be idiopathic or secondary
   3. Secondary aplastic anemia may be caused by
      a. Chemical toxins (e.g., benzene)
      b. Drugs (e.g., chloramphenicol, cytotoxic drugs)
      c. Radiation
      d. Immunologic injury

B. Medical management
   1. Blood transfusions (see page 232): key to therapy until client's own marrow begins to produce blood cells
   2. Aggressive treatment of infections

3. Bone marrow transplantation
4. Drug therapy
   a. Corticosteroids and/or androgens to stimulate bone marrow function and to increase capillary resistance (effective in children but usually not in adults)
   b. Estrogen and/or progesterone to prevent amenorrhea in female clients
5. Identification and withdrawal of offending agent or drug
C. Assessment findings
   1. Fatigue, dyspnea, pallor
   2. Increased susceptibility to infection
   3. Bleeding tendencies and hemorrhage
   4. Laboratory findings: normocytic anemia, granulocytopenia, thrombocytopenia
   5. Bone marrow biopsy: marrow is fatty and contains very few developing cells.
D. Nursing interventions
   1. Administer blood transfusions as ordered.
   2. Provide nursing care for client with bone marrow transplantation.
   3. Administer medications as ordered.
   4. Monitor for signs of infection and provide care to minimize risk.
      a. Maintain neutropenic precautions.
      b. Encourage high-protein, high-vitamin diet to help reduce incidence of infection.
      c. Provide mouth care before and after meals.
   5. Monitor for signs of bleeding and provide measures to minimize risk.
      a. Use a soft toothbrush and electric razor.
      b. Avoid intramuscular injections.
      c. Hematest urine and stool.
      d. Observe for oozing from gums, petechiae, or ecchymoses.
   6. Provide client teaching and discharge planning concerning
      a. Self-care regimen
      b. Identification of offending agent and importance of avoiding it (if possible) in future

Hemolytic Anemia

A. General information
   1. A category of diseases in which there is an increased rate of RBC destruction.
   2. May be congenital or acquired.
      a. Congenital: includes hereditary spherocytosis, G6PD deficiency, sickle cell anemia, thalassemia
      b. Acquired: includes transfusion incompatibilities, thrombotic thrombocytopenic purpura, disseminated intravascular clotting, spur cell anemia
   3. Cause often unknown, but erythrocyte life span is shortened and hemolysis occurs at a rate that the bone marrow cannot compensate for.
   4. The degree of anemia is determined by the lag between erythrocyte hemolysis and the rate of bone marrow erythropoiesis.
   5. Diagnosis is based on laboratory evidence of an increased rate of erythrocyte destruction and a corresponding compensatory effort by bone marrow to increase production.
B. Medical management
   1. Identify and eliminate (if possible) causative factors
   2. Drug therapy
      a. Corticosteroids in autoimmune types of anemia
      b. Folic acid supplements
   3. Blood transfusion therapy
   4. Splenectomy (see below)
C. Assessment findings
   1. Clinical manifestations vary depending on severity of anemia and the rate of onset (acute vs chronic)
   2. Pallor, scleral icterus, and slight jaundice (chronic)
   3. Chills, fever, irritability, precordial spasm, and pain (acute)
   4. Abdominal pain and nausea, vomiting, diarrhea, melena
   5. Hematuria, marked jaundice, and dyspnea
   6. Splenomegaly and symptoms of cholelithiasis, hepatomegaly
   7. Laboratory tests
      a. Hgb and hct decreased
      b. Reticulocyte count elevated (compensatory)
      c. Coombs' test (direct): positive if autoimmune features present
      d. Bilirubin (indirect): elevated unconjugated fraction
D. Nursing interventions
   1. Monitor for signs and symptoms of hypoxia including confusion, cyanosis, shortness of breath, tachycardia, and palpitations.
   2. Note that the presence of jaundice may make assessment of skin color in hypoxia unreliable.
   3. If jaundice and associated pruritus are present, avoid soap during bathing and use cool or tepid water.
   4. Frequent turning and meticulous skin care are important as skin friability is increased.
   5. Teach clients about the nature of the disease and identification of factors that predispose to episodes of hemolytic crisis.

Splenectomy

A. General information
   1. Indications
      a. Rupture of the spleen caused by

trauma, accidental tearing during surgery, diseases causing softening or damage (e.g., infectious mononucleosis)

    b. Hypersplenism: excessive splenic damage of cellular blood components

    c. As the spleen is a major source of antibody formation in children, splenectomy is not recommended during the early years of life; if absolutely necessary, client should receive prophylactic antibiotics post-op

  2. Primary hypersplenism can be alleviated with splenectomy; procedure is palliative only in secondary hypersplenism

B. Nursing interventions: pre-op

  1. Provide routine pre-op care and explain what to expect postoperatively.

  2. Administer pneumococcal vaccine as ordered since client will be at increased risk for pneumococcal infections for several years after splenectomy.

C. Nursing interventions: post-op

  1. Be aware that it is crucial to monitor carefully for hemorrhage and shock as clients with pre-op bleeding tendencies will remain at risk post-op.

  2. Monitor post-op temperature elevation: fever may not be the best indicator of post-op complications such as pneumonia or urinary tract infection, as fever without concomitant infection is common following splenectomy.

  3. Observe for abdominal distension and discomfort secondary to expansion of the intestines and stomach; an abdominal binder may reduce distension.

  4. Know that post-op infection in a child is considered life threatening; administer prophylactic antibiotics as ordered.

  5. Ambulate early and provide chest physical therapy as location of the incision makes post-op atelectasis or pneumonia a risk.

  6. Emphasize to client the need to report even minor signs or symptoms of infection immediately to the physician.

Sickle Cell Anemia

See page 395.

Disorders of Platelets and Clotting Mechanism

Disseminated Intravascular Coagulation (DIC)

A. General information

  1. Diffuse fibrin deposition within arterioles and capillaries with widespread coagulation all over the body and subsequent depletion of clotting factors.

  2. Hemorrhage from kidneys, brain, adrenals, heart, and other organs.

  3. Cause unknown

  4. Clients are usually critically ill with an obstetric, surgical, hemolytic, or neoplastic disease.

  5. May be linked with entry of thromboplastic substances into the blood.

  6. Pathophysiology

    a. Underlying disease (e.g., toxemia of pregnancy, cancer) causes release of thromboplastic substances that promote the deposition of fibrin throughout the microcirculation.

    b. Microthrombi form in many organs, causing microinfarcts and tissue necrosis.

    c. RBCs are trapped in fibrin strands and are hemolysed.

    d. Platelets, prothrombin, and other clotting factors are destroyed, leading to bleeding.

    e. Excessive clotting activates the fibrinolytic system, which inhibits platelet function, causing further bleeding.

  7. Mortality rate is high, usually because underlying disease cannot be corrected.

B. Medical management

  1. Identification and control of underlying disease is key

  2. Blood transfusions: include whole blood, packed RBCs, platelets, plasma, cryoprecipitates, and volume expanders

  3. Heparin administration

    a. Somewhat controversial

    b. Inhibits thrombin thus preventing further clot formation, allowing coagulation factors to accumulate

C. Assessment findings

  1. Petechiae and ecchymoses on the skin, mucous membranes, heart, lungs, and other organs

  2. Prolonged bleeding from breaks in the skin (e.g., IV or venipuncture sites)

  3. Severe and uncontrollable hemorrhage during childbirth or surgical procedures

  4. Oliguria and acute renal failure

  5. Convulsions, coma, death

  6. Laboratory findings

    a. PT prolonged

    b. PTT usually prolonged

    c. Thrombin time usually prolonged

    d. Fibrinogen level usually depressed

    e. Platelet count usually depressed

    f. Fibrin split products elevated

    g. Protamine sulfate test strongly positive

    h. Factor assays (II, V, VII) depressed

D. Nursing interventions

  1. Monitor blood loss and attempt to quantify.

2. Observe for signs of additional bleeding or thrombus formation.
3. Monitor appropriate laboratory data.
4. Prevent further injury.
    a. Avoid IM injections.
    b. Apply pressure to bleeding sites.
    c. Turn and position client frequently and gently.
    d. Provide frequent nontraumatic mouth care (e.g., soft toothbrush or gauze sponge).
5. Provide emotional support to client and significant others.
6. Administer blood transfusions and medications as ordered.
7. Teach client the importance of avoiding aspirin or aspirin-containing compounds.

Hemophilia

See page 397.

Idiopathic Thrombocytopenic Purpura

See page 397.

Immunologic Disorders

Acquired Immune Deficiency Syndrome (AIDS)

A. General information
  1. Characterized by severe deficits in cellular immune function; manifested clinically by opportunistic infections and/or unusual neoplasms
  2. Etiologic factors
    a. Results from infection with human immunodeficiency virus (HIV), a retrovirus that preferentially infects helper T-lymphocytes (T_4 cells)
    b. Transmissible through sexual contact, contaminated blood or blood products, and from infected woman to child in utero or possibly through breast-feeding
    c. HIV is present in an infected person's blood, semen, and other body fluids
  3. Epidemiology is similar to that of hepatitis B; increased incidence in populations in which sexual promiscuity is common and in IV drug abusers
B. Medical management
  1. No effective cure for AIDS at present; several categories of antiretroviral drugs now available
    a. Nucleoside Analogues: Didanosine (Videx) (ddl), Lamivudine (3TC) (Epivir), Stavudine (d4T) (Zerit), Zidovudine (AZT) (Retrovir)
    b. Nucleoside Analogues: Didanosine (Videx) (ddl), Lamivudine (3TC) (Epivir), Stavudine (d4T) (Zerit), Zidovudine (AZT) (Retrovir)
    c. Non Nucleoside Analogues: Delavirdine (DLV) (Rescriptor), Nevirapine (NVP) (Viramune)
    d. Protease Inhibitors: Indinavir (Crixivan), Nelfinavir (Viracept), Ritonavir (Norvir), Saquinavir (Invirase)
  2. Primary goal of treatment is to treat opportunistic infections and cancers that develop and provide supportive care for the effects of the disease, e.g., diarrhea, malnutrition, mental changes, etc.
  3. Drugs used to treat PCP include
    a. PO or IV trimethoprim-sulfamethoxazole (Bactrim, Septra); side effects include rash, leukopenia, fever
    b. IM or IV pentamidine (Pentam 300); side effects include hepatotoxicity, nephrotoxicity, blood sugar imbalances, abscess or necroses at IM injection site, hypotension
C. Assessment findings (see Table 4.18)
  1. Fatigue, weakness, anorexia, weight loss, diarrhea, pallor, fever, night sweats
  2. Shortness of breath, dyspnea, cough, chest pain, and progressive hypoxemia secondary to infection (pneumonia)
  3. Progressive weight loss secondary to anorexia, nausea, vomiting, diarrhea, and a general wasting syndrome; fatigue, malaise
  4. Temperature elevations (persistent or intermittent); night sweats
  5. Neurologic dysfunction secondary to acute meningitis, progressive dementia, encephalopathy, encephalitis
  6. Presence of opportunistic infection, for example
    a. *Pneumocystis carinii* pneumonia
    b. Herpes simplex, cytomegalovirus, and Epstein-Barr viruses
    c. Candidiasis: oral or esophageal
    d. Mycobacterium-avium complex
  7. Neoplasms
    a. Kaposi's sarcoma
    b. CNS lymphoma
    c. Burkitt's lymphoma
    d. Diffuse undifferentiated non-Hodgkin's lymphoma
  8. Laboratory findings: diagnosis based on clinical criteria and positive HIV antibody test—ELISA (enzyme-linked immunosorbent assay) confirmed by Western blot assay. Other lab findings may include
    a. Leukopenia with profound lymphopenia
    b. Anemia
    c. Thrombocytopenia

TABLE 4.18 Classification System for HIV Infection

CD4 + T-cell categories	A Asymptomatic, acute HIV or PGL	B Symptomatic, not (A) or (C) conditions	C AIDS-indicator conditions
(1) 500/uL	A1	B1	C1
(2) 200–499/uL	A2	B2	C2
(3) <200/uL	A3	B3	C3

Clinical Category A	Clinical Category B	Clinical Category C
1 or more of the following, confirmed HIV infection, and without conditions in B and C • Asymptomatic HIV infection • Persistent Generalized Lymphadenopathy (PGL) • Acute (primary) HIV infection with accompanying illness or history of acute HIV infection	• Candidiasis (oral or vaginal), frequent or poorly resistant to therapy • Cervical dysplasia/cervical carcinoma in situ • Fever or diarrhea exceeding 1 month • Hairy leukoplakia, oral • Herpes zoster, involving 2 episodes or more than one dermatome • ITP • PID • Peripheral neuropathy	• Candidiasis of bronchi, trachea, or lungs • Cervical cancer, invasive • Coccidiomycosis • Cryptosporidiosis • Cytomegalovirus • Encephalopathy • Herpes simplex: chronic ulcer - exceeding 1 month duration • Histoplasmosis • Kaposi's sarcoma • Lymphoma • Mycobacterium - avium complex • Mycobacterium tuberculosis • Pneumocystis carinii pneumonia • Salmonella • Toxoplasmosis of brain • Wasting syndrome due to HIV

Adapted from Centers for Disease Control, U.S. Dept. of Health and Human Services, 1993 revised classification system for HIV infections and expanded surveillance case definition for AIDS among adolescents and adults.

    d. Decreased circulatory T_4 lymphocyte cells

    e. Low T_4:T_8 lymphocyte ratio

D. Nursing interventions

1. Administer medications as ordered for concomitant disease; monitor for signs of medication toxicity.
2. Monitor respiratory status; provide care as appropriate for respiratory problems, e.g., pneumonia.
3. Assess neurological status; reorient client as needed; provide safety measures for the confused/disoriented client.
4. Assess for signs and symptoms of fluid and electrolyte imbalances; monitor lab studies; ensure adequate hydration.
5. Monitor client's nutritional intake; provide supplements, total parenteral nutrition, etc., as ordered.
6. Assess skin daily (especially perianal area) for signs of breakdown; keep skin clean and dry; turn q4 hours while in bed.
7. Inspect oral cavity daily for ulcerations, signs of infection; instruct client to rinse mouth with normal saline and hydrogen peroxide or normal saline and sodium bicarbonate rinses.
8. Observe for signs and symptoms of infection; report immediately if any occur.
9. If severe leukopenia develops, institute neutropenic precautions

    a. Prevent trauma to skin and mucous membranes, e.g., avoid enemas, rectal temperatures; minimize all parenteral infections

    b. Do not place client in a room with clients having infections

    c. Screen visitors for colds, infections, etc.

    d. Do not allow fresh fruits, vegetables, or plants in client's room.

    e. Mask client when leaving room for walks, x-rays, etc.

10. Institute blood and body fluid precautions (see page 141)
11. Provide emotional support for client/significant others; help to decrease sense of isolation
12. Provide client teaching and discharge planning concerning

    a. Importance of observing for signs of infections and notifying physician immediately if any occur

    b. Ways to reduce chance of infection

       1) Clean kitchen and bathroom surfaces regularly with disinfectants.

       2) Avoid direct contact with pet's litter boxes or stool, bird cage droppings, and water in fish tanks.

       3) Avoid contact with people with infections, e.g., cold, flu.

      4) Importance of balancing activity
         with rest.
      5) Need to eat a well-balanced diet
         with plenty of fluids.
   c. Prevention of disease transmission
      1) Use safer sex practices, e.g.,
         condoms for sexual intercourse.
      2) Do not donate blood, semen,
         organs.
      3) Do not share razors, toothbrushes,
         or other items that may draw blood.
      4) Inform all physicians, dentists,
         sexual partners of diagnosis.
   d. Resources include Public Health
     Service, National Gay Task Force,
     American Red Cross, local support
     groups

Malignancies

Multiple Myeloma

A. General information
1. A neoplastic condition characterized by the abnormal proliferation of plasma cells in the bone marrow, causing the development of single or multiple tumors composed of abnormal plasma cells. Disease disseminates into lymph nodes, liver, spleen, and kidneys and causes bone destruction throughout the body.
2. Cause unknown, but environmental factors thought to be involved
3. Disease occurs after age 40; affects men twice as often as women
4. Pathophysiology
   a. Bone demineralization and destruction with osteoporosis and a negative calcium balance
   b. Disruption of erythrocyte, leukocyte, and thrombocyte production
B. Medical management
1. Drug therapy
   a. Analgesics for bone pain
   b. Chemotherapy (melphalan [Alkeran] and cyclophosphamide [Cytoxan]) to reduce tumor mass; may intensify the pancytopenia to which these clients are prone; requires careful monitoring of laboratory studies
   c. Antibiotics to treat infections
   d. Gammaglobulin for infection prophylaxis
   e. Corticosteroids and mithramycin for severe hypercalcemia
2. Radiation therapy to reduce tumor mass and for palliation of bone pain
3. Transfusion therapy
C. Assessment findings
1. Headache and bone pain increasing with activity
2. Pathologic fractures

3. Skeletal deformities of sternum and ribs
4. Loss of height (spinal column shortening)
5. Osteoporosis
6. Renal calculi
7. Anemia, hemorrhagic tendencies, and increased susceptibility to infection
8. Hypercalcemia
9. Renal dysfunction secondary to obstruction of convoluted tubules by coagulated protein particles
10. Neurologic dysfunction: spinal cord compression and paraplegia
11. Laboratory tests
   a. Radiologic: diffuse bone lesions, widespread demineralization, osteoporosis, osteolytic lesions of skull
   b. Bone marrow; many immature plasma cells; depletion of other cell types
   c. CBC: reduced Hgb, WBC, and platelet counts
   d. Serum globulins elevated
   e. Bence-Jones protein: positive (abnormal globulin that appears in the urine of clients with multiple myeloma and other bone tumors)
D. Nursing interventions
1. Provide comfort measures to help alleviate bone pain.
2. Encourage ambulation to slow demineralization process.
3. Promote safety as clients are prone to pathologic and other fractures.
4. Encourage fluids: 3000–4000 ml/day to counteract calcium overload and to prevent protein from precipitating in the renal tubules.
5. Provide nursing care for clients with bleeding tendencies and susceptibility to infection.
6. Provide a supportive atmosphere to enhance communication and reduce anxiety.
7. Provide client teaching and discharge planning concerning
   a. Crucial importance of long-term hydration to prevent urolithiasis and renal obstruction
   b. Safety measures vital to decrease the risk of injury
   c. Avoidance of crowds or sources of infection if leukopenic

Polycythemia Vera

A. General information
1. An increase in both the number of circulating erythrocytes and the concentration of Hgb within the blood
2. Three forms: polycythemia vera, secondary polycythemia, and relative polycythemia
3. Classified as a myeloproliferative disorder (bone marrow overgrowth)

4. Cause unknown, but thought to be a form of malignancy similar to leukemia
5. Usually develops in middle age, common in Jewish men
6. Pathophysiology
   a. A pronounced increase in the production of erythrocytes accompanied by an increase in the production of myelocytes (leukocytes within bone marrow) and thrombocytes.
   b. The consequences of this overproduction are an increase in blood viscosity, an increase in total blood volume (2–3 times greater than normal), and severe congestion of all tissues and organs with blood.

B. Assessment findings
1. Ruddy complexion and duskiness of mucosa secondary to capillary congestion in the skin and mucous membranes
2. Hypertension associated with vertigo, headache, and "fullness" in the head secondary to increased blood volume
3. Symptoms of CHF secondary to overwork of the heart
4. Thrombus formation: CVA, MI, gangrene of the extremities, DVT, and pulmonary embolism can occur
5. Bleeding and hemorrhage secondary to congestion and overdistension of capillaries and venules
6. Hepatomegaly and splenomegaly
7. Peptic ulcer secondary to increased gastric secretions
8. Gout secondary to increased uric acid released by nucleoprotein breakdown
9. Laboratory tests
   a. CBC: increase in all mature cell forms (erythrocytes, leukocytes, and platelets)
   b. Hct: increased
   c. Bone marrow: increase in immature cell forms
   d. Bilirubin (indirect): increase in unconjugated fraction
   e. Liver enzymes may be increased
   f. Uric acid increased
   g. Hematuria and melena possible

C. Nursing interventions
1. Monitor for signs and symptoms of bleeding complications.
2. Force fluids and record I&O.
3. Prevent development of DVT.
4. Monitor for signs and symptoms of CHF.
5. Provide care for the client having a phlebotomy.
6. Prevent/provide care for bleeding or infection complications.
7. Administer medications as ordered.
   a. Radioactive phosphorus (^{32}P): reduction of erythrocyte production, produces a remission of 6 months to 2 years
   b. Nitrogen mustard, busulfan (Myleran), chlorambucil, cyclophosphamide to effect myelosuppression
   c. Antigout and peptic ulcer drugs as needed.
8. Provide client teaching and discharge planning concerning
   a. Decrease in activity tolerance, need to space activity with periods of rest
   b. Phlebotomy regimens: outpatient frequency is determined by hct; importance of long-term therapy
   c. High fluid intake
   d. Avoidance of iron-rich foods to avoid counteracting the therapeutic effects of phlebotomy
   e. Recognition and reporting of bleeding
   f. Need to avoid persons with infections, especially in leukopenic clients.

Leukemia

See page 437.

Hodgkin's and Non-Hodgkin's Lymphoma

See page 440.

Sample Questions

53. Ms. C. is admitted to the hospital with a bleeding ulcer. She is to receive 4 units of packed cells. Which nursing intervention is of PRIMARY importance in the administration of blood?
    1. Checking the flow rate.
    2. Identifying the client.
    3. Monitoring the vital signs.
    4. Maintaining blood temperature.
54. Within 20 minutes of the start of transfusion, the client develops a sudden fever. The most appropriate INITIAL response by the nurse is to
    1. force fluids.
    2. continue to monitor the vital signs.
    3. increase the flow rate of IV fluids.
    4. stop the transfusion.
55. Mr. S., 37 years old, is admitted to the hospital with fever, cough, chills, and shortness of breath. A nursing assessment reveals that he has a history of experimenting with IV drugs and has had several intimate relationships with men. A diagnostic work-up reveals that he is HIV positive and that he has *Pneumocystis carinii* pneumonia. When the nurse assessing the client with AIDS has a negative attitude about the client's life-style, which action is most appropriate?
    1. Share these feelings with the client.

2. Develop a written interview form.
3. Cancel the assessment.
4. Tell other health-care professionals the information may be biased.

56. The client at risk for developing AIDS should be advised to
1. abstain from anal intercourse.
2. have an ELISA test for antibodies.
3. have a semen analysis done.
4. inform all sexual contacts.

57. A young man is admitted to the hospital with *Pneumocystic carinii* pneumonia. He is HIV positive. Part of the nursing assessment for this client is an examination of his mouth for which oral problem commonly associated with AIDS?
1. Halitosis.
2. Carious teeth.
3. Creamy white patches.
4. Swollen lips.

58. The nurse is caring for a client who is HIV positive. To prevent the spread of the HIV virus while caring for her, the nurse will implement the Centers for Disease Control and Prevention (CDC) recommendations for
1. universal blood and body fluid precautions.
2. laminar flow rooms during active infection.
3. body systems isolation.
4. needle and syringe precautions.

Answers and Rationales

53. The correct answer is 2. The most important consideration in transfusion therapy is to give the correct blood product to the correct client. Maintaining blood temperature prevents bacterial proliferation, checking flow rate prevents circulatory overload, and monitoring vital signs assesses the client's reaction to therapy. However, giving blood to the wrong client results in ABO and Rh incompatibilities, which can be fatal.

54. The correct answer is 4. Sudden development of fever during a blood transfusion may be indicative of a pyrogenic reaction. The most appropriate nursing action is to discontinue the blood flow to prevent a more severe reaction. The nurse will continue to monitor the vital signs; however, this is not the initial action. Forcing fluids and increasing the flow rate of IV fluids may be appropriate at a later time if hypotension occurs.

55. The correct answer is 4. When obtaining a sexual history it is important to communicate an attitude of trust and acceptance. If the nurse performing the assessment recognizes that personal feelings are biasing the accuracy of the assessment, then it is necessary to share this with other health care professionals. This provides the client with the opportunity to communicate with another nurse who will obtain a more accurate assessment. This strategy also provides the nurse with the opportunity to seek the counsel of others. It would not be appropriate to share these feelings with the client. The nurse should use a nonjudgmental approach to clients. Having the client fill out an interview form is too impersonal and prevents the nurse from developing a therapeutic relationship with the client. The nursing assessment must be obtained.

56. The correct answer is 2. The ELISA test detects the presence of antibodies to the AIDS virus and is a useful screening tool. It is not a definitive diagnostic test but provides additional information for the high-risk individual. It would be recommended that the client refrain from all unprotected intercourse. A semen analysis would tell nothing of HIV status. It would not be necessary to inform all sexual contacts at this time.

57. The correct answer is 3. Creamy white patches indicating an opportunistic infection (candidiasis) are often seen in the client with AIDS. The client may have halitosis (bad breath) due to an oral infection, but this is not commonly associated with AIDS. Cavities may be present in the teeth but this is not commonly associated with AIDS. Swollen lips are not typically associated with AIDS.

58. The correct answer is 1. Universal blood and body fluid precautions, general infection control routines, and disease-specific measures are recommended by the CDC for AIDS and AIDS-related infections. A laminar flow room filters air as it enters the room and provides protective isolation for the immunosuppressed client. This is not necessary to prevent the spread of the HIV virus. There is no such intervention as body systems isolation. Needle and syringe precautions are included in the universal blood and body fluid precautions.

The Respiratory System

OVERVIEW OF ANATOMY AND PHYSIOLOGY

Upper Respiratory Tract

Structures of the respiratory system, primarily an air conduction system, include the nose, pharynx, and larynx. Air is filtered, warmed, and humidified in the upper airway before passing to lower airway (see Figure 4.10).

Nose

A. External nose is a framework of bone and cartilage, internally divided into two passages or *nares* (*nasal cavities*) by the septum; air enters the system through the nares.
B. The septum is covered with a mucous membrane, where the olfactory receptors are located. Turbinates, located internally, assist in warming and moistening the air.
C. The major functions of the nose are warming, moistening, and filtering the air.

Pharynx

A. Muscular passageway commonly called the throat.
B. Air passes through the nose to the pharynx, composed of three sections
   1. *Nasopharynx:* located above the soft palate of the mouth, contains the adenoids and openings to the eustachian tubes.
   2. *Oropharynx:* located directly behind the mouth and tongue, contains the palatine tonsils; air and food enter body through oropharynx.
   3. *Laryngopharynx:* extends from the epiglottis to the sixth cervical level.

Larynx

A. Sometimes called "voice box," connects upper and lower airways; framework is formed by the hyoid bone, epiglottis, and thyroid, cricoid, and arytenoid cartilages. The opening of the larynx is called the glottis.
B. Larynx opens to allow respiration and closes to prevent aspiration when food passes through the pharynx.
C. Vocal cords of larynx permit speech and are involved in the cough reflex.

Lower Respiratory Tract

Consists of the trachea, bronchi and branches, and the lungs and associated structures (see Figure 4.10).

Trachea

A. Air moves from the pharynx to larynx to trachea (length 11–13 cm, diameter 1.5–2.5 cm in adult).
B. Extends from the larynx to the second costal cartilage, where it bifurcates and is supported by 16–20 C-shaped cartilage rings.
C. The area where the trachea divides into two branches is called the *carina*.

Bronchi

A. Formed by the division of the trachea into two branches (bronchi)
   1. *Right mainstem bronchus:* larger and straighter than the left; further divides into

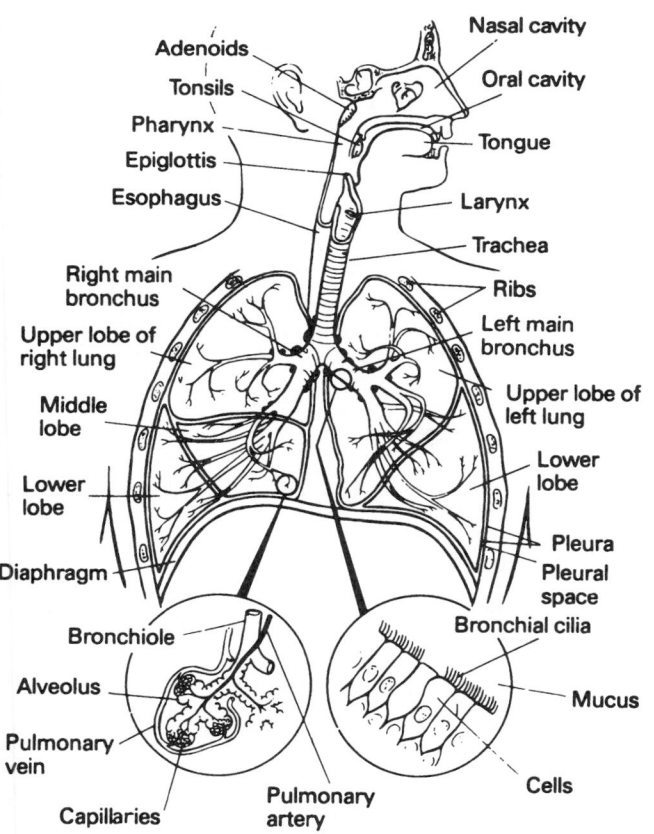

FIGURE 4.10 The respiratory system (Reproduced with permission from Basics of RD, New York, The American Lung Association, 1980)

three lobar branches (upper, middle, and lower lobar bronchi) to supply the three lobes of right lung. If passed too far, endotracheal tube might enter right mainstem bronchus; only right lung is then intubated.
   2. *Left mainstem bronchus:* divides into the upper and lower lobar bronchi, to supply two lobes of left lung.
B. At the point a bronchus reaches about 1 mm in diameter it no longer has a connective tissue sheath and is called a *bronchiole.*

Bronchioles

A. In the bronchioles, airway patency is primarily dependent upon elastic recoil formed by network of smooth muscles.
B. The tracheobronchial tree ends at the terminal bronchioles. Distal to the terminal bronchioles the major function is no longer air conduction, but gas exchange between blood and alveolar air. The *respiratory bronchioles* serve as the transition to the alveolar epithelium.

Lungs (Right and Left)

A. Main organs of respiration, lie within the thoracic cavity on either side of the heart.
B. Broad area of lung resting on diaphragm is called the base; the narrow, superior portion is the apex.
C. Each lung is divided into lobes: three in the right lung, two in the left.
D. *Pleura:* serous membrane covering the lungs; continuous with the parietal pleura that lines the chest wall.
E. Lungs and associated structures are protected by the chest wall.

Chest Wall

A. Includes the rib cage, intercostal muscles, and diaphragm.
B. Parietal pleura lines the chest wall and secretes small amounts of lubricating fluid into the intrapleural space (space between the visceral and parietal pleura). This fluid holds the lung and chest wall together as a single unit while allowing them to move separately.
C. The chest is shaped and supported by 12 pairs of ribs and costal cartilages; the ribs have several attached muscles.
   1. Contraction of the external intercostal muscles raises the rib cage during inspiration and helps increase the size of the thoracic cavity.
   2. The internal intercostal muscles tend to pull ribs down and in and play a role in forced expiration.
D. The *diaphragm* is the major muscle of ventilation (the exchange of air between the atmosphere and the alveoli). Contraction of muscle fibers causes the dome of the diaphragm to descend, thereby increasing the volume of the thoracic cavity. As exertion increases, additional chest muscles or even abdominal muscles may be employed in moving the thoracic cage.

Pulmonary Circulation

A. Provides for reoxygenation of blood and release of CO_2; gas transfer occurs in the pulmonary capillary bed.
B. Pulmonary arteries arise from the right ventricle of the heart and continue to the bronchi and alveoli, gradually decreasing in size to capillaries.
C. The capillaries, after contact with the gas-exchange surface of the alveoli, reform to form the pulmonary veins.
D. The two pulmonary veins, superior and inferior, empty into the left atrium.

Gas Exchange

Alveolar Ducts and Alveoli

A. Alveolar ducts arise from the respiratory bronchioles and lead to the alveoli.
B. *Alveoli* are the functional cellular units of the lungs; about half arise directly from the alveolar ducts and are responsible for about 35% of alveolar gas exchange.
C. Alveoli produce *surfactant,* a phospholipid substance found in the fluid lining the alveolar epithelium. Surfactant reduces surface tension and increases the stability of the alveoli and prevents their collapse.
D. *Alveolar sacs* form the last part of the airway; functionally the same as the alveolar ducts, they are surrounded by alveoli and are responsible for 65% of the alveolar gas exchange.

ASSESSMENT

Health History

A. Presenting problem
   1. Nose/nasal sinuses: symptoms may include colds, discharge, epistaxis, sinus problems (swelling, pain)
   2. Throat: symptoms may include sore throat, hoarseness, difficulty swallowing, strep throat
   3. Lungs: symptoms may include
      a. Cough: note duration; frequency; type (dry, hacking, bubbly, barky, hoarse, congested); sputum (productive vs nonproductive); circumstances related to cough (time of day, positions, talking, anxiety); treatment.

  b. Dyspnea: note onset, severity, duration, efforts to treat, whether associated with radiation, if accompanied by cough or diaphoresis, time of day when it most likely occurs, interference with ALD, whether precipitated by any specific activities, whether accompanied by cyanosis.

  c. Wheezing

  d. Chest pain

  e. Hemoptysis

B. Life-style: smoking (note type of tobacco, duration, number per day, number of years of smoking, inhalation, related cough, desire to quit); occupation (work conditions that could irritate respiratory system [asbestos, chemical irritants, dry-cleaning fumes] and monitoring or protection of exposure conditions), geographical location (environmental conditions that could irritate respiratory system [chemical plants/industrial pollutants]); type and frequency of exercise/recreation.

C. Nutrition/diet: fluid intake per 24-hour period; intake of vitamins

D. Past medical history: immunizations (yearly immunizations for colds/flu; frequency and results of tuberculin skin testing); allergies (foods, drugs, contact or inhalant allergens, precipitating factors, specific treatment, desensitization)

Physical Examination

A. Inspect for configuration of the chest (kyphosis, scoliosis, barrel chest) and cyanosis.

B. Determine rate and pattern of breathing (normal rate 12–18/minute); note tachypnea, hyperventilation, or labored breathing pattern.

C. Palpate skin, subcutaneous structures, and muscles for texture, temperature, and degree of development.

D. Palpate for tracheal position, respiratory excursion (symmetric or asymmetric movement of the chest), and for fremitus.

  1. Fremitus is normally increased in intensity at second intercostal spaces at sternal border and interscapular spaces only.

  2. Increased intensity elsewhere may indicate pneumonia, pulmonary fibrosis, or tumor.

  3. Decreased intensity may indicate pneumothorax, pleural effusion, COPD.

E. Percuss lung fields (should find resonance over normal lung tissue, note hyperresonance or dullness) and for diaphragmatic excursion (normal distance between levels of dullness on full expiration and full inspiration is 6–12 cm).

F. Auscultate for normal (vesicular, bronchial, bronchovesicular) and adventitious (rales or crackles, rhonchi, pleural friction rub) breath sounds (see Figure 4.11).

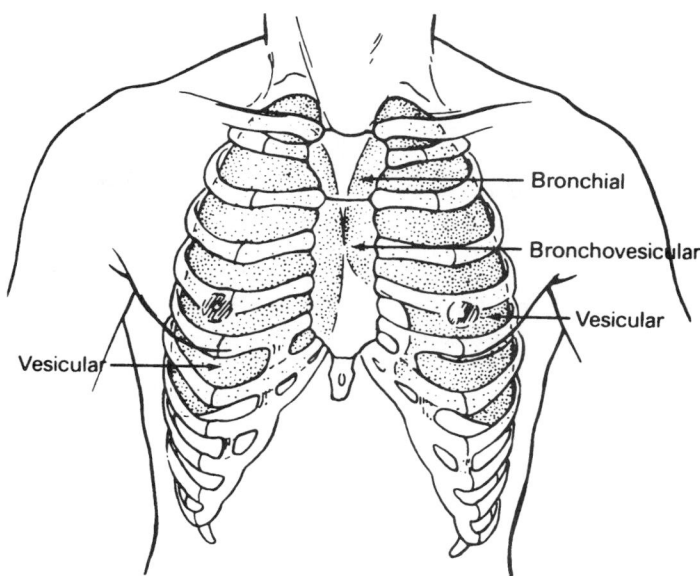

FIGURE 4.11 Locations for hearing normal breath sounds

Laboratory/Diagnostic Tests

A. *Arterial blood gases* (*ABGs*)

  1. Measure base excess/deficit, blood pH, CO_2, total CO_2, O_2 content, O_2 saturation (SaO_2), pCO_2 (partial pressure of carbon dioxide), pO_2 (partial pressure of oxygen)

  2. Nursing care

   a. If drawn by arterial stick, place a 4×4 bandage over puncture site after withdrawal of needle and maintain pressure with two fingers for at least 2 minutes.

   b. Gently rotate sample in test tube to mix heparin with the blood.

   c. Place sample in ice-water container until it can be analyzed.

B. *Pulmonary function studies*

  1. Evaluation of lung volume and capacities by spirometry: tidal volume (TV), vital capacity (VC), inspiratory and expiratory reserve volume (IRV and ERV), residual volume (RV), inspiratory capacity (IC), functional residual capacity (FRC)

  2. Involves use of a spirometer to diagram movement of air as client performs various respiratory maneuvers; shows restriction or obstruction to air flow, or both.

  3. Nursing care

   a. Carefully explaining procedure will help allay anxiety and ensure cooperation.

   b. Perform tests before meals.

   c. Withhold medication that may alter respiratory function unless otherwise ordered.

   d. After procedure assess pulse and provide for rest period.

C. Hematologic studies (ESR, Hgb and hct, WBC)
D. *Sputum culture and sensitivity*
  1. Culture: isolation and identification of specific microorganism from a specimen
  2. Sensitivity: determination of antibiotic agent effective against organism (sensitive or resistant)
  3. Nursing care
     a. Explain necessity of effective coughing.
     b. If client unable to cough, heated aerosol will assist with obtaining a specimen.
     c. Collect specimen in a sterile container that can be capped afterwards.
     d. Volume need not exceed 1–3 ml.
     e. Deliver specimen to lab rapidly.
E. *Tuberculin skin test*
  1. Intradermal test done to detect tuberculosis infection; does not differentiate active from dormant infections
  2. Purified protein derivative (PPD) tuberculin administered to determine any previous sensitization to tubercle bacillus
  3. Several methods of administration
     a. *Mantoux test:* 0.1 ml solution containing 0.5 tuberculin units of PPD-tuberculin is injected into the forearm.
     b. *Tine test:* a stainless steel disc with 4 tines impregnated with PPD-tuberculin is pressed into the skin.
  4. Results: read within 48–72 hours; inspect skin and circle zone of induration with a pencil; measure diameter in mm
     a. Negative: zone diameter less than 5 mm
     b. Doubtful or probable: zone diameter 5–10 mm
     c. Positive: zone diameter 10 mm or more
F. *Thoracentesis*
  1. Insertion of a needle through the chest wall into the pleural space to obtain a specimen for diagnostic evaluation, removal of pleural fluid accumulation, or to instill medication into the pleural space
  2. Nursing care: pretest
     a. Confirm that a signed permit has been obtained.
     b. Explain procedure; instruct client not to cough or talk during procedure.
     c. Position client at side of bed, with upper torso supported on overbed table, feet and legs well supported.
     d. Assess vital signs.
  3. Nursing care: posttest
     a. Observe for signs and symptoms of pneumothorax, shock, leakage at puncture site.
     b. Auscultate chest to ascertain breath sounds.
G. *Bronchoscopy*
  1. Insertion of a fiberscope into the bronchi for diagnosis, biopsy, specimen collection, examination of structures/tissues, removal of foreign bodies
  2. Nursing care: pretest
     a. Confirm that a signed permit has been obtained.
     b. Explain procedure, remove dentures, and provide good oral hygiene.
     c. Keep client NPO 6–12 hours pretest.
  3. Nursing care posttest
     a. Position client on side or in semi-Fowler's.
     b. Keep NPO until return of gag reflex.
     c. Assess for and report frank bleeding.
     d. Apply ice bags to throat for comfort; discourage talking, coughing, smoking for a few hours to decrease irritation.

ANALYSIS

Nursing diagnoses for the client with a respiratory dysfunction may include
A. Impaired gas exchange
B. Ineffective airway clearance
C. Ineffective breathing pattern
D. Impaired verbal communication
E. Activity intolerance
F. Anxiety
G. Altered nutrition: less than body requirements
H. Risk for infection

PLANNING AND IMPLEMENTATION

Goals

A. Adequate ventilation will be maintained.
B. Maintenance of patent airway.
C. Effective breathing patterns will be maintained.
D. Client will communicate in an effective manner.
E. Client will demonstrate increased tolerance for activity.
F. Anxiety will be reduced.
G. Adequate nutritional status will be maintained.
H. Client remains free from infection.

Interventions

Chest Tubes/Water-seal Drainage

A. Insertion of a catheter into the intrapleural space to maintain constant negative pressure when air/fluid have accumulated.
B. Chest tube is attached to underwater drainage to allow for the escape of air/fluid and to prevent reflux of air into the chest.
C. For evacuation of air, chest tube is placed in the second or third intercostal space, anterior or midaxillary line (air rises to the upper chest).
D. For drainage of fluid, chest tube is placed in the eighth or ninth intercostal space, midaxillary line.

E. Chest tube is connected to tubing for the collection system; the distal end of the collection tubing must be placed below the water level in order to prevent atmospheric air from entering the pleural space.

F. Drainage systems: a water-seal drainage system can be set up using one, two, or three bottles; or a commercial, disposable device (e.g., Pleur-evac®) may be used.
    1. *One-bottle system* (Figure 4.12A)
        a. Operates by gravity, not suction; the bottle serves as both collection chamber and water seal.
        b. Two hollow tubes (glass rods) are inserted into the stopper of the bottle; the drainage tube is connected to the glass rod that is submerged approximately 2 cm below the water level; the second glass tube allows for the escape of air.
        c. If considerable drainage accumulates it is difficult for the client to expel air and fluid from the pleural space. If this occurs, the glass rod may be pulled up or a new drainage bottle may be set up (according to physician's orders).
    2. *Two-bottle system* (Figure 4.12B,C)
        a. One bottle serves as a drainage collection chamber, the other as a water seal.
        b. The first bottle is the drainage collection chamber and has two short tubes in the rubber stopper. One of these tubes is attached to the drainage tubing coming from the client; the other is attached to the underwater tube of the second bottle (the water-seal bottle). The air vent of the water-seal bottle must be left open to atmospheric air. If suction is used, the first bottle serves as drainage collection and water-seal chamber, and the second bottle serves as the suction chamber.
    3. *Three-bottle system* (Figure 4.12D)
        a. This system has a drainage collection, a water-seal, and a suction-control bottle.
        b. The third bottle controls the amount of pressure in the system. The suction-control bottle has three tubes inserted in the stopper, two short and one long. One short tube is joined with the tubing to the former air vent of the water-seal bottle; the second short tube is connected to suction. The third (long) tube (or suction-control tube) is located between the short tubes and has one end open to the atmosphere and the other below the water level.
        c. The depth to which the suction-control tube is immersed controls the amount of pressure within the system. The pressure is determined by the physician.

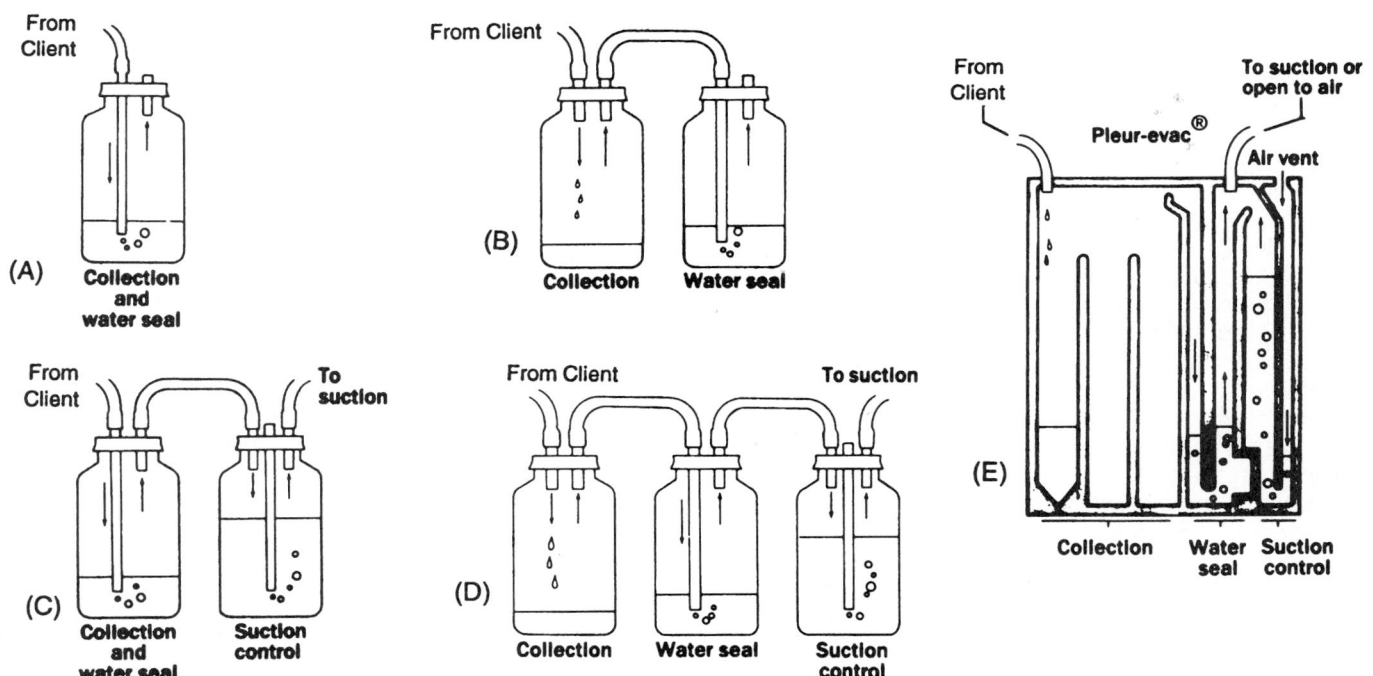

FIGURE 4.12 Water-seal drainage systems: (A) one-bottle system; (B) two-bottle system without suction; (C) two-bottle system with suction; (D) three-bottle system; (E) Pleur-evac®. Adapted from "You can manage chest tubes confidently," by B. Mims, RN, 48(1), 39–44.

4. *Commercial water-seal units:* most popular is *Pleur-evac®* (Figure 4.12E); lightweight, disposable; functions like a three-bottle system, may be used with or without suction.
G. Nursing care: without suction
 1. Prepare the unit for use and connect the chest catheter to the drainage tubing.
 2. Examine the entire system to ensure airtightness and absence of obstruction from kinks or dependent loops of tubing.
 3. Note oscillation of the fluid level within the water-seal tube. It will rise on inspiration and fall on expiration due to changes in the intrapleural pressure. If oscillation stops and system is intact, notify physician.
 4. Check the amount, color, and characteristics of the drainage. If drainage ceases and system is not blocked, assess for signs of respiratory distress from fluid/air accumulation.
 5. Always keep drainage system lower than the level of the client's chest.
 6. Keep Vaseline gauze at bedside at all times in case chest tube falls out.
 7. Encourage coughing and deep breathing to facilitate removal of air and drainage from pleural cavity.
 8. Provide ROM exercises.
H. Nursing care: with suction
 1. Attach suction tubing to suction apparatus, and chest catheter to drainage tubing.
 2. Open suction slowly until a stream of bubbles is seen in the suction chamber. There should be continuous bubbling in this chamber and intermittent bubbling in the water seal. Check for an air leak in the system if bubbling in water seal is constant; notify physician if air leak.
 3. Check drainage, keep drainage system below level of client's chest, keep Vaseline gauze at bedside, encourage coughing and deep breathing, and provide ROM exercises as noted above.
I. Never clamp chest tubes unless a specific order is written by the physician. Clamping the chest tubes of a client with air in the pleural space will cause increased pressure buildup and possible tension pneumothorax.
J. Removal of the chest tube: instruct the client to perform Valsalva maneuver; apply a Vaseline pressure dressing to the site.
K. If the water-seal bottle should break, immediately obtain some type of fluid-filled container to create an emergency water seal until a new unit can be obtained.

Heimlich Flutter Valve

A. This disposable valve allows a unidirectional flow of air and fluid from the pleural space into a drainage bag and prevents any reflux of air or fluid. A water-seal drainage system is not necessary.
B. Controlled suction can be attached if ordered.
C. The valve is encased in clear plastic, which eliminates the possibility of kinks. Its small size, approximately 7 inches, permits greater mobility.

Chest Physiotherapy

A. General information
 1. Used for individuals with increased production of secretions or thick, sticky secretions, and for clients with impaired removal of secretions or with ineffective cough. May also be used as a preventive measure for clients with weakness of the muscles of respiration or a predisposition to increased production or thickness of secretions.
 2. Includes the techniques of postural drainage, percussion, and vibration.
  a. *Postural drainage:* uses gravity and various positions to stimulate the movement of secretions.
   1) postural drainage positions are determined by the areas of involved lung, assessed by chest x-ray and physical assessment findings.
   2) careful positioning is required to help secretions flow from smaller airways into the segmental bronchus and larger airways where secretions can be coughed up.
  b. *Percussion:* involves clapping with cupped hands on the chest wall over the segment to be drained.
   1) the hand is cupped by holding the fingers together so that the shape of the hand conforms with chest wall.
   2) clapping should be vigorous but not painful.
  c. *Vibration:* in this technique the hand is pressed firmly over the appropriate segment of chest wall, and muscles of upper arm and shoulder are tensed (isometric contraction); done with flattened, not cupped hand.
B. Nursing care
 1. Perform procedure before or 3 hours after meals.
 2. Administer bronchodilators about 20 minutes before procedure.
 3. Remove all tight/constricting clothing.
 4. Have all equipment available (tissues, emesis basin, towel, paper bag).
 5. Assist client to correct prescribed position for postural drainage (client to assume each postural drainage position for approximately 3–5 minutes).
 6. Place towel over area to be percussed.
 7. Instruct client to take several deep breaths.

8. Percuss designated area for approximately 3 minutes during inspiration and expiration.
9. Vibrate same designated area during exhalations of 4–5 deep breaths.
10. Assist client with coughing when in postural drainage position; some clients may need to sit upright to produce a cough.
11. Repeat the same procedure in all designated positions.
12. After procedure, assist client to comfortable position and provide good oral hygiene.

Mechanical Ventilation

A. General information
1. Ventilation is performed by mechanical means in individuals who are unable to maintain normal levels of oxygen and carbon dioxide in the blood.
2. Indicated in clients with COPD, obesity, neuromuscular disease, severe neurologic depression, thoracic trauma, ARDS; clients who have undergone thoracic or open-heart surgery are likely to be maintained on mechanical ventilation post-op.
B. Types (positive pressure ventilators)
1. Positive pressure-cycled ventilator: pushes air into the lungs until a predetermined pressure is reached within the tracheobronchial tree; expiration occurs by passive relaxation of the diaphragm.
2. Volume-cycled ventilator: most popular type for intubated adults and older children; delivers air into the lungs until a certain predetermined tidal volume is reached before terminating inspiration.
3. Time-cycled ventilator: terminates inspiration after a preset time; tidal volume is regulated by adjusting length of inspiration and flow rate of pressurized gas.
C. Modes of mechanical ventilation
1. *Assist/control mode:* client's inspiratory effort triggers ventilator, which then delivers breath; may be set to deliver breath automatically if client does not trigger it. The same tidal volume is delivered with each breath.
2. *Intermittent mandatory ventilation* (*IMV*): client may breathe at own rate. IMV breaths are delivered under positive pressure; however, all other respirations taken by the client are delivered at ambient pressure and tidal volume is of client's own determination.
3. *Positive end expiratory pressure* (*PEEP*): ventilator delivers additional positive pressure at the end of expiration, which maintains the alveoli in an expanded state.
4. *Continuous positive airway pressure* (*CPAP*): achieves the same results as PEEP, except CPAP is used on adult clients who are on a T-piece.
D. Nursing care
1. Assess for decreased cardiac output and administer appropriate nursing care.
2. Monitor for positive water balance. Pressure breathing may cause increase in antidiuretic hormone (ADH) and retention of water.
   a. Maintain accurate I&O.
   b. Assess daily weights.
   c. Take PCWP readings as ordered.
   d. Palpate for peripheral edema.
   e. Auscultate chest for altered breath sounds.
3. Monitor for barotrauma (see Tension Pneumothorax, page 254).
   a. Assess ventilator settings every 4 hours.
   b. Auscultate breath sounds every 2 hours.
   c. Monitor ABGs.
   d. Perform complete pulmonary physical assessment every shift.
4. Monitor for GI problems (stress ulcer).
5. Administer muscle relaxants, tranquilizers, analgesics or paralyzing agents as ordered to increase client-machine synchrony by relaxing the client.

Oxygen Therapy

A. Most common therapy for clients with respiratory disease
B. Indications include arterial hypoxemia; COPD; ARDS; tissue, cellular, and circulatory hypoxia
C. Delivery systems
1. *Low-flow system:* delivers oxygen at variable liter flows designed to add to client's inspired air.
   a. *Nasal cannula*
      1) most common mode of oxygen delivery; consists of delivering 100% oxygen through two prongs inserted 1 cm into each nostril; general flow rates of 1–4 liters/minute are used with desired FiO_2 range of 24%–40%.
      2) Nursing care
         a) instruct client to breathe through the nose.
         b) remove cannula and clean nares every 8 hours.
         c) provide mouth care every 2–3 hours.
         d) use gauze pads behind ears to decrease irritation.
         e) assess arterial pO_2 frequently.
   b. *Standard mask*

1) simple face mask that covers the nose and mouth and provides an additional area for oxygen collection; ranges: 6–12 liters/minute; FiO_2: 40%–65%.
2) Nursing care
    a) instruct client to breathe through the nose.
    b) remove and clean mask every 2–3 hours.
    c) monitor carefully in clients who are prone to develop obstructed airways.
    d) replace mask with nasal cannula during meals and reposition mask immediately after eating.
c. Nonrebreathing mask
    1) standard mask with a reservoir bag designed to deliver 90%–100% oxygen; a one-way valve between reservoir bag and mask allows the client to inhale only from the reservoir bag and exhale through separate valves on the side of the mask; ranges: 6–15 liters/minute; FiO_2: 60%–90%.
    2) Nursing care
        a) instruct client to breathe through the nose.
        b) ensure that bag does not collapse completely with each inspiration.
        c) remove and clean mask every 2–3 hours.
2. *High-flow system:* client receives entire inspired gas from the apparatus, flow rates must exceed the volume of air required for a person's minute ventilation; *Venturi mask* commonly used
    a. Provides precise delivery of oxygen concentrations of 24%–50%.
    b. Nursing care
        1) provide supplemental oxygen by cannula during meals and other activities where mask interferes.
        2) remove and clean mask every 2–3 hours.

Tracheobronchial Suctioning

A. Suction removal of secretions from the tracheobronchial tree using a sterile catheter inserted into the airway
B. Catheters may be inserted through various routes: nasopharyngeal, oropharyngeal, or via an artificial airway.
C. Purposes
    1. Maintain a patent airway through removal of secretions.
    2. Promote adequate exchange of oxygen/carbon dioxide
    3. Substitute for effective coughing
    4. Obtain a specimen for analysis

D. Procedure
    1. Gather suctioning equipment (receptacle for secretions, sterile catheter, sterile gloves, and container of sterile normal saline).
    2. Turn vacuum on and test suction system.
    3. Place client in semi- to high-Fowler's position.
    4. Apply sterile glove, fill sterile cup with solution, and attach sterile catheter to connecting tube.
    5. Increase inspired oxygen concentration to highest point and hyperinflate the lungs before and after each catheter insertion by using self-inflating bag; have client deep breathe if able.
    6. Use gloved hand to insert catheter.
        a. Oral route
            1) if oral airway in place, slide the catheter alongside it and back to the pharynx; if no oral airway in place, have client protrude the tongue and guide the catheter into the oropharynx.
            2) insert during inspiration until cough is stimulated or secretion obtained.
        b. Nasal route: advance catheter along the floor of the nares or pass it through an artificial nasal airway until cough is stimulated or secretions obtained.
        c. Artificial airway: insert the catheter into the artificial airway until cough is stimulated or secretions obtained.
    7. Do not cover the thumb control and do not apply suction during insertion of the catheter.
    8. During withdrawal, rotate the catheter while applying intermittent suction.
    9. Whole suctioning procedure including insertion and removal of the catheter should not exceed 10 seconds.
    10. If it is necessary to continue the suctioning process, hyperinflate the lungs, allow the client to rest briefly, and repeat the process.
    11. Discard catheter, glove, and cup; record amount, color, characteristics of the secretions obtained; note client's tolerance of procedure.

Tracheostomy Care

A. Performed to avoid bacterial contamination and obstruction of tracheostomy tube; frequency varies depending on amount of secretions
B. Procedure
    1. Explain procedure and provide reassurance to the client.
    2. If not contraindicated, place client in semi-Fowler's position to promote lung reexpansion.

3. Disconnect ventilator or humidification device.
4. Suction trachea to clear secretions.
5. Reconnect ventilator or humidifier.
6. Remove all tracheostomy dressing.
7. Assemble equipment ("trach care kit").
8. Set up sterile field and put on sterile glove.
   a. For a single-cannula tube
      1) with sterile gloved hand, wipe client's neck under trach tube flanges with presoaked sterile sponge.
      2) wipe skin around tracheostomy with a second sponge until cleansed thoroughly (may use wet cotton-tipped applicators to cleanse around stoma).
      3) use each sponge or applicator only once.
      4) allow area to dry and apply a new sterile dressing (free of lint and fibers).
      5) change tracheostomy ties as needed.
   b. For a double-cannula tube
      1) disconnect ventilator or humidification device and unlock the inner cannula of trach tube using ungloved hand.
      2) place inner cannula in basin containing H_2O_2 to remove encrustations.
      3) if client on a ventilator, insert another inner cannula while old one is being cleaned and reconnect client to ventilator.
      4) cleanse stomal area and trach tube flanges with presoaked gauze sponges.
      5) clean inner cannula.
      6) remove excess liquid by gentle shaking.
      7) if client not on a ventilator, gently reinsert inner cannula into tracheostomy tube and lock in place.
      8) allow area to dry, apply dressing and new tracheostomy ties as described above.

EVALUATION

A. Client demonstrates ABGs within normal limits; absence of dyspnea and cyanosis; usual or improved breath sounds and usual mentation.
B. Client demonstrates effective coughing with expectoration of secretions; absence of dyspnea; rate and depth of ventilation within normal range; improved breath sounds.
C. ABGs within normal range; lungs clear to auscultation; rate and depth of respirations

within client's normal range; effective use of muscles of respiration.
D. Client identifies plans for appropriate alternate speech methods.
E. Client demonstrates increased activity tolerance with absence of dyspnea and excessive fatigue and vital signs within normal limits.
F. Improved rest/sleep patterns; respiratory rate and rhythm within client's normal range; demonstrates effective problem-solving abilities.
G. Client demonstrates behaviors/life-style changes to regain and maintain appropriate body weight. Verbalizes importance of nutrition to general well-being. Stable weight; improved anthropometric measurements.
H. Vital signs within client's normal range; client verbalizes understanding of causative/risk factors and utilizes techniques to promote a safe environment.

DISORDERS OF THE RESPIRATORY SYSTEM

Chronic Obstructive Pulmonary Disease (COPD)

Refers to respiratory conditions that produce obstruction of air flow; includes emphysema, bronchitis, bronchiectasis, and asthma.

Emphysema

A. General information
   1. Enlargement and destruction of the alveolar, bronchial, and bronchiolar tissue with resultant loss of recoil, air trapping, thoracic overdistension, sputum accumulation, and loss of diaphragmatic muscle tone
   2. These changes cause a state of carbon dioxide retention, hypoxia, and respiratory acidosis.
   3. Caused by cigarette smoking, infection, inhaled irritants, heredity, allergic factors, aging
B. Assessment findings
   1. Anorexia, fatigue, weight loss
   2. Feeling of breathlessness, cough, sputum production, flaring of the nostrils, use of accessory muscles of respiration, increased rate and depth of breathing, dyspnea
   3. Decreased respiratory excursion, resonance to hyperresonance, decreased breath sounds with prolonged expiration, normal or decreased fremitus
   4. Diagnostic tests: pCO_2 elevated or normal; pO_2 normal or slightly decreased
C. Nursing interventions

1. Administer medications as ordered.
   a. Bronchiodilators: aminophylline, isoproterenol (Isuprel), terbutaline (Brethine), metaproterenol (Alupent), theophylline, isoetharine (Bronkosol); used in treatment of bronchospasm
   b. Antimicrobials: tetracycline, ampicillin to treat bacterial infections
   c. Corticosteroids: prednisone
2. Facilitate removal of secretions.
   a. Ensure fluid intake of at least 3 liters/day.
   b. Provide (and teach client) chest physical therapy, coughing and deep breathing, and use of hand nebulizers.
   c. Suction as needed.
   d. Provide oral hygiene after expectoration of sputum.
3. Improve ventilation.
   a. Position client in semi- or high-Fowler's.
   b. Instruct client to use diaphragmatic muscle to breathe.
   c. Encourage productive coughing after all treatments (splint abdomen to help produce more expulsive cough).
   d. Employ pursed-lip breathing techniques (prolonged, slow relaxed expiration against pursed lips).
4. Provide client teaching and discharge planning concerning
   a. Prevention of recurrent infections
      1) avoid crowds and individuals with known infection.
      2) adhere to high-protein, high-carbohydrate, increased vitamin C diet.
      3) receive immunizations for influenza and pneumonia.
      4) report changes in characteristics and color of sputum immediately.
      5) report worsening of symptoms (increased tightness of chest, fatigue, increased dyspnea).
   b. Control of environment
      1) use home humidifier at 30%–50% humidity.
      2) wear scarf over nose and mouth in cold weather to prevent bronchospasm.
      3) avoid smoking and others who smoke.
      4) avoid abrupt changes in temperature.
   c. Avoidance of inhaled irritants
      1) stay indoors if pollution levels are high.
      2) use air conditioner with high-efficiency particulate air filter to remove particles from air.
   d. Increasing activity tolerance

1) start with mild exercises, such as walking, and gradually increase amount and duration.
2) use breathing techniques (pursed lip, diaphragmatic) during activities/exercises to control breathing.
3) have oxygen available as needed to assist with activities.
4) plan activities that require low amounts of energy.
5) plan rest periods before and after activities.

Bronchitis

A. General information
   1. Excessive production of mucus in the bronchi with accompanying persistent cough.
   2. Characteristic changes include hypertrophy/hyperplasia of the mucus-secreting glands in the bronchi, decreased ciliary activity, chronic inflammation, and narrowing of the small airways.
   3. Caused by the same factors that cause emphysema.
B. Medical management: drug therapy includes bronchodilators, antimicrobials, expectorants (e.g., Robitussin)
C. Assessment findings
   1. Productive (copious) cough, dyspnea on exertion, use of accessory muscles of respiration, scattered rales and rhonchi
   2. Feeling of epigastric fullness, slight cyanosis, distended neck veins, ankle edema
   3. Diagnostic tests: increased pCO_2, decreased pO_2
D. Nursing interventions: same as for emphysema

Bronchiectasis

A. General information
   1. Permanent abnormal dilation of the bronchi with destruction of muscular and elastic structure of the bronchial wall
   2. Caused by bacterial infection; recurrent lower respiratory tract infections; congenital defects (altered bronchial structures); lung tumors; thick, tenacious secretions
B. Medical management: same as for emphysema.
C. Assessment findings
   1. Chronic cough with production of mucopurulent sputum, hemoptysis, exertional dyspnea, wheezing
   2. Anorexia, fatigue, weight loss
   3. Diagnostic tests
      a. Bronchoscopy reveals sources and sites of secretions

b. Possible elevation of WBC

D. Nursing interventions: same as for emphysema

Asthma

See page 404.

Pulmonary Tuberculosis

A. General information
1. Bacterial infectious disease caused by *M. tuberculosis* and spread via airborne droplets when infected persons cough, sneeze, or laugh
2. Once inhaled, the organisms implant themselves in the lung and begin dividing slowly, causing inflammation, development of the primary tubercle, and eventual caseation and fibrosis.
3. Infection spreads via the lymph and circulatory systems.
4. Half of the cases occur in inner-city neighborhoods, and incidence is highest in areas with a large population of native Americans. Nonwhites affected four times more often than whites. Men affected more often than women. The greatest number of cases occur in persons age 65 and over. Socially and economically disadvantaged, alcoholic, and malnourished individuals affected more often.
5. The causative agent, *M. tuberculosis,* is an acid-fast bacillus spread via droplet nuclei from infected persons.

B. Assessment findings
1. Cough (yellow mucoid sputum), dyspnea, hemoptysis, rales or crackles
2. Anorexia, malaise, weight loss, afternoon low-grade fever, pallor, pain, fatigue, night sweats
3. Diagnostic tests
   a. Chest x-ray indicates presence and extent of disease process but cannot differentiate active from inactive form
   b. Skin test (PPD) positive; area of induration 10 mm or more in diameter after 48 hours
   c. Sputum positive for acid-fast bacillus (three samples is diagnostic for disease)
   d. Culture positive
   e. WBC and ESR increased

C. Nursing interventions
1. Administer medications as ordered (see Table 2.23).
2. Prevent transmission.
   a. Strict isolation not required if client/significant others adhere to special respiratory precautions for tuberculosis.
   b. Client should be in a well-ventilated private room, with the door kept closed at all times.
   c. All visitors and staff should wear masks when in contact with the client and should discard the used masks before leaving the room; client should wear a mask when leaving the room for tests.
   d. All specimens should be labelled "AFB precautions."
   e. Handwashing is required after direct contact with the client or contaminated articles.
3. Promote adequate nutrition.
   a. Make ongoing assessments of client's appetite and do kcal counts for 3 days; consult dietitian for diet guidelines.
   b. Offer small, frequent feedings and nutritional supplements; assist client with menu selection stressing balanced nutrition.
   c. Weigh client at least twice a week.
   d. Encourage activity as tolerated to increase appetite.
4. Prevent social isolation.
   a. Impart a comfortable, confident attitude when caring for the client.
   b. Explain the nature of the disease to the client, significant others, and visitors in simple terms.
   c. Stress that visits are important, but isolation precautions must be followed.
5. Vary the client's routine to prevent boredom.
6. Discuss the client's feelings and assess for boredom, depression, anxiety, fatigue, or apathy; provide support and encourage expression of concerns.
7. Provide client teaching and discharge planning concerning
   a. Medication regimen: prepare a sheet with each drug name, dosage, time due, and major side effects; stress importance of following medication schedule for prescribed period of time (usually 9 months); include significant others
   b. Transmission prevention: client should cover mouth when coughing, expectorate into a tissue and place it in a paper bag; client should also wash hands after coughing or sneezing; stress importance of plenty of fresh air; include significant others
   c. Importance of notifying physician at the first sign of persistent cough, fever, or hemoptysis (may indicate recurrence)
   d. Need for follow-up care including physical exam, sputum cultures, and chest x-rays

    e. Availability of community health services
    f. Importance of high-protein, high-carbohydrate diet with inclusion of supplemental vitamins

Histoplasmosis

A. General information: a systemic fungal disease caused by inhalation of dust contaminated by Histoplasma capsulatum which is transmitted through bird manure.
B. Medical management: antifungal agent Amphotericin B
    1. Very toxic: toxicity includes anorexia, chills, fever, headache, and renal failure
    2. Acetaminophen, Benadryl, and steroids given with Amphotericin B to prevent reactions
C. Assessment findings
    1. Symptoms similar to tuberculosis or pneumonia
        a. Cough
        b. Fever
        c. Joint pain
        d. Malaise
    2. Sometimes asymptomatic
    3. Diagnostic tests
        a. Chest x-ray (often appears similar to tuberculosis)
        b. Histoplasmin skin test (read the same as PPD)
D. Nursing interventions
    1. Monitor respiratory status
    2. Administer medications as ordered; observe for severe side effects of Amphotericin B: fever (acetaminophen given prophylactically), anaphylactic reaction (Benadryl and steroids given prophylactically), abnormal renal function with hypokalemia and azotemia.

Chest Trauma

Fractured Ribs

A. General information
    1. Most common chest injury resulting from blunt trauma
    2. Ribs 4–8 are most commonly fractured because they are least protected by chest muscles. Splintered or displaced fractured ribs may penetrate the pleura and lungs.
B. Medical management: drug therapy consists of narcotics, intercostal nerve block (injection of intercostal nerves above and below the injury with an anesthetic agent) for pain relief
C. Assessment findings
    1. Pain, especially on inspiration
    2. Point tenderness and bruising at injury site, splinting with shallow respirations, apprehensiveness

    3. Diagnostic tests
        a. Chest x-ray reveals area and degree of fracture
        b. pCO_2 elevated; pO_2 decreased (later)
D. Nursing interventions
    1. Provide pain relief/control.
        a. Administer ordered narcotics and analgesics cautiously and monitor effects.
        b. Place client in semi- or high-Fowler's position to ease pain associated with breathing.
    2. Monitor client closely for complications.
        a. Assess for bloody sputum (indicative of lung penetration).
        b. Observe for signs and symptoms of pneumothorax or hemothorax.

Flail Chest

A. General information
    1. Fracture of several ribs and resultant instability of the affected chest wall.
    2. Chest wall is no longer able to provide the bony structure necessary to maintain adequate ventilation; consequently, the flail portion and underlying tissue move paradoxically (in opposition) to the rest of the chest cage and lungs.
    3. The flail portion is sucked in on inspiration and bulges out on expiration.
    4. Result is hypoxia, hypercarbia, and increased retained secretions.
    5. Caused by trauma (sternal rib fracture with possible costochondral separations).
B. Medical management
    1. Internal stabilization with a volume-cycled ventilator
    2. Drug therapy (narcotics, sedatives)
C. Assessment findings
    1. Severe dyspnea; rapid, shallow, grunty breathing; paradoxical chest motion
    2. Cyanosis, possible neck vein distension, tachycardia, hypotension
    3. Diagnostic tests
        a. pO_2 decreased
        b. pCO_2 elevated
        c. pH decreased
D. Nursing interventions
    1. Maintain an open airway: suction secretions/blood from nose, throat, mouth, and via endotracheal tube; note changes in amount, color, characteristics.
    2. Monitor mechanical ventilation (see page 249).
    3. Encourage turning, coughing, and deep breathing.
    4. Monitor for signs of shock.

Pneumothorax/Hemothorax

A. General information

1. Partial or complete collapse of the lung due to an accumulation of air or fluid in the pleural space
2. Types
   a. *Spontaneous pneumothorax:* the most common type of closed pneumothorax; air accumulates within the pleural space without an obvious cause. Rupture of a small bleb on the visceral pleura most frequently produces this type of pneumothorax.
   b. *Open pneumothorax:* air enters the pleural space through an opening in the chest wall; usually caused by stabbing or gunshot wound.
   c. *Tension pneumothorax:* air enters the pleural space with each inspiration but cannot escape; causes increased intrathoracic pressure and shifting of the mediastinal contents to the unaffected side (mediastinal shift).
   d. *Hemothorax:* accumulation of blood in the pleural space; frequently found with an open pneumothorax resulting in a hemopneumothorax.
B. Assessment findings
   1. Sudden sharp pain in the chest, dyspnea, diminished or absent breath sounds on affected side, decreased respiratory excursion on affected side, hyperresonance on percussion, decreased vocal fremitus, tracheal shift to the opposite side (tension pneumothorax accompanied by mediastinal shift)
   2. Weak, rapid pulse; anxiety; diaphoresis
   3. Diagnostic tests
      a. Chest x-ray reveals area and degree of pneumothorax
      b. pCO_2 elevated
      c. pO_2, pH decreased
C. Nursing interventions
   1. Provide nursing care for the client with an endotracheal tube: suction secretions, vomitus, blood from nose, mouth, throat, or via endotracheal tube; monitor mechanical ventilation.
   2. Restore/promote adequate respiratory function.
      a. Assist with thoracentesis and provide appropriate nursing care (see page 246).
      b. Assist with insertion of a chest tube to water-seal drainage and provide appropriate nursing care (see page 246).
      c. Continuously evaluate respiratory patterns and report any changes.
   3. Provide relief/control of pain.
      a. Administer narcotics/analgesics/sedatives as ordered and monitor effects.
      b. Position client in high-Fowler's position.

Atelectasis

A. General information
   1. Collapse of part or all of a lung due to bronchial obstruction
   2. May be caused by intrabronchial obstruction (secretions, tumors, bronchospasm, foreign bodies); extrabronchial compression (tumors, enlarged lymph nodes); or endobronchial disease (bronchogenic carcinoma, inflammatory structures)
B. Assessment findings
   1. Signs and symptoms may be absent depending upon degree of collapse and rapidity with which bronchial obstruction occurs
   2. Dyspnea, decreased breath sounds on affected side, decreased respiratory excursion, dullness to flatness upon percussion over affected area
   3. Cyanosis, tachycardia, tachypnea, elevated temperature, weakness, pain over affected area
   4. Diagnostic tests
      a. Bronchoscopy: may or may not reveal an obstruction
      b. Chest x-ray shows diminished size of affected lung and lack of radiance over atelectic area
      c. pO_2 decreased
C. Nursing interventions (prevention of atelectasis in hospitalized clients is an important nursing responsibility)
   1. Turn and reposition every 1–2 hours while client is bedridden or obtunded.
   2. Encourage mobility (if permitted).
   3. Promote liquification and removal of secretions.
   4. Avoid administration of large doses of sedatives and opiates that depress respiration and cough reflex.
   5. Prevent abdominal distension.
   6. Administer prophylactic antibiotics as ordered to prevent respiratory infection.

Pleural Effusion

A. General information
   1. Collection of fluid in the pleural space
   2. A symptom, not a disease; may be produced by numerous conditions
   3. Classification
      a. Transudative: accumulation of protein-poor, cell-poor fluid
      b. Suppurative (empyema): accumulation of pus
   4. May be found in clients with liver/kidney disease, pneumonia, tuberculosis, lung abscess, bronchial carcinoma, leukemia, trauma, pulmonary edema, systemic

infection, disseminated lupus
erythematosus, polyarteritis nodosa
B. Medical management
  1. Identification and treatment of the
    underlying cause
  2. Thoracentesis
  3. Drug therapy
    a. Antibiotics: either systemic or inserted
      directly into pleural space
    b. Fibrinolytic enzymes: trypsin,
      streptokinase-streptodornase to
      decrease thickness of pus and dissolve
      fibrin clots
  4. Closed chest drainage
  5. Surgery: open drainage
C. Assessment findings
  1. Dyspnea, dullness over affected area upon
    percussion, absent or decreased breath
    sounds over affected area, pleural pain, dry
    cough, pleural friction rub
  2. Pallor, fatigue, fever, and night sweats
    (with empyema)
  3. Diagnostic tests
    a. Chest x-ray positive if greater than 250
      ml pleural fluid
    b. Pleural biopsy may reveal
      bronchogenic carcinoma
    c. Thoracentesis may contain blood if
      cause is cancer, pulmonary infarction,
      or tuberculosis; positive for specific
      organism in empyema
D. Nursing interventions: vary depending on
  etiology
  1. Assist with repeated thoracentesis.
  2. Administer narcotics/sedatives as ordered
    to decrease pain.
  3. Assist with instillation of medication into
    pleural space (reposition client every 15
    minutes to distribute the drug within the
    pleurae).
  4. Place client in high-Fowler's position to
    promote ventilation.

Pneumonia

A. General information
  1. An inflammation of the alveolar spaces of
    the lung, resulting in consolidation of lung
    tissue as the alveoli fill with exudate
  2. The various types of pneumonias are
    classified according to the offending
    organism.
  3. Bacterial pneumonia accounts for 10% of
    all hospital admissions; affects infants and
    elderly most often, and most often occurs
    in winter and early spring
  4. Caused by various organisms: *D.
    pneumoniae, S. aureus, E. coli, H.
    influenzae*
B. Assessment findings
  1. Cough with greenish to rust-colored
    sputum production; rapid, shallow

respirations with an expiratory grunt;
nasal flaring; intercostal rib retraction; use
of accessory muscles of respiration;
dullness to flatness upon percussion;
possible pleural friction rub; high-pitched
bronchial breath sounds; rales or crackles
(early) progressing to coarse (later)
  2. Fever, chills, chest pain, weakness,
    generalized malaise
  3. Tachycardia, cyanosis, profuse
    perspiration, abdominal distension
  4. Diagnostic tests
    a. Chest x-ray shows consolidation over
      affected areas
    b. WBC increased
    c. pO_2 decreased
    d. Sputum specimens reveal particular
      causative organism
C. Nursing interventions
  1. Facilitate adequate ventilation.
    a. Administer oxygen as needed and
      assess its effectiveness.
    b. Place client in semi-Fowler's position.
    c. Turn and reposition frequently clients
      who are immobilized/obtunded.
    d. Administer analgesics as ordered to
      relieve pain associated with breathing
      (codeine is drug of choice).
    e. Auscultate breath sounds every 2–4
      hours.
    f. Monitor ABGs.
  2. Facilitate removal of secretions (general
    hydration, deep breathing and coughing,
    tracheobronchial suctioning as needed,
    expectorants as ordered, aerosol
    treatments via nebulizer, humidification of
    inhaled air, chest physical therapy).
  3. Observe color, characteristics of sputum
    and report any changes; encourage client
    to perform good oral hygiene after
    expectoration.
  4. Provide adequate rest and relief/control of
    pain.
    a. Provide bed rest with limited physical
      activity.
    b. Limit visits and minimize
      conversations.
    c. Plan for uninterrupted rest periods.
    d. Institute nursing care in blocks to
      ensure periods of rest.
    e. Maintain pleasant and restful
      environment.
  5. Administer antibiotics as ordered, monitor
    effects and possible toxicity.
  6. Prevent transmission (respiratory isolation
    may be required for clients with
    staphylococcal pneumonia).
  7. Control fever and chills: monitor
    temperature and administer antipyretics as
    ordered, maintain increased fluid intake,
    provide frequent clothing and linen
    changes.

8. Provide client teaching and discharge planning concerning prevention of recurrence.
   a. Medication regimen/antibiotic therapy
   b. Need for adequate rest, limited activity, good nutrition with adequate fluid intake, and good ventilation
   c. Need to continue deep breathing and coughing for at least 6–8 weeks after discharge
   d. Availability of vaccines (pneumonococcal pneumonia, influenza)
   e. Techniques that prevent transmission (use of tissues when coughing, adequate disposal of secretions)
   f. Avoidance of persons with known respiratory infections
   g. Need to report signs and symptoms of respiratory infection (persistent or recurrent fever; changes in characteristics, color of sputum; chills; increased pain; difficulty breathing; weight loss; persistent fatigue)
   h. Need for follow-up medical care and evaluation.

Bronchogenic Carcinoma

A. General information
   1. The majority of primary pulmonary tumors arise from the bronchial epithelium and are therefore referred to as bronchogenic carcinomas.
   2. Characteristic pathologic changes include nonspecific inflammation with hypersecretion of mucus, desquamation of cells, hyperplasia, and obstruction.
   3. Metastasis occurs primarily by direct extension and via the circulatory or lymphatic system.
   4. Men over age 40 affected most often; 1 out of every 10 heavy smokers; affects right lung more often than left.
   5. Caused by inhaled carcinogens (primarily cigarette smoke but also asbestos, nickel, iron oxides, air silicone pollution; preexisting pulmonary disorders [TB, COPD])

B. Medical management: depends on cell type, stage of disease, and condition of client; may include
   1. Radiation therapy
   2. Chemotherapy: usually includes cyclophosphamide, methotrexate, vincristine, doxorubicin, and procarbazine; concurrently in some combination
   3. Surgery: when entire tumor can be removed

C. Assessment findings
   1. Persistent cough (may be productive or blood tinged), chest pain, dyspnea, unilateral wheezing, friction rub, possible unilateral paralysis of the diaphragm
   2. Fatigue, anorexia, nausea, vomiting, pallor
   3. Diagnostic tests
      a. Chest x-ray may show presence of tumor or evidence of metastasis to surrounding structures
      b. Sputum for cytology reveals malignant cells
      c. Bronchoscopy: biopsy reveals malignancy
      d. Thoracentesis: pleural fluid contains malignant cells
      e. Biopsy of scalene lymph nodes may reveal metastasis

D. Nursing interventions
   1. Provide support and guidance to client as needed.
   2. Provide relief/control of pain.
   3. Administer medications as ordered and monitor effects/side effects.
   4. Control nausea: administer medications as ordered, provide good oral hygiene, provide small and more frequent feedings.
   5. Provide nursing care for a client with a thoracotomy.
   6. Provide client teaching and discharge planning concerning
      a. Disease process, diagnostic and therapeutic interventions
      b. Side effects of radiation and chemotherapy
      c. Realistic information about prognosis

Thoracic Surgery

A. General information
   1. Types
      a. *Exploratory thoracotomy:* anterior or posterolateral incision through the fourth, fifth, sixth, or seventh intercostal spaces to expose and examine the pleura and lung
      b. *Lobectomy:* removal of one lobe of a lung; treatment for bronchiectasis, bronchogenic carcinoma, emphysematous blebs, lung abscesses
      c. *Pneumonectomy:* removal of an entire lung; most commonly done as treatment for bronchogenic carcinoma
      d. *Segmental resection:* removal of one or more segments of lung; most often done as treatment for bronchiectasis
      e. *Wedge resection:* removal of lesions that occupy only part of a segment of lung tissue; for excision of small nodules or to obtain a biopsy
   2. Nature and extent of disease and condition of client determine type of pulmonary resection.

B. Nursing interventions: preoperative
   1. Provide routine pre-op care.

2. Perform a complete physical assessment of the lungs to obtain baseline data.
3. Explain expected post-op measures: care of incision site, oxygen, suctioning, chest tubes (except if pneumonectomy performed)
4. Teach client adequate splinting of incision with hands or pillow for turning, coughing, and deep breathing.
5. Demonstrate ROM exercises for affected side.
6. Provide chest physical therapy to help remove secretions.

C. Nursing interventions: postoperative
1. Provide routine post-op care.
2. Promote adequate ventilation.
    a. Perform complete physical assessment of lungs and compare with pre-op findings.
    b. Auscultate lung fields every 1–2 hours.
    c. Encourage turning, coughing, and deep breathing every 1–2 hours after pain relief obtained.
    d. Perform tracheobronchial suctioning if needed.
    e. Assess for proper maintenance of chest drainage system (except after pneumonectomy).
    f. Monitor ABGs and report significant changes.
    g. Place client in semi-Fowler's position (if pneumonectomy performed, follow surgeon's orders about positioning, often on back or operative side, but not turned to unoperative side).
3. Provide pain relief.
    a. Administer narcotics/analgesics prior to turning, coughing, and deep breathing.
    b. Assist with splinting while turning, coughing, deep breathing.
4. Prevent impaired mobility of the upper extremities by doing ROM exercises; passive day of surgery, then active.
5. Provide client teaching and discharge planning concerning
    a. Need to continue with coughing/deep breathing for 6–8 weeks post-op and to continue ROM exercises
    b. Importance of adequate rest with gradual increases in activity levels
    c. High-protein diet with inclusion of adequate fluids (at least 2 liters/day)
    d. Chest physical therapy
    e. Good oral hygiene
    f. Need to avoid persons with known upper respiratory infections
    g. Adverse signs and symptoms (recurrent fever; anorexia; weight loss; dyspnea; increased pain; difficulty swallowing; shortness of breath; changes in color, characteristics of sputum) and importance of reporting to physician
    h. Avoidance of crowds and poorly ventilated areas.

Acute Respiratory Distress Syndrome (ARDS)

A. General information
1. A form of pulmonary insufficiency more commonly encountered in adults with no previous lung disorders than in those with existing lung disease.
2. Initial damage to the alveolar-capillary membrane with subsequent leakage of fluid into the interstitial spaces and alveoli, resulting in pulmonary edema and impaired gas exchange.
3. There is cell damage, decreased surfactant production, and atelectasis, which in turn produce hypoxemia, decreased compliance, and increased work of breathing.
4. Predisposing conditions include shock, trauma, infection, fluid overload, aspiration, oxygen toxicity, smoke inhalation, pneumonia, DIC, drug allergies, drug overdoses, neurologic injuries, fat emboli.
5. Has also been called shock lung.

B. Assessment findings
1. Dyspnea, cough, tachypnea with intercostal/suprasternal retraction, scattered to diffuse rales/rhonchi
2. Changes in orientation, tachycardia, cyanosis (rare)
3. Diagnostic tests
    a. pCO_2 and pO_2 decreased
    b. Hypoxemia
    c. Hgb and hct possibly decreased
    d. pCO_2 increased in terminal stages

C. Nursing interventions
1. Promote optimal ventilatory status.
    a. Perform ongoing assessment of lungs with auscultation every 1–2 hours.
    b. Elevate head and chest.
    c. Administer/monitor mechanical ventilation with PEEP.
    d. Assist with chest physical therapy as ordered.
    e. Encourage coughing and deep breathing every hour.
    f. Monitor ABGs and report significant changes.
2. Promote rest by spacing activities and treatments.
3. Maintain fluid and electrolyte balance.

Cancer of the Larynx

A. General information
1. Most common upper respiratory malignancy.

2. The majority of laryngeal malignancies are squamous cell carcinomas.
3. Types
    a. Supraglottic (also called extrinsic laryngeal cancer): involves the epiglottis and false cords and is likely to produce no symptoms until advanced stages.
    b. Glottic (also referred to as intrinsic laryngeal cancer): affects the true vocal cords; the most frequently occurring laryngeal cancer; produces early symptoms
4. Occurs most often in white men in middle or later life
5. Caused by cigarette smoking, excessive alcohol consumption, chronic laryngitis, vocal abuse, family predisposition to cancer of larynx

B. Medical management
1. Radiation therapy: may be effective in cases of localized disease, affecting only one vocal cord
2. Chemotherapy: used as adjuvant therapy to help shrink tumor and eradicate metastases (experimental)
3. Surgery
    a. Partial laryngectomy: a lesion on the true cord on one side is removed along with adjoining tissue. Useful in early, intrinsic lesions. Client is able to talk and has a normal airway post-op.
    b. Total laryngectomy (see below)
    c. Radical neck dissection
        1) performed when metastasis from cancer of the larynx is suspected
        2) includes removal of entire larynx, lymph nodes, sternocleidomastoid muscle, internal jugular vein, and spinal accessory nerve
        3) may also involve removal of the mandible, submaxillary gland, part of the thyroid and parathyroid gland
        4) nursing care: same as for total laryngectomy, below

C. Assessment findings
1. Supraglottic: localized throat pain; burning when drinking hot liquids or orange juice; lump in the neck; eventual dysphagia; dyspnea; weight loss; debility; cough; hemoptysis; muffled voice
2. Glottic: progressive hoarseness (more than 2-week duration), eventual dyspnea
3. Enlarged cervical lymph nodes

D. Nursing interventions: provide care for the client with a laryngectomy.

Total Laryngectomy

A. General information: consists of removal of the entire larynx, hyoid bone, pre-epiglottic space, cricoid cartilage, and 3–4 rings of trachea. The pharyngeal opening to the trachea is closed and remaining trachea brought out to the neck to form a permanent tracheostomy. The result is loss of normal speech and breathing and loss of olfaction.

B. Nursing care: preoperative
1. Provide routine pre-op care.
2. Explain expected procedures after surgery including suctioning, humidification, coughing and deep breathing, IV fluids, nasogastric tube feedings, tracheostomy or laryngectomy tube.
3. Reinforce physician's teaching regarding loss of normal speech, breathing patterns, and sense of smell.
4. Encourage client/significant others to talk about fears and hopes following surgery.
5. Introduce client to changes in modes of communication (esophageal speech, artificial larynx).
6. Establish method of communication to be used immediately post-op (Magic Slate, gestures).

C. Nursing interventions: postoperative
1. Promote optimum ventilatory status.
2. Suction nose frequently because of rhinitis.
3. Assess function of tracheostomy/laryngectomy tube and suction as needed.
4. Promote pain relief.
    a. Elevate head of bed to decrease pressure on suture line.
    b. Administer analgesics as needed and monitor effects.
    c. Assist with moving head and turning by supporting back of neck with hands.
5. Promote wound drainage.
    a. Elevate head of bed to promote lymphatic drainage from head.
    b. Monitor amount, characteristics of drainage.
6. Promote nutrition.
    a. Institute and monitor tube feedings as ordered.
    b. Increase fluid intake as tolerated to improve hydration.
    c. Encourage self-feeding.
    d. Advance to normal diet as soon as client able to tolerate.
7. Prevent infection.
    a. Assess WBC and report significant increases.
    b. Take temperature every 4 hours.
    c. Maintain sterile technique when suctioning and performing tracheostomy care.
    d. Observe stoma/suture lines for signs of infection.
    e. Provide frequent oral hygiene.
    f. Monitor sputum and drainage for changes in color, odor, characteristics.
8. Enhance communication.

a. Carry out modes of communication determined pre-op.
b. Assess nonverbal behavior.
c. Allow client time to ask questions and do not anticipate answers.
d. Arrange for volunteer laryngectomee to visit client and assist with esophageal speech/artificial larynx.
e. Consult with speech therapist if needed.
f. Progress to normal diet as soon as possible to regain muscle tone of throat and abdomen.

9. Support client during adaptation to altered physical status.
a. Encourage client to discuss feelings about changes in appearance, body functioning, and life-style; be aware of nonverbal responses to the changes.
b. Assist to identify and use coping techniques that have been helpful in past.
c. Suggest flattering clothing styles that don't emphasize chest or neck configuration.
d. Monitor for and support behaviors indicative of positive adaptation to changes (e.g., interest in appearance).

10. Assess for respiratory complications (dyspnea, cyanosis, tachycardia, tachypnea, restlessness).

11. Provide client teaching and discharge planning concerning
a. Tracheostomy/laryngectomy and stomal care
b. Proper administration of nasogastric tube feedings and maintenance of nasogastric tube (see page 268)
c. Control of dryness/crusting of tongue by brushing tongue regularly with soft toothbrush and toothpaste and using mouthwashes
d. Need for humidified air at home
e. Importance of protecting the stoma with a shield or towel while showering, directing shower nozzle away from stoma
f. Need to use electric razors only for 6 months after surgery as facial area will be numb
g. Need to lean forward when expectorating secretions and to cover stoma when coughing or sneezing
h. Snorkle devices to enable swimming (caution is advised since drowning can occur rapidly in these clients)
i. Need to wear an identification bracelet indicating that client is a neck breather
j. Types of stoma guards available
k. Necessity of installing smoke detectors since sense of smell is lost
l. Information about prosthetic devices, speech therapy, and reconstructive surgery

Sample Questions

59. A 17-year-old male is admitted following an automobile accident. He is very anxious, dyspneic, and in severe pain. The left chest wall moves in during inspiration and balloons out when he exhales. The nurse understands these symptoms are most suggestive of
1. hemothorax.
2. flail chest.
3. atelectasis.
4. pleural effusion.

60. A young man is admitted with a flail chest following a car accident. He is intubated with an endotracheal tube and is placed on a mechanical ventilator (control mode, positive pressure). Which physical finding alerts the nurse to an additional problem in respiratory function?
1. Dullness to percussion in the third to fifth intercostal space, midclavicular line.
2. Decreased paradoxical motion.
3. Louder breath sounds on the right chest.
4. pH of 7.36 in arterial blood gases.

61. The nurse is caring for a client who has had a chest tube inserted and connected to water seal drainage (Pleur-evac®). The nurse determines the drainage system is functioning correctly when which of the following is observed?
1. Continuous bubbling in the water-seal chamber.
2. Fluctuation in the water-seal (U-tube) chamber.
3. Suction tubing attached to a wall unit.
4. Vesicular breath sounds throughout the lung fields.

62. The nurse is caring for a client who has just had a chest tube attached to a water seal drainage system (Pleur-evac®). To ensure that the system functions effectively the nurse should
1. observe for intermittent bubbling in the water seal chamber.
2. flush the chest tubes with 30 to 60 ml of NSS q4 to 6 hours.
3. maintain the client in an extreme lateral position.
4. strip the chest tubes in the direction of the client.

63. The nurse enters the room of a client who has a chest tube attached to a water seal drainage system and notices the chest tube is dislodged from the chest. The most appropriate nursing intervention is to
1. notify the physician.
2. insert a new chest tube.

3. cover the insertion site with petroleum gauze.
4. instruct the client to breathe deeply until help arrives.

64. Mr. Q. is ordered oxygen via nasal prongs. The nurse administering oxygen via this low-flow system recognizes that this method of delivery
   1. mixes room air with oxygen.
   2. delivers a precise concentration of oxygen.
   3. requires humidity during delivery.
   4. is less traumatic to the respiratory tract.

65. An adult is receiving oxygen by nasal prongs. Which statement by the client indicates that client teaching regarding oxygen therapy has been effective?
   1. "I was feeling fine so I removed my nasal prongs."
   2. "I've increased my fluids to six glasses of water daily."
   3. "Don't forget to come back quickly when you get me out of bed; I don't like to be without my oxygen for too long."
   4. "My family was angry when I told them they could not smoke in my room."

66. Mr. A., 64 years old, is diagnosed with tuberculosis. Client teaching for Mr. A. will include prevention of disease transmission. The most common means of transmitting the tubercle bacillus from one individual to another is by
   1. hands.
   2. droplet nuclei.
   3. milk products.
   4. eating utensils.

67. The treatment plan for a client newly diagnosed with tuberculosis is likely to include which of the following medications as initial treatment?
   1. Ethambutol (Myambutol) and isoniazid (INH).
   2. Streptomycin and penicillin G (Crysticillin).
   3. Tetracycline and thioridazine (Mellaril).
   4. Pyridoxine (Beesix) and rifampin (Rifadin).

68. Mr. R., 64 years old, has been smoking since he was 11 years old. He has a long history of emphysema. Mr. R. is admitted to the hospital because of a respiratory infection that has not improved with outpatient therapy. Which finding would the nurse expect to observe during Mr. R.'s nursing assessment?
   1. Electrocardiogram changes.
   2. Increased anterior-posterior chest diameter.
   3. Slow, labored respiratory pattern.
   4. Weight-height relationship indicating obesity.

69. Supplemental low-flow oxygen therapy is prescribed for a man with emphysema. Which is the most essential action for the nurse to initiate?
   1. Anticipate the need for humidification.

2. Notify the physician that this order is contraindicated.
3. Place the client in high-Fowler's position.
4. Schedule nursing care to allow frequent observations of the client.

Answers and Rationales

59. The correct answer is 2. Paradoxical breathing movements (opposite the normal) are characteristic of flail chest. The flail portion is sucked in on inspiration and bulges out on expiration. Flail chest is caused by trauma, which is evident in this case. Chest pain is present in hemothorax but not paradoxical breathing. Hemothorax can also be associated with trauma. Atelectasis is collapse of all or part of a lung due to bronchial obstruction. It may be caused by hypoventilation, intrabronchial obstruction, or endobronchial disease. Paradoxical breathing movements are not seen in atelectasis. Pleural effusion is characterized by pain on inspiration. It is collection of fluid in the pleural space and is a symptom of numerous diseases. It is not usually associated with trauma and is not characterized by paradoxical breathing.

60. The correct answer is 3. Louder breath sounds on the right side of the chest indicate that the endotracheal tube may be misplaced and is aerating only one lung. Dullness to percussion is normal in the third to fifth intercostal spaces as the heart is located there. Decreased paradoxical motion is a desired effect when the client has a flail chest. A pH of 7.36 is within normal limits.

61. The correct answer is 2. Fluctuation in the water-seal chamber demonstrates that the tubing system is patent. Bubbling in the water seal should be intermittent. Vigorous bubbling indicates that air is being pulled into the system and is not normal. The fact that suction tubing is attached to a wall unit provides no information about function. Vesicular breath sounds should not be heard in the upper chest.

62. The correct answer is 1. Intermittent bubbling in the water seal chamber indicates that air is leaving the thoracic cavity. If there is no bubbling in the water seal chamber, it indicates either obstruction of the tubing or reexpansion of the lung. Reexpansion of the lung is unlikely, as the tube has just been inserted. Flushing is contraindicated as it disrupts the airtight system and introduces fluid into the chest cavity. An extreme lateral position may be uncomfortable for the client and does not necessarily maintain patency of the system. Stripping the chest tubes, when

permitted, is done away from and not toward the client.

63. The correct answer is 3. Covering the insertion site with petroleum gauze is a priority nursing measure that prevents air from entering the chest cavity. Notifying the physician should be done after covering the insertion site. Inserting a chest tube is not a nursing action. Instructing the client to breathe deeply will cause air to enter the chest cavity.

64. The correct answer is 1. Low-flow oxygen systems provide an oxygen concentration that is determined by the amount of air drawn into the system and the dilution of oxygen with room air. There is a considerable variation in the concentration of oxygen that can be delivered to the client. Not all systems require humidification. Oxygen therapy given on a short-term basis is usually not traumatic to the respiratory tract.

65. The correct answer is 4. Oxygen is a flammable gas and smoking is not permitted in the area. Compliance with the prescription for oxygen therapy is extremely important to prevent the fluctuation of oxygen levels. Fluid intake is important for clients with respiratory disease to liquefy secretions, but it is not directly related to oxygen therapy. Clients should have portable oxygen therapy if they are moving around the room.

66. The correct answer is 2. The most frequent means of transmission of the tubercle bacillus is by droplet nuclei. The bacillus is present in the air as a result of coughing, sneezing, and expectorating by infected persons. TB can be transmitted from infected cattle to humans through contaminated milk and milk products. The organism responsible for this is *Mycobacterium bovis*. Pasteurization has controlled this mode of transmission. The disease is much less likely to spread by hands, eating utensils, or fomites.

67. The correct answer is 1. Ethambutol, isoniazid, streptomycin, and rifampin are first-line drugs used in the treatment of TB. Penicillin and tetracycline are antibiotics that are not used in the initial treatment of TB. Thioridazine is an antianxiety agent and pyridoxine is a vitamin. Neither are used in the initial treatment of TB. Pyridoxine is given with isoniazid to prevent the side effect of peripheral neuropathy.

68. The correct answer is 2. An increased anterior-posterior chest diameter, commonly referred to as a "barrel chest" is seen in clients with emphysema as a result of chronic hyperinflation of the lungs. EKG changes would not necessarily be seen with emphysema. A rapid, labored respiratory pattern would be seen in a client with emphysema. The client would most likely be thin because of the demanding work of breathing required and because the client would not have the stamina to eat large meals.

69. The correct answer is 4. The stimulus to breathe in a client with emphysema is low oxygen levels rather than rising CO_2 levels. Frequent nursing observations are necessary to see how the client handles low-flow oxygen administration. Humidification will be necessary but this is not the most important nursing intervention. Low-flow oxygen is appropriate for a client with chronic obstructive lung disease. High-Fowler's position may make it easier for the client to breathe. However, the client will assume the position most helpful for him to breathe.

The Gastrointestinal System

OVERVIEW OF ANATOMY AND PHYSIOLOGY

The organs of the digestive system are grouped into the alimentary canal (GI tract), consisting of the mouth, esophagus, stomach, and small and large intestine; and the accessory digestive organs, including the liver, pancreas, gallbladder, and ductal system (Figure 4.13). The primary functions of this system are movement of food, digestion, absorption, elimination, and provision of a continuous supply of nutrients, electrolytes, and water.

Mouth

A. Consists of the lips and oral cavity: provides entrance and initial processing for nutrients and sensory data, such as taste, texture, and temperature.
B. Oral cavity contains the teeth, used for mastication, and the tongue, which assists in deglutition, taste sensation, and mastication.
C. The salivary glands, located in the mouth, produce secretions containing ptyalin for starch digestion and mucus for lubrication.
D. The pharynx aids in swallowing and functions in ingestion by providing a route for food to

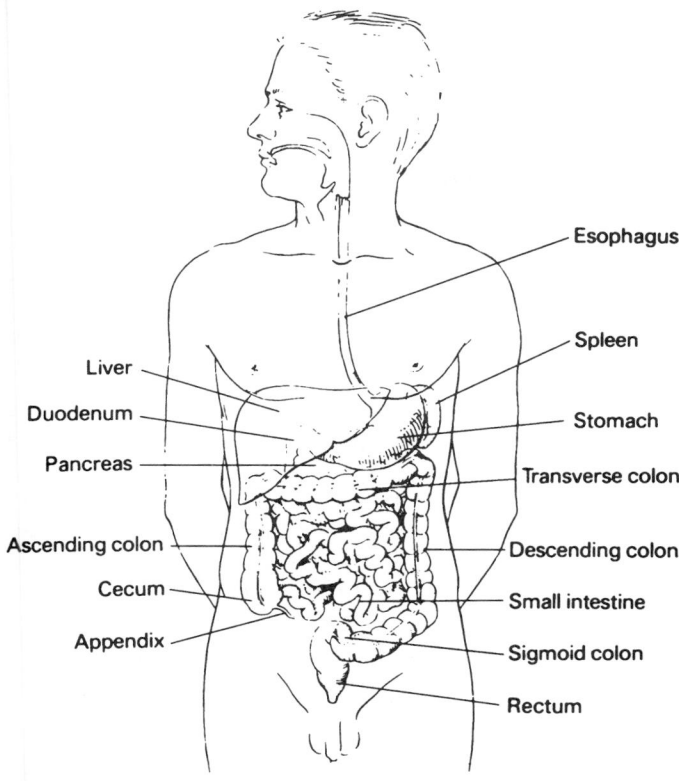

FIGURE 4.13 Anterior view of the structures of the GI tract

Labels: Esophagus, Spleen, Liver, Stomach, Duodenum, Transverse colon, Pancreas, Descending colon, Ascending colon, Small intestine, Cecum, Sigmoid colon, Appendix, Rectum

pass from the mouth to the esophagus (see page 243 for further details).

Esophagus

Muscular tube that receives food from the pharynx and propels it into the stomach by peristalsis.

Stomach

A. Located on the left side of the abdominal cavity, occupying the hypochondriac, epigastric, and umbilical regions.
B. Stores and mixes food with gastric juices and mucus, producing chemical and mechanical changes in the bolus of food.
   1. The secretion of digestive juices is stimulated by smelling, tasting, and chewing food, which is known as the cephalic phase of digestion.
   2. The gastric phase is stimulated by the presence of food in the stomach; regulated by neural stimulation via the PNS and hormonal stimulation through secretions of gastrin by the gastric mucosa.
   3. After processing in the stomach, the food bolus, called *chyme,* is released into the small intestine through the duodenum.
C. Two sphincters control the rate of food passage.

1. *Cardiac sphincter:* located at the opening between the esophagus and stomach
   2. *Pyloric sphincter:* located between the stomach and duodenum
D. Three anatomic divisions: fundus, body, and antrum
E. Gastric secretions
   1. *Pepsinogen:* secreted by chief cells, located in fundus, aids in protein digestion
   2. *Hydrochloric acid:* secreted by parietal cells, functions in protein digestion, released in response to gastrin
   3. *Intrinsic factor:* secreted by parietal cells, promotes absorption of vitamin B_{12}
   4. Mucoid secretions: coat stomach wall and prevent autodigestion

Small Intestine

A. Composed of the duodenum, jejunum, and ileum
B. Extends from the pylorus to the *ileocecal valve,* which regulates flow into the large intestine and prevents reflux into the small intestine.
C. Major functions of the small intestine are digestion and absorption of the end products of digestion.
D. Structural features
   1. *Villi* (functional units of the small intestine): fingerlike projections located in the mucous membrane; contain goblet cells that secrete mucus and absorptive cells that absorb digested foodstuffs.
   2. *Crypts of Lieberkuhn:* produce secretions containing digestive enzymes.
   3. *Brunner's glands:* found in the submucosa of the duodenum, secrete mucus.

Large Intestine

A. Divided into four parts: cecum (with appendix), colon (ascending, transverse, descending, sigmoid), rectum, and anus.
B. Serves as a reservoir for fecal material until defecation occurs; functions to absorb water and electrolytes.
C. Microorganisms present in the large intestine are responsible for a small amount of further breakdown and also make some vitamins.
   1. Amino acids are deaminated by bacteria, resulting in ammonia, which is converted to urea in the liver.
   2. Bacteria in the large intestine aid in the synthesis of vitamin K and some of the vitamin B groups.
D. Feces (solid waste) leave the body via the rectum and anus.
   1. Anus contains internal sphincter (under involuntary control) and external sphincter (voluntary control)

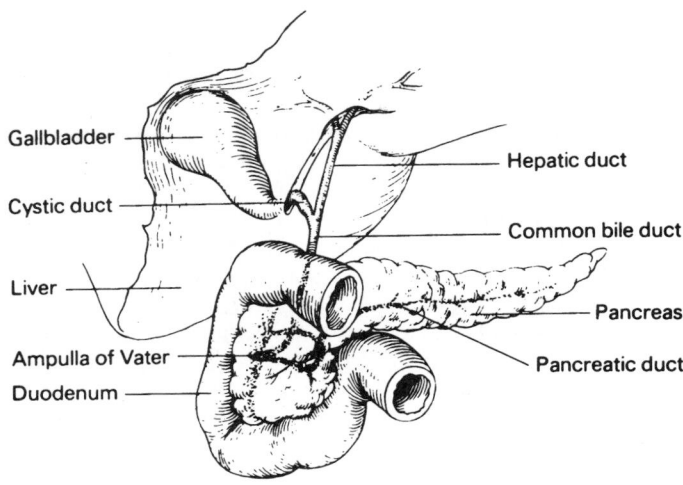

FIGURE 4.14 Gallbladder and ductal system

2. Fecal matter usually 75% water and 25% solid wastes (roughage, dead bacteria, fat, protein, inorganic matter)

Liver

A. Largest internal organ; located in the right hypochondriac and epigastric regions of the abdomen
B. *Liver lobules:* functional units of the liver, composed of hepatic cells
C. Hepatic sinusoids (capillaries) are lined with Kupffer cells, which carry out the process of phagocytosis.
D. Portal circulation brings blood to the liver from the stomach, spleen, pancreas, and intestines.
E. Functions
   1. Metabolism of fats, carbohydrates, and proteins; oxidizes these nutrients for energy and produces compounds that can be stored.
   2. Production of bile
   3. Conjugation and excretion (in the form of glycogen, fatty acids, minerals, fat-soluble and water-soluble vitamins) of bilirubin.
   4. Storage of vitamins A, D, B_{12}, and iron
   5. Synthesis of coagulation factors
   6. Detoxification of many drugs and conjugation of sex hormones

Biliary System

Consists of the gallbladder and associated ductal system (bile ducts), see Figure 4.14.
A. *Gallbladder:* lies on the undersurface of the liver, functions to concentrate and store bile.
B. *Ductal system:* provides a route for bile to reach the intestines.
   1. Bile is formed in the liver and excreted into the hepatic duct.
   2. Hepatic duct joins with the cystic duct

(which drains the gallbladder) to form the *common bile duct.*
   3. If sphincter of Oddi is relaxed, bile enters the duodenum. If contracted, bile is stored in gallbladder.

Pancreas

A. Positioned transversely in the upper abdominal cavity.
B. Consists of a head, body, and tail along with a pancreatic duct, which extends along the gland and enters the duodenum via the common bile duct.
C. Has both exocrine and endocrine functions; function in GI system is exocrine.
   1. Exocrine cells in the pancreas secrete trypsinogen and chymotrypsin for protein digestion, amylase to break down starch to disaccharides, and lipase for fat digestion.
   2. Endocrine function is related to islets of Langerhans (see page 321).

Physiology of Digestion and Absorption

A. Digestion: physical and chemical breakdown of food into absorptive substances
   1. Initiated in the mouth where food mixes with saliva and starch is broken down
   2. Food then passes into the esophagus where it is propelled into the stomach.
   3. In the stomach, food is processed by gastric secretions into a substance called *chyme.*
   4. In the small intestine, carbohydrates are hydrolyzed to monosaccharides, fats to glycerol, and fatty acids and proteins to amino acids to complete the digestive process.
      a. When chyme enters the duodenum, mucus is secreted to neutralize hydrochloric acid; in response to release of *secretin,* pancreas releases bicarbonate to neutralize acid chyme.
      b. *Cholecystokinin and pancreozymin (CCK-PZ)* are also produced by the duodenal mucosa; stimulate contraction of the gallbladder along with relaxation of the sphincter of Oddi (to allow bile to flow from the common bile duct into the duodenum), and stimulate release of pancreatic enzymes.

ASSESSMENT

Health History

A. Presenting problem
   1. Mouth: symptoms may include dental

caries, bleeding gums, dryness or increased salivation, odors, difficulty chewing (note use of dentures)
2. Ingestion: symptoms may include
   a. Changes in appetite: anorexia or hyperorexia; note food preferences/dislikes.
   b. Food intolerances: allergies, fluid, fatty foods.
   c. Weight gain/loss: note symptoms/situations that might interfere with appetite (stress, deliberate weight reduction, dental problems); note average weight and percent gain/loss within past 2–9 months.
   d. Dysphagia: note level of sensation where problem occurs, whether it occurs with foods/fluids.
   e. Nausea: note onset and duration, existence of associated symptoms (weakness, headache, vomiting), occurrence before or after meals.
   f. Vomiting: note onset and duration; foods/fluids that can be maintained; associated symptoms (fever, diarrhea).
   g. Regurgitation (reflux): note whether occurs with ingestion of certain foods, any associated symptoms (vomiting), occurrence with certain positions (supine, recumbent).
3. Digestion/absorption: symptoms may include
   a. Dyspepsia (indigestion): note location of discomfort, whether associated with certain foods, time of day/night of occurrence, associated symptoms (vomiting).
   b. Heartburn (pyrosis): note location, whether pain radiates, whether it occurs before or after meals, time of day when discomfort is most noticeable, foods that aggravate or eliminate symptoms.
   c. Pain: character, frequency, location, duration, distribution, aggravating or alleviating factors.
4. Bowel habits: symptoms may include
   a. Constipation: note number of stools/day or week, changes in size or color of stool, alterations in food/fluid intake, presence of tenesmus, painful defecation, associated symptoms (abdominal pain, cramps)
   b. Diarrhea: note number of stools/day, consistency, quantity, odor, interference with ADL, associated symptoms (nausea, vomiting, flatus, abdominal distension)
5. Hepatic/biliary problems: symptoms may include

   a. Jaundice: note location, duration, notable increase/decrease in degree.
   b. Pruritus: note location, distribution, onset.
   c. Urine changes: note color, onset, notable increase or decrease in color change, associated symptoms (pain).
   d. Clay-colored stools: note onset, number/day, associated symptoms (pain, problems with ingestion/digestion).
   e. Increased bleeding: note ecchymoses, purpura, bleeding gums, hematuria.
B. Life-style: eating behaviors (rapid ingestion, skipping meals, snacking), cultural/religious values (vegetarian, kosher foods), ingestion of alcohol, smoking.
C. Use of medications: note use of antacids, antiemetics, antiflatulents, vitamin supplements; aspirin and anti-inflammatory agents
D. Past medical history: childhood, adult, psychiatric illness; surgery; bleeding disorders; menstrual history; exposure to infectious agents; allergies.

Physical Examination

A. Mouth: inspect/palpate
   1. Outer/inner lips: color, texture, moisture
   2. Buccal mucosa: color, texture, lesions, ulcerations
   3. Teeth/gums: missing teeth, cavities, tenderness, swelling
   4. Tongue: protrusion without deviation, texture, color, moisture
   5. Palates (hard and soft): color
B. Abdomen: divided into regions and quadrants (Figure 4.15); note specific location of any abnormality.
   1. Inspect skin: color, scars, striae, pigmentation, lesions, vascularity.
   2. Inspect architecture: contour, symmetry, distension, umbilicus.
   3. Inspect movement: peristalsis, pulsations.
   4. Auscultate peristaltic sounds.
      a. Normal: bubbling, gurgling, 5–30 times/minute
      b. Increased: may indicate diarrhea, gastroenteritis, early intestinal obstruction
      c. Decreased: may indicate constipation, late intestinal obstruction, use of anticholinergics, post-op anesthesia
   5. Auscultate arterial sounds: note presence or absence of bruits in aorta/renal arteries.
   6. Percuss for tenderness/masses; determine distribution of tympany and dullness
      a. Liver span: normal 6–12 cm dullness at the midclavicular line; determine shifting dullness (ascites)
      b. Stomach: normal tympany

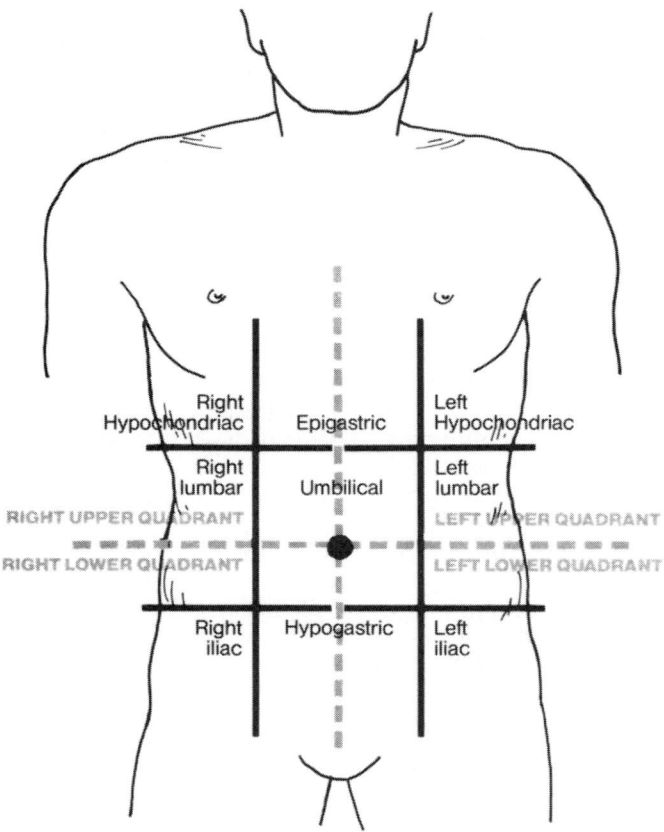

FIGURE 4.15 Abdominal quadrants (broken lines) and regions (solid lines)

Labels within figure:

Right Hypochondriac | Epigastric | Left Hypochondriac
Right lumbar | Umbilical | Left lumbar
RIGHT UPPER QUADRANT | | LEFT UPPER QUADRANT
RIGHT LOWER QUADRANT | | LEFT LOWER QUADRANT
Right iliac | Hypogastric | Left iliac

   c. Spleen: normal tympany, dullness only if enlarged

   d. Small/large intestine: normal tympany

   e. Bladder: normal tympany, dullness if full

7. Palpate to depth of 1 cm (light palpation) to determine areas of tenderness, muscle guarding, and masses

8. Palpate to a depth of 4–8 cm (deep palpation) to identify rigidity, masses, ascites, tenderness, liver margins, spleen

Laboratory/Diagnostic Tests

A. Blood chemistry and electrolyte analysis: albumin, alkaline phosphatase, ammonia, amylase, bilirubin, chloride, LDH, lipase, potassium, SGOT or AST, serum glutamic pyruvic transaminase (SGPT or ALT), sodium.

B. Hematologic studies: Hgb and hct, PT, WBC

C. Serologic studies: carcinoembryonic antigen (CEA), hepatitis-associated antigens, helicobacter pylori

D. Urine studies: amylase, bilirubin

E. Fecal studies: for blood, fat, infectious organisms

   1. A freshly passed, warm stool is the best specimen.

   2. For fat or infectious organisms collect three separate specimens and label day #1, day #2, day #3.

F. Upper GI series (barium swallow)

   1. Fluoroscopic examination of upper GI tract to determine structural problems and gastric emptying time; client must swallow barium sulfate or other contrast medium; sequential films taken as it moves through the system.

   2. Nursing care: pretest

      a. Keep NPO after midnight or 6–8 hours pretest.

      b. Explain that the barium will taste chalky.

   3. Nursing care: posttest: administer laxatives to enhance elimination of barium and prevent obstruction or impaction.

G. Lower GI series (barium enema)

   1. Barium is instilled into the colon by enema; client retains the contrast medium while x-rays are taken to identify structural abnormalities of the large intestine or colon.

   2. Nursing care: pretest

      a. Keep NPO for 8 hours pretest.

      b. Give enemas until clear the morning of test.

      c. Administer laxative or suppository.

      d. Explain that cramping may be experienced during the procedure.

   3. Nursing care: posttest: administer laxatives and fluids to assist in expelling barium.

H. Endoscopy (Esophagogastroduodenoscopy)

   1. Direct visualization of the esophagus, stomach, and duodenum by insertion of a lighted fiberscope

   2. Used to observe structures, ulcerations, inflammation, tumors; may include a biopsy

   3. Nursing care: pretest

      a. Keep NPO for 6–8 hours.

      b. Ensure consent form has been signed.

      c. Explain that a local anesthetic will be used to ease discomfort and that speaking during the procedure will not be possible; the client should expect hoarseness and a sore throat for several days.

   4. Nursing care: posttest

      a. Keep NPO until return of gag reflex.

      b. Assess vital signs and for pain, dysphagia, bleeding.

      c. Administer warm normal saline gargles for relief of sore throat.

I. Colonoscopy

   1. Endoscopic visualization of the large intestine: may include biopsy and removal of foreign substances.

2. Nursing care: pretest
   a. Keep NPO for 8 hours pretest.
   b. Administer laxatives for 1–3 days before the exam, and sometimes enemas until clear the night before the test.
   c. Ensure a consent form has been signed.
   d. Explain to client that when the instrument is inserted into the rectum a feeling of pressure might be experienced.
3. Nursing care: posttest
   a. Observe for rectal bleeding and signs of perforation.
   b. Schedule planned rest periods for the client.
J. Sigmoidoscopy
   1. Endoscopic visualization of the sigmoid colon
   2. Used to identify inflammation or lesions, or remove foreign bodies.
   3. Nursing care: pretest
      a. Offer a light supper and light breakfast.
      b. Do bowel prep.
      c. Explain to client that the sensation of an urge to defecate or abdominal cramping might be experienced.
   4. Nursing care: posttest: assess for signs of bowel perforation.
K. Gastric analysis
   1. Insertion of a nasogastric tube to examine fasting gastric contents for acidity and volume
   2. Nursing care: pretest
      a. Keep NPO 6–8 hours pretest.
      b. Advise client about no smoking, anticholinergic medications, antacids for 24 hours prior to test.
      c. Inform client that tube will be inserted into the stomach via the nose, and instruct to expectorate saliva to prevent buffering of secretions.
   3. Nursing care: posttest: provide frequent mouth care.
L. Oral cholecystogram
   1. Injection of a radiopaque dye and x-ray examination to visualize the gallbladder
   2. Used to determine the gallbladder's ability to concentrate and store the dye and to assess patency of the biliary duct system
   3. Nursing care: pretest
      a. Offer a low-fat meal the evening before the test and black coffee, tea, or water the morning of the exam.
      b. Check for iodine sensitivity and administer dye tablets (Telepaque) as ordered.
   4. Nursing care: posttest: observe for side effects of the dye (nausea, vomiting, diarrhea).

M. Liver biopsy (closed needle)
   1. Invasive procedure where a specially designed needle is inserted into the liver to remove a small piece of tissue for study
   2. Nursing care: pretest
      a. Ensure client has signed consent form.
      b. Keep NPO 6–8 hours pretest.
      c. Instruct client to hold breath during the biopsy.
   3. Nursing care: posttest
      a. Assess vital signs every hour for 8–12 hours.
      b. Place client on right side for a few hours with a pillow against the abdomen to provide pressure on the liver.
      c. Observe puncture site for hemorrhage.
      d. Assess for complications of shock and pneumothorax.

ANALYSIS

Nursing diagnoses for the client with a disorder of the digestive system may include
A. Risk for fluid volume deficit
B. Body image disturbance
C. Altered nutrition: less than body requirements
D. Diarrhea
E. Constipation
F. Pain
G. Ineffective breathing pattern
H. Impaired verbal communication
I. Impaired skin integrity

PLANNING AND IMPLEMENTATION

Goals

A. Restoration of fluid and electrolyte balance.
B. Client will express feelings of self-worth.
C. Adequate nutritional status will be maintained.
D. Client will experience decreased frequency of regular bowel habits.
E. Client will establish regular bowel habits of appropriate amount and consistency.
F. Client will be free from pain.
G. Effective breathing patterns will be maintained.
H. Effective communication methods will be established.
I. Skin integrity will be restored/maintained.

Interventions

Enemas

A. General information
   1. Instillation of fluid into the rectum, usually for the purpose of stimulating defecation. The various types include

a. *cleansing enema* (tap water, normal saline, or soap): used to treat constipation or feces impaction, as bowel cleansing prior to diagnostic procedures or surgery, to help establish regular bowel functions.

b. *retention enema* (mineral oil, olive oil, cottonseed oil): usually administered to lubricate or soften a hard fecal mass to facilitate defecation.

B. Nursing care for a cleansing enema
1. Explain procedure and that breathing through the mouth relaxes abdominal musculature and helps to avoid cramps; explain the need to take adequate time to defecate.
2. Assemble equipment: prepare solution at 105°–110°F and have bedpan, commode, or nearby bathroom ready for use.
3. Position client and drape adequately.
4. Place waterproof pad under buttocks.
5. Lubricate tube and allow solution to fill the tubing, displacing air.
6. Insert rectal tube 4–5 inches without using force; request that client take several deep breaths.
7. Administer 500–100 ml of solution over 5–10 minutes; if cramping occurs slow the speed of instillation.
8. After administration, have the client retain solution until the urge to defecate becomes strong.
9. Document amount, color, characteristics of stool, and client's reaction during procedure.
10. Assess for dizziness, light-headedness, abdominal cramps, nausea.
11. Monitor electrolyte levels if client is to receive repeated enemas.

C. Nursing care for a retention enema: same as for a cleansing enema except
1. Oil is used instead of water (comes prepared in commercial kits and is given at body temperature).
2. Administer 150–200 ml of prepared solution.
3. Instruct client to retain oil for at least 30 minutes in order for it to take effect.

Gastrostomy

A. General information
1. Insertion of a catheter through an abdominal incision into the stomach where it is secured with sutures.
2. Used as an alternative method of feeding, either temporary or permanent, for clients who have problems with swallowing, ingestion, and digestion.

B. Nursing care
1. Maintain skin integrity: inspect and cleanse skin around stoma frequently; keep deep area dry to avoid excoriation.

2. Maintain patency of the gastrostomy tube.
   a. Assess for residual before each feeding (check orders concerning withholding feeding).
   b. Irrigate tube before and after meals.
   c. Measure/record any drainage.
3. Promote adequate nutrition.
   a. Administer feeding with client in high-Fowler's and keep head of bed elevated for 30 minutes after meals to prevent regurgitation.
   b. Maintain feeding at room temperature.
   c. Ensure that prescribed amount of feeding be given within prescribed amount of time.
   d. Weigh client daily.
   e. Monitor I&O until feedings are well tolerated.
   f. Monitor for signs of dehydration.

Nasogastric (NG) Tubes

A. General information
1. Soft rubber or plastic tube inserted through a nostril and into the stomach for gastric decompression, feeding, or obtaining specimens for analysis of stomach contents
2. Types
   a. Levin: single-lumen, nonvented
   b. Salem: a tube within a tube; vented to provide constant inflow of atmospheric air

B. Nursing care
1. Insertion of the tube
   a. Explain the purpose of the tube and the procedure for insertion.
   b. Measure the tube: distance on the tube from the tip of the nose to the ear lobe plus the distance from the ear lobe to the tip of the xiphoid.
   c. Instruct client to bend head forward if possible during insertion.
2. Monitor functioning of system and ensure patency of the NG tube: abdominal discomfort/distension, nausea and vomiting, and little or no drainage in collection bottle are all signs that system is not functioning properly.
   a. Assess the position: aspirate gastric contents to confirm that tube is in stomach; inject 10 ml air through tube and auscultate for rapid influx.
   b. Check that tubing is free of kinks; irrigate as per physician order.
   c. Record amount, color, and odor of drainage.
3. Provide measures to ensure maximal comfort.
   a. Apply water-soluble lubricant to lips to prevent dryness.
   b. Keep nares free from secretions.

    c. Provide periodic warm saline gargles to prevent dryness.

    d. Provide frequent mouth care with toothbrush/toothpaste or flavored mouthwashes.

    e. If allowed, give client hard candy or gum to stimulate the flow of saliva and prevent dryness.

    f. Elevate head and chest during and for 1–2 hours after feedings to prevent reflux (most comfortable position when suction is used).

4. Monitor/maintain fluid and electrolyte balance.

    a. Assess for signs of metabolic alkalosis (suctioning causes excessive loss of hydrochloric acid and potassium).

    b. Administer IV fluids as ordered.

    c. If suction used, irrigate NG tube with normal saline to decrease sodium loss.

    d. Keep accurate I&O.

    e. If suction used provide ice chips sparingly (if allowed) to avoid dilution of electrolytes.

    f. Monitor lab values and electrolytes frequently.

Intestinal Tubes

A. General information

  1. Tube is inserted via a nostril through the stomach and into the intestine for decompression proximal to an obstruction, relief of an obstruction, decompression of post-op edema at the surgical site.

  2. Types

    a. Cantor tube: single lumen

    b. Harris tube: single lumen

    c. Miller-Abbott: double lumen

B. Nursing care

  1. Facilitate placement of the tube.

    a. Position client in high-Fowler's while tube is being passed from the nose to the stomach; then place client on right side to aid in advancing the tube from the stomach to duodenum.

    b. Continuously monitor tube markings.

    c. Tape tube in place only after placement in duodenum is confirmed.

  2. Provide measures for maximal comfort, as for NG tube.

EVALUATION

A. Adequate urine output; stable vital signs; moist mucous membranes; adequate skin turgor and mobility; electrolyte levels within normal range.

B. Client expresses interest in personal well-being; actively participates in ADL, treatments, and care.

C. Stable weight; improved anthropometric measurements; laboratory values within normal limits; client verbalizes types of foods that should be included or eliminated from prescribed diet.

D. Client reports reduction in frequency of stools and return to more normal stool consistency; laboratory values within normal range.

E. Client reports increased frequency with improved consistency of stool.

F. Relaxed facial expression; decreased abdominal distension; healed mouth ulcers.

G. Improved respiratory rate, depth, and rhythm; lungs clear to auscultation; effective use of muscles of respiration.

H. Client effectively uses artificial means of communication (artificial larynx, sign language, or esophageal speech).

I. No redness, irritation, or breakdown; client demonstrates techniques to prevent skin breakdown.

DISORDERS OF THE GASTROINTESTINAL SYSTEM

Nausea and Vomiting

A. General information

  1. *Nausea:* a feeling of discomfort in the epigastrium with a conscious desire to vomit; occurs in association with and prior to vomiting.

  2. *Vomiting:* forceful ejection of stomach contents from the upper GI tract. Emetic center in medulla is stimulated (e.g., by local irritation of intestine or stomach or disturbance of equilibrium), causing the vomiting reflex.

  3. Nausea and vomiting are the two most common manifestations of GI disease.

  4. Contributing factors

    a. GI disease

    b. CNS disorders (meningitis, CNS lesions)

    c. Circulatory problems (CHF)

    d. Metabolic disorders (uremia)

    e. Side effects of certain drugs (chemotherapy, antibiotics)

    f. Pain

    g. Psychic trauma

    h. Response to motion

B. Assessment findings

  1. Weakness, fatigue, pallor, possible lethargy

  2. Dry mucous membrane and poor skin turgor/mobility (if prolonged with dehydration)

  3. Serum sodium, calcium, potassium decreased

  4. BUN elevated (if severe vomiting and dehydration)

C. Nursing interventions
1. Maintain NPO until client able to tolerate oral intake.
2. Administer medications as ordered and monitor effects/side effects.
   a. Phenothiazines: chlorpromazine (Thorazine), perphenazine (Trilafon), prochlorperazine (Compazine), trifluoperazine (Stelazine)
   b. Antihistamines: benzquinamide (Emete-con), dimenhydrinate (Dramimine), diphenhydramine (Benadryl), hydroxyzine (Atarax, Vistaril), cyclizine (Marezine), meclizine (Antivert), promethazine (Phenergan)
   c. Other drugs to help control nausea and vomiting: thiethylperazine (Torecan), trimethobenzamide (Tigan), metoclopramide (Reglan)
3. Notify physician if vomiting pattern changes.
4. Maintain fluid and electrolyte balance.
   a. Administer IV fluids as ordered, keep accurate record of I&O.
   b. Record amount/frequency of vomitus.
   c. Assess skin tone/turgor for degree of hydration.
   d. Monitor laboratory/electrolyte values.
   e. Test NG tube drainage or vomitus for blood, bile; monitor pH.
5. Provide measures for maximum comfort.
   a. Institute frequent mouth care with tepid water/saline mouthwashes.
   b. Remove encrustations around nares.
   c. Keep head of bed elevated and avoid sudden changes in position.
   d. Eliminate noxious stimuli from environment.
   e. Keep emesis basin clean.
   f. Maintain quiet environment and avoid unnecessary procedures.
6. When vomiting subsides provide clear fluids (ginger ale, warm tea) in small amounts, gradually introduce solid foods (toast, crackers), and progress to bland foods (baked potato), in small amounts.
7. Provide client teaching and discharge planning concerning
   a. Avoidance of situations, foods, or liquids that precipitate nausea and vomiting
   b. Need for planned, uninterrupted rest periods
   c. Medication regimen, including side effects
   d. Signs of dehydration
   e. Need for daily weights with frequent anthropometric measurements

Anorexia/Eating Disorders

See page 533.

Diarrhea

A. General information
1. Increase in peristaltic motility, producing watery or loosely formed stools. Diarrhea is a symptom of other pathologic processes.
2. Causes
   a. Chronic bowel disorders
   b. Malabsorption problems
   c. Intestinal infections
   d. Biliary tract disorders
   e. Hyperthyroidism
   f. Saline laxatives
   g. Magnesium-based antacids
   h. Stress
   i. Antibiotics
   j. Neoplasms
   k. Highly seasoned foods
B. Assessment findings
1. Abdominal cramps/distension, foul-smelling watery stools, increased peristalsis
2. Anorexia, thirst, tenesmus, anxiety
3. Decreased potassium and sodium if severe
C. Nursing interventions
1. Administer antidiarrheals: diphenoxylate with atropine (Lomotil), paregoric, loperamide (Imodium), Kaopectate as ordered; monitor effects.
2. Control fluid/food intake.
   a. Avoid milk and milk products.
   b. Provide liquids with gradual introduction of bland, high-protein, high-calorie, low-fat, low-bulk foods.
3. Monitor and maintain fluid and electrolyte status; record number, characteristics, and amount of each stool.
4. Prevent anal excoriation.
   a. Cleanse rectal area after each bowel movement with mild soap and water and pat dry.
   b. Apply A and D ointment or Desitin to promote healing.
   c. Use a local anesthetic as needed.
5. Provide client teaching and discharge planning concerning
   a. Medication regimen
   b. Adherence to prescribed diet and avoidance of foods that are known to produce diarrhea
   c. Importance of perineal hygiene and care and daily assessment of skin changes
   d. Importance of good handwashing techniques after each stool
   e. Need to report worsening of symptoms (increased abdominal cramps, increased frequency or amount of stool)

    f. Need to assess daily weights with frequent anthropometric measurements

Constipation

A. General information
  1. Lengthening of normal (for individual) time period between bowel movements; small volume of dry, hard stool; results from decreased motility of the colon or from retention of feces in the colon or rectum
  2. Causes
    a. Inadequate bulk/liquids in the diet
    b. Lack of physical activity
    c. Retention of barium after radiographic exam
    d. Prolonged use of constipation medications (aluminum-based antacids, anticholinergics, antihistamines, antidepressants, phenothiazines, calcium, iron)
B. Assessment findings
  1. Feeling of abdominal fullness, pressure in the rectum; abdominal distension, dyschezia; increased flatus
  2. Hardened stool upon digital examination
C. Nursing interventions
  1. Promote adequate intake of fluids/foods and dietary modification: increase fluid intake to at least 3000 ml/day; include high-fiber foods in diet.
  2. Administer medications as ordered
    a. Cathartics: milk of magnesia, castor oil, cascara sagrada, senna (Senokot), bisacodyl (Dulcolax), psyllium (Metamucil)
    b. Stool softeners: docusate calcium (Surfak), docusate sodium (Colace)
  3. Prevent accumulation of stool in the colon/rectum.
    a. Instruct client not to suppress urge to defecate.
    b. Gently massage abdomen to promote stimulation and movement of feces.
  4. Provide client teaching and discharge planning concerning
    a. Need to establish and maintain a regular time to defecate
    b. Diet modification
    c. Medication regimen
    d. Need to assume position of comfort when sitting on toilet

Stomatitis

See page 170.

Cancer of the Mouth

A. General information
  1. Cancer of the mouth may occur on the lips or within the mouth (tongue, floor of mouth, buccal mucosa, hard/soft palate, pharynx, tonsils).
  2. Most common type of oral tumor is squamous cell carcinoma; most malignancies occur on the lower lip.
  3. More common in men.
  4. Caused by
    a. Excessive sun exposure
    b. Tobacco (cigar, pipe, cigarette, snuff)
    c. Excessive alcohol intake
    d. Constant irritation (dental caries)
  5. Early detection is very important; most discovered by dentists in routine checkups.
B. Medical management
  1. Radiation therapy: both primary lesion and affected lymph nodes; radioactive implants
  2. Chemotherapy: sometimes indicated, not used as often as radiation therapy and surgery
  3. Surgery: type depends on location and extent of the tumor.
    a. Mandibulectomy: removal of the mandible.
    b. Hemiglossectomy: removal of half the tongue
    c. Glossectomy: removal of the entire tongue
    d. Radical neck dissection
C. Assessment findings
  1. Ulcerations (often painless) on the lip, tongue, or buccal mucosa
  2. Pain or soreness of the tongue upon eating hot or highly seasoned foods
  3. Erythroplakia, leukoplakia
  4. Difficulty chewing/speaking, dysphagia
  5. Positive oral exfoliative cytology
  6. Positive toluidine blue test
D. Nursing interventions
  1. Provide nursing care for the client receiving radiation therapy
  2. Prepare client for surgery: in addition to routine pre-op care
    a. Inform client of expected changes post-op.
    b. Provide explanation of anticipated post-op suctioning, NG tube, drains.
  3. In addition to routine post-op care
    a. Promote drainage.
     1) place in side-lying position initially, then Fowler's.
     2) suction mouth (except for lip surgery).
     3) maintain patency of drainage tubes.
    b. Promote oral hygiene/comfort.
     1) provide mouth irrigations with sterile water, diluted peroxide, normal saline, or sodium bicarbonate.

2) avoid use of commercial mouthwashes, lemon and glycerine swabs.
c. Monitor/promote optimum nutritional status.
   1) provide tube feedings following a hemiglossectomy.
   2) place oral fluids in back of the throat with an asepto syringe.
   3) provide foods/fluids that are nonirritating and facilitate swallowing (yogurt, puddings).
d. Monitor for signs and symptoms of facial nerve damage (drooping, uneven smile, circumoral numbness or tingling).

Cancer of the Esophagus

A. General information
   1. Malignant tumors of the esophagus usually appear as ulcerated lesions, most often in middle and lower portions of the esophagus
   2. Penetration of the muscular layers with extension to the outer wall of the esophagus is commonly found. Metastases may cause eventual esophageal obstruction
   3. More common in men than in women (4:1); usually between ages 50–70
   4. Cause unknown; contributing factors include cigarette smoking, excessive alcohol intake, trauma, poor oral hygiene, achalasia, diverticula, and lye burns.
B. Medical management
   1. Radiation therapy: used for inoperable tumors, has been found to alleviate symptoms
   2. Chemotherapy: not found effective
   3. Surgery
      a. Esophagectomy: removal of part or all of the esophagus using a Dacron graft to replace the resected portion
      b. Esophagogastrostomy: resection of a portion of the esophagus (usually middle third) and anastomosis of the remaining portion of the stomach
      c. Esophagoenterostomy: resection of portion of the esophagus and anastomosis of a segment of colon to the remaining portion
      d. Palliative gastrostomy: done for the purpose of feeding the client
C. Assessment findings
   1. Substernal burning after drinking hot fluids
   2. Pain located in the substernal and epigastric areas; usually intensified with swallowing
   3. Weight loss

4. Barium swallow reveals narrowing of the esophagus at the area of the tumor
5. Diagnostic test: esophagoscopy with a biopsy reveals malignant cells
D. Nursing interventions
   1. Provide nursing care for the client receiving radiation therapy.
   2. Prepare client for surgery: in addition to routine pre-op care
      a. Provide meticulous oral hygiene including teeth, gums, tongue, and mouth.
      b. Explain that client may have a chest tube if thoracic approach is used.
      c. Prepare client for feedings through a gastrostomy.
   3. In addition to routine post-op care
      a. Monitor NG tube: expect bloody drainage for approximately 12 hours with gradual change to green, then to yellow.
      b. Prevent gastric reflux: place client in semi-Fowler's position; maintain upright position for 2 hours after meals when client is able to take fluids/food orally.
   4. Provide emotional support to client/significant others; prognosis is grave.
   5. Provide client teaching and discharge planning concerning
      a. Gastrostomy and proper dietary measures
      b. Importance of cessation of smoking and elimination of alcohol consumption
      c. Maintain good oral hygiene.
      d. Maintain a high-calorie, high-protein diet

Esophageal Varices

See page 284.

Hiatal Hernia

A. General information
   1. Sliding hiatal hernia occurs when a portion of the stomach and vagus nerve slide upward into the thorax through an enlarged hiatus in the diaphragm.
   2. Result is reflux of gastric juices and inflammation of the lower portion of the esophagus.
   3. Occurs more often in women ages 40–70
   4. May be caused by congenital weakening of the muscles in the diaphragm around the esophagogastric opening; increased intra-abdominal pressure (obesity, pregnancy, ascites); trauma
B. Medical management
   1. Drug therapy: antacids to reduce acidity and relieve discomfort, cholinergics

2. Modification of diet: elimination of spicy foods and caffeine
3. Surgery: reduction of the hiatal hernia via an abdominal or thoracic approach

C. Assessment findings
1. Heartburn, especially after meals, at night, or with position changes (particularly recumbent), dysphagia, regurgitation several hours after meals without vomiting
2. Barium swallow displays protrusion of the gastric mucosa through a hiatus
3. Esophagoscopy reveals an incompetent cardiac sphincter

D. Nursing interventions
1. Provide a bland diet with six small feedings/day, as ordered.
2. Administer medications as ordered.
3. Prepare client for surgery: in addition to routine pre-op care
   a. Inform client about chest tubes (if thoracic approach to be used).
   b. Provide information regarding NG intubation.
4. In addition to routine post-op care
   a. Decrease/avoid gastric distension.
   b. Promote pulmonary expansion: chest tubes if a thoracic approach; semi-Fowler's position.
5. Provide client teaching and discharge planning concerning
   a. Modification of diet
   b. Sitting up for meals and for 2 hours after meals will help reduce gastric acid reflux
   c. Use of antacids
   d. Eating small, frequent meals slowly to help prevent gastric distension
   e. Need to avoid carbonated beverages and anticholinergic drugs (and OTC medications that contain them)
   f. Avoidance of heavy lifting (to prevent intra-abdominal pressure); bend, kneel, or stoop instead
   g. Importance of treating persistent cough
   h. Adherence to weight-reduction plan if obese

Gastritis

A. General information
1. An acute inflammatory condition that causes a breakdown of the normal gastric protective barriers with subsequent diffusion of hydrochloric acid into the gastric lumen
2. Results in hemorrhage, ulceration, and adhesions of the gastric mucosa
3. Present in some form (mild to severe) in 50% of all adults
4. Caused by excessive ingestion of certain drugs (salicylates, steroids, Butazolidin), alcohol; food poisoning; large quantities of spicy, irritating foods in diet

B. Assessment findings
1. Anorexia, nausea and vomiting, hematemesis, epigastric fullness/discomfort, epigastric tenderness
2. Decreased Hgb and hct (if anemic)
3. Endoscopy: inflammation and ulceration of gastric mucosa
4. Gastric analysis: hydrochloric acid usually increased, except in atrophic gastritis

C. Nursing interventions
1. Monitor and maintain fluid and electrolyte balances.
2. Control nausea and vomiting (NPO until able to tolerate foods, then bland diet).
3. Administer medications as ordered: antiemetics, antacids, sedatives.
4. Maintain patency of NG tube.
5. Provide client teaching and discharge planning concerning avoidance of foods/medications such as coffee, spicy foods, alcohol, salicylates, ibuprofen, steroids.

Peptic Ulcer Disease

Gastric Ulcers

A. General information
1. Ulceration of the mucosal lining of the stomach; most commonly found in the antrum
2. Gastric secretions and stomach emptying rate usually normal
3. Rapid diffusion of gastric acid from the gastric lumen into gastric mucosa, however, causes an inflammatory reaction with tissue breakdown
4. Also characterized by reflux into the stomach of bile containing duodenal contents
5. Occurs more often in men, in unskilled laborers, and in lower socioeconomic groups; peak age 40–55 years
6. Predisposing factors include smoking, alcohol abuse, emotional tension, and drugs (salicylates, steroids, Butazolidin).
7. Caused by bacterial infection (*Helicobacter pylori*)

B. Medical management
1. Supportive: rest, bland diet, stress management
2. Drug therapy: antacids, histamine (H_2) receptor antagonists, anticholinergics, omeprazole (Prilosec), sucralfate (Carafate); also metronidazole and amoxicillin for ulcers caused by *Helicobacter pylori*
3. Surgery: various combinations of gastric resections and anastomosis

C. Assessment findings

1. Pain located in left epigastrium, with possible radiation to the back; usually occurs 1–2 hours after meals
2. Weight loss
3. Hgb and hct decreased (if anemic)
4. Endoscopy reveals ulceration; differentiates ulcers from gastric cancer
5. Gastric analysis: normal gastric acidity in gastric ulcer, increased in duodenal ulcer
6. Upper GI series: presence of ulcer confirmed

D. Nursing interventions
1. Administer medications as ordered (Table 4.19).
2. Provide nursing care for the client with ulcer surgery.
3. Provide client teaching and discharge planning concerning
   a. Medical regimen
      1) take medications at prescribed times.
      2) have antacids available at all times.
      3) recognize situations that would increase the need for antacids.
      4) avoid ulcerogenic drugs (salicylates, steroids).
      5) know proper dosage, action, and side effects.
   b. Proper diet
      1) bland diet consisting of six small meals/day.
      2) eat meals slowly.
      3) avoid acid-producing substances (caffeine, alcohol, highly seasoned foods).
      4) avoid stressful situations at mealtime.
      5) plan for rest periods after meals.
      6) avoid late bedtime snacks.
   c. Avoidance of stress-producing situations and development of stress-reduction methods (relaxation techniques, exercises, biofeedback).

Duodenal Ulcers

A. General information
1. Most commonly found in the first 2 cm of the duodenum
2. Occur more frequently than gastric ulcers
3. Characterized by gastric hyperacidity and a significant increased rate of gastric emptying
4. Occur more often in younger men; more women affected after menopause; peak age 35–45 years
5. Predisposing factors include smoking, alcohol abuse, psychological stress, bacterial infection (*Helicobacter pylori*)

B. Medical management: same as for gastric ulcers
C. Assessment findings

1. Pain located in midepigastrium and described as burning, cramping; usually occurs 2–4 hours after meals and is relieved by food.
2. Diagnostic tests: same as for gastric ulcer.

D. Nursing interventions: same as for gastric ulcer.

Gastric Surgery

A. General information
1. Surgery is performed when peptic ulcer disease does not respond to medical management or for gastric cancer
2. Types
   a. *Vagotomy:* severing of part of the vagus nerve innervating the stomach to decrease gastric acid secretion
   b. *Antrectomy:* removal of the antrum of the stomach to eliminate the gastric phase of digestion
   c. *Pyloroplasty:* enlargement of the pyloric sphincter with acceleration of gastric emptying
   d. *Gastroduodenostomy* (*Billroth I*): removal of the lower portion of the stomach with anastomosis of the remaining portion of the duodenum
   e. *Gastrojejunostomy* (*Billroth II*): removal of the antrum and distal portion of the stomach and duodenum with anastomosis of the remaining portion of the stomach to the jejunum
   f. *Gastrectomy:* removal of 60%–80% of the stomach
   g. *Esophagojejunostomy* (*total gastrectomy*): removal of the entire stomach with a loop of jejunum anastomosed to the esophagus
3. Dumping syndrome
   a. Abrupt emptying of stomach contents into the intestine
   b. Common complication of these types of surgery
   c. Associated with the presence of hyperosmolar chyme in the jejunum, which draws fluid by osmosis from the extracellular fluid into the bowel. Decreased plasma volume and distension of the bowel stimulates increased intestinal motility.
   d. Signs and symptoms include weakness, faintness, palpitations, diaphoresis, feeling of fullness, or discomfort, nausea, and occasionally diarrhea; appear 15–30 minutes after meals and last for 20–60 minutes

B. Nursing interventions: routine preoperative care
C. Nursing interventions: postoperative
1. Provide routine post-op care.
2. Ensure adequate function of NG tube.

TABLE 4.19 Drug Therapy for Peptic Ulcer

Drug	Action	Side Effects	Nursing Implications
Histamine (H₂) receptor-site antagonists			
Cimetidine (Tagamet)	Inhibits gastric secretion by inhibiting histamine-stimulating effect	Hematopoietic: reversible leukopenia, occasional thrombocytopenia CNS: metabolic encephalopathy, mild restlessness, confusion, hallucinations; agitation, coma Renal: slight increase in creatinine CV: reversible bradycardia GI: transient diarrhea Other: muscle pain, decreased sperm count, impotence, infertility, acnelike rash, gynecomastia Drug interactions: potentiates hypoprothrombinemia in clients taking warfarin (Coumadin)	Administer with meals. Allow at least one hour between cimetidine and antacid administration. Periodic evaluations of blood count, renal, and hepatic function. Advise client to avoid driving and other potentially hazardous activities until reaction to drug is known. Periodic determination of gastric pH.
Ranitidine (Zantac)	Potent histamine H₂ receptor-site antagonist	Hematopoietic: leukopenia, thrombocytopenia CNS: headache, malaise, dizziness GI: liver damage, constipation, nausea, abdominal pain Other: rash	Absorption not affected by food. Periodic evaluations of kidney and liver function. Report severe, persistent headache immediately. Periodic determination of gastric pH.
Famotidine (Pepcid)	Similar to Zantac		
Antacids			
Aluminum-containing antacids (Amphogel, Rolaids)	Neutralizes gastric acid (increases pH) and provides pain relief	Constipation, fecal impaction, interferes with anticholinergic absorption, hypophosphatemia, hypercalcemia	Explain that best time to take antacid is after meals. If administered in tablet form, instruct client to chew thoroughly before swallowing and to follow tablet with ½ glass of water or milk. Note number and consistency of stools.
Magnesium-containing antacids (milk of magnesia)	Neutralizes gastric acid and provides pain relief	Diarrhea, hypermagnesemia, nausea, and vomiting	Explain that best time to take antacid is after meals and at bedtime. Mix suspension with water or follow with sufficient water.
Anticholinergics			
Atropine, dicyclomine (Bentyl), methantheline bromide (Banthine), propantheline bromide (Pro-Banthine), glycopyrrolate (Robinul)	Decreases vagal stimulation of parietal cells; decreases motility and volume of gastric secretions	CNS: headache, insomnia, drowsiness, blurred vision CV: increased pulse, postural blood pressure changes GI: dry mouth, throat; increased thirst; constipation; nausea, paralytic ileus GU: urinary hesitancy; retention, impotence Skin: diaphoresis, urticaria	Advise client that best time to take is 30 minutes before meals. Antacids may interfere with absorption of anticholinergics. Advise client to avoid driving and to change positions slowly. Instruct to drink plenty of fluids; suck hard candy to relieve dryness. Assess for abdominal distension. Advise client to void before each dose. Use cautiously in hot environment.
Antisecretory			
Omeprazole (Prilosec)	Suppresses H⁺-K⁺ ATPase enzyme system of gastric parietal cell decreasing gastric acid production	CNS: headache, dizziness, fatigue GI: diarrhea, abdominal pain, nausea Skin: rash	Instruct client to take capsules before eating, preferably before breakfast and to swallow capsules whole. Antacids can be taken with Prilosec. Lactating women should stop nursing. Instruct client to report severe diarrhea, changes in urinary elimination. Increases blood levels of diazepam (Valium), phenytoin (Dilantin), and warfarin (Coumadin). Monitor urine for blood and protein.
Other			
Sucralfate (Carafate)	Reacts with acid to form "paste" that adheres to GI mucosa and allows ulcer to heal	GI: nausea, gastric discomfort, constipation, diarrhea	Administer one hour before meals and at bedtime. Administer antacids 30 minutes before or after sucralfate.

a. Measure drainage accurately to determine necessity for fluid and electrolyte replacement; notify physician if there is no drainage.
   b. Anticipate frank, red bleeding for 12–24 hours.
3. Promote adequate pulmonary ventilation.
   a. Place client in mid- or high-Fowler's position to promote chest expansion.
   b. Teach client to splint high upper abdominal incision before turning, coughing, and deep breathing.
4. Promote adequate nutrition.
   a. After removal of NG tube, provide clear liquids with gradual introduction of small amounts of bland food at frequent intervals.
   b. Monitor weight daily.
   c. Assess for regurgitation; if present, instruct client to eat smaller amounts of food at a slower pace.
5. Provide client teaching and discharge planning concerning
   a. Gradually increasing food intake until able to tolerate three meals/day
   b. Daily monitoring of weight
   c. Stress-reduction measures
   d. Need to report signs of complications to physician immediately (hematemesis, vomiting, diarrhea, pain, melena, weakness, feeling of abdominal fullness/distension)
   e. Methods of controlling symptoms associated with dumping syndrome
      1) avoidance of concentrated sweets
      2) adherence to six, small, dry meals/day
      3) maintenance of modified diet
      4) refraining from taking fluids during meals but rather 2 hours after meals
      5) Assuming a recumbent position for ½ hour after meals

Cancer of the Stomach

A. General information
   1. Most often develops in the distal third and may spread through the walls of the stomach into adjacent tissues, lymphatics, regional lymph nodes, and other abdominal organs, or through the bloodstream to the lungs and bones.
   2. Affects men twice as often as women; more frequent in African Americans and Orientals; most commonly occurs between ages 50–70
   3. Causes
      a. Excessive intake of highly salted or smoked foods
      b. Diet low in quantity of vegetables and fruits

c. Atrophic gastritis
   d. Achlorhydria
   e. Helicobacterpylori infection
B. Medical management
   1. Chemotherapy
   2. Radiation therapy
   3. Treatment for anemia, gastric decompression, nutritional support, fluid and electrolyte maintenance
   4. Surgery: type depends on location and extent of lesion.
      a. Subtotal gastrectomy (Billroth I or II)
      b. Total gastrectomy
C. Assessment findings
   1. Fatigue, weakness, dizziness, shortness of breath, nausea and vomiting, hematemesis, weight loss, indigestion, epigastric fullness, feeling of early satiety when eating, epigastric pain (later)
   2. Pallor, lethargy, poor skin turgor and mobility, palpable epigastric mass
   3. Diagnostic tests
      a. Stool for occult blood positive
      b. CEA positive
      c. Hgb and hct decreased
      d. SGOT (AST), SGPT (ALT), LDH, serum amylase elevated (if liver and pancreatic involvement)
      e. Gastric analysis reveals histologic changes
D. Nursing interventions
   1. Give consistent nutritional assessment and support.
   2. Provide care for the client receiving chemotherapy.
   3. Provide care for the client with gastric surgery (see Gastric Surgery, page 274).

Hernias

A. General information
   1. Protrusion of a viscus from its normal cavity through an abnormal opening/weakened area
   2. Occurs anywhere but most often in the abdominal cavity
   3. Types
      a. *Reducible:* can be manually placed back into the abdominal cavity.
      b. *Irreducible:* cannot be placed back into the abdominal cavity.
      c. *Inguinal:* occurs when there is weakness in the abdominal wall where the spermatic cord in men and round ligament in women emerge.
      d. *Femoral:* protrusion through the femoral ring; more common in females.
      e. *Incisional:* occurs at the site of a previous surgical incision as a result of inadequate healing postoperatively.

    f. *Umbilical:* most commonly found in children.

    g. *Strangulated:* irreducible, with obstruction to intestinal flow and blood supply.

B. Medical management
   1. Manual reduction, use of a truss (firm support)
   2. Bowel surgery if strangulated
   3. Herniorrhaphy: surgical repair of the hernia by suturing the defect

C. Assessment findings
   1. Vomiting, protrusion of involved area (more obvious after coughing), and discomfort at site of protrusion
   2. Crampy abdominal pain and abdominal distention (if strangulated with a bowel obstruction)

D. Nursing interventions
   1. Observe client for complications such as strangulation.
   2. Prepare client for herniorrhaphy, provide routine pre-op care.
   3. In addition to routine post-op care
      a. Assess for possible distended bladder, particularly with inguinal hernia repair.
      b. Discourage coughing, but deep breathing and turning should be done.
      c. Assist to splint incision when coughing or sneezing.
      d. Apply ice bags to scrotal area (if inguinal repair) to decrease edema.
      e. Scrotal (athletic) support may be ordered in some cases.
   4. Provide client teaching and discharge planning concerning
      a. Need to avoid strenuous physical activities (e.g., heavy lifting, pulling, pushing) for at least 6 weeks.
      b. Need to report any difficulty with urination.

Intestinal Obstructions

A. General information
   1. Mechanical intestinal obstruction: physical blockage of the passage of intestinal contents with subsequent distension by fluid and gas; caused by adhesions, hernias, volvulus, intussusception, inflammatory bowel disease, foreign bodies, strictures, neoplasms, fecal impaction
   2. *Paralytic ileus* (*neurogenic or adynamic ileus*): interference with the nerve supply to the intestine resulting in decreased or absent peristalsis; caused by abdominal surgery, peritonitis, pancreatic toxic conditions, shock, spinal cord injuries, electrolyte imbalances (especially hypokalemia)

   3. Vascular obstructions: interference with the blood supply to a portion of the intestine, resulting in ischemia and gangrene of the bowel; caused by an embolus, atherosclerosis

B. Assessment findings
   1. Small intestine: nonfecal vomiting; colicky intermittent abdominal pain
   2. Large intestine: cramplike abdominal pain, occasional fecal-type vomitus; client will be unable to pass stools or flatus
   3. Abdominal distension, rigidity, high-pitched bowel sounds above the level of the obstruction, decreased or absent bowel sounds distal to obstruction
   4. Diagnostic tests
      a. Flat-plate (x-ray) of the abdomen reveals the presence of gas/fluid
      b. Hct increased
      c. Serum sodium, potassium, chloride decreased
      d. BUN increased

C. Nursing interventions
   1. Monitor fluid and electrolyte balance, prevent further imbalance; keep client NPO and administer IV fluids as ordered.
   2. Accurately measure drainage from NG/intestinal tube.
   3. Place client in Fowler's position to alleviate pressure on the diaphragm and encourage nasal breathing to minimize swallowing of air and further abdominal distension.
   4. Institute comfort measures associated with NG intubation and intestinal decompression.
   5. Prevent complications.
      a. Measure abdominal girth daily to assess for increasing abdominal distension.
      b. Assess for signs and symptoms of peritonitis.
      c. Monitor urinary output.

Chronic Inflammatory Bowel Disorders

Regional Enteritis (Crohn's Disease)

A. General information
   1. Chronic inflammatory bowel disease that can affect both the large and small intestine; terminal ileum, cecum, and ascending colon most often affected
   2. Characterized by granulomas that may affect all the bowel wall layers with resultant thickening, narrowing, and scarring of the intestinal wall
   3. Both sexes affected equally; more common in the Jewish population; two age peaks: 20–30 years and 40–60 years
   4. Cause unknown; contributing factors

include food allergies, autoimmune reaction, psychologic disorders
B. Medical management
1. Diet: high calorie, high vitamin, high protein, low residue, milk free; supplementary iron preparations
2. Drug therapy: antimicrobials (especially sulfasalazine) to prevent or control infection, corticosteroids, antidiarrheals, anticholinergics
3. Supplemental parenteral nutrition
4. Surgery: resection of diseased portion of bowel and temporary or permanent ileostomy
C. Assessment findings
1. Right, lower quadrant tenderness and pain; abdominal distension
2. Nausea and vomiting, 3–4 semisoft stools/day with mucus and pus
3. Decreased skin turgor, dry mucus membranes
4. Increased peristalsis
5. Pallor
6. Diagnostic tests
a. Hgb and hct (if anemic) decreased
b. Sigmoidoscopy negative or reveals scattered ulcers
c. Barium enema shows narrowing with areas of strictures separated by segments of normal bowel
D. Nursing interventions
1. Provide appropriate nutrition while reducing bowel motility.
a. Administer/monitor TPN (see page 139).
b. Provide high-protein, high-calorie, low-residue diet with no milk products (if able to tolerate oral foods/ fluids).
c. Weigh daily, monitor kcal counts, and take periodic anthropometric measurements.
d. Record number and characteristics of stools daily.
e. Administer antidiarrheals, antispasmodics, and anticholinergics as ordered.
f. Provide tepid fluids to avoid stimulation of the bowel.
g. Omit gas-producing foods/fluids from diet.
h. Administer/monitor enteral tube feedings (see page 139) as ordered.
2. Promote comfort/rest: provide good perineal care with frequent washing and adequate drying after each bowel movement; apply analgesic or protective ointment as needed; provide sitz baths as needed.
3. Provide care for the client with bowel surgery (see page 279).

Ulcerative Colitis

A. General information
1. Inflammatory disorder of the bowel characterized by inflammation and ulceration that starts in the rectosigmoid area and spreads upward. The mucosa of the bowel becomes edematous, thickened with eventual scar formation. The colon consequently loses its elasticity and absorptive capabilities.
2. Occurs more often in women and the Jewish population, usually between ages 15–40
3. Cause unknown; contributing factors include autoimmune factors, viral infection, allergies, emotional stress, insecurity
B. Medical management
1. Mild to moderate form
a. Low-roughage diet with no milk products
b. Drug therapy (antimicrobials, corticosteroids, anticholinergics, antidiarrheals, immunosuppressives, hematinic agents)
2. Severe form: client kept NPO with IVs and electrolyte replacements, NG tube with suction, blood transfusions, surgery
C. Assessment findings
1. Severe diarrhea (15–20 liquid stools/day containing blood, mucus, and pus); severe tenesmus, weight loss, anorexia, weakness, crampy discomfort
2. Decreased skin turgor, dry mucous membranes
3. Low-grade fever, abdominal tenderness over the colon
4. Diagnostic tests
a. Sigmoidoscopy reveals mucosa that bleeds easily with ulcer development
b. Hgb and hct decreased
D. Nursing interventions: same as for Crohn's disease

Diverticulosis/Diverticulitis

A. General information
1. A diverticulum is an outpouching of the intestinal mucosa, most commonly found in the sigmoid colon.
2. *Diverticulosis:* multiple diverticula of the colon
3. *Diverticulitis:* inflammation of the diverticula
4. Men affected more often than women, more common in obese individuals; usually occurs between ages 40–45
5. Caused by stress, congenital weakening of muscular fibers of intestine, and dietary deficiency of roughage and fiber

B. Medical management
   1. High-residue diet with no seeds for diverticulosis; low residue diet for diverticulitis
   2. Drug therapy: bulk laxatives, stool softeners, anticholinergics, antibiotics
   3. Surgery (rare): resection of diseased portion of colon with temporary colostomy may be indicated
C. Assessment findings
   1. Intermittent lower left quadrant pain and tenderness over rectosigmoid area
   2. Alternating constipation and diarrhea with blood and mucus
   3. Diagnostic tests
      a. Barium enema indicates an inflammatory process
      b. Hgb and hct decreased (if anemic)
D. Nursing interventions
   1. Administer medications as ordered.
   2. Provide nursing care for the client with bowel surgery.
   3. Provide client teaching and discharge planning concerning
      a. Importance of adhering to dietary regimen.
      b. Prevention of increased intraabdominal pressure.
      c. Signs and symptoms of peritonitis and need to notify physician immediately if they occur.

Cancer of the Colon/Rectum

A. General information
   1. Adenocarcinoma is the most common type of colon cancer and may spread by direct extension through the walls of the intestine or through the lymphatic or circulatory system. Metastasis is most often to the liver.
   2. Second most common site for cancer in men and women; usually occurs between ages 50–60
   3. May be caused by diverticulosis, chronic ulcerative colitis, familial polyposis
B. Medical management: chemotherapy, radiation therapy, bowel surgery
C. Assessment findings
   1. Alternating diarrhea/constipation, lower abdominal cramps, abdominal distension
   2. Weakness, anorexia, weight loss, pallor, dyspnea
   3. Diagnostic tests
      a. Stool for occult blood positive
      b. Hgb and hct decreased
      c. CEA positive
      d. Sigmoidoscopy reveals a mass
      e. Barium enema shows a colon mass
      f. Digital rectal exam indicates a palpable mass

D. Nursing interventions
   1. Administer chemotherapy agents as ordered, provide care for the client receiving chemotherapy.
   2. Provide care for the client receiving radiation therapy.
   3. Provide care for the client with bowel surgery.

Bowel Surgery

A. General information: type of surgery varies depending on location and extent of lesion; may be indicated in Crohn's disease, ulcerative colitis, intestinal obstructions, colon/rectal cancer.
B. Types: see Table 4.20
C. Nursing interventions common to all bowel surgery
   1. In addition to routine pre-op care

TABLE 4.20   Bowel Surgeries

Type	Procedures
Abdominoperineal resection	Distal sigmoid colon, rectum, and anus are removed through a perineal incision and a permanent colostomy is created. Surgery of choice for cancer of the colon/rectum.
Ileostomy	Opening of the ileum onto the abdominal surface; most frequently done for treatment of ulcerative colitis, but may also be done for Crohn's disease.
Continent ileostomy (Kock's pouch)	An intra-abdominal reservoir with a nipple valve is formed from the distal ileum. The pouch acts as a reservoir for fecal material and is cleaned at regular intervals by insertion of a catheter.
Cecostomy	An opening between the cecum and the abdominal base temporarily diverts the fecal flow to rest the distal portion of the colon after some types of surgery.
Temporary colostomy	Usually located in the ascending or transverse colon; most often done to rest the bowel.
Double-barreled colostomy	The colon is resected and both ends are brought through the abdominal wall creating two stomas, a proximal and a distal; done most often for an obstruction or tumor in the descending or transverse colon.
Loop colostomy	Often a temporary procedure whereby a loop of bowel is brought out above the skin surface and held in place by a glass rod. There is one stoma but two openings, a proximal and a distal.
Permanent colostomy	Consists of a single stoma made when the distal portion of the bowel is removed; most often located in the sigmoid or descending colon.
Resection with anastomosis	Diseased part of the bowel is removed and remaining portions anastomosed, allowing elimination through the rectum.

a. Ensure adherence to dietary restrictions.
   1) offer clear liquids only on day before surgery.
   2) provide high-calorie, low-residue diet 3–5 days before surgery.
b. Assist with bowel preparation.
   1) administer antibiotics 3–5 days pre-op to decrease bacteria in intestine.
   2) administer enemas (possibly with added antibiotics) to further cleanse the bowel.
c. Administer vitamins C and K (decreased by bowel cleansing) to prevent post-op complications.
2. In addition to routine post-op care
   a. Promote elimination.
      1) assess for signs of returning peristalsis.
      2) monitor characteristics of initial stools.
   b. Monitor and maintain fluid and electrolyte balance.
D. Additional nursing interventions specific to abdominoperineal resection
   1. Reinforce and change perineal dressings as needed.
   2. Record type, amount, color of drainage.
   3. Irrigate with normal saline or hydrogen peroxide.
   4. Provide warm sitz baths 4 times/day.
   5. Cover wound with dry dressing.
E. Additional nursing interventions specific to colostomy
   1. Prevent skin breakdown.
      a. Cleanse skin around stoma with mild soap and water and pat dry.
      b. Use a skin barrier to protect skin around the stoma.
      c. Assess skin regularly for irritation.
      d. Avoid the use of adhesives on irritated skin.
   2. Control odor, maintain pleasant environment.
      a. Change pouch/seal whenever necessary.
      b. Empty or clean bag frequently, and provide ventilation afterwards; use deodorizer in bag/room if needed
      c. Avoid gas-producing foods.
   3. Promote adequate stomal drainage.
      a. Assess stoma for color and intactness.
      b. Expect mucoid/serosanguinous drainage during the first 24 hours, then liquid type.
      c. Assess for flatus indicating return of intestinal function.
      d. Monitor for changing consistency of fecal drainage.
   4. Irrigate colostomy as needed.
      a. Position client on toilet or in high-Fowler's if client on bed rest.
      b. Fill irrigation bag with desired amount of water (500–1000 ml) and hang bag so the bottom is at shoulder height.
      c. Remove air from tubing and lubricate the tip of the catheter or cone.
      d. Remove old pouch and clean skin and stoma with water.
      e. Gently dilate stoma and insert the irrigation catheter or cone snugly.
      f. Open tubing and allow fluid to enter the bowel.
      g. Remove catheter or cone and allow fecal contents to drain.
      h. Observe and record amount and character of fecal return.
   5. Promote adequate nutrition.
      a. Assess return of peristalsis.
      b. Advance diet as tolerated, add new foods gradually.
      c. Avoid constipating foods.
   6. Provide at least 2500 ml liquid/day.
   7. Encourage client to discuss concerns and feelings about surgery.
   8. Provide client teaching and discharge planning concerning
      a. Recognition of complications and need to report immediately
         1) changes in odor, consistency, and color of stools
         2) bleeding from the stoma
         3) persistent constipation or diarrhea
         4) changes in the contour of the stoma
         5) persistent leakage around the stoma
         6) skin irritation despite treatment
      b. Proper procedure for colostomy irrigation.

Peritonitis

A. General information
   1. Local or generalized inflammation of part or all of the parietal and visceral surfaces of the abdominal cavity
   2. Initial response: edema, vascular congestion, hypermotility of the bowel and outpouring of plasmalike fluid from the extracellular, vascular, and interstitial compartments into the peritoneal space
   3. Later response: abdominal distension leading to respiratory compromise, hypovolemia results in decreased urinary output
   4. Intestinal motility gradually decreases and progresses to paralytic ileus
   5. Caused by trauma (blunt or penetrating), inflammation (ulcerative colitis, diverticulitis), volvulus, intestinal ischemia, or intestinal obstruction
B. Medical management
   1. NPO with fluid replacement
   2. Drug therapy: antibiotics to combat infection, analgesics for pain

3. Surgery
   a. *Laparotomy*: opening made through the abdominal wall into the peritoneal cavity to determine the cause of peritonitis
   b. Depending on cause, bowel resection may be necessary
C. Assessment findings
   1. Severe abdominal pain, rebound tenderness, muscle rigidity, absent bowel sounds, abdominal distension (particularly if large bowel obstruction)
   2. Anorexia, nausea, and vomiting
   3. Shallow respirations; decreased urinary output; weak, rapid pulse; elevated temperature
   4. Diagnostic tests
      a. WBC elevated
      b. Hct elevated (if hemoconcentration)
D. Nursing interventions
   1. Assess respiratory status for possible distress.
   2. Assess characteristics of abdominal pain and changes over time.
   3. Administer medications as ordered.
   4. Perform frequent abdominal assessment.
   5. Monitor and maintain fluid and electrolyte balance; monitor for signs of septic shock.
   6. Maintain patency of NG or intestinal tubes.
   7. Place client in Fowler's position to localize peritoneal contents.
   8. Provide routine pre- and post-op care if surgery ordered.

Hemorrhoids

A. General information
   1. Congestion and dilation of the veins of the rectum and anus; usually result from impairment of flow of blood through the venous plexus
   2. May be internal (above the anal sphincter) or external (outside anal sphincter)
   3. Most commonly occur between ages 20–50
   4. Predisposing conditions include occupations requiring long periods of standing; increased intra-abdominal pressure caused by prolonged constipation, pregnancy, heavy lifting, obesity, straining at defecation; portal hypertension
B. Medical management
   1. Stool softeners, local anesthetics, or anti-inflammatory creams
   2. Diet modification: high fiber, adequate liquids
   3. Hemorrhoidectomy: surgical excision of hemorrhoids indicated when there is prolapse, severe pain, and excessive bleeding
C. Assessment findings

   1. Bleeding with defecation, hard stools with streaks of blood
   2. Pain with defecation, sitting, or walking
   3. Protrusion of external hemorrhoids upon inspection
   4. Diagnostic tests
      a. Proctoscopy reveals presence of internal hemorrhoids
      b. Hgb and hct decreased if bleeding excessive, prolonged
D. Nursing interventions: preoperative
   1. Prepare client for hemorrhoidectomy.
   2. In addition to routine pre-op care, provide laxatives/enemas to promote cleansing of the bowel.
E. Nursing interventions: postoperative
   1. Provide routine post-op care.
   2. Assess for rectal bleeding: inspect rectal area/dressings every 2–3 hours and report significant increases in bloody drainage.
   3. Promote comfort.
      a. Assist client to side-lying or prone position, provide flotation pad when sitting.
      b. Administer analgesics as ordered and monitor effects.
   4. Promote elimination: administer stool softeners as ordered and, if possible, administer analgesic before first post-op bowel movement.
   5. Provide client teaching and discharge planning concerning
      a. Dietary modifications (high fiber and ingestion of at least 2000 ml/day)
      b. Need to defecate when urge is felt
      c. Use of stool softeners as needed until healing occurs
      d. Sitz baths after each bowel movement for at least 2 weeks after surgery
      e. Perineal care
      f. Recognition and reporting immediately to physician of the following signs and symptoms
         1) rectal bleeding
         2) continued pain on defecation
         3) puslike drainage from rectal area

DISORDERS OF THE LIVER

Hepatitis

A. General information
   1. Widespread inflammation of the liver tissue with liver cell damage due to hepatic cell degeneration and necrosis; proliferation and enlargement of the Kupffer cells; inflammation of the periportal areas (may cause interruption of bile flow)
   2. *Hepatitis A*
      a. Incubation period: 15–45 days

b. Transmitted by fecal/oral route: often occurs in crowded living conditions; with poor personal hygiene; or from contaminated food, milk, water, or shellfish
  3. *Hepatitis B*
    a. Incubation period: 50–180 days
    b. Transmitted by blood and body fluids (saliva, semen, vaginal secretions): often from contaminated needles among IV drug abusers; intimate/sexual contact
  4. *Hepatitis C*
    a. Incubation period: 7–50 days
    b. Transmitted by parenteral route: through blood and blood products, needles, syringes
B. Assessment findings
  1. Preicteric stage
    a. Anorexia, nausea and vomiting, fatigue, constipation or diarrhea, weight loss
    b. Right upper quadrant discomfort, hepatomegaly, splenomegaly, lymphadenopathy
  2. Icteric stage
    a. Fatigue, weight loss, light-colored stools, dark urine
    b. Continued hepatomegaly with tenderness, lymphadenopathy, splenomegaly
    c. Jaundice, pruritus
  3. Posticteric stage
    a. Fatigue, but an increased sense of well-being
    b. Hepatomegaly gradually decreasing
  4. Diagnostic tests
    a. All three types of hepatitis
      1) SGPT (ALT), SGOT (AST), alkaline phosphatase, bilirubin, ESR: all increased (preicteric)
      2) leukocytes, lymphocytes, neutrophils: all decreased (pericteric)
      3) prolonged PT
    b. Hepatitis A
      1) hepatitis A virus (HAV) in stool before onset of disease
      2) anti-HAV (IgG) appears soon after onset of jaundice; peaks in 1–2 months and persists indefinitely
      3) anti-HAV (IgM): positive in acute infection; lasts 4–6 weeks
    c. Hepatitis B
      1) HBsAg (surface antigen): positive, develops 4–12 weeks after infection
      2) anti-HBsAG: negative in 80% of cases
      3) anti-HBc: associated with infectivity, develops 2–16 weeks after infection

      4) HBeAg: associated with infectivity and disappears before jaundice
      5) anti-HBe: present in carriers, represents low infectivity
    d. Hepatitis C: no specific serologic tests
C. Nursing interventions
  1. Promote adequate nutrition.
    a. Administer antiemetics as ordered, 30 minutes before meals to decrease occurrence of nausea and vomiting.
    b. Provide small, frequent meals of a high-carbohydrate, moderate- to high-protein, high-vitamin, high-calorie diet.
    c. Avoid very hot or very cold foods.
  2. Ensure rest/relaxation: plan schedule for rest and activity periods, organize nursing care to minimize interruption.
  3. Monitor/relieve pruritus (see Cirrhosis of the Liver).
  4. Administer corticosteroids as ordered.
  5. Institute isolation procedures as required; pay special attention to good hand-washing technique and adequate sanitation.
  6. In hepatitis A administer immune serum globulin (ISG) early to exposed individuals as ordered.
  7. In hepatitis B
    a. Screen blood donors for HBsAg.
    b. Use disposable needles and syringes.
    c. Instruct client/others to avoid sexual intercourse while disease is active.
    d. Administer ISG to exposed individuals as ordered.
    e. Administer hepatitis B immunoglobulin (HBIG) as ordered to provide temporary and passive immunity to exposed individuals.
    f. To produce active immunity, administer hepatitis B vaccine to those individuals at high risk.
  8. In non-A, non-B: use disposable needles and syringes; ensure adequate sanitation.
  9. Provide client teaching and discharge planning concerning
    a. Importance of avoiding alcohol
    b. Avoidance of persons with known infections
    c. Balance of activity and rest periods
    d. Importance of not donating blood
    e. Dietary modifications
    f. Recognition and reporting of signs of inadequate convalescence: anorexia, jaundice, increasing liver tenderness/discomfort
    g. Techniques/importance of good personal hygiene

Cirrhosis of the Liver

A. General information
  1. Chronic, progressive disease characterized

by inflammation, fibrosis, and degeneration of the liver parenchymal cells

2. Destroyed liver cells are replaced by scar tissue, resulting in architectural changes and malfunction of the liver

3. Types
   a. *Laënnec's cirrhosis:* associated with alcohol abuse and malnutrition; characterized by an accumulation of fat in the liver cells, progressing to widespread scar formation.
   b. *Postnecrotic cirrhosis:* results in severe inflammation with massive necrosis as a complication of viral hepatitis.
   c. *Cardiac cirrhosis:* occurs as a consequence of right-sided heart failure; manifested by hepatomegaly with some fibrosis.
   d. *Biliary cirrhosis:* associated with biliary obstruction, usually in the common bile duct; results in chronic impairment of bile excretion.

4. Occurs twice as often in men as in women; ages 40–60

B. Assessment findings
   1. Fatigue, anorexia, nausea and vomiting, indigestion, weight loss, flatulence, irregular bowel habits
   2. Hepatomegaly (early): pain located in the right upper quadrant; atrophy of liver (later); hard, nodular liver upon palpation; increased abdominal girth
   3. Changes in mood, alertness, and mental ability; sensory deficits; gynecomastia, decreased axillary and pubic hair in males; amenorrhea in young females
   4. Jaundice of the skin, sclera, and mucous membranes; pruritus
   5. Easy bruising, spider angiomas, palmar erythema
   6. Muscle atrophy
   7. Diagnostic tests
      a. SGOT (AST), SGPT (ALT), LDH alkaline phosphatase increased
      b. Serum bilirubin increased
      c. PT prolonged
      d. Serum albumin decreased
      e. Hgb and hct decreased

C. Nursing interventions
   1. Provide sufficient rest and comfort.
      a. Provide bed rest with bathroom privileges.
      b. Encourage gradual, progressive, increasing activity with planned rest periods.
      c. Institute measures to relieve pruritus.
         1) do not use soaps and detergents
         2) bathe in tepid water followed by application of an emollient lotion.
         3) provide cool, light, nonrestrictive clothing.
         4) keep nails short to avoid skin excoriation from scratching.
         5) apply cool, moist compresses to pruritic areas.
   2. Promote nutritional intake.
      a. Encourage small frequent feedings.
      b. Promote a high-calorie, low- to moderate-protein, high-carbohydrate, low-fat diet, with supplemental vitamin therapy (vitamins A, B-complex, C, D, K, and folic acid)
   3. Prevent infection.
      a. Prevent skin breakdown by frequent turning and skin care.
      b. Provide reverse isolation for clients with severe leukopenia; pay special attention to hand-washing technique.
      c. Monitor WBC.
   4. Monitor/prevent bleeding.
   5. Administer diuretics as ordered.
   6. Provide client teaching and discharge planning concerning
      a. Avoidance of agents that may be hepatotoxic (sedatives, opiates, or OTC drugs detoxified by the liver)
      b. How to assess for weight gain and increased abdominal girth
      c. Avoidance of persons with upper respiratory infections
      d. Recognition and reporting of signs of recurring illness (liver tenderness, increased jaundice, increased fatigue, anorexia)
      e. Avoidance of all alcohol
      f. Avoidance of straining at stool, vigorous blowing of nose and coughing, to decrease the incidence of bleeding

Ascites

A. General information
   1. Accumulation of free fluid in the abdominal cavity
   2. Most frequently caused by cirrhotic liver damage, which produces hypoalbuminemia, increased portal venous pressure, and hyperaldosteronism
   3. May also be caused by CHF

B. Medical management
   1. Supportive: modify diet, bed rest, salt-poor albumin
   2. Diuretic therapy (see Antihypertensive Drugs, Table 2.17)
   3. Surgery
      a. *Paracentesis:* insertion of a needle into the peritoneal cavity through the abdomen to remove abnormally large amounts of peritoneal fluid.
         1) peritoneal fluid assessed for cell count, specific gravity, protein, and microorganisms.

2) used in clients with acute respiratory or abdominal distress secondary to ascites.
b. *LeVeen shunt* (*peritoneal-venous shunt*): used in chronic, unmanageable ascites
1) permits continuous reinfusion of ascitic fluid back into the venous system through a silicone catheter with a one-way pressure-sensitive valve.
2) one end of the catheter is implanted into the peritoneal cavity and is channeled through the subcutaneous tissue to the superior vena cava, where the other end of the catheter is implanted; the valve opens when pressure in the peritoneal cavity is 3–5 cm of water higher than in superior vena cava, thereby allowing ascitic fluid to flow into the venous system.

C. Assessment findings
1. Anorexia, nausea and vomiting, fatigue, weakness, changes in mental functioning
2. Positive fluid wave and shifting dullness on percussion, flat or protruding umbilicus, abdominal distension/tautness with striae and prominent veins, abdominal pain
3. Peripheral edema, shortness of breath
4. Diagnostic tests
a. Potassium and serum albumin decreased
b. PT prolonged
c. LDH, SGOT (AST), SGPT (ALT), BUN, sodium increased

D. Nursing interventions
1. Monitor nutritional status/provide adequate nutrition with modified diet.
a. Restrict sodium to 200–500 mg/day.
b. Restrict fluids to 1000–1500 ml/day.
c. Promote high-calorie foods/snacks.
2. Monitor/prevent increasing edema.
a. Administer diuretics as ordered and monitor for effects.
b. Measure I&O.
c. Monitor peripheral pulses.
d. Measure abdominal girth.
e. Inspect/palpate extremities, sacrum.
f. Administer salt-poor albumin to replace vascular volume.
3. Monitor/promote skin integrity.
a. Reposition frequently.
b. Apply lotions to stretched areas.
c. Assess for redness, breakdown.
4. Promote comfort: place client in mid- to high-Fowler's and reposition frequently.
5. Provide nursing care for the client undergoing paracentesis.
a. Confirm that client has signed a consent form.
b. Instruct client to empty bladder before the procedure to prevent inadvertent puncture of the bladder during insertion of trocar.
c. Inform client that a local anesthetic will be provided to decrease pain.
d. Place in sitting position to facilitate the flow of fluid by gravity.
e. Measure abdominal girth and weight before and after the procedure.
f. Record color, amount, and consistency of fluid withdrawn and client tolerance during procedure.
g. Assess insertion site for leakage.
6. Provide routine pre- and post-op care for the client with LeVeen shunt.

Esophageal Varices

A. General information
1. Dilation of the veins of the esophagus, caused by portal hypertension from resistance to normal venous drainage of the liver into the portal vein
2. Causes blood to be shunted to the esophagogastric veins, resulting in distension, hypertrophy, and increased fragility.
3. Caused by portal hypertension, which may be secondary to cirrhosis of the liver (alcohol abuse), swallowing poorly masticated food, increased intra-abdominal pressure

B. Medical management
1. Iced normal saline lavage
2. Transfusions with fresh whole blood
3. Vitamin K therapy
4. Sengstaken-Blakemore tube: a three-lumen tube used to control bleeding by applying pressure on the cardiac portion of the stomach and against bleeding esophageal varices. One lumen serves as NG suction, a second lumen is used to inflate the gastric balloon, the third to inflate the esophageal balloon.
5. Intra-arterial or IV vasopressin
6. Injection sclerotherapy
7. Surgery for portal hypertension (decompresses esophageal varices and helps to maintain optimal portal perfusion)
a. Ligation of esophageal and gastric veins to stop acute bleeding
b. *Portacaval shunt:* end-to-side or side-to-side anastomosis of the portal vein to the inferior vena cava
c. *Splenorenal shunt:* end-to-side or side-to-side anastomosis of the splenic vein to the left renal vein
d. *Mesocaval shunt:* end-to-side or use of a graft to anastomose the inferior vena cava to the side of the superior mesenteric vein

C. Assessment findings
1. Anorexia, nausea and vomiting, hematemesis, fatigue, weakness
2. Splenomegaly, increased splenic dullness, ascites, caput medusae, peripheral edema, bruits
3. Diagnostic tests
   a. PT prolonged
   b. Hematest of vomitus positive
   c. Serum albumin, RBC, Hgb, and hct decreased
   d. LDH, SGOT (AST), SGPT (ALT), BUN, increased
D. Nursing interventions
1. Monitor/provide care for client with Sengstaken-Blakemore tube.
   a. Facilitate placement of the tube: check and lubricate tip and elevate head of bed.
   b. Prevent dislodgment of the tube by placing client in semi-Fowler's position; maintain traction by securing the tube to a piece of sponge or foam rubber placed on the nose.
   c. Keep scissors at bedside at all times.
   d. Monitor respiratory status; assess for signs of distress and if respiratory distress occurs cut the tubing to deflate the balloons and remove tubing immediately.
   e. Label each lumen to avoid confusion; maintain prescribed amount of pressure on esophageal balloon and deflate balloon as ordered to avoid necrosis.
   f. Observe nares for skin breakdown and provide mouth and nasal care every 1–2 hours (encourage client to expectorate secretions, suction gently if unable).
2. Promote comfort: place client in semi-Fowler's position (if not in shock); provide mouth care.
3. Monitor for further bleeding and for signs and symptoms of shock; hematest all secretions.
4. Administer vasopressin as ordered and monitor effects.
5. Provide routine pre- and post-op care if the client has portasystemic or portacaval shunt.
6. Provide client teaching and discharge planning concerning
   a. Minimizing esophageal irritation (avoidance of salicylates, alcohol; use of antacids as needed; importance of chewing food thoroughly)
   b. Avoidance of increased abdominal, thoracic, and portal pressure
   c. Recognition and reporting of signs of hemorrhage

Hepatic Encephalopathy

A. General information
1. Frequent terminal complication in liver disease
2. Diseased liver is unable to convert ammonia to urea, so that large quantities remain in the systemic circulation and cross the blood/brain barrier, producing neurologic toxic symptoms.
3. Caused by cirrhosis, GI hemorrhage, hyperbilirubinemia, transfusions (particularly with stored blood), thiazide diuretics, uremia, dehydration
B. Assessment findings
1. Early in course of disease: changes in mental functioning (irritability); insomnia, slowed affect; slow slurred speech; impaired judgment; slight tremor; Babinski's reflex, hyperactive reflexes
2. Progressive disease: asterixis, disorientation, apraxia, tremors, fetor hepaticus, facial grimacing
3. Late in disease: coma, absent reflexes
4. Diagnostic tests
   a. Serum ammonia levels increased (particularly later)
   b. PT prolonged
   c. Hgb and hct decreased
C. Nursing interventions
1. Conduct ongoing neurologic assessment and report deteriorations.
2. Restrict protein in diet; provide high carbohydrate intake and vitamin K supplements.
3. Administer enemas, cathartics, intestinal antibiotics, and lactulose as ordered to reduce ammonia levels.
4. Protect client from injury: keep side rails up; provide eye care with use of artificial tears/eye patch.
5. Avoid administration of drugs detoxified in liver (phenothiazines, gold compounds, methyldopa, acetaminophen).
6. Maintain client on bed rest to decrease metabolic demands on liver.

Cancer of the Liver

A. General information
1. Primary cancer of the liver is extremely rare, but it is a common site for metastasis because of liver's large blood supply and portal drainage. Primary cancers of the colon, rectum, stomach, pancreas, esophagus, breast, lung, and melanomas frequently metastasize to the liver.
2. Enlargement, hemorrhage, and necrosis are common occurrences; primary liver tumors often metastasize to the lung.
3. Higher incidence in men.

4. Prognosis poor; disease well advanced before clinical signs evident.
B. Medical management
1. Chemotherapy and radiotherapy (palliative) to decrease tumor size and pain
2. Resection of liver segment or lobe if tumor is localized
C. Assessment findings
1. Weakness, anorexia, nausea and vomiting, weight loss, slight increase in temperature
2. Right upper quadrant discomfort/ tenderness, hepatomegaly, blood-tinged ascites, friction rub over liver, peripheral edema, jaundice
3. Diagnostic tests: same as cirrhosis of the liver (page 282) plus
   a. Blood sugar decreased
   b. Alpha fetoprotein increased
   c. Abdominal x-ray, liver scan, liver biopsy all positive
D. Nursing interventions: same as for cirrhosis of the liver plus
1. Provide emotional support for client/significant others regarding poor prognosis.
2. Provide care of the client receiving radiation therapy or chemotherapy.
3. Provide care of client with abdominal surgery plus
   a. Preoperative
      1) Perform bowel prep to decrease ammonium intoxication.
      2) Administer vitamin K to decrease risk of bleeding.
   b. Postoperative
      1) Administer 10% glucose for first 48 hours to avoid rapid blood sugar drop.
      2) Monitor for hyper/hypoglycemia.
      3) Assess for bleeding (hemorrhage is most threatening complication).
      4) Assess for signs of hepatic encephalopathy.

DISORDERS OF THE GALLBLADDER

Cholecystitis/Cholelithiasis

A. General information
1. Cholecystitis: acute or chronic inflammation of the gallbladder, most commonly associated with gallstones. Inflammation occurs within the walls of the gallbladder and creates a thickening accompanied by edema. Consequently, there is impaired circulation, ischemia, and eventual necrosis.
2. Cholelithiasis: formation of gallstones, cholesterol stones most common variety
3. Most often occurs in women after age 40, in postmenopausal women on estrogen

therapy, in women taking oral contraceptives, and in the obese; Caucasians and Native Americans are also more commonly affected.
4. Stone formation may be caused by genetic defect of bile composition, gallbladder/bile stasis, infection.
5. Acute cholecystitis usually follows stone impaction, adhesions; neoplasms may also be implicated.
B. Medical management
1. Supportive treatment: NPO with NG intubation and IV fluids
2. Diet modification with administration of fat-soluble vitamins
3. Drug therapy
   a. Narcotic analgesics (Demerol is drug of choice) for pain. Morphine sulfate is contraindicated because it causes spasms of the sphincter of Oddi.
   b. Anticholinergics (atropine) for pain. (Anticholinergics relax smooth muscle and open bile ducts.)
   c. Antiemetics
4. Surgery: cholecystectomy/ choledochostomy
C. Assessment findings
1. Epigastric or right upper quadrant pain, precipitated by a heavy meal or occurring at night
2. Intolerance for fatty foods (nausea, vomiting, sensation of fullness)
3. Pruritus, easy bruising, jaundice, dark amber urine, steatorrhea
4. Diagnostic tests
   a. Direct bilirubin transaminase, alkaline phosphatase, WBC, amylase, lipase: all increased
   b. Oral cholecystogram (gallbladder series): positive for gallstone
D. Nursing interventions
1. Administer pain medications as ordered and monitor for effects.
2. Administer IV fluids as ordered.
3. Provide small, frequent meals of modified diet (if oral intake allowed).
4. Provide care to relieve pruritus.
5. Provide care for the client with a cholecystectomy or choledochostomy.

Cholecystectomy/Choledochostomy

A. General information
1. Cholecystectomy: removal of the gallbladder with insertion of a T-tube into the common bile duct if common bile duct exploration is performed
2. Choledochostomy: opening of common duct, removal of stone, and insertion of a T-tube
3. Cholecystectomy performed via laparoscopy for uncomplicated cases when

client has not had previous abdominal surgery
B. Nursing interventions: routine preoperative care
C. Nursing interventions: postoperative
   1. Provide routine post-op care.
   2. Position client in semi-Fowler's or side-lying positions; reposition frequently.
   3. Splint incision when turning, coughing, and deep breathing.
   4. Maintain/monitor functioning of T-tube.
      a. Ensure that T-tube is connected to closed gravity drainage.
      b. Avoid kinks, clamping, or pulling of the tube.
      c. Measure and record drainage every shift.
      d. Expect 300–500 ml bile-colored drainage first 24 hours, then 200 ml/24 hours for 3–4 days.
      e. Monitor color of urine and stools (stools will be light colored if bile is flowing through T-tube but normal color should reappear as drainage diminishes).
      f. Assess for signs of peritonitis.
      g. Assess skin around T-tube; cleanse frequently and keep dry.
   5. Provide client teaching and discharge planning concerning
      a. Adherence to dietary restrictions
      b. Resumption of ADL (avoid heavy lifting for at least 6 weeks; resume sexual activity as desired unless ordered otherwise by physician); clients having laparoscopy cholecystectomy usually resume normal activity within two weeks.
      c. Recognition and reporting of signs of complications (fever, jaundice, pain, dark urine, pale stools, pruritus)

Appendicitis

See page 414.

DISORDERS OF THE PANCREAS

Pancreatitis

A. General information
   1. An inflammatory process with varying degrees of pancreatic edema, fat necrosis, or hemorrhage
   2. Proteolytic and lipolytic pancreatic enzymes are activated in the pancreas rather than in the duodenum, resulting in tissue damage and autodigestion of the pancreas
   3. Occurs most often in the middle aged

   4. Caused by alcoholism, biliary tract disease, trauma, viral infection, penetrating duodenal ulcer, abscesses, drugs (steroids, thiazide diuretics, and oral contraceptives), metabolic disorders (hyperparathyroidism, hyperlipidemia)
B. Medical management
   1. Drug therapy
      a. Analgesics (Demerol) to relieve pain
      b. Smooth-muscle relaxants (papaverine, nitroglycerin) to relieve pain
      c. Anticholinergics (atropine, propantheline bromide [Pro-Banthine]) to decrease pancreatic stimulation
      d. Antacids to decrease pancreatic stimulation
      e. H_2 antagonists, vasodilators, calcium gluconate
   2. Diet modification
   3. NPO (usually)
   4. Peritoneal lavage
   5. Dialysis
C. Assessment findings
   1. Pain located in left upper quadrant with radiation to back, flank, or substernal area; may be accompanied by difficulty breathing and is aggravated by eating
   2. Vomiting, shallow respirations (with pain), tachycardia, decreased or absent bowel sounds, abdominal tenderness with muscle guarding, positive Grey Turner's spots (ecchymoses on flanks) and positive Cullen's sign (ecchymoses of periumbilical area)
   3. Diagnostic tests
      a. Serum amylase and lipase, urinary amylase, blood sugar, lipid levels: all increased
      b. Serum calcium decreased
      c. CT scan shows enlargement of the pancreas
D. Nursing interventions
   1. Administer analgesics, antacids, anticholinergics as ordered, monitor effects.
   2. Withhold food/fluid and eliminate odor and sight of food from environment to decrease pancreatic stimulations.
   3. Maintain NG tube and assess for drainage.
   4. Institute nonpharmacologic measures to decrease pain.
      a. Assist client to positions of comfort (knee-chest; fetal position).
      b. Teach relaxation techniques and provide a quiet, restful environment.
   5. Provide client teaching and discharge planning concerning
      a. Dietary regimen when oral intake permitted
         1) high-carbohydrate, high-protein, low-fat diet

      2) eating small, frequent meals instead of three large ones
      3) avoiding caffeine products
      4) eliminating alcohol consumption
      5) maintaining relaxed atmosphere after meals
   b. Recognition and reporting of signs of complications
      1) continued nausea and vomiting
      2) abdominal distension with increasing fullness
      3) persistent weight loss
      4) severe epigastric or back pain
      5) frothy/foul-smelling bowel movements
      6) irritability, confusion, persistent elevation of temperature (2 days)

Cancer of the Pancreas

A. General information
   1. Most pancreatic tumors are adenocarcinomas and half occur in the head of the pancreas
   2. Tumor growth results in common bile duct obstruction with jaundice
   3. Occurs more often in men and in the African American and Jewish populations; ages 45–65
   4. Contributing factors: chemical carcinogens, cigarette smoking, high-fat diet, diabetes mellitus
   5. Prognosis generally poor
B. Medical management
   1. Radiation therapy
   2. Whipple's procedure (pancreatoduodenectomy): resection of the proximal pancreas, adjoining duodenum, distal portion of the stomach, and distal segment of the common bile duct
   3. Drug therapy
      a. Pancreatic enzymes; oral hypoglycemic agents or insulin, bile salts necessary after surgery
      b. Chemotherapy may also be used
C. Assessment findings
   1. Anorexia; rapid, progressive weight loss; dull abdominal pain located in upper abdomen or left hypochondriacal region with radiation to the back, related to eating; jaundice
   2. Diagnostic tests
      a. Increased serum lipase (early)
      b. Increased bilirubin (conjugated)
      c. Increased serum amylase
D. Nursing interventions
   1. See Pancreatitis.
   2. Provide care for the client receiving radiation therapy or chemotherapy.
   3. Routine pre- and post-op care (for clients undergoing Whipple's procedure).

   4. Provide emotional support to client/significant others.
   5. Provide client teaching and discharge planning concerning
      a. Need to eat small frequent meals of a low-fat, high-calorie diet with vitamin supplements.
      b. Importance of adhering to medication regimen after surgery.

Sample Questions

70. An adult client has a nasogastric tube in place to maintain gastric decompression. Which nursing action will relieve discomfort in the nostril with the NG tube?
   1. Remove any tape and loosely pin the tube to his gown.
   2. Lubricate the NG tube with viscous xylocaine.
   3. Loop the NG tube to avoid pressure on the nares.
   4. Replace the NG tube with a smaller diameter tube.
71. An adult client has just returned to his room following a bowel resection and end-to-end anastomosis. The nurse can expect the drainage from the NG tube in the early post-op period to be
   1. clear.
   2. mucoid.
   3. scant.
   4. discolored.
72. A 23-year-old man with a long history of ulcerative colitis is experiencing an exacerbation of the disease and is admitted with severe diarrhea, electrolyte disturbances, and severe abdominal pain. He questions the nurse about his prognosis. The best response to this inquiry is
   1. Ask your physician.
   2. It is rarely fatal.
   3. It depends on the form of the disease.
   4. You sound concerned.
73. The physician inserts a central venous catheter; the nurse should assist the client to assume which of the following positions?
   1. Supine.
   2. Trendelenburg.
   3. Reverse Trendelenburg.
   4. High-Fowler's.
74. A 35-year-old man has a history of peptic ulcer disease. He has had numerous bleeding episodes in the past and is admitted to the hospital for evaluation. His physician has prescribed cimetidine (Tagamet). The nurse recognizes that the primary reason this client is taking Tagamet is that it
   1. blocks the secretion of gastric hydrochloric acid.

2. coats the gastric mucosa with a protective membrane.
3. increases the sensitivity of H_2 receptors.
4. releases basal gastric acid.

75. Mr. K. has a Billroth II procedure and does well postoperatively. He is preparing for discharge. Mr. K. recognizes that symptoms of dizziness, sweating, and weakness in the weeks following the surgery are usually associated with
1. afferent loop syndrome.
2. dumping syndrome.
3. pernicious anemia.
4. marginal ulcers.

76. Mr. S., 56 years old, has had a significant problem with alcohol abuse for the past 15 years. His wife brings him to the emergency department because he is increasingly confused and is coughing blood. His medical diagnosis is cirrhosis of the liver. He has ascites and esophageal varices. Assessment of Mr. S. would reveal all of the following changes except
1. bulging flanks.
2. protruding umbilicus.
3. abdominal distension.
4. bluish discoloration of the umbilicus.

77. The major dietary treatment for ascites calls for
1. high protein.
2. increased potassium.
3. restricted fluids.
4. restricted sodium.

78. Which laboratory value would the nurse expect to find in a client as a result of liver failure?
1. Decreased serum creatinine.
2. Decreased sodium.
3. Increased ammonia.
4. Increased calcium.

79. A man is admitted with bleeding esophageal varices. A Sengstaken-Blakemore tube is inserted in an effort to stop the bleeding. After the Sengstaken-Blakemore tube is inserted, the client has difficulty breathing. Based on this information, the first action the nurse should take is to
1. deflate the esophageal balloon.
2. encourage him to take deep breaths.
3. monitor his vital signs.
4. notify the physician.

Answers and Rationales

70. The correct answer is 3. Looping the NG tube will prevent pressure on the nares that can cause pain and eventual necrosis. Pinning the tube to the client's gown would cause irritation of the nares each time he moved and might cause dislocation of the tube. Prior to insertion of an NG tube it is proper to lubricate the tip with viscous xylocaine, but this is not applied to the nostril. A smaller tube might not be large enough to drain the contents of the stomach and intestine, it might still irritate the nose, and it may not be changed without a doctor's order.

71. The correct answer is 4. The drainage following abdominal surgery is discolored as it is evacuating stomach and intestinal contents, not mucoid material. There is a significant amount of drainage.

72. The correct answer is 4. The nurse should explore the client's motivation for posing the question and establish what his current knowledge is. "Ask your physician" is a response that ignores the role of the nurse in dealing with client concerns. The response "It is rarely fatal" is not accurate. "It depends on the form of the disease" is a true statement, but does not give the client an opportunity to express his concerns.

73. The correct answer is 2. The client is placed in Trendelenburg position to aid in the filling of the subclavian veins. Supine, reverse Trendelenburg and high-Fowler's positions do not allow for subclavian filling.

74. The correct answer is 1. Cimetidine (Tagamet) is a histamine antagonist that blocks the secretion of hydrochloric acid. Antacids such as Mylanta and Maalox coat the gastric mucosa. Tagamet does not increase the sensitivity of the histamine receptors; Tagamet blocks the secretion of hydrochloric acid.

75. The correct answer is 2. Signs of dumping syndrome include vertigo, pallor, sweating, palpitations, and weakness. Dumping syndrome occurs after a gastric resection because ingested foods rapidly enter the jejunum without proper mixing and without the normal duodenal processing. It generally subsides in 6–12 months. These are not symptoms of pernicious anemia. However, the client will develop pernicious anemia if parenteral vitamin B_{12} is not administered as prescribed. Dizziness, sweating, and weakness are not signs of an ulcer. A marginal peptic ulcer is an ulcer that develops postoperatively at the surgical anastomosis of the stomach and jejunum.

76. The correct answer is 4. Bluish discoloration of the umbilicus (Cullen's sign) is present in massive gastrointestinal hemorrhage resulting from free blood present in the abdomen. Bulging flanks would be present due to ascites. Protruding umbilicus is secondary to ascites. Abdominal distension would be present due to ascites secondary to portal hypertension.

77. The correct answer is 4. Sodium restriction is most important for a client with cirrhosis

because fluid retention contributes to ascites. A high-protein diet is contraindicated because increased protein in the intestine causes elevated blood ammonia levels. The diseased liver is unable to convert ammonia to urea, thereby leading to possible signs of hepatic encephalopathy. Increased potassium would not be indicated because advancing cirrhosis could lead to hepatorenal disease with resultant renal retention of potassium. Fluids will probably be restricted but sodium restriction is more important.

78. The correct answer is 3. Increased ammonia levels would be seen because ammonia is a byproduct of protein metabolism and a diseased liver is unable to convert ammonia into urea to be excreted in the urine. Serum creatinine might be increased because of impaired renal function. Sodium level would most likely be elevated contributing to portal hypertension and ascites. Serum calcium would likely be decreased as a result of inactivity and bed rest.

79. The correct answer is 1. If the client's airway is obstructed by the Sengstaken-Blakemore tube, the esophageal balloon must be deflated so the client can breathe. Deep breaths will be useless if the airway is occluded. Monitoring vital signs will not solve the problem. Immediate action must be taken by the nurse before the physician is notified.

The Genitourinary System

OVERVIEW OF ANATOMY AND PHYSIOLOGY

The genitourinary system includes the kidneys, ureters, urinary bladder, urethra, and the male and female genitalia. This section discusses only the male genitalia; the female reproductive system is covered in Unit 6.

Urinary System

Kidneys

See Figure 4.16.
A. Two bean-shaped organs that lie in the retroperitoneal space on either side of the vertebral column; adrenal glands located on top of each kidney

B. *Renal parenchyma*
  1. Cortex: outermost layer; site of glomeruli and proximal and distal tubules of nephron
  2. Medulla: middle layer; formed by collecting tubules and ducts

C. *Renal sinus and pelvis*
  1. Papillae: projections of renal tissues located at the tips of the renal pyramids
  2. Calices
    a. Minor calyx: collects urine flow from collecting duct
    b. Major calyx: directs urine from renal sinus to renal pelvis
  3. Urine flows from renal pelvis to ureters

D. *Nephron:* the functional unit of the kidney (Figure 4.17)
  1. Renal corpuscle (vascular system of nephron)
    a. *Bowman's capsule:* a portion of the proximal tubule, surrounds the glomerulus
    b. *Glomerulus:* a capillary network permeable to water, electrolytes, nutrients, and wastes; impermeable to large protein molecules
  2. *Renal tubule:* divided into proximal convoluted tubule, descending loop of Henle, ascending loop of Henle, distal convoluted tubule, and collecting duct

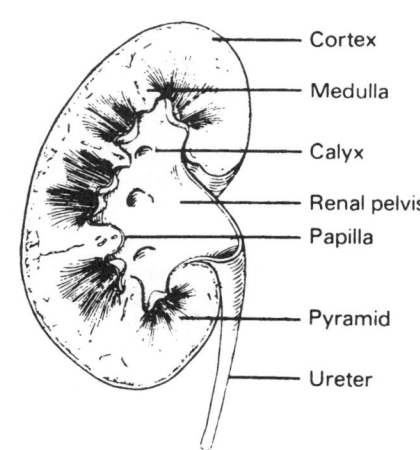

FIGURE 4.16 Anatomy of the kidney

Cortex
Medulla
Calyx
Renal pelvis
Papilla
Pyramid
Ureter

Ureters

A. Two tubes approximately 25–35 cm long
B. Extend from the renal pelvis to the pelvic

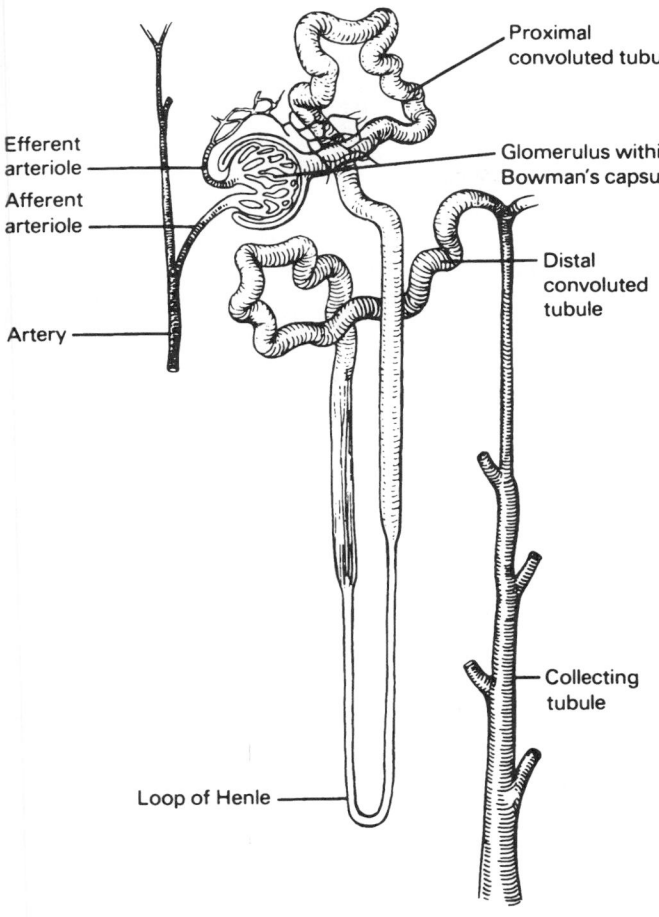

FIGURE 4.17 The nephron

cavity, where they enter the bladder, convey urine from the kidneys to the bladder.
C. Ureterovesical valve prevents backflow of urine into ureters.

Bladder

A. Located behind the symphysis pubis; composed of muscular, elastic tissue that makes it distensible
B. Serves as a reservoir of urine (capable of holding 1000–1800 ml; moderately full bladder usually holds about 500 ml)
C. Internal and external urethral sphincters control the flow of urine; urge to void stimulated by passage of urine past the internal sphincter (involuntary) to the upper part of the urethra. Relaxation of external sphincter (voluntary) produces emptying of the bladder (voiding, micturition).

Urethra

A. A small tube that extends from the bladder to the exterior of the body

B. In females, located behind the symphysis pubis and anterior to the vagina; approximately 3–5 cm long
C. In males, extends the entire length of the penis; approximately 20 cm long

Regulatory Functions of Kidney

Kidneys and urinary system play a major role in maintenance of homeostatic control of the body. Kidneys remove nitrogenous wastes and regulate fluid and electrolyte balance (see page 144) and acid-base balance (see page 146). Urine is the end product of these mechanisms.

Formation of Urine

A. Glomerular filtration
  1. Ultrafiltration of blood by the glomerulus; beginning of urine formation
     a. Requires hydrostatic pressure (supplied by the heart and assisted by vascular resistance [glomerular hydrostatic pressure]) and sufficient circulating volume.
     b. Pressure in Bowman's capsule opposes hydrostatic pressure and filtration; if glomerular pressure insufficient to force substances out of the blood into the tubules, filtrate formation stops.
  2. Glomerular filtration rate (GFR): amount of blood filtrated by the glomeruli in a given time; normal is 125 ml/min
  3. Filtrate formed has essentially same composition as blood plasma without the proteins; blood cells and proteins are usually too large to pass the glomerular membrane.
B. Tubular function: the tubules and collecting ducts carry out the functions of reabsorption, secretion, and excretion. Reabsorption of water and electrolytes is controlled by antidiuretic hormone (ADH), released by the pituitary, and aldosterone, secreted by the adrenal glands (see Table 4.22, page 322).
  1. Proximal convoluted tubule: reabsorption of certain constituents of the glomerular filtrate: 80% of electrolytes and H_2O, all glucose and amino acids, and bicarbonate; secretes organic substances and wastes.
  2. Loop of Henle: reabsorption of sodium and chloride in the ascending limb; reabsorption of water in the descending limb; concentrates/dilutes urine.
  3. Distal convoluted tubule: secretes potassium, hydrogen ions, and ammonia; reabsorbs H_2O (regulated by ADH) and bicarbonate; regulates calcium and phosphate concentrations.
  4. Collecting ducts: receive urine from distal convoluted tubules and reabsorb water (regulated by ADH).

C. Normal adult produces 1 liter/day of urine.

Blood Pressure Control

A. Kidneys regulate blood pressure partly through maintenance of volume (formation/excretion of urine).
B. The renin-angiotensin system is the other kidney-controlled mechanism that can contribute to rise in blood pressure. When blood pressure drops, the cells of the glomerulus release renin, which then activates angiotensin to cause vasoconstriction

Male Reproductive System

See Figure 4.18, page 292.

Penis

A. An external structure that serves as a passageway for urine and semen

B. Capable of distension during sexual excitement
C. Distal portion, glans penis, is covered by a prepuce or foreskin that may or may not be removed (circumcised)

Scrotum

A. Saclike structure that hangs from the root of the penis
B. Contains the testes and epididymis, and helps to regulate temperature conducive to sperm production.

Testes

A. Small oval structures suspended in the scrotum
B. Produce sperm (exocrine function) and male hormones (endocrine function, see Table 4.22, page 322).

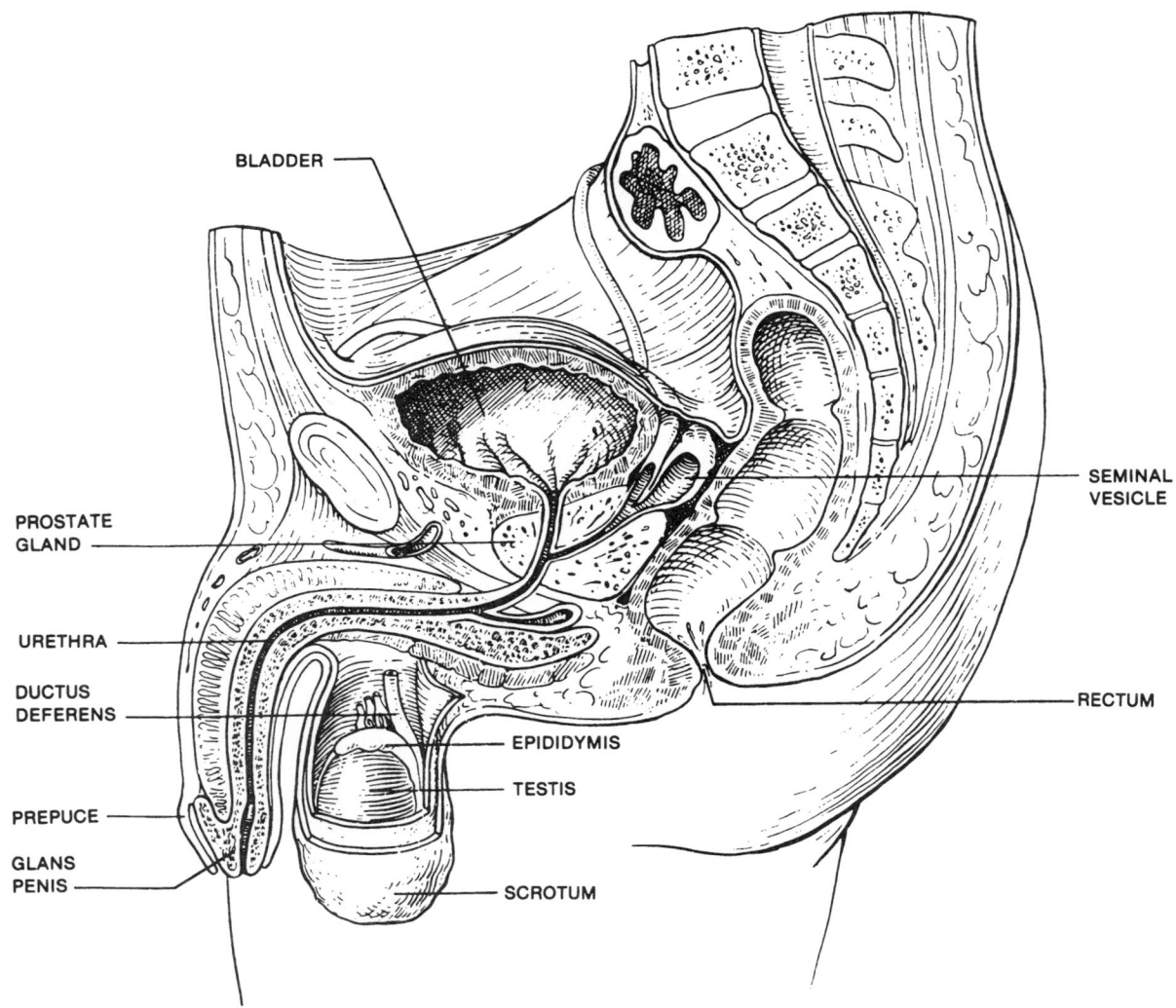

FIGURE 4.18 The male reproductive tract (Delmar Publishers)

Ductal System

A. *Epididymis:* first part of ductal system
1. Soft cordlike structure that lies along the posterolateral surface of each testis
2. Head is attached to the top of the testis, tail is continuous with vas deferens; stores spermatozoa while they mature.
B. *Spermatic cord:* consists of vas deferens, arteries, veins, nerves, and lymphatic vessels. Vas deferens joins the duct of the seminal vesicles to become the ejaculatory duct.

Accessory Glands

A. *Prostate:* located below the bladder and in front of the rectum; approximately 4–6 cm long
1. Enclosed in firm, fibrous capsule; connected to the urethra and ejaculatory ducts
2. Secretes a milky fluid that aids in the passage of spermatozoa and helps keep them viable.
B. *Cowper's glands:* lie on each side of the urethra and just below the prostate; secrete a small amount of lubricating fluid.
C. *Seminal vesicles:* paired structures parallel to the bladder; secrete a portion of the ejaculate and may contribute to nutrition and activation of sperm.

ASSESSMENT

Health History

A. Presenting problem: symptoms may include
1. Pain in flank, groin; dysuria
2. Changes in urination patterns: frequency, nocturia, hesitancy of stream, urgency, dribbling, incontinence, retention
3. Changes in urinary output: polyuria, oliguria, anuria
4. Changes in color/consistency of urine: dilute, concentrated, malodorous; hematuria, pyuria
B. Life-style: occupation (type of employment, exposure to chemicals such as carbon tetrachloride, ethylene glycol); level of activity, exercise
C. Nutrition/diet: water, calcium, dairy product intake
D. Past medical history: hypertension; diabetes mellitus; gout; cystitis; kidney infections; connective tissue diseases (systemic lupus erythematosus); infectious diseases; drug use (prescribed/OTC); previous catheterizations, hospitalizations, or surgery for renal problems
E. Family history: hypertension, diabetes mellitus, renal disease, gout, connective tissue disorders, urinary tract infections (UTIs), renal calculi

Physical Examination

A. Inspect skin for color, turgor, and mobility; purpuric lesions; integrity.
B. Inspect mouth for color, moisture, odor, ulcerations.
C. Inspect face for edema, particularly periorbital edema.
D. Inspect abdomen and palpate bladder for distension; percuss bladder for tympany or dullness (if full).
E. Inspect extremities for edema.
F. Determine rate, rhythm, and depth of respirations.
G. Inspect muscles for tremors, atrophy.
H. Palpate right and left kidneys for tenderness, pain, enlargement; percuss costovertebral angles for tenderness/pain; fist percuss kidneys for tenderness/pain.
I. Palpate flank area for pain and prostate for size, shape, consistency.
J. Auscultate aorta and renal arteries for bruits.

Laboratory/Diagnostic Tests

A. Urine studies
1. Urinalysis: examination to assess the nature of the urine produced
   a. Evaluates color, pH, and specific gravity.
   b. Determines presence of glucose (glycosuria), protein, blood (hematuria), ketones (ketonuria).
   c. Analyzes sediment for cells (presence of WBC called pyuria), casts, bacteria, crystals.
2. Urine culture and sensitivity: diagnoses bacterial infections of the urinary tract
3. Residual urine: amount of urine left in bladder after voiding measured via catheter (permanent or temporary) in bladder
4. Creatinine clearance: determines amount of creatinine (waste product of protein breakdown) in the urine over 24 hours, measures overall renal function.
B. Urine collection methods: nursing care
1. Routine urinalysis: wash perineal area if soiled, obtain first voided morning specimen; send to lab immediately (should be examined within 1 hour of voiding).
2. Clean catch (midstream) specimen for urine culture.
   a. Cleanse perineal area.
      1) females: spread labia and cleanse meatus front to back using antiseptic sponges.
      2) males: retract foreskin (if uncircumsized) and cleanse glans with antiseptic sponges.
   b. Have client initiate urine stream then stop.

c. Collect specimen in a sterile container.
d. Have client complete urination, but not in specimen container.
3. 24-hour specimen (preferred method for creatinine clearance test)
   a. Have client void and discard specimen; note time.
   b. Collect all subsequent urine specimens for 24 hours.
   c. If specimen is accidentally discarded, the test must be restarted.
   d. Record exact start and finish of collection; include date and times.
C. Blood studies
   1. Bicarbonate
   2. BUN: measures renal ability to excrete urea nitrogen
   3. Calcium
   4. Serum creatinine: specific test for renal disorders; reflects ability of kidneys to excrete creatinine
   5. Phosphorus
   6. Potassium
   7. Sodium
   8. Prostate-specific antigen (PSA)
D. KUB/plain film: an abdominal flat-plate x-ray showing the kidneys, ureters, and bladder; may identify the number and size of kidneys with tumors, malformations, and calculi
E. Intravenous pyelogram (IVP)
   1. Fluoroscopic visualization of the urinary tract after injection with a radiopaque dye
   2. Nursing care: pretest
      a. Assess for iodine sensitivity.
      b. Inform client he will lie on a table throughout procedure.
      c. Administer cathartic or enema the night before.
      d. Keep client NPO for 8 hours pretest
   3. Nursing care: posttest: force fluids.
F. Cystoscopy
   1. Use of a lighted scope (cystoscope) to inspect the bladder
      a. Inserted into the bladder via the urethra
      b. May be used to remove tumors, stones, or other foreign material (use of electrical current to remove tumors is called fulguration); or to implant radium, place catheters in ureters
   2. Nursing care: pretest
      a. Explain to client that procedure will be done under general or local anesthesia.
      b. Confirm consent form is signed.
      c. Administer sedatives 1 hour before test, as ordered.
      d. General anesthesia: keep client NPO.
      e. Local anesthesia: offer liquid breakfast.
      f. Give enemas as ordered.
   3. Nursing care: posttest

a. Provide warm sitz baths, mild analgesics to relieve discomfort after test.
b. Monitor I&O and vital signs (especially temperature, as elevation may indicate infection).
c. Expect mild hematuria at first; urine will be pink tinged, subsiding over 24–48 hours; monitor for large clots.
d. Advise client that burning on urination is normal and will subside.
e. Force fluids.

ANALYSIS

Nursing diagnoses for the client with a disorder of the genitourinary system may include
A. Fluid volume excess/deficit
B. Fatigue
C. Risk for injury
D. Altered thought processes
E. Altered oral mucous membrane
F. Altered nutrition: less than body requirements
G. Risk for infection
H. Impaired skin integrity
I. Urinary retention
J. Sexual dysfunction

PLANNING AND IMPLEMENTATION

Goals

A. Fluid imbalance will be resolved.
B. Client will exhibit improved sense of energy.
C. Client will not exhibit unusual bleeding.
D. Thought processes will improve.
E. Integrity of mucous membranes will be maintained.
F. Adequate nutritional status will be maintained.
G. Client will remain free from infection.
H. Adequate skin integrity will be maintained.
I. Client will demonstrate restored urinary flow.
J. Changes in sexual functioning will be accepted.

Interventions

Urinary Catheterization

A. General information
   1. Insertion of a catheter through the external meatus and the urethra into the bladder
   2. Purposes include relief from urinary retention, bladder decompression, prevention of bladder obstruction, instillation of medications into the bladder, and splinting the bladder.
B. Nursing care: insertion
   1. Explain procedure to client and collect necessary equipment (catheter set).

2. Wash hands and position client.
3. Use sterile technique while inserting catheter.
4. Observe for urine return and obtain specimen.
5. Connect drainage tubing to catheter (indwelling) and tape.

C. Nursing care: indwelling catheter
1. Maintain catheter patency: place drainage tubing properly to avoid kinking or pinching.
2. Observe for signs of obstruction (e.g., decreased urine in collection bag, voiding around the catheter, abdominal discomfort, bladder distension).
3. Irrigate catheter as necessary.
4. Ensure comfort and safety: relieve bladder spasms by administering belladonna suppositories (if ordered); ensure adequate fluid intake and provide perineal care.
5. Prevent infection: maintain a closed drainage system and prevent backflow of urine by keeping drainage system below level of bladder.
6. Empty collection bag at least every 8 hours.
7. Promote acidification of the urine with acid-ash diet and ascorbic acid.
8. Change catheter/drainage system only when necessary.

Dialysis

A. General information
1. Removal by artificial means of metabolic wastes, excess electrolytes, and excess fluid from clients with renal failure
2. Principles
   a. *Diffusion:* movement of particles from an area of high concentration to one of low concentration across a semipermeable membrane
   b. *Osmosis:* movement of water through a semipermeable membrane from an area of lesser concentration of particles to one of greater concentration

B. Purposes
1. Remove the end products of protein metabolism from blood
2. Maintain safe levels of electrolytes
3. Correct acidosis and replenish blood bicarbonate system
4. Remove excess fluid from the blood

C. Types: hemodialysis and peritoneal dialysis

Hemodialysis

A. General information
1. Shunting of blood from the client's vascular system through an artificial dialyzing system, and return of dialyzed blood to the client's circulation

2. Dialysis coil acts as the semipermeable membrane; the dialysate is a specially prepared solution.
3. Access routes (see Figure 4.19)
   a. External AV shunt: one cannula inserted into an artery and the other into a vein; both are brought out to the skin surface and connected by a U-shaped shunt.
   b. AV fistula: internal anastomosis of an artery to an adjacent vein in a sideways position; fistula is accessed for hemodialysis by venipuncture; takes 4–6 weeks to be ready for use.
   c. Femoral/subclavian cannulation: insertion of a catheter into one of these large veins for easy access to circulation; procedure is similar to insertion of a CVP line; temporary
   d. Graft: piece of bovine artery or vein, Gore-Tex material, or saphenous vein sutured to client's own vessel; used for clients with compromised vascular systems; provides a segment in which to place dialysis needles.

B. Nursing care: external AV shunt
1. Auscultate for a bruit and palpate for a thrill to ensure patency.
2. Assess for clotting (color change of blood, absence of pulsations in tubing).
3. Change sterile dressing over shunt daily.
4. Avoid performing venipuncture, administering IV infusions, giving injections, or taking a blood pressure with a cuff on the shunt arm.

C. Nursing care: AV fistula.
1. Auscultate for a bruit and palpate for a thrill to ensure patency.
2. Report bleeding, skin discoloration, drainage, and pain.
3. Avoid restrictive clothing/dressings over site.
4. Avoid administration of IV infusions, giving injections, or taking blood pressure with a cuff on the fistula extremity.

D. Nursing care: femoral/subclavian cannulation
1. Palpate peripheral pulses in cannulized extremity.
2. Observe for bleeding/hematoma formation.
3. Position catheter properly to avoid dislodgment during dialysis.

E. Nursing care: before and during hemodialysis
1. Have client void.
2. Chart client's weight.
3. Assess vital signs before and every 30 minutes during procedure.
4. Withhold antihypertensives, sedatives, and vasodilators to prevent hypotensive episode (unless ordered otherwise).
5. Ensure bed rest with frequent position changes for comfort.

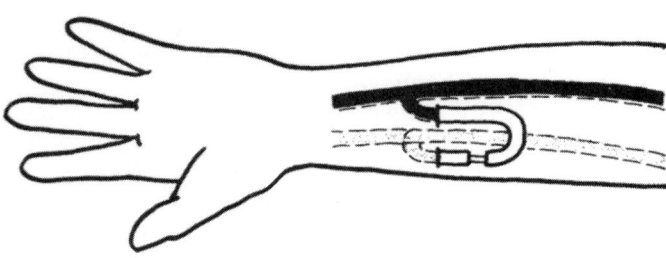

ARTERIOVENOUS SHUNT

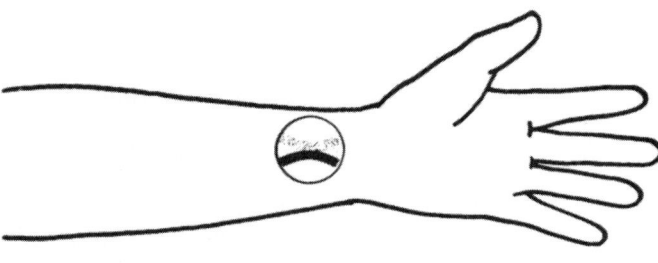

ARTERIOVENOUS FISTULA

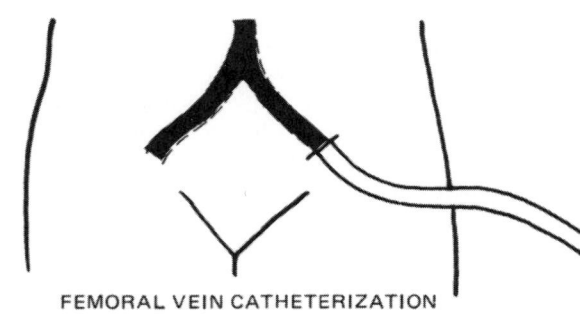

FEMORAL VEIN CATHETERIZATION

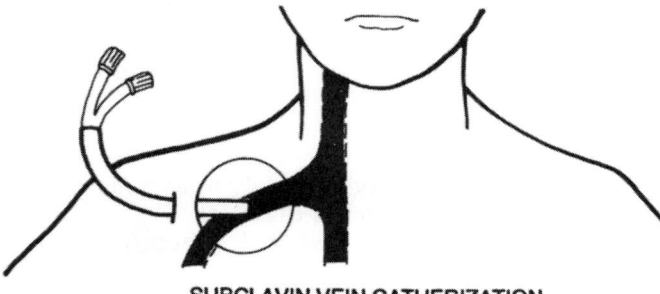

SUBCLAVIN VEIN CATHERIZATION

FIGURE 4.19   Hemodialysis sites (Delmar Publishers)

6. Inform client that headache and nausea may occur.
7. Monitor closely for signs of bleeding since blood has been heparinized for procedure.

F. Nursing care: postdialysis
   1. Chart client's weight.
   2. Assess for complications.
      a. Hypovolemic shock: may occur as a result of rapid removal or ultrafiltration of fluid from the intravascular compartment (see page 149).
      b. Dialysis disequilibrium syndrome (urea is removed more rapidly from the blood than from the brain): assess for nausea, vomiting, elevated blood pressure, disorientation, leg cramps, and peripheral paresthesias.

Peritoneal Dialysis

A. General information: introduction of a specially prepared dialysate solution into the abdominal cavity, where the peritoneum acts as a semipermeable membrane between the dialysate and blood in the abdominal vessels

B. Nursing care
   1. Chart client's weight.
   2. Assess vital signs before, every 15 minutes during first exchange, and every hour thereafter.
   3. Assemble specially prepared dialysate solution with added medications.
   4. Have client void.
   5. Warm dialysate solution to body temperature.
   6. Assist physician with trocar insertion.
   7. Inflow: allow dialysate to flow unrestricted into peritoneal cavity (10–20 minutes).
   8. Dwell: allow fluid to remain in peritoneal cavity for prescribed period (30–45 minutes).
   9. Drain: unclamp outflow tube and allow to flow by gravity.
   10. Observe characteristics of dialysate outflow.
      a. Clear pale yellow: normal
      b. Cloudy: infection, peritonitis
      c. Brownish: bowel perforation
      d. Bloody: common during first few exchanges; abnormal if continues
   11. Monitor total I&O and maintain records.
   12. Assess for complications.
      a. Peritonitis resulting from contamination of solution or tubing during exchange (see page 280).
      b. Respiratory difficulty: may occur from upward displacement of diaphragm due to increased pressure in the peritoneal cavity; assess for signs and symptoms of atelectasis (page 255),

pneumonia (page 256), and bronchitis (page 252)

   c. Protein loss: most serum proteins pass through the peritoneal membrane and are lost in the dialysate fluid; monitor serum protein levels closely

Continuous Ambulatory Peritoneal Dialysis

A. General information
   1. A continuous type of peritoneal dialysis performed at home by the client or significant others.
   2. Dialysate is delivered from flexible plastic containers through a permanent peritoneal catheter.
   3. Following infusion of the dialysate into the peritoneal cavity, the bag is folded and tucked away during the dwell period.
B. Provide client teaching and discharge planning concerning
   1. Need to assess the permanent peritoneal catheter for complications
      a. Dialysate leak
      b. Exit site infection
      c. Bacterial/fungal contamination
      d. Obstruction
   2. Adherence to high-protein (if indicated), well-balanced diet
   3. Importance of periodic blood chemistries
   4. Daily weights

EVALUATION

A. Adequate urinary output with specific gravity/ laboratory studies within client's normal range; stable weight; absence of edema; pulmonary congestion.
B. Client verbalizes increased tolerance for activities.
C. Skin and mucous membranes free from ecchymoses/bleeding; improved laboratory values (CBC, platelet count; clotting factors); no signs of bleeding.
D. Client identifies ways to compensate for cognitive impairment; demonstrates improved problem-solving skills.
E. Oral mucosa pink, moist, and intact; no ulcerations; saliva consistency normal; verbalizes interventions to promote/maintain healthy oral mucosa.
F. Stable weight gain; laboratory values within client's normal range; improved anthropometric measurements.
G. Vital signs within normal range; client identifies measures to prevent/reduce the risk of infection.
H. Skin warm and dry; absence of redness and irritation.

I. Voiding in adequate amounts with no palpable bladder distention; postvoid residuals less than 50 ml; absence of dribbling/overflow.
J. Client identifies acceptable sexual practices and explores alternate methods.
K. Client integrates treatment regimen into ADL; shows increased interest in appearance; actively participates in treatments.

DISORDERS OF THE GENITOURINARY SYSTEM

Disorders of the Urinary Tract

Cystitis

A. General information
   1. Inflammation of the bladder due to bacterial invasion
   2. More common in women
   3. Predisposing factors include stagnation of urine, obstruction, sexual intercourse, high estrogen levels
B. Assessment
   1. Abdominal or flank pain/tenderness, frequency and urgency of urination, pain on voiding, nocturia
   2. Fever
   3. Diagnostic tests: urine culture and sensitivity reveals specific organism (80% *E. coli*)
C. Nursing interventions
   1. Force fluids (3000 ml/day).
   2. Provide warm sitz baths for comfort.
   3. Assess urine for odor, hematuria, sediment.
   4. Administer medications as ordered and monitor effects.
      a. Systemic antibiotics: ampicillin, cephalosporins, aminoglycosides
      b. Sulfonamides: sulfisoxazole (Gantrisin), sulfamethoxazole (Gantanol), trimethoprim-sulfamethoxazole (Bactrim)
      c. Antibacterials: nitrofurantoin (Macrodantin), methenamine mandelate (Mandelamine), nalidixic acid (NegGram)
      d. Urinary tract analgesic: pyridium
   5. Provide client teaching and discharge planning concerning
      a. Importance of adequate hydration
      b. Frequent voiding to avoid stagnation
      c. Proper personal hygiene; women to cleanse from front to back
      d. Voiding after sexual intercourse
      e. Acidification of the urine to decrease bacterial multiplication (acid-ash diet, vitamin C)

f. Need for follow-up urine cultures.

Bladder Cancer

A. General information
  1. Most common site of cancer of the urinary tract
  2. Occurs in men 3 times more often than women; peak age 50–70 years
  3. Predisposing factors include exposure to chemicals (especially aniline dyes), cigarette smoking, chronic bladder infections
B. Medical management: dependent on the staging of cell type; includes
  1. Radiation therapy, usually in combination with surgery
  2. Chemotherapy: considerable research on both agents and methods of administration
    a. Methods include direct bladder instillations, intra-arterial infusions, IV infusion, oral ingestion
    b. Agents include 5-fluorouracil, methotrexate, bleomycin, mitomycin-C, hydroxyurea, doxorubicin, cyclophosphamide, cisplatin; results variable
  3. Surgery: see Bladder Surgery.
C. Assessment findings
  1. Intermittent painless hematuria, dysuria, frequent urination
  2. Diagnostic tests
    a. Cytoscopy with biopsy reveals malignancy
    b. Cytologic exam of the urine reveals malignant cells
D. Nursing interventions: provide care for the client receiving radiation therapy or chemotherapy, and for the client with bladder surgery.

Bladder Surgery

A. General information
  1. *Cystectomy* (removal of the urinary bladder) with one of the various types of urinary diversions is the surgical procedure done for bladder cancer
  2. Types of urinary diversions
    a. *Ureterosigmoidostomy:* ureters are excised from the bladder and implanted into sigmoid colon; urine flows through the colon and is excreted via the rectum
    b. *Ileal conduit:* ureters are implanted into a segment of the ileum that has been resected from the intestinal tract with formation of an abdominal stoma; most common type of urinary diversion
    c. *Cutaneous ureterostomy:* ureters are excised from the bladder and brought through abdominal wall with creation of a stoma

d. *Nephrostomy:* insertion of a catheter into the renal pelvis via an incision into the flank or by percutaneous catheter placement into the kidney
B. Nursing interventions: preoperative
  1. Provide routine pre-op care.
  2. Assess client's ability to learn prior to starting a teaching program.
  3. Discuss social aspects of living with a stoma (sexuality, changes in body image).
  4. Assess understanding and emotional response of client/significant others.
  5. Perform pre-op bowel preparation for procedures involving the ileum or colon.
  6. Inform client of post-op procedures.
C. Nursing interventions: postoperative
  1. Provide routine post-op care.
  2. Maintain integrity of the stoma.
    a. Monitor for and report signs of impaired stomal healing (pale, dark red, or blue-black color; increased stomal height, edema, bleeding).
    b. Maintain stomal circulation by using properly fitted faceplate.
    c. Monitor for signs and symptoms of stomal obstruction (sudden decrease in urine output, increased abdominal tenderness and distension).
  3. Prevent skin irritation and breakdown.
    a. Inspect skin areas for signs of breakdown daily.
    b. Patch test all adhesives, sprays, and skin barriers before use.
    c. Change appliance only when necessary and when production of urine is slowest (early morning).
    d. Place wick (rolled gauze pad) on stomal opening when appliance is off.
    e. Cleanse peristomal skin with mild soap and water.
    f. Remove alkaline encrustations by applying vinegar and water solution to peristomal area.
    g. Implement measures to maintain urine acidity (acid-ash foods, vitamin C therapy, omission of milk/dairy products).
  4. Provide care for the client with an NG tube (see page 268); will be in place until bowel motility returns.
  5. Assist client to identify strengths and qualities that have a positive effect on self-concept.
  6. Provide client teaching and discharge planning concerning
    a. Maintenance of stomal/peristomal skin integrity
    b. Proper application of appliance
    c. Recommended method of cleaning reusable ostomy equipment (manufacturer's recommendations)

d. Information regarding prevention of UTIs (adequate fluids; empty pouch when half full; change to bedside collection bag at night)
e. Control of odor (adequate fluids; avoid foods with strong odor; place small amount of vinegar or deodorizer in pouch)
f. Reporting signs and symptoms of UTIs (see Cystitis, page 297).

Nephrolithiasis/Urolithiasis

A. General information
1. Presence of stones anywhere in the urinary tract; frequent composition of stones: calcium, oxalate, and uric acid
2. Most often occurs in men age 20–55; more common in the summer
3. Predisposing factors
   a. Diet: large amounts of calcium, oxalate
   b. Increased uric acid levels
   c. Sedentary life-style, immobility
   d. Family history of gout or calculi; hyperparathyroidism
B. Medical management
1. Surgery
   a. Percutaneous nephrostomy: tube is inserted through skin and underlying tissues into renal pelvis to remove calculi.
   b. Percutaneous nephrostolithotomy: delivers ultrasound waves through a probe placed on the calculus.
2. Extracorporeal shock-wave lithotripsy: delivers shock waves from outside the body to the stone, causing pulverization
3. Pain management and diet modification
C. Assessment findings
1. Abdominal or flank pain; renal colic; hematuria
2. Cool, moist skin
3. Diagnostic tests
   a. KUB: pinpoints location, number, and size of stones
   b. IVP: identifies site of obstruction and presence of nonradiopaque stones
   c. Urinalysis: indicates presence of bacteria, increased protein, increased WBC and RBC
D. Nursing interventions
1. Strain all urine through gauze to detect stones and crush all clots.
2. Force fluids (3000–4000 ml/day).
3. Encourage ambulation to prevent stasis.
4. Relieve pain by administration of analgesics as ordered and application of moist heat to flank area.
5. Monitor I&O.
6. Provide modified diet, depending upon stone consistency.
   a. Calcium stones: limit milk/dairy products; provide acid-ash diet to acidify urine (cranberry or prune juice, meat, eggs, poultry, fish, grapes, whole grains); take vitamin C.
   b. Oxalate stones: avoid excess intake of foods/fluids high in oxalate (tea, chocolate, rhubarb, spinach); maintain alkaline-ash diet to alkalinize urine (milk; vegetables; fruits except prunes, cranberries, and plums).
   c. Uric acid stones: reduce foods high in purine (liver, brains, kidneys, venison, shellfish, meat soups, gravies, legumes); maintain alkaline urine.
7. Administer allopurinol (Zyloprim) as ordered, to decrease uric acid production; push fluids when giving allopurinol.
8. Provide client teaching and discharge planning concerning
   a. Prevention of urinary stasis by maintaining increased fluid intake especially in hot weather and during illness; mobility; voiding whenever the urge is felt and at least twice during the night
   b. Adherence to prescribed diet
   c. Need for routine urinalysis (at least every 3–4 months)
   d. Need to recognize and report signs/symptoms of recurrence (hematuria, flank pain).

Pyelonephritis

A. General information
1. Inflammation of the renal pelvis; may be unilateral or bilateral, acute or chronic
2. Acute: infection usually ascends from lower urinary tract
3. Chronic: thought to be a combination of structural alterations along with infection, major cause is ureterovesical reflux, with infected urine backing up into ureters and renal pelvises; result of recurrent infections is eventual renal parenchymal deterioration and possible renal failure
B. Medical management
1. Acute: antibiotics, antispasmodics, surgical removal of any obstruction
2. Chronic: antibiotics and urinary antiseptics (sulfanomides, nitrofurantoin); surgical correction of structural abnormality if possible
C. Assessment findings
1. Acute: fever, chills, nausea and vomiting; severe flank pain or dull ache
2. Chronic: client usually unaware of disease; may have bladder irritability, chronic fatigue, or slight dull ache over kidneys; eventually develops hypertension, atrophy of kidneys.

D. Nursing interventions: acute pyelonephritis
  1. Provide adequate comfort and rest.
  2. Monitor I&O.
  3. Administer antibiotics as ordered.
  4. Provide client teaching and discharge planning concerning
    a. Medication regimen
    b. Follow-up cultures
    c. Signs and symptoms of recurrence and need to report
E. Nursing interventions: chronic pyelonephritis
  1. Administer medications as ordered.
  2. Provide adequate fluid intake and nutrition.
  3. Support client/significant others and explain possibility of dialysis, transplant options if significant renal deterioration.

Glomerulonephritis

See page 420.

Nephrosis

See page 419.

Acute Renal Failure

A. General information
  1. Sudden inability of the kidneys to regulate fluid and electrolyte balance and remove toxic products from the body
  2. Causes
    a. Prerenal: factors interfering with perfusion and resulting in decreased blood flow and glomerular filtrate, ischemia, and oliguria; include CHF, cardiogenic shock, acute vasoconstriction, hemorrhage, burns, septicemia, hypotension
    b. Intrarenal: conditions that cause damage to the nephrons; include acute tubular necrosis (ATN), endocarditis, diabetes mellitus, malignant hypertension, acute glomerulonephritis, tumors, blood transfusion reactions, hypercalcemia, nephrotoxins (certain antibiotics, x-ray dyes, pesticides, anesthetics)
    c. Postrenal: mechanical obstruction anywhere from the tubules to the urethra; include calculi, BPH, tumors, strictures, blood clots, trauma, anatomic malformation
B. Assessment findings
    a. Oliguric phase (caused by reduction in glomerular filtration rate)
      1) urine output less than 400 ml/24 hours; duration 1–2 weeks
      2) manifested by hypernatremia, hyperkalemia, hyperphosphatemia, hypocalcemia, hypermagnesemia, and metabolic acidosis
      3) diagnostic tests: BUN and creatinine elevated
    b. Diuretic phase (slow, gradual increase in daily urine output)
      1) diuresis may occur (output 3–5 liters/day) due to partially regenerated tubule's inability to concentrate urine
      2) duration: 2–3 weeks; manifested by hyponatremia, hypokalemia, and hypovolemia
      3) diagnostic tests: BUN and creatinine elevated
    c. Recovery or convalescent phase: renal function stabilizes with gradual improvement over next 3–12 months
C. Nursing interventions
  1. Monitor/maintain fluid and electrolyte balance.
    a. Obtain baseline data on usual appearance and amount of client's urine.
    b. Measure I&O every hour; note excessive losses.
    c. Administer IV fluids and electrolyte supplements as ordered.
    d. Weigh daily and report gains.
    e. Monitor lab values; assess/treat fluid and electrolyte and acid-base imbalances as needed (see Tables 4.5 and 4.6).
  2. Monitor alteration in fluid volume.
    a. Monitor vital signs, PAP, PCWP, CVP as needed.
    b. Weigh client daily.
    c. Maintain strict I&O records.
    d. Assess every hour for hypervolemia; provide nursing care as needed.
      1) maintain adequate ventilation.
      2) decrease fluid intake as ordered.
      3) administer diuretics, cardiac glycosides, and antihypertensives as ordered; monitor effects.
    e. Assess every hour for hypovolemia; replace fluids as ordered.
    f. Monitor ECG and auscultate heart as needed.
    g. Check urine, serum osmolality/osmolarity, and urine specific gravity as ordered.
  3. Promote optimal nutritional status.
    a. Weigh daily.
    b. Maintain strict I&O.
    c. Administer TPN as ordered.
    d. With enteral feedings, check for residual and notify physician if residual volume increases.
    e. Restrict protein intake.
  4. Prevent complications from impaired

mobility (pulmonary embolism, skin breakdown, contractures, atelectasis; see Table 4.21, page 308).
5. Prevent fever/infection.
   a. Take rectal temperature and obtain orders for cooling blanket/antipyretics as needed.
   b. Assess for signs of infection.
   c. Use strict aseptic technique for wound and catheter care.
6. Support client/significant others and reduce/relieve anxiety.
   a. Explain pathophysiology and relationship to symptoms.
   b. Explain all procedures and answer all questions in easy-to-understand terms.
   c. Refer to counseling services as needed.
7. Provide care for the client receiving dialysis if used.
8. Provide client teaching and discharge planning concerning
   a. Adherence to prescribed dietary regime
   b. Signs and symptoms of recurrent renal disease
   c. Importance of planned rest periods
   d. Use of prescribed drugs only
   e. Signs and symptoms of UTI or respiratory infection, need to report to physician immediately

Chronic Renal Failure

A. General information
   1. Progressive, irreversible destruction of the kidneys that continues until nephrons are replaced by scar tissue; loss of renal function gradual
   2. Predisposing factors: recurrent infections, exacerbations of nephritis, urinary tract obstructions, diabetes mellitus, hypertension
B. Medical management
   1. Diet restrictions
   2. Multivitamins
   3. Hematinics
   4. Aluminum hydroxide gels
   5. Antihypertensives
C. Assessment findings
   1. Nausea, vomiting; diarrhea or constipation; decreased urinary output; dyspnea
   2. Stomatitis, hypotension (early), hypertension (later), lethargy, convulsions, memory impairment, pericardial friction rub, CHF
   3. Diagnostic tests: urinalysis
      a. Protein, sodium, and WBC elevated
      b. Specific gravity, platelets, and calcium decreased
D. Nursing interventions
   1. Prevent neurologic complications.

   a. Assess every hour for signs of uremia (fatigue, loss of appetite, decreased urine output, apathy, confusion, elevated blood pressure, edema of face and feet, itchy skin, restlessness, seizures).
   b. Assess for changes in mental functioning.
   c. Orient confused client to time, place, date, and persons; institute safety measures to protect client from falling out of bed.
   d. Monitor serum electrolytes, BUN, and creatinine as ordered.
2. Promote optimal GI function.
   a. Assess/provide care for stomatitis
   b. Monitor nausea, vomiting, anorexia; administer antiemetics as ordered.
   c. Assess for signs of GI bleeding.
3. Monitor/prevent alteration in fluid and electrolyte balance.
4. Assess for hyperphosphatemia (paresthesias, muscle cramps, seizures, abnormal reflexes), and administer aluminum hydroxide gels (Amphojel, AlternaGEL) as ordered.
5. Promote maintenance of skin integrity.
   a. Assess/provide care for pruritus.
   b. Assess for uremic frost (urea crystallization on the skin) and bathe in plain water.
6. Monitor for bleeding complications, prevent injury to client.
   a. Monitor Hgb, hct, platelets, RBC.
   b. Hematest all secretions.
   c. Administer hematinics as ordered.
   d. Avoid IM injections.
7. Promote/maintain maximal cardiovascular function.
   a. Monitor blood pressure and report significant changes.
   b. Auscultate for pericardial friction rub.
   c. Perform circulation checks routinely.
   d. Administer diuretics as ordered and monitor output.
   e. Modify digitalis dose as ordered (digitalis is excreted in kidneys).
8. Provide care for client receiving dialysis.

Kidney Transplantation

A. General information
   1. Transplantation of a kidney from a donor to recipient to prolong the life of person with renal failure
   2. Sources of donor selection
      a. Living relative with compatible serum and tissue studies, free from systemic infection, and emotionally stable
      b. Cadavers with good serum and tissue crossmatching; free from renal disease,

neoplasms, and sepsis; absence of ischemia/trauma.
B. Nursing interventions: preoperative
1. Provide routine pre-op care.
2. Discuss the possibility of post-op dialysis/immunosuppressive drug therapy with client and significant others.
C. Nursing interventions: postoperative
1. Provide routine post-op care.
2. Monitor fluid and electrolyte balance carefully.
   a. Monitor I&O hourly and adjust IV fluid administration accordingly.
   b. Anticipate possible massive diuresis.
3. Encourage frequent and early ambulation.
4. Monitor vital signs, especially temperature; report significant changes.
5. Provide mouth care and nystatin (Mycostatin) mouthwashes for candidiasis.
6. Administer immunosuppressive agents as ordered.
   a. Cyclosporine (Sandimmune): does not cause significant bone marrow depression. Assess for hypertension; blood chemistry alterations (hypermagnesemia, hyperkalemia, decreased sodium bicarbonate); neurologic functioning.
   b. Azathioprine (Imuran): assess for manifestations of anemia, leukopenia, thrombocytopenia, oral lesions.
   c. Cyclophosphamide (Cytoxan): assess for alopecia, hypertension, kidney/liver toxicity, leukopenia.
   d. Antilymphocytic globulin (ALG), antithymocytic globulin (ATG): assess for fever, chills, anaphylactic shock, hypertension, rash, headache.
   e. Corticosteroids (prednisone, methylprednisolone sodium succinate [Solu-Medrol]): assess for peptic ulcer and GI bleeding, sodium/water retention, muscle weakness, delayed healing, mood alterations, hyperglycemia, acne.
7. Assess for signs of rejection. Include decreased urinary output, fever, pain/tenderness over transplant site, edema, sudden weight gain, increasing blood pressure, generalized malaise, rise in serum creatinine, and decrease in creatinine clearance.
8. Provide client teaching and discharge planning concerning
   a. Medication regimen: names, dosages, frequency, and side effects
   b. Signs and symptoms of rejection and the need to report immediately
   c. Dietary restrictions: restricted sodium and calories, increased protein
   d. Daily weights
   e. Daily measurement of I&O

f. Resumption of activity and avoidance of contact sports in which the transplanted kidney may be injured.

Nephrectomy

A. General information
1. Surgical removal of an entire kidney
2. Indications include renal tumor, massive trauma, removal for a donor, polycystic kidneys
B. Nursing interventions: preoperative care
1. Provide routine pre-op care.
2. Ensure adequate fluid intake.
3. Assess electrolyte values and correct any imbalances before surgery.
4. Avoid nephrotoxic agents in any diagnostic tests.
5. Advise client to expect flank pain after surgery if retroperitoneal approach (flank incision) is used.
6. Explain that client will have chest tube if a thoracic approach is used.
C. Nursing interventions: postoperative
1. Provide routine post-op care.
2. Assess urine output every hour; should be 30–50 ml/hour.
3. Observe urinary drainage on dressing and estimate amount.
4. Weigh daily.
5. Maintain adequate functioning of chest drainage system; ensure adequate oxygenation and prevent pulmonary complications.
6. Administer analgesics as ordered.
7. Encourage early ambulation.
8. Teach client to splint incision while turning, coughing, deep breathing.
9. Provide client teaching and discharge planning concerning
   a. Prevention of urinary stasis
   b. Maintenance of acidic urine
   c. Avoidance of activities that might cause trauma to the remaining kidney (contact sports, horseback riding)
   d. No lifting heavy objects for at least 6 months
   e. Need to report unexplained weight gain, decreased urine output, flank pain on unoperative side, hematuria
   f. Need to notify physician if cold or other infection present for more than 3 days
   g. Medication regimen and avoidance of OTC drugs that may be nephrotoxic (except with physician approval)

Disorders of the Male Reproductive System

Epididymitis

A. General information

1. Inflammation of epididymis, one of the most common intrascrotal infections
2. May be sexually transmitted, usually caused by *N. gonorrhoeae, C. trachomatis;* also caused by GU instrumentation, urinary reflux

B. Assessment findings
   1. Sudden scrotal pain, scrotal edema, tenderness over the spermatic cord
   2. Diagnostic test: urine culture reveals specific organism

C. Nursing interventions
   1. Administer antibiotics and analgesics as ordered.
   2. Provide bed rest with elevation of the scrotum.
   3. Apply ice packs to scrotal area to decrease edema.

Prostatitis

A. General information
   1. Inflammatory condition that affects the prostate gland
   2. Several forms: acute bacterial prostatitis, chronic bacterial prostatitis, or abacterial chronic prostatitis
   3. Acute and chronic bacterial prostatitis usually caused by *E. coli, N. gonorrhoeae, Enterobacter* or *Proteus* species, and group D streptococci
   4. Most important predisposing factor: lower UTIs

B. Assessment findings
   1. Acute: fever, chills, dysuria, urethral discharge, prostatic tenderness, copious purulent urethral discharge upon palpation
   2. Chronic: backache; perineal pain; mild dysuria; frequency; enlarged, firm, and slightly tender prostate upon palpation
   3. Diagnostic tests
      a. WBC elevated
      b. Bacteria in initial urinalysis specimens

C. Nursing interventions
   1. Administer antibiotics, analgesics, and stool softeners as ordered.
   2. Provide increased fluid intake.
   3. Provide sitz baths/rest to relieve discomfort.
   4. Provide client teaching and discharge planning concerning
      a. Importance of maintaining adequate hydration
      b. Antibiotic therapy regimen (may need to remain on medication for several months)
      c. Activities that drain the prostate (masturbation, sexual intercourse, prostatic massage)

Benign Prostatic Hypertrophy (BPH)

A. General information

1. Mild to moderate glandular enlargement, hyperplasia, and overgrowth of the smooth muscles and connective tissue
2. As the gland enlarges, it compresses the urethra, resulting in urinary retention.
3. Most common problem of the male reproductive system; occurs in 50% of men over age 50; 75% of men over age 75
4. Cause unknown; may be related to hormonal mechanism

B. Assessment findings
   1. Nocturia, frequency, decreased force and amount of urinary stream, hesitancy (more difficult to start voiding), hematuria
   2. Enlargement of prostate gland upon palpation by digital rectal exam
   3. Diagnostic tests
      a. Urinalysis: alkalinity increased; specific gravity normal or elevated
      b. BUN and creatinine elevated (if longstanding BPH)
      c. Prostate-specific antigen (PSA) elevated. (Normal is <4 ng/ml.)
      d. Cystoscopy reveals enlargement of gland and obstruction of urine flow

C. Nursing interventions
   1. Administer antibiotics as ordered.
   2. Provide client teaching concerning medications
      a. Terazosin (Hytrin) relaxes bladder sphincter and makes it easier to urinate. May cause hypotension and dizziness.
      b. Finasteride (Proscar) shrinks enlarged prostate.
   3. Force fluids.
   4. Provide care for the catheterized client.
   5. Provide care for the client with prostatic surgery.

Cancer of the Prostate

A. General information
   1. Second most common cause of cancer deaths in American males over age 55
   2. Usually an adenocarcinoma; growth related to the presence of androgens
   3. Spreads from the prostate to the seminal vesicles, urethral mucosa, bladder wall, external sphincter, and lymphatic system
   4. Highest incidence is in African American men age 60 or over
   5. Cause is unknown

B. Medical management
   1. Drug therapy: estrogens, chemotherapeutic agents
   2. Radiation therapy
   3. Surgery: radical prostatectomy

C. Assessment findings: same as for BPH above but diagnostic test results are

1. Elevated acid phosphatase (distant metastasis) and alkaline phosphatase (bone metastasis)
2. Bone scan: abnormal in metastatic areas
D. Nursing interventions
   1. Administer medications as ordered and provide care for the client receiving chemotherapy
   2. Provide care for the client receiving radiation therapy.
   3. Provide care for the client with a prostatectomy.

Prostatic Surgery

A. General information
   1. Indicated for benign prostatic hypertrophy and prostatic cancer.
   2. Types
      a. *Transurethral resection (TUR or TURP):* insertion of a resectoscope into the urethra to excise prostatic tissue; good for poor surgical risks, does not require an incision; most common type of surgery for BPH
      b. *Suprapubic prostatectomy:* the prostate is approached by a low abdominal incision into the bladder to the anterior aspect of the prostate; for large tumors obstructing the urethra
      c. *Retropubic prostatectomy:* to remove a large mass high in the pelvic area; involves a low midline incision below the bladder and into the prostatic capsule
      d. *Perineal prostatectomy:* often used for prostatic cancer; the incision is made through the perineum, which facilitates radical surgery if a malignancy is found
B. Nursing interventions: preoperative
   1. Provide routine pre-op care.
   2. Institute and maintain urinary drainage.
   3. Force fluids; administer antibiotics, acid-ash diet to eradicate UTI.
   4. Reinforce what surgeon has told client/significant others regarding effects of surgery on sexual function.
C. Nursing interventions: postoperative
   1. Provide routine post-op care.
   2. Ensure patency of 3-way Foley.
   3. Monitor continuous bladder irrigations with sterile saline solution (removes clotted blood from bladder), and control rate to keep urine light pink changing to clear.
   4. Expect hematuria for 2–3 days.
   5. Irrigate catheter with normal saline as ordered.
   6. Control/treat bladder spasms; encourage short, frequent walks; decrease rate of continuous bladder irrigations (if urine is not red and is without clots); administer anticholinergics (propantheline bromide

[Pro-Banthine]) or antispasmodics (B&O suppositories) as ordered.
   7. Prevent hemorrhage: administer stool softeners to discourage straining at stool; avoid rectal temperatures and enemas; monitor Hgb and hct.
   8. Report bright red, thick blood in the catheter; persistent clots, persistent drainage on dressings.
   9. Provide for bladder retraining after Foley removal.
      a. Instruct client to perform perineal exercises (stopping and starting stream during voiding; pressing buttocks together then relaxing muscles) to improve sphincter control.
      b. Limit liquid intake in evening.
      c. Restrict caffeine-containing beverages.
      d. Withhold anticholinergics and antispasmodics (these drugs relax bladder and increase chance of incontinence) if permitted.
   10. Provide client teaching and discharge planning concerning
      a. Continued increased fluid intake
      b. Signs of UTI and need to report them
      c. Continued perineal exercises
      d. Avoidance of heavy lifting, straining during defecation, and prolonged travel (at least 8–12 weeks)
      e. Measures that promote urinary continence
      f. Possible impotence (more common after perineal resection)
         1) discuss ways of expressing sexuality (massage, cuddling)
         2) suggest alternative methods of sexual gratification and use of assistive aids
         3) discuss possibility of penile prosthesis with physician
      g. Need for annual and self-exams

Sample Questions

80. A 55-year-old man is hospitalized for bladder cancer. He is scheduled for ileal loop surgery to create a urostomy. Which information is most important for the nurse to include in a teaching plan for this client when learning to change his urostomy appliance?
   1. Change the appliance before going to bed.
   2. Cut the wafer ½ inch larger than the stoma.
   3. Cleanse the peristomal skin with soap and water.
   4. Use firm pressure to attach the wafer to the skin.
81. Which nursing intervention best prevents urinary tract infections in a person who has an ileal conduit?

1. Allowing the bag to fill completely.
2. Attaching a larger bag at night.
3. Restricting fluids to less than 1000 ml daily.
4. Changing the appliance every 8 hours.

82. An 84-year-old man has just returned to the nursing unit after a transurethral resection. He has a three-way Foley catheter for continuous bladder irrigation connected to straight drainage. Immediately after surgery, the nurse would expect his urine to be
    1. clear.
    2. light yellow.
    3. pink or dark red.
    4. bright red.

83. An elderly man has just returned to the nursing care unit following a transurethral resection. He has a three-way indwelling catheter with continuous bladder irrigation. He tells the nurse he has to void. The most appropriate nursing action is to
    1. allow him to void around the catheter.
    2. irrigate the catheter.
    3. notify the physician.
    4. remove the catheter.

84. Sally, 17 years old, is admitted to the hospital with a diagnosis of acute renal failure. She is oliguric and has proteinuria. Sally asks the nurse, "How long will it be until I start to make urine again?" A correct nursing response would be to tell her that this phase of renal failure will last for approximately
    1. 1–2 days.
    2. 3–7 days.
    3. 1–2 weeks.
    4. 3–4 weeks.

85. A client who is in acute renal failure develops pulmonary edema. Nursing interventions for this person should include all of the following except
    1. administering oxygen.
    2. encouraging coughing and deep breathing.
    3. placing her in semi-Fowler's position.
    4. replacing lost fluids.

86. The nurse is caring for a person who is admitted in acute renal failure. The appearance of a U wave on the ECG should alert the nurse to check laboratory values for
    1. hyperkalemia.
    2. hypokalemia.
    3. hypernatremia.
    4. hyponatremia.

87. A young man is admitted in chronic renal failure and placed on hemodialysis three times a week. Which is an attainable short-term goal for this person when he is placed on hemodialysis?
    1. Understanding the treatment and its implications.
    2. Independence in the care of the AV shunt.
    3. Self-monitoring during dialysis.

4. Recording dialysate composition and temperature.

88. The nurse is caring for a woman who is on hemodialysis. She has an arteriovenous fistula. Which finding is expected when assessing the fistula?
    1. Ecchymotic area.
    2. Enlarged veins.
    3. Pulselessness.
    4. Redness.

Answers and Rationales

80. The correct answer is 3. Cleansing the peristomal skin is critical to maintenance of skin integrity. The appliance should be changed in the morning when urinary drainage can be expected to be scant. A ½-inch gap between the stoma and the wafer is too large and encourages skin excoriation. Soap should not be used around the stoma. Firm pressure should not be used.

81. The correct answer is 2. Attaching a larger bag at night helps to prevent reflux of urine into the stoma during a period when the bag is emptied less frequently. Allowing the bag to fill completely will cause the seal to be broken but will not prevent urinary tract infection. Fluids should be encouraged, not restricted, in a client with a urinary stoma. Changing an appliance every 8 hours is too frequent and may cause skin irritation.

82. The correct answer is 3. The urine is expected to be pink or dark red for up to 36 hours after a transurethral resection. Some hematuria is usual for several postoperative days. Immediately after surgery the urine will not be light yellow. Bright red blood indicates arterial bleeding. The client's blood pressure may fall and emergency surgical intervention may be necessary.

83. The correct answer is 2. Blood clots clogging the catheter will produce the sensation of needing to void. Irrigation of the catheter will remove the blood clots allowing the urine to run freely. The client will not be able to void around the catheter because the catheter is inserted snugly into the urethra and the urine drains into the lumen of the catheter. It is not necessary to notify the physician at this point. The catheter may not be removed unless ordered by the physician.

84. The correct answer is 3. The oliguric period ranges from 1–2 weeks.

85. The correct answer is 4. The goal of therapy in a client with pulmonary edema is to reduce the amount of fluid in the body. Administration of oxygen as ordered would be an important nursing intervention. Coughing and deep breathing should be

encouraged. Placing the client in a semi-Fowler's position would facilitate breathing and reduce the client's anxiety.

86. The correct answer is 2. U waves on an EKG are associated with hypokalemia. Hyperkalemia shows EKG changes of tall tented T waves, widening QRS, and ST segment depression. Hypernatremia is a greater than normal concentration of sodium in the blood caused by excessive loss of water. Clients with hypernatremia may become confused, experience seizures, and lapse into coma. Replacement of water must be done slowly to avoid other electrolyte imbalances. Hyponatremia is a less than normal concentration of sodium in the blood caused by inadequate excretion of water, or by excessive water in the bloodstream. The client may develop water intoxication with confusion and lethargy, progressing to muscle excitability, convulsions, and coma.

87. The correct answer is 1. Prior to the start of dialysis, the client should fully comprehend its meaning and the changes in life-style required. Independence in the care of the AV shunt is not an expected short-term goal, although the client will need to care for the shunt at home. Monitoring the client during dialysis is a nursing intervention. Recording dialysate composition and temperature is not a client goal. It is a nursing intervention.

88. The correct answer is 2. The leaking of arterial blood into an AV fistula causes the veins to enlarge so they are easier to access for hemodialysis. An AV fistula requires 4–6 weeks to mature before it can be used. Peritoneal dialysis or external shunts may be used while the fistula is maturing. There should not be a marked ecchymotic area. There should be a bounding pulse and a continuous bruit (on auscultation) over the fistula. Redness over the fistula is not an expected finding.

The Musculoskeletal System

OVERVIEW OF ANATOMY AND PHYSIOLOGY

The musculoskeletal system consists of the bones, muscles, joints, cartilage, tendons, ligaments, and bursae. Its major function is to provide a structural framework for the body and to provide a means for movement.

Bones

A. Functions
1. Provide support to skeletal framework
2. Assist in movement by acting as levers for muscles
3. Protect vital organs and soft tissues
4. Manufacture RBCs in the red bone marrow (hematopoiesis)
5. Provide site for storage of calcium and phosphorus
B. Types of bones
1. Long: central shaft (diaphysis) made of compact bone and two ends (epiphyses) composed of cancellous bone (e.g., femur and humerus)
2. Short: cancellous bone covered by thin layer of compact bone (e.g., carpals and tarsals)
3. Flat: two layers of compact bones separated by a layer of cancellous bone (e.g., skull and ribs)
4. Irregular: sizes and shapes vary (e.g., vertebrae and mandible)

Joints

A. Articulation of bones occurs at joints; movable joints provide stabilization and permit a variety of movements
B. Classification (according to degree of movement)
1. Synarthroses: immovable joints
2. Amphiarthroses: partially movable joints
3. Diarthroses (synovial): freely movable joints
   a. Have a joint cavity (synovial cavity) between the articulating bone surfaces
   b. Articular cartilage covers the ends of the bones
   c. A fibrous capsule encloses the joint
   d. Capsule is lined with synovial membrane that secretes synovial fluid to lubricate the joint and reduce friction

Muscles

A. Functions

1. Provide shape to the body
2. Protect the bones
3. Maintain posture
4. Cause movement of body parts by contraction

B. Types of muscles
   1. *Cardiac:* involuntary; found only in heart
   2. *Smooth:* involuntary; found in walls of hollow structures (e.g., intestines)
   3. *Striated (skeletal):* voluntary

C. Characteristics of skeletal muscles
   1. Muscles are attached to the skeleton at the point of origin and to bones at the point of insertion.
   2. Have properties of contraction and extension, as well as elasticity, to permit isotonic (shortening and thickening of the muscle) and isometric (increased muscle tension) movement.
   3. Contraction is innervated by nerve stimulation.

Cartilage

A. A form of connective tissue
B. Major functions are to cushion bony prominences and offer protection where resiliency is required

Tendons and Ligaments

A. Composed of dense, fibrous connective tissue
B. Functions
   1. Ligaments attach bone to bone
   2. Tendons attach muscle to bone

ASSESSMENT

Health History

A. Presenting problem
   1. Muscles: symptoms may include pain, cramping, weakness
   2. Bones and joints: symptoms may include stiffness, swelling, pain, redness, heat, limitation of movement
B. Life-style: usual patterns of activity and exercise (limitations in ADL, use of assistive devices such as canes or walkers), nutrition (obesity) and diet, occupation (sedentary, heavy lifting, or pushing)
C. Use of medications: drugs taken for musculoskeletal problems
D. Past medical history: congenital defects, trauma, inflammations, fractures, back pain
E. Family history: arthritis, gout

Physical Examination

A. Inspect for overall body build, posture, and gait.
B. Inspect and palpate joints for swelling, deformity, masses, movement, tenderness, crepitations.
C. Inspect and palpate muscles for size, symmetry, tone, strength.

Laboratory/Diagnostic Tests

A. Hematologic studies
   1. Muscle enzymes: CPK, aldolase, SGOT (AST)
   2. Erythrocyte sedimentation rate (ESR)
   3. Rheumatoid factor
   4. Complement fixation
   5. Lupus erythematosus cells (LE prep)
   6. Antinuclear antibodies (ANA)
   7. Anti-DNA
   8. C-reactive protein
   9. Uric acid
B. X-rays: detect injury to or tumors of bone or soft tissue
C. Bone scan
   1. Measures radioactivity in bones 2 hours after IV injection of a radioisotope; detects bone tumors, osteomyelitis.
   2. Nursing care
      a. Have client void immediately before the procedure.
      b. Explain that client must remain still during the scan itself.
D. Arthroscopy
   1. Insertion of fiberoptic endoscope (arthroscope) into a joint to visualize it, perform biopsies, or remove loose bodies from the joint
   2. Performed in OR using aseptic technique
   3. Nursing care
      a. Maintain pressure dressing for 24 hours.
      b. Advise client to limit activity for several days.
E. Arthrocentesis: insertion of a needle into the joint to aspirate synovial fluid for diagnostic purposes or to remove excess fluid
F. Myelography
   1. Lumbar puncture used to withdraw a small amount of CSF, which is replaced with a radiopaque dye; used to detect tumors or herniated intravertebral discs
   2. Nursing care: pretest
      a. Keep NPO after liquid breakfast.
      b. Check for iodine allergy.
      c. Confirm that consent form has been signed and explain procedure to client.
   3. Nursing care: posttest (see also Lumbar Puncture, page 180)
      a. If oil-based dye (e.g., iophendylate [Pantopaque]) was used, keep client flat for 12 hours.
      b. If water-based dye (e.g., metrizamide [Amipaque]) was used

1) elevate head of bed 30°–45° to prevent upward displacement of dye, which may cause meningeal irritation and possibly seizures.
2) institute seizure precautions and do not administer any phenothiazine drugs to client, e.g., prochlorperazine (Compazine).

G. Electromyography
1. Measures and records activity of contracting muscles in response to electrical stimulation; helps differentiate muscle disease from motor neuron dysfunction
2. Nursing care: explain procedure to the client and advise that some discomfort may occur due to needle insertion

ANALYSIS

Nursing diagnoses for clients with disorders of the musculoskeletal system may include
A. Risk for injury
B. Risk for disuse syndrome
C. Impaired physical mobility
D. Bathing/hygiene self-care deficit
E. Dressing/grooming self-care deficit
F. Toileting self-care deficit
G. Body-image disturbance
H. Pain

PLANNING AND IMPLEMENTATION

Goals

Client will
A. Be free from injury.
B. Be free from complications of immobility.
C. Attain optimal level of mobility.
D. Perform self-care activities at optimal level.
E. Adapt to alterations in body image.
F. Achieve maximum comfort level.

Interventions

Preventing Complications of Immobility

See Table 4.21, page 308.

Range-of-Motion (ROM) Exercises

A. Movement of joint through its full ROM to prevent contractures and increase or maintain muscle tone/strength
B. Types

TABLE 4.21 Preventing Complications of Immobility

System	Complication	Nursing Intervention
Cardiovascular	Orthostatic hypotension Deep-vein thrombosis and pulmonary embolism Increased workload on heart	Active or passive ROM exercises Plantar-flexion and dorsiflexion foot exercises Quadriceps and gluteal-setting exercises Frequent turning Slow mobilization No pillows behind knees Antiembolism stockings
Respiratory	Decreased chest expansion Accumulation of secretions in respiratory tract	Frequent turning Encourage frequent coughing and deep breathing
Integumentary	Breakdown of skin integrity (abrasions, decubitus ulcers) caused by friction, pressure, or shearing forces	Frequent turning and repositioning Regular inspection of skin for signs of pressure Gentle massage of skin, especially over bony prominences
Gastrointestinal	Constipation	Frequent movement and turning in bed Increase in fluid intake Adequate dietary intake with increase in high-fiber foods Use of stool softeners/laxatives as ordered
Musculoskeletal	Atrophy and weakness of muscles Contractures Demineralization of bone (osteoporosis)	Active and passive ROM and isometric exercises Encourage participation in ADL as much as possible Proper positioning and repositioning of joints
Urinary	Increased calcium excretion from bone destruction (calculi formation) Increased urine pH (alkaline) Stasis of urine in kidney and bladder Urinary infection	Increase in fluid intake Decrease in calcium intake, especially milk and milk products Use of acid-ash foods Use of commode if possible
Neurologic	Sensory deprivation and isolation	Frequent contact by staff Orienting measures (clock, calendar) Diversional activities (television, radio, hobbies) Inclusion of client in decision-making activities

1. Active: carried out by client; increases and maintains muscle tone; maintains joint mobility
2. Passive: carried out by nurse without assistance from client; maintains joint mobility only; body part not to be moved beyond its existing ROM
3. Active assistive: client moves body part as far as possible and nurse completes remainder of movement
4. Active resistive: contraction of muscles against an opposing force; increases muscle size and strength

Isometric Exercises

A. Active exercise through contraction/relaxation of muscle; no joint movement; length of muscle does not change.
B. Client increases tension in muscle for several seconds and then relaxes.
C. Maintains muscle strength and size.

Assistive Devices for Walking

A. Cane
   1. Types: single, straight-legged cane; tripod cane; quad cane.
   2. Nursing care: teach client to hold cane in hand opposite affected extremity and to advance cane at the same time the affected leg is moved forward.
B. Walker
   1. Mechanical device with four legs for support.
   2. Nursing care: teach client to hold upper bars of walker at each side, then to move the walker forward and step into it.
C. Crutches: teaching the client proper use of crutches is an important nursing responsibility.
   1. Ensure proper length
      a. When client assumes erect position the top of crutch is 2 inches below the axilla, and the tip of each crutch is 6 inches in front and to the side of the feet.
      b. Client's elbows should be slightly flexed when hand is on hand grip.
      c. Weight should not be borne by the axillae.
   2. Crutch gaits
      a. Four-point gait: used when weight bearing is allowed on both extremities
         1) advance right crutch.
         2) step forward with left foot.
         3) advance left crutch.
         4) step forward with right foot.
      b. Two-point gait: typical walking pattern, an acceleration of four-point gait
         1) step forward moving both right crutch and left leg simultaneously.
         2) step forward moving both left crutch and right leg simultaneously.
      c. Three-point gait: used when weight bearing is permitted on one extremity only
         1) advance both crutches and affected extremity several inches, maintaining good balance.
         2) advance the unaffected leg to the crutches, supporting the weight of the body on the hands.
      d. Swing-to gait: used for clients with paralysis of both lower extremities who are unable to lift feet from floor
         1) both crutches are placed forward.
         2) client swings forward to the crutches.
      e. Swing-through gait: same indications as for swing-to gait
         1) both crutches are placed forward.
         2) client swings body through the crutches.

Care of the Client with a Cast

A. Types of casts: long arm, short arm, long leg, short leg, walking cast with rubber heel, body cast, shoulder spica, hip spica
B. Casting materials
   1. Plaster of paris—traditional cast
      a. Takes 24–72 hours to dry.
      b. Precautions must be taken until cast is dry to prevent dents, which may cause pressure areas.
      c. Signs of a dry cast: shiny white, hard, resistant.
      d. Must be kept dry since water can ruin a plaster cast.
   2. Synthetic casts, e.g., fiberglass
      a. Strong, lightweight; sets in about 20 minutes.
      b. Can be dried using cast dryer or hair blow-dryer on cool setting; some synthetic casts need special lamp to harden.
      c. Water-resistant; however, if cast becomes wet, must be dried thoroughly to prevent skin problems under cast.
C. Cast drying—plaster cast
   1. Use palms of hands, not fingertips, to support cast when moving or lifting client.
   2. Support cast on rubber- or plastic-protected pillows with cloth pillowcase along length of cast until dry.
   3. Turn client every 2 hours to reduce pressure and promote drying.
   4. Do not cover the cast until it is dry (may use fan to facilitate drying).
   5. Do not use heat lamp or hair dryer on plaster cast.
D. Assessment
   1. Perform neurovascular checks to area distal to cast.

a. Report absent or diminished pulse, cyanosis or blanching, coldness, lack of sensation, inability to move fingers or toes, excessive swelling.
b. Report complaints of burning, tingling, or numbness.
2. Note any odor from the cast that may indicate infection.
3. Note any bleeding on cast in a surgical client.
4. Check for "hot spots" that may indicate inflammation under cast.
E. General care
1. Instruct client to wiggle toes or fingers to improve circulation.
2. Elevate affected extremity above heart level to reduce swelling.
3. Apply ice bags to each side of the cast if ordered.
F. Provide client teaching and discharge planning concerning
1. Isometric exercises when cleared with physician
2. Reinforcement of instructions given on crutch walking
3. Do not get cast wet; wrap cast in plastic bag when bathing or take sponge bath
4. If a cast that has already dried and hardened does become wet, may use blow-dryer on low setting over wet spot; if large area of plaster cast becomes wet, call physician
5. Do not scratch or insert foreign bodies under cast; may direct cool air from blow-dryer under cast for itching
6. Recognize and report signs of impaired circulation or of infection
7. Cast cleaning
a. Clean surface soil on plaster cast with a slightly damp cloth; mild soap may be used for synthetic cast
b. To brighten a plaster cast, apply white shoe polish sparingly

Care of the Client in Traction

A. A pulling force exerted on bones to reduce and/or immobilize fractures, reduce muscle spasm, correct or prevent deformities
B. Types.
1. Skin traction: weights are attached to a moleskin or adhesive strip secured by elastic bandage or other special device (e.g., foam rubber boot) used to cover the affected limb.
a. *Buck's extension*
1) exerts straight pull on affected extremity
2) generally used to temporarily immobilize the leg in a client with a fractured hip

3) shock blocks at the foot of the bed produce countertraction and prevent the client from sliding down in bed
b. *Russell traction*
1) knee is suspended in a sling attached to a rope and pulley on a Balkan frame, creating upward pull from the knee; weights are attached to foot of bed (as in Buck's extension) creating a horizontal force exerted on the tibia and fibula
2) generally used to stabilize fractures of the femoral shaft while client is awaiting surgery
3) elevating foot of bed slightly provides countertraction
4) head of bed should remain flat
5) foot of bed usually elevated by shock blocks to provide countertraction
c. *Cervical traction*
1) cervical head halter attached to weights that hang over head of bed
2) used for soft tissue damage or degenerative disc disease of cervical spine to reduce muscle spasm and maintain alignment
3) usually intermittent traction
4) elevate head of bed to provide countertraction
d. *Pelvic traction*
1) pelvic girdle with extension straps attached to ropes and weights
2) used for low back pain to reduce muscle spasm and maintain alignment
3) usually intermittent traction
4) client in semi-Fowler's position with knee bent
5) secure pelvic girdle around iliac crests
2. Skeletal traction: traction applied directly to the bones using pins, wires, or tongs (e.g., Crutchfield tongs) that are surgically inserted; used for fractured femur, tibia, humerus, cervical spine
3. Balanced suspension traction: produced by a counterforce other than the client's weight; extremity floats or balances in the traction apparatus; client may change position without disturbing the line of traction
4. *Thomas splint and Pearson attachment* (usually used with skeletal traction in fractures of the femur)
a. Hip should be flexed at 20°
b. Use footplate to prevent foot drop
C. Nursing care
1. Check traction apparatus frequently to ensure that

a. Ropes are aligned and weights are hanging freely.
b. Bed is in proper position.
c. Line of traction is within the long axis of the bone.
2. Maintain client in proper alignment.
   a. Align in center of bed.
   b. Do not rest affected limb against foot of bed.
3. Perform neurovascular checks to affected extremity.
4. Observe for and prevent foot drop.
   a. Provide footplate.
   b. Encourage plantarflexion and dorsiflexion exercises.
5. Observe for and prevent deep-vein thrombosis (especially in Russell traction due to pressure on popliteal space).
6. Observe for and prevent skin irritation and breakdown (especially over bony prominences and traction application sites).
   a. Russell traction: check popliteal area frequently and pad the sling with felt covered by stockinette or ABDs.
   b. Thomas splint: pad top of splint with same material as in Russell traction.
   c. Cervical traction: pad chin area and protect ears.
7. Provide pin care for clients in skeletal traction.
   a. Usually consists of cleansing and applying antibiotic ointment, but individual agency policies may vary.
   b. Observe for any redness, drainage, odor.
8. Assist with ADL; provide overhead trapeze to facilitate moving, using bedpan, etc.
9. Prevent complications of immobility.
10. Encourage active ROM exercises to unaffected extremities.
11. Check carefully for orders about turning.
    a. Buck's extension: client may turn to unaffected side (place pillows between legs before turning).
    b. Russell traction and balanced suspension traction: client may turn slightly from side to side without turning body below the waist.
    c. May need to make bed from head to foot.

EVALUATION

A. Client remains free from injury.
B. Client is free from complications of immobility.
   1. Maintains clear, intact skin.
   2. Has regular bowel movements.
   3. Is free from urinary tract infection/retention/calculi.
4. Has clear breath sounds; normal rate, rhythm, and depth of respiration.
5. Demonstrates adequate peripheral circulation.
6. Maintains joint mobility and muscle tone.
7. Remains oriented to time, place, and person.
8. Is active in decision making regarding own care.
C. Optimum level of mobility is attained.
D. Client attains independence in self-care activities; uses assistive devices as necessary.
E. Client successfully adjusts to alterations in body image; exhibits increased self-esteem.
F. Pain is relieved or is more manageable.

DISORDERS OF THE MUSCULOSKELETAL SYSTEM

Rheumatoid Arthritis (RA)

A. General information
   1. Chronic systemic disease characterized by inflammatory changes in joints and related structures
   2. Occurs in women more often than men (3:1); peak incidence between ages 35–45
   3. Cause unknown, but may be an autoimmune process; genetic factors may also play a role.
   4. Predisposing factors include fatigue, cold, emotional stress, infection.
   5. Joint distribution is symmetric (bilateral); most commonly affects smaller peripheral joints of hands and also commonly involves wrists, elbows, shoulders, knees, hips, ankles, and jaw.
   6. If unarrested, affected joints progress through four stages of deterioration: synovitis, pannus formation, fibrous ankylosis, and bony ankylosis.
B. Medical management
   1. Drug therapy
      a. Aspirin: mainstay of treatment, has both analgesic and anti-inflammatory effect.
      b. Nonsteroidal anti-inflammatory drugs (NSAIDs): ibuprofen (Motrin), indomethacin (Indocin), fenoprofen (Nalfon), mefenamic acid (Ponstel), phenylbutazone (Butazolidin), piroxicam (Feldene), naproxen (Naprosyn), sulindac (Clinoril); relieve pain and inflammation by inhibiting the synthesis of prostaglandins
      c. Gold compounds (chrysotherapy)
         1) injectable form: sodium thiomalate (Myochrysine); aurothioglucose (Solganal); given IM once a week;

take 3–6 months to become effective; side effects include proteinuria, mouth ulcers, skin rash, aplastic anemia; monitor blood studies and urinalysis frequently.
   2) oral form: auranofin (Ridaura); smaller doses are effective; take 3–6 months to become effective; diarrhea also a side effect with oral form; blood and urine studies should also be monitored.
   d. Corticosteroids
      1) intra-articular injections temporarily suppress inflammation in specific joints.
      2) systemic administration used only when client does not respond to less potent anti-inflammatory drugs.
   e. Methotrexate, Cytoxan given to suppress immune response; side effects include bone marrow suppression
   2. Physical therapy to minimize joint deformities
   3. Surgery to remove severely damaged joints (e.g., total hip replacement; knee replacement)
C. Assessment findings
   1. Fatigue, anorexia, malaise, weight loss, slight elevation in temperature
   2. Joints are painful, warm, swollen, limited in motion, stiff in morning and after periods of inactivity, and may show crippling deformity in long-standing disease
   3. Muscle weakness secondary to inactivity
   4. History of remissions and exacerbations
   5. Some clients have additional extra-articular manifestations: subcutaneous nodules; eye, vascular, lung, or cardiac problems.
   6. Diagnostic tests
      a. X-rays show various stages of joint disease
      b. CBC: anemia is common
      c. ESR elevated
      d. Rheumatoid factor positive
      e. ANA may be positive
      f. C-reactive protein elevated
D. Nursing interventions
   1. Assess joints for pain, swelling, tenderness, limitation of motion.
   2. Promote maintenance of joint mobility and muscle strength.
      a. Perform ROM exercises several times a day; use of heat prior to exercise may decrease discomfort; stop exercise at the point of pain.
      b. Use isometric or other exercise to strengthen muscles.
   3. Change position frequently; alternate sitting, standing, lying.
   4. Promote comfort and relief/control of pain.

   a. Ensure balance between activity and rest.
   b. Provide 1–2 scheduled rest periods throughout day.
   c. Rest and support inflamed joints; if splints used, remove 1–2 times/day for gentle ROM exercises.
   5. Ensure bed rest if ordered for acute exacerbations.
      a. Provide firm mattress.
      b. Maintain proper body alignment.
      c. Have client lie prone for ½ hour twice a day.
      d. Avoid pillows under knees.
      e. Keep joints mainly in extension, not flexion.
      f. Prevent complications of immobility.
   6. Provide heat treatments (warm bath, shower, or whirlpool; warm, moist compresses; paraffin dips) as ordered.
      a. May be more effective in chronic pain.
      b. Reduce stiffness, pain, and muscle spasm.
   7. Provide cold treatments as ordered; most effective during acute episodes.
   8. Provide psychologic support and encourage client to express feelings.
   9. Assist client in setting realistic goals; focus on client strengths.
   10. Provide client teaching and discharge planning concerning
      a. Use of prescribed medications and side effects
      b. Self-help devices to assist in ADL and to increase independence
      c. Importance of maintaining a balance between activity and rest
      d. Energy conservation methods
      e. Performance of ROM, isometric, and prescribed exercises
      f. Maintenance of well-balanced diet
      g. Application of resting splints as ordered
      h. Avoidance of undue physical or emotional stress
      i. Importance of follow-up care

Osteoarthritis

A. General information
   1. Chronic, nonsystemic disorder of joints characterized by degeneration of articular cartilage
   2. Women and men affected equally; incidence increases with age
   3. Cause unknown; most important factor in development is aging (wear and tear on joints); others include obesity, joint trauma
   4. Weight-bearing joints (spine, knees, hips) and terminal interphalangeal joints of fingers most commonly affected
B. Assessment findings

1. Pain (aggravated by use and relieved by rest) and stiffness of joints
2. Heberden's nodes: bony overgrowths at terminal interphalangeal joints
3. Decreased ROM, possible crepitation (grating sound when moving joint)
4. Diagnostic tests
   a. X-rays show joint deformity as disease progresses
   b. ESR may be slightly elevated when disease is inflammatory
C. Nursing interventions
   1. Assess joints for pain and ROM.
   2. Relieve strain and prevent further trauma to joints.
      a. Encourage rest periods throughout day.
      b. Use cane or walker when indicated.
      c. Ensure proper posture and body mechanics.
      d. Promote weight reduction if obese.
      e. Avoid excessive weight-bearing activities and continuous standing.
   3. Maintain joint mobility and muscle strength.
      a. Provide ROM and isometric exercises.
      b. Ensure proper body alignment.
      c. Change client's position frequently.
   4. Promote comfort/relief of pain.
      a. Administer medications as ordered: aspirin and NSAIDs most commonly used; intra-articular injections of corticosteroids relieve pain and improve mobility.
      b. Apply heat as ordered (e.g., warm baths, compresses, hot packs) or ice to reduce pain.
   5. Prepare client for joint replacement surgery if necessary.
   6. Provide client teaching and discharge planning concerning
      a. Use of prescribed medications and side effects
      b. Importance of rest periods
      c. Measures to relieve strain on joints
      d. ROM and isometric exercises
      e. Maintenance of a well-balanced diet
      f. Use of heat/ice as ordered

Gout

A. General information
   1. A disorder of purine metabolism; causes high levels of uric acid in the blood and the precipitation of urate crystals in the joints
   2. Inflammation of the joints caused by deposition of urate crystals in articular tissue
   3. Occurs most often in males
   4. Familial tendency
B. Medical management
   1. Drug therapy
      a. Acute attack: Colchicine IV or PO (discontinue if diarrhea occurs); NSAIDs such as indomethacin (Indocin), naproxen (Naprosyn), phenylbutazone (Butazolidin)
      b. Prevention of attacks
         1) uricosuric agents (probenecid [Benemid], sulfinpyrazone [Anturane]) increase renal excretion of uric acid
         2) allopurinal (Zyloprim) inhibits uric acid formation
   2. Low-purine diet may be recommended
   3. Joint rest and protection
   4. Heat or cold therapy
C. Assessment findings
   1. Joint pain, redness, heat, swelling; joints of foot (especially great toe) and ankle most commonly affected (acute gouty arthritis stage)
   2. Headache, malaise, anorexia
   3. Tachycardia; fever; tophi in outer ear, hands, and feet (chronic tophaceous stage)
   4. Diagnostic test: uric acid elevated
D. Nursing interventions
   1. Assess joints for pain, motion, appearance.
   2. Provide bed rest and joint immobilization as ordered.
   3. Administer antigout medications as ordered.
   4. Administer analgesics for pain as ordered.
   5. Increase fluid intake to 2000–3000 ml/day to prevent formation of renal calculi.
   6. Apply local heat or cold as ordered.
   7. Apply bed cradle to keep pressure of sheets off joints.
   8. Provide client teaching and discharge planning concerning
      a. Medications and their side effects
      b. Modifications for low-purine diet: avoidance of shellfish, liver, kidney, brains, sweetbreads, sardines, anchovies
      c. Limitation of alcohol use
      d. Increase in fluid intake
      e. Weight reduction if necessary
      f. Importance of regular exercise

Systemic Lupus Erythematosus (SLE)

A. General information
   1. Chronic connective tissue disease involving multiple organ systems
   2. Occurs most frequently in young women
   3. Cause unknown; immune, genetic, and viral factors have all been suggested
   4. Pathophysiology
      a. A defect in body's immunologic mechanisms produces autoantibodies in the serum directed against components of the client's own cell nuclei.

b. Affects cells throughout the body resulting in involvement of many organs, including joints, skin, kidney, CNS, and cardiopulmonary system.
B. Medical management
   1. Drug therapy
      a. Aspirin and NSAIDs to relieve mild symptoms such as fever and arthritis
      b. Corticosteroids to suppress the inflammatory response in acute exacerbations or severe disease
      c. Immunosuppressive agents such as azathioprine (Imuran), cyclophosphamide (Cytoxan) to suppress the immune response when client unresponsive to more conservative therapy
   2. Plasma exchange to provide temporary reduction in amount of circulating antibodies
   3. Supportive therapy as organ systems become involved
C. Assessment findings
   1. Fatigue, fever, anorexia, weight loss, malaise, history of remissions and exacerbations
   2. Joint pain, morning stiffness
   3. Skin lesions
      a. Erythematous rash on face, neck, or extremities may occur
      b. Butterfly rash over bridge of nose and cheeks
      c. Photosensitivity with rash in areas exposed to sun
   4. Oral or nasopharyngeal ulcerations
   5. Alopecia
   6. Renal system involvement (proteinuria, hematuria, renal failure)
   7. CNS involvement (peripheral neuritis, seizures, organic brain syndrome, psychosis)
   8. Cardiopulmonary system involvement (pericarditis, pleurisy)
   9. Increase susceptibility to infection
   10. Diagnostic tests
      a. ESR elevated
      b. CBC; anemia; WBC and platelet counts decreased
      c. ANA positive
      d. LE prep positive
      e. Anti-DNA positive
      f. Chronic false-positive test for syphilis
D. Nursing interventions
   1. Assess symptoms to determine systems involved.
   2. Monitor vital signs, I&O, daily weights.
   3. Administer medications as ordered.
   4. Institute seizure precautions and safety measures with CNS involvement.
   5. Provide psychologic support to client/significant others.

   6. Provide client teaching and discharge planning concerning
      a. Disease process and relationship to symptoms
      b. Medication regimen and side effects
      c. Importance of adequate rest
      d. Use of daily heat and exercises as prescribed for arthritis
      e. Need to avoid physical or emotional stress
      f. Maintenance of a well-balanced diet
      g. Need to avoid direct exposure to sunlight (wear hat and other protective clothing)
      h. Need to avoid exposure to persons with infections
      i. Importance of regular medical follow-up
      j. Availability of community agencies

Osteomyelitis

A. General information
   1. Infection of the bone and surrounding soft tissues, most commonly caused by *S. aureus.*
   2. Infection may reach bone through open wound (compound fracture or surgery), through the blood stream, or by direct extension from infected adjacent structures.
   3. Infections can be acute or chronic; both cause bone destruction.
B. Assessment findings
   1. Malaise, fever
   2. Pain and tenderness of bone, redness and swelling over bone, difficulty with weight bearing; drainage from wound site may be present
   3. Diagnostic tests
      a. CBC: WBC elevated
      b. Blood cultures may be positive
      c. ESR may be elevated
C. Nursing interventions
   1. Administer analgesics and antibiotics as ordered.
   2. Use sterile technique during dressing changes.
   3. Maintain proper body alignment and change position frequently to prevent deformities.
   4. Provide immobilization of affected part as ordered.
   5. Provide psychologic support and diversional activities (depression may result from prolonged hospitalization).
   6. Prepare client for surgery if indicated.
      a. Incision and drainage of bone abscess
      b. Sequestrectomy: removal of dead, infected bone and cartilage
      c. Bone grafting after repeated infections
      d. Leg amputation

7. Provide client teaching and discharge planning concerning
   a. Use of prescribed oral antibiotic therapy and side effects
   b. Importance of recognizing and reporting signs of complications (deformity, fracture) or recurrence

Fractures

A. General information
   1. A break in the continuity of bone, usually caused by trauma
   2. Pathologic fractures: spontaneous bone break, found in certain diseases or conditions (osteoporosis, osteomyelitis, multiple myeloma, bone tumors)
   3. Types
      a. Complete: separation of bone into two parts
         1) transverse
         2) oblique
         3) spiral
      b. Incomplete (partial): fracture does not go all the way through the bone, only part of the bone is broken.
      c. Comminuted: bone is broken or splintered into pieces.
      d. Closed or simple: bone is broken without break in skin.
      e. Open or compound: break in skin with or without protrusion of bone.
B. Medical management
   1. Traction
   2. Reduction
      a. Closed reduction through manual manipulation followed by application of cast
      b. Open reduction
   3. Application of a cast
C. Assessment findings
   1. Pain, aggravated by motion; tenderness
   2. Loss of motion; edema, crepitus (grating sound), ecchymosis
   3. Diagnostic test: x-ray reveals break in bone
D. Nursing interventions
   1. Provide emergency care of fractures (refer to page 151).
   2. Perform neurovascular checks on affected extremity.
   3. Observe for signs of compartment syndrome (swelling causes an increase within muscle compartment which causes edema and more pressure; irreversible neuromuscular damage can occur within 4 to 6 hours); signs include weak pulse, pallor followed by cyanosis, paresthesias and severe pain.
   4. Observe for signs of fat emboli (respiratory distress, mental disturbances, fever, petechiae) especially in the client with multiple long-bone fractures.

5. Encourage diet high in protein and vitamins to promote healing.
6. Encourage fluids to prevent constipation, renal calculi, and UTIs.
7. Provide care for the client in traction, with a cast, or with open reduction.
8. Provide client teaching and discharge planning concerning
   a. Cast care if indicated
   b. Crutch walking (page 309) if necessary
   c. Signs of complications and need to report them

Open Reduction and Internal Fixation

A. General information
   1. Open reduction of fractures requires surgery to realign bones; may include internal fixation with pins, screws, wires, plates, rods, or nails
   2. Indications include
      a. Compound fractures
      b. Fractures accompanied by serious neurovascular injuries
      c. Fractures with widely separated fragments
      d. Comminuted fractures
      e. Fractures of the femur
      f. Fractures of joints
B. Nursing interventions: preoperative
   1. Provide routine pre-op care.
   2. Provide meticulous skin preparation to prevent infection.
C. Nursing interventions: postoperative
   1. Provide routine post-op care.
   2. Maintain affected limb in proper alignment.
   3. Perform neurovascular checks to affected extremity.
   4. Observe for post-op infection.

Fractured Hip

A. General information
   1. Fracture of the head, neck (intracapsular fracture) or trochanteric area (extracapsular fracture) of the femur
   2. Occurs most often in elderly women
   3. Predisposing factors include osteoporosis and degenerative changes of bone
B. Medical management
   1. Buck's or Russell traction as temporary measures to maintain alignment of affected limb and reduce the pain of muscle spasm
   2. Surgery
      a. Open reduction and internal fixation with pins, nails, and/or plates
      b. Hemiarthroplasty: insertion of prosthesis (e.g., Austin-Moore) to replace head of femur
C. Assessment findings
   1. Pain in affected limb

2. Affected limb appears shorter, external rotation
3. Diagnostic test: x-ray reveals hip fracture
D. Nursing interventions
   1. Provide general care for the client with a fracture.
   2. Provide care for the client with Buck's or Russell traction (page 310).
   3. Monitor for disorientation and confusion in the elderly client; reorient frequently and provide safety measures.
   4. Perform neurovascular checks to affected extremity.
   5. Prevent complications of immobility.
   6. Encourage use of trapeze to facilitate movement.
   7. Administer analgesics as ordered for pain.
   8. In addition to routine post-op care for the client with open reduction and internal fixation
      a. Check dressings for bleeding, drainage, infection: empty Hemovac and note output; keep compressed to facilitate drainage.
      b. Assess client's LOC.
      c. Reorient the confused client frequently.
      d. Avoid oversedating the elderly client.
      e. Turn client every 2 hours.
      f. Turn to unoperative side only.
      g. Place 2 pillows between legs while turning and when lying on side.
      h. Institute measures to prevent thrombus formation.
         1) apply elastic stockings.
         2) encourage plantarflexion and dorsiflexion foot exercises.
         3) administer anticoagulants such as aspirin if ordered.
      i. Encourage quadriceps setting and gluteal setting exercises when allowed.
      j. Observe for adequate bowel and bladder function.
      k. Assist client in getting out of bed, usually on first or second post-op day.
      l. Pivot or lift into chair as ordered.
      m. Avoid weight bearing until allowed.
   9. Provide care for the client with a hip prosthesis if necessary (similar to care for client with total hip replacement).

Total Hip Replacement

A. General information
   1. Replacement of both acetabulum and head of femur with prostheses
   2. Indications
      a. Rheumatoid arthritis or osteoarthritis causing severe disability and intolerable pain
      b. Fractured hip with nonunion
B. Nursing interventions
   1. Provide routine pre-op care.

2. In addition to routine post-op care for the client with hip surgery
   a. Maintain abduction of affected limb at all times with abductor splint or 2 pillows between legs
   b. Prevent external rotation (may vary depending on type of prosthesis and method of insertion) by placing trochanter rolls along leg.
   c. Prevent hip flexion.
      1) keep head of bed flat if ordered.
      2) may raise bed to 45° for meals if allowed.
   d. Turn only to unoperative side if ordered; use abductor splint or 2 pillows between knees while turning and when lying on side.
   e. Assist client in getting out of bed when ordered.
      1) usually on second post-op day.
      2) avoid weight bearing until allowed.
      3) avoid adduction and hip flexion; do not use low chair.
3. Provide client teaching and discharge planning concerning
   a. Prevention of adduction of affected limb and hip flexion
      1) do not cross legs.
      2) use raised toilet set.
      3) do not bend down to put on shoes or socks.
      4) do not sit in low chairs.
   b. Signs of wound infection
   c. Exercise program as ordered
   d. Partial weight bearing only until full weight bearing allowed

Herniated Nucleus Pulposus (HNP)

A. General information
   1. Protrusion of nucleus pulposus (central part of intervertebral disc) into spinal canal causing compression of spinal nerve roots
   2. Occurs more often in men
   3. Herniation most commonly occurs at the fourth and fifth intervertebral spaces in the lumbar region
   4. Predisposing factors include heavy lifting or pulling and trauma
B. Medical management
   1. Conservative treatment
      a. Bed rest
      b. Traction
         1) lumbosacral disc: pelvic traction
         2) cervical disc: cervical traction
      c. Drug therapy
         1) anti-inflammatory agents
         2) muscle relaxants
         3) analgesics
      d. Local application of heat and diathermy
      e. Corset for lumbosacral disc

    f. Cervical collar for cervical disc
    g. Epidural injections of corticosteroids
  2. Surgery
    a. Discectomy with or without spinal fusion
    b. Chemonucleolysis
      1) injection of chymopapain (derivative of papaya plant) into disc to reduce size and pressure on affected nerve root
      2) used as alternative to laminectomy in selected cases

C. Assessment findings
  1. Lumbosacral disc
    a. Back pain radiating across buttock and down leg (along sciatic nerve)
    b. Weakness of leg and foot on affected side
    c. Numbness and tingling in toes and foot
    d. Positive straight-leg raise test: pain on raising leg
    e. Depressed or absent Achilles reflex
    f. Muscle spasm in lumbar region
  2. Cervical disc
    a. Shoulder pain radiating down arm to hand
    b. Weakness of affected upper extremity
    c. Paresthesias and sensory disturbances
  3. Diagnostic tests: myelogram localizes site of herniation

D. Nursing interventions
  1. Ensure bed rest on a firm mattress with bed board.
  2. Assist client in applying pelvic or cervical traction as ordered.
  3. Maintain proper body alignment.
  4. Administer medications as ordered.
  5. Prevent complications of immobility.
  6. Provide additional comfort measures to relieve pain.
  7. Provide pre-op care for client receiving chemonucleolysis.
    a. Administer cimetidine (Tagamet) and diphenhydramine HCl (Benadryl) every 6 hours as ordered to reduce possibility of allergic reaction.
    b. Possibly administer corticosteroids before procedure.
  8. Provide post-op care for client receiving chemonucleolysis.
    a. Observe for anaphylaxis.
    b. Observe for less serious allergic reaction (e.g., rash, itching, rhinitis, difficulty in breathing).
    c. Monitor for neurologic deficits (numbness or tingling in extremities or inability to void).
  9. Provide client teaching and discharge planning concerning
    a. Back-strengthening exercises as prescribed
    b. Maintenance of good posture

    c. Use of proper body mechanics, how to lift heavy objects correctly
      1) maintain straight spine.
      2) flex knees and hips while stooping.
      3) keep load close to body.
    d. Prescribed medications and side effects
    e. Proper application of corset or cervical collar
    f. Weight reduction if needed

Discectomy

A. General information
  1. Excision of inter-vertebral disc.
  2. Indications
    a. Most commonly used for herniated nucleus pulposus not responsive to conservative therapy or with evidence of decreasing sensory or motor status
    b. Also indicated for spinal decompression as with spinal cord injury, to remove fragments of broken bone, or to remove spinal neoplasm or abscess
  3. Spinal fusion may be done at the same time if spine is unstable

B. Nursing interventions: preoperative
  1. Provide routine pre-op care.
  2. Teach client log rolling (turning body as a unit while maintaining alignment of spinal column) and use of bedpan.

C. Nursing interventions: postoperative
  1. Provide routine post-op care.
  2. Position client as ordered.
    a. Lower spinal surgery: generally flat
    b. Cervical spinal surgery: slight elevation of head of bed
  3. Maintain proper body alignment; with cervical spinal surgery avoid neck flexion and apply cervical collar as ordered.
  4. Turn client every 2 hours.
    a. Use log-rolling technique and turning sheet.
    b. Place pillows between legs while on side.
  5. Assess for complications.
    a. Monitor sensory and motor status every 2–4 hours.
    b. With cervical spinal surgery client may have difficulty swallowing and coughing.
      1) monitor for respiratory distress.
      2) keep suction and tracheostomy set available.
  6. Check dressings for hemorrhage, CSF leakage, infection.
  7. Promote comfort.
    a. Administer analgesics as ordered.
    b. Provide additional comfort measures and positioning.
  8. Assess for adequate bladder and bowel function.

        a. Monitor every 2–4 hours for bladder distension.
        b. Assess bowel sounds.
        c. Prevent constipation.
    9. Prevent complications of immobility.
    10. Assist with ambulation.
        a. Usually out of bed day after surgery.
        b. Apply brace or corset if ordered.
        c. If client allowed to sit, use straight-back chair and keep feet flat on floor.
D. Provide client teaching and discharge planning concerning
    1. Wound care
    2. Maintenance of good posture and proper body mechanics
    3. Activity level as ordered
    4. Recognition and reporting of signs of complications such as wound infection, sensory or motor deficits

Spinal Fusion

A. General information
    1. Fusion of spinous processes with bone graft from iliac crest to provide stabilization of spine
    2. Performed in conjunction with laminectomy
B. Nursing interventions
    1. Provide pre-op care as for laminectomy.
    2. In addition to post-op care for laminectomy
        a. Position client correctly.
            1) lumbar spinal fusion: keep bed flat for first 12 hours, then may elevate head of bed 20°–30°, keep off back for first 48 hours.
            2) cervical spinal fusion: elevate head of bed slightly.
        b. Assist with ambulation.
            1) time varies with surgeon and extent of fusion.
            2) usually out of bed 3–4 days post-op.
            3) apply brace before getting client out of bed.
            4) apply special cervical collar for cervical spinal fusion.
        c. Promote comfort: client may experience considerable pain from graft site.
    3. In addition to client teaching and discharge planning for laminectomy, advise client that
        a. Brace will be needed for 4 months and lighter corset for 1 year after surgery.
        b. It takes 1 year until graft becomes stable.
        c. No bending, lifting, stooping, or sitting for prolonged periods for 4 months.
        d. Walking without excessive tiring is healthful exercise.

        e. Diet modification will help prevent weight gain resulting from decreased activity.

Harrington Rod Insertion

See page 425.

Amputation of a Limb

See page 225.

Sample Questions

89. Mrs. F. has been diagnosed with rheumatoid arthritis for the past eight years. Her condition is deteriorating despite conservative treatment, and intramuscular gold is prescribed by the physician. When teaching her about gold (chrysotherapy), it is important that the nurse emphasize
    1. Cushing's syndrome is common.
    2. improvement may not occur for 3–6 months.
    3. side effects are rare.
    4. the need to take this drug daily.
90. A woman who has had rheumatoid arthritis for several years is admitted to the hospital. Upon physical examination of the client, the nurse should expect to find
    1. asymmetric joint involvement.
    2. Heberden's nodes.
    3. obesity.
    4. small joint involvement.
91. A 92-year-old woman was found at home lying on the floor of her kitchen. She was unable to move without experiencing severe pain in her right hip. She is admitted to the orthopedic unit with a diagnosis of a right intracapsular hip fracture. Buck's extension traction is employed prior to surgery. She complains of numbness in the right foot. The nurse inspects the foot and notes the traction tapes are lengthwise on opposite sides of the limb. The nurse's response to the client should be
    1. How long has your foot been numb?
    2. I can adjust it for your comfort.
    3. I'll call your doctor about it.
    4. There is nothing wrong with the traction.
92. An elderly woman had an Austin-Moore prosthesis inserted following an intracapsular hip fracture. During the postoperative period the nurse teaches the client about maintaining her hip in the proper position. Which of the following statements indicates that the client understands her instructions?
    1. I shouldn't bend my knees.
    2. Put a pillow between my legs when you turn me.

3. I will be sure to put my shoes on when I go for a walk.
4. Put me on the commode chair for my bowel movement.

93. The nurse is caring for an elderly woman who has had a fractured hip repaired. In the first few days following the surgical repair which of the following nursing measures will best facilitate the resumption of activities for this client?
1. Arranging for a wheelchair.
2. Asking her family to visit.
3. Assisting her to sit out of bed in a chair qid.
4. Encouraging the use of an overhead trapeze.

94. A 90-year-old woman is preparing for transfer to an extended care facility to continue recovery following repair of a fractured hip. She begins to cry and says, "When you're young these things don't happen. Why did I break my hip at this age?" Which response by the nurse indicates the best understanding of risk factors for the elderly?
1. As you age you become less aware of your surroundings and careless about safety.
2. Nothing works as well when we are older.
3. There are no known specific reasons why hip fractures occur more often in your age group.
4. Your age and sex are factors in the loss of minerals from your bones, making them more likely to break.

95. Mr. R. is admitted to the hospital. X-rays reveal a fractured tibia and a cast is applied. Of the following, which nursing action would be most important after the cast is in place?
1. Assessing for capillary refill.
2. Arranging for physical therapy.
3. Discussing cast care with Mr. R.
4. Helping Mr. R. to ambulate.

96. Ms. B., 44 years old, has been complaining of severe back pain that has been treated conservatively for the past year. She is admitted to the hospital for treatment of a herniated disk. A laminectomy with spinal fusion is scheduled. When Ms. B. returns to the unit after surgery, she is afraid to turn. Of the following maneuvers she plans to use to avoid pain, which is unsafe?
1. Log rolling.
2. Asking for pain medication.
3. Placing pillows between her legs.
4. Sitting up in bed.

97. A 48-year-old man has suffered low-back pain and sciatica for over two years. He is admitted to the hospital for evaluation and treatment of this problem. A thorough assessment of his level of discomfort from low-back pain is important primarily because

1. this will provide a baseline for later comparison.
2. this is a method for identifying clients with "low back neurosis."
3. clients who have pain localized to the back and radiating to one extremity are probably not candidates for surgery.
4. surgery is contraindicated for clients who have had pain for less than two years.

98. An adult man is scheduled for a lumbar laminectomy. Preoperative teaching regarding postoperative pain management should include which of the following explanations?
1. Pain and spasm are not expected and therefore there will be minimal need for pain medication.
2. Pain and spasm are expected and pain medication will be provided as needed.
3. Pain and spasm are expected but pain medication will interfere with a neurological assessment and will therefore be given sparingly.
4. Pain and spasm are expected but pain medication will be limited as client tolerance to the medication is feared.

99. Ms. W., 38 years old, is visiting her mother who has been hospitalized for repair of a fractured hip. The physician told her that her mother has severe osteoporosis and that this was a contributing factor to her current problem. Ms. W. has many questions for the nurse regarding her risk for developing osteoporosis. Which statement by Ms. W. indicates that she does not fully understand the relationship between exercise and maintenance of bone mass?
1. I will begin jogging.
2. I will begin jumping rope.
3. I will begin swimming.
4. I will begin walking.

Answers and Rationales

89. The correct answer is 2. Chrysotherapy often requires a 3- to 6-month period before effects are seen. Cushing's syndrome is associated with steroid therapy, which is also utilized in rheumatoid arthritis. Side effects such as blood dyscrasias and renal damage may occur, and the client must be carefully monitored. Daily doses of this drug are usually not required.

90. The correct answer is 4. Small joint involvement is common in rheumatoid arthritis. All of the other symptoms listed (asymmetric joint involvement, Heberden's nodes, and obesity) are symptoms that are seen in osteoarthritis.

91. The correct answer is 1. Numbness is

symptomatic of circulatory or nerve impairment to the extremity. It is important to know the length of time the client has been experiencing this sensation. The traction appears to be correctly applied. Traction may not be altered by the nurse. The nurse should do a neurological and circulatory assessment of the extremity before calling the doctor.

92. The correct answer is 2. A pillow placed between the client's legs will keep the affected leg abducted and in good alignment while the client is being turned. The unaffected knee may be bent. The client should not bend to put her shoes on until the physician gives her permission to do so. Sitting on a commode chair would cause too great a flexion of the hip joint in the early recovery period. A raised toilet seat would be needed.

93. The correct answer is 4. Exercise is important to keep the joints and muscles functioning and to prevent secondary complications. Use of the overhead trapeze prevents hazards of immobility by permitting movement in bed and strengthening of the upper extremities in preparation for ambulation. Sitting in a wheelchair would require too great hip flexion initially. Asking her family to visit would not facilitate the resumption of activities. Sitting in a chair would cause too great hip flexion. The client initially needs to be in a low Fowler's position or taking a few steps (as ordered) with the aid of a walker.

94. The correct answer is 4. Elderly females are prone to hip fractures because the cessation of estrogen production after menopause contributes to demineralization of bone. Elderly individuals do not automatically become less aware of their surroundings and careless about safety. If this is occurring, a medical evaluation may be indicated. There are physiological changes that occur with aging but for the most part the elderly can live a full and productive life. It is known that the cessation of estrogen production in postmenopausal women does increase the risk of hip fractures.

95. The correct answer is 1. Good capillary refill indicates that the cast has not caused a circulatory problem in the extremity. Physical therapy is not indicated at this time. Discussing cast care with the client is not a priority. Ambulation is not indicated following application of a cast.

96. The correct answer is 4. The client returning from a spinal fusion should be kept flat in bed. Log rolling is the proper method to turn a client following a laminectomy and spinal fusion. Asking for pain medication is a proper approach toward pain relief. Placing pillows between the client's legs is an appropriate nursing action.

97. The correct answer is 1. The importance of an accurate history cannot be overemphasized in assessing the character and location of the pain. A baseline assessment of neurological signs is made so that deviation from the data base can be noted. Pain assessment is the first step in determining a client's level of discomfort. Once this has been obtained, a plan for management of the pain can be developed. Clients who have pain localized in the back and radiating to one extremity are candidates for surgery. Surgical management is often used for clients who have had pain for less than two years.

98. The correct answer is 2. Clients can be told that they may experience pain and spasm in the early postoperative period and that pain medication will be provided. Pain and spasm are expected post-operatively. Pain medication will be given in large enough doses to control the pain. Pain medication will not interfere with a neurological assessment. Pain medication will be given in large enough doses to control the pain without concern for client tolerance to it.

99. The correct answer is 3. Physical compression of weight-bearing joints stimulates osteoblastic deposition of calcium. Swimming does not involve this compression. Jogging would be a good weight-bearing exercise if tolerance is built up gradually. Jumping rope is a good weight-bearing exercise if begun slowly and increased gradually. Walking is a good weight-bearing exercise.

The Endocrine System

OVERVIEW OF ANATOMY AND PHYSIOLOGY

The endocrine system is composed of an interrelated complex of glands (pituitary, adrenals, thyroid, parathyroids, islets of Langerhans of the pancreas, ovaries, and testes) that secrete a variety of hormones directly into the bloodstream. Its major function, together with the nervous system, is to regulate body functions.

Hormone Regulation

A. *Hormones:* chemical substances that act as messengers to specific cells and organs (target organs), stimulating and inhibiting various processes; two major categories
   1. Local: hormones with specific effect in the area of secretion (e.g., secretin, cholecystokinin-pancreozymin [CCK-PZ])
   2. General: hormones transported in the blood to distant sites where they exert their effect (e.g., cortisol)
B. *Negative feedback mechanisms:* major means of regulating hormone levels
   1. Decreased concentration of a circulating hormone triggers production of a stimulating hormone from the pituitary gland; this hormone in turn stimulates its target organ to produce hormones.
   2. Increased concentration of a hormone inhibits production of the stimulating hormone, resulting in decreased secretion of the target organ hormone.
C. Some hormones are controlled by changing blood levels of specific substances (e.g., calcium, glucose).
D. Certain hormones (e.g., cortisol or female reproductive hormones) follow rhythmic patterns of secretion.
E. Autonomic and CNS control (pituitary-hypothalamic axis): hypothalamus controls release of the hormones of the anterior pituitary gland through *releasing and inhibiting factors* that stimulate or inhibit hormone secretion.

Structure and Function of Endocrine Glands

See Table 4.22 and Figure 4.20.

Pituitary Gland (Hypophysis)

A. Located in sella turcica at the base of the brain
B. "Master gland" of the body, composed of three lobes
   1. Anterior lobe (adenohypophysis)
      a. Secretes tropic hormones (hormones that stimulate target glands to produce their hormone): adrenocorticotropic hormone (ACTH), thyroid-stimulating hormone (TSH), follicle-stimulating hormone (FSH), luteinizing hormone (LH)
      b. Also secretes hormones that have direct effect on tissues: somatotropic or growth hormone, prolactin
      c. Regulated by hypothalamic releasing and inhibiting factors and by negative feedback system
   2. Posterior lobe (neurohypophysis): does not produce hormones; stores and releases antidiuretic hormone (ADH) and oxytocin, produced by the hypothalamus
   3. Intermediate lobe: secretes melanocyte-stimulating hormone (MSH)

Adrenal Glands

A. Two small glands, one above each kidney
B. Consist of two sections
   1. Adrenal cortex (outer portion): produces mineralocorticoids, glucocorticoids, sex hormones
   2. Adrenal medulla (inner portion): produces epinephrine, norepinephrine

Thyroid Gland

A. Located in anterior portion of the neck
B. Consists of two lobes connected by a narrow isthmus
C. Produces thyroxine (T_4), triiodothyronine (T_3), thyrocalcitonin

Parathyroid Glands

A. Four small glands located in pairs behind the thyroid gland
B. Produce parathormone (PTH)

Pancreas

A. Located behind the stomach
B. Has both endocrine and exocrine functions (see page 264 for further information about the exocrine function of the pancreas)
C. Islets of Langerhans (alpha and beta cells) involved in endocrine function
   1. Beta cells: produce insulin
   2. Alpha cells: produce glucagon

TABLE 4.22 Hormone Functions

Endocrine Gland	Hormones	Functions
Pituitary		
Anterior lobe	TSH	Stimulates thyroid gland to release thyroid hormones.
	ACTH	Stimulates adrenal cortex to produce and release adrenocorticoids.
	FSH, LH	Stimulate growth, maturation, and function of primary and secondary sex organs.
	GH or somatotropin	Stimulates growth of body tissues and bones.
	Prolactin or LTH	Stimulates development of mammary glands and lactation.
Posterior lobe	ADH	Regulates water metabolism; released during stress or in response to an increase in plasma osmolality to stimulate reabsorption of water and decrease urine output.
	Oxytocin	Stimulates uterine contractions during delivery and the release of milk in lactation.
Intermediate lobe	MSH	Affects skin pigmentation.
Adrenal		
Adrenal cortex	Mineralocorticoids (e.g., aldosterone)	Regulate fluid and electrolyte balance; stimulate reabsorption of sodium, chloride, and water; stimulate potassium excretion.
	Glucocorticoids (e.g., cortisol, corticosterone)	Increase blood glucose levels by increasing rate of glyconeogenesis; increase protein catabolism, increase mobilization of fatty acids; promote sodium and water retention; anti-inflammatory effect; aid body in coping with stress.
	Sex hormones (androgens, estrogen, progesterone)	Influence development of secondary sex characteristics.
Adrenal medulla	Epinephrine, norepinephrine	Function in acute stress; increase heart rate, blood pressure; dilate bronchioles; convert glycogen to glucose when needed by muscles for energy.
Thyroid	T_3, T_4	Regulate metabolic rate; carbohydrate, fat, and protein metabolism; aid in regulating physical and mental growth and development.
	Thyrocalcitonin	Lowers serum calcium by increasing bone deposition.
Parathyroid	PTH	Regulates serum calcium and phosphate levels.
Pancreas (Islets of Langerhans)		
Beta cells	Insulin	Allows glucose to diffuse across cell membrane; converts glucose to glycogen.
Alpha cells	Glucagon	Increases blood glucose by causing glyconeogenesis and glycogenolysis in the liver; secreted in response to low blood sugar.
Ovaries	Estrogen, progesterone	Development of secondary sex characteristics in the female, maturation of sex organs, sexual functioning, maintenance of pregnancy.
Testes	Testosterone	Development of secondary sex characteristics in the male, maturation of sex organs, sexual functioning.

Gonads

A. Ovaries: located in pelvic cavity, produce estrogen and progesterone
B. Testes: located in scrotum, produce testosterone

ASSESSMENT

Health History

A. Presenting problem: symptoms may include
  1. Change in appearance: hair, nails, skin (change in texture or pigmentation); change in size, shape, or symmetry of head, neck, face, eyes, or tongue
  2. Change in energy level
  3. Temperature intolerance
  4. Development of abnormal secondary sexual characteristics; change in sexual function
  5. Change in emotional state, thought pattern, or intellectual functioning
  6. Signs of increased activity of sympathetic nervous system (e.g., nervousness, palpitations, tremors, sweating)
  7. Change in bowel habits, appetite, or weight; excessive hunger or thirst
  8. Change in urinary pattern
B. Life-style: any increased stress
C. Past medical history: growth and development (any delayed or excessive growth); diabetes, thyroid disease, hypertension, obesity, infertility

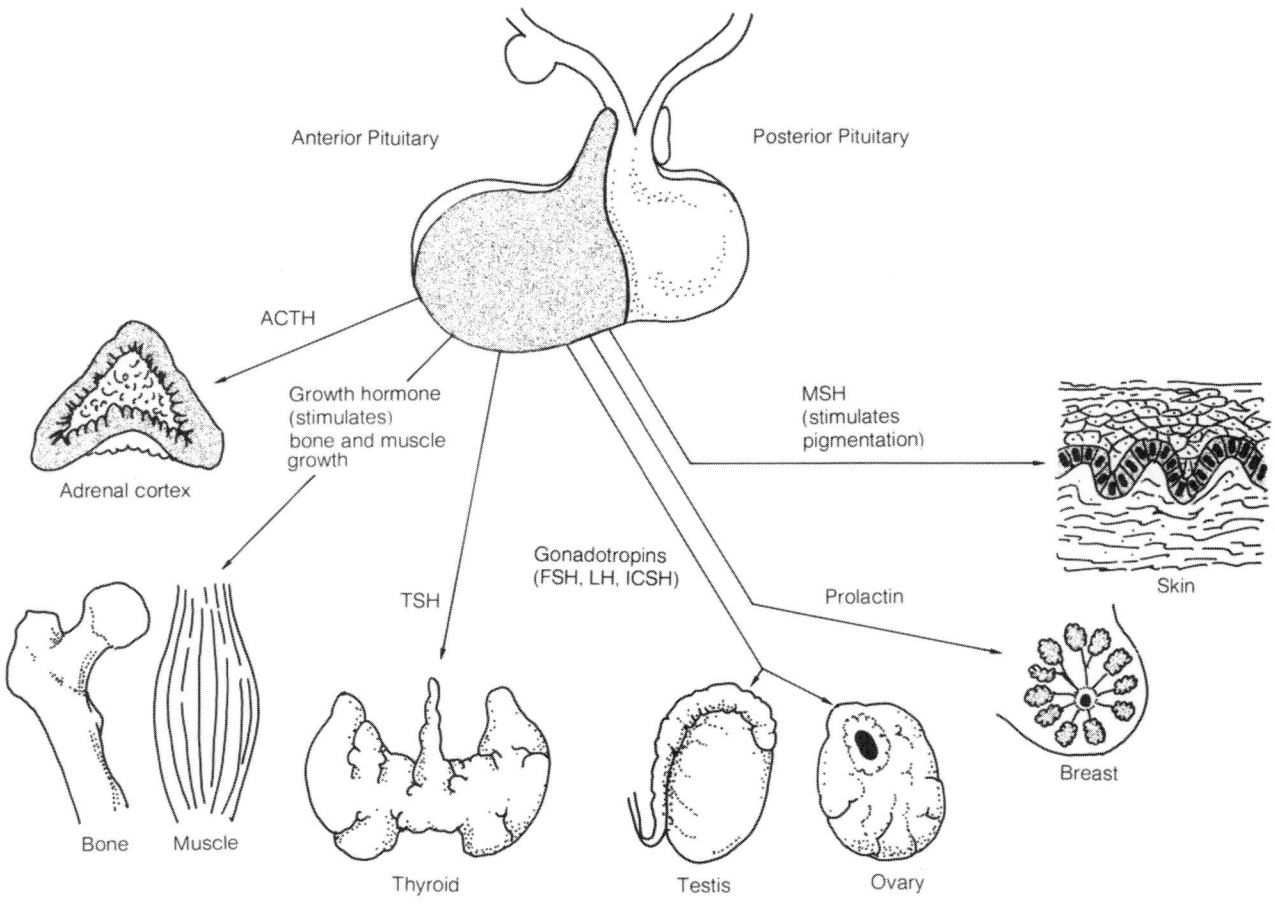

FIGURE 4.20 Hormones secreted by the anterior pituitary gland (Delmar Publishers)

D. Family history: endocrine diseases, growth problems, obesity, mental illness

Physical Examination

A. Check height, weight, body stature, and body proportions.
B. Observe distribution of muscle mass, fat distribution, any muscle wasting.
C. Inspect for hair growth and distribution.
D. Check condition and pigmentation of skin; presence of striae.
E. Inspect eyes for any bulging.
F. Observe for enlargement in neck area and quality of voice.
G. Observe development of secondary sex characteristics.
H. Palpate thyroid gland (normally cannot be palpated): note size, shape, symmetry, any tenderness, presence of any lumps or nodules.

Laboratory/Diagnostic Tests

A variety of tests may be performed to measure the amounts of hormones present in the serum or urine in assessing pituitary, adrenal, and parathyroid functions; these tests will be referred to when appropriate under specific disorders of the endocrine system.

Thyroid Function

A. Serum studies: nonfasting blood studies (no special preparation necessary)
    1. Serum T_4 level: measures total serum level of thyroxine
    2. Serum T_3 level: measures serum triiodothyronine level
    3. TSH: measurement differentiates primary from secondary hypothyroidism
B. Radioactive iodine uptake (RAIU)
    1. Administration of ^{123}I or ^{131}I orally; measurement by a counter of the amount

of radioactive iodine taken up by the gland after 24 hours

  2. Performed to determine thyroid function; increased uptake indicates hyperactivity; minimal uptake may indicate hypothyroidism
  3. Nursing care
     a. Take thorough history; thyroid medication must be discontinued 7–10 days prior to test; medications containing iodine, cough preparations, excess intake of iodine-rich foods, and tests using iodine (e.g., IVP) can invalidate this test.
     b. Assure client that no radiation precautions are necessary.
  C. Thyroid scan
  1. Administration of radioactive isotope (orally or IV) and visualization by a scanner of the distribution of radioactivity in the gland
  2. Performed to determine location, size, shape, and anatomic function of thyroid gland; identifies areas of increased or decreased uptake; valuable in evaluating thyroid nodules
  3. Nursing care: same as RAIU

Pancreatic Function

A. Fasting blood sugar: measures serum glucose levels; client fasts from midnight before the test
B. Two-hour postprandial blood sugar: measurement of blood glucose 2 hours after a meal is ingested
  1. Fast from midnight before test
  2. Client eats a meal consisting of at least 75 g carbohydrate or ingests 100 g glucose
  3. Blood drawn 2 hours after the meal
C. Oral glucose tolerance test: most specific and sensitive test for diabetes mellitus
  1. Fast from midnight before test
  2. Fasting blood glucose and urine glucose specimens obtained
  3. Client ingests 100 g glucose; blood sugars are drawn at 30 and 60 minutes and then hourly for 3–5 hours; urine specimens may also be collected
  4. Diet for 3 days prior to test should include 200 g carbohydrate and at least 1500 kcal/day
  5. During test, assess the client for reactions such as dizziness, sweating, and weakness
D. Glycosylated hemoglobin (hemoglobin A_{1c}) reflects the average blood sugar level for the previous 100–120 days. Glucose attaches to a minor hemoglobin (A_{1c}). This attachment is irreversible.
  1. Fasting is not necessary.
  2. Excellent method to evaluate long term control of blood sugar.

ANALYSIS

Nursing diagnoses for the client with a disorder of the endocrine system may include
A. Altered nutrition: more or less than body requirements
B. Risk for infection
C. Altered urinary elimination
D. Fluid volume excess or deficit
E. Risk for impaired skin integrity
F. Sexual dysfunction
G. Knowledge deficit
H. Ineffective individual coping
I. Sleep-pattern disturbance
J. Body-image disturbance

PLANNING AND IMPLEMENTATION

Goals

Client will
A. Regain optimal nutritional status.
B. Be free from infection.
C. Have adequate urinary elimination and fluid volume.
D. Maintain skin integrity.
E. Experience optimum sexual health.
F. Demonstrate and use knowledge of disease process, prescribed medications, treatments, and complications in order to maintain optimal health.
G. Use positive coping behaviors in dealing with the effects of acute and chronic illness.
H. Attain an optimal balance of rest and activity.

Interventions

Care of the Client on Corticosteroid Therapy

A. General information
  1. Types of preparations include cortisone, hydrocortisone, prednisone, dexamethasone (Decadron)
  2. Indications
     a. Replacement therapy in primary and secondary adrenocortical insufficiency
     b. Symptomatic treatment for anti-inflammatory effect of numerous inflammatory, allergic, or immunoreactive disorders (e.g., arthritis, SLE, bronchial asthma, skin diseases, ocular disorders, allergic diseases, inflammatory bowel disorders, cerebral edema and increased ICP, shock, nephrotic syndrome, malignancies, myasthenia gravis, multiple sclerosis)
  3. Common side effects: salt and water retention, sweating, increased appetite
  4. Adverse reactions
     a. Cardiovascular: hypertension, CHF

b. GI: peptic ulcer, ulcerative esophagitis
   c. Integumentary: petechiae, ecchymoses, purpura, hirsutism, acne, thinning of skin, striae, redistribution of body fat in subcutaneous tissue, abnormal pigmentation, poor wound healing
   d. Endocrine: impaired glucose metabolism, hyperglycemia, menstrual dysfunction, growth retardation
   e. Musculoskeletal: muscle weakness, osteoporosis
   f. Neurologic: personality changes, headache, syncope, vertigo, irritability, insomnia, seizures
   g. Ophthalmologic: cataract formation, glaucoma
   h. Other: hypokalemia, thrombophlebitis, masking of signs of infection, increased susceptibility to infection
   i. Sudden withdrawal may precipitate acute adrenal insufficiency
B. Nursing care
   1. Administer with food or milk; instruct client to report gastric distress (antacids may be necessary).
   2. Give in a single daily dose, preferably before 9 A.M. (corticosteroids suppress adrenal function least when given in early morning, the time of maximal adrenocortical activity).
   3. Instruct client to avoid infections and to report immediately if one is suspected.
   4. Instruct client never to withdraw the drug abruptly, as this may cause acute adrenal insufficiency.
   5. Observe client for any mental changes (e.g., irritability, mood swings, euphoria, depression).
   6. Alert women that menstrual irregularity may develop.
   7. Monitor blood pressure, I&O, weight, blood glucose, and serum potassium.
   8. Advise client to restrict salt intake.
   9. Encourage intake of foods high in potassium.

EVALUATION

A. Client maintains normal weight; no evidence of malnutrition.
B. Client's temperature is within normal limits; no signs of infection.
C. Client has adequate patterns of urinary elimination.
D. Peripheral edema is reduced.
E. Blood pressure and urine output are within normal limits; no signs of dehydration.
F. Skin is intact and free from irritation.
G. Client verbalizes satisfying sexual activity/expression.

H. Client demonstrates and uses knowledge of disease process, prescribed medications, and treatments; reports any complications.
I. Client uses effective coping behaviors to successfully adapt to effects of illness, changes in body image, and loss of function.
J. Client maintains balance between activity and rest.
K. Client demonstrates increased self-esteem.

DISORDERS OF THE ENDOCRINE SYSTEM

Specific Disorders of the Pituitary Gland

Hypopituitarism

A. General information
   1. Hypofunction of the anterior pituitary gland resulting in deficiencies of both the hormones secreted by the anterior pituitary gland and those secreted by the target glands
   2. May be caused by tumor, trauma, surgical removal, or irradiation of the gland; or may be congenital (pituitary dwarfism, see page 429)
B. Medical management: specific treatment depends on cause
   1. Tumor: surgical removal or irradiation of the gland
   2. Regardless of cause, treatment will include replacement of deficient hormones: e.g., cortico-steroids, thyroid hormone, sex hormones, gonadotropins (may be used to restore fertility).
C. Assessment findings
   1. Tumor: bitemporal hemianopia, headache
   2. Varying signs of hormonal disturbances depending on which hormones are being undersecreted (e.g., menstrual dysfunction, hypothyroidism, adrenal insufficiency)
   3. Retardation of growth if condition occurs before epiphyseal closure
   4. Diagnostic tests
      a. Skull x-ray, CT scan may reveal pituitary tumor
      b. Plasma hormone levels may be decreased depending on specific hormones undersecreted
D. Nursing interventions
   1. Provide care for the client undergoing hypophysectomy or radiation therapy if indicated.
   2. Provide client teaching and discharge planning concerning
      a. Hormone replacement therapy
      b. Importance of follow-up care

Hyperpituitarism

A. General information
   1. Hyperfunction of the anterior pituitary gland resulting in oversecretion of one or more of the anterior pituitary hormones
   2. Overproduction of the growth hormone produces acromegaly in adults and gigantism in children (if hypersecretion occurs before epiphyseal closure); see page 430.
   3. Usually caused by a benign pituitary adenoma
B. Medical management: surgical removal or irradiation of the gland
C. Assessment findings
   1. Tumor: bitemporal hemianopia; headache
   2. Hormonal disturbances depending on which hormones are being excreted in excess
   3. Acromegaly caused by oversecretion of growth hormones: transverse enlargement of bones, especially noticeable in skull and in bones of hands and feet; features become coarse and heavy; lips become heavier; tongue enlarged
   4. Diagnostic tests
      a. Skull x-ray, CT scan reveal pituitary tumor
      b. Plasma hormone levels reveal increased growth hormone, oversecretion of other hormones
D. Nursing interventions
   1. Monitor for hyperglycemia and cardiovascular problems (hypertension, angina, CHF) and modify care accordingly.
   2. Provide psychologic support and acceptance for alterations in body image.
   3. Provide care for the client undergoing hypophysectomy or radiation therapy if indicated.

Hypophysectomy

A. General information
   1. Partial or complete removal of the pituitary gland
   2. Indications: pituitary tumors, diabetic retinopathy, metastatic cancer of the breast or prostate, which may be endocrine dependent
   3. Surgical approaches
      a. Craniotomy: usually transfrontal
      b. Transphenoidal: incision made in inner aspect of upper lip and gingiva; sella turcica is entered through the floor of the nose and sphenoid sinuses
B. Nursing care
   1. In addition to pre-op care of the craniotomy client (page 194), explain post-op expectations.

2. In addition to post-op care of the craniotomy client, observe for signs of target gland deficiencies (diabetes insipidus, adrenal insufficiency, hypothyroidism) due to total removal of the gland or to post-op edema.
   a. Perform hourly urine outputs and specific gravities; alert physician if urine output is greater than 800–900 ml/2 hours or if specific gravity is less than 1.004.
   b. Administer cortisone replacement as ordered.
3. If transphenoidal approach used
   a. Elevate the head of the bed to 30° to decrease headache and pressure on the sella turcica.
   b. Administer mild analgesics for headache as ordered.
   c. Perform frequent oral hygiene with soft swabs to cleanse the teeth and mouth rinses; no toothbrushing.
   d. Observe for and prevent CSF leak from surgical site.
      1) warn the client not to cough, sneeze, or blow nose.
      2) observe for clear drainage from nose or postnasal drip (constant swallowing); check drainage for glucose; positive results indicate that drainage is CSF.
      3) if leakage does occur
         a) elevate head of bed and call the physician.
         b) most leaks will resolve in 72 hours with bed rest and elevation.
         c) may do daily spinal taps to decrease CSF pressure.
         d) administer antibiotics as ordered to prevent meningitis.
4. Provide client teaching and discharge planning concerning
   a. Hormone therapy
      1) if gland is completely removed, client will have permanent diabetes insipidus (see below)
      2) cortisone and thyroid hormone replacement
      3) replacement of sex hormones
         a) testosterone: may be given for impotence in men
         b) estrogen: may be given for atropy of the vaginal mucosa in women
         c) human pituitary gonadotropins: may restore fertility in some women
   b. Need for lifelong follow-up and hormone replacement
   c. Need to wear Medic-Alert bracelet
   d. If transphenoidal approach was used

1) avoid bending and straining at stool for 2 months post-op
2) no toothbrushing until sutures are removed and incision heals (about 10 days)

Diabetes Insipidus

A. General information
   1. Hypofunction of the posterior pituitary gland resulting in deficiency of ADH
   2. Characterized by excessive thirst and urination
   3. Caused by tumor, trauma, inflammation, pituitary surgery
B. Assessment findings
   1. Polydipsia (excessive thirst) and severe polyuria with low specific gravity
   2. Fatigue, muscle weakness, irritability, weight loss, signs of dehydration
   3. Tachycardia, eventual shock if fluids not replaced
   4. Diagnostic tests
      a. Urine specific gravity less than 1.004
      b. Water deprivation test reveals inability to concentrate urine
C. Nursing interventions
   1. Maintain fluid and electrolyte balance.
      a. Keep accurate I&O.
      b. Weigh daily.
      c. Administer IV/oral fluids as ordered to replace fluid losses.
   2. Monitor vital signs and observe for signs of dehydration and hypovolemia.
   3. Administer hormone replacement as ordered.
      a. Vasopressin (Pitressin) and vasopressin tannate (Pitressin tannate in oil); given by IM injection
         1) warm to body temperature before giving.
         2) shake tannate suspension to ensure uniform dispersion.
      b. Lypressin (Diapid): nasal spray
   4. Provide client teaching and discharge planning concerning
      a. Lifelong hormone replacement; lypressin as needed to control polyuria and polydipsia
      b. Need to wear Medic-Alert bracelet

Syndrome of Inappropriate Antidiuretic Hormone Secretion (SIADH)

A. General information
   1. Hypersection of ADH from the posterior pituitary gland even when the client has abnormal serum osmolality.
   2. SIADH may occur in persons with bronchogenic carcinoma or other nonendocrine conditions.
B. Medical management

   1. Treat underlying cause if possible
   2. Diuretics and fluid restriction
C. Assessment findings
   1. Persons with SIADH cannot excrete a dilute urine
   2. Fluid retention and sodium deficiency.
D. Nursing interventions
   1. Administer diuretics (furosemide [Lasix]) as ordered
   2. Restrict fluids to promote fluid loss and gradual increase in serum sodium.
   3. Monitor serum electrolytes and blood chemistries carefully
   4. Careful intake and output, daily weight
   5. Monitor neurologic status

Disorders of the Adrenal Gland

Addison's Disease

A. General information
   1. Primary adrenocortical insufficiency; hypofunction of the adrenal cortex causes decreased secretion of the mineralocorticoids, glucocorticoids, and sex hormones
   2. Relatively rare disease caused by
      a. Idiopathic atrophy of the adrenal cortex possibly due to an autoimmune process
      b. Destruction of the gland secondary to tuberculosis or fungal infection
B. Assessment findings
   1. Fatigue, muscle weakness
   2. Anorexia, nausea, vomiting, abdominal pain, weight loss
   3. History of frequent hypoglycemic reactions
   4. Hypotension, weak pulse
   5. Bronzelike pigmentation of the skin
   6. Decreased capacity to deal with stress
   7. Diagnostic tests: low cortisol levels, hyponatremia, hyperkalemia, hypoglycemia
C. Nursing interventions
   1. Administer hormone replacement therapy as ordered.
      a. Glucocorticoids (cortisone, hydrocortisone): to stimulate diurnal rhythm of cortisol release, give ⅔ of dose in early morning and ⅓ of dose in afternoon
      b. Mineralocorticoids: fludrocortisone acetate (Florinef)
   2. Monitor vital signs.
   3. Decrease stress in the environment.
   4. Prevent exposure to infection.
   5. Provide rest periods; prevent fatigue.
   6. Monitor I&O.
   7. Weigh daily.
   8. Provide small, frequent feedings of diet high in carbohydrates, sodium, and protein to prevent hypoglycemia and

hyponatremia and provide proper nutrition.
9. Provide client teaching and discharge planning concerning
    a. Disease process; signs of adrenal insufficiency
    b. Use of prescribed medications for lifelong replacement therapy; never omit medications
    c. Need to avoid stress, trauma, and infections, and to notify physician if these occur as medication dosage may need to be adjusted
    d. Stress management techniques
    e. Diet modification (high in protein, carbohydrates, and sodium)
    f. Use of salt tablets (if prescribed) or ingestion of salty foods (potato chips) if experiencing increased sweating
    g. Importance of alternating regular exercise with rest periods
    h. Avoidance of strenuous exercise especially in hot weather

Addisonian Crisis

A. General information
    1. Severe exacerbation of Addison's disease caused by acute adrenal insufficiency
    2. Precipitating factors
        a. Strenuous activity, infection, trauma, stess, failure to take prescribed medications
        b. Iatrogenic: surgery on pituitary or adrenal glands, rapid withdrawal of exogenous steroids in a client on long-term steroid therapy
B. Assessment findings: severe generalized muscle weakness, severe hypotension, hypovolemia, shock (vascular collapse)
C. Nursing interventions
    1. Administer IV fluids (5% dextrose in saline, plasma) as ordered to treat vascular collapse.
    2. Administer IV glucocorticoids (hydrocortisone [Solu-Cortef]) and vasopressors as ordered
    3. If crisis precipitated by infection, administer antibiotics as ordered.
    4. Maintain strict bed rest and eliminate all forms of stressful stimuli.
    5. Monitor vital signs, I&O, daily weights.
    6. Protect client from infection.
    7. Provide client teaching and discharge planning: same as for Addison's disease.

Cushing's Syndrome

A. General information
    1. Condition resulting from excessive secretion of corticosteroids, particularly the glucocorticoid cortisol

2. Occurs most frequently in females between ages 30–60
3. Primary Cushing's syndrome caused by adrenocortical tumors or hyperplasia
4. Secondary Cushing's syndrome (also called Cushing's disease): caused by functioning pituitary or nonpituitary neoplasm secreting ACTH, causing increased secretion of glucocorticoids
5. Iatrogenic: caused by prolonged use of corticosteroids
B. Assessment findings
    1. Muscle weakness, fatigue, obese trunk with thin arms and legs, muscle wasting
    2. Irritability, depression, frequent mood swings
    3. Moon face, buffalo hump, pendulous abdomen
    4. Purple striae on trunk, acne, thin skin
    5. Signs of masculinization in women; menstrual dysfunction, decreased libido
    6. Osteoporosis, decreased resistance to infection
    7. Hypertension, edema
    8. Diagnostic tests: cortisol levels increased, slight hypernatremia, hypokalemia, hyperglycemia
C. Nursing interventions
    1. Maintain muscle tone.
        a. Provide ROM exercises.
        b. Assist with ambulation.
    2. Prevent accidents or falls and provide adequate rest.
    3. Protect client from exposure to infection
    4. Maintain skin integrity.
        a. Provide meticulous skin care.
        b. Prevent tearing of skin: use paper tape if necessary.
    5. Minimize stress in the environment.
    6. Monitor vital signs; observe for hypertension, edema.
    7. Measure I&O and daily weights.
    8. Provide diet low in calories and sodium and high in protein, potassium, calcium, and vitamin D.
    9. Monitor urine for glucose and acetone; administer insulin if ordered.
    10. Provide psychologic support and acceptance.
    11. Prepare client for hypophysectomy or radiation if condition is caused by a pituitary tumor.
    12. Prepare client for an adrenalectomy if condition is caused by an adrenal tumor or hyperplasia.
    13. Provide client teaching and discharge planning concerning
        a. Diet modifications
        b. Importance of adequate rest
        c. Need to avoid stress and infection
        d. Change in medication regimen (alternate day therapy or reduced

dosage) if cause of the condition is prolonged corticosteroid therapy

Primary Aldosteronism (Conn's Syndrome)

A. General information
1. Excessive aldosterone secretion from the adrenal cortex
2. Seen more frequently in women, usually between ages 30–50
3. Caused by tumor or hyperplasia of adrenal gland
B. Assessment findings
1. Headache, hypertension
2. Muscle weakness, polyuria, polydipsia, metabolic alkalosis, cardiac arrhythmias (due to hypokalemia)
3. Diagnostic tests
   a. Serum potassium decreased, alkalosis
   b. Urinary aldosterone levels elevated
C. Nursing interventions
1. Monitor vital signs, I&O, daily weights.
2. Maintain sodium restriction as ordered.
3. Administer spironolactone (Aldactone) and potassium supplements as ordered.
4. Prepare the client for an adrenelectomy (see page 329) if indicated.
5. Provide client teaching and discharge planning concerning
   a. Use and side effects of medication if the client is being maintained on spironolactone therapy
   b. Signs of symptoms of hypo/ hyperaldosteronism
   c. Need for frequent blood pressure checks and follow-up care

Pheochromocytoma

A. General information
1. Functioning tumor of the adrenal medulla that secretes excessive amounts of epinephrine and norepinephrine
2. Occurs most commonly between ages 25–50
3. May be hereditary in some cases
B. Assessment findings
1. Severe headache, apprehension, palpitations, profuse sweating, nausea
2. Hypertension, tachycardia, vomiting, hyperglycemia, dilation of pupils, cold extremities
3. Diagnostic tests
   a. Increased plasma levels of catecholamines; elevated blood sugar; glycosuria
   b. Elevated urinary catecholamines and urinary vanillylmandelic acid (VMA) levels
   c. Presence of tumor on x-ray
C. Nursing interventions

1. Monitor vital signs, especially blood pressure.
2. Administer medications as ordered to control hypertension.
3. Promote rest; decrease stressful stimuli.
4. Monitor urine tests for glucose and acetone.
5. Provide high-calorie, well-balanced diet; avoid stimulants such as coffee, tea.
6. Provide care for the client with an adrenalectomy (see below) as ordered; observe postadrenelectomy client carefully for shock due to drastic drop in catecholamine level.
7. Provide client teaching and discharge planning: same as for adrenalectomy.

Adrenalectomy

A. General information
1. Removal of one or both adrenal glands
2. Indications
   a. Tumors of adrenal cortex (Cushing's syndrome, hyperaldosteronism) or medulla (pheochromocytoma)
   b. Metastatic cancer of the breast or prostate
B. Nursing interventions: preoperative
1. Provide routine pre-op care.
2. Correct metabolic/cardiovascular problems.
   a. Pheochromocytoma: stabilize blood pressure.
   b. Cushing's syndrome: treat hyperglycemia and protein deficits.
   c. Primary hyperaldosteronism: treat hypertension and hypokalemia.
3. Administer glucocorticoid preparation on the morning of surgery as ordered to prevent acute adrenal insufficiency.
C. Nursing interventions: postoperative
1. Provide routine post-op care.
2. Observe for hemorrhage and shock.
   a. Monitor vital signs, I&O.
   b. Administer IV therapy and vasopressors as ordered.
3. Prevent infections (suppression of immune system makes clients especially susceptible).
   a. Encourage coughing and deep breathing to prevent respiratory infection.
   b. Use meticulous aseptic technique during dressing changes.
4. Administer cortisone or hydrocortisone as ordered to maintain cortisol levels.
5. Provide general care for the client with abdominal surgery.
D. Provide client teaching and discharge planning concerning
1. Self-administration of replacement hormones

    a. Bilateral adrenalectomy: lifelong replacement of glucocorticoids and mineralocorticoids

    b. Unilateral adrenalectomy: replacement therapy for 6–12 months until the remaining adrenal gland begins to function normally

2. Signs and symptoms of adrenal insufficiency
3. Importance of follow-up care

Specific Disorders of the Thyroid Gland

Simple Goiter

A. General information
1. Enlargement of the thyroid gland not caused by inflammation or neoplasm
2. Types
    a. Endemic: caused by nutritional iodine deficiency, most common in the "goiter belt" (midwest, northwest, and Great Lakes regions), areas where soil and water are deficient in iodine; occurs most frequently during adolescence and pregnancy
    b. Sporadic: caused by
      1) ingestion of large amounts of goitrogenic foods (contain agents that decrease thyroxine production): e.g., cabbage, soybeans, rutabagas, peanuts, peaches, peas, strawberries, spinach, radishes
      2) use of goitrogenic drugs: propylthiouracil, large doses of iodine, phenylbutazone, para-amino salicylic acid, cobalt, lithium
      3) genetic defects that prevent synthesis of thyroid hormone
3. Low levels of thyroid hormone stimulate increased secretion of TSH by pituitary; under TSH stimulation the thyroid increases in size to compensate and produces more thyroid hormone.

B. Medical management
1. Drug therapy
    a. Hormone replacement with levothyroxine (Synthroid) (T_4), dessicated thyroid, or liothyronine (Cytomel) (T_3)
    b. Small doses of iodine (Lugol's or potassium iodide solution) for goiter resulting from iodine deficiency
2. Avoidance of goitrogenic foods or drugs in sporadic goiter
3. Surgery: subtotal thyroidectomy (if goiter is large) to relieve pressure symptoms and for cosmetic reasons

C. Assessment findings

1. Dysphagia, enlarged thyroid, respiratory distress
2. Diagnostic tests
    a. Serum T_4 level low-normal or normal
    b. RAIU uptake normal or increased

D. Nursing interventions
1. Administer replacement therapy as ordered.
2. Provide care for client with subtotal thyroidectomy (page 332) if indicated.
3. Provide client teaching and discharge planning concerning
    a. Use of iodized salt in preventing and treating endemic goiter
    b. Thyroid hormone replacement

Hypothyroidism (Myxedema)

A. General information
1. Slowing of metabolic processes caused by hypofunction of the thyroid gland with decreased thyroid hormone secretion; causes myxedema in adults and cretinism in children (see page 429).
2. Occurs more often in women between ages 30–60
3. Primary hypothyroidism: atrophy of the gland possibly caused by an autoimmune process
4. Secondary hypothyroidism: caused by decreased stimulation from pituitary TSH
5. Iatrogenic: surgical removal of the gland or overtreatment of hyperthyroidism with drugs or radioactive iodine
6. In severe or untreated cases, *myxedema coma* may occur
    a. Characterized by intensification of signs and symptoms of hypothyroidism and neurologic impairment leading to coma
    b. Mortality rate high; prompt recognition and treatment essential
    c. Precipitating factors: failure to take prescribed medications; infection; trauma, exposure to cold; use of sedatives, narcotics, or anesthetics

B. Medical management
1. Drug therapy: levothyroxine (Synthroid), thyroglobulin (Proloid), dessicated thyroid, liothyronine (Cytomel)
2. Myxedema coma is a medical emergency.
    a. IV thyroid hormones
    b. Correction of hypothermia
    c. Maintenance of vital functions
    d. Treatment of precipitating causes

C. Assessment findings
1. Fatigue; lethargy; slowed mental processes; dull look; slow, clumsy movements
2. Anorexia, weight gain, constipation

3. Intolerance to cold; dry, scaly skin; dry, sparse hair; brittle nails
4. Menstrual irregularities; generalized interstitial nonpitting edema
5. Bradycardia, cardiac complications (CAD, angina pectoris, MI, CHF)
6. Increased sensitivity to sedatives, narcotics, and anesthetics
7. Exaggeration of these findings in myxedema coma: weakness, lethargy, syncope, bradycardia, hypotension, hypoventilation, subnormal body temperature
8. Diagnostic tests
   a. Serum T_3 and T_4 level low
   b. Serum cholesterol level elevated
   c. RAIU decreased
D. Nursing interventions
1. Monitor vital signs, I&O, daily weights; observe for edema and signs of cardiovascular complications.
2. Administer thyroid hormone replacement therapy as ordered and monitor effects.
   a. Observe for signs of thyrotoxicosis (tachycardia, palpitations, nausea, vomiting, diarrhea, sweating, tremors, agitation, dyspnea).
   b. Increase dosage gradually, especially in clients with cardiac complications.
3. Provide a comfortable, warm environment.
4. Provide a low-calorie diet.
5. Avoid the use of sedatives; reduce the dose of any sedative, narcotic, or anesthetic agent by half as ordered.
6. Institute measures to prevent skin breakdown.
7. Provide increased fluids and foods high in fiber to prevent constipation; administer stool softeners as ordered.
8. Observe for signs of myxedema coma; provide appropriate nursing care.
   a. Administer medications as ordered.
   b. Maintain vital functions: correct hypothermia, maintain adequate ventilation.
9. Provide client teaching and discharge planning concerning
   a. Thyroid hormone replacement
      1) take daily dose in the morning to prevent insomnia.
      2) self-monitor for signs of thyrotoxicosis.
   b. Importance of regular follow-up care
   c. Need for additional protection in cold weather
   d. Measures to prevent constipation

Hyperthyroidism (Grave's Disease)

A. General information
1. Secretion of excessive amounts of thyroid hormone in the blood causes an increase in metabolic processes
2. Overactivity and changes in the thyroid gland may be present
3. Most often seen in women between ages 30–50
4. Cause unknown, but may be an autoimmune process
5. Symptomatic hyperthyroidism may also be called thyrotoxicosis
B. Medical management
1. Drug therapy
   a. Antithyroid drugs (propylthiouracil and methimazole ([Tapazole]): block synthesis of thyroid hormone; toxic effects include agranulocytosis
   b. Adrenergic blocking agents (commonly propanolol [Inderal]): used to decrease sympathetic activity and alleviate symptoms such as tachycardia
2. Radioactive iodine therapy
   a. Radioactive isotope of iodine (e.g., ^{131}I) given to destroy the thyroid gland, thereby decreasing production of thyroid hormone
   b. Used in middle-aged or older clients who are resistant to, or develop toxicity from, drug therapy
   c. Hypothyroidism is a potential complication
3. Surgery: thyroidectomy performed in younger clients for whom drug therapy has not been effective
C. Assessment findings
1. Irritability, agitation, restlessness, hyperactive movements, tremor, sweating, insomnia
2. Increased appetite, hyperphagia, weight loss, diarrhea, intolerance to heat
3. Exophthalmos (protrusion of the eyeballs), goiter
4. Warm, smooth skin; fine, soft hair; pliable nails
5. Tachycardia, increased systolic blood pressure, palpitations
6. Diagnostic tests
   a. Serum T_3 and T_4 levels elevated
   b. RAIU increased
D. Nursing interventions
1. Monitor vital signs, daily weights.
2. Administer antithyroid medications as ordered.
3. Provide for periods of uninterrupted rest.
   a. Assign to a private room away from excessive activity.
   b. Administer medications to promote sleep as ordered.
4. Provide a cool environment.
5. Minimize stress in the environment.
6. Encourage quiet, relaxing diversional activities.

7. Provide a diet high in carbohydrates, protein, calories, vitamins, and minerals with supplemental feedings between meals and at bedtime; omit stimulants.
8. Observe for and prevent complications.
   a. Exophthalmos: protect eyes with dark glasses and artificial tears as ordered.
   b. Thyroid storm: see below.
9. Provide client teaching and discharge planning concerning
   a. Need to recognize and report signs and symptoms of agranulocytosis (fever, sore throat, skin rash) if taking antithyroid drugs
   b. Signs and symptoms of hyper/hypothyroidism

Thyroid Storm

A. General information
   1. Uncontrolled and potentially life-threatening hyperthyroidism caused by sudden and excessive release of thyroid hormone into the bloodstream
   2. Precipitating factors: stress, infection, unprepared thyroid surgery
   3. Now quite rare
B. Assessment findings
   1. Apprehension, restlessness
   2. Extremely high temperature (up to 106°F [40.7°C]), tachycardia, CHF, respiratory distress, delirium, coma
C. Nursing interventions (see also Hyperthermia, page 184)
   1. Maintain a patent airway and adequate ventilation; administer oxygen as ordered.
   2. Administer IV therapy as ordered.
   3. Administer medications as ordered: antithyroid drugs, corticosteroids, sedatives, cardiac drugs.

Thyroidectomy

A. General information
   1. Partial or total removal of the thyroid gland
   2. Indications
      a. Subtotal thyroidectomy: hyperthyroidism
      b. Total thyroidectomy: thyroid cancer
B. Nursing interventions: preoperative
   1. Ensure that the client is adequately prepared for surgery.
      a. Cardiac status is stable.
      b. Weight and nutritional status are normal.
   2. Administer antithyroid drugs as ordered to suppress the production and secretion of thyroid hormone and to prevent thyroid storm.
   3. Administer iodine preparations (Lugol's or potassium iodide solution) to reduce the size and vascularity of the gland and prevent hemorrhage.
C. Nursing interventions: postoperative
   1. Monitor vital signs and I&O.
   2. Check dressings for signs of hemorrhage; check for wetness behind neck.
   3. Place client in semi-Fowler's position and support head with pillows.
   4. Observe for respiratory distress secondary to hemorrhage, edema of the glottis, laryngeal nerve damage, or tetany; keep tracheostomy set, oxygen, and suction nearby.
   5. Assess for signs of tetany due to hypocalcemia secondary to accidental removal of parathyroid glands; keep calcium gluconate available (see Hypoparathyroidism, below).
   6. Encourage the client to rest voice.
      a. Some hoarseness is common.
      b. Check every 30–60 minutes for extreme hoarseness or any accompanying respiratory distress.
   7. Observe for thyroid storm due to release of excessive amounts of thyroid hormone during surgery.
   8. Administer IV fluids as ordered until the client is tolerating fluids by mouth.
   9. Administer analgesics as ordered for incisional pain.
   10. Relieve discomfort from sore throat.
       a. Cool mist humidifier to thin secretions.
       b. Administer analgesic throat lozenges before meals and prn as ordered.
       c. Encourage fluids.
   11. Encourage coughing and deep breathing every hour.
   12. Assist the client with ambulation: instruct the client to place hands behind neck to decrease stress on suture line if added support necessary.
   13. Provide client teaching and discharge planning concerning
       a. Signs and symptoms of hypo/hyperthyroidism
       b. Self-administration of thyroid hormones if total thyroidectomy performed
       c. Application of lubricant to the incision once sutures are removed
       d. Performance of ROM neck exercises 3–4 times a day
       e. Importance of regular follow-up care

Specific Disorders of the Parathyroid Glands

Hypoparathyroidism

A. General information
   1. Disorder characterized by hypocalcemia

resulting from a deficiency of parathormone (PTH) production
2. May be hereditary, idiopathic, or caused by accidental damage to or removal of parathyroid glands during surgery, e.g., thyroidectomy

B. Assessment findings
1. Acute hypocalcemia (tetany)
   a. Tingling of fingers and around lips, painful muscle spasms, dysphagia, laryngospasm, seizures, cardiac arrhythmias
   b. Chvostek's sign: sharp tapping over facial nerve causes twitching of mouth, nose, and eye
   c. Trousseau's sign: carpopedal spasm induced by application of blood pressure cuff for 3 minutes
2. Chronic hypocalcemia
   a. Fatigue, weakness, muscle cramps
   b. Personality changes, irritability, memory impairment
   c. Dry, scaly skin; hair loss; loss of tooth enamel
   d. Tremor, cardiac arrhythmias, cataract formation
   e. Diagnostic tests
      1) serum calcium levels decreased
      2) serum phosphate levels elevated
      3) skeletal x-rays reveal increased bone density

C. Nursing interventions
1. Administer calcium gluconate by slow IV drip as ordered for acute hypocalcemia.
2. Administer medications for chronic hypocalcemia.
   a. Oral calcium preparations: calcium gluconate, lactate, carbonate (Os-Cal)
   b. Large doses of vitamin D (Calciferol) to help absorption of calcium
   c. Aluminum hydroxide gel (Amphogel) or aluminum carbonate gel, basic (Basaljel) to decrease phosphate levels
3. Institute seizure and safety precautions.
4. Provide quiet environment free from excessive stimuli.
5. Monitor for signs of hoarseness or stridor; check for Chvostek's and Trousseau's signs.
6. Keep emergency equipment (tracheostomy set, injectable calcium gluconate) at bedside.
7. For tetany or generalized muscle cramps, may use rebreathing bag to produce mild respiratory acidosis.
8. Monitor serum calcium and phosphate levels.
9. Provide high-calcium, low-phosphorus diet.
10. Provide client teaching and discharge planning concerning

a. Medication regimen; oral calcium preparations and vitamin D to be taken with meals to increase absorption
b. Need to recognize and report signs and symptoms of hypo/hypercalcemia
c. Importance of follow-up care with periodic serum calcium levels

Hyperparathyroidism

A. General information
1. Increased secretion of PTH that results in an altered state of calcium, phosphate, and bone metabolism
2. Most commonly affects women between ages 35–65
3. Primary hyperparathyroidism: caused by tumor or hyperplasia of parathyroid glands
4. Secondary hyperparathyroidism: caused by compensatory oversecretion of PTH in response to hypocalcemia from chronic renal disease, rickets, malabsorption syndrome, osteomalacia

B. Assessment findings
1. Bone pain (especially at back), bone demineralization, pathologic fractures
2. Renal colic, kidney stones, polyuria, polydipsia
3. Anorexia, nausea, vomiting, gastric ulcers, constipation
4. Muscle weakness, fatigue
5. Irritability, personality changes, depression
6. Cardiac arrhythmias, hypertension
7. Diagnostic tests
   a. Serum calcium levels elevated
   b. Serum phosphate levels decreased
   c. Skeletal x-rays reveal bone demineralization

C. Nursing interventions
1. Administer IV infusions of normal saline solution and give diuretics as ordered; monitor I&O and observe for fluid overload and electrolyte imbalances.
2. Assist client with self-care: provide careful handling, moving, and ambulation to prevent pathologic fractures.
3. Monitor vital signs; report irregularities.
4. Force fluids; provide acid-ash juices, e.g., cranberry juice.
5. Strain urine for stones.
6. Provide low-calcium, high-phosphorus diet.
7. Provide care for the client undergoing parathyroidectomy (see Thyroidectomy, page 332).
8. Provide client teaching and discharge planning concerning
   a. Need to engage in progressive ambulatory activities
   b. Increased intake of fluids

c. Use of calcium preparations and importance of high-calcium diet following a parathyroidectomy

Specific Disorders of the Pancreas

Diabetes Mellitus

A. General information
1. Diabetes mellitus represents a heterogenous group of chronic disorders characterized by hyperglycemia.
2. Hyperglycemia is due to total or partial insulin deficiency or insensitivity of the cells to insulin.
3. Characterized by disorders in the metabolism of carbohydrate, fat, and protein, as well as changes in the structure and function of blood vessels.
4. Most common endocrine problem; affects over 11 million people in the U.S.
5. Exact etiology unknown; causative factors may include
   a. genetics, viruses, and/or autoimmune response in type I
   b. genetics and obesity in type II
6. Types
   a. Type I (insulin-dependent diabetes mellitus [IDDM])
      1) secondary to destruction of beta cells in the islets of Langerhans in the pancreas resulting in little or no insulin production; requires insulin injections.
      2) usually occurs in children (see page 428) or in nonobese adults.
   b. Type II (non-insulin-dependent diabetes mellitus [NIDDM])
      1) may result from a partial deficiency of insulin production and/or an insensitivity of the cells to insulin.
      2) usually occurs in obese adults over 40.
   c. Diabetes associated with other conditions or syndromes, e.g., pancreatic disease, Cushing's syndrome, use of certain drugs (steroids, thiazide diuretics, oral contraceptives).
7. Pathophysiology
   a. Lack of insulin causes hyperglycemia (insulin is necessary for the transport of glucose across the cell membrane).
   b. Hyperglycemia leads to osmotic diuresis as large amounts of glucose pass through the kidney; results in polyuria and glycosuria.
   c. Diuresis leads to cellular dehydration and fluid and electrolyte depletion causing polydipsia (excessive thirst).
   d. Polyphagia (hunger and increased appetite) results from cellular starvation.
   e. The body turns to fats and protein for energy; but in the absence of glucose in the cell, fats cannot be completely metabolized and ketones (intermediate products of fat metabolism) are produced.
   f. This leads to ketonemia, ketonuria (contributes to osmotic diuresis), and metabolic acidosis (ketones are acid bodies).
   g. Ketones act as CNS depressants and can cause coma.
   h. Excess loss of fluids and electrolytes leads to hypovolemia, hypotension, renal failure, and decreased blood flow to the brain resulting in coma and death unless treated.
8. Acute complications of diabetes include diabetic ketoacidosis (page 337), insulin reaction (page 337), hyperglycemic hyperosmolar nonketotic coma (page 338).
B. Medical management
1. Type I: insulin, diet, exercise
2. Type II: ideally managed by diet and exercise; may need oral hypoglycemics or occasionally insulin if diet and exercise are not effective in controlling hyperglycemia; insulin needed for acute stresses, e.g., surgery, infection
3. Diet (see Exchange Lists, Appendix)
   a. Type I: consistency is imperative to avoid hypoglycemia
   b. Type II: weight loss is important since it decreases insulin resistance
   c. High fiber, low fat diet also recommended
4. Drug therapy
   a. Insulin: used for Type I diabetes (also occasionally used in Type II diabetes)
      1) types (Table 4.23)
         a) short acting: used in treating ketoacidosis; during surgery, infection, trauma; management of poorly controlled diabetes; to supplement longer-acting insulins
         b) intermediate: used for maintenance therapy
         c) long acting: used for maintenance therapy in clients who experience hyperglycemia during the night with intermediate-acting insulin
      2) various preparations of short-, intermediate-, and long-acting insulins are available (see Table 4.23)
      3) insulin preparations can consist of a mixture of beef and pork insulin,

TABLE 4.23 **Characteristics of Insulin Preparations**

Drug	Synonym	Appearance	Onset	Peak	Duration	Compatible Mixed with
Rapid acting						
Insulin injection	Regular insulin	Clear	½–1	2–4	6–8	All insulin preparations except lente
Insulin, zinc suspension, prompt	Semilente insulin	Cloudy	½–1	4–6	12–16	Lente preparations
Intermediate acting						
Isophane insulin injection	NPH insulin	Cloudy	1–½	8–12	18–24	Regular insulin injection
Insulin zinc suspension	Lente insulin	Cloudy	1–1½	8–12	18–24	Regular insulin and Semilente preparations
Long acting						
Insulin zinc suspension, extended	Ultralente insulin	Cloudy	4–8	16–20	30–36	Regular insulin and Semilente preparations

pure beef, pure pork, or human insulin. Human insulin is the purest insulin and has the lowest antigenic effect.

4) human insulin is recommended for all newly diagnosed Type I diabetics, Type II diabetics who need short-term insulin therapy, the pregnant client, and diabetic clients with insulin allergy or severe insulin resistance.

5) insulin pumps are small, externally worn devices that closely mimic normal pancreatic functioning. Insulin pumps contain a 3 ml syringe attached to a long (42 inch), narrow-lumen tube with a needle or Teflon catheter at the end. The needle or Teflon catheter is inserted into the subcutaneous tissue (usually on the abdomen) and secured with tape or a transparent dressing. The needle or catheter is changed at least every 3 days. The pump is worn either on a belt or in a pocket (see Figure 4.21). The pump uses only regular insulin. Insulin can be administered via the basal rate (usually 0.5–2.0 units/hr) and by a bolus dose (which is activated by a series of button pushes) prior to each meal.

b. Oral hypoglycemic agents (Table 4.24)
1) used for Type II diabetics who are not controlled by diet and exercise
2) increase the ability of islet cells of the pancreas to secrete insulin; may have some effect on cell receptors to decrease resistance to insulin

5. Exercise: helpful adjunct to therapy as exercise decreases the body's need for insulin.
C. Assessment findings
1. All types: polyuria, polydipsia, polyphagia, fatigue, blurred vision, susceptibility to infection
2. Type I: anorexia, nausea, vomiting, weight loss
3. Type II: obesity; frequently no other symptoms
4. Diagnostic tests
   a. Fasting blood sugar
      1) a level of 140 mg/dl or greater on at least two occasions confirms diabetes mellitus

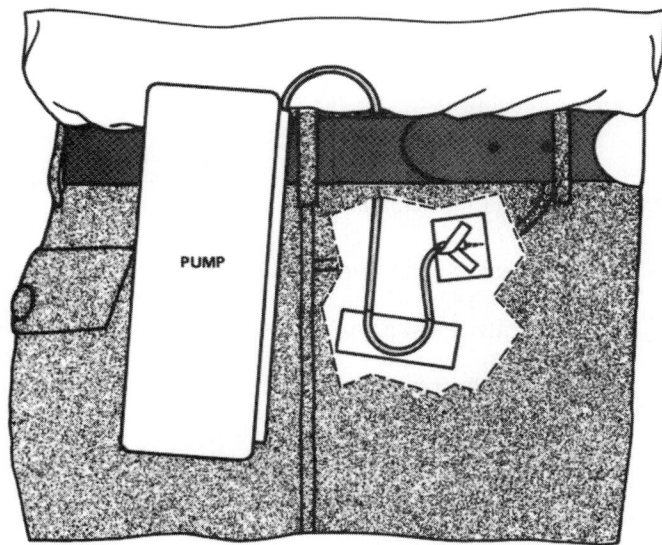

FIGURE 4.21   Insulin infusion pump (Delmar Publishers)

TABLE 4.24 Oral Hypoglycemic Agents

Drug	Onset of Action (hrs)	Peak Action (hrs)	Duration of Action (hrs)	Comments
Oral Sulfonylureas				
Acetohexamide (Dymelor)	1	4–6	12–24	
Chlorpropamide (Diabinase)	1	4–6	40–60	
Glyburide (Micronase, Diabeta)	15 min–1 hr	2–8	10–24	
Oral Biguanides				
Metformin (Glucophage)	2–2.5		10–16	Decreases glucose production in liver; decreases intestinal absorption of glucose and improves insulin sensitivity
Oral Alpha-glucosidose Inhibitor				
Acarbose (Precose)	Unknown	1	Unknown	Delay glucose absorption and digestion of carbohydrates, lowering blood sugar.
Miglitol (Glyset)		2–3		Reduces plasma glucose and insulin. Exact mechanism is unknown. Potentiates action of insulin in skeletal muscle and decreases glucose production in liver.
Troglitazone (Rezulin)	Rapid	2–3	Unknown	

2) may be normal in Type II diabetes
   b. Postprandial blood sugar: elevated
   c. Oral glucose tolerance test (most sensitive test): elevated
   d. Glycosolated hemoglobin (hemoglobin A_{1c}) elevated
D. Nursing interventions
   1. Administer insulin or oral hypoglycemic agents as ordered; monitor for hypoglycemia, especially during period of drug's peak action.
   2. Provide special diet as ordered.
      a. Ensure that the client is eating all meals.
      b. If all food is not ingested, provide appropriate substitutes according to the exchange lists or give measured amount of orange juice to substitute for leftover food; provide snack later in the day.
   3. Monitor urine sugar and acetone (freshly voided specimen).
   4. Perform finger sticks to monitor blood glucose levels as ordered (more accurate than urine tests).
   5. Observe for signs of hypo/hyperglycemia.
   6. Provide meticulous skin care and prevent injury.
   7. Maintain I&O; weigh daily.
   8. Provide emotional support; assist client in adapting to change in life-style and body image.
   9. Observe for chronic complications and plan care accordingly.
      a. Atherosclerosis: leads to coronary artery disease, MI, CVA, and peripheral vascular disease.
      b. Microangiopathy: most commonly affects eyes and kidneys.
      c. Kidney disease
         1) recurrent pyelonephritis

2) diabetic nephropathy
   d. Ocular disorders
      1) premature cataracts
      2) diabetic retinopathy
   e. Peripheral neuropathy
      1) affects peripheral and autonomic nervous systems
      2) causes diarrhea, constipation, neurogenic bladder, impotence, decreased sweating
10. Provide client teaching and discharge planning concerning
    a. Disease process
    b. Diet
       1) client should be able to plan meals using exchange lists before discharge
       2) emphasize importance of regularity of meals; never skip meals
    c. Insulin
       1) how to draw up into syringe
          a) use insulin at room temperature.
          b) gently roll vial between palms of hands.
          c) draw up insulin using sterile technique.
          d) if mixing insulins, draw up clear insulin before cloudy insulin.
       2) injection technique
          a) systematically rotate sites to prevent lipodystrophy (hypertrophy or atrophy of tissue).
          b) insert needle at a 45° or 90° angle depending on amount of adipose tissue.
       3) may store current vial of insulin at room temperature; refrigerate extra supplies.
       4) provide many opportunities for return demonstration.

d. Oral hypoglycemic agents
   1) stress importance of taking the drug regularly.
   2) avoid alcohol intake while on medication.
e. Urine testing (not very accurate reflection of blood glucose level)
   1) May be satisfactory for Type II diabetics since they are more stable.
   2) Use Clinitest, Tes-tape, Diastix for glucose testing.
   3) Perform tests before meals and at bedtime.
   4) Use freshly voided specimen.
   5) Be consistent in brand of urine test used.
   6) Report results in percentages.
   7) Report results to physician if results are greater than 1%, especially if experiencing symptoms of hyperglycemia.
   8) Urine testing for ketones should be done by Type I diabetic clients when there is persistent glycosuria, increased blood glucose levels, or if the client is not feeling well (Acetest, Ketostix).
f. Blood glucose monitoring
   1) Use for Type I diabetic clients since it gives exact blood glucose level and also detects hypoglycemia.
   2) Instruct client in finger-stick technique, use of monitor device (if used), and recording and utilization of test results.
g. General care
   1) perform good oral hygiene and have regular dental exams.
   2) have regular eye exams.
   3) care for "sick days" (e.g., cold or flu)
      a) do not omit insulin or oral hypoglycemic agents since infection causes increased blood sugar.
      b) notify physician.
      c) monitor urine or blood glucose levels and urine ketones frequently.
      d) if nausea and/or vomiting occurs, sip on clear liquids with simple sugars.
h. Foot care
   1) wash feet with mild soap and water and pat dry.
   2) apply lanolin to feet to prevent drying and cracking.
   3) cut toenails straight across.
   4) avoid constricting garments such as garters.
   5) wear clean, absorbent socks (cotton or wool).
   6) purchase properly fitting shoes and break new shoes in gradually.
   7) never go barefoot.
   8) inspect feet daily and notify physician if cuts, blisters, or breaks in skin occur.
i. Exercise
   1) undertake regular exercise; avoid sporadic, vigorous exercise.
   2) food intake may need to be increased before exercising.
   3) exercise is best performed after meals when the blood sugar is rising.
j. Complications
   1) learn to recognize signs and symptoms of hypo/hyperglycemia.
   2) eat candy or drink orange juice with sugar added for insulin reaction (hypoglycemia).
k. Need to wear a Medic-Alert bracelet.

Ketoacidosis (DKA)

A. General information
   1. Acute complication of diabetes mellitus characterized by hyperglycemia and accumulation of ketones in the body; causes metabolic acidosis
   2. Occurs in insulin-dependent diabetic clients
   3. Precipitating factors: undiagnosed diabetes, neglect of treatment; infection, cardiovascular disorder; other physical or emotional stress
   4. Onset slow, may be hours to days
B. Assessment findings
   1. Polydipsia, polyphagia, polyuria
   2. Nausea, vomiting, abdominal pain
   3. Skin warm, dry, and flushed
   4. Dry mucous membranes; soft eyeballs
   5. Kussmaul's respirations or tachypnea; acetone breath
   6. Alterations in LOC
   7. Hypotension, tachycardia
   8. Diagnostic tests
      a. Serum glucose and ketones elevated
      b. BUN, creatinine, hct elevated (due to dehydration)
      c. Serum sodium decreased, potassium (may be normal or elevated at first)
      d. ABGs: metabolic acidosis with compensatory respiratory alkalosis
C. Nursing interventions
   1. Maintain a patent airway.
   2. Maintain fluid and electrolyte balance.
      a. Administer IV therapy as ordered.
         1) normal saline (0.9% NaCl), then hypotonic (0.45% NaCl) sodium chloride
         2) when blood sugar drops to 250 mg/dl, may add 5% dextrose to IV.

   3) potassium will be added when the urine output is adequate.
  b. Observe for fluid and electrolyte imbalances, especially fluid overload, hypokalemia, and hyperkalemia.
 3. Administer insulin as ordered.
  a. Regular insulin IV (drip or push) and/or subcutaneously (SC).
  b. If given IV drip, give with small amounts of albumin since insulin adheres to IV tubing.
  c. Monitor blood glucose levels frequently.
 4. Check urine output every hour.
 5. Monitor vital signs.
 6. Assist client with self-care.
 7. Provide care for the unconscious client if in a coma (page 182).
 8. Discuss with client the reasons ketosis developed and provide additional diabetic teaching if indicated.

Insulin Reaction/Hypoglycemia

A. General information
 1. Abnormally low blood sugar, usually below 50 mg/dl
 2. Usually caused by insulin overdosage, too little food, nutritional and fluid imbalances from nausea and vomiting, excessive exercise
 3. Onset rapid; may develop in minutes to hours
B. Assessment findings
 1. Headache, dizziness, difficulty with problem solving, restlessness, hunger, visual disturbances
 2. Slurred speech; alterations in gait; decreasing LOC; pallor, cold, clammy skin; diaphoresis
 3. Diagnostic test: serum glucose level 50–60 mg/dl or lower
C. Nursing interventions
 1. Administer oral sugar in the form of candy or orange juice with sugar added if the client is alert.
 2. If the client is unconscious, administer 20–50 ml 50% dextrose IV push, or 1 mg glucagon IM, IV, or SC, as ordered.
 3. Explore with client reasons for hypoglycemia and provide additional diabetic teaching as indicated

Hyperglycemic Hyperosmolar Nonketotic Coma (HHNK)

A. General information
 1. Complication of diabetes, characterized by hyperglycemia and a hyperosmolar state without ketosis
 2. Occurs in non-insulin-dependent diabetics or nondiabetic persons (typically elderly clients)

 3. Precipitating factors: undiagnosed diabetes; infections or other stress; certain medications (e.g., Dilantin, thiazide diuretics); dialysis; hyperalimentation; major burns; pancreatic disease
B. Assessment findings
 1. Similar to ketoacidosis but without Kussmaul respirations and acetone breath
 2. Laboratory tests
  a. Blood glucose level extremely elevated
  b. BUN, creatine, hct elevated (due to dehydration)
  c. Urine positive for glucose
C. Nursing interventions: treatment and nursing care is similar to DKA, excluding measures to treat ketosis and metabolic acidosis.

Sample Questions

100. A 57-year-old woman was admitted to the hospital for uncontrolled diabetes. Lab studies reveal a fasting blood sugar of 310. Her admission diagnosis is Type I diabetes mellitus. The client needs to understand that the type of diabetes that she has
 1. is associated with the destruction of beta cells.
 2. usually causes complete fat metabolism.
 3. often occurs in obese individuals.
 4. is rarely controlled.
101. A diabetic client who is taking regular and NPH insulin asks why she must mix the two insulins. The nurse explains that regular and NPH insulins are mixed to ensure
 1. immediate onset of the regular insulin.
 2. onset of the regular insulin within 2 hours.
 3. a peak action of the NPH insulin at 2 hours.
 4. a total duration of action of 24 hours.
102. Ms. A., 45 years old, has a simple goiter. She is being seen by the community health nurse for teaching and follow-up regarding nutritional deficiencies related to her goiter. Ms. A.'s problems are most likely associated with which nutritional deficiency?
 1. Calcium.
 2. Iodine.
 3. Iron.
 4. Sodium.
103. The nurse is teaching a woman who has a simple goiter. The nurse teaches the client that to enhance glandular function, she should eliminate which of the following foods?
 1. Corn.
 2. Milk.
 3. Turnips.
 4. Watermelon.
104. Mr. B., 45 years old, is admitted to the hospital with Addison's disease. He has a

respiratory infection. When Mr. B.'s vital signs are assessed, his blood pressure is 90/40. The nurse should notify the physician immediately because
1. blood gases need to be drawn.
2. seizure activity is imminent.
3. shock may be developing.
4. the reading is atypical.

105. A client who is diagnosed with Addison's disease is admitted to the hospital. Which of the following would the nurse expect to find when assessing the client?
1. Acne.
2. Hyperpigmentation.
3. Moon face.
4. Supraclavicular fat pads.

106. A client who is diagnosed as having Addison's disease is receiving teaching about his disease from the nurse. Which statement the client makes indicates to the nurse that he understands the teaching?
1. "I should avoid strenuous exercise during hot weather."
2. "I should not eat salty foods."
3. "I need to take medication only when I am having symptoms."
4. "I should eat foods such as bananas and oranges several times daily."

107. The nurse is teaching a person who has Addison's disease about drug therapy for his condition. In evaluating the effectiveness of teaching regarding drug therapy, the nurse should expect him to be able to verbalize the need
1. to avoid antibiotics.
2. for lifelong therapy.
3. to taper the steroid dose.
4. to receive alternate-day therapy.

108. Ms. H., 34 years old, is newly diagnosed with Type I diabetes. She is hospitalized for insulin dose stabilization and is being taught insulin administration and self-monitoring of blood glucose (SMBG) levels. The nurse tells Ms. H. that the major benefit of self-monitoring of blood glucose levels is
1. blood glucose is maintained at close to normal levels.
2. materials and laboratory expenses are cost efficient.
3. dependence on the health care system is reduced.
4. larger but fewer doses of insulin are required.

109. The nurse is teaching an adult client who has Type I diabetes mellitus about ketoacidosis. The nurse explains that the primary cause of the development of ketoacidosis is
1. a GI disturbance.
2. an insulin overdosage.
3. omitted meals.
4. not taking insulin regularly.

Answers and Rationales

100. The correct answer is 1. Type I diabetes, also known as insulin-dependent diabetes, occurs in individuals whose pancreatic beta cells do not function at all. Metabolic processes are interfered with in diabetes, therefore fat metabolism is incomplete. Although Type I diabetes can occur in an obese individual, obesity is more characteristic of Type II diabetes. Diet and insulin therapy can be effective in controlling blood sugar.

101. The correct answer is 4. As NPH insulin is an intermediate-acting insulin, the result of mixing regular and NPH insulin is a total duration of action of 24 hours. Onset of the regular insulin is within an hour, regardless of what it is mixed with. NPH insulin peaks in 8–12 hours and lasts for 24 hours.

102. The correct answer is 2. Lack of iodine in the diet is a primary contributor to the development of a simple goiter. A calcium deficiency is likely to be related to osteoporosis. A diet deficient in iron is likely to be related to iron deficiency anemia. A sodium deficiency would likely be related to abnormally large outputs of urine, as seen in diabetes insipidus or untreated diabetes mellitus.

103. The correct answer is 3. Turnips belong to a classification of foods called exogenous goitrogens. Goitrogens are thyroid-inhibiting substances and therefore should be avoided. Other goitrogens include rutabagas, cabbage, soybeans, peanuts, peaches, peas, strawberries, spinach, and radishes. Corn, milk, and watermelon are not goitrogenic.

104. The correct answer is 3. Any emotional or physical stress, such as a respiratory infection, may precipitate acute adrenal crisis with vascular collapse. Blood gases may be ordered, but this is not the most important reason for notifying the physician. Seizure activity would be unlikely. Low blood pressure would be an expected finding in a client with Addison's disease.

105. The correct answer is 2. Addison's disease is characterized by bilateral hypofunction of the adrenal cortex, resulting in a deficient production of adrenal steroids such as cortisol and aldosterone. The cortisol deficiency results when there is a failure to inhibit anterior pituitary secretion of adrenocorticotropic hormone (ACTH) and melanocyte-stimulating hormone (MSH). MSH stimulates the epidermal melanocytes, which manufacture melanin, a dark pigment. Increased MSH stimulation results in increased pigmentation of the skin and mucous membranes. Thus individuals with Addison's disease have increased levels of

ACTH and an "eternal tan" with a peculiar bronze appearance. Acne would be seen in Cushing's syndrome (a metabolic disorder resulting from the chronic and excessive production of cortisol by the adrenal cortex). Moonface and supraclavicular fat pad are seen in Cushing's syndrome as a result of excessive cortisol levels.

106. The correct answer is 1. If he perspires heavily he is prone to become hyponatremic and hypovolemic. He should avoid strenuous exercise during hot weather. Persons with Addison's disease tend to be hypernatremic. He should eat additional sodium in his diet. He will need to take steroid replacements every day of his life. Addison's disease causes hyperkalemia. He should not eat additional foods that are high in potassium such as bananas and oranges.

107. The correct answer is 2. Addison's disease cannot be cured but is controlled with lifelong hormonal replacement. Antibiotics may be prescribed for infections. The steroid dose will not be tapered down. The physician will direct the client to increase the dose in certain circumstances. Steroids must be taken daily.

108. The correct answer is 1. Self-monitoring of blood glucose has become an important part of diabetic management. It provides a direct measurement of blood glucose levels, serving as an aid to making day-to-day decisions about insulin doses, thereby allowing the client to maintain glucose levels as close to normal as possible. Laboratory costs have no relation to the expected health benefits of self-monitoring of blood glucose. Reducing dependence on the health care system is beneficial, but self-monitoring of blood glucose will help maintain as close to normal glucose levels, which will in the long term possibly reduce complications. Monitoring glucose levels will probably necessitate more doses of insulin per day, but a more stable level of blood glucose will result.

109. The correct answer is 4. In order to meet metabolic demands, insulin must be taken on a regular basis. Ketoacidosis occurs when there is a lack of insulin in relation to metabolic demands. A GI disturbance could cause ketoacidosis, but this is not the primary cause. An insulin overdose would cause hypoglycemia and insulin shock. Omitting meals would cause hypoglycemia.

The Integumentary System

OVERVIEW OF ANATOMY AND PHYSIOLOGY

The integumentary system consists of the skin and its appendages, such as hair, nails, and various glands. The integumentary system not only provides a barrier against the external environment, it also plays a role in maintenance of the body's internal environment.

Skin

A. Functions
  1. Protection: barrier to noxious agents (microorganisms, parasites, chemical substances) and to loss of water and electrolytes
  2. Thermoregulation: radiant cooling, evaporation
  3. Sensory perception: touch, temperature, pressure, pain
  4. Metabolism: excretion of water and sodium, production of vitamin D, wound repair

B. Layers (See Figure 4.22)
  1. *Epidermis*
     a. The avascular outermost layer
     b. Stratified into several layers
     c. Composed mainly of keratinocytes and melanocytes
        1) keratinocytes produce *keratin,* responsible for formation of hair and nails
        2) melanocytes produce *melanin,* a pigment that gives color to skin and hair
     d. Appendages (hair and nails, eccrine sweat glands, sebaceous glands, apocrine sweat glands) all derived from epidermis
  2. *Dermis:* layer beneath the epidermis composed of connective tissue that contains lymphatics, nerves, and blood vessels; elasticity of skin results from presence of collagen, elastin, and reticular fibers in the dermis, which also nourish the epidermis
  3. *Subcutaneous layer:* layer beneath the dermis composed of loose connective

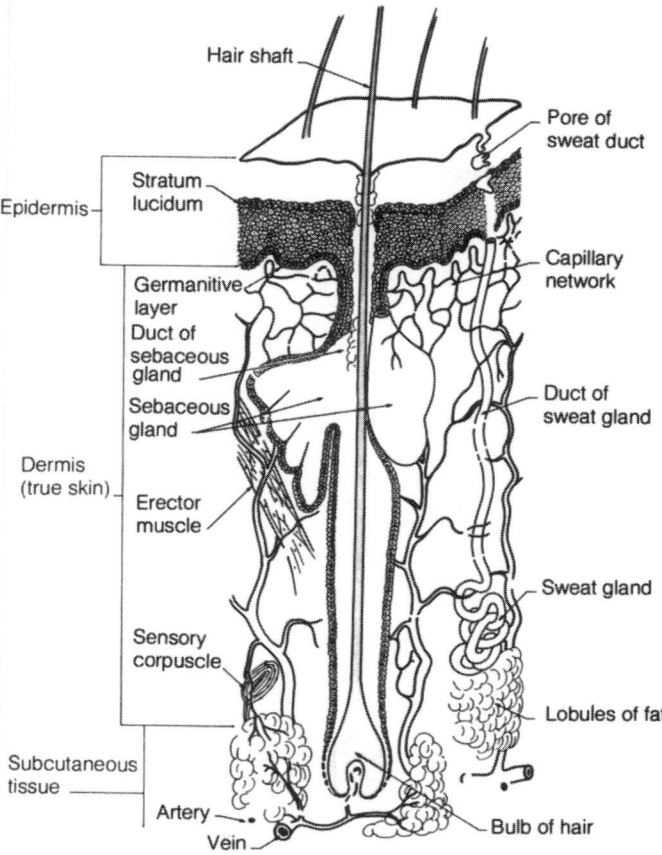

Hair shaft

Pore of
sweat duct

Epidermis

Stratum
lucidum

Capillary
network

Germanitive
layer

Duct of
sebaceous
gland

Sebaceous
gland

Duct of
sweat gland

Dermis
(true skin)

Erector
muscle

Sensory
corpuscle

Sweat gland

Lobules of fat

Subcutaneous
tissue

Artery

Vein

Bulb of hair

FIGURE 4.22 Skin cross section: observe the skin layers and note the location of the glands in the dermal layer (Delmar Publishers)

tissue and fat cells; stores fat; important in temperature regulation

Hair

A. Covers most of the body surface (except palms of hands, soles of feet, lips, nipples, and parts of external genitalia).
B. *Hair follicles:* tube-like structures, derived from epidermis, from which hair grows.
C. Hair functions as protection from external elements and from trauma.
D. Hair growth is controlled by hormonal influences and by blood supply.
E. Loss of body hair is called *alopecia.*

Nails

A. Dense layer of flat, dead cells; filled with keratin
B. Systemic illnesses may be reflected by changes in the nail or its bed; common changes include
   1. *Clubbing:* enlargement of fingers and toes, nail becomes convex; caused by chronic pulmonary or cardiovascular disease

   2. *Beau's line;* transverse groove caused by temporary halt in nail growth because of systemic disorder

Glands

A. *Eccrine sweat glands:* located all over the body; participate in heat regulation
B. *Apocrine sweat glands:* odiferous glands, found primarily in axillary, nipple, anal, and pubic areas; bacterial decomposition of excretions causes body odor.
C. *Sebaceous glands:* oil glands, located all over the body except for palms of hands and soles of feet (abundant on face, scalp, upper chest, and back); produce *sebum.*

ASSESSMENT

Health History

A. Presenting problem: symptoms may include changes in color or texture of skin, hair, nails; pruritus; infections; tumors; lesions; dermatitis; ecchymoses; rashes; dryness
B. Life-style: hygienic practices (skin-cleansing measures, use of cosmetics [type, brand names]); skin exposure (duration of exposure to sun, irritants [occupational], cold weather)
C. Nutrition/diet: intake of vitamins, essential nutrients, water; food allergies
D. Use of medications: steroids, vitamin use, hormones, antibiotics, chemotherapeutic agents
E. Past medical history: renal, hepatic, or collagen diseases; trauma or surgery; food, drug, or contact allergies
F. Family history: diabetes mellitus, allergic disorders, blood dyscrasias, specific dermatologic problems, cancer

Physical Examination

A. Color: note areas of uniform color; pigmentation; redness, jaundice, cyanosis.
B. Vascular changes
   1. Purpuric lesions: note ecchymoses, petechiae.
   2. Vascular lesions: note angiomas, hemangiomas, venous stars.
C. Lesions: note color, type (see page 343), size, distribution, location, consistency, grouping (annular, circular, linear, or clustered).
D. Edema: differentiate pitting from nonpitting.
E. Moisture content: note dryness, clamminess.
F. Temperature: note whether increased or decreased, distribution of temperature changes.
G. Texture: note smoothness, coarseness.
H. Mobility/turgor: note whether increased or decreased.

Laboratory/Diagnostic Studies

A. Blood chemistry/electrolytes: calcium, chloride, magnesium, potassium, sodium
B. Hematologic studies: Hbg, hct, RBC, WBC
C. Biopsy
   1. Removal of a small piece of skin for examination to determine diagnosis
   2. Nursing care: instruct client to keep biopsied area dry until healing occurs
D. Skin testing
   1. Administration of allergens or antigens on the surface of or into the dermis to determine hypersensitivity
   2. Three types: patch, scratch, and intradermal

ANALYSIS

Nursing diagnoses for clients with a disorder of the integumentary system may include
A. Impaired skin integrity
B. Pain
C. Body-image disturbance
D. Risk for infection
E. Ineffective airway clearance
F. Altered peripheral tissue perfusion

PLANNING AND IMPLEMENTATION

Goals

A. Restoration of skin integrity.
B. Client will experience absence of pain.
C. Client will adapt to changes in appearance.
D. Client will be free from infection.
E. Maintenance of effective airway clearance.
F. Maintenance of adequate peripheral tissue perfusion.

Interventions

Skin Grafts

A. Replacement of damaged skin with healthy skin to provide protection of underlying structures or to reconstruct areas for cosmetic or functional purposes
B. Graft sources
   1. *Autograft:* client's own skin
   2. *Isograft:* skin from a genetically identical person (identical twin)
   3. *Homograft or allograft:* cadaver of same species
   4. *Heterograft or xenograft:* skin from another species (such as a porcine graft)
   5. *Human amniotic membrane*
C. Nursing care: preoperative
   1. Donor site: cleanse with antiseptic soap the night before and morning of surgery as ordered.
   2. Recipient site: apply warm compresses and topical antibiotics as ordered.
D. Nursing care: postoperative
   1. Donor site
      a. Keep area covered for 24–48 hours.
      b. Use bed cradle to prevent pressure and provide greater air circulation
      c. Outer dressing may be removed 24–72 hours postsurgery; maintain fine mesh gauze (innermost dressing) until it falls off spontaneously.
      d. Trim loose edges of gauze as it loosens with healing.
      e. Administer analgesics as ordered (more painful than recipient site).
   2. Recipient site
      a. Elevate site when possible.
      b. Protect from pressure (use bed cradle).
      c. Apply warm compresses as ordered.
      d. Assess for hematoma, fluid accumulation under graft.
      e. Monitor circulation distal to graft.
   3. Provide emotional support and monitor behavioral adjustments; refer for counseling if needed.
E. Provide client teaching and discharge planning concerning
   1. Applying lubricating lotion to maintain moisture on surfaces of healed graft for at least 6–12 months
   2. Protecting grafted skin from direct sunlight for at least 6 months
   3. Protecting graft from physical injury
   4. Need to report changes in graft (fluid accumulation, pain, hematoma)
   5. Possible alteration in pigmentation and hair growth; ability to sweat lost in most grafts
   6. Sensations may or may not return

EVALUATION

A. Healing of burned areas; absence of drainage, edema, and pain over graft sites.
B. Relaxed facial expression/body posture; achieves effective rest patterns; participates in daily activities without pain.
C. Incorporates changes into self-concept without negating self-esteem; verbalizes about changes that occurred; demonstrates interest in physical appearance.
D. Achieves wound healing; vital signs within normal range; lungs clear; laboratory studies within normal range.
E. Lungs clear to auscultation; respiratory rate and depth within normal limits; free of dyspnea.

F. Palpable peripheral pulses of equal quality; adequate capillary refill; skin color normal in uninjured areas.

DISORDERS OF THE INTEGUMENTARY SYSTEM

Primary Lesions of the Skin

A. *Macule:* a flat, circumscribed area of color change in the skin without surface elevation, up to 2 cm in diameter
B. *Papule:* a circumscribed solid and elevated lesion, up to 1 cm in size
C. *Nodule:* a solid, elevated lesion extending deeper into the dermis, 1–2 cm in diameter
D. *Wheal:* a slightly irregular, transient superficial elevation of the skin with a palpable margin (e.g., hive)
E. *Vesicle:* circumscribed elevated lesion filled with serous fluid, less than 1 cm in diameter
F. *Bulla:* a vesicle larger than 1 cm in diameter
G. *Pustule:* a vesicle or bulla containing purulent exudate

Contact Dermatitis

A. General information
  1. An irritation of the skin from a specific substance or from a hypersensitivity immune reaction from contact with a specific antigen
  2. Caused by irritants (mechanical, chemical, biologic); allergens
B. Assessment findings
  1. Pruritus
  2. Erythema; localized edema; vesicles (oozing, crusting, and scaling [later])
  3. Diagnostic test: skin testing reveals hypersensitivity to specific antigen
C. Nursing interventions
  1. Apply wet dressings of Burrow's solution for 20 minutes 4 times a day to help clear oozing lesions.
  2. Provide relief from pruritus (see Cirrhosis of the Liver, page 282).
  3. Administer topical steroids and antibiotics as ordered.
  4. Provide client teaching and discharge planning concerning
    a. Avoidance of causative agent
    b. Preventing skin dryness
      1) use mild soaps (Ivory).
      2) soak in plain water for 20–30 minutes.
      3) apply prescribed steroid cream immediately after bath.
      4) avoid extremes of heat and cold.
    c. Allowing crusts and scales to drop off skin naturally as healing occurs

d. Avoidance of wool, nylon, or fur fibers on sensitive skin
e. Need to use gloves if handling irritant or allergenic substances

Psoriasis

A. General information
  1. Chronic type of dermatitis that involves accelerated turnover rate of the epidermal cells
  2. Predisposing factors include stress, trauma, infection; changes in climate may produce exacerbations; familial predisposition to the disease
B. Medical management
  1. Topical corticosteroids
  2. Coal tar preparations
  3. Ultraviolet light
  4. Antimetabolites (methotrexate)
C. Assessment findings
  1. Mild pruritus
  2. Sharply circumscribed scaling placques that are mostly present on the scalp, elbows, and knees; yellow discoloration of nails
D. Nursing interventions
  1. Apply occlusive wraps over prescribed topical steroids.
  2. Protect areas treated with coal tar preparations from direct sunlight for 24 hours.
  3. Administer methotrexate as ordered, assess for side effects.
  4. Provide client teaching and discharge planning concerning
    a. Feelings about changes in appearance of skin (encourage client to cover arms and legs with clothing if sensitive about appearance)
    b. Importance of adhering to prescribed treatment and avoidance of commercially advertised products

Acne

See page 433.

Pediculosis

See page 432.

Skin Cancer

A. General information
  1. Types of skin cancers
    a. *Basal cell epithelioma:* most common type of skin cancer; locally invasive and rarely metastasizes; most frequently located between the hairline and upper lip

b. *Squamous cell carcinoma (epidermoid):* grows more rapidly than basal cell carcinoma and can metastasize; frequently seen on mucous membranes, lower lip, neck, and dorsum of the hands

c. *Malignant melanoma:* least frequent of skin cancers, but most serious; capable of invasion and metastasis to other organs

2. Precancerous lesions
   a. *Leukoplakia:* white, shiny patches in the mouth and on the lip
   b. *Nevi (moles):* junctional nevus may become malignant (signs include a color change to black, bleeding, and irritation); compound and dermal nevi unlikely to become cancerous
   c. *Senile keratoses:* brown, scalelike spots on older individuals

3. Contributing factors include hereditary predisposition (fair, blue-eyed people; redheads and blondes); irritation (chemicals or ultraviolet rays)

4. Occurs more often in those with outdoor occupations who are exposed to more sunlight

B. Medical management: varies depending on type of cancer; surgical excision with or without radiation therapy most common; chemotherapy and immunotherapy for melanoma

C. Assessment findings: characteristics depend on specific type of lesion; biopsy reveals malignant cells

D. Nursing interventions: provide client teaching concerning
   1. Limitation of contact with chemical irritants
   2. Protection against ultraviolet radiation from sun
      a. Wear thin layer of clothing.
      b. Use sun block or lotion containing para-amino benzoic acid (PABA).
   3. Need to report lesions that change characteristics and/or those that do not heal.

Herpes Zoster (Shingles)

A. General information
   1. Acute viral infection of the nervous system
   2. The virus causes an inflammatory reaction in isolated spinal and cranial sensory ganglia and the posterior gray matter of the spinal cord
   3. Contagious to anyone who has not had varicella or who is immunosuppressed
   4. Caused by activation of latent varicella-zoster virus

B. Medical management
   1. Analgesics

2. Corticosteroids
3. Acetic acid compresses
4. Acyclovir (Zovirax)

C. Assessment findings
   1. Neuralgic pain, malaise, itching, burning
   2. Cluster of skin vesicles along course of peripheral sensory nerves, usually unilateral and primarily on trunk, thorax, or face

D. Nursing interventions
   1. Apply acetic acid compresses or white petrolatum to lesions.
   2. Administer medications as ordered.
      a. Analgesics for pain
      b. Systemic corticosteroids: monitor for side effects of steroid therapy (see page 324).
      c. Acyclovir (Zovivax): antivalagent reduces severity when given early in illness.

Herpes Simplex Virus, Type I

A. General information
   1. Causes cold sores or fever blisters, canker sores and herpetic whitlow
   2. Common disorder, frequently seen in women
   3. Primary infection occurs in children, recurrences in adults
   4. Self-limiting virus

B. Assessment findings: clusters of vesicles, may ulcerate or crust; burning, itching, tingling; usually appears on lip or cheek

C. Nursing interventions: keep lesions dry; apply topical antibiotics or anesthetic as ordered.

Burns

A. Types
   1. Thermal: most common type; caused by flame, flash, scalding, and contact (hot metals, grease)
   2. Smoke inhalation: occurs when smoke (particular products of a fire, gases, and superheated air) causes respiratory tissue damage
   3. Chemical: caused by tissue contact, ingestion or inhalation of acids, alkalies, or vesicants
   4. Electrical: injury occurs from direct damage to nerves and vessels when an electric current passes through the body.

B. Classification
   1. *Partial thickness*
      a. Superficial partial-thickness (first degree)
         1) depth: epidermis only
         2) causes: sunburn, splashes of hot liquid
         3) sensation: painful

4) characteristics: erythema, blanching on pressure, no vesicles
  b. Deep partial thickness (second degree)
    1) depth: epidermis and dermis
    2) causes: flash, scalding, or flame burn
    3) sensation: very painful
    4) characteristics: fluid-filled vesicles; red, shiny, wet after vesicles rupture
  2. *Full thickness* (third and fourth degree)
    a. Depth: all skin layers and nerve endings; may involve muscles, tendons, and bones
    b. Causes: flame, chemicals, scalding, electric current
    c. Sensation: little or no pain
    d. Characteristics: wound is dry, white, leathery, or hard
C. Medical management
  1. Supportive therapy: fluid management (IVs), catheterization
  2. Wound care: hydrotherapy, debridement (enzymatic or surgical)
  3. Drug therapy
    a. Topical antibiotics: mafenide (Sulfamylon), silver sulfadiazine (Silvadene), silver nitrate, povidone-iodine (Betadine) solution
    b. Systemic antibiotics: gentamicin
    c. Tetanus toxoid or hyperimmune human tetanus globulin (burn wound good medium for anaerobic growth)
    d. Analgesics
  4. Surgery: excision and grafting
D. Assessment
  1. Extent of burn injury by rule of nines: head and neck (9%); each arm (9%), each leg (18%), trunk (36%), genitalia (1%) (See Figure 4.23)
  2. Lund and Browder method determines the extent of the burn injury by using client's age in proportion to relative body-part size.
  3. Severity of burn
    a. Major: partial thickness greater than 25%; full thickness greater than or equal to 10%
    b. Moderate: partial thickness 15%–25%, full thickness less than 10%
    c. Minor: partial thickness less than 15%; full thickness less than 2%
E. Stages
  1. *Emergent phase*
    a. Remove person from source of burn.
      1) thermal: smother burn beginning with the head.
      2) smoke inhalation: ensure patent airway.
      3) chemical: remove clothing that contains chemical; lavage area with copious amounts of water.
      4) electrical: note victim position, identify entry/exit routes, maintain airway.

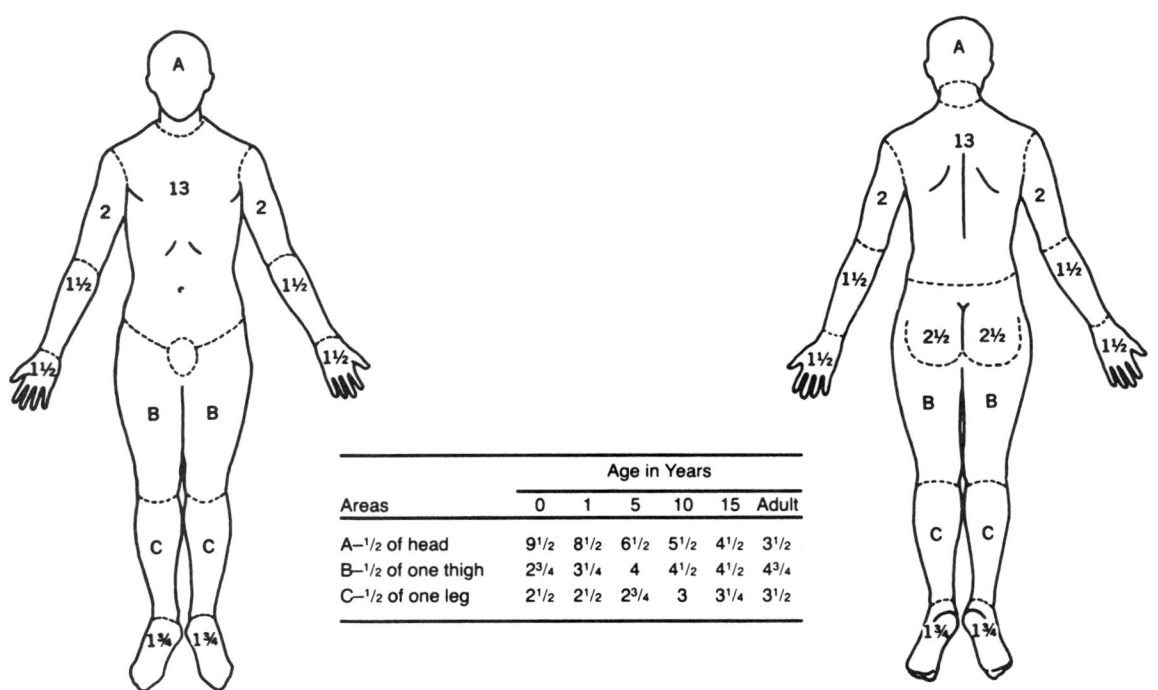

Areas	Age in Years					
	0	1	5	10	15	Adult
A–1/2 of head	9½	8½	6½	5½	4½	3½
B–1/2 of one thigh	2¾	3¼	4	4½	4½	4¾
C–1/2 of one leg	2½	2½	2¾	3	3¼	3½

FIGURE 4.23 Body proportions change with growth. Shown here, in percentage, is the relationship of body area to whole body surface at various ages. This method of determining the extent of the burned area is attributed to Lund and Browder (Delmar Publishers)

b. Wrap in dry, clean sheet or blanket to prevent further contamination of wound and provide warmth.
c. Assess how and when burn occurred.
d. Provide IV route if possible.
e. Transport immediately.

2. *Shock phase* (first 24–48 hours)
   a. Plasma to interstitial fluid shift causing hypovolemia; fluid also moves to areas that normally have little or no fluid (third-spacing).
   b. Assessment findings
      1) dehydration, decreased blood pressure, elevated pulse, decreased urine output, thirst
      2) diagnostic tests: hyperkalemia, hyponatremia, elevated hct, metabolic acidosis

3. *Fluid remobilization or diuretic phase* (2–5 days postburn)
   a. Interstitial fluid returns to the vascular compartment.
   b. Assessment findings
      1) elevated blood pressure, increased urine output
      2) diagnostic tests: hypokalemia, hyponatremia, metabolic acidosis

4. *Convalescent (Rehabilitation) phase*
   a. Starts when diuresis is completed and wound healing and coverage begin.
   b. Assessment findings
      1) dry, waxy-white appearance of full thickness burn changing to dark brown; wet, shiny, and serous exudate in partial thickness
      2) diagnostic test: hyponatremia

F. Nursing interventions
   1. Provide relief/control of pain.
      a. Administer morphine sulfate IV and monitor vital signs closely.
      b. Administer analgesics/narcotics 30 minutes before wound care.
      c. Position burned areas in proper alignment.
   2. Monitor alterations in fluid and electrolyte balance.
      a. Assess for fluid shifts and electrolyte alterations (see Table 4.5, page 146).
      b. Administer IV fluids as ordered (see Table 4.25)
      c. Monitor Foley catheter output hourly (30 ml/hour desired).
      d. Weigh daily.
      e. Monitor circulation status regularly.
      f. Administer/monitor crystalloids/colloids/H_2O solutions.
   3. Promote maximal nutritional status.
      a. Monitor tube feedings/TPN if ordered.
      b. When oral intake permitted, provide high-calorie, high-protein, high-carbohydrate diet with vitamin and mineral supplements.
      c. Serve small portions.
      d. Schedule wound care and other treatments at least 1 hour before meals.
   4. Prevent wound infection.
      a. Place client in controlled sterile environment.
      b. Use hydrotherapy for no more than 30 minutes to prevent electrolyte loss.
      c. Observe wound for separation of eschar and cellulitis.
      d. Apply mafenide (Sulfamylon) as ordered.
         1) administer analgesics 30 minutes before application.
         2) monitor acid-base status and renal function studies.
         3) provide daily tubbing for removal of previously applied cream.

TABLE 4.25 Guidelines and Formulas for Fluid Replacement for Burns

Consensus Formula	Evans Formula	Brooke Army Formula	Parkland/Baxter Formula
Lactated Ringer's: 2–4 ml × wt. in kg × % body surface area (BSA) burned. Half to be given in first 8 hrs after burn; remaining fluid to be given over next 16 hrs.	1. Colloids: 1 ml × wt. kg × % BSA burned 2. Electrolytes (saline): 1 ml × wt. kg × % BSA burned 3. Glucose (5% in water): 2000 ml for insensible loss Day 1: Half to be given in first 8 hrs; remaining half over next 16 hrs. Day 2: Half of previous day's colloids and electrolytes; all of insensible fluid replacement Maximum of 10,000 ml over 24 hours. Second and third degree burns exceeding 50% BSA calculated on basis of 50% BSA.	1. Colloids: 0.5 ml × wt, kg × % BSA burned 2. Electrolytes (lactated Ringer's): 1.5 ml × wt, kg × % BSA burned 3. Glucose (5% in water): 2000 ml for insensible loss Day 1: Half to be given in first 8 hrs; remaining half over next 16 hrs. Day 2: Half of colloids, half of electrolytes, all of insensible fluid replacement Second and third degree burns exceeding 50% BSA calculated on basis of 50% BSA.	Lactated Ringer's: 4 ml × wt, kg × % BSA burned. Day 1: Half to be given in first 8 hours; half to be given over next 16 hours Day 2: Varies; colloid is added.

e. Apply silver sulfadiazine (Silvadene) as ordered.
      1) administer analgesics 30 minutes before application.
      2) observe for and report hypersensitivity reactions (rash, itching, burning sensation in unburned areas).
      3) store drug away from heat.
  f. Apply silver nitrate as ordered.
      1) handle carefully; solution leaves a gray or black stain on skin, clothing, and utensils.
      2) administer analgesic before application.
      3) keep dressings wet with solution; dryness increases the concentration and causes precipitation of silver salts in the wound.
  g. Apply povidone-iodine (Betadine) solution as ordered.
      1) administer analgesics before application.
      2) assess for metabolic acidosis/renal function studies.
  h. Administer gentamicin as ordered: assess vestibular/auditory and renal functions at regular intervals.
5. Prevent GI complications.
  a. Assess for signs and symptoms of paralytic ileus.
  b. Assist with insertion of NG tube to prevent/control Curling's/stress ulcer; monitor patency/drainage.
  c. Administer prophylactic antacids through NG tube and/or IV cimetidine (Tagamet) or ranitidine (Zantac) (to prevent gastric pH of less than 5).
  d. Monitor bowel sounds.
  e. Test stools for occult blood.
6. Provide client teaching and discharge planning concerning
  a. Care of healed burn wound
      1) assess daily for changes.
      2) wash hands frequently during dressing change.
      3) wash area with prescribed solution or mild soap and rinse well with H_2O; dry with clean towel.
      4) apply sterile dressing.
  b. Prevention of injury to burn wound
      1) avoid trauma to area.
      2) avoid use of fabric softeners or harsh detergents (might cause irritation).
      3) avoid constrictive clothing over burn wound.
  c. Adherence to prescribed diet
  d. Importance of reporting formation of blisters, opening of healed area, increased or foul-smelling drainage from wound, other signs of infection
  e. Methods of coping and resocialization

Sample Questions

110. A 37-year-old man is seen in the outpatient clinic for treatment of psoriasis. The nurse should anticipate which of the following findings in this man?
    1. Intense pain.
    2. Discolored nails.
    3. Abdominal lesions.
    4. Hyperpigmented skin.
111. The physician prescribes coal tar preparations as part of the treatment plan for a man who has psoriasis. The nurse should include which statement in the teaching plan for this client?
    1. Avoid sunlight immediately after the treatment.
    2. Ingest the coal tar with liberal amounts of water.
    3. Eat a high-carbohydrate diet.
    4. Restrict activity for 24 hours.
112. A 34-year-old man is involved in many craft projects. While he is burning the paint off some furniture that he is restoring, his shirt catches on fire. In a panic, he runs into his neighbor's yard with his clothes in flames. All the following are appropriate first-aid interventions for this man except
    1. dousing the flames with water.
    2. removing his burned clothing.
    3. removing his jewelry.
    4. rolling him on the ground rapidly.
113. The nurse is caring for a man admitted with severe burns sustained when his clothing caught fire while he was burning leaves. During the acute burn phase, the nurse explains to the man that his nursing care plan is directed toward all of the following except
    1. strict aseptic technique.
    2. proper alignment of all joints.
    3. maintenance of fluid and electrolyte balance.
    4. frequent and routine administration of narcotics.
114. The nurse is planning care for an adult man who is admitted with severe flame burns. Nursing care planning is based on the knowledge that the first 24–48 hours post-burn are characterized by
    1. an increase in the total volume of intravascular plasma.
    2. excessive renal perfusion with diuresis.
    3. fluid shift from interstitial spaces to plasma.
    4. fluid shift from plasma to interstitial spaces.
115. The nurse is caring for a client who was admitted following severe burns sustained in a house fire. The nurse understands that an acceptable range for hourly urine output during the first two days post-burn is

1. 20 ml.
2. 30–50 ml.
3. 50–90 ml.
4. 90–150 ml.
116. The nurse is planning care for a seriously burned woman. Which intervention is least appropriate in preventing the development of wound infection?
   1. Administer hyperimmune tetanus globulin.
   2. Apply topical antibiotics.
   3. Cleanse the wounds.
   4. Place her in protective isolation.

Answers and Rationales

110. The correct answer is 2. A yellow discoloration of the nails is frequently seen in psoriasis. The pain of psoriasis produces discomfort, but it is usually not described as intense. The lesions of psoriasis are usually distributed on the extremities; these lesions are raised macular-papular areas with erythema rather than hyperpigmentation.

111. The correct answer is 1. Sunlight should be avoided after a coal tar treatment. Special diets and other activity restrictions are not required. The coal tar is applied topically, not ingested.

112. The correct answer is 2. Removing burned clothing will cause further trauma to adhering tissue. Dousing the flames with water is a correct intervention. Removing jewelry if possible is a correct intervention. Having the person roll on the ground rapidly is a correct intervention.

113. The correct answer is 4. Narcotics should be given only after careful assessment in this phase due to the danger of shock and respiratory depression. Strict aseptic technique is necessary to prevent infection of the burned area. Proper alignment of all joints will help prevent future deformity. Dramatic fluid shifts following a severe burn make maintenance of fluid and electrolyte balance a nursing priority.

114. The correct answer is 4. The initial fluid alteration following a burn is a plasma-to-interstitial fluid shift. The capillary walls become more permeable and fluid is lost in significant quantities. Following a burn there is a decrease in the total volume of intravascular plasma. Diuresis does not begin until 48 hours after the burn. Following a burn fluid shifts from the plasma to the interstitial spaces.

115. The correct answer is 2. A safe range for the hourly urine output post burn is 30–50 ml. Less than this amount would indicate severely decreased renal arterial perfusion. 20 ml

hourly output would be insufficient to maintain renal function. Diuresis does not begin until 48 hours after the burn.

116. The correct answer is 1. Tetanus is a potential danger in burn clients and is prevented by administration of hyperimmune tetanus globulin; this treatment will not prevent or control other infections. Topical antibiotics will aid in preventing infection. Cleansing the wound will aid in preventing infection. Placing the client in protective isolation will aid in preventing infection.

References and Suggested Readings

Barker, E. (1990). Avoiding increased intracranial pressure. *Nursing '90*, 20(5), 64Q–64RR.

Bates, B. (1995). *A guide to physical examination* (6th ed.). Philadelphia: Lippincott.

Birchenall, J., & Streight, M. (1993). *Care of the older adult* (3rd ed.). Philadelphia: Lippincott.

Black. (1997). *Luckman and Sorenson's medical-surgical nursing* (5th ed.). Philadelphia: Saunders.

Brooker. (1998). *Human structure and function: Nursing Applications in Clinical Practice* (2nd ed.). St. Louis: Mosby.

Burckhardt, C. (1990). Chronic pain. *Nursing Clinics of North America*, 25(4), 863–869.

Carpenito, L. (1997). *Nursing diagnoses—application to clinical practice* (7th ed.). Philadelphia: Lippincott.

Doenges, M. (1995). *Application of Nursing Process and Nursing Diagnosis* (2nd ed.). Philadelphia: F.A. Davis Co.

Donovan, M. (1990). Acute pain relief. *Nursing Clinics of North America*, 25(4), 851–861.

Faden, R., & Beauchamp, T. (1986). *A history and theory of informed consent*. New York: Oxford University Press.

Fischbach, F. (1995). *A manual of laboratory diagnostic tests* (5th ed.). Philadelphia: Lippincott.

Fischbach, F. (1998). *Quick reference to common laboratory and diagnostic tests*. (2nd ed.). Philadelphia: Lippincott.

Flavell, C. (1994). Combating hemorrhagic shock. *RN*, 57(12), 26–30.

Fulmer, T., & Walker, M. (1992). *Critical care nursing of the elderly*. New York: Springer.

Guyton, A. (1997). *Physiologic mechanisms of disease* (6th ed.). Philadelphia: Saunders.

Johannsen, J. (1993). Update: Guidelines for treating hypertension. *American Journal of Nursing*, 93(3), 42–49.

Matteson, M. A., & McConnell, E. (1996). *Gerontological nursing: Concepts and practice*. (2nd ed.). Philadelphia: Saunders.

Metheny, N. (1996). *Fluid and electrolyte balance: Nursing considerations* (3rd ed.). Philadelphia: Lippincott.

Phipps, W., Long, B., Woods, N., & Cass Meyer, V. (1995). *Medical-surgical nursing concepts and clinical practice* (5th ed.). St. Louis: Mosby.

Seeley, R., Tate, P., Stephens, Trent D. (1998). *Essentials of anatomy and physiology* (3rd ed.). St. Louis: Mosby.

Smeltzer. (1996). *Brunner & Suddarth's textbook of medical-surgical nursing* (8th ed.). Philadelphia: Lippincott.

Walbrecker, J. (1995). Start talking about testicular cancer. *RN*, 51(1), 34–35.

Unit 5

Pediatric Nursing

Mary Lou Manning, RN, PhD, CPNP

The challenges today's pediatric nurse faces in providing care for children and their families require skills from a wide spectrum of both technologic and psychosocial arenas. To meet the needs of the child and the family in a variety of settings, the nurse must have a thorough understanding of disease processes, as well as knowledge of emotional, social, cultural, and developmental needs.

To provide this essential knowledge base, this unit begins with a review of growth and development, which is basic to understanding the behavior of children and the influences of illness. The next section, multisystem stressors, emphasizes such topics as fluid, electrolyte, and acid-base imbalance, which are applicable to many pediatric health care problems.

The unit is further divided into specific body systems. For each system, there is an initial review of aspects of anatomy and physiology unique to the child. Each step of the nursing process is then reviewed, followed by discussions of the major health problems of that system.

Throughout the unit, only information specific to children is presented. In many cases, for instance, when lab tests or nursing care do not differ from those for the adult, the content is not repeated. Be sure to refer to Unit 4 for background information when needed.

UNIT OUTLINE

350	Growth and Development
365	Multisystem Stressors
373	The Neurosensory System
385	The Cardiovascular System
394	The Hematologic System
400	The Respiratory System
409	The Gastrointestinal System
418	The Genitourinary System
421	The Musculoskeletal System
427	The Endocrine System
430	The Integumentary System
433	Pediatric Oncology

Growth and Development

GENERAL PRINCIPLES

Definition of Terms

A. *Growth:* increase in size of a structure. Human growth is orderly and predictable, but not even; it follows a cyclical pattern.
B. *Development:* maturation of structures. Development includes growth and is a process that continues over time.
C. *Cephalocaudal:* head-to-toe progression of growth and development
D. *Proximodistal:* trunk-to-periphery (fingers and toes) progression of growth and development
E. *Phylogeny:* development or evolution of a species or group; a pattern of development for a species
F. *Ontogeny:* development of an individual within a species
G. *Critical period:* specific time period during which certain environmental events or stimuli have greatest effect on a child's development.

Rates of Development

Growth and development are not synonymous but are closely interrelated processes directed by both genetic and environmental factors. Although changes in growth and development are more obvious in some periods than others, they are important in all periods.
A. Infancy and adolescence: fast growth periods
B. Toddler through school-age: slow growth periods
C. Fetal period and infancy: the head and neurologic tissue grow faster than other tissues.
D. Toddler and preschool periods: the trunk grows more rapidly than other tissue.
E. The limbs grow most during school-age period.
F. The trunk grows faster than other tissue during adolescence.

Child Development Theorists

Also see Unit 7, pages 519–522.

Sigmund Freud (Psychosexual Theory)

A. 0–6 months: oral passive (development of id; biologic pleasure principle)
B. 7–18 months: oral aggressive (teething); oral satisfaction of needs by mother decreases tension
C. 1½–3 years: anal (toilet training); projection of feelings onto others; elimination and retention as ways to control and inhibit
D. 3–6 years: phallic (love of opposite sex, parent-Oedipal complex); ego development; objective conscious reality
E. 6–12 years: latent; sexual drive repressed; socialization occurs; superego and morality development

Erik Erikson (Psychosocial Theory)

Core stages/psychosocial tasks or crises
A. Birth–1 year: trust vs mistrust
B. 1–3 years: autonomy vs shame and doubt
C. 3–6 years: initiative vs guilt
D. 6–12 years: industry vs inferiority
E. 12–18 years: identity vs role confusion
F. Young adult: intimacy vs isolation
G. Adult: generativity vs stagnation
H. Elderly: ego integrity vs despair

Jean Piaget (Cognitive Theory)

Development of thought
A. 0–2 years: sensorimotor (reflexes, repetition of acts)
B. 2–4 years: preoperational (preconceptual); no cause and effect reasoning; egocentrism; use of symbols; magical thinking
C. 4–7 years: intuitive/preoperational (beginning of causation)
D. 7–11 years: concrete operations
E. 11–15 years: formal operations (reality, abstract thought)

ASSESSMENT

Developmental Tasks

Developmental tasks are accomplishments normally occurring at one stage and having an effect on the development of subsequent stages; fall into three categories
A. Physical tasks (e.g., learning to sit, crawl, walk; toileting)
B. Psychologic tasks (e.g., learning trust, self-esteem)
C. Cognitive tasks (e.g., acquiring concepts of time and space, abstract thought)

Measurement Tools

There are a number of different assessment tools for measuring the progress of growth and development.

A. Chronologic age: assessment of developmental tasks related to birth date
B. Mental age: assessment of cognitive development
  1. Measured by variety of standardized intelligence tests (IQ)
  2. Results from at least two separate testing sessions needed before an assessment is made
  3. Uses toys and language based on mental rather than chronologic age
C. *Denver Developmental Screening Test* (*DDST*)
  1. Generalized assessment tool; measures gross motor, fine motor, language, and personal-social development from newborn–6 years
  2. Does not measure intelligence
D. Growth parameters
  1. Bone age: x-ray of tarsals and carpals determines degree of ossification
  2. Growth charts: norms are expressed as percentile of height, weight, head circumference for age; any child who crosses over multiple percentile lines needs further evaluation

Developmental Stages

Infant (Birth through 12 months)

A. Physical tasks
  1. *Neonate* (*Birth to 1 month*)
    a. Weight: 6–8 lb (2750–3629 g); gains 5–7 oz (142–198 g) weekly for first 6 months
    b. Length: 20 inches (50 cm); grows 1 inch (2.5 cm) monthly for first 6 months
    c. Head growth
      1) head circumference 33–35.5 cm (13–14 inches)
      2) head circumference equal to or slightly larger than chest
      3) increases by ½ inch (1.25 cm) monthly for first 6 months
      4) brain growth related to myelinization of nerve fibers; increase in size of brain reflects this process, reaches ⅔ adult size at 1 year; 90% adult size at 2 years
      5) no control of muscles of the head
    d. Vital signs
      1) pulse: 110–160 and irregular; count for a full minute apically
      2) respirations: 32–60 and irregular; neonates are abdominal breathers, obligate nose breathers
      3) blood pressure: 75/49 mm Hg
      4) poor development of sweating and shivering mechanisms; impaired temperature control
    e. Motor development
      1) behavior is reflex controlled
      2) flexed extremities

      3) can lift head slightly off bed when prone
    f. Sensory development
      1) hearing and touch well developed at birth
      2) sight not fully developed until 6 years
        a) differentiates light and dark at birth
        b) rapidly develops clarity of vision within 1 foot
        c) fixates on moving objects
        d) strabismus due to lack of binocular vision
  2. *1–4 months*
    a. Head growth: posterior fontanel closes
    b. Motor development
      1) reflexes begin to fade (e.g., Moro, tonic neck)
      2) gains head control; balances head in sitting position
      3) rolls from back to side
      4) begins voluntary hand-to-mouth activity
    c. Sensory development
      1) begins to be able to coordinate stimuli from various sense organs
      2) hearing: locates sounds by turning head and visually searching
      3) vision
        a) binocular vision developing; less strabismus
        b) beginning hand-eye coordination
        c) prefers human face
        d) follows objects 180°
        e) ability to accommodate is equal to adult
  3. *5–6 months*
    a. Weight: birth weight doubles; gains 3–5 oz (84–140 g) weekly for next 6 months
    b. Length: gains ½ inch (1.25 cm) for next 6 months
    c. Eruption of teeth begins
      1) lower incisors first
      2) causes increased saliva and drooling
      3) enzyme released with teething causes mild diarrhea, facial skin irritation
      4) slight fever may be associated with teething, but not a high fever or seizures
    d. Motor development
      1) intentional rolling over
      2) supports weight on arms
      3) creeping; pushes backward with hands
      4) can grasp and let go voluntarily
      5) transfers toys from one hand to another
      6) sits with support

e. Sensory development
   1) hearing: can localize sounds above and below ear
   2) vision: smiles at own mirror image and responds to facial expressions of others
   3) taste: sucking needs have decreased and cup weaning can begin; chewing, biting, and taste preferences begin to develop
4. *7–9 months*
   a. Teething continues
      1) 7 months: upper central incisors
      2) 9 months: upper lateral incisors
   b. Motor development
      1) sits unsupported; goes from prone to sitting upright
      2) crawls; may go backwards initially
      3) pulls self to standing position
      4) develops finger-thumb opposition (pincer grasp)
      5) preference for dominant hand evident
   c. Sensory development: vision
      1) can fixate on small objects
      2) beginning to develop depth perception
5. *10–12 months*
   a. Weight: birth weight tripled
   b. Length: 50% increase over birth length
   c. Head and chest circumference equal
   d. Teething
      1) lower lateral incisors erupt
      2) average of eight deciduous teeth
   e. Motor development
      1) creeps with abdomen off floor
      2) walks with help or cruises
      3) may attempt to stand alone
      4) can sit down from upright position
      5) weans from bottle to cup
   f. Sensory development: vision
      1) able to discriminate simple geometric forms
      2) able to follow rapidly moving objects
      3) visual acuity 20/50 or better
      4) binocularity well established; if not, amblyopia may develop
B. Psychosocial tasks
   1. *Neonatal period*
      a. Cries to express displeasure
      b. Smiles indiscriminately
      c. Receives gratification through sucking
      d. Makes throaty sounds
   2. *1–4 months*
      a. Crying becomes differentiated at 1 month
         1) decreases during awake periods
         2) ceases when parent in view
      b. Vocalization distinct from crying at 1 month

   1) squeals to show pleasure at 3 months
   2) coos, babbles, laughs; vocalizes when smiling
   c. Socialization
      1) stares at parents' faces when talking at 1 month
      2) smiles socially at 2 months
      3) shows excitement when happy at 4 months
      4) demands attention, enjoys social interaction with people at 4 months
   3. *5–6 months*
      a. Vocalization: begins to imitate sounds
      b. Socialization: recognizes parents, stranger anxiety begins to develop; comfort habits begin
   4. *7–9 months*
      a. Vocalization: verbalizes all vowels and most consonants
      b. Socialization
         1) shows increased stranger anxiety and anxiety over separation from parent
         2) exhibits aggressiveness by biting at times
         3) understands the word "no"
   5. *10–12 months*
      a. Vocalization: imitates animal sounds, can say only 4–5 words but understands many more (ma, da)
      b. Socialization
         1) begins to explore surroundings
         2) plays games such as pat-a-cake, peek-a-boo
         3) shows emotions such as jealousy, affection, anger, fear (especially in new situations)
C. Cognitive tasks
   1. *Neonatal period: reflexive behavior only*
   2. *1–4 months*
      a. Recognizes familiar faces
      b. Is interested in surroundings
      c. Discovers own body parts
   3. *5–6 months*
      a. Begins to imitate
      b. Can find partially hidden objects
   4. *7–9 months*
      a. Begins to understand object permanence; searches for dropped objects
      b. Reacts to adult anger; cries when scolded
      c. Imitates simple acts and noises
      d. Responds to simple commands
   5. *10–12 months*
      a. Recognizes objects by name
      b. Looks at and follows pictures in book
      c. Shows more goal-directed actions
D. Nutrition
   1. *Birth to 6 months*

a. Breast milk is a complete and healthful diet; supplementation may include 0.25 mg fluoride, 400 IU vitamin D, and iron after 4 months.
b. Commercial iron-fortified formula is acceptable alternative; supplementation may include 0.25 mg fluoride if water supply is not fluoridated.
c. No solid foods before 5 months; too early exposure may lead to food allergies, and protrusion reflex will cause food to be pushed out of mouth.
d. Juices may be introduced at 5–6 months, diluted 1:1 and preferably given by cup.

2. *6–12 months*
a. Breast milk or formula continues to be primary source of nutrition.
b. Introduction of solid foods starts with cereal (usually rice cereal), which is continued until 18 months.
c. Introduction of other food is arbitrary; most common sequence is fruits, vegetables, meats.
   1) introduce one new food a week.
   2) decrease amount of formula to about 30 oz. as foods are added.
d. Iron supplementation can be stopped.
e. Finger foods such as cheese, meat, carrots can be started around 10 months.
f. Chopped table food or junior food can be introduced by 12 months.
g. Weaning from breast or bottle to cup should be gradual during second 6 months.

E. Safety
1. *Birth to 4 months*
a. Use car seat properly. Infants up to 9 kg (20 lb) should face rear.
b. Ensure crib mattress fits snugly; do not use a pillow in the crib.
c. Keep side rails of crib up.
d. Do not leave infant unattended on bed, couch, table.
e. Do not tie pacifier on string around infant's neck; remove bib before sleep.
f. Remove small objects that infant could choke on.
g. Check temperature of bath water and warmed formula or food.
h. Use cool mist vaporizer.
2. *5–7 months*
a. Restrain in high chair or infant seat.
b. Do not feed hard candy, nuts, food with pits.
c. Inspect toys for small removable parts.
d. Be sure paint on furniture does not contain lead.

e. Keep phone number of poison control center readily available.
3. *8–12 months*
a. Keep crib away from other furniture and windows.
b. Keep gates across stairways.
c. Keep safety plugs in electrical outlets.
d. Remove hanging electrical wires and tablecloths.
e. Use child protective caps and cabinet locks.
f. Place cleaning solutions and medications out of reach.
g. Do not let child use fork to self-feed.
h. Do not leave alone in bathtub.

F. Play (Solitary)
1. *Birth to 4 months*
a. Provide variety of brightly colored objects, different sizes and textures.
b. Hang mobiles within 8–10 inches of infant's face.
c. Expose to various environmental sounds; use rattles, musical toys.
2. *5–7 months*
a. Provide brightly colored toys to hold and squeeze.
b. Allow infant to splash in bath.
c. Provide crib mirror.
3. *8–12 months*
a. Provide toys with movable parts and noisemakers; stack toys, blocks; pots, pans, drums to bang on; walker and push-pull toys.
b. Plays games: hide and seek, pat-a-cake.

G. Fears
1. Separation from parents
a. Searches for parents with eyes.
b. Shows preference for parents.
c. Develops stranger anxiety around 6 months.
2. Pain
a. Reacts with generalized body movement and loud crying.
b. Can be distracted with talking, sucking opportunities.

Toddler (12 months to 3 years)

A. Physical tasks: this is a period of slow growth
1. Weight: gain of approximately 11 lb (5 kg) during this time; birth weight quadrupled by 2½ years
2. Height: grows 20.3 cm (8 inches); adult height about 2 times height at 2 years
3. Head circumference: 19½–20 inches (49–50 cm) by 2 years; anterior fontanel closes by 18 months
4. Pulse 110; respirations 26; blood pressure 99/64
5. Primary dentition (20 teeth) completed by 2½ years

6. Develops sphincter control necessary for bowel and bladder control
7. Mobility
   a. Walks alone by 18 months.
   b. Climbs stairs and furniture by 18 months.
   c. Runs fairly well by 2 years.
   d. Jumps from chair or step by 2½ years.
   e. Balances on one foot momentarily by 2½ years.
   f. Rides tricycle by 3 years.
B. Psychosocial tasks
   1. Increases independence; better able to tolerate separation from primary caregiver.
   2. Less likely to fear strangers.
   3. Able to help with dressing/undressing at 18 months; dresses self at 24 months.
   4. Has sustained attention span.
   5. May have temper tantrums during this period; should decrease by 2½ years.
   6. Vocabulary increases from about 10–20 words to over 900 words by 3 years.
   7. Has beginning awareness of ownership (my, mine) at 18 months; shows proper use of pronouns (I, me, you) by 3 years.
   8. Moves from hoarding and possessiveness at 18 months to sharing with peers by 3 years.
   9. Toilet training usually completed by 3 years.
      a. 18 months: bowel control
      b. 2–3 years: daytime bladder control
      c. 3–4 years: nighttime bladder control
C. Cognitive tasks
   1. Follows simple directions by 2 years.
   2. Begins to use short sentences at 18 months to 2 years.
   3. Can remember and repeat 3 numbers by 3 years.
   4. Knows own name by 12 months; refers to self, gives first name by 24 months; gives full name by 3 years.
   5. Able to identify geometric forms by 18 months.
   6. Achieves object permanence; is aware that objects exist even if not in view.
   7. Uses "magical" thinking; believes own feelings affect events (e.g., anger causes rain).
   8. Uses ritualistic behavior; repeats skills to master them and to decrease anxiety.
   9. May develop dependency on "transitional object" such as blanket or stuffed animal.
D. Nutrition
   1. Caloric requirement is approximately 100 calories/kg/day.
   2. Increased need for calcium, iron, and phosphorus.
   3. Needs 16–24 oz milk/day.
   4. Appetite decreases.
   5. Able to feed self.

6. Negativism may interfere with eating.
7. Initial dental examination at 3 years.
E. Safety
   1. Turn pot handles toward back of stove.
   2. Teach swimming and water safety; supervise near water.
   3. Supervise play outdoors.
   4. Avoid large chunks of meat, particularly hotdogs.
   5. Do not allow child to walk around with objects such as lollipops in mouth.
   6. Know when and how to use ipecac.
   7. Use car seats properly. Children greater than 9 kg (20 lb) should be in a forward-facing position in the back seat of the car.
F. Play
   1. Predominantly "parallel play" period.
   2. Imitation of adults often part of play.
   3. Begins imaginative and make-believe play.
   4. Provide toys appropriate for increased locomotive skills: push toys, rocking horse, riding toys or tricycles; swings and slide.
   5. Give toys to provide outlet for aggressive feelings: work bench, toy hammer and nails, drums, pots, pans.
   6. Provide toys to help develop fine motor skills, problem-solving abilities: puzzles, blocks; finger paints, crayons.
G. Fears: separation anxiety
   1. Learning to tolerate and master brief periods of separation is important developmental task.
   2. Increasing understanding of object permanence helps toddler overcome this fear.
   3. Potential patterns of response to separation
      a. Protest: screams and cries when mother leaves; attempts to call her back.
      b. Despair: whimpers, clutches transitional object, curls up in bed, decreased activity, rocking.
      c. Denial: resumes normal activity but does not form psychosocial relationships; when mother returns, child ignores her.
   4. Bedtime may represent desertion.

Preschooler (3 to 5 years)

A. Physical tasks
   1. Slower growth rate continues
      a. Weight: increases 4–6 lb (1.8–2.7 kg) a year
      b. Height: increases 2½ inches (5–6.25 cm) a year
      c. Birth length doubled by 4 years
   2. Vital signs decrease slightly
      a. Pulse 90–100
      b. Respirations 24–25/minute

    c. Blood pressure: systolic 85–100 mm Hg: diastolic 60–70 mm Hg

3. Permanent teeth may appear late in preschool period; first permanent teeth are molars, behind last temporary teeth.

4. Gross motor development
    a. Walks up stairs using alternate feet by 3 years.
    b. Walks down stairs using alternate feet by 4 years.
    c. Rides tricycle by 3 years.
    d. Stands on 1 foot by 3 years.
    e. Hops on 1 foot by 4 years.
    f. Skips and hops on alternate feet by 5 years.
    g. Balances on 1 foot with eyes closed by 5 years.
    h. Throws and catches ball by 5 years.
    i. Jumps off 1 step by 3 years.
    j. Jumps rope by 5 years.

5. Fine motor development
    a. Hand dominance is established by 5 years.
    b. Builds a tower of blocks by 3 years.
    c. Ties shoes by 5 years.
    d. Ability to draw changes over this time
        1) copies circles, may add facial features by 3 years.
        2) copies a square, traces a diamond by 4 years.
        3) copies a diamond and triangle, prints letters and numbers by 5 years.
    e. Handles scissors well by 5 years.

B. Psychosocial tasks
1. Becomes independent
    a. Feeds self completely.
    b. Dresses self.
    c. Takes increased responsibility for actions.
2. Aggressiveness and impatience peak at 4 years then abate; by 5 years child is eager to please and manners become more evident.
3. Gender-specific behavior is evident by 5 years.
4. Egocentricity changes to awareness of others; rules become important; understands sharing.

C. Cognitive development
1. Focuses on one idea at a time; cannot look at entire perspective.
2. Awareness of racial and sexual differences begins.
    a. Prejudice may develop based on values of parents.
    b. Manifests sexual curiosity.
    c. Sexual education begins.
    d. Beginning body awareness.
3. Has beginning concept of causality.
4. Understanding of time develops during this period.
    a. Learns sequence of daily events.
    b. Is able to understand meaning of some time-oriented words (day of week, month, etc.) by 5 years.
5. Has 2000-word vocabulary by 5 years.
6. Can name 4 or more colors by 5 years.
7. Is very inquisitive.

D. Nutrition
1. Caloric requirement is approximately 90 calories/kg/day.
2. May demonstrate strong taste preferences.
3. More likely to taste new foods if child can assist in the preparation.

E. Safety
1. Safety issues similar to toddler
2. Education of children concerning potential dangers important during this period
3. Car safety: lap belt may be used when child is either 40 lb, 40 inches, or 4 years old.

F. Play
1. Predominantly "associative play" period.
2. Enjoys imitative and dramatic play.
    a. Imitates same-sex role functions in play.
    b. Enjoys dressing up, dollhouses, trucks, cars, telephones, doctor and nurse kits.
3. Provide toys to help develop gross motor skills: tricycles, wagons, outdoor gym; sandbox, wading pool.
4. Provide toys to encourage fine motor skills, self-expression, and cognitive development: construction sets, blocks, carpentry tools; flash cards, illustrated books, puzzles; paints, crayons, clay, simple sewing sets.
5. Television, when supervised, can provide a quiet activity; some programs have educational content.
6. Imaginary playmates common during this period.
    a. More prevalent in bright children
    b. Help child deal with loneliness and fears
    c. Abandoned by school age

G. Fears
1. Greatest number of imagined and real fears of childhood during this period.
2. Fears concerning body integrity are common.
    a. Child is able to imagine an event without experiencing it.
    b. Observing injuries or pain in others can precipitate fear.
    c. Magical and animistic thinking allows children to develop many illogical fears (fear of inanimate objects, the dark, ghosts).
3. Exposing child to feared object in a safe situation may provide a degree of conditioning; child should progress at own rate.

School-age (6 to 12 years)

A. Physical tasks
 1. Slow growth continues.
  a. Height: 2 inches (5 cm) per year
  b. Weight: doubles over this period
  c. At age 9, both sexes same size; age 12, girls bigger than boys
 2. Dentition
  a. Loses first primary teeth at about 6 years.
  b. By 12 years, has all permanent teeth except final molars.
 3. Bone growth faster than muscle and ligament development; very limber but susceptible to bone fractures during this time.
 4. Vision is completely mature; hand-eye coordination develops completely.
 5. Gross motor skills: predominantly involving large muscles; children are very energetic, develop greater strength, coordination, and stamina.
 6. Develops smoothness and speed in fine motor control.
B. Psychosocial tasks
 1. School occupies half of waking hours; has cognitive and social impact.
  a. Readiness includes emotional (attention span), physical (hearing and vision), and intellectual components.
  b. Teacher may be parent substitute, causing parents to lose some authority.
 2. Morality develops
  a. Before age 9 moral realism predominates: strict superego, rule dominance; things are black or white, right or wrong.
  b. After age 9 autonomous morality develops: recognizes differing points of view, sees "gray" areas.
 3. Peer relationships
  a. Child makes first real friends during this period.
  b. Is able to understand concepts of cooperation and compromise (assist in acquiring attitudes and values); learns fair play vs competition.
  c. Help child develop self-concept.
  d. Provide feeling of belonging.
 4. Enjoys family activities.
 5. Has some ability to evaluate own strengths and weaknesses.
 6. Has increased self-direction.
 7. Is aware of own body; compares self to others; modesty develops.
C. Cognitive development
 1. Period of industry
  a. Is interested in exploration and adventure.
  b. Likes to accomplish or produce.
  c. Develops confidence.
 2. Concept of time and space develops.
  a. Understands causality.
  b. Masters concept of conservation: permanence of mass and volume; concept of reversibility.
  c. Develops classification skills: understands relational terms; may collect things.
  d. Masters arithmetic and reading.
D. Nutrition
 1. Caloric needs diminish in relation to body size: 85 kcal/kg.
 2. "Junk" food may become a problem; excess sugar, starches, fat.
 3. Obesity is a risk in this age group.
 4. Nutrition education should be integrated into school program.
E. Safety
 1. Incidence of accidents is decreased when compared with younger children.
 2. Motor vehicle accidents most common cause of severe injury and death.
 3. Other common activities associated with injuries include sports (skateboarding, rollerskating, etc.).
 4. Education and supervision are key elements in prevention.
  a. Proper use of equipment
  b. Risk-taking behavior
F. Play
 1. Rules and ritual dominate play; individuality not tolerated by peers; knowing rules provides sense of belonging; "cooperative play."
 2. Team play: games or sports
  a. Help learn value of individual skills and team accomplishments.
  b. Help learn nature of competition.
 3. Quiet games and activities: board games, collections, books, television, painting
 4. Athletic activities: swimming, hiking, bicycling, skating
G. Fears: more realistic fears than younger children; include death, disease or bodily injury, punishment; school phobia may develop, resulting in psychosomatic illness.

Adolescent (12 to 19 years)

A. Physical tasks
 1. Fast period of growth
 2. Vital signs approach adult norms
 3. Puberty
  a. Follows same pattern for all races and cultures.
  b. Is related to hormonal changes.
  c. Results in growth spurt, change in body structure, development of secondary sex characteristics, and reproductive maturity.

d. Girls: height increases approximately 3 inches/year; slows at menarche; stops around age 16.
e. Boys: growth spurt starts around age 13; height increases 4 inches/year; slows in late teens.
f. Boys double weight between 12 and 18, related to increased muscle mass.
g. Body shape changes
   1) boys become leaner with broader chest.
   2) girls have fat deposited in thighs, hips, and breasts; pelvis broadens.
h. Apocrine glands cause increased body odor.
i. Increased production of sebum and plugging of sebaceous ducts causes acne (page 432).

4. Sexual development: girls
   a. Menarche
      1) onset about 2 years after first of pubescent changes
      2) average age 12½ years
      3) first 1–2 years: menses irregular, infertile
   b. Menstrual cycle: controlled by complex interaction of hormones (see page 449).
   c. Development of secondary sex characteristics and sexual functioning under hormonal control (see Table 4.22).
   d. Breast development is first sign of puberty.
      1) bud stage: areola around nipple is protuberant.
      2) breast development is complete around the time of first menses.

5. Sexual development: boys
   a. Development of secondary sex characteristics, sex organs and function under hormonal control (see Table 4.22).
   b. Enlargement of testes is first sign of sexual maturation; occurs at approximately age 13, about 1 year before growth spurt.
   c. Scrotum and penis increase in size until age 18.
   d. Reaches reproductive maturity about age 17, with viable sperm.
   e. Nocturnal emission: a physiologic reflex to ejaculate buildup of semen; natural and normal; occurs during sleep (child should not be made to feel guilty; needs to understand that this is not enuresis).
   f. Masturbation increases (also a normal way to release semen).
   g. Pubic hair continues to grow and spread until mid 20s.
   h. Facial hair; appears first on upper lip.
   i. Voice changes due to growth of laryngeal cartilage.
   j. Gynecomastia: slight hypertrophy of breasts due to estrogen production; will pass within months but causes embarrassment.

B. Psychosocial tasks
   1. Early adolescence: ages 12–14 years
      a. Starts with puberty.
      b. Physical body changes result in an altered self-concept.
      c. Tends to compare own body to others.
      d. Early and late developers have anxiety regarding fear of rejection.
      e. Fantasy life, daydreams, crushes are all normal, help in role play of varying social situations.
      f. Is prone to mood swings.
      g. Needs limits and consistent discipline.
   2. Middle adolescence: ages 15–16 years
      a. Is separate from parents (except financially).
      b. Can identify own values.
      c. Can define self (self-concept, strengths and weaknesses).
      d. Partakes in peer group; conforms to values/fads.
      e. Has increased heterosexual interest; communicates with opposite sex; may form "love" relationship.
      f. Sex education continues.
   3. Late adolescence: ages 17–19 years
      a. Achieves greater independence.
      b. Chooses a vocation.
      c. Participates in society.
      d. Finds an identity.
      e. Finds a mate.
      f. Develops own morality.
      g. Completes physical and emotional maturity.

C. Cognitive development
   1. Develops abstract thinking abilities.
   2. Is often unrealistic.
   3. Is capable of scientific reasoning and formal logic.
   4. Enjoys intellectual abilities.
   5. Is able to view problems comprehensively.

D. Nutrition
   1. Nutritional requirements peak during years of maximum growth: age 10–12 in girls, 2 years later in boys
   2. Appetite increases.
   3. Inadequate diet can retard growth and delay sexual maturation.
   4. Food intake needs to be balanced with energy expenditure.
   5. Increased needs include calcium for skeletal growth; iron for increased muscle mass and blood cell development; zinc for development of skeletal and muscle tissue and sexual maturation.

E. Safety
   1. Accidents are leading cause of death: motor vehicle accidents, sports injuries, firearms accidents.
   2. Safety measures include education about proper use of equipment and caution concerning risk taking.
   3. Drug and alcohol use may be a serious problem during this period.
   4. Adolescent characteristics of poor impulse control and recklessness make prevention complex.
F. Activities: group activities predominate (sports are important); activities involving opposite sex by middle adolescence.
G. Fears
   1. Threats to body image: acne, obesity
   2. Injury or death
   3. The unknown

ANALYSIS

Nursing diagnoses for problems of growth and development may include
A. Altered thought processes
B. Knowledge deficit (specify)
C. Disturbance in self-esteem
D. Social isolation
E. High risk for violence
F. Altered family process
G. Ineffective family coping
H. Altered health maintenance
I. Altered parenting

PLANNING AND IMPLEMENTATION

Goals

A. Child will achieve appropriate developmental level for age.
B. Family/child will adapt successfully to developmental changes.
C. Family/child will cope successfully with crises of illness and hospitalization.
D. Family/child will cope successfully with issues related to death and dying.

Interventions for the Ill or Hospitalized Child

Communicating with Children

A. Speak in quiet, pleasant tones.
B. Bend down to meet child on own level.
C. Use words appropriate to age/communication ability; do not use cliches.
D. Do not explain more than is necessary.

E. Always explain what you are going to do and give the reason for it.
F. Be honest; do not lie about whether something will hurt.
G. Do not make a promise you know you cannot keep.
H. Observe nonverbal behavior for clues to level of understanding.
I. Do not threaten; and when necessary, punish the act, not the child ("I like you, but not what you did.").
J. Never shame a child by using terms like baby or sissy.
K. Allow child to show feelings (hurt and anger); provide therapeutic play, pounding or throwing toys; allow child to cry; encourage creative writing.
L. Provide time to talk; encourage a trusting environment where the child can talk without embarrassment and confide without fear.
M. Provide support to child and parents/family.
N. Teach parents to anticipate next stage of development.
O. If teaching with a child is interrupted, start over from the beginning.
P. Promote independence; allow the child to perform as many self-care activities as possible.
Q. Do not compare child's progress to that of anyone else.
R. Provide praise at every opportunity.
S. Instead of asking what something is, ask child to give it a name or tell you about it.
T. Allow choices where possible, but do not use yes/no questions unless you can accept a "no" answer ("It is time for your medication now; do you want it with milk or juice?" versus "Do you want your medication now?").
U. Involve parents in child's care.
V. Keep routines as much like home as possible (on admission, ask parents about routines such as toileting, eating, sleeping, and names for bowel movements and urination).
W. Allow parents time and opportunities to ask questions and express themselves.
X. If parents cannot stay with child, encourage them to bring in a favorite toy, pictures of family members, or to make a tape to be played for the child.

Play

A. Play is a way to solve problems, become enculturated, express creativity, decrease stress in the environment, prepare for different situations, sublimate sensations, enhance fine and gross motor development as well as social development.
B. Make play appropriate for mental age and physical/disease state (e.g., appropriate for oxygen tents, isolation, hearing or vision defects).
C. Use multisensory stimulation.

D. Provide toys safe for mental age (no points, sharp edges, small parts, loud noises, propelled objects).
E. Offer play specific to age group.
 1. Toddler: enjoys repetition; solitary play, parallel play.
 2. Preschooler: likes to role play and make believe; associative play.
 3. School-age: likes group, organized activities (to enhance sharing); cooperative play, group goals with interaction.

Preparation for Procedures

A. Allow child to play with equipment to be used.
B. Demonstrate procedure first on a doll.
C. Teach child skills that will be needed after the procedure and provide time to practice (crutches, blow bottles).
D. Show the child pictures of staff garb, special treatment room, special machines to be used, etc., before the procedure.
E. Describe sensations the child may experience during or after the procedure.
F. Listen carefully to child to detect misconceptions or fantasies.
G. With younger children, the preparatory information should be simple and as close to the time of the procedure as possible.
H. Parents can often be helpful in preparing child for procedures, but need to be prepared as well.
 1. May need different explanation, away from child.
 2. Should have opportunity to ask questions about what will happen to child.
I. School-age children and adolescents may not wish parents to be present during procedure.
 1. Child's desires should be confirmed.
 2. Parents need to be assured that this is not rejection by child.
J. Inadequate preparation results in heightened anxiety that may result in regressive behavior, uncooperativeness, or acting out.

EVALUATION

A. Child maintains normal developmental level during hospitalization.
B. Parents participate in care of child during hospitalization.

GROWTH AND DEVELOPMENT ISSUES

Health Promotion

A. Immunization schedule (see Table 5.1). (Also see page 106).

B. Types of immunity (see page 131).
C. Considerations concerning immunization schedule
 1. If the immunization schedule is interrupted it is not necessary to reinstitute the entire series. Immunization should occur on the next visit as if the usual interval has elapsed
 2. If immunization status is unknown, children should be considered susceptible and appropriate immunizations administered
 3. For children not immunized during the first year of life and who are less than 7 years old the same immunizations are given but following different time schedule
 4. For children 7 years old and older who are not immunized, Td rather than DTP or DTaP is administered
D. Contraindications for immunization
 1. Severe allergic reaction to a vaccine contraindicates further doses of that vaccine.
 2. Anaphylactic reaction to a vaccine additive contraindicates the use of vaccines containing that substance (e.g., eggs, neomycin, streptomycin).
 3. Immunocompromised persons should not receive live vaccines.
E. Tuberculin testing
 1. The tuberculin skin test is the only practical tool for diagnosing tuberculosis infection.
 2. Tuberculin testing may be done at the same visit at which an immunization is being given.
 3. Routine testing is no longer recommended. Testing is always indicated for individuals with known contact with a person with tuberculosis disease.
 4. Positive reaction signifies infection with *Mycobacterium tuberculosis*.
 5. Positive reaction indicates need for further evaluation.
F. Common childhood communicable diseases (see Table 5.2).

Challenges of Parenting

A. Failure to Thrive (FTT)
 1. General information
  a. A condition in which a child fails to gain weight and is persistently less than the 5th percentile on growth charts.
  b. When related to nonorganic cause, it is usually due to a disrupted maternal-child relationship.
  c. Other pathology (especially absorption problems and hormonal dysfunction) must be ruled out before a disorder can be diagnosed as FTT.

TABLE 5.1 Recommended Schedule for Immunizations, 1999*

Age	Immunization	Comment
Birth–2 months	Hep B-1	Hepatitis B virus vaccine
1–4 months	Hep B-2	
2, 4, and 6 months	DTaP or DPT	Diphtheria and tetanus toxoids and acellular pertussis vaccine (DTaP) is the preferred vaccine. Whole-cell DTP is an acceptable alternative to DTaP.
	Hib	*Haemophilus influenzae* type b conjugate vaccine (three vaccines are licensed for use; check administration guidelines for each prior to use).
2, 4, and 6 months	Rotavirus	Not mandatory; first dose not given before 6 weeks. Rv vaccine series must be started before 7 months and completed by first birthday
2 and 4 months	Polio	Two poliovirus vaccines are licensed for use; inactivated poliovirus vaccine (IPV) and oral poliovirus vaccine (OPV). Check administration guidelines prior to use).
6–18 months	Hep B-3	
	Polio	
12–15 months	Hib	
	MMR	Measles-mumps-rubella
12–18 months	Varicella	Chicken pox
15–18 months	DTaP or DTP	
4 to 6 years	DTaP or DTP	
	Polio	
	MMR	
11–12 years**	Hep B	
	MMR	
	Varicella	Susceptible children aged greater or equal to 13 years should receive two doses of varicella vaccine at least one month apart.
11–16 years	Td	Diphtheria and tetanus toxoids (recommended every 10 years)

*recommendations are constantly changing
**vaccines to be assessed and administered if necessary
Courtesy of American Academy of Pediatrics, Committee on Infectious Disease, January 1999

d. Growth and developmental delay usually improve with appropriate stimulation.
2. Assessment findings
  a. Sleep disturbances; rumination (voluntary regurgitation and reswallowing)
  b. History of parental isolation and social crisis with inadequate support systems
  c. Physical exam reveals delayed growth and development (decreased vocalization, low interest in environment) and characteristic postures (child is stiff or floppy, resists cuddling)
  d. Disturbed maternal-infant interaction may be demonstrated in feeding techniques, amount of stimulation provided by mother, ability of mother to respond to infant's cues
3. Nursing interventions
  a. Provide consistent care.
  b. Teach parents positive feeding techniques.
    1) Provide quiet environment.
    2) Follow child's rhythm of feeding.
    3) Maintain face-to-face posture with child.

    4) Talk to child encouragingly during feeding.
  c. Involve parents in care.
    1) Provide supportive environment.
    2) Give positive feedback.
    3) Demonstrate and reinforce responding to child's cues.
  d. Refer to appropriate community agencies.
B. Child abuse
1. General information
  a. Physical, emotional, or sexual abuse of children: may result from intentional and nonaccidental actions; or may be from intentional and nonaccidental acts of omission (neglect).
  b. In sexual abuse, 80% of children know their abuser.
  c. Problem usually related to parents' limited capacity to cope with, provide for, or relate to a child and/or to each other.
  d. Adults who abuse were often themselves victims of child abuse; although abuser may care about child, pattern of response to frustration and discipline is to be abusive.
  e. Occurs in all socioeconomic groups.

TABLE 5.2 Communicable Childhood Diseases

Disease	Characteristics	Immunization
Diphtheria	A respiratory disease caused by bacteria. Bacteria forms a pseudomembrane across the trachea causing respiratory distress; also produces an exotoxin that causes myocarditis and neurologic problems.	Included in DTP* and DTaP up to 6 years, then in Td,* repeated every 10 years throughout life.
Pertussis (whooping cough)	Respiratory disease caused by bacteria; life threatening in young children. Severe paroxysmal cough results in severe respiratory distress; complications include seizures, pneumonia, encephalopathy and death.	Included in DTP* and DTaP; not given after 6 years because of risk from associated side effects. Do not give pertussis vaccine if child has active neurologic disorder.
Tetanus (lockjaw)	Neurologic disorder caused by bacterial exotoxin affects motor neurons, causing rigidity and spastic muscles; first symptom is stiffness of the jaw (trismus) No immunity is conferred after having the disease; associated mortality 25%–50%.	Included in DTP* and DTaP up to 6 years; included in Td* every 10 years throughout life. May be given with a puncture wound if the wound is dirty and no immunization has been given in 5 years, or if wound is clean but more than 10 years have elapsed since previous immunization.
Measles (rubeola)	Viral infection producing harsh cough, maculopapular rash, photophobia, and Koplik spots; complications may include pneumonia, bacterial superinfections and encephalitis. Incubation period is 8 to 12 days. Care includes keeping room darkened and providing antipruritic measures.	Maternal antibodies last for at least a year, then included in MMR* given at 15 months. Do not give to pregnant women or immunocompromised persons.
German measles (rubella)	Viral infection causing lymphadenopathy and pink maculopapular rash; very mild disease, no specific care needed; complications may include arthralgia or arthritis, especially if occurring in young adults. Greatest danger is if pregnant woman contracts the disease; causes serious congenital anomalies.	Included in MMR*
Mumps (parotitis)	Viral infection causing swelling of the salivary glands with painful swallowing. Ice collar may help relieve discomfort. Complications include orchitis (usually unilateral) if disease occurs after puberty, aseptic meningitis, encephalitis.	Included in MMR*
Poliomyelitis (polio)	Viral infection, 95% of infected patients have no symptoms. Virus multiplies in the GI tract and enters the bloodstream to affect the CNS, resulting in paralysis in less than 2% of infected.	OPU*
Chicken pox (varicella)	Most common communicable childhood disease, caused by the varicella zoster virus. Causes rash that starts on the trunk and spreads. Rash starts as vesicles, which then erupt and crust over. Highly contagious from 2 days prior to rash to 6 days after rash erupts; incubation period 21 days. Once lesions have crusted or scabbed over they are no longer contagious. Care is directed at comfort measures.	Short-term protection from maternal antibodies. Varicella vaccine.

*For immunization schedule and additional information about vaccine see Table 5.1.

    f. Only 10% of abusers have serious psychologic disturbances, but most have low self-esteem, little confidence, low tolerance for frustration.

    g. Abuse is most common among toddlers as they exercise autonomy and parents may sense loss of power.

  2. Assessment findings

    a. History may be indicative of child abuse.

      1) No history to explain injury

      2) Delay in seeking medical attention

      3) History changes with repetition

      4) Injury not consistent with history

    b. Skin injuries (bruises, lacerations, burns) are most common; may show outline of instrument used and may be in varying stages of healing.

    c. Musculoskeletal injuries, fractures (especially chip or spiral fractures), sprains, dislocations are also common; x-rays may show multiple old fractures

    d. Signs of central nervous system (CNS) injuries include subdural hematoma, retinal hemorrhage.

e. Abdominal injuries may include lacerated liver, ruptured spleen.
f. Observation of parents and child may reveal interactional problems.
   1) Does parent respond to child's cues?
   2) Does parent comfort child?
   3) Does child respond to parent with fear?
3. Nursing interventions
   a. In emergency room: tend to physical needs of child first; determination of existence of abuse must wait until child's condition is stable.
   b. Report suspected child abuse to appropriate agency.
   c. Provide a role model for parents in terms of communication, stimulation, feeding, and daily care of child.
   d. Encourage parents to be involved in child's care.
   e. Encourage parents to express feelings concerning abuse, hospitalization, and home situation.
      1) Feelings of fear and guilt should be acknowledged.
      2) Provide reassurance.
   f. Provide family education concerning child care, especially safety and nutrition needs, discipline, and age-appropriate stimulation
   g. Initiate referrals for long-term follow-up (community agencies, pediatric and mental health clinics, self-help groups).
C. Learning disabilities
1. General information
   a. A heterogeneous group of disorders manifested by significant difficulties in acquisition and use of listening, speaking, writing, reasoning, or math skills
   b. Presumed to be due to CNS dysfunction
   c. Children of average or above-average IQ
   d. Affects all aspects of learning, not just academics
   e. Boys affected 6 times more often than girls
   f. Categories include
      1) Receptive/sensory: perceptual problem (dyslexia, visual misperception)
      2) Integrative: difficulty processing information (analysis, organization, sequencing, abstract thought)
      3) Expressive: motor dysfunction (aphasia, writing or drawing difficulties, difficulty in sports or games)
      4) Diffuse: combination of above
2. Assessment findings
   a. Poor attention span
   b. Poor grades, normal IQ

c. Low general information scores on standardized IQ tests
d. Decreased participation in extracurricular activities or hobbies
e. Low self-esteem due to multiple failures
f. Diagnostic tests: specific testing to confirm diagnosis and determine type of defect
3. Medical management: psychostimulants may be prescribed to reduce hyperactivity and frustration and to increase attention span and self-control; side effects include anorexia.
4. Nursing interventions
   a. Environmental manipulation for behavior management
      1) Limit external stimuli.
      2) Maintain predictable routines.
      3) Enforce limits on behavior.
   b. Teaching strategies tailored for child's specific defects
      1) Repeat directions often.
      2) Elicit feedback from child.
      3) Give time to ask questions.
      4) Keep teaching sessions short.
      5) Do not give nonessential information.
D. Sudden infant death syndrome (SIDS)
1. General information
   a. Sudden death of any young child that is unexpected by history and in which thorough postmortem examination fails to demonstrate adequate cause of death
   b. Cannot be predicted; cannot be prevented (unexpected and unexplained)
   c. Peak age: 3 months; 90% by 6 months
   d. Usually occurs during sleep; there is no struggle and death is silent
   e. Diagnosis made at autopsy
   f. Although cause of death is not known, chronic hypoxemia related to periodic apnea has been suggested; suffocation and DTP reactions are *not* causes of SIDS
2. Assessment findings
   a. Incidence higher in preterm infants, twins or triplets, low-birth-weight infants
   b. Infant with abnormalities in respiration, feeding, or other neurologic symptoms at higher risk
3. Nursing interventions
   a. Nursing care is directed at supporting parents/family; parents usually arrive at emergency department.
   b. Provide a room for the family to be alone if possible, stay with them; prepare them for how infant will look and feel (baby will be bruised and blanched due to pooling of blood until death was discovered; also will be cold).
   c. Let parents say good-bye to baby (hold, rock).

d. Reinforce that death was not their fault.
e. Provide appropriate support referrals: clergy, notification of significant others, local SIDS program.
f. Explain how parents can receive autopsy results.
g. Notify family physician or pediatrician.

DEATH AND DYING

Overview

Parental Response to Death

A. Major life stress event
B. Initially parents experience grief in response to potential loss of child
   1. Acknowledgement of terminal disease is a struggle between hope and despair with resultant awareness of inevitable death.
   2. Parents will be at different stages of grief at different times and constantly changing.
C. Parental response is related to age of child, cause of death, available social support, and degree of uncertainty; response might include denial, shock, disbelief, guilt.
D. Parents often confronted with major decisions such as home care versus hospital care, use of investigational drugs, and continuation of life supports.
E. May have long-term disruptive effects on family system
   1. Stress may result in divorce.
   2. May contribute to behavioral problems or psychosomatic symptoms in siblings.
F. Bereaved parents experience intense grief of long duration.

Child's Response to Death

A. Child's concept of death depends on mental age.
   1. Infants and toddlers
     a. Live only in present.
     b. Are concerned only with separation from mother and being alone and abandoned.
     c. Can sense sadness in others and may feel guilty (due to magical thinking).
     d. Do not understand life without themselves.
     e. Can sense they are getting weaker.
     f. Healthy toddlers may insist on seeing a significant other long after that person's death.
   2. Preschoolers
     a. See death as temporary; a type of sleep or separation.
     b. See life as concrete; they know the word "dead" but do not understand the finality.
     c. Fear separation from parents; want to know who will take care of them when they are dead.
     d. Dying children may regress in their behavior.
   3. School-age
     a. Have a concept of time, causality, and irreversibility (but still question it).
     b. Fear pain, mutilation, and abandonment.
     c. Will ask directly if they are dying.
     d. See death as a period of immobility.
     e. Interested in the death ceremony; may make requests for own ceremony.
     f. Feel death is punishment.
     g. May personify death (bogey man, angel of death).
     h. May know they are going to die but feel comforted by having parents and loved ones with them.
   4. Adolescents
     a. Are thinking about the future and knowing they will not participate.
     b. May express anger at impending death.
     c. May find it difficult to talk about death.
     d. Have an accurate understanding of death.
     e. May wish to write something for friends and family, make things to leave, or make a tape.
     f. May wish to plan own funeral.

Nursing Implications

Communicating with Dying Child

A. Use the child's own language.
B. Do not use euphemisms.
C. Do not expect an immediate response.
D. Never give up hope.

Care Guidelines at Impending Death

A. Do not leave child alone.
B. Do not whisper in the room (increases fears).
C. Know that touching child is important.
D. Let the child and family talk and cry.
E. Continue to read favorite stories to child or play favorite music.
F. Let parents participate in care as far as they are emotionally capable.
G. Be aware of the needs of siblings who are in the room with the family.

Sample Questions

1. The nurse has assessed four children of varying ages; which one requires further evaluation?
   1. A 7-month-old who is afraid of strangers.

2. A 4-year-old who talks to an imaginary playmate.
3. A 9-year-old with enuresis.
4. A 16-year-old male who had nocturnal emissions.

2. The nurse is caring for a 5-year-old child who has leukemia and is now out of remission and not expected to survive. The child says to his mother, "Will you take care of me when I am dead the way you do now?" The child's mother asks the nurse how to answer her child. The nurse's response should be based on which of the following understandings of the child's behavior?
   1. The child is denying that he has a terminal illness.
   2. The child may be hallucinating.
   3. Children of this age do not understand the finality of death.
   4. Most 5-year-old children have a great fear of mutilation.

3. The nurse is talking with the mother of a one-year-old child in well-baby clinic. Which statement the mother makes indicates a need for more instruction in keeping the child safe?
   1. "I have some syrup of ipecac at home in case my child ever needs it."
   2. "I put all the medicines on the highest shelf in the kitchen."
   3. "We have moved all the valuable vases and figurines out of the family room."
   4. "My husband put the gates up at the top and bottom of the stairs."

4. Suzy Walker was born 6 weeks prematurely. She is now 2 months old and her mother brings her to the clinic for her checkup. Administration of DTaP will depend on
   1. the presence of sufficient muscle mass.
   2. whether the vaccines are live or inactive.
   3. the Denver Developmental Screening results.
   4. calculating her age by subtracting six weeks from the due date.

5. Fifteen-month-old Anne is brought in for her regular checkup. All of her immunizations are given as recommended. Anne's mother asks the nurse what immunizations her daughter will receive today. The nurse's best response is that she is due for her
   1. third DTaP.
   2. MMR vaccine.
   3. first Hib immunization.
   4. first OPV immunization.

6. The presence of what condition would necessitate a change in the standard immunization schedule for a child?
   1. Allergy to eggs.
   2. Immunosuppression.
   3. Congenital defects.
   4. Mental retardation.

7. Jimmy Wilkins, 2 years old, is brought to the pediatric clinic with an upper respiratory infection. After assessing Jimmy, the nurse informs the physician that she suspects this child may be a victim of child abuse. Physical signs that almost always indicate child abuse are
   1. diaper rash.
   2. bruises on the lower legs.
   3. asymmetrical burns on the legs.
   4. welts or bruises in various stages of healing.

8. Which parent-child interaction does NOT warrant further assessment when child abuse is suspected? The parent who
   1. appears tired and disheveled.
   2. is hypercritical of the child.
   3. pushes the frightened child away.
   4. expresses far more concern than the situation warrants.

9. When child abuse is suspected, the nurse knows that abusive burns will
   1. have a number of scars.
   2. have identifiable shapes.
   3. display an erratic pattern.
   4. be on one side of the body.

Answers and Rationales

1. The correct answer is 3. The child may have a physiologic or psychologic problem; all other answers indicate age-appropriate situations.

2. The correct answer is 3. Preschool children do not understand the finality of death. They often view it as a long sleep. It is common for preschoolers to ask who will take care of them when they die. Preschool children may know the word *dead* but do not really comprehend what it means. The child is not in denial or hallucinating; he is behaving normally for his age. Fear of mutilation is more common among school-age children. The statement as given in the question does not describe mutilation.

3. The correct answer is 2. At one year of age babies are or soon will be climbing on everything. Putting medicines on the highest shelf is not sufficient. All medicines should be put in a locked cabinet. Syrup of ipecac should be in every home in case of accidental poisoning. The poison control center may recommend a dose of syrup of ipecac. The family is wise to "baby proof" the house rather than always saying "no" to the child. Moving breakable valuables removes temptation from the child. Putting gates up at the stairs will help to prevent falls.

4. The correct answer is 1. DTaP is given intramuscularly, therefore administration is dependent on the presence of sufficient muscle mass. The Denver Developmental Screening is an assessment tool. Subtracting six weeks from the due date because of prematurity is done for developmental

assessment, not for immunizations. Administration of either live or inactive vaccines is not contraindicated in prematurity.

5. The correct answer is 2. Current recommendations call for measles, mumps, and rubella combined vaccine (MMR) to be given at 15 months. DTaP is given at 2, 4, and 6 months, followed by a booster 6 to 12 months after the third dose. OPV is given at 2 and 4 months followed by boosters between 12 and 24 months and between 4 and 6 years of age. Hib is given at 2, 4, and 6 months.

6. The correct answer is 2. Immunosuppressed clients may need alteration in immunization protection as they may be overwhelmed by live viruses. Mental retardation and congenital defects would not interfere with the immunization schedule unless neurologic defects were present. MMR vaccine does contain eggs but a child allergic to eggs would receive the vaccine on schedule in very small doses at 20-minute intervals with adrenalin available should anaphylaxis occur.

7. The correct answer is 4. Injuries at various stages of healing are symptomatic of child abuse. Bruises on the lower legs are common occurrences in a healthy active child. Diaper rash may be seen in a well-cared-for child. Burns characteristic of child abuse usually have shapes resembling the item used to burn the child, such as cigarette butts.

8. The correct answer is 1. Being tired and disheveled gives no clue to parent-child interaction. The parent who pushes the frightened child away, who is hypercritical of the child, and who expresses far more concern than the situation warrants exhibits extremes in behavior that are seen frequently in parents who physically abuse their children.

9. The correct answer is 2. Burns typical of child abuse have symmetrical shapes and resemble the shape of the item used to burn the child. When a child is burned accidentally, the burns form an erratic pattern and are usually irregular or asymmetrical. A number of scars is inconclusive evidence of child abuse. When burning is used as a means of physically abusing the child, the burns are usually bilateral.

Multisystem Stressors

GENETIC DISORDERS

A. Genes are functional units of heredity, capable of replication, mutation, and expression.
B. Teratology is the branch of embryology that deals with the study of abnormal development and congenital malformations.
   1. *Congenital disorders:* present at birth, although may not be noticeable until later; may be caused by genetic factors, nongenetic factors, or a combination.
   2. *Genetic disorders:* caused by a single aberrant gene or a deviation in chromosome structure or number.
C. In humans there are normally 46 chromosomes (23 pairs) that contain the genes.
   1. *Genotype:* the gene constitution of an individual
   2. *Phenotype:* the outward visible physical appearance/expression of a person's genes (color, size, allergies)
   3. *Karyotype:* the number and pattern of chromosomes in a cell
   4. *Allele:* one or two or more forms of a gene that controls expression of specific characteristic (e.g., genes for eye color)

   a. *Mendel's law:* for each hereditary property we receive 2 genes, 1 from each parent; 1 is dominant and expressed; 1 is recessive and not expressed.
   b. *Homozygous:* alleles for characteristic are identical; both dominant (DD) or both recessive (dd).
   c. *Heterozygous:* alleles are different (Dd).
D. Normal cell division
   1. *Meiosis:* cell division that produces gametes, each with a haploid set of chromosomes (one-half the number of the parent cell); this is reductional division, occurs in the ova and sperm.
   2. *Mitosis:* cell division that produces two cells (daughter cells), each with a full complement of chromosomes, identical to the composition of the parent cell.

Principles of Inheritance

Traits that are controlled by genes located on autosomes are inherited according to dominant or recessive patterns. Most cases of autosomal inheritance in humans involve traits controlled by one gene.

Autosomal Dominant

A. General information
   1. Allele responsible for the trait (or disease) is dominant.
   2. Only one parent needs to pass on the gene (child may be heterozygous for trait).
   3. Examples of inherited diseases; Huntington's chorea, myotonic muscular dystrophy, night blindness, osteogenesis imperfecta, neurofibromatosis.
B. Genetic counseling: advise parents that if one of them has a disease inherited through autosomal dominant pattern, there is a 50% chance with each pregnancy that the child will have the disease/disorder.

Autosomal Recessive

A. General information
   1. Allele responsible for trait (or disease) will not result in expression if the other allele in the pair is dominant.
   2. Both parents must pass on the gene(s) (child is homozygous for trait).
   3. Examples of inherited diseases: cystic fibrosis, PKU, sickle cell anemia, albinism, Tay-Sachs.
B. Genetic counseling: advise parents that if both are heterozygous for the trait then
   1. There is a 25% chance with each pregnancy of having a child with the disease/disorder.
   2. There is a 50% chance with each pregnancy of having a child who is a carrier of the disease but who will not have the symptoms.
   3. There is a 25% chance with each pregnancy of having a child who will neither have the disease nor be a carrier.

Sex-linked (X-Linked) Inheritance

A. General information
   1. Inheritance of characteristics located on X and Y chromosomes
   2. Only known genetic locus on the Y chromosome is associated with determination of male sex.
   3. X chromosome carries other traits in addition to determination of female sex.
   4. Sex-linked inheritance in males: even a recessive defective gene on X chromosome can manifest itself in males because there is no opposing normal gene on Y chromosome.
   5. Sex-linked inheritance in females: recessive defective gene can be masked by a normal dominant gene.
   6. Examples of sex-linked inherited disorders: color blindness, baldness, hemophilia A and B, Duchenne's muscular dystrophy.

B. Genetic counseling
   1. If a woman is a carrier for a sex-linked disorder and her partner does not have the disorder
      a. There is a 50% chance with each pregnancy that her son will have the disorder.
      b. There is a 50% chance her daughter will become a carrier.
   2. If a man has a sex-linked disorder, all his daughters will be carriers but none will manifest the disease.

Chromosome Alterations

A. General information: deviations from normal chromosome complement may be numeric or structural.
   1. *Mutation:* spontaneous alteration in genetic material not present in previous generation
   2. *Nondisjunction:* failure of a pair of chromosomes to separate during meiosis; results in numeric change called trisomy (47 chromosomes); can be passed on by either parent (one parent would pass 24 chromosomes).
   3. *Translocation:* the transfer of all or part of a chromosome to another location on the same chromosome or to a different chromosome after chromosome breakage
   4. *Mosaicism:* the presence in the same individual of two or more genotypically different cell lines
B. Genetic counseling: varies depending on the origin of the alteration
   1. Random risk: chromosome alterations caused by environmental agents are not likely to occur in subsequent pregnancies. Therefore, the risk of the same defect recurring is no more than for any person in the general population.
   2. High risk: at least one parent carries a chromosomal aberration or mutant gene and passes it on to the offspring (e.g., if a parent is a balanced translocation carrier, the risk of a child being affected is 1 in 4)
   3. Moderate risk: largest group; includes multifactorial disorders. Risk recurrence in these disorders is empiric, based not on genetic theory but on prior experience and observation.

Assessment

History

A. Careful, detailed history is the basis of genetic counseling; can help confirm diagnosis and establish recurrence risk in multifactorial disorders.

B. Family history (pattern of affected family members) is recorded in form of pedigree chart or family tree.
   1. Information about affected child and immediate family: history of this pregnancy and all previous pregnancies, including stillbirths and abortions; information about siblings
   2. Information about maternal relatives
      a. Mother's siblings
      b. Outcome of maternal grandmother's pregnancies
      c. Health status of maternal relatives
   3. Information about paternal relatives: same as maternal

Laboratory/Diagnostic Tests

A. Amniocentesis
   1. Examination of amniotic fluid to screen for
      a. Some inborn errors of metabolism
      b. Chromosomal abnormalities
      c. Some CNS disorders
      d. Sex of infant in sex-related disorders
   2. Indications
      a. One parent is chromosome mosaic or has balanced translocation.
      b. Mother is age 35 or older.
      c. Both parents are heterozygous for an autosomal recessive disorder.
      d. Mother is carrier of an X-linked disorder.
      e. Couple already has an affected child.
B. Karyotyping (chromosomal analysis)
   1. Confirms or refutes probable diagnosis of chromosomal abnormality.
   2. Identifies whether individual is a carrier of chromosomal abnormality.
   3. Determines infant's sex if necessary.
C. Determination of fetal status (see page 457)

Analysis

Nursing diagnoses for the family/individual with a genetic disorder may include
A. Altered thought processes
B. Knowledge deficit (specify)
C. High risk for altered parenting

Planning and Implementation

Goals

A. Child will achieve maximum potential for cognitive and motor development.
B. Family will develop effective coping strategies.

Interventions

A. Provide community health agency referral.
B. Support family in identification of appropriate stimulation programs for child.

C. Communicate with and provide support for parents.
D. Offer genetic counseling (see Principles of Inheritance, page 365).

Evaluation

A. Optimum level of motor and cognitive development is attained.
B. Self-care is performed at satisfactory level.
C. Family is able to function appropriately.
D. Parents demonstrate ability to meet child's physical and developmental needs.
E. Parents derive comfort/satisfaction from parenting affected child.

Chromosome Disorder

Down's Syndrome

A. General information
   1. One of the most common causes of mental retardation; incidence: about 1 in 600 live births
   2. Caused by an extra chromosome 21 (total 47)
      a. Most cases associated with nondisjunction; incidence increased with maternal, and to some degree paternal, age; incidence in women over age 35 markedly increased
      b. Also associated with translocation; hereditary type, incidence not increased with parental age
B. Assessment findings
   1. Head and face
      a. Small head, flat facial profile, broad flat nose
      b. Small mouth, normal-size protruding tongue
      c. Upward slanting palpebral fissure
      d. Low-set ears
   2. Extremities
      a. Short, thick fingers and hands
      b. Simian creases (single crease across palms)
      c. Muscle weakness, lax joints
   3. Associated anomalies and disorders
      a. Congenital heart defects (40% incidence)
      b. GI structural defects
      c. Increased incidence of leukemia
      d. Increased incidence of respiratory infection
      e. Visual defects: strabismus, myopia, nystagmus, cataracts
   4. Retardation usually moderate, IQ 50–70
C. Nursing interventions: see also Mental Retardation, page 531
   1. Provide parent education concerning
      a. Increased susceptibility to respiratory infection

b. Nutritional needs, feeding techniques
  c. Medication administration if necessary
2. Promote developmental progress
3. Provide genetic counseling.

FLUID AND ELECTROLYTE, ACID-BASE BALANCES

General Principles and Variations from Adult

A. Percent body water compared to total body weight
   1. Premature infant: 90% water
   2. Infant: 75%–80% water
   3. Child: 64% water
B. Infant also has a higher percentage of water in extracellular fluid compared to adults (therefore infant has less fluid reserve).
C. Renal function
   1. Concentrating ability of kidney does not reach adult levels until approximately age 2; specific gravity of infant's urine is 1.003.
   2. Glomerular filtration rate does not reach adult levels until approximately age 2.
   3. Average urine output
      a. Infant: 5–10 ml/hour
      b. 1–10 years: 10–25 ml/hour
      c. 35 ml/hour thereafter
D. Metabolic rate in children is 2–3 times that of adults; children therefore have an increased need for nutrients and fluids, and an increased amount of waste to excrete.
E. Fluid is not conserved; there is less reserve, and children more prone to fluid volume deficit than adults; ½ of infant's extracellular fluid is exchanged each day compared with only ⅕ of adult's.
F. Children have faster respiratory rate than adults, causing more water loss through breathing.
G. Infants have a greater body surface area per kg body weight than adults, therefore fluid loss through skin (evaporation) is greater in children.

Assessment

Health History

A. Ascertain age, recent weight, usual feeding habits/patterns, amount and type of daily intake.
B. Determine usual voiding/stooling habits and volume of urine/stool output.
C. Identify any recent illnesses or medications taken.
D. Ascertain usual activity level.

Physical Examination

A. Measure present weight and vital signs.
B. Observe general appearance.
   1. Muscle tone
   2. Reflex responses
   3. Activity level
C. Inspect skin and mucous membranes for turgor, color, temperature.
D. Head and face
   1. Inspect fontanels, eye orbits.
   2. Ascertain presence of tears, saliva.
E. Abdomen/genitalia
   1. Auscultate for bowel sounds, peristaltic waves.
   2. Inspect for diaper rash, urine stream.

Laboratory/Diagnostic Tests

A. Hematologic studies
   1. Hbg and hct
   2. Sodium, potassium, chloride, calcium, magnesium
   3. pCO_2 and CO_2
   4. pH
B. Urine studies: specific gravity, glucose, ketones, osmolarity, pH
C. Stool studies: culture, reducing substances, blood, sodium, potassium, pH

Analysis

Nursing diagnoses for children with fluid/electrolyte and acid-base imbalances may include
A. Diarrhea
B. Pain
C. Fluid volume deficit
D. Altered nutrition
E. Altered oral mucous membrane
F. Impaired skin integrity
G. Altered tissue perfusion
H. Altered urinary elimination

Planning and Implementation

Goals

A. Child will have normal hydration status.
B. Parents will demonstrate knowledge of child's disorder, prescribed treatment, and prevention of complications.

Interventions

A. Maintain strict I&O.
   1. Weigh diapers.
   2. Monitor urine specific gravity.
   3. Hematest stools.
B. Take daily weights.
C. Keep NPO for bowel rest.
D. Administer IV fluids.

1. Maintenance plus replacement
2. Generally use hypotonic solutions (0.25 NSS, 0.33 NSS, or 0.45 NSS)

E. Provide pacifier for infant.
F. Reintroduce oral fluids slowly.
   1. In children under 2 years use Pedialyte, a balanced electrolyte solution.
   2. In children over 2 use weak tea, flat soda.
   3. Do not use
      a. Broth (high sodium)
      b. Milk/formula (high solute)
      c. Water, glucose water, Jell-O (no electrolytes).

Evaluation

A. Child has adequate hydration status.
   1. Adequate I&O
   2. Normal stooling pattern
   3. Good skin turgor
   4. Normal vital signs
   5. Normal serum laboratory values
B. Parents participate in care, demonstrate understanding of signs and symptoms of disorder and treatment.

Disorders

Dehydration

A. The most common fluid and electrolyte disturbance in infants and children
B. Osmotic factors, particularly sodium, control the movement of fluid between extracellular and intracellular compartments and influence the types of dehydration
   1. *Isotonic dehydration: most common*
      a. Plasma sodium level is normal (130–150 mEq/liter).
      b. Water and electrolyte lost in proportionate amounts; net loss is isotonic.
      c. Major loss is from extracellular fluid; loss of circulating blood volume.
      d. Shock may develop if losses are severe.
   2. *Hypotonic dehydration*
      a. Plasma sodium level is less than 130 mEq/liter.
      b. Electrolyte deficit exceeds water deficit.
      c. May occur when fluid and electrolyte losses are replaced with plain or glucose water.
      d. Fluid lost from extracellular compartment; also moves from extracellular to intracellular compartment.
      e. Signs of decreased fluid appear sooner with smaller fluid losses than in isotonic dehydration.
      f. Shock is a frequent finding.
   3. *Hypertonic dehydration*
      a. Plasma sodium exceeds 150 mEq/liter.
      b. Water loss exceeds electrolyte loss; may occur when fluid and electrolyte losses are replaced with large amount of solute (hypertonic formula).
      c. Fluid shifts from the intracellular to the extracellular compartments.
      d. Physical signs of dehydration may be less apparent.
      e. Neurologic symptoms (e.g., seizures) may occur.

Diarrhea

A. General information
   1. A change in consistency and frequency of stool
   2. Very common in young children
   3. Caused by bacteria and viruses, parasites, poisons, inflammation, malabsorption, allergies, abnormal bowel motility, and anatomic alterations
   4. Infants can easily lose 5% of their body weight in 1 day
   5. Intestinal fluids are alkaline; large loss causes metabolic acidosis
   6. Also causes bicarbonate and potassium loss
   7. Body may use its own fat for energy, leading to ketosis
B. Assessment findings
   1. History of frequent stools; child may complain of or indicate abdominal cramping by guarding, weight loss; child may be lethargic and irritable
   2. Decreased urine output, decreased tears and saliva, dry mucous membranes, dry skin with poor tissue turgor
   3. In children less than 18 months, may find depressed anterior fontanel
   4. Soft eyeballs with sunken appearance
   5. Ashen skin color; cold extremities
   6. High-pitched cry
   7. Increased pulse rate and decreased blood pressure
   8. Diagnostic tests
      a. Hct elevated if dehydrated
      b. Serum sodium and potassium decreased
      c. BUN elevated if renal circulation is decreased
      d. CBC will show increased bands if caused by bacterial infection
      e. Low pH and positive sugar with disaccharide intolerance
      f. Stool culture will identify specific microorganism
      g. Leukocytes in stool if caused by enteroinvasive organisms
C. Nursing interventions

1. Keep NPO to rest bowel, if ordered.
2. Administer IV fluid therapy as ordered.
3. Resume oral feedings slowly; provide foods such as bread, rice, tea.
4. Provide skin care to prevent/treat excoriation of diaper area.
5. Test all stool and chart results.
6. Isolation may be ordered with infectious cause.

Vomiting

A. General information
   1. Common symptom during childhood; usually not a cause for concern
   2. Differs from spitting up (dribbling of undigested formula, often with burping)
   3. If prolonged may result in metabolic alkalosis or aspiration
B. Assessment findings: in addition to vomiting, child may have fever, abdominal pain and distension.
C. Nursing interventions
   1. Assist with identification and treatment of underlying cause.
      a. Assess for accompanying diarrhea that may indicate gastroenteritis.
      b. Determine if others in family/school/etc., are also sick; may indicate food poisoning.
      c. Assess for history of anxiety-producing life events.
      d. Assess amount and force of vomitus; forceful, projectile vomiting may indicate pyloric stenosis (page 412)
      e. Determine frequency and character of vomitus (color, whether formula or food, presence of bile or blood), relationship to feeding (new foods, overeating).
   2. Prevent complications: monitor fluid/electrolyte and acid-base status
   3. Administer antiemetics if ordered; trimethobenzamide HCl (Tigan) and promethazine HCl (Phenergan) recommended for children.

ACCIDENTS, POISONINGS, AND INGESTION

A. Accidents are the main cause of death in children over the age of 1 year.
B. 90% of accidents are preventable.
C. Interaction among host (the child), agent (the principle cause), and environment (⅔ of accidents occur in the home); safeguard the host while the agent and environment are made safer.
D. Methods of prevention
   1. Childproofing the environment

2. Educating parents and child
3. Legislation (e.g., seat belts, safe toys)
4. Anticipatory guidance
5. Understanding and applying growth and development principles
   a. Infant: totally dependent on adults for maintenance of safe environment
   b. Toddler: more mobile, impatient; urge to investigate and imitate; climbing, running, jumping
   c. Preschooler: very curious, exploring neighborhood, running, climbing, riding bikes; can accept and respond to teaching but still needs protection
   d. School-age and adolescent: taking dares, sports injuries, peer pressure, learning to drive
E. Precipitating factors
   1. Arguments or tension in the home
   2. Change in routines
   3. Tired child/tired parents
   4. Inadequate babysitting
   5. Hungry child
   6. Illness in immediate family member
F. Potential outcomes include temporary incapacitation, permanent disfigurement, and death

Specific Disorders
Pediatric Poisonings

A. General information
   1. Toddlers and suicidal adolescents most often involved
   2. Deaths have declined due to continued efforts in prevention and the establishment of poison control centers
   3. Modes of exposure: ocular, skin, ingestion (vast majority)
   4. Types of substances ingested: drugs, household products (cleaning agents), garden supplies, plants and berries
   5. Most ingestions are acute in nature and accompanied by a history of invasion of the medicine chest or cabinet where household cleaners are kept
   6. Chronic ingestions result in accumulation of toxic substance, such as lead
B. General assessment findings
   1. Signs vary depending on substance ingested
   2. May evidence bradycardia; tachycardia; tachypnea; slow depressed respiration; hypotension or hypertension; hypothermia or hyperpyrexia
   3. Confusion, disorientation, coma, ataxia, seizures
   4. Miosis, mydriasis, nystagmus
   5. Jaundice, cyanosis
   6. Child may have a distinctive odor: hydrocarbons, alcohol, garlic, sweat

C. General interventions
  1. Resuscitate child and stabilize condition: establish patent airway and provide measures to restore circulation as indicated.
  2. Prevent absorption.
    a. Determine what, when, and how much was ingested; will frequently not be able to identify substance.
    b. Induce emesis.
      1) indicated in all cases *except* caustic material ingestion, or in a child who is comatose, experiencing seizures, or lacking gag reflex
      2) drug of choice is syrup of ipecac.
        a) administer 30 ml for adolescents, 15 ml for children, 10 ml for children under 1 year.
        b) follow with 100–300 ml water.
        c) if no response in 20–30 minutes, repeat dose.
        d) produces vomiting almost 100% of the time.
    c. Gastric lavage: may also be used to prevent absorption
      1) use largest nasogastric (NG) or orogastric tube possible.
      2) aspirate gastric contents.
      3) use water or ½ normal saline.
      4) continue until return is clear.
    d. Activated charcoal: minimizes absorption of toxins by binding them on its surface
      1) administer after vomiting with ipecac treatment
      2) administer 5–10 g for each gram of drug or chemical ingested.
      3) mix charcoal with water to make a syrup that can be given by mouth or NG tube.
    e. Cathartic: may be used after emesis or lavage to speed elimination of ingested substance; recommended agents are sodium or magnesium sulfate.
  3. Provide treatment and prevention information to parents.
    a. Parents should always be instructed to save container, vomitus, spills on clothing for analysis.
    b. Teach parents about safety practices that will decrease chances of accidental poisonings; educate as to use of drugs, labeling, storage, and handling of household products, importance of child-resistant safety packaging.
    c. Stress importance of having syrup of ipecac in the home (30 ml can be purchased over-the-counter) and instruct parents on proper administration.
    d. Advise parents to keep poison control center phone number readily available.
    e. Incorporate anticipatory guidance related to developmental stage of child.
    f. Discuss general first aid measures with parents.

Salicylate Poisoning

A. General information
  1. Toxicity begins at doses of 150–200 mg/kg.
  2. Products include not only aspirin but oil of wintergreen and analgesic cold medicines.
  3. Peak effect of aspirin is 2–4 hours and effects may last 8 hours.
  4. Ingestion may be accidental or due to therapeutic overdosing.
  5. Salicylate ingestion causes
    a. acid-base alterations
    b. respiratory alkalosis
    c. metabolic acidosis
    d. impaired glucose metabolism
    e. an inhibition of prothrombin formation
B. Assessment findings
  1. Hyperventilation, confusion, loss of consciousness
  2. Hyperpnea, hyperpyrexia, dehydration
  3. CNS depression, vomiting, lethargy
  4. Coma, respiratory failure, circulatory collapse
C. Nursing interventions
  1. Assist with emergency management
  2. Administer fluid therapy
  3. Monitor vital signs, BP, urine specific gravity, I&O
  4. Monitor temperature, provide tepid sponging or cooling mattress
  5. Provide emotional support to child and family
  6. Administer vitamin K

Acetaminophen Ingestion

A. General information
  1. Has become a commonly used analgesic-antipyretic
  2. Little associated morbidity or mortality in accidental ingestion
  3. Major risk is severe hepatic damage
B. Assessment findings
  1. Vague and nonspecific initially; nausea, vomiting, anorexia, sweating
  2. Jaundice, liver tenderness, increase in liver enzymes, abdominal pain
  3. Progression to hepatic failure
C. Nursing interventions
  1. Emesis or lavage; do *not* use activated charcoal (will bind antidote).
  2. Administer antidote (acetylcysteine [Mucomyst]): lessens hepatic damage if given within 16 hours of ingestion.

A. General information
   1. Increased blood lead levels resulting from ingestion and absorption of lead-containing substances
   2. Most common source is lead-based paint (used in houses prior to 1950)
   3. Toddlers and preschoolers most often affected; many have pica (tendency to eat nonfood substances)
   4. Lead value of more than 15 μg/dl is considered a health hazard
   5. Symptoms usually appear once level is 70 μg/dl
   6. Lead is absorbed through the GI tract and pulmonary system; it is then deposited in bone, soft tissue, and blood; excretion occurs via urine, feces, and sweat; toxic effects are due to enzyme inhibition.
   7. Low dietary iron and calcium may enhance toxic effects.
   8. Widespread screening programs have diminished severe effects.
B. Assessment findings
   1. Abdominal complaints including colicky pain, constipation, anorexia, vomiting, weight loss
   2. Pallor, listlessness, fatigue
   3. Clumsiness, irritability, loss of coordination, ataxia, seizures
   4. Encephalopathy
   5. Identification of lead in the blood
   6. Erythrocyte protoporphyrin (EP) levels increased
C. Nursing interventions
   1. Administer chelating agents as ordered: dimercaprol (BAL in Oil); edatate calcium disodium (calcium EDTA).
      a. Prepare child for multiple injections; involve parents.
      b. Relieve pain at injection sites by applying warm soaks, rotating sites.
      c. Maintain hydration, measure I&O, encourage fluids (chelation is toxic to kidney).
   2. Provide nutritional counseling.
   3. Aid in eliminating environmental conditions that led to lead ingestion.

Lyme Disease

A. General information
   1. Caused by the spirochete *Borrelia burgdorferi*
   2. Transmitted by a deer tick, requires 24-hour tick attachment
   3. Most prevalent during summer and early fall
   4. Symptoms usually involve the skin, nervous system, and joints
   5. Incubation period is 3 to 32 days
B. Medical management
   1. Blood tests available, but lack sensitivity and specificity, therefore diagnosis is often based on clinical and epidemiologic data.
   2. Antibiotic treatment: if early infection, given for 10–21 days. If neurologic or arthritic symptoms occur, combined treatment for longer duration may be necessary.
C. Assessment findings
   1. Divided into stages on the basis of chronologic relationship to the tick bite
      a. Stage I: Skin rash (erythema migrans) starting 3–32 days past tick bite and lasting about 3 weeks. Most common on thighs, buttock, axilla. Systemic symptoms of malaise, fatigue, headache, stiff neck, fever, arthralgia.
      b. Stage II: Symptoms of late disease may occur months to years after the initial disease. Includes neurologic symptoms such as facial palsies, sensory losses, focal weaknesses, cardiac rhythm abnormalities, and increased arthritis complaints involving multiple joints.
D. Nursing interventions
   1. Medication administration
   2. Prevention
      a. Avoid high-risk areas such as woody, grassy areas
      b. If walking in such areas, wear long pants, long-sleeved shirt, high socks, and sneakers
      c. Use insect repellents for skin and clothing
      d. After every potential exposure, check carefully for ticks
      e. Remove tick by pulling straight out with tweezers

Sample Questions

10. The mother of an eight-year-old brings her child to the physician because the child has a "funny red circle" on his leg. The mother reports that the child went on a camping trip last weekend. The physician draws blood to rule out Lyme disease and prescribes doxycycline for the child. The child's mother asks why an antibiotic is prescribed for a tick bite. The nurse's response is based on which of the following understandings?
    1. Lyme disease weakens the person so they are susceptible to infections.
    2. Lyme disease is caused by a spirochete that is sensitive to doxycycline.
    3. Doxycycline will kill the tick, which may still be in the child.

4. Antibiotics are given to cure the infection at the site of the tick bite.
11. The mother of a three-year-old child calls her nurse neighbor in a panic state, saying that the child swallowed most of a bottle of aspirin. The nurse determines that the child is still alert. In addition to calling the poison control center, the nurse should:
   1. Induce vomiting in the child.
   2. Observe the child carefully until the ambulance arrives.
   3. Immediately start CPR.
   4. Give the child lots of milk to drink.
12. An eight-month-old infant was admitted to the hospital with severe diarrhea and dehydration. Fluid replacement therapy was initiated. Which observation the nurse makes indicates an improvement in the infant's status?
   1. Fontanels are depressed.
   2. Infant has gained 3 oz since yesterday.
   3. Skin remains pulled together after being gently pinched and released.
   4. The infant's hematocrit is greater today than yesterday.
13. Jeffrey, age 17, has Down's syndrome. He is 57 inches tall and weighs 155 pounds. In planning his care, it is most important for the nurse to take into consideration
   1. his mental age.
   2. his chronologic age.
   3. his bone age.
   4. growth chart percentiles.
14. Down's syndrome is caused by
   1. an autosomal recessive defect.
   2. an extra chromosome.
   3. a sex-linked defect.
   4. a dominant gene.

Answers and Rationales

10. The correct answer is 2. Lyme disease is caused by a spirochete that is sensitive to antibiotics. Lyme disease does not make the client more susceptible to infections. The tick will not be in the child. There is not likely to be an infection at the site of the bite. The red bull's eye around the tick bite is not an infection.
11. The correct answer is 1. Since the child is still alert, the nurse should plan to administer syrup of ipecac. If the child was not conscious, he would be lavaged upon arrival at the emergency room. There is no indication that the child is not breathing; CPR is not indicated. It would be better to remove the poison than to dilute it with milk.
12. The correct answer is 2. A weight gain would suggest greater circulating volume. Blood has weight. Depressed fontanels are a sign of dehydration. As the infant improves, the fontanels should no longer be depressed. The skin turgor should improve, not remain poor as described in option 3. Hematocrit rises with dehydration. There is less fluid in the blood and consequently a greater portion of blood is red cells.
13. The correct answer is 1. All Down's syndrome children are retarded and care must be geared to their mental age. The other measurements of age do not reflect the special needs of these children.
14. The correct answer is 2. In Down's syndrome there is an extra chromosome on the 21st pair, which is why the disease is also called trisomy 21. The mutation is spontaneous and not inherited.

The Neurosensory System

VARIATIONS FROM THE ADULT

Brain and Spinal Cord

Size and Structure

A. Rapid head growth in early childhood: brain is 25% of adult weight at birth, 75% at 2½ years, and 90% at 6 years.
B. Head growth results from development of nerve tracts within the brain and an increase in nerve fibers, not an increase in the number of neurons.
C. Infant's skull is not a rigid structure.
   1. Bones of skull are not fused until 18 months.
   2. Head circumference will increase with increase in intracranial volume in infants.
   3. Sutures may separate if there is significant gradual increase in intracranial volume up to age 12.
D. Fontanels ("soft spots"): areas of head not covered by skull
   1. Anterior fontanel
      a. Diamond-shaped opening at junction of parietal and frontal bones
      b. Closes between 9 and 18 months
   2. Posterior fontanel

a. Triangular-shaped opening at junction of occipital and parietal bones
   b. Closes by 2 months
3. Should feel flat and firm
4. May be sunken with severe dehydration
5. Will bulge with increased intracranial pressure (ICP)

Function

A. Cortical functions (e.g., fine motor coordination) are incompletely developed at birth.
B. The autonomic nervous system (ANS) is intact but immature.
   1. Infant has limited ability to control body temperature
   2. Infant's heart rate very sensitive to parasympathetic stimulation
C. Infant's behavior primarily reflexive
   1. Neurologic exam consists of evaluating reflexes
   2. Babinski's reflex normal in infant; disappears after child begins to walk
D. Peripheral neurons not myelinated at birth
   1. Myelination occurs in later infancy
   2. Motor skill development depends on myelinization
E. Infant usually demonstrates a dominance of flexor muscles; extremities will be flexed even when infant is sleeping
F. Small tremors are normal findings during first few months of life: not considered seizure activity if occurring in response to environmental stimuli, if they are not accompanied by abnormal eye movements, and if movements cease with passive flexion

Eye and Vision

A. Vision changes as the eye and eye muscles undergo physiologic change.
B. Visual function becomes more organized.
   1. Binocular vision developed by 4 months
   2. Maturation of eye muscles by 1 year
      a. Nystagmus common in infant
      b. Strabismus (eyes out of alignment when fixating on an object): due to imbalance in extraocular muscles, common up to 6 months
   3. Visual acuity changes
      a. 16 weeks: 20/50 to 20/100
      b. 1 year: 20/50+
      c. 2 years: 20/40
      d. 3 years: 20/30
      e. 4 years: nearly 20/20

Ear and Hearing

A. Hearing is fully developed at birth.
B. Abnormal physical structure of ears may indicate genetic problems (low-set ears often associated with renal problems or mental retardation).

ASSESSMENT

History

A. Most important part of neurologic evaluation
B. Family history: seizure disorders, degenerative neurologic diseases, mental retardation, sensory defects
C. History of pregnancy: maternal illness, placental dysfunction, fetal movements, nuchal cord, intrapartal fetal distress, prematurity, meconium staining, Apgar scores
D. Child's health history: delayed motor or speech development, hypotonia, seizures, childhood illnesses
E. Parental concerns: development, vision, hearing

Physical Examination

A. Inspect size and shape of head: note fontanels in infants, chart head circumference on growth chart.
B. Observe posture and activity: note flexed posture versus hypotonia or opisthotonos, symmetry of movement of extremities, excessive tremors or twitching, abnormal eye movements, ineffective suck or swallow, high-pitched cry.
C. Observe respiratory pattern: note apnea, ataxic breathing, asymmetric or paradoxic chest movement.
D. Determine developmental level with DDST.
E. Vision tests
   1. Binocularity
      a. Corneal light reflex test: performed by shining a light at the bridge of the nose as the child looks straight ahead; light reflex should fall at the same point in both pupils; deviation indicates strabismus
      b. Cover test: performed by getting the child to fixate on an object and then covering one eye and uncovering that eye quickly to determine if child remains fixated on that object; normally both eyes will remain fixated without drifting.
   2. Visual acuity
      a. Snellen E chart for preschoolers
      b. Snellen alphabet chart for older children
   3. Peripheral vision
   4. Color vision
F. Auditory tests
   1. Audiometry: perception of sound
   2. Tympanometry: conduction of sound in middle ear

3. Crib-o-gram: neonatal motor response to sound
4. Conduction tests

Laboratory/Diagnostic Tests

A. Same tests that are used in adults are used in children.
B. Child should be carefully prepared and informed of what to expect during the test.
C. Sedation may be required for tests requiring child to be immobile for extended period.
D. Positioning and immobilization is crucial to the success of lumbar puncture.

ANALYSIS

Nursing diagnoses for the child with a disorder of the nervous system may include
A. Impaired physical mobility
B. Altered thought process
C. Sensory/perceptual alterations (specify)
D. Knowledge deficit (specify)
E. Pain
F. Ineffective family coping: compromised or disabling
G. High risk for injury
H. Impaired verbal communication
I. High risk for impaired skin integrity

PLANNING AND IMPLEMENTATION

Goals

A. Child will be protected from injury.
B. Child will be free from signs and symptoms of increased ICP.
C. Normal respiratory function will be maintained.
D. Optimum developmental level will be achieved.
E. Family will be able to care for child at home.

Interventions

Care of the Child with Increased Intracranial Pressure

A. General information
1. Intracranial volume and pressure can increase as a result of
   a. Increased brain volume (cerebral edema, tumor)
   b. Increased cerebral blood volume (hematoma or hemorrhage)
   c. Increased cerebrospinal fluid (CSF) volume (hydrocephalus)
2. Herniation of brain tissue: most serious complication of increased ICP; may result

in life-threatening deterioration of vital functions
B. Medical management
1. Directed towards reducing intracranial volume and controlling underlying disorder
2. Drug therapy
   a. Osmotic diuretics (mannitol, glycerol) to reduce acute brain edema; for short-term use only
   b. Corticosteroids (dexamethasone) to reduce brain swelling
      1) may be used for longer periods than osmotic diuretics
      2) antacids may be given concomitantly to prevent gastric irritation
3. Fluid restriction, hyperventilation, temperature regulation may all be used to control increased ICP
4. Surgery: if increased ICP caused by obstruction to CSF, shunt procedures may be performed
C. Assessment findings
1. Infants
   a. Lethargy, poor feeding, anorexia, or vomiting
   b. High-pitched cry
   c. Tense, bulging fontanel; increased head circumference; separation of cranial sutures
2. Children
   a. Anorexia, nausea, vomiting, irritability, or lethargy
   b. Headache, blurred vision, papilledema
   c. Separation of cranial sutures
3. Late signs
   a. Altered LOC
   b. Pupil dilation and sluggish response to light
   c. Tachycardia then bradycardia
   d. Altered respiratory rate then apnea
D. Nursing interventions
1. Administer medications as ordered.
   a. With osmotic diuretics, monitor fluid and electrolyte balance carefully.
   b. With corticosteroids, monitor for signs of gastric bleeding.
2. Monitor hydration status carefully.
   a. Administer IV fluids as ordered, assess carefully for fluid overload.
   b. Assess for fluid and electrolyte imbalances.
   c. Monitor for hypovolemic shock if on strict fluid restriction.
3. Assist with hyperventilation if ordered; monitor arterial blood gases (ABGs)
4. Assist with reduction of body temperature as needed.
   a. Administer antipyretics as ordered.
   b. Use sponge baths, hypothermia pads as necessary.

5. Monitor LOC and behavioral/mental changes carefully.
6. Elevate head of bed 30°–45° unless contraindicated (e.g., possible spinal injury); keep neck in neutral alignment and avoid flexion.
7. Arrange nursing care activities to minimize stimulation and keep environment as quiet as possible.
8. Prepare for shunt surgery (see below) if needed.

EVALUATION

A. Head growth progresses normally, fontanels are flat, and seizure activity is controlled.
B. Child maintains an appropriate activity level.
C. Child is placed in an appropriate special program or school, if needed.
D. Parents demonstrate ability to perform treatments and administer appropriate medications.

DISORDERS OF THE NERVOUS SYSTEM

Disorders of the Brain and Spinal Cord

Hydrocephalus

A. General information
1. Increased amount of CSF within the ventricles of the brain
2. May be caused by obstruction of CSF flow or by overproduction or inadequate reabsorption of CSF
3. May result from congenital malformation or be secondary to injury, infection, or tumor
4. Classification
   a. Noncommunicating: flow of CSF from ventricles to subarachnoid space is obstructed.
   b. Communicating: flow is not obstructed, but CSF is inadequately reabsorbed in subarachnoid space.
B. Assessment findings: depend on age at onset, amount of CSF in brain
1. Infant to 2 years: enlarging head size; bulging, nonpulsating fontanels; downward rotation of eyes; separation of cranial sutures; poor feeding, vomiting, lethargy, irritability; high-pitched cry and abnormal muscle tone
2. Older children: changes in head size less common; signs of increased ICP (vomiting, ataxia, headache) common; alteration in consciousness and papilledema late signs
3. Diagnostic tests

a. Serial transilluminations detect increases in light areas
b. CT scan shows dilated ventricles as well as presence of mass; with dye injection shows course of CSF flow
C. Nursing interventions: provide care for the child with increased ICP and for the child undergoing shunt procedures.

Shunts

A. General information
1. Insertion of a flexible tube into the lateral ventricle of the brain
2. Catheter is then threaded under the skin and the distal end positioned in the peritoneum (most common type) or the right atrium; a subcutaneous pump may be attached to ensure patency
3. Shunt drains excess CSF from the lateral ventricles of the brain in communicating or noncommunicating hydrocephalus; fluid is then absorbed by the peritoneum or enters the general circulation via the right atrium
B. Nursing interventions
1. Provide routine pre-op care with special attention to monitoring neurologic status.
2. Provide post-op care.
   a. Maintain patency of the shunt.
      1) position child off the operative site.
      2) pump the shunt as ordered.
      3) observe for signs of infection of the incision.
      4) observe for signs of increased ICP.
      5) position the child with head slightly elevated or as ordered.
3. Instruct parents regarding
   a. Wound care, positioning of infant, and how to pump the shunt
   b. Signs of infection
   c. Signs of increased ICP
   d. Need for repeated shunt revisions as child grows or if shunt becomes blocked or infected
   e. Expected level of developmental functioning
   f. Availability of support groups and community agencies

Spina Bifida (Myelodysplasia)

A. General information
1. Failure of posterior vertebral arches to fuse during embryologic development
2. Incidence: 2 in 1,000 infants in the U.S.
3. Although actual cause is unknown, frequency of the defect is increased if a sibling has had a neural tube defect; radiation, viral, and environmental factors have been suggested as causative.
4. Site of the defect varies

a. Approximately 85% of the defects in the spine involve the lower thoracic lumbar or sacral area.
b. Defects in the upper thoracic and cervical regions make up the remaining 15%.

B. Types
1. *Spina bifida occulta*
a. Spinal cord and meninges remain in the normal anatomic position.
b. Defect may not be visible, or may be identified by a dimple or a tuft of hair on the spine.
c. Child is asymptomatic or may have slight neuromuscular deficit.
d. No treatment needed if asymptomatic; otherwise treatment aimed at specific symptoms.
2. *Spina bifida cystica*
a. *Meningocele*
1) sac (meninges) filled with spinal fluid protrudes through opening in spinal canal; sac is covered with thin skin
2) no nerves in sac
3) no motor or sensory loss
4) good prognosis after surgery
b. *Myelomeningocele/meningomyelocele*
1) same as meningocele except there are spinal nerves in the sac (herniation of dura and meninges).
2) child will have sensory/motor deficit below site of the lesion.
3) 80% of these children have multiple handicaps.

C. Medical management
1. Surgery
a. Closure of the sac within 48 hours of birth to prevent infection and preserve neural tissue
b. Shunt procedure if accompanying hydrocephalus
c. Orthopedic procedures to correct defects of hips, knees, or feet
2. Drug therapy
a. Antibiotics for prevention of infections.
b. Anticholinergic drugs to increase bladder capacity and lower intravesicular pressure.
3. Immobilization (casts, braces, traction) for defects of the hips, knees, or feet

D. Assessment findings
1. Examine the defect for size, level, tissue covering, and CSF leakage.
2. Motor/sensory involvement may include
a. Voluntary movement of lower extremities
b. Withdrawal of lower extremities or crying after pinprick
c. Paralysis of lower extremities
d. Joint deformities
e. Hydrocephalus

f. Evaluate bowel and bladder function. Neurogenic bowel and bladder occur in up to 90% of the children.
4. Diagnostic tests
a. Prenatal
1) ultrasound image of the pregnant uterus shows fetal spinal defect and sac
2) amniocentesis: increased alphafetoprotein (AFP) level prior to 18th week of gestation
b. Postpartal
1) x-ray of spine shows vertebral defect; CT scan of skull may show hydrocephalus
2) myelogram shows extent of neural defect
3) encephalogram may show hydrocephalus
4) urinalysis, culture and sensitivity (C&S) may identify organism and indicate appropriate antibacterial therapy
5) BUN may be increased
6) creatinine clearance rate may be decreased

E. Nursing interventions
1. Prevent trauma to the sac.
a. Cover with sterile dressing soaked with normal saline.
b. Position infant prone or side-lying.
c. Keep the area free from contamination by urine or feces. A protective barrier drape may be necessary.
d. Inspect the sac for intactness or signs of infection.
e. Administer antibiotics as ordered.
2. Prevent complications.
a. Observe for signs of hydrocephalus, meningitis, joint deformities.
b. Clean intermittent urinary catheterization to manage neurogenic bladder.
c. Administer medications to prevent urinary complications as ordered.
d. Perform passive ROM exercises to lower extremities.
3. Provide adequate nutrition: adapt diet and feeding techniques according to the child's position.
4. Provide sensory stimulation.
a. Adjust objects for visual stimulation according to child's position.
b. Provide stimulation for other senses.
5. Provide emotional support to parents/family.
6. Provide client teaching and discharge planning to parents concerning
a. Wound care
b. Physical therapy, range of motion exercises
c. Signs of complications

      d. Medication regimen: schedule, dosage, effects, and side effects

      e. Feeding, diapering, positioning

      f. Availability of appropriate support groups/community agencies/genetic counseling

Meningitis

See page 186.

Encephalitis

See page 186.

Reye's Syndrome

A. General information
1. An acute encephalopathy with fatty degeneration of the liver
2. Reye's syndrome is a true pediatric emergency: cerebral complication may reach an irreversible state
3. Increased ICP secondary to cerebral edema is major factor contributing to morbidity and mortality
4. Early recognition and prompt management reducing mortality
5. Etiology unknown

B. Medical management
1. Proper initial staging essential.
2. Treatment is supportive, based on stage of coma and level of blood ammonia.
3. Treatment should take place in a pediatric intensive care unit.

C. Assessment findings
1. Child appears to be recovering from a viral illness, such as influenza or chickenpox, during which salicylates have been administered; symptoms then appear that follow a definite pattern, which has led to clinical staging.
   a. Stage I: sudden onset of persistent vomiting, fatigue, listlessness
   b. Stage II: personality and behavior changes, disorientation, confusion, hyperreflexia
   c. Stage III: coma, decorticate posturing
   d. Stage IV: deeper coma, decerebrate rigidity
   e. Stage V: seizures, absent deep tendon reflexes, respiratory reflexes, flaccid paralysis
2. Pathophysiologic changes include
   a. Increased free fatty acid level
   b. Hyperammonemia due to reduction of enzyme that converts ammonia to urea
   c. Impaired liver function
   d. Structural changes of mitochondria in muscle and brain tissue
   e. Significant swelling of the brain

D. Nursing interventions (depend on stage)

1. Stage I: assess hydration status: monitor skin turgor, mucous membranes, I&O, urine specific gravity; maintain IV therapy.
2. Stages I–V: assess neurologic status: monitor LOC, pupils, motor coordination, extremity movement, orientation, posturing, seizure activity.
3. Stages II–V
   a. Assess respiratory status: note changing rate and pattern, presence of circumoral cyanosis, restlessness, agitation.
   b. Assess circulatory status: frequent vital signs, note neck vein distension, skin color and temperature, abnormal heart sounds.
   c. Support child/family.
     1) explain all treatments and procedures.
     2) incorporate family members in treatment as applicable.
     3) organize regular family and client-care conferences.
     4) use support services as needed.
   d. Provide additional parental and community education to ensure early recognition and treatment.

Seizure Disorders

A. General information
1. *Seizures:* recurrent sudden changes in consciousness, behavior, sensations, and/or muscular activities beyond voluntary control that are produced by excess neuronal discharge
2. *Epilepsy:* chronic recurrent seizures
3. Incidence higher in those with family history of idiopathic seizures
4. Cause unknown in 75% of epilepsy cases
5. Seizures may be symptomatic or acquired, caused by
   a. Structural or space-occupying lesion (tumors, subdural hematomas)
   b. Metabolic abnormalities (hypoglycemia, hypocalcemia, hyponatremia)
   c. Infection (meningitis, encephalitis)
   d. Encephalopathy (lead poisoning, pertussis, Reye's syndrome)
   e. Degenerative diseases (Tay-Sachs)
   f. Congenital CNS defects (hydrocephalus)
   g. Vascular problems (intracranial hemorrhage)
6. Pathophysiology
   a. Normally neurons send out messages in electrical impulses periodically, and the firing of individual neurons is regulated by an inhibitory feedback loop mechanism

b. With seizures, many more neurons than normal fire in a synchronous fashion in a particular area of the brain; the energy generated overcomes the inhibitory feedback mechanism

7. Classification (Table 5.3)
   a. Generalized: initial onset in both hemispheres, usually involves loss of consciousness and bilateral motor activity
   b. Partial: begins in focal area of brain and symptoms are appropriate to a dysfunction of that area; may progress into a generalized seizure, further subdivided into simple partial or complex partial

B. Medical management
   1. Drug therapy (refer to Anticonvulsants, page 32)
      a. Phenytoin (Dilantin)
         1) often used with phenobarbital for its potentiating effect
         2) inhibits spread of electrical discharge
         3) side effects include gum hyperplasia, hirsutism, ataxia, gastric distress, nystagmus, anemia, sedation
      b. Phenobarbital: elevates the seizure threshold and inhibits the spread of electrical discharge
   2. Surgery: to remove the tumor, hematoma, or epileptic focus

C. Assessment findings
   1. Clinical picture varies with type of seizure (see Table 5.3)
   2. Diagnostic tests
      a. Blood studies to rule out lead poisoning, hypoglycemia, infection, or electrolyte imbalances
      b. Lumbar puncture to rule out infection or trauma
      c. Skull x-rays, CT scan, or ultrasound of the head, brain scan, arteriogram, or pneumoencephalogram to detect any pathologic defects
      d. EEG may detect abnormal wave patterns characteristic of different types of seizures
         1) child may be awake or asleep; sedation is ordered and child may be sleep deprived the night before the test
         2) evocative stimulation: flashing strobe light, clicking sounds, hyperventilation

D. Nursing interventions
   1. During seizure activity
      a. Protect from injury.
         1) prevent falling, gently support head.
         2) decrease external stimuli; do not restrain.

TABLE 5.3   Types of Seizures

Type of Seizure	Clinical Findings
Generalized seizures	
Major motor seizure (grand mal)	May be preceded by aura; tonic and clonic phases. *Tonic phase:* limbs contract or stiffen; pupils dilate and eyes roll up and to one side; glottis closes, causing noise on exhalation; may be incontinent; occurs at same time as loss of consciousness; lasts 20–40 seconds. *Clonic phase:* repetitive movements, increased mucus production; slowly tapers. Seizure ends with postictal period of confusion, drowsiness.
Absence seizure (petit mal)	Usually nonorganic brain damage present; must be differentiated from daydreaming. Sudden onset, with twitching or rolling of eyes; lasts a few seconds.
Myoclonic seizure	Associated with brain damage, may be precipitated by tactile or visual sensations. May be generalized or local. Brief flexor muscle spasm; may have arm extension, trunk flexion. Single group of muscles affected; involuntary muscle contractions; myoclonic jerks.
Akinetic seizure (tonic)	Related to organic brain damage. Sudden brief loss of postural tone, and temporary loss of consciousness.
Febrile seizure	Common in 5% of population under 5, familial, nonprogressive; does not generally result in brain damage. Seizure occurs only when fever is rising. EEG is normal 2 weeks after seizure.
Partial seizures	
Psychomotor seizure	May follow trauma, hypoxia, drug use. Purposeful but inappropriate, repetitive motor acts. Aura present; dreamlike state.
Simple partial seizure	Seizure confined to one hemisphere of brain. No loss of consciousness. May be motor, sensory, or autonomic symptoms.
Complex partial seizure	Begins in focal area but spreads to both hemispheres. Impairs consciousness. May be preceded by an aura.
Status epilepticus	Usually refers to generalized grand mal seizures. Seizure is prolonged (or there are repeated seizures without regaining consciousness) and unresponsive to treatment. Can result in decreased oxygen supply and possible cardiac arrest.

        3) do not use tongue blades (they add additional stimuli).
        4) loosen tight clothing.
    b. Keep airway open.
        1) place in side-lying position.
        2) suction excess mucous.
    c. Observe and record seizure.
        1) note any preictal aura.
           a) affective signs: fear, anxiety
           b) psychosensory signs: hallucinations
           c) cognitive signs: "déjà-vu" symptoms
        2) note nature of the ictal phase.
           a) symmetry of movement
           b) response to stimuli; LOC
           c) respiratory pattern
        3) note postictal response: amount of time it takes child to orient to time and place; sleepiness.
  2. Provide client teaching and discharge planning concerning
    a. Care during a seizure
    b. Need to continue drug therapy
    c. Safety precautions/activity limitations
    d. Need to wear Medic-Alert identification bracelet or carry identification card
    e. Potential behavioral changes and school problems
    f. Availability of support groups/community agencies
    g. How to assist the child in explaining disorder to peers

Cerebral Palsy (CP)

A. General information
  1. Neuromuscular disorder resulting from damage to or altered structure of the part of the brain responsible for controlling motor function
  2. Incidence: 1.5–5 in 1,000 live births
  3. May be caused by a variety of factors resulting in damage to the CNS; possible causes include
    a. Prenatally: genetic, altered neurologic development, or trauma or anoxia to mother (toxemia, rubella, accidents)
    b. Perinatally: during the birth process (drugs at delivery, precipitate delivery, fetal distress, breech deliveries with delay)
    c. Postnatally: kernicterus or head trauma (child falls out of crib or is hit by a car)
B. Medical management
  1. Drug therapy
    a. Antianxiety agents
    b. Skeletal muscle relaxants
    c. Local nerve blocks
  2. Physical/occupational therapy
  3. Speech/audiology therapy

  4. Surgery: muscle- and tendon-releasing procedures
C. Assessment findings: disease itself does not progress once established; progressive complications, however, cause changes in signs and symptoms
  1. Spasticity: exaggerated hyperactive reflexes (increased muscle tone, increase in stretch reflex, scissoring of legs, poorly coordinated body movements for voluntary activities)
    a. Occurs with pyramidal tract lesion
    b. Found in 40% of all CP
    c. Results in contractures
    d. Also affects ability to speak: altered quality and articulation
    e. Loud noise or sudden movement causes reaction with increased spasm
    f. No parachute reflex to protect self when falling
  2. Athetosis: constant involuntary, purposeless, slow, writhing motions
    a. Occurs with extrapyramidal tract (basal ganglia) lesion
    b. Found in 40% of all CP
    c. Athetosis disappears during sleep, therefore contractures do not develop
    d. Movements increase with increase in physical or emotional stress
    e. Also affects facial muscles
  3. Ataxia: disturbance in equilibrium; diminished righting reflex (lack of balance, poor coordination, dizziness, hypotonia)
    a. Occurs with extrapyramidal tract (cerebellar) lesion
    b. Found in 10% of all CP
    c. Muscles and reflexes are normal
  4. Tremor: repetitive rhythmic involuntary contractions of flexor and extensor muscles
    a. Occurs with extrapyramidal tract (basal ganglia) lesion
    b. Found in 5% of all CP
    c. Interferes with performance of precise movements
    d. Often a mild disability
  5. Rigidity: resistance to flexion and extension resulting from simultaneous contraction of both agonist and antagonist muscle groups
    a. Occurs with extrapyramidal tract (basal ganglia) lesion
    b. Found in 5% of all CP
    c. Diminished or absent reflexes
    d. Potential for severe contractures
  6. Associated problems
    a. Mental retardation: the majority of CP clients are of normal or higher than average intelligence, but are unable to demonstrate it on standardized tests; 18%–50% have some form of mental retardation

     b. Hearing loss in 13% of CP clients
     c. Defective speech in 75% of CP clients
     d. Dental anomalies (from muscle contractures)
     e. Orthopedic problems from contractures or inability to mobilize
     f. Visual disabilities in 28% due to poor muscle control
     g. Disturbances of body image, touch, perception
     h. Feelings of worthlessness

D. Nursing interventions
1. Obtain a careful pregnancy, birth, and childhood history.
2. Observe the child's behavior in various situations.
3. Assist with activities of daily living (ADL), help child to learn as many self-care activities as possible; CP clients cannot do any task unless they are consciously aware of each step in the task; careful teaching and demonstration is essential.
4. Provide a safe environment (safety helmet, padded crib).
5. Provide physical therapy to prevent contractures and assist in mobility (braces if necessary).
6. Provide client teaching and discharge planning concerning
     a. Nature of disease: CP is a nonfatal, noncurable disorder
     b. Need for continued physical, occupational, and speech therapy
     c. Care of orthopedic devices
     d. Provision for child's return to school
     e. Availability of support groups/community agencies.

Tay-Sachs Disease

A. General information
1. Degenerative brain disease, caused by absence of hexosaminidase A from all body tissues
2. Autosomal recessive inheritance
3. Occurs predominantly in children of Eastern European Jewish ancestry
4. A fatal disease; death usually occurs before age 4

B. Assessment findings
1. Progressive lethargy in a previously healthy 2- to 6-month-old infant
2. Loss of developmental accomplishments
3. Loss of visual acuity
4. Hyperreflexia, decerebrate posturing, dysphagia, malnutrition, seizures
5. Diagnosis confirmed by classic cherry-red spot on the macula and by enzyme measurements in serum, amniotic fluid, or white cells

C. Nursing interventions

1. Support parents at time of diagnosis; help them cope with feelings of anger and guilt.
2. Assist parents in planning long-term care for the child.
3. Provide genetic counseling and psychologic follow-up as needed.

Disorders of the Eye

Blindness

A. Causes
1. Genetic disorders: Tay-Sach's disease, inborn errors of metabolism
2. Maternal infections during pregnancy: TORCH syndrome
3. Perinatal: prematurity, retrolental fibroplasia
4. Postnatal: trauma, childhood infections

B. Medical management: treatment of causative disorders

C. Assessment findings
1. Vacant stare; obvious failure to look at objects
2. Rubbing eyes, tilting head, examining objects very close to the eyes
3. Does not reach for objects (over 4 months)
4. Does not smile when mother smiles (over 3 months), but does smile in response to mother's voice
5. Crawls or walks into furniture (over 12 months)
6. Does not respond to the motions of others
7. No concept of the look of an object, no concept of color or reflection of self
8. Other senses become more keenly developed to compensate
9. Unable to copy the actions of others; delayed motor milestones in accomplishing tasks but are not mentally handicapped
10. Various degrees (20/200 O.U. and worse)

D. Nursing interventions
1. For hospitalized child, find out parents' usual method of care.
2. Encourage infant to be active; use multisensory stimulation (rocking, water play, musical toys, touch).
3. From ages 2–5 arrange environment for maximum autonomy and safety (e.g., avoid foods with seeds and bones).
4. Speak before you touch the child, announce what you plan to do.
5. Do not rearrange furniture without first telling child.
6. For a partially sighted child
     a. Encourage child to sit in front of classroom.
     b. Speak directly to child's face; do not look down or turn back.
     c. Use large print and provide adequate nonglare lighting.

        d. Use contrasting colors to help locate areas.
    7. Provide client teaching and discharge planning concerning
        a. General child care, with adaptations for safety and developmental/functional level
        b. Availability of support groups/community agencies
        c. Special education programs
        d. Interaction with peers; assist child as necessary

Conjunctivitis

A. General information: infection of membrane covering anterior surface of eye globe and inner surface of eyelid due to multiple causes (bacterial, viral, allergic)
B. Medical management: ophthalmic antibiotics, steroids, anesthetics
C. Assessment findings: weeping eye, reddened conjunctiva, sensitivity to light, eyelid stuck shut with exudate
D. Nursing interventions
    1. Administer medications as ordered: apply ophthalmic antibiotic ointments from inner to outer canthus (do not let container touch eye).
    2. Provide client teaching and discharge planning concerning measures to prevent spread of infection
        a. Very contagious if bacterial or viral; no school until antibiotics have been taken for 24–48 hours
        b. Should not share pillows, tissues, toys
        c. Good hand-washing technique
        d. Medication regimen: schedule, dosage, desired and side effects

Disorders of the Ear

Deafness

A. Causes
    1. Conductive: interference in transmission from outer to middle ear from chronic otitis media, foreign bodies
    2. Sensorineural: dysfunction of the inner ear; damage to cranial nerve VIII (from rubella, meningitis, drugs)
B. Medical management
    1. Treatment of causative disorders
    2. Speech/auditory therapy
    3. Hearing aids
    4. Surgery, depending on the cause
C. Assessment findings
    1. Infant
        a. Fails to react to loud noises (does have a Moro reflex, but not to noise)
        b. Makes no attempt to locate sound

        c. Remains in babbling stage or ceases to babble
        d. Fails to develop speech
        e. Startled by sudden appearances
    2. All children
        a. Respond only when speaker's lips are visible
        b. Cannot concentrate for long on visual images; constantly scan the surroundings for change
        c. May have slow motor development
        d. Appear puzzled or withdrawn, or strain to hear
        e. Use high volume on TV/radio
    3. Audiologic testing
        a. Slight hearing deficit: difficulty hearing faint sounds, very little interference in school, no speech defect, benefits from favorable seating
        b. Mild hearing deficit: can understand conversational speech at 3–5 feet when facing the other person, decreased vocabulary, may miss half of class discussions
        c. Marked hearing deficit: misses most of conversation, hears loud noises, needs special education for language skills
D. Nursing interventions
    1. Speak slowly, not more loudly.
    2. Face child.
    3. Get child's attention before talking; let child see you before performing any care.
    4. Get feedback from child to make sure child has understood.
    5. Decrease outside noises that could interfere with child's ability to discern what you are saying.
    6. Be careful not to cover your mouth with hands.
    7. Teach language through visual cues, touch, and kinesthetics.
    8. Use body demonstrations or use doll play.
    9. Provide appropriate stimulation (puppets and musical toys are inappropriate).
    10. Provide client teaching and discharge planning concerning
        a. General child care, with adaptation for safety and developmental/functional levels
        b. Availability of support groups/community agencies
        c. Special education programs
        d. Care and use of hearing aids
        e. Interaction with peers: assist child as needed

Otitis Media

A. General information
    1. Bacterial or viral infection of the middle ear

2. More common in infants and preschoolers as the ear canal is shorter and more horizontal than in older children; also found in children with cleft lip/palate
3. Blockage of eustachian tube causes lymphedema and accumulation of fluid in the middle ear

B. Medical management
   1. Drug therapy
      a. Systemic and otic antibiotics
      b. Analgesics/antipyretics
   2. Surgery: myringotomy, with or without insertion of tubes (incision into the tympanic membrane to relieve the pressure and drain the fluid)

C. Assessment findings
   1. Dysfunction of eustachian tube
   2. Ear infection usually related to respiratory infection
   3. Increased middle ear pressure; bulging tympanic membrane
   4. Pain; infant pulls or touches ear frequently
   5. Irritability; cough; nasal congestion
   6. Diagnostic tests: C&S of fluid reveals causative organism

D. Nursing interventions
   1. Administer antibiotics as ordered, for a full 10-day course. When administering ear drops pull earlobe up and back for older children and down and back for infants.
   2. Administer acetaminophen for fever and discomfort.
   3. Administer decongestants to relieve eustachian tube obstruction as ordered.
   4. Provide care for child with a myringotomy tube insertion (day surgery)
      a. Child should wear earplugs when showering or having hair washed; do not permit diving.
      b. Be aware that tubes may fall out for no reason.
   5. Provide client teaching and discharge planning concerning
      a. Medication administration
      b. Post-op care, depending on the type of surgery

Sample Questions

15. Louise was born with a myelomeningocele with accompanying hydrocephalus. She has had a shunt procedure to alleviate the hydrocephalus. Louise should be placed in which of the following positions?
    1. Trendelenburg's.
    2. On her back.
    3. With her legs adducted.
    4. On her abdomen.

16. The nurse is caring for an infant who is born with hydrocephalus. She has a shunt inserted. Which of the following signs indicates that the shunt is functioning properly?
    1. The sunset sign.
    2. A bulging anterior fontanel.
    3. Decreasing daily head circumference.
    4 Widened suture lines.

17. Henry is a 13-year-old who has been diagnosed as having epilepsy. A positive sign that Henry is taking his Dilantin properly is
    1. hair growth on his upper lip.
    2. absence of seizures.
    3. lowered hemoglobin and hematocrit.
    4. drowsiness.

18. Jennifer Pine, 3 years old, is admitted with a diagnosis of viral meningitis. During an initial assessment of Jennifer the nurse would expect to find
    1. headache, fever, and petechiae.
    2. seizures, lethargy, and hypothermia.
    3. pallor, anorexia, and bulging fontanels.
    4. fever, irritability, and nuchal rigidity.

19. To meet the sensory need of a child with viral meningitis, nursing strategies should include
    1. minimizing bright lights and noise.
    2. promoting active range of motion.
    3. increasing environmental stimuli.
    4. avoiding physical contact with family members.

20. When addressing the emotional needs of the parents of a young child with meningitis, the primary focus should be on
    1. assuming all responsibility for physical care of the child.
    2. providing reassurance that the symptoms will resolve within the week.
    3. reinforcing information about the child's condition and plan of treatment.
    4. explaining the importance of an optimistic outlook when interacting with their child.

21. Discharge teaching for the parents of a child who had meningitis should include
    1. engaging a tutor to assist with learning problems.
    2. administering the prescribed antibiotic.
    3. notifying the physician if her fever or headache persists more than a few days after discharge.
    4. encouraging Jennifer to resume normal activities immediately.

22. Phillip, 6 years old, is brought to the emergency department unconscious after being hit by a car. The most helpful information for the nurse performing the neurological examination on Phillip is the nurse's knowledge of
    1. normal growth and development.
    2. Phillip's usual behavior and status.

3. Phillip's past medical history.
4. Phillip's growth and developmental progress during infancy.
23. The nurse is assessing a child who has a head injury for the occulocephalic reflex (doll's eyes). The nurse understands that the doll's eye reflex is present if the child's eyes
   1. move in the same direction in which his head is turned.
   2. move in the direction opposite to which his head is turned.
   3. remain midline when his head is turned.
   4. move to the medial aspect of the orbit when his head is turned.
24. Phillip's pupils are dilated and react sluggishly. This is indicative of
   1. barbiturate overdosage.
   2. damage to the diencephalon.
   3. damage to the sympathetic system.
   4. damage to the parasympathetic system.

Answers and Rationales

15. The correct answer is 4. Pressure must be kept off the spinal sac. As there is paralysis of the lower extremities, the legs should be abducted. Trendelenburg's position is contraindicated in hydrocephalus.
16. The correct answer is 3. With improved draining of the CSF, the head circumference should become smaller. All the other signs indicate increased ICP.
17. The correct answer is 2. Dilantin is an antiepileptic drug that controls seizures. All the other signs and symptoms are side effects of the medication.
18. The correct answer is 4. The clinical symptoms of viral meningitis (aseptic meningitis) include fever, irritability, and stiffness of the neck (nuchal rigidity). Other symptoms include drowsiness, photophobia, weakness, painful extremities, and sometimes seizures. Aseptic meningitis usually resolves within two weeks. Headache and fever may be seen in meningitis, but petechiae are not. Seizures and lethargy may be seen in meningitis, but hypothermia is not. Bulging fontanels are a sign of hydrocephalus.
19. The correct answer is 1. Photophobia and hypersensitivity to environmental stimuli are common clinical manifestations of meningeal irritation and infection. Comfort measures include providing an environment that is quiet and has minimal stressful stimuli. Promoting active range of motion at this time would not be beneficial. The client needs rest. Increasing environmental stimuli would only exacerbate the symptoms of photophobia and hypersensitivity. The client needs quiet and rest. Viral meningitis is not contagious so contact with family members is not contraindicated.

20. The correct answer is 3. Successful coping in times of anxiety and stress requires that the nurse be available to provide information that validates parental right to know and participation in their child's care. Honesty, patience, and unhurried repetition of information is necessary to support the family. The parents should not be expected to assume all responsibility for the child's physical care. The symptoms will not necessarily resolve within a week. An optimistic outlook is also important when interacting with the child but it is not the primary focus.
21. The correct answer is 3. Parents should be instructed to contact the physician if the child's symptoms worsen or persist. The child recovering from viral meningitis should show signs of feeling better a week after discharge. A tutor may be necessary if cognitive function was affected by the meningitis but this is not a priority in discharge teaching. Antibiotics are not indicated in the treatment of *viral* meningitis. The client should resume activities as tolerated in time.
22. The correct answer is 2. The child's usual behavior and level of development is what provides critical information about his pretrauma neurological function. This would serve as baseline data, present prior to the injury. It is important to know normal growth and development but it is not individualized to this child. Phillip's past medical history is important but is not the most helpful information when doing the neurological exam.
23. The correct answer is 2. The occulocephalic reflex occurs if, when the head of an unconscious child is turned rapidly in one direction, the eyes move in the opposite direction. In the occulocephalic reflex, the eyes do not move in the same direction in which the head is turned. The eyes do not remain in the midline when the head is turned. The eyes do not move to the medial aspect of the orbit when the head is turned.
24. The correct answer is 4. When dilated pupils react sluggishly or are nonreactive, it is an indication that there has been damage to the parasympathetic nervous system, which controls the pupillary construction response. Damage to the diencephalon would show pupils that are small and reactive to light. Barbiturates cause pupillary dilation. Damage to the sympathetic nervous system would inhibit the normal dilation response and would cause pupils to be constricted.

The Cardiovascular System

VARIATIONS FROM THE ADULT

Fetal Circulation

A. Fetal circulation differs from adult circulation in several ways and is designed to ensure a high-oxygen blood supply to the brain and myocardium.

B. Characteristics
1. Placenta is the source of oxygen for the fetus.
2. Fetal lungs receive less than 10% of the blood volume; lungs do not exchange gas.
3. Right atrium of fetal heart is the chamber with the highest oxygen concentration.

C. Pattern of altered blood flow and facilitating structures
1. Blood is carried from the placenta through the umbilical vein and enters the inferior vena cava through the *ductus venosus.*
2. This permits most of the highly oxygenated blood to go directly to the right atrium, bypassing the liver.
3. This right atrial blood flows directly into the left atrium through the *foramen ovale,* an opening between the right and left atria.
4. From the left atrium, blood flows into the left ventricle and aorta, through the subclavian arteries, to the cerebral and coronary arteries, resulting in the brain and heart receiving the most highly oxygenated blood.
5. Deoxygenated blood returns from the head and arms through the superior vena cava, enters the right atrium, and passes into the right ventricle.
6. Blood from the right ventricle flows into the pulmonary artery, but because fetal lungs are collapsed, the pressure in the pulmonary artery is very high.
7. Because pulmonary resistance is high, most of the blood passes into the distal aorta through the *ductus arteriosus,* which connects the pulmonary artery and the aorta distal to the origin of the subclavian arteries.
8. From the aorta, blood flows to the rest of the body.

Normal Circulatory Changes at Birth

A. When the umbilical cord is clamped or severed, the blood supply from the placenta is cut off, and oxygenation must then take place in the newborn's lungs.

B. As the lungs expand with air, the pulmonary artery pressure decreases and circulation to lungs increases.

C. Structural changes
1. Ductus venosus: after the umbilical cord is severed, flow through the ductus venosus decreases and eventually ceases; it constricts within 3–7 days after birth and eventually becomes ligamentum venosum.
2. Foramen ovale
   a. Functional closure of this valvelike opening occurs when pressure in the left atrium exceeds pressure in the right.
   b. Expansion of the pulmonary artery causes a drop in pulmonary artery pressure and in right atrial and ventricular pressure.
   c. At the same time there is increased pulmonary blood flow to the left atrium and increased aortic pressure (from clamping of the umbilical cord), which in turn raises left ventricular and left atrial pressure.
   d. Anatomic closure of the foramen ovale occurs within the first weeks after birth with the deposit of fibrin.
3. Ductus arteriosus
   a. Increase in aortic blood flow increases aortic pressure and decreases right-to-left shunt through the ductus arteriosus; shunt becomes bidirectional.
   b. Increased pulmonary blood flow increases arterial oxygen, causing vasoconstriction of ductus arteriosus within hours of birth.
   c. Functional closure occurs when this constriction causes cessation of blood flow, usually 24 hours after birth.
   d. Anatomic closure occurs when there is growth of fibrous tissue in the lumen of the ductus arteriosus, by 1–3 weeks.

Abnormal Circulatory Patterns after Birth

A. Normal blood flow in the child may be disrupted as a result of abnormal openings between the pulmonary and systemic circulations.

B. Any time there is a defect connecting systemic and pulmonary circulation, blood will go from high to low pressure (the path of least resistance).

1. Normally pressure is higher in the systemic circulation, so blood will be shunted from systemic to pulmonary (left to right).
2. An obstruction to pulmonary blood flow, however, may cause increased pressure proximal to the site of the obstruction.
3. With an obstruction to pulmonary blood flow, as well as an opening between ventricles, the blood flow may be right to left (if right-sided pressure exceeds left-sided pressure).

ASSESSMENT

Overview

A. Approximately 40,000 babies are born with congenital heart disease (CHD) in the United States yearly.
B. One-third of these babies will be seriously ill at birth, one-third will have problems detected during childhood or later, and one-third never have problems.
C. Etiology is multifactional.

History

A. Family history: parental history of CHD, congenital defects in siblings, history of genetic problems in family.
B. History of pregnancy: rubella, viral infections, medications, x-ray exposure, alcohol ingestion, cigarette smoking.
C. Child's health history
   1. Presenting problem: symptoms may include
      a. Feeding problems: fatigue, irritability, tachypnea, profuse sweating
      b. Failure to thrive
      c. Respiratory difficulties: tachypnea, difficulty breathing, frequent respiratory infections
      d. Color changes: pallor, cyanosis (persistent or intermittent)
      e. Activity intolerance
      f. All presenting symptoms must be explored within a developmental framework
   2. Past medical history: rheumatic fever; associated chromosomal abnormalities (e.g., Down's syndrome)

Physical Examination

A. Plot height and weight on growth chart; measure respiratory rate and rhythm; inspect for chest enlargement or asymmetry.
B. Inspect for presence of cyanosis: lips, mucous membranes, extremities.
C. Inspect for clubbing of fingers (thought to be caused by increased capillary formation and soft tissue fibrosis).
D. Observe for distended veins.
E. Palpate/percuss quality and symmetry of pulses, size of liver and spleen, presence of thrill over heart during expiration.
F. Auscultate for heart rate and rhythm.
G. Auscultate for abnormal heart sounds and murmurs; murmurs are caused by abnormal flow of blood between chambers or vessels; classified as
   1. Innocent: no anatomic or physiologic abnormality
   2. Functional: no anatomic defect, but may be caused by a physiologic abnormality
   3. Organic: caused by a structural abnormality
H. Measure blood pressure in both arm and thigh.
   1. In infants under 1 year, arm and thigh blood pressure should be the same.
   2. In children over 1 year, systolic pressure in leg is usually higher by 10–40 mm Hg.
   3. A wide pulse pressure (greater than 50 mm Hg) or a narrow pulse pressure (less than 10 mm Hg) may be associated with a heart defect.
I. Select proper blood pressure cuff size.
   1. Too small a cuff can give a falsely elevated BP reading
   2. Bladder inside the cuff should be two-thirds the length of the upper arm

Laboratory/Diagnostic Tests

A. Chest x-ray
B. Cardiac fluoroscopy
C. Magnetic resonance imaging (MRI)
D. Electrocardiogram
E. Echocardiography
F. Hematologic testing: polycythemia is often associated with cyanotic heart defects
G. Cardiac catheterization
   1. Femoral vein often used for access
   2. Catheter threaded into right side of the heart since septal defects permit entry into the left side
   3. Nursing care: pretest
      a. Child's preparation should be based on developmental level, level of understanding, and past experience.
      b. Use doll play and pictures as appropriate.
      c. Describe sensations child will feel in simple terms.
      d. Administer medications as ordered.
   4. Nursing care: posttest
      a. Check extremity distal to the catheterization site for color, temperature, pulse, capillary refill.

b. Keep extremity distal to the catheterization site extended for 6 hours.
c. Check pressure dressing over catheterization site for bleeding.
d. Monitor heart rate for signs of bradycardia, tachycardia, and dysrhythmia.
e. Monitor for transient temperature elevation due to physiologic dehydration (NPO, contrast media).
f. Monitor urine output and blood pressure.

ANALYSIS

Nursing diagnoses for the child with a disorder of the cardiovascular system may include
A. Altered growth and development: failure to thrive
B. High risk for injury: physiologic
C. Exercise intolerance
D. Altered nutrition: less than body requirements
E. Fear/anxiety: child and family
F. High risk for infection
G. Knowledge deficit (specify)
H. Decreased cardiac output
I. Fluid volume excess

PLANNING AND IMPLEMENTATION

Goals

A. Tissue will be adequately oxygenated.
B. Child will achieve normal growth and development milestones.
C. Child will be free from symptoms of complications of heart disease.
D. Parents will understand child's condition.
E. Parents will be able to care for child at home.

Interventions

Care of the Child with Congestive Heart Failure (CHF)

A. General information
1. Usually due to a surgically correctable structural abnormality of the heart that results in increased blood volume and pressure
2. A symptom complex reflecting the heart's inability to meet the metabolic demands of the body
B. Medical management
1. Directed toward improvement of cardiac function and energy conservation
2. Drug therapy
a. Digitalis to improve myocardial contractility and slow the heart rate

b. Diuretics to decrease total body water and to increase urine output
c. Potassium supplement if diuretic is potassium depleting
3. High-caloric formula or nasogastric feedings may be required to meet nutritional needs
C. Assessment findings
1. Tachycardia, gallop rhythm, cardiomegaly, decreased peripheral pulses, and mottling of the extremities
2. Tachypnea, retractions, grunting, nasal flaring, cough, cyanosis, orthopnea
3. Hepatomegaly, edema, distended neck and peripheral veins, decreased urine output
4. Failure to thrive, decreased exercise tolerance
D. Nursing interventions
1. Decrease energy expenditure
a. Frequent rest periods
b. Small, frequent feedings
c. Minimize crying
d. Prevent cold stress
2. Provide adequate nutrition
a. Estimate daily caloric requirement
b. Use soft nipple
c. Consider gavage feeding if necessary
3. Monitor fluid status
a. I&O, specific gravity
b. Daily weight
4. Administer medications as ordered
a. Digoxin (see page 55)
1) check dosage with another RN
2) give 1 hour before feeding or 2 hours after feeding
3) take apical pulse for 1 minute; if bradycardia is present, hold dose and contact physician
4) monitor serum potassium levels; if less than 3.5mEq/L, may be contraindicated
5) monitor therapeutic effects; therapeutic serum digoxin levels range from 0.8 to 2.0 µg/L.
6) monitor for toxicity: nausea, anorexia, vomiting, lethargy, bradycardia
7) parent/child teaching
b. Diuretic (see Table 2.17, pages 68–69, Antihypertensive Drugs)
1) intake and output
2) daily weight
3) monitor side effects: dehydration, electrolyte imbalance especially hypokalemia (potentiates digoxin and may lead to toxicity)
4) parent/child teaching
5. Provide adequate rest
6. Prevent infections
7. Promote growth and development
8. Reduce respiratory distress

a. Position in semi- or high-Fowler's position
b. Knee-chest position (squatting) in children with cyanotic heart disease

EVALUATION

A. Child reaches optimum cardiac status.
  1. Normal color
  2. Easy respirations
  3. Increased exercise tolerance
  4. Satisfactory growth
B. No evidence of complications such as signs and symptoms of congestive heart failure (CHF), infection, or electrolyte imbalance.
C. Parents demonstrate ability to care for child, perform necessary treatments, and administer prescribed medications.

DISORDERS OF THE CARDIOVASCULAR SYSTEM

Congenital Heart Defects

See Figure 5.1.

Classification

A. Acyanotic heart defects
  1. Oxygenated blood is shunted from the systemic to pulmonary circulation (left-to-right shunt) and blood leaving the aorta is completely oxygenated.
  2. Increased blood volume on right side of heart results in hypertrophy of right ventricle.
  3. Eventually, most acyanotic heart defects will result in CHF.
B. Cyanotic heart defects
  1. Unoxygenated blood is shunted from the right to the left side of the heart where it mixes with oxygenated blood.
  2. The blood pumped to the peripheral tissues has a much lower oxygen content than normal, causing the bluish color called cyanosis.

Acyanotic Heart Defects

A. General information and medical management
  1. *Atrial septal defect* (*ASD*): abnormal opening in the septum between left and right atria, causing a left-to-right shunt
    a. 15% of CHD
    b. Symptoms depend on size and location of defect
    c. Usually detected after the neonatal period

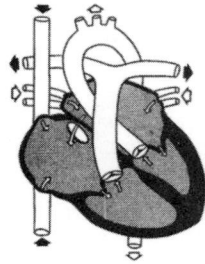

(A) Atrial septal defect

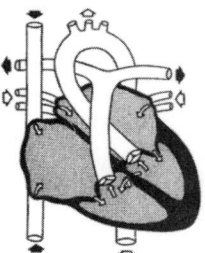

(B) Ventricular septal defect

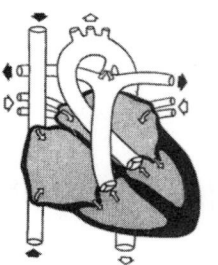

(C) Patent ductus arteriosus

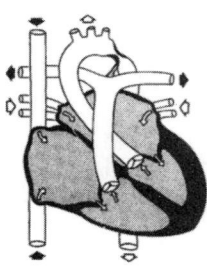

(D) Coarctation of the aorta

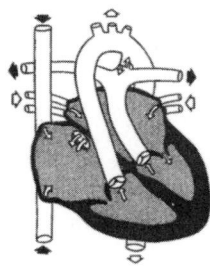

(E) Transposition of the great arteries

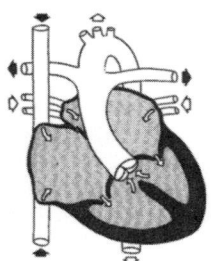

(F) Truncus arteriosus

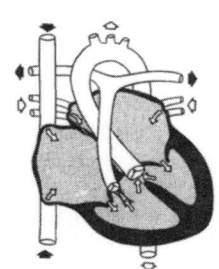

(G) Tetralogy of Fallot

FIGURE 5.1 Congenital heart defects (Courtesy of Ross Laboratories, Columbus, OH, from Clinical Aid, #7)

d. Symptoms include decreased exercise tolerance, dyspnea, and systolic ejection murmur heard best in the upper left sternal border
e. Surgical correction performed between 2 and 4 years of age
  2. *Ventricular septal defect* (*VSD*): opening in the septum between ventricles, causing a left-to-right shunt
    a. 25% of CHD

b. Symptoms depend on size of the defect, child's age, and degree of pulmonary vascular resistance

c. Small VSDs may be asymptomatic; larger defects may result in hypertrophy, potential failure of the right ventricle, and CHF

d. Symptoms include tachycardia, increased respiratory effort, dyspnea, fatigue, FTT, CHF, frequent respiratory infections, systolic murmur heard best at lower left sternal border

e. Surgical correction indicated if medical management fails to diminish symptom or if a child continues to have a persistent shunt by age 3 to 4 years

f. If an infant is a poor surgical risk, pulmonary artery banding (a constricting band around pulmonary artery to reduce blood flow and prevent heart failure) may be performed; complete repair is undertaken when the child is older

3. *Patent ductus arteriosus* (*PDA*): failure to close at birth
   a. 10% of CHD in term infants, higher in premature infants
   b. Allows oxygenated blood pumped into the aorta from the left ventricle to return to the lungs
   c. A small PDA may be asymptomatic; larger PDAs cause excess blood in lungs and volume overload, leading to CHF
   d. Machinery-type murmur best heard at middle to upper left sternal border
   e. In premature infants treatment with indomethacin (prostaglandin inhibitor) sometimes causes closure
   f. Definitive surgery is ligation of PDA (closed-heart procedure), relatively safe at all ages.

4. *Coarctation of aorta*
   a. Narrowing of the aorta usually just beyond the left subclavian artery; 8% of CHD
   b. Causes a significant decrease in blood flow to abdomen and legs, with majority of blood shunted to head and arms
   c. Clinical manifestations depend on degree of narrowing; may include
      1) blood and pulse pressure higher in arms than legs; high pulse pressure in carotid and radial pulses; low pulse pressure in femoral pulses
      2) warm upper body and cool lower body, nosebleeds and headaches (from increased blood pressure in top half of body)
      3) predisposition to strokes

d. Surgical treatment dependent on location of coarctation

5. *Pulmonary stenosis* (*pulmonic valve stenosis*)
   a. Abnormally narrowed valvular orifice.
   b. If stenosis is mild to moderate children may be asymptomatic and require no treatment.
   c. More severe pulmonic valve stenosis can result in right ventricular hypertrophy and even hepatomegaly.
   d. Severe stenosis requires valvotomy.

6. *Aortic stenosis*
   a. Abnormally small valve orifice; valve may be bicuspid rather than tricuspid.
   b. Mild to moderate stenosis may not produce symptoms; more severe stenosis produces left ventricular hypertrophy, left heart failure, decreased cardiac output.
   c. Valvotomy is preferred treatment for children, but valve replacement may be necessary later.

7. *Endocardial cushion defects*
   a. Altered development of the core of the heart from which septum and valves originate
   b. Causes mixing of oxygenated and unoxygenated blood in the heart chambers
   c. Most common cardiac defects in Down's syndrome

B. Assessment findings
   1. Feeding problems such as fatigue, tachypnea, irritability, reflux, profuse sweating
   2. Failure to thrive, poor weight gain
   3. Respiratory problems such as tachypnea, dyspnea, difficulty breathing, retractions, nasal flaring, anoxic spells, frequent respiratory infections, congested cough
   4. Pallor, cyanosis
   5. Activity intolerance such as restlessness, diaphoresis, lethargy
   6. Signs and symptoms of congestive heart failure

C. Nursing interventions
   1. Prepare the child/family for diagnostic studies, surgery
      a. Age-appropriate explanations/play
      b. Address the emotional impact of heart disease
   2. Administer medications as ordered
   3. Ensure adequate nutrition
      a. Anticipate infant's hunger to avoid crying
      b. Small, frequent feedings
      c. Position in a semi-erect position in caregiver's arms
      d. Burp frequently
      e. Observe for vomiting and diarrhea if high-caloric formula ordered

      f. Support the breastfeeding mother

      g. For older children, avoid empty-caloric foods; offer small, well-balanced meals

  4. Monitor vital signs.

  5. Prevent cold stress; maintain body temperature.

  6. Provide adequate rest.

      a. Provide passive age-appropriate play.

      b. Organize care to decrease child's energy expenditure.

      c. Try to anticipate child's needs; prevent crying.

      d. In infants, use soft nipple to decrease work during feeding; gavage feedings may be necessary.

  7. Position child properly.

  8. Prevent infection (excess secretions make child susceptible to respiratory infections).

  9. Promote normal growth and developmental needs.

  10. Antibiotic prophylaxis before certain procedures (e.g., dental work).

Cyanotic Heart Defects

See Figure 5.1.

A. General information and medical management

  1. *Tetralogy of Fallot*

      a. 10% of CHD/most common cyanotic heart defect

      b. Four components: pulmonary stenosis, VSD, overriding aorta, and ventricular hypertrophy

      c. Symptoms depend on the degree of pulmonary stenosis

      d. Aorta sits near core of heart over the VSD and therefore receives blood from both ventricles

      e. Decreased blood flow to lungs; mixture of unoxygenated blood going to aorta causes cyanosis and dyspnea

      f. Symptoms also include activity intolerance, irritability, failure to thrive, polycythemia, harsh systolic murmur best heard along the left sternal border, and TET spells

      g. TET spells

        1) hypoxic episodes caused by transient increase in the obstruction of the right ventricular outflow tract

        2) symptoms include cyanosis, tachypnea, flaccidity, altered level of consciousness; may progress to seizures, CVA, death

        3) episodes may be precipitated by crying, feeding, or defecation

        4) treatment includes positioning in a knee-chest position, oxygen, propranolol, and morphine

      h. Surgical correction

        1) surgical intervention indicated when infant or child becomes symptomatic

        2) palliative procedure

          a) goal: to increase blood flow to the lungs

          b) Blalock-Taussig shunt: anastomosis of the right or left subclavian artery to the pulmonary artery

        3) total repair

          a) patch closure of VSD

          b) correction of pulmonary stenosis

      i. Lifelong antibiotic prophylaxis (to prevent endocarditis) for certain procedures (e.g., dental work)

  2. *Transposition of the great vessels* (*TGA*)

      a. Aorta arises from right ventricle; pulmonary artery arises from left ventricle

      b. Oxygenated blood therefore circulates through left side of heart to lungs and back to left side; unoxygenated blood enters right atrium from body, goes to right ventricle, and back out to the body without being oxygenated.

      c. Child cannot live without a communication between atria or ventricles.

      d. Foramen ovale remains open for short while as pressure in heart is not sufficient to close it.

      e. Poor oxygenation makes these children cyanotic.

      f. Treatment includes surgical incision or balloon septostomy to create an ASD (Rashkind procedure).

      g. When child is old enough, defect will be corrected surgically (Mustard procedure) to redirect blood flow.

      h. An arterial switch is performed when associated with a VSD

  3. *Truncus arteriosus*

      a. Only one vessel exits heart from both ventricles; always associated with a large VSD.

      b. As there is no septum to divide aorta and pulmonary trunk, oxygenated and unoxygenated blood mix, causing cyanosis.

      c. Medical treatment includes digitalis and diuretics; if growth failure occurs despite treatment, surgical intervention is necessary.

      d. Until recently, pulmonary banding was the only surgical option; some centers now perform complete intracardiac repair.

  4. *Hypoplastic left heart syndrome*

      a. Concomitant presence of aortic valve atresia, mitral atresia or stenosis, diminutive or absent left ventricle, severe hypoplasia of ascending aorta, and aortic arch

    b. Usually fatal, few infants survive past 6 weeks

    c. No satisfactory treatment; surgical corrections have had limited success

B. Assessment findings
1. Cyanosis
2. Polycythemia (low oxygen output triggers increase in RBC production to attempt to increase body's oxygen-carrying capacity)
3. Clubbing of digits (poor circulation to extremities)
4. Poor growth and little tolerance for activity
5. Increased pulse and respiratory rate, dyspnea
6. Poor feeding; weak cry
7. Squatting (especially in tetralogy) helps to decrease blood flow to extremities and to keep oxygenated blood for brain and trunk
8. These children at risk for left-sided heart failure, brain infarctions, and blood clots
9. Development of collateral circulation
10. Laboratory tests: hct increased (increased sludging/concentration of blood from increased RBC)

C. Nursing interventions
1. Do not interfere when child is squatting; as long as child appears comfortable, no intervention other than observation required.
2. Organize care to decrease child's expenditure of energy.
3. Administer oxygen as ordered.
4. Meet needs quickly; prevent crying.
5. Provide passive stimulation.
6. Use soft "preemie" nipple to decrease energy in sucking.
7. Provide careful skin care; decreased blood flow to periphery predisposes these children to circulatory problems.
8. Antibiotic prophylaxis for certain procedures (e.g., dental work).

Cardiac Surgery

A. General information
1. Surgical correction of congenital defects within the heart, or surgery of the great vessels in the immediate area surrounding the heart
2. *Open-heart surgery* (uses cardiopulmonary bypass): provides a relatively blood-free operative site; heart-lung machine maintains gas exchange during surgery
3. *Closed heart surgery* does not use cardiopulmonary bypass machine; indicated for ligation of a patent ductus arteriosus or coarctation of the aorta

B. Nursing interventions: preoperative
1. Determine the child's level of understanding; have child draw a picture, tell you a story, or use doll play.
2. Correct misunderstandings/teach the child about the surgery using diagrams and play therapy; use terms appropriate to developmental level.
3. Accompany the child to the operating and recovery rooms and the intensive care unit, explaining the various equipment; allow child to handle/experience it, if possible, and introduce staff and clients, depending on child's developmental/emotional levels.
4. Have child practice post-op procedures (turning, coughing, deep breathing, etc.).
5. Include parents in teaching sessions, but have separate sessions for the parents only.
6. Establish pre-op baseline data for vital signs, activity/sleep patterns, I&O.

C. Nursing interventions: postoperative
1. Prevent injury/complications.
    a. Monitor vital signs and circulatory pressure readings frequently until stable. Monitor EKG.
    b. Assess neurologic status frequently.
    c. Observe surgical site for intactness/drainage.
2. Promote gas exchange (client may be on mechanical ventilation).
    a. Position as ordered.
    b. Administer oxygen at prescribed rate.
    c. Provide humidification.
    d. Suction as necessary.
    e. Perform postural drainage and chest percussion as ordered.
    f. Turn, cough, and deep breathe hourly.
    g. Perform routine care of chest tubes and drainage system, depending on the type of surgery.
3. Monitor I&O.
4. Provide nutrition as ordered.
5. Provide alternative means of communication if mechanical ventilation is used, e.g., picture cards.
6. Provide psychologic support of the child/family.
7. Allow activity as tolerated.
8. Provide client teaching and discharge planning concerning
    a. Need for child/family to express feelings/fears
    b. Resumption of ADL
    c. Assisting child in dealing with peers/returning to school
    d. Referral for parents to support groups/community agencies

Acquired Heart Disease

Rheumatic Fever (RF)

A. General information
  1. An inflammatory disorder that may involve the heart, joints, connective tissue, and the CNS
  2. Peaks in school-age children; linked to environmental factors and family history of disorder
  3. Thought to be an autoimmune disorder
      a. Preceded by an infection of group A beta-hemolytic streptococcus (usually a strep throat); the heart itself is not infected, however.
      b. Antigenic markers for strep toxin closely resemble markers for heart valves; this resemblance causes antibodies made against the strep to also attack heart valves.
  4. Prognosis depends on degree of heart damage
B. Medical management
  1. Drug therapy
      a. Penicillin
          1) used in the acute phase
          2) used prophylactically for several years after the attack
          3) erythromycin substituted if child is sensitive to penicillin
      b. Salicylates: for analgesic, anti-inflammatory, antipyretic effect
      c. Steroids: for anti-inflammatory effect
  2. Decrease cardiac workload: bed rest until lab studies return to normal
C. Assessment findings
  1. Major symptoms (Jones' criteria)
      a. Carditis
          1) seen in 50% of clients
          2) Aschoff nodules (areas of inflammation and degeneration around heart valves, pericardium, and myocardium)
          3) valvular insufficiency of mitral and aortic valves possible
          4) cardiomegaly
          5) shortness of breath, hepatomegaly, edema
      b. Polyarthritis
          1) migratory, therefore no contractures develop
          2) most common in large joints, which become red, swollen, painful
          3) synovial fluid is sterile
          4) no arthralgia
      c. Chorea (Sydenham's chorea, St. Vitus' dance): CNS disorder characterized by abrupt, purposeless, involuntary muscular movements
          1) gradual, insidious onset: starts with personality change or clumsiness
          2) mostly seen in prepubertal girls
          3) may appear months after strep infection
          4) movements increase with excitement
          5) lasts 1–3 months
      d. Subcutaneous nodules
          1) usually a sign of severe disease
          2) occur with active carditis
          3) firm, nontender nodes on bony prominences of joints
          4) lasts for weeks
      e. Erythema marginatum: transient, nonpruritic rash starting with central red patches that expand; results in series of irregular patches with red, raised margins and pale centers (resemble giraffe spots)
  2. Minor symptoms
      a. Reliable history of RF, fever
      b. Recent history of strep infection
      c. Diagnostic tests: erythrocyte sedimentation rate (ESR) and antistreptolysin O (ASO) titer increased; changes on ECG
D. Nursing interventions
  1. Carditis
      a. Administer penicillin as ordered.
          1) used prophylactically to prevent future attacks of strep and further damage to the heart
          2) to be taken until age 20 or for 5 years after attack, whichever is longer
      b. Promote bed rest until ESR returns to normal.
  2. Arthritis: administer aspirin as ordered, change child's position in bed frequently.
  3. Chorea
      a. Decrease stimulation.
      b. Provide a safe environment: no forks with meals, assistance with mobility.
      c. Provide small, frequent meals; increased muscle activity causes increased kcal requirements.
  4. Nodules and rash: none.
  5. Alleviate child's anxiety about the ability of heart to continue to function.
  6. Prevent recurrent infection.
  7. Minimize boredom with age-appropriate sedentary play.
  8. Provide client teaching and discharge planning concerning
      a. Adaptation of home environment to promote bed rest (commode, call bell, diversional activities)
      b. Importance of prophylactic medication regimen

c. Diet modification in relation to decreased activity/cardiac demands
d. Avoidance of reinfections
e. Home-bound education
f. Availability of community agencies

Sample Questions

25. A 4-year-old with tetralogy of Fallot is seen in a squatting position near his bed. The nurse should
    1. administer oxygen.
    2. take no action if he looks comfortable but continue to observe him.
    3. pick him up and place him in Trendelenburg's position in bed.
    4. have him stand up and walk around the room.
26. Christopher, 2 months, is suspected of having coarctation of the aorta. The cardinal sign of this defect is
    1. clubbing of the digits and circumoral cyanosis.
    2. pedal edema and portal congestion.
    3. systolic ejection murmur.
    4. upper extremity hypertension.
27. When assessing the apical heart rate in infants and toddlers, the point of maximal impulse (PMI) is
    1. between the third and fourth left intercostal space.
    2. between the fourth and fifth left intercostal space.
    3. at the fifth intercostal space to the right of the midclavicular line.
    4. in the aortic area.
28. Two-week-old Jonathon has a patent ductus arteriosus. Prior to administering digoxin the nurse should
    1. take the apical pulse for 30 seconds and multiply by 2.
    2. give the medication if his pulse is 92, but notify the physician.
    3. take the radial pulse for 1 full minute.
    4. give the medication after finding that the pulse is 135 beats/minute.
29. The nurse is planning care for a two-week-old infant who has a congenital heart defect. Which of the following actions is not appropriate?
    1. Using a soft "preemie" nipple for feedings.
    2. Providing passive stimulation.
    3. Allowing him to cry to promote increased oxygenation.
    4. Placing him in orthopneic position.
30. Alice White, 10 years old, has been hospitalized for two weeks with rheumatic fever. Alice's mother questions whether her other children can catch the rheumatic fever. The nurse's best response is
    1. The fact that you brought Alice to the hospital early enough will decrease the chance of her siblings getting it.
    2. It is caused by an autoimmune reaction and is not contagious.
    3. You appear concerned that your daughter's disease is contagious.
    4. Your other children should be taking antibiotics to prevent them from catching rheumatic fever.
31. A 10-year-old child is admitted with rheumatic fever. In addition to carditis, the nurse should assess the child for the presence of
    1. arthritis.
    2. bronchitis.
    3. malabsorption.
    4. oliguria.

Answers and Rationales

25. The correct answer is 2. Squatting is a normal response to a cyanotic heart defect. This position increases pulmonary blood flow because it changes the relationship between systemic and pulmonary vascular resistance. The squatting position alone should increase the child's oxygen level, so administration of oxygen will most likely not be necessary. Picking the child up and placing him in a Trendelenburg position (head down) decreases his pulmonary blood flow and makes it harder for him to breathe. His cardiopulmonary status would not allow him to walk around the room at this time.
26. The correct answer is 4. Coarctation of the aorta is characterized by upper extremity hypertension and diminished pulses in the extremities. These signs would be seen in a child with a cyanotic heart defect. Pedal edema and portal hypertension are seen in clients with congestive heart failure secondary to many congenital cardiac disorders. Systolic ejection murmurs are present in a child with atrial septal defect.
27. The correct answer is 1. The heartbeat is most easily counted at the point of maximum impulse. From birth through toddlerhood it is located between the third and fourth left intercostal space. The PMI in an adult is located at the fifth intercostal space inside the left midclavicular line.
28. The correct answer is 4. The apical pulse is taken for 1 full minute and the medication is withheld if the pulse is less than 100 beats/minute.

29. The correct answer is 3. Crying expends already decreased energy. All the other measures help to compensate for the decreased cardiac output.
30. The correct answer is 2. Rheumatic fever is an autoimmune reaction to a streptococcal infection and is limited to the person having the reaction. Rheumatic fever is not a contagious disease.
31. The correct answer is 1. A major symptom of rheumatic fever is arthritis. Bronchitis is not seen with rheumatic fever. Malabsorption is not seen with rheumatic fever. Oliguria is not seen with rheumatic fever.

The Hematologic System

VARIATIONS FROM THE ADULT

A. In the young child all the bone marrow is involved in blood cell formation.
B. By puberty, only the sternum, ribs, pelvis, vertebrae, skull, and proximal epiphyses of femur and humerus are involved.
C. During the first 6 months of life, fetal hemoglobin is gradually replaced by adult hemoglobin, and it is only after this that hemoglobin disorders can be diagnosed.

ASSESSMENT

History

A. Family history: genetic hematologic disorders, anemia, or jaundice
B. History of pregnancy: parents' blood types, anemia, infection or drug ingestion, course of labor and delivery
C. Child's health history
   1. Neonatal course: occurrence, duration, and treatment of jaundice; bleeding episodes; blood transfusions
   2. Accidents, operations, hospitalizations (any blood transfusions or unusual bleeding)
   3. Nutrition: dietary intake of iron and vitamin B_{12}; history of pica
   4. Ingestions: lead-based paint; drugs
   5. Ability to participate in age-appropriate activities

Physical Examination

A. General appearance
   1. Skin: note whether cyanotic, pale, ruddy, jaundiced; note bruises or petechiae, other evidences of hemorrhage; pain, swelling around joints.
   2. Neurologic status: note listlessness or fatigue, irritability, dizziness, or lightheadedness.

B. Measure vital signs; note tachycardia or tachypnea.
C. Plot height and weight on growth chart.
D. Inspect and palpate abdomen; note enlargement of liver and spleen, pain, or tenderness on palpation.

ANALYSIS

Nursing diagnoses for the child with a disorder of the hematologic system may include
A. Activity intolerance
B. Pain
C. Impaired gas exchange
D. Altered tissue perfusion: cardiopulmonary
E. Altered nutrition

PLANNING AND IMPLEMENTATION

Goals

A. Child will have adequate tissue oxygenation.
B. Child will be free from complications associated with hematologic diseases.
C. Child will be free from pain, or have pain controlled.
D. Optimal growth and developmental level will be achieved.
E. Parents will participate in care of child.

Interventions

See pages 232–233.

EVALUATION

A. Serum values of hematologic components are normal.
B. Child is free from signs or symptoms of infection.
C. Child has no abnormal bleeding episodes.
D. Normal activity level is maintained without pain or fatigue.

E. Parents are able to describe symptoms of disease and complications.
F. Parents are able to administer medications and participate in child's care.

DISORDERS OF THE HEMATOLOGIC SYSTEM

Anemias

Iron Deficiency Anemia

A. General information: iron deficiency is most common cause of anemia in children; children whose diet consists mainly of cow's milk, which is low in absorbable iron, are especially vulnerable.
B. Assessment findings
  1. Pallor, fatigue, irritability
  2. History of iron-deficient diet
  3. Diagnostic tests
    a. RBC normal or slightly reduced
    b. Hgb below normal range for child
    c. Hct below normal
C. Nursing interventions
  1. Add iron to formula, food, or by vitamins by age 4–6 months.
    a. Oral iron
      1) give iron with citrus juice and on empty stomach (iron is best absorbed in an acidic environment).
      2) have child use straw if possible, since iron stains teeth and skin.
    b. Administer IM iron if ordered.
  2. Provide iron-rich foods: liver (muscle meats), nuts, dried beans/legumes, dried fruit, dark-green leafy vegetables (spinach), whole grains (farina), egg yolk, potatoes, shellfish.
D. Also see page 234.

Sickle-Cell Anemia

A. General information (see Figure 5.2)
  1. Most common inherited disorder in U.S. African American population; sickle cell trait found in 10% of African Americans
  2. Autosomal recessive inheritance pattern
  3. Individuals who are homozygous for the sickle cell gene have the disease (more than 80% of their hemoglobin is abnormal [HgbS]).
  4. Those who are heterozygous for the gene have sickle cell trait (normal hemoglobin predominates, may have 25%–50% HgbS). Although sickle cell trait is not a disease, carriers may exhibit symptoms under periods of severe anoxia or dehydration.

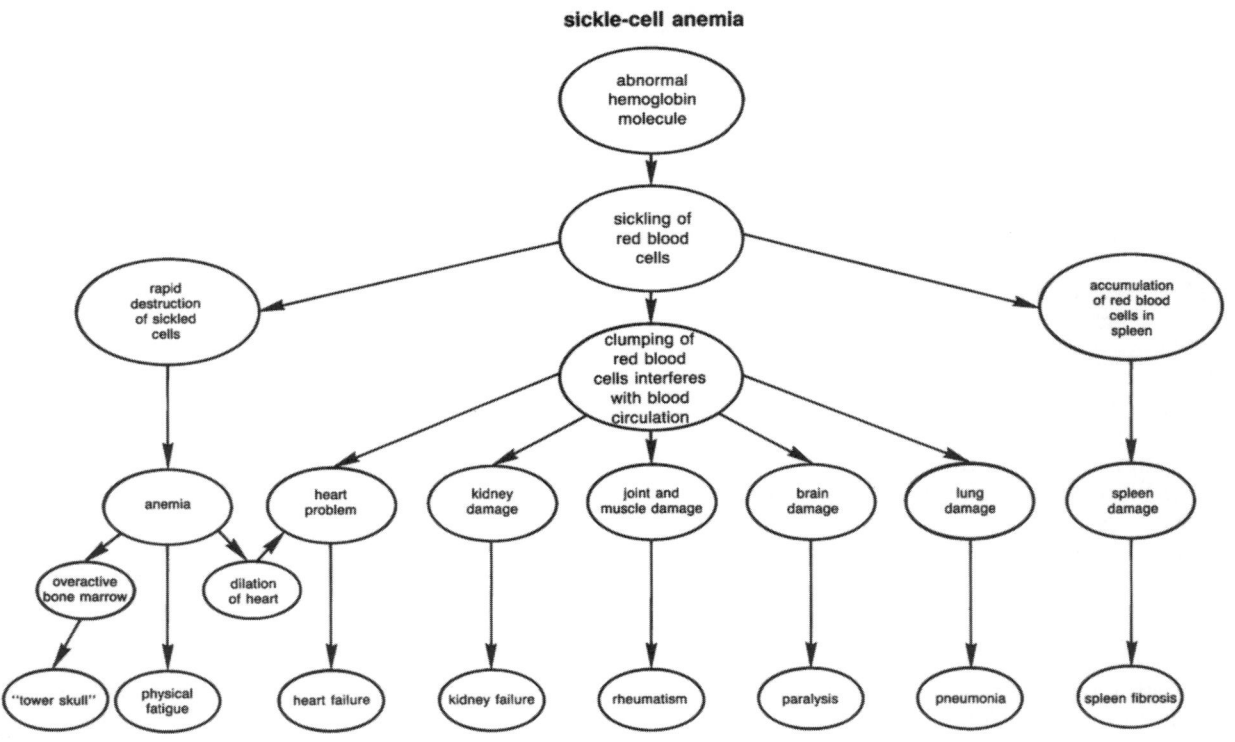

FIGURE 5.2   A series of damages and effects caused by sickle-cell anemia (Delmar Publishers)

5. In this disease, the structure of hemoglobin is changed; the sixth rung of the beta chain changes glutamine for valine.
6. HgbS (abnormal Hgb), which has reduced oxygen-carrying capacity, replaces all or part of the hemoglobin in the RBCs.
7. When oxygen is released, the shape of the RBCs changes from round and pliable to crescent shaped, rigid, and inflexible.
8. Local hypoxia and continued sickling lead to plugging of vessels.
9. Sickled RBCs live for 6–20 days instead of 120, causing hemolytic anemia.
10. Usually no symptoms prior to age 6 months; presence of increased level of fetal hemoglobin tends to inhibit sickling.
11. Death often occurs in early adulthood due to occlusion or infection.
12. *Sickle cell crisis*
    a. Vaso-occlusive (thrombocytic) crisis: most common type
       1) crescent-shaped RBCs clump together; agglutination causes blockage of small blood vessels.
       2) blockage causes the blood viscosity to increase, producing sludging and resulting in further hypoxia and increased sickling.
    b. *Splenic sequestration:* often seen in toddler/preschooler
       1) sickled cells block outflow tract resulting in sudden and massive collection of sickled cells in spleen.
       2) blockage leads to hypovolemia and severe decrease in hemoglobin and blood pressure, leading to shock.
B. Medical management: sickle cell crisis
    1. Drug therapy
       a. Urea: interferes with hydrophobic bonds of the HgbS molecules
       b. Analgesics/narcotics to control pain
       c. Antibiotics to control infection
    2. Exchange transfusions
    3. Hydration: oral and IV
    4. Bed rest
    5. Surgery: splenectomy
C. Assessment findings
    1. First sign in infancy may be "colic" due to abdominal pain (abdominal infarct)
    2. Infants may have dactylitis (hand-foot syndrome): symmetrical painful soft tissue swelling of hands and feet in absence of trauma (aseptic, self-limiting)
    3. Splenomegaly: initially due to hemolysis and phagocytosis; later due to fibrosis from repeated infarct to spleen
    4. Weak bones or spinal defects due to hyperplasia of marrow and osteoporosis
    5. Frequent infections, especially with *H. influenzae* and *D. pneumoniae*
6. Leg ulcers, especially in adolescents, due to blockage of blood supply to skin of legs
7. Delayed growth and development, especially delay in sexual development
8. CVA/infarct in the CNS
9. Renal failure: difficulty concentrating urine due to infarcts; enuresis
10. Heart failure due to hemosiderosis
11. Priapism: may result in impotence
12. Pain wherever vaso-occlusive crisis occurs
13. Development of collateral circulation
14. Diagnostic tests
    a. Hgb indicates anemia, usually 6–9 g/dl
    b. Sickling tests
       1) sickle cell test: deoxygenation of a drop of blood on a slide with a cover slip; takes several hours for results to be read; false negatives for the trait possible.
       2) Sickledex: a drop of blood from a finger stick is mixed with a solution; mixture turns cloudy in presence of HgbS; results available within a few minutes; false negatives in anemia clients or young infants possible.
    c. Hgb electrophoresis: diagnostic for the disease and the trait; provides accurate, fast results.
D. Nursing interventions: sickle cell crisis
    1. Keep child well hydrated and oxygenated.
    2. Avoid tight clothing that could impair circulation.
    3. Keep wounds clean and dry.
    4. Provide bed rest to decrease energy expenditure and oxygen use.
    5. Correct metabolic acidosis.
    6. Administer medications as ordered.
       a. Analgesics: acetaminophen, meperidine, morphine (avoid aspirin as it enhances acidosis, which promotes sickling)
       b. Avoid anticoagulants (sludging is not due to clotting)
       c. Antibiotics
    7. Administer blood transfusions as ordered.
    8. Keep arms and legs from becoming cold.
    9. Decrease emotional stress.
    10. Provide good skin care, especially to legs.
    11. Test siblings for presence of sickle cell trait/disease.
    12. Provide client teaching and discharge planning concerning
       a. Pre-op teaching for splenectomy if needed
       b. Genetic counseling
       c. Need to avoid activities that interfere with oxygenation, such as mountain climbing, flying in unpressurized planes

Disorders of Platelets or Clotting Mechanism

Idiopathic Thrombocytopenic Purpura (ITP)

A. General information
1. Increased destruction of platelets with resultant platelet count of less than 100,000/mm³ characterized by petechiae and ecchymoses of the skin
2. Exact cause unknown; may be an autoimmune mechanism; onset sudden, often preceded by a viral illness
3. The spleen is the site for destruction of platelets; spleen is not enlarged

B. Medical management
1. Drug therapy: steroids and immunosuppressive agents
2. Platelet transfusion
3. Surgery: splenectomy

C. Assessment findings
1. Petechiae: spider-web appearance of bleeding under skin due to small size of platelets
2. Ecchymosis
3. Blood in any body secretions, bleeding from mucous membranes, nosebleeds
4. Diagnostic tests: platelet count decreases, anemia

D. Nursing interventions
1. Control bleeding
   a. Administer platelet transfusions as ordered.
   b. Apply pressure to bleeding sites as needed.
   c. Position bleeding part above heart level if possible.
2. Prevent bruising.
3. Provide support to client and be sensitive to change in body image.
4. Protect from infection.
5. Measure normal circumference of extremities for baseline.
6. Administer medications orally, rectally, or IV, rather than IM; if administering immunizations, give subcutaneously (SC) and hold pressure on site for 5 minutes.
7. Administer analgesics (acetaminophen) as ordered; avoid aspirin.
8. Provide care for the client with a splenectomy (see page 236).
9. Provide client teaching and discharge planning concerning
   a. Pad crib and playpen, use rugs wherever possible.
   b. Provide soft toys.
   c. Sew pads in knees and elbows of clothing.
   d. Provide protective headgear during toddlerhood.
   e. Use soft Toothettes instead of bristle toothbrushes.
   f. Keep weight to low normal to decrease extra stress on joints.
   g. Use stool softeners to prevent straining.
   h. Avoid contact sports; suggest swimming, biking, golf, pool.

Hemophilia

A. General information
1. A group of bleeding disorders where there is a deficit of one of several factors in clotting mechanism
2. Sex-linked, inherited disorder; classic form affects males only
3. Types
   a. *Hemophilia A:* factor VIII deficiency (75% of all hemophilia)
   b. *Hemophilia B* (*Christmas disease*): factor IX deficiency (10%–12% of all hemophilia)
   c. *Hemophilia C:* factor XI deficiency (autosomal recessive, affects both sexes)
4. Only the intrinsic system is involved; platelets are not affected, but fibrin clot does not always form; bleeding from minor cuts may be stopped by platelets.
5. If individual has less than 20%–30% of factor VIII or IX, there is an impairment of clotting and clot is jelly-like.
6. Bleeding in neck, mouth, and thorax requires immediate professional care.

B. Assessment findings
1. Prolonged bleeding after minor injury
   a. At birth after cutting of cord
   b. Following circumcision
   c. Following IM immunizations
   d. Following loss of baby teeth
   e. Increased bruising as child learns to crawl and walk
2. Bruising and hematomas but no petechiae
3. Peripheral neuropathies (due to bleeding near peripheral nerves): pain, paresthesias, muscle atrophy
4. Hemarthrosis
   a. Repeated bleeding into a joint results in a swollen and painful joint with limited mobility
   b. May result in contractures and possible degeneration of joint
   c. Knees, ankles, elbows, wrists most often affected
5. Diagnostic tests
   a. Platelet count normal
   b. Prolonged coagulation time: PTT increased
   c. Anemia

C. Nursing interventions

1. Control acute bleeding episode.
   a. Apply ice compress for vasoconstriction.
   b. Immobilize area to prevent clots from being dislodged.
   c. Elevate affected extremity above heart level.
   d. Provide manual pressure or pressure dressing for 15 minutes; do not keep lifting dressing to check for bleeding status.
   e. Maintain calm environment to decrease pulse.
   f. Avoid sutures, cauterization, aspirin: all exacerbate bleeding.
   g. Administer hemostatic agents as ordered.
      1) fibrin foam
      2) topical application of adrenalin/epinephrine to promote vasoconstriction
2. Provide care for hemarthrosis.
   a. Immobilize joint and control acute bleeding.
   b. Elevate joint in a slightly flexed position.
   c. Avoid excessive handling of joint.
   d. Administer analgesics as ordered; pain relief will minimize increases in pulse rate and blood loss.
   e. Aspirin should not be given because it inhibits platelet function.
   f. Instruct to avoid weight bearing for 48 hours after bleeding episode if bleeding is in lower extremities.
   g. Provide active or passive ROM exercises after bleeding has been controlled (48 hours), as long as exercises do not cause pain or irritate trauma site.
3. Administer cryoprecipitate (frozen factor VIII) as ordered.
   a. Thaw slowly.
   b. Gently rotate bottle; shaking deteriorates antihemophilic factor.
   c. Infuse immediately when thawed; factor VIII deteriorates at room temperature.
4. Provide client teaching and discharge planning concerning
   a. Prevention of trauma (see Idiopathic Thrombocytopenic Purpura)
   b. Genetic counseling
      1) when mother is carrier: 50% chance with each pregnancy for sons to have hemophilia, 50% chance with each pregnancy for daughters to be carriers
      2) when father has hemophilia, mother is normal: no chance for children to have disease, but all daughters will be carriers

   c. Availability of support/counseling agencies

Disorder of White Blood Cells

Infectious Mononucleosis

A. General information
   1. Viral infection that causes hyperplasia of lymphoid tissue and a characteristic change in mononuclear cells of the blood
   2. Affects adolescents and young adults most commonly
   3. Caused by the Epstein-Barr virus, which is not highly contagious, but is transmitted by saliva (the "kissing disease")
   4. Incubation period 2–6 weeks
   5. Pathophysiology: mononuclear infiltration of lymph nodes and other body tissue
B. Assessment findings
   1. Lethargy
   2. Sore throat/tonsilitis
   3. Lymphadenopathy; enlarged spleen, liver involvement
   4. Diagnostic tests
      a. Atypical WBCs increased
      b. Heterophil antibody and Monospot tests positive

Sample Questions

32. The Tates have one child with hemophilia. Mrs. Tate wants to have another child and she asks the nurse what her chances are of having another child with hemophilia. The nurse's best response is
    1. All of your daughters will be carriers of the disease.
    2. If you have another son, there is almost a 100% chance he will have hemophilia.
    3. If you have a son, there is a 50% chance he will have hemophilia but none of your daughters will have it.
    4. There is a 25% chance of having another child with hemophilia.
33. John is 4 years old and has been diagnosed as having iron deficiency anemia. A liquid iron preparation has been prescribed. When administering John's medication the nurse should
    1. ask him if he wants to take his medicine.
    2. mix the medication in his milk bottle and give it to him at nap time.
    3. allow him to sip the medication through a straw.
    4. give the medication after lunch with a sweet dessert to disguise the taste.
34. Todd, age 10, has hemophilia A and is admitted to the hospital for hemarthrosis of

the right knee. He is in a great deal of pain. Which of the following interventions would aggravate his condition?
1. Applying an ice bag to the affected knee.
2. Administering children's aspirin for pain relief.
3. Elevating the right leg above the level of his heart.
4. Keeping the right leg immobilized.

35. Melissa Heller, 17 years old, has had sickle cell anemia since she was a toddler. Her brother has sickle cell trait. The client with sickle cell trait
1. has a chronic form of sickle cell anemia.
2. has the most lethal form of the disease.
3. will transmit the disease to all children.
4. has some normal and some abnormal hemoglobin cells.

36. The mother of a child with sickle cell anemia tells the nurse that, when she was reading about sickle cell anemia, she learned that sickled blood cells do not have as long a life expectancy as normal red cells. The life expectancy of a sickled blood cell is approximately
1. 5 days.
2. 15 days.
3. 30 days.
4. 60 days.

37. The child with sickle cell anemia may exhibit
1. vitiligo.
2. hyperactivity.
3. mild mental retardation.
4. delayed physical development.

38. A child who has sickle cell anemia has developed stasis ulcers on her lower extremities. This is due to
1. poor range of motion.
2. ruptured blood vessels.
3. impaired venous circulation.
4. hypertrophy of muscular tissue.

39. Which complication is associated with sickle cell anemia?
1. Constipation.
2. Hypothyroidism.
3. Addison's disease.
4. Cerebrovascular accidents.

40. Both of Sammy's parents carry the sickle cell anemia trait. Sammy, 8 months old, contracted chickenpox from his brother and now is very weak, febrile, and anorexic, and cries with pain with his wrists and elbows are moved. He is admitted to the hospital with a diagnosis of sickle cell crisis. Sammy's mother asks the nurse why Sammy has not been symptomatic before now. The best response by the nurse would be
1. High fetal hemoglobin protected Sammy against sickling.
2. His red blood cell levels remained normal.
3. Maternal antibodies protected Sammy against sickling.

4. Sickle cell hemoglobin was not present until about 1 year of life.

41. In planning care for a child with newly diagnosed sickle cell anemia, his mother should be taught that vaso-occlusive crises may be prevented by
1. prophylactic administration of acetaminophen.
2. eating food with a high iron content.
3. exercising regularly.
4. promoting hydration.

Answers and Rationales

32. The correct answer is 3. Hemophilia is inherited as an X-linked recessive trait. If this family has another son, there is a 50% chance that he will have the disease. If they have a daughter, she will not have the disease but there is a 50% chance that she will be a carrier of the disease.

33. The correct answer is 3. Iron is given with a straw to prevent staining the teeth. It is best absorbed on an empty stomach in an acidic environment. Do not ask toddlers if they want to take their medication. They are likely to say no.

34. The correct answer is 2. Aspirin interferes with the clotting mechanism. All the other measures listed will help decrease bleeding or alleviate the associated pain.

35. The correct answer is 4. Clients with sickle cell trait inherit only one defective gene. They can synthesize both normal and abnormal hemoglobin chains. If two people with sickle cell trait marry, some of their children may inherit abnormal genes. It is not a lethal form of the disease, nor is it sickle cell anemia.

36. The correct answer is 2. The life span of a sickled cell is 6 to 20 days.

37. The correct answer is 4. Children with sickle cell disease manifest an impairment of growth. They do not experience mental retardation, hyperactivity, or vitiligo (abnormal pigmentation).

38. The correct answer is 3. The tissues of a client with sickle cell disease are constantly vulnerable to microcirculatory interruptions. The vessels do not actually rupture, they are blocked with the defective cells. The stasis ulcers are not related to range of motion. Hypertrophy of muscular tissue does not occur with sickle cell anemia.

39. The correct answer is 4. The sudden appearance of a stroke in sickle cell anemia is related to the microcirculatory interruptions that are caused by the sickled cell. The blood supply to the bowel may be damaged; however, constipation is not a common problem associated with sickle cell disease.

Addison's disease and hypothyroidism are endocrine disorders that are not related to sickle cell disease.

40. The correct answer is 1. High levels of fetal hemoglobin inhibit sickling of red cells prior to the age of 6 months. His red blood cell level may have been normal, but his abnormal blood cells were protected by the fetal hemoglobin. Maternal antibodies do not protect the baby's blood cells from sickling. The baby is still not a year old.

41. The correct answer is 4. Promoting good hydration is a major factor in maintaining the blood viscosity needed to maximize the circulation of red blood cells. Good hydration can help to minimize the severity of symptoms should the child develop sickle cell crisis. Acetaminophen would not be helpful in decreasing the sickling process. Iron administration would be of no value because in sickle cell anemia there is an abnormally shaped hemoglobin. The problem is not due to iron deficiency. Regular exercise is important for children with sickle cell disease, but it will not prevent a vaso-occlusive crisis.

The Respiratory System

VARIATIONS FROM THE ADULT

A. Infants are obligatory nose breathers and diaphragmatic breathers.
B. Number and size of alveoli continue to increase until age 8 years.
C. Until age 5, structures of the respiratory tract have a narrower lumen and children are more susceptible to obstruction/distress from inflammation.
D. Normal respiratory rate in children is faster than in adults.
   1. Infants: 40–60/minute
   2. 1 year: 20–40/minute
   3. 2–4 years: 20–30/minute
   4. 5–10 years: 20–25/minute
   5. 10–15 years: 17–22/minute
   6. 15 and older: 15–20/minute
E. Most episodes of acute illness in young children involve the respiratory system due to frequent exposure to infection and a general lack of immunity.

ASSESSMENT

History

A. Presenting problem: symptoms may include cough, wheezing, dyspnea
B. Medical history: incidence of infections, respiratory allergies or asthma, prescribed and OTC medications, recent immunizations
C. Exposure to other children with respiratory infections or other communicable diseases

Physical Examination

A. Inspect shape of chest; note
   1. Barrel chest: occurs with chronic respiratory disease.
   2. Pectus carinatum (pigeon breast): sternum protrudes outward producing increased A-P diameter; usually not significant.
   3. Pectus excavatum (funnel chest): lower part of sternum is depressed; usually does not produce symptoms; may impair cardiac function.
B. Note pattern of respirations.
   1. Rate
   2. Regularity
      a. Periodic respirations (periods of rapid respirations, separated by periods of slow breathing or short periods of no respirations) normal in young infants
      b. Apnea episodes (cessation of breathing for 20 seconds or more accompanied by color change or bradycardia) an abnormal finding
   3. Respiratory effort
      a. Nasal flaring: attempt to widen airway and decrease resistance
      b. Open-mouth breathing: chin drops with each inhalation
      c. Retractions: from use of accessory muscles
C. Observe skin color and temperature, particularly mucous membranes and peripheral extremities.
D. Note behavior: position of comfort, signs of irritability or lethargy, facial expression (anxiety).
E. Note speech abnormalities: hoarseness or muffled speech.
F. Observe presence and quality of cough: productive; paroxysmal, with inspiratory "whoop" characteristic of pertussis.
G. Auscultate for abnormal breath sounds (auscultation may be more difficult in infants

and young children because of shallowness of respirations).
1. Grunting on expiration
2. Stridor: harsh inspiratory sound associated with obstruction or edema
3. Wheezing: whistling noise during inspiration or expiration due to narrowed airways, common in asthma
4. "Snoring": noisy breathing associated with nasal obstruction

Laboratory/Diagnostic Tests

A. Pulmonary function testing should not be done under age 6 years since children have difficulty following directions.
B. Chest x-rays: avoid unnecessary exposure; protect gonads and thyroid.

ANALYSIS

Nursing diagnoses for the child with a disorder of the respiratory system may include
A. Activity intolerance
B. Altered respiratory functions: ineffective airway clearance, ineffective breathing pattern, impaired gas exchange
C. Anxiety
D. Fatigue
E. Altered oral mucous membrane
F. Altered nutrition
G. Sleep-pattern disturbance

PLANNING AND IMPLEMENTATION

Goals

A. Child will have patent airway and satisfactory oxygenation.
B. Child will be free from symptoms of respiratory distress.
C. Child will have improved ability to tolerate exercise, conserve energy.
D. Parents will participate in caring for child.

Interventions

Oxygen Tent (Croup Tent, Mist Tent, Oxygen Canopy)

A. General information
1. Used when desired oxygen concentration is 40% or less as oxygen concentration can be difficult to control
2. Primarily used for croup, when mist is to be delivered
B. Nursing care
1. Keep sides of plastic down and tucked in.

2. If tent has been opened for a while, increase oxygen flow to raise concentration quickly.
3. If child has been out of the tent, return oxygen concentration to ordered percent before returning child to tent.
4. If tent enclosure gets too warm, add ice to cooling chamber as needed.
5. Mist is usually prescribed in addition to oxygen
   a. Keep reservoir for humidification filled.
   b. Do not allow condensation on tent walls to obstruct view of child.
   c. Keep clothes and bedding dry to avoid chilling.
6. Provide safety measures.
   a. Keep plastic away from child's face.
   b. Avoid toys that produce spark or friction, such as mechanical toys.
   c. Avoid stuffed toys because of tendency to absorb moisture.
   d. Encourage use of one or two favorite toys or transitional object in tent; other toys may be kept outside of tent in child's view.

Vaporizers

A. General information
1. Same principle as oxygen tent
2. Used at home; placed at bedside; mist directed into room around child
3. Usually cool mist
B. Nursing responsibilities: teach parents to clean frequently because bacteria that grow in vaporizer can be dispersed into air.

Chest Physical Therapy

A. Postural drainage: infants and young children do not have enough rib cage for a lower front position
1. Combine side and lower front positions
2. 5 positions: upper front, upper back, lower back, right side and front, and left side and front
3. 2–5 minutes per position
B. Percussion
1. Do not use with clients with an acute attack of asthma or croup (dislodged mucous may cause plugging because of bronchial edema).
2. Use percussion 30 minutes before meals to clear mucus before eating, thus enhancing intake.
3. If aerosol medications are being used, administer immediately before percussion.
4. Percussion is done with cupped hand, never on bare skin, over the rib cage only
   a. Use an underskirt, gown, or diaper over skin.

b. If infant's chest is too small for nurse's hand, a small face mask can be substituted.

c. Be careful to avoid spine and neck during percussion.

d. Infants can be percussed while being held on nurse's lap.

e. If child is unable to cough during and after percussion, suction as needed.

Suctioning

A. Bulb syringes can be used to clear nasal stuffiness.

B. For nasotracheal suction, use low pressure.

Deep Breathing Exercises

A. Encourage use by making exercises into games (e.g., touch toes, sit-ups, jumping jacks, blowing out "flashlight," ping-pong ball games using blowing).

B. Encourage use of toys that require blowing (harmonica, bubbles).

C. Laughing and crying also stimulate coughing and deep breathing.

Apnea Monitor

A. General information: monitors often use same three chest leads for simultaneous cardiac and respiratory rate monitoring

1. Lead placement will differ from that usually prescribed for cardiac monitoring if apnea monitoring is also required.

2. To monitor respiratory rate, chest leads will need to be where chest moves during inspiration.

3. As chest wall movement rather than air entry is monitored, obstruction and dyspnea may not be recognized early.

4. Most useful for early recognition of cessation of breathing.

B. Nursing care: when alarm sounds

1. Note whether cardiac or respiratory rate has triggered alarm.

2. Assess child's color, activity, and presence of respiratory effort.

3. Auscultate cardiac and respiratory sounds.

4. If no physical distress, check lead placement.

EVALUATION

A. Child is satisfactorily oxygenated.

1. Absence of respiratory distress
2. Normal color and activity
3. Decreased need for supplementary oxygen therapy

B. Parents are able to care for child at home.

1. Identify symptoms of increased oxygen need
2. Perform prescribed treatments
3. Have obtained and demonstrated use of necessary equipment

DISORDERS OF THE RESPIRATORY SYSTEM

Tonsillitis

A. General information
1. Inflammation of tonsils often as a result of a viral or bacterial pharyngitis
2. 10%–15% caused by group A beta-hemolytic streptococci

B. Medical management
1. Comfort measures and symptomatic relief
2. Antibiotics for bacterial infection, usually penicillin or erythromycin
3. Surgery: removal of tonsils/adenoids if necessary

C. Assessment findings
1. Enlarged, red tonsils; fever
2. Sore throat, difficulty swallowing, mouth breathing, snoring
3. White patches of exudate on tonsillar pillars, enlarged cervical lymph nodes

D. Nursing interventions
1. Provide soft or liquid diet.
2. Use cool-mist vaporizer.
3. Administer salt water gargles, throat lozenges.
4. Administer analgesics (acetaminophen) as ordered.
5. Administer antibiotics as ordered; stress to parents importance of completing entire course of medication.

Tonsillectomy

A. General information
1. One of the most common operations performed on children
2. Indications for tonsillectomy include recurrent tonsillitis, peritonsillar abscess, airway or esophageal obstruction
3. Indications for adenoidectomy include nasal obstruction due to hypertrophy

B. Nursing interventions: preoperative
1. Make pre-op preparation age-appropriate; child enters the hospital feeling well and will leave with a very sore throat.
2. Obtain baseline bleeding and clotting times.
3. Check for any loose teeth.

C. Nursing interventions: postoperative
1. Position on side or abdomen to facilitate drainage of secretions.

2. Avoid suctioning if possible; if not, be especially careful to avoid trauma to surgical site.
3. Provide ice collar/analgesia for pain.
4. Observe for hemorrhage; signs may include frequent swallowing, increased pulse, vomiting bright red blood (vomiting old dried blood or pink-tinged emesis is normal).
5. Offer clear, cool, noncitrus, nonred fluids when awake and alert.
6. Provide client teaching and discharge planning concerning
   a. Need to maintain adequate fluid and food intake and to avoid spicy and irritating foods
   b. Quiet activity for a few days
   c. Need to avoid coughing, mouth gargles
   d. Chewing gum (but not Aspergum): can help relieve pain and difficulty swallowing and aids in diminishing bad breath
   e. Mild analgesics for pain
   f. Signs and symptoms of bleeding and need to report to physician

Acute Spasmodic Laryngitis (Croup)

A. General information
   1. Respiratory distress characterized by paroxysmal attacks of laryngeal obstruction
   2. Etiology unclear but familial predisposition, allergy, viruses, psychologic factors, and anxious temperament have been implicated
   3. Common in children ages 1–3 years
   4. Attacks occur mostly at night; onset sudden and usually preceded by a mild upper respiratory infection
   5. Respiratory symptoms last several hours; may occur in a milder form on a few subsequent nights
B. Assessment findings
   1. Inspiratory stridor, hoarseness, barking cough, anxiety, retractions
   2. Afebrile, skin cool
C. Nursing interventions
   1. Instruct parents to take the child into the bathroom, close the door, turn on the hot water, and sit on floor of the steamy bathroom with child.
   2. If the laryngeal spasm does not subside the child should be taken to the emergency department.
   3. After the spasm subsides, provide cool mist with a vaporizer.
   4. Provide clear fluids.
   5. Try to keep child calm and quiet.
   6. Assure parents this is self-limiting.

Laryngotracheobronchitis

A. General information
   1. Viral infection of the larynx that may extend into trachea and bronchi
   2. Most common cause for stridor in febrile child
   3. Parainfluenza viruses most common cause
   4. Infection causes endothelial insult, increased mucous production, edema, low grade fever
   5. Affects children less than five years of age
   6. Onset more gradual than with croup, takes longer to resolve; usually develops over several days with upper respiratory infection
   7. Usually treated on outpatient basis; indications for admission include dehydration and respiratory compromise
B. Medical management
   1. Drug therapy
      a. Aerosolized racemic epinephrine
      b. Antibiotics only if secondary bacterial infection present
      c. Steroids: still controversial
   2. Oxygen therapy: low concentrations to relieve mild hypoxia (concentrations greater than 30% may mask signs of obstruction and should not be used)
   3. Oral or nasotracheal intubation for moderate hypoxia
   4. IV fluids to maintain hydration
C. Assessment findings
   1. Fever, coryza, inspiratory stridor, barking cough, tachycardia, tachypnea, retractions
   2. May have difficulty taking fluids
   3. WBC normal
D. Nursing interventions
   1. Instruct parents to take child into steamy bathroom for acute distress.
   2. Keep child calm.
   3. After distress subsides, use cool mist vaporizer in bedroom.
   4. Child can vomit large amounts of mucus after the episode; reassure parents that this is normal.
   5. For hospitalized child
      a. Monitor vital signs, I&O, skin color, and respiratory effort.
      b. Maintain hydration.
      c. Provide care for the intubated child.
      d. Plan care to disturb the child as little as possible.
      e. Avoid direct examination of the epiglottis as it may precipitate spasm and obstruction.

Epiglottitis

A. General information
   1. Life-threatening bacterial infection of epiglottis and surrounding structures

2. Primary organism: *H. influenzae,* type B
3. Often preceded by upper respiratory infection
4. Rapid progression of swelling causes reduction in airway diameter; may lead to sudden respiratory arrest
5. Affects children ages 3–7 years

B. Assessment findings
1. Fever, tachycardia, inspiratory stridor, labored respirations with retractions, sore throat, dysphagia, drooling
2. Irritability, restlessness, anxious-looking
3. Position: sitting upright, head forward and jaw thrust out
4. Diagnostic tests
   a. WBC increased
   b. Lateral neck x-ray reveals characteristic findings

C. Nursing interventions
1. Provide mist tent with oxygen.
2. Administer IV antibiotics as ordered.
3. Provide tracheostomy or endotracheal tube care (page 250); note the following
   a. Restlessness, fatigue, dyspnea, cyanosis, pallor, tachycardia, tachypnea, diminished breath sounds, adventitious lung sounds.
   b. Need for suctioning to remove secretions; note amount, color, consistency.
4. Reassure child through touch, sound, and physically being present.
5. Involve parents in all aspects of care.
6. Avoid direct examination of the epiglottis as it may precipitate spasm and obstruction.
7. Remember this is extremely frightening experience for child and parents; explain procedures and findings; reinforce explanations of physician.

Bronchiolitis

A. General information
1. Pulmonary viral infection characterized by wheezing
2. Usually caused by respiratory syncytial virus
3. Virus invades epithelial cells of nasopharynx and spreads to lower respiratory tract, causing increased mucus production, decreased diameter of bronchi, hyperinflation, and possible atelectasis
4. Affects infants ages 2–8 months
5. Increased incidence of asthma as child grows older

B. Medical management: IV epinephrine (if provides relief, follow with epinephrine suspension [Sus-Phrine], which is longer acting, then theophylline); if no response to epinephrine, all treatment is supportive

C. Assessment findings
1. Difficulty feeding, fever
2. Cough, coryza
3. Wheezing, prolonged expiratory phase, tachypnea, nasal flaring, retractions (intercostal more pronounced than supraclavicular retractions)
4. Diagnostic tests
   a. WBC normal
   b. X-ray reveals hyperaeration

D. Nursing interventions
1. Provide high-humidity environment, with oxygen in some cases (instruct parents to take child into steamy bathroom if at home).
2. Offer small, frequent feedings; clear fluids if trouble with secretions.
3. Provide adequate rest.
4. Administer antipyretics as ordered to control fever.

Asthma

A. General information
1. Obstructive disease of the lower respiratory tract
2. Most common chronic respiratory disease in children, in younger children affects twice as many boys as girls; incidence equal by adolescence
3. Often caused by an allergic reaction to an environmental allergen, may be seasonal or year round
4. Immunologic/allergic reaction results in histamine release, which produces three main airway responses
   a. Edema of mucous membranes
   b. Spasm of the smooth muscle of bronchi and bronchioles
   c. Accumulation of tenacious secretions
5. *Status asthmaticus* occurs when there is little response to treatment and symptoms persist

B. Medical management
1. Drug therapy
   a. Bronchodilators to relieve bronchospasm
      1) Beta-adrenergic agents: rapid onset of action when administered by aerosol (see Figure 5.3)
      2) theophylline: check pulse and blood pressure
   b. Corticosteroids to relieve inflammation and edema
   c. Antibiotics: if secondary infection
   d. Cromolyn sodium: not used during acute attack; inhaled; inhibits histamine release in lungs and prevents attack
2. Physical therapy
3. Hyposensitization
4. Exercise

C. Assessment findings

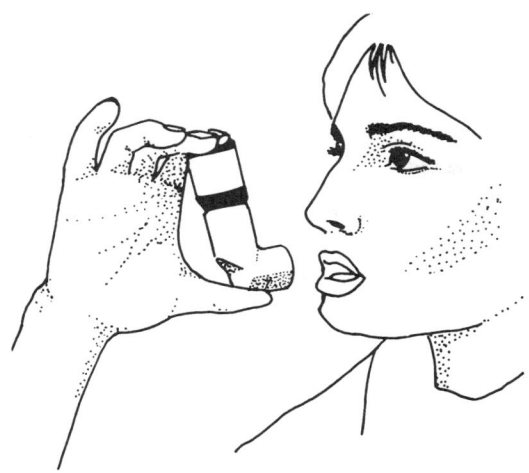

1. Remove the cap from the mouthpiece and shake the inhaler well.
2. Hold the inhaler so the metal canister containing the medication is upside down.
3. Breathe out as fully as possible.
4. Open your mouth and tilt your head back slightly. Hold the inhaler about 2 inches from your mouth.*
5. Firmly press the metal canister down into the mouthpiece. This releases the medication. At the same time, begin to inhale slowly through your mouth.
6. Hold your breath for about 10 seconds.
7. Slowly breathe out through your nose and pursed lips.
8. Wait about 5 minutes, shake the inhaler, and repeat if necessary. Cap and store the inhaler.
9. Rinse your mouth with water or gargle after the last inhalation.
10. Periodically clean the mouthpiece by removing the canister and rinsing the mouthpiece in warm water. Dry it and replace the canister.

*Note: This is a new procedure. Many physicians and pharmacists will teach the client to place the mouthpiece in the mouth. The nurse should reinforce the procedure that has been taught.

FIGURE 5.3 Instructions for use of an oral inhaler (Delmar Publishers)

1. Family history of allergies
2. Client history of eczema
3. Respiratory distress: shortness of breath, expiratory wheeze, prolonged expiratory phase, air trapping (barrel chest if chronic), use of accessory muscles, irritability (from hypoxia), diaphoresis, change in sensorium if severe attack
4. Diagnostic tests: ABGs indicate respiratory acidosis
D. Nursing interventions
1. Place client in high-Fowler's position.

2. Administer oxygen as ordered.
3. Administer medications as ordered.
4. Provide humidification/hydration to loosen secretions.
5. Provide chest percussion and postural drainage when bronchodilation improves.
6. Monitor for respiratory distress.
7. Provide client teaching and discharge planning concerning
   a. Modification of environment
      1) ensure room is well ventilated.
      2) stay indoors during grass cutting or when pollen count is high.
      3) use damp dusting.
      4) avoid rugs, draperies or curtains, stuffed animals.
      5) avoid natural fibers (wool and feathers).
   b. Importance of moderate exercise (swimming is excellent)
   c. Purpose of breathing exercises (to increase the end expiratory pressure of each respiration)

Aspiration of a Foreign Object

A. General information
1. Relatively common airway problem.
2. Severity depends on object (e.g., pins, coins, nuts, buttons, parts of toys) aspirated and the degree of obstruction.
3. Depending on object aspirated, symptoms will increase over hours or weeks.
4. The curious toddler is most frequently affected.
5. If object does not pass trachea immediately, respiratory distress will be evident.
6. If object moves beyond tracheal region, it will pass into one of the main stem bronchi; symptoms will be vague, insidious.
7. Causes 400 deaths per year in children under age 4.
B. Medical management
1. Objects in upper airway require immediate removal.
2. Lower airway obstruction is less urgent (bronchoscopy or laryngoscopy).
C. Assessment findings
1. Sudden onset of coughing, dyspnea, wheezing, stridor, apnea (upper airway)
2. Persistent or recurrent pneumonia, persistent croupy cough or wheeze
3. Object not always visible on x-ray
4. Secondary infection
D. Nursing interventions
1. Perform Heimlich maneuver if indicated.
2. Reassure the scared toddler.
3. After removal, place child in high-humidity environment and treat secondary infection if applicable.

4. Counsel parents regarding age-appropriate behavior and safety precautions.

Cystic Fibrosis (CF)

A. General information
1. Disorder characterized by dysfunction of the exocrine glands (mucus-producing glands of the respiratory tract, GI tract, pancreas, sweat glands, salivary glands)
2. Transmitted as an autosomal recessive trait
3. Incidence: 1 in 1500–2000 live births
4. Most common lethal genetic disease among Caucasians in U.S. and Europe
5. No test to detect carriers
6. Prenatal diagnosis of CF is not reliable
7. Secretions from mucous glands are thick, causing obstruction and fibrosis of tissue
8. Sweat and saliva have characteristic high levels of sodium chloride
9. Affected organs
    a. Pancreas: 85% of CF clients have pancreatic involvement
        1) obstruction of pancreatic ducts and eventual fibrosis and atrophy of the pancreas leads to little or no release of enzymes (lipase [fats], amylase [starch], and trypsin [protein])
        2) absence of enzymes causes malabsorption of fats and proteins
        3) unabsorbed food fractions excreted in the stool produce steatorrhea
        4) loss of nutrients and inability to absorb fat-soluble vitamins causes failure to thrive
    b. Respiratory tract: 99.9% of CF clients have respiratory involvement
        1) increased production of secretions causes increased obstruction of airway, air trapping, and atelectasis
        2) pulmonary congestion leads to cor pulmonale
        3) eventually death occurs by drowning in own secretions
    c. Reproductive system
        1) males are sterile
        2) females can conceive, but increased mucus in vaginal tract makes conception more difficult
        3) pregnancy causes increased stress on respiratory system of mother
    d. Liver: one-third of clients have cirrhosis/portal hypertension
10. The disease is ultimately fatal; average age at death is 20 years; 95% of deaths are from abnormal mucus secretion and fibrosis in the lungs

B. Medical management
1. Pancreatic involvement: aimed at promoting absorption of nutrients
    a. Diet modification
        1) infant: predigested formula
        2) older children: may require high-calorie, high-protein, or low/limited-fat diet, but many CF clients tolerate normal diet
    b. Pancreatic enzyme supplementation: enzyme capsules, tablets, or powders (Pancrease, Cotazym, Viokase) given with meals and snacks
2. Respiratory involvement: goals are to maintain airway patency and to prevent lung infection
    a. Chest physiotherapy
    b. Antibiotics for infection

C. Assessment findings: symptoms vary greatly in severity and extent
1. Pancreatic involvement
    a. Growth failure; failure to thrive
    b. Stools are foul smelling, large, frequent, foamy, fatty (steatorrhea), contain undigested food
    c. Meconium ileus (meconium gets stuck in bowel due to lack of enzymes) in newborns
    d. Rectal prolapse is possible due to greasy stools
    e. Voracious appetite
    f. Characteristic protruding abdomen with atrophy of extremities and buttocks
    g. Symptoms associated with deficiencies in the fat-soluble vitamins
    h. Anemia
    i. Diagnostic tests
        1) trypsin decreased to absent in aspiration of duodenal contents
        2) fecal fat in stool specimen increased
2. Respiratory involvement
    a. Signs of respiratory distress
    b. Barrel chest due to air trapping
    c. Clubbing of digits
    d. Decreased exercise tolerance due to distress
    e. Frequent productive cough
    f. Frequent pseudomonas infections
    g. Diagnostic tests
        1) chest x-ray reveals atelectasis, infiltrations, emphysemic changes
        2) pulmonary function studies abnormal
        3) ABGs show respiratory acidosis
3. Electrolyte involvement
    a. Hyponatremia/heat exhaustion in hot weather
    b. Salty taste to sweat
    c. Diagnostic tests
        1) pilocarpine iontophoresis sweat test: indicates 2–5 times normal amount of sodium and chloride in the sweat
        2) fecal fat elevated

        3) fecal trypsin absent or decreased
D. Nursing interventions
  1. Pancreatic involvement
    a. Administer pancreatic enzymes with meals as ordered: do not mix enzymes until ready to use them; best to mix in applesauce.
    b. Provide a high-calorie, high-carbohydrate (no empty-calorie foods), high-protein, normal-fat diet.
    c. Provide a double dose of multivitamins per day, especially fat-soluble vitamins (A, D, E, K), in water-soluble form.
    d. If low-fat diet required, MCT (medium-chain triglycerides) oil may be used.
  2. Respiratory involvement
    a. Administer antibiotics as ordered (all antibiotics for pseudomonas are given IV; doses may be above recommended levels (for virulent organisms)
    b. Administer expectorants, mucolytics (rarely used) as ordered.
    c. Avoid cough suppressants and antihistamines.
    d. Encourage breathing exercises.
    e. Provide percussion and postural drainage 4 times a day.
    f. Provide aerosol treatments as needed; hand-held nebulizers, mask, intermittent positive pressure breathing (IPPB), mist tent.
  3. Electrolyte involvement
    a. Add salt to all meals, especially in summer.
    b. Give salty snacks (pretzels).
  4. Provide appropriate long-term support to child and family.
  5. Provide client teaching and discharge planning concerning
    a. Genetic counseling
    b. Promotion of child's independence
    c. Avoidance of cigarette smoking in the house
    d. Availability of support groups/community agencies
    e. Alternative school education during extended hospitalization/home recovery

Sample Questions

42. Jimmy had a tonsillectomy performed earlier in the day. He is now 4 hours post-op. Which of the following is an abnormal finding and a cause for concern?
  1. An emesis of dried blood.
  2. Increased swallowing.
  3. Pink-tinged mucus.
  4. Jimmy's complaints of a very sore throat.

43. Kevin is 7 years old and has been diagnosed as having cystic fibrosis. Chest physiotherapy has been ordered. Kevin's chest percussion should be performed
  1. before postural drainage.
  2. ½ hour before meals.
  3. before an aerosol treatment.
  4. after suctioning.

44. The nurse is performing chest physiotherapy on a 6-year-old child who has congestion in his left lower lobe. The nurse should position the child on his
  1. left side in semi-Fowler's position.
  2. right side in semi-Fowler's position.
  3. left side in Trendelenburg's position.
  4. right side in Trendelenburg's position.

45. An infant is being evaluated for possible cystic fibrosis. The sweat test will show an elevation of which electrolyte?
  1. Chloride.
  2. Fluoride.
  3. Potassium.
  4. Calcium.

46. Michael, 2 years old, is admitted to the hospital with cystic fibrosis. As a result of malabsorption, he is small for his age. What dietary suggestions can the nurse recommend to Michael's mother to enhance his growth?
  1. Low-fat, low-residue, and high-potassium diet.
  2. Low-carbohydrate, soft diet with no sugar products.
  3. High-carbohydrate, high-fat diet with extra water between meals.
  4. High-protein, high-calorie meals with skim-milk milkshakes between meals.

47. The nurse is caring for a 2-year-old who has cystic fibrosis. His mother asks why the child developed cystic fibrosis. The nurse explains that cystic fibrosis
  1. develops due to meconium ileus at birth.
  2. is an autosomal recessive genetic defect.
  3. occurs during embryologic development.
  4. results from chromosomal nondysjunction that occurred at conception.

48. A 2-year-old is admitted to the hospital and will need to stay for several days. The child's mother is unable to stay overnight because there is no one to care for her other children. The nurse recommends that she
  1. leave something of hers with Michael and tell him she'll be back in the morning.
  2. leave while he is in the playroom.
  3. leave after he has fallen asleep.
  4. tell him she'll be back in a few minutes after she has dinner.

49. Albert is a 2-year-old who has cystic fibrosis. His mother tells the nurse that the family is planning their first summer vacation with Albert. She wants to know if there are any special precautions needed because he has cystic fibrosis. The nurse should tell her that

children with cystic fibrosis are particularly susceptible to
1. severe sunburn.
2. infectious diarrhea.
3. heat prostration.
4. respiratory allergies.

50. Amy, 4 years old, is admitted to the hospital for the treatment of an acute asthma attack. Her health history reveals that she has been blind since birth and has had four asthma attacks in the past six months. She received epinephrine (Adrenalin) in the emergency department and was transferred to the pediatric unit with an aminophylline infusion. When evaluating Amy for positive effects of the aminophylline treatment, the most significant finding is
1. a decrease in mucous production.
2. a decrease in wheezing.
3. an increase in blood pressure.
4. a sleeping child.

51. Bryan, 12 months old, is hospitalized for a severe case of croup and has been placed in an oxygen tent. Today the oxygen order has been reduced from 35% to 25%. His blood gases are normal. Bryan refuses to stay in the oxygen tent. Attempts to placate him only cause him to become more upset. The most appropriate action for the nurse is to
1. restrain him in the tent and notify the physician.
2. take him out of the tent and notify the physician.
3. take him out of the tent and let him sit in the playroom.
4. tell him it will please his mother if he stays in the tent.

Answers and Rationales

42. The correct answer is 2. Increased swallowing could be a sign of hemorrhage from the surgical site. Vomiting of dried blood would be expected following a tonsillectomy. Pink-tinged mucus would be an expected finding. Complaints of a very sore throat would be expected following surgery.

43. The correct answer is 2. Chest percussion is done prior to meals to prevent vomiting. It follows aerosol therapy and positioning. Suctioning may be needed afterwards to remove thick secretions after they have been loosened by percussion.

44. The correct answer is 4. The affected lobe must be uppermost to be drained by gravity.

45. The correct answer is 1. There is increased excretion of chloride in the sweat of children with cystic fibrosis. A chloride level of over 60 mEq/liter is diagnostic for the disease.

46. The correct answer is 4. A client with cystic fibrosis lacks pancreatic enzymes necessary for fat absorption. A diet high in protein and calories is necessary to meet the child's growth needs. Between-meal snacks of skim-milk milkshakes may be given to provide additional protein, vitamins, and calories. The child needs carbohydrates. A soft diet with sugar restrictions is not necessary. Fat must be restricted in a client with cystic fibrosis.

47. The correct answer is 2. Cystic fibrosis is an autosomal recessive genetic disease. If both parents have the cystic fibrosis trait, each child has a 25% chance of developing the disease, a 50% chance of having the trait (being a carrier), and a 25% chance of not having the disease. Meconium ileus (obstruction of the small intestine in the newborn caused by impaction of thick, dry, tenacious meconium) often occurs but is a result of cystic fibrosis and may be one of the earliest signs. Autosomal disorders are hereditary and depend on the presence or absence of certain genes on the autosomes. It is unrelated to embryological development. Autosomal disorders are hereditary. The abnormal recessive gene was present at conception.

48. The correct answer is 1. Leaving something of his mother's with the child and telling him that she will be back in the morning is the best approach in developing trust between the mother and her child. Sneaking out and not being truthful with the child does not allow the child to develop trust. Lying to the child and giving him false hope that the mother will return after supper is not appropriate.

49. The correct answer is 3. Clients with cystic fibrosis are prone to electrolyte imbalances due to increased loss of sodium and potassium in their sweat. The mother should avoid having her child become overheated and should frequently replenish body fluids with water or fruit juices. A child with cystic fibrosis is no more susceptible to sunburn than any other child. Any young child should be protected with sunscreen when in the sun for long periods of time. A child with cystic fibrosis is no more likely to get infectious diarrhea than any other child, although they do have noninfectious diarrhea. A child with cystic fibrosis is no more likely to have respiratory allergies than any other child. A child with cystic fibrosis will have respiratory problems but they will not necessarily be allergy related.

50. The correct answer is 2. Aminophylline is a bronchodilator. As it exerts its effects, wheezing will decrease. Aminophylline has no effect on mucous production. A toxic effect of

aminophylline is hypotension. A sleeping child does show evidence that the drug worked, but this is not the most significant finding.

51. The correct answer is 2. The energy exerted by the child in resisting the oxygen tent is causing increased respiratory effort. The child should be removed from the tent and closely monitored to be sure that he handles being in room air. The physician should be notified because the oxygen content of room air is only 20%, which is less than that ordered. Restraining him in the oxygen tent would further increase respiratory effort. It would be best to leave him in his room where he can be closely monitored and where the oxygen tent is available if needed. A proper nursing response would help the child deal with the treatment by himself and not just do it to please someone else. The twelve-month-old is moving into the stage of toddlerhood and the development of a sense of autonomy.

The Gastrointestinal System

VARIATIONS FROM THE ADULT

A. Mechanical functions of digestion are immature at birth.
   1. No voluntary control over swallowing until 6 weeks
   2. Stomach capacity decreased
   3. Peristalsis increased, faster emptying time, more prone to diarrhea
   4. Relaxed cardiac sphincter contributes to tendency to regurgitate food
B. Liver functions (glyconeogenesis and storage of vitamins) are immature throughout infancy.
C. Production of mucosal-lining antibodies is decreased.
D. Gastric acidity is low in infants, slowly rises until age 10, and then increases again during adolescence to reach adult levels.
E. Secretory cells are functional at birth, but efficiency of enzymes impaired by lower gastric pH.
F. Infant has decreased saliva, which causes decreased ability to digest starches.
G. Digestive processes are mature by toddlerhood.
H. Completion of myelinization of spinal cord allows voluntary control of elimination.

ASSESSMENT

History

A. Presenting problem: symptoms may include
   1. Vomiting: type, color, amount, relationship to eating or other events
   2. Abnormal bowel habits: diarrhea, constipation, bleeding
   3. Weight loss or growth failure
   4. Pain: location; relationship to meals or other events; effect on sleep, play, appetite
   5. Any other parental concerns
B. Diet/nutrition history: appetite, daily caloric intake, food intolerances, feeding schedule, nutritional deficits

Physical Examination

A. General appearance
   1. Plot height and weight on growth chart.
   2. Measure midarm circumference and tricep skinfold thickness.
   3. Observe color: jaundiced or pale.
B. Mouth
   1. Note level of dentition, presence of dental caries.
   2. Observe mucosal integrity.
C. Abdomen
   1. Observe skin integrity.
   2. Note abdominal distention or visible peristaltic waves (seen in pyloric stenosis).
   3. Inspect for hernias (umbilical, inguinal).
   4. Auscultate for bowel sounds (a sound every 10–30 seconds is normal).
   5. Palpate for tenderness.
   6. Palpate for liver (inferior edge normally palpated 1–2 cm below right costal margin).
   7. Palpate for spleen (may be felt on inspiration 1–2 cm below left costal margin).
D. Vital signs: note presence of fever.

ANALYSIS

Nursing diagnoses for the child with a disorder of the gastrointestinal system may include

A. Altered bowel elimination: constipation, diarrhea
B. Pain
C. High risk for fluid volume deficit
D. Altered nutrition: less than body requirements
E. Altered oral mucous membrane
F. High risk for impaired skin integrity
G. Altered tissue perfusion: gastrointestinal
H. Altered family processes

PLANNING AND IMPLEMENTATION

Goals

A. Child will maintain adequate nutritional intake.
B. Child will be free from complications of inadequate nutritional intake.
C. Pain will be relieved/controlled.
D. Child will reach optimal developmental level.
E. Parents will be able to care for child at home.

Interventions

Nasogastric Tube Feeding

A. Provide continuous NG tube feedings when child needs high-calorie intake.
B. Use infusion pump to ensure sustained intake.
C. Check tube placement every 4 hours.
D. Check residuals and refeed every 4 hours.

Gastrostomy

A. Used for clients at high risk for aspiration.
B. Regulate height of tube so feeding flows in over 20–30 minutes.

Parenteral Nutrition

A. Use central venous line for high dextrose solutions (greater than 10%).
B. Check infusion rate and amount every 30 minutes.
C. Monitor urine sugar and acetone every 4 hours for 24 hours after a solution change, then every 8 hours.
D. Monitor for signs of hyperglycemia (nausea, vomiting, dehydration).
E. Provide sterile care for insertion site.
   1. Change solution and tubing every 24 hours.
   2. Change dressing every 1–3 days.
   3. Apply restraints (if needed) to prevent dislodgement of central line.
F. Provide infants who are not receiving oral feedings with a pacifier to satisfy sucking needs.

EVALUATION

A. Child is receiving adequate nourishment as evidenced by normal growth and development.
B. Skin is intact, free from signs of redness or inflammation.
C. Child is free from infection, diarrhea, or vomiting.
D. Child is free from pain.
   1. Relaxed facial expression
   2. Level of activity
   3. No guarding of abdomen
E. Parents participate in care of child.
F. Child participates in normal daily activities with family and peers.

DISORDERS OF THE GASTROINTESTINAL SYSTEM

Congenital Disorders

Cleft Lip and Palate

A. General information
   1. Nonunion of the tissue and bone of the upper lip and hard/soft palate during embryologic development
   2. Familial disorder, often associated with other congenital abnormalities; incidence higher in Caucasians
      a. Cleft lip/palate: 1 in 1000 births
      b. Cleft palate: 1 in 2500 births
      c. Cleft lip with or without cleft palate affects more boys; cleft palate affects more girls
   3. With cleft palate, the failure of the bone and tissues to fuse results in a communication between the mouth and nose
B. Medical management: team approach for therapy
   1. Speech therapist
   2. Dentist and orthodontist
   3. Audiologist, otolaryngologist, pediatrician (these children are prone to otitis media and possible hearing loss)
   4. Surgical correction
      a. Timing varies with severity of defect; early correction helps to avoid speech defects.
      b. Cheiloplasty: correction of cleft lip
         1) goal is to unite edges to allow lips to be both functional and cosmetically attractive.
         2) usually performed approximately age 2 months (to prepare gums for eruption of teeth) when child is free from respiratory infection.

3) Steri-Strips or Logan bar usually used to take tension off suture line.
   c. Cleft palate repair is usually not done until age 18 months in anticipation of speech development.
      1) between lip and palate repair child is maintained on normal nutritional and respiratory status; also maintains normal immunization schedule.
      2) child should be weaned and able to take liquids from a cup before palate repair.
C. Assessment findings
   1. Facial abnormality visible at birth: cleft lip or palate or both, unilateral or bilateral, partial or complete
   2. Difficulty sucking, inability to form airtight seal around nipple (size of defect may preclude breast-feeding)
   3. Formula/milk escapes through nose in infants with cleft palate
   4. Predisposition to infection because of free communication between mouth and nose
   5. Possible difficulty swallowing
   6. Abdominal distension due to swallowed air
D. Nursing interventions: pre-op cleft lip repair
   1. Feed in upright position to decrease chance of aspiration and decrease amount of air swallowed.
   2. Burp frequently; increased swallowed air causes abdominal distension and discomfort.
   3. Use a large-holed nipple; press cleft lip together with fingers to encourage sucking and to strengthen muscles needed later for speech.
   4. If infant unable to suck, use a rubber-tipped syringe and drip formula into side of mouth.
   5. Administer gavage feeding as ordered if necessary.
   6. Finish feeding with water to wash away formula in palate area.
   7. Provide small, frequent feedings.
   8. Provide emotional support for parents/family.
      a. Demonstrate benefits of surgery by showing before and after pictures.
      b. Reinforce that disorder is not their fault and that it will not affect child's life span or mental ability.
E. Nursing care: post-op cleft lip repair
   1. Maintain patent airway (child may appear to have respiratory distress because of closure of previously open space; adaptation occurs quickly).
   2. Assess color; monitor amount of swallowing to detect hemorrhage.

3. Do not place in prone position or with pressure on cheeks; avoid any pressure or tension on suture line.
4. Avoid straining on suture line by anticipating child's needs.
   a. Prevent crying.
   b. Keep child comfortable and content.
5. Use elbow restraints or pin sleeves of shirt to diaper to keep child's hands away from suture line.
6. Resume feedings as ordered.
. Keep suture line clean; clean after each feeding with saline, peroxide, or water to remove crusts and prevent scarring.
8. Provide pain control/relief.
F. Nursing interventions: pre-op cleft palate repair
   1. Prepare parents to care for child after surgery.
   2. Instruct concerning feeding methods and positioning.
G. Nursing interventions: post-op cleft palate repair
   1. Position on side for drainage of blood/mucus.
   2. Have suction available but use only in emergency.
   3. Prevent injury or trauma to suture line.
      a. Use cups only for liquids; no bottles.
      b. Avoid straws, utensils, Popsicle sticks, chewing gum.
      c. Provide soft toys.
      d. Use elbow restraints.
      e. Provide liquid diet initially, then progress to soft before returning to normal.
      f. Give water after each feeding to clean suture line.
      g. Hold and cuddle these babies to help distract them.

Altered Connections between Trachea, Esophagus, and Stomach

A. General information
   1. Types (Figure 5.4)
      a. *Esophageal atresia:* esophagus ends in a blind pouch; no entry route to stomach
      b. *Tracheoesophageal fistula* (*TEF*): open connection between trachea and esophagus
      c. *Esophageal atresia with TEF:* esophagus ends in a blind pouch; stomach end of esophagus connects with trachea
   2. These deformities are found more often in low-birth-weight or premature infants, and are associated with polyhydramnios in the mother and multiple congenital anomalies.

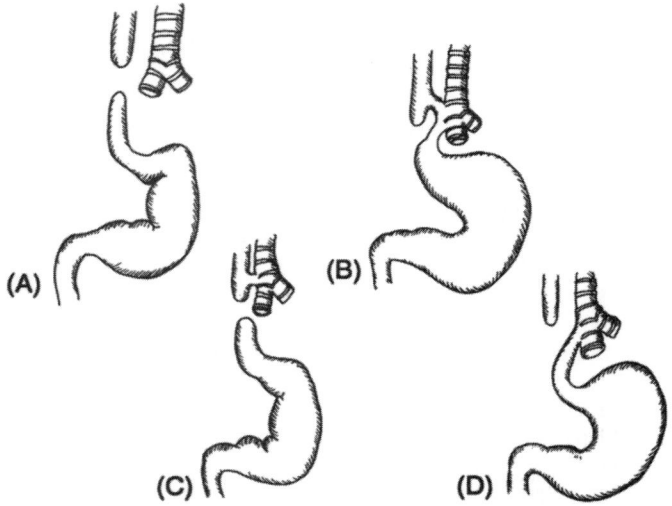

FIGURE 5.4 Esophageal defects: (A) Esophageal atresia; (B) (C) (D) Esophageal atresia with tracheoesophageal fistula

B. Medical management
   1. Drug therapy: antibiotics for respiratory infections
   2. Surgery
      a. Palliative
         1) gastrostomy for placement of a feeding tube
         2) esophagostomy to drain secretions
      b. Corrective
         1) end-to-end anastomosis to correct the defect and restore normal anatomy
         2) colon transplant for defects where there is insufficient tissue for an end-to-end anastomosis
C. Assessment findings
   1. Esophageal atresia
      a. History of polyhydramnios in mother (from infant's inability to swallow and excrete amniotic fluid)
      b. Inability to pass an NG tube
      c. Increased drooling and salivation
      d. Immediate regurgitation of undigested formula/milk when fed
      e. Intermittent cyanosis from choking on aspirated secretions
   2. TEF
      a. Normal swallowing but some food/mucus crosses fistula, causing choking and intermittent cyanosis
      b. Distended abdomen from inhaled air crossing fistula into stomach
      c. Aspiration pneumonia from reflux of gastric secretions into the trachea
   3. Esophageal atresia with TEF
      a. All findings for esophageal atresia

      b. Abdominal distension and aspiration pneumonia from gas and reflux of gastric acids into trachea
   4. Diagnostic tests: fluoroscopy with contrast material reveals type of defect
D. Nursing interventions: preoperative
   1. Maintain patent airway.
      a. Position according to type of defect (usually 30° head elevation).
      b. Provide continuous or prn nasal suctioning.
   2. Keep NPO.
   3. Administer IV fluids as ordered.
E. Nursing interventions: postoperative
   1. Provide nutrition.
      a. Provide gastrostomy tube feedings until the anastomosis site has healed.
      b. Start oral feedings when infant can swallow well.
      c. Progress from glucose water to small, frequent formula feedings.
   2. Promote respiratory function.
      a. Position properly.
      b. Suction as needed.
      c. Provide chest tube care (page 246).
   3. Provide client teaching and discharge planning concerning
      a. Alternative feeding methods
      b. Signs of respiratory distress and suctioning technique

Gastroesophageal Reflux (Chalasia)

A. General information
   1. Reversal of flow of stomach contents into lower portion of esophagus
   2. More common in premature infants due to hypotonia
   3. Caused by relaxed cardiac sphincter or overdistension of stomach by gas or overfeeding
   4. Results in local irritation of the lining of the esophagus from backflow of acidic gastric contents; sometimes causes aspiration pneumonia
B. Assessment findings
   1. Irritability
   2. "Spitting up" (versus vomiting or projectile vomiting); note relationship to feedings
   3. Diagnostic tests
      a. Muscle tone of cardiac sphincter reduced
      b. Esophageal pH: contents acidic
      c. Fluoroscopy: presence of refluxed contrast material not quickly cleared or repeated reflux
C. Nursing interventions
   1. Position with head elevated 30°–45°.
   2. Give small, frequent feedings with adequate burping.

3. Provide client teaching and discharge planning: teach parents how to position and feed infant.

Pyloric Stenosis

A. General information
   1. Hypertrophy (thickening) of the pyloric sphincter causing stenosis and obstruction
   2. Incidence: 5 in 1000 births; more common in Caucasian, firstborn, full-term boys
   3. Cause unknown; possibly familial
B. Medical management
   1. Noninvasive: thickened feedings
   2. Surgery: pyloromyotomy (Fredet-Ramstedt procedure)
C. Assessment findings
   1. Olive-size bulge under right rib cage
   2. Vomiting
      a. As obstruction increases, vomiting becomes more forceful and projectile.
      b. Vomitus does not contain bile (bile duct is distal to the pylorus).
   3. Peristaltic waves during and after feeding (look like rolling balls under abdominal wall)
   4. Failure to thrive, even though infant appears hungry after vomiting
   5. Dehydration: sunken fontanels, poor skin turgor, decreased urinary output
   6. Diagnostic tests
      a. Upper GI series reveals narrowing of the diameter of the pylorus
      b. Sodium, potassium, chloride decreased
      c. Hct increased
      d. Metabolic alkalosis
D. Nursing interventions: preoperative
   1. Administer replacement fluids and electrolytes as ordered.
   2. Prevent vomiting.
      a. Give thickened feedings.
      b. Keep in high-Fowler's position.
      c. Place on right side after feedings.
      d. Minimize handling.
      e. Record strict I&O, daily weights, and urine specific gravity.
   3. Observe for symptoms of aspiration of vomitus.
E. Nursing interventions: postoperative
   1. Advance diet as tolerated.
   2. Place on right side after feeding.
   3. Monitor strict I&O, daily weights.
   4. Observe incision for signs of infection.
   5. Provide client teaching and discharge planning concerning feeding and positioning of infant.

Intussusception

A. General information
   1. Telescoping of bowel into itself (usually at the ileocecal valve) causing edema, obstruction, and possible necrosis of the bowel
   2. Most common at about age 6 months; occurs more often in boys than in girls; associated with cystic fibrosis and celiac disease
   3. Cause unknown
B. Medical management
   1. Barium enema to reduce telescoping by hydrostatic pressure
   2. Surgery if barium enema unsuccessful or if signs of peritonitis
C. Assessment findings
   1. Piercing cry
   2. Severe abdominal pain (pulls legs up)
   3. Vomiting of bile-stained fluid
   4. Bloody mucus in stool
   5. "Currant-jelly" stool
D. Nursing interventions
   1. Provide routine pre- and post-op care for abdominal surgery.
   2. Monitor for fluid and electrolyte imbalance and intervene as needed.
   3. Monitor for peritonitis and intervene as needed.

Hirschsprung's Disease (Aganglionic Megacolon)

A. General information
   1. Absence of autonomic parasympathetic ganglion cells in a portion of the large colon (usually occurs 4–25 cm proximally from anus), resulting in decreased motility in that portion of the colon and signs of functional obstruction
   2. Usually diagnosed in infancy
   3. Familial disease; more common in boys than girls; associated with Down's syndrome
   4. When stool enters the affected part of the colon, lack of peristalsis causes it to remain there until additional stool pushes it through; colon dilates as stool is impacted.
B. Medical management
   1. Drug therapy: stool softeners
   2. Isotonic enemas
   3. Diet therapy: low residue
   4. Surgery
      a. Palliative: loop or double-barrel colostomy
      b. Corrective: abdominal-perineal pull through; bowel containing ganglia is pulled down and anastomosed to the rectum.
C. Assessment findings
   1. Failure or delay in passing meconium
   2. Abdominal distension; failure to pass stool

3. Temporary relief following digital rectal exam
4. Loose stools; only liquid can get around impaction (may also be a ribbonlike stool)
5. Nausea, anorexia, lethargy
6. Possibly bile-stained or fecal vomiting
7. Loss of weight, failure to grow
8. Volvulus (bowel twists upon itself, causing obstruction and necrosis) and enterocolitis due to fecal stagnation
9. Diagnostic tests: rectal biopsy confirms presence of aganglionic cells
D. Nursing interventions
1. Administer enemas as ordered.
   a. Use mineral oil or isotonic saline.
   b. Do not use tap water or soap suds enemas in infants because of danger of water intoxication.
   c. Use volume appropriate to weight of child.
      1) infants: 150–200 ml
      2) children: 250–500 ml
2. Do not treat the loose stools; the child actually is constipated.
3. Administer TPN as ordered.
4. Provide a low-residue diet.
5. Provide client teaching and discharge planning concerning colostomy care and low-residue diet.

Imperforate Anus

A. General information
1. Congenital malformation caused by abnormal fetal development
2. Many variations; anal agenesis most frequent
3. Often associated with fistula formation to rectum or vagina and other congenital anomalies
4. Surgical correction performed in stages with completion at about age 1 year
5. May need temporary colostomy
B. Medical management
1. Manual dilatation
2. Surgery: anoplasty (reconstruction of anus)
3. Prophylactic antibiotics
C. Assessment findings
1. No stool passage within 24 hours of birth
2. Meconium stool from inappropriate orifice
3. Inability to insert thermometer
D. Nursing interventions
1. If suspected, do not take rectal temperature because of risk of perforating wall and causing peritonitis.
2. Perform manual dilatation as ordered; instruct parents in proper technique.
3. After surgery prevent infection; keep anal incisional area as clean as possible.
4. After surgery use side-lying position, or have child lie prone with hips elevated.

Acquired Gastrointestinal Disorders

Celiac Disease

A. General information
1. Malabsorption syndrome characterized by intolerance of gluten, found in rye, oats, wheat, and barley
2. Familial disease, found more commonly in Caucasians
3. Cause unknown; thought to be an inborn error of metabolism or an immunologic disorder
4. Characterized by flat mucosal surface and atrophy of villi of the intestine; reduced absorptive surface causes marked malabsorption of fats
B. Medical management: diet therapy main intervention; gluten-free diet, TPN in children who are severely malnourished
C. Assessment findings
1. Steatorrhea: frothy, pale, bulky, foul-smelling, greasy stools
2. Chronic diarrhea during late infancy and throughout toddlerhood
3. Failure to thrive
4. Grossly distended abdomen; muscle wasting of limbs and buttocks
5. Abdominal pain, irritability, listlessness, vomiting
6. Symptoms of vitamin A, D, E, and K deficiency
7. Diagnostic tests
   a. Pancreatic enzymes and sweat chloride test normal (performed to rule out the possibility of cystic fibrosis)
   b. Jejunal and duodenal biopsies show characteristic atrophy of the mucosa
D. Nursing interventions
1. Monitor gluten-free diet (no wheat, barley, oats, and rye products).
2. Provide supplemental fat-soluble vitamins in water-soluble form
3. Provide client teaching and discharge planning concerning
   a. Gluten-free diet; stress allowed foods and importance of reading labels carefully
   b. Avoidance of infection
   c. Assisting child to feel like a "normal" peer
   d. Importance of adhering to diet even though symptoms are controlled
   e. Importance of long-term follow-up management

Appendicitis

A. General information
1. Inflammation of the appendix that prevents mucus from passing into the cecum; if

untreated, ischemia, gangrene, rupture, and peritonitis occur
2. Most common in school-age children
3. May be caused by mechanical obstruction (fecaliths, intestinal parasites) or anatomic defect; may be related to decreased fiber in the diet
B. Assessment findings
1. Diffuse pain, localizes in lower right quadrant
2. Nausea/vomiting
3. Guarding of abdomen, rebound tenderness, walks stooped over
4. Decreased bowel sounds
5. Fever
6. Diagnostic tests
   a. WBC increased
   b. Elevated acetone in urine
C. Nursing interventions
1. Administer antibiotics/antipyretics as ordered
2. Prevent perforation of the appendix; do not give enemas or cathartics or use heating pad
3. In addition to routine pre-op care for appendectomy
   a. Give support to parents if seeking treatment was delayed.
   b. Explain necessity of obtaining lab work prior to surgery.
4. In addition to routine post-op care
   a. Monitor NG tube (usually with low suction).
   b. Monitor Penrose drains.
   c. Position in semi-Fowler's or lying on right side to facilitate drainage.
   d. Administer antibiotics as ordered.

Parasitic Worms

A. General information
1. A parasite is an organism that lives in, on, or at the expense of the host.
2. Common human GI parasites are pinworms and roundworms.
3. Medication varies depending on type of parasite.
B. Assessment findings
1. Pinworms: anal irritation, itching, disturbed sleep
2. Roundworm: colic, abdominal pain, lack of appetite, weight loss
C. Nursing interventions
1. Obtain stool culture.
2. Observe for worms in all excreta (Scotch-tape test for stool).
3. Instuct parents to change clothing, bed linens, towels and launder in hot water.
4. Clean toilets with disinfectant.
5. Instruct all family members to scrub hands and fingernails prior to eating and after using toilet.

6. Follow specific medication and hygiene orders given by physician.

Constipation

A. General information
1. Decrease in number of bowel movements with large, hard stools
2. May be caused by high fat and protein and low fluid in diet
3. May cause bowel obstruction if severe
B. Medical management
1. Drug therapy: stool softeners, suppositories, enemas
2. Diet therapy: increased fluids and fiber
C. Assessment findings
1. Less frequent stools, difficulty eliminating stool, hard consistency compared to normal pattern (children do not have to stool every day)
2. Bleeding with stooling
3. Abdominal pain
D. Nursing interventions
1. Assess for other pathologic causes of constipation.
2. Dietary modification, increase fiber and fluids.
3. Apply lubricant around anus.
4. Remove stool digitally if possible.
5. Provide prune juice (1 oz); add fruits to diet.
6. Add small amount of Karo syrup to formula.
7. Teach parents methods to prevent further episodes.

Sample Questions

52. Janie, age 9, has celiac disease, which has been in good control since it was diagnosed six years ago. She has now been admitted to the hospital for an emergency appendectomy. Which preoperative procedure should the nurse withhold?
    1. A cleansing enema.
    2. Starting an IV.
    3. Keeping her NPO.
    4. Obtaining a blood sample for a CBC.
53. Alice, age 8, has celiac disease. She had an emergency appendectomy. She is progressing well and is having her first real meal. Which food should the nurse remove from her tray?
    1. Chicken rice soup.
    2. Crackers.
    3. Hamburger patty.
    4. Fresh fruit cup.
54. Barry K., 12 months old, had a cleft lip repaired successfully as an infant. His mother brings him to the clinic for a checkup and his

MMR immunization. While talking to the nurse, Ms. K. reports that her teenage babysitter has just come down with rubeola. The most appropriate plan of treatment for Barry is to
1. administer immune serum globulin.
2. administer prophylactic penicillin.
3. vaccinate him now with MMR.
4. allow him to catch measles from the babysitter in order to develop active immunity.

55. The nurse is caring for a 12-month-old child who has a cleft palate. A cleft lip was repaired when he was 2 months old. His mother asks the nurse when he will be ready for a cleft palate repair. The most appropriate response is that cleft palate repair is usually done
1. prior to development of speech.
2. when the child is toilet trained.
3. when the child is completely weaned from the bottle and pacifier.
4. when a large-holed nipple is ineffective for his feedings.

56. Bobby, 2 years old, has had a cleft palate repair. A priority in the post-op plan of care for Bobby includes teaching his mother
1. to resume toilet training after he is up and around.
2. to use a cup or wide bowl spoon for feeding.
3. that he will be more prone to respiratory infections now that his airway is smaller.
4. that no further treatment will be needed until his adult teeth come in at age 6.

Answers and Rationales

52. The correct answer is 1. Enemas, cathartics, and heat to the abdomen should all be avoided in appendicitis because they may cause perforation of the appendix. All the other measures are appropriate pre-op interventions.

53. The correct answer is 2. The prescribed diet for children with celiac disease is gluten free; crackers contain gluten, but the other foods do not.

54. The correct answer is 1. Administration of immune serum globulin will provide the child with passive immunity to prevent a full-blown case of measles or reduce the severity of symptoms. Penicillin does not prevent or treat a viral infection. Active immunization with MMR should be given at a later time. It takes time for active immunity to develop. It is not appropriate to let the child get a disease with potentially serious complications when the disease can be prevented.

55. The correct answer is 1. Cleft palate repair should be done prior to the development of speech. This allows for the formation of a more normal speech pattern. Being toilet trained has no relation to cleft palate surgery. The child does not have to be completely weaned from the bottle and the pacifier prior to the surgery. However, the child must be able to drink from a cup because a bottle may not be used until the surgical repair is healed. A large holed nipple is generally used for a premature infant with a weak sucking reflex. The child with cleft palate repair is not allowed to suck until the repair is healed.

56. The correct answer is 2. Care must be taken to not put anything in the mouth that could damage the suture line. Toilet training has no relationship to the surgery done. The child may have regressed in toilet training since the surgery but may begin again whenever he seems interested. Now that the repair has been done he should experience fewer respiratory infections. Additional stages of treatment may need to be done prior to age 6.

The Genitourinary System

VARIATIONS FROM THE ADULT

A. Nephrons continue to develop after birth.
B. Glomerular filtration rate is 30% below adult levels at birth; reaches normal level by age 2 years.
C. Tubular functions immature at birth; tubular absorption and secretion reach adult levels by age 2 years.
D. Urethra is shorter in children and more prone to ascending infection (particularly true in girls); the urethra is also closer to anus as source of contamination.

E. Many GU conditions in children become chronic.

ASSESSMENT

History

A. Presenting problem: symptoms may include
1. Change in appearance, color, or smell of urine
2. Change in amount, frequency, or pattern of urination
3. Abdominal or back pain
4. Anorexia, nausea, vomiting, weight loss
5. Headaches, seizures
6. Fatigue, lethargy
7. Excessive thirst
8. Drug use or accidental ingestions
B. Family history: kidney disease, hypertension

Physical Examination

A. General appearance: note presence of edema.
B. Abdomen and genitalia: note abdominal distension, presence of undescended testicle, tenderness to palpation, placement of urinary meatus, urinary stream during voiding.
C. Vital signs: note presence of fever; increased blood pressure (common in renal disease)

ANALYSIS

Nursing diagnoses for the child with a disorder of the genitourinary tract may include
A. Fluid volume excess
B. Altered urinary elimination
C. Pain
D. Activity intolerance
E. Altered family process

PLANNING AND IMPLEMENTATION

Goals

A. Child will have normal urinary function.
B. Child's fluid and electrolyte and acid-base balances will be normal.
C. Child will be free from signs of infection.
D. Child's blood pressure will be within normal limits.
E. Parents will be able to care for child at home.

Intervention

Pediatric Urine Collector (PUC)

A. Used when child is not toilet trained
B. Nursing care

1. Wash genitalia as for clean catch specimens.
2. Apply bag directly to dry skin; do not use powder or creams.
3. If child has not voided within 45 minutes, remove bag and repeat process.

EVALUATION

A. Child is adequately hydrated as evidenced by normal serum electrolyte levels and normal urine output.
B. Child is free from complications such as infection, skin breakdown, or hypertension.
C. Parents demonstrate ability to administer appropriate medications and treatments.

DISORDERS OF THE GENITOURINARY SYSTEM

Urinary Tract Infection (UTI)

A. General information
1. Bacterial invasion of the kidneys or bladder
2. More common in girls, preschool, and school-age children
3. Usually caused by *E. coli;* predisposing factors include poor hygiene, irritation from bubble baths, urinary reflux
4. The invading organism ascends the urinary tract, irritating the mucosa and causing characteristic symptoms.
B. Assessment findings
1. Low-grade fever
2. Abdominal pain
3. Enuresis, pain/burning on urination, frequency, hematuria
C. Nursing interventions
1. Administer antibiotics as ordered; prevention of kidney infection/glomerulonephritis important. (*Note:* obtain cultures before starting antibiotics.)
2. Provide warm baths and allow child to void in water to alleviate painful voiding.
3. Force fluids.
4. Encourage measures to acidify urine (cranberry juice, acid-ash diet).
5. Provide client teaching and discharge planning concerning
   a. Avoidance of tub baths (contamination from dirty water may allow microorganisms to travel up urethra)
   b. Avoidance of bubble baths that might irritate urethra
   c. Importance for girls to wipe perineum from front to back
   d. Increase in foods/fluids that acidify urine.

Vesicoureteral Reflux

A. General information
   1. Regurgitation of urine from the bladder into the ureters due to faulty valve mechanism at the vesicoureteral junction
   2. Predisposes child to
      a. UTIs from urine stasis
      b. Pyelonephritis from chronic UTIs
      c. Hydronephrosis from increased pressure on renal pelvis
B. Assessment findings: same as for urinary tract infections
C. Nursing interventions for surgical reimplantation of ureters
   1. Assist with preoperative studies as needed (IVP, voiding cystourethrogram, cystoscopy).
   2. Provide postoperative care.
      a. Monitor drains; may have one from bladder and one from each ureter (ureteral stents).
      b. Check output from all drains (expect bloody drainage initially) and record carefully.
      c. Observe drainage from abdominal dressing; note color, amount, frequency.
      d. Administer medication for bladder spasms as ordered.

Exstrophy of the Bladder

A. General information
   1. Congenital malformation in which nonfusion of abdominal and anterior walls of the bladder during embryologic development causes anterior surface of bladder to lie open on abdominal wall
   2. Varying degrees of defect
B. Assessment findings
   1. Associated structural changes
      a. Prolapsed rectum
      b. Inguinal hernia
      c. Widely split symphysis
      d. Rotated hips
   2. Associated anomalies
      a. Epispadias
      b. Cleft scrotum or clitoris
      c. Undescended testicles
      d. Chordee (downward deflection of the penis)
C. Medical management: two-stage reconstructive surgery, possibly with urinary diversion; usually delayed until age 3–6 months
D. Nursing interventions: preoperative
   1. Provide bladder care; prevent infection.
      a. Keep area as clean as possible; urine on skin will cause irritation and ulceration.
      b. Change diaper frequently; keep diaper loose fitting.
      c. Wash with mild soap and water.
      d. Cover exposed bladder with Vaseline gauze.
E. Nursing interventions: postoperative
   1. Design play activities to foster toddler's need for autonomy (e.g., Play-Doh, talking toys, books); child will be immobilized for extended period of time.
   2. Prevent trauma; as child gets older and more mobile, trauma more likely; teach parents to avoid areas such as sandboxes.

Undescended Testicles (Cryptorchidism)

A. General information
   1. Unilateral or bilateral absence of testes in scrotal sac
   2. Testes normally descend at 8 months of gestation, will therefore be absent in premature infants
   3. Incidence increased in children having genetically transmitted diseases
   4. Unilateral cryptorchidism most common
   5. 75% will descend spontaneously by age 1 year
B. Medical management
   1. Whether or not to treat is still controversial; if testes remain in abdomen, damage to the testes (sterility) is possible because of increased body temperature.
   2. If not descended by age 8 or 9, chorionic gonadotropin can be given.
   3. Orchipexy: surgical procedure to retrieve and secure testes placement; performed between ages 1–3 years.
C. Assessment findings: unable to palpate testes in scrotal sac (when palpating testes be careful not to elicit cremasteric reflex, which pulls testes higher in pelvic cavity)
D. Nursing interventions
   1. Advise parents of absence of testes and provide information about treatment options.
   2. Support parents if surgery is to be performed.
   3. Post-op, avoid disturbing the tension mechanism (will be in place for about 1 week).
   4. Avoid contamination of incision.

Hypospadias

A. General information
   1. Urethral opening located anywhere along the ventral surface of penis
   2. Chordee (ventral curvature of the penis) often associated, causing constriction
   3. In extreme cases, child's sex may be uncertain
B. Medical management

1. Minimal defects need no intervention
2. Neonatal circumcision delayed, tissue may be needed for corrective repair
3. Surgery performed at age 3–9 months; 2 years of age for complex repairs.
C. Assessment findings
 1. Urinary meatus misplaced
 2. Inability to make straight stream of urine
D. Nursing interventions
 1. Diaper normally.
 2. Provide support for parents.
 3. Provide support for child at time of surgery.
 4. Post-operatively check pressure dressing, monitor catheter drainage, assess pain.

Enuresis

A. General information
 1. Involuntary passage of urine after the age of control is expected (about 4 years)
 2. Types
  a. Primary: in children who have never achieved control
  b. Secondary: in children who have developed complete control and lose it
 3. May occur at any time of day but is most frequent at night
 4. More common in boys
 5. No organic cause can be identified; familial tendency
 6. Etiologic possibilities
  a. Sleep disturbances
  b. Delayed neurologic development
  c. Immature development of bladder leading to decreased capacity
  d. Psychologic problems
B. Medical management
 1. Bladder retention exercises
 2. Behavior modification, e.g., bed alarm devices
 3. Drug therapy: results are temporary; side effects may be unpleasant or even dangerous
  a. Tricyclic antidepressants: imipramine HCI (Tofranil)
  b. Anticholinergics
C. Assessment findings
 1. Physical exam normal
 2. History of repeated involuntary urination
D. Nursing interventions
 1. Provide information/counseling to family as needed.
  a. Confirm that this is not conscious behavior and that child is not purposely misbehaving.
  b. Assure parents that they are not responsible and that this is a relatively common problem.
 2. Involve child in care; give praise and support with small accomplishments.

 a. Age 5–6 years; can strip bed of wet sheets.
 b. Age 10–12 years: can do laundry and change bed.
3. Avoid scolding and belittling child.

Nephrosis (Nephrotic Syndrome)

A. General information
 1. Autoimmune process leading to structural alteration of glomerular membrane that results in increased permeability to plasma proteins, particularly albumin
 2. Course of the disease consists of exacerbations and remissions over a period of months to years
 3. Commonly affects preschoolers, boys more often than girls
 4. Pathophysiology
  a. Plasma proteins enter the renal tubule and are excreted in the urine, causing proteinuria.
  b. Protein shift causes altered oncotic pressure and lowered plasma volume.
  c. Hypovolemia triggers release of renin and angiotensin, which stimulates increased secretion of aldosterone; aldosterone increases reabsorption of water and sodium in distal tubule.
  d. Lowered blood pressure also stimulates release of ADH, further increasing reabsorption of water; together with a general shift of plasma into interstitial spaces, results in edema.
 5. Prognosis is good unless edema does not respond to steroids.
B. Medical management
 1. Drug therapy
  a. Corticosteroids to resolve edema
  b. Antibiotics for bacterial infections
  c. Thiazide diuretics in edematous stage
 2. Bed rest
 3. Diet modification: high protein, low sodium
C. Assessment findings
 1. Proteinuria, hypoproteinemia, hyperlipidemia
 2. Dependent body edema
  a. Puffiness around eyes in morning
  b. Ascites
  c. Scrotal edema
  d. Ankle edema
 3. Anorexia, vomiting, and diarrhea, malnutrition
 4. Pallor, lethargy
 5. Hepatomegaly
D. Nursing interventions
 1. Provide bed rest.
  a. Conserve energy.
  b. Find activities for quiet play.
 2. Provide high-protein, low-sodium diet during edema phase only.
 3. Maintain skin integrity.

  a. Do not use Band-Aids.
  b. Avoid IM injections (medication is not absorbed into edematous tissue).
  c. Turn frequently.
 4. Obtain morning urine for protein studies.
 5. Provide scrotal support.
 6. Monitor I&O, vital signs and weigh daily.
 7. Administer steroids to suppress autoimmune response as ordered.
 8. Protect from known sources of infection.

Acute Glomerulonephritis

A. General information
 1. Immune complex disease resulting from an antigen-antibody reaction
 2. Secondary to a beta-hemolytic streptococcal infection occurring elsewhere in the body
 3. Occurs more frequently in boys, usually between ages 6–7 years
 4. Usually resolves in about 14 days, self-limiting
B. Medical management
 1. Antibiotics for streptococcal infection
 2. Antihypertensives if blood pressure severely elevated
 3. Digitalis if circulatory overload
 4. Fluid restriction if renal insufficiency
 5. Peritoneal dialysis if severe renal or cardiopulmonary problems develop
C. Assessment findings
 1. History of a precipitating streptococcal infection, usually upper respiratory infection or impetigo
 2. Edema, anorexia, lethargy
 3. Hematuria or dark-colored urine, fever
 4. Hypertension
 5. Diagnostic tests
  a. Urinalysis reveals RBCs, WBCs, protein, cellular casts
  b. Urine specific gravity increased
  c. BUN and serum creatinine increased
  d. ESR elevated
  e. Hgb and hct decreased
D. Nursing interventions
 1. Monitor I&O, blood pressure, urine; weigh daily.
 2. Provide diversional therapy.
 3. Provide client teaching and discharge planning concerning
  a. Medication administration
  b. Prevention of infection
  c. Signs of renal complications
  d. Importance of long-term follow-up

Hydronephrosis

A. General information
 1. Collection of urine in the renal pelvis due to obstruction to outflow

 2. Obstruction most common at ureteral-pelvic junction (see Vesicoureteral Reflux, page 417) but may also be caused by adhesions, ureterocele, calculi, or congenital malformation
 3. Obstruction causes increased intrarenal pressure, decreased circulation, and atrophy of the kidney, leading to renal insufficiency
 4. May be unilateral or bilateral; occurs more often in left kidney
 5. Prognosis good when treated early
B. Medical management: surgery to correct or remove obstruction
C. Assessment findings
 1. Repeated UTIs
 2. Failure to thrive
 3. Abdominal pain, fever
 4. Fluctuating mass in region of kidney
D. Nursing interventions: prepare child for multiple urologic studies (see also Vesicoureteral Reflux, page 417).

Sample Questions

57. Tyrone, age 4 years, has just been diagnosed as having nephrotic syndrome. His potential for impairment of skin integrity is related to
 1. joint inflammation
 2. drug therapy
 3. edema
 4. generalized body rash
58. Walter is 20 months old and admitted to the hospital with a diagnosis of cryptorchidism. Surgical correction is performed at this time to prevent
 1. difficulty in urinating.
 2. sterility.
 3. herniation.
 4. peritonitis.
59. Charlie Urich, 3 days old, is diagnosed with hypospadias. His parents are very upset and have been willing listeners as the nurse has explained this problem to them. The nurse explained that in hypospadias, the physical problem is primarily
 1. ambiguous genitalia.
 2. urinary incontinence.
 3. ventral curvature of the penis.
 4. altered location of the urethral meatus.
60. The parents of a newborn who has hypospadias ask about surgical repair. They are told that the preferred time to schedule surgical repair of hypospadias is when the boy is
 1. 9 months old.
 2. 5 years old.
 3. 12 years old.
 4. 17 years old.

61. The parents of a baby boy who was born with hypospadias want to know about the surgical repair. The nurse tells them that they will be able to evaluate the success of hypospadias surgery by
   1. the cosmetic appearance of the penis.
   2. maintaining stable blood pressure in the child.
   3. observing a straight stream when he voids.
   4. his ability to void without discomfort.

Answers and Rationales

57. The correct answer is 3. A child with nephrotic syndrome will have massive edema. A child with edema is prone to skin breakdown. Joint inflammation and generalized body rash are not usually problems in the child with nephrotic syndrome. Drug therapy is usually steroids and diuretics, neither of which is related to impairment of skin integrity.
58. The correct answer is 2. If the testes remain in the abdomen beyond the age of 5, damage resulting from exposure to internal body temperature can result in sterility.
59. The correct answer is 4. In hypospadias, the urethral opening may be anywhere along the underside of the penis. This dislocation may be accompanied by genital edema and fibrous penile dislocation, which may make sexual identification difficult. If uncorrected, the boy will have problems controlling his urinary stream when he has outgrown diapers.
60. The correct answer is 1. Most surgical repairs are scheduled for the child between 6 and 18 months of age. If left until later, body image problems and mutilation/castration anxieties may occur.
61. The correct answer is 3. Observing the child void in a straight stream while standing is the expected successful outcome of hypospadias repair. The penis may be swollen and discolored after surgery and voiding may be uncomfortable initially. Having a stable blood pressure is always important, but its presence does not indicate successful surgical repair of hypospadias.

The Musculoskeletal System

VARIATIONS FROM THE ADULT

Bones

A. Linear growth results from skeletal development
   1. Centers of ossification
      a. Primary centers in diaphyses
      b. Secondary centers in epiphyses
      c. Used in assessment of bone age; number of ossification centers in wrist equals age in years plus 1
      d. Centers appear earlier in girls than in boys
   2. Metaphysis
      a. Cartilaginous plate between diaphysis and epiphysis
      b. The site of active growth in long bones
      c. Disappears over time with bony fusion of diaphysis and epiphysis
      d. Linear growth ends with epiphyseal fusion
      e. Assessment of bone age includes the advancing bone edges
B. Bone circumference growth occurs as new bone tissue is formed beneath the periosteum.
C. Skeletal maturity is reached by age 17 in boys and 2 years after menarche in girls.
D. Certain characteristics of bone in children affect injury and healing, bones are more prone to injury, and injury results from relatively minor accidents.
   1. Metaphysis
      a. Absorbs shock, protects joints from injury.
      b. Traumatic injury or infection to this growth plate can cause deformity.
      c. If not injured, this growth plate participates in healing and straightening of limbs by process of remodeling.
   2. Porous bone
      a. Increases flexibility; absorbs force on impact.
      b. Allows bones to bend, buckle, and break in "greenstick" or incomplete fracture.
   3. Thicker periosteum
      a. More active osteogenic potential
      b. Healing more rapid
         1) neonatal period: may take 2–3 weeks
         2) early childhood: may take 4 weeks
         3) later childhood: may take 6 weeks
         4) adolescence: 8–10 weeks

      c. Stiffness after immobilization is rare unless joint has been injured.

E. Bone growth is affected by Wolff's law: bone will grow in the direction in which stress is placed on it.

Muscles

A. Muscle growth is responsible for a large part of increase in body weight.
B. The number of muscle fibers is constant throughout life; growth results from an increase in the size of the muscle fibers and by an increased number of nuclei per fiber.
C. Muscle growth most apparent in adolescence, influenced by growth hormone, adrenal androgens, and in boys by testosterone.

ASSESSMENT

History

A. Presenting problem: symptoms may include
    1. Delayed motor development
    2. Injury
    3. Pain, loss of sensation, tingling
    4. Muscle weakness, loss of function of an extremity
    5. Interference with normal activity or play
    6. Other parental concerns
B. Family history: genetic disorders, skeletal deformities
C. Inadequate nutrition (e.g., vitamin A deficiency causes rickets)

Physical Examination

A. General appearance: note any asymmetry, visible deformities, swelling (of joints or over bones), quality of movement (ROM, gait, guarding).
B. Measure muscle strength.
C. Identify warmth or tenderness over bones and joints.
D. Assess pain: note type, location, onset, relationship to activity.
E. Perform examination in standing, lying, and sitting positions.

ANALYSIS

Nursing diagnoses for the child with a disorder of the musculoskeletal system may include
A. High risk for activity intolerance
B. Pain
C. Diversional activity deficit
D. High risk for injury
E. Impaired physical mobility
F. Self-care deficit
G. Body image disturbance

H. High risk for impaired skin integrity
I. Altered tissue perfusion: peripheral

PLANNING AND IMPLEMENTATION

Goals

A. Injury or deformity will be identified and treated early.
B. Child will achieve maximum level of mobility.
C. Pain will be relieved/controlled.
D. Child will be free from injury.
E. Parents will be able to care for child at home.

Interventions

Care of the Child with a Cast

Also see pages 309–310.
A. General information
    1. Initial chemical hardening reaction may cause a change in an infant's body temperature; monitor and intervene as needed.
    2. Choose toys too big to fit down cast.
    3. Do not use baby powder near cast since it clumps and provides a medium for bacterial growth.
    4. Prepare for anticipated casting by having child help apply a cast to a doll the day before.
    5. Demonstrate the use of a cast cutter on a doll before using on child to show it does not cut skin.
B. Care of child in hip spica cast (cast encases child from nipples to knees; legs are abducted with a bar between the thighs)
    1. Use firm mattress to allow for increased weight of plaster cast.
    2. Do not lift cast by crossbar.
    3. Protect cast from water and urine.
       a. Put waterproof material over petaling (Chux®, plastic diapers).
       b. Elevate head of bed slightly to prevent urine and stool from seeping under cast; confirm that entire body is on a slant, not just the head.
       c. Use Bradford frame (canvas board with opening near genitalia) and place a bedpan under opening.
    4. Use pillows to support all parts of the cast.
    5. Drape towel across top of chest part of cast during feedings to prevent crumbs from entering cast.
    6. Monitor for pain/pressure points due to growth if cast is on for a long time.

Care of the Child in Traction

Also see page 310.

A. General information
   1. Infants and young toddlers do not have enough body weight to use traditional tractions effectively.
   2. Children do not understand the necessity of maintaining proper body alignment and will need frequent repositioning.
B. Bryant's traction: used primarily in children
   1. Child is own counterweight.
   2. Both legs are at 90° angle to bed.
   3. Buttocks must be slightly off mattress in order to ensure sufficient traction on legs.
   4. Used with children under age 2 years whose weight is too low (under 30 lb [14 kg]) to counterbalance without additional gravitational force.
   5. Used for fractured femur and dislocated hip.
   6. Monitor for vascular injury to feet with frequent neurovascular checks.

Care of the Child with a Brace

A. General information
   1. Orthopedic device made of metal or leather applied to the body, particularly the trunk and lower extremities, to support the weight of the body, to correct or prevent deformities, and to prevent involuntary movements in spastic conditions
   2. Types
      a. Milwaukee brace
         1) steel and leather brace fitted and adapted to child individually
         2) extends from chin cup and neck pad to pelvis
         3) used in scoliosis to correct curvature
         4) worn 23 hours/day, removed once daily for bathing
         5) causes little interference with activity
      b. Rotowalker
         1) used to provide upright mobility in children with lower limb paralysis
         2) child shifts weight to achieve mobility
      c. Leg brace
         1) designed to stabilize extremity and offer support during ambulation
         2) special hinges permit hip, knee, and ankle to flex during sitting
B. Nursing care: provide client teaching and discharge planning concerning
   1. Importance of meticulous skin care
   2. Need to wear protective clothing under brace
   3. Potential problems of ill-fitting braces
      a. Difficulty in balancing
      b. Muscle stress and skin breakdown
   4. Need for frequent checking and adjustment of braces with growth

EVALUATION

A. Child's musculoskeletal development is normal as evidenced by normal growth and activity.
B. Child experiences minimal discomfort.
C. Injuries are prevented.
D. Parents demonstrate ability to identify complications and administer treatments correctly.

DISORDERS OF THE MUSCULOSKELETAL SYSTEM

Congenital Dislocation of the Hip

A. General information
   1. Displacement of the head of the femur from the acetabulum; present at birth, although not always diagnosed immediately
   2. One of the most common congenital malformations; incidence is 1 in 500–1000 live births
   3. Familial disorder, more common in girls; may be associated with spina bifida
   4. Cause unknown; may be fetal position in utero (breech delivery), genetic predisposition, or laxity of ligaments
   5. The acetabulum is shallow and the head of the femur cartilaginous at birth, contributing to the dislodgment.
B. Medical management
   1. Goal is to enlarge and deepen socket by pressure.
   2. The earlier treatment is initiated, the shorter and less traumatic it will be.
   3. Early treatment consists of positioning the hip in abduction with the head of the femur in the acetabulum and maintaining it in position for several months.
   4. If these measures are unsuccessful, traction and casting (hip spica) or surgery may be successful.
C. Assessment findings
   1. May be unilateral or bilateral, partial or complete
   2. Limitation of abduction (cannot spread legs to change diaper)
   3. Ortolani's click (should only be performed by an experienced practitioner)
      a. With infant in supine position (on the back), bend knees and place thumbs on bent knees, fingers at hip joint.
      b. Bring femurs 90° to hip, then abduct.
      c. With dislocation there is a palpable click where the head of the femur snaps over edge of acetabulum.
   4. Barlow's test
      a. With infant on back, bend knees.

      b. Affected knee will be lower because the head of the femur dislocates towards bed by gravity (referred to as telescoping of limb).

   5. Additional skin folds with knees bent, from telescoping

   6. When lying on abdomen, buttocks of affected side will be flatter because head of femur falls toward bed from gravity

   7. Trendelenburg test (used if child is old enough to walk)
      a. Have child stand on affected leg only.
      b. Pelvis will dip on normal side as child attempts to stay erect.

D. Nursing interventions
   1. Maintain proper positioning: keep legs abducted.
      a. Use triple diapering.
      b. Use Frejka pillow splint (jumperlike suit to keep legs abducted).
      c. Place infant on abdomen with legs in "frog" position.
      d. Use immobilization devices (splints, casts, braces).
   2. Provide adequate nutrition; adapt feeding position as needed for immobilization device.
   3. Provide sensory stimulation; adapt to immobilization device and positioning.
   4. Provide client teaching and discharge planning concerning
      a. Application and care of immobilization devices
      b. Modification of child care using immobilization devices.

Clubfoot (Talipes)

A. General information
   1. Abnormal rotation of foot at ankle
      a. Varus (inward rotation): would walk on ankles, bottoms of feet face each other
      b. Valgus (outward rotation): would walk on inner ankles
      c. Calcaneous (upward rotation): would walk on heels
      d. Equinas (downward rotation): would walk on toes
   2. Most common deformity (95%) is talipes equinovarus.
   3. Deformity almost always congenital; usually unilateral
   4. Occurs more frequently in boys than in girls; may be associated with other congenital disorders but cause unknown
   5. General incidence: 1 in 700–1000

B. Medical management
   1. Exercises
   2. Casting (cast is changed periodically to change angle of foot)

   3. Denis Browne splint (bar shoe): metal bar with shoes attached to the bar at specific angle
   4. Surgery and casting for several months

C. Assessment findings: foot cannot be manipulated by passive exercises into correct position (differentiate from normal clubbing of newborn's feet)

D. Nursing interventions
   1. Perform exercises as ordered.
   2. Provide cast care or care for child in a brace.
   3. Child who is learning to walk must be prevented from trying to stand; apply restraints if necessary.
   4. Provide diversional activities.
   5. Adapt care routines as needed for cast or brace.
   6. Assess toes to be sure cast it not too tight.
   7. Provide skin care.
   8. Provide client teaching and discharge planning concerning
      a. Application/care of immobilization device
      b. Preparation for surgery if indicated
      c. Need to monitor special shoes for continued fit throughout treatment.

Tibial Torsion

A. General information
   1. Rotational deformity of tibia (greater than that normally found in newborn)
   2. Types
      a. Internal: knee forward and foot inward
      b. External: knee forward and foot outward (rare, associated with muscle paralysis)
   3. Majority of cases resolve without treatment

B. Medical management
   1. Splinting: use of Denis Browne splint at night
   2. Surgical correction if still evident by age 3 years

C. Assessment findings: with child lying supine, assess for straight line between tibial tuberosity and 2nd toe; in tibial torsion, the line intersects the 4th or 5th toe.

D. Nursing interventions
   1. If no treatment needed, encourage parents to be patient and emphasize that condition usually resolves by itself
   2. If stretching exercises are recommended, teach parents normal ROM exercises and how to carry them out.
   3. Instruct parents on use of Denis Browne splint if needed.

Legg-Calvé-Perthes Disease

A. General information

1. Aseptic necrosis of femoral head due to disturbance of circulation to the area
2. Primarily affects boys ages 4–10 years
3. Stages: lasting from 18 months to a few years
   a. Initial stage: may not be distinguishable from transient synovitis
   b. Avascular stage: often the first stage noticed
   c. Revascularization stage: regeneration of vascular and connective tissue
   d. Regeneration stage: formation of new bone
B. Medical management: goal is to minimize deformity until healing process is completed
   1. Initial bed rest with traction and then an abduction brace
   2. Possible surgery
C. Assessment findings
   1. Limp, limitation of movement
   2. Pain in groin, hip, and referred to knee; often difficult for child to localize pain
   3. Diagnostic test: x-ray reveals opaque ossification center of head of the femur (softened in avascular stage)
D. Nursing interventions
   1. Provide care for a child with a cast or brace.
   2. Provide diversional activities.

Slipped Femoral Capital Epiphysis

A. General information
   1. Spontaneous displacement of proximal femoral epiphysis in a posterior and inferior direction
   2. Onset insidious; usually occurs during fast growth period of adolescence (growth hormones weaken epiphyseal plate)
   3. Occurs most often in very tall and very obese adolescents; boys affected more frequently
B. Medical management
   1. Skeletal traction
   2. Surgical stabilization with pinning
C. Assessment findings
   1. Limp and referred pain to groin, hip, or knee
   2. Limited internal rotation and abduction of hip
D. Nursing interventions
   1. Suggest weight reduction program for obese children to decrease stress on bones.
   2. Provide care for the child with a cast or traction.

Osteogenesis Imperfecta

A. General information
   1. An inherited disorder affecting collagen formation and resulting in pathologic fractures

2. Types
   a. Osteogenesis imperfecta congenita: autosomal recessive, prognosis poor
   b. Osteogenesis imperfecta tarda: autosomal dominant, less severe form, involvement of varying degrees
3. Classic picture includes soft, fragile bones; blue sclera; otosclerosis
4. Severity of symptoms decreases at puberty due to hormone production and child's ability to prevent injury
B. Medical management
   1. Magnesium oxide supplements
   2. Reduction and immobilization of fractures
C. Assessment findings
   1. Osteogenesis imperfecta congenita
      a. Multiple fractures at birth
      b. Possible skeletal deformity due to intrauterine fracture
      c. Bones of skull are soft
      d. Occasional intracranial hemorrhage
   2. Osteogenesis imperfecta tarda
      a. Delayed walking, fractures, structural scoliosis as child grows
      b. Lower limbs more frequently affected
      c. Hypermobility of joints
      d. Prone to dental caries
D. Nursing interventions
   1. Support limbs, do not stretch.
   2. Position with care; use blankets to aid in mobility and provide support.
   3. Instruct parents in bathing, dressing, diapering.
   4. Support parents; encourage expression of feelings of anger or guilt (parents may have been unjustly suspected of child abuse).

Scoliosis

A. General information
   1. Lateral curvature of the spine
   2. Most commonly occurs in adolescent girls
   3. Disorder has a familial pattern; associated with other neuromuscular disorders
   4. Majority of the time (75% of cases) disorder is idiopathic; others causes include congenital abnormality of vertebrae, neuromuscular disorders, and trauma
   5. May be functional or structural
      a. Nonstructural/functional: "C" curve of spine
         1) due to posture, can be corrected voluntarily and disappears when child lies down
         2) not progressive
         3) treated with posture exercises
      b. Structural/progressive: "S" curve of spine
         1) usually idiopathic
         2) structural change in spine, does not disappear with position changes

        3) more aggressive intervention needed
    B. Medical management
        1. Stretching exercises of the spine for nonstructural changes
        2. Milwaukee brace worn for 23 hours/day for 3 years
        3. Plaster jacket cast
        4. Halo-pelvic or halo-femoral traction
        5. Spinal fusion with insertion of Harrington rod
    C. Assessment findings (structural scoliosis)
        1. Failure of curve to straighten when child bends forward with knees straight and arms hanging down to feet (curve disappears with functional scoliosis)
        2. Uneven bra strap marks
        3. Uneven hips
        4. Uneven shoulders
        5. Asymmetry of rib cage
        6. Diagnostic test: x-ray reveals curvature
    D. Nursing interventions
        1. Teach/encourage exercises as ordered.
        2. Provide care for child with Milwaukee brace
            a. Child wears brace 23 hours/day; is removed once a day for bathing.
            b. Monitor pressure points, adjustments may be needed to accommodate increase in height or weight.
            c. Promote positive body image with brace.
        3. Provide cast/traction care.
        4. Assist with modifying clothing for immobilization devices.
        5. Adjust diet for decreased activity.
        6. Provide diversional activities.
        7. Provide care for child with Harrington rod insertion (see below).
        8. Provide client teaching and discharge planning concerning
            a. Exercises
            b. Brace/traction/cast care
            c. Correct body mechanics
            d. Alternative education for long-term hospitalization/home care
            e. Availability of community agencies

Harrington Rod Insertion

    A. General information
        1. Spinal fusion and installation of a permanent steel rod along spine
        2. Used for moderate to severe curvatures
        3. Usually results in increase in height; positive body image changes
    B. Nursing interventions (see also Discectomy, page 317)
        1. Provide general pre-op teaching and care.
        2. In addition to routine post-op care.
            a. Log roll.
            b. Do not raise head of bed.

    c. Discuss adapting home environment to allow for privacy yet interaction with family during long-term recovery.
    d. Discuss alternate methods of education during recovery period.

Muscular Dystrophy

    A. General information
        1. A group of muscular diseases in children characterized by progressive muscle weakness and deformity
        2. Genetic in origin; biochemical defect is suspected
        3. Types
            a. *Pseudohypertrophic (Duchenne type)*: most frequent type
                1) X-linked recessive
                2) affects only boys
                3) usually manifests in first 4 years
            b. *Facioscapulohumeral*
                1) autosomal dominant
                2) mild form, with weakness of facial and shoulder girdle muscles
                3) onset usually in adolescence
            c. *Limb girdle*
                1) autosomal recessive
                2) affects boys and girls
                3) onset usually in adolescence
            d. *Congenital*
                1) autosomal recessive
                2) onset in utero
            e. *Myotonic*
                1) autosomal dominant
                2) more common in boys
                3) onset in infancy or childhood, or adult onset
                4) prognosis in childhood form is guarded
        4. Disease causes progressive disability throughout childhood; most children with Duchenne's muscular dystrophy are confined to a wheelchair by age 8–10 years.
        5. Death occurs by age 20 in 75% of clients with Duchenne's muscular dystrophy.
    B. Assessment findings (Duchenne type)
        1. Pelvic girdle weakness is early sign (child waddles and falls)
        2. Gower's sign (child uses hands to push up from the floor)
        3. Scoliosis (from weakness of shoulder girdle)
        4. Contractures and hypertrophy of muscles
        5. Diagnostic tests
            a. Muscle biopsy reveals histologic changes: degeneration of muscle fibers and replacement of fibers with fat.
            b. EMG shows decrease in amplitude and duration of potentials.
        6. Serum enzymes increased, especially CPK
    C. Nursing interventions
        1. Prepare child for EMG and muscle biopsy.

2. Maintain function at optimal level; keep child as active and independent as possible.
3. Plan diet to prevent obesity.
4. Continually evaluate capabilities.
5. Support child and parents and provide information about availability of community agencies and support groups.

Juvenile Rheumatoid Arthritis

A. General information
  1. Systemic, chronic disorder of connective tissue, resulting from an autoimmune reaction
  2. Results in eventual joint destruction
  3. Affected by stress, climate, and genetics
  4. More common in girls; peak ages 2–5 and 9–12 years
  5. Types
    a. *Mono/pauciarticular JRA*
      1) fewer than 4 joints involved (usually in legs)
      2) asymmetric; rarely systemic
      3) generally mild signs of arthritis
      4) symptoms may decrease as child enters adulthood
      5) prognosis good
    b. *Polyarticular JRA*
      1) multiple joints affected
      2) symmetrical symptoms of arthritis, disability may be mild to severe
      3) involvement of temporomandibular joint may cause earaches
      4) characterized by periods of remissions and exacerbations
      5) prognosis poorer
      6) treatment symptomatic for arthritis: physical therapy, ROM exercises, aspirin
    c. *Systemic disease with polyarthritis* (*Still's disease*)
      1) explosive course with remissions and exacerbations lasting for months
      2) begins with fever, rash, lymphadenopathy, anorexia, and weight loss
B. Medical management, assessment findings, and nursing interventions: see Rheumatoid Arthritis, page 311

Sample Questions

62. Doug, age 3, has a fractured femur and is in Bryant's traction. To evaluate correct application of the traction the nurse should note that
  2. Doug is being continuously and gradually pulled toward bottom of bed.
  2. Doug's buttocks are raised slightly.
  3. Doug's leg is at a 45° angle to the bed.
  4. Doug can move the unaffected leg freely.
63. Ethel, age 14, is in a hip spica cast. To turn her correctly, the nurse should
  1. use the cross bar.
  2. turn her upper body first, then turn the lower body.
  3. log-roll her.
  4. tell her to pull on the trapeze and sit up to help in turning.
64. A routine physical examination on 2-day-old Melissa Carter uncovered evidence of congenital dislocation, or dysplasia, of the right hip. When assessing Melissa, a sign of one-sided hip displacement is
  1. an unusually narrow perineum
  2. pain where her leg is abducted.
  3. symmetrical skin folds near her buttocks and thigh.
  4. asymmetrical skin folds over the buttocks and thigh.
65. An infant is being treated for congenital hip dysplasia with a Pavlik harness. The baby's mother asks if she can remove the harness if it becomes soiled. The best response for the nurse to make is
  1. No, the harness may not be removed.
  2. No, she will only be wearing it a few days.
  3. Yes, just long enough to clean the area.
  4. Yes, just overnight while she is sleeping.
66. 10-year-old Jamie takes aspirin qid for Still's disease (juvenile rheumatoid arthritis). What symptoms would her mother observe that would be indicative of aspirin toxicity?
  1. Hypothermia.
  2. Hypoventilation.
  3. Decreased hearing acuity.
  4. Increased urinary output.

Answers and Rationales

62. The correct answer is 2. In Bryant's traction both legs are in traction at a 90° angle and the buttocks are raised off the mattress. The child's weight provides the countertraction; he should not be pulled down toward the bottom of the bed.
63. The correct answer is 3. The client in a hip spica cast should be turned as a unit. The stabilizing bar should not be handled.
64. The correct answer is 4. Displacement of the hip on one side causes asymmetry of skin folds. The baby will not have an unusually narrow perineum, will not have pain when her leg is abducted, and skin folds near her buttocks and thighs will not be symmetrical.
65. The correct answer is 1. The harness is not to be removed until the hip is stable with 90 degrees of flexion and x-ray confirmation. This usually occurs after about three weeks in a Pavlik harness. No, she cannot remove it, but it

will be in place about three weeks until the hip is stable.

66. The correct answer is 3. Tinnitus or ringing in the ears is a side effect of aspirin therapy. Hypothermia, hypoventilation, and increased urinary output are not signs of aspirin toxicity. In salicylate poisoning, the child will have hyperthermia, hyperventilation to compensate for metabolic acidosis and may develop renal failure.

The Endocrine System

VARIATIONS FROM THE ADULT

A. Adenohypophysis (anterior lobe of pituitary gland)
   1. Growth hormone
      a. Does not affect prenatal growth.
      b. Main effect on linear growth is through increase of cells in skeletal bones.
      c. Maintains rate of synthesis of body protein.
   2. Thyroid-stimulating hormone (TSH)
      a. Important for normal development of bones, teeth, and brain.
      b. Secretion decreases throughout childhood, then increases at puberty.
   3. Adrenocorticotropic hormone (ACTH)
      a. Little is produced throughout childhood.
      b. Becomes active in adolescence.
      c. Stimulates adrenals to secrete sex hormones.
      d. Influences production of gonadotropic hormone by hypothalamus.
         1) gonadotropic hormones activate gonads.
         2) gonads secrete estrogen or testosterone, which stimulate development of secondary sex characteristics.
   4. Estrogen has an inhibitory effect on epiphyseal growth.

ANALYSIS

Nursing diagnoses for the child with a disorder of the endocrine system may include
A. Altered health maintenance
B. Impaired home maintenance management
C. Noncompliance (specify)
D. Disturbance in self-concept: body image, self-esteem

PLANNING AND IMPLEMENTATION

Goals

A. Any endocrine imbalance in childhood will be identified and treated.
B. Child will achieve a normal metabolic state.
C. Child will develop successful coping mechanisms for manifestations of disease.
D. Child will have no signs of complications of the disease.

EVALUATION

A. Child receives appropriate medication, and nutritional requirements are met; symptoms of endocrine disease are controlled.
B. Child is free from complications of disease.
C. Child is achieving growth and developmental tasks on as normal a timetable as possible.
D. Child discusses feelings about body image and uses coping mechanisms that promote a positive self-image.

DISORDERS OF THE ENDOCRINE SYSTEM

Diabetes Mellitus

Also see Diabetes Mellitus, page 334.
A. General information
   1. Most common endocrine disease of children; onset may be at any age
   2. Children typically develop Type I: insulin dependent diabetes mellitus
   3. Possible genetic predisposition to disease
   4. Treatments vary based on rapid growth rate in children, increased incidence of

infections, and dietary fads of peers; all include insulin administration.

5. Risk of complications is high; most commonly retinopathy, neuropathy, nephropathy, skin changes, predisposition to infection

6. Children sometimes have one honeymoon period that occurs shortly after a child is regulated on insulin for the first time
   a. Lasts from 1 month to 1 year.
   b. Represents final effort of pancreas to provide insulin until beta cells are completely destroyed.
   c. Parents may distrust the diagnosis of diabetes and need to be reminded that symptoms will reappear and child will need insulin for life.

B. Medical management
   1. Insulin
   2. Diet therapy
   3. Exercise
   4. Prevention of complications

C. Assessment findings
   1. Rapid onset
   2. Polyuria, polydipsia, polyphagia, fatigue
   3. Weight loss
   4. Ketoacidosis
   5. Dry, flushed skin with hyperglycemia

D. Nursing interventions
   1. Administer insulin (regular and NPH) as ordered.
   2. Force fluids without sugar.
   3. Monitor blood glucose levels daily.
   4. Observe for hypoglycemia (insulin shock): behavior changes, sweating.
   5. Provide client teaching and discharge planning concerning
      a. Daily regimen for home care
      b. Urine and blood glucose monitoring
      c. Nutrition management
      d. Effects of infection and exercise on carbohydrate metabolism
      e. Prevention of acute and chronic complications

Congenital Hypothyroidism (Cretinism)

A. General information
   1. Disorder related to absent or nonfunctioning thyroid
   2. Newborns are supplied with maternal thyroid hormones that last up to 3 months

B. Medical management
   1. Prevention: neonatal screening blood test (mandatory in many states)
   2. Drug therapy: thyroid hormone replacement

3. Without treatment mental retardation and developmental delay will occur after age 3 months

C. Assessment findings
   1. Altered body proportions; short stature with legs shorter than they should be in proportion to trunk
   2. Tongue is enlarged and protrudes from mouth; may result in breathing and feeding difficulties
   3. Hypothermia with cool extremities
   4. Short, thick neck; delayed dentition
   5. Hypotonia
   6. Low levels of T_3 and T_4

D. Nursing interventions
   1. Administer oral thyroxine and vitamin D as ordered to prevent mental retardation.
   2. Provide client teaching and discharge planning concerning
      a. Medication administration and side effects
      b. Importance of continued therapy

HYPOPITUITARISM (PITUITARY DWARFISM)

A. General information
   1. Hyposecretion of growth hormone by the anterior lobe of the pituitary gland
   2. Cause may be unknown or it may be due to craniopharyngioma

B. Medical management: administration of growth hormone (limited in supply since it is rendered from human cadavers)

C. Assessment findings
   1. Newborn is of normal size, but child falls below the third percentile by age 1.
   2. Child is well proportioned, but may be overweight for height.
   3. Underdeveloped jaw, abnormal position of teeth, high voice, delayed puberty
   4. Diagnostic tests
      a. X-rays reveal delayed closing of epiphyseal plates of long bones
      b. Normal IQ

D. Nursing interventions
   1. Interact with child according to chronologic age/developmental level, and not according to physical appearance.
   2. Administer growth hormone as ordered (because of delay in bone development, these children can still grow even when their peers have stopped).
   3. Monitor for signs and symptoms of additional neurologic disorders.
   4. Keep careful records of height and weight.
   5. Encourage child/parents to express feelings.

6. Assist child in learning to interact normally with peers.

HYPERPITUITARISM (GIGANTISM)

A. General information
   1. Hypersecretion of growth hormone (usually related to a tumor of the anterior pituitary) resulting in enlargement of bones of head, hands, and feet, and overgrowth of long bones
   2. Especially noticeable at puberty
B. Medical management
   1. Surgery to remove tumor
   2. Radiation therapy if there is no tumor
C. Assessment findings
   1. Height beyond maximum upper percentile
   2. Proportional weight and muscle growth
   3. Coarse facial features
   4. Signs of increased ICP if caused by a tumor
D. Nursing interventions
   1. Record height and head circumference.
   2. Provide nursing care for a client receiving radiation therapy.
   3. Provide care for the child with a brain tumor.
   4. Assist child in interacting normally with peers.

Sample Questions

67. Jenny, age 8, is newly diagnosed with diabetes mellitus. Which of the following symptoms is different from what you would expect to find in maturity-onset (Type II) diabetes?
    1. Increased appetite.
    2. Increased thirst.
    3. Increased urination.
    4. Weight loss.

68. Jane is 7 years old and newly diagnosed with diabetes mellitus. She had an injection of regular and NPH insulin at 7:30 A.M. At 3:10 P.M. she complains that she does not feel well. She is pale, perspiring, and trembling. The nurse should
    1. tell her to lie down and wait for the dinner trays to arrive.
    2. ask her to give a urine specimen and test it for sugar and acetone.
    3. give her a carbohydrate snack.
    4. administer the afternoon dose of regular insulin.

69. A 10-year-old with diabetes mellitus is learning how to administer her insulin. She asks the nurse why she cannot take pills like her grandmother who also has diabetes. The best response for the nurse to make is
    1. How long has your grandmother been taking oral medication?
    2. You'll be able to stop taking insulin once you stop growing.
    3. You have a different kind of diabetes and you will need to take insulin throughout your life.
    4. You'll be able to switch to pills when you reach your grandmother's age.

Answers and Rationales

67. The correct answer is 4. Weight loss is associated with juvenile diabetes, whereas weight gain develops in maturity-onset diabetes. The other three signs appear in both forms of the disease.
68. The correct answer is 3. She probably is having a hypoglycemic reaction from the NPH insulin and needs an afternoon snack.
69. The correct answer is 3. Juvenile diabetics need lifetime insulin. She will never be able to switch to oral hypoglycemics.

The Integumentary System

VARIATIONS FROM THE ADULT

A. Skin is only 1 mm thick at birth; approximately twice as thick at maturity.
B. Evaporative water loss is greater in infants and small children.
C. Skin is more susceptible to bacterial infection in children.
D. Children are more prone to toxic erythema as a result of drug reactions and skin eruptions.
E. Children's skin is more susceptible to sweat retention and maceration.

ASSESSMENT

History

A. Medical history: previous skin disease, allergic conditions
B. History of present condition: onset, relationship to eating or other activities, medication usage

Physical Examination

A. Lesion type: note petechiae, erythema, ecchymosis; note secondary symptoms from rubbing, scratching, or healing.
B. Observe distribution pattern.
C. Note presence of pain or altered sensation.
D. Check scalp for signs of lice or nits.

ANALYSIS

Nursing diagnoses for the child with a disorder of the integumentary system may include
A. Pain
B. Disturbance in self-concept: body image, self-esteem
C. Sensory-perceptual alteration: kinesthetic
D. Actual and high risk for impaired skin integrity

PLANNING AND IMPLEMENTATION

Goals

A. Child will be free from discomfort.
B. Skin integrity will be restored.
C. Spread of infection and secondary infection will be prevented.

EVALUATION

A. Child is free from discomfort.
  1. Minimal scratching or rubbing
  2. Relaxed facial expression
  3. Minimal restlessness
B. Child's skin is clean, dry, and free from redness or signs of irritation.
C. Child is free from complications such as spread of infection.
D. Parents demonstrate satisfactory hygiene measures when caring for child with disorder of skin or scalp.

DISORDERS OF THE INTEGUMENTARY SYSTEM

Burns

Also see page 344.

A. For children, the rule of nines is modified; the head of a small child is 18%–19%, the trunk 32%, each leg 15%, each arm 9 1/2%.
B. Burns in infants and toddlers are frequently due to spills (pulling hot fluids on them or falling into hot baths); for older children, flame burns are more frequent.

Impetigo

A. General information
  1. Superficial bacterial infection of the outer layers of skin (usually staphylococcus or streptococcus)
  2. Common in toddlers and preschoolers
  3. Related to poor sanitation
  4. Very contagious
B. Medical management: topical and systemic antibiotics
C. Assessment findings
  1. Well-demarcated lesions
  2. Macules, papules, vesicles that rupture, causing a superficial moist erosion
  3. Moist area dries, leaving a honey-colored crust
  4. Spreads peripherally
  5. Most commonly found on face, axillae, and extremities
  6. Pruritus
D. Nursing interventions
  1. Implement skin isolation techniques.
  2. Soften the skin and crusts with Burrow's solution compresses.
  3. Remove crusts gently.
  4. Cover draining lesions to prevent spread of infection.
  5. Administer antibiotics as ordered, both orally and as bacteriocidal ointments.
  6. Prevent secondary infection.
  7. Provide client teaching and discharge planning concerning
    a. Medication administration
    b. Proper hygiene techniques

Ringworm

A. General information
  1. Dermatomycosis due to various species of fungus
  2. Infected sites include
    a. Scalp (tinea capitis)
    b. Body (tinea corporis)
    c. Feet (tinea pedis or athlete's foot)
  3. May be transmitted from person to person or acquired from animals or soil
B. Assessment findings
  1. Scalp
    a. Scaly circumscribed patches on the scalp
    b. Base of hair shafts are invaded by spores of the fungus; causes hair to break off resulting in alopecia

c. Spreads in a circular pattern
d. Detected by Wood's lamp (fluoresces green at base of the affected hair shafts)
2. Skin: red-ringed patches of vesicles; pain, scaling, itching
C. Nursing interventions
1. Prevention: isolate from known infected persons.
2. Apply antifungal ointment as ordered.
3. Administer oral griseofulvin as ordered.

Pediculosis (Head Lice)

A. General information
1. Parasitic infestation
2. Adult lice are spread by close physical contact (sharing combs, hats, etc.)
3. Occurs in school-age children, particularly those with long hair
B. Medical management: special shampoos followed by use of fine-tooth comb to remove nits
C. Assessment findings
1. White eggs (nits) firmly attached to base of hair shafts
2. Pruritus of scalp
D. Nursing interventions
1. Institute skin isolation precautions (especially head coverings and gloves to prevent spread to self, other staff, and clients).
2. Use special shampoo and comb the hair.
3. Provide client teaching and discharge planning concerning
a. How to check self and other family members and how to treat them
b. Washing of clothes, bed linens, etc.; discouraging sharing of brushes, combs, and hats

Allergies

Diaper Rash

A. General information
1. Contact dermatitis
2. Plastic/rubber pants and linings of disposable diapers exacerbate the condition by prolonging contact with moist, warm environment; skin is further irritated by acidic urine
3. May also be caused by sensitivity to laundry soaps used
B. Medical management: exposure of skin to air/heat lamp
C. Assessment findings
1. Erythema/excoriation in the perineal area
2. Irritability
D. Nursing interventions
1. Keep area clean and dry; clean with mild soap and water after each stool and as soon as child urinates.

2. Take off diaper and expose area to air during the day.
3. Use heat lamp as ordered.
4. Provide client teaching and discharge planning concerning
a. Proper hygiene/infant care
b. Diaper laundering methods
c. Need to avoid use of plastic pants or disposable diapers with a plastic lining
d. Need to avoid use of cornstarch (a good medium for bacteria once it becomes wet)
e. Need to avoid use of commercially prepared diaper wipes since they contain chemicals and alcohol, which may be irritating

Poison Ivy

A. General information
1. Contact dermatitis; mediated by T-cell response so rash is not seen for 24–48 hours after contact.
2. Poison ivy is not spread by the fluid in the vesicles; can be spread by clothes and animals that retain the plant resin.
B. Assessment findings: very pruritic impetigo-like lesions
C. Nursing interventions
1. Administer antihistamines and cortisone as ordered.
2. Provide client teaching and discharge planning concerning
a. Plant identification
b. Need to wash with soap and water after contact with plant
c. Importance of washing clothes to get the resin out

Eczema

A. General information
1. Atopic dermatitis, often the first sign of an allergic predisposition in a child; many later develop respiratory allergies
2. Usually manifests during infancy
B. Medical management
1. Drug therapy
a. Topical steroids
b. Antihistamines
c. Coal tar preparations
d. Cautious administration of immunizations
e. Medicated or colloid baths
2. Diet therapy: elimination diet to detect offending foods
C. Assessment findings
1. Erythema, weeping vesicles that rupture and crust over

2. Usually evident on cheeks, scalp, behind ears, and on flexor surfaces of extremities (rarely on diaper area)
3. Severe pruritus; scratching causes thickening and darkening of skin
4. Dry skin, sometimes urticaria
D. Nursing interventions
1. Avoid heat and prevent sweating; keep skin dry (moisture aggravates condition).
2. Monitor elimination diet to detect food cause.
   a. Remove all solid foods from diet (formula only).
   b. If symptoms disappear after 3 days, start 1 new food group every 3 days to see if symptoms reappear.
   c. The food that is suspected of causing the rash is withdrawn again to make sure symptoms go away in 3 days and is then introduced a second time (challenge test).
3. Check materials in contact with child's skin (sheets, lotions, soaps).
4. Avoid frequent baths.
   a. Add Alpha Keri to bath.
   b. Provide lubricant immediately after bath.
   c. Pat dry gently with soft towel (do not rub) and pat in lubricant.
   d. Avoid the use of soap (dries skin).
5. Administer topical steroids as ordered (penetrate better if applied within 3 minutes after bath).
6. Use cotton instead of wool clothing.
7. Keep child's nails short to prevent scratching and secondary infection; use gloves or elbow restraints if needed.
8. Apply wet saline or Burrow's solution compresses.

Acne

A. General information
1. Skin condition associated with increased production of sebum from sebaceous glands at puberty.
2. Lesions include pustules, papules, and comedones.
3. Majority of adolescents experience some degree of acne, mild to severe.
4. Lesions occur most frequently on face, neck, shoulders and back.
5. Caused by a variety of interrelated factors including increased activity of sebaceous glands, emotional stress, certain medications, menstrual cycle.
6. Secondary infection can complicate healing of lesions.
7. There is no evidence to support the value of eliminating any foods from the diet; if cause and effect can be established, however, a particular food should be eliminated.
B. Assessment findings
1. Appearance of lesions is variable and fluctuating
2. Systemic symptoms absent
3. Psychologic problems such as social withdrawal, low self-esteem, feelings of being "ugly"
C. Nursing interventions
1. Discuss OTC products and their effects.
2. Instruct child in proper hygiene (handwashing, care of face, not to pick or squeeze any lesions).
3. Demonstrate proper administration of topical ointments and antibiotics if indicated

Pediatric Oncology

OVERVIEW

A. Cancer is the leading cause of death from disease in children from 1–14 years.
B. Incidence
1. 6000 children develop cancer per year.
2. 2500 children die from cancer annually.
3. Boys are affected more frequently.
C. Leukemia is the most frequent type of childhood cancer, followed by tumors of the CNS.
D. Etiologic factors include environmental agents, viruses, familial/genetic factors, and host factors.

Major Stressful Events

Five events have been identified as major stressors:
A. *Diagnosis:* child is initially hospitalized to determine extent of disease, plan course of treatment, and to educate child and family.
B. *Treatment:* multimodal
1. May include surgery, radiation, chemotherapy
2. Side effects are serious and unpleasant; child/family may complain that the "treatment is worse than the disease."

C. *Remission:* child is without evidence of disease, treatment continues; goals for this period include
  1. Maintenance of normal family patterns: discipline and usual household chores
  2. Maintenance of relationships among family and friends
     a. Parents' marriage may be strained
     b. Siblings may feel neglected or jealous
  3. Attendance at school
     a. Child may fear rejection by peers due to change in appearance or not being able to keep up
     b. Teacher may be unsure as to what to say or how to treat the child
     c. Classmates need to be prepared for child's return; may have fears/concerns about whether the disease is catching and whether their friend will die
D. *Recurrence*
  1. An event of enormous magnitude and a cause of severe disappointment
  2. May occur while still on treatment or after treatment has been completed
E. *Death*

ASSESSMENT

History

A. Family history: some cancers suggest patterns of inheritance
B. Prenatal exposure
C. Children with chromosomal disorders have a higher-than-average incidence of cancer
D. History may elicit symptoms that have been present for a period of time
E. Presenting problems: symptoms may include
  1. Fever, pain, bleeding
  2. Abdominal mass
  3. Night sweats, weight loss
  4. Hematuria, hypertension

Physical Examination

A. General appearance
  1. Skin: note color, bruises, or petechiae
  2. Neurologic status: note fatigue, activity level, behavior, headache, dizziness, gait disturbances
  3. Pain: guarding of any body part, changes in range of motion
B. Measure vital signs including BP
C. Plot height and weight on growth chart
D. Inspect and palpate abdomen; note enlargement of liver and spleen
E. Palpate for enlarged lymph nodes
F. Inspect eyes for nystagmus

Laboratory/Diagnostic Test

A. Blood studies, e.g., CBC
B. X-rays, bone scans, CT scans, MRI, ultrasound
C. Lumbar puncture
D. Bone marrow aspiration

Analysis

Nursing diagnoses for the child with cancer may include
A. High risk for infection
B. High risk for injury
C. Fear/anxiety
D. Body image disturbances
E. Knowledge deficit
F. Altered comfort

Planning and Implementation

Goals

A. Child will be free from infection
B. Child will be free from pain
C. Optimum developmental level will be achieved
D. Family will develop effective coping strategies

INTERVENTIONS

Surgery

A. May be performed for tumor removal, to obtain a biopsy, to determine extent of disease, or for palliation
B. Often used in conjunction with radiation or chemotherapy

Radiation Therapy

A. Primarily used in children to improve prognosis
B. Goal is to achieve maximum effect on tumor while sparing normal tissue
  1. May be used for palliative relief from pain, disfigurement
  2. May be curative, destroys cancer cells/reduces size of tumor
  3. Frequently used as an adjunct to chemotherapy and surgery
  4. Must weigh gain versus risks of permanent damage to normal tissue
  5. Infants particularly susceptible to developing skeletal deformities in later years as a result of radiation
  6. Complications to growing child include scoliosis, arrested skeletal development, and pulmonary fibrosis (depends on site radiated)

7. Dosage range varies; may be as low as 1000 rad to relieve bone pain in a specific area, to as high as 7000 rad to achieve a cure in Ewing's sarcoma
8. Usually performed 5 days a week for 2–6 weeks

Chemotherapy

Almost all pediatric cancer clients receive some form of drug therapy.
A. Childhood cancers are more sensitive and responsive to drugs than are adult cancers.
B. Childhood cancers tend to metastasize early and systemic treatment is needed in addition to localized treatment.

Bone Marrow Transplant

A. General information
   1. Relatively new treatment alternative for a variety of childhood diseases including
      a. Definite: acute lymphoblastic leukemia, acute nonlymphocytic leukemia, severe aplastic anemia, immunodeficiencies, and malignant infantile osteopetrosis
      b. Possible: chronic myelogenous leukemia, solid tumors, some hematologic disorders, and some inherited metabolic disorders
   2. Types
      a. Autologous: client transplanted with own harvested marrow
      b. Syngeneic: transplant between identical twins
      c. Allogeneic: transplant from a genetically nonidentical donor
         1) most common transplant type
         2) sibling most common donor
   3. Procedure
      a. Donor suitability determined through tissue antigen typing; includes human leukocyte antigen (HLA) and mixed leukocyte culture (MLC) typing.
      b. Donor bone marrow is aspirated from multiple sites along the iliac crests under general anesthesia.
      c. Donor marrow is infused IV into the recipient.
   4. Early evidence of engraftment seen during the second week posttransplant; hematologic reconstitution takes 4–6 weeks; immunologic reconstitution takes months.
   5. Hospitalization of 2 or 3 months required.
   6. Prognosis is highly variable depending on indication for use.
B. Complications

   1. Failure of engraftment
   2. Infection: highest risk in first 3–4 weeks
   3. Pneumonia: nonbacterial or interstitial pneumonias are principal cause of death during first 3 months posttransplant
   4. *Graft vs host disease* (*GVHD*): principal complication; caused by an immunologic reaction of engrafted lymphoid cells against the tissues of the recipient
      a. Acute GVHD: develops within first 100 days posttransplant and affects skin, gut, liver, marrow, and lymphoid tissue
      b. Chronic GVHD: develops 100–400 days post-transplant; manifested by multiorgan involvement
   5. Recurrent malignancy
   6. Late complications such as cataracts, endocrine abnormalities
C. Nursing care: pretransplant
   1. Extensive time must be spent with child/parents in preparing for this procedure.
   2. Recipient immunosuppression attained with total body irradiation (TBI) and chemotherapy to eradicate existing disease and create space in host marrow to allow transplanted cells to grow.
   3. Provide protected environment.
      a. Child should be in a laminar air flow room or on strict reverse isolation; surveillance cultures done twice a week.
      b. Encourage use of toys and familiar objects; they must be sterilized before being brought into the room.
      c. Encourage frequent contact with schoolteacher/play therapist.
      d. Introduce new people where they can be seen, but outside child's room so child can see what they look like without isolation garb.
   4. Monitor central lines frequently; check patency and observe for signs of infection (fever, redness around site).
   5. Provide care for the child receiving chemotherapy and radiation therapy to induce immunosuppression.
      a. Administer chemotherapy as ordered, assist with radiation therapy if required.
      b. Monitor side effects and keep child as comfortable as possible.
      c. Monitor carefully for potential infection.
      d. Child will become very ill; prepare parents.
D. Nursing care: posttransplant
   1. Prevent infection.
      a. Maintain protective environment.
      b. Administer antibiotics as ordered.

    c. Assess all mucous membranes, wounds, catheter sites for swelling, redness, tenderness, pain.
    d. Monitor vital signs frequently (every 1–4 hours as needed).
    e. Collect specimens for cultures as needed and twice a week.
    f. Change IV set-ups every 24 hours.

2. Provide mouth care for stomatitis and mucositis (severe mucositis develops about 5 days after irradiation).
    a. Note tissue sloughing, bleeding, changes in color.
    b. Provide mouth rinses, viscous lidocaine, and antibiotic rinses.
    c. Do not use lemon and glycerin swabs.
    d. Administer parenteral narcotics as ordered if necessary to control pain.
    e. Provide care every 2 hours or as needed.

3. Provide skin care: skin breakdown may result from profuse diarrhea from the TBI.

4. Monitor carefully for bleeding.
    a. Check for occult blood in emesis and stools.
    b. Observe for easy bruising, petechiae on skin, mucous membranes.
    c. Monitor changes in vital signs.
    d. Check platelet count daily.
    e. Replace blood products as ordered (all blood products should be irradiated).

5. Maintain fluid and electrolyte balance and promote nutrition.
    a. Measure I&O carefully.
    b. Provide adequate fluid, protein, and caloric intake.
    c. Weigh daily.
    d. Administer fluid replacement as ordered.
    e. Monitor hydration status: check skin turgor, moisture of mucous membranes, urine output.
    f. Check electrolytes daily.
    g. Check urine for glucose, ketones, protein.
    h. Administer antidiarrheal agents as needed.

6. Provide client teaching and discharge planning concerning
    a. Home environment (e.g., cleaning, pets, visitors)
    b. Diet modifications
    c. Medication regimen: schedule, dosages, effects, and side effects
    d. Communicable diseases and immunizations
    e. Daily hygiene and skin care
    f. Fever
    g. Activity

STAGES OF CANCER TREATMENT

A. Induction
    1. Goal: to remove bulk of tumor
    2. Methods: surgery, radiation/chemotherapy, bone marrow transplant
    3. Effects: often the most intensive phase; side effects of treatment are potentially life threatening

B. Consolidation
    1. Goal: to eliminate any remaining malignant cells
    2. Methods: often chemotherapy/radiation therapy
    3. Effects: side effects will still be evident

C. Maintenance
    1. Goal: to keep child disease free
    2. Method: chemotherapy (this phase may last for several years)

D. Observation
    1. Goal: to monitor the child at intervals for evidence of recurrent disease and complications of treatment
    2. Method: treatment is complete; child may continue in this stage indefinitely

E. Late effects of treatment
    1. Impaired growth and development, usually related to radiation of growth centers
    2. CNS damage resulting in intellectual, psychologic, or neurologic sequelae
    3. Impaired pubertal development including hormonal or reproductive problems
    4. Development of secondary malignancy
    5. Psychologic problems (poor self-esteem, depression, anxiety) related to living with a life-threatening disease and complex treatment regimen

Side Effects

A. From combined effects of treatment: nausea, vomiting, diarrhea, alopecia, anemia (low RBCs), increased susceptibility to infection (low WBCs), bleeding (low platelets), stomatitis, mucositis, pain, learning problems
B. From radiation (findings differ according to site radiated): sleepiness, reddened skin
C. From chemotherapy: drug toxicity specific to agents used
D. Developmental: behavior problems, avoidance of school and friends, low self-esteem or self-image

Nursing Interventions

A. Help child cope with intrusive procedures.
    1. Provide information geared to developmental level and emotional readiness.

2. Explain what is going to happen, why it is necessary, and how it will feel.
3. Allow child to handle and manipulate equipment.
4. Use needle play as indicated.
5. Allow child some control in situations (e.g., positioning, selecting injection site).

B. Support child and parents.
1. Maintain frequent clinical conferences to keep all informed.
2. Always tell the truth.
3. Acknowledge feelings and encourage child/family to express them, assure them that feelings are normal.
4. Provide contact with another parent or an organized support group such as Candlelighters.
5. Try to keep daily life as normal as possible.

C. Minimize side effects of treatment.
1. Skin breakdown
   a. Keep clean and dry; wash with warm water, no soaps or creams.
   b. Do not wash off radiation markings.
   c. Avoid exposure to sunlight.
   d. Avoid all topical agents with alcohol (perfumes and powders).
   e. Do not use electric heating pads or hot water bottles.
2. Bone marrow suppression
   a. Decreased RBCs
      1) allow child to determine activities.
      2) provide frequent rest periods.
   b. Decreased WBCs
      1) avoid crowds, isolate from children with known communicable disease.
      2) evaluate any potential site of infection.
      3) monitor temperature elevations.
   c. Decreased platelets
      1) make environment safe.
      2) select activities that are physically safe.
      3) avoid use of salicylates.
   d. Administer transfusions as ordered.
   e. Interpret peripheral blood counts to guide specific interventions and precautions.
3. Nausea and vomiting
   a. Administer antiemetic at least half an hour before chemotherapy; repeat as necessary.
   b. Encourage relaxation techniques.
   c. Eat light meal prior to administration of therapy.
   d. Ensure adequate oral intake or administer IV fluids as necessary.
4. Alopecia
   a. Reduce trauma of hair loss (especially in children over age 5 years).
   b. Buy wig before hair falls out.
   c. Discuss various head coverings with boys and girls.
   d. Avoid exposing head to sunlight.
   e. Discuss feelings.
5. Stomatitis, mucositis (see Bone Marrow Transplant, page 434).
6. Nutrition deficits
   a. Establish baseline prior to start of treatment.
   b. Measure height and weight regularly.
   c. Provide small, frequent meals.
   d. Consult dietitian as needed.
   e. Provide high-calorie, high-protein supplements.
7. Developmental delays
   a. Discuss limit setting, discipline.
   b. Some behavior problems might be side effects of drug therapy.
   c. Facilitate return to school as soon as able.
   d. Realize changing needs of child.

CANCERS

Leukemia

A. General information
1. Most common form of childhood cancer
2. Peak incidence is 3 to 5 years of age
3. Proliferation of abnormal white blood cells that do not mature beyond the blast phase
4. In the bone marrow, blast cells crowd out healthy white blood cells, red blood cells, and platelets, leading to bone marrow depression
5. Blast cells also infiltrate other organs, most commonly the liver, spleen, kidneys, and lymph tissue
6. Symptoms reflect bone marrow failure and associated involvement of other organs
7. Types of leukemia, based on course of disease and cell morphology
   a. Acute lymphocytic leukemia (ALL)
      1) 80–85% of childhood leukemia
      2) malignant change in the lymphocyte or its precursors
      3) acute onset
      4) 95% chance of obtaining remission with treatment
      5) 75% chance of surviving 5 years or more
      6) prognostic indicators include: initial white blood count (less than 10,000/mm³), child's age (2–9 years), histologic type, sex
   b. Acute nonlymphocytic leukemia (ANLL)
      1) includes granulocytic and monocytic types

2) 60–80% will obtain remission with treatment
3) 30–40% cure rate
4) prognostic indicators less clearly defined

B. Medical management
  1. Diagnosis: blood studies, bone marrow biopsy
  2. Treatment stages
    a. Induction: intense and potentially life threatening
    b. CNS prophylaxis: to prevent central nervous system disease. Combination of radiation and intrathecal chemotherapy.
    c. Maintenance: chemotherapy for 2 to 3 years.

C. Assessment findings
  1. Anemia (due to decreased production of RBCs), weakness, pallor, dyspnea
  2. Bleeding (due to decreased platelet production), petechiae, spontaneous bleeding, ecchymoses
  3. Infection (due to decreased WBC production), fever, malaise
  4. Enlarged lymph nodes
  5. Enlarged spleen and liver
  6. Abdominal pain with weight loss and anorexia
  7. Bone pain due to expansion of marrow

D. Nursing interventions
  1. Provide care for the child receiving chemotherapy and radiation therapy.
  2. Provide support for child/family; needs will change as treatment progresses.
  3. Support child during painful procedures (frequent bone marrow aspirations, lumbar punctures, venipunctures needed).
    a. Use distraction, guided imagery.
    b. Allow child to retain as much control as possible.
    c. Administer sedation prior to procedure as ordered.

Brain Tumors

A. General information
  1. A space-occupying mass in the brain tissue; may be benign or malignant
  2. Males affected more often; peak age 3–7 years
  3. Second most prevalent type of cancer in children
  4. Cause unknown; genetic and environmental factors may play a role; familial tendency for brain tumors, which are found with preexisting neurocutaneous disorders.
  5. Two-thirds of all pediatric brain tumors are beneath the tentorium cerebelli (in the posterior fossa), often involving the cerebellum or brain stem.
  6. Three-fourths of brain tumors in children are gliomas (medulloblastoma and astrocytoma).

B. Types
  1. *Medulloblastoma:* highly malignant tumor usually found in cerebellum; runs a rapid course
    a. Findings include increased ICP plus unsteady walk, ataxia, anorexia, early morning vomiting
    b. Treated with radiation since complete removal is impossible
  2. *Astrocytoma:* a benign, cystic, slow-growing tumor usually found in cerebellum
    a. Onset of symptoms is insidious.
    b. Findings include focal disturbances, papilledema, optic nerve atrophy, blindness.
  3. *Ependymoma:* a usually benign tumor that arises in the ventricles of the brain, causing noncommunicating hydrocephalus and damage (by pressure) to other vital tissues of the brain
  4. *Craniopharyngioma:* tumor that arises from remnants of embryonic tissue near the pituitary gland in the sella turcica, causes pressure on the third ventricle
    a. Decreased secretion of ADH causes diabetes insipidus (these children may need Pitressin).
    b. Additional symptoms include altered growth pattern, visual difficulties, difficulty regulating body temperature.
  5. *Brain stem glioma:* slow-growing tumor, indicated by cranial nerve palsies, ataxia

C. Medical management
  1. Surgery: some tumors entirely or partially resected; others are not amenable to surgery because of proximity to vital brain parts
  2. Radiation therapy: often used to shrink tumors
  3. Chemotherapy: vincristine, lomustine, procarbazine, intrathecal methotrexate; not as effective with brain tumors as with other childhood cancers

D. Assessment findings
  1. Symptoms dependent on location and type of tumor.
  2. A definite diagnosis is difficult in children because of the elasticity of child's skull and generally poor coordination of the young child.
  3. A decrease in school performance may be the first sign.
  4. Increased ICP
    a. Morning headache

b. Morning vomiting without nausea; vomiting without relation to feeding schedule; projectile vomiting
c. Personality changes
d. Diplopia
  1) difficult to assess in young children
  2) observe child for tilting of head, closing or covering one eye, rubbing the eyes, or impaired eye-hand coordination
e. Papilledema: a late sign
f. Increased blood pressure with decreased pulse: also a late sign
g. Cranial enlargement
  1) more readily noticeable prior to 18 months when suture lines are still open
  2) bulging, tense, pulsating fontanels
  3) widened suture lines
  4) 90% or more on head circumference chart
5. Focal signs and symptoms
  a. Ataxia
    1) in cerebellar tumors
    2) may not be readily identified because of uncoordinated movements of young children
  b. Muscle strength
    1) weakness with cerebellar tumors
    2) weakness, spasticity, and paralysis of lower extremities with cerebral or brain stem tumors
    3) change in handedness, posture, or manual coordination: may be early signs
  c. Head tilt
    1) in posterior fossa tumors
    2) early sign of visual impairment
    3) associated with nuchal rigidity
    4) due to traction on the dura
  d. Ocular signs
    1) nystagmus: corresponds to the same side as the infratentorial lesion
    2) diplopia/strabismus: from palsy of cranial nerve VI with brain stem glioma or increased ICP
    3) visual field deficit (child does not react to activity on periphery of vision): with craniopharyngiomas
  e. Seizures: with cerebral tumors
6. Diagnostic tests
  a. Skull x-ray reveals presence and location of tumor
  b. CT scan (with or without contrast dye) reveals position, consistency, size of tumor, and effect on surrounding tissue
  c. EEG may show seizure activity
E. Nursing interventions
  1. Obtain baseline vital signs and perform thorough neurologic assessment; monitor vital signs and neurologic status frequently.

2. Prevent injury/complications.
  a. Institute seizure precautions.
  b. Monitor for fluid and electrolyte imbalance from vomiting.
  c. Observe for increased ICP.
  d. Provide safety measures (bed rails up).
3. Promote comfort/relief of headache.
  a. Decrease environmental stimuli.
  b. Administer analgesics as ordered.
4. Prevent constipation (straining increases ICP).
  a. Provide appropriate foods and fluids as ordered.
  b. Provide stool softeners as ordered.
  c. Avoid enemas, which increase ICP.
5. Provide care for the child undergoing brain surgery.
6. Provide care for the child undergoing radiation or chemotherapy.
7. Provide client teaching and discharge planning concerning
  a. Diagnostic tests (instruction needs to be appropriate to the child's developmental level)
    1) machines will make clicking sounds
    2) wires attached to the head for an EEG will not electrocute child
    3) head is immobilized for a CT scan
    4) the use of contrast dye and expected sensations if used
    5) need to lie still with the technician out of the room for most tests (younger children will be sedated for fuller cooperation)
  b. Importance of family discussion of fears/anxiety about surgery and prognosis
  c. Need to assist in implementing child's interaction with peers
  d. Available support groups and community agencies

Brain Surgery

A. General information
  1. Indications
    a. Removal of a tumor
    b. Evacuation of a hematoma
    c. Removal of a foreign body or skull fragments resulting from trauma
    d. Aspiration of an abscess
    e. Insertion of a shunt
B. Nursing interventions: preoperative
  1. Assess the child's understanding of the procedure; have the child draw a picture, tell a story; observe doll play.
  2. Explain the procedure in terms according to the child's developmental level.
  3. Allow the child to visit the operating room/intensive care unit, if permitted, depending on the child's emotional and developmental levels.

4. Explain that pre-op symptoms such as headache and ataxia may be temporarily aggravated.
5. Advise child/parents that blindness may result, depending on the location of the tumor.
6. Inform the child/parents that the head will be shaved; long hair may be saved; hats or scarves may be used to cover the head once the dressings are removed.
7. Support the child/family if a tumor cannot be totally removed.
8. Provide instruction about radiation and chemotherapy (may need to be delayed since detail may be overwhelming).
9. Explain to the child/parents about the post-op dressing, monitoring devices, and possibility of facial edema.

C. Nursing interventions: postoperative
 1. Prevent injury/complications.
   a. Monitor vital signs and neuro status frequently until stable.
   b. Apply hypothermia blanket as ordered.
   c. Assess respiratory status/signs of infection.
   d. Observe the dressing for discharge/hemorrhage.
   e. Close or cover eyes, apply ice, instill saline drops or artificial tears.
   f. Position as ordered according to the location of the tumor and type of surgery.
   g. Assess for increased ICP.
   h. Institute seizure precautions.
 2. Promote comfort.
   a. Decrease environmental stimuli.
   b. Administer analgesics as ordered, first assessing LOC.
 3. Promote adequate nutrition.
   a. Administer fluids as ordered.
   b. Monitor I&O.
   c. Provide diet as ordered.
 4. Provide emotional support and encourage child/family to discuss prognosis.
 5. Provide client teaching and discharge planning concerning
   a. Wound care
   b. Signs of increased ICP
   c. Activity level
   d. Sensation and time period of hair growth
   e. Peer acceptance
   f. Radiation/chemotherapy, if indicated
   g. Availability of support groups/community agencies

Hodgkin's Lymphoma

A. General information
 1. Malignant neoplasm of lymphoid tissue, usually originating in localized group of lymph nodes; a proliferation of lymphocytes
 2. Metastasizes first to adjacent lymph nodes
 3. Cause unknown
 4. Most prevalent in adolescents; accounts for 5% of all malignancies
 5. Prognosis now greatly improved for these children; influenced by stage of disease and histologic type
 6. Long-term treatment effects include increased incidence of second malignancies, especially leukemia and infertility

B. Medical management
 1. Diagnosis: extensive testing to determine stage, which dictates treatment modality
   a. Lymphangiogram determines involvement of all lymph nodes (reliable in 90% of clients); is helpful in determining radiation fields
   b. Staging via laparotomy and biopsy
     1) stage I: single lymph node involved; usually in neck; 90%–98% survival
     2) stage II: involvement of 2 or more lymph nodes on same side of diaphragm; 70%–80% survival
     3) stage III: involvement of nodes on both sides of diaphragm; 50% survival
     4) stage IV: metastasis to other organs
   c. Laparotomy and splenectomy
   d. Lymph node biopsy to identify presence of Reed-Sternberg cells and for histologic classification
 2. Radiation: used alone for localized disease
 3. Chemotherapy: used in conjunction with radiation therapy for advanced disease

C. Assessment findings
 1. Major presenting symptom is enlarged nodes in lower cervical region; nodes are nontender, firm, and movable
 2. Recurrent, intermittent fever
 3. Night sweats
 4. Weight loss, malaise, lethargy
 5. Pruritus
 6. Diagnostic test: presence of Reed-Sternberg cells

D. Nursing interventions
 1. Provide care for child receiving radiation therapy.
 2. Administer chemotherapy as ordered and monitor/alleviate side effects.
 3. Protect client from infection, especially if splenectomy performed.
 4. Provide support for child/parents; specific needs of adolescent client must be considered.

Non-Hodgkin's Lymphoma

A. General information
 1. Tumor originating in lymphatic tissue

2. Significantly different from Hodgkin's lymphoma
    a. Control of primary tumor is difficult
    b. Disease is diffuse, cell type undifferentiated
    c. Tumor disseminates early
    d. Includes wide range of disease entities: lymphosarcoma, reticulum cell sarcoma, Burkitt's lymphoma
3. Primary sites include GI tract, ovaries, testes, bone, CNS, liver, breast, subcutaneous tissues
4. Affects all age groups.
B. Medical management
    1. Chemotherapy: multiagent regimens including cyclophosphamide (Cytoxan), vincristine, prednisone, procarbazine, doxorubicin, bleomycin
    2. Radiation therapy: primary treatment in localized disease
    3. Surgery for diagnosis and clinical staging
C. Assessment findings
    1. Depend on anatomic site and extent of involvement
    2. Rapid onset and progression
    3. Many have advanced disease at diagnosis
D. Nursing interventions: provide care for child receiving chemotherapy, radiation therapy, and surgery.

Wilm's Tumor (Nephroblastoma)

A. General information
    1. Large, encapsulated tumor that develops in the renal parenchyma, more frequently in left kidney (usually unilateral)
    2. Originates during fetal life from undifferentiated embryonic tissues
    3. Peak age of occurrence: 1–3 years
    4. Prognosis good if there are no metastases.
B. Medical management
    1. Nephrectomy, with total removal of tumor
    2. Postsurgical radiation in treatment of stages II, III, and IV; stage I disease does not usually require radiation, but it may be used if the tumor histology is unfavorable.
    3. Postsurgical chemotherapy: vincristine and daunorubicin, doxorubicin
C. Assessment findings
    1. Staging
        a. Stage I: limited to kidney
        b. Stage II: tumor extends beyond kidney, but is completely encapsulated
        c. Stage III: tumor confined to abdomen
        d. Stage IV: tumor has metastasized to lung, liver, bone, or brain
        e. Stage V: bilateral renal involvement at diagnosis
    2. Usually mother notices mass while bathing or dressing child; nontender, usually midline near liver

3. Hypertension and possible hematuria, anemia, and signs of metastasis
4. Diagnostic test: IVP reveals mass
D. Nursing interventions
    1. Do not palpate abdomen to avoid possible dissemination of cancer cells.
    2. Handle child carefully when bathing and giving care.
    3. Provide care for the client with a nephrectomy; usually performed within 24–48 hours of diagnosis.
    4. Provide care for the child receiving chemotherapy and radiation therapy.

Neuroblastoma

A. General information
    1. A highly malignant tumor that develops from embryonic neural crest tissue; arises anywhere along the craniospinal axis, usually from the adrenal gland
    2. Incidence
        a. One in 10,000
        b. Males slightly more affected
        c. From infancy to age 4
    3. Staging
        a. Stage I: tumor confined to the organ of origin
        b. Stage II: tumor extends beyond primary site but not across midline
        c. Stage III: tumor extends beyond midline
        d. Stage IV: tumor metastasizes to skeleton (bone marrow), soft tissue (liver), and lymph nodes
B. Medical management: depends on the staging of tumor and age of child; includes surgery, radiation therapy, chemotherapy
C. Assessment findings vary, depending on the tumor site and stage
    1. If in the abdomen, may initially resemble Wilm's tumor
    2. Local signs and symptoms caused by pressure of the tumor on surrounding tissue
    3. Metastatic manifestations
        a. Ocular: supraorbital ecchymosis, periorbital edema, exophthalmos
        b. Cervical or supraclavicular lymphadenopathy
        c. Bone pain: may or may not occur with bone metastasis
        d. Nonspecific complaints; pallor, anorexia, weight loss, irritability, weakness
    4. Diagnosis usually made after metastasis has occurred
    5. Diagnostic tests
        a. X-rays of the head, chest, or abdomen reveal presence of primary tumor or metastases

     b. IVP: if tumor is adrenal, shows a downward displacement of the kidney on the affected side

     c. Bone marrow aspiration: to rule out metastasis; neuroblasts have a clumping pattern

     d. CBC: RBCs and platelets decreased

     e. Coagulation studies: abnormal due to thrombocytopenia

     f. Catecholamine excretion: VMA levels in urine increased

        1) child must not ingest vanilla, chocolate, bananas, or nuts for 3 days prior to the test

        2) 24-hour urine specimen needed

D. Nursing interventions: same as for leukemia (page 437) and brain tumors.

Bone Tumors

Osteogenic Sarcoma

A. General information
1. Primary bone tumor arising from the mesenchymal cells and characterized by formation of osteoid (immature bone)
2. Invades ends of long bones, most frequently distal end of femur or proximal end of tibia
3. Occurs more often in boys, usually between ages 10–20 years
4. Lungs most frequent site of metastasis
5. 5-year survival rate is 10%–20%

B. Medical management
1. Surgery: treatment of choice
    a. Amputation: temporary prosthesis used immediately after surgery; permanent one usually fitted a few weeks later
    b. Limb salvage procedures
    c. Lung surgery if there are metastases
2. Radiation: only in areas where tumor is not accessible to surgery
3. Chemotherapy: adjuvant therapy being studied

C. Assessment findings
1. Insidious pain, increasing with activity, gradually becoming more severe
2. Tender mass, warm to touch; limitation of movement
3. Pathologic fractures

D. Nursing interventions
1. Prepare child for amputation: discuss fears, concerns, and facts of procedure; answer questions regarding prosthetic devices, limited activity
2. Assure child that phantom limb pain will subside

Ewing's Sarcoma

A. General information
1. Primary tumor arising from cells in bone marrow
2. Invades bone longitudinally, destroying bone tissue; no new bone formation
3. Femur most frequently affected site
4. More common in males, between ages 5–15 years
5. Lungs most frequent site of metastasis

B. Medical management
1. High-dose radiation is primary treatment
2. Chemotherapy
3. Value of surgery presently being reassessed

C. Assessment findings
1. Pain and swelling
2. Palpable mass, may be tender, warm to touch
3. 15%–35% of clients have metastatic disease at time of diagnosis

D. Nursing interventions
1. Promote exercise of affected limb to maintain function.
2. Avoid activities that may cause added stress to affected limb.

Sample Questions

70. A 10-year-old is being prepared for a bone marrow transplant. The nurse can assess how well he understands this treatment when he says
1. I'll be much better after this blood goes to my bones.
2. I won't feel too good until my body makes healthy cells.
3. This will help all of the medicine they give me to work better.
4. You won't have to wear a mask and gown after my transplant.

71. Susan, age 4, has leukemia. Her mother understands the white count involvement in this disease but doesn't understand why her child has bruises and anemia. The nurse explains that
1. all blood cells are made in the bone marrow and therefore all types will be affected.
2. the anemia is because her child hasn't been eating well; the bruises are from the multiple needle sticks.
3. they are related to inactivity.
4. this is indicative that the end is near.

72. 14-year-old Louise has had an exacerbation of acute lymphocytic leukemia. The primary effect of leukemia on the bone marrow is

1. crowding out of normal bone marrow cells.
2. proliferation of cells producing blood components.
3. a selective reduction in the number of neutrophils.
4. leukopenia, thrombocytopenia, and anemia.

73. A 14-year-old girl has acute lymphocytic leukemia and is admitted. She is terminally ill. An appropriate nursing action would be to
   1. leave her alone as much as possible and whisper when in her room in order not to disturb her.
   2. assist her in giving away her possessions to friends and family.
   3. encourage Louise's parents to explain to her 5-year-old sister that Louise will be asleep for a long time.
   4. reduce emotional stress by not having Louise's parents/family participate in her care.

74. Jack is 10 years old and is receiving cranial irradiation for a brain tumor. He has developed alopecia. Which of the following is an appropriate nursing intervention?
   1. Have Jack identify famous movie stars and sports heroes who are bald.
   2. Assure Jack that his hair will grow in before he leaves the hospital.
   3. Wrap a bandage around his head.
   4. Help him select a variety of hats.

Answers and Rationales

70. The correct answer is 2. The goal of a bone marrow transplant is to have the donor cells produce functioning blood cells for the client. In a bone marrow transplant, blood is not transfused into the client. Instead bone marrow is given to the person in the hopes that it will begin producing normal, healthy blood cells. A bone marrow transplant is not done to increase the effectiveness of medication therapy. A mask and gown will still be worn until the client begins to produce normal white blood cells.

71. The correct answer is 1. In leukemia, bone marrow is replaced by blast cells, resulting in decreased white cells, red cells, and platelets. The bruises are due to the child's decreased platelet count.

72. The correct answer is 1. Since leukemia cells are capable of an increased rate of production and a long cell life, they crowd out all of the normal bone marrow cells. Cells producing blood components are then unable to reproduce. There is no selective reduction, although the neutrophils, too, may be crowded out in nonmylocytic leukemias. Leukopenia is an absolute decrease in the number of white blood cells in the peripheral circulation; in leukemia, the white blood cell count rises.

73. The correct answer is 2. Adolescents may want to give away their belongings. The other interventions are all inappropriate and may increase Louise's fears and anxiety.

74. The correct answer is 4. Selecting hats to cover his head will help Jack deal with the change in his body image. The other suggestions are all inappropriate.

References and Suggested Readings

American Academy of Pediatrics, Committee on Infectious Diseases (1997). Report of the Committee on Infectious Diseases (24th edition). Elk Grove Village, Illinois.

Bowden, V. R., Dickey, S. B., Greenberg, C. S. (1998). *Children and their families: The continuum of care* (1st ed.). Philadelphia: WB Saunders.

Jaffe, M. (1998). *Pediatric Nursing Care Plans*. El Paso, Texas: Roth Publications.

Petrillo, M., & Sanger, S. (1981). *Emotional care of hospitalized children* (2nd ed.). Philadelphia: Lippincott.

Wong, D., Hockenberry-Eaton, M., Wilson, D., Winkelstein, M. L., Ahmann, E., DeVito-Thomas, P. A. (1999). *Whaley and Wong's nursing care of infants and children* (6th ed.). St. Louis: Mosby.

Unit 6

Maternity and Female Reproductive Nursing

Charlotte D. Kain, RNC, EdD
Judith M. Hall, RNC, MSN, IBCLC

This section covers the health care needs of females from adolescence through late adulthood. Emphasis is placed on the childbearing cycle and the normal neonate, and frequently encountered health care problems. Cultural differences are addressed.

The unit begins with a review of the anatomy and physiology of the female reproductive system as a basis for understanding the entire childbearing process. Nursing process is emphasized throughout, and nursing diagnoses are used to identify the client's health care needs and to select nursing interventions.

Nursing process always must be implemented with an awareness of the interrelationship, during childbearing, of the maternal and fetal needs and their manifestations. The nurse needs to keep in mind that interventions for the mother may have an impact on the developing fetus, and vice versa. Medications for maternal conditions may affect the fetus, and fetal distress may require that the mother undergo surgery.

In this unit, a major assertion is that childbearing, for most women, is a normal, healthy life event. Discomforts and complications of childbearing also are covered, and these conditions are presented after the content that reviews the natural progression of events in pregnancy and childbearing. In this manner, the factors that alter pregnancy from a normal life event to a life crisis can be clearly identified.

In addition to childbearing, the unit includes a review of frequently encountered health care conditions of women. These conditions usually involve the reproductive system or its accessory organs and include normally occurring states, such as menopause, as well as pathologic conditions, such as gynecologic cancer.

UNIT OUTLINE

446 Overview of Anatomy and Physiology of the Female Reproductive System
450 The Childbearing Cycle
455 The Antepartal Period
468 Labor and Delivery
485 The Postpartum Period
492 The Newborn
499 The High-Risk Infant
506 Conditions of the Female Reproductive System

445

Overview of Anatomy and Physiology of the Female Reproductive System

ANATOMY

External Structures

See Figure 6.1.

A. *Mons veneris:* rounded, soft, fatty, and loose connective tissue over the symphysis pubis. Dark, curly pubic hair growth in typical triangular shape begins here one to two years before the onset of menstruation.

B. *Labia majora:* lengthwise fatty folds of skin extending from the mons to the perineum that protect the labia minora, the urinary meatus, and the vaginal introitus.

C. *Labia minora:* thinner, lengthwise folds of hairless skin, extending from the clitoris to the fourchette.
   1. Glands in the labia minora lubricate the vulva.
   2. The labia minora are very sensitive because of their rich nerve supply.
   3. The space between the labia minora is called the vestibule.

D. *Clitoris:* small erectile organ located beneath the arch of the pubis, containing more nerve endings than the glans penis; sensitive to temperature and touch; secretes a fatty substance called smegma.

E. *Vestibule:* area formed by the labia minora, clitoris, and fourchette, enclosing the openings to the urethra and vagina, Skene's and Bartholin's glands; easily irritated by chemicals, discharges, or friction.
   1. *Urethra:* external opening to the urinary bladder
   2. *Skene's glands* (also called *paraurethral glands*): secrete a small amount of mucus; especially susceptible to infections

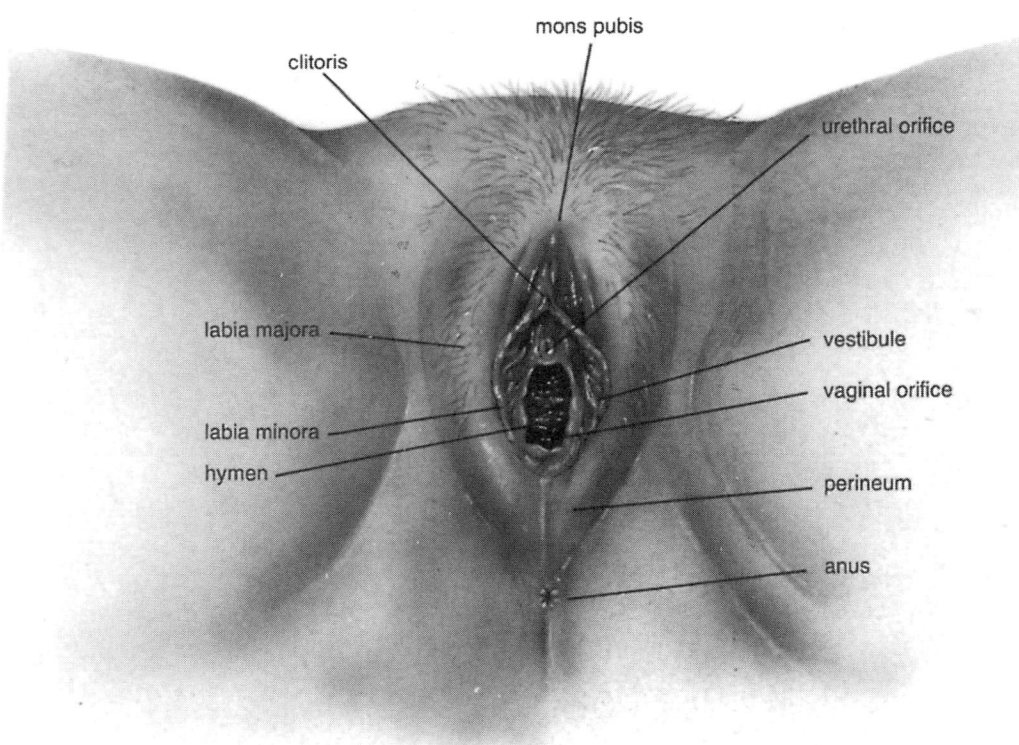

FIGURE 6.1   External structures of the female reproductive system (*Delmar Publishers*)

3. *Bartholin's glands:* located on either side of the vaginal orifice; secrete clear mucus during sexual arousal; susceptible to infection, as well as cyst and abscess formation
4. *Vaginal orifice* and *hymen:* elastic, partial fold of tissue surrounding opening to the vagina

F. *Fourchette:* thin fold of tissue formed by the merging of the labia majora and labia minora, below the vaginal orifice.

G. *Perineum:* muscular, skin-covered area between vaginal opening and anus.
1. Underlying the perineum are the paired muscle groups that form the supportive "sling" for the pelvic organs, capable of great distension during the birth process.
2. An episiotomy can be made in the perineum if necessary during the birth process.

Internal Structures

See Figure 6.2.

A. *Fallopian tubes:* paired tubules extending from the cornu of the uterus to the ovaries that serve as the passageway for the ova. Mucosal lining of tubes resembles that of vagina and uterus, therefore infection may extend from lower organs.

B. *Uterus:* hollow, pear-shaped muscular organ, freely movable in pelvic cavity, comprised of *fundus, corpus, isthmus,* and *cervix.* Cervix has internal and external os, separated by the cervical canal. Wall of uterus has three layers.
1. *Endometrium:* inner layer, highly vascular, shed during menstruation and following delivery
2. *Myometrium:* middle layer, comprised of smooth muscle fibers running in three directions; expels fetus during birth process, then contracts around blood

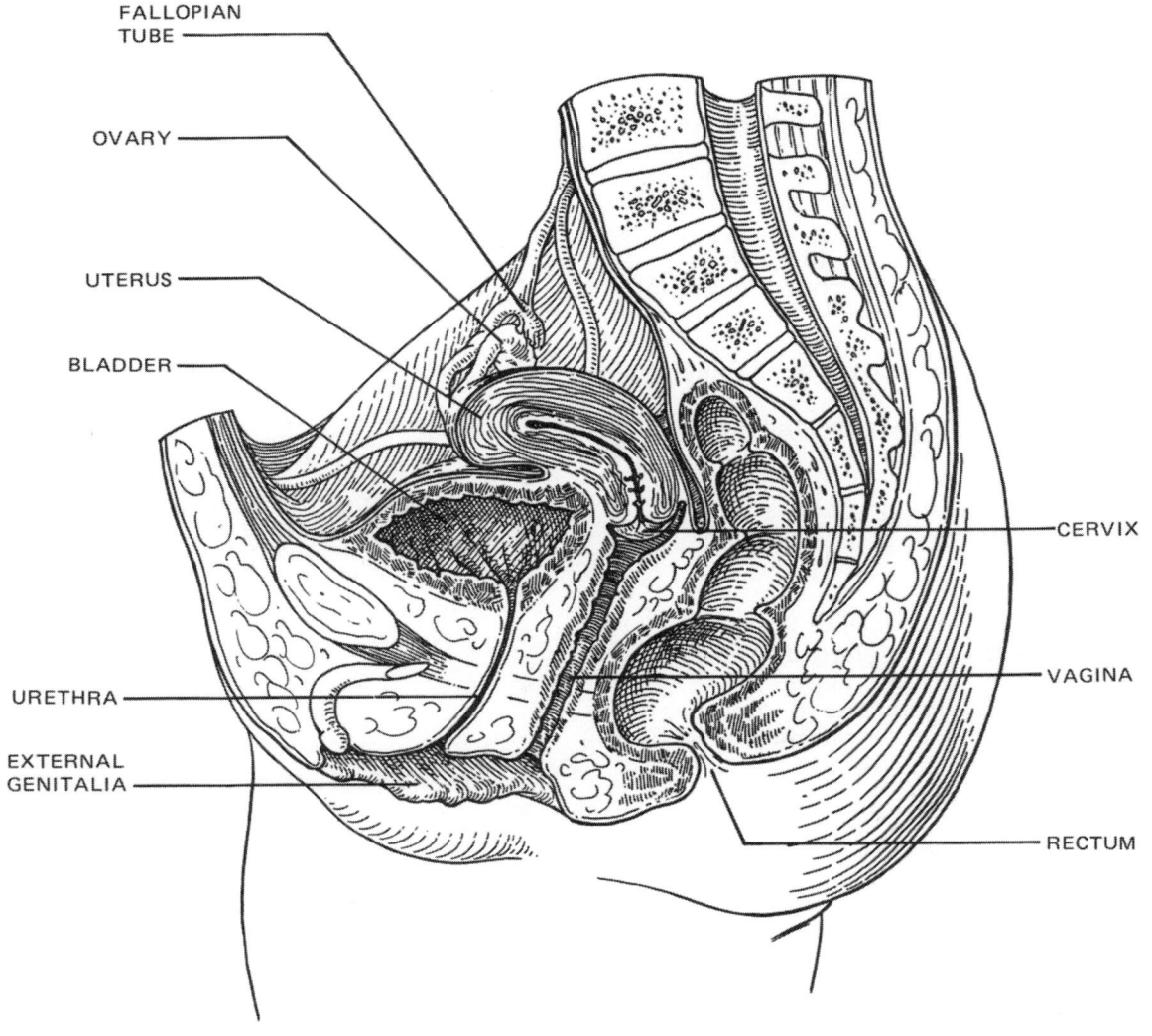

FALLOPIAN TUBE

OVARY

UTERUS

BLADDER

URETHRA

EXTERNAL GENITALIA

CERVIX

VAGINA

RECTUM

FIGURE 6.2 Internal structures of the female reproductive system (*Delmar Publishers*)

process, then contracts around blood vessels to prevent hemorrhage
   3. *Parietal peritoneum:* serous outer layer
C. *Ovaries:* oval, almond-sized organs on either side of the uterus that produce ova and hormones.
D. *Vagina:* Muscular, distensible tube connecting perineum and cervix; the birth canal.

The Pelvis

Right and left innominate bones, sacrum, and coccyx form the bony passage through which the baby passes during birth. Relationship between pelvic size/shape and baby may affect labor or make vaginal delivery impossible.
A. Pelvic measurements
   1. True conjugate: from upper margin of symphysis pubis to sacral promontory, should be at least 11 cm; may be obtained by x-ray or ultrasound.
   2. Diagonal conjugate: from lower border of symphysis pubis to sacral promontory; should be 12.5–13 cm; may be obtained by vaginal examination.
   3. Obstetric conjugate: from inner surface of symphysis pubis, slightly below upper border, to sacral promontory, it is the *most important pelvic measurement;* can be estimated by subtracting 1.5–2 cm from diagonal conjugate.
   4. Intertuberous diameter: measures the outlet between the inner borders of the ischial tuberosities; should be at least 8 cm.
B. Pelvic shapes
   1. Android: narrow, heart shaped; male-type pelvis
   2. Anthropoid: narrow, oval shaped; resembles ape pelvis
   3. Gynecoid: classic female pelvis; wide and well rounded in all directions
   4. Platypelloid: wide but flat; may still allow vaginal delivery.
C. Pelvic divisions
   1. False pelvis: shallow upper basin of the pelvis; supports the enlarging uterus, but not important obstetrically
   2. Linea terminalis: plane dividing upper or false pelvis from lower or true pelvis
   3. True pelvis: consists of the pelvic inlet, pelvic cavity, and pelvic outlet. Measurements of true pelvis influence the conduct and progress of labor and delivery.

The Breasts

A. Paired mammary glands on the anterior chest wall, between the second and sixth ribs, comprised of glandular tissue, fat, and connective tissue.

B. Nipple and areola are darker in color than breasts.
C. Responsible for lactation after delivery.

PHYSIOLOGY

Menarche

Onset of the menstrual cycle; puberty.

Menstrual Cycle

See Figure 6.3.
A. Complex pituitary/ovarian/uterine interaction.
B. Controls ripening and release of an ovum on a regular basis, and preparation for its fertilization and implantation in a thickened uterine lining (endometrium).
C. When fertilization/implantation do not occur, the endometrium is shed (menstruation), and the cycle begins again, due to follicle-stimulating hormone (FSH) and luteinizing hormone (LH) from the anterior pituitary.
D. Stages of cycle
   1. *Menstruation:* first days of cycle when endometrium is shed.
   2. *Proliferative phase:* major hormone involved is estrogen, which influences build-up of endometrium; also called *follicular phase.*
   3. *Ovulation:* release of ovum, usually 14 days (plus or minus 2) before end of cycle.
   4. *Secretory phase:* major hormone is progesterone, which influences myometrium (decreased irritability); also called *luteal phase.*

Menopause (Climacteric)

A. Decline in ovarian function and hormone production.
B. Characterized by menstrual cycle irregularity and, in some women, by vasomotor instability and loss of bone density.
C. See also Menopause, page 513.

Sexual Response in the Female: Four Phases

A. Excitement phase: vaginal lubrication and vasocongestion of external genitals.
B. Plateau phase: formation of orgasmic platform in vagina.
C. Orgasmic phase: strong rhythmic contractions of vagina and uterus.
D. Resolution phase: cervix dips into seminal pool in vagina; all organs return to previous condition.

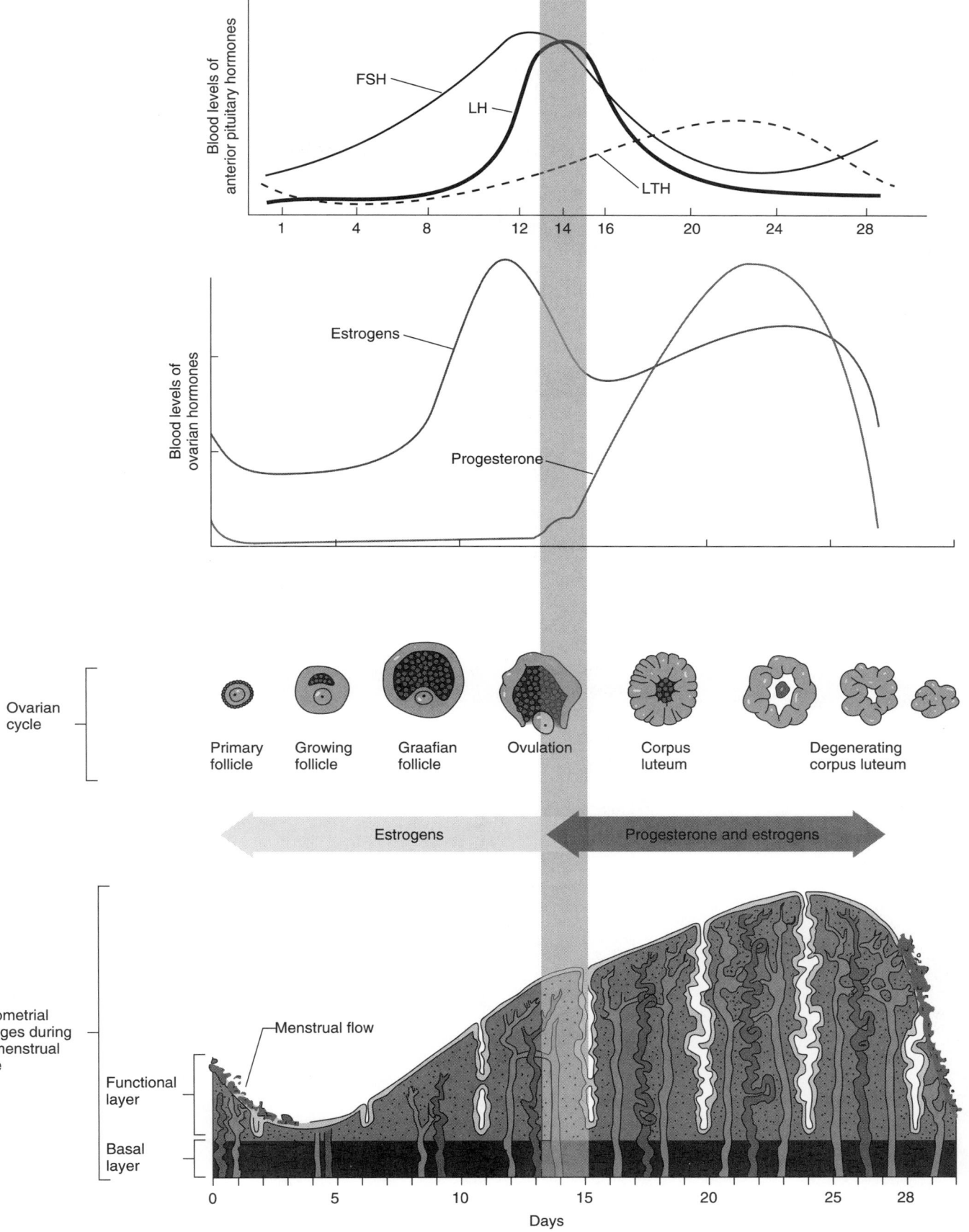

FIGURE 6.3 Menstrual cycle illustrating the levels of pituitary and ovarian hormones, ovarian cycle, and endometrial changes (*Delmar Publishers*)

The Childbearing Cycle

CONCEPTION

See Figure 6.4.
A. The penetration of one ovum (female gamete) by one sperm (male gamete) resulting in a fertilized ovum (zygote). Each gamete has haploid number of chromosomes (23). Zygote has diploid number (46) with one of each pair from each parent.
B. Sex of child is determined at moment of conception by male gamete. If X-bearing male gamete unites with ovum, result is a female child (X + X). If Y-bearing male gamete unites with ovum, result is a male child (X + Y).
C. Usually occurs in the outer third of the fallopian tube.
D. Multiple pregnancies result from
   1. Two or more fertilized ova (fraternal or dizygotic)
   2. Single fertilized ovum that divides - always same sex, only 1 chorion (identical or monozygotic)

NIDATION (IMPLANTATION)

A. Burrowing of developing zygote into endometrial lining of uterus.
B. May take place 7–10 days after fertilization, while zygote develops to trophoblastic stage.
C. Chorionic villi appear on surface of trophoblast and secrete human chorionic gonadotropin (HCG), which inhibits ovulation during pregnancy by stimulating continuous production of estrogen and progesterone. This secretion of HCG forms the basis of the various tests for pregnancy.

DEVELOPMENTAL STAGES

Fertilized Ovum

A. From conception through first two weeks of pregnancy.
B. Nidation complete by the end of this period.

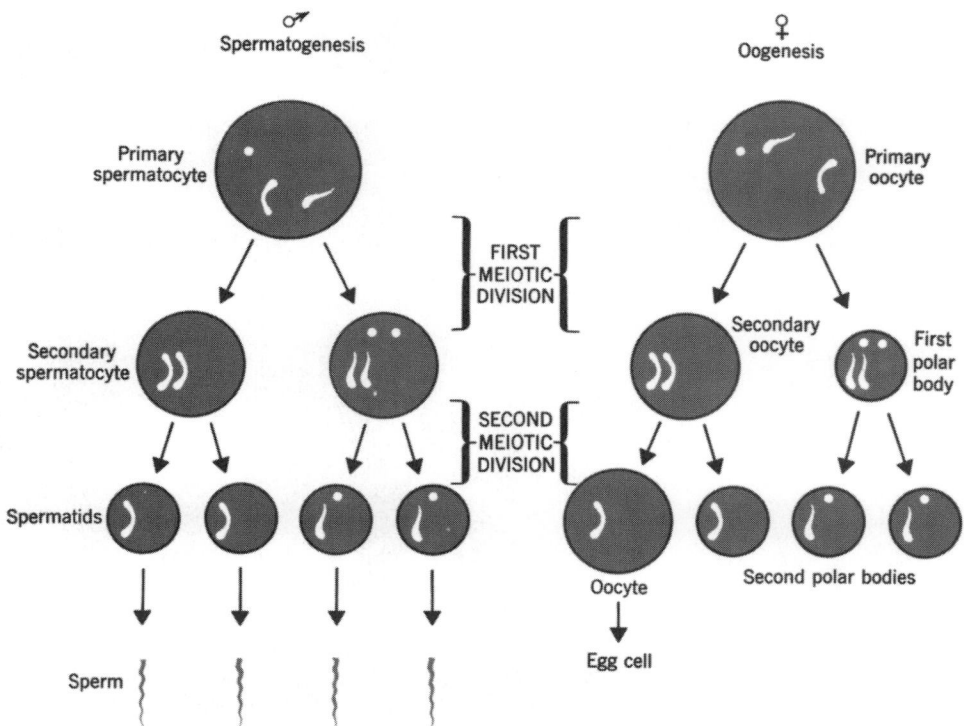

FIGURE 6.4 Spermatogenesis and oogenesis. A primary spermatocyte produces four sperm, but only one egg results from meiosis of a primary oocyte. The polar bodies are functionless. (*Delmar Publishers*)

Embryo

A. From end of second week through end of eighth week (also called period of organogenesis).
B. Critical time in development; embryo most vulnerable to teratogens (harmful substances or conditions), which can result in congenital anomalies.

Fetus

A. From end of eighth week to termination of pregnancy.
B. Continued maturation of already-formed organ systems.

SPECIAL STRUCTURES OF PREGNANCY

Fetal Membranes

A. Arise from the zygote.
B. Inner (amnion) and outer (chorion).
C. Hold the developing fetus as well as the amniotic fluid.

Amniotic Fluid

A. Clear, yellowish fluid surrounding the developing fetus.
B. Average amount 1000 ml.

C. Protects fetus.
  1. Allows free movement.
  2. Maintains temperature.
  3. Provides oral fluid.
D. Can be aspirated and tested for various diseases and abnormalities during pregnancy.
E. Alkaline pH: can be tested when membranes rupture to distinguish from urine.

Umbilical Cord

A. Connecting link between fetus and placenta.
B. Contains two arteries and one vein supported by mucoid material (Wharton's jelly) to prevent kinking and knotting.
C. There are no pain receptors in the umbilical cord.

Placenta

See Figure 6.5.
A. Transient organ allowing passage of nutrients and waste materials between mother and fetus.
B. Also acts as an endocrine organ and as a sieve which allows smaller particles through and holds back larger molecules. Passage of materials in either direction is effected by:
  1. Diffusion: gases, water, electrolytes.
  2. Facilitated transfer: glucose, amino acids, minerals.
  3. Pinocytosis: movement of minute particles (e.g., fats).

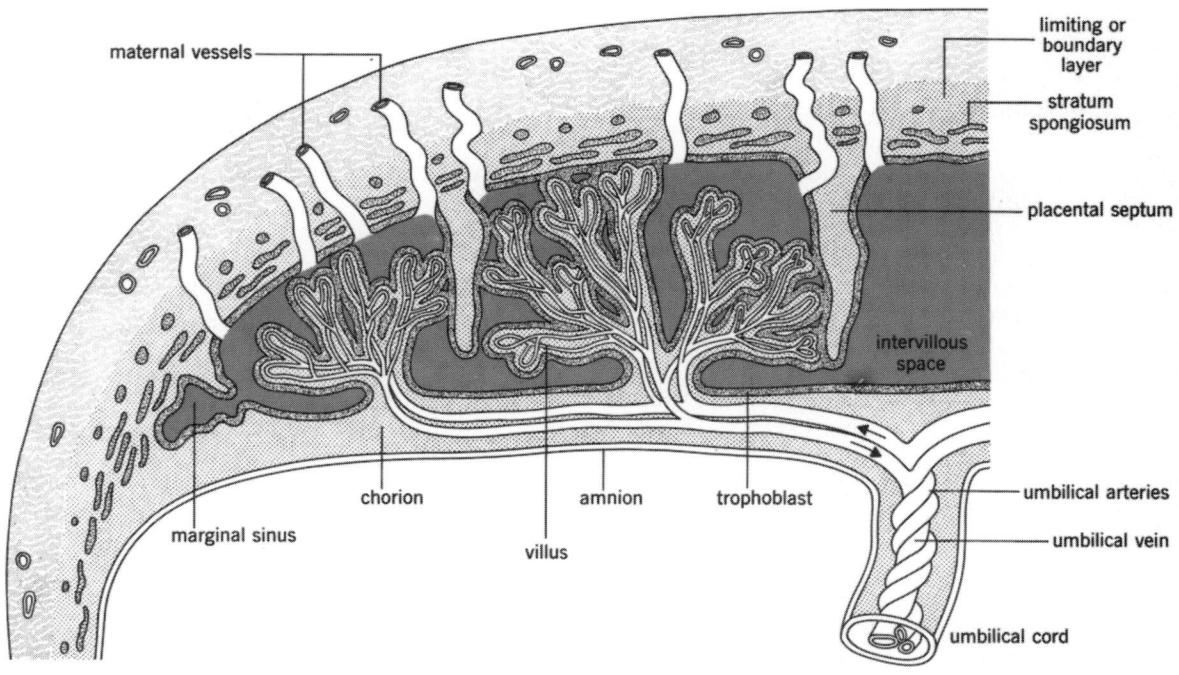

FIGURE 6.5 Placental circulation. Through the placenta, the fetus gets nourishment and excretes wastes. (*Delmar Publishers*)

4. Leakage: caused by membrane defect; may allow maternal and fetal blood mixing.

C. Mother also transmits immunoglobulin G (IgG) to fetus through placenta, providing limited passive immunity.

D. Hormones produced by the placenta include
   1. HCG: early in pregnancy, responsible for continued action of corpus luteum, is basis of pregnancy tests.
   2. Human chorionic somato-mammotropin/human placental lactogen (HCS/HPL): similar to growth hormone; affects maternal insulin production; prepares breasts for lactation.
   3. Estrogen and progesterone: necessary for continuation of pregnancy.

Fetal Circulation

A. Arteries in cord and fetal body carry deoxygenated blood.

B. Vein in cord and those in fetal body carry oxygenated blood.

C. Ductus venosus connects umbilical vein and inferior vena cava; bypassing portal circulation; closes after birth.

D. Foramen ovale allows blood to flow from right atrium to left atrium, bypassing lungs. Closes functionally at birth because of increased pressure in left atrium; anatomic closure may take several weeks to several months.

E. Ductus arteriosus allows blood flow from pulmonary artery to aorta, bypassing fetal lungs; closes after delivery.

Fetal Growth and Development

A. Organ systems develop from three primary germ layers.
   1. Ectoderm: outer layer, produces skin, nails, nervous system, and tooth enamel.
   2. Mesoderm: middle layer, produces connective tissue, muscles, blood, and circulatory system.
   3. Endoderm: inner layer, produces linings of gastrointestinal and respiratory tracts, endocrine glands, and auditory canal.

B. Timetable (Table 6.1 and Figure 6.6).

C. Measurements of length of pregnancy
   1. Days: 267–280
   2. Weeks: 40, plus or minus 2
   3. Months (lunar): 10
   4. Months (calendar): 9
   5. Trimesters: 3

D. Estimated due date/estimated date of confinement (*Nägele's rule*); see Figure 6.7. This calculation is an estimation only. Most women deliver: due date + or − 2 weeks. Sonogram dating used to confirm dates.

TABLE 6.1   Markers in Fetal Development

Date*	Development
4 weeks	All systems in rudimentary form; heart chambers formed and heart is beating. Embryo length about 0.4 cm; weight about 0.4 g.
8 weeks	Some distinct features in face; head large in proportion to rest of body; some movement. Length about 2.5 cm, weight 2 g.
12 weeks	Sex distinguishable; ossification in most bones; kidneys secrete urine; able to suck and swallow. Length 6–8 cm, weight 19 g.
16 weeks	More human appearance; earliest movement likely to be felt by mother; meconium in bowel; scalp hair develops. Length 11.5–13.5 cm, weight 100 g.
20 weeks	Vernix caseosa and lanugo appear; movement usually felt by mother; heart rate audible; bones hardening. Length 16–18.5 cm, weight 300 g.
24 weeks	Body well proportioned; skin red and wrinkled; hearing established. Length 23 cm, weight 600 g.
28 weeks	Infant viable, but immature if born at this time. Body less wrinkled; appearance of nails. Length 27 cm, weight 1100 g.
32 weeks	Subcutaneous fat beginning to deposit; L/S ratio in lungs now 1.2:1; skin smooth and pink. Length 31 cm, weight 1800–2100 g.
36 weeks	Lanugo disappearing; body usually plump; L/S ratio usually 2:1; definite sleep/wake cycle. Length 35 cm, weight 2200–2900 g.
40 weeks	Full-term pregnancy. Baby is active, with good muscle tone; strong suck reflex; if male, testes in scrotum; little lanugo. Length 40 cm, weight 3200 g or more.

*Dates are approximate, but developmental level should have been reached by the end of the time period specified.

PHYSICAL AND PSYCHOLOGIC CHANGES OF PREGNANCY

Reproductive System

A. External structures: enlarged due to increased vascularity.

B. Ovaries
   1. No ovulation during pregnancy
   2. Corpus luteum persists in early pregnancy until development of placenta is complete

C. Fallopian tubes: elongate as uterus rises in pelvic and abdominal cavities.

D. Vagina
   1. Increased vascularity (*Chadwick's sign*)
   2. Estrogen-induced leukorrhea
   3. Change in pH (less acidic) may favor overgrowth of yeastlike organisms
   4. Connective tissue loosens in preparation for distention of labor and delivery.

E. Cervix

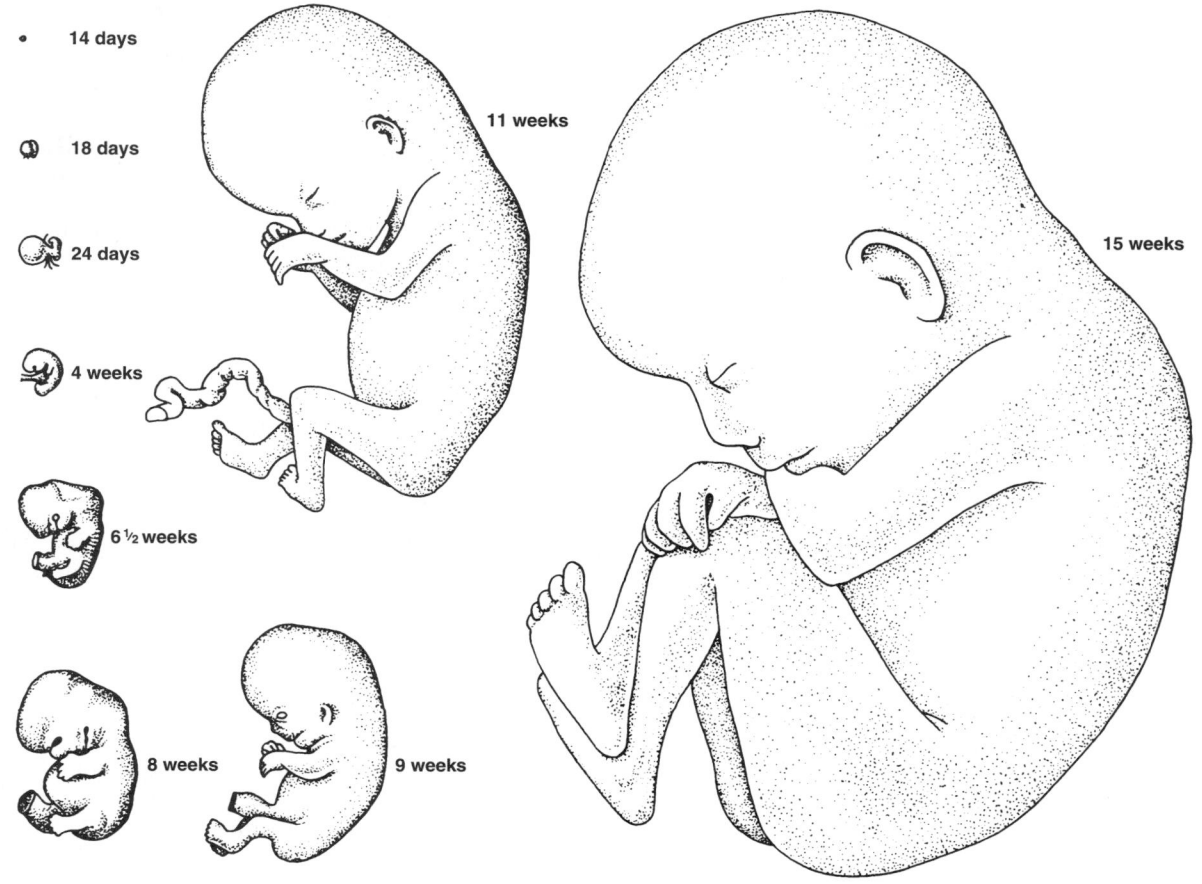

14 days

18 days

24 days

4 weeks

6 ½ weeks

8 weeks

9 weeks

11 weeks

15 weeks

FIGURE 6.6 Changes in the body size of the embryo and fetus during development in the uterus (all figures natural size) (*Delmar Publishers*)

1. Softens and loosens in preparation for labor and delivery (*Goodell's sign*).
2. Mucous production increases, and plug (operculum) is formed as bacterial barricade.
F. Uterus
   1. Hypertrophy and hyperplasia of muscle cells
   2. Development of fibroelastic tissue that increases ability to contract
   3. Shape changes from pearlike to ovoid

- Add 7 days to the first day of the last normal menstrual period
- Subtract 3 months
- Add 1 year

Example:
      1st day of LNMP = September 16, 1998
      Add 7 days = September 23
      Subtract 3 months = June 23
      Add 1 year = June 23 1999, will be estimated due date

FIGURE 6.7 Nägele's rule

4. Rises out of pelvic cavity by 16th week of pregnancy
5. Increased vascularity and softening of isthmus (*Hegar's sign*)
6. Mild contractions (*Braxton Hicks' sign*) beginning in the fourth month through end of pregnancy.
G. Breasts
   1. Increased vascularity, sensitivity, and fullness
   2. Nipples and areola darken
   3. Nipples become more erectile
   4. Proliferation of ducts and alveolar tissue evidenced by increased breast size.
   5. Production of colostrum by the second trimester

Cardiovascular System

A. Blood volume expands as much as 50% to meet demands of new tissue and increased needs of all systems.
B. Progesterone relaxes smooth muscle, resulting

in vasodilation and accommodation of increased volume.

C. RBC volume increases as much as 30%; may be slight decline in hematocrit as pregnancy progresses because of this relative imbalance (physiologic anemia).
D. Stroke volume and cardiac output increase.
E. WBCs increase.
F. Greater tendency to coagulation.
G. Blood pressure may drop in early pregnancy; should not rise during last half of pregnancy.
H. Heart rate increases; palpitations possible.
I. Blood flow to uterus and placenta is maximized by side-lying position.
J. Varicosities may occur in vulva and rectum as well as lower extremities.

Respiratory System

A. Increased vascularity of mucous membranes of this system gives rise to symptoms of nasal and pharyngeal congestion and fullness in the ears.
B. Shape of thorax shortens and widens to accommodate the growing fetus.
C. Slight increase in respiratory rate.
D. Dyspnea may occur at end of third trimester before engagement or "lightening."
E. Increased respiratory volume by 40 to 50%.
F. Oxygen consumption increases by 15%.

Renal System

A. Kidney filtration rate increases as much as 50%.
B. Glucose threshold drops; sodium threshold rises.
C. Water retention increases as pregnancy progresses.
D. Enlarging uterus causes pressure on bladder resulting in frequency of urination, especially during first trimester; later in pregnancy relaxed ureters are displaced laterally, increasing possibility of stasis and infection.
E. Presence of protein (not an expected component of maternal urine) indicates possible renal disease or pregnancy-induced hypertension.

Integumentary System

A. Increased pigmentation of nipples and areolas.
B. Possible appearance of *chloasma* (mask of pregnancy): darkening of areas on forehead and cheekbones.
C. Appearance of *linea nigra*, darkened line bisecting abdomen from symphysis pubis to top of fundus.
D. Striae (stretch marks): separation of underlying connective tissue in breasts, abdomen, thighs, and buttocks; fade after delivery.
E. Greater sweat and sebaceous gland activity.

Musculoskeletal System

A. Alterations in posture and walking gait caused by change in center of gravity as pregnancy progresses.
B. Increased joint mobility as a result of action of ovarian hormone (relaxin) on connective tissue.
C. Possible backache.
D. Occasional cramps in calf may occur with hypocalcemia.

Neurologic System

A. Few changes with a typical pregnancy.
B. Pressure on sciatic nerve may occur later in pregnancy due to fetal position.

Gastrointestinal System

A. Bleeding gums and hypersalivation may occur.
B. Tooth loss due to demineralization should *not* occur.
C. Nausea and vomiting in first trimester due to rising levels of HCG.
D. Appetite usually improves.
E. Cravings or desires for strange food combinations may occur.
F. Progesterone-induced relaxation of muscle tone leads to slow movement of food through GI tract; may result in heartburn.
G. Constipation may occur as water is reabsorbed in large intestine.
H. Emptying time for gallbladder may be prolonged; increased incidence of gallstones.

Endocrine System

A. Pituitary: FSH and LH greatly decreased; oxytocin secreted during labor and after delivery; prolactin responsible for initiation and continuation of lactation.
B. Progesterone secreted by corpus luteum until formation of placenta.
C. Principal source of estrogen is placenta, synthesized from fetal precursors.
D. HCS/HPL produced by placenta; similar to growth hormone, it prepares breasts for lactation; also affects insulin/glucose metabolism. May overstress maternal pancreas.
E. Ovaries secrete relaxin during pregnancy.
F. Slight increase in thyroid activity and basal metabolic rate (BMR).
G. Pancreas may be stressed due to complex interaction of glucose metabolism, HCS/HPL, and cortisol, resulting in diminished effectiveness of insulin, and demand for increased production.

Psychosocial Changes

A. First trimester

1. Mother needs accurate diagnosis of pregnancy.
2. Works through characteristic ambivalence of early pregnancy.
3. Mother is self-centered, baby is "part" of her.
4. Grandparents are usually the first relatives to be told of the pregnancy.
B. Second trimester
   1. Mother demonstrates growing realization of baby as separate and needing person.
   2. Fantasizes about unborn child.
C. Third trimester
   1. "Nesting" activity appears as due date approaches.
   2. Desire to be finished with pregnancy.
D. Anxiety over "safe passage" for self and baby through labor and delivery.
E. Reactions of father-to-be may parallel those of mother (e.g., ambivalence, anxiety). Additionally, as mother's pregnancy progresses he may experience similar physical changes.
F. Preparation of siblings varies according to their age and experience.

Transcultural Concerns in Pregnancy

A. Dominant philosophy concerning pregnancy and birth may differ in non-U.S. cultures. May view this as "healthy" time, with little or no insight concerning potential complications.
B. Biological variations may occur, e.g., higher rate of complications in women with sickle cell trait or gene; diabetes mellitus seen with more frequency in pregnant American Indians; increase in parasitic infections and hepatitis in women from Southeast Asia.
C. Behaviors during pregnancy (eating, sleeping, bathing, sexual activity, etc.) will differ from culture to culture.
D. Superstition, taboos, and "old wives tales" may play an important role.
E. Most cultures consider childbirth to be the province of women; men's roles may be limited or excluded. This may include caregivers.
F. Perception of discomfort/pain will vary; may be influenced by cultural expectations as well as mother's own experiences.
G. Despite culture, many women prefer upright position for labor and birth, rather than lying down. Additionally, many women prefer to have the freedom to move around during labor, whenever possible.
H. After delivery, cultural rituals may refer to rest, seclusion, and purification. The postpartum women may be considered vulnerable. Applications of heat or cold, in air or water, need to be specially assessed.
I. Other areas of culturally related practices may be: nutrition, clothing, activity, resumption of contact with the community, resumption of sexual activities, and return to work.
J. Infant care (feeding, cord care, circumcision, clothing, sleeping arrangements) will vary among differing cultures.
K. Control of future fertility may vary from natural methods such as breastfeeding to the use of any available means.

The Antepartal Period

ASSESSMENT

Classification of Pregnancy

Gravida - number of times pregnant, regardless of duration, including the present pregnancy.
A. Primagravida - pregnant for the first time
B. Multigravida - pregnant for second or subsequent time
Para - number of pregnancies that lasted more than 20 weeks, regardless of outcome.
A. Nullipara - a woman who has not given birth to a baby beyond 20 weeks gestation.
B. Primipara - a woman who has given birth to one baby more than 20 weeks gestation.
C. Multipara - Woman who has had two or more births at more than 20 weeks gestation . . . twins or triplets count as 1 para.

D. TPAL - Para subdivided to reflect births that went to Term, Premature births, Abortions, and Living children

Determination of Pregnancy

Diagnosis of pregnancy is based on pregnancy-related physical and hormonal changes and are classified as presumptive, probable, or positive.

Presumptive Signs and Symptoms (Subjective)

These changes may be noticed by the mother/health care provider but are *not* conclusive for pregnancy.
A. Amenorrhea (cessation of menstruation)
B. Nausea and vomiting

C. Urinary frequency
D. Fatigue
E. Breast changes
F. Weight change
G. Skin changes
H. Vaginal changes including leukorrhea
I. Quickening

Probable Signs and Symptoms (Objective)

These changes are usually noted by the health care provider but are *still not conclusive* for pregnancy.
A. Uterine enlargement
B. Changes in the uterus and cervix from increased vascularity
C. Ballottement: fetus rebounds against the examiner's hand when pushed gently upwards.
D. Braxton Hicks' contractions: occur early in pregnancy, although not usually sensed by the mother until the third trimester.
E. Laboratory tests for pregnancy
   1. Most tests rely on the presence of HCG in the blood or urine of the woman.
   2. Easy, inexpensive, but may give false readings with any handling error, medications, or detergent residue in laboratory equipment.
   3. Exception is the radioimmunoassay (RIA), which tests for the beta subunit of HCG and is considered to be so accurate as to be diagnostic for pregnancy.
F. Changes in skin pigmentation.

Positive Signs and Symptoms

These signs emanate from the fetus, are noted by the health care provider, and *are conclusive* for pregnancy.
A. Fetal heartbeat: detected as early as eighth week with an electronic device; after 16th week with a more conventional auscultory device.
B. Palpation of fetal outline.
C. Palpation of fetal movements.
D. Demonstration of fetal outline by either ultrasound (after sixth week) or x-ray (after 12th week).

ANALYSIS

Nursing diagnoses for the antepartal period *may* include
A. Knowledge deficit: information on the following topics needs to be given and reinforced
   1. Danger signals of pregnancy to be reported
   2. Dangerous behaviors during pregnancy (e.g., smoking, using drugs [especially alcohol], use of nonprescription medications)

B. Alteration in nutrition potential: individualized nutritional information will be needed
C. Activity intolerance: need for additional rest and benefits of a moderate exercise program
D. Anxiety
E. Constipation, potential
F. Body image disturbance
G. Alteration in comfort
H. Individual coping, ineffective
I. Powerlessness
J. Noncompliance
K. High risk for fluid volume deficit
L. Health-seeking behaviors

PLANNING AND IMPLEMENTATION

Goals

A. Establish a diagnosis of pregnancy.
B. Gather initial data to form the basis for comparison with data collected as pregnancy progresses.
C. Identify high-risk factors.
D. Propose realistic and necessary interventions.
E. Promote optimal health for mother and baby, providing any needed information.
F. Provide needed information for prepared childbirth.

Interventions

Prenatal Care

A. Time frame
   1. First visit: may be made as soon as woman suspects she is pregnant; frequently after first missed period.
   2. Subsequent visits: Every month until the 8th month, every 2 weeks during the 8th month, and weekly during the 9th month; more frequent visits are scheduled if problems arise.
B. Conduct of initial visit
   1. Extensive collection of data about client in all pertinent areas in order to form basis for comparison with data collected on subsequent visits and to screen for any high-risk factors
      a. Menstrual history: menarche, regularity, frequency and duration of flow, last period
      b. Obstetrical history: all pregnancies, complications, outcomes, contraceptive use, sexual history
      c. Medical history: include past illnesses, surgeries; current use of medications
      d. Family history/psychosocial data
      e. Information about the father-to-be may also be significant
      f. Current concerns

2. Complete physical examination, including internal gynecologic exam and bimanual exam
3. Laboratory work, including CBC, urinalysis, Pap test, blood type and Rh, rubella titer, testing for sexually transmitted diseases (STD), other tests as indicated (e.g., TB test, hepatitis viral studies, EKG, etc.)
C. Conduct of subsequent visits
   1. Continue collection of data, especially weight, blood pressure, urine screening for glucose and protein, evaluation of fetal development through auscultation of fetal heart rate (FHR) and palpation of fetal outline, measurement of fundal height as correlation for appropriate progress of pregnancy.
   2. Prepare for any necessary testing.
      a. Have client void (clean catch).
      b. Collect baseline data on vital signs.
      c. Collect specimen.
      d. Monitor client and fetus after procedure.
      e. Provide support to client.
      f. Document as needed.

Nutrition during Pregnancy

A. Weight gain
   1. Variable, but 25 lb usually appropriate for average woman with single pregnancy.
   2. Woman should have consistent, predictable pattern of weight gain, with only 2–3 lb in first trimester, then average 12 oz gain every week in second and third trimesters.
   3. Gains mostly reflect maternal tissue in first half of pregnancy, and fetal tissue in second half of pregnancy.
B. Specific nutrient needs
   1. *Calories:* usual addition is 300 kcal/day, but there will be specific guidelines for those beginning pregnancy either over- or underweight (never less than 1800 kcal/day).
   2. *Protein:* additional 30 g/day to ensure intake of 74–76 g/day; very young pregnant adolescents and those with multiple pregnancies will need more protein.
   3. *Carbohydrates:* intake must be sufficient for energy needs, using fresh fruits and vegetables as much as possible to derive additional fiber benefit; teach to avoid "empty" calories.
   4. *Fats:* high-energy foods, which are needed to carry the fat-soluble vitamins.
   5. *Iron:* needed by mother as well as fetus; reserves usually sufficient for first trimester, supplementation recommended after this time; iron preparations should be taken with source of vitamin C to promote absorption.
   6. *Calcium:* 1200 mg per day needed; dairy products most frequent source, with supplementation for those with lactose intolerance.
   7. *Sodium:* contained in most foods; needed in pregnancy; should not be restricted without serious indication.
   8. *Vitamins:* both fat- and water-soluble are needed in pregnancy; essential for tissue growth and development, as well as regulation of metabolism. Generally not synthesized by body, nor stored in large amounts (folic acid - special concern as deficiency may cause fetal anomalies and bleeding complications).
C. Dietary supplements: many health care providers supplement the pregnant woman's diet with an iron-fortified multivitamin to ensure essential levels.
D. Special concerns
   1. Religious, ethnic, and cultural practices that influence selection and preparation of foods
   2. Pica (ingestion of nonedible or nonnutritive substances)
   3. Vegan vegetarians - no meat products, may need B12 supplement.
   4. Adolescence
   5. Economic deprivation
   6. Heavy smoking, alcohol consumption, drugs
   7. Previous reproductive problems

Education for Parenthood

A. Provision of information about pregnancy, labor and delivery, the postpartum period, and lactation.
B. Usually taught in small groups, may be individualized.
C. Topics can be grouped into early and late pregnancy, labor and delivery, and postdelivery/newborn care.
D. Emphasis placed on both physical and psychosocial changes seen in childbearing cycle.
E. Preparation for childbirth: intended to provide knowledge and alternative coping behaviors in order to diminish anxiety and discomfort, and promote cooperation with the birth process; see Table 6.2 for specific methodologies.

Determination of Fetal Status and Risk Factors

A. Fetal diagnostic tests
   1. Used to
      a. Identify or confirm the existence of risk factor(s)
      b. Validate pregnancy

TABLE 6.2 Methods of Childbirth

Read method	The so-called "natural" childbirth method. Underlying concept: knowledge diminishes the fear that is key to pain. Classes include information as well as practice in relaxation and abdominal breathing techniques for labor.
Lamaze method	Psychoprophylactic method based on utilization of Pavlovian conditioned response theory. Classes teach replacement of usual response to pain with new, learned responses (breathing, effleurage, relaxation) in order to block recognition of pain and promote positive sense of control in labor.
Bradley method	Husband-coached childbirth. A modification of the Read method emphasizing working in harmony with the body.
Other methods	Hypnosis, yoga, the Wright method, and the Kitzinger method.

c. Observe progress of pregnancy
d. Identify optimum time for induction of labor if indicated
e. Identify genetic abnormalities

2. Types
   a. *Chorionic villi sampling* (*CVS*): earliest test possible on fetal cells; sample obtained by slender catheter passed through cervix to implantation site.
   b. *Ultrasound:* use of sound and returning echo patterns to identify intrabody structures. Useful early in pregnancy to identify gestational sac(s); later uses include assessment of fetal viability, growth patterns, anomalies, fluid volume, uterine anomalies, and adnexal masses. Used as an adjunct to amniocentesis; safe for fetus (no ionizing radiation).
   c. *Amniocentesis:* location and aspiration of amniotic fluid for examination; possible after the 14th week when sufficient amounts are present. Used to identify chromosomal aberrations, sex of fetus, levels of alphafetoprotein and other chemicals indicative of neural tube defects and inborn errors of metabolism, gestational age, Rh factor.
   d. *X-ray:* can be used late in pregnancy (after ossification of fetal bones) to confirm position and presentation; not used in early pregnancy to avoid possibility of causing damage to fetus and mother.
   e. *Alpha-fetoprotein Screening:* Maternal serum screens for open neural tube defects. Alpha-fetoprotein is glucoprotein produced by fetal yolk sac, GI tract, and liver. Test done between 16 and 18 weeks gestation.
   f. *L/S ratio:* uses amniotic fluid to ascertain fetal lung maturity through measurement of presence and amounts of the lung surfactants lecithin and sphingomyelin. At 35–36 weeks, ratio is 2:1, indicative of mature levels; once ratio of 2:1 is achieved, newborn less likely to develop respiratory distress syndrome. Phosphatidylglycerol (PG) is found in amniotic fluid after 35 weeks. In conjunction with the L/S ratio, it contributes to increased reliability of fetal lung maturity testing. May be done in laboratory or by "shake" test.
   g. *Creatinine level:* estimates fetal renal maturity and function, uses amniotic fluid.
   h. *Bilirubin level:* high early in pregnancy; drops after 36 weeks gestation; uses amniotic fluid.
   i. Fetal movement count: teach mother to count 2–3 times daily, 30–60 minutes each time, should feel 5–6 movements per counting time. Mother should notify care giver immediately of abrupt change or no movement.
   j. PUBS (percutaneous umbilical blood sampling): uses ultrasound to locate umbilical cord. Cord blood aspirated and tested. Used in second and third trimesters.
   k. Biophysical profile: a collection of data on fetal breathing movements, body movements, muscle tone, reactive heart rate, and amniotic fluid volume. A score of 0 to 2 is given in each category, and the summative number interpreted by the physician. Primary suggested use is to identify fetuses at risk for asphyxia.

B. Electronic Monitoring
   1. Nonstress test (NST) (see Table 6.3)
      a. Accelerations in heart rate accompany normal fetal movement

TABLE 6.3 Nonstress Test (NST)

Result	Interpretation	Significance
Reactive	2 or more accelerations of 15 beats/min lasting 15 sec or more in 20-min period (associated with each fetal movement)	High-risk pregnancy allowed to continue if twice weekly NSTs are reactive.
Nonreactive	No FHR acceleration, or accelerations less than 15 beats/min or lasting less than 15 sec through fetal movement	Need to attempt to clarify FHR pattern; implement CST and continue external monitoring.
Unsatisfactory	FHR pattern not able to be interpreted	Repeat NST or do CST.

TABLE 6.4 Contraction Stress Test (CST)

Result	Interpretation	Significance
Negative	3 contractions, 40–60 sec long, within 10-min period, no late decelerations	Fetus should tolerate labor if it occurs within 1 week.
Positive	Persistent/consistent late decelerations with more than ½ contractions	Fetus at increased risk. May need additional testing, may try induction or cesarean birth.
Suspicious	Late decelerations in less than ½ contractions	Repeat CST in 24 hr, or other fetal assessment tests.
Unsatisfactory	Inadequate pattern or poor tracing	Same as for suspicious.

  b. In high-risk pregnancies, NST may be used to assess FHR on a frequent basis in order to ascertain fetal well-being.
  c. Non-invasive
 2. Contraction stress test (CST) (see Table 6.4)
  a. Based on principle that healthy fetus can withstand decreased oxygen during contraction, but compromised fetus cannot.
  b. Types
    1) nipple-stimulated CST: massage or rolling of one or both nipples to stimulate uterine activity and check effect on FHR.
    2) oxytocin challenge test (OCT): infusion of calibrated dose of IV oxytocin "piggybacked" to main IV line; controlled by infusion pump; amount infused increased every 15–20 minutes until three good uterine contractions are observed within 10-minute period.
    3) CST never done unless willing to deliver fetus.

EVALUATION

A. Maternal/fetal assessment data remain within acceptable limits; fetus maintains growth and development pattern appropriate to gestational age (evidenced by maternal weight gain, normal increments in fundal height, fetal activity level, other antepartal tests).
B. No complications of pregnancy are evident.
  1. Pregnant woman receives prenatal care (initial and subsequent visits).
  2. Maternal blood pressure, weight gain, and other lab test findings are within normal range.
C. Pregnant woman/family have received adequate educational instruction.

 1. Pregnant woman/family express understanding of childbirth experience and begin transition to role of parenting.
 2. Any necessary testing procedures carried out completely and correctly; client/fetus in stable condition.

COMPLICATIONS OF PREGNANCY

Pregnancy can be complicated by situations unique to childbearing (e.g., placental bleeding), or by long-standing conditions predating pregnancy and continuing into the childbearing process (e.g., age socioeconomic status, cardiac problems); for common discomforts of pregnancy, see Table 6.5.

TABLE 6.5 Common Discomforts During Pregnancy

Discomfort	Trimester	Intervention
Morning sickness	First	Eat dry carbohydrate in AM; avoid fried, odorous, and greasy foods; small meals rather than large.
Fatigue	First	Rest frequently, as needed.
Urinary frequency	First, end of third	Kegel exercises, perineal pad for leakage.
Heartburn	Second, third	Small meals, bland foods, antacids if ordered.
Constipation	Second, third	Sufficient fluids, foods high in roughage, regular bowel habits. No laxatives unless ordered, including mineral oil.
Hemorrhoids	Third	Avoid constipation; promote regular bowel habits.
Varicosities	Third	Avoid crossing legs and long periods of sitting or standing; rest with feet and hips elevated; avoid elastic garters and other constrictive clothing.
Backache	Third	Use good posture and body mechanics; low-heeled shoes; exercises to strengthen back muscles.
Insomnia	Third	Conscious relaxation; supportive pillows as needed; warm shower before retiring.
Leg cramps	Third	Flex toes toward knees for relief; ensure adequate calcium in diet.
Supine hypotensive syndrome	Third	Left side-lying position.
Vaginal discharge	Second	Correct personal hygiene, refer to physician. Do not douche.
Skin changes, dryness, itching	All	Interventions are symptomatic; cool baths, lotions, oils as indicated.

General Nursing Responsibilities

A. Teach danger signals of pregnancy early in prenatal period so that client is aware of what needs to be reported to health care provider on an immediate basis (see Table 6.6).
B. Be aware that early teaching allows the client to participate in the identification and reporting of symptoms that can indicate a problem in her pregnancy.
C. Early recognition and reporting of danger signals usually results in diminishing the risk and controlling the severity of maternal/fetal complications.
D. Interventions are specific for the individual risks.
E. Evaluation centers around whether or not the risk was controlled or eliminated, and how the maternal/fetal reaction was controlled.

First Trimester Bleeding Complications

Abortion

A. General information
   1. Loss of pregnancy before viability of fetus; may be spontaneous, therapeutic, or elective (for additional information on therapeutic and elective abortions see Control of Fertility, page 507). (Clients may use term "miscarriage" for spontaneous abortion.)
   2. Types
      a. Threatened abortion
         1) cervix closed
         2) some bleeding and contractions
         3) fetus not expelled
      b. Inevitable
         1) cervix open
         2) heavier bleeding and stronger contractions
         3) loss of fetus usually not avoidable
      c. Incomplete
         1) expulsion of fetus incomplete
         2) membranes or placenta retained
      d. Complete: all products of conception expelled.
      e. Missed: fetus dies in uterus, but is not expelled

TABLE 6.6 Danger Signals of Pregnancy

- Any bleeding from vagina
- Gush of fluid from vagina (clear, not urine)
- Regular contractions occurring before due date
- Severe headaches or changes in vision
- Epigastric pain
- Vomiting that persists and is severe
- Change in fetal activity patterns
- Temperature elevation, chills, or "sick" feeling indicative of infection
- Swelling in upper body, especially face and fingers

   f. Habitual
      1) three pregnancies in a row culminating in spontaneous abortion
      2) may indicate need for investigation into underlying causes.
B. Assessment findings
   1. Vaginal bleeding (observing carefully for accurate determination of amount, saving all perineal pads)
   2. Contractions, pelvic cramping, backache
   3. Lowered hemoglobin if blood loss significant
   4. Passage of fetus/tissue
C. Nursing interventions
   1. Save all tissue passed.
   2. Keep client at rest and teach reason for bed rest.
   3. Increase fluids PO or IV.
   4. Prepare client for surgical intervention (D&C or suction evacuation) if needed (see also Termination of Pregnancy, page 509).
   5. Provide discharge teaching about limited activities and coitus after bleeding ceases.
   6. Observe reaction of mother and others, provide emotional support, and give opportunity to express feelings of grief and loss.
   7. Administer Rhogam if mother Rh negative (see page 502).

Incompetent Cerical Os (Premature Dilation of Cervix)

A. General information: painless condition in which the cervix dilates without uterine contractions and allows passage of the fetus; usually the result of prior cervical trauma.
B. Medical management: may be treated surgically to cerclage (placement of fascia or artificial material to constrict the cervix in a "purse-string" manner). When client goes into labor, choice of removal of suture and vaginal delivery, or cesarean birth.
C. Assessment findings
   1. History of repeated, relatively painless abortions
   2. Early and progressive effacement and dilation of cervix
   3. Bulging of membranes through cervical os
D. Nursing interventions
   1. Continue observation for contractions, rupture of membranes, and monitor fetal heart tones.
   2. Position client to minimize pressure on cervix.

Ectopic Pregnancy

A. General information
   1. Any gestation outside the uterine cavity

2. Most frequent in the fallopian tubes, where the tissue is incapable of the growth needed to accommodate pregnancy, so rupture of the site usually occurs before 12 weeks.
3. Any condition that diminishes the tubal lumen may predispose a woman to ectopic pregnancy

B. Assessment findings
1. History of missed periods and symptoms of early pregnancy
2. Abdominal pain, may be localized to one side
3. Rigid, tender abdomen; sometimes abnormal pelvic mass
4. Bleeding; if severe may lead to shock
5. Low hemoglobin and hematocrit, rising white cell count
6. HCG titers usually lower than in intrauterine pregnancy

C. Nursing interventions
1. Prepare client for surgery.
2. Institute measures to control/treat shock if hemorrhage severe; continue to monitor postoperatively.
3. Allow client to express feelings about loss of pregnancy and concerns about future pregnancies.

Hydatidiform Mole (Gestational Trophoblastic Disease)

A. General information
1. Proliferation of trophoblasts; embryo dies. Unusual chromosomal patterns seen (either no genetic material in ovum, or 69 chromosomes). The chorionic villi change into a mass of clear, fluid-filled grapelike vessels.
2. More common in oriental women and women over 40.
3. Cause essentially unknown

B. Assessment findings
1. Size of uterus disproportionate to length of pregnancy
2. High levels of HCG with excessive nausea and vomiting
3. Dark red to brownish vaginal bleeding after 12th week
4. Anemia often accompanies bleeding
5. Symptoms of preeclampsia before usual time of onset
6. No fetal heart sounds or palpation of fetal parts
7. Ultrasound shows no fetal skeleton

C. Nursing interventions
1. Provide pre- and postoperative care for evacuation of uterus (usually suction curettage).
2. Teach contraceptive use so that pregnancy is delayed for at least one year.
3. Teach client need for follow-up lab work to

detect rising HCG levels indicative of choriocarcinoma.
4. Provide emotional support for loss of pregnancy.
5. Teach about risk for future pregnancies, if indicated.

Second Trimester Bleeding Complications

There are few unique causes of bleeding in the second trimester. Bleeding may be a late manifestation of condition usually seen in first trimester, such as spontaneous abortion or incompetent cervical os.

Third Trimester Bleeding Complications

Placental problems are the most frequent cause of bleeding in the third trimester.

Placenta Previa

A. General information
1. Low implantation of the placenta so that it overlays some or all of the internal cervical os.
2. Cause uncertain, but uterine factors (poor vascularity, fibroid tumors, multiple pregnancies) may be involved.
3. Amount of cervical os involved classifies placenta previa as marginal, partial, or complete.

B. Assessment findings
1. Bright red vaginal bleeding after seventh month of pregnancy is cardinal indicator. Bleeding may be intermittent, in gushes, or continuous.
2. Uterus remains soft.
3. FHR usually stable unless maternal shock present.
4. No vaginal exam by nurse, may result in severe bleed, if done by physician, double set-up used
5. Diagnosis by sonography.

C. Nursing interventions
1. Ensure complete bed rest.
2. Maintain sterile conditions for any invasive procedures (including vaginal examination).
3. Make provision for emergency cesarean birth (double set-up procedure).
4. Continue to monitor maternal/fetal vital signs.
5. Measure blood loss carefully.
6. Assess uterine tone regularly.

Abruptio Placentae

A. General information
1. Separation of placenta from part or all of

normal implantation site, usually accompanied by pain
   2. Usually occurs after 20th week of pregnancy
   3. Seen frequently in women with hypertension, previous abruptio placentae, late pregnancies, and multigravidas, but cause essentially unknown
B. Assessment findings
   1. Painful vaginal bleeding
   2. Tender, boardlike uterus (especially if concealed hemorrhage, then no vaginal bleeding)
   3. Fetal bradycardia and late decelerations, absent FHT in complete abruption
   4. Additional signs of shock
C. Nursing interventions
   1. Ensure bed rest.
   2. Check maternal/fetal vital signs frequently.
   3. Prepare for IV infusions of fluids/blood as indicated.
   4. Monitor urinary output.
   5. Anticipate coagulation problems (DIC).
   6. Provide support to parents as outlook for fetus is poor.
   7. Prepare for emergency surgery as indicated.

Hyperemesis Gravidarum

A. General information
   1. Excess nausea and vomiting of early pregnancy leads to dehydration and electrolyte disturbances, especially acidosis.
   2. Causes: possible severe reaction to HCG, not psychological, greater risk in conditions where HCG levels increased. HCG levels peak around 6 weeks after conception, plateau, then begin to decline after the 12th week. Symptoms often improve later in pregnancy, but may last entire time.
B. Assessment findings
   1. Nausea and vomiting, progressing to retching between meals
   2. Weight loss
C. Nursing interventions
   1. Begin NPO and IV fluid and electrolyte replacement. (Correction of F&E balance will decrease nausea, NPO will rest the stomach)
   2. Monitor I&O
   3. Gradually re-introduce PO intake, monitor amounts taken and retained
   4. Monitor TPN and central line placement if unable to eat.
   5. Provide mouth care.
   6. Offer emotional support—very demoralizing and depressing to client.
   7. Refer to home health as appropriate for continued IV or TPN therapy.

Pregnancy-Induced Hypertension

General Information

A. Refers to condition unique to pregnancy where vasospastic hypertension is accompanied by proteinuria and edema; maternal or fetal condition may be compromised.
   1. Probable cause: gradual loss of normal pregnancy-related resistance to angiotensin II
   2. May also be related to decreased production of some vasodilating prostaglandins
B. Onset after 20th week of pregnancy, may appear in labor or up to 48 hours postpartum.
C. Characterized by widespread vasospasm.
D. Cause essentially unknown, but incidence is high in primigravidas, multiple pregnancies, hydatidiform mole, poor nutrition, essential hypertension; familial tendency.
E. Occurs in 5%–7% of all pregnant women.
F. Usual clinical classification of hypertensive disorders in pregnancy is as follows:
   1. Pregnancy-induced hypertension (PIH)
      a. Hypertension
      b. Preeclampsia
         1) Mild
         2) Severe
      c. Eclampsia
   2. Chronic hypertension
   3. Chronic hypertension with superimposed PIH
      a. Superimposed preeclampsia
      b. Superimposed eclampsia
G. Classic triad of symptoms includes edema/weight gain, hypertension, and proteinuria. Eclampsia includes convulsions and coma.
H. Possible life-threatening complication: HELLP syndrome (hemolysis, elevated liver enzymes, lowered platelets).
I. Only known cure is delivery.

Mild Preeclampsia

A. Assessment findings
   1. Appearance of symptoms between 20th and 24th week of pregnancy
   2. Blood pressure of 140/90 or +30/+15 mm Hg on two consecutive occasions at least 6 hours apart
   3. Sudden weight gain (+3 lb/month in second trimester; +1 lb/week in third trimester; or +4.5 lb/week at any time)
   4. Slight generalized edema, especially of hands and face
   5. Proteinuria of 300 mg/liter in a 24-hour specimen (+1)
B. Nursing interventions
   1. Promote bed rest as long as signs of edema

or proteinuria are minimal, preferably side-lying.
2. Provide well-balanced diet with adequate protein and roughage, no Na^+ restriction.
3. Explain need for close follow-up, weekly or twice-weekly visits to physician

Severe Preeclampsia

A. Assessment findings
   1. Headaches, epigastric pain, nausea and vomiting, visual disturbances, irritability
   2. Blood pressure of 150–160/100–110
   3. Increased edema and weight gain
   4. Proteinuria (5 g/24 hours) (4+)
B. Medical management: magnesium sulfate
   1. Magnesium sulfate acts upon the myoneural junction, diminishing neuromuscular transmission.
   2. It promotes maternal vasodilation, better tissue perfusion, and has anticonvulsant effect.
   3. Nursing responsibilities
      a. Monitor client's respirations, blood pressure, and reflexes, as well as urinary output frequently.
      b. Administer medications either IV or IM.
   4. Antidote for excess levels of magnesium sulfate is calcium gluconate or calcium chloride.
C. Nursing interventions
   1. Promote complete bed rest, side-lying.
   2. Carefully monitor maternal/fetal vital signs.
   3. Monitor I&O, results of laboratory tests.
   4. Take daily weights.
   5. Do daily fundoscopic examination.
   6. Institute seizure precautions.
      a. Restrict visitors.
      b. Minimize all stimuli.
      c. Monitor for hyperreflexia.
      d. Administer sedatives as ordered.
   7. Instruct client about appropriate diet.
   8. Continue to monitor 24–48 hours postdelivery.
   9. Administer medications as ordered; vasodilator of choice usually hydralazine (Apresoline).

Eclampsia

A. Medical management (see Severe Preeclampsia).
B. Assessment findings
   1. Increased hypertension precedes convulsion followed by hypotension and collapse.
   2. Coma may ensue.
   3. Labor may begin, putting fetus in great jeopardy.
   4. Convulsion may recur.

C. Nursing interventions
   1. Minimize all stimuli.
      a. Darken room.
      b. Limit visitors.
      c. Use padded bedsides and bed rails.
   2. Check vital signs and lab values frequently.
   3. Have airway, oxygen, and suction equipment available.
   4. Administer medications as ordered.
   5. Prepare for C-section when seizures stabilized.
   6. Continue observations 24–48 hours postpartum.

PRE- AND COEXISTING DISEASES OF PREGNANCY

Cardiac Conditions

General Information

A. May be the result of congenital heart disease or the sequelae of rheumatic fever/heart disease.
B. May affect pregnancy, but are definitely affected by pregnancy.
C. Classification
   1. Class 1: no limitation of activity
   2. Class 2: slight limitation of activity
   3. Class 3: considerable limitation of activity
   4. Class 4: symptoms present even at rest

Prenatal Period

A. Assessment findings
   1. Evidence of cardiac decompensation especially when blood volume peaks (weeks 28–32)
   2. Cough and dyspnea
   3. Edema
   4. Heart murmurs
   5. Palpitations
   6. Rales
B. Nursing interventions
   1. Promote frequent rest periods and adequate sleep, decreased stress.
   2. Teach client to recognize and report signs of infection, importance of prophylactic antibiotics.
   3. Compare vital signs to baseline and normal values expected during pregnancy.
   4. Instruct in diet to limit weight gain to 15 lbs., low Na^+.
   5. Explain rationale for anticoagulant therapy (heparin used in pregnancy) if ordered.
   6. Teach danger signals for individual client.

Intrapartal Period

A. Labor increases risk of congestive heart failure: milking effect of contractions and delivery increases blood volume to heart.

B. Nursing interventions
1. Monitor maternal EKG and FHT continuously.
2. Explain to client that vaginal delivery is preferred over C-section.
3. Monitor client's response to stress of labor and watch for signs of decompensation.
4. Administer oxygen and pain medication as ordered, epidural preferable.
5. Position client in side-lying/low semi-Fowler's position.
6. Provide calm atmosphere.
7. Encourage "open-glottal" pushing during second stage of labor, forceps or vacuum extractor used to minimize pushing.

Postpartal Period

A. Nursing interventions
1. Monitor vital signs, any bleeding, strict I&O, lab test values, daily weight, rest and diet.
2. Promote bed rest in appropriate position (see Intrapartal Period above).
3. Assist with activities of daily living (ADL) as needed.
4. Prevent infection.
5. Facilitate nonstressful mother/baby interactions.
6. Help mother plan for rest and activity patterns at home, as well as household help if indicated.

Endocrine Conditions

Diabetes Mellitus

A. General information
1. Chronic disease caused by improper metabolic interaction of carbohydrates, fats, proteins, and insulin.
2. Interaction of pregnancy and diabetes may cause serious complications of pregnancy.
3. Classifications of diabetes mellitus (see also Unit 4, page 334)
   a. Type 1: formerly called juvenile-onset or insulin-dependent diabetes; onset before age 40
   b. Type 2: formerly called maturity-onset or non-insulin-dependent; onset after age 40
   c. Type 3: formerly called gestational; onset during pregnancy; reversal after termination of pregnancy
   d. Type 4: formerly called secondary; occurs after pancreatic infections or endocrine disorders.
4. Significance of diabetes in pregnancy
   a. Interaction of estrogen, progesterone, HCS/HPL, and cortisol raise maternal resistance to insulin (ability to use glucose at the cellular level).

b. If the pancreas cannot respond by producing additional insulin, excess glucose moves across placenta to fetus, where fetal insulin metabolizes it, and acts as growth hormone, promoting macrosomia.
   c. Maternal insulin levels need to be carefully monitored during pregnancy to avoid widely fluctuating levels of blood glucose.
   d. Dose may drop during first trimester, then rise during second and third trimesters.
   e. Higher incidence of fetal anomalies and neonatal hypoglycemia (good control minimizes).

B. Assessment findings: signs of hyperglycemia
1. Polyuria
2. Polydipsia
3. Weight loss
4. Polyphagia
5. Elevated glucose levels in blood and urine. Urine tests for elevated blood glucose less reliable in pregnancy. Blood tests (more accurate) used as follows
   a. 1-hour glucose tolerance test: usually done for screening on all pregnant women 24–28 weeks pregnant.
   b. 3-hour glucose tolerance test: used where results from 1 hour GTT > 140 mg/dl.
   c. HbA_{1c}: glycosylated hemoglobin; reflects past 4–12 week blood levels of serum glucose.

C. Nursing interventions
1. Teach client the effects and interactions of diabetes and pregnancy and signs of hyper- and hypoglycemia.
2. Teach client how to control diabetes in pregnancy, advise of changes that need to be made in nutrition and activity patterns to promote normal glucose levels and prevent complications.
3. Advise client of increased risk of infection and how to avoid it.
4. Observe and report any signs of preeclampsia.
5. Monitor fetal status throughout pregnancy.
6. Assess status of mother and baby frequently
   a. Monitor carefully fluids, calories, glucose, and insulin during labor and delivery.
   b. Continue careful observation in postdelivery period.

Renal Conditions

Urinary Tract Infections (UTI)

A. General information
1. Affect 10% of all pregnant women.

2. Dilated, flaccid, and displaced ureters are a frequent site.
3. *E. coli* is the usual cause.
4. May cause premature labor if severe, untreated, or pyelonephritis develops.

B. Assessment findings
  1. Frequency and urgency of urination
  2. Suprapubic pain
  3. Flank pain (if kidney involved)
  4. Hematuria
  5. Pyuria
  6. Fever and chills

C. Nursing interventions
  1. Encourage high fluid intake.
  2. Provide warm baths to relieve discomfort and promote perineal hygiene.
  3. Administer and monitor intake of prescribed medications (antibiotics, urinary analgesics).
  4. Stress good bladder-emptying schedule.
  5. Monitor for signs of premature labor from severe or untreated infection.

Other Infections

A. General information
  1. Pregnancy is not a prevention against pre- or coexisting infections.
  2. *Toxoplasmosis, other infections, rubella, cytomegalovirus,* and *herpes* (*TORCH infections*) are especially devastating to the fetus, causing abortions, malformations, and even fetal death.
  3. Rubella titer is assessed during early prenatal visit. If mother is deficient in rubella antibodies (titer less than 1.0), rubella virus vaccine is recommended in immediate postpartum period.

B. General nursing interventions
  1. Instruct the pregnant woman in signs and symptoms that indicate infection, especially fever, chills, sore throat, localized pain, or rash.
  2. Caution pregnant women to avoid obviously infected persons and other sources of infection, as danger exists for the fetus in all maternal infections.
  3. May affect delivery options.

AIDS and Pregnancy

A. General information
  1. Transmission of the human immunodeficiency virus authenticated through blood, semen, vaginal secretions, and breast milk.
  2. Can be transmitted from mother to fetus during pregnancy.
  3. Cesarean delivery will not avert mother-to-fetus transmission.
  4. Breast-feeding not currently recommended for seropositive mothers.

5. Increase in prematurity, premature rupture of membranes, low birth weight, and coexistent STDs.
6. Pregnancy-altered immune states may result in the acceleration of opportunistic diseases, such as *Candida albicans,* herpes, and toxoplasmosis.
7. Treatment of the mother with AZT during pregnancy decreases the risk of transmission of the virus to the fetus.

B. Nursing implications
  1. Thorough review of history and any physical symptoms.
  2. Close attention to lab studies, especially CBC, leukocyte count, T-cell count, and urinalysis indicated.
  3. Strict attention to universal precautions as appropriate.
  4. Protective coverings in delivery room.
  5. Wear gloves to handle all infants until they are bathed.
  6. Suction newborn with bulb or wall suction devices only.
  7. Special assessments: respiratory, neurologic, psychosocial.

Other Conditions of Risk in Pregnancy

Adolescence

A. General information
  1. Pregnancy is a condition of both physical and psychologic risk.
  2. Adolescent is frequently undernourished and not yet completely matured either physically or psychosocially.
  3. Adolescent is uniquely unsuited for the stresses of pregnancy.
  4. Frequency of serious complications increases in adolescent pregnancy, particularly toxemia and low-birth-weight infants.

B. Nursing interventions
  1. Encourage adequate prenatal care.
  2. Provide health teaching to prepare for pregnancy, labor and delivery, and motherhood.
  3. Provide nutritional counseling.
  4. Teach coping skills for labor and delivery.
  5. Teach child care skills.

Disseminated Intravascular Coagulation (DIC)

A. General information
  1. Also known as *consumptive coagulopathy*
  2. A diffuse, pathologic form of clotting, secondary to underlying disease/pathology.
  3. Occurs in critical maternity problems such as abruptio placenta, dead fetus syndrome, amniotic fluid embolism, preeclampsia/

eclampsia, hydatidiform mole, and hemorrhagic shock
  4. Mechanism
    a. Precoagulant substances released in the blood trigger microthrombosis in peripheral vessels and paradoxical consumption of circulating clotting factors.
    b. Fibrin-split products accumulate, further interfering with the clotting process.
    c. Platelet and fibrinogen levels drop.
B. Assessment findings
  1. Bleeding may range from massive, unanticipated blood loss to localized bleeding (purpura and petechiae)
  2. Presence of special maternity problems
  3. Prolonged prothrombin and partial thromboplastin times
C. Nursing interventions
  1. Assist with medical management of underlying condition.
  2. Administer blood component therapy (white blood cells, packed cells, fresh frozen plasma, cryoprecipitate) as ordered.
  3. Observe for signs of insidious bleeding (oozing IV site, petechiae, lowered hematocrit).
  4. Institute nursing measures for severe bleeding/shock if needed.
  5. Provide emotional support to client and family as needed.

Anemia

A. General information
  1. Low red cell count may be underlying condition
  2. May or may not be exacerbated by physiologic hemodilution of pregnancy
  3. Most common medical disorder of pregnancy
B. Assessment findings
  1. Client is pale, tired, short of breath, dizzy
  2. Hgb is less than 11 g/dl; hct less than 37%.
C. Nursing interventions
  1. Encourage intake of foods with high iron content.
  2. Monitor iron supplementation.
  3. Teach sequelae of iron ingestion.
  4. Assess need for parenteral iron.

Prenatal Substance Abuse

A. General information
  1. Incidence: probably underestimated in our society.
  2. Morbidity/mortality: related to chemical used, timing, and route of administration.
B. Assessment findings
  1. Alcohol
    a. elevates the mood, depresses the central nervous system

    b. affects every other system in the body of the mother
    c. displaces other nutritional food intake
    d. greatest risk from high blood alcohol levels
    e. no safe level of maternal alcohol use in pregnancy has been established
    f. fetus may display IUGR (intrauterine growth retardation), CNS dysfunction, and craniofacial abnormalities (fetal alcohol syndrome).
  2. Cocaine
    a. powerful stimulant; very addictive
    b. causes vasoconstriction, elevated BP, tachycardia
    c. may precipitate seizures
    d. affects ability to transport O_2 into the blood
    e. may cause spontaneous abortion, fetal malformation, placenta abruptio, neural tube defects
    f. newborn may display irritability, hypertonicity, poor feeding patterns, increased risk of SIDS.
  3. Opiates
    a. produce analgesia, euphoria, respiratory depression
    b. if used IV, foreign substance contamination may cause pulmonary emboli or infections
    c. if used IV, places mother at greater risk of contracting HIV, then passing it on to fetus
    d. newborns experience withdrawal within 24–72 hours after delivery
    e. high-pitched cry, restlessness, poor feeding seen in the newborn
  4. Other chemicals
    a. may include tranquilizers, prescription medications, paint thinners, other aerosols, etc.
    b. major danger is overdose, with accompanying cardiac/respiratory arrest
C. Nursing interventions
  1. Treatment during pregnancy may include in- or outpatient care. Alcoholics Anonymous-based programs are widely utilized.
  2. Treatment may include family therapy.
  3. Efforts to treat the chemical abuse/dependency should be maximized during pregnancy. Withdrawal is best accomplished with competent, professional help.

Sample Questions

1. Mary G. is 22 years old and has missed two of her regular menstrual periods. Her doctor confirms an early, intrauterine pregnancy.

She is married and works as a salesperson in a local department store. This is her first pregnancy. To determine Mary's expected due date, which of the following assessments is most important?
1. Dates of first menstrual period.
2. Date of last intercourse.
3. Dates of last normal menstrual period.
4. Age at menarche.

2. A 24-year-old woman is pregnant with her first baby. During her seventh month, she complains of backache. The nurse teaches her to
1. sleep on a soft mattress.
2. walk barefoot at least once/day.
3. perform Kegel exercises once/day.
4. wear low-heeled shoes.

3. Anne T. is hospitalized for the treatment of severe preeclampsia. Which of the following represents an unusual finding for this condition?
1. Convulsions.
2. Blood pressure 160/100.
3. Proteinuria 3+.
4. Generalized edema.

4. A woman is admitted with severe preeclampsia. What type of room should the nurse select for this woman?
1. A room next to the elevator.
2. The room farthest from the nursing station.
3. The quietest room on the floor.
4. The labor suite.

5. The action of hormones during pregnancy affects the body by
1. raising resistance to insulin.
2. blocking the release of insulin from the pancreas.
3. preventing the liver from metabolizing glycogen.
4. enhancing the conversion of food to glucose.

6. Vicki F., 28 years old, has had diabetes mellitus since she was an adolescent. She is 8 weeks pregnant. Hyperglycemia during Vicki's first trimester will have what effect on the fetus?
1. Hyperinsulinemia.
2. Excessive fetal size.
3. Malformed organs.
4. Abnormal positioning.

7. The nurse is caring for a young diabetic woman who is in her first trimester of pregnancy. As the pregnancy continues the nurse should anticipate which change in her medication needs?
1. A decrease in the need for short-acting insulins.
2. A steady increase in insulin requirements.
3. Oral hypoglycemic drugs will be given several times daily.
4. The variable pattern of insulin absorption

throughout the pregnancy requires constant close adjustment.

8. A glycosylated hemoglobin level is ordered for a pregnant diabetic because it
1. is the most accurate method of determining present insulin levels.
2. will predict how well the pancreas can respond to the stress of pregnancy.
3. indicates mean glucose level over a 1- to 3-month period.
4. gives diagnostic information related to the peripheral effects of diabetes.

9. Mrs. Alice Sloane, 25 years old, has been coming to the prenatal clinic on a regular basis. She is five months pregnant. She suffered from morning sickness early in her pregnancy and is now concerned because the vomiting has continued and she is feeling weak and exhausted. Diagnosed as having hyperemesis gravidarum, she is hospitalized and parenteral fluid therapy is started. Mrs. Sloane has vomited twice within the last hour. The first appropriate nursing intervention would be to
1. assist her with mouth care.
2. notify the physician.
3. change the IV infusion to Ringer's lactate.
4. warm her tray and serve it to her again.

10. A woman in her seventh month of pregnancy has a hemoglobin of 10.5 g. The nurse teaches the woman about proper nutrition during pregnancy. Which statement made by the client indicates to the nurse that teaching was effective?
1. I eat liver once a week.
2. I have an orange for breakfast.
3. I eat six small meals a day.
4. I have a green leafy vegetable occasionally.

Answers and Rationales

1. The correct answer is 3. The dates of the last menstrual period, especially the first day of that period, will be used in applying Nägele's rule to determine the estimated date of delivery. The other information may be gathered as part of a general health history.
2. The correct answer is 4. A frequent cause of backache in the third trimester of pregnancy is the combined effect of relaxation of the sacroiliac joints and the change in the center of gravity of the pregnant woman due to the enlarging uterus. Wearing low-heeled shoes, especially when on her feet for extended periods of time, will help to minimize this discomfort.
3. The correct answer is 1. Convulsions are associated with an eclamptic condition. The other findings are usual for severe preeclampsia.

4. The correct answer is 3. A quiet room, in which stimuli are minimized and controlled, is essential to the nursing care of the severely preeclamptic client. Because she will need continuous monitoring, the room farthest from the nursing station is inappropriate. Additionally, this client may not need to be in the labor suite; the first goal of care is to prevent the condition from worsening.

5. The correct answer is 1. Hormonal influences during pregnancy cause a resistance to insulin utilization at the cellular level. It allows sufficient glucose for placental transport to the fetus, and also prevents the blood sugar in the nondiabetic client from falling to dangerous levels. In the diabetic client, it requires increases in her insulin doses. It does not affect the release of insulin. Gluconeogenesis is not altered. The conversion of food to glucose is not the problem in pregnancy; the problem is, rather, the utilization of the glucose.

6. The correct answer is 3. Major congenital malformations are noted in the insulin-dependent diabetic mother with poor metabolic control. Excessive fetal size develops as a result of high maternal levels of glucose over the course of the entire pregnancy. Abnormal positioning is not a common problem for the baby of a diabetic mother. Hyperinsulinemia in the fetus occurs in the third trimester.

7. The correct answer is 2. During the first trimester of pregnancy, there is little change in insulin requirements. In the second trimester, gradually increasing amounts of insulin are needed, with the insulin dose doubling by the end of the gestation period. Oral hypoglycemic agents pass through the placenta and can cause fetal damage. Insulin absorption is not the problem.

8. The correct answer is 3. Glycosylated hemoglobin measurements can be used to assess prior glycemic control. They have no predictive capacity. They provide a more accurate clinical picture of diabetic control but not its complications. They are not used for current blood glucose levels.

9. The correct answer is 1. Frequent vomiting irritates the oral mucosa and leaves the mouth very dry. The first nursing action should be aimed at relieving irritation and drying of the mouth by providing mouth care. The physician could be notified next if an antiemetic by injection or suppository had not yet been ordered. Changing the IV solution is not an independent nursing action. Her stomach needs to calm down before giving more food or liquid by mouth.

10. The correct answer is 1. Liver contains more iron than any other food source. The client should be eating 4–6 servings of fruit per day, particularly in light of the fact that iron is better absorbed when taken with foods high in vitamin C. Six small meals a day may be easier for the client to digest at this state of pregnancy, but there is no mention of what the meals consist of. Two or three servings of green leafy or other vegetable should be eaten daily.

Labor and Delivery

OVERVIEW

Five Factors of Labor (Five Ps)

Passenger

The size, presentation, and position of the fetus.
A. Fetal head (Figure 6.8)
   1. Usually the largest part of the baby; it has profound effect on birthing process.
   2. Bones of skull are joined by membranous sutures, which allow for overlapping or "molding" of cranial bones during birth process.
   3. *Anterior* and *posterior fontanels* are the points of intersection for the sutures and are important landmarks.
      a. Anterior fontanel is larger, diamond-shaped, and closes about 18 months of age.
      b. Posterior fontanel is smaller, triangular, and usually closes about 3 months of age.
   4. Fontanels are used as landmarks for internal examinations during labor to determine position of fetus.
B. Fetal shoulders: may be manipulated during delivery to allow passage of one shoulder at a time.
C. Presentation: that part of the fetus which enters the pelvis in the birth process (Figure 6.9). Types of presentation are
   1. Cephalic: head is presenting part; usually vertex (*occiput*), which is most favorable

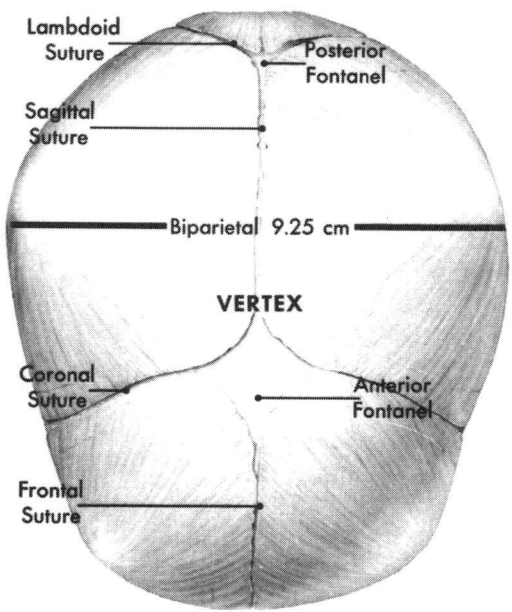

FIGURE 6.8 The fetal head (*Reprinted with permission of Ross Laboratories, Columbus, OH, from* Clinical Education Aid #13)

for birth. Head is flexed with chin on chest.
2. Breech: buttocks or lower extremities present first. Types are
   a. Frank: thighs flexed, legs extended on anterior body surface, buttocks presenting
   b. Full or complete: thighs and legs flexed, buttocks and feet presenting (baby in squatting position)
   c. Footling: one or both feet are presenting
3. Shoulder: presenting part is the scapula, and baby is in horizontal or transverse position. Cesarean birth indicated.
D. Position: relationship of reference point on fetal presenting part to maternal bony pelvis (Figure 6.10).
   1. Maternal bony pelvis divided into four quadrants (right and left anterior; right and left posterior). Relationship is expressed in a three-letter abbreviation: first the maternal side (R or L), next the fetal presentation, and last the maternal quadrant (A or P). Most common positions are

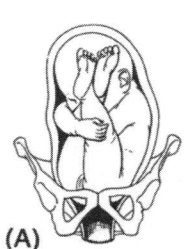
(A)

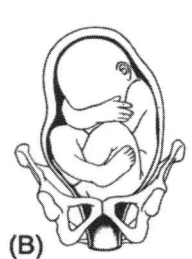
(B)

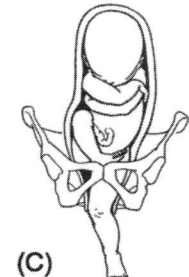
(C)

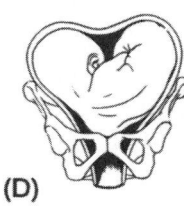
(D)

FIGURE 6.9 Malpresentations (A) frank breach; (B) full or complete breach; (C) footing; (D) shoulder. (*Reprinted with permission of Ross Laboratories, Columbus, OH, from* Clinical Education Aid #18)

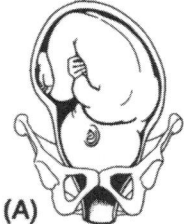
(A)

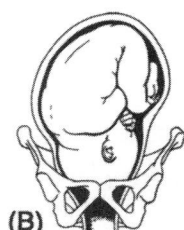
(B)

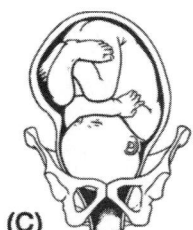
(C)

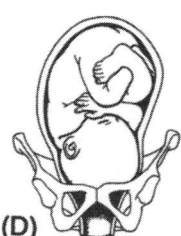
(D)

FIGURE 6.10 Positions (A) LOA; (B) ROA; (C) LOP; (D) ROP. (*Reprinted with permission of Ross Laboratories, Columbus, OH,* from Clinical Education Aid #18)

a. LOA (left occiput anterior): fetal occiput is on maternal left side and toward front, face is down. This is a favorable delivery position.
b. ROA (right occiput anterior): fetal occiput on maternal right side toward front, face is down. This is a favorable delivery position.
c. LOP (left occiput posterior): fetal occiput is on maternal left side and toward back, face is up. Mother experiences much back discomfort during labor; labor may be slowed; rotation usually occurs before labor to anterior position, or health care provider may rotate at time of delivery.
d. ROP (right occiput posterior): fetal occiput is on maternal right side and toward back, face is up. Presents problems similar to LOP.

2. Assessment of fetal position can be made by
   a. *Leopold's maneuvers:* external palpation (4 steps) of maternal abdomen to determine fetal contours or outlines. Maternal obesity, excess amniotic fluid, or uterine tumors may make palpation less accurate.
   b. Vaginal examination: location of sutures and fontanels and determination of relationship to maternal bony pelvis.
   c. Rectal examination: now virtually completely replaced by vaginal examination.
   d. Auscultation of fetal heart tones and determination of quadrant of maternal abdomen where best heard. (Correlate with Leopold maneuvers)

Passageway

Shape and measurement of maternal pelvis and distensibility of birth canal (see also Overview of Anatomy and Physiology, page 446).
A. Engagement: fetal presenting part enters true pelvis (inlet). May occur two weeks before labor in primipara; usually occurs at beginning of labor for multipara.
B. Station: measurement of how far the presenting part has descended into the pelvis. Referrant is ischial spines, palpated through lateral vaginal walls.
   1. When presenting part is at ischial spines, station is 0.
   2. If presenting part is above ischial spines, station expressed as a negative number (e.g., −1, −2).
   3. If presenting part is below ischial spines, station expressed as a positive number (e.g., +1, +2).

4. "High" or "floating" terms used to denote unengaged presenting part.
C. Soft tissue (cervix, vagina): stretches and dilates under the force of contractions to accommodate the passage of the fetus.

Powers

Forces of labor, acting in concert, to expel fetus and placenta. Major forces are
A. Uterine contractions (involuntary)
   1. Frequency: timed from the beginning of one contraction to the beginning of the next
   2. Regularity: discernible pattern; better established as pregnancy progresses
   3. Intensity: strength of contraction; a relative assessment without the use of a monitor. May be determined by the "depressability" of the uterus during a contraction. Described as mild, moderate, or strong.
   4. Duration: length of contraction. Contractions lasting more than 90 seconds without a subsequent period of uterine relaxation may have severe implications for the fetus and should be reported.
B. Voluntary bearing-down efforts
   1. After full dilation of the cervix, the mother can use her abdominal muscles to help expel the fetus.
   2. These efforts are similar to those for defecation, but the mother is pushing out the fetus from the birth canal.
   3. Contraction of levator ani muscles.

Placenta

A. As the placenta usually forms in the fundus of the uterus, it seldom interferes with the progress of labor.
B. A low-lying, marginal, partial, or complete placenta previa may require medical intervention to complete the birth process (see also Placenta Previa and Abruptio Placentae, page 461).

Psychologic Response

A woman who is relaxed, aware, and participating in the birth process usually has a shorter, less intense labor. A woman who is fearful has high levels of adrenaline which slows uterine contractions.

The Labor Process
Causes

Actual cause unknown. Factors involved include
A. Progressive uterine distension
B. Increasing intrauterine pressure

C. Aging of the placenta
D. Changes in levels of estrogen, progesterone, and prostaglandins
E. Increasing myometrial irritability

Mechanisms (Vertex Presentation)

A. Engagement
   1. The biparietal diameter of the head passes the pelvic inlet.
   2. The head is fixed in the pelvis.
B. Descent: progress of the presenting part through the pelvis
C. Flexion: chin flexed more firmly onto chest by pressure on fetal head from maternal soft tissues (cervix, vaginal walls, pelvic floor)
D. Internal rotation
   1. Fetal skull rotates along axis from transverse to anteroposterior at pelvic outlet.
   2. Head passes the midpelvis.
E. Extension: head passes under the symphysis pubis and is delivered, occiput first, followed by face and chin.
F. External rotation: head rotates to full alignment with back and shoulders for shoulder delivery mechanisms.
G. *When entire body of baby has emerged from mother's body, birth is complete. This time is recorded as the time of birth.*

Stages of Labor

A. Definitions
   1. Stage 1: from onset of labor until full dilation of cervix
      a. Latent phase: from 0–4 cm
      b. Active phase: 4–8 cm
      c. Transition: 8–10 cm
   2. Stage 2: from full dilation of cervix to birth of baby
   3. Stage 3: from birth of baby to expulsion of placenta
   4. Stage 4: time after birth (usually 1–2 hours) of immediately recovery
B. Cervical changes in first stage of labor
   1. Effacement
      a. Shortening and thinning of cervix.
      b. In primipara, effacement is usually well advanced before dilation begins; in a multipara, effacement and dilation progress together.
   2. Dilation
      a. Enlargement or widening of the cervical os and canal
      b. Full dilation is considered 10 cm.

Duration of Labor

A. Depends on
   1. Regular, progressive uterine contractions

   2. Progressive effacement and dilation of cervix
   3. Progressive descent of presenting part
B. Average length
   1. Primipara
      a. Stage 1: 12–13 hours
      b. Stage 2: 1 hour
      c. Stage 3: 3–4 minutes
      d. Stage 4: 1–2 hours
   2. Multipara
      a. Stage 1: 8 hours
      b. Stage 2: 20 minutes
      c. Stage 3: 4–5 minutes
      d. Stage 4: 1–2 hours

ASSESSMENT DURING LABOR

Fetal Assessment

Auscultation

Auscultate FHR at least every 15–30 minutes during first stage and every 5–15 minutes during second stage (depends on risk status of client).
A. Normal range 120–160 beats/minute
B. Best recorded during the 30 seconds immediately following a contraction

Palpation

Assess intensity of contraction by manual palpation of uterine fundus.
A. Mild: tense fundus, but can be indented with fingertips.
B. Moderate: firm fundus, difficult to indent with fingertips.
C. Strong: very firm fundus, cannot indent with fingertips.

Electronic Fetal Monitoring

A. Placement of ultrasound transducer and tocotransducer to record fetal heartbeat and uterine contractions and display them on special graph paper for comparison and identification of normal and abnormal patterns.
B. Can be applied externally to mother's abdomen, or internally, within uterus.
   1. External application
      a. Less precise information collected
      b. May be affected by maternal movements
      c. Noninvasive: rupture of membranes not required, can be widely used
      d. Little danger associated with use
   2. Internal application
      a. More precise information collected
      b. Cervix must be dilated and membranes ruptured to be utilized

    c. Physician applies scalp electrode and uterine catheter
    d. Sterile technique must be maintained during application to reduce risk of intrauterine infection
    e. Can yield specific short-term variability.

C. Pattern recognition
  1. Nurse is responsible for assessing FHR patterns, implementing appropriate nursing interventions, and reporting suspicious patterns to physician.
  2. Baseline FHR: 120–160, when uterus is not contracting.
  3. Variability is normal, indicative of intact fetal nervous system. Variability is result of interaction of sympathetic and parasympathetic nervous systems. Two types of variability are
    a. Short-term (beat-to-beat): assessed as present/absent.
    b. Long-term (rhythmic fluctuations): classified according to number of cycles/minute. Average is 6/minute.
  4. Tachycardia
    a. FHR more than 160 beats/minute, lasting longer than 10 minutes.
    b. May have multiple causes.
    c. Oxygen may be administered.
  5. Bradycardia
    a. FHR less than 120 beats/minute lasting longer than 10 minutes.
    b. May have multiple causes.
    c. Oxygen may be administered.
  6. Early deceleration
    a. Deceleration of FHR begins early in contraction, stays within normal range, returns to baseline by end of contraction.
    b. Believed to be the result of compression of fetal head against cervix.
    c. Not an ominous pattern, no nursing interventions required.
  7. Late deceleration
    a. Deceleration of FHR begins late in contraction; depth varies with strength of contraction; does not return to baseline by end of contraction.
    b. May be occasional or consistent. Gradual increase in number is always suspicious and MUST be reported/charted.
    c. Believed to be the result of uteroplacental insufficiency.
    d. **An ominous pattern.**
    e. Nurse should change maternal position, administer oxygen, discontinue any oxytocin infusion, assess variability, prepare for immediate delivery if pattern remains uncorrected.
  8. Variable deceleration
    a. Onset of deceleration not related to uterine contraction.
    b. Swings in FHR abrupt and dramatic, return to baseline frequently rapid.
    c. Believed to be the result of compression of the umbilical cord.
    d. **Although not an ominous pattern, continued nursing assessment required.**
    e. Nurse should change maternal position to relieve pressure on cord; if no improvement seen, administer oxygen, discontinue oxytocin if infusing, prepare client for vaginal exam to assess for prolapsed cord (see also Prolapsed Umbilical Cord, page 477).
    f. If cord is prolapsed, relieve pressure on cord; do not attempt to replace cord.
    g. Cesarean delivery will be needed.

Maternal Assessment

Premonitory Assessment

Physiologic changes preceding labor
A. Lightening (engagement): occurs up to two weeks before labor in primipara; at beginning of labor for multipara
B. Braxton Hicks' contractions: may become more noticeable; may play a part in ripening of cervix
C. Easier respirations from decreased pressure on diaphragm
D. Frequent urination, from increased pressure on bladder
E. Restlessness/poor sleeping patterns, "nesting" behaviors.

True vs False Labor

A. True labor
  1. Contractions increased in frequency, intensity, and duration
  2. Progressive cervical changes
  3. Bloody show
  4. Progressive fetal descent
  5. Walking intensifies contractions
  6. Discomfort begins in back then radiates to abdomen
B. False labor
  1. Irregular, inefficient contractions not causing the progressive changes associated with true labor
  2. No bloody show
  3. Discomfort primarily in abdomen, may be relieved by walking
  4. Need to assess client over period of time to differentiate from true labor

FIRST STAGE OF LABOR

Latent Phase (0–4 cm)

Assessment

A. Contractions: frequency, intensity, duration
B. Membranes: intact or ruptured, color of fluid
C. Bloody show
D. Time of onset
E. Cervical changes
F. Time of last ingestion of food
G. FHR every 15 minutes; immediately after rupture of membranes
H. Maternal vital signs
   1. Temperature every 2 hours if membranes ruptured, every 4 hours if intact
   2. Pulse and respirations every hour or prn as indicated
   3. Blood pressure every half hour or prn as indicated
I. Progress of descent (station)
J. Client's knowledge of labor process
K. Client's affect
L. Client's birth plan

Analysis

Nursing diagnoses for the latent phase of first stage of labor may include
A. Anxiety
B. Ineffective breathing pattern
C. Pain
D. Knowledge deficit

Planning and Implementation

A. Goals
   1. Complete all admission procedures.
   2. Labor will progress normally.
   3. Mother/fetus will tolerate latent phase successfully.
B. Interventions
   1. Administer perineal prep/enema if ordered/appropriate.
   2. Assess vital signs, blood pressure, fetal heart, contractions, bloody show, cervical changes, descent of fetus as scheduled.
   3. Maintain bed rest if indicated or required.
   4. Reinforce/teach breathing techniques as needed.
   5. Support laboring woman/couple based on their needs.
   6. Have client attempt to void every 1–2 hours.
   7. Apply external fetal monitoring if indicated or ordered.

Evaluation

A. Admission procedures complete
B. Progress through latent stage normal, cervix dilated

C. Mother/fetus tolerate latent phase well, mother as comfortable as possible, vital signs normal. FHR maintained in response to contractions

Active Phase (4–8 cm)

Assessment

A. Cervical changes
B. Bloody show
C. Membranes
D. Progress of descent
E. Maternal/fetal vital signs
F. Client's affect

Analysis

Nursing diagnoses for the active phase of first stage of labor may include
A. Ineffective individual coping
B. Alteration in oral mucous membranes
C. Knowledge deficit
D. Pain
E. Altered tissue perfusion
F. High risk for injury

Planning and Implementation

A. Goals
   1. Progress will be normal through active phase.
   2. Mother/fetus will successfully complete active phase.
B. Interventions
   1. Continue to observe labor progress.
   2. Reinforce/teach breathing techniques as needed.
   3. Position client for maximum comfort.
   4. Support client/couple as mother becomes more involved in labor.
   5. Administer analgesia if ordered or indicated.
   6. Assist with anesthesia if given and monitor maternal/fetal vital signs.
   7. Provide ice chips or clear fluids for mother to drink if allowed/desired.
   8. Keep client/couple informed as labor progresses.
   9. With posterior position, apply sacral counterpressure, or have father do so.

Evaluation

A. Labor progressing through active phase, dilation progressing
B. Mother/fetus tolerating labor appropriately
C. No complications observed

Transition (8–10 cm)

Assessment

A. Progress of labor

B. Cervical changes
C. Maternal mood changes: if irritable or aggressive may be tiring or unable to cope
D. Signs of nausea, vomiting, trembling, crying, irritability
E. Maternal/fetal vital signs
F. Breathing patterns, may be hyperventilating
G. Urge to bear down with contractions

Analysis

Nursing diagnoses for the transition phase of first stage of labor may include
A. Ineffective breathing pattern
B. Powerlessness
C. Ineffective individual coping

Planning and Implementation

A. Goals
   1. Labor will continue to progress through transition.
   2. Mother/fetus will tolerate process well.
   3. Complications will be avoided.
B. Interventions
   1. Continue observation of labor progress, maternal/fetal vital signs.
   2. Give mother positive support if tired or discouraged.
   3. Accept behavioral changes of mother.
   4. Promote appropriate breathing patterns to prevent hyperventilation.
   5. If hyperventilation present, have mother rebreathe expelled carbon dioxide to reverse respiratory alkalosis.
   6. Discourage pushing efforts until cervix is completely dilated, then assist with pushing.
   7. Observe for signs of delivery.

Evaluation

A. Mother/fetus progressed through transition
B. No complications observed
C. Mother/fetus ready for second stage of labor

SECOND STAGE OF LABOR

Assessment

A. Signs of imminent delivery
B. Progress of descent
C. Maternal/fetal vital signs
D. Maternal pushing efforts
E. Vaginal distension
F. Bulging of perineum
G. Crowning
H. Birth of baby

Analysis

Nursing diagnoses for the second stage of labor may include
A. High risk for injury
B. Noncompliance related to exhaustion
C. Knowledge deficit

Planning and Implementation

A. Goals
   1. Safe delivery of living, uninjured fetus.
   2. Mother will be comfortable after tolerating delivery.
B. Interventions
   1. If necessary, transfer mother carefully to delivery table or birthing chair; support legs equally to prevent/minimize strain on ligaments.
   2. Carefully position mother on delivery table, in delivery chair, or birthing bed to prevent popliteal vein pressure.
   3. Help mother use handles or legs to pull on as she bears down with contractions.
   4. Clean vulva and perineum to prepare for delivery.
   5. Continue observation of maternal/fetal vital signs.
   6. Encourage mother in sustained (5–7 seconds) pushes with each contraction.
   7. Support father's participation if in delivery area.
   8. Catheterize mother's bladder if indicated.
   9. Keep mother informed of delivery progress.
   10. Note time of delivery of baby.

Evaluation

A. Delivery of healthy viable fetus
B. Mother comfortable after procedure
C. No complications during procedure

THIRD STAGE OF LABOR

Assessment

A. Signs of placental separation
   1. Gush of blood
   2. Lengthening of cord
   3. Change in shape of uterus (discoid to globular)
B. Completeness of placenta
C. Status of mother/baby contact for first critical 1–2 hours
   1. Baby's Apgar scores (see Table 6.7)
   2. Blood pressure, pulse, respirations, lochia, fundal status of mother

TABLE 6.7   Apgar Scoring

Category	0	1	2	Score
Heart rate	Absent	<100	>100	_____
Respiratory effort	Absent	Slow, irregular	Good cry	_____
Muscle tone	Absent/limp	Some flexion	Active motion	_____
Reflex irritability	No response	Grimace	Cry	_____
Color	Blue, pale	Body pink, extremities blue	All pink	_____
			Total Score	_____

Analysis

Nursing diagnoses for the third stage of labor may include
A. Pain
B. Potential fluid volume deficit

Planning and Implementation

A. Goals
  1. Placenta will be delivered without complications.
  2. Maternal blood loss will be minimized.
  3. Mother will tolerate procedures well.
B. Interventions
  1. Palpate fundus immediately after delivery of placenta; massage gently if not firm.
  2. Palpate fundus at least every 15 minutes for first 1–2 hours.
  3. Observe lochia for color and amount.
  4. Inspect perineum.
  5. Assist with maternal hygiene as needed.
    a. Clean gown.
    b. Warm blanket.
    c. Clean perineal pads.
  6. Offer fluids as indicated.
  7. Promote beginning relationship with baby and parents through touch and privacy.
  8. Administer medications as ordered/needed (pitocin added to IV if present).

Evaluation

A. Placenta delivered without complications
B. Minimal maternal blood loss
C. Mother tolerated procedure well

FOURTH STAGE OF LABOR

Assessment

A. Fundal firmness, position
B. Lochia: color, amount
C. Perineum
D. Vital signs
E. IV if running
F. Infant's heart rate, airway, color, muscle tone, reflexes, warmth, activity state
G. Bonding/family integration

Analysis

Nursing diagnoses for the fourth stage of labor may include
A. Pain
B. High risk for fluid volume deficit
C. High risk for altered family processes

Planning and Implementation

A. Goal: critical first hour(s) after delivery will pass without complications for mother/baby.
B. Interventions
  1. Palpate fundus every 15 minutes for first 1–2 hours; massage gently if not firm.
  2. Check mother's blood pressure, pulse, respirations every 15 minutes for first 1–2 hours or until stable.
  3. Check lochia for color and amount every 15 minutes for first 1–2 hours.
  4. Inspect perineum every 15 minutes for first 1–2 hours.
  5. Apply ice to perineum if swollen or if episiotomy.
  6. Encourage mother to void, particularly if fundus not firm or displaced.
    a. Use nursing techniques to encourage voiding.
    b. If client unable to void, get order for catheterization.
    c. Measure first voiding.
  7. Encourage early bonding; through breast-feeding if desired.

Evaluation

A. Mother's vital signs stable, fundus and lochia within normal limits
B. Evidence of bonding; parents cuddle, touch, talk to baby
C. No complications observed for mother or baby during crucial time.

COMPLICATIONS OF LABOR AND DELIVERY

Premature/Preterm Labor

A. General information
  1. Labor that occurs before the end of the 37th week of pregnancy.

2. Cause is frequently unknown, but the following conditions are associated with premature labor
   a. Cervical incompetence
   b. Preeclampsia/eclampsia
   c. Maternal injury
   d. Infection
   e. Multiple births
   f. Placental disorders
3. Preterm labor: Prevention
   a. Minimize or stop smoking: a major factor in preterm labor and birth.
   b. Minimize or stop substance abuse/chemical dependency.
   c. Early and consistent prenatal care.
   d. Appropriate diet/weight gain.
   e. Minimize psychological stressors.
   f. Minimize/prevent exposure to infections.
   g. Learn to recognize signs and symptoms of preterm labor.
4. Incidence of preterm labor is between 5% and 10% in all pregnancies and is a major cause of perinatal mortality.

B. Medical management
1. Unless labor is irreversible, or a condition exists in which the mother or fetus would be jeopardized by the continuation of the pregnancy, or the membranes have ruptured, the usual medical intervention is to attempt to arrest the premature labor (tocolysis).
2. Medications used in the treatment of premature labor
   a. Magnesium sulfate
      1) Stops uterine contractions with fewer side effects than beta-adrenergic drugs.
      2) Interferes with muscle contractility.
      3) Administered IV for 12 to 24 hours, PO form of magnesium may be used for maintenance.
         a) Loading dose of 4–6 grams IV over 20 to 30 minutes.
         b) 1–4 g maintenance dose IV (2–3 g/hr)
         c) Must monitor patient for magnesium toxicity
      4) Few serious side effects; initially patient feels hot, flushed, may c/o headache, nausea, diarrhea, dizziness, nystagmus, and lethargy.
      5) Most common fetal side effect is hypotonia.
   b. Beta-adrenergic drugs—Terbutaline and Ritodrine.
      1) Decreases effect of calcium on muscle activation to slow or stop uterine contractions.
      2) Initially given IV, then p.o. brethine (terbutaline) for maintenance.
      3) Terbutaline:

         a) 1–8 mg/min × 8–12 hrs.
         b) 2.5 to 5 mg PO q 4–8 hrs.
      4) Ritodrine
         a) 0.05–0.1 mg/min increased to 0.35 mg/min until contractions stop.
         b) 10–20 mg q 2 h for 24 hours
      5) Side effects: increased heart rate, nervousness, tremors, nausea and vomiting, decrease in serum K+ level, cardiac arrhythmias, pulmonary edema.
   c. Nifedipine
      1) calcium channel blocker
      2) 10–30 mg loading dose, oral or sublingual; second dose may be given in 30 min if contractions persist; 10–20 mg orally q 4–6 hr for maintenance.
      3) Side effects: facial flushing, mild hypotension, reflex tachycardia, headache, nausea.
   d. Indomethacin
      1) Prostaglandin synthetase inhibitor
      2) Loading dose: 50–100 mg PO or rectally: 25 mg q 4–6 hr for 24–48 hr maintenance.
      3) Side effects: nausea, vomiting, dyspepsia
3. When premature labor cannot or should not be arrested and fetal lung maturity needs to be improved, the use of betamethasone (Celestone) can improve the L/S ratio of lung surfactants. It is administered IM to the mother, usually every 12 hrs times 2, then weekly until 34 weeks gestation.

C. Nursing interventions
1. Keep client at rest, side-lying position.
2. Hydrate the patient and maintain with IV or PO fluids.
3. Maintain continuous maternal/fetal monitoring.
   a. Maternal/fetal vital signs every 10 minutes; be alert for abrupt changes.
   b. Monitor maternal I&O.
   c. Monitor urine for glucose and ketones.
   d. Watch cardiac and respiratory status carefully.
   e. Evaluate lab test results carefully.
4. Administer drugs as ordered/indicated.
   a. Terbutaline
      1) position client on side as much as possible.
      2) apply external fetal monitor.
      3) complete maternal/fetal assessment before each increase in dosage rate.
      4) special maternal assessment includes respiratory status, blood pressure, pulse, I&O, lab values.
      5) notify physician of significant changes.

6) support client through stressful period of treatment and uncertainty.
7) teach client necessity of continuing oral medication at home if discharged.
  b. Magnesium sulfate: carefully monitor respirations, reflexes, and urinary output (see also Severe Preeclampsia, page 463).
4. Keep client informed of all progress/changes.
5. Identify side effects/complications as early as possible.
6. Carry out activities designed to keep client comfortable.

Postmature/Prolonged Pregnancy

A. General information
1. Defined as those pregnancies lasting beyond the end of the 42nd week.
2. Fetus at risk due to placental degeneration and loss of amniotic fluid (cord accidents).
3. Decreased amounts of vernix also allow the drying of the fetal skin, resulting in a dry, parchmentlike skin condition.
B. Medical management
1. Directed toward ascertaining precise fetal gestational age and condition, and determining fetal ability to tolerate labor
2. Induction of labor and possibly cesarean birth
C. Assessment findings
1. Measurements of fetal gestational age for fetal maturity
2. Biophysical profile
D. Nursing interventions
1. Perform continual monitoring of maternal/fetal vital signs.
2. Support mother through all testing and labor
3. Assist with amnio-infusion if ordered to increase cushion for cord.

Prolapsed Umbilical Cord

A. General information
1. Displacement of cord in a downward direction, near or ahead of the presenting part, or into the vagina
2. May occur when membranes rupture, or with ensuing contractions
3. Associated with breech presentations, unengaged presentations, and premature labors
4. Obstetric emergency: if compression of the cord occurs, fetal hypoxia may result in CNS damage or death.
B. Assessment findings: vaginal exam identifies cord prolapse into vagina
C. Nursing interventions

1. Check fetal heart tones immediately when membranes rupture, and again after next contraction, or within 5 minutes; report decelerations.
2. If fetal bradycardia, perform vaginal examination and check for prolapsed cord.
3. If cord prolapsed into vagina, exert upward pressure against presenting part to lift part off cord, reducing pressure on cord.
4. Get help to move mother into a position where gravity assists in getting presenting part off cord (knee-chest position or severe Trendelenburg's).
5. Administer oxygen, and prepare for immediate cesarean birth.
6. If cord protrudes outside vagina, cover with sterile gauze moistened with sterile saline while carrying out above tasks. Do not attempt to replace cord.
7. Notify physician.

Premature Rupture of Membranes

A. General information
1. Loss of amniotic fluid, prior to term, unconnected with labor.
2. Dangers associated with this event are prolapsed cord, infection, and the potential need for premature delivery.
B. Assessment findings
1. Report from mother/family of discharge of fluid.
2. pH of vaginal fluid will differentiate between amniotic fluid (alkaline) and urine or purulent discharge (acidic).
C. Nursing interventions
1. Monitor maternal/fetal vital signs on continuous basis, especially maternal temperature.
2. Calculate gestational age.
3. Observe for signs of infection and for signs of onset of labor.
   a. If signs of infection present, administer antibiotics as ordered and prepare for immediate delivery.
   b. If no maternal infection, induction of labor may be delayed.
4. Observe and record color, odor, amount of amniotic fluid.
5. Examine mother for signs of prolapsed cord.
6. Provide explanations of procedures and findings, and support mother/family.
7. Prepare mother/family for early birth if indicated.

Fetal Distress

A. General information: common contributing factors are
1. Cord compression.

2. Placental abnormalities.
3. Preexisting maternal disease.
B. Assessment findings
   1. Decelerations in FHR
   2. Meconium-stained amniotic fluid with a vertex presentation
   3. Fetal scalp sampling (may be needed for a definitive diagnosis)
C. Nursing interventions
   1. Check FHR on appropriate basis, institute fetal monitoring if not already in use.
   2. Conduct vaginal exam for presentation and position.
   3. Place mother on left side, administer oxygen, check for prolapsed cord, notify physician.
   4. Support mother and family
   5. Prepare for emergency birth if indicated.

Dystocia

A. General information
   1. Any labor/delivery that is prolonged or difficult
   2. Usually results from a change in the interrelationships among the 5 Ps (factors in labor/delivery): *passenger, passage, powers, placenta,* and *psyche* of mother.
   3. Frequently seen causes include
      a. Disproportion between fetal presentation (usually the head) and maternal pelvis (cephalopelvic disproportion [CPD]).
         1) if disproportion is minimal, vaginal birth may be attempted if fetal injuries can be minimized or eliminated.
         2) cesarean birth needed if disproportion is great.
      b. Problems with presentation
         1) any presentation unfavorable for delivery (e.g., breech, shoulder, face, transverse lie)
         2) posterior presentation that does not rotate, or cannot be rotated with ease.
         3) cesarean birth is the usual intervention.
      c. Problems with maternal soft tissue
         1) a full bladder may impede the progress of labor, as can myomata uteri, cervical edema, scar tissue, and congenital anomalies.
         2) emptying the bladder may allow labor to continue; the other conditions may necessitate cesarean birth.
      d. Dysfunctional uterine contractions
         1) contractions may be too weak, too short, too far apart, ineffectual.
         2) progress of labor is affected; progressive dilation, effacement, and descent do not occur in the expected pattern.
         3) classification
            a) primary: inefficient pattern present from beginning of labor; usually a prolonged latent phase.
            b) secondary: efficient pattern that changes to inefficient or stops; may occur in any stage.
B. Assessment findings
   1. Progress of labor slower than expected rate of dilation, effacement, descent for specific client
   2. Length of labor prolonged
   3. Maternal exhaustion/distress
   4. Fetal distress
C. Nursing interventions
   1. Individualized as to cause.
   2. Provide comfort measures for client.
   3. Provide clear, supportive descriptions of all actions taken.
   4. Administer analgesia if ordered/indicated.
   5. Prepare oxytocin infusion for induction of labor if ordered.
   6. Monitor mother/fetus continuously.
   7. Prepare for cesarean birth if needed.

Precipitous Labor and Delivery

A. General information
   1. Labor of less than 3 hours.
   2. Emergency delivery without client's physician or midwife
B. Assessment findings
   1. As labor is progressing quickly, assessment may need to be done rapidly.
   2. Client may have history of previous precipitous labor and delivery.
   3. Desire to push.
   4. Observe status of membranes, perineal area for bulging, and for signs of bleeding.
C. Nursing interventions (see Table 6.8)

Amniotic Fluid Embolism

A. General information
   1. Escape of amniotic fluid into the maternal circulation, usually in conjunction with a pattern of hypertonic, intense uterine contractions, either naturally or oxytocin induced.
   2. Obstetric emergency: may be fatal to the mother and to the baby.
B. Assessment findings
   1. Sudden onset of respiratory distress, hypotension, chest pain, signs of shock
   2. Bleeding (DIC)
   3. Cyanosis
   4. Pulmonary edema
C. Nursing interventions
   1. Initiate emergency life support activities for mother.

TABLE 6.8 Emergency Delivery of an Infant

If you have to deliver the baby yourself

■ Assess the client's affect and ability to understand directions, as well as other resources available (other physicians, nurses, auxiliary personnel).

■ Stay with client at all times; mother must not be left alone if delivery is imminent.

■ Do not prevent birth of baby.

■ Maintain sterile environment if possible.

■ Rupture membranes if necessary.

■ Support baby's head as it emerges, preventing too-rapid delivery with gentle pressure.

■ Check for nuchal cord, slip over head if possible.

■ Use gentle aspiration with bulb syringe to remove blood and mucus from nose and mouth.

■ Deliver shoulders after external rotation, asking mother to push gently if needed.

■ Provide support for baby's body as it is delivered.

■ Hold baby in head-down position to facilitate drainage of secretions.

■ Promote cry by gently rubbing over back and soles of feet.

■ Dry to prevent heat loss.

■ Place baby on mother's abdomen.

■ Check for signs of placental separation.

■ Check mother for excess bleeding; massage uterus prn.

■ Hold placenta as it is delivered.

■ Cut cord when pulsations cease, if cord clamp is available; if no clamps, leave intact.

■ Wrap baby in dry blanket, give to mother; put to breast if possible.

■ Check mother for fundal firmness and excess bleeding.

■ Record all pertinent data.

■ Comfort mother and family as needed.

---

    a. Administer oxygen
    b. Utilize CPR in case of cardiac arrest.
  2. Establish IV line for blood transfusion and monitoring of CVP.
  3. Administer medications to control bleeding as ordered.
  4. Prepare for emergency birth of baby.
  5. Keep client/family informed as possible.

Induction of Labor

A. General information: deliberate stimulation of uterine contractions before the normal occurrence of labor.
B. Medical management: may be accomplished by
  1. Amniotomy (the deliberate rupture of membranes)
  2. Oxytocins, usually Pitocin
  3. Prostaglandin (PGE$_2$) in gel/suppository form
C. Assessment findings
  1. Indications for use
    a. Postmature pregnancy
    b. Preeclampsia/eclampsia
    c. Diabetes

    d. Premature rupture of membranes
  2. Condition of fetus: mature, engaged vertex fetus in no distress
  3. Condition of mother: cervix "ripe" for induction, no CPD
D. Nursing interventions
  1. Explain all procedures to client.
  2. Prepare appropriate equipment and medications.
    a. Amniotomy: a small tear made in amniotic membrane as part of sterile vaginal exam
      1) explain sensations to client.
      2) check FHR immediately before and after procedure; marked changes may indicate prolapsed cord (see page 477).
      3) additional care as for woman with premature rupture of membranes (page 477).
    b. Oxytocin (Pitocin): IV administration, "piggybacked" to main IV
      1) usual dilution 10 mU/1000 ml fluid, delivered via infusion pump for greatest accuracy in controlling dosage.
      2) usual administration rate is 0.5–1.0 mU/min, increased no more than 1–2 mU/min at 40–60-minute intervals until regular pattern of appropriate contractions is established (every 2–3 minutes, lasting less than 90 seconds, with 30–45 second rest period between contractions.)
  3. Know that continuous monitoring and accurate assessments are essential.
    a. Apply external continuous fetal monitoring equipment.
    b. Monitor maternal condition on a continuous basis: blood pressure, pulse, progress of labor.
  4. Discontinue oxytocin infusion when
    a. Fetal distress is noted.
    b. Hypertonic contractions occur.
    c. Signs of other obstetric complications (hemorrhage/shock, abruptio placenta, amniotic fluid embolism) appear.
  5. Notify physician of any untoward reactions.

ANALGESIA AND ANESTHESIA

Analgesia for Labor

General Information

A. Definition: the easing of pain or discomfort by the administration of medication that blocks

pain recognition or the raising of the pain recognition threshold.
B. Sources of pain/discomfort
  1. First stage of labor: stretching of cervix and uterine contractions
  2. Second stage of labor: stretching of birth canal and perineum
C. Examples of medications used systemically for labor analgesia
  1. Sedatives: help to relieve anxiety; may use secobarbital (Seconal), sodium pentobarbital (Nembutal), phenobarbital.
  2. Narcotic analgesics: help to relieve pain; may use morphine, meperidine (Demerol), butorphanol (stadol), sublimaze (fentanyl), nalbuphine hydrochloride (Nubain).
  3. Narcotic antagonists: given to reverse narcotic depression of mother or baby; may use naloxone (Narcan), levallorphan (Lorfan).
  4. Analgesic potentiating drugs: given to raise desired effect of analgesic without raising dose of analgesic drug; may use promethazine (Phenergan), promazine (Sparine), propiomazine (Largon), hydroxyzine (Vistaril)
D. Medication administration
  1. IV: the preferred route; allows for smaller doses, better control of administration, better prediction of action.
  2. IM: still widely used; needs larger dose, absorption may be delayed or erratic.
  3. SC: used occasionally for small doses of nonirritating drugs.

Assessment

A. Client's perception of pain/discomfort
B. Baseline vital signs for later comparison
C. Known allergies
D. Current status of labor: medications best given in active phase of first stage of labor
E. Time of previous doses of medications

Analysis

Nursing diagnoses for labor analgesia may include
A. Pain
B. Ineffective individual coping
C. Knowledge deficit

Planning and Implementation

A. Goals
  1. Medication will relieve maternal discomfort.
  2. Maternal comfort will be achieved with least effect of medication on fetus.
B. Interventions
  1. Administer medications on schedule to maximize maternal effect and minimize fetal effect.

2. Continue to observe maternal/fetal vital signs for side effects.
3. Explain to client that she must remain in bed with side rails up.
4. Record accurately drug used, time, amount, route, site, and client response.

Evaluation

A. Medication exerts intended effect.
B. Mother reports positive response to medication.
C. Fetus shows no ill effects from medication.
D. Labor is not affected by medication.

Anesthesia for Labor and Delivery

General Information

A. Removal of pain perception by the administration of medication to interrupt the transmission of nerve impulses to the brain.
B. May be administered by inhalation, IV, or regional routes.
C. All methods of labor and delivery anesthesia have their drawbacks; no one method is perfect.
D. Types of labor and delivery anesthesia
  1. Inhalation: mother inhales controlled concentration of gaseous medication.
    a. Administered by trained personnel only
    b. Methoxyflurane (Penthrane) and nitrous oxide commonly used
    c. Dangers include regurgitation and aspiration, uterine relaxation, and hemorrhage postdelivery.
  2. IV: rarely used in uncomplicated vaginal deliveries; may be used for cesarean birth (as induction anesthesia).
    a. Administered by trained personnel only
    b. Sodium pentothal commonly used
  3. Regional: medication introduced to specific areas to block pain impulses
    a. Always administered by skilled personnel
    b. Medications used include tetracaine (Pontocaine), lidocaine, bupivacaine (Marcaine), mepivacaine (Carbocaine)
    c. May block nerve at the root or in a peripheral area
      1) nerve root blocks
        a) *lumbar epidural:* may be given continuously or intermittently during labor, or at time of delivery; medication is injected over dura through lumbar interspace; absorption of drug is slower, with less hypotension; client should have no postspinal headache

b) *caudal:* may be given intermittently through labor, or at time of delivery; medication is injected through sacral hiatus into peridural space; client should have no postspinal headache

c) *subarachnoid (low spinal, saddle block):* given when delivery is imminent; medication is injected into spinal fluid; mother may experience postdelivery headache; keep flat for at least 6–8 hours postspinal and encourage oral fluids postdelivery to facilitate reversal of headache.

2) peripheral nerve blocks

a) *paracervical:* instillation of medication into cervix; rarely used during labor because of effect on fetus; useful only in first stage of labor.

b) *pudendal:* medication injected transvaginally to affect pudendal nerve as it passes behind ischial spines on either side of vagina; useful for delivery and episiotomy if needed.

c) *perineal (local):* injected into the perineum at the time of delivery in order to perform an episiotomy

Assessment

A. Status of labor progress
B. Maternal/fetal vital signs
C. Allergies
D. Effects of medication on client (she may need help pushing)
E. Level of anesthesia
F. Return of sensation after anesthesia

Analysis

Nursing diagnoses for anesthesia during labor and delivery may include
A. Impaired physical mobility
B. High risk for alteration in tissue perfusion
C. Knowledge deficit
D. High risk for altered urinary elimination

Planning and Implementation

A. Goals
  1. Pain relief will be obtained.
  2. Healthy maternal/fetal status will be maintained.
B. Interventions
  1. Assist client to empty bladder.
  2. Assist client to assume appropriate position.

a. Inhalation anesthesia: supine with wedge under right hip to displace gravid uterus off inferior vena cava
b. Pudendal and perineal: on back or left side
c. Other regional types: on left side or sitting up

3. Check maternal blood pressure and fetal heart rate every 3–5 minutes until stable, then every 15 minutes or prn.
4. If blood pressure drops, turn client on left side, administer oxygen, and notify physician.

Evaluation

A. Client experiences expected pain relief.
B. Fetus exhibits no untoward effects, FHTs remain relatively stable.
C. Labor and delivery carried out as expected.
D. Client's vital signs remain within normal limits.

OPERATIVE OBSTETRICAL PROCEDURES

Episiotomy

A. General information
  1. Incision made in the perineum to enlarge the vaginal opening for delivery
  2. Client usually anesthetized in some manner
  3. Types
    a. Midline or median: from posterior vaginal opening through center of perineum toward anal sphincter.
      1) most frequently used
      2) easily done, least discomfort for client
      3) danger of extension into anal sphincter
    b. Mediolateral: begins at posterior vaginal opening but angles off to left or right at 45 degree angle (rarely in U.S.).
      1) done when need for additional enlargement of vaginal opening is a possibility
      2) mediolateral episiotomy usually more uncomfortable than median
  4. Advantages of episiotomy are
    a. Enlarging of vaginal opening
    b. Second stage of labor shortened
    c. Stretching of perineal muscles minimized
    d. Tearing of perineum may be prevented.
  5. Those opposed to episiotomies argue
    a. Kegel exercises can prepare the perineum to stretch for delivery.
    b. Lacerations may occur anyway.
  6. Side-lying delivery minimizes the strain on the perineum and may, if used, reduce incidence of episiotomies.

B. Nursing interventions
1. Apply ice packs to perineal area in first 12 hours to help alleviate pain and swelling.
2. Help promote healing with warm sitz baths after first 12 hours.
3. Observe episiotomy site for signs of infection or hematoma.
4. Instruct client about perineal hygiene.

Forceps Delivery

A. General information
1. Obstetrician's use of special spoon-shaped instruments to effect the delivery of the baby and shorten the second stage of labor
2. Types
   a. Low or outlet: presenting part at vaginal introitus
   b. Mid forceps: presenting part is at or below ischial spines; often a difficult procedure; rarely done.
   c. High forceps: presenting part above ischial spines. This procedure has been replaced by cesarean birth.
3. Requirements for application of forceps
   a. Fully dilated cervix
   b. Presenting part engaged
   c. Vertex or face presentation
   d. Ruptured membranes
   e. No pelvic contractures or disproportions
   f. Bowel and bladder emptied
4. Situations necessitating use
   a. Maternal exhaustion
   b. Fetal distress
   c. Failure of internal rotation
   d. Nerve root anesthesia (client cannot push)
   e. Maternal heart disease
   f. Poor descent of fetus through birth canal
B. Nursing interventions
1. Anticipate request for forceps if possible.
2. Monitor FHTs continuously.
3. Explain procedure to client if awake, advise mother/family about possible presence of slight bruising that will go away.

Cesarean Birth

General Information

A. Delivery of the baby through an incision into the abdominal wall and uterus
B. Indications
1. Cephalopelvic disproportion (most frequent reason)
2. Fetal distress
3. Breech presentation, especially in a primipara
4. Placenta previa/placenta abruptio
5. Prolapsed cord
6. Ineffective uterine contractions
7. Maternal diabetes
8. Malpresentations
9. Multiple births
10. Previous cesarean births
11. Other obstetric emergencies and conditions
C. Types
1. Classical: vertical incisions made into both abdomen and uterus
   a. Used when rapid delivery is important, as in fetal distress, prolapsed cord, placenta abruptio
   b. Maternal bleeding greater with this method; client may have increased risk of uterine rupture of scar tissue with future pregnancies; not usually a candidate for vaginal birth in future pregnancies.
2. Low cervical/low segment: transverse incisions made in abdomen (above pubic hairline) and in uterus
   a. Most common method used
   b. Procedure may take longer than classic because of need to deflect bladder, but blood loss is lessened and adhesions are fewer.
   c. Vaginal birth after this type of cesarean birth (VBAC) is a possibility.

Preoperative

A. Assessment
1. Maternal/fetal responses to labor
2. Indications for cesarean birth
3. Blood and urine test results
B. Analysis: nursing diagnoses for the preoperative phase of cesarean birth may include
1. Fear
2. Knowledge deficit
3. Powerlessness
4. Disturbance in self-concept
C. Planning and implementation
1. Goals
   a. Client prepared for surgery carefully and competently.
   b. Client will have procedures explained to her.
2. Interventions
   a. Shave/prep abdomen and pubic area.
   b. Insert retention catheter into bladder.
   c. Administer preoperative medications as ordered.
   d. Explain all procedures to client.
   e. Provide emotional support to client/family as needed.
   f. Complete all preoperative charting responsibilities.
D. Evaluation
1. Client adequately prepared for surgery

2. Client understands all procedures

Postoperative

A. Assessment
   1. Maternal vital signs
   2. Observation of incision for signs of infection
   3. I&O
   4. Level of consciousness/return of sensation
   5. Fundal firmness and location
   6. Lochia: color, amount, clots, odor
B. Analysis: nursing diagnoses postoperatively for cesarean birth may include
   1. Alteration in comfort: pain
   2. High risk for fluid volume deficit
   3. High risk for alteration in parenting
   4. Altered family processes
C. Planning and implementation
   1. Goals
      a. Healing will be promoted.
      b. Bonding between mother/couple and baby will be promoted.
      c. No complications will ensue.
   2. Interventions
      a. Implement general postsurgical care (see page 165), and general postpartum care (see pages 485–492).
      b. Assist client with self-care as needed.
      c. Assist mother with baby care and handling as needed.
      d. Encourage client to verbalize reaction to all events.
      e. Reinforce any special discharge instructions from physician.
D. Evaluation
   1. Mother and baby tolerated procedures well
   2. No postoperative complications or infection
   3. Maternal/newborn bonding occurring

Sample Questions

11. The nurse is caring for a woman who is admitted to the hospital in active labor. What information is most important for the nurse to assess to avoid respiratory complications during labor and delivery?
    1. Family history of lung disease.
    2. Food or drug allergies.
    3. Number of cigarettes smoked daily.
    4. When the client last ate.
12. Jane S. is a gravida 1, in the active phase of stage 1 labor. The fetal position is LOA. When Jane's membranes rupture, the nurse should expect to see
    1. a large amount of bloody fluid.
    2. a moderate amount of clear to straw-colored fluid.

3. a small amount of greenish fluid.
4. a small segment of the umbilical cord.
13. The nurse is caring for a woman in stage 1 labor. The fetal position is LOA. When her membranes rupture, the nurse's first action should be to
    1. notify the physician.
    2. measure the amount of fluid.
    3. count the fetal heart rate.
    4. perform a vaginal examination.
14. Mary W.'s baby has just been delivered, and he weighs 9 lb 10 oz. After the delivery, the nurse notices that Mary is chilly and that her fundus has relaxed. The nurse administers the oxytocin that the physician orders. The nurse knows that it has had the expected effect when
    1. Mary states that she feels warmer now.
    2. Mary falls asleep.
    3. the baby cries.
    4. the uterus becomes firm.
15. Mary had a midline episiotomy performed at delivery. The primary purpose of the episiotomy is to
    1. allow forceps to be applied.
    2. enlarge the vaginal opening.
    3. eliminate the possibility of lacerations.
    4. eliminate the need for cesarean birth.
16. Ms. L. is admitted to the hospital in labor. Vaginal examination reveals that she is 8 cm dilated. At this point in her labor, which of the following statements would the nurse expect her to make?
    1. I can't decide what to name my baby.
    2. It feels good to push with each contraction.
    3. Take your hand off my stomach when I have a contraction.
    4. This isn't as bad as I expected.
17. The nurse is caring for a woman who is in labor. She is 8 cm dilated. To support her during this phase of her labor, the nurse should
    1. leave her alone most of the time.
    2. offer her a back rub during contractions.
    3. offer her sips of oral fluids.
    4. provide her with warm blankets.
18. Ms. L. is placed on an external fetal monitor. The nurse notices that the fetal heart rate is erratic during contractions but returns to baseline at the end of each contraction. This should be recorded as
    1. early decelerations.
    2. variable decelerations.
    3. late decelerations.
    4. fetal distress.
19. During labor, the nurse observes variable decelerations on the external fetal monitor. The best action for the nurse to take at this time is to
    1. apply an oxygen mask.
    2. change the woman's position to left side-lying.

3. get the woman out of bed and walk her around.
4. move the woman to the delivery room.
20. During delivery, a mediolateral episiotomy is performed and Ms. L. delivers a 7 lb 8 oz girl. To detect postpartum complications in Ms. L. as soon as possible, the nurse should be particularly alert for all of the following except
1. a foul lochial odor.
2. discomfort while sitting.
3. ecchymosis and edema of the perineum.
4. separation of the episiotomy wound edges.

Answers and Rationales

11. The correct answer is 4. Gastric motility is decreased in pregnancy. Food eaten several hours prior to the onset of labor may still be in the stomach undigested. This will influence the type of anesthesia the client may receive. Client history of lung disease would be more important than family history at this time. Information on food or drug allergies will not help avoid respiratory complications during labor. Information on the number of cigarettes smoked per day will not help avoid respiratory complications during labor.
12. The correct answer is 2. With the baby in a vertex, LOA presentation and no other indicators of distress, amniotic fluid should have a clear to straw-colored appearance. Too much or too little amniotic fluid may be an indication of congenital anomalies in the fetus.
13. The correct answer is 3. Immediately after the rupture of membranes, fetal heart tones are checked, then checked again after the next contraction or after 5–10 minutes. With the fetus in a LOA presentation, there is less chance for a prolapsed cord. However, if the FHR drops significantly at any of the above times, a sterile vaginal exam is indicated.
14. The correct answer is 4. Oxytoxic medications such as Pitocin, Methergine, and Ergotrate are administered to stimulate uterine contractility and reverse fundal relaxation in the postdelivery client.
15. The correct answer is 2. An episiotomy is an incision made in the perineum to enlarge the vaginal opening, allowing additional room for the birth of the baby. An episiotomy reduces the likelihood of perineal lacerations but does not eliminate it. Cesarean birth for women with large babies is related to the size of the pelvis not the size of the vaginal opening.

16. The correct answer is 3. At 8 cm dilated the client is in the transition stage of her labor. Many women experience hyperesthesia of the skin at this time and would not want to be touched during a contraction. Transition is the most difficult stage of labor. The client would not be trying to decide what to name the baby at this time. The client would not be instructed to push until the cervix is fully dilated.
17. The correct answer is 2. The counterpressure of a back rub during a contraction may relieve discomfort. The nurse should stay with the client at this time. The client should not be having sips of water by mouth at this time. She will most likely be getting IV fluids. The client will most likely be hot because of the increased metabolic demands of labor.
18. The correct answer is 2. Variable decelerations are frequently caused by transient fetal pressure on the cord and are not a sign of fetal distress. A change in the mother's position will usually relieve the problem. Early deceleration is normal. It is characterized by a drop in fetal heart rate early in the contraction, typically due to head compression. Late deceleration is characterized by a drop in fetal heart rate late in the contraction. This is indicative of placental insufficiency. The client should be turned on her left side and prepared for possible C-section. The client's monitor does not indicate fetal distress. Late deceleration would indicate fetal distress.
19. The correct answer is 2. Changing the position of the mother will relieve transient pressure on the umbilical cord. The fetus is not in distress at this time so there is no need for oxygen. Labor has progressed too far to permit ambulation. The client is not ready for the delivery room because she is only 8 cm dilated. Progression to full dilation might still take two hours for a primipara; variable time for a multipara.
20. The correct answer is 2. Discomfort while sitting is normal following an episiotomy. A foul lochial odor could be a sign of infection. Ecchymosis and edema of the perineum might indicate a prolonged labor, an unusually large infant, a difficult fetal lie or presentation, or forceps delivery. In such instances recovery would be prolonged. Separation of the episiotomy wound edges might be due to infection or trauma. In this case the episiotomy wound would have to heal by second (wound left open to heal) or third (wound resutured) intention.

The Postpartum Period

OVERVIEW

Physical Changes of the Postpartum Period

A. The postpartum period is defined as that period of time, usually six weeks, in which the mother's body experiences anatomic and physiologic changes that reverse the body's adaptation to pregnancy; may also be called *involution*.

B. Begins with the delivery of the placenta and ends when all body systems are returned to, or nearly to, their prepregnant state.

C. May or may not include the return of the ovulatory/menstrual cycle.

Specific Body System Changes

Reproductive System

A. Uterus: a rapid reversal in size
1. Palpated after delivery below the umbilicus, the uterus regresses approximately 1 fingerbreadth (1 cm) per day until, by the end of the second week postpartum it is a pelvic organ and cannot be palpated through the abdominal wall.
2. The process is accomplished by cell size reduction.
3. The endometrial surface is sloughed off as *lochia,* in three stages
   a. *Lochia rubra:* dark red color, days 1–3 after delivery; consists of blood and cellular debris from decidua.
   b. *Lochia serosa:* pinkish brown, days 4–10; mostly serum, some blood, tissue debris.
   c. *Lochia alba:* yellowish white, days 11–21; mostly leukocytes, with decidua, epithelial cells, mucus.
4. Lochia has a particular, musty odor. Foul-smelling lochia, however, may indicate infection. Some small clots may be normal immediately after delivery; large clots signify the need for close investigation.
5. The placental site heals by means of exfoliative shedding, a process that allows the upward growth of the new endometrium and the prevention of scar tissue at the old placental site. This process may take six weeks.

B. Cervix
1. Flabby immediately after delivery; closes slowly.
2. Admits one fingertip by the end of one week after delivery.
3. Shape of external os changed by delivery from round to slitlike opening

C. Vagina
1. Edematous after delivery
2. May have small lacerations
3. Smooth-walled for 3–4 weeks, then rugae reappear
4. Hypoestrogenic until ovulation and menstruation resume

D. Ovulation/menstruation
1. First cycle is usually anovulatory.
2. If not lactating, menses may resume in 4–6 weeks.
3. If lactating, menses less predictable; may resume in 12–24 weeks.

E. Breasts
1. Nonlactating woman
   a. Prolactin levels fall rapidly.
   b. May still secrete colostrum for 2–3 days.
   c. Engorgement of breast tissue resulting from temporary congestion of veins and lymphatic circulation occurs on third day, lasts 24–36 hours, usually resolves spontaneously.
   d. Client should wear tight bra to compress ducts and use cold applications to reduce swelling.
2. Lactating woman
   a. High level of prolactin immediately after delivery of placenta continued by frequent contact with nursing baby.
   b. Initial secretion is colostrum, with increasing amounts of true breast milk appearing between 48–96 hours.
   c. Milk "let-down" reflex caused by oxytocin from posterior pituitary released by sucking.
   d. Successful lactation results from the complex interaction of infant sucking reflexes and the maternal production and let-down of milk.

Abdominal Wall/Skin

A. May need six weeks to reestablish good muscle tone.

B. Stretch marks gradually disappear or fade to silvery appearance.

Cardiovascular System

A. Normal blood loss in delivery of single infant is less than 500 cc (up to 1000 cc normal blood loss for a c-section).

B. Hematocrit usually returns to prepregnancy value within 4–6 weeks.
C. WBC count increases.
D. Increased clotting factors remain for several weeks leaving woman at risk for problems with thrombi.
E. Varicosities regress.

Urinary System

A. May have difficulty voiding in immediate postpartum period as a result of urethral edema.
B. Voiding reflex may be altered.
C. Marked diuresis begins within 12 hours of delivery; increases volume of urinary output as well as perspiration loss.
D. Lactosuria may be seen in nursing mothers.
E. Many women will show slight proteinuria during first 1–2 days of involution.

Gastrointestinal System

A. Mother usually hungry after delivery; good appetite is expected.
B. May still experience constipation from lack of muscle tone in abdomen and intestinal tract, and perineal soreness.

Other

All other systems experience normal and rapid regression to prepregnancy status.

POSTPARTAL PSYCHOSOCIAL CHANGES

Adaptation to Parenthood

Motor Skills

New parents must learn new physical skills to care for infant (e.g., feeding, holding, burping, changing diapers, skin care).

Attachment Skills

A. *Bonding:* the development of a caring relationship with the baby. Behaviors include
   1. Claiming: identifying the ways in which the baby looks or acts like members of the family.
   2. Identification: establishing the baby's unique nature (assigning the baby his or her own name).
   3. Attachment is facilitated by positive feedback between baby and caregivers.
B. Sensual responses enhance adaptation to parenthood.

1. Touch: from fingertip, to open palm, to enfolding; touch is an important communication with the baby.
2. Eye-to-eye contact: a cultural activity that helps to form a trusting relationship.
3. Voice: parents await the baby's first cry; babies respond to the higher-pitched voice that parents use in talking to the baby.
4. Odor: babies quickly identify their own mother's breast milk by odor.
5. Entrainment: babies move in rhythm to patterns of adult speech.
6. Biorhythm: babies respond to maternal heartbeats.

Maternal Adjustment

Takes place in three phases.

Dependent/"Taking In"

A. 1–2 days after delivery.
B. Mother's needs predominate; mother passive and dependent.
C. Mother needs to talk about labor and delivery experiences to integrate them into the fabric of her life.
D. Mother may need help with everyday activities, as well as child care.
E. Food/sleep important.

Dependent/Independent/"Taking Hold"

A. By third day mother begins to reassert herself.
B. Identifies own needs, especially for teaching and help with her own and baby's needs.
C. Some emotional lability, may cry "for no reason."
D. Mother requires reassurance that she can perform tasks of motherhood.

Independent/"Letting Go"

A. Usually evident by fifth or sixth week.
B. Shows pattern of life-style that includes new baby but still focuses on entire family as unit.
C. Reestablishment of father-mother bond seen in this period.
D. Mother may still feel tired and overwhelmed by responsibility and conflicting demands on her time and energies.

ASSESSMENT

Physical

A. Vital signs
   1. Individual protocol until stable, then at least once every 8 hours.

2. Temperature over 100.4°F (37.8°C) after first 24 hours, lasting more than 48 hours, indicative of infection.
B. Fundus
   1. Should be firm, in midline, slightly below umbilicus immediately after delivery.
   2. After 12 hours should rise to level of umbilicus, or 1 cm above.
   3. Should regress 1 cm/day thereafter until end of second week.
   4. Assessment should always be done with client's bladder empty.
C. Lochia: color, amount, clots, odor
D. Perineum
   1. Healing of episiotomy
   2. Hematoma formation
   3. Development of hemorrhoids
E. Breasts: firmness, condition of nipples
F. Elimination patterns: voiding, flatus, bowels
G. Legs: pain, warmth, tenderness indicating thrombosis
H. Perform foot dorsiflexion (Homan's sign)

Psychosocial Adjustment

A. Overall emotional status of parents
B. Parents' knowledge of infant needs
C. Previous experience of parents
D. Physical condition of infant
E. Ethnocultural background and financial status of parents
F. Additional family support available to parents

ANALYSIS

Nursing diagnoses for the postpartum period may include
A. Alteration in bowel elimination: constipation
B. Knowledge deficit
C. Self-care deficit
D. Alteration in pattern of urinary elimination
E. Alteration in family process
F. High risk for alteration in parenting
G. Disturbance in self-concept: role performance
H. Pain

PLANNING AND IMPLEMENTATION

Goals

A. Involution and return to prepregnancy state will be accomplished without complication.
B. Parental role(s) will be successfully assumed.
C. New baby will be successfully integrated into family structure.
D. Successful infant feeding patterns (bottle- or breast-feeding) will be established

Interventions

Physical Care

A. Assess mother according to individual needs during first critical hours after delivery; implement nursing interventions as needed.
B. Implement routine postpartum care after first hours.
   1. Administer medications as ordered (e.g., antilactational, oxytocins, analgesics).
   2. Teach perineal care.
   3. Perform other care as needed (e.g., heat, cold applications).
   4. Measure first voiding for sufficiency, observe I&O for first 24 hours.
   5. Assist with breast-feeding as needed.
C. Encourage measures to promote bowel function: roughage in diet, ambulation, sufficient fluids, attention to urge to defecate. Reassure about integrity of episiotomy.

Adjustment to Parenthood

A. Provide time for parents to be alone with baby in crucial early time after delivery.
B. Identify learning needs of parents.
C. Plan teaching to include both parents where possible.
D. Help parents realize that fatigue is normal at this time.
E. Help parents identify and strengthen their own coping mechanisms.
F. Help parents identify resources available to them.
G. Promote positive self-esteem on part of parents as they learn new role(s).
H. Provide anticipatory guidance for after discharge.
I. Provide information about contraception if requested.
J. Prepare for discharge: reinforce physician's instructions about activities, rest, diet, drugs, exercise, resumption of sexual intercourse, return for postpartum examination.

Infant Feeding

The first year of life is a time of rapid growth and development, necessitating sufficient and appropriate intake of nutrients. The goals of infant nutrition are to provide these nutrients without subjecting the newborn to undue stress.
A. Choices in newborn nutrition
   1. Breast-feeding: also called lactation; provides exact type and distribution of nutrients needed by human newborn in amounts needed.
      a. Initiated by prolactin, which stimulates milk production.
      b. Also affected by oxytocin, which

causes "let-down" or delivery of milk to nursing baby.

2. Formula-feeding (bottle-feeding): utilizes modified cow's milk, goat's milk, or soy formulas as basis for provision of 20 kcal/oz.

   a. Formulas are widely available in ready-to-feed, concentrated, and powdered forms.

   b. They have supplemental vitamins; may also contain added iron.

   c. Concentrated and powdered forms require addition of prescribed amounts of water for appropriate reconstitution.

   d. Sterilization of prepared formulas may be recommended; methods are
      1) terminal heating method: formula and bottles prepared using clean technique; entire batch sterilized at end of preparation
      2) aseptic method: sterile technique and sterile water used to prepare individual bottles and formula

B. Nursing measures to promote successful infant feeding

   1. Assess previous experience and knowledge of process of infant feeding.
   2. Demonstrate how to hold baby for breast-feeding and for feeding with formula.
   3. Show how to burp baby.
   4. Allow time for practice with selected feeding method.
   5. Provide positive reinforcement for successful actions.
   6. Give written instructions for at-home reference.
   7. Help parents identify progress and pleasure in feeding infant.
   8. If bottle-feeding, demonstrate how to prepare formula using appropriate method.
   9. If breast-feeding, assess breasts for tenderness or discomfort, and examine nipples for cracks, bleeding, soreness, and erectility.
   10. Assist mother with preparation: clean hands, comfortable position, support as needed (extra pillows). Demonstrate alternate infant positioning, e.g., "football hold."
   11. Bring infant to nurse as soon as possible after delivery.
   12. Demonstrate positioning of baby at breast, initiate rooting reflex, place entire nipple and as much of areola as possible into baby's mouth, depress fleshy part of breast away from baby's nose if needed.
   13. Allow baby to nurse in short frequent periods, lengthening gradually in later days. Alternate breast offered first.
   14. Help mother release baby from nipple by

TABLE 6.9 Tips for Successful Breast-Feeding

Breast care	Do not use soap on nipples or areola. Expose nipples to air to toughen them. Know how to pump breast milk if necessary and how to store expressed breast milk.
Nutrition	Need for good maternal nutrition while nursing. ■ Additional 500 kcal/day ■ 2–3 liters fluid/day Know that certain foods may make the baby fussy and will need to be avoided.
Comfort	Wear well-fitting bra; use absorbent pads without plastic coating if leaking occurs. Mild uterine cramping during nursing normal at first.
Medications	Avoid medications excreted in breast milk (mother should check with physician before taking any drug while nursing). Birth control pills should not be taken while nursing (decreases milk production).
Sources of help	Inform mother of community support groups available for nursing mothers.

breaking suction of baby on nipple. Check for nipple trauma.

15. Help mother move baby to alternate breast if needed.
16. Remain with mother at each feeding until she feels confident: see also Table 6.9 for additional information on breast-feeding.
17. Assist bottle-feeding mother with suppression of lactation, accomplished primarily by mechanical inhibition.

    a. Mechanical inhibition: usually takes 48–72 hours
       1) snug breast binder for 2–3 days postdelivery
       2) applications of cold (ice packs) and analgesia to relieve discomfort
       3) avoidance of heat or other stimuli to breasts that increase milk production (including breast pumps)
       4) a well-fitting bra until lactation is suppressed

    b. No approved medications to suppress lactation.

EVALUATION

A. Involution successfully initiated and progressing without complication
B. Parents begin to assume new role behaviors and identities
C. Beginning integration of newborn into family structure; bonding established
D. Infant feeding techniques mastered; infant growing and developing appropriately
E. Parents comfortable about infant care techniques and can demonstrate knowledge

Teaching: Postpartum/Discharge

A. Postpartum
  1. Normal events of postpartum period: physical, psychosocial
  2. Information about feeding her infant
  3. Basic infant care, including cord care, bathing, circumcision care, dressing, handling, signs of illness
  4. Safety needs of infant
  5. Recommendations concerning activities
  6. Specific teaching about any medications
B. Discharge
  1. Reinforcement of all postpartum teaching, allowing parent(s) time to ask questions.
  2. Referrals to professional assistance (MD, CNM, hospital's maternity unit, etc.).
  3. Referrals to appropriate community assistance groups (Nursing Mothers, Mothers of Twins, etc.) that meet individual needs.
  4. Scheduled appointments for postpartal examination/newborn's first well-baby examination.
  5. Literature to reinforce all teaching. Excitement and anxiety of discharge may interfere with learning; literature will be available for quick reference.

COMPLICATIONS OF THE POSTPARTUM PERIOD

Postpartum Hemorrhage

A. General information
  1. A major cause of maternal death
  2. Loss of more than 500 ml blood at the time of delivery or immediately thereafter is considered postpartum hemorrhage.
  3. Major causes include
    a. Uterine atony: loss of muscle tone in the uterus; may be the result of overdistension (large baby, multiple pregnancy, polyhydramnios), overmassage, maternal exhaustion, inhalation anesthesia
    b. Laceration of the birth canal (cervix, vagina, labia, perineum)
    c. Retained placental fragments or incomplete expulsion of placenta (usually the cause of late postpartum hemorrhage)
    d. Placenta accreta: penetration of the myometrium by the trophoblast, resulting in abnormal adherence of the placenta to the uterine wall. Rare; requires manual removal of the placenta
B. Assessment findings
  1. "Boggy" uterus, relaxed state indicating atony
  2. If uterus is firm with excess bleeding, may indicate lacerations.
  3. Dark red blood, with clots
    a. Large amounts with atony
    b. Steady trickle with lacerations
  4. Hemorrhage immediately after delivery with atony or lacerations
  5. With retained placental fragments, delay of up to two weeks
  6. With severe blood loss, signs and symptoms of shock
  7. Full bladder may displace uterus and prevent it from contracting firmly.
C. Nursing interventions
  1. Identify clients at risk for condition.
  2. Monitor fundus frequently if bleeding occurs; when stable, every 15 minutes for 1–2 hours, then at appropriate intervals.
  3. Monitor maternal vital signs for indications of shock.
  4. Administer medications, IV fluids as ordered.
  5. Measure I&O.
  6. Remain with client for support and explanation of procedures.
  7. Keep client warm.
  8. Prepare for client's return to delivery room if needed for repair of laceration or removal of placental fragment.
  9. Monitor for signs of DIC.

Thrombophlebitis

A. General information
  1. Formation of a thrombus when a vein wall is inflamed
  2. May be seen in the veins of the legs or pelvis
  3. May result from injury, infection, or the normal increase in circulating clotting factors in the pregnant and newly delivered woman.
B. Assessment findings
  1. Pain/discomfort in area of thrombus (legs, pelvis, abdomen)
  2. If in the leg, pain, edema, redness over affected area
  3. Elevated temperature and chills
  4. Peripheral pulses may be decreased
  5. Positive Homan's sign
  6. If in a deep vein, leg may be cool and pale
C. Nursing interventions
  1. Maintain bed rest with leg elevated on pillow. Never raise knee gatch on bed.
  2. Apply moist heat as ordered.
  3. Administer analgesics as ordered.
  4. Provide bed cradle to keep sheets off leg.
  5. Administer anticoagulant therapy as ordered (usually heparin), and observe client for signs of bleeding.
  6. Apply elastic support hose if ordered, with daily inspection of legs with hose removed.

7. Teach client *not* to massage legs.
8. Allow client to express fears and reactions to condition.
9. Observe client for signs of pulmonary embolism.
10. Continue to bring baby to mother for feeding and interaction.

Subinvolution

A. General information
   1. Failure of the uterus to revert to prepregnant state through gradual reduction in size and placement
   2. May be caused by infection, retained placental fragments, or tumors in the uterus
B. Assessment findings
   1. Uterus remains enlarged
   2. Fundus higher in the abdomen than anticipated
   3. Lochia does not progress from rubra to serosa to alba
   4. If caused by infection, possible leukorrhea and backache
C. Nursing interventions
   1. Teach client to recognize unusual bleeding patterns.
   2. Teach client usual pattern of uterine involution.
   3. Instruct client to report abnormal bleeding to physician.
   4. Administer oxytoxic medications if ordered.

Postpartum Infection

A. General information
   1. Any infection of the reproductive tract, associated with giving birth, usually occurring within 10 days of the birth
   2. Predisposing factors include
      a. Prolonged rupture of membranes
      b. Cesarean birth
      c. Trauma during birth process
      d. Maternal anemia
      e. Retained placental fragments
   3. Infection may be localized or systemic
B. Assessment findings
   1. Temperature of 100.4°F (37.8°C) or more for 2 consecutive days, excluding the first 24 hours
   2. Abdominal, perineal, or pelvic pain
   3. Foul-smelling vaginal discharge
   4. Burning sensation with urination
   5. Chills, malaise
   6. Rapid pulse and respirations
   7. Elevated WBC count (may be normal for postpartum initially), positive culture/sensitivity report for causative organism
C. Nursing interventions

1. Force fluids: client may need more than 3 liters/day.
2. Administer antibiotics and other medications as ordered.
3. Treat symptoms as they arise (e.g., warm sitz bath for infection in episiotomy).
4. Encourage high-calorie, high-protein diet to promote tissue healing.
5. Position client in semi- to high-Fowler's to promote drainage and prevent reflux higher into reproductive tract.
6. Support mother if isolated from baby.

Mastitis

A. General information
   1. Infection of the breast, usually unilateral
   2. Frequently caused by cracked nipples in the nursing mother
   3. Causative organism usually hemolytic *S. aureus*
   4. If untreated, may result in breast abscess.
B. Assessment findings
   1. Redness, tenderness, or hardened area in the breast
   2. Maternal chills, malaise
   3. Elevated vital signs, especially temperature and pulse
C. Nursing interventions
   1. Teach/stress importance of hand washing to nursing mother, and wash own hands before touching client's breast.
   2. Administer antibiotics as ordered.
   3. Apply ice if ordered between feedings.
   4. Empty breast regularly: baby may continue to nurse or have mother use hospital-grade pump.

Urinary Tract Infection

A. General information: may be caused postpartally by coliform bacteria, coupled with bladder trauma during the delivery, or a break in technique during catheterization.
B. Assessment findings
   1. Pain in the suprapubic area or at the costovertebral angle
   2. Fever
   3. Burning, urgency, frequency on urination
   4. Increased WBC count and hematuria
   5. Urine culture positive for causative organism
C. Nursing interventions
   1. Check status of bladder frequently in postpartum client.
   2. Use nursing measures to encourage client to void.
   3. Force fluids: may need minimum of 3 liters/day.
   4. Catheterize client if ordered, using sterile technique.
   5. Administer medications as ordered.

6. Monitor status of progress through continuing lab tests.
7. Support mother with explanations of interventions.
8. No need for baby to be separated from mother.

Sample Questions

21. On the second day postpartum, the nurse asks the new mother to describe her vaginal bleeding. The nurse should expect her to say that it is
    1. red and moderate.
    2. red with clots.
    3. scant and brown.
    4. thin and white.
22. Ms. S. delivers a 6 lb 4 oz (2835 g) baby boy. Which of the following statements would indicate to the nurse that the mother has begun to integrate her new baby into the family structure?
    1. All this baby does is cry. He's not like my other child.
    2. I wish he had curly hair like my husband.
    3. My parents wanted a granddaughter.
    4. When he yawns, he looks just like his brother.
23. Ms. D., a diabetic, plans to breast-feed her baby. The nurse explains that, if she is hyperglycemic,
    1. the glucose content of her breast milk may be high.
    2. the production of milk may be impaired.
    3. her baby will receive insulin in the milk.
    4. her blood sugar will be extremely difficult to manage.
24. Gerry C. and her roommate, Anne B., each delivered a child two days ago. Gerry is breast-feeding; Anne is using formula. Which of the following instructions can the nurse give to both mothers?
    1. Wear a good, well-supporting bra.
    2. Apply warm compresses to breast if too full.
    3. Apply cold compresses to breast if too full.
    4. Do not apply any soap to your nipples.
25. Because this is Gerry's third child, the nurse should not be surprised if Gerry complains of
    1. chest pain.
    2. afterbirth cramps.
    3. burning on urination.
    4. chills.
26. Connie A. delivered a male infant yesterday. While caring for her on her first postpartum day, which of the following behaviors would you expect?
    1. Asking specific questions about home care of the infant.
    2. Concern about when her bowels will move.

3. Frequent crying spells for unexplained reasons.
4. Acceptance of the nurse's suggestions about personal care.
27. Connie delivered this morning. Because this is Connie's first child, which of the following goals is most appropriate?
    1. Early discharge for mother and baby.
    2. Rapid adaptation to role of parent.
    3. Effective education of both parents.
    4. Minimal need for expression of negative feelings.
28. A new mother is going to breast-feed her baby. What is the best indication that the let-down reflex has been achieved in a nursing mother?
    1. Increased prolactin levels.
    2. Milk dripping from the opposite breast.
    3. Progressive weight gain in the infant.
    4. Relief of breast engorgement.
29. To prevent cracked nipples while she is breast-feeding, the mother should be taught to
    1. apply lanolin prior to feedings.
    2. nurse at least 20 minutes on each breast the first day.
    3. use plastic bra liners.
    4. wash her nipples with water only.
30. What is the best indication that the breast-fed baby is digesting the breast milk properly?
    1. The baby does not experience colic.
    2. The baby passes dark green, pasty stools.
    3. The baby passes soft, golden-yellow stools.
    4. The baby sleeps for several hours after each feeding.

Answers and Rationales

21. The correct answer is 1. Lochia rubra is moderate red discharge, present for the first 2–3 days postpartum. Multiple clots are a sign of lack of tone in the uterine musculature. Scant, brown discharge (lochia serosa) would be present 7–10 days after delivery. Thin, white discharge (lochia alba) begins around the tenth day and ends about three weeks following delivery.
22. The correct answer is 4. Family identification of the newborn is an important part of attachment. The first step in identification is defined in terms of likeness to family members. In 1, the mother is emphasizing a negative characteristic of the baby and comparing him unfavorably to her other child. In 2, the mother is wishing that he had curly hair like her husband; she is not looking at a positive characteristic of the baby that will fit in with the family. In 3, the mother is thinking that the baby should have been a girl instead of a boy.

23. The correct answer is 1. Glucose can be transferred from the serum to the breast, and hyperglycemia may be reflected in the breast milk. The production of milk will not be impaired because the mother is hyperglycemic. The baby will not receive insulin in the milk. If the mother is hyperglycemic her blood sugar will be no more difficult to manage. However, the nurse must stress the importance of keeping the blood sugar as close to normal as possible at all times.

24. The correct answer is 1. A well-fitting, supportive bra with wide straps can be recommended for both the nursing and the nonnursing mother, for the support of the breasts and for comfort. The nursing mother's bra should have front flaps over each breast for easy access during nursing periods.

25. The correct answer is 2. Afterbirth cramps are most common in nursing mothers and multiparas. Gerry falls into both of these categories. The release of oxytocin from the posterior pituitary for the "let-down" reflex of lactation causes the afterbirth cramping of the uterus. The other choices represent potentially pathologic symptoms on the second day postpartum and require further investigation.

26. The correct answer is 4. During the first few days after delivery, the mother is in a dependent phase, initiating little activity herself, and is usually content to be directed in her activities by a health care provider. The other choices represent behaviors that are seen after this dependent phase.

27. The correct answer is 3. Both parents will need education about the new baby: how to care for the baby, information about the baby, and how to be a parent. This education will have an information component, a skills component, and a psychologic component.

28. The correct answer is 2. The nursing infant will stimulate let-down, resulting in milk dripping from the other breast. Prolactin levels will be increased but this is not the best indicator of the let-down reflex. This is a long-term indicator of milk let-down. Breast engorgement will ultimately be relieved.

29. The correct answer is 4. Nipples should be washed with water (no soap) only to prevent drying. Lanolin should be applied after feeding. Twenty minutes on each breast the first day is much too long. The nursing mother should begin with 5 minutes on each breast, increasing to 10 minutes on each breast as tolerated. The breasts should be left open to air as much as possible. A plastic bra liner would create and hold in moisture.

30. The correct answer is 3. Breast-fed babies will pass 6–10 small, loose, yellow stools per day. There is no relationship between breast-fed babies and babies who experience colic. Dark green, pasty stools are seen in formula-fed infants. Sleeping relates more to the components of the milk and the fact that the baby is satisfied than the fact that the milk has been digested properly.

The Newborn

PHYSIOLOGIC STATUS OF THE NEWBORN

Circulatory

A. Umbilical vein and ductus venosus constrict after cord is clamped; these will become ligaments (2–3 months).

B. Foramen ovale closes functionally as respirations are established, but anatomic or permanent closure may take several months.

C. Ductus arteriosus constricts with establishment of respiratory function; later becomes ligament (2–3 months).

D. Heart rate averages 140 beats/minute at birth, with changes noted during sleep and activity.

E. Heart murmurs may be heard; usually have little clinical significance.

F. Average blood pressure is 78/42 mm Hg.

G. Peripheral circulation established slowly; may have mottled (blue/white) appearance for 24 hours (acrocyanosis).

H. RBC count high immediately after birth, then falls after first week; possible physiologic anemia of infancy.

I. Absence of normal flora in intestine of newborn results in low levels of vitamin K; prophylactic dose of vitamin K given on first day of life.

Respiratory

A. "Thoracic squeeze" in vaginal delivery helps drain fluids from respiratory tract; remainder of fluid absorbed across alveolar membranes into capillaries.

B. Adequate levels of surfactants (lecithin and sphingomyelin) ensure mature lung function; prevent alveolar collapse and respiratory distress syndrome.

C. Normal respiratory rate is 30–60 breaths/minute with short periods of apnea (<15 seconds); change noted during sleep or activity.

D. Newborns are obligate nose breathers.

E. Chest and abdomen rise simultaneously; no seesaw breathing.

Renal

A. Urine present in bladder at birth, but newborn may not void for first 12–24 hours; later pattern is 6–10 voidings/day, indicative of sufficient fluid intake.

B. Urine is pale and straw colored; initial voidings may leave brick-red spots on diaper from passage of uric acid crystals in urine.

C. Infant unable to concentrate urine for first three months of life.

Digestive

A. Newborn has full cheeks due to well-developed sucking pads.

B. Little saliva is produced.

C. Hard palate should be intact; small raised white areas on palate (*Epstein's pearls*) are normal.

D. Newborn cannot move food from lips to pharynx; nipple needs to be inserted well into mouth.

E. Circumoral pallor may appear while sucking.

F. Newborn is capable of digesting simple carbohydrates and protein but has difficulty with fats.

G. Immature cardiac (esophageal) sphincter may allow reflux of food when burped; place newborn on right side after feeding to prevent regurgitation.

H. Stomach capacity varies; approximately 50–60 ml.

I. First stool is meconium (black, tarry residue from lower intestine); usually passed within 12–24 hours after birth.

J. Transitional stools are thin and brownish green in color; after three days, milk stools are usually passed—loose and golden yellow for the breast-fed infant, formed and pale yellow for the formula-fed infant. Stools may vary in number from 1 every feeding to 1–2/day.

K. Feeding patterns vary; newborn may nurse vigorously immediately after birth, or may need as long as several days to learn to suck effectively. Provide support and encouragement to new mothers during this time as infant feeding is a very emotional area for new mothers.

Hepatic

A. Liver responsible for changing hemoglobin (from breakdown of RBC) into unconjugated bilirubin, which is further changed into conjugated (water-soluble) bilirubin that can be excreted.

B. Excess unconjugated bilirubin can permeate the sclera and the skin, giving a jaundiced or yellow appearance to these tissues.

C. The liver of a mature infant can maintain the level of unconjugated bilirubin at less than 12 mg/dl. Higher levels indicate a possible dysfunction and the need for intervention.

D. This physiologic jaundice is considered normal in early newborns. It begins to appear after 24 hours, usually between 48–72 hours (see page 501 for additional information on interventions for physiologic jaundice).

Temperature

A. Heat production in newborn accomplished by
   1. Metabolism of "brown fat," a special structure in newborn that is source of heat.
   2. Increased metabolic rate and activity.

B. Newborn cannot shiver as an adult does to release heat.

C. Newborn's body temperature drops quickly after birth; cold stress occurs easily (see page 495 for interventions to prevent heat loss).

D. Body stabilizes temperature in 8–10 hours if unstressed.

E. Cold stress increases oxygen consumption; may lead to metabolic acidosis and respiratory distress.

Immunologic

A. Newborn has passive acquired immunity from IgG from mother during pregnancy and passage of additional antibodies in colostrum and breast milk.

B. Newborn develops own antibodies during first three months, but is at risk for infection during first six weeks.

C. Ability to develop antibodies develops sequentially (see Table 5.1, page 359, for typical immunization schedule).

Neurologic/Sensory

Six States of Consciousness

A. Deep sleep

B. Light sleep: some body movements

C. Drowsy: occasional startle; eyes glazed

D. Quiet alert: few movements, but eyes open and bright

E. Active alert: active, occasionally fussy with much facial movement

F. Crying: much activity, eyes open or closed

Periods of Reactivity

A. First (birth through first ½ hour): newborn alert with good sucking reflex, irregular R/HR.
B. Second (4–8 hours after birth): may regurgitate mucus, pass meconium, and suck well
C. Equilibrium usually achieved by 8 hours of age.

Sleep Cycle

Newborn usually sleeps 17 hours/day.

Hunger Cycle

Varies, depending on mode of feeding.
A. Breast-fed infant may nurse every 2–3 hours.
B. Bottle-fed infant may be fed every 3–4 hours.

Special Senses

A. Sight: eyes are sensitive to light; newborn will fix and gaze at objects, especially those with black and white, regular patterns, but eye movements are uncoordinated.
B. Hearing: can hear before birth (24 weeks); newborn seems best attuned to human speech and its cadences.
C. Taste: sense of taste established; prefers sweet-tasting fluids; derives satisfaction as well as nourishment from sucking.
D. Smell: sense is developed at birth; newborn can identify own mother's breast milk by odor.
E. Touch: newborn is well prepared to receive tactile messages; mother demonstrates touch progression in initial bonding activities.

ASSESSMENT

Physical Examination

A. Weight
 1. Average between 2750 and 3629 g (6–8 lb) at term
 2. Initial loss of 5%–10% of body weight normal during first few days; should be regained in 1–2 weeks
B. Length: average 45.7–55.9 cm (18–22 in)
C. Head circumference: average 33–35.5 cm (13–14 in); remeasure after several days if significant molding or caput succedaneum present
D. Chest circumference: average 1.9 cm (¾ in) less than head
E. Abdominal girth may be measured if indicated. Consistent placement of tape is important for comparison, identification of abnormalities. Measurement is best done before feeding, as abdomen relaxes after a feeding.
F. Skin
 1. Color in Caucasian infants usually pink; varies with other ethnic backgrounds.
 2. Pigmentation increases after birth.
 3. Skin may be dry.
 4. Acrocyanosis of hands and feet normal for 24 hours; may develop "newborn rash" (erythema toxicum neonatorum).
 5. Small amounts of lanugo and vernix caseosa still seen.
G. Fontanels
 1. Anterior: diamond shaped
 2. Posterior: triangular
 3. Should be flat and open.
H. Ears
 1. Should be even with canthi of eyes.
 2. Cartilage should be present and firm.
I. Eyes
 1. May be irritated by medication instillation, some edema/discharge present.
 2. Color is slate blue.
J. Nodule of tissue present in breasts.
K. Female genitalia
 1. Vernix seen between labia.
 2. Blood-tinged mucoid vaginal discharge (pseudomenstruation) from high levels of circulating maternal hormones.
L. Male genitalia
 1. Testes descended or in inguinal canal
 2. Rugae cover scrotum
 3. Meatus at tip of penis
M. Legs
 1. Bowed
 2. No click or displacement of head of femur observed when hips flexed and abducted
N. Feet
 1. Flat
 2. Soles covered with creases in fully mature infant
O. Muscle tone
 1. Predominantly flexed
 2. Occasional transient tremors of mouth and chin
 3. Newborn can turn head from side to side in prone position
 4. Needs head supported when held erect or lifted
P. Reflexes present at birth
 1. Rooting, sucking, and swallowing.
 2. Tonic neck, "fencing" attitude.
 3. Grasp: newborn's fingers curl around anything placed in palm.
 4. *Moro reflex:* symmetric and bilateral abduction and extension of arms and hands; thumb and forefinger form a C; the "embrace" reflex.
 5. *Startle reflex:* similar to Moro, but with hands clenched.
 6. *Babinski's sign:* flare of toes when foot stroked from base of heel along lateral edge to great toe.
Q. Cry
 1. Loud and vigorous.
 2. Heard when infant is hungry, disturbed, or uncomfortable.

Apgar Scoring

A. Used to evaluate the newborn in five specific categories at 1 and 5 minutes after birth (see Table 6.7, page 475).
B. The 1-minute score reflects transitional values.
C. The composite score at 5 minutes provides the best direction for the planning of newborn care.
D. Composite score interpretations
   1. 0–4: prognosis for newborn is grave.
   2. 5–7: infant needs specialized, intensive care.
   3. 7 or above: infant should do well in normal newborn nursery.

Gestational Age Assessment

After birth, direct examination of the infant leads to an accurate assessment of maturity. This is important, as complications may vary with maturity level: pre- and postmature infants, in general, have greater difficulty adapting to extrauterine life.
A. Physical examination
   1. Skin: thickens with gestational age; may be dry/peeling if postmature.
   2. Lanugo: disappears as pregnancy progresses.
   3. Sole (plantar) creases: increase with gestational age (both depth and number).
   4. Areola of breast: at term, 5–10 mm in diameter.
   5. Ear: cartilage stiffens, recoil increases, and curvature of pinna increases with advancing gestational age.
   6. Genitalia: in the male, check for descended testicles and scrotal rugae; in the female, look for the labia majora to cover the labia minora and clitoris.
B. Neuromuscular assessment (best done after 24 hours)
   1. Resting posture: relaxed posture (extension) seen in the premature; flexion increases with maturity.
   2. Square window angle: flex hand onto underside of forearm, identify angle at which you feel resistance. Angle decreases with increasing gestational age.
   3. Arm recoil: flex infant's arms, extend for 5 seconds, then release. Note angle formed as arms recoil. Decreases with increasing gestational age.
   4. Popliteal angle: place infant on back, extend one leg, and measure angle at point of resistance. Angle becomes more acute as gestation progresses.
   5. Scarf sign: draw one arm across chest until resistance is felt; note relation of elbow to midline of chest. Resistance increases with advancing gestational age.
   6. Heel to ear: attempt to raise foot to ear, noting point at which foot slips from your grasp. Resistance increases with gestational age.

In performing gestational age assessments, the use of a specific form usually facilitates the ease and accuracy of the process.

ANALYSIS

Nursing diagnoses for the normal newborn are related to the potential for dysfunction in transition period and first few days of life.

PLANNING AND IMPLEMENTATION

Goals

A. Newborn will adapt to extrauterine life.
   1. Body temperature will be maintained.
   2. Normal breathing and adequate oxygenation will be established.
   3. Cardiovascular function will be stable.
   4. Nutrition and promotion of growth will be established.
B. Positive parent-infant relationship will be established.
C. Potential dysfunctions will be identified early.
D. Needed interventions will be implemented early.

Interventions

Delivery Room

A. Perform Apgar scoring at 1 and 5 minutes after birth.
B. Perform rapid, overall physical and neurologic exam.
   1. Identify obvious congenital anomalies.
   2. Count vessels in cord.
   3. Identify injuries from birth trauma.
C. Prevent heat loss.
   1. Dry infant immediately after birth.
   2. Wrap newborn warmly, cover head, or place in specially warmed area.
   3. Place newborn on warm surfaces (mother's body) or cover cool surfaces (e.g., scale).
   4. Minimize placement of newborn near cooler areas (windows, outside walls).
D. Maintain established respirations and heartbeat.
E. Identify mother and infant with matching bands.
F. Perform cord clamping if physician has not done so.
G. Allow parents to hold infant, or place in warmed area in Trendelenburg's position to facilitate drainage of mucus.
H. Suction gently prn with bulb syringe.

I. Administer oxygen prn.
J. Promote bonding through early nursing if mother so desires, or by having parents hold newborn.
K. Transfer to nursery at appropriate time.

Nursery

A. Continue actions to prevent heat loss (temperature done rectally on admission then axillary, tympanic not accurate on infants).
B. When temperature stabilizes, perform complete physical and neurologic exam.
C. Administer medications as ordered.
   1. To prevent ophthalmia neonatorum, administration of 0.5% erythromycin or 1% tetracycline into conjunctival sac(s).
   2. Vitamin K: prophylactic dose to prevent hemorrhage.
   3. Hepatitis B vaccine in first 12 hrs.
D. Measure and weigh newborn.
E. After temperature has stabilized, bathe and dress newborn, place in open crib.
F. Institute daily care routine.
   1. Take weight.
   2. Monitor temperature, apical pulse, respirations at least every shift.
   3. Suction prn.
   4. Bathe daily if ordered.
   5. Give diaper area care after each change.
   6. Continue assessment for anomalies.
   7. Clean cord with alcohol at each diaper change (triple dye may be applied at birth).
   8. Institute feeding schedule as ordered; may offer sterile water before formula is begun.
   9. Note voidings and stools on daily basis.
G. Assess for physiologic jaundice (see also Hyperbilirubinemia, page 501).
   1. First manifests in the head area (test by depressing skin over bridge of nose) then progresses to chest (depress skin over sternum).
   2. Early feedings promote excretion of bilirubin in urine and stool, diminishing incidence of jaundice.
   3. Prevention of cold stress in newborn diminishes incidence of jaundice.
   4. Loose, greenish stools and green-tinged urine are normal for these infants; advise mother.
   5. These infants need extra fluids to prevent dehydration and replace fluids being excreted.
   6. Advise parents that breast-fed infants may have increased jaundice.
      a. May not feed frequently enough in first 2 days and become dehydrated
      b. True breast-milk jaundice may occur only after 7–10 days. Breastfeeding may be discontinued for 24 hours to confirm diagnosis.

H. Provide phototherapy if ordered, not usually required in physiologic jaundice.
I. Monitor for pathologic jaundice.
   1. Appears at birth or in the first 24 hours.
   2. Bilirubin levels over 12 mg/dl (see Hyperbilirubinemia, page 501).
J. Male infants may need circumcision care.
   1. Observe for bleeding.
   2. Note first voiding after circumcision.
   3. Clean area appropriately.
   4. Vaseline to penis to prevent sticking to diaper.
K. Perform screening tests before discharge (PKU, hypothyroidism, etc.).
L. Provide teaching and demonstrations as indicated for parents (e.g., feeding, burping, holding, diapering, bathing, positioning, safety).

EVALUATION

A. Newborn progress continually observed, normal vital signs for newborn maintained
B. No dysfunctional patterns discerned
C. No congenital anomalies identified
D. Parents comfortable with infant, have initiated bonding
E. Parents comfortable with newborn care
F. All necessary tests carried out at correct time
G. Evidence for continued growth and development at home is positive

VARIATIONS FROM NORMAL NEWBORN ASSESSMENT FINDINGS

Some variations from the normal assessment findings in the newborn are not indicative of any disorders; others, however, provide information about likely gestational age or the possibility of the existence of a more serious disorder.

Weight

A. Under 2500 g (5½ lb): small for gestational age (SGA)
B. Over 4100 g (9 lb): large for gestational age (LGA)

Length

A. Under 45.7 cm (18 in): SGA
B. Over 55.9 cm (22 in): LGA

Head Circumference

A. Under 31.7 cm (12½ in): microcephaly/SGA
B. Over 36.8 cm (14½ in): hydrocephaly/LGA

Blood Pressure

A. Variation with activity: normal
B. Major difference between upper and lower extremities: possible aortic coarctation

Pulse

A. Persistently under 120: possible heart block
B. Persistently over 170: possible respiratory distress syndrome (see page 504)

Temperature

A. Elevated: possible dehydration or infection
B. Temperature falls with low environmental temperature, late in cold stress, sepsis, cardiac disease.

Respirations

A. Under 25/minute: possibly result of maternal analgesia
B. Over 60/minute: possible respiratory distress

Skin

A. Milia (blocked sebaceous glands, usually on nose and chin) are essentially normal.
B. "Stork bites"
   1. Capillary hemangiomas above eyebrows and at base of neck under hairline are essentially normal.
   2. Raised capillary hemangiomas on areas other than face or neck are *not* normal findings.
C. Newborn rash (erythema toxicum neonatorum) is normal.
D. Mongolian spots (darkened areas of pigmentation over sacral area and buttocks) are normal and fade in early childhood. (Seen in Asian and African-American babies.)
E. Fingernail scratches are normal.
F. Excess lanugo: possible prematurity.
G. Vernix
   1. Decreases after 38 weeks, full-term usually has only in creases
   2. Excess: prematurity

Head

A. Fontanels
   1. Depressed: dehydration
   2. Bulging: increased intracranial pressure
B. Hair: coarse or brittle, possible endocrine disorder
C. Scalp: edema present at birth (*caput succedaneum*) from pressure of cervix against presenting part; crosses suture lines; disappears in 3–4 days without intervention.
D. Skull: collection of blood between a skull bone and its periosteum (*cephalhematoma*) from pressure during delivery; does not cross suture line; appears 12–24 hours after delivery; regresses in 3–6 weeks.
E. Eyes
   1. Edema from medications not uncommon
   2. Strabismus (occasional crossing of eyes) is normal
   3. Wide space between eyes is seen in Fetal Alcohol Syndrome
F. Ears
   1. Lack of cartilage: possible prematurity
   2. Low placement: possible kidney disorder or Down's syndrome
G. Nose: copious drainage associated with syphilis
H. Mouth
   1. Thrush: appears as white patches in mouth; candida infection passed from mother during passage through birth canal.
   2. Tongue movement and excess salivation: possible esophageal atresia (see page 411).

Neck

Webbing; masses in muscle

Chest

Breast enlargement and milky secretion from breasts (witch's milk) is result of maternal hormones; self-limiting.

Cord

Fewer than three vessels may indicate congenital anomalies.

Female Genitalia

Pseudomenstruation is normal.

Male Genitalia

Misplaced urinary meatus
A. *Epispadias:* on upper surface of penis
B. *Hypospadias:* on under surface of penis

Upper Extremities

A. Extra fingers
B. Webbed fingers
C. Asymmetric movement: possible trauma or fracture

Lower Extremities

A. Extra toes
B. Webbed toes
C. Congenital hip dysplasia

D. Few creases on soles of feet: prematurity

Spine

Tuft of hair: possible occult spina bifida; assess pilonidal area for fistula.

Anus

Lack of meconium after 48 hours may indicate obstruction.

Sample Questions

31. Which nursing action should be included in the care of the infant with a caput succedaneum?
    1. Aspiration of the trapped blood under the periosteum.
    2. Explanation to the parents about the cause/prognosis.
    3. Gentle rubbing in a circular motion to decrease size.
    4. Application of cold to reduce size.
32. Baby girl J. was born at 9:15 A.M. At 9:20 A.M. her heart rate was 132 beats/minute, she was crying vigorously, moving all extremities, and only her hands and feet were still slightly blue. The nurse should enter her Apgar score as
    1. 7.
    2. 8.
    3. 9.
    4. 10.
33. Which of the following findings in a newborn baby girl does not indicate pathology?
    1. Passage of meconium within the first 24 hours.
    2. Respiratory rate of 70/minute at rest.
    3. Yellow skin tones at 12 hours of age.
    4. Bleeding from umbilicus.
34. Ms. S. delivers a 6 lb 5 oz (2863 g) boy. The nursery nurse carries the baby into his mother's room. Ms. S. states, "I think my baby's afraid of me. Every time I make a loud noise, he jumps." The nurse should
    1. encourage Ms. S. not to be so nervous with her baby.
    2. reassure her that this is a normal reflexive reaction for her baby.
    3. take the baby back to the nursery for a neurologic evaluation.

4. wrap the baby more tightly in warm blankets.
35. Ms. S. asks how much her 3-day-old baby weighs. When the nurse tells her 5 lb 11 oz (2580 g), she starts to cry because the baby is losing weight. The baby weighed 6 lb 5 oz (2863 g) at birth. What is the expected weight loss pattern in a newborn?
    1. None
    2. 5%
    3. 5%–10%
    4. 10%–15%

Answers and Rationales

31. The correct answer is 2. Caput succedaneum (scalp edema) will regress in a few days without interventions such as rubbing or applications of cold. Parents need to have this explained to them as well as what caused it, how it will regress without residual damage, etc. They also need time to express their feelings about this occurrence.
32. The correct answer is 3. Acrocyanosis, where hands and feet are still slightly blue for the first 24 hours, is a normal variant in the newborn, but it rates a 1 on the Apgar scale. All the other descriptors are rated 2 on the Apgar scale, giving this newborn a total of 9.
33. The correct answer is 1. Meconium is usually passed during the first 24 hours of life. The respiratory rate at rest is usually between 30 and 60; early jaundice indicates RBC breakdown before birth, and umbilical bleeding should not be occurring.
34. The correct answer is 2. The startle reflex, normally present in neonates, is characterized by symmetric extension and abduction of the arms with fingers extended. The parent perceives this response as jumping. The nurse should encourage the client to express concerns and ask questions about her baby. The baby does not need a neurological examination because the startle reflex is normal in newborns. The startle reflex is not related to the baby being cold. Wrapping the baby in warm blankets is not a proper approach.
35. The correct answer is 3. Within 3–4 days of birth, a weight loss of 5%–10% is normal.

The High-Risk Infant

OVERVIEW

High-risk infants are those whose incidence of illness or death is increased because of prematurity, dysmaturity, postmaturity, physical problems, or birth complications. They are frequently the result of a high-risk pregnancy.

ASSESSMENT

A. History of high-risk pregnancy or other factor possibly affecting fetal development
B. Apgar scores in the delivery room
C. Head-to-toe assessment of the infant (see Assessment of the normal newborn, page 494)
D. Determination of gestational age

ANALYSIS

A. Alteration in respiratory function
B. Alteration in nutrition: less than body requirements
C. High risk for impaired skin integrity
D. Alteration in tissue perfusion
E. High risk for injury
F. Impaired gas exchange
G. Ineffective thermoregulation
H. For parents of high-risk infants
   1. Ineffective family coping
   2. Knowledge deficit
   3. Anticipatory grieving
   4. Powerlessness
   5. Social isolation

PLANNING AND IMPLEMENTATION

Goals

A. Needs of infant for physical care will be met.
   1. Oxygen: respiratory functioning will be maintained.
   2. Humidity and warmth: temperature will be regulated and cold stress prevented.
   3. Adequate nutrition will be provided.
   4. Tender handling: newborn will receive proper skin care and positioning.
B. Infection or other complications will be prevented.
C. Normal growth and development will be promoted.

D. Needs of parents for closeness with infant will be met; attachment/bonding will be promoted.

Interventions

A. Constantly monitor infant for subtle changes in condition and intervene promptly when necessary.
B. Conserve infant's energy and decrease physiologic stress.
C. Provide appropriate stimulation for infant growth and development.
D. Allow parents to express their reactions and feelings and assist them in attachment behaviors.
E. Teach parents care of infant in preparation for discharge.

EVALUATION

A. Infant's physical condition stabilized and improved on a steady basis
B. Infant's growth and development steady and appropriate
C. Parents demonstrated acceptance of and comfort with infant's condition
D. Parents demonstrated comfort and confidence with infant care at discharge

HIGH-RISK DISORDERS

The Premature Infant

A. General information
   1. Any infant born before the end of the 37th week of pregnancy
   2. Weight usually less than 2500 g (5½ lb)
   3. Causes include
      a. Maternal factors: age, smoking, poor nutrition, placental problems, preeclampsia/eclampsia
      b. Fetal factors: multiple pregnancy, infection
      c. Other: socioeconomic status, environmental exposure to harmful substance
   4. Severity of problems related to level of maturity: the earlier the infant is born, the greater the chance of complications.
   5. Major complicating conditions
      a. Respiratory distress syndrome
      b. Thermoregulatory problems
      c. Conservation of energy

      d. Infection
      e. Hemorrhage

B. Assessment findings
  1. Respiratory system
    a. Insufficient surfactant
    b. Apneic episodes
    c. Retractions, nasal flaring, grunting, seesaw pattern of breathing, cyanosis
    d. Increased respiratory rate
  2. Thermoregulation: body temperature fluctuates easily (premature newborn has less subcutaneous fat and muscle mass)
  3. Nutritional status
    a. Poor sucking and swallowing reflexes
    b. Poor gag and cough reflexes
  4. Skin: lack of subcutaneous fat; reddened; translucent
  5. Drainage from umbilicus/eyes
  6. Cardiovascular
    a. Petechiae caused by fragile capillaries and prolonged prothrombin time
    b. Increased bleeding at injection sites
  7. Neuromuscular
    a. Poor muscle tone
    b. Weak reflexes
    c. Weak, feeble cry

C. Nursing interventions
  1. Maintain respirations at less than 60/minute, check every 1–2 hours.
  2. Administer oxygen as ordered; check concentration every 2 hours to avoid retrolental fibroplasia while providing adequate oxygenation.
  3. Auscultate breath sounds to assess lung expansion.
  4. Encourage breathing with gentle rubbing of back and feet.
  5. Suction as needed.
  6. Reposition every 1–2 hours for maximum lung expansion and prevention of exhaustion.
  7. Monitor blood gases and electrolytes.
  8. Maintain thermoneutral body temperature; prevent cold stress.
  9. Maintain appropriate humidity level.
  10. Monitor for signs of infection; these infants have little antibody production and decreased resistance.
  11. Feed according to abilities.
  12. Monitor sucking reflex; if poor, gavage feeding indicated. Most preterm infants require at least some gavage feeding as it diminishes the effort required for sucking while improving the caloric intake.
  13. Use "preemie" nipple if bottle-feeding.
  14. Monitor I&O, weight gain or loss; these infants are easily dehydrated, with poor electrolyte balance.
  15. Monitor for hypoglycemia and hyperbilirubinemia.
  16. Handle carefully; organize care to minimize disturbances.
  17. Provide skin care with special attention to cleanliness and careful positioning to prevent breakdown.
  18. Monitor heart rate and pattern at least every 1–2 hours; listen apically for 1 full minute.
  19. Monitor potential bleeding sites (umbilicus, injection sites, skin); these infants have lowered clotting factors.
  20. Monitor overall growth and development of infant; check weight, length, head circumference.
  21. Provide tactile stimulation when caring for or feeding infant.
  22. Provide complete explanations for parents.
  23. Encourage parental involvement in infant's care.
  24. Provide support for parents; refer to self-help group or other parents if necessary.
  25. Promote parental confidence with infant care before discharge.

The Dysmature Infant (SGA)

A. General information
  1. Birth weight in the lowest 10th percentile at term
  2. Causes: discounting heredity, possibly intrauterine growth retardation, infections, malformations

B. Assessment findings
  1. Skin: loose and dry, little fat, little muscle mass
  2. Small body makes skull look larger than normal
  3. Sunken abdomen
  4. Thin, dry umbilical cord
  5. Little scalp hair
  6. Wide skull sutures
  7. Respiratory distress; may have had hypoxic episodes in utero
  8. Hypoglycemia
  9. Tremors
  10. Weak cry
  11. Lethargic
  12. Cool to touch

C. Nursing interventions
  1. Care of SGA infant is similar in many instances to care of preterm infant.
  2. Tailor high-level nursing care to meet specific needs of infant with regard to functioning of all body systems, psychologic growth and development, parental support and teaching, and prevention of complications.

The Postmature Infant

A. General information
  1. Born after the completion of 42 weeks of pregnancy

2. Problems caused by progressively less efficient actions of placenta

B. Assessment findings
1. Skin
   a. Vernix and lanugo completely disappeared
   b. Dry, cracked, parchmentlike appearance of skin
   c. Color: yellow to green from meconium staining
2. Depleted subcutaneous fat; old looking
3. Hard nails extending beyond fingertips
4. Signs of birth injury or poor tolerance of birth process

C. Nursing interventions
1. Nursing care of the postmature infant has many characteristics in common with the care given to the premature infant.
2. Design high-level nursing care to identify the infant's specific physical and psychologic needs; monitor functioning of all body systems, growth and development, parental support and teaching, and prevention of complications.

SPECIAL CONDITIONS IN THE NEONATE

Hyperbilirubinemia

A. General information
1. Elevated serum level of bilirubin in the newborn results in jaundice or yellow color of body tissues.
2. In physiologic jaundice, average increase from 2 mg/dl in cord blood to 6 mg/dl by 72 hours; not exceeding 12 mg/dl
3. Level at which a newborn will sustain damage to body cells (especially brain cells) from high concentrations of bilirubin is termed pathologic.
4. May result from immaturity of liver, Rh or ABO incompatibility, infection, birth trauma with subsequent bleeding (cephalhematoma), maternal diabetes, hypothermia, medications.
5. Breast milk hormone, pregnanedial, is also thought to contribute to hyperbilirubinemia by inhibiting the conjugation of bilirubin (after 7 days).
6. Major complication is *kernicterus* (brain damage caused by high levels of unconjugated bilirubin).

B. Assessment findings
1. Pathologic jaundice usually appears early, up to 24 hours after birth; represents a process ongoing before birth
2. Usual pattern of progression is from head to feet. Blanch skin over bony area or look at conjunctiva and buccal membranes in dark-skinned infants
3. Pallor
4. Dark, concentrated urine
5. Behavior changes (irritability, lethargy)
6. Polycythemia
7. Increased serum bilirubin (direct, indirect, and total)

C. Nursing interventions
1. Identify conditions predisposing to hyperbilirubinemia, especially positive coombs test (test on cord blood for presence of maternal antibodies).
2. Prevent progression or complications of jaundice.
3. Assess jaundice levels (visually, lab tests) as needed.
4. Prevent conditions that contribute to development of hyperbilirubinemia (e.g., cold stress, hypoxia, acidosis, hypoglycemia, dehydration, infection).
5. Provide adequate hydration.
6. Implement phototherapy if ordered; use of blue lights overhead or in blanket-device wrapped around infant. (Wallaby)
   a. Overhead unit
      1) Unclothe infant for maximum skin exposure; minimal diaper
      2) Cover eyes to prevent retinal damage
      3) Change infant's position every 2 hours for maximum exposure
      4) Monitor temperature carefully
      5) Remove and uncover eyes for feedings
      6) Insure feedings every 3 hours
   b. Wallaby blanket
      1) Baby at bedside - explain care of unit to mother
      2) Keep unit on for feedings, eyes remain uncovered
      3) Other care as above
7. Explain all tests and procedures to parents.
8. Assist with exchange transfusion if ordered.
   a. Keep infant warm and restrained.
   b. Check blood for correct identification, age, and temperature.
   c. Have oxygen and suction equipment available.
   d. Aspirate infant's stomach to prevent vomiting and aspiration.
   e. Obtain baseline vital signs; repeat every 15 minutes throughout procedure.
   f. Monitor amount of transfused blood given via umbilical catheter and time of procedure.
   g. Monitor infant posttransfusion.
      1) assess for bleeding, cold stress, any irregular behavior.
      2) check vital signs.

    h. Keep umbilical cord moist in event of need for further transfusions.
  9. Support parents with information on procedures.

Hemolytic Disease of the Newborn (Erythroblastosis Fetalis)

A. General information
  1. Characterized by RBC destruction in the newborn, with resultant anemia and hyperbilirubinemia
  2. Possibly caused by Rh or ABO incompatibility between the mother and the fetus (antigen/antibody reaction)
  3. Mechanisms of Rh incompatibility
    a. Sensitization of Rh-negative woman by transfusion of Rh-positive blood
    b. Sensitization of Rh-negative woman by presence of Rh-positive RBCs from her fetus conceived with Rh-positive man
    c. Approximately 65% of infants conceived by this combination of parents will be Rh positive.
    d. Mother is sensitized by passage of fetal Rh-positive RBCs through placenta, either during pregnancy (break/leak in membrane) or at the time of separation of the placenta after delivery.
    e. This stimulates the mother's immune response system to produce anti-Rh-positive antibodies that attack fetal RBCs and cause hemolysis.
    f. If this sensitization occurs during pregnancy, the fetus is affected in utero; if sensitization occurs at the time of delivery, subsequent pregnancies may be affected.
  4. ABO incompatibility
    a. Same underlying mechanism
    b. Mother is blood type O; infant is A, B, or AB.
    c. Reaction in ABO incompatibility is less severe.
B. Rh incompatibility
  1. First pregnancy: mother may become sensitized, baby rarely affected
  2. Indirect Coombs' test (tests for anti-Rh-positive antibodies in mother's circulation) performed during pregnancy at first visit and again about 28 weeks gestation. If indirect Coombs' test is negative at 28 weeks, a small dose (MicRho gam) is given prophylactically to prevent sensitization in the third trimester. Rhogam may also be given after second trimester amniocentesis.
  3. If positive, levels are titrated to determine extent of maternal sensitization and potential effect on fetus.

  4. Direct Coombs' test done on cord blood at delivery to determine presence of anti-Rh-positive antibodies on fetal RBCs.
  5. If both indirect and direct Coombs' tests are negative (no formation of anti-Rh-positive antibodies) and infant is Rh positive, then Rh-negative mother can be given Rhogam (Rho[D] human immune globulin) to prevent development of anti-Rh-positive antibodies as the result of sensitization from present (just-terminated) pregnancy.
  6. In each pregnancy, an Rh-negative mother who carries an Rh-positive fetus can receive Rhogam to protect future pregnancies if the mother has had negative indirect Coombs' tests and the infant has had a negative direct Coombs' test.
  7. If mother has been sensitized (produced anti-Rh-positive antibodies), Rhogam is not indicated.
  8. Rhogam must be injected into unsensitized mother's system within 72 hours of delivery of Rh-positive infant.
C. ABO incompatibility
  1. Reaction less severe than with Rh incompatibility
  2. Firstborn may be affected because type O mother may have anti-A and anti-B antibodies even before pregnancy.
  3. Fetal RBCs with A, B, or AB antigens evoke less severe reaction on part of mother, thus fewer anti-A, anti-B, or anti-AB antibodies are produced.
  4. Clinical manifestations of ABO incompatibility are milder and of shorter duration than those of Rh incompatibility.
  5. Care must be taken to observe for hemolysis and jaundice.
D. Assessment findings
  1. Jaundice and pallor within first 24–36 hours
  2. Anemia
  3. Erythropoiesis
  4. Enlarged placenta
  5. Edema and ascites
E. Nursing interventions
  1. Determine blood type and Rh early in pregnancy.
  2. Determine results of indirect Coombs' test early in pregnancy and again at 28–32 weeks.
  3. Determine results of direct Coombs' test on cord blood (type and Rh, hemoglobin and hematocrit).
  4. Administer Rhogam IM to mother as ordered.
  5. Monitor carefully infants of Rh-negative mothers for jaundice.
  6. Implement phototherapy/exchange transfusion for any hyperbilirubinemia (see page 501).

7. Support parents with explanations and information.

Neonatal Sepsis

A. General information
   1. Associated with the presence of pathogenic microorganisms in the blood, especially gram-negative organisms (*E. coli, Aerobacter, Proteus,* and *Klebsiella*), and gram-positive group B beta-hemolytic streptococci.
   2. Contributing factors
      a. Prolonged rupture of membranes (more than 24 hours)
      b. Prolonged or difficult labor
      c. Maternal infection
      d. Infection in hospital personnel
      e. Aspiration at birth or later
B. Assessment findings
   1. Behavioral changes: lethargy, irritability, poor feeding
   2. Frequent periods of apnea
   3. Jaundice
   4. Low-grade fever
   5. Vomiting, diarrhea
C. Nursing interventions
   1. Perform cultures as indicated/ordered.
   2. Administer antibiotics for 3 days till 72 hour cultures back if negative, discontinue; if positive, continue with full course of specific antibiotics
   3. Prevent heat loss.
   4. Administer oxygen as indicated.
   5. Maintain hydration.
   6. Monitor vital signs (temperature, pulse, respirations) frequently.
   7. Weigh daily.
   8. Stroke back and feet gently to stimulate breathing if infant is apneic.
   9. Promote parental attachment and involvement in newborn care.

Hypoglycemia

A. General information
   1. Less-than-normal amount of glucose in the blood of the neonate
   2. Common in infants of diabetic mothers (IDM), especially type III: these infants usually LGA (macrosomic) due to high maternal glucose levels that have crossed placenta, stimulating the fetal pancreas to secrete more insulin, which then acts as growth hormone.
   3. At birth, with loss of supply of maternal glucose, newborn may become hypoglycemic.
   4. Large size may have caused traumatic vaginal birth, or may have necessitated cesarean birth.
   5. Hypoglycemia can also occur in infants who are full term, SGA, postterm, septic, or with any condition that subjects the infant to stress.
B. Assessment findings
   1. May be born prematurely due to complications
   2. Although LGA, IDMs may be immature/dysmature
   3. Higher incidence of congenital anomalies in IDMs
   4. General appearance
      a. Puffy body
      b. Enlarged organs
   5. Tremors, feeding, difficulty, irregular respirations, lethargy, hypothermia
   6. Hypocalcemia and hyperbilirubinemia
   7. Respiratory distress
   8. Blood glucose levels below 40 mg/dl (20 mg/dl in premature infant) using Dextristix
C. Nursing interventions
   1. Provide high-level nursing care similar to that for premature/dysmature infant.
   2. Assess blood glucose level at frequent intervals, beginning ½–1 hour after birth.
   3. Feed hypoglycemic infant according to nursery protocol (formula or breast preferred) if suck/swallow reflex present and coordinated.
   4. Poor suck-swallow or lack of serum response to PO feeding, administer IV glucose.

Infant Born to Addicted Mother

A. General information
   1. Substance may be alcohol, heroin, morphine, or any other addictive drug.
   2. Mother usually seeks prenatal care only when labor begins and has frequently taken a dose of addictive substance before seeking help, delaying withdrawal symptoms 12–24 hours.
   3. Withdrawal symptoms in the neonate may be noticed within 24 hours.
B. Assessment findings
   1. Infants born to alcohol-abusing mothers will have facial anomalies, fine-motor dysfunction, genital abnormalities (especially females), and cardiac defects; may be SGA (also called the *fetal alcohol syndrome*)
   2. Hyperirritability and hyperactivity
   3. High-pitched cry common
   4. Respiratory distress, tachypnea, excessive secretions
   5. Vomiting and diarrhea
   6. Elevated temperature
   7. Other signs of withdrawal: sneezing; sweating; yawning; short, nonquiet sleep; frantic sucking
C. Nursing interventions

1. Reduce external stimuli.
2. Handle minimally.
3. Swaddle infant and hold close when handling.
4. Monitor infant's vital signs.
5. Suction/resuscitate as required.
6. Feed frequently, with small amounts.
7. Measure I&O.
8. Provide careful skin care.
9. Administer medications if ordered (may use phenobarbital or paragoric).
10. Involve parents in care if possible.
11. Inform parents of infant's condition/progress.

Respiratory Distress Syndrome (RDS)

A. General information
   1. Symptoms found almost exclusively in the preterm infant; also known as hyaline membrane disease (HMD).
   2. Deficiency of surfactant is implicated in the condition, but underlying cause still unknown.
   3. When premature labor cannot be arrested, betamethasone may be administered to enhance surfactant.
   4. Additional factors: hypoxia, hypothermia, acidosis
   5. Sequelae of RDS may include
      a. Hyperbilirubinemia (see page 501)
      b. Retrolental fibroplasia: retinal changes, visual impairment and eventually blindness, resulting from too-high oxygen levels during treatment
      c. Bronchopulmonary dysplasia (BPD): damage to the alveolar epithelium of the lungs related to high oxygen concentrations and positive pressure ventilation. May be difficult to wean infant from ventilator, but most recover and have normal x-rays at 6 months to 2 years.
      d. Necrotizing enterocolitis (opposite).
B. Assessment findings
   1. Respiratory rate of over 60/minute
   2. Retractions, grunting, cyanosis, nasal flaring, chin lag
   3. Increased apical pulse
   4. Hypothermia
   5. Decreased activity level
   6. Elevated levels of carbon dioxide
   7. Metabolic acidosis
   8. X-rays show atelectasis and density in alveoli.
C. Nursing interventions
   1. Maintain infant's body temperature at 97.6°F (36.2°C).
   2. Provide sufficient caloric intake for size, age, and prevention of catabolism (usually IV glucose with gradual increase in feedings); nasogastric tube may be used.

3. Organize care for minimal handling of infant.
4. Administer oxygen therapy as ordered.
   a. Monitor oxygen concentration every 2–4 hours; maintain less than 40% concentration if possible.
   b. Oxygen may be administered by hood, nasal prongs, intubation, or mask.
   c. Oxygen may be at atmospheric or increased pressure.
   d. Continuous positive air pressure (CPAP) or positive end-expiratory pressure (PEEP) may be used.
   e. Oxygen should be warmed and humidified.
5. Monitor infant's blood gases.
6. If intubated, suction (for less than 5 seconds) prn using sterile catheter.
7. Auscultate breath sounds.
8. Provide chest physiotherapy, postural drainage, and percussion if ordered.
9. Encourage parental involvement in care (visiting, stroking infant, talking).
10. Administer surfactant via endotracheal tube and other medications as ordered.

Necrotizing Enterocolitis (NEC)

A. General information
   1. An ischemic attack to the intestine resulting in thrombosis and infarction of affected bowel, mucosal ulcerations, pseudomembrane formation, and inflammation.
   2. Bacterial action (*E. coli, Klebsiella*) complicates the process, producing sepsis.
   3. May be precipitated by any event in which blood is shunted away from the intestine to the heart and brain (e.g., fetal distress, low Apgar score, RDS, prematurity, neonatal shock, and asphyxia).
   4. Average age at onset is 4 days.
   5. Now that severely ill infants are surviving, NEC is encountered more frequently.
   6. May ultimately cause bowel perforation and death.
B. Medical management
   1. Parenteral antibiotics
   2. Gastric decompression
   3. Correction of acidosis and fluid electrolyte imbalances
   4. Surgical removal of the diseased intestine
C. Assessment findings
   1. History indicating high-risk group
   2. Findings related to sepsis
      a. Temperature instability
      b. Apnea, labored respirations
      c. Cardiovascular collapse
      d. Lethargy or irritability
   3. Gastrointestinal symptoms
      a. Abdominal distension and tenderness
      b. Vomiting or increased gastric residual

    c. Poor feeding
    d. Hematest positive stools
    e. X-rays showing air in the bowel wall, adynamic ileus, and bowel wall thickening

D. Nursing interventions
1. Carefully assess infants at risk for early recognition of symptoms.
2. Discontinue oral feedings, insert nasogastric tube.
3. Prevent trauma to abdomen by avoiding diapers and planning care for minimal handling.
4. Maintain acid-base balance by administering fluids and electrolytes as ordered.
5. Administer antibiotics as ordered.
6. Stroke infant's hands and head and talk to infant as much as possible.
7. Provide visual and auditory stimulation.
8. Inform parents of progress and support them in expressing their fears and concerns.

Phenylketonuria (PKU)

A. General information
1. Inability to metabolize phenylalanine to tyrosine because of an autosomal recessive inherited disorder causing an inborn error of metabolism
2. Phenylalanine is a composite of almost all proteins: **the danger to the infant is immediate.**
3. High levels of phenylketones affect brain cells, causing mental retardation.
4. Initial screening for diagnosis of PKU is made via the Guthrie test, done after the infant has ingested protein for a minimum of 24 hours.
5. Secondary screening
    a. Done when the infant is about 6 weeks old.
    b. Test fresh urine with a Phenistix, which changes color.
    c. Parents send in a prepared sheet marking the color.
6. These tests, mandatory in many states, allow the early diagnosis of the disorder, and dietary interventions to minimize or prevent complications.

B. Assessment findings
1. Phenylalanine levels greater than 8 mg/dl are diagnostic for PKU.
2. Newborn appears normal; may be fair with decreased pigmentation.
3. Untreated PKU can result in failure to thrive, vomiting, and eczema; by about 6 months, signs of brain involvement appear.

C. Nursing interventions
1. Restrict protein intake.
2. Substitute a low-phenylalanine formula (Lofenalac) for either mother's milk or formula.
3. Provide special food lists for parents.

Sample Questions

36. In differentiating physiologic jaundice from pathologic jaundice, which of the following facts is most important?
1. Mother is 37 years of age.
2. Infant is a term newborn.
3. Unconjugated bilirubin level is 6 mg/dl on third day.
4. Appears at 22 hours after birth.

37. Ms. S. delivers a 6 lb 5 oz (2863 g) boy. Because his serum bilirubin level is elevated, the baby is receiving phototherapy. To meet the safety needs of the baby while he is undergoing phototherapy, the nurse would
1. limit fluid intake.
2. cover the infant's eyes while he is under the light.
3. keep him clothed to prevent skin burns.
4. make sure the light is not closer than 24 inches.

38. The morning temperature on a newborn is 97.6°F (36.4°C). In order to prevent cold stress, which nursing action should be included in the plan of care? Teach the mother to
1. keep the baby's head covered.
2. keep the baby unwrapped.
3. turn up the thermostat in the nursery.
4. use warm water for the bath.

39. Cynthia, a diabetic, has a problem-free prenatal course and she delivers a full-term 9 lb 2 oz girl. At 1 hour after birth, Cynthia's baby exhibits tremors. The nurse performs a heel stick and a Dextrostix test. The result is 40 mg/dl. The nurse concludes that these symptoms are most likely caused by
1. hypoglycemia.
2. hypokalemia.
3. hypothermia.
4. hypercalcemia.

Answers and Rationales

36. The correct answer is 4. Time is one of the most important criteria in differentiating physiologic from pathologic jaundice. Physiologic jaundice appears after 24 hours. When jaundice appears earlier, it may be pathologic. No matter what the cause, the newborn must be observed closely for rising bilirubin levels so that appropriate interventions may be implemented.

37. The correct answer is 2. The infant receiving phototherapy should have patches applied over closed eyes to prevent damage to the retina. Fluid intake should be increased in the baby to aid in decreasing the bilirubin level. The baby should not be clothed. The procedure involves exposing the infant's bare skin to intense fluorescent light. The blue range of light accelerates the excretion of bilirubin in the skin, decomposing it by photo-oxidation. The light should be 60 cm (24 inches) away from the baby.

38. The correct answer is 1. Stabilization of the infant's body temperature is accomplished by keeping the baby wrapped in warm blankets and keeping the head covered. Keeping the baby unwrapped will lower the baby's body temperature. Turning up the thermostat would warm the baby too much. The bath could be postponed until the baby's temperature is stabilized.

39. The correct answer is 1. Tremors, as well as convulsions, listlessness, periods of respiratory distress, and feeding difficulties, are symptoms of the neonatal hypoglycemia. The newborn's insulin supply is large in response to the mother's hyperglycemia. Once the baby leaves the uterus this large supply of insulin can easily cause hypoglycemia in the infant. Immediate administration of IV glucose is indicated as ordered. Symptoms of hypokalemia would include an abnormal electrocardiogram, weakness, and flaccid paralysis. Signs of hypothermia would be shivering. Symptoms of hypercalcemia would include confusion, anorexia, abdominal pain, and muscle pain and weakness.

Conditions of the Female Reproductive System

FERTILITY AND INFERTILITY

Infertility

General Information

A. Inability to conceive after at least one year of unprotected sexual relations
B. Inability to deliver a live infant after three consecutive pregnancies
C. For the male, inability to impregnate a female partner within the same conditions
D. May be primary (never been pregnant/never impregnated) or secondary (pregnant once, then unable to conceive or carry again)
E. Affects approximately 10%–15% of all couples
F. Tests for infertility can include:
   1. For the female
      a. Examination of basal body temperature and cervical mucus and identification of time of ovulation
      b. Plasma progesterone level: assesses corpus luteum
      c. Hormone analysis: endocrine function
      d. Endometrial biopsy: receptivity of endometrium
      e. Postcoital test: sperm placement and cervical mucus
      f. Hysterosalpingography: tubal patency/uterine cavity
      g. Rubin's test: tubal patency (uses carbon dioxide)
      h. Pelvic ultrasound: visualization of pelvic tissues
      i. Laparoscopy: visual assessment of pelvic/abdominal organs; performance of minor surgeries
   2. For the male
      a. Sperm analysis: assesses composition, volume, motility, agglutination.
      b. There are fewer assessment tests as well as interventions and successes for male infertility.

Medical Management

A. Infertility of female partner, causes and therapy
   1. Congenital anomalies (absence of organs, improperly formed or abnormal organs): surgical treatment may help in some situations but cannot replace absent structures.
   2. Irregular/absent ovulation (ovum released irregularly or not at all): endocrine therapy with clomiphene citrate (Clomid)/menotropins (Pergonal) may induce ovulation; risk of ovarian hyperstimulation and release of multiple ova.
   3. Tubal factors (fallopian tubes blocked or scarred from infection, surgery, endometriosis, neoplasms): treatment may include antibiotic therapy, surgery, hysterosalpingogram.
   4. Uterine conditions (endometrium unreceptive, infected): removal of an IUD,

antibiotic therapy, or surgery may be helpful.
5. Vaginal/cervical factors (hostile mucus, sperm allergies, altered pH due to infection): treatment with antibiotics, proper vaginal hygiene, or artificial insemination may be utilized.

B. Infertility of male partner, causes and therapy
1. Impotence: may be helped by psychologic counseling/penile implants, medication.
2. Low/abnormal sperm count (fewer than 20 million/ml semen, low motility, more than 40% abnormal forms): there is no good therapy, use of hormone replacement therapy has had little success.
3. Varicocele (varicosity within spermatic cord): ligation may be successful.
4. Infection in any area of the male reproductive system (may affect ability to impregnate): appropriate antibiotic therapy is advised.
5. Social habits (use of nicotine, alcohol, other drugs; clothes that keep scrotal sac too close to warmth of body): changing these habits may reverse low/absent fertility.

C. Alternatives for infertile couples include
1. Artificial insemination by husband or donor
2. In vitro fertilization
3. Adoption
4. Surrogate parenting
5. Embryo transfers

D. Accepting childlessness as a life-style may also be necessary; support groups (e.g., Resolve) may be helpful.

Nursing Interventions

A. Assist with assessment including a complete history, physical exam, lab work, and tests for both partners.
B. Monitor psychologic reaction to infertility.
C. Support couple through procedures and tests.
D. Identify any existing abnormalities and provide couple with information about their condition(s).
E. Help couple acknowledge and express their feelings both separately and together.

Control of Fertility

Voluntary prevention of conception through various means, some of which employ devices or medications.

Methods of Conception Control

A. Natural methods
1. Natural family planning
a. Periodic abstinence from intercourse when ovulating

b. Uses calculations intended to identify those days of the menstrual cycle when coitus is avoided.
1) basal body temperature: identification of temperature drop before ovulation, then rise past ovulation; identifies days on which coitus is avoided to avoid conception.
2) cervical mucus method: identification of changes in cervical mucus; when affected by estrogen and most conducive to penetration by sperm, cervical mucus is clear, stretchy, and slippery; when influenced by progesterone, cervical mucus is thick, cloudy, and sticky and does not allow sperm passage; coitus is avoided during days of estrogen-influenced mucus.
3) sympto-thermal: combination of basal body temperature and cervical mucus method to increase effectiveness
2. Coitus interruptus
a. Withdrawal of the penis from the vagina before ejaculation.
b. Not very safe; pre-ejaculatory fluids from Cowper's glands may contain live, motile sperm.
c. Demands precise male control.

B. Chemical barriers
1. Use of foams, creams, jellies, and vaginal suppositories designed to destroy the sperm or limit their motility
2. Available without a prescription, widely used, especially in conjunction with the diaphragm and the condom
3. Need to be placed in the vagina immediately before each act of intercourse; messy
4. Some people may have allergic reaction to the chemicals

C. Mechanical barriers: diaphragm, condom, cervical cap, contraceptive sponge
1. Diaphragm: shallow rubber dome fits over cervix, blocking passage of sperm through cervix
a. Efficiency increased by use of chemical barrier as lubricant
b. Woman needs to be measured for diaphragm, and refitted after childbirth or weight gain/loss of 10 lb
c. Device needs to be left in place 6–8 hours after intercourse.
d. Woman needs to practice insertion and removal, and to be taught how to check for holes in diaphragm, store in cool place.
2. Condom: thin stretchable rubber sheath worn over penis during intercourse
a. Widely available without prescription

b. Applied with room at tip to accommodate ejaculate
c. Applied to erect penis before vaginal penetration
d. Man is instructed to hold on to rim of condom as he withdraws from female to prevent spilling semen.

3. Cervical cap: cup-shaped device that is placed over cervical os and held in place by suction.
   a. four sizes; client needs to be fitted
   b. women need to practice insertion and removal
   c. spermicidals increase effectiveness
   d. may be left in place for up to 24 hours

4. Contraceptive sponge: small, soft insert, with indentation on one side to fit over cervix; contains spermicide
   a. moistened with water and inserted with indentation snugly against cervix
   b. may be left in place up to 24 hours
   c. no professional fitting required
   d. may also protect against STDs
   e. should not be used by women with history of toxic shock syndrome
   f. problems include cost, difficulty in removal, and irritation

D. Hormone therapy (oral contraceptives, birth control pills)
   1. Ingestion of estrogen and progesterone on a specific schedule to prevent the release of FSH and LH, thus preventing ovulation and pregnancy.
   2. Causes additional tubal, endometrial, and cervical mucus changes.
   3. Available in combined or sequential types.
   4. Usually taken beginning on day 5 of the menstrual cycle through day 25, then discontinued.
   5. Withdrawal bleeding occurs within 2–3 days.
   6. Contraindications
      a. History of hypertension or vascular disorders
      b. Age over 35
      c. Cigarette smoking (heavy)
   7. Women using oral contraceptives need to be sure to get sufficient amounts of vitamin B as metabolism of this vitamin is affected.
   8. Minor side effects may include
      a. Weight gain
      b. Breast changes
      c. Headaches
      d. Vaginal spotting
   9. Report vision changes/disorders immediately.

E. Intrauterine devices (IUD)
   1. Placement of plastic or nonreactive device into uterine cavity
   2. Mode of action thought to be the creation of a sterile endometrial inflammation, discourages implantation (nidation).
   3. Does not affect ovulation or conception.
   4. Device is inserted during or just after menstruation, while cervix is slightly open.
   5. May cause cramping and heavy bleeding during menses for several months after insertion.
   6. Tail of IUD hangs into vagina through cervix; woman taught to feel for it before intercourse and after each menses.
   7. A distinct disadvantage is the increased risk of pelvic infection (PID) with use of the IUD.

F. Surgical sterilization
   1. Bilateral tubal ligation in the female to prevent the passage of ova.
   2. Bilateral vasectomy in the male to prevent the passage of sperm.
   3. Both of these operations should be considered permanent.
   4. Female will still menstruate but will not conceive.
   5. Male will be incapable of fertilizing his partner after all viable sperm ejaculated from vas deferens (6 weeks or 10 ejaculations).
   6. There should be no effect on male capacity for erection or penetration.
   7. Hysterectomy also causes permanent sterility in the female.

G. Steroid implants: approved in 1990 by FDA; biodegradable rods containing sustained-release, low-dose progesterone. Inhibits LH (luteinizing hormone) release necessary for ovulation. Effective over 5-year time frame. Need minor surgical procedure for insertion and removal. Removal causes total reversibility of effect.

H. Injectable progestin-same action as G; lasts 3 months

Nursing Responsibilities in Control of Fertility

A. Assess previous experience of couple or individual.
B. Obtain health history and perform physical examination.
C. Identify present needs for contraception.
D. Determine motivation regarding contraception.
E. Assist the client/couple in receiving information desired; advise about the various methods available.
F. Ensure that client/couple selects method best suited to their needs.
   1. Support choice of client/couple as right for them.
   2. Provide time for practice with method chosen, if applicable.
   3. Instruct in side effects/potential complications.
G. Encourage expression of feelings about contraception.

Termination of Pregnancy

General Information

A. Deliberate interruption of a pregnancy in a pre-viable time. Legal in all states since Supreme Court ruling of January 1973, as follows
  1. First trimester: determined by pregnant woman and her physician.
  2. Second trimester: determined by pregnant woman and her physician; state can regulate the circumstances to ensure safety.
  3. Third trimester: conditions determined by state law.
B. Indications may be physical or psychologic, socioeconomic or genetic.
C. Techniques vary according to trimester.
  1. First trimester: *vacuum extraction* or *dilatation and curettage* (*D&C*)
    a. Cervix dilated
    b. Products of conception either aspirated or scraped out
    c. Procedure is short, usually well tolerated by client, and has few complications.
  2. Second trimester
    a. *Saline abortion*
      1) amniotic fluid aspirated from uterus, replaced with same amount 20% saline solution.
      2) contractions begin in 12–24 hours; may be induced by oxytocin (Pitocin)
      3) client is hospitalized; infection or hypernatremia possible complications
    b. *Prostaglandins*
      1) injection of prostaglandin into uterus
      2) contractions initiated in under 1 hour
      3) side effects may include nausea and vomiting
    c. *Hysterotomy*
      1) incision into uterus to remove fetus.
      2) may also be used for sterilization.
      3) client is hospitalized.
      4) care is similar to that for cesarean birth.
  3. Third trimester: same as second trimester, if permitted by state law.

Assessment

A. Vaginal bleeding
B. Vital signs
C. Excessive cramping

Analysis

A. High risk for fluid volume deficit
B. High risk for injury
C. High risk for disturbance in self-concept
D. Knowledge deficit

Planning and Implementation

A. Goals
  1. Recovery from procedure will be free from complications.
  2. Client will be supported in her decision.
B. Interventions
  1. Explain procedure to client.
  2. Administer medications as ordered.
  3. Assist with procedure as needed.
  4. Monitor client carefully during procedure.
  5. Monitor client postprocedure.
  6. Administer postprocedure medications as ordered (analgesics, antibiotics, oxytocins, Rhogam if mother Rh negative).
  7. Provide contraceptive information as appropriate.

Evaluation

A. Procedure tolerated without complications; vital signs stable, no hemorrhage, products of conception evacuated, no infection
B. Client supported through procedure; emotionally stable

MENSTRUAL DISORDERS

Menstruation is the periodic shedding of the endometrium when there has been no conception. Onset is menarche (age 11–14); cessation is menopause (average age 50).

Assessment

A. Menstrual cycle for symptoms and pattern
B. Client discomfort with cycles
C. Knowledge base about menses

Analysis

A. Knowledge deficit
B. Alteration in health maintenance
C. Disturbance in self-concept

Planning and Implementation

A. Goals
  1. Client will receive necessary information.
  2. Client will choose treatment/options best suited to her needs.
B. Interventions
  1. Explain menstrual physiology to client.
  2. Explain options for treatment to client.
  3. Provide time for questions.
  4. Reinforce good menstrual hygiene.
  5. Administer medications if ordered.

Evaluation

Client demonstrates knowledge of condition and treatment options.

Specific Disorders

Dysmenorrhea

A. Pain associated with menstruation
B. Usually associated with ovulatory cycles; absent when ovulation suppressed
C. Intensified by stress, cultural factors, and presence of an IUD
D. High levels of prostaglandins found in menstrual flow of women with dysmenorrhea
E. Treatment my include rest, application of heat, distraction, exercise, analgesia (especially anti-prostaglandins: NSAID's)

Amenorrhea

A. Absence of menstruation.
B. Possibly caused by underlying abnormality of endocrine system, rapid weight loss, or strenuous exercise.
C. Treatment is individualized by cause.

Menorrhagia

A. Excessive menstrual flow
B. Possibly caused by endocrine imbalance, uterine tumors, infection
C. Treatment individualized by cause

Metrorrhagia

A. Intercyclic bleeding
B. Frequently the result of a disease process
C. Treatment individualized by cause

Endometriosis

A. Endometrial tissue is found outside the uterus, attached to the ovaries, colon, round ligaments, etc.
B. This tissue reacts to the endocrine stimulation cycle as does the intrauterine endometrium, resulting in inflammation of the extrauterine sites, with pain and fibrosis/scar tissue formation as the eventual result.
C. Actual cause is unknown.
D. May cause dysmenorrhea, dyspareunia, and infertility.
E. Treatment may include the use of oral contraceptives to minimize endometrial buildup or medications to suppress menstruation (Danocrine, Synarel).
F. Pregnancy and lactation may also be recommended as means to suppress menstruation.
G. Surgical intervention (removal of endometrial implants) may be helpful.

H. Hysterectomy and salpingo-oophorectomy are curative.

INFECTIOUS DISORDERS

Sexually Transmitted Diseases (STD)

Infections occurring predominantly in the genital area and spread by sexual relations.

Assessment

A. Sexual history/social practices
B. Physical examination for signs and symptoms of specific disorder

Analysis

A. Knowledge deficit
B. High risk for injury
C. Alteration in health maintenance

Planning and Implementation

A. Goals
  1. Disease process will be identified and treated.
  2. Affected others will be identified and treated.
  3. Complications will be prevented.
B. Interventions
  1. Collect specimens for tests.
  2. Implement isolation technique if indicated.
  3. Teach transmission/prevention techniques.
  4. Assist in case finding.
  5. Administer medications as ordered.
  6. Inform client of any necessary life-style changes.

Evaluation

A. Client receiving treatment appropriate to specific disorder, understands treatment regimen.
B. Client demonstrates knowledge of disease process and transmission.
C. Affected others have been identified and treated.

Specific Disorders

Herpes

A. Genital herpes is caused by herpes simplex virus type 2 (HSV_2).
B. Causes painful vesicles on genitalia, both external and internal.
C. There is no cure.
D. Treatment is symptomatic.
E. If active infection at the end of pregnancy, cesarean birth may be indicated, since virus

may be lethal to neonate who cannot localize infection.

F. Recurrences of the condition may be caused by infection, stress, menses.

G. Acyclovir (Zovirax) reduces severity and duration of exacerbation.

Chlamydia

A. Currently most common STD
B. Symptoms similar to gonorrhea (cervical/vaginal discharge) or may be asymptomatic
C. Can be transmitted to fetus at birth, causes neonatal ophthalmia
D. Treated with erythromycin, prophylactic treatment of neonate's eyes
E. If untreated, can lead to pelvic inflammatory disease (PID)

Gonorrhea

A. Caused by *N. gonorrhoeae*.
B. Symptoms may include heavy, purulent vaginal discharge, but often asymptomatic in female.
C. May be passed to fetus at time of birth, causing ophthalmia neonatorum and sepsis.
D. Treatment is penicillin; allergic clients may be treated with erythromycin or (if not pregnant) the cephalosporins.
E. All sexual contacts must be treated as well, to prevent "ping-pong" recurrence.

Syphilis

A. Caused by *Treponema pallidum* (spirochete)
B. Crosses placenta after 16th week of pregnancy to infect fetus.
C. Initial symptoms are chancre and lymph-adenopathy and may disappear without treatment in 4–6 weeks.
D. Secondary symptoms are rash, malaise, and alopecia; these too may disappear in several weeks without treatment.
E. Tertiary syphilis may recur later in life and affect any organ system, especially cardiovascular and neurologic systems.
F. Diagnosis is made by dark-field exam and serologic tests (VDRL).
G. Treatment is penicillin, or erythromycin if penicillin allergy exists.

Other Genital Infections

Cervical and vaginal infections may be caused by agents other than those associated with STDs. For all female clients with a vaginal infection, nursing actions should include teaching good perineal hygiene.

Trichomonas vaginalis

A. Caused by a protozoan

B. Major symptom is profuse foamy white to greenish discharge that is irritating to genitalia.
C. Treatment is metronidazole (Flagyl) for woman and all sexual partners.
D. Treatment lasts seven days, during which time a condom should be used for intercourse.
E. Alcohol ingestion with Flagyl causes severe gastrointestinal upset.

Candida albicans

A. Caused by a yeast transmitted from GI tract to vagina.
B. Overgrowth may occur in pregnancy, with diabetes, and with steroid or antibiotic therapy.
C. Vaginal examination reveals thick, white, cheesy patches on vaginal walls.
D. Treatment is topical application of clotrimazole (Gyne-Lotrimin), nystatin (Mycostatin), or gentian violet.
E. *Candida albicans* causes thrush in the newborn by direct contact in the birth canal.

Bacterial Vaginitis

A. Caused by other bacteria invading the vagina
B. Foul or fishy-smelling discharge
C. Treatment is specific to causative agent, and usually includes sexual partners for best results

AIDS (see pages 238–240, 561–562)

Female Reproductive System Neoplasia

The nursing diagnoses, general goals and interventions, and evaluation for the client with cancer of the reproductive system are similar to those for any client with a diagnosis of cancer. Only nursing care specific to the disorder will be discussed here.

Fibrocystic Breast Disease

A. Most common benign breast lesion.
B. Cyst(s) may be palpated; surgical biopsy indicated for differential diagnosis.
C. Treatment includes surgical removal of cysts, decreasing or removing caffeine from diet, and medication to suppress menses.

Procedure for Breast Self-Examination (BSE)

See Figure 6.11.
A. Age: routine BSE should begin as early in a woman's life as possible. Adolescence is not too early.
B. Timing: regularly, on a monthly basis, 3 to 7 days after the end of the menses, when breasts are least likely to be swollen or tender. After

• Why Do The Breast Self-Exam?

There are many good reasons for doing a breast self-exam each month. One reason is that it is easy to do and the more you do it, the better you will get at it. When you get to know how your breasts normally feel, you will quickly be able to feel any change, and early detection is the key to successful treatment and cure.

Remember: A breast self-exam could save your breast—and save your life. Most breast lumps are found by women themselves, but, in fact, most lumps in the breast are not cancer. Be safe, be sure.

• When To Do Breast Self-Exam?

The best time to do breast self-exam is right after your period, when breasts are not tender or swollen. If you do not have regular periods or sometimes skip a month, do it on the same day every month.

• Now, How To Do Breast Self-Exam

1. Lie down and put a pillow under your right shoulder. Place your right arm behind your head.

2. Use the finger pads of your three middle fingers on your left hand to feel for lumps or thickening. Your finger pads are the top third of each finger.

3. Press firmly enough to know how your breast feels. If you're not sure how hard to press, ask your health care provider. Or try to copy the way your health care provider uses the finger pads during a breast exam. Learn what your breast feels like most of the time. A firm ridge in the lower curve of each breast is normal.

4. Move around the breast in a set way. You can choose either the circle (A), the up and down line (B), or the wedge (C). Do it the same way every time. It will help you to make sure that you've gone over the entire breast area, and to remember how your breast feels.

5. Now examine your left breast using right hand finger pads.

6. If you find any changes, see your doctor right away.

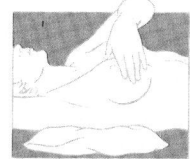 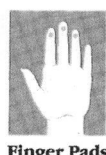
Finger Pads

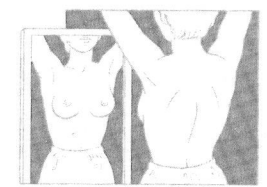

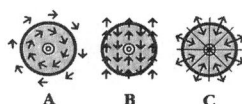
A   B   C

• For Added Safety:

You should also check your breasts while standing in front of a mirror right after you do your breast self-exam each month. See if there are any changes in the way your breasts look: dimpling of the skin, changes in the nipple, or redness or swelling.

You might also want to do a breast self-exam while you're in the shower. Your soapy hands will glide over the wet skin making it easy to check how your breasts feel.

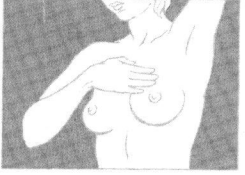

FIGURE 6.11 Breast self-examination. Each breast is to be examined systematically. (*Courtesy of the American Cancer Society, Atlanta, GA*)

menopause, BSE should be done on one particular day/date every month.

C. Procedure
   1. Inspection: stand before mirror and visually inspect with arms at sides; raised over head; hands on hips with muscles tightened; then leaning forward. Assessment should include size, symmetry, shape, direction, color, skin texture and thickness, nipple size and shape, rashes or discharges. Unusual findings should be reported to health care provider.
   2. Palpation: to examine left breast, woman should be lying down, with left hand behind head and small folded towel or pillow under left shoulder. Using flattened fingertips of right hand and a rotary motion, palpate along lines of concentric circles from outer edges of breast to nipple area, or from outer edge to nipple area following wedge or wheel-spoke lines. Also palpate in the left axillary area where multiple lymph nodes are present, as well as a "tail" of breast tissue. The nipple should be gently squeezed to assess for discharges.
      a. To examine right breast, positions are reversed.
      b. Palpation activities are repeated for each breast with the woman in the sitting position.
      c. Unusual findings are reported to the health care provider.
      d. Breast self-examination (BSE) and mammograms as indicated by age and risk are primary screening tools.

Breast Cancer

A. General information
   1. Most common neoplasm in women
   2. Leading cause of death in women age 40–44
B. Medical management
   1. Usually surgical excision; options are simple lumpectomy, simple mastectomy, modified radical mastectomy, and radical mastectomy.
   2. Adjuvant treatment with chemotherapy, radiation, and hormone therapy.
C. Assessment findings
   1. Palpation of lump (upper outer quadrant most frequent site) usually first symptom
   2. Skin of breast dimpled
   3. Nipple discharge
   4. Asymmetry of breasts
   5. Surgical biopsy provides definitive diagnosis
D. Nursing interventions
   1. Assess breasts for early identification and treatment.
   2. Support client through recommended/chosen treatment.
   3. Prepare client for mastectomy if necessary.

Mastectomy

A. General information
   1. Lumpectomy: removal of lump and surrounding breast tissue; lymph nodes biopsied.
   2. Simple mastectomy: removal of breast only, lymph nodes biopsied.
   3. Radical mastectomy: removal of breast, muscle layer down to chest wall, and axillary lymph nodes.

B. Nursing interventions
   1. Provide routine pre- and post-op care (see pages 162–167).
   2. Elevate client's arm on operative side on pillows to minimize edema.
   3. Do not use arm on affected side for blood pressure measurements, IVs, or injections.
   4. Turn only to back and unaffected side.
   5. Monitor client for bleeding, check under her.
   6. Begin range-of-motion exercises immediately on unaffected side.
   7. Start with simple movements on affected side: fingers and hands first, then wrist, elbow, and shoulder movements.
   8. Make abduction the last movement.
   9. Coordinate physical therapy if ordered.
   10. Teach client about any necessary life-style changes (special care of arm on affected side, monthly breast self-examination on remaining breast, use of prosthesis).
   11. Encourage/arrange visit from support group member.
C. Medical Therapy
   1. Hormonal therapy: tamoxifen, anti-estrogen effect.
   2. Chemotherapy
   3. Radiation
   4. Chemotherapy and radiation used with lumpectomy.

Cancer of the Cervix

A. Detected by Pap smear, followed by tissue biopsy.
   1. Class I - normal pap smear
   2. Class II - atypical cells
   3. Class III - moderate dysplasia
   4. Class IV - severe dysplasia, cancer-in-situ
   5. Class V - Squamous cell carcinoma, invasive Ca
B. Preinvasive conditions may be treated by cryosurgery, laser surgery, cervical conization, or hysterectomy.
C. Invasive conditions are treated by radium therapy and radical hysterectomy.

Cancer of the Uterus

A. May affect endometrium or fundus/corpus risk increased by unopposed estrogen.
B. Cardinal symptom: abnormal uterine bleeding, either pre- or postmenopause
C. Diagnosis: by endometrial biopsy or fractional curettage; cells washed from uterus under pressure may also be used for diagnosis
D. Usual intervention: total hysterectomy and bilateral salpingo-oophorectomy
E. Radium therapy and chemotherapy may also be used.

Cancer of the Ovary

A. Etiology unknown.
B. Few early symptoms; palpation of ovarian mass is usual first finding.
C. Treatment of choice is surgical removal with total hysterectomy and bilateral salpingo-oophorectomy.
D. Chemotherapy may be used as adjuvant therapy.

Cancer of the Vulva

A. Begins as small, pruritic lesions
B. Diagnosed by biopsy
C. Treatment is either local excision or radical vulvectomy (removal of entire vulva plus superficial and femoral nodes).

Hysterectomy

A. General information
   1. Total hysterectomy: removal of uterine body and cervix only
   2. Subtotal hysterectomy: removal of uterine body leaving cervix in place (seldom performed)
   3. Total abdominal hysterectomy with bilateral salpingo-oophorectomy (TAH-BSO): removal of uterine body, cervix, both ovaries, and both fallopian tubes
   4. Radical hysterectomy: removal of uterine body, cervix, connective tissue, part of vagina, and pelvic lymph nodes
B. Nursing interventions
   1. Institute routine pre- and post-op care. (See pages 162–167.)
   2. Assess for hemorrhage, infection, or other postsurgical complications (e.g., paralytic ileus, thrombophlebitis, pneumonia).
   3. Support woman and family through procedure, encourage expression of feelings and reactions to procedure.
   4. Explain implications of hysterectomy.
      a. No further menses.
      b. If ovaries also removed, will have menopause and may need estrogen replacement therapy.
   5. Allow woman (and partner) to verbalize concerns about sexuality postsurgery.
   6. Provide discharge teaching.

Menopause

The time in a woman's life when menstruation ceases. Fertility usually ceases, and symptoms associated with changing hormone levels may occur. Reactions to menopause may be influenced by culture, age at menopause, reproductive and menstrual history, and complications.

Assessment Findings

A. Symptoms related to hormone changes
   1. Vasomotor instability (hot flashes and night sweats)
   2. Emotional disturbances (mood swings, irritability, depression), fatigue, and headache
B. Physical changes include
   1. Atrophy of genitalia
   2. Dyspareunia
   3. Urinary changes (frequency/stress incontinence)
   4. Constipation
   5. Possibly uterine prolapse

Interventions

A. Estrogen replacement therapy (ERT)
   1. Used to control symptoms, especially vasomotor instability and vaginal atrophy, and to prevent osteoporosis
   2. Women with family histories of breast or uterine cancer, hypertension, thrombophlebitis, or cardiac dysfunction are not good candidates for ERT.
   3. Women may need information about contraception, as ovulation and ability to conceive may continue for up to 12 months after menses cease.
   4. Sold under many pharmaceutical trade names; may be taken orally, or applied transdermally (patch).
B. Alternatives to ERT include
   1. Vitamin E: from dietary sources and supplements
   2. Herbs: varied relief with combinations of roots and herbs, such as licorice and dandelion
   3. Other medications: Bellergal (phenobarbital, ergotamine tartrate, and belladonna)
   4. Kegel exercises for genital atrophy: alternating constriction and relaxation of pubococcygeal muscles (muscles controlling the flow of urine) done at least three times/day
   5. Vaginal lubricants for genital atrophy: water-soluble lubricants can diminish dyspareunia
   6. Maintenance of good hydration: at least 8 glasses of water/day
   7. Good perineal hygiene

Complications of Menopause

Osteoporosis

A. Increased porosity of the bone, with increased incidence of spontaneous fractures.

B. Other symptoms in the postmenopausal woman include loss of height, back pain, and dowager's hump.
C. Diagnosis by x-ray is not possible until more than 50% of bone mass has already been lost.
D. Decreased bone porosity is inextricably linked with lowered levels of estrogen in the postmenopausal woman. Estrogen plays a part in the absorption of calcium and the stimulation of osteoclasts (new-bone-forming cells).
E. Treatment includes
   1. ERT unless contraindicated
   2. Supplemental calcium to slow the osteoporotic process (1 g taken daily at HS)
   3. Increased fluid intake (2–3 liters/day will help avoid formation of calculi)
   4. High-calcium/high-phosphorus diet with avoidance of excess protein
   5. Some exercise on a regular basis
F. Prevention includes
   1. Not smoking
   2. Regular weight-bearing exercise
   3. Good nutrition, including sources of calcium and vitamin D
   4. Minimal use or exclusion of alcohol
   5. Regular physical examination

Cystocele/Rectocele

A. Herniations of the anterior and posterior (respectively) walls of the vagina.
B. Usually the sequelae of childbirth injuries.
C. Herniation allows the bulging of the bladder and the rectum into the vagina.
D. Treatment is surgical repair of these conditions: anterior and posterior *colporrhaphy*.

Prolapse of the Uterus

A. Usually the result of childbirth injuries or relaxation of the cardinal ligaments.
B. Allows the uterus to sag backward and downward into the vagina, or outside the body completely.
C. Vaginal hysterectomy is the preferred surgical intervention.
D. If condition does not warrant surgery, the insertion of a *pessary* (supportive device) will help to support and stabilize the uterus.

Sample Questions

40. In collecting data for a health history of Peggy L., an infertility client, which of the following findings is most important?
   1. She is 5 ft 8 in tall and weighs 105 lb.
   2. She has never used any form of contraception.
   3. She has been married for three years.
   4. She has no brothers or sisters.

41. The teaching plan for Mary A., who has just been fitted with her first diaphragm, must include
    1. specific amount of spermicide to be used with diaphragm.
    2. insertion at least 8 hours before intercourse.
    3. specific cleaning techniques.
    4. storage in the refrigerator.
42. Mrs. Jane M. is 64 years old, postmenopausal, and takes calcium supplements on a daily basis. She can reduce the danger of renal calculi by the simple action of
    1. chewing her calcium tablets rather than swallowing them whole.
    2. swallowing her calcium tablets with cranberry juice.
    3. eliminating other sources of calcium from her diet.
    4. drinking 2–3 quarts of water daily.
43. Mrs. Frances D. is 57 years old and having a routine physical exam. Which of the following assessments would yield critical information as to her postmenopausal status?
    1. Asking about weight loss of more than 5 lb in the last year.
    2. Asking about her nightly sleep patterns.
    3. Asking about her cultural background.
    4. Asking about her last pregnancy.
44. Ms. S., 46 years old, is admitted to the hospital for a panhysterectomy. Which nursing strategy should be included in the nursing care plan for Ms. S. to meet her body-image perception changes?
    1. Allowing her time to work out her feelings on her own.
    2. Discouraging fears about weight gain.
    3. Helping her verbalize her concerns about her femininity.
    4. Insisting that she look at the scar.
45. Following a panhysterectomy, the woman is placed on estrogen replacement therapy. The primary purpose of estrogen replacement therapy following surgical menopause is to prevent
    1. arthritis.
    2. pregnancy.
    3. breast cancer.
    4. vasomotor instability.
46. Ms. T., 39 years old, has advanced cancer of the breast. She is admitted to the medical unit for nutritional evaluation. She weighs 101 lb and is 5 ft 8 in tall. She is started on leucovorin (Wellcovorin). Assessment of Ms. T.'s nutritional health would include all the following except
    1. a diet history.
    2. anthropometric measurements.
    3. food preferences.
    4. serum protein studies.
47. The nurse's primary role relating to sexually transmitted disease is

    1. case reporting.
    2. sexual counseling.
    3. diagnosis and treatment.
    4. recognizing symptoms and teaching clients.
48. Jamie S., 17 years old, comes to the local health clinic because her boyfriend was recently diagnosed as having gonorrhea. Jamie asks the nurse what would have happened to her if she had gone without treatment. The nurse explains that the possible consequences of lack of treatment could result in
    1. disseminated systemic infections.
    2. minor problems such as skin rashes.
    3. the need for delivery by cesarean section.
    4. sterility, birth defects, and miscarriage.
49. Several adolescent girls are discussing sexual activity with the nurse at the STD clinic. Which comment indicates to the nurse that the client has not understood the teaching regarding safe sexual practices?
    1. "We use KY jelly on condoms."
    2. "I douche after intercourse."
    3. "I shower with my boyfriend."
    4. "We use condoms and birth control pills."
50. When discussing safe sex, which information about the use of condoms would be most helpful?
    1. Lambskin condoms do not interfere with sensation.
    2. Latex condoms prevent the transmission of germs.
    3. Condoms are often inconvenient and unnecessary.
    4. Condoms prevent STDs but they are a poor choice for birth control.

Answers and Rationales

40. The correct answer is 1. Because of the complex interaction between the hypothalamus, the ovary, and the amount of body fat, women who are underweight or who engage in strenuous physical activity over prolonged periods of time may experience changes in their menstrual cycle and their fertility.
41. The correct answer is 3. The client must be instructed to clean the diaphragm with mild, plain soap and warm water, dust it lightly with cornstarch, and store it in a cool, dry place. She should also be instructed to check it regularly for perforations or defects.
42. The correct answer is 4. The ingestion of sufficient amounts of water by a woman taking calcium supplements is crucial to the prevention of renal calculi.
43. The correct answer is 2. Postmenopausal women who are experiencing vasomotor instability may have night sweats and

interrupted sleep. Some physicians prescribe estrogen replacement therapy (ERT) for women with severe postmenopausal vasomotor instability.

44. The correct answer is 3. Loss of the organs of reproduction are often equated with a loss of femininity. The client should be encouraged to explore her feelings and to adapt to body changes. Allowing the client time to work on her feelings alone does not allow for the nurse's input and encouragement. The nurse should let the client talk about her fears regarding weight gain. The nurse should not insist that she look at the scar. In talking to the client, the nurse may determine that the scar itself has no relationship to her perception of body image changes.

45. The correct answer is 4. Low-dose estrogen therapy is used to relieve the vasomotor symptoms of menopausal women. Estrogen replacement is not a treatment to prevent arthritis. Estrogen replacement therapy does not prevent pregnancy. There may be a link between estrogen replacement therapy and increased incidence of breast or endometrial cancer. The physician's decision to use estrogen replacement therapy must take into consideration the advantages and the potential dangers for each individual.

46. The correct answer is 3. Food preferences are considered when planning a program to meet the client's nutritional requirement after the nutritional assessment has been completed. A diet history is part of a nutritional assessment. Anthropometric measurements are precise measurements of body mass in various parts of the body and are a part of a nutritional assessment. Serum protein studies are necessary to identify protein deficiencies.

47. The correct answer is 4. Early recognition of sexually transmitted diseases (STDs) reduces the risk of serious sequelae. The primary role of the nurse is to recognize symptoms of STDs in order to teach clients how to comply with treatment and how to prevent reinfection. Case reporting is not the primary nursing responsibility. Sexual counseling is not a nursing responsibility. Diagnosis and treatment of STDs is not a nursing responsibility.

48. The correct answer is 4. Lack of treatment or inadequate treatment of gonorrhea can result in serious sequelae such as sterility, birth defects, and miscarriage. Untreated gonorrhea does on rare occasions spread via the bloodstream (hematogenous) to distant organs, including joints, skin, heart valves,

and brain. This relatively infrequent complication most likely occurs during pregnancy or menstruation. Skin lesions may appear with gonococcal hematogenous dissemination and are very serious. Treatment includes large doses of penicillin or alternative drugs over an extended period of time. Cesarean sections may be indicated if an STD is active at the time of delivery.

49. The correct answer is 2. Douching is a practice that does not protect against infection and damages the natural protective barriers. Condoms do help prevent transmission of STDs.

50. The correct answer is 2. Condoms can prevent the transmission of many STDs. Condoms may be inconvenient, but they are necessary to prevent transmission of STDs. Condoms are highly effective contraceptives, particularly when used in combination with a spermicide cream.

References and Suggested Readings

Bobak, I. M., Lowdermilk, D. L., & Jensen, M. D. (1995). *Maternity nursing* (4th ed.). St. Louis: Mosby.

Boyle, J. S., & Andrews, M. M. (1998). *Transcultural concepts in nursing care* (2nd ed.). Philadelphia: Lippincott-Raven.

Cella, J., & Watson, J. (1995). *Nurse's manual of laboratory tests* (2nd ed.). Philadelphia: F.A. Davis.

Dickason, E. J., Silverman, B. L., & Kaplan, J. A. (1998). *Maternal-infant nursing care* (3rd ed.). St. Louis: Mosby-Yearbook.

Gorrie, T. M., McKinney, E. M., & Murray, S. S. (1998). *Foundations of maternal-newborn nursing* (2nd ed.). Philadelphia: Saunders.

Kain, C., Reilly, N., & Schultz, E. (1990). A comparative assessment. *Nursing Clinics of North America*, 24(4).

Ladewig, P. W., London, M. L., & Olds, S. B. (1998). *Maternal-newborn nursing care* (4th ed.). Menlo Park, CA: Addison-Wesley.

Lowdermilk, D. L., Perry, S. E., & Bobak, I. M. (1997). *Maternity and women's health care* (6th ed.). St. Louis: Mosby.

Lowdermilk, D. L., Perry, S. E., & Bobak, I. M. (1999). *Maternity nursing* (5th ed.). St. Louis: Mosby.

May, K. A., & Mahlmeister, L. R. (1994). *Maternal and neonatal nursing: Family-centered care* (3rd ed.). Philadelphia: Lippincott.

Nichols, F., & Zwelling, E. (1997). *Maternal-newborn nursing*. Philadelphia: Saunders.

Olds, S. B., London, M. L., & Ladewig, P. W. (1996). *Maternal-newborn nursing: A family centered approach* (5th ed.). Menlo Park, CA: Addison-Wesley.

Pilliterri, A. (1999). *Maternal and child health nursing* (3rd ed.). Philadelphia: Lippincott.

Reeder, S. J., Martin, L. L., & Koniak-Griffen, D. (1997). *Maternity nursing: Family, newborn, and women's health care* (18th ed.). Philadelphia: Lippincott-Raven.

Psychiatric-Mental Health Nursing

Jeanne Gelman, RN, MSN

An important aspect of professional nursing is the use of therapeutic intervention for clients who are experiencing emotional distress. A client does not have to have a psychiatric diagnosis to be in emotional distress, and often clients and their families may respond to illness or injury with anxiety and fear that can be manifested in a variety of behaviors. The principles of psychiatric-mental health nursing and therapeutic interventions can be applied to any client, family, or group in need.

To plan appropriate interventions, nurses need to have an understanding and knowledge of personality development and other theories to analyze behaviors of the client or others. Theories, principles, and treatment modalities are the *science* of psychiatric-mental health nursing.

The manner the nurse selects to use the science of mental health nursing is based in part on that nurse's personal attributes. Personal experiences, the ability to implement principles and theories, and the willingness to use therapeutic communication constitute the *art* of psychiatric-mental health nursing. This creative aspect of each nurse is the therapeutic use of self involved in planning and implementing effective nursing interventions for dealing with clients who are experiencing emotional distress.

Implementing the art of psychiatric-mental health nursing is an important way to convey to clients the *caring* aspect of nursing. Perceiving clients' concerns and responding therapeutically will encourage clients to share more information with the nurse. Awareness of the client's attitudes, values, and fears will enable the nurse to individualize client care. Physical, psychological, social, and spiritual needs should be the concern of a nurse who wants to provide holistic care. Nurses can determine specific client needs by assessing verbal and nonverbal behaviors. Application of the nursing process to meet client needs will ensure comprehensive nursing care.

The following principles of psychiatric-mental health nursing help form the basis of the therapeutic use of self.

- Be aware of your own feelings and responses.
- Maintain objectivity while being aware of your own needs.
- Use empathy (recognizing/identifying somewhat with client's emotions to understand behavior), not sympathy (close identification/ duplication of client's emotions).
- Focus on the needs of the client, not on your own needs; be consistent and trustworthy.
- Accept clients as they are; be nonjudgmental.

UNIT OUTLINE

519 Overview of Psychiatric- Mental Health Nursing

530 Psychiatric Disorders (DSM IV)

556 Psychologic Aspects of Physical Illness

- Recognize that emotions influence behaviors.
- Observe a client's behaviors to analyze needs/problems.
- Accept client's needs to use defenses/behaviors to deal with emotional distress.
- Accept client's negative emotions.
- Avoid verbal reprimands, physical force, giving advice, or imposing your own values on clients.
- Avoid intimate relationships while maintaining a caring attitude.
- Assess clients in the context of their social/cultural group.
- Recognize that client communication patterns (verbal and nonverbal) vary with different cultural groups.
- Teach/explain on client's level of capability.
- Treat clients with respect, caring, and compassion.

Asking yourself, "What is this client's need at this time?" can assist you in determining the best response to questions.

Overview of Psychiatric-Mental Health Nursing

THEORETICAL BASIS

Medical-biologic Model

A. Emotional distress is viewed as illness.
B. Symptoms can be classified to determine a psychiatric diagnosis.
C. DSM IV*
  1. Description of disorders
  2. Criteria (behaviors) that must be met for diagnosis to be made
  3. Axis: the dimensions and factors included when assessing a client with a mental disorder
    a. I and II: clinical syndromes (e.g., bipolar, antisocial personality, mental retardation)
    b. III: physical disorders and symptoms (e.g., cystic fibrosis, hypertension)
    c. IV: psychosocial and environmental problems: acute and long-term severity of stressors
    d. V: functioning of client, rating of symptoms and their effect on activities of daily living (ADL) or violence to self/others
D. Diagnosed psychiatric illnesses are within the realm of medical practice and have a particular course, prognosis, and treatment regimen.
E. Treatment can include psychotropic drugs, electroconvulsive therapy (ECT), hospitalization, and psychotherapy.
F. There is no proven cause, but theory is that biochemical/genetic factors play a part in the development of mental illness. Theories with schizophrenia and affective disorders include
  1. Genetic: increased risk when close relative (e.g., parent, sibling) has disorder
  2. Possible link to neurotransmitter activity

Psychodynamic/Psychoanalytic Model (Freud)

A. Instincts (drives) produce energy.
B. There are genetically determined drives for sex and aggression.
C. Human behavior is determined by past experiences and responses.
D. All behavior has meaning and can be understood.
E. Emotionally painful experiences/anxiety motivate behavior.

---

*American Psychiatric Association (1994). *Diagnostic and Statistical Manual of Mental Disorders* (4th ed.)

F. Client can change behavior and responses when made aware of the reasons for them.
G. Freud's theory of personality
  1. *Id:* present at birth; instinctual drive for pleasure and immediate gratification, unconscious. *Libido* is the sexual and/or aggressive energy (drive). Operates on pleasure principle to reduce tension or discomfort (pain). Uses *primary process* thinking by imagining objects to satisfy needs (hallucinating).
  2. *Ego:* develops as sense of self that is distinct from world of reality; conscious, preconscious, and unconscious. Operates on reality principle which determines whether the perception has a basis in reality or is imagined. Uses *secondary process* thinking by judging reality and solving problems.
    a. Functions of the ego
      1) control and regulate instinctual drives
      2) mediate between id drives and demands of reality; id drives vs superego restrictions
      3) reality testing: evaluate and judge external world
      4) store up experiences in "memory"
      5) direct motor activity and actions
      6) solve problems
      7) use defense mechanisms to protect self
    b. Levels of awareness
      1) Preconscious: knowledge not readily available to conscious awareness but can be brought to awareness with effort (e.g., recalling name of a character in a book)
      2) Unconscious: knowledge that cannot be brought into conscious awareness without interventions such as psychoanalysis, hypnotism, or drugs
      3) Conscious: aware of own thoughts and perceptions of reality
  3. *Superego:* develops as person unconsciously incorporates standards and restrictions from parents to guide behaviors, thoughts, and feelings. Conscious awareness of acceptable/unacceptable thoughts, feelings, and actions is "conscience."
H. Freud's psychosexual developmental stages
  1. *Oral*
    a. 0–18 months

    b. Pleasure and gratification through mouth

    c. Behaviors: dependency, eating, crying, biting

    d. Distinguishes between self and mother

    e. Develops body image, aggressive drives

2. *Anal*
    a. 18 months–3 years
    b. Pleasure through elimination or retention of feces
    c. Behaviors: control of holding on or letting go
    d. Develops concept of power, punishment, ambivalence, concern with cleanliness or being dirty

3. *Phallic/Oedipal*
    a. 3–6 years
    b. Pleasure through genitals
    c. Behaviors: touching of genitals, erotic attachment to parent of opposite sex
    d. Develops fear of punishment by parent of same sex, guilt, sexual identity

4. *Latency*
    a. 6–12 years
    b. Energy used to gain new skills in social relationships and knowledge
    c. Behaviors: sense of industry and mastery
    d. Learns control over aggressive, destructive impulses
    e. Acquires friends

5. Genital
    a. 12–20 years
    b. Sexual pleasure through genitals
    c. Behaviors: becomes independent of parents, responsible for self
    d. Develops sexual identity, ability to love and work

Psychosocial Model (Erikson)

A. Emphasis on psychosocial rather than psychosexual development

B. Developmental stages have goals (tasks)

C. Challenge in each stage is to resolve conflict (e.g., trust vs mistrust)

D. Resolution of conflict prepares individual for next developmental stage

E. Personality develops according to biologic, psychologic, and social influences

F. Erikson's psychosocial development tasks
  1. *Trust vs mistrust*
    a. 0–18 months
    b. Learn to trust others and self vs withdrawal, estrangement
  2. *Autonomy vs shame and doubt*
    a. 18 months–3 years
    b. Learn self-control and the degree to which one has control over the

environment vs compulsive compliance or defiance

3. *Initiative vs guilt*
    a. 3–5 years
    b. Learn to influence environment, evaluate own behavior vs fear of doing wrong, lack of self-confidence, overrestricting actions

4. *Industry vs inferiority*
    a. 6–12 years
    b. Creative; develop sense of competency vs sense of inadequacy

5. *Identity vs role diffusion*
    a. 12–20 years
    b. Develop sense of self; preparation, planning for adult roles vs doubts relating to sexual identity, occupation/career

6. *Intimacy vs isolation*
    a. 18–25 years
    b. Develop intimate relationship with another; commitment to career vs avoidance of choices in relationships, work, or life-style

7. *Generativity vs stagnation*
    a. 21–45 years
    b. Productive; use of energies to guide next generation vs lack of interests, concern with own needs

8. *Integrity vs despair*
    a. 45 years to end of life
    b. Relationships extended, belief that own life has been worthwhile vs lack of meaning of one's life, fear of death

Interpersonal Model (Sullivan)

A. Behavior motivated by need to avoid anxiety and satisfy needs

B. Sullivan's developmental tasks
  1. *Infancy*
    a. 0–18 months
    b. Others will satisfy needs
  2. *Childhood*
    a. 18 months–6 years
    b. Learn to delay need gratification
  3. *Juvenile*
    a. 6–9 years
    b. Learn to relate to peers
  4. *Preadolescence*
    a. 9–12 years
    b. Learn to relate to friends of same sex
  5. *Early adolescence*
    a. 12–14 years
    b. Learn independence and how to relate to opposite sex
  6. *Late adolescence*
    a. 14–21 years
    b. Develop intimate relationship with person of opposite sex

Therapeutic Nurse-Client Relationship (Peplau)

A. Based on Sullivan's interpersonal model
B. Therapeutic relationship is between nurse (helper) and client (recipient of care). The goal is to work together to assist client to grow and to resolve problems.
C. Differs from social relationship where both parties form alliance for mutual benefit.
D. Therapeutic use of self
   1. Focus is on client needs but nurse is also aware of own needs.
   2. Self-awareness enables nurse to avoid having own needs influence perception of client.
   3. Determine what client/family needs are at the time.
E. Three phases of nurse-client relationship
   1. *Orientation*
      a. Nurse explains relationship to client, defines both nurse's and client's roles.
      b. Nurse determines what client expects from the relationship and what can be done for the client.
      c. Nurse contracts with client about when and where future meetings will take place.
      d. Nurse assesses client and develops a plan of care based on appropriate nursing diagnoses.
      e. Limits/termination of relationship are introduced (e.g., "We will be meeting for 30 minutes every morning while you are in the hospital.").
   2. *Working phase*
      a. Client's problems and needs are identified and explored as nurse and client develop mutual acceptance.
      b. Client's dysfunctional symptoms, feelings, or interpersonal relationships are identified.
      c. Therapeutic techniques are employed to reduce anxiety and to promote positive change and independence.
      d. Goals are evaluated as therapeutic work proceeds, and changed as determined by client's progress.
   3. *Termination*
      a. Relationship and growth in nurse and client are summarized.
      b. Client may become anxious and react with increased dependence, hostility, or withdrawal.
      c. These reactions are discussed with client.
      d. Feelings of nurse and client concerning termination should be discussed in context of finiteness of relationship.
F. Transference and countertransference

1. *Transference:* occurs when client transfers conflicts/feelings from past to the nurse. *Example:* Client becomes overly dependent, clinging to nurse who represents (unconsciously to client) the nurturing client desires from own mother.
2. *Countertransference:* occurs when nurse responds to client emotionally, as if in a personal, not professional/therapeutic, relationship. Countertransference is a normal occurrence, but must be recognized so that supervision or consultation can keep it from undermining the nurse-client relationship. *Example:* Nurse is sarcastic and judgmental to client who has history of drug abuse. Client represents (unconsciously to nurse) the nurse's brother who has abused drugs.
3. Interventions
   a. Reflect on reasons for behaviors of client or nurse.
   b. Establish therapeutic goals for this relationship.
   c. If unable to control these occurrences, transfer client to another nurse.

Human Motivation/Need Model (Maslow)

A. Hierarchy of needs in order of importance
   1. Physiologic: oxygen, food, water, sleep, sex
   2. Safety: security, protection, freedom from anxiety
   3. Love and belonging: freedom from loneliness/alienation
   4. Esteem and recognition: freedom from sense of worthlessness, inferiority, and helplessness
   5. Self-actualization: aesthetic needs, self-fulfillment, creativity, spirituality
B. Primary needs (oxygen, fluids) need to be met prior to dealing with higher-level needs (esteem, recognition).
C. Focus on provision of positive aspects such as feeling safe, having someone care, affiliation

Behavioral Model (Pavlov, Skinner)

A. Behavior is learned and retained by positive reinforcement.
B. Motivation for behavior is not considered.
C. Behaviors that are not adequate can be replaced by more adaptive behaviors.

Community Mental Health Model

A. Emotional distress stems from personal and social factors
   1. Family problems (e.g., divorce, single parenthood)

2. Social factors (e.g., unemployment, lack of support groups, changing mores)
B. Health care a right
C. Decreased need for hospitalization, increased community care
D. Collaboration of social and health care services
E. Comprehensive services
   1. Emergency care
   2. Inpatient/outpatient services
   3. Substance-abuse treatment
   4. Transitional living arrangements (temporary residence instead of inpatient care)
   5. Consultation and education to increase knowledge of mental health
F. Prevention
   1. Primary prevention
      a. Minimize development of serious emotional distress: promote mental health, identify persons at risk.
      b. Anticipate problems such as developmental crises (e.g., birth of first child, midlife crisis, death of spouse).
   2. Secondary prevention: early case finding and treatment (drug therapy, outpatient, short-term hospitalization).
   3. Tertiary prevention: restore client to optimal functioning; facilitate return of client to home and community by use of social agencies.

NURSING PROCESS

A. Applies to all clients, not only to those with psychiatric diagnosis; incorporates holism.
B. Utilized in a unique manner for psychosocial assessment.
C. Sets goals (with client, whenever possible) that can be measured in behavioral terms (e.g., client will dress self and eat breakfast before 9 A.M.).
D. Uses principles of therapeutic communication for interventions.
E. Evaluates whether, how well goals were met.

Physical Assessment

A. Subjective reporting of health history
B. Objective data (general status and appearance)
   1. Age: client's appearance in relation to chronologic age
   2. Attire: appropriateness of clothing to age/ situation
   3. Hygiene: cleanliness and grooming, or lack thereof
   4. Physical health: weight, physical distress
   5. Psychomotor: posture, movement, activity level
   6. Sleep and rest
C. Neurologic assessment/level of consciousness

Mental Status Assessment

Emotional Status Assessment

Observation of mood (prolonged emotion) and affect (physical manifestations of mood). That is, sad mood may be evidenced by crying or downcast appearance; joyful mood may be expressed by smiling or happy affect.
A. Appropriateness
B. Description: flat, sad, smiling, serious
C. Stability
D. Specific feelings and moods

Cognitive Assessment

Evaluation of thought, sensorium, intelligence
A. Intellectual performance
   1. Orientation to person, place, and time
   2. Attention and concentration
   3. Knowledge/educational level
   4. Memory: short and long term
   5. Judgment
   6. Insight into illness
   7. Ability to use abstraction
B. Speech
   1. Amount, volume, clarity
   2. Characteristics: pressured, slow or fast, dull or lively
   3. Specific aberrations, i.e., echolalia (imitating and repeating another's words or phrases) or neologisms (making up of own words that have special meaning to client).
C. Thoughts
   1. Content and clarity
   2. Characteristics: spontaneity, speed, loose associations, blocked, flight of ideas, repetitions

Social/Cultural Considerations

A. Age: assess for developmental tasks and developmental crises, age-related problems.
   1. 0–18 months: development of trust and sense of self, dependency
   2. 18 months–3 years: development of autonomy and beginning self-reliance, toilet training
   3. 3–6 years: development of sexual identity, relationships with peers, adjustment to school
   4. 6–12 years: mastery of skills, beginning self-esteem, identification with others outside family, social relationships
   5. 12–18 years: sense of self solidifies, separation and individuation often follow some disorganization and rebellion, substance abuse
   6. 18–25 years: identification with peer group, setting of personal and career goals to master future

7. 25–38 years: take place in adult world, commitments made relating to career, marriage, parenthood
8. 38–65 years: review of past accomplishments; may set new and reasonable goals; midlife crises when present achievements have not met goals set in earlier stages of development
9. 65/70 to death: loss of friends/spouse, retirement, loss of some social/physical functions
B. Family/community relationships
    1. Role of client in family
    2. Family harmony, family support for or dependency on client
    3. Client's perception of family
    4. Availability of community support groups to client (include government social agencies; religious, ethnic, and volunteer agencies)
C. Socioeconomic group/education
    1. Factors that relate to how client is approached and how client perceives own present state
    2. Determination of level of teaching and need for social services
D. Cultural/spiritual background
    1. Assess behaviors in context of client's culture.
    2. Avoid stereotyping persons as having attributes of their culture/subculture.
    3. Note client's religious/philosophic beliefs.

ANALYSIS

Select nursing diagnoses based on collected data. Decide which is most important. Specific nursing diagnoses will be given when discussing particular disorders, but those nursing diagnoses generally appropriate to the client with psychiatric-mental health disorders include

A. Anxiety
B. Ineffective family coping
C. Ineffective individual coping
D. Decisional conflict
E. Fatigue
F. Fear
G. Hopelessness
H. Knowledge deficit
I. Powerlessness
J. Sleep pattern disturbances
K. Altered thought processes
L. Risk for violence
M. Impaired verbal communication
N. Impaired social interaction
O. Altered role performance
P. Spiritual distress
Q. Self-esteem disturbance
R. Social isolation
S. Altered family processes
T. Defensive coping
U. Ineffective denial
V. Noncompliance
W. Body image disturbance
X. Risk for self-mutilation
Y. Rape-trauma syndrome
Z. Impaired adjustment

PLANNING AND IMPLEMENTATION

Goals

A. Client will
    1. Participate in treatment program.
    2. Be oriented to time, place, and person and exhibit reality-based behavior.
    3. Recognize reasons for behavior and develop alternative coping mechanisms.
    4. Maintain or improve self-care activities.
    5. Be protected from harmful behaviors.
B. There will be mutual agreement of nurse and client whenever possible.
C. Short-term goals are set for immediate problems; they should be feasible and within client's capabilities.
D. Long-term goals are related to discharge planning and prevention of recurrence or exacerbation of symptoms.

Interventions

The nurse will use therapeutic intervention and the nurse-client relationship to help the client achieve the goals of therapy. Interventions must be geared to the level of the client's capability and must relate to the specific problems identified for the individual client, family, or group.

Therapeutic Communication

A. Facilitative: use the following approaches to intervene therapeutically
    1. Silence: client able to think about self/problems; does not feel pressure or obligation to speak.
    2. Offering self: offer to provide comfort to client by presence (*Nurse:* "I'll sit with you." "I'll walk with you.").
    3. Accepting: indicate nonjudgmental acceptance of client and his perceptions by nodding and following what client says.
    4. Giving recognition: indicate to client your awareness of him and his behaviors (*Nurse:* "Good morning, John. You have combed your hair this morning.").
    5. Making observations: verbalize what you perceive (*Nurse:* "I notice that you can't seem to sit still.").
    6. Encouraging description: ask client to verbalize his perception (*Nurse:* "Tell me when you need to get up and walk around." "What is happening to you now?").

7. Using broad openings: encourage client to introduce topic of conversation (*Nurse:* "Where shall we begin today?" "What are you thinking about?").
8. Offering general leads: encourage client to continue discussing topic (*Nurse:* "And then?" "Tell me more about that.").
9. Reflecting: direct client's questions/statements back to encourage expression of ideas and feelings (*Client:* "Do you think I should call my father?" *Nurse:* "What do you want to do?").
10. Restating: repeat what client has said (*Client:* "I don't want to take the medicine." *Nurse:* "You don't want to take this medication?").
11. Focusing: encourage client to stay on topic/point (*Nurse:* "You were talking about. . . .").
12. Exploring: encourage client to express feelings or ideas in more depth (*Nurse:* "Tell me more about. . . ." "How did you respond to . . . ?").
13. Clarification: encourage client to make idea or feeling more explicit, understandable (*Nurse:* "I don't understand what you mean. Could you explain it to me?").
14. Presenting reality: report events/situations as they really are (*Client:* "I don't get to talk to my doctor." *Nurse:* "I saw your doctor talking to you this morning.").
15. Translating into feelings: encourage client to verbalize feelings expressed in another way (*Client:* "I will never get better." *Nurse:* "You sound rather hopeless and helpless.").
16. Suggesting collaboration: offer to work with client toward goal (*Client:* "I fail at everything I try." *Nurse:* "Maybe we can figure out something together so that you can accomplish something you want to do.").

B. Ineffective communication styles: the following nontherapeutic approaches tend to block therapeutic communication and are sometimes used by nurses to avoid becoming involved with client's emotional distress; often a protective action on part of nurse.
1. Reassuring: telling client there is no need to worry or be anxious (*Client:* "I'm nervous about this test." *Nurse:* "Everything will be all right.").
2. Advising: telling client what you believe should be done (*Client:* "I am going to. . . ." *Nurse:* "Why don't you do . . . instead?" or "I think you should do. . . .").
3. Requesting explanation: asking client to provide reasons for his feelings/behavior. The use of "why" questions should be avoided (*Nurse:* "Why do you feel, think, or act this way?").

4. Stereotypical response: replying to client with meaningless clichés (*Client:* "I hate being in the hospital." *Nurse:* "There's good and bad about everything.").
5. Belittling feelings: minimizing or making light of client's distress or discomfort (*Client:* "I'm so depressed about. . . ." *Nurse:* "Everyone feels sad at times.").
6. Defending: protecting person or institutions (*Client:* "Ms. Jones is a rotten nurse." *Nurse:* "Ms. Jones is one of our best nurses.").
7. Approving: giving approval to client's behavior or opinion (*Client:* "I'm going to change my attitude." *Nurse:* "That's good.").
8. Disapproving: telling client certain behavior or opinions do not meet your approval (*Client:* "I am going to sign myself out of here." *Nurse:* "I'd rather you wouldn't do that.").
9. Agreeing: letting client know that you think, feel alike; nurse verbalizes agreement.
10. Disagreeing: letting client know that you do not agree; telling client that you do not believe he is right.
11. Probing: questioning client about a topic he has indicated he does not want to discuss.
12. Denial: refusing to recognize client's perception (*Client:* "I am a hopeless case" *Nurse:* "You are not hopeless. There is always hope.").
13. Changing topic: letting client know you do not want to discuss a problem by introducing a new topic (*Client:* "I am a hopeless case." *Nurse:* "It's time to fill out your menu.").

Therapeutic Groups

A. Groups of clients meet with one or more therapists. They work together to alleviate client problems in
1. Interpersonal relations/communication
2. Coping with particular stressors (e.g., ostomy groups)
3. Self-understanding
B. Purposes
1. Increase self-awareness
2. Improve interpersonal relationships
3. Make changes in behavior
4. Deal with particular stressors
5. Enhance teaching/learning
C. Structure of groups
1. Leader(s) chosen
2. Selection of members
3. Size: 5 to 10 members
4. Physical arrangements
5. Time/place of meetings
6. Open: accept members anytime

7. Closed: do not add new members
D. Group dynamics
 1. System of interactions
 2. Collective activity
 3. Process: all activities/interactions
 4. Content: topics discussed
E. Stages of group development
 1. Beginning stage
  a. Anxiety in new situation
  b. Information given
  c. Group norms established
 2. Middle stage
  a. Group cohesiveness
  b. Members confronting each other
  c. Reliance on group member leading to self-reliance
  d. Sense of trust established
 3. Termination stage
  a. Individual member may leave abruptly
  b. Group decides work is done
  c. Ambivalence felt about termination
  d. Ideally, group members have met goals
F. Role of the nurse
 1. Explain purpose and rules of group
 2. Introduce group members
 3. Promote group cohesiveness
 4. Focus on problems of group and group process
 5. Encourage participation
 6. Role model
 7. Facilitate communication
 8. Set limits
   Table 7.1 lists types of therapeutic groups.

Family Therapy

A. Client is whole family, although a family member may be "identified client."
B. Purposes
 1. Improve relationships among family members
 2. Promote family function
 3. Resolve family problem(s)
C. Process
 1. Problem(s) are identified by each family member.

2. Members discuss their involvement in problem(s).
3. Members discuss how problem(s) affect them.
4. Members explore ways each of them can help resolve problem(s).
D. Role of the nurse
 1. Assess interactions among family members
 2. Make observations to family members
 3. Encourage expression of feelings by family members to one another
 4. Assist family in resolving problems

Milieu Therapy

A. Total environment (milieu) has an effect on individual's behavior, including
 1. Physical environment (i.e., cleanliness, noise, colors, fresh air, light)
 2. Relationships of staff to staff, staff to clients, and client to clients
 3. Atmosphere of safety, caring, mutual respect (e.g., client-run community meeting, community-set standards for behaviors)
B. Purposes
 1. Improve client's behavior
 2. Involve client in decision making of unit
 3. Increase client's sense of autonomy
 4. Increase communication among clients and between clients and staff
 5. Set structure of unit and behavioral limits
 6. Form a sense of community
C. Role of the nurse
 1. Involve clients in decision making
 2. Promote involvement of all staff
 3. Promote development of social skills of individual clients (e.g., nurse serves as role model)
 4. Encourage sense of community in staff and clients

Crisis Intervention

A. Client cannot resolve problem with usual problem-solving skills. Problem is so serious that functioning (homeostasis) is threatened. Crisis can be developmental (e.g., birth of first child) or situational (e.g., home destroyed by fire). Generally lasts for a few days but can continue for weeks; is usually limited to 6 weeks
B. Purposes
 1. Support client during time of crisis
 2. Resolve crisis
 3. Restore client at least to precrisis level of functioning
 4. Allow client to attain higher level of functioning through acquiring greater skill in problem solving

TABLE 7.1 Types of Therapeutic Groups

Type	Goal(s)	Example
Task	Accomplish outcome	Select field trip
Teaching/ learning	Gain knowledge/skills	Identify side effects of medications
Social/support	Give and receive support	Postmastectomy clients
Psychotherapy	Insight/behavioral change	Overcome shyness
Activity	Increase social interaction/self-esteem	Grooming, manicures

C. Process
1. Crisis event occurs: client unable to solve problem.
2. Increase in level of client's anxiety.
3. Client may use trial and error approach.
4. If problem unresolved, anxiety escalates and client seeks help.
D. Role of the nurse
1. Assess client's perception of problem: realistic/distorted
2. Determine situational supports (e.g., family, neighbors, agencies)
3. Explore previous coping behaviors of client
4. Offer support in resolving crisis
5. Enlist help of situational supports
6. Help client develop new, more effective coping behaviors
7. Convey hope to client that crisis can be resolved
8. Work with client as he resolves crisis

Behavior Modification

A. Based on theory that all behavior is learned as a result of positive reinforcement. Behaviors can be changed by substituting new behaviors.
B. Purpose: change unacceptable or maladaptive behaviors
C. Process
1. Determine the unacceptable behavior.
2. Identify more adaptive behavior to replace the unacceptable behavior.
3. Apply learning principles.
   a. Respond to unacceptable behavior by negative reinforcement (punishment) or by withholding positive reinforcement (ignore behavior).
   b. Determine what client views as reward.
4. When desired behavior occurs, present positive reinforcement (reward).
5. Consistently reward desired behavior.
6. Consistently respond to unacceptable behavior with negative reinforcement/ ignoring behavior.
D. Types
1. *Counterconditioning:* specific stimulus evokes a maladaptive response that is replaced with a more adaptive response.
2. *Systematic desensitization*
   a. Expose to small amount of stimulus while ensuring relaxation (client cannot be anxious and relaxed at same time).
   b. Continue relaxing client while increasing amount of stimulus.
   c. Fear response to stimulus is eventually extinguished.
3. *Token economy:* Tokens (rewards such as candy) are used to reinforce desired behaviors.

Psychotropic Medications

A variety of agents is used to control disordered thinking, anxiety, and mood disorders. Effects, side effects, and nursing implications are summarized with each disorder.

EVALUATION

A. How well have goals been met? If not met, why not?
1. Review prior steps of nursing process.
   a. Do you need more assessment data?
   b. Were nursing diagnoses prioritized?
   c. Were goals feasible and measurable?
   d. Were interventions appropriate?
2. Revise goals as necessary.
B. Client
1. Enrolled/participates in appropriate treatment program.
2. Expresses concerns/needs and develops a therapeutic relationship with nurse.
3. Identifies causes for behavior; learns and uses alternative coping mechanisms.
4. Demonstrates ability to care for self at optimum level and to identify areas where assistance is needed.
5. Does not engage in harmful behaviors; shows increased ability to control destructive impulses.
C. Client's behavior demonstrates optimal orientation to reality (e.g., can state name, place); interacts appropriately with others.

BEHAVIORS RELATED TO EMOTIONAL DISTRESS

Anxiety

A. General information
1. One of the most important concepts in psychiatric-mental health nursing.
2. Anxiety is present in almost every instance where clients are experiencing emotional distress/have a diagnosed psychiatric illness.
3. Experienced as a sense of emotional or physical distress as the individual responds to an unknown threat or thwarting of unmet needs.
4. The ego protects itself from the effects of anxiety by the use of defense mechanisms (see Table 7.2).
5. Physiologic responses are related to autonomic nervous system response and to level of anxiety.

TABLE 7.2 Defense Mechanisms

Type	Characteristics	Examples
Denial	Refusal to acknowledge a part of reality	A client on strict bed rest is walking down the hall; shows refusal to acknowledge need to stay in bed because of illness. A client states admission to the mental hospital is for reasons other than mental illness.
Repression	Threatening thoughts are pushed into the unconscious, anxiety and other symptoms are observed; client unable to have conscious awareness of conflicts or events that are source of anxiety.	"I don't know why I have to wash my hands all the time, I just have to."
Suppression	Consciously putting a threatening/distressing thought out of one's awareness.	A nurse must study for the NCLEX, but she has had a heated argument with her boyfriend. She decides not to think about the problem until she finishes studying, then she will attempt to resolve it.
Rationalization	Developing an acceptable, justifiable (to self) reason for behavior	A friend tells you that he has been in an automobile accident because the car skidded on wet leaves in the road; you go to the scene of the accident, but there are no leaves; friend admits to you and to self that he was probably driving too fast.
Reaction-formation	Engaging in behavior that is opposite of true desires	A man has an unconscious desire to view pornographic films; he circulates a petition to close the theater where such films are shown.
Sublimation	Anxiety channeled into socially acceptable behavior	A student is upset because she received a failing grade on a test; she knows that she will feel better if she goes jogging and runs a few miles.
Compensation	Making up for a deficit by success in another area	A young man who cannot make any varsity teams becomes the chess champion in his school.
Projection	Placing own undesirable trait onto another; blaming others for own difficulty	A student who would like to cheat on an exam states that other students are trying to cheat; a paranoid client claims that the FBI had him committed to the mental hospital.
Displacement	Directing feelings about one object/person toward a less threatening object/person	The head nurse reprimands you; you do not argue even though you do not agree with her reprimand; when you return home that evening you are hostile towards your roommate.
Identification	Taking onto oneself the traits of others that one admires	You greatly admire the clinical specialist in your hospital; unconsciously you begin to use the approaches she uses with clients.
Introjection	Symbolic incorporation of another into one's own personality	John becomes depressed when his father dies; John's feelings are directed to the mental image he has of his father.
Conversion	Anxiety converted into a physical symptom that is motor or sensory in nature	A young woman unconsciously desires to strike her mother; she develops sudden paralysis of her arms.
Symbolization	Representing an idea or object by a substitute object or sign.	A man who was spurned by a librarian develops a dislike of books and reading.
Dissociation	Separation or splitting off of one aspect of mental process from conscious awareness.	A student who prides herself on being prompt does not recall the times that she arrived late for class.
Undoing	Behavior that is opposite of earlier unacceptable behavior or thought	Joan tells an ethnic joke to a coworker, Sally; Sally, a member of that ethnic group, is offended; the following week Joan offers to work the weekend for Sally.
Regression	Behavior that reflects an earlier level of development. Adults hospitalized with serious illnesses sometimes will engage in regressive behaviors.	When a new baby is brought home, 5-year-old Billy begins to wet his pants although he had not done this for the past 2½ years.
Isolation	Separating emotional aspects of content from cognitive aspects of thought.	A client discusses his terminal diagnosis in clinical terms. He does not express any emotion.
Splitting	Viewing self, others, or situations as all good or all bad.	A client tells you that you are the best nurse. Later tells you that you are incompetent and she will report you.

a. Subjective: client experiences feelings of tension, need to act, uneasiness, distress, and apprehension or fear.
b. Objective: client exhibits restlessness, inability to concentrate, tension, dilated pupils, changes in vital signs (usually increased by sympathetic nervous system response, may be decreased by parasympathetic reactions).
6. Anxiety can be viewed positively (motivates us to change and grow) or negatively (interferes with problem-solving ability and affects functioning).
a. *Trait anxiety:* individual's normal level of anxiety. Some people are usually rather intense while others are more relaxed; may be related to genetic predisposition/early experiences (repressed conflicts).
b. *State anxiety:* change in person's anxiety level in response to stressors (environmental or any internal threat to the ego).
7. Levels of anxiety
a. *Mild:* increased awareness; ability to solve problems, learn; increase in perceptual field; minimal muscle tension
b. *Moderate:* optimal level for learning, perceptual field narrows to pay attention to particular details, increased tension to solve problems or meet challenges
c. *Severe:* sympathetic nervous system (flight/fight response); increase in blood pressure, pulse, and respirations; narrowed perceptual field, fixed vision, dilated pupils, can perceive scattered details or only one detail; difficulty in problem solving
d. *Panic:* decrease in vital signs (release of sympathetic response), distorted perceptual field, inability to solve problems, disorganized behavior, feelings of helplessness/terror
B. Nursing interventions
1. Determine the level of client's anxiety by assessing verbal and nonverbal behaviors and physiologic symptoms.
2. Determine cause(s) of anxiety with client, if possible.
3. Encourage client to move from affective (feeling) mode to cognitive (thinking) behavior (e.g., ask client, "What are you thinking?"). Stay with client. Reduce anxiety by remaining calm yourself; use silence, or speak slowly and softly.
4. Help client recognize own anxious behavior.
5. Provide outlets (e.g., talking, psychomotor activity, crying, tasks).

6. Provide support and encourage client to find ways to cope with anxiety.
7. In panic state nurse must make decisions.
a. Do not leave client alone.
b. Encourage ventilation of thoughts and feelings.
c. Use firm voice and give short, explicit directions (e.g., "Sit in this chair. I will sit here next to you.").
d. Engage client in motor activity to reduce tension (e.g., "We can take a brisk walk around the day room. Let's go.").

Defense Mechanisms

Usually unconscious processes used by ego to defend itself from anxiety and threats (see Table 7.2.).

Disorders of Perception

Occur with increased anxiety, disordered thinking/impaired reality testing
A. *Illusions*
1. General information: stimulus in the environment is misperceived (e.g., car backfiring is perceived as a gunshot; a bathrobe in an open closet is perceived as a person in the closet); may be visual, auditory, tactile, gustatory, olfactory.
2. Nursing intervention: show/explain stimulus to client to promote reality testing.
B. *Delusions*
1. General information: fixed, false set of beliefs that are real to client.
a. Grandiose: false belief that client has power, wealth, or status or is famous person
b. Persecutory: false belief that client is the object of another's harassment or harmful intent
c. Somatic: false belief that client has some physical/physiologic defect
2. Nursing interventions
a. Avoid arguing: client cannot be convinced, even with evidence, that the belief is false.
b. Determine client's need (grandiose delusion may indicate low self-esteem; provide opportunities to succeed at task that will enhance self-concept).
c. Reduce anxiety to encourage decreased need to use delusions.
d. Accept client's need for delusion, present (but do not insist that client accept) reality.
e. After therapeutic relationship has been established, you can express doubt about delusions to client.

f. Direct client's attention to nondelusional, nonthreatening topics (e.g., current events, client's hobbies or interests).

C. *Ideas of reference*
1. General information: belief that events or behaviors of others relate to self (e.g., telephone rings in nurse's station, client believes "they" are calling for him; two nurses are talking and laughing, client believes nurses are talking/laughing at him).
2. Nursing interventions are the same as for delusions.

D. *Hallucinations*
1. General information: sensory perceptions that have no stimulus in environment; most common hallucinations are auditory and visual (e.g., hearing voices; seeing persons, animals, objects).
2. Nursing interventions
   a. Encourage client to describe hallucination.
   b. Accept that this is a real experience for client.
   c. Present reality.
   d. Example: nurse sees client in listening attitude or responding to auditory hallucinations. *Nurse:* "You seem to be listening/talking." *Client:* "The voices are telling me to hurt myself." *Nurse:* "I don't hear the voices. Tell me what the voices are saying to you."

Withdrawal

A. General information: withdrawal from social interaction by not talking, walking away, turning away, sleeping or feigning sleep
B. Nursing interventions
1. Use silence.
2. Offer self.
3. Discuss nonthreatening topics that will not provoke increased anxiety.
4. Be consistent; keep promises, promote trust.

Hostility and Aggression

A. General information
1. Hostile behavior: responding to nurse with anger, insults, threats.
2. Assaultive behavior: attempting to physically harm others.
3. Usually nurse is not real object of client's anger, but is convenient target for angry feelings/verbalizations.
B. Nursing interventions
1. Hostility
   a. Recognize own response of anger or defensiveness.
   b. Determine source of client's anger.

c. Accept angry feelings.
d. Attempt to have client verbalize feelings and channel into acceptable behaviors.
2. Physical aggression/assaultive behaviors (client may act on increased anxiety by throwing objects or attempt to physically harm others)
   a. Assess for increased anxiety.
   b. Maintain distance, at least arm's length.
   c. Attempt to have client verbalize feelings.
   d. Talk client down.
   e. Obtain help if client becomes assaultive.

Self-mutilation

A. General information: behaviors cause physical injury but are not motivated by the desire to die.
B. Nursing interventions
1. Assess for suicide risk.
2. Offer support.
3. Protect client from carrying out self-mutilation actions.
4. Remove objects that can be used for self-harm.
5. Observe for changes in behaviors and attitudes.

Suicide

A. General information
1. Ideation: verbalization of wish to die (overt or disguised)
2. Gestures: engaging in nonlethal behaviors (e.g., superficial scratches, ingestion of medication in amounts that are not likely to cause serious injury/death)
3. Actions: engaging in behaviors or planning to engage in behaviors that have potential to cause death
4. May or may not be associated with a psychiatric disorder
5. Groups at risk (see Table 7.3)
B. Assessment findings

TABLE 7.3 Groups at Increased Risk for Suicide

- Adolescents/young adults (ages 15–24)
- Elderly
- Terminally ill
- Persons who have experienced loss/stress
- Survivors of persons who have committed suicide
- Individuals with bipolar disorders
- Depressed persons (when depression begins to lift)
- Substance abusers
- Persons who have attempted suicide previously
- More women attempt suicide; more men complete suicide

---

1. Verbal cues
   a. Overt: "I'm going to kill myself."
   b. Disguised: "I have the answer to my problems."
2. Behavioral cues
   a. Giving away prized possessions
   b. Getting financial affairs in order, making a will
   c. Suicidal ideation/gestures
   d. Indications of hopelessness, depression
   e. Behavioral and attitudinal changes (e.g., neat person becomes sloppy, depressed person suddenly becomes alert/positive, increased use of drugs and/or alcohol, alcohol withdrawal).
3. For lethality assessment, see Table 7.4.
C. Nursing interventions
   1. Contract with client to report suicide attempt.
   2. Assess suicide risk.
      a. Ask client if he thinks about, intends to harm himself.
      b. Ask client if he has formulation of plan; if details are worked out, when? where? how?
      c. Check availability of method (e.g., gun, pills).
   3. Keep client under constant observation.
   4. Remove any objects that can be used in suicide attempt (e.g., shoe laces, sharp objects).
   5. Therapeutic intervention
      a. Support aspects of wish to live; clients often ambivalent: wish to live and wish to die.
      b. Use one-to-one nurse/client relationship (let client know you care for him).

TABLE 7.4 Lethality Assessment

- Plans for suicide: when? where? how?
- Means available: what will be used? Is it available to client?
- Lethality of means (e.g., tranquilizers are less lethal when used alone than when combined with alcohol; guns are more lethal than plan to cut wrists)
  - Most lethal: gunshot, hanging, jumping from high places, carbon monoxide, potent poisons (e.g., cyanide)
  - Less lethal: nonprescription drugs, wrist cutting, tranquilizers without CNS depressants
  - Males tend to use more lethal means
- Possibility of "rescue"
- Support systems available or sense of isolation
- Availability of alcohol or drugs
- Severe/panic level of anxiety
- Hostility
- Disorganized thinking
- Preoccupation with thought of suicide plan
- Prior suicide attempts

   c. Allow client to express feelings of hopelessness, helplessness, worthlessness.
   d. Provide hope.
   e. Provide diversionary activities.
   f. Utilize support groups (e.g., family, clergy).
6. Following a suicide
   a. Encourage survivors to discuss client's death, their feelings and fears.
   b. Provide anticipatory guidance to family who may experience problems at holidays, anniversaries.
   c. Hold staff meetings to ventilate feelings.

Psychiatric Disorders (DSM IV)

DISORDERS OF INFANCY, CHILDHOOD, AND ADOLESCENCE

Overview

A. A specific group of disorders beginning in infancy, childhood, or adolescence.
B. Clients in these age groups may also evidence other disorders such as depression or schizophrenia.
C. Intellectual, behavioral, and/or emotional dysfunction of the young client also has an effect on the family, which may require nursing intervention.

Assessment

Newborn/Infants

A. Maturation
B. Developmental level
C. Sensorimotor capabilities
D. Bonding
E. Response to cuddling

Children/Adolescents

A. Motor skills
B. Communication abilities
C. Vocational/academic skills

D. Social and behavioral problems
E. Behavioral changes
F. Growth and development: physical/emotional
G. Self-concept
H. Knowledge of disorder

Parent/Family

A. Response to infant/child/adolescent with disorder
B. Guilt, sense of loss
C. Sibling jealousy/resentment
D. Knowledge of disorder
E. Expectations
F. Plans for future (home care/institutionalization)

Analysis

Nursing diagnoses for a child/family with a psychiatric-mental health disorder may include
A. Client
   1. Anxiety
   2. Total incontinence
   3. Ineffective individual coping
   4. High risk for injury
   5. Knowledge deficit
   6. Self-care deficits
   7. Self-esteem disturbance
   8. Sensory-perceptual alterations
   9. Sexual dysfunction
   10. High risk for violence
B. Parents/family
   1. Anxiety
   2. Disabling, ineffective family coping
   3. Altered family process
   4. Anticipatory grieving
   5. Knowledge deficit
   6. Altered parenting

Planning and Implementation

Goals

A. Client will
   1. Communicate thoughts and feelings about self-concept.
   2. Perform tasks at optimal level of capability.
   3. Develop trusting relationship with care givers.
B. Parents/family will
   1. Communicate feelings and responses to child and to disorder.
   2. Demonstrate knowledge of disorder.
   3. Formulate plans for child's care.

Interventions

A. Client
   1. Establish a therapeutic relationship by accepting client and client's limitations.
   2. Promote communication by use of therapeutic techniques, play therapy.
   3. Encourage independence in task performance with guidance and support.
B. Parents/family
   1. Promote communication by accepting family responses.
   2. Provide information about disorder.
   3. Contact appropriate person/agency for consultation with family about care and assistance with the child.

Evaluation

Client

A. Demonstrates trust in care givers.
B. Relates feelings about self verbally or symbolically.
C. Performs activities of daily living (ADL) and tasks at optimal level.

Parents/Family

A. Relate positive/negative responses to child.
B. Demonstrate understanding of disorder and child's potential.
C. With consultant, formulate a plan for child's care.

Specific Disorders

Mental Retardation

A. General information
   1. Significant subaverage intelligence (IQ of 70 or below) resulting in maladaptive behaviors with onset before age of 18 years
   2. Etiology
      a. Heredity 5%
      b. Early alterations in embryonic development 30%
      c. Perinatal problems 10%
      d. Acquired in infancy/early childhood 5%
      e. Environmental/other mental disorders 15%–20%
      f. Unknown etiology 30%–40%
   3. Degrees of retardation
      a. Mild mental retardation (IQ 50–70)
         1) 85% of cases
         2) educable to 6th grade level
         3) able to become self-supporting
      b. Moderate mental retardation (IQ 35–49)
         1) 10% of cases
         2) educable to 2nd grade level
         3) able to perform skills but will need supervision at work
      c. Severe mental retardation (IQ 20–34)
         1) 3%–4% of cases
         2) may learn to talk/communicate
         3) able to perform simple tasks and elementary hygiene

        d. Profound mental retardation (IQ below
            20)
            1) 1%–2% of cases
            2) some speech/communication
                possible
    B. Assessment findings
        1. Intellectual impairment (determine degree)
        2. Sensorimotor impairment
        3. Communication, social, behavioral
            impairment
        4. Lack of self-esteem and poor self-image
        5. Sense of loss, guilt, nonacceptance or
            unrealistic expectations on part of
            parents/family
    C. Nursing interventions
        1. Promote optimal functioning in ADL and
            feelings of accomplishment, self-worth.
        2. Provide opportunities for client/family to
            communicate thoughts, feelings.
        3. Provide positive reinforcement for every
            success.
        4. Accept client's limitations and set goals
            accordingly.
        5. Provide support and information about
            disorder to family.
        6. Accept family's response to client.

Other Disorders of Childhood/Adolescence

    A. General information
        1. *Separation anxiety:* excessive anxiety and
            worry about being separated from
            person(s)/places to which child has
            become attached (e.g., refusal to leave
            mother/home to attend school)
        2. *Reactive/attachment disorder:* reluctance to
            enter social relationships with others,
            creating an interference with social growth
        3. *Overanxious disorders:* pervasive,
            unrealistic worry or concern about
            competency; somatic complaints without
            physical basis
    B. Assessment findings: excessive anxiety related
        to separation, social interaction, and
        achievements
    C. Nursing intervention: provide information
        regarding available mental health services for
        child and family.

Disorders with Physical Manifestations

    A. General information
        1. Important to rule out any physiologic
            cause
        2. Often related to stress or conflict in the
            family
        3. May affect child's family/social interactions
            and development
    B. Assessment findings
        1. *Enuresis:* urinary incontinence
            (bedwetting) after age 5 not caused by
            physical disorder

        2. *Encopresis:* fecal incontinence after age 4
            not caused by physical disorder
        3. *Tics:* involuntary, repetitive movements
        4. *Stuttering:* repetition of sounds, words or
            frequent hesitations in speaking
    C. Nursing interventions
        1. Provide information about the disorders
            and emphasize that they are treatable.
        2. Determine whether family therapy may be
            indicated, as well as individual therapy for
            child.
        3. Offer support and help child/family
            overcome feelings of shame or guilt.
        4. For enuresis and encopresis, utilize toilet
            training techniques.
        5. Encourage discussion of client/family
            response to symptoms.

PERVASIVE DEVELOPMENTAL DISORDERS

Autistic Disorder

    A. General information
        1. Develops prior to 3 years of age.
        2. Child does not relate to people, but may
            become attached to objects.
        3. This is a rare disorder, may have a
            physiologic basis.
        4. Chronic disorder, more than ⅔ of these
            children remain severely handicapped and
            dependent on care givers.
        5. Special education is necessary.
        6. Family may choose institutionalization for
            optimum care.
    B. Assessment findings
        1. Infant not responsive to cuddling; may
            even show an aversion to being touched
        2. No eye contact or facial responsiveness
        3. Impaired or no verbal communication
        4. Echolalia (repetition of words/phrases
            spoken by others)
        5. Inability to tolerate change
        6. Ritualistic behavior
        7. Fascination with movement, spinning
            objects
        8. Labile moods
        9. Unresponsive or overresponsive to
            stimuli
        10. High risk for developing seizure disorders
    C. Nursing interventions
        1. Provide parents/family with support and
            information about the disorder,
            opportunities for therapy and education
            for the child.
        2. Assist child with ADL.
        3. Promote reality testing.
        4. Encourage child to develop a relationship
            with another person.
        5. Maintain regular schedule for activities.

6. Provide constant routine for child (place for eating, sitting, sleeping).
7. Protect child from self-injury.
8. Provide safe environment.
9. Institute seizure precautions if necessary.

Eating Disorders

A. General information
   1. Gross disturbances in eating behaviors
   2. *Pica:* persistent eating of substances such as plaster, paint, or sand
   3. *Bulimia nervosa:* binge eating; the ingestion of large amounts of food in short time, often followed by self-induced vomiting. May be accompanied by affective disorders and fear of being unable to stop this behavior. Manifested by fluctuations in weight caused by binges of eating and fasting.
   4. *Anorexia nervosa:* refusal to eat or aberration in eating patterns resulting in severe emaciation that can be life threatening. Characterized by a fear of becoming fat, and a body-image disturbance where clients claim to feel fat even when extremely thin. This disorder is most common (95%) in adolescent and young adult females. There is a mortality rate of 15%–20%.

B. Assessment findings (anorexia nervosa)
   1. Weight loss of 15% or more of original body weight
   2. Electrolyte imbalance
   3. Depression
   4. Preoccupation with being thin; inability to recognize degree of own emaciation (distorted body image)
   5. Social withdrawal and poor family and individual coping skills
   6. History of high activity and achievement in academics, athletics
   7. Amenorrhea

C. Nursing interventions
   1. Monitor vital signs.
   2. Measure I&O.
   3. Weigh client 3 times/week at the same time (check to be sure client has not hidden heavy objects or water loaded before being weighed, weigh in hospital gown).
   4. Do not comment on weight loss or gain.
   5. Set limits on time allotted for eating.
   6. Record amount eaten.
   7. Stay with client during meals, focusing on client, not on food.
   8. Accompany client to bathroom for at least ½ hour after eating to prevent self-induced vomiting.
   9. Individual/family therapy may be necessary.
   10. Encourage client to express feelings.
   11. Help client to set realistic goal for self and to reduce need for being perfect.
   12. Encourage client to discuss own body image; present reality; do not argue with client.
   13. Teach relaxation techniques.
   14. Help client identify interests and positive aspects of self.

Sample Questions

1. Eddie, 6 years old, has been diagnosed with enuresis after tests revealed no organic cause of bed wetting. Eddie's mother is upset and blames the problem on his father. "It's all his father's fault!" Your initial response is
   1. Why do you say that?
   2. It's usually nobody's fault.
   3. You seem really upset by this.
   4. Why are you blaming Eddie's father?
2. Kara, 17 years old, is admitted with anorexia nervosa. You have been assigned to sit with her while she eats her dinner. Kara says to you, "My primary nurse trusts me. I don't see why you don't." Your best response is
   1. I do trust you, but I was assigned to be with you.
   2. It sounds as if you are manipulating me.
   3. OK. When I return, you should have eaten everything.
   4. Who is your primary nurse?
3. Alicia, 15 years old, is hospitalized for the treatment of anorexia nervosa. She is 64 inches tall and weighs 100 pounds. The primary objective in the treatment of the hospitalized anorexic client is to
   1. decrease the client's anxiety.
   2. increase insight into the disorder.
   3. help the mother to relinquish control.
   4. get the client to eat and gain weight.
4. Fifteen-year-old Alicia is hospitalized for treatment of anorexia nervosa. While admitting Alicia, the nurse discovers a bottle of pills that Alicia calls antacids. She takes them because her stomach hurts. The nurse's best initial response is
   1. Tell me more about your stomach pain.
   2. These do not look like antacids. I need to get an order for you to have them.
   3. Tell me more about your drug use.
   4. Some girls take pills to help them lose weight.
5. A nursing intervention based on the behavior modification model of treatment for anorexia would be
   1. role playing the client's interactions with her parents.
   2. encouraging the client to vent her feelings through exercise.
   3. providing a high-calorie, high-protein diet with between-meal snacks.

4. restricting the client's privileges until she gains three pounds.

Answers and Rationales

1. The correct answer is 3. Upon hearing her son's diagnosis, Eddie's mother is experiencing emotional turmoil and projecting blame. Acknowledging her feelings would build further trust and encourage her to discuss her thoughts and feelings.

2. The correct answer is 2. Clients diagnosed with eating disorders have difficulty establishing trust. Confronting the client's manipulation assists the client to deal with this maladaptive behavior.

3. The correct answer is 4. Because the anorexic client is experiencing physiologic responses to the starvation process, the client's well-being is dependent on establishing an adequate nutritional state to avert the potentially fatal effects of starvation. Therefore, eating the gaining weight is the primary goal of hospitalization. Anxiety is the basis of the client's eating disorder and must be addressed as well during the hospitalization. Long-term psychotherapy will hopefully increase the client's insight into the disorder. Helping the mother with control issues may be a part of family therapy but is not the primary objective.

4. The correct answer is 1. While there might be concern that the client is abusing drugs and possibly using drugs to induce further weight loss, the primary concern is that the client is experiencing abdominal pain. This may be a clue to impending medical crisis, which requires further assessment. Choices 3 and 4 might be appropriate later in the discussion or relationship when more information has been gathered. The question asked for the best initial response.

5. The correct answer is 4. Behavior modification involves creating positive and negative consequences for desirable and undesirable behavior. The benefit of gaining weight is additional privileges. Role playing and venting feelings are not part of behavior modification. Providing appropriate meals is desirable but is not behavior modification.

DELIRIUM, DEMENTIA, AND OTHER COGNITIVE DISORDERS

Overview

A. A group of disorders with a known or presumed etiology.

B. Frequently manifest as dementia or delirium.
C. May be substance induced (drugs or alcohol) or caused by a disease process; etiology may be unknown.
D. It is important for the nurse to assess behaviors rather than focus on medical diagnoses.
E. Behaviors related to impaired brain functioning may be temporary or permanent, with increasing degeneration and eventual loss of brain function.
F. Not exclusive to old age, may complicate illnesses in any age group.

Types

A. *Delirium/Rapid Development*
   1. Manifested by reduced awareness of environment, disorders of perception, thought, speech, and attention deficits.
   2. Usually of brief duration.
   3. May occur postoperatively or following head injury, intoxication from drugs/alcohol, acute disease, or injury.
B. *Dementia/Gradual Development*
   1. Loss of intellectual abilities resulting in impaired social and occupational functioning.
   2. May be temporary, or progressive loss may occur.
   3. Found predominantly in elderly.
   4. Personality changes are usually an exaggeration of former character traits (e.g., suspicious, nontrusting person becomes paranoid); but alteration can also occur (e.g., formerly neat and orderly person pays no attention to hygiene, becomes sloppy and dirty).
   5. Memory impairment; short-term memory loss may be most obvious.
   6. Organic etiology may be known; conditions include intoxication, infections, tumors, circulatory disorders (cerebral atherosclerosis), trauma, Huntington's chorea, Korsakoff's syndrome, Creutzfeld-Jakob disease, neurosyphilis.
   7. Specific etiology may not be known (e.g., Alzheimer's disease, Pick's disease).
   8. Frequently these clients cannot perform basic ADL.

Assessment

A. Mental status assessment, especially orientation to time and place, memory, and judgment
B. Nutritional status
C. Ability to perform ADL, self-care
D. Presence of confabulation (making up information to fill in memory gaps)
E. Behavioral/social changes
F. Disorders of perception
G. Impaired motor skills, coordination

H. Change in sleep patterns
I. Elimination: constipation/incontinence
J. Family response to client's condition

Analysis

Nursing diagnoses for clients with these disorders may include
A. Anxiety
B. Impaired verbal communication
C. Ineffective individual/family coping
D. Altered family processes
E. High risk for fluid volume deficit
F. High risk for injury
G. Nutrition less than body requirements
H. Self-care deficits
I. Self-esteem disturbance
J. Sleep pattern disturbance
K. Altered thought processes
L. High risk for violence

Planning/Implementation

Goals

A. Client will
   1. Be protected from injury.
   2. Retain optimal cognitive function and self-care abilities.
   3. Have fear/anxiety minimized.
   4. Maintain adequate nutrition/hydration.
B. Family will communicate feelings about client.

Interventions

A. Institute safety measures: side rails, frequent checks, restraints only as last resort and for protection of client as ordered by physician.
B. Maintain reality orientation.
   1. Client may not be capable of reality testing.
   2. Continue to address client by name.
   3. Maintain awareness of client's limitations in this area.
   4. Do not tell client to "remember"; severe memory loss may make client incapable of memory.
C. Assist/support with self-care needs; arrange for necessary assistive devices, help with feeding; encourage fluids.
D. Avoid "insight" therapy and discussion of impaired mental functioning as this may increase anxiety.
E. Provide spouse/family with information about client's capabilities.
F. Provide support for spouse/family; encourage continued interaction with client.

Evaluation

A. Client
   1. Remains free from injuries.

   2. Retains cognitive functions and self-care ability as far as possible; interacts with others appropriately.
   3. Maintains appropriate weight.
B. Family
   1. Expresses sense of loss or frustration related to client's condition.
   2. Continues contact with client.

Sample Questions

6. Millie R., aged 74, was recently admitted to a nursing home because of confusion, disorientation, and negativistic behavior. Her family states that Millie is in good health. Millie asks you, "Where am I?" The best response for the nurse to make is
   1. Don't worry, Millie. You're safe here.
   2. Where do you think you are?
   3. What did your family tell you?
   4. You're at the community nursing home.
7. Which of the following would be an appropriate strategy in reorienting a confused client to where her room is?
   1. Place pictures of her family on the bedside stand.
   2. Put her name in large letters on her forehead.
   3. Remind the client where her room is.
   4. Let the other residents know where the client's room is.
8. Millie R., aged 74, was recently admitted to a nursing home because of confusion, disorientation, and negativistic behavior. Which activity would you engage Millie in at the nursing home?
   1. Reminiscence groups.
   2. Sing-alongs.
   3. Discussion groups.
   4. Exercise class.
9. Millie R., aged 74, was recently admitted to a nursing home because of confusion, disorientation, and negativistic behavior. Millie has had difficulty sleeping since admission. Which of the following would be the best intervention?
   1. Provide her with a glass of warm milk.
   2. Ask the physician for a mild sedative.
   3. Do not allow Millie to take naps during the day.
   4. Ask her family what they prefer.

Answers and Rationales

6. The correct answer is 4. Responding factually provides the client with reality orientation. The alternative responses belittle the client.
7. The correct answer is 3. The nurse should be

someone a confused client can turn to for direction and guidance.

8. The correct answer is 4. Millie's short-term memory loss may increase her frustration and anxiety during the other activities. Providing her with structured exercises permits her to release tension.

9. The correct answer is 4. Including the family in the plan of care ensures a more effective plan.

SUBSTANCE USE DISORDERS

Overview

A. The use of chemical agents (alcohol and drugs) to change behavior and mood
B. Abuse: continued use despite problems (social, occupational, psychologic) that are caused by substance or continued use in hazardous situations (e.g., operating machinery, driving)
C. Dependence
  1. Need for larger amounts (tolerance)
  2. Unsuccessful attempts to decrease/discontinue use
  3. Inability to function as usual in work, social activities
  4. Withdrawal symptoms (psychologic/physical distress when substance is reduced/discontinued)
D. Addiction: compulsive use of a substance; physiologic and psychologic dependence

PSYCHOACTIVE SUBSTANCE-INDUCED ORGANIC MENTAL DISORDERS

The use of substances that result in intoxication or withdrawal syndromes, delirium, hallucinations, delusions, mood disorders.

Assessment

A. Determine substances used, amount and last time taken, and if combined with other drugs
B. Pupillary changes, changes in vital signs or level of consciousness
C. Presence of dehydration
D. Presence of nutritional and vitamin deficiencies
E. Suicide potential: ideation, gestures
F. Level of anxiety
G. Use of denial/projection
H. Symptoms of overdose (will be drug-specific; see Table 7.5)
I. Drug-use patterns: what, when, why substances are used

Analysis

Nursing diagnoses for clients with a psychoactive substance abuse disorder may include
A. Anxiety
B. Ineffective individual/family coping
C. Fear
D. High risk for fluid volume deficit
E. High risk for injury
F. Nutrition less than body requirements
G. Self-care deficit
H. Self-esteem disturbance
I. Sensory-perceptual alterations
J. Sleep pattern disturbance
K. Altered thought processes
L. High risk for violence
M. Ineffective denial

Planning and Intervention

Goals

Client will
A. Be protected from injury.
B. Receive adequate hydration and nutrition.
C. Terminate use of substance being abused without withdrawal symptoms; emergency care will be provided if symptoms cannot be avoided.
D. Have decreased feelings of anxiety.
E. Receive information and consider help for substance-abuse disorder

Interventions

A. Assess drug use pattern: identity, recent use, and frequency of use of prescription and nonprescription drugs, other substances (e.g., alcohol, nicotine).
B. Support client during acute phase of detoxification or withdrawal.
  1. Stay with client; reassure that current manifestations are temporary.
  2. Monitor vital signs, level of consciousness.
  3. Institute suicide precautions.
  4. Administer medications (to prevent withdrawal) as ordered.
  5. If client is experiencing panic, talk down, possibly with assistance of family/friends.
  6. If client is hallucinating, reinforce reality, speak in a calm voice.
  7. Confront client's use of denial.
  8. Monitor your own responses of sympathy/anger.
  9. Be aware of transference/countertransference.
  10. Maintain course of action in plan of care; client must follow plan.
  11. Involve staff in negotiating care plan revisions.
C. Rehabilitation/longer-term care
  1. Provide nonthreatening environment.

TABLE 7.5 Commonly Abused Drugs

Drug	Effect	Dependence	Assessment Findings	Overdose	Nursing Interventions for Overdose
Barbiturates					
Antianxiety drugs, hypnotics	Reduction in anxiety, escape from stress	Psychologic at first, then physiologic; withdrawal similar to alcohol withdrawal, to point of delirium. Cross-tolerance to other depressants	Irritability, weight loss, changes in mood or motor coordination	Slurred speech, lethargy, respiratory depression, coma; use combined with alcohol can be lethal	Keep person awake and moving to prevent coma; maintain airway.
Opioids/Narcotics					
Heroin, morphine, meperidine, methadone	Euphoria, dysphoria, and/or apathy	Psychologic dependence rapidly leading to physical; signs of withdrawal: cramps, nausea, vomiting, diarrhea; sleep disturbance, chills and shaking	Pinpoint pupils, mental clouding, lethargy, impaired memory and judgment, evidence of needle tracks, inflamed nasal mucosa if drug is snorted	Depressed consciousness and respirations, dilated pupils with anoxia or polydrug use	Provide emergency support of vital functions. In withdrawal, administer methadone or Narcan as ordered.
Stimulant					
Cocaine/Crack	Increased self-esteem, energy, sexual desire, euphoria; decreased anxiety	Dopamine deficiency results in psychologic dependency to produce feelings of well-being	Increased vital signs, headache, chest pain, depression and/or paranoia, inflamed nasal passages if snorted	Delirium, tremors, high fever (106+) convulsions, cardiac/respiratory arrest	Emergency support of vital functions, reduce CNS stimulation.
Amphetamines					
Amphetamine, dextro-amphetamine, methamphetamine	Depressed appetite; increased activity, awareness, sense of well-being	Long-term use or high doses may produce delirium, paranoid-like delusions, withdrawal, depression, fatigue, sleep disturbances	Same as cocaine, plus suicidal ideation	Same as cocaine	Same as cocaine, plus suicide precautions. Observe for increased anxiety to panic, which may potentiate assaultive behavior.
Phencyclidine (PCP)	Euphoria, psychomotor agitation, emotional lability	Not reported	Vomiting, hallucinations, paranoid ideation, agitation	Violent behavior, suicide, respiratory arrest, delirium, coma, increased blood pressure and pulse	Monitor vital signs. Observe for suicidal or assaultive behavior. Provide nonthreatening environment, reality orientation, support.
Hallucinogens					
LSD, mescaline	Disordered perceptions, depersonalization	Not reported	"Bad trip," high anxiety to panic; hallucinations may occur long after drug has been metabolized; flashbacks may produce long-lasting psychotic disorders	Reduced LOC	Same as PCP, plus talk client down.
Cannabis					
Marijuana, hashish, THC	Euphoria, intense perceptions, relaxation, lethargy	Not reported	Increased pulse rate and appetite; impaired judgment and coordination	Panic reaction, nausea, vomiting, depression and disorders of perception	In panic, talk down. In severe depression, institute suicide precautions.

2. Set limits on unacceptable behavior.
3. Provide adequate diet and fluids.
4. Provide information relating to substance abuse and rehabilitation programs.

Evaluation

A. Client experienced no injury.
B. Vital signs are stable.
C. Withdrawal proceeded without symptoms; client remains drug/alcohol free.
D. Client can discuss substance-abuse problem and requests or agrees to consider rehabilitation/therapy for problem.

Specific Disorders

Alcohol Abuse/Dependence

A. General information
   1. Alcohol is a legal substance and there are millions of social drinkers.
   2. Alcohol is classified as a central nervous system depressant.
   3. Alcohol abuse/dependence is a major problem in this country with over 18 million adults identified as alcohol abusers.
   4. Only approximately 5% of alcohol abusers are the "skid row" type.
   5. Incidence is increasing in women and adolescents.
   6. Considered a disease that can be arrested but not cured.
   7. Important to assess history of alcohol consumption for clients admitted to hospital for non-alcohol-related disorders, because they may go into withdrawal.
   8. Socioeconomic as well as a physiologic problem, resulting in increased health care costs and loss of productivity if ability to maintain a job is impaired.
   9. Alcohol used with other substances (barbiturates, antianxiety drugs) may have lethal consequences.
   10. Long-term use may result in loss of health (gastritis, pancreatitis, cirrhosis, hepatitis, malnutrition, cardiac and neural disorders) and life (suicide, automobile accidents).
   11. Directly related problems include withdrawal, delirium tremens, and alcohol-related dementia
      a. *Withdrawal*
         1) alcohol consumption reduced/discontinued following continuous consumption for many days or longer
         2) withdrawal is progressive and has four stages:
            I: at least 8 hours after last drink; symptoms include mild tremors, tachycardia, increased blood pressure, diaphoresis, nervousness
            II: gross tremors, hyperactivity, profound confusion, loss of appetite, insomnia, weakness, disorientation, illusions, auditory and visual hallucinations
            III: 12–48 hours after last drink: symptoms include (in addition to those found in I and II) severe hallucinations, grand mal seizures
            IV: 3–5 days after last drink (24–72 hours if untreated): delirium tremens, confusion, agitation, severe psychomotor activity, hallucinations, insomnia, tachycardia
         3) withdrawal may last less than a week or may evolve into alcohol withdrawal delirium (delirium tremens).
         4) 10%–15% mortality rate from hypoglycemia/electrolyte imbalances.
      b. *Delirium tremens (DTs)*
         1) history of alcohol abuse usually for more than 5 years.
         2) may be preceded by seizures.
         3) symptoms occur 2–3 days after alcohol reduced/discontinued.
         4) signs include tachycardia, increased blood pressure, agitation, delusions, hallucinations.
      c. *Alcohol hallucinosis:* hallucinations only
      d. *Alcohol-related dementia:* caused by poor nutrition
         1) Korsakoff's psychosis is sometimes preceded by *Wernicke's encephalopathy.* Confusion and ataxia are predominant symptoms.
         2) thiamine deficiency results in *Korsakoff's dementia/psychosis;* symptoms include chronic disorientation, confabulation. It is irreversible.
         3) large doses of thiamine may prevent the development of Korsakoff's psychosis. See Table 7.6.
B. Medical management
   1. Vitamin and nutrition therapy
   2. Antianxiety drugs (Librium or Valium)
   3. Disulfiram (Antabuse)
      a. Produces unpleasant reaction (thirst, sweating, palpitations, vomiting, dyspnea, respiratory and cardiac failure) when taken with alcohol.
      b. 500 mg/day for 1–2 weeks; usual maintenance dose is 250 mg/day.
      c. Duration of action is ½ to several hours;

TABLE 7.6   Phases of Alcohol Addiction

Phase	Features
Prealcoholic	Drink almost every day to reduce tension Increase in amount of alcohol ingested
Addiction	Blackouts Secret drinking Large amounts ingested
Dependence	Physical craving for alcohol Makes up reasons for drinking Reduced nutrition Aggressive behavior Pressure from family and/or employer to reduce/stop drinking
Chronic	Long periods of intoxication Impaired thinking Less alcohol produces sedation tremors

no alcohol should be taken at least 12 hours before taking drug.

   d. Increases effects of antianxiety drugs and oral anticoagulants.

   e. Side effects include headache, dry mouth, somnolence, flushing.

   f. Nursing responsibilities
   1) teach client the nature of severe reaction and importance of avoiding all alcohol (including cough medicine, foods prepared with alcohol, etc.).
   2) teach client to carry an identification card in case of accidental alcohol ingestion.
   3) monitor effects of antianxiety drugs if being taken at the same time.
   4) monitor for bleeding if taking oral anticoagulants.

4. High doses of chlordiazepoxide (Librium) to control withdrawal in acute detoxification.

C. Assessment findings
1. Dependent personality; often using denial as a defense mechanism
2. Tendency to minimize and underreport amount of alcohol consumed
3. Intoxication: blood alcohol level 0.15 (150 mg alcohol/100 ml blood). Legal level 0.08–0.10.
4. Signs of impaired judgment, motor skills, and slurred speech
5. Behavior may be boisterous and euphoric or aggressive, or may be depressed and withdrawn
6. Signs of withdrawal, DTs, or alcohol-related dementias

D. Nursing interventions
1. Stay with client.
2. Monitor vital signs and blood sugar levels.
3. Observe for tremors, seizures, increased agitation, anxiety, disorders of perception.
4. Administer medications as ordered; observe effects/side effects of tranquilizers carefully.
5. If disorders of perception occur, explain that these are part of the withdrawal process.
6. Provide fluids, adequate nutrition, and quiet environment.
7. When client is stable, provide information about rehabilitation programs (Alcoholics Anonymous); at this stage client may be willing to consider a program to stop drinking.
8. Provide information about Alanon (for spouse and adult family members), Alateen (for children), and ACOA (for adult children of alcoholics).

Psychoactive Drug Use

A. General information
1. Drugs abused may be prescription or "street" drugs
2. Types of drugs frequently abused
   a. Barbiturates, antianxiety drugs, hypnotics
   b. Opioids (narcotics): heroin, morphine, meperidine, methadone, hydromorphone
   c. Amphetamines: amphetamine, dextroamphetamine, methamphetamine (speed), some appetite suppressants
   d. Cocaine, hydrochloride cocaine (crack)
   e. Phencyclidine (PCP)
   f. Hallucinogens: LSD, mescaline, DMT
   g. Cannabis: marijuana, hashish, THC

B. Assessment findings and nursing interventions for overdoses vary with particular drug; see Table 7.5, page 537

C. Polydrug abusers
1. Common pattern of drug use
2. Synergistic effect: drugs interact so that effect is greater than if each drug is taken separately
3. Additive effect: two or more drugs with same action are taken together (e.g., barbiturates with alcohol will result in heavy sedation).

Impaired Nurses

A. General information
1. Most nursing licenses are suspended or revoked for substance abuse while on duty.
2. Substances include alcohol and/or prescription drugs pilfered from unit drug stocks.
3. Stealing drugs may result in criminal prosecution.

4. Work-related stress and easy access to drugs are factors relating to nurses' substance abuse.
5. Substance use results in impaired judgment and psychomotor abilities, resulting in unsafe nursing practice.

B. Assessment of impairment
1. Alcohol odor on breath
2. Frequent lateness/absences
3. Shortages in narcotics
4. Clients do not obtain pain relief after "receiving" pain reduction medication from nurse
5. Nurse makes frequent trips to bathroom/locker room
6. Changes in locomotion, psychomotor skills, pupil size, and mood/affect

C. Nurses' responsibilities related to impaired nurse colleague
1. Client safety is first priority.
2. ANA code of ethics (and some state laws) require nurse to safeguard clients.
3. Interventions for suspected substance abuse by co-worker
   a. Obtain information about legal issues, treatment options, and institutional policies.
   b. Document observations related to behaviors and narcotic charting.
   c. If possible, have other co-workers verify your information.
   d. Arrange meeting with peer(s), nurse, supervisor, nurse advocate (where possible) and confront nurse with documentation.
   e. Let nurse know you care about him/her and will help.
   f. Help nurse work through denial.
   g. Provide plan to offer recovery program (e.g., include "recovering" nurse buddy).
   h. Offer hope, support (moral and financial) to aid nurse in treatment.
   i. Explain institutional policies regarding future employment.
   j. If nurse continues to deny substance abuse, consider following steps
      1) advocate should protect nurse's rights.
      2) suspension/dismissal from job.
      3) report to licensing board.
      4) if theft of drug from unit has occurred, report to law enforcement agency.

Sample Questions

10. Mr. J.W., 46 years old, is on the verge of losing his job because of a drinking problem. He voluntarily enters an alcohol detoxification program. The most important information for Mr. W. to accurately relate to the staff when admitted for detoxification is the amount, type, and
    1. time substances were taken over the past 24 hours.
    2. frequency of substances taken over the past week.
    3. frequency of substances taken over the past two weeks.
    4. frequency of substances taken over the past month.
11. A characteristic common to most substance abusers is difficulty in effectively
    1. coping with stress and anxiety.
    2. interacting socially.
    3. performing in work-related settings.
    4. setting limits.
12. Signs and symptoms that a client is developing impending alcohol withdrawal delirium include diaphoresis, tremors,
    1. bradycardia, and hypertension.
    2. bradycardia, and hypotension.
    3. tachycardia, and hypertension.
    4. tachycardia, and hypotension.
13. The most widely accepted treatment modality for substance abuse is
    1. individual therapy with a psychodynamically oriented therapist.
    2. individual therapy with a systems-oriented therapist.
    3. group therapy with others with personality disorders.
    4. group therapy with other substance abusers.

Answers and Rationales

10. The correct answer is 1. Although a complete substance abuse history is necessary eventually, on admission the most important information to determine is the type and amount of substances taken by the client in the past 24 hours. This is vital so that the nursing and medical staff can provide an optimally safe detoxification for the client.
11. The correct answer is 1. While the substance abuser has difficulty in all areas listed, problems handling stress and anxiety underlie all the others. Difficulty handling stress and anxiety is often a presubstance abuse characteristic.
12. The correct answer is 3. Delirium tremens is characterized by increased blood pressure, pulse, and respirations, and an increase in psychomotor activity.
13. The correct answer is 4. While some have found treatment on an individual basis with therapists of varying orientations to be beneficial, group therapy with other

substance abusers is the most highly prescribed treatment modality. It is the model of Alcoholics Anonymous, upon which many other groups have been based. Individual therapy consists of a series of private contacts between the client and a professionally trained therapist. A psychodynamic approach emphasizes the influences of intrapsychic forces on observable behavior. Illness is defined in terms of behavior disorders that originate in conflicts before age six among the id, ego, superego, and environment. This is not the best method of treatment for the substance abuse client. Individual therapy with a systems-oriented therapist has not been found to be helpful in substance abuse clients. Group therapy with clients with other personality disorders would not provide the same cohesiveness as it would if all members of the group were substance abusers. All clients with substance abuse problems demonstrate many of the same behavioral characteristics and can provide support to one another.

SCHIZOPHRENIA AND OTHER PSYCHOTIC DISORDERS

Overview

A. Characterized by disordered thinking, delusions, hallucinations, depersonalization (feeling of being strange, not oneself), impaired reality testing (psychosis), and impaired interpersonal relationships.
B. Regression to the earliest stages of development is often noted (e.g., incontinence, mutism).
C. Onset is usually in adolescence/early adulthood (15 to 35 years of age).
D. Client may be seriously impaired and unable to perform ADL.
E. Etiology is not known; theories include
   1. Genetic: 1% of population.
   2. Biochemical: neurotransmitter dysfunction i.e. dopamine, serotonin.
   3. Interaction of predisposing risk and environmental stress.
F. Prior to onset (premorbid) client may have been suspicious, eccentric, or withdrawn.

Classifications

A. *Disorganized:* incoherent; delusions are not organized; social withdrawal; affect blunted, silly, or inappropriate
B. *Catatonic:* psychomotor disturbances
   1. Stupor: mute, little reaction or movement
   2. Excitement: purposeless, excited motor activity

3. Posturing: voluntary, inappropriate, bizarre postures
C. *Paranoid:* delusions and hallucinations of persecution/grandeur
D. *Undifferentiated:* disorganized behaviors, delusions, and hallucinations

Assessment

A. Four A's
   1. Affect: flat, blunted
   2. Associative looseness: verbalizations are disorganized
   3. Ambivalence: cannot choose between conflicting emotions
   4. Autistic thinking: thoughts on self, extreme withdrawal, unable to relate to outside world
B. Any changes in thoughts, speech, affect
C. Ability to perform self-care activities, nutritional deficits
D. Suicide potential
E. Aggression
F. Regression
G. Impaired communication

Analysis

Nursing diagnoses for clients with schizophrenic disorders may include
A. Anxiety
B. Impaired verbal communication
C. Ineffective individual/family coping
D. High risk for injury
E. Altered nutrition
F. Powerlessness
G. Self-care deficit
H. Self-esteem disturbance
I. Sensory-perceptual alteration
J. Sleep pattern disturbance
K. Social isolation
L. High risk for violence

Planning and Implementation

Goals

Client will
A. Develop a trusting/therapeutic relationship with nurse.
B. Be oriented, able to test reality.
C. Be protected from injury.
D. Be able to recognize impending loss of control.
E. Adhere to medication regimen.
F. Participate in activities.
G. Increase ability to care for self.

Interventions

A. Offer self in development of therapeutic relationship.
B. Use silence.

C. Set time for interaction with client.
D. Encourage reality orientation but understand that delusions/hallucinations are real to client.
E. Assist with feeding/dressing as necessary.
F. Check on client frequently, remove potentially harmful objects.
G. Contract with client to tell you when anxiety is becoming so high that loss of control is possible.
H. Administer antipsychotic medications as ordered (see Table 7.7 for side effects and dosages); observe for effects.
   1. Reduction of hallucinations, delusions, agitation
   2. Postural hypotension
      a. Obtain baseline blood pressure and monitor sitting/standing.
      b. Client must lie prone for 1 hour following injection.
      c. Teach client to sit up or stand up slowly.
      d. Elevate client's legs while seated.
      e. Withhold drug if systolic pressure drops more than 20–30 mm Hg from previous reading.
   3. Photosensitivity
      a. Advise use of sun screen.
      b. Avoid exposure to sunlight.
   4. Agranulocytosis
      a. Instruct client to report sore throat or fever.
      b. Institute reverse isolation if necessary.
   5. Elimination
      a. Measure I&O.
      b. Check bladder distention.
      c. Keep bowel record.
   6. Sedation
      a. Avoid use of heavy machinery.
      b. Do not drive.
   7. Extrapyramidal symptoms
      a. Dystonic reactions
         1) sudden contractions of face, tongue, extraocular muscles
         2) administer antiparkinson agents prn (e.g., benztropine [Cogentin] 1–8 mg or diphenhydramine [Benadryl] 10–50 mg), which can be given PO or IM for faster relief; trihexyphenidyl [Artane] 3–15 mg PO only, can also be used prn).
         3) remain with client; this is a frightening experience and usually occurs when medication is started.
      b. Parkinson syndrome
         1) occurs within 1–3 weeks

TABLE 7.7 Antipsychotic Medications

Drug	Acute Symptoms	Maintenance/Day	Range/Day	Profound Side Effects
Chlorpromazine (Thorazine)	25–100 mg IM q1–4h prn	200–600 mg PO	25–2000 mg PO	Sedation Anticholinergic effects: dry mouth, blurred vision, constipation, urinary retention, postural hypotension
Thioridazine (Mellaril)	200–600 mg PO in divided doses	150–300 mg PO	50–800 mg PO	Sedation
Fluphenazine HCl (Prolixin, Permitil)	1.25 mg IM, max 10 mg IM, divided doses	1–5 mg PO	1–30 mg PO	Extrapyramidal effects: dystonic reactions (muscular contractions of tongue, face, throat; opisthotonos); tremors, rigid posture; akathisia (restlessness); tardive dyskinesia
Fluphenazine decanoate/enanthate (Prolixin, Permitil)	—	25 mg IM q2wk	25–100 mg IM	Extrapyramidal
Trifluoperazine (Stelazine)	1–2 mg IM q4h; 2–4 mg PO, max 10 mg qd	2–4 mg PO	2–80 mg PO	Extrapyramidal
Perphenazine (Trilafon)	5–10 mg IM q6h, max 30 mg IM qd	16–64 mg PO	4–64 mg PO	Extrapyramidal
Haloperidol (Haldol)	2–10 mg IM in divided doses	2–8 mg PO	1–100 mg PO	Extrapyramidal
Thiothixene (Navane)	8–16 mg IM in divided doses	6–10 mg PO	6–60 mg PO	Extrapyramidal
Loxapine (Loxitane)	—	60–100 mg PO	30–250 mg PO	Extrapyramidal
Clozapine (Clozaril)	—	300–450 mg PO	75–700 mg PO	Agranulocytosis; sedation
Risperidone (Risperdal)	—	4–8 mg PO	4–8 mg PO	Insomnia, extrapyramidal

      2) tremors, rigid posture, masklike facial appearance
      3) administer antiparkinson agents prn.
    c. Akathisia
      1) motor restlessness
      2) need to keep moving
      3) administer antiparkinson agents.
      4) do not mistake this for agitation; do not increase antipsychotic medication.
      5) reduce medications to see if symptoms decrease.
      6) determine if movement is under voluntary control.
    d. Tardive dyskinesia
      1) irreversible involuntary movements of tongue, face, extremities
      2) may occur after prolonged use of antipsychotics
    e. Neuroleptic malignant syndrome
      1) occurs days/weeks after initiation of treatment in 1% of clients
      2) elevated vital signs, rigidity, and confusion followed by incontinence, mutism, opisthotonos, retrocollis, renal failure, coma, and death
      3) discontinue medication, notify physician, monitor vital signs, electrolyte balance, I&O
    f. Elderly clients should receive doses reduced by one-half to one-third of recommended level
I. Encourage participation in milieu, group, art, and occupational therapies when client able to tolerate them.

Evaluation

Client
A. Stays with nurse prescribed period of time.
B. Is oriented to reality, can state name, place, and date.
C. Can feed/dress self with specified amount of assistance.
D. Has not attempted/will not attempt to injure self or others.
E. Adheres to medication regimen with minimal side effects.
F. Participates in activities.

Sample Questions

14. Ronald, 23 years old, was voluntarily admitted to the inpatient unit with a diagnosis of paranoid schizophrenia. As the nurse approaches Ronald, he says, "If you come any closer, I'll die.' This is an example of
    1. hallucination.
    2. delusion.
    3. illusion.
    4. idea of reference.
15. The nurse is approaching an adult client who is admitted with a diagnosis of paranoid schizophrenia. As the nurse approaches the client, he says, "If you come any closer, I'll die." The best response for the nurse to make to this behavior is
    1. How can I hurt you?
    2. I'm the nurse.
    3. Tell me more about this.
    4. That's a silly thing to say.
16. Ronald, a young man admitted with a diagnosis of paranoid schizophrenia, is pacing the halls and is agitated. The nurse hears him saying, "I have to get away from those doctors! They are trying to commit me to the state hospital!" The nurse's continued assessment should include
    1. clarifying information with the doctor.
    2. observing Ronald for rising anxiety.
    3. reviewing history of involuntary commitment.
    4. checking dosage of prescribed medication.
17. When communicating with a paranoid client, the main principle is to
    1. use logic and be persistent.
    2. provide an anxiety-free environment.
    3. express doubt and do not argue.
    4. encourage ventilation of anger.
18. An appropriate activity for the nurse to recommend for a client who is extremely agitated is
    1. competitive sports.
    2. Bingo.
    3. Trivial Pursuit.
    4. daily walks.

Answers and Rationales

14. The correct answer is 2. A delusion is a fixed false belief.
15. The correct answer is 2. The nurse needs to present reality to the client and not encourage the delusion.
16. The correct answer is 2. Assessing increasing signs of anxiety and agitation gives clues to the client's ability to maintain control and suggests further nursing interventions to protect the client and others.
17. The correct answer is 3. Paranoid clients develop this delusional system to defend against anxiety. Arguing with the client would increase his anxiety.
18. The correct answer is 4. Daily walks provide time for the nurse to develop trust. The alternative activities are too competitive and would increase the client's paranoia.

MOOD DISORDERS

Overview

A. Characterized by disturbance in mood (affect) that is either depression or elation (mania); occur in a variety of patterns, alone or together (see Figure 7.1). Disturbance is beyond normal range of mood experienced by most people.
B. *Bipolar disorder:* components of both depression and elation (formerly called manic-depression)
C. *Cyclothymic disorder:* milder symptoms of both mania and depression, often separated by long periods of normal mood
D. *Dysthymic disorder:* long-standing symptoms of depression alternating with short periods of normal mood; client usually able to maintain roles in job, school, etc.
E. Etiology is unknown; theories include
   1. Genetic: approximately 7% of general population; risk is 20% if a close relative has depression
   2. Biochemical: dysregulation in norepinephrine and serotonin
   3. Psychoanalytic: anger turned inward (i.e., anger toward significant other is turned into anger toward self)

Assessment

A. Mood: dysphoric; blue/sad or elated/aggressive
B. Presence of psychomotor agitation, retardation, or hyperactivity
C. Disorders of cognition: narrowed perception and interests, impaired concentration, grandiose delusions, flight of ideas in elation stage
D. Sexual functioning changes
E. Appropriateness of appearance/dress
F. Appetite
G. Potential for suicide

Analysis

Nursing diagnoses for clients with affective disorders may include
A. Constipation
B. Impaired verbal communication
C. Ineffective individual coping
D. High risk for injury
E. Nutrition less than body requirements
F. Self-care deficit
G. Self-esteem disturbance
H. Sleep pattern disturbance
I. Altered thought processes

Planning and Implementation

Goals

Client will

A. Be protected from injury.
B. Receive adequate rest and sleep.
C. Maintain adequate intake of fluids and nutrients, regular elimination.
D. Develop trusting/therapeutic relationship with nurse.
E. Be oriented to reality.
F. Participate in planned activities.

Interventions

A. Assess for suicide potential.
B. Encourage verbalization of feelings of hopelessness and helplessness.
C. Provide quiet environment for rest and sleep.
D. Provide small, attractive meals; encourage intake of fluids.
E. Maintain bowel record.
F. Use silence and broad openings, focus on client's verbal/nonverbal behaviors.
G. Present reality but accept client's need for delusions.
H. Accept client's negative responses, hostility.
I. Provide activities and tasks to raise client's self-esteem.
J. Assist with self-care as needed.
K. If client is agitated
   1. Work with client on a one-to-one basis.
   2. Walk with client; provide some diversional activity.
   3. Reduce environmental stimuli (e.g., put in a quiet room, dim lights).

Evaluation

Client
A. Has gained or maintained weight.
B. Reports any suicidal ideation.
C. Sleeps a specified number of hours.
D. Can meet own needs for ADL.
E. Has realistic appraisal of self.

Specific Disorders

Bipolar Disorder (Manic Episode)

A. General information
   1. Onset usually before age 30
   2. Characterized by hyperactivity and euphoria that may become sarcasm or hostility
B. Assessment findings
   1. Hyperactivity to the point of physical exhaustion
   2. Flamboyant dress/makeup
   3. Sexual acting out
   4. Impulsive behaviors
   5. Flight of ideas: inability to finish one thought before jumping to another
   6. Loud, domineering, manipulative behavior
   7. Distractibility

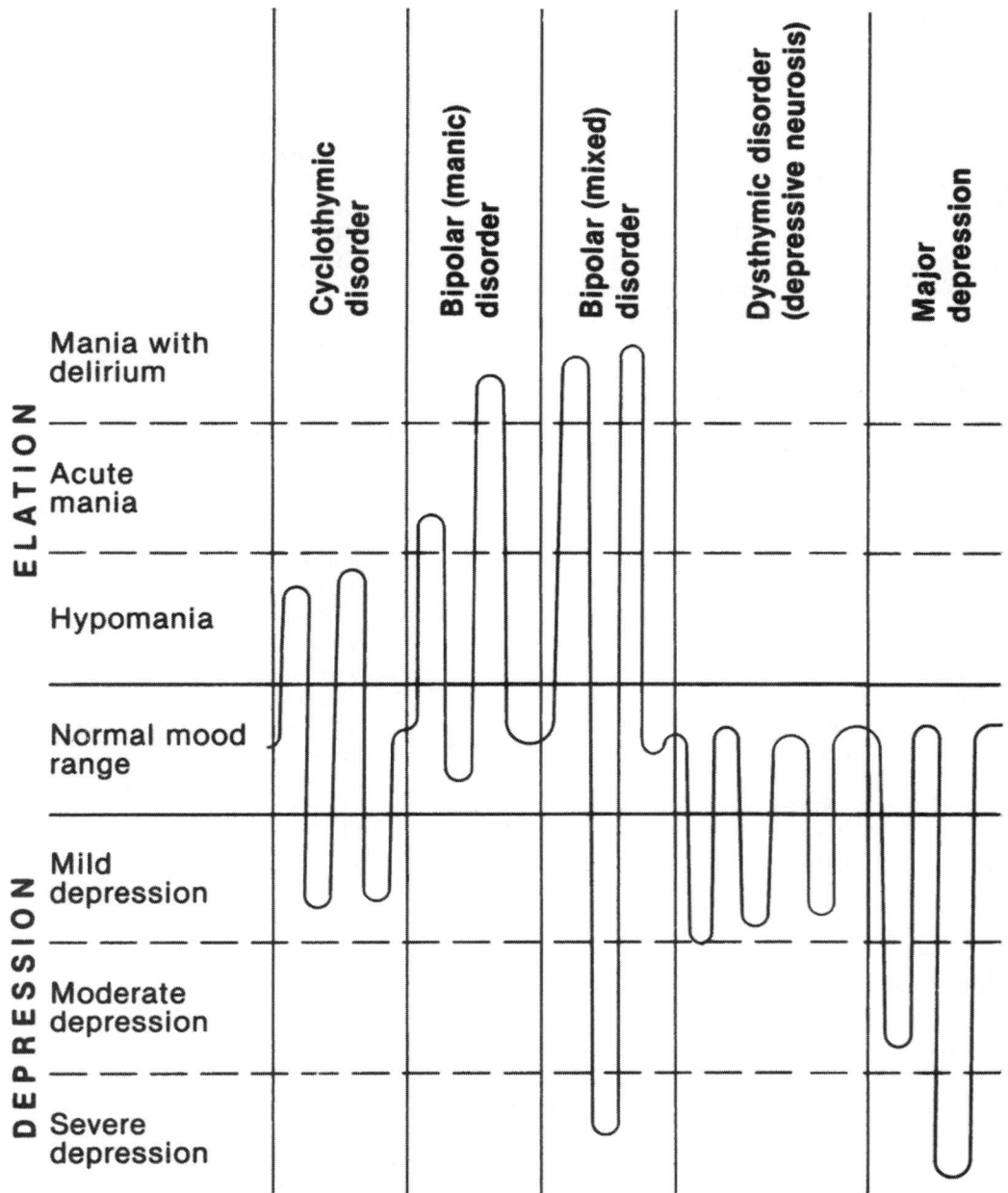

Mania with delirium: persecutory delusions, grandiose delusions, hallucinations
Acute mania: flight of ideas, impulsive behavior, bizarre dress and behavior, distractibility
Hypomania: decreased sleep, inflated self-esteem, increased activity, irritability
Mild depression: sadness, irritability, sleep disorders, social withdrawal, crying and tearful, low energy
Moderate depression: recurring thoughts of suicide, hopelessness, helplessness
Severe depression: delusions, hallucinations, psychomotor retardation and stupor, agitation (in depression with melancholia)

FIGURE 7.1 Patterns of mood disturbances in affective disorders

8. Dehydration, nutritional deficits
9. Delusions of grandeur
10. Possible short-term depression (risk of suicide)
11. Hostility, aggression

C. Medical management
1. Lithium carbonate (Eskalith, Lithane, Lithotabs)
   a. Initial dosage levels: 600 mg tid, to maintain a blood serum level of 1.0–1.5 mEq/liter; blood serum levels should be checked 12 hours after last dose, twice a week.
   b. Maintenance dosage levels: 300 mg tid/qid, to maintain a blood serum level of 0.6–1.2 mEq/liter; checked monthly.
   c. Toxicity when blood levels higher than 2.0 mEq/liter: tremors, nausea and vomiting, thirst, polyuria, coma, seizures, cardiac arrest
2. Antipsychotics may also be given for hyperactivity, agitation, psychotic behavior. Chlorpromazine (Thorazine) and haloperidol (Haldol) are most commonly used (see Table 7.7, page 542).

D. Nursing interventions
1. Determine what client is attempting to tell you; use active listening.
2. Assist client in focusing on a topic.
3. Offer finger foods, high-nutrition foods, and fluids.
4. Provide quiet environment, decrease stimuli.
5. Stay with client, use silence.
6. Remove harmful objects.
7. Be accepting of hostile statements.
8. Do not argue with client.
9. Use distraction to divert client from behaviors that are harmful to self or others.
10. Administer medications as ordered and observe for effects/side effects.
    a. Teach clients early signs of toxicity.
    b. Maintain fluid and salt intake.
    c. Avoid diuretics.
    d. Monitor lithium blood levels.
11. Assist in dressing, bathing.
12. Set limits on disruptive behaviors.

Major Depression

A. General information
1. Characterized by loss of ambition, lack of interest in activities and sex, low self-esteem, and feelings of boredom and sadness.
2. Etiology may be physiologic or response to an actual or perceived loss.
3. These clients are at high risk for suicide, especially when depressed mood begins to lift and/or energy level increases.

B. Medical management
1. Tricyclic antidepressants: amitriptyline HCl (Elavil), doxepin (Sinequan), imipramine (Tofranil); see Table 7.8
2. Monoamine oxidase inhibitors (MAOIs): isocarboxazid (Marplan), tranylcypromine (Parnate); see Table 7.8

TABLE 7.8   Antidepressant Medications

Drug	Initiating	Dosage Maintenance	Side Effects
Tricyclics			
Amitriptyline (Elavil, Endep)	75–100 mg PO	50–150 mg PO at bedtime; 80–100 mg IM in divided doses	Constipation, blurred vision, drowsiness, orthostatic hypotension, urinary retention, dry mouth
Amipramine (Tofranil)	75 mg PO tid	50–150 mg PO	As above
Amoxapine (Asendin)	50-mg PO tid	75–200 mg PO	As above
Doxepin (Sinequan)	75–150 mg PO	50–150 mg PO	As above
Clomipramine (Anafranil)	75–250 mg PO in divided doses	50–150 mg PO	Oversedation, anticholinergic effects, sexual dysfunction, tremors
Monoamine Oxidase Inhibitors (MAOIs)			
Isocarboxazid (Marplan)	30 mg PO in divided doses	10–30 mg PO	As for tricyclics, plus angina, hypoglycemia, hypertensive crisis precipitated by ingestion of foods with tyramine or concurrent use of tricyclics
Phenalizine (Nardil)	60 mg PO in divided doses	30–60 mg PO	As above
Tranylcypromine (Parnate)	20 mg PO in divided doses	10–30 mg PO	As above
Atypical Antidepressants			
Trazadone (Desyrel)	150 mg PO in divided doses	100–400 mg PO in divided doses	Hypotension, priapism, drowsiness, anxiety
Fluoxetine (Prozac)	20 mg PO	20–40 mg per day	Nausea, headache, anxiety
Sertraline (Zoloft)	50 mg PO	50–200 mg per day	Headache, nervousness

3. Selective serotonin reuptake inhibitors (SSRI): fluoxetin (Prozac), sertraline (Zoloft)
4. Electroconvulsive therapy (ECT)

C. Assessment findings
1. Feelings of helplessness, hopelessness, worthlessness
2. Reduction in normal activities or agitation
3. Slowing of body functions/elimination
4. Loss of appetite
5. Inappropriate guilt
6. Self-deprecation, low self-esteem
7. Inability to concentrate, disordered thinking
8. Poor hygiene
9. Slumped posture
10. Crying, ruminating (relates same incident over and over)
11. Dependency
12. Depressed children: possible separation anxiety
13. Elderly clients: possible symptoms of dementia
14. Somatic and persecutory delusions and hallucinations

D. Nursing interventions
1. Monitor I&O.
2. Weigh client regularly.
3. Maintain a schedule of regular appointments.
4. Remove potentially harmful articles.
5. Contract with client to report suicidal ideation, impulses, plans; check client frequently.
6. Assist with dressing, hygiene, and feeding.
7. Encourage discussion of negative/positive aspects of self.
8. Encourage change to more positive topics if self-deprecating thoughts persist.
9. Administer antidepressant medications (see Table 7.8) as ordered.
   a. Tricyclic antidepressants (TCAs)
      1) effectiveness increased by antihistamines, alcohol, benzodiazepines
      2) effectiveness decreased by barbiturates, nicotine, vitamin C
   b. Monoamine oxidase inhibitors (MAOIs)
      1) effectiveness increased with anti-psychotic drugs, alcohol, meperidine
      2) avoid foods containing tyramine (e.g., beer, red wine, aged cheese, avocados, caffeine, chocolate, sour cream, yogurt); these foods or MAOIs taken with TCAs may result in hypertensive crisis.
   c. Be sure client swallows medication. If side effects disappear suddenly, cheeking/hoarding may have occurred. These medications can be used to attempt suicide.
   d. Antidepressant medications do not take effect for 2–3 weeks. Encourage client to continue medication even if not feeling better. Be aware of suicide potential during this time.
   e. Warn client not to take any drugs without consulting physician.
10. Assist with ECT as ordered.
    a. Give normal pre-op preparation, including informed consent (see Perioperative Nursing, pages 161–167).
    b. Remove all hairpins, dentures.
    c. Ensure client is wearing loose clothing.
    d. Check vital signs after the procedure.
    e. Reorient and assure that any memory loss is temporary.
    f. Assist to room or to care of responsible party if outpatient.

Dysthymic Disorder

A. General information: chronic mood disturbance of at least two years' duration for adults, one year for children
B. Assessment findings
1. Normal moods for a period of weeks, followed by depression
2. Insomnia/hypersomnia
3. Social withdrawal
4. Loss of interest in activities
5. Recurrent thoughts of suicide and death
C. Nursing interventions: same as for major depression.

Sample Questions

19. The nurse knows that the major factor that distinguishes a bipolar from a unipolar disorder is the
    1. higher incidence in women.
    2. severity of the depression.
    3. genetic etiology.
    4. presence of mania.
20. Mr. B., 34 years old, is hospitalized with bipolar disorder. At 2 A.M. the nurse finds him phoning friends all across the country to discuss his new plan for eradicating world hunger. His excited explanations are keeping the entire unit awake, but he won't quiet down. The nurse caring for Mr. B. knows the drug most likely to be prescribed for this client is
    1. a tricyclic antidepressant.
    2. an MAO-inhibitor antidepressant.
    3. lithium carbonate (Eskalith).
    4. an antianxiety drug.
21. Supportive therapy for a client who is exhibiting manic behavior may include all of the following except
    1. psychoanalysis.

2. cognitive therapy.
3. interpersonal therapy.
4. problem-solving therapy.

22. Ms. F., 38 years old, was admitted to the psychiatric service after a failed suicide attempt by drug overdose. She had been in treatment with a clinical psychologist on a biweekly basis for six weeks. Ms. F. sought help when her husband informed her of his decision to leave her and the children after 19 years of marriage. Ms. F.'s suicide attempt was made after she and her husband had had a fierce argument about property settlement. Upon initial contact with the nurse, the client looked exhausted, affect was sad, movements and responses were slowed, and self-care impairments were evident. She is convinced that a blemish on her face is a melanoma that is invading her brain and eating away at the tissue. Ms. F.'s disorder is best classified as
1. bipolar disorder.
2. depression with melancholia.
3. dysthymic disorder.
4. major depression.

23. Ms. H. is admitted to the psychiatric service after a failed suicide attempt by drug overdose. She presents with a sad affect and moves and responds slowly. Which nursing diagnosis is of greatest priority at the time of her admission?
1. Alteration in nutrition: less than body requirements.
2. Ineffective individual coping.
3. Potential for violence: self-directed.
4. Bathing/hygiene self-care deficit.

24. Ms. J. is admitted following a suicide attempt. She took sleeping pills. She has been receiving therapy for depression since her husband left her after 23 years of marriage. Upon admission Ms. J. looks very tired, has a sad affect and moves slowly. In attempting to stabilize her activities of daily living in an optimally therapeutic way, she and the nurse would most likely plan to
1. allow her to catch up on lost sleep for the first three days of her hospitalization.
2. have her fully involved in all therapeutic activities.
3. have her husband visit for brief periods of time.
4. schedule balanced periods of rest and therapeutic activity.

Answers and Rationales

19. The correct answer is 4. Although both unipolar and bipolar disorders include episodes of depression, the diagnosis of bipolar disorder is given to persons who also experience manic episodes. There is a higher incidence of bipolar disease in men than in women. There is a depressive phase to both unipolar and bipolar disease. It is the presence of a manic phase that differentiates the two. The causes of a bipolar disorder are multiple and complex, often involving biological, psychological, interpersonal, social, and cultural factors. There may be a genetic factor as well, but this does not differentiate unipolar from bipolar disease.

20. The correct answer is 3. The drug of choice for manic clients is lithium carbonate (Eskalith). A tricyclic antidepressant may be used for a client with a bipolar disorder if for some reason the physician thinks that the client could not tolerate the side effects or manage the close followup required by a client taking lithium. MAO Inhibitors are used in depression but require major dietary restrictions and may not be taken together with tricyclic antidepressants. Antianxiety drugs are used in obsessive-compulsive disorders, phobias, and somatoform disorders and in clients suffering from panic attacks.

21. The correct answer is 1. Psychoanalysis is an in-depth, insight-oriented psychotherapy, not appropriate in treatment of bipolar disorders. Cognitive therapy is shown to be useful in bipolar disorders. Cognitive therapy is a method of treatment that helps clients change attitudes, perceptions, and patterns of thinking. Interpersonal therapy would also be helpful. This is a form of psychotherapy that views faulty communications, interactions, and interrelationships as basic factors in maladaptive behavior. Problem-solving therapy helps the client learn new methods of coping and problem-solving techniques.

22. The correct answer is 4. The client shows many signs of classic depression as evidenced by psychomotor retardation, impairment of self-care, inability to sleep, a suicide attempt, and somatic delusions. There is no indication of mood swings. Depression with melancholia has many of the characteristics of a major depression in that there are early morning wakenings and psychomotor retardation. However, depression with melancholia is not triggered by a loss and the client is not delusional. Typically, dysthymic disorders are chronic and nonpsychotic. They are related to a loss that occurred over two years earlier and the client shows normal periods followed by periods of depression.

23. The correct answer is 3. The priority at this time is maintenance of client safety. This client is at particular risk for self-directed violence because of her recent failed suicide attempt and her obsession with what she perceives to be her impending death. Alteration in nutrition is an important

diagnosis but not the primary one. Ineffective individual coping is an important diagnosis but not the primary one. Self-care deficit is an important diagnosis but not the primary one.

24. The correct answer is 4. While the client is probably exhausted, the optimum environment would be provided by scheduling balanced periods of rest and therapeutic activity. Allowing the client to sleep and rest for three days would not be therapeutic. It is too soon for the client to be fully involved in unit activities. Having her husband visit would have no beneficial effect and the husband would probably not want to visit his wife.

NEUROTIC DISORDERS

In DSM IV, the disorders formerly categorized as neurotic disorders are included in Anxiety, Somatoform, and Dissociative Disorders. Reality testing is intact.

ANXIETY DISORDERS

Overview

A. Common element is anxiety, manifested in a variety of behaviors (see also Behaviors Related to Emotional Distress, page 526).
B. Therapy relates to reduction of anxiety; when anxiety is reduced, the symptoms will be alleviated.
C. Types include generalized anxiety disorder, panic disorder, phobic disorders, and obsessive-compulsive disorders.

Assessment

A. Level of anxiety: may be to point of panic
B. Vital signs: may be elevated
C. Reality testing: should be intact; can recognize that thoughts are irrational but cannot control them
D. Physical symptoms: no organic basis
E. Memory: possible memory loss or loss of identity
F. Pattern of symptoms: chronic with a pattern of waxing and waning or sudden onset

Analysis

Nursing diagnoses for the client with an anxiety disorder may include
A. Anxiety
B. Fear
C. Ineffective individual coping
D. Powerlessness
E. Disturbance in self-concept

F. Sleep pattern disturbance
G. Altered thought processes

Planning and Implementation
Goals

Client will
A. Develop a trusting/therapeutic relationship with nurse.
B. Recognize causes of anxiety and develop alternative coping mechanisms.
C. Reduce/alleviate symptoms of anxiety.

Interventions

A. Encourage discussion of anxiety and relationship to symptoms.
B. Provide calm, accepting atmosphere.
C. Administer antianxiety medications (for short-term use only) as ordered and monitor effects/side effects.
   1. Diazepam (Valium): 5–20 mg PO daily; 2–10 mg IM or IV daily
   2. Chlordiazepoxide (Librium): 20–100 mg PO daily; 50–100 mg IM or IV daily
   3. Alprazolam (Xanax) 0.75–4 mg PO daily
   4. Oxazepam (Serax) 30–120 mg PO daily
   5. Triazolam (Halcion) 0.25–0.5 mg HS
   6. Side effects
      a. Client may become addicted.
      b. Additive effect with alcohol.
      c. Dizziness may occur when treatment initiated.
      d. Lower doses for elderly client.
      e. Do not stop abruptly; taper doses.
D. Teach client about self-medication regimen and side effects.

Evaluation

Client
A. Can discuss causes of anxiety with nurse.
B. Demonstrates constructive coping mechanisms and ability to reduce anxiety.
C. Demonstrates knowledge of effects and hazards of antianxiety medications.

Specific Disorders
Phobic Disorders

A. General information
   1. Irrational fears resulting in avoidance of objects or situations.
   2. Repressed conflicts are projected to outside world and eventually are displaced onto an object or situation.
   3. Client can recognize that fear of these objects/situations is irrational, but cannot control emotional response when

confronting or thinking about confronting the particular object/situation.
B. Assessment findings
1. *Agoraphobia:* most serious phobia; fear of being alone or in public places; may reach point where client panics at thought of being in public places and cannot leave home.
2. *Social phobias:* fear of being in situations where one may be scrutinized and embarrassed by others.
3. *Specific phobias:* irrational fear of specific objects/situations (e.g., snakes, insects, heights, closed places).
C. Nursing interventions
1. Know that behavior modification and systematic desensitization most commonly used; client cannot be "reasoned" out of behavior.
2. Do not force contact with feared object/situation, may result in panic.
3. Administer antianxiety medications (diazepam [Valium], imipramine [Tofranil]) as ordered.
4. Instruct in and encourage use of relaxation techniques.

Generalized Anxiety Disorder

A. General information
1. Persistent anxiety for at least one month
2. Cannot be controlled by client or displaced, remains free-floating and diffuse
B. Assessment findings
1. Motor tensions: trembling, muscle aches, jumpiness
2. Autonomic hyperactivity: sweating, palpitations, dizziness, upset stomach, increased pulse and respirations
3. Affect: worried and fearful of what might happen
4. Hyperalert: insomnia, irritability
C. Nursing interventions
1. Stay with client.
2. Encourage discussion of anxiety and its source.
3. Provide calm, relaxing atmosphere.
4. Administer antianxiety drugs, as ordered.
5. Observe for effects and side effects.
6. Monitor vital signs.
7. Assess for level of anxiety.

Panic Disorder (with/without Agoraphobia)

A. General information: acute, panic-like attack lasting from a few minutes to an hour.
B. Assessment findings
1. Sudden onset of intense fear/terror
2. Symptoms: include dyspnea, palpitations, chest pain, sensation of smothering or choking, faintness, fear of dying, dizziness

3. When severe, symptoms mimic acute cardiac disease that must be ruled out.
4. Client may be seen in ER.
C. Nursing interventions: same as for generalized anxiety disorder.

Obsessive-compulsive Disorder (OCD)

A. General information
1. *Obsession*
   a. Recurrent thoughts that client cannot control; often violent, fearful, or doubting in nature (e.g., fear of contamination).
   b. Client cannot keep thoughts from intruding into consciousness; eventually resort to defense of undoing (performing ritual behavior).
2. *Compulsion*
   a. Action (ritual behavior) that serves to reduce tension from obsessive thought.
   b. Client may not desire to perform behavior but is unable to stop, as this is the only relief from distress.
   c. May interfere with social/occupational functioning.
B. Nursing interventions
1. Allow compulsive behavior, but set reasonable limits.
2. Permit client to complete behavior once started; aggression may result if behavior is not allowed or completed.
3. Engage client in alternative behaviors (client will not be able to do this alone).
4. Provide opportunities to perform tasks that meet need for perfectionism (e.g., stacking and folding linens).
5. As compulsive behavior decreases, help client to verbalize feelings, concerns.
6. Help client to make choices, participate in decisions regarding own schedule.
7. Administer clomipramine (Anafranil) as ordered. Gradual decrease in symptoms may take 2–3 months. Often used with behavior modification therapy (see Table 7.8, page 546).

Posttraumatic Stress Disorder (PTSD)

A. General information
1. Disturbed/disintegrated response to significant trauma
2. Symptoms occur following crisis event such as war, earthquake, flood, airplane crash, rape, or assault
3. Reexperiencing of traumatic event in recollections, nightmares
B. Assessment findings
1. Psychic numbing: not as responsive to persons and events as to the traumatic experience

2. Sleep disturbances (e.g., nightmares)
  3. Avoidance of environment/activities likely to arouse recall of trauma
  4. Symptoms of depression
  5. Possible violent outbursts
  6. Memory impairment
  7. Panic attacks
  8. Substance abuse
C. Nursing interventions
  1. Arrange for individual or group psycho-therapy with others who experienced same trauma (e.g., Vietnam war veterans).
  2. Provide crisis counseling, family therapy as needed.
  3. Provide referrals.

Sample Questions

25. The nurse suspects a client is denying his feelings of anxiety. When assessing this client, the nurse must be particularly alert to
  1. restlessness.
  2. tapping of the feet.
  3. wringing of the hands.
  4. his or her own anxiety level.

26. Lillian, 46 years old, is admitted to the hospital because her family is unable to manage her constant hand-washing rituals. Her family reports she washes her hands at least 30 times each day. The nurse noticed Lillian's hands are reddened, scaly, and cracked. The main nursing goal is to
  1. decrease the number of hand washings a day.
  2. limit the number of hand washings.
  3. provide good skin care.
  4. eliminate the hand-washing rituals.

27. Ruth is an adult admitted to the psychiatric hospital for hand washing rituals. The day after admission she is scheduled for lab tests. To assure that the client is there on time, the nurse should
  1. remind Ruth several times of her appointment.
  2. limit the number of hand washings.
  3. tell her it is her responsibility to be there on time.
  4. provide ample time for her to complete her rituals.

28. Lana is an adult who is hospitalized with an obsessive-compulsive disorder. She washes her hands many times a day. Which of the following is an appropriate treatment for this client?
  1. An unstructured schedule of activities.
  2. A structured schedule of activities.
  3. Intense counseling.
  4. Negative reinforcement every time she performs the ritual.

29. A woman is admitted to the psychiatric hospital. She was found walking on a highway. She is unkempt and appears thin and dirty. The most thorough way to conduct a nursing assessment of her nutritional status is to
  1. observe her at mealtime.
  2. request a medical consult.
  3. explore her recent dietary intake.
  4. compare current weight with her usual weight.

30. Ms. D., 34 years old, is admitted to the psychiatric unit after she was brought to the hospital emergency department by the state police. She had been wandering on a major four-lane highway with no regard for her safety. On first contact with Ms. D., the nurse observes that her face and hands are very red and excoriated, her hair is matted and dirty, her clothing is dirty, and she is quite thin. According to Ms. D., she had been living in a motel with a truck driver, whom she knew by first name only. They had been in the motel for a week, but the truck driver went back to work, and she has been alone for three days. Ms. D. cannot specifically relate her activities for those three days. Once the assessment interview was over, Ms. D. asked to be excused, went directly to her room, and washed her hands and face. Within a very short while, it became apparent to the nurse that the hand and face washing was quite repetitive and ritualistic and occupied a major portion of Ms. D.'s time. However, she refused to bathe or wash her clothing. The nursing diagnosis that describes the most prominent difficulty that Ms. D. is experiencing is
  1. impaired skin integrity.
  2. altered thought processes.
  3. ineffective individual coping.
  4. social isolation.

31. Ms. A. is admitted because of ritualistic behavior. She is also constipated and dehydrated. Which nursing intervention would Ms. A. be most likely to comply with?
  1. Drinking Ensure between meals.
  2. Drinking extra fluids with meals.
  3. Drinking 8 oz water every hour between meals.
  4. Drinking adequate amounts of fluid during the day.

32. Ms. G. is admitted because of excessive hand and face washing rituals. The most effective way for the nurse to intervene with Ms. G.'s hand and face washing is to
  1. allow her a certain amount of time each shift to engage in this behavior.
  2. interrupt the activity briefly and frequently.
  3. lock the door to her room and restrict access to the bathroom.

4. tell her to stop each time she is observed doing it.

33. Ms. D. was admitted for ritualistic behavior involving frequent hand and face washing. Upon admission she was also dehydrated and underweight. The nurse and Ms. D. will know that discharge planning is appropriate when Ms. D
   1. regains her normal body weight.
   2. expresses a desire to leave the hospital.
   3. is able to start talking about her guilt and anxiety.
   4. limits her hand and face washing to a few times a day.

Answers and Rationales

25. The correct answer is 4. Clients who are unaware of, or denying their feelings of anxiety, are less likely to exhibit overt behavioral symptoms. The nurse should rely on the emphatic, contagious communication of anxiety from client to nurse. Restlessness might be a sign of anxiety in the client. Tapping of the feet might be a sign of anxiety in the client. Wringing of the hands might be a sign of anxiety in the client.

26. The correct answer is 1. Obsessive-compulsive behavior represents displacement of anxiety. A concrete, measurable goal is to decrease the number of hand washings.

27. The correct answer is 4. Providing ample time for Lillian to complete her hand-washing rituals will lessen her anxiety.

28. The correct answer is 2. Planning a structured schedule of activities provides the client with other ways to decrease anxiety.

29. The correct answer is 4. Current weight as it relates to usual weight is the best determinant of nutritional status and weight change when the client is unable to be specific about recent activities and eating habits. This is a good method for determining current eating habits but is not the best indicator of nutritional status. Obtaining a medical consult would not be helpful in conducting a nursing assessment of the client's nutritional status. The client is unable to relate her recent dietary intake.

30. The correct answer is 3. Ineffective individual coping encompasses all of the other nursing diagnoses. This area will be the primary focus of nursing interventions and positive changes in the client's ability to cope will be the criteria for discharge readiness. Interventions for the client's impaired skin integrity will be developed, but this problem will hopefully decline as the client's coping ability improves. The history given on the client does not identify altered thought processes as a major difficulty at this time. As coping skills improve

the client will be better able to relate to others.

31. The correct answer is 3. Building the intake of a specific amount of liquid into a daily schedule of activities is very consistent with the obsessive/compulsive client's need to control as many aspects of her life as possible. Ensure is a high calorie nutritional supplement and not a treatment for dehydration and constipation. "Drinking extra fluid with meals" is not a measurable intervention. "Adequate" amounts of fluids are not defined specifically.

32. The correct answer is 1. Allowing the client a certain amount of time to engage in the activity alleviates some of the client's anxiety. Then other activities geared to more positive coping behaviors can be engaged in. Interrupting the activity will increase the client's anxiety. Restricting the client's use of the bathroom will increase the client's anxiety. Stopping the client each time she is seen washing her hands and face will increase the client's anxiety.

33. The correct answer is 4. The major issue is control of behavior and thoughts. When the client is able to control her compulsive behavior (i.e., limit her hand and face washing to a few times a day), she will then be able to resume normal activities of daily living. Compulsive behavior is often episodic and relates to repression and anxiety. Regaining body weight does not mean that the compulsive behavior is under control. Likewise, the desire to leave the hospital does not mean that the compulsive behavior is under control. This does not mean that she is ready to leave the hospital.

SOMATOFORM DISORDERS

Overview

A. Anxiety is manifested in somatic (physical) symptoms.
B. There is organic pathology but no organic etiology.
C. Symptoms are real and not under voluntary control of the client.
D. Defense used is somatization or conversion: anxiety is transformed to a physical symptom.

Specific Disorders

Somatization Disorder

A. General information
   1. Multiple, recurrent somatic complaints (fatigue, backache, nausea, menstrual cramps) over many years

2. No organic etiology for these complaints
B. Assessment findings
 1. Complaints chronic but fluctuating
 2. History of seeking medical attention for many years
 3. Symptoms of anxiety and depression
 4. Somatic complaints may involve any organ system
C. Nursing interventions
 1. Be aware of own response (irritation/impatience) to client.
 2. Rule out organic basis for current complaints.
 3. Focus on anxiety reduction, not physical symptoms.
 4. Minimize secondary gain.

Conversion Disorder

A. General information
 1. Sudden onset of impairment or loss of motor or sensory function.
 2. No physiologic cause.
 3. Defenses used are repression and conversion; anxiety is converted to a physical symptom.
 4. Temporal relationship between distressing event and development of symptom (e.g., unconscious desire to hit another may produce paralysis of arm).
 5. Primary gain: client is not conscious of conflict. Anxiety is converted to a symptom that removes client from anxiety-producing situation.
 6. Secondary gain: gain support and attention that was not previously provided. Tends to encourage client to maintain symptoms.
B. Assessment findings
 1. Sudden paralysis, blindness, deafness, etc.
 2. "La belle indifférence": inappropriately calm when describing symptoms
 3. Symptoms not under voluntary control
 4. Usually short term; symptoms will abate as anxiety diminishes
C. Nursing interventions
 1. Focus on anxiety reduction, not physical symptom.
 2. Use matter-of-fact acceptance of symptom.
 3. Encourage client to discuss conflict.
 4. Do not provide secondary gain by being too attentive.
 5. Provide diversionary activities.
 6. Encourage expression of feelings.

Pain Disorder

A. General information: complaint of severe and prolonged pain
B. Assessment findings
 1. Pain impairs social/occupational function
 2. Pain often severe

3. Sleep may be interrupted by experience of pain
C. Nursing interventions
 1. Pain management
 2. Encourage participation in activities

Hypochondriasis

A. General information
 1. Unrealistic belief of having serious illnesses.
 2. Belief persists despite medical reassurance.
 3. Defenses used are regression and somatization.
B. Assessment findings
 1. Preoccupation with bodily functions, which are misinterpreted.
 2. History of seeing many doctors, many diagnostic tests.
 3. Dependent behavior: desires/demands great deal of attention.
C. Nursing interventions
 1. Rule out presence of actual disease.
 2. Focus on anxiety, not physical symptom.
 3. Set limits on amount of time spent with client.
 4. Reduce anxiety by providing diversionary activities.
 5. Avoid negative response to client's demands by discussing in staff conferences.
 6. Provide client with correct information.

DISSOCIATIVE DISORDERS

Overview

A. Sudden change in client's consciousness, identity, or memory.
B. Loss of memory, knowledge of identity, or how individual came to be in a particular place.
C. Defenses are repression and dissociation.

Specific Disorders

Dissociative Amnesia

A. General information: inability to recall information about self with no organic reason
B. Assessment findings
 1. No history of head injury
 2. Retrograde amnesia, may extend far into past
C. Nursing interventions
 1. Rule out organic causes.
 2. Reassure client that his/her identity will be made known to him/her.
 3. Provide safe environment.
 4. Establish nurse-client relationship to reduce anxiety.

Dissociative Fugue

A. General information
 1. Client travels to strange, often distant place; unaware of how he traveled there, and unable to recall past.
 2. May follow severe psychologic stress.
B. Assessment findings
 1. Memory loss
 2. May have assumed new identity
 3. No recall of fugue state when normal functions return
C. Nursing interventions: same as for psychogenic amnesia.

PERSONALITY DISORDERS

Overview

A. Patterns of thinking about self and environment become maladaptive and cause impairment in social or occupational functioning or subjective distress.
B. Usually develop by adolescence.
C. Most common is borderline personality disorder.

Specific Disorders

Borderline Personality Disorder

A. General information: clients are impulsive and unpredictable, have difficulty interacting; characterized by behavior problems
B. Assessment findings
 1. Unstable, intense interpersonal relationships
 2. Impulsive, unpredictable, manipulative behavior; prone to self-harm
 3. Marked mood shifts from anger to dysphoric
 4. Uncertainty about self-image, gender identity, values
 5. Chronic intolerance of being alone, feelings of boredom
 6. Splitting: distinct separation of love and hate. Views others as *all* good or *all* bad.
 7. Use of projection and regression
C. Nursing interventions
 1. Protect from self-mutilation, suicidal gestures.
 2. Establish therapeutic relationship, be aware of own responses to manipulative behaviors.
 3. Maintain objectivity.
 4. Use a calm approach.
 5. Set limits.
 6. Apply plan of care consistently.
 7. Interact with clients when they demonstrate appropriate behavior.
 8. Teach relaxation techniques.

Antisocial Personality Disorder

A. General information
 1. Chronic history of antisocial behaviors (e.g., fighting, stealing, aggressive behaviors, substance abuse, criminal behaviors).
 2. These behaviors usually begin before the age of 15 and continue into adult life.
 3. May be hospitalized for injuries.
B. Assessment findings
 1. Manipulative behavior, may try to obtain special privileges, play one staff member against another
 2. Lack of shame or guilt for behaviors
 3. Insincerity and lying
 4. Impulsive behavior and poor judgment
C. Nursing interventions
 1. Provide model for mature, appropriate behavior.
 2. Observe strict limit-setting by all staff.
 3. Monitor own responses to client.
 4. Demonstrate concern, interest in client.
 5. Reinforce positive behaviors (socialization, conforming to limits).
 6. Avoid power struggles.

Sample Questions

34. Mr. K., 24 years old, was admitted on a voluntary basis to psychiatric services. He had agreed to inpatient care as an alternative to a 30-day jail sentence for reckless driving, driving under the influence, and speeding. He has been under psychiatric care for three years, has a long history of petty crimes, and was able, with the help of his therapist, to convince the judge that a higher level of psychiatric care would be in everyone's best interest. Once on the unit, Mr. K. is difficult to manage because he is arrogant and manipulative. When a scheduled group therapy session is announced, he refuses to go and the nurse has to resort to pleading with him to attend. He uses other clients to his own ends and often pioneers causes that are disruptive to the milieu. The diagnostic title that best describes Mr. K.'s behavior is
 1. antisocial personality disorder.
 2. borderline personality disorder.
 3. passive-aggressive personality disorder.
 4. passive-dependent personality disorder.
35. Mr. J. is admitted to a psychiatric unit with a diagnosis of antisocial personality disorder. In planning care for Mr. J. it is important for the nurse to recognize that all of the following are likely to occur except
 1. staff and client agree when setting treatment goals.

2. staff and client are in a constant struggle for control of the milieu.
3. staff and client feel threatened by one another.
4. staff and client use the same defense mechanisms when interacting.

36. Key interventions for a client with an antisocial personality disorder include all of the following except
   1. assisting him to identify and clarify his feelings.
   2. changing staff assigned to Mr. Kile at his request.
   3. making expectations about his behavior clear as well as consequences for same.
   4. setting firm limits with clear consequences.

37. Mr. L. is a 26-year-old man who has been hospitalized with an antisocial personality disorder. He was admitted on a voluntary basis as an alternative to serving a jail sentence. At the time of discharge the nurse understands that Mr. L. is most likely to
   1. be committed to another facility for a longer length of stay.
   2. be committed to a virtuous and socially acceptable life-style.
   3. discontinue treatment with the outpatient therapist.
   4. revert to prehospitalization behaviors.

38. Ms. B., 28 years old, is admitted to the psychiatric unit under an involuntary petition after a perceived suicide attempt. Ms. B. cut the palmar aspect of her arm from the antecubital space to the hand. Immediately before this episode, she had flown across the country to return to her parents' home after her husband of one and a half years left her. Initially, she presented as very tearful and highly anxious. Her affect was more that of intense anger than of sadness. As the staff became more familiar with her, it became apparent that she had had many episodes of self-mutilation and would do so "so I can feel something." While Ms. B. could appear quite intact most of the time, when stressed she would respond very impulsively, report hearing voices of a depreciative nature, and require a high level of observation. As the end of her hospitalization neared, she became increasingly angry, anxious, and hostile, saying, "You people (the staff) are useless. You can't help anyone get better. Look at me, I'm no better than when I came in." This client's symptoms can best be described as fitting which of the following diagnostic categories?
   1. Antisocial personality disorder.
   2. Borderline personality disorder.
   3. Passive-aggressive personality disorder.
   4. Passive-dependent personality disorder.

39. Ms. A. is admitted to the psychiatric unit with a diagnosis of borderline personality disorder. All of the following components of a nursing history/data base are extremely important to explore with this client except
   1. ego-strength assessment.
   2. social history.
   3. cognitive aspect of mental status exam.
   4. past psychiatric treatment history.

40. Ms. C. was admitted to the psychiatric unit after cutting herself on the forearm. She has numerous scars which are from prior self-mutilation. Should Ms. C. attempt self-mutilation while in the hospital, the plan for the nurse to implement is
   1. focus on the how, when, and where of the injury.
   2. care for the injury and explore Ms. C.'s activities and feelings immediately before the episode.
   3. care for the injury and leave Ms. C. alone for a while to let her settle down.
   4. care for the injury and seclude, and possibly restrain, Ms. C. to prevent further injury.

41. Ms. D. is a young woman who was admitted with a borderline personality disorder following an episode of self-mutilation. Her husband recently left her. She seems angry much of the time. She reports that she has injured herself in the past so she could feel something. In evaluating her as she nears discharge, the nurse would identify the major issues during this hospitalization to be all of the following except
   1. cognition.
   2. identity.
   3. dealing with anger.
   4. separation/individuation.

Answers and Rationales

34. The correct answer is 1. A long history of petty crimes, a high level of manipulative behavior, use of other clients to his own end, and fostering behavior that is disruptive to the milieu are all signs of the diagnosis of antisocial personality disorder. A client with a borderline personality disorder will display impulsive and unpredictable behavior, unstable and intense interpersonal relationships, and suicidal gestures. A client with a passive-aggressive personality disorder will display chronic lateness, procrastination, complaining and blaming behavior, and fear of authority. A client with a passive-dependent personality disorder will avoid major decisions and will be self-conscious and overly compliant to the needs of others.

35. The correct answer is 1. The staff and client will most likely disagree when setting treatment goals. All the other responses

describe the relationship between an antisocial client and the staff that make it so difficult to work with the antisocial client therapeutically. This is likely to happen between the staff and the client. The staff and client will most likely feel threatened by each other. The staff and client are likely to use the same defense mechanisms when interacting.

36. The correct answer is 2. The client will compare and attempt to "split" staff so it is very important to keep staff assignments as consistent as possible. Allowing the client to request specific staff members would put him in control, which would be counter-productive to his therapeutic goals. Assisting him to identify and clarify his feelings would be a helpful goal. Expecting the client to behave in a certain way is a helpful goal. Consistent limit setting is essential in the management of a manipulative client.

37. The correct answer is 4. People who have this type of personality disorder typically seek psychiatric care as a lesser of two evils. In this case in-hospital care is preferable to jail. The chances of this client making any great change in his lifestyle as a result of this short-term hospitalization are slim. The client will likely be committed to another facility when he is again arrested for deviant behavior. In light of the client's long psychiatric history, change to a socially acceptable lifestyle would be unlikely. The client may continue outpatient care for a short time but is then most likely to continue antisocial behaviors.

38. The correct answer is 2. The clustering of self-mutilation, impulsivity, transient psychosis, intense anger, and feeling empty is most typically found in the borderline personality disorder. A client with an antisocial behavior disorder would exhibit superficial charm, manipulative, often seductive behavior, a

history of substance abuse, and a history of thefts, vandalism, and multiple arrest. A client with a passive-aggressive personality disorder would exhibit intentional inefficiency, chronic lateness, procrastination, complaining and blaming behavior, and a fear of authority. A client with a passive-dependent personality disorder would exhibit a self-conscious, overly compliant, clinging behavior. This client would avoid making major decisions and would be subordinate to the needs of others.

39. The correct answer is 3. The mental status exam is conducted when the nurse suspects the client is disoriented. The client with a borderline personality disorder has, for the most part, intact reality testing. Assessment of ego strength is very important in light of the client's self-mutilation behavior. The client's social history would be important data to obtain. History of past psychiatric treatment is of course vital for planning future care.

40. The correct answer is 2. A matter-of-fact approach to the injury with emphasis on the events leading to the episode of mutilation is the most therapeutic approach. Focusing on how or when she did it doesn't help the client explore her feelings regarding the injury. Caring for the injury and then leaving her alone is not a therapeutic approach. Restraining the client or putting her in seclusion is a punitive approach to the self-mutilation.

41. The correct answer is 1. Impairments involving cognition are most commonly found in psychoses. Identity is a major issue with this client. Feelings of anger are a major issue with this client. Separation/individuation is the most basic issue with clients with borderline personality disorders.

Psychologic Aspects of Physical Illness

STRESS-RELATED DISORDERS

Overview

A. Actual physiologic change in structure/function of organ or system
B. May be referred to as psychosomatic or psychophysiologic disorders
C. Theorized that client's response to stress is a factor in etiology of disease
D. Stress/anxiety not the sole cause but may be a

causative factor in the development/exacerbation of physical symptoms
E. See Table 7.9 for types of disorders with a stress component.

Assessment

A. Health history, family history
B. Physical symptoms
C. Social/cultural considerations
D. Coping behaviors

TABLE 7.9   Types of Stress-Related Disorders

Systems	Examples
Respiratory	Asthma, common cold
Circulatory	Hypertension, migraine headaches
Digestive	Peptic ulcers, colitis
Skin	Hives, dermatitis
Musculoskeletal	Rheumatoid arthritis, chronic backache
Nervous	Fatigue
Endocrine	Dysmenorrhea, diabetes mellitus

Analysis

Nursing diagnoses for stress-related disorders may include any nursing diagnosis specific to the physiologic problem as well as
A. Ineffective individual coping
B. Knowledge deficit
C. Health-seeking behaviors

Planning and Implementation

Goals

Client will
A. Receive appropriate treatment for any physical symptoms (e.g., maintenance of blood pressure within normal range).
B. Recognize relationship of stress to physical symptom(s).
C. Acknowledge coping patterns that may affect recurrence of physical symptoms.
D. Recognize relationship of self-concept, self-esteem, role performance to disorder.
E. Develop alternative coping behaviors.

Interventions

A. Provide nursing care specific to physical symptoms.
B. Establish nurse-client relationship.
C. Encourage discussion of psychosocial problems.
D. Explain relationship of stress to physiologic symptoms.
E. Encourage client to devise alternative coping behaviors, changes in environment, attitude.
F. Role play new behaviors with client.

Evaluation

A. Goals specific to client's physical symptoms have been met.
B. Client
1. Is able to relate stress to physical symptoms.
2. Develops alternative coping behaviors.
3. Engages in role playing of new behaviors.

VICTIMS OF ABUSE

Overview

A. Abuse is physical or sexual assault, emotional abuse, or neglect.
B. Victims are helpless or powerless to prevent the assault on their bodies or personalities.
C. Sometimes victims blame themselves for the assault.
D. The abusers often blame the victims, have poor impulse control, and use their power (physical strength or weapon) to subject victims to their assaults.
E. Victims include children, spouse, elderly, or rape victims; each will be described separately.

Child Abuse

Overview

A. Over one million cases reported each year
B. Suspected child abuse must be reported
C. Abusing adults (parents) often have been victims of abuse, substance abusers, have poor impulse control
D. Battered-child syndrome: multiple traumas inflicted by adult
E. Sexual abuse/incest: common types of child abuse
F. Health care workers often experience negative feelings toward abuser
G. (see Child Abuse, Unit 5, pages 360–362).

Assessment

A. Physical signs/behaviors or physical/sexual abuse (see Table 7.10)
B. Signs of neglect: hunger, poor hygiene/nutrition, fatigue
C. Signs of emotional abuse: habitual behaviors (thumb sucking, rocking, head banging), conduct/learning disorders

Analysis

A. Situational low self-esteem
B. Fear

TABLE 7.10   Symptoms of Child Abuse

Physical Abuse	Sexual Abuse
Pattern of bruises/welts	Pain/itching of genitals
Burns (cigarette, scalds, rope)	Bruised/bleeding genitals
Unexplained fractures/ dislocations	Stains/blood on underwear
Withdrawn or aggressive behavior	Withdrawn or aggressive behavior
Unusual fear of parent/desire to please parent	Unusual sexual behaviors

C. Pain
D. Altered parenting
E. Posttrauma response
F. Powerlessness
G. High risk for injury

Planning and Implementation

A. Goals
  1. Client (child) will be safe until home assessment made by child welfare agency.
  2. Child will participate with nurse (therapist) for emotional support.
  3. Client (parent(s)) will be able to contact agencies to deal with own rage/helplessness.
  4. Parent(s) will participate in therapy (group or other required).
B. Interventions
  1. Provide nursing care specific to physical/emotional symptoms.
  2. Conduct interview in private with child and parent(s) separated.
  3. Inform parent(s) of requirement to report suspected abuse.
  4. Do not probe for information or try to prove abuse.
  5. Be supportive and nonjudgmental.
  6. Provide referrals for assistance and therapy.
C. Evaluation
  1. Physical symptoms have been treated.
  2. Child safety has been ensured.
  3. Parent(s) have agreed to seek help.

Spouse Abuse

Overview

A. Estimates of five million women assaulted by mate each year
B. Stages
  1. Tension builds: verbal abuse, minor physical assaults
    a. Abuser: often reduces tension with alcohol/drugs
    b. Abused: blames self
  2. Acute battering: brutal beating
    a. Abuser: does not recall incident
    b. Abused: depersonalizes, may seek separation/divorce
       Both parties in shock
  3. Honeymoon: make-up stage
    a. Abuser: apologizes and promises to control self
    b. Abused: feels loved/needed; forgives/believes abuser
  4. Cycle repeats with subsequent battering usually more severe

Assessment

A. Headache
B. Injury to face, head, body, genitals

C. Reports "accidents"
D. Symptoms of severe anxiety
E. Depression
F. Insomnia

Analysis

A. High risk for injury
B. Anxiety
C. Pain
D. Ineffective, disabling family coping
E. Ineffective individual coping
F. Spiritual distress

Planning and Implementation

Goals: Client will
A. Admit self and/or children are victims of abuse
B. Describe plan(s) for own/children's safety
C. Name agencies that will assist in maintaining a safe environment
Interventions
A. Crisis stage
  1. Provide safe environment
  2. Treatment of physical injuries; document
  3. Encourage verbalization of actual home environment
  4. Provide referral to shelters
  5. Encourage decision making
B. Rebuilding stage: therapy (individual, family and/or group)

Evaluation

Client will be protected from further injury

Elder Abuse

Overview

A. Estimates one-half million to over one million cases per year.
B. Women, over age 70, with some physical/psychological disability are most frequent victims.
C. Neglect is most common, followed by physical abuse, financial exploitation, and sexual abuse/abandonment.
D. Victims do not always report abuse because of fear of more abuse/abandonment by caretaker(s).

Assessment

A. Malnutrition
B. Poor hygiene, decubiti
C. Omission of medication/overmedication
D. Welts, bruises, fractures

Analysis

A. High risk for injury
B. Fear

C. Anxiety
D. Nutrition less than body requirements
E. Powerlessness
F. Situational low self-esteem

Planning and Implementation

Goals
A. Client will be free from injury.
B. Client will receive adequate nutrition, hydration, prescribed medication.
C. Client will notify nurse if further abuse takes place.
D. Caregiver will verbalize plans to meet own needs.
E. Caregiver will seek assistance to meet client's needs when necessary.
Interventions
A. Refer to state laws for reporting elder abuse and nurse's liability.
B. Obtain client's consent for treatment and/or transfer.
C. Document physical/emotional condition of client.
D. Refer client/caregiver to agencies for assistance.
E. Encourage client and caregiver to discuss problems.
F. Encourage communication between client and caregiver.

Evaluation

A. Client will remain free of injury, effects of neglect.
B. Caregiver will utilize support systems for self.

Rape

Overview

A. Estimates of occurrence vary; only ten percent reported
B. Most victims are female between ages of 15–24 years
C. Response to rape
    1. Shock: panic to overly controlled
    2. Outward adjustment: "manages" life but may make drastic changes (e.g., moves, leaves school/job)
    3. Integration: acknowledges response (e.g., depression, fear, rage)

Assessment

A. Physical injury
B. Emotional response: controlled/hysterical

Analysis

A. Rape trauma syndrome
    1. Acute: immediate to two weeks (anger, fear, self-blame)

2. Long-term: nightmares, phobias, seeks support
B. Silent reaction: anxiety, changes in relationships with men, physical distress, phobias
C. Posttrauma response

Planning and Implementation

Goals: Client will
A. Express response to assault
B. Verbalize plan to handle immediate needs
C. Seek assistance from rape counselor
D. Discuss need for follow-up counseling
E. Report (long-term) reduction of physical and emotional symptoms.
Interventions
A. Give emotional support in nonjudgmental manner.
B. Maintain confidentiality: client must give consent for reporting rape and for medical examination.
C. Listen to client, encourage expression of feelings.
D. Document physical findings. Put evidentiary garments in paper bag.
E. Provide referral to rape counselor and follow-up care.

Evaluation

A. Client seeks support from family/agencies.
B. Client verbalizes emotional response to rape.
C. Long-term: client reports return to prerape life-style.

CRITICAL ILLNESS

Overview

A. Individuals in critical life-threatening situations have realistic fears of death or of permanent loss of function.
B. Clients and their families may respond to these crises with denial, anger, hostility, withdrawal, guilt, and/or panic.
C. Loss of control and a sense of powerlessness can be overwhelming and detrimental to chance of recovery.

Assessment

A. Physiologic needs (first priority)
B. Anxiety level of client/family
C. Client/family fears
D. Coping behaviors of client/family
E. Social and cultural considerations

Analysis

Nursing diagnoses for the psychologic component of critical illness may include
A. Anxiety
B. Hopelessness
C. Ineffective individual/family coping
D. Knowledge deficit
E. Fear
F. Powerlessness
G. Altered self-concept

Planning and Implementation

Goals

A. Client will
   1. Receive treatment for physiologic problems.
   2. Experience decrease in level of anxiety/fear.
   3. Discuss anxiety/fears with nurse.
B. Family will
   1. Be informed of client's condition on regular basis.
   2. Discuss anxiety/fears with nurse.
   3. Provide appropriate support to client.

Interventions

A. Provide nursing care specific to physiologic problems.
B. Stay with client.
C. Explain all procedures slowly, clearly, concisely.
D. Provide opportunities for client to discuss fears.
E. Provide opportunities for client to make decisions, have as much control as possible.
F. Encourage family to ask questions.
G. Recognize negative family responses as coping behaviors.
H. Encourage family members to support each other and client.

Evaluation

A. Goals specific to client's physiologic status have been met.
B. Client
   1. Demonstrates a decrease in anxious behaviors.
   2. Is able to express fears verbally.
   3. Has participated in decisions whenever possible.
C. Family members
   1. Have discussed fears.
   2. Demonstrate support for each other and for client.

Sample Questions

42. Tammy, 18 months old, has been admitted for second-degree burns surrounding the genital area. Her mother told the nurse that Tammy grabbed for the hot coffee cup and spilled it on herself. The nurse is required by law to
    1. testify in court on the injuries.
    2. report suspected child abuse.
    3. have the mother arrested.
    4. refer the mother to counseling.

43. A toddler was admitted for second degree burns surrounding the genital area. Her mother told the nurse that the child grabbed the hot coffee cup and spilled it on herself. The toddler's mother is 17 years old. In which of the areas would the nurse provide health teaching?
    1. Normal growth and development.
    2. Bonding techniques.
    3. How to childproof the apartment.
    4. Parenting skills.

44. Marilyn was returning home from work late and was sexually assaulted. She was brought to the emergency room upset and crying. The nurse's main goal in caring for Marilyn is to
    1. assist Marilyn in crisis.
    2. notify the police of the alleged assault.
    3. understand Marilyn will have a long recovery period.
    4. provide support and comfort.

45. The nurse caring for a young woman who was sexually assaulted. Which of the following is indicative of successful adjustment to the trauma?
    1. She moves to another city.
    2. She resumes her work and activities.
    3. She takes classes in the martial arts.
    4. She remains silent about the assault.

Answers and Rationales

42. The correct answer is 2. Legal statutes require health professionals to report suspected cases of child abuse.
43. The correct answer is 4. Because the toddler's mother is only 17 years old, she needs information and role modeling on how to provide an emotionally and physically safe environment for her child.
44. The correct answer is 1. A sexual assault is a crisis situation that requires immediate intervention.
45. The correct answer is 2. The goal of adjustment is to have the woman return to her precrisis level of functioning.

CHRONIC ILLNESS

Overview

A. Chronic illnesses, such as diabetes mellitus, multiple sclerosis, or illnesses/injuries resulting in loss of function or loss of a body part necessitate adaptation to the inherent changes imposed.

B. Clients/families may respond to the losses associated with chronic illness with a variety of behaviors and defenses, including recurrent depression, anger and hostility, denial, or acceptance.

Assessment and Analysis

Same as stress-related disorders (page 556) as well as
A. Ineffective family coping
B. High risk for violence, self-directed
C. Spiritual distress

Planning and Intervention

Goals

A. Client will
  1. Receive appropriate treatment for any physiologic symptoms.
  2. Be able/willing to discuss responses to illness.
  3. Recognize effect of illness on aspects of self-concept.
  4. Develop realistic plans for activities and role functions.
  5. Contract with nurse to report depression/ suicidal ideation.
B. Family will
  1. Be able to discuss responses to client illness.
  2. Develop plans to deal with alterations in client's behaviors and functions.

Interventions

A. Provide nursing care specific to physiologic problems.
B. Develop nurse/client relationship through active listening, acceptance of positive and negative client responses.
C. Encourage client to plan activities within present capabilities.
D. Provide information about illness, suggestions for activities.
E. Contract with client to request support in times of depression and to report suicidal ideation.
F. Encourage family members to discuss their response to client's illness.
G. Be accepting and nonjudgmental of negative responses (e.g., anger, hopelessness).
H. Support family efforts to develop plans for their participation in client's care.

Evaluation

A. Client
  1. Receives appropriate treatment for any physiologic problems.

  2. Recognizes/discusses positive and negative responses to illness.
  3. Understands effects of feelings about body image, self-esteem, role function.
  4. Agrees to report depression or suicidal thoughts.
B. Family
  1. Discusses positive and negative responses to client's illness.
  2. Plans/engages in appropriate activities with client.

AIDS

Overview

A. In the U.S., many thousands of reported cases and deaths, estimates between 1 and 2 million infected.
B. Highest risk populations: homosexual/bisexual men, I.V. drug users and their sexual partners, hemophiliacs, newborns from infected mothers.
C. Approximately 60% of persons with AIDS develop neurological symptoms.
D. Health care workers may have difficulty caring for these clients because of fear of contagion, knowledge deficit, bias against life-style, or burnout.
E. Families/partners will require support, education, and/or counseling.

Assessment

A. Physical symptoms
  1. Fever
  2. Fatigue
  3. Weight loss
  4. Diarrhea
  5. Opportunistic infections
B. Neurological and emotional responses
  1. Depression
  2. Panic disorders
  3. Paranoid reaction
  4. HIV dementia complex
C. See AIDS (Unit 4, pages 238–240) for other physical assessment findings.

Analysis

A. Anxiety
B. Fear
C. Ineffective denial
D. Anticipatory grieving
E. Ineffective individual coping
F. Powerlessness
G. High risk for violence, self-directed
H. Social isolation

Planning and Implementation

Goals

A. Client will
   1. Communicate responses (physical and psychologic) to disease process
   2. Maintain ADL as long as possible
   3. Report suicidal ideation/impulses
B. Family/partners will
   1. Seek support and education relating to care of HIV-positive client
   2. Communicate responses to client's illness to nurse/support group
C. Health care workers will
   1. Discuss feelings of homophobia, addictophobia, and fear of infection
   2. Attend groups for education and support

Interventions

A. Monitor cognitive and affective domain.
B. Encourage communication of fears and concerns.
C. Maintain nonjudgmental attitude.
D. Assist client/family through grieving process.
E. Provide opportunities for decision making to client and/or caregivers.

Evaluation

A. Client participates in care decisions.
B. Client and caregivers discuss responses to illness.
C. Client expresses anger but does not harm self.

DEATH AND DYING

Overview

A. One of the most difficult issues in nursing practice
B. Often difficult for nurses to maintain objectivity because of identification and response to death based on own value system and personal experiences

Assessment

A. Stage of dying (Kubler-Ross); see Table 7.11
B. Physical discomfort

TABLE 7.11   Stages of Dying

1. Denial and isolation
2. Anger
3. Bargaining
4. Depression
5. Acceptance

C. Emotional reaction (withdrawal, anger, acceptance) and stage of dying
D. Desire to discuss impending death, value of own life
E. Level of consciousness
F. Family needs

Analysis

Nursing diagnoses for the dying client may include
A. Anxiety
B. Pain
C. Ineffective individual/family coping
D. Fear
E. Anticipatory grieving
F. Hopelessness
G. Impaired mobility
H. Powerlessness
I. Self-care deficit
J. Social isolation

Planning and Implementation

Goals

A. Client will
   1. Be maintained in optimum comfort.
   2. Not be alone.
   3. Have opportunity to discuss what death means and to progress through stages of dying.
B. Family will have opportunity to be with client as much as they desire.

Interventions

A. Recognize clients/families have own way of dealing with death and dying.
B. Support clients/families as they work through dying process.
C. Accept negative responses from clients/families.
D. Encourage clients/families to discuss feelings related to death and dying.
E. Support staff and seek support for self when dealing with dying client and grieving family.

Evaluation

A. Client
   1. Takes opportunity to discuss feelings about impending death and eventually acknowledges inevitable outcome.
   2. Is comfortable and participates in self-care for as long as possible.
B. Family discusses feelings about loss of loved one.

GRIEF AND MOURNING

Overview

A. Response to loss (person, body part, role)
B. Biologic, psychologic, social implications
C. Family system effects
D. Mourning is process to resolve grief
   1. Shock, disbelief are short term
   2. Resentment, anger
   3. Concentration on loss
      a. Possible auditory, visual hallucinations
      b. Possible guilt
      c. Possible fear of becoming mentally ill
   4. Despair, depression
   5. Detachment from loss
   6. Renewed interest, investment in others/interests

Assessment

A. Weight loss
B. Sleep disturbance
C. Thoughts centered on loss
D. Dependency, withdrawal, anger, guilt
E. Suicide potential

Analysis

A. Ineffective individual/family coping
B. Hopelessness
C. Sleep pattern disturbance
D. Altered thought processes
E. High risk for violence, self-directed

Planning and Implementation

Goals

Client/family will
A. Discuss responses to loss.
B. Resume normal sleeping/eating patterns.
C. Resume ADL as they accept loss.

Interventions

A. Encourage client/family to express feelings.
B. Accept negative feelings/defenses.
C. Employ empathic listening.
D. Explain mourning process and relate to client/family responses.
E. Refer client/family to support groups.

Evaluation

Client/family
A. Express feelings.
B. Progress through mourning process.
C. Seek necessary support groups.

Sample Questions

46. Larry, aged 27, has recently begun experiencing forgetfulness, disorientation, and occasional lapses in memory. Larry, who is gay, was diagnosed with AIDS dementia. Larry's family began sobbing on hearing the diagnosis. The nurse's initial response would be
    1. You must never give up hope.
    2. He was in a high-risk group for AIDS.
    3. I can understand your grief.
    4. This must be very difficult for you.
47. Larry, 27 years old, was diagnosed with AIDS dementia. The nurse is planning care for Larry. The primary goal in his care is to
    1. enhance the quality of life.
    2. teach him about AIDS.
    3. discuss his future goals.
    4. provide him with comfort and support.
48. One of the major fears experienced by people with AIDS is
    1. dying.
    2. debilitation.
    3. stigma.
    4. poverty.

Answers and Rationales

46. The correct answer is 4. AIDS is an illness that generates intense emotional reactions and fears. Acknowledging these feelings allows the family to discuss them with the nurse in a nonthreatening environment.
47. The correct answer is 1. Because Larry's illness has no cure and the progression is dependent on the body system affected, the primary goal is to ensure his personal dignity and make plans to fulfill personal goals.
48. The correct answer is 2. Research has found that many clients with AIDS are most fearful of the debilitating effects of the disease.

References and Suggested Readings

American Psychiatric Association (1994). *Diagnostic and statistical manual of mental disorders* (4th ed.). Washington, DC: Author.

Burgess, A. (1997). *Psychiatric nursing: promoting mental health.* Stamford, CT: Appleton & Lange.

Deglen, J., & Vallerand, A. (1997). *Davis's drug guide for nurses* (5th ed.). Philadelphia: F.A. Davis.

Doenges, M., Townsend, M., & Moorehouse, M. (1997). *Psychiatric care plans* (3rd ed.). Philadelphia: Davis.

Frisch, N., & Frisch, L. (1998). *Psychiatric mental health nursing.* Albany, NY: Delmar Publishers.

Glod, C. (1998). *Contemporary psychiatric mental health nursing: The brain-behavior connection*. Philadelphia: F.A. Davis.

Gorman, L., Sulton, D., & Raines, M. (1996). *Davis's manual of psychosocial nursing for general patient care*. Philadelphia: F.A. Davis.

Johnson, B. (1997). *Psychiatric-mental health nursing: Adaptation and growth*. Philadelphia: Lippincott.

McBride, A., & Austin, J. (1996). *Psychiatric mental health nursing: Integrating the behavioral and biological sciences*. Philadelphia: W.B. Saunders.

Restak, R. (1994). *Receptors*. New York: Bantam.

Rosenthal, N. (1998). *Winter blues: Seasonal affective disorder, what it is and how to overcome it*. New York: Guilford Press.

Schultz, J., & Videbeck, S. (1998). *Manual of psychiatric nursing care plans* (5th ed.). Philadelphia: Lippincott.

Wilson, H., & Kneisl, C. (1996). *Psychiatric nursing*. Menlo Park, CA: Addison-Wesley.

Appendix

Special Diets

Theresa Marie Giglio, RD, MS
Judith C. Miller, RN, MSN

APPENDIX OUTLINE

566 Exchange Lists for Meal Planning
569 High-Fiber Diet
569 1500-Kilocalorie Diet
571 1000-Milligram Sodium-Restricted Diet
572 Bland Diet
573 Low-Residue Diet
574 20-Gram Fat-Restricted Diet
575 Fat-Controlled Diet

EXCHANGE LISTS FOR MEAL PLANNING

Food Exchange Lists[1]

List	Measure	Carbohydrates g	Protein g	Fat g	Energy kcal
Milk, nonfat (list 1)	1 cup	12	8	trace	80
Milk, whole (list 1)	1 cup	12	8	9	160
Vegetables (list 2)	½ cup	5	2		25
Fruits (list 3)	Varies	10			40
Breads, cereals, and starchy vegetables (list 4)	Varies	15	2		70
Meat, low fat (list 5)	1 oz		7	2.5	50
Meat, medium fat (list 5)	1 oz		7.5	5	75
Meat, high fat (list 5)	1 oz		7	7.5	95
Fat (list 6)	Varies			5	45

[1]Resource: Committees of the American Diabetes Association, Inc., and the American Diatetic Association: Exchange Lists for Meal Planning. Chicago: The American Dietetic Association and the American Diabetes Association, in cooperation with the National Institute of Arthritis, Metabolism and Digestive Diseases and the National Heart, Blood and Lung Institute, Public Health Service, U.S. Department of Health, Education and Welfare, 1976.

List 1: Milk Exchanges

Milk (nonfat, fortified)

Use only this list for diets restricted in saturated fat.

	Amount to Use
Skim or nonfat milk	1 cup
Powdered (nonfat dry)	⅓ cup
Canned, evaporated, skim	½ cup
Buttermilk made from skim milk	1 cup
Yogurt, made from skim milk, plain, unflavored	1 cup

Milk (low fat, fortified)

1% fat, fortified (omit ½ fat exchange)	1 cup
2% fat, fortified (omit 1 fat exchange)	1 cup
Yogurt made from 2% fortified, plain, unflavored (omit 1 fat exchange)	1 cup

Milk (whole)

Whole milk	1 cup
Canned evaporated	½ cup
Buttermilk made from whole milk	1 cup
Yogurt made from whole milk, plain, unflavored	1 cup

List 2: Vegetable Exchanges

One-half cup equals one exchange.

Asparagus*
Bean sprouts
Beets
Broccoli*†
Brussels sprouts*
Cabbage*
Carrots†
Celery
Cauliflower*
Cucumbers
Eggplant
Greens*†
   Beet greens
   Chard
   Collards
   Dandelion greens
   Kale
   Mustard greens
   Spinach
   Turnip greens

Mushrooms
Okra
Onions
Rhubarb
Rutabaga
Sauerkraut
String beans, green or yellow
Summer squash
Tomatoes*
Tomato juice
Turnips
Vegetable juice cocktail
Zucchini

These vegetables can be used as desired: chicory, Chinese cabbage, endive, escarole, lettuce, parsley, radishes, and watercress. *See List 4, Bread Exchanges, for starchy vegetables.*

*Good sources of ascorbic acid
†Good sources of vitamin A

List 3: Fruit Exchanges

	Amount to Use
Apple	1 small
Apple juice	⅓ cup
Applesauce (unsweetened)	½ cup
Apricots, fresh†	2 medium
Apricots, dried†	4 halves
Bananas	½ small
Blackberries	½ cup
Blueberries	½ cup
Raspberries	½ cup
Strawberries	¾ cup
Cherries	10 large
Cider	⅓ cup
Dates	2
Figs, fresh	1
Figs, dried	1
Grapefruit*	½
Grapefruit juice	½ cup
Grapes	12
Grape juice	¼ cup
Mango*†	½ small
Cantaloupe*	¼ small
Honeydew*	⅛ medium
Watermelon	1 cup
Nectarine	1 medium
Orange*	1 small
Orange juice*	½ cup
Papaya*†	¾ cup
Peach†	1 medium
Pear	1 small
Persimmon	1 medium
Pineapple	½ cup
Pineapple juice	⅓ cup
Plums	2 medium
Prunes	2 medium
Prune juice	¼ cup
Raisins	2 tbsp
Tangerine*	1 large

Cranberries may be used as desired if no sugar is added.

*Good sources of ascorbic acid

†Good sources of vitamin A

List 4: Bread, Cereal, and Starchy Vegetable Exchanges

	Amount to Use
Bread	
White (including French and Italian)	1 slice
Whole wheat	1 slice
Rye or pumpernickel	1 slice
Raisin	1 slice
Bagel, small	½
English muffin, small	½
Frankfurter roll	½
Hamburger bun	½
Plain roll (bread)	1
Dry bread crumbs	3 tbsp
Tortillas, 6 in	1
Cereal	
Bran flakes	½ cup
Other ready-to-eat unsweetened cereal	¾ cup
Puffed cereal, unfrosted	1 cup
Cereal, cooked	½ cup
Grits, cooked	½ cup
Rice or barley, cooked	½ cup
Pastas, cooked	½ cup
Popcorn, popped	3 cups
Cornmeal, dry	2 tbsp
Flour	2½ tbsp
Wheat germ	½ cup
Crackers	
Arrowroot	3
Graham, 2½ inch	2
Matzoh, 4 × 6 inch	½
Oyster	20
Pretzels, 3⅛ inch × ⅛ inch	15
Rye wafers, 2 × 3½ inch	3
Saltines	6
Soda, 2½ inch square	4
Dried Beans, Peas, and Lentils	
Dried beans, peas, and lentils cooked	½ cup
Baked beans, no pork	¼ cup
Starchy Vegetables	
Corn	⅓ cup
Corn on cob	1 small
Lima beans	½ cup
Parsnips	⅔ cup
Peas (green, fresh, canned, or frozen)	½ cup
Potato, white	1 small
Potato, mashed	½ cup
Pumpkin	¾ cup
Winter squash, acorn or butternut	½ cup
Yam or sweet potato	¼ cup
Prepared Foods	
Biscuit, 2 inch diam. (omit 1 fat exchange)	1
Cornbread, 2 × 2 × 1 inch (omit 1 fat exchange)	1
Corn muffin, 2 inch diam. (omit 1 fat exchange)	1
Crackers, round, butter type (omit 1 fat exchange)	5
Muffin, plain, small (omit 1 fat exchange)	1
Pancake, 5 × ½ inch (omit 1 fat exchange)	1
Potatoes, french fried, 2 inch to 3½ inch (omit 1 fat exchange)	15
Waffle, 5 × ½ inch (omit 1 fat exchange)	1

List 5: Meat and Protein-Rich Exchanges

Lean Meat, Protein-Rich Exchanges

Use only this list for diets low in saturated fat and cholesterol.

	Amount to Use
Beef	
Baby beef (very lean), chipped beef, chuck, flank steak, tenderloin, plate ribs, plate skirt steak, round (bottom, top), all cuts rump, spare ribs, tripe	1 oz
Lamb	
Leg, rib, sirloin, loin (roast and chops), shank, shoulder	1 oz
Pork	
Leg (whole rump, center shank), smoked ham (center slices)	1 oz
Veal	
Leg, loin, rib, shank, shoulder, cutlets	1 oz
Poultry without skin	
Chicken, turkey, Cornish hen, guinea hen, pheasant	1 oz
Fish, any fresh or frozen	
Canned crab, lobster, mackerel, salmon, tuna	¼ cup
Clams, oysters, scallops, shrimp	5 or 1 oz
Sardines, drained	3
Cheeses containing less than 5% butterfat	1 oz
Cottage cheese: dry or 2% butterfat	¼ cup
Dried peas and beans (omit 1 bread exchange	½ cup

Medium-Fat Meal, Protein-Rich Exchanges

Beef	
Ground, 15% fat; corned beef, canned; rib eye, round, ground (commercial)	1 oz
Pork	
Loin, all cuts tenderloin, shoulder arm (picnic); shoulder blade; Boston butt; Canadian bacon; boiled ham	1 oz
Liver, heart, kidney, and sweetbreads (high in cholesterol)	1 oz
Cottage cheese, creamed	¼ cup
Cheese	
Mozzarella, ricotta, farmer's, Neufchâtel	1 oz
Parmesan	3 tbsp
Eggs (high in cholesterol)	1
Peanut butter (omit 2 fat exchanges)	2 tbsp

High-Fat Meal, Protein-Rich Exchanges

Beef brisket; corned beef brisket; ground beef (over 20% fat); hamburger (commercial); chuck, ground (commercial); rib roast, club and rib steak	1 oz
Lamb, breast	1 oz
Pork; spare ribs; loin (back ribs); pork, ground; country style ham, deviled ham	1 oz
Veal, breast	1 oz
Poultry: capon, duck (domestic), goose	1 oz
Cheese: cheddar type	1 oz
Cold cuts, 4½ × ⅛ inch	1 slice
Frankfurter	small

List 6: Fat Exchanges

For a diet low in saturated fat and higher in polyunsaturated fat, select only from this list.

	Amount to Use
Margarine: soft, tub, or stick (made with corn, cottonseed, safflower, soy, or sunflower oil)	1 tbsp
Avocado, 4 in diam.	⅛
Nuts	
Almonds*	10 whole
Peanuts*	
Spanish	20 whole
Virginia	10 whole
Pecans*	2 large, whole
Walnuts	6 small
Other nuts*	6 small
Oil, corn, cottonseed, safflower, soy, sunflower	1 tsp
Oil, olive or peanut*	1 tsp
Olives*	5 small
Salad dressings, if made with corn, cottonseed, safflower or soy oil	
French dressing	1 tbsp
Italian dressing	1 tbsp
Mayonnaise	1 tsp
Salad dressing, mayonnaise type	2 tsp

*Fat content is primarily monounsaturated

The following fats should not be used on a diet low in saturated fat.

Margarine, regular stick	1 tsp
Butter	1 tsp
Bacon fat	1 tsp
Bacon, crisp	1 strip
Cream, light	2 tbsp
Cream, sour	2 tbsp
Cream, heavy	1 tbsp
Cream cheese	1 tbsp
Lard	1 tsp
Salad dressings (permitted on restricted diets if made with allowed oils)	
French dressing	1 tbsp
Italian dressing	1 tbsp
Mayonnaise	1 tsp
Salad dressing, mayonnaise type	2 tsp
Salt pork	¾ inch cube

HIGH-FIBER DIET

Description

The diet is essentially a normal diet with increased amounts of cellulose, hemicellulose, lignin, and pectin. It increases the volume and weight of the stool; increases gastrointestinal motility; and decreases intraluminal colonic pressure in clients suffering from increased pressure, including clients with constipation, hemorrhoids, and long-term management of diverticulosis.

General Characteristics

Consume a regular diet with increased fiber content
1. Include raw fruits and vegetables instead of canned or cooked ones.
2. Substitute whole-grain bread and cereals for refined grains.
3. Include dried fruits and nuts in meals. (Nuts may be eliminated in clients with diverticulosis.)
4. Prepare soups with high-fiber vegetables.
5. Eat a fresh vegetable or fruit salad daily.
6. Add 1–2 tablespoons of bran to other foods daily.
7. Initiate the high-fiber diet gradually to prevent gas and loose stools.

Possible Complications

1. Osmotic diarrhea.
2. Decreased serum levels of minerals, such as iron, calcium, magnesium, etc.

1500-KILOCALORIE DIET

Description

A 1500 kcal diet will permit a steady weight loss of body fat without loss of body tissue and other essential body components. The diet meets the Recommended Dietary Allowances for the adult for protein, minerals, and vitamins.

Food Preparation

Foods should be prepared without added sugar and flour, using only that amount of fat allowed in the diet. Meats may be broiled, braised, stewed, or roasted. All visible fat should be trimmed. The measure or weight of food refers to the food in its cooked form.

Diet Guidelines
Food Exchange Lists

	Daily Allowance
List 1: Milk: 1 serving = 8 ounces	2 cups
Skim milk (1% fat)	
Buttermilk (1% fat)	
Yogurt made from skim milk	

List 2: Vegetables: 1 serving = ½ cup — 3 servings

Asparagus	Green peppers
Bean sprouts	Mushrooms
Beets	Okra
Broccoli	Onions
Brussels sprouts	Sauerkraut
Cabbage	String beans
Carrots	Summer squash
Cauliflower	Tomatoes
Celery	Tomato/
Eggplant	vegetable juice
Greens	Turnips
Zucchini	

List 3: Fruits (fresh or unsweetened) — 5 servings

Small apple	12 grapes
⅓ cup apple juice	⅛ honeydew melon
2 apricots	Small orange
½ small banana	½ cup orange juice
½ cup berries	Medium peach
¾ cup strawberries	½ cup pineapple
¼ cantaloupe	⅓ cup pineapple juice
10 cherries	2 plums
2 dates	2 prunes
½ grapefruit	¼ cup prune juice
½ cup grapefruit juice	1 cup watermelon
2 tbsp raisins	Medium tangerine

List 4: Bread, Cereal, Starchy Vegetables — 6 servings

1 slice bread	2 graham crackers
½ bagel	6 saltine crackers
½ English muffin	½ matzoh
½ hamburger roll	25 small pretzels
¾ cup dry cereal	(3⅛ long,
½ cup cooked cereal	⅛ inch diam)
½ cup rice, grits	3 cups popcorn
½ cup peas, beans	½ cup pastas
¼ cup baked beans	1 small potato
¼ cup sweet potato	⅓ cup corn

List 5: Meat and Poultry Foods
Lean — 3 oz total or ¾ cup

1 oz beef: leg, round, chipped, rump, loin
1 oz lamb: leg, rib, loin, sirloin
1 oz veal: leg, loin, rib, cutlets
1 oz pork: leg, rump, center slice
1 oz poultry: without skin (no duck or goose)
¼ cup tuna, salmon, crab, shrimp, lobster
¼ cup dry cottage cheese

Medium Fat 3 oz total or ¾ cup
- 1 oz ground beef (15% fat)
- 1 oz pork shoulder, boiled ham,
  Canadian bacon
- 1 oz liver
- 1 egg
- 1 oz mozzarella, ricotta, farmer's cheese
- ¼ cup cottage cheese

List 6: Fats 5 servings
- 1 tsp butter
- 1 tsp margarine
- 1 tsp oil
- 1 tbsp French
  dressing
- 1 tbsp Italian
  dressing
- 10 peanuts
- ¾ inch cube salt pork
- 1 tbsp cream cheese
- 2 tbsp cream
- 1 slice crisp bacon
- 1 tsp bacon fat
- 5 small olives
- 1 tsp mayonnaise
- 1 tsp lard

Foods Allowed as Desired
Cucumbers, dill pickles, Chinese cabbage, endive, escarole, lettuce, parsley, radishes, bouillon, unflavored gelatin, coffee, tea, spices

1000-MILLIGRAM SODIUM-RESTRICTED DIET

Description

The aim of this diet is to promote the loss of excess sodium and water from the extracellular fluid compartments of the body. It is used primarily for clients with ascites/edema associated with advanced liver or renal disease, clients in congestive heart failure, as a treatment for essential hypertension, and with clients receiving adrenocorticosteroids.

Food Preparation

All food should be prepared without the addition of salt, regular baking powder, and baking soda. No salt should be used at the table.

General Principles

Select foods that have not been processed or preserved with large amounts of salt. Include all fruits and fruit juices, fresh, canned, frozen, dried. Use only unsalted snack foods.

Diet Guidelines

Type of Food	Allow	Avoid
Milk	Whole or skim milk Limit: 2 cups/day	Milk shakes, malted milk, commercial chocolate, or buttermilk
Eggs	Any form prepared without the addition of salt. Limit: 4/week	
Cheese	Dry cottage cheese and low-sodium American cheese	All types except those allowed
Meat, fish, poultry	Meat or poultry without added salt or sodium products. Fresh or canned fish without added salt. Unsalted peanut butter.	Lunchmeat, sausage, hot dogs, shellfish organ meats, bacon, ham, corned beef, dried beef, canned meat, anchovies salted canned fish, dried cod

Type of Food	Allow	Avoid
Soups and sauces	All made with allowed milk and vegetables	Broth, bouillon, gravy, canned soup, consomme, and cream sauce
Vegetables Potatoes	Fresh, frozen or canned white and sweet potatoes without added salt	Potato chips
Other vegetables	Unsalted asparagus, green beans, wax beans, corn, fresh or canned lima beans, eggplant, endive escarole, lettuce, mushrooms, fresh or canned peas, squash, tomatoes. Also, if tolerated: broccoli, Brussels sprouts, cabbage, cauliflower, turnips, onions, parsnips, radishes, rutabagas, and cucumbers Following vegetables should be limited to one serving per day: beets, carrots, celery, spinach, or turnips	Beet greens, kale, frozen lima beans, olives, frozen peas, pickles, sauerkraut, Swiss chard, mustard greens, dandelion greens
Cereals	Puffed rice, puffed wheat, shredded wheat, and regular cooked whole-grain or enriched cereals	All other ready-to-eat cereals. Quick cream of wheat, quick-cooking farina, hominy
Bread	Regular white, whole wheat, or rye. Limit: 3 slices/day. If additional bread is desired, use low-sodium bread.	All others
Crackers	Unsalted crackers	All others
Other cereal	Macaroni, spaghetti products, noodles, rice	
Fats	Unsalted butter, margarine, oil	Salted butter or margarine, salad dressings, salt pork, bacon fat

BLAND DIET

Description

This diet excludes foods that may be chemically or mechanically stimulating or irritating to the gastrointestinal tract. Small, frequent meals may be indicated. Prescribed for clients with ulcers and postoperatively after some types of surgery.

Food Preparation

Meats may be baked, broiled, stewed, or roasted, but not fried. Fruits and vegetables should be cooked or canned. Avoid meat extracts, pepper, and chili powder.

Diet Guidelines

Type of Food	Allow	Avoid
Milk	Milk, buttermilk, cocoa, milk beverages	None
Eggs	Soft cooked, hard cooked, poached, steam scrambled	Fried, deviled
Cheese	Cottage cheese, cream, mild cheddar in sauces or in combination dishes	Strongly flavored cheese
Meat, fish, poultry	Tender beef, lamb, pork, liver, poultry, veal, fish, crisp bacon	Smoked, salted, or fatty meat or fish
Vegetables Potatoes	Baked (without skin), boiled, creamed, escalloped, or mashed white potatoes	Sweet potatoes, fried potatoes
Other vegetables	Cooked asparagus tips, beets, carrots, peas, chopped spinach, winter	All others

Type of Food	Allow	Avoid
	squash, green beans, mushrooms, waxed beans, strained corn pudding	
Cereals	Cream of rice, cream of wheat, farina, cornmeal, hominy grits, strained oatmeal, cornflakes, puffed rice, Rice Krispies, Special K	Bran, whole-grain cereals
Breads	White, Italian, French, rye bread without seeds, melba toast	Whole-grain breads
Crackers	Soda crackers, saltines	Graham crackers, crackers with seeds
Other cereal products	Macaroni, noodles, rice, spaghetti	
Fats	Butter, margarine, cream, salad oil	All others
Fruits	Avocado, ripe bananas, canned peaches, pears, Royal Anne cherries, peeled apricots, applesauce, baked apple (no skin),all strained fruit juices	Raw fruits except avocado and bananas; berries, figs, pineapple
Desserts	Plain sugar cookies, vanilla wafers, lady fingers, angel food cake, sponge cake, plain sherbet, plain ice cream, custard, Jell-O, Junket, Bavarian cream, simple puddings, fruit whips	Any containing fruits, nuts, or spices; pastries, pies, doughnuts
Beverages	Decaffeinated beverages	Caffeine-containing soft drinks, coffee, tea; alcohol

LOW-RESIDUE DIET

Description

The low-residue diet is low in fiber, soft in texture, and easily digested. It decreases the weight and bulk of the stool.

Food Preparation

Fruits and vegetables should be well cooked and pureed. Meats may be baked, broiled, stewed, or roasted. The meats that must be ground may be made from cooked meats that have had the gristle and excess fat removed, or ground meats may be purchased and made into patties or meatloaf. The food may be mildly seasoned.

Diet Guidelines

Type of Food	Allow	Avoid
Milk	1 pint	Any additional
Eggs	Hard cooked, soft cooked, steam scrambled, poached	All others
Cheese	Cottage, cream, mild American	All others
Meat, fish, poultry	Ground lean beef, lamb, veal, liver Sliced white meat of chicken or turkey Fish, crisp bacon Smooth peanut butter	Luncheon meats, sausages; smoked, highly seasoned or highly salted meats and fish
Vegetables Potatoes	White potato, strained sweet potato	Potato chips or fried potatoes
Other vegetables	Cooked and pureed: beets, peas, lima beans, squash, string beans, spinach, asparagus, pumpkin Whole asparagus tips and carrots cooked tender, mushrooms Tomato juice	
Cereals	Cream of rice, cream of wheat, farina, cornmeal, strained oatmeal, cornflakes, puffed rice, Rice Krispies, Special K	Whole-grain cereals
Breads	White bread, melba toast, zwieback	All others
Crackers	Soda crackers, saltines	All others
Other cereal products	Macaroni, noodles, refined rice, spaghetti	Whole-grain rice
Fats	Butter, margarine, cream, mayonnaise, salad oil, shortening	All others
Fruits	All canned or strained fruit juices. Cooked or canned applesauce, Royal Anne cherries, peeled apricots, peaches, pears, bananas, peeled baked apple	All others
Desserts	Simple puddings, ice cream, sherbet, plain cakes and cookies, flavored gelatin, custards	All others. Allowed desserts with nuts, seeds, or coconut
Beverages	Coffee, tea, Postum, Sanka, carbonated beverages, fruit juices Milk in allowed amount	All others

20-GRAM FAT-RESTRICTED DIET

Description

The 20-g fat-restricted diet is designed for clients with an acute intolerance for fat and for clients with high serum cholesterol levels. Lean meat is the only source of fat. For a 40-g fat-restricted diet, add any combination of 4 teaspoons of the following: butter, margarine, shortening oil, mayonnaise.

Diet Guidelines

Type of Food	Allow	Avoid
Yogurt, milk	Skim milk, skim milk yogurt, skim milk buttermilk	Whole milk, buttermilk, yogurt
Eggs	Egg whites only	Whole eggs and egg yolks
Cheese	Dry cottage cheese, skim milk cheese	Whole milk cheese
Meat, fish, poultry	Two 2-oz servings of lean beef, veal, pork, lamb, poultry, liver, or fish	Corned beef, sausages, goose, duck, fish canned in oil such as sardines, tuna fish, and salmon Fried meats, fish, and poultry
Vegetables Potatoes	Sweet or white	Those prepared with fat
Other vegetables	All prepared without fat, oil, or cream	Frozen vegetables in butter or cream sauces, au gratin; potato chips; casseroles
Cereals	Cooked and ready-to-eat cereals	None

Type of Food	Allow	Avoid
Bread	White, whole wheat, and rye bread Hard, water rolls, simple yeast buns	All others
Crackers	Saltine and graham	All others
Other cereal products	Macaroni, noodles, rice, and spaghetti	
Fats	None	All
Fruits	Any fruit or juice	Olives, avocados
Desserts	Fruit ices and sherbets, gelatin desserts, puddings prepared with skim milk, fruit whips made with egg whites, and angel food cake	Pies, cakes, pastries, chocolate, rich desserts, ice cream, any containing nuts, whole milk, cream, or butter
Beverages	Coffee, tea, carbonated beverages	All beverages made with whole milk
Sauces	Tomato sauce and white sauce made with skim milk Gravy made with fat-free broth or drippings	Gravies with fat Cheese sauces, meat sauces, rich dessert sauces
Soups	Fat-free broth soups and creamed soups made with skim milk	Soups made with whole milk, cream, or additional fat
Condiments and miscellaneous	In moderation: salt, pepper, spices, herbs, flavoring extracts	Chocolate, nuts
Sweets	Sugar, jelly, honey, jams, syrups, molasses, plain hard candy	Candy with chocolate and nuts

FAT-CONTROLLED DIET

Description

The fat-controlled diet limits foods containing cholesterol and saturated fatty acids and increases foods high in polyunsaturated fatty acids. (Cholesterol intake should be limited to 300 mg daily if diet is followed.)

Food Preparation

Only lean meats, fish, and poultry are used. The allowed vegetable oils may be used in preparing meats, fish, or poultry; used in salad dressings; or in baked products. A portion of the total fat is allowed in the form of margarine each day. Margarine labels should be read carefully to ensure that the one selected contains liquid polyunsaturated oils, preferably corn, soy, or safflower.

Diet Guidelines

Type of Food	Allow	Avoid
Milk	Yogurt made from skim milk, skim milk, skim buttermilk	Whole milk and cream; creamed buttermilk
Eggs	Three whole eggs per week; egg whites as desired	Those prepared with fats other than vegetable oils
Cheese	Dry cottage cheese, skim milk cheese	All others Whole milk cheese
Meat, fish, poultry	Lean beef, veal, lamb, and pork limited to 9 oz/week; fish, poultry without skin	Fat meats such as bacon, duck, goose, sausages, luncheon meats, frankfurters, and spareribs Glandular and organ meats, caviar, and shrimp
Vegetables Potatoes	Sweet or white	Those prepared with fats other than a special margarine or vegetable oil

Type of Food	Allow	Avoid
Other vegetables	All	None
Cereals	All	None
Bread	White or whole grain, hot breads made with vegetable oil	Breads made with other shortenings and egg yolk
Crackers	Soda and graham	All others
Other cereal	Macaroni, rice, and spaghetti	Noodles made with egg
Fats	Margarine (polyunsaturated), corn oil, safflower oil, soybean oil; salad dressings made with these oils	Butter, mayonnaise, cream, lard, hydrogenated vegetable shortening, olive oil, coconut oil
Fruits	All	None
Desserts	Fruit ices, gelatin, fruits, angel food cake, puddings prepared with skim milk, fruit whips made with egg whites, and baked products made with allowed oils	Ice cream; sherbet; baked products made with egg yolk, shortening (other than vegetable oil) or cream Other desserts prepared with same
Beverages	Coffee, tea made with skim milk, carbonated beverages	Beverages made with whole milk or cream
Sauces	Tomato sauce and sauces made with skim milk	Gravies, meat sauces, and rich dessert sauces
Soups	Homemade fat-free soups made with allowed ingredients	Soups made with cream and whole milk
Condiments	All desired	No restrictions
Sweets	All except chocolate	Chocolate

Comprehensive Practice Tests

This section contains eight 100-question tests similar in structure and content to those you will find on the NCLEX-RN™ examination. At the end of each test are the correct answers and the rationales for the correct answers, as well as rationales explaining the incorrect answers. Also included are identifiers for the phases of the nursing process, the categories of client needs, and the cognitive level for each question.

   Following the directions for test taking described in Unit 1, allow 100 minutes for each practice test. The following codes are used in the answers and rationales to categorize the test items.

NP	**= PHASES OF THE NURSING PROCESS**		**CL**	**= COGNITIVE LEVEL**	
As	= Assessment		K	= Knowledge	
An	= Analysis		Co	= Comprehension	
Pl	= Planning		Ap	= Application	
Im	= Implementation		An	= Analysis	
Ev	= Evaluation				

CN	**= CLIENT NEED**			
Sa	= Safe Effective Care Environment	**Ph**	= Physiological Integrity	
Sa/1	= Management of Care	Ph/7	= Basic Care and Comfort	
Sa/2	= Safety and Infection Control	Ph/8	= Pharmacological and Parenteral Therapies	
He	= Health Promotion and Maintenance			
He/3	= Growth and Development Through the Life Span	Ph/9	= Reduction of Risk Potential	
He/4	= Prevention and Early Detection of Disease	Ph/10	= Physiological Adaptation	
Ps	= Psychosocial Integrity			
Ps/5	= Coping and Adaptation			
Ps/6	= Psychosocial Adaptation			

The above categories are discussed in more detail in Unit 1.
The following sample answer should help you understand how to interpret these codes. The correct answer is listed first and is printed in **bold print.**

ANSWER	RATIONALE	NP	CN	CL
#1. 4.	**Hemorrhagic reactions are a result of banked blood that is low in platelets and coagulation factors.**	An	Ph/8	Co
1.	Allergic reactions may result from antibodies in either the donor or the recipient.			
2.	Hemolytic reactions result from ABO or RH incompatibility and use of dextrose solutions.			
3.	Circulatory overload results from too rapid infusion in susceptible persons.			

The elements are as follows:
   #1 is the question or item number in the test; 4 is the correct answer.
   The first rationale explains the correct answer and is in bold print.
   The remaining rationales explain the incorrect answers.
   The phase of the nursing process is analysis.
   The category of client need is physiologic integrity; pharmacological and parenteral therapies.
   The cognitive level is comprehension.

Practice Test 1

1. Mrs. F. has a fractured right hip with 5 lb of Buck's traction. The bed that Mrs. F. is in is broken. How should the nurse best direct the team to move Mrs. F. to the new bed?
   1. Slowly lift the traction to release the weight, support the right leg, and lift Mrs. F. to the new bed.
   2. Slowly lift the 5 lb weight from the traction set up, and apply 10 lb of manual traction during the move.
   3. It is not safe to move Mrs. F. with Buck's traction. Support her position changes with pillows until traction is no longer needed.
   4. Decrease the weight of traction over a two-hour period; then discontinue the traction and move Mrs. F. into the new bed.

2. An adult client sustained a fractured tibia three hours ago. A long leg cast was applied. Now the client is complaining of increasing pain. The pain is more intense with passive flexion of the toes. The nurse suspects the client is developing compartment syndrome. Which initial action should the nurse take?
   1. Prepare for emergency fasciotomy.
   2. Administer the ordered narcotic IV, then reassess the client's pain in 15 minutes.
   3. Raise the casted leg above the heart, apply ice, and notify the physician.
   4. Raise the casted leg to the level of the heart, notify the physician, and prepare to split the cast.

3. Andy, two years old, begins to scream, kick, and wave his arms angrily when the nurse lowers his siderails to take his temperature and other vital signs. The child and nurse are alone in the room. What is the best action for the nurse to take?
   1. Leave Andy alone until his mother comes to visit and can be there to help hold him on her lap for the procedures.
   2. Immediately call another nurse to come and help hold Andy still for the procedures.
   3. Hold Andy and talk calmly while showing him something of interest and explain what is going to be done.
   4. Tell Andy he will be left alone for two minutes without his toys and he must quiet down during that time.

4. An adult client has had a cataract extraction with a lens implant performed on an outpatient basis. The nurse is discussing his postoperative instructions with him prior to his discharge from the surgery center. Which statement by the client indicates a need for further instruction before he is discharged?
   1. "I need to sleep with this metal eye shield at night, but I can wear my glasses during the day."
   2. "I should avoid coughing, sneezing, and vomiting."
   3. "It's okay to bend over to pick something up from the floor as long as I put the eye shield on."
   4. "I should call the doctor for any bad pain in my eyes that the pain medicine doesn't help, or if I start seeing double or light flashes."

5. An adult client has a fractured right ankle, which was casted in the emergency room. Before the client is discharged, the nurse must teach crutch walking skills. Which is the correct technique?
   1. "Lift both crutches, advance a short distance and swing through with both legs."
   2. "Advance crutches and the right leg, then swing through and touch down with the left leg."
   3. "Advance left leg, then lift and advance crutches, and swing right leg."
   4. "Hold both crutches under one arm, advance crutches up stairs. Hold onto rail, lift body, and touch down one step with left leg."

6. A woman who has cystitis is receiving Pyridium 200 mg po tid. Which assessment best indicates to the nurse that the medication is effective?
   1. The client's urine is reddish-orange in color.
   2. There is a decrease in pain and burning on urination.
   3. There is a decrease in the client's temperature.
   4. The client's white blood cell count has returned to normal.

7. An adult client is now ready for discharge following a bilateral adrenalectomy for treatment of Cushing's syndrome. Which statement the client makes indicates to the nurse that further discharge teaching is needed?
   1. "I will begin to look more normal soon."
   2. "I should not lift heavy objects for six weeks."
   3. "I will gradually discontinue the hormone pills in a few months when I feel better."

4. "I will not go grocery shopping or run the vacuum cleaner until the doctor says I can."

8. An adult woman is recovering from a mastectomy for breast cancer. She appears depressed and is frequently tearful when she is alone. The nurse's approach should be based on which of these understandings?
   1. Clients need a supportive person to help them grieve for the loss of a body part.
   2. The client's family should take the leadership in providing the support she needs.
   3. The nurse should explain to the client that breast tissue is not needed by the body.
   4. The client should focus on the cure of her cancer rather than the loss of the breast.

9. Mr. L. has been hospitalized for one week for severe depression and suicidal thinking. Last night, his wife visited and they spent a long time alone in his room. Mr. L. was tearful and withdrawn immediately after the visit, but this morning he is much more relaxed and says, "Now I have it all figured out. I know exactly what I'm going to do." It is important that the nurse act on the understanding that
   1. a sudden lifting of depression may indicate that the client has formed a suicide plan.
   2. support from his wife may have convinced Mr. L. that life is worth living.
   3. antidepressant drugs may require several weeks before an effect is felt.
   4. an absence of sadness and the ability to plan may indicate improvement in depression.

10. An adult male is admitted to the psychiatric unit with a diagnosis of obsessive-compulsive disorder. His hands are red and rough and he tells the nurse that he washes them many times a day. Which would be an appropriate short-term goal for him? The client
    1. explains why his hand washing is inappropriate.
    2. is prevented from accessing the sink in his room.
    3. records the number of times he washes his hands each day.
    4. verbalizes the anxiety underlying each episode of hand washing.

11. The nurse is evaluating a new mother feeding her newborn. Which observation indicates the mother understands proper feeding methods for her newborn?
    1. Holding the bottle so the nipple is always filled with formula.
    2. Allowing her seven-pound baby to sleep after taking 1½ ounces from the bottle.
    3. Burping the baby every ten minutes during the feeding.
    4. Warming the formula bottle in the microwave for 15 seconds and giving it directly to the baby.

12. The nurse is assessing a woman admitted for a possible ectopic pregnancy. The nurse should ask the client about the presence of which of the following?
    1. Profuse, bright-red vaginal bleeding.
    2. Right or left colicky abdominal pain.
    3. Nausea and vomiting.
    4. Dyspareunia.

13. A 19-year-old woman is admitted with a diagnosis of anorexia nervosa. Which of the following should the nurse include in the care plan?
    1. Allow her as much time as she needs for each meal.
    2. Explain the importance of an adequate diet.
    3. Observe her during and one hour after each meal.
    4. Use a random pattern for surprise weights.

14. A 28-year-old client with schizophrenia is sitting alone in his room. He alternates quiet, listening behaviors with agitated talking. The nurse enters his room and observes this behavior. What should the nurse say first?
    1. "You need to come out to the day area with the group now."
    2. "Why are you hearing voices again?"
    3. "You appear to be listening to something."
    4. "I know you hear something but there is no one here."

15. Mr. H. is standing in the day room. His anxiety level has been increasing all morning and now he is shouting, "I want out of here. I want out right now!" The initial response by the nurse should be to
    1. position him/herself in front of Mr. H. and make eye contact.
    2. stand behind Mr. H. and say, "You need to quit shouting now."
    3. approach Mr. H. from the side and say, "You're feeling pretty angry."
    4. obtain sufficient help and escort Mr. H. to the seclusion room.

16. A 28-year-old client with schizophrenia has been taking a phenothiazine drug, chlorpromazine (Thorazine) 50 mg po qid for four days. Which observation by the nurse indicates a desired effect of the drug? The client
    1. reports fewer episodes of hallucinations.
    2. sleeps ten hours at night plus a two-hour afternoon nap.
    3. reports feelings of stiffness in his neck and face.
    4. is increasingly responsive to his delusional system.

17. When a male client with chronic schizophrenia and a history of noncompliance with medication programs was first admitted

to the hospital, he refused medication and argued with the nurse about his need for it. Which observation by the nurse is the best indication that his goal of compliance with the medication routine has been achieved? The client

1. requests his medication at scheduled times.
2. verbalizes the need for medication while in the hospital.
3. takes his medication when offered by the nurse.
4. describes reasons that compliance is important.

18. The nurse is caring for a client who has just returned to the surgical unit following a femoral arteriogram. Which initial assessment by the nurse is most essential?
    1. Auscultating the lungs.
    2. Obtaining a blood pressure.
    3. Palpating the carotid pulse.
    4. Inspecting the groin area.

19. The nurse is caring for a client who is scheduled for an MRI (magnetic resonance imaging) study. Which statement made by the client warrants further assessment by the nurse?
    1. "I am allergic to iodine and seafood."
    2. "I had a total hip replacement five years ago."
    3. "I've been taking a blood thinner and bleed easily."
    4. "My doctor told me never to take laxatives."

20. The nurse is to give medication to an infant. What is the best way to assess the identity of the infant?
    1. Ask the mother what the child's name is.
    2. Look at the sign above the bed that states the client's name.
    3. Compare the bed number with the bed number of the care plan.
    4. Compare the ankle band with the name on the care plan.

21. The nurse is caring for a client who has been placed in cloth wrist restraints. To ensure the client's safety, the nurse should
    1. remove the restraints every two hours and inspect the wrists.
    2. wrap each wrist with gauze dressing beneath the restraints.
    3. keep the head of the bed flat at all times.
    4. tie the restraints using a square knot.

22. An adult client is scheduled for gallbladder x-rays in the morning for suspected cholelithiasis. While preparing the client for the x-rays, it is most important for the nurse to ask the client if he
    1. has ever had trouble with uncontrolled bleeding.
    2. has any known allergies.
    3. received teaching regarding a low-fat diet.

4. understands the procedure for local anesthesia.

23. A client is referred to the outpatient clinic to have a glucose tolerance test (GTT) and glycosylated hemoglobin assay (Hgb A_{1c}) to assess for questionable diabetes mellitus. The client requests clarification from the clinic nurse regarding these tests. The nurse differentiates between a glucose tolerance test (GTT) and glycosylated hemoglobin assay (Hgb A_{1c}) by explaining that the Hgb A_{1c}
    1. is used to diagnose diabetes mellitus.
    2. involves administration of an oral glucose load.
    3. measures serum glucose at 30 minute, 1-, 2-, and 3-hour intervals.
    4. reflects blood glucose level over a 2–3 month period.

24. An adult male client is admitted with a diagnosis of acute M.I. (myocardial infarct). He is attached to a cardiac monitor and has an IV catheter in place. His cardiac rhythm has been normal sinus rhythm with occasional PVCs. The nurse notes a sudden change on the cardiac monitor screen to a very irregular, chaotic-looking pattern. The client appears to be sleeping. The most appropriate action on the part of the nurse is to
    1. administer a precordial thump.
    2. obtain the defibrillator.
    3. begin cardiopulmonary resuscitation.
    4. check the client's ECG electrodes.

25. An adult client presents with the sudden onset of the appearance of "floating black spots" in her right eye. The client sees a black shadow in her peripheral vision. There is no pain but the client is very frightened. What should the nurse expect to do in the care of this client?
    1. Place patches on both eyes and plan for strict bed rest.
    2. Patch the right eye and let the client resume activity after 24 hours.
    3. Plan for emergency surgery as the client is in danger of losing her eyesight.
    4. Administer a cholinergic eye drop (Pilocarpine) to decrease intraocular pressure.

26. The nurse is caring for a woman in labor. When she is 8 cm dilated she tells her support person she wants "to go home for a few hours of sleep." The nurse helps the support person realize that this statement reflects the woman's desire to
    1. have others tell her what she needs.
    2. have a soothing back rub.
    3. be rid of this difficult situation.
    4. be left alone.

27. A 22-year-old woman comes into the obstetrics clinic requesting oral contraceptives. Which item in the nursing

history would indicate that she is not a good candidate for this method of contraception?
1. She has a history of heavy menstrual periods.
2. She has diabetes mellitus.
3. The client reports a broken leg when she was ten years old.
4. The client had a baby six months ago.

28. The nurse is caring for a client who has just had a craniotomy. The client has an intracranial pressure monitor in place and is becoming more lethargic. The intracranial pressure is high. How should the nurse position the client?
1. Elevate the head of the bed 90 degrees. Position the client upright with pillow support under the head.
2. Place the client flat in bed with the legs elevated 15 degrees on pillows.
3. Position the client on the left side with pillow support to the back.
4. Elevate the head of the bed 30 degrees with a pillow under the head.

29. Mrs. L. will be administering daily insulin to her 84-year-old blind grandfather. The insulin dose is 15 u NPH, 5 u regular every morning at 0745. Which statement best indicates that Mrs. L. needs further instruction in insulin administration prior to her grandfather's discharge from the hospital?
1. "The regular insulin acts quickly. NPH insulin is milky colored and lasts longer, usually the whole day."
2. "I need to keep track of where I give his insulin so that I don't use the same site over and over."
3. "If I can't get to Granddaddy's house until lunch time occasionally, I can give him a little more insulin in case his sugar went up in the morning."
4. "It's very important to keep insulin shots on schedule and for him to eat at regular times."

30. An elderly woman received digoxin 0.25 mg for treatment of her congestive heart failure. Which of the following physiological responses indicates that the digoxin is having the desired effect?
1. Increased heart rate.
2. Decreased cardiac output.
3. Increased urine output.
4. Decreased myocardial contraction force.

31. An adult is admitted to the hospital with anorexia, weight loss, and ascites. Serum SGOT (AST), SGPT (ALT), LDH, and total bilirubin are significantly elevated. Based on the lab results, the nurse performing an admission assessment will expect to find
1. pallor.
2. dry mucous membranes.
3. jaundice.
4. peripheral edema.

32. The nurse is preparing a client for an IVP tomorrow. The client tells the nurse that she gets a rash and becomes short of breath after eating lobster. Given this information, the nurse knows that the client
1. should be visited by a dietitian while in the hospital.
2. is not a candidate for IVP.
3. is at risk for an allergic reaction.
4. will require an antihistamine before her IVP.

33. An elderly client requiring abdominal wound packing tid complains about his wound care to the nurse making morning rounds. He states that "everyone does it differently and at any time they feel like it." He is angry at being awakened at night for this procedure. The best response for the nurse to make is
1. "The wound care is being done as ordered by your doctor."
2. "I understand you're upset at losing sleep. You can have medication to help you get back to sleep."
3. "Tell me what's really bothering you."
4. "After rounds I'll be back and we can plan your wound care."

34. The nurse is planning care for a client with cervical radiation implants. Which nursing intervention will be included in the plan of care?
1. Implement strict isolation protocol.
2. Provide a lead apron for the client.
3. Use only disposable supplies and equipment in the client's room.
4. Limit visitors to 30 minutes per day.

35. The nurse reviews a client's laboratory data and notes the following hematology values: hematocrit (hct) 43%; hemoglobin (Hgb) 15 g/dl; RBCs 5 million; WBCs 7,500; platelet count 30,000. What nursing care is indicated in relation to these lab values?
1. Plan a diet high in iron.
2. Plan for frequent rest periods throughout the day.
3. Avoid invasive procedures and injections.
4. Implement protective isolation precautions.

36. The nurse is planning care for a client who is having a gastroscopy performed. Included in the plan of care for the immediate postgastroscopy period will be
1. maintain nasogastric tube to intermittent suction.
2. assess gag reflex prior to administration of fluids.
3. assess frequently for pain and medicate according to orders.
4. measure abdominal girth every four hours.

37. An elderly client has suffered a cerebrovascular accident (CVA) and as a result has left homonymous hemianopia.

Based on this fact, what measure will be nurse include in this client's plan of care?
1. Supporting the client's left arm and hand with pillows.
2. Applying a patch to the client's left eye.
3. Encouraging the client to use his right hand for activities of daily living.
4. Placing the client's meal on the right side of the overbed table.

38. A toddler is admitted with a history of vomiting and diarrhea for two days, accompanied by abdominal pain. The admitting diagnosis is gastroenteritis. What type of room assignment should the nurse make?
1. A room near the nurses' station so that he can be checked frequently and heard if he vomits.
2. A single room with a sink near the doorway for isolation use.
3. A double room with another toddler who also has vomiting and diarrhea.
4. A bed in the pediatric intensive care unit, in case dehydration develops.

39. The nurse is caring for a client who is to have a lumbar puncture (L-P). How should the client be positioned during the procedure?
1. Prone with head turned to the left.
2. Side-lying in a fetal position.
3. Sitting at the edge of the bed.
4. Trendelenburg position.

40. The physician has ordered a Schilling's test for a client with possible pernicious anemia. Implementation of the test will require the nurse to
1. administer a mild laxative.
2. initiate a 24-hour urine collection.
3. administer an intramuscular dose of iron.
4. insert an intravenous catheter.

41. The nurse has given discharge instructions on how to care for a newly applied cast to an adult client. Which statement indicates the client understands the instructions?
1. "I should pack the casted leg in ice for 24 hours to help it dry."
2. "I can use my hair dryer to help the cast dry faster."
3. "A good way to relieve the itching under the cast is to gently scratch under the cast with a soft knitting needle."
4. "Putting the casted leg up on fabric-covered pillows is the best way to dry the cast."

42. The nurse is caring for a client who has just had a bone marrow biopsy. What is essential for the nurse to do at this time?
1. Apply firm pressure over the puncture site.
2. Maintain the client on bed rest for 24 hours.
3. Apply an occlusive dressing to the puncture site.
4. Refrigerate the biopsy specimen.

43. An adult client is one day post subtotal thyroidectomy. The nurse planning care for the day knows that it is most important to
1. carry out range of motion exercises to the neck and shoulders every shift.
2. maintain bed rest with client in supine position at all times.
3. ask client questions every hour or two to assess for hoarseness.
4. provide tracheostomy care every shift and suction PRN to maintain a patent airway.

44. An adult client is four hours post-op abdominal hysterectomy. She has an IV at 125 ml per hour, an indwelling catheter that has drained 100 ml since surgery, and her pain is "3" out of "10." Which would be the priority nursing diagnosis?
1. Alteration in comfort, pain.
2. Alterations in patterns of elimination.
3. Disturbance in self-concept, body image.
4. Fluid volume deficit, actual or risk for.

45. An adult client has meperidine HCl (Demerol) 50 mg–100 mg IM every 3–4 hours ordered. He received Demerol 50 mg IM three hours ago but he's still complaining of pain at "8 out of 10." The client is asking for pain medication even before it is due and refuses to get out of bed "because of the pain." He was heard telling jokes to the cleaning personnel. What is the best action for the nurse to take?
1. Give the client 50 mg of Demerol IM now.
2. Wait one hour and give the client 75 mg of Demerol IM.
3. Give the client 100 mg of Demerol IM now and repeat 100 mg Demerol IM in three hours if the pain is still greater than "5 out of 10."
4. Do not medicate the client now. Laughing and joking behavior indicate the pain is not as severe as the client claims.

46. An elderly male with undiagnosed respiratory symptoms is to receive a diagnostic test for histoplasmosis. The nurse giving a histoplasmin skin test will
1. apply a patch to the skin on the forearm.
2. make a shallow scratch on the skin surface.
3. use a 25-gauge needle placed parallel to the skin.
4. use a 19-gauge needle and Z track injection.

47. A 35-year-old woman is admitted for treatment of depression. Which of these symptoms would the nurse be least likely to find in the initial assessment?
1. inability to make decisions.
2. feelings of hopelessness.
3. family history of depression.
4. increased interest in sex.

48. An adult male, who appears about 40 years old, is admitted to the psychiatric unit for alcohol detoxification. He is tremulous and irritable, and complains of nervousness and

nausea. Which information is most important for the admitting nurse to obtain?
1. The amount of alcohol and other drugs usually taken and the type and amount taken in the last few days.
2. The events prompting the client to seek treatment.
3. The factors that trigger the client's drinking episodes.
4. Any work, legal, or family problems that relate to his use of alcohol.

49. A woman who is nine months pregnant is attending a luncheon and fashion show. Suddenly, her membranes rupture and contractions come so rapidly that she yells, "The baby is coming." What is the most appropriate action for the nurse to take?
1. Ask for boiled water, towels, string, and scissors.
2. Ask someone to call her doctor.
3. Take her via cab to the nearest hospital.
4. Have her lie on her left side in a less-crowded area and be prepared to help with the delivery.

50. While attending a basketball game, a woman who is nine months pregnant suddenly goes into labor and delivers her baby within five minutes. What is the most appropriate course of action for the nurse to take?
1. Tie the cord with a shoelace and cut the cord with a penknife.
2. Have the mother's friend hold the baby until an ambulance arrives.
3. Place the naked baby on the mother's bare chest, cover both, and encourage breast feeding.
4. Ask people to clear the area so more air can circulate around the mother and baby.

51. A young man with newly diagnosed acquired immune deficiency syndrome (AIDS) is being discharged from the hospital. The nurse knows that teaching regarding prevention of AIDS transmission has been effective when the client:
1. verbalizes the role of sexual activity in spread of the disorder.
2. states he will make arrangements to drop his college classes.
3. acknowledges the need to avoid all contact sports.
4. says he will avoid close contact with his three-year-old niece.

52. A client in the intensive care unit is on a volume-cycled mechanical ventilator. The high pressure alarm (PAP) begins to sound repeatedly. The client is sleeping quietly. What is the most appropriate initial response by the nurse?
1. Call the respiratory therapist to check the ventilator.
2. Turn the client to stimulate coughing.

3. Obtain arterial blood for blood gas analysis.
4. Check the ventilator tubing.

53. A 27-year-old woman is 4 cm dilated and wants to walk about the labor and delivery nursing unit. Which of the following criteria will help the nurse determine whether she should walk?
1. Whether her membranes are intact.
2. Her contraction frequency.
3. The fetal position.
4. The fetal station.

54. When reviewing the guidelines for diaphragm use, the nurse knows the client has a good understanding of this contraceptive device when she tells her partner that this device
1. is good for five years.
2. has to be used with a condom.
3. must be left in place for at least six hours after intercourse.
4. has to be removed between each sexual intercourse encounter.

55. The nurse is caring for a woman four hours following a cesarean birth. Because there are surgical effects that hinder the woman's resumption of eating, the nurse should include which of the following in the plan of care?
1. Ambulation at this time.
2. Applying an abdominal binder.
3. Administering a Dulcolax suppository.
4. Listening for bowel sounds.

56. An adult client is admitted to the nursing care unit with intestinal obstruction and has a Miller-Abbott tube in place. How should the nurse assess for proper placement and function of the tube?
1. Inject air and auscultate over the stomach.
2. Aspirate the tube for stomach contents.
3. Check the distance markings on the tube.
4. Assess for signs of respiratory compromise.

57. An adult client who has rheumatoid arthritis reports that the pain and stiffness are greatest upon arising early in the morning. What advice should the nurse give to help the client decrease the pain?
1. Keep the salicylate medication at the bedside and take before getting out of bed.
2. Take a hot tub bath or shower upon arising.
3. Ask the physician to order splints to be worn at night to maintain anatomical position.
4. Increase activity to work out the stiffness.

58. An adult client has a central line placed for IV fluids. When the nurse enters the room the IV bottle is empty, the IV line is full of air, and the client is dyspneic. What is the best initial nursing action?

1. Notify the physician and administer oxygen via nasal cannula immediately.
2. Hang another IV bag as soon as possible, then remove the air from the IV line.
3. Clamp the tubing and place the client on the left side with head down.
4. Begin CPR and call the code team.

59. The nurse is caring for a client who has just returned to the nursing unit following a left above-the-knee amputation. How should the client be positioned?
1. Place the stump on a pillow to decrease edema.
2. Place the stump flat on the bed to prevent contractures.
3. Place the client in a prone position to prevent contractures.
4. Place the client in reverse Trendelenburg position to promote arterial flow.

60. The nurse is planning care for a diabetic child. Which concept is essential to include when developing the care plan?
1. Most of the family and child education about diabetes and its management takes place in the first three or four days after the initial diagnosis is made.
2. The morning short-acting insulin dosage is usually determined by the previous day's late morning and noon blood glucose levels.
3. The majority of the total daily dose of insulin is given in the evenings to cover the day's intake of food.
4. Snacks for diabetic children should be given during an exercise episode, rather than before it.

61. An adult has had diabetes mellitus for many years. When the nurse enters the room to administer the morning dose of regular and NPH insulin, the client complains of dizziness, diaphoresis, and nausea. The nurse does a blood glucose, which is 30. What is the next nursing action?
1. Give the usual dose of regular insulin and get the client's breakfast tray.
2. Hold the NPH insulin but give the regular insulin.
3. Hold the regular and NPH insulin and call the physician.
4. Give the client a glass of orange juice, hold all insulin, and call the physician.

62. An adult had a thyroidectomy this morning. The client begins to complain of circumoral tingling. The nurse assesses a positive Chovstek's sign and a positive Trousseau's sign. The nurse understands that the most common cause of these symptoms is which of the following?
1. Inadvertent removal of the parathyroid glands during the thyroidectomy surgery.
2. Overuse of radioactive iodine given preoperatively to clients undergoing thyroidectomy.

3. A history of insufficient intake of iodine.
4. Overstimulation of parathormone during the thyroid surgery.

63. The nurse is to begin bladder training with a young woman who has a T-2 spinal cord injury. What should the nurse plan to do?
1. Teach her to change the indwelling catheter drainage bag to a leg bag at night.
2. Plan a consistent intermittent catheterization schedule with her and teach her self-catheterization technique as she is able.
3. Plan to place her on the bedside commode to void every two hours until consistent urination is achieved.
4. Clamp the indwelling catheter for longer periods of time each day until a bladder capacity of 1500 ml is achieved.

64. An adult client has a comminuted fracture of the ulnar bone. He asks the nurse what type of fracture this is. The nurse's response is based on which of these understandings?
1. The ulnar bone has been crushed and broken in several places.
2. The two ends of the fractured ulnar bone are pulled apart and separated from each other.
3. The ulnar bone has been broken in two and one end of the bone broke through the skin.
4. Only one side of the ulnar bone is broken.

65. The nurse is caring for several clients with fractures. Which client is most at risk for fat embolus?
1. A four-year-old with a wrist fracture.
2. A 20-year-old with a femur fracture.
3. A 35-year-old with an ulnar fracture.
4. A 75-year-old with rib fractures.

66. A man with a ten-year history of asthma presents with respiratory distress with labored breathing, use of accessory muscles, and audible inspiratory and expiratory wheezes. Which of the following would indicate his condition is worsening?
1. Audible expiratory wheezes with lessening inspiratory wheezes.
2. Increasing expectoration of thick, tenacious sputum with decreasing wheezing lung sounds.
3. Absence of audible inspiratory and expiratory wheezes with increasing somnolence.
4. Decreasing respiratory rate with decreased use of accessory muscles.

67. The nurse has instructed an adult in crutch-walking technique. Which statement best indicates that the client understands the proper way to bear weight on crutches while ambulating?
1. "I should bear my weight on my hands while walking."

2. "It's OK to lean on my crutches, bearing the weight under my arms, as long as I don't walk like that."
3. "I should bear weight on my underarms while I walk."
4. "I should avoid bearing weight on the crutch that is on my injured side as much as possible."

68. An adult has undergone a total hip replacement and is now ready for discharge. Which of his statements indicates good understanding of what activities are allowed and not allowed?
   1. "I can't wait to see my daughter. She lives eight hours away and until now my hip hurt too much to travel such a long distance."
   2. "I will really have to be careful not to cross my legs. That's the way I used to sit all the time."
   3. "It will be great to be able to put on my socks and shoes by myself."
   4. "As soon as I get home, I won't have to use this walker."

69. The nurse is giving discharge instructions to an adult client who is to be discharged taking hydantoin (Dilantin). Which of the following is correct and must be included in the discharge teaching?
   1. If there are problems with taking Dilantin orally, the drug is easily given intramuscularly.
   2. Alcohol interferes with the absorption of Dilantin. Do not drink alcohol while taking Dilantin.
   3. Dilantin builds up in the body and achieves blood levels that prevent seizures. Skipping a day or two will not affect the Dilantin blood levels.
   4. Slurred speech and confusion are side effects of Dilantin and are normal while taking Dilantin.

70. Mrs. C. underwent an exploratory laparotomy 24 hours ago. The nurse assesses her abdominal incision and observes a bulging area at the lower part of the midline abdominal incision. This finding most likely indicates which of the following?
   1. Normal postoperative incisional edema.
   2. A hematoma beneath the skin.
   3. Abdominal distention.
   4. Impending wound infection with purulent drainage.

71. An adult client is to receive a unit of whole blood. The client's vital signs before starting the transfusion are BP 120/70, P 80, and T 98.4°F. Five minutes after the transfusion was started the vital signs are: BP 100/70, P 100, and T 99.4°F. What should the nurse do initially?
   1. Slow down the rate of the transfusion, reassess the client in 15 minutes.

2. Stop the transfusion, keep vein open with normal saline.
   3. Slow down the infusion, notify the physician immediately.
   4. Administer acetaminophen (Tylenol), continue to monitor closely throughout the transfusion.

72. A woman is in the outpatient clinic to have a pelvic sonogram for a suspected ovarian mass. In preparation for the sonogram the nurse will ask her to
   1. sign a permit.
   2. drink several glasses of water.
   3. take a mild sedative.
   4. completely empty her bladder.

73. The community health nurse is making an initial home visit for an elderly client. During this visit, the nurse must assess the client's ability to provide self-care in the home. Which one of the following areas of concern should be assessed for determining the client's ability to remain at home?
   1. Elimination.
   2. Cognitive abilities.
   3. Exercise.
   4. Metabolism.

74. Prior to administering a dose of digitalis, the nurse assesses the client's apical pulse by placing the stethoscope at the
   1. left fifth intercostal space, midclavicular line.
   2. right second intercostal space, midclavicular line.
   3. site of carotid pulsation.
   4. left third intercostal space, sternal border.

75. The nurse is assessing a person with long-standing chronic obstructive pulmonary disease (COPD). Which findings would the nurse expect to find?
   1. Low-grade fever.
   2. Weak, thready pulse.
   3. Increased chest diameter.
   4. Crepitus.

76. The nurse is assessing a 34-year-old housewife who says she has gained a lot of weight recently, feels cold all the time, is always tired, and can't get anything done. In addition she reports her hair is falling out. Given the signs and symptoms, which of the following disorders is the woman most likely to have?
   1. Addison's disease.
   2. Cushing's syndrome.
   3. Myxedema.
   4. Grave's disease.

77. The nurse is caring for a client who underwent a total hip replacement yesterday. Which of the following assessments is not indicated for this client at this time?
   1. Presence of Homan's sign.
   2. Ability to flex and adduct affected hip.
   3. Temperature.

    4. Complaints of pain.

78. A 65-year-old male is admitted to the hospital with the diagnosis of gout. What is the man most likely to relate when the history is taken?
    1. A slow gradual onset of pain, redness, swelling, and warmth of the affected joint.
    2. Recent trauma, alcohol ingestion, drugs, surgical stress, or illness.
    3. No recent alcohol ingestion or dietary changes.
    4. A gradual onset of discomfort, redness, and swelling of the affected joint, occurring mostly during waking hours.

79. The nurse is caring for a person during a seizure. What is the priority assessment at this time?
    1. Presence of an aura.
    2. Length of the seizure.
    3. What precipitated the seizure.
    4. Type and progression of seizure activity.

80. The school nurse initiates a screening program for pediculosis capitis. When searching for nits clinging to the hair shafts, the nurse might also observe
    1. bites, pustules, and excoriated areas on the scalp from scratching.
    2. pruritic, scaling, erythematous papules, plaques, and patches with well-defined borders.
    3. beefy-red erythematous areas with a few surrounding papules and pustules.
    4. an inflammation of the hair follicles with pus-filled nodules.

81. An eight-year-old girl suffered a partial thickness scald burn over most of her anterior thigh and lower leg. What admission assessment would give the nurse the most data about the probability of shock occurring?
    1. Edema, weeping blisters, high serum potassium, low serum sodium.
    2. Tachycardia, hyperventilation, and a pale appearance.
    3. Variations in hyperthermia and hypothermia, and decreased gastric motility.
    4. Anemia from red blood cell loss through damaged capillaries.

82. The nurse is caring for a client on a hypothermia blanket. The nurse turns the client every two hours for which of the following reasons?
    1. The client will accept the treatment more readily if allowed to change positions.
    2. Turning frequently helps to prevent shivering.
    3. Frequent turning helps the client's auto-regulatory mechanism to reestablish itself.
    4. Hypothermia causes vasoconstriction, which may result in skin damage.

83. The nurse is assessing a 26-year-old man whose diagnosis is schizophrenia. Which

statement the client makes indicates he is experiencing hallucinations?
    1. "I don't get along very well with my mother."
    2. "I hear my mother talking to me when I'm alone."
    3. "That picture on the wall looks like my mother."
    4. "I think my mother plans to get rid of me."

84. A woman who is 32 years old and 35 weeks pregnant has had rupture of membranes for eight hours and is 4 cm dilated. Since she is a candidate for infection, the nurse should include which of the following in the care plan?
    1. Universal precautions.
    2. Oxytocin administration.
    3. Frequent temperature monitoring.
    4. More frequent vaginal examinations.

85. A man is hospitalized with probable bacterial pneumonia. The physician has ordered a sputum specimen for culture and sensitivity. In order to obtain a good specimen, the nurse should
    1. teach the client deep breathing and coughing techniques.
    2. use nasotracheal suction.
    3. obtain the specimen after starting antibiotics.
    4. withhold food and fluid 30 minutes prior to specimen collection.

86. The nurse is caring for a mother and her newborn son. Which statement the mother makes indicates understanding of newborn care?
    1. "The face and neck are washed first, then the eyes, going from the outer corners inward."
    2. "As soon as the cord looks dried, my baby can sit in a tub bath instead of being sponged."
    3. "After applying alcohol to the cord once a day with the bath, the diaper is applied over the umbilicus to keep it dry."
    4. "The yellow-white covering over the end of the penis is part of the healing process and should not be removed, but washed gently with water."

87. The pregnant diabetic on insulin needs to be evaluated for correct medication dosage. What is the most effective method to assist the nurse in determining the client's need for insulin management?
    1. Home serum glucose testing.
    2. Weight gain.
    3. Daily dietary diary.
    4. Home urine glucose monitoring.

88. An adult is admitted for further evaluation of a very high white blood cell count, which may indicate leukemia. A bone marrow aspiration and biopsy are scheduled. The nurse knows that this test will

1. determine whether Reed-Sternberg cells are present in the marrow.
2. identify the number and type of white blood cells in all stages of development.
3. determine whether Epstein-Barr virus is present in the marrow.
4. identify metastatic changes in the bone structure that are characteristic of leukemia.

89. A four-year-old boy with acute epiglottitis is admitted to the emergency room. He has a fever of 102°F, is agitated, drools, and insists upon sitting up and leaning forward with the chin thrusting outward. The nurse expects which of the following?
     1. Intravenous fluids and an antibiotic will be started before anything else is done.
     2. The child will cry and resist lying supine when he needs to be examined and x-rayed.
     3. The child will be intubated in the emergency room or operating room and then transferred to the pediatric intensive care unit.
     4. A croup tent with an oxygen source available will be ordered on the regular pediatric unit.

90. Susie and her friends play house in the tall grass and brush on their neighborhood hillside. A few days ago the girls had red, swollen, itchy, poison ivy lesions that are now becoming fluid-filled vesicles. Which statement from Susie demonstrates that she understands how to keep from getting poison ivy again?
     1. "If I'm careful not to touch the leaves of the plant, I can play with the berries and pretend I'm baking."
     2. "My shoes, clothes, and dolls all have to be washed to get the poison ivy off them so I won't get sores from touching them."
     3. "Our dog doesn't get poison ivy when she lies in the plants, so I can hug her all I want."
     4. "When I come inside from playing house, I have to scrub myself with soap and hot water."

91. A 78-year-old female is being seen in a neighborhood clinic for an annual health checkup. During the physical assessment the nurse notes the following findings: pupils that constrict more slowly in bright light and dilate more slowly in dim light, elongated earlobes, localized hyperpigmentation of the skin on the anterior surface of the hand and on the face, kyphosis, difficulty locating the apical impulse, the presence of an S_4 heart sound, decreased respiratory rate, hyperactive deep-tendon reflexes, and sluggish bowel sounds. Which of the findings noted during the physical assessment is of greatest concern to the nurse?
     1. Altered pupillary constriction and dilation.
     2. Sluggish bowel sounds.
     3. Kyphosis.
     4. Hyperactive deep-tendon reflexes.

92. When working with groups of older clients in a day care setting, the nurse can promote socialization best by implementing which of the following interventions?
     1. Grouping clients together by age and gender to encourage the development of friendships based on a common characteristic.
     2. Assign a different nurse to group activities each day to familiarize client with staff.
     3. Avoid discussion of client's life outside the day care setting to encourage participation in current activities.
     4. Get to know the clients and accompany them to group events such as singing, crafts, communal meals, etc.

93. A 75-year-old male client with diabetes mellitus and severe cataracts has been started on insulin therapy because of an increasingly poor response to 15 years of oral sulfonylurea therapy. He has been hospitalized several times in the past for control of his diabetes and associated complications. He will be discharged today on insulin therapy. Which of the following client behaviors signals to the nurse that he has a need for assistance with administration of his insulin?
     1. He uses a magnifier to read the insulin syringe.
     2. He states he will pinch the skin at the site and inject the insulin at a 90 degree angle.
     3. He mixes NPH and Regular insulins by drawing up the NPH first.
     4. He rotates sites only after using all available areas within each site.

94. The nurse is teaching a client with an L-3 spinal cord injury regarding a bladder training regimen. Which of the following instructions should be included in the bladder training process?
     1. Drink 1200 to 1500 ml of liquid a day.
     2. Drink adequate fluids until 10:00 P.M. at night.
     3. Tighten the abdominal muscles to void.
     4. Pour cool water on the perineum.

95. A 48-year-old female was diagnosed with breast cancer twelve weeks ago. She was admitted to the hospital four days ago and is undergoing chemotherapeutic treatment of her cancer. Since her admission, she has communicated very little with the staff, stays in her room, eats almost none of the food provided, and is occasionally seen punching her pillow. While caring for her today, the nurse also finds out that she has not been sleeping and feels as though she is "somehow being punished for not doing regular self-breast exams." Based on the observations

noted above, which of the following nursing diagnoses should the nurse select as most appropriate for this client?
1. Anticipatory grieving.
2. Fear.
3. Ineffective individual coping.
4. Anxiety.

96. The nurse is reviewing the breast self-exam with a client who is being discharged after a spontaneous vaginal delivery. She is breast feeding. The nurse should determine that the client understands which of the following?
1. Breast self-exam should not be done during lactation.
2. Breast should be examined between the 4th and 7th day after menstrual bleeding begins or at least once a month.
3. Breast self-exam should be done with the woman lying flat on her back.
4. The breasts must be checked in a circular method and assessed for any lumps or bumps.

97. An adult has been placed on coumadin therapy after prosthetic valve replacement. The nurse knows the client understands teaching about coumadin when she states
1. "If I miss a dose, I will double the next dose."
2. "I should eat plenty of green and leafy vegetables."
3. "If my arthritis flares up again, I'll take only two aspirins every 6 hours."
4. "I will use a soft toothbrush and stop flossing my teeth."

98. A 17-year-old female has been admitted with a diagnosis of anorexia nervosa. What is the most appropriate short-term nursing goal? The client will
1. admit she has a fear of weight gain.
2. adhere to a nutritionally balanced diet appropriate for her age.
3. identify her problems and develop new coping methods to deal with them.
4. accept herself as having self-worth.

99. The nurse is evaluating the nursing care a client is receiving. The client has right hemiplegia as a result of a cerebrovascular accident. What finding indicates that the caregivers understand the importance of positioning a client with hemiplegia?
1. The right shoulder is adducted and internally rotated.
2. The right hip is externally rotated with knee flexion.
3. The right foot shows plantar flexion.
4. The right fingers are extended with the thumb abducted.

100. An adult is to have a pulse oximeter applied to assess arterial oxygen saturation level. The nurse knows that correct application includes
1. placement over the apical area of the chest.
2. covering the probe with an opaque material.
3. insertion of an arterial catheter.
4. insertion of a venous catheter.

Answers and Rationales for Practice Test 1

ANSWER	RATIONALE	NP	CN	CL
#1. 1.	**5–8 lb of traction is applied temporarily to provide immobilization prior to surgery. Buck's traction should be removed every eight hours to assess the skin under the traction device. Skeletal traction should not be released unless there is a life-threatening emergency.**	Im	Ph/9	Ap
2.	It is not necessary to maintain manual traction, especially at twice the weight, to move a person in Buck's traction.			
3.	It is safe to move persons with Buck's traction and would be uncomfortable to use pillow support for position changes.			
4.	Once the weight of traction has been established as effective, the weight should be maintained until it is no longer needed.			
#2. 4.	**To decrease the pressure within the compartment, raise the affected extremity only to the level of the heart and remove any constrictive dressing or cast. If this does not work to decrease the pressure, a fasciotomy may be necessary.**	Im	Ph/10	Ap
1.	Fasiotomy is performed if compartment pressure cannot be relieved.			
2.	Pain from compartment syndrome does not respond well to pain medicine.			

ANSWER	RATIONALE	NP	CN	CL

3. Placing the extremity above the level of the heart increases compartment pressure and should be avoided.

#3. 3. A two-year-old may respond to distraction to regain some sense of control so he can listen to the explanation of what the nurse wants him to do. Even if he cannot listen, he will sense that the nurse cares and understands the emotion he's trying to communicate and that comfort will be there after the procedure.

Im   He/3   Ap

1. Toddlers tolerate nursing procedures much more easily if not threatened with separation from the parent. Having the mother assist as part of the team gives control to both the child and parent. However, vital signs often need to be done in the parent's absence, as in this case.

2. Getting the help of another nurse may get the procedure done quickly and efficiently but may produce more unreleased anger in the child. It may also give the child a sense of having been abused and misunderstood.

4. Time-out should be set for one minute per year of age. Time-out discipline requires that the child understand what behavior is incorrect and what is desired. There is no evidence in the question that Andy is aware of this. Leaving the room could be a way of ignoring the temper tantrum. Discipline the child understands should be initiated as soon as the child misbehaves. Telling him "I'm sorry you don't like this, but I have to see what your temperature is now" would start to inform him of what is expected.

#4. 3. Bending over should be avoided as it increases intraocular pressure.

Ev   Ph/9   An

1. The client understands the need to sleep with the eye shield at night to protect the eye from accidental injury during sleep.

2. The client indicates an understanding of the need to avoid coughing, sneezing, or vomiting, which may increase intraocular pressure.

4. The physician should be notified of severe pain in the eyes not relieved by pain medication, any visual changes, headaches, inflammation or discharge.

#5. 2. The three-point gait is used when one leg cannot bear weight. The body weight is supported by the hands on the crutches and on the unaffected extremity (three points).

Im   Ph/7   Ap

1. Walking as described could only be achieved with a walker.

3. This is not a correct gait.

4. This describes the technique for stair climbing, which the client may need to know but is not what the question asked.

#6. 2. Pyridium acts locally on the urinary tract mucosa to produce analgesia or local anesthetic effects. If the medication is effective there should be a decrease in the pain and burning the client has been experiencing when urinating.

Ev   Ph/8   An

1. Pyridium will turn the client's urine reddish-orange. This is a side effect, not a therapeutic effect.

3. Pyridium is a nonnarcotic analgesic acting directly on the urinary tract. It has no antimicrobial effects and will not decrease the client's temperature. The client will also have an antimicrobial prescribed.

4. Pyridium is a nonnarcotic analgesic acting directly on the urinary tract. It has no antimicrobial effects and will not decrease the white blood cell count. The client will also have an antimicrobial prescribed.

#7. 3. Clients undergoing a bilateral adrenalectomy require lifelong glucocorticoid and mineralocorticoid replacement. The client's statement that hormones will be gradually discontinued after a few months indicates a need for further discharge instructions.

Ev   Ph/9   An

1. The client should gradually lose the Cushing syndrome features following surgery and adjustment of her hormone replacement.

2. The client, like all who have had major abdominal surgery, should not lift heavy objects for six weeks following surgery.

4. The client, like all who have had major abdominal surgery, should not engage in strenuous activities until given approval to do so by the physician.

#8. 1. The nurse must support the client through the steps of grief by encouraging discussion of the loss, its meaning to the client, the reactions of others, and the ways of compensating. — An — Ps/5 — Co

2. The family will need support in working through their feelings before they can support the client.

3. Breasts symbolize femininity and sexual attractiveness, and the loss of that image is threatening to self-esteem.

4. Minimizing the importance of a loss hinders grief work.

#9. 1. Reassessment for suicide risk is essential when depression suddenly improves, as the client may appear to feel better once the decision to commit suicide has been made. The words "now I have it all figured out" sound like he may be considering suicide as the answer. — An — Ps/5 — An

2. It is possible that the wife's visit may have significantly decreased the depression, but not likely. Reassessment of suicide risk is vital.

3. It is true that the action of antidepressant drugs may be delayed but the priority is reassessment of suicide risk when depression improves and verbal clues are given.

4. These characteristics may occur when depression lifts, but suicide is also a possibility and requires assessment.

#10. 3. The client's participation in obtaining baseline data is the first step to decreasing that behavior. — Pl — Ps/6 — An

1. Clients with compulsive behavior usually know that the behavior is inappropriate but cannot stop it without an increase in anxiety.

2. When compulsive behavior is physically prevented, the client may experience a panic attack or resort to other methods to carry out the compulsion. It is not uncommon for a client who is denied access to the sink to use water from the toilet to wash.

4. Identifying and dealing with the underlying anxiety are long-term goals in obsessive-compulsive behavior and are usually reached through psychotherapy.

#11. 1. Holding the bottle so the nipple is always filled with formula prevents the baby from sucking air. Sucking air can cause gastric distention and intestinal gas pains. — Ev — He/3 — An

2. A seven-pound baby should be getting 50 calories per pound: 350 calories per day. Standardized formulas have 20 calories per ounce. This seven-pound baby needs 17.5 ounces per day. 17.5 ounces per day divided by 6–8 feedings equals 2–3 ounces per feeding.

3. A normal newborn without feeding problems could be burped halfway through the feeding and again at the end. If burping needs to be at intervals, it should be done by ounces or half ounces, not minutes.

4. Microwaving is not recommended as a method of warming due to the uneven heating of the formula. If used, the formula should be shaken after warming and the temperature then checked with a drop on the wrist. The recommended method of warming is to place the bottle in a pan of hot water to warm, and then check the temperature on the wrist before feeding.

#12. 2. In ectopic pregnancy, the abdominal pain is usually on one side, is vague, cramping, or colicky from tubal distention, and lasts from one day to a week or longer. — As — He/3 — An

1. In ectopic pregnancy, there is intermittent vaginal spotting and it is dark red as the uterine decidua is sloughed off.

3. Nausea and vomiting occur, especially if rupture has occurred, but this is not a first complaint.

4. The stress of intercourse can weaken the site in the fallopian tube, but dyspareunia is not a complaint.

ANSWER	RATIONALE	NP	CN	CL

#13. 3. **Left alone at mealtime, clients with anorexia nervosa may hide or discard food, or induce vomiting after a meal. The client should be watched during and one hour after each meal.**   Pl   Ps/5   Ap

    1. Without a time limit, meals for clients with anorexia nervosa may become lengthy sessions providing attention for maladaptive behaviors.

    2. The problem is not a knowledge deficit. In fact, clients with eating disorders may be knowledgeable about nutrition. Discussions of food may provide reinforcement for maladaptive behaviors.

    4. To be accurate, weights must be done at the same time each day. Manipulation of weight is avoided by having the client wear a hospital gown and void prior to weighing.

#14. 3. **This response shares the nurse's observation and allows for validation by the client. This should be the initial response.**   Im   Ps/6   Ap

    1. The nurse needs initially to validate what is happening to the client. Directing the client to another activity avoids dealing with his symptoms. This client may be too ill for group participation at this time.

    2. "Why" questions should not be used. Why implies blame. The inference that the client is hallucinating needs validation before any exploration takes place.

    4. The inference that the client is hallucinating should be validated and the content of the hallucination determined before confronting the client with reality.

#15. 3. **A sidewise approach is less threatening than approaching in front or behind the client. An empathetic statement that acknowledges the angry feelings may allow the client to discuss his anger more calmly.**   Im   Ps/6   Ap

    1. A frontal approach and direct eye contact may be perceived as threatening and make the nurse the target for the client's anger.

    2. Standing behind the client and making direct commands increase his feelings of being out of control and may escalate the situation.

    4. Seclusion may be required but verbal intervention should be tried first. There is no evidence that anyone is in immediate danger.

#16. 1. **Phenothiazine drugs, like chlorpromazine, are antipsychotic drugs. The desired action is to reduce the symptoms of psychosis such as hallucinations.**   Ev   Ps/6   Ap

    2. Drowsiness is a common side effect of phenothiazine drugs early in the course of treatment and should diminish with time.

    3. Stiffness in the neck and face may be signs of a dystonic reaction, one of the extrapyramidal side effects of phenothiazine drugs. If a dystonic reaction is developing, treatment with an antiparkinson drug such as Cogentin will be needed.

    4. Increased response to delusions indicates that the psychosis may be worsening in spite of the drug.

#17. 1. **Requesting the medication when it is due is good evidence of understanding and participating in the medication program. The nurse must also be sure he actually takes the medication.**   Ev   Ps/6   Ap

    2. Talking about the need for medication is not as good evidence of compliance as actually requesting the medication.

    3. Requesting the medication before it is offered is better evidence of compliance than simply taking it when offered by the nurse.

    4. Talking about reasons for compliance is not as good evidence of actual compliance as requesting his medication.

#18. 4. **Bleeding at the site of arterial puncture is a serious potential problem for several hours following femoral arteriogram.**   As   Ph/9   Ap

    1. The arteriogram procedure does not increase the client's risk for pulmonary complications. A general anesthetic is not given during this procedure.

    2. Hypotension could occur with significant bleeding, but obvious

bleeding would be the initial assessment finding.

3. Changes in the pulse are not complications associated with an arteriogram except in the case of thrombus formation at the puncture site, in which case the femoral, not carotid pulse, would be affected.

#19. 2. Implanted medical devices (pacemaker, screws, pins, etc.) may render the client unsuitable for the MRI procedure. Metal devices may heat up from absorption of energy. As Ph/9 An

1. No contrast media is utilized for MRI, so there is no possibility of allergic reaction.
3. No puncture of vessels or skin is necessary with MRI, therefore there is no bleeding risk.
4. A bowel prep is not required for MRI imaging.

#20. 4. Making sure that the client's name is the same as the name on the medication plan is the only safe way to administer medications. As Sa/1 Ap

1. Asking the parent could be appropriate if the identification band could not be found and the medication had to be given immediately. Ask the parent to state the child's name, rather than asking them whether a certain name is the name of the child. This eliminates misunderstandings from hearing deficits. As soon as possible, a new identification band should be put on the infant's ankle or wrist.
2. There should be a sign above the bed, but it could be from the last client who occupied the bed. This is not as safe a method as asking the parent the child's name.
3. Mistakes in bed numbers can be made in admitting, on the unit, and in writing care plans or medication card.

#21. 1. Wrists must be inspected for signs of skin breakdown or trauma. As Sa/2 Ap

2. Wrist restraints are soft and padded already; no further padding is necessary.
3. Position of the head of the bed has no relationship to safety with use of restraints.
4. Method for tying restraints is important for ease of removal, but does not, in itself, affect safety.

#22. 2. Iodine contrast media is used for gallbladder x-rays. The client must be assessed for history of allergy to iodine. As Sa/9 Ap

1. This is not an invasive study and will not precipitate bleeding.
3. Although the client will receive a low-fat diet the evening before the study, this is not a priority assessment.
4. Local anesthesia is not used during gallbladder x-rays.

#23. 4. The Hgb A$_{1c}$ assay provides information about long-term control of diabetes mellitus. The assay reflects glucose level within erythrocytes, providing an average level over the 2–3 months preceding the test. An Ph/9 An

1. The assay is used to evaluate control of diabetes; GTT is used to diagnose diabetes.
2. Oral glucose load is administered for the GTT.
3. The GTT measures serum glucose at various time intervals.

#24. 4. Sudden bizarre-looking ECG patterns may be a result of loose electrodes (artifact) rather than a lethal arrhythmia. The client and electrodes should be checked as the safest initial intervention. An Ph/10 An

1. A precordial thump can cause injury and would not be utilized until it has been determined that the client had a lethal dysrhythmia.
2. Defibrillation can cause injury and would not be utilized until it has been determined that the client had a lethal dysrhythmia.
3. Cardiopulmonary resuscitation can cause injury and would not be utilized until it has been determined that the client had a lethal dysrhythmia.

#25. 1. The client is displaying signs of a detached retina, which requires Pl Ph/10 An

        patching of both eyes to minimize eye movement and bed rest with a flat or slightly raised head of the bed to prevent separation of the retina and choroid layers.

2. Both eyes need to be patched to prevent tracking (movement of one eye when the other one moves), and activity must be curtailed to prevent complete detachment.

3. Emergency surgery is not the initial plan of care but scleral buckling or laser reattachment surgery are options for treatment.

4. Cholinergic eye drops (Pilocarpine) are for treating narrow angle glaucoma.

#26. 3. **The pain may be unbearable at this time and she wishes to get away from it.**   An   He/3   An

1. She does not want to have others tell her what she needs. She wishes to remain in control.

2. Back rubs are good in early labor, but not in transition when she does not wish to be touched.

4. She wants help but turns inward and shuts out extraneous stimuli. She does not wish to be left alone.

#27. 2. **Diabetes is a contraindication for taking oral contraceptives. Diabetics have a high incidence of cardiovascular disease.**   As   Ph/8   An

1. Oral contraceptives decrease menstrual flow and may help to regulate periods and reduce chances of anemia.

3. The broken leg was too long ago to pose a problem. A long leg cast at the present time or a major injury to the lower leg would be a concern because of the danger of thrombus formation.

4. There is a concern if the baby is only a few days old as the pills may predispose to cardiovascular problems, but her baby is six months old.

#28. 4. **Elevation to 30 degrees has been shown to promote optimum venous outflow causing reduction in intracranial pressure. Pillows may cause head flexion, which decreases venous outflow, so pillows should be avoided.**   Im   Ph/10   Ap

1. 90 degrees is too much elevation for a lethargic post-op craniotomy client with an intracranial monitor in place.

2. Elevating legs increases venous return to the heart, which increases blood flow to the brain, which increases intracranial pressure.

3. Side lying is not effective in lowering intracranial pressure.

#29. 3. **It is important not to change the insulin dosage or time without consulting the physician. This statement indicates that the client needs further instruction before her grandfather leaves the hospital.**   Ev   Ph/8   An

1. The client is correct. Regular insulin onset is usually ½ to 1 hour while NPH onset is 3 to 4 hours with a duration of 20–24 hours.

2. The client understands that site rotation is important. This will prevent localized changes in fatty tissue.

4. The client understands the importance of keeping her grandfather's insulin administration on schedule and having him eat regularly scheduled meals to keep his blood sugar controlled.

#30. 3. **Urine output increases due to the increased cardiac output and myocardial contraction force, increasing perfusion of the kidney. Increase in urine output helps to decrease edema.**   Ev   Ph/8   An

1. Digoxin decreases the heart rate and makes it more effective.

2. Cardiac output is increased, not decreased.

4. Digoxin increases myocardial contraction force. This increases the effectiveness of the pumping action.

#31. 3. **The lab values, elevated liver enzymes and total bilirubin, along with the symptoms, anorexia, weight loss and ascites, all suggest liver disease. Jaundice occurs with liver disease because of the inability of diseased liver cells to clear bilirubin from the blood.**   An   Ph/9   An

Bile is deposited in the skin and sclera, producing the yellow discoloration.

1. Pallor is an indication of anemia, which does not correspond to the lab work results. The client will be jaundiced, not pale.
2. Dry mucous membranes are found with dehydration. The lab results given reflect liver function, not hydration status.
4. Ascites, rather than peripheral edema, is a common finding with hepatic failure. The lab results indicate hepatic dysfunction.

#32. 3. People who are allergic to shellfish (iodine) are at risk for allergic reactions to the contrast material (iodine) used for an IVP.   An   Ph/9   An

1. An allergic response to shellfish suggests an allergic reaction to iodine. The primary concern is the client's safety during the procedure using an iodine dye.
2. The test probably won't be canceled, but a substitute, less allergenic contrast material will be used or the client will be given steroids and/or antihistamines before the test.
4. The nurse does not make the decision about administering antihistamines. The data in the questions only tells us the client is at risk for an allergic reaction.

#33. 4. The nurse arranges to plan wound care with the client, thereby allowing him to participate in his own care and addressing the source of his anger.   An   Sa/1   Ap

1. This reply discounts the client's feelings and concerns.
2. This response only addresses part of the problem with suggestion of an inappropriate solution.
3. This response reflects a misunderstanding of the client's complaints as a symptom of another problem.

#34. 4. Limited time in the client's room reduces exposure to radiation for nursing staff and visitors.   Pl   Sa/2   Ap

1. Strict isolation is not appropriate. Only time and distance limits need to be instituted.
2. A lead apron may be worn by visitors or health care workers, not by the client.
3. Disposable supplies and equipment are not necessary. Bed linens and dressings will be handled according to radiation protocol.

#35. 3. The platelet count is low. Normal platelet count is 150,000–500,000. A low platelet count places the client at risk for bleeding. Trauma, injections, and invasive procedures should be avoided.   Pl   Ph/9   Ap

1. The hct, Hgb, and RBCs are all within normal limits so the client is not anemic and will not require supplemental iron.
2. The hct, Hgb, and RBCs are all within normal limits so the client is not anemic and will not require rest periods for fatigue.
4. The WBC is normal so the client is not at risk for infection.

#36. 2. Because a local anesthetic is used to numb the pharyngeal area for gastroscopy, the nurse must be certain the client is able to swallow before giving food or fluids. It may take two to four hours for the gag reflex and swallowing ability to return.   Pl   Ph/9   Ap

1. Clients will not have a nasogastric tube in place following a gastroscopy.
3. The client should have no pain following this procedure. Pain is an indication of a complication.
4. Measuring abdominal girth is not indicated following gastroscopy.

#37. 4. This disorder involves blindness involving the left half of the visual field of both eyes. Therefore, the client can only see objects placed within the right visual field.   Pl   Ph/9   Ap

1. Supporting the client's left arm and hand with pillows is appropriate for a client who has left hemiplegia. This client may have left hemiplegia but we are not given this information. The question asks the action related to left homonymous hemianopia.

2. Applying a patch to one eye is an appropriate intervention for diplopia (double vision) but this is not the condition this client has.

3. Encouraging the client to use his right hand for activities of daily living may be an appropriate intervention for the CVA client but is not related to hemianopia.

#38. 2. The child should be placed on enteric isolation until the lab reports no contagious organisms in the stool. If the stool is infected, isolation is continued after the antibiotics are completed until three consecutive daily stool specimens are negative.   Pl   Sa/2   Ap

1. A room near the nurses' station is a good idea, but does not address the problem of communicability.

3. Another child with the same clinical manifestations may be afflicted with an entirely different organism. Placing these two together would facilitate the exchange of organisms from poor hand washing by caregivers and use of the same equipment in the room.

4. Even if dehydration develops, it can be handled on the regular pediatric unit without the psychologic and financial stressors of an intensive care unit. Only severe dehydration is treated in the pediatric intensive care unit.

#39. 2. The fetal position (flexion) increases space between lumbar vertebrae facilitating easier entry of the needle into the subarachnoid space.   Im   Ph/9   Co

1. The prone position would make access to intervertebral spaces difficult.

3. Sitting at the edge of the bed is used for thoracentesis. Sometimes epidural anesthesia is started in this position. However, cerebrospinal fluid is not withdrawn. An upright position might cause spinal headache if utilized for L-P.

4. Trendelenburg position is used for insertion of central catheters and sometimes for shock states.

#40. 2. A Schilling's test measures the percent of vitamin B_{12} excreted in a 24-hour urine sample following an intramuscular "loading" dose of vitamin B_{12} and a radioactive oral dose of vitamin B_{12}.   Im   Ph/9   Co

1. Laxatives should not be administered during the test, since increased gastrointestinal motility may interfere with oral B_{12} absorption.

3. An intramuscular dose of vitamin B_{12}, not iron, is given. Iron is given to treat iron deficiency anemia.

4. An intravenous catheter is not required for this test.

#41. 4. Cloth-covered pillows or blankets are breathable materials that allow the cast to air dry. No plastic should be used.   Pl   Ph/9   Ap

1. Ice should be applied for 20 minutes, then removed for 20 minutes, to help prevent edema of the casted extremity.

2. Hair dryers, fans, and heat lamps should not be used to dry a cast. The inside of the cast would remain damp while the outside would dry.

3. No objects of any kind should be inserted under the cast.

#42. 1. Bleeding may occur from the puncture site. Firm pressure is required for several minutes to prevent this.   Im   Ph/9   Ap

2. The client can resume normal activity once sedation has worn off.

3. An occlusive dressing is not required for the puncture site.

4. The biopsy specimen is sent to the lab immediately after the procedure.

#43. 3. Damage to the recurrent laryngeal nerve is a major complication of thyroid surgery. Hoarseness immediately following surgery is often related to intubation during surgery. However, persistent or worsening hoarseness must be reported immediately to the physician because it may be the first sign of nerve injury.   Pl   Ph/9   Ap

1. Tension on the suture line should be avoided. Teach the client to support the head and neck when turning or changing position.

    2. Semi-Fowler's position should be maintained to promote respiratory function and the head should be supported in a neutral position with pillows.

    4. A tracheostomy is not routinely performed during a thyroidectomy. An emergency tracheostomy set should be available on the unit for use if the client develops respiratory impairment and obstruction due to laryngeal edema.

#44. 4. All abdominal surgery clients have a potential for third-spacing of fluids, causing a fluid volume deficit. Post-op urine output should be maintained at least 30 ml per hour. 100 ml in four hours indicates a beginning deficit.   Pl   Ph/10   Ap

    1. Alteration in comfort, pain is a working diagnosis. However, fluid volume deficit is the highest priority.

    2. Alterations in patterns of elimination is a working diagnosis. However, fluid volume deficit is the highest priority.

    3. Disturbance in self-concept, body image is a working diagnosis. However, fluid volume deficit is the highest priority.

#45. 3. Pain research has validated the need for nurses to adequately medicate clients in pain. Pain is what the person says it is and occurs when the person says it does. Nurses often undermedicate persons in pain and look for obvious signs of pain, i.e., grimacing, clenched teeth, crying, etc. The client said the pain was "8 out of 10," which validates the nurse giving 100 mg Demerol IM.   Pl   Ph/8   Ap

    1. 50 mg Demerol IM did not adequately control the client's pain. The nurse should increase the dose since the order allows the nurse to make this judgment.

    2. The client is in pain now and needs to be medicated now. The order allows pain medication in three hours.

    4. People use various forms of coping mechanisms to deal with pain including laughing, joking, sleeping, or even exercising.

#46. 3. Intradermal injections are given using a small-gauge needle inserted between skin layers by angling the needle parallel to the skin of the forearm.   Im   Ph/9   Co

    1. Histoplasmin antigen is administered by intradermal injection, not by means of a patch. Drugs such as nitroglycerin may be given by transcutaneous patch.

    2. Shallow scratches on the skin are used for administration of antigen for allergy testing.

    4. Histoplasmin antigen is administered by intradermal injection, not by Z track IM injection. Imferon (iron) is given by Z track injection.

#47. 4. Interest in sex is markedly decreased in depression.   As   Ps/6   Co

    1. Indecisiveness and fear of being wrong are common in depression.

    2. Depression creates feelings that nothing will ever improve.

    3. The risk of depression is increased when there is a family history.

#48. 1. Knowledge of the type and amounts of alcohol and other drugs consumed is necessary to plan the program of detoxification and anticipate physical complications.   As   Ps/6   An

    2. The client's motivation for treatment will become more important as treatment progresses and he passes the detoxification stage.

    3. Several weeks of therapy may be necessary before the client can successfully identify the factors that precipitate drinking bouts.

    4. The social problems created by the client's drinking are not a priority during detoxification but will require consideration as later treatment is planned.

#49. 4. Lying on the left side provides the best perfusion to the uterus and the infant while waiting for delivery. The nurse should have the mother in as clean and uncrowded a place as possible.   Im   He/3   Ap

    1. The cord can be tied with clean cloths, but not cut if hospital care is likely within one hour.

ANSWER	RATIONALE	NP	CN	CL

2. Asking someone to call the doctor is appropriate but not of highest priority. The highest priority is to be prepared to assist the woman with the baby while waiting for the ambulance.
3. It is safer for her to stay where she is and wait for the ambulance than to be in transit during the delivery.

#50. 3. Skin-to-skin contact is recommended so that the mother's warm body will warm the infant. Covering both will help keep them warm. Breastfeeding will help contract the mother's uterus and reduce bleeding.   Im   He/3   Ap
1. The cord should only be tied with a clean or sterile item and the cord cut only with a sterile implement. If the mother will get to a hospital within the next hour, cutting the cord is not necessary.
2. Mother and baby should be together for warmth, safety, and breastfeeding.
4. The area should be kept warm to prevent hypothermia in the mother and baby. Clearing the area may be appropriate to provide privacy and reduce germs but is not the highest priority.

#51. 1. The AIDS virus is spread through direct contact with body fluids such as blood and through sexual intercourse.   Ev   Sa/2   An
2. Casual contact with other people does not pose a risk of transmission of AIDS. Unless the client is feeling very ill, there is no need for him to drop his college classes.
3. Contact sports are not contraindicated unless there is a significant chance of bleeding and direct contact with others.
4. Casual contact with other people does not pose a risk of transmission of AIDS. There is no need to limit casual contact with children.

#52. 4. Unless the client is coughing, has decreased airway compliance, or has an airway obstruction, a high pressure alarm usually indicates water collection in or kinking of ventilator tubing. The tubing should be checked first.   Ev   Ph/9   An
1. The RN should be able to do initial checking of the ventilator. This problem can probably be corrected by the RN.
2. There is no evidence of airway obstruction or excess mucus and, therefore, no indication to stimulate coughing.
3. There is no indication that arterial blood gas analysis is needed (i.e., no respiratory distress or indication of low oxygenation).

#53. 4. If the fetus is engaged, that is at 0 station or +1 or more, cord prolapse will be prevented whether her membranes are ruptured or not.   As   He/3   Co
1. Cord prolapse can occur if the membranes rupture when the fetus is not engaged. The most important criterion is the fetal station.
2. Contractions will continue while walking, and she and her support person can be given guidelines on position and breathing while walking.
3. The baby's position—vertex, transverse, or breech—is not a factor in determining if the woman can ambulate.

#54. 3. For effective action, the diaphragm must be left in place for six to eight hours after intercourse.   Ev   He/3   An
1. The device needs to be inspected for holes. It often lasts around three years, but the woman should inspect the diaphragm regularly.
2. The diaphragm can be used alone. Contraceptive effectiveness will increase with condom usage but diaphragm plus spermicidal jelly can be effective even though the expected failure rate is 18%.
4. The diaphragm has to be removed at least once in a 24-hour period but must be left in place if sexual intercourse occurs more than once during a sexual encounter.

#55. 4. Bowel sounds indicate a beginning return of gastrointestinal function. Bowel sounds are a requisite for resumption of eating.   Pl   Ph/9   Ap
1. Ambulation helps get rid of gas and improves respiratory function,

but is not the indicator for return of gastrointestinal function and resumption of eating.

2. An abdominal binder provides support to the area and may make it easier for the woman to move about but does not indicate return of gastrointestinal function.

3. A Dulcolax suppository is not necessary. The nurse needs to assess for return of peristalsis, not promote evacuation of the bowel.

#56. 3. The Miller-Abbott tube is a double lumen intestinal tube weighted with mercury inserted to decompress the small intestine. As the tube moves through the intestine, progress can be assessed by comparing distance marks on the tube.   Ev   Ph/9   Co

1. Injecting air and auscultating over the stomach is done to assess correct placement of an gastric tube (i.e., Salem sump or feeding tube).

2. Aspirating the tube for stomach contents is done to assess correct placement of a gastric tube (i.e., Salem sump or feeding tube).

4. Signs of respiratory distress would signal malposition of the esophageal balloon on a Blakemore tube, which is used for bleeding esophageal varices.

#57. 2. A hot tub bath or shower upon arising helps to shorten the period of stiffness.   Im   Ph/7   Ap

1. Salicylates should not be taken on an empty stomach.

3. Rheumatoid joints should not stay in one position for long periods so splints are contraindicated.

4. The client may need to decrease activity when the pain is severe.

#58. 3. Air embolism occurs frequently with central lines with sudden onset of dyspnea, hypotension, chest pain, and cyanosis. The best initial nursing action is to clamp the IV line and turn the client to the left side to trap the air in the right side of the heart so it does not enter the pulmonary artery. Then call the physician and administer oxygen.   Im   Ph/10   Ap

1. The second action for the nurse to take is to notify the physician and administer oxygen via nasal cannula immediately.

2. Clamping the IV is the highest priority. Another bag of fluids will not be hung while there is air in the tubing.

4. CPR is not necessary yet, but should be anticipated.

#59. 1. Elevating the stump will decrease edema. However, elevation on a pillow is indicated only for the first day because prolonged hip flexion can lead to contractures. Following that, the foot of the bed should be elevated on shock blocks.   Im   Ph/9   Co

2. Elevating the stump will decrease edema, which is especially likely in the immediate postoperative period.

3. The prone position will decrease contractures and should start early after surgery but elevation of the stump has a higher priority at this time.

4. Reverse Trendelenburg position is contraindicated for this client. That would promote venous congestion.

#60. 2. The morning short-acting insulin dosage is usually determined by the previous day's late morning and noon blood glucose levels. To depend upon today's blood glucose levels to determine today's dose of regular insulin would put the child into a situation of constant overtreatment or undertreatment.   Pl   Ph/8   Ap

1. It takes three or four days for families and children to work through their shock and denial and to be ready to learn new information. It is unrealistic for the nurse to expect all teaching to be finished when the child is discharged from the hospital. Reinforcement must be given at home from an ongoing support system. Proper referrals need to be made if indicated.

3. The majority of the day's total dose of insulin is given in the mornings

ANSWER	RATIONALE	NP	CN	CL
	to cover the food the child will eat during the day. Insulin needs to be given before food is eaten, not after.			
4.	Since exercises uses up glucose stores, the supplemental calories should be available to the body before the exercise begins.			
#61. 4.	**The symptoms indicate hypoglycemia. Ten grams of rapidly absorbed carbohydrate is the treatment for hypoglycemia. This should be repeated in five minutes if the client does not feel better. The physician should be notified for new orders if glucose and insulin parameters have not already been determined.**	Pl	Ph/8	Ap
1.	The client needs rapidly absorbed carbohydrate first, then the next scheduled meal. The insulin should not be given while the client is hypoglycemic.			
2.	The nurse should treat the hypoglycemia. Regular insulin acts quickly and will make the hypoglycemia worse.			
3.	The nurse will hold the insulins but should administer concentrated carbohydrate before calling the physician.			
#62. 1.	**The symptoms suggest hypocalcemia. The four pea-sized parathyroid glands, which regulate calcium and phosphorous balance, are imbedded in the thyroid. Inadvertent removal during thyroidectomy is a common cause of postoperative hypocalcemia.**	An	Ph/10	Ap
2.	Radioactive iodine is used to shrink the thyroid gland and usually causes hypothyroidism, not hypoparathyroidism.			
3.	Insufficient iodine intake may cause a goiter but is not a cause of hypocalcemia.			
4.	Overstimulation of the parathyroid gland causes hypercalcemia, not hypocalcemia, which this client's symptoms indicate.			
#63. 2.	**Early intermittent catheterization is essential in bladder training. A high thoracic spinal cord injury may have some arm, shoulder, and hand movement that would enable the client to learn self-catheterization techniques.**	Pl	Ph/9	Ap
1.	An indwelling catheter should be removed as soon after injury as possible to begin early intermittent catheterization. Changing to a leg bag is unnecessary.			
3.	A high thoracic spine injury usually leaves an atonic, areflexic, neurogenic bladder, so unassisted voiding is unlikely.			
4.	An areflexic neurogenic bladder distends to accommodate a large volume of urine. Clamping the indwelling catheter is not the method of choice for bladder training.			
#64. 1.	**A comminuted fracture usually results from a crush injury and results in fractured and crushed bones. The bone is broken in several places.**	An	Ph/10	Co
2.	A displaced bone occurs when the two ends of the fractured bone are pulled apart and separated from each other.			
3.	A compound or open fracture occurs when the bone has been broken in two and one end of the bone breaks through the skin.			
4.	A greenstick or incomplete fracture is when only one side of the bone is broken. A greenstick fracture happens in children whose bones are still soft.			
#65. 2.	**Fat embolism occurs most often in the client with long bone lower extremity fractures or multiple fractures, despite age.**	An	Ph/9	Co
1.	Fat embolism occurs most often in the client with long bone lower extremity fractures. A wrist is not a long bone and is not a lower extremity.			
3.	Fat embolism occurs most often in the client with long bone lower extremity fractures. The ulnar bone is in the arm.			
4.	Fat embolism occurs most often in the client with long bone lower extremity fractures. The ribs are not long bones.			
#66. 3.	**Absence of audible wheezes can be a sign of improvement.**	An	Ph/10	An

ANSWER	RATIONALE	NP	CN	CL

However, when coupled with somnolence, a sign of hypercapnia, absence of wheezing is a sign of worsening bronchospasm. This is a respiratory emergency.

1. Decreasing respiratory wheezes indicates improved passage of air.
2. Expectoration of sputum is encouraged. Decreased respiratory wheezes indicates improved passage of air.
4. Decreasing respiratory rate with decreased use of accessory muscles both indicate improved passage of air.

#67. 1. The client should be taught to support his weight on the crutch hand pieces. Ev Ph/7 Ap

2. This statement indicates a need for further instruction. It is not acceptable to lean on the crutches bearing weight on the arms. Pressure on the axilla can damage the brachial plexus nerves, producing "crutch paralysis."
3. This statement indicates a need for further instruction. It is not acceptable to lean on the crutches, bearing weight on the arms. Pressure on the axilla can damage the brachial plexus nerves, producing "crutch paralysis."
4. This statement indicates a need for further instruction. There is no need to avoid bearing weight on the crutch that is on the injured side. Weight bearing should be distributed evenly in order to ensure maximum stability.

#68. 2. The client should not cross his legs or adduct them or assume any positions that require acute flexion of more than 90 degrees. Ev Ph/9 An

1. Traveling long distances should be avoided as the person remains in hip flexion for extended periods of time.
3. Putting on socks and shoes may require acute flexion or adduction. He may need assistance.
4. Ambulatory aides such as a walker or crutches will be needed for a period of time until sufficient muscle tone has developed so that the client can maintain a normal gait without pain or discomfort.

#69. 2. Alcohol interferes with Dilantin and causes it to remain at a subtherapeutic level causing the client to be prone to seizure activity. Im Ph/8 Co

1. The intramuscular route for Dilantin should be avoided as it causes inconsistent absorption, necrosis at the site, and pain.
3. Dilantin should be taken regularly and consistently to maintain a therapeutic blood level.
4. It is not normal to experience slurred speech and confusion. Side effects also include ataxia, nystagmus, hypotension, rash, gingival hyperplasia, and ventricular fibrillation.

#70. 2. A hematoma beneath the skin may cause the skin to bulge. This may require evacuation of the hematoma so that healing may take place. Ev Ph/9 An

1. The incision may be somewhat edematous at this point in the recovery period. However, it should not have a bulging area; it should be more uniform.
3. Abdominal distention will not usually cause a single bulging area of the incision.
4. The description of the wound does not contain information suggesting wound infection. A wound infection is very unlikely 24 hours after surgery. It usually takes 72 hours for the development of a wound infection.

#71. 2. The symptoms suggest transfusion reaction. The priority nursing action for a client with symptoms of an acute hemolytic reaction to a blood transfusion is to stop the transfusion immediately. Other signs suggesting transfusion reaction include chills, increased respiration, flushing, low back or thigh pain, headaches, pleuritic chest pain, dyspnea, abnormal bleeding, hemoglobinuria, and shock. Im Ph/8 An

1. The transfusion should be stopped, not slowed down. The transfusion reaction will continue.
3. The transfusion should be stopped, not slowed down. The transfusion reaction will continue. The physician should be notified after the transfusion has been stopped.
4. The transfusion should be stopped. Administration of acetaminophen is not a priority action.

#72. 2. **The bladder should be full for a pelvic sonogram to serve as a reference point and sonic window to the pelvic organs.**   Ev   Ph/9   Ap
1. A permit is not required for a sonogram since it is not an invasive procedure.
3. No sedation is required for a pelvic sonogram.
4. The bladder should be full for a pelvic sonogram to serve as a reference point and sonic window to the pelvic organs.

#73. 2. **Alzheimer's disease is the most common cognitive impairment affecting older adults. As the disease progresses, it requires ongoing assessment to determine the client's ability to maintain himself in the home environment.**   As   He/3   Ap
1. With good cognitive abilities, the client may well be able to develop ways of meeting elimination needs.
3. Cognitive abilities are more related to ability to remain at home than the amount of exercise the client has. With good cognitive abilities, the client may well be able to develop ways of meeting exercise needs.
4. Cognitive abilities are more related to ability to remain at home than metabolic needs. With good cognitive abilities, the client may well be able to develop ways of meeting metabolic needs.

#74. 1. **The left fifth intercostal space, midclavicular line is the site of maximum ventricular impulse (PMI) during systole in most people.**   As   He/4   Co
2. The right second intercostal space, midclavicular line is the auscultatory site for the aortic heart sound.
3. The site of carotid pulsation is the site utilized for palpation of the carotid pulse.
4. The left third intercostal space, sternal border is the site known as Erb's point for auscultation of first and second heart sounds and murmurs.

#75. 3. **The anterior posterior diameter of the chest increases over time as compensation for chronic hypoxemia.**   As   Ph/9   An
1. Fever is present with pneumonia, but not with COPD unless infection is also present.
2. A weak, thready pulse is usually associated with shock states, not COPD.
4. Crepitus is a popping or crunching feeling on palpation secondary to accumulation of air under the skin, as with pneumothorax. Crepitus is not present with COPD.

#76. 3. **Myxedema is a condition of the thyroid gland in which there is thyroid hypofunction. Classic signs and symptoms include extreme fatigue, hair loss, brittle nails, and dry skin with severe hypothyroidism. Weight gain with no increased caloric intake is present, and temperature and pulse rate may fall.**   As   Ph/9   Co
1. Addison's disease is hypofunction of the adrenal cortex and is characterized by low blood sugar, low blood volume, low blood pressure, and a bronze color to the skin.
2. Cushing's syndrome is hyperfunction of the adrenal cortex and is characterized by high blood sugar, hypertension, buffalo hump, moon face, and hirsutism.
4. Grave's disease is hyperfunction of the thyroid gland. It is characterized by weight loss, tremors, tachycardia, and tachypnea. The client feels hot.

ANSWER	RATIONALE	NP	CN	CL

#77. 2. The client should not flex and adduct the affected joint 24 hours after surgery. Usually an abductor pillow maintains the hip in slight abduction to prevent dislocation.   As   Ph/9   Co

    1. Persons undergoing lower extremity surgery are at high risk for developing deep vein thrombosis. Advancing age and immobilization are also risk factors.

    3. Temperature monitoring can provide important information. Generally temperature elevations in the first 24 to 48 hours are related to atelectasis or other respiratory problems. Elevations in the next few days may be attributed to urinary tract infections. In five to nine days the temperature elevation may be caused by superficial wound infections.

    4. Pain may be due to wound hematoma or general postsurgical pain.

#78. 2. Recent trauma, alcohol ingestion, drugs, surgical stress, or illness can all trigger an acute gout attack.   As   Ph/9   An

    1. The onset of pain, redness, swelling, and warmth is usually abrupt.

    3. Alcohol ingestion and dietary changes can trigger an acute gout attack.

    4. The abrupt onset of symptoms usually occurs at night with the client awakening to the severe pain, redness, swelling, and warmth in the affected joint.

#79. 4. The nurse should observe the type and progression of seizure activity that occurs. It is also important to ensure the client is safe and does not injure himself during the seizure.   As   Ph/10   An

    1. An aura is a warning sign that some clients experience prior to a seizure. It can include dizziness, numbness, or visual or auditory disturbances. This is not a priority assessment during a seizure. However, it can be very useful information to elicit from the client to help predict forthcoming seizure activity.

    2. It is important to record the length of the seizure after the seizure.

    3. It is important to record what precipitated the seizure after the seizure.

#80. 1. The scalp itches from the crawling and saliva of the adult louse. The child's fingernails scratch the skin, leaving red marks.   As   Ph/9   Co

    2. Pruritic, scaling, erythematous papules, plaques, and patches with well-defined borders describe tinea capitis (ringworm), a fungal parasitic infection.

    3. Beefy-red erythematous areas with a few surrounding papules and pustules describe candidiasis, which is usually located in dark moist areas.

    4. An inflammation of the hair follicles with pus-filled nodules is folliculitis, which is usually caused by staphylococci.

#81. 1. Shifts in fluids and electrolytes are caused by the loss of fluid and proteins through damaged tissues and blood vessels. Loss of protein causes the interstitial area to fill with fluid, decreasing the intravascular volume. Broken cells release potassium into the circulation. Sodium is retained when aldosterone is released into the blood stream in response to stress. From the blood stream it goes to the interstitial spaces through broken capillaries, thus lowering serum levels and drawing more fluid from the circulating volume. Shock is a major complication during the first one to two days.   As   Ph/10   An

    2. Pain can increase heart and respiratory rates, as well as change peripheral color.

    3. Burned tissue can no longer maintain temperature balance. Any temperature fluctuation increases nutritional and calorie demands on the body. When hypovolemia occurs, the major volume of blood is directed to the brain and heart, while the gastrointestinal and renal systems receive less blood volume, decreasing motility and outputs.

4. Anemia occurs around four to seven days after the injury when hemoconcentration is corrected and the red cell loss from the burn injury can be accurately measured.

#82. 4. **Hypothermia causes vasoconstriction, which can result in skin damage and even frostbite. Turning frequently reduces skin damage.**   An   Ph/9   An
   1. Client acceptance is not a major reason for frequent turning.
   2. Turning frequently will probably not prevent shivering. The client should shiver as this is the body's temperature-raising mechanism.
   3. Frequent turning does not help the body's autoregulatory mechanism.

#83. 2. **A hallucination is a sensory experience with no stimuli, as in hearing voices when alone.**   As   Ps/6   An
   1. Difficulty with authority figures is a common symptom of schizophrenia, but no sensory experience is indicated.
   3. Misinterpretation of stimuli is an illusion. A hallucination occurs when there is a sensory experience with no stimuli.
   4. False beliefs are delusions. A sensory experience is required for a hallucination.

#84. 3. **Temperature elevation will indicate beginning infection. This is the most important measure to help assess the client for infections, since the lost mucous plug and the ruptured membranes increase the potential for ascending bacteria from the reproductive tract. This will infect the fetus, membranes, and uterine cavity.**   Pl   He/3   Ap
   1. Universal precautions are necessary for all clients but a specific assessment of the client's temperature will give an indication the client is becoming infected.
   2. Oxytocin may be needed to induce labor if it is not progressing, but it is not done initially.
   4. More frequent vaginal examinations are not recommended, as frequent vaginal exams can increase chances of infection.

#85. 1. **Deep breathing and coughing are essential for obtaining mucus from the bronchi.**   Im   Ph/9   Ap
   2. Deep suctioning is used for collection of airway mucus only when other methods fail. Suctioning may cause injury to the client.
   3. Specimens for culture should be obtained before antibiotics are started if possible.
   4. There is no reason to withhold food or fluids. Have the client rinse his mouth before collecting the specimen.

#86. 4. **The yellow-white covering over the end of the penis is part of the healing process and should not be removed, but washed gently with water. Rubbing or the use of soap on the area will cause irritation. Any bleeding or other exudate needs to be reported to the physician.**   Ev   He/3   An
   1. The face and neck are washed after the eyes, so that a completely clean washcloth can be used for the eyes. The eyes are washed from the inner canthus outward, to prevent blockage of the tear ducts with exudate and transference of organisms into the nasal passages from the eyes.
   2. The cord must not only look dry, but must have fallen off and the area underneath completely healed before it can safely be soaked with water containing fecal organisms, etc.
   3. Alcohol, or another drying agent prescribed, should be applied several times a day. The diaper should never cover the unhealed cord because of the urinary and fecal organisms that could come in contact with the cord.

#87. 1. **Home serum glucose testing is the best method as it indicates metabolism of food and the body's response to intake.**   Pl   Ph/9   An

2. Weight gain results from adequate nutrition but glucose levels are not determined.

3. A diary records what the client has eaten. This does not ensure proper intake. Proper dietary intake helps maintain glucose levels, but metabolism and the body's response to intake are not determined by food but by serum glucose level.

4. All pregnant women spill glucose in their urine and urine monitoring is unreliable in diabetics.

#88. 2. Leukemia is diagnosed by identifying abnormal white blood cells and their precursors in the bone marrow and noting how many of these cells are present.   An   Ph/9   Co

1. Reed-Sternberg cells are found in lymphatic tissue of persons having Hodgkin's lymphoma.

3. Epstein-Barr virus may be associated with some types of lymphoma, but has not been shown to have a direct relationship to leukemia.

4. Since the primary site for the malignancy in leukemia is the bone marrow, metastases would not be found by biopsying bone marrow. Common sites of metastasis for leukemias include the brain and lymphatic tissues.

#89. 3. Epiglottitis is always a medical emergency. Intubation is best facilitated in the operating room where all equipment is readily available, and where the epiglottis could safely be visualized with a laryngoscope.   An   Ph/10   An

1. After the airway is established, the antibiotic is the next concern for the nurse. Epiglottitis is commonly caused by *Haemophilus influenzae* type B, which is usually sensitive to ampicillin or chloramphenicol. The IV is started after the intubation to prevent laryngospasm as a result of crying.

2. The child with epiglottitis should never be made to move from a sitting position, usually on his mother's lap. Fear, crying, and supine positioning could all cause laryngospasm and complete airway obstruction. Intubation equipment must be kept with the child at all times. Portable x-ray equipment can be brought to the client to decrease movement.

4. A croup tent is indicated for a child with croup. The child with epiglottitis will most likely be intubated.

#90. 2. Shoes, toys, and clothes can all transfer the oil (urushiol) to the skin, where it sets up an immediate reaction. Items that have touched ANY part of the plant should be washed in hot water and detergent.   An   He/4   Ap

1. All parts of the plant are poisonous, even dried leaves. Even when burning brush that contains poison ivy plants, care should be taken not to allow the skin or lungs to be exposed to the smoke. Susie should not even be near the plants.

3. It's true that animals seem to be unaffected themselves by the plants. However, their fur carries the plant oils and becomes a source of contamination, so the dog needs a bath before hugs.

4. Susie's skin and clothes need to be gently rinsed with cool water within 15 minutes of contact with the plant irritant. This neutralizes the urushiol before it can bond to the skin and does not irritate the skin from scrubbing. If she scrubs with soap and water, the protective oils are removed from her skin, and the urushiol may dilute and spread to irritate more areas.

#91. 4. Hyperactive deep-tendon reflexes are not a normal finding in any client and may result in the phenomena called clonus. Sustained clonus suggests the presence of central nervous system disease and should be thoroughly investigated by the physician. The normal aging process often produces less reactive reflexes in older clients, which may also be cause for concern regarding safety issues.   An   He/4   An

ANSWER	RATIONALE	NP	CN	CL
	1. The alterations in pupil reaction described are a result of the normal process of aging.			
	2. Sluggish bowel sounds are a result of the normal process of aging.			
	3. Kyphosis is a result of the normal process of aging.			
#92. 4.	**Social isolation is a phenomena that may result from feelings of not belonging and hopelessness about one's life situation. It may be self-imposed or environmentally imposed by a lack of contact with support systems. In day care settings, be they with older clients or with children, socialization with other group members is fostered when nurses and other caregivers take time to talk with clients and show a genuine concern for the well-being of the new member. As a rule, most people appreciate efforts made to include them in the group and will commonly respond by repeating these inclusionary behaviors for other new members over time.**	Pl	He/3	Ap
	1. With the older adult there is no need to separate by age and gender.			
	2. The same nurse should be assigned so that the clients and the nurse can get to know one another better.			
	3. The nurse should encourage the clients to talk about their life outside the day care center.			
#93. 3.	**When mixing insulins, air equal to the amount of insulin to be removed from the vial is first injected into each vial. Next, Regular insulin equal to the prescribed amount is always drawn into the syringe first, followed by withdrawal of the designated amount of NPH insulin from its vial. The short-acting Regular insulin is drawn first to keep the vial free of potential "contamination" by intermediate-acting NPH insulin. Remember "clear before cloudy." Regular is clear and NPH is cloudy.**	An	Ph/8	An
	1. Using a magnifier to read the insulin syringe is appropriate behavior to help this visually impaired person draw up the correct amount of insulin.			
	2. Pinching the skin and injecting insulin at a 90 degree angle are appropriate behaviors.			
	4. The client should use all available areas within one site, i.e., thigh, before moving to another site.			
#94. 3.	**Clients with injuries to the lumbosacral area usually have a lower motor neuron (flaccid) bladder. Clients with this type of bladder may achieve emptying of the bladder by performing a Valsalva maneuver or tightening the abdominal muscles.**	Im	Ph/9	Ap
	1. The client should drink 2000 ml to 2500 ml of fluid daily.			
	2. The client should decrease fluid intake after 6 P.M.			
	4. Pouring warm water on the perineum may help clients with upper motor neuron injuries but is not likely to be helpful to this spinal cord injury client.			
#95. 1.	**Anticipatory grieving is the state in which an individual or group experiences feelings in response to an expected significant loss. In this case, the client's diagnosis of a form of cancer produces behavioral manifestations of grieving. These behaviors include decreased activity levels, withdrawal from socialization, altered patterns of nutrition and sleep, and anger. In addition, clients experiencing anticipatory grieving often communicate their perceived loss by expressing feelings of guilt through self-deprecating comments and/or by acting out their anger.**	An	Ps/5	An
	2. The behaviors described are more consistent with anticipatory grieving than with fear.			
	3. The behaviors described are more consistent with anticipatory grieving than with ineffective individual coping.			
	4. The behaviors described are more consistent with anticipatory grieving than with anxiety.			
#96. 2.	**The best time to perform breast self-exam is between the 4th**	Ev	He/4	Ap

and 7th day after menstrual bleeding begins. At this time, hormones have the least effect on the breasts, making them easier to examine. If not menstruating, breasts should be examined once a month.

1. Although it may be more difficult during lactation due to the fullness of the breasts, breast self-exam should still be done.
3. The procedure should be done both in an upright and a lying position. When in the lying position, the person should be lying down with a pillow or folded towel under the shoulder on the side that is being examined.
4. The breasts can be examined using one of three methods: circular, vertical strip, or wedge, whichever the woman is most comfortable with.

#97. 4. **Clients taking the anticoagulant coumadin should be cautious about any injuries, especially to mucous membranes or soft tissue, which bleed easily.**   Ev   Ph/8   Ap

1. The client should not increase the dose of coumadin without authorization from the physician. This could cause a bleeding episode.
2. Green and leafy vegetables such as broccoli and spinach contain vitamin K, which is the antidote for coumadin. These should not be eaten in large amounts when the person is taking coumadin.
3. The client should not take any salicylate drugs such as aspirin without the permission of the physician. Salicylates are anticoagulants and will cause bleeding.

#98. 1. **To aid in promoting positive expectations regarding body image, fears must be discussed openly before management can be approached.**   Pl   Ps/6   Ap

2. Adhering to a nutritionally balanced diet is a long-term goal.
3. There are two goals in the statement. Identifying problems is a short-term goal and developing new coping methods is a long-term goal.
4. Accepting herself as having self-worth is a long-term goal.

#99. 4. **When a cerebrovascular accident causes one-sided paralysis (hemiplegia) the weaker extensor and abductor muscles can be overcome by the spasms in the flexors and adductors, resulting in flexion and adduction contractures. Proper positioning of joints in an extended, abducted position prevents contractures. The hand tends to form a fist around the thumb unless properly positioned in a semi-extended position.**   Ev   Ph/9   Ap

1. To prevent shoulder adduction, a pillow should be placed in the axilla when there is limited external rotation.
2. A trochanter roll is used to prevent external hip rotation. The bed should be flat to prevent knee flexion.
3. In plantar flexion, the foot is curled up. A posterior splint may be used at night to keep the foot in good alignment.

#100. 2. **The pulse oximeter is a painless noninvasive procedure. The probe is attached over a pulsating vascular bed, such as the finger. Inaccurate readings may be caused by the effect of bright external light. Covering the probe with an opaque material is often recommended.**   Im   Ph/9   Ap

1. The probe is attached over a pulsating vascular bed such as the finger.
3. The pulse oximeter is a noninvasive procedure. The probe is attached over a pulsating vascular bed such as the finger.
4. The pulse oximeter is a noninvasive procedure. The probe is attached over a pulsating vascular bed such as the finger.

Practice Test 2

1. The nurse is administering medication in an extended care facility. The client answers to Mr. Smith and Mr. Brown. What is the best way for the nurse to correctly identify the client before administering the medications?
   1. Check with the picture identification on file.
   2. Check the arm band.
   3. Check the name on the bed.
   4. Check the name on the room door.
2. An adult is scheduled to undergo an exploratory laparotomy in one hour. The nurse has just received the order to administer his preoperative medication. What assessment is essential for the nurse before administering the medication?
   1. The client's ability to cough and deep breathe.
   2. Any drug hypersensitivity or allergy.
   3. The client's understanding of the surgical procedure.
   4. Whether the client's family is present and supportive.
3. The nurse is assessing a male client who has been admitted for treatment of alcoholism. Which question by the nurse is least appropriate?
   1. "How much do you drink?"
   2. "What other drugs do you use?"
   3. "How is your general health?"
   4. "Why do you drink so much?"
4. The nurse is planning care for a client who has a phobic disorder manifested by a fear of elevators. Which goal would need to be accomplished first? The client
   1. demonstrates the relaxation response when asked.
   2. verbalizes the underlying cause of the disorder.
   3. rides the elevator in the company of the nurse.
   4. role plays the use of an elevator.
5. Which statement would be least expected when the nurse assesses a client with posttraumatic stress disorder?
   1. "Sometimes my heart pounds and I can't get my breath."
   2. "I have nightmares about my time in the war."
   3. "I can't concentrate at work but I do fine at home."
   4. "My wife worries that I am drinking more now."
6. Mr. K. comes to the nurses' station complaining of shortness of breath, choking, dizziness, and nausea. He says, "I think I'm going crazy or dying or something. I don't know what happened. Help me, help me." When the nurse tries to ask about what happened, Mr. K. can only say, "Help me, help me." The best interpretation for the nurse to make regarding his level of anxiety is
   1. mild.
   2. moderate.
   3. severe.
   4. panic.
7. A woman completes a session with her psychotherapist and becomes increasingly anxious. The nurse talks with her and the physician orders Xanax (alprazolam) 0.25 mg po. Which action by the nurse is appropriate for evaluating the effectiveness of this drug?
   1. Ask her if she remembers not to drive or use alcohol.
   2. Assess her anxiety level one hour after giving the drug.
   3. Encourage her to use a relaxation tape along with the medication.
   4. Ask her if the medication caused her to be nauseated.
8. The nurse is assessing a client who was raped a month ago. The client cannot describe any feelings related to her rape. She focuses on the need for better law enforcement and rape prevention programs. The client is using which defense?
   1. Denial.
   2. Conversion.
   3. Introjection.
   4. Isolation.
9. Mr. P. confides to the nurse that he is being pursued by the Federal Bureau of Investigation because he has access to information that will prevent future wars. This behavior most likely represents which of the following?
   1. Ideas of reference.
   2. Delusions.
   3. Hallucinations.
   4. Dissociation.
10. A 40-year-old woman is admitted in the manic phase of bipolar disorder. She has eaten very little food from her meal trays and has lost two pounds in the three days since admission. Which approach by the nurse is most likely to meet her nutritional needs?
    1. Provide frequent snack foods that are high in nutrition.
    2. Limit her intake of between-meal snacks.

3. Allow her to eat in the cafeteria and choose her own foods.
4. Set up a system in which greater intake is rewarded by privileges.

11. Mr. T. was admitted to the psychiatric unit three days ago with a diagnosis of schizophrenia. Today the nurse finds him facing the window, and he seems to be talking and listening. After validating that Mr. T. is hallucinating, which is the best action by the nurse?
1. Allow him to continue his conversation without interruption.
2. Offer him a choice of IM or PO for his PRN medication.
3. Tell him that his behavior is inappropriate and should stop.
4. Involve him in some concrete game or other activity.

12. The nurse is evaluating a woman who has been treated for major depression for three weeks. Which is the best indication that her depression is improving?
1. She takes her medication as prescribed.
2. She says, "I think I can set more realistic goals now."
3. Her husband demonstrates more understanding of his wife's condition.
4. She ventilates about how sad and hopeless she feels.

13. The nurse enters the room of a depressed client to find the client poorly responsive and an empty pill bottle and water pitcher on the night stand. What is the best initial action by the nurse?
1. Determine if the client is on suicide precautions.
2. Check the client's level of consciousness and vital signs.
3. Ask the client what precipitated his overdose.
4. Find out how many pills were in the bottle.

14. During her first trimester, a woman experiences many physiological changes that lead her to think she is pregnant. Which of the following changes will the nurse most likely tell her are normal for an eight-week pregnancy?
1. Dysuria.
2. Colostrum secretion.
3. Nosebleeds.
4. Dependent edema.

15. The nurse is assessing a healthy neonate upon admission to the newborn nursery. Which characteristic, if observed by the admitting nurse, is normal?
1. Hypertonia.
2. Irregular respiratory rate of 50 breaths/minute.
3. Head circumference measuring 31 cm.
4. High-pitched or shrill cry.

16. Following her baby's birth, the woman's uterine fundus is soft, midline, 2 cm above the umbilicus, and she has saturated two pads within 30 minutes. The nurse knows the client's condition shows that she has an immediate need to
1. be cleaned and have another pad change.
2. empty her bladder.
3. have an increase in her intravenous fluids of Ringer's lactate.
4. have her fundus massaged.

17. The nurse is caring for a child with hemophilia who is actively bleeding. Which nursing action is most important in the prevention of the crippling effects of bleeding?
1. Active range of motion.
2. Avoidance of all dental care.
3. Encourage genetic counseling.
4. Elevate and immobilize the affected extremity.

18. The nurse is planning care for an infant with Hirschsprung's disease who is admitted to the hospital prior to surgery. Which would not be included in the nursing care plan?
1. Measure abdomen every four hours.
2. Administer tap water enemas until clear results.
3. Begin colostomy care teaching with the parents.
4. Complete daily intake and output.

19. The nurse is developing a care plan for a woman with cystitis. Which is most appropriate to include in the care plan?
1. Testing urine for protein with a dipstick.
2. Promoting elimination of excess fluid by maintaining NPO.
3. Encouraging voiding every two to three hours.
4. Telling her to take a tub bath to sooth the urethra.

20. A man underwent an exploratory laparotomy yesterday. He is on strict intake and output. Calculate his intake and output for an eight-hour period.

Intake	Output
IV - D_5LR at 125 ml/hr	Foley urine output 850 ml
PO–1 ounce ice chips	NG tube–200 ml
NG irrigant–NS 15 ml q 2 hr.	

1. I = 170 ml; O = 1050 ml
2. I = 1090 ml; O = 1050 ml
3. I = 141 ml; O = 1000 ml
4. I = 1000 ml; O = 990 ml

21. Mr. A. is receiving Coumadin (warfarin) 5 mg po qd for treatment of a resolving deep vein thrombosis. The nurse is ready to administer his daily dose of Coumadin when she observes several ecchymotic areas on the client's extremities. When asked, the client

states his gums have been bleeding when he brushes his teeth. Which nursing action is most appropriate?

1. Administer the daily dose of Coumadin, then notify the physician so tomorrow's dose can be adjusted.
2. Administer the daily dose of Coumadin. These are the expected side effects of Coumadin.
3. Hold the Coumadin and notify the physician of the assessment findings.
4. Hold the Coumadin until the next daily dose is due.

22. A 75-year-old male has had Parkinson's disease for several years. He exhibits all of the typical signs and symptoms of advanced Parkinson's. He is being discharged to his home with his 70-year-old wife as his primary caregiver. Which statement best indicates that his wife understands his symptoms and needs?

1. "Since my husband is on Levodopa, I need to watch him closely for things like facial grimacing and involuntary movements of his trunk, legs, and arms."
2. "It is very important for my husband to rest in bed or his chair most of the day."
3. "My husband may have bad diarrhea due to his Parkinson's."
4. "My husband may be embarrassed by his difficulties with eating so we should not go out like we used to do."

23. A client with a head injury is moaning and complaining of head pain. The family requests that some pain medication be given. The nurse explains that most pain medications are usually not given to clients with head injuries. The family says, "A couple of aspirin won't hurt." The best rationale for withholding aspirin from clients with head injuries is that aspirin may cause

1. gastrointestinal distress.
2. tinnitus, making neuro assessments more difficult.
3. increased likelihood of intracranial bleeding.
4. constriction of the pupils, making pupil assessment more difficult.

24. A client has a closed head injury. Vital signs are T 103°F rectally; pulse 100; respirations 24; B.P. 110/84. Hourly urine output is 200 ml/hr. What is the best understanding of the cause of these findings?

1. Damage to the hypothalamus resulting in decreased hormone production.
2. Movement of fluid from the tissue into the intravascular space, resulting from sepsis.
3. An increase in antidiuretic hormone (ADH) as a result of injury to the hypothalamus.
4. Fluid shifts from the tissue into the intravascular space due to administration

of normal saline used during fluid resuscitation.

25. An adult client has been on bed rest for several months. Which statement best describes the relationship between complications of prolonged bed rest and nursing interventions to prevent these complications?

1. Turning and positioning will help decrease the potential for calcium loss from bones.
2. Adequate fluid intake is vital to decrease the risk of brittle bones.
3. Leg exercises are important to decrease the loss of calcium from the bones and the risk of pathological fractures.
4. Encouraging milk intake will help decrease the loss of calcium from the bones.

26. An adult client had an exploratory laparotomy three days ago. The nurse assesses the client's incision and observes the following: edges of incision well approximated; a small amount of edema noted entire length of incision; moderate amount of serosanguinous drainage. The nurse understands that these findings indicate

1. that the wound is likely to develop an infection.
2. an abnormal amount of wound drainage.
3. a healthy postoperative wound.
4. that the wound is infected.

27. An order is written to start an IV on a 75-year-old client who is getting ready to go to the operating room for a total hip replacement. What gauge of catheter would best meet the needs of this client?

1. 18
2. 20
3. 21 butterfly
4. 25

28. An adult client is taking Prednisone. Which statement by the client best indicates understanding of the possible side effects of Prednisone therapy?

1. "I really need to limit how much potassium I take in since hyperkalemia is a side effect of this medicine."
2. "I must take this medicine exactly as my doctor ordered it. I shouldn't skip doses or double up on them if I should forget."
3. "This medicine will protect me from getting any colds or infections."
4. "Since I'm taking Prednisone, my incision will heal much faster."

29. The nurse is inserting an indwelling urinary catheter. Which action is essential to decrease the risk of complications associated with catheter insertion?

1. Cleanse the female client using betadine-soaked 4 × 4s, cleaning from the rectal area to the clitoris.

2. Utilize a catheter that is slightly larger than the external urinary meatus.
3. Utilize clean technique.
4. Test the retention balloon prior to insertion.

30. A woman who is receiving tamoxifen (Tamofen) 20 mg po bid asks the nurse why she is receiving this medication and what side effects are possible. The best response for the nurse to make is
   1. "Tamoxifen is a vasodilator-antihypertensive. It will lower your blood pressure. The main side effects include dizziness, headache, nasal congestion, and nausea."
   2. "Tamoxifen will help you manage your nausea and vomiting associated with chemotherapy. It may cause you to be a little sleepy and constipated, and to have dry eyes."
   3. "Tamoxifen is used to treat your breast cancer. It will help stop the tumor from growing. You may have some nausea, vomiting, and hot flashes from this drug."
   4. "Tamoxifen is an antiulcer medication. Constipation is the major side effect."

31. An adult has terminal cancer. She is receiving morphine sulfate by PCA. She is grimacing and moaning occasionally. She sleeps for short intervals. Her respiratory rate is 20, heart rate 100, and BP 140/90. Which is the most accurate assessment of this client's pain?
   1. As long as the client is sleeping for short periods, the pain is manageable.
   2. The client may be hurting some, but her respirations should not be depressed any further.
   3. The client may need additional pain medication or an increase in dosage.
   4. As long as the client does not voice complaints of pain, the nurse can assume she is comfortable.

32. A nine-year-old child fell off her bicycle and was seen in the emergency room for a mild concussion. The x-rays and physical exam were normal and the child was discharged. Which statement indicates the parents have a need for further instruction?
   1. "I should let her sleep as much as possible since she needs the rest."
   2. "I should report any vomiting episodes."
   3. "She should be seen in one or two days for a follow-up exam."
   4. "I can give her Tylenol (acetaminophen) as needed for pain."

33. Ms. B. is seen in the outpatient medical clinic for an upper respiratory infection. The physician prescribes erythromycin 500 mg po q 8h. Which statement indicates Ms. B. understands the possible side effects of erythromycin?

1. "I may have to increase my theophylline dose while I'm taking this medication."
2. "Erythromycin is supposed to cause constipation, so I should take it with a glass of fruit juice."
3. "Taking antibiotics may cause me to get a yeast infection."
4. "This drug may cause me to feel lightheaded when I stand up."

34. An infant is being treated for talipes equinovarus. Which statement by the child's mother indicates the best understanding of the casting process?
   1. "My child will have successive casts until the desired results are achieved."
   2. "Wearing a cast is very painful, so I'll need to medicate her every four hours."
   3. "Once the cast is on, it will remain on until the deformity is corrected."
   4. "My child will be immobilized and confined to an infant seat."

35. The nurse is caring for an adult client with cirrhosis. The best explanation for the development of edema is that it is due to
   1. shunting of the blood from the portal vessels into vessels with lower pressure.
   2. inadequate formation, use, and storage of vitamins A, C, and K.
   3. decreased concentration of plasma albumin.
   4. decreased production of aldosterone, causing sodium and water retention.

36. A man is admitted to the nursing care unit with a diagnosis of cirrhosis. He has a long history of alcohol dependence. During the late evening following his admission, he becomes increasingly disoriented and agitated. Which of the following would the client be least likely to experience?
   1. Diaphoresis and tremors.
   2. Increased blood pressure and heart rate.
   3. Illusions.
   4. Delusions of grandeur.

37. The nurse is caring for an adult client who is scheduled for an intravenous pyelogram (IVP). Which nursing intervention is most essential?
   1. Encourage large amounts of fluids prior to the test.
   2. Assess for any indications of allergies.
   3. Administer a laxative.
   4. Restrict fluids only in clients with marginal renal reserve or uncontrolled diabetes.

38. Jenny, age seven, has the chickenpox. Her mother calls a nurse friend to find out when Jenny can return to school. What is the best response for the nurse to make?
   1. All the lesions must be completely gone before contact with others is resumed.
   2. Within two to three weeks, the itching should be under control and good hand

washing established so that contact with others can be started.

3. Jenny can return six days after the first lesions appear, because the crusts will be formed.

4. Jenny must first learn to cough with her mouth covered, put tissues in the trash, and wash her hands after touching her nose and mouth.

39. A one-year-old child has a staph skin infection. Her brother has also developed the same infection. Which behavior by the children is most likely to have caused the transmission of the organism?
1. Bathing together.
2. Coughing on each other.
3. Sharing pacifiers.
4. Eating off the same plate.

40. The nurse is caring for a client who has a nasogastric tube attached to low wall suction. The suction is not working. Which is the nurse least likely to note when assessing the client?
1. Client vomits.
2. Client has a distended abdomen.
3. There is no nasogastric output in the last two hours.
4. Large amounts of nasogastric output.

41. Mr. I. was placed in four-point restraints three hours ago after he attempted to hit a nurse. Which observation by the nurse is the best indication that Mr. I.'s restraints could be discontinued?
1. Mr. I. has had one hand and one leg free for the past hour and has made no aggressive moves.
2. Mr. I. apologizes to the nurse and explains that he doesn't want to hurt anyone.
3. The nurse has explained the importance of not striking out in anger and Mr. I. verbalized understanding.
4. The medication administered to Mr. I. has been effective and he is now sleeping.

42. The nurse is planning care for a client who has just had a renal biopsy. Which would the nurse expect?
1. The client's urine will be red.
2. The client will experience severe excruciating pain in the flank that radiates to the groin.
3. The client will be encouraged to drink at least 3000 ml of fluid per day.
4. The client will ambulate four hours after the procedure.

43. The nurse is planning care for an adult client who has just undergone a liver biopsy. Which nursing action is of highest priority?
1. Making sure the client can void right away.
2. Measuring and recording the client's blood pressure, pulse, and respiratory rate every 10 to 20 minutes.

3. Positioning the client on his left side with a pillow placed under his costal margin.
4. Ambulating the client to the chair, placing a pillow against his abdomen.

44. The following clients are on a medical surgical nursing care unit:
359–1) Mr. A., 59, had an exploratory laparotomy with permanent colostomy two days ago. He has an IV, PCA, indwelling urinary catheter, and nasogastric drainage to low wall suction. He is receiving IV push Decadron.
359–2) Mr. B., 85, suffered a cerebrovascular accident one week ago. He has a private sitter because he is confused. He has left-sided paralysis.
360–1) Mrs. C., 35, is a 23-hour admit for a myelogram. She is ready for discharge.
360–2) Miss D., 29, has severe asthma. She is experiencing some respiratory difficulty. She is on an aminophylline drip and IV steroids.
361–1) Mrs. E., 75, a newly diagnosed diabetic, requires reinforcement about insulin administration.
361–2) Mrs. F., 95, was admitted from a nursing home with dehydration and hypokalemia. She will be receiving KCl 10 mEq IV in 50 ml D5W × 3.
These clients will be assigned to one LPN and one RN. Which is the best assignment?
1. RN: 359–1, 359–2, 360–1;
   LPN: 360–2, 361–1, 361–2.
2. RN: 359–1, 360–2, 361–2;
   LPN: 359–2, 360–1, 361–1.
3. RN: 360–2, 361–1, 361–2;
   LPN: 359–1, 359–2, 360–1.
4. RN: 360–1, 360–2, 361–1;
   LPN: 359–1, 359–2, 361–2.

45. Zantac is ordered for an adult client. The nurse mistakenly administered Xanax. What is the most appropriate action for the nurse to take?
1. Notify the physician and document in the nurse's notes that the physician was notified of the error.
2. Notify the supervisor, complete a medication error incident report, and document in the nurse's notes that an incident report was completed.
3. Notify the house supervisor, assess client carefully, and document only if adverse or untoward effects occur.
4. Notify the physician, complete an incident report, and document the notification of the physician and any assessments made.

46. A client who has ascites is admitted to the hospital and will be undergoing a paracentesis. What should be included in the nursing care plan?
1. Monitor client closely for evidence of vascular collapse.

2. Place client in Trendelenburg position for the procedure.
3. Encourage client to drink plenty of fluids to distend the bladder prior to the procedure.
4. Have client remain on bed rest for 24 hours following the procedure.

47. An adult underwent an exploratory laparotomy two days ago. The physician has just written an order for a soft diet. The nurse assessed the client and did not hear bowel sounds in any quadrant. What is the best nursing action?
1. Follow the physician's order and feed the client.
2. Cancel the physician's order and make the client NPO.
3. Order clear liquids for the client.
4. Notify the physician that the client does not have bowel sounds at this time.

48. Mr. C. is receiving O_2 at 3 liters per nasal cannula. His roommate lights a cigarette and tosses the match, catching the curtain on fire. What is the priority action for the nurse?
1. Turn off the oxygen.
2. Sound the fire alarm.
3. Try to extinguish the flames.
4. Remove the clients from the room.

49. An 84-year-old male patient has been bedridden for two weeks. Which of the following complaints by the patient indicates to the nurse that he is developing a complication of immobility?
1. Stiffness of the right ankle joint.
2. Soreness of the gums.
3. Short-term memory loss.
4. Decreased appetite.

50. Mrs. J. has been diagnosed with cervical cancer and will be undergoing internal radiation in addition to surgery. The nurse is planning Mrs. J.'s nursing care. Which is least appropriate in maintaining a safe environment?
1. Minimizing staff contact with the client.
2. Utilizing required shielding.
3. Encouraging staff to stay at the foot of the bed or at the entrance to the room.
4. Wearing isolation gowns when entering the room.

51. The lab results of a 68-year-old male reveal an elevated titer of *Helicobacter pylori*. Which of the following statements, if made by the nurse, indicates an understanding of this data?
1. "Treatment will include Pepto-Bismol and antibiotics."
2. "No treatment is necessary at this time."
3. "This result indicates a gastric cancer caused by the organism."
4. "Surgical treatment is indicated."

52. Which of the following nursing interventions indicate an understanding on the part of the nurse concerning proper care of pressure ulcers?

1. Rub reddened skin to increase circulation.
2. Use a heat lamp four times a day to dry the wound surface.
3. Cleanse a noninfected pressure ulcer with isotonic saline.
4. Cleanse a noninfected pressure ulcer with povodone-iodine.

53. Mrs. A. is scheduled for a mammogram. The nurse calls her the day before the test to reinforce mammogram preparation information and answer any questions. Which statement made by Mrs. A. best indicates that she understands the proper preparation for a mammogram?
1. "I know that I can't use deodorant, so I will use powder instead that morning."
2. "I should eat a low-fat diet today and drink extra water."
3. "I should not use deodorant, powders, or creams under my arms."
4. "The technician will be able to tell me immediately if my mammogram is okay."

54. A client has been placed in blood and body fluid isolation. The nurse is instructing auxiliary personnel in the correct procedures. Which statement by the nursing assistant indicates the best understanding of the correct protocol for blood and body fluid isolation?
1. Masks should be worn with all client contact.
2. Gloves should be worn for contact with nonintact skin, mucous membranes, or soiled items.
3. Isolation gowns are not needed.
4. A private room is always indicated.

55. Autonomic dysreflexia may be manifested by flushed skin above the level of the lesion, pallor below; severe hypertension; tachycardia; and piloerection. These symptoms may best be explained by:
1. parasympathetic nervous system stimulation with release of epinephrine.
2. sympathetic nervous system hyperactivity with release of norepinephrine.
3. disruption in the communication between upper motor neurons and lower motor neurons.
4. Muscles served by a lower motor neuron no longer receive stimuli and are unable to contract.

56. An adult client is to participate in a double-blind research study of a new medication. Which statement by the client indicates that the client does not understand the study risks?
1. "I can drop out of the study at any time."
2. "I must sign an informed consent form to be in the study."
3. "They will tell me exactly what medication I am getting."

4. "My confidentiality will be protected in the study."

57. Mrs. M. underwent a D&C under general anesthesia. She was placed in lithotomy position during surgery. Because she was placed in lithotomy position, what assessment is essential in the immediate postoperative period?
   1. Check pulses.
   2. Check presence of sensation in lower extremities.
   3. Check for foot drop.
   4. Check blood pressure.

58. Mrs. C. will have to change the dressing on her injured right leg twice a day. The dressing will be a sterile dressing, using 4 × 4s, normal saline irrigant, and abdominal pads. Which statement best indicates that Mrs. C. understands the importance of maintaining asepsis?
   1. "If I drop the 4 × 4s on the floor, I can use them as long as they are not soiled."
   2. "If I drop the 4 × 4s on the floor, I can use them if I rinse them with sterile normal saline."
   3. "If I question the sterility of any dressing material, I should not use it."
   4. "I should put on my sterile gloves, then open the bottle of saline to soak the 4 × 4s."

59. Mr. T., a 16-year-old client, has his arm in suspension traction. Which nursing assessment is highest priority?
   1. Skin integrity.
   2. Neurovascular status of the affected extremity.
   3. Level of discomfort.
   4. Knowledge about his injury.

60. A 74-year-old client has been admitted with a three-day history of severe diarrhea. The nurse is assessing for fluid volume deficit. Which findings are seen in the client with a fluid volume deficit?
   1. Pedal edema.
   2. Orthostatic hypotension and tachycardia.
   3. Increased urine output.
   4. Elastic skin turgor.

61. The nurse is assessing a client who is developing slow progressive hydrocephalus. Which is the nurse least likely to find in the assessment?
   1. Client reports a headache.
   2. Client reports blurred vision.
   3. Rapid thready pulse.
   4. Decreased level of consciousness.

62. While assessing the client with a history of allergic asthma, the nurse questions the client about what precipitates an attack. Which is the client's response least likely to include?
   1. Climate changes.
   2. Exposure to animal dander.
   3. Exposure to high pollen and mold counts.

4. Seasonal changes.

63. A four-year-old child is admitted with acute epiglottitis. Which is of highest priority as the nurse plans care?
   1. Assessing the airway frequently.
   2. Turning, coughing, and deep breathing.
   3. Administering cough medicine as ordered.
   4. Encouraging the child to eat.

64. A young child with bronchial asthma is admitted for the second time in one month. Cystic fibrosis is suspected. Which physiological assessment is most likely to be seen in the child with cystic fibrosis?
   1. Expectoration of large amounts of thin, frothy mucus with coughing, and bubbling rhonchi for lung sounds.
   2. High serum sodium chloride levels and low sodium chloride levels in the sweat.
   3. Large, loose, foul-smelling stools with normal frequency or a chronic diarrhea of unformed stools.
   4. Obesity from malabsorption of fats and polycythemia from poor oxygenation of tissues.

65. Mrs. B.'s physician has prescribed tetracycline 500 mg po q6h. While assessing Mrs. B.'s nursing history for allergies, the nurse notes that Mrs. B. is also taking oral contraceptives. What is the most appropriate initial nursing intervention?
   1. Administer the dose of tetracycline.
   2. Notify the physician that Mrs. B. is taking oral contraceptives.
   3. Tell Mrs. B. she should stop taking oral contraceptives since they are inactivated by tetracycline.
   4. Tell Mrs. B. to use another form of birth control for at least two months.

66. A client with an acute exacerbation of rheumatoid arthritis is admitted to the hospital for treatment. Which drug, used to treat clients with rheumatoid arthritis, has both an anti-inflammatory and immunosuppressive effect?
   1. Gold sodium thiomalate (Myochrysine)
   2. Azathioprine (Imuran)
   3. Prednisone (Deltasone)
   4. Naproxen (Naprosyn)

67. Which finding would alert the nurse to potential problems in a newly delivered term infant of a mother whose blood type is O negative?
   1. Pallor.
   2. Negative direct Coombs.
   3. Infant's blood type is O negative.
   4. Resting heart rate of 155.

68. A ten-year-old is admitted to the hospital with sickle cell crisis. Which client goal is most appropriate for this child? The client will
   1. participate in daily aerobic exercise program.

2. take an antibiotic until the temperature is 98.6°F.
3. increase fluid intake.
4. utilize cold compresses to control pain.

69. The nurse is caring for a client who has had a total gastrectomy. The client complains of weakness, palpitations, cramping pains, and diarrhea. He is also experiencing reactive hypoglycemia. What is the best explanation for these signs and symptoms?
   1. Rapid distention of the jejunal loop anastomosed to the stomach.
   2. Lack of fluid intake at mealtime.
   3. There is only a small opening from the gastric remnant to the jejunum.
   4. The hypotonic intestinal contents draw extracellular fluid from the circulating blood volume into the jejunum to dilute the high concentration of electrolytes and sugars.

70. An adult presents with severe rectal bleeding, 16 diarrheal stools a day, severe abdominal pain, tenesmus, and dehydration. Because of these symptoms the nurse should be alert for complications associated with which of these diseases?
   1. Crohn's disease.
   2. Ulcerative colitis.
   3. Diverticulitis.
   4. Peritonitis.

71. Mr. B. underwent a below-the-knee amputation four days ago. He is complaining of burning, crushing pain in his amputated foot. What is the best action for the nurse to take in relation to administering his ordered pain medication?
   1. Explain to Mr. B. that he really is not having pain and encourage him to wait until later for his pain medication.
   2. Acknowledge Mr. B.'s pain and administer the pain medication.
   3. Acknowledge Mr. B.'s pain but tell him he really shouldn't use pain medication for his pain.
   4. Explain to Mr. B. that he really is not having pain and administer his pain medication.

72. Mr. C. underwent a right below-the-knee amputation two days ago. He tells the nurse, "I must be crazy, my right foot hurts so bad. It's cramping and burning. I can't stand it. I must be crazy." What is the most appropriate nursing action?
   1. Tell Mr. C. that this is temporary and it will eventually go away.
   2. Explain to Mr. C. that he really is not having pain and ask if he'd like to see a chaplain to help him deal with the loss of his limb.
   3. Explain to Mr. C. that phantom pain is a frequently occurring complication

following amputation and reassure him that he is not crazy.
   4. Reassure him that he is not going crazy and that this phantom pain will go away.

73. An adult has undergone surgery for a detached retina. What is essential to include in the postoperative care plan?
   1. Up ad lib with assistance.
   2. Notify physician of severe pain that does not respond to pain medication, and/or severe nausea and vomiting.
   3. Bed rest with bed flat.
   4. Notify physician of any mucoid discharge.

74. A ten-year-old is admitted to the rehabilitation center for gait training and use of adaptive devices. He has cerebral palsy and a history of falls related to spasticity. Which of the following nursing goals has highest priority?
   1. Prevent deformity.
   2. Prevent physical injury.
   3. Establish locomotion.
   4. Ensure a balanced diet.

75. A two-year-old is admitted to the hospital with meningitis. In planning his care, the nurse's highest priority is to
   1. inform the parents of the child's condition.
   2. maintain a quiet environment.
   3. monitor for changes in intracranial pressure.
   4. maintain bed rest.

76. Which of the following statements, if made by a 43-year-old female, would indicate to the nurse in a cancer health screening clinic that further follow-up is needed?
   1. "My diet is low in fat and high in residue."
   2. "My mother and uncle died of colon cancer."
   3. "I have a yearly rectal exam."
   4. "I was born and raised in suburbia."

77. A two-and-a-half-year-old child is hospitalized for severe otitis media. He was toilet trained prior to being hospitalized but is having "accidents" now that he is in the hospital. What is the best explanation for this change in behavior?
   1. It is unrealistic for a child at age two and a half to be toilet trained.
   2. The nurse did not show the child where the bathroom is located.
   3. A child of this age needs a parent available to assist with toileting.
   4. It is normal for a child to experience regressive behavior due to the stress of hospitalization.

78. The nurse has been instructing the parents of a toddler about nutrition. Which of the following statements best indicates the parents' understanding of an appropriate diet for a toddler?

1. "It's unusual for a toddler to be a picky eater."
2. "A multivitamin each day will meet my child's nutritional needs."
3. "A toddler needs servings from each food group daily."
4. "Toddlers should still be eating prepared junior foods."

79. The nurse is caring for a woman who is having labor induced with an oxytocin (Pitocin) drip. Which assessment of the client indicates there is a problem?
    1. The fetal heart rate is 160 beats per minute.
    2. The woman has three contractions in five minutes.
    3. Contraction duration is 60 seconds.
    4. Early fetal heart rate decelerations are occurring.

80. Mr. and Mrs. M. attended Lamaze childbirth classes. Mrs. M. is now in labor. During transition, her husband has her take three cleansing breaths followed by four slow, deep breaths with each contraction. She is experiencing much discomfort with her contractions. Because she is uncomfortable, what action is most appropriate for the nurse?
    1. Demonstrate to Mrs. M. a different breathing pattern during contractions.
    2. Ask the physician for an order for pain medication.
    3. Have Mr. M. take a break and instruct Mrs. M. in another breathing pattern.
    4. Leave the couple alone as they have their routine established.

81. The nurse is teaching childbirth education classes. What topic should be included during the second trimester?
    1. Overview of conception.
    2. Medication usage and breastfeeding.
    3. Infant care.
    4. Strategies to relieve the discomforts of pregnancy.

82. A woman 30 weeks pregnant is admitted to the hospital with a diagnosis of placenta previa. She and the fetus are stable. To help achieve the goal of avoiding premature delivery, the nurse anticipates the client will
    1. receive a blood transfusion.
    2. be placed on bed rest.
    3. receive betamethasone.
    4. avoid sexual intercourse upon discharge.

83. A 37-week-gestation neonate has just been born to a woman with insulin-dependent diabetes mellitus and is admitted to the term nursery. Which of the following is most essential when planning immediate care for the infant?
    1. Glucose monitoring.
    2. Daily weights.
    3. Supplemental formula feedings.

4. An apnea monitor.

84. The nurse is caring for a woman in labor who suddenly complains of dizziness, becomes pale, and has a 30-point drop in her blood pressure with an increase in pulse rate. The most appropriate initial nursing action is to
    1. turn her to her left side.
    2. have her breathe into a paper bag.
    3. notify her physician.
    4. increase her intravenous fluids.

85. A client on the labor and delivery unit has spontaneous rupture of membranes at 2 cm dilation. The nurse notes that the fetal heart rate has dropped to 80 and suspects a prolapsed cord. The most appropriate immediate action for the nurse is to
    1. call for an emergency cesarean section.
    2. place the woman in knee chest position.
    3. place the expelled cord back into the vagina.
    4. open up the main intravenous line.

86. A 23-year-old woman is 25% over her ideal weight of 140 pounds. She would like to lose weight before becoming pregnant. The woman is two months into her weight loss program. Which indicates she is following proper weight management principles? The woman
    1. carefully selects only carbohydrate and fat choices for meals.
    2. has lost a total of four pounds.
    3. is now 5% over her ideal weight.
    4. goes to beginning aerobics three times a week.

87. The nurse is caring for a client admitted with herpes zoster, or shingles. What should the nurse expect to find during the initial assessment?
    1. Rhinorrhea, small red lesions including some with vesicles that are widespread over the face and body.
    2. A painful vesicular eruption following a nerve pathway.
    3. Blisters on the lips and in the corners of the mouth.
    4. Painful fluid-filled vesicles in the genital area.

88. The mother of a four-month-old who received his second DTP immunization yesterday calls the office nurse to report he has a temperature of 104°F and a hard red area as big as a quarter on his thigh. The best interpretation of these data is that the child
    1. is reacting normally to the immunization.
    2. may be allergic to the vaccine.
    3. is developing symptoms of the disease.
    4. has developed a secondary infection.

89. The nurse is administering insulin to an adult client. Which is the correct method of administering insulin?

1. Administer via intramuscular injection holding the needle at a 90° angle.
2. Inject via Z track intramuscular injection.
3. Use a ½ inch 27-gauge needle at a 90° angle into subcutaneous tissue.
4. Inject at a 10° angle into the intradermal area.

90. The nurse is caring for a client from an Asian culture. The client refuses to look at the nurse and does not maintain eye contact. The best interpretation of this behavior is that
   1. the client is angry at the nurse.
   2. the nurse is not effective in communicating with the client.
   3. the client does not understand English.
   4. the client is treating the nurse with respect.

91. A 58-year-old male client tells the office nurse that his wife does not let him change his colostomy bag himself. Which response by the nurse indicates an understanding of the situation?
   1. "Your wife's need to help you is a reality you should accept."
   2. "Do you think your wife might benefit from counseling?"
   3. "You feel you need privacy when changing your colostomy?"
   4. "Have you discussed the situation with your doctor?"

92. Which of the following nursing interventions would the nurse perform prior to administering a tube feeding?
   1. Check for placement by aspirating for gastric contents with a syringe and test pH with Testape.
   2. Advance the tube 3–5 inches prior to the feeding.
   3. Instruct the client to swallow.
   4. Instill 30 ml of sterile water into the tube.

93. The nurse is caring for an adult who is one-day post-op following an abdominal cholecystectomy. Which finding by the nurse indicates the patient-controlled analgesia (PCA) is controlling her pain?
   1. The client's vital signs have returned to preoperative status.
   2. The client is observed laughing and talking with her family.
   3. The client rates her pain as 8 on a 0–10 pain scale.
   4. The client states that she is comfortable.

94. An adult male is admitted to a medical floor with a diagnosis of "sepsis, dehydration." Which finding by the nurse indicates that he is now rehydrated within normal limits?
   1. His urine output is 40 ml per hour.
   2. His skin "tents" when it is pinched.
   3. The specific gravity of his urine is 1.001.
   4. His apical pulse is 120 and his blood pressure is 70/40.

95. Which statement by a 57-year-old postoperative client suggests that he is ready to learn how to care for his new ileostomy?
   1. "I think I'll be able to wear one of those pouches my doctor told me about without any problems. What do you think, Nurse?"
   2. "I want to know all about my ileostomy, right after you give me my pain medication."
   3. "I suppose I have to learn how to take care of this thing eventually, but it sure is disgusting."
   4. "My wife's always been the one to do the nursing in our house. She'll come in and learn how to take care of it and I'll watch."

96. An adult who is one day post abdominal cholecystectomy complains to the nurse that she is having abdominal pain. The nurse goes in to assess her pain utilizing a visual analog scale. Which action by the nurse would be initially most important?
   1. Have the client describe the type and location of pain.
   2. Check the chart for the pain medication order.
   3. Assess the client's abdomen.
   4. Ask the client to locate the pain on a linear scale.

97. An 87-year-old widow was hospitalized for treatment of chronic renal disease. She lives with her daughter and son-in-law and their family, who are very supportive. She is now ready for discharge. The doctor has ordered a high-carbohydrate, low-protein, low-sodium diet for her and the family has asked for assistance in planning low-sodium meals. Which of the following choices best reflects the predischarge information the nurse should provide for the client's family regarding the low-sodium diet?
   1. Avoid canned and processed foods, do not use salt replacements, substitute herbs and spices for salt in cooking, and when seasoning foods, call a dietitian for help.
   2. Use potassium salts in place of table salt when cooking and seasoning foods, read the labels on packaged foods to determine sodium content, and avoid snack foods.
   3. Limit milk and dairy products, cook separate meals that are low in sodium, and encourage increased fluid intake.
   4. Avoid eating in a restaurant, soak vegetables well before cooking to remove sodium, omit all canned foods, and remove salt shakers from table.

98. An adult client is being treated in the burn unit for partial and full-thickness burns of the left foot, ankle, and leg. Skin autografts are taken from the right thigh and a skin graft is performed. The nurse planning care for the client on return from the operating room includes which of the following nursing interventions?

1. Change dressing on graft sites every shift.
2. Cover donor site with fine mesh gauze and expose to air.
3. Lubricate donor site with skin cream every shift.
4. Hydrotherapy to graft sites daily.

99. A client with antisocial personality uses manipulation to gain access to a vending room close to the entrance of the hospital, where he attempts to leave the hospital grounds. Which is the best nursing intervention for manipulative behavior?
   1. Place client in restraints for attempting to escape.
   2. Help client identify patterns of manipulative behavior and the consequences as determined by the team plan.
   3. Deal with each incident of client manipulation on an individualized basis, dependent on the context of the situation and the nurse involved.
   4. Restrict the client from all unit activities, to provide time for reflection on social behavior.

100. A 67-year-old was admitted with a diagnosis of left-sided heart failure. Furosemide (Lasix) 80 mg was given slowly by IV push. The nurse is assessing the client following administration of the medication. Which finding indicates that the furosemide (Lasix) is not having the desired effect?
   1. Oliguria.
   2. Decrease in blood pressure.
   3. Absence of rales.
   4. Polydipsia.

Answers and Rationales for Practice Test 2

ANSWER	RATIONALE	NP	CN	CL
#1. 1.	**Having a picture ID for each resident allows the nurse to positively identify the client. This helps to decrease errors in a population that may not always be able to respond appropriately.**	As	Sa/1	Ap
2.	Arm bands are helpful but residents may remove them.			
3.	Residents in nursing homes frequently wander and get in the wrong beds.			
4.	Names on the room door are not the most appropriate way to identify residents in a nursing home. Residents in nursing homes frequently wander and get in the wrong beds.			
#2. 2.	**A complete drug history on every perioperative client is essential because of potential reactions to drugs. Drug hypersensitivity and allergic reactions must be assessed before preoperative medications are administered.**	As	Ph/9	Co
1.	His ability to cough and deep breathe should be assessed earlier so that further teaching can take place if needed. Once preoperative medications are administered, the client's ability to retain information is impaired.			
3.	The client's understanding should be assessed earlier so the nurse can do further teaching if indicated.			
4.	While it is optimal to have the family present, medication should be given as ordered so that the timing of the peak action is most beneficial to the client.			
#3. 4.	**"Why" questions are challenging and often appear blaming.**	As	Ps/6	An
1.	The nurse should open discussion on the amount of alcohol consumed.			
2.	Multiple drug use is common and must be included in the assessment.			
3.	Clients who use alcohol may have a variety of physical illnesses, and that information must be included in the assessment.			
#4. 1.	**The ability to use relaxation is basic to treatment of phobia.**	Pl	Ps/6	Ap
2.	Clients with phobias are resistant to insight therapy.			
3.	Riding the elevator accompanied by the nurse is an appropriate long-term goal.			

		NP	CN	CL
	4. Role playing may be appropriate after the client has learned relaxation.			
#5. 3.	**Work and family life are usually both affected by posttraumatic stress disorder.**	As	Ps/6	An
	1. Symptoms of anxiety and panic are common with posttraumatic stress disorder.			
	2. Recurrent dreams about the traumatic event are a cardinal symptom of posttraumatic stress disorder.			
	4. Alcohol or drug abuse is a common symptom of posttraumatic stress disorder.			
#6. 4.	**Mr. K. has typical symptoms of a panic attack; especially indicative of panic is his inability to focus on the nurse's questions or other current events.**	An	Ps/5	An
	1. Mild anxiety enhances reasoning ability.			
	2. Moderate anxiety may reduce the ability to focus attention but is manageable.			
	3. Severe anxiety impairs problem solving, but behavior focused on obtaining relief is possible.			
#7. 2.	**Since alprazolam is given to decrease anxiety, assessment of the client's anxiety level is an appropriate evaluation.**	Ev	Ps/5	Ap
	1. Asking Ms. D. if she remembers not to drive or use alcohol evaluates the client's knowledge of the side effects of alprazolam, not the effectiveness of the drug.			
	3. Using a relaxation tape may be desirable for Ms. D., but suggesting a tape does not evaluate the effectiveness of the drug.			
	4. Establishing the presence or absence of side effects such as nausea does not tell whether the drug is effective.			
#8. 4.	**Isolation is separating unacceptable feelings from one's thoughts.**	An	Ps/5	An
	1. Clients using denial refuse to acknowledge that a stressful event has occurred. This client is isolating the feelings, not denying the event.			
	2. Conversion is changing unacceptable feelings into physical symptoms.			
	3. Introjection is taking in feelings or attitudes of another. There is no evidence that the client has done this.			
#9. 2.	**Delusions are fixed false beliefs. They occur when the client's unacceptable feelings are projected and rationalized.**	An	Ps/5	An
	1. Ideas of reference occur when the client assumes that events such as a news broadcast are directly related to him. There is no evidence that this has occurred here, although it would not be uncommon for a client such as Mr. P.			
	3. Hallucinations involve sensory perceptions without stimuli. There is no evidence that Mr. P. is hallucinating.			
	4. Dissociation involves a change in the consciousness such as amnesia. There is no evidence that Mr. P. has amnesia.			
#10. 1.	**The nutritional problem in mania is the client's decreased attention span and difficulty sitting still long enough to eat. Snack foods that are easy to eat and have good nutritional value may prevent malnutrition until the client is in better control.**	Pl	Ps/6	Ap
	2. The problem is decreased attention span, not decreased appetite at meals. Limiting snacks will not help the client eat better at meals and may limit opportunities to provide adequate nutrition.			
	3. The cafeteria offers too much stimuli for a client with mania and may further increase distractibility and decrease intake.			
	4. A client in the manic phase of bipolar disorder usually lacks the attention span to carry through with goal-directed behavior, even when a reward is offered.			
#11. 4.	**Involvement in reality may decrease Mr. T.'s preoccupation with his hallucinations.**	Im	Ps/5	Ap
	1. The nurse needs to make an effort to help Mr. T. regain contact with reality, not continue with his hallucination.			

2. Medication is indicated only if the client becomes more agitated and poses a danger to himself or others. Other interventions should be tried first.

3. A judgmental approach doesn't solve the problem and may increase Mr. T.'s hallucinations and agitation. He needs involvement in a real world more pleasant than his hallucinations.

		NP	CN	CL
#12. 2.	**Clients with depression often have unrealistic expectations for themselves and cannot set goals that are possible to reach. Severely depressed clients may be unable to visualize any future and thus are unable to set any goals.**	Ev	Ps/6	An

1. Compliance with the medication program does not necessarily indicate improvement in the depression.

3. Support by the client's spouse is desirable but does not indicate improvement in the client.

4. Ventilation will be helpful for clients with depression but may not indicate improvement. Even severely depressed clients talk about hopelessness.

#13. 2.	**Baseline data are needed to assess the seriousness of the client's condition and determine the next actions.**	Im	Ph/10	Ap

1. Whether the client is on precautions is irrelevant at this time. Priority must be given to emergency treatment.

3. When the immediate emergency care is done and the client is stable, it is appropriate to assess precipitating factors. It is not the first priority in this situation.

4. To determine the amount of medication consumed would be helpful in the emergency treatment, but assessing the client is the first priority. The pill bottle should be saved and sent with the client to the emergency facility. Once the client is assessed and emergency care is under way, efforts should be made to ascertain how much medication was available to the client.

#14. 3.	**Epistaxis (nosebleed) occurs in the first trimester. It is related to capillary dilation.**	As	He/3	An

1. Frequency is a common complaint due to bladder neck stretching and pressure from the uterus. Dysuria is seen with a urinary tract infection and is not normal.

2. Colostrum secretion may occur, but not until 16 weeks gestation.

4. Dependent edema may occur in the third trimester of pregnancy from an increase in venous pressure and a decrease in venous return.

#15. 2.	**The normal respiratory rate is between 30 and 60, characterized by shallow, irregular breaths, often interrupted by short periods of apnea lasting 5 to 15 seconds.**	As	He/3	An

1. Hypertonia is an abnormal finding and may indicate neurologic impairment or drug withdrawal.

3. The average normal head circumference is 33–35 cm. Microcephaly is to be considered with less than 32.5 cm.

4. A lusty cry should be evident but a high-pitched or shrill cry may indicate neurologic impairment or drug withdrawal.

#16. 4.	**Massaging the fundus is most important since her uterus is soft and higher than normal. Fundal massage causes uterine contractions leading to vasoconstriction, which will lead to decreased bleeding. Complete saturation of two pads within one hour suggests hemorrhage.**	An	He/3	An

1. She needs a pad change for an infection-free environment, but immediate care is to reduce the bleeding through massage.

2. There is inadequate information to indicate whether her bladder is full, which can be associated with increased bleeding. However, the fundus is soft but not deviated. The fundus is often deviated to one side when the bladder is full.

3. Intravenous fluids are important to replace lost volume, but bleeding must be controlled first.

ANSWER	RATIONALE	NP	CN	CL

#17. 4. **Repeated hemarthrosis may result in flexion contractures and joint fixation. During bleeding episodes, the affected joint must be elevated and immobilized in order to prevent the crippling effects of bleeding.**   Pl Ph/9 Ap

    1. Passive range of motion exercises are helpful in preventing contractures. Active range of motion is contraindicated during a bleeding episode.

    2. The child should have prophylactic dental care to prevent the need for operative dentistry. This is not a priority action during a bleeding episode.

    3. Genetic counseling is appropriate for families. However, it is not a priority action during a bleeding episode.

#18. 2. **Tap water enemas are contraindicated in children, as the hypotonic solution can cause rapid fluid shift and fluid overload.**   Pl Ph/7 Ap

    1. Abdominal measurements every four hours should be a part of the plan of care to determine abdominal distention due to fecal retention secondary to lack of parasympathetic innervation to the large intestine.

    3. The surgery usually performed for an infant with Hirschsprung's disease is a colostomy. It is appropriate to start teaching the parents about colostomy care.

    4. Intake and output are essential for this infant, who does not pass stool normally.

#19. 3. **Encouraging voiding every two to three hours prevents overdistention of the bladder and a compromised blood supply to the bladder wall.**   Pl Ph/9 Ap

    1. Testing urine for protein with a dipstick is not appropriate. Cystitis is an inflammatory process with bacteria in the urine. Protein is not present in the urine in the client with cystitis.

    2. The woman with cystitis should be encouraged to drink plenty of fluids to flush out the bacteria. NPO is contraindicated.

    4. Showers are preferred to tub bathing because bacteria in the bath water may enter the urethra.

#20. 2. **125 ml/hr of D_5LR (125 ml × 8 hr) is 1000 ml. 1 ounce of ice chips is 30 ml. NG irrigant 15 ml q 2 hr (15 ml × 4) is 60 ml for a total of 1090 ml. Output is 850 ml urine and 200 ml of nasogastric drainage for a total of 1050 ml.**   Im Ph/7 Ap

    1. You forgot to multiply the hourly IV rate times eight hours and the NG irrigant times 4.

    3. You forgot to multiply the hourly IV rate times eight hours and the NG irrigant times 4 and convert the ounce of ice chips to ml. You added the output incorrectly.

    4. You subtracted the NG irrigant from the output and counted it as intake.

#21. 3. **The physician should be notified prior to administration of the Coumadin since ecchymotic areas and bleeding gums are adverse effects of Coumadin and may indicate overdose.**   Im Ph/8 Ap

    1. The daily dose should not be given until the physician is notified. Ecchymotic areas and bleeding gums are adverse effects of Coumadin and may indicate overdose.

    2. The daily dose should not be given until the physician is notified. Ecchymotic areas and bleeding gums are adverse effects of Coumadin and may indicate overdose.

    4. The physician must be notified when an ordered dose is withheld. Ecchymotic areas and bleeding gums are adverse effects of Coumadin and may indicate overdose.

#22. 1. **Dyskinesias (abnormal involuntary movements) are fairly common side effects of Levodopa. These can include facial grimacing, rhythmic jerking movements of the hands, head bobbing, chewing and smacking movements, and involuntary**   Ev Ph/8 Ap movements of the hand and extremities. **This is most likely due to the body's failure to readjust to disappearance of dopamine. The client may need his dose of Levodopa adjusted.**

2. A progressive program of exercise is important to increase muscle strength and prevent muscle contractures. The person with Parkinson's tends to get stiffer the longer he sits.

3. A client with Parkinson's may have problems with constipation. This may be caused by muscle weakness, lack of exercise, decreased autonomic nervous system activity, and inadequate fluid intake.

4. Clients with Parkinson's may have difficulty eating, be very slow, or have saliva buildup or drooling while eating. However, it is vital that the client be an active participant in social or recreational programs to ward off depression and withdrawal, which are very common in clients with Parkinson's. If the client enjoyed going out to eat previously, arrangements should be made for this to continue if at all possible.

#23. 3. Aspirin is an anticoagulant and increases the client's potential for further bleeding.   An   Ph/8   An

1. Gastrointestinal distress may result from large doses of aspirin, but this is not the reason aspirin is withheld in the head-injured person.

2. Large doses of aspirin may cause tinnitus, but this is not the rationale for withholding aspirin in the head-injured person.

4. Aspirin does not cause constriction of the pupils. Narcotic analgesics cause pupil constriction.

#24. 1. Injury to the hypothalamus usually leads to decreased secretion of antidiuretic hormone (ADH), which is manifested by large amounts of very dilute urine output. The hypothalamus also controls temperature. Injury causes a very high temperature.   An   Ph/10   An

2. Sepsis is unlikely with a closed head injury. The assessments are classic for hypothalamus injury.

3. Injury to the hypothalamus usually leads to decreased secretion of antidiuretic hormone (ADH), which is manifested by large amounts of very dilute urine output. The hypothalamus also controls temperature. Injury causes a very high temperature.

4. Normal saline is isotonic and would not cause these fluid shifts.

#25. 3. Leg exercises are important to help prevent calcium loss from the bones. The ideal exercises will have some resistance or weight bearing as tolerated.   An   Ph/9   An

1. Turning and positioning is vital for maintenance of skin integrity but will not prevent calcium loss from bones.

2. Fluid intake is important to help mobilize pulmonary secretions and decrease the risk of kidney stones but will not prevent brittle bones.

4. The increased milk intake may predispose the client to formation of calcium kidney stones and will not decrease loss of calcium from the bones as the calcium loss is caused by lack of weight bearing, not lack of dietary calcium.

#26. 3. The findings are typical of a healing, healthy incision.   Ev   Ph/9   An
1. There are no data to suggest the beginnings of wound infection.
2. A moderate amount of serosanguinous wound drainage may be seen at this point in the postoperative course.
4. These findings are not typical of an infected wound. An infected wound has purulent drainage and marked inflammation.

#27. 1. Clients going to the operating room ideally should have an 18-gauge catheter. This is large enough to handle blood products safely and to allow rapid administration of large amounts of fluid if indicated during the perioperative period.   Im   Ph/8   Ap

2. An 18-gauge catheter is recommended. A 20-gauge catheter is a second choice.

3. A 21-gauge needle is too small and a butterfly too unstable for a client going to surgery.

    4. A 25-gauge needle is too small.

#28. 2. Prednisone should be taken exactly as ordered. It is very important not to skip doses. Stopping the medication suddenly may result in adrenal insufficiency manifested by anorexia, nausea, fatigue, weakness, hypotension, dyspnea, and hypoglycemia. If these appear, the physician should be notified immediately as this can be life threatening. Ev Ph/8 An

    1. Prednisone may cause hypokalemia. The client should eat a diet high in protein, calcium, and potassium and low in sodium.

    3. Prednisone causes immunosuppression and may mask symptoms of infection. The client should avoid people with known contagious illnesses.

    4. The anti-inflammatory effects of prednisone may cause slowed wound healing.

#29. 4. The balloon should be checked for inflation and leaks prior to insertion, preventing repeated catheterization if the balloon fails. Im Ph/9 Ap

    1. The female client should be cleansed from front to back.

    2. The catheter should be slightly smaller than the external urinary meatus to minimize trauma and to allow secretions to drain out alongside the catheter.

    3. Strict aseptic technique should be employed.

#30. 3. Tamoxifen is indicated for use in palliative or adjunctive treatment of breast cancer, suppressing tumor growth. Tamoxifen is given following mastectomy to prevent recurrence. The most frequent side effects are nausea, vomiting, hypercalcemia, and hot flashes. Confusion, edema, and bone pain may also occur. Ev Ph/8 Ap

    1. Tamoxifen is not a vasodilator antihypertensive.

    2. Tamoxifen is not an antinausea drug.

    4. Tamoxifen is not an antiulcer medication.

#31. 3. The client is grimacing and moaning. In combination with her elevated heart rate and blood pressure, this may indicate that she has not had adequate pain relief with PCA. It could be due to her inability to activate the machine or the dose may be inadequate. If the nurse feels the client is in pain, the client should be assessed and the physician notified. Ev Ph/8 An

    1. Short intervals of sleep do not indicate that pain relief is obtained.

    2. The respiratory rate is acceptable for an adult.

    4. The client may not complain of pain for several reasons (cultural, doesn't want to be a burden, etc.) so the nurse should not assume that she is comfortable.

#32. 1. A child with a concussion should be aroused every two hours and evaluated for responsiveness. Her parents need to understand how important this is. Ev Ph/9 Ap

    2. Vomiting is a sign of rising intracranial pressure and should be reported. This statement indicates understanding.

    3. The child needs to be evaluated for delayed signs of rising intracranial pressure. This statement indicates understanding.

    4. Tylenol (acetaminophen) is the only analgesic the child can have. This statement indicates understanding.

#33. 3. Erythromycin may lead to superimposed infections including yeast infection. Ev Ph/8 Ap

    1. Erythromycin increases blood levels of theophylline and may increase toxicity from theophylline. The dose of theophylline may have to be decreased while receiving erythromycin.

    2. Erythromycin usually causes diarrhea, not constipation. The medication can be taken with food if gastrointestinal upset occurs, but fruit juices should be avoided.

    4. Feeling light-headed is not an expected side effect of erythromycin. Feeling light-headed occurs frequently with antihypertensives.

#34. 1. An appropriate treatment for talipes equinovarus is serial Ev Ph/9 An casting. **Parents should be prepared for repeat cast changes throughout the course of treatment.**

2. Although casts may feel heavy, they should not cause pain. Continuous pain needs to be reported to the physician.

3. Casts are changed every week or two until the desired results are achieved.

4. The child will not be immobile due to the cast. Activity that is appropriate for age and development should be encouraged.

#35. 3. **The late symptoms of cirrhosis can be attributed to chronic failure of liver function. The concentration of plasma albumin is reduced, leading to formation of edema.** An Ph/10 An

1. The shunting of blood into vessels with lower pressure is due to fibrotic changes in the liver. This causes development of collateral vessels, which can form varices or hemorrhoids depending on the location.

2. Inadequate function, use, and storage of vitamins A, C, and K cause signs and symptoms of deficiency, including the hemorrhagic phenomena associated with vitamin K deficiency. Vitamin K is a clotting factor.

4. Overproduction of aldosterone causes sodium and water retention.

#36. 4. **Delusions of grandeur are symptomatic of manic clients, not clients withdrawing from alcohol. The symptoms and history of alcohol abuse suggest this client is in alcohol withdrawal.** As Ps/6 Co

1. Diaphoresis and tremors occur in the first phase of alcohol withdrawal.

2. The blood pressure and heart rate increase in the first phase of alcohol withdrawal.

3. Illusions are common in persons withdrawing from alcohol. Illusions occur most often in dim artificial lighting where the environment is not perceived accurately.

#37. 2. **The client should be assessed for allergic reactions to iodine, i.e., shellfish allergy or previous allergic reaction to contrast dye materials.** As Ph/9 Ap

1. Liquids may be restricted eight to ten hours prior to the test to concentrate the urine.

3. Laxatives are sometimes administered the night before the test; however, this is not essential. Determining if the client is allergic to iodine is a much higher priority.

4. Fluids are generally not restricted in clients with marginal renal reserve, elderly clients, or clients with uncontrolled diabetes as they may not tolerate dehydration.

#38. 3. **Varicella zoster, the chickenpox virus, is found in the respiratory secretions of infected persons and also in the skin lesions that are not scabbed over. Scabs are not infectious. By six days after the rash first appears, all the lesions will be scabbed over.** Im He/4 Co

1. Brownish lesions may remain on the skin for a while after the crusts have disappeared. It is not necessary to wait that long before returning to school. Good hand washing will help to prevent the spread of the disease to others, since it is carried through respiratory secretions.

2. The itching is very severe with chickenpox and can be the cause of secondary infections of the skin and also scarring. It has no relationship to communicability.

4. Good respiratory hygiene is a good precaution with any disease spread by respiratory secretions. To prevent transmission of the disease, her lesions must also be crusted over.

#39. 1. **Direct contact is the mode of transmission for staphylococcus.** An Sa/2 An

2. Staph is not spread by coughing.

3. Staph is not spread through oral secretions. Direct contact is required.

    4. Staph is not spread through oral secretions.

#40. 4. If the nasogastric suction is not working, the nurse would not expect to see large amounts of nasogastric output.   As   Ph/9   Ap

    1. Vomiting is common because the stomach becomes overdistended.

    2. The abdomen may become distended as fluid and air build up in the stomach.

    3. If the suction is not working, there will be no nasogastric output.

#41. 1. Mr. I.'s ability to control his behavior while only partially restrained is the best indication of his ability to remain in control if he is released from the remaining restraints.   An   Sa/2   Ap

    2. Apologizing for past behavior is not the best indication of the client's ability to control future behavior.

    3. Verbalizing understanding of the need for different ways of handling aggression is an important beginning, but it is not the best indication of his ability to control his behavior now.

    4. The fact that Mr. I. has been medicated and is sleeping offers no indication of what his behavior will be when he awakens.

#42. 3. The fluid intake is maintained at 3000 ml/day to decrease hematuria, unless the client has renal insufficiency. Renal insufficiency is an indication for limiting fluid intake.   Pl   Ph/9   Ap

    1. All urine should be closely examined and compared to a prebiopsy specimen for evidence of bleeding. Gross hematuria, unless present prior to the procedure, is not usually expected.

    2. Severe flank pain radiating to the groin is usually caused by a clot in the ureter.

    4. Clients are usually kept on bed rest for 24 hours following a renal biopsy.

#43. 2. Vital signs should be checked every 10 to 20 minutes for the prescribed period or until stable. Any increase in pulse or respiration or decrease in blood pressure should be reported. The nurse should also report any complaints of pain or signs of apprehension. These signs could indicate hepatic bleeding, a frequent complication following a liver biopsy. Remember that the liver is a very vascular organ.   Pl   Ph/9   Ap

    1. Voiding immediately is not a high priority.

    3. The client should be placed on the right side with a pillow under his costal margin.

    4. The client is kept on bed rest for several hours to decrease the risk of bleeding.

#44. 2. The RN should assume care for 359-1 as he is receiving recurring IV push medication and requires teaching about his colostomy; 360-2 because of the acute problems with asthma requiring very close respiratory assessment, IV aminophylline, and steroids; 361-2 as she will be receiving IV runs of potassium and must be observed closely for signs and symptoms of fluid and electrolyte imbalances. The LPN should assume care for 359-2, 360-1, and 361-1. The LPN can teach the client going home from a myelogram and can reinforce diabetic teaching.   Pl   Sa/1   Ap

    1. The LPN can not give IV medications the client in 360-2 requires. The client in 361-2 is a newly diagnosed diabetic with teaching needs and is more appropriately assigned to the RN.

    3. The LPN can not give the IV push medication required by the client in 359-1.

    4. The LPN can not give the IV push medication required by the client in 359-1. The client in 361-2 is a newly diagnosed diabetic with teaching needs and is more appropriately assigned to the RN.

#45. 4. The physician must be notified of the medication error. An incident report should be completed. However, no record of the incident report should appear in the nurse's notes. The nurse   Im   Sa/1   Ap should document that the physician was notified and any assessments completed.

1. In addition to notifying the physician and documenting it, the nurse should complete an incident report.
2. The physician must be notified. An incident report should be completed. However, no record of the incident report should appear in the nurse's notes.
3. The physician must be notified. An incident report should be completed. However, no record of the incident report should appear in the nurse's notes.

#46. 1. Removing large amounts of fluid may cause hypotension leading to vascular collapse. The client should be monitored closely for decrease in blood pressure, increase in pulse and pallor.   Pl   Ph/9   Ap

2. The client is usually placed in an upright position on the edge of the bed or in a chair.
3. The client should be encouraged to void immediately prior to the procedure to decrease the risk of bladder puncture.
4. The client is not usually kept on bed rest for 24 hours following a paracentesis.

#47. 4. Solid food should not be given until the client has bowel sounds. The nurse should notify the physician of the assessment findings prior to feeding this client.   Im   Ph/7   Ap

1. Solid food should not be given until the client has bowel sounds. The nurse should notify the physician of the assessment findings prior to feeding this client.
2. The nurse cannot cancel a physician's order.
3. The nurse cannot cancel a physician's order.

#48. 1. Oxygen itself does not burn, but supports combustion, so a fire burns more readily in the presence of oxygen. If the client is not engulfed in flames, the nurse's priority action should be to turn off the oxygen.   Im   Sa/2   Ap

2. After the oxygen is discontinued, the RACE format should be followed: Rescue, Alarm, Contain or Extinguish, Evaluate if necessary.
3. After the oxygen is discontinued, the RACE format should be followed: Rescue, Alarm, Contain or Extinguish, Evaluate if necessary.
4. After the oxygen is discontinued, the RACE format should be followed: Rescue, Alarm, Contain or Extinguish, Evaluate if necessary.

#49. 1. Stiffness of a joint may indicate the beginning of a contracture and/or early muscle atrophy.   As   Ph/7   Co

2. Soreness of the gums is not related to immobility.
3. Short-term memory loss is not related to immobility.
4. Decreased appetite is unlikely to be related to immobility.

#50. 4. Isolation gowns offer no protection against radiation. The other choices are all correct.   Pl   Ph/9   Ap

1. Radiation is cumulative. Limiting the amount of time with the client limits the nurse's exposure to radiation.
2. Shielding decreases the amount of radiation exposure. Shielding must be made of a heavy metal.
3. The foot of the bed and the entrance to the room limit the amount of radiation exposure.

#51. 1. *Helicobacter pylori* is the organism believed to cause most peptic ulcers. The organism has multiple flagella allowing it to move through the mucous layer of the stomach thereby interfering with the local protection of the gastric mucosa against acid. Treatment with bismuth compounds (Pepto-Bismol), antibiotics and an acid-suppressing drug (ranitidine [Zantac] or omiperazole [Prilosec])   An   Ph/9   Co

ANSWER	RATIONALE	NP	CN	CL

is indicated to prevent chronic atrophic gastritis (a predisposition to cancer).

2. Treatment with bismuth, antibiotics, and acid suppressing drugs is indicated when the *H. pylori* titer is elevated.

3. An elevated *H. pylori* does not by itself indicate cancer. An untreated infection predisposes to cancer. Cancer is diagnosed with a biopsy. Most people with elevated *H. pylori* do not have gastric cancer.

4. Surgical treatment of an ulcer is indicated when medical approaches fail and the client has a bleeding ulcer.

#52. 3. A noninfected pressure ulcer should be cleansed gently with a nonionic cleanser such as isotonic saline to prevent disruption of healing. Im Ph/7 Ap

1. Rubbing reddened skin may cause breakdown of skin.

2. Pressure ulcers heal better in a moist environment. Heat lamps are no longer used in the treatment of pressure ulcers.

4. There is no need to use an antiseptic on a noninfected pressure ulcer.

#53. 3. Because aluminum chlorhydrate (found in many deodorants, powders, and creams) may mimic calcium clusters, the client is discouraged from using these the morning of the exam. Ev Ph/9 Ap

1. Because aluminum chlorhydrate (found in many deodorants, powders, and creams) may mimic calcium clusters, the client is discouraged from using these the morning of the exam.

2. There are no dietary restrictions prior to a mammogram.

4. Generally, the technician will not be able to share results of the mammogram immediately. The client usually receives results from her physician.

#54. 2. Gloves should be worn for all contact with blood and body fluids, nonintact skin and mucous membranes; for handling soiled items; and for performing venipuncture. Ev Sa/2 An

1. Masks should only be worn during procedures that are likely to cause splashes of blood or body fluid.

3. Gowns should be worn during procedures that are likely to cause splashes of blood or body fluids.

4. A private room is only indicated if the client's hygiene is poor.

#55. 2. Autonomic dysreflexia is usually seen in spinal cord injuries above the level of the 6th thoracic vertebra. This results from uninhibited sympathetic discharge with release of norepinephrine. An Ph/9 An

1. Sympathetic nervous stimulation does occur.

3. Disruption in communication between the upper motor neurons and the lower motor neurons is what happens with spinal shock.

4. Flaccid paralysis results when muscles served by a lower motor neuron receive stimuli and are unable to contract.

#56. 3. A double-blind research study of a new medication generally will have a placebo and a test drug. The client will not know which drug is being administered. Ev Sa/1 An

1. The client is free to stop participating at any time.

2. The client must sign a consent form to participate in the study.

4. The client will remain anonymous throughout the study.

#57. 4. Hypotension is common after lowering the client's legs. The blood pressure should be assessed. As Ph/9 An

1. Pulses should be checked after the blood pressure is taken to ensure adequate circulation.

2. Checking sensation is important. However, the client who has had general anesthesia may be unable to respond to the nurse's assessment of sensation.

3. Foot drop usually occurs when pressure is placed on the peroneal nerve. This is not likely to happen in lithotomy position.

#58. 3. If there is ever any doubt about the sterility of an instrument or dressing, it should not be used. Ev Sa/2 An

ANSWER	RATIONALE	NP	CN	CL

1. Anything dropped on the floor is no longer sterile and should not be used. The statement indicates lack of understanding.
2. Anything dropped on the floor is no longer sterile and should not be used. The statement indicates lack of understanding.
4. The 4 × 4s should be soaked prior to donning the sterile gloves. Once the sterile gloves touch the bottle of normal saline they are no longer sterile. This statement indicates a need for further instruction.

#59. 2. **It is essential to assess the neurovascular assessment (color, temperature, capillary refill, edema, pulses, sensations, ability to move) frequently and compare to the unaffected extremity.**   As   Ph/9   Ap
1. Skin integrity will be assessed but is not highest priority.
3. Discomfort will be assessed but is not highest priority.
4. Client's knowledge will be assessed but is not highest priority.

#60. 2. **Orthostatic hypotension and tachycardia are seen in the volume-depleted person.**   As   Ph/10   An
1. Edema will not usually be present in the volume-depleted client unless other disease processes are involved.
3. Urine output decreases in fluid volume deficit.
4. Skin turgor will become nonelastic as the client becomes dehydrated.

#61. 3. **A rapid thready pulse is a sign of shock, not hydrocephalus, which causes increased intracranial pressure.**   As   Ph/10   An
1. Signs and symptoms of slow progressive hydrocephalus include headache, decreased level of consciousness, irritability, blurred vision, and urinary incontinence.
2. Signs and symptoms of slow progressive hydrocephalus include headache, decreased level of consciousness, irritability, blurred vision, and urinary incontinence.
4. Signs and symptoms of slow progressive hydrocephalus include headache, decreased level of consciousness, irritability, blurred vision, and urinary incontinence.

#62. 1. **Exacerbation triggered by climate changes (cold air, air pollution) are most often associated with nonallergic asthma.**   As   Ph/9   An
2. Exposure to animal dander is a precipitating factor for allergic asthma.
3. Environmental factors such as seasonal changes, pollen, and mold are associated with allergic asthma.
4. Environmental factors such as seasonal changes, pollen, and mold are associated with allergic asthma.

#63. 1. **Frequent airway assessment is vital. Airway occlusion frequently occurs with epiglottitis.**   Pl   Ph/9   Ap
2. Turning, coughing, and deep breathing is not a high priority for this child who is in danger of airway occlusion.
3. Administering cough medicines is not a high priority for this child who is in danger of airway occlusion.
4. The child should not be encouraged to eat at this time.

#64. 3. **The obstruction of the pancreatic duct with thick mucus prevents digestive enzymes from entering the duodenum, thus preventing digestion of food. Undigested food (mainly fats and proteins) are excreted in the stool, increasing the bulk to twice the normal amount.**   As   Ph/9   An
1. Expectoration is very difficult because the excess mucus produced is tenacious and viscous. It settles in the bronchioles and is a good culture medium for bacterial growth. The cough is dry and nonproductive. Bubbling rhonchi are not common, because the mucus does not move about with respiratory movements. Wheezes are more common due to partially blocked airways.
2. Elevated sweat chlorides above 69 mEq/liter is diagnostic of cystic fibrosis. The low serum levels of sodium and chloride during hyperthermic conditions can cause alkalosis.

4. Failure to thrive (weight below the 5th percentile) is the usual pattern because of malabsorption of nutrients from lack of enzymes. Anemia develops, not polycythemia.

#65. **2. The physician should be notified. Tetracycline decreases the effectiveness of oral contraceptives. There may be an equally effective antibiotic available that can be prescribed. Note on the client's chart that the physician was notified.**   Im   Ph/8   An

    1. The nurse should be aware that tetracyclines decrease the effectiveness of oral contraceptives. The physician should be notified.

    3. The nurse should be aware that tetracyclines decrease the effectiveness of oral contraceptives. The nurse should not tell the client to stop taking oral contraceptives unless the physician orders this.

    4. The nurse should be aware that tetracyclines decrease the effectiveness of oral contraceptives. If the physician chooses to keep the client on tetracycline, the client should be encouraged to use another form of birth control. The first intervention is to notify the physician.

#66. **3. Prednisone is used to treat persons with acute exacerbations of rheumatoid arthritis. This medication is given for its anti-inflammatory and immunosuppressive effects.**   An   Ph/8   K

    1. Gold sodium thiomalate is usually used in combination with aspirin and nonsteroidal anti-inflammatory drugs to relieve pain. Gold has an immunosuppressive affect.

    2. Azathioprine is used for clients with life-threatening rheumatoid arthritis for its immunosuppressive effects.

    4. Naproxen is a nonsteroidal anti-inflammatory drug. Immunosuppression does not occur.

#67. **1. When maternal sensitization occurs, maternal antibodies destroy the fetus's red blood cells, leading to anemia and pallor.**   An   Ph/9   An

    2. Negative direct Coombs indicates that maternal antibodies have not developed and there is no destruction of the neonate's red blood cells. With incompatibilities, the direct Coombs is positive.

    3. No incompatibility exists if the infant's blood type is the same as the mother's (in this case O negative). Rh incompatibility occurs when the mother's blood is negative and the infant's blood is positive. ABO incompatibility occurs when the mother is O and fetus is A, B, or AB; mother is A and the fetus is B; or if the mother is B and the fetus is A.

    4. A resting heart of 155 is normal in a newborn. Neonates severely affected by the hemolytic process manifest cardiovascular collapse with a sustained resting heart rate of 190 or more.

#68. **3. Adequate hydration is needed to prevent sickling and to delay the stasis-thrombosis-ischemic cycle.**   Pl   Ph/9   Ap

    1. A child with sickle cell crisis should avoid strenuous physical activity such as aerobic exercises since it causes increased cellular metabolism.

    2. Antibiotics are given for a course of therapy, such as 10–14 days, and are not stopped when the temperature returns to normal.

    4. Applying cold compresses to any area affected with pain is contraindicated because cold enhances sickling and vasoconstriction.

#69. **1. The signs, symptoms, and history suggest dumping syndrome. The pathophysiology underlying this disorder is not completely understood. Most likely it is due to the rapid distention of the jejunal loop anastomosed to the stomach.**   An   Ph/9   An

    2. Usually ingestion of fluids at mealtime increases signs and symptoms.

    3. The gastric remnant is connected to the jejunum with a large opening.

    4. Intestinal contents are hypertonic.

#70. **2. The signs and symptoms described are characteristic signs and symptoms of ulcerative colitis.**   An   Ph/10   An

1. Signs and symptoms of Crohn's disease include less frequent diarrhea, crampy abdominal pain, and formation of abscesses and fistulas. Bleeding can occur, but usually does not.
3. Common signs and symptoms of diverticulitis include bowel irregularity, crampy pain, and a low-grade fever.
4. Signs and symptoms of peritonitis include abdominal pain, rigidity, loss of bowel sounds, and rectal bleeding.

#71. 2. Phantom limb pain is a commonly occurring complication of amputation. The pain is probably caused by the brain misinterpreting pain from the stump and labeling it limb pain. The nurse should recognize that the pain is real to the client and administer pain medication as ordered.   Im   Ph/9   Ap

1. It is not therapeutic for the nurse to tell the client that he is not hurting or to withhold pain medication.
3. Pain medication should be given as ordered.
4. It is not therapeutic for the nurse to tell the client that he is not having pain. Clients describe the pain as severe, burning, crushing, or cramping and/or experience numbness and tingling in the removed limb.

#72. 3. The nurse should recognize that the client's pain is very real and explain that phantom pain is very common and that he is not crazy.   Im   Ph/9   Ap

1. The client may complain of phantom pain immediately after surgery and it may occur sporadically on a long-term basis. The pain can be triggered by touching the stump, concurrent illness, fatigue, or stress.
2. The nurse must acknowledge the client's pain. Calling the chaplain is not the most appropriate nursing action when the client states he feels he is going crazy. The nurse needs to provide support and reassurance.
4. The client should be reassured, but phantom pain may not go away, so the client should not be told it will.

#73. 2. The physician should be notified of any severe pain that does not respond to therapy, severe nausea, vomiting, swelling, cloudy vision, halo around lights, purulent or excessive mucoid drainage, or any symptoms of retinal detachment.   Pl   Ph/9   /Ap

1. Postoperative activity may be restricted to bed rest with bathroom privileges.
3. It is important that the client does not assume a flat, supine position, especially if there is a gas bubble in the eye being used to tamponade the retinal break. If the client assumes a flat position the gas bubble will rise and push the iris forward, causing acute glaucoma in clients who have had the lens removed.
4. The physician should be notified of any excessive purulent or mucoid drainage.

#74. 2. All of the responses are important for a child with cerebral palsy. However, since he has a history of falls and spasticity, the most important is to prevent physical injury.   Pl   Ph/9   Ap

1. Preventing deformity is important for a child with cerebral palsy. However, since he has a history of falls and spasticity, the most important is to prevent physical injury.
3. Establishing locomotion is important for a child with cerebral palsy. However, since he has a history of falls and spasticity, the most important is to prevent physical injury.
4. Ensuring a balanced diet is important for a child with cerebral palsy. However, since he has a history of falls and spasticity, the most important is to prevent physical injury.

#75. 3. All of the choices are important aspects of planning care for this child. However, changes in intracranial pressure can be life threatening so monitoring for changes is the highest priority.   Pl   Ph/9   An

ANSWER	RATIONALE	NP	CN	CL

1. It is important to inform parents of the child's condition, but this is not the highest priority.
2. Maintaining a quiet environment is important but is not the highest priority.
4. Maintaining bed rest is important but is not the highest priority.

#76. 2. **A family history of colon cancer is a known risk factor for colon cancer. Susceptibility to some forms of colon cancer is inherited.**   As   He/4   An
1. A low-fat, high-fiber diet is the diet to help prevent many cancers. High-fat diets have been linked to breast and colon cancers. High-fiber diets seem to prevent many types of cancer.
3. An annual rectal exam and stool for occult blood is indicated to help detect colon cancer. Persons with a family history of colon cancer should have a colonoscopy and if normal should have one every 5–10 years.
4. Suburbia is not a particular risk factor for cancer. Living in a highly industrialized urban society is a risk factor for several forms of cancer.

#77. 4. **Regressive behavior is frequently seen in children who are under stress.**   An   He/3   Ap
1. Children at age two and a half are frequently toilet trained.
2. It is possible that this is true, but the best explanation for the behavior is that regression is common in children who are hospitalized.
3. Two-and-a-half-year-old children may need some assistance with toileting but it need not be a parent. The best explanation for the behavior is that regression is common in children who are hospitalized.

#78. 3. **Toddlers present a challenge to parents since they are picky eaters. They need servings from each food group daily.**   Ev   He/3   An
1. Toddlers are picky eaters.
2. Although toddlers may be given a multivitamin, it will not meet all of the child's nutritional needs.
4. Toddlers should be eating table foods.

#79. 2. **When contractions occur more frequently than one every two minutes, oxytocin should be discontinued. Three contractions in five minutes is an indication to stop oxytocin.**   Ev   Ph/8   Ap
1. The normal fetal heart rate is 120 to 160 beats per minute.
3. The normal contraction duration is 40 to 90 seconds.
4. Early decelerations indicate fetal head compression and do not indicate fetal distress. They are normal during labor.

#80. 1. **Appropriate demonstration does not belittle Mr. M. or diminish his wife's confidence in him. The guidance through demonstration is helpful.**   Im   He/3   Ap
2. Better control may be reached with a better pattern of breathing. The breathing should be tried before suggesting pain medication.
3. Dismissing the husband and teaching the wife another breathing pattern interferes with his control and is inappropriate.
4. Leaving the couple alone is not helpful. Suggesting another approach to manage contractions of active labor is needed.

#81. 4. **Strategies to relieve the discomforts of pregnancy is the most important issue. Many discomforts arise during the second trimester, and information regarding relief will make pregnancy much more comfortable.**   Pl   He/3   Ap
1. The woman is pregnant so an overview of conception is not relevant to her current concerns.
2. Medication usage and breastfeeding is an important topic, but women may not have yet made the decision to breast feed. This is more relevant closer to delivery.
3. Second trimester is too soon for the couple to discuss infant care. Psychologically the couple may not be ready to be concerned about

ANSWER	RATIONALE	NP	CN	CL
	providing physical care. This is more appropriate in the third trimester or after delivery.			
#82. 2.	**Restricted activity is the most important measure to minimize stress on the cervix and reduce chances of premature labor.**	Pl	He/3	Ap
1.	It is important to replace lost blood if the woman has hemorrhaged but this does not prevent premature labor and delivery.			
3.	Betamethasone is given to a woman who is in premature labor to stimulate fetal lung maturity. Betamethasone does not prevent premature labor.			
4.	Discharge teaching should include avoiding sexual intercourse as it can cause further separation of the placenta. However, the question deals with preventing premature labor in a hospitalized client.			
#83. 1.	**Glucose monitoring identifies the glucose level and is a guideline for treatment. Since the infant is no longer exposed to the mother's high circulating glucose levels and its own pancreas is still secreting insulin in response to the glucose, the infant is subject to hypoglycemia.**	Pl	He/3	Ap
2.	Daily weights may be done to check for weight loss, but are not necessary and do not indicate the serum glucose level. Daily weights are not a priority in planning immediate care.			
3.	Supplemental feedings may be implemented but may not be necessary if glucose levels are adequate.			
4.	Respiratory distress is more common in preterm infants with immature lung development. This infant is admitted to the term nursery, not the neonatal intensive care unit.			
#84. 1.	**The signs and symptoms described are those of vena caval syndrome. It is most important to remove the gravid uterus from the inferior vena cava and the aorta. Turning the woman to the left side will accomplish this.**	Im	He/3	Ap
2.	Breathing into a paper bag is the appropriate action for hyperventilation. Signs and symptoms of hyperventilation include becoming light-headed and tingling in the hands, but blood pressure and pulse are unaffected. The signs and symptoms described are those of vena caval syndrome.			
3.	The signs and symptoms described are those of vena caval syndrome. Notifying the physician is not necessary because nursing measures can manage the situation.			
4.	The signs and symptoms described are those of vena caval syndrome. Increasing intravenous fluids is important and is the second step if position changes are not effective.			
#85. 2.	**Knee chest position removes pressure from the cord, which is caught between the presenting part and the woman's pelvis.**	Im	He/3	Ap
1.	A cesarean section will likely be done, but first the knee chest position relieves the pressure on the cord and the provider will attempt to manually push the presenting part away from the cord.			
3.	Replacing the expelled cord is not done as it may interfere with the circulation in the cord.			
4.	The intravenous infusion drip rate may be increased but the first action is to remove the pressure.			
#86. 4.	**Traditional weight loss programs combine dieting, exercise, psychosocial support, and behavior modification.**	Ev	He/4	An
1.	Protein is missing from this diet. Muscle wasting may occur.			
2.	Four pounds is inadequate weight loss for two months.			
3.	Weight loss has occurred too rapidly.			
#87. 2.	**Herpes zoster (shingles) produces painful vesicular eruptions along a nerve pathway.**	As	Ph/10	An
1.	Chickenpox, caused by the herpes virus, is characterized by initial runny nose and lesions that occur over the entire body. Herpes zoster (shingles) produces painful vesicular eruptions along a nerve pathway.			

3. Cold sores or fever blisters, also known as herpes simplex I, are characterized by lesions on the lips and the corners of the mouth. Herpes zoster (shingles) produces painful vesicular eruptions along a nerve pathway.

4. Herpes simplex II or genital herpes is characterized by lesions in the genital area.

#88. 2. **The description sounds like an adverse reaction to the immunization. The child may be allergic to the vaccine.** An He/4 An

1. A high temperature and large local reaction are not a normal reaction to the vaccine.

3. A high temperature and large local reaction are not symptoms of diphtheria, tetanus, or pertussis (whooping cough). They are symptoms of an adverse reaction to the vaccine.

4. A secondary infection at the injection site would not occur the day after the injection. It would take more time for a secondary infection to develop.

#89. 3. **Insulin is administered via a short needle at a 90-degree angle into the subcutaneous tissue. In a person with very little adipose tissue, it can be administered at a 60-degree angle, but it should always be administered into subcutaneous tissue.** Im Ph/8 Ap

1. Insulin is given at a 90° angle into the subcutaneous tissue, not the intramuscular tissue.

2. Insulin is given at a 90° angle into the subcutaneous tissue, not the intramuscular tissue and not via Z track. Imferon is given via Z track IM.

4. Insulin is given at a 90° angle into the subcutaneous tissue. Skin tests are given via intradermal injection.

#90. 4. **In many Asian cultures a person does not look directly at a person who is in a position of authority or who is greatly respected.** An Sa/1 An

1. There is no evidence the client is angry at the nurse. This behavior in many Asian cultures indicates respect.

2. In many Asian cultures a person does not look directly at a person who is in a position of authority or who is greatly respected.

3. In many Asian cultures a person does not look directly at a person who is in a position of authority or who is greatly respected. There is nothing in the question to indicate the client does not understand English. The nurse would want to assess this further.

#91. 3. **This type of communication technique, making an observation, enables the nurse to acknowledge that something exists or has changed in some way. This acknowledgment made by the nurse should open communication with the client.** An Ps/5 Ap

1. With this answer the nurse makes assumptions and jumps to a solution to the problem without involving the client.

2. This response also makes assumptions and jumps immediately to a possible solution without involving the client. This response also focuses on the wife and not the client in the question.

4. The nurse should be able to discuss this problem with the client and not immediately refer it to the physician.

#92. 1. **Prior to administering a tube feeding the nurse must check for placement of the tube in the stomach. The most effective methods include: (1) aspirating for gastric contents with a syringe and testing pH with Testape and (2) placing a stethoscope over the stomach and rapidly injecting 5–10 ml of air through the tubing. A swooshing sound is heard as the air enters the stomach.** As Ph/9 Ap

2. Once the tube is originally placed in the stomach there should be no need to advance the tube. It would never be done without first assessing placement.

3. As the tube is initially passed through the oropharynx the client is asked to swallow. Asking the client to swallow is not a part of assessing placement of the tube.

ANSWER	RATIONALE	NP	CN	CL

4. The nurse would not administer water into the tube until placement has been assessed.

#93. **4. The only true evidence that a client's pain is controlled is that the client says it is controlled.** — Ev — Ph/9 — An

   1. The body's compensatory mechanisms will stabilize the vital signs when the initial phase of the acute pain episode is over.

   2. The client may well be cheerful with her family because she does not want them to know she is in pain. Most people mask pain with a "happy face" from time to time.

   3. A pain rating scale goes from 0 (no pain) to 10 (the worst pain imaginable). A pain rating of 8 indicates severe pain.

#94. **1. A normal urinary output is indicative of adequate hydration and renal perfusion. Urine output for adults should approximate 0.5 ml/kg/hr.** — Ev — Ph/10 — An

   2. "Tenting" skin indicates poor skin turgor, a sign of dehydration.

   3. The specific gravity of water is 1.000. A specific gravity of 1.001 suggests far too much dilution and the possibility of overhydration.

   4. These vital signs are seen in hypovolemic shock, another indication of severe dehydration. They may also be seen in septic shock. The question asked which finding indicated adequate rehydration.

#95. **1. The concept of readiness for learning involves physical readiness, such as not being in pain, emotional readiness, and experiential readiness; (his wife appears to have these, but the client does not). However, by thinking in a future tense (anticipating that he will be able to wear a pouch) and soliciting the nurse's opinion, the client is indicating that he is ready to learn.** — As — Ps/5 — An

   2. Pain indicates that the client is not physically ready to learn how to care for his ileostomy.

   3. Stating that the ileostomy is disgusting indicates that the client is not emotionally ready to learn how to care for it.

   4. This answer indicates the client is placing the responsibility for ileostomy care onto his wife. It does not indicate he is ready to learn to care for his ileostomy.

#96. **4. A visual analog pain scale is a line indicating the intensity of pain with visual anchors at either end, one indicating the worst possible pain and the other end indicating no pain.** — As — Ph/9 — Ap

   1. Having the client describe the type and location of pain is part of pain assessment but is not using a visual analog scale.

   2. Before preparing to administer pain medication the nurse should assess the client.

   3. The nurse may need to assess the client's abdomen but that is not the visual analog scale as asked about in the question.

#97. **1. Salt is used as a preservative in most canned and processed foods. These foods should be avoided, as should any food that has a salty taste right out of the package. Salt replacements often contain potassium salts, which are usually contraindicated in chronic renal failure. The use of herbs and spices to replace salt in cooking and in seasoning foods is recommended as it enhances flavor of foods.** — Pl — Ph/7 — Ap

   2. Potassium salts are usually contraindicated in persons with chronic renal failure. The other parts of the answer are correct.

   3. Milk is high in sodium and protein and will need to be limited. However, it is not necessary to cook separate meals. The whole family will benefit from a low-sodium diet. High fluid intake is contraindicated in advanced chronic renal failure.

   4. With care, the client may be able to eat in a restaurant. Soaking vegetables before cooking may help to remove sodium and potassium. The client should avoid canned foods with the exception of some canned fruits.

#98. **2. The donor site may be treated in a variety of ways but the most** — Pl — Ph/9 — Ap common method is to cover the wound with a fine mesh gauze or an impregnated gauze that is opened to the air or exposed to a heat lamp to allow the wound to dry.

1. The grafted site is generally covered with a large occlusive dressing to hold the skin graft in place; the dressing remains in place for 48–72 hours.
3. The donor site is an open wound that is treated using aseptic technique. It is often exposed to the air to promote drying. The healed wound is generally lubricated to reduce drying and itching.
4. Hydrotherapy is useful in cleaning wounds and removing eschar and necrotic tissue, but autografts are delicate and would be dislodged by the currents.

#99. 2. Help the client to develop a relationship between his behavior and the consequences. Do address the client with a consistent team plan to minimize manipulation.   Im   Ps/6   Ap

1. The client does not need to be in restraints unless his behavior is excessively aggressive.
3. All members of a mental health team must have a consistent plan to deal effectively with the manipulative behavior. This assists in the client understanding limits and learning to live within the structure of those limits.
4. Restriction of unit activities would not have a therapeutic outcome. The client needs opportunities to interact with staff and peers to gain here-and-now experiences in terms of his behavioral style and consequences of his behavior.

#100. 1. Furosemide (Lasix) is a loop diuretic which should increase urinary output. Oliguria is decreased urinary output.   Ev   Ph/8   Ap

2. As the extracellular fluid (ECF) volume decreases, the blood pressure should also decrease.
3. Rales should decrease as the ECF decreases.
4. Polydipsia, thirst, is more likely to occur with diuresis, which would occur when furosemide is effective.

Practice Test 3

1. A woman is admitted for a suspected duodenal ulcer. The nurse is interviewing her for an admission history. Which description of her pain would be most characteristic of a duodenal ulcer?
   1. Aching in the epigastric area that wakens her from sleep.
   2. Right upper quadrant pain that increases after meals.
   3. Sharp pain in the epigastric area that radiates to the right shoulder.
   4. A sensation of painful pressure in the midsternal area.
2. The nurse is playing with a two-year-old child with tetralogy of Fallot, who suddenly squats on the floor. The best initial nursing action to take is to
   1. return the child to bed immediately.
   2. allow the child to remain in that position.
   3. place the child in a chair.
   4. call the physician immediately.
3. The nurse is caring for a client with cirrhosis of the liver who has developed esophageal varices. The nurse understands that the best explanation for development of esophageal varices is which of the following?
   1. Chronic low serum protein levels result in inadequate tissue repair, allowing the esophageal wall to weaken.
   2. The enlarged liver presses on the diaphragm, which in turn presses on the esophageal wall, causing collapse of blood vessels into the esophageal lumen.
   3. Increased portal pressure causes some of the blood that normally circulates through the liver to be shunted to the esophageal vessels, increasing their pressure and causing varicosities.

4. The enlarged liver displaces the esophagus toward the left, tearing the muscle layer of the esophageal blood vessels, which allows small aneurysms to form along the lower esophageal vessels.

4. An adult with esophageal varices begins to experience severe gastrointestinal bleeding. The plan of care to meet the client's fluid needs should include, as a priority, strategies for
   1. accommodating his frequent need for the bedpan.
   2. maintaining the gastric pH.
   3. monitoring vital signs on an hourly basis.
   4. rapid blood and fluid administration.

5. An adult has just had a broken left ankle casted in the emergency department. He will be going home to a second floor apartment. When teaching him to walk with his crutches the nurse should instruct him to go up the stairs by
   1. resting his weight on his right foot while he lifts the crutches and his left foot to the next step, then resting his weight on the crutches while he brings his right foot up onto the same step.
   2. resting his weight on the crutches while he lifts his right foot to the next step, then moving the crutches and his left foot to the same step.
   3. holding both crutches with his left arm and using the crutches to bear part of his weight while he lifts his right foot to the next step, then moving his crutches and his left foot to the same step.
   4. sitting on the steps and using his right leg and left arm to lift his weight and place his buttocks on the next step, while pulling the crutches with his right hand.

6. John, age 6, has cerebral palsy and is hospitalized for corrective surgery for muscle contractures. The most important immediate postoperative goal for John is to
   1. ambulate using adaptive devices.
   2. demonstrate optimal oxygenation.
   3. verbalize pain control.
   4. complete daily self-care needs.

7. A five-year-old child with a terminal illness is talking to the nurse. Which of the following best reflects a five-year-old's understanding of death?
   1. "I'll see Grandma in heaven."
   2. "Will it hurt when I die?"
   3. "Can Mommy go with me?"
   4. "It isn't fair. Why me? I'm too young to die."

8. The nurse is teaching the parents of a child who is being treated in clinic for otitis media. Which of the following statements is essential to include in the teaching?
   1. "Do not take acetaminophen as this is contraindicated."

2. "Take the medication until the pain and fever are gone."
   3. "Do not apply heat to the ear."
   4. "Take all of the medication as ordered."

9. The nurse is planning care for a child who must remain in a croup tent continuously. Which goal is of highest priority?
   1. The tent will remain closed, except for feedings and hygiene.
   2. The child will maintain normal body temperature and have dry linens.
   3. The tent will deliver mist and cooled air simultaneously while the child is inside.
   4. The child will find entertainment within the tent to encourage compliance.

10. A 28-year-old woman comes to the prenatal clinic because she thinks she might be pregnant. She tells the nurse that her menstrual periods are irregular but, since her last menses seven weeks ago, she's noticed some physiologic changes in her body. Which finding should the nurse expect when assessing the woman for a probable sign of pregnancy?
    1. Morning sickness.
    2. Urinary frequency.
    3. A positive pregnancy test.
    4. Auscultation of fetal heart sounds.

11. A woman in prenatal clinic tells the nurse that the first day of her last normal menstrual period was June 15th. The nurse uses Nägele's rule to calculate the due date as being about
    1. March 8th.
    2. March 15th.
    3. March 22nd.
    4. March 29th.

12. A woman who is six months pregnant is seen in antepartal clinic. She states she is having trouble with constipation. To minimize this condition, the nurse should instruct her to
    1. increase her fluid intake to three liters/day.
    2. request a prescription for a laxative from her physician.
    3. stop taking iron supplements.
    4. take two tablespoons of mineral oil daily.

13. A woman who is eight months pregnant is being seen in the physician's office. She has been working as a salesperson throughout her pregnancy and would like to continue working until the middle of her ninth month. She now weighs 150 lb. and is 5 ft. 6 in. tall, and reports that her back hurts at the end of the day. What advice should the nurse give to increase the woman's comfort level?
    1. Lose weight.
    2. Quit her job.
    3. Wear low-heeled shoes.
    4. Rest with her legs elevated at all times.

14. The nurse is caring for a woman in labor. The woman is irritable, complains of nausea and vomits, and has heavier show, and the

membranes rupture. The nurse understands that this indicates that
1. the woman is in transition stage of labor.
2. the woman is having a complication and the doctor should be notified.
3. labor is slowing down and the woman may need oxytocin.
4. the woman is emotionally distraught and needs assistance in dealing with labor.

15. The nurse is caring for a woman who had a vaginal delivery an hour ago without complications. She has a boggy fundus after voiding 500 ml. The nurse caring for this woman should give highest priority to
1. massaging the fundus until it is firm.
2. assessing the lochia.
3. adding Pitocin to the intravenous solution being administered.
4. calling the health care provider.

16. A client who is having a saline abortion is being cared for on the labor floor. The client's vital signs are temperature 101°F, pulse 100, respirations 24, blood pressure 120/90. The nurse most appropriately interprets these data to mean
1. the blood pressure is elevated from receiving the saline injection.
2. the vital signs are within normal limits for a client undergoing saline abortion.
3. the client is at extreme risk for shock.
4. the client may be developing an infection, such as chorioamnionitis.

17. A woman who is taking oral contraceptives tells her nurse neighbor that she is experiencing a vaginal discharge. The most appropriate action for the nurse is to advise the woman to
1. purchase an over-the-counter remedy.
2. change undergarments.
3. see the physician as soon as possible.
4. stop taking the oral contraceptives.

18. The nurse is assessing a woman for sexually transmitted diseases. Which symptom would be most apt to be present in a woman with a *Trichomonas vaginalis* vaginal infection?
1. A profuse white bubbly discharge.
2. White cheese-like patches in the vagina.
3. A perineal deformity.
4. An ulcer or lesion of the vulva or vagina.

19. The nurse is assessing a newborn five minutes after birth. He has full flexion of the extremities, is acrocyanotic, has a heart rate of 124, a full, lusty cry, and resists the suction catheter. The nurse should record which Apgar score?
1. 9.
2. 8.
3. 7.
4. 6.

20. A client in the active phase of labor has just been given continuous epidural anesthesia. Which assessment finding indicates to the

nurse that the client is experiencing a common side effect of this type of anesthesia?
1. Blood pressure of 50/30.
2. Uterine pain.
3. Fetal heart rate of 140.
4. Euphoria.

21. Ms. C. has had a CVA (cerebrovascular accident) and has severe right-sided weakness. She has been taught to walk with a cane. The nurse is evaluating her use of the cane prior to discharge. Which of the following reflects correct use of the cane?
1. Holding the cane in her left hand, Ms. C. moves the cane forward first, then her right leg, and finally her left leg.
2. Holding the cane in her right hand, Ms. C. moves the cane forward first, then her left leg, and finally her right leg.
3. Holding the cane in her right hand, Ms. C. moves the cane and her right leg forward, then moves her left leg forward.
4. Holding the cane in her left hand, Ms. C. moves the cane and her left leg forward, then moves her right leg forward.

22. The nurse is caring for a client who has just had a splenectomy. When planning care in the immediate postoperative period the nurse should avoid using which position?
1. Left side lying.
2. Right side lying.
3. Semi-Fowler's.
4. Supine.

23. Harry, 23 years old, is admitted to the hospital after having taken LSD. What should the nurse assess for?
1. Dilated pupils, flushing, and tremors.
2. Pupillary constriction, constipation, and sleepiness.
3. Tremors, muscular weakness, and mask-like face.
4. Vertical and horizontal nystagmus.

24. A group of eight psychiatric clients have been together in group therapy for twelve sessions. There has been an expression of warm feelings, self-disclosure, and an awareness of events in the here and now. The group finds it difficult to deal with two members who must now join the group. The nurse recognizes that group members are experiencing which phase of the group process?
1. Beginning phase.
2. Transition phase.
3. Middle phase.
4. Termination phase.

25. Mr. T. has been informed that he needs surgery for rectal cancer. His response is, "There's nothing wrong with me. I just have hemorrhoids." The nurse knows this response to be which defense mechanism?
1. Projection.
2. Repression.
3. Denial.

4. Displacement.
26. Mrs. G., 25, is hospitalized for depression. One evening after an argument with her husband, Mrs. G. discusses with the evening nurse her intent to cut her wrists. Her husband has threatened to divorce her and retain custody of the children. The most appropriate initial action for the nurse to take is to
   1. attempt to convince Mrs. G. of the need to address her husband's threats instead of using self-destructive behavior.
   2. place Mrs. G. on suicide precautions, which restrict her leaving the nursing unit.
   3. place Mrs. G. on suicide precautions requiring close observation and one to one monitoring by nursing staff.
   4. recognize the suicidal remarks as less serious since Mrs. G. is in a safe environment.
27. A 17-year-old male is brought to the emergency room in a semi-conscious state. The friend who accompanies him reports that he fell while playing ball. He appeared to be unconscious, his respirations were deep and rapid but never stopped. The nurse assesses the client and notes Kussmaul respirations, hypotension, tachycardia, decreased reflexes, and an acetone odor to his breath. Which question does the nurse appropriately ask the friend at this time?
   1. "Does he have diabetes?"
   2. "Does he have epilepsy?"
   3. "Did he hit his head?"
   4. "Did he use drugs?"
28. An adult client has been passing blood in his feces. The best way for the nurse to assess if the hematochezia is a symptom of gastric bleeding is to
   1. ask him how long he has been bleeding.
   2. check his vital signs.
   3. monitor his laboratory results.
   4. obtain his complete past medical history.
29. A construction worker complains of low back pain that increases when he bends over, coughs, or lifts objects. A diagnosis of herniated disc is made. He asks the nurse to explain the cause of his pain. The nurse's response is based on knowledge that pain associated with a herniated disc results from
   1. compression of the spinal nerve root.
   2. spasms of the paraspinal muscles.
   3. a friction rub created by degeneration of vertebrae.
   4. edema and swelling of nerve endings.
30. The nurse is caring for a client who is being transfused for severe gastrointestinal bleeding. The nurse can decrease the danger of hypothermia by
   1. administering blood with normal saline.
   2. administering blood products through a central line.

3. giving only packed cells.
   4. warming blood to body temperature before administering.
31. A 55-year-old complains of a sudden onset of pain in the ankle, which is swollen, red, and extremely sensitive to pressure. A diagnosis of acute gout is made. The client asks the nurse about gout. The nurse teaches him that gout is
   1. a metabolic disorder that results in elevated serum uric acid levels.
   2. an infection of the synovial membrane by microorganisms, resulting in inflammation.
   3. a disease of cartilage resulting in destruction of the cartilage and the underlying bone, causing severe pain.
   4. inflammation of the bursal sac accompanied by formation of large calcium deposits, which cause swelling and joint pain.
32. A 71-year-old is admitted to the hospital with congestive heart failure. She has shortness of breath and a +3–4 peripheral edema. The care plan to reduce the client's edema should include nursing strategies for
   1. establishing limits on activity.
   2. fostering a relaxed environment.
   3. identifying goals for self-care.
   4. restricting IV fluids.
33. An elderly woman admitted with congestive heart failure and +3–4 peripheral edema complains that she is always tired. Which of the following would be the most appropriate suggestion by the nurse while the client is still on bed rest?
   1. Continue to exercise your legs.
   2. Try not to think about the fatigue.
   3. Eat larger meals.
   4. Sleep as much as possible.
34. An adult is admitted with early left-sided congestive failure. Which symptom should the nurse expect to find?
   1. Bradycardia.
   2. Rales.
   3. Liver engorgement.
   4. Jugular vein distention.
35. An adult is given digoxin (Lanoxin) 0.25 mg daily. The nurse should teach the client that the signs of digitalis toxicity include
   1. auditory hallucinations and bradycardia.
   2. dry mucous membranes and diarrhea.
   3. heart block and brittle hair and nails.
   4. visual disturbances and premature heartbeats.
36. Which serum potassium level reported for an adult requires no immediate nursing intervention?
   1. 3.2 mEq/liter.
   2. 4.0 mEq/liter.
   3. 5.7 mEq/liter.
   4. 6.0 mEq/liter.
37. The mother of a newborn learns that her

infant son has lost eight ounces since his birth two days ago. The nurse explains that this weight loss is normal. The nurse's answer is based on the understanding that the weight loss is probably the result of
1. feeding infants every four hours instead of every three hours.
2. loss of fluid from the cord stump.
3. limited food intake since birth.
4. regurgitation of feedings.

38. A 16-year-old Type I (insulin-dependent) diabetic, takes his morning dose of insulin and leaves for school. At 10 A.M. he feels faint and is brought to the nurse's office. He has tachycardia and diaphoresis and is unresponsive. The most appropriate intervention by the nurse at this time is to administer
1. 5 units regular insulin S.C.
2. 8 ounces of orange juice.
3. Glucagon S.C.
4. Glucose 50% IV push.

39. The mother of a three-year-old child calls the clinic and states that her child has just swallowed an unknown amount of baby aspirin. What is the best initial action for the nurse to take?
1. Call the physician.
2. Instruct the mother to bring the child to the emergency room as soon as possible.
3. Discuss with the mother observable changes for which she should watch the child.
4. Tell the mother to give ipecac to the child and then come to the emergency room.

40. The nurse in well-baby clinic is assessing a 12-month-old child. He is 30 inches tall and weighs 30 lb. The nurse interprets this as
1. normal height, increased weight.
2. normal height, decreased weight.
3. small for age, normal weight.
4. tall for age, but weight appropriate for height.

41. The nurse has been discussing promotion of growth and development with a family whose 15-month-old son has a cyanotic heart defect. Which statement by the father indicates a need for further teaching?
1. "I need to feed him slowly and allow frequent rest periods."
2. "I need to play quiet games and activities with my son."
3. "I need to provide highly nutritious foods."
4. "I need to limit my son's interactions with other children."

42. A ten-year-old child with hemophilia cut his hand while working on a craft project in the hospital play room. The initial nursing action to take is to
1. apply pressure to the bleeding area for at least ten to fifteen minutes.
2. apply an ice pack.

3. cover the wound with a sterile dressing.
4. notify the physician immediately.

43. The nurse is caring for a woman in the fourth stage of labor. The nursing care plan should include monitoring the woman for
1. uterine contractions.
2. cervical dilation.
3. birth of the baby and delivery of the placenta.
4. readjustment to the nonpregnant state.

44. A 54-year-old woman is diagnosed with somatization disorder. She experiences palpitations, nausea, abdominal pain, and headaches. Physical exam and diagnostic tests do not reveal pathology. The client comes to the nurse stating she has palpitations. Which plan of care by the nurse best reduces secondary gain?
1. After investigation of her palpitations, do not continue to take her vital signs with each complaint of the problem.
2. Inform her that the palpitations are not real and she must learn to relax.
3. Convey an intense interest in her palpitations by encouraging her to talk about her symptoms.
4. Reassure her that she will be assisted in meeting her dependency needs.

45. The nurse is assessing a client with border-line personality disorder. It is most important for the nurse to assess for behavior indicating
1. aggression.
2. depression.
3. sleep disturbances.
4. splitting.

46. A 72-year-old woman is addicted to pain killers prescribed for her arthritis. She denies it is a problem since it was prescribed by her physician. What is the best interpretation of the client's view of her addiction?
1. The client is using rationalization to support her denial.
2. The client really does not have a problem; it is the physician who does.
3. The client is transferring blame by denying she has a problem.
4. The client is an uneducated woman so she couldn't understand her problem.

47. An adult is prepared for discharge following a bilateral adrenalectomy. The nurse determines that the client understands her discharge instructions when she states,
1. "The surgery cured my disease, now I won't have to take any medications."
2. "I should wear a Medic-alert bracelet or necklace at all times."
3. "I will need to take replacement doses of steroids daily for one to two months."
4. "I will probably develop a round face and gain weight now that I will take cortisol daily."

48. Sandra, an R.N., reports to work looking unkempt. Nancy, another R.N., approaches when she notices her using uncoordinated movements. Sandra's breath reeks of peppermints and Nancy suspects Sandra may be intoxicated. What is the best initial nursing action for Nancy to take?
    1. Call the supervisor and report Sandra.
    2. Confront Sandra, saying that she feels she is intoxicated, and relieve her of her nursing duties immediately.
    3. Ignore the situation.
    4. Give Sandra a lecture about substance abuse and do nothing else.

49. An adult is experiencing a panic attack. The nurse intervenes by escorting him to his room, using short sentences, and conveying a calm demeanor. Which action by the client indicates the nursing interventions are effective? The client
    1. releases his anxiety by punching his fist on a bedside table.
    2. states he wants to be alone to deal with his feelings.
    3. expresses verbally his demands to the nurse.
    4. makes connections between events and his anxious response.

50. A 22-year-old is readmitted to the rehabilitation unit after a T4 incomplete spinal cord injury that occurred six months ago. He is about to begin an intensive rehabilitation program. Which of the following statements made by this client best indicates that he understands the extent of his injury?
    1. "I want to use an electric wheelchair."
    2. "My goal is to be independent in transfers."
    3. "Soon I'll be walking."
    4. "There is little I can do, but I will try."

51. The nurse is caring for an adult with a T4 spinal cord transaction. Which activity by the client indicates adequate learning regarding urinary tract care?
    1. Avoiding the Valsalva maneuver when the bladder is full.
    2. Cleaning the urinary meatus every two hours.
    3. Checking the bladder distention frequently.
    4. Limiting fluids to 100 ml per 24 hours.

52. To evaluate the effectiveness of bowel training for an adult with a T6 spinal cord injury, the nurse should expect him to be able to
    1. avoid laxatives and stool softeners.
    2. experience no incontinence.
    3. move his bowels daily.
    4. resume previous bowel habits.

53. The nurse is caring for a client with severe back strain. The nurse administers diazepam (Valium) 10 mg qid. Which observation is

most indicative of the need to reassess this order?
    1. Drowsiness.
    2. Hyperesthesia of the arms.
    3. Loss of appetite.
    4. Severe muscle spasms.

54. An adult has been receiving physical therapy following a cerebrovascular accident. His left leg is weak and he is instructed in the use of a cane. The nurse evaluates the client's ability to use the cane and documents that he uses the cane correctly when he
    1. holds the cane in his left hand.
    2. leans his body toward the cane when walking.
    3. advances the left leg and cane simultaneously.
    4. advances the right leg and cane simultaneously.

55. The nurse is caring for a client who is hypertensive. To facilitate the client's ability to lower his blood pressure to a normal range, the nurse should teach him to avoid which of the following foods?
    1. Cooked cereal.
    2. Broccoli.
    3. Catsup.
    4. Sugar.

56. An adult client has hypertension. The nurse takes his blood pressure in lying and standing positions. The nurse explains to him that this is a test for
    1. central nervous system depression.
    2. malignant hypertension.
    3. orthostatic hypotension.
    4. vascular insufficiency.

57. The nurse is formulating a teaching plan for an adult client with severe emphysema. The nurse should instruct him to select activities that primarily
    1. avoid movement.
    2. build strength.
    3. conserve energy.
    4. test his limits of tolerance.

58. Nursing interventions to facilitate breathing for a client with chronic obstructive lung disease are considered effective if the client
    1. deemphasizes expirations.
    2. increases his respiratory rate.
    3. reduces the use of his diaphragm.
    4. utilizes abdominal breathing.

59. An adult is hospitalized for treatment of deep electrical burns. Burn wound sepsis develops and mafenide acetate 10% (Sulfamylon) is ordered bid. While applying the Sulfamylon to the wound, it is important for the nurse to prepare the client for expected responses to the topical application, which include
    1. severe burning pain for a few minutes following application.
    2. possible severe metabolic alkalosis with continued use.

3. black discoloration of everything that comes in contact with this drug.
4. chilling due to evaporation of solution from the moistened dressings.

60. A 56-year-old is admitted to the burn unit with partial and full thickness burns of both legs, which occurred when a charcoal grill tipped over on her. The burn area is edematous. Blister formation and a large amount of fluid exudate is noted. Urine output is 30 ml/hr, BP 90/60, and pulse 110. A primary nursing diagnosis during the initial 48–72 hours following the burn is
   1. body image disturbance related to disfiguring burns of both legs.
   2. high risk for infection related to skin breakdown.
   3. potential for ineffective airway clearance related to smoke inhalation.
   4. fluid volume deficit related to increased capillary permeability.

61. While assessing the client with burns on the back and trunk, the nurse notes areas that are not painful, grayish-white in color, and leathery in appearance. The nurse documents that these burns are
   1. superficial burns.
   2. superficial partial thickness burns.
   3. deep partial thickness burns.
   4. full thickness burns.

62. A middle-aged woman has no memory of her past. She assumed the name Blanche as she created a new identity during her hospital stay. The nurse feels it was important for her to do this because
   1. it decreased the client's anxiety level.
   2. all people need a name and a history.
   3. the hospital needs to have a name for its records for payment purposes.
   4. it increased the client's self-esteem by developing a possible self.

63. A 15-year-old high school student with a history of sexual abuse was admitted to the psychiatric unit experiencing depersonalization. An appropriate short-term goal for the nurse is to
   1. help the client develop coping skills.
   2. orient the client to the staff and unit.
   3. place the client on q 15 minute checks.
   4. teach the client about her medications.

64. A delusional client is admitted to the hospital. The most appropriate action for the nurse to take is to
   1. attempt to disprove the client's delusion.
   2. focus on the reality aspects of the client's communication.
   3. place the client on room restriction to decrease stimuli.
   4. agree with the delusion until psychotropic medications take effect, then focus on reality.

65. The nurse evaluates a delusional client for improvement. Which of the following statements indicates a positive outcome for a delusional client?
   1. Client states he/she hears voices, but only when alone.
   2. Client states people are observing him but are not talking about him.
   3. Client expresses less fear in using the public phone on the hospital unit.
   4. Client states he/she can now use the unit shower room because he/she realizes the shoe left by another client is not a rat.

66. A child who is two years and six months old has had one bout of nephrosis (nephrotic syndrome). His mother suspected a recurrence when she observed swelling around his eyes. The nurse helps to confirm this condition by recognizing what additional symptom?
   1. Blood pressure of 140/90.
   2. Marked proteinuria.
   3. Cola-colored urine.
   4. A history of positive streptococcal infection.

67. The nurse is evaluating a child who is being treated for nephrosis. Which observations indicate successful treatment of nephrosis?
   1. Diuresis and weight loss.
   2. Improved appetite and weight gain.
   3. Increase in the sedimentation rate and urine specific gravity.
   4. Return of temperature to normal and indications that the child is more comfortable.

68. The mother of a two-year-old tells the nurse that her son has temper tantrums, demanding cookies in the supermarket, and asks how she can best handle these temper tantrums. The nurse should suggest to the mother that she
   1. buy one box of cookies for each shopping trip.
   2. leave him home while she goes shopping.
   3. remain calm and ignore his behavior.
   4. discipline the child immediately when he demands cookies.

69. A 25-year-old woman is in her fifth month of pregnancy. She has been taking 20 units of NPH insulin for diabetes mellitus daily for six years. Her diabetes has been well controlled with this dosage. She has been coming for routine prenatal visits, during which diabetic teaching has been implemented. Which of the following statements indicates that the woman understands the teaching regarding her insulin needs during her pregnancy?
   1. "Are you sure all this insulin won't hurt my baby?"
   2. "I'll probably need my daily insulin dose raised."
   3. "I will continue to take my regular dose of insulin."

4. "These finger sticks make my hand sore. Can I do them less frequently?"

70. A woman who delivered a healthy baby 18 hours ago has just been given Rho (D) immune globulin. Which finding indicates the need for administration of this medication?
    1. The mother is Rho (D) negative with Rho (D) antibodies.
    2. The infant is Rho (D) positive.
    3. There is a positive indirect Coombs test of cord blood.
    4. The mother is Rho (D) positive.

71. In evaluating the effectiveness of IV pitocin for a client with secondary dystocia (uterine inertia), the nurse should expect
    1. a precipitate delivery.
    2. cervical effacement without delivery.
    3. infrequent contractions lasting longer than 90 seconds.
    4. progressive cervical dilation with contractions lasting less than 90 seconds.

72. A class B diabetic delivered a 3700-gram live girl via cesarean delivery for a breech position 15 minutes ago. She wishes to breastfeed as soon as possible. The nurse caring for the infant makes the following assessments of vital signs: T 98.8°F, P 148, respirations 22, color pink with tremors and irritability. What is the best nursing intervention at this time?
    1. Feed the infant 5% dextrose water via gavage.
    2. Take the infant to the mother to feed immediately.
    3. Check the infant's blood sugar.
    4. Ask a coworker to call the pediatrician immediately.

73. When caring for a client with a casted extremity, frequent assessments of neurologic and circulatory status of the affected extremity are required. Which of the following assessment findings should be recognized by the nurse as abnormal?
    1. Client reports the extremity feels "like it's asleep."
    2. Capillary refill time is less than five seconds.
    3. The area distal to the cast is warm to touch.
    4. Client reports dull aching in the casted extremity.

74. An adult is receiving peritoneal dialysis. His acid-base balance and electrolytes are now within normal limits. Which of the following best explains the mechanism of action for peritoneal dialysis?
    1. Hypotonic fluid is instilled into the peritoneal cavity and waste products passively diffuse into it.
    2. Sodium and bicarbonate from the dialysate in the peritoneal cavity are exchanged for excess potassium and hydrogen ions from the blood.

3. Increased intra-abdominal pressure caused by the dialysate solution in the abdomen creates a filtration pressure similar to that in the kidney, causing wastes and electrolytes to move out of the blood.
4. Glucose added to the dialysate solution increases the osmotic pressure of the dialysate, causing fluid to move from the blood into the dialysate along with wastes and electrolytes.

75. An adult with chronic renal failure is receiving peritoneal dialysis. His acid-base balance and electrolyte levels are now within normal limits. His hemoglobin is 9.2 and his hematocrit is 30. The most likely cause of his anemia is
    1. hemodilution secondary to fluid retention.
    2. eating insufficient protein due to taste changes that occur with dialysis.
    3. failure of his kidneys to produce the hormone necessary to stimulate bone marrow to produce red blood cells.
    4. hemolysis of red blood cells as they move past the membrane containing the dialysis solution.

76. An adult is scheduled for an intravenous pyelogram (IVP). Before sending her to have the test the nurse should
    1. ask if she is allergic to barium.
    2. ask if she is allergic to shellfish.
    3. give her a full glass of water.
    4. instruct her not to urinate until after the test.

77. A child is recovering from chickenpox. At what point will he be allowed to return to school?
    1. After he has been on antibiotics for 48 hours.
    2. After his temperature is normal and the itching has subsided.
    3. When all lesions are crusted and scabbed.
    4. When his skin is clear of all lesions.

78. A woman calls her neighbor, who is a nurse, to say that her five-year-old has had a stomach virus with vomiting for 24 hours. The doctor recommended the child eat nothing for four to six hours. There has been no vomiting during that time and now she wants to know what is best to give him. Her neighbor recommends
    1. broth and water.
    2. flat ginger ale and tea.
    3. Jell-O and a soft boiled egg.
    4. skim milk and dry toast.

79. The nurse is assessing a child who is admitted with pyloric stenosis. Which of the following findings is most likely to be reported/observed?
    1. The child has greenish-yellow mucus-like emesis that has a strong odor.

2. The vomiting began gradually and then increased until there is no retention of feedings.
3. The infant is content between feedings and shows hesitancy to feed.
4. There is a palpable lump in the epigastrum directly under the xyphoid process.

80. The S. family is planning a camping trip. Mrs. S. calls the clinic to obtain information regarding Lyme disease. Which information would not be appropriate for the nurse to give?
    1. Wear long pants and long-sleeved shirts when hiking.
    2. Use a tick repellent.
    3. Inspect hair and skin daily for signs of bites.
    4. Look for bites that cause a fine petechial rash.

81. Ms. L. is scheduled for a liver biopsy. When planning her postprocedure care, the nurse should include
    1. administering narcotic analgesics every three to four hours for the first 24 hours.
    2. positioning her on her right side for at least the first two hours.
    3. monitoring for pain referred to the left arm.
    4. changing the dressing over the puncture site frequently, until bile leakage has stopped.

82. The nurse is evaluating whether nonprofessional staff understand how to prevent transmission of HIV. Which of the following behaviors indicates correct application of universal precautions?
    1. A lab technician rests his hand on the desk to steady it while recapping the needle after drawing blood.
    2. An aide wears gloves to feed a helpless client.
    3. An assistant puts on a mask and protective eye wear before assisting the nurse to suction a tracheostomy.
    4. A pregnant worker refuses to care for a client known to have AIDS.

83. Mr. A. is ready for discharge following creation of a sigmoid colostomy. Which of the following statements by Mr. A. should be evaluated by the nurse as an indication that he has understood his discharge instructions correctly?
    1. "I will irrigate the colostomy with tap water every day."
    2. "I can eat anything as long as I chew thoroughly."
    3. "I will change the pouch every day."
    4. "I should not drink more than six glasses of fluid a day."

84. The nurse is caring for a 33-week premature baby girl who is five days old and weighs 2000 grams. Which should be included in the nursing care plan?
    1. Teach her parents how to do gavage feedings, since the baby has no sucking reflex.
    2. Allow the mother to breastfeed when she visits.
    3. Inform the parents that the infant will need to stay in an isolette until she is discharged.
    4. Instruct the parents on how to take rectal temperatures.

85. The mother of an infant who has had a cleft lip repair has been taught the postoperative care needed. When evaluating the mother's understanding of this care, the nurse hopes to see the mother
    1. positioning the child on his abdomen to facilitate drainage of oral secretions.
    2. comforting the child as soon as he starts to fuss, to prevent his crying.
    3. using a regular bottle nipple to feed the infant in a semi-reclining position.
    4. cleaning the suture line with warm water and a wash cloth once a day.

86. The school nurse is assessing a child who has fallen in the gymnasium. The child exhibits all of the following. Which finding indicates to the nurse that the child most likely has a fracture in addition to soft tissue injury?
    1. Localized swelling.
    2. Abnormal motion.
    3. Ecchymosis.
    4. Pain.

87. The nurse is planning care for a three-year-old child who has just returned to the unit following a cardiac catheterization. The nurse should include which of the following on the care plan?
    1. Monitor for response to general anesthetic.
    2. Bed rest for 24 hours.
    3. NPO for 12 hours.
    4. Observe for severe pain and medicate as needed.

88. The school nurse is assisting a school teacher to understand the classroom capabilities of a child with athetoid cerebral palsy. The nurse explains that the child most probably will demonstrate
    1. exaggerated hyperactive reflexes.
    2. normal intelligence levels.
    3. slow, worm-like, writhing movements.
    4. unsteady gait and clumsy, uncoordinated upper extremity function.

89. A woman with severe pregnancy-induced hypertension was delivered two hours ago. Which nursing action should be included in the plan of care for her postpartum hospital stay?
    1. Continuing to monitor blood pressure, respirations, and reflexes.

2. Encouraging frequent family visitors.
3. Keeping her NPO.
4. Maintaining an IV access to the circulatory system.

90. An adult has received one unit of packed red blood cells after sustaining severe trauma to his legs with profuse bleeding. To evaluate whether the transfusion has been effective the nurse should
1. take his blood pressure.
2. auscultate lung sounds.
3. check hemoglobin and hematocrit results.
4. take his temperature.

91. An 80-year-old woman who underwent a right total hip replacement arrived on the nursing unit from the post anesthesia care unit at 2 P.M. What should be the initial assessment by the 3 to 11 nurse during initial rounds at change of shift?
1. The dressing.
2. Urine output.
3. Circulation to the leg.
4. Breath sounds.

92. An adult who had gastric surgery is passing large amounts of blood via nasogastric suction. Which finding, if assessed by the nurse, is an early sign of shock?
1. Distended neck veins.
2. Rapid shallow breathing.
3. Bradycardia.
4. Constricted pupils.

93. The nurse is administering tracheostomy care to an adult. Which of the following should be included in the procedure?
1. Soaking the outer cannula with saline solution.
2. Performing the procedure utilizing medical asepsis.
3. Soaking the inner cannula in half-strength hydrogen peroxide solution.
4. Cutting a sterile gauze pad to place between the neck and the tracheostomy tube.

94. Which of the following teaching should the nurse include when establishing a bowel training regimen for a 62-year-old with chronic constipation?
1. Avoid laxatives.
2. Decrease exercise.
3. Increase the fiber content of your diet.
4. Increase fluid intake 4500 to 5000 ml.

95. Medicare will pay for a limited number of home care visits for clients with hypertension. The nurse visiting an elderly hypertensive client must assess the client regularly for
1. ability to ambulate.
2. dehydration.
3. effectiveness of medication.
4. awareness of advanced directives.

96. The clinic nurse is teaching the client about breast cancer. Which one of the following risk factors for breast cancer should be assessed regularly by the nurse?
1. Dietary habits.
2. Socioeconomic status.
3. Early menarche.
4. Being over 30 years of age.

97. The home health nurse is visiting a 90-year-old man who lives with his 88-year-old wife. He is legally blind and suffered a broken hip five years ago. He ambulates with difficulty with the aid of a walker. The highest priority nursing diagnosis for him is
1. self-care deficit, toileting.
2. knowledge deficit regarding blindness.
3. high risk for injury.
4. impaired adjustment.

98. A client with Guillain-Barré syndrome has been on a ventilator for three weeks, and can communicate only with eye blinks because of quadriplegia. The intensive care nursing staff sometimes have no time for this tedious communication process. The client's family comes infrequently since they run a family-owned restaurant that does not close until visiting hours are over. How should the nurse respond to the family's request for exemption from visiting hours?
1. Arrange for a volunteer to stay with the client during the day to provide for socialization needs and to facilitate communication with staff.
2. Explain to the family that consistency in enforcing rules is important to prevent complaints from the families of other clients.
3. Suggest that the family visit in shifts during the normal visiting hours, since the client needs to sleep at night.
4. Make an exception to visiting regulations because of the long-term nature of the client's recovery and the need for family support.

99. An adult client has congestive heart failure and is receiving spironolactone (Aldactone). Which of the following is least appropriate for the nurse to teach the client about his medication?
1. Use calcium-based salt substitutes.
2. Swelling and tenderness of the breasts may occur with long-term therapy.
3. Take the medicine in the morning if possible.
4. Include high-potassium foods in the diet to decrease the possibility of hypokalemia.

100. A one-year-old child is admitted to the hospital with Tay-Sachs disease. The nurse can expect that this child will be placed on
1. seizure precautions.
2. a cooling blanket.
3. strict intake and output.
4. protective isolation.

Answers and Rationales for Practice Test 3

ANSWER	RATIONALE	NP	CN	CL

#1. 1. **Pain from a duodenal ulcer is often aching or burning in character. Pain occurs when the stomach is empty. In addition, persons who develop duodenal ulcers often hypersecrete gastric acid during REM sleep, with a resulting increase in pain that wakens them from sleep.**   As   Ph/9   An

    2. Duodenal ulcer pain is likely to be in the mid upper abdomen (epigastric) not the right upper quadrant. Food in the stomach buffers the excess acid and reduces the pain from an ulcer.

    3. Sharp pain in the epigastric area radiating to the right shoulder is characteristic of gallbladder disease, not ulcers.

    4. Painful pressure in the midsternal area is characteristic of cardiac problems, not ulcers.

#2. 2. **Allowing the child to remain in a squatting position serves to decrease venous return by occluding the femoral vein through hip flexion, to lessen the workload on the right side of the heart, and to increase arterial oxygen saturation.**   Im   Ph/9   Ap

    1. Returning the child to bed is not the best initial nursing action. Allowing the child to remain in a squatting position serves to decrease venous return by occluding the femoral vein through hip flexion, to lessen the workload on the right side of the heart, and to increase arterial oxygen saturation.

    3. Placing the child in a chair is not the best initial nursing action. Allowing the child to remain in a squatting position serves to decrease venous return by occluding the femoral vein through hip flexion, to lessen the workload on the right side of the heart, and to increase arterial oxygen saturation.

    4. There is no need to call the physician. The child is assuming the position that is best for her.

#3. 3. **The fibrosed liver obstructs flow through portal vessels, which normally receive all blood circulating from the gastrointestinal tract. The increased pressure in portal vessels shunts some of the blood into the lower pressure veins around the lower esophagus. Since these veins are not designed to handle the high-pressure portal blood flow, they develop varicosities, which often rupture and bleed.**   An   Ph/10   An

    1. While low serum albumin is common with liver disease, it does not weaken the existing structures of the body. Weakness of the esophageal wall is not the problem. Since the esophageal vessels lie close to the surface, under the mucous membranes, the esophageal wall does not support them at the inner surface.

    2. The liver is located to the right of the esophagus. When it enlarges, it is more likely to compromise expansion of the right lung than to affect the esophagus.

    4. Enlargement of the liver does not displace the esophagus.

#4. 4. **Administration of blood and fluid is vital in maintaining blood volume in a client with severe gastrointestinal bleeding.**   Pl   Ph/10   An

    1. Accommodating the client's frequent needs to use the bedpan has no effect on the client's fluid needs.

    2. Maintaining the gastric pH has nothing to do with meeting the client's fluid needs.

    3. Vital signs need to be monitored more frequently than hourly.

#5. 2. **When going up steps the client must always provide for either the crutches or the unaffected leg to be bearing his weight at all times. Moving the unaffected leg up first allows the strong leg**   Im   Ph/7   Im

ANSWER	RATIONALE	NP	CN	CL

muscles of the unaffected leg to do the lifting to raise him to the next step.

1. Moving the crutches up to the next step before the unaffected leg would place the arms in a raised position from which they could not possibly lift the client's body weight. The arms are not as strong as the unaffected leg and should not be used to lift the body weight.

3. Placing both crutches on the same side would cause the client to lean to one side, throwing him off balance, and increasing his risk of falling.

4. It would be very difficult and awkward to lower himself to a sitting position so close to the ground and to raise himself from the floor at the top of the stairs back to a standing position. He would be off balance at least part of the time while doing this and in danger of falling.

#6. 2. Oxygenation is the most important immediate postoperative goal. Remember the ABC's of client care. — Pl — Ph/9 — Im

1. Ambulating using adaptive devices is an appropriate goal for a child with cerebral palsy, however, it is not the most important immediate postoperative goal.

3. Verbalizing pain control is an appropriate goal for a child who has had surgery, however, it is not the most important immediate postoperative goal.

4. Completing daily self-care needs is an appropriate goal for a child with cerebral palsy, however, it is not the most important immediate postoperative goal.

#7. 3. Children ages three to five often think of death as sleep or a departure. To them, death is reversible. — An — He/3 — An

1. Children ages five to nine begin to view death as irreversible and permanent. They develop generalizations based on observable facts.

2. Children ages seven to ten view death as inevitable, universal, and final. Death becomes associated with pain.

4. Teenagers view death as a final, universal, and personal experience. Adolescents view life in the present and can become very angry at the injustice of death.

#8. 4. To prevent reinfection, the entire prescribed antibiotic needs to be taken. The course of treatment is usually seven to ten days. — Im — Ph/8 — Ap

1. Acetaminophen is the drug of choice for fever or pain. Aspirin is contraindicated.

2. All of the medication must be taken.

3. Heat may be applied to the ear to decrease pain.

#9. 3. If the air intake tubings are not delivering room air and/or oxygen, the carbon dioxide level in the tent will increase, causing hypoxia. If the humidity reservoir is allowed to run dry, the blowing air will dry the mucous membranes and cause more edema. — Pl — Ph/9 — Ap

1. The tent can also be left open and used as a humidity source for the entire room. This method is used for the child who is totally noncompliant, with the understanding that the treatment will not be as effective.

2. Keeping the child unchilled will decrease oxygen needs. This is the second priority in nursing care.

4. A child who can play and rest contentedly inside the tent will recuperate faster than one who receives less "tent time." However, this is not the highest priority.

#10. 3. Probable signs of pregnancy are objective signs seen on physical examination. A positive urine test is a probable sign of pregnancy. — As — He/3 — An

1. Morning sickness is a subjective sign of pregnancy and a possible sign of pregnancy.

2. Urinary frequency is a possible sign of pregnancy, but it could also be a sign of urinary tract disease.

4. Auscultation of fetal heart tones is a positive sign of pregnancy. Fetal heart tones could not be auscultated at this stage of gestation.

#11. 3. Nägele's rule for calculating EDC (estimated date of confinement) is to add seven days to the first day of the last menstrual period, subtract three months, and add one year. The EDC calculates to March 22.   An   He/3   An

1. You subtracted seven days instead of adding seven days.

2. You forgot to add seven days.

4. You added 14 days instead of seven.

#12. 1. In pregnancy, constipation results from decreased gastric motility and increased water reabsorption in the colon caused by increased levels of progesterone. Increasing fluid intake to three liters a day will help prevent constipation.   Pl   He/3   Ap

2. The client should increase fluid intake, increase roughage in the diet, and increase exercise as tolerated. Laxatives are not recommended because of the possible development of laxative dependence or abdominal cramping.

3. Iron supplements are necessary during pregnancy, as ordered, and should not be discontinued.

4. The client should increase fluid intake, increase roughage in the diet, and increase exercise as tolerated. Laxatives are not recommended because of the possible development of laxative dependence or abdominal cramping. Mineral oil is especially bad to use as a laxative because it decreases the absorption of fat-soluble vitamins (A, D, E, K) if taken near mealtimes.

#13. 3. Backache in the late months of pregnancy may be relieved by wearing shoes with low heels that provide a wide base when walking. The growth of the fetus and uterus in late pregnancy alter the client's center of gravity and put a strain on the back muscles.   Pl   He/3   Co

1. The client's weight seems to be within normal limits but, even if it were not, attempting to lose weight during pregnancy would not be safe for the fetus. Weight in itself is not the cause of the backache in the later stages of pregnancy. The altered center of gravity is the problem.

2. It should not be necessary to quit her job to help relieve her backache.

4. Resting with legs elevated is good for varicosities but is not the recommended treatment for backache. Also, notice that the answer says at all times. This is impossible.

#14. 1. The signs and symptoms describe the transition phase of labor.   An   He/3   Co

2. The signs and symptoms describe the transition phase of labor. Transition is a normal phase of labor.

3. The signs and symptoms describe the transition phase of labor. There is nothing to indicate a need for oxytocin.

4. The signs and symptoms describe the transition phase of labor.

#15. 1. Gentle massage of the uterine fundus is indicated. If uterine atony is due to a full bladder, the bladder will protrude into the abdomen; if due to retained products of conception, clots will be expelled from the vagina; if due to an infection, a foul lochia will be noted.   Im   He/3   Ap

2. Priority is given to attempting to perform external uterine fundal massage in order to determine uterine response. Further evaluation of lochia is done after attempted uterine massage.

3. Initial fundal massage noting uterine response is indicated. Pitocin may be prescribed by the physician or midwife after nursing assessments and nursing interventions are made and results of uterine massage are relayed to the health care provider.

    4. The nurse performs the initial assessment of the uterus and does uterine fundal massage. The bladder, lochia, and fundal firmness and placement should be assessed. If uterine atony is not resolved, the physician or midwife should be called for further evaluation.

#16. 4. There is risk of infection from saline abortion because saline is injected into the amniotic sac. The woman also may labor at length with ruptured membranes.   An Ph/9 An

    1. Her diastolic blood pressure could be elevated from pain. Only 150 to 250 ml of fluid is injected and should not cause elevation in blood pressure. The client's baseline blood pressure is unknown.

    2. A temperature of 101°F is not normal and may be indicative of infection.

    3. Vital signs for the client in shock would include an increased pulse and decreased blood pressure.

#17. 3. Chlamydia growth is enhanced by oral contraceptives. The primary symptoms of chlamydia infection are vaginal discharge and pruritis. Chlamydia is often seen in conjunction with other infections such as gonorrhea or trichomonas. Cultures and blood studies are indicated for diagnosis and treatment. Contacting a physician is necessary.   Im Ph/8 Ap

    1. The woman is at risk for development of an infection. Over-the-counter remedies should not be prescribed until a diagnosis is made.

    2. Changing of undergarments will not cure a sexually transmitted disease.

    4. Oral contraceptives are a very effective method of birth control. Careful assessment, diagnosis, and treatment of the vaginal discharge should be done before terminating the pill.

#18. 1. Clients harboring *Trichomonas vaginalis* usually exhibit a profuse, bubbly, foul-smelling discharge.   As Ph/9 Co

    2. Clients harboring *Trichomonas vaginalis* may experience painful urination and some perineal inflammation in addition to the foul-smelling discharge. White cheese-like patches in the vagina are characteristic of monilia infection.

    3. A perineal deformity is not present in trichomonas. Warts may alter the appearance of the genitalia as in condyloma acuminata.

    4. Ulcers or lesions of the vagina or vulva are usually seen in herpes simplex virus types I and II and in syphilis.

#19. 1. The Apgar scoring system was designed to initially evaluate the physical condition of the newborn. The total score ranges from 0 to 10 based on two points being assigned to each of the following categories: heart rate, respiratory effort, muscle tone, reflex irritability, and color. One point was deducted for the baby's color. All other parameters are given a score of 2 for a total of 9 points.   As He/3 Ap

    2. Full flexion is assigned a score of two; acrocyanosis, a score of one; heart rate, a score of two; full, lusty cry is a score of two for respiratory effort and two for reflex irritability.

    3. Full flexion is assigned a score of two; acrocyanosis, a score of one; heart rate, a score of two; full, lusty cry is a score of two for respiratory effort and two for reflex irritability.

    4. A score of six usually indicates a moderately depressed neonate. The baby described is normal. Full flexion assigned a score of two; acrocyanosis, a score of one; heart rate, a score of two; full, lusty cry is a score of two for respiratory effort and two for reflex irritability.

#20. 1. The most common side effect of epidural anesthesia is a sudden drop in maternal blood pressure, which can compromise fetal blood flow.   Ev Ph/8 An

    2. Uterine pain occurs if the anesthesia is not evenly distributed over the nerve roots or if there is incorrect placement of the epidural.

    3. A fetal heart rate of 140 is within the normal range.

4. The objective of administering epidural anesthesia is to provide relief from the discomfort of uterine contractions. The relief that the client experiences may help her cope with labor. The epidural does not produce an alteration in the client's perception of reality.

#21. 1. When a person with weakness on one side uses a cane, there should always be two points of contact with the floor. When Ms. C. moves the cane forward, she has both feet on the floor, providing stability. As she moves the weak leg, the cane and the strong leg provide support. Finally, the cane, which is even with the weak leg, provides stability while she moves the strong leg. Ev   Ph/7   An

2. She should not hold the cane with her weak arm. The use of the cane requires arm strength to ensure that the cane provides adequate stability when standing on the weak leg.

3. The cane should be held in the left hand, the hand opposite the affected leg.

4. If Ms. C. moved the cane and her strong foot at the same time, she would be left standing on her weak leg at one point. This would be unstable at best; at worse, impossible.

#22. 4. The supine position allows abdominal organs to rise, permitting less space for lung expansion. With a high abdominal incision, such as is used for splenectomy, incisional pain and irritation at the surgical site predispose the client to respiratory complications. The pressure of abdominal organs that occurs in the supine position increases this risk. Pl   Ph/9   Co

1. Although the incision in a nonemergency splenectomy is to the left of midline, there is no contraindication to lying on the left side.

2. Since the operative site is on the left, the right side is not contraindicated.

3. A semi-Fowler's or higher position is beneficial for the splenectomy client, since it allows the abdominal organs to drop lower in the abdominal cavity, leaving more space for adequate lung expansion.

#23. 1. Dilated pupils, flushing, and tremors are seen in persons taking hallucinogens. As   Ps/6   An

2. Pupillary constriction, constipation, and sleepiness are seen in persons taking opiates.

3. Tremors, muscular weakness, and mask-like face are signs and symptoms of Parkinson's disease.

4. Vertical and horizontal nystagmus is indicative of PCP use and/or intoxication.

#24. 3. The middle phase of group therapy is one in which cohesiveness is built. Self-disclosure and warm feelings promote group cohesion. Joining or leaving the group at this point results in strong emotions due to disruption of group cohesiveness and sharing. An   Ps/5   An

1. During the beginning phase group members are learning to know one another, have a sense of their problems being universal with other members, are generally unsure as to what to say, and are more "I" focused.

2. Transition is not a phase in group process.

4. Group members may have many reactions to termination of the group. However, the date of termination known in advance may help clients feel more secure.

#25. 3. Denial is the blocking out of thoughts or feelings perceived as painful. Mr. T. is blocking the news that he has rectal cancer and needs surgery. As   Ps/5   Co

1. Projection is blaming others for one's own shortcomings or unacceptable thoughts and feelings about the self.

2. Repression is a forgotten memory that cannot be brought into awareness. Repressed thoughts are anxiety producing and are often produced by trauma.

ANSWER	RATIONALE	NP	CN	CL

4. Displacement is the expression of emotion onto someone or some object that is less dangerous than the original person. Pent-up feelings are usually hostile ones expressed in a safer environment, since to express it to the original person is unacceptable or too dangerous.

#26. 3. Suicide attempts are more common on evenings or night shift and weekends when unit structure is lessened. Mrs. G. is at high risk because of her husband's threats to cut off financial resources and access to her children. She is depressed and is experiencing "tunnel vision" in regards to her situation. Mrs. G.'s safety needs must be met. The suicidal intent must be taken seriously. She has an intent to follow through with a plan and needs close observation, preferably one on one with the nurse. Im   Ps/6   Ap

1. Safety is the nurse's first concern. Therapeutic sessions will address the marital relationship, coping strategies, and problem solving at a later time.
2. Mrs. G.'s safety may not be secure as she could possibly find some object with which to cut herself.
4. All suicidal remarks and gestures must be taken seriously. Clients can find a multitude of ways to commit or attempt to commit suicide while hospitalized.

#27. 1. Kussmaul respirations, acetone odor to breath, hypotension, tachycardia, decreased reflexes, and loss of consciousness in a young client all suggest diabetic ketoacidosis. The nurse should ask if the client is known to have diabetes. However, a negative answer does not rule out diabetes. It is estimated that 15–30% of all hospital admissions for diabetic ketoacidosis occur in undiagnosed diabetics. An   Ph/10   An

2. Epilepsy denotes a group of neurological disorders characterized by the repeated occurrence of any of several forms of seizures. Seizures, or convulsions, are paroxysmal episodes in which there is a disturbance in consciousness, behavior, sensation, or autonomic function. They may include recurrent contractions of muscles. The seizure is usually transitory with full recovery of function.
3. General effects of moderate to severe head trauma include cerebral edema, sensorimotor deficits, and increased intracranial pressure. Manifestations of cerebral edema and increased intracranial pressure include changes in level of consciousness, slow, labored respirations, bradycardia, pupillary dysfunction, and changes in motor function.
4. Responses to drug overdose vary according to the substance used. Signs of opiate overdose include slow, shallow respirations, often with periods of apnea, constricted pupils, and circulatory collapse.

#28. 4. Hematochezia (blood in the stool) may come from a source in either the upper or lower gastrointestinal tract. The client's past medical history will aid in determining the location of the bleeding. As   Ph/9   An

1. Finding out the duration of the bleeding will not help determine the location of the bleeding.
2. Vital signs will help determine the amount of the bleeding, but will not determine the location of the bleeding.
3. Laboratory results will show that bleeding is present but will not identify the site of the bleeding.

#29. 1. The intervertebral disc is a cartilaginous plate that forms a cushion between the vertebral plates. In herniation of the disc, the nucleus of the disc protrudes into the annulus (the fibrous ring around the disc) with subsequent compression of the spinal nerve as it emerges from the spinal column. This causes pain in the area of nerve distribution. An   Ph/10   Co

2. In herniation of the disc the nucleus of the disc protrudes into the annulus (the fibrous ring around the disc) with subsequent

compression of the spinal nerve as it emerges from the spinal column. This causes pain in the area of nerve distribution.

3. In herniation of the disc the nucleus of the disc protrudes into the annulus (the fibrous ring around the disc) with subsequent compression of the spinal nerve as it emerges from the spinal column. This causes pain in the area of nerve distribution.

4. In herniation of the disc the nucleus of the disc protrudes into the annulus (the fibrous ring around the disc) with subsequent compression of the spinal nerve as it emerges from the spinal column. This causes pain in the area of nerve distribution.

#30. 4. Hypothermia with cardiac arrhythmias may occur when infusing the large quantities of blood needed in GI bleeding. Blood-warming equipment should be used to prevent this problem. Im Ph/8 Ap

1. Blood should always be administered with saline, but this will not prevent hypothermia.

2. Running blood through a central line would only increase the danger of hypothermia. Blood is not given through a central line.

3. Packed cells are not any warmer than whole blood. Packed cells are indicated when oxygen-carrying capacity is needed and volume is not. The client who is hemorrhaging needs whole blood.

#31. 1. Gout, or gouty arthritis, is a systemic disease in which urate crystals are deposited in joints and other body tissues. Elevated uric acid levels occur as a result of improper metabolism of purines, resulting in excessive production of uric acid, which the kidneys are unable to adequately eliminate. This causes hyperuricemia and leads to formation of sodium urate crystals, which are deposited in the synovium and other tissues. An Ph/9 Co

2. Elevated uric acid levels occur as a result of improper metabolism of purines, resulting in excessive production of uric acid, which leads to formation of sodium urate crystals. The crystals are deposited in the synovium and other tissues, resulting in severe inflammatory response.

3. Gout, or gouty arthritis, is a systemic disease in which urate crystals deposit in joints and other body tissues, causing a severe inflammatory response with joint pain and swelling. Degeneration of cartilage and bone is characteristic of osteoarthritis.

4. Gout, or gouty arthritis, is a systemic disease in which urate crystals are deposited in joints and other body tissues, causing a severe inflammatory response. Inflammation of the bursa is bursitis and may be acute or chronic. It is usually the result of trauma or strain to the joint.

#32. 4. Restriction of both oral and IV fluids is necessary to reduce the excess vascular volume in congestive heart failure. Pl Ph/9 Ap

1. Activity will be restricted, but this does nothing to relieve the edema.

2. Fostering a relaxed environment is an important objective but it is not specific to edema.

3. Identifying goals for self-care is an appropriate nursing objective, but is not specific to the client's edema.

#33. 1. Active and passive leg exercises are important for client on bed rest as a method for preventing thrombophlebitis. As Ph/9 An

2. Trying not to think about the fatigue doesn't help the fatigue in any way and it doesn't allow the client to talk about her feelings regarding her symptoms of fatigue.

3. Eating larger meals would likely increase the client's feeling of fatigue. Meals should be smaller.

4. Rest is important to a client's recovery, but it must be combined with proper exercise and activity.

#34. 2. Left-sided failure is caused by ventricular dysfunction, resulting in increased pressure in the pulmonary veins, which leads to the development of rales. As Ph/10 An

1. Tachycardia, not bradycardia, is present in left-sided failure.
3. Liver engorgement is present in right-sided failure.
4. Jugular vein distention is present in right-sided failure.

#35. 4. Visual disturbances and arrhythmias are signs of digitalis toxicity.   Ev   Ph/8   Ap
1. Bradycardia is a sign of digitalis toxicity, but auditory hallucinations are not.
2. Dry mucous membranes and diarrhea are not signs of digitalis toxicity.
3. Heart block and brittle hair and nails are not signs of digitalis toxicity.

#36. 2. Normal serum potassium levels are 3.5–5.3 mEq/liter. Only 4.0 mEq/liter is within normal limits and requires no immediate intervention.   An   Ph/9   An
1. 3.2 mEq/l indicates hypokalemia. The physician should be notified at once.
3. 5.7 mEq/l indicates hyperkalemia. The physician should be notified.
4. 6.0 mEq/l indicates serious hyperkalemia. The client should be monitored for arrhythmias and the physician should be notified at once.

#37. 3. Weight loss occurs through excessive extracellular fluid loss, meconium loss, and limited food intake. Infants take in small amounts of feedings, and energy expenditure exceeds intake.   An   He/3   An
1. Feedings every three to four hours are adequate to meet infant needs. Breast-fed infants will nurse between six and ten times a day. Formula-fed infants may feed six to eight times a day.
2. The cord stump has a minimal amount of Wharton's jelly in it and does not contribute to weight loss through drying.
4. Regurgitation may occur but it is very limited. This is very different from vomiting every feeding, which is pathologic and would contribute to weight loss.

#38. 3. Glucagon is the drug of choice in the treatment of hypoglycemia due to excess insulin when the client cannot safely take glucose by mouth. Glucagon begins to raise the blood sugar within five minutes, usually increasing the level of consciousness sufficiently to allow the client to eat carbohydrates, including complex carbohydrates needed to restore liver glycogen supplies.   Im   Ph/8   Ap
1. The symptoms presented are indicative of hypoglycemia, a common complication of insulin overdose or insufficient food intake. Insulin is not indicated.
2. Sweetened juice or other source of oral simple carbohydrates is the treatment of choice when the client with hypoglycemia is fully conscious. A reduced level of consciousness increases the risk of aspiration with intake of oral food or fluids. Glucagon should be administered to elevate glucose levels sufficiently to allow oral intake.
4. IV glucose is used when glucagon is unable to raise the blood glucose sufficiently to raise the level of consciousness. Most schools are not equipped for IV drug administration and an ambulance would be called to transport the client to the hospital for treatment.

#39. 4. The first line of treatment is ipecac. The child should be seen as soon as possible after that. The child has just swallowed the aspirin and is not described as being unconscious. Ipecac is contraindicated if the child is unconscious.   Im   Ph/10   Ap
1. The physician should be notified once the child is en route to the emergency room.
2. The mother should bring the child to the emergency room, but first should give ipecac.
3. Since the child took an unknown amount of aspirin, it would be inappropriate to have the child remain at home. The child should be evaluated by a health care worker.

#40. 1. Normal height for a twelve-month-old ranges from 29–32 inches; normal weight for a twelve-month-old ranges from 19–27 lb. This   An   He/3   An child's height is within normal limits for his age, but his weight is above normal for his age.

2. The child has a normal height, but he does not have a decreased weight.

3. The child is a normal height but his weight is above normal.

4. The child is normal height but is above normal in weight.

#41. 4. The parents should be encouraged to foster normal socialization of their child. Parents may need additional information regarding fears they may have.

Ev He/3 An

1. Feeding slowly and allowing frequent rest periods help reduce energy expenditure and are appropriate activities.

2. Playing quiet games and activities help reduce energy expenditure and are appropriate activities.

3. Maintaining a good diet fosters growth and development.

#42. 1. Applying pressure allows for clot formation. A child with hemophilia will require ten to fifteen minutes for clot formation.

Im Ph/10 Ap

2. Applying an ice pack will be beneficial for vasoconstriction. However, pressure is the initial action, not an ice pack.

3. Covering the wound with a sterile dressing is not the initial nursing action when a person with hemophilia is injured. Stopping the bleeding takes priority.

4. It is not necessary to notify the physician immediately unless the nurse is unable to control bleeding with pressure.

#43. 4. The fourth stage of labor is the first hour or two after delivery and is a critical period for maternal systems to stabilize after giving birth.

Pl He/3 An

1. Uterine contractions mark the beginning of the first stage of labor, not the fourth.

2. Cervical dilation is characteristic of the first and second stages of labor, not the fourth.

3. The third stage of labor is characterized by the delivery of the baby and the placenta.

#44. 1. The plan is to reduce secondary gain, which is the avoidance of an unpleasant activity. Focusing on symptoms only promotes secondary gain.

Pl Ps/6 Ap

2. Somatic symptoms are perceived as real and are not under voluntary control.

3. It is best to convey interest in the client and not the client's symptoms.

4. The plan is to reduce secondary gain and the dependency inherent in it. The nurse wants to foster independence.

#45. 4. Splitting is the primitive defense mechanism seen in clients with borderline personality disorder. There is an inability to integrate both good and bad aspects of self and others into an integrated whole. This results in both an idealization and a devaluation of others and self.

As Ps/6 An

1. Aggressive behavior is seen in many psychiatric disorders. Borderline clients may act out and become aggressive, but aggressive behavior is not as diagnostic of borderline as splitting.

2. Depressive symptoms are exhibited as "abandonment depression," however, it is not the most important assessment.

3. Sleep disturbances occur with many mental illnesses, especially with regards to mood disorders and anxiety, but are not a key assessment in borderline personality disorders.

#46. 1. Denial is often used for maintaining self-esteem when control is lost. The client may rationalize her behavior to support her denial.

An Ps/5 An

2. The client definitely has a problem with addiction. The physician is at fault for not monitoring the situation to prevent it before it occurred.

3. The client is not assuming blame nor is she blaming her physician.

4. There is no information provided regarding her education.

ANSWER	RATIONALE	NP	CN	CL

#47. 2. **The Medic-alert bracelet is essential to warn health care providers that the adrenals have been removed and that glucocorticoid and mineralocorticoid replacement is essential for life. Failure to supply replacement doses will precipitate severe hypotension, shock, coma, and vasomotor collapse.** Ev Ph/9 An

    1. Bilateral adrenalectomy is removal of the adrenal glands and requires life-long replacement of the glucocorticoids and mineralocorticoids usually secreted by these glands.

    3. Glucocorticoids and mineralocorticoids will need to be taken for life as they are normally produced only by the glands that have been removed and are essential for life.

    4. If the dose of replacement hormones is carefully adjusted, the client should not experience signs of overdose such as "moon face," weight gain, and edema.

#48. 2. **When another nurse is unable to perform her nursing duties due to substance abuse, she should not be allowed to continue them, as client safety is a primary concern.** Im Sa/1 Ap

    1. Calling the supervisor is a secondary measure after confronting the nurse and relieving the nurse of her duties. You cannot always assume the supervisor will be immediately available, and client safety should be addressed first.

    3. Ignoring the situation is against the professional code of conduct for nurses.

    4. Sandra needs to be relieved of her duties. She probably would not benefit from a lecture in her condition.

#49. 4. **With reduced levels of anxiety, the client's perceptual field broadens, allowing the client to focus on the cause of anxiety and to connect the cause with his anxious response. He is able to learn from the experience. High levels of anxiety prevent this from occurring.** Ev Ps/5 Ap

    1. Repetitive, tiring tasks may reduce anxiety. However, for safety concerns, punching the bedside table is unacceptable. It shows increased psychomotor agitation.

    2. Anxiety often increases when a client is left alone.

    3. Anxiety is seen in demanding verbal responses. Unmet needs or expectations create anxiety.

#50. 2. **Clients with a T4 injury will have sufficient upper extremity strength to master the technique of independent transfer.** As Ph/9 An

    1. The client will not need an electric wheelchair. He will have strength in his upper body.

    3. Given the level of the spinal injury, he will not be walking.

    4. Saying, "there is little I can do" does not indicate an understanding that he will be able to do a great deal.

#51. 3. **Checking for bladder distention frequently will prevent distention of the ureters and renal pelvis. If the client is on intermittent self-catheterization, this must be done at least every three to four hours. Bladder distention may cause urinary tract infections because the pressure exerted on the bladder wall will impair the blood supply to the bladder. A full bladder is often the cause of autonomic dysreflexia.** Im Ph/9 Ap

    1. The bladder should not remain full. A Valsalva maneuver is any forced respiratory effort against a closed airway as when an individual holds his breath and tightens his muscles in a concerted effort to move a heavy object or to change positions in bed. A Valsalva maneuver can be dangerous for clients with cardiovascular disease.

    2. The urinary meatus only needs to be cleaned two to three times a day.

    4. 3000 ml of fluid per day is recommended.

#52. 2. **The goal with this client is to prevent incontinence by having the client control defecation.** Ev Ph/9 An

ANSWER	RATIONALE	NP	CN	CL

1. The client should not need laxatives or stool softeners.
3. The client will not necessarily have a daily bowel movement.
4. It is unrealistic to expect him to resume previous bowel habits.

#53. 4. Severe muscle spasms indicate that the Valium is not effective as a muscle relaxant.   Ev   Ph/8   An
1. Drowsiness is an expected side effect of Valium.
2. Hyperesthesia of the arms is not usually seen following administration of Valium.
3. Loss of appetite is a possible side effect of Valium.

#54. 3. The cane should be held in the hand opposite the affected leg and should be advanced at the same time the weak leg is advanced to maximize support.   Ev   Ph/7   An
1. A cane is used to help the client walk with greater balance and support. The cane should be held in the hand opposite the involved leg (on the good side). In normal ambulation the opposite arm and leg move forward together. Holding the cane on the opposite side reinforces normal body mechanics, widens the base of support, and provides support to the weakened leg.
2. The cane should be held fairly close to the body to prevent leaning. The client should maintain an erect posture to reduce the chance of losing his balance and falling.
4. The cane should be held in the hand opposite the affected leg and should be advanced at the same time the weak leg is advanced to maximize support. The cane should be held in the hand opposite the involved leg (on the good side). In normal ambulation the opposite arm and leg move forward together.

#55. 3. Catsup, like all canned tomato products, is very high in sodium and should be avoided.   Pl   Ph/7   Ap
1. Cooked cereal such as oatmeal or cream of wheat is not very high in sodium.
2. Broccoli is high in vitamins A and K, calcium, and fiber and should be eaten regularly.
4. Sugar may be restricted if the client is on a weight reduction diet or has diabetes.

#56. 3. Assessments are made of lying and standing blood pressures to detect orthostatic hypotension, which is characterized by a decrease in systolic blood pressure when the client moves from a lying to a standing position.   Im   He/4   Co
1. Assessment for central nervous system depression includes vital signs and a neurological exam.
2. Malignant hypertension is characterized by severely elevated blood pressure in both standing and lying positions. Malignant hypertension commonly damages the intima of small vessels, the brain, retina, heart, and kidneys.
4. Vascular insufficiency is inadequate peripheral blood flow caused by occlusion of vessels with atherosclerotic plaques, thrombi, or emboli. Diagnosis is made by checking and comparing peripheral pulses and skin temperature on opposite extremities.

#57. 3. Activities should be planned to conserve energy as the client must work so hard to breathe. It is important to plan care in a manner that does not increase breathlessness.   Pl   Ph/9   Ap
1. The client must continue to move to avoid the complications of immobility.
2. For this client maintenance of strength is more appropriate than increasing strength.
4. Testing limits of tolerance will fatigue the client needlessly.

#58. 4. Abdominal breathing elevates the diaphragm, thereby improving breathing effectiveness in clients with emphysema.   Ev   Ph/9   An
1. Expirations should be prolonged to remove as much CO_2 as possible.
2. The client's respiratory is already rapid.

ANSWER	RATIONALE	NP	CN	CL

3. The use of the diaphragm should be increased.

#59. **1.** **Mafenide acetate 10% (Sulfamylon) does cause burning on application. An analgesic may be required before the ointment is applied.** Im Ph/8 Co

2. Mafenide acetate 10% (Sulfamylon) is a strong carbonic anhydrase inhibitor that affects the renal tubular buffering system, resulting in metabolic acidosis.

3. Mafenide acetate 10% (Sulfamylon) does not cause discoloration. Silver nitrate solution, another topical antibiotic used to treat burn sepsis, has the disadvantage of turning everything it touches black.

4. Mafenide acetate 10% (Sulfamylon) is an ointment that is applied directly to the wound. It has the ability to diffuse rapidly through the eschar. The wound may be left open or dry dressing may be applied. Silver nitrate solution is applied by soaking the wound dressings and keeping them constantly wet, which may cause chilling and hypotension.

#60. **4.** **Since this client is not at high risk for pulmonary complication (her burns are lower extremity and occurred outdoors), the most urgent need is to replace lost fluids and prevent irreversible shock. The first 48–72 hours after the burn is characterized by a rapid shift of fluid from the vascular compartment into interstitial spaces as a result of vasodilation and increased capillary permeability.** An Ph/10 Hn

1. The primary goal of the emergent or shock phase of burn care is to maintain life. Interventions to prevent later complications are initiated at this stage but are not the primary concern. Dealing with the psychological aspects of a burn is a long-term goal.

2. The primary goal of the emergent or shock phase of burn care is to maintain life. Interventions to prevent later complications are initiated at this stage but are not the primary concern. Care of the burn wound and prevention of infection becomes the primary goal in the acute or intermediate phase of care, which begins 48–72 hours after the burn once the client has been stabilized.

3. About 30% of all persons with burns develop inhalation injuries due to smoke, heat, or toxic substances. Persons at risk for pulmonary damage include those with burns of the face and neck, burns that occurred in enclosed area, and exposure to smoke. A charcoal burn sustained outdoors is unlikely to cause pulmonary complications.

#61. **4.** **Full thickness burns destroy the epidermis and dermis. The nerve endings are destroyed, resulting in a painless wound that appears dry, pale, and leathery and ranges from white to charred in appearance.** An Ph/10 An

1. First-degree burns, also called superficial partial thickness burns, look like a severe sunburn. They are red, blanch with pressure, and are very painful. Skin texture may be normal to firm.

2. Superficial partial thickness burns, also called first-degree burns, look like a severe sunburn. They are red, blanch with pressure, and are very painful. Skin texture may be normal to firm.

3. Deep partial thickness burns involve the epidermis and part of the dermis. The presence of blisters often indicates a deep partial thickness burn. The wound is red, weeps fluid, and may become edematous.

#62. **4.** **By developing an identity the client is able to reckon with negative and positive feelings to establish self-esteem. This should provide motivation to cope.** An Ps/6 An

1. Decreasing the client's anxiety level is important to aid the client to cope with her problem but it is not the motivating force to enable her to cope.

2. It is true that people need a name and a history, however, it is not an appropriate interpretation of this client's behavior.

3.   It is true that the hospital needs a name for its records, however, it is not an appropriate interpretation of this client's behavior.

#63. 2.   The client experiencing depersonalization sees herself as changed or the situation as unreal. It is essential to orient the client to the unit to create a sense of reality and security in her environment.   Pl   Ps/6   Ap

1.   The client who is not experiencing reality cannot develop coping skills.
3.   The nurse needs more information to determine if 15-minute checks are sufficient or other measures are necessary.
4.   A client not based in reality cannot focus on education.

#64. 2.   Delusions are fixed false beliefs. The nurse focuses on reality aspects of communications in an effort to promote health rather than focus on delusions, which could become further entrenched.   Im   Ps/5   Ap

1.   Attempts to disprove the client's delusions often lead to tension. The client tends to defend and hold onto his delusions when they are attacked.
3.   Room restriction is not necessary for a delusional client, unless delusional behaviors prove harmful to the client or others.
4.   To agree with the delusional thinking reinforces the delusion. The nurse may also become part of the client's delusional system.

#65. 2.   The intensity of the ideas of reference has diminished, showing improvement in the client's delusional thinking.   Ev   Ps/5   An

1.   Hearing voices refers to auditory hallucinations, not the delusions the client is exhibiting.
3.   Less fear in using the public phone is evidence of improvement in a phobic client, not a delusional client.
4.   Correctly interpreting environmental stimuli reflects improvements in a client who experiences illusions.

#66. 2.   In nephrotic syndrome (nephrosis) plasma proteins are excreted in the urine due to an abnormal permeability of the glomerular basement membrane of the kidney to protein molecules, particularly albumin. The cause of nephrosis is unknown. The average age of onset is two and a half years and it is more common in boys than girls.   As   Ph/10   An

1.   Blood pressure is generally not elevated in nephrotic syndrome except in a child with severe renal insufficiency. A normal blood pressure in a two-and-a-half-year-old should be between 80 and 85 systolic and 50 and 60 diastolic.
3.   Dark urine is not seen in nephrotic syndrome.
4.   A history of a streptococcal infection is associated with glomerulonephritis.

#67. 1.   The primary goal in the treatment of nephrotic syndrome is to control edema. Diuretics are used to promote diuresis and subsequent weight loss. Corticosteroids are also given.   Ev   Ph/10   An

2.   Successful treatment will show improved appetite with weight loss instead of weight gain because of the reduction in edema.
3.   Successful treatment will show a decrease in the sedimentation rate and a decrease in the urine specific gravity.
4.   Temperature is not elevated with nephrotic syndrome.

#68. 3.   The best technique for handling temper tantrums includes being consistent, remaining calm, and ignoring the behavior.   Im   He/3   Ap

1.   Bribery (buying cookies for each trip) is not appropriate. Rewards may be given on occasion for good behavior.
2.   Leaving him home is not the best action. It does not give the child a chance to learn impulse control.
4.   Disciplining the child in a public place is difficult. No matter what form of discipline the mother uses, the child is getting additional attention. This will reinforce the child's behavior.

#69. 2.   As a result of placental maturation and placental production of   Ev   Ph/8   An

ANSWER	RATIONALE	NP	CN	CL

lactogen, insulin requirements begin increasing in the second trimester and may double or quadruple by the end of pregnancy.

1. The client starts to need increased insulin in the second trimester. This statement indicates a lack of understanding.
3. The client starts to need increased insulin in the second trimester. This statement indicates a lack of understanding.
4. Insulin doses depend on blood glucose levels. Finger sticks for glucose levels must be continued.

#70. 2. Rho (D) immune globulin is given to prevent maternal sensitization by promoting destruction of Rh positive red blood cells circulating in the mother's blood stream. Two of the criteria for administration of the Rho (D) immune globulin are: Rho (D) negative mother without Rh antibodies (nonsensitized) and an Rho (D) positive infant.   An   Ph/8   An

1. Only nonsensitized Rh negative mothers receive Rho (D) immune globulin.
3. Rho (D) immune globulin is given when the indirect Coombs test of cord blood is negative.
4. The Rho (D) immune globulin is given to Rho (D) negative mothers.

#71. 4. IV Pitocin for a client with secondary dystocia should produce progressive cervical dilation with contractions lasting no longer than 90 seconds.   Ev   Ph/8   An

1. A precipitate delivery would be dangerous to the mother and baby.
2. IV Pitocin should produce cervical effacement and cervical dilation with subsequent delivery.
3. Contractions lasting over 90 seconds would be dangerous to the unborn baby.

#72. 3. The infant has signs of hypoglycemia: tremors, irritability, and a decreased respiratory rate, which may be related to hypoglycemia. Checking the blood sugar is necessary to determine if hypoglycemia is the problem.   Im   Ph/9   Ap

1. The nurse should check the infant's blood sugar first. Dextrose may be indicated after checking the blood sugar.
2. The nurse should check the infant's blood sugar first. Dextrose may be indicated after checking the blood sugar.
4. The nurse should check the infant's blood sugar first. The pediatrician will want to know the infant's blood sugar.

#73. 1. Paresthesias, such as numbness or tingling (often described by the client as "feeling like it's asleep"), occur when compression of the tissues deprives the nerves of part of their circulation or when something presses directly on the nerve. This is an indication of both neurologic and circulatory problems.   Ev   Ph/9   An

2. This is a normal finding. It would be abnormal to find capillary refill time prolonged beyond five seconds. Capillary refill time is assessed by pressing the nail bed, or tissue beside a nail, long enough to blanch it, and observing how long it takes color to return to normal when the pressure is released.
3. The skin distal to the cast should be warm. Coolness would indicate a problem.
4. Dull aching of an extremity that has been fractured is not unusual. The pain with circulatory impairment is characteristically localized in one specific part of the extremity and is described as stabbing or throbbing.

#74. 4. Glucose is added to the dialysate for peritoneal dialysis to provide sufficient osmotic pressure to remove fluid. The osmotic pressure in the dialysate must be greater than the osmotic pressure exerted by blood proteins and electrolytes or fluid will not be removed. Wastes and electrolytes will diffuse passively into dialysate that has lower concentrations of these substances than blood.   An   Ph/10   An

1. While wastes might passively diffuse into a hypotonic fluid, water would diffuse out of it into the blood, worsening the fluid overload. The fluid used as dialysate must have an osmotic pressure greater than blood components.
2. The peritoneal membranes do not provide for active exchange of electrolytes or other ions. The exchange process in dialysis is a passive one that depends on concentration gradients.
3. If the increased pressure inside the abdomen were to create filtration pressure, it would force substances into the bloodstream, not out of it. Substances move from areas of greater pressure to areas of lesser pressure.

#75. 3. Erythropoietin produced by the kidneys is necessary to stimulate the bone marrow to produce red blood cells. In chronic renal failure this hormone is not produced.   An   Ph/10   An

1. Hemodilution can produce a drop in hematocrit. However, if the cause of the decrease in hematocrit were fluid retention, one would expect to find corresponding decreases in serum sodium. If the dialysis has corrected the electrolyte balance, it is unlikely that the client would retain sufficient fluid to cause this drop in hematocrit. Hemodilution does not usually produce such a drop in hemoglobin.
2. The cause of anemia in persons with chronic renal failure is lack of erythropoietin.
4. Hemolysis does not occur with peritoneal dialysis because red blood cells do not move outside the client's own blood vessels, so there are no mechanical forces to harm them.

#76. 2. Dye is injected intravenously for an IVP. The dye contains iodine. Allergy to shellfish often reflects iodine allergy and would therefore indicate that the client is at high risk for an allergic reaction to the dye.   As   Ph/9   Ap

1. Barium is not used in an IVP.
3. There would be no reason for giving a glass of water before the test and some radiologists require that the person be NPO prior to the test.
4. A full bladder is not necessary for the IVP. This measure would be used in preparation for ultrasound of the bladder.

#77. 3. Once chickenpox lesions are crusted and scabbed, they are no longer infectious to others.   Ev   Sa/2   Ap

1. Antibiotics are not given in the treatment of chickenpox.
2. The criteria for communicability is that there be no lesions that are in the vesicle stage. His temperature could be normal and itching subsided but the lesions could still be infectious.
4. It is not necessary to wait until all the lesions have faded. It may take several weeks.

#78. 2. Flat ginger ale and tea are well tolerated and not irritating to the GI tract after a stomach virus.   Pl   Ph/7   Ap

1. The broth may be irritating to the stomach.
3. The egg may be difficult to digest at this time.
4. Milk is difficult to digest.

#79. 2. Although there is variability in the pattern and type of vomiting, it usually starts gradually, rather than suddenly, and becomes more projectile (1–4 feet away) and more frequent with the tightening and further obstruction of the pyloric channel. It takes about four to six weeks for complete obstruction to occur.   As   Ph/10   An

1. Greenish-yellow, mucus-like, strong-smelling emesis is indicative of an obstruction below the level of the stomach that allows reflux of intestinal contents into the stomach.
3. Infants with pyloric stenosis are ravenously hungry and will take an entire replacement feeding after vomiting. They do not seem to suffer from nausea or pain, except when obstruction causes gastric distention.

ANSWER	RATIONALE	NP	CN	CL

4. The olive-shaped tumor of hypertrophied muscle is located just to the right of the umbilicus and is easily felt when the abdomen is relaxed during a feeding or after vomiting.

#80. 4. Tick bites associated with Lyme disease can be distinguished by a papule at the bite site, which progresses to large circumferential ring with a raised border.   Pl   He/4   An

    1. Keeping the skin covered in areas where ticks are likely to be helps to prevent tick bites.

    2. Tick repellent helps to prevent tick bites.

    3. It is important to detect tick bites early so treatment can be started immediately. Early treatment with doxycycline can prevent Lyme disease.

#81. 2. Ms. L. will need to be positioned on her right side for the first two hours, or longer, to put pressure on the liver. Persons with liver problems often have coagulation defects and are at high risk for bleeding from the biopsy site. Pressure on the liver will decrease the bleeding from the very vascular liver and also reduce leakage of bile into the peritoneal cavity.   Pl   Ph/9   Ap

    1. Some pain in the right upper quadrant, or referred to the right shoulder, is expected, but PRN analgesics should be sufficient to manage it. The pain should not persist as long as 24 hours, nor should it be severe enough to require narcotics every 3 or 4 hours.

    3. Pain from the liver is referred to the right shoulder, not the left arm. Referred pain in the left arm reflects a cardiac problem, which is not a common complication of liver biopsy.

    4. The dressing over the puncture site is usually a pressure dressing and should not be disturbed. Leakage of bile from the puncture site would be abnormal.

#82. 3. Masks and protective eye wear are indicated anytime there is great potential for splashing of body fluids that may be contaminated with blood. Suctioning of a tracheostomy almost always stimulates coughing, which is likely to generate droplets that may splash the health care worker. Clients who are suctioned frequently or have had an invasive procedure like a tracheostomy are likely to have blood in the sputum.   Ev   Sa/2   Ap

    1. Needles that have been used to draw blood should not be recapped. If it is necessary to recap them, an instrument such as a hemostat should be used to recap. The hand should never be used.

    2. Gloves are not necessary when feeding, since there is no contact with mucus membranes. Although saliva may have small amounts of HIV in it, the virus does not invade through unbroken skin. There is no evidence in the question to indicate broken skin.

    4. There is no reason to restrict pregnant workers from caring for persons with AIDS as long as they utilize universal precautions.

#83. 2. The presence of a colostomy does not require any dietary restrictions. However, it is important that food be thoroughly chewed to prevent obstruction by inadequately digested foods. This is especially likely to occur with partially cooked or raw vegetables. Clients may choose to limit gas-forming foods to reduce flatulence, but this is a matter of personal choice, not a dietary order.   Ev   Ph/9   Ap

    1. Irrigation is not recommended for management of ostomy drainage. The colostomy irrigation should be viewed as an enema and used for the same reasons an enema would be used.

    3. Daily pouch changes will strip the skin under the faceplate, predisposing it to excoriation. The pouch should be changed when the faceplate begins to loosen or when it is no longer possible to keep it clean and odor free. A pouch should last an average of three to five days.

    4. If there are no contraindications due to other medical problems, the

client should force fluids. Not doing so can lead to constipation and allow the drainage to become more concentrated and therefore more likely to damage skin.

#84. 2. At 33 weeks, the infant's sucking reflex is developed and breastfeeding should be encouraged if this is the mother's wish. Pl He/3 Ap

1. The sucking reflex is apparent from approximately 32 weeks on and it is often seen earlier.
3. The infant must be weaned to a crib at least several days prior to discharge so the infant's ability to maintain her temperature can be evaluated. The infant is of adequate size and gestational age to be moved to a crib.
4. Rectal temperatures are not recommended due to the risk of anal perforation. Axillary temperatures are recommended.

#85. 2. Crying pulls the edges of the suture line, and may widen the scar line. The baby should be prevented from crying as much as possible by keeping the infant's needs met and providing postoperative analgesia. Ev Ph/9 Ap

1. The prone position is contraindicated because it allows the child to move the face back and forth on the bed, putting tension on the suture line and Logan bar. Drainage of secretions is done by oral suction with a bulb syringe or by positioning the infant on his side.
3. Special nipples and feeders are available to allow the infant to close his jaws around the nipple without damaging the lip repair. He should always be positioned upright for feedings to prevent choking and should be burped often.
4. The cleansing procedure should be kept as sterile as possible with the use of cotton applicators dipped in saline (as ordered). An antibiotic ointment is sometimes ordered also. The suture line should be cleaned after every meal and at any other time that exudate forms or soiling has occurred. Small cleansing devices are used, rather than washcloths, to prevent movement of the protective device (Logan bar) around the suture lines.

#86. 2. Following a fracture or break in a bone, the extremity cannot be used and tends to move unnaturally instead of remaining rigid as it normally would. As Ph/10 An

1. Swelling due to inflammation or effusion accompanies trauma to soft tissue and is present following sprains, strains, contusions, and other soft tissue injuries. Swelling may be present in a fracture because there is often accompanying soft tissue damage. However, swelling does not differentiate between fracture and soft tissue injury.
3. Ecchymosis is hemorrhage into the injured part due to the rupture of many small blood vessels and is a common occurrence following soft tissue injury. Ecchymosis may occur following a fracture and related soft tissue damage. However, ecchymosis does not differentiate between fracture and soft tissue injury.
4. Pain is a common response to many kinds of injury including fractures. However, pain does not differentiate between fracture and soft tissue injury.

#87. 2. Children are usually kept in bed for 24 hours after a cardiac catheterization to prevent bleeding at the catheter insertion site. Pl Ph/9 Ap

1. General anesthetic is not used for a cardiac catheterization.
3. Usual diet as tolerated is ordered following a cardiac catheterization.
4. Severe pain is not expected. There should be only slight discomfort at the insertion site.

#88. 3. Athetoid cerebral palsy is characterized by involuntary, purposeless, slow writhing motions. As Ph/9 Co

1. Hyperactive reflexes are seen in a child with spastic cerebral palsy.
2. The intellectual function of some children with cerebral palsy may be affected, but many children with athetoid cerebral palsy have normal

intelligence. Not enough information is given to determine the intelligence level of this child.

4. Unsteady gait and clumsy, uncoordinated upper extremity function are seen in a child with spastic cerebral palsy.

#89. 1. **Postdelivery management of the mother with severe pregnancy-induced hypertension includes close observation for blood pressure elevations, CNS irritability, and respiratory function. The client is at risk for seizures for 24 hours after delivery.**   Pl   He/3   Co

2. Visitors are limited to decrease central nervous system stimulation and risk of seizures.

3. There is no need to keep the woman NPO. She should have small meals as tolerated.

4. Once the immediate postdelivery fluids have infused, there is no need to continue an IV just because of the pregnancy-induced hypertension.

#90. 3. **Hemoglobin and hematocrit are expected to rise as a result of transfusion of packed red blood cells.**   Ev   Ph/8   An

1. Packed red blood cells do not provide volume expansion and therefore might not raise blood pressure significantly.

2. While improving the oxygen-carrying capacity of the blood might reduce shortness of breath, it is not expected to change lung sounds.

4. Elevation in temperature is a sign of a transfusion reaction, not an effective transfusion.

#91. 4. **Respiratory function is always of prime importance in assessing a postoperative client.**   As   Ph/9   Ap

1. The nurse will assess the dressing but this will be done after assessing breath sounds.

2. The nurse will assess urine output but this will be done after assessing breath sounds.

3. The nurse will assess circulation to the leg but this will be done after assessing breath sounds.

#92. 2. **Rapid respirations typically occur during shock due to decreased tissue perfusion. The respiratory rate increases because the accumulation of excessive amounts of CO_2 stimulates the respiratory center.**   As   Ph/10   Ap

1. Distended neck veins are a sign of fluid overload (extracellular fluid volume excess) and are not seen in hypovolemic shock where the extracellular fluid volume deficit is decreased.

3. Tachycardia, not bradycardia, is seen in shock.

4. Constricted pupils are not an early sign of shock.

#93. 3. **The inner cannula is removed utilizing sterile gauze and is soaked in half-strength hydrogen peroxide solution. Clean the inner cannula with a small brush or pipe cleaners. Rinse in sterile saline or water and replace after the outer cannula has been suctioned.**   Im   Ph/9   Ap

1. The outer cannula is not removed for tracheostomy care.

2. Sterile technique should be used, not medical asepsis (clean technique).

4. Never use gauze dressings that have been cut with scissors. There is a danger of gauze filaments working their way into the stoma.

#94. 3. **The purpose of a bowel training program is to manipulate factors within the person's control (food and fluid intake, exercise, time for defecation) to produce the elimination of a soft formed stool at regular intervals. The increase of fiber in the diet as well as an increase of fluids to 2500 to 3000 ml and an increase of exercise will help the effectiveness of a bowel training program.**   Im   Ph/7   Ap

1. Laxatives should be used as little as possible but the nurse should start the teaching with diet and exercise.

2. Exercise stimulates peristalsis and should be increased to promote bowel function.

ANSWER		RATIONALE	NP	CN	CL

    4.   The fluid intake should be increased to 2500 to 3000 ml. 5000 ml may be too much for a 62-year-old.

#95. 3.   In clients with cardiovascular disease, the effectiveness of medication, as well side effects, should be monitored. This is the highest priority.   As   He/4   Ap

    1.   Ability to ambulate is important but is not specifically related to the management of hypertension.

    2.   Signs of dehydration are important but not specifically related to the management of hypertension.

    4.   The nurse should be aware of advanced directives but this is not specifically related to the management of hypertension.

#96. 1.   Dietary habits is the only risk factor that can be assessed regularly. A high-fat diet puts the woman at risk for breast cancer as well as other cancers. A high-fiber, low-fat diet lowers risk.   As   He/4   Ap

    2.   Socioeconomic status may be a risk factor but is one that the nurse and often the client can do little about.

    3.   Early menarche is a risk factor, but cannot be changed.

    4.   Breast cancer incidence increases with age. The woman, however, cannot change her age.

#97. 3.   The facts that the client is legally blind and has difficulty ambulating place him at extreme risk for injury.   An   Sa/2   Ap

    1.   There are no data to support this diagnosis.

    2.   There are no data to support this diagnosis.

    4.   There are no data to support this diagnosis.

#98. 4.   Guillain-Barré syndrome is characterized by the onset of ascending paralysis, which may include respiratory muscles. Persons with Guillain-Barré syndrome may remain ventilator-dependent for weeks, but have full consciousness. The prognosis for recovery from Guillain-Barré syndrome is good, but is very much dependent upon the level of supportive care during the acute stage.   Im   Sa/1   Ap

    1.   The need for family support is vital to prevent discouragement and depression. A volunteer will not take the place of family.

    2.   The need for family support is vital to prevent discouragement and depression, even at the risk of offending the families of other patients.

    3.   Loss of a breadwinner during the lengthy recovery process may add financial problems for the family.

#99. 4.   Spironolactone is a potassium-sparing diuretic so dietary potassium should be limited, not increased.   Pl   Ph/8   An

    1.   Calcium-based salt substitutes should be used rather than potassium-based salt substitutes because spironolactone is a potassium-sparing diuretic.

    2.   Swelling and tenderness of the breasts may occur with long-term therapy.

    3.   Diuretics should be taken in the morning if possible so the client will not be up all night urinating.

#100. 1.   Tay-Sachs disease is a degenerative neurologic disorder. It is often characterized by seizures.   Pl   Ph/9   An

    2.   Fevers that would necessitate a cooling blanket are not typical of Tay-Sachs disease.

    3.   Strict intake and output is not indicated for a child with Tay-Sachs unless there is a secondary disease present.

    4.   Protective isolation is not indicated for a child with Tay-Sachs unless there is a secondary disease present.

Practice Test 4

1. An adult woman is seen in the clinic for treatment of a minor burn. While assessing the woman the nurse obtains data suggesting that the client has developed hyperthyroidism. Which data are most suggestive of hyperthyroidism?
   1. Nervousness, frequent crying, weight loss, and tachycardia.
   2. Intolerance to cold, cool clammy skin, and bradycardia.
   3. Weight gain, puffiness around eyes, and extreme fatigue.
   4. Dry skin, constipation, and memory defects.
2. Randy, age 8, is admitted with rheumatic fever. Which clinical finding indicates to the nurse that Randy needs to continue taking the salicylates he had received at home?
   1. Chorea.
   2. Polyarthritis.
   3. Subcutaneous nodules.
   4. Erythema marginatum.
3. The nurse is caring for a client with advanced cancer of the breast. She complains of hypoguesia. The nurse should recommend
   1. eating dry crackers.
   2. monitoring intake and output.
   3. using spices to enhance food flavors.
   4. weighing her before and after meals.
4. An adult is admitted to the hospital to undergo a stapedectomy for the treatment of otosclerosis. Which findings elicited during physical assessment are most indicative of otosclerosis?
   1. Bone conduction is greater than air conduction.
   2. Bone conduction is equal to air conduction.
   3. Air conduction is greater than bone conduction.
   4. Sound lateralizes to the unaffected ear.
5. The nurse is caring for a client who has had a stapedectomy. Postoperative communications will be effective if the nursing personnel
   1. overarticulate.
   2. shout in the affected ear.
   3. speak at a moderate rate.
   4. use long, easily understood phrases.
6. Four-year-old Amy has been blind since birth. She has been attending a nursery program for the visually impaired. To continue independence in her activities of daily living, when her lunch tray arrives, the nurse will
   1. offer to feed her.
   2. explain that foods on her tray are set up like a clock.

3. put food on her fork and hand her the fork.
4. tell her that two foods are in front of her, one at the top of the tray and one at the bottom.
7. Bumping into a crib, the nurse notices that the newborn infant demonstrates the Moro (startle) reflex. This is seen as
   1. alternate flexion, adduction, and extension of the legs.
   2. extension of one side of the body while the other side is flexed.
   3. abduction, extension, and adduction of arms to an embracing position.
   4. flexion of the knees and hips with movement of the legs upward.
8. The nurse realizes that the discharge instructions given to a woman with placenta previa are understood when the nurse overhears the client tell her husband,
   1. "We can't have sex."
   2. "I have to return in a few days for a vaginal exam."
   3. "I will have to have a cesarean for this and other pregnancies."
   4. "I can go back to part-time work beginning tomorrow."
9. Miss R. is an 88-year-old client at a long-term care facility. Prior to administering any medication or treatment to this client the nurse must confirm identity by
   1. asking the client if she is Miss R.
   2. reading the client's identification bracelet.
   3. reading the client's medical record.
   4. asking the roommate to state the client's name.
10. A young adult is involuntarily admitted to the psychiatric unit in a manic state. Upon arrival on the unit he is unable to sit, and it is very difficult to follow what he is saying because of the rate and content of speech. He is very provocative and refuses to eat or drink. The area of disturbance that poses the greatest physical danger to this client is
    1. activity.
    2. perceptual.
    3. sensory.
    4. social.
11. A young man was arrested by the police for indecent exposure, loitering, and disturbing the peace. Prior to his arrest he had visited his mother's grave (she has been deceased for 12 years), where he became hyperactive, stripped off his clothes, and terrorized people living in the area near the cemetery. He was then admitted to the psychiatric unit. Upon admission he was speaking very rapidly, and

moved quickly around the unit, never sitting. He refused to eat or drink. The nursing diagnosis that would most appropriately describe the behavior that is of greatest concern is
1. anxiety.
2. potential for violence.
3. spiritual distress.
4. alteration in nutrition: less than body requirements.

12. A young woman with a history of bipolar disorder is admitted to the psychiatric unit. She is talking excitedly and walking rapidly around the unit. During the initial period of hospitalization, the nurse would most likely
1. encourage the client to participate in group and therapeutic activities.
2. observe the client closely until she calms down.
3. place the client in four-point restraints for protection of self and others.
4. place the client in seclusion but maintain frequent one-to-one contact with her.

13. Which of the following is least likely to influence the potential for a client to comply with lithium therapy after discharge?
1. The impact of lithium on the client's energy level and life-style.
2. The need for consistent blood level monitoring.
3. The potential side effects of lithium.
4. What the client's friends think of his need to take medication.

14. Ms. E., 16 years old and 20 weeks pregnant, has attended a prenatal nutrition course at her high school. The next day, the nurse knows she needs more instruction regarding proper protein intake because she has chosen the following for lunch:
1. roast chicken sandwich and ice cream cone.
2. roast beef sandwich and vanilla pudding.
3. fruit salad with cottage cheese and frozen yogurt.
4. bacon, lettuce, and tomato sandwich and an apple.

15. The nurse in the delivery room is caring for the newborn. Which action is the most important and most immediate action for the nurse to take?
1. Do the Apgar score.
2. Dry the baby completely.
3. Place identification bracelets on the infant and the mother.
4. Prevent infection by doing eye care.

16. The nurse caring for Ms. F., who is breastfeeding her full-term two-day-old baby boy, instructed Ms. F. on proper breast care this morning and wishes to evaluate her learning. Which of the following would demonstrate that the mother has an adequate knowledge base?

1. Ms. F. states she should not be concerned if hard lumps develop in her breasts at home because engorgement may cause lumps.
2. Ms. F. states she will continue to feed the infant as she has been, even if mild skin breakdown occurs on the nipple.
3. Ms. F. assesses her nipples carefully before and after each feeding.
4. Ms. F. states she does not have to worry about good hand washing because her baby is not premature.

17. The nurse is caring for a 30-week baby girl who is currently receiving 15 ml of breast milk via oral gastric tube every three hours. As part of the routine assessment the nurse should assess which of the following?
1. Assess for heme in the stool at each bowel movement.
2. Assess abdominal girth once every three days.
3. Assess for residual once per shift.
4. Assess for tube placement once every 24 hours.

18. The nurse is caring for Baby M., age two weeks, who is showing clinical manifestations of heart murmur, widened pulse pressure, cardiomegaly, bounding pulses, and tachycardia. The assessment findings indicate that which of the following shunt systems from fetal circulation has failed to close?
1. Ductus venosus.
2. Ductus arteriosus.
3. Ligamentum arteriosum.
4. Foramen ovale.

19. The nurse is caring for a 48-hour full-term infant whose mother abused cocaine and heroin throughout pregnancy. The mother does not wish to go into rehabilitation at this time. The nursing care plan should include which of the following?
1. Feeding the infant whenever it cries or acts hungry.
2. Allowing extra time to assist the woman with breastfeeding and promote attachment.
3. Organizing all necessary care around feeding times.
4. Covering the baby loosely with a blanket to prevent irritation.

20. A mother brings her baby in for his one-month check up. The mother reports that she has difficulty spreading the baby's right leg when she is diapering him. The nurse suspects a dislocated hip. Further assessment of this child for the possibility of a dislocated hip on the right side would include observing for
1. absence of Ortolani's sign.
2. presence of Trendelenburg's sign.
3. an increase in skin folds on the unaffected side.

4. shortening of the affected femur when supine with knees bent.

21. The nurse is caring for a client receiving intravenous therapy for correction of a fluid volume deficit. The nurse evaluates the effectiveness of the therapy. Which observation by the nurse indicates infiltration of the IV has occurred?
   1. Pallor at the infusion site.
   2. Increased temperature at the infusion site.
   3. Erythema around the infusion insertion device.
   4. Seepage of blood around the infusion insertion device.

22. An adult woman is admitted to an isolation unit in the hospital after tuberculosis was detected during a pre-employment physical. Although frightened about her diagnosis, she is anxious to cooperate with the therapeutic regimen. The teaching plan includes information regarding the most common means of transmitting the tubercle bacillus from one individual to another. Which contamination is usually responsible?
   1. Hands.
   2. Droplet nuclei.
   3. Milk products.
   4. Eating utensils.

23. An adult is receiving rifampin (Rifadin). Teaching by the nurse should include alerting the client to which of the following common side effects?
   1. Vertigo.
   2. Skin rash.
   3. Tingling in the feet.
   4. Orange-tinged body fluids.

24. The nurse is caring for an elderly woman who has been admitted to the hospital. The woman is upset and confused and repeatedly tells the nurse she is worried about being constipated while in the hospital. To elicit information effectively about the client's bowel status, the nurse should ask,
   1. "Do you realize you are confused?"
   2. "What laxative do you take at home?"
   3. "When was your last bowel movement?"
   4. "Why are you so worried about your bowels?"

25. An 84-year-old woman is awaiting surgery for repair of a fractured left hip. Buck's traction is being applied using a foam Buck's traction boot. While developing the plan of care for the client, the nurse must be sure to include which of the following?
   1. Turn from side to side every two hours.
   2. Maintain high Fowler's position.
   3. Remove boot every shift.
   4. Use footboard to position left foot.

26. The nurse is caring for a client who has just returned to the nursing unit from the recovery room (postanesthesia care unit) after surgery. The first action for the nurse to perform is to
   1. take vital signs.
   2. administer pain medication.
   3. connect drainage systems.
   4. check dressings.

27. An adult client received a kidney transplant eight days ago. Because he is in the period when acute rejection of the kidney is most likely, the nurse should continue assessing him for
   1. increased output of very dilute urine.
   2. hypotension.
   3. anemia.
   4. fever.

28. What advice by the school nurse would ensure a safe health care environment for the child with impetigo?
   1. "You need to see your doctor this week to get started on some antibiotics so the sores on your face will clear up."
   2. "It's O.K. to share personal items, such as towels, with the rest of the family, because good hand washing will prevent the spread of impetigo."
   3. "Be sure to drink 6 to 8 glasses of fluid each day and let me know right away if your urine turns dark like the color of cola."
   4. "If the itching bothers you, put some rubbing alcohol on your face several times a day."

29. A 68-year-old man is admitted to the emergency department with a medical diagnosis of closed-angle glaucoma. He is placed on miotic therapy and receives 75% glycerin (Glycol). In planning care for the client, which of the following should be a teaching priority during the acute phase of his illness?
   1. Eyedrop administration.
   2. Eye patch changes every hour.
   3. Measuring intake and output.
   4. Keeping bright lights on in the room.

30. Which nursing action represents unsafe nursing care for a client with closed-angle glaucoma?
   1. Administering morphine sulfate 8 mg IM prn for pain.
   2. Allowing him to ambulate to the bathroom with assistance.
   3. Occluding the puncta during the administration of eyedrops.
   4. Wearing unsterile gloves when examining the eye.

31. The primary purpose of medications such as pilocarpine (Pilocar) used in the treatment of glaucoma is
   1. control of increased intraocular pressure.
   2. improvement of vision.
   3. relief of pain.
   4. restoration of peripheral vision.

32. An 80-year-old man has closed-angle glaucoma. He tells the nurse that he has heard that glaucoma may be hereditary. He is concerned about his children, a son age 45 and a daughter age 38. The most appropriate response by the nurse is to ask,
    1. "Are your children complaining of eye problems?"
    2. "There is no need for concern because glaucoma is not a hereditary disorder."
    3. "There may be a genetic factor with glaucoma and your children should be screened."
    4. "Your son should be evaluated because he is over 40."

33. Ms. S. develops disseminated intravascular coagulation (DIC) following childbirth. Lab studies show she has elevated prothrombin time (PT), elevated activated partial thromboplastin time (APTT), and decreased platelet count and fibrinogen level. The nurse understands that these changes have occurred because
    1. Formation of clots in small blood vessels throughout the body has used up her clotting factors.
    2. Damage to her liver during childbirth has resulted in impaired production of clotting factors.
    3. Exposure to fetal blood of a type different from hers has caused Ms. S. to form antibodies, which are attacking her bone marrow.
    4. Internal bleeding has resulted in loss of the clotting factors from the intravascular space into the interstitial spaces.

34. A four-year-old girl was in a car accident with her family. Upon arrival in the emergency room, she is noted to have lacerations on her head and arms, a temperature of 39° C, BP 158/102, pulse 60, and sluggish pupil reactions. She is crying and does not recognize her family. The nurse recognizes these manifestations as possible evidence of
    1. elevated intracranial pressure.
    2. Reye's syndrome.
    3. Guillain-Barré syndrome.
    4. anxiety attack related to being in a strange environment.

35. An adult male is admitted in alcohol withdrawal. The nurse plans his care to include all of the following. What is the most important goal to approach first? The client will
    1. be able to identify reality.
    2. remain free from injury.
    3. remain free of alcohol use.
    4. maintain optimal nutrition intake.

36. Mr. B., 34, is admitted with a diagnosis of antisocial personality. Mr. B. has a long history of fights, incarcerations for stealing

and forgery, lying, lack of remorse for his actions, inconsistent employment, and impersonal relationships with others. As a child, he was often truant, in trouble with school officials, and cruel to his family dog. Based on Mr. B.'s background, which statement provides the nurse with the best understanding of the client? Antisocial personality stems from
    1. a low I.Q.
    2. Failure to develop a stabilized and socialized ego and superego during early childhood.
    3. Rebelliousness despite parental discipline and moral values in the home.
    4. Poverty and resulting need to meet basic needs independent of family.

37. Sarah, 25 years old, suffered from depression and was withdrawn when admitted to the unit. She has responded well to treatment and, though still depressed, now attends unit group meetings. How can the nurse best determine if the client's condition has improved?
    1. The client has been compliant with her medications.
    2. Ask another client if Sarah has improved in her participating in the milieu.
    3. Observe whether or not she socializes appropriately with other clients outside of unit group meetings.
    4. Observe that the client attends unit group meetings.

38. A child is admitted with idiopathic thrombocytopenic purpura with a platelet count of 18,000/mm³. The nurse can expect that this child will have
    1. aspirin every four hours.
    2. seizure precautions.
    3. restricted activity level.
    4. tracheostomy set at bedside.

39. Mrs. B., a 68-year-old client with arthritis, is experiencing increased alterations in mobility. In planning her care, which of the following measures would be the best approach for the nurse to safeguard the client?
    1. Using a vest restraint at all times.
    2. Teaching crutch walking.
    3. Removing excess room furniture and clutter.
    4. Placing the bedside table away from the client.

40. An adult client states that it hurts too much to cough and deep breathe following abdominal surgery. Which of the following approaches would the nurse take first?
    1. Inform the client that coughing is not a matter of choice and must be done.
    2. Call the respiratory therapist in to talk with the client.

3. Notify the surgeon that the client refuses to cough.
4. Coordinate a pain medication and respiratory exercise schedule.

41. An adult client has been admitted to the psychiatric unit. She is convinced that a blemish on her face is a malignant melanoma. By the end of the third day of hospitalization, her fear of dying from the melanoma has reached psychotic proportions. The most adaptive way she might try to deal with this would be to
    1. attempt thought-control methods to decrease pervasiveness of thoughts.
    2. request PRN medication whenever such thoughts intrude.
    3. share her concerns with another client whenever they arise.
    4. withdraw to her room whenever such thoughts arise.

42. Several clients are participating in group therapy. Which is least likely to be a benefit of group therapy for clients?
    1. Focusing strictly on personal situations.
    2. An increase in the sense of belonging and worthiness.
    3. A decrease in isolation and an increase in reality testing.
    4. The opportunity to ventilate and problem solve.

43. The nurse is caring for a woman who is 35 weeks pregnant. She comes to the emergency department with painless vaginal bleeding. This is her third pregnancy and she states that this has never happened to her before. In caring for this woman, the nurse should avoid
    1. allowing her husband to stay with her.
    2. keeping her at rest.
    3. shaving the perineum.
    4. performing a vaginal examination.

44. The nurse is caring for a woman with a placenta previa who has been hospitalized for several weeks. She is now at 38 weeks gestation and her membranes have ruptured. The amniotic fluid has a greenish color and the woman has started to bleed again. The nurse should plan to
    1. administer oxygen.
    2. place her in Trendelenburg's position.
    3. call the physician and prepare for a cesarean birth.
    4. move her to the delivery room immediately.

45. A child has been brought to the emergency room with an asthma attack. What signs and symptoms would the nurse expect to see?
    1. A prolonged inspiratory time and a short expiratory time.
    2. Frequent productive coughing of clear, frothy, thin mucus progressing to thick, tenacious mucus heard only on auscultation.
    3. Hypoinflation of the alveoli with resulting poor gas exchange from increasingly shallow inspirations.
    4. Swelling of the bronchial mucosa, with wheezes starting on expiration and spreading to continuous.

46. A mother brings her baby to well-baby clinic for his two-month checkup. She reports that he is doing well except that he has a rash on his cheeks, trunk, and extremities that won't heal. A diagnosis of infantile eczema is made and the nurse reviews the care for this problem with the mother. The mother returns for the baby's three-month checkup. Reporting what activity indicates she has been properly caring for his skin?
    1. She bathes him twice a day to remove crusts.
    2. She leaves his skin exposed to air whenever possible.
    3. She gently pats lubricant into the skin.
    4. She uses only natural fibers against his skin.

47. The parents of a two-month-old infant who has an apnea monitor are visiting the pediatrician for a checkup. When asked how the monitoring is going at home, the parents indicate dissatisfaction with the process, saying it keeps everyone awake and on edge while the baby is okay. What can the nurse do to promote a safe, effective health care environment for this infant?
    1. Order another monitor for them, since there are several brands to choose from.
    2. Ask the parents to apply the monitor and turn it on, so the nurse can see what happens.
    3. Stress the importance of continuation of monitoring during the first year for all high-risk infants.
    4. Recommend that the infant's crib be placed beside the parent's bed so the baby can be heard if any distress occurs.

48. The nurse is caring for a woman who has had a lumbar laminectomy with a spinal fusion. Immediately after surgery, which of the following should the nurse expect the client to manifest?
    1. Absence of lower extremity movement.
    2. Response to pin-prick sensation.
    3. Severe muscle spasms.
    4. Weak pedal pulses.

49. The nurse is caring for a client who has had a spinal fusion. The donor site for the graft begins to hemorrhage and then ooze blood. The most appropriate way to determine if nursing interventions to stop bleeding have been effective is by
    1. monitoring output.

2. taking hourly vital signs.
3. asking the client if she feels dizzy.
4. outlining drainage on the dressing and noting the time.

50. A woman who has had a lumbar laminectomy and a spinal fusion is getting out of bed for the first time. The teaching plan can be considered effective if she
   1. bends only from the waist.
   2. moves rapidly.
   3. thinks through every movement.
   4. refuses to use a walker.

51. A 16-year-old client has acute infectious mononucleosis. Which statement by the client indicates to the nurse that he understands the necessary home care?
   1. "I'm excited about going to the football game tonight."
   2. "My friends are coming over here to help me with my school work."
   3. "I plan to work out with the swim team tomorrow."
   4. "I have to stay in bed all the time."

52. Mrs. M., a 70-year-old woman with severe macular degeneration, is admitted to the hospital the day before scheduled surgery. The nurse's preoperative goals for Mrs. M. would include
   1. independently ambulating around the unit.
   2. reading the routine preoperative education materials.
   3. maneuvering safely after orientation to the room.
   4. using a bedpan for elimination needs.

53. The nurse is caring for a client with a newly implanted pacemaker. When monitoring pacemaker functioning, which of the following should the nurse initially assess?
   1. Electrocardiogram.
   2. Pulse.
   3. Blood pressure.
   4. Incision site.

54. The nurse is assessing a child with conjunctivitis (pink eye). Which of the following findings would the nurse most likely observe?
   1. Serous drainage from the eyes.
   2. Crusting of the eyelids.
   3. Severe eye pain.
   4. Only one eye is affected.

55. An adult client is receiving cancer chemotherapy. Which action the client makes indicates a need for further instruction to prevent stomatitis?
   1. Brushing teeth with a soft bristle brush.
   2. Lubricating lips with petroleum jelly.
   3. Avoiding hard or spicy foods.
   4. Rinsing with an alcohol-based mouthwash.

56. The nurse is conducting a mental status examination. The component of the examination that tests for the client's ability to abstract as well as reason is the use of

1. proverbs.
2. item identification.
3. presidents' names.
4. serial sevens.

57. A 24-year-old man was seen in the outpatient clinic by the psychiatric nurse clinician for an assessment interview. In establishing the data base, the client related that he hears the voice of his former girlfriend calling to him to help her. In an attempt to find her, he breaks into various buildings and enters homes other than his own uninvited. He rarely sleeps and has lost a job because he is afraid he will miss a visit or telephone call from her. The client lives with his parents, who are very upset by his behavior and have threatened to evict him from the house if he does not get help. Which of the following nursing diagnoses is least appropriate?
   1. Altered thought processes.
   2. Bathing hygiene self-care deficit.
   3. Sensory/perceptual alterations.
   4. Sleep pattern disturbance.

58. A young adult was seen in outpatient clinic. He states he hears the voice of a former girlfriend calling to him to help her. He does not sleep and has lost his job because he is afraid he will miss a visit or a phone call. Using the community mental health model the nurse would plan to
   1. encourage the client to admit himself to a community hospital psychiatric unit.
   2. file a petition for involuntary commitment.
   3. maintain the client in treatment in a community-based setting.
   4. refer the client to a psychiatrist for medication as sole treatment.

59. A young adult is being seen in outpatient clinic. He states he hears the voice of a former girlfriend calling to him to help her. He does not sleep and has lost his job because he is afraid he will miss a visit or a phone call. After six weeks of biweekly therapy sessions, the client secured full-time minimum-wage employment. Within the first week of working, it became apparent that the client was not able to get out of bed in time for work and was jeopardizing his employment. A realistic, initial client-oriented goal that the client might negotiate with the nurse therapist is to get to work
   1. on time four out of five days with his parents' assistance.
   2. every day with his parents' assistance.
   3. on time every day independently.
   4. on time two out of five days independently.

60. Mr. T., 35, is admitted for bipolar illness, manic phase, after assaulting his landlord in an argument over Mr. T. staying up all night playing loud music. Mr. T. is hyperactive, intrusive, and has rapid, pressured speech. He has not slept in three days and appears

thin and disheveled. Which of the following is the most essential nursing action at this time?
1. Providing a meal and beverage for Mr. T. to eat in the dining room.
2. Providing linens and toiletries for Mr. T. to attend to his hygiene.
3. Consulting with the psychiatrist to order a hypnotic to promote sleep.
4. Providing for client safety by limiting his privileges.

61. The nurse is assessing a two-year-old child with tetralogy of Fallot. Which of the following is most characteristic of a child with this condition?
1. Normal growth and development.
2. Hypotonia of upper extremities.
3. Epistaxis.
4. Assuming a squatting position.

62. The nurse is caring for a 51-year-old man who has a 13-year history of heavy alcohol consumption. He has been smoking two packs of cigarettes a day since he was 15 years old. He complains of a sore throat, weight loss, and increasing hoarseness. After an extensive medical workup, a diagnosis of cancer of the larynx is made. The client is scheduled for a radical neck dissection. When he returns to the nursing unit after surgery, he is having difficulty breathing. Secretions are visible in the laryngectomy tube. The initial nursing intervention is to
1. obtain the vital signs.
2. notify the physician.
3. remove the secretions.
4. start oxygen via a tracheostomy collar.

63. The nurse is caring for a client who has had a total laryngectomy. The nursing management in the early postoperative period is primarily directed toward
1. alleviation of pain.
2. decreasing the client's concern about appearance.
3. improving the nutritional status of the client.
4. observing the client for hemorrhage.

64. The nurse is caring for a toddler who has infantile eczema. What will be included in the nursing care plan?
1. Applying the emollient preparation to the skin before allowing the child to sit in the bathtub to protect the skin from water damage.
2. Removing the gloves, cotton stockings, or elbow protector devices when the child is sleeping.
3. Measures to protect the family from the child's lesions.
4. Teaching the parents that permanent remission will usually take place around age two or three.

65. The nurse is assessing a newborn baby girl and finds the following: in a supine position with hips and knees flexed, the right knee is higher than the left; there are more gluteal and thigh folds on the left than the right. The best interpretation of these data is that
1. the right hip is dislocated.
2. the left hip is dislocated.
3. both hips are dislocated.
4. the baby has normal newborn joint laxity.

66. A client with schizophrenia is admitted to the hospital experiencing auditory hallucinations that others are after him and intend to harm him. The nursing plan of care should include
1. seclusion until hallucinations lessen.
2. placement in a reality-oriented therapy group.
3. advising the client that antipsychotic drugs will cure him.
4. presenting reality by stating that the nurse does not hear the voices.

67. An adult man underwent a cardiac catheterization to evaluate the condition of his coronary arteries. Significant atherosclerotic plaque formations were seen. His blood work revealed an elevated serum cholesterol with low HDL levels. After a session with the dietitian, the client tells the nurse, "I can eat red meat as long as I don't see any fat on it." Which of the following nursing diagnoses is most appropriate related to the client's statement?
1. Altered nutrition: risk for more than body requirements.
2. Altered nutrition: dysfunctional eating behaviors.
3. Knowledge deficit: lack of information.
4. Knowledge deficit: information misinterpretation.

68. One liter of fluid every six hours is ordered for an adult client. Which flow rate indicates the IV calculations are correct for an administration set that delivers 10 gtts/ml?
1. 22 gtts/minute.
2. 28 gtts/minute.
3. 32 gtts/minute.
4. 36 gtts/minute.

69. The nurse is caring for a woman who is one day post radical mastectomy. What must be included in the care plan?
1. Elevate the arm on the operative side for 24 to 48 hours.
2. Maintain complete bed rest or 24 to 48 hours.
3. Do not allow the client to perform any self-care activities for 48 hours.
4. Maintain the client NPO for 24 hours.

70. A 19-year-old woman comes to the gynecology clinic to be fitted for a diaphragm. Which nursing action would best prevent incorrect placement of a diaphragm when the client is inserting it for the first time?
1. Allowing her supervised practice time.
2. Providing a brochure.

3. Teaching her to lie on her back.
4. Teaching her sex partner to insert it.

71. The nurse in the gynecology clinic is assessing a young woman. The client states that she gets her menstrual period every 18 days. She states that her flow is very heavy and lasts six days. The nurse identifies this pattern as
1. dysmenorrhea.
2. dyspareunia.
3. menorrhagia.
4. metrorrhagia.

72. A young woman is seen in the woman's clinic. She states that she has "many little blisters on my privates." After examining her labia and perineum, the nurse finds multiple vesicles, some ruptured and crusted over. There is no unusual vaginal discharge. The nurse should suspect
1. chlamydia.
2. gonorrhea.
3. herpes.
4. syphilis.

73. A six-year-old child is admitted to the hospital with a diagnosis of Reye's syndrome. Which of the following would the nurse expect to see in the child's history?
1. Temperature elevations of 103° or higher in the past eight hours.
2. Enlarged spleen.
3. Influenza one week ago.
4. Family history of Reye's syndrome.

74. A 75-year-old man with a ten-year history of Parkinson's disease is admitted to the hospital because his condition is deteriorating. The symptom of Parkinson's disease that would be most obvious during the admission assessment is
1. confusion.
2. intention tremor.
3. pallor.
4. "pill rolling."

75. Amantadine hydrochloride (Symmetrel) is prescribed for a client with Parkinson's disease. The client asks how the drug works. In formulating a response, the nurse recalls that the drug
1. allows accumulation of dopamine.
2. corrects mineral deficiencies.
3. elevates the client's mood.
4. replaces enzymes.

76. The nurse is planning care for an elderly client who has severe Parkinson's disease. Which of the following is of highest priority?
1. Positioning.
2. Encouraging independence.
3. Increasing activity.
4. Preventing aspiration.

77. In planning care for a client with advanced Parkinson's disease, which activity is most likely to be effective in alleviating fatigue?
1. Getting him to bed on time.

2. Avoiding high carbohydrate foods.
3. Collaborating with him when scheduling activities.
4. Providing for morning and afternoon naps while he is in the hospital.

78. When planning care for the client with multiple myeloma the nurse should include
1. fluid restriction.
2. administration of potassium supplements.
3. assisting with mobility.
4. administration of aspirin to control bone pain.

79. The nurse is evaluating a client who has been in a long leg cast for three weeks. Which finding indicates the client is free of neurological or circulatory complications?
1. The toes on the casted foot are cool to the touch.
2. The nail beds have a blue tinge when pressed lightly.
3. The client reports pain under the cast near the fracture site.
4. The dorsalis pedis pulse is palpable and regular.

80. A fifteen-year-old is treated in the emergency room for a fractured right ankle. A plaster walking cast is applied and the client is instructed to walk with the aid of crutches once the cast has dried. While instructing the client to ambulate with crutches the nurse most appropriately teaches the client to
1. place the crutches under the arms, bear weight on the axilla, and position both crutches 8–10 inches in front of the body.
2. move crutches and feet in the following sequence: right crutch, left foot, left crutch, right foot.
3. move both crutches and the right foot forward simultaneously followed by the left foot.
4. move the right foot and left foot forward together followed by the left foot and right crutch.

81. Mrs. B. is admitted to the hospital with a femoral neck fracture of the left leg. A total hip replacement is performed. While planning care for Mrs. B. two days following the surgery, the nurse includes which of the following nursing interventions?
1. Ambulate in room with weight bearing on both legs for five minutes.
2. Out of bed in the chair for one hour, elevating both legs on another chair.
3. Turn from side to side q 2 h, support upper leg with pillows from thigh to heel.
4. Turn from supine to right side q 2 h while maintaining the left leg in abduction.

82. An 85-year-old widow was admitted to the hospital following complaints of oliguria, extreme fatigue, and difficulty breathing, which have resulted in her inability to carry out activities of daily living. During the

admission database, the client tells the nurse she has no appetite and has recently felt as though she has "had enough of living." Vital signs are temperature 100.2°F (oral); pulse 62, weak and irregular; respirations 28, shallow and irregular; and blood pressure 152/94. The nurse notes 3+ bilateral pedal edema, crackles in bases of both lungs, expectoration of yellow-green sputum, finger-stick blood glucose of 115, hypoactive bowel sounds, right-sided weakness, and a 1 cm pressure sore on the lateral aspect of the left ankle. When caring for this client, the nurse assigns the highest priority to which of the following nursing diagnoses?
1. Activity intolerance.
2. Ineffective breathing patterns.
3. Situational low self-esteem.
4. Skin integrity impairment.

83. An adult client is hospitalized for treatment of diabetes insipidus. The nurse is performing the initial assessment. Which finding should the nurse expect?
1. Daily urine output of 10 liters.
2. Urine specific gravity of 1.050.
3. Serum sodium levels of 120 mEq/L.
4. Daily fluid intake of one to two liters.

84. A one-day-old infant is admitted to the intensive care nursery. She is suspected of having esophageal atresia. What assessment findings should the nurse expect to find?
1. Bile-stained vomitus and a weak cry.
2. Diarrhea and colicky abdominal pain.
3. Excessive drooling and immediate regurgitation of feedings.
4. Visible peristaltic waves and projectile vomiting.

85. The nurse is assessing a six-month-old child. Which developmental skills are normal and should be expected?
1. Speaks in short sentences.
2. Sits alone.
3. Can feed self with a spoon.
4. Pulling up to a standing position.

86. The parents of a one-year-old are discussing the safety needs of their daughter with the nurse. Which statement indicates a need for further education on safety practices?
1. "We should fence in our yard soon."
2. "One of us will always be with her while she is in the bathtub."
3. "We don't need the stair gate anymore; she's so good at walking."
4. "The safest position for her car seat is in the middle of the back seat."

87. The nurse is caring for a client with Raynaud's phenomenon. The nurse should instruct the client to avoid which of the following situations?
1. Living in a warm climate.
2. Active exercising.
3. Exposure to cold temperatures.

4. Alcohol consumption.

88. The nurse is caring for an elderly client who has been diagnosed as having sundown syndrome. He is alert and oriented during the day but becomes disoriented and disruptive around dinnertime. He is hospitalized for evaluation. The nurse asks the client and his family to list all of the medications, prescription and nonprescription, he is currently taking. What is the primary reason for this action?
1. Multiple medications can lead to dementia.
2. The medications can provide clues regarding his medical background.
3. Ability to recall medications is a good assessment of the client's level of orientation.
4. Medications taken by a client are part of every nursing assessment.

89. Mr. P., a 65-year-old client who has just retired, expresses concerns of loneliness due to the loss of his job and coworkers. Which response by the nurse is most therapeutic?
1. "You need to take a vacation."
2. "Do you know about the local senior citizen group?"
3. "But now you can finally relax and enjoy life."
4. "Why don't you go in to work and visit with your old friends?"

90. An adult has continued slow bleeding from the graft after repair of an abdominal aortic aneurysm. Because of the client's unstable condition, he is in the intensive care unit where visitors are limited to the family. The client insists on having a visit from a medicine man whom the family visits regularly. How should the nurse interpret this request?
1. The principle of justice prohibits giving one client a privilege that other clients are not permitted.
2. Faith healers do not meet the standards for clergy exemption from visitation rules.
3. Medicine men are not approved by the hospital as legitimate health care providers.
4. Provision of holistic care requires that the client's belief system is honored.

91. The nurse is caring for a 45-year-old who had a left knee replacement. The nurse is adjusting the passive motion device on his 3rd post-op day. Which of the following indicates correct technique?
1. Allow passive motion prn as desired.
2. Monitor pressure at hinged joint of machine.
3. Monitor pressure areas on shins.
4. Allow client to choose speed and degree of extension.

92. An adult is admitted to the surgical floor with a diagnosis of a tumor, right lung. Upon return to the surgical unit following a right

pneumonectomy, the nurse should place the client in which position?
1. Left lateral decubitus.
2. Right lateral decubitus.
3. Semi-Fowler's.
4. High-Fowler's.

93. An adult comes to the clinic because she has a productive cough. She smokes two packs of cigarettes a day and has a family history of lung cancer and emphysema. Using the principles of health promotion, the nurse would make what interpretation of the client's behavior? She is
1. using denial to deal with being at high risk for lung cancer.
2. not assuming self-responsibility for her health.
3. exhibiting a laissez-faire attitude toward smoking and her risk of cancer.
4. demonstrating passive suicidal tendencies.

94. The nurse is teaching an adult who has ulcerative colitis. In developing the teaching plan which of the following foods should the nurse plan to instruct the client to avoid?
1. Roast chicken and cooked spinach.
2. Broiled liver and white rice.
3. Cottage cheese and canned apricots.
4. Pork chop and brown rice.

95. A 46-year-old female with chronic constipation is assessed by the nurse for a bowel training regimen. Which factor indicates further information is needed by the nurse?
1. The client's dietary habits include foods high in bulk.
2. The client's fluid intake is between 2500–3000 ml per day.
3. The client engages in moderate exercise each day.
4. The client's bowel habits were not discussed.

96. A 26-year-old obese female is assessed for a weight reduction diet by a clinic nurse. Which of the following findings by the nurse is of most concern? The client has
1. an understanding of the food pyramid.
2. a social support system.
3. a history of periodic weight loss and weight gain.
4. no history of medical problems.

97. Mr. C. suffered a traumatic amputation of his left arm in a factory accident about seven months ago and has had severe chronic phantom pain for the last six months. Which statement, if made by Mrs. C., who assists her husband with his daily care, indicates an understanding of this client's pain?
1. "Phantom pain is not real pain; his body is just tricked into thinking he has pain."
2. "Because he lost his arm so long ago, his pain must be caused by something besides his injury."
3. "I believe he is having pain and I want to help him deal with it."
4. "If he continues taking pain medication, he will become a drug addict even though he really has pain."

98. The nurse is assessing a client following hemodialysis. Which of the following findings indicates the treatment was effective?
1. Hypertension.
2. Hyperkalemia.
3. Fluid volume decrease.
4. Cardiac dysrhythmias.

99. The nurse is discontinuing an intravenous catheter. When performing this procedure, the nurse should
1. apply a tourniquet proximal to the catheter insertion site.
2. flush the catheter with a heparin solution to ensure patency of the catheter before removal.
3. assess the insertion site for signs of infiltration or inflammation.
4. wear only sterile gloves to perform the procedure.

100. The nurse is preparing to administer two units of packed red blood cells. The nurse should
1. prime the blood administration tubing with 3% saline solution.
2. administer the prescribed intravenous drugs through the blood administration tubing to ensure proper distribution throughout the body.
3. understand that blood transfusion reactions usually do not occur until the client has received 500 ml of the packed red blood cells.
4. use a special blood filter and an 18-gauge needle to administer the packed red blood cells.

ANSWER	RATIONALE	NP	CN	CL

#1. 1. Excess output of the thyroid hormones increases the metabolic rate and increases sympathetic (adrenergic) activity, resulting in nervousness, hyperexcitability, palpitations, and a pulse that is abnormally elevated even at rest. The client usually demonstrates a fine tremor of the hands and intolerance to heat.   As   Ph/9   An

2. The increased metabolic rate that results from increased thyroid hormone secretion causes heat intolerance, flushing of the skin and warm, moist skin.

3. These responses are indicative of hypothyroidism or myxedema and relate to the reduced metabolic rate and reduced cardiac output often accompanying serum cholesterol levels.

4. The client with hyperthyroidism usually has moist skin, and may have constipation or diarrhea. Dry skin, constipation and memory defects are often seen in clients with hypothyroidism.

#2. 2. Polyarthritis is characterized by swollen, painful, hot joints that respond to salicylates.   An   Ph/8   An

1. Chorea is the restless and sudden aimless and irregular movements of the extremities suddenly seen in persons with rheumatic fever, especially girls.

3. Subcutaneous nodules are nontender swellings over bony prominences sometimes seen in persons with rheumatic fever.

4. Erythema marginatum is a skin condition characterized by nonpruritic rash, affecting trunk and proximal extremities, seen in persons with rheumatic fever.

#3. 3. It is thought that hypoguesia (altered taste sensation) occurs when cancer cells release substances that resemble amino acids and stimulate the bitter taste buds. Spices and seasoning can mask the taste alterations that are occurring.   As   Ph/7   Ap

1. Eating dry crackers does not help altered taste sensation. Dry crackers are more appropriate for nausea.

2. Monitoring intake and output is more appropriate for someone with nausea and vomiting.

4. Weighing the client is not related to altered taste sensation.

#4. 1. Otosclerosis is the formation of spongy bone in the capsule of the ear labyrinth. As otosclerosis advances, it causes progressive fixation of the footplate of the stapes. Normally, as the footplate of the stapes rocks in the oval window, sound is transmitted directly to the perilymph of the inner ear. With oval window obstruction by otosclerosis, hearing by air conduction is reduced, since sound pressure is no longer effectively transmitted to the hair cells.   As   Ph/10   An

2. Otosclerosis reduces hearing by air conduction.

3. Otosclerosis reduces hearing by air conduction.

4. In otosclerosis sound does not lateralize to the unaffected ear.

#5. 3. Speaking at a moderate rate allows the client to observe the lips of the speaker and to hear normal voice tones.   Ev   Ph/9   Ap

1. Overarticulating may make it more difficult for the client to read the lips of the speaker.

2. Excessive loudness distorts the voice and makes understanding more difficult.

4. The best approach is to use short phrases and speak slowly and distinctly.

#6. 4. Placing the food in a recognizable location fosters autonomy as well as reinforcing independence with activities of daily living.   As   Ph/7   Ap

    1. Feeding the child fosters dependence.

    2. A four-year-old is too young to understand the clock method.

    3. Putting food on the fork fosters dependence.

#7. 3. The Moro (startle) reflex is demonstrated by abduction, extension, and adduction of arms to an embracing position.   As   He/3   An

    1. The crossed extension reflex includes alternate flexion, adduction, and extension of the legs.

    2. The tonic neck reflex is evidenced by extension of one side of the body while the other side is flexed.

    4. The stepping reflex includes flexion of the knees and hips with movement of the legs upward.

#8. 1. Sexual intercourse is avoided as it causes uterine contractions, contributing to further placental separation. Depending upon where the placenta is lying, sexual intercourse may dislodge the placenta.   Ev   He/3   An

    2. Vaginal examinations can cause further separation of the placenta from the cervix, lacerate the placenta, and result in more bleeding.

    3. A cesarean birth may be indicated but will be evaluated later on in the pregnancy. Having a cesarean now does not mean that she always has to have one. An incision in the upper uterine segment can cause uterine rupture during successive labors. Vaginal delivery may be possible if the incision is in the lower uterine segment.

    4. Rest, especially bed rest, is important in the treatment of placenta previa. Working is contraindicated.

#9. 2. Reading the name on the client's ID bracelet is the most accurate way to confirm identity.   Im   Sa/1   Ap

    1. An alert, oriented client should be asked to state her full name so that there is no confusion in identity. The ID bracelet will confirm identity when the client is not alert or oriented to person.

    3. Reading the client's medical record will not confirm identity.

    4. The roommate is not an accurate source for client identification.

#10. 1. The client's high activity level poses the most danger because it can lead to absence of food, fluid, and rest with resultant dehydration, electrolyte imbalance, and physical collapse.   An   Ps/6   An

    2. The client does have altered perception of normal behavior, but this does not pose the greatest physical danger.

    3. The client may have sensory overload, but this does not pose the greatest physical danger.

    4. The client's disturbed social behavior does not pose the greatest physical threat.

#11. 2. Many characteristics of a client who is manic (i.e., irritability, excitement, agitation, provocative behavior) contribute to the potential for violence. Maintaining the safety of the client and those around him is the greatest priority.   An   Ps/6   An

    1. Anxiety is a nursing diagnosis but not the one with greatest priority at this time.

    3. The client's spiritual distress is not of greatest concern. Potential violence is of greater concern.

    4. Alteration in nutrition: less than body requirements is second in priority to potential for violence.

#12. 4. Manic clients cannot calm down without assistance. Decreasing the level of sensory stimulation is of paramount importance and provides the greatest therapeutic effect until proper medication levels (often lithium) are established.   Im   Ps/6   Ap

    1. The client is not ready for group activities yet.

    2. The client is not able to calm himself down.

    3. Restraints further agitate the client.

#13. 4. While the client's social network can influence the client in terms of compliance, the influence is typically secondary to that of the other factors listed.   Ev   Ph/8   An

1. The impact of lithium on the client's energy level and life style are great determinants to compliance.
2. The frequent blood level monitoring required is difficult for clients to follow for a long period of time.
3. Potential side effects such as fine tremor, drowsiness, diarrhea, polyuria, thirst, weight gain, and fatigue can be disturbing to the client.

#14. 4. There is very little protein in a bacon, lettuce, and tomato sandwich and an apple.   Ev   Ph/7   An
1. Poultry is a good source of protein as is ice cream.
2. Meat and puddings are recommended and good sources of protein.
3. Cheese and yogurt are good sources of protein.

#15. 2. Drying the baby completely is the most important part of newborn care, because it prevents heat loss and reduction of body temperature.   Im   He/3   Ap
1. This assessment scale evaluates the condition of the newborn baby at 1 and 5 minutes of age. The score indicates the infant's adaptation to extrauterine existence, but drying the baby is crucial to preventing heat loss.
3. Identification is important but can wait for several minutes while the nurse makes sure heat loss is not occurring and that the infant is stable.
4. Eye care is important to prevent infection from potential vaginal infections from the mother, but one hour is an acceptable time period to allow for interaction between parents and baby.

#16. 3. Careful assessment of the breasts before and after each feeding is extremely important for noting any early skin breakdown, which can get infected.   Ev   He/3   An
1. A hard lump in her breast can signify a clogged duct, which can lead to mastitis.
2. Mild skin breakdown can rapidly become worse. The woman should be instructed to use other positions or possibly use a shield to protect her breast from further trauma.
4. Hand washing should always be encouraged prior to breastfeeding no matter what the infant's status.

#17. 1. Heme in the stool can be an early warning sign of necrotizing enterocolitis.   As   Ph/9   An
2. Abdominal girth should be assessed prior to each feeding. Increased abdominal girth can be an early sign of necrotizing enterocolitis.
3. The nurse should check for residual prior to each tube feeding to assess how the infant tolerated and digested the prior feeding.
4. The nurse should check for tube placement prior to each tube feeding.

#18. 2. Baby M. shows clinical manifestations of patent ductus arteriosus (PDA): failure of the fetal ductus arteriosus to completely close after birth.   An   Ph/9   An
1. The ductus venosus is a major blood channel that develops through the embryonic liver from the left umbilical vein to the inferior vena cava.
3. Normally the ductus arteriosus closes shortly after birth. Anatomic closure of the ductus arteriosus occurs when there is growth of fibrous tissue in the lumen of the ductus arteriosus, by 1–3 weeks. The remains of the ductus arteriosus are called the ligamentum arteriosus.
4. The foramen ovale is the septal opening between the atria in the fetal heart. The opening closes at birth. Failure to close causes an atrial septal defect which is manifested by decreased exercise tolerance, dyspnea, and systolic ejection murmur heard in the upper left sternal border.

#19. 3. Since infants born to addicted mothers are highly irritable, it is   Pl   He/3   Ap

best to organize all care around the feedings and then try to disturb them as little as possible in between.
1. Infants born to addicted mothers often have strong sucking reflex and are very irritable. Frequent vomiting is also common. Overfeeding will only accentuate the problem.
2. Because the mother is using cocaine and heroin and is not entering rehabilitation, breastfeeding should not be recommended. The drugs will cross into the breast milk.
4. Infants born to addicted mothers are prone to temperature instability. Keep the infant wrapped snugly to maintain temperature.

#20. 4. **Gravity will cause the head of the femur to drop toward the bed, causing the affected thigh to appear shorter.** As | Ph/9 | An
1. Ortolani's sign (a popping sensation felt when the examiner attempts to internally and externally rotate the hip joint) will be present.
2. Trendelenburg's sign is seen in persons with an abnormality of the pelvis associated with congenital hip dislocation. When the client stands on the involved foot, the opposite (normal) gluteal fold falls rather than rises.
3. There would be an increase in skin folds in the affected thigh.

#21. 1. **Infiltration is the infusion of fluid into tissue. The accumulation of fluid causes pressure, which reduces circulation to the area, resulting in pallor.** Ev | Ph/8 | An
2. Increased temperature is an indication of inflammation and indicates the presence of phlebitis. An area of infiltration feels cool to the touch due to the reduced blood supply to the area.
3. Increased redness is a sign of inflammation and infection and often is accompanied by swelling, heat, and pain.
4. An area of infiltration may appear swollen and pale and feels cool to the touch. Blood seeping around the needle or intracath may occur when a client is receiving heparin or coumadin and may indicate an overdose of anticoagulant.

#22. 2. **The most frequent means of transmission of the tubercle bacillus is by droplet nuclei. The bacillus is present in the air as a result of coughing, sneezing, and expectoration of sputum by an infected person.** Pl | Sa/2 | Co
1. Hands are the primary method of transmission of the common cold.
3. The tubercle bacillus is not transmitted by means of contaminated food. Contact with contaminated food or water could cause outbreaks of salmonella, infectious hepatitis, typhoid, or cholera.
4. The tubercle bacillus is not transmitted by eating utensils. Some exogenous microbes can be transmitted via reservoirs such as linens or eating utensils.

#23. 4. **A side effect of rifampin is orange-tinged urine and body fluids.** Im | Ph/8 | Co
1. Vertigo is not a side effect of rifampin.
2. A skin rash is not a major side effect of rifampin.
3. Tingling in the feet is a side effect of isoniazid (INH), not rifampin.

#24. 3. **Determining when the client had her last bowel movement provides baseline data as a first part of a bowel history.** As | Ph/7 | Ap
1. Assessing orientation level does not relate to the client's bowel status.
2. History of laxative use is important information. However, it does not give information about her current bowel status.
4. Beginning a question with the word "why" may be threatening to the client. Even if the client told why she is worried about her bowels, that information will not indicate her current bowel status.

#25. 3. **The boot should be removed at least once a shift for skin care and to assess for skin breakdown and nerve damage. The left leg must be immobilized by one person and traction applied while the second person removes the boot, provides the skin care, and performs the assessment.** Pl | Ph/7 | Ap

ANSWER	RATIONALE	NP	CN	CL

1. The client may not be turned from side to side because movement may cause bone fragments to move against one another and result in damage to blood vessels and nerves in the area. Encourage the client to use a trapeze to lift herself off the bed and to cough and deep breathe to prevent complications of immobility.

2. The person in Buck's traction needs to be maintained flat or in Trendelenburg's position to provide countertraction. Special low-pressure mattresses may be used to prevent skin breakdown. Coughing and deep breathing can help prevent respiratory problems.

4. The Buck's traction boot helps to maintain the foot in alignment and to prevent contractures. The use of a footboard reduces the pull of traction on the extremity and interferes with the desired effects.

#26. 1. Monitoring vital signs is the most important aspect of assessing cardiovascular and respiratory status in the postoperative period. This is the first action taken. — Im — Ph/9 — Ap

2. Administering pain medication can be done if needed after initial assessments.

3. Connecting drainage systems is not the first action. Take vital signs first.

4. The dressings are not checked until after vital signs are taken.

#27. 4. Signs and symptoms of acute rejection include temperature of 100°F or greater, enlarged tender kidney, fluid retention, increased blood pressure, fatigue, and lethargy. — As — Ph/9 — Co

1. Anuria or oliguria occurs with acute rejection. Increased urine output occurs in the early stages of chronic renal failure.

2. Blood pressure increases due to the fluid overload.

3. Anemia is a symptom of chronic renal failure and would not be connected with acute rejection.

#28. 3. Several weeks after the lesions have healed, the child who had a beta-hemolytic streptococci infection is at risk for acute glomerulonephritis. Puffiness around the eyes would also be seen. Medical referral is needed promptly. — Im — Ph/9 — Im

1. The antibiotic should be started as soon as the lesions are discovered, because the usual organisms are streptococci or staphylococci. The penicillin or erythromycin will need to be taken for 7 to 10 days.

2. The client's personal items do need to be separated from the rest of the family's belongings, because secretions can harbor the organisms. Good hand washing is also very necessary.

4. Alcohol would cause extreme pain in the open lesions. Instead, a topical antibiotic ointment, such as Neosporin or Mycitracin, would be ordered for application several times a day after washing the lesions with soap and water.

#29. 3. Because glycerin, a rapid-acting osmotic diuretic, is being used to treat the client's glaucoma, a priority nursing intervention is to monitor the intake and output. — Pl — Ph/8 — Ap

1. During the acute phase the teaching priority is intake and output, which is an immediate need. Teaching about the administration of eyedrops is a long-term need. It will be needed but is not high priority during the acute phase.

2. Eye patches are not changed every hour. The client may not have eye patches.

4. Bright lights are irritating to the eyes of a client with glaucoma.

#30. 1. Morphine is contraindicated for a client with glaucoma because it is constipating. Straining at stool raises intraocular pressure. — An — Ph/8 — Ap

2. It would be appropriate to assist the client to the bathroom.

3. The punta is a tiny opening in the margin of each eyelid that leads into the lacrimal duct. Occluding the opening when administering eyedrops prevents the eye medication from entering the systemic circulation. It also prevents tearing.

ANSWER	RATIONALE	NP	CN	CL

4. Unsterile gloves can be worn when examining the eye to prevent exposure of the examiner to viruses that may be in the eye.

#31. 1. Pilocarpine is a cholinergic agent that reduces intraocular pressure by producing miosis (constriction of the pupil), thus increasing outflow of aqueous humor.   An   Ph/8   Co

2. Medications used for glaucoma will not bring back vision that has already been lost.
3. Pilocarpine does not relieve pain.
4. Pilocarpine does not restore peripheral vision.

#32. 3. There is a strong hereditary factor in glaucoma. Therefore, family members should have intraocular pressures measured yearly.   Im   He/4   Co

1. Chronic glaucoma is thought to be hereditary. Family members should be evaluated yearly whether or not they have symptoms. Early glaucoma has few symptoms.
2. Chronic glaucoma is thought to be hereditary.
4. Family members of a client with glaucoma should be evaluated yearly at all ages.

#33. 1. The pathophysiology of DIC includes formation of multiple microscopic clots in very small vessels, which uses up the clotting factors, leaving the client vulnerable to bleeding from other sites.   An   Ph/9   An

2. A damaged liver does not produce sufficient thromboplastin or prothrombin, resulting in bleeding tendencies. Platelets are not formed by the liver and are not affected. If the clotting factors were decreased because the liver was not making them, there would not be clot formation in the small vessels.
3. Antibodies induced by exposure to blood of a different type would not attack one's own bone marrow.
4. Internal bleeding would result in loss of all blood components equally, so that no individual components would appear reduced in comparison to others. PT and APTT would not be altered as a result of bleeding.

#34. 1. Head injury is one situation that may cause elevated intracranial pressure. Clinical manifestations include the ones listed in the question.   An   Ph/10   An

2. Reye's syndrome affects the central nervous system. It is caused by taking aspirin when a viral infection is present. It is not related to trauma.
3. Guillain-Barré syndrome is a condition probably caused by a virus, in which the person develops an ascending paralysis that usually ascends. If the person has been well supported during the time of paralysis he may not have much residual functional loss.
4. A child may cry and be very anxious in a strange environment. However, elevated temperature and sluggish pupil reactions would not occur.

#35. 2. Safety is the highest priority. A client in withdrawal suffers from altered cognition and/or sensory disturbances, as well as tremors, which increase potential for injury.   Pl   Ps/6   Ap

1. If a client is able to identify reality, it assists in ability to restore normal function. However, this is not the highest priority during withdrawal.
3. Remaining free of alcohol use is a long-range goal for the client in alcohol withdrawal.
4. It is important to maintain food and fluid intake as the client can tolerate. However, this is not the priority goal during withdrawal.

#36. 2. The psychodynamic view says that antisocial personality stems from a failure to develop a stabilized and socialized ego and superego during early childhood.   An   Ps/6   An

1. A low I.Q. is not correlated with antisocial personality. Many have above-average intelligence.

ANSWER	RATIONALE	NP	CN	CL

3. Antisocial personality can result from lack of consistent and effective discipline at home. Fragmented and stressed families may not provide an atmosphere to introject society morals and values.
4. Poverty is not a direct link to antisocial personality.

#37. 4. Client's attendance displays that client is a participant in her treatment and has made a step forward from her withdrawn behavior.   Ev   Ps/6   An

1. Being compliant with medications does not display an improvement in her depression.
2. It is inappropriate to ask other clients if a client has improved.
3. It is important to observe that the client socializes outside group meetings. However, that fact alone is not the best indicator of improvement in the client.

#38. 3. Prevention of injury, bruising, and bleeding is high priority when the platelet count is low. Normal platelet count is 150,000–500,000/mm³. This child's count is very, very low.   Pl   Ph/9   Ap

1. Aspirin is contraindicated in bleeding disorders.
2. There is no reason for seizure precautions. Thrombocytopenic purpura is not a central nervous system disorder.
4. The child with thrombocytopenic purpura is not at risk for airway obstruction. There is no reason to keep a tracheostomy set at the bedside.

#39. 3. Removing excess room furniture and clutter is the best way to safeguard the client because this measure can reduce the chance of injury by ensuring clearer access for walking and movement.   Pl   Ph/7   Ap

1. Use of a restraint is not appropriate.
2. Crutch walking may not be appropriate and may be difficult to do because of the arthritis. Stress to the joints may be painful.
4. Bedside tables should be close to the client so as to prevent overreaching and the chance of injury or falling.

#40. 4. The first step is to relieve or lessen pain so the client can cooperate and achieve the goal of coughing and deep breathing. A planned schedule for pain medication can help achieve this goal.   Pl   Ph/9   Ap

1. This is an overly aggressive statement.
2. The nurse should be able to handle the situation initially. Consultation with the respiratory therapist may be appropriate later.
3. The nurse should try nursing approaches before notifying the physician.

#41. 1. Thought-control methods are applicable to this situation and are the least restrictive method of achieving symptom control.   Im   Ps/5   An

2. Use of PRN medications is not the best way to reduce the frequency of such thoughts. Medication may be helpful in the long run but will not work immediately.
3. Sharing her concerns with another client will not alleviate the fear of dying.
4. Being alone in her room is likely to increase her psychotic fears and have no beneficial effect.

#42. 1. A strict focus on the individual's personal situation is not appropriate in group therapy. This is handled in individual therapy.   An   Ps/6   An

2. An increase in a client's sense of worth and belonging is a beneficial goal of group therapy.
3. A decrease in isolation and greater opportunity for reality testing is a beneficial goal of group therapy.
4. An opportunity to ventilate feelings and to problem solve is a beneficial goal of group therapy.

#43. 4. Painless vaginal bleeding is symptomatic of a placenta previa. Vaginal exams are contraindicated before 36 weeks unless done in the delivery room set up for emergency cesarean section if needed.   Im   He/3   Ap

1. Allowing the client's husband to stay is beneficial.
2. She should be kept on bed rest.
3. There is no reason not to shave her perineum. This may or may not be done, depending on the physician and agency policies.

#44. 3. Green amniotic fluid is indicative of fetal distress. This combined with bleeding from the placenta previa may require a cesarean section.   Pl   He/3   Ap

1. Oxygen administration might also be done to increase oxygenation of the fetus.
2. Trendelenburg's position might be indicated for prolapsed cord but is not indicated in placenta previa.
4. The client may be moved to the delivery room as determined by the physician's assessment of the client.

#45. 4. The wheeze starts during the expiratory phase because of the extreme narrowing of the bronchus on exhalation. As obstruction increases, wheezes become more high pitched and continuous.   As   Ph/10   Co

1. Bronchi normally expand and lengthen during inspiration and shorten during expiration. Asthma causes spasm of the smooth muscles in the bronchi and bronchioles, resulting in an even tighter airway on exhalation and prolonged exhalation. Inspirations increase in rate in an effort to relieve hypoxia.
2. At the beginning of the attack, the cough is nonproductive and results from bronchial edema. Then the mucus becomes profuse and rattly, with a cough producing frothy, clear sputum.
3. Gas trapping is the central feature of asthma. It is caused by allowing more air to enter alveoli than can escape from them through the narrowed airways. Gas trapping also causes an increased depth and rate of respirations.

#46. 3. Lubricants applied to the skin after bathing seal in moisture and rehydrate, lubricate, and moisturize the skin.   Ev   Ph/9   Ap

1. Bathing the baby twice a day is not necessary and will increase skin dryness.
2. Leaving the skin exposed to the air may excessively dry the skin.
4. Babies with eczema should not have wool clothing; wool is a natural fiber.

#47. 2. Watching how the leads are positioned and held in place by the parents will rule out the problem of faulty technique and will give the nurse more data about how the parents work with the equipment. When monitors frequently alarm for breathing infants, it is usually due to loose leads or low batteries.   Ev   Ph/9   Ap

1. Ordering another monitor is a good intervention after fully assessing that the monitor is faulty. There is no evidence of that yet.
3. The parents are obviously trying to use the equipment. Reteaching the importance of using the monitor, before acknowledging their problems with it, shows a lack of perception of the problem on the part of the nurse.
4. Sleeping in the same room with the baby will not prevent apnea episodes from occurring. Infant respirations cannot be easily heard, especially when the parents are sleeping also. Training the infant to sleep in the same room with the parents causes feelings of abandonment when the child is finally moved to its own room at a later age.

#48. 2. There should be a normal response to pin-prick sensation following a laminectomy.   As   Ph/9   An

1. The client should be able to move the lower extremities. Inability to do so indicates nerve damage during the surgery.
3. Severe muscle spasms are indicative of nerve damage during surgery.
4. The client should have normal pedal pulses.

ANSWER	RATIONALE	NP	CN	CL

#49. 4. Outlining drainage on the dressing provides a quantitative measure of bleeding. — Ev — Ph/9 — An

1. Monitoring output is not effective. By the time output is decreased due to shock the client will be in serious difficulty. There would be other indicators of hemorrhage.
2. Bleeding that is enough to cause blood pressure and pulse changes is extensive. The nurse should be able to pick this up before the vital signs change. Vital signs should, however, be monitored every 15 minutes if there is a hemorrhage.
3. There can be many causes of dizziness. This is not a good indicator of whether the bleeding has stopped.

#50. 3. The client should think through each movement to maintain good body alignment and avoid sudden moves. — Ev — Ph/7 — Ap

1. The client should not bend from the waist as it would dangerously flex the spine. The goal of nursing intervention is to prevent strain at the surgical site. When the client is ready to get out of bed, as ordered by the physician, raise the head of the bed as the client lies on her side. Support the client's head and shoulders while she pushes up to a sitting position, while another person eases her legs over the side of the bed. Then instruct the client to move from sitting to standing position in one smooth motion.
2. The client should not move, twist, or turn quickly as this would strain the spine.
4. A walker may or may not be indicated for this client. Refusing to use a walker does not indicate effective teaching.

#51. 2. Rest is a primary treatment for mononucleosis. However, adolescents have a great need for socialization and contact with peers. It is appropriate to encourage the client to have friends visit. — Ev — Ph/9 — Ap

1. Clients with mononucleosis should restrict activity during the acute phase. Going to the football game is not appropriate.
3. Clients with mononucleosis should restrict activity during the acute phase. Working out with the swim team is not appropriate.
4. Bed rest is not a must. Rather, a client's energy level will influence the amount of rest needed.

#52. 3. Maneuvering safely after orientation to the room is a realistic goal for a person with impaired vision. Orienting the client to the room should help the client to move safely. — Pl — Sa/2 — Ap

1. Independently ambulating around the unit is not appropriate because the unit environment can change and injury could result. Assistance is necessary because of the client's visual deficit.
2. It is unlikely the client can see well enough to read the materials.
4. Using the bedpan is an unnecessary restriction on the client as she can be oriented to the bathroom or to call for assistance.

#53. 1. The ECG reflects the heart rate and rhythm. Pacer spikes and dysrhythmias will be visible. It is the initial and most informative step in assessing pacemaker functioning. — As — Ph/9 — Ap

2. The pulse should be taken but not initially, as it will not provide all of the information that an ECG will.
3. Blood pressure is not an initial assessment.
4. Incision site assessment is not an initial pacemaker function assessment.

#54. 2. Crusting of the eyelids is associated with purulent drainage, a characteristic of bacteria conjunctivitis. — As — Ph/9 — Ap

1. Serous drainage is characteristic of a viral infection.
3. Severe eye pain is characteristic of conjunctivitis associated with a foreign body.
4. Conjunctivitis is usually bilateral.

#55. 4. An alcohol-based mouthwash will tend to dry and break down the oral tissues. — Ev — Ph/9 — Ap

ANSWER	RATIONALE	NP	CN	CL

1. A soft bristle brush helps to prevent trauma and removes oral debris that could cause breakdown of oral tissues.
2. Lubrication keeps lips soft, which helps prevent irritation.
3. Avoiding hard or spicy foods helps to prevent irritation of the oral tissues.

#56. 1. The use of proverbs tests for the client's ability to abstract meaning as well as reason.   As   Ps/5   Co
2. Item identification tests knowledge of objects in the environment.
3. Presidents' names tests long-term memory.
4. Serial sevens tests calculation ability.

#57. 2. There is nothing in the case information to support the diagnosis of a self-care deficit.   An   Ps/6   An
1. The client has altered thought processes.
3. The client has a sensory perceptual alteration; he hears his girlfriend calling him.
4. The client has a sleep pattern disturbance; he rarely sleeps.

#58. 3. The community mental health model is based on the philosophy that mental health care can best be delivered within the community and focuses on prevention. This client would best be cared for in a community-based setting such as partial hospitalization, community support, or outpatient care.   Pl   Ps/6   Ap
1. The client is unlikely to agree to admit himself to a psychiatric unit.
2. Filing a petition for involuntary commitment would be a last resort.
4. The client needs psychotherapy as well as treatment with medication.

#59. 1. In light of his past behavior it would probably be unrealistic to get to work every day, even with his parents' assistance. Four out of five days is a good initial goal.   Pl   Ps/6   Ap
2. It is highly unlikely that this client will be able to get to work, either on time or late, without assistance. To expect him to get there on time every day with assistance is probably unrealistic. Because of the ambivalence that pervades much of the schizophrenic client's life, this client will be hesitant to consistently accept his parents' help and to consistently accept the responsibilities of the adult role of wage earner.
3. It is unrealistic to expect the client to get to work independently. He has already proved that he cannot do this.
4. It is unrealistic to expect the client to get to work independently. He has already proved that he cannot do this.

#60. 4. Mr. T. has been assaultive with the landlord and it is reasonable to expect that he may be with peers and staff. His mental illness produces a hyperactive state and poor judgment and impulse control. External controls such as limiting of unit privileges will assist in feelings of security and safety.   Im   Ps/6   Ap
1. Food and fluids are necessary. However, Mr. T.'s hyperactivity does not allow him to sit quietly to eat. Finger foods "on the run" will provide needed nourishment.
2. When hyperactivity decreases, then approach Mr. T. regarding hygiene and grooming needs.
3. Medications will be ordered. However, a thorough evaluation must be done first.

#61. 4. Assuming a squatting position allows for relief of dyspnea. This is a classic manifestation of tetralogy of Fallot. The child assumes this position to improve the hemodynamics.   As   Ph/9   Ap
1. Children with tetralogy have poor growth.
2. Hypotonia may be present in situations with progressive heart failure, but this is not the most characteristic manifestation.
3. Epistaxis may be present in older children but is not the most characteristic finding.

#62. 3. The secretions visible in the tube may be partially occluding the airway and should be removed immediately.   Im   Ph/9   Ap

ANSWER	RATIONALE	NP	CN	CL

1. Get the vital signs after the airway has been cleared.
2. Clear the airway and then notify the physician if the client is still having difficulty breathing.
4. After the secretions are removed oxygen could be started as ordered.

#63. 4. Observation for life-threatening problems of hemorrhage and breathing difficulties are priorities in the immediate postoperative period.   Pl   Ph/9   Ap
1. Alleviation of pain is important to allow the client to rest more comfortably, but this is not the first priority. Life-threatening events always take priority.
2. Decreasing the client's concern over his appearance is important, but it is not the primary concern in the early postoperative period.
3. Planning with the physician and dietitian to improve the client's nutritional status are vital aspects of care, but they are not the primary focus in the immediate postoperative period.

#64. 4. Permanent remission usually takes place around age two or three. Until the time of spontaneous permanent remission, there will be many exacerbations and remissions. Sometimes these children develop asthma-type respiratory reactions or other allergies when infantile eczema subsides.   Pl   Ph/9   Ap
1. Management of eczema with frequent baths requires that the emollient be applied immediately after the bath while the skin is still slightly moist. This prevents drying of the skin. Applying the preparation before the bath is futile. The water will wash it away.
2. Because children usually scratch during sleep, the protectors are not removed at this time. A safe time to remove the protectors is during the bath, when the skin areas are soothed by the water, or after an antipyretic medication has been given and the child is free from pruritis temporarily.
3. Secondary infection is common and occurs because the scratching is not sufficiently controlled. Eczema runs in families.

#65. 2. The shorter leg is on the affected side, because the femur head slips further upward into the acetabulum. This causes the extra skin folds in the thigh on the affected side.   An   Ph/9   An
1. Most congenital hip dislocations are unilateral and on the left side, with a higher incidence in girls than boys.
3. Dislocation of both hips causes a widening of the perineum, which has not been mentioned in the data.
4. Newborn joint laxity is often blamed for lack of detection of congenital hip in the newborn period. However, there are two clear manifestations of dislocation in this child that can be tested by the nurse.

#66. 4. The nurse needs to present reality to the client to decrease his fear, which results from internal stimuli.   Pl   Ps/6   An
1. Seclusion is not planned because isolation will enhance the intensity of the hallucinations.
2. Placement in any group setting initially will be too threatening. Hallucinations prevent the client from interacting in and concentrating on group process.
3. Antipsychotic medications help to control symptoms but do not cure schizophrenia and the hallucinations that are a symptom of the illness.

#67. 4. The client does not want to understand (denial) or has misinterpreted the information given to him by the dietitian. Red meat contains hidden fat which is not visible. He should eat no red meat.   An   Ph/7   An
1. He may be overweight, but there are insufficient data to justify this diagnosis.
2. There are no data to suggest dysfunctional eating behaviors.

ANSWER	RATIONALE	NP	CN	CL

3. The question states that he had a session with the dietitian, therefore, the cause for knowledge deficit is not likely to be lack of information, but rather denial or misinterpretation of information.

#68. 2. Using the formula: amount of solution in ml ÷ time in minutes × the drop factor, the correct rate of flow is 28 gtts/minute.

Ev   Ph/8   Ap

6 hrs × 60 min. = 360 min.

$$\frac{1000\ ml}{360} = 2.8 \times 10 = 28$$

1. The answer 22 gtts/minute is the calculation for 1 liter of fluid to run over 8 hours instead of 6 hours.
3. The answer 32 gtts/minute may have been calculated on a drip factor of 12 instead of 10.
4. The answer 36 may just have been an error in calculation.

#69. 1. The arm of the affected side should be elevated for 24 to 48 hours post surgery. It is elevated and placed at a right angle to the chest.

Pl   Ph/9   Ap

2. Early ambulation and resumption of activity is encouraged to promote functioning of all body systems.
3. Early postoperative arm exercises are recommended and should be started within 24 hours. The client is encouraged to feed herself, comb her hair, and wash her face, being careful not to abduct the affected arm.
4. Promoting early food and fluid intake are immediate objectives and will enhance the functioning of all body systems.

#70. 1. Correct placement of the diaphragm is accomplished best if the client is allowed time to practice insertion of the device under professional supervision.

Im   He/3   Ap

2. A brochure should also be provided but practice at the clinic or doctor's office is best so she could ask questions and ensure proper placement.
3. It is not essential for the client to lay on her back to insert the diaphragm.
4. The client needs to take the responsibility for proper insertion. She may elect to involve her sex partner, but the responsibility is still hers.

#71. 3. Menorrhagia is abnormally profuse or excessive menstrual flow.

As   Ph/9   K

1. Dysmenorrhea is painful menstruation.
2. Dyspareunia is painful intercourse.
4. Metrorrhagia is uterine bleeding other than that caused by menstruation.

#72. 3. Genital herpes is characterized by multiple little blisters on the cervix, vagina, vulva, and buttocks that rupture and crust over in two to six weeks. Genital herpes causes severe morbidity and recurs. There is no cure, but oral acyclovir helps to reduce the number of recurrences. It is highly contagious.

As   Ph/9   Co

1. Chlamydia is characterized by a thin, whitish, nonodorous discharge, but can be asymptomatic. It is sensitive to antibiotics. Chlamydia leads to salpingitis and subsequent infertility.
2. Gonorrhea is characterized in women by a greenish or yellow-green discharge and irritation of the vulva with onset one to fourteen days after sexual contact with an infected person. Sometimes the person develops a sore throat and swollen glands. The treatment is penicillin.
4. Syphilis symptoms appear 9 to 90 days after sexual contact with an infected individual. The primary stage is characterized by a painless chancre (sore) that appears at the spot where the syphilis spirochete entered the body. It disappears in one to five weeks without treatment. The secondary stage is characterized by a rash, flulike symptoms, mouth sores, and patchy balding. It also disappears after a few months even without treatment. Tertiary syphilis occurs years later when the spirochetes attack internal organs including the

vascular system and brain. The treatment is penicillin, ideally at the primary stage.

#73. 3. Reye's syndrome follows a common viral illness such as influenza or varicella.

As   Ph/9   Co

   1. Temperature elevations may be present in Reye's syndrome. However, 103° or higher indicates bacterial infection.

   2. An enlarged liver is seen in Reye's syndrome, not an enlarged spleen.

   4. There does not appear to be a genetic predisposition to Reye's syndrome.

#74. 4. Rhythmic flexion and contraction of the muscles cause a characteristic tremor called a pill-rolling tremor. This is characteristic of Parkinson's disease.

As   Ph/9   Ap

   1. Confusion is not usually seen in a person with Parkinson's disease.

   2. Persons with Parkinson's disease are apt to have tremors at rest that disappear with motion.

   3. Pallor is not a characteristic of Parkinson's disease. The client will have a staring, mask-like facial expression because of muscle tension.

#75. 1. Amantadine hydrochloride (Symmetrel) is a synthetic antiviral agent with an unknown mechanism of action that allows dopamine to accumulate in extracellular or synaptic sites. Parkinson's disease is characterized by a dopamine deficiency.

An   Ph/8   Ap

   2. Amantadine does not correct mineral deficiencies. Mineral deficiencies are not known to be related to Parkinson's disease.

   3. Amantadine does not elevate the client's mood. Parkinson's disease is not a mood disorder.

   4. Amantadine does not replace enzymes. Parkinson's disease is not due to enzyme deficiency.

#76. 4. Persons with advanced Parkinson's disease usually have difficulty swallowing and are in danger of choking. Aspiration pneumonia must be prevented and is the highest priority.

Pl   Ph/9   Ap

   1. Proper positioning and frequent changes in position are important in preventing and relieving stiffness, but are not of highest priority.

   2. Encouraging independence is important in the care plan but is not highest priority.

   3. Increasing activity to the extent possible is important. The client may need assistance or walking aids to prevent falls. However, activity is not the highest priority.

#77. 3. Scheduling activities in collaboration with the client will allow him to proceed at his own pace and maximize his strength.

Pl   Ph/9   Ap

   1. Adequate nighttime sleep is important. However, this client needs rest times during the day.

   2. High-carbohydrate foods will provide energy.

   4. The client needs to find an appropriate schedule of activities he can tolerate both in the hospital and at home. This may include naps or rest times during the day, which should be planned in collaboration with the client.

#78. 3. Mobility is important for the client with multiple myeloma. Weight bearing promotes movement of calcium back into weakened bones, helping to maintain their strength. This will also reduce the risk of hypercalcemia, which is a common complication of multiple myeloma. The client will need assistance with mobility because the bones are weak.

Pl   Ph/9   Ap

   1. Fluids are forced when the client has multiple myeloma to prevent renal failure due to the high levels of uric acid released as plasma cells are destroyed.

   2. Potassium levels are not a primary consideration in multiple myeloma. Calcium levels are of greater concern.

   4. Aspirin is normally avoided during treatment for multiple myeloma, since the chemotherapy agents used decrease platelet count and predispose to bleeding.

ANSWER	RATIONALE	NP	CN	CL

#79. 4. **The casted extremity should have palpable pulses and feel warm to the touch, and the toes should be able to move freely.**   Ev Ph/9 Ap

    1. The toes should feel warm to the touch. The temperature of the casted foot is compared to that of the uninjured foot in order to determine the normal temperature. Coolness of an extremity may indicate poor tissue perfusion.

    2. The nail beds are normally pink in color. The blanch test is performed by pressing lightly on the nail bed and then releasing. The pink color should return almost instantly. A blue tinge indicates venous impairment while white toes may indicate arterial insufficiency.

    3. Localized pain is expected soon after the fracture. If pain continues the cast may be exerting pressure on a nerve, blood vessel or bony prominence and is a warning of complications.

#80. 3. **This is the three-point gait, which is used when one leg is injured or weak and the other leg is capable of supporting the client's full body weight. Most of the body weight is placed on the crutches when the fractured leg is moved forward.**   Im Ph/7 Ap

    1. Weight should be borne by the hands; weight borne by the axilla can cause damage to the brachial plexus nerves and can cause crutch paralysis.

    2. This is the four-point gait and it is taught when the client can move each leg separately and can bear considerable weight on each of them.

    4. This is a two-point gait and is used by persons capable of bearing weight on both legs. It permits faster ambulation than the four-point gait, which could also be used.

#81. 4. **Positioning activities that will maintain the femoral head component in the acetabular cup are essential to prevent dislocation of the prosthesis. The leg must be maintained in abduction and the hip is not to be flexed more than 45–60 degrees.**   Pl Ph/9 Ap

    1. When the client is initially allowed out of bed, limited flexion is permitted and abduction is maintained. The client is taught to transfer by pivoting on the nonoperative leg. Ambulation is permitted when ordered and only partial weight bearing is permitted. Ambulatory aids such as a walker are used for a time until sufficient muscle tone has developed to allow full weight bearing.

    2. The hip is not to be flexed more than 45–60 degrees. The client's bed may not be elevated more than 60 degrees and sitting in a chair or on a commode is not permitted.

    3. The client may not be positioned on the operative hip because it would require the hip to be placed in adduction which could cause dislocation of the prosthesis. The operative leg must be maintained in abduction at all times.

#82. 2. **According to models like Maslow and Kalish, the need for air is more basic than the need for activity, self-esteem, or skin integrity. While lack of care at any level may interfere with the client's overall health, failure to meet basic physiologic human needs, is necessary before higher level needs may be addressed. The data suggest the client may have congestive failure.**   An Ph/9 An

    1. Activity intolerance is a diagnosis for this client. However, it is not the priority diagnosis. According to models like Maslow and Kalish, the need for air is more basic than the need for activity, self-esteem, or skin integrity.

    3. Situational low self-esteem is a nursing diagnosis. It is not the priority diagnosis. According to models like Maslow and Kalish, the need for air is more basic than the need for activity, self-esteem, or skin integrity.

    4. Impairment in skin integrity is a nursing diagnosis for this client. However, it is not the priority nursing diagnosis. According to

ANSWER	RATIONALE	NP	CN	CL

models like Maslow and Kalish, the need for air is more basic than the need for activity, self-esteem, or skin integrity.

#83. 1. Diabetes insipidus is a disorder of water metabolism caused by deficiency of vasopressin (the antidiuretic hormone secreted by the posterior pituitary gland). Clinical manifestations include marked polyuria, extreme dilution of the urine resulting in a specific gravity of 1.000–1.005, polydipsia (fluid intake of 4–40 liters daily), high serum osmolarity, and hypernatremia.   As   Ph/9   Co

   2. Diabetes insipidus is a disorder of water metabolism caused by a deficiency of vasopressin, which results in production of a highly dilute urine with a specific gravity of 1.000–1.005 and polyuria.

   3. Diabetes insipidus is a disorder of water metabolism caused by a deficiency of vasopressin, which results in production of a highly dilute urine and polyuria resulting in high serum osmolarity and hypernatremia. Serum sodium levels often exceed 145 mEq/L.

   4. Diabetes insipidus is a disorder of water metabolism caused by a deficiency of vasopressin, which results in marked polyuria and causes an increase in serum osmolarity. This in turn triggers the thirst center, resulting in polydipsia with fluid intake over 4 liters (4–30 liters) daily.

#84. 3. In atresia of the esophagus, the esophagus, instead of being an open tube from the throat to the stomach, is closed at some point, and there is a fistula to the trachea. Because of the blockage, excessive mucus builds up in the nasopharynx and the child has difficulty breathing and becomes cyanotic. When the mucus is suctioned, the baby becomes pink again. If the newborn's condition is not recognized and he is fed, the feeding will immediately be expelled through the nose and mouth, and the infant will choke and cough and likely aspirate the feeding.   As   Ph/9   Co

   1. Bile-stained vomitus might indicate a bowel obstruction. Bile in the vomitus means the vomitus comes from the intestines. With esophageal atresia there is no connection between the mouth and the stomach.

   2. The infant with esophageal atresia is not getting food to the intestine. Diarrhea and colicky abdominal pain would not be seen.

   4. Visible peristaltic waves and projectile vomiting are indicative of pyloric stenosis.

#85. 2. A six-month-old child is learning to sit alone.   As   He/3   K

   1. The child develops language skills between the ages of one and three.

   3. The child begins to use a spoon at 12–15 months of age.

   4. The baby pulls himself to a standing position about ten months of age.

#86. 3. Most children at 12 months of age are not proficient walkers. They may know how to climb up stairs but not how to come down stairs. Their sense of balance is not stable. They have no judgment.   Ev   Sa/2   Ap

   1. The yard should be fenced for the now-mobile child. This indicates that the parents understand safety issues.

   2. Children can easily drown in a bathtub. This indicates understanding of safety needs.

   4. The car seat should be in the middle of the back seat. This indicates understanding of safety needs.

#87. 3. Raynaud's phenomenon (excessive and prolonged painful vasoconstriction of the extremities, especially the hands) is precipitated by exposure to cold and aggravated by smoking.   Im   Ph/9   Ap

   1. Warm weather is ideal for this client who is sensitive to the cold.

   2. Exercise does not cause an attack.

   4. Alcohol consumption by itself does not seem to cause an attack.

#88. 1. Drugs commonly used by elderly people, especially in combination, can lead to dementia.   An   Ph/8   An

2. Assessment of the medication taken may or may not provide information on the client's medical background. However, this is not the primary reason for assessing medications in a client who is exhibiting sundown syndrome.

3. Ability to recall medications may indicate short-term memory and recall. However, that is not the primary reason for assessing medications in a client with sundown syndrome.

4. Medication history should be a part of the nursing assessment. In this client there is an even more important reason for evaluating the medications taken.

#89. 2. **Becoming involved in an organization assists the retired adult in resocialization, which is beneficial to clients who depended on their employment for social interaction.**   Im   He/3   Ap

1. Going away on vacation may cause more isolation or be only a temporary solution.

3. This is not a therapeutic response as the client is experiencing social isolation.

4. Suggesting he go back to the work environment is not a therapeutic suggestion as it does not provide for resocialization and long-term adjustment.

#90. 4. **The client's spiritual needs must be met within the framework of his personal belief systems, even if those beliefs differ from those of the nursing staff.**   An   Sa/1   An

1. The client's spiritual needs must be met within the framework of his personal belief systems, even if those beliefs differ from those of the nursing staff.

2. The client's spiritual needs must be met within the framework of his personal belief systems, even if those beliefs differ from those of the nursing staff.

3. The client's spiritual needs must be met within the framework of his personal belief systems, even if those beliefs differ from those of the nursing staff.

#91. 2. **Careful alignment of the knee at the hinged joint must not be overlooked when the leg is placed in the continuous passive motion machine (CPM). Observation at frequent intervals regarding maintenance of correct position is also important.**   Im   Ph/9   Ap

1. Passive motion is maintained as ordered by the physician. Frequently it is maintained for several hours at a time with resting intervals or it may be maintained during the day with a knee immobilizer used at night.

3. There are no pressure areas on the shins. The leg rests in the CPM machine so the pressure is on the calves and the back of the legs.

4. The speed and degree of extension is determined by the physician and physical therapist.

#92. 3. **A semi-Fowler's position is indicated to promote respiratory function. Some authorities recommend placing the client on the affected side to prevent mediastinal shift and some authorities believe positioning on the affected side may put pressure on the surgical site on the main stem bronchus. All agree the client should be in the semi-Fowler's position.**   Im   Ph/9   Ap

1. Clients with limited respiratory function may not be able to breathe when placed on their unaffected side. Placement on the unaffected side tends to promote mediastinal shift following the removal of an entire lung. Decubitus means lying down.

2. The client should be on his back following a pneumonectomy but not in the decubitus or lying down position. The client should be in semi-Fowler's position.

4. High-Fowler's position is too high and will probably be too fatiguing for the client.

ANSWER	RATIONALE	NP	CN	CL
#93. 2.	There are four principles of health promotion: self-responsibility, nutrition, stress management, and exercise. Self-responsibility includes avoiding high risk behaviors such as abusing alcohol or drugs, overeating, driving while intoxicated, engaging in sexual practices which put the client at risk for disease, and smoking. Although any of the answers could be true, this is the only answer which addresses the question of health promotion principles.	An	He/4	An
1.	It may be that the client is in denial; however, there are no data to support that conclusion. In addition, denial does not address the question of health promotion principles.			
3.	The client may have a laissez-faire attitude, however, there are no data to support that conclusion. In addition, a laissez-faire attitude does not address the question of health promotion principles.			
4.	The client may be demonstrating passive suicidal tendencies; however, there are no data to support that conclusion. In addition, that conclusion does not address the question of health promotion principles.			
#94. 4.	Persons with ulcerative colitis should be on a low-fiber (low-residue) diet. This diet will provide the essential nutrients and is limited in high roughage content which stimulates peristalsis and makes symptoms of ulcerative colitis worse. Foods to be avoided include whole grains, nuts, raw fruits and vegetables, caffeine, alcohol, tough meats, pork, and highly spiced meats.	Pl	Ph/7	Co
1.	Chicken is considered a mild meat and is acceptable as long as it does not have highly spiced sauces. Cooked spinach is acceptable but a spinach salad would not be.			
2.	Broiled liver is acceptable as is white rice.			
3.	Cottage cheese is acceptable and canned apricots are allowed. Fresh apricots are not allowed on a low-residue diet.			
#95. 4.	To assess the client for a bowel training program the factors causing the bowel alteration should be assessed. A routine for bowel elimination should be based on the client's previous bowel habits and alterations in bowel habits that have occurred because of illness or trauma. The client and the family should assist in the planning of the program which should include foods high in bulk, adequate exercise, and fluid intake of 2500–3000 ml.	An	Ph/7	Co
1.	Foods high in bulk are appropriate.			
2.	2500–3000 ml fluid intake is appropriate.			
3.	Exercise should be a part of a bowel training regimen.			
#96. 3.	To design an effective care plan for an obese client the nurse should be aware of any medical diagnoses and the metabolic aberrations. The nurse should also assess the history of weight gain, extent of obesity (body mass index, skin-fold measurements), family attitudes, role in the family, emotional and psychological status, eating behaviors, activity and exercise habits, social relationships, motivation, and reasons for desiring weight loss.	An	Ph/7	Ap
1.	A knowledge of the food pyramid will help in planning the needed dietary changes.			
2.	A social support system is important when undertaking life style changes. The nurse should utilize this in planning the weight reduction program.			
4.	The nurse should assess any medical problems such as diabetes that might have a bearing on the weight reduction program.			
#97. 3.	The only real evidence that someone understands a client's pain is when that person states that he or she believes the pain is real. Fear that pain will not be accepted as real increases the perception of pain by increasing anxiety and tension.	Ev	Ph/9	Ap

1. Since pain cannot be measured objectively, nurses and caregivers must realize that pain is whatever the client says it is, and that pain is present whenever the client says it is present.
2. Phantom pain can last for many years without another causative agent.
4. Clients on narcotic analgesics may become physically dependent on them, but this is not the same as being addicted to them. Addiction is the seeking of drugs for their psychic, not physical, actions.

#98. 3. One of the cardiovascular manifestations of chronic renal failure and uremia is fluid volume excess. Hemodialysis should result in fluid volume decrease.   Ev   Ph/9   Co
1. The blood pressure should decrease following hemodialysis.
2. The serum potassium should decrease following hemodialysis.
4. The heart rate and rhythm should be stable following hemodialysis. Hemodialysis should normalize electrolytes which might cause dysrhythmias when elevated.

#99. 3. Extravasation of intravenous fluids may cause tissue ischemia or necrosis. The nurse should assess for this possible complication.   Im   Ph/8   Ap
1. There is no need to apply a tourniquet during the removal of an intravenous catheter. A tourniquet is applied when the catheter is inserted.
2. Flushing the catheter with a heparin solution may be done when the client has a heparin lock in place, but is not part of the removal process.
4. An IV catheter can be removed wearing clean gloves to protect the nurse.

#100. 4. The large bore needle prevents lysis of the red blood cells. The special blood filter prevents emboli or contaminated matter from flowing into the bloodstream.   Im   Ph/8   Ap
1. A normal saline solution (0.9%) is used to prime the tubing, not 3%.
2. Medications are not administered through the same tubing used to administer blood.
3. The greatest risk for blood transfusion reactions is during the first hour of the transfusion.

Practice Test 5

1. A fifty-year-old woman is admitted to the hospital with a diagnosis of tuberculosis. Which room assignment is most appropriate for a client with active tuberculosis?
   1. A semiprivate room.
   2. A room with laminar flow.
   3. A reverse isolation unit.
   4. A private room vented to the outside.
2. A sputum specimen is ordered for a client. The most important factor for the nurse to consider when obtaining a sputum specimen for culture is that
   1. a copious amount must be collected.
   2. sputum collected must not be diluted.
   3. it should be coughed up from deep in the lungs.

4. the specimen must be refrigerated immediately.
3. An adult client with tuberculosis asks the nurse if she needs to follow any special diet. Which suggestion would be most appropriate for the nurse to give?
   1. Eat a high-carbohydrate diet.
   2. Eat a low-calorie, low-protein diet.
   3. Eat frequent small, high-calorie meals.
   4. Consume only high-carbohydrate liquids.
4. Ms. J. is a client in the burn unit three days following second- and third-degree burns of both legs. The nurse plans to assess Ms. J. for indications of the complication that is the major cause of death in this period and includes which of the following?

1. Monitor arterial blood gases daily.
2. Monitor intake and output every shift.
3. Monitor results of wound cultures daily.
4. Monitor daily caloric intake.

5. Mr. J. is admitted to the surgical ICU following a left adrenalectomy. He is sleepy but easily aroused. An IV containing hydrocortisone is running. The nurse planning care for Mr. J. knows it is essential to include which of the following nursing interventions at this time?
   1. Monitor blood glucose levels every shift to detect development of hypo- or hyperglycemia.
   2. Keep flat on back with minimal movement to reduce risk of hemorrhage following surgery.
   3. Administer hydrocortisone until vital signs stabilize, then discontinue the IV.
   4. Teach Mr. J. how to care for his wound since he is at high risk for developing postoperative infection.

6. When ten-year-old Johnny went to see the school nurse about a circle of ringworm on his scalp, he was asked some questions for a data base. Which of his environmental factors most likely contributed to John's acquisition of ringworm?
   1. He rides a public bus to and from school each day and likes to sit behind the driver so they can talk about baseball.
   2. He has a pet kitten that stays outside during the day but comes inside to sleep with him at night.
   3. He loaned his baseball hat to a friend last week but hasn't gotten it back yet.
   4. He forgets to wash his hair sometimes, and his mother has to remind him.

7. When planning immediate postoperative care for the adolescent with a Harrington rod insertion, the nurse should particularly focus upon
   1. assessment of paralytic ileus.
   2. cast care and repair of rough edges.
   3. neurological assessments.
   4. vital signs and urinary output.

8. When a five-year-old vomits a bright-red liquid several hours after a tonsillectomy, the nurse needs to determine whether or not the child is bleeding from the operative site. Which nursing action would be most informative?
   1. Visualizing the posterior throat with use of a tongue depressor and flashlight.
   2. Asking if the child had received red Koolaid for oral intake during the last hour.
   3. Taking vital signs, including the blood pressure, and checking oral mucus membranes for color changes.
   4. Staying with the child and watch to see if he is swallowing frequently.

9. The nurse has been teaching the family of a child with croup about emergency care. Which statement made by the parent indicates that teaching was effective?
   1. "If he wakes up coughing a barky cough, I'll try sitting in a steamy bathroom with him. If he isn't better in an hour, I'll bring him to the hospital for an aerosol of epinephrine."
   2. "If the x-ray shows no swelling of the epiglottis, we can probably go back home and use the humidifier there."
   3. "Symptoms of breathing hard, inward movement of the ribs and neck with breathing, and a continuous loud breathing noise, are usual signs of spasmodic croup and can be treated at home."
   4. "If he has an episode of loud, labored breathing and retractions, becomes frightened, sweaty, and thrashes around, then falls asleep, the croup attack is over."

10. The nurse is assisting a child with congestive heart failure. Which of the following would the child be least likely to manifest?
    1. Weakness and fatigue.
    2. Dyspnea.
    3. Tachycardia.
    4. Oliguria.

11. A woman is scheduled for radiation therapy following a mastectomy. The nurse can expect that this client may have
    1. more energy during therapy.
    2. an increased appetite.
    3. skin changes at the radiation site.
    4. diarrhea.

12. The nurse is assessing an 84-year-old woman. She wears glasses and a hearing aid and is in generally good health. The nurse knows that a common theme in the physical assessment and evaluation of the elderly client is
    1. decline is avoidable.
    2. reserve capacity is diminished.
    3. changes are usually related to disease.
    4. clients with good health habits experience few age-related changes.

13. The nurse is performing a cardiovascular assessment on an elderly client. What findings would be expected?
    1. A bounding radial pulse.
    2. An early systolic murmur.
    3. First-degree heart block.
    4. Frequent bursts of tachycardia.

14. When caring for an elderly client it is important to keep in mind the changes in color vision that may occur. What colors are apt to be most difficult for the elderly to distinguish?
    1. Red and blue.
    2. Blue and gold.
    3. Red and green.
    4. Blue and green.

15. Ms. T., a Type II diabetic, has been attending

group classes related to self-care and prevention of complications of diabetes. The nurse who teaches the course questions Ms. T. about her understanding of diabetic foot care and determines that Ms. T. needs further instruction when she states:

1. "I should use a mirror to examine all surfaces of my feet for cuts, cracks, or redness."
2. "I should wear shoes that fit well and allow room for my toes to wiggle."
3. "I should use a bath thermometer to ensure that my bath water is between 85 and 90 degrees before I step into the tub."
4. "I should remove corns and calluses by using the special medicated pads available at the drugstore."

16. Mrs. W., 88 years old, is diagnosed as having sick sinus syndrome and is being prepared for the insertion of a demand pacemaker. When explaining to Mrs. W. how the demand pacemaker works, the nurse relates that it
    1. senses changes in blood pressure.
    2. stimulates the SA node at 60 beats per minute.
    3. beats when there is decreased coronary blood flow.
    4. senses the heart rate and starts a beat as needed.

17. Which information would be most accurate when describing pacemakers to a client who is to receive a pacemaker?
    1. Batteries are no longer necessary.
    2. Today's pacemakers are smaller than earlier models.
    3. The generator will be implanted in the upper arm.
    4. Modern pacemakers can be inserted in the client's room.

18. Which information should the nurse include in the discharge teaching plan of a client who had a pacemaker implanted?
    1. Remember to take all medications as directed.
    2. Avoid sudden changes in temperature.
    3. Keep the pacemaker insertion site covered.
    4. Follow a low-cholesterol diet carefully.

19. The nurse is teaching a client about symptoms of pacemaker failure. Which would not be included?
    1. Nausea.
    2. Syncope.
    3. Dizziness.
    4. Palpitations.

20. An adult male is admitted for evaluation of back pain. He has a two-year history of back pain and sciatica. Which of the following is he least likely to report having been included during conservative therapy for his back problem?
    1. Analgesics.
    2. Enzymes.

3. Muscle relaxants.
4. Anti-inflammatory agents.

21. In dealing with the client who has pain, the nurse knows that even though pain is a subjective experience, an objective approach for eliciting the severity of the pain experience is
    1. asking the client to describe the pain on a 0–10 scale, record the information, and base future assessments on it.
    2. asking the client to compare the current pain experience to that of previous experiences.
    3. not helpful as the pain experience is a subjective one and not amenable to a standardized assessment approach.
    4. not helpful and the best approach is to medicate the client sufficiently to control the pain.

22. When assessing the client with polycythemia vera, the nurse should expect to find
    1. pallor.
    2. tachycardia.
    3. leg pain with exercise.
    4. shortness of breath.

23. Which of the following actions should the nurse take in assisting an above-the-knee amputee who is two weeks post-op and experiencing phantom pain?
    1. Provide and encourage client activities.
    2. Keep the client on bed rest.
    3. Tell the client the pain will disappear in one week.
    4. Instruct the client to ignore the pain.

24. A mother brings her six-month-old daughter to the well-baby clinic for her regular checkup. When discussing childhood immunizations, the nurse explains that routine childhood immunizations protect against
    1. poliomyelitis, *Haemophilus influenzae* type b, and mononucleosis.
    2. measles, mumps, rubella, and herpes simplex.
    3. diphtheria, tetanus, and Calmette-Guérin bacillus.
    4. poliomyelitis, *Haemophilus influenzae* type b, and pertussis.

25. The mother of a child in well-baby clinic asks the nurse which immunizations contain live virus. The nurse's best response is
    1. MMR and OPV.
    2. Hib and MMR.
    3. DTaP and OPV.
    4. DTaP and Hib.

26. A six-month-old child is seen in well-baby clinic. The child has had the routine immunizations up to this point. At this visit, which immunizations should the nurse expect to administer?
    1. OPV.
    2. MMR.

3. DTaP.
4. Smallpox.

27. Nursing interventions prior to electroconvulsive therapy (ECT) should include
    1. providing an opportunity for the client to ask questions and express concerns about ECT.
    2. telling the client that it is not helpful to concentrate on the therapy.
    3. reassuring the client that ECT is no worse than having a venipuncture.
    4. telling the client she will recover completely as a result of ECT.

28. The nurse is discussing electroconvulsive therapy (ECT) with a client who asks how long it will be before she feels better. The nurse explains that the beneficial effects of ECT usually occur within
    1. one week.
    2. three weeks.
    3. four weeks.
    4. six weeks.

29. Nursing assessment before electroconvulsive therapy (ECT) is aimed at establishing parameters that reflect the client's mental and physical status. Which is not a part of the assessment before ECT therapy?
    1. Activity level.
    2. Bowel habits.
    3. Pain tolerance.
    4. Sleep habit.

30. The nurse caring for a client following electroconvulsive therapy (ECT) would expect the side effects of therapy to include
    1. cardiac arrhythmias, elevated SED rate, and fractures of the spine.
    2. an increase in norepinephrine at synapses of the brain, an increase in MAO platelet levels, and euphoria.
    3. slowing of electrical impulses in the brain, temporary amnesia, and confusion.
    4. mild organic changes in the neurons of the brain, dementia, and mild aphasia.

31. The nurse is planning care for a client who has had a bowel resection. It is important for the nurse to assess the client for which complication seen in all clients having this type of surgery?
    1. Atelectasis.
    2. Parotitis.
    3. Temporary ileus.
    4. Transient ischemia.

32. The nurse is to irrigate a nasogastric tube every two hours. Which solution should the nurse select to irrigate the tube?
    1. Normal saline.
    2. Tap water.
    3. Ringer's lactate.
    4. Half-strength peroxide.

33. To prevent postoperative pulmonary complications, which of the following will be most effective in helping a client who has had abdominal surgery to breathe deeply?
    1. Oxygen via nasal prongs.
    2. Incentive spirometry.
    3. Periodic ambulation.
    4. Verbal encouragement.

34. An adult has received albumin to treat ascites secondary to cirrhosis. To evaluate whether this therapy has been effective, the nurse should
    1. assess whether pedal edema has decreased.
    2. observe whether the client is less short of breath.
    3. measure the client's abdominal girth.
    4. check lab study results for an increase in serum albumin.

35. An adult who has had an abdominal perineal resection asks the nurse when he can expect his bowel function to return. The nurse explains that the earliest that normal bowel function can be expected to return postoperatively is
    1. six hours.
    2. twelve hours.
    3. three days.
    4. one week.

36. Mrs. M., 89, is dying from heart failure after a heart attack and two hospitalizations for congestive heart failure. Mrs. M.'s daughter attempts to keep a "stiff upper lip" and to smile so as not to upset her mother, but she cries when alone with the nurse. She also states, "My mother says God should take her" and that "she is ready for the garbage heap." In evaluating this situation, which statement made by the daughter indicates to the nurse that the daughter is adjusting to the dying process her mother is experiencing?
    1. "I'm so depressed. I try to do my best but I find myself crying a lot of the time."
    2. "My mother isn't dying. She has so many relatives to live for."
    3. "I really don't know what I would do if mother died."
    4. "We don't talk about death. It's a morbid topic."

37. The nurse is caring for an adult client who had an abdominal resection. On the fourth postoperative day, the client's wound dehisces. The safest nursing intervention when this occurs is to
    1. cover the wound with sterile, moist saline dressings.
    2. approximate the wound edges with tape.
    3. irrigate the wound with sterile saline.
    4. hold the abdominal contents in place with a sterile, gloved hand.

38. Ms. G., 34 years old, has been experiencing double vision and frequent headaches. She has noticed some forgetfulness and mood swings. The diagnosis of a right frontal lobe

lesion was made and she is admitted to the hospital for a craniotomy. During the admission interview, Ms. G. reviews her outpatient diagnostic work-up. Which diagnostic procedure most likely confirmed the presence of her brain tumor?
  1. A CT scan.
  2. A myelogram.
  3. Skull x-rays.
  4. A lumbar puncture.

39. The nurse is caring for an adult admitted with a diagnosis of a brain tumor. Shortly after her admission, the client suffers a seizure. The nurse's initial intervention must be directed toward
  1. controlling the seizure.
  2. protecting the client.
  3. restraining the client.
  4. reducing circulation to the brain.

40. Following a craniotomy, the client asks the nurse why a bone flap is necessary. The nurse explains that the purpose for removing the bone flap is to
  1. allow for the insertion of an ICP bolt.
  2. accommodate postoperative brain swelling.
  3. allow free flow of fluid into the Jackson-Pratt drain.
  4. permit reoperation if necessary as access will be easier.

41. The nurse is caring for a client who had a craniotomy performed this morning. Positioning the client's head is most important to
  1. maintain a patent airway.
  2. facilitate venous drainage.
  3. provide for client comfort.
  4. prevent hemorrhage from the suture line.

42. Following craniotomy, which of the following measures is contraindicated for postoperative pulmonary toilet?
  1. Coughing.
  2. Deep breathing.
  3. Turning.
  4. Suctioning.

43. The glucocorticoid dexamethasone (Decadron) is given following craniotomy because
  1. it creates a feeling of euphoria, which is beneficial in the early postoperative period.
  2. it promotes excretion of water, which aids in reducing ICP.
  3. it enhances venous return and thus reduces ICP.
  4. it reduces cerebral edema, thus reducing ICP.

44. Joe, 35 years old, is diagnosed as having psychogenic amnesia. The nurse would find which of the following symptoms during the assessment?

  1. Client states he feels detached from his body.
  2. Client states he can recall some things, but not everything.
  3. Client states he can't move his arm since he saw a man killed.
  4. Client states he's told he does things that he can't remember.

45. A newly admitted client with a conversion disorder says he cannot move his legs. What is the best nursing response?
  1. "The physical tests and examinations state no physiological reason for your paralysis."
  2. "Let me help you out of bed to the wheelchair. I will show you where the dining room is. Dinner is served at 5:30 P.M. I'll be telling you more about the typical routine later."
  3. "I'm sorry to hear this. I'll plan to have your meals served to you in bed. Because of your physical problem you will receive special privileges."
  4. "You are here to get an understanding of how your physical symptoms related to the conflicts in your personal life. Maybe you should reflect on this a while and I'll be back in one hour to discuss it with you."

46. Which of the following assessments made by the nurse would be essential in understanding behavior of a client with a conversion disorder?
  1. Physical symptoms are not under voluntary control.
  2. Physical symptoms are under voluntary control but without intent to reduce secondary gain.
  3. Physical symptoms are experienced as a means to manipulate others to meet narcissistic needs.
  4. Physical symptoms are produced through purposeful means to reduce anxiety and maintain dependency.

47. A young woman witnesses an accident between a construction truck and a railroad car in which the driver of the truck was killed. She suddenly reports changes in her vision and claims to be developing blindness. Physical work-up reveals no damage to the eyes. A conversion disorder is diagnosed. Which of the following responses by family members indicate to the nurse that they understand their daughter's symptoms?
  1. "She's afraid to get involved as a witness of the event, so she claims to be blind."
  2. "She's trying to avoid her civic responsibilities, so she's manipulating the situation and being childish."
  3. "Seeing the accident was very traumatic for her."
  4. "Perhaps the physical examinations aren't true. Maybe glass splinters are in her eyes and are too small to be seen."

48. Which of the following would best indicate to the nurse that a depressed client is improving?
    1. Reduced levels of anxiety.
    2. Changes in vegetative signs.
    3. Compliance with medications.
    4. Requests to talk to the nurse.
49. In assessing a client for posttraumatic stress disorder, which symptoms would the nurse perceive as key in the client's response to trauma?
    1. Emotional numbing and detachment followed by irritability, anxiety, aggressiveness, and hyperalertness.
    2. Depression and social withdrawal.
    3. Intrusive, hyperactive behavior and use of alcohol to soothe symptoms.
    4. Drug-seeking behavior and sexual promiscuity as a means to cope.
50. The nurse is talking with a young woman client in the health clinic who is concerned she may have a sexually transmitted disease. The nurse commends her for seeking medical care. The nurse explains that the major reason treatment of the majority of STDs is delayed is because
    1. the client is embarrassed.
    2. symptoms are thought to be caused by something else.
    3. symptoms are ignored.
    4. the client never has symptoms.
51. A young woman tells the nurse in the health clinic that her boyfriend has gonorrhea. He told her about his disease after their last sexual experience three days ago. She wants to know when she can expect symptoms. The nurse replies that the unusual time between initial infection with *Neisseria gonorrhoeae* and the onset of symptoms is
    1. two to five days.
    2. five to seven days.
    3. one to two weeks.
    4. two to three weeks.
52. A client with gonorrhea asks the nurse if it can cause cancer. The nurse tells her that the organism associated with up to 90% of cervical malignancies and may be linked to other genital cancers is
    1. *Neisseria gonorrhoeae*.
    2. *Chlamydia trachomatis*.
    3. Human papilloma virus.
    4. Herpes simplex virus.
53. The nurse is teaching a client about the treatment for gonorrhea. The nurse explains that follow-up cultures will be taken after treatment has been completed to
    1. evaluate for complications.
    2. check the lab's work.
    3. validate eradication of the infection.
    4. provide an opportunity for sexual counseling.
54. The nurse is teaching clients in the diabetes clinic. A woman with newly diagnosed Type I diabetes asks when she will need to test her urine for ketones. The nurse tells her she will need to test her urine for ketones when
    1. she is overhydrated.
    2. she begins to gain weight.
    3. the glucometer reading is abnormal.
    4. her blood glucose level is more than 240 mg/dl for six hours.
55. The nurse is discussing ketones with a newly diagnosed Type I diabetic. In answering the client's question about how ketones will affect her, the nurse should base the answer on which concept?
    1. The diabetic is no different from others in the capacity to handle ketones.
    2. Ketones overpower the diabetic's adaptive mechanisms.
    3. Most diabetic clients are allergic to the byproducts of ketone metabolism.
    4. It is impossible to predict the reaction to ketones.
56. Which special precaution must the nurse take when assisting a client with self-monitoring of blood glucose?
    1. Give the client a machine for his use only.
    2. Wear gloves when performing the test.
    3. Rinse the lancet between uses.
    4. Recalibrate the glucometer before each use.
57. An adult client's insulin dosage is 10 units of regular insulin and 15 units of NPH insulin in the morning. The client should be taught to expect the first insulin peak
    1. as soon as food is ingested.
    2. in two to four hours.
    3. in six hours.
    4. in ten to twelve hours.
58. Dietary teaching for a Type I diabetic includes information on the glycemic impact of a meal. The nurse knows that the client has a good understanding when the client says,
    1. "Foods high in protein raise blood sugar rapidly."
    2. "Simple sugars or carbohydrates cause a predictable rise in blood sugar."
    3. "The protein, fat, and carbohydrate composition of a meal affect the blood glucose level."
    4. "Dairy beverages contain lactose, which dramatically increases the need for insulin."
59. Teaching an insulin-dependent diabetic will include guidelines for managing sick days. If an insulin dependent diabetic is nauseated, she should
    1. take the prescribed insulin.
    2. go to the emergency department.
    3. administer her regular insulin only.
    4. take nothing by mouth if she thinks she'll vomit.

60. An adult Type I diabetic tells the clinic nurse that she plans to accompany her husband on a business trip. When traveling, the client can use which food or beverage as a substitute for a delayed meal?
   1. Diet cola.
   2. Raisins.
   3. A candy bar.
   4. A glass of wine.
61. An adult Type I diabetic tells the nurse that she would like to lose 15 pounds. The best way for the client to lose weight is to
   1. increase her insulin dosage.
   2. reduce calories and walk daily.
   3. do an aerobic exercise program daily.
   4. reduce calories by at least 100 kcal daily.
62. The nurse is caring for a woman who has been taking insulin for eight months. Which diagnostic study is the most valuable in evaluating long-term management of a diabetic client?
   1. A two-hour postprandial test.
   2. A six-hour glucose tolerance test.
   3. A glycosolated hemoglobin test.
   4. The diary of glucometer test results.
63. A known diabetic is brought to the emergency department with complaints of fever, vague abdominal pain, nausea, and vomiting for the past several days. A diagnostic work-up reveals that she is in ketoacidosis. When eliciting a history from the client, one of the subtle signs of ketoacidosis that the nurse should be particularly observant for is
   1. polyuria.
   2. abnormal reflexes.
   3. increased thirst.
   4. mental deterioration.
64. The nurse is assessing a client admitted in ketoacidosis. The nurse can expect the client's skin to be
   1. clammy.
   2. flushed.
   3. diaphoretic.
   4. silky.
65. The nurse is caring for a client who is admitted in diabetic ketoacidosis. The client was diagnosed ten months ago. This is the first episode of ketoacidosis since the client was diagnosed. The care should focus on dealing with
   1. an extremely poor prognosis.
   2. the client's noncompliance.
   3. reinforcement of client teaching.
   4. the potential for a long, painful, chronic disorder.
66. The nurse is doing discharge teaching with a client who had diabetic ketoacidosis. The client should be reminded that
   1. the symptoms of ketoacidosis are variable; therefore all changes in status should be monitored.

2. weight loss and fatigue are early symptoms of ketoacidosis.
   3. headache is a serious diagnostic sign of ketoacidosis.
   4. in ketoacidosis mucous membranes will be pale.
67. In assessing clients for early signs of cancer, which of the following findings reported to the nurse would indicate a priority for follow-up?
   1. Bowel movements twice a day for the past five years.
   2. Monthly breast self-exam.
   3. Lingering cough one week after a cold.
   4. Mole that has become larger in the past four weeks.
68. The nurse is caring for the mother of a newborn. The nurse recognizes that the mother needs more teaching regarding cord care because she
   1. keeps the cord exposed to the air.
   2. washes her hands before sponge bathing her baby.
   3. washes the cord and surrounding area well with water at each diaper change.
   4. checks it daily for bleeding and drainage.
69. To minimize discomfort and embarrassment when assessing an adolescent girl, the nurse should
   1. make sure a parent is present.
   2. provide a gown and private area.
   3. examine two adolescents at the same time.
   4. postpone the exam until the adolescent is older.
70. A ten-month-old child is brought to the clinic for the first time. During the assessment interview, the mother states that her baby is allergic to eggs. This is important because the child will need testing before receiving
   1. DTaP.
   2. smallpox vaccine.
   3. OPV.
   4. MMR.
71. An elderly man is admitted to the hospital. He was alert and oriented during the admission interview. However, his family states that he becomes disruptive and disoriented around dinnertime. One night he was shouting furiously and didn't know where he was. He was sedated and the next morning he was fine. At dinnertime the disruptive behavior returned. The client is diagnosed as having sundown syndrome. The client's son asks the nurse what causes sundown syndrome. The nurse's best response is that it is attributed to
   1. an underlying depression.
   2. inadequate cerebral flow.
   3. changes in the sensory environment.
   4. fluctuating levels of oxygen exchange.
72. When an elderly client with sundown syndrome becomes mildly disoriented, the nurse should

1. ignore the disorientation.
2. prepare a normal saline IV.
3. turn off the lights in the room.
4. remind him where he is and why he is there.

73. The nurse places a large calendar in the room of a client with sundown syndrome to
   1. improve the appearance of the room.
   2. encourage independence.
   3. enhance time orientation.
   4. promote visual stimulation.

74. Which evening activity would be most helpful to a client with sundown syndrome?
   1. Lying in bed.
   2. Attending a unit party.
   3. Watching a favorite TV show.
   4. Looking out the window.

75. When planning the care of a client with sundown syndrome, which instruction would be most helpful to his family?
   1. Visit early in the day.
   2. Bring gifts when you visit.
   3. Visit in the evenings.
   4. Don't visit unless you see improvement.

76. What should the nurse include in the care plan for a client with sundown syndrome regarding his room environment during his sleeping hours?
   1. Keep the room brightly lit.
   2. Use subdued lighting.
   3. Keep the room dark with a night light.
   4. Ask the client how he is most comfortable.

77. The nurse is caring for a client who is having a panic attack. Which symptom will the client be least likely to exhibit?
   1. Bradycardia.
   2. Choking.
   3. Chest pain.
   4. Fear of going crazy.

78. The nurse is caring for a man who has angina. He complains of chest pain. Nitroglycerin is given because it
   1. slows and strengthens the heart rate.
   2. assists smooth muscles to contract.
   3. increases venous return to the heart.
   4. reduces both preload and afterload.

79. A man who received nitroglycerin for chest pain says that the nitroglycerin had no taste or sensation. What is the most appropriate response by the nurse?
   1. "That is good, it can be unpleasant."
   2. "I'll get a fresh supply of tablets."
   3. "Maybe we should switch to another brand."
   4. "Many improvements have been made in nitroglycerin."

80. Discharge teaching for a client with angina includes a complete review of nitroglycerin usage. The nurse tells the client that sublingual nitroglycerin can be used after the vial has been opened for up to
   1. one week.

2. one month.
3. four months.
4. six months.

81. What advice should the nurse give a client who takes a sublingual nitroglycerin tablet without relief of pain?
   1. Go to the emergency department.
   2. Take another tablet sublingually.
   3. Take two more tablets orally.
   4. Double the strength of the next dose.

82. What special precautions are necessary for a client with angina to take if he must go out in cold weather?
   1. Drink plenty of orange juice.
   2. Take a warm bath first.
   3. Walk as quickly as possible.
   4. Wear a scarf over his mouth.

83. When assessing the client with iron deficiency anemia, the nurse should expect to find
   1. bradycardia.
   2. jaundice.
   3. hunger.
   4. fatigue.

84. The nurse has been teaching self-care to a client who is receiving external radiation therapy to the facial area. Which of the following client actions indicates a need for further teaching?
   1. Sitting next to his wife and holding hands.
   2. Applying lotion and powder to the radiated site.
   3. Gently cleaning mouth and teeth with a sponge.
   4. Resting between activities.

85. The nurse is caring for a 28-week premature infant on a ventilator. Which action is essential for the nurse to take?
   1. Assess the oxygen saturation of the infant once per eight-hour shift using a pulse oximeter.
   2. Notify the physician if the oxygen saturation falls below 95% on the pulse oximeter, and plan to increase the oxygen settings.
   3. Notify the physician if the oxygen saturation is continually above 95%.
   4. Suction the infant every two hours around the clock.

86. To prevent complications for a client who has developed thrombocytopenia secondary to radiation therapy, the nurse instructs the client to
   1. brush the teeth with a hard bristle brush.
   2. shave with an electric razor.
   3. continue with sports activities.
   4. continue with intramuscular pain medications.

87. A laboring client has just been told that she will be delivering her baby by cesarean birth because of a contracted pelvis. To ensure a positive outcome for the parents, the nurse

preparing the client for cesarean delivery should give the highest priority to
1. keeping the woman clean and dry.
2. keeping the woman informed.
3. escorting the husband to the waiting room.
4. maintaining comfort.

88. Following circumcision of a one-day-old infant, the nurse knows that the most effective strategy for ensuring urinary elimination is
1. feeding the infant.
2. having nonconstrictive gauze over the penis.
3. keeping the infant on his side.
4. checking for first void postcircumcision.

89. Mr. J., a 45-year-old businessman, is scheduled for gallbladder surgery in four weeks. During his preadmission office visit he states that he smokes two packs of cigarettes a day. The nurse planning Mr. J.'s preoperative teaching will need to include instructions to
1. continue smoking.
2. try to decrease smoking.
3. stop smoking now.
4. join a nonsmoker's group and reschedule surgery.

90. Mr. D. had abdominal surgery two days ago. Which of the following statements would indicate to the nurse that normal bowel peristalsis is returning?
1. "My belly seems bigger this afternoon."
2. "I keep burping."
3. "I passed some rectal gas today."
4. "I feel like vomiting."

91. A 52-year-old man was admitted to the medical intensive care unit with a diagnosis of left-sided cerebrovascular accident. He was placed on hardwire cardiac monitoring. The predominant dysrhythmia demonstrated a baseline characterized by irregular undulations without discernible P waves. The QRS complex was normal, but the ventricular rhythm was irregular with a rate of between 100 to 180 beats per minute. This supraventricular arrhythmia often associated with the occurrence of a cerebrovascular accident is identified as
1. wide complex junctional tachycardia.
2. sinus tachycardia.
3. second-degree AV block referred to as Wenckebach.
4. atrial fibrillation initiated by an ectopic focus outside the SA node.

92. An adult is admitted with a diagnosis of probable Graves' disease with thyrotoxic crisis. Which of the following assessments will provide the nurse with the best measure of the severity of the client's disease?
1. Blood glucose.
2. Heart rate.
3. Urine output.
4. Blood pressure.

93. An adult with diabetes mellitus has a glycosolated hemoglobin (hemoglobin A_{1c}) reading that is elevated, while the blood glucose reading is 100 mg%. How should the nurse proceed?
1. Ask the client for daily blood glucose monitoring records, and ask the client to describe self-care practices.
2. Congratulate the client on the excellent level of diabetic control achieved and suggest that the client continue the present regimen.
3. Observe the client for the signs and symptoms of diabetic ketoacidosis and refer the client to the physician immediately.
4. Observe the client for signs and symptoms of hypoglycemia and provide orange juice immediately.

94. An elderly client with Type II diabetes mellitus lives alone. The client eats only one meal a day consisting mostly of carbohydrate foods, even though the client can afford more healthy meal choices. The nurse notes that the client wears poorly fitting shoes and often goes barefoot. The client is receptive to the nurse's offer to assist with a change in these behaviors. Select the most appropriate nursing diagnosis for the plan of care.
1. Impaired home maintenance management related to declining health.
2. Activity intolerance related to pedal pain.
3. Feeding self-care deficit related to poor food choices.
4. Altered health maintenance related to inadequate health teaching.

95. An adult client with hemiplegia and right hemianopia expresses concern about how to operate the vacuum cleaner and washing machine at home. Which of the following nursing diagnoses is appropriate for this client?
1. High risk for injury related to right-sided weakness.
2. Impaired home maintenance management related to paralysis and visual impairment.
3. Altered health management related to altered mobility and sensory perception.
4. Hygiene and self-care deficit related to inability to keep house clean.

96. Which techniques are most important for a nurse to assess a 60-year-old client with a family history of diabetes mellitus?
1. Palpation of pedal pulses and auscultation for carotid bruit.
2. Palpation of liver and observation of sclera.
3. Palpation of spleen and pulse oximetry.
4. Palpation of abdomen and auscultation of breath sounds.

97. The nurse is teaching a male client to examine his testicular area for abnormal masses.

Which of the following would be included in the appropriate assessment of the scrotum?
1. Observing that the right side is lower than the left.
2. Including the inguinal and femoral areas for bulges.
3. Requesting he inhale during the exam.
4. Holding the penis down during the exam.

98. The nurse is discussing risk factors for osteoporosis with a 45-year-old woman. Which assessment finding indicates a risk factor for osteoporosis? The client
1. has lactose intolerance and does not drink milk, but eats cheese and dark green vegetables.
2. is 5 feet 2 inches tall and weighs 90 pounds.
3. participates in aerobics classes twice weekly.
4. has been taking estrogen since her ovaries were removed two years ago.

99. The nurse is performing a breast examination for a nonpregnant woman during her annual gynecological visit. The nurse will be concerned if which one of the following findings is present?
1. Nipple discharge.
2. Tail of Spence.
3. Soft axilla.
4. Consistent patterns of veins.

100. The nurse is assessing a client who has had a kidney transplant. Which of the following assessment findings would indicate to the nurse that the client might be developing acute rejection of the kidney?
1. Oliguria or anuria.
2. Temperature range of 37.2 to 37.7° C.
3. Decreased blood pressure.
4. Stabilization of urine and blood chemistry values.

Answers and Rationales for Practice Test 5

ANSWER	RATIONALE	NP	CN	CL
#1. 4.	**Isolation for the client with tuberculosis requires a private room with a closed door and special ventilation.**	Pl	Sa/2	Ap
1.	A semiprivate room is not safe for the other client.			
2.	A laminar flow is an alternative to protective isolation. In a laminar flow environment air is filtered as it enters the room and flows horizontally at 90 feet per second, creating a totally sterile environment. A laminar flow room is not necessary with tuberculosis.			
3.	A reverse (protective) isolation unit is indicated if the client's immune system is suppressed. This protects the client from exogenous bacteria from staff and visitors.			
#2. 3.	**The client must use a deep explosive cough in order to obtain a suitable specimen.**	Im	Ph/9	Ap
1.	A copious amount of sputum is not needed.			
2.	Sputum collected is not diluted. It is put on an appropriate culture medium and incubated for at least 24 hours.			
4.	The specimen does not need to be refrigerated.			
#3. 3.	**The client with tuberculosis requires a diet that will maintain normal weight or allow for weight gain. This can be achieved best by eating a well-balanced, high-carbohydrate diet. Most clients tolerate small, frequent meals best.**	Pl	Ph/7	Ap
1.	The client needs a high-calorie die to help regain weight lost with tuberculosis. This choices does not include frequent meals, which are necessary for most people.			
2.	The client needs a diet high in protein.			
4.	The client needs more than liquids.			
#4. 3.	**Infection is the major cause of death in persons in the intermediate stage of a burn episode. The infection begins in the burn wound and travels into the bloodstream. Cultures are taken to monitor the colonization of the wound by organisms. Early detection permits treatment with antimicrobials to prevent the development of septicemia.**	Pl	Ph/9	Ap

1. Infection is the primary cause of death in persons who survive the first few days following extensive burns. Airway obstruction and edema continue to be threats to the client and changes in blood gases serve as indicators for the need for intubation and mechanical ventilation. Inhalation injuries are a major cause of death in fire victims in the emergent period immediately following the burn.

2. Fluid overload is a major complication of this period and it is important to monitor intake and output. Fluid movement three days after a burn is from the interstitial tissue back into the vascular system, and cardiotonics and diuretics may be necessary to prevent congestive heart failure. However, infection is the primary cause of death in persons who survive the first few days following extensive burns, and prevention of wound sepsis is the most important nursing activity at this time.

4. The client with severe burns requires a high-calorie, high-protein diet to meet the increased needs due to the increased metabolic rate and wound healing. Caloric intake must be documented. However, infection is the primary cause of death in persons who survive the first few days following extensive burns, and prevention of wound sepsis takes priority at this time.

#5. 1. Hydrocortisone promotes gluconeogenesis and elevates blood glucose levels. Following adrenalectomy the normal supply of hydrocortisone is interrupted and must be replaced to maintain the blood glucose at normal levels.   Ev   Ph/8   Ap

2. Care for the client following adrenalectomy is similar to that for any abdominal operation. The client is encouraged to change position, cough, and deep breathe to prevent postoperative complications such as pneumonia or thrombophlebitis.

3. Maintenance doses of hydrocortisone will be administered IV until the client is able to take it by mouth and will be necessary for six months to two years or until the remaining gland recovers.

4. The client undergoing an adrenalectomy is at increased risk for infection and delayed wound healing and will need to learn about wound care, but not at this time while he is in the ICU.

#6. 2. It is common for children to acquire ringworm from their pets, especially if the pets are outside during the day and only spend the night in the house. His pet needs to be assessed thoroughly for ringworm lesions.   An   He/4   Ap

1. Ringworm is a fungus that can live in dead skin and hair cells left on headrests by occupants of public forms of transportation. Since Johnny is busy talking, from a position behind the bus driver, it is likely that he is leaning forward most of the time, rather than backward against the headrest.

3. If Johnny is in the habit of loaning hats, scarves, or combs to other children he will most likely transmit or receive other infections. Since he loaned, rather than borrowed, the baseball hat, his friend should also be checked for ringworm now.

4. Most ten-year-old children need reminding about hygiene needs, because these concerns are not uppermost in their minds at this age. As long as his mother is monitoring this, it is probably not the cause of the current infection.

#7. 3. Any sign of paresthesia or paralysis needs to be reported promptly. Spinal nerve damage is a risk and may require emergency removal of the instrumentation.   Pl   Ph/9   Ap

1. Paralytic ileus is common postoperatively and is treated with nasogastric intubation, NPO, and assessment of returning bowel sounds. Paralytic ileus is not an immediate complication.

2. Cast care and repair of rough edges is a priority 8–12 days postoperatively, when the child is removed from the immobilization of the Stryker frame bed and receives a plaster jacket to wear for six months.

ANSWER	RATIONALE	NP	CN	CL

4. Any decrease in kidney perfusion during surgery from excessive blood loss with this procedure could cause acute renal failure. This answer is a good second choice, since strict intake and output measurements are needed postoperatively.

#8. 1. The definitive action is to look for oozing of blood from the back of the throat, since the operative site can be visualized with good lighting and a tongue depressor. Im Ph/9 Ap

2. Red dye in Koolaid can stain stomach contents a red color that does not darken with time, as bloody drainage darkens. This is a helpful assessment to make if no bleeding is observed from the throat.

3. Vital sign changes would be a later sign of bleeding, after blood loss has made a difference in the circulating blood volume.

4. The child who is experiencing postpharyngeal bleeding will be swallowing frequently to decrease the fluid in the back of the throat, so this is a good assessment to make. However, nausea, with resultant salivation, could also cause frequent swallowing.

#9. 1. This is correct procedure for spasmodic croup and may also be used for LTB, as long as the parent recognizes worsening signs of respiratory distress and acts promptly. Racemic epinephrine is the drug of choice in causing vasoconstriction and a reduction of airway swelling. It should be monitored in the hospital setting because of its side effects and its ability to wear off in a few hours, causing rebound of signs and symptoms. Ev Ph/9 Ap

2. There is no swelling of the epiglottis with laryngotracheobronchitis, but it can be life threatening, depending upon signs and symptoms. Monitoring of airway patency and hypoxia is best done in the hospital setting.

3. The mother has just described stage II of the progression of symptoms of LTB. Constant stridor, use of accessory muscles and retractions, along with labored breathing, will fatigue the child unless the airway is opened more with medications and cool mist. He needs to be observed in a croup tent, along with an oximeter to indicate oxygenation status.

4. Airway obstruction and unconsciousness are pending. The child is fatigued from trying to breathe through closing airways. Intubation equipment should be handy and the physician called.

#10. 4. Oliguria is not usually seen in congestive heart failure. Diuretics are a mainstay treatment in congestive heart failure. The nurse would expect urine output. Weakness, fatigue, dyspnea, and tachycardia are clinical manifestations of congestive heart failure. As Ph/10 Ap

1. Weakness and fatigue are common in congestive heart failure.

2. Dyspnea is common in congestive heart failure.

3. Tachycardia is common in congestive heart failure.

#11. 3. Changes in skin at the radiation site are common. Pl Ph/10 Ap

1. Fatigue is a general side effect of radiation therapy.

2. Anorexia is a general side effect of radiation therapy.

4. Diarrhea would be a common side effect if the intestinal area were being radiated.

#12. 2. Body organs experience a decrease in functional capacity as the individual ages. The cardiac and respiratory system are particularly vulnerable to decline. As He/3 Ap

1. Physiological changes associated with aging will ultimately occur if the person lives long enough. There is no fountain of youth that can prevent the physiologic changes associated with aging.

3. Changes in the elderly are not always associated with disease. The elderly have decreased physiological reserve, less flexible homeostatic processes, and less effective defense mechanisms, making them more susceptible to infectious diseases.

ANSWER	RATIONALE	NP	CN	CL

4. Clients with good health habits still experience the physiological changes of aging, but good health habits may help prevent disease.

#13. 2. The cardiac valves thicken and stiffen with age. This increased stiffness at the bases of the aortic cusps is thought to be the cause of the common systolic murmur heard in the elderly.   As   He/3   An

  1. A bounding radial pulse is not typical of the elderly. The pulse may be weaker with age.

  3. First-degree heart block is not related specifically to aging.

  4. Frequent bursts of tachycardia are not related specifically to tachycardia.

#14. 4. The elderly have poor blue-green discrimination. The effects of age are greatest on short wavelengths. These changes are related to the yellowing of the lens with age.   An   He/3   K

  1. The elderly are better able to distinguish between red and blue because of the difference in wavelengths.

  2. The elderly are better able to distinguish between blue and gold because of the difference in wavelengths.

  3. The elderly are better able to distinguish between red and green because of the difference in wavelengths. Red and green color blindness is an inherited disorder that is unrelated to age.

#15. 4. Ms. T. did not learn the importance of seeing a podiatrist for the treatment of corns or calluses or other problems resulting from pressure on the foot. Special shoes may be necessary to prevent recurrence of these problems in order to prevent possible skin breakdown and infection.   Ev   Ph/9   Ap

  1. This is a correct statement by Ms. T. and indicates that she has understood the fact that diabetics are at high risk for infection and that early treatment of cuts, scratches, and irritations can prevent ulceration.

  2. This is a correct statement by Ms. T. and indicates that she has understood that proper shoe fit is very important in preventing irritation and trauma to the feet and reduces the risk of skin breakdown.

  3. This is a correct statement by Ms. T. and indicates that she has understood that diabetics often develop reduced sensitivity to temperatures due to neuropathy.

#16. 4. A pacemaker is an electronic device that provides repetitive electrical stimuli to the heart muscle for the control of heart rate. A demand pacemaker is either inhibited by ventricular response or initiated by the atria and will respond as needed. It is set at a rate determined individually for each client.   Im   Ph/9   Ap

  1. A demand pacemaker is not regulated by changes in blood pressure.

  2. A demand pacemaker is not set at a certain rate and does not compete with the heart's basic rhythm. The pacemaker stimulates the heart when a normal ventricular contraction does not occur or if the heart rate drops below a specified rate.

  3. The demand pacemaker does not sense the coronary blood flow. It senses the heart rate and starts a beat as needed.

#17. 2. Pulse generators are much smaller in size than those used a few years ago.   Im   Ph/9   Ap

  1. Batteries are still needed. They are usually lithium cell units with a projected life of 8 to 12 years.

  3. The generator is usually implanted in the upper right chest.

  4. Insertion of a pacemaker must be done under fluoroscopic control in a cardiovascular laboratory or operating room. It is inserted either by a transvenous approach, during which the client is awake, or by direct application of the pacing electrode to the epicardial surface during a thoracotomy.

#18. 1. Many clients will require cardiac medication following the   Im   Ph/9   Ap insertion of a pacemaker. They may feel well but should recognize the importance of taking all medications as prescribed.

2. There is no need to avoid sudden changes in temperature.
3. The insertion site does not need to be covered once it has healed.
4. The client should follow the diet prescribed. If the client's cholesterol is within normal limits, cholesterol restrictions are not necessary.

#19. 1. **Nausea is not usually associated with pacemaker failure.** Ev Ph/9 An
2. Syncope is due to a lack of oxygen to the brain and is often a sign of pacemaker failure.
3. Dizziness may be due to a lack of blood and oxygen to the brain and is often a sign of pacemaker failure.
4. Palpitations or other arrhythmias are signs of pacemaker failure.

#20. 2. **Conservative treatment of a back problem would not include enzyme therapy. Chemonucleolysis, a surgical procedure, is the injection of an enzyme into the nucleus pulposus of the intravertebral disc.** As Ph/9 An
1. Analgesics are part of a conservative therapy regimen.
3. Muscle relaxants are part of a conservative therapy regimen.
4. Anti-inflammatory medications are part of a conservative therapy regimen.

#21. 1. **A numerical scale can be used as long as the same scale is used with that client each time. It is important to obtain an accurate description, record it, and use it to compare with future assessments.** Im Ph/9 Ap
2. Asking the client to compare current pain with past experiences is too subjective and not reliable.
3. A standardized assessment scale can be helpful in determining the level of pain.
4. The goal of pain management is to use as little medication as possible to control the pain. Alternative methods of pain management such as progressive relaxation, abdominal breathing, distraction, expression of feelings, behavior modification, and physical comfort measures should be used in conjunction with drug-induced analgesia.

#22. 4. **Symptoms of polycythemia vera are caused by increased blood viscosity, which may make circulation through capillary beds sluggish. This results in decreased oxygenation of the tissues, leading to shortness of breath as the body tries to compensate. Other signs and symptoms include headache, thrombosis, and paresthesias. Platelet deficiencies with associated bleeding tendencies also occur.** As Ph/9 Ap
1. A ruddy complexion often occurs. Pallor would not be associated with polycythemia vera.
2. Changes in heart rate are not characteristic of polycythemia.
3. Leg pain with exercise is characteristic of arterial insufficiency. If leg pain occurs at all in polycythemia it would most likely be in the form of paresthesias.

#23. 1. **Phantom pain (pain in an amputated extremity), like all pain, may be decreased by keeping the client active.** Im Ph/9 Ap
2. Keeping the client inactive may increase the frequency of phantom pain.
3. Phantom pain may occur up to two to three months after amputation.
4. Phantom pain is real and should be acknowledged by the client and the nurse.

#24. 4. **Routine childhood immunizations are given to prevent poliomyelitis, diphtheria, pertussis, tetanus, *Haemophilus influenzae* type b, measles, mumps, and rubella.** Pl He/4 Ap
1. There is no effective vaccine for mononucleosis at this time.
2. There is no vaccine for herpes simplex.

3.   Calmette-Guérin bacillus is BCG vaccine given in some countries to protect against tuberculosis. BCG is not given routinely in the United States.

#25. 1.   **The measles, mumps, and rubella vaccine (MMR) and oral Sabin polio vaccine (OPV) contain live virus.**   An   He/4   Ap

2.   Hib does not contain live virus.

3.   DTaP does not contain live virus.

4.   DTaP and Hib do not contain live virus.

#26. 3.   **At six months of age, a child on a normal immunization schedule would receive the third immunization for diphtheria, tetanus, and pertussis (whooping cough). DTaP is given at two, four, and six months of age, at eighteen months, and between four and six years of age. At six months of age, the baby would also be given *Haemophilus influenzae* b (Hib). Hib vaccine is given at two, four, six, and fifteen months.**   Im   He/4   Ap

1.   OPV is given at two, four, and eighteen months of age, and between four and six years of age.

2.   MMR is given at fifteen months and between 11 and 12 years of age.

4.   Smallpox vaccine is no longer given.

#27. 1.   **The opportunity to ask questions helps to reduce anxiety and misinformation regarding electroconvulsive therapy. This prepares the client and family and enlists their support and cooperation in the treatment.**   Im   Ps/6   Ap

2.   The client should not be discouraged from thinking about the therapy.

3.   Comparing ECT to a venipuncture is not helpful. She will have a venipuncture but the experience involves more than a simple venipuncture.

4.   The nurse can not assure the client that ECT will give her a complete recovery from depression. ECT often results in significant reduction in depression, but results cannot be guaranteed.

#28. 1.   **Beneficial effects of ECT usually are evident after the first several treatments. Since treatments are administered at intervals of 48 hours, these effects are apparent after one week of therapy.**   Ev   Ps/6   K

2.   Beneficial effects of ECT therapy are usually seen before three weeks. It takes three to four weeks for tricyclic antidepressants to take effect.

3.   Beneficial effects of ECT therapy are usually seen before four weeks. It takes three to four weeks for tricyclic antidepressants to take effect.

4.   Beneficial effects of ECT therapy are usually seen after the first few treatments.

#29. 3.   **There is no pain associated with ECT, therefore pain tolerance is not an assessment factor.**   As   Ps/6   An

1.   Activity level is a measure of the client's physical and mental status. Activity level usually increases as depression lifts.

2.   Bowel habits reflect client's physical and mental status.

4.   Depression may cause either insomnia or hypersomnia. As depression lifts more normal patterns are seen.

#30. 3.   **Common side effects of ECT include slowing of electrical impulses in the brain and temporary confusion and amnesia.**   As   Ph/9   Co

1.   Cardiac arrhythmias, elevated sedimentation rate, and fractures of the spine are not typical side effects of ECT therapy.

2.   The real mechanism of action of ECT is not known. ECT may increase the level of the neurotransmitter serotonin in the brain. ECT is not thought to affect norepinephrine levels in the brain.

4.   ECT does not cause mild organic changes in the neurons of the brain, dementia, or mild aphasia.

#31. 3.   **Temporary ileus is a result of bowel manipulation during surgery and is found in all clients to a degree.**   As   Ph/9   An

1.   Atelectasis is certainly possible in clients who have had abdominal

surgery. However, all clients who have had bowel resections will develop some degree of ileus.

2. Parotitis is inflammation of the parotid gland. This is not a common complication of abdominal surgery.

4. A transient ischemic attack is an episode of cerebrovascular insufficiency due to a partial obstruction of an artery. This is not a likely complication of abdominal surgery.

#32. 1. Normal saline is used to irrigate an NG tube since it will not cause a loss of sodium when it is removed by suction. Saline is an isotonic solution which has the same osmotic pressure as that found across the semi-permeable membrane within the cell. Pl Ph/9 K

2. Tap water is a hypotonic solution which has less osmotic pressure than blood serum, thus causing the cells to swell. When the fluid is suctioned from the NG tube, the client will lose sodium.

3. Ringer's lactate is an isotonic solution that contains sodium, potassium, chloride, calcium, and lactate. This is not an appropriate solution to use for irrigation of an NG tube. Ringer's lactate is a fluid and electrolyte replenisher that is prescribed for correction of extracellular volume deficit.

4. Hydrogen peroxide is a solution used to cleanse open wounds. It is not indicated for internal use.

#33. 2. Incentive spirometry helps the client to breathe deeply by providing visual reinforcement to the breathing effort. An Ph/9 Ap

1. Oxygen does not help the client breathe more deeply.

3. Periodic ambulation will help prevent respiratory complications, but it will not have as great an effect on respiratory excursion as spirometry.

4. Verbal encouragement has no measurable parameters.

#34. 3. Since ascites is accumulation of fluid in the abdominal cavity, measuring abdominal girth before and after treatment will be the most effective way to determine whether treatment has been effective. Ev Ph/9 An

1. While the client with cirrhosis may have pedal edema, it is not related to evaluation of ascites and would not be treated with salt-poor albumin.

2. Ascites can cause shortness of breath but does not always do so. Therefore, a decrease in shortness of breath is not a reliable indicator of reduction of ascites.

4. Salt-poor albumin will increase the serum albumin level but knowing that serum albumin level has increased will not tell the nurse that the ascites has decreased. Raising the serum albumin level might not have diminished the ascites.

#35. 3. Peristalsis usually returns to all segments of the bowel three to four days after surgery. Ev Ph/9 An

1. Normal bowel function does not return in six hours after surgery; that is too soon.

2. Normal bowel function does not return in twelve hours after surgery; that is too soon.

4. Normal peristalsis has usually returned three to four days after surgery.

#36. 1. Depression is a response to an impending loss, chronic illness, or death. The daughter recognizes this as a healthy response in adjusting to this life event. Ev Ps/5 Ap

2. The daughter is not adjusting. She is continuing to deny the situation.

3. The daughter is not adjusting well to the eventual separation of her and her mother due to her mother's impending death.

4. To suppress the topic of death prevents the pair from evaluating life and the joys and sorrows they have shared in the past. The mother may have a need to discuss death, yet the daughter is unable to do so.

ANSWER	RATIONALE	NP	CN	CL
#37. 1.	**The wound should be covered with a sterile, moist dressing to prevent infection and drying of the wound until the physician arrives.**	Im	Ph/10	Ap
2.	Once dehiscence has occurred, the wound edges cannot be pulled together. Attempting to do this may injure the wound and cause contamination.			
3.	Irrigating the wound with sterile saline should not be done until the physician has decided on a plan of action.			
4.	Holding the abdominal contents in place is not necessary. The wound should be covered with a sterile, moist dressing to prevent it from drying out.			
#38. 1.	**Computerized tomography (CT scan or CAT scan) is a highly accurate neurological diagnostic test using computer analysis or x-ray data. It provides definitive information on presence, size, and location of brain tumors.**	An	Ph/9	An
2.	A myelogram is an x-ray taken following the injection of a radiopaque medium into the subarachnoid space to demonstrate any distortions of the spinal cord, spinal nerve roots, and the subarachnoid roots.			
3.	Skull x-rays may still be done to demonstrate bone structure changes, such as damage, healing, and calcification. However, to identify a brain tumor the far superior CT scan would be done.			
4.	A lumbar puncture is the introduction of a hollow needle into the subarachnoid space of the lumbar portion of the spinal cord. Diagnostic indications for the test include the measurement of cerebrospinal fluid (CSF) pressure, obtaining CSF for laboratory analysis, and evaluating the canal for the presence of a tumor.			
#39. 2.	**The first priority of care during a seizure is to protect the client from injury.**	Im	Ph/9	Ap
1.	It is not possible to control the course of a seizure once it has started.			
3.	Restraining the client during a seizure can lead to further injuries.			
4.	Reducing circulation to the brain is not therapeutic.			
#40. 2.	**An intact cranium and vertebral canal together with the relatively inelastic dura form a rigid container. A bone flap allows for accommodation of postoperative brain tissue swelling.**	An	Ph/10	An
1.	To insert an ICP bolt or subarachnoid screw it is not necessary to remove a bone flap. The ICP bolt is inserted through the skull into the subarachnoid space. Measurement of intracranial pressure is transmitted through the brain tissue and is less accurate than direct intraventricular monitoring.			
3.	A Jackson-Pratt suction drain may be surgically inserted if a large cavity remains after removal of a tumor or large hematoma. A bone flap does not need to be removed to allow free flow of fluid into the Jackson-Pratt drain.			
4.	A bone flap is not removed to permit reoperation. The bone flap is removed to accommodate postoperative brain swelling. Following some craniotomies, a protective prosthesis made of methyl methacrylate is later surgically inserted.			
#41. 2.	**Placing a pillow under the head and shoulders while elevating the head of the bed 30–45 degrees promotes venous return and improves cerebrospinal circulation, thus minimizing the most serious potential problem of increased intracranial pressure.**	Im	Ph/9	Ap
1.	This is one case where maintenance of a patent airway is second priority to facilitating venous drainage.			
3.	Providing for client comfort is an important nursing intervention. The client should be made as comfortable as possible within the limits of position requirements.			
4.	The nurse must frequently assess for hemorrhage from the suture line.			
#42. 1.	**Coughing or sneezing will elevate intra-abdominal or**	Pl	Ph/9	Co

intrathoracic pressure. The increase in pressure from these areas is transmitted through the spinal subarachnoid space to the intracranial subarachnoid space. Venous return from the cranial vault is impeded, resulting in increased intracranial pressure.

2. Deep breathing is important to maintain lung function.
3. Turning from side to side and moving to a chair when able is important for mobilizing secretions and promoting good lung function.
4. Following a craniotomy suctioning should not be done through the nose. A tear in the nasal membrane could cause a leak of the cerebral spinal fluid (CSF), leading to infection. Priority nursing care following a craniotomy is to avoid hypercapnia (high blood CO_2) and to ensure maximal oxygenation to the brain. When suctioning the oral cavity, the catheter should be in place no longer than 10–15 seconds at a time, with oxygenation between each pass of the catheter. Prolonged suctioning increases thoracic pressure, which in turn increases intracranial pressure.

#43. 4. The mechanism of action of dexamethasone (Decadron) is unclear but its anti-inflammatory action is effective in reducing cerebral edema, which reduces ICP.   An   Ph/8   An

1. Decadron, like most steroids, may cause a feeling of euphoria. However, this is not the reason for administering it following a craniotomy.
2. Decadron does not promote excretion of water.
3. Decadron does not act to enhance venous return.

#44. 2. Recalling some things but not everything is selective amnesia, which is a form of psychogenic amnesia.   As   Ps/6   An

1. Feeling detached from the body is depersonalization.
3. Losing a body function after an emotionally traumatic experience is a conversion reaction as there is no organic reason for his inability to move his arm.
4. Being told he does things that he cannot remember could be symptomatic of a multiple personality disorder.

#45. 2. Explanation of normal routine reduces anxiety and decreases secondary gain.   Im   Ps/6   Ap

1. Confronting the client is nontherapeutic in that it does not build trust and minimizes the client's feelings.
3. Providing special privileges enhances secondary gain from the paralysis. The nurse should not give secondary gains.
4. This response does not reduce anxiety or build trust. It is too early in the relationship to uncover the conflict underlying the conversion.

#46. 1. Conversion disorder is loss or alteration in physical functioning due to psychological causes, but the symptoms are not produced on a conscious level. Symptoms cannot be explained as resulting from an organic physical disorder.   As   Ps/6   An

2. Symptoms in conversion disorders are involuntary in nature.
3. Since conversion disorders are unconscious, manipulation is not operating.
4. Intentional production of symptoms on a conscious level are called factitious disorders.

#47. 3. This response shows an understanding of the traumatic event and the conflict she feels in terms of the consequences of being a witness to it.   Ev   Ps/6   Ap

1. This response indicates that the client has voluntary control over the symptoms.
2. This response also indicates a voluntary control and the need to manipulate, thus showing lack of knowledge of conversion disorder.
4. This statement contributes to the behavior and the lack of understanding as to the cause of the blindness.

ANSWER	RATIONALE	NP	CN	CL

#48. 2. **Vegetative signs such as insomnia, anorexia, psychomotor retardation, constipation, diminished libido, and poor concentration are biological responses to depression. Improvement in these signs indicate a lifting of the depression.**   Ev   Ps/6   Co

    1. Reduced levels of anxiety do not indicate an improvement in depressive symptoms.

    3. Compliance with medications does not indicate improvement in depression.

    4. Requests to talk to the nurse vary. Requests may show trust in the nurse but are not a sign that depression has diminished.

#49. 1. **Psychic numbing and detachment are followed by somatic and cognitive symptoms.**   An   Ps/6   Ap

    2. Depression and social withdrawal can occur in other disorders and are not key to this assessment.

    3. Alcohol use is common in response to posttraumatic stress disorders, but intrusive and hyperactive behavior is more typical of manic depressive illness.

    4. These two behaviors are not key assessments to posttraumatic stress disorder. Substance abuse may soothe the emotions of PTSD, but sexual acting out is not a symptom.

#50. 4. **Chlamydia is the #1 STD. Many women who harbor chlamydia in the cervix are asymptomatic. As many as 15%–50% of females and 5%–25% of males with _Neisseria gonorrhoeae_ infection are asymptomatic carriers. In women, the primary chancre of syphilis may be on the endocervix and thus be undetected.**   Ev   He/4   An

    1. Embarrassment may play a role in treatment delay, but it is not the major reason.

    2. It is possible that symptoms may be thought to be caused by something else, but it is not the major reason for delay in treatment.

    3. Some people do ignore symptoms, but this is not the major reason for delay of treatment.

#51. 1. **The usual incubation period between infection with _Neisseria gonorrhoeae_ and onset of symptoms is two to five days.**   An   Ph/9   K

    2. The usual incubation period for _Neisseria gonorrhoeae_ is two to five days.

    3. The usual incubation period for _Neisseria gonorrhoeae_ is two to five days.

    4. The usual incubation period for _Neisseria gonorrhoeae_ is two to five days.

#52. 3. **Human papilloma virus (genital warts) has been strongly linked to cervical malignancies. Warts may appear on the external genitalia, anorectal area, urethra, vagina, cervix, or mouth. Treatment is generally the application of podophyllin in a tincture of benzoin compound.**   An   He/4   An

    1. There is no known link between _Neisseria gonorrhoeae_ and cancer.

    2. There is no known link between _Chlamydia trachomatis_ and cancer.

    4. Herpes simplex virus type II or herpes virus hominis type II is related to a higher incidence of cancer of the cervix and vulva. Women who engaged in sexual intercourse at an early age and who have multiple sex partners are at a greater risk.

#53. 3. **A repeat culture is important to validate eradication of disease, thus preventing spread of infection. Repeat culture also documents successful treatment.**   Ev   He/4   An

    1. Complications following treatment for gonorrhea are few. This is not the reason for a follow-up visit.

    2. Checking the lab's work is not the reason for follow-up.

    4. Providing an opportunity for sexual counseling is not the reason for follow-up cultures. However, the visit can be used to answer any questions the client may have.

#54. 4. **The urine should be tested for ketone bodies when there is a**   Ev   Ph/9   An

ANSWER	RATIONALE	NP	CN	CL

persistent increase in the blood sugar. Ketones in the urine signal that the body is breaking down fat stores for energy.

1. Overhydration does not cause the development of ketone bodies. The client who is in ketoacidosis will be dehydrated.

2. Weight gain does not cause the development of ketone bodies. However, dramatic weight loss over a short period of time may cause the development of ketones as a result of the body breaking down fat stores for energy.

3. It is not necessary to test for ketones every time the glucometer reading is abnormal. Persistently high glucometer readings are the indication.

#55. 2. A lack of insulin stimulates ketoacidosis. The hyperglycemia of ketoacidosis produces large fluid losses (polyuria) and the client becomes thirsty (polydipsia). The body is unable to compensate for the renal losses and dehydration results.   An   Ph/9   An

1. The diabetic is different from the nondiabetic in producing and handling ketones.

3. Diabetics are not allergic to the byproducts of ketone metabolism.

4. All persons act in a very predictable way to the development of ketoacidosis.

#56. 2. The nurse should wear gloves, and protective clothing if necessary, any time contact with blood or body fluids is anticipated.   Pl   Sa/2   Ap

1. The machine can be used by other clients. The only thing that is contaminated with the client's blood is the lancet and this is never reused.

3. The lancet is never used more than once.

4. The glucometer does not need to be recalibrated before each use.

#57. 2. Regular insulin is classified as rapid acting and will peak two to four hours after administration. The second peak will be eight to twelve hours after the administration of NPH insulin. This is why a snack must be eaten mid-morning and also three to four hours after the evening meal.   Ev   Ph/8   An

1. The first insulin peak will occur two to four hours after administration of regular insulin.

3. The first insulin peak will occur two to four hours after administration of regular insulin.

4. The first insulin peak will occur two to four hours after administration of regular insulin. The second peak will occur eight to twelve hours after the administration of NPH insulin.

#58. 3. The glycemic index is the result of research that revealed that factors other than chemical composition impact on the blood glucose level. The protein and fat composition of a meal appears to delay gastric emptying, resulting in a slower rise in blood sugar.   Ev   Ph/7   Ap

1. Foods high in protein raise blood sugar slowly.

2. Simple sugars cause a rapid and unpredictable rise in blood sugar.

4. Lactose does not dramatically increase the need for insulin.

#59. 1. Sick-day procedure includes taking insulin as usual because insulin decreases the blood sugar level. Insulin is needed even in the presence of a reduced oral intake.   Pl   Ph/8   Ap

2. The client should keep in touch with the physician if the illness persists for several days, but it is not necessary to go to the emergency department.

3. The client needs long-acting insulin as well as regular insulin.

4. The client needs to at least drink liquids. If vomiting is not manageable, the physician should be notified.

#60. 2. Nonperishable foods such as raisins are the most appropriate food to serve as a substitute for a delayed meal. One-quarter cup of raisins provides 1 fruit exchange, containing 10 grams of carbohydrate and 40 calories.   Pl   Ph/7   Ap

1. Diet cola does not provide simple sugar or sustained carbohydrates.
3. A candy bar is a simple sugar, which quickly elevates the blood sugar, but it is not a sustained rise.
4. Alcohol causes a rapid increase in glucose level, followed by a rebound hypoglycemia, so it should be used with discretion in the diabetic.

#61. 2. Clients who need to lose weight should have a reduced-calorie diet plan. Exercise must be carefully selected and should be used in combination with diet control. For some individuals, walking may be the best form of exercise. Pl Ph/7 Ap
1. Increasing her insulin dose would not help the client lose weight. It might cause hypoglycemia with resultant diaphoresis, pallor, tachycardia, and changes in level of consciousness progressing to coma if not treated promptly.
3. The best weight loss occurs with both exercise and reduction in caloric intake.
4. A maintenance diet for a person with a sedentary life style would be at least 1500 kcalories per day as prescribed by the physician. A low-calorie reducing diet will be individually prescribed based on weight, activity, age, etc. It will probably be 1200 kcalories per day or less.

#62. 3. A glycosolated hemoglobin test shows the pattern of blood glucose levels over a three-month period. Ev Ph/9 An
1. A two-hour postprandial test will give evidence of only one glucose testing.
2. A six-hour glucose tolerance test gives evidence of one six-hour period of glucose readings following a glucose dose.
4. A glucometer test is not as accurate as a glycosolated hemoglobin test.

#63. 4. The buildup of ketone bodies causes a decline in tissue perfusion, resulting in hypoxia. Cerebral hypoxia will be manifested by mental deterioration. Early detection of cerebral hypoxia is achieved by evaluating orientation to person, place, and time, and the appropriateness of answers to simple questions and commands. Identifying subtle changes in these areas can facilitate the early diagnosis and treatment of ketoacidosis and prevent progression to coma. As Ph/10 An
1. Polyuria may be present but it is not a subtle sign.
2. Slowed reflexes are a late sign of ketoacidosis.
3. Increased thirst will be present but is not a subtle sign.

#64. 2. Ketoacidosis causes dehydration that results in flushed, dry skin. As Ph/10 Co
1. Cool, clammy skin is seen in hypoglycemia.
3. Diaphoresis is seen in hypoglycemia.
4. Silky skin is not seen in ketoacidosis.

#65. 3. Since this is the first time in ten months that this client has had any problems, reinforcement of client teaching is the priority to avoid future episodes of ketoacidosis. Pl Ph/9 Ap
1. There are not enough data to suggest a poor prognosis. The client seems to have done well in managing the disease for ten months.
2. The client has done well for a long time. There is no evidence to support noncompliance.
4. Focusing on diabetes as a long, painful, chronic disorder is not appropriate. The client has adapted well to dealing with the disease for a considerable period of time at this point.

#66. 2. Weight loss and fatigue are early symptoms of ketoacidosis. Im Ph/9 Ap
1. The symptoms of ketoacidosis are very specific.
3. Headache is a sign of hypoglycemia.
4. In ketoacidosis mucous membranes are flushed.

#67. 4. Obvious changes in moles are a cancer warning signal and would be a priority for follow-up. As He/4 Ap

    1. This finding does not indicate a change in bowel habits and therefore is not a cancer warning.

    2. Breast self-exam is a recommended action to detect early signs of breast cancer.

    3. This cough is most likely the result of the respiratory infection and would not be a priority for follow-up related to cancer.

#68. 3. Washing the surrounding area is fine but wetting the cord keeps it moist and predisposes it to infection.   Ev   He/3   Ap

    1. Exposure to air helps dry the cord.

    2. Good hand washing is the prime mechanism for preventing infection.

    4. It is important to check for complications of bleeding and drainage that might occur.

#69. 2. To ensure that privacy needs are met, the nurse should give the client a gown and provide a private area for changing.   Im   He/4   Ap

    1. Because of the privacy needs of an adolescent it is best not to have the parent present.

    3. The adolescent is self-conscious about her body image. It is best to examine her alone.

    4. The exam is not postponed until the adolescent is older.

#70. 4. The MMR vaccine contains eggs. Any child who is allergic to eggs should receive a skin test before receiving the vaccine. If the child tests positive, the vaccine would be given in very small doses at 20-minute intervals with adrenaline available should anaphylaxis occur.   An   He/4   Ap

    1. The DTaP (diphtheria, tetanus, pertussis) vaccine does not contain eggs.

    2. Smallpox vaccine is no longer given.

    3. The oral polio vaccine does not contain eggs.

#71. 3. Sundown syndrome is related to environmental and sensory abnormalities that lead to acute confusion.   Ev   Ps/6   K

    1. An underlying depression does not cause sundown syndrome.

    2. There is not sufficient evidence to suggest he has inadequate cerebral blood flow. Because the confusion occurs at sundown, the cause is probably changes in the sensory environment.

    4. Fluctuating levels of oxygen exchange do not cause sundown syndrome.

#72. 4. When the client's cognitive level declines, the nurse should provide clear and simple explanations and cues to minimize confusion and disorientation.   Im   Ps/6   Ap

    1. Ignoring the disorientation is not helpful to the client.

    2. Starting an IV is not indicated. The client is not dehydrated.

    3. Turning off the lights in the room will only add to the client's confusion.

#73. 3. A prominently displayed calendar will improve orientation to time.   Im   Ps/6   Ap

    1. The placement of a large calendar in the client's room is not to improve the appearance of the room.

    2. The calendar does encourage client independence.

    4. The primary purpose of the calendar is not to promote visual stimulation.

#74. 3. Diversionary activities in the evening help the client to avoid overstimulation or misinterpretation of the environment. A favorite TV show will provide enjoyment from a familiar routine.   Pl   Ps/6   Ap

    1. Lying in bed will provide no sensory stimulation.

    2. Attending a unit party may be overstimulating.

    4. Looking out the window provides little sensory stimulation.

#75. 3. Family members should be encouraged to maintain contact with the elderly individual.   Pl   Ps/6   Ap

    1. The client will be more alert early in the day. Visiting in the evening will help more with orientation.

ANSWER	RATIONALE	NP	CN	CL

2. Bringing gifts will not necessarily improve the level of orientation.
4. The client needs visitors even if no improvement is seen.

#76. 3. **The lighting in the room should be adjusted to provide for normal circadian rhythm. Darkening the room and using a night light is an important safety measure to prevent disorientation and to prevent falls.** Pl Sa/2 Ap
1. Keeping the room brightly lit will keep the client awake at night.
2. Use of subdued lighting could add to the client's confusion.
4. Asking the client questions is not helpful because the client is at his most confused state in the evening.

#77. 1. **A panic attack stimulates the sympathetic nervous system, resulting in an increased heart rate.** An Ps/6 An
2. A feeling of choking is a sign of a panic attack.
3. Chest pain is frequently seen in a panic attack.
4. People having a panic attack often fear they are going crazy.

#78. 4. **Nitrates cause venous pooling, resulting in reduced blood return to the heart. This reduces preload. The systemic arterial bed is also relaxed, causing a fall in blood pressure. The result is decreased afterload.** An Ph/8 Ap
1. Digitalis preparations slow and strengthen the heart.
2. Nitroglycerine does not assist smooth muscles to contract.
3. Nitroglycerine reduces the venous return to the heart.

#79. 2. **Nitroglycerin should cause a slight burning or tingling sensation when placed under the tongue. If this does not occur, the tablets may not be fresh and should be discarded.** Ev Ph/8 An
1. Nitroglycerin should cause a tingling or burning sensation when placed under the tongue if it is potent.
3. Nitroglycerin should cause a tingling or burning sensation when placed under the tongue if it is potent.
4. Nitroglycerin should cause a tingling or burning sensation when placed under the tongue if it is potent.

#80. 4. **Nitroglycerin may be used up to six months after the vial is opened. It should, however, be kept in a cool, dark place.** Im Ph/8 Ap
1. Nitroglycerin can be used for up to six months if it is kept in a dark, cool place.
2. Nitroglycerin can be used for up to six months if it is kept in a dark, cool place.
3. Nitroglycerin can be used for up to six months if it is kept in a dark, cool place.

#81. 2. **Up to three sublingual nitroglycerin tablets should be taken at five-minute intervals before the client seeks further medical intervention for the relief of pain.** Ev Ph/8 Ap
1. Going to the emergency room is not necessary at this point.
3. Sublingual nitroglycerin should not be taken orally.
4. Only one nitroglycerin tablet should be taken at a time at five-minute intervals.

#82. 4. **A scarf worn over the mouth will help to warm the inhaled air.** An Ph/9 An
1. Drinking orange juice is not a precaution for going out in the cold.
2. Taking a warm bath is not a precaution for going out in the cold.
3. The client should only walk as fast as he can tolerate and should stop at once if chest pain occurs.

#83. 4. **Fatigue is often the only symptom of iron deficiency anemia in its early stages. Inadequate iron stores result in inadequate production of red blood cells. This decreases the amount of oxygen carried to all tissues. When tissues receive inadequate oxygen a decrease in activity tolerance and the subjective experience of fatigue result.** As Ph/9 Ap
1. When anemia is severe enough to affect heart rate, the change is to tachycardia. Heart rate increases in an effort to increase the amount of oxygen reaching the tissues.

    2. Jaundice does not occur with iron deficiency anemia. Jaundice is due to destruction of excessive numbers of red blood cells, such as might occur in hemolytic anemia or sickle cell anemia.

    3. Anorexia, not hunger, is seen in anemia.

#84. **2.** **Lotions, powders, and soaps are not applied to the radiation site as they may cause skin irritation.**   Ev   Ph/9   Ap

    1. Clients receiving external radiation therapy are not radioactive, therefore contact with others is appropriate.

    3. Oral mucosa is susceptible to radiation changes; therefore, oral hygiene is done gently to prevent irritation.

    4. Fatigue is a systemic side effect of radiation therapy; therefore, the client may need to take frequent rests.

#85. **3.** **If the infant continually has high pulse oxygenation readings and other vital signs are stable, the infant may be ready to be weaned to lower oxygen settings. Hyperoxemia increases the potential for retrolental fibroplasia.**   Im   Ph/9   Ap

    1. The oxygen saturation should be monitored on an hourly basis at minimum.

    2. The pulse oxygenation reading can drop if the probe is not on properly or if the baby is moving. Any pulse oxygenation in the 90's is within normal limits, provided other vital signs are stable.

    4. Infants only need to be suctioned when needed. Breath sounds should be assessed prior to suctioning to determine the need.

#86. **2.** **All precautions to prevent bleeding must be taken. Using an electric razor should not cut the face.**   Im   Ph/9   Ap

    1. To decrease the chance of bleeding, a soft bristle brush or sponge should be used for oral hygiene.

    3. To decrease the chance of spontaneous bleeding, joints and extremities should be handled gently and risk of falls or trauma should be minimized. Sports activities should be stopped.

    4. Intramuscular pain medications should be discontinued because the client will have bone marrow suppression and decreased platelets as a result of radiation therapy.

#87. **2.** **Often, a couple is prepared for cesarean delivery at the last minute. The nurse should make the birth experience a positive one by making collaboration between client and staff a priority.**   Im   He/3   Ap

    1. Maintaining the client's comfort is important. However, the highest priority even while performing the simplest skills requires informing the client of what is being done.

    3. Escorting the husband to the waiting room is not the highest priority. Keeping the couple informed is highest priority.

    4. Priority is given to keeping the client informed. Some preoperative procedures like venipuncture and insertion of indwelling catheter may be uncomfortable along with the contractions of the laboring process. Informing the client may help to alleviate some anxiety.

#88. **1.** **The infant has had feeding restrictions prior to the circumcision so feeding him afterwards will satisfy his nutritional needs and provide him with fluid to help him void.**   Pl   Ph/9   Ap

    2. The gauze is placed there to aid in wound healing and prevent irritation/friction from covers on the penis. There is no interference with the urinary meatus.

    3. Side-lying position helps prevent irritation/friction to the penis but has no influence on the urethra.

    4. It is important to check for voiding, but this is an evaluative measure and does not lead to voiding.

#89. **3.** **All clients should be encouraged to stop smoking 4–6 weeks before surgery.**   Pl   Ph/9   Ap

    1. To continue smoking could increase the chances of respiratory complications during and after surgery.

    2.   Trying to decrease smoking is better than continuing to smoke, but the better goal is to stop smoking.

    4.   To cancel surgery, wait for the client to join a support group, and stop smoking would delay necessary surgery and possibly lead to other complications.

#90. 3.   **Passage of flatus is usually a sign of full peristaltic activity.**   Ev   Ph/9   Ap

    1.   This statement indicates distention, which is an accumulation of gas in a bowel that is not being moved by peristaltic activity.

    2.   Burping indicates an accumulation of air and secretions in the stomach, which are not being moved into the intestine.

    4.   Nausea indicates an accumulation of food, air, and secretions in the stomach, which are not getting moved into the intestine.

#91. 4.   **Atrial fibrillation is the most rapid of atrial dysrhythmias. The atria beat chaotically at rates of 350 to 600 beats per minute. Cardiac output is reduced due to loss of atrial kick. Mural thrombi tend to form, resulting in pulmonary or cerebral thrombosis. Atrial fibrillation is characterized by no definite P wave and an irregular ventricular rhythm.**   An   Ph/10   An

    1.   Junctional rhythm is an escape rhythm, or safety mechanism, that occurs when the SA node fails to pace the heart. Junctional tachycardia can result from digoxin toxicity or acute inferior myocardial infarction. It is characterized by P waves that may be absent, upright, or inverted in Lead II. QRS complexes are normal and alike. This is not the rhythm described in the question.

    2.   Sinus tachycardia is characterized by rapid but normal P waves and QRS complexes. This is not the rhythm described in the question.

    3.   Second-degree AV block known as Wenckebach is also called AV Heart Block Type I and Mobitz I. The atrial rate is usually normal while the ventricular rate is irregular and less than the atrial rate. There are more P waves than QRS complexes. The PR interval gets longer and longer until a P does not conduct to the ventricles. This is not the rhythm described in the question.

#92. 2.   **The metabolic rate is elevated in Graves' disease (hyperthyroidism).**   As   Ph/9   Co
The client's heart rate increases to provide the additional oxygen required to meet metabolic demands. Thyrotoxic crisis (thyroid storm) is a state of extreme hyperthyroidism characterized by a heart rate over 130 beats per minute. Because it can be fatal if untreated, the nurse must recognize the onset of thyrotoxicosis immediately. The body temperature also increases when excessive thyroid hormone is produced.

    1.   Blood glucose is not a measure of thyroid activity. Blood glucose is critical in assessing clients who have diabetes mellitus.

    3.   Urine output is not a measure of thyroid activity. Urine output is important in assessing diabetes insipidus and diabetes mellitus.

    4.   Blood pressure is not the best indicator of thyroid activity.

#93. 1.   **Glycosolated hemoglobin is formed each time blood glucose levels**   An   Ph/9   Ap
are elevated and remains attached to the red blood cell for up to 120 days. Since glycosolated hemoglobin reflects the average level of diabetic control achieved over the past two or three months, the client's blood glucose level must have been elevated repeatedly during that time even though it is normal today. A review of daily blood glucose records and diabetic control practices may reveal the cause of the poor control. Though more expensive than blood glucose tests, glycosolated hemoglobin provides more accurate information about daily diabetic self-care.

    2.   An elevated hemoglobin A_{1c} does not indicate good control.

    3.   The normal blood glucose at the present time rules out diabetic ketoacidosis, which would be characterized by elevated blood glucose levels.

ANSWER	RATIONALE	NP	CN	CL

4. The normal blood glucose at the present time rules out hypoglycemia.

#94. 4. The nursing diagnosis altered health maintenance is used when a client expresses a desire to learn better health management techniques. Poor nutrition and unsafe foot care habits place a client with Type II diabetes at risk for complications of diabetes, such as infection, vascular disease, hyperglycemic hyperosmolar nonketotic coma, nephropathy, neuropathy, and retinopathy. An Ph/9 Ap

1. Defining characteristics for impaired home maintenance include difficulty in maintaining home hygiene and safety or a lack of sufficient finances. This client does not have these characteristics.
2. There is no evidence of either activity intolerance or pedal pain.
3. Defining characteristics for feeding self-care deficit include being unable to cut food or open packages or being unable to bring food to mouth. This client does not have these characteristics.

#95. 2. Hemiplegia is one-sided paralysis. Hemianopia is the loss of one-half of the visual field in each eye. Impaired home maintenance management is an appropriate diagnostic statement when a client with impaired vision or mobility expresses concern about ability to maintain the home properly. An Ph/9 Ap

1. While high risk for injury is a possible diagnosis, the data given in the question support the diagnosis of impaired home maintenance. Concern about operating the vacuum cleaner and washing machine are related to impaired home maintenance.
3. Altered health maintenance is the state in which an individual or group experiences or is at risk of experiencing a disruption in health because of an unhealthy lifestyle or lack of knowledge to manage a condition.
4. Hygiene self-care deficit is a state in which the individual experiences an impaired ability to perform or complete hygiene activities for oneself. This refers to personal hygiene, not house cleaning.

#96. 1. Type II diabetes is more frequent in persons with a family history of diabetes, especially as they age. The vascular complications of diabetes may be present at the time of diagnosis, since the symptoms of Type II diabetes mellitus may be so mild that detection of the disease is delayed. Pedal pulses may be absent in the presence of peripheral vascular disease of the lower limbs. The presence of a carotid bruit may indicate partial occlusion of the carotid artery related to arteriosclerosis. Other organs typically affected in diabetes mellitus include the eye, kidney, and nerves. As He/4 Ap

2. Liver complications are not common in diabetes. The eye changes in diabetes are on the retina, not the sclera.
3. Palpation of the spleen and pulse oximetry are not screening tests for diabetes and do not pick up common complications of diabetes.
4. Abdominal changes and respiratory complications are not indicative of diabetes.

#97. 2. In teaching the client to examine the scrotal area, it is important to also inspect the inguinal and femoral areas for bulges that indicate herniation. Im He/4 Ap

1. The left testicle is usually lower than the right.
3. He should not inhale during the exam. That makes it more difficult to palpate the area.
4. The penis is held up during the exam.

#98. 2. Women who are short and slender are at increased risk for osteoporosis. An He/4 Ap

1. Lactose intolerance could be a risk factor because the client is likely not to drink milk, which is a major source of calcium. However, cheese and dark green vegetables are also good sources of calcium.
3. Weight-bearing exercise reduces risk of osteoporosis as it helps to keep calcium in the bones.

4.   Lack of estrogen has been linked to osteoporosis. Taking estrogen following removal of ovaries will help to prevent osteoporosis.

#99. 1.   **Nipple discharge in a woman who is not pregnant or lactating is an abnormal finding during breast examination and should be further evaluated.**   As   He/4   Ap

2.   The Tail of Spence is the tissue of the mammary gland that extends into the axillary region. It is a normal structure which may become enlarged premenstrually and during lactation.

3.   The axilla should be soft.

4.   Consistent patterns of veins are normal.

#100. 1.   **Acute rejection of a kidney transplant can be differentiated from chronic rejection. Oliguria or anuria are signs of acute rejection. Signs of rejection include signs of organ failure.**   As   Ph/9   An

2.   37°C is normal temperature. A low-grade fever is not a sign of acute rejection. It could be a sign of infection secondary to immunosuppressant drugs.

3.   The person with a functioning kidney transplant should have normalization of blood pressure. Persons with chronic renal failure are usually hypertensive. Decreased blood pressure may indicate the kidney is functioning well.

4.   Following a kidney transplant the urine and blood chemistry values should stabilize.

Practice Test 6

1. The nurse is caring for a 48-year-old woman whose blood pressure over the past two months has ranged between 140/88 and 148/94. The nurse explains to her that her pressure is considered elevated because the current upper limit for normal systolic pressure is
   1. 110 mm Hg.
   2. 120 mm Hg.
   3. 140 mm Hg.
   4. 160 mm Hg.
2. The nurse in a hypertension clinic is working with a woman who has had mildly elevated blood pressure for the last several months. The clinic follows the recommendations of the Joint National Committee on Detection, Evaluation, and Treatment of High Blood Pressure. Which of the following studies would not be ordered for this client?
   1. An EKG.
   2. A urinalysis.
   3. Serum calcium levels.
   4. White blood cell count.
3. A 50-year-old woman has been referred to the hypertension clinic because, in the past two months, her blood pressure has ranged between 142/90 to 148/96. She is 55 pounds overweight for her height and age. What life-

style change should the nurse suggest for this woman?
   1. Lose weight as rapidly as possible.
   2. Plan a gradual exercise program.
   3. Begin vigorous exercise immediately.
   4. Avoid exercise until your blood pressure is within the normal range.
4. The nurse in a hypertension clinic is caring for a woman who has just been diagnosed as having primary hypertension. She asks the nurse what causes primary hypertension. The nurse's best response is
   1. atherosclerosis.
   2. renal disease.
   3. diabetic vessel changes.
   4. the cause is unknown.
5. The nurse is discussing dietary teaching with an overweight woman who has mild hypertension. The nurse should advise the woman to
   1. eat fewer vegetables.
   2. reduce calcium intake.
   3. read contents labels on processed foods.
   4. add a water softening system for drinking water.
6. Ms. T. tells the nurse she is going to buy a blood pressure machine so she can monitor her own blood pressure. When teaching Ms.

T. how to measure her blood pressure, she should be taught that the cuff should surround how much of her upper arm?
1. One-third.
2. Two-thirds.
3. Three-fourths.
4. The entire circumference of the arm.

7. A woman who has mild hypertension asks if she needs blood pressure medicine. The nurse explains that pharmacologic therapy is usually added to the therapeutic regime
1. when symptoms appear.
2. any time a client is noncompliant with diet therapy.
3. when the history indicates the client is at risk for cardiovascular disease.
4. when the difference between systolic and diastolic blood pressure is greater than 60 mm Hg.

8. The nurse is teaching a client who has mild hypertension. The teaching plan should include the information that the major goal of treatment for an adult with hypertension is
1. control of the disease.
2. a healthier life-style.
3. avoidance of renal complications.
4. restoration of her prior state of health.

9. The gynecologist has referred a young couple to the infertility clinic. They have been married for five years, are in their late twenties, and have been trying to conceive a child for over a year. A primary tool in the initial assessment of this infertile couple will be
1. a complete history and physical.
2. a psychological examination.
3. an explanation of all surgical options.
4. hormonal assessment of ovulatory function.

10. The nurse in an infertility clinic explains to a couple under evaluation that a semen analysis is done to evaluate for
1. chromosomal disorders.
2. hormone levels.
3. sperm motility.
4. temperature.

11. The nurse in an infertility clinic is discussing tests that will be done to evaluate an infertile couple. The nurse should include in the teaching plan that a simple method of determining ovulatory function is
1. laparoscopy.
2. cervical mucous testing.
3. postcoital sampling.
4. testing urine LH levels.

12. the nurse in an infertility clinic is discussing the treatment routine. The nurse advises the couple that the major stressor for couples being treated for infertility is usually
1. having to tell their families.
2. the cost of the interventions.
3. the inconvenience of multiple tests.

4. the right scheduling of sexual intercourse.

13. A woman who is being evaluated and treated for infertility is instructed to graph her ovulatory function by taking her basal body temperature when she awakens each morning. In addition to recording her waking body temperature, she should also document
1. all food consumed.
2. her daily weight.
3. the temperature of the room.
4. the presence of a sore throat.

14. A two-day-old infant is diagnosed as having congenital hip dysplasia of the right hip. The infant is fitted with a Pavlik harness. Which of the following would not be included in the instructions for home care for the parents?
1. Turn her every three to four hours.
2. Keep her off the affected side.
3. Watch for signs of skin breakdown.
4. Give her sponge baths, not tub baths.

15. A newborn is being treated for congenital hip dysplasia. After six weeks in the Pavlik harness, the baby's hip does not become stabilized and she is scheduled for more aggressive treatment. Prior to having an open reduction under general anesthesia, she is hospitalized in Bryant's traction for a week or two to bring the femoral head fully into position. The baby's mother needs to understand that, while in Bryant's traction, her daughter's
1. hips will be flexed at a 45° angle.
2. buttocks will be flat.
3. buttocks will be slightly elevated off the bed.
4. knees will be bent.

16. An infant who has congenital hip dysplasia not responding to a Pavlik harness is placed in Bryant's traction prior to surgery. The baby's mother asks the nurse if she can take the baby out of traction for feeding. The best response for the nurse to make is
1. "Yes, but only for feedings."
2. "Yes, this is intermittent traction."
3. "No, parenteral feedings will be given."
4. "No, continuous traction is necessary to bring the femoral head fully into position."

17. The nurse is caring for an infant who has had a hip spica cast applied. To keep the cast as free of urine and stool as possible the nurse should
1. use a Bradford frame.
2. use a Denis Browne splint.
3. catheterize the baby prn.
4. insert an indwelling catheter.

18. The nurse is caring for an infant who is in a hip spica cast. Which action is least appropriate for the nurse to take to prevent skin irritation at the edges of the baby's cast?
1. Give meticulous skin care.
2. Petal the edges with moleskin.
3. Use baby powder around the edges.

4. Tuck plastic wrap under the edges.

19. Clients with acute pancreatitis often have H_2 blockers or antacids ordered. The primary purpose of giving these drugs to a client with pancreatitis is to
    1. coat the stomach to protect it from the effects of bile reflux.
    2. reduce gastric pH to inactivate digestive enzymes.
    3. counteract excessive gastric acid secretion stimulated by release of gastrin from the damaged pancreas.
    4. Raise gastric pH to decrease stimulation of excessive release of pancreatic enzymes.

20. In caring for a client with varicose veins, which of the following measures is most essential for the nurse to include in the plan of care?
    1. Discussing cosmetic techniques to improve appearance.
    2. Discouraging stair climbing or walking.
    3. Teaching activities to promote circulation.
    4. Encouraging activities that cause venous stasis.

21. After swallowing a dime, a 22-month-old toddler is brought to the emergency room by her frightened mother. What assessment would alert the nurse to the possibility of esophageal blockage?
    1. Dim breath sounds in upper right lobe.
    2. Choking, gagging, wheezing, and coughing.
    3. Increased salivation, painful swallowing.
    4. Inability to speak, cyanosis, and collapse.

22. Which of the following manifestations indicates to the nurse that an infant needs further fluid therapy for dehydration?
    1. Fontanel level with skull and sutures.
    2. Liquid, loose stools.
    3. Specific gravity of 1.010.
    4. Urinary output 1–2 ml/kg/hour.

23. The nurse is caring for a client with chronic venous insufficiency. He now has deep, draining, foul-smelling ulcers on his legs. The nurse can anticipate that the client is likely to be given which of the following vitamins?
    1. Vitamin A.
    2. B complex vitamins.
    3. Vitamin C.
    4. Vitamin D.

24. The treatment of a client with chronic venous insufficiency and severe leg ulcers includes the application of a gelatin bandage around the stasis ulcers. This is
    1. a Jobst stocking.
    2. An Unna's paste boot.
    3. a specialized ace bandage.
    4. a plaster of Paris bandage.

25. Discharge instructions for a client who has chronic venous insufficiency will include instructions to avoid
    1. walking.

2. sexual intercourse.
3. elevating the legs.
4. standing for long periods.

26. The nurse is discussing the prevention of osteoporosis with a group of clients. The nurse explains factors required to keep bones strong. Which is not included in the nurse's discussion?
    1. An adequate calcium intake.
    2. Maintenance of a low weight.
    3. Sufficient estrogen levels.
    4. Weight-bearing exercise.

27. A client whose mother has developed osteoporosis asks the nurse if there was anything she could have been aware of that would have indicated that her mother had osteoporosis. The nurse's best response is,
    1. "Did she experience cramps after exercising?"
    2. "Were her nails and hair brittle?"
    3. "Is she shorter now than she was in the past?"
    4. "Had she been eating less and still gaining weight?"

28. When teaching about osteoporosis, the nurse stresses the importance of prevention. The nurse suggests that the client's diet should include adequate amounts of
    1. Vitamin A.
    2. Vitamin D.
    3. Vitamin E.
    4. Vitamin K.

29. The nurse is teaching a woman about osteoporosis. The woman reports all of the following. Which should the nurse recommend she stop doing to help reduce the risk of osteoporosis?
    1. Smoking.
    2. Overeating.
    3. Biting her nails.
    4. Skipping breakfast.

30. The nurse has been teaching a client about factors to reduce the risk of development of osteoporosis. Adding which food to her diet indicates that the client understands the role of nutrition in preventing osteoporosis?
    1. Oatmeal.
    2. Peaches.
    3. Canned salmon.
    4. Poached flounder.

31. An 85-year-old man was admitted for surgery for benign prostatic hypertrophy. Preoperatively he was alert, oriented, cooperative, and knowledgeable about his surgery. Several hours after surgery, the evening nurse found him acutely confused, agitated, and trying to climb over the protective side rails on his bed. The most appropriate nursing intervention that will calm an agitated client is
    1. limit visits by staff.
    2. encourage family phone calls.

3. position in a bright, busy area.
4. speak soothingly and provide quiet music.

32. A 25-year-old woman is admitted to the eating disorders clinic for treatment of bulimia. The nurse caring for the client knows that the primary issue for the bulimia client is
1. delusions.
2. depersonalization.
3. fear and suspicion of others.
4. poor impulse control.

33. The nurse is assessing a client with bulimia. Which characteristic is least likely to be evident in the history?
1. Repeated crash dieting.
2. Repeated weight fluctuations.
3. Rigorous exercise regimens.
4. Self-induced vomiting.

34. In planning care for a client with bulimia, the nurse expects that the client may be given which pharmacologic agent?
1. An anticonvulsant.
2. An antidepressant.
3. A major tranquilizer.
4. A minor tranquilizer.

35. The nurse is caring for a client admitted with severe diarrhea. The nurse should observe this client for hyponatremia because
1. sodium is concentrated in gastrointestinal fluid.
2. water lost in diarrhea causes sodium to follow it.
3. diarrhea triggers renal mechanisms to waste sodium.
4. hyponatremia occurs as a result of treatment for diarrhea.

36. Mr. S., 68 years old, has had Type I diabetes mellitus for many years. When he went to his diabetologist for a regular checkup, he presented complaints that led to his referral to a specialist for evaluation of peripheral arterial disease. Mr. S. would most likely have described his discomfort as
1. incapacitating.
2. throbbing.
3. mild.
4. aching weakness in the lower extremities.

37. An older adult with a long history of Type I diabetes mellitus is being evaluated for peripheral arterial disease. The nurse assesses his feet after elevating them for 30 seconds and notes the color is pale. The nurse most correctly interprets this as
1. normal.
2. dependent rubor.
3. pregangrenous.
4. cadaveric pallor.

38. The nurse is examining the feet of an older man suspected of having peripheral arterial disease. Which finding indicates an inadequate nutritional supply to the feet?
1. coarse body hair.
2. muscle hypertrophy.

3. thick, ridged nails.
4. rough, reddened skin.

39. The nurse is having difficulty assessing peripheral pulses. The most appropriate action for the nurse to take is to
1. ask him to lie on his stomach.
2. have him do 20 jumping jacks.
3. ask him to flex and extend his foot.
4. ask him to elevate his leg.

40. An adult with a long history of diabetes mellitus is being evaluated for peripheral vascular disease. The nurse understands that a person with a long history of diabetes is at increased risk for developing peripheral arterial disease due to
1. hypoglycemic episodes.
2. capillary rupture.
3. early atherosclerotic changes.
4. fluctuating levels of insulin.

41. The nurse is caring for a client with peripheral arterial disease and long term diabetes mellitus. If the client should develop diabetic neuropathy the risk of complications of peripheral arterial disease increases because diabetic neuropathy
1. dilates peripheral vessels.
2. decreases sensation.
3. increases cardiac output.
4. alters renal function.

42. The nurse is caring for a client with long-standing diabetes. Which finding is most consistent with damage to the autonomic nervous system?
1. Flushed, warm extremities.
2. Dry, cracked skin.
3. Absent pulses.
4. Burning sensation on the soles of the feet.

43. The nurse is teaching a client with diabetes mellitus and peripheral arterial disease how to care for his feet. Which instruction should the nurse include?
1. Avoid deodorant soaps.
2. Examine your feet weekly.
3. Use only hot water.
4. Soak your feet daily.

44. The nurse is caring for a client who is scheduled for surgery tomorrow. It is expected that he will have patient-controlled analgesia (PCA) following surgery. The nurse tells the client that the primary reason for using PCA is that it
1. is very cost effective.
2. requires less pain medication.
3. makes nursing care easier to manage.
4. allows clients to control their own pain.

45. The nurse knows that which criteria is most important in determining whether a client is a good candidate for PCA?
1. He is alert.
2. He is not overweight.
3. His pain will be constant.

4. His surgical procedure will be relatively short.

46. In discussing PCA and possible side effects with the client, the nurse tells the client that the risk of respiratory depression with PCA is reduced because
   1. it eliminates peaks in serum drug levels.
   2. it uses drugs without respiratory side effects.
   3. it requires very little medication for pain relief.
   4. there are intervals when the client receives no medication.

47. The nurse is caring for a client who is at risk for developing deep vein thrombosis. Which nursing care measure is not appropriate?
   1. Careful leg massages.
   2. Elastic stockings.
   3. Elevating the legs.
   4. Leg exercises.

48. The nurse is caring for a client who has a deep vein thrombosis. Which nursing care measure is not appropriate?
   1. Nursing measures to help the client avoid straining at stool.
   2. Telling the client to avoid sudden movements.
   3. Assisting the client to dangle on the side of the bed three times a day.
   4. Teaching the client to avoid bumping the legs against other objects.

49. A client with deep vein thrombosis is started on heparin therapy. Which nursing action is not indicated during heparin administration?
   1. Having vitamin K available if bleeding occurs.
   2. Observing for hematomas at IV puncture sites.
   3. Suggesting that the client use a soft bristled toothbrush.
   4. Using an IV control device for drug administration.

50. Two days after admission with deep vein thrombosis, an adult client develops a cough with slight hemoptysis and complains of shortness of breath and sharp pain under his right shoulder blade. A pulmonary embolus is suspected and a ventilation/perfusion scan of the lungs is ordered. The ventilation/perfusion scan of a client with pulmonary embolism who has no other pulmonary disease demonstrates
   1. decreased ventilation; decreased perfusion.
   2. decreased ventilation; normal perfusion.
   3. normal ventilation; decreased perfusion.
   4. normal ventilation; normal perfusion.

51. The nurse is caring for a small child. Child abuse is suspected. The nurse understands that children are most frequently abused by a
   1. babysitter.
   2. relative.
   3. teacher.

4. casual acquaintance.

52. In evaluating risk factors for child abuse, the nurse understands that the child at least risk for being abused is one whose family
   1. moves frequently.
   2. owns their own home.
   3. has experienced divorce.
   4. has problems with chronic illnesses.

53. The nurse is assessing a 4-year-old girl who has been brought to the emergency room with a high fever. Child abuse is suspected. Which test is least likely to indicate that the child has been sexually abused?
   1. A Pap smear.
   2. Urine culture.
   3. Throat culture.
   4. Vaginal culture.

54. When interviewing a child suspected of being sexually abused, the nurse should
   1. ask leading questions.
   2. have the parents present.
   3. have a security guard present.
   4. use the child's words to describe body parts.

55. Children who survive physical abuse are least likely to become
   1. depressed.
   2. drug abusers.
   3. abusive parents.
   4. academic achievers.

56. A 4-year-old girl is brought to the emergency room with a high fever. She has been irritable for several days and is clinging to two dolls. Her mother says she refuses to eat. Playing with her dolls while in the examining room, she has them engaging in explicit sexual behavior. The nurse should know that
   1. she is mimicking behavior seen on TV.
   2. she is acting out a personal experience.
   3. such play is a healthy expression of sexual development.
   4. she needs to be directed to more appropriate play.

57. When child abuse is suspected, the least appropriate nursing action is to
   1. take a wait-and-see position.
   2. call a local social service agency for help.
   3. prevent the child's return to a dangerous environment.
   4. confront the parent with security present.

58. Which question is least useful in the assessment of a client with AIDS?
   1. Are you a drug user?
   2. Do you have many sex partners?
   3. What is your method of birth control?
   4. How old were you when you became sexually active?

59. When planning care for the client with *Pneumocystis carinii* pneumonia (PCP), the nurse should recognize that
   1. it is usually fatal.
   2. the client has few symptoms.

3. it is highly contagious.
4. treatment is more successful now than in the past.
60. The drug of choice for the treatment of *Pneumocystis carinii* pneumonia is
1. amphotericin B (Fungazone).
2. ethambutol (Myambutol).
3. pentamidine (Pentam).
4. zidovudine (Retrovir).
61. The nurse is planning care for an adult client who has *Pneumocystis carinii* pneumonia and AIDS. The nurse knows that the IV drug abuser is at risk for infective endocarditis due to
1. HIV-associated arrhythmias.
2. increased workload on the heart.
3. resistance of bacteria to antibiotics.
4. introduction of bacteria into the bloodstream.
62. The nurse is planning care for an HIV-infected drug abuser. Which goal is unrealistic?
1. Quitting the drug addiction.
2. Cooperating with unit goals.
3. Learning to clean drug equipment.
4. Remaining for the full treatment course.
63. The nurse is assessing a client who has infective endocarditis secondary to AIDS. Which symptoms indicate that the client is experiencing endocarditis?
1. A pronounced S_1 and S_2.
2. Chronic low-grade fever.
3. Tachycardia and hypertension.
4. Shortness of breath and chest pain.
64. A six-year-old is brought to the emergency department unconscious after having been hit by a car. Which of the following will not be included when the nurse performs a baseline neurologic exam?
1. Motor function.
2. Visual acuity.
3. Vital signs.
4. Level of consciousness.
65. A 27-year-old woman has Type I diabetes mellitus. She and her husband want to have a child so they consulted her diabetologist, who gave her information on pregnancy and diabetes. Of primary importance for the diabetic woman who is considering pregnancy should be
1. a review of the dietary modifications that will be necessary.
2. early prenatal medical care.
3. adoption instead of conception.
4. understanding that this is a major health risk to the mother.
66. A young woman who had Type I diabetes mellitus is pregnant. She asks the nurse how much weight she can gain during her pregnancy. The nurse's best response is
1. 10 to 15 pounds.
2. 25 to 30 pounds.
3. less than 40 pounds.

4. the weight of the baby plus 3 pounds.
67. The nurse is teaching a pregnant woman who is also diabetic about her diet during pregnancy. The nurse knows that the client understands her dietary needs when she says
1. "I will eat a low-protein low-salt diet."
2. "I will continue my normal intake of simple carbohydrates."
3. "I will increase my water consumption."
4. "I will eat lots of fruits, vegetables, and grains."
68. The nurse is caring for a pregnant woman who is also diabetic. The nurse knows that she understands the management of her diabetes during pregnancy when she says, "My blood sugar level should be
1. 80 to 110 mg/dl."
2. 150 to 200 mg/dl."
3. 200 to 250 mg/dl."
4. no greater than 300 mg/dl."
69. The nurse is assessing a pregnant diabetic for signs and symptoms of hyperglycemia. Which symptom does not indicate hyperglycemia?
1. Lethargy.
2. Polyuria.
3. Thirst.
4. Sweating.
70. A pregnant woman asks the nurse if there are any special problems that she might encounter during labor and delivery because she has diabetes. The nurse responds that during labor and delivery, diabetic mothers may develop
1. hypoglycemia.
2. hyperglycemia.
3. metabolic alkalosis.
4. hyperosmolar nonketotic coma.
71. Mr. T., 45, is admitted with a diagnosis of manic depressive illness, manic episode. Mr. T. is euphoric, intrusive, has pressured, rapid speech, and experiences delusions of grandeur. Mr. T. states, "My name is T. I'm quite well known. I've also got 3 PhDs, in chemistry, philosophy, and theology." When Mr. T. describes himself in this manner, the nurse interprets this behavior as
1. due to high anxiety levels.
2. a response to noncompliance with anxiolytic signs.
3. a need to feel important so as to minimize the stigma of mental illness.
4. indicative of Mr. T.'s biochemical mental disorder.
72. A short-term goal (to be met in one week following admission) planned by the nurse for a delusional client is for the client to
1. reduce the frequency and intensity of the delusional thinking.
2. verbalize why he/she uses delusions to deal with life.
3. communicate in only reality-oriented terms.

4. recognize his delusions as nonreality-based statements.

73. The nurse and a severely depressed client mutually plan a short-term goal regarding self-esteem needs. Which of the following would be appropriate to meet in one week?
   1. The client will be able to describe one positive attribute about himself to the nurse.
   2. The client will be able to attend the fully participate in all groups and therapeutic activities.
   3. The client verbalizes to the nurse that he is now able to solve his problems.
   4. The client verbalizes to the nurse that he feels good enough to run the next community meeting.

74. Ms. J., 40, states, "That TV newsman is talking about me." The nurse recognizes this type of thought process as
   1. thought broadcasting.
   2. delusion of reference.
   3. thought insertion.
   4. delusion of persecution.

75. A college student was at the airport waiting for his flight home when a terrorist bomb exploded nearby, killing several people. He developed selective psychogenic amnesia and was admitted to the hospital for treatment. He is cooperative and compliant. However, he remembers nothing regarding his experience and when questioned becomes very anxious. What is the best nursing intervention?
   1. Plan a trip with the client to the airport to jar his memory.
   2. Help the client develop coping skills to deal with his anxiety.
   3. Be firm with the client and insist he try to remember.
   4. Tell the client, "It is all right to be anxious and we'll talk another time."

76. Which of the following behaviors indicates to the nurse that the client with agoraphobia is improving?
   1. Client is able to offer complaints to the boss regarding the workload.
   2. Client is able to travel five flights on an elevator.
   3. Client is able to shop alone at a local mall without intense anxiety.
   4. Client is able to resist washing hands after touching a dirty object.

77. Albert, a 60-year-old man, has just completed the detoxification process and is due for discharge. His nurse must evaluate his comprehension of the long-term nature of his addiction. Which statement indicates the best understanding?
   1. "I can have a social drink for special holidays without a problem."
   2. "I must attend 90 AA meetings in 90 days."
   3. "I know I must never drink alcohol again."

4. "Once I finish the 12 stages I'm cured."

78. Ms. D. has been taking tricyclic medication for a week with no improvement in mood. The nurse's best explanation for this situation is
   1. The client has been ordered an antidepressant that is ineffective due to client insensitivity.
   2. The client should consider electroconvulsive therapy for a more rapid change in mood.
   3. The client needs to wait longer because drug onset takes seven to ten days.
   4. The client requires a second opinion with regards to her medical diagnosis and treatment.

79. A client with a spinal cord injury develops the signs and symptoms of autonomic dysreflexia. The initial action the nurse takes is to
   1. administer an analgesic to relieve the headache.
   2. instruct the client on preventive measures.
   3. examine the rectum for a fecal mass.
   4. sit the client up to lower the blood pressure.

80. A client who is scheduled for a bowel resection tomorrow has just completed preoperative teaching by the nurse. Which of the following statements to the nurse indicates the client needs further instruction on postoperative care?
   1. "I know I'll have pain after surgery, but I can call the nurses for medicine."
   2. "They will be taking my pulse and blood pressure many times after the operation."
   3. "The intravenous needle will come out in the recovery room."
   4. "I'll show you how I can deep breathe and cough."

81. An 11-year-old girl is ready for hospital discharge after being newly diagnosed with Type I diabetes mellitus. Which statement by the child alerts the nurse to do further teaching before the child leaves?
   1. "I never know when my sugar is low, because I don't feel any different, so I guess I'll really have to use my blood glucose monitor on schedule."
   2. "On my constant carb diet I can have a dessert every day, as long as I eat it at the same time each day."
   3. "I need to pinch up my skin for the injections because if the insulin gets into my muscle instead of fat it won't work right."
   4. "I think I'll have Mom get me some of those glucose tablets to carry with me, because I won't be tempted to eat them for snacks, like I would with Life Savers."

82. Ms. F. has acute cholecystitis secondary to cholelithiasis. Which factor in Ms. F.'s history is most often associated with cholelithiasis?
   1. Low-fat diet for many years.

2. A period of unusually strenuous exercise.
3. Use of oral hypoglycemic drugs.
4. A history of gallbladder disease in family members.

83. Ms. P. is discharged following treatment for partial and full thickness burns of the upper body. An elastic pressure garment is prescribed. The nurse examines the wounds when Ms. P. returns for a clinic visit one year later and documents that the wounds are healing without complications when the wound appears
   1. red, raised, and hard.
   2. pink, flat, and soft.
   3. hard, raised, and shiny.
   4. open, pink, and draining.

84. A child with head lice is seen in the clinic and receives home care instructions. The child's mother indicates understanding of the teaching if she says
   1. "I'm really embarrassed about this situation, because our home isn't a dirty place."
   2. "I guess we'll have to wash all the towels and sheets in the house, along with all your clothes!"
   3. "I'll have to get seven bottles of this special shampoo and use one every day for a week on my child's hair. Then she can return to school."
   4. "I'm supposed to leave this special shampoo on her for 10 minutes, rinse, and then comb out the nits with a fine-toothed comb."

85. Knowing that a test for phenylketonuria (PKU) is conducted on all babies in the United States, the nurse instructs the mother to
   1. keep the infant NPO before the test.
   2. maintain the infant's feeding schedule.
   3. request that it be done within 8 hours of delivery.
   4. give the infant water before the test.

86. The nurse has just completed education with parents of a newborn recently diagnosed with phenylketonuria. Which statement the parents make indicates the best understanding of phenylketonuria?
   1. The child only needs to be on a special diet until the age of one year.
   2. The child must eat a diet low in phenylalanine.
   3. There is medicine that the child can take to avoid being on any special diet.
   4. The child must avoid all foods that contain phenylalanine.

87. The nurse has just completed teaching with Ms. B. regarding the use of the diaphragm and is assessing her understanding. Which statement demonstrates correct learning by the client?
   1. "I will use Vaseline to lubricate the rim of the diaphragm prior to insertion."

2. "I should get refitted for the diaphragm if I gain or lose more than 5 pounds."
3. "I should put spermicide only on the rim of the diaphragm before insertion."
4. "I will leave the diaphragm in place at least six hours after intercourse."

88. An elderly client has reported to a local health department to receive a flu shot. The nurse should make which one of the following assessments prior to administering the flu vaccine?
   1. Mental status.
   2. Gastrointestinal system.
   3. Integumentary system.
   4. Egg allergies.

89. While teaching self-testicular examination, the nurse instructs the client that the best time to perform the exam may be
   1. after a warm bath or shower.
   2. in the morning before getting out of bed.
   3. at bedtime.
   4. after exercise.

90. The nurse is administering CPR. Which is most important for the nurse to evaluate to determine whether the procedure is being done effectively?
   1. Feeling the carotid pulse during compressions.
   2. Observing the chest rise and fall during rescue breathing.
   3. Monitoring arterial blood gases.
   4. Monitoring the electrocardiogram rhythm.

91. The nurse is assessing an elderly client in a long-term care facility. Which finding is a normal finding?
   1. Deposits of melanin.
   2. Thickening of the epidermis.
   3. Increase in hair follicles.
   4. Increase in subcutaneous tissue.

92. An adult has had a left hip replacement. He is now three days post-op. Which parameter should the nurse monitor to determine if the client is meeting goals related to the nursing diagnosis of high risk for infection?
   1. Nutrition status.
   2. Hemoglobin and hematocrit.
   3. Vital signs every four hours.
   4. Amount and character of drainage from incision.

93. The nurse suspects a complication in a client who is receiving peritoneal dialysis. Which of the following observations would support this evaluation?
   1. Pain during the inflow of dialysate.
   2. Occasional diarrhea.
   3. Cloudy or opaque effluent.
   4. Clear or light yellow effluent.

94. The clinic nurse is administering tuberculin skin tests. The nurse should administer the skin test by injecting the purified protein derivative (PPD) at a
   1. 90-degree angle into the deltoid.

2. 45-degree angle into the subcutaneous tissue of the arm.
3. 60-degree angle into the hypodermal space of the gluteal.
4. 10-degree angle into the forearm.

95. An adult who has recently arrived in the United States from Honduras had a PPD planted 72 hours ago. The nurse assesses the region where the PPD was planted and finds an erythematous circle of 10 mm in diameter and an induration of 1.5 mm. The nurse correctly interprets these findings as
   1. meaningless. The test must be read at 24 and 48 hours; these results are too old.
   2. exposure to tuberculosis because of the size of the erythema but not active disease, because the induration is small.
   3. conclusive for active tuberculosis because there is an induration and the client comes from a part of the world where tuberculosis is common.
   4. indicative of no tuberculosis because the induration is small.

96. A tracheostomy was performed and mechanical ventilation instituted on an adult. Tracheal suctioning by the nurse should include
   1. wearing clean gloves, goggles, and a mask.
   2. applying constant suction while inserting the catheter.
   3. hyperoxygenating the client with 100% oxygen only after the procedure is completed.
   4. applying intermittent suction and rotating the catheter as the suction catheter is drawn from the tracheostomy tube.

97. The physician has ordered total parenteral nutrition to be delivered through the central venous line of an adult admitted to the medical intensive care unit. When changing the tubing to institute the TPN, the nurse should perform which of the following activities to prevent the occurrence of an air embolism?
   1. Cleanse the central line insertion site with povidone-iodine ointment.
   2. Wrap sterile Vaseline gauze around the hub of the open central venous line while priming the TPN line.

3. Clamp the central venous line while connecting the primed TPN administration set.
4. Place an alcohol wipe over the open end of the central venous catheter while preparing to insert the primed TPN tubing.

98. A 55-year-old adult was admitted to the coronary care unit (CCU) for complaints of substernal chest pain of one hour duration unrelieved by nitroglycerin. Hardwire cardiac monitoring was instituted using lead sites for MCL[1]. To properly locate the correct sites for electrode placement, the nurse should identify the
   1. McBurney's point.
   2. Angle of Louis.
   3. suprasternal notch.
   4. costovertebral angle.

99. The nurse is instructing a woman in a low-fat, high-fiber diet. Which of the following food choices, if selected by the client, indicate an understanding of a low-fat, high-fiber diet?
   1. Tuna salad sandwich on whole wheat bread.
   2. Vegetable soup made with vegetable stock, carrots, celery, and legumes served with toasted oat bread.
   3. Chef's salad with hard boiled eggs and fat-free dressing.
   4. Broiled chicken stuffed with chopped apples and walnuts.

100. A 38-year-old woman asks the nurse why she should have a mammogram. The best response for the nurse to make is
   1. "Mammograms can diagnose breast cancer with nearly 100% accuracy."
   2. "Every sexually active woman needs to have a mammogram, since there is a correlation between sexual intercourse and breast cancer."
   3. "You are 38 years old. This is the appropriate time to have a baseline mammogram done."
   4. "The dye, or contrast medium, used when you have a mammogram helps the radiologist see the difference between a tumor and a cyst."

Answers and Rationales for Practice Test 6

ANSWER	RATIONALE	NP	CN	CL

#1. 3. **The normal range for blood pressure is between 95 and 140 mm Hg systolic pressure and between 60 and 90 mm Hg diastolic pressure. Ms. T.'s systolic pressure is above 140.**   Im   He/4   Co
  1. A systolic pressure of 110 mm Hg is within normal limits.
  2. A systolic pressure of 120 mm Hg is within normal limits.
  4. A systolic pressure of 160 mm Hg is above normal and signifies hypertension.

#2. 4. **A white blood cell count is not necessary for the evaluation of a client with hypertension. The JNC recommends a complete urinalysis, hemoglobin and hematocrit, serum potassium, calcium, creatinine, and plasma cholesterol levels.**   An   He/4   An
  1. An EKG is part of the evaluation of high blood pressure.
  2. Complete urinalysis is part of evaluation of high blood pressure.
  3. Serum calcium should be included in the evaluation.

#3. 2. **An exercise program should be carefully planned and begun gradually.**   Pl   He/4   Ap
  1. Rapid weight loss is not healthy and if eating habits are not altered, all the weight lost and more, will return when the client stops dieting.
  3. The cardiovascular system might not be able to handle vigorous exercise right away. There must be a gradual buildup to the level of exercise desired.
  4. Moderate exercise may be begun before the blood pressure is within the normal range. The client's blood pressure range listed is not that severe.

#4. 4. **Primary hypertension is a disorder in which the cause of the hypertension cannot be identified.**   An   He/4   Co
  1. Atherosclerosis causes hypertension, but it is not the cause of primary hypertension.
  2. Renal disease can cause hypertension, but it is not the cause of primary hypertension.
  3. Diabetic vessel changes can cause hypertension, but it is not called primary hypertension.

#5. 3. **Salt and fat in the diet should be limited. Processed foods usually have a high sodium and fat content.**   Im   He/4   Ap
  1. The client should increase the amount of vegetables eaten. Vegetables are low in sodium and fat.
  2. The client should increase calcium intake because a high calcium diet is thought to lower blood pressure.
  4. Water softening systems usually use sodium and add sodium to the water. Persons with hypertension should not have a water softening system.

#6. 2. **The blood pressure cuff should surround two-thirds of the arm.**   Im   He/4   Ap
  1. The blood pressure cuff should surround two-thirds of the arm. A blood pressure cuff that is too small will give a higher than actual reading.
  3. The blood pressure cuff should surround two-thirds of the arm. A blood pressure cuff that is too large will give a lower than actual reading.
  4. The blood pressure cuff should surround two-thirds of the arm. A blood pressure cuff that is too large will give a lower than actual reading.

#7. 3. **First-line drugs used in the management of hypertension are added when the client is considered to be a high risk for cardiovascular disease.**   Ev   Ph/8   An

    1. Hypertension has few symptoms. Waiting for symptoms to appear is too late. Clients with primary hypertension are generally asymptomatic.

    2. Some clients who comply with dietary therapy also need antihypertensive medication.

    4. The difference between the systolic and the diastolic blood pressure does not determine the need for antihypertensive medication. Medication is used in the management of hypertension when the client history and physical exam suggest a high risk for cardiovascular disease.

#8. 1. The major goal in the treatment of clients with hypertension is control of the disease.   Pl   He/4   Ap

    2. Management of the disease with increased exercise and a well-balanced diet leads to a healthier life-style.

    3. Control of hypertension aids in avoiding renal complications.

    4. Hypertension can be controlled through diet, exercise, and possible medication therapy, but it cannot be cured.

#9. 1. The basic work-up should be initiated with a thorough history, physical exam, and sexual history.   As   He/3   Ap

    2. A psychological evaluation is not part of the initial assessment. It may be done at some point because of the pressure the couple may be experiencing. Both partners need support in expressing concerns and fears about infertility. Failure to conceive may threaten their individual self-concepts, sex roles, and sexual interaction. One or both partners may blame themselves.

    3. Once an infertility work-up is completed, possible surgical intervention will be discussed with the couple. It is not part of the initial assessment.

    4. Assessment of ovulatory function will be a determining factor for possible medical and/or surgical interventions. However, it is not the initial assessment.

#10. 3. Motile sperm should compose at least 50% of the specimen sent for analysis.   Ev   He/3   Ap

    1. Presence of chromosomal abnormalities will not help determine fertility.

    2. Hormone levels alone are not enough to determine fertility. Number of sperm (20–120 million per ml) and motility of sperm determine fertility.

    4. Semen analysis does not include the temperature of the sperm.

#11. 4. Ovulation occurs 16–30 hours after the LH (luteinizing hormone) surge. Testing the urine on a daily basis throughout the cycle helps to pinpoint the time of ovulation.   Pl   He/3   Ap

    1. Laparoscopy is a surgical intervention and does not determine ovulatory function.

    2. Cervical mucous testing gives an indication of when ovulation occurs but is not as accurate as testing urine for LH levels.

    3. Postcoital sampling does not determine ovulation. It gives indication of sperm count and whether the sperm and female secretions are compatible.

#12. 4. Sexual activity "on demand" is the major cause of stress for most infertile couples.   Im   He/3   Ap

    1. Having to tell families may also be a factor contributing to stress but is not the major stressor.

    2. Cost may also be a contributing factor to stress but is not usually the major factor.

    3. The inconvenience of multiple tests may also be a factor contributing to stress but is not usually the major factor.

#13. 4. A sore throat may be indicative of a cold or other infection that could affect body temperature, distorting the interpretation of the graph.   Ev   He/3   An

ANSWER	RATIONALE	NP	CN	CL

1. Food eaten by the client does not affect her basal body temperature.
2. Daily weight does not affect the client's basal body temperature.
3. The temperature of the room does not affect the body temperature of the client.

#14. 2. The infant in a Pavlik harness can be turned from back to abdomen but should not be positioned on either side.   Pl   Ph/9   Ap

1. The baby should be turned every three to four hours.
3. Skin should be assessed daily for signs of skin breakdown.
4. The child should have sponge baths rather than tub baths.

#15. 3. The buttocks need to be raised slightly off the bed to maintain Bryant's traction.   Im   Ph/9   Ap

1. The hips of the child in Bryant's traction are flexed at a 90° angle, not a 45° angle.
2. The buttocks are elevated slightly off the bed, not flat.
4. The knees will be straight and the buttocks raised slightly off the bed.

#16. 4. Continuous traction is needed to bring the femoral head into position. The child easily learns to play with toys tied to the crib and to eat in this position.   Im   Ph/7   Ap

1. Bryant's traction is continuous traction. The baby may not be removed for feeding.
2. Bryant's traction is not intermittent traction. It is continuous traction.
3. Parenteral feedings need not be given. The baby easily learns to eat in this position. Parenteral feedings are not necessary.

#17. 1. The Bradford frame facilitates collection of urine and stool for an infant or child in a hip spica cast.   Im   Ph/9   Ap

2. The Denis Browne splint is a splint used for the correction of club foot.
3. Intermittent catheterization is not indicated.
4. An indwelling catheter is not indicated.

#18. 3. Baby powder coats the skin and causes skin irritation. It is also not advised in infants as it can cause respiratory irritation.   Im   Ph/9   Ap

1. Meticulous skin care is essential for a child in a cast.
2. Petaling the edges of the cast will prevent irritation of the skin by the rough edges of the skin.
4. Tucking plastic wrap under the edges of the cast will prevent seepage of urine under the cast.

#19. 4. In acute pancreatitis, the pancreas itself is exposed to the digestive action of pancreatic enzymes. During the acute phase it is desirable to remove the stimulation to release these enzymes and thus reduce autodigestion. NPO and H_2 blockers are also commonly ordered for this reason.   An   Ph/8   An

1. Bile reflux into the stomach is not a result of acute pancreatitis. It occurs with pyloric sphincter incompetence, a common sequela of removal of part of the stomach.
2. A lower pH reflects gastric acidity. Gastric acid activates pepsin, the digestive enzyme, so lowering the pH would increase the activity of digestive enzymes.
3. Amylase and lipase, which are digestive enzymes, are usually elevated in acute pancreatitis. There is no evidence that hormones from the pancreas, including astrin, are released in greater quantities when the pancreas is inflamed.

#20. 3. When planning care for a client with varicose veins the most essential measure is to teach the client activities that promote circulation and to avoid activities that decrease circulation.   Pl   Ph/9   Ap

1. Teaching about cosmetic techniques to improve appearance might be done but is not the most essential measure.
2. If there are no contraindications, clients with varicose veins should be encouraged to walk and climb stairs to promote circulation.
4. Activities that cause venous stasis should be discouraged.

ANSWER	RATIONALE	NP	CN	CL

#21. 3. A dime-size object usually can pass through the gastrointestinal tract and be eliminated in the stool within a week. However, if it occludes the esophagus, the child will not be able to swallow saliva effectively and will begin drooling. Swallowing causes pain from the tightening motion of esophageal tissues around the coin.

As Ph/10 Ap

 1. Collapse of a lobe or blockage of the air flow in the lobe would cause dim breath sounds.
 2. Choking, gagging, wheezing, and coughing are the initial signs of a foreign body in the air passages. This might occur if the child were to vomit the coin upwards and then aspirate it.
 4. A child who is choking and cannot speak has a blocked airway and needs to have back blows and the Heimlich maneuver initiated.

#22. 2. Liquid, loose stools contribute to dehydration in infants and warrant further liquid therapy.

Ev Ph/10 Ap

 1. Fontanel level with the skull and sutures is normal and indicates adequate hydration.
 3. Specific gravity of 1.010 is normal for an infant.
 4. Urine output of 1–2 ml/kg/hour is normal for an infant.

#23. 3. Vitamin C, the healing vitamin, will aid wound healing through a mechanism that maintains capillary integrity.

Pl Ph/9 An

 1. Vitamin A is essential for skeletal growth, maintenance of normal mucosal epithelium, and visual acuity. Vitamin A is not indicated for this client.
 2. The B complex includes thiamine (B_1), riboflavin (B_2), pyridoxine (B_6), and cyanocobalamin (B_{12}). Thiamine is essential for normal metabolism and for the health of the cardiovascular and nervous system. Riboflavin is important in the prevention of some visual disorders, primarily cataracts. Pyridoxine functions as an essential coenzyme for the synthesis and breakdown of amino acids, the conversion of tryptophan to niacin, the breakdown of glycogen to glucose, the production of antibodies, the formation of heme in hemoglobin, and the maintenance of the balance of sodium and potassium, which regulates body fluids and the functioning of the nervous and musculoskeletal systems. Cyanocobalamin is essential for the metabolism of protein, fats, and carbohydrates; normal blood formation; and neural function. Deficiency of cyanocobalamin is usually due to an absence of the intrinsic factor, which is necessary for its absorption. Lack of absorption of cyanocobalamin results in pernicious anemia. The B complex vitamins are not indicated for this client.
 4. Vitamin D is essential for the normal formation of bones and teeth and for the absorption of calcium and phosphorus from the gastrointestinal tract. Vitamin D is not indicated for this client.

#24 2. An Unna's paste boot is a gelatin-based bandage that is frequently used to treat the stasis ulcers that occur in a client with venous insufficiency.

An Ph/9 K

 1. A Jobst stocking is a custom-made support hose used to prevent venous stasis.
 3. An ace bandage also provides support to the extremity.
 4. A plaster of Paris bandage is a composition of a liquid and powder that hardens when it dries. It is used in shaping a cast to support a fractured bone as it heals.

#25. 4. Standing for long periods of time aggravates venous insufficiency and causes pain and venous congestion.

Im Ph/9 Ap

 1. Walking as tolerated is encouraged to promote venous return.
 2. There is no contraindication for sexual intercourse.
 3. Elevating the legs promotes venous return and should be done regularly as prescribed.

ANSWER	RATIONALE	NP	CN	CL

#26. 2. **Low weight is not a requirement for bone strength. It is indicated for persons with osteoarthritis.**   Pl   He/4   An

    1. Adequate calcium intake is necessary for bone strength at all ages but particularly in the elderly. Calcium intake should be started in childhood.

    3. Estrogen levels in premenopausal women play a role in preventing osteoporosis. Small amounts of estrogen may be taken after menopause as prescribed by the physician.

    4. Weight-bearing exercise is vital to maintaining bone strength. If there is no weight bearing, the calcium moves out of the bones.

#27. 3. **There is a loss of height in clients with osteoporosis.**   As   He/4   An

    1. Cramps after exercising do not relate to osteoporosis. Leg cramps related to exercising may indicate arterial insufficiency.

    2. Brittle hair and nails might be a sign of a nutritional deficiency such as iron deficiency anemia.

    4. Eating less food and still gaining weight is not seen with osteoporosis. It might indicate hypothyroidism. Many persons with osteoporosis are thin.

#28. 2. **Vitamin D is a fat-soluble vitamin essential for the normal formation of bones and teeth and for the absorption of calcium and phosphorus from the gastrointestinal tract. The vitamin is present in saltwater fish, sardines, organ meats, fish liver oils, and egg yolk. However, requirements are usually met from vitamin D fortified breads, milk, and dairy products, and by exposure to sunlight.**   Pl   He/4   An

    1. Vitamin A is a fat-soluble vitamin essential for skeletal growth, maintenance of normal mucosal epithelium, and visual acuity. It is derived from carotene and is present in leafy green vegetables, yellow fruits and vegetables, and fish, liver, milk, cheese, butter, and egg yolk.

    3. Vitamin E consists of a group of fat-soluble vitamins essential for normal reproduction, muscle development, and resistance of erythrocytes to hemolysis. Dietary sources are wheat germ, soybean, cottonseed, peanut and corn oils, margarine, raw seeds and nuts, eggs, butter, liver, sweet potato, and the leaves of many vegetables. Vitamin E is stored in the body for long periods of time, so deficiency is rare.

    4. Vitamin K is a group of fat-soluble vitamins essential for the synthesis of prothrombin in the liver and of several related proteins involved in the clotting of blood. Vitamin K is found in leafy green vegetables, pork liver, yogurt, egg yolk, alfalfa, and molasses.

#29. 1. **Smoking causes a decrease in bone density.**   As   He/4   Ap

    2. The client should also be encouraged to maintain a normal weight to avoid further stress on her bone structure. However, most persons with osteoporosis are thin.

    3. Nail biting is not related to osteoporosis.

    4. Skipping breakfast is not a good habit for anyone. A nutritious breakfast provides energy to begin the day and prevents the client from becoming famished and overeating at the next meal. However, it does not relate to the development of osteoporosis.

#30. 3. **Canned salmon is a good source of calcium if the bones are not removed.**   Ev   He/4   An

    1. Oatmeal is high in grains and roughage, but not calcium.

    2. Peaches are high in vitamin A and vitamin C, but not calcium.

    4. Flounder would be a good source of protein and vitamin A, but not calcium.

#31. 4. **The environment is an important factor in the prevention of injuries. Talking softly and providing quiet music have a calming effect on the agitated client.**   Pl   Sa/2   An

1. The client needs frequent visits by the staff to orient him and to assess his safety.
2. Phone calls from his family will not help a client who is trying to climb over the side rails and may even add to his danger.
3. Putting the client in a bright, busy area would probably add to his confusion.

#32. 4. The bulimic client's awareness of the inappropriateness of the eating pattern coupled with the client's inability to control eating activity indicate a lack of impulse control. — An — Ps/6 — An

1. The client with bulimia is not delusional. A paranoid client is delusional. Bulimia is a substance abuse problem where the abused substance is food.
2. Depersonalization is a feeling of strangeness or unreality concerning one's self or the environment. Bulimic clients do not have a feeling of depersonalization. Persons with schizophrenia may experience depersonalization.
3. Bulimic clients do not have a paranoid feeling of fear and suspicion of others.

#33. 3. Rigorous exercise regimens are seen in anorexia nervosa and are less likely in persons with bulimia. — As — Ps/6 — An

1. Crash dieting is common in bulimia.
2. Repeated weight fluctuations are common in persons with bulimia.
4. Self-induced vomiting is a characteristic of bulimia. Persons with bulimia engage in a repeated pattern of binge eating and purging (self-induced vomiting).

#34. 2. Antidepressants have been found to be the most promising pharmacologic treatment for bulimia. — Pl — Ph/8 — Ap

1. Anticonvulsant drugs are prescribed for seizure disorders and various neuropathies but are not indicated in bulimia.
3. Major tranquilizers, such as Thorazine, are given to persons with psychotic disorders such as schizophrenia. They are not indicated for bulimia.
4. Minor tranquilizers, such as Valium, are given to clients with anxiety disorders but are not indicated in the treatment of bulimia.

#35. 1. Gastrointestinal fluid has a high concentration of sodium. — As — Ph/10 — Ap
2. Water loss follows sodium loss, not the other way around.
3. Diarrhea is a problem in the intestinal tract. It does not trigger a reaction in the renal system.
4. Hyponatremia does not occur as a result of treatment of diarrhea. Treatment for diarrhea helps restore electrolyte balance.

#36. 4. The pain of arterial insufficiency is usually described by the client as an aching weakness in the lower extremities. — As — Ph/9 — An
1. The pain of arterial insufficiency is generally not incapacitating.
2. Symptoms usually include a sharp, cramping pain during exercise and even at rest.
3. The pain of arterial insufficiency is usually not described as mild. Aching weakness in the lower extremities is the most common description.

#37. 4. When the extremities of a client with peripheral arterial disease are elevated for 30 seconds, a cadaverous pallor (skin color is pale gray) often results. — An — Ph/9 — An
1. Persons with peripheral arterial disease do not have a normal color.
2. Dependent rubor is a sign of peripheral vascular disease (PVD).
3. Pregangrenous assessment would show cyanosis, cold skin, and absent pulses.

#38. 3. The nails of a client with PAD are often thick and hardened due to a lack of nutrients to the area. — As — Ph/9 — An
1. Skin over the extremities in a client with PAD would be thin, shiny, and hairless.
2. The client would have muscular atrophy.

ANSWER	RATIONALE	NP	CN	CL
4.	The skin would not be rough or reddened.			
#39. 1.	**Asking the client to lie in the prone position will provide greater exposure to the popliteal space and thereby make assessment easier.**	An	He/4	An
2.	The client probably will not be able to do jumping jacks.			
3.	Flexing and extending the foot may obliterate the pulse.			
4.	Elevating the leg in the presence of peripheral arterial disease would make assessment of the pulse more difficult.			
#40. 3.	**The diabetic client often experiences early atherosclerotic changes due to alterations in fat and carbohydrate metabolism.**	An	Ph/9	An
1.	Frequent hypoglycemic episodes do not cause vessel disease.			
2.	Capillary rupture does not cause peripheral arterial disease.			
4.	Fluctuating levels of insulin do not cause arterial disease.			
#41. 2.	**Decreased sensation can lead to injury or the client may be unaware of injury. Healing is slow in persons with peripheral arterial disease.**	An	Ph/9	An
1.	Diabetic neuropathy does not cause peripheral vessel dilation.			
3.	Diabetic neuropathy does not increase cardiac output.			
4.	Diabetic neuropathy does not alter renal function. Diabetic nephropathy is renal damage due to diabetes.			
#42. 2.	**The blood vessels of the skin constrict in response to impulses from the autonomic nervous system. This can result in dry, cracked skin when vascular constriction is of a long-standing nature.**	As	Ph/9	An
1.	Autonomic nerve damage includes decreased sweating. Peripheral vasoconstriction is caused by damage to autonomic nervous system. This results in pallor, not flushed, warm extremities.			
3.	Absent pulses indicate major arterial damage and may be present in advanced arterial disease.			
4.	Burning sensation on the soles of the feet is indicative of diabetic neuropathy with damage to the central nervous system.			
#43. 1.	**To prevent drying and cracking, only mild soaps should be used on the feet of the diabetic client.**	Pl	Ph/9	Ap
2.	Feet should be examined every day. Use a hand mirror for the bottom of the feet.			
3.	Feet should not be soaked in hot water because of the danger of burning the feet, especially since the client may have decreased sensation. Water temperature should be assessed by the elbow or an area of the body that has normal sensation to temperature, or with a bath thermometer.			
4.	Feet should be soaked in warm, not hot, water. There is no need to soak feet daily. Prolonged frequent soaking makes the skin too soft. Feet should be dried carefully, especially between the toes.			
#44. 4.	**The primary purpose of PCA is to allow clients to control their own IV pain medication. Current research shows that pain medication is more effective when it is given before the client's pain gets too intense.**	Pl	Ph/8	Ap
1.	Cost effectiveness is not the primary reason for its use.			
2.	Persons receiving PCA often require less pain medication because they are medicated before the pain is too intense. This is true but not the primary reason for its use.			
3.	The primary reason for using PCA is not to make nursing care easier to manage. The nurse must still assess the client for pain, pain control, and side effects of the pain medication.			
#45. 1.	**PCA requires that the client be alert enough to activate the system. A client who is mentally confused is not a good candidate for PCA.**	Pl	Ph/8	An
2.	The weight of the client has no relationship to ability to utilize PCA. Analgesic dosage can be determined to accommodate various weights.			

ANSWER	RATIONALE	NP	CN	CL

3. PCA is ideal for persons with intermittent pain because the person can activate the system and be medicated when it is needed. Constant pain is not a criteria for use of PCA.

4. The length of the surgical procedure has no bearing on whether the client can use PCA.

#46. 1. The risk of respiratory depression in a client receiving PCA is minimal because small doses are being given continuously, thus eliminating peaks in the serum drug levels.   An   Ph/8   An

2. PCA uses the usual postoperative analgesic drugs, which do have respiratory side effects.

3. The client may receive less total medication. However, the primary reason for reduced risk of respiratory depression is the elimination of peaks that occur when IM medication is given.

4. There may be intervals when the client receives no medication. This is not the reason that the risk of respiratory depression is decreased.

#47. 1. Leg massages are contraindicated for deep vein thrombosis or persons at risk for deep vein thrombosis because of the danger of dislodging part of the clot and causing it to become an embolus.   Pl   He/4   Ap

2. Elastic stockings are appropriate to help prevent deep vein thrombosis.

3. Elevating the legs aids venous return to the heart and helps prevent venous stasis and deep vein thrombosis.

4. Active or passive leg exercises should be done regularly to help prevent deep vein thrombosis. However, if the nurse suspects thrombosis, the client should be placed on bed rest.

#48. 3. Clients with deep vein thrombosis must be on bed rest. Dangling on the side of the bed would promote movement of the clot and formation of additional clots by putting pressure on the leg veins.   Im   Ph/9   Ap

1. Straining at stool causes Valsalva maneuver, which could dislodge the clot from the vessel wall.

2. Sudden movements may dislodge the clot.

4. The legs should not be jarred or bumped as this may dislodge the clot.

#49. 1. Protamine sulfate is the antidote for heparin. Vitamin K is the antidote for Coumadin.   Im   Ph/8   Ap

2. The nurse should observe for hematomas at IV puncture sites. Heparin is an anticoagulant. Hematoma formation indicates overdose.

3. Heparin is an anticoagulant. Using a soft bristled toothbrush will reduce the likelihood of bleeding gums.

4. Heparin must be administered via an IV control device to prevent overdose.

#50. 3. Pulmonary embolism causes a decrease in perfusion due to obstruction of the vascular system from the clot. Ventilation will be normal.   An   Ph/9   An

1. Ventilation will be normal in the absence of other lung disease.

2. Pulmonary embolism causes a decrease in perfusion due to obstruction of the vascular system from the clot. Ventilation will be normal.

4. Pulmonary embolism causes a decrease in perfusion due to obstruction of the vascular system from the diet. Ventilation will be normal.

#51. 2. In 90% of child physical abuse cases, the abuser is a relative whom the child trusts.   An   Ps/6   An

1. Children are not most frequently abused by a babysitter.

3. Children are not most frequently abused by a teacher.

4. Children are not most frequently abused by a casual acquaintance.

#52. 2. **The family that owns their own home provides some stability and is less likely to be at risk for abusing their children.** | As | Ps/6 | An

    1. Risk factors in child abuse include isolation, unemployment, geographic changes, poverty, and homelessness.

    3. A family in which there is separation or divorce is at higher risk for child abuse.

    4. A setting where a family member has a chronic illness exhibits a greater risk of child abuse.

#53. 1. **A Pap smear does not detect sexual abuse. A Pap smear detects changes in cells that may indicate cancer and precancer changes.** | As | Ps/6 | An

    2. A urinalysis is done to detect hematuria, and a urine culture is done to detect the presence of STDs.

    3. A throat culture is done to detect the presence of sperm and STDs.

    4. Cultures of the vagina, urethra, and rectum are done to detect sperm and STDs.

#54. 4. **Using words the child uses to describe body parts ensures that the child understands what is being said.** | Im | Ps/6 | Ap

    1. The nurse should ask the child to describe things in her own words.

    2. The parents should not be present during the interview. If the parents are the abusers, the child will not feel free to speak out.

    3. No one should be present during the interview except the nurse so the child will feel free to express her feelings.

#55. 4. **The child who survives physical abuse is likely to develop into a dysfunctional adult. These children are generally not academic achievers.** | An | Ps/6 | An

    1. Children who have survived physical abuse often show signs of depression.

    2. Children who have survived physical abuse often become drug abusers.

    3. Children who have survived physical abuse are highly likely to become abusive parents because this is the only model of discipline that they have known growing up.

#56. 2. **Demonstrating explicit sexual activity is not within the normal four-year-old's realm of understanding. These are acts that could only have been known through actual experience.** | An | Ps/6 | An

    1. If the child had seen this acted out on TV she would not have understood it well enough to act it out in play.

    3. This type of play is not a healthy expression of sexual development in any age child.

    4. Observation of this action will help the nurse be able to explore feelings with the child.

#57. 1. **The primary goal is to prevent further abuse and to ensure the child's safety. Taking a wait-and-see stance can prove deleterious to the child.** | Im | Ps/6 | An

    2. Calling a local social service agency for help is an appropriate nursing intervention.

    3. Preventing a child's return to a dangerous environment is an appropriate nursing intervention.

    4. When the situation indicates, the nurse may confront the parent in a nonjudgmental, nonpunitive manner with a security guard present.

#58. 4. **The age at which sexual activity began it not relevant as it does not usually provide information that identifies the presence of risk factors for AIDS.** | As | Sa/2 | Ap

    1. Drug use is a risk factor for AIDS.

    2. Multiple sex partners is a risk factor for AIDS.

    3. Birth control methods are important to prevent a baby from being born with the AIDS virus.

#59. 4. **Great progress has been made recently in the treatment of PCP, and research is continuing.** | Pl | Ph/9 | An

    1.   PCP can usually be treated successfully now.

    2.   The client has typical symptoms of pneumonia, which are even more severe due to the client's immune deficiencies.

    3.   It is not highly contagious in a person with an intact immune system.

#60. 3.   Pentamidine (Pentam) is used in the treatment of *Pneumocystis carinii* pneumonia.   Pl   Ph/8   An

    1.   Amphotericin B (Fungazone) is an antifungal drug used in treating histoplasmosis, candidiasis, meningitis, septicemia, and other skin infections.

    2.   Ethambutol (Myambutol) is an antitubercular drug used in combination with other drugs in the treatment of pulmonary tuberculosis.

    4.   Zidovudine (formerly asidothymidine or AZT) is an antiviral drug that inhibits replication of the HIV virus by interfering with the transcription of RNA and DNA. Zidovudine is used in symptomatic HIV infections.

#61. 4.   The direct introduction of bacteria into the bloodstream increases the risk of the IV drug user developing infective endocarditis.   An   Ph/9   An

    1.   Arrhythmias would not increase the risk of endocarditis.

    2.   Increasing the workload of the heart does not increase the risk of endocarditis.

    3.   This would not increase the client's chance of getting endocarditis. It makes it more difficult to treat.

#62. 1.   Counseling may be insufficient to obtain desired behaviors when the negative consequences seem distant. Objectives must take into consideration the life-style of the individual and where changes can be made with the client's cooperation. Therefore, quitting the drug addiction can be unrealistic or inappropriate for clients seeking only care for their medical problems.   Pl   Ps/6   An

    2.   The client should be able to cooperate with goals while at the facility.

    3.   The client should be able to learn to clean the drug equipment, but there is of course no guarantee that he will continue to do so in the future.

    4.   It would be appropriate for the client to remain for the full treatment course.

#63. 4.   The signs of endocarditis include shortness of breath and chest pain.   As   Ph/9   An

    1.   Infective endocarditis includes bacterial endocarditis (ABE) and subacute bacterial endocarditis (SBE). Murmurs are often present in SBE. These murmurs are usually mild to moderate in intensity and change in character from day to day. These variations represent the growth and fragmentation of the valvular vegetations.

    2.   A high fever would generally be present in endocarditis.

    3.   Endocarditis is characterized by tachycardia but not hypertension.

#64. 2.   Visual acuity is not assessed during a baseline neurological exam. Moreover, it is impossible to assess visual acuity in an unconscious client.   As   Ph/9   An

    1.   Assessment of motor function is part of a neurological exam.

    3.   Vital signs are part of a neurological exam.

    4.   Level of consciousness should be assessed, including pupillary response to light and ocular movements.

#65. 2.   Pregnancy makes metabolic control of diabetes more difficult. It is essential that the client start prenatal care early so that potential complications can be controlled or minimized by the efforts of the client and health care team.   Pl   He/3   An

    1.   A review of dietary modifications is important once the woman is pregnant. However, it is not of primary importance when considering pregnancy.

3. The alternative of adoption is not necessary just because the client is a diabetic. Many diabetic women have pregnancies with successful outcomes if they receive good care.

4. While there is some risk to the pregnant diabetic woman, it is not considered a major health risk. The greater risk is to the fetus.

#66. 2. The woman of average size should gain between 25 and 30 pounds during her pregnancy.   Pl   He/3   Ap

1. Ten to 15 pounds is not enough weight to gain to support an average-sized baby of between 6 and 9 pounds.

3. Forty pounds is too much weight to gain and would make the pregnancy more difficult for the mother.

4. The weight of the baby plus 3 pounds is not enough weight. This means the mother is actually losing weight because there is additional weight in the placenta, amniotic fluid, and mother's increased blood volume.

#67. 4. The recommended diet for diabetes is high-fiber, low-fat. The pregnant diabetic should follow a high-fiber, moderate-fat diet with adequate amounts of protein.   Ev   Ph/7   Ap

1. She should not eat a low-protein, low-salt diet. Pregnant women need significant amounts of protein for the growth of the baby. Sodium is not restricted.

2. Additional complex carbohydrates need to be added throughout the pregnancy. Her intake of simple carbohydrates should be limited.

3. Increased water is a good idea during pregnancy to prevent constipation but is not the primary understanding she needs.

#68. 1. The goal of insulin administration in a diabetic is to maintain the client's blood sugar as near to a normal level as possible, 80 to 110 mg/dl.   Ev   Ph/9   Ap

2. 150 to 200 mg/dl is too high a blood glucose level and is dangerous for the baby.

3. 200 to 250 mg/dl is too high a blood glucose level and is dangerous for the baby.

4. 300 mg/dl is too high a blood sugar level.

#69. 4. Sweating is a symptom of hypoglycemia. Pregnant women also perspire because of the increased metabolic rate during pregnancy.   An   Ph/9   An

1. Lethargy is a sign of hyperglycemia.

2. Polyuria is a sign of hyperglycemia.

3. Thirst is a sign of hyperglycemia.

#70. 1. The metabolic demands on the mother during labor and delivery are great, and glucose may be insufficient to meet these demands. Blood sugars will be monitored every hour during labor and delivery to detect hypoglycemia.   An   Ph/9   An

2. The metabolic demands of labor and delivery are likely to produce hypoglycemia rather than hyperglycemia.

3. Although it would be very unlikely, a diabetic mother could develop metabolic acidosis because of the buildup of acetone from fat metabolism, but she would not develop metabolic alkalosis.

4. The client would not develop hyperosmolar nonketotic coma (HHNK). The insulin-dependent diabetic develops acidosis due to buildup of ketone bodies when hyperglycemia occurs. HHNK is seen in Type II diabetics, not Type I, and occurs with hyperglycemia rather than hypoglycemia, which usually occurs during labor.

#71. 4. Manic depressive illness is a biochemically related mental disorder that responds well to antimanic drugs such as Lithium and Tegretol. Delusions of grandeur such as seen in Mr. T. are common symptoms of this brain disorder.   An   Ps/6   An

1. High levels of anxiety in persons without bipolar illness do not cause delusions.

2. Compliance with medications such as Lithium, Tegretol, and a combination of such drugs with antipsychotics help to control delusions. Anxiolytics (anti-anxiety agents) do not affect delusional thinking.

3. Delusions of grandeur are not due to a conscious desire to impress others but are a symptom of bipolar illness. The defense mechanism of reaction formation is operating in this case.

#72. 1. **Within one week, there may be minimal to moderate changes in thought process, depending on the client's diagnosed mental illness. An appropriate goal is for the client to feel less threatened and less anxious, lessening the requirement for delusional thought. If the client is compliant with psychotropic medications, he/she may respond positively by decreased frequency and intensity of delusions after one week of medications.** Pl Ps/5 Ap

2. Verbalizing why delusions are used to deal with life is a long-term goal. It also requires insight. Depending on the mental illness, insight may or may not be possible because it calls for abstract thinking.

3. Communicating only in reality-oriented terms is unrealistic for a short-term goal of one week. In some clients, this may never be fully achieved.

4. Recognizing delusions as nonreality-based statements is not an appropriate short-term goal. Perhaps it can be achieved as a long-term goal.

#73. 1. **Within one week, the client should be able to describe one positive attribute of himself. There is an emphasis on being rather than doing.** Pl Ps/5 Ap

2. It may not be possible for the client to attend and fully participate in all groups and therapeutic activities due to symptoms of depression such as decreased concentration, a markedly diminished interest in pleasurable activities, and psychomotor retardation or agitation.

3. Verbalizing to the nurse the ability to solve problems is unrealistic for one week and may take a long time to accept due to altered thoughts of failure and pessimism.

4. Verbalizing to the nurse that he feels good enough to run the next community meeting is unrealistic in one week. However, it may be possible later as self-esteem improves. Activities such as community involvement provide opportunities to enhance self-esteem.

#74. 2. **A delusion of reference is a fixed false belief that events or people are directly related to the individual person.** As Ps/5 An

1. Thought broadcasting is a disturbance in thought pattern in which the individual thinks everyone can hear his thoughts.

3. Thought insertion is a disturbance in thought patterns in which the client thinks thoughts of others are being placed in his mind.

4. A delusion of persecution is a fixed false belief that others are attempting to harm a person.

#75. 2. **If the client can develop coping skills to deal with his anxiety, it is more likely he will be able to gradually recall his trauma.** Im Ps/6 Ap

1. Planning a trip to the airport is an interdisciplinary staff decision. It is not an appropriate nursing decision.

3. Insisting that a client with amnesia try to remember is not therapeutic and may traumatize the client more.

4. Telling the client it is all right to be anxious and doing nothing does not help the client adjust to the situation or reduce the anxiety.

#76. 3. **Agoraphobia is the fear of open or public places. The client is improving when he/she can shop alone at a mall without anxiety, which usually accompanies the disorder.** Ev Ps/6 Ap

1. Being able to offer complaints to the boss regarding workload is an example of improvement in a social phobia.

ANSWER	RATIONALE	NP	CN	CL

2. Being able to travel five flights on an elevator is an example of improvement of a simple phobia.

4. Not washing hands after touching a dirty object is an example of improvement of a compulsion.

#77. 3. Stating he knows he must never drink alcohol again shows that the client is aware that he must remain abstinent for life. This is essential to his recovery.   Ev   Ps/6   Ap

1. Stating he can drink on special holidays indicates he does not understand that he should never drink again.

2. Attending 90 AA meetings in 90 days may be a part of his recovery. However, it is short range. It does not indicate understanding of the long-term nature of his addiction.

4. An alcoholic is never cured. He may be rehabilitated, but the disease is still present.

#78. 3. Drug onset with tricyclic antidepressants begins between seven and ten days after initial treatment with full effects taking up to one month. Gradual improvements will take place during the month of treatment in clients who will respond to tricyclic antidepressants.   An   Ph/8   Ap

1. It is too early to decide if the client will not respond to the tricyclic medication.

2. Electroconvulsive therapy is not recommended at this time. Adequate time to determine a positive effect with medications is the conservative treatment of choice.

4. Sufficient time for a response to medications has not been allowed, thus a second opinion is not yet warranted.

#79. 4. Autonomic dysreflexia is an emergency situation and the priority is to lower the blood pressure. The initial action is to place the client in a sitting position, which lowers the blood pressure.   Im   Ph/10   Ap

1. A major symptom is severe headache due to the hypertension. The initial action is to lower the blood pressure, not treat the headache.

2. Instruction on prevention of further episodes is given after the acute episode is treated and the client is safe. It is not the initial action.

3. The rectum will be examined for a fecal mass that may be causing the problem after the symptoms have subsided. Examining the rectum may aggravate the symptoms.

#80. 3. Intravenous fluids are necessary post-op to maintain fluid and electrolyte balance and as a route for medications. The intravenous infusion will be left in until fluids can be taken by mouth.   Ev   Ph/9   Ap

1. The client can anticipate pain but knows that medication will be available to relieve it.

2. Vital signs are taken frequently post-op as part of assessment.

4. Deep breathing and coughing are done post-op to promote lung ventilation, blood oxygenation, and mobilization of lung secretions.

#81. 2. The principle of the constant carbohydrate diet is to keep the CHO intake consistent by times of day, each day. But the "dessert" may differ considerably in content from day to day. This part of her statement needs correction or clarification.   Ev   Ph/9   Ap

1. Most children can detect low blood sugar by symptoms but can also find behavior changes frustrating, since it appears in the early stages of both hypo- and hyperglycemia. The girl has found a safe way to manage the problem.

3. She has described correct insulin injection techniques and indicates a correct understanding of the reason for pinching the skin. If she needs to use areas of her body that have fewer fat cells, she could change the angle of the injection to more of a 45-degree than a 90-degree angle.

4. A quick glucose source needs to be easily accessible for the child. Life Savers and regular soft drinks from machines require having money

available to use. Good-tasting candies are tempting at times other than during hypoglycemia episodes. She has described a good plan.

#82. 4.   **A positive family history is a risk factor for gallbladder disease, including cholecystitis and cholelithiasis.**   As   Ph/9   Ap

    1.   A high-fat, or high-cholesterol, diet is a risk factor. A low-fat diet is often ordered as conservative treatment for gallbladder disease. Fasting is contraindicated, however, as it allows stasis of gallbladder contents, increasing the risk of stone formation.

    2.   Sedentary life-style contributes to the risk of gallbladder disease. Exercise reduces the risk. A change in the pattern of exercise would not change the level of risk.

    3.   Oral contraceptives and other forms of estrogen increase the risk of gallbladder disease, as does pregnancy. Oral hypoglycemic agents are not known to alter the risk of gallbladder disease.

#83. 2.   **The continuous use of the elastic pressure garment is designed to reduce vascularity and cellularity of the scar tissue and promote the growth of soft, pale scar tissue that is free of collagen nodules.**   Ev   Ph/9   Ap

    1.   A red, raised wound indicates the development of hypertrophic scars. The continuous use of the elastic pressure garment is designed to reduce vascularity and cellularity and promote growth of soft, pale scar tissue.

    3.   A hard, raised shiny scar that may extend beyond the wound area is characteristic of keloid formation. Keloids tend to occur in darkly pigmented persons and may recur following surgical excision.

    4.   An open, pink, and draining wound indicates failure to heal. Inadequate nutrition often is a factor in failure to heal.

#84. 4.   **The shampoo loosens the nits and kills the adult lice. The fine-toothed comb pulls the nit from the hair shaft. If there are nits remaining after the combing, tweezers or fingernails can be used to dislodge them.**   Ev   He/4   An

    1.   People from all socioeconomic groups, ages, and environments get head lice.

    2.   It is only necessary to wash articles and linens with which the child has had contact. Water temperature should be around 140°F. Clothes can be put into the dryer on a hot cycle.

    3.   One shampoo is sufficient with some brands of pediculocides; others require one shampoo followed by another one 7–10 days later. After the initial shampoo and nit removal, the child can resume school but needs daily inspection for newly laid nits for 2 weeks after the shampoo treatment.

#85. 2.   **The infant's feeding schedule should be maintained since phenylalanine is an essential amino acid that is converted into tyrosine by the enzyme phenylalanine hydroxylase. Therefore, protein in the diet is necessary to see if phenylalanine is converted.**   Im   He/4   An

    1.   The infant should not be NPO. A diet containing protein must be ingested before the test.

    3.   The test cannot be done within 8 hours of delivery. The infant must have eaten protein. The recommendation is that the neonate be tested after it is 72 hours old.

    4.   Water may be given if the infant wants it, but it is not a prerequisite. Protein via formula or breast milk is needed.

#86. 2.   **A diet low in phenylalanine is necessary for an indefinite period of time. Experts vary as to how long the diet must be continued: at least 6 years and maybe for life.**   Ev   He/4   Ap

    1.   Experts vary as to how long the diet must be continued: at least 6 years and maybe for life. The disease is an inborn error of metabolism and will never be cured.

ANSWER	RATIONALE	NP	CN	CL

3. There is currently no medicine available to treat phenylketonuria.

4. The diet must be very low in phenylalanine. Some phenylalanine is necessary for growth. It is extremely difficult to eliminate all phenylalanine from the diet.

#87. 4. The diaphragm should be left in at least six hours after the last intercourse to let the spermicidal cream or jelly work. Ev He/3 Ap

1. Vaseline should not be used with latex-based products because it can cause breakdown of the latex.

2. The diaphragm should be refitted after a weight loss or gain of 25 pounds or more.

3. Spermicide should be applied around the rim of the diaphragm and at least one tablespoonful should be placed inside the dome.

#88. 4. Because of the albumin in the influenza vaccine, it should not be given to individuals who are allergic to eggs or egg products. As He/4 Co

1. Mental status is not essential to assess before administering a flu shot.

2. It is not essential to assess the gastrointestinal system before administering a flu shot.

3. It is not essential to assess the skin (integumentary system) before administering a flu shot.

#89. 1. The exam should be performed when the scrotum is relaxed. After a warm bath or shower may be the most convenient time. Im He/4 Ap

2. The scrotum may not be relaxed enough to perform an accurate exam. The client cannot visualize the testes in a mirror while in bed. This is part of the exam.

3. The scrotum may not be relaxed enough to perform an accurate exam.

4. The scrotum may not be relaxed enough to perform an accurate exam.

#90. 2. If the airway is open and breaths are being delivered correctly, then the chest is rising and falling. Oxygen must be delivered to the lungs. This is the most important factor during CPR. Ev Ph/10 Ap

1. Feeling the carotid pulse may be an indication of correct cardiac compression technique, but airway and breathing must be established first so that oxygen can be circulated with compressions.

3. Blood gases give indications of oxygen status, but they do not directly indicate the effectiveness of CPR technique and are less important while administering CPR.

4. The ECG rhythm may show cardiac compressions, but the airway and delivery of oxygen are the more important factors.

#91. 1. As the skin ages, there is an increase in melanin. These are commonly called "age spots." As He/3 Co

2. The epidermis thins as a person ages.

3. The number of hair follicles decreases with aging.

4. There is less subcutaneous tissue as a person ages.

#92. 3. Monitoring for infection includes several steps. When the client has had a total joint replacement, the nurse must place high priority on careful monitoring of vital signs as a means of detecting infection that is not otherwise visible or obvious. Ev Ph/9 Ap

1. Nutritional status is not the best indicator of infection.

2. Hemoglobin and hematocrit give information about bleeding but are not the best indicators of infection.

4. Drainage from the incision might be indicative of infection; however, temperature changes would occur more quickly and more consistently than wound drainage.

#93. 3. The major complication of peritoneal dialysis is peritonitis. Cloudy or opaque effluent is the earliest sign of peritonitis. Other signs of infection include fever, rebound abdominal tenderness, malaise, nausea, and vomiting. Ev Ph/9 Ap

1. Pain during inflow of dialysate is common during the first few exchanges. It gets less with time. Warming dialysate bags helps to relieve discomfort.
2. Constipation is a major cause of inflow and outflow disturbances. Clients should be on a high-fiber diet and stool softeners. Occasional diarrhea is not a symptom of a complication of dialysis.
4. The effluent in peritoneal dialysis should be clear or light yellow.

#94. 4. A PPD skin test should be given intradermally. When injected properly, the PPD will form a tense, white wheal just beneath the surface of the skin. If a wheal does not form, the inoculate was injected too deeply and the test results will be invalid. Im He/4 Co
1. A 90-degree angle is appropriate for an intramuscular injection.
2. A 45-degree angle is appropriate for a subcutaneous injection.
3. This is totally inappropriate for anything.

#95. 4. Indurations of 10 mm or more are considered significant and highly suggestive of tuberculosis. The client needs further assessment before the disease can be confirmed or ruled out. Indurations of 5–9 mm are inconclusive and should probably be repeated in another site. If the client is at high risk for tuberculosis, these may be interpreted as suspicious. Indurations less than 5 mm are not significant and erythema is always insignificant. Im He/4 An
1. PPD tests are read at 48 and 72 hours.
2. Indurations less than 5 mm are considered insignificant. Erythema is always insignificant.
3. Tuberculosis is common in Honduras, but that does not mean the client has it. Indurations less than 5 mm are considered insignificant.

#96. 4. Suctioning should only be applied when withdrawing the catheter from the airway while rotating the catheter to prevent damage to the tracheal mucosa. Im Ph/9 Ap
1. Suctioning a tracheostomy is a sterile procedure, not a clean procedure.
2. The suction should not be applied while inserting the suction catheter. It should only be applied when withdrawing the catheter from the airway while rotating the catheter to prevent damage to the tracheal mucosa.
3. The client should be hyperoxygenated both before and after suctioning.

#97. 3. Clamping the central venous line tubing when changing tubing prevents air embolism and blood backup. Im Ph/9 Ap
1. Cleaning the insertion site may help to prevent infection but does not prevent air embolism.
2. The TPN line is primed before the tubing is attached to the existing line.
4. Clamping the central venous line tubing when changing tubing prevents air embolism and blood backup. Placing an alcohol wipe over the end of the tubing does not prevent air embolism.

#98. 2. The sternal notch or Angle of Louis identifies the second rib and thereby assists in locating the fourth intercostal space where the lead should be placed. Im Ph/9 Ap
1. McBurney's point is in right lower abdominal quadrant where the appendix is at the junction of the ileum and the cecum.
3. The suprasternal notch, above the sternum, is not the site of electrode placement for this lead.
4. Costovertebral angle refers to the joining of a rib and a vertebra. These sites on the back are not the site for electrode placement.

#99. 2. This choice shows a low-fat soup (which would have been higher in fat if made with chicken or beef stock) and high-fiber bread and soup contents (both the vegetables and the legumes). Ev Ph/7 An

1. Mayonnaise in tuna salad is high in fat. The whole wheat bread has some fiber.
3. Salad is high in fiber, but hard boiled eggs are high in fat.
4. There is some fiber in the apples and walnuts. The walnuts are high in fat, as is the chicken.

#100. 3. The schedule for mammogram testing recommended by the American Cancer Society is a baseline between the ages of 35–40; once every 1–2 years between 40 and 50; and every year after age 50.   Im   He/4   Co

1. Mammograms can detect tumors and other breast lesions when they are still too small to be palpated (i.e., smaller than 1 cm). There is a documented false negative rate of 5–10%. A client should not be promised nearly 100% accuracy.
2. There is no known correlation between sexual activity and breast cancer. A sexually active woman under 35 would not need a mammogram unless there was a strong family history of cancer or she had symptoms.
4. Mammograms do not use contrast media.

Practice Test 7

1. An adult client has been taking aluminum hydroxide (Amphojel) for hyperphosphatemia. It is most important for the nurse to teach the client
   1. to inform the physician if he has constipation.
   2. the tablets tend to be more effective than the liquid.
   3. to take large amounts of water to ensure passage of the medication to the stomach.
   4. to report signs of muscle weakness, anorexia, and malaise.

2. An adult client has chronic idiopathic hypoparathyroidism. Which of the following is not appropriate to include in the nursing care plan?
   1. Low-calcium, high-phosphorus diet.
   2. Oral calcium (Os-Cal) for chronic hypocalcemia.
   3. Seizure precautions.
   4. Private room to reduce environmental stimuli.

3. Ms. E. has hyperthyroidism and is scheduled for a thyroidectomy. The physician has ordered Lugol's solution for the client. The nurse understands that the primary reason for giving Lugol's solution preoperatively is to
   1. decrease the risk of agranulocytosis postoperatively.
   2. prevent tetany while the client is under general anesthesia.
   3. reduce the size and vascularity of the thyroid and prevent hemorrhage.
   4. potentiate the effect of the other preoperative medication so less medicine can be given while the client is under anesthesia.

4. The nurse is caring for a client who had a thyroidectomy this morning. The nurse must monitor for possible adverse effects. Which of the following is least likely to occur in this client?
   1. Chovstek's sign.
   2. Laryngeal damage.
   3. Brudzinski's sign.
   4. Trousseau's sign.

5. Mrs. M. is a 68-year-old widow whose husband died six months ago. Which of the following actions best indicates to the nurse that Mrs. M. is making progress in resocialization?
   1. She does biweekly grocery shopping.
   2. She has stopped attending a widow support group.
   3. She babysits her two grandchildren whenever asked.
   4. She participates in a local senior citizen group.

6. Mrs. M. is a 68-year-old resident in a long-term care facility with a medical diagnosis of organic brain syndrome. Her mental status assessment documents an untidy, suspicious,

easily agitated woman who speaks in nonsense syllables. In caring for Mrs. M., the nurse should anticipate which of the following nursing actions to promote socialization?
1. Limiting visitation by family and friends.
2. Utilizing the pet-animal companion program.
3. Discussing the need for a speech therapist.
4. Touching the client only when necessary.

7. In completing an assessment of an elderly client who has been a victim of abuse, the nurse knows that the elder who is at highest risk is
1. a Caucasian female who is physically or cognitively impaired.
2. a Caucasian male who has a physical disability.
3. an African-American female whose physical or mental conditions cause dependency on family members.
4. an African-American male whose cognitive impairment causes behavioral problems.

8. Which of the following would best indicate to the nurse that a client is depressed?
1. Feelings of worthlessness.
2. Poor hygiene and grooming.
3. Intense anxiety.
4. Thought insertion.

9. The nurse in an outpatient mental health clinic has identified marital discord as a significant problem for one of the clients. A client with this type of problem would be most likely to be dealing with issues in which developmental phase?
1. Trust vs. mistrust.
2. Identity vs. role confusion.
3. Intimacy vs. isolation.
4. Generativity vs. stagnation.

10. Which of the following statements best indicates that the client understands the nurse's teaching about effective coping mechanisms?
1. "Talking to you really helped me put things into perspective."
2. "Talking to you really helped me solve my problems."
3. "I don't have time at home to do the relaxation techniques."
4. "The relaxation techniques helped me to go right to sleep."

11. A 45-year-old male was admitted to the chemical dependency unit with a history of daily alcohol use for the past 15 years. Which of the following nursing diagnoses should the admitting nurse select to be the primary focus during the initial phase of his treatment?
1. Sensory/perceptual alteration related to withdrawal seizures secondary to alcohol cessation.
2. High risk for injury related to suicidal thoughts secondary to alcohol cessation.
3. Ineffective denial related to inability to identify effect of alcohol on life secondary to alcohol use.
4. High risk for injury related to withdrawal seizures secondary to alcohol cessation.

12. The labor and delivery unit called report on Ms. A., who delivered a full-term live baby girl 2 hours ago via spontaneous vaginal delivery. She had a first-degree laceration, which was repaired. She plans to breast feed. Both mother and infant will be coming to the mother baby unit. What should the nurse expect will be included in the care plan?
1. Keep the client NPO for 24 hours.
2. An order for ice packs to the breasts.
3. An order for ice packs to the perineum PRN for 4 hours.
4. An indwelling catheter that will remain in place for 12 hours.

13. The nurse has been giving a mother who is at risk for having a baby with Rh incompatibility instruction about preventing isoimmune hemolytic disease in future neonates. Which statement indicates that she understands the need for Rho(D) immune globulin in the future?
1. The mother asks when her baby will get the shot.
2. The mother verbalizes a need for a shot after donating blood.
3. The mother verbalizes a need for a shot after giving birth to an Rh-positive baby.
4. The mother verbalizes a need for a shot after breast feeding.

14. A client who is 25 weeks pregnant with no previous medical or obstetrical problems is admitted to the hospital in premature labor. The nurse can expect that orders for this client, in addition to bed rest, will include which of the following?
1. A fetal monitor and a tocolytic.
2. A fetal monitor and a tranquilizer.
3. A maternal cardiac monitor and fluid therapy.
4. A fetal monitor and a maternal cardiac monitor.

15. Upon admission, a 64-year-old woman tells the nurse that she has "weak blood" but doesn't know the name of her disease. She has been taking vitamin B_{12} injections for five years. The nurse explains that vitamin B_{12} is the drug management for which type of anemia?
1. Iron deficiency anemia.
2. Aplastic anemia.
3. Pernicious anemia.
4. Hemolytic anemia.

16. A 56-year-old woman has been admitted with possible pernicious anemia. Various diagnostic tests are ordered. The nurse

understands that the definitive test for pernicious anemia is
1. a positive Schilling test.
2. a gastric analysis with decreased free HCl acid.
3. a bone marrow biopsy showing abnormal erythrocyte and defective leukocyte maturation.
4. an elevated LDH.

17. An adult male is hospitalized for urolithiasis. A stone he passed in his urine was sent to the laboratory this morning. The lab identifies the stone as an oxalate stone. Which of the following modifications should the nurse teach him to make in his diet?
1. Limit milk and dairy products.
2. Limit his intake of tea, chocolate, and spinach.
3. Eat an acid ash diet to keep his urine acidic.
4. Limit food high in purine.

18. The nurse is teaching a 17-year-old male how to perform a testicular self-exam. Which of the following is an abnormal finding that indicates he should see his physician?
1. His left testis hangs lower than his right testis.
2. His testes feel smooth, rubbery, and oval shaped.
3. His left testis is larger than his right testis.
4. His testes are slightly tender when he examines them.

19. An adult is in acute renal failure and must undergo hemodialysis. Of the following medications, which one must the nurse withhold prior to dialysis?
1. NPH insulin.
2. Pilocarpine.
3. Dipyridamole (Persantine).
4. Cholestyramine (Questran).

20. The nurse is monitoring an adult who is undergoing hemodialysis. The client suddenly becomes cyanotic and complains of dyspnea and chest pain. His blood pressure is 70/40 and his pulse is weak and rapid. The nurse calls the physician immediately because the signs and symptoms suggest which complication of dialysis?
1. Disequilibrium syndrome.
2. Air embolism.
3. Internal bleeding.
4. Hemorrhage at the shunt.

21. Mr. R. has urolithiasis and is being treated conservatively in hopes that surgery will not be necessary. The nurse should plan to
1. provide fluid intake of 3000 ml or more.
2. restrict citrus juices and milk products.
3. insert an indwelling catheter as ordered.
4. administer ordered narcotic analgesics whenever the client requests them.

22. Prior to discharge, the client with COPD will need to be taught self-care. The nurse should plan to include which of the following in the instructions given to the client?
1. Increase the oxygen flow rate to 4 l/min. when you plan to exercise.
2. Stay indoors if possible when the weather is very cold.
3. Limit fluid intake to 200 ml or less.
4. When short of breath, sit in a recliner chair with the backrest at a 45- to 60-degree angle.

23. Mr. S. has developed dumping syndrome following a subtotal gastrectomy. Which of the following should the nurse include in the plan of care for Mr. S.?
1. Sit upright for at least 30 minutes after meals.
2. Take sips of fluid between bites of solid food.
3. Eat something every 2 to 3 hours.
4. Reduce the amount of simple carbohydrate in the diet.

24. An adult client is scheduled for a variety of tests for diarrhea and other gastrointestinal complaints. The doctor has ordered an antacid PRN for upset stomach. Which antacid is least likely to be ordered for this client because it may have a laxative effect?
1. Aluminum hydroxide (Amphogel).
2. Kaopectate.
3. Magnesium hydroxide (MOM).
4. Dihydroxy-aluminum sodium carbonate (Rolaids).

25. An adult client is admitted for bowel surgery. The nurse teaches the client what to expect in preparation for surgery. Which is least likely to be included in the nurse's explanation?
1. Cleansing enemas will be given the night before surgery.
2. Antibiotics are given three to five days preoperatively to decrease bacteria in the intestine.
3. A nasogastric tube will be inserted on the morning of surgery.
4. Laxatives will be given the morning of surgery to relax the bowel.

26. An adult woman is recovering from rectal surgery. She tells the nurse that she has always eaten a lot of bran to help keep her bowel movements regular and does not understand why she needs to take any medicine for her bowels. The nurse explains that the doctor has ordered Colace, which acts to
1. attract and hold large amounts of fluids, thereby increasing the bulk of stools.
2. coat the feces with an oily film and prevent the colon from reabsorbing water from the feces.
3. prevent straining during defecation and prevent constipation by decreasing surface tension of feces.
4. stimulate peristalsis.

27. An adult client is diagnosed with a hiatal hernia. He has listed all of the following on his admission form. Which activity is most likely to be aggravating his condition?
    1. Experiencing added stress because he gave up smoking recently.
    2. Lying down and falling asleep on the couch after a big dinner each evening.
    3. Taking an antacid before and after each meal.
    4. Eating six small meals a day.
28. When planning care for the client during the immediate postoperative period after a total laryngectomy, it is most important for the nurse to include
    1. provision of a nonverbal means of communication.
    2. positioning the client on the side with the head of the bed flat.
    3. administering cough suppressants.
    4. suctioning the tracheostomy every 4 hours.
29. The nurse is planning care for an adult client who is receiving chemotherapy for cancer. Which side effect should the nurse anticipate because it is the most common for clients receiving cancer chemotherapy?
    1. Nausea and vomiting.
    2. Cardiac arrhythmias.
    3. Paralytic ileus.
    4. Diuresis.
30. An adult suffered a detached retina of the right eye while playing racquetball. He presents in the emergency department with which of the following symptoms?
    1. Sharp pain OD.
    2. Redness OU.
    3. Increase in intraocular pressure OD.
    4. Blank areas in the field of vision.
31. An adult has undergone surgery to correct a detached retina. The postoperative care plan includes which of the following?
    1. Turn, cough, and deep breathe every 2 hours.
    2. Position on the operative side to keep the retina next to the choroid.
    3. A patch over the operative eye to prevent further detachment.
    4. Administer Pilocarpine eye drops for pupil constriction.
32. The nurse is admitting a client with probable Ménière's disease. Which of the following symptoms is the client most likely to exhibit?
    1. Vertigo, nystagmus, tinnitus.
    2. Vertigo, tinnitus, deafness.
    3. Tinnitus, nausea, blurred vision.
    4. Deafness, nystagmus, vertigo.
33. An adult female has Ménière's disease. Which statement she makes indicates that she needs more teaching about the management of her disease?
    1. "I was trying to stop smoking anyway, so I'm glad to have to now."

2. "I have to remember to move slower even when I'm in a hurry on my job."
3. "I'm going to miss using a lot of salt on my food."
4. "I'll have to fit in the extra fluid I need to drink throughout the day so I don't feel bloated all at once."

34. A term newborn is admitted to the nursery with excessive drooling, coughing, and sneezing. To assess for an esophageal atresia the nurse should
    1. check the mother's prenatal record for a history of oligohydramnios.
    2. pass a catheter gently into the esophagus to detect resistance.
    3. give 10 ml of glucose water to check for swallowing and color changes with feeding.
    4. place the infant with the head in a downward position to drain mucus.
35. The nurse performs a cardiovascular assessment on an elderly client which reveals a blood pressure of 162/86. The nurse's assessment finding is most likely a result of
    1. less muscle mass.
    2. calcification of arteries.
    3. dehydration.
    4. impaired lung capacity.
36. A two-year-old child with congestive heart failure has been receiving digoxin for one week. The nurse needs to recognize that an early sign of digitalis toxicity is
    1. bradypnea.
    2. failure to thrive.
    3. tachycardia.
    4. vomiting.
37. A five-year-old child is being discharged to home after a bone marrow transplant. Which of the following statements to the nurse by the child's mother indicates understanding of home care for this child?
    1. "My child needs to wear a mask when contact with others is necessary."
    2. "My child can return to school tomorrow."
    3. "My child should stay in bed."
    4. "My child will need a nurse 24 hours a day."
38. The nurse working in the newborn nursery notices that baby boy S. has one foot that curves inward. The nurse knows that congenital clubfoot
    1. rarely occurs in boys and is usually a bilateral defect.
    2. can be manipulated to various range-of-motion positions if muscle stretching exercises are performed first.
    3. will not need to be actually diagnosed until the infant is ready to be dismissed from the hospital.
    4. is most commonly of the equinovarus type with plantar flexion and inversion of the ankle and foot.

39. Ms. S. is a graduate nurse assigned to the orthopedic ward for the first time. She takes report on four clients in traction. Of the four, which client's traction is intermittent and can be released?
    1. A one-and-a-half-year-old in Bryant's traction for hip dislocation.
    2. A 24-year-old in Russell traction for a fractured femur.
    3. A 40-year-old in Buck's extension traction for a fractured hip.
    4. A 32-year-old in cervical traction for cervical disc disease.
40. The nurse is caring for an obese male client who has had a herniorrhaphy for a strangulated hernia. Important postoperative care and teaching includes which of the following?
    1. Turn, cough, and deep breathe every 2 hours, making sure to splint the incision.
    2. Assess for a distended bladder.
    3. Place a heating pad on the scrotal area to reduce the swelling.
    4. Restrict physical activities for 2 weeks.
41. Ms. J. has brought her daughter Andrea to the pediatrician's office for her nine-month checkup. The nurse assesses the baby and finds all of the following data. Which finding would cause the nurse to be concerned about developmental delay?
    1. Andrea plays with a toy for only a few minutes, then moves on to something else.
    2. Andrea cannot pull herself up to a standing position.
    3. She does not sit up without assistance.
    4. When something is taken away from her, she cries and protests.
42. Six-year-old Timmy is in the hospital for surgery. He has preoperative medications ordered by injection. When the nurse brings it to him, Timmy cries, "No, I won't be bad! Don't give me a shot!" The nurse's best response is,
    1. "Timmy, you have to have this shot, but if you are good, there won't be any more."
    2. "Timmy, what have you done that makes you say you are bad?"
    3. "You need this shot to get ready for your operation. It has nothing to do with being good or bad."
    4. "I know you try to be good. I'll call the doctor and ask if you really have to have this shot."
43. Four-year-old Sam is admitted to the hospital with rheumatic fever. He is placed on bed rest with intravenous antibiotics. His mother must go home at night because she has a one-year-old child at home. Sam doesn't want his father to stay with him. "I want Mommy. I am going to marry Mommy!" His mother is embarrassed, saying, "I don't know where he

gets such ideas." The nurse most appropriately responds
    1. "It's pretty normal behavior for a four-year-old."
    2. "Are you and your husband having difficulties in your marriage?"
    3. "If you discipline him when he says that, he will stop and eventually forget about it."
    4. "Have you considered getting counseling for Sam? It is not normal to want to marry your mother."
44. A two-month-old infant is admitted to the pediatric unit in congestive heart failure. He has a history of ventricular septal defect diagnosed at birth. He is placed on digoxin by mouth in liquid form. When administering this medication, it is appropriate for the nurse to
    1. place the medication in a small amount of formula and have the infant suck.
    2. take the apical heart rate and withhold if the rate is below 70.
    3. draw the medication up in a syringe and verify the correctness with a second nurse.
    4. give the medication when the mother is available to hold the infant and prevent him from spitting it out.
45. Matthew is two months old and is admitted with a history of vomiting for the last two weeks. His mother states it has become "like a missile" and goes across the room. Pyloric stenosis is the probable diagnosis. The nurse's admission assessment finds an infant who has gone from a birth weight of 8 pounds to a current weight of 9 pounds. He appears emaciated. He acts very hungry and is crying. Given this data, a priority nursing diagnosis is
    1. alteration in growth and development related to poor food intake.
    2. alteration in fluid and electrolyte balance due to vomiting and poor intake.
    3. potential for altered family process related to situational crisis.
    4. nutritional deficit.
46. For a school nurse in a junior high school, it is important to check young teenage girls for scoliosis. One way to assess this is to
    1. have each girl walk in a straight line.
    2. have each girl bend over and measure shoulder height.
    3. run fingers down the spine to feel for abnormalities.
    4. watch as each girl does physical education activities to see if any abnormality is evident.
47. A five-year-old boy is admitted in acute respiratory distress. He is sitting upright, drooling, unable to swallow, and looking panicky. A tentative diagnosis of epiglottitis is given. The nurse plans to place which essential equipment at the bedside?
    1. Croup tent.

2. Padded bedsides for seizure precautions.
3. Tracheotomy set.
4. Suction.

48. A ten-year-old boy has been admitted to the hospital for the tenth time with leukemia. He has been out of remission for the past 2 years and all treatments have been ineffective in stopping the course of the disease. He has been admitted this time to make him comfortable while he dies. His parents cry frequently and have a hard time staying in the room with him. When they are gone, he frequently talks about them and how hard they are taking the fact that he is going to die. An appropriate nursing diagnosis related to the care of this child is
   1. anxiety due to fear of dying.
   2. altered family process.
   3. body image disturbance.
   4. knowledge deficit.

49. Ms. J. is an 18-year-old who has been sexually active for two years. She has used condoms or foam sporadically for birth control. She has come to the clinic for birth control pills. One of the nursing goals in caring for this client is for her to choose effective birth control. Her history states that she is about 15 pounds underweight, a nonsmoker, exercises 3 to 4 times per week, and has numerous sexual partners. Which of the following would be the least appropriate birth control device?
   1. Oral contraceptives.
   2. Condoms and foam.
   3. Intrauterine device.
   4. Diaphragm.

50. Ms. S. has just been admitted to the postpartum unit after delivery of a baby girl. The nurse brings her baby in and prepares to assist her in breast feeding. Ms. S. says she doesn't want to try yet. She begins to talk about her labor and delivery and how difficult it was. The nurse recognizes this behavior is indicative of
   1. high risk for alteration in parenting related to the mother's lack of interest in her baby's needs.
   2. fatigue from labor and delivery.
   3. inability to accept the reality of parenthood.
   4. normal developmental phase of taking-in during the early puerperium.

51. While caring for a newborn baby boy, the nurse notices the foreskin on the penis cannot be retracted. The baby's mother asks if this means her baby must be circumcised immediately. The best response for the nurse is
   1. "It is normal for a newborn. You cannot retract the foreskin until he is older."
   2. "Yes, the foreskin should retract or bacteria can grow and cause infection."

3. "It is a good indication he'll need to be circumcised, but there is no hurry."
4. "Discuss this with your pediatrician. Circumcision is controversial."

52. A client who is 24 hours post cesarean delivery has orders to advance diet as tolerated. She has been on full liquids and asks if she can have real food. Which question is most appropriate for the nurse to ask before changing her to a regular diet?
   1. "Have you had a bowel movement yet?"
   2. "Are you passing gas?"
   3. "Do you notice rumblings in your belly?"
   4. "Are you still hungry after eating your liquid tray?"

53. A client is admitted to labor and delivery for an induction of labor. She is receiving pitocin and has progressed to 5 cm dilation. Her contractions have steadily become stronger and longer until the nurse notices a contraction lasting two minutes. The best initial action for the nurse is to
   1. assess the fetal heart rate and observe a little longer.
   2. turn the client on her left side and encourage transition breathing.
   3. give the client oxygen through a nasal cannula and decrease the rate of the infusion.
   4. stop the pitocin infusion.

54. Ms. J. is 30 weeks pregnant and has been diagnosed with gestational diabetes. Her physician has ordered a 2000-calorie ADA diet, moderate exercise, and weekly appointments for prenatal care. She is very upset and wants to know everything about her condition and how she can have a healthy baby. Which of the following is an appropriate goal for Ms. J. at this time? The client will
   1. discuss how pregnancy causes diabetes.
   2. demonstrate insulin injections.
   3. keep a food diary for 48 hours.
   4. identify risks to her fetus if she doesn't follow her diet rigidly.

55. Ms. T. is admitted to the antepartal unit with pregnancy-induced hypertension. She is 34 weeks gestation and is admitted with a blood pressure of 160/100, 3+ protein in her urine, generalized edema, and headache, and is seeing spots before her eyes. She is concerned about her two preschool children being cared for by a neighbor. The priority nursing diagnosis for Ms. T. at this time is
   1. alteration in fluid volume.
   2. powerlessness.
   3. ineffective family coping.
   4. alteration in tissue perfusion.

56. Ms. S. has been in labor for 8 hours. She has been pushing for an hour and a half without making progress. The fetus remains at minus one station. Ms. S. is extremely tired and

discouraged. The nurse suggests changing to a nontraditional position. Which assessment is most important to make before proceeding?
1. The condition of the fetal membranes.
2. The level of maternal fatigue.
3. Effacement and dilatation.
4. Status of maternal bladder.

57. A newborn is admitted to the nursery 20 minutes after birth. His vital signs are stable. He is crying vigorously. The nurse begins the admission procedure. Which of the following is most appropriate?
1. Wear latex gloves during the admission.
2. Do the admission in an open crib with good light.
3. Wear mask and gown when approaching the infant.
4. Perform the admission procedures while the infant is asleep.

58. An infant has just been delivered with a myelomeningocele. The infant is immediately transferred to the nursery. The nurse should place the infant in what position?
1. Semi-sitting with support of an infant seat.
2. Side-lying with his head lower than the rest of his body to promote drainage.
3. Supine to place counterpressure on the defect.
4. Prone to reduce the risk of rupture and infection.

59. Shortly after administering Prolixin (fluphenazine) 10 mg PO to a client who has schizophrenia, the nurse notices that he is pacing, appears restless, is drooling, and complains that his tongue feels thick. Which of the following PRN orders would the nurse administer to alleviate these symptoms?
1. Ativan (lorazepam) 2 mg IM.
2. Atropine 4 mg IM.
3. Cogentin (benztropine mesylate) 2 mg IM.
4. Thorazine (chlorpromazine hydrochloride) 50 mg IM.

60. The nurse is evaluating the effectiveness of antipsychotic medication 2 weeks after starting treatment in a client who has paranoid schizophrenia. If the medication is effective, the nurse would expect to see
1. decreased hallucinations and decreased sleep.
2. increased sleep and improved personal hygiene.
3. decreased suspiciousness and increased appetite.
4. decreased hallucinations and decreased suspiciousness.

61. Sara, a physically abused wife, says to her nurse, "I'd be nothing without my husband." To increase Sara's self-esteem, the nurse would most appropriately say
1. "I see you as a survivor in a difficult situation."
2. "No, you're not. I think you're important."

3. "Your husband should be the one who is a nothing."
4. "I can see that you're upset."

62. The nurse is planning nursing interventions for parents who abuse their children. It is important for the nurse to recall that these parents
1. plan ahead as to when and how to abuse their children.
2. ask for help generally only after feeling overwhelmed with the problem.
3. usually feel no guilt concerning the abuse.
4. are always a product of abuse themselves.

63. The nurse is caring for a client with antisocial personality. What behavior exhibited by the client would indicate an improvement?
1. Attending therapeutic groups daily.
2. Compliance with antipsychotic medications.
3. Abiding by hospital rules and regulations.
4. Interacting with peers in the day room.

64. The nurse is caring for an adult client who is to undergo a cystoscopy in the morning. Preparation of the client should include
1. explaining that this is a painless test.
2. instructing the client to drink several glasses of water prior to the test.
3. giving instructions to breathe rapidly and deeply throughout the procedure.
4. telling the client to administer a small package enema in the evening before the test.

65. A young woman is to undergo a Tensilon test. The nurse is explaining the test to the client. Which statement the client makes indicates the best understanding of the test?
1. "A positive test will be evident within 1 minute of the Tensilon injection."
2. "The test is of diagnostic value in only about 20% of persons with myasthenia gravis."
3. "If the test is positive I will feel an immediate decrease in muscle strength."
4. "Tensilon acts by blocking the action of acetylcholine at the myoneural junction."

66. An adult client is scheduled for a CT scan of the abdomen and pelvis. The client asks the nurse why it is necessary to have a serum creatinine and BUN drawn before the scan. The best answer for the nurse to give is
1. "These tests will determine if you are allergic to iodine contrast media."
2. "The tests determine if the kidneys are functioning and can eliminate contrast media."
3. "The tests serve as baseline information to determine if the scan has caused damage."
4. "The blood tests give additional information about the presence of possible tumors."

67. The nurse is performing an ophthalmologic examination on an elderly client. The client

states, "my peripheral vision is decreased." The nurse's best response to this client during the exam is
1. "You should be grateful you are not blind."
2. "As one ages, peripheral vision decreases. This is normal."
3. "You should rest your eyes frequently."
4. "You may be able to improve your vision if you move slowly."

68. Ms. J. is admitted post CVA (cerebral vascular accident) with right-sided paralysis. Upon assessment, she is awake and alert but has difficulty speaking because of impairment of the facial muscles involved with production of speech. When documenting Ms. J.'s speech, the nurse notes that she has
1. semantic aphasia.
2. receptive aphasia.
3. dysarthria.
4. dysphagia.

69. The nurse is assessing a client for local inflammation following an injury. The cardinal signs the nurse should observe for are
1. pain, swelling, heat, redness, fever.
2. fever, redness, swelling, impaired function, pain.
3. swelling, heat, redness, impaired function, pain.
4. fever, chills, sweating, malaise, pain.

70. The nurse is caring for a client who is scheduled for a ureterosigmoidostomy. Which information is inappropriate and will not be a part of the preoperative teaching plan?
1. Liquid diet for 24 hours prior to the surgery.
2. Assessment of the adequacy of the rectal sphincter.
3. Administration of neomycin sulfate for 3 days prior to surgery.
4. application of full-length elastic stockings.

71. Mr. A. is an adult who has chronic obstructive lung disease and needs frequent monitoring of arterial blood gases. Following the drawing of arterial blood gases it is essential for the nurse to do which of the following?
1. Encourage the client to cough and deep breathe.
2. Apply pressure to the puncture site for 5 minutes.
3. Shake the vial of blood before transporting it to the lab.
4. Keep the client on bed rest for 2 hours.

72. The nurse is caring for a client with chronic obstructive lung disease. An order is written for oxygen by nasal cannula at 2 liters per minute. Which assessment is most useful in assessing the adequacy of the oxygen therapy?
1. Respiratory rate.

2. Color of mucous membranes.
3. Pulmonary function tests.
4. Arterial blood gases.

73. The nurse is interpreting the results of a blood gas analysis performed on an adult client. The values include pH of 7.35, pCO_2 of 60, HCO_3 of 35, and O_2 of 60. Which interpretation is most accurate?
1. The client is in metabolic acidosis.
2. The client is in compensated metabolic alkalosis.
3. The client is in respiratory alkalosis.
4. The client is in compensated respiratory acidosis.

74. The nurse is caring for an elderly woman who fell at her home. Following X-rays she is admitted with a diagnosis of fractured left hip. During the nursing assessment the nurse would expect to see which of the following?
1. The client cannot move her left leg but can wiggle her toes.
2. The left leg will have internal rotation and appear longer.
3. The client can voluntarily move the left leg without pain.
4. The left leg will have involuntary tremors.

75. The nurse is evaluating the care given to a client who has had a total hip replacement. Which position indicates the client has been positioned appropriately?
1. The affected leg is abducted and externally rotated.
2. The affected leg is adducted and externally rotated.
3. The affected leg is abducted and internally rotated.
4. The affected leg is adducted and internally rotated.

76. The nurse is admitting an adult male to the nursing care unit. He has severe weakness in the lower extremities and is only able to stand with assistance. He is complaining of numbness in both hands and is extremely anxious. He had a mild upper respiratory infection several weeks ago but has otherwise been in excellent health. A diagnosis of Guillain-Barré syndrome is made. When he is admitted the priority nursing action is to
1. raise the head of the bed to high-Fowler's to prevent increased intracranial pressure.
2. place respiratory support equipment at the bedside.
3. reassure the client that in time the strength will return to his legs.
4. place the client in reverse isolation to prevent spreading the virus.

77. The nurse is assessing Mr. V., who has a cataract in his right eye. What symptoms is the client likely to exhibit?
1. Acute eye pain.
2. Redness and itching in the right eye.

3. Gradual blurring of vision.
4. Severe headaches and dizziness.

78. Mr. W. is scheduled for an MRI (magnetic resonance imaging) test because of a back injury. Which question is it essential for the nurse to ask Mr. W. before the procedure?
1. "Are you allergic to iodine or shellfish?"
2. "Are you afraid of heights?"
3. "Do you get dizzy easily?"
4. "Do you have any metal in your body?"

79. Ms. A. had a tuberculin skin test as part of an employment physical. A positive result is seen. The client suggests to the nurse that the reason she has a positive skin test and a negative chest X-ray is that she was born and raised in another country and received BCG vaccine as a child. The nurse's response is based on the understanding that
1. the only cause for a positive skin test and negative chest X-ray is exposure to the tubercle bacillus without development of tuberculosis infection.
2. the skin test is only a screening test.
3. BCG vaccine is not effective against tuberculosis.
4. BCG vaccine stimulates formation of antibodies against tuberculosis.

80. Ms. W. has had a low-sodium, low-fat diet prescribed for heart disease. The nurse is evaluating her understanding of the diet. Which statement she makes indicates a need for further instruction?
1. "Whenever I go out to eat at a restaurant, I get the salad bar and use vinegar for a dressing."
2. "When I eat chicken, I take the skin off and broil the chicken in the oven."
3. "I like to put catsup on my noodles."
4. "We use skim milk for drinking and cooking."

81. The nurse is administering eye drops to an elderly client. Which action is least appropriate for the nurse to take?
1. Inform the client that the drops may cause blurred vision and difficulty focusing for a period of time.
2. Apply gentle pressure to the nasolacrimal canal for 1 to 2 minutes after instillation to prevent systemic absorption.
3. Encourage the client to lie down with eyes closed after instillation to prevent systemic absorption.
4. Gently pull the lower lid down and place the medicine in the center of the lid.

82. Ms. R. is admitted for internal radiation for cancer of the cervix. The nurse knows the client understands the procedure when she makes which of the following remarks the night before the procedure?
1. She says to her husband, "Please bring me a hamburger and french fries

tomorrow when you come. I hate hospital food."
2. "I told my daughter who is pregnant to either come to see me tonight or wait until I go home from the hospital."
3. "I understand it will be several weeks before all the radiation leaves my body."
4. "I brought several craft projects to do while the radium is inserted."

83. The nurse is teaching auxiliary staff on the unit about universal precautions. Which statement made by one of the aides indicates the best understanding of the procedure?
1. "I should wear gloves when I give an enema to a client who can't hold it."
2. "If I see a blood spill I will get iodine immediately and wipe up the spill."
3. "When I see used needles in the treatment room or the client's room, I will recap them and put them in the Sharps box."
4. "I will wear a gown and mask whenever I go into the room of a person with AIDS."

84. The nurse is caring for a client who has patches on both eyes following eye surgery. When entering the room the nurse should do which of the following?
1. Announce presence and name clearly before entering the room.
2. Speak in a louder tone than usual.
3. Enter the room quietly and touch the client before speaking.
4. Refrain from saying things like "I see" to the client.

85. An adult client is admitted following a knife fight. Among other injuries he has a pneumothorax. A chest tube is inserted and attached to a Pleurevac drainage system. Immediately following insertion of the chest tube, which observation by the nurse best indicates the drainage system is functioning adequately?
1. There is no bubbling in the water seal chamber.
2. The fluid level in the suction control chamber fluctuates with each respiration.
3. The collection chambers are filling with sanguinous drainage.
4. The client reports pain relief.

86. Mr. Y. is admitted to the medical unit with symptoms of angina. Nitroglycerin is administered. Which assessment indicates the client is responding positively to the administration of nitroglycerin?
1. The client's blood pressure drops.
2. Mr. Y. reports he has developed a headache.
3. Mr. Y. asks to be discharged because his pain is relieved.
4. Mr. Y. reports he has developed nausea.

87. The nurse is caring for several clients. Which client may need an order for wrist restraints?

1. An elderly woman who is confused and pulls out her intravenous line.
2. An adult man who refuses to have an intravenous line started.
3. A one-year-old child who keeps pulling herself up in the crib and tries to climb out.
4. An adult who is supposed to be on bed rest following surgery who tried to get up during the night.

88. The nurse is to administer an intramuscular injection to a one-year-old child. Which site is most appropriate for the nurse to select?
    1. Dorsal gluteal.
    2. Ventral gluteal.
    3. Ventral forearm.
    4. Vastus lateralis.

89. An adult client is being treated for hypertension. A low-sodium, low-fat diet is prescribed. The nurse knows the client understands his diet when he selects which of the following menus?
    1. Fried chicken, mashed potatoes, green beans, and milk.
    2. Macaroni and cheese casserole, tossed salad with dressing, and hot chocolate.
    3. Baked chicken, steamed broccoli and cauliflower, steamed rice, and hot tea.
    4. Steak, baked potato, peas, and hot coffee.

90. An adult client is to have a pelvic sonogram today to diagnose possible ovarian cysts. When she arrives in the clinic area which question is it most important for the nurse to ask?
    1. "When was your last menstrual period?"
    2. "What have you had to drink this morning?"
    3. "When was your last bowel movement?"
    4. "Did you use powder or deodorant today?"

91. A registered nurse (RN) is in charge of the care of eight clients, assisted by a nursing assistant (nurse aide). The following clients need care that must be given at 10 A.M.: an adult with an infected decubitus ulcer needs the wound cleaned and dressed; an adult needs to be ambulated for the first time following an appendectomy; an adult who has returned from extensive shoulder surgery needs to have an ice bag placed on the incision. How should the nurse proceed?
    1. Ask the nursing assistant to apply the ice bag and ambulate the client while the RN performs the decubitus ulcer care.
    2. Ask the nursing assistant to perform decubitus care and ambulate the client while the RN applies the ice bag.
    3. Ask the nursing assistant to ambulate the client while the RN performs decubitus care and applies the ice bag.
    4. Ask the nursing assistant to perform decubitus care while the RN applies the ice bag and ambulates the client.

92. A client has been trying for several months to become pregnant. At long last, the nurse receives the results of the laboratory tests that confirm the pregnancy, and, at the request of the physician, telephones the client to tell her the good news. The client's husband answers the phone, stating that his wife is not home. The nurse congratulates him on his impending fatherhood, and asks that his wife call as soon as she returns. When the wife calls later that day, she is distant and cool to the nurse. How can the nurse best interpret this behavior?
    1. The wife may be having second thoughts about the pregnancy.
    2. Depression is common in early stages of pregnancy due to hormonal changes.
    3. The stresses of long-awaited pregnancy often place a strain on a marriage.
    4. The nurse violated the client's privacy by telling her husband the test results.

93. A 37-year-old man whose secondary hypertension has not responded to lifestyle modifications over the last five weeks is admitted to undergo treatment in an effort to bring the hypertension under control. During the hospitalization he is being treated using the stepped-care approach. The medications which are part of his therapy are furosemide (Lasix) and quinipril hydrochloride (Accupril). What types of information should the nurse include in the discharge plan for this client?
    1. Cholesterol restriction, weight reduction, limited activity, drug use, and side effects.
    2. Potassium restriction, increased activity, drug use, and self-blood pressure monitoring.
    3. Sodium restriction, increased activity, drug action, tobacco avoidance, and reduced stress.
    4. Magnesium restriction, drug use and side effects, limited alcohol intake, and rest periods.

94. The nurse is caring for an adult male whose renal disease has progressed so that he will now need dialysis therapy. After discussing his options with his physician, the client decided to use continuous ambulatory peritoneal dialysis (CAPD) as his treatment option. In order to discharge him on CAPD, the nurse must know that he understands the essential components of the procedure. Which of the following choices best reflects the information the nurse should include in the CAPD teaching plan for this client?
    1. Review of anatomy and physiology, hand washing, how to perform the exchange procedure, low-sodium diet, Foley catheter care, complications, and responses.
    2. Low-protein/high-carbohydrate diet, hand washing, how to perform the exchange

procedure, measurement of apical pulse, and care of the A-V shunt site.

3. Review of disease process, performing the procedure, CAPD catheter care, measurement of vital signs, complications and responses, and aseptic technique.

4. Oral fluid restrictions, auscultation for bruit over fistula, measurement of vital signs, aseptic technique, how to perform the exchange procedure, complications, and responses.

95. A 66-year-old man has been admitted to the coronary care unit with the diagnosis of an anterior wall myocardial infarction. He is on hardwire cardiac monitoring. He has a history of left-sided heart failure complicated by early signs of renal insufficiency. His rhythm strip demonstrates frequent premature ventricular beats as well as occasional episodes of second-degree heart block episodes. The physician is most likely to prescribe an alternative drug to suppress the ventricular ectopic beats with most likely would be
1. atenolol (Tenormin).
2. calcium gluconate.
3. verapamil (Calan).
4. diltiazem (Cardizem).

96. The nurse is assisting a client who has a broken ankle with crutch walking. The nurse knows the client understands the instructions when the client
1. advances both crutches and the unaffected leg at the same time.
2. puts partial weight on the affected leg.
3. advances both crutches and the affected leg at the same time.
4. leans on the crutch pads to relieve pressure on the affected foot.

97. An adult is receiving a transfusion of whole blood. The client has undergone head trauma and is unconscious. The nurse assesses the client and finds a weak pulse, fever, and hypotension. The best initial action by the nurse is
1. notify the physician.
2. stop the blood transfusion.
3. recheck the vital signs.
4. check the amount of urine output.

98. The nurse is caring for an adult who has had an acute myocardial infarction. The nurse finds him very restless with a heart rate of 110, respiratory rate of 28, and blood pressure 80/50. The most appropriate nursing action is
1. prepare for administration of vasoconstrictive drugs.
2. limit IV intake to 100 ml the first two hours.
3. prepare for insertion of CVP or pulmonary artery catheter.
4. prepare to apply MAST trousers/suit.

99. The nurse is visiting a client at home and is assessing him for risk of a fall. The most important factor to consider in this assessment is
1. illumination of the environment.
2. amount of regular exercise.
3. the resting pulse rate.
4. status of salt intake.

100. A 72-year-old who is alert and oriented is being treated for polyarthritis, primary biliary cirrhosis, mild hypertension, and glaucoma. As part of his treatment he must take four medications, some of which are once a day and some twice a day at different times of the day. He is being seen in the neighborhood blood pressure clinic for a follow-up visit. The nurse inquires about possible side effects of the various medications prescribed and the client says "I'm not used to taking all these medicines and frequently miss taking them all." Which of the following suggestions should the nurse make to this client to most effectively promote adherence to the prescribed medication regimen?
1. Purchase a pill sorting box to arrange dosages and associate medication administration with some other regular daily task, such as brushing your teeth, washing your face, etc.
2. Make arrangements to have the public health nurse visit daily to prepare the day's drugs and to administer the first dose.
3. Require family members to organize and administer medications on a daily basis.
4. Explain the importance of these medicines and tell the client he needs to find a better way of remembering.

Answers and Rationales for Practice Test 7

ANSWER	RATIONALE	NP	CN	CL

#1. 4. Muscle weakness, anorexia, and malaise are symptoms of hypophosphatemia that may occur with prolonged use of Amphojel.   Pl   Ph/8   Ap

    1. Constipation is the expected side effect of Amphojel. It needs to be reported to the physician only if it is not manageable.

    2. The liquid tends to be more effective than the tablets.

    3. Small amounts of milk or water are given to ensure passage of the medication to the stomach. Too much liquid will dilute the medicine.

#2. 1. Hypoparathyroidism results in decreased calcium and increased phosphorus levels. The client will be on a high-calcium, low-phosphorus diet.   Pl   Ph/9   Ap

    2. The client has hypocalcemia and will receive oral calcium.

    3. Seizure precautions are necessary because acute hypocalcemia can precipitate seizures.

    4. A quiet environment is necessary because acute hypocalcemia causes nerve irritability and can precipitate seizures.

#3. 3. The client may receive iodine solution (Lugol's solution) for 10 to 14 days before surgery to decrease vascularity of the thyroid and thus prevent excess bleeding.   An   Ph/8   Ap

    1. Doses of over 30 mg/day may increase the risk of agranulocytosis.

    2. Lugol's solution does not act to prevent tetany. Calcium is used to treat tetany.

    4. Lugol's solution does not potentiate any other preoperative medication.

#4. 3. Brudzinski's sign is flexion at the hip and knee in response to forward flexion of the neck and may be present in the client with meningitis.   As   Ph/9   Co

    1. Chovstek's sign is assessed to check for neuromuscular irritability due to hypocalcemia if the parathyroid glands have been inadvertently removed. A positive Chovstek's is hyperirritability of the facial nerve. When the facial nerve is tapped, a spasm occurs.

    2. Laryngeal nerve damage is assessed by asking the client to speak. If the client suddenly develops hoarseness, the laryngeal nerve may be damaged. The laryngeal nerve is sometimes damaged during thyroid surgery.

    4. Trousseau's sign is assessed to check for neuromuscular irritability due to hypocalcemia if the parathyroid glands have been inadvertently removed. To test for Trousseau's sign the nurse applies a blood pressure cuff. A carpopedal spasm that causes thumb adduction and phalangeal extension is a positive Trousseau's sign.

#5. 4. Participating in a senior citizen group best indicates positive resocialization and expansion of her social network.   Ev   Ps/5   Ap

    1. Grocery shopping is a necessity and does not necessarily expand the social network.

    2. Not attending the support group may be a sign of withdrawal and therefore is not the best indicator of resocialization.

    3. Babysitting the grandchildren whenever asked could limit and does not expand the social network. It is not the best indicator of progress in resocialization.

#6. 2. Pets can provide an opportunity for touching and can promote socialization.   Pl   Ps/5   Ap

    1. Family and friends should be encouraged to visit. This provides opportunities for socialization.

ANSWER		RATIONALE	NP	CN	CL

	3.	Nonsense syllables are a symptom of the progression of organic brain syndrome and cannot be corrected by speech therapy.			
	4.	Touching helps to maintain contact with the client. Tactile stimulation is easiest to interpret.			
#7.	1.	**According to Hirst and Miller (1986) as cited in Wilson, H., & Kneisl (1992),** *Psychiatric Nursing,* **the elderly Caucasian female who has physical and/or cognitive impairment is at greatest risk for elder abuse by a family member.**	As	Ps/6	Co
	2.	The elderly Caucasian female who has physical and/or cognitive impairment is at greatest risk for elder abuse by a family member.			
	3.	The elderly Caucasian female who has physical and/or cognitive impairment is at greatest risk for elder abuse by a family member.			
	4.	The elderly Caucasian female who has physical and/or cognitive impairment is at greatest risk for elder abuse by a family member.			
#8.	1.	**Depressive symptoms include exaggerated feelings of sadness, dejection, worthlessness, hopelessness, and emptiness.**	As	Ps/5	Co
	2.	Poor grooming and hygiene are signs of mental decompensation in several mental illnesses such as dementia, schizophrenia, and depression.			
	3.	Intense anxiety alone is not a symptom of depression.			
	4.	Thought insertion is a symptom of schizophrenia.			
#9.	3.	**According to Erickson's developmental stages intimacy vs. isolation is the stage that targets intimate relationships.**	An	Ps/5	Ap
	1.	Trust vs. mistrust is the developmental stage in which infants learn to trust the world by having their basic needs met in a consistent manner.			
	2.	Identity vs. role confusion is the developmental stage in which adolescents face the issues of "who am I" and "what am I going to do with my life." This stage does not target relationship issues specifically.			
	4.	Generativity vs. stagnation is the middle adult stage in which persons are concerned with being productive and contributing to the greater society. This stage does not target relationship issues specifically.			
#10.	1.	**The client learned a method to use in dealing with problems/ stressors such as verbalization rather than looking to quick and sometimes superficial answers to problems.**	Ev	Ps/5	Ap
	2.	This response indicates an immediate and possibly superficial answer to problems rather than a coping mechanism to be used.			
	3.	This is a negative response to the teaching and may indicate a block to accepting it.			
	4.	This response indicates an immediate and possibly superficial answer to problems rather than a coping mechanism to be used.			
#11.	4.	**Using Maslow's hierarchy of needs as well as basic concepts of alcohol detoxification, the nurse needs to initially assess and attend to the potential for physical problems associated with withdrawal.**	An	Ps/6	Ap
	1.	Sensory/perceptual alteration related to withdrawal seizures secondary to alcohol cessation is an appropriate nursing diagnosis for this client. However, high risk for injury has a higher priority during the initial phase of treatment.			
	2.	There are no data to support a diagnosis of suicidal thoughts.			
	3.	Ineffective denial is also an appropriate diagnosis for a client with alcohol addiction. It will be the focus later in treatment after safe detoxification has been achieved.			
#12.	3.	**An ice pack applied to the perineum in the first few hours after delivery helps to soothe the area by constricting vessels and reducing inflammation.**	Pl	He/3	Ap
	1.	Following vaginal delivery it is not necessary for a woman to be NPO. After a cesarean a woman is NPO until bowel sounds are audible.			

2. Ice packs to the breasts suppress lactation and are not appropriate for a woman who plans to breast feed.

4. Following a normal vaginal delivery an indwelling catheter is not necessary. An indwelling catheter is usually in place until the first postpartum day in a woman undergoing a cesarean section so the bladder is continually emptied during surgery and bed rest can be maintained during the initial postpartum period.

#13. 3. Rho(D) should be given within 72 hours of delivery when the mother is Rho(D) negative and the infant is Rho(D) positive.   Ev   Ph/8   Ap

1. Rho(D) immune globulin is administered to the mother, not the infant.

2. Rho(D) immune globulin is not needed after donating blood since the client has not been sensitized by receiving any Rho(D) blood or blood product.

4. Rho(D) immune globulin is not needed after breast feeding. Rho(D) immune globulin is indicated following the termination of a pregnancy, after amniocentesis, after abdominal trauma during pregnancy, and after receiving a transfusion of Rho(D) positive blood.

#14. 1. Monitoring fetal heart rate assesses fetal well-being and fetal distress. A tocolytic is administered to relax the smooth muscles of the uterus and inhibit uterine contractility.   Pl   He/3   Ap

2. Monitoring fetal heart rate assesses fetal well-being and fetal distress. A tranquilizer is not indicated as it can depress the neonate's respiratory center.

3. A maternal cardiac monitor is not necessary unless there is a history of maternal cardiac disease or compromise. Fluid therapy is appropriate as it helps promote uterine perfusion.

4. Monitoring fetal heart rate assesses fetal well-being and fetal distress. A maternal cardiac monitor will not be used unless the client experiences serious side effects, such as cardiac arrhythmias or tachycardia, from the tocolytic agent.

#15. 3. Vitamin B_{12} injections must be taken for life by the person who has pernicious anemia. Persons with pernicious anemia are unable to absorb vitamin B_{12} from the gastrointestinal tract.   An   Ph/8   Ap

1. Iron preparations are given for the treatment of iron deficiency anemia.

2. Aplastic anemia is medically managed with blood transfusions and corticosteroids, which stimulate red blood cell production. Persons with aplastic anemia have bone marrow failure and do not make red blood cells, white blood cells, or platelets.

4. Hemolytic anemia is medically managed with blood transfusions and corticosteroids which stimulate red blood cell production. Persons with hemolytic anemia break down red blood cells too quickly.

#16. 1. Although all of the assessment findings occur in the client with pernicious anemia, only the Schilling test provides a definitive diagnosis of pernicious anemia.   An   Ph/9   Co

2. A gastric analysis with decreased free HCl acid is seen in pernicious anemia and also in stomach cancer, and so does not provide a definitive diagnosis.

3. A bone marrow biopsy showing increased abnormal erythrocyte and defective leukocyte maturation may be seen in a person with pernicious anemia but can also be seen in persons with other blood disorders, and so does not provide a definitive diagnosis.

4. An elevated LDH may be seen in persons with pernicious anemia but is also seen in persons with a myocardial infarction or liver disease, so the test is not definitive for pernicious anemia.

#17. 2. With an oxalate stone the client should limit excess intake of foods high in oxalate and maintain an alkaline ash diet for alkaline urine. Tea, chocolate, and spinach are high in oxalates.   Pl   Ph/9   Ap

1. Milk and dairy products leave an alkaline ash and are appropriate for

this client. A calcium stone would necessitate limiting milk and dairy products and keeping an acid urine.

3. This client needs an alkaline ash diet, not an acid ash diet. An acid ash diet is indicated for an alkaline-based stone.

4. Limiting foods high in purine is indicated for persons with uric acid stones or gout.

#18. 3.	**The warning signs of testicular cancer are a slight enlargement or a change in the consistency of the testes.**	Ev	He/4	An

1. It is normal for the left testis to hang lower than the right.
2. Smooth, rubbery, and oval-shaped testes are normal.
4. It is normal for the testes to be slightly tender when examined.

#19. 3.	**Persantine is a peripheral vasodilator and should be withheld before dialysis, along with antihypertensives and sedatives, to prevent a hypotensive episode.**	Im	Ph/8	Ap

1. There is no contraindication to giving NPH insulin before dialysis.
2. Pilocarpine is used to treat glaucoma and is given in the form of eye drops. It is not contraindicated before dialysis.
4. Questran is an antilipemic and is not contraindicated before dialysis.

#20. 2.	**Air embolism is a potentially fatal complication characterized by sudden hypotension, dyspnea, chest pain, cyanosis, and weak, rapid pulse.**	An	Ph/10	Ap

1. Symptoms of disequilibrium syndrome include headache, muscle twitching, backache, nausea, vomiting, and seizures.
3. Internal bleeding presents as apprehension; restlessness; pale, cold, clammy skin; excessive thirst; hypotension; rapid, weak, thready pulse; and increased respirations. Sudden onset of chest pain and dyspnea are not characteristic of internal bleeding.
4. Hemorrhage at the shunt has visible blood loss as well as apprehension; restlessness; pale, cold, clammy skin; excessive thirst; hypotension; rapid, weak, thready pulse; and increased respirations. Sudden onset of chest pain and dyspnea are not characteristic of bleeding at the shunt.

#21. 1.	**Since the goal of conservative treatment is for the client to pass the stone without the need for invasive procedures, fluids will be forced to help flush the stone through the urinary tract quickly and to dilute the urine to reduce the risk of forming additional stones or enlarging the existing one. If obstruction were present, forcing fluids would be undesirable since urine would be accumulating behind the obstruction. Conservative treatment would never be selected in the presence of obstruction.**	Pl	Ph/9	Ap

2. Restricting citrus juices and milk products would make the urine acid, which would help prevent formation of alkaline-based stones. The nurse will not know whether the stones are of this type until the client has passed them and they are analyzed. This intervention is premature. If the client's stones are of a type that form in acid urine these measures would be contraindicated.
3. An indwelling catheter would not be of help in this situation, since the stone is most likely in the kidney or the ureter. Once the stone moves out of the ureter, which has the smallest diameter, it usually moves fairly rapidly through the rest of the urinary tract. The small openings of the indwelling catheter tip would only obstruct the progress of the stone.
4. Narcotic analgesics will be required for the severe pain of urolithiasis. However, narcotics should be administered on a regular schedule. Waiting until the client requests them allows the pain to become severe and harder to relieve.

#22. 2.	**Very cold air, especially if it is dry, is likely to cause bronchospasms, which make breathing even more difficult for the person with COPD.**	Pl	Ph/9	Ap

1. COPD clients should never increase the oxygen flow rate over 2–3

l/min since high oxygen levels can reduce the hypoxic drive to breathe, resulting in cessation of breathing.

3. Fluids should be increased to 2500 to 3000 ml daily to help liquefy secretions and make them easier to clear from the airways. Fluid restriction is indicated if the client also has CHF, but the question does not indicate that this is the case.

4. To help relieve shortness of breath the client needs to be in a forward-leaning position. Sitting up with the upper body leaning over a table that has been padded with pillows for support, or with the arms resting on the knees for support, is best. Reclining in a backward-leaning position is likely to cause a sensation of smothering.

#23. 4. **Large amounts of simple carbohydrate in the diet produce a high osmotic pressure within the intestine, which draws fluid into the intestine from surrounding cells, causing the early dumping syndrome. The hypoglycemic effect noted in late dumping syndrome is produced by production of large amounts of insulin when the intestinal contents are high in simple carbohydrates. Reducing dietary carbohydrate and using primarily complex carbohydrates helps to control dumping syndrome. Increasing fat and protein in the diet delays gastric emptying time.**   Pl   Ph/9   Ap

1. Lying down, especially on the left side, is helpful in slowing gastric emptying. It is rapid emptying of stomach contents into the intestine that causes the dumping syndrome.

2. To help prevent dumping syndrome, fluids should not be taken at meal times. This allows the food in the stomach to remain more solid, slowing gastric emptying.

3. Eating six small meals rather than three large ones will help reduce dumping syndrome. Eating every 2 to 3 hours would keep the stomach full at all times and would tend to increase the length of time that the intestinal contents are exerting osmotic pressure to pull fluids into the intestine.

#24. 3. **Antacids containing magnesium have diarrhea as a side effect.**   An   Ph/8   Co

1. Aluminum hydroxide causes constipation.

2. Kaopectate is an antidiarrheal, not an antacid.

4. Rolaids may cause constipation.

#25. 4. **Laxatives are given, if needed, the night before surgery to help cleanse the bowel.**   Im   Ph/9   Ap

1. Cleansing enemas will be given the night before surgery to be sure the bowel is empty.

2. An antibiotic, such as neomycin, that is poorly absorbed from the gastrointestinal tract is given preoperatively to kill the bacteria that are normal inhabitants of the bowel.

3. A nasogastric tube is inserted the morning of surgery.

#26. 3. **Colace is a stool softener and the laxative of choice for clients who should not strain during defecation.**   An   Ph/8   Ap

1. Saline cathartics attract and hold large amounts of fluids and increase the bulk of stools.

2. Lubricant laxatives coat the feces with an oily film and prevent the colon from reabsorbing water from the feces.

4. Stimulant laxatives such as Dulcolax stimulate peristalsis.

#27. 2. **A hiatal hernia is a structural defect of a weakened diaphragm and is aggravated by reclining and activities that cause an increase in intra-abdominal pressure. The client should be instructed to wait at least 2 hours after eating before lying down.**   An   Ph/9   Ap

1. Hiatal hernia is a structural defect of a weakened diaphragm and is not influenced by stress. Clients with hiatal hernia are advised to give up smoking.

3. Antacids help to neutralize the gastric contents that are refluxed into the esophagus.

ANSWER	RATIONALE	NP	CN	CL

4. Clients with hiatal hernia are advised to eat small, frequent, bland meals and to avoid smoking, coffee, and alcohol.

#28. 1. The client who has had a total laryngectomy loses the ability to speak. It will be important to plan ahead for an alternate method of communication so that the client can communicate needs in the postoperative period.   Pl   Ph/9   Ap

2. The client should be positioned with the head elevated at least 30 degrees to lower the abdominal organs so that the pressure on the suture line is reduced and the work of breathing lessened.

3. Coughing and deep breathing will be especially important for this client to maintain a patent airway and must be encouraged. Cough suppressants could result in retention of secretions in the lungs and development of pneumonia as a postoperative complication.

4. The tracheostomy must be suctioned every hour in the early postoperative period to remove the copious secretions that develop in the immediate postoperative period. Every 4 hours is not frequent enough.

#29. 1. Nausea and vomiting are the most common side effects of cancer chemotherapy.   Pl   Ph/8   Ap

2. Cardiac arrhythmias are not common. However, the antitumor antibiotics may cause irreversible cardiac toxicities.

3. Paralytic ileus is not common. However, the plant alkaloids can cause neurologic damage including paralytic ileus.

4. Diuresis is unlikely, and in fact adequate fluid hydration must be maintained to prevent damage to the kidneys.

#30. 4. There is no pain, bilateral redness, or increase in intraocular pressure with a detached retina. Symptoms include gaps in vision, flashes of light, floating particles before the eyes, a curtain over the field of vision, and blindness if not treated.   As   Ph/10   An

1. Detached retina is not characterized by sharp pain. Sharp pain is more typical of a foreign object in the eye.

2. Redness in both eyes could be caused by infection or irritation by a noxious substance but is not characteristic of detached retina.

3. Increase in intraocular pressure is characteristic of glaucoma, not detached retina.

#31. 2. Positioning to keep the retina next to the choroid and the area of detachment dependent is important postoperatively. This may be on the operative or the nonoperative side depending on the position of the detachment.   Pl   Ph/9   Ap

1. The client should not cough after eye surgery. Coughing may cause increased intraocular pressure.

3. The client is put on bed rest with both eyes patched to minimize eye movement.

4. Mydriatics to dilate the pupil and cycloplegics to paralyze the eye muscles are give postoperatively.

#32. 2. Ménière's disease is a chronic disease of the inner ear characterized by recurrent episodes of vertigo, tinnitus, and progressive unilateral nerve deafness. Nausea may result from the vertigo the client is experiencing.   As   Ph/9   An

1. Nystagmus is not characteristic of Ménière's disease. Ménière's disease is a chronic disease of the inner ear characterized by recurrent episodes of vertigo, tinnitus, and progressive unilateral nerve deafness.

3. Ménière's disease is a chronic disease of the inner ear characterized by recurrent episodes of vertigo, tinnitus, and progressive unilateral nerve deafness. Nausea may result from the vertigo the client is experiencing. Blurred vision is not seen.

4. Ménière's disease is a chronic disease of the inner ear characterized by recurrent episodes of vertigo, tinnitus, and progressive unilateral nerve deafness. Nystagmus is not characteristic of Ménière's disease.

#33. 4. Clients with Ménière's disease are on a restricted fluid intake and may also be on diuretics.   Ev   Ph/9   Ap

     1. Management of Ménière's disease includes stopping smoking.

     2. Management of Ménière's disease includes moving slowly to promote safety.

     3. Management of Ménière's disease includes a low-sodium diet.

#34. 2. The catheter should be sufficiently stiff so as not to coil in the esophageal pouch and should never be forced when resistance is felt. Air can be instilled into the stomach or gastric contents aspirated to confirm a patent esophagus.   As   Ph/9   Ap

     1. The history would more likely show polyhydramnios. Amniotic fluid does not reach the gastrointestinal tract of the fetus with an esophageal atresia, thus causing a gradual increase in the volume of amniotic fluid throughout the pregnancy.

     3. As the esophageal pouch fills with fluid, it will overflow into the trachea and bronchus, causing laryngospasm and respiratory distress.

     4. Placing the infant with the head in a downward position is an intervention rather than an assessment. If the defect is the most common type (upper atresia with lower fistula into the trachea), air will collect in the stomach with crying, causing pressure upward on the diaphragm. Since air rises, the infant's head should be elevated to reduce gastric distention from air. Continuous suction of the pouch with a catheter in place keeps the mucus away from the upper trachea.

#35. 2. Increased systolic pressure is a result of fibrosis of blood vessels and calcification and elongation of arteries, which frequently occur in aging.   As   He/3   An

     1. Less muscle mass does not cause increased systolic pressure.

     3. Dehydration does not cause increased systolic pressure. It is apt to cause hypotension.

     4. Impaired lung capacity is not the most likely cause of systolic hypertension.

#36. 4. The earliest sign of digitalis toxicity is vomiting, although one episode does not warrant discontinuing medication.   Ev   Ph/8   Ap

     1. Bradypnea (slow breathing) is not associated with digitalis toxicity. Bradycardia is associated with digitalis toxicity.

     2. Although children with congestive heart failure often have a related condition of failure to thrive, it is not directly related to digitalis administration. It is more related to chronic hypoxia.

     3. Tachycardia is not a sign of digitalis toxicity. Bradycardia is a sign of digitalis toxicity.

#37. 1. Following a bone marrow transplant, it is of the utmost importance to protect the child from infections.   Ev   Ph/9   Ap

     2. Until the child starts producing leukocytes, he should stay at home and avoid crowded areas such as school, malls, etc.

     3. There is no reason to confine the child to bed. His own energy level can dictate his activity.

     4. There is no reason for 24-hour nursing care. Family members can learn specifics of care needed by the child.

#38. 4. Talipes equinus refers to plantar flexion, which lowers the toes below the level of the heel. Talipes varus refers to the inversion of the whole foot. Notice that the defect involves the ankle and whole foot, rather than just the toes and forefoot (which would be metatarsus adductus or pigeon toes).   As   Ph/9   An

     1. Boys have a 2:1 higher incidence of clubfoot than girls. Unilateral defects are slightly more common.

     2. True clubfoot cannot be rotated to a neutral position because the ankle and foot bones have formed in utero into a rigid defect.

ANSWER	RATIONALE	NP	CN	CL

However, the statement is true of metatarsus adductus, which is a flexible inversion of the toes and forefoot.

3. Manipulation and casting are usually begun immediately upon discovery of the defect. The infant's bones are most flexible during the newborn period. Early treatment has resulted in fewer long-term complications with tendons, ligaments, and muscles.

#39. 4. Cervical traction can be intermittent.   Im   Ph/9   An
1. Bryant's traction is continuous traction.
2. Russell traction is continuous traction.
3. Buck's traction is continuous traction.

#40. 2. The two major complications of a herniorrhaphy are a distended bladder and scrotal swelling. It is important to assess for difficulty in urinating postoperatively.   Im   Ph/9   Ap
1. The herniorrhaphy client is instructed to turn and deep breathe but not to cough, as coughing may cause increased pressure on his incision.
3. Ice bags, not heat, are applied to his scrotal area to reduce swelling and pain.
4. No strenuous physical activities are allowed for 6 to 8 weeks postoperatively.

#41. 3. The nine-month-old should easily sit up without support.   An   He/3   Ap
1. The attention span of a nine-month-old is very short. Playing with a toy for only a few minutes is normal behavior.
2. Some nine-month-old children can pull themselves to a standing position, but being unable to do so is not a cause for concern.
4. Crying when something is taken away from her is normal behavior for a nine-month-old.

#42. 3. The nurse is firm in carrying out the order and separating it from behavior.   Im   He/3   Ap
1. The nurse cannot promise there won't be any more shots. This response also ties shots to behavior, which the nurse should not do.
2. The response in choice 2 deals with behavior as a cause for injections and is inappropriate.
4. The child needs the medication. The nurse should not try to shift the blame to the physician.

#43. 1. It is normal for a child of this age to want to marry the parent of the opposite sex. It is known as the oedipal stage. The child will outgrow this and only needs to be reminded that he can't marry his mother.   Im   He/3   Ap
2. Asking about marital difficulties is inappropriate, especially in light of the child's normal behavior.
3. The child is exhibiting normal behavior. He does not need discipline.
4. The child is exhibiting normal behavior and does not need counseling.

#44. 3. A syringe is used for accuracy. A second nurse should always verify potent drugs that require measurement.   Im   Ph/8   Ap
1. It is inappropriate to put the medication in formula. The medication will alter the taste of the formula and the infant may refuse it. There is also no way of knowing how much of the medication the infant actually gets if he does not drink all of the formula.
2. The apical rate below which digoxin is not given is 100 to 110 for a young infant.
4. The mother is not responsible to the hospital. The nurse must demonstrate how to give medications to the infant as part of discharge teaching.

#45. 2. All of the diagnoses are relevant at some point in the care of this child. Alteration in fluid and electrolyte balance is the most immediate concern.   An   Ph/9   Ap
1. Growth will improve following surgery.

ANSWER	RATIONALE	NP	CN	CL

3.   Potential for altered family process related to situational crisis is a possible diagnosis. However, it is of lesser importance than the actual physiologic problem related to fluid and electrolyte balance.

4.   Nutritional deficit is a high priority but secondary to fluid and electrolyte balance.

#46. 2.   A quick assessment is to look for uneven shoulders. Ask the girl to bend over and look at bra strap marks to see if one side is deeper.   As   He/4   An

    1.   Scoliosis is a lateral curvature. Girls with scoliosis may well be able to walk a straight line.

    3.   The nurse is unlikely to detect scoliosis by running the fingers down the spine.

    4.   Watching the girls as they do physical education activities is unrealistic and not as likely to pick up a potential problem as checking each girl individually.

#47. 3.   The biggest risk to this child is that his airway will close off. If this occurs, a tracheotomy will be necessary to save his life.   Pl   Ph/9   Ap

    1.   A croup tent may be used but is of lesser importance than a tracheotomy set.

    2.   The child is not in danger of having seizures.

    4.   Suction would be handy but can be dangerous to use in the child with epiglottitis, as it may irritate, increase swelling, and cause complete blockage of the airway.

#48. 2.   Altered family process is a priority diagnosis as this child needs to be able to talk with his family and they need to be able to support him through his death.   An   Ps/5   An

    1.   The child may have some anxiety about dying but the data show him to be dealing reasonably with his coming death. His parents seem to have the greater problem.

    3.   There are no data to support body image disturbance. It is possible that chemotherapy has altered his appearance, but those data are not presented.

    4.   There are no data to support the diagnosis of a knowledge deficit.

#49. 3.   An intrauterine device is least appropriate. With a history of numerous partners, she is at increased risk of infection, a common problem with IUDs.   An   He/3   Ap

    1.   There are no risk factors presented that would contraindicate the use of oral contraceptives.

    2.   Condoms and foam would be harmless and might give some protection against sexually transmitted diseases.

    4.   The diaphragm is not contraindicated. It does, however, require motivation to use.

#50. 4.   Reva Rubin identified the phases of adjustment following delivery as taking-in, taking-hold, and letting-go. Lack of interest in infant care and the need to talk about herself are perfectly normal in this initial phase of taking-in.   An   He/3   An

    1.   Lack of interest in infant care and the need to talk about herself are perfectly normal at this point in her puerperium.

    2.   Fatigue is not the best answer. Although she may be fatigued, the behavior does not indicate this.

    3.   It is too soon after delivery to suggest the woman is unable to accept the reality of parenthood. Her behavior is normal for this point in time.

#51. 1.   It is rare to be able to retract the foreskin of a newborn. This does not indicate a need for circumcision.   Im   He/3   An

    2.   The foreskin of an infant may not retract. This statement is not correct in regards to an infant. An older child will be taught to retract and clean when the foreskin can be easily retracted. It is never forced.

    3.   Inability to retract the foreskin of a newborn is not an indication the child will need to be circumcised.

ANSWER	RATIONALE	NP	CN	CL

4. Referring the mother to the pediatrician is not the best answer. It does not deal with the mother's question about the foreskin not being retractable.

#52. 2. It is appropriate to ask about passing flatus as this would indicate normal peristaltic activity.   As   Ph/7   Ap

1. She would be unlikely to have a bowel movement so soon. It is not necessary to have a bowel movement before eating solids.
3. The nurse assesses bowel sounds with a stethoscope, not by asking the client to describe them.
4. The client is hungry as she has asked for real food. Hunger is not an indication of return of peristalsis. If she has no bowel sounds and is not passing gas, hunger alone is not a criterion for beginning solid foods.

#53. 4. A contraction lasting longer than 90 seconds increases the risk of fetal distress and uterine rupture. Safe practice requires the nurse to immediately discontinue the pitocin.   Im   Ph/8   Ap

1. Although fetal heart rate is an important indicator, stop the drip first, then assess fetal heart. It is dangerous to wait longer.
2. Turning the client on her left side and encouraging transition breathing is inadequate intervention. The pitocin must be discontinued.
3. The pitocin must be stopped. It is not safe to merely decrease the rate of the infusion.

#54. 3. She has a 2000-calorie ADA diet prescribed. The best way to begin is to see what her normal eating habits are. Then the diet can be individualized to her needs and compliance will be better.   Pl   Ph/9   An

1. She needs to know about her problem, but dietary compliance is most appropriate at this time.
2. Insulin injections are not necessary at this time. She may not need insulin.
4. Diets must be flexible. Identifying risks to her fetus at this time will put too much pressure on the client.

#55. 4. Given the degree of symptoms, this client is at risk of seizures and probably is already suffering intrauterine growth retardation. Her physical well-being and that of the fetus are in jeopardy. The other three choices are appropriate but less important.   An   Ph/10   An

1. Alteration in fluid volume is appropriate but less important than alteration in tissue perfusion.
2. Powerlessness is appropriate but less important than alteration in tissue perfusion.
3. Ineffective family coping is appropriate but less important than alteration in tissue perfusion.

#56. 4. Before any further intervention, it is essential to check if the bladder is full. A full bladder may hold the fetus back.   As   He/3   An

1. The condition of the fetal membranes is not likely to be a problem. Most likely they are ruptured, but, unlike the bladder, this is not holding up descent.
2. We already know that she is tired, but the baby must be delivered and this assessment will not help us with that goal.
3. The cervix is completely effaced and dilated or she would not be pushing.

#57. 1. Wearing latex gloves is part of universal precautions. This is essential because the newborn is coated with amniotic fluid.   Im   Sa/2   Ap

2. It is not appropriate to keep the infant in an open crib. The newborn must be kept warm, so the admission is usually done under a warmer.
3. A mask and gown are not necessary.
4. It would be easier to perform the admission procedures while the infant is asleep. However, this is not practical. The infant will not sleep through the whole procedure. It is better to obtain heart rate and respiratory rate while the infant is quiet.

ANSWER	RATIONALE	NP	CN	CL

#58. 4. **Prone is the best position for minimal pressure on the defect. Rupture presents a surgical emergency and all efforts are taken to avoid it.** — Im — Ph/9 — An

   1. Semi-sitting in an infant seat would put direct pressure on the sac. This position is contraindicated.

   2. Side-lying with head lower than the rest of his body increases pressure on the defect and is contraindicated.

   3. Supine is the worst position as the sac would be very likely to rupture.

#59. 3. **The symptoms described are side effects of antipsychotic medication and are not the symptoms of agitation often seen in a schizophrenic client. Cogentin is the only medication listed that will decrease the side effects of the antipsychotic medication.** — Im — Ph/8 — An

   1. The symptoms described are side effects of antipsychotic medication and are not the symptoms of agitation often seen in a schizophrenic client. Ativan would be administered for psychotic agitation but would not treat the side effects of antipsychotic medications.

   2. Atropine is an anticholinergic medication and is not used to treat side effects of antipsychotic medications.

   4. The symptoms described are side effects of antipsychotic medication and are not the symptoms of agitation often seen in a schizophrenic client. Thorazine would make the side effects worse.

#60. 4. **Because DSM-IV criteria for paranoid schizophrenia focus on delusions and suspiciousness, a decrease in these symptoms would be the expected outcome from antipsychotic medication.** — Ev — Ph/8 — An

   1. Sleep may be affected with paranoid schizophrenia, however, it is not a hallmark symptom. The nurse would expect to see decreased hallucinations.

   2. Appetite may be affected with paranoid schizophrenia, however, it is not a hallmark symptom. Personal hygiene may be improved but is not a hallmark symptom.

   3. Appetite may be affected with paranoid schizophrenia, however, it is not a hallmark symptom. The nurse would expect to see decreased suspiciousness.

#61. 1. **This response points out the client's strength in a realistic manner and is an attempt to improve the client's self-concept.** — Im — Ps/6 — Ap

   2. This response is the nurse's opinion only.

   3. This is a judgmental and nontherapeutic response.

   4. This response is therapeutic and empathetic but is not geared toward self-esteem. The question asked for a response that would increase the client's self-esteem.

#62. 2. **Abusive behavior often occurs when parents lose control or feel overwhelmed.** — Pl — Ps/6 — An

   1. Abusive parents usually do not plan their abuse.

   3. Abusive parents usually do feel guilt.

   4. Abusive parents are not always the product of abuse themselves.

#63. 3. **The most important improvement would be the client's ability to live within the guidelines, rules, and regulations of the psychiatric hospital environment, as well as a decrease in testing limits.** — Ev — Ps/6 — An

   1. Attendance at therapeutic groups does not indicate improvement in an antisocial client. The client may well attend groups and continue to manipulate people and test limits.

   2. Clients with antisocial personalities are not psychotic and are not routinely medicated with antipsychotic drugs.

   4. Antisocial clients may well socialize with peers. The quality of the interactions needs to be evaluated.

#64. 2. **The client should drink several glasses of water prior to the test.** — Pl — Ph/9 — Ap

   1. A cytoscopy is not painless. A local anesthetic is usually used.

ANSWER		RATIONALE	NP	CN	CL
	3.	Breathing rapidly and deeply during the procedure would cause respiratory alkalosis. The client should not do this.			
	4.	An enema is not necessary before a cytoscopy.			
#65.	1.	**A Tensilon test yields immediate results. If positive, the client almost immediately has an increase in muscle strength.**	Ev	Ph/9	An
	2.	The test is accurate in nearly all persons with myasthenia gravis.			
	3.	Tensilon causes an increase in muscle strength.			
	4.	Tensilon acts to increase the amount of acetylcholine available.			
#66.	2.	**Serum creatinine and BUN (blood urea nitrogen) are tests of kidney function. Before giving contrast media, it is essential to be sure the kidneys can excrete the dyes.**	An	Ph/9	An
	1.	Renal function tests do not determine if the person is allergic to iodine.			
	3.	The CT scan is very unlikely to cause renal damage.			
	4.	BUN and serum creatinine do not give additional information about the presence of possible tumors.			
#67.	2.	**As one ages, the eyes undergo changes including a decreased ability to focus on near objects, increased difficulty with color discrimination and a lessened field of peripheral vision.**	As	He/4	Ap
	1.	This is poor communication.			
	3.	Resting the eyes will not increase peripheral vision.			
	4.	Moving slowly will not increase peripheral vision. Moving slowly might be relevant if the client had a detached retina.			
#68.	3.	**Dysarthria is the term used to describe difficulty speaking when muscle impairment is present.**	As	Ph/9	Ap
	1.	Semantic aphasia is the inability to understand the meaning of words.			
	2.	Receptive aphasia is the inability to understand spoken or written words.			
	4.	Dysphagia is difficulty swallowing.			
#69.	3.	**Swelling, heat, redness, impaired function, and pain are cardinal signs of local inflammation.**	As	Ph/9	An
	1.	Fever is a sign of systemic inflammation. Pain, swelling, heat, and redness are signs of local inflammation.			
	2.	Fever is a sign of systemic inflammation. Pain, swelling, heat, and redness are signs of local inflammation.			
	4.	Fever, sweating, chills, and malaise are signs of systemic inflammation.			
#70.	1.	**A liquid diet should be given for 5 days prior to surgery to ensure adequate cleansing of the bowel before surgery.**	Pl	Ph/9	Ap
	2.	Adequacy of rectal sphincter should be assessed by giving enemas in increasing amounts. This also helps to increase sphincter control.			
	3.	Neomycin decreases intestinal flora.			
	4.	There is increased risk of thrombophlebitis in pelvic surgery. Elastic stockings are an important preventive measure.			
#71.	2.	**It is essential to apply pressure to the puncture site for 5 minutes to ensure the client does not bleed from the arterial puncture.**	Im	Ph/9	Ap
	1.	Coughing and deep breathing are indicated for this client but this is not related to the drawing of arterial blood gases.			
	3.	The nurse should not shake the vial of blood as this will bring atmospheric oxygen into the blood and make the analysis inaccurate.			
	4.	There is no need for bed rest because the client had arterial blood gases drawn.			
#72.	4.	**Arterial blood gases give the most specific information about the adequacy of the oxygen therapy.**	Ev	Ph/9	An
	1.	Respiratory rate is not the most useful in assessing the adequacy of oxygen therapy. Factors other than oxygen therapy can affect the respiratory rate.			
	2.	The color of the mucous membranes is not the best method to assess the adequacy of oxygen therapy. Many things can affect the mucous membranes.			

3. Pulmonary function tests are useful in differentiating between obstructive and restrictive lung diseases and in quantifying the degree of obstructive or restrictive lung disorders.

#73. 4. A pH of 7.35 is on the acid side of normal. All of the other values are abnormal so the client is compensated. The CO_2 is sharply elevated and will lower the pH. The HCO_3 is also elevated and is responsible for bringing the pH up to the normal range. An abnormal O_2 suggests that the problem is a respiratory one. An Ph/9 An

1. Metabolic acidosis would have a low HCO_3 level as well as a low pH.
2. Compensated metabolic alkalosis would have a higher pH and a high HCO_3.
3. Respiratory alkalosis would have a higher pH and a low CO_2.

#74. 1. The client will probably be unable to move the injured leg but should be able to move the toes. As Ph/10 Ap

2. The injured extremity will appear shorter and be in external rotation.
3. The injured leg will be painful if moved. She will have difficulty voluntarily moving the leg.
4. Involuntary tremors are not usually seen in a client with a hip fracture.

#75. 1. The affected leg should be kept abducted and externally rotated to keep the hip in the socket. Ev Ph/9 An

2. The affected leg should be kept abducted and externally rotated to keep the hip in the socket. Adduction will encourage the hip to pop out of the socket.
3. The affected leg should be kept abducted and externally rotated to keep the hip in the socket. Internal rotation allows the hip to pop out of the socket.
4. The affected leg should be kept abducted and externally rotated to keep the hip in the socket. Adduction and internal rotation allow the hip to pop out of the socket.

#76. 2. Guillian-Barré syndrome is characterized by an ascending paralysis that usually paralyzes the respiratory muscles before descending. Im Ph/9 Ap

1. High-Fowler's position is not indicated for this client with an ascending paralysis. The client does not have increased intracranial pressure.
3. Guillain-Barré syndrome is characterized by a paralysis that ascends and paralyzes the respiratory muscles. If the client receives good respiratory support the paralysis will descend after a few days. If the client has received good supportive nursing care and receives good care and physical therapy he may have return of nearly all function. However, this is not the priority action.
4. Guillain-Barré syndrome is thought to be an autoimmune response following a viral infection. The client is no longer infectious. The viral infection occurred in the past.

#77. 3. Gradual blurring and clouding of vision are symptomatic of cataracts. As Ph/10 An

1. Acute eye pain is characteristic of a foreign body in the eye or acute glaucoma.
2. Redness and itching in the eye indicate infection or allergic reaction.
4. Severe headaches and dizziness are not characteristic of cataracts. They might suggest migraine headaches.

#78. 4. Metal in the body such as pacemakers, aneurysm clips, and hip prostheses can affect the magnetic field. As Ph/9 Ap

1. MRI does not use an iodine dye.
2. The client should be asked if he has claustrophobia, fear of small spaces, as the MRI chamber is very small and confined.
3. There is no movement of the client during the procedure. Dizziness is not a concern.

ANSWER	RATIONALE	NP	CN	CL

#79. 4. **BCG vaccine is given in many parts of the world to immunize against tuberculosis. It causes formation of antibodies and consequently a positive reaction to a tuberculin skin test, which is an antigen-antibody test. A positive skin test for tuberculosis in the person who has had BCG vaccine indicates the vaccine is working and producing antibodies.**   An   Sa/4   An

    1. A positive skin test and negative chest X-ray is seen in persons who have been immunized against tuberculosis.

    2. It is true that the skin test is only a screening test. However, this is not the key understanding the nurse needs to respond to the client.

    3. BCG vaccine is effective against tuberculosis.

#80. 3. **Catsup is high in sodium and should not be used on a low-sodium diet. The nurse should suggest a better substitute than catsup for gravy.**   Ev   Ph/7   Ap

    1. The client can select a low-sodium, low-fat diet at the salad bar. Using vinegar only will give the salad flavor without adding oil and sodium. The nurse should be sure the client understands that not all foods on the salad bar are low in fat and sodium.

    2. Removing the skin from chicken reduces the fat content. Broiling is a good way to cook meat without adding fat or sodium.

    4. Skim milk contains no fat and is appropriate for this client. Milk does contain sodium and should be used in limited amounts on a low-sodium diet.

#81. 3. **There is no reason for the client to lie down following administration of eye drops.**   Im   Ph/8   Ap

    1. Eye drops may cause blurred vision and difficulty focusing for a period of time.

    2. Applying gentle pressure to the nasolacrimal canal for 1 to 2 minutes after instillation will prevent the medication from entering the lacrimal duct and causing systemic absorption or tearing.

    4. Eye drops should be placed in the conjunctival sac by pulling the lower lid down and placing the medicine in the center of the lid.

#82. 2. **People who are pregnant should not come in close contact with someone who has internal radiation therapy. The radioactivity could possibly damage the fetus.**   Ev   Sa/2   An

    1. The client will be on a clear liquid or very low residue diet. Hamburgers and french fries are not allowed.

    3. This statement is not true. As soon as the radiation source is removed (probably 36 to 72 hours after insertion), the client is no longer contaminated with radioactivity.

    4. Craft projects usually require the client to sit. The client must remain flat with very little head elevation during the time the rods are in place.

#83. 1. **The nurse aide should wear gloves when giving an enema to a client. Fecal material is certainly a body fluid and could transmit AIDS or, more likely, hepatitis.**   Ev   Sa/2   Ap

    2. Blood spills should be cleaned with chlorine bleach, not iodine.

    3. Needles should never be recapped. The number one cause of needle sticks has been recapping needles.

    4. It is not necessary to wear a gown and mask just to be in the same room with a person with AIDS. All persons should avoid contact with body fluids from a person infected with AIDS.

#84. 1. **Before entering the room the nurse should announce his/her name clearly so the client is not startled.**   Im   Sa/2   Ap

    2. There is no need to speak in a louder tone. The client is unable to see, not deaf.

    3. Before entering the room the nurse should announce his/her name clearly so the client is not startled. The nurse should speak before touching the client.

4. The nurse should speak normally to the client. Most persons will be more uncomfortable if people try to avoid all reference to sight than if they continue to use the normal figures of speech.

#85. 3. Filling of the collection chambers with sanguinous (bloody) drainage indicates the drainage system is functioning. The purpose of chest drainage is to remove fluid and air in the thoracic cavity. — Ev — Ph/9 — Ap

1. If the drainage system is functioning there should be intermittent bubbling in the water seal chamber. Bubbling in the water seal chamber is caused by air leaving the thoracic cavity. Absence of bubbling shortly after the chest tube is inserted indicates an obstruction in the tubing.

2. The fluid level in the suction control chamber does not fluctuate with respiration. Fluctuation with respiration may occur in the fluid in the water seal chamber.

4. The client may report relief of pain as air and fluid are removed from the thoracic cavity, however, this is not the best indicator that the system is functioning effectively. The client will probably also have received pain medication.

#86. 3. The purpose of administering nitroglycerin is to improve blood flow to the myocardium and relieve chest pain. — Ev — Ph/8 — Ap

1. Nitroglycerin may cause blood pressure to drop because it dilates peripheral vessels. However, that is not the primary purpose for administering nitroglycerin. Increased perfusion of the myocardium and resultant relief of pain is the desired effect. If the client is having a myocardial infarction rather than angina his blood pressure may drop even though he does not have increased myocardial perfusion and pain relief.

2. A headache indicates the cerebral vessels have dilated as a result of the nitroglycerin. However, that is not the primary purpose for administering nitroglycerin. Increased perfusion of the myocardium and resultant relief of pain is the desired effect. If the client is having a myocardial infarction rather than angina he may develop a headache even though he does not have increased myocardial perfusion and pain relief.

4. The development of nausea does not indicate increased myocardial perfusion and pain relief. Nausea may indicate his condition is getting worse.

#87. 1. Wrist restraints may be indicated for a confused client who is pulling out an IV line. The least restraint possible should be used for the shortest period of time. — As — Sa/2 — Ap

2. A client's refusal of treatment is not sufficient basis for the use of restraints. The description says nothing about the client being confused. A person has the right to refuse treatment.

3. Netting over the crib would be more appropriate for a one-year-old child who is trying to climb out of the crib. Wrist restraints are not indicated. The least restraint possible should be used.

4. Side rails would be more appropriate for an adult who gets out of bed during the night. There is no need for wrist restraints. The least restraint possible should be used.

#88. 4. The vastus lateralis is the most appropriate site for a child of this age. The gluteal sites are not used until the child has been walking for some time. — Im — Ph/8 — Ap

1. The gluteal sites are not used until the child has been walking for some time. The infant does not have enough muscle at this site. There is danger of hitting vessels and nerves.

2. The gluteal sites are not used until the child has been walking for some time. The infant does not have enough muscle at this site. There is danger of hitting vessels and nerves.

ANSWER		RATIONALE	NP	CN	CL

	3.	The ventral forearm is used for skin tests, not intramuscular injections.			
#89.	3.	**Baked chicken, steamed broccoli and cauliflower, steamed rice, and hot tea are all low in sodium and low in fat.**	Ev	Ph/7	Ap
	1.	Fried chicken is high in fat. Milk is high in sodium and fat.			
	2.	Macaroni and cheese casserole, salad dressing, and hot chocolate are high in both fat and sodium.			
	4.	Steak is high in fat and sodium. A baked potato is acceptable unless the client puts butter, cheese, or sour cream on it.			
#90.	2.	**Persons who are having a pelvic sonogram should drink several glasses of water before the procedure so the bladder is full.**	As	Ph/9	Ap
	1.	The client may be asked this question. However, there is no x-ray exposure during a pelvic sonogram so the procedure is safe even if the woman is pregnant.			
	3.	There is no bowel prep required for this procedure. This question is irrelevant.			
	4.	It is important to ask about the use of powders and deodorants in the woman who is having a mammogram but this is not relevant to a pelvic sonogram.			
#91.	1.	**The RN should delegate routine care to nonprofessional staff. Complex wound care requires the assessment and problem-solving skill possessed by the RN. The nursing assistant has the knowledge and skill to ambulate a postoperative client for the first time. The least comprehensive task is the application of an ice bag, which can be delegated to the nursing assistant.**	An	Sa/1	Ap
	2.	See rationale for choice #1.			
	3.	See rationale for choice #1.			
	4.	See rationale for choice #1.			
#92.	4.	**The ethical principle of autonomy is the basis for the client's right to expect that the nurse will hold personal information in confidence, even when the news is good.**	As	Sa/1	An
	1.	There are no data to support this interpretation.			
	2.	Mood swings are common in pregnancy. However, there are no data to support this interpretation.			
	3.	The statement may be true, but again there are no data to support this interpretation.			
#93.	3.	**Secondary hypertension occurs in response to one or more underlying causative factors such as specific disease processes (i.e., renal disease, primary aldosteronism, etc.), or in response to a combination of modifiable risk factors such as obesity, smoking, excessive sodium intake, high alcohol intake, low potassium intake, physical inactivity, and high stress levels. The stepped-care approach focuses on control of modifiable risk factors first, followed by medication therapy tailored to meet the client's specific needs. Reducing the sodium in the diet, losing weight, increasing exercise, avoiding tobacco use, and reducing stress are all within the client's control and must be emphasized in a discharge plan of care along with clear, specific information regarding the actions and side effects of drug therapy being used to treat the client's hypertension.**	Pl	Ph/9	Ap
	1.	There is no need to limit activity.			
	2.	There is no need to restrict potassium.			
	4.	There is no need to restrict magnesium and probably not a need for rest periods.			
#94.	3.	**In addition to review of the disease process, a brief review of anatomy and physiology is needed. Clients should be taught the importance of good hand washing as a preface to the use of strict aseptic technique while performing the exchange procedure. Clients should be taught to monitor vital signs before starting**	Pl	Ph/9	Ap

ANSWER	RATIONALE	NP	CN	CL

the exchange procedure and when the procedure is complete. An awareness of possible complications and appropriate responses, along with specific measures for maintaining peritoneal catheter sterility are essential parts of the teaching plan. Clients need current information regarding dietary modifications and oral fluid intake. Commonly these modifications result in protein and carbohydrate restrictions and no fluid restrictions, but each client's diet is tailored to meet individual needs.

1. The client does not have an indwelling Foley catheter.
2. The client does not have an A-V shunt with CAPD. An A-V shunt may be in place in the client with hemodialysis.
4. There is no fistula with CAPD.

#95. 1. A cardioselective beta blocker is less likely to cause or worsen the heart block while still effectively suppressing the ventricular ectopic beats.   Ev   Ph/8   Co

2. Calcium gluconate is contraindicated in ventricular fibrillation.
3. Verapamil is contraindicated in A-V block.
4. Diltiazem is contraindicated in second degree heart block.

#96. 3. The 3-point gait is the appropriate gait for someone with a broken ankle as it allows no weight bearing on the affected leg. The client advances both crutches and the unaffected leg at the same time. The client then swings the involved extremity to the crutches while the body's weight is supported by the crutches and the unaffected leg.   Ev   Ph/7   Ap

1. This would involve bearing weight on the affected leg.
2. The client should bear no weight on the affected leg.
4. Weight should be borne by the hands and not the armpits.

#97. 2. The nurse's assessment reveals symptoms of a transfusion reaction. When a transfusion reaction is suspected, the transfusion should be stopped and the IV line should be kept open with normal saline. After stopping the transfusion, the nurse should notify the physician.   Im   Ph/8   An

1. The physician should be notified after the infusion is stopped.
3. The nurse should trust his/her ability to take vital signs. The nurse should not wait before stopping the transfusion.
4. The amount of urine output will be checked as further indication of possible shock, but not until the transfusion has been stopped.

#98. 3. CVP or pulmonary artery catheter will be inserted by the physician to monitor fluid levels in the blood. This enables early detection of high or low levels and promotes management of complication.   Im   Ph/10   An

1. The client might receive vasoconstrictive drugs, but initially the CVP or pulmonary artery catheter will be inserted to monitor the client.
2. Depending upon the client's status, fluids may or may not be restricted.
4. MAST trousers are applied when the client has severe abdominal bleeding. They are not appropriate for the client in cardiogenic shock.

#99. 1. To prevent falls, the environment should be well lighted. Night lights should be used if necessary. Other factors to assess include removing loose scatter rugs, removing spills, and installing handrails and grab bars as appropriate.   As   Sa/2   An

2. The amount of regular exercise is not the most important factor to assess. It is only indirectly related.
3. The resting pulse rate is not related to preventing falls.
4. The salt intake is not directly related to preventing falls.

#100. 1. Older adults make medication administration errors for many reasons, the most common of which is forgetfulness. As with any new behavior, incorporation into the daily scheme of events requires patience and repetition, and is more easily   Pl   Ph/9   Ap accomplished if associated with some other regular, familiar, daily activity. **Pill boxes come in an assortment of styles, are very useful in organizing dosages, and are used for any client who is taking several medications either daily or more than once each day.**

2. The client should be able to be responsible for his own medication routine since he is alert and oriented.
3. The client should be responsible for his own medication routine since he is alert and oriented.
4. Encouragement, understanding, teaching, and follow-up are important in promoting adherence to medication regimens.

Practice Test 8

1. The nurse is assessing an elderly client. Which finding is most apt to be seen in the elderly client with dementia?
   1. Good hygiene and grooming.
   2. Rapid mood swings.
   3. Agnosia.
   4. Phobias and unwanted thoughts and behaviors.

2. A middle-aged adult is being treated for second and third degree burns over 25% of his body and is now ready for discharge. The nurse evaluates his understanding of discharge instructions relating to wound care and is satisfied that he is prepared for home care when he makes which statement?
   1. "I will need to take sponge baths at home to avoid exposing the wounds to unsterile bath water."
   2. "If any healed areas break open I should first cover them with a sterile dressing and then report it."
   3. "I must wear my Jobst elastic garment all day and can only remove it when I'm going to bed."
   4. "I can expect occasional periods of low-grade fever and can take Tylenol every 4 hours."

3. The nurse is developing a care plan for a two-year-old girl with Hirschsprung's disease. Which of the following is least appropriate and would not be included on the care plan?
   1. Administer stool softeners.
   2. Give isotonic enemas.
   3. Have client follow a low-fiber diet.
   4. Place on fluid restriction.

4. Two-year-old James is admitted to the hospital with the flu and dehydration. The mother states that he has been running high fevers, which she brought down with baby aspirin. She has given him decongestants and leftover amoxicillin ordered by the pediatrician the last time the child had an ear infection. He has taken almost no food or fluid for several days and has slept almost constantly. His weight has dropped from 30 pounds to 21 pounds. On admission, his temperature is 101.2°F, heart rate 100, respiratory rate 26. In analyzing the above data, which fact increases his risk for Reye's syndrome?
   1. The use of aspirin.
   2. His prolonged high fevers.
   3. The use of antibiotics previously prescribed.
   4. Severe dehydration as evidenced by weight loss.

5. Three-year-old Sally has been admitted with a diagnosis of suspected child abuse. Her parents brought her to the emergency room with a fractured arm, which they say she sustained when she fell down the stairs. Which of the following would the nurse expect to find in the assessment of Sally if she has been abused?
   1. A child who is very trusting of her nurse since she has not been able to trust her parents.
   2. Sally will be constantly asking for her parents to comfort her even if they abused her.
   3. A child who doesn't cry much and who responds very little to her environment.
   4. Sally will be bouncing around, feeling safe and happy to be away from an abusive home.

6. A pregnant woman is diagnosed as being anemic. Her physician has told her to eat an iron-rich diet and to take iron supplements

BID. What instruction should the nurse plan to give about taking iron?
1. Iron should be taken on an empty stomach at least 1 hour before meals.
2. It is good to increase consumption of dairy products while taking iron.
3. Citrus juice taken with iron will increase absorption.
4. Iron supplements often cause diarrhea and should be discontinued if diarrhea develops.

7. During parenting classes, the nurse teaches parents the importance of immunizations and the schedule that will be implemented. Which of the following findings indicate the nurse's teaching has been effective?
1. The parents are able to list three reasons to immunize and when to begin immunization.
2. Taking the infant for his first immunization at 2 weeks of age.
3. The parents state their intent to follow a printed immunization schedule.
4. By 6 months of age, the infant has received the recommended immunizations.

8. Ms. K. delivered her first baby 12 hours ago. She calls the nurse in tears stating that she has been unable to get the baby to nurse. "All she does is cry when I try to get her to nurse." The nurse comes to assist Ms. K. The best initial action for the nurse is to
1. explain the basics of breast feeding to the client.
2. assess Ms. K.'s nipples and the measures she has tried.
3. demonstrate proper positioning of mother and baby.
4. find out if Ms. K. really wants to breast feed or would rather bottle feed.

9. A postpartum client complains of sore nipples, a sore bottom, cramping, fatigue, and lack of ability to satisfy her newborn, who is crying. Based on these data, which of the following would be an appropriate nursing diagnosis?
1. Ineffective parenting.
2. Alteration in comfort.
3. Anxiety related to new role of parenting.
4. Knowledge deficit.

10. A client in labor has been taught to use breathing to help her cope with the discomfort of contractions. To evaluate the effectiveness of the teaching, the nurse would
1. ask the client to demonstrate each of the techniques and state the appropriate time in labor to use it.
2. observe the client's use of breathing with contractions.
3. have the client list the two main respiratory techniques and the variations.
4. identify the client's request for pain medications or refusal as evidence of good breathing.

11. The nurse is to give Coumadin (warfarin) 10 mg po. The nurse is comparing the anticoagulants Coumadin and heparin. Which statement is not correct?
1. Heparin dose is measured in units; Coumadin dose is measured in mg.
2. Both heparin and Coumadin can be given IV.
3. Heparin therapy is monitored by APTT; Coumadin therapy is monitored by PT.
4. Heparin dissolves existing clots; Coumadin does not.

12. Mr. S. is post-op abdominoperineal resection (AP resection) for colon and rectal cancer. Which of the following statements indicates to the nurse that he requires further teaching concerning his recovery?
1. "I'm glad this colostomy is only temporary."
2. "I'll have to cut back on eating coleslaw, my favorite type of salad."
3. "The warm sitz baths relieve the discomfort I feel from the incision on my bottom."
4. "This T-binder helps support my abdominal incision."

13. Ms. S. had a tuberculin skin test, which the nurse reads as positive. Which of the following is true about the tuberculin skin test?
1. The intradermal test does not differentiate active tuberculosis from dormant infections.
2. The induration is measured in cm.
3. A positive test has a diameter of 5 mm.
4. Results of a tuberculin skin test must be read within 24 hours.

14. A man fractured his femur yesterday. In writing his care plan, the nurse notes to observe for a fat embolism from the long-bone fracture. Which of the following is least likely to be seen with a fat embolism?
1. Altered level of consciousness.
2. Rash.
3. Bradycardia.
4. Tachypnea.

15. Ms. A. has chronic renal failure. She begins complaining to the nurse of increasing numbness of her right hand and leg cramps. The nurse checks her reflexes and finds they are abnormal. Of the following medications ordered for Ms. A., which is the appropriate medication for the nurse to administer to help alleviate these symptoms?
1. Lasix.
2. Amphojel.
3. Dilantin.
4. Magnesium sulfate.

16. Ms. A. had a barium enema for complaints of chronic diarrhea, right lower quadrant pain, weight loss, and weakness. The barium enema revealed the characteristic string sign,

a marked narrowing of the bowel separated by normal bowel. The client asks what this means. In formulating a response the nurse understands that this is characteristic of which inflammatory disorder?
1. Ulcerative colitis.
2. Crohn's disease.
3. Diverticulosis.
4. Gastritis.

17. A baby boy who is 8 hours old is in his mother's room. Which finding by the nurse indicates the newborn needs his environment altered to promote adjustment to extrauterine life?
1. The baby just regurgitated his formula.
2. Petechiae are present on his head.
3. His hands and feet have a blue-tinged color.
4. His axillary temperature is 96.8°F.

18. A three-year-old child has been diagnosed with Wilm's tumor and is scheduled for surgery. The nurse performing the preoperative assessment must modify the usual procedure. Which procedure will be omitted in this child?
1. Auscultation of the lungs.
2. Assessment of parents' understanding of the child's condition.
3. Measurement of vital signs.
4. Palpation of abdomen.

19. A 70-year-old is being treated for chronic open-angle glaucoma. Which medication is contraindicated for her?
1. Pilocarpine eye drops.
2. Diamox.
3. Mannitol.
4. Neo-Synephrine eye drops.

20. The nurse is caring for an adult male who has just returned to the nursing care unit following a radical neck dissection for squamous cell carcinoma of the mouth. Which nursing action would be inappropriate during the early postoperative period?
1. Provide mouthwash and lemon and glycerin swabs at the bedside to maintain the client's comfort and oral hygiene.
2. Place the client in a side-lying position initially, then in Fowler's position.
3. Place oral fluids in the back of the throat with an asepto syringe.
4. Monitor for facial drooping and circumoral numbness or tingling.

21. A client's health is gradually failing from chronic renal failure and a kidney transplant that is in the process of rejection. When told that kidney dialysis is the next treatment of choice, the client states, "I'm not going on that machine. My kidneys can hold out until I find another kidney." The nurse recognizes this defense mechanism as
1. rationalization.

2. intellectualization.
3. denial.
4. suppression.

22. Charlie, eight months old, is totally unresponsive to his parents talking to him or being cuddled by them. The nurse performs an assessment. What will the nurse most likely find if his behavior is a product of infant autism?
1. Charlie is responsive to other adults.
2. Babble is less than usual.
3. He will not rock back and forth as he tries to crawl.
4. Though he won't cuddle, his body is relaxed when picked up.

23. Karen is a 25-year-old who has had repeated psychiatric hospitalizations for exacerbation of psychotic symptoms related to noncompliance with antipsychotic medications. She was brought to the hospital today by the police, who found her intoxicated and wandering down the middle of the highway. The admitting nurse on the psychiatric unit knows that Karen would be least apt to be at increased risk for which of the following?
1. Alcohol withdrawal symptoms.
2. Cholinergic crisis.
3. Sensory/perceptual symptoms.
4. Suicidal crisis.

24. When a client who is experiencing a conversion disorder exhibits paralysis, the nurse should provide which therapeutic approach?
1. Develop trust through a therapeutic one-to-one relationship in which acceptance of the disorder is conveyed.
2. Confront the client gently about the fact that no physical basis exists for the conversion.
3. Probe into the nature of the recent conflict-producing event and the resultant paralysis.
4. Provide a treatment approach in which the paralysis receives negative reinforcement so the client will eventually give up the symptom.

25. In planning care for a newly admitted schizophrenic client, it would be important for the nurse to provide
1. an environment that makes minimal demands on the client.
2. an environment that provides maximal stimulation for the client.
3. a climate in which the client can reflect on her problems.
4. a climate of social relatedness for the client.

26. A 45-year-old male is newly admitted to the psychiatric service following an overdose of prescribed antidepressant medication. During individual sessions with him the nurse learns

that he is concerned about his job being phased out and that he would "rather die" than be faced with unemployment. The most appropriate short-term goal for him is
1. to look at the help-wanted ads in the local newspaper every day.
2. to identify one new adaptive coping mechanism by the end of the week.
3. to contract for safety while on the unit.
4. to contact his supervisor at work to discuss job possibilities within the company by the time of his discharge.

27. An appropriate short-term goal for a client with borderline personality disorder, as mutually agreed upon by client and nurse, would be for the client to
    1. discuss feelings of self-destruction with the nurse rather than to act out impulses.
    2. state ability to use problem solving as a means to deal with life problems.
    3. control impulses through use of PRN medications.
    4. identify the process of splitting before acting out the behaviors.

28. Edward is a cocaine addict who was admitted to the psychiatric service 1 week ago with complaints of depression and cocaine intoxication. He relates that because his wife left him and he was fired from his job he became depressed. Which nursing intervention would best target Edward's use of denial of the effect of cocaine on his life?
    1. "Tell me what happened the last time you got high?"
    2. "Don't you think your cocaine use led to your wife leaving you?"
    3. "You must feel overwhelmed."
    4. "I think you're denying the effects of cocaine on your life."

29. The nurse is assessing a 17-year-old female who is admitted to the eating disorders unit with a history of weight fluctuation, abdominal pain, teeth erosion, receding gums, and bad breath. She states that her health has been a problem but there are no other concerns in her life. Which of the following assessments will be the least useful as the nurse develops the care plan?
    1. Information regarding recent mood changes.
    2. Family functioning using a genogram.
    3. Ability to socialize with peers.
    4. Whether she has a sexual relationship with a boyfriend.

30. The mother of a six-day-old breast-fed infant calls the nurse and asks how she can be sure her baby is getting enough milk since she cannot see how much milk there is. He is breast feeding approximately every 3 hours. To best evaluate the effectiveness of his breast feeding the nurse would have the mother
    1. weigh the baby before and after feedings.

2. offer the baby water after a feeding to determine if he is still hungry.
3. compare the amount of time the baby cries with his contented time.
4. see if the baby has at least six wet diapers in 24 hours.

31. The nurse is caring for an eight-year-old child who is admitted to the hospital. Which statement is the eight-year-old most apt to make during the admission process?
    1. "I don't want to be away from my friends."
    2. "I know all about the hospital."
    3. "I want to be a doctor."
    4. "I don't like going to the hospital."

32. The nurse is interviewing the mother of a child who is scheduled for a tonsillectomy. Which question is it most essential for the nurse to ask the mother?
    1. "Have you had your tonsils out?"
    2. "Does your child get colds easily?"
    3. "Does your child have any bleeding tendencies?"
    4. "Has your child ever had an operation?"

33. The nurse is preparing a seven-year-old child for a tonsillectomy. The nurse is discussing what to expect postoperatively. All of the following information may be given to the child. The nurse should give which information first?
    1. He may vomit blood.
    2. He will have a sore throat.
    3. An ice collar will be used.
    4. Where he will wake up.

34. A two-year-old is to be admitted to the pediatric unit. His diagnosis is febrile seizures. In preparing for his admission, which of the following is the most important nursing action?
    1. Order a stat admission CBC.
    2. Place a urine collection bag and specimen cup at the bedside.
    3. Place a cooling mattress on his bed.
    4. Pad the side rails of his bed.

35. The nurse is caring for a two-year-old who is admitted for febrile seizures. Which of the following is the primary goal of nursing care following admission?
    1. Recognition of abnormal signs or behavior indicative of a neurological deficit.
    2. Early detection and recognition of elevated temperatures.
    3. Identification of the etiology of the child's febrile condition.
    4. Promotion of rest and comfort in an atmosphere of limited stimulation.

36. The nurse is caring for a two-year-old child who has had febrile seizures. His temperature rises to 104.6°F rectally. The nurse gives him a Tylenol (acetaminophen) suppository as ordered by the physician. Which of the following is the next most appropriate action for the nurse to implement?

1. Request that stat blood cultures be drawn while the temperature is elevated.
2. Retake the temperature in 30 minutes.
3. Ask his mother to report any seizure activity.
4. Notify the physician immediately concerning the highly elevated temperature.

37. The nurse is caring for a two-year-old who is admitted for febrile seizures. The nurse dresses him in only a diaper and does not cover him with a blanket. This action is based on the understanding that heat loss for this client can best be enhanced by which of the following?
    1. Radiation, conduction, and evaporation.
    2. Conduction, radiation, and a decrease in metabolic rate.
    3. Convection, evaporation, and radiation.
    4. Evaporation, convection, and a reduction in metabolic rate.

38. When implementing any method to reduce a child's fever, chilling should be avoided. Which of the following best explains the reason for this principle?
    1. Chilling makes the child irritable and uncooperative.
    2. Chilling causes peripheral vasodilation.
    3. Chilling can lead to shivering.
    4. Chilling can lessen the child's ability to fight infection.

39. The nurse is caring for a client admitted with pneumococcal pneumonia in the left lower lobe. Percussion of the client's left lower lobe would most likely produce which of the following findings?
    1. Rales.
    2. Rhonchi.
    3. Hyperresonance.
    4. Dullness.

40. Percussion and vibration are ordered as part of chest physical therapy for a client who has pneumonia. The nurse understands that percussion should be performed
    1. intermittently during postural drainage.
    2. at each bronchopulmonary segment immediately prior to postural drainage.
    3. at each bronchopulmonary segment immediately following postural drainage.
    4. only during the expiratory phase of respirations.

41. Ms. J. calls the emergency room, stating she found her seven-year-old daughter, Sue, taking children's aspirin. She suspects that she took 8 or 10 aspirin. Sue is awake. The nurse tells Ms. J. to bring Sue to the emergency room immediately. The most important instruction for the nurse to give Ms. J. before bringing Sue to the emergency room is
    1. "Give Sue a glass of milk."
    2. "Administer 1 Tbs. of syrup of ipecac."
    3. "Give Sue a Fleet's enema."
    4. "Let Sue rest quietly in the car."

42. A seven-year-old child has taken approximately 10 children's aspirin. The physician places a nasogastric tube in the child and administers activated charcoal. The mother asks the nurse what the charcoal is used for. The best response for the nurse to make is that charcoal will
    1. induce vomiting.
    2. correct electrolyte imbalances.
    3. adsorb the aspirin in the stomach.
    4. prevent bleeding tendencies.

43. A child who has swallowed several aspirin is admitted to the emergency room. Aquamephyton is ordered. The nurse explains to the child's mother that it is given to
    1. promote metabolism of aspirin.
    2. prevent bleeding.
    3. decrease absorption of aspirin.
    4. prevent hepatotoxicity.

44. The nurse is giving instructions to a client who has a prescription for penicillin V potassium (Pen Vee K) 500 mg tablets to be given 4 times a day. Which statement by the client indicates the best understanding of the instructions regarding taking this medication?
    1. "I will take the pill with a full glass of orange juice to make it work better."
    2. "I will call my doctor when I feel better so I can stop taking the medicine."
    3. "I should take the pill 1 or 2 hours before meals or 2 to 3 hours after meals."
    4. "I know I could get a rash, so I won't worry if I start to itch."

45. The nurse is caring for a client who had major abdominal surgery. At 3:00 P.M. the day following surgery the client's temperature is 102.6°F. To determine the most likely cause of the temperature elevation the nurse should first
    1. auscultate the lungs.
    2. obtain a urine sample for culture.
    3. culture the wound.
    4. ask the client about exposure to communicable diseases.

46. The charge nurse observes a new staff nurse who is changing a dressing on a surgical wound. After carefully washing her hands the nurse dons sterile gloves to remove the old dressing. After removing the dirty dressing, the nurse removes the gloves and dons a new pair of sterile gloves in preparation for cleaning and redressing the wound. The most appropriate action for the charge nurse is to
    1. interrupt the procedure to inform the staff nurse that sterile gloves are not needed to remove the old dressing.
    2. congratulate the nurse on the use of good technique.

3. discuss dressing change technique with the nurse at a later date.
4. interrupt the procedure to inform the nurse of the need to wash her hands after removal of the dirty dressing and gloves.

47. An adult male is scheduled for exploratory surgery this morning. After he is premedicated for surgery the nurse reviews his chart and discovers that he has not signed a consent form. The nurse's action is based on which of the following understandings?
1. Since the client came to the hospital consent is implied even if the consent for the surgery has not been signed.
2. All invasive procedures require a consent form.
3. The nurse should have him sign a consent form immediately.
4. The nurse should have the next of kin sign the necessary consent form.

48. The nurse has administered an intramuscular injection. Following the procedure which is the best technique to use for disposal of the needle and syringe?
1. Recap the needle and discard in the waste container in the client's room.
2. Recap the needle and dispose of the entire unit in a special container in the utility room.
3. Carefully break the needle before placing the needle in a needle box and the syringe in a plastic-lined container.
4. Do not recap the needle, and place syringe with needle attached in a puncture-resistant container.

49. The nurse is evaluating the infection control procedures on the unit. Which finding indicates a break in technique and the need for education of staff?
1. The nurse aide is not wearing gloves when feeding an elderly client.
2. A client with active tuberculosis is asked to wear a mask when he leaves his room to go to another department for testing.
3. A nurse with open, weeping lesions of the hands puts on gloves before giving direct client care.
4. The nurse puts on a mask, a gown, and gloves before entering the room of a client on strict isolation.

50. A 19-year-old is admitted to the emergency room. He is comatose. Initial assessment shows a pulse of 90 and respirations of 32 and deep. His face is flushed and his skin is dry. He is wearing a medical alert bracelet identifying him as a diabetic. The nurse should expect that initial orders for this client will include
1. administration of glucagon.
2. oxygen at 6 liters/minute.
3. administration of sweetened orange juice.
4. starting an IV of normal saline.

51. A young adult is admitted to the emergency room with a rapid pulse, rapid, deep respirations, flushed face, and dry skin. He is known to be a diabetic. He responds to treatment and regains consciousness. Which statement he makes is most likely related to the onset of his current problem?
1. "I've been eating at a lot of restaurants since I moved into my own apartment."
2. "I like my new job at the manufacturing plant."
3. "I recently joined the health club and I work out three times a week."
4. "I have a new kitten that I like a lot."

52. A diabetic who was admitted in ketoacidosis receives 30 units of regular insulin at 7:30 A.M. When is he most likely to experience a hypoglycemic reaction?
1. Midmorning.
2. At the midday meal.
3. Midafternoon.
4. At the evening meal.

53. The nurse is caring for a diabetic client. One morning at 10:00 he becomes very irritable to the nurse. The nurse's first priority is to determine
1. what is upsetting the client.
2. when he took his insulin and if he ate his breakfast.
3. how well he slept the previous night.
4. which behavior on the part of the nurse is upsetting the client.

54. The nurse is teaching a young adult who is diabetic about management of his disease. Which statement indicates the greatest need for further instruction?
1. "I'm glad I'll be able to eat out sometimes."
2. "I will take a snack when I go to the health club to exercise."
3. "I'll be glad when I get off the shots and start the pills."
4. "It's hard for me to remember to read labels on cans and boxes."

55. An adult woman had a cystectomy with ileal conduit for a diagnosis of bladder cancer. During the first 48 hours post-op which symptoms should be reported to the physician?
1. Absence of urinary output over a period of 1 to 2 hours.
2. Swelling of the abdominal stoma.
3. Pain along the incision site.
4. Absent bowel sounds.

56. The nurse is teaching an adult who had a cystectomy and ileal conduit. Which statement made by the client indicates a need for further instruction?
1. "Now that I've had the surgery, I'll have to be careful that I don't get frequent urinary tract infections."
2. "My stoma is 1½ inches in size now, but I understand it will get smaller. Therefore, I

will need to measure it again in several weeks."

3. "I'm glad that once I get home and am better regulated, I will only have to wear an appliance at night."

4. "I certainly don't want the stoma to close up so I will gently dilate it with my finger once a week."

57. An adult client has an IV infusing. The current fluid order is for Ringer's lactate 1000 ml to run in over an 8-hour period. The drop factor is 12 gtts/ml. What is the drip rate?
1. 25 gtts/min.
2. 42 gtts/min.
3. 83 gtts/min.
4. 125 gtts/min.

58. An adult client is admitted with a diagnosis of urinary tract calculi. The physician's orders read: vital signs every shift, morphine 10 mg for pain, Probanthine (propantheline bromide) 15 mg PO with meals, OOB as tolerated, limit fluid intake to 1000 ml/24 hours, strain all urine. Which medical order should the nurse question?
1. Morphine 10 mg.
2. Limit fluid intake.
3. OOB as tolerated.
4. Strain all urine.

59. An adult client is scheduled for a magnetic resonance imaging test. Before scheduling the test it is most essential for the nurse to ask the client which question?
1. Are you afraid of heights?
2. Do you have any metal in your body?
3. Are you allergic to shellfish?
4. Are you pregnant?

60. A 24-hour urine specimen is ordered for an adult client. The nurse goes to the client at 8:00 A.M. to start the specimen collection. The nurse instructs the client to
1. empty her bladder and save the specimen. Collect all urine until 8:00 A.M. tomorrow.
2. empty her bladder and discard the specimen. Collect all urine for 24 hours including that voided at 8:00 A.M. tomorrow.
3. drink large amounts of fluid during the test. Collect all urine for the next 24 hours.
4. note the time when she next voids and collect urine for 24 hours from that time. Notify the nurse when the collection is completed.

61. A 67-year-old man had a stapedectomy. He has just returned to the nursing care unit following an uneventful stay in the postanesthesia care unit. What is essential for the nurse to include in his care plan?
1. Instruct the client to ask for help when he wants to get out of bed.
2. Encourage the client to drink plenty of fluids during the day.

3. Remind the client to remain in bed for 24 hours.
4. Tell the client to speak only when it is essential for the next 24 hours.

62. The nurse is performing an admission assessment on a client admitted for outpatient surgery today. In addition to obtaining vital signs what information is it most essential for the nurse to obtain?
1. Time and amount the client last voided.
2. Characteristics of client's stools.
3. When the client last had anything to eat or drink.
4. The client's understanding of the surgical procedure to be performed.

63. The nurse is performing an admission assessment on a client admitted with a diagnosis of pernicious anemia. Which assessment findings is the nurse most likely to find?
1. Pallor, gingivitis, and fever.
2. Jaundice, hepatomegaly, and fatigue.
3. Ruddy complexion, ecchymotic areas, and distended veins.
4. Glossy red tongue, paresthesias, and fatigue.

64. Anne was born 3 months ago to a mother who was diagnosed with syphilis late in her pregnancy. Which information would be most useful in determining if Anne has congenital syphilis?
1. Irritability.
2. Red rash around anus.
3. Rhinitis.
4. Positive serology.

65. The nurse is caring for an infant who has congenital syphilis. The baby is started on penicillin. Which statement is true about the baby's ability to transmit the disease now that treatment is started?
1. She will not be contagious after 48 hours of penicillin therapy.
2. After 10 days of antibiotic therapy she will not be contagious.
3. She will always be infected and be contagious.
4. Congenital syphilis is not contagious.

66. The nurse is caring for an infant who is being treated for congenital syphilis. The baby develops vesicular lesions on the soles of her feet and has a rash on her face. What is the most appropriate initial intervention for the nurse?
1. Call the physician immediately.
2. Apply Neosporin ointment to the rash.
3. Cover the infant's hands with mittens.
4. Give Benadryl (diphenhydramine) by mouth.

67. The nurse is caring for a child who has eczema. To prevent infection, it is important for the nurse to administer good personal hygiene and give baths with

1. baby oil.
2. tepid water.
3. bubble bath.
4. perfumed soap.

68. The nurse is caring for a four-year-old child who has eczema. Which toy is most appropriate to give to this child while she is in the hospital?
    1. Fuzzy teddy bear.
    2. Tabletop toy piano.
    3. Stuffed doll.
    4. 1,000-piece jigsaw puzzle.

69. A 16-year-old girl is admitted in sickle cell crisis. She is anemic, has painful joints, abdominal pain, a leg ulcer, and hematuria. What should the nurse expect to include in the nursing care plan during the acute stage?
    1. Promotion of hydration.
    2. Application of cold to swollen and painful joints.
    3. Administration of aspirin for pain.
    4. Active exercises to involved joints.

70. An adult client is scheduled for a colonoscopy under anesthesia. Which statement the client makes indicates he understands the prescribed preparation regimen?
    1. "All I need to do is give myself a packaged enema the morning of the procedure."
    2. "I will eat only jello and drink clear liquids for 2 days before the test."
    3. "I will take the dye tablets with water the night before the test."
    4. "All I have to do is not eat anything after midnight the night before the test."

71. The nurse is caring for a woman who had a vaginal hysterectomy 2 days ago. The indwelling catheter has been removed. The nurse has performed a catheterization for residual urine. Which finding indicates the client does not have a problem? The urine volume obtained was
    1. 30 ml.
    2. 150 ml.
    3. 300 ml.
    4. 500 ml.

72. An eleven-month-old infant is brought to the pediatric clinic. The nurse suspects that the child has iron deficiency anemia. Because iron deficiency anemia is suspected, which of the following is the most important information to obtain from the infant's parents?
    1. Normal dietary intake.
    2. Relevant sociocultural, economic, and educational background of the family.
    3. Any evidence of blood in the stools.
    4. A history of maternal anemia during pregnancy.

73. The nurse is assessing a six-month-old infant. He has acquired all the expected developmental milestones. Which will he have acquired most recently?

1. Imitates sounds.
2. Balances head well in a sitting position.
3. Smiles at mirror image.
4. Is able to grasp objects voluntarily.

74. The nurse is assessing a two-month-old infant. The mother says the baby has colic. Which of the following is the most appropriate initial step in managing colic.
    1. Obtain a detailed history of normal daily events surrounding the infant.
    2. Eliminate cow's milk from the infant's diet or from the diet of the lactating mother.
    3. Request that the physician prescribe antispasmodic and antiflatulent medication and instruct the mother on its use.
    4. Identify the mother's feelings regarding mothering and the infant.

75. The nurse is talking with the parents of a normal two-month-old. Which of the following should be included in anticipatory guidance for the next month of life?
    1. Stranger anxiety will begin.
    2. The posterior fontanel will close.
    3. The first tooth will erupt.
    4. The child will begin to show awareness of strange situations.

76. The clinic nurse is performing anticipatory guidance with parents of a two-month-old infant. Instruction aimed at the prevention of accidents would best be planned with which of the following as a reference?
    1. Mouthing of objects is very prominent.
    2. Grasps and manipulates objects well.
    3. Dislikes being restrained.
    4. Crawling and Moro reflexes are present.

77. A 25-year-old woman had surgery today. Her father, a physician but not her surgeon, enters the nursing station and asks for her chart. The best action for the nurse to take is
    1. to give him the chart as requested.
    2. not to allow him to read the chart.
    3. to ask the attending surgeon if it is permissible for him to read the chart.
    4. to ask the client if she wants him to read her chart.

78. An adult client is being prepared for abdominal surgery. She refuses to remove her plain gold wedding band before going to surgery. What is the best action for the nurse to take?
    1. Firmly insist that it must be removed or surgery cannot be performed.
    2. Ask her husband to assist you in discussing this with his wife.
    3. Cover the wedding band with adhesive tape and tape it to her finger.
    4. Premedicate her and remove the wedding band after she falls asleep.

79. The client has had a central venous access device (Hickman catheter) inserted. Correct placement has been confirmed by X-ray. The

nurse is to set up parenteral nutrition to be connected to the Hickman catheter. The nurse should place the client in which position for the procedure?

1. Trendelenburg.
2. Semi-Fowler's.
3. Side lying.
4. Supine.

80. An adult client has an order for a nasogastric tube. Before inserting the tube the nurse measures the amount of tube needed. To determine the amount of tube needed the nurse should

1. measure from the forehead to the ear and from the ear to the umbilicus.
2. measure from the chin to the back of the throat and from the back of the throat to the umbilicus.
3. measure from the mouth to the xiphoid process and add 2 inches.
4. measure from the tip of the client's nose to his earlobe and from the earlobe to the xiphoid process.

81. An adult client is admitted with an asthma attack. Aminophylline IV is prescribed. The nurse caring for the client knows the desired results have been achieved when the client's

1. pulse rate increases.
2. breathing effort is less.
3. pain is relieved.
4. respiratory rate increases.

82. An adult client has just returned to the nursing care unit following a gastroscopy. Which notation is essential for the nurse to include on the nursing care plan?

1. Throat lozenges PRN for sore throat.
2. Supine position for 6 hours.
3. NPO for 4 hours.
4. Clear liquid diet for 24 hours.

83. Mr. G. has myasthenia gravis and is admitted in myasthenic crisis. The nurse should include which of the following on the nursing care plan immediately after admission?

1. Suction equipment at bedside.
2. Active exercises qid.
3. Give medicines following meals.
4. Prepare client for the Tensilon test.

84. The nurse is evaluating a client who is receiving TPN (total parenteral nutrition) therapy. Which observation best indicates the client is having the desired therapeutic effects from TPN?

1. The client has regular bowel movements.
2. The client maintains blood sugars in the normal range.
3. The client is gaining weight.
4. The client has normal urine output.

85. Mr. A. fractured his right ankle, which was casted in the emergency room. Before discharge from the emergency room the nurse gives him instructions for his care.

Which statement he makes indicates a need for further instruction?

1. "I will keep my foot elevated when I go home."
2. "My wife's hair dryer should work well to dry the cast."
3. "I won't let anyone sign my cast for a couple of days."
4. "It is okay to wiggle my toes on my right foot."

86. Ms. C., 40 weeks pregnant, is admitted to the labor suite. While the nurse is assessing Ms. C., her membranes rupture. The nurse immediately performs a vaginal exam. During the exam the nurse feels a loop of cord protruding into the vagina. The best immediate action for the nurse to take is

1. attempt to lift the fetal head off the cord.
2. prepare for immediate vaginal delivery.
3. call the physician.
4. place the tocometer on the mother's abdomen.

87. Mr. L. is in acute renal failure secondary to hemorrhagic shock. Which statement his wife makes best indicates to the nurse that she understands her husband's condition?

1. "I understand my husband will need dialysis for the rest of his life."
2. "I need to watch our son for evidence of renal failure as he grows up."
3. "My husband will be on a special diet for a long time."
4. "My husband has a good chance to recover normal kidney function."

88. The nurse is planning care for an adult who has just had a liver biopsy. The care plan includes a notation to position the client

1. on his left side.
2. on his right side.
3. in semi-Fowler's.
4. prone.

89. Ms. A. is to have a pelvic sonogram tomorrow. The nurse knows the client understands preprocedure instruction when she makes which of the following statements?

1. "I won't eat for 12 hours before the procedure."
2. "I will take a laxative the night before the procedure."
3. "I will empty my bladder immediately before the test."
4. "I will drink several glasses of water just before I come."

90. Ms. M. has had a total hip replacement and is to be discharged home. Ms. M. can ambulate with a walker. The nurse is evaluating the home care environment. Which finding alerts the nurse to a potential safety problem?

1. The bathroom has a shower but not a tub.
2. The bathroom door is narrow.
3. The kitchen is equipped with a microwave.

4. There are scatter rugs on the floor in the entrance hall and the living room.

91. A 25-year-old is admitted for treatment of a broken right arm, ruptured spleen, increased intracranial pressure, and damage to the spinal cord at the level of C-5 and C-6 which he incurred in a motor vehicle accident. His Glasgow Coma Scale Score is 10 and he is aphasic at present. His right arm is casted and he has Crutchfield tongs inserted through burr holes in his head to stabilize the neck injuries. He has been placed on a Stryker frame with instructions to turn him every two hours around the clock. When designing a plan of care for him, the nurse should assign the highest priority to which of the following diagnoses?
    1. Impaired verbal communication.
    2. Self-care deficit: level IV.
    3. High risk for infection.
    4. Decreased intracranial adaptive capacity.

92. A 43-year-old woman who has been experiencing vertigo and severe headaches for the past three weeks is admitted to the hospital for control of hypertension. The physician has prescribed furosemide (Lasix) and quinapril hydrochloride (Accupril) to augment treatment of the modifiable risk factors associated with her secondary hypertension. What specific drug information should the nurse include in the discharge plan for this client?
    1. Take Accupril only if not feeling well but take Lasix every day, reduce dietary sodium intake, increase exercise level gradually, and take medications at bedtime.
    2. Monitor blood pressure while taking medication, change positions slowly, increase dietary potassium intake, take medications in the morning, and increase fluid intake.
    3. Discontinue medication therapy once blood pressure is within normal range, take medications in the early morning, decrease potassium intake, and increase rest periods.
    4. Take both medications daily, expect some lightheadedness for the first week, increase sodium intake, increase fluid intake, and monitor blood pressure only monthly.

93. An adult was admitted to the respiratory floor with COPD. The nurse finds him extremely restless, incoherent, and showing signs of acute respiratory distress. He is using accessory muscles for breathing and is diaphoretic and cyanotic. The best initial action by the nurse is to
    1. administer oxygen as ordered.
    2. assess vital signs and neural vital signs.
    3. administer medication which has been ordered for pain.

4. call respiratory therapy for a prescribed ABG (arterial blood gas) analysis.

94. The nurse is evaluating a 70-year-old with respiratory disease. Which finding, if observed, indicates compliance with breathing exercises?
    1. Decreased use of pursed lip breathing.
    2. Decreased coughing after exhalation when using resisted breathing exercises.
    3. Increased coughing after exhalation when using resisted breathing exercises.
    4. Inhaling through the mouth and exhaling through the nose.

95. The nurse is caring for a client who has an order for a cooling blanket. Before starting the procedure it is essential for the nurse to assess
    1. if the client is improperly exposed.
    2. the skin for areas of breakdown.
    3. the amount of shivering that the client exhibits.
    4. skin color for cyanosis.

96. The nurse is instructing a homebound client how to apply a warm compress to her wrist. Which comment by the client indicates to the nurse that she understands the safety aspects of the procedure?
    1. "I will take my temperature before and after applying the compress."
    2. "If the pain is not reduced by the compress I will call the nurse."
    3. "I will make sure the water temperature is not over 100°F."
    4. "If the compress begins to get cool, I can warm it up by putting my arm under the hot water faucet."

97. The nurse is visiting an 80-year-old woman at home. She is mildly hypertensive, takes no medications, ambulates with a cane, and lives by herself in her own home. The woman complains of constipation and asks the nurse how to prevent it. Before making suggestions, the nurse assesses the client further. Which of the following assessments will most help the nurse in devising a strategy to help this client?
    1. Determining the time and amount of the last bowel movement.
    2. Assessing the dietary habits of the client.
    3. Obtaining a drug history.
    4. Evaluating the mobility status of the client.

98. The nurse is assessing a 75-year-old woman. Which statement by the client indicates an abnormal finding and one that needs to be further evaluated?
    1. "I move a little slower these days."
    2. "I can't seem to remember what's going on now."
    3. "I enjoy reading, but have to use a magnifying glass."
    4. "My skin is thin and dry and there are little brown spots on my hands."

99. The nurse is instructing a client how to perform Kegel's exercises. Which is most appropriate for the nurse to include in the instructions?
   1. Squeeze your buttocks.
   2. Hold your urine as long as possible before voiding.
   3. Push down on your lower abdomen while holding your breath.
   4. Practice stopping your urine in midstream.
100. The school nurse is called to the playground where an 8-year-old child is lying on the ground with bright red blood spurting from a wound in his thigh. He says he was climbing on the swings when he caught his leg on something. The most appropriate initial action for the nurse to take is
   1. Assess the child's level of consciousness.
   2. Apply an ice pack.
   3. Call the rescue squad.
   4. Apply firm pressure to the bleeding leg.

Answers and Rationales for Practice Test 8

ANSWER	RATIONALE	NP	CN	CL
#1. 3.	**Agnosia, the inability to identify familiar objects, is a key finding in dementia. For example, the client may not be able to recognize a pencil or a watch and may not know what they do.**	As	Ps/6	Ap
1.	Good hygiene and grooming are seen in clients with delirium because of the rapid onset. Poor grooming is seen in clients with depression or dementia, conditions that take longer to onset.			
2.	Rapid mood swings are often seen in delirium (i.e., rage to euphoria to tears).			
4.	Phobias and obsessive thoughts and behaviors are representative of severe depression in the elderly.			
#2. 2.	**The client is taught to report changes in wound healing such as blister formation, signs of infection, and opening of a previously healed area. Sterile dressings are applied until the wound is assessed and a plan of care developed.**	Ev	Sa/2	Ap
1.	Bathing or showering in the usual manner is permitted, using a mild detergent soap such as Ivory Snow. This cleanses the wounds, especially those that are still open, and removes dead tissue.			
3.	The Jobst garment is designed to place constant pressure on the new healthy tissue that is forming to promote adherence to the underlying structure in order to prevent hypertrophic scarring. In order to be effective, the garment must be worn for 23 hours daily. It is removed for wound assessment and wound care and to permit bathing.			
4.	The client must be aware that infection of the wound may occur; signs of infection, including fever, redness, pain, warmth in and around the wound and increased or foul smelling drainage must be reported immediately.			
#3. 4.	**Fluid restriction is inappropriate and would not help her condition.**	Pl	Ph/9	An
1.	Stool softeners are appropriate for this child, who does not have parasympathetic innervation to part of her colon.			
2.	Isotonic enemas will be administered to promote bowel evacuation. Isotonic solution is used to prevent fluid and electrolyte imbalance.			
3.	This client should follow a low-fiber diet to reduce the bulk of the stool.			
#4. 1.	**Aspirin ingestion associated with flu or chickenpox increases the risk of Reye's syndrome. Reye's syndrome is thought to occur when a person who has a viral infection receives aspirin.**	An	Ph/9	An
2.	Prolonged high fevers are not directly related to Reye's syndrome.			
3.	Using antibiotics previously prescribed is not a good thing to do.			

However, it is not directly related to the development of Reye's syndrome.

    4. The client is severely dehydrated, but that is not directly related to the development of Reye's syndrome.

#5. 3.   **The abused child doesn't cry because that has probably resulted in more abuse for her. She has learned to turn inward and not expect good things from her environment.**   As   Ps/6   An

    1. It is hoped that the child will develop trust, but that will take time.

    2. An abused child usually does not constantly ask the parents for comfort. She may fear her parents and won't expect comfort from them.

    4. Sally is not likely to be bouncing around. She will most likely be withdrawn and fearful. If she does bounce around, it would lend credence to her injury being spontaneous.

#6. 3.   **Vitamin C taken with iron increases absorption.**   Pl   Ph/8   An

    1. Iron should be taken with meals to avoid gastrointestinal distress. Iron is more readily absorbed when taken on an empty stomach. However, it frequently causes GI distress.

    2. Dairy products should not be taken at the same time as iron as they decrease absorption. Dairy products contain no iron. Iron intake does not increase the need for dairy products.

    4. The most common side effect of iron is constipation.

#7. 4.   **The best way to evaluate that teaching has been effective is to see the desired behavior.**   Ev   He/4   An

    1. Verbalizing reasons for immunizing a child is desirable behavior but not as strong an indicator of learning as seeing the desired behavior demonstrated.

    2. The first immunization is given at 2 months of age. The teaching was not effective if the parents took the child for an immunization at 2 weeks of age.

    3. Verbalizing intent to follow an immunization schedule is desirable behavior but not as strong an indicator of learning as seeing the desired behavior demonstrated.

#8. 2.   **The nurse needs to know what the client has tried and if her nipples are flat or inverted before planning the appropriate intervention.**   As   He/3   Ap

    1. The nurse may explain the basics of breast feeding to the woman but only after the nurse has assessed the client.

    3. The nurse may demonstrate proper positioning of mother and baby but only after the nurse has assessed the client.

    4. This response is not appropriate. The client has not given any indication that she does not want to breast feed.

#9. 2.   **There are specific data (sore nipples, sore bottom, crying) to support the diagnosis of alteration in comfort (sore nipples, sore bottom, crying).**   An   He/3   An

    1. There are no data to support the diagnosis of ineffective parenting.

    3. There are insufficient data to support the diagnosis of anxiety related to the new role of parenting.

    4. There may be a knowledge deficit, but these data are not the best choice. The prevailing nursing diagnosis is alteration in comfort.

#10. 2.   **The best way to evaluate the effectiveness of teaching breathing techniques during labor is to watch the client use them.**   Ev   He/3   Ap

    1. Asking the client to demonstrate each of the techniques might be appropriate in a prenatal class but not during labor when the client is too busy dealing with contractions.

    3. Listing the two main respiratory techniques might be appropriate in a prenatal class but not during labor when the client is too busy dealing with contractions.

    4. Request for pain medication is not the correct criterion. The client may use breathing well and still need or want medications.

ANSWER	RATIONALE	NP	CN	CL

#11. 4. **Neither heparin nor Coumadin dissolve clots.** · An · Ph/8 · An
    1. This statement is true. Heparin is measured in units. Coumadin is measured in mg.
    2. Although rarely used IV, Coumadin is available for IV use. Heparin is given either IV or subcutaneously.
    3. Heparin therapy is monitored by APTT and Coumadin therapy is monitored by PT.

#12. 1. **The distal sigmoid colon, rectum, and anus are removed and a permanent colostomy is created following an AP resection.** · Ev · Ph/9 · Ap
    2. The client is taught to avoid gas-producing foods. Cabbage (coleslaw) is gas forming.
    3. Warm sitz baths and a T-binder are used for the discomfort of the two incisions.
    4. A T-binder is used for the discomfort of the two incisions.

#13. 1. **The tuberculin skin test measures the presence of antibodies against tuberculosis. Both dormant and active infections will give a positive skin test.** · An · He/4 · An
    2. The induration is measured in mm.
    3. A positive test shows an induration of 10 mm or more.
    4. Results of a tuberculin skin test are read in 48 to 72 hours.

#14. 3. **A fat embolism occurs 12 to 48 hours after injury with typical symptoms of fever, rash, tachycardia, tachypnea, blood-tinged sputum, cyanosis, anxiety, restlessness, altered level of consciousness, convulsions, and coma.** · Pl · Ph/9 · Ap
    1. Altered level of consciousness occurs with a fat embolus.
    2. A petechial rash is often seen with a fat embolus.
    4. Tachypnea is usually seen with a fat embolus.

#15. 2. **Paresthesias, muscle cramps, abnormal reflexes, and seizures are symptoms of hyperphosphatemia. Aluminum hydroxide (Amphojel) binds phosphate in the GI tract and is used in renal failure to help control hyperphosphatemia.** · An · Ph/8 · An
    1. Lasix (furosemide) is a potassium-depleting diuretic. It does not relieve the symptoms described in this case.
    3. Dilantin (hydantoin) is an anticonvulsant. It does not relieve the symptoms described in this case.
    4. Magnesium sulfate is given to women who have pregnancy-induced hypertension. It does not relieve the symptoms described in this case.

#16. 2. **A barium enema showing the characteristic string sign supports the diagnosis of Crohn's disease. The client's other symptoms are all characteristic of Crohn's disease.** · An · Ph/9 · Co
    1. Ulcerative colitis is characterized by inflammatory ulcerations in the mucosa and submucosa of the colon. Ulcerative colitis is also characterized by frequent loose stools containing mucous and blood.
    3. In diverticulosis there are sacs or pouches in the colon that can become inflamed, causing diverticulitis.
    4. Gastritis is inflammation of the stomach. A barium swallow or upper GI series, not a barium enema, might be done. A person with gastritis would have nausea and vomiting rather than diarrhea and right lower quadrant pain.

#17. 4. **A temperature of 96.8°F is below the normal range of 97 to 99°F and may indicate a cold environment.** · Ev · He/3 · An
    1. An infant may regurgitate formula if too much air is ingested while feeding or if he was not burped during the feeding.
    2. The skin color is normally pink but petechiae, which are hemorrhagic spots on the skin from increased intravascular pressure in capillaries, may result from pressure on the presenting part at delivery.
    3. This is normal. Acrocyanosis is characterized by bluish discoloration of the hands and feet and is caused by a normal condition of vasomotor instability and poor peripheral circulation found in the newborn.

ANSWER	RATIONALE	NP	CN	CL

#18. 4. **Palpation of the abdomen is contraindicated in children with Wilm's tumor, which is an encapsulated tumor. Palpation may cause the tumor to rupture and scatter cancer cells in the abdomen.**   As   Ph/9   Ap

    1.   The lungs should be auscultated.

    2.   It is essential to assess the parents' understanding of the child's condition.

    3.   Vital signs must be assessed.

#19. 4. **Neo-Synephrine is a mydriatic and not used in the treatment of open-angle glaucoma. Treatment of open-angle glaucoma includes drugs that constrict the pupil and increase the outflow of aqueous humor. Neo-Synephrine is contraindicated.**   Im   Ph/8   Co

    1.   Pilocarpine eye drops are used in the treatment of open-angle glaucoma to facilitate outflow of aqueous humor by constricting the pupil.

    2.   Diamox decreases the production of aqueous humor, thereby lowering intraocular pressure.

    3.   Mannitol is an osmotic diuretic that is used to force fluid from the eye by making the blood hypertonic.

#20. 1. **Mouthwashes and lemon and glycerin swabs would be chemically irritating to the client's mouth. Postoperatively the nurse would provide mouth irrigations with sterile water, diluted peroxide, normal saline, or sodium bicarbonate.**   Im   Ph/9   Ap

    2.   The client is positioned side-lying until he is alert and then in Fowler's position to reduce tension on the suture line and to decrease edema.

    3.   Swallowing will be difficult following a radical neck dissection. Placing fluids in the back of the throat with an asepto syringe will assist the client as he starts back on oral fluids.

    4.   Neuromuscular checks for facial drooping and circumoral numbness or tingling will be done at frequent intervals to assess for possible nerve or circulatory damage as a result of surgery or edema.

#21. 3. **Denial is occurring because the news of a chronic course to this client's illness is too painful to address at this time. Denial helps cushion the news and protect the client in the short term until the client can better handle the situation.**   As   Ps/5   An

    1.   Rationalization is the attribution of plausible reasons for one's behavior so as to justify or deal with disappointment.

    2.   In intellectualization there is separation of emotion from the event. Intellectualization is not being used. There is too much emotion in the client's statement.

    4.   Suppression is a conscious attempt to forget about something until a later time when it can be addressed. Suppression is not operating in this situation.

#22. 2. **Infants with autism do not communicate well. Babble, an early form of communication, is less than usual in autistic children.**   As   Ps/6   An

    1.   Children with autism treat people as inanimate objects and do not respond.

    3.   Rocking is a stereotypic behavior associated with autism.

    4.   The child with autism stiffens his body when picked up.

#23. 2. **The client has a history of noncompliance with antipsychotic medications. Because of this a cholinergic crisis is not a high risk for her. If she had been taking the prescribed antipsychotic medications regularly there would be a risk of cholinergic crisis.**   An   Ps/6   An

    1.   Alcohol withdrawal is considered a risk as the client was intoxicated upon admission.

    3.   Sensory/perceptual symptoms are possible due to the alcohol use as well as the history of psychotic symptoms.

    4.   Suicide is a risk due to withdrawal as well as sensory/perceptual alterations.

#24. 1. **The nurse must first accept the client where he is. Conversion**   An   Ps/6   An reactions are due to a conflict-producing situation and are involuntary in nature. Presence of paralysis assists the client in avoiding some unpleasant situation. This needs to be brought out in psychotherapy at the client's pace. Analysis of the relationship between anxiety and conversion symptoms helps the nurse choose the correct response.

2. Confrontation is not effective as it does not get to the root of the conflict-producing situation.

3. Conversion reactions are involuntary and thus the client needs to eventually face the conflict on his own timetable. Symptoms allow the client to get assistance from the environment; thus, when he feels safer, he may be able to face the conflict.

4. The conversion reaction is experienced as real. The underlying conflict needs to be addressed since the paralysis in this case is both symbolic of and a solution to a conflict. It will not disappear due to negative reinforcement.

#25. 1. **A newly admitted schizophrenic client needs decreased stimulation/demands due to sensory perceptual alterations and an inability to process information correctly.**   Pl   Ps/6   An

2. A newly admitted schizophrenic client needs decreased stimulation due to sensory perceptual alterations and an inability to process information correctly.

3. A newly admitted schizophrenic client is not able to reflect on problems. That requires too much of the client in light of the difficulty processing information.

4. A newly admitted schizophrenic client needs decreased stimulation due to sensory perceptual alterations and an inability to process information correctly.

#26. 3. **Using Maslow's hierarchy of needs, the issue of physical safety is the only appropriate short-term goal. The nurse is concerned about a possible suicide attempt and should have the client contract to notify the nurse if he feels like harming himself.**   Pl   Ps/6   Ap

1. Looking at help-wanted ads is a long-term goal and would be appropriate later in the treatment process.

2. Identifying a new adaptive coping mechanism is appropriate for later but is not the most appropriate short-term goal.

4. Contacting his supervisor at work is a long-term goal.

#27. 1. **Clients with borderline personality need to remain in a safe environment and learn to discuss self-destructive feelings rather than acting out self-destructive impulses.**   Pl   Ps/6   Ap

2. Using problem solving as a means to deal with life problems is a long-term goal. Clients with borderline personality disorder overrespond to stress and act impulsively rather than use a problem-solving approach.

3. Although PRN medications may be given for severe anxiety, the nurse will want the client to attempt problem solving instead of relying only on medications.

4. Splitting is an unconscious defense mechanism. Insight into behavior may be possible and, as a long-term goal, splitting may be avoided as a means to cope with stress in interpersonal relationships.

#28. 1. **This approach leads the client to make the connection between substance use and its consequences on his own.**   Im   Ps/6   An

2. This approach is too argumentative and may lead to a defensive response.

3. This approach is empathic and therapeutic, however, it does not focus on the client's denial process.

4. This approach is too argumentative and may lead to a defensive response.

#29. 4. **It is inappropriate to ask about her sexual relationships.**   An   Ps/6   An

1. Information about mood changes is important to assess, as bulimia is often associated with affective disorders.
2. Family functioning is the most essential point to assess, as it reveals if binge eating is triggered by conflict within the family.
3. Information about ability to socialize with peers is important to assess, as it is possible the problem initiated with peer relationships.

#30. 4. Six wet diapers in 24 hours means the baby is adequately hydrated and is getting enough milk.   Ev   He/3   Ap
1. Weighing the baby before and after feedings is neither practical nor accurate. It sets up a tendency to be constantly worried.
2. It is inappropriate to offer the baby water after a feeding. Many babies, even if getting enough milk, would take water. Giving the baby water might reduce the amount of milk he gets from mother and reduce the milk production.
3. Comparing crying time to contented time is not appropriate. Babies cry for many reasons other than hunger.

#31. 1. The school-age child is very concerned about separation from school and peers.   An   He/3   An
2. The eight-year-old is more concerned about separation from school and peers than knowing all the answers.
3. The eight-year-old is concerned about separation from school and peers. A given child might want to be a doctor, but this would not be generally expected.
4. The child may not like going to the hospital but is more concerned about separation from school and friends.

#32. 3. Bleeding tendencies are especially significant in a child who is to have a tonsillectomy. The most common complication following tonsillectomy is hemorrhage.   As   Ph/9   Ap
1. It is not necessary to know if the mother has had her tonsils out.
2. It might be nice to know if the child gets infections easily but this is not the priority information. Hemorrhage, not infection, is the primary complication of tonsillectomy.
4. It is nice to know if the child has had previous experience with surgery. However, this is not the most essential data for the nurse to obtain.

#33. 4. It is important to be honest with any child. The child needs to know where he will be to reduce fear. He may need to be shown the recovery area. The unknown is frightening.   Pl   Ph/9   Ap
1. The child may vomit blood. However, this is not the first information the nurse should give the child.
2. Explaining to the child that he will have a sore throat is important. The nurse should be honest and tell him this after the concerns about the unknown are addressed.
3. Explaining to the child that he will have an ice collar may be done. This is not the first information that the nurse should give the child.

#34. 4. The child has a diagnosis of febrile seizures. Precautions to prevent injury and promote safety should take precedence.   Pl   Sa/2   Ap
1. Preparing for routine laboratory studies is not as high a priority as preventing injury and promoting safety.
2. Preparing for routine laboratory studies is not as high a priority as preventing injury and promoting safety.
3. A cooling blanket must be ordered by the physician and is usually not used unless other methods for the reduction of fever have not been successful.

#35. 2. Febrile seizures occur in association with a fever and are a common transient neurologic disorder of childhood. The height and rapidity of temperature elevation are important factors in the onset of a febrile seizure. Seizures are more likely to occur during a rise in temperature rather than after it has been elevated for a prolonged period. Early detection and reduction of   Pl   Ph/9   Ap rising temperatures helps to prevent a febrile seizure and is the primary goal.

1. The nurse will be alert to abnormal signs or behavior indicative of a neurological deficit but this is not the highest priority.
3. Efforts will be made to determine the etiology of the fevers but the child's safety is a higher priority.
4. Febrile seizures are caused by fever. It is more important to detect fevers early than it is to limit stimulation. Limiting stimulation is more important in a child with seizures due to meningitis than febrile seizures.

#36. 2. The nurse must recheck the temperature in 30 minutes to determine the effectiveness of the Tylenol suppository. If there is little or no response, alternative methods for the reduction of temperature need to be employed. If the temperature continues to rise, the physician should be notified.   Im   Ph/9   Ap

1. It is not appropriate to obtain blood cultures after Tylenol is administered.
3. It is inappropriate to rely on the child's mother to observe and report seizure activity. This is a nursing responsibility.
4. The physician should be notified if the temperature does not respond to the Tylenol suppository. Other temperature control methods may need to be utilized.

#37. 3. Light-weight, loose clothing and the removal of heavy blankets and coverings enhance the movement of air and facilitate the reduction of core temperature through convection. The less dense warm air coming from the body is lost through the movement of more dense cooler air circulating in the surrounding environment. Increasing air flow to the body allows for heat loss through radiation because more heat is radiated from the body than to the body when core and skin temperature are greater than surrounding air. Heat is lost through evaporation when air flow comes in contact with perspiration on the skin.   An   Ph/9   An

1. Conduction heat loss is the loss of heat from object to object. Removing blankets and clothing does not promote heat loss by conduction.
2. Removing blankets and clothing does not decrease the metabolic rate.
4. Removing blankets and clothing does not decrease the metabolic rate.

#38. 3. Shivering can be precipitated by chilling. Shivering is a normal compensatory mechanism used by the body to warm itself by increasing the body heat. Therefore, allowing the child to become chilled and shiver defeats the purpose of fever reduction activities.   An   Ph/9   An

1. The child may become irritable but this is not the reason for avoiding chilling. Chilling causes shivering, which is the body's temperature-raising mechanism.
2. Chilling causes vasoconstriction, not vasodilation. Chilling causes shivering, which is the body's temperature-raising mechanism.
4. Chilling does not lessen the child's ability to fight infection. Chilling causes shivering, which is the body's temperature-raising mechanism.

#39. 4. When pneumonia is localized in a single lobe, consolidation or infiltration of exudate into the alveoli can be expected. Dullness is revealed by percussion over the lobe where consolidation has occurred.   As   Ph/9   An

1. Rales are the sounds produced by air passing through liquid in the smaller air passages and alveoli.

2. Rhonchi are dry, coarse rales caused by air passing through wet and swollen airways.

3. Hyperresonance is exaggerated resonance on percussion. This is caused by excessive air in the lungs. Hyperresonance may occur in COPD when air is trapped in the alveoli. Pneumonia causes consolidation and dullness.

#40. 1. The technique of postural drainage is made more effective when used in conjunction with percussion and vibration. Percussion performed intermittently during postural drainage loosens tenacious secretions so that they will flow more freely from the segment to be drained.   Im   Ph/9   Ap

2. It is better to do percussion intermittently during postural drainage rather than prior to postural drainage.

3. The purpose of percussion is to loosen secretions so they can be removed more easily. Percussion following postural drainage does very little good.

4. Percussion does not have to be done during a particular phase of respiration.

#41. 2. It is important to induce vomiting and to empty the stomach of the aspirin. It is also important to keep Sue alert and not let her fall asleep. Ipecac would not be given if the child was unconscious because aspiration of vomitus could occur.   Im   Ph/10   Ap

1. It is better to induce vomiting than to try to neutralize the poison.

3. Giving the child an enema would accomplish nothing except delaying appropriate treatment. Vomiting should be induced to remove the poison.

4. It is important to keep Sue alert and not let her fall asleep. Vomiting should be induced to remove the poison.

#42. 3. Charcoal is an adsorbent and will adsorb the aspirin in the stomach.   An   Ph/8   Ap

1. Ipecac is used to induce vomiting. Charcoal is an adsorbent and will adsorb the aspirin in the stomach.

2. Charcoal is an adsorbent and will adsorb the aspirin in the stomach. It does not correct electrolyte imbalances.

4. Charcoal is an adsorbent and will adsorb the aspirin in the stomach. It does not correct bleeding tendencies.

#43. 2. Aquamephyton is vitamin K, which promotes clotting. Aspirin is an anticoagulant.   An   Ph/8   An

1. Aquamephyton is vitamin K, which promotes clotting.

3. Aquamephyton is vitamin K, which promotes clotting. It does not decrease absorption of aspirin. Charcoal will decrease absorption of aspirin.

4. Aquamephyton is vitamin K, which promotes clotting. It does not prevent hepatotoxicity. Removing the poison is the best way to prevent hepatotoxicity.

#44. 3. Food may interfere with absorption. Penicillin should be given 1 to 2 hours before meals or 2 to 3 hours after meals.   Ev   Ph/8   Ap

1. Each dose should be taken with a full glass of water, not juice or carbonated beverage. Acid will inactivate the drug.

2. The client should take all of the medicine prescribed, even if he feels better, to prevent development of drug-resistant organisms.

4. Allergic reactions to penicillin are relatively common. However, itching and a rash could be early signs of a more serious reaction and should be reported immediately.

#45. 1. The most likely cause of a low-grade temperature elevation 24 to 48 hours after surgery is pulmonary infection. The nurse should auscultate the lungs for presence of rales or rhonchi.   As   Ph/9   An

2. The most likely cause of a low-grade temperature elevation 24 to 48 hours after surgery is pulmonary infection. Temperature elevation from a urinary tract infection more typically occurs 48 to 72 hours

after surgery. The client would most likely have had either a straight catheter or an indwelling catheter inserted.

3. The most likely cause of a low-grade temperature elevation 24 to 48 hours after surgery is pulmonary infection. Wound infections usually do not occur until 72 hours following surgery.

4. The most likely cause of a low-grade temperature elevation 24 to 48 hours after surgery is pulmonary infection. Communicable disease is an unlikely cause of a low-grade postoperative fever. However, if other causes were ruled out, this would be a possibility.

#46. 4. **The staff nurse is doing two things incorrectly. Nonsterile gloves are adequate to remove the old dressing. However, the use of sterile gloves does not put the client in danger so discussion of this can wait until later. However, the nurse should wash her hands after removing the soiled dressing and before donning sterile gloves to clean and dress the wound. Not doing this compromises client safety and should be brought to the immediate attention of the nurse.**   Im   Sa/2   Ap

1. Nonsterile gloves are adequate to remove the old dressing. However, the use of sterile gloves does not put the client in danger so discussion of this can wait until later.

2. The staff nurse is doing two things incorrectly. Nonsterile gloves are adequate to remove the old dressing. The nurse should wash her hands after removing the soiled dressing and before donning sterile gloves to clean and dress the wound.

3. The nurse should wash her hands after removing the soiled dressing and before donning the sterile gloves to clean and dress the wound. Not doing this compromises client safety and should be brought to the immediate attention of the nurse.

#47. 2. **All invasive procedures require informed consent. The surgery is prescheduled and described as exploratory and therefore is not an emergency. If the client is an adult and has not been declared incompetent the client must sign the form. This client should not have surgery performed without written consent. The nurse must notify the physician immediately.**   An   Sa/1   Ap

1. It cannot be legally assumed that the client consents to a procedure for which he has not given consent. This is not legally defensible.

3. The client has been premedicated for surgery and is not alert. He cannot give legal consent when under the influence of mind-altering drugs.

4. The client is an adult and there is no evidence that he has been declared incompetent to make his own decisions. The surgery is exploratory. There is no indication it is for an immediately life-threatening condition. It is not appropriate to ask the next of kin to sign his consent form.

#48. 4. **The proper procedure is not to recap the needle and to place the syringe with needle attached in a puncture-resistant container. Breaking or recapping the needle exposes the nurse to the danger of a needle stick and possible exposure to blood-borne infections.**   Im   Sa/2   Ap

1. The proper procedure is not to recap the needle and to place the syringe with needle attached in a puncture-resistant container. Breaking or recapping the needle exposes the nurse to the danger of a needle stick and possible exposure to blood-borne infections. The waste basket in the client's room is never used to dispose of contaminated material.

2. The proper procedure is not to recap the needle and to place the syringe with needle attached in a puncture-resistant container. Breaking or recapping the needle exposes the nurse to the danger of a needle stick and possible exposure to blood-borne infections.

3. The proper procedure is not to recap the needle and to place the

syringe with needle attached in a puncture-resistant container. Breaking or recapping the needle exposes the nurse to the danger of a needle stick and possible exposure to blood-borne infections. The container should be puncture resistant. Plastic lined is not sufficient.

#49. 3. Persons with exudative lesions or weeping dermatitis should not give direct client care or handle client-care equipment until the condition resolves.   Ev   Sa/2   An

1. There is no need to wear gloves when feeding a client. However, universal precautions (treating all blood and body fluids as if they are infectious) should be observed in all situations.
2. A client with active tuberculosis should be on respiratory precautions. Having the client wear a mask when leaving his private room is appropriate.
4. Strict isolation requires the use of mask, gown, and gloves.

#50. 4. Initial assessment of this client reveals classic signs of hyperglycemia and metabolic ketoacidosis: Kussmaul respirations, flushed skin, and dehydration. Normal saline does not contain glucose. Administration of a nonglucose solution is appropriate initial therapy.   Pl   Ph/10   An

1. Glucagon is indicated for a client having an insulin reaction.
2. Oxygen is not indicated. In fact, he needs to blow off carbon dioxide to compensate for metabolic acidosis.
3. The client is comatose and so will not get oral fluids. His symptoms are those of hyperglycemia and metabolic ketoacidosis, not hypoglycemia.

#51. 1. Hyperglycemia and ketoacidosis may be caused by a change in eating patterns. Restaurant food is apt to be high in carbohydrates and fats.   An   Ph/10   Ap

2. There is no information that suggests his job is excessively stressful, which might contribute to the onset of hyperglycemia.
3. Exercise is apt to cause hypoglycemia, not hyperglycemia.
4. Hyperglycemia and ketoacidosis are not caused by allergic reactions to animals.

#52. 1. Regular insulin is a short-acting insulin. Peak action is 2 to 4 hours after administration. Hypoglycemia is most apt to occur at peak action of insulin.   Pl   Ph/8   Ap

2. Regular insulin is a short-acting insulin. Peak action is 2 to 4 hours after administration. Hypoglycemia is most apt to occur at peak action of insulin.
3. Regular insulin is a short-acting insulin. Peak action is 2 to 4 hours after administration. Hypoglycemia is most apt to occur at peak action of insulin. NPH insulin peaks in 6 to 8 hours and would be apt to cause hypoglycemia in midafternoon if given in the morning.
4. Regular insulin is a short-acting insulin. Peak action is 2 to 4 hours after administration. Hypoglycemia is most apt to occur at peak action of insulin.

#53. 2. Irritability is a classic sign of hypoglycemia. The time suggests it might be hypoglycemia due to insulin reaction. The nurse must assess when he took his insulin and if he ate his breakfast.   As   Ph/8   Ap

1. Assessment of a likely physiologic cause for the irritability should be done first. Irritability is a classic sign of hypoglycemia. The time suggests it might be hypoglycemia due to insulin reaction. The nurse must assess when he took his insulin and if he ate his breakfast.
3. Assessment of a likely physiologic cause for the irritability should be done first. Irritability is a classic sign of hypoglycemia. The time suggests it might be hypoglycemia due to insulin reaction. The nurse must assess when he took his insulin and if he ate his breakfast.
4. Assessment of a likely physiologic cause for the irritability should be done first. Irritability is a classic sign of hypoglycemia. The time suggests it might be hypoglycemia due to insulin reaction. The nurse

ANSWER	RATIONALE	NP	CN	CL

must assess when he took his insulin and if he ate his breakfast. The nurse should not assume responsibility for a client's irritable behavior.

#54. 3. **Diabetes that onsets in adolescence is almost always Type I (insulin-dependent diabetes mellitus). A Type I diabetic does not produce insulin and will always need insulin replacement. He will not be able to take oral hypoglycemic agents that stimulate the pancreas and increase cell utilization of insulin. His statement indicates a lack of understanding.** Ev Ph/9 Ap

   1. Using food groups should enable him to eat out sometimes. This statement indicates good understanding.

   2. He should take a snack before exercising. Exercising tends to cause hypoglycemia. This response indicates understanding.

   4. Reading labels to detect hidden sugar and fat is important. Admitting it is difficult indicates he is aware of the need to do this.

#55. 1. **Absence of urine indicates poor renal perfusion. Thirty ml/hr is the minimum acceptable urine output. Below that is considered shock.** As Ph/9 Ap

   2. Swelling of the abdominal stoma is normal during the first 48 hours postop.

   3. Pain along the incision site is normal during the first 48 hours postop.

   4. Absent bowel sounds are normal during the first 48 hours postop.

#56. 3. **An ileal conduit drains urine continuously. An appliance must be worn at all times. The client does not understand about the ileal conduit.** Ev Ph/9 An

   1. Urinary tract infections are apt to be more frequent. This statement indicates understanding.

   2. The stoma will shrink in time. This is a true statement.

   4. The stoma should be dilated by the client every week to keep it patent. This is a true statement.

#57. 1. **To calculate the drip rate, first determine the number of ml per hour.** Im Ph/8 Ap

$$\frac{1000 \text{ ml}}{8 \text{ hrs}} = 125 \text{ ml/hr.}$$

Next, divide 125 ml/hr by 60 min per hour and multiply by the drop factor of 12 gtts/ml. The correct answer is 25 gtts/min.

   2. The wrong drop factor was used.

   3. You calculated incorrectly. You divided 1000 ml by the drop factor instead of the hours.

   4. You did not finish the calculation. 125 gtts/min is really the number of ml per hour.

#58. 2. **The nurse should encourage fluids to 3000 ml to 5000 ml in 24 hours to help flush the stones out of the urinary system.** An Ph/9 An

   1. Morphine is an appropriate analgesic. Urinary calculi are very painful.

   3. The client can be out of bed as tolerated. In fact, walking may help relieve the pain and may help the stone to pass.

   4. All urine should be strained to detect any calculi that may be passed in the urine.

#59. 2. **MRI testing is based on magnetic fields that are affected by and can affect metal in the body such as pacemakers, hip prosthesis, skull plates, etc. It is essential to ask this question. Depending on the type of metal and the part of the body being imaged the person with metal may not be a candidate for MRI.** As Ph/9 Co

   1. The client should be asked about claustrophobia—fear of small places. During the MRI the client is placed in a cylinder, which can be frightening for persons with claustrophobia. There is no reason to ask about fear of heights.

   3. No contrast media is used with MRI and therefore no worry about allergy to iodine.

4. MRI does not use radiation. There are no known teratogenic effects of MRI.

#60. 2. **The bladder should be emptied and the specimen discarded at the beginning of the 24-hour collection. Urine in the bladder was made prior to the start of the 24-hour period. All urine is collected for 24 hours. The bladder should be emptied at the end of 24 hours and that urine saved, as it was made during the 24-hour period. Remember, the bladder is simply a storage facility for urine made by the kidneys.**   Im   Ph/9   Ap

1. Urine in the bladder at the beginning of the collection was produced by the kidneys at an earlier time. It should be discarded.
3. Unless specifically ordered, there is no need to drink large amounts of fluid.
4. The collection should start and end at a specific time.

#61. 1. **A stapedectomy is removal of the stapes (the small bone in the ear next to the inner ear) and insertion of a prosthesis. Because of the proximity to the inner ear and the balance mechanism the client is very apt to be dizzy when he changes position or ambulates. He should have assistance in ambulating to prevent falling.**   Pl   Ph/9   Ap

2. There is no particular need to encourage fluid intake.
3. There is no need for the client to remain in bed. He should have assistance when ambulating to prevent falling because of the vertigo associated with surgery in the ear.
4. A stapedectomy is removal of the stapes (the small bone in the ear next to the inner ear) and insertion of a prosthesis. There is no need to avoid speaking. Voice rest is appropriate for a client who has had a laryngectomy.

#62. 3. **It is essential for the nurse to determine if the client has maintained NPO status for at least 6 to 8 hours prior to surgery to prevent the possibility of aspiration.**   As   Ph/9   Ap

1. Time and amount of last voiding is information that is nice to know. However, it is not as essential as time of last oral intake. The client should be asked to empty the bladder immediately prior to being sent to surgery, no matter when he last voided.
2. Characteristics of stool is not priority information in the immediate preoperative period.
4. It is nice to know if the client understands the surgical procedure to be performed. However, in the immediate preoperative period information about NPO status is of greater priority.

#63. 4. **A glossy red tongue is characteristic of pernicious anemia. Persons with pernicious anemia lack intrinsic factor, which is necessary for absorption of vitamin B_{12}. Vitamin B_{12} is necessary for the manufacture of red blood cells and for proper functioning of the nervous system. Paresthesias, changes in sensation, are frequently seen in pernicious anemia. Fatigue occurs because the oxygen-carrying capacity is diminished when the red blood cell count is decreased.**   As   Ph/9   Co

1. Pallor will be present because of the diminished red count. The client is more apt to have a sore mouth and glossy red tongue than sore gums. Fever is not likely to be present.
2. Jaundice and hepatomegaly are seen in hemolytic anemias such as sickle cell anemia. Rapid destruction of red blood cells increases the amount of bilirubin to be processed by the liver. Fatigue is common to all types of anemia.
3. Ruddy complexion, ecchymotic areas, and distended veins are common in persons with polycythemia vera, a condition in which there is excessive production of red blood cells.

#64. 4. **Congenital syphilis is difficult to diagnose until the infant develops**   As   Ph/9   An her own antibodies. **A positive serology confirms the diagnosis of congenital syphilis.**

    1. Irritability is seen in an infant with syphilis but can be present in other conditions as well.

    2. A red rash around the anus is seen in infants with syphilis but does not confirm the diagnosis of syphilis.

    3. Rhinitis is seen in infants with syphilis but does not confirm the diagnosis.

#65. 1. **After 48 hours of penicillin therapy the infant should not be contagious. Until that time she should be in isolation.**   An   Sa/2   Ap

    2. After 48 hours of penicillin therapy the infant should not be contagious.

    3. After 48 hours of penicillin therapy the infant should not be contagious.

    4. Congenital syphilis is contagious. The spirochete is present in the blood and in fluid in the vesicles.

#66. 3. **Covering the infant's hands will minimize trauma to her skin from scratching.**   Im   Sa/2   Ap

    1. The nurse will notify the physician but the immediate action is to protect the infant from further injury.

    2. Applying Neosporin ointment to the rash is not an independent nursing action. It is also not the appropriate treatment. The rash is probably related to the diagnosis of syphilis. Neosporin will not relieve the itching and will not treat the rash.

    4. Giving Benadryl (diphenhydramine) by mouth is not an independent nursing action. Benadryl is helpful in the management of severe itching.

#67. 2. **Tepid water is the best substance to use when bathing someone who has eczema. The other substances are irritating and may cause the child to scratch and develop an infection.**   Im   Ph/7   Ap

    1. Baby oil can be irritating and may cause scratching. Baby oil also makes it difficult for lesions to heal.

    3. Bubble bath is very irritating to the skin and may cause scratching.

    4. Performed soap is very irritating to the skin and may cause scratching.

#68. 2. **A tabletop toy piano is age appropriate and also appropriate for the diagnosis. The child with eczema should not have fuzzy, stuffed toys that may be allergenic.**   Im   He/3   Ap

    1. A fuzzy teddy bear is age appropriate but not disease appropriate. The child with eczema should not have fuzzy, stuffed toys that may be allergenic.

    3. A stuffed doll is age appropriate but not disease appropriate. The child with eczema should not have fuzzy, stuffed toys that may be allergenic.

    4. A 1,000-piece jigsaw puzzle is not age appropriate. It is too difficult for a four-year-old child.

#69. 1. **Hydration is very important. Dehydration causes sickle cell crisis. The client will be hydrated, usually with both IV and PO fluids.**   Pl   Ph/9   Ap

    2. Application of cold is contraindicated in the client with sickle cell crisis. The abnormally shaped red blood cells clump and obstruct circulation. Heat is indicated to dilate vessels and promote circulation.

    3. Aspirin (acetylsalicylic acid) is contraindicated in the client with sickle cell anemia. Acidosis causes red cells to sickle in the client with sickle cell anemia. Aspirin may cause the blood to become more acidic.

    4. Painful joints should not be exercised during the acute period of the disease.

#70. 2. **The client is given laxatives for 2 days before the procedure and**   Ev   Ph/9   Ap must have only clear liquids during this time. He will be NPO the night before the procedure.

1. Administration of a packaged enema the morning of the procedure is appropriate for a sigmoidoscopy in which only the sigmoid colon is to be visualized. A colonoscopy under anesthesia will visualize the entire colon.

3. There are no dye tablets given before a colonoscopy. Dye tablets are given as preparation for a gall bladder X-ray.

4. The client will be NPO after midnight the night before the test but will also have to have a bowel prep, so the answer is not correct. The client is given laxatives for 2 days before the procedure and must have only clear liquids during this time.

#71. 1. The urine volume obtained during a catheterization for residual urine should be 50 ml or less.   Ev   Ph/9   Ap

2. 150 ml is too much. The urine volume obtained during a catheterization for residual urine should be 50 ml or less.

3. 300 ml is too much. The urine volume obtained during a catheterization for residual urine should be 50 ml or less.

4. 500 ml is too much. The urine volume obtained during a catheterization for residual urine should be 50 ml or less.

#72. 1. Iron deficiency anemia occurs commonly in children 6 to 24 months of age. For the first 4 to 5 months of infancy iron stores laid down for the baby during pregnancy are adequate. When fetal iron stores are depleted, supplemental dietary iron needs to be supplied to meet the infant's rapid growth needs. Iron deficiency may occur in the infant who drinks mostly milk, which contains no iron, and does not receive adequate dietary iron or supplemental iron.   As   Ph/7   An

2. Daily dietary intake is much more related to the diagnosis of iron deficiency anemia than is sociocultural, economic, and educational background of the family.

3. Iron deficiency anemia in an infant is very unlikely to be related to gastrointestinal bleeding.

4. Anemia during pregnancy is unlikely to be the cause of the infant's iron deficiency anemia. Fetal iron stores are drawn from the mother even if she is anemic.

#73. 1. A six-month-old will begin to imitate sounds.   As   He/3   Ap

2. A four-month-old can balance his head well while in a sitting position.

3. A five-month-old will smile at his mirror image.

4. A five-month-old is able to grasp objects voluntarily.

#74. 1. The initial step in the management of colic should be an investigation of identifying factors that contribute to the cause of colic. The best way to accomplish this is to obtain a detailed history of the normal daily routine with an emphasis on such areas as diet of the infant and the lactating mother, frequency and time of attacks with their relationship to feeding, activity of the mother surrounding the time of attacks and presence of others, and measures that can be taken to alleviate or minimize the problem. The nurse should assess the overall situation and then begin to focus on a specific area of concern.   As   Ph/9   Ap

2. Elimination of foods from the diet is not the initial step. It might need to be done as the investigation proceeds, but is not the initial step.

3. Medication is not the initial step in the assessment of an infant with colic. Assess first, then treat.

4. The mother's feelings may be assessed but as a part of the initial assessment.

#75. 4. Showing awareness of strange situations is something parents should expect to occur with their three-month-old infant.   Pl   He/3   Ap

1. Stranger anxiety usually begins about 6 to 8 months of age.

2. The posterior fontanel usually closes at 2 months of age.

3. The first tooth usually erupts at 5 to 6 months of age.

#76. 4. One of the bases for accident prevention for a very young infant should be the fact that the Moro and crawling reflexes are present. These reflexes can propel the infant forward unexpectedly, causing injury from falling.   Pl   He/4   Ap

1. Mouthing of small objects becomes a serious concern about 4 months of age.

2. Infants start to grasp voluntarily at 4 or 5 months of age.

3. The 8-month-old dislikes being restrained.

#77. 2. Since he is not the client's physician and does not have a medical need to see her chart, he should not be allowed to read the chart without written permission from the client, who is above the age of majority.   Im   Sa/1   Ap

1. The nurse must maintain the client's right of confidentiality. Since he is not the client's physician and does not have a medical need to see her chart, he should not be allowed to read the chart without written permission from the client, who is above the age of majority.

3. It is not the attending surgeon who can give permission for him to review the chart, it is the client.

4. The client must give written permission for unauthorized persons to review her chart. This client had surgery today and is probably not alert enough to give legal permission, which must be written.

#78. 3. It is preferred that all jewelry be removed before surgery and either sent home with family or placed in the hospital safe for safekeeping. However, if a client who has a plain wedding band with no stones wants to keep the ring on, it can be covered with adhesive tape and taped to the finger. A ring with stones in it should not be taped as the tape could loosen the stones when it is removed. If the client is to have surgery that might involve swelling of the hand on which the ring is worn, the ring must be removed before surgery.   Im   Sa/2   Ap

1. It is preferred that all jewelry be removed before surgery and either sent home with family or placed in the hospital safe for safekeeping. However, if a client who has a plain wedding band with no stones wants to keep the ring on, it can be covered with adhesive tape and taped to the finger.

2. It is not necessary to add to the stress of the situation by involving the husband in this situation.

4. The nurse should never remove jewelry from a sleeping or unconscious client unless it is an emergency situation. It leaves the nurse open to a lawsuit.

#79. 1. Placing the client in Trendelenburg's position reduces the likelihood of an air embolism occurring during the procedure.   Im   Ph/9   Ap

2. Placing the client in Trendelenburg's position reduces the likelihood of an air embolism occurring during the procedure.

3. Placing the client in Trendelenburg's position reduces the likelihood of an air embolism occurring during the procedure.

4. Placing the client in Trendelenburg's position reduces the likelihood of an air embolism occurring during the procedure.

#80. 4. The best way to determine the amount of tube needed to reach the pylorus is to measure from the tip of the client's nose to his earlobe and from the earlobe to the xiphoid process.   Im   Ph/9   Ap

1. The best way to determine the amount of the tube needed to reach the pylorus is to measure from the tip of the client's nose to his earlobe and from the earlobe to the xiphoid process.

2. The best way to determine the amount of tube needed to reach the pylorus is to measure from the tip of the client's nose to his earlobe and from the earlobe to the xiphoid process.

ANSWER	RATIONALE	NP	CN	CL

3. The best way to determine the amount of tube needed to reach the pylorus is to measure from the tip of the client's nose to his earlobe and from the earlobe to the xiphoid process.

#81. 2. Aminophylline is a bronchodilator. When it is effective, the breathing effort is less.   Ev   Ph/9   An

    1. Aminophylline will increase the pulse rate but this is not the desired effect in the client who has asthma. Aminophylline is a bronchodilator. When it is effective, the breathing effort is less.

    3. Aminophylline is a bronchodilator. Respiratory distress, not pain, is the primary problem with asthma.

    4. Aminophylline is a bronchodilator. When it is effective, the breathing effort is less.

#82. 3. Because a local anesthetic is used during the procedure, the client must be NPO until the gag reflex returns. This usually takes 2 to 4 hours.   Pl   Ph/9   Ap

    1. Throat lozenges are not allowed until the gag reflex returns as the client may aspirate. This usually takes 2 to 4 hours.

    2. The client should be in semi-Fowler's position to facilitate drainage of saliva and prevent aspiration.

    4. The client will be NPO until the gag reflex returns.

#83. 1. The person in myasthenic crisis will likely need vigorous respiratory support including possibly a tracheotomy, positive pressure breathing, and vigorous suctioning.   Pl   Ph/10   Ap

    2. Myasthenia gravis causes extreme muscle weakness. During crisis he will not be able to do active exercises. When he is stable, exercises should be done when his activity level is highest, usually in the morning.

    3. Medicines should be administered 20 to 30 minutes before meals to facilitate chewing and swallowing.

    4. The Tensilon test is used in diagnosing myasthenia gravis. In myasthenic clients, muscle function improves within 30 to 60 seconds and lasts up to 30 minutes.

#84. 3. The client should gain weight if he is getting adequate nutrition. Most clients who receive TPN have a condition in which they are unable to adequately digest food. Weight gain indicates adequate nutrition.   Ev   Ph/8   Ap

    1. Regular bowel movements are not the best indicator that TPN is having the desired results. Bowel movements are not always regular with TPN.

    2. Persons receiving TPN may have hypoglycemia if too much insulin is given or hyperglycemia from rapid administration of high sugar solution into the central circulation.

    4. Normal urine output does not necessarily mean the client is getting the desired results from TPN.

#85. 2. The cast should be allowed to air dry. Using a hair dryer will cause the cast to dry from the outside in, rather than the correct way, from the inside out. This statement indicates a need for further instruction.   Ev   Ph/9   Ap

    1. The foot should be kept elevated. This statement indicates understanding.

    3. The cast should not be handled or touched in a way that could cause indentations until after it is dry. This statement indicates understanding.

    4. The client should wiggle his toes several times a day to assess neurologic functioning. This statement indicates understanding.

#86. 1. Keeping the fetal head from compressing the cord will allow circulation through the cord to the fetus to continue and save the baby's life.   Im   He/3   Ap

    2. The baby will be delivered as soon as possible by cesarean section.

ANSWER	RATIONALE	NP	CN	CL

3. The physician should be called but the highest priority is to keep the fetal head from compressing the cord. The nurse should keep her hand in the vagina and have someone else call the physician.

4. The tocometer may well be used but this is not the highest priority. The highest priority is to keep the fetal head from compressing the cord.

#87. 4. Persons with acute renal failure secondary to hemorrhagic shock have a good chance of complete recovery if well cared for during the acute renal failure episode. Ev Ph/10 Ap

1. Persons with acute renal failure secondary to hemorrhagic shock have a good chance of complete recovery if well cared for during the acute renal failure episode. The chances are good that he will not need dialysis the rest of his life.

2. Acute renal failure caused by hemorrhagic shock is usually not due to any hereditary condition. The son is not at particular risk.

3. If he recovers from acute renal failure, he will probably not need a special diet. Dietary limitations for this man are apt to be for a brief period of time.

#88. 2. The person who has had a liver biopsy should be positioned on his right side immediately following the procedure to provide hemostasis and reduce the likelihood of bleeding. Remember, the liver is on the right. Pl Ph/9 Ap

1. The client is on his left side during a liver biopsy. Immediately following the biopsy, he should be positioned on his right side to provide hemostasis and reduce the likelihood of bleeding.

3. The person who has had a liver biopsy should be positioned on his right side immediately following the procedure to provide hemostasis and reduce the likelihood of bleeding.

4. The person who has had a liver biopsy should be positioned on his right side immediately following the procedure to provide hemostasis and reduce the likelihood of bleeding.

#89. 4. The client who is having a pelvic sonogram should have a full bladder. The bladder acts as a landmark and reflects sound waves. Drinking several glasses of water will assure the bladder is full. Ev Ph/9 Ap

1. It is not necessary to be NPO before a pelvic sonogram.

2. It is not necessary to take a laxative the night before the test.

3. The client must not empty her bladder until the test is completed. The client who is having a pelvic sonogram should have a full bladder. The bladder acts as a landmark and reflects sound waves.

#90. 4. Scatter rugs are a hazard for anyone, but especially for a person with a walker. The rugs either need to be secured to the floor or, preferably, removed. Ev Sa/2 Ap

1. It will be easier for the client to shower than take a tub bath. Getting in and out of a tub can be difficult and hazardous. This finding is a positive one.

2. The fact that the bathroom door is narrow is not a problem for a person with a walker. It could be a serious problem if the client is wheelchair dependent.

3. A microwave does not present a problem to a client with a hip replacement. It could be a potential hazard if the client had a pacemaker. The microwave may make it easier to prepare meals.

#91. 4. Prioritization of nursing diagnosis is aimed at meeting basic physiologic needs for survival before meeting higher level needs. The client's intracranial adaptive mechanisms have been damaged by the auto accident, thereby altering the pressures within the cranial vault and placing him at high risk for alterations in basic body functioning secondary to pressure on brain tissue. Once the intracranial pressure has been stabilized, Pl Ph/10 An a review of the priority of nursing diagnoses should be undertaken.

1. This is not the highest priority. See rationale for correct answer.
2. This is not the highest priority. See rationale for correct answer.
3. This is not the highest priority. See rationale for correct answer.

#92. 2. Furosemide (Lasix) is a potent loop diuretic which can cause potassium depletion unless dietary supplements are given. Early morning administration is recommended so that sleep is not disturbed by nocturia. Both quinapril hydrochloride (Accupril) and furosemide (Lasix) may cause lightheadedness and orthostatic hypotension because of vasodilation and decreased vascular volume. Increased oral fluid intake often helps correct this and assists in flushing excess sodium from the body. Blood pressure should be monitored daily at first and at least weekly after the first follow-up visit to prevent syncopal episodes resulting from too-low blood pressure. Pl Ph/9 Co

1. The medications should be taken daily as ordered and should be taken in the morning.
3. The client should only discontinue medication upon the physician's order and should increase potassium intake.
4. The client should not increase sodium intake and should monitor blood pressure daily at first and weekly thereafter.

#93. 1. The client's symptoms are indicative of hypoxemia. Oxygen administration is required whenever hypoxemia occurs. Im Ph/10 Ap

2. The nurse may assess vital signs after starting oxygen.
3. His primary problem is hypoxemia, not pain.
4. ABGs may be indicated, but are not the first priority.

#94. 3. Resisted breathing is one kind of breathing exercise that can be taught to clients with respiratory disease. Noncompliance is common and is suspected when clients do not have typical results. One of the expected results is a cough after the exhalation phase of resisted breathing. Ev Ph/9 Co

1. Clients with respiratory disease should use pursed lip breathing.
2. The client should have a cough after exhalation when using resisted breathing exercises.
4. The client should inhale through the nose and exhale through the mouth.

#95. 2. The cooling blanket will cause vasoconstriction which decreases the peripheral blood supply. Frequent skin care and inspection of the skin every hour helps prevent skin breakdown. The cooling blanket also should be covered with a sheet or blanket to prevent direct exposure to the skin. As Ph/9 Ap

1. The client should not be unduly exposed, but this is not essential.
3. Shivering is likely to occur after the cooling blanket is started, not before. Shivering is the body's mechanism for raising body temperature and is not desired when a cooling blanket is in use.
4. The nurse should assess skin color, especially after the blanket has been started. A white area may suggest frostbite.

#96. 3. The client should make sure the temperature of the compress does not exceed 37.8°C or 100°F. Ev Ph/9 Ap

1. There is no need to take her temperature before and after applying the compress. It is the temperature of the compress that is important. A wrist compress is unlikely to raise the body temperature significantly.
2. This answer does not relate to the safety issue. Pain may not be immediately relieved.
4. It is dangerous to put the arm under the hot water faucet as the water temperature may easily exceed 100°F and burn the arm.

#97. 2. The nurse should assess this client for dietary habits. A diet that is high in fiber helps to prevent constipation. It is not unusual for As Ph/7 An the elderly and those living by themselves not to eat fresh fruits and vegetables.

1. The nurse may want to obtain this information. However, it is not the most important factor. Diet has to take priority.
3. The question states the client is hypertensive and takes no medications. A drug history may be helpful, particularly if the client was taking narcotics, calcium, or iron, which tend to be constipating. However, the question tells us she takes no medications.
4. Immobility may tend to cause constipation and activity helps to prevent constipation. The question gives the information that the client ambulates with a cane and lives alone. Therefore, further evaluation of mobility status will not be most helpful.

#98. 2. Recent memory loss can be a sign of organic brain disease. It needs to be further evaluated.   An   He/3   An

1. It is normal for the aging client to move more slowly.
3. As a person ages, near vision becomes more difficult. A magnifying glass or reading glasses are needed by most people as they age.
4. Thinning and drying of the skin with the development of lentigo ("liver spots" or "age spots") are normal as a person ages.

#99. 4. Stopping the urine while voiding requires the use of the pubococcygeus (PG) muscle—the muscle Kegel's exercises are designed to strengthen. Stopping the urine while voiding helps the client to identify the PG muscle so she can learn to contract and relax the muscle.   Im   Ph/9   Ap

1. If the client is squeezing her buttocks, the wrong muscle is being used. The PG muscle does not work the buttocks.
2. Holding the urine as long as possible is not part of Kegel's exercises.
3. Kegel's exercises are designed to strengthen the PG muscle, not the abdominal muscles. Pushing on the lower abdomen is part of the Crede maneuver sometimes used to help empty the bladder.

#100. 4. Bright red blood spurting from a wound signals arterial bleeding. Firm pressure is necessary to stop the bleeding and is the appropriate initial action.   Im   Ph/10   Ap

1. The question describes the child as telling the nurse what happened. This is adequate initial assessment of neurological status when the child also has an arterial bleed which must take priority.
2. Ice promotes vasoconstriction but when there is an arterial bleed, firm pressure is needed initially.
3. The rescue squad should be called. However, the nurse must first apply pressure to the arterial bleed. The nurse should delegate someone else to call the rescue squad.

Review Tests

Review Test 1

Universal Principles of Nursing Care Management

1. Mr. L. is homeless and has gangrene on his foot. The physician has recommended hospitalization and surgery. Mr. L. has refused. The nurse knows which of the following is true? The client
   1. can be restrained if one physician declares him incompetent.
   2. cannot be hospitalized against his will.
   3. cannot choose which treatment to refuse.
   4. may sign against medical advice (AMA).

2. Ms. R. has been medicated for her surgery. The operating room (OR) nurse, when going through the client's chart, realizes that the consent form has not been signed. Which of the following is the best action for the nurse to take?
   1. Assume it is emergency surgery and the consent is implied.
   2. Get the consent form and have the client sign it.
   3. Tell the physician that the consent form is not signed.
   4. Have a family member sign the consent form.

3. A licensed nurse in one state receives a job offer as a nurse in an adjoining state. Which of the following should the nurse do first?
   1. Contact the first state's board of nursing to cancel his/her license.
   2. Contact the hospital s/he wants to work in and ask them to contact its state board of nursing.
   3. Contact the new state's board of nursing and ask for reciprocity.
   4. Take the examining test in the new state.

4. Mr. O. has just returned to the unit from surgery. The nurse transferred him to his bed but did not put up the siderails. The client fell and was injured. What kind of liability does the nurse have?
   1. None.
   2. Negligence.
   3. Intentional tort.
   4. Assault and battery.

5. Company AZ asks the nurse to endorse a product that guarantees weight loss without exercise or diet changes with no side effects. Which of the following is the best response for the nurse to take according to the American Nurses Association (ANA) code for nurses?
   1. Endorse the product.
   2. Ask for proof of claims.
   3. Decline the offer.
   4. Report the product to the appropriate authorities.

6. The nurse is in the hospital's public cafeteria and hears two nursing assistants talking about Ms. B., in 406. They are using her name and discussing intimate details about her illness. Which of the following actions is best for the nurse to take?
   1. Go over and tell the nursing assistants that their actions are inappropriate, especially in a public place.
   2. Wait and tell the assistants later that they were overheard discussing the client. Otherwise, they might be embarrassed.
   3. Tell the nursing assistants' supervisor about the incident. It is the supervisor's responsibility to address the issue.
   4. Say nothing. It is not the nurse's job and s/he is not responsible for the assistants' actions.

7. The nurse is about to medicate a woman for breast cancer lumpectomy. The client says, "I'll be glad when the surgery is over. It will eliminate all the cancer from my body." Which of the following is the best action for the nurse to take?
   1. Medicate the client and tell the physician.
   2. Correct the client's misconceptions.
   3. Call the doctor without medicating the client.
   4. Give the medication to the client and note her comment in the chart.

8. Mr. T. is a client on your medical-surgical unit. His cousin is a physician and wants to see the chart. Which of the following is the best response for the nurse to take?
   1. Hand the cousin the client's chart to review.
   2. Ask Mr. T. to sign an authorization, and have someone review the chart with the cousin.
   3. Call the attending physician and have the doctor speak with the cousin.
   4. Tell the cousin that the request cannot be granted.

9. A nurse comes upon a motor vehicle accident when driving to work. The nurse administers care to the people involved. Under the Good Samaritan Act, the nurse could be liable
   1. for nothing, any action is covered.
   2. for gross negligence.
   3. for not providing the standard of care found in a hospital.
   4. for not stopping and offering care.

10. The nurse is supervising a newly trained certified nurse aide (CNA). An adult has just arrived on the unit after surgery. Which of the following is the most appropriate task for the nurse to delegate to the CNA and under what type of supervision?
    1. Taking the client's vital signs while the nurse watches.
    2. Suctioning the client's tracheostomy and reporting back to the nurse.
    3. Changing the client's postoperative (post-op) surgical dressing then describing it to the nurse.
    4. Testing urine with a reactant strip, and recording and reporting the results.

11. The nurse is making the assignment for the floor. There is one LPN and three RNs. Which of the following rooms should the LPN be assigned to?
    1. Ms. A., intubated and Ms. E., a newly diagnosed diabetic.
    2. Mr. V., a recent transfer from the ICU and Mr. W., a person with AIDS.
    3. Mr. T., awaiting a nursing home bed and Mr. E., one day post-hernia repair.
    4. Ms. C., a new admission for cholecystectomy and Ms. D., one day post-op mastectomy.

12. Which of the following clients should the nurse deal with first?
    1. Ms. E., who needs her dressing changed.
    2. Mr. J., who needs to be suctioned.
    3. Mr. Y., who needs to be medicated.
    4. Ms. W., who is incontinent and needs to be cleaned.

13. Which of the following clients should the nurse observe first?
    1. Mr. S., who has just returned from the OR.
    2. Ms. H., whose call light is not working.
    3. Mr. I., who has Alzheimer's disease.
    4. Ms. R., who is receiving a heating pad treatment.

14. Four clients have signaled with their call bells for the nurse. Who should be seen first?
    1. Mr. L., who needs to use the toilet.
    2. Mr. W., who does not have his glasses or hearing aid.
    3. Ms. A., who has just been given morphine.
    4. Mr. K., in a geri chair with a restraint vest on.

15. Ms. L. is admitted to the floor. She is in the terminal stages of AIDS. During the admission assessment, the nurse would ask her if she had which of the following?
    1. A will.
    2. A do not resuscitate (DNR) order.
    3. An organ donation card.
    4. Healthcare proxy.

16. The nurse enters a room and finds a fire. Which is the best initial action?
    1. Evacuate any people in the room, beginning with the most ambulatory and ending with the least mobile.
    2. Activate the fire alarm or call the operator, depending on the institution's system.
    3. Get a fire extinguisher and put out the fire.
    4. Close all the windows and doors, and turn off any oxygen or electrical appliances.

17. The nurse is unfamiliar with a new piece of OR equipment that is scheduled to be used today. What is the best course of action?
    1. Ask another nurse for instructions on how to use it.
    2. Wait until s/he has attended a class on using the equipment before using it.
    3. Get another nurse who is familiar with the equipment to operate it.
    4. Read the instructions provided with the equipment.

18. It is the first home care visit for Mr. E. He is in an electric hospital bed with an oxygen tank behind it. The bed's three-prong, grounded electric cord is connected to a frayed, two-prong extension cord. What is the most appropriate first action for the nurse to take?
    1. Turn off the oxygen supply, so as not to accelerate any spark into a fire.
    2. Turn off the electricity, so as to maintain the oxygen supply to the nonrebreather mask.
    3. Leave everything as it is and replace the extension cord as soon as possible.
    4. Unplug the bed immediately and have it replaced with a manual model as soon as possible.

19. As a nurse in a skilled nursing facility/nursing home, you are supervising several CNAs. Which CNA best understands the use of restraints? The CNA who
    1. places all clients in bed with the siderails up.
    2. applies a jacket restraint for the client who pulls out IV lines.
    3. fastens the ends of the restraint(s) to the siderails.
    4. fastens the restraints with a half bow knot to an area the client cannot reach.

20. Ms. R. has had both wrists restrained because she is agitated and pulls out her IV lines. Which of the following would the nurse observe if Ms. R. is not suffering any ill effects from the restraints? That
    1. she has difficulty moving her fingers and making a fist.
    2. her skin is reddened where the mitts were tied around her wrist.
    3. Ms. R.'s capillary refill is less than two seconds.
    4. the client complains of numbness and tingling in her hand.

21. Ms. K. is to be placed in a knee-chest position for an exam by a new staff member. Which of the following should the nurse observe?
    1. The arms are at the client's side.
    2. The head and upper chest are supported with a pillow.
    3. The lower legs are supported with a pillow.
    4. The back supports the client's weight.
22. Mr. E. has been placed in a right side-lying position by the CNAs. Which of the following should the nurse observe?
    1. The right arm is flat under the hip.
    2. The left leg is extended at the hip and knee.
    3. The right leg is flexed at the hip and knee.
    4. The left arm is supported by a pillow.
23. The nurse is evaluating whether the CNAs are correctly log rolling Mr. W. in bed. Which of the following should the nurse observe? That the CNAs
    1. use a draw sheet to aid the turning.
    2. do not place a pillow behind the head.
    3. do not put a pillow between the client's legs.
    4. place the bed in the lowest position.
24. Mr. I. is supine. Which of the following can the nurse do to prevent external rotation of the legs?
    1. Put a pillow under the client's lower legs.
    2. Place a pillow directly under the client's knees.
    3. Use a trochanter roll alongside Mr. I.'s upper thighs.
    4. Lower the client's legs so that they are below the hips.
25. Mr. T. is a C4 quadriplegic. He has slid down in the bed. Which of the following is the best method for the nurse to use to reposition him?
    1. One nurse lifting under his buttocks while he uses the trapeze.
    2. Two people lifting him up in bed with a draw sheet.
    3. Two people log rolling the client from one side to the other.
    4. One nurse lifting him under his shoulders from behind.
26. Ms. B. is to have a pelvic exam. Which of the following should the nurse do first?
    1. Have the client remove all her clothes and her socks and shoes.
    2. Have the client go to the bathroom and void, saving a sample.
    3. Place the client in a lithotomy position on the exam table.
    4. Assemble all the equipment needed for the examination.
27. Mr. U. had a left, above-the-knee amputation two weeks ago. The nurse places him in a prone position three times a day because this
    1. prevents pressure ulcers on the sacrum.
    2. helps the prosthesis to fit correctly.
    3. prevents flexion contractures.

    4. allows better blood flow to the heart.
28. Ms. L. has a chest tube placed and is in a semi-Fowler's position. The nurse knows the client is in this position because it
    1. is necessary to prevent pulmonary emboli.
    2. allows the nurse to have access to the chest tube.
    3. promotes comfort and drainage.
    4. is the only position a chest tube will work in.
29. Mr. B. is to have a rectal examination. In which of the following positions should the nurse position the client?
    1. Supine.
    2. Prone.
    3. Sims.
    4. Right lateral.
30. Mr. Y. has just returned to the unit from the OR where he spent more than two hours in the lithotomy position. Which of the following assessments should the nurse make because of the positioning during the surgery?
    1. Lower extremity pulses, paresthesias, and pain.
    2. The presence of bowel sounds.
    3. Upper extremity pulses, paresthesias, and pain.
    4. Ability to walk.
31. Mr. L. has been in a motor vehicle accident and is going into shock. Before placing the client in a modified Trendelenburg position, the nurse should assess the client for
    1. long bone fractures.
    2. air embolus.
    3. head injury.
    4. thrombophlebitis.
32. The client has been placed in the Trendelenburg position. The nurse knows the effects of this position on the client include which of the following?
    1. Increased blood flow to the feet.
    2. Decreased blood pressure.
    3. Increased pressure on the diaphragm.
    4. Decreased intracranial pressure.
33. The nurse knows the difference between the left lateral and the Sims position is that the
    1. Sims position is semiprone, halfway between lateral and prone.
    2. lateral position places the client's weight on the anterior upper chest and the left shoulder.
    3. Sims position places the weight on the right shoulder and hip.
    4. lateral position places the weight on the right hip and shoulder.
34. Ms. B. needs to be placed in position for a pelvic exam. Which of the following describes how the nurse should position the client?
    1. Supine with knees and hips bent and thighs abducted.
    2. Lying on her back, extremities moderately flexed.

3. Kneeling with arms, upper chest, and head resting on a pillow.
4. Lying on her left side with right knee and thigh flexed toward her chest.

35. Ms. L. is bedridden. The nurse knows which of the following should be included in the plan of care?
1. Asking the client about comfort prior to positioning.
2. Instituting a four-hour turning schedule.
3. Planning range of motion exercises every two hours.
4. Using support devices to maintain alignment.

36. Ms. O. is bedridden. The nurse is evaluating whether the family members understand how to position the client correctly. Which of the following should the nurse observe?
1. Lower arm and leg are always supported in the lateral positions.
2. The extremities should always be extended to prevent contractures.
3. The spine should have maximal lordosis in almost all positions.
4. The family should change the position at least every two hours.

37. A victim of a motor vehicle accident is brought to the emergency room via ambulance in hypovolemic shock. When placing the client in a modified Trendelenburg position, the nurse should place the client
1. with the legs only elevated above the heart.
2. supine, with the head of the bed lowered.
3. prone, with the head of the bed elevated.
4. supine, tilting the bed so the head is above the heart.

38. Ms. O. is bedridden and positioned on her right side. There is a pillow beneath her head. Her right arm is extended near her hip. Her left leg is extended and parallel with the right leg. Which of the following is correct?
1. The client's right leg should be flexed at the hip and knee.
2. Ms. O.'s right arm should be flexed at the shoulder and elbow.
3. There should not be a pillow under her head.
4. She should be semiprone with the weight on her upper chest.

39. The nurse uses a wide stance when moving a heavy box of supplies. Which of the following is the best reason the nurse would do this? Because it
1. avoids back strain.
2. contracts the muscles.
3. lowers the center of gravity.
4. increases stability.

40. Ms. S. is brought in after a motor vehicle accident. She has suffered a head injury and possible spinal injury. When moving her from the stretcher to the bed, the nurse should
1. have the client move segmentally.
2. sit Ms. S. up and transfer her to the bed.
3. move Ms. S. with a draw sheet.
4. log roll the client.

41. Mr. T. is a C4 quadriplegic in a nursing home. Which of the following techniques would the nurse use to transfer him from bed to wheelchair?
1. One nurse dangling the client, then using a transfer belt.
2. Two people, one at Mr. T.'s knees, the other under his arms.
3. Two nurses using a mechanical lifting device (Hoya).
4. Two nurses, one on either side, lifting Mr. T. with a sheet.

42. The nurse is dangling Ms. S. prior to transferring her from the bed to a wheelchair. Which of the following assessments is essential for the nurse to make before moving the client?
1. Taking the client's pulse and respiration.
2. Ensuring that the bed is in the highest position.
3. Assessing the client's height and range of motion.
4. Enlisting the help of another nurse or a CNA.

43. Mr. C. has just been admitted for acute asthma exacerbation and placed in a high Fowler's position. The nurse knows this position is best because it
1. facilitates maximal ventilation.
2. is required for the aerosol treatments to work.
3. allows for chest physiotherapy.
4. is the position for the chest X-ray.

44. Ms. L. is to go home with her family. The nurse is evaluating that the family members can correctly move Ms. L. from the bed to a chair. Which of the following should be seen?
1. The transfer belt is placed loosely around the waist.
2. There is no pause while the client is standing.
3. The family member leans forward from the waist.
4. The client has one foot slightly in front of the other.

45. Ms. F. suffered a stroke and has right-sided hemiparesis. The nurse is going to transfer her from bed to wheelchair. Which of the following is the best method?
1. Have the client put her arms around the nurse's neck.
2. Position the wheelchair closer to the weaker foot.
3. Place the wheelchair about a foot away from the bed.
4. Put the wheelchair at a 45° angle to the bed.

46. The nurse knows which of the following is the proper technique for medical asepsis?

1. Gloving for all client contact.
2. Changing hospital linen weekly.
3. Using your hands to turn off the faucet after handwashing.
4. Gowning to care for a one-year-old child with infectious diarrhea.

47. The nurse is conducting a class on aseptic technique and universal precautions. Which of the following statements is correct and should be included in the discussion?
    1. Universal precautions are designed to reduce the number of potentially infectious agents.
    2. Medical asepsis is designed to decrease exposure to bloodborne pathogens.
    3. Medical asepsis is designed to confine microorganisms to a specific area, limiting the number, growth, and transmission of microorganisms.
    4. The term universal precautions is synonymous with disease or category-specific isolation precautions.

48. The nurse is to open a sterile package from central supply. Which is the correct direction to open the first flap?
    1. Toward the nurse.
    2. Away from the nurse.
    3. To the nurse's left or right.
    4. It does not matter as long as the nurse only touches the outside edge.

49. For which procedure would the nurse use aseptic technique and which would require the nurse to use sterile technique?
    1. Aseptic technique for changing the client's linen and sterile technique for placing a central line.
    2. Aseptic technique for urinary catheterization in the hospital and sterile technique for cleaning surgical wounds.
    3. Aseptic technique for a spinal tap and sterile technique for surgery.
    4. Aseptic technique for food preparation and sterile technique for starting an IV line.

50. Ms. W. has a draining pressure ulcer on her sacrum and is to be discharged to her daughter's care. The nurse has taught Ms. W.'s daughter to perform dressing changes. Which observation by the nurse indicates the daughter's technique is done correctly? The daughter
    1. uses only sterile gloves to remove the old dressing.
    2. irrigates the wound from the bottom up.
    3. places the forceps used to remove the old dressing on the sterile field.
    4. washes her hands before each gloving and after the procedure is done.

51. Ms. P. is transferred to a skilled nursing facility from the hospital because she is unable to ambulate due to a left femoral fracture. The nurse knows Ms. P.'s greatest

risk factor for developing a pressure ulcer is that she
    1. is 5 ft 4 in tall, 130 lb, and eats more than half of most meals.
    2. is apathetic but oriented to person, place, and time.
    3. has slightly limited mobility and needs assistance to move from bed to chair.
    4. has good skin turgor, no edema, and her capillary refill is less than three seconds.

52. An elderly male client is transferred to a skilled nursing facility from the hospital because he is unable to ambulate due to a left femoral fracture. When doing a skin assessment, the nurse notices a 3-cm, round area partial thickness skin loss that looks like a blister on the client's sacrum. The nurse knows this is a
    1. stage I pressure ulcer.
    2. stage II pressure ulcer.
    3. stage III pressure ulcer.
    4. stage IV pressure ulcer.

53. When planning for the care of a client with a pressure ulcer on the sacrum, the nurse would include which of the following?
    1. Positioning the client with a donut around the area to relieve pressure on the ulcer.
    2. Massaging the sacrum, concentrating on the bony prominences and reddened areas.
    3. Using a heat lamp twice a day to dry the wound.
    4. Having a pressure-relieving device such as an egg crate mattress or gel flotation pad.

54. The nurse is to apply a dressing to a stage II pressure ulcer. Which of the following dressings is best?
    1. Dry gauze dressing.
    2. Wet gauze dressing.
    3. Wet to dry dressing.
    4. Moisture-vapor permeable dressing.

55. When evaluating a client with a pressure ulcer, the nurse understands that the best response to treatment of the sacral pressure ulcer on a client with a hip fracture would be indicated by
    1. the client's nutritional status including adequate protein; carbohydrates; fats; vitamins A, B, C, and K; and minerals including copper, iron, and zinc.
    2. the client's skin status including length, width, depth, condition of the wound margins, and stage of the ulcer as well as the integrity of the surrounding skin.
    3. increased mobility including the ability to reposition self in bed or wheelchair and walking with assistance.
    4. absence of clinical signs of infection including redness, warmth, swelling, pain, odor, and exudate.

56. Mr. D. has a disorder of the hypothalamus and is on a hypothermia blanket. The nurse

should make which of the following assessments?
1. Document the client's ability to sweat.
2. Ensure the client's skin is warm and dry.
3. Record baseline vital signs, neurologic status, and skin integrity.
4. Confirm that the client is alert and oriented.

57. When Mr. C. is placed on a hypothermia blanket, which of the following should be included in the nursing care plan?
1. Taking frequent vital signs, and doing skin assessments.
2. Ensuring the hypothermia blanket continues to cool until the client's temperature reaches 98.6° F.
3. Placing the client directly on the blanket.
4. Monitoring Mr. C.'s temperature through the hypothermia machine's rectal probe.

58. The physician's orders for Mr. C. include warm compresses to the left leg three times a day for treatment of an open wound. The nurse should
1. use medical aseptic techniques throughout the procedure.
2. wet the compress and apply it directly to the area.
3. place both a dry covering and waterproof material over the compress.
4. remove the compress after about five minutes.

59. Ms. H. is receiving a hot soak to her right arm. What assessments would the nurse make?
1. The water temperature at the start of the treatment is 120° F (48° C).
2. That the water basin is placed at shoulder height.
3. Throughout the treatment, the water remains at approximately the same temperature.
4. The client's baseline and after-treatment temperature.

60. Mr. H. has chronic lower back pain and receives hot packs three times a week. The nurse knows the treatment is given for which of the following reasons?
1. To help remove debris from the wound.
2. To keep the client warm and raise his temperature.

3. To improve the client's general circulation.
4. To relieve muscle spasm and promote muscle relaxation.

61. While giving an adult a tepid sponge bath to reduce his temperature, the nurse notes that the client is shivering. The nurse correctly interprets this to mean that the
1. sponge bath is being given too slowly.
2. client has a decreased metabolic demand.
3. body is trying to warm itself.
4. temperature of the water is below 90° F (32° C).

62. Ms. B. is giving a tepid sponge bath to her invalid mother who has a fever. When evaluating Ms. B. to ensure the procedure is being given correctly, the nurse would note which of the following? That Ms. B.
1. tests the water temperature on the inside of her wrist.
2. rubs each area with the wet sponge.
3. sponges one part of the body, and then another.
4. rubs her mother's skin dry after each area is sponged.

63. Mr. S. is to have a tepid sponge bath to lower his fever. What temperature should the nurse make the water?
1. 65° F (18° C).
2. 90° F (32° C).
3. 110° F (43° C).
4. 105° F (40.5° C).

64. Mr. A. has sprained his ankle. The physician would order cold applied to the injured area to
1. reduce the body's temperature.
2. increase circulation to the area.
3. aid in reabsorbing the edema.
4. relieve pain and control bleeding.

65. Mr. A. is going home from the emergency room with directions to apply a cold pack to his ankle sprain. He asks how he will know if the cold pack has worked. The nurse tells him
1. after the first application, the swelling will be decreased.
2. he will notice the red-blue bruises will turn purple.
3. there should be less pain after applying the cold pack.
4. that the skin will be blanched and numb afterward.

Universal Principles of Nursing Care Management

ANSWER	RATIONALE	NP	CN	CL

#1. 4. **A competent client may decide which treatments and procedures to accept or refuse.**   An   Sa/1   Ap

    1. Although state laws differ slightly, most have a provision that allows two physicians to examine the client and if deemed incompetent, or a risk to self or others, allow a person to be held against his/her wishes.

    2. If a court order is given or an emergency situation exists (as defined by law), then a client may be hospitalized against the client's will.

    3. As long as the client is competent and understands the risks, the hospital is unable to force him to be hospitalized or receive treatment including surgery.

#2. 3. **It is the physician's responsibility to obtain the consent and to ensure that the signer is competent. A medicated client generally is not deemed competent and the surgery may have to be postponed.**   Im   Sa/1   Ap

    1. The nurse has an obligation to report the lack of a signed consent form. It is rare that a hospitalized client cannot have a signed form.

    2. It is the physician's responsibility to obtain the consent and answer any questions. The nurse may witness the consent or the signature only.

    4. A physician is responsible for having the consent form signed, not the nurse. Only if the client is not competent (medicated, unconscious, or otherwise unable to) can a family member sign in his/her stead.

#3. 3. **Endorsement by one state because a person is licensed in another is often done.**   Im   Sa/1   Co

    1. It is not necessary to cancel the present license. It is still valid and will prove the nurse is licensed.

    2. Although the new hospital can verify the employment, it is the nurse's responsibility to contact the new state board of nursing.

    4. Once a nurse is licensed in one state, reciprocity is generally given by other states without having to take the examination again.

#4. 2. **The nurse has been negligent and can be liable for malpractice.**   An   Sa/1   Co

    1. The nurse is responsible for providing a safe environment for the client. Leaving a client who has just returned from surgery with the siderails down is a breach of duty and a causal relationship between the injury and breach can be shown.

    3. Intentional tort involves the commission of a prohibited act, willfully and deliberately. The nurse is guilty of unintentional tort or negligence.

    4. The nurse did not threaten to (assault) or actually (battery) touch the client unjustifiably. Raising siderails for a client immediately post-op is the standard of care.

#5. 4. **The product is misleading and potentially harmful to the public. It should be reported to the proper authorities to protect the public.**   An   Sa/1   An

    1. The product is deceptive and potentially dangerous to the public. The ANA code for nurses states that the nurse should participate in protecting the public from misinformation and misrepresentation and maintain the integrity of nursing.

    2. At this point, there is no product that can make these claims. It is deceptive at the least, and potentially harmful or dangerous to prospective users. It should be reported to authorities.

3. Declining the offer does not protect the public. It should be reported to the proper authorities.

#6. 1. The client has a right to confidentiality and her case should not be discussed in a public place. Im Sa/1 Ap

2. Action should be taken right away. The cafeteria is public and the information could be heard by others.

3. The supervisor should address the issue, but immediate action should be taken.

4. The nurse has a responsibility as a patient advocate to take action. The cafeteria is a public place and the client has a right to confidentiality.

#7. 3. Medicating the client can cloud her judgment and should be withheld. The doctor is the person to clarify the misconceptions. Im Sa/1 Ap

1. The client seems to misunderstand the surgery. Medicating her can cloud her judgment prior to having the physician clarify the procedure.

2. The physician obtained the consent, not the nurse. The physician should be the person to clarify the client's misconceptions.

4. If the nurse judges the client has misconceptions about the surgery, it is the responsibility of the nurse as a patient advocate to act on it. Putting a note in the chart after medicating the client does not solve the misconception.

#8. 2. The client must agree to and sign an authorization before others can review the chart, including insurance companies. Most institutions require someone on staff to review the chart with the client or client representative. Im Sa/1 Ap

1. The hospital chart is confidential and cannot be released without permission.

3. The attending physician must also keep the client's information confidential unless given permission.

4. The patient bill of rights allows Mr. T. and/or his representative access to his records and an explanation of them.

#9. 2. Actions that a reasonable, prudent person with the same level of skill and training would have provided are covered, but gross negligence is not. Im Sa/1 An

1. Gross negligence usually involves further harm or injury and is not covered.

3. Because the equipment and resources are generally greater at a hospital, the nurse is held to the standard of what a reasonable prudent person with the same training and skills would do in the same situation.

4. Most state statutes do not require healthcare workers to stop. It is an ethical rather than legal duty to do so.

#10. 4. Testing urine via reactant strips (Dip stix) and recording the results is usually within the scope of a CNA's training. The CNA should also report the results to the nurse, especially if they are abnormal. Pl Sa/1 Ap

1. If the CNA has been properly trained, then vital signs need not be directly observed.

2. While a few places allow CNAs to suction, assessment and evaluation of the procedure is the nurse's responsibility, and therefore the nurse should be at the bedside while the procedure is done.

3. The nurse should change the dressing to establish a baseline, evaluate healing, or note complications.

#11. 3. These clients are the least sick and require the least amount of highly skilled nursing care. Pl Sa/1 Ap

1. A client who is intubated requires high-level, skilled nursing and should not be assigned to an LPN. A newly diagnosed diabetic requires a great deal of patient education.

    2. Mr. V. is not the most stable client and remains in need of high level nursing care as does a hospitalized person with AIDS.

    4. A client scheduled for surgery requires a great deal of patient education, as does the client with a major loss, like a breast for cancer.

#12. 2. Any client with a potential compromise of the airway should be dealt with first.   Pl   Sa/1   Ap

    1. A dressing change can be delayed with little injury to the client, whereas someone with a blocked airway can suffer damage after four minutes.

    3. Although clients should be medicated for pain promptly, this would not supersede someone with a potential airway problem.

    4. This client needs to be seen, but Mr. J. should be suctioned first.

#13. 1. A client who has just returned from the OR is at highest risk for potential problems.   Pl   Sa/1   Ap

    2. Although the client needs to be assessed, the client returning from the OR has a higher priority.

    3. This client needs to be observed frequently, but the client returning from the OR should come first.

    4. Although this client is at risk for burns, the client returning from the OR has a higher priority need.

#14. 3. An adverse reaction to any drug can be life-threatening and should be dealt with first.   Pl   Sa/1   Ap

    1. This client needs to be seen, but does not have a life-threatening problem.

    2. Although this client needs to be assessed, Ms. A. should be seen first.

    4. This client may be at risk, but the priority should be with Ms. A.

#15. 4. A living will, durable power of attorney for healthcare, or a healthcare proxy is an important part of an admission assessment, especially for a terminally ill client.   As   Sa/1   Ap

    1. A will is not something the admission assessment should focus on. A living will is important for the nurse to know about.

    2. Only a physician may write a DNR order. The client can specify his/her wishes in an advance directive such as a living will.

    3. A person with HIV or AIDS is not an appropriate organ donor.

#16. 1. Rescue and evacuate any people in the room first. Begin with those who are able to walk, then those in wheelchairs, finally those who are nonambulatory in stretchers or beds.   Im   Sa/2   Ap

    2. Rescue and evacuate is generally the first step, while activating the fire alarm if nearby or calling the operator.

    3. The first step should be to clear the room of any people. Extinguishing the fire is the last step.

    4. Containment of the fire occurs after people have been removed from the area and the fire system has been activated.

#17. 3. Only those with knowledge of the equipment should operate it.   Pl   Sa/2   Ap

    1. If there were an emergency, you would not have the knowledge base to trouble-shoot the problem.

    2. It is important to learn how to operate the equipment, but it is essential to have someone knowledgeable operate it today.

    4. Although reading the instructions is important, hands-on practice before using it for the first time is better.

#18. 4. Because any electrical (or gas) appliance is a hazard around oxygen, it is better to unplug the dangerous cord and replace the appliances with nonelectrical ones.   Im   Sa/2   Ap

    1. If the client is on oxygen, it should not be removed hastily. It would be better to keep the oxygen flowing and replace potential electrical hazards.

    2. Turning off the electricity is a drastic step. It is better to unplug the bed and other electrical hazards in the area.

    3. The frayed, nongrounded extension cord is a definite hazard but it

ANSWER	RATIONALE	NP	CN	CL
	would be better to remove all electrical (or gas) appliances around the oxygen.			
#19. 4.	**The half bow knot is a secure knot that will not loosen, but can be easily released by the nurse in an emergency.**	Ev	Sa/2	Ap
1.	Not all clients need the siderails up. Many falls are associated with clients climbing over the siderails while trying to get out of bed.			
2.	It is best to use a restraint that restricts as little as possible. It would be better to use mitt restraints for a client with a tendency to pull out IV lines rather than a chest restraint that prevents falling or walking.			
3.	The ends of the restraints should be fastened to the bed frame, which is more stable than the siderails.			
#20. 3.	**A normal capillary refill is less than three seconds, which would indicate good circulation.**	Ev	Sa/2	Ap
1.	The client's difficulty in moving her hand and making a fist often indicates that there is impaired circulation.			
2.	The reddened area would indicate that the skin is being chafed by the restraints and there could be skin breakdown.			
4.	Numbness and tingling indicate a neurologic impairment, and should be investigated.			
#21. 2.	**A pillow can be given to the client for comfort.**	Ev	Ph/7	Ap
1.	The arms should be bent and around the client's head.			
3.	The lower legs are flat on the table or bed.			
4.	The genupectoral or knee-chest position has the client on the knees, not on the back.			
#22. 4.	**The upper arm is supported with a pillow or other device to prevent internal rotation.**	Ev	Ph/7	Ap
1.	The lower arm should be flexed at the shoulder and elbow so the body does not rest on it.			
2.	The upper leg should be supported and flexed at the hip and knee.			
3.	The lower leg is extended, not flexed.			
#23. 1.	**A draw sheet helps to maintain tension along the back and allows the body to be turned as one.**	Ev	Ph/7	Ap
2.	A pillow or the client's arm should be under the client's head to maintain cervical spine alignment.			
3.	A pillow or other support should be between the legs as the client is log rolled.			
4.	The bed should be in a comfortable position for the CNAs to limit back strain. This is not the lowest position.			
#24. 3.	**A blanket roll along side of the hips down to the mid thighs helps to prevent external rotation.**	Pl	Ph/7	Ap
1.	This does not prevent external rotation of the legs, yet it does relieve pressure on the heels.			
2.	The pillow will not prevent external rotation of the legs and can occlude the popliteal artery.			
4.	This will not prevent the legs from rotating outward.			
#25. 2.	**A draw sheet is the easiest and most effective method to lift a client up in bed.**	Im	Ph/7	Ap
1.	Mr. T. cannot use the trapeze. It should be used by those clients who can aid in lifting their own weight.			
3.	Log rolling a client moves a client laterally, not vertically.			
4.	This position places a great deal of strain on the nurse's back. It is better to use two people.			
#26. 2.	**The client should have an empty bladder, reserving a sample for analysis if needed.**	Im	He/4	Ap
1.	The client need not remove her socks and shoes. The client should be asked to void first.			
3.	Although this is the correct position, Ms. B. should void first.			
4.	The nurse should assemble the equipment, not have the client do so.			
#27. 3.	**Flexion contractures can be prevented by positioning and exercise.**	An	Ph/7	Co

    1.   To prevent pressure ulcers, the client should be encouraged to change positions frequently. The prone position helps to stretch the flexor muscles and prevents contractures.

    2.   Wrapping the stump helps to shape the residual limb for a prosthesis.

    4.   Trendelenburg promotes lower extremity blood flow. Prone position helps to prevent flexion contractures.

#28. 3.   This position facilitates drainage, and is generally most comfortable.   An   Ph/9   An

    1.   This position will not prevent a pulmonary embolus.

    2.   The nurse should have access to the chest tube no matter its location or client position.

    4.   A chest tube is connected to suction. A closed chest drainage system will work in any position, assuming there are no kinks or occlusions.

#29. 3.   The rectum is easily accessed when the hip is bent at a right angle.   Pl   He/4   Co

    1.   Placing the client in the supine position does not allow easy access to the rectum.

    2.   Access to the rectum is difficult in the prone position.

    4.   With the client's legs straight, access to the rectum is more difficult.

#30. 1.   The lithotomy position places pressure on the nerves and blood vessels of the legs.   As   Ph/9   Ap

    2.   The positioning during surgery does not affect the bowel. Also, it is not likely that the bowel will be active immediately after colon surgery.

    3.   The lithotomy position does not generally place additional pressure on the upper extremities. It does put pressure on the lower extremities.

    4.   The ability to walk should not be assessed until assessment of the pulses, paresthesias, and pain is done. Most general surgery clients do not ambulate for a period of time.

#31. 3.   Head injuries and chest injuries are contraindications for the Trendelenburg position.   As   Ph/9   Ap

    1.   Long bone fractures are not a contraindication for the Trendelenburg position, which is often used for clients in shock with or without long bone fractures.

    2.   A client with an embolus is often placed in a left-lying Trendelenburg position.

    4.   Thrombophlebitis is not a contraindication for the Trendelenburg position.

#32. 3.   The chest cavity is pushed by the pressure from the abdominal contents.   An   Ph/9   Co

    1.   The legs and feet have less blood in them as they are raised above the heart.

    2.   The blood pressure is raised because of the increased return from the legs.

    4.   The intracranial pressure is increased not decreased. This is why head injury is a contraindication for the Trendelenburg position.

#33. 1.   The Sims position is halfway between the left lateral position and the prone position.   An   Ph/7   Co

    2.   The Sims position places the weight on the upper anterior chest and hip.

    3.   The left lateral position places the weight on the left hip and shoulder. With the Sims position, the weight is forward because the client is halfway prone.

    4.   The left lateral position has the weight on the left shoulder and hip.

#34. 1.   The dorsal lithotomy position is used for most pelvic exams.   Im   He/4   Ap

    2.   The dorsal recumbent position does not allow the greatest ease, comfort, or access for pelvic exams.

    3.   The genupectoral or knee-chest position is generally not used for pelvic exams because access for bimanual palpation is limited.

ANSWER		RATIONALE	NP	CN	CL
	4.	The Sims position is not used for pelvic exams because of difficulty with access.			
#35.	4.	**Support devices like pillows, special mattresses, trochanter rolls, and foot boards help to maintain alignment and prevent contractures.**	Pl	Ph/7	Ap
	1.	A correctly aligned client may still be uncomfortable. Therefore, ask the client if the new position is comfortable.			
	2.	The client should be turned every two hours at least, not four hours. This helps to prevent pressure ulcers.			
	3.	Range of motion exercises are usually scheduled for twice a day.			
#36.	4.	**Position changes should occur at least every two hours, more often if needed.**	Ev	Ph/7	Ap
	1.	The upper arm and leg, not the lower, should be supported, usually with a pillow.			
	2.	Not all positions require the extremities to be extended. The side-lying and Sims position should have the upper arm and leg bent. Range of motion exercises aid in preventing contractures.			
	3.	Lordosis is the excessive concavity of the back. It should be avoided and the spine kept in alignment.			
#37.	1.	**The modified Trendelenburg position raises the legs only.**	Im	Ph/10	Ap
	2.	The modified Trendelenburg position puts only the legs above the heart. The regular or traditional Trendelenburg position either raises the foot of the bed or lowers the head of the bed.			
	3.	In the Trendelenburg position, the client is supine, not prone.			
	4.	The reverse Trendelenburg position elevates the head of the bed or lowers the foot of the bed. The modified Trendelenburg raises only the legs above the heart.			
#38.	2.	**The lower arm should be flexed, so the body does not rest on it.**	An	Ph/7	Au
	1.	The upper leg should be bent. This would be her left, not right leg.			
	3.	A pillow helps to maintain the cervical spine in alignment.			
	4.	The Sims position is not necessary. The client should be realigned in the lateral position.			
#39.	4.	**The greater the stability, the less chance of injury. When increasing the base of support, the nurse helps to maintain balance.**	An	Ph/2	Ap
	1.	Using the large muscle groups in the arms and legs helps to avoid back strain by distributing the workload away from the back.			
	2.	Preparatory isometric tensing or contractions lessen the energy required to move it, and reduce the likelihood of injury.			
	3.	Lowering the center of gravity would be when the nurse bends or squats, not necessarily from widening the stance.			
#40.	4.	**Log rolling a client would protect the spinal column and keep the body in alignment.**	An	Ph/9	Ap
	1.	A person with a spinal cord injury should be kept as straight as possible.			
	2.	Sitting up a client with a spinal injury is contraindicated because it places additional stress on the cord.			
	3.	Using a draw sheet requires the client to maintain his/her own head alignment. A person should keep the head in alignment.			
#41.	3.	**A mechanical lifting device (Hoya, Hoyer) helps to transfer clients and prevents back injury to the nurses.**	Pl	Ph/7	Ap
	1.	One nurse is not enough and a transfer belt is inadequate for a client who cannot bear his own weight.			
	2.	Although acceptable in an emergency, a better method would be to use a mechanical lifting device.			
	4.	This method can lift the client up in bed but is not used to transfer to a wheelchair.			
#42.	1.	**The client must be assessed before and after dangling to gather a baseline and reaction to the procedure.**	As	Ph/7	Ap
	2.	The bed should be in the lowest position to prevent straining.			

3.   Neither of these assessments is essential, although helpful to know.

4.   Dangling only requires one person, although two people may be used if needed.

#43. **1.** **A high Fowler's position allows maximal chest expansion and decreases hypoxia.**   An   Ph/9   Co

2.   Although the nebulizer works best in a vertical position, it is not necessary.

3.   Chest physiotherapy requires multiple positions and is generally not performed with acute asthma attacks.

4.   Although a chest X-ray might be ordered, it is not necessary to keep a client in a high Fowler's position for this reason.

#44. **4.** **Both the family member and the client should have one foot slightly in front of the other. This allows for a greater base of support and helps when rocking to achieve a standing position.**   Ev   Ph/7   Ap

1.   The transfer belt should be secured snugly around the client's waist, not loosely.

2.   A few moments in the standing position allows the client and family member to extend the joints and provides a chance to ensure that the client is alright prior to further movement.

3.   The family member should lean only slightly from the hips, so that there is minimal strain on the back.

#45. **4.** **This position is best for clients who have difficulty walking. The client can pivot into the chair and lesson the amount of body rotation.**   Im   Ph/7   Ap

1.   Grasping of the neck can injure the nurse. Better to have the client put her hands on the nurse's waist or shoulders.

2.   The stronger foot should be closer to the wheelchair to allow better pivoting, and so that the client can bear more of her own weight.

3.   The wheelchair should be placed as close to the bed as possible to make transfer as easy as possible.

#46. **4.** **Gowns should be worn when the nurse's clothing is likely to be soiled by infected material.**   Im   Sa/2   Kn

1.   Gloves are not needed for all client contact, only when there is potential for infection from pathogens.

2.   Hospital linen should be changed every day or more often if soiled, wet, or otherwise needed.

3.   If there are no elbow, knee, or foot pedals, the nurse should use a towel to turn off the faucet.

#47. **3.** **Medical asepsis should be practiced everywhere. It includes such things as handwashing.**   An   Sa/2   Ap

1.   Universal precautions are designed to prevent exposure to bloodborne pathogens like hepatitis B and C, as well as HIV.

2.   Medical asepsis is designed to reduce the number of potentially infectious agents, whereas universal precautions help to limit exposure to bloodborne pathogens.

4.   Universal precautions are not the same as disease or category-specific precautions such as AFB, respiratory, contact, or enteric precautions.

#48. **2.** **This allows for the least possible potential for contamination while opening the package.**   Im   Sa/2   Ap

1.   The first flap should open away from the nurse, so as to prevent reaching across the sterile field later when opening the other flaps.

3.   The second and third flaps should open to either side. The first flap should open away from the nurse.

4.   While opening the package, the nurse should only touch the outside edge, but the first flap should open away from the nurse.

#49. **1.** **Changing linen should be done with aseptic technique, whereas putting in central lines requires sterile technique.**   Pl   Sa/2   An

2.   In the hospital, sterile technique is used for urinary catheterization, although aseptic technique is often used by clients in their home.

ANSWER	RATIONALE	NP	CN	CL

3. A spinal tap requires sterile technique as does surgery.

4. Putting in an IV line requires asepsis not sterile technique.

#50. 4. Handwashing should occur before donning the nonsterile gloves, when changing from nonsterile to sterile gloves, and after the procedure. This prevents the spread of microorganisms.   Ev   Sa/2   An

1. Sterile gloves are not needed to remove the old dressing, just for applying the new dressing. A better alternative is to use clean gloves.

2. Wounds are cleaned from the top down; this ensures that microorganisms are washed away with the solution. If the nurse washes from the bottom up, the area cleaned first will be exposed to the microorganisms from the top of the wound as the solution flows with gravity.

3. The forceps are considered contaminated after removing the old dressing. Placing them on the sterile field renders the field nonsterile.

#51. 3. The fact that Ms. P. is chair-bound has the greatest impact on her developing pressure ulcers.   As   Ph/7   An

1. The client has adequate nutrition, eating more than half of most meals, with a weight appropriate to her height.

2. Although the client is apathetic, a mild risk factor, she is oriented, and therefore only at slight risk for pressure ulcers.

4. These findings are normal and do not increase the risk for the client to develop pressure ulcers.

#52. 2. A stage II pressure ulcer may look like a blister, abrasion, or shallow crater and only involve a partial thickness skin loss of the epidermis and/or dermis.   An   Ph/9   An

1. A stage I pressure ulcer is defined as a nonblanchable erythema of intact skin. The client's skin integrity is broken.

3. A stage III pressure ulcer is a full thickness skin loss involving damage to or necrosis of subcutaneous tissue that may extend down to, but not through, underlying fascia. It generally looks like a deep crater.

4. A stage IV pressure ulcer is a full thickness skin loss with extensive destruction, tissue necrosis, or damage to muscle, bone, or supporting structures.

#53. 4. Any supportive device that protects bony prominences aids in relieving pressure. This can include egg crates, gel flotation devices, sheepskins, alternating pressure mattresses, and various air loss beds.   Pl   Ph/9   Ap

1. Donuts increase pressure and damage tissues. They are not used in the treatment of pressure ulcers.

2. Massage can cause additional trauma and is therefore not used.

3. Heat lamps dry the skin and decrease tissue tolerance. They should not be used for pressure ulcers.

#54. 4. Moisture-vapor permeable dressings help stage II ulcers heal faster than saline dressings.   Im   Ph/9   Co

1. Dry dressings help to wick drainage away from the wound surface, but are used on stage III and IV pressure ulcers, not stage I or II.

2. Although common, wet or saline dressings applied to stage II pressure ulcers are less likely to heal than those ulcers with moisture-vapor permeable dressings.

3. Wet to dry dressings debride necrotic and healthy tissue alike and are not used for stage I or II pressure ulcers.

#55. 2. The best clinical indicator of healing is observation of the skin and evaluation of the pressure ulcer.   Ev   Ph/9   An

1. The client's nutritional status is very important for prevention and healing, but is not the best method to evaluate wound healing.

3. Although limited mobility is one of the most important factors for developing the pressure ulcer, healing is best measured through skin assessment.

    4. Although prevention of infection is important, absence alone does not indicate wound healing.

#56. 3. Baseline vital sign assessment is necessary to document against those taken during and after the treatment.   As   Ph/9   Ap

    1. The client's ability to sweat does not alter the hypothermia blanket's ability to cool Mr. D.

    2. The skin will probably become moist or clammy during the procedure. Dry the client and replace any wet linen.

    4. The client need not be alert and oriented to be placed on a hypothermia blanket. The nurse, however, should be even more vigilant when the client has an altered mental status.

#57. 1. Frequent vital signs and skin assessments are necessary to ensure that the treatment is working and there are no adverse effects.   Pl   Ph/9   Ap

    2. The machine generally shuts off a few degrees above the desired temperature because the client's temperature will drift down (continue to cool).

    3. A bath blanket or sheet should be placed between the client and the cooling blanket.

    4. The client's temperature should be assessed by a rectal thermometer to ensure the machine probe's accuracy.

#58. 3. The layers act as insulators and prevent moisture loss. Some nurses prefer placing the waterproof layer next to the compress and then covering with a dry cover, whereas others reverse the order, putting the waterproof layer on the outside.   Im   Sa/2   Ap

    1. Surgical asepsis (sterile technique) is used when dealing with an open wound.

    2. The compress should be wrung out to remove excess liquid, and then shaken to incorporate air, thus allowing better temperature control.

    4. Compresses are generally applied for at least 15 minutes up to 30 minutes. If the client has an adverse effect after five minutes, remove the compress, and evaluate the reason.

#59. 3. The nurse should check the temperature every five minutes or so, and replace some of the water with a hotter solution. Care should be taken to stir the basin while adding the additional water so as not to burn the client.   As   Ph/9   Ap

    1. This water temperature is too hot and can burn the client.

    2. Placing the basin at shoulder height will cause poor body alignment and is uncomfortable for the client.

    4. A local application of heat to the arm should not dramatically raise the core body temperature. A comparison of after-treatment with baseline temperature should be taken for those procedures that cause systemic effects.

#60. 4. Most people with chronic lower back pain find relief with applications of heat.   An   Ph/7   An

    1. Although warm soaks and compresses help to remove debris from a wound, Mr. H.'s skin is intact.

    2. Applications involving heat can warm a client and help to raise his/her body temperature, but this is not why Mr. H. receives hot packs.

    3. Heat will promote circulation to the area in which it is applied, but a hot pack to Mr. H.'s back will not improve his general circulation.

#61. 3. Shivering indicates that the body is trying to warm itself and conserve heat.   An   Ph/9   An

    1. A sponge bath should take approximately 30 minutes to be most effective at allowing the body to cool.

    2. Shivering increases the body's metabolic demand and can increase the client's temperature.

    4. Although the temperature of the water should remain at approximately 90° F (32° C) during a tepid sponge bath, shivering itself does not indicate the water temperature is too low.

ANSWER	RATIONALE	NP	CN	CL
#62. 3.	**Each area is sponged slowly and gently. The face and forehead, the neck, arms, and legs for three to five minutes, and the back for 10 minutes.**	Ev	Ph/9	Ap
1.	Testing the water on the inside of the wrist is generally reserved for warm applications, not to cool the body.			
2.	Each area is sponged not rubbed as rubbing may increase heat production.			
4.	The skin should be covered, not dried, during the bath, and afterward the client should be patted dry, not rubbed, which can cause skin irritation.			
#63. 2.	**Unlike a cooling sponge bath where the temperature begins at this point and gradually is lowered to 65° F (18° C) at the end, this is the temperature that the water begins and ends at for a tepid sponge bath.**	Pl	Ph/9	Co
1.	This is the end temperature for a cooling sponge bath and is reached by adding ice cubes to 90° F (32° C) water.			
3.	This is the temperature for a sitz bath, and would be too warm for a tepid sponge bath designed to lower a fever.			
4.	This is the temperature for a warm compress. It would not decrease a fever as effectively as water at a lower temperature.			
#64. 4.	**Cold will produce an anesthetic effect and help to reduce pain as well as control bleeding by constricting blood vessels.**	An	Ph/7	Co
1.	The client's body temperature does not need to be lowered, nor does a local application reduce core body temperature significantly.			
2.	Cold does not increase circulation; rather it constricts blood vessels in the application area.			
3.	Cold does not aid in the reabsorption of fluid because it reduces the amount of blood flow to the area. It can limit future edema.			
#65. 3.	**Cold produces an anesthetic effect and can relieve pain.**	Ev	Ph/7	Ap
1.	Any edema present before the application will remain. Future swelling may be decreased.			
2.	Bruises will occur as blood collects from the broken vessels. The color change from red-blue to purple will occur naturally, whether or not cold is applied.			
4.	Blanched, mottled skin and numbness are indications of excessive cold.			

Review Test 2

Adult Health

1. An adult has just been brought in by ambulance after a motor vehicle accident and has moderate anxiety. When assessing the client, the nurse would expect which of the following from sympathetic nervous system stimulation?
   1. A rapid pulse and increased respiratory rate.
   2. Decreased physiologic functioning.
   3. Rigid posture and altered perceptual focus.
   4. Increased awareness and attending.
2. Mr. V. has received an injection of immunoglobulin. The nurse knows that he will develop which of the following types of immunity?
   1. Active natural immunity.
   2. Active artificial immunity.
   3. Passive natural immunity.
   4. Passive artificial immunity.
3. The nurse knows which of the following is true about immunity?
   1. Antibody-mediated defense occurs through the T-cell system.
   2. Cellular immunity is mediated by antibodies produced by the B-cells.
   3. Antibodies are produced by the B-cells.

4. Humoral or circulating immunity is lost with AIDS.
4. An adult is on a clear liquid diet. The nurse can offer him
   1. milk.
   2. Jello.
   3. freshly squeezed orange juice.
   4. ice cream.
5. An adult is being taught about a healthy diet. The nurse explains that the food pyramid can guide him
   1. by indicating exactly how many servings of each group to eat.
   2. on how many calories he should have.
   3. in making daily food choices.
   4. to divide food into four basic groups.
6. Before administering a tube feeding the nurse knows to perform which of the following assessments?
   1. The gastrointestinal (GI) tract, including bowel sounds, last BM, and distention.
   2. The client's neurologic status, especially gag reflex.
   3. The amount of air in the stomach.
   4. That the formula is used directly from the refrigerator.
7. The nurse knows which of the following indicates protein deficiency?
   1. Negative nitrogen balance.
   2. Koilonychia (spoon-shaped nails).
   3. Magenta tongue.
   4. Bleeding gums.
8. The nurse knows that a client understands a low residue diet when he selects which of the following from a menu?
   1. Rice and lean chicken.
   2. Eggs and bacon.
   3. Pasta with vegetables.
   4. Tuna casserole.
9. An adult is receiving total parenteral nutrition (TPN). The nurse knows which of the following assessments is essential?
   1. Evaluation of the peripheral intravenous (IV) site.
   2. Confirmation that the tube is in the stomach.
   3. Assessment of the GI tract, including bowel sounds.
   4. Fluid and electrolyte monitoring.
10. The nurse knows which of the following statements about TPN and peripheral parenteral nutrition (PPN) is true?
    1. TPN is usually indicated for clients needing short-term (less than three weeks) nutritional support, while PPN is for long-term maintenance.
    2. A client needing more than 3000 calories would receive PPN, whereas TPN is given to those requiring less than 3000 calories.
    3. TPN is often given to those with fluid restrictions, whereas PPN is used for those without constraints on their fluid intake.
    4. TPN is given to those who need to augment oral feedings, whereas PPN is used for those who are nothing by mouth (NPO).
11. When administering TPN, the nurse makes sure the
    1. IV site is kept aseptic while infusing the solution.
    2. feeding is poured into a pouch and then infused.
    3. solution is only hung for a maximum of eight hours at a time.
    4. new formula is added to the partially used solution so the line does not run dry.
12. Mr. T. has been treated for pulmonary tuberculosis (TB) and is being discharged home with his wife and two young children. Mr. T.'s wife asks how TB is passed from one person to another so she can prevent any one else from catching it. The nurse responds,
    1. "You should wear gloves when handling his linen and bedding, because you can get TB by touching the germs."
    2. "You should keep the windows and doors closed so as not to spread the droplets."
    3. "He must be careful to cough into a handkerchief that is washed in hot water or discarded."
    4. "Make sure to boil all milk before drinking or using it."
13. The nurse is evaluating a certified nursing assistant (CNA). Which of the following CNAs understands universal precautions? The CNA who
    1. wears gloves during all client contact.
    2. cleans blood spills with soap and water.
    3. pours bulk blood and other secretions down a drain connected to a sanitary sewer.
    4. carries blood sample to the lab in an open basket.
14. An adult is on long-term aspirin therapy and is experiencing tinnitus. The nurse best interprets this to mean
    1. the aspirin is working correctly.
    2. the client ingested more medicine than was recommended.
    3. the client has an upper GI bleed.
    4. he is experiencing a mild overdosage.
15. An adult is receiving a nonsteroidal anti-inflammatory drug (NSAID). The nurse is to assess him for side-effects. Which of the following would the nurse observe if the client is experiencing no side-effects?
    1. The client is somnolent and hard to arouse.
    2. The client is having dark, tarry stools.
    3. There is no complaint of nausea or vomiting.
    4. The pain is still a 6 on a scale of 1–10.
16. An adult is to receive an intramuscular (IM) injection of morphine for post-op pain. Which of the following is necessary for the nurse to assess prior to giving a narcotic analgesic?

1. The client's level of alertness and respiratory rate.
2. The last time the client ate or drank something.
3. The client's bowel habits and last bowel movement.
4. The client's history of addictions.

17. An adult is to receive narcotic analgesic via a patient-controlled analgesia (PCA). The nurse is evaluating the client's understanding of the procedure. Which of the following statements by the client indicates that she understands PCA?
    1. "When I press this button the machine will always give me more medicine."
    2. "I will press the button whenever I begin to experience pain."
    3. "I should press this button every hour so the pain doesn't come back."
    4. "With this machine I will experience no more pain."

18. An adult suffered second and third degree burns over 20% of his body two days ago. The nurse knows that the best way to assess fluid balance is to
    1. maintain strict records of intake and output.
    2. weigh the client daily.
    3. monitor skin turgor.
    4. check for edema.

19. Mr. H., 78-years-old, has been working on his lawn for two days, although the temperature has been above 90° F. He has been on thiazide diuretics for hypertension. His lab values are: K 3.7 mEq/L, Na 129 mEq/L, Ca 4.9 mEq/L, and Cl 95 mEq/L. When planning for his care the nurse would
    1. make sure he drinks eight glasses of water a day.
    2. monitor for fatigue, muscle weakness, restlessness, and flushed skin.
    3. look for signs of hyperchloremia.
    4. observe for neurologic changes.

20. Ms. H. has gastroenteritis and is on digitalis. Her lab values are: K 3.2 mEq/L, Na 136 mEq/L, Ca 4.8 mEq/L, and Cl 98 mEq/L. The nurse puts which of the following on the client's plan of care?
    1. Monitor for hyperkalemia.
    2. Avoid foods rich in potassium.
    3. Observe for digitalis toxicity.
    4. Observe for Trousseau's and Chvostek's signs.

21. Mr. D. is a hemodialysis patient who is complaining of muscle weakness and numbness in his legs. His lab results are: Na 136 mEq/L, K 5.9 mEq/L, Cl 100 mEq/L, Ca 4.5 mEq/L. The nurse knows Mr. D. is suffering from
    1. hyperkalemia.
    2. hypernatremia.
    3. hypocalcemia.

4. hypochloremia.

22. Ms. C. has breast cancer that has metastasized to her bones. She is complaining of increased thirst, polyuria, and decreased muscle tone in her legs. Her lab values are: Na 139 mEq/L, K 4.0 mEq/L, Cl 103 mEq/L, and Ca 4.0 mEq/L. The nurse's best interpretation of the data is
    1. hypocalcemia.
    2. hypercalcemia.
    3. hyperkalemia.
    4. hypochloremia.

23. Mr. B. is anxious and hyperventilating. His blood gases are: pH 7.47, $PaCO_2$ 33. What is the best initial action for the nurse to take?
    1. Try to have the client breathe slower or into a paper bag.
    2. Monitor the client's fluid balance.
    3. Give O_2 via nasal cannula.
    4. Administer sodium bicarbonate.

24. Mr. G. has had gastroenteritis with vomiting for three days. He has taken baking soda without relief. His blood gases are as follows: pH 7.49, $PaCO_2$ 45, and HCO_3 30. The nurse would expect which of the following to be included in the plan of care?
    1. Have the client drink at least eight glasses of water in the first day.
    2. Administer $NaHCO_3$ IV as per physician's orders.
    3. Continue sodium bicarbonate for nausea.
    4. Monitor electrolytes for hypokalemia and hypocalcemia.

25. Ms. A.'s blood gas results are: pH 7.31, $PaCO_2$ 49, and HCO_3 24. The nurse interprets this as
    1. respiratory acidosis.
    2. respiratory alkalosis.
    3. metabolic acidosis.
    4. metabolic alkalosis.

26. An adult who is a diabetic has infectious diarrhea. His arterial blood gases are: pH 7.30, $PaCO_2$ 35, and HCO_3 of 19. The nurse would monitor the client for which of the following?
    1. Trousseau's sign.
    2. Hypokalemia.
    3. Hypoglycemia.
    4. Respiratory changes.

27. An adult has an IV line in his right forearm infusing D5 1/2NS with 20 mEq of potassium at 75 ml/h. The nurse evaluating the client with no adverse reactions would expect to find which of the following?
    1. The area around the needle insertion is cool, blanched, and swollen.
    2. Redness and warmth at the needle site.
    3. An empty drip chamber and tubing.
    4. No blood in the IV tubing.

28. An adult has a central venous line. Which of the following should the nurse include in the care plan?

1. Frequent monitoring of blood values including complete blood count (CBC) and electrolytes.
2. Regular serial chest X-rays to ensure proper placement of the central line.
3. Continuous infusion of a solution at a keep vein open rate.
4. Any signs of infection, air embolus, and leakage or puncture.

29. An adult has a Hickman type central venous catheter and needs to have blood drawn from it. Which of the following is the nurse going to do first?
1. Use sterile technique to assemble the supplies needed.
2. Aspirate and discard the first 5 ml of the blood.
3. Flush the catheter with normal saline according to hospital policy.
4. Remove the cap on the catheter and replace it with a new one.

30. An adult has a central line in his right subclavian vein. The nurse is to change the tubing. Which of the following should be done?
1. Use the old solution with the new tubing.
2. Connect the new tubing to the hub prior to running any fluid through the tubing.
3. Close the roller clamp on the new tubing after priming it.
4. Irrigate the hub prior to inserting the new tubing.

31. An adult suffered a diving accident and is being brought in by an ambulance intubated and on a backboard with a cervical collar. What is the first action the nurse would take on arrival in the hospital?
1. Take the client's vital signs.
2. Insert a large bore IV line.
3. Check the lungs for equal breath sounds bilaterally.
4. Perform a neurologic check using the Glasgow scale.

32. An adult has been shot. His vital signs are blood pressure (BP) 90/60, pulse (P) 120 weak and thready, respirations (R) 20. During the initial assessment, he is placed in a modified Trendelenburg position. If the position change has the desired effect the nurse would expect
1. an increase in the client's blood pressure.
2. an increase in the client's heart rate.
3. an increase in the client's respiratory rate.
4. a faster capillary refill time in the toes.

33. An adult has been stung by a bee and is in anaphylactic shock. An epinephrine (adrenaline) injection has been given. The nurse would expect which of the following if the injection has been effective?
1. The client's breathing will become easier.
2. The client's blood pressure will decrease.
3. There will be an increase in angioedema.

4. There will be a decrease in the client's level of consciousness.

34. An adult has been in a motor vehicle accident. She has a 4-in laceration on her forehead that is bleeding profusely. Her left ankle has an obvious deformity and is splinted. Her vital signs are BP 100/60, P 110, and R 16. What is the first action the nurse should take?
1. Start an IV line.
2. Place a Foley catheter.
3. Get an ECG.
4. Check her neurologic status.

35. An adult is brought in by ambulance after a motor vehicle accident. He is unconscious, on a backboard with his neck immobilized. He is bleeding profusely from a large gash on his right thigh. What is the first action the nurse should take?
1. Stop the bleeding.
2. Check his airway.
3. Take his vital signs.
4. Find out what happened from eyewitnesses.

36. A 74-year-old, widowed client is hospitalized for cataract surgery. During his admission interview, he repeatedly talks about how he wishes he was as strong and energetic as he was when he was younger. In planning care for this client, the nurse should include which of the following?
1. Use of the intervention reminiscence.
2. Confrontation of the client about being so grim.
3. Changing the topic whenever he brings it up.
4. Incorporation of a humorous view of the normal loss of strength.

37. A 74-year-old woman is hospitalized for dehydration. During the admission interview, she admits to the nurse that she is depressed. The nurse would expect this client to exhibit which of the following symptoms?
1. Increased energy level.
2. Increased anxiety.
3. Increased autonomy and independence.
4. Increased socialization.

38. Knowing the difference between normal age-related changes and pathologic findings, which finding should the nurse identify as pathologic in a 74-year-old client?
1. Increase in residual lung volume.
2. Decrease in sphincter control of the bladder.
3. Increase in diastolic blood pressure.
4. Decreased response to touch, heat, and pain.

39. Mrs. V. is a sexually active 63-year-old client. She complains of painful intercourse secondary to vaginal dryness. Which information is most important for the nurse to include in a teaching plan for this client?

1. Instruct Mrs. V. to reflect on all medications, including over-the-counter drugs, that she has taken in the past month in order to determine a possible etiology for the dryness.
2. Teach Mrs. V. alternative methods of intimacy in the form of touch.
3. Instruct Mrs. V. to use an artificial water-based lubricant in the vagina to decrease the discomfort of intercourse.
4. Prepare Mrs. V. for a vascular work-up since the dryness is often related to vascular deficiencies.

40. Mr. Z., an elderly, medically controlled manic-depressive and asthmatic, has been under the care of his primary physician for many years. Recently, a cardiologist prescribed cardiac medications for congestive heart failure. He complains to the home care nurse that he is nauseated. It would be justifiable for the nurse to reach which of the following conclusions as to the cause of Mr. Z.'s nausea?
    1. The reaction between the new medication regime and the foods caused Mr. Z.'s nausea.
    2. The problem of polypharmacy may exist as Mr. Z.'s symptomatology may be a result of multiple drug interactions.
    3. The nausea could be psychosomatic and related to Mr. Z.'s depression over having to take new medications.
    4. Mr. Z. may be taking too much of his new medications, which may contribute to his symptoms.

41. An elderly client has several medications ordered and has difficulty swallowing them. What strategy should the nurse use to administer these medications?
    1. Hide the medication by placing them in meat.
    2. Crush the medication and mix them with soft foods.
    3. Substitute injectable medications.
    4. Dissolve medications in liquid.

42. Which of the following measures is necessary to incorporate into a plan of care for a client who is diagnosed with senile dementia?
    1. Because these clients are easily bored, they need to be challenged with new activities.
    2. Environmental stimuli need to be eliminated.
    3. Communicate in simple words, short sentences, and a calm tone of voice.
    4. Schedule more demanding activities later in the day.

43. Mr. B., a 76-year-old client who is a resident in an extended care facility, is in the late stages of Alzheimer's disease. He tells his nurse that he has sore back muscles from all the construction work he has been doing all day. Which response by the nurse is most appropriate?
    1. "Mr. B., you know you don't work in construction anymore."
    2. "What type of motion did you do to precipitate this soreness?"
    3. "Mr. B., you're 76-years-old and you've been here all day. You don't work in construction anymore."
    4. "Would you like me to rub your back for you?"

44. An 86-year-old male with senile dementia has been physically abused and neglected for the past two years by his live-in caregiver. He has since moved and is living with his son and daughter-in-law. Which response by the client's son would cause the nurse great concern?
    1. "How can we obtain reliable help to assist us in taking care of Dad? We can't do it alone."
    2. "Dad used to beat us kids all the time. I wonder if he remembered that when it happened to him?"
    3. "I'm not sure how to deal with Dad's constant repetition of words."
    4. "I plan to ask my sister and brother to help my wife and me with Dad on the weekends."

45. Mrs. J. is an alert and oriented 84-year-old client who is receiving home care services following a cerebrovascular accident (CVA) that has left her with right-sided hemiparesis. She lives with her middle-aged daughter and son-in-law. The nurse suspects she is being physically abused by her daughter. To elicit information effectively, the nurse should do which of the following?
    1. Directly ask the client if she has been physically struck or hurt by anyone.
    2. Wait until enough trust has been developed to enable the client to approach the nurse first.
    3. Confront the daughter with the suspicions.
    4. Interview the son-in-law to gain his perspective of the situation.

46. An adult male is scheduled for surgery and the nurse is assessing for risk factors. Which of the following are the greatest risk factors?
    1. He is 5 ft 4 in tall and weighs 125 lb.
    2. He expresses a fear of pain in the post-op period.
    3. He is 5 ft 4 in tall, weighs 360 lb, and is diabetic.
    4. He expresses a fear of the unknown.

47. The nurse in an outpatient department is interviewing an adult one week prior to her scheduled elective surgery. In planning for the surgery, which of the following should the nurse include in her teaching?
    1. The client will be able to return home alone following the surgery.

2. Limitations of oral intake the day of the procedure.
3. The laboratory studies ordered do not need to be done until after the surgery.
4. The client should not take any of her routine medications the morning of the surgery.

48. The nurse enters Mrs. M.'s room to administer 10 mg Valium PO, the ordered pre-op medication for her hysterectomy. During the conversation, Mrs. M. tells the nurse that she and her husband are planning to have another child in the coming year. The best action for the nurse to take is which of the following?
1. Do not administer the pre-op medication, notify the nursing supervisor and the physician.
2. Go ahead and administer the medication as ordered.
3. Check to see if the patient has signed a surgical consent.
4. Send the patient to the operating room (OR) without the medication.

49. The nurse administers 10 mg intramuscular (IM) morphine as a pre-op medication, and then discovers that there is no signed operative permit. The best action for the nurse to take is to
1. send the patient to surgery as scheduled.
2. notify the nursing supervisor, the OR, and the physician as the effects of the drug must be allowed to wear off before the consent can be obtained.
3. cancel the surgery.
4. obtain the needed consent.

50. Ms. D. received atropine sulfate (Atropine) as a pre-op medication 30 minutes ago and is now complaining of dry mouth and her pulse rate is higher than before the medication was administered. The nurse's best interpretation of these findings is that
1. the patient is having an allergic reaction to the drug.
2. the patient needs a higher dose of this drug.
3. this is a normal side-effect of Atropine.
4. the patient is anxious about the upcoming surgery.

51. Mr. L. has chronic obstructive pulmonary disease (COPD), is scheduled for surgery and the physician has recommended an epidural anesthetic. The nurse should know that general anesthesia was not recommended for this client because
1. there is too high a risk for pressures sores developing.
2. there is less effect on the respiratory system with epidural anesthesia.
3. central nervous system control of vascular constriction would be affected with general anesthesia.

4. there is too high a risk of lacerations to the mouth, bruising of lips, and damage to teeth.

52. Ms. J. had a bunion removed under an epidural block. In the immediate post-op period, the nurse plans to assess Ms. J. for side-effects of the epidural block that include which of the following?
1. Headache.
2. Hypotension, bradycardia, nausea, and vomiting.
3. Hypertension, muscular rigidity, fever, and tachypnea.
4. Urinary retention.

53. Mr. T. received droperidol and fentanyl (Innovar) during surgery. In planning his care, the nurse will need to monitor for which of the following during the immediate post-op period?
1. Restlessness and anxiety.
2. Delirium.
3. Dysrhythmias.
4. Respiratory depression.

54. An adult has just arrived on the general surgery unit from the Post Anesthesia Care Unit (PACU). Which of the following needs to be the initial intervention the nurse takes?
1. Assess the surgical site, noting the amount and character of drainage.
2. Assess for amount of urinary output and the presence of any distention.
3. Allow the family to visit with the patient to decrease the anxiety of the patient.
4. Take vital signs, assessing first for a patent airway and the quality of respirations.

55. Ms. R. is receiving morphine via a PCA pump after her surgery. The best method for the nurse to use to evaluate her level of pain is to ask the client
1. to rate her pain on a scale of 1–10.
2. if the morphine is working for her.
3. if she is feeling any pain.
4. if she needs her morphine level increased.

56. A 58-year-old smoker underwent major abdominal surgery two days ago. During the respiratory assessment, the nurse notes he is taking shallow breaths and breath sounds are decreased in the bases. The best interpretation of these findings is that the patient is experiencing post-op
1. pneumonia.
2. atelectasis.
3. hemorrhage.
4. thromboembolism.

57. To prevent thromboembolism in the post-op patient the nurse should include which of the following in the plan of care?
1. Place a pillow under the knees and restrict fluids.
2. Use strict aseptic technique including handwashing and sterile dressing technique.

3. Assess bowel sounds in all four quadrants on every shift and avoid early ambulation.
4. Assess for Homan's signs on every shift, encourage early ambulation, and maintain adequate hydration.

58. It is 10:00 P.M. and the nurse notes that Mr. P., who returned from the PACU at 2:00 P.M., has not voided. The patient has an out of bed order, but has not been up yet. The best action for the nurse to take is
1. insert a Foley catheter.
2. straight-catheterize Mr. P.
3. assist Mr. P. to stand at the side of his bed and attempt to void into a urinal.
4. encourage Mr. P. to lie on his left side in bed and attempt to void into a urinal.

59. When assessing a post-op patient, the nurse notes a nasogastric tube to low constant suction, the absence of a bowel movement since surgery, and no bowel sounds. The most appropriate plan of care based on these findings is to
1. increase the patient's mobility and ensure he is receiving adequate pain relief.
2. increase coughing, turning, and deep breathing exercises.
3. discontinue the nasogastric tube as the patient does not need it any more.
4. assess for bladder pain and distention.

60. On the second post-op day following an inguinal herniorrhaphy, the nurse assessing a client's wound would expect to find
1. a small amount of serous drainage, edges approximated, and a pink color.
2. a large amount of sanguineous drainage and edges pink in color.
3. no drainage, the edges brown and coming apart.
4. a Penrose drain putting out large amounts of serosanguineous drainage.

61. Mr. D. says to the nurse, "I don't understand how my wife could have come down with cancer. She doesn't smoke or drink. How do people get cancer, anyway?" The nurse's best response is based on the knowledge that which of the following has *not* been implicated in the etiology of cancer?
1. Bacteria.
2. Viruses.
3. Dietary factors.
4. Genetic and familial factors.

62. Mrs. B. has breast cancer. Her physician has just told her that her cancer has been staged as "T2, N1, M0," and Mrs. B. asks the nurse what this means. The nurse's answer is based on the understanding that
1. the primary tumor is 2 cm in diameter, she has one positive lymph node, and no metastasis.
2. there are two primary tumors, one involved lymph node chain, and no metastasis.

3. the primary tumor is between 2–5 cm in size, she has metastasis to one movable lymph node, and no distant metastasis.
4. there is carcinoma in situ, no regional lymph node metastasis, and the presence of distant metastasis cannot be assessed.

63. The nurse at a senior citizen center is teaching a class on the early warning signals of cancer. Which of the following will be a part of the teaching plan for this class?
1. Reduction in the amount of dietary fat.
2. Stop cigarette smoking.
3. Avoid overexposure to the sun.
4. Practice monthly breast self-exam (BSE).

64. Which statement by Mr. I. tells the nurse that he needs further information about testicular self-examination (TSE)?
1. "The best time to perform TSE is immediately before sexual intercourse."
2. "It's normal to find one testis lower than the other."
3. "I should have my doctor examine any lumps I find, even though they might be benign."
4. "That cord-like thing that I feel on the top and back of the testicle is not something to be worried about."

65. Which of the following actions is vital for the nurse to perform when assessing a patient receiving chemotherapy?
1. Checking complete vital signs every eight hours.
2. Taking rectal temperatures every four hours to check for infection.
3. Testing emesis for blood.
4. Avoiding fresh fruits and vegetables if absolute white blood count (WBC) is less than 1000/mm^3.

66. Miss E. asks the nurse how the chemotherapy that she is receiving for her lung cancer works. The nurse's best response is based on the knowledge that chemotherapeutic drugs
1. block the sodium-potassium pump in the cell wall and cause cellular death due to an excess of intracellular potassium.
2. prevent the entry of oxygen into the cell and cause cellular death due to cellular anoxia.
3. shrink the size of the existing tumor, which causes the release of antitumor metabolites that are toxic to further tumor cell growth.
4. destroy enough of the tumor so that the body's immune system can eradicate the remaining cells.

67. Mr. G., diagnosed with multiple myeloma, is receiving cyclophosphamide (Cytoxan). The nurse must include which of the following interventions in the nursing care plan of this patient?
1. High-flow oxygen delivery to combat interstitial pneumonitis, which routinely develops with cyclophosphamide therapy.

2. Encouraging the patient to empty his bladder every two to three hours to prevent development of hemorrhagic cystitis.
3. Application of an ice cap to reduce or prevent alopecia.
4. Antiemetic therapy for 7–10 days after cyclophosphamide administration, or until blood studies show nadir is reached.

68. Mrs. F. is receiving cancer chemotherapy and demonstrates alteration in her oral mucous membranes. Which of the following should be included in her plan of care?
1. Brushing teeth and flossing after every meal and at bedtime.
2. Using normal saline mouth rinses every two hours while awake.
3. No use of dentures until mucous membranes have healed.
4. Bland, mechanical, soft diet until mucous membranes have healed.

69. Ten days ago, Mr. A. received chemotherapy for his non-Hodgkin's lymphoma, stage IV. Drugs administered through his vascular access device ("Port-a-cath") included doxorubicin, cyclophosphamide, vincristine, and prednisone (CHOP protocol). This morning, his blood work is as follows: WBC: 1500/mm^3; hemoglobin (Hgb): 7.6 gm/dl; RBC 3,000,000/mm^3; hematocrit (Hct) 22.3%, platelets 20,000/mm^3. The nurse knows that Mr. A.'s plan of care will include which of the following interventions?
1. Insertion of two extra IV lines for blood administration.
2. Cutting fingernails and toenails to prevent scratching that could lead to bleeding or infection.
3. Providing Mr. A. with a low residue diet.
4. Using a soft toothbrush and avoiding dental floss.

70. Miss C., receiving external radiation therapy for Hodgkin's disease, makes all of the following statements to her nurse. Which statement tells the nurse that Miss C. needs further teaching about the care she requires because of her radiation therapy?
1. "I will check my mouth frequently for signs of irritation."
2. "I know that if I get tired easily, it may be from the radiation and doesn't necessarily mean my Hodgkin's disease is getting worse."
3. "I will use a good quality lotion on my skin to keep the radiation from burning it."
4. "I may lose some of my hair during radiation and foods may not taste right."

71. Mrs. E. asks the nurse to explain how the radiation therapy she will be receiving for her neck cancer is effective. The nurse's best response is based on the knowledge that

1. radiation causes breakage in the strands of the DNA helix, which leads to cell death.
2. radiation is antagonistic to glucose, which cells need for energy and replication; radiation prevents glucose from entering cells, leading to cell death.
3. cell walls are broken down by gamma rays during radiation therapy, leading to cell death.
4. oxygen cannot enter cells that have been irradiated, so the cell converts to anaerobic metabolism that causes its death.

72. The nurse manager on the oncology unit is assessing the knowledge level of the staff in regard to safety requirements for the patient receiving internal radiation therapy. Which observation by the nurse manager indicates that further instruction is necessary?
1. The physical therapist is ambulating the patient in the hall.
2. The nurse uses rubber gloves when emptying the bedpan.
3. The dietitian provides a low residue diet for the patient.
4. The housekeeping staff calls for Radiation Safety personnel to inspect the room before the patient is discharged.

73. Mrs. G. is receiving internal radiation therapy for cancer of the cervix. Which statement by Mrs. G. indicates to the nurse that the patient understands precautions necessary during her treatment?
1. "I should get out of bed and walk around in my room at least every other hour."
2. "My seven-year-old twins should not come to visit me while I'm receiving treatment."
3. "I will try not to cough, because the force might make me expel the applicator."
4. "I know that my primary nurse has to wear one of those badges like the people in the X-ray department wear, but they aren't necessary for anyone else who comes in here."

74. An adult is receiving internal radiation therapy for cancer of the cervix. Her radiation source, a rod, becomes dislodged. The nurse's best first action is to
1. notify the Radiation Safety personnel at once and wait further information.
2. use long-handled forceps to remove the rod and place in a lead-lined container.
3. apply two sets of rubber gloves and pick up the rod; place it in a white plastic "biohazard" bucket and call Radiation Safety personnel for a special pick-up.
4. use long-handled forceps to pick up rod; clean with normal saline, and reinsert into patient's vagina, stopping when the rod meets resistance. This indicates that it is against the cervix.

75. In caring for the patient receiving external

radiation therapy, the nurse assesses for which of the following side-effects?
1. Extravasation injury at the IV site used for contrast media injection.
2. Generalized or local edema.
3. Infection and bleeding.
4. Allergic reactions, particularly anaphylaxis.

76. The nurse is assessing reflexes on a client. A positive Babinski's reflex is
1. extension of the elbow and contraction of the triceps tendon.
2. supination and flexion of the forearm.
3. dorsiflexion of the great toe with fanning of the other toes.
4. flexion of the arm at the antecubital fossa and contraction of the biceps.

77. The nurse is assessing the optic nerve of a client. Which of the following is a correct method to evaluate cranial nerve (CN) II, the optic nerve?
1. Inspect the pupils for reaction.
2. Test extraocular movements.
3. Use of a Snellen chart.
4. Test for a corneal reflex.

78. Which of the following tests or tools could the nurse use to assess CN VIII, the acoustic nerve?
1. Romberg.
2. Rosenbaum chart.
3. Inspection of pupils.
4. Audiometry.

79. A nurse is obtaining a Glasgow Coma Score on a client. The score is as follows:
    Best eye opening   3
    Best motor response   6
    Best verbal response   4
The nurse interprets these findings as the client
1. opens eyes to speech, obeys verbal commands, and is confused.
2. opens eyes to pain, decorticates to pain, and does not speak.
3. opens eyes to pain, no motor response, and has inappropriate speech.
4. opens eyes spontaneously, obeys verbal commands, and is oriented × 3.

80. A nurse is preparing a client for an MRI. Which of the following conditions would *exclude* a client from an MRI?
1. Wearing jewelry.
2. Cardiac pacemaker.
3. Claustrophobia.
4. Allergy to iodine.

81. A nurse is assessing a client who has returned from a cerebral arteriogram. The left carotid was the site punctured. Which of the following indicates complications?
1. Difficulty in swallowing.
2. Puncture site is dry and red.
3. BP 120/82, HR 86, RR 22.

4. No swelling or hematoma at the site.

82. A client with a closed head injury is confused, drowsy, and has unequal pupils. Which of the following nursing diagnosis is *most important* at this time?
1. Altered level of cognitive function.
2. High risk for injury.
3. Altered cerebral tissue perfusion.
4. Sensory perceptual alteration.

83. A client is admitted with a head injury. To monitor hypothalamic function, the nurse should monitor what parameters?
1. Temperature and urinary output.
2. Gastric aspirate and BP.
3. Heart rate and pupillary responses.
4. Respiratory rate and skin integrity.

84. Which of the following is the best way for the nurse to assist a blind client in ambulation?
1. Allow client to take nurse's arm with the nurse walking slightly ahead of the client.
2. Allow client to walk beside the nurse with the nurse's hand on the client's back.
3. Allow client to walk down the hall with his or her hand along the wall.
4. Push the client in a wheelchair.

85. Which of the following is the best way for the nurse to communicate with the hearing impaired client?
1. Talk directly into the impaired ear.
2. Speak directly and clearly facing the person.
3. Shout into the good ear.
4. Write out all communication.

86. A nurse is assessing a client who is unable to extend the legs without pain, has a temperature of 103° F, and on flexion of the neck also flexes the hip and knee. Based on this assessment, the nurse suspects the client has (a)
1. meningitis.
2. brain abscess.
3. brain tumor.
4. epilepsy.

87. A client has a fever of 103° F, nuchal rigidity, pain on extension of the legs, and opisthotonos. Based on these findings, the *most important* nursing diagnosis is
1. pain.
2. altered cerebral perfusion.
3. anxiety.
4. high risk for injury.

88. A client presents with symptoms of increased intracranial pressure, papilledema, and headache. No history of trauma is found. Vital signs are: BP 110/60, HR 80, T 98.9° F, RR 24. Based on this assessment, the nurse suspects the client has a(n)
1. brain tumor.
2. meningitis.
3. skull fracture.
4. encephalitis.

89. What should the nurse include in the plan of care for a newly admitted client with an infratentorial craniotomy for a brain tumor?
    1. Keep the head of the bed elevated 30–45° and a large pillow under the client's head and shoulder.
    2. Keep the head of the bed flat with a small pillow under the nape of the neck.
    3. Assess vital signs and pupils every four hours.
    4. Flex neck every two hours to prevent stiffness.

90. The home health nurse observes an aide who is transferring a client with hemiplegia from a sitting position in the bed to the wheelchair. Which action by the aide requires correction? The aide transfers the client by
    1. grasping the client's arms to pull the client to a standing position.
    2. reminding the client to lean forward before rising.
    3. moving the client toward the unaffected side.
    4. bracing the affected knee and foot to assist the client to stand.

91. When comparing a cerebrovascular accident (CVA) to a transient ischemic attack (TIA), the nurse understands that a TIA is
    1. permanent with long-term focal deficits.
    2. intermittent with spontaneous resolution of the neurologic deficit.
    3. intermittent with permanent motor and sensory deficits.
    4. permanent with no long-term neurologic deficits.

92. The nurse is teaching a client with transient ischemic attacks about aspirin therapy. Which statement by the client indicates understanding of the reason for his aspirin therapy?
    1. "I must take the aspirin regularly to prevent the headache that many people have with this disorder."
    2. "If I take aspirin, I am less likely to develop bleeding in my brain."
    3. "The aspirin will help to prevent me from having a stroke."
    4. "Taking aspirin regularly will reduce my chances of having a heart attack."

93. A client with Parkinson's disease is receiving combination therapy with levodopa (L-dopa) and carbidopa (Sinemet). Which of the following manifestations indicates to the nurse that an adverse drug reaction is occurring?
    1. Involuntary head movement.
    2. Bradykinesia.
    3. Shuffling gait.
    4. Depression.

94. A nurse is teaching the family of a client with Parkinson's disease. Which of the following statements by the family reflects a need for more education?
    1. "We can buy lots of soups for Dad."
    2. "We are teaching Dad posture exercises."
    3. "Dad is going to do his range of motion (ROM) exercises three times a day."
    4. "The bath bars will be installed before Dad comes home."

95. A 36-year-old female reports double vision, visual loss, weakness, numbness of the hands, fatigue, tremors, and incontinence. On assessment, the nurse notes nystagmus, scanning speech, ataxia, and muscular weakness. Based on these findings, the nurse suspects the client has
    1. Parkinson's disease.
    2. myasthenia gravis (MG).
    3. amyotrophic lateral sclerosis (ALS).
    4. multiple sclerosis (MS).

96. Which nursing diagnosis is of the *highest priority* when caring for a client with myasthenia gravis (MG)?
    1. Pain.
    2. High risk for injury related to muscle weakness.
    3. Ineffective coping related to illness.
    4. Ineffective airway clearance related to muscle weakness.

97. The nurse has explained the use of neostigmine methylsulfate (Prostigmin) to a client with myasthenia gravis. Which comment by the client indicates the need for further instruction?
    1. "I need to take the medication regularly, even when I feel strong."
    2. "I should take the medication once daily at bedtime."
    3. "If I take too much medication, I can become weak and have breathing problems."
    4. "I may have difficulty swallowing my saliva if I take too much medication."

98. A nurse is assessing a client with a head injury. The client has clear drainage from the nose and ears. How can the nurse determine if the drainage is cerebrospinal fluid (CSF)?
    1. Measure the pH of the fluid.
    2. Measure the specific gravity of the fluid.
    3. Test for glucose.
    4. Test for chloride.

99. The nurse is caring for a confused client who sustained a head injury resulting in a subdural hematoma. The client's blood pressure is 100/60 mmHg and he is unresponsive. Select the most effective position for the client as the nurse transports him to the operating room.
    1. Semi-Fowler's.
    2. Trendelenburg.
    3. High-Fowler's.
    4. Supine.

100. A client who has been treated in the emergency room for a head injury is preparing for discharge. The nurse is teaching the family about the signs of complications that may occur within the first 24 hours and the appropriate action to take if a complication is suspected. Which statement by the client's spouse would require further teaching by the nurse?
1. "I'm not looking forward to checking on my husband all night long."
2. "If he can just get a long nap, I'm sure that my husband will be fine."
3. "I'll call the doctor immediately if my husband starts to vomit."
4. "If my husband has trouble talking, I'll bring him to the hospital."

101. A client is admitted postcraniotomy. Decadron 4 mg IV is ordered every six hours. The nurse understands the Decadron is ordered to
1. stabilize the blood sugar.
2. decrease cerebral edema.
3. prevent seizures.
4. maintain the integrity of the gastric mucosa.

102. A client is admitted with a C7 complete transection. In the *immediate* postinjury period, the nurse must plan for
1. bladder and bowel training.
2. possible ventilatory support.
3. complications of autonomic dysreflexia.
4. diaphragmatic pacing.

103. A client fell backward over a stair rail to the floor below, and is not breathing. After calling for assistance, how should the nurse proceed?
1. Initiate rescue breathing by performing a chin tilt maneuver and administering two breaths.
2. After determining absence of breathing, administer 15 chest compressions at the rate of 60 per minute.
3. Initiate rescue breathing by performing a jaw thrust maneuver and administering two breaths.
4. After determining pulselessness, administer five chest compressions at the rate of 60 per minute.

104. A client with a cervical spine injury was placed in Halo traction yesterday. When the client complains of discomfort around the pins, what action should the nurse take?
1. Carefully loosen the pins and notify the physician immediately.
2. Cleanse the skin around the pin sites and dry the area thoroughly.
3. Give the ordered analgesic and reassure the client that the pain is temporary.
4. Loosen the pins immediately and maintain the head in a neutral position.

105. A client with a C6 spinal cord injury two months ago now complains of a pounding headache. The pulse is 64 and the blood pressure is 220/110 mmHg. Which of the following actions should the nurse take first?
1. Give the analgesic as ordered.
2. Check for fecal impaction.
3. Elevate the client's head and lower the legs.
4. Notify the physician.

106. The nurse is evaluating the ability of a client with trigeminal neuralgia to implement the treatment that has been suggested. Which of the following behaviors by the client will be most effective in controlling manifestations? The client
1. exercises the facial muscles at least twice daily.
2. puts the affected arm through full range of motion daily.
3. avoids extremes in temperature of food and drink.
4. uses proper body mechanics in sitting and bending.

107. A client with Bell's palsy asks the nurse why artificial tears were ordered by the physician. Select the best reply by the nurse.
1. "When your affected eye fails to make tears, the eye can become irritated and ulcerated."
2. "Because your eye remains closed, foreign matter can be trapped beneath the lid."
3. "Artificial tears will remove the purulent drainage from your eye, which speeds healing."
4. "Because you cannot blink the affected eye, it can become dry and irritated."

108. A nurse is caring for a client with Guillain-Barré syndrome. Which of the following strategies is of the *most importance* in the plan of care?
1. Range of motion exercises three to four times per day.
2. Frequent measurement of vital capacity.
3. Use of artificial tears.
4. Starting an enteral feeding.

109. The nurse has presented information about amyotrophic lateral sclerosis (ALS) to a newly diagnosed client. Which question by the client indicates that he understands the nature of the disease?
1. "How can I avoid infecting my family with the virus?"
2. "How can I execute a living will?"
3. "How can I prevent an exacerbation of the disease?"
4. "How many people achieve remission with chemotherapy?"

110. A client reports gradual painless blurring of vision. On assessment, the nurse notes a

cloudy opaque lens. Based on this assessment, the nurse suspects the client has
1. glaucoma.
2. cataracts.
3. retinal detachment.
4. diabetic retinopathy.

111. Which of the following risk factors would the nurse assess for in a client with glaucoma?
1. Family history, increased intraocular pressure, and age of 45–65.
2. History of diabetes and age greater than 50.
3. Female gender, cigarette smoking, age greater than 65.
4. Myopia, history of diabetes, and sudden severe physical exertion.

112. The nurse has been planning for home care with the family of a client who will undergo extracapsular lens extraction with an intraocular lens implant. Because the client and family speak very little English, the nurse takes extra care to evaluate their understanding. Which behavior by the client and/or family shows progress in understanding post-op home care instructions?
1. Using a chart showing various sleeping positions, the client points to a person lying on the affected side.
2. The family demonstrates that the eye should be cleaned with a washcloth, soap, and water.
3. The client demonstrates medication instillation by carefully dropping the solution on the cornea.
4. The family shows the nurse the sunglasses they have purchased for the client to wear post-op.

113. A nurse is admitting a client who reports vision loss. To determine if a client has glaucoma or a detached retina, the nurse understands that a client with glaucoma will report
1. seeing floating spots.
2. eye pain.
3. seeing flashing lights.
4. sudden loss of vision.

114. Which of the following techniques should the nurse use to evaluate a client's understanding of self-care for chronic (primary) open angle glaucoma?
1. The nurse measures the client's blood pressure at each visit.
2. The nurse measures hearing acuity at each visit.
3. The nurse observes the client's technique for monitoring blood glucose.
4. The nurse observes the client's administration of eye drops.

115. A client is admitted with a detached retina of the left eye. The nurse patches both eyes. What is the rationale for patching both eyes?

1. To prevent eye infections.
2. To decrease eye movement.
3. To prevent photophobia.
4. To prevent nystagmus.

116. A neighbor splashes chlorine bleach in her eyes and calls the nurse for immediate help. The *first* action the nurse should take is to
1. lift the upper lid over the lower lid of each eye.
2. close and patch both eyes with a loose bandage.
3. continuously flush the eyes with tap water for 20 minutes.
4. instill an over-the-counter anti-irritant solution, such as Visine.

117. A client reports bilateral hearing loss. On assessment of the ear, the nurse observes chalky white plaques on the eardrum and the eardrum appears pinkish orange in color. The Rinne test favors bone conduction. Based on this assessment, the nurse suspects the client has (a)
1. cholesteatoma.
2. actinic keratosis.
3. external otitis.
4. otosclerosis.

118. The nurse is teaching a post-op stapedectomy client. What should be included in the teaching?
1. Work can be resumed the next day.
2. Gently sneeze or cough with the mouth closed.
3. Blow the nose gently one side at a time.
4. Resume exercise in one week.

119. A client reports very loud, overpowering ringing in the ears, fluctuating hearing loss on the right side with severe vertigo accompanied by nausea and vomiting, and a feeling of fullness in the right ear. The nurse suspects the client has (a)
1. Ménière's disease.
2. acoustic neuroma.
3. otosclerosis.
4. cholesteatoma.

120. What is the *priority* nursing diagnosis for a client with very loud overpowering ringing in his ears, fluctuating hearing loss on the right side with severe vertigo accompanied by nausea and vomiting and a feeling of fullness in the right ear?
1. Knowledge deficit related to the disease process.
2. Anxiety.
3. Impaired physical mobility.
4. Pain.

121. A client is being assessed to rule out cardiovascular problems. The nurse understands that some of the common symptoms associated with cardiovascular disease are
1. shortness of breath, chest discomfort, palpitations.

2. dyspnea, chest discomfort, sputum production.
3. fatigue, weight changes, mood swings.
4. mood swings, headaches, fainting.

122. Which of the following assessment findings by the nurse is abnormal?
   1. S_1 heard at the fourth-fifth left intercostal space in a 35-year-old man.
   2. S_2 heard at the second-third left intercostal space in a 40-year-old female.
   3. S_4 heard at the apex in an 80-year-old male.
   4. S_3 heard at the apex in a 15-year-old female.

123. Which of the following instructions should the nurse give to a client prior to an exercise electrocardiogram?
   1. Avoid coffee, tea, and alcohol the day of the test.
   2. Smoking is permitted up to the time of the test.
   3. Allow only three hours of sleep the night prior to the test.
   4. Take all medications as prescribed prior to the test.

124. To prevent possible complication, which of the following questions should a nurse ask a client prior to a cardiac catheterization?
   1. "Have you ever had a cardiac catheterization before?"
   2. "Can you eat shellfish?"
   3. "Do you understand the procedure?"
   4. "Have you ever had a heart attack?"

125. Which of the following should the nurse include in the plan of care for a post-op coronary arteriogram client?
   1. Assess pedal pulses.
   2. Assess lung sounds.
   3. Provide early ambulation.
   4. Monitor vital signs every eight hours.

126. A client has the following rhythm. The client has no pulse or blood pressure.

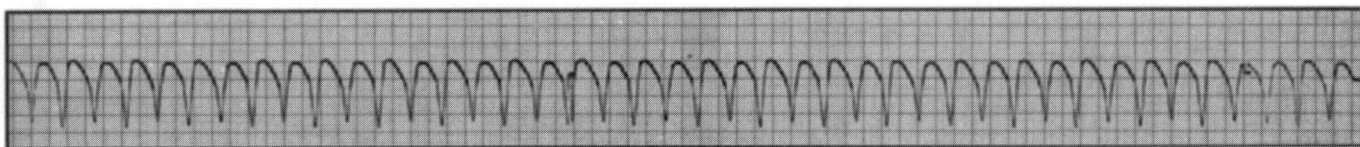

The nurse interprets the rhythm as
1. ventricular tachycardia.
2. ventricular fibrillation.
3. sinus tachycardia.
4. supraventricular tachycardia.

127. A client has the following rhythm. The client has no pulse or blood pressure.

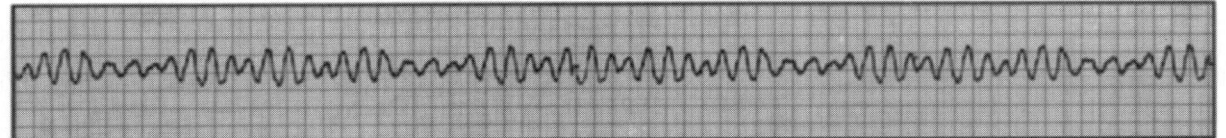

The nurse interprets the rhythm as
1. ventricular tachycardia.
2. ventricular fibrillation.
3. sinus tachycardia.
4. supraventricular tachycardia.

128. A client had a myocardial infarction yesterday. His cardiac monitor shows six to eight PVCs per minute, with occasional couplets. The best action by the nurse at this time is to
   1. monitor the client for development of ventricular tachycardia.
   2. administer the ordered prn dose of lidocaine.
   3. perform a precordial thump.
   4. initiate manual chest compressions.

129. A client is admitted in cardiogenic shock. To *best* evaluate the heart's hemodynamic performance, the nurse anticipates the insertion of a(n)
   1. intra-arterial line.
   2. pulmonary artery catheter.
   3. intra-aortic balloon pump (IABP).
   4. central venous pressure line (CVP).

130. Which of the following statements by a client to the nurse indicates a risk factor for coronary artery disease?
   1. "I exercise four times a week."
   2. "No one in my family has heart problems."
   3. "My cholesterol is 189."
   4. "I smoke 1½ packs of cigarettes per day."

131. An adult female has a history of coronary artery disease and angina pectoris. After walking to the bathroom, she complains of aching substernal pain that radiates to her left shoulder. The nurse should
   1. assist her to lie down and elevate her legs.
   2. administer a prn dose of nitroglycerin sublingually.

3. use pillows to support and immobilize the left shoulder.
4. administer a prn dose of aspirin or acetaminophen (Tylenol).

132. A nitroglycerin transdermal patch was prescribed six weeks ago for an adult to treat angina pectoris. The nurse knows that the patch has been effective if
   1. the client's serum cholesterol level has decreased.
   2. the client's pressure is within normal limits.
   3. the client reports no episodes of chest pain.
   4. pulse oximetry shows the client's oxygen saturation is improved.

133. Ms. F. has developed angina pectoris secondary to coronary artery disease. A low fat, low cholesterol diet is prescribed for her. The nurse should praise Ms. F. for a wise choice if she selected which of the following for an evening snack?
   1. Cheese cubes and crackers.
   2. Half tuna salad sandwich.
   3. Yogurt with fresh strawberries.
   4. Jello mold with fruit slices.

134. Lidocaine is mixed 2 g in 500 ml D_5W. The nurse prepared to start an infusion at 2 mg/h using a 60-drop tubing. Which of the following is the correct rate to start the infusion on a pump?
   1. 15 ml.
   2. 30 ml.
   3. 45 ml.
   4. 60 ml.

135. An adult male is transferred to the step-down unit on the third day after a myocardial infarction. Which of the following should the nurse include in his care plan at this time?
   1. Enforcing complete bedrest.
   2. Supervising short walks in the hallway.
   3. Performing passive range of motion exercises.
   4. Having him sit on the side of the bed and dangle his legs.

136. A 55-year-old man with a history of angina pectoris, complains of chest pain radiating to the jaw. After taking three nitroglycerin gr 1/150 tablets he is still having the chest pain. His skin is cool and pale and he is diaphoretic and mildly short of breath. The best initial action for the nurse to take is to
   1. auscultate heart and lung sounds.
   2. administer another nitroglycerin tablet.
   3. initiate telemetry monitoring.
   4. assist him to a supine position.

137. An adult male is being discharged from the hospital following a myocardial infarction. The nurse knows that he understands the guidelines for resuming sexual activity if he states that
   1. bedtime is the best time to have intercourse.

2. he should exercise for 10–15 minutes before intercourse, to "warm up."
3. he should take a nitroglycerin before intercourse to prevent chest pain.
4. it is best to avoid having intercourse when the stomach is empty.

138. Ms. G. is scheduled for a percutaneous transluminal coronary angioplasty (PTCA). She says to the nurse, "Can you tell me again what the doctor is going to do? I don't remember exactly what she told me." The most appropriate response by the nurse would be,
   1. "A clot dissolving drug is administered through a catheter into the blocked section of your artery."
   2. "A piece of vein from your leg is used to bypass the blocked section of your artery."
   3. "A tiny rotating blade is used to scrape off the plaque that is blocking your artery."
   4. "A balloon is placed next to the plaque blocking your artery, then the balloon is inflated to crush the plaque."

139. Mr. P. is being discharged following coronary artery bypass graft surgery (CABG). The nurse recognizes that Mr. P. needs additional teaching if he makes which of the following statements?
   1. "I'll be going to a support group to help me quit smoking."
   2. "I need to use a golf cart instead of walking around the course."
   3. "I should bake or broil my chicken instead of frying it."
   4. "I've learned a breathing exercise to help me calm down if I get upset."

140. Which of the following assessment findings by the nurse indicates right ventricular failure in a client?
   1. Pink frothy sputum.
   2. Paroxysmal nocturnal dyspnea.
   3. Jugular venous distention.
   4. Crackles.

141. A nurse is assessing a client with fatigue, tachycardia, crackles, and pink frothy sputum. Which nursing diagnosis is of the most importance?
   1. Impaired skin integrity.
   2. Impaired gas exchange.
   3. Potential for injury.
   4. Anxiety.

142. Mr. P. is admitted with an acute exacerbation of congestive heart failure. His vital signs are: T 99, P 115, R 32, BP 154/100. His ankles are edematous and crackles are auscultated at the bases of both lungs, 0.5 mg of digoxin (Lanoxin) IV and 40 mg of furosemide (Lasix) IV are administered immediately. The nurse recognizes that the medications are having a therapeutic effect if
   1. Mr. P.'s pulse rate decreases below 100.

2. Mr. P. has an increased urine specific gravity.
3. Mr. P. expectorates frothy sputum.
4. Mr. P.'s lungs are clear to auscultation.

143. A client is admitted with pulmonary edema. The nurse is preparing to administer morphine sulfate. What beneficial effect does morphine have in pulmonary edema?
    1. Decreases anxiety, work of breathing, and vasodilates.
    2. Decreases respiratory rate.
    3. Provides an analgesic and sedative effect.
    4. Decreases anxiety and vasoconstricts.

144. An adult female is being discharged after having a ventricular demand pacemaker inserted. The nurse should include which of the following in the teaching plan for this client?
    1. She should not use remote control devices (e.g., TV channel selector).
    2. She must leave the room while a microwave oven is in operation.
    3. She will need to avoid air travel.
    4. She should not pass through metal detectors.

145. Ms. T. has a ventricular demand pacemaker that is set at 72 beats per minute. The nurse knows that Ms. T.'s pacemaker is functioning correctly if which of the following appears on the ECG?
    1. Pacemaker spikes instead of QRS complexes.
    2. Pacemaker spikes followed by QRS complexes.
    3. Pacemaker spikes before each P wave.
    4. Pacemaker spikes appearing only if the heart rate is over 72.

146. Which strategy by the nurse provides safety during a defibrillation attempt?
    1. A verbal and visual check of "all clear."
    2. No lubricant on the paddles.
    3. Placing paddles lightly on the chest.
    4. Standing in alignment with the bed while administering the shock.

147. An adult client has experienced a cardiac arrest and the nurse is performing CPR. The correct position of the nurse's hands on the client's chest is
    1. over the upper half of the sternum.
    2. two finger widths below the sternal notch.
    3. two finger widths above the xiphoid process.
    4. over the xiphoid process.

148. A client with a history of a myocardial infarction two days ago reports chest pain that is worse on inspiration but is relieved on sitting forward. Based on this finding, the nurse suspects the client is experiencing the pain of
    1. endocarditis.
    2. angina pectoris.
    3. pericarditis.

4. recurrent myocardial infarction.

149. Mr. J. has prazocin hydrochloride (Minipress) prescribed to treat hypertension. The nurse should instruct him to
    1. take the medication with meals.
    2. take the first dose at bedtime.
    3. report a pulse rate below 50 to the physician.
    4. check his ankles daily for edema.

150. An adult has essential hypertension. She is being treated with a thiazide diuretic and dietary and lifestyle modifications. The nurse knows that she understands the treatment if she makes which of the following statements?
    1. "I will use soy sauce or mustard instead of salt on my food."
    2. "I need to cut back to two, four-ounce glasses of wine a day."
    3. "I will stop riding my bike because vigorous exercise will raise my blood pressure."
    4. "Smoking helped cause my hypertension, but quitting won't reverse the damage."

151. Ms. R. has chlorothiazide (Diuril) prescribed to treat high blood pressure. The nurse knows that Ms. R. understands the dietary modifications she needs to make if she states that she will increase her intake of
    1. fresh oranges.
    2. cold cereals.
    3. cola drinks.
    4. cranberry juice.

152. A client reports an aching pain and cramping sensation that occurs while walking. The pain disappears after cessation of walking. The pain is in both legs. Based on these clinical findings, the nurse suspects the client has (a)
    1. deep vein thrombosis (DVT).
    2. Raynauds' disease.
    3. arteriosclerosis obliterans.
    4. thrombophlebitis.

153. Ms. M. has severe arteriosclerosis obliterans and complains of intermittent claudication after walking 20 feet. How should the nurse plan to position Ms. M. when she is in bed?
    1. Supine with legs elevated.
    2. In semi-Fowler's position with knees extended.
    3. In reverse Trendelenburg position.
    4. In Trendelenburg position.

154. An adult female experiences painful arterial spasms in her hands due to Raynaud's phenomenon. Which of the following should the nurse include in the teaching plan for her?
    1. Drink a hot beverage, such as tea or coffee, to relieve spasms.
    2. Reduce intake of high fat or high cholesterol foods.
    3. Raise the hands above the head to relieve spasms.
    4. Wear gloves when handling refrigerated foods.

155. Which assessment finding by the nurse would indicate an abdominal aortic aneurysm?
    1. Knifelike pain in the back.
    2. Pulsatile mass in the abdomen.
    3. Unequal femoral pulses.
    4. Boardlike rigid abdomen.

156. A nurse is assessing a post-op femoral popliteal bypass client. Which of the following assessment findings indicates a complication?
    1. BP 110/80, HR 86, RR 20.
    2. Small amount of dark-red blood on dressing.
    3. A decrease in pulse quality in the operated leg.
    4. Swelling of the operative leg.

157. An adult has just returned to the surgical unit after a femoral-popliteal bypass on the right leg. The nurse should place the client in what position?
    1. Fowler's position with the right leg extended.
    2. Supine with the right knee flexed 45°.
    3. Supine with the right leg extended and flat on the bed.
    4. Semi-Fowler's position with the right leg elevated on two pillows.

158. The client has a large, venous stasis ulcer on her left ankle. Wound care is performed three times a week by a home health nurse. The nurse should teach her to
    1. dangle the legs for 5–10 minutes several times a day.
    2. wear heavy cotton or wool socks when going outdoors.
    3. soak the feet in tepid water three or four times daily.
    4. take frequent rest periods with her legs elevated.

159. An adult is hospitalized with deep vein thrombophlebitis. During the first few days of therapy, the nurse should
    1. keep the client in Trendelenburg position.
    2. apply ice packs three or four times daily to relieve pain.
    3. massage the affected leg once a shift.
    4. encourage the client to perform active range of motion exercises with both legs each shift.

160. Ms. R. is being discharged after treatment of deep vein thrombosis. Coumadin (warfarin) 2.5 mg daily is prescribed for her. The nurse recognizes that which of the following statements by Ms. R. indicates that she understands the effects of Coumadin?
    1. "I'll use an electric razor to shave my legs."
    2. "I'll have a podiatrist cut my toenails."
    3. "I need to eat more salads and fresh fruits."
    4. "I will take aspirin instead of Tylenol for headaches."

161. An adult, who was admitted four hours ago with thrombophlebitis in the left leg, suddenly becomes confused and dyspneic. She begins coughing up blood-streaked sputum and complains of chest pain that worsens on inspiration. The nurse should first
    1. apply soft restraints to prevent excessive movement.
    2. perform a Heimlich maneuver.
    3. place her in bed in semi-Fowler's position.
    4. place her in Trendelenburg position on her left side.

162. A client is admitted to rule out pulmonary embolism (PE) from a deep vein thrombosis. A Dextran 70 infusion is ordered for the client. The nurse understands the Dextran is administered to
    1. increase blood viscosity.
    2. decrease platelet adhesion.
    3. decrease plasma volume.
    4. increase the hemoglobin.

163. A client reports aching, heaviness, itching, and moderate swelling of the legs. On assessment, the nurse notes dilated tortuous skin veins. Based on this assessment, the nurse suspects the client has
    1. thrombophlebitis.
    2. venous thrombosis.
    3. varicose veins.
    4. chronic venous insufficiency.

164. Mr. B. had an above-the-knee amputation of the left leg two days ago. The nurse should include which of the following in the care plan for him?
    1. Resting in a prone or supine position with the stump extended several times a day.
    2. Using a rolled towel or small pillow to elevate the stump at all times.
    3. Applying warm soaks to the stump to reduce phantom limb pain.
    4. Avoiding turning to the left side until the stump has healed completely.

165. An adult male had a below-the-knee amputation of the right foot two days ago. He is complaining of pain in his right foot. The best response by the nurse is to
    1. explain to him that this is a common sensation after amputation.
    2. remind him that that foot was amputated and therefore cannot have pain.
    3. tell him that such pain is a common psychological response to loss of a limb.
    4. show him the stump so he will realize his right foot is gone.

166. Mr. J. has been diagnosed with some type of anemia. The results of his blood tests showed: Decreased WBC, normal RBC, decreased Hct, decreased Hgb. Based on these data, which of the following nursing diagnoses should the nurse prioritize as being the most important?
    1. Potential for infection.
    2. Alteration in nutrition.
    3. Self-care deficit.
    4. Fluid volume excess.

167. A client has the following blood lab values
    platelets 50,000/ul
    RBCs 3.5 ($\times 10^6$)
    Hemoglobin 10 g/dl
    Hematocrit 30%
    WBCs 10,000/ul
    Which nursing instruction should be included in the teaching plan?
    1. Bleeding precautions.
    2. Seizure precautions.
    3. Isolation to prevent infection.
    4. Control of pain with analgesics.
168. A hospitalized client has the following blood lab values:
    WBC 3,000/ul
    RBC 5.0 ($\times 10^6$)
    platelets 300,000
    Nursing interventions should be aimed at
    1. preventing infection.
    2. controlling blood loss.
    3. alleviating pain.
    4. monitoring blood transfusion reactions.
169. Mr. L.'s blood type is AB and he requires a blood transfusion. To prevent complications of blood incompatibilities, the nurse knows that this client may receive
    1. type A or B blood only.
    2. type AB blood only.
    3. type O blood only.
    4. either type A, B, AB, or O blood.
170. Which nursing intervention is appropriate for the nurse to take when setting up supplies for a client who requires a blood transfusion?
    1. Add any needed IV medication in the blood bag within one half hour of planned infusion.
    2. Obtain blood bag from laboratory and leave at room temperature for at least one hour prior to infusion.
    3. Prime tubing of blood administration set with 0.9% NS solution, completely filling filter.
    4. Use a small-bore catheter to prevent rapid infusion of blood products that may lead to a reaction.
171. A client who is receiving a blood transfusion begins to experience chills, shortness of breath, nausea, excessive perspiration, and a vague sense of uneasiness. The best action for the nurse to initially take is to
    1. report the signs and symptoms to the physician.
    2. stop the transfusion.
    3. monitor the client's vital signs.
    4. assess respiratory status.
172. A client with iron deficiency anemia is ordered parental iron to be given intramuscularly. Which of the following actions should the nurse take in the preparation/administration of this medication?
    1. Use the same large (19–20) gauge needle

for drawing up the medication and injecting it.
    2. Massage the site after the injection is given to promote absorption.
    3. Use a 1-in needle to administer the medication.
    4. Use the Z-track technique to administer the medication.
173. The nurse has been teaching Ms. T., who has iron deficiency anemia, about those foods that she needs to include in her meal plans. Which of the following, if selected by Ms. T., would indicate to the nurse that she understands the dietary instructions?
    1. Citrus fruits and green leafy vegetables.
    2. Bananas and nuts.
    3. Coffee and tea.
    4. Dairy products.
174. In assessing clients for pernicious anemia, the nurse should be alert for which of the following risk factors?
    1. Positive family history.
    2. Acute or chronic blood loss.
    3. Infectious agents or toxins.
    4. Inadequate dietary intake.
175. Mr. S. is a client who has been scheduled for a Schilling's test. The nurse should instruct the client to
    1. take nothing by mouth for 12 hours prior to the test.
    2. collect his urine for 12 hours.
    3. administer a fleets enema the evening before the test.
    4. empty his bladder immediately before the test.
176. A 40-year-old woman with aplastic anemia is prescribed estrogen with progesterone. The nurse can expect that these medications are given for which of the following reasons?
    1. To stimulate bone growth.
    2. To regulate fluid balance.
    3. To enhance sodium and potassium absorption.
    4. To promote utilization and storage of fluids.
177. Which of the following lab value profiles should the nurse know to be consistent with hemolytic anemia?
    1. Increased RBC, decreased bilirubin, decreased hemoglobin and hematocrit, increased reticulocytes.
    2. Decreased RBC, increased bilirubin, decreased hemoglobin and hematocrit, increased reticulocytes.
    3. Decreased RBC, decreased bilirubin, increased hemoglobin and hematocrit, decreased reticulocytes.
    4. Increased RBC, increased bilirubin, increased hemoglobin and hematocrit, decreased reticulocytes.
178. In planning care for a client who has had a

splenectomy, the nurse should be aware that this client is most prone to developing
1. infection.
2. congestive heart failure.
3. urinary retention.
4. viral hepatitis.

179. Mr. C. is diagnosed with disseminated intramuscular coagulation (DIC). The nurse should identify that Mr. C. is at risk for which of the following nursing diagnoses?
1. Risk for increased cardiac output related to fluid volume excess.
2. Diminished sensory perception related to bleeding into tissues.
3. Alteration in tissue perfusion related to bleeding and diminished blood flow.
4. High risk for aspiration related to constriction of the respiratory musculature.

180. The nurse should understand that a heparin order for a client with DIC is given to
1. prevent clot formation.
2. increase blood flow to target organs.
3. increase clot formation.
4. decrease blood flow to target organs.

181. Mr. H. is a 34-year-old client diagnosed with AIDS. His pharmacologic management includes zidovudine (AZT). During a home visit, Mr. H. states, "I don't understand how this medication works. Will it stop the infection?" The nurse's best response is
1. "The medication helps to slow the disease process, but it won't cure or stop it totally."
2. "The medication blocks reverse transcriptase, the enzyme required for HIV replication."
3. "Don't you know? There aren't any medications to stop or cure HIV."
4. "No, it won't stop the infection. In fact, sometimes the HIV can become immune to the drug itself."

182. Which statement, from a participant attending a class on AIDS prevention, indicates an understanding of how to reduce transmission of HIV?
1. "Mothers who are HIV-positive should still be encouraged to breast feed their babies because breast milk is superior to cow's milk."
2. "I think a needle exchange program, where clean needles are exchanged for dirty needles, should be offered in every city."
3. "Orgasms are necessary for the heterosexual transmission of the virus."
4. "It's okay to use natural skin condoms since they offer the same protection as the latex condoms."

183. What should be included in the teaching plan to young adults about the spread of AIDS?
1. Heterosexual transmission of HIV is on the rise.

2. The increase of HIV in children is primarily attributed to the rise in sexual abuse.
3. The greatest increase of HIV infection is by homosexual transmission.
4. Transmission of HIV by IV drug users is prominent even when sterile equipment is used.

184. In planning care for a client with multiple myeloma, the nurse should be aware that the client may have orders for
1. bedrest.
2. corticosteroid therapy.
3. fluid restrictions.
4. calcium replacement therapy.

185. Which client statement would indicate to the nurse that the client with polycythemia vera is in need of further instruction?
1. "I'll be flying overseas to see my son and grandchildren for the holidays."
2. "I plan to do my leg exercises at least three times a week."
3. "I'm going to be walking in the mall every day to build up my strength."
4. "At night when I sleep, I like to use two pillows to raise my head up."

186. The nurse is assessing the breath sounds of a patient. The nurse hears a sound described as a rustling, like the sound of the wind in the trees over the peripheral lung fields. The breath sounds are
1. crackles.
2. rhonchi.
3. wheezes.
4. vesicular.

187. The nurse's assessment of a client with lung cancer reveals the following: copious secretions, dyspnea, and cough. Based on these findings the most appropriate nursing diagnosis is
1. impaired gas exchange.
2. ineffective airway clearance.
3. pain.
4. altered tissue perfusion.

188. Mr. B. has just had arterial blood gases drawn. When handling the specimen, the nurse's best action is to
1. gently shake the syringe.
2. place the sample in a syringe of warm water.
3. aspirate 0.5 ml of heparin into the syringe.
4. have the specimen analyzed immediately.

189. The nurse is to obtain a sputum specimen from a client. Select the correct set of statements instructing the patient in the proper technique for obtaining a sputum specimen.
1. "Collect the specimen right before bed. Spit carefully into the container."
2. "Brush your teeth, then cough into the container. Do this first thing in the morning."

3. "Right after lunch, cough and spit into the container."
4. "Spit into the container, then add two tablespoons of water."

190. The nurse is checking tuberculin skin test results at a health clinic. One client has an area of induration measuring 12 mm in diameter. The nurse is aware that this indicates that
1. this finding is a normal reading.
2. this finding indicates active TB.
3. this is a positive reaction and can indicate exposure to TB.
4. this patient needs to come back in two more days and let the nurse look at the area of induration again.

191. An adult has undergone a bronchoscopy. Which assessment findings indicate to the nurse that he is ready for discharge?
1. Use of accessory muscles for breathing, decreased lung sounds.
2. Stable vital signs, return of gag and cough reflex.
3. Hemoptysis, rhonchi.
4. Development of tachycardia with occasional PVCs, able to eat and drink.

192. Mr. E. has a chest tube to a Pleur-evac® drainage system attached to a wall suction. An order to ambulate Mr. E. has been received. To ambulate Mr. E. safely, the nurse should:
1. clamp the chest tube and carefully ambulate Mr. E. a short distance.
2. question the order to ambulate Mr. E.
3. carefully ambulate Mr. E., keeping the Pleur-evac lower than Mr. E.'s chest.
4. disconnect the Pleur-evac from Mr. E.'s chest tube, leave it attached to the bed, ambulate Mr. E., and then reconnect the chest tube when he is returned to bed.

193. The nurse is assessing a client who has a chest tube to water seal drainage with a one-bottle drainage system. Which statement best indicates proper functioning of the chest drainage system?
1. The nurse observes bubbling from the straw in the bottle when the client coughs.
2. The nurse observes no fluctuations in the straw in the bottle with respiration.
3. The nurse observes rising and falling of fluid in the bottle's straw with respiration.
4. The nurse observes the air vent is clamped off.

194. The nurse will perform chest physiotherapy (CPT) on Mrs. Y. every four hours. It is important for the nurse to
1. gently slap the chest wall.
2. use vibration techniques to move secretions from affected lung areas during the inspiration phase.
3. perform CPT at least two hours after meals.

4. plan apical drainage at the beginning of the CPT session.

195. A client is on a ventilator. The ventilator alarm goes off. The nurse assesses the patient and observes increased respiratory rate, use of accessory muscles, and agitation. The nurse's best initial action is to
1. remove the client from the ventilator and ambu bag the patient, while continuing to assess to determine the cause of the client's distress.
2. call respiratory therapy to check the ventilator.
3. notify the physician.
4. turn off the alarm.

196. A patient with respiratory failure is on a ventilator. The alarm goes off. The nurse's initial reaction should be to
1. notify the physician.
2. assess the patient to determine the cause of the alarm.
3. turn off the alarm.
4. disconnect the patient and use the ambu bag to ventilate the patient.

197. A nurse is setting up oxygen for an adult male. He is to receive oxygen at 2 L per nasal cannula. It is important for the nurse to
1. adjust the flow rate to keep the reservoir bag inflated ⅔ full during inspiration.
2. monitor the patient carefully for risk of aspiration.
3. make sure the valves and rubber flaps are patent, functional, and not stuck.
4. remind the client and his wife of the smoking policy.

198. Mrs. C., a long term COPD patient, is receiving oxygen at 1 L/minute. Her visiting cousin decides Mrs. C. "doesn't look too good" and increases her oxygen to 7 L/minute. What should the nurse's initial action be?
1. Thank Mrs. C.'s cousin and continue to observe Mrs. C.
2. Immediately decrease the oxygen.
3. Notify the physician.
4. Elevate Mrs. C.'s head and take her vital signs.

199. An adult is receiving oxygen per face mask at 40%. The nurse should include which of the following in her plan of care?
1. Provide good skin care, making sure the mask fits well.
2. Provide water-soluble jelly to the nares.
3. Instruct the client's husband to smoke away from the bed.
4. Assess for signs and symptoms of oxygen toxicity.

200. Mr. E. has a new tracheostomy in place. He has a small amount of thin, white secretions. The stoma is pink with no drainage noted. The nurse should expect to provide trach care for Mr. E. every:

1. four hours.
2. eight hours.
3. 24 hours.
4. hour.

201. A 64-year-old female is admitted to the hospital. She has smoked two packs per day for 30 years. While providing her history, she becomes breathless, pauses frequently between words, and appears very anxious. She has a cough with thick white sputum production. Her chest is barrel shaped. Based on this data, the nurse will need to develop a plan of care for a client with
1. pneumonia.
2. chronic obstructive pulmonary disease.
3. tuberculosis.
4. asthma.

202. Mr. B., a 68-year-old male, is being admitted to the hospital for an exacerbation of his COPD. The nurse is developing his plan of care. The nurse can expect that this client will
1. be placed on 10 L of oxygen per nasal cannula.
2. be placed in respiratory isolation.
3. require frequent rest periods throughout the day.
4. be placed on fluid restriction.

203. A client with suspected tuberculosis will most likely relate which clinical manifestations?
1. Fatigue, weight loss, low grade fevers, night sweats.
2. Dyspnea, chest pain, cough.
3. Rapid shallow breathing, prolonged labored expiration, stridor.
4. Dyspnea, hypoxemia, decreased pulmonary compliance.

204. An adult is being admitted to the nursing unit with a diagnosis of pneumonia. She has a history of arrested TB. When planning care for this client, the nurse's initial action should be to
1. place the client in respiratory isolation.
2. encourage cough and deep breathing.
3. force fluids.
4. administer O_2.

205. An adult is being followed in the outpatient clinic for a diagnosis of active TB. She is receiving isoniazid 200 mg po qd, rifampin 500 mg po qd, and streptomycin 1500 mg IM twice weekly. Which statement by the client best indicates she understands her therapeutic regime?
1. "I'm glad I only have to take these drugs for a couple of weeks."
2. "I need to take these two drugs every day and come back to the clinic once a week for the shot."
3. "It may work best to take these pills in the evening right before bed."
4. "I'm glad my birth control pills aren't affected by these drugs—the doctor told me not to get pregnant!"

206. The nurse is counseling the family of Ms. C., 18-years-old, a patient with active TB, about measures to prevent transmission of the disease. Which statement by the family best indicates understanding of these instructions?
1. "I won't let Ms. C. and her sister share clothes."
2. "We will have to keep her in her room."
3. "We all need to wash our hands carefully, but especially Ms. C."
4. "We cannot get TB from exposure to Ms. C.'s sputum."

207. Mrs. P., 86-years-old, has fallen and broken her eighth rib on her left side. the nurse should include which of the following when developing Mrs. P.'s plan of care?
1. Bind Mrs. P.'s chest with a 6-in Ace bandage.
2. Keep Mrs. P. on bedrest for three days.
3. Encourage Mrs. P. to use her incentive spirometer and cough and deep breathe.
4. Administer large doses of narcotic analgesic so that Mrs. P. will be able to more fully participate in pulmonary care.

208. Mr. Z. is injured in an industrial accident. The industrial nurse assesses Mr. Z. and observes use of accessory muscles, severe chest pain, agitation, shortness of breath. The nurse also notices one side of his chest moving differently than the other. The nurse suspects flail chest. Based on these observations, the nurse's best initial action is to
1. apply a sandbag to the flail side of his chest.
2. prepare for intubation and mechanical ventilation.
3. prepare for chest tube placement.
4. administer pain medication.

209. A patient with a pleural effusion most often presents to the hospital with
1. pain.
2. swelling.
3. dyspnea.
4. increased sputum production.

210. An 86-year-old female was admitted to the hospital two days ago with pneumonia. She now has an order to be up in the chair as much as possible. The nurse plans to get her up and help her with her morning care. The best plan to accomplish this would be to
1. get her up before breakfast. Have her eat in the chair, then bathe while still up.
2. allow her to eat breakfast in bed, rest for 30 minutes, get up in the chair, and rest for a few minutes. Allow her to wash her hands and face—nurse to complete bath.
3. Allow her to eat in bed, get her up, and provide her with a pan of water for her to bathe.

4. get her up before breakfast, have her bathe before breakfast, eat in the chair, then a rest in the chair.

211. A client has been admitted to the hospital. Lung assessment reveals the following: bronchial breath sounds over (L) lower lobe, diminished breath sounds (L) lower lobe, tactile fremitus present, percussion dulled in this area. Based on the assessment findings the nurse can expect to plan care for a client with
   1. pneumonia.
   2. asthma.
   3. emphysema.
   4. early left-sided heart failure.

212. A nurse is teaching a class in a community center about lung cancer. Which statement best demonstrates the client's understanding of the risk factors for lung cancer?
   1. "My husband smokes, but I don't! So, I really don't need to worry about getting lung cancer."
   2. "I guess I will need to eat more green and yellow vegetables."
   3. "Just because I have COPD doesn't mean that I have a higher risk."
   4. "I've worked with asbestos all my life and have never had any problems."

213. An adult male was diagnosed with lung cancer 18 months ago. He is now in the terminal stages and is experiencing severe generalized pain. He has ordered morphine sulfate 10 mg IM q 4–6 h prn. When planning his care, the nurse's best action is to
   1. teach him that the pain medicine prescribed will take away all his pain and he will have no discomfort.
   2. counsel him about the addictive qualities of his prescribed narcotic.
   3. inform him that he may only ask for the pain medicine every four hours and there is nothing else you can offer in between medication times.
   4. encourage him to ask for the pain medicine before the pain becomes too severe.

214. A 52-year-old patient is admitted to the nursing unit from the recovery room follow-ing a left pneumonectomy. When planning his care, the nurse can expect this patient to
   1. have a chest tube to water seal.
   2. have a chest tube to suction.
   3. be monitored closely for respiratory and cardiac complications.
   4. have his left arm maintained in a sling to prevent pain and discomfort.

215. Mr. B. has had a right thoracotomy for a wedge resection of his lung. He repeatedly refuses to do breathing or arm exercises because of the pain. What should the nurse include on Mr. B.'s plan of care?
   1. Offer Mr. B. pain medication immediately after arm exercises are completed.

2. Offer Mr. B. sips of ice water prior to a deep breathing and coughing session.
3. Schedule Mr. B.'s activity 30–45 minutes after his IM injection of pain medication.
4. Have Mr. B. hold a pillow against his abdomen for support.

216. The nurse may expect a client with suspected early ARDS to exhibit which of the following?
   1. PaO_2 of 90, PCO_2 of 45, X-ray showing enlarged heart, bradycardia.
   2. Thick green sputum production, PaO_2 of 75, pH 7.45.
   3. Restlessness, suprasternal retractions, PaO_2 of 65.
   4. Wheezes, slow deep respirations, PCO_2 of 55, pH of 7.25.

217. The nurse caring for a patient who has had a removal of the larynx and a permanent opening made into the trachea will plan care for a patient who has undergone a
   1. total laryngectomy.
   2. tracheostomy.
   3. radical neck dissection.
   4. partial laryngectomy.

218. An adult will undergo a total laryngectomy tomorrow. She is concerned about communicating post-op. The nurse should plan for her to communicate by which method the first 24–48 hours after surgery?
   1. Using the artificial larynx.
   2. Writing or pointing on a communication board.
   3. Using esophageal speech.
   4. Using a voice button.

219. Mrs. S. has had a total laryngectomy. The nurse is discussing options for verbal communication with Mrs. S. Which statement by Mrs. S. indicates her understanding of the available options for verbal communication?
   1. "Because of the arthritis in my hands, I think the voice button method would be easiest to use."
   2. "By the time I leave the hospital, I will be able to talk."
   3. "If I use the esophageal speech, my voice will be high pitched and soft."
   4. "Using an artificial larynx will make me sound sort of monotone."

220. An adult is ready for discharge after undergoing a total laryngectomy. The nurse is discussing safety aspects of his home care. Which statement by the client best indicates that he understands the safety aspects of his care at home?
   1. "It is okay to swim as long as I'm careful."
   2. "I should use paper tissues to cover my stoma when I'm coughing."
   3. "I should not wear anything to cover my stoma."
   4. "I will need to use a humidifier in my home."

221. Mr. R., a 35-year-old, is scheduled for a esophagoduodenoscopy. In planning for Mr. R.'s postprocedural care, the nurse recognizes that the *most effective* nursing action for preventing respiratory complications is to
1. keep Mr. R. positioned on his left side for 8–10 hours.
2. assess for a gag reflex before offering Mr. R. anything to eat or drink.
3. provide throat lozenges for complaints of a sore throat.
4. position Mr. R. in high Fowler's until he is fully awake and alert.

222. Mr. O., 52-years-old, is being evaluated for cancer of the colon. In preparing Mr. O. for a barium enema, the nurse can expect that Mr. O. will be
1. placed on a low residue diet one to two days before the study.
2. given an oil retention enema the morning of the study.
3. instructed to swallow six radiopaque tablets the evening before the study.
4. positioned in a high Fowler's position immediately following the procedure.

223. Mr. P., a 45-year-old, complains of excessive weight loss and anorexia. Laboratory studies show that Mr. P. is anemic. Hepatocellular carcinoma is suspected. A liver biopsy is performed at the bedside. The nurse can expect that after the procedure Mr. P. will be
1. encouraged to ambulate to prevent the formation of venous thrombosis.
2. asked to turn, cough, and deep breathe every two hours for the next eight hours.
3. placed in a high Fowler's position to maximize thoracic expansion.
4. positioned on his right side with a pillow under the costal margin, and immobile for several hours.

224. A client has a fecal impaction. The physician orders an oil-retention enema followed by a cleansing enema. The nurse would administer the oil-retention enema initially to
1. lubricate the walls of the intestinal tract.
2. soften the fecal mass and lubricate the walls of the rectum and colon.
3. reduce bacterial content of the fecal mass.
4. coat the walls of the intestines to prevent irritation by the hardened fecal mass.

225. Mr. M., 30-years-old, has amyotrophic lateral sclerosis. His neurologic status has continued to deteriorate. He is receiving enteral feedings through a gastrostomy tube. The nurse recognizes that the *priority* assessment before administering a bolus feeding is
1. check the expiration date of the prepared enteral feeding.
2. confirm the presence of a gag reflex.
3. check placement of feeding tube.
4. review laboratory studies for indications of electrolyte imbalances.

226. Mr. L. is eight hours post-op a Billroth II (gastric resection) for an intractable gastric ulcer. The drainage from his nasogastric decompression tube is thickened and the volume of secretions has dramatically reduced in the last two hours. Mr. L. complains that he feels like he is going to vomit. The *most* appropriate nursing action is to
1. reposition the nasogastric tube by advancing it gently.
2. notify the physician of your findings.
3. irrigate the nasogastric tube with 50 ml of sterile normal saline.
4. discontinue the low-intermittent suctioning.

227. Ms. P., a 47-year-old, is receiving chemotherapy for cancer of the liver. Her physician has prescribed metoclopramide for the nausea and vomiting associated with the chemotherapy. Metoclopramide has anticholinergic and extrapyramidal side-effects. The nurse recognizes that these side-effects put Ms. P. at high risk for
1. hyperglycemia related to increased gastric emptying.
2. injury related to decreased visual acuity and ataxia.
3. decreased cardiac output related to reduced heart rate.
4. fluid volume deficit related to frequent episodes of diarrhea.

228. Mr. K. develops diarrhea secondary to hyperosmolar enteral therapy. The care plan now includes giving Mr. K. water every four to six hours and after feedings. Which of the following findings would indicate that fluid therapy was effective?
1. Dry mucous membranes.
2. Hyperactive bowel sounds.
3. Increased urinary output.
4. Hypokalemia.

229. An elderly client complains of frequent episodes of constipation. An effective strategy for preventing constipation is
1. reducing fluid intake to encourage bulk formation in the intestinal lumen.
2. use of laxatives daily to establish a regular elimination pattern.
3. a regimen of exercises directed at toning the abdominal muscles.
4. setting a routine for bowel elimination just before bedtime.

230. Mr. W., a 55-year-old, is scheduled for a resection of the lower thoracic esophagus to remove a malignant tumor. In planning for Mr. W.'s postoperative care, the nurse would expect to
1. keep Mr. W. in a supine position to encourage thoracic expansion.
2. carefully advance the nasogastric tube past the anastomosis site.
3. frequently assess Mr. W.'s breath sounds.

4. provide a regular diet high in protein.

231. Ms. N., a 46-year-old, has been experiencing frequent episodes of "heartburn" and regurgitation of acrid, sour-tasting fluid. These episodes tend to occur especially after a heavy meal. Ms. N. is diagnosed with a hiatal hernia. The nurse knows that Ms. N. had a good understanding of her treatment regimen when Ms. N. states she will
1. elevate her legs when she is sleeping.
2. increase the roughage in her diet.
3. drink more fluids with her meals.
4. avoid caffeine, alcohol, and chocolate.

232. Mr. J., a 35-year-old stockbroker, has recently been diagnosed with peptic ulcer disease. Diagnostic studies confirm the presence of the gram-negative bacteria *Helicobacter pylori* in his gastrointestinal tract. If Mr. J. has a duodenal ulceration, the nurse would expect Mr. J. to describe the "ulcer pain" as
1. located in the upper right epigastric area radiating to his right shoulder or back.
2. relieved by vomiting.
3. occurring two to three hours after a meal, often awakening him between 1:00 and 2:00 A.M.
4. worsening with the ingestion of food.

233. A 42-year-old has been diagnosed with peptic ulcer disease. Her medication regimen includes misoprostol. The nurse understands that misoprostol exerts its therapeutic effect by
1. neutralizing excess gastric acid.
2. inhibiting gastric acid production.
3. increasing mucous production and bicarbonate levels.
4. increasing gastric emptying time.

234. Mr. T., a 56-year-old, has Billroth II (gastrojejunostomy) for intractable peptic ulcer disease. The nurse is instructing Mr. T. concerning the potential complication of dumping syndrome. The nurse can expect that Mr. T.'s dietary and activity instructions would include
1. a high carbohydrate diet.
2. exercise after mealtime to promote the digestive process.
3. limit drinking fluids with meals.
4. a protein-restricted diet.

235. Mr. H. is a 45-year-old who underwent a total gastrectomy for gastric cancer. The nurse has been giving Mr. H. post-op instructions about his diet, activities, and medications. Which of the following statements made by Mr. H. indicates that he understands his post-op care?
1. "I should take a walk after meals to aid my digestion."
2. "Drinking more water with my meals will prevent indigestion."
3. "I need more carbohydrates in my diet for an extra energy source."

4. "The visiting nurse will come monthly to give an injection of vitamin B_{12}."

236. Mrs. A., 72-years-old, has a direct inguinal hernia. The nurse caring for Mrs. A. should be alert for
1. hypoactive bowel sounds.
2. passage of semi-liquid, brown stools.
3. vomiting of bile-stained gastric contents.
4. complaints of constant, localized abdominal pain.

237. Mr. L. has developed peritonitis related to a perforated duodenal ulceration. During the nursing assessment of Mr. L., the nurse would expect to find
1. decreased or absent bowel sounds.
2. colicky abdominal pain.
3. high-pitched bowel sounds.
4. alternating episodes of constipation and diarrhea.

238. A nursing diagnosis appropriate for a client who has ulcerative colitis is
1. abdominal pain, related to decreased peristalsis.
2. diarrhea related to hyperosmolar intestinal contents.
3. fluid volume excess related to increased water absorption by intestinal mucosa.
4. activity intolerance related to fatigue.

239. Mr. D. is a 26-year-old recently diagnosed with ulcerative colitis. The nurse has been giving dietary instructions to Mr. D. to help prevent exacerbation of his inflammatory bowel disease. Which dietary choice indicates that Mr. D. understands the dietary instructions?
1. apple.
2. celery.
3. refined cereals.
4. hard cheeses.

240. When a client is diagnosed with ulcerative colitis, the nurse should be alert for the complication of
1. intestinal obstruction.
2. toxic megacolon.
3. malnutrition from malabsorption.
4. fistula formation.

241. A client with diverticulosis is admitted to the hospital. The nurse can expect that this client will be placed on
1. a bland, low residue diet.
2. a low protein, high carbohydrate diet.
3. a soft, but high fiber diet.
4. saline cathartics to increase intestinal peristalsis.

242. Mr. H. has been diagnosed with colon cancer. The nursing assessment would *most* likely reveal
1. epigastric pain that intensifies when the stomach is empty.
2. stools that are fatty and foul-smelling.
3. alternating episodes of diarrhea and constipation.

4. a rigid, board-like abdomen.

243. The nurse has been instructing a client regarding identifying and alleviating the risk factors associated with colon cancer. The nurse recognizes that the client has a good understanding of the means to reduce the chances of colon cancer when he states,
   1. "I will exercise daily."
   2. "I will include more red meat in my diet."
   3. "I will have an annual chest X-ray."
   4. "I will include more fresh fruits and vegetables in my diet."

244. Mr. T. has a sigmoid colostomy. The nurse is performing peristomal skin care and changing the stoma pouch. The most appropriate nursing action is to
   1. empty the ostomy pouch when it is full.
   2. pull flange and pouch off together to prevent spillage of stomach pouch contents.
   3. leave 1/4 in of skin exposed around stoma when determining size to cut new skin barrier.
   4. apply liquid deodorant to mucous membrane of protruding stoma.

245. Mr. D. has a double-barreled, transverse colostomy. The nurse has formulated the nursing diagnosis: risk for impaired skin integrity related to irritation of the peristomal skin by the effluent. The most appropriate nursing action relevant to this nursing diagnosis is
   1. strict measurement and recording of intake and output.
   2. assessing for bowel sounds when changing ostomy appliance.
   3. wash peristomal skin with an astringent solution to reduce bacterial contamination.
   4. apply skin barrier before applying flange and ostomy pouch.

246. Mr. J. is brought to the emergency room with severe, constant, localized abdominal pain. Abdominal muscles are rigid and rebound tenderness is present. Peritonitis is suspected. Mr. J. is hypotensive and tachycardiac. The nursing diagnosis most appropriate to Mr. J.'s signs/symptoms is
   1. fluid volume deficit related to depletion of intravascular volume.
   2. altered thought process related to toxic effects of elevated ammonia levels.
   3. abdominal pain related to increased intestinal peristalsis.
   4. altered nutrition, less than body requirements, related to malabsorption.

247. Ms. L., 28-years-old, has had a hemorrhoidectomy. The nurse recognizes that Ms. L. understands her post-op discharge instructions when Ms. L. states that she will
   1. reduce her fluid intake for several weeks after her surgery.

   2. include more fresh fruits and vegetables in her diet.
   3. vigorously clean her perianal area with soap and water after every bowel movement.
   4. limit her activities to bedrest for at least six hours a day.

248. The client with hepatitis may be anicteric and symptomless. The nurse recognizes that if symptoms are present early in the hepatic inflammatory disorder, the most likely symptom/sign is
   1. dark urine.
   2. ascites.
   3. occult blood in stools.
   4. anorexia.

249. Ms. S., a 22-year-old, visits her physician with flu-like symptoms that have persisted for nearly a month. She complains of headaches, malaise, anorexia, and fever. Ms. S. is a child care worker at a local daycare center with children ranging in ages from six months to five years. Based on the associated risk factors and mode of transmission, the nurse recognizes that Ms. S. is most likely experiencing
   1. hepatitis A.
   2. hepatitis B.
   3. hepatitis C.
   4. hepatitis D.

250. Mr. C., a 25-year-old, is a laboratory technician in a community health clinic. For the past two months he has been experiencing fatigue, headaches, diminished appetite, and a yellowish discoloration of his sclera. He is diagnosed with hepatitis B. Mr. C. asks the nurse how he contracted hepatitis. The nurse's most appropriate response is
   1. airborne droplets carry the infectious hepatitis B virus.
   2. the hepatitis B virus is transmitted parenterally and through intimate contact.
   3. an individual may contract hepatitis B by using contaminated eating utensils.
   4. hepatitis B may be transmitted through eating shellfish from contaminated water sources.

251. Mr. G. is a 56-year-old with hepatic cirrhosis related to 10-year history of alcohol abuse. Mr. G. is at risk for injury related to portal hypertension. The most appropriate nursing action to decrease his risk of injury is
   1. keep Mr. G.'s fingernails short.
   2. offer small, frequent feedings.
   3. observe stools for color and consistency.
   4. assess for jaundice of skin and sclera.

252. Mr. L., a 52-year-old, is diagnosed with Laennec's cirrhosis. He has massive ascites formation. His respirations are rapid and shallow. The physician decides to perform a paracentesis. The nurse caring for Mr. L.

during the procedure gives the *highest priority* to
1. gathering the appropriate sterile equipment.
2. labeling samples of abdominal fluid and sending them to the laboratory.
3. positioning Mr. L. upright on the edge of the bed.
4. measuring and recording blood pressure and pulse frequently during the procedure.

253. Mr. L. has a seven-year history of hepatic cirrhosis. He was brought to the emergency room because he began vomiting large amounts of dark-red blood. A Sengstaken-Blakemore tube was inserted to tamponade the bleeding esophageal varices. While the balloon tamponade is in place, the nurse caring for Mr. L. gives the highest priority to
1. assessing his stools for occult blood.
2. evaluating capillary refill in extremities.
3. performing frequent mouth care.
4. auscultating breath sounds.

254. Mr. L., a 52-year-old, is experiencing advanced hepatic cirrhosis now complicated by hepatic encephalopathy. He is confused, restless, and demonstrating asterixis. The nurse has formulated the nursing diagnosis: altered thought processes related to
1. massive ascites formation.
2. increased serum ammonia levels.
3. fluid volume excess.
4. altered clotting mechanism.

255. Mr. N., a 45-year-old, has choledocholithiasis. During the nursing admission, the nurse notes that Mr. N.'s sclera and skin are jaundiced. He also complains of abdominal distention, and pain which he is *most likely* to describe as
1. an intermittent, colicky pain in his left flank.
2. pain which awakens him during the night, and is relieving by eating.
3. a vise-like pressure over his sternum.
4. right upper quadrant pain that often radiates to his right shoulder.

256. Ms. C. is a 40-year-old who is admitted to the hospital for acute cholecystitis. She is six hours post-op abdominal cholecystectomy with a choledochostomy. Ms. C. has a T-tube in place. The nurse understands that proper management of the T-tube includes
1. hanging the T-tube drainage below the bed.
2. notifying the physician if T-tube drainage is 75 ml for the first 24 hours after surgery.
3. irrigating the T-tube with sterile normal saline q2h to prevent obstruction.
4. clamping the T-tube if Ms. C. develops sudden, severe abdominal pain.

257. Mr. T., a 40-year-old, has experienced repeated episodes of acute pancreatitis. He has continued to consume alcohol. The nurse observes that Mr. T. is doubled-over, rocking back-and-forth in pain. The nurse understands that morphine and morphine derivatives are contraindicated for the pain associated with acute pancreatitis because
1. it causes severe respiratory depression.
2. depression of GI peristalsis may cause constipation.
3. spasms of the sphincter of Oddi may occur.
4. it is rapidly metabolized by the liver.

258. Mr. G., a 56-year-old, has a five-year history of alcohol abuse. He appears acutely ill. He is vomiting bile-stained emesis. The nurse notes signs of severe, hemorrhagic pancreatitis that is accurately documented as
1. the presence of a positive fluid wave in the abdominal area.
2. a yellowish color of the sclera and skin.
3. ecchymosis in the flank and around the umbilical area.
4. bloody, foul-smelling stools.

259. Mr. B. is a 66-year-old with a 10-year history of alcohol abuse. He has recently been diagnosed with chronic pancreatitis. The physician has prescribed pancrelipase, a pancreatic enzyme replacement, for Mr. B. The nurse will recognize that Mr. B. understands his medication regimen when he states,
1. "I will take this medication with a glass of milk."
2. "If my stools appear yellowish with a foul odor, I will call my doctor."
3. "I will take my medication with some antacid so it will not bother my stomach."
4. "I will be sure to thoroughly chew the capsule contents before swallowing the medication."

260. Mr. P., a 60-year-old, has been diagnosed with a malignant tumor of the head of the pancreas. A pancreatoduodenectomy (Whipple's procedure) was done to resect the tumor. The nurse recognizes that hemorrhage is a potentially major complication of a Whipple procedure. Which of the following assessment findings suggest this complication?
1. Jaundice of the skin and sclera.
2. Hyperglycemia.
3. Oliguria.
4. Bradycardia.

261. A female client is to have a urine culture collected. The nurse instructs the client on the procedure for collecting a clean catch urine specimen by telling the client to
1. separate the labia, clean from front to back with the three wipes impregnated with the cleaning solution, and then start to void in the toilet. Stop, and finally continue to void into the sterile container.

2. retract the foreskin, cleanse with the three cleansing sponges, and start to void. Stop, and finally continue to void into the sterile container.
3. separate the labia, clean from back to front with the three wipes impregnated with the cleaning solution, and then start to void in the toilet. Stop, and finally continue to void into the sterile container.
4. retract the foreskin, clean with soap and water, and then start to void. Stop, and finally continue to void into the sterile container.

262. The nurse is to collect a urine culture specimen from a catheterized client. Which one of the following statements describes the nurse's actions for this procedure?
1. With a sterile syringe the nurse aspirates 50 ml of urine from the silicone catheter tubing.
2. With a sterile syringe, the nurse aspirates 1–3 ml from the distal end of the catheter after first cleaning the sampling port with alcohol.
3. With a sterile syringe, the nurse aspirates 1–3 ml from the distal end of the catheter after first cleaning the sampling port with soap and water.
4. The nurse disconnects the catheter from the tubing and allows a small volume of urine to drain into a sterile container.

263. The nurse is ordered to perform a urinary catheterization for post-void residual volume (PVR) on a patient with urinary incontinence. Several minutes after the patient voids, the nurse obtains a residual urine of 30 ml. The nurse interprets this residual volume of urine to be
1. adequate bladder emptying.
2. inadequate bladder emptying.
3. decreased urethral pressure.
4. increased urethral pressure.

264. Post cystoscopy, which one of the following assessment findings would the nurse expect to find?
1. Gross hematuria and pain.
2. Pink-tinged urine and burning on voiding.
3. Colicky pain and bladder distention.
4. Flank pain and bladder distention.

265. A post-op client is unable to void and is ordered to have an indwelling catheter inserted immediately. The nurse performing the catheterization is extremely concerned with
1. teaching the client deep breathing techniques to decrease post-op pain, preprocedure.
2. maintaining strict aseptic technique.
3. medicating the client for pain, before the procedure.

4. teaching the client the signs and symptoms of urinary tract infection.

266. The nurse is assessing a client with an indwelling catheter and finds the catheter is not draining and the client's bladder is distended. The nurse should immediately plan to
1. notify the physician.
2. assess the catheter tubing for kinks and position so downhill flow is initiated.
3. change the catheter.
4. aspirate urine for culture.

267. The nurse is teaching a client about the concept of dialysis and how it works for the body. It is the nurse's understanding that dialysis is a technique that
1. will move blood through a semipermeable membrane into a dialysate that is used to remove waste products as well as correct fluid and electrolyte imbalances.
2. will add electrolytes and water to the blood when passing through a semipermeable membrane to correct electrolyte imbalances.
3. will increase potassium to the blood when passing through a semipermeable membrane to correct electrolyte imbalances.
4. allows the nurse to choose to use either diffusion osmosis or ultrafiltration to correct the client's fluid and electrolyte imbalance.

268. A client with end-stage renal disease (ESRD) receives hemodialysis three times a week. The nurse concludes that dialysis is effective when
1. the client does not have a large weight gain.
2. the client has no signs and symptoms of infection.
3. the client expresses he or she can catch up on rest while on dialysis.
4. the client is able to return to employment.

269. The nurse is caring for a client going to hemodialysis three times a week. The client receives the following medications every morning: hydrochlorothiazide (Hydrodiuril), nitroglycerin patch (Minitran), vancomycin, and allopurinol (Zyloprim). The nurse expects to withhold which of the above medications until after hemodialysis?
1. Hydrochlorothiazide (Hydrodiuril) and vancomycin.
2. Hydrochlorothiazide (Hydrodiuril) and nitroglycerin patch (Minitran).
3. Nitroglycerin (Minitran) and allopurinol (Zyloprim).
4. Vancomycin and allopurinol (Zyloprim).

270. The nurse is caring for a client receiving peritoneal dialysis. The nurse is completing the exchange by draining the dialysate and

notices the dialysate is cloudy. The nurse best interprets this finding as
1. the normal appearance of draining dialysate.
2. a sign of infection.
3. an indication of an impending lower back problem.
4. a sign of a vascular access occlusion.

271. The nurse knows the client on continuous ambulatory peritoneal dialysis (CAPD) understands his treatment when the client states,
1. "I must increase my carbohydrate intake daily."
2. "I must maintain a positive nitrogen balance by decreasing proteins."
3. "I must take prophylactic antibiotics to prevent infection."
4. "I must be aware of the signs and symptoms of peritonitis."

272. A woman presents to the urgent care center with dysuria and hematuria. The woman reveals that she has a history of cystitis. The nurse should also assess for which of the following clinical manifestations suggesting cystitis?
1. Frequency and urgency of urination, flank pain, nausea, and vomiting.
2. Abscess formation and flank pain.
3. Frequency and urgency of urination, suprapubic pain, and foul smelling urine.
4. Fever, nausea, vomiting, and flank pain.

273. A three-day post-op client for a ureterosigmoidostomy is complaining of cramping in lower extremities and occasional dizziness. The nurse should give highest priority to
1. assessing for electrolyte imbalance.
2. assessing for cardiac dysrhythmias.
3. observing the client's response to surgery.
4. verifying the temperature of the client's lower extremities.

274. The nurse who is caring for a client with a Kock's pouch should plan to teach the client about
1. decreasing the client's sexual encounters.
2. adhering to catheterization schedules.
3. decreasing fluid intake to avoid embarrassing situations.
4. decreasing fluid intake to manage the urinary diversion.

275. A 35-year-old male presents to the ER with hematuria, flank pain, fever, nausea, and vomiting. He is admitted and passes a "stone." The stone is sent to the laboratory and is found to be composed of uric acid. The client is placed on allopurinol (Zyloprim). The nurse understands that the allopurinol (Zylopri) is prescribed to
1. decrease the client's serum creatinine.

2. reduce the urinary concentration of uric acid.
3. acidify the urine.
4. bind oxalate in the gastrointestinal tract.

276. The nurse is caring for a client who has just been given discharge instruction for kidney stones. Which statement by the client indicates a need for further instruction?
1. "I will decrease my intake of all foods on the list you gave me that are high in purine, calcium, or oxalate."
2. "I will decrease my fluid intake."
3. "I will take my medication daily."
4. "I will return to my doctor in one week for follow-up."

277. Medication will be used in the management of a client with urolithiasis. Based on knowledge of urolithiasis, the nurse should include which of the following in planning nursing care for the client?
1. Place the client in bed with siderails up as a narcotic will be given.
2. Keep the client NPO so there will be no experience of nausea with medication administration.
3. Increase intake of purine-, calcium-, and oxalate-rich food.
4. Add Probenecid to the narcotic to prevent renal tubular excretion of the narcotic.

278. The nurse is performing discharge teaching for a client who was admitted with pyelonephritis. The client asks the nurse, "What is pyelonephritis?" Based on the nurse's knowledge of pyelonephritis the best response would be,
1. "Pyelonephritis is an inflammation of the bladder."
2. "Pyelonephritis is a rupture of the bladder."
3. "Pyelonephritis is an infection of the kidney."
4. "Pyelonephritis is an infection of the lower urinary tract."

279. On a medical-surgical unit, a client is admitted with acute renal failure. The nurse must continually assess for
1. hyponatremia and hyperkalemia.
2. decreased BUN and creatinine.
3. alkalosis.
4. hypercalcemia.

280. The client with chronic renal failure complains of irritating white crystals on his skin. The nurse recognizes this finding as uremic frost and takes which of the following nursing actions?
1. Administers an antihistamine because the doctor would prescribe one to relieve itching.
2. Increases fluids to prevent crystal formation and decrease itching.

3. Provides skin care with tepid water and applies lotion on the skin to relieve itching.
4. Permits the client to soak in a bathtub to remove crystals.

281. The nurse has been working with a client with chronic renal failure. Which of the following behaviors would indicate to the nurse that the client understands his dietary regimen?
1. He reports eating two bananas for breakfast, rice and beans for lunch, and fruit salad, green beans, and an 8 oz. T-bone steak for dinner.
2. He reports eating bacon and eggs for breakfast, hot dogs and sauerkraut for lunch, and baked canned ham with green beans for dinner.
3. He reports eating an apple and oatmeal for breakfast, homemade tomato soup for lunch, and pasta with fish for dinner.
4. He reports eating half a honeydew melon and three eggs for breakfast, a baked potato with processed cheese spread and broccoli for lunch, and chicken, yams, pinto beans, squash, and 8 oz. of pecans for dinner.

282. A client who has been in intensive care, for cardiogenic shock related to a myocardial infarction, is recovering. He is transferred to the renal unit in renal failure. The client's spouse asks the nurse "Is this acute or chronic renal failure?" Based on knowledge of this client's history the nurse's best response is,
1. "Don't worry this is an excellent renal unit, so we can treat either acute or chronic failure."
2. "Acute renal failure always progresses to chronic renal failure."
3. "Acute renal failure is glomerular degeneration whereas chronic renal failure is the result of cardiovascular collapse."
4. "Acute renal failure generally results from decreased blood to the kidneys, nephrotoxicity, or muscle injury. The myocardial infarction caused extensive heart muscle damage decreasing blood to the kidneys."

283. A client immediately post kidney transplant should be assessed by the nurse for
1. fluid and electrolyte imbalances.
2. infection.
3. hepatotoxicity.
4. respiratory complications.

284. K. had a renal transplant, as a result of glomerulonephritis, and is at the physician's office for a follow-up visit. K. tells the office nurse "I am not worried about rejection. I am not going to come here weekly." The nurse interprets his reaction to constant follow-up care as an example of
1. projection.
2. intellectualization.
3. denial.

4. regression.

285. The prudent nurse will complete which one of the following initial assessments on the client immediately post-op nephrectomy?
1. Performing cardiovascular assessment.
2. Ordering laboratory studies monitoring renal functions and electrolytes.
3. Inspecting the incision site for bleeding.
4. Obtaining a urine culture.

286. The nurse is completing an admission assessment on a client with benign prostatic hyperplasia (BPH). The nurse should obtain an in-depth assessment about
1. laboratory studies.
2. urinary patterns.
3. electrocardiograms.
4. internal bleeding.

287. A client with BPH is at the clinic for follow-up. Which of the following statements indicates to the nurse his understanding of management of his condition?
1. "As soon as I finish this visit I won't ever have to worry about BPH again."
2. "I don't know how I am going to get used to voiding every two to three hours."
3. "I will wear an athletic supporter while I am awake."
4. "I am going to avoid fluids while at work to prevent dribbling."

288. A client who is eight hours posttransurethral resection prostatectomy (TURP) asks the nurse "Why is my urine in the bag clotting like blood?" The nurse's best interpretation of this finding is that
1. after all surgery bleeding is normal.
2. it is common for blood clots to be irrigated from the bladder for a day or so.
3. the physician needs to be called as the patient is hemorrhaging.
4. the client is tugging on the catheter causing irritation to the bladder mucosa.

289. A 68-year-old client, 48 hours post-transurethral resection prostatectomy asks "How will my sex life be affected?" The nurse's best response would be,
1. "I will get the physician to determine if your sex life was affected during surgery."
2. "Only your doctor can answer that. Why don't you ask him prior to discharge."
3. "A transurethral prostatectomy does not usually result in erectile dysfunction."
4. "Don't you remember, before surgery you were told that you would not be able to engage in sexual intercourse but you can express your love for your spouse by alternate acts such as cuddling."

290. Following a prostatectomy, the client has a three-way, indwelling catheter for continuous bladder irrigation. During evening shift, 2400 ml of irrigant was instilled. At the end of the shift, the drainage bag was drained of 2900 ml

of fluid. The nurse calculates the urine output to be
1. 5300 ml.
2. 2900 ml.
3. 240 ml.
4. 500 ml.

291. In preparing a teaching plan for an adult who has had an arthroscopy, the nurse will include which of the following?
1. Client should check extremity for color, mobility, and sensation at least every two hours after procedure.
2. Client may return to regular activities immediately after procedure.
3. Remove compression dressing six to eight hours after procedure.
4. Keep extremity in flexion for 24 hours after procedure.

292. The nursing care plan for an adult who has had a myelogram using an oil-based contrast medium should include which intervention by the nurse?
1. Give the client a light meal immediately before the myelogram, to help prevent nausea or lightheadedness.
2. Restrict fluids for 12 hours after the myelogram.
3. Keep the client in a recumbent position for 12–24 hours after the myelogram.
4. Assure the client that stiff neck or photophobia are expected side-effects of the contrast medium used during the myelogram.

293. Which statement by the family tells the nurse that they understand how to perform passive range of motion exercises on bed-bound Mrs. C.?
1. "We should put each joint through a full series of exercises until Mother tells us she's fatigued."
2. "Every day, we should try to move all of her joints a degree or two further than they naturally go."
3. "If Mother has a muscle spasm, we should stop exercising that limb for a day or two."
4. "To exercise Mother's elbow, we would hold her upper arm still, and move her forearm."

294. Miss G. is learning how to use a cane. The nurse knows that Miss G. can use the cane safely when observing which of the following?
1. The cane is held on the unaffected side; the cane and affected leg are moved forward, then the unaffected leg comes forward.
2. The cane is held on the affected side; the cane is moved forward, then the unaffected leg, then the affected leg.
3. The cane is held on the unaffected side; the cane is moved forward, then the unaffected leg, then the affected leg.

4. The cane is held on the affected side; the cane and unaffected leg are moved forward, then the affected leg comes forward.

295. An adult who has had a total hip replacement is learning how to walk with a standard (not reciprocal) walker. Which description below tells the nurse that he is using the walker correctly?
1. One side of the walker is simultaneously advanced with the opposite foot; the process is repeated on the other side.
2. Each time he steps on his nonaffected side, the patient advances the walker; when moving his affected side, he steps into the walker and lifts his nonaffected foot.
3. The patient balances on both feet, most weight on his nonaffected side, and lifts the walker forward; he then balances on the walker and swings both feet forward into the walker.
4. The patient lifts the walker in front while balancing on both feet, then walks into the walker, supporting his body weight on his hands while advancing his affected side.

296. Mr. D. has sprained his knee and the emergency nurse is fitting him with crutches. If Mr. D. is measured while he is lying down, how does the nurse ensure the correct crutch length?
1. Measure patient from anterior axillary fold to sole of foot and add two inches.
2. Add six inches to the length of the patient's foot and measure the distance from that point to the patient's axilla.
3. Measure from the patient's axilla to his palm to get the length from the top of the crutch to the hand piece. Measure from palm to sole to determine length of lower part of crutch.
4. Subtract 24 inches from patient's height to determine length of crutch from top to tip.

297. The nurse is teaching a client with a broken left ankle how to go up stairs when using crutches. Which statement by the nurse is correct?
1. "Place both crutches on the next step, stand on the right foot and place the left foot on the step next to the crutches."
2. "Place the left crutch and right foot on the next step and push off with both arms then lift the left foot up to the step."
3. "Place the right foot on the next step, then move the crutches and the left foot onto the step."
4. "Place the right crutch and left foot on the next step; move the right crutch up onto the step, then swing the right foot up."

298. Seventeen-year-old Jack E. sprained his left ankle playing football. The emergency nurse is teaching Jack ambulation with crutches

using a four-point gait. Which sequence correctly describes this gait?
1. Weight on both crutches and right foot; crutches and left foot move forward while weight stays on right foot; all weight transferred to crutches, then to right foot; crutches advanced forward for next step.
2. Weight on both crutches and both feet; right crutch advances forward, then left foot is advanced as weight shifts to right foot and both crutches; weight is distributed to both feet and right crutch as left crutch is advanced; right foot is advanced with weight on left foot and both crutches.
3. Weight on both crutches and both feet; left foot and right crutch are advanced simultaneously and weight transferred to them; right foot and left crutch are advanced simultaneously and weight transferred to them; the pattern is continued.
4. Weight on both feet and crutches; both crutches are advanced while weight remains on feet; weight transfers to crutches as feet swing forward and land with heels on line with the crutches; both crutches are advanced and the pattern is continued.

299. Which of the following findings would alert the nurse to notify the physician of a serious complication for the client with a cast on his leg?
1. Itching under the cast.
2. Poor capillary refill of the toes.
3. Ability of client to move toes without difficulty.
4. Pain relieved by application of ice bag to cast.

300. Which intervention below would be appropriate for the nurse to teach the client with a cast on his left arm?
1. "Cover your plaster cast with plastic before taking a long bath or shower."
2. "Repair breaks in the cast with super-glue or epoxy."
3. "Remove surface dirt on your cast with a damp cloth."
4. "If your fiberglass cast gets wet, dry it with the warm setting on your blowdryer."

301. An adult is in Russell traction. It is appropriate for the nurse to make which of the following assessments because of the client's treatment modality?
1. Make sure sling under the affected knee is smooth and doesn't apply pressure in the popliteal space.
2. Ensure that both buttocks clear the mattress.
3. Check that the leg in traction is on the mattress, not elevated.

4. Assess for numbness and tingling of one or more fingers, suggesting radial, ulnar, or median nerve pressure.

302. Mr. Y.'s family asks why Mr. Y. has been put into pelvic traction for low back pain. The best response for the nurse to give is,
1. "He really needs bedrest; the traction will force him to stay in bed."
2. "By pulling on either side of the pelvis, the lower back muscles are stretched and this gives relief from the crampy back muscles."
3. "Traction helps to relieve compression of the roots of the nerves."
4. "By holding the pelvis still, the back muscles can relax and start to heal."

303. Miss R.'s left leg is in Buck's extension traction. She complains of burning under the traction boot and the toes on that foot are cool. The nurse's best first action is to
1. ask Miss R., "What do you mean by 'burning'?"
2. notify the physician at once.
3. remove the boot, then reapply and reassess.
4. apply an ice pack to the boot for 15 minutes.

304. Mr. Q., a client whose left leg is in balanced suspension traction for a femur fracture, needs to be moved to a new bed. The nurse understands that this can be safely done as long as
1. all weights are removed from the ends of the traction ropes so the leg moves freely before the move is attempted.
2. the left leg is kept above the level of the heart.
3. sufficient time is given to the client to move himself to the new bed at his own rate of tolerance.
4. the line of pull is maintained on the left leg.

305. Which statement below best describes the nurse's assessment of the client with rheumatoid arthritis?
1. Assessment is done of the musculoskeletal, cardiac, pulmonary, and renal systems.
2. Pain is best assessed by monitoring the client's facial expression during exam and by observing limitations in the client's own movement.
3. Vital signs are an adequate assessment of the acuity of the client's level of pain.
4. The client's health history is not nearly as important as the nurse's findings on physical examination.

306. Mr. K. is admitted to the medical unit with an acute exacerbation of rheumatoid arthritis. Which of the following will the nurse include on his nursing care plan?
1. "Administer analgesics for pain when systolic blood pressure increases 20

mmHg or more or pulse increases 20% or more."
2. "Develop plan with client to meet self-care needs."
3. "Instruct client to stop taking iron supplements that lead to constipation."
4. "Schedule hygiene activities together in one block to provide longer rest periods before and after care."

307. Miss J. has rheumatoid arthritis and is taking prednisone. In creating a teaching plan for Miss J., the nurse will be certain to include which of the following?
1. "You should expect to be on corticosteroids for the rest of your life."
2. "It will take three to six months for you to notice any effect from this medication."
3. "Notify your physician of any stomach upset you may have."
4. "Avoid bananas and spinach while you are taking this drug."

308. Which statement by an adult with osteoarthritis indicates to the nurse that she understands her therapeutic regimen?
1. "I will wait until my pain is very bad before I take my pain medication, or else further on in my disease, the medication won't help at all."
2. "Jogging for short distances is better for my arthritis than walking for longer distances."
3. "It would probably be a good idea for me to lose the 30 pounds my doctor recommended I lose."
4. "I should do all my house cleaning on one day, so I can rest for the remainder of the week."

309. In preparing a teaching plan for the client with osteoarthritis, the nurse would include which of the following?
1. Application of cold packs to affected joints to decrease swelling.
2. Patient education regarding self-administration of medications.
3. Progressively increasing activity to point of muscle fatigue to build muscle bulk and improve rate of metabolism.
4. Teaching client that degenerative changes are progressive and that pain is a natural sequela of age.

310. The nurse, assessing a client with systemic lupus erythematosus can expect to find which of the following?
1. Dysphagia.
2. Decreased visual acuity or blindness.
3. Dryness or itching of genitalia.
4. Abnormal lung sounds.

311. Mrs. I., a client with systemic lupus erythematosus, is taking gold. Which of the following interventions would the nurse include in the teaching plan for this client?

1. "Stop taking your anti-inflammatory medication as long as you are taking gold preparations."
2. "You will give yourself intramuscular injections of gold preparations every day for two to four weeks, then taper down to one injection every two months."
3. "You will be taking a large dose when you start taking gold capsules, and will taper down to a smaller dose as the therapy becomes effective."
4. "Stay away from crowds during flu season and have your blood tested after every other gold injection."

312. In assessing the client with osteomyelitis, the nurse would expect to find which of the following?
1. Pale, cool, tender skin at site.
2. Decreased white blood cell count.
3. Positive wound cultures.
4. Decreased erythrocyte sedimentation rate.

313. Mrs. V. has a fractured left radius, which has been casted. While performing an assessment of this client, the nurse will correctly identify which of these findings as *emergent*?
1. Pain at the fracture site.
2. Swelling of fingers of left hand.
3. Diminished capillary refill of fingers of left hand.
4. Warm, dry fingers of left hand.

314. Which intervention by the emergency nurse is critical in caring for the patient with a fractured tibia and fibula?
1. Cutting away clothing on the injured leg.
2. Palpation of the dorsalis pedis pulses.
3. Administration of analgesic medications as ordered.
4. Initiating two, large-bore IV catheters and warmed normal saline at a fast rate.

315. Sharon V., 20-years-old, was brought to the emergency department after an auto accident. There is a strong scent of alcohol about her, and she states she had three beers over three hours. Her only injury is an open fracture of the left humerus. Which assessment finding by the emergency nurse is critical?
1. Status of client's tetanus immunization.
2. Current blood alcohol level.
3. Support systems available at home to assist with care.
4. Last time client voided.

316. Mr. U. is a firefighter who fell off a roof while fighting a house fire and fractured his femur. Approximately 24 hours after the incident, the nurse finds Mr. U. dyspneic, tachypneic, with scattered crackles in his lung fields; he is coughing up large amounts of thick, white sputum. The nurse correctly interprets this as

1. respiratory compromise related to inhalation of smoke.
2. pneumonia related to prolonged bedrest.
3. fat embolism syndrome related to femur fracture.
4. hypovolemic shock related to multiple trauma.

317. Mr. S. has had a total right hip replacement. The nurse understands that his operative hip is kept in extension and abduction because this position
    1. reduces the risk for the development of thromboemboli.
    2. promotes circulation to the operative site, reducing the risk of avascular necrosis.
    3. helps to prevent dislocation of the hip prosthesis.
    4. facilitates the drainage of blood and fluid at the operative site.

318. Mrs. T. has had a total right hip replacement and asks the nurse about "moving around in this bed." The nurse's best response is based on the knowledge that
    1. the client should remain supine for 48 hours after surgery, with affected leg in a slightly inward-rotation position.
    2. although the client must remain supine, she can cross her legs to change position for comfort.
    3. a side-lying position is undesirable, but the head of the bed can be elevated 60–75° to shift weight off of back and buttocks.
    4. the client will be repositioned using an abductor pillow between the legs.

319. Which statement by Miss W., who has had an open reduction/internal fixation of her fractured left hip, indicates to the nurse that the client understands her care?
    1. "My nephew will move my bed down to the first floor so I won't have to go up stairs when I get home."
    2. "I should expect my surgical site to be swollen and red for a week or two after I get home."
    3. "The night nurse will take off these thigh-high stockings at bedtime, and the day nurse will put them back on at breakfast time."
    4. "I need to limit my fluid intake so I won't be getting on and off the bedpan so often; it's not good for my hip."

320. The nurse teaches an adult woman that because she has osteoporosis, she must take safety precautions to prevent falls, "because you could break a hip." The client asks the nurse what one has to do with the other, and the nurse's best response is based on the knowledge that
    1. osteoporosis yields brittle bones which break easily.
    2. osteoporosis causes changes in balance,

which makes the client more susceptible to falls that could lead to hip fractures.
    3. hips are the primary sites of calcium loss in osteoporosis, making them more susceptible to fracture.
    4. both osteoporosis and hip fractures are common in elderly women.

321. Mrs. N. is diagnosed with a herniated nucleus pulposus at the C5-C6 interspace, and a second at the C6-C7 interspace. Which of the following findings would the nurse expect to discover during the assessment?
    1. Constant, throbbing headaches.
    2. Numbness of the face.
    3. Clonus in the lower extremities.
    4. Pain in the scapular region.

322. Mr. A. has undergone a cervical laminectomy. Because of the potential complications associated with this procedure, the nurse must perform which of the following assessments?
    1. Assess for wheezes and stridor.
    2. Check pupils for response to direct and consensual light.
    3. Assess gag reflex.
    4. Assess shoulder shrug and neck strength.

323. Mrs. H. is post-op for a cervical laminectomy. The nurse knows that the patient will most likely be maintained in what position?
    1. Left lateral decubitus with neck flexed to 30°.
    2. Supine, with no pillows under the head.
    3. Flat, with a neck roll under the neck.
    4. Modified Trendelenburg, with a soft cervical collar in place.

324. Miss B. is being discharged after a lumbar laminectomy. Which statement by Miss B. indicates to the nurse that the patient understands her discharge teaching?
    1. "I can't wait to sit in my own recliner and rest while I watch my soaps!"
    2. "I'll be able to man the refreshment stand at my nephew's baseball game next weekend, won't I?"
    3. "My friend is getting me a footstool for in front of my sink."
    4. "I have to buy a soft mattress so my spine won't be subjected to any extra pressure."

325. The nurse is planning post-op care for a patient undergoing a laminectomy. The nurse needs to know whether or not a spinal fusion is also performed because
    1. the contrast medium used to check the fusion site for grafting could cause an allergic reaction.
    2. the patient whose laminectomy is performed with a spinal fusion will be on bedrest longer than the patient who does not undergo spinal fusion.
    3. patients undergoing spinal fusion will be in long torso casts for six to eight weeks after surgery.

4. the patient whose laminectomy is performed with a spinal fusion is at greater risk for spontaneous pneumothorax than the patient who does not undergo spinal fusion.

326. A client is to have the following diagnostic procedures: serum T_3 and T_4, carotid arteriogram, and thyroid scan. In what order should the nurse schedule the tests?
1. Arteriogram, serum T_3 and T_4, scan.
2. Serum T_3 and T_4, scan, arteriogram.
3. Arteriogram, scan, serum T_3 and T_4.
4. Serum T_3 and T_4, arteriogram, scan.

327. After reading about the procedure for his upcoming thyroid scan, a client expresses concern about the dangers of being "radioactive" after the test. Which understanding about the test should guide the nurse's response?
1. There is no danger since the thyroid scan no longer involves the use of a radioactive isotope.
2. The radioactive isotope is only a tracer dose, which is not harmful to the client or others close to him.
3. The client must avoid close contact with others for five days following the test.
4. Wearing a lead shield during the test will protect the client from radioactivity.

328. The nurse is explaining to a client about a radioactive iodine uptake test. Which of the following over-the-counter medications should the nurse advise the client to avoid prior to the test?
1. Antiflatulents.
2. Poison ivy remedies.
3. Cough syrups.
4. Antifungal agents.

329. Select the most accurate explanation by the nurse to a client who is to have an oral glucose tolerance test and needs to understand the procedure.
1. "You will go to the laboratory and your blood will be drawn."
2. "After you drink a concentrated glucose solution, you cannot eat or drink anything until your blood is drawn."
3. "You will eat a large meal and your blood will be drawn two hours later."
4. "Your blood will be drawn, you will drink a concentrated glucose solution, and your blood will be drawn again."

330. An adult is suffering from adrenocortical insufficiency and is placed on glucocorticoid therapy. The nurse plans to include which of the following administration directions?
1. "You will need to take the large dose of the medication at bedtime and the smaller dose in the morning until the prescription is finished."
2. "You will need to take the medication at bedtime for life."
3. "You will need to take the medication in the morning until the prescription is finished."
4. "You will need to take the large dose of the medication in the morning and the smaller dose in the afternoon for life."

331. Which assessment is most important for the nurse to make when monitoring a client with a pituitary tumor that secretes ACTH?
1. Height.
2. Blood pressure.
3. Pulse rate.
4. Output.

332. The nurse is caring for a client who underwent surgical hypophysectomy. Which of the following assessments is most essential for the nurse to make immediately post-op?
1. Blood pressure.
2. Serum calcium levels.
3. Breath sounds.
4. Bowel sounds.

333. Mr. P. has had a hypophysectomy with a complete removal of the pituitary gland. Which of the following statements represents to the nurse the most complete understanding of follow-up care?
1. I will need to wear a Medic-Alert bracelet.
2. I will need to take hormone replacements for the next two months.
3. I will need to wear a Medic-Alert bracelet and take hormone replacements for the next year.
4. I will need to have lifelong follow-up, to take hormone replacement therapy for the rest of my life, and to wear a Medic-Alert bracelet.

334. A 62-year-old female is admitted with a posterior pituitary tumor and is experiencing diabetes insipidus, a complication of that tumor. The nursing diagnosis most appropriate for this client is
1. fluid volume excess.
2. fluid volume deficit.
3. incontinence, bowel.
4. diarrhea.

335. A client who has been taking prednisone to treat lupus erythematosus has discontinued the medication because of lack of funds to buy the drug. When the nurse becomes aware of the situation, which assessment is most important for the nurse to make first?
1. Breath sounds.
2. Capillary refill.
3. Blood pressure.
4. Skin integrity.

336. An adult is readmitted to the medical/surgical care unit in addisonian crisis. He is exhibiting signs of tachycardia, dehydration, hyponatremia, hyperkalemia, and hypoglycemia. The nurse should expect that the initial orders for this client will include
1. administration of oxygen via 100% nonrebreathing mask.

2. starting an IV solution of saline and dextrose.
3. administering potassium chloride.
4. preparing for an emergency tracheostomy.

337. A 29-year-old female is suffering from Cushing's syndrome. She is constantly lashing out at her coworkers and family. Her husband informs the nurse of this behavior. The nurse's best interpretation of this behavior is
   1. mineralocorticoid excess.
   2. glucocorticoid excess.
   3. activity intolerance.
   4. sensory-perceptual alterations.

338. A nurse at a weight loss center assesses a client who has a large abdomen and a rounded face. Which additional assessment finding would lead the nurse to suspect that the client has Cushing's syndrome rather than obesity from imbalance of food intake and body need?
   1. Large thighs and upper arms.
   2. Pendulous abdomen and large hips.
   3. Abdominal striae and ankle enlargement.
   4. Posterior neck fat pad and thin extremities.

339. A client has primary aldosteronism. Which assessment findings would the nurse expect to find initially?
   1. Decreased serum sodium and potassium.
   2. Decreased blood glucose and elevated temperature.
   3. Tachycardia and albuminuria.
   4. Hypertension and decreased serum potassium.

340. A client who is suspected of having a pheochromocytoma complains of sweating, palpitations, and headache. Which assessment is essential for the nurse to make first?
   1. Pupil reaction.
   2. Hand grips.
   3. Blood pressure.
   4. Blood glucose.

341. J. is to have an adrenalectomy. The nurse is performing preoperative teaching. The client asks the nurse "What will I look like and behave like after surgery?" The nurse's best response is,
   1. "Don't worry about that now. You need to concentrate on the surgery."
   2. "You will only have a small incision."
   3. "I know you are worried, maybe we should resume the education session later."
   4. "After surgery you may not respond to any stressors, so we will do our best to help decrease stimuli and help you through it. Your appearance will not change immediately after the surgery."

342. Ms. O. has undergone a bilateral adrenalectomy. Which of the following demonstrates to the nurse the best understanding of long-term care needs?

   1. When I run out of the medication the doctor gave me, I can stop taking the hormones.
   2. I can take the steroid replacement therapy once every three days.
   3. I need to take the steroid replacement therapy every day. I should not alter the dose or stop taking it.
   4. I can take the dose of the medication I feel I need.

343. An adult is admitted to the hospital for removal of a simple goiter. The nurse understands that a simple goiter is caused by
   1. low intake of fat-free foods.
   2. excessive thyroid-stimulating hormone (TSH) stimulation.
   3. excessive adrenocorticotropic hormone (ACTH) stimulation.
   4. low intake of goitrogenic foods.

344. An adult is currently being treated at the clinic for Graves' disease. It is essential for the nurse to assess for which of the following signs immediately?
   1. Goiter.
   2. Tachycardia.
   3. Constipation.
   4. Hypothermia.

345. A 35-year-old female visits her managed care physician for an annual physical examination. Routine laboratory studies reveal thyroxine (T_4) and triiodothyronine (T_3) levels are elevated, whereas the thyroid-stimulating hormone (TSH) level was undetectable. The nurse's understanding of these diagnostic tests is the client is experiencing
   1. hypothyroidism.
   2. addisonian crisis.
   3. hypoparathyroidism.
   4. hyperthyroidism.

346. An adult who is newly diagnosed with Graves' disease asks the nurse "Why do I need to take propranolol (Inderal)?" Based on the nurse's understanding of the medication and Graves' disease, the best response would be,
   1. "The medication will limit thyroid hormone secretion."
   2. "The medication will inhibit synthesis of thyroid hormones."
   3. "The medication will relieve the symptoms of Graves' disease."
   4. "The medication will increase the synthesis of thyroid hormones."

347. The nurse is preparing a room to receive a client immediately post-thyroidectomy. The nurse should be sure that which of the following equipment is available at the bedside?
   1. Nasogastric tray.
   2. Central venous tray set-up.
   3. Tracheostomy tray.

4. Lumbar puncture tray.

348. An adult had a total thyroidectomy. Which statement by the client demonstrates to the nurse an adequate understanding of long-term care?
1. "I will need to take replacement hormones for the rest of my life."
2. "I should try to avoid stress and be alert for signs of recurrent hyperthyroidism."
3. "Thank goodness this is over, I will never have to worry about thyroid problems again!"
4. "I should increase my caloric intake to replace what I lost during the surgery."

349. The nurse is caring for a client who is status postthyroidectomy. The client is exhibiting hyperreflexia, muscle twitching, and spasms. The first action the nurse should perform is to
1. assess for additional signs of tetany.
2. prepare to send a blood sample to the laboratory for a calcium level.
3. place the client in semi-Fowler's position.
4. administer post-op pain medication.

350. An adult who has Grave's disease just received a dose of sodium ^{131}I. Which of the following statements made to the nurse best demonstrates an understanding of immediate care needs?
1. "I should be able to go home after about two hours if I don't have any vomiting."
2. "I have my belongings with me to stay in the isolation room for the next 24 hours."
3. "My daughter is pregnant, so I told her I will not be able to see her for the next month."
4. "I brought my antithyroid drug with me so I will not miss a dose."

351. An adult has had hypoparathyroidism for 20 years. The client has come in to the center for a check-up. The nurse should assess the client for
1. hypothermia.
2. hyperthermia.
3. tetany.
4. hypertension.

352. A 45-year-old newly diagnosed type I diabetic asks the nurse "Why can't I take a pill for my diabetes like my 62-year-old neighbor?" The nurse understands that the primary difference between type I diabetes and type II diabetes is
1. that type I diabetes and type II diabetes can be controlled with injections of antibodies.
2. that type I diabetes is the result of autoimmune destruction of beta cell function in the pancreas, whereas type II diabetes is the result of the lack of responsiveness of beta cells to insulin.
3. that type I diabetes insulin production is a circadian function, whereas in type II diabetes, insulin production depends on serum glucose levels.

4. that type I diabetes has a complication known as hyperglycemic hyperosmolar nonketosis, whereas type II diabetes has a complication known as diabetic ketoacidosis.

353. The nurse administers the client's morning dose of regular insulin at 7:30 A.M. The nurse should anticipate to observe the client for a hypoglycemic reaction at which of the following times?
1. Immediately.
2. 10:00 A.M.
3. 1:00 P.M.
4. 7:30 P.M.

354. The nurse is planning an education session for a newly diagnosed diabetic. Which concept is essential to include when developing the plan of care?
1. All diabetic teaching needs to be accomplished within 20 hours before discharge.
2. Insulin injection sites should be cleaned with iodine prior to injection.
3. Snacks should be ingested prior to physical exercise.
4. Urine sugar levels should be checked prior to insulin administration.

355. The nurse is attending a bridal shower for a friend when another guest starts to tremble and complains of dizziness. The nurse notices a medical alert bracelet for diabetes. The best action for the nurse to take is to
1. encourage the guest to eat some baked ziti.
2. call the guest's personal physician.
3. offer the guest a peppermint.
4. give the guest a glass of orange juice.

356. Ms. F. usually administers her NPH insulin at 6:00 A.M. but she plans to attend a banquet and fashion show next week, at which lunch will be served at 2:00 P.M. rather than noon when she usually eats lunch. Which of the following statements by Ms. F. demonstrates to the nurse an understanding of peak action of NPH and risk for hypoglycemia?
1. "I will administer the insulin at my regular time, it is important to adhere to my schedule."
2. "I will take the insulin at 8:00 A.M. that day, as the insulin peaks in 6–12 hours."
3. "I will not take any insulin until they serve the lunch at the banquet."
4. "I will take the insulin at 10:00 A.M. that day as the peak action of NPH is four hours after administered."

357. Mr. T. is hospitalized for an infected foot ulcer. At 11:00 A.M. his blood glucose is 460 mg/dl and he has been up to the bathroom seven times this morning to urinate. The best action for the nurse to take is to
1. administer regular insulin according to the physician's sliding scale order.

2. administer NPH insulin according to the physician's sliding scale order.
3. notify the physician.
4. make sure Mr. T.'s urinal is close to the bed so he does not have to keep getting up.

358. A 35-year-old diabetic is displaying signs of irritability and irrational behavior during an office visit. The nurse observes visible tremors in the client's hands. Based on the client's history and the nurse's understanding of diabetes mellitus, the nurse interprets these findings to be signs of
1. hyperglycemia.
2. diabetic ketoacidosis (DKA).
3. hyperglycemic hyperosmolar nonketosis (HHNK).
4. hypoglycemia.

359. Which statement by a woman newly diagnosed with NIDDM demonstrates to the nurse an adequate understanding of dietary needs?
1. "I need to stick to the meal plan the dietician explained to me."
2. "I usually have two to three drinks with dinner and I understand its okay to continue doing this."
3. "I should only buy foods that are labeled 'dietetic' from now on."
4. "It is okay to skip lunch on my shopping days as I never have time to eat."

360. The client came to the diabetic clinic for follow-up teaching on the complications of diabetes. The nurse explains that neuropathy is the result of
1. microangiopathies or metabolic defects that cause by-products to accumulate in the nerve tissues.
2. microvascular damage to the retina.
3. macroangiopathy in the extremities.
4. end-stage renal disease.

361. The nurse is teaching a type II, noninsulin-dependent diabetic about the acute metabolic complications. The primary reason a type II diabetic does not usually develop diabetic ketoacidosis is
1. that there is no insulin available for the state of hyperglycemia.
2. that the type II diabetic has no protein or fat reserves.
3. that there is sufficient insulin to prevent the breakdown of protein and fatty acid for metabolic needs.
4. that there is insufficient serum glucose concentrations.

362. Mrs. D. is the primary caretaker for Mr. D. who was recently started on an oral hypoglycemic agent. Mrs. D. should know to watch for which of the following symptoms of hypoglycemia?
1. High blood sugar readings (greater than 250 mg/dl).
2. Presence of ketones in the urine.

3. Significant increase in urine output.
4. Cold sweats, weakness, and trembling.

363. Which of the following statements by Mr. E., who has diabetes mellitus, shows the nurse that he has an adequate understanding of special foot care needs?
1. "I am looking forward to the summer when I can go barefoot in my house and at the beach."
2. "I like to use a heating pad at night as I always have cold feet."
3. "I used to take a shower every other night but now I am going to wash and examine my feet every night."
4. "I have a corn on my left foot, so I am going to go to the pharmacy to get something for it right away."

364. Ms. F. took her usual NPH insulin dose at 6:00 A.M., her lunch is delayed until 1:00 P.M., and she begins to feel weak. Which of the following actions demonstrates to the nurse an adequate understanding?
1. Ms. F. administers an extra four units of regular insulin.
2. Ms. F. administers an additional four units of NPH insulin.
3. Ms. F. goes and takes a nap.
4. Ms. F. drinks a cup of milk and then eats her lunch.

365. The nurse is teaching a client about diabetic management. The client asks the nurse "What is a hemoglobin A1c test?" The most appropriate answer for the nurse to give is,
1. "The hemoglobin A1c is a blood test that evaluates glycemic control over a three-month time period by measuring the glucose attached to hemoglobin."
2. "The hemoglobin A1c is a blood test that measures the glucose attached to hemo-globin molecule over the last seven days."
3. "The hemoglobin A1c test is a blood test that measures protein to evaluate glucose control over the last seven days."
4. "The hemoglobin A1c test is a urine test that measures protein to evaluate glucose control over the last few months."

366. The nurse is to perform a scratch test for allergy. Which statement best describes this procedure?
1. The antigen is directly applied to the skin and covered with a gauze dressing.
2. The allergen is applied superficially to a small cut of the outer layer of skin.
3. A small amount of allergen is injected into the intradermal layer of skin.
4. Suspected food allergy items are scratched from the diet, one at a time, until all allergy symptoms are no longer present.

367. Mr. B. has undergone a skin graft from his left buttock to his right upper thigh. When caring for Mr. B.'s recipient site, the nurse can expect to

1. apply silver sulfadiazine to promote rapid healing.
2. assess for bleeding and large amounts of fluid accumulation beneath the graft.
3. encourage Mr. B. to ambulate and do leg lifts on return from the OR.
4. encourage Mr. B. to take frequent soaking baths to relieve his soreness and discomfort.

368. A client with a skin graft has undergone a full-thickness skin graft from her right upper thigh to her upper chest area. The most appropriate nursing action in caring for her *donor* site is to
1. keep the fine mesh gauze dressing on her chest soaked with normal saline.
2. completely immobilize her right upper thigh area.
3. maintain the compression bandage on her right upper thigh for several days.
4. remove the nylon fabric adhered to the donor site no later than two to three days after grafting has taken place.

369. A patient has undergone a skin graft. Which finding most likely indicates that complications with the recipient site may exist?
1. Small amounts of blood beneath the graft.
2. Small amounts of serum beneath the graft.
3. A meshed pattern in the graft.
4. Continuous bleeding beneath the graft.

370. Mrs. P., a 42-year-old homemaker, has been diagnosed with atopic dermatitis. She has severe pruritis. Which interventions are most appropriate to include in Mrs. P.'s plan of care?
1. Soak in a hot water bath at least once a day for 15–20 minutes.
2. Avoid use of air conditioning when possible.
3. When symptoms are worse, decrease bathing.
4. Use superfatted soaps or soap for sensitive skin.

371. The nurse is developing a teaching plan for a patient with psoriasis. What information would the nurse need to know when developing the teaching plan?
1. It is a chronic disorder resulting in the development of blisters; an autoimmune disorder caused by circulating IgG antibodies. Management includes steroids and immunosuppressives. Nursing management focuses on self-concept and pain management.
2. It is a superficial inflammatory dermatitis occurring when two skin surfaces rub together, causing erythema, maceration, itching, and burning. Management includes liberal application of talc, or cellulose-containing powder, or corticosteroids.
3. It is a chronic recurrent, erythematous, inflammatory disorder involving keratin synthesis. Severe scaling and itching occurs. Management includes sunlight, tar preparation, and use of anthralin. Nursing management includes teaching patients about UV light therapy, and assisting with altered self-concept.
4. It is an area of very dry skin. Sometimes shallow ulcers occur. Itching, brown stained skin may occur. Management includes elevation of affected extremity, lotion, and support hose.

372. The nurse has been giving instructions to Mrs. S., a 35-year-old white female, about preventing skin cancer. Which statement best indicates Mrs. S.'s understanding of skin cancer risk factors?
1. "I guess because I am dark complected I will be more prone to developing skin cancer."
2. "I used to lay in the sun all the time—now I just go to the tanning bed."
3. "My father was treated for melanoma, but my mom says not to worry."
4. "I really need to use sunscreen—even in winter."

373. A 60-year-old farmer presents with a diagnosis of basal cell epithelioma. The lesion would most likely be described as
1. dome shaped, shiny, with a well defined border.
2. poorly marginated, flat red area.
3. red, dark blue or purple macules.
4. erythema, edema, and blisters.

374. While providing a nursing history, a client with suspected malignant melanoma will most often relate which of the following?
1. A history of intense sunlight exposure.
2. Complaints of frequently occurring irregularly shaped, flat macules with overlying hard scale.
3. Consistent use of sunscreen agents.
4. Complaints of several lesions with a raised border and flattened center.

375. Mrs. K., a 37-year-old school teacher presents with the following symptoms: clusters of vesicles on her right flank, constant pain, burning, itching, and discomfort in her flank area. She ranks her pain as a 5, with 5 being most severe. Which of the following diagnoses would be a priority when developing a plan of care for Mrs. K.?
1. Pain, related to herpes simplex.
2. Pain, related to herpes zoster.
3. Pain, related to herpetic whitlow.
4. Pain, related to staphylococcal cellulitis.

376. When planning care for a client with herpes zoster, the nurse should include
1. teaching the client to avoid sexual contact during outbreaks.

2. administering analgesics and evaluating the efficacy.
3. informing the client that people who have not had chickenpox will not develop them from exposure to the client.
4. Scheduling several diagnostic tests to confirm the presence of herpes zoster.

377. Which client statement best indicates the client understands how herpes simplex is transmitted?
1. "It is okay to share towels as long as it is a family member."
2. "I really don't need to use a condom, unless I have a sore."
3. "Once I'm over this spell, I won't need to worry about it again."
4. "I shouldn't have sex if some of those sores are around."

378. Mr. B., a 78-year-old man, is admitted with severe flame burns resulting from smoking in bed. The nurse can expect his room environment to include
1. strict isolation techniques and policies.
2. a semi-private room.
3. liberal unrestricted visiting.
4. equipment shared between Mr. B. and the other burn patient in the unit.

379. Mr. L., a 23-year-old factory worker, was burned severely in an industrial accident. He has second degree burns on his right leg and arm and on his back. He has third degree burns on his left arm. The triage nurse, using the rule of nines, estimates the extent of Mr. L.'s burns as:
1. 18%
2. 36%
3. 45%
4. 54%

380. Mrs. C. was burned in a house fire 16 hours ago. She suffered second and third degree burns over 65% of her body. She is receiving lactated Ringer's at 200 ml/h. Which intervention is a *priority* at this time?
1. Monitoring hourly urine output.
2. Assessing for signs and symptoms of infection.
3. Performing range of motion q 1–2 h.
4. Meeting the high caloric needs of the patient.

381. A nurse is providing care for a severely burned patient during the shock phase of the burn injury. Which assessment findings would indicate that the patient is receiving adequate fluid volume replacement?
1. Urine output 20 ml/h, CVP 3, weak pulses, K+ level of 5.3.

2. Urine output 50 ml/h, BP 100/60, oriented to person and place.
3. Weak thready pulses, BP 70/40, pulse 130, Hct 52%.
4. Restlessness, confusion, urine output 15 ml/h, rapidly increasing weight.

382. A client with severe burns is receiving IV Zantac. Which statement best explains the reason for administration of this medication in this situation?
1. The client was treated for gastritis several years ago.
2. The medication will reduce hypoxemia in burn clients.
3. The medication is an H₂ receptor antagonist and will decrease acid secretion.
4. The medication will aid in removal of pulmonary secretions.

383. Miss P., 18-years-old, was burned six weeks ago. She is now ready for discharge. Select the statement best reflecting Miss P.'s and her family's understanding of her discharge care.
1. "I will be so glad to get home so that I don't have to wear this pressure thing anymore."
2. "I will need to call my doctor if my temperature goes up or this burn area starts draining and oozing."
3. "I really need to stick to that low calorie, low protein diet at home like I have been here."
4. "To prevent that area of new skin from feeling so tight, I can rub ice and baby oil on it."

384. A patient has suffered a chemical burn. The best initial action is to
1. roll the patient in a blanket.
2. secure lead-lined gloves and move the patient away from the chemical.
3. flush the area with copious amounts of water or normal saline.
4. if the chemical is an acid, neutralize with a base.

385. Mr. B., a 25-year-old electrical worker, has come in contact with a live power line. He is unconscious and is lying across the power line. The best initial action is to
1. move Mr. B. away from the power line using a wooden pole.
2. cover Mr. B. with a blanket.
3. grab Mr. B. and pull him away from the power lines.
4. flush Mr. B. with copious amounts of water.

Adult Health

ANSWER	RATIONALE	NP	CN	CL
#1. 1.	**The sympathetic nervous system during moderate anxiety will increase the pulse and respirations.**	As	Ph/10	Co
2.	If there is any decreased physiologic functioning, it is from the parasympathetic nervous system and not the sympathetic.			
3.	Both a rigid posture and either fixed or scattered perceptual focus indicate severe anxiety or panic, not moderate stress.			
4.	The increased awareness and attending as well as the ability to focus on most of what is really happening is a sign of mild anxiety. Learning can take place during mild anxiety.			
#2. 4.	**Passive artificial immunity occurs when antibodies are produced by another person or animal and injected into the recipient.**	An	He/4	Kn
1.	Active natural immunity refers to when the body produces antibodies in response to an active infection.			
2.	Active artificial immunity is developed when antigen, either vaccine or toxoids, are administered to stimulate antibody response.			
3.	Passive natural immunity occurs when antibodies are transferred from an immune mother to a baby through the placenta or colostrum.			
#3. 3.	**Antibodies or immunoglobulins are produced by the B-cells and are part of the body's plasma proteins.**	An	He/4	Kn
1.	Cell-mediated defense or cellular immunity occurs through the T-cell system.			
2.	Antibody-mediated defense or humoral or circulating immunity is mediated by antibodies produced by the B-cells.			
4.	Cell-mediated defenses or cellular immunity is lost with HIV infection and thus the client becomes increasingly defenseless against infections.			
#4. 2.	**Plain gelatins can be given on a clear liquid diet, as well as tea, coffee, ginger ale, or 7-Up.**	Im	Ph/7	Co
1.	Milk is not permitted on a clear liquid diet, but is allowed on a full liquid diet.			
3.	The only fruit juices allowed on a clear liquid diet are those that are strained and clear (able to be seen through).			
4.	Ice cream is allowed with a full liquid diet, not a clear liquid diet.			
#5. 3.	**The pyramid helps to guide the client in choosing a variety of foods to obtain the nutrients he needs. It also aids in eating more of some groups (bread, cereal, rice, and pasta) and less of others (fats, oils, and sweets).**	Pl	Ph/7	Co
1.	Each person differs in nutritional needs according to age, activity level, size, and other factors. Therefore the pyramid serves as a guide.			
2.	The food pyramid does not indicate caloric count. It can serve to guide eating patterns.			
4.	The pyramid replaces the old basic four, by dividing food into six groups: bread, cereal, rice, and pasta; fruit; vegetables; milk, yogurt, and cheese; meat, poultry, fish, dry beans, eggs, and nuts; and fats, oils, and sweets. It also indicates to eat more of some foods and less of others.			
#6. 1.	**The GI tract should be assessed before each feeding to ensure functioning and minimal problems.**	As	Ph/9	Ap
2.	An altered neurologic status can be the reason for tube feedings, the gag reflex need not be present as the tube provides the conduit although it can be a significant risk factor for aspiration.			

3. The gastric residue can be checked to evaluate gastric emptying. If there is more than 100 ml, then the feeding is often held and the physician contacted.
4. The formula is administered at room temperature to avoid cramping, which can occur if the formula is cold.

#7. 1. A negative nitrogen balance indicates that protein catabolism exceeds protein anabolism. A positive nitrogen balance indicates intake exceeds output.   As   Ph/7   Co
2. Koilonychia indicates iron deficiency, not protein deficiency.
3. Magenta tongue indicates riboflavin (vitamin B_2) deficiency.
4. Although bleeding gums can be caused by several different agents, the most common nutritional cause is vitamin deficiency, not protein deficiency.

#8. 1. A low residue diet includes rice, lean meats, and eggs.   Ev   Ph/7   Ap
2. Lean meats are acceptable on a low residue diet, but bacon is not lean.
3. Vegetables are not generally low residue.
4. Rice rather than pasta with a sauce would be a better choice.

#9. 4. Clients receiving TPN can experience electrolyte imbalances, hypo- or hyperglycemia, as well as difficulties with fluid balance.   As   Ph/8   Ap
1. TPN is given through a central IV line, usually the subclavian or internal jugular vein.
2. TPN is given through a central line. It is not given through an NG tube into the stomach.
3. TPC can be given to rest the bowel and does not require elimination through the GI tract.

#10. 3. TPN can provide a greater concentration of calories than PPN. Therefore, TPN is given to those with fluid restrictions.   An   Ph/8   Co
1. TPN is usually reserved for long-term care, whereas PPN is given to those with short-term needs.
2. TPN can provide a greater number of calories, whereas PPN can only support approximately 3000 calories per day.
4. PPN can supplement oral feedings, whereas TPN is usually reserved for those clients who are NPO.

#11. 1. The IV site must be kept aseptic. It is a central line and the TPN with its high concentration of glucose provides an ideal medium for pathogens.   Im   Ph/8   Ap
2. TPN solutions are usually formulated by a pharmacy and are given using sterile technique similar to an IV. NG or gastric tubes often use pouches to infuse the feeding.
3. Tube feedings, not TPN are only hung for a limited period of time. TPN is often given around the clock.
4. TPN is replaced like IV solution. The nurse does not add more solution to that which is already infusing.

#12. 3. TB is spread through residue of evaporated droplets and may remain in the air for long periods of time. Thus care should be given when coughing or sneezing.   Pl   Sa/2   Co
1. Gloves will not prevent the spread of TB, as it is spread through droplet nuclei.
2. Ventilation is extremely important. TB is most often transmitted in poorly ventilated or closed rooms.
4. In developing countries, milk must be boiled to prevent transmission of TB, but that is not necessary in the United States. Boiling milk will not prevent transmission from the client to another family member.

#13. 3. Bulk blood and other secretions like suctioned fluids are carefully poured down a drain connected to a sanitary sewer.   Ev   Sa/2   Ap
1. Gloves are not needed for all client contact, only when handling items or surfaces soiled with blood or body fluids, or invasive procedures.
2. Blood spills are cleaned with a chemical germicide or diluted bleach in a 1:10 solution with water.

ANSWER	RATIONALE	NP	CN	CL

4.   Blood and other body fluid samples are transported in a container with a lid to avoid possible leakage.

#14. 4.   **Tinnitus is a classic sign of aspirin overdosages, either from too much ingestion or limited excretion.**   An   Ph/8   An

1.   Tinnitus or ringing in the ears is a sign of an overdosage and the aspirin should be stopped to allow the tinnitus to clear.

2.   Although the client has an overdosage, it does not mean that he took too much medicine. A build-up can occur, especially among those with limited liver or kidney function.

3.   Although aspirin can cause GI irritation and bleeding, tinnitus or ringing in the ears is a sign of aspirin overdosage.

#15. 3.   **NSAIDs often cause nausea or vomiting. This can be alleviated by taking the medicine with food, milk, or antacids.**   As   Ph/8   An

1.   NSAIDs do not cause sedation. They can relieve pain to allow for sleep, but the client should be arousable.

2.   These are signs of upper GI bleeding. NSAIDs can increase bleeding time and provoke ulcers.

4.   NSAIDs should decrease or relieve pain. If the pain continues, then the medication needs to be evaluated for dosage, timing, or augmentation.

#16. 1.   **A decreasing level of alertness can signal early respiratory depression and a significant drop in the respiratory rate is a warning sign. Both should be taken prior to giving the medication for baseline purposes.**   As   Ph/8   Ap

2.   The last meal is important for surgery, but narcotic analgesics can be given after eating or drinking as long as care is given to avoid vomiting and aspiration.

3.   Although constipation is a common side-effect of narcotics, it should not prohibit the administration of the drug.

4.   A history of addictions does not preclude a client from receiving the analgesic.

#17. 2.   **PCA allows the client to administer more analgesic before the pain becomes severe, thus allowing better pain control.**   Ev   Ph/8   Ap

1.   The machine will only give the analgesic after a preset time has elapsed. This is designed to prevent overdosing. The client can see this by the ready light on the machine and the beep that accompanies the delivery of the medicine.

3.   The client should press the button only when experiencing pain. This is not necessarily every hour.

4.   The client may experience pain, although using the PCA pump correctly. If this happens, she should notify the nurse immediately.

#18. 2.   **This is the best way to assess fluid balance, especially acute changes in those with large losses or acutely ill.**   As   Ph/10   Ap

1.   Although inputs and outputs are important, they do not take into account other losses (especially through the wound) which can be significant.

3.   Skin turgor can assist in assessing fluid balance, but daily weights can provide a better measure for the burn victim.

4.   Edema informs the nurse about fluid in the interstitial spaces, but would not reflect the vascular component.

#19. 4.   **Neurologic changes can occur from hyponatremia. They include confusion, disorientation, lethargy, seizures, and coma.**   Pl   Ph/10   Ap

1.   Although water loss is important, Mr. H. has hyponatremia. A better action would be to have him drink fluids that are rich in sodium, so as not to increase the hyponatremia through excess water.

2.   These are signs of hypernatremia. This client has hyponatremia and should be observed for signs indicating his situation has worsened from too little sodium.

3.   Hypochloremia, not hyperchloremia, often occurs with

hyponatremia. For Mr. H., the thiazide diuretics has probably caused the sodium to be proportionally lower than the chloride.

		NP	CN	CL
#20. 3.	**Hypokalemia enhances digitalis toxicity, and must be observed for carefully.**	Pl	Ph/8	An
1.	The client has hypokalemia, not hyperkalemia, and needs to be observed for problems related to too little potassium.			
2.	Ms. H.'s problem is hypokalemia, too little potassium. She needs to increase the amount in her diet, not limit it.			
4.	These signs indicate hypocalcemia or hypomagnesemia. This client has hypokalemia.			
#21. 1.	**Potassium is normally 3.5–5.5 mEq/L. Clients with renal failure are prone to hyperkalemia.**	An	Ph/10	An
2.	Mr. D.'s sodium is normal, generally 135–145 mEq/L.			
3.	The client's problem is not with calcium, which is the normal range of 4.5–5.5 mEq/L, rather with the potassium.			
4.	Normal chloride levels are generally 95–105 mEq/L.			
#22. 1.	**The client's calcium is low. The normal values are 4.5–5.5 mEq/L. Hypocalcemia is common among those with bone cancer.**	An	Ph/10	An
2.	Mr. C.'s calcium is low, 4.0 mEq/L, not high as it would be with hypercalcemia (above 5.5 mEq/L).			
3.	The client's problem is with calcium, which has the normal range of 4.5–5.5 mEq/L, not potassium.			
4.	The chloride levels are normal, generally 95–105 mEq/L. The problem is with calcium.			
#23. 1.	**The client is in respiratory alkalosis, and needs to increase the carbon dioxide. The easiest way to do this is to try and calm the client and/or have him breathe in and out of a paper bag, thus inhaling the exhaled carbon dioxide.**	Im	Ph/10	An
2.	Fluid loss, especially vomiting and diarrhea will often result in metabolic alkalosis. This client's problem is respiratory alkalosis and would not be corrected through fluid administration.			
3.	The problem is not too little oxygen as much as it is too much exhalation of carbon dioxide.			
4.	There is not too little bicarbonate (which occurs with metabolic acidosis), rather too little carbonic acid.			
#24. 4.	**Hypokalemia and hypocalcemia are both common with metabolic alkalosis as a result of cellular buffering.**	Pl	Ph/10	An
1.	The fluids, although needed, should be given IV rather than by mouth, especially with vomiting.			
2.	Bicarbonate of sodium would cause further metabolic alkalosis and should be avoided.			
3.	Sodium bicarbonate added to the metabolic alkalosis and would worsen the situation.			
#25. 1.	**A low pH indicates acidosis, whereas the high $PaCO_2$ indicates the problem is respiratory rather than metabolic.**	An	Ph/10	An
2.	The pH is below 7.35, which indicates acidosis. If the pH is above 7.45 then it is alkalosis.			
3.	Although the pH indicates acidosis, the $PaCO_2$ is above 45. If the problem had been metabolic, then the $PaCO_2$ would be normal or low, and the bicarbonate would be low.			
4.	The problem is neither acidosis (low pH) nor metabolic (an alteration of HCO_3).			
#26. 4.	**The client is in metabolic acidosis and the body will try to compensate through the respiratory system, although it cannot completely correct the problem.**	Pl	Ph/10	An
1.	Trousseau's sign is often seen in respiratory alkalosis. This client is in metabolic acidosis.			
2.	Metabolic acidosis often results in hyperkalemia and can be lethal if not treated.			

3. A diabetic with an infection often requires additional insulin. Insulin also serves as an important component when trying to correct hyperkalemia, which is a common occurrence with metabolic acidosis.

#27. **4. Although blood return indicates the catheter is in a vein, it should not be in the tubing. The nurse should find the reason and attempt to correct it.**   Ev   Ph/8   An

1. Coolness, blanching, and swelling at the needle site suggest infiltration, a complication that must require the removal of the IV.
2. Phlebitis, inflammation of the vein, is a problem that requires the removal of the IV. Signs and symptoms often include redness, warmth, and pain.
3. Air in the tubing can lead to emboli and should be prevented. Asking the client to notify the nurse before the bag is empty can help.

#28. **4. All of these are potential problems for those with a central line, which the nurse needs to be observant for.**   Im   Ph/8   Ap

1. The condition the client has that necessitated the central venous line might require frequent blood analysis, but the fact that he has a central line does not necessarily indicate this need.
2. An X-ray is done after placing the central line to ensure proper placement, but unless there are complications, serial films are not necessary.
3. Central venous lines need not always be connected to an infusion. They may be accessed sporadically for blood drawing or chemotherapy as well as other conditions.

#29. **2. The first 5 ml are drawn off and discarded. Lab values can be altered by the solution remaining in the catheter from the infusion or flush.**   Im   Ph/8   Ap

1. Medical asepsis is needed, not surgical asepsis or sterile technique.
3. Flushing the catheter is done last after the blood is drawn. Depending on institutional policy, normal saline or heparin is used.
4. If the client is not receiving an infusion through the catheter, the nurse can draw the blood through the cap with a needle or exchange it for a needleless system depending on institutional policy.

#30. **3. The roller clamp should be closed after priming, otherwise the fluid will continue to flow. Open the roller clamp after inserting the tubing into the hub.**   Im   Ph/8   Ap

1. If the solution is contaminated, the new tubing is contaminated. Therefore, when changing the tubing, change the bottle with the solution as well.
2. There should be fluid in the tubing before running into the hub. Otherwise, the air in the line will enter the vein causing an embolus.
4. Irrigating the tubing can push a blood clot into the circulation. If the IV is running sluggishly, call a physician to remove and restart the IV.

#31. **3. The airway is provided by the endotracheal tube. The nurse should assess breathing, the next step in the ABCs.**   Im   Ph/10   Ap

1. This step is done after ensuring the ABCs of airway, breathing, and circulation.
2. Although needed, an IV comes after checking the ABCs of airway, breathing, and circulation.
4. The neurologic status is important, especially with a potential spinal injury and shock, but ABC is first.

#32. **1. The Trendelenburg position increases the blood return from the legs, thereby raising the blood pressure.**   Ev   Ph/10   An

2. The client is hypovolemic, and the position change would allow greater return, thus lowering the pulse rate if successful.
3. The respiratory rate would decrease if the position change helps in preventing/reversing shock.
4. The Trendelenburg position raises the legs above the heart, thereby decreasing the capillary refill time in the toes.

ANSWER	RATIONALE	NP	CN	CL

#33. **1.** **The epinephrine would help to ease the client's respiratory distress.** ... Ev ... Ph/8 ... An

2. In shock, the blood pressure decreases. A further decrease indicates that the adrenaline is not working effectively.
3. Continued or increasing angioedema would indicate that the epinephrine has not corrected the reaction.
4. A decreased level of consciousness would indicate that shock is becoming worse, not better.

#34. **1.** **Her vital signs indicate that she is probably going into shock. Fluids are the first action to do after assessing ABCs.** ... Im ... Ph/10 ... Ap

2. A foley catheter will probably be placed early in the resuscitation to monitor urinary output and perfusion, but it does not supersede fluids.
3. An ECG will in all likelihood be done shortly after initial stabilization, but it would not be done before starting an IV line, especially given her vital signs.
4. Assessment of neurologic status should be done soon, but the client's vital signs indicate shock is likely and an IV line needs to be started immediately.

#35. **2.** **Airway is the first step of ABCs.** ... As ... Ph/10 ... Ap

1. Although important, the nurse will always think of ABCs first. Check the airway, breathing, and circulation.
3. Vital signs are important and should be taken soon after arrival, but the first steps are always ABCs.
4. A history of what happened is important, but the client should always be evaluated prior to obtaining information.

#36. **1.** **Assisting the older adult in reminiscing, or engaging in a "life review" process, is one way to assist the individual to accomplish his/her developmental tasks. One such task, adjusting to decreasing physical strength, needs to be met to establish and preserve ego integrity.** ... Pl ... He/3 ... Ap

2. For him to complete the developmental task of adjusting to decreased physical strength, which needs to be met to establish and preserve ego integrity vs despair, he needs to be able to express his feelings and concerns. Instead of attempting to help the person not to be so "morbid," the nurse must understand that each stage of life has specific developmental tasks to achieve and it is normal for the older adult to talk about the physiologic changes that occur with aging.
3. When an older person is talking about things of the past that no longer exist, it is part of the developmental tasks appropriate for this age group. In this case, instead of hampering with the achievement of the developmental task of adjusting to his decreasing physical strength, the nurse should be facilitating it. Unresolved losses can otherwise lead to despair.
4. Although humor is an effective way to release tension, it can be inappropriate if the individual does not respond positively to it. What can be meant as a lighthearted, playful interaction could be interpreted as denial of the painful, real losses experienced by the older adult. It is normal for the older adult to talk about the physiologic changes that occur with aging. The nurse must understand that in each stage of life there are specific developmental tasks to achieve. If humor prevents dealing with the developmental task of adjusting to physiologic changes, it would not be appropriate.

#37. **2.** **Many psychosocial symptoms occur with depression, including feelings of hopelessness, helplessness, and increased anxiety, which contributes to despair rather than ego integrity.** ... As ... Ps/5 ... An

1. Many psychosocial symptoms occur with depression. Rather than an increased energy level, common symptoms include the feelings of malaise, fatigue, and lack of interest which contributes to despair rather than ego integrity.

ANSWER	RATIONALE	NP	CN	CL

3. Rather than increased autonomy and independence, elders with depression frequently have feelings of increased dependence on others. Feeling a burden to others affects the elder's self-esteem, which can lead to an increased level of despair.

4. Rather than increase their socialization, people with depression tend to withdraw from those people and interests they have enjoyed in the past, which contributes significantly to their level of despair.

#38. 3. A modest increase in systolic blood pressure, not diastolic blood pressure, is an expected age-related change due to an increase in vascular resistance and vessel rigidity. An increase in diastolic blood pressure, however, is not an expected age-related change. It is pathologic and needs to be monitored.   An   He/3   An

1. An increase in residual lung volume is a normal age-related change.

2. Decreased sphincter control resulting in increased frequency, urgency, and nocturia is an expected age-related change.

4. Normally, in the aging process, sensory receptors are decreased and the ability to respond to heat and cold and to feel light touch is decreased. Cutaneous pain sensitivity also declines.

#39. 3. The decrease in vaginal secretions, which contributes to vaginal dryness and subsequent painful intercourse, is a normal age-related change. Using a lubricant will decrease or eliminate this discomfort.   Pl   He/3   Ap

1. Vaginal dryness is a normal age-related change and is not related to medications.

2. The problem of vaginal dryness, which is a normal age-related change, can and should be dealt with directly. Although alternative methods of intimacy can be explored, there is no reason that sexual intercourse, without discomfort, cannot be achieved.

4. Vaginal dryness is a normal age-related change that is not pathologic.

#40. 2. Polypharmacy is the prescription, use, or administration of five or more medications. If not coordinated, different physicians, each focusing on a specific disease process, contribute to polypharmacy. The background data indicate such may be the case.   An   Ph/8   An

1. Although food and medication ingestion often require specific timing, and if it is off, can contribute to such a symptom, it is more likely, from the data given, that the cause is due to multiple drug interactions.

3. Although this explanation cannot be ruled out, from the data presented, it is more likely that the cause is due to multiple drug interactions. Further assessment data would need to be obtained to rule out psychosomatic variables.

4. Although it is necessary to further assess Mr. Z.'s adherence to his medication regime, there are no data presented to suggest this. On the other hand, there are data that support multiple drug interactions, which is likely to contribute to his nausea.

#41. 2. Medications, crushed and mixed with soft foods, are easier to digest for persons who have difficulty swallowing.   Pl   He/3   Ap

1. For clients with dysphagia, meat is difficult to ingest. Furthermore, this could be dangerous, as the client could aspirate the food when unknowingly trying to swallow the medicine.

3. This is not the best strategy for administering medications. It is uncomfortable to have to have several injections throughout the day, which would be necessary since the medications could not be mixed as one injection. It is not a realistic long-term solution.

4. Medications dissolved in liquid are not always fully ingested and absorbed, thus precipitating underdosage.

#42. 3. Keep communications simple and concrete. Close-ended questions are more beneficial than open-ended questions, which may require complex answers that serve only to confuse the   Pl   Ps/5   Ap

client. Even if the client isn't able to fully comprehend communications, a calm tone of voice may alleviate any stress.

1. Consistency and stability needs to be maintained to identify expectations in behaviors and prevent sensory overload.
2. Environmental stimuli may be decreased but not totally eliminated. Mental stimulation should be provided. Tasks and activities should be consistent and stable to prevent the client from becoming too frustrated.
4. Such activities should generally be scheduled earlier in the day when the client is more rested. A phenomenon called the "sundown syndrome" is applied to a client who experiences agitation and restlessness that occurs late in the day. It is apparent that there is an increased sensitivity to stress at this time of day. Therefore activities that are demanding should be scheduled earlier.

#43. 4. In the late stages of Alzheimer's disease, it is better to go along with the client's reality rather than confront him with logic and reasoning. Asking close-ended, simple questions that relate to his reality is nonthreatening and calming. Note that the nurse responds in a way that is congruent with his main concern, which is his sore back.   Im   Ps/5   Ap

1. In the late stages of Alzheimer's disease, reasoning or logic is ineffective. Confrontation is inappropriate. It is better to go along with the client's reality and attempt to change behaviors that are disturbing rather than cognitive perception.
2. Even though it is better to go along with the client's reality in the late stages of Alzheimer's disease, asking open-ended questions that require complex answers serves only to confuse the client further. In addition, the word "precipitate" may not be understood by the client. Words used to communicate should be simple and concrete.
3. Although reality orientation may be appropriate in the earlier stages of Alzheimer's disease, when the disease has progressed, it is best to go along with the client's reality.

#44. 2. This statement is a cause for concern. Victims of abuse may alternate between generations. Abusive patterns are highly likely to be passed from parents to children. When children grow up and move into positions where they are caring for their aged parents (role reversal), the abusive behavior can surface.   Ev   Ps/6   An

1. The nurse has no reason for concern. The acceptance of outside intervention and support services is a healthy response.
3. The nurse should not be overly concerned. Although there is a risk for abuse whenever an elder is dependent on another for care, the son is realistically requesting information to help him to deal with his concerns. The nurse's role is to provide teaching and counseling.
4. The nurse has no reason to be concerned. The son is realistically seeking respite care to assist him in his father's care.

#45. 1. Direct questioning, in an open and accepting manner, is important. Abused elders are often reluctant to report abuse and will not volunteer the information on their own. Clients need to feel free to indicate the existence of an activity about which they may feel embarrassment and shame.   As   Ps/6   Ap

2. Although disclosure of such intimate information is, in part, dependent on the development of a trusting relationship between the client and nurse, the nurse should not wait for the client to be the first one to approach the topic. Valuable time is lost and the client, who is often reluctant to report the abuse, may not do so. Direct questioning by the nurse is the best approach.
3. It is unwise to confront the suspected abuser without attempting to verify the abuse with the client first. In this case, the client is alert and oriented and direct questioning is the best approach.

ANSWER	RATIONALE	NP	CN	CL

4. The best approach would be to question the client, herself, directly. A family assessment can and should be done following the client assessment.

#46. 3. Obesity and diabetes are major risk factors with the potential for complications related to anesthesia.   As   Ph/9   An
1. This is a normal height and weight, not a risk factor.
2. This is a normal fear that is commonly associated with surgery and anesthsia.
4. This is a normal fear that is commonly associated with surgery and anesthsia.

#47. 2. Instructions should be given to the patient regarding limitations of oral intake to avoid nausea and vomiting from the anesthesia.   Pl   Ph/9   Ap
1. The patient must be accompanied home by a responsible adult who can provide adequate homecare in the immediate post-op period.
3. Laboratory studies are usually done pre- and post-op.
4. Medications need to be evaluated on an individual basis, patients who have IDDM will still need to take some insulin the morning of the procedure.

#48. 1. No patient should be administered the pre-op medication until the informed consent has been obtained. Informed consent means that the patient understands the information about the surgery. Even if the consent form is signed, the nurse should withhold sedating medication. This client clearly does not understand the planned procedure.   Im   Sa/1   Ap
2. The medication cannot be administered because the patient obviously does not have an understanding of the procedure.
3. The consent is important, but the more important action is for the nurse not to administer the medication because the patient does not have an adequate understanding of the procedure.
4. The patient may be sent to the OR without the medication if there is not a signed consent, but the next action of the nurse before sending the patient down would be to inform the physician of the patient's lack of understanding of the procedure.

#49. 2. If a narcotic, sedative, or tranquilizing drug has been administered before signing of the consent, the drug's effects must be allowed to wear off before consent can be given.   Im   Sa/1   Ap
1. Before transferring the patient to surgery, the record must be complete. Required documentation includes the consent forms.
3. The surgery may not need to be cancelled, but just rescheduled for later in the day to allow for the effects of the drug to wear off and the consent to be obtained.
4. To be valid, the consent must be signed before the pre-op medication is administered.

#50. 3. These are normal side-effects; adverse side-effects would include ECG changes, constipation, and urinary retention.   An   Ph/8   An
1. This is not an adverse reaction, but normal side-effects of the drug.
2. These side-effects indicate an appropriate dose of the drug.
4. The Atropine should act as a CNS depressant and decrease the anxiety level of the patient.

#51. 2. Epidural anesthesia does not cause respiratory depression, but general anesthesia can, especially in a client with COPD.   An   Ph/9   Ap
1. Pressure sores develop if circulation to the skin is inadequate and epidural and general anesthesia both affect circulation.
3. Both general and regional anesthesia reduce central nervous system control of vascular constriction.
4. These are all possible complications that can occur with general anesthesia, but this client has COPD so the respiratory system is a much higher concern.

#52. 2. These are all symptoms of sympathetic nervous system blockade, so the patient should be closely monitored for these.   Pl   Ph/9   Co

ANSWER	RATIONALE	NP	CN	CL

1. Headache is more common with spinal vs. epidural anesthesia.
3. These are signs of malignant hyperthermia, a rare, life-threatening disorder that may be triggered by drugs commonly used in anesthesia.
4. Urinary retention can occur following any type of anesthesia and is not specific to epidural blocks.

#53. 4. Depression of respiratory rate has been reported and tends to last longer than the analgesic effect when Innovar is used during surgery.   Pl   Ph/8   Ap
1. Restlessness and anxiety are not characteristic side-effects of Innovar.
2. Delirium occurs most commonly with ketamin hydrochloride (Ketalar).
3. Dysrhythmias are not characteristic side-effects of Innovar.

#54. 4. A specific assessment priority is the evaluation of a patent airway and respiratory and circulatory adequacy.   Im   Ph/9   Ap
1. Assessing for signs and symptoms of hemorrhage is important, but the first priority is airway assessment.
2. Urinary distention may occur, but the patient's physiologic status at the time of admission to the unit should be the priority, maintaining a patent airway is the first priority.
3. The family should be encouraged to visit once the nurse has determined the physiologic stability of the patient.

#55. 1. The patient should obtain relief from pain, and using a scale to assess this is a more objective measure.   Ev   Ph/8   Ap
2. Using a 1–10 scale gives the nurse a more objective measure of the level of pain relief.
3. The expectation that the client will be totally pain free is unrealistic.
4. Asking the client if she needs more narcotics is inappropriate. Using a scale to rate pain is a more objective measure.

#56. 2. Atelectasis occurs commonly after abdominal surgery, especially in smokers. This occurs when mucus blocks the bronchioles and causes decreased breath sounds and shallow breathing.   An   Ph/9   An
1. With pneumonia, the microorganisms in the lung grow in the stagnant mucus and infection develops. The patient would be exhibiting signs and symptoms of infection such as fever with pneumonia.
3. Hemorrhage is indicated by bleeding and changes in vital signs.
4. Thromboembolism is indicated by redness, swelling, pain, and increased warmth along the path of a vein or a positive Homan's sign.

#57. 4. Thromboembolism can be related to dehydration and immobility. These measures help prevent hypovolemia and subsequent sludging of cells. A positive Homan's sign is often associated with thromboembolism.   Pl   Ph/9   Ap
1. To prevent thromboembolism, pressure under the knees from bed or pillows should be avoided as they put pressure on veins and constrict circulation.
2. These are good interventions to avoid infection, but are not directly related to the formation of a thromboembolism.
3. Assessment of breath sounds is not related to thromboembolism, and ambulation should be encouraged unless contraindicated.

#58. 3. Nursing interventions to facilitate voiding include ambulation and normal positioning for voiding. The normal voiding position for the male is standing.   Im   Ph/9   Ap
1. Inserting an indwelling catheter has the highest infection rate for the patient and, therefore, should be used only when all other measures fail.
2. Intermittent catheterization can be performed to relieve urinary distention once other more conservative measures have been tried and failed.

ANSWER	RATIONALE	NP	CN	CL

4. Interventions to facilitate voiding include normal positioning for voiding and most males do not normally void lying down in bed.

#59. 1. Paralytic ileus can be related to immobility and inadequate pain medication as well as bowel manipulation and the anesthetic used during surgery. Pl Ph/9 Ap

2. These interventions are directed at the respiratory system and will not help the patient recover from a paralytic ileus.

3. The patient has a paralytic ileus and needs the nasogastric tube to prevent nausea and vomiting.

4. Bladder pain and distention occur with urinary retention, not paralytic ileus.

#60. 1. An inguinal herniorrhaphy should have only minimal serous drainage (straw colored) during the post-op period. Ev Ph/9 Ap

2. Sanguineous (red) drainage may be normal after certain types of surgery (chest for example) but not after an inguinal herniorrhaphy.

3. Separation and disruption of previously joined wound edges may indicate a complication such as wound dehiscence.

4. A Penrose drain would be more common following major abdominal surgery. Even if one were present by day two, it should not be putting out large amounts of serosanguineous (pink) drainage, but a small amount of serous (straw colored) drainage if any.

#61. 1. Bacteria have not currently been implicated in carcinogenesis, although bacteria can be extremely harmful to a patient with cancer whose immune system has been altered by disease, radiation therapy, or chemotherapy. An Ph/9 Co

2. Viruses are thought to insinuate themselves into the genetic structure of cells, thereby altering future generations of that cell. For example, Epstein-Barr is strongly implicated in the development of Burkitt's sarcoma.

3. Approximately 40–60% of all environmental cancers are thought to have links to dietary factors such as fats, alcohol, foods containing nitrates/nitrites, and salt-cured or smoked meats.

4. Genetic and familial factors are involved in cancer cell development: damage to the DNA in certain populations of cells may lead to mutant cells being transmitted to future generations. Examples of cancers associated with familial inheritance include breast, colon, and rectal cancers.

#62. 3. In the TNM staging classification system, T refers to the primary tumor, and T2 is between 2–5 cm without extension to chest wall or skin. The N refers to regional lymph node involvement, with N1 indicating spread to an ipsilateral movable node. N0 indicates no regional lymph node spread; N2 indicates metastasis to an ipsilateral axillary node fixed to another node or other structure. M refers to distant metastasis, with MX indicating that metastasis cannot be assessed, M0 that there is no distant spread, and M1 that there is spread present. An He/4 An

1. In the TNM staging classification system, T refers to the primary tumor and T2 is between 2–5 cm without extension to chest wall or skin. The "2" does not refer to a specific size. The N refers to regional lymph nodes, with N1 indicating spread to an ipsilateral node that is movable. M refers to metastasis, and M0 does mean no distant spread.

2. In the TNM staging classification system, T refers to the primary tumor and T2 is between 2–5 cm without extension to chest wall or skin. The "2" does not refer to two primary tumors. The N refers to regional lymph nodes, with N1 indicating spread to an ipsilateral node that is movable. M refers to metastasis, and M0 does mean no distant spread.

4. In the TNM staging classification system, T refers to the primary tumor and T2 is between 2–5 cm without extension to chest wall or

skin. Carcinoma in situ would be indicated by "Tis." The N refers to regional lymph nodes, with N1 indicating spread to an ipsilateral node that is movable. (No regional spread would be indicated by N0.) The M refers to metastasis, and M0 means no distant spread; MX means distant metastasis cannot be assessed.

#63. 4. Only this answer, practicing breast self-exam, will yield a "warning signal of cancer" (i.e., a breast lump). Be certain that your response answers the question, not just that it contains factual information.   Pl   He/4   Co

   1. Reducing the amount of fat in one's diet refers to cancer prevention; the question asks about a teaching plan for the early warning signals of cancer. Always be certain that your response answers the question, not just that it supplies correct information.

   2. Smoking cessation refers to cancer prevention; the question asks about a teaching plan for the early warning signals of cancer. Always be certain that your response answers the question, not just that it supplies correct information.

   3. Avoiding overexposure to the sun refers to cancer prevention; the question asks about a teaching plan for the early warning signals of cancer. Always be certain that your response answers the question, not just that it supplies correct information.

#64. 1. Mr. I. is mistaken (and needs more teaching) if he says that testicular self-exam should be performed immediately prior to sexual intercourse. The best time to do TSE is when the scrotum is relaxed, such as after a warm bath or shower.   Ev   He/4   An

   2. Mr. I. shows comprehension when he says that it is normal to find one testis lower than the other.

   3. Mr. I. shows comprehension of your teaching when he says that any lump should be examined by a physician; a pea-sized lump could be due to an infection, but it could also indicate a tumor.

   4. Mr. I. does not need to worry about that "cord-like thing," which is the epididymis; the function of the epididymis is to store and transport sperm.

#65. 3. Because of the bleeding disorders common in patients receiving chemotherapy, all body secretions, including emesis, should be assessed for obvious and occult blood.   As   Ph/8   Ap

   1. Frequent vital signs are necessary, since infection is always a risk for the patient receiving chemotherapy, but every eight hours is insufficient. Signs should be taken at least every four hours.

   2. Bleeding disorders are common in patients receiving chemotherapy, and for this reason, rectal temperatures are to be avoided.

   4. It is true that fresh fruits and vegetables may contain bacteria that are not removed by washing, which can contribute to a patient's risk for developing an infection. However, the question asks for an *assessment* action by the nurse; this answer does not address the parameter of assessment.

#66. 4. Each time the tumor is exposed to the chemotherapeutic drug, a certain percentage of cells are killed. (The exact percentage is determined by the drug dosage used.) Because a *percentage* of tumor is killed, a part of tumor will remain (there is no percentage—except for zero—which yields zero) after therapy. It is up to the body's immune system to destroy the remaining tumor, which an intact immune system may be able to do if the tumor is made small enough.   An   Ph/8   Co

   1. Chemotherapeutic agents have no effect on the sodium-potassium pump in the cell wall.

   2. Chemotherapeutic agents are not involved in oxygen utilization by or transport to the cell.

   3. Anti-tumor metabolites that are toxic to further tumor cell growth do not exist; this is a nonsense answer.

ANSWER	RATIONALE	NP	CN	CL

#67. 2. If the metabolites of cyclophosphamide are allowed to accumulate in the bladder, the subsequent irritation of the bladder wall capillaries will cause hemorrhagic cystitis. This condition is preventable; if it develops, one of its serious sequelae is bladder fibrosis. In addition to monitoring BUN and creatinine prior to administration, the nurse must promote hydration of at least 3 liters a day and frequent voiding.   Pl   Ph/8   Ap

    1. Interstitial pneumonitis is a rare manifestation of pulmonary toxicity and high-flow oxygen delivery would be an insufficient intervention.

    3. Ice caps are no longer recommended for alopecia prevention: their usefulness is controversial, and they decrease the blood flow to the head—including the flow containing the chemotherapeutic agent.

    4. Nausea and vomiting, common with cyclophosphamide administration, begin two to four hours after the dose is given, peak at 12 hours and usually subside within 24 hours. Antiemetic therapy for 7–10 days is not needed.

#68. 2. The patient will use normal saline mouth rinses every two hours while awake and every six hours at night to aid in the removal of thick secretions, debris, and bacteria.   Pl   Ph/7   Ap

    1. Brushing teeth after meals and at bedtime is a good intervention, but flossing should be limited to once every 24 hours to limit trauma to gums.

    3. Dentures can and should be worn during mealtimes if they are not exacerbating the problem with the oral mucosa, but they are to be removed between meals; dentures must fit well so as not to add to the oral trauma.

    4. A bland, mechanical soft diet is not necessary, but the patient should avoid foods that are difficult to chew or excessively spicy, as these can further irritate the mucosa. Otherwise, foods pleasing to the patient can and should be offered.

#69. 4. By using a soft toothbrush and avoiding dental floss, the patient promotes a healthy oral cavity without risking bleeding or disruption of skin integrity, which could lead to infection.   Pl   Ph/8   Ap

    1. The patient is severely anemic, thrombocytopenic, and leukopenic; he will most likely require blood administration, but has an intact central venous access device, so additional IV lines are not needed. Indeed, further venipuncture should be avoided because of the low platelet count (there is a risk of uncontrolled bleeding).

    2. Although fingernails and toenails should be short to prevent excoriation, they should be filed, not cut (sharp edges from cutting could tear skin).

    3. Thrombocytopenic patients should be instructed to have regular bowel movements to prevent constipation; a low-residue diet will not provide enough fiber to stimulate normal bowel movements.

#70. 3. It is important to protect skin from irritation, and lotions, creams, powders, and ointments can all contribute to skin problems. Patients are advised to consult their radiation oncologists for troublesome skin problems, and should be advised that after treatment, reepithelialization will occur.   Ev   Ph/10   An

    1. This statement by Miss C. is correct and appropriate. Even if radiation therapy is not directed at the mouth, changes in oral mucosa can occur.

    2. This statement by Miss C. is correct and appropriate. Fatigue is often a sequelae of radiation therapy, and the course of the disease cannot be measured by the degree of fatigue.

    4. This statement by Miss C. is correct and appropriate. Alopecia is likely to occur, particularly in areas that receive direct irradiation. Even if radiation is not directed at the mouth, changes in taste are common.

#71. 1. There are two types of ionizing radiation: electromagnetic rays   An   Ph/10   Co and particulate radiation. **Either of these can cause tissue disruption, the most harmful of which is the alteration in the structure of the cell's DNA molecules; this will lead to cell death.**

2. Radiation is not implicated in glucose metabolism within the cell.
3. Radiation is not implicated in cell wall destruction.
4. Radiation is not implicated in oxygen metabolism by the cell.

#72. 1. The patient will be restricted to her room to minimize exposure of staff, visitors, and other patients to the radiation source. Ev Sa/2 An

2. Rubber gloves are appropriately used to dispose of contaminated material. Rubber gloves would be *inappropriate* if the radiation source had to be handled; long forceps would need to be used.
3. A low residue diet is appropriate for preventing frequent bowel movements that will be uncomfortable for the patient with an applicator in place.
4. It is appropriate for the Radiation Safety personnel to survey the room before the patient is discharged, to ensure that all sources of radiation have been removed.

#73. 2. Visitors younger than 18 years of age, and pregnant visitors, are not allowed during internal radiation therapy. Ev Sa/2 An

1. The patient will be on strict bedrest, although she may move from side to side and the head of the bed may be elevated 45°. Because of her relative immobility, this patient will require back care (integrated into the time scheduled at the bedside by the primary nurse).
3. Because of her relative immobility (the patient is on strict bedrest during therapy), she should be encouraged to cough and deep breathe to promote adequate gas exchange and keep respiratory secretions mobile. The likelihood of dislodging the applicator is very small.
4. All members of the healthcare team who are involved with the patient's care should have film badges or pocket ion chambers to monitor their exposure to the radiation source.

#74. 2. Long-handled forceps and a lead-lined container (sometimes called a "lead pig") must be kept in the room of any patient receiving internal radiation therapy for this very occurrence. Im Sa/2 Ap

1. The radiation source must not be left in the open, as its nonchanneled radioactivity is dangerous both to the patient and staff.
3. Radiation sources must never be handled directly; rubber gloves provide no protection from radiation.
4. The nurse cannot reinsert the rod; insertion is a surgical procedure requiring general or local anesthesia.

#75. 3. If bone marrow-producing sites are included in the field being irradiated, anemia, leukopenia (low white blood cells), and thrombocytopenia (low platelets) may occur; these may lead to infection and/or bleeding. As Ph/10 Ap

1. No contrast medium is used in radiation therapy, so there is no IV site involved in care.
2. Radiation therapy does not facilitate the development of edema.
4. No foreign substances are introduced into the body, so allergic reactions—reactions to allergens—are not developed.

#76. 3. Babinski reflex is abnormal in an adult. It signifies an upper motor neuron lesion. As He/4 Kn

1. This is a tendon reflex.
2. This is a brachioradialis reflex.
4. This is a biceps reflex.

#77. 3. To correctly test cranial nerve II, the optic nerve, use a Snellen chart to assess visual acuity. As He/4 Kn

1. Cranial nerves III, IV, and VI are assessed by the inspection of the pupils.
2. Cranial nerves III, IV, and VI are assessed by testing the extraocular movements.

ANSWER	RATIONALE	NP	CN	CL

    4. Cranial nerves III, IV, and VI are responsible for a corneal reflex.

#78. 4. An audiometry test tests different pitches and sounds.   As   He/4   Kn
    1. The Romberg test is used to test cerebellar and vestibular intactness.
    2. The Rosenbaum chart is used to test visual acuity.
    3. Inspection of the pupils tests cranial nerves III, IV, and VI.

#79. 1. 3 points are given for opening eyes to speech, 6 points are given for obeying verbal commands related to motor response, and 4 points are given for best verbal response when client is confused.   An   Ph/10   An
    2. 2 points are given when client opens eyes to pain, 4 points are given when the client has a decorticate response to painful stimuli, and 1 point is given when there is no verbal response.
    3. 2 points are given when the client only opens eyes to pain, 1 point is given when there is no motor response, and 3 points are given when there is inappropriate speech.
    4. 4 points are given when the client opens eyes spontaneously, 6 points are given when the client obeys verbal command, and 5 points are given when the client is oriented in all spheres.

#80. 2. Pacemakers and cerebral aneurysm clips are the exclusions for an MRI.   As   Ph/9   Ap
    1. Jewelry or other metal has to be removed, but does not exclude the client.
    3. Claustrophic clients can be given a mild sedative prior to the procedure.
    4. Iodine dye is not used in an MRI.

#81. 1. Difficulty swallowing occurs from a hematoma developing and pushing on the trachea.   Ev   Ph/9   An
    2. This is the normal appearance of an arteriogram site.
    3. These vital signs are normal. A high blood pressure could cause bleeding.
    4. This is a normal finding.

#82. 3. The client is manifesting symptoms of increased intracranial pressure.   An   Ph/9   An
    1. The client does have an altered level of cognitive function, but it is related to the increased intracranial pressure.
    2. The client does have a risk for injury, but if cerebral perfusion is maximized, injury can be decreased.
    4. The client does have a sensory perceptual deficit, but it is related to the increased intracranial pressure.

#83. 1. Increased intracranial pressure causes hypothalamic dysfunction creating hypo/hyperthermia, SIADH, and diabetes insipidus. The hypothalamus regulates body temperature, osmolality of body fluids, hunger, and satiety.   An   Ph/9   Ap
    2. In a patient with a head injury, the nurse needs to check the gastric aspirate for blood. It is common for head injury clients to get stress ulcers. Blood pressure is controlled by the brainstem.
    3. Heart rate is controlled by the brainstem. Pupillary response is dependent on the area of edema in the brain.
    4. Respiratory rate is controlled by the brainstem.

#84. 1. This method allows the client to have a feeling of control.   Im   Ph/7   Ap
    2. This does not provide balance and stability.
    3. This provides no support physically.
    4. This does not facilitate independence or self-esteem in the client.

#85. 2. Facing the person and speaking clearly is the best way to communicate with the hearing impaired.   Im   Ph/7   Ap
    1. It is best to speak into the nonimpaired ear.
    3. Shouting overuses normal speaking tones and may cause distortion and be too loud for the person with sensorineural damage.
    4. It is best to speak first directly and clearly then write all communication if the person does not understand.

ANSWER	RATIONALE	NP	CN	CL
#86. 1.	**These are some of the symptoms of meningitis.**	As	Ph/10	An
2.	The symptoms of a brain abscess are headache, drowsiness, and confusion.			
3.	The symptoms of a brain tumor include paralysis, weakness, disorientation, and speech and visual problems.			
4.	The characteristic symptom of epilepsy is seizures.			
#87. 2.	**The altered cerebral perfusion is related to the increased intracranial pressure and inflammatory process.**	An	Ph/10	An
1.	Clients with meningitis do have pain, but this is not the most important nursing diagnosis.			
3.	Anxiety may occur, but if the disease process is controlled the anxiety should resolve.			
4.	This is important, but cerebral perfusion takes priority. If cerebral perfusion is maximized, the chance for injury is decreased.			
#88. 1.	**These findings are consistent with a brain tumor.**	An	Ph/10	An
2.	Meningitis is accompanied by fever, headache, nuchal rigidity, and Kernig's and Brudzinski's signs.			
3.	There is no history of head trauma.			
4.	The symptoms of encephalitis include headache, fever, vomiting, and meningeal signs.			
#89. 2.	**This is the correct position for an infratentorial approach.**	Pl	Ph/9	Ap
1.	This position is for a supratentorial approach.			
3.	Vital signs and pupils should be checked every 30 minutes to one hour after surgery.			
4.	Flexing the neck can cause disruption of the suture line.			
#90. 1.	**Pulling the client's paralyzed arm can result in shoulder subluxation and pain. The client's unaffected hand must be free to reach for the arm of the wheelchair.**	Ev	Ph/7	An
2.	Leaning the patient forward is a correct transfer technique that shifts the center of gravity to enable the client to rise from the bed.			
3.	Moving the client toward the unaffected side is a correct transfer technique that permits the strong arm and leg to accomplish the transfer safely.			
4.	The aide correctly braces the affected knee and foot, which may buckle during the transfer.			
#91. 2.	**A TIA is a temporary loss of function due to cerebral ischemia.**	An	Ph/10	Kn
1.	A TIA is not permanent and does not have long-term neurologic deficits. A cerebrovascular accident may cause long-term deficits.			
3.	A TIA is intermittent, but does not leave permanent damage.			
4.	A TIA is not permanent and does not have long-term neurologic deficits.			
#92. 3.	**Platelet-inhibiting drugs such as aspirin are taken prophylactically to prevent cerebral infarction secondary to embolism and thrombosis.**	Ev	Ph/8	An
1.	Headache is not a common manifestation in transient ischemic attack and is not the rationale for aspirin therapy.			
2.	Platelet-inhibiting drugs such as aspirin can increase the chances of intracranial hemorrhage, especially if dosage is excessive.			
4.	Although aspirin therapy is used to prevent myocardial infarction, this client is taking the drug to decrease chances of cerebral infarction.			
#93. 4.	**Depression, confusion, and hallucinations are adverse effects that can occur after prolonged use of L-dopa. A "drug holiday" under medical supervision may restore drug effectiveness.**	Ev	Ph/8	An
1.	Involuntary head movement is one of the many dyskinesias that are side-effects of L-dopa. The development of dyskinesias, although annoying, does not indicate drug toxicity.			
2.	Bradykinesia is a common manifestation of Parkinson's disease. The demonstration of slowing of movement may indicate noncompliance			

with the treatment plan, inadequate dosage, or poor response to the drug.

3. A shuffling gait is a common manifestation of Parkinson's disease that may not entirely disappear with medication therapy. Dosage may be inadequate or the client may not be taking the drug as prescribed.

#94. 1. The client should have semisolid, thickened food. Soup is thin in texture and could be aspirated by the client. Ev Ph/9 An
2. Posture exercises help to relieve muscle stiffness and rigidity.
3. Range of motion exercises reduce muscular stiffness.
4. Safety during bathing is imperative. The placement of bath bars, a bath bench, and non-skid appliances are required.

#95. 4. These are the symptoms of MS, which is more common in women ages 20–40. As Ph/10 An
1. The symptoms of Parkinson's include masklike appearance to the face, drooling, slow speech, and shuffling gait.
2. The symptoms of MG include weakness, fatigue, drooling, and ptosis.
3. The symptoms of ALS include progressive muscle weakness, atrophy, fasciculations, dysphagia, and spasticity of the flexor muscles.

#96. 4. Clients with MG have respiratory muscle failure. Pl Ph/9 An
1. Clients with MG do not usually have pain.
2. This is important, but airway is always the highest priority.
3. This is not a priority.

#97. 2. The client is confused about the timing of medication administration. The anticholinesterase medication should be taken 30 minutes prior to meals to enhance the muscle strength needed for chewing and swallowing. Ev Ph/8 An
1. The client's comment does not indicate the need for further instruction. A regular schedule of taking the anticholinesterase medication will help the client to maintain muscle strength.
3. This comment does not indicate the need for further instruction. The client is accurately describing two of the manifestations of cholinergic crisis, which arises from toxicity from the anticholinesterase medication.
4. This comment does not indicate the need for further instruction. Anticholinergic drug toxicity can cause difficulty in swallowing. Atropine sulfate is used to decrease saliva production during the cholinergic crisis resulting from drug toxicity.

#98. 3. Cerebrospinal fluid is positive for glucose. As Ph/9 Ap
1. The most effective way to determine if the fluid is CSF is to test for glucose.
2. The most effective way to determine if the fluid is CSF is to test for glucose.
4. The most effective way to determine if the fluid is CSF is to test for glucose.

#99. 1. The client's head should be elevated about 30° to lower the intracranial pressure, which may be dangerously elevated in a subdural hematoma. The venous blood pressure begins to decline as intracranial pressure rises. Im Ph/10 Ap
2. Trendelenburg position is contraindicated for clients with possible increased intracranial pressure. The client's lowered blood pressure may indicate brain compression.
3. High Fowler's position may compromise the airway of clients who are not fully conscious. Sudden seizure activity may develop in head-injured clients, who can fall over the siderails if they are in a sitting position.
4. Head elevation is needed to decrease intracranial pressure. The client's lowered blood pressure may indicate brain compression.

#100. 2. The wife may not understand that she must interrupt the client's Ev Ph/9 An sleep to detect early signs of increased intracranial pressure caused by contusion or hematoma development.

1. The wife knows that she must check on the client frequently during the first night to detect early signs of increased intracranial pressure caused by contusion or hematoma development.
3. The wife knows that vomiting is a sign of increased intracranial pressure caused by contusion or hematoma development. Immediate action is necessary.
4. The wife knows that motor deficits may develop when intracranial pressure rises as a result of contusion or hematoma development. Immediate action is indicated.

#101. 2. Cerebral edema is common after surgery. Decadron (a corticosteroid) is given to decrease the edema. An Ph/8 Co
1. Corticosteroids elevate the blood sugar.
3. Steroids are not given for seizures.
4. Steroids can create gastric ulcers.

#102. 2. Edema above the area of the lesion can cause respiratory depression and arrest. Pl Ph/10 Ap
1. Bowel and bladder training usually occurs in the rehabilitation phase.
3. Autonomic dysreflexia is usually a complication in the rehabilitation phase.
4. A C7 patient does not usually require a diaphragmatic pacer.

#103. 3. When initiating rescue breathing for a client with a suspected spinal injury, the jaw thrust maneuver is used with rescue breathing at the rate of 12 breaths per minute. Im Ph/10 Ap
1. The chin tilt maneuver is not used when a client may have a spinal injury.
2. Before administering chest compressions, the airway must be established, and rescue breathing is initiated.
4. Before administering chest compressions, the airway must be established and rescue breathing is initiated.

#104. 3. Discomfort at the pin sites is expected for several days after application of the Halo device. The pain can be controlled with mild analgesic medication. The client can benefit from the reassurance that the pain will not continue for the weeks that the traction will be in place. Im Ph/9 Ap
1. Loosening the pins will disrupt the traction that is stabilizing the spinal fracture. Spinal cord damage can result.
2. Whereas the pin sites should be kept clean and dry, this action does not relieve the client's pain.
4. Loosening the pins will disrupt the traction that is stabilizing the spinal fracture. Spinal cord damage can result.

#105. 3. The client is showing signs of autonomic dysreflexia. Placing the client in a sitting position will allow blood to pool in the legs, which should lower the blood pressure and prevent possible hypertensive hemorrhage. Im Ph/10 Ap
1. The client's high blood pressure takes priority over comfort needs.
2. While fecal impaction can cause autonomic dysreflexia, assessing for fecal impaction may elevate the blood pressure even higher. The blood pressure must be lowered before such an assessment takes place.
4. The blood pressure needs to be reduced immediately and the client assessed before the physician is notified.

#106. 3. Extremes of temperature of food or drink can trigger paroxysms of severe facial pain along the pathways of the trigeminal nerve. Meals are better tolerated if served at room temperature. Ev Ph/9 An
1. Facial movement can trigger paroxysms of severe facial pain along the pathways of the trigeminal nerve. Some clients have difficulty with chewing and talking.

2. Trigeminal neuralgia does not affect the arm. The branches of this cranial nerve are in the face.

4. While good body mechanics can prevent many musculoskeletal problems, the severe facial pain of trigeminal neuralgia is triggered by stimulation of facial structures.

#107. 4. Bell's palsy may cause paralysis of the eyelid and loss of the blink reflex on the affected side. The eye may not close completely. These problems render the eye susceptible to drying and irritation from dust or other debris.   Im   Ph/8   Co

1. The ability to make tears is not impaired in Bell's palsy.

2. Persons with Bell's palsy have difficulty closing the affected eye.

3. Bell's palsy is not characterized by primary infection of the eye, although secondary infection may occur if the eye is not kept moist with artificial tears.

#108. 2. Clients with Guillain-Barré have respiratory muscle weakness and respiratory failure.   Pl   Ph/9   Ap

1. Range of motion is important to prevent contractures but is not the most important.

3. Clients with Guillain-Barré may not be able to blink their eyes, at the height of the disease but this is not the most important diagnosis.

4. This is important, but the measurement of vital capacity will take precedence.

#109. 2. Clients with ALS often experience respiratory failure as the disease progresses, and need to communicate their wishes regarding ventilator support. The nurse should explore the client's wishes and facilitate discussion within the family. Arranging for the client to sign a living will, if the client wishes to do so, is also a nursing responsibility.   Ev   Ph/10   An

1. ALS is not considered to be an infectious disease. The cause is unknown.

3. ALS is characterized by a steady decline in muscle strength. Clients do not have the exacerbations and remissions that are typical of multiple sclerosis.

4. ALS does not respond to antineoplastic chemotherapy.

#110. 2. These are the assessment findings of cataracts.   As   Ph/10   An

1. Glaucoma is characterized by increased intraocular pressure and peripheral vision loss.

3. Retinal detachment symptoms are floating spots, flashes of light, and vision loss.

4. Diabetic retinopathy can only be found by ophthalmoscopic exam. Findings are tortuous vessels, exudate, and new vessel formation.

#111. 1. These are common risk factors for glaucoma.   As   Ph/10   Ap

2. The most common eye disorder seen in diabetes is retinopathy.

3. These are the risk factors for macular degeneration.

4. These are the risk factors for retinal detachment.

#112. 4. Sunglasses should be worn post-op for comfort and protection when outdoors.   Ev   Ph/9   An

1. Pressure on the operative site is reduced by sleeping on the unaffected side.

2. To avoid infection, the eye is cleansed with sterile cotton balls or pads that have been moistened with sterile water or saline.

3. Instilling eye drops on the cornea can cause damage. The drops should be instilled on the conjunctiva.

#113. 2. Eye pain is present with open and narrow angle glaucoma, but not with a detached retina.   An   Ph/10   Co

1. Floating spots are seen with a detached retina, with glaucoma the client sees halos.

3. Flashing lights are common with retinal detachment.

    4.   Vision loss with a detached retina is quick, but vision loss with glaucoma is gradual.

#114. 4. Glaucoma is usually treated with eye drops, such as betaxolol (Timoptic), a beta-adrenergic antagonist. The eye can be damaged when eye drops are used incorrectly.   Ev   Ph/9   An

    1.   Blood pressure is not altered in glaucoma or by glaucoma therapy.

    2.   Hearing is not affected by glaucoma or its treatment.

    3.   Self-care techniques for glaucoma do not include blood glucose monitoring, unless the client also has diabetes mellitus.

#115. 2. Eye movements can increase the amount of detachment.   An   Ph/9   Co

    1.   Antibiotics would be administered to decrease eye infections.

    3.   Photophobia does not occur in detached retina.

    4.   Nystagmus does not occur in detached retina.

#116. 3. Immediate irrigation with copious amounts of water or normal saline solution may reduce alkaline burns of the cornea and conjunctiva. Any delay in initiating the irrigation can result in serious damage to eye structures.   Im   Ph/10   Ap

    1.   This method is used to remove a nonpenetrating foreign body from the eye.

    2.   Patching is used only after the caustic chemical is removed from the eye.

    4.   Anti-irritant products are not designed for removal of caustic chemicals, and may worsen the chemical damage.

#117. 4. These are classic signs of otosclerosis.   As   Ph/10   An

    1.   A cholesteatoma causes hearing loss, painless fetid pearly white otorrhea, and perforation of the tympanic membrane.

    2.   Actinic keratosis is a precancerous lesion commonly on the auricle.

    3.   Pain and pruritis with a normal appearing tympanic membrane are the symptoms of external otitis.

#118. 3. The client should blow the nose gently one side at a time to prevent pressure changes in the ear.   Pl   Ph/9   Ap

    1.   Work is resumed one week later.

    2.   The client must sneeze or cough with the mouth open.

    4.   Exercise can be resumed in three weeks.

#119. 1. These are classic signs of Ménière's disease.   As   Ph/10   An

    2.   An acoustic neuroma's symptoms are unilateral hearing loss, tinnitus in the affected ear, and intermittent vertigo.

    3.   Otosclerosis is characterized by white chalky plaques on the eardrum with hearing loss.

    4.   A cholesteatoma causes hearing loss, painless fetid pearly white otorrhea, and perforation of the tympanic membrane.

#120. 1. This client most likely has Ménière's disease. In Ménière's disease, patient education is paramount. The client needs to be taught that with the increased volume of hydrolymph, excessive fluid intake increases the volume even more and exacerbates the disease. They should also be taught not to ambulate or make extreme movements during the acute attacks.   An   Ph/9   An

    2.   Anxiety may occur, but if the client understands the disease and treatment required to control the disease s/he should be able to control the anxiety.

    3.   There is no impairment of physical mobility with Ménière's. The client may be dizzy.

    4.   Pain does not usually accompany Ménière's disease, only a feeling of fullness in the ear.

#121. 1. Some of the most common clinical manifestations of cardiovascular disease are shortness of breath, chest pain or discomfort, dyspnea, palpitations, fainting, and peripheral skin changes such as edema.   As   Ph/9   Co

2. Some of the most common clinical manifestations of respiratory disease are cough, sputum production, dyspnea, hemopytosis, wheezing, and chest pain.

3. Some of the most common clinical manifestations of endocrine disorders are fatigue, depression, decreased energy, sleep pattern disorders, weight changes, altered mood, changes in the condition of the skin and hair, sexual dysfunction.

4. Some of the most common clinical manifestations of neurologic disorders are behavior changes, mood swings, loss of consciousness, seizures, memory deficits, motor and sensory function problems.

#122. 3. S_4 is an abnormal heart sound. It is indicative of decreased ventricular compliance.   As   He/4   An

1. Normal location of S_1.
2. Normal location of S_2.
4. S_3 is normal in children and some adults over 50.

#123. 1. Avoid any stimulants such as coffee, tea, or a depressant such as alcohol.   Im   Ph/9   Ap

2. Smoking should be avoided at least two hours prior to the test.
3. The client needs adequate rest prior to the test.
4. Consult with the physician about what medications to take prior to the exam. Some medications such as Digitalis, Inderal, and vasodilators may affect the results.

#124. 2. Shellfish contains iodine, which is also in the contrast media used during a catheterization. It is _imperative_ to obtain information regarding iodine allergies.   As   Ph/9   Ap

1. Client teaching can enforce new material but does not reduce complications.
3. Anxiety can be reduced by client education, but this does not reduce complications.
4. Past history is important; however, this information will not prevent life-threatening complications.

#125. 1. Assessment of pedal pulses is imperative after a cardiac catheterization. Evaluation of presence and quality of pulses indicates blood flow to the catheterized extremity.   Pl   Ph/9   Ap

2. Lung assessment is important but not imperative.
3. The catheterized extremity must be immobilized for four to six hours, making ambulation impossible until approximately 24 hours after the catheterization.
4. Vital signs should be checked every 15–30 minutes to assess for complications.

#126. 1. The above rhythm is ventricular tachycardia.   An   Ph/10   An

2. Ventricular fibrillation has no discernible waveforms and a chaotic baseline.
3. Sinus tachycardia has discernible P, ORS, and T waves. It is a regular rhythm.
4. Supraventricular tachycardia is a very fast rate with discernible T waves and QRS complexes.

#127. 2. The above rhythm is ventricular fibrillation.   An   Ph/10   An

1. Ventricular tachycardia is usually regular and fast with wide, bizarre QRS complexes.
3. Sinus tachycardia has discernible P, QRS, and T waves. It is a regular rhythm.
4. Supraventricular tachycardia is a very fast rate with discernible T waves and QRS complexes.

#128. 2. Lidocaine, a class I antidysrhythmic drug, is indicated when the client has six or more PVCs per minute, multifocal PVCs, couplets or triplets, or PVCs occurring on the downslope of the T wave. Any of these situations is likely to progress to the more   Im   Ph/8   Ap

dangerous ventricular tachycardia or ventricular fibrillation if not treated immediately.

1. Because this client has six or more PVCs per minute and couplets, he is at risk for development of ventricular tachycardia. He must be treated immediately to prevent this progression.
3. A precordial thump is sometimes administered if the change to ventricular tachycardia is observed. This client has not progressed to ventricular tachycardia, so a precordial thump is inappropriate and could be dangerous.
4. Chest compressions are indicated only when there is no pulse (e.g., cardiac arrest or ventricular fibrillation). They would be dangerous for this client.

#129. 2. A pulmonary artery catheter will show all right and left heart hemodynamic pressures and provide for cardiac output measurements.   An   Ph/10   Ap

1. An arterial line will only show blood pressure.
3. An IABP will help to augment blood flow to the coronary arteries.
4. A CVP will measure preload to the right heart only; CVP only measures the right heart.

#130. 4. Smoking has been determined to increase the risk of coronary heart disease.   As   He/4   An

1. Exercise has been shown to decrease the risk of coronary artery disease.
2. Heredity is a risk factor for heart disease.
3. A normal serum cholesterol is 189.

#131. 2. Nitroglycerin dilates peripheral veins, reducing venous return to the heart. This immediately decreases cardiac workload, relieving ischemia and chest pain. It also dilates coronary arteries, improving oxygen supply to the heart.   Im   Ph/8   Ap

1. Lying down and elevating the legs would increase venous return to the heart, which would increase cardiac workload. This could worsen the angina.
3. The left shoulder pain is referred pain from the heart. Immobilizing the shoulder will not help to relieve the pain.
4. The pain of angina is due to cardiac ischemia. Aspirin and acetaminophen would not reduce cardiac workload or improve coronary blood flow, so they would not be effective in relieving the chest pain.

#132. 3. Nitroglycerin reduces cardiac workload and improves myocardial oxygenation. This prevents episodes of anginal pain.   Ev   Ph/8   An

1. Nitroglycerin does not lower cholesterol levels. This would be an expected effect of antilipemic drugs such as cholestyramine (Questran).
2. Vasodilation due to nitroglycerin produces hypotension as a side-effect. This is not an indication of therapeutic effectiveness.
4. Oxygen saturation is a measure of respiratory function. Nitroglycerin does not affect respiratory function, so oxygen saturation does not measure its effectiveness.

#133. 4. Most fruits and vegetables are low in fat and cholesterol-free. Jello also has no fat or cholesterol.   Ev   Ph/7   An

1. Cheese is high in fat and cholesterol, unless it is labeled as a skim milk or reduced fat product.
2. Tuna is low in fat and cholesterol, but tuna salad is made with mayonnaise or salad dressing, which add large amounts of fat.
3. Regular yogurt is made with whole milk and therefore has as much fat as an equal amount of whole milk. Clients often mistakenly believe that products such as yogurt, which are considered "healthy," will be low in fat.

#134. 2. 30 ml is 2 mg/h.   Pl   Ph/8   Ap
        1000 mg = 1 g. 2 g is 200 mg.

$2000\text{mg}:500\text{ml}::2\text{mg}: x$ ml

$2000\,x = 1000$

$\qquad x = 0.5$ ml/hr

60 drops = 1 ml. 60 drops $\times$ 0.5 ml. = 30 ml/hr.

1. 15 ml is 1 mg/h.
3. 45 ml is 3 mg/h.
4. 60 ml is 4 mg/h.

#135. 2. To improve activity tolerance, supervised walks for gradually increasing distances are encouraged when the client is transferred out of the coronary care unit.   Pl   Ph/9   Ap

1. Complete bedrest is only indicated for the first 24 hours after an uncomplicated MI.
3. As soon as the client's condition stabilizes, passive range of motion exercises are started. When the client is transferred to the stepdown unit, active exercise is encouraged.
4. Dangling is indicated on the first or second day after the MI. After the first day, the client may be allowed to be out of bed for 15–20 minute periods. By the third day, self-care and short walks are encouraged.

#136. 1. Assessment is important to identify the probable cause of the pain so that definitive intervention can be planned. Dysrhythmias are a common complication of MI. Crackles in the lungs and an S$_3$ gallop may indicate heart failure.   Im   Ph/10   An

2. No more than three nitroglycerin tablets should be taken, because more could lower the blood pressure dangerously and compromise circulation.
3. A 12-lead ECG is indicated to determine whether the client is having an MI. Telemetry monitoring may be initiated once a diagnosis is made, but it is not an immediate intervention.
4. Chest pain is indicative of myocardial ischemia. The supine position would increase venous return to the heart, which would increase cardiac workload. A high Fowler's or semi-Fowler's position would be appropriate.

#137. 3. Nitroglycerin is used prophylactically before activities that are known to cause chest pain, including sexual intercourse.   Ev   Ph/9   An

1. The best time to have intercourse is when the client is well rested. This is more likely to be in the morning than at night.
2. Intercourse should not occur immediately after a period of exercise. Performing multiple activities that increase cardiac workload may place excessive demands on the heart. He should wait about 90 minutes after exercise before beginning sexual activity.
4. It is actually preferable to have intercourse when the stomach is empty. After meals, the digestive system puts additional demands on the heart until the meal is digested. Intercourse should be avoided when other demands have already increased cardiac workload.

#138. 4. PTCA is also called balloon angioplasty because a balloon-tipped catheter is used. When the balloon is inflated, the plaque is compressed, leaving the artery unobstructed.   Im   Ph/9   Co

1. This describes thrombolytic therapy.
2. This describes coronary artery bypass grafting (CABG).
3. This describes a coronary atherectomy. Remember that the suffix "-ectomy" is used in the names of procedures that involve cutting.

#139. 2. Aerobic exercise, such as walking, helps to slow formation of atherosclerotic plaques in coronary artery disease. Mr. P. needs to make the necessary lifestyle changes to prevent further progression of his disease. Riding instead of walking would not provide aerobic exercise. Therefore this statement shows that Mr. P. needs further teaching.   Ev   Ph/9   An

1. Smoking is one of the major risk factors for coronary artery disease. Mr. P. should seek support to help him quit because it is very difficult to break the habit alone.

3.   Mr. P. is correct. Baking and broiling allow fat to drain out of meat. Frying adds extra fat. A low fat diet is important to reduce coronary artery disease risk.

4.   Effective stress management is an important lifestyle change to slow progression of coronary artery disease. This statement shows Mr. P. has understood what he was taught about reducing his risk.

#140. 3.   **Jugular venous distention is seen in right ventricular failure as volume overload occurs. This overload is reflected upward into the jugulars.**   As   Ph/10   An

1.   Pink frothy sputum is indicative of pulmonary edema seen in left-sided heart failure.

2.   Paroxysmal nocturnal dyspnea is a symptom commonly seen in left heart failure.

4.   Crackles are heard in left ventricular failure.

#141. 2.   **With left ventricular heart failure, carbon dioxide and oxygen exchange is impaired due to fluid overload and leads to hypoxia.**   An   Ph/10   An

1.   This is not the most important nursing diagnosis.

3.   Potential for injury is not the most important.

4.   Anxiety can occur but usually results from the disease process. Not the most important diagnosis.

#142. 4.   **Crackles in the lungs are a sign of pulmonary edema due to CHF. Improved cardiac output due to digoxin and reduced extracellular fluid volume due to furosemide should result in reduction of pulmonary edema.**   Ev   Ph/8   An

1.   Digoxin will most likely reduce the pulse rate. Decreased heart rate is not an indication that cardiac output has improved, which is the desired effect in this case. It is a side-effect, not the therapeutic effect.

2.   If digoxin and furosemide are effective, Mr. P. will excrete an increased amount of fluid. Because the urine will be more dilute, the specific gravity will decrease.

3.   Pulmonary edema initially produces a nonproductive cough. Production of frothy sputum indicates worsening pulmonary edema. Digoxin and furosemide should reduce the pulmonary edema.

#143. 1.   **This is the beneficial effect of morphine in pulmonary edema.**   An   Ph/8   Kn

2.   Decreasing the respiratory rate is a side-effect to be alert for.

3.   Morphine has analgesic effects, but does not have sedative effects.

4.   Morphine does decrease anxiety, but does not vasoconstrict.

#144. 4.   **Metal detectors generate strong magnetic fields that can alter pacemaker settings or produce interference that causes malfunction.**   Pl   Ph/9   Ap

1.   Remote control devices do not produce strong magnetic fields and are, therefore, not likely to affect the pacemaker.

2.   In the past, clients were taught to avoid microwave ovens. Modern microwave ovens do not produce electromagnetic fields that would disturb pacemaker function. Some clients may have heard this information and may need to be reassured.

3.   Air travel is not a problem for the person with a pacemaker. She will need to communicate that she has a pacemaker so that she does not have to pass through airport metal detectors.

#145. 2.   **The ventricular pacemaker stimulates the ventricle if no atrial impulse is transmitted through the AV node. The appearance of the QRS complex shows that the ventricle has responded to the stimulus.**   Ev   Ph/10   An

1.   The absence of a QRS complex would indicate a problem called "loss of capture," meaning the stimulus from the pacemaker has not produced a ventricular response.

3.   An atrial pacemaker would produce pacemaker spikes followed by P waves. The atrial pacemaker stimulates the atria, whose response is indicated by the P wave.

4.   Demand pacemakers fire when the heart rate drops below the preset

rate. They do not fire as long as the heart rate is above the preset rate, which in this case is 72.

		NP	CN	CL
#146. 1.	**The nurse must make sure both verbally and visually that all healthcare providers are clear.**	Im	Ph/9	Ap
2.	No lubricant on the paddles can burn the client's skin.			
3.	Placing the paddles lightly on the chest can produce an electrical arc. Paddles should be placed firmly on the chest.			
4.	The person doing the defibrillating must stand back and not touch the bed to prevent also getting shocked.			
#147. 3.	**This hand position would depress the lower half of the sternum, which would compress the heart effectively.**	Im	Ph/10	Ap
1.	This hand position would not compress the heart because it is located behind the lower half of the sternum.			
2.	This could place the hands too high on the sternum to compress the heart effectively.			
4.	This could result in lacerations of the liver with potentially fatal bleeding should circulation be restored. It is too low to adequately compress the heart.			
#148. 3.	**The pain of pericarditis is exacerbated with respirations. Rotating the trunk and sitting up frequently relieves the pain.**	As	Ph/10	An
1.	Chest pain is not a symptom of endocarditis.			
2.	Angina is not associated with respiratory patterns and is not relieved by position changes.			
4.	The pain of a myocardial infarction is not relieved by position changes and is usually constant.			
#149. 2.	**First dose syncope occurs with prazocin. To reduce the risk of fainting, the client should take the first dose at bedtime.**	Pl	Ph/8	Ap
1.	Prazocin does not need to be taken with food.			
3.	This is appropriate for a beta-blocking drug. Alpha-blocking drugs such as prazocin do not cause bradycardia.			
4.	Edema may occur with central sympatholytics such as methyldopa (Aldomet) or calcium channel blockers such as nifedipine (Procardia). It is not a common problem with alpha blockers like prazocin.			
#150. 2.	**Moderation in alcohol intake is an important lifestyle change for controlling high blood pressure. Alcohol adds empty calories to the diet and elevates arterial blood pressure.**	Ev	He/4	An
1.	Soy sauce and mustard contain significant amounts of sodium. They would not be good substitutes for salt in a reduced sodium diet.			
3.	Aerobic exercise improves cardiovascular fitness. The client need not discontinue existing aerobic exercise but should start new exercises gradually. Isometric exercise (e.g., weight lifting, rowing) must be avoided.			
4.	Clients should be encouraged to stop smoking. Tobacco use causes vasoconstriction, raising blood pressure, and alters blood lipid levels. These are reversible changes.			
#151. 1.	**Oranges are high in potassium. Thiazide diuretics, such as Diuril, deplete body potassium by increasing urinary excretion, so potassium intake should be increased.**	Ev	Ph/8	Co
2.	Cold cereals are not high in potassium. They are high in sodium, which should be limited by clients with high blood pressure.			
3.	Brewed coffee is high in potassium. Cola drinks are not. Most good sources of potassium are fruits or vegetables.			
4.	Cranberry juice is low in potassium. It helps to prevent urinary tract infections, but is not useful in preventing adverse effects of diuretics.			
#152. 3.	**Intermittent claudication is the main symptom of narrowing of the arteries.**	An	Ph/10	An
1.	Pain, edema, and increased circumference of the affected limb are symptoms of DVT.			
2.	Chronically cold hands and feet, especially in the winter months, are			

ANSWER	RATIONALE	NP	CN	CL

characteristic of Raynaud's. The hands usually have pallor and cyanosis.

4. Pain, tenderness, redness, and a palpable induration along the course of the vein are characteristic of thrombophlebitis.

#153. 3. Gravity facilitates improved arterial blood flow. The reverse Trendelenburg position, in which the feet are below heart level, is used to improve circulation to the lower extremities.   Pl   Ph/9   Ap

1. If the legs are elevated, gravity further impedes circulation to the lower extremities. Rest pain may result.
2. The semi-Fowler's position does nothing to improve circulation to the legs. Extending the knees may be uncomfortable. Many clients prefer flexing the knees slightly.
4. The Trendelenburg position would place the feet above heart level. Gravity would impede blood flow to the lower extremities.

#154. 4. Cold induces arterial spasms. When the hands will be exposed to cold, warm gloves or mittens should be worn.   Pl   Ph/9   Ap

1. Caffeine should be avoided. Its vasoconstricting action can precipitate arterial spasms.
2. A low fat, low cholesterol diet is useful in treating atherosclerosis. Raynaud's phenomenon is due to arterial spasms, not atherosclerosis, so this diet change would not be helpful.
3. Elevating the hands does not relieve arterial spasms. The effects of gravity would reduce circulation to the hands even further. Immersing the hands in warm water is the best method for relieving spasms.

#155. 2. A pulsating abdominal mass is a common finding of an abdominal aortic aneurysm.   As   Ph/10   An

1. This pain is typical of a dissecting aortic aneurysm.
3. Unequal pulses is not seen with an abdominal aortic aneurysm.
4. A board-like, rigid abdomen is found in peritonitis.

#156. 3. A decrease in pulse quality signifies a decrease in the patency of the artery.   As   Ph/10   An

1. These are normal vital signs.
2. Dark-red blood is old. A small amount can be expected after surgery.
4. Swelling of the leg is common after surgery.

#157. 3. The best position for the affected leg is extended and flat in the bed. Elevating the leg would allow gravity to impede circulation. Having the leg dependent would promote development of edema, which could also impair circulation.   Im   Ph/9   Ap

1. Fowler's position would cause hip flexion, which constricts femoral vessels, reducing circulation to the leg.
2. Knee flexion would impede circulation to the calf and foot by constricting vessels in the popliteal space.
4. Elevating the leg would allow gravity to impede circulation. Placing the leg on pillows can cause pressure on the popliteal space, constricting vessels.

#158. 4. Elevating the legs improves venous drainage and reduces edema, which will promote wound healing.   Im   Ph/9   Ap

1. Dangling the legs reduces venous return and promotes edema formation. The legs should be elevated as much as possible.
2. Warm socks would be helpful in arterial disorders because cold worsens arterial insufficiency. Wearing warm socks has no special benefit in venous insufficiency.
3. Soaking the feet will not improve wound healing. Frequent soaks can cause maceration of the skin, which increases the risk of further breakdown. The dressing must be kept dry between changes.

#159. 1. Elevation of the legs by raising the foot of the bed 6 inches (Trendelenburg position) reduces venous stasis, decreasing the risk of further thrombus formation.   Im   Ph/9   Ap

ANSWER	RATIONALE	NP	CN	CL

2. Moist heat is applied to relieve pain and promote resolution of the inflammation. Ice would cause vasoconstriction and would not relieve inflammation.

3. The leg should never be massaged. Massage could dislodge the thrombus, resulting in pulmonary emboli.

4. Bedrest with minimal leg movement is indicated during the first few days when the risk of embolization is high. Leg movement could dislodge the thrombus, resulting in embolization.

#160. 1. Warfarin is an anticoagulant, which increases the risk of bleeding from any injury. Use of an electric razor reduces the risk of a cut, which might bleed excessively.   Ev   Ph/8   An

2. This is not necessary for clients taking warfarin. It would be appropriate if the client has arterial disease or diabetes because any injury might not heal.

3. This would be appropriate if constipation were likely as a side-effect. Warfarin is more likely to cause diarrhea. Clients taking warfarin should not change their normal eating habits because increased vitamin K can antagonize the drug. Dark green, leafy vegetables are high in vitamin K.

4. Aspirin is contraindicated while taking warfarin because it potentiates the anticoagulant effect, increasing the risk of bleeding.

#161. 3. Her symptoms suggest that the client has pulmonary emboli. Her activity should be limited to prevent further embolization and her head should be elevated to promote lung expansion and ease dyspnea.   Ev   Ph/10   Ap

1. Restraints will increase the client's anxiety, exacerbating the dyspnea. Because her oxygen supply will be decreased by the inability to circulate blood through the blocked pulmonary vessels, the client needs to be kept calm to reduce her oxygen demand.

2. The Heimlich maneuver is performed to remove a foreign body that is obstructing the airway. Signs of obstruction include absence of air movement and inability to speak or cough. The client's symptoms suggest pulmonary emboli.

4. This position is appropriate if air embolism is suspected because it will trap air in the right atrium. The client's history and symptoms suggest embolization of the clots from her leg. Since the emboli are solid, not air, a left Trendelenburg position will not prevent them from entering lung vessels.

#162. 2. Dextran coats the platelet surface to decrease adhesion. In doing so, the plasma volume expands, and viscosity is decreased.   An   Ph/8   An

1. Dextran decreases blood viscosity. Increasing blood viscosity would increase the chance of a pulmonary embolism.

3. Dextran increases plasma volume.

4. Dextran does not effect hemoglobin.

#163. 3. This describes varicose veins.   An   Ph/10   An

1. Thrombophlebitis is a raised, red, slightly indurated warm tender cord along a vein.

2. Thrombosis creates pain in the affected area. There is swelling distal to the site, with redness.

4. Venous insufficiency creates swollen limbs and thick coarse brown skin.

#164. 1. It is essential to prevent contractures of the hip joint so that Mr. B. will be able to walk with a prosthesis. Lying supine or prone with the stump extended helps to prevent hip contractures.   Pl   Ph/9   Ap

2. The stump is elevated for the first 24 hours after surgery to prevent edema. After this, the hip should be extended whenever possible to prevent contractures.

3. Warm soaks relax muscles. Because phantom limb pain is not caused by muscle tension or stiffness, warm soaks are unlikely to relieve it.

4. It is not necessary to avoid turning to the affected side after amputation. This would be indicated after some types of hip surgery to avoid disrupting the surgical site.

#165. 1. Phantom limb pain is common after amputation. It is a real sensation and needs to be acknowledged by the nurse.   Im   Ph/9   Ap

2. The sensation the client feels is real. He needs to know the nurse believes him, and he needs to be assured the sensation is not abnormal.

3. Phantom limb pain is a real physiologic response. It is not a psychological reaction.

4. The client may know his right foot is not there and still experience phantom limb pain. He needs to know this is not abnormal.

#166. 1. These blood values are consistent with a diagnosis of aplastic anemia in which the nurse's primary goals are to prevent complications from infection and hemorrhage. Whenever WBC blood levels are low, this should cue the nurse to recognize that the client's immune system is weakened and the potential for infection is great.   An   Ph/9   An

2. Because the WBC count is low, this should cue the nurse in to the fact that the client's immune system is weakened and the potential for infection is great. The blood values are consistent with a diagnosis of aplastic anemia. With other types of anemia, i.e., iron deficiency anemia, nutrition is altered and may be a primary concern. If that were the case, however, these blood values would be altered.

3. Although a weakened immune system, which is evident by the decreased WBC lab value, could precipitate a state of fatigue and weakness that could subsequently lead to a self-care deficit, priority should be given to the potential for infection.

4. There is no indication from these lab values that fluid volume excess would exist. The lab values are associated with aplastic anemia, which, as indicated by the low WBC lab values, should alert the nurse to the fact that the client's immune system is weakened and that there is a high potential for infection. A fluid volume deficit, vs excess, may be indicative of other types of anemias. In such cases, however, the lab values would be altered.

#167. 1. The RBCs are decreased (normal 4.5–5.0), which is associated with either the decreased production of RBCs, increased destruction of RBCs, or blood loss. Both hemoglobin (normal 12–18) and hematocrit (normal 38–54) values are subsequently decreased. Low platelets (normal 150,000–400,000) are most frequently associated with a tendency to bleed. These factors support the need for the nurse to monitor the client closely for bleeding problems.   Pl   Ph/9   Ap

2. These lab values do not indicate any need for seizure precautions.

3. The need for isolation to prevent infection is indicated when WBCs are low. In this case, the WBCs are within normal limits.

4. These values do not indicate that the client is in need of pain control. To rule this out, the client would have to be clinically assessed.

#168. 1. The WBC is very low (normal 4,000–11,000). This indicates that the client's immune system is deficient and the client is subject to infection.   Im   Ph/9   An

2. The RBCs are within normal limits (4.0–5.0 million). There is no indication of bleeding.

3. The platelet count is within normal limits (150,000–400,000) and there is neither any indication that the client is bleeding nor in pain.

4. Blood transfusions are not indicated for these lab values.

#169. 4. Persons with type AB blood, because they are universal blood recipients, are able to receive either type A, B, AB, or O blood. People with any blood type other than AB, are restricted as to the type of blood they can receive.   An   Ph/8   Ap

1. Persons with type AB blood are called "universal blood recipients." This means that they are able to receive blood from donors who are either blood type A, B, AB, or O. People with any blood type other than AB, are restricted as to the type of blood they can receive.
2. Persons with type AB blood are called "universal blood recipients." This means that they are able to receive blood from donors who are either blood type A, B, AB, or O. People with any blood type other than AB, are restricted as to the type of blood they can receive.
3. Persons with type AB blood are called "universal blood recipients" and are able to receive A, B, AB, or O blood. People with any blood type other than AB, are restricted as to the type of blood they can receive.

#170. 3. **The tubing is primed with 0.9% NS solution. If the filter is not completely primed, debris will coagulate in the filter and the transfusion will be slowed. In addition, saline is prepared to infuse in case a transfusion reaction occurs.** | Im | Ph/8 | Ap

1. Intravenous medications cannot be added to a blood bag. An additional IV site is required if IV meds need to be administered.
2. Blood should be hung 15–30 minutes after it is released from the laboratory.
4   A large-bore catheter is used to prevent hemolysis of cells.

#171. 2. **The signs and symptoms the client is experiencing are indicative of a transfusion reaction and the transfusion must first be discontinued.** | Im | Ph/8 | Ap

1. The signs and symptoms the client is experiencing are indicative of a transfusion reaction and the transfusion must first be discontinued. The physician and blood bank are to be notified after this initial step is taken.
3. The signs and symptoms the client is experiencing are indicative of a transfusion reaction and the transfusion must first be discontinued prior to the monitoring of vital signs.
4. The signs and symptoms the client is experiencing are indicative of a transfusion reaction and the transfusion must first be discontinued. The client's status can then be further assessed.

#172. 4. **A Z-track injection technique should be used to prevent leakage of the iron to subcutaneous tissues.** | Im | Ph/8 | Ap

1. Because IM iron solutions may stain the skin, separate needles should be used for withdrawing the solution and for injecting the medication. The needle should be a large gauge (19–20) size.
2. The site is not massaged after administration.
3. The solution should be injected deep IM in the upper outer quadrant of the buttocks with a 2–3 in needle.

#173. 1. **Dark, leafy green vegetables (as well as meats, eggs, legumes, and whole-grain or enriched breads and cereals) are rich in iron. In addition, both citrus foods and green leafy vegetables are high in vitamin C, which aids in iron absorption.** | Ev | Ph/7 | An

2. Bananas are well known for their potassium and vitamin B_6; however, neither bananas nor nuts have significant levels of iron or vitamin C, the latter of which is necessary for iron absorption.
3. Both coffee and tea are high in caffeine. Neither are sources of iron or vitamin C, the latter of which is necessary for iron absorption.
4. Dairy products are well known for their calcium and fortified vitamins; however, neither have significant amounts of iron or vitamin C, the latter of which is necessary for iron absorption.

#174. 1. **There is a familial predisposition for pernicious anemia, and although the disease cannot be prevented, it can be controlled if detected and treated early. Pernicious anemia occurs as a result of the lack of the protein intrinsic factor that is secreted by the gastric mucosa.** | As | Ph/9 | Co

2. Although blood loss is a significant factor contributing to many types

of anemia, pernicious anemia occurs as a result of the lack of the protein intrinsic factor that is secreted by the gastric mucosa.

3. Although infectious agents and toxins can precipitate anemia caused by increased erythrocyte destruction, pernicious anemia occurs as a result of the lack of the protein intrinsic factor that is secreted by the gastric mucosa.

4. Although a deficient dietary intake may be related to iron deficiency anemia, pernicious anemia occurs as a result of a lack of the protein intrinsic factor that is normally secreted by the gastric mucosa.

#175. 1. The client is to fast for 12 hours prior to the test. No food or drink is permitted. Following administration of the vitamin B_{12} dose, food is delayed for three hours.   Im   Ph/9   Ap

2. Urine is collected for a minimum of 24 hours. Because the most common source of error in performing the test is incomplete collection of urine, some labs require a 48-hour collection period to allow for a small margin of error.

3. Bowel evacuation is not required for this test. Should there be fecal contamination of the urine, the test may be invalid.

4. It is not necessary that the bladder be emptied prior to the test. The test examines the urine from the time the client receives the injection of B_{12}. Whether or not the bladder is empty or full at the time of the injection is not important.

#176. 1. In aplastic anemia, the bone marrow elements (erythrocytes, leukocytes, and platelets) are suppressed. Treatments include, but are not limited to, bone marrow transplantation, transfusions to reduce symptomatology, and drugs to stimulate bone marrow function. Drugs like estrogen and progesterone work to stimulate bone growth. Estrogen and progesterone also stop menstruation so there is less blood loss.   An   Ph/8   An

2. These drugs work to stimulate bone growth, which is suppressed in aplastic anemia. They do not function to regulate fluid balance.

3. These drugs work to stimulate bone growth, which is suppressed in aplastic anemia. They do not function to enhance sodium and potassium absorption.

4. These drugs work to stimulate bone growth, which is suppressed in aplastic anemia. They do not function to promote utilization and storage of fluids.

#177. 2. Decreased RBCs are a result of the excessive destruction of the red blood cells. With this destruction, there is a subsequent decrease in both hemoglobin and hematocrit. In addition, this increased destruction causes an elevation in bilirubin levels. The reticulocyte count is high because the numbers of immature RBCs are increased when RBCs are being destroyed. This count reflects the bone marrow activity, which is active in producing RBCs to compensate for the destruction.   An   Ph/9   An

1. Hemolytic anemia is associated with a decrease in RBCs due to their destruction, rather than an increase. Bilirubin levels subsequently increase, whereas hemoglobin and hematocrit decrease. The reticulocyte count is high because the numbers of immature RBCs are increased when RBCs are being destroyed.

3. Whereas hemolytic anemia is associated with decreased RBCs as a result of their destruction, bilirubin is increased rather than decreased, hemoglobin and hematocrit are decreased rather than increased, and reticulocytes are increased rather than decreased.

4. Whereas hemolytic anemia is associated with increased bilirubin levels, RBCs are decreased rather than increased, hemoglobin and hematocrit are decreased rather than increased, and the reticulocyte count is increased rather than decreased.

#178. 1. Following a splenectomy, immunologic deficiencies may develop, and vulnerability to infection is greatly increased. The   Pl   Ph/9   Ap

postsplenectomy client is highly susceptible to infection from organisms such as *Pneumococcus*. A preventive measure is immunization with Pneumovax.

2. The nurse is responsible for closely monitoring the client after any type of surgery. Following a splenectomy, however, the client is most prone to developing infection subsequent to immunologic deficiency, not congestive heart failure.

3. The nurse is responsible for closely monitoring the client after any type of surgery. Following a splenectomy, however, the client is most prone to developing infection subsequent to immunologic deficiency, not urinary retention.

4. The nurse is responsible for closely monitoring the client after any type of surgery. Following a splenectomy, however, the client is most prone to developing infection subsequent to immunologic deficiency. Viral hepatitis, rather than being a complication of surgery, is a possible cause for splenomegaly, which may necessitate surgery.

#179. 3. **Cerebral, cardiopulmonary, and peripheral tissue perfusion is affected by DIC. The many clots can cause obstruction to blood flow and tissue damage can subsequently occur.** An   Ph/10   An

1. In DIC, there is a fluid volume deficit and hypotension, which contribute to decreased cardiac output. The treatment is directed toward fluid replacement.

2. In DIC, there is great potential for pain related to this bleeding. Sensory perception remains acute rather than decreased.

4. Although multisystem organ dysfunction is commonly associated with the development of DIC, respiratory aspiration is not a high risk problem.

#180. 1. **In DIC, the paradoxical events of hemorrhage and clotting occur. Although it may seem counterproductive to administer heparin while a client is bleeding, it is necessary to prevent the clotting that is simultaneously occurring in the microcirculation. It is critical that the client be monitored closely.** An   Ph/10   Ap

2. Although increased blood flow may be a subsequent action of heparin administration, it is not the primary goal. Heparin is ordered for the purpose of preventing clot formation. Although it may seem counterproductive to administer heparin while a client is bleeding, it is necessary to prevent the clotting which is simultaneously occurring.

3. Heparin is ordered for the purpose of preventing clot formation. It does not act to increase clot formation even though this may be a paradoxical goal when treating clients with DIC. In DIC, the paradoxical events of hemorrhage and clotting occur together. Therefore, seemingly conflicting treatments may be used.

4. Heparin is ordered for the purpose of preventing clot formation. It does not decrease blood flow nor would one wish to do so because this is already a primary factor in the diminished tissue perfusion that occurs in DIC.

#181. 1. **This statement answers Mr. H.'s question in a simple, matter of fact manner that is truthful and to the point.** Im   Ph/8   Ap

2. Although the content of this statement is true, it is not the best response for the nurse to make because the pharmacologic explanation may not be understood by the client. Furthermore, it does not answer the question he asked.

3. Although the content of this statement is true at the current time, it is too direct and harsh. In addition, the words, "Don't you know?" are condescending and should be avoided.

4. The content of these statements are correct. HIV can become refractory to such drugs; however, communicating this to the client in this manner conveys a sense of hopelessness. This can be harmful for someone with an incurable and terminal disease.

#182. 2. **Although needle exchange programs are very controversial, it is evident the transmission of HIV can be significantly reduced when needle exchange programs are introduced.**   Ev   Sa/2   An

     1.   HIV-positive mothers are encouraged to refrain from breast feeding their infants because studies have shown that the virus can be passed from the mother to the infant via breast milk.

     3.   The presence of an orgasm is irrelevant to the transmission of HIV. This is a myth, much like the one used by many teens who believe orgasm is necessary for pregnancy to occur.

     4.   Natural skin condoms do not afford the protection that latex and polyurethane condoms do. The natural skin condoms have pores that are large enough for HIV to penetrate.

#183. 1. **Heterosexual transmission of HIV is a concern, especially in this age group. It is on the rise and this is often overlooked because the more known transmissions take place among homosexuals and IV drug abusers.**   Pl   Sa/2   Ap

     2.   Although children can be infected with HIV via sexual contact, the primary etiology of AIDS in children is by contracting it in the womb from their HIV-positive mother.

     3.   Although homosexual transmission accounts for how the majority of HIV-positive individuals have contracted the virus, the homosexual community has been well educated. Currently, the greatest increase in transmission is a result of engaging in other risky behaviors, namely sharing of contaminated needles and heterosexual activity with an infected partner.

     4.   Transmission of HIV by IV drug users is prominent whenever contaminated needles are shared or other unsterile equipment is used. Transmission is significantly decreased and often eliminated when clean, sterile equipment is used. Results from cities that have clean needle exchange programs can attest to the decrease in transmission rates.

#184. 2. **Corticosteroids may be added to the chemotherapy regime because of their antitumor effect. In addition, they assist in the excretion of calcium, which helps to treat the hypercalcemia that occurs in clients who have multiple myeloma.**   Pl   Ph/8   Ap

     1.   Ambulation, not bedrest, is necessary to treat the hypercalcemia, that occurs in clients with multiple myeloma. Weight bearing helps the bones to reabsorb calcium.

     3.   Adequate hydration is necessary to treat hypercalcemia, hyperuricemia, and dehydration. Fluids dilute calcium and prevent protein particles from blocking the renal tubules. Fluids are administered to attain a urinary output of 1.5–2 L per day.

     4.   Although calcium is lost from the bones, eventually this causes hypercalcemia. The therapeutic regime is aimed at decreasing blood levels of calcium, rather than increasing it.

#185. 1. **With polycythemia vera, maintaining oxygenation is critical. High altitudes can precipitate hypoxia. This client needs further instruction.**   Ev   Ph/9   An

     2.   This statement does not indicate that the client needs further instruction. Passive or active leg exercises should be maintained to decrease the chance of thrombus formation.

     3.   Walking is a good exercise to decrease the chance of thrombus formation. By selecting walking as an exercise, and by avoiding inclement weather by walking indoors, the client can avoid situations that are associated with an insufficient supply of oxygen. This client does not need further instruction.

     4.   If lying flat might contribute to hypoxia, it is helpful to either raise the head of the bed or use pillows to assist the person to obtain an upright position. There is no need for concern.

ANSWER	RATIONALE	NP	CN	CL

#186. 4. This is a description of the normal vesicular breath sounds. They are low pitched, soft sounds heard over the peripheral lung fields where air flows through smaller bronchioles.   As   He/4   Ap

   1. Crackles are audible when there is a sudden opening of small airways containing fluid. Crackles are usually heard during inspiration and do not clear with cough.

   2. Rhonchi sound like gurgles. Heard on expiration, they may clear with cough.

   3. A wheeze is a musical noise that results from the passage of air through a narrowed airway. A wheeze is commonly associated with asthma, bronchoconstriction, and edema.

#187. 2. A patient with lung cancer demonstrating the assessment findings provided would indicate a nursing diagnosis of ineffective airway clearance. The goal for this patient is that the patient will breathe without dyspnea or discomfort and maintain a patent airway.   An   Ph/9   An

   1. Based on the provided information, the diagnosis of impaired gas exchange cannot be made. If the patient exhibited cyanosis, respiratory distress, or use of accessory muscles the impaired gas exchange could be made.

   3. Based on the given data, this diagnosis cannot be made. However, pain could potentially be a realistic diagnosis for a patient with lung cancer.

   4. Based on the provided information, this diagnosis cannot be made. The nurse would need to observe cyanosis, decreased pulses, and decreased skin temperature to make the diagnosis of altered tissue perfusion.

#188. 4. The sample must be analyzed within 20 minutes, or if the patient has leukocytosis immediately, to ensure accurate results.   As   Ph/9   Ap

   1. By shaking the syringe, air bubbles may form in the sample. The results may then be altered—increased PO_2, decreased PCO_2, and increased pH.

   2. The sample should be placed in ice water immediately. If it is not the results may be altered—decreased PO_2, increased PCO_2, decreased pH.

   3. Heparin's anticoagulant effects decrease the sample's pH. Heparin should not be added to the sample.

#189. 2. Teeth are brushed to reduce contamination, then the patient coughs into the container. Sputum is best collected in the morning when it is more plentiful.   Im   Ph/9   Ap

   1. Sputum is best collected in the morning when it is more plentiful and concentrated from pooling during the night. The client should also be encouraged not to spit, but to cough so that sputum is obtained.

   3. Immediately after eating is not a good time to obtain a sputum specimen, as food particles left in the mouth may contaminate the specimen. Spitting should be avoided—deep coughing is encouraged. The best time to obtain a sputum specimen is first thing in the morning.

   4. The client should be encouraged to cough, not spit, so that sputum rather than saliva is obtained. *Nothing* should be added to the sputum specimen.

#190. 3. A positive reaction is present when the induration is greater than 10 mm in diameter. The positive reaction indicates exposure to TB or the presence of inactive disease, not active disease.   An   He/4   An

   1. Induration measuring greater than 10 mm in diameter indicates exposure to TB. Further follow-up of this client is indicated.

   2. Although this reaction is positive (any area of induration greater than 10 mm in diameter is considered positive), a positive reaction does

not mean that active disease is present, but indicates exposure to TB or the presence of dormant disease.

    4.   Tuberculosis skin test results must be read within 48 hours to ensure accuracy. By waiting two additional days, nothing would be accomplished. The client should be referred for further follow-up at this time.

#191. 2.   Vital signs are taken frequently. Nothing is given by mouth until the cough and swallow reflexes have returned. Both are important criteria for discharge.   Ev   Ph/9   An

    1.   The client should be observed for signs and symptoms of respiratory distress including dyspnea, changes in respiratory rate, use of accessory muscles, and change in or absent lung sounds. If the client is exhibiting these findings, he or she is not ready for discharge.

    3.   If the client is having hemoptysis, this is considered an adverse reaction and the physician should be notified (unless an excision has taken place, then there may be a small amount of hemoptysis expected). Development of adventitious breath sounds should be reported to the physician, also.

    4.   Development of arrhythmias and tachycardias need to be reported to the physician immediately. It is positive that the patient is able to eat and drink, but due to the development of the arrhythmias, the patient's discharge would be held.

#192. 3.   The Pleur-evac must not be raised above chest level because it can cause back flow of the fluid into the pleural space precipitating collapse of the lung or mediastinal shift. The Pleur-evac must remain upright and the chest tube should not have traction on it.   Im   Ph/9   Ap

    1.   The chest tube should not be clamped for ambulation. Chest tubes should not be clamped unless there an order to do so is present.

    2.   There is no reason to question the order to ambulate Mr. E. Presence of chest tubes is not a contraindication for ambulation.

    4.   The Pleur-evac chest tube connection should never be disconnected. Atmospheric air will enter the pleural space through the chest tube.

#193. 3.   Fluctuations of 5–10 cm during normal breathing are common. These fluctuations provide continuous manometer of pressure changes in the pleural space and are a reliable indicator of overall respiratory effort.   Ev   Ph/9   An

    1.   Bubbling from the straw when the client exhales or coughs indicates an air leak. Further observation and assessment of the client and the system should take place.

    2.   Fluctuations of 5–10 cm during normal breathing are common. Absence of fluctuation could indicate the client lying on the chest tube, the tube being obstructed by a kink, or dependent fluid filling a loop of the tubing.

    4.   An air vent is placed through the stopper in the bottle so that incoming pleural air can not build up, and further air entry is prevented. The air vent should not be clamped off.

#194. 3.   Chest physiotherapy should be performed at least two hours after meals to reduce the risk of vomiting and aspiration.   Im   Ph/9   Ap

    1.   Chest percussion is performed by clapping on the chest wall with a cupped hand. The cupped hand will capture a pocket of air as it strikes the chest promoting loosened secretions.

    2.   Vibration is the use of energy waves from the hand to move the secretions from the affected lung areas during *expiration* phase of respiration.

    4.   Apical drainage is accomplished in the sitting position. Plan this phase of CPT during the middle of the session, allowing the client to rest.

#195. 1.   The nurse's best initial action should be to remove the client from the ventilator, ventilating the client with an ambu bag. Obviously,   Im   Ph/10   Ap the client is experiencing respiratory distress and is not receiving adequate ventilation. The nurse should continue to closely assess to determine the cause and determine if the respiratory distress is related to ventilator malfunction or change in patient status.

2. The best initial response is not to call respiratory therapy. The nurse should provide care to the client first, then follow up with a call if needed.

3. This is not the best initial action. The nurse should carefully assess and ventilate the client; if there is no response and the ventilator has been deemed functioning properly, then the physician should be notified of the change in patient status.

4. Alarms on a ventilator should never be disabled.

#196. 2. It is important for the nurse to quickly assess the patient and determine the cause of the alarm. Once the cause has been determined, the nurse must intervene promptly to prevent complications. See below for examples of causes of ventilator alarms. As Ph/10 Ap

1. The physician should not be notified every time the alarm goes off. The alarm can be triggered by the client becoming disconnected from the ventilator, a kink in the tubing, or the patient needing suctioning. These are all things that the nurse can take care of without notifying the physician.

3. The alarm should *never* be disabled.

4. Initial reaction should be to quickly assess the client and determine the cause of the alarm. If the nurse is unable to determine the cause of the alarm, then the client is removed from the ventilator and ventilated with an ambu bag.

#197. 4. Oxygen supports combustion. Smoking is not permitted in the room while O_2 is set up or being administered. A sign should be posted to that effect. Im Ph/9 Ap

1. This is appropriate for a client with a partial rebreather mask. The flow rate of the oxygen is adjusted to meet the respiratory pattern of the client.

2. This is more appropriate for a client with a face mask because the face mask limits the client's ability to clear the mouth if vomiting occurs.

3. This is appropriate for a patient with a non-rebreather mask. The valves should open during expiration and close during inhalation to prevent a dramatic decrease in FiO_2. It is possible for suffocation to occur if the reservoir bag kinks or the O_2 source becomes disconnected.

#198. 2. The COPD client's drive to breathe is hypoxia. In COPD the CO_2 level gradually rises over time and central chemoreceptors are no longer sensitive to high CO_2 levels. Instead, the peripheral chemoreceptors found in the carotid and aortic arch bodies become the major stimuli for breathing. When the client with COPD receives high levels of O_2, the hypoxic drive to breathe is eliminated. The client experiences respiratory depression that may lead to apnea. Im Ph/9 An

1. Visitors should not be encouraged to manipulate medical equipment. By increasing Mrs. C.'s oxygen flow rate, the cousin may have decreased Mrs. C.'s hypoxic drive to breathe. The hypoxic drive to breathe is common in COPD patients; they require only low doses of oxygen. Seven liters is too much.

3. The physician should be notified, but only after the O_2 level has been decreased and careful assessment has taken place.

4. Again, this is an appropriate action; however, the oxygen should be decreased first.

#199. 1. The mask must fit properly as a poor fitting mask reduces the Pl Ph/9 Ap amount of oxygen delivered. **The mask may also cause skin breakdown, so it is very important to provide skin care. Loosen the strap holding the mask frequently and assess the skin.**

2. This intervention is appropriate for a patient receiving oxygen per nasal cannula.
3. Smoking is not allowed in the room in which oxygen is being administered. Oxygen supports combustion.
4. Oxygen toxicity is possible for a patient receiving oxygen therapy at a concentration of greater than 50%, administered continuously for more than 24–48 hours.

#200. 2. Trach care should be provided once every eight hours. Pl Ph/9 An

1. Trach care is performed to keep the trach tube and stoma free from secretions and mucus, prevent infection, and maintain a patent airway. The recommendation is to provide trach care every eight hours. Trach care may be done more often if the client has a large amount of secretions or the stoma has drainage or exudate.
3. In a client with a new trach in place, the recommendation is to provide trach care every eight hours. Some clients with an older trach, or in the home setting may provide care once a day.
4. A client may need to be suctioned every hour if a large amount of secretions are present, but total trach care should not be required.

#201. 2. These are signs and symptoms of COPD. The nurse would also need to evaluate breathing rate/pattern, use of accessory muscles for breathing, cyanosis, capillary refill, and clubbing of fingernails. An Ph/10 An

1. Generally, the sputum production with pneumonia is yellow or green. Other signs and symptoms include fever, chills, sweats, headache, fatigue, and cough.
3. Tuberculosis may be present with progressive fatigue, lethargy, nausea, anorexia, weight loss, low grade fevers, and night sweats. A cough may be noted with mucoid, blood-tinged sputum.
4. Asthma is an intermittent airway narrowing. It affects the airways, not the air sacs and is reversible. Barrel chest is not common.

#202. 3. A major goal for the COPD client is that the client will use a breathing pattern that does not lead to tiring and to plan activities so that the client does not become overtired. Care should be spaced, allowing frequent rest periods, and preventing fatigue. Pl Ph/9 Ap

1. Oxygen is used to treat symptoms of hypoxia or hypoxemia. In either case, the goal is to use the lowest FiO_2 possible. The amount of oxygen required is extremely precise, because the high levels of oxygen can be fatal to a COPD client. Usually the range for a COPD client is between 1–6 L/minute. Remember the principle respiratory drive for COPD clients is hypoxia!
2. This is not indicated at this time. Respiratory isolation is not routinely required for COPD clients.
4. It is very important that the COPD patient drink adequate amounts to help liquefy secretions, aiding in mobilization and removal of secretions.

#203. 1. Typically, the client with TB will present with fatigue, lethargy, nausea, anorexia, weight loss, low grade fever, and night sweats. As Ph/10 Co

2. Dyspnea in TB is uncommon unless there is massive pleural effusion.
3. There are not typical signs and symptoms of TB. More likely is a pulmonary obstruction such as a tumor.
4. These signs and symptoms are not typical of TB. Dyspnea, hypoxemia, and decreased pulmonary compliance can be associated with ARDS.

#204. 1. The client should be placed in respiratory isolation until active TB is ruled out. TB is spread by droplet infection, thus her sputum should be handled according to respiratory isolation protocol. Pl Ph/9 Ap

ANSWER	RATIONALE	NP	CN	CL

2. Encouraging the client to cough and deep breathe is very important, but not the initial action.

3. Fluids should be encouraged to keep a client with pneumonia well hydrated, thinning secretions aiding in mobilization of the secretions. However, this is not the nurse's initial action.

4. The client may require O_2 at some point, but this is not the nurse's initial action.

#205. 3. These medications frequently cause nausea. The nausea may be decreased if the medications are taken at bedtime. — Ev — Ph/8 — An

1. Generally, therapy for TB is usually between 6–24 months. The average length of therapy is 9–12 months. The medication regime and dosage is based on patient response and compliance.

2. The order for the 2 po drugs is daily, the injection is twice weekly, so the client would have to come to the clinic two times a week, not once.

4. Rifampin affects the action of several drugs including inactivation of birth control pills. The client should be counseled regarding alternative birth control methods to use while she is on this medication.

#206. 3. Handwashing is the best tool for prevention of infection. Ms. C. should wash her hands very carefully after any contact with body substances, masks, or soiled tissues. The family should also use good handwashing techniques. — Ev — Sa/2 — An

1. Tuberculosis is transmitted by droplet infection and is not carried on items such as clothing.

2. Clients with TB are no longer isolated for long periods of time as they were in the past, as long as compliance with therapy is maintained.

4. Sputum is highly contaminated. Ms. C. should cough into paper tissues and dispose of them properly.

#207. 3. Pulmonary care is a vital part of the management of this type of client. Measures are taken to prevent stasis of secretions and promote chest expansion, preventing complications such as atelectasis and pneumonia. — Pl — Ph/9 — An

1. Binding is not recommended. Binding inhibits chest expansion, impairing respiratory function, and promoting complications associated with hypoventilation.

2. Mrs. P. should be mobilized as soon as possible to prevent complications associated with bedrest and hypoventilation. Activity helps prevent stasis of secretions and promotes chest expansion.

4. Although pain management and control is an important part of caring for a patient with a rib fracture, large doses of narcotics most likely will oversedate an elderly patient like Mrs. P. The goal is to achieve a delicate balance between pain relief and sedation to avoid hypoventilation. To participate in pulmonary care, the patient must be awake, yet comfortable.

#208. 2. Based on Mr. Z.'s symptoms the nurse suspects impending respiratory failure and should prepare for intubation and mechanical ventilation. — Im — Ph/10 — Ap

1. Never apply sandbags on the patient's chest. They may provide some comfort by acting as a splint, but will inhibit chest expansion impairing respiratory function.

3. At this time a chest tube is not indicated.

4. Mr. Z. has signs and symptoms of respiratory failure. Pain medicine would not be administered at this time because it may further impair his respiratory status.

#209. 3. With pleural effusions, lung expansion may be restricted and the patient will experience dyspnea, primarily on exertion. — As — Ph/10 — Co

1. Pleural pain is a very common pulmonary symptom associated with pleural effusion. The pain arises from the parietal pleura, which is

richly supplied with sensory nerve endings. However, it is not the most often occurring presenting symptom.

2. A pleural effusion is the accumulation of fluid in the pleural space—swelling is not a presenting symptom.

4. Increased sputum production is not a common sign/symptom of pleural effusion.

#210. 2. This plan allows frequent rest periods for the client. The patient should not rush through morning care activities as rushing will increase hypoxemia, dyspnea, and fatigue. Pl Ph/7 Ap

1. This regime would exhaust the client. It is imperative to space activities with frequent rest periods. Activity intolerance related to fatigue is very common in this type of patient.

3. It is not realistic to expect this client to be able to sit up in the chair and provide her own care the first time she is up. She will become too fatigued.

4. By getting this client up and bathing before breakfast, she may become very fatigued. She may be too tired to eat properly. Proper nutrition is very important in the healing process.

#211. 1. In a patient with pneumonia, bronchial breath sounds are heard over areas of density or consolidation. Breath sounds are diminished when the airflow is decreased as is typical with pneumonia. Tactile fremitus is increased over the affected area. Percussion is dulled. In pneumonia, the alveoli fill with fluid, red cells, and white cells creating consolidation. An Ph/10 An

2. The presented findings are not characteristic of asthma. Typically, a lung assessment of a patient with asthma would demonstrate wheezes obscuring normal breath sounds, decreased tactile fremitus, and percussion would be normal to diffusely hyperresonant. Asthma occurs when the bronchi respond excessively to stimuli causing restriction to airflow and hyperinflation of the alveoli.

3. In emphysema, the distal air sacs are enlarged and the lungs are hyperinflated. Normal breath sounds are decreased to absent. Tactile fremitus is decreased. Crackles, wheezes, and rhonchi may be present. Percussion is hyperresonant.

4. Early (L) sided heart failure is caused by the increasing pressure in the pulmonary veins causing congestion and edema around the alveoli. Lung assessment reveals resonant percussion, normal breath sounds, normal tactile fremitus, and late inspiration crackles in the dependent portion of the lungs can occur.

#212. 2. Research has shown that there may be a correlation between vitamin A deficiency in the diet and the development of lung cancer. Daily consumption of green and yellow vegetables is encouraged. Ev He/4 An

1. Cigarette smoke may be inhaled actively by smoking or passively (second hand smoke). Both types of inhalation are positively correlated with development of lung cancer.

3. Clients with chronic respiratory diseases are at higher risk for development of lung cancer.

4. Lung cancer has a higher incidence in industrial areas. Coal tar, radioactive ore, asbestos, nickel, silver, arsenic and plastics have been found to be carcinogenic. Asbestos exposure is a definite risk factor for development of lung cancer.

#213. 4. A preventive approach to pain control provides a more consistent level of relief and reduces client anxiety, which in turn can reduce discomfort and pain. Ph Ph/8 Ap

1. Most pain medications will not afford the patient complete and total pain relief, but will make the pain more manageable and decrease the severe discomfort.

2. At this point in his car, it is more important for pain relief to be obtained than to have concern with addiction problems. By talking

with him about becoming addicted, he may not use the medication he needs to alleviate his suffering and pain.

3. It is more important to have the patient inform the nurse regarding the degree of relief obtained from the medication. If relief is not obtained, perhaps additional pain medication could be ordered or his current medication changed. Also, remember to use alternative methods of pain relief such as relaxation techniques, back rubs, and guided imagery.

#214. 3. **Post-op respiratory insufficiency may result from an altered level of consciousness related to anesthesia, pain medications, decreased respiratory effort secondary to pain, or inadequate airway clearance. So, the client must be monitored very closely with frequent vital sign checks and respiratory assessments.** `Pl  Ph/9  Ap`

1. In an pneumonectomy, the entire lung is removed and the pleural space is left empty. Closed chest drainage is generally not used because it is helpful for serous fluid to accumulate in the empty space to prevent an extensive mediastinal shift.

2. In an pneumonectomy, the entire lung is removed and the pleural space is left empty. Closed chest drainage is generally not used because it is helpful for serous fluid to accumulate in the empty space to prevent an extensive mediastinal shift.

4. It is very important that the client move the arm on the affected side. Generally the pain is due to muscle dissection and restricted positioning while the patient is in the OR. Encouraging use of analgesics and arm exercises will help decrease discomfort.

#215. 3. **Thirty or forty-five minutes after the administration of IM pain medication is the time when the pain medication is most effective. Thus, this is the best time to schedule coughing and deep breathing and arm exercises.** `Pl  Ph/9  Ap`

1. It would be more beneficial to Mr. B. to offer him pain medication prior to the activity rather than after the exercise. Mr. B. would be able to better participate if the medication were given prior to the activity with sufficient time allowed for the medication to work.

2. This will not decrease the pain; however, sips of warm water can aid relaxation and produce more effective coughing.

4. Mr. B.'s incision is not on his abdomen. Splinting provides support of the incision promoting comfort. It is also reassuring to the client who may be fearful that the incision may come "undone." The nurse may have to help Mr. B. hold a pillow to splint to achieve maximum benefit.

#216. 3. **It is common for the client to have suprasternal and intercostal retractions as the client loses lung capacity. The nurse should anticipate restlessness, apprehension, agitation, sluggishness, disorientation, and tachycardia.** `As  Ph/10  An`

1. Early blood gas analysis (on room air), reveals PaO_2 less than 70 mmHg, $PaCO_2$ less than 35 mmHg, and respiratory alkalosis. The X-ray will demonstrate a normal heart size with diffuse, bilateral lung infiltrates. Tachycardia is common.

2. Secretions associated with ARDS are usually thin and frothy. PaO_2 is less than 70 mmHg, pH is greater than 7.45.

4. The most common adventitious breath sounds are crackles or diminished breath sounds caused by pulmonary edema. These blood gas findings are compatible with late ARDS. Respiratory pattern is shallow and rapid breathing progressing to dyspnea.

#217. 1. **A total laryngectomy is the removal of the larynx and formation of the tracheostomy. The esophagus remains attached to the pharynx. No air will enter through the nose. The patient will breathe through the tracheostomy. The procedure is indicated for large glottic tumors with fixation of vocal cords.** `An  Ph/9  Kn`

2. A tracheostomy is a surgical opening made into the trachea for airway management with a creation of a stoma. This procedure can be indicated for (but not limited to) long-term airway management, upper airway obstruction, altered level of consciousness, sleep apnea, airway burns.

3. Radical neck dissection is the removal of the lymphatic drainage channels and nodes, sternicleodomastoid muscle, spinal accessory nerve, jugular vein, and submandibular area. This procedure is indicated when metastasis occurs to the cervical lymph nodes from tumors in the upper aerodigestive tract.

4. A partial laryngectomy is removal of half or more of the larynx. This procedure is performed for cancer of the vocal cords.

#218. 2. For the first few days after surgery, the client should communicate by writing. If the client is very tired, a communication board may be used allowing the client to point to statements. Pl Ph/9 Ap

1. The artificial larynx may be used three to four days after surgery. The electronic device is held along the neck with vibration producing a mechanical speech.

3. Esophageal speech is a technique that requires the client to swallow air, holding it in the upper esophagus and controlling the release to produce speech. This technique requires practice and is not appropriate in the immediate post-op period.

4. A voice button is used with a tracheoesophageal puncture. A fistula is made in the upper tracheostoma to the cervical esophagus. Once this is healed, a valve is inserted. By occluding the valve, the client may speak. This technique is not appropriate in the immediate postoperative period.

#219. 4. An artificial larynx is an electronic device held along the neck and vibration produces mechanical speech. The speech quality is monotone and artificial. Ev Ph/9 An

1. The tracheoesophageal puncture is a surgical method that may restore speech. Once healed, a small, one-way valve or voice button is inserted. Air can be shunted into the esophagus, producing speech. These devices require maintenance and only clients who are highly motivated, able to perform self-care, and have good manual dexterity are successful with this procedure. Because Mrs. S. suffers from arthritis in her hands, this most likely is not the best option for her.

2. All of the techniques to restore speech require much time. The client will be seen by a speech therapist following discharge. It is a long process and the client will require much support and encouragement.

3. Esophageal speech is a technique requiring the client to swallow and hold air in the upper esophagus. By controlling the flow of air, the client can speak 6–10 words at a time. The voice is deep and loud once the technique is mastered.

#220. 4. To substitute for the nose and pharynx, where air is usually warmed and humidified, a humidifier, pans of water, or houseplants should be used to increase the humidity in the home. Ev Sa/2 An

1. Swimming should be avoided and care should be taken when showering to prevent water from entering the stoma and causing airway obstruction.

2. The stoma should be covered with a handkerchief or gauze when coughing, not tissues since the paper tissues can adhere to the stoma and cause obstruction.

3. A stoma guard or loose clothing should cover the stoma to protect the stoma from foreign substances.

#221. 2. The client's throat is sprayed with a local anesthetic agent. Until the anesthetic agent wears off, the client is at high risk for aspiration. Pl Ph/9 Ap

1. It is not necessary to position the client on his left side for an extended period of time.

3. Throat lozenges for complaint of a sore throat is not an intervention that addresses respiratory complication.

4. A high Fowler's position is not indicated when the client remains drowsy from the IV sedation.

#222. 1. **A low residue diet one to two days before the study aids in evacuating the lower intestinal tract of all fecal matter.**   Pl   Ph/9   Co

2. A cleansing enema until clear will most likely be administered the morning of the study.

3. Orally administering radiopaque tablets with iodine-based dye is a procedure for preparing the client for an oral cholecystogram.

4. There is no indication that the client needs to be placed in a high Fowler's position. He is at no risk for aspiration with a barium enema.

#223. 4. **The client experiencing a liver biopsy is at risk for bleeding or hemorrhage related to penetration of the liver capsule. Positioning on the right side acts as a tamponade against the puncture site discouraging bleeding from the site.**   Pl   Ph/9   Ap

1. Clients are to remain immobile on bedrest for several hours post liver biopsy.

2. Turning the client side to side is contraindicated; bleeding from the puncture site is encouraged.

3. High Fowler's position does not provide pressure against the puncture site, which would discourage bleeding.

#224. 2. **Oil retention enemas are given to soften the hardened fecal mass and lubricate the walls of the rectum and colon. Cleansing enemas stimulate intestinal peristalsis, thus eliminating the softened fecal mass.**   Im   Ph/7   Co

1. Lubrication of the intestinal walls is only a partial explanation for oil retention enema.

3. Oil retention enemas are not effective for reducing intestinal bacterial count. Antibiotic enemas, such as neomycin, are used to reduce bacterial count.

4. Lubrication of the walls of the rectum and colon are only a partial explanation for an oil retention enema.

#225. 3. **A client with altered central nervous system functioning is at high risk for aspiration. Checking for the placement of the feeding tube using several different methods, i.e., aspiration of gastric contents for residual volume, determining pH of aspirated gastric contents, and auscultating for gurgling sounds with injection of air bolus, is the priority nursing assessment to ensure client safety.**   As   Ph/9   Ap

1. Whereas checking the expiration date of the prepared enteral feeding is correct, it is not the priority assessment before administering the feeding.

2. The client is receiving enteral tube feedings because of his deteriorated neurologic status. Checking for the presence of a gag reflex would be critical to an individual taking fluids or food orally.

4. It is correct to carefully monitor the client's electrolyte balance while receiving enteral feedings; however, it is not the priority intervention before administering the feeding.

#226. 2. **The nasogastric tube for gastric decompression after a gastric resection is never irrigated without a specific order from the physician. Irrigating the nasogastric tube may rupture the suture line and hemorrhaging may occur.**   Im   Ph/9   Ap

1. A nasogastric tube for gastric decompression after a gastric resection is never irrigated without a specific order from the physician.

3. Nasogastric tubes for gastric decompression after a gastric resection are not irrigated without specific orders from the physician.

4. Discontinuing the nasogastric suctioning may result in increased gastric distention and pressure on the gastric suture lines.

ANSWER	RATIONALE	NP	CN	CL

#227. 2. **Metoclopramide blocks dopamine receptors in the chemoreceptor trigger zone (CTZ). This action results in the extrapyramidal and anticholinergic side-effects that include sedation, dilated pupils and parkinsonian effects.** — An — Ph/8 — An

   1. Increased gastric emptying increases the risk of hypoglycemia, not hyperglycemia.

   3. Anticholinergic side-effects may result in a rapid heart rate.

   4. Anticholinergic side-effects include constipation, not diarrhea.

#228. 3. **Increased urinary output is related to the resolved dehydration state. Adding fluid to the enteral feedings reduced the osmolarity of the gastrointestinal contents.** — Ev — Ph/10 — An

   1. Dry mucous membranes are a major sign of dehydration related to the hyperosmolarity of the enteral feedings resulting in the diarrhea.

   2. Hyperactive bowels sounds often accompany increased intestinal peristalsis associated with diarrhea.

   4. Hypokalemia results from excessive gastrointestinal losses. Diarrhea often results in the electrolyte imbalance hypokalemia.

#229. 3. **Exercises to strengthen the abdominal muscles are appropriate to aiding the defecation process.** — Pl — Ph/7 — Ap

   1. Increasing fluid intake is indicated. Restricting fluid intake may cause the stool to become hardened and a fecal impaction to form.

   2. Becoming dependent on laxatives to evacuate the bowel daily may actually increase the episodes of constipation.

   4. The most favorable time to encourage bowel evacuation is after meals.

#230. 3. **Surgical resection of the esophagus has a relatively high mortality rate related to pulmonary complications.** — Pl — Ph/9 — Ap

   1. Post-op clients experiencing esophageal resections are positioned in a semi-Fowler's position to help prevent reflux of gastric contents.

   2. Nasogastric tubes of clients with an esophageal resection should not be manipulated.

   4. Clients with an esophageal resection when beginning to take food orally would have a liquid or soft diet.

#231. 4. **These substances aggravate the episodes of heartburn (pyrosis) and gastroesophageal eflux.** — Ev — Ph/9 — An

   1. Elevation of the head of the bed discourages gastroesophageal reflux.

   2. A bland diet with small, frequent feedings is the appropriate therapeutic diet.

   3. Fluid with meals increases the feeling of fullness and bloating.

#232. 3. **Duodenal ulcer pain characteristically occurs two to three hours after a meal, often awakening the client in the very early morning hours.** — As — Ph/10 — Ap

   1. This pain is typical of the pain associated with cholecystitis.

   2. Vomiting is more frequently associated with a gastric ulcer.

   4. Pain that worsens with the ingestion of food is more often associated with gastric ulcers.

#233. 3. **Misoprostol, a synthetic prostaglandin, is a cytoprotective agent. By increasing mucous production and bicarbonate levels, the mucosal barrier better resists the erosive action of the gastric acid-pepsin complex.** — An — Ph/8 — Co

   1. Antacids neutralize gastric acid.

   2. Gastric acid pump inhibitors, such as omeprazole, inhibit gastric acid production.

   4. Cispride, often used to treat gastroesophageal reflux (GER) increases gastric emptying time.

#234. 3. **Fluids with meals cause rapid emptying of the gastric contents. Fluids with meals should be limited.** — Pl — Ph/9 — Ap

   1. A high carbohydrate diet increases the osmolarity of the chyme, thus increasing the gastric emptying time.

ANSWER	RATIONALE	NP	CN	CL

<table>
<tr><td></td><td>2.</td><td>Resting after meals, not exercising, helps prevent the rapid emptying of the stomach.</td><td></td><td></td><td></td></tr>
<tr><td></td><td>4.</td><td>A high protein diet is indicated for adequate nutrition and tissue repair.</td><td></td><td></td><td></td></tr>
<tr><td>#235.</td><td>4.</td><td>A total gastrectomy results in a loss of intrinsic factor which is necessary for the absorption of vitamin B₁₂.</td><td>Ev</td><td>Ph/9</td><td>An</td></tr>
</table>

#235. 4. **A total gastrectomy results in a loss of intrinsic factor which is necessary for the absorption of vitamin B_{12}.**   Ev   Ph/9   An

1. Walking after meals will exacerbate the occurrence of dumping syndrome.
2. Taking fluids with meals increasing the risk of dumping syndrome.
3. A high carbohydrate diet increases the osmolarity of the food bolus, thus increasing the risk of dumping syndrome.

#236. 3. **A direct inguinal hernia is most likely to cause a small bowel obstruction. Therefore, the nurse must monitor closely for the signs/symptoms of a small bowel mechanical obstruction, including vomiting of bile-stained gastric contents from reverse peristalsis.**   An   Ph/9   Ap

1. A small bowel mechanical obstruction would most likely result in high-pitched, hyperactive bowel sounds proximal to the obstruction.
2. Passage of blood and mucus is more characteristic of a small bowel obstruction related to the inguinal hernia. No fecal matter or flatus is passed.
4. A mechanical small bowel obstruction would most likely produce crampy pain, which is wavelike and colicky in nature.

#237. 1. **A paralytic ileus is related to disturbance of the neural stimulation of the bowel. There is decreased or absence of bowel sounds.**   As   Ph/10   Ap

2. Colicky abdominal pain is a characteristic of a mechanical intestinal obstruction. The pain associated with a paralytic ileus is continuous abdominal pain.
3. High-pitched bowel sounds are characteristic of mechanical intestinal obstruction.
4. Alternating episodes of constipation and diarrhea are signs related to inflammatory bowel disease.

#238. 4. **Anorexia, weight loss, fever, vomiting, and blood loss are conditions that will cause the client to become easily fatigued. Activities are planned or restricted to conserve energy.**   An   Ph/9   An

1. The abdominal pain and cramping associated with ulcerative colitis is associated with increased intestinal peristalsis and massive inflammation of intestinal mucosa.
2. The diarrhea commonly associated with ulcerative colitis is a result of a massive inflammatory response.
3. The more appropriate diagnosis is fluid volume deficit related to anorexia, nausea, diarrhea, and rectal bleeding. The client may experience 10–20 liquid stools daily.

#239. 3. **Oral fluids and a low residue, high protein, and high calorie diet are prescribed to meet nutritional requirements.**   Ev   Ph/7   An

1. Apples are high residue foods.
2. Celery is a high residue food item.
4. Hard cheeses are high residue food items.

#240. 2. **Toxic megacolon is a serious complication of ulcerative colitis. Excessive dilation of the colon may lead to intestinal perforation and death.**   An   Ph/9   Ap

1. Intestinal obstruction is a complication of Crohn's disease related to transmural involvement and stricture formation.
3. Malnutrition from malabsorption is a more likely complication of Crohn's disease, which often involves the right ileum and right colon.
4. Because Crohn's disease has transmural involvement of the intestinal wall, stricture is more likely to develop. Ulcerative colitis does not result in narrowing of the colon.

#241. 3. **A soft, high fiber diet is indicated to increase the bulk of the stool,**   Pl   Ph/7   Ap

thereby promoting defecation. Fluid intake of 2 L/day is recommended unless otherwise contraindicated. Seeds are not allowed.

1. A low residue diet is a risk factor for the development of diverticulosis.
2. A low protein, high carbohydrate diet is not appropriate for diverticulosis.
4. Bulk-forming laxatives such as metamucil, not saline laxatives, are recommended for diverticulosis.

#242. 3. A change in bowel habits such as alternating episodes of diarrhea and constipation is a common manifestation of colon cancer.   As   Ph/9   Ap

1. Epigastric pain that intensifies when the stomach is empty is indicative of peptic ulcer disease. It is an upper gastrointestinal tract symptom.
2. Steatorrhea, fatty, foul-smelling stools, is associated with biliary tract disease or malabsorption syndrome, which involves the small intestines.
4. A rigid, board-like abdomen is associated with the onset of peritonitis, inflammation of the peritoneum.

#243. 4. A diet low in fiber is a major risk factor for colon cancer. Fresh fruits and vegetables increase the fiber content of the diet, thereby, reducing the risk of colon cancer.   Ev   He/4   An

1. Although an exercise program may improve overall health, it does not address the specific risk factors for colon cancer.
2. A diet high in proteins, especially red meats, has been indicated as a risk factor for colon cancer.
3. Annual chest X-ray has not been identified as a means for early detection of colon cancer. In fact, many medical authorities believe that frequent exposure to this type of radiation is, in many instances, contraindicated.

#244. 3. Leaving 1/4 inch of skin exposed around stoma when determining size to cut skin barrier prevents trauma to stoma.   Im   Ph/9   Ap

1. The ostomy pouch should be emptied when it is half full. A full, heavy ostomy pouch will break the seal and cause leakage.
2. Pulling the stoma pouch and skin barrier off together may cause trauma (abrasion, skin irritation) to the stoma as well as peristomal skin.
4. The liquid deodorant should be placed in stoma pouch, either on a piece of tissue or directly into pouch. Deodorant should not be applied directly to the mucous membrane of the stoma.

#245. 4. A skin barrier applied helps prevent enzymatic activity, which is a risk for peristomal skin breakdown.   Im   Ph/9   An

1. Monitoring intake and output is important in the management of fluid and nutrition status, but does not impact directly on peristomal skin care.
2. Bowel sounds assessment is appropriate intervention when caring for a client with an ostomy. However, it does not directly address the issue of preventing peristomal skin breakdown.
3. The peristomal skin should be cleansed with mild soap and warm water. An astringent may dry skin and promote skin breakdown.

#246. 1. Hypovolemia occurs because massive amounts of fluid and electrolytes move from intestinal lumen into peritoneal cavity and deplete intravascular volume. Hypotension and tachycardia are manifestations of this massive fluid shift.   An   Ph/10   An

2. Altered thought processes related to elevated ammonia levels is associated with hepatic encephalopathy. There is no evidence to support this nursing diagnosis.
3. The immediate response of the intestinal tract to the peritonitis is hypermotility, soon followed by paralytic ileus, with an accumulation of air and fluid in the bowel.

ANSWER	RATIONALE	NP	CN	CL
4.	Altered nutrition, less than body requirements, related to malabsorption is associated with inflammatory bowel disease involving the small intestines.			
#247. 2.	**Post-hemorrhoidectomy diet is modified to include increased fluid and fiber intake. This promotes regular bowel elimination and reduces the occurrence of constipation.**	Ev	Ph/9	An
1.	Reducing fluid intake will encourage the occurrence of constipation. Constipation is a risk factor for hemorrhoids.			
3.	The perianal area should be cleansed gently with mild soap and water, then patted dry with cotton balls. Sitz baths may be given three to four times a day and/or after each bowel movement.			
4.	The client is encouraged to ambulate as soon as possible. Moderate exercise is encouraged. Sedentary activities encourage constipation.			
#248. 4.	**Anorexia is often an early and severe symptom of hepatitis.**	As	Ph/10	Ap
1.	Dark urine is associated with the later icteric stage of hepatitis.			
2.	Ascites is associated with hepatic cirrhosis.			
3.	Occult blood in the stools is associated with GI tract bleeding, which may have several different etiologies.			
#249. 1.	**Hepatitis A is transmitted through the fecal-oral route. Childcare workers are in a high risk group because of potentially poor hygiene/sanitation practices.**	An	Ph/10	An
2.	Hepatitis B is transmitted parenterally.			
3.	Hepatitis C is transmitted through exposure to contaminated blood sources.			
4.	Hepatitis D is transmitted in a manner similar to hepatitis B.			
#250. 2.	**Hepatitis B is transmitted parenterally or through intimate sexual contact with a carrier.**	An	Ph/10	Ap
1.	Hepatitis B is not transmitted through airborne droplets.			
3.	Hepatitis B is transmitted parenterally, not through eating utensils used by a carrier.			
4.	Hepatitis A and E are transmitted through the fecal-oral route.			
#251. 3.	**Portal hypertension puts the client at risk for injury related to bleeding/hemorrhaging esophageal varices. Monitoring stools permits early detection of bleeding in the GI tract.**	Im	Ph/9	Ap
1.	This intervention is more appropriate for the nursing diagnosis related to impaired skin integrity, at risk for.			
2.	This intervention is more appropriate for the nursing diagnosis related to altered nutrition, less than body requirements.			
4.	This intervention is more appropriate for the nursing diagnosis related to impaired skin integrity, at risk for.			
#252. 4.	**A serious complication of a paracentesis is hypovolemic shock or vascular collapse. Early detection of this cardiovascular complication through monitoring blood pressure and pulse is a nursing priority intervention.**	Im	Ph/9	Ap
1.	This is an appropriate intervention, but not the priority to prevent serious injury.			
2.	This is an appropriate intervention, but not the priority intervention to prevent serious injury.			
3.	This is an appropriate intervention, but not the priority intervention.			
#253. 4.	**Airway obstruction and aspiration of gastric contents are potential serious complications of balloon tamponade. Frequent assessment of the client's respiratory status is the priority.**	Im	Ph/9	Ap
1.	Stools positive for occult blood may indicate slow leaking varices. Important, but not the priority intervention.			
2.	Tissue oxygenation assessment is important, but not the priority assessment.			
3.	Frequent mouth care should be performed, but is not the priority intervention.			
#254. 2.	**Hepatic cirrhosis leads to elevated serum ammonia levels, which have an adverse toxic effect on cerebral metabolism.**	An	Ph/10	An

ANSWER	RATIONALE	NP	CN	CL

1. Ascites formation is related to portal hypertension, hypoalbuminemia, and hyperaldosteronism.
3. Fluid volume excess is related to ascites and edema formation.
4. Altered clotting mechanism is related to decreased production of prothrombin and synthesis of other substances necessary for blood coagulation.

#255. 4. Pain related to gallstones in the common duct is located in the right upper quadrant and often radiates to the right shoulder or back.   As   Ph/10   An
1. This pain is associated with renal calculi.
2. This pain is associated with a duodenal ulceration.
3. This pain is typical of cardiac pain associated with a myocardial infarction.

#256. 2. The T-tube usually drains 200–500 ml in the first 24 hours. Decreased bile drainage may indicate an obstruction to bile flow or bile may be leaking into the peritoneum.   Ev   Ph/9   Ap
1. The T-tube should be hung at abdominal level to prevent excessive bile loss.
3. Routine irrigation of T-tubes is contraindicated.
4. Sudden, severe abdominal pain may indicate spillage of bile into the peritoneum causing peritonitis.

#257. 3. Morphine sulfate causes spasms of the sphincter of Oddi, which will exacerbate the episode of acute pancreatitis.   An   Ph/8   An
1. Respiratory depression is an expected adverse effect of morphine sulfate. The client's respiratory status must be monitored closely.
2. Decreased gastrointestinal peristalsis is an expected side-effect of morphine sulfate. GI assessment must be done to prevent complications.
4. Morphine sulfate is normally metabolized by the liver.

#258. 3. Bruising (ecchymosis) in the flank and umbilical area is known as Cullen's sign, which indicates severe, hemorrhagic pancreatitis.   As   Ph/10   Ap
1. A positive fluid wave indicates the presence of ascites.
2. Jaundice presents as a yellowish color of the sclera and skin.
4. Bloody, foul-smelling stools is an indication of an inflammatory bowel disease.

#259. 2. The presence of steatorrhea indicates that the dosage of pancrelipase needs to be adjusted.   Ev   Ph/8   An
1. Pancreatic enzyme replacement should not be taken with milk.
3. Pancreatic enzyme replacement should not be taken with antacids.
4. The contents of the capsule form of pancreatic enzyme replacement should not be chewed.

#260. 3. Oliguria is a primary sign of hypovolemic shock related to hemorrhage.   As   Ph/9   An
1. Jaundice indicates biliary obstruction or hepatic disease.
2. Hyperglycemia is related to insulin deficit, which this client may experience.
4. Tachycardia, not bradycardia, would be a compensatory neuroendocrine response to the complication of hemorrhage.

#261. 1. Women should separate the labia, clean from front to back, and then proceed to void into the toilet. Stop, and finally continue to void into the sterile container.   Im   Ph/9   Ap
2. This statement describes the correct method for obtaining a clean catch urine specimen from a male.
3. Women should never wipe from back to front because this will increase the risk of infection.
4. Soap and water is not used to cleanse the urinary meatus. Generally, the iodine solution provided in the clean catch kit should be used unless otherwise ordered.

#262. 2. Several ml's of urine for culture can be aspirated with a 21-gauge needle and 3-ml syringe after the sampling port or the distal   Im   Ph/9   Ap catheter has been swabbed with alcohol or iodine swabs. The urinary catheter and drainage system should remain a closed system to prevent infection.

1. A urine culture only requires 1–3 ml of urine for completion.
3. To use the sampling port to obtain a urine culture, it is first cleaned with iodine or alcohol.
4. The urinary drainage system should not be opened as this increases the risk of infection.

#263. 1. Measurement of post-void residual volume (PVR) should be performed for all patients with urinary incontinence. Catheterization is performed several minutes after the patient voids. A residual of less than 50 ml signifies adequate bladder emptying.   An   Ph/9   An

2. Urine residual of 200 ml or more indicates inadequate bladder functioning.
3. Urethral pressure can only be measured by urodynamic studies and not PVR.
4. Urethral pressure can only be measured by urodynamic studies and not PVR.

#264. 2. Pink-tinged urine and burning on voiding for a day or two following the procedure are expected.   As   Ph/9   Co

1. Gross hematuria and pain may indicate bladder perforation or infection.
3. Bladder distention and colicky pain may indicate complications of bladder perforation, urinary retention, infection, and dysrhythmias. These signs should be monitored and reported.
4. Flank pain and bladder distention may indicate bladder perforation or infection and should be reported.

#265. 2. Strict aseptic technique is vital to prevent urinary tract infection. The patient is positioned on the back with heels flat on the bed with legs separated. The meatus is cleansed with an iodine solution. The catheter is lubricated with a water-soluble jelly and is inserted through the urethra into the bladder until urine starts to flow. The balloon is inflated and the catheter is taped securely to the leg.   Im   Sa/2   Ap

1. Teaching deep breathing techniques for post-op pain reduction is not a priority in this situation.
3. Medicating the patient for pain before the procedure is not necessary because the procedure produces minimum discomfort.
4. Teaching is not a priority nursing intervention in an urgent situation.

#266. 2. Possible signs of indwelling catheter obstruction can be pain, distention, and no urinary output. Possible causes of obstruction include blood clots, mineral sediment, or mucous plugs in the catheter or tubing. The most effective strategies to promote drainage are to place the tubing so downhill flow is unobstructed and to empty the collection system regularly. Irrigation and catheter changes should be performed when all other means fail as they are associated with a high potential for infection.   Pl   Ph/9   Ap

1. Notifying the physician should only be done if all other methods to restore drainage have been unsuccessful.
3. The catheter should not be changed unless all other methods to return patency of the drainage system are unsuccessful.
4. Obtaining a urine culture will not relieve an obstruction.

#267. 1. Dialysis allows substances to move from the blood through a semipermeable membrane into a dialysis solution (dialysate) to correct fluid and electrolyte imbalances as well as remove waste products that accumulate when the client is in renal failure. The principles of dialysis include diffusion, osmosis, and ultrafiltration.   An   Ph/10   Co

    2.   Dialysis does not add water or electrolytes to the blood, but rather removes these products across concentration gradients.

    3.   Potassium is removed from the blood of a renal client because s/he is usually in a state of hyperkalemia.

    4.   The nurse cannot choose which principle of dialysis to employ for a treatment. Dialysis uses all these principles: diffusion, osmosis, and ultrafiltration.

#268. 4. It is imperative for the client to maintain an adequate fluid status as evidenced by normal weight and also remain infection free. The primary nursing goal is to help the client maintain a positive self-image and continue to be a productive member of society.   Ev   Ph/9   An

    1.   Some weight gain is expected between hemodialysis treatments. The purpose of dialysis is to correct fluid and electrolyte balance.

    2.   If proper technique is used during the dialysis treatment, the risk of infection should be minimized.

    3.   A client may sleep through dialysis treatment as a result of changes in metabolic status and temporary hypovolemia.

#269. 2. The morning of dialysis antihypertensives, nitrates, and sedatives are usually withheld as they may precipitate hypotensive episodes.   Pl   Ph/8   An

    1.   Vancomycin is an antibiotic and should be given the same time each day to maintain therapeutic levels. Vancomycin is given IV and circulated rapidly in the blood and would not be affected by dialysis.

    3.   Allopurinol (Zyloprim) is a drug utilized to decrease uric acid or treat gout. Dialysis would not be affected by it.

    4.   Neither vancomycin nor allopurinol (Zyloprim) would affect dialysis by producing hypotension.

#270. 2. Peritonitis is usually caused by *Staphylococcus*. The first indication of peritonitis is cloudy dialysate.   An   Ph/9   An

    1.   Dialysate should always appear clear no matter what phase of the exchange.

    3.   Increased intra-abdominal pressure from the dialysate may cause lower back pain but cloudy dialysate will not cause back pain.

    4.   In peritoneal dialysis there is no vascular access device. Vascular access devices are needed for hemodialysis.

#271. 4. Peritonitis is a life-threatening complication of CAPD, which is manifested by abdominal pain and distention, diarrhea, vomiting, and fever. Clients are given antibiotics orally or parenterally as necessary not prophylactically.   Ev   Ph/9   An

    1.   Few dietary restrictions are needed with CAPD. Usually the client must increase protein to maintain positive nitrogen balance and decrease carbohydrate intake to compensate for dialysate glucose absorption.

    2.   An increase in protein is usually necessary to maintain a positive nitrogen balance as protein is lost during dialysis because the peritoneal membrane is permeable to amino acid and proteins.

    3.   Antibiotics are usually only given during periods of infection as antibiotic use decreases the normal flora in one's body, thus making one susceptible to organisms.

#272. 3. The signs and symptoms of cystitis are frequency and urgency of urination, suprapubic pain, dysuria, foul-smelling urination, and sometimes pyuria. Some clients with cystitis may be asymptomatic.   As   Ph/10   Ap

    1.   Flank pain, nausea, and vomiting usually indicate pyelonephritis.

    2.   Abscess formation and flank pain are not signs of cystitis.

    4.   Fever, flank pain, nausea, and vomiting usually indicate pyelonephritis.

#273. 1. In this surgical procedure, the client's ureters are anastomosed to the sigmoid colon. This results in the client having drainage   As   Ph/10   Ap from the rectum, which often leads to acidosis and electrolyte imbalance involving potassium, chloride, and magnesium.

2. Cardiac dysrhythmias would not cause leg cramps.

3. The client's response to surgery is not high priority under these circumstances.

4. Assessing the temperature of the lower extremities would not provide useful data for this condition.

#274. 2. The client with a Kock's pouch should be taught about living with a stoma, how to self-catheterize and irrigate the appliance, increasing fluid intake to dilute urine to prevent irritation of the stoma, and lastly stoma care. The client will need to self-catheterize at regular intervals. Pl Ph/9 Ap

1. There need not be any change in the client's sexuality as long as it does not produce discomfort at the stoma.

3. If the client adheres to a strict catheterization schedule, the client will not have embarrassing situations. Decreasing fluids may result in the client's stoma being irritated from concentrated urine.

4. A high fluid intake is recommended to dilute the urine and decrease its irritating effects.

#275. 2. Allopurinol (Zyloprim) reduces the urinary concentration of uric acid to decrease the recurrence of uric acid stones. An Ph/8 Co

1. Allopurinol (Zyloprim) has no effect on creatinine.

3. Allopurinol (Zyloprim) does not acidify urine. A client with uric acid stones should be taught to increase the alkalinity of urine.

4. Kidney stones can be composed of uric acid, calcium oxalate or phosphate, struvite or cystine. Calcium lactate precipitates oxalate in the gastrointestinal tract.

#276. 2. A high fluid intake of at least 3000 ml/day is needed to remove minerals prior to precipitation. Ev Ph/9 Hp

1. Foods high in purine, calcium, or oxalate need to be avoided or decreased to prevent stone formation.

3. Medication schedules should be strictly followed to prevent the recurrence of stones.

4. Follow-up care is necessary to encourage the patient's adherence to fluid and dietary recommendations and evaluate the patient for signs of infection.

#277. 1. Nursing care priorities for the patient with urolithiasis include pain relief and prevention of urinary tract obstruction and recurrence of stones. The nurse can expect to administer narcotics and maintain client safety. Pl Ph/8 Hp

2. High fluid intake prevents urinary stasis, which is a nursing care priority.

3. Purine, calcium, and oxalate foods are decreased to prevent further recurrence of stones.

4. Probenecid is added to penicillin when treating sexually transmitted diseases to prevent renal tubular excretion of penicillin.

#278. 3. Pyelonephritis is an inflammation or infection of the kidney or kidney pelvis. An Ph/10 Co

1. Cystitis is an inflammation of the bladder.

2. Pyelonephritis is not a rupture of the bladder. A bladder rupture is usually the result of trauma.

4. Cystitis is an infection of the lower urinary tract.

#279. 1. The most common findings in acute renal failure include elevations in BUN and creatinine, metabolic acidosis, hyponatremia, hyperkalemia, hypocalcemia, and hypophosphatemia. As Ph/9 Ap

2. Acute renal failure causes elevations in BUN and creatinine.

3. A client with acute renal failure is usually in metabolic acidosis because the serum bicarbonate level is less than 15 mEq/L. The kidneys regulate the body's buffer system.

4. A client with acute renal failure usually experiences hypocalcemia due to the decreased gastrointestinal absorption of calcium. Calcium absorption only occurs in the presence of vitamin D. The kidney is responsible for the activation of vitamin D.

#280. 3. Skin care should be provided for the client by bathing with tepid water and oils to reduce dryness and itching. Im Ph/9 Ap

1. Administering antihistamines without a physician's order is a violation of the Nurse Practice Act.
2. Clients with chronic renal failure are usually placed on fluid restrictions.
4. Permitting clients to soak in a tub will further promote drying and itching of skin.

#281. 3. A patient with chronic renal failure needs to adhere to a low protein, low sodium, and low potassium diet. This meal plan would fall into these restrictions. Ev Ph/7 An

1. Each banana contains more than 350 mg K, beans are high in protein, as is the large steak.
2. This menu reflects a high sodium diet. Sodium should be restricted in clients with chronic renal failure.
4. This menu reflects foods that are high in either potassium or protein. Both potassium and protein are restricted in a chronic renal failure client's diet.

#282. 4. A myocardial infarction causes decreased cardiac output, which may cause acute renal failure. The other mechanisms responsible for acute renal failure are nephrotoxicity, trauma, burns, sepsis, and mismatched blood. Chronic renal failure results from irreversible damage to the nephrons and glomeruli. Diseases commonly responsible for chronic renal failure are diabetes, hypertension, and kidney infections. An Ph/10 Ap

1. This response does not answer the client's spouse's question and it assumes the client's spouse is worried.
2. Acute renal failure does not always progress to chronic renal failure.
3. Acute renal failure is a reversible syndrome caused by an abrupt disruption in renal functioning, whereas chronic renal failure is the progressive irreversible destruction of the glomeruli.

#283. 1. The immediate assessments to be performed for a kidney recipient are fluid and electrolyte status, intake and output, and hypotension. As Ph/10 Ap

2. Signs of infection and rejection should be assessed but these do not immediately develop.
3. Hepatotoxicity is a side-effect of cyclosporine (Sandimmune) given to prevent rejection.
4. As with any surgical client, respiratory complications may develop.

#284. 3. Denial is disowning intolerable thoughts. The client is denying his feelings of anxiety and the seriousness of potential rejection of the organ. An Ps/5 An

1. Projection is the act of attributing one's own thoughts to another. This is not occurring here.
2. Intellectualization is excessive reasoning to avoid feeling. K. is not reasoning or rationalizing anything in this situation.
4. Regression is retreating to an earlier stage of development. K. is not regressing to any earlier stage of development by not wanting follow-up care.

#285. 3. The renal system is highly vascular; the client is at risk for post-op bleeding. As Ph/9 Ap

1. Performing a cardiovascular assessment is important but not an initial concern.
2. Ordering laboratory studies is not an independent nursing function.
4. Urine culture is performed prior to discharge.

#286. 2. Benign prostatic hyperplasia (BPH) is the growth of new cells in As Ph/9 Ap

the prostate gland resulting in urinary obstruction; therefore assessment of the obstructive symptoms are: decrease in the force of the urinary stream; hesitancy in initiation of urine; dribbling; urinary retention; incomplete bladder emptying; nocturia; dysuria; and urgency.
  1. Laboratory studies require a physician's order.
  3. Performing an electrocardiogram requires a physician's order.
  4. Internal bleeding is generally not a symptom of BPH.

#287. 2. Clients with BPH should void every two to three hours to flush the urinary tract. Ev Ph/9 An
  1. Clients with BPH even after surgery require yearly rectal examinations as hyperplasia and/or cancer can occur in any remaining prostatic tissue unless all of the prostate is removed.
  3. Athletic supporters are not necessary for clients with BPH. Supporters are usually required for hernia management.
  4. Incontinence may be experienced in clients with BPH. Avoiding fluids will not decrease dribbling.

#288. 2. Blood clots are normal after a prostatectomy for the first 36 hours. Large quantities of bright red blood may indicate hemorrhage. An Ph/9 Ap
  1. Bleeding is not a common result of all surgery.
  3. The physician need only be called if the client is hemorrhaging. An assessment of the patient and the continuous bladder irrigation system should always be performed prior to calling a physician.
  4. Some bleeding after TURP is normal and is not the result of the client tugging on the catheter.

#289. 3. Prior to surgery, the client should be informed that his sexual functioning will not be hampered other than retrograde ejaculation, which is not physically harmful. Im Ph/9 Ap
  1. This response suggests physician error in surgery. Two days post-TURP would not be enough time to determine the return of sexual functioning.
  2. This response does not meet the client's need for an immediate answer.
  4. This is not a therapeutic or accurate response, as following TURP a client's erectile functioning is not altered.

#290. 4. Urine output is calculated by subtracting the amount of irrigant instilled from the total fluid removed from the drainage bag (2900 ml drainage − 2400 ml irrigant = 500 ml urine). Im Ph/10 Co
  1. Urine output is calculated by subtracting the amount of irrigant instilled from the total fluid removed from the drainage bag.
  2. Urine output is calculated by subtracting the amount of irrigant instilled from the total fluid removed from the drainage bag.
  3. Urine output is calculated by subtracting the amount of irrigant instilled from the total fluid removed from the drainage bag.

#291. 1. Because the joint is distended with saline and the arthroscope is introduced into the joint area, the potential for neurovascular damage exists. Color (indicating adequate vascular perfusion), sensation, and mobility (indicating intact neurologic status) should be assessed, although mobility assessment will likely be limited to "wiggling the digits." Pl Ph/9 Ap
  2. Rest for 24–48 hours is essential for protection of the traumatized joint; after this, gradual resumption of activities is permitted.
  3. The compression dressing should remain in place for 24–48 hours to decrease edema and provide some support for the joint.
  4. To facilitate circulation and protect the joint structures, the extremity is kept in extension; to minimize edema and facilitate drainage, it is elevated.

#292. 3. If an oil-based contrast medium is used, the client will be kept in a recumbent position for 12–24 hours to reduce cerebrospinal fluid leakage, and thus decrease the likelihood of developing a Pl Ph/9 Ap postprocedure headache. If a water-soluble medium is used, the client will usually remain in bed, with the head elevated 15–30° (to minimize the upward migration of the medium), but some physicians may allow these patients to ambulate.

1. The meal that would normally be eaten immediately prior to the procedure is omitted because anxiety, discomfort, or an adverse reaction to the contrast medium could stimulate nausea or vomiting.

2. The client needs to replace fluids lost via cerebrospinal fluid leakage (this will help stave off postprocedure headache) and for rehydration. Fluids should be liberally provided.

4. These are signs of bacterial or chemical meningitis, and should be reported to the physician at once. Other significant findings are changes in vital signs, especially fever, and an inability to void.

#293. 4. To perform passive range of motion, the joint is supported, the bones above the joint are stabilized, and the body part distal to the joint is exercised through the range of motion. The family's description of how to maneuver the elbow illustrates this well.   Ev   Ph/7   Ap

1. It is recommended that each joint be put through its range of motion three times, twice a day. Exercising to the point of fatigue is used when building muscle, but this is not the purpose of range of motion exercises.

2. The purpose of range of motion exercises is to preserve the mobility present, not to increase mobility. In addition, pushing a joint past its natural range could permanently damage the joint structures.

3. Muscle spasms are painful, but the spasm can be eased by moving the joint to the point of resistance, and then exerting a gentle, steady pressure until the muscle is relaxed; at that time, the motion can be continued.

#294. 1. The cane, held on the unaffected side, will provide a wider base of support for the affected side while the unaffected limb is moving. The patient should keep the cane close to the body to prevent leaning.   Ev   Ph/7   Ap

2. The cane and affected leg should be moved forward simultaneously, with the cane ready to provide support when the unaffected leg is advanced.

3. The cane and affected leg should be moved forward simultaneously, with the cane ready to provide support when the unaffected leg is advanced.

4. The cane should be held on the unaffected side and advanced when the affected leg is advanced. The process described in this incorrect answer would leave the patient balancing unsupported on the affected leg.

#295. 4. The sequence for using a walker is balance on both feet, lift the walker and place in front of you, walk into the walker (using it for support when standing on affected limb) and then balance on both feet before repeating the sequence.   Ev   Ph/7   Ap

1. This describes the process for ambulating with a reciprocal walker, a device with a hinge mechanism that allows one side of the walker to be advanced ahead of the other side.

2. Following this description would leave the patient with all weight on the unaffected leg while the walker and affected limb are in the air. When using the walker, either it or both feet must be on the ground to provide maximum stability.

3. Swinging the legs forward is dangerous; balance could be easily lost. In addition, the patient has one nonoperative leg that does not need to be "favored" during ambulation, but should be used to provide stability.

#296. 1. Although measuring the patient while he is lying down is not the preferred method of fitting crutches, this formula may be used successfully.   Im   Ph/7   Ap

ANSWER	RATIONALE	NP	CN	CL

2. This complicated formula may suggest that the nurse is determining the length of the crutch dependent of the crutch's forward swing, but this calculation will yield no useful information.

3. It is impossible to determine the length of the crutch this way. In addition, the hand piece should be adjusted with the elbow flexed 20° or 30°, not with the elbow straightened, as described here.

4. Crutch length can be approximated by subtracting 16 in (40 cm) from the patient's height; 24 in (60 cm) will be too short.

#297. 3. **The unaffected limb is advanced to the next step, then the crutches and the affected limb move to that step (weight stays on crutches or foot of unaffected side). A handy mnemonic for patients is, "Up with the good leg, down with the bad," meaning the "good" leg is used first when going up stairs, and the crutches and "bad" leg go to the new step first when going down stairs.**   Im   Ph/7   Ap

1. If the patient puts his left foot on the step before his right, he will be bearing weight on his broken ankle while he lifts his unaffected foot up to the step.

2. This maneuver would have the patient attempting to walk up the steps in a diagonal—and very unsafe—manner.

4. With this pattern, the weight is borne on the affected (broken) ankle, and the strong ankle is protected. Also, "swinging" on stairs is extremely unsafe.

#298. 2. **A four-point gait is used when partial weight bearing is called for; it provides maximal support.**   Ev   Ph/7   Ap

1. This describes a three-point gait, used when one leg is non-weight bearing; it requires arm strength and good balance and is a faster gait.

3. This describes a two-point gait, used in partial weight bearing situations, but providing less support than a four-point gait.

4. This describes the "swing through," the most advanced gait requiring arm strength, coordination, and balance and full weight bearing ability.

#299. 2. **Poor capillary refill (a "pinking up" of the toes after the nailbeds are blanched by compression, which takes more than 3 seconds) is indicative of a circulatory compromise. In this scenario, the likely cause is compartment syndrome: an increase of pressure within the cast ("compartment"). Other signs/symptoms include pain unrelieved by usual modalities, disproportional swelling, and inability to move digits.**   As   Ph/10   Ap

1. Although extremely irritating, itching under the cast is not a sign of a serious complication. Teach the client not to try to scratch the skin under the cast, because he could possibly break the skin and cause the formation of a cast sore. Instead, cool air from a blowdryer may relieve the itch.

3. The client should be able to move toes without difficulty; in fact, this is one of the assessment findings indicating no neurologic compromise.

4. Pain relieved with an ice bag is likely related to the initial trauma (the fracture). Pain that is unrelieved by cold applications, elevations, and analgesics would alert the nurse to the possibility of the development of compartment syndrome, a condition requiring immediate physician attention.

#300. 3. **A damp, not wet, cloth can be used to remove superficial dirt. Stained areas can be covered with a thin layer of white shoe polish.**   Im   Ph/9   Ap

1. Moisture, from condensation, collects under rubber or plastic; moisture destroys the hardness of plaster casts. The client should avoid baths or showers during the period that he has a plaster cast.

2. Breaks in the cast must be repaired by a physician, who may elect to

ANSWER	RATIONALE	NP	CN	CL

replace the defective cast. The client may, however, cushion rough edges of the cast with tape.

4. A fiberglass cast can be dried by using the cool setting—not the warm one—of a blowdryer. Using the warm setting can cause skin problems.

#301. 1. Russell traction is a modification of Buck extension, used for a femur fracture that is not appropriate for internal fixation. The modification occurs when a sling is placed under the affected knee, giving more comfort to the patient, and preventing some of the rotation tendencies. — As · Ph/9 · Ap

2. Only the affected leg is elevated with Russell traction, and the buttock stays on the mattress. This incorrect answer refers to Bryant traction, a form of skin traction used to treat congenital hip dislocations.

3. With Buck extension, the leg in traction is kept on the mattress without a pillow under the leg; Russell traction, a modification of Buck extension, adds a sling under the knee of the affected limb.

4. Russell traction is used for femur fractures. This incorrect answer describes side arm traction and 90-90 arm traction, used with supracondylar fractures of elbow, humerus, and shoulder.

#302. 3. Although this information may be a bit technical for the lay members of Mr. Y.'s family, it is the only answer that provides correct information. Increased lumbar flexion relieves compression of the lumbar nerve roots, which is why the head of the bed is elevated 30° and the knees are flexed; 15–30 lb of traction increases lumbar flexion and facilitates relief. — An · Ph/10 · Co

1. Although it is true that clients with low back pain often need to be reminded to maintain bedrest (answering the phone, getting the mail, etc. are not permitted, although bathroom privileges are), traction is not a "leash" to keep the client tied to the bed.

2. The pelvic traction does not pull laterally across the pelvis; rather, weights at the end of the bed provide a downward pull on the pelvis for additional lumbar flexion.

4. Pelvic traction does not hold the pelvis still; in fact, most clients in pelvic traction decide for themselves when to release it for self-care activities. Do not mistake pelvic traction with a form of skeletal traction.

#303. 2. These are signs of potential neurovascular compromise, an orthopedic emergency. Additionally, the nurse would check the capillary refill of the toes, any peripheral pulses present, and the sensation and mobility of the foot. In addition, the nurse would compare findings on the affected side with those on the nonaffected side. — Im · Ph/9 · Ap

1. Any complaint by the client of discomfort must be further assessed, but asking for more descriptive words would waste valuable time. Neurovascular compromise can manifest as burning, and time is of the essence to salvage the limb.

3. Although the boot may be applied incorrectly, these signs and symptoms, suggesting neurovascular compromise, must be assessed by a physician. Reapplying the boot and reassessing the extremity may be ordered by the physician, but the decision to take the time to do this should not be a nursing judgment. In addition, manipulating the boot is a complicated activity, requiring more than one person.

4. These are signs and symptoms of potential neurovascular compromise; ice will further impair circulation that may already be altered.

#304. 4. A vertical transfer is permitted, as long as manual traction is applied to maintain the "line of pull," that is, the direction of the traction, or "pull," which the balanced suspension device supplied. — Pl · Ph/9 · Ap

1. The important concept of balanced suspension traction is that the pull—accomplished by the weights, ropes, and pulley system—is maintained. Removing the weights and allowing the leg to move freely eliminates the required pull.

2. The height of the leg during the transfer is not as important as maintaining the pull in the correct direction. The purpose is not to reduce edema (associated with the elevation of an extremity above the level of the heart), but to continue the traction on the extremity in an upward and outward direction.

3. The client cannot move himself safely, although he should be encouraged to participate in the move to his tolerance. He will need assistance, and one person will be needed to hold manual pull on the affected leg while it is disconnected from the traction device.

#305. 1. Rheumatoid arthritis is a condition with multisystem effects. The cardiopulmonary and renal systems must be assessed, as well as the obvious assessment of the musculoskeletal system. Because some of the medications used in treating rheumatoid arthritis can have serious systemic effects (e.g., gold therapy, corticosteroids), this is especially true of the client on aggressive pharmacotherapy.   As   Ph/10   Ap

2. The human body learns to adapt to severe chronic pain; although the pain is still experienced, the facial expression will not change accordingly and movement may appear to be without pain. A better assessment tool is simply to ask the client about his pain.

3. The human body learns to adapt to severe chronic pain; although the pain is still experienced, the vital signs will not change accordingly. A better assessment tool is simply to ask the client about his pain.

4. Health history from a client is always a vital part of nursing assessment, and this is especially true for this client. Unusual fatigue, weakness, morning stiffness, pain, and anorexia are just some of the things about which the nurse must question the client.

#306. 2. Although this is an exacerbation of an existing problem, it is always appropriate to formulate a plan—with the client's input— as how best to meet his self-care needs. The plan will need to address protection of joints, conservation of energy, and methods to simplify work tasks. Correct use of assistive devices may also be involved in the plan.   Pl   Ph/9   Ap

1. The client's assessment of his pain is always a more sufficient rationale for administering ordered analgesics than a change in vital signs, and this is especially true with a patient in chronic pain, where the body learns to accommodate for pain (and thus vital signs do not change when pain increases).

3. Fatigue and activity intolerance are often due to anemia related to the disease process. Clients should increase iron intake, by diet or supplement, and the potential for constipation should be managed with increased fiber and/or stool softeners.

4. To decrease fatigue, rest periods should be incorporated into all care activities. Blocking activities together to create longer "rest" periods will only lead to overstimulation and greater fatigue. Brief periods of activity interspersed with rest periods are more beneficial.

#307. 3. High dosage or long-term use of corticosteroids is associated with the development of gastric ulcers. Other adverse effects associated with this treatment include hypertension, hyperglycemia, infection susceptibility, and psychiatric disorders.   Pl   Ph/8   Ap

1. Steroids are ideally used for a short period and are tapered to as low a maintenance dose as possible. Long-term use of steroids is associated with toxic effects and/or large numbers of adverse effects.

2. Onset of action is considered rapid with corticosteroids; usually the client reports effects within the first week.

ANSWER		RATIONALE	NP	CN	CL

	4.	Hypokalemia, not hyperkalemia, is seen with long-term or high-dose steroid use; these foods, high in potassium, should not be restricted.			
#308.	3.	**Weight reduction can reduce stress on weight bearing joints; because the client's physician has recommended it, we can believe that she will benefit from weight loss.**	Ev	Ph/9	An
	1.	Many clients believe that pain medication will be less effective for severe pain if it is taken frequently for more tolerable pain, but this is incorrect. The client should take her medication as prescribed; anti-inflammatory drugs will likely be taken around the clock, to prevent acute pain rather than to "cure" acute pain episodes.			
	2.	Jogging puts tremendous strain on joints; the bouncing from impact is detrimental to the weight bearing parts of the body. Walking produces less wear and tear on the joints.			
	4.	It is important for the client to intersperse strenuous activities with rest periods to avoid fatigue and provide an opportunity for stressed joints to recover.			
#309.	2.	**Anti-inflammatory medications including salicylates and nonsteroidal anti-inflammatories will be taken by the client indefinitely. The client must understand the regimen; ways to monitor for (and when possible diminish) adverse effects must also be taught.**	Pl	Ph/9	Ap
	1.	Heat is applied to decrease the stiffness associated with osteoarthritis; gentle range of motion exercises can also decrease stiffness.			
	3.	The goal for this client is not to build bulky muscles, but to exercise to maintain current mobility and strength. Balancing exercise with adequate rest periods is essential.			
	4.	Clients with osteoarthritis often assume that pain and loss of function are natural outcomes of the aging process, but this is not so. Degenerative changes do not need to be progressive and clients are encouraged to develop coping mechanisms and elicit support of significant others.			
#310.	4.	**Abnormal lung sounds are indicative of respiratory insufficiency from pleural effusions or infiltrations. Pleural effusions may occur with myocarditis, which might manifest as a pericardial friction rub assessed during the cardiovascular exam.**	As	Ph/10	Co
	1.	The rheumatic disorder associated with dysphagia is myositis.			
	2.	The rheumatic disorder associated with vision changes or blindness is temporal arteritis. Regardless of the associated condition, loss of or changes in sight require immediate medical attention!			
	3.	The rheumatic disorder associated with dryness or itching of the genitalia is Sjogren's syndrome.			
#311.	4.	**Signs of gold toxicity include bone marrow suppression and hematuria, proteinuria, diarrhea, and stomatitis. The client receiving parenteral gold should expect to have blood and urine monitored after every other injection.**	Pl	Ph/8	Ap
	1.	The client will continue to take anti-inflammatory medications along with the gold preparations until the benefits from the gold are achieved. This may take three to six months.			
	2.	Intramuscular preparations are initially given every week, then decreased to one injection every two to four weeks. The regimen in this answer would lead to toxicity.			
	3.	The oral dose of gold preparations remains constant, unlike the parenteral dose which decreases with time.			
#312.	3.	**Positive wound cultures are used to help determine the causative organisms and indicate which antibiotic therapy is appropriate. Blood cultures may also be positive.**	As	Ph/10	Co
	1.	Osteomyelitis is an infection and is accompanied by traditional signs of infection: redness, warmth, swelling at the site, and fever.			

2. Osteomyelitis is an infection and is accompanied by an elevated white blood cell count.

4. The speed at which erythrocytes settle after spinning is elevated in infection, pregnancy, and some forms of cancer. Osteomyelitis is an infectious process.

#313. 3. Diminished capillary refill suggests vascular compromise, an emergency condition.   As   Ph/9   An

1. Pain at the fracture site is to be expected. The nurse would, however, be alert for increasing pain or pain that is unrelieved by analgesics, both of which could indicate neurovascular compromise.

2. Swelling of the fingers of the affected hand is expected following a forearm fracture; ice packs can control edema and the pain that accompanies it.

4. Warm, dry fingers are a normal finding; cool skin would suggest vascular compromise and would require immediate attention.

#314. 2. Neurovascular compromise is possible with fracture; distal pulses should be palpated to ensure circulation is adequate; the dorsalis pedis pulses in both feet should be assessed for comparison purposes. Likewise color, sensation, and mobility should be assessed. These interventions are also to be repeated at frequent intervals during the emergent phase, and especially after any intervention (i.e., splinting, casting).   Im   Ph/9   Ap

1. Clothing may well be cut off the affected extremity, although if clothing is first removed from the unaffected side, it is seldom necessary to cut to finish the removal. However, this intervention, even if needed, is not a priority. When a question asks about "critical" or "immediate" interventions, think "airway," "breathing," "circulation," "disability/neurologic" to get your best answer.

3. Analgesic administration is certainly important, but assessing airway, breathing, circulation, and disability/neurologic status must be done first; pain relief should be provided as rapidly as possible thereafter.

4. This intervention is to replace lost fluids; while fluids can be lost rapidly with a long-bone (e.g., femur) fracture, this is not a problem with tibia/fibula fractures. Intravenous access and fluid replacement may be needed later, but this is not a critical step at this time.

#315. 1. There is a strong risk of infection with an open fracture (a fracture with an open wound through skin surface to bone injury), and the nurse will expect the client to be given antibiotics prophylactically; in addition, tetanus immunization status must be assessed, and tetanus prophylaxis given if needed, or if the status cannot be determined.   As   Ph/9   An

2. The current blood alcohol level may be of interest if the client is exhibiting alterations in neurologic status, but the stem of the question clearly states that the open fracture is the client's only injury. Do not read more into a question than that which is stated.

3. Support systems at home will be significant in planning for the client's discharge, but the question asks which assessment is critical for the nurse to make; preventing infection is more important at this stage than assessing support systems.

4. The time of the patient's last void could be important (because she admits to three beers before the crash) if there were reason to suspect bladder or abdominal trauma, but the stem of the question clearly states that the client's only injury is the fracture. Do not read more into a question than what is clearly stated.

#316. 3. These are classic observations of the patient with fat embolism syndrome, seen within 48 hours of a long-bone fracture. Onset of symptoms is rapid, and often fatal. Any respiratory difficulties, personality changes, or chest pain in patients with recent long-bone fractures must be assessed with fat embolism syndrome in mind.   An   Ph/10   An

ANSWER	RATIONALE	NP	CN	CL

1. These are classic signs of fat embolism syndrome. Respiratory compromise related to smoke inhalation would have developed earlier, and the sputum would most likely be soot-tinged.

2. The client has only been on bedrest for 24 hours; before this he was fighting a fire! Pneumonia would not manifest this quickly. In addition, sputum from the person with pneumonia would more likely be yellow or green than white.

4. We do not know if Mr. U. in fact has other injuries (vis-à-vis "multiple trauma"). However, even if he were in hypovolemic shock due to multiple trauma, these are not the manifestations of shock. One would expect to find hypotension, pale, cool, clammy skin, and tachycardia. The signs and symptoms described here are classically those of fat embolism syndrome.

#317. 3. Positioning the patient in extension and abduction helps to ensure that the femoral head part of the prosthesis remains in the acetabular cup. The use of wedge pillows or abduction splints helps in maintaining correct position. — An — Ph/9 — Co

1. The incidence of deep vein thrombosis after hip replacement is 45–70%, with approximately 2% developing into fatal pulmonary emboli. Positioning, however, is not a factor in thrombosis development; rather, the nurse can decrease venous stasis by correctly using sequential compression devices or elastic stockings as ordered, and by promoting position changes and movement as permitted by physician.

2. Avascular necrosis (death of bone due to loss of blood supply) is a rare complication associated with hip replacement, but the abduction/extension position does not prevent its development.

4. Wound drainage is usually accomplished with a portable suction device; 200–500 ml in the first 24 hours is not uncommon, but the amount tapers off quickly after that. Positioning will not facilitate drainage.

#318. 4. To maintain the femoral component of the prosthesis in the acetabular cup, an abductor pillow may be used to keep the legs separate; this must be maintained in all repositioning activities. The patient is always encouraged to assist with repositioning, as long as the integrity of the hip position is maintained. — Pl — Ph/9 — Ap

1. The client will be repositioned during the post-op period to improve circulation and prevent skin complications. The affected leg will never be inwardly rotated because this could cause prosthesis dislocation; the leg will be kept in abduction and extension.

2. The client will not remain supine, but will be repositioned to promote circulation and prevent skin complications. Crossing the legs is to be avoided, as such a maneuver could dislocate the head of the prosthesis.

3. To prevent dislocation of the prosthesis, acute flexion of the hip (with the head of the bed at or greater than 45°) is avoided.

#319. 1. The client will need to refrain from climbing stairs in the early recovery phase, except as guided during physical therapy sessions. Moving to the first floor is a prudent decision. — Ev — Ph/9 — An

2. The surgical site should be clean and free of redness and swelling, both of which indicate an infected site and should be reported at once to the physician.

3. Thigh-high elastic stockings or sequential compression devices should be worn continuously (except for two 20-minute periods per day for skin care); otherwise their purpose, to promote venous return and adequate circulation, is defeated.

4. Hydration is important to promote healing, prevent hemoconcentration and prevent constipation, and provide for adequately liquefied pulmonary secretions to stave off respiratory

complications. Using a fracture pan should minimize discomfort associated with bedpan use following a hip fracture.

#320. 1. **Osteoporosis is a disorder in which bone formation is slower than bone resorption. The outcome of this disequilibrium is bones that are increasingly porous, brittle, and fragile. Any bone can be broken, but the trauma associated with falls frequently leads to hip fractures in osteoporosis clients.**   An   Ph/9   Co

2. Osteoporosis is not linked to alterations in balance (although a change in bone mass may change the individual's center of gravity; however, this change is gradual enough that the client will develop compensatory mechanisms).

3. Osteoporosis is seen frequently in the thoracic and lumbar spine in which compression fractures are common. Also common are fractures of the femur, Colles' fractures of the wrist, and fractures of the neck. Also, osteoporosis is *bone mass* loss, not calcium loss.

4. The accuracy of this statement is debatable; either way, the statement does not answer the question of why having osteoporosis puts one at risk for hip fractures.

#321. 4. **Sometimes misinterpreted by the client as a heart attack or bursitis, pain with cervical disc herniation at this level may occur between the scapulae, in the neck or the top of the shoulders. Stiffness, paresthesias, or numbness in upper extremities is also possible.**   As   Ph/10   Co

1. Headaches are not associated with cervical intervertebral disc herniations.

2. Numbness of the face is associated with damage to the fifth or seventh cranial nerves (CN V or CN VII), both of which exit from the brainstem, not the cervical spine.

3. Clonus—the abnormal rhythmic "beating" of the foot when it is sharply dorsiflexed—is indicative of central nervous system disease; it is not a response mediated by cervical disc injury.

#322. 1. **The patient is assessed for respiratory distress that would be caused by cord edema. The nurse would also look for signs of interstitial edema and/or hematoma.**   As   Ph/9   Ap

2. Pupillary responses are mediated by the third cranial nerve (CN III), located in the brainstem, and well above the level of the cervical spine. The nurse would not expect a cervical laminectomy to affect the pupils.

3. The gag reflex is mediated by the ninth and tenth cranial nerves (CN IX and CN X), neither of which would be affected by cervical laminectomy.

4. Shoulder shrug and neck strength are assessed to test the functioning of the eleventh cranial nerve (CN XI), which would not be affected by a cervical laminectomy. Also, it is important to keep the neck immobile after this procedure; neck strength, tested by having the patient try to move his head against the pressure of your hand, would be contraindicated.

#323. 2. **This position will maintain spinal alignment. Occasionally, the physician will approve the use of a pillow under the head, or the head of the bed raised 30° if a soft cervical collar is used, and if the surgical approach was posterior.**   Im   Ph/9   Ap

1. To maintain alignment of the spine, the patient is usually kept flat in bed after cervical spine surgery.

3. To maintain alignment of the spine, the patient is usually kept flat in bed after cervical spine surgery. If the patient's surgical approach was posterior, a neck roll would put undue, even dangerous, stress on the operative site.

4. To maintain alignment of the spine, the patient is usually kept flat in bed after cervical spine surgery. Modified Trendelenburg is a position

used when a patient is in shock, where the head, thorax, and abdomen are flat, and the legs are raised; this facilitates blood flow to the vital organs, away from the extremities.

#324. 3. When standing (for example, while washing dishes at the sink), the patient should place one foot on a stool, thus alternating the weight between the feet.   Ev   Ph/9   An

    1. The patient must avoid sitting in soft or low chairs; use of a straight-backed chair is recommended.

    2. Running a refreshment stand requires a great deal of standing in one place, something to be avoided by patients who have had lumbar laminectomies.

    4. Physicians may recommend the use of a firm mattress, but a soft mattress would not give adequate support to the back and should be avoided.

#325. 2. Because the bone graft used for fusion is taken from the iliac crest or fibula, the patient will have pain and the potential for complications at those sites as well as complications from the laminectomy. Bedrest may be maintained for longer periods of time; lumbar support may be used once the patient is ambulating, and pain relief must be directed at the graft site as well as the laminectomy site.   Pl   Ph/9   Ap

    1. There is no process performed by which contrast medium is used to check the fusion site.

    3. Patients having spinal fusions are not put into casts after their surgery. The sites for the graft (the iliac crest or the fibula) are not immobilized, although the patient is kept on bedrest.

    4. The graft for the spinal fusion comes from the iliac crest or the fibula; the torso (and thus the lungs) are not involved, so there is no greater risk of pleural pathology.

#326. 2. The blood work can be done quickly without preparation, while the remaining tests must be scheduled in advance. The scan must precede the arteriogram, since the arteriogram dye contains iodine that will interfere with the scan.   Pl   Ph/9   Ap

    1. Infusion of the iodine dye used for arteriograms will interfere with the thyroid scan.

    3. Infusion of the iodine dye used for arteriograms will interfere with the thyroid scan.

    4. Infusion of the iodine dye used for arteriograms will interfere with the thyroid scan.

#327. 2. The tracer dose used is much smaller than a therapeutic dose, and is not harmful. The client can resume contact with others immediately following the test.   Im   Ph/9   Ap

    1. A radioactive isotope is used for the test.

    3. Isolation from others is not necessary following the test.

    4. Wearing a lead shield is not necessary for the client.

#328. 3. Many cough syrups contain iodine, which interferes with the test. Other over-the-counter drugs to be avoided include salicylates, multivitamins, and some iodine-containing preparations found in health food stores.   Im   Ph/9   Ap

    1. These medications do not interfere with the test.

    2. These medications do not interfere with the test.

    4. These medications do not interfere with the test.

#329. 4. A fasting blood glucose is drawn before Glucola is administered. The client can drink only water as blood samples are obtained at designated intervals.   Im   Ph/9   Ap

    1. This is the procedure for a random blood glucose, not a glucose tolerance test.

    2. The client is permitted to drink water during the glucose tolerance test.

    3. This is the procedure for a two-hour post-prandial blood glucose test.

ANSWER	RATIONALE	NP	CN	CL

#330. 4. **Adrenal insufficiency requires lifelong glucocorticoid replacement therapy. Glucocorticoids are given in divided doses, two-thirds in the morning and one-third in the afternoon to reflect the body's own circadian rhythm, which decreases the side-effects of therapy.** Pl Ph/8 Ap

   1. Glucocorticoid therapy for adrenal insufficiency is usually needed lifelong.

   2. Glucocorticoid therapy is given in divided doses during the day to decrease side-effects.

   3. Glucocorticoid therapy is lifelong for adrenal insufficiency.

#331. 2. **ACTH-secreting tumors can cause Cushing's syndrome, which can elevate the blood pressure to dangerously high levels.** As Ph/10 Co

   1. Growth hormone-secreting tumors can stimulate the growth of long bones and increase height, but ACTH-secreting tumors do not affect height.

   3. TSH-secreting tumors can cause hyperthyroidism, with resulting tachycardia. ACTH-secreting tumors do not increase the pulse rate.

   4. The syndrome of inappropriate ADH (SIADH) can diminish urinary output, but ACTH-secreting tumors do not alter output substantially.

#332. 1. **Hypophysectomy (removal of the pituitary gland) interferes with the secretion of both glucocorticoids and antidiuretic hormone, both of which are essential to maintain fluid balance and blood pressure. Careful monitoring of blood pressure is essential to ensure that hormone replacement therapy is adequate.** As Ph/9 Ap

   2. Removal of the pituitary gland does not substantially affect serum calcium levels. The pituitary gland does not stimulate the parathyroid glands, which regulate serum calcium.

   3. Although assessment of breath sounds is routinely carried out in the immediate post-op period, this is not the most essential assessment for the nurse to make.

   4. Although assessment of bowel sounds is routinely carried out post-op, this is not the most essential assessment for the nurse to make.

#333. 4. **Hormone replacement and follow-up care are needed for the rest of his life because the pituitary gland has been removed. This is the master gland that secretes trophic hormones that stimulate target glands to produce their hormones. A Medic-Alert bracelet is needed to alert others of his condition.** Ev Ph/9 An

   1. Mr. P. will need a Medic-Alert bracelet, but he will also need lifelong follow-up and hormone replacement for the rest of his life.

   2. Hormone replacement will be needed for the rest of his life because the pituitary gland has been removed and this is the master gland that secretes trophic hormones that stimulate target glands to produce their hormones.

   3. Hormone replacement will be needed for the rest of Mr. P.'s life, not only one year because the pituitary gland has been removed and this is the master gland that secretes trophic hormones that stimulate target glands to produce their hormones.

#334. 2. **Diabetes insipidus is characterized by polydipsia and polyuria. It occurs with lesions of the hypothalamus and pituitary. Because antidiuretic hormone synthesis is affected, the client is at high risk for dehydration, which is life-threatening.** An Ph/10 Ap

   1. Fluid volume excess is an appropriate diagnosis for a client experiencing the syndrome of inappropriate antidiuretic hormone (SIADH).

   3. Diabetes insipidus has no direct effect on the client's ability to control the bowel.

   4. Because diabetes insipidus causes dehydration the client would experience constipation not diarrhea.

#335. 3. **Withdrawal from glucocorticoid therapy can precipitate** As Ph/8 An addisonian crisis, which is characterized by circulatory collapse and shock. Hypotension is a major manifestation of addisonian crisis and must be treated vigorously.

1. Breath sounds are not initially affected in most clients during drug withdrawal.
2. There are many problems that can impair capillary refill. The nurse needs to select a more direct measurement of circulatory function to use first.
4. While undertreatment of lupus erythematosus may result in the development of the classic butterfly rash of lupus, a more life-threatening problem can occur in drug withdrawal.

#336. 2. Management of addisonian crisis includes glucocorticoid management. Intravenous replacement of sodium and dextrose is also necessary.   Pl   Ph/8   An

1. Oxygen would only be administered at a dose required to manage the client's level of shock. It is not routinely given at 100%.
3. The client is in a state of hyperkalemia; therefore, the nurse should not anticipate administering potassium chloride.
4. If the client were in severe shock there would possibly be a need for an emergency endotracheal intubation but not a tracheostomy.

#337. 1. Cushing's syndrome is caused by excessive corticosteroids. Excessive mineralocorticoid produces hypertension, acne, changes in secondary sex characteristics, and mood disturbances such as irritability, anxiety, euphoria, insomnia, irrationality, and psychosis.   An   Ph/10   An

2. Excessive glucocorticoids produces increases in adipose tissue in the trunk, face, and cervical area.
3. Activity intolerance is a result of muscle wasting and weakness due to excessive glucocorticoids. Activity intolerance would not cause mood disturbance.
4. Mood disturbances are not caused by sensory-perceptual alterations. Cushing's syndrome does not cause sensory-perceptual alterations.

#338. 4. Clients with Cushing's syndrome exhibit central obesity, with a "buffalo hump," a heavy trunk, and thin extremities. The accumulation of fat on the cheeks makes the face moon-shaped, or rounded.   As   Ph/10   An

1. Clients with Cushing's syndrome typically have thin extremities.
2. Although clients with Cushing's syndrome may have a pendulous abdomen, the hips and extremities are thin.
3. Striae may develop any time tissue is stretched, as occurs in the central obesity of Cushing's syndrome. However, the extremities are thin.

#339. 4. Hypertension and hyperkalemia are the classic manifestations of primary aldosteronism, in which the adrenal cortex secretes excessive mineralocorticoid.   As   Ph/10   Co

1. Serum sodium is normal or elevated, while the potassium is diminished from the excessive secretion of mineralocorticoid by the adrenal cortex.
2. Body temperature is not affected. The blood glucose may be elevated, rather than decreased.
3. Pulse rate and urinary excretion of albumin are not affected initially in primary aldosteronism. If the characteristic hypertension continues, renal damage can result in albuminuria and renal failure.

#340. 3. Clients with pheochromocytoma can experience episodes of life-threatening hypertension when the adrenal tumor secretes catecholamines that stimulate the sympathetic nervous system. These attacks are often accompanied by sweating, palpitations, and headache.   As   Ph/9   Ap

1. Pupil reaction is affected only if untreated pheochromocytoma results in cerebral hemorrhage.

ANSWER	RATIONALE	NP	CN	CL
2.	Hand grips are affected only if untreated pheochromocytoma results in cerebral hemorrhage.			
4.	Although blood glucose can be elevated in pheochromocytoma, it is not the first assessment the nurse should make.			
#341. 4.	**The client cannot cope with stress because the client cannot produce corticosteroids.**	Im	Ph/9	Ap
1.	This response does not address the client's concerns.			
2.	This response does not address the client's concern related to behavior.			
3.	This response does not immediately meet the client's need for information.			
#342. 3.	**Without adrenal glands there is a lifelong need for a constant dose for replacement therapy daily.**	Ev	Ph/9	An
1.	Long-term management of this illness requires lifelong steroid replacement therapy.			
2.	Steroid replacement therapy needs to be taken every day without fail.			
4.	Altering the drug dosage could precipitate an acute adrenal crisis.			
#343. 2.	**A simple goiter is an enlargement of the thyroid gland caused by excess thyroid-stimulating hormone (TSH) stimulation, growth-stimulating hormones, or excessive intake of goitrogenic foods.**	An	Ph/10	Co
1.	The absence or presence of goiter is not affected by the intake of fat free foods. A heart-healthy diet consists of decreasing fat in the diet.			
3.	Excessive ACTH is responsible for Cushing's disease.			
4.	High (not low) intake of goitrogenic foods is associated with goiter. Goitrogenic foods include turnips, rutabagas, soybeans, green leafy vegetables, peanuts, and some fruits.			
#344. 2.	**The client with Graves' disease is at risk for tachycardia, shock, hyperthermia, weight loss, and nervousness.**	As	Ph/9	Ap
1.	A client with Graves' disease does not always have a goiter. Graves' disease is an autoimmune disease characterized by increased thyroid hormone.			
3.	A client in hyperthyroid crisis may experience diarrhea not constipation.			
4.	A client in hyperthyroid crisis would experience hyperthermia not hypothermia.			
#345. 4.	**Thyroxine and triiodothyronine levels are usually elevated and thyroid-stimulating hormone levels may be normal or undetectable in hyperthyroidism.**	An	Ph/9	An
1.	In hypothyroidism the thyroxine and triiodothyronine levels are usually low. The serum thyroid-stimulating hormone is utilized to determine the etiology of the hyperthyroidism.			
2.	Addisonian crisis is a life-threatening emergency caused by insufficient adrenocortical hormones. The diagnostic test is the ACTH stimulation test.			
3.	Hypoparathyroidism is due to decreased parathyroid hormone (PTH). It is characterized by hypocalcemia.			
#346. 3.	**Propranolol (Inderal) is a beta-adrenergic blocker that will relieve the symptoms of Graves' disease caused by increased circulating thyroid hormone. The symptoms are heat intolerance, palpitations, nervousness, tachycardia, and tremors.**	An	Ph/8	Ap
1.	Propranolol (Inderal) has no effect on thyroid hormone secretion. Thyroid hormone secretion is inhibited by propylthiouracil (PTU), methimazole (Tapazole), and iodine (Lugol's solution).			
2.	Propranolol (Inderal) has no effect on thyroid hormone secretion. Thyroid hormone secretion is inhibited by propylthiouracil (PTU), methimazole (Tapazole), or iodine (Lugol's solution).			
4.	Propranolol (Inderal) has no effect on thyroid hormone secretion. Radioactive iodine (radiodine) limits thyroid hormone secretion.			
#347. 3.	**Oxygen, suction equipment, and a tracheostomy tray should be available in case airway obstruction occurs.**	Pl	Ph/9	Ap

1. Nasogastric tubes are usually not necessary for intestinal decompression status post-thyroidectomy.
2. The client is returning from the operating room and therefore should have an established IV or central line site.
4. A thyroidectomy is the removal of the thyroid gland. Removal of the thyroid is independent of the spinal column.

#348. 1. **The administration of thyroid hormone is needed after surgery because there is no thyroid gland to perform the usual functions.**   Ev   Ph/9   An
2. Hyperthyroidism will not recur because there is no thyroid gland left.
3. The client who has undergone thyroid surgery still needs to be alert for symptoms of hypothyroidism if the dose of medication is inadequate.
4. Caloric intake should be reduced, not increased, after surgery to prevent weight gain.

#349. 2. **During a thyroidectomy it is possible for the parathyroid glands to be removed or damaged. If the parathyroid glands are disturbed, hypocalcemia may result.**   Im   Ph/9   Ap
1. Muscle twitching and spasms are already indicative of tetany after a thyroidectomy; therefore, a calcium level should be drawn and calcium given to correct a life-threatening emergency.
3. After a thyroidectomy, placing a client in semi-Fowler's position will avoid flexing the neck and decrease the choking sensations, but it will not relieve hyperreflexia or muscle spasm due to decreased calcium.
4. Pain medication will relieve discomfort and decrease anxiety, but will not relieve hyperflexia and spasms.

#350. 1. **The client remains in the outpatient department for about two hours to be monitored for vomiting.**   Ev   Ph/9   Ap
2. Only very high-dose therapy necessitates hospitalization for isolation. Normally the client has to remain in the outpatient department for about two hours.
3. The client should avoid close body contact with infants, young children, or pregnant women during the first 24 hours, although the radiation risk is minimal.
4. Antithyroid drugs need to be discontinued at least five days before treatment.

#351. 3. **The signs and symptoms of hypoparathyroidism are due to low serum calcium levels. A decrease in serum calcium may produce tetany. Tetany produces tingling in lips, fingers, and feet. Severe tetany is associated with muscle spasms.**   As   Ph/9   Ap
1. Hypothermia is associated with hypothyroidism.
2. Hyperthermia is associated with hyperthyroidism due to decreased thyroid hormone.
4. Hypertension is associated with hyperthyroidism due to increased thyroid hormone.

#352. 2. **Type I diabetes arises from the destruction of the beta cells, which results in little or no insulin production. Type II diabetes is the result of tissues being unresponsive to insulin, which eventually exhausts the production of insulin. Type II diabetics tend to be older than 35 years and overweight.**   An   Ph/10   Co
1. Type I diabetes requires insulin administration, whereas type II diabetes is treated with oral hypoglycemic agents known as sulfonylureas.
3. Insulin is released continuously into the blood with increased release following food ingestion. Diabetes is the result of the decreased secretion of insulin or decreased activity of insulin.
4. The complication usually associated with type I diabetes is diabetic ketoacidosis (DKA), whereas the complication usually associated with type II diabetes is hyperglycemic hyperosmolar nonketosis (HHNK).

#353. 2. **The peak action for regular insulin occurs in two to four hours**   Pl   Ph/8   Ap after administration. If regular insulin is administered at 7:30 A.M., then the client should be observed for hypoglycemia between 9:30 A.M. and 11:30 A.M.

1. Usually a diabetic client is hyperglycemic on rising not hypoglycemic.
3. Regular insulin would be heading toward the end of its duration at 1:00 P.M., if administered at 7:30 A.M. Regular insulin has a duration of six to eight hours.
4. Regular insulin administered at 7:30 A.M. would no longer be working.

#354. 3. **Snacks should be eaten prior to any exercise so glucose is readily available for the body's use.** Pl Ph/9 Ap

1. If diabetic teaching is not accomplished prior to discharge, most insurance companies will cover outpatient or home instruction.
2. Iodine is very caustic to the skin and should never be used as a skin preparation agent prior to insulin administration.
4. Urine glucose levels reflect the serum glucose levels two to six hours prior and therefore should not be utilized to determine insulin need. Capillary blood glucose monitoring is a reliable method for determining glucose levels.

#355. 4. **A conscious patient experiencing hypoglycemia needs 5–20 grams of simple carbohydrates immediately. A 4–6 oz glass of orange juice would provide enough glucose to counteract hypoglycemia.** Im Ph/10 Ap

1. Baked ziti is a long acting carbohydrate and would not provide immediate glucose.
2. At a bridal shower, the personal physician may not be able to be contacted immediately and hypoglycemia is a life-threatening condition.
3. A peppermint would not supply 5–20 grams of carbohydrates. It would take approximately six candies to relieve hypoglycemia.

#356. 2. **The peak action for NPH is six hours after administration; therefore delaying the administration two hours in the morning will allow the patient to safely eat lunch at 2:00 P.M.** Ev Ph/8 Ap

1. The patient is likely to experience hypoglycemia if she waits to eat lunch eight hours after taking NPH.
3. The patient needs a balanced diet, medication, and activity in IDDM, but can never omit insulin.
4. The peak action for NPH is six, not four hours following administration.

#357. 1. **At the first sign of diabetic ketoacidosis (elevated blood glucose and frequent urination) the nurse should administer insulin per physician's order to stabilize the blood glucose level.** Im Ph/9 Ap

2. Regular insulin is always used for sliding scale because it is the fastest acting and the immediate need is to lower the patient's blood sugar level.
3. It may be appropriate later to notify the physician, but if a sliding scale has been ordered, the appropriate first action is to administer the insulin.
4. Putting the urinal close to the bed does nothing to lower the blood sugar, which is the immediate concern.

#358. 4. **Hypoglycemia or low blood glucose occurs when there is more insulin than glucose in the serum or when blood glucose levels drop too rapidly. The signs of hypoglycemia include irritability, irrational behavior, dizziness, tremors, or loss of consciousness.** An Ph/9 An

1. Hyperglycemia is an elevation of blood glucose levels. The signs of hyperglycemia include increase in urination and appetite, weakness, headache, glycosuria, and nausea.
2. Diabetic ketoacidosis (DKA) is the result of hyperglycemia accompanied by little insulin causing starvation of cells due to no glucose for cellular energy. In response to too little energy available

to the body for metabolism, stored fats and proteins are broken down to provide energy.

   3. Hyperglycemic hyperosmolar nonketosis occurs when diabetes produces enough insulin to prevent diabetic ketoacidosis but not enough to prevent hyperglycemia.

#359. 1. The patient needs to adhere to the meal plan that has been prescribed, as this is individualized according to the dietary needs.   Ev   Ph/7   An

   2. Alcohol should be avoided as it is high in calories, yet has no nutritive value.

   3. Dietetic foods are expensive, can be confusing, and although convenient, are not necessary.

   4. The diabetic patient should never skip meals. Omission or delay of meals can result in hypoglycemia.

#360. 1. Neuropathy is one of the most common complications of diabetes caused by microangiopathies or metabolic defects that cause waste to build up in the nerves resulting in demyelinization.   An   Ph/9   Co

   2. Microangiopathy of the retina is known as retinopathy.

   3. Macroangiopathy is a disease of the medium and large vessels, which results in atherosclerosis.

   4. Diabetic nephropathy is the cause of end-stage renal disease.

#361. 3. A type II diabetic is more likely to have hyperglycemic hyperosmolar nonketosis because there is sufficient insulin to prevent the metabolism of protein and fats for basic energy needs.   An   Ph/10   Co

   1. Diabetic ketoacidosis is the result of insufficient insulin available for glucose metabolism so the body breaks down proteins and fats to produce energy at the cellular level. This breakdown results in excessive ketone production which alters pH and results in acidosis.

   2. Type II diabetics tend to be overweight middle-aged adults; therefore, protein and fat reserves are adequate.

   4. Diabetes mellitus produces elevations in serum glucose levels. Diabetic ketoacidosis is a hyperglycemic state.

#362. 4. The cardinal signs of hypoglycemia are cold sweats, weakness, and trembling. Additional signs include nervousness, irritability, pallor, increased heart rate, confusion, and fatigue.   Ev   Ph/8   Ap

   1. This is a sign of hyperglycemia, not hypoglycemia.

   2. The presence of ketones in the urine indicates diabetic ketoacidosis that can occur in untreated hyperglycemia.

   3. An increase in urine output occurs with hyperglycemia.

#363. 3. The diabetic patient should wash the feet daily and examine for cuts, blisters, swelling, and any red, tender spots.   Ev   Ph/9   An

   1. The patient with diabetes mellitus should not go barefoot, as small cuts may occur that the patient is not aware of.

   2. Using a heating pad or water bottle at night is not recommended; socks should be used for warmth if needed.

   4. Commercial remedies should not be used to remove calluses or corns.

#364. 4. Ms. F. is experiencing low blood sugar or hypoglycemia; ingesting a quick-acting carbohydrate source is the best action.   Ev   Ph/9   Ap

   1. Ms. F. would take regular insulin for hyperglycemia not the hypoglycemia that she is experiencing.

   2. NPH insulin is an intermediate-acting insulin and would not help her hypoglycemia.

   3. Ms. F. is not tired, so a nap will not help.

#365. 1. Glyosylated hemoglobin, also known as the hemoglobin A_{1c} test, is used to determine glycemic control over time. Glucose attaches to hemoglobin and remains there for the life of the blood cell (120 days); therefore, the test indicates the overall glucose level of 120 days.   An   Ph/9   Co

2. The hemoglobin A1c test is a measurement of glycemic control over 120 and not seven days.

3. The hemoglobin A1c test measures glucose control over the last 120 days and is not a protein analysis.

4. The hemoglobin A1c test is a blood test that measures glycemic control over the last 120 days and is not a urine protein calculation.

#366. 2. The allergen is applied to a small superficial scratch that cuts the outer layer of the skin.   Im   Ph/9   Co

   1. This describes patch allergy testing.

   3. This describes intradermal testing. This type of testing is usually the most accurate type of testing, but carries the highest risk of severe allergic reaction.

   4. This is simply not a true statement. A scratch test is application of the allergen through a small scratch that cuts the outer layer of skin. Food allergies can be tested by the challenge test or by a skin test. The challenge test provides suspected foods to the client in progressively larger doses until a reaction is evoked.

#367. 2. Bleeding and large amounts of fluid accumulation beneath the graft may prevent successful adherence of the graft.   Pl   Ph/9   Ap

   1. Silver sulfadiazine would not be indicated in the situation.

   3. Quite frequently grafts are immobilized after surgery allowing the graft time to adhere well to the wound bed.

   4. Soaking in a bath is not indicated at this time. This may decrease the adherence of the graft. It may also increase the risk of infection. To help Mr. B.'s discomfort, try positioning and/or administration of medications as ordered.

#368. 3. Compression bandages are often applied in the operating room on top of a synthetic, semipermeable polyurethane film. This dressing allows the polyurethane film to adhere to the donor site, reducing accumulation of fluid.   Im   Ph/9   Ap

   1. This is not appropriate. Her donor site is her right upper thigh—her recipient site is her chest. In addition, a fine mesh gauze dressing is usually allowed to dry.

   2. This is not appropriate. Often the recipient site may be immobilized to allow the graft to adhere, not the donor.

   4. This is not appropriate. Donor sites may be dressed with a nylon fabric that may be sutured, stapled, or taped in place. It is covered with a compression dressing for at least 48 hours post-op. The nylon fabric remains adhered to the donor site and is peeled away once reepithelialization has occurred—usually 10–14 days.

#369. 4. Continuous bleeding beneath a graft may prevent adherence of the graft.   As   Ph/9   An

   1. This is common. Small amounts of blood and serum may be removed by gently rolling the blood from the center of the graft to the edges where it may be absorbed with a sterile 4 × 4 gauze pad.

   2. This is common. Small amounts of blood and serum may be removed by gently rolling the blood from the center of the graft to the edges where it may be absorbed with a sterile 4 × 4 gauze pad.

   3. The meshed pattern results from a meshed graft. It contains many little slits allowing expansion of the donor skin. This technique allows coverage of larger areas, irregularly shaped wounds, and drainage of the wound beds.

#370. 4. If a drying soap is used it will increase the pruritis. Superfatted soaps are less alkaline, therefore less drying.   Pl   Ph/9   Ap

   1. Hot water causes vasodilatation, which increases pruritis. Warm water is preferred for bathing.

   2. A cooler environment will decrease pruritis. Air conditioning will also decrease aeroallergen exposure.

   3. When symptoms increase, taking more warm (not hot) baths may help relieve symptoms by hydrating the epidermis.

ANSWER	RATIONALE	NP	CN	CL

#371. 3. **This is information the nurse would need prior to developing the teaching plan.** — An | Ph/10 | Co

   1. These symptoms are typical for pemphigus.
   2. These symptoms are typical for intertrigo.
   4. These are symptoms of stasis dermatitis.

#372. 4. **Almost all cases of basal and squamous cell skin cancer diagnosed each year in the United States are considered to be sun-related.** — Ev | He/4 | An

   1. Fair skinned, fair headed people are more prone to the development of skin cancer.
   2. History of excessive sunbathing/sunburn and exposure to UV light predispose to the development of skin cancer.
   3. Family history of melanoma is a strong risk factor.

#373. 1. **The most common presentation of BSE is a nodular lesion that is dome-shaped papules with well-defined borders. The lesions can have a pearly or shiny appearance because it does not keratinize.** — As | Ph/10 | Co

   2. This is a typical description of squamous cell cancer.
   3. These characteristics describe the lesions associated with Kaposi's sarcoma.
   4. These are characteristics of a second degree sunburn.

#374. 1. **The majority of malignant melanoma appears to be associated with the intensity of sunlight exposure rather than the duration.** — As | Ph/10 | Co

   2. These features are descriptive of lesions occurring with actinic keratosis.
   3. See above, also UV light continues to be one of the causes of malignant melanoma. Sunscreen use decreases incidence.
   4. This is a lesion usually associated with basal cell carcinoma.

#375. 2. **Pain is a significant problem with herpes zoster. Topical solutions, cooling soaks, and use of analgesics are usually incorporated into the plan of care.** — An | Ph/9 | Ap

   1. These symptoms describe herpes zoster, not herpes simplex. Herpes simplex lesions usually appear in the genitalia or face.
   3. Herpetic Whitlow is a form of the herpes simplex virus occurring on the fingertips of healthcare providers who have come in contact with viral secretions.
   4. Staph cellulitis does not present with these symptoms.

#376. 2. **Pain is usually present and can be quite severe. It is important to help the patient obtain relief. Cool compresses, analgesics, and topical antipruritic preparations may be used.** — Pl | Ph/9 | Ap

   1. This intervention is indicated for clients with herpes simplex.
   3. Herpes zoster is less communicable than varicella (chickenpox), but people who have not had varicella may develop it after exposure to a client with herpes zoster.
   4. Diagnostic tests are usually not necessary because of the specific characteristics of herpes zoster.

#377. 4. **Sexual contact should be avoided during the initial and recurring infections. The client should also avoid touching the infected area, as it may be transferred to the eyes or face. Good handwashing is vital.** — Ev | He/4 | Co

   1. Infected clients should have separate personal articles.
   2. The use of condoms during latent phases is encouraged because the disease may be transmitted even when symptoms are not present.
   3. The major problem with herpes simplex virus is recurrence. The client will need to take preventive measures even when the disease is not active.

#378. 1. **Isolation is thought by some clinicians to reduce the incidence of cross contamination significantly. However, methods vary drastically from one center to another. The single most effective technique to prevent transmission of infection is handwashing!** — Pl | Sa/2 | Ap

   2. Private rooms are almost exclusively used.

ANSWER	RATIONALE	NP	CN	CL

3. Visitors are usually restricted when the patient is immunosuppressed. Ill persons and small children are encouraged not to visit routinely.

4. Equipment should not be shared among clients. Disposable items are used as much as possible. All equipment must be cleaned thoroughly after use on one client and before use on another.

#379. 4. The rule of nines is a quick assessment scale used to estimate the extent of burn injury. The basis of the rule is to divide the body into areas each representing 9% or a multiple of 9% of the total body surface area. Mr. L.'s injuries were assigned the following percentages: R arm 9%, L arm 9%, R leg 18%, back 18%, total 54%. An Ph/10 Ap

1. See rationale for correct answer.
2. See rationale for correct answer.
3. See rationale for correct answer.

#380. 1. Urine output is the most readily available and reliable indicator for determining the adequacy of fluid resuscitation. Urine output should be monitored every hour and maintained between 30–50 ml/h. An Ph/10 Ap

2. It is important to assess for infection; however, during the shock phase of burn injury, adequacy of fluid resuscitation should be the priority.

3. Range of motion is an important part of caring for the burn patient, but not a priority at this time.

4. Again, this is important but not at this critical time.

#381. 2. 50 ml/h of urine is adequate, BP is stable, clear sensorium is another positive sign that adequate fluid volume replacement is occurring. Pulses should also be easily palpable. Ev Ph/10 An

1. These findings would indicate that fluid replacement is not adequate. Urine output should be at least 30–50 ml/h, CVP should range from 7–10, pulses should be easily palpable, and K+ level should be returning to normal.

3. Pulses should be palpable. The BP is too low, heart rate too fast, the Hct is high. These could indicate too little volume replacement.

4. Restlessness and confusion could demonstrate respiratory distress. The given urine output is not adequate. The weight increase indicates possible fluid shifts.

#382. 3. Burn patients are very susceptible to development of stress ulcers. Routinely they receive Zantac to help prevent this complication. An Ph/8 Ap

1. This is not the reason for administration of the drug.
2. The drug has no effect on hypoxemia.
4. Zantac has no effect on secretions.

#383. 2. This statement demonstrates that Miss P. realizes she must be alert to the signs and symptoms of infection and notify her physician if they do occur. Ev Ph/9 An

1. Pressure garments, used to decrease scar formation, may be worn up to two years post-burn.

3. The recommended diet for burn patients is high calorie, high protein to promote healing.

4. A lanolin-rich lotion is recommended to decrease itching and dryness. Rubbing ice directly on her new skin could cause damage.

#384. 3. Water will neutralize most chemicals while decreasing the heat reaction. Im Ph/9 Ap

1. This would be the initial action with a flame burn.
2. Lead-lined protective devices are appropriate for emergency care of patients experiencing radiation accidents.
4. Not appropriate. Water will neutralize most chemicals.

#385. 1. Emergency treatment starts with separating the patient from Im Ph/10 Ap

the power source. It is important to use nonconductive
implements such as wooden poles to prevent injury to the
rescuer.

2.   Not very helpful unless it is very cold and there is no hope of rescue.
     Not an initial action.
3.   Don't touch Mr. B.!! You too could receive the electrical current.
4.   No!! Water is conductive to electrical energy. This would make rescue
     even more dangerous. Flushing with water is the treatment of choice
     for chemical burns.

Review Test 3

Pediatric Nursing

1. The nurse is testing reflexes in a four-month-
    old infant as part of the neurologic
    assessment. Which of the following findings
    would indicate an abnormal reflex pattern
    and an area of concern in a four-month-old
    infant?
    1. Closes hand tightly when palm is touched.
    2. Begins strong sucking movements when
       mouth area is stimulated.
    3. Hyperextends toes in response to stroking
       sole of foot upward.
    4. Does not extend and abduct extremities in
       response to loud noise.

2. The mother of a three-month-old infant asks
    the nurse when she can start feeding her baby
    solid food. Which of the following should the
    nurse include in teaching this mother about
    the nutritional needs of infants?
    1. Infant cereal can be introduced by spoon
       when the extrusion reflex fades.
    2. Solid foods should be given as soon as the
       infant's first tooth erupts.
    3. Pureed food can be offered when the infant
       has tripled his birth weight.
    4. Infant formula or breast milk provides
       adequate nutrients for the first year.

3. The nurse is assessing a six-month-old infant
    during a well child visit. The nurse makes all
    of the following observations. Which of the
    following assessments made by the nurse is
    an area of concern indicating a need for
    further evaluation?
    1. Absence of Moro reflex.
    2. Closed posterior fontanel.
    3. Three pound weight gain in two months.
    4. Moderate head lag when pulled to sitting
       position.

4. The nurse is giving anticipatory guidance
    regarding safety and injury prevention to the
    parents of an 18-month-old toddler. Which of
    the following actions by the parents indicates

understanding of the safety needs of a
toddler?
1. Supervise the child in outdoor, fenced play
   areas.
2. Teach the child swimming and water
   safety.
3. Use automobile booster seat with lap belt.
4. Allow child to cross the street with four-
   year-old sibling.

5. The community health nurse is making a
    newborn follow-up home visit. During the
    visit the two-year-old sibling has a temper
    tantrum. The parent asks the nurse for
    guidance in dealing with the toddler's temper
    tantrums. Which of the following is the most
    appropriate nursing action?
    1. Help the child understand the rules.
    2. Leave the child alone in his bedroom.
    3. Suggest that the parent ignore the child's
       behavior.
    4. Explain that the toddler is jealous of the
       new baby.

6. The parent of a three-year-old child brings the
    child to the clinic for a well child checkup. The
    history and assessment reveals the following
    findings. Which of these assessment findings
    made by the nurse is an area of concern and
    requires further investigation?
    1. Unable to ride a tricycle.
    2. Has ability to hop on one foot.
    3. Uses gestures to indicate wants.
    4. Weight gain of four pounds in last year.

7. The parents of a four-year-old child tell the
    nurse that the child has an invisible friend
    named "Felix." The child blames "Felix" for
    any misbehavior and is often heard scolding
    "Felix," calling him a "bad boy." The nurse
    understands that the best interpretation of
    this behavior is which of the following?
    1. A delay in moral development.
    2. Impaired parent-child relationship.

3. A way for the child to assume control.
4. Inconsistent parental discipline strategies.

8. The nurse is caring for a five-year-old child who is in the terminal stages of acute leukemia. The child refuses to go to sleep and is afraid that his parents will leave. The nurse recognizes that the child suspects he is dying and is afraid. Which of the following questions about death is most likely to be made by a five-year-old child?
1. "What does it feel like when you die?"
2. "Who will take care of me when I die?"
3. "What will my friends do when I die?"
4. "Why do children die if they're not old?"

9. The parents of an eight-year-old child bring the child into the clinic for a school physical. The nurse makes all of the following assessments. Which assessment finding is an area of concern and needs further investigation?
1. Complains of a stomach ache on test days at school.
2. Has many evening rituals and resists going to bed at night.
3. Refers to self as being too dumb and too small during the exam.
4. Has lost three deciduous teeth and has the central and lateral incisors.

10. The nurse is performing a neurologic assessment on an eight-year-old child. As part of this neurologic assessment the nurse is assessing how the child thinks. Which of the following abilities best illustrates that the child is developing concrete operational thought?
1. Able to make change from a dollar bill.
2. Describes a ball as both red and round.
3. Tells time in terms of after breakfast and before lunch.
4. Able to substitute letters for numbers in simple problems.

11. The nurse is caring for a 10-year-old child during the acute phase of rheumatic fever. Bedrest is part of the child's plan of care. Which of the following diversional activities is developmentally appropriate and meets the health needs of this child in the acute phase of rheumatic fever?
1. Using hand-held computer video games.
2. Sorting and organizing baseball cards in a notebook.
3. Playing basketball with a hoop suspended from the bed.
4. Using art supplies to make drawings about the hospital experience.

12. The nurse is caring for a 13-year-old who has been casted following spinal instrumentation surgery to correct idiopathic scoliosis. The nurse is helping the teen and family plan diversional activities while the teen is in the cast. Which of the following activities would be most appropriate to support adolescent development while the teen is casted?
1. Take the teen shopping at the mall in a wheelchair.
2. Plan family evenings playing a variety of board games.
3. Have teen regularly attend special school activities for own class.
4. Encourage siblings to spend time with teen watching television and movies.

13. A two-month-old infant is in the clinic for a well baby visit. Which of the following immunizations can the nurse expect to administer?
1. TD, Varicella, IPV.
2. DTaP, Pneumovax.
3. DTaP, MMR, Menomune.
4. DTaP, Hib, OPV, HBV.

14. An 18-month-old child with a history of falling out of his crib has been brought to the emergency room by the parents. Examination of the child reveals a skull fracture and multiple bruises on the child's body. Which of the following findings obtained by the nurse is most suggestive of child abuse?
1. Poor personal hygiene of the child.
2. Inability of the parents to comfort the child.
3. Conflicting explanations about the accident from the parents.
4. Cuts and bruises on the child's lower legs in various stages of healing.

15. The nurse is discussing the risk of sudden infant death syndrome (SIDS) in infants with the parents whose second baby died of SIDS six months ago. The parents express fear that other children will die from SIDS since they have already had one baby die. Which of the following statements made by the parents indicate their understanding of the relationship of future children and the risk of SIDS?
1. "Any new baby will be on home monitoring for one year to prevent SIDS."
2. "There is a 99% chance that we will not have another baby die of SIDS."
3. "Genetic testing is available to determine the likelihood of another baby dying from SIDS."
4. "There is medicine that can be used to stimulate the heart rate while the baby is sleeping."

16. A ten-day-old baby is admitted with 5% dehydration. The nurse notes which of the following signs?
1. Tachycardia.
2. Bradycardia.
3. Hypothermia.
4. Hyperthermia.

17. The nurse is asked why infants are more prone to fluid imbalances than adults. The response is

1. adults have a greater body surface area.
2. adults have a greater metabolic rate.
3. infants have functionally immature kidneys.
4. infants ingest a lesser amount of fluid per kilogram.

18. A 10-month-old weighs 10 kg and has voided 100 ml in the past four hours. The nurse determines normal urine output based on the fact that normal urine output is
   1. 1–2 ml/kg/hour.
   2. 3–5 ml/kg/hour.
   3. 7–9 ml/kg/hour.
   4. 10 ml/kg/hour.

19. A three-month-old is NPO for surgery. The nurse attempts to comfort him by
   1. administering acetaminophen.
   2. encouraging parents to leave so the child can rest.
   3. offering pacifier.
   4. giving 10 cc Pedialyte.

20. An 11-year-old is admitted for treatment of lead poisoning. The nurse includes which of the following in the plan of care?
   1. Oxygen.
   2. Strict intake and output.
   3. Heme-occult stool testing.
   4. Calorie counts.

21. A two-month-old is admitted with diarrhea. What is the best room assignment for the nurse to make?
   1. Semi-private room with no roommate.
   2. Private room with no bathroom.
   3. Semi-private room with 10-year-old who has acute lymphocytic leukemia.
   4. Open ward.

22. The nurse is discussing safety measures to prevent poisoning with the mother of a one-year-old. The nurse knows the mother understands safety precautions when she states,
   1. "I have child protection locks on my cabinet under the sink."
   2. "My child is not potty-trained, so the bathroom is safe."
   3. "I keep all poisons and cleaners above the fridge."
   4. "I don't think I have any poisons in my house."

23. A mother calls her local emergency room (ER) and tells the nurse, "My four-year-old just swallowed a bottle of aspirin. What should I do?" After verifying that the child is still awake and alert, the triage nurse would give what advice to the mother?
   1. Call 911, then give one glass milk to protect the esophagus.
   2. Call 911, then give syrup of ipecac.
   3. Bring child to local pediatrician.
   4. Call a poison control center.

24. A 16-year-old admits to her mother that she tried to commit suicide by swallowing a bottle of Tylenol (acetaminophen) 16 hours ago. Her mother brings the girl to the ER. The nurse implements treatment of choice, which is
   1. ipecac syrup.
   2. activated charcoal.
   3. mucomyst.
   4. milk and observation.

25. The nurse would include which of the following nursing diagnoses for a 10-year-old patient with stage I Lyme disease?
   1. Decreased cardiac output.
   2. Impaired mobility.
   3. Altered cerebral tissue perfusion.
   4. Alteration in skin integrity.

26. A four-year-old female is admitted to the pediatric intensive care unit (PICU) after suffering a severe closed head injury following a car accident. An intracranial pressure (ICP) monitor is in place and reveals an ICP of 40 mmHg. In an effort to lower the ICP, the nurse knows the best position for the patient would be
   1. supine with the head turned to the right.
   2. supine with the head turned to the left.
   3. supine with the head midline.
   4. side-lying on the right with the head turned to the left.

27. A five-year-old female is admitted to the PICU after being hit by a car while riding her bike. She sustained a severe closed head injury and has an ICP monitor in place. Her ICP is 40 mmHg and mannitol is ordered. What is the rationale for administering mannitol for a child with an increased ICP?
   1. It will produce a rise in the intravascular osmolality, resulting in a shift of free water from the interstitial and cellular spaces to the intravascular space, thus decreasing the ICP.
   2. It will produce a decrease in the intravascular osmolality, resulting in a shift of free water from the interstitial and cellular spaces to the intravascular space, thus decreasing the ICP.
   3. It will produce a rise in the intravascular osmolality, resulting in a shift of free water from the intravascular space to the cellular space, thus decreasing the ICP.
   4. It will produce a decrease in the intravascular osmolality, resulting in a shift of free water from the interstitial space to the cellular space thus decreasing the ICP.

28. An infant who has a ventriculoperitoneal (VP) shunt in place for treatment of hydrocephalus is hospitalized for potential shunt malfunction. When developing the plan of care, which of the following assessment findings would the nurse list as a positive sign of shunt malfunction?
   1. Overriding sutures.
   2. Bulging, tense anterior fontanel.
   3. Flat, soft anterior fontanel.

4. Consistent head circumference.
29. A male newborn was just admitted to the pediatric floor with a myelomeningocele. When developing the preoperative plan of care, the nurse lists "high risk for infection of and trauma to the nonepithelialized lesion" as the diagnosis of most concern. The *most effective* strategy to prevent infection and trauma to the lesion would be to
   1. leave the lesion uncovered and open to the air and place the baby supine.
   2. cover the lesion with sterile, saline-soaked gauze and place the baby prone.
   3. apply lotion to the lesion and place the baby on his side.
   4. cover the lesion with dry sterile gauze and place the baby supine.
30. The nurse has been giving instructions to parents on measures to prevent Reye's syndrome. When questioning the parents on a safe medication to provide to their child during a viral illness, which choice indicates that they understand steps toward Reye's syndrome prevention?
   1. Pepto-Bismol.
   2. Acetaminophen (Tylenol).
   3. Children's aspirin.
   4. Adult aspirin.
31. The nurse is caring for a five-year-old boy with a known seizure disorder. On entering his room, the nurse sees that he is experiencing a generalized, tonic-clonic seizure. The *first* intervention for the nurse would be to
   1. immediately leave the room to retrieve intravenous (IV) phenobarbital.
   2. place a metal spoon between his teeth to prevent him from biting his tongue.
   3. position him on his side to maintain a patent airway.
   4. try to hold the patient down.
32. When assessing a patient who is taking hydantoin (Dilantin), the nurse would recognize which of the following findings as side-effects?
   1. Drowsiness and irritability.
   2. Slurred speech and increased salivation.
   3. Hair loss and tremor.
   4. Gum hyperplasia and nystagmus.
33. A 12-year-old girl with cerebral palsy has severe language deficits and poor muscle coordination. However, she can voluntarily turn her head from side to side and her mother reports that she has normal intelligence. The nurse is concerned with the child's ability to call when help is needed. Considering the child's abilities, which of the following would be the *best* way for her to call the nurse?
   1. Kick the siderails of the bed.
   2. Scream loudly.
   3. Press the call bell with her fingers.

4. Press a large, padded call bell with her cheek.
34. When teaching a child measures to prevent spread of conjunctivitis, the nurse would recognize that *further* instruction is necessary when the child states the following,
   1. "It is important that I wash my hands regularly."
   2. "I can use a tissue to clean my eyes, but must throw it away immediately."
   3. "I need to use my own washcloth and towel, not my sister's."
   4. "My Dad said he would carry a handkerchief with him so I could wipe my eyes with it during the day."
35. Mrs. B. brings her daughter to the pediatric clinic because she is concerned that the child has otitis media. On examination, the nurse would recognize which of the following findings as the *most common* positive sign of otitis media?
   1. Temperature of 39° C and loss of appetite.
   2. Pearly gray tympanic membrane and rhinorrhea.
   3. Pain on pressure on the tragus and edema within the canal.
   4. Feeling of "fullness" in the ear and a popping sensation during swallowing.
36. An infant's blood pressure is reported to be very high. What is the most appropriate nursing action to take?
   1. Take it again in 20 minutes.
   2. Call the house officer.
   3. Measure the cuff width to the infant's arm.
   4. Prepare to give an antihypertensive.
37. Prior to discharge from the newborn nursery at 48 hours old, the nurse knows that murmurs are frequently assessed and are most often due to which factor?
   1. A ventricular septal defect.
   2. Heart disease of the newborn period.
   3. Transition from fetal to pulmonic circulation.
   4. Cyanotic heart disease.
38. A 10-year-old with a ventricular septal defect (VSD) is going to have a cardiac catheterization. Which of the following needs to be a high priority for the nurse to assess?
   1. Capillary refill.
   2. Breath sounds.
   3. Arrhythmias.
   4. Pedal pulses.
39. An infant with congestive heart failure (CHF) is admitted to the hospital. Which goal has the highest priority when planning nursing care?
   1. The infant will maintain an adequate fluid balance.
   2. The infant will have digoxin at the bedside.
   3. Skin integrity will be addressed.
   4. Administer medications on time.

40. An infant on the ward is receiving digoxin and diuretic therapy. The nurse knows that which of the following choices indicates no toxicity?
    1. Heart rate less than 100, no dysrhythmias.
    2. Heart rate of 80–100.
    3. Heart rate greater than 100, no dysrhythmias.
    4. Vomiting.
41. An infant with cardiac disease has been admitted to the nursery from the delivery room. Which finding helps the nurse to differentiate between a cyanotic and an acyanotic defect?
    1. Infants with cyanotic heart disease feed poorly.
    2. The pulse oximeter does not read above 93%.
    3. Infants with cyanotic heart disease usually go directly to the operating room.
    4. Cyanotic heart disease causes high fevers.
42. A child with tetralogy of Fallot has been admitted. What equipment is most important to have at the bedside?
    1. Morphine.
    2. A blood pressure cuff.
    3. A thermometer.
    4. An oxygen setup.
43. A nine-year-old boy has been transferred back to the floor after cardiac surgery. Which of the following does the nurse need to include in the plan of care to evaluate that the fluid needs are being appropriately met?
    1. Call if the heart rate falls below 60 per minute.
    2. Place a Foley catheter.
    3. Prepare to assist with an arterial line to monitor blood pressure.
    4. Calculate the daily maintenance fluid requirements and ensure correct delivery.
44. A nine-year-old girl with rheumatic fever is asking to play. Which diversional activity is the nurse likely to offer?
    1. Walking to the gift store.
    2. Coloring books and crayons.
    3. A 300 piece puzzle.
    4. A dancing contest.
45. A 10-year-old has been diagnosed with rheumatic fever and is now being discharged. What statement made by the parents shows an understanding of long-term care?
    1. "She will need penicillin each day."
    2. "She will need antibiotic prophylaxis when she has dental work."
    3. "We will have yearly checkups."
    4. "The murmur will always go away by adolescence."
46. How could the nurse evaluate if parents are giving their child with iron deficiency anemia iron as prescribed?
    1. Parents state they offer orange juice when they give the medication.
    2. Parents state the child has greenish black stools.
    3. Parents state the child experiences nausea with the iron preparation.
    4. Parents state they are giving the iron as prescribed.
47. Parents of a child who has sickle-cell anemia want to know why their child did not have the first episode until he was approximately a year old. The best reply for the nurse to make is,
    1. "Are you sure your child has sickle-cell anemia and not sickle-cell trait?"
    2. "Affected children can be asymptomatic in infancy because of high levels of fetal hemoglobin that inhibit sickling."
    3. "Have you asked your doctor about this?"
    4. "Your child probably had a crisis and you did not realize it."
48. A five-year-old is admitted to the nursing care unit in vaso-occlusive crisis from sickle cell anemia. What is the priority nursing intervention?
    1. Teaching the family about sickle cell anemia and home care needs.
    2. Managing the child's pain.
    3. Encouraging a high protein, high calorie diet.
    4. Administering oxygen via nasal cannula.
49. A three-year-old with a recent history of chickenpox is admitted to the unit with idiopathic thrombocytopenic purpura. His platelet count is 15,000 mm^3/dl. His lesions are enlarging. Which of the following nursing actions best provides for the child's safety?
    1. Supervised outdoor play.
    2. Set times of rest periods.
    3. Only allowing him to have soft stuffed toys to play with.
    4. Keeping him on complete bedrest.
50. A child is admitted to the pediatric unit with hemarthrosis secondary to hemophilia. The most appropriate nursing intervention would be?
    1. Daily bleeding times.
    2. Prophylactic antibiotic therapy.
    3. Elevating and immobilizing the affected joint.
    4. Encouraging active range of motion of affected joint.
51. The nurse should recognize which of the following respiratory findings as normal in a 10-month-old infant?
    1. Respiratory rate of 60 at rest.
    2. Use of accessory muscles to assist in respiratory effort.
    3. Respiratory rate of 32 at rest.
    4. Diaphoresis with shallow respirations.
52. An 18-month-old presents with nasal flaring, intercostal and substernal retractions, and a respiratory rate of 50. What is the most appropriate nursing diagnosis?

1. Knowledge deficit.
2. Ineffective breathing pattern.
3. Ineffective individual coping.
4. High risk for altered body temperature: hyperthermia.

53. An 11-month-old is admitted to the hospital with bronchiolitis. He is currently in a croup tent with supplemental oxygen. Which toy is most appropriate for the nurse to recommend to the child's parents?
    1. A stuffed animal made from a washable fabric.
    2. A soft plastic stacking toy with multicolored rings.
    3. A set of wooden blocks.
    4. A pull toy.

54. Which of the following statements best assures the nurse that the parents understand the safety concerns related to use of a vaporizer at home?
    1. "I have a high dresser in the bedroom on which to place the vaporizer. The cord will be concealed behind the dresser."
    2. "I plan to put the vaporizer on a stool next to the bed so that my child will get the most benefit from the cool mist."
    3. "I purchased a warm mist vaporizer because I don't want my child to get chilled from the mist in her face."
    4. "I thought I could just set the vaporizer on the floor next to the bed."

55. A four-year-old is experiencing an acute asthma attack. Why should the nurse avoid chest percussion with this child?
    1. Chest percussion may lead to increased bronchospasm and more respiratory distress.
    2. Chest percussion may cause mucous plugging of the alveoli.
    3. Chest percussion is useful in removing airway secretions and should be used.
    4. Chest percussion will produce increased coughing and thereby enhance respiratory distress.

56. A five-month-old has severe nasal congestion. What is the best way for the nurse to clear his nasal passages?
    1. Administer saline nose drops and use a bulb syringe to clear passages.
    2. Ask him to blow his nose and keep tissues handy.
    3. Place him in a mist tent with 40% oxygen.
    4. Administer vasoconstrictive nose drops before meals and at bedtime.

57. A 30-week gestation infant who had apnea of prematurity is ready for discharge and will be going home on apnea monitoring. What should the nurse teach the parents for proper use of the monitor?
    1. The monitor is only used when the child is awake. It is not indicated at night or during naps.

2. The alarms on the monitor should be turned off when an attendant is with the infant.
3. The monitor should be kept on at all times except when the infant is being bathed. Careful attention to skin integrity and hygiene is important.
4. It is best for the parents to have 24-hour home health supervision to watch the infant while monitoring is required.

58. A three-year-old underwent a tonsillectomy this morning. As the nurse giving discharge instructions, which comment by the child's mother suggests that she understands the care requirements?
    1. "I plan to take her back to her play group tomorrow. I know she won't want to stay home."
    2. "I have bought fruit popsicles to give her later today."
    3. "I will give her aspirin if she gets irritable."
    4. "She is just waiting for the ice cream we promised her before she came to the hospital."

59. A three-year-old boy presents in the ER with dysphagia, drooling, and respiratory difficulty that has increased significantly over the past six hours. The nurse should know that these findings are suggestive of which of the following conditions?
    1. Croup.
    2. Pneumonia.
    3. Bronchopulmonary dysplasia.
    4. Epiglottitis.

60. A two-year-old presents to an urgent care center with respiratory distress and cyanosis. Parents report an initial episode of choking. What is the best initial action for the nurse to take?
    1. Call 911 and have parents wait for an ambulance to transport the child to a pediatric hospital.
    2. Administer oxygen by face mask and call the child's pediatrician.
    3. Perform abdominal thrusts as described in the Heimlich maneuver.
    4. Start CPR after the child loses consciousness.

61. What is the appropriate feeding technique for the nurse to use with an infant who has a cleft palate?
    1. Suction patient prior to feeding.
    2. Feed in sitting position.
    3. Have the nurse feed the patient during hospitalization.
    4. Bubble patient after feed to reduce risk of aspiration.

62. How would you evaluate that the new nurse is using appropriate technique to feed a three-day-old with a cleft lip?
    1. NG tube is patent.
    2. Infant is seated in upright position.

3. The nurse uses a Nuk nipple.
4. The nurse adds rice to formula.
63. A baby girl is born prematurely to a mother with polyhydramnios. The baby is diagnosed with esophageal atresia with tracheoesophageal fistula. What assessment finding would the nurse be likely to note?
   1. Jaundice, high bilirubin.
   2. Seedy yellow stools.
   3. Projectile emesis.
   4. Frothy saliva, drooling.
64. A five-month-old girl is admitted with gastroesophageal reflux. Her signs and symptoms include emesis, poor weight gain, hemepositive stools, irritability, and gagging with feeds. The nurse would include which intervention?
   1. Urine dipstick each void.
   2. Appropriate feeding positioning.
   3. Bi-weekly weights.
   4. Monitor white blood count as indicator for infection.
65. A four-week-old is admitted for observation. Her assessment reveals projectile vomiting, visible gastric peristalsis, and an olive-shaped mass in the epigastrium. Which nursing diagnosis is of highest best priority?
   1. Altered nutrition.
   2. Self-care deficit.
   3. Impaired gas exchange.
   4. Fluid volume deficit.
66. The nurse would find which stool characteristic consistent with a diagnosis of intussusception?
   1. Yellow seedy stools.
   2. Currant jelly-like stools.
   3. Mucous-like stools.
   4. Hard black stools.
67. A six-month-old boy is treated at home with saline enemas due to his Hirschsprung's disease. His mother asks if she can use tap water to reduce costs. The nurse responds,
   1. "Yes, tap water is as effective as saline, just be sure to boil it first."
   2. "No, saline enemas must be used to maintain his electrolyte balance."
   3. "Yes; you can use tap water after letting it run for one minute to clear any lead from the pipes."
   4. "No; tap water enemas are not allowed, but soap suds enemas are just as effective."
68. A five-year-old boy has celiac disease. During a routine clinic visit, the nurse knows he is following his diet when he states,
   1. "I had hot dogs and french fries for lunch."
   2. "I ate chicken and vegetables for dinner."
   3. "I had macaroni and cheese for lunch."
   4. "I ate soup and crackers for dinner."
69. A 14-year-old is admitted to your unit following an emergency appendectomy. What is the nurse's goal for this patient?
   1. Pain related to inflamed appendix.

2. Patient will experience minimized risk of spread of infection.
3. Maintain NG tube decompression until bowel motility returns.
4. Child demonstrates resolution of peritonitis.
70. A nine-year-old girl comes into the clinic with a diagnosis of pinworms. What is it essential for the nurse to teach?
   1. Check for pinworms every morning for a week with a scotch tape test.
   2. Save the girl's next bowel movement to check for pinworms.
   3. Follow-up with local doctor in six months to check for recurrence.
   4. Scrub hands and fingernails thoroughly before each meal and after each use of the toilet.
71. The nurse is teaching parents about post-op care of their child who has had an orchiopexy. The nurse states,
   1. "You must tighten the rubber band around the scrotum every four hours to maintain the testicle."
   2. "You must increase tension on the rubber band every four hours."
   3. "You must check the rubber band every four hours to check for disconnection."
   4. "Cut the rubber band after 24 hours."
72. A baby boy is born with a hypospadias. The parents decide to wait until the child is six months old for the repair. The father asks the nurse why the doctor said not to have the baby circumcised. The nurse's best response is,
   1. "It is best to wait until the baby is older and understands the surgery."
   2. "Circumcision carries a high infection rate and that may delay his hypospadias repair."
   3. "The foreskin may be used during the hypospadias repair."
   4. "He will need the foreskin to help anchor the Foley catheter after the repair."
73. The nurse is planning care for a two-year-old who has nephrotic syndrome and is in remission. What type of diet would the nurse plan to feed this child?
   1. High protein, low calorie.
   2. High calorie, low protein.
   3. Low sodium, low fat.
   4. Regular diet, no added salt.
74. A five-year-old girl recovered from a strep infection two weeks ago. She now presents with loss of appetite, dark colored urine, and orbital edema. What is the nurse's assessment?
   1. Nephrotic syndrome.
   2. Glomerulonephritis.
   3. Renal tubular acidosis.
   4. Hemolytic uremic syndrome.
75. A four-year-old boy is admitted with

glomerulonephritis. His mother asks why his eyes are so puffy. The nurse responds,
1. "This is a common finding due to circulatory congestion in the kidneys."
2. "Children cry a lot with glomerulonephritis and the puffiness should subside when he feels better."
3. "Has he been rubbing his eyes excessively?"
4. "Periorbital edema is associated with hypertension."

76. Which of the following would the nurse include in a plan of care for a toddler with a newly applied hip spica cast?
1. Petal the cast around the perineum area with waterproof tape.
2. Teach the parents care of the child just before discharge.
3. Give the child small blocks and beads to promote eye-hand coordination.
4. Check neurovascular status every shift.

77. The mother of a six-year-old asks why she was told not to use powder under her child's long leg cast. Which of the following is the most accurate basis for the nurse's response?
1. Promoting adequate circulation is a top priority.
2. Drying the cast is very important.
3. Assessing the smell of a cast is a top priority.
4. Preserving skin integrity is of the utmost importance.

78. In examining a newborn, the nurse notes the following: asymmetric gluteal folds, shortened right leg, and limited abduction of the right thigh. The nurse would correctly interpret these observations as which of the following?
1. Right congenital dislocated hip.
2. Spastic cerebral palsy.
3. Left hip dysplasia.
4. Myelodysplasia.

79. An infant with congenital hip dysplasia is placed in a Pavlik harness. In the nurse's teaching plan for the mother, which of the following would be important to include?
1. Adjustment of daily care routines as the harness is worn 24 hours a day.
2. Clothing should not be worn under the harness.
3. The harness should be removed for bathing and diapering only.
4. The infant should be confined to the crib.

80. In assessing a newborn for talipes equinovarus, the nurse would note which of the following?
1. The feet turn inward when the infant lies still, but they are flexible.
2. The feet are rigid and cannot be manipulated to a neutral position.
3. Uneven knee length occurs when both knees are flexed.

4. Limited abduction is observed when performing the Ortolani maneuver.

81. The nurse would evaluate that the parents correctly understand the care of their infant being treated for talipes equinovarus if the parents said which of the following?
1. "We will unwrap the cast every night and massage his feet with lotion to prevent skin breakdown."
2. "We'll petal the cast around the baby's groin to protect it from urine and bowel movements."
3. "Every day we'll check the baby's toes for movement and color after we squeeze them."
4. "We're so glad that the casts will cure his club feet."

82. Which of the following comments by the school nurse would be most appropriate in screening for scoliosis of a 13-year-old?
1. "You may leave your shirt on, but stand erect and turn to the side."
2. "Do you have any back pain?"
3. "Remove your clothes from the waist up and bend over at your waist."
4. "Have you noticed that your skirts don't hang evenly?"

83. A child is admitted to the hospital for a spinal fusion and Harrington rod insertion. A nursing priority in the first eight hours postoperatively will be to
1. give fluids and fiber to promote bowel elimination.
2. check neurovascular function in extremities.
3. log roll every four hours.
4. monitor hourly urine output.

84. The nurse would evaluate that a child understood the effective use of her Milwaukee brace for her scoliosis if she said which of the following?
1. "I'm so glad that I don't have to sleep in this brace."
2. "I've toughened my skin so I can wear the brace right next to my skin."
3. "I can't believe that I'm not allowed to chew gum anymore."
4. "I'm going to look forward to my bath time each day without this brace."

85. A four-year-old has recently been diagnosed with Duchenne's muscular dystrophy. His parents ask if their two-year-old daughter will get the disease. The nurse's best response would be which of the following?
1. "Every child you have has a 25% chance of developing the disease and a 50% chance of being a carrier."
2. "Sons are affected 50% of the time, whereas 50% of the time daughters will become carriers who have no symptoms."
3. "Only your sons have a 25% chance of developing the disease."

4. "Every child has a 50% chance of developing the disease."

86. A two-year-old was recently found to have impetigo. What measures should be given the highest priority to prevent its spread while in the hospital?
   1. Keeping it covered.
   2. Good handwashing.
   3. Applying A&D ointment.
   4. Placing the child in isolation.

87. A seven-year-old boy has a loss of scalp hair and is diagnosed with ringworm. What question will the nurse most likely ask?
   1. Whether the family owns any pets.
   2. From what economic background is the family.
   3. Whether other children in his classroom have ringworm.
   4. Whether the child can read the medicine directions.

88. Three school children have pediculosis capitus. The school nurse has been instructing the parents of all three students on prevention. Which statement made by one mother indicates an understanding of prevention?
   1. "I will put all of the stuffed animals in plastic bags for two weeks."
   2. "Since the sheets are now clean, the kids can share beds, too."
   3. "Once I cut her hair, all the nits should be gone."
   4. "I will now bathe my child every day to prevent reinfection."

89. Prior to discharge home with their new baby, the nurse knows that the parents understand diaper rash prevention when
   1. they articulate that the baby should be checked for wet diapers every half an hour.
   2. they are observed wiping with soap and water at diaper changes.
   3. the mother discusses needs to use tight rubber pants to keep diapers from leaking.
   4. the father wipes carefully and uses a mild ointment to protect the skin.

90. A three-year-old girl has had eczema since four months of age. Which statement made by her father indicates to the nurse that he understands the management of eczema?
   1. "Benadryl should be given every night before bedtime."
   2. "It's beneficial to keep her in the bubble bath for as long as possible each day."
   3. "Typical eruption areas that need to be treated include flexor surfaces of joints."
   4. "Hot water is better in which to bathe."

91. A six-year-old girl is newly diagnosed with acute lymphoid leukemia (ALL). During your assessment, which of the following signs and symptoms would you expect?
   1. Fever, pallor, bone and joint pain.
   2. Fever, ruddy complexion, petechiae.

3. Abdominal pain, cystitis, swollen joints.
   4. Enlarged lymph nodes, low grade fever, night sweats.

92. A 12-year-old girl with ALL is receiving induction therapy with vincristine, prednisone, and L-asparaginase. She presents with paresthesia, alopecia, and moon face. Which of the following nursing diagnoses would be most appropriate for this child?
   1. High risk for injury.
   2. Impaired physical mobility.
   3. Body image disturbance.
   4. Altered nutrition: less than body requirements.

93. You are caring for a 10-year-old with ALL who underwent a bone marrow transplant. To provide a safe, effective care environment, what would be included in a plan of care?
   1. Rectal temperature every four hours to monitor for infection.
   2. Encouraging the child to go to the playroom to limit isolation.
   3. Use of egg crate or other pressure reducing mattress.
   4. Inserting a Foley catheter to monitor output.

94. A 15-year-old girl with ALL has been on maintenance therapy for six months. She is receiving chemotherapy of L-asparaginase, methotrexate, and cytarabine. Her absolute neutrophil count is 500/mm³. In planning for her care, which of the following would be included in a nursing care plan?
   1. Good handwashing by visitors and staff.
   2. Daily CBCs drawn.
   3. Daily physical therapy.
   4. Restriction of activity.

95. A five-year-old boy is newly diagnosed with an astrocytoma brain tumor. His symptoms include headache, nausea, and seizures. Based on this information, which nursing diagnosis would be most appropriate for him?
   1. High risk for infection.
   2. High risk for injury.
   3. Anticipated grief.
   4. Impaired physical mobility.

96. Which of the following statements made by parents of an eight-year-old boy who just had surgery for a brain tumor reflect understanding of safety needs?
   1. "We will obtain a tutor to teach him at home."
   2. "We will not allow him to participate in sports anymore."
   3. "We will tell our other children to let him have his way and not upset him."
   4. "He will wear a helmet for sports."

97. A 16-year-old boy is admitted with Hodgkin's lymphoma. Which assessment finding would you expect?

1. Small, tender lymph nodes in the groin.
2. Enlarged, firm nontender nodes in the supraclavicular area.
3. Enlarged, tender nodes all over the body.
4. Small, nontender, nonmoveable nodes in the cervical area.

98. A three-year-old with a Wilms' tumor is returning to the unit after surgery to remove the tumor. Which of the following actions have the highest priority in caring for this child?
1. Maintaining NPO.
2. Frequent blood pressure.
3. Turning every four hours.
4. Administering pain medication every four hours.

99. A child is to receive radiation therapy following surgery for Wilms' tumor. Which of the following measures would be important to include in the care plan prior to radiation therapy?
1. Give compazine every six hours for nausea.
2. Place a sign over the bed that reads "no needle punctures."
3. Practice lying in the required position.
4. Encourage play appropriate to age.

100. A six-year-old boy with Ewing's sarcoma has just finished his course of chemotherapy. Which of the following statements by his parents indicate they understand the signs of complications from the chemotherapy?
1. "He will be playing football next week."
2. "We will keep him on a liquid diet until he feels better."
3. "We understand he is more susceptible to infections; we will keep him away from any sick family members."
4. "He will wear a baseball hat to bed."

Answers and Rationales for Review Test 3

Pediatric Nursing

ANSWER		RATIONALE	NP	CN	CL
#1.	1.	**The palmar grasp is present at birth. The palmar grasp lessens by age three months and is no longer reflexive. The infant is able to close hand voluntarily.**	As	He/3	Ap
	2.	The sucking reflex is present at birth and persists throughout infancy, even with and without stimulation, such as seen during sleep.			
	3.	The Babinski reflex is present at birth. The Babinski reflex disappears after one year of age.			
	4.	The startle or Moro reflex is present at birth. This reflex is strongest during the first two months of life and disappears after three to four months of age.			
#2.	1.	**Infant cereal is generally introduced first because of its high iron content. The infant is able to accept spoon feeding at around four to five months when the tongue thrust or extrusion reflex fades.**	Pl	He/3	Co
	2.	Solid food can be offered even if the baby does not have any teeth. The first primary teeth usually erupt at approximately six to eight months.			
	3.	The infant usually triples his birth weight by the age of one year. The infant is capable of eating solid foods before this time. Doubling of birth weight is one of the readiness indicators to begin solid foods.			
	4.	Breast milk or commercial iron-fortified formula is recommended for the first year of life. Whole milk should not be introduced to infants until after one year of age. Solid foods should be offered to assist the infant in coordination and motor development and as well as essential nutrients.			
#3.	4.	**By four to six months, head control is well established. There should be no head lag when infant is pulled to a sitting position by the age of six months.**	As	He/3	Ap
	1.	The Moro reflex is present at birth. The Moro reflex is strongest during the first two months of life and disappears after three to four months.			

    2. The posterior fontanel is closed by two months of age.

    3. The infant gains 1½–2 pounds per month for the first five months of life. A three pound weight gain in the last two months is a normal weight gain.

#4. 1. The child has great curiosity and has the mobility to explore. Toddlers need to be supervised in play areas. Play areas with soft ground cover and safe equipment need to be selected.   Ev   Sa/2   An

    2. Swimming and water safety lessons are possible at this age; however, they are not a substitute for protection. The toddler is helpless in water and unaware of danger.

    3. Boosters are not restraint systems like the convertible devices because they depend on the vehicle belts to hold the child and booster in place. The rule of four serves as a guide: if the child weighs 40 pounds or is 40 inches or is four years old, then the child restraint can be replaced by the car's regular restraint system.

    4. The four-year-old child does not have the cognitive ability to keep himself safe or to protect the 18-month-old child. These children are often unable to recognize danger.

#5. 3. The best approach toward extinguishing attention-seeking behavior is to ignore it as long as the behavior is not inflicting injury.   Im   He/3   Ap

    1. Reasoning is an ineffective discipline technique to use for toddlers related to their limited cognitive ability.

    2. Using the bedroom as a punishment should be avoided. The bedroom is often a stimulating environment. The bedroom should be a safe and secure place.

    4. The toddler may be jealous of the new baby; however, the parent is asking for guidance in dealing with the temper tantrum at this time.

#6. 3. This behavior indicates a delay in language and speech development. The child may not be able to hear. The child should have a vocabulary of about 900 words and use complete sentences of three to four words.   As   He/3   An

    1. While a child of three years of age is expected to have the gross motor ability to ride a tricycle, this finding would not be an area of concern and need for referral or further investigation.

    2. The child is expected to have the gross motor ability to hop on one foot by the age of four years. This ability is still considered normal.

    4. Usual weight gain at the age of three years is four to six pounds per year. A four pound weight gain in one year is normal.

#7. 3. Imaginary friends are a normal part of development for many preschool children. These imaginary friends often have many faults. The child plays the role of the parent with the imaginary friend. This becomes a way of assuming control and authority in a safe situation.   An   He/3   An

    1. This is expected moral development for this age group. In the punishment and obedience orientation (ages two to four), children judge an action as good or bad depending on rewards or punishment.

    2. There are no data to support that there is an alteration in the parent-child relationship. The active imagination of the preschool child support the appearance of imaginary friends.

    4. There are no data to support that the parents are inconsistent in discipline strategies or have unrealistic behavioral expectations of this four-year-old child.

#8. 2. The greatest fear of preschool children is being left alone and abandoned. Preschool children still think as though they are alive and need to be taken care of.   An   He/3   Co

    1. This is an expected response of a school-age child who wants to know concretely what it feels like to experience death. School-age children often ask if it hurts when you die.

ANSWER	RATIONALE	NP	CN	CL

3. This is an expected response of a school-age child who is interested in peer relationships and has lost some of their egocentric thinking. School-age children can think of how something will affect others.

4. This is an expected response of a school-age child. School-age children know that everyone dies; however, they think death happens to old people and not people they know or love.

#9. 3. The school-age years are very important in the development of a healthy self-esteem. These statements by the eight-year-old child indicate a risk for development of a sense of inferiority and need further assessment.   As   He/3   Co

1. The school-age child often experiences stress related to school in physical complaints. The school-age child is afraid of getting poor grades and afraid of failing.

2. Bedtime resistance is a common characteristic during the middle school-age years. For some children it is related to normal fears of their age. These children use delay tactics to avoid going to bed.

4. This is a normal pattern of permanent teeth eruption. Eruption of permanent teeth begins at approximately six years of age. The eruption of the secondary teeth follow the same order as the primary teeth and follow shedding of the deciduous teeth.

#10. 1. This ability illustrates the concept of conservation, which is one of the major cognitive tasks of school-age children.   As   He/3   An

2. The ability to understand two characteristics of an object is attained during the preschool period and is an example of preoperational thought.

3. This is an example of egocentric thought. The child understands time in terms of how it relates to himself. Egocentrism is a characteristic of the preschool child.

4. This is an example of formal operations or abstract thinking in using letters to represent numbers as used in the math concepts of algebra. School-age children can serialize and use combinational skills to manipulate numbers and to learn the skills of addition, subtraction, multiplication, and division.

#11. 2. The middle childhood years are times for collections. The collections of middle to late school-age children become orderly, selective, and neatly organized in scrapbooks. This quiet activity supports the development of industry and concrete operational thought as well as the physical restrictions related to the rheumatic fever.   Pl   He/3   Ap

1. The disease process of rheumatic fever may prevent the child from having the fine motor skill to utilize the hand-held computer game and increase the child's frustration.

3. The basketball hoop demands high level of physical energy for the child and although it provides an important physical outlet for the school-age child, the activity increases the workload of the heart during the acute phase of rheumatic fever.

4. The disease process of rheumatic fever including the effects on the central nervous system interferes with the child's fine motor ability. Drawing with art supplies may be too difficult for the child during the acute stage.

#12. 3. Early adolescents have a strong need to fit in and be accepted by their peers. Attending school activities helps the teen continue peer relationships and develop a sense of belonging.   Pl   He/3   Ap

1. This activity supports the dependent relationship. The teen does not like to look different, which is emphasized by both the cast and the wheelchair.

2. The young teen is beginning to separate from the family. The young teen enjoys spending more time with friends than the family.

4. Sibling rivalry is very intense during the adolescent years. The

siblings may resent the attention of the teen who is ill and do not want the caregiving responsibility.

#13. 4. Healthy infants at two months of age receive diphtheria, tetanus, and pertussis (DTP); hemophilus influenza (Hib); oral polio vaccine (OPV); and hepatitis B virus (HBV). — Pl — He/4 — Ap

    1. The tetanus, diphtheria is given between the ages of 14–16 years, the varicella or chickenpox has no current recommendation by CDC, and inactivated poliovirus vaccine (IPV) is given for immunocompromised children.

    2. The DTP is given; however, the pneumovax is given to children two years and older who have sickle cell disease, asplenia, nephrotic syndrome, HIV infection, and Hodgkin's disease before beginning cytoreduction therapy.

    3. The diphtheria, tetanus, and acellular pertussis is given as the third dose of the DTP. The MMR is given after the infant's first birthday. The Menomune is recommended for children two years and older with terminal complement deficiencies and anatomic or functional asplenia.

#14. 3. Incompatibility between the history and the injury is probably the most important criterion on which to base the decision to report suspected abuse. — An — Ps/6 — An

    1. Poor personal hygiene may be a sign of neglect and lack of resources and other environmental factors. Nurses need to avoid stereotyping parents and children in an attempt to predict or diagnose abuse.

    2. The stress of the injury and the environment may affect the parents' ability to comfort the child. This is an important observation, however, it does not indicate abuse.

    4. Cuts and bruises on the child's lower legs are normal findings in a child of this age. Unusual areas of bruising include the face, back, and buttocks. The nurse needs to look for object patterns or hand patterns to the bruising.

#15. 2. Whether subsequent siblings of the SIDS infant are at risk is unclear. Even if the increased risk is correct, families have a 99% chance that their subsequent child will not die of SIDS. — Ev — He/4 — An

    1. Home monitoring is not recommended for subsequent siblings. Home infant monitoring does not prevent SIDS.

    3. No genetic link has been identified as a causative risk factor in SIDS.

    4. Theophylline is used in neonatal apnea as a cardiac stimulant to reduce bradycardiac events. There is no medication to prevent or reduce the risk of SIDS.

#16. 1. Tachycardia is associated with dehydration. — As — Ph/10 — Co

    2. Bradycardia is not noted until the patient is greater than 25% dehydrated.

    3. Hypothermia is not associated with dehydration.

    4. Hyperthermia is not always associated with dehydration.

#17. 3. Infant kidneys are unable to concentrate or dilute urine, to conserve or secrete sodium, or to acidify urine. — An — Ph/10 — Co

    1. Infants have a greater BSA that allows larger quantities of fluid to be lost through the skin.

    2. Infants have a greater metabolic rate related to their larger BSA.

    4. Infants excrete a greater amount of fluid per kilogram of body weight than do older children or adults.

#18. 1. Normal urine output is 1–2 ml/kg/hour. — An — Ph/10 — Co

    2. Normal urine output is 1–2 ml/kg/hour.

    3. Normal urine output is 1–2 mg/kg/hour.

    4. Normal urine output is 1–2 ml/kg/hour.

#19. 3. Non-nutritive sucking will help console and pacify him. — Pl — He/3 — Ap

    1. There is no basis to administer any meds.

    2. The nurse should encourage family to stay.

    4. Patient is NPO.

ANSWER		RATIONALE	NP	CN	CL

#20. 2. CaNaEDTA (treatment for lead poisoning) is nephrotoxic and strict intake and output records need to be kept.   Pl   Ph/10   Ap

    1. Oxygen is not indicated for treatment of lead poisoning.

    3. This is not indicated for treatment of lead poisoning.

    4. This is not indicated for treatment of lead poisoning.

#21. 2. A bathroom is irrelevant with an infant in diapers. A private room is necessary.   Pl   Sa/2   Ap

    1. Diarrhea is considered infectious until proven otherwise. There is a potential for infection of a roommate.

    3. Immunocompromised patients should also be in a private room.

    4. Infant diarrhea is considered infectious until proven otherwise so this is an inappropriate assignment.

#22. 3. All cleaners and poisons should be kept in high locked cabinets.   Ev   Sa/2   Ap

    1. Child protection locks are not child-proof and all cleaners/poisons should be kept in high cabinets.

    2. Developmentally, this child will explore all surroundings, including the bathroom cabinets.

    4. Poisons are prevalent in many household products including cleaners, pool chemicals, cosmetics, and over-the-counter medications.

#23. 4. Phone numbers for poison control centers are located in the blue pages of phone books nationwide.   Im   Ph/10   Ap

    1. Give nothing by mouth.

    2. Vomiting is a toxic effect of aspirin; if ipecac syrup is given, professionals won't know if child is having toxic effect or reacting to ipecac.

    3. It is too time consuming to call the pediatrician.

#24. 3. Mucomyst is the treatment of choice to bind with acetaminophen and help reduce levels.   An   Ph/10   Ap

    1. Ingestion was too many hours ago for ipecac to be helpful.

    2. Ingestion was too many hours ago for charcoal to be effective.

    4. This treatment is ineffective.

#25. 4. Stage I consists of tick bite followed by small erythematous papules that may be described as burning.   Pl   Ph/9   Co

    1. This is associated with stage II.

    2. This is associated with stage III.

    3. This is associated with stage II.

#26. 3. The patient's head must be kept in midline to facilitate venous return. Patients with a severe closed head injury have low intracranial compliance and turning of the head may result in an increase of ICP of 10–15 mmHg. The head of bed (i.e., 30°) should be determined individually for each patient based on the ICP and cerebral perfusion pressure (CPP) as well as the clinical appearance.   Pl   Ph/9   Ap

    1. The head must be kept in midline to facilitate venous return from the head, therefore decreasing the ICP. Patients with a severe closed head injury have low intracranial compliance and turning of the head may result in a rise in ICP of 10–15 mmHg.

    2. The head must be kept in midline to facilitate venous return from the head, therefore decreasing the ICP. Patients with a severe closed head injury have low intracranial compliance and turning of the head may result in a rise in ICP of 10–15 mmHg.

    4. Although a head-injured patient can be turned from side to side, the neck must be maintained in midline to facilitate venous return. Patients with a severe closed head injury have low intracranial compliance and turning of the head may result in an ICP of 10–15 mmHg.

#27. 1. A shift in fluid from the interstitial and cellular space to the intravascular space will occur with a rise in intravascular   An   Ph/8   Ap osmolality, the fluid will then be diuresed resulting in a decreased ICP.

2. Mannitol will cause a rise in the intravascular osmolality that allows fluid to shift from the interstitial and cellular spaces to the intravascular space. A decrease in intravascular osmolality will encourage fluid to shift into the interstitial and cellular space thus increasing the ICP.

3. A rise in intravascular osmolality will cause a shift of free water from the interstitial and cellular space to the intravascular space. This shift will result in a decreased ICP.

4. Mannitol will cause a rise in the intravascular osmolality. This will then cause a shift of free water from the interstitial and cellular space to the intravascular space, thus decreasing the ICP.

#28. 2. This is a common sign of shunt malfunction. The best way to assess an infant's fontanel is when the infant is upright and calm. In this position, a fontanel that is bulging and firm to light palpation is considered abnormal.   Pl   Ph/9   Ap

1. Split sutures are a sign of increased intracranial pressure secondary to accumulation of cerebrospinal fluid (CSF) in the brain. The soft bones of the infant skull will begin to separate as the ICP increases. Split sutures are a sign of shunt malfunction. If sutures are overriding, this indicates that the ICP is at a normal level and the shunt is functioning properly.

3. This is a normal fontanel and indicates the shunt is functioning properly.

4. An infant with a shunt malfunction will have an increasing head circumference (HC). It is important to document the position of the infant when the HC is measured (i.e., lying down or upright) because consistency in measurement technique is imperative.

#29. 2. The lesion must be kept moist with sterile, saline-soaked gauze. The prone position should be maintained preoperatively to prevent tension on the lesion and minimize trauma.   Pl   Sa/2   Ap

1. The lesion must be kept moist with sterile, saline-soaked gauze and the infant must be placed in a prone position to prevent trauma.

3. Lotion should not be applied because it may cause trauma to the lesion. Only sterile, saline-soaked gauze should be applied. The prone position should be maintained preoperatively to prevent tension and trauma to the lesion. A side-lying position can be used postoperatively.

4. Dry sterile gauze will allow the lesion to become dry. Sterile, saline-soaked gauze must be applied to prevent drying of the lesion. A prone position should be maintained to prevent tension to the lesion.

#30. 2. Acetaminophen does not contain salicylates, which have been suspected as an ingredient that can lead to Reye's syndrome.   Ev   He/4   Ap

1. Pepto-Bismol contains salicylates, which have been suspected as an ingredient that can lead to Reye's syndrome.

3. Children's aspirin contains salicylates, which have been suspected as an ingredient that can lead to Reye's syndrome.

4. Adult aspirin contains salicylates, which have been suspected as an ingredient that can lead to Reye's syndrome.

#31. 3. The first priority is to maintain a patent airway. The best position for the client during a seizure is on his side.   Im   Ph/9   Ap

1. The nurse should stay with the client to protect him from injury. Although IV medication would be an appropriate intervention, maintaining the client's airway would be the first intervention. The nurse should call another nurse to deliver the IV anticonvulsant.

2. One should never place a solid object between the teeth, because this could harm the client or the nurse. Instead, place the client on his side to maintain a patent airway.

ANSWER	RATIONALE	NP	CN	CL

4. One should never try to forcefully restrain the client during a seizure because this could injure the client or the nurse. Instead, place the client on his side and place a blanket or pillow under his head. Pad the bedrails.

#32. 4. Hydantoin (Dilantin) may cause gum hyperplasia and nystagmus. Other side-effects include hirsutism, ataxia, diplopia, anorexia, nausea, nervousness, and folate deficiency. — As — Ph/8 — Co

1. Phenobarbital (Luminal) generally causes these side-effects. Drowsiness does not occur after Dilantin administration.
2. Clonazepam (Klonopin) causes these side-effects.
3. Divalproex sodium, valproate, and valproic acid (Depakene, Depakote) cause these side-effects.

#33. 4. She is able to control her head movements voluntarily. A large padded call bell could easily be pressed when she turns her head to the side. — As — Ph/9 — Ap

1. Because of her poor coordination, she may not be able to consistently perform this task. Additionally, it may cause her injury and is simply not an appropriate and effective way of indicating a need for help.
2. Because of her severe language deficits, she may not be able to reliably or voluntarily perform this task. The nurse may not hear it. It may disturb the other patients.
3. She may not be able to perform this task consistently and reliably due to her poor muscle control.

#34. 4. The eye should be wiped with disposable tissues after a single use and no other individual should be exposed to items that come in contact with the infected eye. — Ev — Sa/2 — Ap

1. Handwashing is an important means of preventing spread of infection.
2. A tissue can be used to clean the eyes, but needs to be discarded after a single use.
3. Children must not share their washcloth and towel with others because this would promote the spread of infection.

#35. 1. Common signs of otitis media include fever (as high as 40° C), postauricular and cervical lymph gland enlargement, rhinorrhea, vomiting, diarrhea, loss of appetite, and red tympanic membrane. Infants become irritable, hold their ears, and roll their head from side to side. Young children verbally complain of pain. A concurrent respiratory or pharyngeal infection may also be present. — As — Ph/10 — Co

2. A normal tympanic membrane is pearly gray. Rhinorrhea that accompanies this finding suggests a viral illness. Further assessment would be necessary.
3. These are common signs of otitis externa or infection of the external ear. The most common symptom is pain on manipulation of the pinna, especially pressure on the tragus. The pain often may be accompanied by a tender, edematous external canal or fever.
4. These are common signs of otitis media with effusion (OME) in which exudate accumulates in the middle ear causing a feeling of "fullness" and a popping sensation. Severe pain and fever are usually absent in OME.

#36. 3. The cuff should be approximately two-thirds the length of the humerus. — Im — He/4 — Ap

1. This should be done, but only with correctly sized equipment.
2. The house officer should not be called until correct equipment is used to measure the blood pressure.
4. This is not done unless the measurement is correct.

#37. 3. As the transition occurs, the murmurs may become loud, and then resolve. — As — He/3 — Ap

1. Ventricular septal defects have distinct murmurs, and the infant would not likely be discharged.

ANSWER	RATIONALE	NP	CN	CL

    2. Frank heart disease may cause an infant to be more ill than having a heart murmur.

    4. These babies are cyanotic at birth and are not discharged early.

#38. 4. The nurse needs to know the baseline pedal pulses.   As   Ph/9   Ap

    1. Pedal pulses are the assessment priority after the catheterization so baseline values are essential.

    2. Breath sounds are important, but this is an invasive procedure to the vascular system, which makes pulses the assessment priority.

    3. The question asks for an assessment priority prior to the procedure; arrhythmias typically occur during or after the procedure.

#39. 1. This is a major priority for CHF patients.   Pl   Ph/9   Ap

    2. Digoxin may be administered, but does not need to be at the bed.

    3. Whereas this is important, it is not the highest priority.

    4. This is also important, but not the highest priority.

#40. 3. Infants' heart rates need to be greater than 100, with no rhythm disturbances.   Ev   Ph/8   Ap

    1. Heart rates below 100 are considered toxic in infants.

    2. Heart rates in this range for infants are considered toxic.

    4. Vomiting is a key sign of toxicity.

#41. 2. Cyanotic heart disease is unlikely to produce a reading above 93%.   An   Ph/10   An

    1. Most babies with heart disease feed poorly.

    3. Many babies are not diagnosed until after 48 hours of life.

    4. Cyanotic heart disease does not cause high fevers.

#42. 4. This is used emergently in a Tet spell.   Pl   Ph/9   Ap

    1. This is a necessary drug, but should not be at the bedside.

    2. It is necessary equipment, but need not be at the bedside.

    3. This, too, is necessary equipment that need not be nearby.

#43. 4. It is vital for pediatric nurses to know exactly how much fluid should be delivered each 24 hours to evaluate proper fluid needs.   Ev   Ph/10   Ap

    1. This symptom reflects more of a cardiac problem than a fluid status problem.

    2. Foley catheters may be too invasive and urine may be assessed in a nine-year-old with a "hat" in the toilet or urinal.

    3. Arterial lines are too invasive to monitor fluid status on a ward.

#44. 3. This will be quiet, yet stimulating.   Pl   He/3   Ap

    1. Walking may be too strenuous.

    2. This is for the younger patient.

    4. This is too strenuous.

#45. 2. This will be necessary for many years.   Ev   Ph/9   An

    1. She will need prophylaxis, not daily doses.

    3. She will need checkups approximately every two months.

    4. Some, but not all, murmurs may go away during adolescence.

#46. 2. When an adequate dosage of iron is reached, the stools usually turn a greenish black. Absence of this color stool usually gives a clue to poor compliance.   Ev   Ph/8   Ap

    1. Iron is better absorbed by the body when given with citrus juice; however, this doesn't help evaluate if the iron is being given as prescribed.

    3. Nausea is a side-effect of iron preparation. This may be a reason why parents are not compliant.

    4. Parents need to be evaluated on how they give the iron preparation. Just telling you they do it is not enough to evaluate compliance.

#47. 2. Children with sickle-cell anemia are often asymptomatic until at least four to six months of age. A crisis is usually precipitated by an acute upper respiratory or gastrointestinal infection.   Im   Ph/10   Ap

    1. This answer questions the parents' knowledge of their child's disease.

    3. You should answer the parents' questions based on solid knowledge of pathophysiology and not dismiss their concerns.

ANSWER	RATIONALE	NP	CN	CL
4.	This statement is not true and may alienate the parents from voicing further concerns.			
#48. 4.	**During a vaso-occlusive crisis, tissue hypoxia and ischemia cause pain. By delivering oxygen at the prescribed rate, further tissue hypoxia can be avoided.**	Im	Ph/9	Ap
1.	Discharge teaching should be implemented as soon as possible before discharge but it is not the highest priority at this time.			
2.	Pain management in sickle cell crisis is very important; however, the highest priority would be to prevent additional tissue hypoxia and ischemia, which cause pain.			
3.	Adequate nutrition is essential to promote growth but is not the highest priority.			
#49. 4.	**Initially when his platelets are below 20,000 mm³/dl and he is experiencing active bleeding or progression of lesions, activity is restricted.**	Im	Ph/9	An
1.	His platelets are low and he is at risk for bleeding. His activity will be restricted at this time.			
2.	The best answer to prevent injury from further bleeding is "4." Rest periods are important but there is no indication of the activity he would be doing between the rest periods.			
3.	He is at risk for bleeding, but he could play with a variety of toys while maintaining bedrest.			
#50. 3.	**During bleeding episodes, hemarthrosis is managed by elevating and immobilizing the joint and applying ice packs.**	Im	Ph/9	Ap
1.	It is important to avoid all venipunctures except for factor replacement therapy when caring for a child with a bleeding disorder.			
2.	The child has bleeding into the joints. Prophylactic antibiotic therapy is not necessary.			
4.	During the active bleeding episode, the joint is immobilized. Range of motion exercises can begin once the bleeding is controlled to prevent flexion contractures.			
#51. 3.	**Rates of 20–40 breaths per minute are normal at this age.**	As	He/3	Co
1.	A resting rate of 60 breaths per minute is an abnormal finding in a 10-month-old. Respiratory rates of 20–40 are characteristic of this age.			
2.	Use of accessory muscles to assist in respiration is an abnormal finding and suggests increased work of breathing.			
4.	Diaphoresis is an abnormal finding associated with increased respiratory effort. Shallow respirations by themselves may not be abnormal, however, when associated with diaphoresis, this is an abnormal finding.			
#52. 2.	**The findings on assessment suggest respiratory distress. Ineffective breathing pattern is an appropriate diagnosis with the information now available.**	An	Ph/10	Ap
1.	There is nothing in the scenario that suggests a knowledge deficit for this child. Although the parents may have a knowledge deficit, this is not the most important consideration.			
3.	This diagnosis is most often used when the client is not coping with the information or diagnosis provided. It is not a consideration in this case.			
4.	Although infection may have produced the respiratory symptoms described, there is insufficient information to support this diagnosis.			
#53. 2.	**Stacking toys with bright, large, colored plastic rings provide age-appropriate activity that is safe within the croup tent environment. The large rings can be held or stacked. They can be wiped down if damp. The size of the objects prevent them from creating any environmental hazards if the child is not continuously supervised.**	Pl	Sa/2	Ap

1. Although a stuffed animal is an age-appropriate toy, the moist environment of the croup tent makes it a poor choice.
3. Wooden blocks would be safe in the croup tent, but they are not the most age-appropriate selection for an 11-month-old infant.
4. A pull toy is not age appropriate for a child who is not yet walking. This toy would also not be appropriate to a child confined in a croup tent.

#54. 1. It is best to keep the vaporizer out of the child's way. Concealing the cord and placing the appliance on a high surface is preferable.   Ev   Sa/2   An
2. Although cool mist vaporizers are safer than warm mist ones, they are still electrical appliances. Placing the vaporizer next to the bed may tempt a young child to explore.
3. Warm mist vaporizers are more dangerous than cool mist vaporizers because scalding may occur as well as electrical injuries.
4. Placing the vaporizer next to the bed may subject the young child to potential electrical injury from chewing or playing with electrical cords.

#55. 1. During the course of an acute asthma attack, bronchospasm is a significant problem. Chest percussion can enhance the bronchospasm, leading to more pronounced respiratory distress.   An   Ph/9   An
2. Chest percussion is used to facilitate removal of secretions.
3. Although chest percussion is useful in removing secretions, it is contraindicated due to the degree of airway irritability in an acute asthma attack.
4. Although chest percussion may produce increased coughing, this is not the most important reason to avoid percussion in this case.

#56. 1. Saline nose drops will help loosen secretions. The bulb syringe is necessary because the child is not old enough to effectively blow his nose.   Im   Ph/9   Ap
2. Generally it is difficult to get a child under 18 months to cooperate and effectively clear nasal passages by independently blowing the nose.
3. A mist tent with oxygen supplementation is not appropriate to clear the nasal passages. Depending on the cause of the condition, it might be a part of therapy for alteration in oxygenation.
4. Although vasoconstrictive and decongestant nose drops may be useful in an older child, this is not the most appropriate nursing action for a child as young as this.

#57. 3. Although apneic episodes are most common during sleep, they can occur at other times. Initially, it is particularly advisable to use the monitor continually except when bathing the infant.   Im   Ph/9   Ap
1. The most likely time for apneic episodes to develop are during sleep time. Using only while awake defeats the purpose of monitoring.
2. Alarms should not be disabled at any time while monitoring is in progress.
4. Although parents may display anxiety about the monitoring, home health supervision is not necessary. Careful instruction and follow-up can allay anxiety.

#58. 2. Clear liquids are a good choice during the first 24 hours after surgery. Popsicles are appealing to children while providing fluids. They are less likely to irritate the surgical site than juices.   Ev   Ph/9   Ap
1. It is a good idea to restrict the child's activity for the first week after surgery to allow the clot to form and to minimize bleeding.
3. Aspirin is contraindicated after tonsillectomy because it increases the chances of bleeding.
4. Although ice cream is frequently promised after tonsillectomy, it produces tenacious secretions and is not the best choice.

#59. 4. Epiglottitis is a medical emergency. The drooling and dysphagia   As   Ph/10   Ap are most often diagnostic of this condition.

1. Children with croup do not present with drooling and dysphagia. The barking cough is most characteristic of this illness.
2. Although young children with pneumonia do have respiratory distress, the drooling and dysphagia are not characteristic of lower respiratory tract illness.
3. Bronchopulmonary dysplasia is a disease found in infants and young children who have had respiratory disease in the newborn period. A three-year-old will not manifest this disease for the first time.

#60. 3. The reported episode of choking and the child's condition suggest foreign body aspiration. The Heimlich maneuver should be attempted as an initial action to remove the object. — Im — Ph/10 — Ap

1. This is an emergency situation. The nurse cannot wait for an ambulance to take initial action.
2. Although oxygen might relieve cyanosis, if the airway is obstructed, the therapy will be ineffective.
4. Although CPR may be required at some point, this is not the best initial action. The nurse must recognize that the obstruction will need to be relieved first.

#61. 2. This position reduces the risk of aspiration. — Im — Ph/9 — Ap

1. Children with cleft palates do not need routine suctioning.
3. The family should begin feeding as soon as possible so they become adept in feeding technique before discharge.
4. Bubble patient frequently during feed to reduce risk of aspiration.

#62. 2. This position reduces the risk of aspiration. — Ev — Ph/9 — Ap

1. Children with cleft lips do not routinely have NG tubes.
3. Nipples are generally modified to facilitate feeds or special nipples (Asepto, Breck feeder) are used.
4. Rice cereal is not used for a three-day-old child.

#63. 4. Infants with esophageal atresia (EA) with tracheoesophageal fistula (TEF) have difficulty handling their secretions. — As — Ph/10 — Ap

1. Jaundice is not a symptom of EA with TEF. Jaundice is a symptom of biliary atresia.
2. Seedy yellow stools are not a symptom of EA with TEF.
3. This is a symptom of pyloric stenosis.

#64. 2. It may be a challenge to find the optimum position. Best positions include upright prone and 30° head of bed elevation. — Im — Ph/9 — Ap

1. This is not necessary for this diagnosis.
3. This patient needs to be weighed at least every day.
4. Gastroesophageal reflux is not associated with changes in white blood count.

#65. 4. Infants with pyloric stenosis are at high risk for electrolyte imbalance and these need to be corrected prior to a pyloromyotomy. — An — Ph/10 — An

1. Although the child may have weight loss related to the pyloric stenosis, it is more important to correct potential electrolyte imbalances caused by the fluid volume deficit.
2. All infants have self-care deficits.
3. Does not apply to infant with pyloric stenosis.

#66. 2. The obstruction causes bloody mucus known as currant jelly stools. — As — Ph/10 — Co

1. Yellow seedy stools are consistent with breast fed babies.
3. Mucous stools are consistent with a child with cystic fibrosis.
4. Hard black stools are consistent with constipation.

#67. 2. Repeated water enemas cause electrolyte dilution. — An — Ph/10 — Ap

1. Tap H_2O is effective for enemas but not in maintaining electrolyte integrity in a Hirschsprung's patient.
3. There is no correlation between lead poisoning and Hirschsprung's.
4. Saline enemas are isotonic; soap suds enemas do not contain electrolytes.

ANSWER	RATIONALE	NP	CN	CL

#68. 2. Chicken and vegetables do not contain gluten. Gluten is in barley, rye, oats, and wheat.   Ev   Ph/9   An
1. Hot dogs contain gluten.
3. Macaroni contains gluten.
4. Soup and crackers contain gluten.

#69. 2. This is an appropriate goal.   Pl   Ph/9   Ap
1. This is a nursing diagnosis.
3. This is a nursing intervention.
4. This is an expected outcome.

#70. 4. Handwashing prevents reinfection and/or new infections in other people.   Im   Sa/2   Ap
1. Diagnosis has already been made and this is no longer necessary.
2. Diagnosis has already been made and this is no longer necessary.
3. Follow-up is not necessary unless symptoms recur.

#71. 3. The Torek procedure attaches a rubber band from the testicle to the scrotal sac to the thigh to maintain the testicle in the pouch. The family must check the rubber band every four hours and call the doctor if the rubber band breaks or becomes disconnected.   Im   Ph/9   Ap
1. This would lead to ischemia.
2. This would lead to great discomfort and ischemia.
4. The rubber band is not cut off until the follow-up visit.

#72. 3. The foreskin is frequently used as a flap during the repair.   Im   Ph/9   Ap
1. Circumcision is best done at birth prior to the infant developing a castration complex.
2. Circumcision has a relatively low infection rate.
4. A Foley catheter is kept in place with a balloon.

#73. 4. The child who is in remission is allowed a regular diet; salt is restricted in the form of no added salt at the table and excluding foods with very high salt content.   Pl   Ph/7   Ap
1. There is no evidence that a high protein diet is beneficial or alters the outcome of the disease.
2. There is no evidence that altering the protein content in a diet will influence the outcome of the disease.
3. Children need the RDA of fat per day. A low sodium diet is only indicated during periods of exacerbation. A low sodium diet will not decrease the amount of edema already present but may reduce the rate of increase.

#74. 2. Acute poststreptococcal glomerulonephritis is the most common of the noninfectious renal diseases in children.   As   Ph/10   An
1. Nephrotic syndrome does not follow a strep infection.
3. Edema is not a symptom of renal tubular acidosis.
4. Hemolytic uremic syndrome occurs primarily in children six months to three years of age and predominantly in white children.

#75. 1. Periorbital edema is often associated with circulatory congestion in the kidneys.   An   Ph/10   An
2. Edema associated with crying clears 30 minutes after the child stops crying. Periorbital edema does not.
3. Excessive eye rubbing is not consistent with prolonged periorbital edema.
4. Hypertension is a sign of glomerulonephritis, but not a cause of periorbital edema.

#76. 1. It is important to protect the cast from urine and stool to prevent skin and cast breakdown.   Pl   Ph/9   Ap
2. Parents need generous amounts of time and practice to learn care of a child in a spica cast. Teaching should begin as soon as plans for spica casting are made.
3. Play materials should be large enough not to be hidden in the cast to prevent skin breakdown. Adequate play materials are an appropriate part of the plan.

4. Neurovascular checks should be done hourly until normal and then a minimum of every four hours until the cast is dry for early detection of swelling and neurovascular compromise.

#77. 4. Powder may irritate the skin leading to skin breakdown and infection. An Ph/9 Ap
  1. Use or nonuse of powder will not affect circulation.
  2. Using powder under the cast will not promote drying.
  3. Although assessing for a foul odor that might indicate infection is important, there are odorless powders and this is nto the primary rationale for not using powder.

#78. 1. These are all signs of right congenital dislocated hip in a newborn. An Ph/10 An
  2. These signs are inconsistent with spastic cerebral palsy. Increased muscle tone, hyperactive stretch reflex, and muscle spasms or motor weakness might be seen.
  3. Congenital hip dysplasia and congenital dislocated hip are the same. However, signs of shortened leg and limited abduction are on the affected side.
  4. These signs are inconsistent with myelodysplasia, which are congenital malformations of the vertebral column, spinal meninges, and spinal cord.

#79. 1. The harness is worn 24 hours a day so that parents must learn how to manage daily care (sponging and dressing the baby) with the harness on. Pl Ph/9 Ap
  2. Clothing is worn under the harness to prevent skin breakdown.
  3. The harness is worn 24 hours a day.
  4. The baby is physically normal and should be moved about as any normal infant to promote optimum development. Because the harness is visible, explanations may be required.

#80. 2. Talipes equinovarus is a rigid deformity with forefoot adduction, inversion of the heel, and plantar flexion of the feet. As Ph/10 Co
  1. This observation suggests metatarsus adductus, in which the feet readily correct to a neutral position with passive manipulation.
  3. This is an assessment for congenital hip dysplasia.
  4. This is an assessment for congenital hip dysplasia.

#81. 3. Parents should be taught to assess neurovascular status of the toes because babies grow quickly and may outgrow the casts. Ev Ph/9 An
  1. The casts are not bivalved so this is not an option. Casts should remain on until changed.
  2. Infants usually have short leg casts, so petaling is not a priority. Casts are changed every one to two weeks to accommodate the baby's rapid growth.
  4. This answer does not give any indication as to how the parents will care for their infant.

#82. 3. This is part of the screening process for scoliosis. The nurse is checking for rib hump and flank asymmetry. Also included is visual inspection of frontal and dorsal posture, observation for uneven hip and shoulder levels as well as for muscular disproportion. As He/4 Ap
  1. This is not the proper position for screening for scoliosis.
  2. Back pain is not an early symptom of scoliosis so would not be used in screening.
  4. Although this comment might lead one to suspect scoliosis, this is not an accurate method for screening for scoliosis. Incorrect posture might also be the reason for this.

#83. 2. One of the greatest risks of spinal surgery is of paralysis if the spinal cord is injured or compressed by swelling. Monitoring for sensation and movement is the top priority. As Ph/9 Ap
  1. This is not a priority because the child will be NPO or on clear liquids for several days until the return of bowel sounds.

3. Log rolling should be done every two hours to promote effective breathing and prevent skin breakdown.

4. The child will have an indwelling catheter for the first 48 hours postoperatively which will promote urinary elimination. An hourly check is not a top priority.

#84. 4. For best results in correction, the brace should be worn for 20–23 hours a day and only removed for hygiene and skin care.   Ev   Ph/9   An

1. Clients need to wear their brace for 20–23 hours a day for maximum correction including at night while sleeping.

2. A cotton undershirt/T shirt and/or bra should be worn under the brace so the brace is not next to the skin. Underpants should be worn over the brace.

3. Chewing gum is not restricted but rather encouraged to promote jaw mobility. Sugarless gum is advised.

#85. 2. Duchenne's muscular dystrophy is an X-linked recessive disorder. The defective gene is transmitted through carrier females to affected sons 50% of the time depending on which X is transmitted. Daughters have a 50% chance of becoming carriers.   Im   Ph/10   Ap

1. This occurs with autosomal recessive disorders when both parents are carriers of the given trait. This is not how this disorder is transmitted.

3. Because this disorder is X-linked recessive, there is a 50% chance of sons receiving the mutant gene.

4. This would be true if the disorder were either autosomal dominant (one parent had the disorder) or X-linked dominant, which it is not. There is also no evidence that one of the child's parents is affected.

#86. 2. Good handwashing is of paramount importance in preventing its spread.   Im   Sa/2   Ap

1. Keeping it covered may not prevent its spread and is impractical.

3. Bactroban is more appropriate to use as A&D ointment does not work on the infection.

4. All patients are on universal isolation, but handwashing is by far the most important step.

#87. 1. Pets are known to be carriers of ringworm.   As   Sa/2   Ap

2. Although lower income families are more often affected, this is an inappropriate question.

3. This is important, but does not affect this child's treatment plan.

4. Medicine directions need to be given to adults to maintain safety.

#88. 1. Stuffed animals can harbor eggs and cause reinfection.   Ev   Sa/2   An

2. Not only do sheets need to be cleaned, but also the eggs and nits on each infected person need to be resolved with medicine.

3. Cutting hair does not guarantee resolution of nits and eggs.

4. Cleanliness does not prevent infection.

#89. 4. Careful cleansing on delicate skin and use of ointments helps to preserve the skin's integrity.   Ev   He/4   Ap

1. Diapers can be checked every two hours.

2. Soap is too drying and can promote tissue breakdown.

3. If using cloth diapers, loose rubber pants are more appropriate.

#90. 3. These are the joint areas typically affected in the childhood years.   Ev   Ph/9   An

1. Benadryl is more appropriately used when exacerbations occur.

2. Bubble baths promote drying of the skin and make symptoms worse.

4. Hot water washes off essential oil on the skin making it drier.

#91. 1. The signs and symptoms of leukemia are a result of infiltration of the bone marrow. These include fever, pallor, fatigue, anorexia, petechiae, and bone and joint pain.   As   Ph/10   Ap

2. Although fever and petechiae are signs of leukemia, children have anemia which gives them a pallor to their complexion.

3. Abdominal pain can be caused by areas of inflammation from normal flora within the intestinal tract in leukemia but cystitis and swollen joints are not.

    4. These are signs and symptoms of Hodgkin's disease.

#92. 3. **This may be especially true for this child as she is entering adolescence. Her loss of hair and "fat face" will make her different from her friends. Adolescents need to belong and be accepted by a group of peers.** An   Ps/5   Ap

    1. The side-effects she is experiencing now do not increase her risk of injury.

    2. Although she is experiencing paresthesia, there are insufficient data to support a diagnosis of impaired physical mobility.

    4. Nausea, vomiting, and anorexia are all common side-effects of chemotherapy that would support a diagnosis of altered nutrition. This client, however, is not experiencing these side-effects at this time.

#93. 3. **Skin breakdown and impaired healing are common with bone marrow transplant. This is a preventive measure for the integrity of the skin.** Pl   Sa/2   Ap

    1. The child with bone marrow transplant is immunosuppressed and has a tendency to bleed. A rectal temperature would increase the risk of bleeding.

    2. Although isolation is a problem with bone marrow transplant, contact with other sick children would increase the risk of infection in a child who is immunosuppressed.

    4. A Foley catheter is not necessary and would increase the risk of infection in a child who is immunosuppressed.

#94. 1. **Because of the maintenance therapy and neutrophil count, this client may have bone marrow suppression, which increases her risk for infection. Good handwashing is essential to help prevent infection.** Pl   Sa/2   Ap

    2. Generally on maintenance therapy, complete blood counts are drawn only weekly-monthly.

    3. She doesn't need physical therapy.

    4. There is no reason to restrict her activity. If her neutrophil count were lower than 500/mm^3, she would need to keep away from crowded places such as the mall, shopping center, school, etc.

#95. 2. **Seizure precautions should be instituted to prevent an injury.** An   Ph/9   An

    1. There is no evidence at this time that he is at high risk for infection.

    3. Although there is only a 75–85% five-year survival rate for low-grade astrocytomas, there is no evidence presented that the parents are experiencing anticipating grief at this time.

    4. This tumor does not affect his physical mobility. The signs and symptoms of astrocytoma include headache, nausea, seizures, staring spells, or automatic movements and visual disturbances.

#96. 4. **To protect the skull while it is healing, a child may need to wear a padded helmet for active sports.** Ev   Sa/2   An

    1. The ultimate goal is to return child to a normal life as soon as possible; going to school is part of the normalcy and should resume as soon as possible.

    2. The child should resume normal activities within tolerable limits as soon as possible.

    3. Families need help to cope effectively with serious childhood illness. This child should not receive any special treatment.

#97. 2. **The most common symptom of Hodgkin's disease is enlarged, firm, nontender moveable nodes in the supraclavicular area.** As   Ph/10   Co

    1. The nodes are enlarged and nontender. Involvement of the inguinal lymph nodes is less frequent.

    3. Hodgkin's disease usually arises in a single lymph node or an anatomic group of lymph nodes.

    4. The involvement in Hodgkin's disease causes enlarged, nontender moveable nodes usually in the supraclavicular area, but could also be in cervical area.

ANSWER	RATIONALE	NP	CN	CL

#98. 2. Frequent blood pressure measurements are needed to watch for signs of shock and as an indication of the functioning of the remaining kidney. — Pl, Ph/9, Ap

1. Once the client is awake and alert, sips of clear liquids may be given if ordered; fluid must be monitored to prevent hypovolemia after surgery.
3. Gentle handling and frequent repositioning (at least every two hours) will improve comfort and prevent postop complications.
4. Although pain management is important postsurgery, the highest priority postop for Wilms' tumor is the monitoring of the blood pressure.

#99. 3. The child may stay in a fixed position during each therapy session, which may last 10–20 minutes. Having the child practice the required position prior to beginning radiation therapy can be helpful. — Pl, Ph/10, Ap

1. Most nausea comes from chemotherapy, not radiation.
2. A child who is immunosuppressed has bleeding tendencies. This is not appropriate at this time.
4. Appropriate play is important for all hospitalized children but it's not as important as practicing the correct position for radiation.

#100. 3. This client is likely to have bone marrow suppression, which increases his risk for infection and bleeding. — Ev, Ph/8, An

1. Although he should return to normal activities as soon as he is able, this is too soon and will increase his risk for injury.
2. This child should be encouraged to eat whatever he likes to maintain weight. The nausea associated with chemotherapy will cease now that chemotherapy is finished.
4. Alopecia is a side-effect of chemotherapy. This client needs to protect his scalp when out in the sun, not while going to bed.

Review Test 4

Maternity and Female Reproductive Nursing

1. Mr. and Mrs. W. recently arrived in the United States from East Asia. Mr. W. brings his wife to the hospital in late labor; his mother and Mrs. W.'s sister are also present. As the nurse directs Mr. W. to the dressing room to change into a scrub suit, Mrs. W. anxiously states, "No, he can't come with me. Get my sister and mother-in-law!" The nurse's best response is,
   1. "I'm sorry, but our hospital only allows the father into the delivery."
   2. "I'll ask the doctor if that's OK."
   3. "When I talk to your husband, I'm sure he'll want to be with you."
   4. "That's fine. I'll show your husband the waiting area."

2. During an initial prenatal visit, a woman states that her last menstrual period began on November 21; she also reports some vaginal bleeding about December 19. The nurse would calculate that this client's expected date of birth (EDB) would be
   1. July 21.
   2. August 28.
   3. September 26.
   4. October 1.

3. A 24-year-old woman comes to the clinic because she thinks she is pregnant. Which of the following is a probable sign of pregnancy that the nurse would expect this client to have?
   1. Fetal heart tones.
   2. Nausea and vomiting.
   3. Amenorrhea.
   4. Chadwick's sign.

4. A married 25-year-old housewife is six weeks gestation and is being seen for her first prenatal visit. In relation to normal maternal acceptance of pregnancy, the nurse would expect that the client feels

1. some ambivalence now that the pregnancy is confirmed.
2. overwhelmed by the thought of future changes.
3. much happiness and enjoyment in the event.
4. detached from the event until physical changes occur.

5. A woman is entering the 20th week of pregnancy. Which normal change would the nurse expect to find on assessment?
   1. Fundus just below diaphragm.
   2. Pigment changes in skin.
   3. Complaints of frequent urination.
   4. Blood pressure returning to prepregnancy level.

6. Ms. W., blood type A+, rubella negative, hemoglobin 12 g, hematocrit 36%, is a primigravida in the first trimester. During her second prenatal visit she complains of being very tired, experiencing frequent urination, and a white vaginal discharge; she also states that her nausea and occasional vomiting persists. Based on these findings, the nurse would select which of the following nursing diagnoses?
   1. Activity intolerance related to nutritional deprivation.
   2. Alteration in elimination related to a possible infection.
   3. High risk for injury related to hematologic incompatibility.
   4. Alteration in physiologic responses related to pregnancy.

7. Ms. R. had her pregnancy confirmed and has completed her first prenatal visit. Considering that all data were found to be within normal limits, the nurse would plan that the next visit should be in
   1. one week.
   2. two weeks.
   3. one month.
   4. two months.

8. Which statement by a pregnant client would indicate to the nurse that diet teaching has been effective?
   1. "The most important time to take my iron pills is during the early weeks when the baby is forming."
   2. "I don't like milk, but I'll increase my intake of cheese and yogurt."
   3. "I'll be very careful about using salt while I'm pregnant."
   4. "Because I'm overweight to begin with, I can continue my weight loss diet."

9. Mrs. C., age 40, gravida 3 para 2, is eight weeks pregnant. She is a full-time office manager, states she "usually unwinds with a few glasses of wine" with dinner, smokes about five cigarettes a day, and was "surprised" by this pregnancy. After the assessment, which of the following would

the nurse select as the priority nursing diagnosis?
   1. High risk for an alteration in bonding related to an unplanned pregnancy.
   2. High risk for injury to the fetus related to advanced age.
   3. Ineffective individual coping related to low self-esteem.
   4. Knowledge deficit related to effects of substance abuse.

10. A young couple has just completed a preconception visit in the maternity clinic. Before leaving, the woman asks the nurse why she was instructed not to take any over-the-counter medications. The nurse should reply
    1. "Research has found that many of these drugs have been linked to problems with getting pregnant."
    2. "At conception, and in the first trimester, these drugs can be as dangerous to the fetus as prescription drugs."
    3. "You should only take drugs that the physician has ordered during pregnancy."
    4. "Any drug is dangerous at this time; later on in pregnancy it won't matter."

11. The pregnant couple asks the nurse what is the purpose of prepared childbirth classes. The nurse's best response would be
    1. "The main goal of most types of childbirth classes is to provide information that will help eliminate fear and anxiety."
    2. "The desired goal is childbirth without the use of analgesics."
    3. "These classes help to reduce the pain of childbirth by exercise and relaxation methods."
    4. "The primary aim is to keep you and your baby healthy during pregnancy and after!"

12. A woman in her 38th week of pregnancy is to have an amniocentesis to evaluate fetal maturity. The L/S (lecithin/sphingomyelin) ratio is 2:1. The nurse knows that this finding indicates
    1. fetal lung maturity.
    2. that labor can be induced.
    3. the fetus is not viable.
    4. a non-stress test is indicated.

13. Mrs. T. is having a contraction stress test (CST) in her last month of pregnancy. When assessing the fetal monitor strip, the nurse notices that with most of the contractions, the fetal heart rate uniformly slows at mid-contraction and then returns to baseline about 20 seconds after the contraction is over. The nurse would interpret the test result to be
    1. negative: normal.
    2. reactive negative.
    3. positive: abnormal.
    4. unsatisfactory.

14. Mrs. P., 36 weeks gestation, is having a CST with an oxytocin IV infusion pump. After two

contractions, the uterus stays contracted. The best initial action of the nurse is to
1. help the client turn on her left side.
2. turn off the infusion pump.
3. wait three minutes for the uterus to relax.
4. administer prn terbutaline sulfate (Brethine).

15. A pregnant woman, in the first trimester, is to have a transabdominal ultrasound. The nurse would include which of the following instructions?
1. Nothing by mouth (NPO) from 6:00 A.M. the morning of the test.
2. Drink one to two quarts of water and do not urinate before the test.
3. Come to the clinic first for injection of the contrast dye.
4. No special instructions are needed for this test.

16. Mrs. F., pregnant for the first time, calls the clinic to say she is bleeding. To obtain important information, the nurse should next ask,
1. "When did you last feel the baby move?"
2. "How long have you been pregnant?"
3. "When was your pregnancy test done?"
4. "Are you having any uterine cramping?"

17. Ms. Y. is hospitalized with a possible ectopic pregnancy. In addition to the classic symptoms of abdominal pain, amenorrhea, and abnormal vaginal bleeding, the nurse knows that which of the following factors in Ms. Y.'s history may be associated with this condition?
1. Multiparity.
2. Age under 20.
3. Pelvic inflammatory disease (PID).
4. Habitual spontaneous abortions.

18. Ms. C. is being discharged after treatment for a hydatidiform mole. The nurse should include which of the following in the discharge teaching plan?
1. Do not become pregnant for at least one year.
2. Have blood pressure checked weekly for six months.
3. RhoGAM must be received with next pregnancy and delivery.
4. An amniocentesis can detect a recurrence of this disorder in the future.

19. Mrs. T., 40 weeks gestation, is admitted to the labor and delivery unit with possible placenta previa. On the admission assessment, the nurse would expect to find
1. signs of a Couvelaire uterus.
2. severe lower abdominal pain.
3. painless vaginal bleeding.
4. a board-like abdomen.

20. Mrs. S., 30 weeks gestation, is being discharged to home care with a diagnosis of placenta previa. The nurse knows that the client understands her care at home when the client states,
1. "As I get closer to my due date I will have to remain in bed."
2. "I can continue with my office job because it's mostly sitting."
3. "My husband won't be too happy with this 'no sex' order."
4. "I'm disappointed that I will need a cesarean section."

21. A teenage patient, 38 weeks gestation, is admitted with a diagnosis of pregnancy-induced hypertension (PIH). Data include: blood pressure 160/100, generalized edema, weight gain of 10 pounds in last 2 weeks, and proteinuria of +3; the patient is also complaining of a headache and nausea. In planning care for this client, the nurse would set the following priority goal. The client will
1. demonstrate a decreased blood pressure within 48 hours.
2. not experience a seizure prior to delivery.
3. maintain a strict diet prior to delivery.
4. comply with medical and nutritional regimen.

22. Mrs. S., 32 weeks gestation, has developed mild PIH. The nurse evaluates that the client understands her treatment regimen when the client states,
1. "It is most important not to miss any of my blood pressure medication."
2. "I will watch my diet restrictions very carefully."
3. "I will spend most of my time in bed, on my left side."
4. "I'm happy that this only happens during a first pregnancy."

23. A pregnant client with class 3 cardiac disease is seen during an initial prenatal visit. The nurse selects which of the following priority nursing diagnoses?
1. Knowledge deficit related to self-care during pregnancy.
2. Fear; client and family, related to pregnancy outcome.
3. Alteration in nutrition related to sodium-restricted diet.
4. Activity intolerance related to compromised cardiac status.

24. The nurse includes the importance of self-monitoring of glucose in the care plan for a diabetic client planning a pregnancy. The goal of this monitoring is to prevent
1. congenital malformations in the fetus.
2. maternal vasculopathy.
3. accelerated growth of the fetus.
4. delayed maturation of fetal lungs.

25. After a prenatal class on healthy behaviors during pregnancy, the nurse can evaluate that learning has occurred when a client states,

1. "Alcohol in the first trimester of pregnancy is very dangerous, later it's OK."
2. "Drinking alcohol during pregnancy is the most preventable cause of mental retardation."
3. "Alcohol is bad during pregnancy, but a little with breast feeding helps with let-down."
4. "Problems for the baby usually only occur with heavy drinking of alcohol."

26. Mrs. D. is 36 weeks gestation and the nurse is talking with her during a prenatal visit. Which statement indicates that Mrs. D. understands the onset of labor?
   1. "I need to go to the hospital as soon as the contractions become painful."
   2. "If I experience bright red vaginal bleeding I know that I am about to deliver."
   3. "I need to go to the hospital when I am having regular contractions and bloody show."
   4. "My labor will not start until after my membranes rupture and I gush fluid."

27. Using Leopold's maneuvers to determine fetal position, the nurse finds that Mrs. L.'s fetus is in a vertex position with the back on the left side. Where is the best place for the nurse to listen for fetal heart tones?
   1. In the right upper quadrant of the mother's abdomen.
   2. In the left upper quadrant of the mother's abdomen.
   3. In the right lower quadrant of the mother's abdomen.
   4. In the left lower quadrant of the mother's abdomen.

28. Which of the following is the best way for the nurse to assess contractions in a client presenting to the labor and delivery area?
   1. Place the client on the electronic fetal monitor with the labor toco at the fundus.
   2. Ask the client to describe the frequency, duration, and strength of her contractions.
   3. Use Leopold's maneuvers to determine the quality of the uterine contractions.
   4. Place the fingertips of one hand on the fundus to determine frequency, duration, and strength of contractions.

29. As the nurse assigned to Mrs. Q., you are listening to fetal heart tones. Which of the following findings would you consider abnormal for a patient in active labor?
   1. A rate of 160 with no significant changes through a contraction.
   2. A rate of 130 with accelerations to 150 with fetal movement.
   3. A rate that varies between 120 and 130.
   4. A rate of 170 with a drop to 140 during a contraction.

30. Ms. K. arrives at the birthing center in active labor. On examination, the cervix is 5 cm dilated, membranes intact and bulging, and the presenting part at −1 station. Ms. K. asks if she can go for a walk. What is the best response for the nurse to give?
   1. "I think it would be best for you to remain in bed at this time because of the risk of cord prolapse."
   2. "It's fine for you to walk, but please stay nearby. If you feel a gush of fluid, I will need to check you and your baby."
   3. "It will be fine for you to walk because that will assist the natural body forces to bring the baby down the birth canal."
   4. "I would be glad to get you a bean bag chair or rocker instead."

31. Mrs. M., a primigravida, presents to the labor room with rupture of membranes at 40 weeks gestation. Her cervix is 2 cm dilated and 100% effaced. Contractions are every 10 minutes. What should the nurse include in the plan of care?
   1. Allow Mrs. M. to ambulate as desired as long as the presenting part is engaged.
   2. Assess fetal heart tones and maternal status every five minutes.
   3. Place Mrs. M. on an electronic fetal monitor for continuous assessment of labor.
   4. Send Mrs. M. home with instructions to return when contractions are every five minutes.

32. Mrs. B. is in active labor at 4 cm dilated, 100% effaced, and 0 station. As she is ambulating she experiences a gush of fluid. What is the most appropriate initial action for the nurse to take?
   1. Send a specimen of the amniotic fluid to the laboratory for analysis.
   2. Have Mrs. B. return to her room and place her in Trendelenburg position to prevent cord prolapse.
   3. Have Mrs. B. return to her room so that you can assess fetal status, including auscultation of fetal heart tones for one full minute.
   4. Call Mrs. B.'s physician because a cesarean delivery will be required.

33. The nurse is providing care to Ms. C. During the most recent vaginal examination the nurse feels the cervix 6 cm dilated, 100% effaced, with the vertex at −1 station. What is the best interpretation of this information? The woman is in
   1. active labor with the head as presenting part not yet engaged.
   2. transition with the backside as presenting part fully engaged.
   3. latent phase labor with the backside as presenting part fully engaged.
   4. active labor with the head as presenting part fully engaged.

34. Mrs. M. is completely dilated and at +2 station. Her contractions are strong and last 50–70 seconds. Based on this information, the nurse should know that Mrs. M. is in which stage of labor?
   1. First stage.
   2. Second stage.
   3. Third stage.
   4. Fourth stage.

35. A 28-year primigravida is admitted to the labor room. She is 2 cm dilated, 90% effaced, and the head is at 0 station. Contractions are every 10 minutes lasting 20–30 seconds. Membranes are intact. Admitting vital signs are: blood pressure 110/70, pulse 78, respirations 16, temperature 98.8° F, and fetal heart rate 144. The nurse plans to monitor
   1. blood pressure and contractions hourly and fetal heart rate every 15 minutes.
   2. temperature, blood pressure, and contractions every 4 hours and fetal heart rate hourly.
   3. contractions, effacement, and dilation of cervix, and fetal heart rate every hour.
   4. contractions, blood pressure, and fetal heart rate every 15 minutes.

36. Mrs. H.'s cervix is completely dilated with the head at −2 station. The head has not descended in the past hour. What is the most appropriate initial assessment for the nurse to make?
   1. Assess to determine if Mrs. H.'s bladder is distended.
   2. Send Mrs. H. for x-rays to determine fetal size.
   3. Notify the surgical team so that an operative delivery can be planned.
   4. Assess fetal status, including fetal heart tones, and scalp pH.

37. Ms. N. has been in labor for six hours. She is now 9 cm dilated and has intense contractions every one to two minutes. Ms. N. is anxious and feels the need to bear down with her contractions. What is the best action for the nurse to take?
   1. Allow Ms. N. to push so that delivery can be expedited.
   2. Encourage panting breathing through contractions to prevent pushing.
   3. Reposition Ms. N. in a squatting position to make her more comfortable.
   4. Provide back rubs during contractions to distract Ms. N.

38. A newborn, at one minute after vaginal delivery, is pink with blue hands and feet, has a lusty cry, heart rate 140, prompt response to stimulation with crying, and maintains minimal flexion, with sluggish movement. The nurse should know that this newborn's Apgar score is
   1. ten.
   2. nine.

   3. eight.
   4. seven.

39. Mrs. G. delivered a 7 lb boy by spontaneous vaginal delivery 30 minutes ago. Her fundus is firm at the umbilicus and she has moderate lochia rubra. Which nursing diagnosis is highest priority as the nurse plans care?
   1. Risk for infection related to episiotomy.
   2. Constipation related to fear of pain.
   3. Potential for altered urinary elimination related to perineal edema.
   4. Knowledge deficit related to lack of knowledge regarding newborn care.

40. Mrs. G. is in the fourth stage of labor. She and her new daughter are together in the room. What assessments are essential for the nurse to make during this time?
   1. Assess the pattern and frequency of contractions and the infant's vital signs.
   2. Assess Mrs. G.'s vital signs, fundus, bladder, perineal condition, and lochia. Assess the infant's vital signs.
   3. Assess Mrs. G.'s vital signs, fundus, bladder, perineal condition, and lochia. Return the infant to the nursery.
   4. Assess the infant for obvious abnormalities. Assess Mrs. G. for blood loss and firm uterine contraction.

41. Mrs. P., G3 P2, was admitted at 32 weeks gestation contracting every 7–10 minutes. Her cervix is 2 cm dilated and 70% effaced. What should the nurse include in the plan of care for this client?
   1. Discuss with Mrs. P. the need to stop working after her discharge from the hospital.
   2. Monitor Mrs. P. and her fetus for response to impending delivery.
   3. Assess Mrs. P.'s past pregnancy history to determine if she has experienced preterm labor in the past.
   4. Start oral terbutaline to stop the contractions.

42. Mrs. P. was admitted in premature labor contracting every five minutes. Her cervix is 3 cm dilated and 100% effaced, IV magnesium sulfate at 1 g per hour is infusing. How will the nurse know the drug is having the desired effect?
   1. The contractions will increase in frequency to every three minutes, although there will be no further cervical changes.
   2. Mrs. P. will be able to sleep through her contractions due to the sedative effect of the magnesium sulfate.
   3. The contractions will diminish in frequency and finally disappear.
   4. Mrs. P. will have diminished deep tendon reflexes and her body pressure will decrease.

43. Mrs. K. has just received an epidural for anesthesia during her labor. What should the

nurse include in the plan of care because of the anesthesia?
1. Assist Mrs. K. in position changes and observe for signs of labor progress.
2. Administer 500–1000 ml of a sugar-free crystalloid solution.
3. Place a Foley catheter as soon as the anesthesia has been administered.
4. Offer Mrs. K. a back rub to reduce the discomfort of her contractions.

44. Mrs. K. delivered her infant son three hours ago. She had an episiotomy to facilitate delivery. As the nurse assigned to care for Mrs. K., which of the following would be the most appropriate action?
1. Place an ice pack on the perineum.
2. Apply a heat lamp to the perineum.
3. Take Mrs. K. for a sitz bath.
4. Administer analgesic medication as ordered.

45. Mrs. C. is scheduled for a cesarean section delivery due to a transverse fetal lie. What is the best way for the nurse to evaluate that Mrs. C. understands the procedure?
1. Ask Mrs. C. about the help she will have at home after her delivery.
2. Give Mrs. C. a diagram of the body and ask her to draw the procedure for you.
3. Ask Mrs. C. to tell you what she knows about the scheduled surgery.
4. Provide Mrs. C. with a booklet explaining cesarean deliveries when she arrives at the hospital.

46. Which of the following observations in the postpartum period would be of most concern to the nurse?
1. After delivery, the mother touches the newborn with her fingertips.
2. The new parents asked the nurse to recommend a good baby care book.
3. A new father holds his son in the en face position while visiting.
4. A new mother sits in bed while her newborn lies awake in the crib.

47. Mrs. N. has just delivered her first baby who will be breast fed. The nurse should include which of the following instructions in the teaching plan?
1. Try to schedule feedings at least every three to four hours.
2. Wash nipples with soap and water before each feeding.
3. Avoid nursing bras with plastic lining.
4. Supplement with water between feedings when necessary.

48. A woman's prenatal antibody titer shows that she is not immune to rubella and will receive the immunization after delivery. The nurse would include which of the following instructions in the teaching plan?
1. Pregnancy must be avoided for the next three months.

2. Another immunization should be administered in the next pregnancy.
3. Breast feeding should be postponed for five days after the injection.
4. An injection will be needed after each succeeding pregnancy.

49. A woman had a normal vaginal delivery 12 hours ago and is to be discharged from the birthing center. The nurse evaluates that the woman understands the teaching related to the episiotomy and perineal area when she states,
1. "I know the stitches will be removed at my postpartum clinic visit."
2. "The ice pack should be removed for 10 minutes before replacing it."
3. "The anesthetic spray, then the heat lamp, will help a lot."
4. "The water for the Sitz bath should be warm, about 102–105° F."

50. Mrs. B. is bottle feeding her newborn. The nurse evaluates that the client understands how to safely manage formula when Mrs. B. states,
1. "Prepared formula should be used within 48 hours."
2. "All bottles, caps, and nipples must be sterilized."
3. "A dishwasher is not sufficient for proper cleaning."
4. "Prepared formula must be refrigerated until used."

51. Mrs. P. delivered her baby 12 hours ago. During the postpartum assessment, the uterus is found to be boggy with a heavy lochia flow. The initial action of the nurse is to
1. notify the physician or nurse midwife.
2. administer prn oxytocin.
3. encourage the woman to increase ambulation.
4. massage the uterus until firm.

52. A breast feeding mother is visited by the home health nurse two weeks after delivery. The woman is febrile with flulike symptoms; on assessment the nurse notes a warm, reddened, painful area of the right breast. The best initial action of the nurse is to
1. contact the physician for an order for antibiotics.
2. advise the mother to stop breast feeding and pumping.
3. assess the mother's feeding technique and knowledge of breast care.
4. obtain a sample of breast milk for culture.

53. Mrs. P. had a vaginal delivery of her second child two days ago. She is breast feeding the baby without difficulty. During a postpartum assessment on Mrs. P., the nurse would expect the following normal finding.
1. Complaints of afterpains.
2. Pinkish to brownish vaginal discharge.
3. Voiding frequently, 50–75 ml per void.

4. Fundus 1 cm above the umbilicus.

54. A mother who had a vaginal delivery of her first baby six weeks ago is seen for her postpartum visit. She is feeling well and is bottle feeding her infant successfully. During the physical assessment, the nurse would expect to find the following normal data.
    1. Fundus palpated 6 cm below the umbilicus.
    2. Breasts tender, some milk expressed.
    3. Striae pink but beginning to fade.
    4. Creamy, yellow vaginal discharge.

55. A nurse collects the following data on a woman 26 hours after a long labor and a vaginal delivery: temperature 101° F (38.3° C), blood pressure 110/70, pulse 90, some diaphoresis, output 1000 ml per eight hours, ankle edema, lochia moderate rubra, fundus 1 cm above umbilicus and tender on palpation. The client also asks that the infant be brought back to the nursery. In the analysis of this data, the nurse would select which of the following priority nursing diagnoses?
    1. Alteration in parenting related to material discomfort.
    2. High risk for injury related to spread of infection.
    3. Fluid volume excess related to urinary retention.
    4. Knowledge deficit related to uterine subinvolution.

56. Which of the following findings in a three-hour-old, full-term newborn would the nurse record as abnormal when assessing the head?
    1. Two "soft spots" between the cranial bones.
    2. Asymmetry of the head with overriding bones.
    3. Head circumference 32 cm, chest 34 cm.
    4. A sharply outlined, spongy area of edema.

57. The nurse collects the following data while assessing the skin of a six-hour-old newborn: color pink with bluish hands and feet, some pale yellow papules with red base over trunk, small white spots on the nose, and a red area at the nape of the neck. The nurse's next action would be to
    1. document findings as within normal range.
    2. isolate infant pending diagnosis.
    3. request a dermatology consultation.
    4. document as indicators of malnutrition.

58. While performing the discharge assessment on a two-day-old newborn, the nurse finds that after blanching the skin on the forehead, the color turns yellow. The nurse knows that this indicates
    1. a normal biologic response.
    2. an infectious liver condition.
    3. an Rh incompatibility problem.
    4. jaundice related to breast feeding.

59. Baby Y. is two-days-old and is being breast fed. The nurse finds that yesterday her stool was thick and tarry, today it's thinner and greenish brown; she voided twice since birth with some pink stains noted on the diaper. The nurse knows that these findings indicate
    1. marked dehydration.
    2. inadequate initial nutrition.
    3. normal newborn elimination.
    4. a need for medical consultation.

60. The nurse notes the following behaviors in a six-hour-old, full-term newborn: occasional tremors of extremities, straightens arms and hands outward and flexes knees when disturbed, toes fan out when heel is stroked, and tries to walk when held upright. The nurse knows that these findings indicate
    1. signs of drug withdrawal.
    2. abnormal uncoordinated movements.
    3. asymmetric muscle tone.
    4. expected neurologic development.

61. While assessing a newborn, the nurse notes that the areola is flat with less than 0.5 cm of breast tissue. This finding indicates
    1. that infant is male.
    2. maternal hormonal depletion.
    3. intrauterine growth retardation.
    4. preterm gestational age.

62. The nurse's initial care plan for a full-term newborn includes the nursing diagnosis "risk of fluid volume depletion related to absence of intestinal flora." A related nursing intervention would be to
    1. administer glucose water or put to breast.
    2. assess first void and passing of meconium.
    3. administer vitamin K injection.
    4. send cord blood to lab for Coombs' test.

63. In the time immediately following birth, the nurse may delay instillation of eye medication primarily to
    1. check prenatal record to determine if prophylactic treatment is needed.
    2. ensure that initial eye saline irrigation is completed.
    3. enable mother to breast feed the infant in the first hour of life.
    4. facilitate eye contact and bonding between parents and newborn.

64. The nurses should include which of the following instructions in the care plan for a new mother who is breast feeding her full-term newborn?
    1. Put to breast when infant shows readiness to feed.
    2. Breast feed infant every three to four hours until discharge.
    3. Offer water feedings between breast feedings.
    4. Feed infant when he shows hunger by crying.

65. In the delivery area, after ensuring that the newborn has established respirations, the next priority of the nurse should be to
    1. perform the Apgar score.
    2. place plastic clamp on cord.

3. dry infant and provide warmth.
4. ensure correct identification.
66. During the bath demonstration, Mrs. A. asks the nurse if it is OK to use baby powder because warm weather is coming. The nurse should respond
   1. "Just dust in on the diaper area only."
   2. "It's best not to use powder on infants."
   3. "First use baby oil, then the powder."
   4. "If the baby is just in a diaper he'll be cool."
67. Which of the following muscles would the nurse choose as the preferred site for a newborn's vitamin K injection?
   1. Gluteus medius.
   2. Mid-deltoid.
   3. Vastus lateralis.
   4. Rectus femoris.
68. The nurse knows that Mrs. T. understands proper cord care for her newborn when the client
   1. views a videotape on newborn hygiene care.
   2. reads a booklet on care of the newborn's cord stump.
   3. says she will apply Bacitracin ointment three times per day.
   4. cleans the cord and surrounding skin with an alcohol pad.
69. The nurse knows that more instruction on care of the circumcised infant is needed when the mother states,
   1. "I know to gently retract the foreskin after the area is healed."
   2. "At each diaper change I will squeeze water over the penis and pat dry."
   3. "I know not to disturb the yellow exudate that will form."
   4. "For the first day or so I'll apply a little A&D ointment."
70. The nurse knows that Ms. Y. has a basic understanding of bottle feeding her infant when the client states,
   1. "I know not to prop the bottle until my baby is older."
   2. "With these little bottles, he should be able to finish them."
   3. "When I hold the bottle upside down, drops of milk should fall."
   4. "I should burp the baby about every 5–10 minutes."
71. Baby G. weighs 1450 g, has weak muscle tone, with extremities in an extended position while at rest. The pinna is flat and does not readily recoil. Very little breast tissue is palpable. The soles have deep indentations over the upper one-third. Based on these data, what should the nurse know about Baby G.'s gestational age?
   1. Full-term infant, 38–42 weeks gestation.
   2. Premature infant, less than 24 weeks gestation.

3. Premature infant, 29–33 weeks gestation.
4. Post-term infant greater than 42 weeks gestation.
72. A premature infant at six hours old, has respirations of 64, mild nasal flaring, and expiratory grunting. She is pink in room air, temperature is 36.5° C. The baby's mother ruptured membranes 36 hours prior to delivery. Which measures should the nurse include in the plan of care?
   1. Have respiratory therapy set up a respirator since respiratory failure is imminent. Get blood gases every hour.
   2. Encourage mother/infant interaction. Rooming in as soon as stable. Monitor vital signs every eight hours.
   3. Observe for signs of sepsis. Cultures if ordered. Monitor vital signs at least every two hours for the first 24 hours. Encourage family interaction with infant.
   4. Radiant warmer for first 48 hours. Vital signs every hour. Restrict visitation due to risk of infection.
73. During the assessment of a two-day-old infant with bruising and a cephalhematoma, the nurse notes jaundice of the face and trunk. The baby is also being breast fed. Bilirubin level is 10 mg/dl. What is the most likely interpretation of these findings?
   1. Hyperbilirubinemia due to the bruising and cephalhematoma.
   2. Pathologic jaundice requiring exchange transfusion.
   3. Breast milk jaundice.
   4. Hyperbilirubinemia due to blood group incompatibility.
74. A six-hour-old newborn has been diagnosed with erythroblastosis fetalis. The nurse understands that this condition is caused by
   1. ABO blood group incompatibility between the father and infant.
   2. Rh incompatibility between the mother and infant.
   3. ABO blood group incompatibility between the mother and infant.
   4. Rh incompatibility between father and infant.
75. Mrs. K. is an Rh negative mother who has just given birth to an Rh positive infant. She had a negative indirect Coombs' test at 38 weeks gestation and her infant had a negative direct Coombs' test. What should the nurse know about these tests?
   1. Although Mrs. K.'s infant is Rh positive, she has no antibodies to the Rh factor. RhoGAM should be given.
   2. Mrs. K. has demonstrated antibodies to the Rh factor. She should not have any more children.
   3. Mrs. K. has formed antigens against the Rh factor. RhoGAM must be given to the infant.

4. Since Mrs. K.'s infant is Rh positive, the Coombs' tests are meaningless.

76. Baby G. was born at 38 weeks gestation to a heroin-addicted mother. At birth, Baby G. had Apgar scores of 5 at one minute and 6 at five minutes. Birthweight was at the 10th percentile for gestational age. What should the nurse include in Baby B.'s plan of care?
   1. Administer methadone to diminish symptoms of heroin withdrawal.
   2. Promote parent-infant attachment by encouraging rooming-in.
   3. Observe for signs of jaundice because this is a common complication.
   4. Place in a quiet area of the nursery and swaddle with hands near mouth to promote more organized behavioral state.

77. Baby L. is a 36-week-gestation infant who had tachypnea, nasal flaring, and intercostal retractions that increased over the first six hours of life. Baby L. was treated with IV fluids and oxygen. Which of the following assessments suggests to the nurse that Baby L. is improving?
   1. Baby L. has see-saw respirations with coarse breath sounds.
   2. Baby L.'s respiratory rate is 50 and pulse is 136, no nasal flaring is observed.
   3. Baby L. has a pH of 6.97 and pO_2 of 61 on 40% oxygen.
   4. Baby L. has gained 150 g in the 12 hours since birth.

78. You are caring for an infant. During your assessment you note a flattened philtrum, short palpebral fissures, and birth weight and head circumference below the fifth percentile for gestational age. The infant has a poor suck. Which of the following is the best interpretation of this data?
   1. Down syndrome.
   2. Fetal alcohol syndrome.
   3. Turner's syndrome.
   4. Congenital syphilis.

79. A two-week-old premature infant with abdominal distention, significant gastric aspirate prior to feeding, and bloody stools has also had episodes of apnea and bradycardia and temperature instability. What should the nurse include in the plan of care for this infant?
   1. Increase feeding frequency to every two hours.
   2. Place the infant on seizure precautions.
   3. Place the infant in strict isolation to prevent infection of other infants.
   4. Monitor infant carefully including blood pressure readings and measurements of abdominal girth.

80. Mrs. L. is taking her newborn home from the hospital at 18 hours after birth. As the nurse giving discharge instructions, which response by Mrs. L. best validates her understanding of PKU testing?
   1. "I know you stuck my baby's heel today for that PKU test and that my doctor will recheck the test when I bring her for her one month appointment."
   2. "After I start my baby on cereal, I will return for a follow-up blood test."
   3. "I will have a visiting nurse come to the house each day for the first week to check the PKU test."
   4. "I will bring my baby back to the hospital or doctor's office to have a repeat PKU no later than one week from today."

81. Mr. and Mrs. A. have come to your clinic because they have not been able to achieve a pregnancy after trying for two years without using any form of birth control. Which of the following tests could determine that Mrs. A. is ovulating regularly?
   1. Hysterosalpingogram.
   2. Serial basal body temperature graph.
   3. Postcoital test.
   4. Semen analysis.

82. Mrs. J. is preparing to take Clomid to induce ovulation so she can have an in vitro fertilization. She asks if she should expect any side-effects from the drug. Your *best* answer should include which of the following?
   1. Weight gain with increased appetite and constipation.
   2. Tingling of the hands and feet.
   3. Alopecia (hair loss).
   4. Stuffy nose and cold-like symptoms.

83. Mr. and Mrs. M. have been using a diaphragm for contraception. Which of the following statements indicates they are using it correctly?
   1. "We use K-Y jelly around the rim to help with insertion."
   2. "I wash the diaphragm each time and hold it up to the light to look for any holes."
   3. "I take the diaphragm out about one hour after intercourse because it feels funny."
   4. "I douche right away after intercourse."

84. Ms. B., who is 25-years old, wishes to take oral contraceptives. When taking her history, which of the following questions would determine if she is an appropriate candidate for this form of birth control?
   1. "Do you currently smoke cigarettes and, if so, how many?"
   2. "Have you had any recent weight gain or loss?"
   3. "Do you douche regularly after intercourse?"
   4. "Is there any family history of kidney or gallbladder disease?"

85. Ms. K., who is 18-weeks pregnant, is scheduled for a saline injection to terminate

her pregnancy. She asks the nurse what she should expect. Your *best* answer is,
1. "Contractions will begin immediately after the instillation of saline and will be mild."
2. "An amniocentesis will be performed with amniotic fluid removal and saline replacement."
3. "A tube will be inserted through the cervix and warm saline will be administered by continuous drip."
4. "The baby will be born alive but will die a short time later."

86. Mrs. C. comes to the office complaining of the following symptoms: fatigue, weight gain, pelvic pain related to menstruation, heartburn, and constipation. Which of the above symptoms might indicate a diagnosis of endometriosis?
1. Weight gain and fatigue.
2. Heartburn.
3. Constipation.
4. Pelvic pain related to menstruation.

87. Miss D. has been diagnosed with *Candida albicans*. Which of the following types of vaginal discharge would you expect to find?
1. Thin, greenish yellow with a foul odor.
2. Either a yellowish discharge or none at all.
3. Thick and white, like cottage cheese.
4. Thin, grayish white with a fishy odor.

88. Ms. G. has just been diagnosed with genital herpes for the first time. You can expect which of the following treatments to be part of her plan of care?
1. Vaginal soaks with saline to keep the area moist.
2. Acyclovir 200 mg five times daily for 7–10 days.
3. Ceftriaxone 125 mg IM times 1 dose.
4. Topical application of podophyllin to the lesions.

89. Ms. E. is 10 weeks pregnant and tested positive for syphilis but has no symptoms. She asks you why she needs to be treated since she feels fine? Your *best* response to her would include which of the following?
1. "Syphilis can be transmitted to the baby and may cause it to die before birth if you are not treated."
2. "If you do not receive treatment before the baby is born, your baby could become blind."
3. "If syphilis is untreated, the baby may be mentally retarded at birth."
4. "Syphilis may cause your baby to have a heart problem when it is born."

90. Miss H. has been diagnosed with fibrocystic breast disease. Which of the following should be included in the teaching plan for her?
1. Limiting breast self-examinations to every three months because it may be painful.
2. Wearing a bra as little as possible because pressure on the breast may be painful.
3. Limiting caffeine and salt intake.
4. Using heat to the tender areas of the breast.

91. The local YWCA is having a series of seminars on health-related topics. You are invited to discuss breast self-examination (BSE) with the group. Which of the following would be appropriate to teach regarding when BSE should be performed by women of reproductive age?
1. At the end of each menstrual cycle.
2. At the beginning of each menstrual cycle.
3. About 7–10 days after the beginning of each menstrual cycle.
4. About 7–10 days before the end of the menstrual cycle.

92. You have been discussing breast self-examination (BSE) with Miss N. Which of the following statements would *best* indicate she is doing BSE correctly?
1. "I begin to examine my breasts by placing the palm of my right hand on the nipple of the left breast."
2. "I don't like to press very hard because my breasts are very tender."
3. "I use the tips of the middle three fingers of each hand to feel each breast."
4. "I feel for lumps in my breasts standing in front of a mirror."

93. Ms. I., who is 32-years-old, had a simple mastectomy this morning. Which of the following should be included in your plan for her care?
1. Complete bedrest for the first 24 hours.
2. NPO with IV fluids for the first 48 hours.
3. Positioning on the operative side for the first 24 hours.
4. Keep patient-controlled anesthesia (PCA) controller within easy reach for the first 48 hours.

94. The nurse is teaching a woman who had a simple mastectomy. Which of the following would be appropriate to tell her?
1. She should wait to be fitted for a permanent prosthesis until the wound is completely healed.
2. Since she had a simple mastectomy, she will probably not feel the need to attend Reach for Recovery meetings.
3. She will have very little pain and the incision will heal very quickly.
4. She should refrain from seeking male companionship since she will be seen as less than a woman.

95. A group of women have gathered at the local library for a series of seminars about women's health issues. In discussing cancer of the cervix, which of the following would be accurate?

1. This cancer is very rapid growing, so early detection is difficult to achieve.
2. A cervical biopsy is the screening test of choice for early detection of cervical cancer.
3. All women have an equal chance to develop cervical cancer because there are no high risk factors.
4. An annual Pap smear may detect cervical dysplasia, a frequent precursor of cervical cancer.

96. The nurse is talking to a woman who has been diagnosed with cancer of the ovary. She asks you what she could have done so that the cancer would have been found earlier. The best response should include which of the following?
    1. She should have had more frequent, twice a year, Pap smears.
    2. A yearly complete blood count (CBC) could have provided valuable clues to detect ovarian cancer.
    3. Detection of ovarian cancer is easier if a yearly proctoscopy is done.
    4. There is little more she could have done for earlier detection.

97. The nurse is caring for a woman who has had a vaginal hysterectomy and an indwelling Foley catheter. After removal of the catheter, she is unable to void and has little sensation of bladder fullness. She is also constipated and is experiencing some perineal pain. The *most* appropriate nursing diagnosis is altered urinary elimination related to
    1. infection as evidenced by inability to void with frequency and urgency.
    2. retention as evidenced by inability to void and urinary distention.
    3. gastrointestinal functioning as evidenced by inability to void and constipation.
    4. dysuria as evidenced by inability to void and loss of bladder sensation.

98. Mrs. F., age 42, has had a simple vaginal hysterectomy without oophorectomy, due to uterine fibroids. You have completed your discharge teaching and she is preparing to go home. Which of the following statements indicates Mrs. F. understands the physical changes she will experience?

1. "I hope my husband will still love me since we can't have sexual intercourse anymore."
2. "I was hoping to stop having periods, but I guess that will need to wait a few more years."
3. "It will be so nice to not need to use birth control any more."
4. "I just don't think I will ever feel feminine again since I can no longer experience orgasm."

99. The nurse has been discussing menopause with a 50-year-old woman who is experiencing some bodily changes indicative of the perimenopausal period. Which of the following statements indicates the client understands what is happening to her body?
    1. "Even though I am only having periods every few months, I should continue to use birth control until at least six months after my periods have stopped."
    2. "I am very upset to think that I will continue to have these hot flashes for the rest of my life."
    3. "Now that I am an old woman, I guess I'll be sick most of the time, so I should plan to move to a retirement home."
    4. "I may continue to bleed on and off throughout the next 25 years."

100. A 55-year-old woman who has ceased having menses has a family history of osteoporosis and increasing cholesterol levels over the past several years. Hormone replacement therapy (HRT) has been prescribed with estrogen and progesterone. She asks you why she should take the pills since she feels quite well. The nurse's answer would be
    1. HRT is thought to help protect women from heart disease and osteoporosis.
    2. HRT will help to reestablish the menstrual cycle, thus providing natural protection against heart disease and osteoporosis.
    3. even though she feels well now, she will soon begin having major health problems and HRT will protect her against those problems.
    4. she will be protected from breast cancer by HRT.

Answers and Rationales for Review Test 4

Maternity and Female Reproductive Nursing

ANSWER	RATIONALE	NP	CN	CL

#1. 4. Within the traditional East Asian family, roles are clearly defined. One consideration is the East Asian husband's lack of involvement during pregnancy and birth; this is a mutually agreeable separation of men's and women's roles.
    Im   Sa/1   Ap

    1. The client's cultural background must be integrated into any management strategy; referring to policy does not ensure culturally sensitive care.

    2. The nurse is responsible for assessing cultural factors and integrating strategies into the client's plan of care.

    3. The nursing profession, as the profession most involved in providing holistic care to individuals, must be knowledgeable about and skilled in values, beliefs, and health-illness practices of different cultures; omission of cultural factors is a major obstacle to providing quality care.

#2. 2. If a woman has a menstrual period every 28 days and was not taking oral contraceptives, Nagele's rule may be a fairly accurate determiner of her predicted birth date. To use this method, begin with the first day of the last menstrual period, subtract three months, and add seven days.
    An   He/3   Co

    1. To use Nagele's rule, begin with the first day of the last menstrual period, subtract three months and add seven days.

    3. To use Nagele's rule, begin with the first day of the last regular menstrual period, subtract three months and add seven days; some women do experience some vaginal bleeding around the time of what would have been their next period even though they are pregnant.

    4. To use Nagele's rule, begin with the first day of the last menstrual period, subtract three months and add seven days.

#3. 4. Probable signs of pregnancy are the result of physiologic changes in the pelvic organs and hormonal influences; for example, the mucous membranes of the vulva, vagina, and cervix become bluish (Chadwick's sign) as a result of hyperemia and proliferation of cells.
    As   He/3   Ap

    1. Detection of fetal heart tones is a positive sign (clearly demonstrates the presence of a fetus) of pregnancy that can be detected, with a Doppler instrument, as early as 10 weeks.

    2. Nausea and vomiting is a presumptive symptom of pregnancy because it can be caused by factors other than pregnancy.

    3. Amenorrhea is a presumptive symptom of pregnancy because it can be caused by factors other than pregnancy.

#4. 1. During the first trimester of pregnancy, women normally experience ambivalence about being pregnant. It is estimated that around 80% of women initially reject the idea of pregnancy; even women who planned pregnancy may respond at first with surprise and shock.
    As   He/3   Ap

    2. Feelings of being overwhelmed by changes related to pregnancy (physical, lifestyle, etc.) are an indicator of lack of acceptance of the pregnancy and are not considered normal.

    3. Feeling happiness and enjoyment about being pregnant does occur in some women initially; however, it is not the predominant finding.

    4. By the end of the first trimester, most women accept pregnancy but research has not found a direct relationship between this acceptance

and the physical changes; these changes are related more to the reality of the fetus than the pregnancy.

#5. 2. **From 20–24 weeks gestation, pigment changes in skin may occur from actions of hormones. These include the linea nigra, melasma on the face, and striae gravidarum (stretch marks).**   As   He/3   Ap

    1. Uterine growth in pregnancy follows a pattern; by the 20th week the fundus should reach the umbilicus, at about the 38th week it is just below the diaphragm until *lightening* (uterus drops into true pelvis) occurs before labor.

    3. Frequency of urination occurs in the first trimester (weeks 0–12) and again in the last trimester (weeks 28–40) from pressure of the gravid uterus on the bladder.

    4. Blood pressure in the first 24 weeks usually decreases 5–10 mmHg systolic and 10–15 mmHg diastolic due to relaxation of the vascular smooth muscle and the formation of new peripheral vascular beds. The blood pressure usually rises to prepregnancy levels by the time labor begins.

#6. 4. **All of the data stated are within the normal expected range for a first trimester pregnancy. These factors are related to hormonal changes and the growing uterus.**   As   He/3   Ap

    1. The findings of fatigue, nausea and vomiting, and the hemoglobin and hematocrit count are all within the norm for a first trimester pregnancy.

    2. Frequency of urination, from pressure of the growing uterus on the bladder, and a white vaginal discharge, from increased activity of cervical and vaginal cells, are all normal findings for a first trimester pregnancy.

    3. There are no data to support this nursing diagnosis; a blood type of O, or if the woman was Rh negative, would increase the risk for this type of injury to the fetus.

#7. 3. **In a low-risk pregnancy, the recommended frequency of prenatal visits is: every 4 weeks for the first 28 weeks, every 2 weeks until the 36th week, then every week until birth.**   Pl   He/3   Co

    1. For a low-risk pregnancy, this sequence of visits would be too frequent and unnecessary.

    2. For a low-risk pregnancy in the early weeks, this sequence of visits would be too frequent and unnecessary.

    4. Even in a low-risk pregnancy, this sequence of visits would be inadequate to detect danger signs of complications or administer needed care and assessments.

#8. 2. **To meet increased calcium needs, pregnant women need to increase their intake of dairy products or consider a calcium supplement that provides 600 mg of calcium per day; it is not necessary to drink milk.**   Ev   He/3   Ap

    1. The fetus stores iron during the last trimester of pregnancy; because of this, and other increased needs for iron during pregnancy, an additional daily supplement of 30–60 mg of ferrous salts is recommended beginning about 12 weeks gestation.

    3. Because of the extra requirements for sodium storage in the body, sodium intake should not be restricted during pregnancy; rigid sodium restriction has been observed to lead to neonatal hyponatremia.

    4. Although the ideal weight gain for obese pregnant women appears to be less than that recommended for normal-weight women, pregnancy is not the time to diet to lose weight; in weight loss, ketones are formed and these may lead to neurologic damage to the fetus.

#9. 4. **Evidence exists that smoking, consuming alcohol, or using social drugs during pregnancy may be harmful to the fetus.**   An   He/3   Ap

1. Initially, even if the pregnancy is planned, there is an element of surprise that conception has occurred. This feeling of ambivalence does not, in itself, indicate that acceptance and normal bonding will not occur.

2. A major risk for the older expectant couple relates to the increased incidence of Down syndrome in children born to women over age 35 or 40; however, the risk for injury to the fetus is greater from substance abuse.

3. No data support this nursing diagnosis.

#10. 2. It is best to avoid any medication when planning a pregnancy and during the first trimester; the greatest potential for gross abnormalities in the fetus occurs during the first trimester, when fetal organs are first developing. The greatest danger extends from day 31 after the last menstrual period to day 71.   Im   He/3   Ap

1. Problems with fertility have been linked to many areas, such as smoking, alcohol (in male infertility), and pelvic inflammatory disease; this connection has not been found with most common over-the-counter medications.

3. Even prescription drugs may have a teratogenic effect (cause serious defects) on the fetus; the rule to follow is that the advantage of using a particular medication must outweigh the risks.

4. Even though the most dangerous time for the fetus is conception and the first trimester of pregnancy, some medications have teratogenic effects (cause serious defects) when taken in the second and third trimesters.

#11. 1. All programs in prepared childbirth have some similarities; all have an educational component to help eliminate fear.   Im   He/3   Ap

2. Expectant parents are taught that childbirth preparation classes do not exclude the use of analgesics but that they often reduce the amount necessary. To set childbirth without pain relief as a goal can be extremely destructive to the woman's self-concept.

3. Most prepared childbirth classes do teach the mother *coping* strategies to deal with the pain and discomforts of birth; these may not directly reduce the pain itself and also other methods may be used instead of exercises and relaxation, such as hypnosis.

4. Maintaining a healthy pregnancy with a positive outcome for mother and newborn is a goal of prenatal care by a physician, nurse midwife, or other qualified health care provider; childbirth education classes are not a substitute for this important intervention.

#12. 1. Lecithin and sphingomyelin are phospholipids produced by the type II alveolar cells. The L/S ratio increases with gestation and a ratio of 2:1 indicates lung maturity.   An   Ph/9   An

2. An L/S ratio of 2:1 indicates lung maturity but there are several potential problems with this indicator; thus other parameters must also be measured. Meconium or blood in amniotic fluid alters the ratio and, despite a mature ratio in pregnancies complicated by diabetes, the neonate may still develop respiratory distress syndrome.

3. Viability refers to the fetus being capable of living outside the womb, now considered to be 25 weeks gestation due to advanced technology; L/S ratio is not used to measure viability.

4. A non-stress test is used to identify the fetus who may not be adapting well to the intrauterine environment; it does not indicate fetal maturity.

#13. 3. The CST subjects the fetus to uterine contractions that compress the arteries supplying the placenta, thus reducing placental blood flow and the flow of oxygen to the fetus; the fetus with minimal metabolic reserve will have late decelerations where the fetal heart rate does not return to the baseline until the contraction ends. Fetal compromise is therefore suggested.   An   Ph/9   An

1. In a negative normal CST there are no late decelerations occurring with contractions. This indicates fetal well-being related to uteroplacental function.
2. A reactive negative result refers to a normal non-stress test in which the fetal heart rate accelerates with fetal movement.
4. This term refers to a test that cannot be read adequately, for example, inability to stimulate at least three contractions in 10 minutes or unsatisfactory tracings related to positioning or fetal movement.

#14. 2. When IV oxytocin is being used to stimulate uterine contractions in a contraction stress test, the oxytocin infusion is stopped if contractions occur more often than every two minutes or last longer than 60 seconds, if uterine tetany (remains contracted) takes place, or if continued fetal heart rate decelerations are noted. Im Ph/8 Ap

1. Turning a client, in late pregnancy, on her left side will relieve pressure of the gravid uterus on the inferior vena cava; it will have no effect on a contracted uterus.
3. A contracted uterus reduces placental blood flow and the flow of oxygen to the fetus; this condition can result in fetal hypoxia so it must be resolved immediately.
4. It is possible that this tocholytic drug may be given to inhibit uterine contractions, but first the cause of the contraction must be eliminated.

#15. 2. To obtain clearer images during the first trimester, women are required to drink one to two quarts of clear fluid to fill the urinary bladder and thereby push the uterus higher into the abdomen where it can be more accurately scanned. Im Ph/9 Ap

1. There are no diet restrictions necessary to prepare for an ultrasound.
3. Ultrasound is a technique that involves the use of high-frequency sound waves; the sound waves bounce off tissues of differing acoustic density. No contrast dye is needed.
4. There are special instructions needed when a woman in the first trimester is to have a transabdominal ultrasound.

#16. 2. When a pregnant woman is bleeding vaginally, the nurse should first ask her how many weeks or months pregnant she is; management of bleeding differs in an early pregnancy contrasted with bleeding in late pregnancy. Additional information would include if tissue amniotic fluid was discharged and what other symptoms, such as cramps or pain, are present. As He/3 An

1. Feeling fetal movement is a good indicator of fetal well-being in late pregnancy. If this client were in the third trimester, this would be additional information obtained.
3. The actual timing of a pregnancy test does not relate to the length of pregnancy; testing can be done at any time.
4. Careful assessment is required to determine whether the cause of the bleeding is a threatened abortion; this would include other symptoms, such as cramps or abdominal pain, that may be present. The nurse must *first* determine the length of gestation.

#17. 3. The incidence of ectopic pregnancy in the United States has increased by a factor of 4.9 during recent years. This is attributed primarily to the growing number of women of childbearing age who experience PID and endometriosis, who use intrauterine devices, or who have had tubal surgery. As He/3 An

1. Multiparity (having had two or more children) has not been found to be a factor in the incidence of ectopic pregnancy; infertile women treated with assisted reproductive technology are at higher risk.
2. The incidence of ectopic pregnancy increases with age; youth is not an individual factor.

4. A history of therapeutic abortions has been found to be a factor in ectopic pregnancy, not spontaneous abortions (miscarriage).

#18. 1. The follow-up protocol of critical importance after a molar pregnancy is the assessment of serum chorionic gonadotropin (hCG); hCG is considered a highly specific tumor marker for gestational trophoblastic disease (GTD). The hCG levels are assayed at intervals for one year; a rise or plateau necessitates further diagnostic assessment and usually treatment. Pregnancy would obscure the evidence of choriocarcinoma by the normal secretion of hCG.
Pl Ph/9 Ap

2. Pregnancy-induced hypertension (PIH) may be seen earlier than the usual 20 weeks of gestation when there is a molar pregnancy; after evacuation of the mole there is no need for long-term blood pressure assessment.

3. The administration of RhoGAM is indicated to prevent hemolytic disease of the newborn as seen in a Rh-negative pregnancy.

4. In a molar pregnancy, cell differentiation is halted and trophoblastic tissue proliferates; the disorder becomes evident in the first trimester, there is no growing embryo, and immediate evacuation is indicated. An amniocentesis, usually performed at 16+ weeks of pregnancy, is not related to this disorder.

#19. 3. Placenta previa, when the placenta is implanted in the lower uterine segment, often is characterized by the sudden onset of bright red bleeding in the third trimester. Usually this bleeding is painless and may or may not be accompanied by contractions.
As He/3 Ap

1. A Couvelaire uterus can occur in severe abruptio placentae when blood extravasates into the uterine musculature and prevents contraction of the uterus after delivery.

2. Severe lower abdominal pain, especially in a woman in labor, can be a sign of a ruptured uterus.

4. This sign can be part of the classic presentation of abruptio placenta, which also includes constant abdominal pain and uterine tenderness on palpation.

#20. 3. In placenta previa, any sexual arousal is contraindicated because it can cause the release of oxytocin, which can cause the cervix to pull away from the low-lying placenta; this results in bleeding and potential jeopardy to the fetus.
Ev He/3 An

1. For women with placenta previa whose condition is stable, but the fetus is premature, a regimen of restricted activity and bedrest is indicated.

2. For women with placenta previa whose condition is stable, but the fetus is premature, a regimen of restricted activity and bedrest is indicated.

4. In placenta previa, if the woman's condition is stable, and the previa is less than 30% (a partial or marginal previa), a vaginal delivery may be possible with careful monitoring.

#21. 2. Preeclampsia may progress to eclampsia, the convulsive phase of PIH. Symptoms that herald the progression include headache, visual disturbances, epigastric pain, nausea or vomiting, hyperreflexia, and oliguria; classical signs of PIH also intensify.
Pl He/3 An

1. In this disorder, placental perfusion is already compromised, decreasing maternal blood pressure can further reduce perfusion and stress the fetus; if the diastolic pressure exceeds 110 mmHg, an antihypertensive drug may be administered.

3. Weight gain in advancing PIH is an indication of progressive water retention and not a sign of an inappropriate diet; a weight gain exceeding 1.5 kg per week during the third trimester is a sign of PIH.

4. The signs described here are indicators of progressive PIH; the data do not support noncompliance.

#22. 3. Modified bedrest in the left lateral position may be advised for
Ev He/3 An

the client with mild PIH. **This position improves venous return and placental and renal perfusion; urine output increases, and blood pressure may stabilize or decrease.**

1. If diastolic pressure exceeds 110 mmHg, an antihypertensive drug may be administered IV in more severe PIH; in PIH placental perfusion is already compromised and lowering maternal blood pressure can further reduce perfusion and stress the fetus.
2. Dietary restrictions are no longer advised, and the client may follow a regular, well-balanced diet as tolerated.
4. Previous PIH predisposes to recurrence of PIH.

#23. 4.   **Once pregnancy is established, the focus of management is on minimizing any extra cardiac demands on the pregnant woman. In class 3 cardiac disease, the client experiences fatigue, palpitation, dyspnea, or angina when she undertakes less than ordinary activity. Physical activity is markedly restricted; this includes bedrest throughout the pregnancy.**   Ph   Ph/9   An

1. Pregnant women with cardiac disease do need to learn self-care to minimize the risk of complications; this, however, does not take priority over physiologic safety.
2. Pregnancies with serious complications instill fear in the client and family; however, physiological needs take priority.
3. Pregnant women with cardiac disease are likely to be placed on a sodium-restricted diet; however, this does not take priority over the risk of cardiac decompensation.

#24. 1.   **There is increasing evidence that the degree of control for an insulin-dependent diabetic woman prior to conception greatly affects the fetal outcome. Studies find that poor maternal glucose control underlies the incidence of congenital malformations in the infants of diabetic mothers.**   Pl   Ph/9   Ap

2. In a diabetic woman with vascular disease, White's class D, or one who has had diabetes for at least 20 years, even careful control of glucose at this point will not prevent these cardiovascular changes.
3. Macrosomia, excessive fetal growth, can occur in infants of diabetic mothers from hyperinsulinism; however, this is a concern in later pregnancy, not at conception.
4. Infants of diabetic mothers have a higher incidence of respiratory distress syndrome because hyperinsulinism has a delaying effect on fetal lung maturation; however, this is a concern in later pregnancy.

#25. 2.   **Prenatal alcohol exposure is a preventable cause of birth defects and neurodevelopmental deficits; it is the leading most preventable cause of mental retardation.**   Ev   He/3   An

1. Research confirms that infants suffer more severe abnormalities the earlier alcohol consumption occurs during gestation; but alcohol consumption in late pregnancy is also associated with intrauterine growth retardation and preterm delivery.
3. Women should not drink any alcohol when breast feeding. It can cause drowsiness, weakness, decrease in linear growth, and abnormal weight gain in the infant; it may also decrease milk ejection.
4. No safe level has been determined for alcohol consumption during pregnancy.

#26. 3.   **Regular contractions coupled with bloody show suggest that cervical changes are occurring as a result of contractions.**   Ev   He/3   An

1. Perception of pain with contractions is not a reliable indicator of true labor.
2. Bright red vaginal bleeding is a sign of a complication, not the onset of labor.
4. Rupture of membranes does not necessarily occur prior to the onset of labor.

#27. 4.   **The left lower quadrant is the correct location since the back is on the left and the vertex is in the pelvis.**   An   He/3   Ap

ANSWER	RATIONALE	NP	CN	CL
	1. The right upper quadrant would be the place to auscultate if the back were on the right and the breech were in the pelvis.			
	2. The left upper quadrant would be the place to auscultate if the back were on the left and the breech were in the pelvis.			
	3. The right lower quadrant would be the place to auscultate if the back were on the right side.			
#28. 4.	**The fingertips of one hand allow the nurse to feel when the contraction begins and ends and to determine the strength of by the firmness of the uterus.**	As	He/3	Ap
	1. Although the electronic fetal monitor can yield useful information as the patient continues to labor, it is not the best way for initial assessment to occur.			
	2. Self-report by the patient may be used to supplement the nurse's assessment, but should not replace it.			
	3. Leopold's maneuvers are used to determine fetal position prior to auscultation of heart rate. They do not provide information about contractions.			
#29. 4.	**A rate of 170 is suggestive of fetal tachycardia. A drop to 140 during a contraction represents some periodic change, which is not a normal finding.**	An	He/3	An
	1. A rate of 160 is normal. The absence of changes during contractions is a reassuring finding.			
	2. A rate of 130 is normal. Accelerations with fetal movement are a reassuring finding.			
	3. Baseline variability between 120 and 130 is a normal finding.			
#30. 2.	**Although there is always some risk of complications when membranes rupture, it is safe for Ms. K. to ambulate as long as she is rechecked if rupture of membranes occurs.**	Im	He/3	Ap
	1. Although cord prolapse can occur when the presenting part is not fully engaged, the incidence is highest with malpresentation, grand multiparity, multiple gestation, and low birthweight.			
	3. Although ambulation does support natural labor progress, this response is not the best one without anticipatory guidance.			
	4. Although the nurse may not feel comfortable allowing Ms. K. to walk, this response does not provide the client with any rationale for the nurse's response and is therefore inappropriate.			
#31. 1.	**Ambulation will help Mrs. M.'s contractions more effectively dilatethe cervix. As long as the presenting part is engaged, there is not increased risk of cord prolapse.**	Pl	He/3	Ap
	2. Assessments every five minutes are made during the second stage of labor. They are not required during latent phase of first stage labor.			
	3. Although periodic assessments of mother and fetus are required, continuous monitoring is not indicated.			
	4. Although many patients in latent phase are sent home with instructions to return when contractions become more frequent, Mrs. M.'s ruptured membranes are a contraindication to that action.			
#32. 3.	**The most important nursing action after rupture of the membranes is careful fetal assessment, including fetal heart tones counted for one minute.**	Im	He/3	Ap
	1. There is no known reason based on the available information to request amniotic fluid analysis. Therefore, not only is this not an appropriate initial action, it is not required at all.			
	2. The presenting part is at 0 station. At this station, it is unlikely that a cord prolapse would occur. Trendelenburg would be used only if an assessment confirmed this complication.			
	4. There is no information suggesting that Mrs. B. will require operative delivery. It is more important to assess the client than anything else at this time.			
#33. 1.	**At 6 cm dilation and complete effacement, active labor is**	An	He/3	An

occurring. A station of −1 indicates that the vertex is above the ischial spines and not fully engaged.

2. Transition does not begin until 8 cm of cervical dilation. The vertex is the head, not backside and −1 station is above the ischial spines and not fully engaged.

3. Latent phase ends by the time the cervix is 4 cm dilated. The vertex is the head, not backside and −1 station is above the ischial spines and not fully engaged.

4. Although Ms. C. is in active labor with the head as presenting part, a −1 station is not fully engaged since the head is above the ischial spines.

#34. 2. The second stage of labor extends from complete cervical dilation to delivery of the infant.   An   He/3   An

1. The first stage of labor extends until the cervix is fully dilated.

3. The third stage of labor extends from delivery of the fetus to delivery of the placenta.

4. The fourth stage of labor extends from delivery of the placenta through the early postpartum period.

#35. 1. During early labor, blood pressure and contractions should be monitored hourly and fetal heart rate every 15 minutes.   Pl   He/3   Ap

2. During early labor, temperature is monitored every 4 hours, blood pressure every hour and contractions every half hour to hour. Fetal heart rate is monitored every 15 minutes.

3. During early labor, contractions are monitored every half hour or hour, cervical effacement and dilation are assessed when there is a change in condition. Fetal heart rate is monitored every 15 minutes.

4. During early labor, contractions are monitored every half hour to hour and blood pressure is monitored hourly. Fetal heart rate is monitored every 15 minutes.

#36. 1. A full bladder may prevent the head from moving down into the pelvic inlet. Often clients do not have the sensation of a full bladder late in labor, despite significant distention.   As   He/3   Ap

2. Although fetal size may contribute to failure of the head to descend, this is not the initial assessment required.

3. Notification of a surgical team is not an assessment. There is also no evidence that an operative delivery is required at this time.

4. Although continuous assessment of fetal well-being is important, there is no indication for scalp pH. Therefore, these assessments are not the most appropriate ones to be made.

#37. 2. Since Ms. N. is still in transition and not ready to deliver, encouraging her to pant will diminish the urge to push.   Im   He/3   Ap

1. Pushing prior to complete dilation of the cervix may increase edema and make delivery more difficult.

3. Although a squatting position may be useful as delivery approaches, it will not help diminish the urge to push prior to complete cervical dilation.

4. During transition, many women do not like to be touched, even if this action was perceived as helpful earlier in labor.

#38. 3. This infant has two points for heart rate, respiratory effort, and reflex irritability. One point is awarded for color and muscle tone for a total of eight.   As   He/3   Ap

1. A score of 10 would result if all five criteria received a maximum of two points. This infant does not have two points for color or for muscle tone.

2. A score of nine would result if four criteria received a maximum of two points and one received one point. This infant does not have two points for color or for muscle tone.

4. A score of seven would result if there was a total of three points off from the five criteria. This infant has a total of two points off.

#39. 3. Perineal edema may affect urinary elimination. If allowed to   Pl   He/3   Ap continue, it may also lead to excessive postpartum bleeding because the uterus cannot stay firmly contracted when the bladder is excessively full.

1. Although this diagnosis may be appropriate during the postpartum period, it is not the highest priority.
2. Concerns about constipation are more often seen after the first 24 hours.
4. There is no information to suggest that this client has a knowledge deficit regarding newborn care. Even if she does, physiologic needs are of higher priority during the first hour after birth.

#40. 2. Assessment of the mother during fourth stage includes elements related to her recovery from childbirth. Infant assessment focuses on stability and transition to extrauterine life. — As — He/3 — Ap

1. This information is not appropriate to fourth stage for the mother. She should not experience a pattern of contractions after delivery, although afterpains are a part of the involutional process. Infant assessment information is correct.
3. Although the information related to maternal assessment is correct, there is no reason to return the infant to the nursery.
4. These assessments would be appropriate during the third stage of labor.

#41. 3. As a G3 P2, Mrs. P.'s past pregnancy history may provide some important information that may shape the care rendered at this time. — Pl — He/3 — Ap

1. Although Mrs. P. may need to reduce her activity level if she continues with preterm labor, this is not the most appropriate plan at this time.
2. Although the nurse should monitor Mrs. P. and her fetus, this is not with the expectation of impending delivery.
4. Although tocolytic agents may be required, a physician's order is necessary. The IV therapy is usually initiated first, with a switch to oral agents after contractions cease.

#42. 3. If the magnesium sulfate is effective you would expect the contractions to decrease and then disappear. You would not continue to perform vaginal exams if the desired result is occurring. — Ev — Ph/8 — Ap

1. Magnesium sulfate is a central nervous system depressant. Smooth muscle relaxation will occur, hence contractions will not increase in frequency.
2. Although magnesium sulfate is a central nervous system depressant, it is not a sedative. Therefore, you would not expect Mrs. P. to fall asleep.
4. Although magnesium sulfate is used to treat preeclampsia, diminished deep tendon reflexes and decreased blood pressure would not tell the nurse that the drug is having the desired effect in premature labor.

#43. 1. Epidural anesthesia may diminish Mrs. K.'s sensation of painful stimuli and movement. Assistance and frequent assessment are therefore essential. — Pl — Ph/8 — Ap

2. A bolus infusion of fluid is usually administered prior to placement of an epidural. It is not a part of the plan after administration of the anesthesia.
3. Although patients receiving epidural anesthesia may have difficulty in voiding, that is not a reason to place a Foley.
4. If the epidural is working satisfactorily, Mrs. K. should experience minimal discomfort from her contractions. Although a back rub is not contraindicated, the rationale is not correct.

#44. 1. Ice during the first 12 hours after delivery causes vasoconstriction and thereby prevents edema. Ice also provides pain relief through numbing of the area. — Ev — He/3 — Ap

ANSWER	RATIONALE	NP	CN	CL

2. Heat is not an appropriate initial action because it may increase edema formation and does not aid the early healing process.

3. Although sitz baths may be used later in the course of recovery, the heat is not desirable in the first 12 hours because it may enhance edema formation.

4. Although analgesic agents may be required for pain relief, this is not the most appropriate action based on the information available.

#45. 3. Asking for clarification of what Mrs. C. knows is the best way to evaluate what she understands of the procedure. If the client has additional questions, the nurse can then clarify or amplify the information. — Ev · He/3 · Ap

1. Although it is important to have some help after discharge, this question will not elicit information about her understanding of the procedure.

2. This technique is useful in preparing young children for surgery, but is inappropriate for a normal adult.

4. Although written information may be helpful to explain cesarean birth, providing it at the time of admission does not allow the nurse the opportunity to evaluate that the patient understands the procedures.

#46. 4. During the early postpartum period, evidence of maladaptive mothering may include limited handling or smiling at the infant; studies have shown that a predictable group of reciprocal interactions, between mother and baby, should take place with each encounter to foster and reinforce attachment. — An · He/3 · Ap

1. Shortly after birth, the new mother examines her baby's body with her fingertips looking for cues from the infant; fingertip touch causes the newborn to turn toward the touch.

2. Concern for ability to care for their newborn is an indicator of positive bonding and attachment.

3. For parents, the need for the newborn to open its eyes is nearly universal. Babies held in the face-to-face (*en face*) position attempt to focus on the eyes of the holder; this strongly evokes parental feeling.

#47. 3. Although plastic linings protect clothing from leaking milk, the nipples may become sore and prone to infection from trapped moisture; disposable nursing pads can be used to protect clothing. — Pl · He/3 · Ap

1. Successful lactation is fostered by feeding soon after delivery and then feeding when the newborn is ready to nurse; signs of infant readiness include a wakeful state and rooting and sucking motions.

2. Mothers are advised to simply wash their hands before breast feeding; washing the nipples is not necessary. The use of powders, creams, and soap is discouraged.

4. In a normal term infant who is being breast fed, supplemental water feedings are not needed; in fact, these feedings may impede breast feeding by decreasing the volume of breast milk required and also by creating "nipple confusion" in the infant.

#48. 1. To prevent intrauterine infection, which can result in miscarriage, stillbirth, and congenital rubella syndrome in the fetus, women who are immunized should be advised not to become pregnant for three months. — Pl · He/4 · Ap

2. One immunization should result in the woman becoming immune to rubella; rubella vaccine is never administered during pregnancy because of the serious dangers to the fetus.

3. Receiving a rubella vaccination in the postpartum period is not a contraindication to breast feeding.

4. One immunization should result in the woman becoming immune to rubella; another antibody titer will be done in subsequent pregnancies for validation.

#49. 2. To attain the maximum effect of reducing edema and providing — Ev · He/3 · Ap numbness of the tissues, the ice pack should remain in place approximately 20 minutes and then be removed for about 10 minutes before replacing it.

1. Stitches used for an episiotomy are absorbable and do not require removal.

3. Because of the danger of tissue burns, a woman must be cautioned not to apply anesthetic spray before using a heat lamp.

4. Recently, cool sitz baths have gained popularity because they are effective in reducing perineal edema; therefore, it may be best to offer the woman a choice.

| #50. 4. | **Extra bottles of prepared formula are stored in the refrigerator and should be warmed slightly before feeding.** | Ev | Sa/2 | Ap |

1. Bottles may be prepared individually, or up to one day's supply of formula may be prepared at one time.

2. Cleanliness is essential, but sterilization is necessary only if the water source is questionable.

3. Bottles may be effectively prepared in dishwashers or washed thoroughly in warm soapy water and rinsed well; nipples should be washed and rinsed by hand.

| #51. 4. | **A soft, boggy uterus should be massaged until firm; clots may be expressed during massage and this often tends to contract the uterus more effectively.** | Im | He/3 | Ap |

1. If the uterus continues not to contract well or the bleeding is excessive, the physician or nurse midwife should be contacted; however, this is not the initial action of the nurse.

2. If the uterus continues not to contract well or the bleeding is excessive, the physician or nurse midwife may order that oxytocin be administered; however, this is not the initial action of the nurse.

3. Ambulation is advised in the immediate postpartum period; however, this intervention is not related to the emergency situation described.

| #52. 1. | **These symptoms are signs of infectious mastitis, usually caused by *Staphylococcus aureus;* a 10-day course of antibiotics is indicated.** | Im | He/3 | Ap |

2. In mastitis, an improved outcome, a decreased duration of symptoms, and decreased incidence of breast abscess result if the breasts continue to be emptied by either nursing or pumping.

3. It is important that breast feeding technique and knowledge be assessed when mastitis has occurred because there have been found to be contributing factors for this complication; however, it is not the best initial action of the nurse.

4. Diagnosis and treatment of mastitis are usually based on symptoms and physical examination, even while waiting for laboratory results; if there is a recurrence of the mastitis, most experts agree that a culture should be obtained.

| #53. 1. | **Afterpains occur more commonly in multiparas than in primiparas and are caused by intermittent uterine contractions. Because oxytocin is released when the infant suckles, breast feeding also increases the severity of the afterpains.** | As | He/3 | Ap |

2. Lochia (term for vaginal discharge after birth) serosa occurs from about the third until the tenth day after delivery and would not be observed on the second day; it is a pinkish to brownish color.

3. Catheterization would be required when the bladder is distended and the woman cannot void or when she is voiding small amounts (<100 ml) frequently.

4. After birth, the top of the fundus remains at the level of the umbilicus for about half a day; it then descends approximately one fingerbreadth per day until it can no longer be palpated on about the tenth day.

| #54. 3. | **At two weeks postpartum, striae (stretch marks) are pink and** | As | He/3 | Ap |

obvious; by six weeks they are beginning to fade but may not achieve a silvery appearance for several more weeks.

1. The uterus is no longer palpable abdominally by 10 days to two weeks postpartum.
2. In a non-nursing mother, breasts would not be tender and no milk would be expressed by two weeks postpartum.
4. The final discharge, termed lochia alba, is creamy or yellowish and persists from about the tenth day to two to three weeks after delivery; by six weeks, there would be no vaginal discharge or menses may be resumed.

#55. 2. The classic definition of puerperal morbidity resulting from infection is a temperature of 100.4° F (38.0° C) or higher on any of the first 10 days postpartum exclusive of the first 24 hours; additional signs are increased pulse rate, uterine tenderness, foul-smelling lochia, and subinvolution (uterus remains enlarged).   An   He/3   An

1. The postpartum client needs additional rest and an isolated request for the newborn to be cared for in the nursery should not be interpreted as an alteration in parenting or bonding.
3. In the first 48 hours after birth, a postpartum diuresis takes place and the woman will frequently urinate as much as 3000 ml per day; there may also be profuse sweating (diaphoresis) and gradually diminishing of edema of the extremities.
4. After delivery, the uterus should descend below the umbilicus at the rate of 1–2 cm per day; failure to do so may be termed subinvolution and the cause must be determined. The client's lack of knowledge about this condition would not be the first priority.

#56. 3. The circumference of the newborn's head should be approximately 2 cm greater than the circumference of the chest at birth and will remain in this proportion for the next few months. Any differences in head size may indicate microcephaly (abnormal smallness of head) or hydrocephalus (increased cerebrospinal fluid within the ventricles of the brain).   As   He/3   Ap

1. Two "soft spots" (fontanels) may be palpated on the newborn's head. These are openings at the juncture of the cranial bones; the anterior fontanel closes within 18 months, the posterior fontanel within 8–12 weeks.
2. The head may appear asymmetric in the newborn of a vertex delivery. This is called *molding* and is caused by overriding of the cranial bones during labor and birth; it diminishes within a few days.
4. Caput succedaneum is a localized, easily identifiable soft area of the scalp, generally resulting from a long and difficult labor or vacuum extraction; the fluid is reabsorbed within 12 hours to a few days after birth.

#57. 1. These findings of acrocyanosis (bluish discoloration of the hands and feet), erythema toxicum (newborn rash), milia, and a nevus flammeus (port wine stain) are all within the normal range for a full-term newborn.   As   He/3   An

2. The findings described do not indicate that the infant has an infectious condition that would require isolation.
3. The findings described do not require further medical intervention.
4. Intrauterine malnutrition is mainly manifested by low birth weight and internal physiologic changes.

#58. 1. Physiologic jaundice occurs after the first 24 hours of life and is caused by accelerated destruction of fetal red blood cells (RBCs), impaired conjugation of bilirubin, and increased bilirubin reabsorption from the intestinal tract; there is no pathologic basis.   An   He/3   An

2. Hepatitis B virus (HBV), if transmitted to the fetus, increases the risk

of prematurity and perinatal morbidity; infants who subsequently test positive for HBV surface antigen are rarely symptomatic.

3. Hemolytic disease of the newborn caused by Rh incompatibility with the mother's blood may cause jaundice that most often appears at birth or in the first 24 hours of life.

4. Breast feeding jaundice, found in 1–5% of newborns being breast fed, appears after the first week of life when the mother's mature milk has come in.

#59. 3. **Normal term newborns pass meconium within 8–24 hours of life; meconium is formed in utero and is thick, tarry, black (or dark green) in appearance. Transitional stool is a thinner brown to green. Normal voiding is two to six times daily; there may be innocuous pink stains ("brick dust spots") on the diaper from urates.**   An   He/3   An

1. Dehydration in a newborn may be indicated by an increased temperature or a depressed fontanel; normal urinary output is often limited and the voidings may be scanty.

2. Following birth, caloric intake is often insufficient for weight gain and during this time there may be a weight loss of 5–10%; normal newborn elimination criteria takes this phenomenon into consideration.

4. The findings described here do not indicate a need for medical interventions.

#60. 4. **Tremors are common in the full-term newborn; when a newborn is startled s/he will exhibit the Moro reflex, that is, s/he will straighten arms and hands outward while the knees flex; in a newborn the Babinski reflex is displayed by a fanning and extension of the toes (in adults the toes flex); and when held upright with feet lightly touching a surface, the newborn will put one foot in front of the other and "walk."**   An   He/3   An

1. The signs of drug withdrawal include hyperactivity, hyperirritability (persistent high-pitched cry), exaggerated tremors and reflexes, and seizures.

2. The movements of a newborn are normally uncoordinated; the findings described are not ones of uncoordination.

3. When awake the newborn may exhibit purposeless, uncoordinated bilateral movements of the extremities, if asymmetric (one-sided) neurologic dysfunction should be suspected; these are not the type of movements described.

#61. 4. **At term gestation, the breast bud tissue will measure between 0.5 and 1 cm (5–10 mm).**   As   He/3   An

1. At birth, both male and female newborns may have enlarged breasts from maternal estrogen; decreased breast tissue would not be expected in either male or female.

2. Maternal hormonal influences may cause the newborn's breast to become engorged, but not reduced in size.

3. Intrauterine growth retardation (IUGR), or an infant who is small-for-gestational age (SGA), is a newborn at or below the tenth percentile for weight on the newborn classification chart.

#62. 3. **The newborn is at a high risk for hemorrhage due to an absence of intestinal flora (bacteria). Vitamin K, needed for the formation of prothrombin and proconvertin for blood coagulation, is usually synthesized by these bacteria in the colon; however, they are absent in the newborn's sterile gut. This problem is prevented by the administration of vitamin K following birth.**   Pl   He/3   Ap

1. Newborns should be fed by bottle or breast shortly after birth; however, this is not related to the newborn's lack of intestinal flora.

2. Usually the first void and passing of meconium is noted in the first 24 hours of life and should be documented by the nurse; this is not related to the listed nursing diagnosis.

4. A Coombs' test is performed on a newborn's cord blood if hemolytic disease of the newborn is suspected, as in Rh incompatibility; this is not related to the listed nursing diagnosis of fluid depletion.

#63. 4. The initial parental-newborn attachment period can be enhanced if the care providers keep routine investigations to a minimum, delay instillation of ophthalmic antibiotic for one hour, keep the room dim, and provide privacy; eye prophylaxis medication can cause chemical conjunctivitis, which may interfere with the baby's ability to focus on the parents' faces. Pl He/3 Ap

1. Prophylactic eye treatment for *Neisseria gonorrhoea*, which may have infected the infant of an infected mother during the birth process, is legally required for all newborns.

2. Before instillation of ophthalmic ointment, the eyes should be gently cleaned with a moist cotton ball; irrigations, before or after medication administration, should not be done.

3. Breast feeding of newborns should be encouraged as soon as possible after birth; however, this is not a reason to delay eye prophylaxis.

#64. 1. It is important for the new mother to learn and respond to her infant's early feeding cues. Early cues that indicate a newborn is interested in feeding include hand-to-hand or hand-passing-mouth motion, whimpering, sucking, and rooting. Pl He/3 Ap

2. In the past it was typical to establish artificial, every three to four hour schedules for feeding after the initial feeding; this schedule failed to recognize the individual needs of the newborn infant and presented difficulties for the new mother just establishing lactation.

3. Using supplementary bottle feedings for the breast feeding infant may weaken or confuse the suckling reflex or decrease the infant's interest in nursing; bottles should be avoided until breast feeding is well established.

4. Crying is a late sign of hunger; it has also been shown to delay the transition to extrauterine life by causing unoxygenated blood to be shunted into systemic circulation through the foramen ovale and ductus arteriosus.

#65. 3. After birth, the first priority is to maintain respirations, the second priority is to provide and maintain warmth; the newborn's temperature may fall 2–3° C after birth due mainly to evaporative losses; this triggers cold-induced metabolic responses and heat production. Pl He/3 Ap

1. The Apgar score, an immediate evaluation of the newborn's physical condition, is rated one minute after birth and again in five minutes; however, it is not the second priority of care.

2. The cord is clamped with two Kelly clamps and then cut at delivery; it is not a priority to replace the clamps with a plastic clamp immediately.

4. To ensure correct identification, the nurse places ID bands on the mother and infant before they leave the birth area; however, this is not the second priority of care.

#66. 2. Powders and oils are not recommended for the neonate's skin; oils may clog the pores, and the small particles of powders may be inhaled by the neonate. Im He/3 Ap

1. Powders are not recommended for the neonate because the small particles may be inhaled.

3. Powders and oils are not recommended for the neonate's skin; oils may clog the pores, and the small particles of powders may be inhaled by the neonate.

4. Even in a hot environment, an infant should have a layer of clothing, so excess moisture will be absorbed and the body cooled.

#67. 3. The middle third of the vastus lateralis muscle in the thigh is the preferred site for an intramuscular injection in the newborn. Im Ph/8 Ap

1. Children below the age of three do not have sufficient muscle development in the gluteal muscle group (buttocks) to withstand injections at this site.
2. Children below the age of three do not have sufficient muscle development in the deltoid muscle group (upper arm) to withstand injections at this site.
4. The middle third of the rectus femoris in the thigh is an alternate site, but its proximity to major vessels and the sciatic nerve necessitates caution in using this site for injections in the newborn.

#68. 4. Before discharge, parents should demonstrate proper cleaning of the cord stump by wiping it with an alcohol pad; they should know to do this two to three times a day until the cord falls off in 7–14 days. Ev He/3 Ap
1. Viewing a videotape does not indicate that learning or understanding has occurred.
2. Reading a booklet does not indicate that learning or understanding has occurred.
3. Various preparations such as triple dye, Betadine, and Bacitracin are used for newborn cord care in nurseries to promote drying and provide a bactericidal effect; this is not necessary after discharge.

#69. 1. A circumcision is the surgical removal of the prepuce or foreskin from the tip of the penis; any foreskin that remains should not be retracted. Ev Ph/9 Ap
2. The parents should be instructed to squeeze water gently over the penis and pat it dry after each diaper change for two to three days or until healing has occurred.
3. A whitish yellow exudate that adheres to the glans is granulation tissue and should not be removed.
4. After the circumcision, A&D ointment is placed on the penis to keep the diaper from adhering to the site; new ointment is applied at each diaper change for at least 24–48 hours.

#70. 3. The nipple should have a hole big enough to allow milk to flow in drops when the bottle is inverted; too large an opening may cause regurgitation, too small an opening can exhaust and upset the infant. Ev He/3 Ap
1. Bottles should always be held, not propped; positional otitis media may develop when the infant is fed horizontally because milk and nasal mucus may occlude the eustachian tube.
2. Parents should be encouraged to avoid overfeeding or feeding infants every time they cry; infants should be allowed to set their own pace once feedings are established.
4. The infant should be burped at intervals, preferably at the middle and end of the feeding; too frequent burping may confuse a newborn who is attempting to coordinate sucking, swallowing, and breathing simultaneously.

#71. 3. A birth weight of 1450 g is the mean weight for an infant at 30 weeks gestation, but falls within the 10–90th percentiles for infants between 29 and 33 weeks gestation. The diminished muscle tone and extension of extremities at rest are also characteristic of this gestational age. The sole creases described are actually most characteristic of an infant between 32 and 34 weeks gestation. An He/3 An
1. Full-term infants generally have birth weights of greater than 3000 g, with a range of 2700–4000 g.
2. The infant cannot be less mature than 24 weeks gestation based on all of the assessment data presented. Generally, at less than 24 weeks gestation, weight would be 500–700 g at most, breast tissue would be absent, and the areola might not be discernible. Sole creases would not be present.

4. The post-term infant would be expected to weigh at least 2700 g, be tightly flexed at rest, and have abundant sole creases, large and well-defined breast buds, and a pinna that readily recoils.

#72. 3. Prolonged rupture of membranes places this premature infant at risk for sepsis. Frequent monitoring of vital signs, color, activity level, and overall behavior is particularly important because changes may provide early cues to a developing infection. Family interaction with the infant should always be a part of the nursing plan.   Pl   He/3   An

1. Although the infant is exhibiting signs of mild respiratory distress, there is no sign that respiratory failure is imminent. Blood gas frequency is determined by physician order.

2. Although this infant will probably do very well, she must be monitored more frequently than every eight hours. Rooming in would not be a priority at this time.

4. Although the infant has some mild hypothermia, there is no evidence that a warmer will be needed for 48 hours. Vital signs should be monitored frequently, but are not required on an hourly basis. Limitation of visitors with obvious infections may be appropriate; however, restrictions are not needed.

#73. 1. Although hyperbilirubinemia is common in newborns, certain factors increase the likelihood of early appearance of visible jaundice. Cold stress, bruising at delivery, cephalhematoma, asphyxiation, prematurity, breast feeding, and poor feeding are all factors that may lead to hyperbilirubinemia in otherwise normal infants.   An   Ph/10   An

2. Although jaundice at this age may be pathologic, exchange transfusion is reserved for situations that cannot be managed with more conservative measures such as continued monitoring, supplemental feeding, and/or phototherapy first.

3. Although the infant is being breast fed, true breast milk jaundice does not develop until four to seven days after birth.

4. There is no information to suggest blood group incompatibility.

#74. 2. Erythroblastosis fetalis results when an Rh negative woman makes antibodies against her Rh positive fetus. The antibodies attack fetal red cells.   An   Ph/10   An

1. Although ABO blood group incompatibility may lead to jaundice, it does not result in erythroblastosis fetalis. Blood group incompatibility between father and infant will not produce problems for the infant.

3. ABO incompatibility will not lead to erythroblastosis fetalis although it may result in fetal hemolysis and jaundice of the newborn.

4. Although erythroblastosis is an Rh-related disorder, it is not produced by any relationship between the father's and infant's blood types.

#75. 1. Since the indirect and direct Coombs' tests were negative, antibodies to Rh have not developed. Mrs. K. should have RhoGAM to prevent antibody formation.   An   He/4   Co

2. Negative tests indicate that antibodies have not developed to the Rh factor.

3. Rh is an antigen. If Mrs. K. was sensitized, she would have developed antibodies to the Rh antigen. RhoGAM would be given to the mother to prevent antibody development.

4. The Coombs' tests indicate the presence or absence of antibodies to the Rh antigen. Since Mrs. K. is Rh negative and her infant is positive, these tests are important.

#76. 4. Neonatal withdrawal is a common occurrence in heroin addiction. Placing Baby G. in a quiet area and swaddling may promote state organization and minimize some symptoms. Medication may be needed to control hyperirritability.   Pl   Ph/9   Ap

ANSWER	RATIONALE	NP	CN	CL

1. Although neonatal withdrawal may be a problem, methadone is contraindicated because it may cause addiction in the newborn.
2. Although parent-infant attachment is important, this infant is not stable enough for rooming-in.
3. Infants born to heroin-addicted mothers experience early liver maturation and a lower incidence of jaundice than other newborns.

#77. 2. Baby L.'s respiratory rate and pulse are within normal limits and the nasal flaring is no longer present.   Ev   Ph/9   Ap

1. See-saw respirations and coarse breath sounds suggest that Baby L. continues with significant respiratory distress.
3. A pH of 6.97 suggests significant acidosis. A pO_2 of 61 on 40% oxygen is suggestive of significant hypoxia. Neither of these findings suggests improvement.
4. A weight gain of 150 g in the first 12 hours of life is suggestive of edema. Edema often accompanies respiratory distress in infants.

#78. 2. Although a medical diagnosis cannot be made from the assessment data, all of the findings noted are commonly seen in infants with fetal alcohol syndrome.   An   Ph/10   An

1. Infants with Down syndrome do not exhibit the flattened philtrum or short palpebral fissures. Most do not manifest any growth abnormalities at birth.
3. Turner's syndrome is very rarely identified in infants due to the limited manifestations until later in childhood.
4. Although infants with congenital syphilis may have intrauterine growth retardation, the other symptoms described are not usually present.

#79. 4. The infant's prematurity is the major risk factor for necrotizing enterocolitis, which effects 1–15% of all infants in NICU. Usual nonsurgical treatment includes antibiotic therapy, making the infant NPO, frequent monitoring, and respiratory and circulatory support as needed.   Pl   Ph/10   Ap

1. The infant described most likely has a condition known as necrotizing enterocolitis. In this situation the infant is placed NPO. Continued feedings may lead to perforation of the intestines.
2. The infant described most likely has a condition known as necrotizing enterocolitis. These infants are not at increased risk for seizures, hence, seizure precautions are not needed.
3. Necrotizing enterocolitis is not directly transmitted from one infant to the next; therefore, isolation is not required.

#80. 4. One additional PKU test within the first week of life will validate whether PKU disease is present. The infant should have been on breast milk or formula for 48 hours prior to the test.   Ev   He/4   Ap

1. Although Mrs. L. understands that one test has already been done, waiting until one month of age would be too late if the infant had this disorder.
2. PKU is a disease of abnormal protein metabolism. Waiting until the infant starts cereal would be of no use. If PKU exists, the milk feedings of the first months of life would produce brain damage.
3. The PKU test needs to be repeated only once after the infant has been on milk feedings for at least 48 hours.

#81. 2. Serial basal body temperature graphs are a baseline for determining when ovulation has taken place during a menstrual cycle. If ovulation has occurred, the temperature will be higher the second half of the cycle and lower the first half.   As   He/3   Co

1. Hysterosalpingogram is an X-ray visualization of the uterus and fallopian tubes with the aid of a dye to determine tubal patency.
3. The postcoital test determines the effects of the cervical environment on the sperm.
4. Semen analysis determines the number, motility, and condition of sperm at ejaculation.

#82. 1. **Weight gain associated with increased appetite and constipation are fairly common side-effects of Clomid.** — Im, Ph/8, Ap
2. There is no connection between Clomid and changes in sensation of hands and feet.
3. Alopecia is associated with chemotherapy, not ovulatory therapy.
4. Stuffy nose and cold-like symptoms are associated with allergies, not Clomid.

#83. 2. **The diaphragm should be washed and dried and inspected for holes before being put away.** — Ev, He/3, Ap
1. A spermicide should be used in the center of the diaphragm as well as around the rim for added protection as well as insertion ease.
3. The diaphragm should be left in place at least six hours after intercourse. If it feels "funny" it should be checked by the healthcare provider for proper fit.
4. Douching, even with the diaphragm in place, will lessen its effectiveness. Douching after intercourse is unnecessary.

#84. 1. **Cigarette smoking significantly increases a woman's risk for circulatory complications and may contraindicate oral contraceptive use.** — As, Ph/8, Ap
2. Weight gain or loss is insignificant for oral contraceptive users but important for diaphragm users.
3. Douching is unrelated to oral contraceptive use but may indicate a lack of knowledge regarding other forms of birth control.
4. Kidney or gallbladder disease is not a contraindication for oral contraceptive use, although diabetes, liver disease, and heart disease are.

#85. 2. **The procedure begins with an amniocentesis where amniotic fluid is withdrawn and replaced with saline solution.** — Im, Ph/10, Ap
1. Contractions begin 24–48 hours after saline is administered and then contractions are very strong.
3. Insertion of fluid through the cervix is done for amnioinfusion, not saline injection.
4. Saline injection causes death to the fetus before contractions begin, usually in one to two hours.

#86. 4. **Pelvic pain related to menstruation is the most common symptom of endometriosis. The pain usually ends following cessation of menses.** — As, Ph/10, An
1. Weight gain and fatigue have no relationship to endometriosis.
2. Heartburn has no relationship to endometriosis, which is bleeding of endometrial tissue located outside the uterus.
3. Some women complain of pain with defecation, but not constipation.

#87. 3. **Thick, white cottage cheese-like discharge is consistent with** *Candida albicans.* — As, Ph/10, Ap
1. Thin, greenish yellow discharge with a foul odor is consistent with trichomoniasis.
2. Yellowish discharge or no discharge is consistent with gonorrhea.
4. Thin, grayish white discharge with a fishy odor is consistent with bacterial vaginosis.

#88. 2. **This is the correct drug and dosage for an initial infection of genital herpes.** — Pl, Ph/8, Ap
1. The area should be kept as dry as possible to promote drying of the lesions.
3. This is an antibiotic and is used as part of the treatment for gonorrhea.
4. Podophyllin is used to remove venereal warts (condyloma acuminata).

#89. 1. **Syphilis is associated with stillbirth, premature birth, and neonatal death.** — An, Ph/9, Ap
2. Blindness in infants is most often caused by untreated gonorrhea when prophylactic eye care is not given.

ANSWER	RATIONALE	NP	CN	CL

3.   Mental retardation is associated with cytomegalovirus but not syphilis.

4.   Heart defects are most often associated with rubella, not syphilis.

#90. 3.   Most women benefit from caffeine and salt restriction because this reduces fluid retention and increases comfort. — Pl   Ph/9   Ap

1.   Breast self-examination should be done every month so the woman can become more familiar with her breasts and, therefore, more readily identify any irregularities.

2.   A supportive bra that fits well should be worn both day and night because support will relieve symptoms.

4.   Ice is more beneficial when breasts are sore than is heat.

#91. 3.   The breasts are softer, less tender, and swelling is reduced about a week after the beginning of the menstrual cycle. — Im   He/4   Ap

1.   The end of the menstrual cycle is the beginning of menses when the breasts are the most tender and edematous.

2.   The beginning of the menstrual cycle is the beginning of menses when the breasts are the most tender and edematous.

4.   As the end of the menstrual cycle approaches, the breasts become more tender and edematous.

#92. 3.   The ends of the three middle fingers are the most sensitive and should be used for BSE. — Ev   He/4   Ap

1.   The palms of the hands are not at all sensitive and will be very inaccurate.

2.   If the breasts are very tender, the exam is being done at the wrong time of the menstrual cycle. She should be pressing firmly to feel the deep tissue.

4.   She should be lying down for palpation or standing in the shower. It is important to inspect the breasts in the mirror for changes in shape, nipples, and dimpling of the skin.

#93. 4.   Adequate pain relief is important and the use of PCA allows the client to control her own pain relief. — Pl   Ph/9   Ap

1.   Ambulation is encouraged as soon as the effects of anesthesia are gone and fluids are tolerated.

2.   Fluids are encouraged as soon as the effects of the anesthesia have worn off.

3.   Positioning should be changed frequently and should not include the operative side.

#94. 1.   The incisional site may change with time and healing, so a permanent prosthesis should be purchased only after complete healing has occurred. — Im   Ph/9   Ap

2.   Reach to Recovery is a support group that will help her in many ways and should be encouraged.

3.   Many women are surprised at the amount of incisional pain and the length of time required for healing.

4.   She should continue her relationships with both men and women because mastectomy does not change who she is. With the help of a prosthesis, no one will know of her mastectomy unless she reveals it.

#95. 4.   Cervical dysplasia is frequently a forerunner of cervical cancer and is readily detected by Pap smear; thus follow-up Pap smears allow for early detection and treatment of cervical cancer. — Im   He/4   Ap

1.   Cervical cancer is a slow-growing disease, so regular Pap smears have a good chance to detect it before it becomes invasive.

2.   A cervical biopsy may be required to confirm or rule out cancer from suspicious cervical tissue identified by culposcopy.

3.   There are numerous high-risk factors for cervical cancer such as multiple sex partners, history of STDs and dysplasia, and intrauterine DES (diethylstilbesterol) exposure.

#96. 4.   Detection of ovarian cancer is very difficult because it gives only vague, subtle symptoms and there are no diagnostic screening tests. — Im   He/4   Ap

    1. Biannual pelvic exams may be recommended for women with a family history of ovarian cancer. Pap smears only detect cervical changes.

    2. There are no cancer markers identifiable with a CBC.

    3. While vague gastrointestinal symptoms may be early symptoms, a proctoscopy will not visualize the ovaries.

#97. 2. Retention of urine is common following vaginal hysterectomy due to stretching of musculature and proximity of the surgery to the bladder and its enervation.   An   Ph/9   An

    1. Although infection is a potential problem, there is no evidence, such as urgency or frequency, that the client has an infection.

    3. The constipation experienced by the client may be related to the surgery, but is not related to the urinary problem.

    4. There is no evidence that the client has dysuria, pain when urinating. The perineal pain is related to the surgery, but not the urinary retention.

#98. 3. After the loss of the uterus, pregnancy is unachievable and birth control is not needed even if the ovaries remain.   Ev   Ph/9   Ap

    1. Intercourse may be resumed after the tissues in the vaginal area have healed and an active, satisfying sex life may continue, although there may be some changes in sensations.

    2. Mrs. F. will never have a menstrual period again since there is no uterine lining to be shed.

    4. Orgasm is a function of the clitoris, not the uterus, so orgasm is still possible following hysterectomy.

#99. 1. Even though ovulation is erratic and many periods are anovulatory, birth control should be continued for at least six months after the last menses.   Ev   He/3   An

    2. Symptoms of menopause such as hot flashes and mood swings gradually subside and disappear by the time menses have stopped for a full year.

    3. Menopause is not an illness and most women do not experience a decline in health related to this process.

    4. Menopause is usually completed by age 54–60. Any bleeding after menses has stopped for a full year is considered abnormal and requires evaluation.

#100. 1. HRT appears to help protect many women from heart disease and osteoporosis if used with exercise and calcium supplements.   Im   Ph/8   Ap

    2. HRT may cause spotting and some bleeding for the first six months, but will not reestablish the menstrual cycle.

    3. There is no indication of declining health in the menopausal woman with or without HRT.

    4. Actually, the risk of breast cancer increases in susceptible women with the use of HRT.

Review Test 5

Psychiatric–Mental Health Nursing

1. The nurse is talking with a mother to assess her child. A positive response to which question would indicate the child is in the anal stage of psychosexual development as described by Freud?
   1. "Does he put everything in his mouth?"
   2. "Does he say 'No!' to everything you say?"
   3. "Does he like to dress up and pretend to be his father?"
   4. "Does he seem jealous when you show affection to his father?"

2. The nurse is assessing a 70-year-old woman. Which statement by the client indicates that she has achieved integrity according to Erickson's stages of personality development?
   1. "My life has been wasted."
   2. "My children no longer visit me. I am just waiting to die."
   3. "I was a good nurse when I was younger, but now I am nothing."
   4. "I have a good life and I still enjoy it, but I feel ready to go when it is time."

3. Which cognitive skill would the nurse expect a six-year-old child to be in the process of developing?
   1. Understanding of basic rules.
   2. Ability to understand abstract concepts.
   3. Recognition of object permanence.
   4. Imitation of others' actions.

4. The nurse is meeting a new client on the unit. Which action, by the nurse, is most effective in initiating the nurse-client relationship?
   1. Introduce self and explain the purpose and the plan for the relationship.
   2. Describe the nurse's family and ask the client to describe his/her family?
   3. Wait until the client indicates a readiness to establish a relationship.
   4. Ask the client why s/he was brought to the hospital.

5. Mr. P. has just been brought to the psychiatric unit and is pacing up and down the hall. The nurse is to admit him to the hospital. To establish a nurse-client relationship, which approach should the nurse try first?
   1. Assign someone to watch Mr. P. until he is calmer.
   2. Ask Mr. P. to sit down and orient him to the nurse's name and the need for information.
   3. Check Mr. P.'s vital signs, ask him about allergies, and call the physician for sedation.
   4. Explain the importance of accurate assessment data to Mr. P.

6. The nurse is beginning to establish a nurse-client relationship with Ms. E. who was referred for help in managing her children. Ms. E. arrives late for appointments and focuses on her busy schedule, the difficulty in parking, and other reasons for being late. The nurse best interprets this behavior as
   1. transference.
   2. counter-transference.
   3. identification.
   4. resistance.

7. Mrs. F. has remained close to the nurse all day. When the nurse talked with other clients during dinner, Mrs. F. tried to regain the nurse's attention and then began to shout, "You're just like my mother. You pay attention to everyone but me!" The best interpretation of this behavior is that
   1. Mrs. F. is exhibiting resistance.
   2. Mrs. F. has been spoiled by her family.
   3. The nurse has failed to meet Mrs. F.'s needs.
   4. Mrs. F. is demonstrating transference.

8. A nurse is part of a community task force on teenage suicide. The task force is considering all of the following steps in an effort to reduce teen suicide. Which action represents primary prevention?
   1. Encourage emergency room staff to request psychiatric consultation for adolescents who overdose.
   2. Educate teachers, counselors, and school nurses in recognition and early intervention with suicidal teens.
   3. Provide community programs, such as Scouts, which increase self-esteem for children and adolescents.
   4. Increase the number of inpatient adolescent psychiatric beds available in the community.

9. Two nurses are discussing plans for their client group. What should be in the plan to promote group cohesiveness?
   1. Let the group know which clients are behaving in ways approved by the nurses.
   2. Help the group identify group goals that are consistent with the individual members' goals.
   3. Make most decisions about the group in advance and make each group member aware of the nurses' decisions.
   4. Seat the most talkative members nearest the nurses where they can be more clearly heard by the group.

10. The nurse is the leader of a client group. The members relate superficially, test each other and the group rules, and compete for the nurse's attention. This behavior is typical of which stage of group development?
    1. Orientation.
    2. Working.
    3. Feedback.
    4. Termination.
11. The M. family was referred to family therapy after their teenage son experienced behavioral problems in school. Which statement by Mr. M. indicates that he understands the purpose of family therapy?
    1. "Our son will realize the consequences of his actions and try harder to behave."
    2. "It will help us learn to communicate and problem solve better as a group."
    3. "I expect the therapist to tell my wife to quit babying our son."
    4. "The therapist will tell us how to make our son behave better in school."
12. A client walks in to the mental health outpatient center and states, "I've had it. I can't go on any longer. You've got to help me." The nurse asks the client to be seated in a private interview room. Which action should the nurse take next?
    1. Reassure the client that someone will help him soon.
    2. Assess the client's insurance coverage.
    3. Find out more about what is happening to the client.
    4. Call the client's family to come and provide support.
13. The nurse is caring for a client with anorexia nervosa who is to be placed on behavior modification. Which is appropriate to include in the nursing care plan?
    1. Remind the client frequently to eat all the food served on the tray.
    2. Increase phone calls allowed the client by one per day for each pound gained.
    3. Include the family with the client in therapy sessions two times per week.
    4. Weigh the client each day at 6:00 A.M. in hospital gown and slippers after she voids.
14. Mr. G. is pacing about the unit and wringing his hands. He is breathing rapidly and complains of palpitations and nausea and he has difficulty focusing on what the nurse is saying. He says he is having a heart attack but refuses to rest. The nurse would interpret his level of anxiety as
    1. mild.
    2. moderate.
    3. severe.
    4. panic.
15. Each time Ms. H. is scheduled for a therapy session she develops headache and nausea. The nurse might interpret this behavior as
    1. conversion.

2. reaction formation.
3. projection.
4. suppression.
16. Mr. J. is admitted to the intensive care unit with chest pain, an abnormal ECG, and elevated enzymes. When the significance of this is explained to him, he says, "I can't be having a heart attack. No way. You must be mistaken." The nurse suspects the client is using which defense mechanism?
    1. Sublimation.
    2. Regression.
    3. Dissociation.
    4. Denial.
17. Mr. K. is admitted for panic attacks. He frequently experiences shortness of breath, palpitations, nausea, diaphoresis, and terror. What should the nurse include in the care plan for Mr. K. when he is having a panic attack?
    1. Calm reassurance, deep breathing, and medication as ordered.
    2. Teach Mr. K. problem solving in relation to his anxiety.
    3. Explain the physiologic responses of anxiety.
    4. Explore alternate methods for dealing with the cause of his anxiety.
18. A client on an inpatient psychiatric unit refuses to eat and states that the staff is poisoning her food. Which action should the nurse include in the client's care plan?
    1. Explain to the client that the staff can be trusted.
    2. Show the client that others eat the food without harm.
    3. Offer the client factory-sealed foods and beverages.
    4. Institute behavior modification with privileges dependent on intake.
19. Mrs. R. is being treated on the inpatient unit for depression. She tells the nurse, "I don't see how I can go on. I've been thinking of ways to kill myself. I can see several ways to do it." The best initial action for the nurse is to
    1. call the physician for orders.
    2. explain to Mrs. R. the consequences of suicide on her family.
    3. see that someone is with Mrs. R. at all times.
    4. help Mrs. R. identify alternate means of coping.
20. An adult male has been admitted to the inpatient unit with a diagnosis of depression. He states that he continues to think of suicide and will be looking for a way to kill himself in the hospital. Which is most essential for the nurse to include in his nursing care plan?
    1. Encourage the client to participate in all unit activities.
    2. Explain to the client how suicide will affect his family.

3. Allow the client time alone to relax and think.
4. Have someone stay with the client 24 hours a day.

21. While collecting data about a seven-year-old boy, the school nurse learned that he has minimal verbal skills and expresses his needs by acting out behaviors. The communication capabilities of this boy indicate which of the following levels of mental retardation?
1. Mild
2. Moderate.
3. Severe.
4. Profound.

22. The nursing care for Tim, a four-year-old boy with severe autistic disorder, is most likely to include
1. psychotropic medications.
2. social skills training.
3. play therapy.
4. group therapy.

23. The nurse makes the following assessment of a 14-year-old gymnast: underweight, hair loss, yellowish skin, facial lanugo, and peripheral edema. These findings are suggestive of which of the following disorders?
1. Anorexia nervosa.
2. Bulimia nervosa.
3. Acquired immunodeficiency.
4. Ulcerative colitis.

24. J., a 15-year-old gymnast presents in the eating disorders clinic severely emaciated, with sallow skin color, 20% body weight loss, amenorrhea for the past 12 months, and facial lanugo. Based on these findings, which one of the following nursing diagnoses would be most appropriate for the nurse to make?
1. Altered nutrition: less than body requirements.
2. Impaired tissue integrity.
3. Ineffective individual coping.
4. Knowledge deficit, nutritional.

25. Which observation of the client with anorexia indicates the client is improving?
1. The client eats meals in the dining room.
2. The client gains one pound per week.
3. The client attends group therapy sessions.
4. The client has a more realistic self-concept.

26. A client with severe Alzheimer's disease has violent outbursts, wanders, and is incontinent. He can no longer identify familiar people or objects. In developing the nursing care plan, the nurse would give highest priority to which nursing diagnosis?
1. High risk for injury.
2. Impaired verbal communication.
3. Self-care deficits.
4. Altered pattern of urinary elimination: incontinence.

27. A client with Alzheimer's disease has a self-care deficit related to his cognitive impairment. He has difficulty dressing himself. The best action for the nurse to take is to
1. have the client wear hospital gowns.
2. explain to the client why he should dress himself.
3. give the client step-by-step instructions for dressing himself.
4. allow enough time for the client to dress himself.

28. The family of a client with Alzheimer's disease indicates to the nurse an understanding of the prognosis when they say,
1. "Does another hospital have a better treatment?"
2. "Will a change in diet help his memory?"
3. "Won't his new medicine cure him?"
4. "What supports are available for the long haul?"

29. A 75-year-old man was brought to the emergency room confused, incoherent, and agitated after painting his lawn furniture earlier in the day. He has no current history of illness. Which one of the following interpretations would be appropriate for the nurse to make about his condition?
1. Depression related to aging.
2. Dementia related to organic illness.
3. Delirium related to toxin exposure.
4. Distress related to unaccomplished tasks.

30. A student with a history of barbiturate addiction is brought to the infirmary with suspected overdose. Which of the following assessments is the nurse likely to make?
1. Watery eyes, slow and shallow breathing, clammy skin.
2. Dilated pupils, shallow respirations, weak and rapid pulse.
3. Constricted pupils, respirations depressed, nausea.
4. Responsive pupils, increased respirations, increased pulse and blood pressure.

31. A 16-year-old girl is admitted to a detoxification unit with a history of cocaine abuse. Her pupils are dilated and she complains of nausea and feeling cold. She states that she is not addicted, but uses cocaine occasionally with friends. Which one of the following nursing diagnoses is appropriate for the nurse to make?
1. Impaired verbal communication related to substance use as evidenced by giving untrue information.
2. Altered growth and development related to substance use as evidenced by age of client.
3. Perceptual alteration related to substance use as evidenced by distortion of reality.
4. Ineffective denial related to substance use as evidenced in refusal to admit problem.

32. The nursing care plan for a client in early alcohol withdrawal is most likely to include

1. using physical restraints.
2. providing environmental stimulation.
3. taking pulse and blood pressure.
4. administering antipsychotic medications.

33. A client in a detox program is being manipulative by trying to split staff and ingratiating himself with certain clients. The best response of the nurse to being told he or she is the "best" staff member on the unit is to
   1. thank the client for the compliment.
   2. identify the client's manipulative behavior.
   3. ignore the client's comment.
   4. ask the client why he feels that way.

34. In developing a teaching plan for adolescents on the topic of cocaine abuse, the nurse would highlight which of the following?
   1. Cocaine is a naturally occurring depressant.
   2. Cocaine's physical effects differ according to the method of ingestion.
   3. The body's peak reaction occurs 30 minutes after it is taken.
   4. Taking cocaine by injection is particularly dangerous to the cardiovascular system.

35. A 14-year-old male client is admitted to the emergency room after ingesting a high dose of PCP and subsequently injuring himself in a fall. An effective action for the nurse to take is to
   1. attempt to talk the client down.
   2. withhold fluids.
   3. place the client in a quiet, dimly lit room.
   4. administer a prn phenothiazine.

36. Miss O., the nurse on a medical unit, observes that the relief nurse seems to be under the influence of alcohol. Miss O. smells alcohol and notices that the relief nurse's words are slurred and she is giggling inappropriately. The best initial action for Miss O. to take is to
   1. double assign the nurse's clients.
   2. ask the relief nurse if she has been drinking.
   3. report the nurse to the licensing board.
   4. refer the nurse to an employee assistance program.

37. Mr. L., a staff nurse, observes another nurse diverting meperidine (Demerol) ordered for a client and injecting it into herself. The nurse denies that she has done anything wrong and pleads with Mr. L. to remain quiet. Mr. L.'s best action is to
   1. agree to remain quiet if the nurse promises to enter treatment.
   2. notify the nurse manager/supervisor.
   3. notify a family member of the nurse.
   4. send the nurse home without saying anything.

38. The nurse evaluates that Mrs. C. may be ready for discharge from the substance abuse unit when she says,
   1. "I'll take my Antabuse when I need it."

2. "I can't wait to hang out with my old buddies."
3. "I'll drink in moderation and only on the weekend."
4. "Attending daily AA meetings will help me not drink again."

39. Which of the following assessment findings would the nurse observe in a client with schizophrenia?
   1. Associative looseness, affect disturbance, ambivalence, autistic thinking.
   2. Euphoria, distractibility, dramatic mannerisms, energetic.
   3. Argumentative, anhedonia, poor judgment, manipulative.
   4. Psychomotor retardation, intense sadness, loss of energy, suicidal.

40. A client with a diagnosis of paranoid schizophrenia reports to the nurse that he hears a voice that says, "Don't take those poisoned pills from that nurse!" Which one of the following nursing diagnoses would it be appropriate for the nurse to make regarding this statement?
   1. Sensory perceptual alteration: auditory, related to anxiety as evidenced by auditory hallucination.
   2. Altered thought processes related to anxiety as evidenced by delusions of persecution.
   3. Defensive coping related to impaired reality testing as evidenced by paranoid ideation.
   4. Impaired verbal communication related to disturbances in form of thinking as evidenced by use of symbolic references.

41. Mrs. W. is admitted with a diagnosis of catatonic schizophrenia, excited phase. She shouts and paces continuously and seems to be responding to internal stimuli. A realistic short-term goal for the nurse to formulate is
   1. Mrs. W. will groom self daily.
   2. Mrs. W. will maintain adequate nutrition.
   3. Mrs. W. will sleep eight hours per night.
   4. Mrs. W. will attend unit social activities.

42. A client with schizophrenia stops talking mid sentence and tilts her head to one side. The nurse suspects that the client is experiencing auditory hallucinations. The best initial action is for the nurse to
   1. ask the client what she is experiencing.
   2. change the topic of conversation.
   3. explain that hallucinations are not real.
   4. deny that she hears anything.

43. In teaching a client for whom clozapine (Clozaril) has been prescribed, the nurse would include which of the following?
   1. The drug will be given every four weeks by intramuscular injection.
   2. The drug will probably cause weight reduction.

3. There is a high incidence of extra pyramidal side-effects.
4. The signs and symptoms of blood dyscrasia.

44. Mr. P. is to go on a three-day pass and has his maintenance supply of chlorpromazine (Thorazine). Which statement indicates to the nurse that he understands instructions regarding his medication?
    1. "I'll take my pills when I hear those voices."
    2. "I'll drink beer but no wine while I'm away."
    3. "I'll cover up when I go to the beach."
    4. "I'll stop taking it if my mouth stays dry."

45. Which of the following behaviors indicates to the nurse that the client's antipsychotic medication is having a desired effect?
    1. The client states that her "voices" are not as threatening.
    2. The client reports having inner feelings of restlessness.
    3. The client sleeps all day.
    4. The client reports muscular stiffening in her face and arms.

46. A client taking trifluoperazine (Stelazine) exhibits severe extrapyramidal symptoms, a temperature of 105° F, and diaphoresis. The nurse suspects neuroleptic malignant syndrome. The best action of the nurse is to
    1. administer an antiparkinsonism medication.
    2. stop the neuroleptic medication.
    3. withhold fluids.
    4. administer an antianxiety medication.

47. Mr. W., a client with paranoid schizophrenia, has a delusion of persecution. He tells the nurse, "The CIA is out to get me. They're spying on me." The nurse's best initial response is,
    1. "Mr. W., I don't want to hurt you."
    2. "Mr. W., how would they spy on you here?"
    3. "Mr. W., tell me how they're trying to get you."
    4. "Mr. W., I know the CIA wouldn't want to hurt you."

48. Which of the following statements indicates to the nurse that a client with obsessive-compulsive disorder has developed insight into her problem?
    1. "I realize that the dangers are more in my mind."
    2. "I don't hear the voices anymore."
    3. "I check on my family 12 times every day."
    4. "I slept eight hours last night."

49. An adult is brought to the emergency room after he attempted to walk across the roof of a building in an attempt to "fly like a jet plane." In addition to impulsiveness, which of the behaviors identified below would the nurse assess in a client diagnosed as bipolar, manic type?

1. Hallucinations and delusions.
2. Euphoria and increased motor activity.
3. Paranoia and ideas of reference.
4. Splitting and manipulation.

50. During the focused assessment of a client with major depression, the nurse may ask which of the following questions?
    1. "You seem to have a lot of energy; when did you last have six or more hours of sleep?"
    2. "You seem to be angry with your family now; when was it that you last got along?"
    3. "Have you had any thoughts of harming yourself?"
    4. "You seem to be listening to something. Could you tell me about it?"

51. Which of the following nursing diagnoses would be most appropriate for a client who is diagnosed as bipolar I disorder, single manic episode and is intrusive, argumentative, and severely critical of peers?
    1. Impaired social interaction related to narcissistic behavior as evidenced by inability to sustain relationships.
    2. Risk for injury related to extreme hyperactivity as evidenced by increased agitation and lack of control over behavior.
    3. Social isolation related to feelings of inadequacy in social interaction as evidence by problematic interaction with others.
    4. Defensive coping related to social learning patterns as evidenced by difficulty interacting with others.

52. An adult is in an acute manic phase of bipolar disorder. He talks and paces incessantly, frequently shouting and threatening other clients. The nurse expects the client's care plan to include which of the following?
    1. Monitor blood lithium levels.
    2. Monitor client during phototherapy.
    3. Monitor client after electroconvulsive therapy.
    4. Teach client to avoid foods with tyramine.

53. The nurse is preparing to administer lithium (Eskalith) to a client with bipolar disorder. The client complains of nausea and muscle weakness, and his speech is slurred. His lithium level is 1.6 mEq/L. The best action for the nurse to take is to
    1. chart the client's symptoms after giving the lithium.
    2. explain that these are common side-effects.
    3. withhold the client's lithium.
    4. administer a prn antiparkinsonism drug.

54. Which of the following behaviors indicates to the nurse that the client understands her teaching related to lithium treatment? The client
    1. takes her lithium one hour after meals.

2. states she will stop taking her lithium when her mania subsides.
3. goes on a low salt diet to counter weight gain.
4. states she will withhold her lithium if she experiences diarrhea, vomiting, and diaphoresis.

55. An adult is recovering from a severe depression. Which of the following behaviors alerts the nurse to a risk for suicide?
    1. The client sleeps most of the day.
    2. The client has a plan to kill herself.
    3. The client loses five pounds.
    4. The client does not attend unit activities.

56. Mr. P. has been severely depressed for two weeks. He had mentioned "ending it all" prior to admission. Which of the following questions should the nurse ask during the prescreen assessment?
    1. "How long have you thought about harming yourself?"
    2. "What is it that makes you think about harming yourself?"
    3. "How has your concentration been?"
    4. "What specifically have you thought about doing to harm yourself?"

57. M., age 19, recently broke off her one year engagement. Her mother states, "She does nothing but cry and sit and stare into space. I can't get her to eat or anything!" M. feels she can't go on without her boyfriend. The nurse should make which priority nursing diagnosis for M.?
    1. Altered nutrition: less than body requirements.
    2. Dysfunctional grieving.
    3. Risk for self-directed violence.
    4. Social isolation.

58. Miss O. is admitted for treatment of a major depression. She is withdrawn, appears disheveled and states, "No one could ever love me." The nurse can expect Miss O. to be placed on
    1. antiparkinsonism medication.
    2. suicide precautions.
    3. a low salt diet.
    4. phototherapy.

59. Mr. S.'s wife complains that his depression isn't any better after one week on amitriptyline (Elavil). The nurse's best response is to
    1. tell Mrs. S. she will contact the physician.
    2. question Mrs. S. about what response she expects.
    3. explain that it may take one to three weeks to see any improvement.
    4. suggest that Mr. S. change antidepressants.

60. Which of the following behaviors indicates to the nurse that Mr. Y.'s major depression is improving? Mr. Y.
    1. displays a blunted affect.

2. has lost an additional two pounds.
3. states one "good" thing about himself.
4. sleeps about 16 hours per day.

61. Mrs. W. is hospitalized for treatment of her obsessive-compulsive disorder (OCD). The nurse recognizes which of the following as an indication that Mrs. W.'s sertraline (Zoloft) is having the desired effect?
    1. Mrs. W. experiences nervousness and drowsiness.
    2. Mrs. W.'s delusions are less entrenched.
    3. Mrs. W. engages in fewer rituals.
    4. Mrs. W. sleeps four hours per night.

62. Mr. L., a client with major depression, is scheduled for electroconvulsive therapy (ECT) tomorrow. The nurse would plan for which of the following activities?
    1. Force fluids six to eight hours before treatment.
    2. Administer succinylcholine (Inestine, Anectine) during pretreatment care.
    3. Encourage Mr. L.'s wife to accompany him.
    4. Reorient Mr. L. frequently during posttreatment care.

63. Mr. T., a severely depressed client, received ECT this morning. Which of the findings listed below would the nurse *least* expect to assess posttreatment?
    1. Headache.
    2. Memory loss.
    3. Ileus.
    4. Disorientation.

64. A client for whom Nardil was prescribed for depression is brought to the ER with severe occipital headaches after eating pepperoni pizza for lunch. Which of the following interpretations is it important for the nurse to make regarding these findings?
    1. Allergic reaction related to ingestion of processed food.
    2. Hypertensive crisis related to drug and food reaction.
    3. Panic anxiety related to unresolved issues.
    4. Conversion disorder related to uncontrolled anxiety.

65. The nurse understands that the major difference between neurotic disorders and psychotic disorders is that in psychotic disorders the clients
    1. are aware that their behaviors are maladaptive.
    2. are aware they are experiencing distress.
    3. experience no loss of contact with reality.
    4. exhibit a flight from reality.

66. The nurse realizes that Mr. L., a client taking buspirone hydrochloride (BuSpar), needs additional medication teaching when he says,
    1. "I'll take my drugs as soon as I feel anxious."
    2. "I won't drink any alcohol."
    3. "I'll report any troubles with my heart or seeing."

4. "I'll have my blood checked every month."
67. In teaching a client about her new antianxiety medication, alprazolam (Xanax), the nurse should include which of the following?
    1. Caution the client to avoid foods with tyramine.
    2. Caution the client not to drink alcoholic beverages.
    3. Instruct the client to take the Xanax one hour after meals.
    4. Instruct the client to double up a dose if she forgets to take her medication.
68. A client experiencing thanataphobia is afraid to leave her aging, ailing husband alone for any reason. She has not left her husband alone since her mother and sister died four years ago. Which of the following statements would be appropriate for the nurse to make during the initial assessment of this client?
    1. "Are you afraid that your husband might die while you are away from him?"
    2. "There must be someone you are able to trust to stay with your husband."
    3. "Don't you have children who are willing to stay with your husband when you need to be away?"
    4. "It must be very confining to have constantly attended to your husband for so long."
69. Miss B., a newly admitted client, is fearful of elevators. She needs to take one in 10 minutes to attend therapy on the 10th floor. Which of the following actions would be best for the nurse to take?
    1. Explain to Miss B. that she needs to attend therapy.
    2. Have another client go with Miss B.
    3. Accompany Miss B. to the 10th floor.
    4. Explore with Miss B. why she is afraid of elevators.
70. A man, with a family of five, was recently laid off and now has financial concerns. He is experiencing muscle tension, breathlessness, and sleep disturbances. Which one of the following nursing diagnoses would be appropriate for the nurse to make regarding his condition?
    1. Post-trauma response related to loss of economic support as evidenced by job loss.
    2. Parental role conflict related to perceived inability to meet his family's economic and physical needs as evidenced by job loss.
    3. Ineffective individual coping related to recent unemployment as evidenced by physical manifestations.
    4. Powerlessness related to inability to deal with anxiety as evidenced by physical manifestations.
71. Miss R. appears to be having a panic attack during group therapy. She is agitated, pacing rapidly, and not responding to verbal stimuli. The best initial nursing intervention is to

1. remove Miss R. from the group.
2. encourage Miss R. to express her feelings.
3. facilitate Miss R. recognizing her anxiety.
4. ignore Miss R.
72. The nurse is assessing a client who presents with OCD. In addition to gathering information about the client's anxiety and rituals, which of the following assessments should the nurse make?
    1. Hand-wringing and foot-tapping behaviors.
    2. Use of abusive substances and gambling.
    3. Tics, stuttering, or other unusual speech patterns.
    4. Diaphoresis and rapid breathing.
73. Which of the following statements by a client with delusions indicates to the nurse that the client is improving?
    1. "I don't feel those crawling bugs anymore."
    2. "I won't talk about my crazy thoughts at work."
    3. "I feel less jumpy inside."
    4. "I must check my room for bugs."
74. During the assessment phase of the nurse-client interaction, which of the following statements made by the client is suggestive of posttraumatic stress disorder?
    1. "My dad had trouble swallowing before he died and I always feel as if I have a lump in my throat."
    2. "After I contracted meningitis on vacation last summer, I can't control this horrible thought that all people who work in park restaurants are dirty."
    3. "I continue to have the same dream over and over again. At least once a month."
    4. "I had another horrible nightmare last night and went through the same trauma and anxiety all over again."
75. Miss T., a client with OCD, has an elaborate handwashing and touching ritual that interferes with her activities of daily living. She misses meals and therapy sessions. The nurse recognizes that an effective strategy to limit Miss T.'s ritual is to
    1. teach thought stopping techniques.
    2. prevent the ritualistic behavior.
    3. use adjunctive therapies for distraction.
    4. facilitate her insight regarding the need for the ritual.
76. Mrs. P. is a client with an OCD who has checking rituals and thoughts that her family will be harmed. Which of the following indicates to the nurse that Mrs. P. is improving? Mrs. P.
    1. obsesses about her family's health.
    2. adheres to the unit schedule.
    3. loses two pounds in one week.
    4. awakens eight times during the night.
77. A four-year-old girl, who is a victim of a bomb blast that demolished the building which housed her daycare, constantly builds block

houses and blows them up. She also has nightmares frequently. Which one of the following diagnoses is appropriate for the nurse to make regarding this child?
1. Post-trauma response related to terrorist attack as evidenced by destructive behaviors and sleep disturbances.
2. Explosive disorder related to dysfunctional personality as evidenced by destructive behaviors.
3. Sleep disturbance related to emotional trauma as evidenced by nightmares.
4. Ineffective individual coping related to internal stressors as evidenced by destructive behaviors and nightmares.

78. The nurse recognizes that the client with posttraumatic stress disorder (PTSD), is improving when he
1. states he feels "numb" most of the time.
2. drinks alcohol to cope with his feelings.
3. talks about a benefit of the traumatic experience.
4. attends weekly group therapy.

79. Miss P. is found wandering on campus after a fraternity party. She is disheveled and does not know who she is. She has no recollection of the evening. At the student health service she is diagnosed with dissociative amnesia subsequent to a rape. The most appropriate nursing diagnosis for the nurse to formulate is
1. ineffective individual coping.
2. personal identity disturbance.
3. anxiety related to alteration in memory.
4. high risk for violence, self-directed.

80. The nurse finds, during the initial assessment of the star player on the basketball team, that he is not concerned about the sudden paralysis of his "shooting arm." This behavior is known as
1. secondary gain.
2. la belle indifference.
3. malingering.
4. hypochondriasis.

81. Mr. M.'s family brought him into the hospital because of his many somatic complaints. He has been seen by many medical specialists in the past without discovery of organic pathology. The nurse assesses that Mr. M. is experiencing which of the following problems?
1. Conversion disorder.
2. Body dysmorphic disorder.
3. Malingering.
4. Hypochondriasis.

82. Mrs. W. is hospitalized for treatment of a conversion disorder. She complained of paralysis of her right side after her husband threatened to leave her and their children. She seems unconcerned about her paralysis. An appropriate long-term goal for the nurse to formulate is that Mrs. W. will

1. cope effectively with stress without using conversion.
2. identify stressors.
3. express feelings about the conflict.
4. develop an increased sense of relatedness to others.

83. Mr. T. has hypochondriasis—believing he is dying of stomach cancer despite repeated and extensive diagnostic testing that has all been negative. He has become reclusive and is preoccupied with his physical complaints. The nurse would include which of the following in Mr. T.'s nursing care plan? Mr. T. will
1. focus on the signs and symptoms of stomach cancer.
2. attend a support group for persons with cancer.
3. complete a contract to attend social and diversional activities daily.
4. receive secondary gain from his physical symptoms.

84. A man is brought into the police station after he ran toward a boy who resembled his son. At the police station he was unable to recall any personal information. The prescreening nurse inferred that the man has which one of the following dissociative disorders?
1. Amnesia.
2. Fugue.
3. Personality disorder.
4. Stress disorder.

85. Which of the behaviors listed below would assist the nurse in establishing the diagnosis of borderline personality disorder?
1. Impulsivity.
2. Hallucinations.
3. Self-mutilation.
4. Narcissism.

86. Miss T. is admitted to the unit with a diagnosis of borderline personality disorder. She has angry outbursts and is impulsive and manipulative. She has lacerations on her arm from self-mutilation. The priority nursing diagnosis for the nurse to formulate is
1. ineffective individual coping.
2. body image disturbance.
3. personal identity disturbance.
4. high risk for violence to self.

87. A client with borderline personality disorder tells the nurse she hates her doctor because he denied her a pass because she returned "high" from her last pass. The best nursing action for the nurse is to
1. ask the client why she is feeling so angry.
2. suggest that the client bring it up in community meeting.
3. offer to contact the doctor and discuss the situation.
4. set limits and point out that the denial is a consequence of her inappropriate behavior.

88. The nurse would formulate which of the

following outcome criteria for a client with borderline personality disorder? The client
1. displays anger frequently.
2. acts out her neediness.
3. experiences troubling thoughts without self-mutilation.
4. idolizes her nurse.

89. Mr. P., a client with antisocial personality disorder, is charming, seductive, and highly manipulative. He has a history of multiple jobs and marriages, which have all failed, and problems with the law. Which of the following is an appropriate short-term goal for the nurse to formulate in relation to a nursing diagnosis of ineffective individual coping? Mr. P. will
1. avoid situations that provoke aggressive acts.
2. adhere to unit rules.
3. assume a leadership role in unit governance.
4. acknowledge manipulative behaviors pointed out by staff.

90. Which of the following indicates to the nurse that Mr. C., a client with antisocial personality disorder, is improving? Mr. C.
1. compliments the nurse for her outstanding job on the unit.
2. tests the limits on his behavior.
3. acknowledges some manipulative behavior.
4. sleeps eight hours per night.

91. A school nurse is assessing a second grade child for symptoms of sexual abuse. Which of the following behavioral symptoms would support the possibility of sexual abuse?
1. Enuresis, impulsivity, decline in school performance.
2. Thumb sucking, isolating self from peers on playground, excessive fearfulness.
3. Hyperactivity, rocking, isolating self from peers on playground.
4. Stuttering, rocking, impulsivity.

92. A 21-year-old college student is seen in the ER following an incident of date rape. During the nursing assessment, the patient describes the entire chain of events with a blank facial expression. She ends her comments by saying, "It's like it didn't happen to me at all." Which of the following statements most accurately explains that patient's reaction?
1. This patient is using dissociation/isolation as a defense mechanism to cope with the attack.
2. This patient is using denial as a defense mechanism to cope with the attack.
3. This patient is in the shock phase of a crisis and is repressing feelings associated with the traumatic event.
4. This patient is using reaction formation to manage the hostility she feels toward the attacker.

93. A 38-year-old mother of three children is seen in the medical clinic with complaints of chronic fatigue. The woman looks sad, makes only brief eye contact, and startles easily. The nurse acknowledges these observations and the woman says, "My husband has started to hold a gun to my head when I don't do exactly what he wants." Which of the following is the most appropriate response by the nurse?
1. "What is it you won't do that makes him do this?"
2. "Tell me what has influenced your decision to stay with your husband?"
3. "That is abusive behavior; there are resources which can help you."
4. "How often does this happen?"

94. Which of the following statements made by a victim of spouse abuse would indicate to the nurse that the woman was admitting that she was a victim of spouse abuse?
1. "It would be nice to be out of the situation, but I cannot afford to leave. I have no skills."
2. "My husband has never visited me when I've been in the hospital. He even said he will take me out more often."
3. "Last time it happened I tried to talk to his mother. She said he was never like this growing up."
4. "I have the shelter number and I've decided to work on my high school diploma while the kids are in school each day."

95. A 78-year-old male with a history of cancer of the prostate is admitted to the medical unit for the fourth time in six weeks. On admission, the patient is confused and has a decubitis ulcer the size of a fifty cent piece on the sacral area. The patient did not have this breakdown on discharge 10 days ago. The nurse also notes what appear to be friction burns on both wrists. Which of the following nursing diagnosis statements takes priority in the care of this patient?
1. Skin integrity, impaired.
2. Thought processes, altered.
3. Health maintenance, altered.
4. Injury, risk for.

96. A 27-year-old is admitted to the medical unit with severe abdominal pain, dehydration, and renal insufficiency associated with substance abuse. The patient's admitting chest X-ray shows diffuse interstitial infiltrates and the physician asks that the patient give consent for HIV testing. The patient consents and the test returns positive. After learning of the positive results, the patient says to the nurse, "I never thought this would happen to me. I don't know if I can go through this." Which of the following nursing diagnosis statements is of highest priority for this patient?
1. Grieving, anticipatory.

2. Risk for infection.
3. Risk for self-directed violence.
4. Thought process, altered.

97. The nurse is changing the dressing on a patient who has had a modified radical mastectomy two days ago. The patient refuses to look in the direction of the nurse or the operative site. The nurse notices a tear running down the patient's cheek. Which of the following responses would most appropriately facilitate the patient's grief resolution?
1. "You look very sad, it might help you feel better if you let yourself cry."
2. "Tell me what's the worst part about losing your breast."
3. "Everything is going to be all right; you can be fitted for a new bra and no one will notice."
4. "Are you crying because you are concerned about how your partner will respond?"

98. A 42-year-old male is admitted to the medical unit for insertion of an access site for hemodialysis. The patient relates that his transplant graft failed, he has lost his job due to corporate downsizing, and his wife left him recently. He has now moved back into his parents' home. Which of the following nursing diagnosis statements takes priority in planning nursing care for this patient?
1. Fluid volume deficit.
2. Ineffective denial.
3. Tissue perfusion altered; renal.
4. Powerlessness.

99. The condition of a patient diagnosed with chronic obstructive pulmonary disease (COPD) and cor pulmonale is deteriorating. The patient is very hypoxemic, obtunded, and easily fatigued by any activity. The nurse who has been working with this patient through-out this hospitalization is repositioning the patient. Which of the following remarks made by the patient indicates that the patient has come to terms with death?
1. "It is finally spring and that is my favorite time of year."
2. "Am I going to die?"
3. "I'm very tired, but content and ready to go."
4. "I'm feeling stronger by the moment today."

100. A family member whose mother is terminally ill asks to speak to the nurse. Which of the following statements made by this family member should indicate to the nurse that this family member understands the emotional response to death and dying?
1. "Mother seems very comfortable; so we're able to recall some of our good times spent together."
2. "My mother is irate because she says you all told her she had to have an advanced directive."
3. "My mother is talking about redoing her bedroom when she's discharged. Doesn't she know she's dying?"
4. "My mother is crying so much these days. Where's all this sadness coming from?"

Answers and Rationales for Review Test 5

Psychiatric–Mental Health Nursing

ANSWER	RATIONALE	NP	CN	CL
#1. 2.	**Negativism is common to the toddler in the anal stage of development (age one to three) who is learning to assert his independence and mastery.**	As	Ps/5	An
1.	Testing everything with the mouth is part of the oral stage (birth to one year).			
3.	Identification with the same-sex parent occurs in the oedipal stage (ages three to six).			
4.	Children in the oedipal stage (ages three to six) often show jealousy of the same-sex parent.			
#2. 4.	**Integrity includes acceptance of changes; a sense of continuity of past, present, and future; and acceptance of death.**	As	Ps/5	An
1.	Despair, the failure to achieve integrity in old age, is characterized by feelings of worthlessness and futility.			
2.	Loneliness and resignation result from despair, the failure to achieve integrity in old age.			

ANSWER	RATIONALE	NP	CN	CL
	3. Lack of a reason to continue living is characteristic of despair.			
#3. 1.	**Preoperational-preconceptual children (five to seven years old) are learning to integrate concepts based on relationships and can comprehend the basic rules.**	As	Ps/5	Co
	2. The ability to understand abstract concepts does not occur until the formal operations stage (12–15 years).			
	3. Object permanence is part of the sensorimotor period (birth to two years).			
	4. Imitation of others is common in the sensorimotor period (birth to two years).			
#4. 1.	**The client needs orientation to the nurse and the situation. An open, honest approach in sharing this initial data will set the tone for the relationship.**	Im	Ps/5	Ap
	2. Describing the nurse's family focuses the relationship on the nurse, when it should be focused on the client.			
	3. The nurse must take the initiative in the relationship; psychiatric clients usually have problems relating to others and cannot be expected to take the initiative.			
	4. Why questions are rarely appropriate. Any questions should wait until the nurse has established a relationship.			
#5. 2.	**Many clients are anxious at the time of admission and are often reassured by a calm, competent professional approach, which should always be tried first. If the client is unable to respond to this, then other measures, such as medication, may be necessary.**	Im	Ps/5	Ap
	1. Mr. P. needs intervention, not observation, at this point.			
	3. The nurse should attempt to establish a relationship with Mr. P. before touching him or asking questions.			
	4. This client is too anxious to respond to detailed explanations.			
#6. 4.	**Resistance is characterized by conscious or unconscious actions that sabotage the relationship and thus help the client avoid confronting issues that may increase anxiety.**	An	Ps/5	Ap
	1. Transference involves the client responding to the therapist as to someone in the past, usually a parent or sibling.			
	2. In counter-transference, the therapist responds to the client as he or she did to someone in a past relationship.			
	3. In identification, the client attempts to be like the therapist.			
#7. 4.	**Transference is the unconscious transfer of qualities originally associated with another relationship to the nurse. These are often qualities associated with a parent or sibling and may provoke responses from the client that are not appropriate to the situation.**	An	Ps/5	Ap
	1. Resistance is characterized by conscious or unconscious actions by the client which sabotage the relationship. There is no clear evidence of resistance in this situation.			
	2. There is no evidence of "spoiling" in this situation. The client actually suggests that she felt neglected at home.			
	3. There is no evidence of neglect by the nurse in the situation.			
#8. 3.	**Primary prevention involves making changes in the community that promote health and prevent disease.**	Im	Ps/5	Co
	1. Actions that limit the disability from illness after it occurs are tertiary prevention.			
	2. Recognition and early intervention when a problem is suspected are secondary prevention.			
	4. Provision for better treatment of existent illness is tertiary prevention.			
#9. 2.	**Goals that are best met by a group and that are consistent with the goals of the individual members foster cohesive groups.**	Pl	Ps/6	Ap
	1. The group should be encouraged to establish its own norms and to let clients know how their behavior affects them.			

3. Lack of decision making by the group will decrease group cohesion. The nurses should help the group set its own goals.

4. The nurses need to guide the group to set its own limits and to encourage every member of the group to participate and to be heard.

#10. 1. During the orientation phase, group members demonstrate these behaviors as they try to identify and develop trust with the group.   An   Ps/6   Co

2. In the working phase, members develop trust, discuss feelings, and listen to each other.

3. In the termination phase, members indicate their goals have been met and begin to separate from each other.

4. Feedback is not a phase of group development, but a healthy process of sharing perceptions within the group.

#11. 2. Family therapy is aimed at improving communication and problem solving within the family group. The focus is on the family as a group, not on correcting the behavior of any one.   Ev   Ps/6   Ap

1. The focus of family therapy is not to correct the behavior of any one individual but to increase communication within the family. The son may realize how his behavior affects the others in his family as they learn to communicate more clearly with one another.

3. The goal of family therapy is for the family to discuss this issue together, not for the therapist to point blame.

4. Family therapy should help the family function better together, but the goal is not to correct the behavior of any one family member. All member of the family will probably make changes as a result of family therapy.

#12. 3. The nurse must assess the client and his situation before the appropriate action can be determined.   As   Ps/6   Ap

1. This client needs immediate attention. The nurse cannot be sure that he can be helped until more data are gathered about the situation.

2. This is not the primary need at this time.

4. Calling the client's family may be a realistic intervention, but more data are needed first.

#13. 2. In behavior modification, rewards are tied to specific goals.   Pl   Ps/6   Ap

1. Clients with anorexia nervosa need to focus away from food and weight. They do not benefit from reminders to eat. Behavior modification substitutes specific goals and rewards for reminders and nagging.

3. Family therapy may benefit this client, but that is not a part of the behavior modification program.

4. It is usually recommended that clients with anorexia be weighed weekly rather than daily. This response does not set any goals or rewards.

#14. 4. Terror, physiologic changes, and inability to focus on the real world are characteristic of the most extreme form of anxiety, panic.   An   Ps/5   Ap

1. Mild anxiety is characterized by a relaxed body, feelings of security, and an open perceptual field.

2. Moderate anxiety involves feelings of challenge focused on selected stimuli and some sympathetic nervous system activation.

3. Severe anxiety includes further restriction of perceptual capacity, agitation, and sympathetic activation.

#15. 1. Conversion changes anxious feelings into somatic symptoms.   An   Ps/5   Ap

2. Reaction formation is demonstration of attitudes opposite those really felt.

3. Projection attributes the client's own feelings to others.

4. Suppression is conscious exclusion of unwanted thoughts or feelings.

#16. 4. Denial helps the person escape unpleasant or intolerable reality by refusing to perceive the facts. It can serve as a normal   An   Ps/5   Ap

ANSWER	RATIONALE	NP	CN	CL

protection in the early stages of crisis, but if the denial persists it will prevent the client from coping.

   1. Sublimation is diversion of unacceptable impulses to an acceptable outlet.

   2. Regression is a return to an earlier stage of development.

   3. Dissociation is separation or compartmentalization of painful feelings.

#17. 1. Before any other interventions can be used, the client in panic must reduce his anxiety to a manageable level. The other interventions might be used when the client is less anxious.   Pl   Ps/6   Ap

   2. This is a long-term goal, not possible or appropriate when the client is having a panic attack.

   3. During a panic attack, the client cannot comprehend explanations of any kind of detail.

   4. While the client is in acute panic, he cannot respond to explorations. This is a long-term goal.

#18. 3. The client may be able to eat food that the staff has not handled.   Pl   Ps/6   Ap

   1. Telling the client that the staff can be trusted most likely will increase his suspicion.

   2. Because delusions persist in spite of logical evidence to the contrary, explanations and demonstration only increase the client's suspicion that the staff will cause harm.

   4. Coercion to comply with the staff requests will only increase the client's anxiety and suspicion.

#19. 3. Maintaining client safety is the first priority. When a client is actively suicidal, one to one observation is necessary.   Im   Ps/6   Ap

   1. If this is a new development, the physician should be notified, but only after the client's safety is ensured.

   2. Explaining the consequences of suicide usually only increases guilt and worthlessness but does not act as a deterrent to the acutely suicidal individual.

   4. Identification of other means of coping is a long-term goal to be pursued when the client is not acutely suicidal.

#20. 4. The client who is actively suicidal needs constant observation to prevent him from carrying out his plan.   Pl   Ps/6   Ap

   1. When a client is this depressed, participation is too great a burden.

   2. Rational explanation may only increase his feelings of worthlessness.

   3. While the client should not be pushed into participation, he should not be left alone (for his own safety). He should be reassured of his worth and be discouraged from rumination over shame and guilt.

#21. 3. Individuals with severe mental retardation possess minimal verbal skills. They often communicate wants and needs by acting our behaviors.   As   Ps/5   Co

   1. In mild mental retardation, a child is capable of developing social skills.

   2. In moderate mental retardation, the child may experience some limitation in speech communication.

   4. In profound mental retardation, the child will exhibit little, if any, speech development.

#22. 3. Play therapy would be most effective for Tim given his developmental level and autism. In autistic disorder, communication with others is severely impaired. Through one to one play therapy, the therapist may establish rapport through nonverbal play.   Pl   Ps/6   Co

   1. Psychotropic medications are used less frequently with children because of side-effects, also they are not highly effective in autistic disorder.

   2. Tim does not have the capabilities to engage in social skills training at this time. The goal of this training is to increase the ability to handle stressful interpersonal situations.

4.   Tim does not have the ability to engage in activity-oriented or verbal group process.

#23. 1.   **Anorexia nervosa, usually occurring in individuals ages 13–22 years, is an eating disorder characterized by self-starvation, weight loss (25% below normal weight), disturbance in body image, and physiologic and metabolic changes.**   As   Ps/5   Co

    2.   Although bulimia nervosa is also an eating disorder, the characteristics are chipmunk faces, chronic hoarseness, dental caries, dehydration, electrolyte imbalance.

    3.   In acute HIV infection, the characteristic symptoms are fever, myalgia, sore throat, lymphadenopathy, anorexia, skin rash, and diarrhea.

    4.   Ulcerative colitis, a chronic mucosal inflammatory disease of the colon and rectum presents with diarrhea (15–20 liquid stools per day); the stools may contain blood, mucus, and pus. There is fever, anorexia, weight loss, nausea, and vomiting.

#24. 1.   **The assessment data and history of the client support the diagnosis of altered nutrition related to anorexia.**   An   Ps/6   Ap

    2.   The client is high risk for impaired tissue integrity owing to poor nutrition and dehydration. However, the data support a primary diagnosis of altered nutrition.

    3.   There are insufficient data to support an ineffective coping diagnosis.

    4.   The client may have a knowledge deficit regarding nutrition; however, the data do not support this diagnosis.

#25. 2.   **Weight gain is the best indication that the client's anorexia is improving. A realistic expectation is for the client to gain one pound per week.**   Ev   Ps/6   Ap

    1.   This does not necessarily indicate that the client's anorexia is improving. She may purge after eating.

    3.   This behavior is not an indication of improvement for anorexia.

    4.   A disturbance in body image, a component of self-concept, is a factor in anorexia, but is not the best indicator of improvement.

#26. 1.   **Safety is of highest concern for this client. His wandering and memory loss pose hazards for accidents, falls, and injuries.**   Pl   Ps/6   An

    2.   Although communicating with a client with Alzheimer's disease becomes progressively more difficult, it is not the highest priority.

    3.   The inability to engage in self-care is characteristic in late-stage dementia, but is not the highest priority for intervention.

    4.   The client's incontinence supports this diagnosis, but it is not the priority concern.

#27. 3.   **The client may need step-by-step instructions so he can focus on small amounts of information. This allows him to perform at his optimal level. Clients with dementia may not remember how to dress themselves.**   Im   Ps/6   Ap

    1.   To maintain dignity and identity, the client should wear his own clothing, which should be labeled. Clothing should have elastic or Velcro fastenings.

    2.   This action is inappropriate and inconsistent with his capabilities.

    4.   This action would not be effective because the client needs assistance in dressing.

#28. 4.   **This response indicates that the family is expecting to need support during the process of the client's increasing cognitive impairment.**   Ev   Ps/6   An

    1.   There is no specific treatment for Alzheimer's disease.

    2.   The memory deficits increasingly worsen and are not affected by diet.

    3.   There is currently no cure for Alzheimer's disease.

#29. 3.   **Delirium is a state of mental confusion and excitement. The mind wanders, speech is incoherent, and the client is often in a state of continual, aimless physical activity. The onset is rapid (hours to days). Paint is a toxin that could cause delirium.**   An   Ps/6   An

ANSWER		RATIONALE	NP	CN	CL
	1.	Although the onset of depression may be rapid (weeks to months) there is usually a sad, depressed affect.			
	2.	Dementia is a global impairment of intellectual functions, which is usually progressive.			
	4.	Distress is a subjective response to internal or external stimuli that is threatening or perceived as threatening to self.			
#30.	2.	**The effects of overdose of barbiturates are shallow respirations, cold and clammy skin, dilated pupils, weak and rapid pulse, coma, and possible death.**	As	Ps/6	Co
	1.	Watery eyes, runny nose, yawning, slow and shallow breathing, and clammy skin are the effects of withdrawal and overdose of narcotics.			
	3.	These are the possible effects of narcotic use.			
	4.	Hyperalertness and increased vital signs are suggestive of stimulant (cocaine) use.			
#31.	4.	**Denial is the minimizing or disavowing of symptoms or a situation to the detriment of health.**	An	Ps/6	An
	1.	The client is in denial.			
	2.	There is insufficient evidence to support this diagnosis.			
	3.	There is insufficient evidence to support the distortion of reality.			
#32.	3.	**Pulse and blood pressure should be checked hourly for the first 8–12 hours after admission. They are usually elevated during withdrawal and the pulse is a good indication of progress through withdrawal. Elevation may indicate impending alcohol withdrawal delirium.**	Pl	Ps/6	Ap
	1.	People in withdrawal are usually terrified and anxious. Physical restraint is contraindicated.			
	2.	Clients in withdrawal need a quiet, consistent, and secure environment. Excess stimulation may exacerbate illusions and hallucinations.			
	4.	The medications of choice are cross-dependent sedatives such as the benzodiazepines, diazepam (Valium), and chlordiazepoxide hydrochloride (Librium).			
#33.	2.	**A priority in intervening in manipulative behavior is to identify it and then set limits by stating expected behaviors.**	Im	Ps/6	Ap
	1.	This response is inappropriate because it would reinforce the client's manipulation.			
	3.	Ignoring the client's comment does not facilitate his responsibility for his manipulative behavior.			
	4.	This response is inappropriate in relation to his reason for manipulation and reinforces it.			
#34.	4.	**A total cardiac collapse may occur. Freebasing is the method that most often leads to myocardial infarction.**	Pl	Ps/6	Ap
	1.	Cocaine is a central nervous system stimulant.			
	2.	Cocaine's physical effects are identical. Differences include the speed, strength, and duration of effects.			
	3.	The peak reaction occurs about five minutes after ingestion.			
#35.	3.	**Environmental stimuli need to be reduced for the client in PCP intoxication to reduce danger to self, paranoia, delusions, and hallucinations. These clients are sensitive to stimuli and quickly become combative and assaultive.**	Im	Ps/6	Ap
	1.	Reassurance, verbal support, and touch are rarely useful and, in fact, may trigger agitation and combativeness. Only one staff member should interact minimally with the client.			
	2.	Clients in PCP intoxication may lose a lot of fluids due to diaphoresis and hyperpyrexia. Acidic fruit juices increase the excretion of PCP from the body.			
	4.	Phenothiazines are contraindicated because they potentiate the anticholinergic actions of PCP. Diazepam (Valium) and haloperidol (Haldol) may be used.			
#36.	2.	**There is usually a chain of command policy that begins with a**	Im	Sa/1	Ap

direct discussion of the involved parties. **If the relief nurse denies drinking, Miss O. has a duty to intervene.**

   1.   This action is inappropriate and does not directly deal with the problem. It violates the duty to intervene if the safety of clients is at risk.

   3.   This would not be the initial action. Most states do require reporting of impaired or incompetent colleagues. This is not usually the first step in a chain of command policy.

   4.   This may be an intervention appropriate later for the nurse's rehabilitation, but does not protect the safety of the clients at the present time.

#37. 2.   **The hospital's chain of command policy must be followed. The duty to intervene to protect patients from harm must be followed in light of the nurse's poor judgment, etc.**   Im   Sa/1   Ap

   1.   This action violates the duty to intervene and colludes with the nurse.

   3.   This action may be warranted at some point, but fails to uphold the duty to intervene to protect clients from harm.

   4.   While the nurse should not remain on duty, this action violates the duty to intervene.

#38. 4.   **Daily attendance at AA meetings is necessary for most discharged clients to remain sober and continue their rehabilitation.**   Ev   Ps/6   An

   1.   Antabuse must be taken daily for it to be effective in maintaining sobriety.

   2.   Most clients need to resocialize and avoid old friends who are associated with drinking. An entirely new lifestyle must be developed.

   3.   Most clients need to avoid ingesting any alcohol to maintain sobriety.

#39. 1.   **Eugen Bleuler's 4 As of schizophrenia are loosening of associations (L.O.A.), which are representative of thought disorders, disturbance in effect, ambivalence, and autistic thinking.**   As   Ps/6   Co

   2.   These are the emotional, cognitive, behavioral, and physical manifestations of bipolar disorder.

   3.   These are the behavioral, emotional, cognitive, and interpersonal behaviors of borderline personality disorder.

   4.   These are the physical and emotional manifestations of depression.

#40. 1.   **Hallucinations are sensory experiences of perception without corresponding stimuli in the environment.**   An   Ps/6   An

   2.   Although the content of the statement is delusional in nature, the statement itself is an hallucinatory experience.

   3.   The statement suggests that the client fears that the pills will harm him; however the statement is an hallucinatory experience.

   4.   There are no data to support symbolic reference.

#41. 2.   **It is important for the nurse to monitor dietary intake and weight so the person does not lose calories and fluids due to hyperactivity. "Finger foods" may need to be provided, e.g., sandwiches and fruit.**   Pl   Ps/6   An

   1.   At this stage, Mrs. W. will probably need help in grooming and other self-care activities.

   3.   In this phase of hyperactivity, it is unrealistic to expect that Mrs. W. will sleep eight hours per night. Frequent rest periods should be provided to prevent exhaustion and fatigue.

   4.   At this stage, Mrs. W. may be too overstimulated by large group activities. One to one activities or activities involving large muscle groups would be more effective.

#42. 1.   **The best initial action is to focus on the cues and elicit the client's description of her experience. It is important for the nurse to determine that she is hallucinating and the content. This is vital in relation to safety issues and command hallucinations.**   Im   Ps/5   Ap

ANSWER	RATIONALE	NP	CN	CL

2. This is inappropriate and does not meet the client's needs nor heighten the nurse's understanding.

3. This is not the best initial response. The nurse would indicate to the client that she understands the voices are real to her but are not heard by the nurse.

4. The nurse would indicate later that she does not hear the voices. This would reinforce reality, but the nurse should not argue about their existence.

#43. 4. Symptoms of blood dyscrasias such as sore throat, fever, malaise, unusual bleeding, need to be taught. Weekly white blood cell counts may be required.   Pl   Ph/8   Co

1. Clozapine is given orally in daily doses of usually 300–450 mg.

2. Weight reduction is not common for clients taking clozapine.

3. Clozapine has a very low incidence of extrapyramidal side-effects.

#44. 3. Mr. P. should avoid the sun or cover up and use sunscreen to protect himself from severe photosensitivity.   Ev   Ph/8   An

1. Mr. P. should take his maintenance dose on a daily basis and not as a "prn."

2. Mr. P. should avoid all alcoholic beverages because they could enhance the drug's central nervous system depression.

4. Dry mouth is a common autonomic side-effect. The drug should not be discontinued.

#45. 1. A desired effect of the antipsychotics is to reduce the disturbing quality of hallucinations and delusions.   Ev   Ph/8   An

2. This reaction is probably akathisia, an extrapyramidal side-effect.

3. The sedation effects of the antipsychotics may be desirable early in treatment, but are a liability if the client is too sedated to engage in therapy.

4. This reaction is probably pseudoparkinsonism, an extrapyramidal side-effect.

#46. 2. The neuroleptic should be immediately discontinued. Medical treatment should be instituted because this is a potentially fatal syndrome.   Im   Ph/8   Ap

1. This is not an effective medication for neuroleptic malignant syndrome.

3. The client will probably require oral and IV fluids.

4. This is not an effective treatment for neuroleptic malignant syndrome.

#47. 1. The nurse should first clarify her intent and then empathize with the underlying feeling.   Im   Ps/6   Ap

2. The nurse should not discuss the content of the delusion nor try to use logic to refute it.

3. The nurse should not reinforce the delusion by discussing the content.

4. This response is inappropriate in trying to use logic and sounds like false reassurance.

#48. 1. This statement indicates that the client has some insight into the underlying reason for her rituals.   Ev   Ps/6   An

2. Auditory hallucinations are not a common feature of obsessive-compulsive disorder.

3. This statement acknowledges her compulsive behavior but does not indicate insight.

4. Sleep disturbance may occur in obsessive-compulsive disorder related to preoccupation with the obsession and compulsions. Sleeping through the night, however, does not indicate insight.

#49. 2. The client diagnosed as bipolar, manic exhibits behaviors of elation, euphoria, and is full of energy, which may lead to exhaustion.   As   Ps/6   Co

1. Hallucination and delusions are the hallmarks of schizophrenia.

ANSWER	RATIONALE	NP	CN	CL

3. Although the client diagnosed as bipolar, manic may present paranoid and delusional, especially if psychotic, these behaviors are often not present.

4. These behaviors are associated with borderline personality disorder.

#50. 3. Clients with major depression are often suicidal. The first concern of assessment is the risk of suicide potential in the immediate future.   As   Ps/6   Ap

1. This question would be more appropriate for the client who is hypo manic.

2. This question would be appropriate for the client with borderline personality disorder who uses splitting as a defense.

4. This question would be appropriate for the client who appears to be hallucinating.

#51. 2. The client who invades the space of others, creates arguments, and attacks others is at risk for injury by those in the environment.   An   Ps/6   An

1. The impaired social relationship is related to the client's hypomanic behavior.

3. Although social interaction may be a problem, the problem of risk for injury is more appropriate for the behavior described.

4. There are insufficient data to support the diagnosis of defensive coping.

#52. 1. Lithium is the drug of choice for manic clients with an antimanic effectiveness of 78%. It reduces the intensity, duration, and frequency of manic and depressive episodes. Blood levels are monitored for therapeutic levels in the acute phase (1.0–1.5 mEq/L) and during maintenance.   Pl   Ps/6   Ap

2. Phototherapy is used for clients with seasonal affective disorder.

3. Electroconvulsive therapy is primarily used for depressed clients.

4. Foods with tyramine are contraindicated for clients taking Monoamine oxidase inhibitor (MAOI) antidepressants.

#53. 3. The client is exhibiting symptoms and signs of lithium toxicity. Another blood level should be drawn and the dose evaluated.   Im   Ph/8   Ap

1. A priority is to withhold the medication because of signs of toxicity. The symptoms should be recorded.

2. These are signs of lithium toxicity.

4. This is not an accurate intervention.

#54. 4. These are early signs of lithium toxicity. The drug should be withheld and a lithium blood level drawn and evaluated to determine an appropriate dosage.   Ev   Ph/8   An

1. Lithium is irritating to the gastric mucosa. Therefore, it should be taken with meals.

2. A maintenance dose of lithium must be taken to maintain an adequate blood level and prevent relapse.

3. A low sodium intake causes an increase in lithium retention, which could lead to toxicity.

#55. 2. Having a suicide plan is a risk factor. The lethality needs to be assessed. When a depression is "lifting," the client may have the energy and resources to carry out a plan. Behavioral, somatic, and emotional cues may be overt or covert.   An   Ps/6   An

1. This may indicate sleep disturbance in depression but is not indicative of a suicide risk.

3. This may be related to altered nutrition secondary to the anorexia of depression but is not indicative of a suicide risk unless the weight loss is significant.

4. Social isolation and withdrawal are common in depression and do not necessarily indicate a suicide risk.

#56. 4. This question assists in determining suicidal intent and lethality.   As   Ps/6   Ap

1. The length of time that the client has entertained suicidal ideation

ANSWER	RATIONALE	NP	CN	CL

helps to determine duration of the depression, but does not address intent and lethality.

2. This question is nontherapeutic. It requires the client to consider an external source of power.

3. Although the client with major depression has difficulty concentrating, this question does not address suicidal intent.

#57. 3. The depressed client often feels hopeless and helpless with self-directed anger. Suicidal ideations are often expressed and warrant immediate intervention. — An · Ps/6 · An

1. Although M. is not eating, suicidal ideations take priority at this time.
2. M. is depressed due to loss; however, the potential for self-harm is a priority.
4. M. is withdrawn; however, the potential for self-harm is a priority.

#58. 2. Maintaining safety for Miss O. is a priority because she may have suicidal ideation and/or a plan. — Pl · Ps/6 · Ap

1. Miss O. would probably be placed on an antidepressant medication.
3. A low salt diet is not indicated for Miss O.
4. Phototherapy is a treatment of choice for clients with seasonal affective disorder.

#59. 3. Mr. S. may need to take Elavil one to three weeks before any improvement or a therapeutic effect is noticed. — Im · Ph/8 · Ap

1. This is not an effective action due to the length of time expected before improvement occurs.
2. This is not effective in relation to Mrs. S.'s knowledge deficit.
4. Another antidepressant would be used after waiting one to three weeks for a therapeutic effect.

#60. 3. This behavior may indicate an increase in self-esteem that accompanies an improvement in depression. A depressed person often cannot problem solve or acknowledge any positive aspects of their lives. — Ev · Ps/6 · An

1. This behavior may indicate that Mr. Y. has a severe depression in which clients often feel no emotion or feel empty (anhedonia).
2. This behavior may indicate a severe depression in which Mr. Y. has no appetite (anorexia), resulting in altered nutrition.
4. This behavior is indicative of sleep disturbance (hypersomnia) in severe depression.

#61. 3. Zoloft is a selective serotonin reuptake inhibitor (SSRI) that is effective in treating clients with obsessive compulsive disorder. Using fewer rituals would indicate an improvement. — Ev · Ph/8 · Ap

1. These are common side-effects of the SSRIs.
2. Zoloft is not effective in treating delusional content.
4. This behavior may indicate insomnia, a common sleep disturbance in depressed clients.

#62. 4. Common side-effects of bilateral treatment include confusion, disorientation, and short-term memory loss. The nurse should provide frequent orientation statements that are brief, distinct, and simple. — Pl · Ph/9 · Ap

1. Fluids are withheld for six to eight hours before treatment.
2. Anectine, thiopental (Pentathol), and oxygen are administered during treatment.
3. Mr. L. is taken to a special room for the treatment and recovery. It is inappropriate for his wife to accompany him.

#63. 3. ECT is treated as an operative procedure; however, ileus (intestinal obstruction, especially failure of peristalsis) frequently accompany peritonitis and usually result from disturbances in the bowel. — As · Ph/9 · Co

1. Headache is commonly seen following ECT.
2. Memory loss is commonly seen following ECT.
4. Disorientation is commonly seen following ECT.

#64. 2. Severe occipital and/or temporal pounding headaches, — An · Ph/8 · An manifestations of hypertensive crisis, occur when processed meats are eaten by individuals currently taking nardil (MAOI).

1. The client may be allergic to something eaten, however, the first interpretation is a drug/food reaction given the client's history.
3. There are insufficient data to support panic anxiety attack.
4. There are insufficient data to support conversion disorder.

#65. 4. In psychotic responses to anxiety, clients escape from reality into hallucination and/or delusional behavior.   An   Ps/5   Co

1. Persons with neurotic disorders are aware that their behaviors are maladaptive; persons with psychotic disorders are not.
2. Persons with neurotic disorders are aware they are experiencing distress; persons with psychotic disorders are not.
3. Persons with neurotic disorders experience no loss of contact with reality; persons with psychotic disorders exhibit a flight from reality.

#66. 1. BuSpar must be taken as a maintenance drug, not as a prn response to symptoms. Improvement may be noted in 7–10 days, but it may take three to four weeks to note therapeutic effects.   Ev   Ph/8   An

2. Alcoholic beverages should be avoided by clients taking BuSpar.
3. These are less common side-effects of BuSpar, which should be reported.
4. Liver, renal, and blood count tests should be done regularly on clients on long-term therapy.

#67. 2. The depressant effects of alcohol and alprazolan will be potentiated and may cause harmful sedation.   Im   Ph/8   Ap

1. This caution is appropriate for clients on MAOI antidepressants.
3. Medication should be taken with or soon after meals to minimize gastric discomfort.
4. The client should not increase the dose or frequency without prior approval.

#68. 1. Confronting fear diminishes the phobic response and the anticipatory anxiety that precedes it.   As   Ps/5   Ap

2. This statement does not help the client confront her fear.
3. This statement does not help the client confront her fear.
4. This statement does not help the client confront her fear.

#69. 3. This is the best action because the nurse is conveying her support of Miss B. and her needs. Later, she would need to further assess Miss B.'s fear of elevators and respond accordingly.   Im   Ps/6   Ap

1. This action does not respond to Miss B.'s fear of the elevator. Knowing the importance of attending therapy will not affect her fear nor support her.
2. This action is inappropriate until the nurse conducts a further assessment.
4. This is not a timely action and probably would not reduce Miss B.'s fear in the short term.

#70. 2. Parental role conflict is the state in which a parent experiences role confusion and conflict in response to crisis. Loss of economic base constitutes a crisis state.   An   Ps/6   An

1. There are insufficient data to support a posttrauma response.
3. Even though the client has generalized anxiety, there are insufficient data to support ineffective individual coping.
4. There are insufficient data to support powerlessness.

#71. 1. The nurse should remove Miss R. from the group to provide a safe environment for her and others. The nurse should stay with Miss R. and provide comfort and reality orientation.   Im   Ps/6   Ap

2. This is an unrealistic expectation at this point. Later, the nurse would attempt to have Miss R. link her feelings prior to the attack to its onset.
3. This is a realistic and important intervention after Miss R.'s anxiety has lowered.

ANSWER	RATIONALE	NP	CN	CL
4.	This response would not meet Miss R.'s need nor the needs of group members.			
#72. 3.	**There is comorbidity between Tourette's syndrome and obsessive-compulsive disorder.**	As	Ps/6	Ap
1.	Hand-wringing and foot-tapping behaviors are characteristic of generalized anxiety.			
2.	Substance abuse and gambling are often characteristic of borderline personality disorder.			
4.	Diaphoresis and rapid breathing are characteristics of generalized anxiety.			
#73. 2.	**Improvement in relation to delusional content includes a reduction in the disturbing quality of the delusion and the client's ability to control and/or not respond to them.**	Ev	Ps/6	An
1.	This would indicate a response to a tactile hallucination.			
3.	This would not be a feature of delusions and may indicate agitation or akathisia.			
4.	This would indicate that the client is responding to a delusional belief that his room is "bugged."			
#74. 4.	**Symptoms of posttraumatic stress disorder range from emotional "numbness" to vivid nightmares in which the traumatic event is recalled.**	As	Ps/6	An
1.	This statement is a defining characteristic of somatoform disorders.			
2.	This statement is representative of obsessive thinking.			
3.	The content of the statement is not related to a stressful event.			
#75. 1.	**Thought stopping techniques, flooding, and response prevention have proven effective in treating clients with OCD. Clients may shout or think "stop" or snap a rubber band on their wrist to dismiss the obsessive thought.**	Pl	Ps/6	Ap
2.	Preventing the ritualistic behavior is likely to increase Miss T.'s anxiety to the panic level.			
3.	Using therapies for distraction is both inappropriate and ineffective.			
4.	Gaining insight usually has little effect on an OCD client's need for the performance of rituals.			
#76. 2.	**If Mrs. P. adheres to the unit schedule, it is likely that her obsessions and compulsive rituals have lessened. They no longer preoccupy her to the point of interfering with activities.**	Ev	Ps/6	An
1.	This would indicate that Mrs. P. continues to have obsessive thoughts.			
3.	It is likely that Mrs. P.'s rituals would have interfered with her food intake and a weight gain would indicate improvement.			
4.	This would indicate sleep disturbance related to obsessive thoughts.			
#77. 1.	**Posttrauma response is the state of an individual experiencing a sustained painful response to an overwhelming traumatic event.**	An	Ps/6	An
2.	There is insufficient evidence to support dysfunctional personality.			
3.	Although there is evidence to support sleep disturbance, the most appropriate diagnosis is posttraumatic response, which is supported by the data.			
4.	Posttrauma victims cope by reliving the experience in a variety of ways.			
#78. 3.	**Cognitive treatment for PTSD includes redefining the event by considering benefits of the experience and finding meaning in the experience.**	Ev	Ps/6	An
1.	Psychic numbness, constricted effect, and avoidance behavior are common features of PTSD. Continued numbness does not indicate improvement.			
2.	Clients with PTSD may use alcohol to maintain control and blunt emotions. This would not indicate improvement.			
4.	This would not necessarily indicate an improvement in the client.			
#79. 2.	**Miss P.'s behavior is indicative of personal identity disturbance**	An	Ps/6	An

related to a traumatic event, the rape. Miss P. is unable to recall her identity, which is a factor in dissociative disorders. The person loses the ability to integrate consciousness, memory, identity, or motor behavior.

1. Miss P.'s behavior does not indicate maladaptive coping subsequent to the amnesia.
3. Miss P.'s behavior does not indicate symptoms of anxiety due to loss of memory.
4. Miss P.'s behavior does not indicate poor impulse control or suicidal thoughts.

#80. 2. **This lack of concern is identified as "la belle indifference" and is often a clue that the problem may be psychological rather than physical.**   As   Ps/6   Co

1. Secondary gains are the advantages clients derive from their illness.
3. Malingering is the presentative of false or exaggerated physical or psychological symptoms to accomplish conscious goals.
4. Hypochondriasis is excessive preoccupation with one's physical health, without organic pathology.

#81. 4. **Hypochondriasis is excessive preoccupation with one's physical health, without organic pathology.**   As   Ps/6   An

1. Conversion disorder is the repression of an emotional problem by replacing it with a physical symptom.
2. Body dysmorphic disorder is characterized by the exaggerative beliefs that the body is deformed or defective in some specific way.
3. Malingering is the presentation of false or exaggerated physical or psychological symptoms to accomplish conscious goals.

#82. 1. **This is an appropriate long-term goal related to Mrs. W.'s ineffective coping (use of conversion symptom, paralysis) related to unresolved conflicts and anxiety.**   Pl   Ps/6   An

2. This would be an appropriate short-term goal related to ineffective coping.
3. This would be an appropriate short-term goal related to ineffective coping.
4. This would be an appropriate short-term goal related to ineffective coping.

#83. 3. **This goal is related to Mr. T.'s impaired social interaction in response to his preoccupation with illness.**   Pl   Ps/6   Ap

1. It is important for Mr. T. to have an intellectual understanding of stomach cancer and realize that his fear is unrealistic, but he should not focus on his physical complaints.
2. This is an inappropriate goal because Mr. T. does not have cancer.
4. The receiving of secondary gains such as attention or less responsibility should not be reinforced.

#84. 1. **In dissociative amnesia, an individual is unable to recall important personal information such as name, occupation, and relatives.**   As   Ps/6   Ap

2. Dissociative fugue is characterized by sudden, unexpected travel away from one's home or customary place of work, with an inability to recall one's past.
3. Dissociative identity (multiple personality disorder) is when the individual must demonstrate two or more distinct personality disorders.
4. Stress disorder is not dissociative in nature.

#85. 3. **Self-mutilation is characteristic of borderline personality disorder.**   As   Ps/6   Co

1. Although impulsivity is present in borderline personality, it is also characteristic of bipolar-manic disorder.
2. Hallucinations are characteristic of the client diagnosed as psychotic.
4. Narcissism is characteristic of the client diagnosed as narcissistic personality disorder.

ANSWER	RATIONALE	NP	CN	CL

#86. 4. A safe environment for Miss T. is a priority. Her self-mutilation, poor impulse control, and temper are characteristic of persons with borderline personality disorder who have self-directed violence. — An — Ps/6 — An

   1. While Miss T.'s manipulation, impulsivity, and maladaptive behaviors may indicate ineffective coping, the self-directed violence is the priority nursing diagnosis.

   2. Body image disturbance is not indicated by Miss T.'s behavior.

   3. Miss T.'s behavior is not indicative of personality identity disturbance.

#87. 4. Miss T.'s acting out and demanding behavior indicates her need for ego boundaries and control, which the nurse provides. — Im — Ps/6 — Ap

   1. Miss T. has already explained why she is angry. A priority is to set limits on her demanding behavior.

   2. This is an inappropriate strategy and avoids dealing with the current situation.

   3. This is an inappropriate strategy that avoids dealing with the behavior and it may promote "splitting the staff."

#88. 3. Clients with borderline personality disorder frequently engage in impulsive suicidal or self-mutilating behaviors. The behavior described in choice 3 indicates less "acting-out" of feelings and less impulsiveness in response to more effective coping. — Ev — Ps/6 — Ap

   1. Angry outbursts are common and would not indicate improvement.

   2. This is a common feature and would not indicate improvement.

   4. Alternating between extremes of overidealization and devaluation is common and would not indicate improvement.

#89. 4. This is an appropriate short-term goal for Mr. P. in relation to his use of manipulative behavior to meet his needs. — Pl — Ps/6 — Ap

   1. This goal is inappropriate and is relevant to high risk for violence.

   2. This goal is an appropriate long-term goal related to ineffective coping.

   3. This goal is inappropriate in treating Mr. P.'s manipulative behavior.

#90. 3. This would indicate that Mr. C. may be improving related to recognizing his manipulative behavior. This is a first step in reducing the need for manipulation and attaining more effective coping strategies. — Ev — Ps/6 — An

   1. This behavior is probably an attempt of Mr. C. to verbally manipulate the nurse.

   2. This behavior does not indicate improvement.

   4. Sleep disturbance is not a common feature in antisocial personality disorder.

#91. 2. Behavioral symptoms of children who are victims of sexual abuse include: regression–thumb sucking would be regressive behavior in second grade child who is probably around 7 years old, disturbed sleep patterns, clinging behaviors, lack of peer friendships, sexual acting out, running away or threats to do so, and suicide attempts. — As — Ps/6 — Co

   1. Enuresis in children is considered an elimination disorder; impulsivity is most often seen in children with attention deficit hyperactivity disorder; and declining school performance is most often seen in children who are depressed.

   3. Hyperactivity and impulsivity are most often seen in children with attention deficit hyperactivity disorder; rocking is considered part of a stereotypic movement disorder.

   4. Stuttering is a symptom commonly seen in communication disorders in children; it represents a disturbance in normal timing and fluency of speech. Rocking is part of a stereotypic movement disorder. Impulsivity is seen in children with attention deficit hyperactivity disorder.

#92. 1. **One of the defense mechanisms that a person can use to manage the anxiety associated with an attack/rape is dissociation/isolation in which the client strips an event of its emotional significance and affective content.**   An   Ps/6   An

    2. If the client were using denial, her statement would more likely say, "I wasn't raped." Using denial could result in the victim's failure to report the incident at all and the accompanying feeling of personal responsibility for what happened.

    3. Although it is accurate that the client is in the shock phase of a crisis, if she were using repression she would be unable to recount the sequence of events.

    4. Clients who have been raped do often experience anger and hostility. If the victim were using reaction formation, she would talk about all the wonderful attributes of her date and the evening they spent together.

#93. 3. **This response identifies the husband's behavior as abusive and offers help for the wife if she is ready to consider other options. It does not cast judgment on her or question why she stays.**   Im   Ps/6   Ap

    1. This response sides with the abuser and conveys that the wife is the cause of abuser's behavior, which she is not. Power and control issues are often central to the abuse cycle.

    2. It seems obvious in this case that the woman fears for her life if she leaves or stands up to her husband. There are numerous reasons why a woman might stay in an abusive relationship. The nurse should not question a person's motives or cast judgment.

    4. Although determining the frequency may be important, even one such instance of what this woman describes is abuse and needs to be labeled as such by the nurse for the client.

#94. 4. **This statement acknowledges that the victim has admitted the need for protection in case of emergency and is making plans to work on establishing some degree of autonomy, which is a factor that keeps many women in abusive relationships.**   Ev   Ps/6   An

    1. This statement indicates that the victim maintains a sense of hope that the abuser will change and no longer behave abusively.

    2. This statement indicates that the victim believes that the abuser has changed and will maintain this new behavior.

    3. This statement indicates that the victim continues to believe that she is responsible for the abuse and is also willing to accept this view from others.

#95. 4. **The highest priority for this client based on the available data is the increased risk for injury because of confusion. The nurse's immediate concern must be the client's safety in the present environment.**   Pl   Ph/7   An

    1. It is correct that the nurse will want to plan interventions to promote tissue repair and healing and prevention of further breakdown, but the client's safety takes priority. The client is at risk for injury due to confusion.

    2. This client's altered thought processes related to confusion may or may not clear rapidly and will continue to pose an increased risk for injury and the need for the nurse to maintain the client's safety as the priority.

    3. Once discharged, this client is having difficulty maintaining any gains achieved through hospitalization. The nurse should initiate a report to Adult Protective Services to evaluate the home environment for abuse. If abuse is found an alternate placement will be needed. The nurse may also want to initiate a referral to the hospital's Social Services Department to facilitate discharge planning.

#96. 3. **Based on the patient's comment, the highest priority of care for**   An   Ps/6   An

ANSWER	RATIONALE	NP	CN	CL

this client immediately is the risk of suicide. He states he doesn't know if he can go through this. Suicide is a common reaction of persons who learn they are HIV-positive, which is associated with stigma and many losses. The client does not have a history of positive coping, which increases the risk of suicide.

1. Although it is true that this client is in a state of anticipatory grieving of his own death, the safety risk posed by the veiled suicidal comment must be taken seriously.

2. The client already has an infection, *pneumocystis carinii pneumonia* by chest X-ray, and subsequent infections must be prevented as much as possible to prevent worsening of the patient's HIV-positive status. The greatest immediate risk is suicide. The nurse must protect the client from these impulses.

4. As this client's HIV-positive status progresses, the client will most likely develop AIDS dementia and alterations in thought processes such as confusion, forgetfulness, decreased concentration, loss of balance, and regressive behaviors will occur.

#97. 1. This acknowledges the client's mood and gives her permission to cry. Crying puts the client in touch with the sadness/pain over the loss. Offering permission to cry facilitates expression of feelings related to the loss.   Im   Ps/6   Ap

2. It is too early in the grief process for this type of response, which facilitates problem solving and enhanced coping with the loss and its permanency. The nurse must first facilitate expression of feelings about the loss.

3. This response offers false reassurance and minimizes the extent of the patient's pain and sadness related to the loss.

4. This response is an assumption on the part of the nurse about the nature of the patient's concerns. This response does not encourage the patient to start where she is most comfortable.

#98. 4. Powerlessness, or feelings of uncertainty about the future, may be present in this patient due to the uncertainty about his future in several areas: job, another transplant, long-term hemodialysis, reconciliation in his marriage, whether he will have to be dependent on parents long term, and concern about their own possible declining health.   Pl   Ps/5   Ap

1. A critical concern with hemodialysis patients is fluid volume excess, not deficit. Failed kidneys produce little to no urine and water and other toxic waste products build up in the patient's blood.

2. There are no data in this situation to indicate that this patient is in denial about his losses; in fact, he discloses them freely.

3. Once the graft is rejected, all perfusion to the kidney is eliminated. Only a new graft (transplant) can restore perfusion to the (new) kidney. Hemodialysis will substitute for the kidneys until a new graft can be found.

#99. 3. This response indicates that the patient is exhausted and ready to let the natural processes take their course. The patient is at peace.   Ev   Ps/5   An

1. This response is an avoidance response to discussing impending death.

2. This response is asking for self-disclosure from the nurse and reassurance. It sounds panicky.

4. This response is clearly denial because the patient's condition is actually deteriorating.

#100. 1. This statement indicates that the family member and mother have been able to reminisce about good times together, acknowledging that there may be few remaining times to share these memories. This sharing indicates both have accepted death of mother and its finality.   Ev   Ph/5   An

2. This response sounds like the family member is accusing the staff of angering his/her mother. Anger is a normal response to death and dying. In this case, it seems as though it was aroused by the staff asking the patient to make some preparation for death.
3. This statement indicates that the family member does not realize that denial is a normal part of the response to death and dying.
4. This response indicates that the family member does not understand the depression and its accompanying feeling of sadness can be overwhelming and long term in its duration.

Index

A

Abbokinase, 65
Abdominal aortic aneurysm, 222
ABG (Arterial blood gas), 245
Abortion, 460
    methods of, 509
Abruptio placentae, 461–462
Absence seizure, 379t
Absorption, physiology of, 264
Absorptive dressings, for pressure
        sores, 124
Abuse
    child, 360–362, 557–558
    of elderly, 159–160
    stress of, 557–559
Acarbose, 336t
Accidents, children's, 370–373
Accumulation, of drugs, 11
ACE inhibitors, 67
Acetaminophen, 27, 142
Acetazolamide, 71
    for seizures, 33
Acetohexamide, 336t
Acetylcholine chloride, 43, 55
Acetylcholinesterase inhibitors, 43
Acetylcysteine, 75
Acetylsalicylic acid, 27, 142
Achromycin IV, 89–90
Acid-base imbalances, 146–147
    in children, 368–370
Acidosis, 147t
Acne, 433
Acquired immune deficiency syndrome
        (AIDS), 238–240
    and pregnancy, 465
    psychologic stress of, 561–562
Actinomycin D, 99t
Activase, 65
Acupuncture, 144
Acute respiratory distress syndrome
        (ARDS), 258
Acyclovir, 94–95
Adaptation syndrome, 130
Addisonian crisis, 328
Addison's disease, 327–328
ADH (antidiuretic hormone), 49, 322t
Adjuvants, to analgesics, 142–143
Admission of client, to hospital, 115–
        116
Adolescents
    development of, 356–358
    pregnancy in, 465
    psychiatric disorders (DSM IV) of,
        530–532
Adrenalectomy, 329–330
Adrenal glands, 321
    disorders of, 327–330
        Addison's disease, 327–328
        adrenalectomy, 329–330
        Conn's syndrome, 329
        Cushing's syndrome, 328
        pheochromocytoma, 329

        primary aldosteronism, 329
    hormones secreted by, 50–51
Adrenaline chloride, 38
Adrenergic blockers, 41–42
    alpha, 66
    beta, 42, 62, 68t
    peripheral, 67
Adrenergics, 38–41
    direct-acting, 38–40
    mixed-acting, 40–41
Adrenocorticotropic hormone (ACTH),
        49, 322t
Adriamycin, 98–99
Adsorbent diarrheals, 79
Advil, 28t
Aganglionic megacolon, 413
Aging, 154–161
    assessment of client, 156–158
    biologic theories of, 154
    chronic vs. acute disease in, 157t
    disease patterns in, 156
    evaluation of client, 158–160
    health patterns in, 156
    physical changes of, 155t–156t
    planning nursing care, 158
    psychosocial changes of, 154, 156
Agoraphobia, 550
AIDS (Acquired immune deficiency
        syndrome), 238–240
    and pregnancy, 465
    psychologic stress of, 561–562
Akinetic seizure, 379t
Alcohol bath, 121
Alcohol dependence, 538–539
Aldactone, 68t, 71–72
Aldomet, 66, 68t
Aldosterone, 50–51, 322t
Aldosteronism, primary, 329
Alkalosis, 147t
Alkylating agents, 97–98
Allergies, 432–433
    medications for, 74–75
        nonsedating, 74
Allopurinol, 84–85, 313
Alopecia, 341
Alpha adrenergic blockers, 66
Alpha agonists, 38–39
Alpha fetoprotein screening, 458
Alpha glucoside inhibitor, 336t
Alprazolam, 32t
Altepase, 65
Aluminum hydroxide, 78t
Aluminum-magnesium combinations,
        78t
Alupent, 40
Alveoli, 244
Alzheimer's dementia, 159
Amenorrhea, 510
Americaine, 26t
Amikacin, 86
Amikin, 86
Aminoglycosides, 86

Aminopenicillins, 87
Aminophylline, 73–74
Amiodarone, 62
Amitriptyline, 36, 142, 546t
Amnesia, dissociative, 553–554
Amniocentesis, 367, 458
Amniotic fluid, 451
Amniotic fluid embolism, 478–479
Amobarbital sodium, 31t
Amoxapine, 546t
Amphojel, 78t
Amphotericin B, 95
Amputation of limb, 225–226
Amyotrophic lateral sclerosis, 199
Amytal, 31t
Anafranil, 546t
Analgesics, 27–30
    adjuvants to, 142–143
    for labor, 479–480
    narcotic, 28–30, 142
    nonnarcotic, 27–28
    patient-controlled, 143
Anaphylactic shock, 149t
Ancef, 87–88
Androgens, 322t
    adrenal, 50–51
Anemia
    during pregnancy, 466
    types of, 234–237, 395–396
Anesthesia
    adjuncts to, 164
    epidural, 164t
    general, 163–164
    for labor, 480–481
    local, 26–27, 26t
    regional, 164, 164t
    stages of, 163t
Aneurysms, cardiovascular, 221–223
Angina pectoris, 211–212
    medications for, 56–59
Angiotensin converting enzyme (ACE)
        inhibitors, 67
Angles of injections, 17
Anorexia, 533
Antacids, 77–78, 78t
Antagonists
    heavy metal, 105
    histamine, 76–77
    narcotic, 30
Antepartal period, 455–468
Anthelmintics, 96
Antiarrhythmic agents, 57t, 60–62
Antibiotics
    antineoplastic, 98–100
    penicillin, 86–87
    for shock, 150t
Anticholinergics, 44–45, 44t, 45t
    gastrointestinal, 77
Anticoagulants, 63–64
Anticonvulsants, 32–33
Antidepressants
    administration of, 546t

Antidepressants (continued)
  atypical, 546t
  monoamine oxidase inhibitors
    (MAOIs), 36–37, 546t
  tricyclic, 36, 546t
Antidiarrheal agents, 79, 79t
Antidiuretic hormone (ADH), 49, 322t
Antidotes, to anticoagulants, 63
Antiemetics, 80–82
Antifungal agents, 95
Antihistamines, 74–75
  nonsedating, 74
Antihypertensives, 66–69, 68t–69t
  beta adrenergic blocking agents, 68t
  central acting, 66, 68t
  diuretics, 68t–69t
  vasodilators, 69t
Antilipemic agents, 65
Antimalarials, 84
Antimetabolites, 98
Antimicrobials, 85–94
  aminoglycosides, 86
  anti tubercular drugs, 93–94
  cephalosporins, 87–89
  chloramphenicol, 90
  ciprofloxacin, 92–93
  erythromycins, 89
  penicillin, 86–87
  sulfonamides, 90–91
  tetracyclines, 89–90
  urinary antiinfectives, 91–92
  vacomycin, 92
Antiminth, 96t
Antineoplastic agents, 97–102
  alkylating agents, 97–98
  antibiotics, 98–100
  antimetabolites, 98
  hormones, 100–101
  miscellaneous, 102
  vinca alkaloids, 101–102
Antipsychotics, 34–37
  administration of, 542t
Antipyretics, 27–28
Antitubercular agents, 93–94
Antivert, 81
Antiviral agents, 94–95
Anturane, 313
Anxiety
  medications for
    administration of, 546t
    atypical, 546t
    monoamine oxidase inhibitors,
      36–37, 546t
    tricyclic, 36, 546t
Anxiety disorders, 549–551
Aortic aneurysms, 222
Aortography, 209
Apgar scoring, of newborn, 495
Aphasia, 188
Aplastic anemia, 235–236
Apnea monitoring, 402
Apneustic breathing, 179–180
Apocrine glands, 341
Apomorphine, 82
Appendicitis, 414–415
Apraxia, 189
Apresoline, 67, 69t
Aralen, 84

Aramine, 41
Arlidin, 40
Arrhythmias, 212–213
  medications for, 57t, 60–62
Artane, 45
Arterial blood gas (ABG), 245
Arteriosclerosis obliterans, 220–221
Arteriovenous fistula, 296
Arteriovenous shunt, 296
Arthritis
  drugs for, 83–85
  rheumatoid, 311–312
Ascites, 283–284
Asepsis
  defined, 122
  practices and principles of,
    122–123
L-Asparaginase, 102
Aspirin, 27, 142
Assistive devices, for walking, 309
Astemizole, 74
Asthma, 404–405
  medications for, 73–74
Astrocytoma, 438
Atarax, 142
Ataxic breathing, 180
Atelectasis, 255
Ateriography, coronary, 209
Atherosclerosis, 211
Atrial fibrillation, 212
Atropine, 44, 54, 63
Auranofin, 83–84
Aurothioglucose, 84, 311
Autistic disorder, 532–533
Autonomic dysreflexia, 197
Autonomic nervous system, 176
  drugs acting on, 38–46
    adrenergic blocking agents, 41–
      42
    adrenergic drugs, 38–41
    anticholinergic agents, 44–45
    antiparkinson agents, 45–46
    cholinergics, 43
  effects of, 177t
Autonomy, defined, 113
Aventyl, 36
Axid, 77t
Azathioprine, 103
AZT, 95
Azulfidine, 91

B
Bacillus Calmette-Guérin (BCG) vaccine,
  106
Baclofen, 33
Bacteria, drugs acting on, 85–94
Baking soda, 78t
BAL in oil, 105
Barbiturates, 31, 31t
  for seizures, 32
Bartholin's glands, 446–447
Basal cell epithelioma, 343
Basophils, 229
BCG (Bacillus Calmette-Guérin) vaccine,
  106
Beau's line, 341
Bedsores, 123–124

Behavior, client, 526–530
  anxiety, 526–528
  defense mechanisms, 527t, 528
  hostility-aggression, 529
  perception disorders, 528–529
  self-mutilation, 529
  suicide, 529–530
  withdrawal, 529
Behavioral techniques, for pain control,
  144
Bell's palsy, 198
Benadryl, 74–75
Benemid, 313
Benylin DM, 75
Benzocaine, 26t
Benzodiazepines, 31–32, 32t
  for seizures, 32
Benztropine mesylate, 45t
Beta adrenergic blocking agents, 42, 62,
  68t
Beta adrenergic drugs
  for premature labor, 476
Beta agonists, 39–40
  nonselective, 38–40
  selective, 40
Beta blockers, 42, 62, 68t
Betamethasone, 50–51
Bethanechol chloride, 43
Biguanides, 336t
Biliary system, 264
Bilirubin, of fetus, 458
Bipolar disorder, 544–545
Birth control methods, 507–508
Birth control pills, 52–53
Bisacodyl, 81t
Bismuth subsalicylate, 79t
Bladder, 291
Bladder cancer, 297
Bladder surgery, 297–298
Bland diet, 139
Blenoxane, 99t
Bleomycin, 99t
Blindness, in children, 381–382
Blocadren, 62
Blood, 228
  cellular components of, 228–229
  coagulation of, 229
  disorders of, see Hematologic system
Blood component therapy, 232–233
Blood groups, 229
Blood transfusion, 232–233
  complications of, 230t
Blood vessels, 207
Body mechanics, in moving client,
  118–119
Body surface, nomogram for
  determining, 24
Bone marrow, 228
Bone marrow transplant, 171–172
  pediatric, 435–436
Bones, 306, see also Musculoskeletal
  system
  tumors of, 442
Bowel disorders, chronic inflammatory,
  277–279
Bowel surgery, 279–280
Braces, children in, 423
Bradley method, of childbirth, 458t

Bradycardia, sinus, 212
Brain, 174–176, *see also* Neurosensory
    system, drugs acting on, 26–38,
    38–46
Brain abscess, 186
Brain scan, 181
Brain stem glioma, 438
Brain tumors, 186–187, 438–439
Breast cancer, 512
Breasts, female, 448
  changes in pregnancy, 453
Breast self examination (BSE), 169,
    511–512
Brethine, 40
Bretylium, 62
Bretylol, 62
Brevibloc, 62
Bromocriptine, 46t
Bronchi, 243–244
Bronchiectasis, 252–253
Bronchioles, 244
Bronchiolitis, 404
Bronchitis, 252
Bronchogenic carcinoma, 257
Bronchoscopy, 246
Bronkephrine, 40
Buck's extension, 310, 311
Buerger's disease, 221
Bulk-forming laxatives, 80, 81t
Bulla, in skin, 343
Bumetanide, 68t, 70–71
Bumex, 68t, 70–71
Buprenex, 29
Buprenorphone, 29
Bupropion, 37
Burns, 344–347, 431
  classification of, 344–345
  client care, 345–347
    fluid replacement in, 346t
  types of, 344
Busulfan, 98t
Butabarbital sodium, 31t
Butazolidin, 311, 313
Butisol, 31t
Butorphanol, 29

C
CAD (Coronary artery disease), 211
Calan, 57t, 59
Calcium, in nutrition, 134t
Calcium alginates, for pressure sores, 124
Calcium carbonate, 78t
Calcium channel blockers, 59
  for premature labor, 476
Calcium EDTA, 105
Calculations, for medications, 20–25
  conversions, 20–21
  dosages, 21–25
Cancer
  cell characteristics of, 168
  classification of, 168–169
  diagnosis of, 168–169
  drugs acting on, 97–102, *see also*
    Cancer treatment
    alkylating agents, 97–98
    antibiotics, 98–100
    antimetabolites, 98
    hormones, 100–101

    miscellaneous, 102
    vinca alkaloids, 101–102
  etiology of, 168
  evolution of, 168
  genetics of, 168
  immunologic factors in, 168
  stages of, 169
  types of
    bladder, 297
    bone, 442
    brain, 186–187, 438–440
    breast, 512
    bronchogenic, 257
    cervical, 513
    colon, 279
    esophageal, 272
    hematologic, 240–241
    hepatic, 285–286
    laryngeal, 258–259
    liver, 285–286
    mouth, 271–272
    ovarian, 513
    pancreatic, 288
    pheochromocytoma, 329
    prostate, 303–304
    rectal, 279
    skin, 343–344
    stomach, 276
    uterine, 513
    vulval, 513
  warning signs of, 169
Cancer treatment, 169–172
  bone marrow transplant, 171–172
  chemotherapeutic, 169–170
  pediatric, 433–442
    stages of, 436–437
    surgery for, 439–440
    types of, 434–436
  radiation, 170–171
Candida albicans, 511
Capoten, 67, 69t
Captopril, 67, 69t
Carafate, 82–83
Carbachol, 55
Carbamazepine, for seizures, 33
Carbidopa/levodopa, 46t
Carbocaine, 26t
Carbohydrates, 132
Carbonic anhydrase inhibitors, 71
Carcinoma, bronchogenic, 257
Cardiac arrest, 217–218
Cardiac conditions, during pregnancy,
    463–464
Cardiac drugs, 55–69
Cardiac glycosides, 55–56
Cardiac stimulants, 62–63
Cardiac surgery, in children, 391
Cardiac tamponade, 219
Cardiogenic shock, 149t
Cardiopulmonary resuscitation (CPR),
    218
Cardiovascular drugs, 55–69
  antianginal drugs, 56–59
  antiarrhythmics, 60–62
  anticoagulants, 63–64
  antihypertensives, 66–69
  antilipemic agents, 65
  beta blockers, 62

  cardiac glycosides, 55–56
  cardiac stimulants, 62–63
  peripheral vasodilators, 59–60
  thrombolytic drugs, 64–65
Cardiovascular system, 205–227
  anatomy of, 205–207
  assessment of, 207–209
  blood vessel disorders of, 219–227
  children's, 385–394
    acquired heart disease, 392–394
    assessment in, 386–387
    congenital heart defects, 388–392,
      388t
    disorders of, 387–394
    surgery, 391
  client care
    interventions in, 210–211
    planning for, 209–210
  diagnostic testing of, 208–209
  disorders of, 211–227
    aneurysms, 221–223
    angina pectoris, 211–212
    arteriosclerosis obliterans, 220–221
    Buerger's disease, 221
    cardiac arrest, 217–218
    cardiac tamponade, 219
    cardiogenic shock, 149t
    congestive heart failure, 215–216
    coronary artery bypass surgery,
      214–215
    coronary artery disease, 211
    dysrhythmias, 212–213
    endocarditis, 218
    hypertension, 219–220
    myocardial infarction, 213–214
    pacemakers, 216–217
    percutaneous transluminal coronary
      angioplasty, 214
    pericarditis, 219
    peripheral circulation, 225–226
    pulmonary edema, 216
    pulmonary embolism, 224–225
    Raynaud's phenomenon, 221
    thromboangiitis obliterans, 221
    thrombophlebitis, 223–224
    varicose veins, 225
    venous stasis ulcers, 223
  of elderly clients, 155t
  medication for, *see* Cardiovascular
    drugs
  monitoring, 210–211
  physiology of, 205–207
  postpartum changes in, 485–486
  during pregnancy, 453–454
Cardizem, 57t
Care, of client, 115–117
  age, drug action and, 11
  asepsis, 122
  assigning delivery of, 116–117
  body mechanics in, 118–119
  cold application, 121–122
  examples of, 124–127
  external heat application, 122
  moving patient, 118–119
  positioning client, 118–121
  pressure sores, 123–124
  priorities of, 115–116
  psychologic aspects of, 556–563

Care, of client, (continued)
  restraints in, 118
  safety practices in, 117–119
Carisoprodol, 33
Cartilage, 307
Cascara sagrada, 81t
Castor oil, 81t
Casts
  care of client with, 309–310
  children in, 422
Catapres, 66, 68t
Cataracts, 199
Catheterization
  cardiac, 209
  femoral vein, 296
  subclavian vein, 296
  urinary, 294–295
Caudal anesthesia, 164t
Cefazolin sodium, 87–88
Cefepine, 88–89
Cefotaxime, 88–89
Cefoxitin sodium, 88–89
Celestone, 50–51
Celiac disease, 414
CellCept, 103
Central line, intravenous, 147–148
  care of client with, 148–149
Central nervous system, 174–176
  disorders of, 185–197
  drugs acting on, 26–38
    anticonvulsants, 32–33
    antipsychotic agents, 34–37
    antipyretics, 27–28
    hypnotics, 30–32
    local anesthetics, 26–27
    narcotic analgesics, 28–30
    narcotic antagonists, 30
    nonnarcotic analgesics, 27–28
    sedatives, 30–32
    skeletal muscle relaxants, 33–34
Central neurogenic hyperventilation, 179
Central venous pressure (CVP), 210
Cephalocaudal, 350
Cephalosporins, 87–89
Cerebral aneurysm, 189
Cerebral angiography, 181
Cerebral palsy, 380–381
Cerebrovascular accident (CVA),
  187–189
Cervical tongs, 195
Cervical traction, 310, 311
Cervix
  cancer of, 513
  changes in pregnancy, 452–453
  premature dilation of, 460
Cesarean birth, 482–483
CF (Cystic fibrosis), 406–407
Chadwick's sign, 452
Chalasia, 412–413
Chemotherapy, 169–170
  in pediatric oncology, 435
Chest physical therapy, for children,
  401–402
Chest trauma, 254–255
Chest wall, 244
Cheyne-Stokes respiration, 179
CHF (Congestive heart failure), 215–216
  in children, 387–388

Chicken pox, 361t
Child abuse, 360–362, 557–558
Childbearing cycle
  antepartal period, 455–468
  labor and delivery, 468–483
  newborn, 492–499
  postpartum period, 485–492
  pregnancy, 450–455
Childbirth, methods of, 458t
Child development, 350–365
  analysis of problems of, 358
  assessment of, 350–351
  defined, 350
  health promotion in, 359–360
  parenting in, 360–363
  rates of, 350
  stages of, 351–358
  theories of, 350
Children
  abuse of, 360–362
  cancer in, 433–442
  cardiovascular system of, 385–394
  communicable diseases of, 361t
  death and dying, 363–365
  development of, 350–365
  endocrine system of, 428–430
  gastrointestinal system of, 409–416
  genitourinary system of, 416–421
  growth and development of, 350–
    365
  hematologic system of, 394–400
  hospitalized, 358–359
  immunization of, 359–360
  integumentary system of, 430–433
  musculoskeletal system of, 421–428
  neurosensory system of, 373–385
  preparation for procedures, 359
  psychiatric disorders (DSM IV),
    530–532
  respiratory system of, 400–409
  stressors of, 365–373
Chlamydia, 511
Chloral hydrate, 32
Chlorambucil, 98t
Chloramphenicol, 90
Chlorine, in nutrition, 134t
Chloromycetin, 90
Chloroquine, 84
Chlorothiazide, 68t, 70
Chlorpheniramine, 74–75
Chlorpromazine, 34–35, 542t
Chlorpropamide, 336t
Chlorthalidone, 68t, 70
Chlor-Trimeton, 74–75
Cholecystectomy, 286–287
Cholecystitis, 286
Choledochostomy, 286–287
Cholelithiasis, 286
Cholesterol, drugs for high, 65
Cholestyramine, 65
Choline magnesium trisalicylate
  (Trilisate), 142
Cholinergics, 43
Chorionic villi sampling, 458
Chromosome disorders, 367–368
Chromosomes, human, 365–366
Chronic illness, psychologic stress of,
  560–561

Chronic obstructive pulmonary disease
  (COPD), 251–254
Chronic vs. acute disease, in aging, 157t
Chrysotherapy, 311
Cibalith-S, 36
Cimetidine, 76–77
Cipro, 92–93
Ciprofloxacin, 92–93
Circulatory system, see Cardiovascular
  system
Cirrhosis, 282–283
Cisplatin, 98t
Citroma, 81t
Citrucel, 81t
Claforan, 88–89
Claritin, 74
Clear liquid diet, 138
Cleft lip, 410–411
Cleft palate, 410–411
Client, rights of, 115
Client behavior, 526–530
  anxiety, 526–528
  defense mechanisms, 527t, 528
  hostility-aggression, 529
  perception disorders, 528–529
  self-mutilation, 529
  suicide, 529–530
  withdrawal, 529
Client care, 115–117
  age, drug action and, 11
  asepsis, 122
  assigning delivery of, 116–117
  body mechanics in, 118–119
  cold application, 121–122
  examples of, 124–127
  external heat application, 122
  moving patient, 118–119
  positioning client, 118–121
  pressure sores, 123–124
  priorities of, 115–116
  psychologic aspects of, 556–563
  restraints in, 118
  safety practices in, 117–119
Client needs
  care environment, 2
  health promotion/maintenance, 2
  physiologic adaptation compromises,
    3
  physiologic integrity, 2–3
  psychosocial integrity, 2
  reduction of risk potential
    compromises, 3
Climacteric, 448
Clinoril, 85, 311
Clitoris, 446
Clomipramine, 546t
Clonidine, 66, 68t
Clorazepate, 32t
Clotting, of blood, 229
Clotting disorders, 237–238, 397–398
Clozapine, 542t
Clozaril, 542t
Clubbed nails, 341
Clubfoot, 424
Cluster breathing, 180
Coagulation, of blood, 229
Coagulation disorder, medications for,
  63–64

Codeine, 29t, 75
Codes for nurses (ANA, 1985), 113
Cogentin, 45t
Cognex, 43
Cognitive ability, levels of, and testing, 3
Cognitive disorders, 534–536
Cognitive psychiatric disorders (DSM IV), 534–536
Cognitive theory, 350
Colace, 81t
Colchicine, 84–85, 313
Cold application, 121–122
Colestid, 65
Colestipol, 65
Cologel, 81t
Colon cancer, 279
Commitment of client, defined, 114
Communicable diseases, of children, 361t
Compazine, 80–81
Competence, defined, 114
Computed tomography (CT), 180
Conception, 450
Congestive heart failure (CHF), 215–216
  in children, 387–388
Conjunctivitis, 382
Conn's syndrome, 329
Constipation, 271
  in children, 415
Contact dermatitis, 343
Contraceptives, oral, 52–53
Contraconception, methods of, 507–508
Contraction stress test (CST), of fetus, 459
Conversion disorder, 553
Conversions, in medication calculation, 20–21
COPD (Chronic obstructive pulmonary disease), 251–254
Cordarone, 62
Corgard, 62, 68t
Coronary artery bypass surgery, 214–215
Coronary artery disease (CAD), 211
Correctol, 81t
Corticosteroids, 50–51
  for shock, 150t
Corticosteroid therapy, 324–325
Corticosterone, 322t
Corticotropin, 49
Cortisol, 50–51, 322t
Cortrosyn, 49
Cosyntropin, 49
Coumadin, 63–64
Cowper's glands, 293
Cozaar, 67
CPR (Cardiopulmonary resuscitation), 218
Cranial nerves, 176t
Craniopharyngioma, 438
Creatinine level, of fetus, 458
Cretinism, 429
Crimes and torts, examples of, 114
Critical illness, psychologic stress of, 559–560
Crohn's disease, 277–278
Cromolyn sodium, 73–74
Croup, 403

Cryptorchidism, 418
CST (Contraction stress test), of fetus, 459
CT (Computed tomography), 180
Cushing's syndrome, 328
CVA (Cerebrovascular accident), 187–189
CVP (Central venous pressure), 210
Cyclandelate, 60t
Cyclogyl, 54
Cyclopentolate, 54
Cyclophosphamide, 97–98
Cycloplegics, 54
Cyclospasmol, 60t
Cyclosporine, 103–104
Cystic fibrosis (CF), 406–407
Cystitis, 296
Cystocele, of uterus, 514
Cytarabine, 98
Cytomel, 51–52, 330
Cytosar-U, 98
Cytoxan, 97–98, 312

D
Dactinomycin, 99t
Dalmane, 32t
Dantrium, 33–34
Dantrolene, 33–34
Daunomycin, 99t
Daunorubicin, 99t
DDAVP (Desmopressin), 49
Deafness, in children, 382
Death and dying
  of children, 363–365
  psychologic stress of, 562
Debridement, of pressure sores, 124
Decadron, 50–51
Decubitus ulcers, 123–124
Deep breathing exercises, for children, 402
Deferoxamine mesylate, 105
Defibrillation, 218
Dehydration, in children, 369
Delalutin, 52–53
Delirium, 534–536
Delta-Cortef, 50–51
Deltasone, 50–51
Dementia, 534–536
  senile, 159
Demerol, 29t
Depakene, for seizures, 33
DepoTestosterone, 100t
Depression
  major, 546–547
  medications for, 546t
    atypical, 546t
    MAOIs, 36–37, 546t
    tricyclic antidepressants, 36, 546t
Dermal ulcers, 123–124
Dermatitis, contact, 343
Dermis, 340–341
DES (Diethylstilbestrol), 100–101
Desiccated thyroid, 51–52
Desmopressin (DDAVP), 49
Desoxycorticosterone acetate (DOCA), 50–51
Desyrel, 546t
Detached retina, 201–202

Development, of children, 350–365
  analysis of problems of, 358
  assessment of, 350–351
  defined, 350
  health promotion in, 359–360
  hospitalization and, 358–359
  implementation of, 358–359
  parenting in, 360–363
  rates of, 350
  stages of, 351–358
Developmental disorders, psychiatric, 532–534
Dexamethasone, 50–51
Dextromethorphan, 75
Diabeta, 336t
Diabetes, medications for, 47–49
Diabetes insipidus, 327
Diabetes mellitus, 334–338, 428–429
  complications of, 337–338
  medical management of, 334–336
  during pregnancy, 464
  type I and type II, 334
Diabetic diet, 138
Diabinase, 336t
Dialysis, 295–297
Diamox, 71
Diaper rash, 432
Diapid, 49
Diarrhea, 270
  in children, 369–370
  medications for, 79, 79t
Diazepam, 31
Diazoxide, 67
DIC (Disseminated intravascular coagulation), 237–238
  in pregnancy, 465–466
Dietary guides, 136
Diethylstilbestrol (DES), 100–101
Diets, special, 137–140
Diflunisal, 142
Digestion, physiology of, 264
Digitalis, 57t
Digitalis preparations
  for shock, 150t
Digoxin, 55–56
Dihydroxyaluminum sodium carbonate, 78t
Dilantin, 32–33, 61t
Dilatation and curettage, for abortion, 509
Dilaudid, 29t
Diltiazem, 57t
Dimenhydrinate, 80–81
Dimercaprol, 105
Diphenhydramine, 74–75
Diphenoxylate, with atropine, 79t
Diphtheria, 361t
Diphtheria, tetanus toxoid and pertussis (DPT) vaccine, 106
Dipyridamole, 59–60
Direct-acting adrenergics, 38–40
Direct-acting vasodilators, 67
Disalcid, 142
Discectomy, 317–318
Discharge of client, from hospital, 116–117
Disease, drug action and, 11
Disopyramide, 57t

Disseminated intravascular coagulation
    (DIC), 237–238
  in pregnancy, 465–466
Dissociative anesthetics, 164
Dissociative disorders, 553–554
Distributive justice, 113
Diuretics, 68t, 69–72
Diuril, 68t
Diverticulitis, 278–279
Diverticulosis, 278–279
DKA (Ketoacidosis), 337–338
Dobutamine, 40
  for shock, 150t
Dobutrex, 40
  for shock, 150t
DOCA (Desoxycorticosterone acetate),
    50–51
Docusate sodium, 81t
Dolobid, 142
Dolophine, 29t
Dopamine, 40
  for shock, 150t
Dopaminergic agents, 45, 46t
Dorsal column stimulator, 143
Dorsal lithotomy position, 121
Dosage calculations, medication,
    21–25
Double effect, principle of, 113
Down's syndrome, 367–368
Doxepin, 546t
Doxorubicin, 98–99
Doxycycline, 90
DPT vaccine, 106
Dramamine, 80–81
Drug abuse disorders, 536–541
  alcohol dependence, 538–539
  impaired nurses, 539–540
  and newborn, 503–504
  during pregnancy, 466
  psychoactive drug use, 539
Drugs
  abuse of, see Drug abuse disorders
  action of, factors affecting, 10–12
  administration of, 12–25
    calculations, 20–25
      conversions, 20–21
      dosage calculations, 21–25
  commonly abused, 537t
  definition of, 10
  types of, see Medications
Dulcolax, 81t
Duodenal ulcers, 274
Dymelor, 336t
Dyrenium, 71–72
Dysmature infant (SGA), 500
Dysmenorrhea, 510
Dysphagia, 188
Dysreflexia, autonomic, 197
Dysrhythmias, 212–213
  medications for, 57t, 60–62
Dysthymic disorder, 547
Dystocia, 478

E
Ear
  assessment of, 178, 180
  diagnostic testing of, 180–181
  disorders of, 202–203

    children's, 382–383
    Ménière's disease, 203
    otosclerosis, 202
    stapedectomy, 202–203
  irrigation of, 184–185
  structures of, 177–178
Eating disorders, 533
Eccrine glands, 341
ECG (Electrocardiogram), 208–209, 210
Echocardiogram, 209
Echothiophate, 55
Eclampsia, 463
Ecotrin, 142
Ectopic pregnancy, 460–461
Eczema, 432–433
Edecrin, 68t, 70–71
Edetate calcium disodium, 105
Edrophonium chloride, 43
EEG (electroencephalography), 181
Effexor, 37
Elavil, 36, 142, 546t
Elder abuse, 159–160, 558–559
Electrical stimulation, for pain, 143
Electrocardiogram (ECG), 208–209,
    210
Electroencephalography (EEG), 181
Electrolytes and fluid imbalances,
    144–146
  in children, 368–370
Elixophyllin, 73–74
Elspar, 102
Embryo, 451
  changes in size of, 453
Emetics, 82
Emotional distress
  behavior under, 526–530
    anxiety, 526–528
    defense mechanisms, 527t, 528
    hostility-aggression, 529
    perception disorders, 528–529
    self-mutilation, 529
    suicide, 529–530
    withdrawal, 529
  theories of, 519–522
    behavioral (Pavlov, Skinner), 521
    community mental health, 521–522
    human need (Maslow), 521
    interpersonal (Sullivan), 520
    medical-biological, 519
    psychoanalytic (Freud), 519–520
    psychosocial (Erikson), 520
    therapeutic nurse-client relationship
        (Peplau), 521
Emphysema, 251–252
Emulsoid, 81t
E-Mycin, 89
Enalapril, 67, 69t
Encephalitis, 186
Endep, 546t
Endocarditis, 218
Endocrine system, 321–340, 427–430; see
        also Hormones
  anatomy and physiology of, 321–322
  assessment of, 322–324
  children's, 428–430
    assessment of, 428
    disorders of, 428–430
  client care, 322–325

    evaluation of, 325
    interventions in, 324–325
  diagnostic testing of, 323–324
  disorders of, 325–340
    Addison's disease, 327–328
    adrenalectomy, 329–330
    Conn's syndrome, 329
    Cushing's syndrome, 328
    diabetes insipidus, 327
    diabetes mellitus, 334–338
    goiter, simple, 330
    Graves' disease, 331–332
    hyperparathyroidism, 333–334
    hyperpituitarism, 326
    hyperthyroidism, 331–332
    hypoparathyroidism, 332–333
    hypophysectomy, 326–327
    hypopituitarism, 325
    hypothyroidism, 330–331
    myxedema, 330–331
    pheochromocytoma, 329
    primary aldosteronism, 329
    syndrome of inappropriate
        antidiuretic hormone secretion,
        327
    thyroidectomy, 332
    thyroid storm, 332
  drugs acting on, 47–53
    antidiabetic agents, 47–49
    corticosteroids, 50–51
    oxytocics, 53–54
    pituitary hormones, 49–50
    progestogens (progestins), 52–53
    thyroid antagonists, 51–52
    thyroid hormones, 51
  of elderly clients, 156t
  pregnancy
    changes during, 454
    disorders during, 464
  regulation of, 321
Endometriosis, 510
Endometrium, 447
Enemas, 267–268
Energy metabolism, 133
Enflurane, 163
Engerix-B vaccine, 106
Enteral nutrition, 139
Enuresis, 418–419
Environmental factors, in cancer, 168
Eosinophils, 229
Ependymoma, 438
Ephedrine, 40–41
Epidermis, 340–341
Epidermoid, 343
Epididymis, 293
Epididymitis, 302–303
Epidural anesthesia, 164t
Epiglottitis, 403–404
Epilepsy, 378–380
Epinephrine, 26, 38, 322t
Ergomar, 42
Ergonovine, 53t
Ergot alkaloids, 53t
Ergotamine tartrate, 42
Ergotrate, 53t
Erikson, Erik, 350
ERT (Estrogen replacement therapy), 514
  alternatives to, 514

Erythroblastosis fetalis, 502
Erythrocytes, 228
Erythromycins, 89
Esidrex, 68t
Eskalith, 35–36
Esmolol, 62
Esophageal varices, 284–285
Esophagus, 263
  defects of, 412
Estinyl, 100t
Estrogen, 322t
  adrenal, 50–51
Estrogen replacement therapy (ERT),
    514
  alternatives to, 514
Ethacrynic acid, 68t, 70–71
Ethambutol, 94t
Ethical concepts, of nursing practice,
    113
Ethical dilemma, defined, 113
Ethics, defined, 113
Ethosuximide, 33
Ethrane, 163
Ethyl norepinephrine, 40
Ethynyl estradiol, 100t
Etoposide, 101t
Ewing's sarcoma, 442
Excretion, drug, 11
ExLax, 80, 81t
Exopthalmos, 331
Expectorants and antitussives, 75–76
Exstrophy of bladder, 418
Eye
  assessment of, 178, 180
  diagnostic testing of, 180–181
  disorders of, 199–202
    cataracts, 199
    children's, 381–382
    detached retina, 201–202
    elderly clients, 155t
    eye injuries, 202
    glaucoma, 200–201
  injury of, emergency care, 202
  medications for, 54–55
    administration of, 14–15
  structures of, 176–177
Eyesight, diminished, 184

F
Failure to thrive (FTT), 360
Fallopian tubes, 447
Famotidine, 77t
Fat-restricted diets, 138
Febrile seizure, 379t
Feen-a-Mint, 81t
Feldene, 28t, 142, 311
Female reproductive system, 446–450
  anatomy of, 446–448
  changes during pregnancy, 452–453
  disorders of, 506–516
    breast cancer, 512
    cervical cancer, 513
    fibrocystic breast disease, 511
    hysterectomy, 513
    infertility and infertility, 506–509
    menopause, 513–514
    menstrual disorders, 509–510
    neoplasia, 511

ovarian cancer, 513
    sexually transmitted diseases,
      510–511
    uterine cancer, 513
  external structures, 446–447
  internal structures, 447–448
  mammary glands, 448
  menarche, 448
  menopause, 448, 513–514
  menstrual cycle, 448, 449
  neoplasia of, 511
  pelvis, 448
  physiology of, 448
  postpartum changes in, 485
  sexual response, 448
Femoral capital epiphysis, slipped, 425
Femoral popliteal bypass surgery,
    222–223
Femoral vein catheterization, 296
Fenoprofen, 311
Fertility, 506–507
Fetus, 451
  bilirubin of, 458
  biophysical profile of, 458
  changes in size of, 453
  circulation of, 385–386, 452
  contraction stress test (CST) of, 459
  creatinine level of, 458
  delivery of, 468–483, see also Labor
      and delivery
  electronic monitoring of, 458–459,
      471–472
  growth and development of, 452, 452t
  head of, 469
  membranes of, 451
  movement of, 458
  percutaneous umbilical blood
      sampling (PUBS) of, 458
  risk factors of, 457–458
  status of, 457–458
  ultrasound of, 458
  X-ray of, 458
Fever, drugs acting on, 27–28
Fibrillation, atrial, 212
Fibrocystic breast disease, 511
Field block anesthesia, 164t
Fire safety and preparedness, 117–118
Five factors of labor (five Ps), 468–470
Flail chest, 254
Florinef, 50–51
Fludrocortisone, 50–51
Fluid and electrolyte imbalances,
    144–146
  in children, 368–370
5-Fluorouracil, 98
Fluothane, 163
Fluoxetine, 37, 546t
Fluoxymesterone, 100t
Fluphenazine, 35t, 542t
Fluphenazine decanoate/enanthrate,
    542t
Flurazepam, 32t
Foams, for pressure sores, 124
Folic acid, in nutrition, 135t
Follicle stimulating hormone (FSH), 322t
Food consistency, modification of,
    138–139
Forceps delivery, 482

Foreign object, choking on, 405
Fourchette, 447
Fowler's position, 119
Fractures, 315–316
  hip, 315–316
    open reduction and internal fixation,
      315
  ribs, 254
Freud, Sigmund, 350
FTT (Failure to thrive), 360
Fugue, dissociative, 554
Full liquid diet, 138
Fungal infections, medications for, 95
Fungizone, 95
Furosemide, 68t, 70

G
Gall bladder, 264
  disorders of, 286–287
Gantanol, 91
Gantrisin, 91
Garamycin, 86
Gas exchange, 244
Gastric surgery, 274, 276
Gastric ulcers, 273–274
Gastritis, 273
Gastroesophageal reflux, 412
Gastrointestinal anticholinergics, 77
Gastrointestinal system, 262–290,
    409–416
  anatomy and physiology of, 262–264
  assessment of, 264–267
  children's, 409–416
    acquired disorders of, 414–416
    assessment of, 409–410
    congenital disorders of, 410–411
    defective connections in, 411–412
    disorders of, 410–416
    gastroesophageal reflux (chalasia),
      412
    Hirschsprung's disease (aganglionic
      megacolon), 413
    imperforate anus, 414
    intussusception, 413
    pyloric stenosis, 413
  client care
    evaluation of, 268
    interventions in, 267–268
    planning of, 267
  diagnostic testing of, 266–267
  disorders of, 269–290
    anorexia/eating disorders, 533
    appendicitis, 414–415
    ascites, 283–284
    bowel surgery, 279–280
    cholecystectomy, 286–287
    cholecystitis, 286
    choledochostomy, 286–287
    cholelithiasis, 286
    cirrhosis, 282–283
    colon cancer, 279
    constipation, 271
    Crohn's disease, 277–278
    diarrhea, 270
    diverticulitis, 278–279
    diverticulosis, 278–279
    duodenal ulcers, 274
    esophageal varices, 284–285

Gastrointestinal system, (continued)
  gastric surgery for, 274, 276
  gastric ulcers, 273–274
  gastritis, 273
  hemorrhoids, 281
  hepatic encephalopathy, 285
  hepatitis, 281–282
  hernias, 276–277
  hiatal hernia, 272–273
  intestinal obstructions, 277
  liver cancer, 285–286
  mouth cancer, 271–272
  nausea and vomiting, 269–270
  pancreatic cancer, 288
  pancreatitis, 287–288
  peritonitis, 280–281
  rectal cancer, 279
  regional enteritis, 277–278
  stomach cancer, 276
  stomatitis, 170
  ulcerative colitis, 278
  drugs acting on, 76–83
    antacids, 77–78
    antidiarrheal agents, 79
    antiemetics, 80–82
    emetics, 82
    gastrointestinal anticholinergics, 77
    histamine antagonists, 76–77
    laxatives, 80
    sucralfate, 82–83
  of elderly clients, 156t
  female, changes during pregnancy,
    454
  postpartum changes in, 486
Gastrostomy, 268, 410
Gels/hydrogels, for pressure sores, 124
Genetic disorders, 365–368
Genetics
  of cancer, 168
  principles of, 365–366
Genital infections, 510–511
Genitourinary system, 290–306, 416–420
  anatomy and physiology of
    female reproductive system, 446–448
    male reproductive system, 292–293
    urinary system, 290–292
  children's, 416–421
    assessment of, 416–417
    disorders of, 417–420
  client care, 293–294
    evaluation of, 297
    interventions in, 294–297
  disorders of, 296–306, see also Genital
    infections
    acute renal failure, 300–301
    bladder cancer, 297
    bladder surgery, 297–298
    chronic renal failure, 300–301
    cystitis, 296
    glomerulonephritis, acute, 420
    kidney transplantation, 301–302
    nephrectomy, 302
    nephrolithiasis, 299
    nephrosis, 419–420
    pyelonephritis, 299–300
    urolithiasis, 299
Gentamicin, 86, 345

German measles, 361t
Gestational age assessment, 495
GH (Growth hormone), 49–50, 322t
Gigantism, 430
Glasgow coma scale, 179, 179t
Glaucoma, 200–201
Glomerulonephritis, acute, 420
Glucagon, 322t
Glucocorticoids, 50–51, 322t
Glucophage, 336t
Glyburide, 336t
Glycerin, 81t
Glycerol, 81t
Glycopyrrolate, 44t
Glyset, 336t
Goiter, simple, 330
Gold sodium thiomalate, 84
Gonads, 322
Gonorrhea, 511
Goodell's sign, 453
Good Samaritan Doctrine, 114
Gout, 313
  medications for, 84–85
Graft vs. host disease, 172
Grand mal seizure, 379t
Granulocytes, 229
Graves' disease, 331–332
Grief and mourning, psychologic stress
    of, 56
Grisactin, 95
Griseofulvin, 95
Growth and development, human,
    350–365
  analysis of problems of, 358
  assessment of, 350–351
  critical period of, 350
  defined, 350
  health promotion in, 359–360
  hospitalization and, 358–359
  parenting in, 360–363
  rates of, 350
  stages of, 351–358
Growth hormone (GH), 49–50, 322t
Guaifenesin, 75
Guanethidine, 67
Guillain-Barré syndrome, 198–199

H
Hair, 341
Halcion, 32t
Haldol, 35t, 542t
Haloperidol, 35t, 542t
Halotestin, 100t
Halothane, 163
Halo traction, 195
Harrington rod insertion, 426
Headache, 185–186
Head injury, 193–194
Head lice, in children, 431, 432
Health promotion, in children, 359–360
Hearing impairment
  in aging, 155t
  communicating with client with, 184
Heart, 382–383; see also Cardiovascular
    system
  anatomy and physiology of, 205–207
  children's, 385–394

acquired heart disease, 392–394
  assessment of, 386–387
  congenital heart defects, 388–392,
    388t
  disorders of, 387–394
  surgery, 391
circulation of, 206–207
conduction system of, 206
congenital defects of, 388–392,
    388t
diagnostic testing of, 208–209
disorders of, 211–219
  acquired, 392–394
  blood vessel, 219–227
of elderly clients, 155t
medication for, 55–69, see also
    Cardiovascular drugs
monitoring, 210–211
Heat application, external, 122
Heavy metal antagonists, 105
Helicobacter pylori, 77, 273–274
Hematocrit, 228
Hematologic system, 227–242, 394–399
  anatomy and physiology of, 227–231
  assessment of, 231–232
  children's, 394–400
    assessment of, 394–395
    disorders of, 395–400
  client care
    evaluation in, 233
    interventions in, 232–233
    planning of, 232
  diagnostic testing of, 232
  disorders of, 234–242
    acquired immune deficiency
      syndrome, 238–240
    aplastic anemia, 235–236
    disseminated intravascular
      coagulation, 237–238
    hemolytic anemia, 236
    hemophilia, 397–398
    Hodgkin's lymphoma, 440
    idiopathic thrombocytopenic
      purpura, 397
    iron-deficiency anemia, 234
    leukemia, 437–438
    multiple myeloma, 240
    non-Hodgkin's lymphoma, 439–440
    pernicious anemia, 234–235
    polycythemia vera, 240–241
    sickle-cell anemia, 395–396
    splenectomy, 236–237
Hemiplegia, 188, 189
Hemodialysis, 295–296
Hemodynamic monitoring, 210
Hemolysis, 228
Hemolytic anemia, 236
Hemolytic diseases, neonatal, 502–503
Hemophilia, 397–398
Hemophilus influenza B vaccine, 106
Hemorrhage, postpartum, 489
Hemorrhoids, 281
Hemothorax, 254–255
Heparin, 63–64
Hepatic cancer, 285–286
Hepatic encephalopathy, 285
Hepatitis, 281–282

Hepatitis B immune globulin, human, 106
Hepatitis B vaccine, 106
Hernias, 276–277
Herniated nucleus pulposus (HNP), 316–317
Herpes, genital, 510–511
Herpes simplex Type I, 344
Herpes zoster, 344
HHNK (Hyperglycemic hyperosmolar nonketotic coma), 338
Hiatal hernia, 272–273
Hib titer vaccine, 106
High blood pressure, medications for, 66–69
 beta adrenergic blocking agents, 68t
 central acting, 66, 68t
 diuretics, 68t-69t
 vasodilators, 69t
High Fowler's position, 119
High-risk infant, 499–506
 disorders in
  dysmature infant, 500
  postmature infant, 500-501
  premature infant, 499–500
 special conditions in, 501–505
  addiction in mother, 503–504
  hemolytic diseases, 502–503
  hyperbilirubinemia, 501–502
  hypoglycemia, 503
  necrotizing enterocolitis, 504–505
  phenylketonuria, 505
  respiratory distress syndrome, 504
  sepsis, 503
Hip dislocation, congenital, 423–424
Hip fractures, 315–316
Hip replacement, 316
Hiprex, 92t
Hirschsprung's disease, 413–414
Hismanal, 74
Histamine antagonists, 76–77
Histoplasmosis, 254
HIV infection, 238–240, *see also* AIDS
 classification of, 239t
HNP (Herniated nucleus pulposus), 316–317
Hodgkin's lymphoma, 440
Homatropine, 54
Homonymous hemianopsia, 188
Hormones
 as antineoplastic agents, 100–101, 100t
 function of, 322t
 of menstrual cycle, 448, 449
 placental, 452
 regulation of, 321
 secreted by anterior pituitary, 323
Hospitalization, of children, 358–359
Humalog, 47
Humatropel, 49–50
Hydantoins, for seizures, 32–33
Hydatidiform mole, 461
Hydralazine, 67, 69t
Hydrea, 102
Hydrocephalus, 376
Hydrochlorothiazide, 68t, 69–70
Hydrocortisone, 50–51, 328
Hydrodiuril, 68t, 69–70

Hydrolromide, 44t
Hydromorphone, 29t
Hydronephrosis, 420
Hydroxychloroquine, 84
Hydroxyprogesterone, 52–53
Hydroxyurea, 102
Hydroxyzine, 81, 142
Hygroton, 68t, 70
Hymen, 447
Hyperbilirubinemia, neonatal, 501–502
Hypercalcemia, 147t
Hyperemesis gravidarum, 462
Hyperglycemic hyperosmolar nonketotic coma (HHNK), 338
Hyperkalemia, 145t
Hypermagnesemia, 147t
Hypernatremia, 145t
Hyperparathyroidism, 333–334
Hyperpituitarism, 326, 430
Hyperstat, 67
Hypertension, 219–220
Hypertension, pregnancy-induced, 462–463
Hyper-Tet, 106
Hyperthermia, 184
Hyperthyroidism, 331–332
Hypervolemia, 145t
Hypnosis, for pain control, 144
Hypnotics, 30–32
Hypocalcemia, 147t
Hypochondriasis, 553
Hypodermoclysis, 18
Hypoglycemia, 338
 neonatal, 503
Hypoglycemic agents, oral, 336t
Hypokalemia, 145t
Hypomagnesemia, 147t
Hyponatremia, 146t
Hypoparathyroidism, 332–333
Hypophysectomy, 326–327
Hypophysis, 321
Hypopituitarism, 325, 429–430
Hypospadias, 418–419
Hypothyroidism, 330–331
 congenital, 429
Hypovolemia, 145t
Hypovolemic shock, 149t
Hysterectomy, 513
 for abortion, 509

I
Ibuprofen, 28t, 142, 311
ICP (Intracranial pressure), increased, 182–184
 in children, 375–376
Idiopathic thrombocytopenic purpura (ITP), 397
Illness, psychologic aspects of, 556–563
Ilosone, 89
Ilotycin, 89
IM (Intramuscular) drug administration, 18
Imipramine, 36, 546t
Immune response, 130–131
Immune serum globulin, 106
Immune serums, 106–107

Immunity
 acquired, 105–106, 131
 alterations in, 131
 natural, 105, 131
 passive, 106
Immunization, of children, 359–360, 361t
 schedule for, 359t
Immunoglobulin, 106
Immunosuppressant drugs, 103–104
Imodium, 79t
Impaired nurses, 539–540
Imperforate anus, 414
Impetigo, 431
Implantation, of ovum, 450
Imuran, 103
Incompetent cervix os, 460
Inderal, 62, 68t
Indocin, 28t, 142, 311, 313
Indomethacin, 28t, 142, 311, 313
 for premature labor, 476
Infants, 492–498
 Apgar scoring of, 495
 assessment of, 494–495
  variations from normal, 496–498
 care of, 492–499
 consciousness of. six states of, 493
 development of, 351–353
 disorders in, 499–501, 501–505
  addiction in mother, 503–504
  dysmature infant, 500
  hemolytic diseases, 502–503
  hyperbilirubinemia, 501–502
  hypoglycemia, 503
  necrotizing enterocolitis, 504–505
  phenylketonuria, 505
  postmature infant, 500–501
  premature infant, 499–500
  respiratory distress syndrome, 504
  sepsis, 503
 feeding, 487–488
 gestational age assessment of, 495
 immunologic status of, 493
 interventions for, 495–496
 neurologic/sensory status of, 493–494
 physiologic status of, 492–493
 psychiatric disorders (DSM IV), 530–532
 senses of, 494
Infections, 140–141
 bacterial, drugs for, 85–94
 fungal, drugs for, 95
 medications for
  antineoplastic, 98–100
  penicillin, 86–87
  for shock, 150t
 postpartum, 490
 during pregnancy, 465
 prevention of spread of, 141
Infectious mononucleosis, 398
Infertility, 506–507
Inflammatory response, 130
Informed consent, 162
Inhaled anesthesia, 163
Inhaled drugs, administration of, 14, 405
Inhaler, use of, 14, 405
Inheritance, principles of, 365–366
Injection angles, 17

Injection sites, 17–19
Insanity, defined, 114
Insanity defenses, 114–115
Insulin, 47–48, 322t
   analog of, 47
   infusion pump for, 335
   preparations of, 335t
Insulin reaction, 338
Insulin therapy, 334–336
   insulin preparations, 335t
   oral hypoglycemic agents, 336t
Intal, 73–74
Integumentary system, 340–348, 430–433
   anatomy and physiology of, 340–341
   children's, 430–433
   client care
      assessment in, 341–342
      interventions in, 342
   disorders of, 343–348
      acne, 433
      burns, 344–347
      contact dermatitis, 343
      eczema, 432
      Herpes simplex Type I, 344
      Herpes zoster, 344
      pediculosis, 432
      primary lesions, 343
      psoriasis, 343
      shingles, 344
      skin cancer, 343
   of elderly clients, 155t
   in pregnancy, 454
Intestinal obstructions, 277
Intestinal tubes, 269
Intestine, 263
Intracranial pressure (ICP), increased,
   182–184
   in children, 375–376
Intracranial surgery, 194–195
Intradermal drug administration, 18
Intramuscular (IM) drug administration,
   18
Intraspinal narcotic infusion, 143
Intravenous (IV) anesthesia, 164
Intravenous (IV) drug administration,
   18–20
Intravenous (IV) therapy, 147–149
   complications of, 148t
   interventions in, 147
   types of, 147–149
Intropin, 40
   for shock, 150t
Intussusception, 413
Involuntary commitment, defined, 114
Iodine, in nutrition, 134t
Ipecac syrup, 82
Iron, in nutrition, 134t
Iron deficiency anemia, 234, 395
Ismelin, 67
Isocarboxazid, 546t
Isometric exercises, 309
Isoniazid, 93–94, 94t
Isoproterenol, 39–40, 63
   for shock, 150t
Isoptin, 57t, 59
Isopto Atropine, 54
Isopto Carbachol, 55

Isopto Carpine, 55
Isopto Homatropine, 54
Isordil, 58–59
Isosorbide dinitrate, 58–59
Isoxsuprine, 40, 59–60, 60t
Isuprel, 39–40, 63
   for shock, 150t
ITP (Idiopathic thrombocytopenic
   purpura), 397
IV (Intravenous) anesthesia, 164
IV (Intravenous) drug administration,
   18–20
IV (Intravenous) therapy, 147–149
   complications of, 148t
   interventions in, 147
   types of, 147–149

J
Joints, 306

K
Kanamycin, 86
Kantrex, 86
Kaolin and pectin, 79t
Kaopectate, 79t
Karyotyping, 367
Kayexalate, 72
Ketoacidosis (DKA), 337–338
Ketorolac, 28t
Kidneys, 290
   drugs acting on, 69–72
   function of, 291
Kidney transplantation, 301–302
Kussmaul respirations, 338

L
Labia, majora and minora, 446
Labor and delivery, 468–483
   amniotic fluid embolism, 478–479
   analgesia and anesthesia in, 479–481
   assessment of fetal position, 470
   duration of, 471
   dystocia, 478
   emergency, 479t
   fetal assessment in, 471–472
   fetal distress in, 477–478
   five factors of labor (five Ps), 468–470
   induction of, 479
   LOA presentation, 469t, 470
   LOP presentation, 469t, 470
   malpresentations, 469t
   maternal assessment in, 472–473
   medical management of, 476
   nursing interventions in, 476–477
   precipitous, 478
   premature rupture of membranes, 477
   process of, 470–471
   prolapsed umbilical cord, 477
   prolonged, 477
   ROA presentation, 469t, 470
   ROP presentation, 469t, 470
   stages of, 471, 473–477
   surgical procedures in, 481–483
   true vs. false, 472
Lamaze method, of childbirth, 458t
Lanoxin, 55–56
Large intestine, 263

Larodopa, 68t
Laryngeal cancer, 258–259
Laryngectomy, total, 259–260
Laryngotracheobronchitis, 403
Larynx, 243
Lasix, 68t, 70
Lateral position, 120
Laxatives, 80, 81t
Lead poisoning, of children, 372
Learning disabilities, 362
Legal concepts, of nursing practice,
   113–115
Legal responsibilities, of nurse, 115
Legg-Calvé-Perthes disease, 424–425
Leopold's maneuvers, 470
Leukemia, 437–438
Leukeran, 98t
Leukocytes, 229
Leukoplakia, 343–438
Leukotriene inhibitors, 73–74
Level of consciousness (LOC), 179
Levodopa, 46t, 68t
Levophed, 38–39
   for shock, 150t
Levothyroxine, 51–52
LH (Luteinizing hormone), 322t
Licensure, 114
Lidocaine, 26, 57t, 61–62
   drugs related to, 61t
Lioresal, 33
Liothyronine sodium, 51–52
Lipid emulsions, 140
Lipids, 132
Lisinopril, 67
Lithium carbonate, 35–36
Lithium citrate, 36
Liver, 264
   disorders of, 281–286
      ascites, 283–284
      cirrhosis, 282–283
      esophageal varices, 284–285
      hepatic encephalopathy, 285
      hepatitis, 281–282
      liver cancer, 285–286
   hematologic function of, 231
Liver cancer, 285–286
LOA presentation, 469t, 470
LOC (Level of consciousness), 179
Local anesthetics, 26–27, 26t
Local infiltration block anesthesia, 164t
Lockjaw, 361t
Log rolling, 119
Lomotil, 79t
Loniten, 67
Loop diuretics, 68t, 70
Loperamide, 79t
LOP presentation, 469t, 470
Loratidine, 74
Losarten, 67
Lou Gehrig's disease, 199
Lovastatin, 65
Low residue diet, 139
Loxapine, 542t
Loxitane, 542t
L/S ratio, 458
Lubricant laxatives, 81t
Lumbar puncture, 180

Luminal, 31
Lungs, 244, *see also* Respiratory system
  circulation of, 244
  edema of, 216
  embolism in, 224–225
  pulmonary function studies, 245
  tuberculosis, 253–254
Lupus erythematosus, systemic, 313–314
Luteinizing hormone (LH), 322t
Lyme disease, 372
Lymphocytes, 229
Lypressin spray, 49

M
Macrodantin, 92t
Macule, in skin, 343
Mafenide, 345, 346
Magaldrate, 78t
Magnesium, in nutrition, 134t
Magnesium citrate, 81t
Magnesium hydroxide, 78t, 81t
Magnesium sulfate, for premature labor,
  476
Magnetic resonance imaging (MRI),
  180–181
Major depression, major, 546–547
Malaria, drugs for, 84
Male reproductive system
  disorders of, 302–306
    benign prostatic hypertrophy, 303
    epididymitis, 302–303
    prostate cancer, 303–304
    prostate surgery, 304
    prostatitis, 303
Malpractice, defined, 114
Malpresentations, in labor, 469t
Mammary glands, 448
  in pregnancy, 453
Mandelamine, 92t
Manic episode, 544–545
Mannitol, 72
MAOIs (Monoamine oxidase inhibitors),
  36–37, 546t
Marplan, 546t
Maslow's hierarchy of needs, 115–116
Mastectomy, 512–513
Mastitis, postpartum, 490
Maternity nursing, 450–506
  antepartal period, 455–468
  labor and delivery, 468–483
  newborn, 492–499
  postpartum period, 485–492
  pregnancy, 450–455
Matulane, 102
Maxipine, 88–89
Measles, 361t
Measles, mumps, rubella (MMR)
  vaccine, 106
Mebendazole, 96
Mechlorethamine, 98t
Meclizine, 81
Medications
  abuse of, *see* Drug abuse
  action of, factors affecting, 10–12
    absorption, 10
    accumulation of, 11
    age, 11

diseases, 11
distribution, 10–11
excretion, 11
metabolism, 11
administration of, 12–25
  calculations, 20–25
    conversions, 20–21
    dosage calculations, 21–25
  inhalants, 14
  intravenous (IV), 18–20
  nasal, 14
  ophthalmic, 14–15
  oral, 13
  otic, 15–16
  parenteral, 16–18
  principles of, 12–13
  rectal, 13–14
  topical, 16
  vaginal, 16
commonly abused, 537t
definition of, 10
distribution of, 10
for elderly clients, 158
metabolism of, 11
for treatment of
  arthritis, 83–85
  autonomic nervous system
    disorders, 38–46
  cancer, 169
  cardiovascular system disorders,
    55–69
  central nervous system disorders,
    26–38
  endocrine system disorders, 47–53
  eye disorders, 54–55
  gastrointestinal system disorders,
    76–83
  renal system disorders, 69–72
  respiratory system disorders, 73–76
  shock, 150t
types of
  anthelminthics, 96
  antiarrhythmics, 57t, 60–62
  anticholinergics, 44–45, 77
  anticoagulants, 63–64
  anticonvulsants, 32–33
  antidepressants, 36, 546t
  antidiarrheals, 79, 79t
  antiemetics, 80–82
  antifungal agents, 95
  antihistamines, 74–75
  antihypertensives, 66–69
  antilipemic agents, 65
  antimalarials, 84
  antimetabolites, 98
  antimicrobials, 85–94
  antineoplastic agents, 97–102
  antipsychotics, 542t
  antiviral agents, 94–95
  immunosuppressants, 103–104
  ophthalmic agents, 54–55
  vaccines and toxoids, 105–107
  vitamins and minerals, 104–105
Medroxyprogesterone, 52–53
Medulloblastoma, 438
Mefenamic acid, 311
Mefoxin, 88–89

Melanocyte stimulating hormone (MSH),
  322t
Mellaril, 35t, 542t
Menarche, 448
Ménière's disease, 203
Meningitis, 186
Menopause, 448, 513–514
Menorrhagia, 510
Menstrual cycle, 448, 449
Menstrual disorders, 509–510
Mental retardation, 531–532
Meperidine, 29t
Mepivacaine, 26t
Mercaptopurine, 98
Mestinon, 43
Metabolic acidosis, 147t
Metabolic alkalosis, 147t
Metabolism of drugs, 11
Metal antagonists, heavy, 105
Metamucil, 81t
Metaproterenol, 40
Metaraminol, 41
Metastasis, 168
Metformin, 336t
Methadone, 29t
Methenamine, 92t
Methergine, 53t
Methimazole, 51–52
Methotrexate, 98, 312
Methoxamine, 39
Methoxyflurane, 163
Methylcellulose, 81t
Methyldopa, 66, 68t
Methylergonovine, 53t
Methylprednisolone, 50–51
Metoclopramide, 81–82
Metolazone, 68t, 70
Metrorrhagia, 510
Mevacor, 65
Micronase, 336t
Midazolam, 32t
Miglitol, 336t
Milk of Magnesia, 78t, 81t
Mineralocorticoids, 50–51, 322t
Mineral oil, 81t
Minerals, 104–105, 133, 134t
Minipress, 66–67
Minocin, 90
Minocycline, 90
Minoxidil, 67
Mintezol, 96t
Miochol, 43, 55
Miotics, 54–55
Mithramycin, 99t
Mitomycin, 99t
Mixed-acting adrenergics, 40–41
MMR vaccine, 106
Modified Trendelenburg position, 120
Moles, 343
Monoamine oxidase inhibitors (MAOIs),
  36–37, 546t
Monocytes, 229
Mononucleosis, infectious, 398
Mons veneris, 446
Mood disorders, 544–549
  bipolar disorder, 544–545
  drugs for, 546t

Mood disorders, drugs for, (continued)
  atypical, 546t
    MAOIs, 36–37, 546t
    tricyclic, 36, 546t
  dysthymic disorder, 547
  major depression, 546–547
Morals, defined, 113
Morphine, 28–29
Motrin, 28t, 142, 311
Mouth, 262–263
Mouth cancer, 271–272
Moving client, 118–119
MRI (Magnetic resonance imaging), 180–181
MSH (Melanocyte stimulating hormone), 322t
Mucolytics, 75
Mucomyst, 75
Multiple myeloma, 240
Multiple sclerosis, 191–192
Multiple trauma, 150–151
Multisystem stressors, 130
Mumps, 361t
Muscle relaxants, skeletal, 33–34
Muscles, 306–307
Muscular dystrophy, 426–427
Musculoskeletal system, 306–320, 421–428
  anatomy and physiology of, 306–307
  assessment in, 307–308
  children's, 421–428
    assessment of, 421–422
    disorders of, 423–428
  client care, 307–311
  client in traction, 310–311
  client with cast, 309–310
  disorders of, 311–321
    discectomy, 317–318
    fractures, 315–316
    gout, 313
    Harrington rod insertion, 426
    herniated nucleus pulposus, 316–317
    hip replacement, 316
    limb amputation, 225
    osteoarthritis, 312–313
    osteomyelitis, 314–315
    rheumatoid arthritis, 311–312
    spinal fusion, 318
    systemic lupus erythematosus, 313–314
  of elderly clients, 155t
  evaluation of, 311
  female, changes during pregnancy, 454
  preventing complications of immobility, 308–309, 308t
Mustargen, 98t
Mutamycin, 99t
Myambutol, 94t
Myasthenia gravis, 192–193
Mycophenolate, 103
Mycostatin, 95
Mydriatics, 54
Myelodysplasia, 376–377
Myleran, 98t
Myocardial infarction (MI), 213–214
Myochrysine, 84, 311

Myoclonic seizure, 379t
Myometrium, 447
Myxedema, 330–331

N
Nadolol, 62, 68t
Nagel's rule, 453
Nails, 341
Nalbuphine, 29
Nalfon, 311
Nalidixic acid, 92t
Naloxone, 30
Naltrexone, 30
Naprosyn, 28t, 85, 311, 313
Naproxen, 28t, 85, 311, 313
Narcan, 30
Narcotic agonist/antagonists, 29
Narcotic analgesics, 28–30, 29t, 142
  for labor, 480
Narcotic antagonists, 30
  for labor, 480
Narcotic infusion, intraspinal, 143
Nardil, 36–37, 546t
Nasalcrom, 73–74
Nasal drug administration, 14
Nasogastric (NG) tubes, 268–269
  in children, 410
Nausea and vomiting, 269–270
Navane, 542t
Nebcin, 86
Necrotizing enterocolitis (NEC), neonatal, 504–505
Needs, of client, 2–3
  care environment, 2
  health promotion/maintenance, 2
  physiologic adaptation compromises, 3
  physiologic integrity, 2–3
  psychosocial integrity, 2
  reduction of risk potential compromises, 3
Negative feedback mechanisms, 321
Neg Gram, 92t
Neglect, of elderly, 159–160
Negligence, defined, 114
Neisseria gonorrhoeae, 511
Nembutal, 31t
Neobiotic, 86
Neoloid, 81t
Neomycin, 86
Neonates, see Newborns
Neoplasms, see Cancer
Neostigmine, 43
Neo-Synephrine, 39
Nephrectomy, 302
Nephroblastoma, 441
Nephrolithiasis, 299
Nephron, 291
Nephrosis, 419–420
Nephrotic syndrome, 419–420
Nervous system, see Neurosensory system
Neuroblastoma, 441–442
Neurogenic bladder, 196
Neurogenic hyperventilation, central, 179
Neurogenic shock, 149t

Neuroleptic anesthetics, 164
Neurologic examination, 178–180
Neurons, 174
Neurosensory system, 174–202
  assessment of, 178–182
  autonomic, 176, 177t
  central, 174–176
    disorders of, 185–197
  children's, 373–385
    assessment of, 374–375
    disorders of, 375–384
  client care, 178–185
    evaluation of, 185
    interventions in, 182–185
    planning of, 182
  diagnostic testing of, 180–181
  disorders of, 185–204
    amyotrophic lateral sclerosis, 199
    Bell's palsy, 198
    brain abscess, 186
    brain tumors, 186–187
    cerebral aneurysm, 189
    cerebrovascular accident (CVA), 187–189
    encephalitis, 186
    epilepsy, 378–380
    Guillain-Barré syndrome, 198–199
    headache, 185–186
    head injury, 193–194
    Lou Gehrig's disease, 199
    meningitis, 186
    multiple sclerosis, 191–192
    myasthenia gravis, 192–193
    Parkinson's disease, 189–191
    spinal cord injuries, 195–197
    tic douloureux, 197–198
    trigeminal neuralgia, 197–198
  of elderly clients, 155t
  peripheral, 176
    disorders of, 197–199
  in pregnancy, 454
  surgery of, 194–195
Neurosurgery, for pain control, 143–144
Neutrophils, 229
Nevi, 343
Newborns, 492–498
  Apgar scoring of, 495
  assessment of, 494–495
    variations from normal, 496–498
  care of, 492–499
  consciousness of, six states of, 493
  disorders in, 499–501
    dysmature infant, 500
    postmature infant, 500–501
    premature infant, 499–500
  disorders of, 501–505
    addiction in mother, 503–504
    hemolytic diseases, 502–503
    hyperbilirubinemia, 501–502
    hypoglycemia, 503
    necrotizing enterocolitis, 504–505
    phenylketonuria, 505
    respiratory distress syndrome, 504
    sepsis, 503
  gestational age assessment of, 495
  immunologic status of, 493
  interventions for care of, 495–496

neurologic/sensory status of, 493–494

physiologic status of, 492–493

psychiatric disorders (DSM IV), 530–532

senses of, 494

Niacin, in nutrition, 135t

Nidation, 450

Nifedipine, 57t

for premature labor, 476

Nipride, 67

for shock, 150t

Nitrites, 58–59

Nitrites, proper use of, 212

Nitro-Bid, 58–59

Nitro-Dur, 58–59

Nitrofurantoin, 92t

Nitroglycerin, 58–59

Nitroprusside, 67

Nitrostat IV, 58–59

Nizatidine, 77t

Noctec, 32

Nodule, in skin, 343

Nonbenzodiazepines, 32

Non-Hodgkin's lymphoma, 440–441

Nonnarcotic analgesics, 27–28

Nonsedating antihistamines, 74–75

Nonselective agonists, 38–39

Nonstress test (NST), of fetus, 458–459

Norepinephrine, 322t

for shock, 150t

Norepinephrine bitartrate, 38–39

Norpace, 57t

Nortriptyline, 36

Nose, 243

Novocain, 26t

Novocolchine, 84–85

NSAIDs (Nonsteroidal anti-inflammatory drugs), 28t, 142

NST (Nonstress test), of fetus, 458–459

Nubain, 29

Nurses, impaired, 539–540

Nursing, 109–127

adult, 130–348, see also Aging; Oncologic nursing; Perioperative nursing; Stressors

care management, 115–117

asepsis, 122

body mechanics, 118–119

cold application, 121–122

examples of, 124–127

external heat application, 122

fire safety and preparedness, 117–118

moving client, 118–119

positioning client, 119–121

pressure sores, 123–124

restraints, 118

of elderly clients, 154–161, see also Aging

ethical aspects of, 113–115

legal aspects of, 113–115

legal responsibilities of, 115

maternity, 450–506, see also Childbearing cycle

oncologic, 168–174, see also Oncologic nursing

pediatric, 350–443; see also Children

perioperative, 161–167, see also Perioperative nursing

psychiatric/mental health, 517–563, see also Psychiatric nursing

standards of practice, 110–112

Nutrition, 132–140

carbohydrates, 132

dietary guides, 136

energy metabolism, 133

enteral, 139

food consistency, modification of, 138–139

lipids, 132

minerals, 133, 134t

parenteral, 139–140

planning, 137

principles of, 132

proteins, 132–133

status of client

assessment of, 136–137

interventions in, 136–140

during pregnancy, 457

vitamins, 133, 135t

water, 136

Nylidrin, 40

Nystatin, 95

O

Obsessive-compulsive disorder (OCD), 550

Obstetrical procedures, operative, 481–483

Omeprazole, 77

Oncologic nursing, 168–174

Oncology

adult, 168–172

pediatric, 433–443

Oncovin, 101–102

Ontogeny, 350

Oogenesis, 450

Open reduction and internal fixation, 315

Ophthalmic drugs, 54–55

administration of, 14–15

Opiate diarrheals, 79

Opium tincture, 79t

OPV (Oral polio vaccine), 106

Oral alpha-glucosidase inhibitor, 336t

Oral biguanides, 336t

Oral contraceptives, 52–53

Oral drug administration, 13

Oral feeding, 139

Oral polio vaccine (OPV), 106

Oral sulfonylureas, 336t

Oretic, 68t

Orinase, 48–49

Ortho-Novum contraceptives, 52–53

Osmitrol, 72

Osmotic diuretics, 72

Osteoarthritis, 312–313

Osteogenesis imperfecta, 425

Osteogenic sarcoma, 442

Osteomyelitis, 314–315

Osteoporosis, 514

Otic drug administration, 15–16

Otitis media, 382–383

Otosclerosis, 202

Ovaries, 448

cancer of, 513

changes in pregnancy, 452

as endocrine glands, 322

Ovum, development of, 450–451

Oxycodone, 29t

Oxygen tent, for children, 401

Oxytocics, 53–54

Oxytocin, 53–54, 322t

for induction of labor, 479

Oxytocin-related drugs, 53t

P

Pacemakers, 216–217

Paclitaxel, 102

Pain, 141–144

acute and chronic, 141

assessment of, 142t

gate control theory, 141

interventions in, 141–142

therapies for, 142–144

Pain disorder, 553

Pancreas, 264, 321–322

disorders of, 287–288

diabetes mellitus, 334–338

Pancreatic cancer, 288

Pancreatic function testing, 324

Pancreatitis, 287–288

Panic disorder, 550

Papaverine, 60t

Papule, in skin, 343

Paral, 32

Paraldehyde, 32

Paraplegia, 195

Parasitic worms, 415

Parathyroid glands, 321

disorders of, 332–334

Parathyroid hormone (PTH), 322t

Paregoric, 79t

Parenteral drug administration, 16–18

in children, 410

hypodermoclysis, 18

intradermal, 18

intramuscular, 18

subcutaneous, 17–18

Parenteral nutrition, 139–140, 410

Parenting, 360–363

adaptation to, 486

education for, 457

Parietal peritoneum, 448

Parkinson's disease, 189–191

medications for, 45–46, 45t, 46t

Parlodel, 46t

Parnate, 37, 546t

Parotitis, 361t

Paroxetine, 37

Partial seizures, 379t

Paternalism, defined, 113

Pathologic reflex, 179

Patient care, see Client care

Patient-controlled analgesia (PCA), 143

Pavabid, 60t

Paxil, 37

PCA (Patient-controlled analgesia), 143

Pediatric nursing, 350–432; see also Children

Pediatric oncology, 433–443
  assessment in, 434
  cancer treatment in
    stages of, 436–437
    types of, 434–436
  interventions in, 434–436
Pediatric urine collector (PUC), 417
Pediculosis, 432
Pelvis, female, 448
Penicillin, 86–87
  extended-spectrum, 87
  penicillinase-resistant, 87
Penicillin/beta-lactamase inhibitor
    combinations, 87
Penis, 292
Pentazocine, 29
Penthrane, 163
Pentids, 86–87
Pentobarbital sodium, 31t
Pentothal sodium, 31t
Pepcid, 77t
Peptic ulcers, 273–276
  medications for, 275t
PeptoBismol, 79t
Percocet, 29t
Percodan, 29t
Percorten, 50–51
Percutaneous transluminal coronary
    angioplasty (PTCA), 214
Percutaneous umbilical blood sampling
    (PUBS), of fetus, 458
Pericarditis, 219
Perineum, 447
Perioperative nursing, 161–167
  anesthesia, 163–164
  client care, 161
    postoperative, 164–166
    preoperative, 162, 163
  in labor and delivery, 481–483
  legal responsibilities, 162–163
  pediatric
    brain, 434, 439–440
    cancer, 439, , 439–440, 442
    cardiac, 391
Peripheral adrenergic blocking agents,
    67
Peripheral nervous system, 176, see also
    Neurosensory system
  disorders of, 197–199
    amyotrophic lateral sclerosis, 199
    Bell's palsy, 198
    Guillain-Barré syndrome, 198–199
    Lou Gehrig's disease, 199
    tic douloureux, 197–198
    trigeminal neuralgia, 197–198
Peripheral vasodilators, 59–60
Peripheral vein parenteral nutrition
    (PPN), 140
Peritoneal dialysis, 296–297
Peritonitis, 280–281
Permitil, 542t
Pernicious anemia, 234–235
Perphenazine, 542t
Persantine, 59–60
Personality disorders, 554–556
Pertussin, 75
Pertussis, 361t
Petit mal seizure, 379t

Pharynx, 243
Phenazopyridine, 92t
Phenelzine, 36–37, 546t
Phenergan, 35t, 74–75, 80–81
Phenobarbital sodium, 31
Phenolphthalein, 81t
Phenothiazine, 34–35, 35t, 80–81
Phentolamine, 39, 42
Phenylbutazone, 311, 313
Phenylephrine, 39
Phenylketonuria (PKU), neonatal, 505
Phenytoin, 32–33, 61t
Pheochromocytoma, 329
Phonocardiogram, 209
Phospholine Iodine, 55
Phosphorus, in nutrition, 134t
Phylogeny, 350
Physiologic readiness, for testing, 5–6
Piaget, Jean, 350
Pilocar, 55
Pilocarpine, 55
Pinolol, 62
Pitocin, 53–54
  for induction of labor, 479
Pitressin, 68t
Pituitary dwarfism, 429–430
Pituitary gland, 321
  disorders of, 325–340
    diabetes insipidus, 327
    hyperpituitarism, 326
    hypophysectomy, 326–327
    hypopituitarism, 326
    syndrome of inappropriate
      antidiuretic hormone secretion,
      327
  hormones secreted by, 49–50, 323
PKU (Phenylketonuria), neonatal, 505
Placenta, 451–452
Placental circulation, 451
Placenta previa, 461
Plaquenil, 84
Plasma, 228
Platelets, 229
  disorders of, 237–238, 397–398
Platinol, 98t
Pleural effusion, 255–256
Plicamycin, 99t
Pneumonia, 256–257
Pneumothorax, 254–255
Poisonings, of children, 370–373
  acetaminophen, 371
  lead, 372
  salicylate, 371
Poison ivy, 432
Poliomyelitis, 361t
Polycythemia vera, 240–241
Ponstel, 311
Positioning client, 119–121
  dorsal lithotomy position, 121
  general principles, 119
  high Fowler's position, 119
  lateral position, 120
  modified Trendelenburg position,
    120
  prone position, 120
  semi-Fowler's position, 119
  Sim's position, 120

  supine position, 120
  Trendelenburg position, 120
Postmature infant, 500–501
Postoperative care, 164–165
  complications of surgery, 165–166
Postpartum hemorrhage, 489
Postpartum period, 485–492
  assessment in, 486–489
  complications of, 489–492
  discharge teaching, 489
  physical changes in, 485–486
  psychosocial changes in, 486
Posttraumatic stress disorder (PTSD),
    550–551
Potassium, in nutrition, 134t
Potassium removing resin, 72
Potassium sparing diuretics, 68t, 71–72
PPN (Peripheral vein parenteral
    nutrition), 140
Prazosin, 66–67
Precose, 336t
Prednisolone, 50–51
Prednisone, 50–51
Preeclampsia, 462–463
Pregnancy
  assessment of, 455–456
  classification of, 455
  complications of, 459–463
    common discomforts, 459t
    first trimester bleeding, 460–461
    hyperemesis gravidarum, 462
    hypertension, 462–463
    pre- and coexisting conditions,
      463–468
    second trimester bleeding, 461
    third trimester bleeding, 461–462
  danger signs in, 460t
  ectopic, 460–461
  familial adjustment to, 454–455
  fetus, 451
    changes in size of, 453
    circulation of, 385–386, 452
    delivery of, 468–483
    electronic monitoring of, 458–459
    growth and development of, 452, 452t
    membranes of, 451
    monitoring of, 458–459
    movement of, 458
    risk factors of, 457–458
    status of, 457–458
  interventions in, 456–458
  nursing responsibilities in, 460
  nutrition during, 457
  ovum, development of, 450–451
  physical changes of, 452–455
  psychologic changes of, 452–455
  psychosocial changes in, 454–455
  special structures of, 451–452
  termination of, 460, 509
  transcultural concerns, 455
Premature infant, 499–500
Premature ventricular contractions
    (PVCs), 213
Prenatal care, 456–457
Preschooler development, 354–355
Pressure sores
  defined, 123
  general care of, 123

prevention of, 123
specific wound care, 123–124
stages of, 123
Prilosec, 77
Primary lesions, of skin, 343
Probenecid, 313
Procainamide, 57t
Procaine, 26t
Procarbazine, 102
Procardia, 57t
Prochlorperazine, 80–81
Progesterone, 322t
Progestins, 52–53
Progestogens, 52–53
Prograf, 103–104
Prolapse, of uterus, 514
Prolixin, 35t, 542t
Proloid, 51–52, 330
Promethazine, 35t, 74–75, 80–81
Prone position, 120
Pronestyl, 57t
Propranolol, 62, 68t
Propylthiouracil, 51–52
Prostaglandins
   for abortion, 509
   for induction of labor, 479
Prostate cancer, 303–304
Prostate gland, 293
Prostate surgery, 304
Prostatic hypertrophy, benign, 303
Prostatitis, 303
Prostigmen, 43
Protamine, 63
Protein modified diet, 138
Proteins, 132–133
Proton pump inhibitor, 77
Provera, 52–53
Prozac, 37, 546t
Psoriasis, 343
Psychiatric disorders (DSM IV), 530–556
   in adolescence, 530–532
   anxiety disorders, 549–552
   autistic disorder, 532–533
   childhood, 530–532
   cognitive, 534–536
   delirium, 534–536
   dementia, 534–536
   developmental disorders, 532–534
   dissociative disorders, 553–554
   eating disorder, 533
   in infancy, 530–532
   mood disorders, 544–549
      bipolar disorder, 544–545
      dysthymic disorder, 547
      major depression, 546–547
   neurotic disorders, 549–552
   personality disorders, 554–556
   psychotic disorders, 541–543
   schizophrenia, 541–543
   somatoform disorders, 552–553
   substance abuse disorders, 536–541
      alcohol dependence, 538–539
      impaired nurses, 539–540
      psychoactive drug use, 539
Psychiatric nursing, 519–529
   client care in, 522–526
      analysis, 523
      assessment, 522–523

evaluation, 526
implementation, 523–526
emotional distress
   behavior under, 526–530
   theories of, 519–522
interventions of, 523–526
   behavior modification, 526
   crisis intervention, 525–526
   family therapy, 525
   groups, types of, 525t
   milieu therapy, 525
   psychotropic medications, 526
   therapeutic communication, 523–524
   therapeutic groups, 524–525
Psychoactive drug use, 539
   disorders of, 536–541
Psychologic stress, 556–557
   of abuse, 557–559
   of AIDS, 561–562
   of chronic illness, 560–561
   of critical illness, 559–560
   of death and dying, 562
   of grief and mourning, 56
   of pregnancy, 452–455
   before testing, 5–6
Psychomotor seizure, 379t
Psychosexual theory, 350
Psychosocial theory, 350
Psychotic disorders, 541–543
Psychotropic medications, 526
Psyllium hydrophilic muciloid, 81t
PTCA (Percutaneous transluminal
   coronary angioplasty), 214
PTH (Parathyroid hormone), 322t
PTSD (Posttraumatic stress disorder),
   550–551
PUBS (Percutaneous umbilical blood
   sampling), of fetus, 458
PUC (Pediatric urine collector), 417
Pulmonary circulation, 244
Pulmonary edema, 216
Pulmonary embolism, 224–225
Pulmonary function studies, 245
Pulmonary tuberculosis, 253–254
Purinethol, 98
Pustule, in skin, 343
PVCs (Premature ventricular
   contractions), 213
Pyelonephritis, 299–300
Pyloric stenosis, 413
Pyrantel, 96t
Pyrazinamide, 94t
Pyridium, 92t
Pyridostigmine, 43

Q
Quadriplegia, 195
Questran, 65
Quibron, 73–74
Quinaglute, 57t, 60–61
Quinidine, 57t, 60–61

R
RA (Rheumatoid arthritis), 311–312
   juvenile, 427
Radiation therapy
   for cancer, 170–171
   for pediatric cancer, 434–435

Range-of-motion (ROM) exercises,
   308–309
Ranitidine, 77t
Rape, 559
Raynaud's phenomenon, 221
RDS (Respiratory distress syndrome),
   504
Read method, of childbirth, 458t
Rectal cancer, 279
Rectal drug administration, 13–14
Rectocele, of uterus, 514
Regional enteritis, 277–278
Regitine, 39, 42
Reglan, 81–82
Regonol, 43
Renal failure
   chronic, 300–301
   femoral vein, 300–301
Renal system, see also Kidneys; Urinary
   system
   during pregnancy, 464–465
Renin-angiotensin system, drugs acting
   on, 69t
Reproductive system
   female, 446–450
      anatomy, 446–448
      changes during pregnancy, 452–453
      disorders of, 506–516
      external structures, 446–447
      internal structures, 447–448
      mammary glands, 448
      menarche, 448
      menopause, 448
      menstrual cycle, 448, 449
      neoplasia of, 511
      pelvis, 448
      physiology, 448
      postpartum changes in, 485
      sexual response, 448
   of female elderly clients, 156t
   infections of, 510–511
   male, 292–293
      disorders of, 302–306
   of male elderly clients, 156t
   sexually transmitted diseases, 510–511
Reserpine, 67
Respiratory acidosis, 147t
Respiratory alkalosis, 147t
Respiratory distress syndrome (RDS),
   neonatal, 504
Respiratory system, 243–262, 400–409
   anatomy and physiology of, 243–244
   assessment of, 244–246
   children's, 400–409
      assessment of, 400–402
      disorders of, 402–408
   diagnostic testing of, 245–246
   disorders of, 251–260
      acute respiratory distress syndrome
         (ARDS), 258
      asthma, 404–405
      atelectasis, 255
      bronchiectasis, 252–253
      bronchitis, 252
      bronchogenic carcinoma, 257
      emphysema, 251–252
      flail chest, 254
      fractured ribs, 254

Respiratory system, *(continued)*
  hemothorax, 254–255
  histoplasmosis, 254
  laryngeal cancer, 258–259
  laryngectomy, total, 259–260
  pleural effusion, 255–256
  pneumonia, 256–257
  pneumothorax, 254–255
  pulmonary tuberculosis, 253–254
  thoracic surgery, 257–258
  of elderly clients, 155t
  evaluation of, 251
  interventions in, 246–251
    chest physiotherapy, 248–249
    chest tubes/water-seal drainage,
      246–248
    Heimlich flutter valve, 248
    mechanical ventilation, 249
    oxygen therapy, 249–250
    tracheobronchial suctioning, 250
    tracheostomy care, 250–251
  medications for, 73–76
    antiasthmatic drugs, 73–74
    antihistamines, 74–75
    expectorants and antitussives, 75–76
    mucolytics, 75
  planning, 246
  pregnancy and changes in, 454
Restraints, 118
Retina, detached, 201–202
Retrovir, 95
Reye's syndrome, 378
Rezulin, 336t
Rheumatic fever (RF), 392–393
Rheumatoid arthritis, 311–312
  juvenile, 427
RhoGAM, 107
Rho (D) immune globulin, human, 107
Rh typing, 229
Ribavirin, 95
Ridaura, 83–84
Rifadin, 94t
Rifampin, 93–94, 94t
Rights of clients, 115
Right to know, defined, 113
Rimactane, 93–94, 94t
Ringworm, 431–432
Riopan, 78t
Risperdal, 542t
Risperidone, 542t
Ritodrine, for premature labor, 476
ROA presentation, 469t, 470
Robinul, 44t
Robitussin, 75
Rolaids, 78t
ROM (Range-of-motion) exercises,
  308–309, 312, 313
ROP presentation, 469t, 470
Rubella, 361t
Rubeola, 361t
Russell traction, 310, 311

S
Saddle block anesthesia, 164t
Salicylates, 27, 142
Saline abortion, 509
Saline laxatives, 81t
Sandimmune, 103–104

Sarcomas, 442
SC (Subcutaneous) drug administration,
  17–18
Schizophrenia, 541–543
School-age development, 356
Scoliosis, 425–426
Scopolamine, 44t
Scrotum, 292
Sebaceous glands, 341
Secobarbital sodium, 31t
Seconal, 31t
Sedatives, 30–32
  for labor, 480
Seizure disorders, 378–380, 379t
  medications for, 32–33
Selective agonists, 39–40
Selective serotonin reuptake inhibitors
  (SSRIs), 37
Self-needs analysis, for test preparation,
  4–5
Selye, Hans, 130
Semi-Fowler's position, 119
Senile dementia, 159
Senile keratoses, 343
Senna, 81t
Senokot, 81t
Sensory disorders, of aging, 155t
Sensory/perceptual deficits, 188–189
Sepsis, neonatal, 503
Septic shock, 149t
Serpasil, 67
Sertraline, 37, 546t
Sex hormones, 322t
Sex-linked inheritance, 366
Sexual response, female, 448
SGA (Dysmature infant), 500
Shingles, 344
Shock, 149–150
  classification of, 149t
    drug treatment of, 150t
    spinal, 195
Sickle-cell anemia, 395–396
SIDS (Sudden infant death syndrome),
  362
Silvadene, 345
Silver nitrate, 345
Silver sulfadiazine, 345
Sim's position, 120
Sinemet, 46t
Sinequan, 546t
Sinus bradycardia, 212
Sinus tachycardia, 212
Skeletal muscle relaxants, 33–34
Skene's glands, 446–447
Skin, *see* Integumentary system
Skin cancer, 343
Skin grafts, 342
  sources of, 342
Skin testing, 342
SLE (Systemic lupus erythematosus),
  313–314
Slow-Bid Gyro caps, 73–74
Small intestine, 263
Sodium, in nutrition, 134t
Sodium carbonate/bicarbonate, 78t
Sodium nitroprusside
  for shock, 150t
Sodium polystyrene sulfonate, 72

Sodium thiomalate, 311
Soft diet, 138–139
Solganal, 84
Solu-Cortef, 328
Solu-Medrol, 50–51
Soma, 33
Somatization disorder, 552–553
Somatotropin, 49–50, 322t
Somophyllin, 73–74
Spasmodic laryngitis, 403
Spasticity, 197
Special diets, 137–140
Spermatic cord, 293
Spermatogenesis, 450
Spina bifida, 376–377
Spinal anesthesia, 164t
Spinal cord, 174–176, *see also*
  Neurosensory system
Spinal cord injuries, 195–197
Spinal fusion, 318
Spinal shock, 195
Spironolactone, 68t, 71–72
Spleen, 231
Splenectomy, 236–237
Sponge bath, 121
Spouse abuse, 558
Sputum culture, 246
Squamous cell carcinoma, 343
Stadol, 29
Standards
  defined, 113–114
  of nursing practice, 110–112
Stapedectomy, 202–203
Status epilepticus, 379t
Stelazine, 542t
Stimulant laxatives, 81t
Stomach, 263
  defects of, 412
Stomach cancer, 276
Stomatitis, 170
Stool softeners, 81t
Streptase, 64–65
Streptokinase, 64–65
Streptomycin, 86, 94t
Stress, 556–557
  of abuse, 557–559
  and adaptation, 130
  of AIDS, 561–562
  of chronic illness, 560–561
  of critical illness, 559–560
  of death and dying, 562
  of grief and mourning, 56
  management of, 130
  of pregnancy, 452–455
  before testing, 5–6
Stressors, 130–153
  acid-base imbalances, 146–147
  of children, 365–373
    accidents, 370–373
    acid-base imbalance, 368–370
    fluid and electrolyte imbalance,
      368–370
    genetic disorders, 365–368
    poisonings, 370–373
  defined, and characteristics of, 130
  fluid and electrolyte balance, 144–146
  immune response, 130–131
  infections, 140–141

inflammatory response, 130
intravenous therapy, 147–149
multiple trauma, 150–151
nutrition, 132–140
pain, 141–144
shock, 149–150
Subclavian vein catheterization, 296
Subcutaneous (SC) drug administration, 17–18
Subinvolution, postpartum, 490
Substance abuse
  and newborn, 503–504
  during pregnancy, 466
Substance abuse disorders, 536–541
  alcohol dependence, 538–539
  impaired nurses, 539–540
  psychoactive drug use, 539
Succinimides, for seizures, 33
Sucralfate, 82–83
Suctioning, respiratory, 402
Sudden infant death syndrome (SIDS), 362
Sulfamethoxazole, 91
Sulfasalazine, 91
Sulfisoxazole, 91
Sulfamylon, 345, 346
Sulfinpyrazone, 313
Sulfonamides, 90–91
Sulfonylureas, 336t
Sulfur, in nutrition, 134t
Sulindac, 85, 311
Supine position, 120
Surgery
  anesthesia during, 163–164
  client care
    postoperative, 164–166
    postoperative complications, 165–166
    preoperative, 162
    preoperative preparation, 163
  effect on client, 161
  legal responsibilities of medical staff, 162–163
  pediatric
    brain, 434, 439–440
    cancer, 434, 439–440, 442
    cardiac, 391
  risks of, 161–162
  types of
    adrenalectomy, 329–330
    bladder, 297–298
    bowel, 279–280
    cataracts, 199–200
    cholecystectomy, 286–287
    choledochostomy, 286–287
    coronary artery bypass, 214–215
    discectomy, 317–318
    femoral-popliteal bypass, 222–223
    gastric, 274, 276
    gastrostomy, 268
    Harrington rod insertion, 426
    hip replacement, 316
    hypophysectomy, 326–327
    intracranial, 194–195
    labor and delivery, 481–483
    limb amputation, 225
    nephrectomy, 302
    pain control, 143–144

prostate, 304
thoracic, 257–258
thyroidectomy, 332
Swan-Ganz catheter, 210
Sweat glands, 341
Syndrome of inappropriate antidiuretic hormone (SIADH), 327
Synthroid, 51–52, 330
Syphilis, 511
Syringes, examples of, 22
Systemic lupus erythematosus (SLE), 313–314

T
T3 (Triiodothyronine), 322t, 331
T4 (Tetraiodothyronine), 322t, 331
Tachycardia
  sinus, 212
  ventricular, 213
Tacrine, 43
Tacrolimus, 103–104
Tagamet, 76–77
Talipes, 424
Talwin, 29
Tapazole, 51–52
Taxol, 102
Tay-Sachs disease, 381
TBI (Total body irradiation), 172
Td toxoid, 106
Tegretol, for seizures, 33
Tendons and ligaments, 307
Tensilon, 43
TENS unit, 143
Terbutaline, 40
  for premature labor, 476
Terpin hydrate elixir, 75
Testes, 292
  as endocrine glands, 322
Testicles, undescended, 418
Testicular self-examination (TSE), 169
Testing
  preparation for nursing exam, 1–7
  psychologic stress of, 5–6
Testosterone, 322t
Testosterone cypionate, 100t
Tetanus, 361t
Tetanus immune globulin, human, 106
Tetanus toxoid, adult, 106
Tetracyclines, 89–90
Tetraiodothyronine (T4), 322t
TheoDur, 73–74
Theophylline, 73–74
Thiabendazole, 96t
Thiazine diuretics, 68t, 69–70
Thiopental sodium, 31t
Thioridazine, 35t, 542t
Thiotepa, 98t
Thiothixene, 542t
Thomas splint, and Pearson attachment, 310, 311
Thoracentesis, 246
Thoracic aortic aneurysm, 222
Thoracic squeeze, of newborn, 492–493
Thoracic surgery, 257–258
Thorazine, 34–35, 542t
Thromboangiitis obliterans, 221
Thrombocytes, 229
Thrombolytic drugs, 64–65

Thrombophlebitis, 223–224
  postpartum, 489–490
Thyrocalcitonin, 322t
Thyroglobulin, 51–52
Thyroid antagonists, 51–52
Thyroidectomy, 332
Thyroid function testing, 323–324
Thyroid gland, 321
  disorders of, 330–332
    goiter, simple, 330
    Graves' disease, 331–332
    hyperthyroidism, 331–332
    hypothyroidism, 330–331
    myxedema, 330–331
    thyroidectomy, 332
    thyroid storm, 332
  hormones secreted by, 51
Thyroid stimulating hormone (TSH), 322t
Thyroid storm, 332
TIA (Transient ischemic attack), 187–188
Tibial torsion, 424
Tic douloureux, 197–198
Timolol, 42, 62
Timoptic, 42
Tobramycin, 86
Tocainide, 61t
Toddler development, 353–354
Tofranil, 36, 546t
Tolbutamide, 48–49
Tonic seizure, 379t
Tonocard, 61t
Tonsillectomy, 402–403
Tonsillitis, 402
Topical anesthetics, 164t
Topical drug administration, 16
Toradol, 28t
Total body irradiation (TBI), 172
Total parenteral nutrition (TPN), 139–140
Toxoids, 105–107
TPN (Total parenteral nutrition), 139–140
Trachea, 243
  defects of, 412
Traction
  care of client in, 310–311
  children in, 422–423
Transient ischemic attack (TIA), 187–188
Tranxene, 32t
Tranylcypromine, 37, 546t
Trauma, multiple, 150–151
Trazodone, 546t
Trendelenburg position, 120
Trexan, 30
Triamterene, 71–72
Triazolam, 32t
Trichomonas vaginalis, 511
Tricyclic antidepressants, 36, 546t
Trifluoperazine, 542t
Trigeminal neuralgia, 197–198
Trihexyphenidyl, 45
Triiodothyronine (T3), 322t
Trilafon, 542t
Trilisate, 142
Troglitazone, 336t
Trophoblastic disease, gestational, 461
TSE (Testicular self-examination), 169

TSH (Thyroid stimulating hormone), 322t
Tube feeding, 139
Tuberculin skin testing, 246
  in children, 360
Tuberculosis
  medications for, 93–94
  pulmonary, 253–254
Tumor growth, *see* Cancer
Tums, 78t
Tylenol, 27, 142

U
Ulcerative colitis, 278
Ulcers
  decubitus, 123–124
  dermal, 123–124
  duodenal, 274
  gastric, 273–274
  peptic, 273–276
  venous stasis, 223
Ultrasound, of fetus, 458
Umbilical cord, 451
  prolapsed, 477
Unconscious client, 182
Undescended testicles, 418
Urecholine, 43
Ureters, 290–291
Urethra, 291, 446
Urinary catheterization, 294–295
Urinary system, 290–292, *see also*
      Genitourinary system
  disorders of, 296–306, *see also* Urinary
      tract infection
    acute renal failure, 300–301
    bladder cancer, 297
    bladder surgery, 297–298
    chronic renal failure, 300–301
    cystitis, 296
    glomerulonephritis, acute, 420
    kidney transplantation, 301–302
    nephrectomy, 302
    nephrolithiasis, 299
    nephrosis, 419–420
    pyelonephritis, 299–300
    urolithiasis, 299
  of elderly clients, 156t
  female, 446–448
    changes during pregnancy, 454
  male, 292–293
  medications for, 69–72
  postpartum changes in, 486
Urinary tract infection (UTI), 417
  drugs acting on, 91–92, 92t
  postpartum, 490–491
  during pregnancy, 464–465

Urine, formation of, 291
Urine collector, pediatric, 417
Urokinase, 65
Urolithiasis, 299
Uterus, 447
  cancer of, 513
  changes in pregnancy, 453
  cystocele/rectocele of, 514
  prolapse of, 514

V
V-16, 101t
Vaccines and toxoids, 105–107
  for children, 359–360, 361t
    schedule for, 359t
  immune serums, 106–107
Vacomycin, 92
Vagina, 448
  changes in pregnancy, 452
  drug administration into, 16
  orifice of, 447
Vaginitis, bacterial, 511
Valium, 31
Valproic acid, for seizures, 33
Values, defined, 113
Vancocin, 92
Vaporizers, for children, 401
Varicella, 361t
Varicose veins, 225
Vascular system, 207
Vasoconstrictors, for shock, 150t
Vasodilan, 40, 59–60, 60t
Vasodilators, 69t
  direct-acting, 60t, 67
  for shock, 150t
  peripheral, 59–60
Vasopressin, 68t
Vasospan, 60t
Vasotec, 67, 69t
Vasoxyl, 39
Velban, 101t
Venlafaxine, 37
Venous stasis ulcers, 223
Ventricular tachycardia, 213
VePesid, 101t
Verapamil, 57t, 59
Vermox, 96
Versed, 32t
Vertex presentation, 471
Vesicle, in skin, 343
Vesicoureteral reflux, 418
Vestibule, 446
Vibramycin, 90
Vinblastine, 101t
Vinca alkaloids, 101–102
Vincristine, 101–102

Virazole, 95
Viruses
  and cancer, 168
  drugs acting on, 94–95
Visken, 62
Vistaril, 81, 142
Vitamins, 104–105, 133, 135t
  in nutrition
    vitamin A, 135t
    vitamin B_1, 135t
    vitamin B_2, 135t
    vitamin B_6, 135t
    vitamin B_{12}, 135t
    vitamin C, 135t
    vitamin D, 135t
    vitamin E, 135t
    vitamin K, 63, 135t
Voluntary commitment, defined, 114
Vomiting
  in children, 369–370
  and nausea, 269–270
Vulva, cancer of, 513

W
Warfarin sodium, 63–64
Water, 136
Water deficit sydromes, 145t
Water excess syndromes, 145t
Weight control diet, 137–138
Wellbutrin, 37
Wheal, in skin, 343
White blood cell disorders, 398
Whooping cough, 361t
Wilm's tumor, 441
Worm infestations, 415
  medications for, 96
Wound care, 123–124
  surgical, 165–166

X
Xanax, 32t
X-rays, 180
  of fetus, 458
Xylocaine, 26, 57t, 61–62

Z
Zantac, 77t
Zarontin, 33
Zaroxolyn, 68t, 70
Zestril, 67
Zidovudine, 95
Zileutron, 73–74
Zoloft, 37, 546t
Zovirax, 94–95
Zyflo, 73–74
Zyloprim, 84–85, 313

Set-Up Instructions

NSNA NCLEX Study DIsk

1. Insert disk into CD ROM player
2. From the Start Menu, choose *RUN*
3. In the *Open* text box, enter **d: setup.exe** then click the *OK* button.(Substitute the letter of your CD ROM drive for **d:**)
4. Follow the installation prompts from there.